The CAMBRIDGE WORLD HISTORY of FOOD

EDITORS
Kenneth F. Kiple
Kriemhild Coneè Ornelas

VOLUME TWO

CAMBRIDGE
UNIVERSITY PRESS

PUBLISHED BY THE PRESS SYNDICATE OF THE UNIVERSITY OF CAMBRIDGE
The Pitt Building, Trumpington Street, Cambridge, United Kingdom

CAMBRIDGE UNIVERSITY PRESS
The Edinburgh Building, Cambridge CB2 2RU, UK
40 West 20th Street, New York, NY 10011-4211, USA
10 Stamford Road, Oakleigh, VIC 3166, Australia
Ruiz de Alarcón 13, 28014 Madrid, Spain
Dock House, The Waterfront, Cape Town 8001, South Africa

http://www.cambridge.org

© Cambridge University Press 2000

First published 2000
Reprinted 2000

Printed in the United States of America

Typeface Garamond Book 9.5/10.25 pt.   *System* QuarkXPress®   [GH]

The following illustrations in Part II are from the LuEsther T. Mertz Library, The New York Botanical Garden, Bronx, New York: Corn, Sorghum.

The following illustrations in Parts II and III are from the General Research Division, The New York Public Library, Astor, Lenox and Tilden Foundations: Banana plant, White potato, Prickly sago palm, Taro, Early onion, Lentil, Cabbage, Brussels sprouts, Cucumber, Watermelon, Field mushroom, Long white squash, Tomato, Chestnut, Peanut, Sesame, Soybean, Coriander, Peking duck, Geese, Goat, Cacao, Kola.

The following illustrations in Parts II and III are from the Rare Book and Manuscript Library, Columbia University: Oat, Olive, Sugar, Reindeer, Cattle, Turkey, Coffee.

A catalog record for this book is available from the British Library.

Library of Congress Cataloging in Publication Data

The Cambridge world history of food / editors, Kenneth F. Kiple, Kriemhild Coneè Ornelas.
     p. cm.
  Includes bibliographical references and index.
   ISBN 0-521-40214-X (v. 1) – ISBN 0-521-40215-8 (v. 2) – ISBN 0-521-40216-6
(slipcase set)
    1. Food–History. I. Kiple, Kenneth F., 1939– II. Ornelas, Kriemhild Coneè.

TX353.C255 2000
641.3'09–dc21   00-057181

ISBN   0 521 40214 X (Volume 1)
ISBN   0 521 40215 8 (Volume 2)
ISBN   0 521 40216 6 (Set)

CONTENTS

VOLUME ONE

VOLUME TWO

PART V

Food and Drink around the World

Part V comprises a history of food and drink around the world, from the beginnings of agriculture in the Near East to recent excitement generated by the "Mediterranean diet." It is divided chronologically as well as geographically, which invariably creates anomalies and overlap that invite explanation. Illustrative is the treatment together of South Asia and the Middle East in view of the culinary impact of Islam on both regions. Or again, because of an abundance of available authorities on food and drink in the various European countries (and their many regions), that section could easily have mushroomed to the point of giving lie to a title that promised "world history." Thus, we have dealt with Greece, Italy, and the Iberian countries under the rubrics of "The Mediterranean" and "Southern Europe."

For the Americas, we have two Caribbean entries, which might seem somewhat disproportionate. But it should be noted that the chapter that provides a pre-Columbian historical background for the Caribbean region does so for South America and lowland Central America as well, whereas the chapter treating the period since 1492 reveals the mélange of cultures and cuisines of the region, in which those of Africa blended with others of Europe and Asia, even though the dishes often centered on plants originally cultivated by the region's indigenous peoples.

In Part V, alarm about the danger of the demise of national and regional cuisines is sometimes expressed – triggered, at least in part, by fast-food chains, born in the United States but now reproducing wildly across the globe from Mexico City to Moscow, Bridgetown to Brussels, and Phnom Penh to Paris. It is interesting to note how the standardized nature of fast foods contrasts so starkly with the usage of foods in an earlier period of globalization, which took place during the centuries following the Columbian voyages. Then, burgeoning nationalism ensured that although various cultures adopted most of the same foods, they prepared them differently, just as regional cuisines arose in similar fashion to proclaim a distinctiveness from the metropolis.

Yet, even though nationalism has faded in the West, the ongoing globalization of everything from economics to politics seems once again, in the case of foods, to be provoking a like reaction, doubtless because the homogenization process appears paradoxically to spur a need for cultural autonomy. Thus, although fast food has its place in a world in a hurry, it is almost certainly not the harbinger of planetary food uniformity it stands accused of being. Indeed, it is probably best to conceive of food globalization as a process of expanding the availability of more and more foods, reaching the point at which the ingredients of the national dishes of the world are increasingly available to anyone anywhere. Another comforting indication that national cuisines are not on the verge of extinction is the vital and rapidly expanding field of culinary history, discussed in the last chapter of Part V.

V.A

The Beginnings of Agriculture: The Ancient Near East and North Africa

The Sumerians may have said it best: "Food: That's the thing! Drink: That's the thing!" (Gordon 1959: 142). From bread and beer to wine and cheese, the people of the ancient Near East and North Africa developed a rich cuisine based on a set of crops and livestock domesticated in Southwest Asia, and a sophisticated technology of food preparation and preservation. This chapter traces the history of diet and foods of hunter-gatherers who lived at the end of the Stone Age in the Near East and North Africa, the impact of the development and spread of agriculture, and the social context of food and drink in early Mesopotamian and Egyptian civilization.

Geographical Background

Patterns of subsistence in any society reflect geography and cultural development. The civilizations of the ancient Near East and North Africa developed in a complex environmental mosaic that encompassed coasts and inland plateaus, high mountains and lands below sea level, barren deserts, fertile plains, and dense woodlands. The boundaries of the environmental zones have shifted over the years because the region has known both dry periods and moister phases.

People, too, have wrought changes on the land as they assisted the movement of plants and animals from their original homelands. Over the millennia, humans have turned deserts into gardens with irrigation, and have transformed naturally productive lands into deserts by overgrazing and fuel cutting. Specifying the environmental picture at any particular place and time is not an easy task.

Elevation has also had a profound influence on vegetation and climate in the Near East and, ultimately, the productive capacity of the land. Levantine mountains form the western border of the Fertile Crescent, and the Taurus-Zagros chain lies to the north and east, from Mediterranean Anatolia to southwestern Iran. The winter months bring the snow and rain that support forests and grasslands. The three main vegetational zones are forests in the mountains and hill zones surrounding the Fertile Crescent, steppe at slightly lower elevations, and desert in the lowlands.

The natural forest and steppe forest formations are dominated by oaks. Conifers of various types occur throughout. Pistachio is common in both the Mediterranean forests and the southern Zagros (Zohary 1973). This band of hilly country borders undulating grasslands and shrubby steppe to the south. Lying south of the steppe are the hot deserts of Arabia. The Tigris and Euphrates river systems originate in the mountains in the north, run through Mesopotamia, and drain into the Persian Gulf, providing a distinct riparian habitat, as well as an important source of water for irrigation. During the last 15,000 years, the margins of these environmental zones have shifted back and forth with drier and moister climatic phases (Zeist and Bottema 1991).

North Africa has a less hospitable environment than the Near East. The Sahara desert spans the continent; on its southern margins are the dry Sahel grasslands, and along its northern periphery are more semiarid lands. The immense Sahara has a varied terrain with scattered oases, depressions, high ground, rugged hills along the Red Sea coast, and mountains in the central region. Higher mountains lie to the northwest in the Maghreb. Along the North African coast, light winter rains sustain a narrow band of green. The Nile Valley is the lushest region in North Africa because of the river water derived from Equatorial Africa, but the desert lies just beyond the river valley.

The Near East

Foragers

Fourteen thousand years ago, human populations throughout this region were mobile hunter-gatherers who relied on wild plants and animals for sustenance (Table V.A.1). Little is known of the full range of foods eaten by these people. There is scant evidence of the plant foods consumed even though nuts, starchy seeds, and tubers were probably important contributors to the diet (Colledge 1991). But the skeletal remains of forest and steppe animals attest to a variety of game that was eaten, including several types of deer and gazelle, wild cattle, pigs, sheep, goats, and onagers (Hesse 1995).

Table V.A.1. *Chronology of the Near East and Egypt*

Near East			Egypt	
Calibrated date B.C.		Uncalibrated date B.C.		Calibrated date B.C.
Literate civilizations of Mesopotamia			**Pharaonic state**	
3,100	–	2,600	–	3,100
	Early states		Predynastic	
3,500	–	2,800	Later villages & towns	
	Later villages & proto-urban societies	3,000	–	3,750
			Early predynastic villages	
		3,700	–	4,500
			Semisedentary farmers/foragers	
		6,300	–	5,200
	Pottery Neolithic			
6,900	–	6,000	–	
Aceramic Neolithic			**Mobile foragers**	
10,200	–	8,300	–	
	Sendentary and semisedentary foragers			
12,000	–	10,000	–	
	Mobile foragers			

Source: Adapted from Evin (1995) for the Near East and Hassan (1985) for Egypt. Calibrated dates interpreted from Stuiver et al. (1986, fig. 7) and uncalibrated dates based on Libby half-life (5,568 years).

Note on Chronology: Scientists have developed ways to calibrate radiocarbon dates so that they more accurately reflect calendar years. Most of the reports and papers cited here, however, use uncalibrated radiocarbon dates for periods before the early states. In order to be consistent, we have decided to use calibrated and historical dates throughout (cf. Evin 1995). We hope this does not cause confusion for readers who investigate some of our source material.

By 12,000 B.C., seeds and nuts had become an important part of the diet (Flannery 1973). At this time, foraging populations in the more favorable areas became less mobile and began to stay in settlements for extended periods. People living in the steppe and steppe forest began to concentrate on a few main species of animals and plants. The faunal evidence is fairly straightforward; at sites from the Levant to the Syrian steppe, gazelle appears to have been the primary source of animal protein (Garrard 1984). At Abu Hureyra, for example, gazelle constitutes about 80 percent of the animal bone (Legge 1975). Depending on local availability, the meat diet in other areas also seemed to focus on only one or two wild ungulates, like sheep, goat, pig, and onager (Hesse 1995).

As the climate changed during this period, the habitat of wild grasses expanded. Analysis of isotopes in human bone from archaeological sites suggests that people were now eating more plant foods. The most extensive collection of archaeological plant remains comes from the site of Abu Hureyra. Though Gordon C. Hillman, Susan M. Colledge, and David R. Harris (1989) suggest that the Abu Hureyrans consumed a wide array of plants, some of the plant remains they have turned up as evidence may have derived from animal dung burned as fuel, and so may not fairly represent human food choices (Miller 1996). Slightly later samples from nearby Mureybit (Zeist and Bakker-

Heeres 1984) have a few concentrations of seeds that are more likely to be human food remains, especially those of wild einkorn.

Accompanying the shift to a settled lifestyle were advances in food technology that probably contributed to a more stable food supply and population growth. In addition to cooking, which probably had been practiced for about a million years, archaeological evidence points to improvements in grinding and storage technology. Without grinding and cooking, the digestibility of wild cereals and pulses would have been low, but with such techniques, even pulses that are toxic when fresh could be nutritious, and, consequently, the amount of food available from a given tract of land would have been increased. Moreover, storing food in pits reduced both intra- and interannual variation in food availability.

These technological changes encouraged an increase in sedentism as well as in population during the early village period. Food, a welcome addition to most social interactions, probably also became important for greasing the wheels of human relations. Feasting, practiced on a grand scale in later periods, was doubtless begun for a variety of reasons, ranging from the cementing of alliances to the attracting of labor. Such activities would have encouraged sedentary foragers to accumulate surplus beyond bare subsistence needs (Bender 1978).

Farmers

Sometime after 12,000 B.C., sedentary hunter–gatherer communities in the Levant, followed slightly later by inhabitants of Anatolia and parts of the Zagros Mountains, embarked on a path that led to the domestication of plants and animals and, ultimately, food production. This shift in subsistence that archaeologists refer to as the "Neolithic Revolution" was the most profound change in human history and one that still has a far-reaching impact on the planet.

Current consensus is that plant domestication in the Near East began in the Jordan Valley around 9500 B.C. (Zeist 1988), and animal husbandry started about the same time or a little later in the Zagros Mountains and, possibly, North Africa (Hole 1984; Rosenberg et al. 1995). By the middle of the ninth millennium B.C., domesticated plants could also be found in Anatolia and the Zagros. Even with advances in agriculture, however, wild plant gathering and hunting continued to play an important role in the economy. In fact, it is probable that the ancestors of the first domesticated plants in the Near East – emmer, einkorn, and barley – had been important food plants for local foraging populations.

Domesticated plants entered the archaeological record at different times and places. For example, emmer wheat originated in the Jordan Valley, but bitter vetch is probably Anatolian. The earliest farming villages did not use pottery or domestic animals and, like their forebears, stored grain in pits. As early as the ninth and eighth millennia B.C., the ability to store surplus food enabled small, undifferentiated settlements of farmers to develop into larger communities of more complex social and economic organization. Changes are evidenced by public architecture (shrines), differences in wealth as reflected in the goods accompanying burials, specialized occupations for a few, and elaborate mortuary cults (see Voigt 1990). Some of the communities were also vastly larger than the earliest villages and may have housed a thousand or more inhabitants.

Nomadic foragers who followed herds of goat and sheep in the mountains of Iran began managing wild herds about 12,000 years ago, and pigs may have been domesticated at about that time as well (Rosenberg et al. 1995). Cattle were domesticated in Anatolia about 7000 B.C. By determining the age and sex of the animals slaughtered, faunal analysts can infer herd management strategies. For example, if the bone assemblage includes both adult males and females, it is unlikely that milk production was the goal; whether hunted or herded, the primary product supplied by the animals of the early herders was meat.

By 6700 B.C., a fully agricultural economy that relied almost entirely on farming and herding was established over much of the Near East. The staple crops grown over a broad area were cereals (emmer, einkorn, durum wheat, bread wheat, and two- and six-row barley) and pulses (lentil, bitter vetch, and chickpea). It is likely that these crops were eaten, even toxic ones (like bitter vetch) because they are sometimes found in concentrations in roasting pits. Whereas cereals satisfied much of the caloric needs of the early villagers, the addition of domesticated pulses and livestock helped satisfy protein needs. A variety of wild plants, including such nuts as pistachio, almond, and acorn, continued to enhance the diet as well (see, for example, Mason 1995).

Farming spread to the hot, dry lowlands of Mesopotamia where techniques for water management developed. Late in the sixth millennium B.C., the Near Eastern complex of crops and livestock also spread to the Nile Valley, where still other irrigation techniques emerged to take advantage of the Nile floods. Farming villages proliferated as the new subsistence systems proved to be highly productive and capable of supporting a burgeoning population. After the initial phase of domestication, such fruits as grape, olive, fig, and date were domesticated. Their dietary and economic potential, however, was not fully realized until relatively late.

The Near Eastern agro-pastoral subsistence system proved very productive, initially supporting ever-increasing populations. Although one might think the domesticated pulses would be the perfect dietary complement to the cereals, the inclusion of domestic animals in a mixed economy had several advantages lacking in a purely plant-based system. First, animals provided ready access to dietary fat; aside from wild nut trees (especially pistachio and almond), oil plants (olive, flax, and sesame) do not appear to have been utilized at this early date. Second, land marginal for agriculture could have been used productively for pasture. Third, animals convert inedible pasture plants into tasty meat, which would have increased the food supply. Finally, domestic animals may have been traded with other groups to "set up reciprocal obligations and maximize sharing during lean years" (Flannery 1969: 87).

In the short run, the new farming methods seem to have been successful in evening out seasonal and year-to-year fluctuations in the food supply. On a theoretical level, the combined effect of plant and animal husbandry should have been a more stable food supply for growing populations (Raish 1992; Redding 1993). Yet the land could not continue to support expanding populations without some change in management (Köhler-Rollefson 1988). In fact, the first half of the sixth millennium B.C. saw a fairly widespread abandonment of settlements and the reestablishment of smaller communities on other sites, and faunal assemblages from Iran to Syria show a renewed emphasis on hunted animals (Buitenhuis 1990, Zeder 1994). Overgrazing and inadequate fallowing may have exacerbated a long-term impact of fuel cutting by village farmers, with inevitable results.

It was the development of new techniques of chemically transforming food that allowed the theoretical advantages of the agro-pastoral system to be realized. Pottery, widespread by 6000 B.C., permitted new forms of storage and cooking possibilities (though stone boiling in animal skins would have been possible even in prepottery days) (Moore 1995). Fermentation allowed farmers to transform grain and fruits into psychotropic substances; though alcohol is itself not digested, the fermentation process makes many nutrients more available.

Fermented grapes could also have yielded vinegar, a pickling agent. In the Near East, the earliest evidence for fermentation comes from Iran – wine residues at Hajji Firuz, around 5500 B.C., and beer (and wine) residues at Godin Tepe, around 3500 B.C. (Michel, McGovern, and Badler 1993; McGovern et al. 1996); it did not take long for people to appreciate the added value of fermentation. Beer became a convenient and pleasant way to consume grain's carbohydrates and vitamins. It is probably no accident that olives, which must be cured before eating, were domesticated in this era, and olive oil would have been a welcome addition to the diet.

Early Near Eastern farmers did not just experiment with plants. Although we do not know when adults in these populations lost at least some of their inability to absorb lactose (Simoons 1979), at some point they probably began to consume milk from their herds. Cheese, ghee, yoghurt, and other cultured milk products were most likely innovations of the later village societies. Based on the age of slaughter, the zooarchaeologist Simon Davis (1984) suggests that dairy products were not emphasized until relatively late, around 4500 to 4000 B.C. in western Iran. In the Levant, ceramic vessels considered to be churns date to this time (Kaplan 1954). And in the earliest archaic texts from Mesopotamia (before 3000 B.C.), mention of an elaborate array of storable dairy products that were produced in institutional quantities suggest strongly that these items had long been part of the culinary repertoire (Nissen, Damerow, and Englund 1993).

Finally, the period of the later villages seems to have been the time when people began to use salt as a food preservative, although the mineral may have been used for animal hide preparation as early as the seventh millennium B.C. Archaeological evidence for the production and procurement of salt at this time is not available (Potts 1984), but it is difficult to imagine that the large quantities of fish placed as offerings in the fifth millennium B.C. temple at Eridu were fresh! Certainly by the third millennium, drying and salting were well-known techniques of food preservation (see Reiner 1980). In summary, it seems that the major food-transforming technologies developed and spread between about 5500 and 3500 B.C.

By about 3500 B.C., orchard crops began to make a noticeable contribution to the diet. Grape and olive in the Mediterranean region and date in Mesopotamia, so important to the earliest civilizations, had been domesticated. Such fruits as fig, pomegranate, and apple came under cultivation, too. By this time domesticated livestock had almost completely replaced their wild relatives and other hunted animals. The ability to preserve large quantities of varied foods permitted surplus accumulation that, in turn, provided an impetus toward the developments we associate with civilization: urbanization, a high degree of economic specialization, and social inequality (Sherratt 1981; Redding 1993).

The First States

Productive surplus-generating agriculture may not have caused the changes set in motion, but it certainly permitted them to occur. Towns began to appear across Mesopotamia and the northern plains, which individually, as well as collectively, had all the trappings of a society more complex than any previously seen in the Near East. Among them were monuments and temples, full-time craft specialists, social stratification, and large populations.

Specialized nomadic pastoralists who began to share the landscape with settled agricultural populations joined in feeding the growing urban populations, and by 3500 B.C. the trend toward larger and more complex communities culminated in the emergence of the literate civilizations of Mesopotamia and, around 3100 B.C., in the appearance of a state in Egypt. Such social and cultural changes accompanying the rise of complex societies also had profound implications for foodways.

In earlier times, differences in consumption patterns had resulted from seasonal and local resource availability. But these early civilizations were now composed of people divided by wealth, class, occupation, and ethnicity, and their diets varied accordingly. Social status, in other words, had become an additional factor in determining who ate what.

Moreover, the basic Near Eastern crop complex was joined by a few new plants, as indicated by the archaeological record of the third and second millennia B.C. (see Miller 1991). For example, a grave offering included dried apples at Ur (Ellison et al. 1978), and coriander, fruits, and garlic cloves have been uncovered at Tell ed-Der (Zeist 1984). Plants originally domesticated beyond the borders of the Near East also began to appear, including millets, sesame, and rice (Zohary and Hopf 1993). Wild plants continued to add variety to the diet, as evidenced by occasional finds in food-related contexts: a jar of caper buds and fruits at Sweyhat (Zeist and Bakker-Heeres 1985), *Prosopis* seeds at Nimrud (Helbaek 1966), and *Chenopodium* at Shahr-i Sokhta (Costantini n.d.).

Deposits in cesspits provide direct evidence of diet, but they are not commonly found. A mineralized cess deposit from the third millennium B.C. city of Malyan, however, produced dozens of grape seeds and incompletely digested seeds of wheat and barley (Miller 1984). Most plant remains found are charred, however, so they do not directly represent food remains. Rather, they reflect fuel use, trash disposal, and cooking accidents. Archaeobotanical analysis is, therefore, not the primary means of understanding class or ethnic distinctions in human food consumption, but the situation is different for faunal remains.

As in earlier times, the major food animals were sheep, goat, cattle, and pig. Such domesticates as donkey, horse, and camel became more common, but they do not appear to have been eaten to any great extent. A variety of wild animals, such as gazelle, small game, birds, turtles, and fish, are frequent but minor contributors to faunal assemblages (Hesse 1995).

Several studies of the pattern of animal bone disposal on urban sites demonstrate the strategies employed to ensure a steady access to animal products, as well as social differences among the inhabitants. On most Near Eastern sites, the bulk of the bone is from sheep or goat, yet a fluctuating percentage of pig bone consistently appears. Pigs do well in forest and thickets, and can only survive harsh summers with shade and water. Generally then, pork-consuming regions are ecologically suited to the pig (Hesse 1995: 215).

The distribution of pigs in the later periods probably reflects the economics of pig production; they are a fine animal for town dwellers because they reproduce quickly and eat garbage. Thus, in Mesopotamia, the town residents of al-Hiba ate more pork than their rural counterparts in the community of Sakheri Sughir (Mudar 1982: 33). The difficulty in managing large numbers of pigs was another variable in pork consumption. At Lahav, in Israel, their numbers increased when the site was occupied by relatively isolated independent households. But when the settlement was integrated into a regional economy and, presumably, pig raising was more strictly regulated, production declined (Zeder 1995a). Faunal studies have not yet detected specific evidence for the Jewish prohibition on pork consumption because it is difficult to segregate ecological and economic from symbolic values reflected in archaeological bone remains (Hesse 1995: 215).

The dietary impact of wealth is exhibited at al-Hiba, a site where residents of the temple precinct had greater access to domestic animals, and residents of the lower town ate relatively more wild animals, along with pork (Mudar 1982). At Leilan, too, the lower town residences of poorer people had relatively large quantities of pig bones (Zeder 1995b). At Malyan, differential distribution of species and of meat-bearing elements across the site suggests that some residents had more direct access to the herds of sheep and goat than others, and some higher-status households appear to have had greater access to choicer cuts than did lower-status ones (Zeder 1991: 199).

Our sources of evidence for food multiply after the advent of complex society. Visual representations of food and texts concerning its production, distribution, preparation, and consumption fill out a picture constructed with more ubiquitous archaeological remains like seeds and bones. Writing, glyptic, and monumental art are associated with the upper strata of society and comprise evidence that begins to overshadow the archaeological plant remains among the literate societies. Animal bones, however, continue to be the primary source of information about meat consumption.

Among the earliest written signs in Mesopotamia is the one for beer, a necked jar (Green and Nissen 1987: 229). Even after the pictograph was transformed into a more abstract cuneiform sign, the image of two people sitting opposite each other and drinking (beer) with reed straws out of a necked vessel became one of the major elements in banquet scenes on seals (Selz 1983). Bread baking, beer brewing, and other food procurement and preparation scenes give some idea of the vast establishment that was necessary to support the major palace and temple institutions (Strommenger n.d.).

Plants of any sort are rarely depicted in the art of the ancient Near East, as either landscape elements or food. In contrast, images of animals are relatively common. There is no reason to suppose, however, that they are literal symbols of food sources, even when the subject is a food animal. Stylized animal representations in clay figurines are a normal part of assemblages from the aceramic Neolithic on. Although they frequently show important food species (bovids, caprids, and dogs), the animal taxa do not occur in proportion to bone refuse. The famous installations and wall paintings of Çatal Hüyük (eighth to seventh millennium B.C.) depict cattle, but they also depict vultures (Mellaart 1967). The pottery of some late farming cultures includes stylized birds and caprids, but again, there is no direct correlation with the faunal remains.

Depictions of animals in the art of the early civilization of Mesopotamia include many different life forms: scorpions, fish, turtles, birds, and wild and domestic mammals, along with imaginary creatures (Strommenger n.d.). Files of animals on cylinder seals and wall art seem to show sheep, goat, and cattle heading toward byres and are probably depictions of offerings to temple or palace. Haunches of meat and other comestibles are also elements in offering scenes. Portrayals of capture, such as men fishing with nets, sometimes suggest food procurement, but at other times, sport, as with the Assyrian royal lion hunts. A victory stela, showing human captives caught in a net, illustrates a new use for an old technology (Strommenger n.d.: 67), further demonstrating that pictorial evidence cannot be taken at face value. Moreover, scenes directly reflecting diet or dining only refer to a small segment of society. Their symbolic message is more significant than their documentary value.

Mesopotamians began keeping records on clay toward the end of the fourth millennium B.C. In the third millennium, the Sumerians developed writing for a variety of additional purposes. Hundreds of plant and animal names, many of which were used as foods and medicines, occur in ancient Sumerian and Akkadian texts from Mesopotamia (see, for example, Powell 1984; Stol 1985, 1987; Waetzoldt 1985, 1987; Postgate 1987). Economic and literary texts from Mesopotamia point to the importance of wheat, barley (and beer), date (and date wine), cattle, goat, sheep, dairy products, fish, and some fowl. Onion, garlic, and leek were the most important condiments. Different types of food preparation, such as roasting, brewing, and baking, are mentioned, as are names for many types of beer, cheese, and the like (Civil 1964; Ellison 1984; Bottéro 1985).

With textual evidence, it becomes easier to assess geographical, cultural, and social dietary variations. For example, although the staple plant foods of the Near East continued over a wide area, they had overlapping distributions. Cultural preference within the irrigation civilizations of southern Mesopotamia favored barley and beer, as well as date and date wine, whereas wheat and grape wine prevailed in the hilly regions and were joined by olive oil around the Mediterranean (see Powell 1995). Many regional differences are a function of ecology – grapes are more suited to a Mediterranean regime, and dates cannot be grown in the cooler climes. But these "natural" explanations for food preferences do not exclude cultural differences in attitudes toward various kinds of food. Wine, for example, came to have a religious significance in the Mediterranean civilizations that carries through to this day.

Distribution of food in the urban societies of lower Mesopotamia reflected social distinctions. It would seem that in the stratified societies of the ancient Near East, meat was a less important part of the diet for those of the lower classes. Economic texts from some of the major third millennium institutions show that careful track was kept of food provided to workers. Barley comprised the bulk of the rations for people working for the state or temple, although oil, malt products, meat, and other animal products were also distributed. Amounts varied according to the age and sex of the recipients, but scholars still disagree about whether daily ration for a worker constituted his or her whole diet or just a part of it (Gelb 1965; Ellison 1981).

Palace and temple archives also give a glimpse of herd management and production, but they deal exclusively with the large institutional herds of cattle, sheep, and goats. It has long been recognized that such archives tell only part of the story. Illustrative is sheep milk. Textual evidence suggests that only cattle and goats were milk producers, and sheep were grown for their wool and meat (Stol 1993). Yet sheep milk is high in fat and protein and would hardly have been wasted. Perhaps shepherds were allowed to milk the herds directly, or, as is ethnographically attested, sheep milk was mixed with cow's milk, but not recorded separately. Similarly, although quantities of fish were frequently deposited in temple and palace storehouses, no mention is made of fish preservation; because large quantities of fresh fish spoil rapidly, it seems likely that fish preservation and processing (for oil) was carried out by the private sector (Potts 1984).

Textual evidence of food preparation is slender. Perhaps best known is a hymn to the Mesopotamian beer goddess, which describes how *bappir,* an aromatic-flavored dough, is mixed with barley malt and fermented with herbs and other flavorings to make beer (Civil 1964). Three culinary texts from the second millennium B.C. (Bottéro 1985, 1995) contain recipes of sorts, although they are by no means step-by-step cooking instructions. Jean Bottéro, the Assyriologist who has studied them, considers them to be a codification of court cuisine that sets down general guidelines. Although the texts do not contain materials representative of the entire range of foods eaten by the upper stratum of society, let alone ordinary people, a few things are worth noting. The recipes include words for a variety of birds. They also contain words for meats and a method of cooking that included repeated washing of meat at different stages of food preparation. The number of plant types mentioned is relatively low, and those that have been identified appear to have been cultivated (with the possible exception of the potherbs). Finally, Mesopotamian cuisine was based on the use of sauces, which, as Bottéro points out, permitted the blending of subtle flavors unavailable with less elaborate forms of food preparation.

In earliest times, subsistence depended on wild resources available locally. The advent of agriculture brought together plants and animals from different regions and led to the creation of the Near Eastern agricultural complex of wheat and barley, pulses, sheep, goat, cattle, and pig. People of the Near East came to depend on domesticates, but wild plants and animals always constituted at least a minor portion of the diet. Advances in food preparation and storage technologies transformed agriculture into a highly productive and reasonably stable food procurement system, and effective food preservation techniques, in turn, permitted dense populations in towns and cities. Allowing for differences rooted in geography and culture, the diet and cuisine of Egyptian civilization developed along a similar path.

Egypt and North Africa

Beginning some 11,000 to 12,000 years ago, North Africa experienced a moist phase that lasted until historic times, although it was broken by several brief arid spells. During this period, summer rains produced seasonal lakes and dry grasslands, and the boundary of the Sahel shifted hundreds of kilometers north of its present location (Grove 1993). Hunter-gatherers who had been living on the margins of the Sahara began moving out onto what had been desert to subsist on wild plants, such fauna as gazelle and hare, and, in some cases, even fish (Muzzolini 1993).

By the seventh millennium B.C., these groups were growing larger and becoming more settled, as in the Near East. At Nabta Playa in southwestern Egypt, there were seasonal settlements that included storage pits, wells, and oval huts arranged in rows. Archaeological remains of plant foods indicate that the inhabitants gathered wild grasses, especially sorghum *(Sorghum)* and millet *(Pennisetum),* as well as Christ's-thorn fruits *(Zizyphus spina-christi)* and other wild fruits and seeds.

They cooked the plant foods in vessels, possibly made of hide, set in the sand of the hut floors (Wasylikowa et al. 1993). They may have also used the grinding stones that have been found in abundance at these sites to process grain. By the sixth millennium B.C., the Nabta Playa folk herded domestic cattle, sheep, and goats. The cattle were probably kept mainly for milk and blood, rather than meat (Wendorf and Schild 1984, 1994). Some scholars believe they were herded as early as 8000 B.C., but others reject this very early date (Gautier 1987; Muzzolini 1993; Wendorf and Schild 1994).

Livestock raising was gradually adopted by various groups of hunter-gathers in the Sahara and surrounding regions. Eventually pastoralism, combined with the gathering of wild plants, became a common pattern across North Africa, persisting in some areas until Roman conquerors introduced farming (Muzzolini 1993). In fact, in some regions of the desert, pastoralism and plant gathering are still practiced, although by 3,000 to 4,000 years ago, much of the Sahara had become far too arid to support any life (Grove 1993). It is believed that the African cereals, such as millet and sorghum, were domesticated in the Sahel, but little archaeological evidence of these plants has been collected (Harlan 1992). In contrast, the Egyptian Nile Valley has yielded a rich archaeological record of food and diet.

Nile Valley Hunter-Gatherers

Just off the Nile Valley in Wadi Kubbaniya, investigation of a series of 18,000-year-old camps has revealed one of the most detailed records of a hunting and gathering diet in the Old World (Wendorf and Schild 1989). Root foods from wetland plants, such as tubers, rhizomes, corms of sedges, rushes, and cattails, were dietary staples. The most important of these was purple nutgrass *(Cyperus rotundus)* (Hillman, Madeyska, and Hather 1989), which grows abundantly in wet ground and can be easily harvested with a digging stick. Young tubers are simply prepared by rubbing off the outer skin and roasting. Although older nutgrass tubers become woody and bitter with toxic alkaloids, grinding and washing renders them palatable. All of the archaeological specimens were found charred, suggesting roasting as the method for preparing young tubers. Aging tubers were probably prepared with the grinding stones found scattered across the Kubbaniyan sites (Hillman et al. 1989). Root foods were abundant through the fall and winter but became woody and eventually inedible by summer. Seeds of wetland plants helped fill the gap, but during the summer, the Nile's annual inundation restricted plant foods to wild dates and dom (or doom) palm fruits (Hillman et al. 1989).

The flood also brought catfish, the main source of animal protein for the Kubbaniyans. Catfish would have been exceptionally easy to catch at the onset of the inundation, when they spawned (Gautier and van Neer 1989). As the Nile waters moved across the floodplain, catfish would move to shallow water, where they congregated in dense masses and where they were doubtless readily taken with baskets, nets, spears, clubs, and even by hand. At the Kubbaniyan campsites, catfish were prepared for storage by drying or smoking after their heads had been removed. The vast quantities of catfish bones that littered the campsites suggest that they may have been eaten for some months after having been caught. Fish were supplemented with migratory waterfowl and small quantities of gazelle, hartebeest, and aurochs (Gautier and van Neer 1989).

The Nilotic adaptation, focused on root foods and catfish, appears to have persisted up until the beginnings of agriculture in Egypt, though the scant record of diet throughout these millennia does not provide incontrovertible evidence for either stability or change (Wetterstrom 1993). There are clues, however. Fishing gear and catfish bones are common at late hunter-gatherer sites. Fishing may have become even more important in the diet as fishing techniques apparently improved. Three fish of the deep Nile channel (Nile perch, *Bagrid,* and *Synodontes*) became common at sites after about 9,000 to 10,000 years ago (Neer 1989). The bones of aurochs, hartebeest, and gazelle indicate that they were the most abundant mammals. Occasional finds of other animals, such as hippopotamus or wild sheep, suggest rare catches.

Evidence of plant use for this period in the Nile Valley has not been collected systematically except at one site – a camp in the Fayum. Here, seeds of wetland plants were recovered, but no root foods were found, probably because preservation was poor (Wetterstrom 1993). The only other clue to the use of root foods is the fact that many sites during this period were located in ideal situations for collecting wetland tubers – next to embayments where the marshlike conditions necessary for wetland plants would have prevailed.

The Early Farmers of Egypt

The earliest traces of domestic plants and animals in Egypt are dated to roughly 5000 B.C. at a series of campsites in the Fayum Depression and in the oldest level of Merimde, a site on the western edge of the delta (Wetterstrom 1993). The Fayum data suggest that local forager groups adopted a few domestic crops and livestock but continued subsisting on wild plants and animals (Caton-Thompson and Gardiner 1934). Merimde, slightly younger than the early Fayum sites, may have been farther along in this transition. Although the settlement was probably only used seasonally, livestock bones found there are far more abundant than those of wild fauna (Driesch and Boessneck 1985). At this point, however, crops may not have supplied the bulk of the plant foods, as the facilities necessary for storing harvests were very limited (Wetterstrom 1993).

It is not clear when ancient Egyptians finally crossed the threshold from foraging to farming, shifting the balance in their diet from wild products to crops and livestock, but this appears to have occurred within a few centuries after domesticates were taken into the economy. Before 4400 B.C., Merimde had become a substantial village with abundant settlement debris and capacious storage facilities, while similar sites began to appear elsewhere, first in the north and later in the south. By 4000 to 3800 B.C., full-time farmers lived in permanent villages in the south as well as the north (Wetterstrom 1993).

The Near Eastern crop complex was the source of Egypt's first domesticates, and it formed the core of the agricultural economy through later periods (emmer wheat, six-row barley, lentils, peas, and flax, along with sheep, goats, cattle, and pigs). All of these, except perhaps cattle, probably came to Egypt from the Levant by way of the Sinai. As noted, cattle could have been independently domesticated in North Africa. The Near Eastern crops, all adapted to the Mediterranean climate, were planted in the fall after the annual flood had receded. As in the Near East, domesticated crops and livestock probably evened out the large seasonal fluctuations in the diet. Stored food may also have reduced the impact of year-to-year variations in Nile floods.

After Egyptians had become dependent on farming, they doubtless continued to supplement their diet with wild foods (Wetterstrom 1993). Fish were an important resource in many communities year-round, as were migratory waterfowl in the winter months. Larger animals, like gazelle, hippopotamus, and crocodile, occasionally show up among archaeological remains. But hunting was probably a rare adventure by this time. Where bone remains have been collected, wild fauna are extremely uncommon, as is hunting gear.

The archaeological evidence for wild plant foods is also unfortunately very limited. A small number of types have been recovered from archaeological sites, including the fruits of Christ's-thorn *(Zizyphus spina-christi)*, sycamore fig *(Ficus sycamorus)*, dom palm *(Hyphaene thebiaca)*, and balanites *(Balanites aegyptiaca)*, which has an edible oil in its seed. The small nutlike tubers of nutgrass *(Cyperus esculentus)* have been recovered from a variety of contexts: burials, inside a pot at a settlement, and from the stomach of a body mummified by the desert sands. This sedge, related to the *Cyperus* eaten at Wadi Kubbaniya, has been cultivated for its tubers since pharaonic times (Täckholm and Drar 1950). Seeds of grasses, sedges, vetches, and other wild plants have also been found at pre-Dynastic sites, although it is not clear if these were all used as foods. A variety of wild plants that do not preserve very well, if at all, were probably also gathered, including leafy vegetables and the stalk and rhizome of papyrus that we know were eaten in later periods (Täckholm and Drar 1950).

How prehistoric Egyptians prepared these foods and combined them into meals is very difficult to determine. Without the texts or representations of foods, so abundant in later periods, pre-Dynastic foodways must be inferred from a meager archaeological record. Cuts of meat – ribs, blades, legs – found in pre-Dynastic burial pots (Brunton 1928, 1937) hint at simple cooking techniques: boiling in pots or roasting over a fire. Headless remains of fish found in pots at settlements (Brunton 1928) suggest that fish were boiled after beheading. Fish may have also been smoked for storage as in earlier times, but there is no clear evidence of this.

Perhaps the easiest way to use cereals is in porridge, and this dish was probably on the early Egyptian farmer's menu. Bread is another simple way to turn grain into food. There is abundant documentation of bread in the Pharaonic Period, but for prehistoric periods, the evidence is limited to coarse loaves found in graves and settlement sites. At one site, a charred piece of bread was made of flour described as "more crushed than ground grain" (Debono 1948: 568). Though the pre-Dynastic breads seem crude, some may have been leavened with yeast, as they are porous (Brunton 1928). This would not necessarily have required any sophisticated understanding of baking techniques; a simple sourdough can easily be produced if flour and water are left to sit and collect wild yeast from the air. Fermentation could also have been readily discovered when grain and water or fruit juices were allowed to sit for a while. Egyptians certainly realized early the potential of fermentation, as attested to by traces of beer dregs found in the bottoms of vessels (Lucas and Harris 1962; Helck 1975a). Beginning around 3500 to 3400 B.C., formal brewery installations appeared at a number of sites (Geller 1989), associated with increasing economic specialization in Egypt.

Like Mesopotamia before it, Egypt, after the mid–fourth millennium B.C., was transformed from a society of simple autonomous villages into an organized, hierarchical state. In southern Egypt, burials showed marked differences in wealth and status among different groups, as well as individuals (Trigger 1983, Bard 1994). Large centers with temple and palace complexes and industrial and residential areas began to appear in southern Egypt. By around 3100 B.C., a centralized state had emerged with domain over the whole Nile Valley from the delta south to the First Cataract near Aswan (Bard 1994).

Pharaonic Egypt

The Pharaonic Period in Egypt, which spanned nearly 3,000 years, was an extraordinarily stable, conservative era (Map V.A.1.). From the beginning, a strong centralized government ruled Egypt as a single polity. The reign of the pharaohs was disrupted only three times when the power of that government broke down as a result of civil war or foreign invasion. Following these three so-called "intermediate" periods between the Old, Middle, and New Kingdoms and the Late Period, the central government was reestablished (Table V.A.2.).

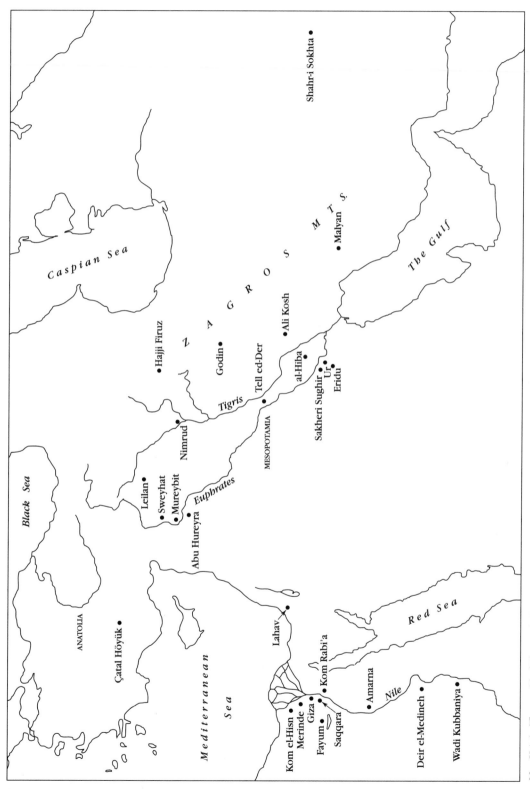

Map V.A.1. The world of Pharaonic Egypt.

Table V.A.2. *Pharaonic Egypt*

Period	Dynasties	Dates
Early Dynastic	1–2	c. 3100–2686 B.C.
Old Kingdom	3–6	c. 2686–2181 B.C.
First Intermediate	7–10	c. 2181–2040 B.C.
Middle Kingdom	11–12	c. 2133–1786 B.C.
Second Intermediate	13–17	c. 1786–1567 B.C.
New Kingdom	18–20	c. 1567–1085 B.C.
Third Intermediate	21–25	c. 1085–664 B.C.
Late Dynastic	26–31	c. 664–332 B.C.

Source: Bienkowski and Tooley (1995), p. 16.

Like early Mesopotamian civilization, pharaonic Egypt had a complex economic and social organization. People were divided by wealth, class, and occupation. Whereas the pharaoh, a divine king, presided at the top of the hierarchy, most of the people belonged to the lowest classes, working in myriad trades and as farmers and laborers (O'Connor 1983). In theory, the pharaoh owned all of Egypt; in practice, much of the land was held by the crown, but there were also large private estates. Crown-land harvests and taxes in kind from private lands supported the state bureaucracy, the military, and the conscripted laborers. Some land was also held as trusts, which supplied food to mortuary cults and temples (O'Connor 1983; Trigger 1983).

Pharaonic foods and diet are documented by a wealth of sources. These include artistic depictions in tombs, food offerings and offering lists in tombs and temples, tomb models, texts, and archaeological remains (Helck 1975b). Artistic depictions of everyday life, including food preparation, are common in Old and Middle Kingdom tombs, but less common in those of the New Kingdom. They are a rich source of information but can be difficult to interpret, as Egyptians tended to use a highly standardized iconography (Weeks 1979; Samuel 1989, 1993a, 1993b, 1994). Tomb models, most frequent in Middle Kingdom contexts, pose some of the same problems. Offerings and offering lists present a selective set of foods, the significance of which may elude present-day observers (Weeks 1979). Texts dealing with economic matters are abundant for the New Kingdom but less common for earlier periods. In addition, many words in the texts, including names of foods, are not yet understood (Janssen 1975).

Popular tales from the Middle and New Kingdoms offer clues to diet, but they are limited in scope. Archaeological data provide actual evidence of foods, allowing proper taxonomic identification in many cases, and may be useful in refining insights gained from textual sources and representations in tombs. Unfortunately, for the Pharaonic Period most archaeological material comes from tomb and temple contexts, with very little recovered from settlements. Other kinds of archaeological evidence, such as ovens, bakeries, and hearths, indicate something of

food processing and preparation, but the precise ways in which they were used is not always apparent. Recently, archaeologists have tried to test insights and theories gained from tomb depictions and other evidence by experimenting with baking, milling, and brewing techniques (Samuel 1989, 1993a, 1993b, 1994; Lehner 1994, 1997).

What emerges from the assorted lines of evidence is that all members of Egyptian society shared the same basic foods, with the upper strata having access to larger quantities and greater variety. At the core of the ancient Egyptian diet were bread and beer, consumed as staples by pharaoh and peasant alike throughout pharaonic history. Indeed, bread and beer were the basic wages, along with oils, grain, and clothing, paid to workmen on public and private projects (Eyre 1987). They were also the foods mentioned most often in popular tales, such as in the Middle Kingdom "Tale of the Eloquent Peasant" (Darby, Ghalioungui, and Grivetti 1977). As the hero set out on a trip, he commanded his wife, "[Y]ou shall make for me the six measures of barley into bread and beer for every day on which [I shall be traveling]" (Simpson 1973: 31).

Bread and beer were also fit for a king, however. An economic text from the Thirteenth Dynasty recorded a daily delivery of 1,630 loaves and 130 jugs of beer to the king's court (Scharff 1922). Bread and beer were also delivered to the temples every day and were viewed as essentials for the afterlife. The elite placed offerings of bread and beer in their tombs and enumerated them on offering lists. For example, Pharaoh Tutankhamen's tomb was stocked with bread (Hepper 1990).

Bread was produced in modest village kitchens (Janssen 1975) and in the large "commissaries" of elite households, the court, temples, and civic projects (Helck 1975b; Samuel 1993a, 1993b). Whereas the village breads that have been recovered are simple round loaves baked in an oven (Darby et al. 1977), professional bakers used a variety of techniques. Ceramic molds, which first appeared in late pre-Dynastic times, were commonly employed in the Old and Middle Kingdoms to bake offering breads and probably also rations for workmen (Jacquet-Gordon 1981; Lehner 1994). These coarse, thick-walled molds, shaped like flowerpots, were used as a kind of portable oven for baking in open pits (Lehner 1994). By the time of the New Kingdom, molded breads appear to have been made for special purposes and were baked in ovens in long, narrow, cylindrical molds (Samuel 1989, 1993b).

In addition to the mold-made loaves, a wide assortment of other breads and cakes were prepared for the temple and for the elite, employing a variety of techniques, temperatures, and grains (Drenkhahn 1975; Wild 1975; Samuel 1994). This was especially true during the New Kingdom, when loaf shapes proliferated; tomb art depicts spirals, cows, human figures, and other fanciful forms (Wreszinski 1926). Forty different kinds of breads and cakes were known at this time, compared to about a dozen in the Old Kingdom (Wild 1975). Emmer flour appears to have been the main ingredient in Egyptian bread, but other ingredients were also used (Grüss 1932; Täckholm, Täckholm, and Drar 1941), such as barley flour, ground nutgrass *(Cyperus esculentus)* tubers (Wilson 1988b), and sprouted wheat, which gave bread a slightly sweet flavor (Samuel 1994). Bakers sometimes added honey, dates, figs, and other fruits (Wilson 1988a; Samuel 1993a). For example, bread found in Tutankhamen's tomb was flavored with Christ's-thorn fruits (Hepper 1990).

Like bread, beer was brewed in modest households and in commissaries. Little is known of home-brewed beer, but breweries are frequently depicted in tomb scenes and models (Montet 1925). Archaeological traces of them have been found at a number of sites, as have vats and jars with beer residues (Lutz 1922; Lucas and Harris 1962; Helck 1975a; Geller 1992a, 1992b). The brewing process carried on at these ancient breweries, however, has not been well understood (Nims 1958; Geller 1992a; Samuel 1993a). The depictions are often ambiguous and the texts accompanying them subject to various interpretations because of difficulties in translating the language.

Delwen Samuel (1996) sidestepped these problems by turning to the direct evidence of brewing – ancient beer dregs and brewing by-products from the New Kingdom. Using scanning electron microscopy, she examined the microscopic structure of the starch granules in the residues and determined the processes they were subject to while being transformed into beer. It appears that Egyptians prepared grains intended for brewing in several different ways. After the grain was malted, or sprouted, some of the moist malt was heated while the rest was dried gently. The latter would have provided active enzymes for breaking down starch granules into simple sugars, which would support the yeast or lactic acid that is essential for producing alcohol. The roasted malted grains would have imparted a pleasant flavor and yielded a gelatinized starch that would be particularly susceptible to enzymatic attack. In addition, unsprouted, cooked grains may also have been used to make some beers. A large variety of named beers may have been produced by using different kilning and cooking techniques to prepare malted or unsprouted grains prior to brewing (Samuel 1996).

Both emmer and barley were used for beer in institutional breweries (Samuel 1996). In modest households, though, barley seems to have been the choice for brewing; as suggested in the "Tale of the Eloquent Peasant" and the evidence at Deir el-Medineh, a New Kingdom artisans' village, beer was brewed from barley rations (Lucas and Harris 1962; Janssen 1975). Bread, which has long been regarded as an essential ingredient of Egyptian brewing (Faltings 1991), played no role in these beers, according to the evidence that Samuel examined. As for flavorings in ancient Egyptian beer, there is little substantial evidence (Samuel 1996), although dates have often been propounded as a basic ingredient (Faltings 1991). As for Old Kingdom brewing techniques, Samuel's findings for the New Kingdom may well apply. No comparable studies have been conducted on beer dregs of the former period, and the archaeological evidence poses the ambiguities noted.

While bread and beer were basic subsistence to ancient Egyptians, vegetables and fruits were apparently regarded as above the level of basic needs. They were sometimes distributed as wages but were also depicted in market scenes, indicating that they could have been acquired through barter (Eyre 1994). The lower classes probably saw only the most common fruits and vegetables. The high labor costs of watering fruits and vegetables would have put many of them out of the reach of the poor (Eyre 1994). For the elite, on the other hand, "a variety and abundance of fresh produce was the mark of a luxury diet, emphasized by the elaboration of the fruits and vegetables recorded as offerings on the walls of tombs and temples" (Eyre 1994: 73).

Common vegetables in ancient Egypt included lettuce, leeks, onions, garlic, cucumbers, and radishes (Helck 1975b). Other names are listed in texts, but they have not yet been translated (Janssen 1975). How vegetables were prepared is not clear; they are shown as fresh produce in temple and tomb depictions. For lower classes, vegetables probably served mainly as condiments, as suggested by a New Kingdom tomb scene in which a workmen eats a lunch of bread, cucumber, and onion (Wilson 1988a).

The lower classes may have also supplemented their diet with wild plants. A host of weedy plants found in the fields and gardens, such as amaranth, chenopod, knotweed, sheep's sorrel, and wild grasses, could have been used as potherbs and grains. Their seeds have been found in settlement sites, such as Kom el-Hisn, an Old Kingdom community in the delta (Moens and Wetterstrom 1988), and Kom Rabi'a, a Middle and New Kingdom artisans' village at Memphis (Murray 1993), but it is not known for certain that these were actually consumed; many probably arrived at settlements as contaminants of cereal harvests. Still, many of these herbs have edible greens and/or seeds, which, ethnographic accounts indicate, have been used by others as foods (Fernald and Kinsey 1958; Nicolaisen 1963; Goodman and Hobbs 1988; Harlan 1989; Facciola 1990).

A number of fruits were known in ancient Egypt. Starting in the Old Kingdom with a short list – sycamore fig, dom palm, balanites, date, Christ's-thorn, and grape – the assortment grew as new types were introduced. Early additions were the true fig *(Ficus carica)*, melon *(Cucumis melo)*, persea, and a small watermelon *(Citrullus lunatus)* cultivated for its seeds (Germer 1985). Later, cordia *(Cordia myxa)*, pomegranate, and olive were adopted. During the

New Kingdom, exotic tropical fruits, such as grewia *(Grewia tenex),* were imported, as were pinenuts and almonds (Hepper 1990).

For peasants, the most important fruits were probably those that grew in Egypt with little or no care, such as Christ's-thorn, sycamore fig, and dom palm, as they would have been relatively cheap. Pomegranate, grape, and olive, on the other hand, all require tending and watering and were probably the prerogative of the elite. In tomb paintings and reliefs, fruits were usually displayed in large, overflowing baskets, perhaps to be consumed fresh, but fruits were also enjoyed dried, or cooked, and used as ingredients in other dishes. At Saqqara, a funerary meal laid out in a Second Dynasty tomb belonging to an elderly woman included plain Christ's-thorn berries placed on a plate and figs (probably *Ficus sycamorus*) prepared as a stew (Emery 1962). Fruits, particularly grapes, were also used to prepare wines imbibed by the elite (Janssen 1975). Wine production, which required substantial labor and skill, took place primarily in the delta and oases. But wine was also imported from Palestine, starting, perhaps, as early as pre-Dynastic times (Stager 1992). Often listed as an offering, wine was frequently depicted in New Kingdom funerary banquet scenes and was included in the funerary meal at Saqqara just discussed (Emery 1962).

Animal products were highly valued in the ancient Egyptian diet and together constituted the third most frequently mentioned food item in popular tales, after bread and beer (Darby et al. 1977). But they were not considered basic for subsistence, as indicated by the fact that meat was not given as rations. Market scenes in tombs show peasants buying pieces of meat through barter (Harpur 1987). For the well-to-do, meat figures prominently in tomb scenes, offering lists, and actual food offerings in tombs. The Saqqara funerary meal included four plates of meat out of a total of twelve dishes (Emery 1962).

Cattle were the most highly valued livestock in ancient Egypt, serving as draft animals and sacrificial beasts, as well as a source of food. Associated with the bovine deity Hathor (a mother goddess), they were considered sacred. Costly to raise, cattle were the premier choice for sacrifice at temples and tombs. Countless tomb paintings and reliefs show scenes of cattle husbandry, sacrificial processions, and the sacrifice of young, well-fed oxen. Beef consumption was almost certainly a prerogative of the elite, and the priests who butchered the cattle may have eaten the largest share (Darby et al. 1977). At the pyramid complex of Giza, for example, cattle bones from animals under two years of age predominate among the faunal remains (Redding 1992). The "middle classes," however, were not entirely excluded from enjoying beef. At Deir el-Medineh, cattle were delivered for feast days and periodically at other times for butchering, providing an occasional, but not rare, treat for the king's artisans (Janssen 1975).

For the lowest classes, beef was probably an extremely rare luxury. At Kom el-Hisn, for example, there is almost no bovine bone among the abundant faunal remains, although cattle were raised there (Moens and Wetterstrom 1988; Wenke 1990; Redding 1992). Kom el-Hisn peasants consumed only the occasional elderly or very young animal that died of natural causes, although they raised cattle destined for sacrifice at major ceremonial centers, such as the pyramid complex at Giza (Redding 1992).

Small livestock (sheep, goat, and pig) were more important sources of protein for lower classes. Bones of sheep and goats are common at settlement sites (Redding 1992). At Kom el-Hisn, peasants may have maintained their own small flocks while raising sacrificial cattle (Redding 1992). Pig remains are even more abundant at Kom el-Hisn and other settlement sites, such as the workmen's village at Amarna (Hecker 1982). Richard W. Redding (1991) proposes that peasants in rural areas raised small numbers of pigs for their own consumption, particularly in marginal regions where grain agriculture was not important.

Small livestock apparently played a minor role in the diet of the well-to-do. Large herds of sheep and goat were kept primarily for wool, hair, and milk. They were seldom depicted as sacrificial animals or placed in tombs as offerings. On the other hand, the Saqqara funerary repast did include a pair of kidneys from a small domestic animal (Emery 1962), and texts indicate that goats were occasionally sacrificed for certain festivals (Darby et al. 1977).

Relatively little is known about how meat was prepared, but food offerings placed in tombs during the Old Kingdom provide clues. Ribs and legs of beef found in the Saqqara funerary meal were most likely boiled or roasted. A dish that could not be identified (perhaps a stew) included ribs of beef among its ingredients (Emery 1962). A kitchen scene from a Fifth Dynasty tomb shows a cook cutting chunks of ox meat into pieces that were placed in a large cauldron. The hieroglyphic label underneath reads "cooking meat" (Hayes 1953: 97). Texts and a few tomb scenes indicate that beef was roasted as well (Darby et al. 1977).

While domestic livestock played an important role in ancient Egyptian life, the major sources of animal protein for rich and poor appear to have been fish and wild fowl. Both were abundant, and because little investment was required to produce them, they were probably inexpensive, compared with domestic animals. Texts from Deir el-Medineh indicate that they were very cheap at the time (Nineteenth Dynasty), with fish nearly as cheap as bread and beer (Janssen 1975). Fish are often shown in market scenes being purchased by barter (Eyre 1987). At Deir el-Medineh, fish were apparently a major source of protein, because they were distributed as rations (Janssen 1975). At Kom Rabi'a, abundant fish bones suggest that fish were an important source of food there as well (Ghaleb 1993).

As virtually the entire population lived close to the Nile waters, nearly everyone would have had some access to fish, at least during the flood season.

Poor Egyptians would, likewise, have had access to waterfowl during the winter migration. Fish and fowl were also common foods of the elite, who included them in tomb offerings and, particularly during the Old Kingdom, depicted fishing and fowling on their tomb walls (Montet 1925; Harpur 1987). Tomb scenes of food preparation indicate that fish were usually sun dried, pickled, or salted, whereas fowl was commonly roasted on a spit (Montet 1925). Wild fowl were also kept and fattened for consumption. The funerary meal from the Saqqara tomb included a cooked fish, cleaned, dressed, and beheaded, as well as a pigeon "stew" (Emery 1962).

Wild mammals were another potential source of meat, but hunting, already on the decline during the pre-Dynastic Period, had become an insignificant source of food by Old Kingdom times. At settlement sites, bones of wild mammals are rare; at Kom el-Hisn, for example, gazelle and hartebeest accounted for only 3 percent of the total faunal remains (Wenke 1990).

The traditional "poor man's meat" – pulses – were probably eaten by most of the people of ancient Egypt, although there is scant documentation. Pulses do not appear as tomb offerings or art, nor are they mentioned with any frequency in texts. But there are scattered archaeological finds, hinting at their importance. Lentils, for example, occur frequently in Tutankhamen's tomb as a contaminant of baskets of food offerings, suggesting that they were a common crop in ancient Egypt (Vartavan 1990, 1993). At Giza, lentils were found in trash left by workmen (Wetterstrom unpublished data). In Zoser's Third Dynasty tomb at Saqqara, lentils occurred in straw fill (Lauer, Täckholm, and Åberg 1950). They are also common in Middle and New Kingdom deposits at Kom Rabi'a (Murray 1993).

Records of other pulses in Egypt are few (scattered reports of lupine and fava beans [see, for example, Germer 1988]). Peas occasionally appear in archaeological contexts, such as Kom el-Hisn (Moens and Wetterstrom 1988). Chickpeas were apparently introduced in New Kingdom times; a few occurred in Tutankhamen's tomb as contaminants (Vartavan 1990, 1993). They are mentioned in texts from the Eighteenth Dynasty on but do not occur as offerings.

Dietary oil was considered an essential food, as indicated by the fact that it was among the rations allotted. Flaxseeds, castor beans, moringa nuts *(Moringa aptera)*, olives, and, in later periods, sesame and safflower were all sources of oil (Germer 1985). Sesame seeds occur as offerings in Tutankhamen's tomb (Vartavan 1990), but they were not restricted to the elite; at Deir el-Medineh, artisans were given rations of sesame oil (Janssen 1975). In contrast, olive oil, most of which was imported from Palestine beginning in pre-Dynastic times (Stager 1992), was food for the elite.

The first cultivated spice found in Egypt is fenugreek, dated to 3000 B.C. (Renfrew 1973). From the New Kingdom on, and perhaps earlier, a wider range of seasonings was available in Egypt. In Tutankhamen's tomb, black cumin *(Nigella sativa)* and coriander occurred frequently as contaminants among baskets of foods, suggesting that they were grown widely and, therefore, were popular condiments (Vartavan 1990). Dill and cumin were also known in New Kingdom Egypt (Germer 1985). How these seasonings were used is not known, as recipe texts from ancient Egypt have yet to be found.

Honey and fruits were the only sweeteners known in ancient Egypt. In the Old Kingdom, honey, a scarce and costly resource, was under Pharaoh's control. Still expensive by the Middle Kingdom, honey was a frequent offering in private tombs and was employed extensively in temple rituals (Kueny 1950). It is unlikely that lower classes ever saw honey, relying instead on fruits and fruit juices as sweeteners. Sweetened breads and flavored beers, however, were probably a rare treat among the poorest classes.

During the 3,000 years of pharaonic history, it appears that the diet changed slowly, showing great conservatism and stability, like other aspects of Egyptian culture. The most visible changes relate to the introduction of new crops, new technologies, and new imports. Although the core of the agricultural system remained unchanged, with emmer wheat and barley the dominant crops, improvements in water management made it possible to grow fruits and vegetables in orchards and plantations (Eyre 1994) and, probably, to raise many of the new introductions, such as olives. While bread and beer retained their place as staples, baking and brewing technologies became more sophisticated.

Changes in the diet and the rewards of new technologies were probably not universally experienced. Initially, the diets of rich and poor were likely not vastly different. The elite would have had access to greater quantities of food, particularly meat, and sole access to a few costly goods, such as wine and olive oil. The elite may also have eschewed some low-status foods, such as pulses. But by New Kingdom times, and perhaps earlier, the gulf between rich and poor diets may have expanded into a chasm. The upper classes, undoubtedly, had greater access, and in some cases exclusive access, to new crops and imports, such as pine nuts, almonds, and pomegranates. In addition, tomb art and textual evidence suggest an elaboration of cooking techniques among the well-to-do during the New Kingdom.

Conclusion

In this chapter we have traced the history of food and diet over a heterogeneous territory and through a long time period that extended from the end of the Stone Age to the first civilizations. This era saw what are arguably the most significant changes ever to occur in the human diet, establishing the food patterns that still sustain people today.

With the adoption of farming and herding, peoples in the Near East and Egypt abandoned their diverse hunting-gathering diet and came to rely on the Near Eastern complex of domesticated plants and animals. After the shift to agriculture, both areas followed similar cultural trajectories, which involved the development of larger and more complex communities and, eventually, the emergence of civilizations. In both regions, improvements in food production and food storage technologies led to surplus accumulation and permitted the growth of large, dense populations and urban centers.

With the advent of complex society, people no longer had equal access to all types of food. An elite class ultimately controlled the production and distribution of much of the food supply. Some foods even became their sole prerogative, particularly exotic imports and those requiring extensive labor to produce. Most of the population, however, subsisted mainly on grain and grain products as earned wages in kind. In both Egypt and the Near East, the diet was based on plants, primarily cereal products like bread and beer, supplemented with vegetables, fish, and meat. For the lower classes, meat was probably a rare commodity except for the pigs that households could raise without interference from state authorities. Yet, although Egypt and the Near East followed similar social trajectories and shared the same core diet, they developed their own distinctive cuisines. Today much of the world shares that same core diet based on the Near Eastern domesticates, and variations on it are still developing.

Naomi F. Miller
Wilma Wetterstrom

Bibliography

Bard, Kathryn. 1994. The Egyptian Predynastic: A review of the evidence. *Journal of Field Archaeology* 21: 265–88.

Bender, Barbara. 1978. Gatherer-hunter to farmer: A social perspective. *World Archaeology* 10: 204–22.

Bienkowski, Piotr, and Angela M. J. Tooley. 1995. *Gifts of the Nile.* London.

Borowski, Oded. 1987. *Agriculture in Iron Age Israel.* Winona Lake, Ind.

Bottéro, Jean. 1985. The cuisine of ancient Mesopotamia. *Biblical Archaeologist* 48: 36–47.

1995. *Textes culinaires Mésopotamiens.* Winona Lake, Ind.

Brunton, Guy. 1928. The Badarian civilization, Part. I. In *The Badarian civilization and Predynastic remains near Badari,* ed. Guy Brunton and Gertrude Caton-Thompson, 1–68. London.

1937. *Mostagedda and the Tasian culture.* London.

Buitenhuis, Hijlke. 1990. Archaeozoological aspects of late Holocene economy and environment in the Near East. In *Man's role in the shaping of the eastern Mediter-*

ranean landscape, ed. S. Bottema, J. Entje-Neiborg, and W. van Zeist, 195–205. Rotterdam.

Caton-Thompson, Gertrude, and E. W. Gardiner. 1934. *The desert Fayum.* London.

Civil, M. 1964. A hymn to the beer goddess and a drinking song. In *Studies presented to A. Leo Oppenheim,* ed. Anon., 67–89. Chicago.

Colledge, Susan M. 1991. Investigations of plant remains preserved on epipalaeolithic sites in the Near East. In *The Natufian culture in the Levant,* ed. O. Bar-Yosef and F. R. Valla, 391–8. Ann Arbor, Mich.

Costantini, Lorenzo. N.d. Le piante. In *La città bruciata del deserto salato,* ed. Giuseppe Tucci, 159–228. Venice.

Darby, William J., Paul Ghalioungui, and Louis Grivetti. 1977. *Food: The gift of Osiris.* 2 vols. London and New York.

Davis, Simon J. M. 1984. The advent of milk and wool production in western Iran: Some speculations. In *Animals and archaeology: Early herders and their flocks,* ed. J. Clutton-Brock and C. Grigson, 265–78. Oxford.

Debono, Fernand. 1948. Helouan-el Omari: Fouilles du Service des Antiquités, 1943–1945. *Chronique d'Égypte* 21: 561–83.

Drenkhahn, Rosemarie. 1975. Brot. *Lexikon der Ägyptologie* 1: 871.

Driesch, Angela von den, and Joachim Boessneck. 1985. *Die Tierknochenfunde aus der neolithischen Siedlung von Merimde-Benisalame am westlichen Nildelta.* Deutsches Archäologisches Institut, Abteilung Kairo. Munich.

Ellison, Rosemary. 1981. Diet in Mesopotamia: The evidence of the barley ration texts c. 3000–1400 B.C. *Iraq* 43: 35–45.

1984. Methods of food preparation in Mesopotamia (c. 3000–600 B.C.). *Journal of the Economic History of the Orient* 27: 89–98.

Ellison, R., J. Renfrew, D. Brothwell, and N. Seeley. 1978. Some food offerings from Ur, excavated by Sir Leonard A. Woolley, and previously unpublished. *Journal of Archaeological Science* 5: 167–77.

Emery, W. B. A. 1962. *A funerary repast in an Egyptian tomb of the Archaic Period.* Leiden, the Netherlands.

Evin, J. 1995. Possibilité et nécessité de la calibration des datations C-14 de l'archéologie du proche-orient. *Paléorient* 21: 5–16.

Eyre, Christopher J. 1987. Work and the organization of work in the Old Kingdom. In *Labor in the ancient Near East,* ed. Marvin A. Powell, 5–47. New Haven, Conn.

1994. The water regime for orchards and plantations in pharaonic Egypt. *Journal of Egyptian Archaeology* 80: 57–80.

Facciola, Stephen. 1990. *Cornucopia: A sourcebook of edible plants.* Vista, Calif.

Faltings, Dina. 1991. Die Bierbrauerei in AR. *Zeitschrift für Ägyptische Sprache und Altertumskunde* 118: 104–16.

Fernald, Merrit L., and Alfred C. Kinsey. 1958. *Edible wild plants of eastern North America.* Revised by Reed C. Rollin. New York.

Flannery, Kent V. 1969. Origins and ecological effects of early domestication in Iran and the Near East. In *The domestication and exploitation of plants and animals,* ed. P. J. Ucko and G. W. Dimbleby, 73–100. Chicago.

1973. The origins of agriculture. *Annual Review of Anthropology* 2: 271–310.

Garrard, Andrew N. 1984. The selection of south-west Asian animal domesticates. In *Animals and archaeology 3. Early herders and their flocks,* ed. J. Clutton-Brock and C. Grigson, 117–39. Oxford.

Gautier, Achille. 1987. Prehistoric men and cattle in North Africa: A dearth of data and a surfeit of models. In *Pre-*

history of arid North Africa: Essays in honor of Fred Wendorf, ed. Angela E. Close, 163-87. Dallas, Tex.

Gautier, Achille, and Wim van Neer. 1989. Animal remains from the Late Paleolithic sequence at Wadi Kubbaniya. In *The Prehistory of Wadi Kubbaniya, Vol. 2, Palaeoeconomy, Environment and Stratigraphy,* ed. Angela E. Close, comp. Fred Wendorf and Romuald Schild, 119-58. Dallas, Tex.

Gelb, I. J. 1965. The ancient Mesopotamian ration system. *Journal of Near Eastern Studies* 24: 230-43.

Geller, Jeremy. 1989. Recent excavations at Hierakonpolis and their relevance to Predynastic production and settlement. *Cahier de recherches de l'Institut de Papyrologie et d'Égyptologie de Lille* 11: 41-52.

1992a. Bread and beer in fourth-millennium Egypt. *Food and Foodways* 5: 1-13.

1992b. From prehistory to history: Beer in Egypt. In *The followers of Horus: Studies dedicated to Michael Allen Hoffman.* Egyptian Studies Association Publication No. 2, ed. Renee Friedman and Barbara Allen, 19-26. Oxford.

Germer, Renate. 1985. *Flora des pharaonischen Ägypten.* Deutsches Archäologisches Institut, Abteilung Kairo, Sonderschrift 14. Munich.

1988. *Katalog der altägyptischen Pflanzenreste der Berliner Museen.* Wiesbaden.

Ghaleb, Barbara. 1993. Aspects of current archaeozoological research at the ancient Egyptian capital of Memphis. In *Biological anthropology and the study of ancient Egypt,* ed. V. Vivian Davies and Roxie Walker, 186-90. London.

Goodman, Steven M., and Joseph J. Hobbs. 1988. The ethnobotany of the Egyptian Eastern Desert: A comparison of common plant usage between two culturally distinct Bedoui groups. *Journal of Ethnopharmacology* 23: 73-89.

Gordon, Edmund I. 1959. *Sumerian proverbs.* Philadelphia, Pa.

Green, M. W., and H. J. Nissen. 1987. *Zeichenliste der archäischen Texte aus Uruk.* Berlin.

Grove, A. T. 1993. Africa's climate in the Holocene. In *The archaeology of Africa: Food, metal and towns,* ed. Thurstan Shaw, Paul Sinclair, Bassey Andah, and Alex Okpoko, 32-42. London.

Grüss, Johannes von. 1932. Untersuchung von Broten aus der ägyptischen Sammlung der staatlichen Museen zu Berlin. *Zeitschrift für Ägyptische Sprache und Altertumskunde* 68: 79-80.

Harlan, Jack. 1989. Wild-grass seed harvesting in the Sahara and the Sub-Sahara of Africa. In *Foraging and farming: The evolution of plant exploitation,* ed. D. R. Harris and G. C. Hillman, 79-98. London.

1992. *Crops and man.* Madison, Wis.

Harpur, Yvonne. 1987. *Decoration in Egyptian tombs of the Old Kingdom: Studies in orientation and scene content.* London.

Hassan, Fekri. 1985. A radiocarbon chronology of Neolithic and Predynastic sites in Upper Egypt and the Delta. *African Archaeological Review* 3: 95-116.

Hayes, William C. 1953. *The scepter of Egypt, Part I: From earliest times to the end of the Middle Kingdom.* New York.

Hecker, Howard M. 1982. A zooarchaeological inquiry into pork consumption in Egypt from prehistoric to New Kingdom times. *Journal of the American Research Center in Egypt.* 19: 59-71.

Helbaek, Hans. 1966. The plant remains from Nimrud. In *Nimrud and its remains,* Vol. 2, ed. M. E. L. Mallowan, 613-20. 3 vols. London.

Helck, Wolfgang. 1975a. Bier. *Lexikon der Ägyptologie* 1: 789-92.

1975b. Ernährung. *Lexikon der Ägyptologie* 1: 1267-71.

Hepper, F. Nigel. 1990. *Pharaoh's flowers: The botanical treasures of Tutankhamun.* London.

Hesse, Brian. 1995. Animal husbandry and human diet in the ancient Near East. In *Civilizations of the ancient Near East,* ed. J. Sasson, 203-22. New York.

Hillman, Gordon C., Susan M. Colledge, and David R. Harris. 1989. Plant food economy during the epipaleolithic period at Tell Abu Hureyra, Syria: Dietary diversity, seasonality, and modes of exploitation. In *Foraging and farming, the evolution of plant exploitation,* ed. D. R. Harris and G. C. Hillman, 240-68. London.

Hillman, Gordon C., Eva Madeyska, and Jonathan G. Hather. 1989. Wild plant foods and diet at Late Paleolithic Wadi Kubbaniya: The evidence from charred remains. In *The prehistory of Wadi Kubbaniya, Vol. 2, Palaeoeconomy, environment and stratigraphy,* ed. Angela E. Close, comp. Fred Wendorf and Romuald Schild, 159-242. Dallas, Tex.

Hoffner, Harry A. Jr. 1974. *Alimenta Hethaeorum; food production in Hittite Asia Minor.* New Haven, Conn.

Hole, F. 1984. A reassessment of the Neolithic revolution. *Paléorient* 19: 49-60.

Jacquet-Gordon, Helen. 1981. A tentative typology of Egyptian bread moulds. In *Studien zur altägyptischen Keramik,* ed. Dorothea Arnold, 11-24. Mainz.

Janssen, J. J. 1975. *Commodity prices from the Ramessid period: An economic study of the village of the necropolis workmen at Thebes.* Leiden, the Netherlands.

Kaplan, J. 1954. Two Chalcolithic vessels from Palestine. *Palestine Exploration Quarterly* 86: 97-100.

Köhler-Rollefson, I. 1988. The aftermath of the Levantine Neolithic revolution in the light of ecological and ethnographic evidence. *Paléorient* 14: 87-93.

Kueny, G. 1950. Scènes apicoles dans l'ancienne Égypte. *Journal of Near Eastern Studies* 9: 84-93.

Lauer, J. P., V. Laurent Täckholm, and E. Åberg. 1950. Les plantes découvertes dans les souterraines de l'enceinte du roi Zoser. *Bulletin de l'Institut d'Égypte* 32: 121-52.

Legge, Anthony J. 1975. Appendix B. The fauna of Tell Abu Hureyra: Preliminary analysis. *Proceedings of the Prehistoric Society* 41: 74-7.

Lehner, Mark. 1994. Giza. In *The Oriental Institute 1993-1994 Annual Report,* ed. William M. Sumner, 26-30. Chicago.

1997. Replicating an ancient bakery. *Archaeology* 30: 36.

Lucas, A., and H. J. Harris. 1962. *Ancient Egyptian materials and industries.* Third edition. London.

Lutz, H. F. 1922. *Viticulture and brewing in the ancient orient.* Leipzig.

Mason, Sarah. 1995. Acornutopia? Determining the role of acorns in past human subsistence. In *Food in antiquity,* ed. J. Wilkins, D. Harvey, and M. Dobson, 12-24. Exeter, England.

McGovern, Patrick E., Donald L. Glusker, Lawrence J. Exner, and Mary M. Voigt. 1996. Neolithic resinated wine. *Nature* 381: 480-1.

Mellaart, James. 1967. *Çatal Hüyük: A Neolithic town in Anatolia.* New York.

Michel, Rudolph H., Patrick E. McGovern, and Virginia R. Badler. 1993. The first wine and beer: Chemical detection of ancient fermented beverages. *Analytical Chemistry* 65: 408A-13A.

Miller, Naomi F. 1984. The use of dung as fuel: An ethnographic example and an archaeological application. *Paléorient* 10: 71-9.

1991. The Near East. In *Progress in Old World palaeoethnobotany,* ed. W. van Zeist, K. E. Behre, and K. Wasylikowa, 133-60. Rotterdam.

1996. Seed-eaters of the ancient Near East: Human or herbivore? *Current Anthropology* 37: 521-8.

Moens, Marie-Francine, and Wilma Wetterstrom. 1988. The agricultural economy of an Old Kingdom town in Egypt's West Delta: Insights from the plant remains. *Journal of Near Eastern Studies* 47: 159-73.

Montet, Pierre. 1925. *Scènes de la vie privée dans les tombeaux égyptiens de l'ancien empire.* Strasbourg.

Moore, Andrew M. T. 1995. The inception of potting in western Asia and its impact on economy and society. In *The emergence of pottery,* ed. W. K. Bennett and J. W. Hoopes, 39-53. Washington, D.C.

Mudar, Karen. 1982. Early Dynastic III animal utilization in Lagash: A report on the fauna of Tell al-Hiba. *Journal of Near Eastern Studies* 41: 23-34.

Murray, Mary Anne. 1993. Recent archaeobotanical research at the site of Memphis. In *Biological anthropology and the study of ancient Egypt,* ed. V. Vivian Davies and Roxie Walker, 165-8. London.

Muzzolini, A. 1993. The emergence of a food-producing economy in the Sahara. In *The archaeology of Africa: Food, metal and towns,* ed. Thurstan Shaw, Paul Sinclair, Bassey Andah, and Alex Okpoko, 227-39. London.

Neer, Wim van. 1989. Fishing along the prehistoric Nile. In *Late prehistory of the Nile Basin and the Sahara,* ed. L. Krzyzaniak and M. Kobusiewicz, 49-56. Poznan, Poland.

Nicolaisen, Johannes. 1963. *Ecology and culture of the pastoral Tuareg.* Nationalmuseets Skrifter Ethnografisk Raekke IX. Copenhagen.

Nims, Charles F. 1958. The bread and beer problem in the Moscow mathematical papyrus. *Journal of Egyptian Archaeology* 44: 56-65.

Nissen, Hans J., Peter Damerow, and Robert K. Englund. 1993. *Archaic bookkeeping,* trans. Paul Larsen. Chicago.

O'Connor, David. 1983. New Kingdom and Third Intermediate Period, 1552-664 B. C. In *Ancient Egypt: A social history,* ed. B. G. Trigger, B. J. Kemp, D. O'Connor, and A. B. Lloyd, 183-271. Cambridge.

Postgate, J. N. 1987. Notes on fruit in the cuneiform sources. *Bulletin on Sumerian Agriculture* 3: 115-44.

Potts, Daniel. 1984. On salt and salt gathering in ancient Mesopotamia. *Journal of the Economic and Social History of the Orient* 27: 225-71.

Powell, Marvin A. 1984. Sumerian cereal crops. *Bulletin on Sumerian Agriculture* 1: 48-72.

1995. Wine and the vine in ancient Mesopotamia: The cuneiform evidence. In *The origins and ancient history of wine,* ed. P. E. McGovern, S. J. Fleming, and S. H. Katz, 97-122. New York.

Raish, Carol. 1992. *Domestic animals and stability in prestate farming societies.* Oxford.

Redding, Richard W. 1991. The role of the pig in the subsistence system of ancient Egypt: A parable on the potential of faunal data. In *Animal use and culture change,* ed. P. J. Crabtree and K. Ryan, 20-30. MASCA Research Papers in Science and Archaeology 8, Supplement: 20-30. Philadelphia, Pa.

1992. Egyptian Old Kingdom patterns of animal use and the value of faunal data in modeling socioeconomic systems. *Paléorient* 18: 99-107.

1993. Subsistence security as a selective pressure favoring increasing cultural complexity. *Bulletin on Sumerian Agriculture* 7: 77-98.

Reiner, Erica, ed. 1980. *The Assyrian dictionary of the Oriental Institute of the University of Chicago,* Vol. 2. Chicago.

Renfrew, Jane. 1973. *Palaeoethnobotany.* New York.

Rosenberg, Michael, R. Mark Nesbitt, Richard W. Redding, and Thomas F. Strasser. 1995. Hallan Çemi Tepesi: Some preliminary observations concerning early Neolithic subsistence behaviors in eastern Anatolia. *Anatolica* 21: 1-12.

Samuel, Delwen. 1989. Their staff of life: Initial investigations of ancient Egyptian bread baking. *Amarna Reports* 5: 253-90.

1993a. Ancient Egyptian bread and beer: An interdisciplinary approach. In *Biological anthropology and the study of ancient Egypt,* ed. V. Vivian Davies and Roxie Walker, 156-64. London.

1993b. Ancient Egyptian cereal processing: Beyond the artistic record. *Cambridge Archaeological Journal* 3: 276-83.

1994. A new look at bread and beer. *Egyptian Archaeology: Bulletin of the Egypt Exploration Society* 4: 9-11.

1996. Archaeology of ancient Egyptian beer. *Journal of the American Society of Brewing Chemists* 54: 3-12.

Scharff, Alexander. 1922. Ein Rechnungsbuch des königlichen Hofes aus der 13. Dynastie (Papyrus Boulaq #18). *Zeitschrift für Ägyptische Sprache und Altertumskunde* 57: 53-8.

Selz, Gudrun. 1983. *Die Bankettszene, Entwicklung eines "überzeitlichen" Bildmotivs in Mesopotamien.* Wiesbaden.

Sherratt, Andrew. 1981. Plough and pastoralism: Aspects of the secondary products revolution. In *Pattern of the past,* ed. I. Hodder, G. Isaac, and N. Hammond, 261-305. Cambridge.

Simoons, Frederick J. 1979. Dairying, milk use, and lactose malabsorption in Eurasia: A problem in culture history. *Anthropos* 74: 61-80.

Simpson, William Kelly. 1973. *The literature of ancient Egypt.* New Haven, Conn.

Stager, Lawrence. 1992. The periodization of Palestine from Neolithic through Early Bronze times. In *Chronologies in Old World archaeology.* Third edition, ed. Robert W. Ehrich, 22-41. Chicago.

Stol, Marten. 1985. Beans, peas, lentils and vetches in Akkadian texts. *Bulletin on Sumerian Agriculture* 2: 127-39.

1987. Garlic, onion, leek. *Bulletin on Sumerian Agriculture* 3: 57-80.

1993. Milk, butter, and cheese. *Bulletin on Sumerian Agriculture* 7: 99-113.

Strommenger, Eva. N.d. *5000 years of the art of Mesopotamia.* New York.

Stuiver, M., B. Kromer, B. Becker, and C. W. Ferguson. 1986. Radiocarbon age calibration back to 13,300 years B.P. and the 14C age matching of the German oak and U.S. bristlecone pine chronologies. *Radiocarbon* 28: 969-79.

Täckholm, Vivi, and Mohammed Drar. 1950. *Flora of Egypt,* Vol. 2. Bulletin of the Faculty of Science 23. Cairo.

Täckholm, Vivi, Gunnar Täckholm, and Mohammed Drar. 1941. *Flora of Egypt,* Vol. 1. Bulletin of the Faculty of Science 17. Cairo.

Trigger, Bruce. 1983. The rise of Egyptian civilization. In *Ancient Egypt: A social history,* ed. B. G. Trigger, B. J. Kemp, D. O'Connor, and A. B. Lloyd, 1-70. Cambridge.

Vartavan, C. de. 1990. Contaminated plant-foods from the tomb of Tutankhamun: A new interpretative system. *Journal of Archaeological Science.* 17: 473-94.

1993. Analyse plurisystématique pour l'interprétation des restes végétaux de la tombe de Toutankhmon. *Annales de la Fondation Fyssen* 8: 9-22.

Voigt, Mary M. 1990. Reconstructing neolithic societies and economies in the Middle East: An essay. *Archaeomaterials* 4: 1-14.

Waetzoldt, H. 1985. Ölpflanzen und Pflanzenöle im 3. Jahrtausend. *Bulletin on Sumerian Agriculture* 2: 77-96.

1987. Knoblauch und Zwiebeln nach den Texten des 3 JT. *Bulletin on Sumerian Agriculture* 3: 23-56.

Wasylikova, K., J. R. Harlan, J. Evans, et al. 1993. Examination of botanical remains from early neolithic houses at Nabta Playa, Western Egypt, with special reference to sorghum grains. In *The archaeology of Africa: Food, metal and towns,* ed. Thurstan Shaw, Paul Sinclair, Bassey Andah, and Alex Okpoko, 154-64. London.

Weeks, Kent R. 1979. Egypt and the comparative study of early civilizations. In *Egyptology and the social sciences,* ed. Kent R. Weeks, 59-81. Cairo.

Wendorf, Fred, and Romuald Schild. 1984. Conclusions. In *Cattle-keepers of the eastern Sahara: The Neolithic of Bir Kiseiba.* ed. Angela E. Close, comp. Fred Wendorf and Romuald Schild, 404-28. Dallas, Tex.

1989. Summary and synthesis. In *The prehistory of Wadi Kubbaniya, Vol. 3, Late Paleolithic archaeology,* ed. Angela E. Close, comp. Fred Wendorf and Romould Schild, 768-824. Dallas, Tex.

1994. Are the early Holocene cattle in the eastern Sahara domestic or wild? *Evolutionary Anthropology* 3: 118-27.

Wenke, Robert. 1986. Old Kingdom community organization in the west Egyptian Delta. *Norwegian Archaeological Review* 19: 15-33.

1990. Excavations at Kom el-Hisn: The 1988 season. *Newsletter of the American Research Center in Egypt* 149: 1-6.

Wetterstrom, Wilma. 1993. Foraging and farming in Egypt: The transition from hunting and gathering to horticulture in the Nile Valley. In *The archaeology of Africa: Food, metal and towns,* ed. Thurstan Shaw, Paul Sinclair, Bassey Andah, and Alex Okpoko, 165-226. London.

Wild, Henri. 1966. Brasserie et panification au tombeau de Ti. *Bulletin de l'Institut Français d'Archéologie Orientale* 64: 95-120.

1975. Backen. *Lexikon der Ägyptologie* 1: 594-8. Wiesbaden.

Wilson, Hilary. 1988a. *Egyptian food and drink.* Aylesbury, England.

1988b. A recipe for offering loaves? *Journal of Egyptian Archaeology* 74: 214-17.

Wreszinski, Walter von. 1926. Bäckerei. *Zeitschrift für Ägyptische Sprache und Altertumskunde* 61: 1-15.

Zeder, Melinda A. 1991. *Feeding cities.* Washington, D.C.

1994. After the revolution: Post-Neolithic subsistence strategies in northern Mesopotamia. *American Anthropologist* 96: 97-126.

1995a. The role of pigs in Near Eastern subsistence from the vantage point of the southern Levant. In *Retrieving the past: Essays on archaeological research and methodology in honor of Gus van Beek,* ed. J. D. Seger, 297-312. Winona Lake, Ind.

1995b. The archaeobiology of the Khabur Basin. *Bulletin of the Canadian Society for Mesopotamian Studies* 29: 21-32.

Zeist, W. van. 1984. Palaeobotanical investigations of Tell ed-Der. In *Tell ed-Der IV,* ed. L. de Meyer, 119-43. Leuven, Belgium.

1988. Some aspects of early neolithic plant husbandry in the Near East. *Anatolica* 15: 49-67.

Zeist, W. van, and J. A. H. Bakker-Heeres. 1984. Archaeobotanical Studies in the Levant 3. Late paleolithic Mureybit. *Palaeohistoria* 26: 171-99.

1985. Archaeobotanical Studies in the Levant 4. Bronze Age sites on the north Syrian Euphrates. *Palaeohistoria* 27: 247-316.

Zeist, W. van and S. Bottema. 1991. Late Quaternary vegetation of the Near East. In *Beiheft zum Tübinger Atlas des vorderen Orients,* Reihe A nr. 18. Wiesbaden.

Zohary, Daniel, and Maria Hopf. 1993. *Domestication of plants in the Old World.* Second edition. Oxford.

Zohary, Michael. 1973. *Geobotanical foundations of the Middle East.* 2 vols. Stuttgart.

V.B

The History and Culture
of Food and Drink in Asia

V.B.1 ❧ The Middle East and South Asia

Although the regions we call the Middle East and South Asia constitute a very wide area, their collective culture has been shaped by a shared history from the conquest of Alexander the Great to the Islamic empires. The precepts of Islam have been adopted in most of the countries in the area under scrutiny, if not always by the majority, as in India. There are, therefore, many similarities in their cultures and especially in their preparation of foods. Each country, region, and town has its own cooking traditions, but it is easy to spy the similarities behind the differences.

This region of the world is socially traditional; therefore, women stay at home most of the time and are in charge of the kitchen. Food is often prepared in the company of other women in Muslim houses, which makes it a time for socializing. Professional cooks (always male) are employed for special occasions in wealthier homes.

The cooking is done mostly on a stove. The process is very long and slow, resulting in a very tender meat or vegetable, literally ready to disintegrate. The people of the Middle East and South Asia have no liking for red meat (even pieces of meat or kebabs for roasting are cooked previously or at least marinated).

Food is almost never cooked in water alone. Rather, it is first fried, then simmered or boiled, and finally enriched with fat. There is also a wide consumption of street food, fried or grilled. Savory pastries, such as *borek, samossa,* and *brik,* are popular.

Meat is an important item of the diet for those (except for the vegetarians) who can afford it, and it is used as often as possible, even as part of a stuffing or in a broth. Lamb is the favorite meat, although the less expensive chicken dominates in poorer houses. Because of the Islamic influence, pork is avoided, except by minorities, such as the Goanese Christians, for example.

The cookery is also characterized by the use of many pulses, clarified butter (*samn* or *ghee,* mainly from buffalo's milk), and fresh yoghurt (as a drink and a cooking liquid). Unlike in the Far East, milk, milk products, and milk sweets are important here, and all the people of the region rely on a basic cereal, mostly rice or wheat. Food is very colorful as well as flavorful because of the use of such spices as saffron and turmeric. Spices are used extensively, even if only in small quantities. There is a spice street in every bazaar in the Middle East and South Asia. All the countries of the region are on the same spice route, which begins in Asia, with the Middle East a conduit for spices on the way to Africa and Europe.

Scents are also typical of this exotic cookery: Rose, amber, musk, camphor, santal, orange blossom, jasmine, and orchid are used in many a sherbet and dish. People share a fondness for sour things: Lemon or lime, vinegar, tamarind, sumac, pomegranate juice, and sour cherries add zest to meat dishes.

Spices are also used for their assumed medicinal properties, and the composition and preparation of foods is often explained in terms of health needs created by climatic conditions. In fact, another similarity between the cultures of South Asia and the Middle East is a belief in medico-magic properties of food. This, in turn, encourages secrecy in cooking, and the preparation of aphrodisiacs and other potions at times tends to blur the tasks of cook and alchemist.

The History and Culture of Food in the Middle East

The Middle East encompasses a large area stretching from the Arabian Peninsula to Afghanistan and includes the border states of the eastern Mediterranean. It is divided into many countries: Turkey, Syria, Lebanon, Jordan, Israel, Egypt, Saudi Arabia, Iraq, and Iran. The people of the Middle East are of several racial types and have embraced different religions. Geographic and climatic conditions are extremely diverse in the region. Nonetheless, the Middle East can be described as a single cultural entity. Islam has played a unifying role in the area through the building of vast "Islamic" empires that rule over most of these people and the conversion of a vast majority of the population.

There is, therefore, a Middle Eastern civilization with a collection of several culinary traditions, each of which will be given due attention (although the food of the minorities of the region, Coptic, for example, or the cosmopolitan cuisine of Israel will be ignored for the sake of coherence). Overriding similarities in tastes and manners, however, will also be pointed out.

Before the Arrival of Islam

Long before dwellers in Europe could imagine the possibilities of fire, the civilizations of the Middle East had invented agriculture, cattle breeding, and numerous ways of preparing and enjoying foods.

Pre-Islamic Arabia. The diet of pre-Islamic Arabia was the typical diet of a pastoral people in a desert region. It was simple and monotonous, with the most important roles played by dairy foods. According to ancient poems and the *Koran,* milk, milk products, and dates were the main items of the diet. Camel milk was most frequently used, but goat and sheep milk were also available. The milk could be diluted with water and was used in the preparation of a sort of cheese and of clarified butter *(samn)* for cooking.

The oases provided the nomads with dates, which were sometimes the only food available. Dates supplied energy, were easy to carry, and, over time, acquired a symbolic value. They were served at festivals, and the Prophet Mohammed later stressed their importance by making them one of his favorite foods, especially for the breaking of fasts.

Meat was seldom eaten, except for festive occasions, when sheep were frequently consumed and especially appreciated for their fatty tails. Camels, sometimes slaughtered and their coagulated blood shaped into sausages to be cooked, were another source of animal protein. Beef, pork, or fowl were quite unknown. Hare, bustard, large lizards, and grasshoppers could become food in harsh environments.

Cereals were scarce. The Prophet ate cakes of coarse barley with a little vinegar, oil, and perhaps a few dates. Dried barley was also made into a meal that was easily cooked into a gruel with the addition of water and fat. Another type of gruel *(harira)* was prepared from flour cooked in milk. A richer gruel could be made with bran and meat.

A number of vegetables were also available throughout the settled communities of the desert. Cucumbers, vegetable marrows, beets, chicory, and olives were common, as well as leeks, onions, and garlic. Lemons, pomegranates, and grapes or raisins were the main fruits, although figs and apples are mentioned in some texts. By combining all these products, the Arabs could prepare a few elaborate dishes. *Tharid* was one: bread pieces soaked in a meat and vegetable broth. *Hayes* was another. Made of milk, butter, and dates, it is said to

have been another favorite of the Prophet. These dishes and the more common broths were quite bland. The nomads preferred to sell the spices they had rather than use them themselves. Imported wine was a luxury, but the Arabs were familiar with fermented drinks, prepared from dates, barley, honey, or raisins.

Pharaonic Egypt. Thanks to numerous archeological remains, it is possible to imagine how the kings and people of ancient Egypt would dine. Cattle and sheep were slaughtered in the palace and then might be roasted whole or grilled in pieces. Lamb chops were a delicacy, and fowl was also served, as were different types of bread and pastries. The food was seasoned with cream and, perhaps, imported olives from Greece. Lentils and fish constituted a simpler diet, and beverages consisted of beer, milk, and wine. Beer was prepared from the fermentation of barley, wheat, and dates. The country was so rich in wheat that during its Roman period (30 B.C. to A.D. 395) it became the empire's granary.

Ancient Mesopotamia. It was in ancient Mesopotamia that agriculture and cattle breeding were invented, and we can infer much about the diet of these early inventors from that of the people living in the region today. The staple food for this population of agriculturists was bread made of barley rather than wheat. Barley was often eaten in the form of gruel as well.

The banks of the Mediterranean are famous for their olives and grapes. The whole of the region that was once ancient Mesopotamia is very fertile: Cucumbers, turnips, onions, leeks, fennels, herbs, lentils, and chickpeas are among the vegetables grown. Many types of fruit can also be found, most importantly, dates, figs, and pomegranates. Fish is sometimes served, but meat is scarce. In the past, a sheep or goat was occasionally slaughtered for sacrifice or in honor of a guest. But as a rule, beef and pork, along with fowls and pigeons, were rarely eaten. Apart from pulses, most of the protein came from eggs, milk, and milk products, which included curd and cheese. Honey was and is a common treat. Olive and sesame oils are abundant. The common beverages were water, milk, or beer. The rich, however, enjoyed palm or grape wine.

Cooking was done on a stove. For the poor this consisted (and still consists) of a simple cavity, dug in the ground of a house or courtyard, and coated with clay in which embers were piled. These hearths are sometimes built in raised fashion along a wall, and some are ovens entirely of clay.

The arrangement of ovens designed for the baking of the bread is quite complex. They are built in the shape of beehives, with a side opening to introduce the embers. The bread cakes are placed against the hot walls inside and cook very quickly. These ovens are located in a courtyard or in empty ground between houses, where the meal is usually prepared by grinding grain with hand millstones made out of a long, flat stone and a pestle, or by pounding meal in three-legged stone mortars.

General Features of Food in the Middle East

The Imprint of Islam

In pre-Islamic Arabia, there were few prohibitions on food, although certain holy families did not eat meat, and each tribe had customs that might prohibit the eating of a certain part of an animal. Wine was drunk quite often and sometimes ritually. But, even before the time of the Prophet, certain Arabs had been influenced by Judaism and Christianity. Thus, they abstained from eating animals not ritually slaughtered or those sacrificed to idols and, perhaps, refrained from drinking alcohol. The Prophet, however, established what was lawful (*halal*) and unlawful (*haram*) to eat. Prohibitions in some instances included blood, the flesh of an animal that had died, or that of an animal not properly slaughtered. In addition, pork was proscribed, along with a few marginal animals that were snakelike in appearance or wild.

Mohammed insisted that the restrictions for his people were not as excessive as they were for Jews. He also stressed that food should be regarded as a divine blessing and, therefore, thoroughly appreciated. The Koran at first praised the virtue of wine but soon showed reservations about it and, finally, forbade it. In addition to these rules, Islam decreed a periodic general fast during the month of Ramadan.

Middle Eastern Table Manners

Food is traditionally eaten with three fingers of the right hand, from dishes or trays that can be shared by four to eight people. The thumb, index and middle fingers are used to pick up the food. It is polite to take the piece of food nearest to you in the serving dish. Pieces of meat or vegetables are usually taken with the help of a piece of bread, and fingers are licked after the meal.

The "table" is laid in a simple manner: Cloth is spread on the floor, or a large tray is placed on a low stool to form a table. Today, people sit cross-legged around these arrangements, although Pierre Belon, a sixteenth-century observer, noted that Arabs rested on their heels while eating and Turks sat on the floor. Dishes for those dining are displayed in front of them, usually all at the same time. If there is dessert, it is brought after the meal, and coffee follows in many Middle Eastern countries. Hands are washed with the help of a basin and a flask and dried on towels before and after meals.

The meals are inaugurated in Islam with an invocation of God. Islam dislikes the mixing of the sexes, and so in traditional homes, women and men usually eat apart. Everyone stops eating at the same time, and it is polite to nibble until your neighbors are finished. The choicest parts are offered to special guests. A

host can also honor a guest by offering him a good morsel from his hand. There is a strong sense of hospitality, and the expected, or unexpected, guest will always be offered something to drink and eat.

Basic Ingredients and Cooking Techniques

Much of the Middle East is desert, with only about 10 percent of the land useful for cultivation. As a consequence, the common diet can be quite monotonous. Chickpeas and lentils have been part of Middle Eastern cuisine for thousands of years, along with a number of vegetables and fruits. The aubergine (eggplant), for example, is omnipresent on Middle Eastern tables. The Turks claim they know more than 40 ways of preparing this vegetable. It can be smoked, roasted, fried, or mashed for a "poor man's caviar." According to a Middle Eastern saying, to dream of three aubergines is a sign of happiness.

Because of the shortage of pasture land, sheep, goats, and chickens are the main animals raised. Pork is not eaten by Muslims and, generally, beef is not much appreciated. Animals are slaughtered by Muslim ritual; the throat is slit quickly, cutting through the trachea and the esophagus. Thus, the animal does not suffer. At the moment of cutting, the name of God is invoked. Ideally, the animal will have its left side facing Mecca at the moment of death.

Barley has become increasingly neglected in favor of wheat and rice. Wheat is used as flour in many leavened and unleavened breads. So too is *burghul* or cracked wheat, a preparation in which the whole grains are partially cooked, then dried and cracked. Three sizes of burghul are available, medium and large grains found in pilafs and stuffings, and a fine variety that is preferred for salads and *kibbeh*. Medium and large grains must be soaked before use.

Rice arrived in the Middle East later than wheat and is used mainly by urban populations, whereas wheat is the staple food of the countryside. Many types of rice are available, with the best and longest grains coming from Iran. It is prepared differently in every region, although rice is soaked everywhere. In Syria, it is boiled for 2 minutes in the same water it was soaked in, then simmered for 20 minutes until the water is absorbed. Melted butter is poured on it and the rice left to stand for a few minutes before eating. In Lebanon, water and butter are boiled together. In Egypt, the rice is fried in fat, then simmered. Iranians claim to have the best method of cooking rice: They parboil for 6 to 8 minutes, then steam with butter in a sealed dish. The rice is fluffy and flavorful, with a golden crust at the bottom of the pan.

Milk is widely used, especially in the form of thin or thick yoghurt. It is also churned into clarified butter (*samn*). Other cooking oils are derived from olives, cottonseeds, nuts, corn and sesame seeds. Olive oil is often associated with fish and salad dishes. A very sought-after delicacy is the rendered fat of sheep tails.

Because the region has long been involved in spice trading, some spices, mostly of Indian origin, are part of the diet. These include turmeric, cumin, coriander, and cinnamon. If they can be afforded, nuts are widely used in cooking (walnuts in Iran and pine nuts in Lebanon, for example). A few exotic items in a Middle Eastern pantry are *sumac,* a red spice with a sour lemony flavor that is the powder of dried, round berries and gives color and taste to many dishes (in Iran it is sprinkled on rice or kebabs); *tahina,* which is sesame seed paste; and *mahlab,* the powder of black cherry stones. Rose and orange blossom water, mastic, and powdered orchid root are also used, but more rarely.

Traditional cooking is done on a stove or *fatayel,* with bread usually baked by a professional. Moreover, in the past, the baker's oven also served as a public oven. Families sent their pans or dishes to be placed in the oven for very slow cooking. Today domestic ovens play this role most of the time. Middle Eastern cooking is a painstaking and slow process, made possible on an everyday basis because most women of the Middle East spend the day at home. For this reason, these women are able to carry on cooking traditions and people remain very much attached to the dishes of the past.

There is a considerable pride of craftsmanship that goes into Middle Eastern cookery. Miniature foods (like miniature paintings) are favorites, stuffings can be incredibly elaborate, and mock dishes are sometimes invented to puzzle the guests. Pastries are elaborate and reflect craftsmanship, as do the numerous finger foods, such as small pizzas, stuffed grape leaves, fried meat balls with delicate moist fillings, and confections that are jewel-like.

Coffee was first popular in Yemen and Saudi Arabia, then spread throughout the region. There is no ceremony, no bargaining, nor any counseling session without coffee. Cups are small and made of different materials, which vary from country to country. The sugar is usually boiled together with the coffee in water (although Egyptians like their coffee unsweetened). When the water boils, sugar and coffee are thrown into the pot. The beverage is stirred, simmered briefly, then poured, still frothy, into cups. In Lebanon, coffee is often flavored with orange blossom water.

Other Middle Eastern favorites are pickled vegetables or fruit (raw or lightly cooked and soaked in a salt-and-vinegar marinade) and fruit syrups (sherbet) of many kinds: orange, rose water, quince, apricot, and tamarind (in Egypt). A meat and wheat soup is usually served, especially for celebrations. Meat is often minced or hand pounded before cooking. If not, it is cubed, or at least cooked so as to be easily torn to pieces, because it is eaten with the fingers. A typical salad dressing in the Middle East is a simple mixture of olive oil and lemon juice, seasoned with salt, pepper, garlic, and herbs.

The dietary similarities of Middle Eastern countries reflect the long unification and acculturation process under Arab, "Islamic," and Ottoman domination. Under the Abbassids, for example (ninth to twelfth century), during the Golden Age of Islam, there was one single empire from Afghanistan to Spain and the North of Arabia. The size of the empire allowed many foods to spread throughout the Middle East. From India, rice went to Syria, Iraq, and Iran, and eventually, it became known and cultivated all the way to Spain. The use of sugar was common among wealthy people, along with spices from Asia, coffee from Arabia, olive oil from Syria, cheese from Crete, saffron from Tuscany, and even wine from the south of France. Dried and salted fish, honey, and hazelnuts also reached the Middle East from Russia and the Slavic countries.

To keep the products from deteriorating in transit, different techniques were used. Melons from Transoxiana were packed in ice inside lead boxes before they were sent to Baghdad. Nuts and desert truffles were dried. The crystallizing of fruit in honey or sugar, an old process developed in ancient Rome, was also employed, and milk was often preserved in the form of cheese.

Cooks also traveled; those from Egypt and Bolu, in Turkey, were the most famous and in the most demand. In addition, recipes spread, making Iranian and, later on, Turkish dishes fashionable. The culinary arts were considerably elevated early on under the Caliph Hârûn-al-Rashîd (786–801). The gastronomy of the time is depicted in poetry, as well as in medical treatises on food hygiene. The caliphs of Baghdad were renowned for their lavish and sophisticated tables. The rulers liked to converse about food and encouraged people to write about it and experiment with it. Manuals on good manners stressed that the well-bred man of the time could not ignore the culinary arts.

Palace food was characterized by its expense (plenty of meat, spices, sugar, rice), complexity (elaborate combinations of flavors, as well as stuffings), beauty (rich colors), and mock dishes. Palace doctors offered advice in the choice and preparation of food, as dietetics was important for the elite.

Many dishes of that period are still prepared today with ingredients available to the common people. Some of these are vinegar preserves, roasted meat, and cooked livers, which could be bought in the streets, eaten in the shops, or taken home. Such dishes considerably influenced medieval European and Indian cookery; for example, *paella,* which evolved from *pulao,* and pilaf and meat patties that started out as *samosa* or *sambusak.*

Despite the rich and relatively coherent cultural area created by the Muslim conquest, three main types of Middle Eastern cookery can subsequently be distinguished. One is that of Iran, another that of the Fertile Crescent, and the last that of Turkey. Each of these will be examined in turn.

Iranian Cookery

General Features

Iran is a vast land of varied climatic conditions. The coast of the Caspian Sea is known for its heavy rainfall and a verdant vegetation. But such a climate precludes the growing of long-grain rice and citrus fruits, such as oranges, tangerines, lemons, and limes. The region along the Persian Gulf is one of extreme heat, suitable for palm trees and the production of dates. Wheat is grown everywhere except on the Caspian coast, and the whole of the country produces tea, olives, peaches, apricots, pomegranates, pistachios, and walnuts. The famous red and white Damask roses, cultivated in Iran, yield an excellent rose water. The melons and grapes of Iran are also renowned. Although alcohol is prohibited in the Islamic religion, Iran was known in the past for good wines, especially those from Shiraz.

Sheep and goats are raised in large areas of Iran, with the main breed of sheep having fat tails and lean meat (fat is concentrated in the tail). These animals also provide milk from which large quantities of yoghurt are made.

Iranian dishes have changed little over the centuries, and many of them are somewhat unique in the Middle East because sweet and savory ingredients are often cooked together. A lamb stew with spinach and prunes is one example and duck in a sour cherry or pomegranate sauce is another.

Another feature of Iranian dishes is the wide use of fresh herbs, such as parsley, dill, coriander, mint, and cress, and a bowl of fresh herbs can play the role of a salad. Herbs mixed with rice flavor the green *sabzi pollo.* Iranian dishes are very subtly and lightly spiced. Saffron and cinnamon are among the most commonly used spices, dill and coriander seeds among the herbs most frequently employed.

Rice is an Iranian specialty, with many different kinds available, ranging from the longest and most flavorful to the quite ordinary. Rice is used in various ways: as *chilau* (white) or as *pollos* (with different meats and vegetables), and as a dessert (a *shol-e-zard* or saffron rice pudding served, among other occasions, for the annual observance of the martyrdom of Imam Hassan).

There is an Iranian legend explaining the high value of rice. When the Prophet Mohammed was accidentally conveyed into paradise, he sweated with terror at the idea of facing the throne of the Almighty. Six drops of his precious sweat came to earth from paradise. The second of these became a grain of rice.

As noted, Iranians have a unique method of preparing rice. This method is designed to leave the grains separate and tasty, making the rice fluffy and very flavorful. After soaking, parboiling, and draining, the rice is poured into a dish smeared with melted butter. The lid is then sealed tightly with a cloth and a paste of flour and water. The last stage is to steam it on low heat for about half an hour, after which the rice is removed and fluffed. The golden crust on the bottom of the pan, or *tah-dig,* is crumbled on top or served separately.

In addition to *pollo,* other typical Iranian preparations are *koresht* (stews of meat or fowl to be served with rice, such as chicken in walnut-lemon sauce or lamb in pomegranate sauce); *khorak* (eggplant casserole); and kebabs (pieces of roasted meat or game).

Iran is also famous for its soups, which include meat broth with chickpeas, typical rice and spinach soup, and hot yoghurt soup. Spinach originated in Iran and is used in many dishes. In a *kookoo,* or Iranian omelette, for example, the eggs are beaten and sometimes enhanced with a little baking soda so that the result is a very thick souffle, quite unlike an ordinary omelette. This versatile preparation comes in many variations, as does yoghurt, which when combined with fruit, herbs, and nuts is a common side dish, called *borani.* Their *dolmehs,* or stuffed vegetables, the Iranians borrowed from Turkey. Bread, in the past, served as a plate to hold food but today is employed in the Western way, on the side.

Historical Background

The early Persian empire (500 B.C.) was influenced by the Macedonians, Greeks, Romans, and Parthians. At the time of the Achaemenids, the king and the 1,500 individuals who generally dined with him had a great assortment of animal flesh from which to choose, including camels and ostriches. The satraps, or governors, also had to feed many guests. The satrap in Jerusalem, Nehemiah, often fed up to 150 notables at each meal. Food was prepared by a number of specialists, including chefs, bakers, pastry makers, drink mixers, and wine attendants. Tablecloths spread on the floor were of costly fabrics, and gold and silver vessels were in use among the nobility. Indeed, the Persians had such a passion for gold cups that Darius III once lost three or four tons of them, made of gold and encrusted with gems, to an enemy.

Like Nebuchadnezzar and the Assyrian kings before him, the Persian monarch enjoyed the special Helbon wine, from the vineyards on the slopes above Damascus, as well as wheat from Assos, salt from the oases of Ammon, oil from Karmanice, and water from the Nile and Danube.

With Alexander the Great (330 B.C.), links were established between India and Persia, that created common features in their cooking traditions. Under the Sassanids (third to seventh century), Persians seem to have become masters in the art of fine living. A Pahlavi text notes that the study of gastronomy was part of the education of a well-bred boy at the time of the Khusraus (end of sixth and early seventh century). Many of the words used in Middle Eastern cooking are of Persian origin and were popularized during this period. The cookery book of the Roman Apicius gives two recipes "in the Parthian manner." Both include *asafoetida,* a resin, appreciated as a condiment in spite of its unpleasant smell, which used to be important in Persian cooking. One of these recipes is a chicken dish; another uses kid or lamb, flavored with ground pepper, rue, onion, and stoned damson plums. Clearly, Iranian taste for sweet and sour combinations was already apparent at this early date.

During the reign of Khusrau II (early seventh century), a very lavish and sumptuous cookery was invented to satisfy the appetites of the monarch who had conquered Antioch, Damascus, Jerusalem, and Alexandria. It consisted of hot (grilled on a spit or fried) and cold meats, stuffed grape leaves, and marinated chicken. Other foods included mutton in pomegranate juice and rice pudding rich with honey, butter, and eggs. Young kid was popular, as was beef cooked with spinach and vinegar. Meat was marinated in spiced yoghurt, as it is today. Jams of quince, almond pastries, and dates stuffed with almonds and walnuts were served for dessert. *Rishta,* a kind of pasta similar to tagliatelle, was also known in ancient Persia.

In his twelfth-century writings, Marco Polo was impressed with the region and its wealth of foodstuffs: pomegranates, peaches, quince, and big fat sheep. But he noted that whereas the people of the countryside ate meat and wheat bread, those of Ormuz dined on dates, salted fish, and onions. Some 600 years later, John Bell, a visitor to Ispahan, took part in a big dinner:

> The entertainment consisted mostly of different kinds of rice boiled with butter, fowls, mutton, boiled and roasted lamb. The whole was served in large gold or china dishes and placed in the baskets, which stood on a long cloth spread above the carpets. The dishes were interspaced with saucers filled with aromatic herbs, sugar, and vinegar. [In addition to] the common bread, [there were] some very large thin cakes, which were used instead of napkins to wipe our fingers. They were made of wheat flour. (Bell 1965)

Sherbet was served cooled with ice, the latter from water frozen in the winter, then kept in cellars.

Food in the Arab Countries

General Features

In contrast to the Iranians, the Arabs have subsisted on a fairly rustic diet. Its origin is in the simple food of the Bedouins, which has not evolved much. The wealthy prefer rice; bread is the staple food of the common people. Bread of millet is made in the Aden protectorate; elsewhere, it is more generally of wheat, with sour or sweet fresh dough. It can be baked or fried on a griddle. Porridge and wheat gruel are still popular, as they were in ancient Arabia.

Fresh dates are a staple food in the poorest houses and are common everywhere. Individuals who consume *meshwi,* or meat grilled or roasted on a spit, betray tribal origins. Those who cannot afford lamb eat chicken or eggs often baked in an *eggah* or thick omelette. This is a versatile preparation that can be flavored with all kinds of vegetables, herbs, or meat. It is very close to the Spanish *tortilla* or the Iranian *kookoo.* Arab dishes of bread broken in pieces and soaked in stock, with various toppings, are reminiscent of *tharid,* the Prophet's favorite.

In coastal areas, fresh and dried fish are pounded and cooked with clarified butter and onions, or broken into pieces for easy consumption. Milk products are somewhat rare, with sour milk a common drink among the wealthy but not the common people. The mixture of milk, butter, and dates that Mohammed enjoyed is still prepared today. Spices and condiments, such as salt, pepper, chillies, tamarind, coriander, cloves, and cinnamon, are sometimes used.

A *mansaf,* or normal dinner, in a Bedouin family is simple, but served in a festive manner. Women cook huge wheat "pancakes" *(shrak)* on an iron plate. Several of these are piled on top of each other on a tray, then covered with rice and lamb, with butter poured over the top. A more elaborate meal for special occasions is a whole roasted lamb stuffed with rice, onions, nuts, and spices, and surrounded with mounds of rice, with hard-boiled eggs as a decoration. This meal is considered magnificent if the lamb is stuffed with a chicken, which, in turn, is stuffed with eggs and rice.

Meat balls *(kofte)* are another typical way of serving meat in Arab countries. They can be stewed in a soup, simmered in their own juice, or fried, and rice and spinach can be added to stretch the meat if it is scarce.

A meal is usually followed by one to three cups of boiling hot coffee. In the Aden protectorate, a kind of coffee prepared from the husks of the bean is a popular drink. It is not sweetened but flavored with ginger. A raisin tea made with boiled raisins and cinnamon is a specialty in Saudi Arabia.

Historical Background

Some travelers have left vivid written images of the foods and table manners of seventeenth-century Arabia. Among other things, their writings show how food was served. A large skin or woolen cloth was spread on the floor and dishes were placed on top. On great occasions, more than 10 dishes were offered and served six or seven times. In the middle of the table was placed the spectacular whole lamb or sheep with its trimmings. Arabs of rank ate at a small table 1 foot high with a large plate of tinned copper on it. Their food was served in copper dishes, tinned within and without. Instead of napkins, they used long linen cloths placed on their knees.

Western observers stressed the fraternity around these "tables." Sir Thomas Roe noted that Arabs make no great differences among table guests – the king and common soldiers, masters, and slaves, sat together and took food from dish (Roe 1926). Such fraternity is a value in Islam and still a tradition in Arabia. Travelers remarked, however, that women ate apart.

They also stressed the simplicity of the meals. Arabs had only a few cooking utensils of copper and big wooden bowls to use as large dishes or for kneading bread dough. They were reported to be fond of fresh bread and said to have baked it in a number of ways. Three examples of baking techniques are the use of an earthen pot in which a fire of charcoal was kindled (the bread was cooked on the sides of the pot), the placing of the dough on a heated plate of iron, and baking directly on charcoal.

In the desert, however, even the "more eminent schiechs *[sic]*," wrote Carsten Niebuhr, "eat of nothing but pilau or boiled rice. It is served up in a very large wooden plate" (Pinkerton 1811). A little mutton was consumed on occasion, but pastries were rare.

Most Arabs in poorer circumstances dined on bread and onions, sometimes with a little sour milk, salt, cheese, or oil. "But the most plenty and useful of all their fruits are their dates, which support and sustain many millions of people," wrote Roe (1926). Travelers, such as Roe, were also impressed by the use of coffee: "As soon as everyone is seated a servant brings a pot of coffee. It is very hot and poured in tiny cups. They are filled two, even three times, then a pipe of tobacco is presented" (Roe 1926).

Even though Islamic regulations were strictly observed and prayers said before and after meals, some inquisitive foreigners remarked that Muslims sometimes drank alcohol privately at night. Notwithstanding these "mistakes," the travelers gave the picture of a very traditional and modest food consumed by the Arabs, the same food that the Prophet himself had eaten.

Food in Egypt

General Features
Dishes served in Egypt constitute another type of old and simple tradition that goes back to pharaonic times, like the *melokhia* soup, a broth with the leaves of *corchorus olitorius,* (Tussa jute) which imparts a glutinous texture. Also old is the *batarekh,* or salted dried roe of the gray mullet, served sliced with bread. Pulses play an important role in the diet. Lentil soup is common, and the national dish is *ful medames,* brown Egyptian beans boiled and seasoned with olive oil, lemon juice, and parsley. To eat *ful medames* according to custom, one must first eat some of the beans whole, then mash some in the juice, and finally crush the rest with a hard-boiled egg placed on top of the dish. Cooked white broad beans, shaped into patties *(falafel),* spiced, and fried, are another favorite of the Egyptians, especially when eaten in a pita, or hollow flat bread.

Egypt is not a country where people consume animal protein in large amounts, but *hamud,* a chicken soup with lemon, is very popular. It is traditionally served with rice, cooked in the Egyptian way, fried then boiled. A kind of *kibbeh* (pounded meat and cereal) is prepared in Egypt, with ground rice instead of cracked wheat as in the Fertile Crescent. Fish kebabs are also quite common, and pigeons are frequently consumed. Couscous, a North African dish of a sort of semolina prepared with meat and vegetables, is served in Egypt as a dessert, topped with butter and fried raisins.

Nonetheless, the diet of the *fellahs,* or peasants, is mostly vegetarian. They usually have three meals a day, *futour* at sunrise, *ghada* taken while working in the fields, and a hot meal in the evening called *acha.* All of these meals consist mainly of raw or stewed vegetables.

Historical Background
In a fifteenth century Egyptian market, all kinds of foodstuffs could be purchased. Among them were wheat, barley, rice, beans, peas, chickpeas, carrots, cucumbers, lemons, watermelons, beef, mutton, chicken, goose, camel flesh, sugar, olive oil, sesame oil, clarified butter, and white cheese.

Pierre Belon du Mans, visiting in the sixteenth century, noted that Egyptians knew how to preserve foodstuffs. Lamb, for example, was cubed and boiled, cut in very small pieces, and boiled again in fat with cooked onions. Then the preparation was salted, spiced, and stored in barrels for up to two weeks. The French traveler also mentioned other preservation techniques, such as olives in brine, dried sea bream, salted gray mullet roe, and dried cheese (Belon 1557). These are not particularly sophisticated techniques, but they do show that Egyptians were able to make good and prolonged use of the products of their land.

Food in the Fertile Crescent
Syria, Jordan, and Lebanon have similar culinary traditions because all three were influenced by early Greek and Roman civilizations. In addition, Lebanon has recently been the recipient of a strong French influence, which is said to have enhanced the quality of its cookery.

This region is marked by the use of *burghul,* or cracked wheat, which is often consumed in the form of the traditional *tabouleh,* an herb salad with burghul and lemon juice. Burghul also plays an important role in another specialty of the area, *kibbeh,* which is said to have been mentioned in ancient Assyrian and Sumerian writings. Certainly, archeological evidence indicates that all the utensils and products necessary for this dish were on hand in the region long before Islam put its imprint upon it.

Kibbeh is made by pounding lamb with burghul, onions, and a little cinnamon; it is a mixture that can be eaten raw *(kibbeh naye),* grilled, or fried. Stuffed kibbeh is a variation that has become an art in Syria. A kibbeh shell is shaped around the finger of the cook as evenly and thinly as possible. It is then filled with meat, nuts, and herbs and sealed. Once fried, it becomes crisp with a moist inside. Kibbeh is one of the many possible items one can choose as a typical snack *(mezze),* along with a variety of olives, nuts, small pizzas, and pies. In Syria, a favorite is *muhamara,* a mixture of chopped nuts with hot pepper sauce. In Lebanon, another favorite is *mankoush,* a spicy herb flat bread. Lebanese people can spend hours nibbling these sorts of snacks while enjoying a drink of *arak,* an anise-flavored liquor. Local specialties include rice with almond sauce (Damascus), brown lentils and rice (Lebanon), bean salad (Lebanon), and lamb with yoghurt (Jordan). *Fattoush,* or bread salad, with a dressing of olive oil, onions, and lemon juice is common throughout the region.

Turkish Food

General Features

In Turkish food, one encounters the same differences between country food and the palace cookery that we have seen in other countries and regions once parts of the Ottoman empire. A classic Turkish meal starts with hot or cold yoghurt soup. In some villages the soup is made on baking day in a pit oven. A Turkish menu also offers *mezzes* (appetizers), such as sausage, vegetables in oil, cheese, *pastirma* (dried pressed meat cured with garlic and spices), or *borek* (flaky pastries with different fillings). A classic Turkish menu will feature soup, a meat dish, a borek, a vegetable dish, and a dessert.

Meat is a very important item in Turkish cookery. It comes in dozens of varieties of kebabs. Mutton and lamb are favorites, especially minced or pounded. Meat is even used in fruit dishes and puddings; examples include stewed apricots or quinces with lamb and a pudding of chicken breast. For big parties, a whole kid is roasted on a spit. Minced meat is the filling for the numerous *dolmasi,* or stuffed vegetables, such as peppers, tomatoes, vegetable marrow, and grape leaves.

Eggs are an important item of food, and many Turks raise chickens in their backyard. There are more than 130 varieties of fish available in the Bosporus Straits, with mackerel the most popular. A kind of unleavened flat bread made at home is the Turk's staple food. The baker offers many varieties of white bread, the most famous of which is the ring-shaped *simit.*

Turkey is well known for its pilafs, or rice dishes, made from long-grain rice, pounded ripe wheat *(dogme),* toasted unripe wheat *(firik),* and bulgur, or couscous. They are enriched with meat, dried fruit, vegetables, spices, and yoghurt.

Yoghurt is used in two forms in Turkey, one semiliquid and the other firm. The latter is often eaten with jam or used for cooking, while the former, as a yoghurt drink *(ayran),* is often served with meals.

A very special Turkish drink is *salep,* which is made with the infusion of a powder from the root of the salep orchid in milk and served hot. Coffee has been prepared and served in coffeehouses in Turkey since the fifteenth century. It is offered black and strong, usually with confections. Turks are very proud of their sweets, and a confectionery in Istanbul can feature more than 100 sorts of halvah (sweetmeats), such as plain and rose *lokum* and almond and pistachio marzipan.

In the past, vendors made and sold all kinds of foods on the streets. Today, these individuals are not so numerous, but sesame-sprinkled *simits* are still sold everywhere, the water or juice seller is still seen, and the streets of Istanbul still often smell of grilled fresh mackerel or roasted lamb.

Regional differences are important in Turkish food. The Aegean region is renowned for its fish and seafood. The Mediterranean region is rich in vegetables, with aubergines, peppers, tomatoes, and garlic featured in many stews. People of the Black Sea region enjoy cabbage soup and anchovies in many dishes, including a pilaf. Anatolia is the home of the best Turkish roast meat. Bursa is the town that gave birth to the world-famous *doner kebab,* meat roasted on a vertical revolving spit.

Historical Background

The nomadic period (before the eleventh century). In the Turkish city of Konya, people ate bulgur and lentils and knew how to use the pit oven, or tandor, 7,000 to 8,000 years ago. Turks in central Asia probably drank soups of *tarhana* (dried curd and cereals) and, when still nomads, they relied on mutton and horse meat, unleavened bread, milk, and milk products. *Manti* (a kind of ravioli) and *corek* (ring-shaped buns) were probably also known.

The Seljuk sultans and principalities period (1038–1299). During these centuries, the nomads were drawn from their steppes into the armies of the caliphate. They began to settle down, ruled a number of local dynasties, and as they did so, acquired more refined manners and tastes. Dishes of the period reveal that cooking was becoming an art. In an eleventh-century dictionary, for example, there is mention of a layered pastry, of noodle soup, grape syrup, and a corn-flour halvah.

Mowlavi Jalâl-al-Dîn Rumi, founder of the order of Whirling Dervishes, was a philosopher who, nonetheless, showed great interest in the subject of food. Thus, it is possible to infer from his writings the types of comestibles consumed in the thirteenth century. A few examples include saffron rice, homemade noodles with meat, *kadayif* (layered nut filled pastry), all kinds of halvah, wine, and fruit syrups. Within the order, strict rules were established concerning the organization of the kitchen and tables manners. Among other things, such rules show that social distinctions were made among those involved in food preparation, from sherbet makers to coffee masters to waiters, dishwashers, and cooks.

The Ottoman period (1299-1923). One group of nomads, the Osmanlis, or Ottomans, came to control the Islamic empire. Their rulers were cosmopolitan, having previously been slaves (or descendants of slaves) in all parts of the known world as far north as Russia and western Europe. These new rulers first took Persia as a model for their court life, then developed their own, including the culinary arts, borrowing from all over their empire.

The first Turkish cooks employed in the palace came from Bolu, the region where the sultans did their hunting. The men of Bolu were accustomed to leaving their land to learn this craft at the palace. Food was so important to the sultans that the insignia of their renowned janissary force was a pot and a spoon, symbols of their higher standard of living. The titles of janissary officers were drawn from the camp kitchen, such as "first maker of soup" and "first cook." The sacred object of the regiment was the stew pot around which the soldiers gathered to eat and take counsel.

When Sultan Mehmet II, the Conqueror, captured Constantinople (1453), he laid down the rules for food preparation, to be followed at the court for a long time to come. The palace kitchen was divided into four main areas: the king's kitchen; the sovereign's kitchen (responsible for food for his mother, the princes, and privileged members of the harem); the harem kitchen; and a kitchen for the palace household. That there was a movement toward culinary specialization seems clear in that the kitchen staff included bakers, confection and pastry makers, a yoghurt maker, and a pickle maker.

Ottaviano Bon (1653) has provided us with a good account of the kitchen in the seraglio in the seventeenth century, which shows how complex the organization had become. Food was prepared by the *Ajomoglans* (Christian renegades) and 200 cooks and scullions who began their work before daybreak.

The sultan would eat three or four times a day, commonly dining at 10 in the morning and 6 in the evening, with snacks in between. He ate cross-legged, with an expensive towel upon his knees and another hanging on his left arm. Three or four kinds of white bread and two wooden spoons were placed before him (one for soup, one for dessert) upon a piece of Bulgar leather. The sultan's ordinary diet consisted of roasted pigeons, geese, lamb, hens, chickens, mutton and sometimes wild fowl. He would eat fish only when he was at the seaside. Preserves and syrups were always on the "table," though pies were "after their fashion, made of flesh" (Bon 1653). Sherbet followed the meal, since the ruler had adopted Islam and could not take wine.

When he finished, the leftover food was given to high officers. Lesser officers ate from a different kitchen where the food was of lesser quality. Odah youths (young Christians or Turks raised to become officers of the sultan) were fed on two loaves of bread a day, boiled mutton, and a thin pudding of rice with butter and honey. Queens had the same food as the sultan but consumed more sweets and fruit, reflective of their sweet and delicate nature. They drank their sherbet mixed with snow in the summer.

The hierarchy in the palace may be seen in many ways. Four kinds of bread were baked, the best for the sultan (with flour from Bursa), middle-quality loaves for ordinary officers, and a black and coarse bread for the servants; sailors received only sea biscuits.

Reaching the sultan's kitchen were luxury items from all over the empire. Alexandria sent rice, lentils, spices, pickled meats, and sugar, as well as prunes and dates. The latter were used in the dressing of roasted or boiled meats. Although few spices were used in Turkish cooking, an incredible amount of sugar was invested in pies, sherbets, and confections. Even common people offered each other sweets.

In addition, Valachia, Transylvania, and Moldavia sent honey to be used in broth, sherbets, and meat stews. Olive oil arrived from Greece and butter from the Black Sea region.

Bon noted that Turks used the flesh of calves in the same way that Christians used pork in puddings, pies, and sausages. They also dried the meat to make *basturma*. The serai kitchen was lavish in its use of meat, with 200 sheep, 100 kids, 10 calves, 50 geese, 200 hens, 100 chickens, and 200 pigeons slaughtered daily.

This aristocratic tradition of opulent dining that Bon depicted in the seventeenth century would continue into twentieth-century Turkey. Every meal of wealthy families would feature seven courses: fish, egg or *borek,* meat or fowl, cold vegetables in oil, hot vegetables with butter, pilaf, and pastry or pudding. Such meals were certainly not the democratic and rustic affairs of the Arabs.

The History and Culture of Food in the Indian Subcontinent

The Indian subcontinent is a huge triangle extending from the Himalayas to Cape Comorin and from the Baluchistan deserts to the rice fields of Bengal. It is divided into the countries of India, Bangladesh, Pakistan, Sri Lanka, and the Himalayan states. A diversity of physical environment in this area explains the diversity of the various agrarian civilizations and, in turn, the diversity of cookery traditions. The obvious contrast between the wheat eaters of the North and the rice eaters of the South is but one of numerous possible means of classification. Opposition is also found in the vegetarian ideal of Hinduism and the Muslims' fondness for meat. But it is interesting to note that the art of cooking unites, rather than divides, the people of the peninsula. This is an art that has evolved into a very rich and complex affair called "Indian cookery."

Indian Cookery: A Kaleidoscope

Three Cereals

As noted, we can divide the subcontinent into agricultural zones in which either wheat, rice, or millets are predominant. Although cereals are supplemented by various plants and pulses, they nonetheless constitute the staple food in each zone.

Rice is eaten everywhere in the Indian world, but it is the staple food only of the South and of Bengal, where it is boiled and served with a *dahl* (made from one of the many pulses of the peninsula), or perhaps with different curries and fresh yoghurt. When rice is ground and parboiled with split peas *(urad dahl)*, it becomes a batter that the cooks of Tamil Nadu leave to ferment and to steam in molds to make the spongy *idlis*. The same batter can be shaped into small doughnuts and fried, or spread on the griddle to make a crispy pancake called *dosa*. All these preparations are served with chutney, a spicy vegetable curry, or a souplike *sambar.*

Millets like *jowar* (sorghum), *bajra*, or *ragi* are cultivated on the poorest soils and are found mainly in the Dekkan, Western Ghats, Gujerat, and Rajputana. They have been the staple food of the peasants, although "richer" cereals are increasingly becoming more preferred.

Wheat is mainly cultivated in the northern provinces. Most of the time it is used as bleached and unbleached flour. When mixed with water and salt (and for richer loaves, with milk, butter, or oil), it is the basis for the numerous Indian breads.

Roti or *chapati,* a thin whole-wheat griddle bread, is the daily accompaniment of *dahl.* With butter in the dough or on the pan, it becomes a golden *paratha.* Deep fried, it turns into a puffy *puri.* But thanks to the Muslim influence, northern India and Pakistan also know oven bread in its various forms. The most commonly found are the unleavened oblong *nan* or the round and soft *shirmal,* which is smeared with saffron milk. Lucknow and Hyderabad are also famous for their sourdough square breads or *kulchas.* All these oven breads are made of white flour and traditionally baked on the sides of the tandoor, the central Asian clay oven.

Such bread goes well, and is best associated, with the nonvegetarian cookery of the North, which includes kebabs and rich stews *(kormas)* of lamb or chicken.

North and South

Like the differing architecture of their temples and linguistic features, the North and South of the subcontinent have separate staple foods, and there are many differences between their cookeries.

With the curries, for example, the *masalas* (spice mixtures) that give each dish its character are not the same. In the North, the spices are dried, ground, and then dry-roasted or fried before being added to a dish. The dishes themselves are often nonvegetarian, due to a stronger Muslim influence, and tend to be dry so that food can be scooped up with bread. In the South, fresh spices are pounded with a liquid into a paste. The dishes these pastes flavor are mostly vegetarian, and rather liquid, to moisten the plain rice that generally is an important part of the meal.

Northern cooks will, therefore, have many dry spices on hand, such as cardamom, ginger, turmeric, black pepper, chillies, coriander, cumin, and, sometimes, dried vegetables or fruits that could not endure in the humid climate of the South. They use *ghee* (clarified butter) to cook the meat and oil (mustard oil, if possible) for the vegetables. Among the many pulses employed is the chickpea, which is a favorite in the North. Green tea in Kashmir and black tea, elsewhere, is boiled with water and sugar, spiced with ginger and cardamom, and whitened with rich buffalo milk.

By contrast, southerners use few dried spices and no dried vegetables. Rather, the latter are bought fresh on a day-to-day basis. Fruit and vegetables are preserved, however, in oil and chillies *(achar)* and in vinegar (pickles). In addition to jars of these relishes, a good kitchen will have different varieties of rice, some for everyday use, others for festivals and desserts, and still others for the servants. Rice flour will be present, as well as many types of pulses. In the vegetarian South, pulses are a major source of protein. Ghee is seldom used, but sesame and coconut oils are common.

The South, in tropical Asia, is also a land of coconuts and many other exotic products, such as mangoes, limes, bananas, "drumsticks," *moringa oleifera,* and jackfruit, all of which are often part of the diet. Coffee, introduced by the Arabs, is preferred to tea in the South, where it is prepared with milk and sugar. Now it is also found everywhere in its instant form.

Cooking utensils differ from north to south, although the *chula* (square hearth), the *tawa* (griddle), and the *karkhai* (deep frying pan) are common to the entire peninsula. In the North, the dry spices are ground on a grindstone *(chakki),* and in the South, the fresh ingredients are pounded with a mortar and pestle. The coconut grater is also typical of the South. Food is served on individual metal trays *(thali)* in the North, but on a clean banana leaf in the South. Finally, although all people of the subcontinent eat with their right hand, northerners tend to use the tips of the fingers, whereas southerners will dip their whole hand into the food.

More Regional Variations

The diversity of the culture of food and drink in the Indian world is much more complex, however, than simply differences between north and south. There are many interesting variations within the vast regions.

For example, the valley of Kashmir in the northernmost part of India has a somewhat cold climate, which is perfect for growing fruits, walnuts, and cumin, and for breeding sheep. Thus, as one might expect, the cookery is more closely related to that of central Asia. The tea there is made in a samovar and is a green tea, as in Tibet. The bread is closer to that made in Afghanistan than to Indian *chapatis* and is generally baked in clay ovens by professionals.

In Rajasthan, culture has dictated other food habits. Historically, their men have been warriors and, thus, have long been accustomed to outdoor cooking. For this reason, many of their dishes include marinated and grilled meats (including game), often prepared by males.

In contrast to this rugged fare, a Maharashtran meal starts with a sweet, eaten with a *puri* or *chapati*. Maharashtra is rich in seafood and coconuts, and both are often blended together. Every morning the ladies of many houses begin their day by grinding coconut and spices on a grinding stone. The milk of the coconut is also present in practically every dish, even in *pulao* (flavored rice, the Indian rendition of the Turkish pilaf).

Bengali food is reputed to be quite plain, but the sweets of the region (*sandesh, rasmalai, gulab jamen,* and all-milk sweets soaked in syrup) are famous. The waters of the Bay of Bengal yield hundreds of varieties of fish and shellfish. In fact, the "vegetarian" Brahmans of the region, who theoretically should avoid seafood, eat it nonetheless, calling it "vegetables of the sea."

The Portuguese, in their quest for empire, settled in Goa as well as in other places. Thus, personal names, architecture, and festivals, along with the foods of the region, reveal this influence. Indeed, Goanese food is Portuguese food, save for the lavish inclusion of red chillies and coconut milk. The use of onions and tomatoes in many soups is very Portuguese, and the Goanese consumption of pork is unique in India. Vinegar gives many dishes a typical sour-hot taste. Sweets include a lot of egg yolks and almonds. Thus, dishes such as *caldine, bife, souraca,* and *assada* are all reminders of the colonial past.

Malabar Muslim cookery constitutes another example of a blending of local and foreign traditions in India. Kerala Muslims are supposed to have descended from intermarriage between local Kerala women and Arab traders who settled there. Malabar food has a great deal in common with food elsewhere in Kerala in that it testifies to an extensive employment of coconuts, coconut oil, and rice. But the Arab influence is evident in dishes such as *alisa* (a wheat and meat porridge), or stuffed chicken. Another dish *(byriani)* shows the linkage with the Muslims of northern India, although it contains coconut and prawns. A Muslim love for bread is reflected in the Moplah specialty called *pathiri*, which is a rice *chapati*.

Cultural Background

The four major religions of India are Hinduism, Buddhism, Jainism, and Islam. The Islamic influence, which arrived in the eighth century, placed great emphasis on the enjoyment of food because it was considered a reward from God to the believer. Yet food is not a petty matter in the view of other dominant religions either. "All doings come from food" is an Indian saying. For the traditional Hindu, cooking and eating are not just matters of survival but moral investments and rituals as well. The *Mahabharata,* one of the sacred books, refers to the necessity of ensuring purity in food and drink as one of the ten essential disciplines of life; and even in the big cities, a majority of Indians still live according to such age-old customs.

Vegetarianism is a precept of the three Indian religions although, of course, the people of India were not always vegetarian. The first humans who appeared near the basin of the river Indus around 15,000 B.C. ate meat along with rice, molasses, spices, and betel leaves. It was not before the Vedic era (1500–800 B.C.) that an aversion toward meat consumption appeared in ancient texts. At this time, milk acquired a symbolic value and the cow was described as a "gift." Little by little, animals were replaced by clay or flour figurines for sacrifices, and instead of consuming the cows that constituted much of their wealth, the people of India began revering them.

It was the new religions of Buddha and Mahavira Jina (sixth century B.C.), however, which provided the decisive impulse to the vegetarian doctrine. Both prescribed nonviolence *(ahimsa)* and the abstinence from meat. This ideal is still subscribed to by the orthodox Hindus, whereas Jains go so far as not to touch foods that resemble meat, such as tomatoes, beet roots, and so forth.

However, there has always been an ambivalence in the Hindu attitude toward meat consumption. If Brahmans avoided it, it was recommended to the *Kshatriyas* (kings and warriors) and was not forbidden to the castes of merchants, agriculturists, and servants. All this suggests that the Hindu concepts on food were elaborated for a whole society, in which everyone had duties and a diet suited to those duties. Those who lived close to the world and its violence were urged to eat meat to gain energy. By contrast, the Hindu priests and Brahmans embraced vegetarianism; indeed, those who prayed were enjoined to avoid everything exciting to the senses, even onions.

Each individual can follow many diets. Hindus believe that a perfect life is lived in the four stages of student, householder, hermit, and ascetic. A man, therefore, might be vegetarian while single, then be nonvegetarian, and finish his life in abstinence and fasts.

The cow is still held sacred, its products considered excellent for health, as well as religious purposes. Pure *ghee* (clarified butter) is highly esteemed, and many Indians still feed the newborn baby with a spoonful of ghee after the Brahman ritual. They also give ghee to sick individuals and, although very expensive, it is still considered the best cooking medium.

While vegetarian doctrine was being elaborated, concepts of pure and impure foods were being developed as well. A ritual is organized around the meal to ensure its purity, which includes bathing and the wearing of clean clothes for both the cook and those who dine. The kitchen must be as clean as a temple and separated by a little wall from the rest of the house, far from the refuse area and near the prayer room. It is often swept and washed, and, traditionally, the floors are covered with cow dung, a sacred substance and one regarded as an antiseptic.

Purity also shapes the whole Hindu society as a hierarchical structure with the Brahmans at the top. An exchange of food is traditionally prohibited among the segments or castes of this society, especially from the lowest (most impure) to the highest (Brahmins). Even in the same family, it is considered "unclean" to touch food that has been touched by someone else, which is why the food is served directly from the cooking vessels onto the *thalis* (leaves). This also explains why there is no tradition of dining out in India. The quest for purity is too strong.

These age-old principles are still professed by most Hindus, but orthodoxy is sometimes sacrificed for the sake of health (diets low in fat, sugar, and spices), diversity (new recipes), status (for example, the Western habit of going to restaurants), and convenience (ready-made food).

As we have noted, Islam also strongly imposed itself on the cookery of the subcontinent for religious, as well as for purely gastronomic, reasons. Although a late cultural and religious arrival, Islam came to India via many channels. Arab traders, Afghan and Turk soldiers, along with Iranian administrators, all settled down there and made converts to their religion, as well as to portions of their culture.

If Hinduism has given a high spiritual content to the meal, it has paid little attention to the art of cooking. Boiled cereals and griddle bread, stewed vegetables, and pulses had been the usual diet since the beginning of Indian civilization. Islam gave to Indian cookery its masterpiece dishes from the Middle East. These include *pilau* (from Iranian pollo and Turkish pilaf), *samossa* (Turkish *sambussak*), *shir kurma* (dates and milk), kebabs, sherbet, stuffed vegetables, oven bread, and confections (halvah). Such dishes became so well acclimated in India that vegetarian versions of them were elaborated. It is this cross-cultural art that is now acclaimed all around the world.

Delphine Roger

Bibliography

Bell, J. 1965. *A journey from St. Petersburg to Pekin*, ed. J. L. Stevenson. Edinburgh.

Belon, P. 1557. *Portraits d'oyseaux, animaux, serpens, herbes, arbres, hommes et femmes, d'Arabie & Égypte*. Paris.
Bon, O. 1653. *A description of the grand signor's seraglio or Turkish emperours court*, trans. Robert Withers, ed. John Greaves. London.
Daumas, F. 1965. *La civilisation de l'Égypte pharaonique*. Paris.
Deshayes, J. 1969. *Les civilisations de l'Orient ancien*. Paris.
Foster, W., ed. 1968. *Early travels in India*. London.
Halici, N. 1989. *Turkish cookbook*. London.
Miquel, A. 1968. *L'islam et sa civilisation*. Paris.
Pinkerton, J. 1811. *A general collection of the best and most interesting voyages and travels in all parts of the world*. London.
Polo, M. 1926. *The book of Marco Polo, the Venetian, concerning the kingdoms and marvels of the East*, trans. and ed. Henry Yule. New York.
Popper, W. 1957. *Egypt and Syria under the Circassian sultans*. Berkeley, Calif.
Purchas, S. 1619. *Purchas his pilgrim. Microcosmus; or, The historie of man. . . .* London.
Ramazani, N. 1982. *Persian cooking*. Charlottesville, Va.
Ridgwell, J. 1990. *Middle Eastern cooking*. London
Roden, C. 1985. *A new book of Middle Eastern food*. London.
Roe, T. 1926. *The embassy of Sir Thomas Roe to India, 1615-19*, ed. William Foster. London.
Rumi, Jaelal-Din R-um-ii Poet and Mystic, 1207-73. *Selections from his writings*, trans. Reynold A. Nicholson. Oxford 1995.
Sauneron, S., ed. 1970. *Voyage en Égypte de Pierre Belon du Mans*. Cairo.

V.B.2 ‘ Southeast Asia

Southeast Asia, geographically and culturally diverse, stretches from Burma (Myanmar), through Thailand and the Indochinese and Malay peninsulas, to islanded Indonesia. Some would include the Philippines and Indonesian New Guinea as parts of Southeast Asia, but this study adds only the Philippines. European scholars called the region "Farther India" for its location "beyond the Ganges" (Coedes 1968). It is separated from China by the Himalayas and their eastern extension. Each country in the region has other mountain chains, channeling rivers to the South China, Java, Celebes, and other Indonesian seas, and to the Indian Ocean. Lowland plains south of the highest ranges of the mainland are home to most of the populations of Burma, Thailand, Malaysia, Cambodia (Kampuchea), Laos, and Vietnam. The region is also insular: Indonesia has over 13,000 islands, spreading some 5,400 kilometers (3,300 miles). Most people live on or near oceans or river deltas.

Southeast Asia is in the tropical belt along the equator, with little temperature variation – about 15.5 to 24 degrees Celsius (60 to 75 degrees Fahrenheit) in winter to 29 to 32 degrees Celsius (85 to 90 degrees Fahrenheit) in the dry summer months (Hanks 1972).

This is monsoon Asia, and annual rainfall amounts to several hundred millimeters (over 100 inches). North Pacific winds bring rain from the northeast down the South China Sea from October until March, and there is a southwesterly monsoon in summer from May to September (Jin-Bee 1963). Rain is not constant, but brief showers or thunderstorms are always imminent. Temperatures and precipitation are noticeably lower in higher parts of the region. Europeans early recognized the comfort of the foothills and built hill-station retreats where their accustomed temperate plants – fruits, flowers, trees, and vegetables – all flourished.

The mountains, rivers, plains, seas, climate, and laterite, "red-earth" soil have combined to influence what foods are grown or have been available for the choosing since human beings first dwelt there. But despite northern mountain barriers and north–south mountain chains that hinder passage within and beyond the region and keep hill-tribe people (with their different agricultures and religions) apart from lowland dwellers, outside influences have managed to modify behavior and material objects, including what there is to eat. In other words, historically, political, economic, and social factors have frequently resulted in new technologies, products, foodstuffs, and behaviors.

European exploitation of Southeast Asia began with the Portuguese during the Western Age of Exploration in the sixteenth century. But Indians had ventured there much earlier, perhaps in prehistoric times (Jin-Bee 1963; Burling 1965), and had founded kingdoms and introduced Buddhism (Coedes 1968). China has also had a long history and influential relationship with Southeast Asia. Northern Vietnam was part of the Chinese empire for a thousand years until the tenth century A.D. (Burling 1965). Malacca, commanding the waterway through which ships passed from the west to China or the Spice Islands, came under Chinese control in the fifteenth century as a hub of trade. But by the fourteenth century, Islam had been introduced to Southeast Asia by Gujarat Indians, Arabian merchants, or both.

Later colonizers included the Portuguese, Dutch, British, Germans, French, and, in the Philippines, Spaniards and North Americans. All of these cultures influenced foods and the implements for producing and eating them, as indicated among other things by Romanized names for both foods and implements in the languages of the region. It is interesting to note, however, that the World War II occupation of much of the area by Japan had little effect on food practices.

And finally, increased air travel, tourism, commercial marketing, television, advertising, and imported foodstuffs have certainly made the diets of indigenous people more complex, although not necessarily more nutritionally or culturally worthy (Wilson 1994).

Obviously, then, from the foregoing, much of the history of food and drink in Southeast Asia is the history of introductions, some of which can only be guessed at. Written records of the movements of peoples and their political and religious struggles were first made by early Chinese regimes (Coedes 1968). Pre-Aryanized, preliterate kingdoms (Cambodia and Burma) are known to have had complex material cultures, irrigated rice, domesticated cattle and plants, ancient belief systems, temples, and art objects, and also to have bestowed important roles on women. Archaeological records are intermittent, with imprecise dating (Burling 1965; Coedes 1968), so the written Chinese records provide most of our knowledge of early history. But other clues come from linguistic changes, plant distributions, local lore and myth, and, for recent centuries, reports of administrators, travelers, and ethnographers.

Despite the region's diversity, a basic eating pattern common throughout Southeast Asia is a heavy reliance on white rice, consumed with smaller quantities of an accompanying side dish, most often fish, prepared with a sauce from grated coconut meat and a variety of spices, many of which originated in the region (Wilson 1975).

Staples

Rice

Rice *(Oryza sativa)* belongs to the family of grasses, Gramineae. The cultivated species is chiefly *O. sativa,* which, some authorities believe, originated from wild rices native to southeastern Asia (Burkill 1966). *Oryza sativa* is polymorphic, responding with changes in structure to altered environmental growth conditions. This trait earlier led to reports of many different genuses and species until plant genetic studies showed which species were fertile when crossed and which were sterile. Botanists reduced the number of distinct species to 25, but hundreds or thousands of varieties (also termed races) of *O. sativa* exist, having different growing seasons, or responding with inflorescence to less sunlight or drier soils (Burkill 1966; Hanks 1972).

Rice will grow on dry uplands, which may have been the site of its first cultivation in late Mesolithic or early Neolithic times (Coedes 1968; Hanks 1972). The early cultivators could also have accidentally created new species by tying awns of different varieties together to prevent lodging. However, present species and races could also have developed in nature because they grow under similar conditions in the same places and readily interbreed. Quite likely, the process goes on at present when different races are planted for specific characteristics, as suggested by Douglas E. Yen (cited in Crawford 1992).

Rice is a plant of warm, damp areas and, hence, is climate-dependent. It grows satisfactorily in the tropical and subtropical belt from Asia through Africa to warm, moist parts of North and South America. Recognition of its reliability must have been gradual, and the initial understanding of its potential for dependable growth again and again in the same locale (initiated by inserting seeds in the ground) was probably fortuitous suggested when ungathered seeds germinated in a rain-fed field. A liking for the taste of this intermittent crop probably led to efforts to husband its growth, though when and how rice cultivation dawned as a regular agricultural pursuit can only be guessed at (Hanks 1972).

Based on archaeological finds (shards and tools) made in this century (Coedes 1968), together with recent techniques of carbon dating and ethnobotanical research, it has been estimated that the "first" crops of rice appeared some 10,000 to 15,000 years before the present. But "primitive" rice culture continues in some remote areas today, and its ecological and economic consequences that have been recorded also provide insights into early rice cultivation (Conklin 1957).

Rice requires moisture, warmth, and soil with organic matter. The soils of Southeast Asia, like those of much of the tropics, are lateritic, from iron compounds above underlying clay that oxidize upon exposure to air. For plants to grow, a top layer of organic matter, humus, is needed. This may be deposited naturally as fallen detritus in forests or as silt brought by rivers to the deltas. Many of Asia's rice bowls are located between inland forests and coastal mangrove swamps that hold these deposits.

But "dry" rice, which preceded irrigated rice, is still grown in Southeast Asia's upland forest areas, as well as in small dooryard plots (Wilson 1970). Most dryland rice involves shifting cultivation, for the plant removes much of the soil's nutrients, and considerable fallow time must be allowed before a new crop can be nourished (Hanks 1972).

Early growers had to be keenly aware of and attuned to the rhythms of the seasons and plants before regularizing their planting activities. These began by cutting forest growth well ahead of the onset of the rainy season, then drying and burning it. The latter tended to destroy competing plants, and the ash provided phosphates and potassium otherwise lacking in the soil. Still before the rains, seeds were planted through the ash. Such soil could produce crops for two years; after this, the agriculturists would either select another nearby area to plant or move on. Overpopulation and continued land use could lead to erosion and incursion of hardy weeds, and with prolonged soil use, trees would not be able to regenerate to restore the forest.

The other principal method of rice culture is wet-rice cultivation, with its use of shallow water to kill off competing plants. In all countries where rice constitutes the "bulk of consumption" (Wilson 1985), each step in rice raising, from selecting grains for the next year's crop to harvest, storage, and husking for cooking, is accompanied by rituals of worship. People from Burma to the Philippines have long felt that this paramount food is the homesite of a potent god and have made it central to civil and religious rites.

Indeed, beliefs regarding the efficacy and supernatural or curative properties of rice antedate the introduction of organized religions to the region (Geertz 1960; Rosemary Firth 1966; Wilson 1970).

Varieties in which the endosperm starch is partially replaced by soluble starch and dextrin produce glutinous, "sticky" rice that is sweeter, but less easily digested, than ordinary rice (Burkill 1966). Dyed yellow with turmeric (formerly saffron, which is the color of royalty in Southeast Asia), glutinous rice is served for ceremonial occasions as part of the meal or made into sweetmeats exchanged at religious holidays (Geertz 1960; Rosemary Firth 1966; Wilson 1985). One of the most popular of these "cakes" is Malay-Indonesian *ketupat*, usually made of steamed glutinous rice (white, red, or black) mixed with coconut cream and recooked in a woven or folded leaf (Wilson 1985). In Sumatra this mixture is called *lemang* and may be served with fruits or with festival meats such as *sate* or *rendang*. The rice sometimes is made into a fermented liquidlike toddy.

Despite the widespread visibility of wet-rice paddy fields, they are a relatively recent phenomenon. Wet rice was not extensively cultivated in Indonesia, the Philippines, Thailand, or Burma until the latter part of the nineteenth century. Its cultivation coincided with the opening of the Suez Canal and a greatly expanded trade to the area, at a time when colonial powers were encouraging increased food production for growing populations (J. N. Anderson, personal communication).

A continuous need for water and its control has increased sensitivity to seasonal fluctuations in the rains and has also encouraged an elaborate technology to harness and store it – all accompanied by rituals similar to those used for the rice that grows in the water. Where hillside erosion prevented regular upland cropping, terracing was introduced and is still used. Terraces require substantial investments of time and energy because effective structures can be realized only gradually. Notable examples of terracing are to be found in Java and Bali. It has been suggested that the terraces of the northern Philippines were constructed for earlier propagation of taro and other root crops, which may have preceded rice planting (Pollock 1992).

Dry-rice growers practice various means to delay fallowing and maintain soil fertility, including intercropping, a common technique among shifting cultivators. Indonesians, for example, have recently introduced peanuts (*Arachis hypogaea*) in some areas. Moreover, at the International Rice Research Institute in the Philippines, and elsewhere, high-yielding, fast-growing, more highly nutritious strains of rice have been bred to meet increasing demand.

This "Green Revolution" was technically successful, but preexisting races cultivated by small growers were often preferred for taste or for aroma, and when hand-hulled by pounding in a mortar, they retained much of the germ removed by machine hulling. The new strains that replaced them, however, required greater input in terms of time, technology, fertilizers, and water control, and have, therefore, proven too expensive for many small cultivators. Because of these developments, some compromises have ensued, and gene banks for rice now recognize the value of older varieties.

Root Crops

In addition to rice, or as a substitute, Southeast Asians have eaten a variety of other starchy staples (chiefly root vegetables) that are indigenous as well as introduced. Notable among them are yams of the *Dioscorea* species, chiefly *Dioscorea alata,* the greater yam, and *Dioscorea esculenta,* the lesser yam, both of which are ancient plants thought to have been domesticated several thousand years ago in Southeast Asia (Burkill 1966; Pollock 1992). *Dioscorea alata,* is a cultigen unknown in the wild, whereas *D. esculenta,* still has wild varieties. Robert Dentan (1968) notes that the Semai (Malaysian aborigines) tend wild yam patches, which may give us a glimpse of how agriculture began. The plants have climbing vines and starchy tubers that can be stored in the ground. Now chiefly famine foods, these roots, propagated by cuttings, contain alkaloids and other toxins not yet identified, among them acrid substances used by indigenous peoples as fish poisons (Heiser 1990). Consequently, those who rely upon wild yams are careful to boil or roast them before eating.

Another root that may have preceded rice as a staple is *Colocasia esculenta,* together with other members of this family, *Alocasia macrorrhiza, Cyrtosperma chamissonis,* and *Xanthosoma sagittifolium,* that are collectively known as taro. Except for *Xanthosoma,* which is American in origin, taros are Asian or Pacific plants. *Alocasia* and *Colocasia* have been cultivated "from remote times" throughout Southeast Asia (Burkill 1966). *Colocasia,* unknown as a wild plant (Herklots 1972), probably originated in northern India. Its common names are *dasheen, eddo, cocoyam,* or *keladi* (Malay). Taros have not been relied on as a starch food in much of Southeast Asia for many years. They contain crystals of calcium oxalate that must be leached out before the corms are cooked. Occasionally, however, the stems and leaves are boiled or fried in coconut oil.

Two other starchy roots, introduced to Southeast Asia, are the white potato *(Solanum tuberosum)* and manioc (cassava, yuca) *(Manihot utilissima),* both of South American origin. The potato was probably brought by the Spaniards to the Philippines in the sixteenth century and by the Dutch to Java in the following century (Burkill 1966). A taste for it has been slow to develop, but the same cannot be said of manioc. Of the family that includes figs *(Ficus)* and other latex-producing species, manioc was widespread in tropical America (Jones 1959). It was noted by voyagers who followed Christopher Columbus and was taken early to Africa; it reached Asia much later, however, and although the date of its arrival in Southeast Asia is not certain (Burkill 1966), it may have been as late as the eighteenth century.

According to Robert Hefner (1990), in the nineteenth century the Dutch colonial government introduced manioc to Java, where rural people resisted its cultivation until a serious food crisis was experienced in the 1880s. Although a comparative latecomer, manioc is now ubiquitous throughout the region. The roots may be left in the ground for long periods, and because manioc produces more food per unit of land than any other crop, it is increasingly relied upon as a famine food. Yet manioc is nutritionally inferior to most other foods, and it drains soils of nutrients without contributing any. Moreover, most races contain hydrogen cyanide (prussic acid), and South American techniques for removing this poison by boiling or roasting did not accompany manioc to Africa and the East. In Java (Burkill 1966), Malaysia, and other parts of the region, sun-dried strips of manioc are sold and consumed as snacks. In both countries, parboiled tubers are fermented several days with locally produced yeast to make an inexpensive *tapai* (Burkill 1966; Wilson 1986). In addition, the young leaves are sometimes used as a vegetable.

Grain Staples

Another New World staple, maize *(Zea mays),* caught on considerably more swiftly in Southeast Asia than did manioc and the potato. Lucien Hanks (1972) quotes the European traveler Nicholas Gervaise, who wrote, in 1688, that the grain had first been sown just 12 to 15 years earlier in Siam, yet it already covered the upland plains. Maize was also relied upon as a staple by upland dwellers in precolonial Java (Hefner 1990) – before Dutch rule in the nineteenth century. Although the Semai adopted it (together with manioc) as a staple food (Dentan 1968), it has tended to be a substitute grain in the region, and despite introduction of newer varieties, it is used primarily as feed for animals or as a snack, roasted or boiled, for humans.

Some staple grains of importance elsewhere also grow in Southeast Asia. Foxtail, or Italian millet *(Setaria italica),* and some other races have been food sources for tribal peoples (Burkill 1966). Wheat *(Triticum vulgare)* flour is of some importance in bread, biscuits, crackers, and cookies. Wheat was introduced following European settlement and used to make, among other things, noodles, which came to Southeast Asia from China (Chang 1977). Noodles are made and eaten in all the countries of the region, often as snack foods (Wilson 1986). Bread is of some importance in Vietnam and is increasingly common in other parts of the region. Bakeries in major urban centers produce bread and rolls that are sold in shops and markets and by itinerant salespeople. Such baked goods are usually consumed as morning snacks but are considered inferior to rice in relieving hunger.

Palm Staples

The sago palms (*Metroxylon sagu* or *Metroxylon rumphii*) yield a starch from the inner parts of the trunk after they are grated and soaked. This starch is a fallback food, consumed when rice supplies are short in the region. The trees are cut at maturity, about 9 to 15 years after planting, when the starch is at its peak (Burkill 1966). Sago flour is also used in making snack foods.

Another palm, the lontar (*Borassus flabellifer,* also known as the palmyra), grows from India eastward to the Celebes and yields sugar and toddy (wine) in the juices of its trunk. The time required for the lontar to reach maturity is similar to that of the sago (Burkill 1966). The tip of the tree is cut, and the juice collects in a vessel. It may be tapped for several months with daily cuts. J. J. Fox (1977) studied an Indonesian group on the island of Roti, Lesser Sundas, who subsist largely on this juice. Vinegar is made from overfermented lontar toddy (Burkill 1966), and the leaves have long been used in Indonesia for writing; books of leaves fastened together are known as *lontar.*

Staple Qualities

Southeast Asians believe that foods have inherent qualities that affect the body. Such beliefs stem from the humoral systems of Ayurvedic (Indian), Chinese, and Islamic medicine, all of which have influenced these populations over the last millennium (Hart, Rajadhon, and Coughlin 1965; Hart 1969; Lindenbaum 1977; Laderman 1983). Although with ethnic and individual differences, objects, physiological states (including disease), weather, and behaviors are categorized as having degrees of "hot," "cold," and "neutral." Most staple foods are defined as "neutral" among these populations. Manioc, however, is "hot," and eating it is thought to make the body hot, a situation also brought about by consuming animal protein, salt, and some anomalous fruits and seeds. The definition of manioc as "hot" may indicate recognition of the toxic chemical in the raw tuber.

Fish, Meat, and Fowl

Fish

There is little disagreement among experts (Raymond Firth 1966; Hanks 1972) that the dietary staples of Southeast Asians during the historical era have been primarily rice and fish. But the archaeological record is less clear regarding the presence of fish in diets of prehistoric hunter-gatherers, in large part because archaeological research in the area is far from complete. Finds in northern Vietnam of middens of mollusk shells in Hoabhinian-era levels (Burling 1965) indicate an early reliance on foods from the sea, and E. N. Anderson (1988) writes of rich sources of fish and game for central and southern China in Neolithic times. For later periods, Ying-Shi Yu (1977) has noted

the finding of several species of fish in the tomb of a Han aristocrat who died in the first century before the present era in Hunan Province (southern China).

The bony fishes antedate mammals by several hundred million years. When the continents reached their present-day positions, land masses blocked fish migration through the tropical seas, but species found in Southeast Asia range throughout these latitudes as far as Africa or Australia. Relatively few comprehensive listings have been compiled, yet Raymond Firth (1966) cites C. N. Maxwell, who described 250 species of marine food fishes for Malaya, and J. S. Scott (1959) lists 294, including the skate, shark, and ray family, and the dolphin, *Coryphaena hippurus,* as sea fishes of Malaya. Though many are edible, the list of favored marine fish is shorter. Raymond Firth (1966) notes that over 20 types were landed at a Malay village in amounts greater than 1,000 tons. Most were of the mackerel family, *Scombroidii,* including herring (*Clupea* spp.) and small horse mackerel (*Scomberomerus* spp.) (Scott 1959). Of deepwater fish feeding near the surface Firth notes dorab or wolf herring (*Chirocentrus dorab*), shad (*Clupea kanagurta*), sprat or whitebait (*Stolephorus* spp.), and anchovies (*Anchoviella* and *Thrissocles* spp.). Bottom feeders taken in quantity during Firth's research included jewfish (among which are numbered croaker, *Umbrina dussumierii, Corvina* spp., *Otolithes ruber,* and several types of *Johnius*), sea bream (*Synagris* spp.), sea perch (*Lates calcarifer*), snapper (*Lutianus* spp.), gray mullet (*Mugil* spp.), and flatfish (including sole, flounder, *Pseudorhombus,* and *Synaptura* spp.) (Scott 1959; Raymond Firth 1966). This list is echoed by Thomas Fraser (1960), Carol Laderman (1983), and Christine S. Wilson (1983).

Other fish common to the region and mentioned by Raymond Firth include pomfret (*Stromateus* spp., generally prized in Southeast Asia), catfish (*Chilinus* spp., not a popular food), sardines (*Sardinella* spp.), bluefish (*Pomatomus salatrix*), grouper (*Epinephelus* spp.), pike (*Sphyraena* spp.), and scad (*Caranx leptolepis*). Fish have been caught with indigenous methods developed over time, chiefly by nets from shore or small boats, or by handline. Before the existence of motorized transport, these activities were local and subsistent, but commercial trade of sea products seems to have begun with Chinese embassies early in the first millennium (Fraser 1960).

Additional sea animals eaten by Southeast Asians include squid or cuttlefish (*Loligo* and *Sepia* spp.) (Burkill 1966), crabs (*Charybdis* spp.), prawns and crayfish (*Penaeus, Penaeopsis, Parapenaeopsis* spp. and *Peneus semisulcatus;* the spiny lobsters *Panulirus*), and the lobsterlike *Squilla.* Shrimp (*Acetes erythraeus*) (Burkill 1966) and other crustaceans caught in tidal nets are the source of a fermented paste eaten as a side relish with rice meals (Wilson 1970).

A fish of continuing commercial value, used in dishes such as cooked vegetables, is the small whitebait or anchovy (*Stolephorus* spp.). The green sea turtle (*Chelonia mydas*) (Burkill 1966) provides meat occasionally and widely prized eggs seasonally. Mollusks – cockles (*Cardium*), clams, mussels (*Mytilus* spp.), and oysters (*Ostrea edulis* and *Ostrea rivularis*) – are collected along shorelines, often by women and children (Burkill 1966).

Sharks and rays, the Elasmobranchs, are widely found in tropical seas. The gelatinous skeletons are prized by the Chinese, and members of the Carcharidae and Dasybatidae families provide income to fishermen who sell the valued fins (Burkill 1966). The dogfish (*Scoliodon sorrakowah C.*), and other members of this class, are usually eaten by poorer people (Scott 1959; Burkill 1966). Salting (curing in brine) and drying fish have long been practiced. Before ice machines and mechanical refrigeration, these preservation methods permitted the sale of surplus fish at a distance and storage for monsoon months when fishing was unsafe.

Animal Meats

Meat – the flesh of mammals – is chiefly reserved for feasts and special occasions (Geertz 1960; Kirsch 1973; Volkman 1985). Often the flesh is that of the water buffalo (*Bubalus bubalis*) (Burkill 1966), that ancient ricefield plough-laborer. A native of Asia, the water buffalo is said to have been domesticated in many locales, but at present the best evidence points to southern China some time around 5000 B.C. (Hoffpauir, this work). Buffalo milk is higher in fat than that of most cattle, about 7 percent (Heiser 1990), but is little used in Southeast Asia because the populations exhibit high incidences of primary adult lactose intolerance (Simoons 1970).

Other *Bos* species have been domesticated in the region, such as the *seladang (Bos gaurus)* of Malaysia, the *mithan (Bos frontalis)* of Indochina, and the *banteng (Bos sondaicus)* of Java. Some cattle (*Bos taurus*), the species common in the West, are found in the region – mainly in Java and the Philippines (Burkill 1966). *Zebu,* Indian cattle, though well adapted to the climate are relatively rare.

Another ruminant of the bovine family, the goat (*Capra hiracus*), is widespread throughout the region, where it has substituted for more expensive meat species despite its strong flavor. Its Malay name, *kambing,* is well known throughout the region and is applied locally to sheep – *kambing biri-biri* – as well. Rural people neutralize goats' destructive grazing with fences or by staking. Archaeological remains of domesticated sheep have been dated from 9000 B.C.; goat domestication probably was almost that early (Heiser 1990). K. C. Chang (1977) indicates that goats were introduced to China from western Asia in prehistoric times.

The pig (*Sus scrofa*) is said to have been domesticated in the Near East (Anderson 1988; Heiser 1990) around 7000 to 5000 B.C., when villages developed, although Frederick Simoons (1994) suggests that pigs were first domesticated in Southeast Asia. When Islam came to Southeast Asia, its prohibition against eating pork stopped pig raising among many peoples, although others who were not converted continued the practice. Wild pigs are native to Asia as they are to Europe, and it has been suggested that in rural Asian Muslim countries, the animals may be called something other than "pigs" by the natives and, thus, may be hunted and eaten.

Although many wild mammals and birds are protected by legislation (Medway 1969), some are still hunted for meat, particularly by aboriginal peoples. Well liked by all inhabitants of Southeast Asia is another local ruminant, the deer (*Cervus unicolor*) (Medway 1969), along with the mouse deer or chevrotain (*Tragulus javanicus* and *Tragulus napu*). The flesh of this smallest of hoofed mammals is said to be excellent and is salted, dried, and smoked (jerked) throughout Malaysia. Other wild animals that have acted as occasional food sources include the large fruit-eating flying fox or fruit bat (*Pteropus edulis* or *Pteropus vampyrus*) (Burkill 1966; Medway 1969). In addition, jungle tribes may hunt birds, monkeys, and other small animal species for food.

Poultry or Fowl

Chickens (*Gallus gallus*) are generally the most important domestic fowl in Southeast Asia and may have been domesticated there. The archaeological record is not clear, and experts differ as to whether this Asian jungle bird was first domesticated in India or Southeast Asia (Heiser 1990). Yet there is general agreement with I. H. Burkill (1966) that the chicken was early selected for gaming as well as divination, in which both entrails and thigh bones were and still are used (Heiser 1990). Chickens are kept for meat and eggs in rural areas, with the meat often prepared for feasts (Geertz 1960), along with other animal meats. Clifford Geertz and other anthropologists (e.g., Fraser 1960) have noted the frequency of *kenduri* or *slametan,* special feasts of a familial or community nature, with curried chicken dishes to accompany the glutinous rice. Chicken is generally liked and is sometimes a meal-saver during monsoon months when fresh fish is not obtainable.

Fowl eggs have also been valued for use in divination. Simoons (1994), for example, has commented on their use in this capacity by hill-tribe peoples from Assam eastward, while also noting their avoidance (along with fowl meat) because of beliefs associating them with fertility. Others (Rosemary Firth 1966; Strange 1981) have noted the symbolic use of eggs as fertility symbols that are given to female guests at weddings and as spirit offerings to launch a boat or enter a new house.

Simoons (1994) notes a particular preference in this region for brooded eggs, with the embryo well developed – these are especially relished in the

Philippines. He hypothesizes that the practice may have originated, before domestication, in the gathering of wild fowl eggs, which, if they contained half-hatched chicks as recognizable forms of life, were judged as not dangerous to eat. Other poultry kept by Southeast Asians include ducks (the *Anas* species, related to the mallard), which were domesticated independently in both Europe and China (Burkill 1966). In Indonesia, ducks are part of an ecological system that includes rice fields and irrigation ditches containing fish. The ducks subsist on the rice (after threshing) as well as on the fish, while providing eggs and meat for their caretakers. Geese (*Anser anser,* the European domestic species, or an Indian hybrid, *Anser cygnoides*) (Burkill 1966) sometimes play similar roles in rural Southeast Asia. The goose probably reached the region via India.

Nonstaple Plant Foods

Vegetables
Although Western visitors to Southeast Asia have noted native plants sometimes used as food (for example, Burbidge 1989; Wallace 1989), and have commented on "curries" for main meals without always specifying their components (Lewis 1991), nutritionists and anthropologists have been those most concerned with the importance of vegetable foods in Southeast Asian diets. Rosemary Firth (1966), for example, has noted that for Malay fishing people, vegetables are a marginal need. The sandy soil near the sea is not conducive to vegetable propagation, and the people who might have time for such an effort, and who play significant roles in rice raising, have no tradition of gardening. Before the advent of motorized transport, the attitude toward vegetables seemed to be that they made a nice addition to a meal but were not essential to it (Wilson 1988).

Traditionally, the growers of vegetables for market in Southeast Asia have been the Chinese. But others living in rural areas long ago learned of wild plants growing on empty lands and in the forests, including wild ferns, and well into this century, older women made gathering trips to bring these wild plants back for consumption (Wilson 1970). Burkill (1966) lists a number of edible ferns, such as *Diplazium esculentum* and *Stenochlaena palustris,* although most of the species cited are used for making woven objects or for medicinal purposes.

During colonial times, Europeans introduced a number of Western vegetables to the hill stations at higher altitudes. The carrot – *Daucus carota sativus* – is an example: It was carried from Persia to India and then China in the thirteenth century (Herklots 1972). (The Dutch introduced quick-maturing cultivars in Indonesia during the nineteenth century, but roots such as carrots do best at higher elevations.)

Laderman (1983) lists three dozen vegetables that she identified as collected or purchased in an East Coast Malay village. Among those eaten occasionally that are grown locally are many types of spinach, gucil *(Antidesma ghaesembilla),* sweet shoot *(Sauropus androgynus),* and bamboo shoots (*Bambusa* spp.) (Burkill 1966). Several species of amaranths *(Amaranthus gangeticus)* (Herklots 1972) are ancient potherbs here, native to the region and eaten like spinach. Another local spinach abundant in the region is *kangkung (Ipomoea reptans)* (Burkill 1966; Herklots 1972). It grows on or near water, has a peppery taste like watercress, and is also called swamp cabbage.

The Western view that Southeast Asians have little interest in eating vegetables probably results from the climatically difficult enterprise of raising temperate species. Those that are grown are often natives of China or India, such as *Brassica chinensis,* Chinese cabbage, and *Brassica juncea* (Burkill 1966). Among the leguminous plants that are found is the long bean *(Vigna sinensis),* which became a cultigen during ancient times in Asia or Africa and has pods that may measure 1 meter in length (Burkill 1966). Another legume, *Psophocarpus tetragonolobus,* the winged or four-angled bean, was noted in the seventeenth century in the Moluccas as introduced from elsewhere. On the basis of its Malay name, *kachang botor (botor* means lobe in Arabic), Burkill (1966) infers that it was brought by Arabs from the African side of the Indian Ocean. The pods and beans are eaten raw or cooked, as is the root. This plant has received international attention in recent decades thanks to its high protein content, along with some derogatory comments because of preparation difficulties (National Academy of Sciences 1975; Henry, Donachie, and Rivers 1985; Sri Kantha and Erdman 1986).

Another legume is the yam bean *(Pachyrhizus erosus).* A native of tropical America, this bean was brought by the Spaniards to the Philippines in the sixteenth century. From there it quickly spread as far as Indochina and Thailand and soon grew wild (Burkill 1966; Herklots 1972). Both young pods and the starchy root are eaten.

Several other leguminous seed pods that originated in Africa or Asia have added protein and variety to Southeast Asian diets. Examples are the gram beans: red *(Cajanus indicus),* the Indian *dhal* (sometimes known as the pigeon pea), green or mung *(Phaseolus aureus),* and black, also known as mung or *dhal (Phaseolus mungo* L.) (Burkill 1966; Herklots 1972). Sprouts as well as vegetable cheese have been prepared from both *dhal* beans.

The other bean-cheese source for the region is the soybean, *Glycine max,* which has been cultivated by the Chinese for at least 4,500 years (Herklots 1972). In addition to sprouts and oil, the beans have been fermented to produce *tempe* or tofu and soy sauce, a fermented product soaked in brine and exposed to the sun (Burkill 1966).

The South American groundnut or peanut *(Arachis*

hypogaea) may have reached Asia early by western as well as eastern routes (Burkill 1966). A variety of races have developed over the last two centuries, some of which have been selected for oil content. Peanut oil production has been a Southeast Asian industry for over a century, with the oil (chemically similar to olive oil) sold in the region. Nuts, ground into paste, cooked with onions, peppers, and other spices, are served with curries, roasted meat, and in fresh fruit and vegetable salads in several Southeast Asian countries.

Two leguminous trees of the *Parkia* and *Pithecolobium* genera provide seeds that are eaten with meals as a relish and also used as diuretics (Burkill 1966). *Parkia biglobosa* is also found in Africa, where the seeds are eaten after roasting, but the preferred species in Southeast Asia is *Parkia speciosa*, the *petai*. *Pithecolobium* species are found in Asia and America. *Pithecolobium jiringa*, the *jering*, is the seed of choice for both medicinal and food purposes. It may be boiled or roasted. Both seeds smell and taste like garlic, and the odor lingers on the eater's breath.

One vegetable seemingly native to the region is eggplant (also called *brinjal* and *aubergine*, or *terong* in Malay). *Solanum melongena*, related to the potato and tomato, reached India, Africa, and Europe via Spain (Burkill 1966). Charles Heiser (1990) and G. A. C. Herklots (1972) believe it originated in India, reaching Spain and Africa via the Arabs and Persians. The latter authority notes its mention in a Chinese work on agriculture of the fifth century. The plant produces large, egg-shaped fruits, ranging in color from white through golden to green and blackish purple.

Another vegetable – this one has been cultivated in the region for at least two millennia and may, indeed, have originated there – is the climbing snake gourd *(Trichosanthes anguina* or *Trichosanthes cucumerina)* (Burkill 1966; Herklots 1972). The Chinese obtained it from the south, presumably Malaysia, suggesting that it was cultivated there at least from the early Christian era. Another native gourd is the wax gourd *(Benincasa cerifera)* (Burkill 1966; Herklots 1972). Bitter melon or cucumber (*Momordica charantia* L.), a long, green, warty-looking gourd (Herklots 1972) with seeds inside bright red arils, has long been an ingredient in curries (Burkill 1966). It is probably African in origin. The bottle gourd *(Lagenaria leucantha)* may also have originated in Africa; known to the Egyptians, it reached China sometime during the past 2,000 years (Burkill 1966). Other gourds of ancient origin, such as the *Luffah* species, have also served as vegetables (Herklots 1972).

The Chinese or Japanese radish *(Raphanus sativus)*, a cultigen of eastern Asia with a long white root, has origins similar to the European radish (Burkill 1966; Herklots 1972). Okra, or "lady's fingers" *(Hibiscus esculentus)*, a vegetable assumed to be of African origin (Burkill 1966), is sometimes named a bean in local languages; the Malay term *bendi* is from Hindi (Burkill 1966; Herklots 1972).

The tomato *(Lycopersicum esculentum)* (Burkill 1966) was brought from America to Europe and thence to Asia more than 300 years ago. Eaten raw or cooked, it is also the source of bottled sauces called in many lands *kichap* – the name usually given in Malay to soy sauce. (A Malay calls catsup *sos tematu*.)

Edible toadstools or mushrooms *(Volvariella volvacea)* are grown and eaten in some countries of Southeast Asia (Burkill 1966). With the advent of refrigeration and tinned foods in the twentieth century, a variety of Western vegetable foods became available to people in money economies, particularly in urban locales.

Fruits

Southeast Asia has a wealth of native fruits, as well as some introduced from other regions. Best known is the banana (*Musa* species). Heiser (1990) believes that *Musa acuminata*, the wild banana of Malaysia, was the progenitor of all other banana species. In fact, Heiser feels that Southeast Asia was the original home of all bananas, although Betty Allen (1967) suggests that the place of origin may have been India.

Cultivated bananas may be small or large, red- as well as yellow-skinned, and sweet or tart. Plantains have always been eaten cooked; some other races, cultivated for centuries, are dipped in batter and fried. Flowers from banana plants of a Philippine race are served as a vegetable. For millennia the leaves have been used as wrappings for food and as temporary rain cover.

Citrus fruits are also of Asian origin, although grapefruit may be an exception (Burkill 1966; Heiser 1990). Species have been cultivated in subtropical climes from before the time of Alexander the Great. *Citrus microcarpa* (Burkill 1966) is a small, round, green ball of a fruit (sometimes called the music lime) long used in cooking and making drinks, as is *Citrus aurantifolia* (much like the West Indian lime). *Citrus nobilis* (Burkill 1966) is the Mandarin orange or sweet lime, not to be confused with *Citrus sinensis*, the sweet or Chinese orange familiar to Western palates, though both may have originated in China. The rind of the Mandarin orange, green to orange in color, peels easily like that of a tangerine, and the segments are readily removed. Native to Southeast Asia is *Citrus maxima* or *Citrus grandis* (Burkill 1966; Allen 1967), the sweet pomelo, as large as a grapefruit. It reached Europe in the twelfth century (Eiseman and Eiseman 1988) and is now sold in U.S. markets. It is highly valued in Southeast Asia, where it is associated with the Chinese New Year.

Garcinia is a genus of trees of the rubber family in the Old World tropics (Burkill 1966). A number of species have edible fruits, and several yield dyes, ink, or watercolor paint. *Garcinia mangostana*, the mangosteen, is a favorite throughout Southeast Asia and has been known elsewhere since the voyages of exploration; it is also famous for having earned the admiration of Queen Victoria. The small, round fruit has a ¼-inch (0.635 centimeter), dark red to purple rind, and five or more white, fleshy segments of edible matter with a delicate, slightly tart flavor. F. W. Burbidge (1989) was enthusiastic about the mangosteen when he wrote in 1880, as was Alfred Wallace (1989: 148), who commented in his mid-1850s report on the Malay Archipelago that "those celebrated fruits, the mangosteen and . . . durion . . . will hardly grow" elsewhere. *Garcinia atroviridis,* a bright yellow-orange, acid-astringent, fluted fruit about 3 to 4 inches (8 to 9 centimeters) in diameter, and eaten as a relish (Burkill 1966), is native to Malaysia and Burma and common in Thailand (Allen 1967).

Several members of the Sapindaceae family have a tart-sweet pulp, with the best known, *rambutan (Nephelium lappaceum),* named for the hairlike cilia extending from its red or yellow rind. Native to the region, it is widely cultivated, but wild forest specimens are also found (Burkill 1966). Also native is *Nephelium malaiense* ("cat's eyes"), which is small with a buff skin (Allen 1967). The litchi (lychee) from southern China *(Litchi chinensis)* is cultivated as well (Burkill 1966).

Other fruits with refreshing pulp include the langsat *(Lansium domesticum)* – an indigenous fruit that is now cultivated. It was noted by the Chinese in Java in the fifteenth century (Burkill 1966). *Salak (Zalacca edulis)* is a similar fruit from a palm that grows throughout Southeast Asia. Its thin, brown skin looks like that of a lizard (Burkill 1966; Eiseman and Eiseman 1988).

Two members of the rubber and castor oil family produce pleasant fruits. One, *Cicca acida* (Burkill 1966; Allen 1967), known in English and Malay as *chermai,* the Malay or Otaheite gooseberry, is a very tart tree fruit. Although it has been cultivated for centuries, its place of origin is not known. The other fruit, *rambai (Baccaurea motleyana),* is a Southeast Asian native and has long been cultivated there (Allen 1967).

Perhaps the most famed Southeast Asian fruit is durian *(Durio zibethinus)* (Burkill 1966), which grows on trees too tall to climb (70 to 80 meters or more). Ovoid or round, variable in size, each fruit may weigh several kilograms. The thick, green rind has sharp spines that cushion its fall. Inside are four or five arils of soft pulp surrounding seeds. Durian smells and tastes like onion, garlic, or cheese. The fruit is edible for only a few days after dehiscing, after which it undergoes rapid chemical change (Wilson 1970). Most Southeast Asians and some Europeans relish this seasonal fruit, and the seeds are roasted and eaten as well. Durian conserves, sweet or salty, have been made by local people, and in recent decades durian ice cream has been developed.

The mango *(Mangifera indica)* is the most famous member of its family, which originated in India (Burkill 1966). Other species grow throughout Southeast Asia. It has been known for more than 4,000 years (Allen 1967) and was one of the earliest tree fruits to be cultivated (Eiseman and Eiseman 1988). Fruits may be 17 centimeters (7 inches) long, and about 7 centimeters (3 inches) in diameter. When ripe, the flesh is yellow to reddish, sweet, aromatic, and much prized. *Mangifera odorata,* called *kuini* in Malay, is also sweet when ripe, with a resinous smell. The horse mango, *Mangifera foetida,* is inedible until ripe. Both *M. odorata* and *M. foetida* are fibrous and are sometimes eaten to help remove intestinal parasites.

A New World member of this family, *Anacardium occidentale* – the cashew – was brought by the Portuguese in the sixteenth century to become one of the first American trees cultivated in Southeast Asia (Burkill 1966; Allen 1967). The tart fruit, a greenish pedicel the size of an apple, which is rich in ascorbic acid, and its appended nut are both well liked. The nut must be boiled or roasted to remove an irritant chemical, cardol. In rural areas, monkeys and fruit bats vie with human consumers for the fruit, which otherwise serves as a cooked relish with a rice meal.

Two members of the Urticaceae family, *Artocarpus integra* and *Artocarpus champeden* (jackfruit and chempedak), are native to Asia, the jackfruit coming from India (Burkill 1966). Both have large fruits as long as 30 centimeters (1 foot), with mottled green, bumpy rinds and yellowish, creamy flesh surrounding seeds that are boiled before eating. The fruits are used to make sweetmeats. Historically very popular, they were known to Pliny. *Artocarpus communis* (breadfruit), a member of this family, is less common and not much consumed.

Two small trees native to Malaysia produce acid fruits that are cooked and used as tart, refreshing relishes, *Averrhoa bilimbi* and *Averrhoa carambola* (Burkill 1966). The latter, brought to the West by early explorers, is known in Western countries as starfruit because of its shape when cut horizontally. In Asia, both are called *belimbing.* Four tropical American fruits, *Annona muricata* (soursop, or "Dutch durian"), *Annona reticulata* (custard apple or bullock's heart), *Annona cherimola* (cherimoya), and *Annona squamosa* (sweetsop), were brought very early to Southeast Asia (Burkill 1966).

Eugenia, found throughout the tropics, has more than two dozen species in south India and Southeast Asia that have grown wild and been cultivated for centuries for their valued fruits. One, *Eugenia aromatica,* produces cloves. Others have pearlike, rosy or pink-tinted fruits, about 5 to 7 or more centimeters long (2 to 3 inches), that are called *jambu* in Malay, and "apples" by English speakers: *Eugenia aquea* (or *Eugenia jambos*) are water or rose apples, *Eugenia malaccensis* is the Malay apple, and *Eugenia javanica* is the Java apple (Burkill 1966). Also of this Myrtaceae family is the guava, *Psidium guajava,* an American native brought by the Spanish across both the Atlantic and Pacific at an early date (Burkill 1966). The thin, green skin becomes yellow and soft at maturity;

the pulp is white, greenish, or rose, with many small seeds. They are good eaten raw and make excellent juice drinks.

Other well-liked, early introductions from the Americas are papaya *(Carica papaya)*, pineapple *(Ananas comosus)*, and passion fruit *(Passiflora laurifolia)*. Papaya reached Southeast Asia via the West Indies before the sixteenth century (Burkill 1966; Allen 1967). A large herb, it is fast-growing, producing fruit in six months. Ever-bearing, the papaya is a useful dooryard plant, rich in nutrients, green-skinned until ripe, with yellow to red flesh, and 15 to 35 centimeters (6 to 14 inches) in length.

Pineapple was cultivated in America from remote times, and the Europeans brought it around the world to all parts of Asia before the seventeenth century (Burkill 1966). A pineapple plantation industry was developed during the nineteenth century in Malaysia, Indonesia, and the Philippines, when canning was introduced (Allen 1967). Passion fruit, a climbing herb of tropical America, was also introduced to India and other Asian countries in the nineteenth century (Burkill 1966).

Fruits of purple *Passiflora edulis* and yellow *Passiflora laurifolia* are sweet in smell and taste and suitable for both eating or juice. *Passiflora quadrangularis,* the grenadilla, is popular in Indonesia. Unripe it serves as a vegetable and is also preserved in sugar. Not a fruit but a similar snack is sugarcane *(Saccharum officinarum)*, a grass eaten by chewing the cane, or drunk as pressed juice (Burkill 1966). It was domesticated in New Guinea or Indonesia during remote times (Heiser 1990). Burkill (1966) has documented its spread through Asia, and Sidney Mintz (1985) has provided its later history. Early Indian references to the crystallized form of sugar date from several hundred years B.C., and Alexander the Great noted it during his voyages (Burkill 1966). The watermelon *(Citrullus vulgaris)*, an African plant known to the Egyptians (Burkill 1966), reached China via India in the tenth century and is grown in some Southeast Asian countries. The fruits resemble North American varieties in color and character.

Fruits native to the region but less well known because they are seldom marketed are cultivated in dooryards for local consumption. Among these are *Sandoricum indicum* (the *sentul*) (Burkill 1966) and *Erioglossum rubiginosum (mertajam)*, a tree with small red to black astringent fruits, called *kerian* by Malays. The *kundungan (Bouea macrophylla)* is a small tree related to the cashew that is cultivated in villages (Burkill 1966). It is native to Malaysia and much of Indonesia, with a sour-to-sweet taste. Further north, it is called *setar* for the capital of Kedah, Alor Star (Allen 1967).

Kemuntung, or rose myrtle, a shrub of the Myrtaceae family *(Rhodomyrtus tomentosa)*, produces small, wild fruits prized by children. Still other fruits have been available since refrigerated shipping began;

pears, grapes, and oranges are enjoyed by rural people who can afford market prices. Some grow in hill stations or at high altitudes. A few wild species of *Prunus,* relatives of the peach *(Prunus persica),* as well as species of *Pyrus,* related to the pear *(Pyrus communis)* and the apple *(Pyrus malus),* are grown, but most are of European origin (Burkill 1966).

Spices and Seasonings

Southeast Asia encompasses the Spice Islands, whose lure motivated the fifteenth- and sixteenth-century European voyages of discovery. Most sought after were pepper *(Piper nigrum)*, cloves *(Eugenia aromatica),* and nutmeg *(Myristica fragrans)* (Reid 1993). Although clove and nutmeg trees are Southeast Asian natives and have been cultivated for centuries, their early history is dim (Burkill 1966). Clove was known to the Chinese by 300 B.C.; it was in Egypt by the first century A.D. and reached the Mediterranean by the fourth century. Arabs brought nutmeg to Europe in the sixth century. Nutmeg, which is also the source of mace, is made into a sweet by boiling to remove tannin before adding sugar (Burkill 1966). Before the twentieth century, it was candied for sale in Europe.

Piper is a genus of many species that grow in moist, warm parts of the world (Burkill 1966). *Piper nigrum,* with both black and white berries, was apparently first cultivated in India; its name in countries to which it subsequently spread are cognates of the Sanskrit *pippah.* By the sixteenth century, it became an export plantation crop in Dutch-controlled Sumatra and in other countries (Andaya 1993). Supplanting the Portuguese, the Dutch assured their profit by allowing cultivation only in areas they controlled by treaty with local rulers. All these spices remain important cuisine condiments and, thus, important commercial crops (Steinberg 1970).

Cinnamon *(Cinnamomum zeylanicum),* the bark of a tree of eastern and southeastern Asia, is another aromatic spice of ancient origin (Burkill 1966). The genus was once common in Europe and was known to the Egyptians, Hebrews, and Aryans. *Cinnamomum cassia,* a Chinese tree known over the last two millennia, provides cassia, an alternate form of cinnamon in Southeast Asia. *Cinnamomum zeylanicum* grows wild at high elevations in western India and Sri Lanka (Ceylon) and still produces the best cinnamon (Burkill 1966). Both cassia and cinnamon are known in Malay as *kayu manis* ("sweet wood") and are used medicinally as well as for seasoning.

Ginger *(Zingiber* species) is an herb native to tropical Asia and the Pacific (Burkill 1966), where several species and races grow wild. *Zingiber officinale* was cultivated in India and China before the Christian era (Yu 1977). The fresh rhizomes are used medicinally and as flavoring and are also dried and candied. Another family member, galangal *(Zingiber galanga)*

(Burkill 1966), is also native to tropical Asia and India and has been extensively used in Malaysia and Java. Its history and use compare to that of ginger.

Turmeric *(Curcuma domestica),* from the same family, is a Southeast Asian native as well and was used as a condiment (a substitute for saffron) and dye long before the Aryans reached India (Burkill 1966). Its color was the same as the royal color of India and the Indianized states of Southeast Asia, and turmeric was used in weddings and to tint ceremonial rice (Rosemary Firth 1966). Cardamom *(Amomum kepulaga)* (Burkill 1966), still one more herb of the ginger family, grows wild in Java and is cultivated as a breath sweetener and for use in curries.

Other important seasonings in general use have reached Southeast Asia from the outside world. Chief among these are members of the lily family *(Allium* species, such as onions, garlic, shallots, leeks, and chives) and chilli peppers *(Capsicum* species, which are natives of the Americas). Alliums are northern plants, mainly from the Mideast, where they have been grown since ancient times (Burkill 1966). But garlic *(Allium sativum)* and others were also cultivated long ago in India, spreading east from there. Bulbs of the *Allium* species (for example, shallot – *Allium ascalonicum)* are grown for market in hilly parts of Indonesia and the Philippines; most, however, are imported from India. All are ingredients in curries and used as seasonings, and most have also been employed medicinally for generations (Skeat 1967; Gimlette and Thomson 1971). Shallots are eaten raw individually or in salads along with other vegetables and are pickled in brine. Garlic is more prominent in areas closer to China. *Allium cepa,* the white or red onion, may be shredded and deep-fried as a condiment for other foods, as may shallots.

Columbus brought *Capsicum* (the chilli pepper) to Europe, whereupon writers of the time commented on its introduction (Burkill 1966). But less than 50 years later it was termed the "pepper of Calicut," a misnomer that ignored its New World origin. Chilli peppers have long been cultivated in Central and South America, and their European names reflect Spanish versions of the Mexican term *aji* as well as the desire of Dutch black pepper traders to save their own product from confusion by means of another Spanish translation, *"chilli."* Early on, naturalists distinguished over a dozen races, but the main species remain *Capsicum frutescens,* the sweeter, less pungent type represented by bell peppers, and *Capsicum annuum,* the very hot, small perennial known as bird pepper, which is the source of tabasco.

A number of races of both grow in Southeast Asia. *Capsicum baccatum* var. *baccatum,* the source of cayenne (Herklots 1972), has been used medicinally and for arrow poisons in Asia as it was in South America (Burkill 1966). Certainly the chillies are much appreciated in Southeast Asia. Burkill has noted that Malays prefer *Capsicum* to "black" pepper in cookery, and Westerners have long commented on the fiery nature of Thai cuisine (Steinberg 1970). The active principle in peppers is capsaicin, an alkaloid known to irritate skin and mucous membranes (Burkill 1966). It is also said to be addicting (Pangborn 1975), which may explain its lengthy history of use in Southeast Asia as well as in America (Rozin and Schiller 1980). Chillies have long been dried for market sale throughout Southeast Asia.

Tamarind, a leguminous tree with pulp-filled pods, was known to Greeks in the fourth century B.C. Although it probably originated in Africa or India, it was early cultivated in Southeast Asia (Burkill 1966). The pulp of *Tamarindus indica,* which is sweet to tart, looks in its marketable form like dates, which prompted Arabs and Persians to call it *tamar,* the Indian date (Burkill 1966). It is used as a relish and in cooking, and the flowers are sometimes eaten as well. In Java, the pulp is salted and made into balls that are steamed for preservation. Tamarind has also been used for medicinal purposes, to fix dyes, and to clean metal.

A grass native to the region, *Cymbopogon citratus* – lemon or citronella grass – has been cultivated as a food flavoring, a liquor spice, and a tea (Burkill 1966). In Java it is part of a spicy sherbet drink, and in Malay it plays a role in medicine and magic. The Portuguese took it to Madras in the seventeenth century, and it subsequently spread to all the tropics (Skeat 1967).

Three herbs of the temperate Old World or Levant, caraway, coriander, and cumin *(Carum carvi, Coriandrum sativum, Cuminum cyminum),* have been seasonings in Southeast Asia since their introduction at about the beginning of the Christian era. Because they have a past prior to written records (Burkill 1966), they are sometimes thought of as interchangeable, and anise *(Pimpinella anisum),* another family member, has been associated with them because of its odor and flavor. Anise was known to the Egyptians and, within the past thousand years, was carried by Arabs or Persians to China and India. In Malay, anise, caraway, and cumin are all called *jintan* (Winstedt 1966). Fresh coriander leaves (cilantro, or Chinese parsley) are used to flavor soups, meat, and fish dishes; the Thais, in particular, have a passion for them uncooked in many dishes.

Basil *(Ocimum basilicum* and *Ocimum canum),* an herb of the warmer parts of the world, has religious or symbolic roles as well as seasoning and medicinal ones in Southeast Asia (Burkill 1966). The Hindus, to whom it is sacred, may have introduced *Ocimum* species to Southeast Asia during "Indianization" (Coedes 1968). Mint *(Mentha arvensis* and other species), a similarly fragrant herb, is cultivated at higher elevations and used for flavoring and for medicines (Burkill 1966).

Salt has been a substance of physical as well as economic need (to produce dried seafoods) in Southeast Asia and, therefore, has been an item of commerce as well (Kathirithamby-Wells 1993). The salt trade probably antedates written records. Seacoast areas have long been local sources, and sea salt from solar evaporation has been produced in Thailand, Indonesia, and Vietnam for export as well as domestic use (ICNND 1960, 1962; Raymond Firth 1966); in addition, Thailand has salt deposits in the northeast (ICNND 1962).

Unfortunately, the local salt is not iodized, and iodine-deficiency diseases are a health problem in several of these countries (ICNND 1962) despite reliance on seafood, which is a good source of the mineral. The incidence of goiter on Bali, for example, may result from the Balinese preference for pork instead of seafood.

Although honey was undoubtedly the earliest sweetener, the boiling of the inflorescence of the nipa palm *(Nipa fruticans)* to make sugar has been an enduring cottage industry (Burkill 1966; Winstedt 1966). Refined white cane sugar has been much prized for hot drinks, but although refining was done in Java and other locales from early colonial times (Burkill 1966), it has proved too expensive for rural people, even in recent decades (Rosemary Firth 1966). Perhaps unfortunately, however, it has become a dietary essential (Wilson 1970, 1988).

Vinegar has been made from both palm and cane sugar, as well as from rice and fruit pulp (Burkill 1966). It occurs naturally if palm or fruit syrup is allowed to ferment more than 40 days. It is used in food preparation, and much of it has been imported from China in recent decades.

Soy sauce and the fish soy of Vietnam, *nuoc mam,* have already been briefly discussed. *Nam pla* or *pla-ra* (ICNND 1962) is the Thai version. Malay coastal villagers make *budu* by salting small fish, such as anchovies, in vats until the mixture ferments (Wilson 1986). A Philippine version is called *patis* (Steinberg 1970). A similar product, *gnapi,* is made in Burma by allowing fish to decay in the open (Lewis 1991). Shrimp paste is similarly made in most of these countries. The Malay version is *belacan,* the Indonesian *terasi,* and the Philippine *bagung.* These products are relishes or side dishes, often enlivened with fresh raw chillies; all are excellent sources of calcium and protein (Wilson 1986) and, with the chillies, of vitamin C.

Although not a condiment or a seasoning, yeast for household cooking is locally made (Wilson 1986). Burkill (1966) reports that the Javanese use their word for yeast, *tapai* (of Arabic origin), to include the Malaysian preparation *ragi* (from the Hindu) (Winstedt 1970). To rice flour and several spices, *Aspergillus* fungi as well as *Saccharomyces* spores are added, some adventitiously. This combination results in the fermented glutinous rice cakes, *tapai* (Wilson 1986), and also toddy.

Cooking Fats and Oils

Until the past few decades, the cooking mediums in Southeast Asia have been water, oils, sauces, and coconut milk. To save fuel, most cooking was done over wood fires, as quickly as possible, and long, slow roasting was done over coals. The premium oil has been coconut *(Cocos nucifera).* The nut of this palm is the seed of the fruit, and its grated ripe flesh, squeezed in water, also provides coconut milk *(santan* in Malay), the base for the curries of the region. This "most useful of trees" (Heiser 1990) requires warmth and moisture to grow well, and seacoasts provide the best climate. Southeast Asia produces 90 percent of the world's coconuts.

When the coconut was domesticated is not known (Heiser 1990). Its importance to Southeast Asians can be seen in the Malay names given it at every stage of development (Burkill 1966). It is planted by human effort at house sites, and when the trunk has formed, it will fruit in 4 or 5 years, yielding about 50 fruits a year for decades. The nut reaches full size before the meat forms and is fully ripe in one year. People generally pick coconuts, but the Malays and Thais also train the macaque, or "pig-tailed," monkey *(Macacus nemestrina)* to climb the trees and gather ripe fruits when they are ready to fall (Wilson 1970).

The water inside can be drunk for refreshment before the fruit ripens, but it is astringent. The endosperm of a 10-month fruit is eaten with a spoon as a delicacy, whereas the meat of the ripe endosperm is grated for consumption. It is also sun- or heat-dried to make copra, which is pressed for oil as both a cottage and commercial industry. The oil, milk, and meat of coconuts were used in cooking long before the arrival of Europeans. In addition, the husk provides coir for rope, and the shell is both employed as a utensil and made into charcoal. Different parts of the coconut at different development stages are used in pregnancy, in childbirth, and in magical rites (Burkill 1966). The immature inflorescence of the tree is bound in anticipation of later tapping for toddy production.

The oil palm *(Elaeis guineensis)* (Burkill 1966) was brought to Southeast Asia from West Africa as a plantation crop in the nineteenth century by colonial powers, and new plantations have continued to be planted. Most production goes into oil for commercial export to make soap and margarine as well as cooking oil. Palm oil is chemically similar to coconut oil. Other vegetable oils, such as that of the soybean, are imported from China and India.

Beverages

The most important beverages for early humans in Southeast Asia, as elsewhere, were water from rain, streams, ponds, and lakes, and liquids that could be obtained from fresh fruits (Robson 1978). All other drinkables are introductions, although tea (*Camellia sinensis*) is grown in the region. Anderson (1988) indicates that tea probably originated somewhere in the Burma–India border country and was taken to China by Buddhist monks, to become a passion there before the middle of the first millennium A.D. Burkill (1966), however, relying on earlier writers, suggests that tea did not reach western Asia before the thirteenth century. The Dutch and British independently established a sea trade in green tea, and in the eighteenth and nineteenth centuries, the plant was introduced to India and to various locales in Southeast Asia. Basic tea flavors come from postharvest processing of the leaves. Green tea is dried and rolled; black tea is fermented before drying (Burkill 1966).

Coffee originated around the Red Sea (Heiser 1990), where it still grows wild (Burkill 1966). As its Latin name, *Coffea arabica,* suggests, the Arabs were the first to use it as a drink (in the thirteenth century), but whether this was done before or after the technique of roasting (to enhance the flavor and aroma) was developed is unclear. Coffee beans (like some tea leaves) are fermented before roasting. Use of the beverage spread, with the drink reaching Europe in the seventeenth century. The first planting of coffee outside Arabia was in Java in 1696, under Dutch direction. In the next century, the plant radiated to all parts of the world's tropics and had become an industry in Java by the 1800s. Early in that century, Dutch administrators enforced greater cultivation of the shrub, particularly at higher elevations in Java, and entire forest ecosystems were replaced in the process (Hefner 1990).

Smaller plantations in other countries of the region were begun at about this time. A number of species have been cultivated in Southeast Asia, with some, including *C. arabica,* susceptible to the fungus *Hemileia vastatrix,* which spread from Ceylon in the mid–nineteenth century (Burkill 1966). The fungus drove some planters to Malaya, and one resistant species, *Coffea liberica,* was introduced at that time. Coffee (like tea) has generally been drunk hot, often with sugar and sweetened condensed milk.

Adoption of both tea and coffee no doubt owes much to their stimulating effects (Heiser 1990), but how this became recognized is not known, for processing is needed to make their action noticeable. The alkaloids causing the effects are caffeine and similar compounds. Cocoa, another beverage containing a related substance, theobromine, is much less used in Southeast Asia, although the tree, *Theobroma cacao,* was introduced in several locales by planters as a replacement for coffee destroyed by the fungus. Originating in the New World, cacoa trees were in the Philippines by the seventeenth century and in Malacca during the following century. Thus, Spaniards, Portuguese, and Dutch all took part in its dissemination. The cocoa bean is fermented and roasted (like coffee) to produce the powdered material from which the drink is made.

Commercial bottled or tinned beverages are recent introductions. Rosemary Firth (1966) has commented that soft drinks and sweetened condensed milk were considered luxuries in Kelantan, Malaya, in 1963, and prior to World War II were largely unknown. By the late 1960s, however, colas and other carbonated beverages had reached remote villages and, by the mid-1980s, advertisements for well-known brands were common. Local or regional industries produced bottled soy milk for adult consumption. By then, bovine milk processed to remain fresh without refrigeration, and packaged in cardboard containers, had reached village shops, as had similarly processed and packaged fruit drinks. Instant coffee and juice powders, for reconstitution with water, also became available.

Alcoholic Beverages

Muslims are forbidden alcohol-containing beverages, but non-Islamic Southeast Asians have produced local beers and wines as well as toddy. Early dwellers probably sampled sap and other fermentable products and learned how to encourage the process (Burkill 1966). Toddy, the most common of old Southeast Asian drinks, is made from palm sap. Fermented glutinous rice (*tapai*) produces wine during processing that is 3 percent alcohol (ICNND 1964). Spirits had become familiar in Southeast Asia before the end of the sixteenth century, when the Chinese began distilling alcohol in Java (Burkill 1966).

Nonnutritive Ingestants and Inhalants

Oral activity may take place for behavioral or physiological reasons not related to nutrition (Oswald, Merrington, and Lewis 1970). Southeast Asians' most common nonnourishing oral activities involve the substances betel nut and tobacco, which are often chewed together (Burkill 1966; Reid 1985).

Areca nut (*Areca catechu*) is the seed of a native Malaysian palm (called the betel palm) that spread to India and East Africa between A.D. 1000 and 1400. Betel is also the name of the leaf of the pepper (*Piper betel*), also Malaysian, in which the quid is wrapped (Burkill 1966). The nuts are sun- or heat-dried, split, and cut into pieces for the chew. The active principles are alkaloids affecting the nervous system, as does nicotine (Burkill 1966). The quid usually includes lime (calcium carbonate from seashells) that helps to release the stimulants. When these substances came into use in Southeast Asia is unclear, but their oral use was known in southern China by the fourth century A.D. (Anderson 1988). Ash of the nut has been used as tooth powder, and the nut itself is used medicinally, magically, and ceremonially (Wilson 1970).

Christine S. Wilson

Bibliography

Allen, Betty M. 1967. *Malayan fruits. An introduction to the cultivated species.* Singapore.

Andaya, Barbara W. 1993. Cash cropping and upstream-downstream tensions. In *Southeast Asia in the early modern era,* ed. Anthony Reid, 91-122. Ithaca, N.Y.

Anderson, E. N. 1988. *The food of China.* New Haven, Conn.

Burbidge, F. W. [1880] 1989. *The gardens of the sun.* Singapore.

Burkill, I. H. 1966. *A dictionary of the economic products of the Malay Peninsula,* Vols. 1-2. Kuala Lumpur, Malaysia.

Burling, Robbins. 1965. *Hill farms and paddy fields.* Englewood Cliffs, N.J.

Chang, K. C. 1977. *Food in Chinese culture.* New Haven, Conn.

Coedes, G. 1968. *The Indianized states of Southeast Asia.* Honolulu.

Conklin, Harold C. 1957. Hanunoo agriculture, a report on an integral system of shifting cultivation in the Philippines. *FAO Forestry Development Paper No. 12.* Rome.

Crawford, Gary W. 1992. Prehistoric plant domestication in East Asia. In *The origins of agriculture,* ed. C. W. Cowan and P. J. Watson. Washington, D.C.

Dentan, Robert K. 1968. *The Semai.* New York.

Eiseman, Fred, and Margaret Eiseman. 1988. *Fruits of Bali.* Berkeley, Calif.

Firth, Raymond. 1966. *Malay fishermen.* London.

Firth, Rosemary. 1966. *Housekeeping among Malay peasants.* London.

Fox, J. J. 1977. *Harvest of the palm: Ecological change in eastern Indonesia.* Cambridge, Mass.

Fraser, Thomas M. 1960. *Rusembilan: A Malay fishing village in southern Thailand.* Ithaca, N.Y.

Geertz, Clifford. 1960. *The religion of Java.* New York.

Gimlette, John D. 1971. *Malay poisons and charm cures.* Kuala Lumpur, Malaysia.

Gimlette, John D., and H. W. Thomson. 1971. *A dictionary of Malayan medicine.* Kuala Lumpur, Malaysia.

Hanks, Lucien M. 1972. *Rice and man.* Chicago.

Hart, Donn V. 1969. *Bisayan Filipino and Malayan humoral pathologies.* Southeast Asia Program Data Paper No. 76. Ithaca, N.Y.

Hart, Donn V., Phya Anuman Rajadhon, and Richard J. Coughlin. 1965. *Southeast Asian birth customs.* New Haven, Conn.

Hefner, Robert W. 1990. *The political economy of mountain Java.* Berkeley, Calif.

Heiser, Charles B. 1990. *Seed to civilization: The story of food.* New edition. Cambridge, Mass.

Henry, C. J. K., P. A. Donachie, and J. P. W. Rivers. 1985. The winged bean. Will the wonder crop be another flop? *Ecology of Food and Nutrition* 16: 331-8.

Herklots, G. A. C. 1972. *Vegetables in South-East Asia.* London.

Hobhouse, Henry. 1987. *Seeds of change.* New York.

ICNND (Interdepartmental Committee on Nutrition for National Defense). 1960. *Republic of Vietnam nutrition survey.* Washington, D.C.

1962. *The kingdom of Thailand nutrition survey.* Washington, D.C.

1964. *Federation of Malaya nutrition survey.* Washington, D.C.

Jin-Bee, Ooi. 1963. *Land, people and economy in Malaya.* London.

Jones, W. O. 1959. *Manioc in Africa.* Stanford, Calif.

Kathirithamby-Wells, Jeyamalar. 1993. Restraints on the development of merchant capitalism in Southeast Asia before c. 1800. In *Southeast Asia in the early modern era,* ed. Anthony Reid, 123-48. Ithaca, N.Y.

Kirsch, A. Thomas. 1973. *Feasting and social oscillation.* Southeast Asia Program Data Paper No. 92. Ithaca, N.Y.

Laderman, Carol. 1983. *Wives and midwives.* Berkeley, Calif.

Lewis, Norman. 1991. *Golden earth. Travels in Burma.* London.

Lindenbaum, Shirley. 1977. The "last course": Nutrition and anthropology in Asia. In *Nutrition and anthropology in action,* ed. T. K. Fitzgerald, 141-55. Assen, the Netherlands.

Medway, Lord. 1969. *The wild animals of Malaya and off-shore islands including Singapore.* London.

Mintz, Sidney W. 1985. *Sweetness and power.* New York.

National Academy of Sciences. 1975. *The winged bean.* Report. Washington, D.C.

Oswald, I., J. Merrington, and H. Lewis. 1970. Cyclical "on demand" oral intake by adults. *Nature* 225: 959-60.

Pangborn, Rosemarie M. 1975. Cross-cultural aspects of flavor preference. *Food Technology* 26: 34-6.

Pollock, Nancy J. 1992. *These roots remain.* Honolulu.

Reid, Anthony. 1985. From betel-chewing to tobacco-smoking in Indonesia. *Journal of Asian Studies* 44: 529-47.

1993. Introduction: A time and a place. In *Southeast Asia in the early modern era,* ed. Anthony Reid, 1-9. Ithaca, N.Y.

Robson, John R. K. 1978. Fruit in the diet of prehistoric man and of the hunter-gatherer. *Journal of Human Nutrition* 32: 19-6.

Rozin, Paul, and D. Schiller. 1980. The nature and acquisition of a preference for chili pepper by humans. *Motivation and Emotion* 4: 77-101.

Scott, J. S. 1959. *An introduction to the sea fishes of Malaya.* Kuala Lumpur, Malaysia.

Simoons, Frederick J. 1970. The traditional limits of milking and milk use in southern Asia. *Anthropos* 65: 547-93.

1994. *Eat not this flesh.* Second edition. Madison, Wisc.

Skeat, Walter. 1961. *Fables and folk tales from an eastern forest.* Singapore.

1967. *Malay magic.* New York.

Sri Kantha, Sachi, and John W. Erdman. 1986. Letter to the editor, Is winged bean a flop? *Ecology of Food and Nutrition* 18: 339-41.

Steinberg, Rafael. 1970. *Pacific and Southeast Asian cooking.* New York.

Strange, Heather. 1981. *Rural Malay women in tradition and transition.* New York.

Volkman, Toby Alice. 1985. *Feasts of honor.* Illinois Studies in Anthropology No. 16. Chicago.

Wallace, Alfred R. 1989. *The Malay archipelago.* Singapore.

Wilson, Christine S. 1970. Food beliefs and practices of Malay fishermen. Ph.D. thesis, University of California, Berkeley.

1975. Rice, fish and coconuts – the bases of Southeast Asian flavors. *Food Technology* 29: 42-4.

1983. Malay fishers of protein and other nutrients. Unpublished paper presented at the Eleventh International Congress of Anthropological and Ethnological Sciences, Vancouver, B.C.

1985. Staples and calories in Southeast Asia. In *Food energy in tropical ecosystems,* ed. Dorothy J. Cattle and Karl H. Schwerin, 65–81. New York.

1986. Social and nutritional context of "ethnic foods": Malay examples. In *Shared wealth and symbol: Food, culture, and society in Oceania and Southeast Asia,* ed. Lenore Manderson, 259–72. Cambridge.

1988. Commerciogenic food habit changes in a modernizing society. Unpublished paper presented at the Second Annual Meeting, Association for the Study of Food and Society, Washington, D.C.

1994. Traditional diets; their value and preservation. *Ecology of Food and Nutrition* 32: 89–90.

Winstedt, Richard O. 1966. *An unabridged English–Malay dictionary.* Kuala Lumpur, Malaysia.

1970. *An unabridged Malay–English dictionary.* Kuala Lumpur, Malaysia.

Yu, Ying-Shih. 1977. Han. In *Food in Chinese culture,* ed. K. C. Chang, 53–83. New Haven, Conn.

V.B.3 ⁓ China

Legend has it that when Emperor Tang, the founder of the Shang dynasty (sixteenth to eleventh centuries B.C.), appointed his prime minister, he chose Yi Yin, a cook widely renowned for his great professional ability. Indeed, in the Chinese classics (the oldest of which date from the eighth and seventh centuries B.C.) the art of proper seasoning and the mastery of cooking techniques are customary metaphors for good government (Chang 1977: 51; Knechtges 1986). Moreover, in certain contexts the expression *tiaogeng,* literally "seasoning the soup," must be translated as "to be minister of state"!

That government should be likened to the cooking process is not really surprising, considering that the foremost task of the emperor was to feed his subjects.[1] Seeing the sovereign, the intermediary between heaven and earth, in the role of provider of food is in keeping with a mythical vision of primeval times. According to legend, the first humans, clad in animal skins, lived in caves or straw huts and fed on raw animals, indiscriminately devouring meat, fur, and feathers in the same mouthful. Shennong, the Divine Farmer, one of the mythical Three August Sovereigns and founders of civilization, taught men to cultivate the five cereals and acquainted them with the blessings of agriculture (Zheng 1989: 39) after Suiren had taught them to make fire for cooking their foods. In mythology, cooking is associated with the process of civilization that put an end to the disorder of the earliest ages and led to a distinction between savagery and civilized human behavior.

Throughout Chinese history, the cooking of foodstuffs and the cultivation and consumption of cereals were considered the first signs of the passage from barbarity to culture. Thus the Chinese of the Han ethnic group set themselves apart from surrounding nationalities who, they said, had no knowledge of agriculture or did not know about the cooking of food (Legge 1885: 223; Couvreur 1950, 1: 295; Chang 1977).

Cooking and food, then, were assigned a major role in ancient China. This is very clear in the *Zhou Ritual,* a compendium describing the idealized administration of the Zhou dynasty (1066–771 B.C.). Written in the fifth century B.C., this compendium indicates that half of the personnel of the imperial palace were occupied in the preparation of food, meaning that more than 2,000 persons were involved in handling the food of the sovereign and his family (Knechtges 1986: 49).

In the third century B.C., the authors of the *Lüshi chunqiu,* a compendium of the cosmological and philosophical knowledge of the time, credited cook and prime minister Yi Yin with inventing a theory of cuisine and gastronomy that became a major point of reference for posterity. The culinary principles of Emperor Tang's minister (in fact a set of rules of good government) were to remain the implicit standard adopted by all the subsequent authors of culinary works. Yi Yin classifies all foodstuffs according to their origin, categorizes flavors, indicates the best sources of supply and the best products, and stresses the importance of the mastery of cooking techniques and the harmony of flavors. He points out that raw foods, whether they belong to the vegetable, animal, or aquatic kingdom, have a naturally disagreeable odor, which can be corrected or intensified by the combination of the five flavors and the mastery of the three elements, water, fire, and wood. These techniques make it possible to create, at will, balanced sweetness, sourness with acidity, saltiness without an excess of brine, sharp flavor that does not burn, and delicate but not insipid tastes (Chen Qiyou 1984; Knechtges 1986).

To this day, cuisine in China is implicitly defined as the art of using cooking and seasoning to transform ingredients steeped in savagery – as their unique smells indicate – into edible dishes fit for human beings living in society. Dishes cooked in this manner are not only edible but healthful. In ancient China, all foodstuffs were considered both nutriment and medicine. In principle, the dietary regime was supposed to provide all that was needed to maintain the body's vital energy. It was – and still is – believed that the first step in treating an illness must be a change of diet and that medications should be brought to bear only if diet proves ineffectual. Foodstuffs were, therefore, classified by their "nature" (hot, cold, temperate, cool) and their flavor (salty, sour, sweet, bitter, acrid) as part of a humoral medicine founded on matching, contrasting, or combining these qualities with those of the illness to be treated. Although there is some controversy as to where ideas of hot and cold foods originated (with Greece and India leading candidates along with China), it is a credit to the great originality of the Chinese that they invented what one might call a "medicinal gastronomy," which, still in vogue, endeavors to heal by using the pharmacopoeia without sacrificing the aesthetics or the tastes of high-class cuisine.

The Importance of Cereals

Although emperors and the princes enjoyed the privilege of savoring the very finest dishes, they, like everybody else, could not get along without cooked cereals. For in ancient as in modern China, cereals have been assigned the function of nourishing and sustaining life, which has given birth to the model of the Chinese meal, whose antiquity is suggested by the classic texts. When Confucius asserted, for instance, that a little coarse rice washed down with water was enough to make him happy, he meant to indicate that he was humble and modest, but he also was making the point that no one can survive without these two ingredients. In normal times, Confucius liked to eat his rice accompanied by fine dishes and complemented by wine. But he made it clear that the quantity of meat should never exceed that of rice. Underlying this recommendation is the norm that makes cereal the centerpiece of the meal (Legge 1893).

Cereal, or more precisely starch, remains the basic ingredient of the daily meal in China, and despite an increased meat consumption of late in urban areas, a very large majority of the population continues to derive almost 90 percent of its proteins from vegetable foods.

An ordinary meal consists of a starch cooked in water or steamed and a choice of several dishes prepared with meat, fish, eggs, vegetables, and products derived from soybeans. Such a pattern is not peculiar to China. This kind of meal was also the norm in preindustrial Europe and still exists in many countries where foods such as couscous, corn tortillas, polenta, and bread are considered the staff of life. The dishes or sauces that accompany them are more a matter of seasoning and gastronomic pleasure than of dietary bulk.

In China, not all staples have the same status. Two of them, rice and wheat, are the most highly valued, with millet and maize less appreciated. Tuberous plants, such as taros, yams, and white and sweet potatoes, are generally disliked and considered poor substitutes for the prestigious cereals.[2]

From an agricultural point of view, wheat, various millets, and maize are the typical cereals of the north,[3] whereas rice is characteristic of the regions south of the Yangtze River and of western China. But that more wheat buns are eaten in Beijing than in certain poor country places of Guangdong Province is not simply a matter of climate and geography. When

in the past the prince and his entourage enjoyed ravioli made of fine wheat flour, the peasant, the soldier in the field, and the hermit made do with gruel, in keeping with their social status (Sabban 1990). Access to "fancy" cereals still depends on a family's economic situation. Sometimes the inequalities are stark. Whereas prosperity and city living attenuate the differences by offering wide food choices to the inhabitants of Beijing, Shanghai, or Canton (Guangzhout), who thus do not experience the constraints of local supply, poorer people and peasants living far from urban centers have access only to the cheapest local products.

It is, therefore, only on festive occasions that ordinary people treat themselves to a good banquet, during which they almost dismiss the tyranny of the daily cereal. On such occasions cooked dishes become the center of the meal, and when rice or steamed buns are served at the end, the guests will casually take only a mouthful or two. For once, they have filled up on dishes that ordinarily only complement the meal. Such short-lived disdain for a foodstuff that is venerated in day-to-day life is a way of expressing one's pleasure and satisfaction.

The Historical Roots of the Different Chinese Cuisines

In an area larger than that of Europe, the territory of China stretches some 5,000 kilometers from the Siberian border in the north to the tropics in the south and a similar distance from the Pamir Mountains in the west to the shores of the Yellow Sea in the east. This climatic and geographical diversity makes for a variety of Chinese cuisines. However, the division of China into gastronomic regions is relatively recent and does not obscure the ancient contrast between North and South China, which is as pertinent as ever.

As already suggested, the production of different cereals as basic staples has made North China and South China two distinct entities with identifiable political, cultural, and economic roots. Throughout Chinese history the location of the capital has moved back and forth between the north and the south, and with it the court and the decision-making bodies. Such shifts also meant that each new capital became the center of innovation in fashions and taste, and on such occasions the other part of the Chinese world was made to adopt the values and views of the capital.

This struggle for preeminence has always been mirrored in the cuisine and food habits of the Chinese. A political exile, for instance, might evoke a specific food to signify his homesickness and indignation about the injustice he is suffering. Or, again, one who has betrayed an unfamiliarity with foods peculiar to the "other" China gives a reason for others to stigmatize his or her ignorance, or naivete, or haughtiness.

The strong allusive value of some foodstuffs that assumed the rank of regional emblems thus made deep or nuanced comparisons unnecessary.[4]

As we have seen, wheat was to the north what rice was to the south. Most characteristically northern, however, were the breads, cakes, and wheat-based noodles, all subsumed under the generic term *bing* until the end of the Tang (A.D. 618–907) (Sabban 1990). These foodstuffs were highly appreciated by the aristocracy and identified those who ate them as "northerners," as did mutton and milk products.

The cuisine of the south, by contrast, was characterized by rice and also by pork, vegetables, and fish. Indeed, as shown by archaeological findings from ancient times and supported by more recent texts, fish have long occupied an important dietary role for the Chinese, who very early developed techniques of pisciculture. But even more important than pond-raised aquatic animals were the freshwater fish and shellfish present in the rice paddies of the lower Yangtze River. In this area, covered with rivers, lakes, and streams, large carp grew naturally along with an abundance of vegetables.

If before the Song (A.D. 960–1279), the northerners with their noodles, butter, and milk tended to elevate their own preferences as the standard of taste, the southerners were occasionally able to defend their indigenous products. King Wu of Jin who reigned from A.D. 266 to 290, for instance, unfavorably compared *lao* – a kind of yoghurt made from the milk of sheep and highly prized for its excellence in the north at the time – with a soup made of young aquatic plants growing in the southern lakes (Xu Zhen'e 1984).

Between the end of the Tang and the beginning of the Song, the center of gravity of Chinese civilization shifted from the north to the south. Subsequently, the Song period marked the rise of a new urban society and of a nationwide economy based on a network of transportation and distribution (Shiba 1970). Kaifeng and Hangzhou, the respective capitals of the northern and southern Song dynasties, were the scenes of an unprecedented mixing of populations, for it was here that inhabitants of north and south, as well as people from Sichuan, met and mingled. In this encounter, each group became conscious of its own food habits. Once they were recognized as distinct, the culinary styles of the north, the south, and Sichuan could be combined and finally become the cuisine of the capital.

In a parallel development, the discourse on cooking and food habits assumed new dimensions. The food of the emperor and his entourage had always been commented upon, and it was understood that the governing class and the well-to-do ate choice dishes (and sometimes too much of them), whereas the rest of the population, in keeping with its rank, consumed coarse cereals and vegetables. Before the Song period, testimonies to these contrasting habits were rare and widely scattered. Only the recipes of the agricultural treatise *Qimin yaoshu*, written in the fourth century by a northern notable, provided a glimpse of the tastes of the contemporary elites (Shi Shenghan 1982).

In the Song period, the discourse on food practices began to take a larger view. Although the opposition between north and south remained at its core, some attention was now paid to other, more remote and even foreign regions, and, at times, value judgments yielded to quasi-ethnological descriptions. In this way, the customs and cuisines of foreign peoples came to be considered as legitimate as those of the Chinese. Thus, the culinary part of a household encyclopedia of the early fifteenth century contains a list of Muslim recipes and another of Jürchet (also Juchen or Jurchen) recipes (Qiu Pangtong 1986).[5] It is true that beginning in the late thirteenth century, the Mongol domination added impetus to the greater openness that had emerged in the Song period. A diet book containing many recipes, visibly influenced by foreign customs practiced in central Asia and India, was written in Chinese by the court dietician and presented to Emperor Tuq Temür in 1330 (Sabban 1986a).

In the sixteenth century, the literati Wang Shixing commented on the proverb "[t]hose who dwell on the mountain live off the mountain, those who haunt the seashore live off the sea" by noting that

> the inhabitants of the southern seashore eat fish and shrimp, whose odor makes the people of the north sick, while the men of the northern frontiers consume milk and yoghurt that southerners find nauseating. North of the Yellow River, people eat onions, garlic, and chives, which do them much good, whereas south of the Yangzi people are chary of spicy foods. (Wang Shixing 1981: 3)

Then he tolerantly and wisely concluded: "These are ways peculiar to different regions, and any attempt to make them uniform by force would be useless."

Beginning with the Qing or Manchu dynasty (A.D. 1644–1912), regional differences of cuisine were no longer perceived as the traceable consequences of geographic and climatic diversity but rather as veritable styles defined by a series of criteria involving the nature of the ingredients, seasonings, and types of preparation. The schema founded on three culinary styles, and supplemented by the cuisine of Sichuan dating from the Song period, gave rise to the notion of a China divided into four major gastronomical regions. But as the country's frontiers expanded as a result of the Manchu domination, what was called the "North" stretched even farther north, reaching as far as Shandong, Beijing, and Tianjin; the "South" came to include Zhejiang and Jiangsu, as well as Anhui, with the region of Canton becoming the country's "Deep South." The West still meant Sichuan but also came to include Guizhou, Yunnan, Hunan, and Hubei.

This division is still recognized today, although the limits of these four regions are often drawn very loosely. For example, the cuisine of Canton is seen as including that of Fujian Province and Taiwan, which may not be altogether justified.[6] Nonetheless, once travelers from Beijing have crossed the Yangtze River, they are in the south, and everything is different for the palate.

A regional cuisine is defined by certain dishes, by the frequent use of certain modes of cooking, by the use of specific ingredients, and especially by its condiments and spices – in short, by the tastes that set the one Chinese cuisine apart from all the others.

North of the Yellow River, garlic and onions have always been in favor, as Wang Shixing said long ago. Peking duck, with its fat and crunchy skin, must absolutely be eaten with a garnish of raw scallions and sweet sauce, *tianmianjiang*. The aroma of mutton blends with that of garlic, and the taste of balsamic vinegar cleanses these strong flavors with its tempered acidity.

Sichuan has the strongest condiments and spices, and the sharpest among them, chilli pepper and fagara, or Sichuan pepper *(Xanthoxylum Piperitum)*, are highly prized. Together with sesame oil or puree and fermented broad bean paste *(doubanjiang)*, they are used to flavor dishes and produce harmonies of flavors bearing such evocative names as "strange flavor" *(guai wei)*, "family flavor" *(jiachang wei)*, or "hot-fragrant" flavor *(xiangla wei)*.[7]

The inhabitants of the low-lying plains of the Yangtze, a land of fish and rice, produce the most tender vegetables and raise the biggest carp and the fattest crabs. They slowly simmer dishes of light and subtle flavor enlivened by the presence of refreshing ginger and the fillip of Shaoxing wine. This is the only region of China where gentle flavors and sweet-and-sour tastes are truly appreciated and beautifully cooked.

The complexity and richness of Cantonese cuisine cannot be reduced to a few dominant flavors, for the art of the Cantonese cook is characterized by mastery in blending different flavors or, alternatively, permitting each one of them to stand out on its own. Seafood, however, is one of the main features of this cuisine. Its preparation emphasizes freshness by, for instance, simply steaming a fish au naturel. Oyster sauce is used to season poached poultry, fish, and briefly blanched green vegetables. But Canton is also famous for its roasted whole suckling pigs and its lacquered meats hung up as an appetizing curtain in the windows of restaurants.

China's culinary diversity can also be seen in the streets, where itinerant vendors sell small specialties *(xiaochi)* to hungry passersby at all hours of the day. Soups, fritters, skewers, fried, cooked, or steamed ravioli, cakes, crepes, tea, fruit juice – the choices seem infinite, though they depend, of course, on the season and the region. In the streets of Beijing, skewers of caramelized haws are offered in winter, whereas ruby-red slices of watermelon appear on the hottest days of summer.

To this mosaic of practices, habits, and tastes, one must add the cuisines of some 50 ethnic minorities. Among these are those of Turkish origin living in the autonomous region of Xinjiang and the Hui families, who in every other way are indistinguishable from the Han Chinese disseminated throughout the territory. These Islamic communities have developed a "Chinese" cuisine from which pork and all its derivatives are absent but are replaced with mutton and beef, which are consumed after Islamic ritual slaughtering.

Nor must one forget *su* cooking, which goes back very far and was already highly regarded under the Song. Based on the exclusion of all animal foods, this cuisine was adopted by the Buddhists and others who wished to eat a meatless or light diet. In their gastronomic version, *su* dishes bear the names of normal meat-containing dishes, and the cook's art consists of using vegetable ingredients to reproduce the taste, consistency, and shape of the meat normally included in these dishes.

Such diversity might make it appear as if there were no Chinese cuisine but several Chinese cuisines, and it is true that there is no haute cuisine without regional roots or affiliation with a genre (be it *su*, Islamic, or even traditional court cooking) that imparts its rhythm, its style, and its specific flavors to a gourmet meal. Nonetheless, everyday cooking is the same from one end of China to the other in its principles and its results. Throughout the territory, people use the same flavoring agents, namely soy sauce, ginger, scallions, and chilli peppers, supplemented, to be sure, by local condiments. Moreover, certain originally regional dishes, among them "Mother Ma's soy curds," "vinegar carp of the Western Lake," and "sweet-sour pork," have become so widely known that they are on the menu of ordinary restaurants in all parts of the country.

The Principles of Cooking Technique

The Chinese word for "to cook" is *pengtiao*, composed of two morphemes signifying, respectively, "to cook" and "to season." In China, cooking foods and combining their flavors are thus two equally important operations.

Certain condiments, as well as mastery of the techniques of chopping and cooking – which, in turn, are related to the use of specialized tools such as the wok and chopsticks – are indispensable in the practice of Chinese cooking. In other words, there is a close connection between the manners of the eater and the work of the cook. Small pieces and foods that can be broken up without using a knife are better suited to the use of chopsticks than any other food. But it would be naive to attribute the functioning of the Chinese culinary system merely to the way food is served and eaten, for Chinese cooking developed out of the interaction of all its constituent parts.

A clear distinction must be made, however, between day-to-day cooking designed to feed a family as economically as possible and professional cooking by specialists highly trained in every technique. The endeavors of the latter have nothing to do with necessity and are exclusively concerned with providing satisfaction and pleasure to the senses.

Home Cooking

Characteristic of cooking in the home is the chopping of ingredients into uniform small pieces, followed by their rapid cooking, usually sautéing in a semispherical iron skillet or wok.[8] The cooking is done with little fat but with a gamut of seasonings dominated by soy sauce, fresh ginger, scallions, sesame oil, Chinese vinegar, fagara, and chilli peppers. Such preparation of food makes for a remarkable economy of equipment. In addition to a rice cooker,[9] all that is needed to prepare any dish is a chopping board – a simple tree "slice" 5 to 10 centimeters in thickness – a cleaver, the wok, and a cooking spatula.

In the city most people cook on a gas ring; in the countryside they have a brick stove with several holes in the top so that the wok can be placed directly over the flame. Since fuel is scarce and expensive, it is always used sparingly, which has given rise to the widespread practice of quick stir-frying over high heat. Sometimes the cook will make use of the heat generated by cooking the rice to steam one of the dishes of the meal above the rice on the rice cooker. Several different dishes are cooked in the same wok, one right after the other, but this is done so rapidly that they have little time to cool. And even if they do cool, the rice, always served piping hot, will provide a balance.

Professional Cooking

Becoming a professional cook demands long years of apprenticeship under the watchful eye of a great chef, and before the aspiring kitchen boy can himself become a chef, he must pass through all the work stations. If he chooses the specialty of meat and vegetable cooking, he will go to the "red work bench" *(hongan),* where he will learn all about chopping and carving, composing, cooking techniques, and seasoning. If he prefers the white vest of the "pastry cook" he will go to the "white work bench" *(baian)* to learn the meticulous art of preparing little dishes made from flours and cereals, including the proper cooking times for pasta products.

A great chef does not, of course, have to be concerned with economy, for he is called upon to use ingredients to their best advantage and to bring out their quintessential flavor by treating them according to the rules of the subtle and difficult techniques he has mastered. He will, thus, use the hump or the heels of a camel without worrying about the rest of the animal when asked to create two of the great dishes of the haute cuisine of North China. Nor is there any economy in the use of fat, a great deal of which is used for deep frying, a practice generally absent from family cooking. Ovens, which are unknown in private homes, are part of the equipment of professional kitchens, particularly in restaurants located in such culinary regions as Beijing or Canton, where roast meat is a specialty.

Even though the same basic principles inform both the great gastronomy and the home cooking of China, professional practice gives cooking a scope and a complexity that cannot possibly be achieved at home. And so one usually turns to a restaurant if one wants to taste the grand specialties prepared with rare, costly, and such delicate ingredients as shark fins, bird's nests, sea cucumbers, abalones, shark's skin, and mountain mushrooms.

A Rich Repertory of Products and Condiments

Because most Chinese enjoy such a wide variety of foods, it is often asserted that there are no food taboos in China. In fact, the Chinese make the claim themselves,[10] even though they recognize that China's Muslims avoid pork and devout Buddhists reject all flesh as well as garlic and onions. Doubtless, such a claim stems, in part, from the popular understanding that a number of unexpected animal species such as the cat, the dog, the snake, and even the anteater end up as a ragout under the chopsticks of Cantonese food lovers, and from the knowledge that Chinese cooks do not, in principle, shun any edible product as long as they are able to prepare it according to the rules of the art. Indeed, haute cuisine calls for "the precious fruits of sea and mountain," essentially animal by-products whose consumption is limited because they are so rare and costly. If their strangeness strikes the imagination, they are not the only gustatory exotica that speak to the originality and the history of China's culinary repertory.

Such consumption of animal foods has a long history in China despite the frequent assertion that the country was traditionally a kind of "vegetal kingdom." Neither hunting nor pastoral activities were proscribed in ancient China and both classical written sources and archaeological findings testify to the importance of cattle breeding in ancient and medieval China. The first millennium of the Christian era probably paralleled the "golden age" of domestication in China in which the utilization of draft animals and the production of meat products gave rise to increasing leisure (and increasing warfare). It has only been in more recent times that activities leading to meat production and to specialized breeding of animals for hunting have become progressively marginalized (Cartier 1993; Elisseeff 1993).

China also stands out for the exceptional richness of vegetal species grown and eaten there – many times more than the fruits and vegetables known in the West. Moreover, these plants are used in an intensive manner, and roots, stems, leaves, shoots, seeds, and sometimes flowers are all exploited for their respective qualities.

The original stock of plants in China was later supplemented by large numbers of new plants, which were very quickly assimilated. As early as the first century B.C. the Chinese acclimatized plants imported from central Asia (which had mostly reached there from the Near East, India, and Africa) such as cucumbers, coriander, peas, sesame, onions, grapes, and pomegranates. Under the Tang (618–907), spinach was acquired from Persia. This was a time when there was great interest in the exotic, and in North China, fresh fruits that grew in faraway southern countries were highly prized. Thus we know that citrus fruit and litchi were carried from Lingnan (today in the Canton region) by special courier for Empress Yang Guifei.

Finally, in the mid–sixteenth century under the Ming, the "American plants" appeared in the coastal areas of Fujian and Guangdong, with the Portuguese and their ships instrumental in bringing maize, sweet potatoes, and peanuts to China. The tomato did not become known until the following century, and the chilli pepper had to await the eighteenth century. These new arrivals became highly popular in China, and scholars subsequently went so far as to attribute the country's population growth in the eighteenth century to the availability of maize and the sweet potato (Ho Ping-ti 1955). The chilli pepper wrought a deep change in the fundamental taste of the cuisines of Sichuan, Hunan, and Yunnan, which are known today for their highly spiced character.

To these expanding natural resources must be added a large number of "processed" foods made from meat, fish, vegetables, and fruit and subsequently used in the culinary process as basic ingredients or condiments. These processed foods have their own history, for their production is predicated on the availability of the appropriate technologies. The oldest texts (of the fourth and fifth centuries B.C.) mention the names of forcemeats, *coulis,* and seasoning sauces, as well as vinegars, pickled and fermented vegetables, and "smoked and salted meats," all of which shows beyond a doubt that aside from day-to-day cooking there was already a whole food "industry" founded on foresight and the stockpiling or conservation of foodstuffs.

The oldest example of this kind of organization is provided by the description of the ideal functioning of the imperial household of the Zhou in the *Zhou Ritual.* The household administration naturally included brigades of pigtailed officials in charge of preparing the daily meals, along with pork butchers *(laren),* the wine steward *(jiuzheng),* and the employees of the manufactory of spiced preserves *(yanren)* and of vinegar *(xiren)* (Biot 1851; Lin Yin 1985).

For the period before the sixth century of the current era we have no idea what these functions involved or, rather, what items were produced under the supervision of these officials. A weighty agricultural treatise of this period devotes a fourth of its space to food preparation. This section contains as many cooking recipes in the narrow sense as it does recipes pertaining to brewing, pickling, malting, and preserving. All of these recipes testify to great expertise and to the widespread use of preserved foods (Shih Sheng-han 1962). The most remarkable, and probably the oldest, of these recipes are those for making seasoning sauces by fermenting grains and legumes and the more than 20 recipes for different vinegars, which are also obtained by subjecting cooked cereals to acetic fermentation. In addition, this text contains a large number of recipes for pickled vegetables, "smoked and salted meats," and, of course, alcoholic beverages, the role and importance of which in Chinese culture we shall examine next.

Contrary to what one might expect, however, this treatise does not even allude to certain products that are today considered the very emblems of Chinese cooking. An example is soy sauce, which is so universally used in our day. Then it was probably perceived as nothing more than the residual liquid of a spicy paste until the Song period, when it became clearly identified with its own name. Similarly, the clotting of soy milk for a curd called *doufu* (tofu) seems to have been unknown in the written sources until the tenth century, when the first reference to this subject can be found (Hong Guangzhu 1987: 8).[11]

Conversely, some foods that have almost disappeared today seem to have enjoyed a certain vogue in the past. *Lao,* for example, which is a kind of fermented milk, and butter were luxury foods highly prized by the upper classes of society, at least until the end of the Song (Sabban 1986b). The reputation of these products (and the taste for them) lasted until the Qing period, although they were probably difficult to obtain outside of court circles, which had access to cows and ewes as well as to a "dairy" that produced for the emperor and his entourage. Perhaps the popularity of the Beijng yoghurt today and the recent fashion of "dairy cafés" offering traditional sweets made of milkcurd are vestiges of these ancient and prestigious treats.

This entire food "industry" was predicated on a remarkable knowledge of the phenomenon of fermentation, which is still used in the production of popular ready-to-use condiments such as soy sauce *(jiangyou),* salted black beans *(douchi),* sweet-salty sauce *(tianmianjiang),* and fermented broad bean paste *(doubanjiang).*

In addition to these condiments produced by fermentation, the Chinese developed original techniques for turning plant materials into edible substances much sought after for their consistency, their malleability, and their taste. In this category one finds a considerable variety of noodles made with cereal or leguminous plant flours. *Mianjin,* or "gluten," is a kind of firm but elastic dough obtained by rinsing a sponge of wheat flour. Also used are all the secondary products of soy milk, such as fresh or dried curd and its skin and gelatin. The textures of these particular substances have stimulated the imaginations of many cooks; thus, they not only have played a vital role in the development of *su* cooking diffused by Buddhist temples but also have made their mark on home cooking and on the cuisine of great restaurants. In this area the Chinese developed a technical prowess that may well be unmatched by other societies (Sabban 1993).

A Culture of Alcoholic Beverages

China is known as the land of tea, but in fact alcohol has been drunk there longer than the brew of the plant that has conquered the world. Yet tea has come to overshadow the other Chinese beverages called *jiu.* Difficult to translate into Western languages, this word *jiu* designates today all alcoholic liquids, from the lightest beer to the strongest distilled alcohol, with wines made from grapes and rice and sweet liqueurs in the middle.[12]

Before the advent of distillation, which is generally assumed to have occurred around the fourteenth or fifteenth century, *jiu* meant all alcoholic beverages obtained through the fermentation of cereals. But these were not beers whose fermentation was induced by malt, such as are found in several other ancient societies, but rather beverages with alcohol contents of between 10 and 15 percent obtained through a "combined fermentation" that called for the preliminary production of an ad hoc ferment that subsequently started the fermenting process in a mash of cooked cereals (Needham 1980; Sabban 1988). Each of these two processes involved fairly lengthy preparation and maturation. The cereal, the water, and the ferment *(qu)* were so indissolubly associated that the Chinese sometimes compared the *jiu* that had resulted from their transmutation to a body in which the cereal occupied the place of the flesh and muscle, the ferment that of the skeleton, and the water, like blood, irrigated all the veins.

This original technique, which subsequently spread to Japan, Korea, and all of Southeast Asia, has existed in China for a very long time. The first texts that have come down to us allude to the precise fermenting time of the *qu* needed for making *jiu* (Hong Guangzhu 1984). The "invention" of this precious liquid is attributed to Du Kang, a legendary figure venerated as the "immortal of *jiu*" who is the object of a cult in several villages of North China. He is supposed to have lived at the end of the Shang dynasty (1324–1066 B.C.). We do know from the texts and from an abundance of magnificent utensils found in archaeological sites that the Shang aristocrats loved to

drink, and there is evidence that some of their predecessors had also succumbed to this passion. In fact, the production of alcoholic beverages in China seems to go all the way back to the end of the Neolithic and perhaps even further. The site of Dawenkou in Shandong (4000 B.C.) has yielded a great variety of earthen vessels used for preserving, storing, and consuming alcoholic beverages.

There is no question that since the presumed time of their appearance alcoholic beverages have enjoyed considerable popularity in China. The sixth-century agricultural treatise *Qimin yaoshu* gives more than 30 recipes, each one for a specific beverage identified by its mode of production, its ingredients, and its flavor, color, strength, and so forth (Shi Shenghan 1982). We also learn from the texts that these beverages played an important role at all levels of society. Their production was controlled by the institution of state monopolies in the course of the first dynasties, and there were times when their consumption was forbidden. Every ritual involved alcoholic beverages as offerings to the gods or the ancestors. But alcohol was regularly used for more mundane purposes, and families were consequently ruined and promising careers cut short. In a word, it is clear that alcoholic beverages were present at every moment of people's lives. In the sixteenth century 70 kinds of *jiu* were counted (Du Shiran et al. 1982), and to this profusion should be added the exotic "grape wines" imported from central Asia, which became very fashionable in court circles under the Han and the Tang.

Alcoholic beverages maintain their importance in the present. No banquet, for example, would be complete without them. Indeed, the ceremony of marriage is referred to by the expression *he xijiu* or "drinking the wine of happiness," and each of the guests is invited to raise a glass in honor of the bride. The latter, as she was already enjoined to do in the ritual books of the third and fourth centuries B.C., must exchange a goblet with the groom. To testify to their mutual commitment, betrothed couples no longer drink out of the two halves of the same gourd but now cross their arms and give to each other the goblet they hold in their hands.

In eastern Zhejiang, a region where the production of a renowned rice wine is a tradition, people would bury several earthenware jars of good wine at the birth of a child and not open them until the day of his or her marriage. A family celebration without alcoholic beverages is unthinkable, and even on the occasion of a funeral it is customary to offer a drink to friends who have come to salute the deceased for the last time. Seasonal and religious festivities as well have always included generous libations, and until the advent of the republic in 1912 the winter solstice was celebrated with libations to heaven performed by the emperor and his ministers, whereas families made offerings of alcohol to their ancestors.

Alcoholic beverages are also items of gastronomy

consumed for no particular reason at a drinking party or to accompany a meal. Drinking with friends is a social activity mentioned in the oldest literature. In grave no. 1 of the Mawangdui site dating from the Eastern Han period (about 168 B.C.), where the spouse of the Marquis of Dai is buried, the arrangement of the objects contained in the northernmost funerary chamber is thought to represent the deceased seated at a lacquered table laden with meat dishes and goblets containing two kinds of wine. There is little doubt that this scene depicts either a drinking party or the first part of a banquet devoted, as usual, to the drinking of alcoholic beverages (Pirazzoli-t'-Serstevens 1991).

Although drinking parties sometimes had a political function, for instance when the seating arrangements concretely showed patterns of social hierarchy (Yü Ying-shih 1979), they were mainly moments of joy and exaltation. Almost all the poets have devoted some of their writings to the celebration of wine and the inspiring inebriation it brings. Poets of the Tang and Song period felt that wine was as necessary as paper, brush, and ink, and there was no lack of hardened drinkers among the rhymesters. It is even said that once when the great Li Bai (701–62) was in his cups, he thought that he could catch the moon when he saw its quivering reflection in the river and so perished by drowning. Perhaps it was a befitting end for a poet who, certain of his modern confreres do not hesitate to say, was permanently steeped in alcohol.

Drinking in China is a form of entertainment and a way to shed inhibitions. Sometimes it also gives rise to games and contests that make the losers drink more and more. At popular banquets the game of *morra* marks the time for drinking amid peals of laughter and screams of excitement. The famous eighteenth-century novel *The Dream in the Red Pavilion* furnishes a fine example of the jousts associated with wine drinking in literary circles: Any participant who did not succeed in improvising a song or poem with prearranged constraints within a limited time was made to drain his cup on the spot.

Although getting drunk is the admitted aim of these drinking bouts, drinking without eating is unthinkable. In order to "make the wine go down" *(xiajiu),* one must sip it while nibbling at some tidbits or little dishes that not only fill the stomach but also sharpen one's thirst, although they should never distract the drinker from the appreciation of the wine.

The social standing of the drinker determines how fancy these indispensable accompaniments can be. A small bowl of fennel-toasted beans is all there was for poor Kong Yiji, the hero of a novel of Lu Xun, who occasionally treated himself to a nice bowl of warm wine at the corner tavern (Yang and Yang 1972). By contrast, goose braised in marc, pork of five flavors, fish with crayfish eggs, and the finest specialties of Suzhou carefully selected to go with the drinks were enjoyed by Zhu Ziye, the gourmet of the recent novel by Lu Wenfu (Lu Wenfu 1983). A contemporary of poor Kong Yiji, Zhu Ziye was vastly more wealthy.

The prewar taverns no longer exist, and the wine of Shaoxing is now rarely served warm, but people never fail to drink at a banquet or any other celebration. The choice of beverages has become wider: There are now clear alcohols made of rice or sorghum like the famous *maotai* and wines made of glutinous rice, the best of which is probably the yellow wine of Shaoxing. In addition, there is osmanthus-flavored liqueur, grape wines, which are now produced in China, and also port wine and even cognac.

Beer has been regularly consumed ever since it was introduced by the Europeans early in this century. "Qingdao," the best known and most renowned brand, is manufactured at Qingdao in Shandong, a town and region taken over in 1897 by the Germans, who established a brewery there in 1903 (Wang Shangdian 1987). Today, beer is the first alcoholic beverage people will buy if they are looking for a little treat.

The Art of Making Tea

Appearing much later than alcoholic beverages, tea began to acquire considerable importance in the Tang period, when its use became widespread. At first it was perceived as a serious competitor of wine, which it implicitly is to this day. Certain "weak natures" who could not tolerate alcohol very well actually replaced wine with tea when they attended official drinking parties. A *Discourse on Tea and Wine* (Wang Zhongmin 1984) from the late Tang period pits Tea against Wine in a debate that allows each of them to argue and preach in favor of his own brotherhood. Wine calls himself more precious than his opponent and better able to combat death, whereas Tea accuses Wine of causing the ruin of families and prides himself on being a virtuous drink of beautiful color that clears away confusion. But in the end Wine and Tea make peace when Water reminds them that without her neither of them amounts to much and that they should get along, since tea often helps to dissipate the vapors of drunkenness. And it is true that infusions of tea were first used for medicinal purposes (Sealy 1958; Chen Chuan 1984). Tea, however, very quickly became much more than a mere remedy.

Part of its enormous success can be attributed to its commercial value both within and without the borders of China, in nearby regions, and throughout the world. Of the three stimulating beverages – coffee (from Ethiopia and Yemen), tea (from China), and cocoa (from the New World) – that the Europeans "discovered" in the late Renaissance, tea was the most widely disseminated and is still the most commonly consumed today. China gave us this custom of drinking tea, which also took root in Japan, Korea, and northern India. It should be noted that all of the tea consumed in western Europe was initially imported from China until the

British broke this monopoly by launching their highly successful tea plantations in Ceylon and India toward the end of the nineteenth century.

Sichuan was the cradle of the decoction of a bitter plant thought to be tea, which was probably first used toward the end of the Western Han period (206–23). The names employed at the time are still somewhat doubtful, but the plant was clearly *Camellia sinensis*. At that time tea was not infused but prepared in decoction, perhaps seasoned with salt, onions, ginger, or citrus peels, and its leaves were sometimes simmered in cooked dishes. Clearly this was a far cry from what we call "tea" today. Two factors are thought to have facilitated the spread of tea throughout China to its northernmost frontiers, beginning with the Sui (581–618) and the Tang (618–907). One is that tea soon came to be an item of tribute and, thus, became known and appreciated in court circles. The other has to do with the vigorous growth of Buddhism between the beginning of the Christian era and the Tang period. It is reported that tea was a great help to Buddhist monks, whose religion prohibited the drinking of "intoxicating" beverages like wine and whose practice of meditation demanded fasting and staying awake for many hours at a time. Tea plantations therefore followed the founding of Buddhist temples in the mountains.

Most would agree, however, that it was Lu Yu, author of the famous *Classic of Tea* (Carpenter 1974; Lu Yu 1990), who in the middle of the eighth century provided the Chinese culture of tea with its veritable birth certificate. The Tang period, moreover, marks the beginning of the "tea policy" adopted by the Chinese government. More or less successful, depending on the period, this policy, which lasted until the Qing period, regulated the monopoly, the tribute, and the taxation of tea and monitored an official trade in which tea was exchanged for "barbarian" horses on the country's northern and northeastern frontiers. Doubtless the vast scope of tea consumption and the potential profits of its cultivation played a decisive role in the elaboration of this policy. Lu Yu himself probably only codified and formally described the practices and the techniques peculiar to his time and to the literati. His work in three chapters was devoted to the origins, the cultivation, the processing, and the drinking of tea. It had enormous influence on the rise of the culture of tea, which developed not only in China but in Japan as well.

Lu Yu's work gave rise to an endless number of treatises that either followed in the same vein or provided more elaborate information. It is important to note that in China – unlike Japan, where tea was associated with a Zen discipline – the art of tea was always in the realm of practical "know-how," somewhat ritualized but only done so to encourage a more thorough enjoyment of life. Lu Yu explains the comparative merits of different beverages in perfectly straightforward terms: "To quench one's thirst, one should drink water; to dissipate sadness and anger, one should drink wine; to drive away listlessness and sleepiness, one should drink tea" (Fu Shuqin and Ouyang Xun 1983: 37). But despite such straightforwardness, he insists that the processing, preparation, and drinking of tea must be done according to the rules, and he heaps scorn on those who, believing that they are drinking tea, settle for "stuff that has washed out of the rain spout" (Fu Shuqin and Ouyang Xun 1983: 37).

It goes without saying that although Lu Yu was sometimes worshiped as the "God of Tea," planters, processors, and lovers of the divine brew have gone beyond the master's instructions. As processing techniques evolved, they led to modifications in the preparation of tea and changes in the consumers' tastes. As early as the Tang period, "steam wilting" was discovered, a technique that made it possible to free the brew of its "green taste." Then, under the Song, planters began to wash the leaves before wilting them, and loose-leaf tea replaced the kind that had hitherto been pressed into "cakes" that had to be crumbled before being used in decoctions. In the early Ming period the growing taste for loose-leaf tea spelled the victory of infusions over decoctions. The leaves of *C. sinensis* were now mixed with fragrant flower petals whose scent is imparted to the infusion. Today the best known of these infusions is jasmine tea.

In the Tang period, several local teas had already acquired a great reputation, and by the Song period 41 kinds of tea were considered worthy of serving as tributes. Today there are three major types of Chinese teas: green tea, oolong tea, and black tea. Green tea, which is the kind most frequently consumed in China and Japan, is not made to undergo fermentation, whereas oolong tea, most popular in the southern provinces, is semifermented. Black teas, mainly produced for export, are called "fermented."

Drinking and serving tea today are such commonplace activities that they do not elicit any commentary. Wherever they might be, people can expect to find a thermos of boiling hot water, covered mugs, and tea leaves ready to be steeped. In any waiting or reception area, the visitor is offered tea. Tea is never drunk with the meal.[13] But when invited to share a meal, visitors are always received with a cup of tea. And this little offering is repeated to mark the end of the meal. On all such occasions this gesture must be made, whether or not the tea is actually drunk.

Every Chinese worker – blue or white collar – and every traveler carries a glass receptacle whose lid is tightly closed over some hot water in which a small handful of tea is steeping. In the course of the day more water is added and the liquid becomes paler and paler. This type of consumption, which in Taiwan is facilitated by automatic dispensers, is suited to the normal use of tea conceived as a mildly stimulating internal lubricant that will aid the digestion. The tea used throughout the day is usually of rather poor quality and in principle affordable for everyone. In lean times, the habit continues even without tea and people drink hot water, calling it "tea."

Along with such routine tea drinking in all parts of the country, the southern provinces have developed a veritable culture of tea. Every town or village has its "tea house," which can be quite modest, where people go to relax, to talk to their friends, and to share and comment on the latest news. These "tea parlors" have a long history in China. Indeed, those of the capitals of the northern and southern Song have become legendary thanks to the authors of the *Descriptions of the Capital* (Gernet 1962), who vaunted their lively and refined character.

In Canton and its region, however, and in Hong Kong, too, tea drinking is a more serious matter, as is everything that involves food. In Canton, the gastronomic capital of China, there are vast numbers of establishments that from morning until midafternoon offer tea lovers the opportunity to order a large pot of their favorite tea along with, if they choose, an incredible variety of "little dishes" – ravioli, fritters, dumplings, tartlets, pâtés, noodles, and so forth – all of them especially designed to accompany tea without overpowering its taste.

Françoise Sabban
(translated by Elborg Forster)

Notes

1. This assertion is according to the hallowed expression taken from the *History of the Han* (compiled in the first century of our era): *Wangzhe yi min wei tian, er min yi shi wei tian,* "The most important thing(s) in the world for the prince are his subjects, for whom nothing is more important than food."

2. In the food trade, a distinction is made between "fine cereals," *xiliang,* that is to say, rice and wheat, and "coarse cereals," *culiang,* meaning all the others. Counted among the latter are the tuberous vegetables, which are the mainstay of the diet in the poorest regions and in times of shortage.

3. To this list should be added sorghum, which can also be consumed as the mainstay of the diet when nothing else is available but which is generally used for the production of alcoholic beverages.

4. Until the Tang (618–907), North China, the cradle of Chinese civilization, imposed its values on the rest of the territory and hot and humid South China remained a neglected part of the huge empire, to cite Jacques Gernet (1962). But as a result of the continuous onslaught of nomadic barbarians from central Asia, who made increasing inroads on the great northern plain, the Yangtze Basin assumed ever greater importance. Under the Song, when South China had become conscious of its strength, it developed a refined urban civilization, which in turn gave birth to a genuine national cuisine based on the recognition of three major regional cuisines.

5. The Jürchet were a Tungusic tribe of the present Heilongjian Province in northeastern China who adopted the dynastic name of Jin in 1115. They were neighbors of the northern Song, with whom they concluded an alliance to attack the Liao empire. But they eventually turned on the

Song, whom they finally annexed when they conquered their capital of Kaifeng in 1126.

6. The present literature on Chinese cuisine contains a great many typologies of regional cuisines, but all of them are based on the historical division into four major zones. Certain specialists assign different culinary schools to eight geographic regions. In reality, each province lays claim to its own cuisine and every provincial publishing house has published works devoted to the cooking of its own provincial cuisine.

7. Here are two of the most typical flavor combinations of Sichuan: One is *yuxiang wei,* literally "fish flavor," which does not contain a single fish-based ingredient but consists of a mixture of chilli pepper, fermented broad bean paste, soy sauce, scallions, and so forth. The other is *mala wei,* literally "numbing hot flavor," which, consisting essentially of chilli pepper and fagara, or Sichuan pepper, is said to produce in the mouth a blended sensation of numbness, relaxation, and heat.

8. "Wok" is the Cantonese pronunciation of the word for this utensil, pronounced *huo* in standard Chinese. In North China this type of skillet is given another word, pronounced *guo.*

9. Today, this is often an automatic electric cooker.

10. This assertion holds except with respect to certain combinations of foods whose consumption during the same meal is not recommended for reasons of health. Works on diet, but also peasant calendars, contain lists of pernicious, that is, poisonous, "combinations" of foodstuffs, although not without indicating the corresponding antidotes. Their presence in calendars makes it seem likely that in addition to medical reasons, considerations of a magic and religious nature are also involved here.

11. See also the arguments of Chen Wenhau (1991), who advances the hypothesis that tofu was a much earlier invention dating back to the end of the Eastern Han period (25–220).

12. Although fully aware of the inadequacy of this choice, I shall here translate *jiu* as "wine" or "alcoholic beverage," as a matter of convenience. But it does seem better than the word "beer," which today designates a product that has nothing to do with the Chinese *jiu,* since it has always involved the use of malt. This is not the case for various Chinese *jiu,* which are produced by "combined fermentation" with ferments from cereal mashes. (In this connection see the essay by Ankei Takao 1986.) The few available recipes from the sixth century actually indicate that malt, though well known in China, was by that time used only to make "cereal sugars" or "maltoses."

13. One must be clear about what is called a "meal." An implicit classification defines the standard meal by its composition, namely, a staple cereal accompanied by its cooked dishes and often a light soup, and by the time at which it is eaten, essentially at noon and in the evening. If, in Guangdong, tea sometimes appears as part of a "snack" that might be considered a meal – for the "Cantonese breakfast" can be eaten any time between the morning and early afternoon – such a snack is really a matter of drinking tea and eating some accompanying dishes, even though it might take the place of a meal by virtue of the quantity of food and even the time when it is eaten.

Bibliography

Anderson, Eugene N. 1988. *The food of China.* New Haven, Conn., and London.

Ankei Takao. 1986. Discovery of SAKE in central Africa: Mold fermented liquor of the Songola. *Journal d'Agriculture et de Botanique Appliquée* 33: 30.

Biot, Edouard, trans. 1851. *Rites des Tcheou*, Vol. 1. Paris.

Bray, Francesca. 1984. Part II: Agriculture. In *Science and civilisation in China*, ed. Joseph Needham. Vol. 6, *Biology and Biological Technology*. Cambridge and London.

Buck, John Lossing. 1956. *Land utilization in China.* . . . Facsimile reprint of vol. 1 of the original 1937 edition. New York.

Carpenter, Francis Ross, trans. 1974. *The classic of tea*. Boston, Mass., and Toronto.

Cartier, Michel. 1993. La marginalisation des animaux en Chine. *Anthropozoologica* 18: 7–16.

Chang K. C. 1977. Ancient China. In *Food in Chinese culture*, ed. K. C. Chang, 23–52. New Haven, Conn., and London.

Chen Chuan. 1984. *Chaye tongshi*. Beijing.

Chen Qiyou, ed. 1984. *Lüshi chunqiu jiaoshi*, Vol. 14. Shanghai.

Chen Wenhua. 1991. Doufu qiyuan yu heshi. *Nongye kaogu* 1: 245–8.

Couvreur, Séraphin, trans. 1950. *Mémoires sur les bienséances et les cérémonies. Li Ki* (Liji), 2 vols. Paris.

Du Shiran et al. 1982. *Zhongguo kejishu shigao*, Vol. 1. Beijing.

Elisseeff, Danielle. 1993. Des animaux sous une chape de plomb. *Anthropozoologica* 18: 17–28.

Epstein, Helmut. 1969. *Domestic animals of China*. Edinburgh.

Fu Shuqin and Ouyang Xun, eds. 1983. *Lu Yu chajing shizhu*. Hubei.

Gernet, Jacques. 1962. *Daily life in China in the eve of the Mongol invasion, 1250–1276*, trans. H. M. Wright. New York.

Ho Ping-ti. 1955. The introduction of American food plants into China. *American Anthropologist* 57: 191–201.

Hong Guangzhu. 1984. *Zhongguo shipin keji shi gao*. Beijing.

1987. *Zhongguo doufu*. Beijing.

Knechtges, David R. 1986. A literary feast: Food in early Chinese literature. *Journal of the American Oriental Society* 106: 49–63.

Knightley, David N., ed. 1983. *The origins of Chinese civilization*. Berkeley, Calif.

Laufer, Berthold. 1919. Sino-Iranica: Chinese contributions to the history of civilization in ancient Iran. *Field Museum of Natural History, Anthropological Series* 15: 185–630.

Legge, James, trans. 1885. The Lî Kî. In *The sacred books of China*, Part 3, Oxford (The royal regulations, Sect. III/14).

1893. Confucian analects. In *The Chinese classics*, Vol. 1. Oxford.

Lin Yin. 1985. *Zhouli jinzhu*. Beijing.

Lu Wenfu. 1983. *The gourmet*, trans. Yu Fanqin. Beijing.

Lu Yu. 1990. *Il canone del tè*, trans. Marco Ceresa. Milan.

Needham, Joseph. 1980. *Science and civilisation in China*, Vol. 5. Cambridge.

Pirazzoli-t'-Serstevens, Michèle. 1991. The art of dining in the Han period: Food vessels from tomb no. 1 at Mawangdui. *Food and Foodways* 3 and 4: 209–19.

Qiu Pangtong, ed. 1986. *Jujia biyong shilei quanji*. Beijing.

Sabban, Françoise. 1986a. Court cuisine in fourteenth-century imperial China: Some culinary aspects of Hu Sihui's *Yinshan Zhengyao*. *Food and Foodways* 2: 161–96.

1986b. Un savoir-faire oublié: Le travail du lait en Chine ancienne. *Zinbun [Memoirs of the Research Institute for Humanistic Studies]*. Kyoto, 21: 31–65.

1988. Insights into the problem of preservation by fermentation in 6th-century China. In *Food Conservation. Ethnological Studies*, ed. A. Riddervold and A. Ropeid, 45–55. London.

1990. De la main à la pâte: Réflexion sur l'origine des pâtes alimentaires et les transformations du blé en Chine ancienne (3e siècle av. J.-C.-6e siècle ap. J.-C.). *L'Homme* 31: 102–37.

1993. La viande en Chine. Imaginaire et usages culinaires. *Anthropozoologica* 18: 79–90.

Sealy, Robert. 1958. *A revision of the genus Camellia*. London.

Shiba Yoshinobu. 1970. *Commerce and society in Sung China*, trans. Mark Elvin. Ann Arbor, Mich.

Shih Sheng-han. 1962. *A preliminary survey of the book "Ch'i Min Yao Shu," an agricultural encyclopaedia of the sixth century*. Beijing.

Shi Shenghan. 1982. *Qimin yaoshu jiaoshi*. Beijing.

Simoons, Frederick J. 1991. *Food in China: A cultural and historical inquiry*. Boca Raton, Fla.

Wang Shangdian, ed. 1987. *Zhongguo shipin gongye fazhan jianshi*. Taiyuan.

Wang Shixing. [1597] 1981. *Guangzhiyi*. Beijing.

Wang Zhongmin, ed. 1984. Chajiu lun. In *Dunhuang bianwenji*. Beijing.

Xu Zhen'e, ed. 1984. *Shishuo xinyu jiaojian*, Vol. 1. Beijing.

Yang Hsien Yi and Gladys Yang, trans. 1972. Kung I-chi. In *Selected stories of Lu Hsun*. Third edition. Beijing.

Yü Ying-shih. 1979. Han. In *Food in Chinese culture*, ed. K. C. Chang, 53–83. New Haven, Conn., and London.

Zheng, Chantal. 1989. *Mythes et croyances du monde chinois primitif*. Paris.

V.B.4 ❧ Japan

Rice and Staple Food

Rice has long been the main staple of the traditional Japanese diet. It is not only consumed daily as a staple food but also used to brew sake, a traditional alcoholic drink. Japanese cuisine has developed the art of providing side dishes to complement consumption of the staple food. Table manners were also established in the quest for more refined ways of eating rice and drinking sake at formal ceremonial feasts. The history of the Japanese diet, which is inseparable from rice, started therefore with the introduction of rice cultivation.

Subsistence during the Neolithic period in Japan (known as the Jōmon era, beginning about 12,000 years ago) was provided by hunting and gathering. Agriculture did not reach the Japanese archipelago until the very end of the Neolithic period. Collecting nuts (especially acorns and chestnuts) and hunting game were common activities, and a large variety of marine resources was intensively exploited throughout the period. The Jōmon era, however, ended with a shift from hunting and gathering to sedentary agriculture.

The Yangtze delta in China is considered to be the original source for the practice of rice cultivation in Japan. Continuous waves of migrants bearing knowledge of the technique reached Japan from the continent around 2,400 years ago via two major routes. One was through the Korean peninsula and the other was a direct sea route from China. Rice production techniques were accompanied by the use of metal tools, which provided high productivity and a stable supply. Population increased rapidly, and localized communities appeared in the following Yayoi era (1,700 to 2,400 years ago). Paddy-field rice cultivation was then under way except in the northern Ainu-dominated region of Hokkaido and in the southern Okinawa islands, an island chain between Kyūmshū (the southernmost main island of Japan) and Taiwan.

From the beginning of cultivation, only short-grain rice was known in Japan. Although long-grain rice was common in Southeast Asia and India, its absence from Japan caused the Japanese to develop prejudices about rice that persist until today. For them, rice means exclusively the short-grain variety; the long-grain type is regarded as inferior and unpalatable.

Traditionally, a meal consists of boiled plain rice, called *gohan* or *meshi,* and seasoned side dishes, called *okazu.* Cooked rice has always been the staple of a meal, so much so that the words *gohan* and *meshi* are used colloquially as synonyms for the word "meal." Side dishes complement rice consumption with their seasoned flavors, and as a rule, the sophistication and variety of such dishes has betokened the affluence of those who served them.

Peasants living in mountain areas with low rice productivity, along with poor people in general, formerly mixed millet with rice. The sweet potato, introduced in the eighteenth century, also became popular as a staple in the south of Japan, where it supplemented a low yield of rice. However, even the poor cooked pure boiled rice and pounded rice cake from pure glutinous rice for important meals. Pounded rice cakes *(mochi),* prepared by pounding steamed glutinous rice with a mortar and pestle, have been indispensable food items for Japanese ceremonial feasts. People thought that the essence – the sacred power of rice – was made purer by pounding, and *mochi* was believed to contain the "spirit of rice." Naturally this was and is the most celebrated form of rice and therefore the most appropriate food for feasts. Thus, New Year's day, the principal annual feast in Japan, sees *mochi* always consumed as a ceremonial food.

In a census record of 1873, nutritional information for the Hida Region (Gife Prefecture, Central Honsyū) shows that rice was the most important food, notwithstanding the general unsuitability of the area for the crop's cultivation (Koyama et al. 1981: 548–51). The same data reveal a typical daily intake of nutriments for premodern Japanese people. The recorded population of this mountainous region was about 90,000, and these people are thought to have maintained the highest dependency in Japan on millet as a rice substitute. The average daily energy intake per capita was 1,850 kilocalories (kcal) (in 1980 it was 2,600 kcal), of which 55 percent was supplied by rice, which also supplied 39 percent of the protein.

Both rice and millet, when served as a staple, have always been either boiled or steamed. Milling, however, was not developed generally, and processed powder was used only for cakes or snacks and not for bread. Later, noodle products made from the powder became popular. The oldest form of the noodles, *sakubei,* produced by adding rice powder to flour, was introduced from China in the eighth century.

Noodles made from flour as a light lunch or snack became popular during the fourteenth and fifteenth centuries, and consumption increased considerably after the seventeenth century, when a processing technique for buckwheat noodles *(soba)* was developed in Edo, now Tokyo. Since then, *soba* has become popular mainly in eastern Japan, where Tokyo is located, whereas *udon* noodles (made from flour) have always been popular in western Japan (Ishige 1991a).

Meat and Fish

A unique feature of Japanese dietary history has been the country's various taboos on meat eating. The first recorded decree prohibiting the eating of cattle, horses, dogs, monkeys, and chickens was issued by Emperor Temmu in A.D. 675. Similar decrees, based on the Buddhist prohibition of killing, were issued repeatedly by emperors during the eighth and ninth centuries. The number of regulated meats increased to the point that all mammals were included except whales, which, given their marine habitat, were categorized as fish.

The taboo against the consumption of animal flesh developed further when the Japanese aboriginal religion, Shintō, adopted a philosophy similar to that of the Buddhists. This did not mean, however, that meat eating was totally banned in Japan. Professional hunters in mountain regions ate game (especially deer and wild boar), and it was not uncommon for hunted bird meat to be consumed. However, a lack of animal breeding for meat kept its consumption very low. Indeed, it was only during the fifteenth century and its aftermath that the tradition of eating both the meat and eggs of domestic fowl was revived. Fowls, until then, had been regarded in Shintō as God's sacred messengers and were reared to announce the dawn rather than as a mere food resource.

Milk and other dairy products failed to become popular in Japan, China, and Korea. In fact, the only Japanese dairy product known to history was *so,* produced between the eighth and fourteenth centuries. Milk was boiled down to yield this semisolid product. But even this food, consumed at the court and among the noble class, disappeared as a result of the demise of the aristocracy. Cattle were raised only for drawing carts or plowing fields. To utilize them for meat or even for milk was, until relatively recently, a long-forgotten practice.

Lack of meat and dairy products in the Japanese diet produced an aversion to oily tastes, so that even vegetable oil was not commonly used for cooking. Tempura, fish or vegetables fried in a vegetable oil, is one of the best-known Japanese dishes today, but it became popular only after the mid–eighteenth century.

The lack of meat products also minimized spice utilization. Pepper and cloves were known from the eighth century and were imported either via China or directly from Southeast Asia, and garlic was also grown on a small scale. But these spices were used mainly to make medicines and cosmetics.

In the coastal seas of Japan, warm and cold currents mix to provide bountiful fishing grounds. This favorable natural environment and the traditional exclusion of fish from the meat taboo meant an extensive exploitation of marine resources. The Japanese developed a special liking for fish, and most people enjoyed a variety, although consumption was still largely forbidden for Buddhist monks.

Fish dishes, with a higher status as well as a more attractive taste than vegetable dishes, were formerly considered indispensable at feasts. However, before the introduction of modern delivery systems, the difficulty of preserving and transporting fresh marine fish minimized consumption in inland areas where freshwater fish were commonly eaten instead.

The basic concept of fish preparation in Japan is suggested by the following proverb: "Eat it raw first of all, then grill it, and boil it as the last resort." To amplify, it is felt that the taste and texture of fish is best appreciated when it is very fresh and eaten raw. If the fish is a little less than fresh then its best taste will be produced by sprinkling it with salt and grilling it. If the fish is not fresh, then it is better boiled with seasonings, such as soy sauce *(shoyu)* or soybean paste (miso).

The consumption of fish raw has been traditional since ancient times. *Namasu,* or the eating of thinly sliced raw fish dipped in a sauce with a vinegar base, is a typical example. However, the better-known sashimi has been popular only since the seventeenth century – its popularity increasing as the general consumption of soy sauce increased. Delicately sliced raw fish of the utmost freshness and quality is eaten after being dipped in soy sauce flavored with a small amount of grated wasabi *(Wasabia japonica),* which is similar to horseradish.

As a rule, the philosophy of cooking aims at the creation of new tastes that do not exist naturally – such creation is a result of imposing artificial processes on food materials. But Japanese cooking methods are antithetical to this philosophy. The ideal of Japanese cooking is to retain the natural tastes of food with the minimum of artificial processes. Thus sashimi, for example, can be viewed as a representative product of the Japanese cooking philosophy.

Nigiri-sushi, prepared by putting a slice of raw fish onto a bite-size portion of hand-rolled, vinegar-flavored rice, has recently become internationally popular. But sushi originated as a means of preserving fish by fermenting it in boiled rice. Fish that are salted and placed in rice are preserved by lactic acid fermentation, which prevents proliferation of the bacteria that bring about putrefaction. A souring of flavor occurs during the process, and the fish is eaten only after the sticky decomposed rice has been cleaned off.

This older type of sushi is still produced in the areas surrounding Lake Biwa in western Japan, and similar types are also known in Korea, southwestern China, and Southeast Asia. In fact, the technique first originated in a preservation process developed for freshwater fish caught in the Mekong River and is thought to have diffused to Japan along with the rice cultivation.

A unique fifteenth-century development shortened the fermentation period of sushi to one or two weeks and made both the fish and the rice edible. As a result, sushi became a popular snack food, combining fish with the traditional staple food, rice. Sushi without fermentation appeared during the Edo period (1600–1867), and sushi was finally united with sashimi at the end of the eighteenth century, when the hand-rolled type, *nigiri-sushi,* was devised. Various styles of hand-rolled sushi were developed, such as *norimaki,* in which vinegar-flavored rice and seasoned boiled vegetables are rolled in paper-thin layers. In addition, sushi restaurants became popular during this era. They offered ready-made rice prepared with vinegar and other seasonings and rolled with different toppings according to the taste of the guests. In this manner, sushi has changed from its original character as a preserved food to that of a fast food (Ishige and Ruddle 1990: 21-94).

Vegetable Food

In daily meals, vegetables have generally constituted the main ingredients of side dishes and soups accompanying rice. Among these vegetables are a variety of sea plants that have been utilized since ancient times and remain a unique feature of Japanese cooking even today. Sea plants are usually dried and soaked in water before cooking. Sea tangle has been the most important of all. It is commonly used to prepare broth, and owing to its rich content of glutamic acid, it enhances the original taste of the foodstuffs with which it is boiled.

Traditionally, salted vegetables have been an indispensable part of the daily diet of even the poorest classes of people. Some several hundred varieties of salted vegetables are known in Japan; however, the method of pickling common in the West, using vinegar, has not developed there.

Of all beans, the soybean is the most significant. It is a good source of vegetable protein, and its importance in the Japanese diet is surpassed only by that of rice. Varieties of soya in a processed state, such as tofu and *natto,* have played an extremely prominent dietary role over the ages. Tofu, or soybean curd, which diffused from China and is first mentioned in Japan in an eleventh-century document, has been one of the most widespread of the processed foods. A cookbook providing 100 different recipes for tofu cooking was published in 1782 and became so popular that a second volume, containing another 138 recipes, was issued the following year. Many of these recipes were devised by Buddhist monks, who abstained from eating meat for doctrinal reasons and relied heavily on tofu as a source of protein.

Bacillus subtilis bacteria, which grow on rice straw, are cultivated on boiled soybeans to produce *natto. Natto* has a unique sticky consistency and is usually seasoned with soy sauce and mustard before eating; minced *natto* is used as an ingredient of soybean-paste soup. *Natto* contains abundant protein and vitamin B_2 and has been popular as a breakfast food because it is easily digestible.

Vegetarian diets, or *shojin-ryori,* rely on a variety of foods processed from soybeans. These include tofu, *abura-age* (fried tofu), *kori-dofu* (freeze-dried tofu), and *yuba* (paper-thin processed tofu), as well as mushrooms, sea plants, sesame, walnuts, and, of course, vegetables. *Fu,* which is produced by condensing wheat gluten, has also been a popular foodstuff. *Shojin-ryori* has generally been served during periods of mourning, for Buddhist rituals, and on the anniversary of the death of close kin.

From a dietetic point of view, the Japanese vegetarian diet is both well balanced and quite rational. It supplies protein from tofu and similar products, fat from sesame, walnuts, and vegetable oil, vitamins from vegetables, and minerals from sea plants. Such a diet not only is nutritious but also offers many palatable recipes, which have been refined by such techniques as employing a broth made from dried sea tangle and mushrooms as a base for cooking. Vegetable oils, which are extensively used, were especially developed by those Zen Buddhist monks who had maintained contacts with China.

Seasonings and Flavorings

Because of an absence of rock salt in Japan, salt made from seawater has been prevalent since the Neolithic era. But a salty residue fermented from soybeans has traditionally been used as a basic and versatile seasoning in Japan (as well as in China and Korea). Miso (soybean paste) and *shoyu* (soy sauce), the two major products of this residue, have been used to season boiled dishes and as ingredients in the preparation of various sauces.

Of the *koji* fungi that are employed as starters for soybean fermentation, *Aspergillus oryzae,* which grows on rice grains, is the most common. The fermented products of soybeans were first recorded in

a law book called the *Taiho-ritsuryo,* compiled in A.D. 702. But it is known that by that time a type of miso was already being produced, using a technique thought to have been introduced from Korea. The indigenous Japanese processing method, which employs artificially cultivated starters like *koji* and combines soybeans with rice and barley, was devised later. It differs from the Korean method, which relies on natural bacteria in the air to ferment pure soybeans, to which salt is added.

The traditional Japanese method of processing miso is to mash boiled or steamed beans while the *koji* fungus is cultured on boiled or steamed rice or barley. All these ingredients are then mixed together with salt and placed in a container. After a maturation period of more than a year, the mixture changes into miso, a pastelike substance. The liquid that oozes out in the maturation container is sometimes used as a type of soy sauce. Other types of miso are also made; these all vary by region in processing techniques.

Similarly, the general method of processing *shoyu* (soy sauce) is to culture *koji* fungus on pounded, preparched wheat grains and then to mix this with boiled beans and a large amount of salt water in a maturation container. The mixture is stirred occasionally, and fermentation is completed within three or four months. During the maturation period following fermentation, the contents intensify in color and flavor, owing to chemical reactions among the ingredients. After one year of maturation, the liquid obtained by squeezing the contents is pasteurized and becomes *shoyu.* As with miso, *shoyu* also has many regional varieties.

The use of the liquid by-product of miso processing as a seasoning has been known for a long time, but commercial production of *shoyu* dates only from the sixteenth century. Propagation of recipes from major cities where *shoyu* was employed extensively during the Edo period gave *shoyu* national status as a seasoning, and more than 70 percent of present-day Japanese recipes employ it in some way. In contrast to *shoyu,* miso has decreased in importance as a seasoning for both boiled dishes and sauces, and its daily use has generally been restricted to soup.

Rice is employed to make the traditional Japanese vinegar. In addition, a type of sake with a strong sweet taste, called *mirin* (which is processed in a slightly different way from the usual brew), serves as a cooking wine.

Another unique feature of Japanese food culture is the extensive development of dried foods for the preparation of soup stock (broth), or *dashi.* Dried sea tangle *(konbu),* dried bonito *(katsuo-bushi),* and dried brown mushrooms *(shiitake)* are some examples. They are not only used for *dashi* but also often added to boiling vegetables.

Katsuo-bushi, or dried bonito, is produced by boiling the fish, after which it is heat-dried and cooled. This process is repeated more than 10 times until the water content of the fish is reduced to less than 20 percent and the surface is covered by "tar." The covering of "tar" and fat is scraped off and the remaining meat is placed in a wooden box and left for two weeks to propagate an artificially planted fungus of the genus *Aspergillus*. After two weeks the surface is cleaned, and the fungus-planting process is repeated four more times.

At completion, a majority of the remaining contents are protein and flavor essence. Water content is reduced to 15 percent of the original, and the final product, *katsuo-bushi,* appears dry and hard like a block of wood. The fungus-planting process, which yields a better flavor and helps extract the water, was invented in the seventeenth century, although the rest of the process has been known since ancient times.

When used, small amounts of very thin flakes of *katsuo-bushi* are shaved from the block with a specially designed plane, then placed in boiling water to extract their flavor. When the water is strained it becomes a pure soup stock, and the flakes are usually discarded except in rare cases when they are combined with soy sauce to prepare a salty side dish. *Konbu* and *shiitake* are similarly boiled to prepare soup stocks yielding their particular flavors.

Dried foods for making *dashi* were developed essentially to add subtle and enhancing flavors to traditional dishes that consisted mainly of vegetables with little intrinsic taste. But the traditional interest in such products led Japanese scientists to conduct chemical analyses of their flavors. The analyses found that inosinic acid from *katsuo-bushi,* monosodium glutamate from *konbu,* and guanylic acid from *shiitake* were the sources of their natural tasty flavors. This research was the forerunner of Japan's modern natural and artificial flavor research industry.

Table Manners and Tableware

As is the case in China and Korea, Japanese food is usually served in sizes suitable for picking up by chopsticks, the use of which is thought to have been introduced from China in the seventh century. That the Japanese ate with the fingers prior to the introduction of chopsticks was recorded by a Chinese mission in the early third century. Spoons, however, although common in China and Korea, did not catch on in Japan, perhaps because the habit of sipping soup from handheld wooden bowls made the use of spoons superfluous. Japan's abundant forest resources meant that wooden tableware was more readily available than ceramic ware, and a wooden bowl can be more comfortably held than a ceramic or metal one.

Traditionally, only lacquered wooden ware was used for formal feasts. Chinaware remained unpopular until the seventeenth century, when mass production became possible as a result of new manufacturing techniques learned from Korea. The more widespread use of china caused a functional division between wooden and chinaware to evolve for daily use. Chinaware was used for rice and side dishes, whereas boiling hot soup was served in wooden lacquered bowls.

As a rule, every individual has his or her own chopsticks and a set of tableware. An extra set of chopsticks is used to serve food from a communal food vessel to each individual vessel. If extra chopsticks are not provided with the communal food vessel, then individuals reverse their own chopsticks and use them to transfer food to their own vessels. This practice, however, reflects more a psychological cleanliness derived from Shintoism (in order to prevent one's spoiled spirit from passing to others through shared foods) than it does practical sanitary concerns.

No chairs were used in Japan before the general adoption of dining tables in the latter half of the twentieth century. Diners sat either on tatami (straw mats) or on the wooden floor. Vessels containing food were served on a small, low, portable table called a *zen*. Usually, each dish was set on a *zen* in the kitchen and then brought to and placed in front of the diner. Several *zen* tables were used for each person at a formal feast, as the numerous separate dishes could not all be placed on just one. The number of small tables at a feast consequently became a standard for evaluating the event as well as the host. One unique feature of a Japanese meal is that all the dishes are served simultaneously. The only exceptions are meals served as part of a tea ceremony, in which dishes arrive in an orderly manner one after the other.

As a diner's personal table is very low, vessels containing food are handheld and lifted close to the mouth, to which the food is delivered with chopsticks. When sipping soup it is not considered bad manners to make a slurping sound. Modern Japanese table manners, for the most part, originated at the formal feasts of the samurai warrior class during the sixteenth and seventeenth centuries. From these feasts evolved the rituals and complicated manners for using tableware and chopsticks that are still commonly practiced today.

A big change, however, has occurred in the traditional table setting during the twentieth century. During the first half of the century, a larger portable table called *cyabu-dai,* on which there is space enough to place all the diners' dishes, gradually replaced the traditional personal table. Family members sat on tatami mats and surrounded the dining table for their daily meals. But the biggest change has been the increasing use of Western-style tables and chairs in ordinary households during the last few decades. This has drastically westernized Japanese dining settings: About 70 percent of all households now use a table and chairs for meals (Ishige 1991b).

Tea and Liquor

The first record of tea in Japan mentions an offering of prepared tea to the Emperor Saga, in A.D. 815, by a Buddhist monk who had studied in China. This particular tea was prepared by pounding a roasted block of compacted tea leaves into powder and then boiling it in water. The emperor became fond of it and ordered the planting of tea trees. Tea drinking quickly became fashionable among the aristocracy but, for some unknown reason, lost popularity in the tenth century. The taste and flavor may have been too strong for the Japanese palate at that time.

In the thirteenth century, tea drinking again became a popular custom as a result of the reintroduction of the tree, on the one hand, and on the other a new method of tea preparation, brought from China by a Buddhist monk called Yōsai. Yōsai's book, which recommended tea as healthful, caused a strong revival of interest in tea drinking among aristocrats and monks, and the popularity of tea has continued undiminished until the present. After its reintroduction, steamed tea sprouts were dried and then ground to produce powder, which was mixed with boiling water in a tea bowl, a method basically the same as that which continues today as the tea ceremony.

The tea ceremony, or *cha-dou*, was established in the sixteenth century by Rikyu, who refined the custom to an aesthetic form based on Zen philosophy. It was an attempt to create an aesthetic whole, unifying architecture, gardening, fine arts, crafts, religion, philosophy, literature, food preparation, and presentation. The meal that accompanies the ceremony, called *kaiseki-ryōri*, has come to be regarded as the most refined form of cuisine and is still served in the best Japanese restaurants today.

The drinking of powdered tea, however, did not achieve general popularity owing to the intricate preparation and drinking etiquette required. Even today it is limited to the tea ceremony or other special occasions. The popular green tea is a leaf-type tea, or *sen-cha*, which is prepared by pouring boiling water on dried tea leaves in a teapot. Neither milk nor sugar are added. Drinking of this type of tea started in China during the Ming dynasty, and in the seventeenth century was introduced to Japan, where it became a custom widespread throughout the population and, thus, was incorporated into the Japanese way of life. People who had drunk only hot water prior to the introduction of tea now finished meals with it, had tea breaks, and served tea to welcome guests. That this tradition has survived is evident in the free tea service still offered in virtually every Japanese restaurant.

Only in recent times have alcoholic drinks such as wine or beer (produced by the saccharification of cereal germination) existed in Japan. The oldest-known such beverage, mentioned in eighth-century literature, utilized the starch saccharification potential of saliva. Raw or boiled rice was chewed and expectorated into a container where it mixed with saliva. This primitive technique survived until the beginning of the twentieth century in Okinawa. By tradition, virgins prepared this type of liquor for special religious ceremonies. Another practice – that of applying *kōji* fungus to rice as an initiator of fermentation (introduced from China) – has also been in general use since ancient times.

Rice wine or sake, which was homemade by farmers, is a result of the alcoholic fermentation of a simple mixture of steamed rice, *kōji*, and water. Professional brewers would prepare sake by adding low-alcohol sake to newly mixed steamed rice and *kōji* without previous filtering. This process causes saccharification and alcoholic fermentation at the same time and increases the alcoholic strength of the mixture. In contemporary commercial production, such a process is repeated three times to increase the amount of alcohol to nearly 20 percent. The mixture is then placed in a cloth bag and squeezed with a press. The pasteurization of the clear liquid from the press is the last part of the process.

The latter technique was first mentioned in A.D. 1568, in the *Tamonin-nikki*, the diary of a Buddhist monk, indicating its practice in Japan some 300 years before Louis Pasteur. In China, the first country in East Asia to develop the technique, the earliest record of the process dates from A.D. 1117 (Yoshida 1991).

Today, sake is normally served by warming it to nearly 50 degrees centigrade in a china bottle immersed in boiling water, after which it is poured into a small ceramic cup. This popular procedure began in the seventeenth century, although at that time hot sake was regarded as appropriate only in autumn and winter.

Shōchū, a traditional distilled liquor first mentioned in a sixteenth-century record, uses rice, sake lees, or sweet potatoes as a base material. A similar distillate from Okinawa, *awamori*, employs rice exclusively. In this case, the production technique is thought to have been diffused from Thailand in the fifteenth century, but the true forerunner of Japanese *shōchū* has yet to be firmly identified. One theory regards Okinawa and its *awamori* as the origin, whereas another insists that China was the source. We do know that *shōchū* was produced mainly in southern Kyūshū and Okinawa, where the hot climate made the brewing of good-quality sake difficult, and the liquor has been consistently consumed there since the Edo period. In other regions, *shōchū* has been regarded as a drink for the lower classes, who wanted a stronger (and cheaper) beverage than the more expensive sake.

Establishing Traditional Food Culture

As already mentioned, since the introduction of rice cultivation, various foods and their processing or cooking techniques have reached Japan from both China and Korea. In addition, European foods, brought by Portuguese traders and missionaries, started to flow into Japan between the late fifteenth and the early seventeenth centuries. But European styles of cooking, which mainly used meat, were not accepted by the mostly Buddhist Japanese, who were banned from eating meat by religious decree. Nonetheless, Western desserts and sweet snacks were welcomed, and some of the techniques of preparing these were adopted locally and still survive today. A typical example is a sponge cake called *kasutera* that derived from the Portuguese *bolo de Castelo,* a cake from the Castelo region of Portugal (Etchū 1982: 78–9).

Fearing that the propagation of Christianity by Western missionaries was merely a pretext to disguise Western attempts to colonize Japan, the Tokugawa Shogunate banned Christianity and closed the country to outsiders in 1639. The resulting near-total isolation from the rest of the world, lasting until 1854, brought domestic peace during the Edo period (named for the Shogunate's city). Domestic social stability, combined with isolation, tended to lend an unchanging quality to Japanese culture, including the culture of food. Indeed, most traditional dishes served in homes and restaurants today had their origins in the Edo period.

During the Edo period, Japanese food culture was developed and refined among wealthy urban middle-class merchants and artisans. This was a situation much different from that of many other countries, the food cultures of which, including styles of cooking, preparation techniques, table settings, and manners, were first developed and refined in the social life of the court and aristocracy before they diffused to the general society. But the Imperial Court in Kyoto had only a symbolic status at that time, with little political, economic, or social influence. The warrior class that supported the shogunate administration adopted the ritualized court cuisine of former times, which placed great emphasis on an intricate etiquette of food consumption, rather than on the food itself. The ruling class that regulated its members through ascetic morals had little interest in developing better or different flavors and tastes in their cuisine, whereas the majority of the peasants lived in poverty and were scarcely able to sustain themselves on the meanest of foods.

Wealthy merchants controlled (at least economically) Edo society, and Japanese haute cuisine restaurants came into being about the middle of the eighteenth century to cater to them. These restaurants were mostly located in the three major cities of Edo, Osaka, and Kyoto, and were similar to those established in Paris for the French bourgeoisie. With their superb interior decorations and ornamental gardens, such restaurants made every effort to serve refined, palatable dishes that were utterly different from those offered at the formal banquets of the court and the warrior class. The new and innovative recipes and food preparation techniques gradually spread to influence eating habits nationwide and ultimately became the core of today's traditional Japanese cuisine.

The emphasis on aesthetic food presentation in contemporary Japanese cuisine also originated in these restaurants with presentation devices of *kaiseki-ryōri.* The Japanese philosophy of food presentation seeks to reflect the Japanese view of nature in the elimination of anything artificial from the plate. Thus, symmetrical presentation, for example, is the antithesis of this philosophy, which would rather have imbalance and a blank space on a plate. This approach provides an elegant appearance, whereas to cover a whole plate with various foods is considered vulgar, even though it gives an affluent impression at first glance. Conceptually similar to an empty space in an India ink oriental painting, this deliberately proportioned space becomes an integral part of the art of food presentation. The representation of a season of the year in the display of a dish (by utilizing specific materials such as bonito fish in May or the taro potato in August – both lunar months) is also an important dimension of this philosophy.

Along with the haute cuisine restaurants, inexpensive eating houses and pubs for craftsmen and store employees also appeared in big cities. Not only did various noodles, along with sushi and tempura, become popular snacks in these eating houses, but other specialty restaurants and stalls serving only specific items proliferated. One *soba* shop and two sushi shops to a block was a common sight in the center of Edo, even in the eighteenth century, and according to the 1804 census, 6,165 eating houses existed in the city. This meant that there was one eating house for every 170 persons in the population, not counting peddlers' stalls and eating houses in the red-light district, which were excluded from the census. Another record (which again excluded peddlers' stalls) shows that in 1860, representatives of 3,763 *soba* shops from all over Edo held a meeting to discuss raising prices to meet the increased cost of ingredients.

Restaurant guidebooks for urban gourmets and visitors from the country became popular from the late eighteenth century, corresponding to the rapid increase of dining-out facilities in big cities. Indeed, there were urban bourgeoisie who enjoyed restaurant hunting in Japanese cities with help from guidebooks nearly a century before the publication of the *Michelin Guide* in France (Ishige 1990). Cookbook publication was also brisk, with about 130 originals and several hundred later editions of the originals known to have been printed.

Modernization of Foods

The Meiji Restoration, which put an end to the Tokugawa Shogunate in 1868, gave expression to the need for rapid social modernization. The government-led industrial revolution introduced Western technology and culture and developed a capitalistic economy with the ultimate goal of enriching and strengthening the Japanese nation in the world. A change of eating habits, which occurred in accordance with social improvements, can be seen in government encouragement of meat eating and milk drinking so as to make the physique of Japanese people comparable to that of Western people.

The change began with a public report in 1872, which mentioned that Emperor Meiji enjoyed beef dishes. Following this declaration, it became a custom of the court to entertain international guests with formal dinner parties at which French cuisine was served, and the traditional taboo against meat eating disappeared rather quickly. The first popular meat dish was boiled, thinly sliced meat served with tofu and leeks. It was seasoned with soy sauce and sugar and later became known as sukiyaki. Yet Western cuisine in general was reserved for special occasions and was prepared exclusively by professional chefs; thus, although the number of Western restaurants in big cities increased, Western cuisine was not commonly adopted in Japanese homes for a long time to come.

Milk drinking, although introduced by resident Westerners and repeatedly praised as nutritious by the government, met nonetheless with stubborn resistance from a general public unwilling to accept it as part of the normal diet. Indeed, until the mid-twentieth century, milk was regarded as either a medicine or a special health drink for the sick or persons of weak constitution. Except for canned condensed milk, welcomed by nursing mothers as a supplement to breast milk, few people adopted the custom of consuming dairy products (such as butter and cheese) before the general introduction of bread as a breakfast food in the 1960s. Yet even in the present, the limited consumption of dairy products in the home is another of the features that set Japanese eating habits apart from those of other developed countries.

It is interesting to note that although Western cuisine became progressively more popular after the Meiji Restoration, Chinese cuisine was largely ignored, even though it shared with Japanese cuisine a common food element (rice) and eating method (chopsticks) and had long influenced Japanese food culture. Western cuisine was regarded as a symbol of modernization, whereas the late nineteenth century Japanese victory in the Sino-Japanese War over Korea strengthened contempt for the Chinese people and their culture. Such factors delayed the Japanese patronage of Chinese restaurants until the 1920s, though there were many such restaurants in Japan, catering to Chinese merchants and students. The Japanese maintained a similar prejudice against Korean cuisine, arrogantly disregarding the culture of a people whom they had annexed. But also at the time, the spicy flavor of Korean food created by the use of garlic and pepper was contrary to the traditional plain taste of Japanese food. Korean barbecues and pickles have, however, subsequently become common in Japanese homes.

The production of beer and wine began in the early Meiji era. Beer, despite its bitter and unfamiliar taste, soon became popular, while sake drinking also continued. The government tried to promote a wine industry for export, but the project was destroyed by phylloxera, which raged through European vineyards at that time and reached Japan in 1884 via imported vine stock. After the devastation, only artificially sweetened wine, consumed as a nourishment for the sick or by people of weak constitution, was produced – and this on a small scale. However, quite recently a resumption of domestic table wine production has occurred in Japan to meet a demand that has increased since the 1970s. This development has paralleled Japanese economic growth and with it a growth of interest in European and Californian wines. But although wine was unpopular until recently, by the 1920s beer, whiskey, coffee, and black tea were regularly drunk at an increasing number of bars, beerhouses, cafés, and teahouses in the big cities.

The modernization of Japanese food culture after the Meiji Restoration was interrupted by the rise of militarism and World War II. Following the Manchurian incident of 1931, 15 years of war and large-scale mobilizations, along with trade sanctions by Western nations, caused food imports to decline severely and slowed domestic agricultural production as well. Consequently, major food items, including meat and dairy products, were rationed under government control. Even fish was in short supply as war destroyed the fishing industry, and a return to the traditional meal of rice with vegetable side dishes was strongly encouraged by the government.

As the war progressed, even the minimum food ration could not be distributed regularly, and malnutrition became a serious problem. People were forced to supplement their rations by growing sweet potatoes (as a rice substitute) and other vegetables in home gardens; even after the defeat in 1945, it took 10 years for the nation to regain its prewar level of agricultural output. However, as a result of the rapid growth of the Japanese economy since the 1960s, diets previously concentrated on carbohydrates and poor in fat and animal protein have greatly improved. As foreign foods and styles of cooking have been embraced for cooking in the home, with their original tastes altered to conform with Japanese preferences, a large-scale fusion of foreign and traditional cuisines has taken place.

Thus, annual per capita rice consumption, which reached a maximum of 171 kilograms (kg) in 1962, has since declined and has remained at around 70 kg since the late 1980s. The consumption of sweet potatoes and barley as rice substitutes has declined drastically, and only a few people still eat them regularly. Such traditional carbohydrate foods have been largely supplanted by bread, which school-lunch programs made popular. These programs served bread made from American flour to schoolchildren. The flour had been received as food aid during the postwar food shortage.

Today, about 30 percent of the adult population

eats bread for breakfast, but very few people eat bread at lunch or dinner. In contrast with the laborious preparation needed for rice, timesaving bread is suitable for the breakfast needs of a developing urban society in which many people commute and so have less time for meals.

Although there has been a rapid increase in the consumption of previously rare foods, such as meat, eggs, dairy products, and fats, the consumption of traditional foods, like fish and vegetables, has also increased. People in Japan no longer maintain the attitude that meals are merely a source of energy for labor and that a staple food is the most efficient source of such energy. Now people enjoy the meal itself through the various tastes of side dishes, and a greater emphasis on side dishes than on staple foods has kept pace with increases in the national income.

A large variety of foreign foods and cuisines are now part of the household menu. But they have become popular only as it was determined that their flavors complement rice, soy sauce, green tea, and so on. Moreover, their tastes and preparation have often been adapted to moderate flavors, and their size or form has been arranged for use with chopsticks. In other words, such modifications should be viewed as part of an expansion of Japanese eating habits and cuisine, rather than a headlong adoption of foreign dietary patterns.

The Japanese intake of the chief nutrients reached an almost ideal level by the end of the 1970s, except for a little too much salt and a lack of calcium. The general physique has improved accordingly and the average life span has become the longest in the world. This ideal situation, however, may not continue long, as the generation now being raised in this affluent society on a high-protein diet may later pay a stiff price in geriatric diseases as a result of overnutrition – a problem that is becoming acute in other developed nations.

Naomichi Ishige

Bibliography

Etchū, Tetsuya. 1982. *Nagasaki no seiyō ryōri-yōshoku no yoake.* Tokyo.

Ishige, Naomichi. 1990. Développement des restaurants Japonais pendant la périod Edo (1603-1867). In *Les restaurants dans le monde et à trâvers les ages,* ed. A. H. de Lamps and Jean-Robert Pitte. Paris.

1991a. *Bunka menruigaku kotohajime.* Tokyo.

1991b. Shokutaku bunkaron. In *Bulletin of the National Museum of Ethnology,* Special Issue No. 16: 3-51.

Ishige, Naomichi, and Kenneth Ruddle. 1990. *Gyoshō to narezushi no kenkyū.* Tokyo.

Koyama, Shūzō, et al. 1981. Hidagofudoki ni yoru shokuryōshigen no keiryōteki kenkyū. In *Bulletin of the National Museum of Ethnology* 6 (3): 363-596.

Yoshida, Hajime. 1991. *Nihon no shoku to sake - chūsei matsu no hakkōgijutsu wo chūsin ni.* Kyoto.

V.B.5 ✍ Korea

Historical Background

If the history of a dietary culture is, in many ways, the history of a people, then the evolution of Korea's dietary traditions clearly reflects that nation's turbulent history. Geography and environment play a decisive role in determining the foundation of a nation's dietary culture, whereas complex political, economic, and social conditions and interactions with other cultures contribute to further development.

Traditional dietary strategies must balance the need for sufficient calories and specific nutrients with the need to avoid or minimize diseases associated with foods that are contaminated, spoiled, or otherwise unhealthy. An account of traditional diets should, therefore, deal with food- and waterborne diseases as well as with typical foods and cooking methods. Once dietary habits and food preferences have been established, they become a central part of the culture and are highly resistant to change.

It is not uncommon, however, to find that in the course of exchanges between cultures, foreign foods have become so thoroughly adapted to local conditions that their origins are quite forgotten. In a rapidly changing and interdependent world, it is important to understand the historical background of traditional diets and the impact of modernization in order to maintain and develop dietary strategies that balance cherished traditions with new circumstances. An understanding of the traditional foods of Korea, therefore, requires a brief overview of Korean geography and history.

Korea occupies the mountainous peninsula south of Manchuria; the Yellow Sea separates Korea from mainland China to the west. Japan is only 206 kilometers (km) away across the southern Korea Straits. Because of its strategic location, Korea has a history that has been intimately linked to developments in China, Japan, and other Asian countries. The total size of the peninsula is about that of the state of New York. It was artificially divided along the 38th parallel as the result of World War II and the Korean War, with the area of the northern zone about 122,370 square kilometers (sq km) and that of the Republic of Korea about 98,173 sq km. The peninsula is approximately 1,000 km in total north-south length and 216 km wide at its narrowest point, with a rugged coastline about 17,269 km long. Korea has long been a cultural bridge and a mediator between China and Japan and often the target of their territorial ambitions and aggression. Devastated and exhausted by centuries of conflict, the "Hermit Kingdom" during the sixteenth century embarked on a policy of isolationism that kept Korea virtually unknown to the West until the last decades of the nineteenth century.

Only vague outlines of Korea's early history have been reconstructed. Old Choson – the first of the periods of Korean history – is traditionally, but unreliably, dated from 2333 to 562 B.C. Ancient sources recall a period of settled village life in which the people cultivated the five grains, domesticated the six animal species, and harvested foods from the sea.

The Three Kingdoms period encompassed the era of Koguryo (37 B.C. to A.D. 688), Paekche (18 B.C. to A.D. 660), and Silla (57 B.C. to A.D. 935). Since the fourth century A.D., Buddhism has provided a sense of spiritual unity for the peninsula, despite conflicts among the Three Kingdoms.

The period from A.D. 618 to 935 is known as the time of Unified Silla. The Koryo dynasty lasted from 918 to 1392 and was followed by the establishment of Modern Choson under the rule of the Yi dynasty (1392–1910), whose bureaucratic and administrative structures were based on Confucian principles. During the Three Kingdoms period, the adaptation of the Chinese writing system to the Korean language stimulated state-supported compilation of national histories, but none of these annals survive. Extracts from the annals compiled during the Koryo era are the oldest extant Korean historical texts.

Korean Foodways

Staples

As might be predicted from what we know of Korea's long history and the struggles of its people to maintain their independence and their unique culture, Korean dietary patterns, traditions, and customs can be described as deeply rooted and not easily changed. Some modern Korean nutritionists not very modestly proclaim that traditional Korean foods constitute the perfect diet, outstanding in nutrition, taste, appearance, and variety. In sum, Korean cuisine is said to provide a nutritious, well-balanced answer to the weight and cholesterol problems that plague the developed world. Moreover, presenting traditional foods in the proper manner is said to promote a sense of peace and well-being that enhances the stability of the family and the nation.

The Korean diet is about 70 percent carbohydrate, 13 percent fat, and 14 to 17 percent protein. The European diet, in contrast, is usually about 40 percent carbohydrate, 30 to 40 percent fat, 15 to 20 percent protein, and 10 to 15 percent sugar. Scientific studies of traditional Korean foods, however, find both good and bad aspects. On the positive side, by combining and mixing a variety of materials, Korean cooks have been able to balance the nutritional qualities of available foods. On the other hand, traditional foods and seasonings provide a very high salt intake. Rice is regarded as the staple food, and other foods are described as subsidiary. Of course, although rice may satisfy hunger, it is not a complete food, and essential elements must be added to the diet to avoid malnutri-

tion. Korea's famous fermented vegetable preparations, known as kim-chee, almost invariably accompany each meal.

The traditional arts of cooking and presentation are said to be fundamental aspects of Korean culture; the proper preparation of food is considered a noble art as well as a science. Although it is difficult to precisely analyze and describe the special "Korean taste," preserving special dietary traditions and transmitting them to future generations is highly valued. Beyond nostalgia, Korean nutritionists are also concerned with the scientific analysis of the many components of the Korean diet and methods of preparation.

Historically, Korean food components and methods of preparation have been adapted to the four distinct seasons of the year and the different regions. Seasonal and regional adaptations bring out the best tastes in available foods and provide the balance needed to supply the body's nutritional requirements. Food etiquette is inextricably linked to food preparation and presentation, which is expressed in terms of rules for the placement of food on the table and rules for facing the table. Although the original Korean low food table, around which diners sit on the floor, has been largely displaced by Western-type tables and chairs, the etiquette of food presentation has not been forgotten.

Generally, the traditional Korean diet features three meals a day in which the foods are divided into two parts: the main dish or staple food – almost invariably boiled rice – and subsidiary foods or side dishes, such as soup, bean curd, cooked meat or fish, cooked vegetables, and fermented vegetables. Proper meal planning dictates diversity in methods of preparation and ingredients. The simplest meal has three side dishes, whereas more elaborate meals are characterized by an increasing number of side dishes. An ordinary everyday meal might consist of a serving of rice and soup for each person and a series of shared side dishes. The table setting shows a clear distinction between the main and the subsidiary dishes. For rituals and festivals, the table setting becomes more elaborate and includes a variety of appetizers, soups, noodles, vegetables, rice cakes, pastries, and beverages.

The evolution of Korea's traditional grain-based diet required the development of farming techniques as well as tools for hulling and pulverizing the grains. The evolution of the house, the kitchen, and the utensils for cooking, serving, and eating food was also part of this process. Cereals, such as millet and sorghum *(kaoliang),* were cultivated in Korea from about 2000 B.C. Excavations at ancient sites have yielded stone farming tools and the remains of different kinds of millet. Millet is probably the only grain native to the whole peninsula, but rice has long been the most important component of the Korean diet, with short-grain rice ultimately the favorite staple.

Rice was introduced from China, perhaps as early as 2000 B.C., although, according to some accounts, a

Chinese nobleman brought rice to Korea in 1122 B.C. Though small in area, the Korean peninsula has an extremely varied climate, so other cereals predominated in regions not suited to rice farming. In southern areas, rice was the mainstay, whereas millet was the staple grain in the north. Barley was introduced to Korea earlier than wheat, but the exact date is unknown. Barley was grown mainly in the southeastern region, where it was consumed as a staple in combination with rice. Wheat was not cultivated until about the first or second century A.D. It was probably introduced into Korea from China around the first century, but it has never been considered a staple. Even in the 1930s, the area devoted to wheat farming was only about half that occupied by barley.

During the Three Kingdoms era, Koguryo, Paekche, and Silla all engaged in land-reform policies, expanded irrigation systems, and actively encouraged the propagation of improved iron farming implements. Rice became the staple food of Paekche, whereas the people of Silla still depended on barley, and millet remained as important as rice in Koguryo. During the Unified Silla period, further developments in land use and farming techniques led to significant increases in rice production. But other important crops, in addition to barley, millet, and sorghum, were soybeans, red beans, mung beans, and buckwheat. Policies that increased farming productivity and land use were of primary importance to the government of Koryo. Rice reserves were maintained for emergency use, and the price of grain was regulated in order to increase rice production.

The soybean, a legume, is the most widely eaten plant in the world and is used in many forms, especially in China, Korea, and Japan. With only slight exaggeration, the ancients called the soybean a treasurehouse of life, well suited to sustain, restore, and enrich the soil and the human body. The nutritious quality and versatility of the soybean make it an important part of the diet in areas like Korea, where adults do not drink milk and dairy products are not used. Soybeans can be eaten fresh, dried, ground, fermented, sprouted, or processed into bean curd and various pastes and sauces. Both soybeans and mung beans yield bean sprouts, a good source of vitamin C.

The soybean is also an excellent source of oil, although sesame oil is a favorite component in Korean cooking, and both toasted sesame seeds and sesame oil are important flavoring agents. Many different kinds of vegetables, fruits, and nuts have been part of the Korean diet since ancient times, among them radishes, turnips, lotus roots, taro, leeks, lettuce, green onions, garlic, cucumbers, eggplants, pears, peaches, chestnuts, pine nuts, and hazelnuts. In addition, there are wild plants, such as bamboo shoots, ferns, mushrooms, ginseng, and the broad bellflower obtained from the mountains and fields. During the Koryo era, radishes and pears were especially grown for the preparation of kim-chees that were said to be superior in taste to the fermented vegetables of the Three Kingdoms period. Vegetable leaves were also used as wrapping for little packages of rice or meat.

Agricultural techniques developed further during the Choson era, and practical farming manuals, stressing methods appropriate to Korea, were written during this period. The Yi dynasty actively encouraged an expansion of the trade in exotic foreign drugs and foods that had begun during the Koryo era. For example, the great king Sejong (reigned 1418-50) supported attempts to grow orange and grapefruit trees in several provinces in order to determine whether these fruit trees could be established in Korea. These and other experiments made it possible for Korean farmers to cultivate various foreign plants and trees.

New Foods

Somewhat later, important foods from the Americas, including chilli peppers, pumpkins, sweet potatoes, white potatoes, maize, and tomatoes, were introduced. The sweet potato reached Korea from Japan in 1763 with an official returning from a diplomatic mission. Originally regarded as a famine-prevention food, it eventually became a popular part of the diet. The white potato was introduced by way of China about 1840. It proved well suited to cultivation in the northern regions.

Chilli peppers and tobacco were brought to Korea about the time of the devastating war with Japan known as the Hideyoshi Invasion (1592-8). But today it is impossible to imagine Korean food without chilli peppers, which constitute the main seasoning in most Korean dishes, especially in kim-chee and hot soybean paste.

One of the early names for the plant was "Japanese mustard," because the Japanese had acquired knowledge of the chilli pepper, and probably its seeds as well, from Portuguese Catholic priests. King Sonjo (reigned 1567-1608) made numerous requests to Japan and even to China in attempts to obtain the seeds. Unwilling to lose their monopoly, however, the Japanese claimed that the pepper plant could grow only in foreign tropical areas, and that even if seeds could be obtained, they would not necessarily grow in Korea. They also claimed that the foreigners who sold peppers always boiled the seeds so that they would be useless in attempts to grow new plants. The Korean king countered that various other plants and animals that had been brought to Korea from foreign lands had flourished, and after the difficulties in obtaining the seeds had finally been overcome, the pepper plant was easily adapted to Korea.

Some authorities thought that chilli peppers contained a powerful poison, but the new food quickly became widely used as a seasoning and even was sold in winehouses, where drinkers added it to liquor for a sensation of hotness. Presumably, given the eager acceptance of chilli peppers, Korean cuisine had not been bland before their arrival. And, in fact, Koreans had previously used a hot spice from China, which was probably similar to the Sichuan peppercorn. The ancients thought that pepper was valuable in the cure of fever, whereas modern admirers of the chilli pepper claim that its active agent strengthens the stomach, offers protection against dysentery, and prevents the oxidation of fats.

Cooking and Eating

Bowl-shaped earthenware pots were used for cooking in Korea from the beginning of the farming period. But steaming was thought to improve the quality of the food, and earthenware steamers for cooking grains have been found in Bronze Age shell mounds that date from 1000 to 300 B.C. Koguryo wall paintings in third-century tombs depict food cooked in an earthenware steamer. The kinds of food cooked in the steamer apparently included five-grain rice (a mixture of rice, millet, soybeans, red beans, and barley or sorghum), steamed rice cakes, and glutinous rice cakes. Sauteed rice cakes or sorghum pancakes were also consumed. Cast-iron kettles for rice cooking did not become common until the later part of the Three Kingdoms era, and the traditional chinaware and brassware used for serving foods developed during the Choson period. One interesting example is a special large dish with nine compartments that was used to hold an assortment of side dishes placed in the individual compartments. Wealthy people used this dish for outdoor meals and picnics.

Ideas about the ideal configuration of the house reflect the importance of the kitchen and the proper handling of rice. According to custom and classical texts, the house with the most auspicious configuration was one that faced south and had a mountain behind it. The mountain protected the house from the northeasterly winter winds and the sun could shine into the front of the house. The kitchen would be located to the west so that when the rice was scooped out of the pot, the flat wooden spoon faced the inside of the house. If the kitchen faced east, the spoon would face the outside; this was thought likely to bring bad fortune.

A unique aspect of Korean table manners is that Koreans, unlike the other peoples of East Asia, use spoons for soup and rice and came to believe, unlike the Chinese, that it was rude to bring bowls up to their mouths. In the northern parts of the Korean peninsula, where staple foods included millet and barley, it was found that the grains of these cereals (especially when mixed with nonglutinous rice) were not easily managed with chopsticks. Thus, bronze spoons as well as chopsticks have been found in fifth- and sixth-century royal tombs.

Bronze spoons from the Unified Silla Kingdom (618–935) differed in shape from spoons found in China in that they were bent, thin, and long, and were apparently used together with chopsticks in sets (the shape of Korean chopsticks is also different from

those of the Chinese and Japanese). Silver spoons were used at court and by the ruling class. In addition to being elegant, silver was supposed to detect poison in food.

The short-grain sticky rice favored in Korea can readily be picked up with chopsticks, but the use of the spoon is essential in dealing with the ubiquitous soups, stews, and porridgelike preparations found at almost every meal. Another important utensil is the *chori,* a bamboo strainer used to separate rice from sand and stones. Because the *chori* sifts good from bad it has been used as a symbol of good fortune.

It was during the Choson period that Confucianism came to exert a profound impact on political and moral standards, family structure, rituals, and ceremonies. Under the influence of Confucian ideals, the rules concerning food for the extended family and for ceremonial occasions became increasingly strict and rigid. Some concept of the most elaborate cuisine of this time period can be obtained through studies of the foods prepared in the palaces of the kings of Choson. Although the rituals and regulations governing royal cuisine were not common knowledge, some aspects of the art of royal cuisine influenced the dietary culture of the ruling class and diffused beyond the palace walls.

By the end of the Choson period, the art of royal cooking was on the verge of disappearing, and in 1970, when only one former palace chef still remained alive, royal cuisine was designated a major cultural property. Chef Han Hi-san, who had served King Kojong, King Sunjong, and Queen Yun, was awarded the title of Human Cultural Property of Royal Cuisine in 1971. After Han died, Professor Hwang Hye-song, who had studied with Chef Han, inherited the title. Hwang published many books on Korean cooking, established a research institute for royal cuisine, and held exhibitions to bring royal cuisine to the attention of the general public.

Traditions

A grain-based diet need not be bland or totally monotonous, even when boiled rice remains the single most important component. Thus, cereals were also made into gruel, noodles, and dumplings. Well-cooked porridge-like dishes, especially those made of millet, are still considered particularly nourishing and appropriate to the needs of the sick. Another simple, nourishing ancient food product called *misu karu* was made by washing, drying, roasting, and pounding cereal grains into a fine powder that could be mixed with water and used as an instant food. The roasted flour of assorted grains was useful for travelers, students, and others who needed a simple, ready-to-eat food.

Noodles and dumplings are such an ancient and popular part of the traditional Korean diet that, like China, Italy, Japan, Germany, and France, Korea also claims to have invented pasta (Korea has not, however, asserted this claim as passionately as Italy).

Dumplings and noodles have been made from rice and barley and prepared by boiling, steaming, or frying. They were usually served as main dishes for lunch or on special occasions. Noodles were considered especially appropriate for birthdays because they are a symbol of long life. Various kinds of noodles were made of wheat, buckwheat, rice, soya, or mung beans. Steamed wheat-flour buns were first brought from China and also became very popular for festive occasions.

Many different kinds of rice cakes and pancakes have been associated with holidays and festivals ever since the Koryo period. Steamed rice cakes were made with regular or glutinous rice and flavored with chestnuts, honey, jujubes, sorghum, and mugwort. Rice cakes, flavored with mugwort leaves or flowers, are a specialty of the southern provinces, and many therapeutic virtues have been attributed to mugwort (*Artemisia vulgaris*), which is also known as *moxa*. *Moxa* is supposed to increase the user's level of energy and ward off disease. Mugwort is dried and used in making *moxa* for cauterization (*moxibustion*) and other medicines. Rice cakes made with mugwort paste are traditionally served at the *Tano* festival.

Mugwort figures prominently in the foundation myth of Old Choson. According to ancient sources, the King of Heaven, leader of the gods of wind, rain, and clouds, ruler of grains of all kinds, who presided over life, disease, punishment, and goodness and evil, established his Holy City at the summit of Mount Taebaeksan. The god was approached by a bear and a tiger who beseeched him to make them human. The god gave them each a stick of *moxa* and 20 cloves of garlic and told them to eat them and avoid the sun for 100 days. The tiger failed to follow these instructions, but the bear did and became a woman. The god married her and she had a son called Tan-gun, the founder of Old Choson. Thus, both *moxa* and garlic were regarded as powerful drugs and foods in early times.

Among the most treasured traditional Korean foods are those associated with holidays, ceremonies, and seasons. Traditionally, Korean women prepared special dishes for folk holidays according to the lunar calendar. During the Choson period, with the rise of Confucianism, great attention was paid to rituals attached to holidays, including the preparation of foods thought to supply nutrition appropriate to each season. Such foods were a part of the ceremonies that expressed the hope of good harvests and harmony within the family and the village. Special holiday foods are often described as particularly nourishing and are said to encourage harmony between man and nature. Among these are rice cake soup, dumpling soup, cakes made of glutinous rice, rice cakes steamed on a layer of pine needles, five-grain rice, rice gruel prepared with red beans, sweet rice beverages, and seasoned dried vegetables. Cooking methods and ingredients have varied with regional customs, products, and increasing modernization.

The custom of making a red bean porridge with small dumplings of glutinous rice to mark the winter solstice has been practiced since the Koryo era, and sharing this dish with neighbors has also been part of the tradition. Eating certain foods on holidays was said to prevent different kinds of misfortune: For example, consuming red bean porridge on the day of the winter solstice was supposed to ensure good health, prevent colds, and drive away ghosts.

Five-grain rice and nine kinds of vegetables are typical holiday fare for the first full moon of the lunar year; rice cake soup was eaten on New Year's Day; crescent-shaped rice cakes were prepared for the second lunar month; azalea flower pancakes for the third lunar month; and grilled wheat cakes for the sixth lunar month. In the heat of mid-July, holiday foods that included chicken broth with ginseng, red dates and glutinous rice, and croaker stews were thought to revive the appetite and ward off illness. Foods appropriate to the August harvest moon festival have included taro soup, wine, rice cakes, and new fruits such as pears and persimmons.

Food and flower customs expressed the theme of seeking harmony with nature and incorporating its beauty in delicacies. A document from the Choson period describes an especially fragrant delicacy made by boiling together apricot petals, melted snow, and white-rice porridge. It was customary to go on "flower outings" several times a year, and while admiring the beauty of the flowers, participants would eat foods that incorporated them, such as chrysanthemum pancakes, chrysanthemum wines, chestnut balls, and citron tea.

Different kinds of rice cakes still retain symbolic value. For the ceremonial feast on a child's 100th day of life, steamed rice cakes represent purity and cleanliness; glutinous rice cakes, coated with mashed red beans, represent endurance; rice cakes steamed on a layer of pine needles represent generosity; and stuffed rice cakes represent intelligence. Collectively, the ceremonial foods represent longevity, purity, and divinity. At the feast held for a child's first birthday, there are, in addition to rice cakes, cakes made with cinnamon bark, steamed rice balls rolled in colored powders, and even a steamed, layered, rainbow rice cake that represents the parents' hope that the child will enjoy a wide range of accomplishments.

Seafood

Because Korea is surrounded by the sea on three sides and has many large rivers, its supply of seafood has been plentiful and varied. The remains of abalone, clams, oysters, snails, mackerel, pike, shark, and sea urchins have been found in ancient shell mounds. Different kinds of seaweed were also harvested, dried, and prepared in various ways. For example, seaweed can be made into paper-thin sheets, called *laver*, which are usually seasoned with hot sauce and wrapped around small portions of rice, vegetables, and meat. Seaweed soup is still considered essential for women recovering from the birth of a baby. At the ceremonial feast held when the baby is 100 days old, the mother again eats seaweed soup.

By the Three Kingdoms period, shipbuilding skills had been highly developed, so that many kinds of seafoods could be harvested. The challenge of storing highly perishable aquatic animals led to the development of methods for preserving them by fermentation. Fresh shrimp, fish, and other seafoods were salted and allowed to ferment. Pickled fish were often added to winter kim-chee.

During the Choson period, fishing techniques were further developed, fisheries became significant enterprises, and the production of herring, anchovies, pollack, codfish, and croakers increased rapidly. So, too, did the production of seaweed, and particular kinds were cultivated and processed on offshore islands.

All these products of the sea were dried, salted, or fermented and sold throughout the peninsula. Some were regarded in China as valuable medicines and desirable exotics. Chinese physicians were very interested, for example, in the properties of a certain mollusk that was eaten by the people of Silla; the medical men thought that a soup made from this mollusk and seaweed would cure "knotted-up breath."

Meat

Although geographic conditions in Korea were not suitable for livestock farming, cows, pigs, and hens were raised on a small scale, and, thus, some meat also entered the diet. Wild game could be found in the mountains, and the Koguryo people were known as skillful hunters of pheasants, roe deer, and wild boar. The people of Silla kept semiwild livestock on nearby islands. Cattle, hens, pigs, horses, and oxen were raised by the people of Paekche.

During the early Koryo period, when the influence of Buddhism was especially strong, kings and commoners alike generally refrained from eating meat, but pickled fish and shellfish were often served as side dishes. By the middle of the Koryo period, cattle were being raised on Cheju Island, and those whose religion and finances permitted it ate beef, pork, lamb, chicken, pheasant, and swan meat. Wealthy people might have their meats cooked whole, but cooking thinly sliced pieces of meat became popular during this time. Among the favorite meat dishes of the Koryo period were roasted ribs and bone and tripe soup. Significant changes in dietary customs developed during the Choson era, including increased (and perhaps guilt-free) consumption of beef, pork, chicken, and pheasant.

Fermented Food and Drink

Korea's famous pickled cabbage, kim-chee, has probably been an important side dish since agriculture began, but the first appearance of the word "kim-chee" occurred in the collected poems of Lee Kyu-bo (1168–1241), an eminent Koryo poet. Fermented vegetables were essential parts of the diet during the long, harsh Korean winter, when fresh vegetables were not available. Kim-chee is said to retain all the nutrition of almost any fresh vegetable.

Making kim-chee for the winter was a major annual event for each household. Traditionally, relatives and neighbors took turns helping each other, sharing the ingredients and the freshly made kim-chee. Originally, kim-chee contained only simple vegetables, but eventually a large number of regional and seasonal variations evolved, including those flavored with fermented seafoods, such as shrimp, anchovies, cuttlefish, crabs, and oysters. When hot chilli peppers were introduced in the middle of the Yi dynasty, the method of making this traditional food underwent substantial changes and improvements.

Although kim-chee is eaten as an essential side dish throughout the year, different ingredients and methods of preparation are associated with the changing seasons and different regions. Almost all varieties include Chinese cabbage, radishes, red pepper, and garlic. Salted shrimp provides the special flavor characteristic of the kim-chee preferred by residents of Seoul; salted anchovy is used in southern regions, and various kinds of fish are favored in northern regions, but the art of making kim-chee can be applied to an almost endless variety of basic ingredients, spices, and flavorings. Even the stems of the sweet potato vine can be turned into kim-chee.

Today, except for rice, kim-chee is the most important and popular food in the Korean diet. Another interesting fermented food, however, is made from a mixture of chopped fish, rice, radishes, and malt. This preparation is said to ward off indigestion, especially during festivals when overindulgence is likely to occur. Similar health-promoting benefits have been ascribed to kim-chee. There is no doubt that it is a good source of vitamins, including ascorbic acid, which protects against scurvy. Kim-chee is also said to regulate body fluids and intestinal fermentation, prevent constipation, and stimulate the appetite. Certainly, fermented foods add taste, texture, and important nutrients to the bland main dish of rice and other grains. They are said to provide the five different tastes: sweet, salty, hot, sour, and bitter.

In addition, wine and soy sauce are important products of fermentation. The production of alcoholic beverages from fermented grains probably developed during the early stages of farming. Similarly, soy sauce and hot soybean pastes, made by processing soybeans, have long been used as seasonings and condiments that contribute to the characteristic flavor of Korean foods. Techniques for making wine and soy sauces became highly advanced in the Three Kingdoms period, but the art of making soybean paste was revolutionized by the addition of the hot chilli pepper. Soy sauce and hot soybean pastes are still indispensable seasoning agents in Korean cooking. Koreans consider Japanese soybean sauces excessively sweet in comparison to their own, which they characterize as salty, light, simple, and refreshing. Each household traditionally prepared soy sauce and soybean pastes in the spring or autumn and stored them in large earthenware jars on special terraces. Recent health claims have been made for soy sauces: It is suggested that they not only prevent the oxidation of dietary fats but also contain anticancer factors.

Various kinds of rice wine were made during the Koryo period, including several that served for medicinal purposes. Other wines derived from sources as diverse as roots, barks, irises, chrysanthemums, and bamboo leaves. Many of these were made at home – an important task for the housewife. Farmers and laborers traditionally drank rice wine from a gourd before and after meals and with their midmorning snack to wet the throat and clear away the kim-chee aftertaste.

Exactly when techniques for the distillation of hard liquor were imported into Koryo is unknown. However, records of the time of King Kongmin, who reigned from 1351 to 1374, suggest that hard liquor was already being used and misused. During the twentieth-century Japanese occupation (1910–45), Japanese wines, grape wines, and Western liquors gradually became popular. After liberation from Japan in 1945, Western liquor and beer became widely available, and cocktails and mixed drinks were commonly served at social functions, especially in the cities.

Hot Beverages

In Korea, hot beverages have been collectively referred to as *ch'a,* or tea. Green tea, made of dried tea leaves steeped in hot water, was introduced to Korea in the eighth century by a Buddhist monk from China. Ancient Chinese texts associated tea with Taoist philosophy and referred to tea as the elixir of immortality. Tea plants and the seeds of tea bushes arrived from China in the ninth century. At first, tea drinking was associated primarily with Buddhist temples, the court, and the aristocracy. Drinking the beverage was said to soothe the mind and refresh the spirit while cleansing and improving the body. But it soon became popular among the common people as well, and offerings of tea and tea-drinking ceremonies were part of all national rites. Buddhist temples operated large tea plantations and sponsored tea-brewing competitions.

With the establishment of the Yi dynasty, the custom of tea drinking declined among members of the upper class, who were now professing Confucianism. The Choson government denounced Buddhism and levied high taxes on tea plantations. Alcoholic beverages, such as rice wine, generally took the place of tea in official ceremonies. But despite government repression, tea drinking remained popular, and people cultivated small tea gardens near their homes. Buddhist monks and nuns also continued to drink tea, which was always included in offerings to the Buddha, and men of letters associated tea drinking with artistic endeavors and the contemplation of nature.

The opinions of tea-loving scholars, monks, and poets profoundly influenced Korean culture, especially those of the Buddhist monk and scholar Ch'o Ui (1786–1866), who is credited with reviving interest in the rituals and traditions of tea drinking. In his *Eulogy to Oriental Tea* (1837), Ch'o asserted, among other things, that Korean tea was superior to Chinese tea in taste, fragrance, and medicinal virtues.

In addition to green tea, other such drinks, made from barley, corn, rice, sesame seeds, ginseng, ginger, cinnamon bark, citron, quince, dates, pears, strawberries, cherries, watermelon, and peaches, are also popular. Even the pollen of pine tree flowers can be mixed with honey and made into a sweet tea. Sweet beverages based on honey or fruits are often accompanied by rice or barley cakes. Indeed, many pastries were developed as accompaniments for tea, including fried honey cookies, fried cookies made from glutinous rice, small cakes made with green tea, and candied fruits.

Another important traditional beverage is the scorched-rice tea served with everyday family meals. It is made by pouring water over the rice that sticks to the bottom of the pot in which the rice was cooked. Boiling this rice with water creates a fragrant drink, and rice that is not consumed with the meal can also be mixed with this tea. Making such a beverage also has the virtue of making it easier to clean the spoon, rice bowl, and rice kettle.

Since the 1940s, coffee has become very popular in Korea, but King Kojong, who reigned from 1864 to 1906, appears to have been the first Korean king with the coffee-drinking habit. He was introduced to coffee by the Russian consul general in Seoul. In 1898 Kojong's enemies tried to murder him along with the crown prince by putting poison in their morning coffee. Fortunately, Kojong noticed a peculiar odor and did not drink his coffee. The prince was not so observant, but he vomited the tainted brew before it could do him significant harm.

Famine and Food-Related Disease

Famine

Ancient sources refer to famines and epidemics, floods, severe droughts, and grasshoppers that consumed all the grain. Early agricultural societies were very vulnerable to crop failures and famines. The importance of agriculture in the early Three Kingdoms period is reflected in references to Paekche kings punished for crop failures by removal from the throne, or even by death.

Other sources mention the Koryo relief system and the efforts made by these kings to deal with famines and epidemics. Warehouses were established in various provinces and opened as needed to ward off mass starvation. Government officials were charged with aiding and feeding the poor, and they provided a set measure of millet per day per person. During the Choson period, food reserves were maintained for use during natural disasters and for famine relief. To prepare for famine years, farmers were ordered to gather various edible roots, flowers, fruits, and leaves. Texts written in the sixteenth century describe hundreds of different kinds of foods that could be stored for famine relief. In order to disseminate such information to the general population, books on famine relief were written in the Korean alphabet, the script for the people, rather than in scholarly Chinese characters. Other texts provided discussions of the relationship between diet and health.

Food-Related Disease

Thirteenth-century texts dealing with traditional Korean medicine describe food poisoning that was variously attributed to the consumption of domestic animals, fish, crabs, mushrooms, alcohol, medicines, and miscellaneous chemicals. Given the age-old problem of contaminated food and water, it is not surprising that dysentery was historically one of Korea's more common diseases, to which even members of the royal family fell victim.

Despite the many virtues ascribed to kim-chee, including those of preventing everything from scurvy to dysentery, the symptoms of some vitamin deficiency diseases seem to have been described in early Korean medical texts. One recurrent condition suggests the possibility of beriberi. The symptoms described included swelling of the lower limbs, followed by swelling of the heart and stomach, difficulty in urination, weakness in the feet, and dizziness. However, early accounts are vague, and the symptoms of beriberi are not easily differentiated from those of other diseases.

According to Koryo sources, the Chinese apparently believed that beriberi could be cured by wearing shoes made from the skin of a remarkable fish found in Korea. The skin of this fish was said to be similar to that of the cow. Beriberi was probably rare in Korea, when compared to other parts of Asia, because few Koreans subsisted on a thiamine-deficient polished white rice diet. But the disease was noted among Japanese living in Korean cities because the Japanese were more likely to consume polished rice. During World War II, polished rice became more common in Korea, and beriberi was sometimes observed even in villages. Scurvy and pellagra seem to have been rare, but anemia was not uncommon, and symptoms that suggest rickets, including a condition referred to as "turtle chest," appear in the pediatric sections of ancient medical texts. Classic descriptions of "gentle wind" disease probably refer to osteomalacia, a form of adult rickets. In modern Korea, osteo-

malacia, a gradual deformation of improperly calcified bones, is fairly common among older women.

Parasitic infections are widespread in Asia, and presumably always have been, but ancient texts are too ambiguous to provide specific diagnostic clues as to the agents involved or the specific sources of infection, although various herbal remedies were prescribed to remove parasites. Gastritis seems to have been the major disease in the category of digestive disorders, but symptoms are also described that suggest gastric ulcers, intestinal disorders, and parasitic infestations.

Paragonimiasis (or pulmonary distomiasis) is caused by infection with members of the genus *Paragonimus,* and references to a disorder characterized by rusty-brown mucus are suggestive of this disease, which could have been acquired by eating contaminated raw crabmeat or other seafoods. The developing parasites lodge in the lungs and cause an intense inflammatory reaction that results in the production of the rusty-brown sputum.

Other parasites were still widespread in the early twentieth century. Infestation with flukes was generally caused by eating raw fish and crustaceans contaminated with the lung fluke *(Paragonimus westermani),* the liver fluke *(Clonorchis sinensis),* or the intestinal fluke *(Metagonimus yokogawai).* Until recent times, contaminated food and water were also a constant source of intestinal diseases such as bacillary and amebic dysentery. The custom of drinking tea or water boiled in the rice kettle provided some protection, as did the use of kim-chee instead of fresh vegetables. Noting that Korean patients recovered from dysentery more easily than Japanese patients, early-twentieth-century medical missionaries advised the latter to eat kim-chee.

Nutritional Status Today

The history of disease in twentieth-century Korea illustrates the remarkable impact of improved sanitary conditions, public-health measures, land reform, and economic development. Despite the devastation caused by World War II and the Korean War, and the repatriation of millions of Koreans from Manchuria, China, and Japan, many epidemic and endemic diseases have been virtually eliminated.

Since land reform policies were put in place in 1948, South Korean agricultural policy has encouraged the development of small, intensively worked farms. This policy was vindicated by the achievement of self-sufficiency in rice production and an increased food output that has kept pace with population growth. South Korea, Japan, and Taiwan have among the world's highest per-acre rice yields. Because much of the peninsula is mountainous and unsuitable for farming, agricultural development policy has focused on maximizing yields by means of high-yield crop varieties. Today, genetic engineering is seen as a principal means of increasing crop yields.

In addition, in the 1960s, South Korea embarked on a vigorous and highly successful program of economic development, and since 1962 the Korean economy has grown at one of the fastest rates in the world. In a remarkably short period of time, South Korea's traditionally agrarian society has undergone a major structural transformation, and the country has become one of the key industrialized nations of the Pacific Rim.

Since the late 1940s, numerous studies of the nutritional status of the South Korean people have addressed the question of shortages in the quantity and quality of the food supply. Most of these investigations reached the same general conclusions, despite some relatively minor regional differences. Overall, the traditional South Korean diet is high in carbohydrates and low in protein and fats. Studies of the state of nutrition in Korea undertaken in 1946 found that over 90 percent of foods consumed came from plant sources.

When similar studies were conducted in the 1960s, the proportion of grains consumed had been somewhat reduced. Rice, however, remained the main food, which may reflect a reaction to years of food rationing and shortages during the Japanese occupation. But rice shortages from 1960 to 1975 led the government to establish rice conservation measures, such as the increased production of wheat, the importation of American surplus foods, and attempts to create two "rice-free days" each week, during which, as a patriotic duty, wheat products would be eaten instead of rice. Bread was used in school lunches, restaurants were ordered to use wheat-flour foods, and a nationwide mass communication campaign was launched to encourage the consumption of wheat products. Although resistance to these attempts to change dietary habits was quite strong, at least students and some white-collar workers seem to have adopted the custom of eating bread for breakfast. Nevertheless, Korea remains primarily a rice-eating culture.

Although self-sufficiency in rice production was attained in the 1980s, imports of wheat products and maize were still essential. In fact, increased demand for wheat flour, used in bread and instant noodles, reflects a significant change in South Korean dietary patterns. Beef imports have also increased, whereas the production of traditional cattle has decreased. Fish and other seafoods have become increasingly important sources of protein.

In general, the intake of animal protein has significantly increased since the 1970s, and the growth in the amount of protein consumed was accompanied by a threefold jump in fat intake between 1962 and 1982. Consumption of beef and pork increased about two times; chicken consumption increased almost five times, and the use of milk and other dairy products also increased about five times. Although the intake of some minerals, particularly calcium, increased significantly, that of iron did not, and many Korean women have exhibited symptoms of iron-deficiency anemia. Investigations of infant and child nutrition in different regions during the 1970s led nutritionists to urge mothers to increase the use of eggs, fish, and vegetables as supplemental foods. One problem with the typical Korean diet is a very high intake of salt and hot chilli peppers; these factors appear to be linked to high blood pressure and a high incidence of gastroenteritis and stomach cancer. Researchers report that the use of great amounts of salt becomes habitual for South Koreans prior to reaching 6 years of age.

It is interesting to note that studies of nutritional status and dietary patterns conducted in the 1960s indicated that at that point, despite changes associated with rapid industrialization, many people had maintained traditional food habits. Indeed, the Korean dietary pattern seems to have been remarkably stable from the early beginnings of Korean history to the end of the Yi dynasty and beyond. Researchers have found little evidence of changes in the basic ingredients and cooking methods used by Korean families other than an increase, in urban areas, in the consumption of dairy products such as butter and cheese.

Between 1970 and 1990, however, the combination – already mentioned – of urbanization, modernization, industrialization, socioeconomic development, and the influence of Western culture wrought significant changes in the typical South Korean diet. In addition, factors such as the 1988 Seoul Olympic Games, the expansion of the fast-food industry, and the influence of mass media have helped accelerate such changes. South Korean nutritionists predict that in coming years, the pattern of food consumption in South Korea will involve a continuing decrease in the amount of grains used and an increase in the consumption of foods of animal origin. Consequently, they urge the development of a national health and nutrition policy that will focus on the prevention of the kinds of diseases associated with these new dietary patterns. Since the 1970s, the pattern of major diseases and causes of death in South Korea has become that of the Western world, whereby cardiovascular diseases, circulatory problems, and stroke are the most important killers. Those who value Korea's unique historical culture warn against losing the harmony and balance encapsulated in the traditional dietary culture and etiquette of the table.

Lois N. Magner

Work on this chapter was supported in part by NIH Grant R01 LM 04175 from the National Library of Medicine.

Bibliography

Handelman, Howard, ed. 1981. *The politics of agrarian change in Asia and Latin America.* Bloomington, Ind.

Han Woo-keun. 1970. *The history of Korea*, trans. Lee Kyung-shik, ed. Grafton K. Mintz. Seoul.

Im Dong-kwon. 1994. Village rites. A rich communal heritage. *Koreana: Korean Art and Culture* (Special Issue) 8: 6-11. (Special issue entitled *Village rites and festivals: Celebrating the spirits, feasting the gods.*)

Kim Tu-jong. 1966. *A history of Korean medicine* (in Korean). Seoul.

Korean Nutrition Society. 1989. *Korean nutrition resource data.* Seoul.

Lee, Florence C., and Helen C. Lee. 1988. *Kimchi: A natural health food.* Elizabeth, N.J.

Lee Ki-baik. 1984. *A new history of Korea,* trans. Edward W. Wagner. Cambridge, Mass.

Lee, K. Y. 1985. Korean food life 100 years (1880-1980). (One hundred years of Korean food habits, main dishes and side dishes): Evaluation and trends in dietary status (in Korean). *Yonsei Nonchong* (Korea) 21: 297-318.

Magner, Lois N. 1993. Diseases of antiquity in Korea. In *The Cambridge world history of human disease,* ed. Kenneth F. Kiple, 389-92. Cambridge and New York.

Marks, Copeland, with Manjo Kim. 1993. *The Korean kitchen: Classic recipes from the Land of the Morning Calm.* San Francisco.

Medical News Company, ed. 1984. *Centennial of modern medicine in Korea (1884-1983)* (in Korean). Seoul.

Miki, Sakae. 1962. *History of Korean medicine and of disease in Korea* (in Japanese). Japan.

Mo, Sumi. 1991. Present-day dietary patterns of Korea, influenced by social, economic and technological forces, and cultural processes. *Journal of the Asian Regional Association for Home Economics* (Supplement) 1: 87-95.

Ravenholt, Albert. 1981. Rural mobilization for modernization in South Korea. In *The politics of agrarian change in Asia and Latin America,* ed. Howard Handelman, 48-62. Bloomington, Ind.

Sohn, Kyunghee. 1991. A review of traditional Korean food. *Journal of the Asian Regional Association for Home Economics* (Supplement) 1: 81-6.

Yu Geh-won. 1976. *Season and food table* (in Korean). 4 vols. Seoul.

Yun Seo-Seok. 1993. History of Korean dietary culture. *Koreana: Korean Art and Culture* (Special Issue) 7: 7-11. (Special issue entitled *Traditional food: A taste of Korean life.*)

The History and Culture
of Food and Drink in Europe

V.C.1 ❧ The Mediterranean
(Diets and Disease Prevention)

The basic elements of healthful diets are well established (USDHHS 1988; National Research Council 1989; USDA/USDHHS 1995). They provide adequate amounts of energy and essential nutrients, reduce risks for diet-related chronic diseases, and derive from foods that are available, affordable, safe, and palatable. A very large body of research accumulated since the mid-1950s clearly indicates that healthful diets are based primarily on fruits, vegetables, and grains, with smaller quantities of meat and dairy foods than are typically included in current diets in the United States and other Western countries (James 1988; USDHHS 1988; National Research Council 1989).

Throughout the course of history, societies have developed a great variety of ways to combine the foods that are available to them (as a result of geography, climate, trade, and cultural preferences) into characteristic dietary patterns. In some areas, typical diets have developed patterns so complex, varied, and interesting in taste that they have come to be identified as particular cuisines. Some of these, most notably those of Asia and the Mediterranean, seem to bless the populations that consume them with substantially lower levels of coronary heart disease, certain cancers, diabetes mellitus, and other chronic diseases than those suffered by other peoples. Consequently, such apparent relationships between cuisines and health have created much interest in traditional dietary patterns.

Illustrative is the current interest in Mediterranean diets that has been stimulated by the unusually low levels of chronic diseases and the longer life expectancies enjoyed by adults residing in certain regions bordering the Mediterranean Sea (WHO 1994). Such good health cannot be understood within the context of those factors usually associated with disease prevention in industrialized countries, such as educational levels, financial status, and health-care expenditures. Indeed, the percentages of those who are poor in

Mediterranean regions are often quite high relative to those of more developed economies (World Bank 1993). To explain this paradox, researchers have focused on other lifestyle characteristics associated with good health, and especially on the various constituents of the typical Mediterranean diet.

Data from the early 1960s best illustrate the intriguing nature of the paradox. At that time, the overall life expectancy of Greeks at age 45 exceeded that of people in any other nation reporting health statistics to the World Health Organization (WHO/FAO 1993). Subsequently, the ranking of life expectancy in Greece has declined somewhat, at least partly because of undesirable changes in dietary practices that have occurred (Kafatos et al. 1991). But even with such changes, in 1991 life expectancy at age 45 in Greece was an additional 32.5 years, second in rank only to the 33.3 years yet available to Japanese people. By comparison, in the same year, life expectancy at age 45 for adults in the United States, United Kingdom, and Canada was respectively 30.8, 30.9, and 32.1 years (WHO 1994).

Even these brief observations raise interesting historical questions. For example: What, precisely, is a "Mediterranean" diet? When and under what circumstances did it develop? What are the health effects of specific dietary patterns? In what ways do diets change, and what are the health implications of such changes? Should – and could – a Mediterranean-style diet be adopted elsewhere, and if such a diet were to be adopted in, for example, the United States, what would be the impact on agriculture, the food economy, and health patterns? Because such questions address fundamental issues of food and nutrition research and policy, the Mediterranean diet constitutes an especially useful model for studying healthful dietary patterns (Nestle 1994).

Historical Antecedents

Diets of the Ancient Mediterranean
In the absence of written records, knowledge of ancient diets must be inferred from other kinds of evidence. Fortunately, evidence related to Mediterranean

diets is extraordinarily abundant, including a vast and extensively documented archaeological record of food debris and a large quantity of food-related art, pottery, tools, and inscribed tablets excavated from prehistoric, Neolithic, Bronze Age, and later sites throughout the region (Fidanza 1979). The evidence also includes information derived from scholarly analyses of the writings of Homer and other classical authors. (The many and varied sources of information about the diets of ancient Egyptians, for example, are summarized in Table V.C.1.1.)

Inferences based on such sources must, however, be tempered by consideration of the difficulties inherent in evaluation: poor preservation of materials, incomplete fragments, errors of oversight, biased opinions, false information, and problems of translation, classification, dating, and interpretation (Darby, Ghalioungui, and Grivetti 1977). Nonetheless, scholars have used these sources over the years to firmly establish the availability in ancient times of an astonishing variety of plant and animal foods, breads, spices, sweets, and beers and wines (Seymour 1907; Vickery 1936; Vermeule 1964).

Discovery of the presence of various foods in a region suggests – but does not prove – that people ate those foods on a routine basis. Reports of actual dietary intake in ancient times are scanty and are especially lacking for the diets of the general population. When classical authors described foods at all, they wrote almost exclusively about those consumed by warriors or noblemen. Such accounts do not seem entirely credible; the writings of Homer, for example, leave the impression that Hellenic heroes consumed nothing but meat, bread, and wine (Seymour 1907). Homeric texts mention vegetables and fruits only rarely, perhaps because such foods were considered

inadequate to the dignity of gods and of heroes (Yonge 1909), and olive oil is mentioned only in the context of its use as an unguent (Seymour 1907).

Perhaps as a result of such research, scholars have concluded that the typical diet of the common people in ancient times must have been rather sparse, based mainly on plant foods and bread, with meat and seafood only occasional supplements. In fact, such a diet was characteristic of the Mediterranean region even in the early twentieth century (Seymour 1907; Vickery 1936). However, a second- to third-century A.D. review of the food writings of classical poets and authors has provided a vivid contrast. It described foods and drinks in great detail, classifying them by flavor and aroma, means of preparation, and contribution to meals and banquets, suggesting that people of all classes ate and enjoyed a vast array of foods and ingredients (Yonge 1909).

Modern scholars have related dietary practices to the health of ancient Mediterranean populations through inferences from examinations of prehistoric skeletal remains, analyses of sepulchral inscriptions, and other kinds of evidence, as indicated by the listings in Table V.C.1.1. Some of this evidence provides insights into dental lesions, anemia, and other diseases, and taken together, it all suggests that the average life span in ancient Greece and Rome was probably on the order of 20 to 30 years (Wells 1975). The evidence also indicates, however, that this brief life expectancy had much more to do with infection and civil conflict than with malnutrition and starvation (Darby et al. 1977).

Modern History: The Rockefeller Study

The first systematic attempt to investigate dietary intake in the Mediterranean region took place shortly after the end of World War II. In 1948, the government of Greece, concerned about the need to improve the economic, social, and health status of its citizens, invited the Rockefeller Foundation to conduct an epidemiological study on the island of Crete. The aim was to identify factors that would best contribute to raising the standard of living of the Greek population, and Leland Allbaugh, an epidemiologist, was appointed to oversee the study. Allbaugh and his colleagues designed and conducted an extraordinarily comprehensive survey of the demographic, economic, social, medical, and dietary characteristics of the members of 1 out of each 150 households on the island, a sample chosen through a carefully designed randomization process. The foundation published the results of these investigations as a monograph in the early 1950s (Allbaugh 1953).

The report of the survey was remarkable in several important respects. It was, for example, extraordinarily thorough. It included a 75-page appendix that contained descriptions and critical evaluations of statistical methods and a 50-page compendium of the questionnaires used to obtain information. The sur-

Table V.C.1.1. *Sources of information about diets in ancient Egypt*

Archaeology (preserved remains of animals and plants)
    Stomach and intestines of human mummies
    Tombs (sealed and opened)
    Mud bricks

Art (depictions of foods, food preparation, domestic animals)
    Temple and tomb paintings and reliefs
    Statues, models, dioramas

Literature
    Papyrus, tomb, or temple texts
        Daily food allowances
        Lists of food offerings
        Foods in medical prescriptions
        Cosmology and mythology texts
    Greek, Roman, and Arabic texts
    Religious texts
    Descriptive accounts by travelers, historians, naturalists

Source: Adapted from Darby, Ghalioungui, and Grivetti (1977), 1:23.

vey's numerous dietary components included a review of agricultural data on the Greek food supply; the administration to 128 households of several distinct questionnaires examining cooking practices, daily menus, food expenditures, household food production, and food handling and consumption practices; and three dietary-intake surveys: one of pregnant women and nursing mothers, another of children and adolescents aged 7 to 19 years, and yet another of children aged 1 to 6, with the information in the latter obtained from the parents. These multiple surveys, however, constituted only the most peripheral components of the overall dietary probe.

The core of the survey's dietary sections consisted of 7-day weighed food inventories collected from the 128 households, 7-day dietary-intake records obtained from more than 500 individuals in those households, and food-frequency questionnaires administered to 765 households. These extensive dietary investigations were conducted in the early fall by volunteer nurses from the Greek Red Cross who, after 5 full days of training, went to live in the survey communities for periods of 7 to 10 days and made daily visits to the sample households. The work of these nurses was closely supervised and their data cross-checked in several ways. Given the extent, complexity, and comprehensiveness of these investigations, it is difficult to imagine that anything like a survey of this magnitude could be initiated – or funded – today.

Table V.C.1.2 compares selected data on Cretan dietary practices obtained through the various dietary survey methods. The methods yielded substantial agreement about the daily amount of energy consumed by the population – an average of 2,500 kilocalories per day – and the amounts of meat and dairy foods consumed on an average day. Agricultural food "balance" data, which represented the amounts of food available throughout the entire country of Greece on a per capita daily basis, indicated a higher intake of cereals and sugar and a lower intake of potatoes, pulses, nuts, oils, and fats than did data derived from the Crete surveys. However, as is discussed later in this chapter, these differences can be attributed to sources of random and systematic error inherent in methods of dietary-intake measurement. Data on alcohol consumption best illustrate the nature of such errors. Allbaugh was able to explain the discrepancy between the small amount reported in the dietary-intake records and the much larger amount indicated by food balance or household inventory data as a result of systematic underreporting. This was confirmed by his own observations as well as by "an expressed feeling by the respondents that the visiting Americans might be expected to frown upon heavy wine consumption where food was short" (Allbaugh 1953: 106).

A comparison of the food sources of energy in the diets of people in Crete, Greece, and the United States, as reported in the Rockefeller study, may be found in

Table V.C.1.2. *Dietary intake in Crete in 1948 as estimated by three methods*

	Greece	Crete	
	Food balance 1948-9	7-day diet record	Household inventory[a]
Energy, MJ (kcal)/d	10.2 (2,443)	10.7 (2,547)	10.7 (2,554)
Foods, kg/person/y			
Cereals	158.2	127.7	128.2
Potatoes	30.9	59.1	38.6
Sugar, honey	9.1	5.5	5.5
Pulses, nuts	15.0	20.0	23.2
Vegetables, fruits, olives	120.5	175.9	132.3
Meat, fish, eggs	23.2	28.6	27.7
Milk, cheese	35.0	25.5	34.5
Oils, fats	15.0	30.9	30.9
Wine, beer, spirits	37.7	10.0	38.6

Source: Adapted from Allbaugh (1953), p. 107.

[a]Adjusted for information obtained from food-frequency questionnaires.

Table V.C.1.3. It displays data derived from dietary-intake surveys for Crete and reports data taken from food-supply surveys for Greece and the United States, even though these types of data are not truly comparable. The results indicate that plant foods – cereals, pulses, nuts, potatoes, vegetables, and fruits – comprised 61 percent of total calories reported as consumed by people in Crete, whereas plant foods comprised 74 percent of the energy available in the Greek food supply (although not necessarily consumed in the Greek diet) and 37 percent of the energy in the U.S. food supply (again, available but not necessarily consumed).

Table V.C.1.3. *Percentage of total energy contributed by major food groups in the diet of Crete as compared to their availability in the food supplies of Greece and the United States in 1948-9*

	Crete (7-day record)	Greece (food balance)	U.S. (food balance)
Total energy, MJ (kcal)/d	10.7 (2,547)	10.4 (2,477)	13.1 (3,129)
	Energy (%)		
Food group			
Cereals	39	61	25
Pulses, nuts, potatoes	11	8	6
Vegetables, fruits	11	5	6
Meat, fish, eggs	4	3	19
Dairy products	3	4	14
Table oils, fats	29	15	15
Sugar, honey	2	4	15
Wine, beer, spirits	1	–[a]	–[a]

Source: Adapted from Allbaugh (1953), p. 132.

[a]Data not available.

Similarly, foods of animal origin – meat, fish, eggs, and dairy products – comprised only 7 percent of energy in the Cretan diet, in contrast to 19 percent of the energy in the Greek food supply and 29 percent of the energy in the U.S. food supply, but table oils and fats were reported to contribute 29 percent of the energy in the Cretan diet, whereas they constituted only 15 percent of that in the Greek and U.S. food supplies. In Crete, however, 78 percent of the table fats derived from olives and olive oil. The total amount of fat from all sources in the Cretan diet, including that "hidden" in animal foods, was reported as 107 grams per day, or an estimated 38 percent of total energy, a percentage similar to that in the U.S. food supply in the late 1940s (USDA 1968) and considerably higher than that recommended today as a means to reduce chronic disease risk factors (Cannon 1992; USDA 1992; USDA/USDHHS 1995).

The data in Tables V.C.1.2 and V.C.1.3 constitute the basis for the conclusion of the Rockefeller report that "olives, cereal grains, pulses, wild greens and herbs, and fruits, together with limited quantities of goat meat and milk, game, and fish have remained the basic Cretan foods for forty centuries . . . no meal was complete without bread . . . Olives and olive oil contributed heavily to the energy intake . . . food seemed literally to be 'swimming' in oil" (Allbaugh 1953: 100). The Rockefeller survey data also indicated that wine was frequently consumed at all meals – midmorning, noon, and evening.

Whether olive oil made such a contribution to the diet for 40 centuries, however, is doubtful. At least one analysis of tree cultivation in southern Italy suggests that olive oil must have been a scarce commodity until at least the sixteenth century and that its principal use in medieval times was in religious rituals (Grieco 1993).

Thus, in attempting to correlate his current observations of dietary intake with the nutritional and general health of the population, Allbaugh noted certain limitations of his study. Few data were available on the nutrient and energy composition of Cretan foods, and virtually no information was available on the clinical and biochemical status of the Cretan population. Nevertheless, the study reported few serious nutritional problems in Crete; those that existed "were limited to a relatively small number of households, living under conditions of very low income and little home production of food" (Allbaugh 1953: 124). Diets generally were nutritionally adequate as measured against the U.S. Recommended Dietary Allowances of that time (National Research Council 1948). The investigators concluded that the diets and food consumption levels observed for most individuals "were surprisingly good. On the whole, their food pattern and food habits were extremely well adapted to their natural and economic resources as well as their needs" (Allbaugh 1953: 31).

This favorable conclusion, however, was one not necessarily shared by the study subjects. Allbaugh

reported that only one out of six of the interviewed families judged the typical diet to be satisfactory. He quoted one family as complaining: "We are hungry most of the time" (Allbaugh 1953: 105). When asked what they would most like to eat to improve their diets, survey respondents listed meat, rice, fish, pasta, butter, and cheese, in order of priority. A large majority of respondents (72 percent) listed meat as the favorite food. On the basis of such views, Allbaugh concluded that the diet of Crete could best be improved by providing more foods of animal origin – meat, fish, cheese, eggs – on a daily basis.

Ancel Keys and the Seven Countries Study

Despite the great wealth of information provided by the Rockefeller report, interest in the health implications of Mediterranean diets is more often thought to have begun with the work of Ancel Keys, an epidemiologist from the University of Minnesota. In 1952, impressed by the low rates of heart disease that he had observed on vacations in the Mediterranean (Keys 1995), Keys initiated a series of investigations of dietary and other coronary risk factors with colleagues in seven countries. Keys and his wife, Margaret, have reported the genesis of these investigations in vivid detail:

> Snowflakes were beginning to fly as we left Strasbourg on the fourth of February. All the way to Switzerland we drove in a snowstorm . . . On the Italian side the air was mild, flowers were gay, birds were singing, and we basked at an outdoor table drinking our first espresso coffee at Domodossola. We felt warm all over. (Keys and Keys 1975: 2)

The two were particularly impressed by the difference between the diet they were eating in Italy and the typical diet consumed by people in the United States. As they described it, the Italian diet included:

> [H]omemade minestrone . . . pasta in endless variety . . . served with tomato sauce and a sprinkle of cheese, only occasionally enriched with some bits of meat, or served with a little local sea food . . . a hearty dish of beans and short lengths of macaroni . . . lots of bread never more than a few hours from the oven and never served with any kind of spread; great quantities of fresh vegetables; a modest portion of meat or fish perhaps twice a week; wine of the type we used to call "Dago red". . . always fresh fruit for dessert. Years later, when called on to devise diets for the possible prevention of coronary heart disease we looked back and concluded it would be hard to do better than imitate the diet of the common folk of Naples in the early 1950s. (Keys and Keys 1975: 4)

Keys and his colleagues published the results of their Neapolitan investigations, which found Italian diets to be remarkably low in fat – 20 percent of energy, or just half the proportion observed in the diets of comparable American groups (Keys et al. 1954). By that time (and long before such ideas became commonplace), Keys had associated the typical American diet, rich in meat and dairy fats, with higher levels of blood cholesterol and, therefore, with increased risk of coronary heart disease.

In 1959, the the principal lines of evidence for these associations were reviewed in a cookbook designed to help the general public reduce risks for coronary heart disease (Keys and Keys 1959). In a foreword to this volume, the eminent cardiologist Paul Dudley White, who had made several expeditions with the authors "to study the health and the ways of life of native populations" in southern Italy and Crete, extolled both the health benefits and the taste of the lowfat foods – and the wine – that they had routinely consumed during their Mediterranean travels.

In this cookbook, perhaps the first of the "healthy heart" genre, the authors summarized their "best advice" for lifestyle practices to reduce coronary risk (Keys and Keys 1959: 40). Table V.C.1.4 lists their precepts in comparison to the 1995 U.S. dietary guidelines for health promotion and disease prevention (USDA/USDHHS 1995). As is evident, the guidelines closely follow the 1959 advice that Ancel and Margaret Keys derived from their observations of diet and coronary risk in southern Italy and Crete. This comparison demonstrates that the Mediterranean diet of the 1950s can be considered to constitute the original prototype for development of current dietary guidance policy in the United States.

Beginning in the early 1950s, and for more than 20 years thereafter, Keys and his colleagues identified dietary and other risk factors for coronary heart disease through a large-scale study of nearly 13,000 middle-aged men from 7 countries distributed among 16 cohorts (Keys 1970; Keys et al. 1980). The overall results of the Seven Countries Study provided strong epidemiological evidence for the effects of fat and various fatty acids on serum cholesterol levels and on coronary heart disease risk (Kromhout, Menotti, and Blackburn 1994).

Dietary-intake data for foods and food components other than fat, however, were published in English for the first time only in 1989 (Kromhout et al. 1989). That report compared the 16 cohorts in the 7 countries with respect to their intake of bread, cereals, various vegetables, fruit, meat, fish, eggs, dairy foods, table fats, pastries, and alcoholic beverages. These data confirmed that Mediterranean diets in the early 1960s were based primarily on foods from plant sources, but that some versions were higher in fat – mainly olive oil – than might be expected in a population with such good health. The Seven Countries' data, as confirmed by subsequent investigations (Cresta et al. 1969; Kafatos et al. 1991; Trichopoulou et al. 1992), constituted the principal research basis for the pro-

Table V.C.1.4. *Ancel and Margaret Keys' 1959 dietary advice for prevention of coronary heart disease compared to the 1995 U.S. dietary guidelines*

The Keyses' "best advice"	1995 dietary guidelines
	Eat a variety of foods.
Do not get fat; if you are fat, reduce. Get plenty of exercise and outdoor recreation.	Balance the food you eat with physical activity – maintain or improve your weight.
Restrict saturated fats, the fats in beef, pork, lamb, sausages, margarine, solid shortenings, fats in dairy products. Prefer vegetable oils to solid fats, but keep total fats under 30 percent of your diet energy.	Choose a diet low in fat, saturated fat, and cholesterol.
Favor fresh vegetables, fruits, and nonfat milk products.	Choose a diet with plenty of grain products, vegetables, and fruits.
Avoid heavy use of salt and refined sugar.	Choose a diet moderate in salt and sodium. Choose a diet moderate in sugars.
Be sensible about cigarettes, alcohol, excitement, business strain.	If you drink alcoholic beverages, do so in moderation.

Sources: Adapted from Keys and Keys (1959) and USDA/USDHHS (1995).

portions of foods from plant and animal sources proposed recently as a Mediterranean diet pyramid (Willett et al. 1995) or a Greek column (Simopoulos 1995).

The EURATOM Study

One additional large-scale study, from a rather unexpected source, yielded comparative information about dietary intake in the Mediterranean and other regions of Europe. From 1963 to 1965, the European Atomic Energy Commission (EURATOM) examined household food consumption among 3,725 families in 11 regions of 6 European countries in an effort to identify the foods among those most commonly consumed that were likely to be sources of radioactive contaminants. Investigators conducted dietary interviews for 7 consecutive days in each of the selected households and weighed all foods present in the households on those days. After applying several correction factors, the researchers converted the data on household food consumption to daily average amounts of food consumed per person. These data were published in 1969 (Cresta et al. 1969).

Of the regions selected by EURATOM for the study, nine were in the north of Europe and two in the south. One of the northern regions was in Italy (Friuli).

Because both of the southern regions also were in Italy (Campania and Basilicata), the data could be used to compare the typical dietary intake of the Italian north – which was quite similar to dietary patterns throughout the rest of northern Europe – with that of the Mediterranean regions. A detailed comparative analysis of these data is now available (Ferro-Luzzi and Branca 1995).

The EURATOM study revealed distinct differences in dietary-intake patterns between the northern and southern Italian regions. Diets in the Mediterranean areas were characterized by a much greater intake of cereals, vegetables, fruit, and fish, but a much smaller intake of potatoes, meat and dairy foods, eggs, and sweets. Although no consistent differences were observed in overall consumption of table fats, the foods contributing to total fat intake were quite different. Consumption of butter and margarine was much higher in the north, whereas in the south, the principal fat was olive oil, and margarine was not consumed at all. Taken together, the results of the EURATOM study provide further evidence that the Mediterranean diet of the mid-1960s was based predominantly on plant foods and included olive oil as the principal fat.

Recent Observations
In the years following these investigations, the Keys' description of the role of diet in coronary risk has become more widely accepted (James 1988; USDHHS 1988; National Research Council 1989). Along with this acceptance has come increasing recognition that the traditional dietary patterns of many cultures meet current dietary guidelines and that the cuisines of these cultures – especially those of Mediterranean and Asian countries – could serve as models for dietary improvement (Nestle 1994). In recent years, reports of investigations of the scientific basis and health implications of Mediterranean diets have been published in at least five edited collections of papers (Helsing and Trichopoulou 1989; Spiller 1991; Giacosa and Hill 1993; Serra-Majem and Helsing 1993; Nestle 1995). Public interest in Mediterranean diets has been stimulated by numerous articles in the popular press (Kummer 1993; Hamlin 1994), and their palatability has been celebrated in cookbooks emphasizing the dual themes of good taste and good health (Shulman 1989; Goldstein 1994; Jenkins 1994; Wolfert 1994).

Historical and Research Issues

As noted previously, studies of Mediterranean dietary patterns raise research issues that are also applicable to a more general understanding of the role of diet in health.

Definition of the Mediterranean Diet
The peoples of the 16 or more countries that border the Mediterranean Sea vary greatly in culture, ethnicity, religion, economic and political status, and other factors that might influence dietary intake, and their food supplies vary widely in the quantity used of every item that has been examined. Thus, the identification of common dietary elements within the region has proved a challenging task to researchers (Ferro-Luzzi and Sette 1989; Giacco and Riccardi 1991; Varela and Moreiras 1991; Giacosa et al. 1993).

Because the studies of Ancel Keys found the typical dietary pattern of the Greek island of Crete in the 1950s and 1960s to be associated with especially good health, this pattern has come to be viewed as the model, and because olive oil was a principal source of fat in the Cretan diet, the model has been extended to include diets consumed in olive-producing Mediterranean regions. In this manner, the generic term "Mediterranean diet" has come to be used, in practice, as referring to dietary patterns similar to those of Crete in the early 1960s and other regions in the Mediterranean where olive oil is the principal source of dietary fat (Willett et al. 1995).

Dietary Epistemology: Research Methods
Knowledge of the content of Mediterranean diets in the early 1960s – or at present – necessarily depends upon the reliability of methods used to determine the typical food intake of the population. National diet surveys, such as those that are conducted regularly in the United States, have not been generally available in Mediterranean countries. The Rockefeller study of Crete was a notable exception, remarkable by any standard of epidemiological investigation (see Table V.C.1.2) in its use of multiple methods, lengthy personal interviews, and critical analysis of results to attempt to define dietary intake (Allbaugh 1953). The Seven Countries Study also used multiple methods. For most of the 16 cohorts, Keys and his colleagues obtained 7-day diet records from small subsamples of each group and corroborated these records by analyzing the energy and nutrient composition of weighed, duplicate meals. For a few cohorts, investigators collected dietary data from 24-hour recalls as verified through food-frequency questionnaires (Keys 1970). Finally, the EURATOM study attempted to corroborate daily reports of household food intake by weighing all foods present in the house on each of the seven consecutive interview days (Cresta et al. 1969).

These investigations were designed to overcome fundamental flaws in each of the methods commonly used to evaluate the dietary intake of individuals and populations; all provide opportunities for random and systematic errors in reporting food intake, estimating serving sizes, and determining nutrient content (Mertz 1992; Buzzard and Willett 1994; Young and Nestle 1995). Such problems are compounded in studies that attempt to compare dietary-intake data from one country to another, or within one country over time. If the methods for determination of dietary intake differ, their results are not strictly comparable – a situation similar to comparing apples to oranges (see Tables V.C.1.2 and V.C.1.3).

For purposes of international comparison, investigators must often rely on food-balance data – agricultural data on specific commodities present in the food supply from one year to the next. As already noted, these data are distinctly different from those that describe dietary intake. They reflect the amounts of specific foods produced in a country during a given year, with imports of foods added and food exports subtracted, expressed on a per capita basis through dividing by the population total on a defined day of the year.

Such data are also known by other names: food supply, food availability, food disappearance, and food consumption. Among these terms, "consumption" is a misnomer, because food-balance data are only an indirect estimate of dietary intake. A food that is produced but then wasted, fed to animals, or used for industrial purposes is not consumed; for many foods, therefore, food-balance data overestimate dietary intake. In the case of foods produced at home, however, food-balance data underestimate consumption. The average annual per capita availability of a food commodity only rarely – and accidentally – is an accurate measure of actual consumption by an individual man, woman, or child. These limitations may explain observed discrepancies in study results, and they emphasize the need for caution in interpreting comparative data such as those presented in Tables V.C.1.2 and V.C.1.3.

Despite such limitations, food-balance data are often the best – or only – data available to estimate time trends in dietary practices, and they are used frequently in comparative descriptions of Mediterranean diets (Ferro-Luzzi and Sette 1989; Helsing 1995). Three agencies of the United Nations (UN) produce such data. The Organization of Economic Cooperation and Development (OECD) has published data for the supply and use in 23 countries of specific food items, such as pork, cheese, or olive oil, from 1979 to 1988 (OECD 1991).

The Food and Agriculture Organization (FAO) publishes individual food-balance sheets for 145 countries that include data for per capita supply of major food groups (e.g., meat, legumes, alcohol); its most recent edition provides data in 3-year averages from 1961–3 through 1986–8 (FAO 1991). The World Health Organization (WHO) Regional Office for Europe has established a comprehensive computerized database that incorporates FAO food-balance data as well as the WHO annual health statistics since 1961 for each of the countries that supply such data to the UN (WHO/FAO 1993). This program makes it possible to generate an immediate display of the relationship between the availability of any food and the disease rates in any country of interest (Ferro-Luzzi and Sette 1989; Helsing 1995).

Health Impact

By the definition used here, the Mediterranean diet can be considered a near-vegetarian diet. As such, it would be expected to produce the well-established health benefits of vegetarian diets and to solve any deficiencies of energy or micronutrients (especially vitamin B_{12}) that are occasionally associated with such diets (Johnston 1994). Vegetarian or near-vegetarian diets are especially plentiful in key nutrients, particularly antioxidant vitamins, fiber, and a variety of phenolic compounds that have been identified as protective against cancer and other chronic diseases (Dwyer 1994; Kushi, Lenart, and Willett 1995a, 1995b). Researchers, however, have yet to establish the relative contribution of any single nutrient or food component, the foods that contain such factors, or physical activity and lifestyle patterns – alone or in combination – to the favorable health indices observed in the Mediterranean region.

In this context, the role of olive oil is of particular interest. The Greek diet, for example, contains a higher proportion of fat than is usually recommended. Yet much of this fat is olive oil, and the diet is associated with very good health. Diets rich in olive oil are associated with exceptionally low rates of coronary heart disease, even when blood cholesterol levels are high (Verschuren et al. 1995). The traditional Greek diet is also associated with an exceptionally low risk for breast cancer (Trichopoulou et al. 1995).

Changing Dietary Patterns

If it is indeed true that Mediterranean diets of the 1960s protected adult populations against premature death, it would seem highly desirable to preserve the protective elements of those diets. Evidence from dietary-intake surveys and from food-balance data indicates, however, that dietary patterns throughout the region are changing rapidly, and generally in an undesirable direction. For example, one dietary-intake study of an urban population on Crete (obtained by 24-hour diet recalls corroborated by food models, photographs, and clinical and biochemical measurements) reported an increase in the intake of meat, fish, and cheese but a decrease in the intake of bread, fruit, potatoes, and olive oil (Kafatos et al. 1991) from levels reported by Keys and his colleagues in the early 1960s (Kromhout, Keys, Aravanis, et al. 1989). Similar changes have been observed in Italy (Ferro-Luzzi and Branca 1995). Food-balance data also document large increases in the availability of meat, dairy foods (FAO 1991), and animal fats (Serra-Majem and Helsing 1993) throughout the region since the early 1960s. Given this situation, the traditional Mediterranean diet may well become a historical artifact.

Increasing evidence suggests that the recent changes in Mediterranean dietary patterns have been accompanied by increases in chronic disease risk factors among the populations. These risk factors include a decline in levels of physical activity, along with higher levels of serum cholesterol (Kafatos et al. 1991), hypertension, and obesity (Spiller 1991). Associated with these changes in risk factors are reports of rising rates of coronary heart disease, diabetes (Spiller 1991), and several types of diet-related cancers (LaVecchia et al. 1993) in several Mediterranean countries. These trends confirm well-established relationships between diet and chronic disease risk (James 1988; USDHHS 1988; National Research Council 1989) and suggest the need to reverse current practices through widespread efforts at preserving and promoting traditional diets within the region (Nestle 1994).

Preservation and Adaptation

Overall dietary patterns in a country are the result of an ongoing interaction between culturally determined food traditions and the assimilation of new foods through economic improvement, foreign contact, or international food marketing. Education also has a role in influencing personal food preferences and dietary change (Heimendinger and Van Duyn 1995). Until recently, Mediterranean dietary patterns were quite resistant to change. Allbaugh and Keys both remarked on the similarity of the foods commonly eaten in Italy and Crete to those produced and consumed in those areas in the ancient past. Despite suggestions that traditional dietary patterns are beginning to be abandoned (Alberti-Fidanza et al. 1994), such foods are still routinely consumed by at least some older population groups (Trichopoulou, Katsouyanni, and Cnardellis 1993).

Issues related to the assimilation of Mediterranean dietary patterns within other countries are best illustrated by the adaptation of southern Italian foods to American tastes (Levenstein and Conlin 1990). Italian immigrants of the late nineteenth and early twentieth centuries retained many of their food traditions despite North American–held views of their diets as insufficiently nutritious, indigestible, unsanitary, and inadequate in amounts of milk and meat. Such views, however, began to change during the economic restrictions of World War I, when Italian pastas became popular as inexpensive, well-balanced alternatives to meat, and since the 1920s, Italian food products have been widely marketed in the United States (Levenstein 1985). But today many Italian-style foods have been "Americanized" to the point that they are far higher in energy, fat, cholesterol, and sodium than the traditional foods from which they were derived (Hurley and Liebman 1994).

Policy Implications

Policies designed to encourage consumption of traditional diets within their country of origin, or to promote the adaptation of traditional models to new locations, will have to address many well-defined cultural, economic, and institutional barriers (Nestle 1994). They will also need to recognize that diet is only one of a great many behavioral factors that influence health and that other determinants may command higher national priorities for action (Jamison

and Mosley 1991). Moreover, the transfer of traditional Mediterranean dietary patterns to a country such as the United States would be likely to affect agriculture, the food industry, the overall economy, and the environment in highly complex ways, some of which may be beneficial, but others undesirable (Gussow 1994, 1995; O'Brien 1995).

The role of the Mediterranean diet in U.S. dietary guidance policy is of particular interest. As is demonstrated in Table V.C.1.4, the Mediterranean observations of Keys' led directly to the formulation of dietary guidelines for the prevention of coronary heart disease. In turn, such guidelines eventually encompassed more general advice for health promotion and disease prevention in American statements of dietary guidance policy, as expressed in the Dietary Guidelines for Americans (USDA/USDHHS 1995). Because animal foods are principal sources of fat, saturated fat, and cholesterol in American diets (Gerrior and Zizza 1994), dietary guidelines necessarily should promote predominantly plant-based diets similar to those traditionally consumed in the Mediterranean region or in Asia. That this may not be evident from standard American food guides (USDA 1992) is, at least in part, a result of political pressures from producers of meat and dairy foods to ensure that their products retain a dominant position in the American food supply and diet (Nestle 1993). Such pressures may well have resulted in dietary recommendations that are ambiguous and confusing to the public (Nestle 1995a).

Research Directions

Traditional Mediterranean diets appear to have been based mainly on plant foods, to contain foods from animal sources in very small amounts, to use olive oil as the principal dietary fat, to feature alcohol in moderation, and to balance energy intake with energy expenditure. Substantial research – in quantity and quality – supports the very great health benefits of just such dietary and activity patterns (Willett 1994; Kushi et al. 1995a, 1995b).

Mediterranean diets are consistent with current food guide recommendations for public-health promotion and disease prevention, as well as with recommendations for nutritionally adequate vegetarian diets (Haddad 1994). Because they also are appreciated for their gastronomic qualities, they are well worth further study as a cultural model for dietary improvement. Several areas of historical and applied research related to Mediterranean diets seem especially worthy of additional investigation; these are listed in Table V.C.1.5. While awaiting the results of such studies, immediate efforts should be instituted to preserve the ancient – and healthful – dietary traditions within the Mediterranean region and to encourage greater consumption of plant foods among industrialized populations as a means to improve health.

Table V.C.1.5. *Suggestions for further historical and applied research on the health impact of Mediterranean diets*

Historical research needs

Identification of methods to determine the typical dietary intake of individuals and populations in Mediterranean countries in the past, present, and future.

Identification of methods to determine time trends in Mediterranean dietary patterns.

Determination of the impact of dietary changes on nutritional status and health risks in Mediterranean countries in the past and present.

Identification of cultural, behavioral, economic, and environmental determinants of dietary change in Mediterranean countries in the past and present.

Determination of the impact of dietary changes on the agriculture, food industry, economy, and environment of Mediterranean countries in the past and present.

Determination of the impact of adoption of Mediterranean foods or dietary patterns on the agriculture, food industry, economy, and environment of countries outside the Mediterranean region in the past and present.

Applied research needs

Identification of the roles of specific plant foods characteristic of Mediterranean diets – fruits, vegetables, legumes, cereals, nuts, oils, wine – in health promotion and disease prevention.

Identification of the roles of specific plant-food nutrients – vitamins, minerals, monounsaturated fatty acids, linolenic acid, fiber, alcohol, phytochemicals – in the low rates of chronic diseases observed in Mediterranean countries.

Determination of the proportions of plant and animal foods in Mediterranean diets optimal for reducing disease risk.

Determination of the proportion of energy from fat and specific fatty acids in Mediterranean diets associated with the lowest risk of disease.

Development of dietary recommendations and food guides that best reflect current scientific knowledge of the health benefits of Mediterranean diets.

Identification of effective methods to educate the public in Mediterranean countries about traditional dietary practices that best promote health.

Marion Nestle

This chapter was adapted from the author's "Mediterranean Diets: Historical and Research Overview," which appeared in the *American Journal of Clinical Nutrition* 61 (Supplement), June 1995, pp. 1313s-20s.

Bibliography

Alberti-Fidanza, A., C. A. Paolacci, M. P. Chiuchiù, et al. 1994. Dietary studies on two rural Italian population groups of the Seven Countries Study. 1. Food and nutrient intake at the thirty-first year follow-up in 1991. *European Journal of Clinical Nutrition* 48: 85-91.

Allbaugh, L. G. 1953. *Crete: A case study of an undeveloped area.* Princeton, N.J.

Buzzard, I. M., and W. C. Willett, eds. 1994. First international conference on dietary assessment methods: Assessing diets to improve world health. *American Journal of Clinical Nutrition* 59 (Supplement): 143s-306s.

Cannon, G. 1992. *Food and health: The experts agree.* London.

Cresta, M., S. Ledermann, A. Garnier, et al. 1969. *Étude des consommations alimentaires des population de onze régions de la Communauté Européenne en vue de la détermination des niveaux de contamination radioactive.* Rapport établi au Centre d'Étude Nucléaire de Fontenay-aux-Roses, France EUR 4218 f. Bruselles.

Darby, W. J., P. Ghalioungui, and L. Grivetti. 1977. *Food: The gift of Osiris.* 3 vols. London.

Dwyer, J. T. 1994. Vegetarian eating patterns: Science, values, and food choices – where do we go from here? In Second International Congress on Vegetarian Nutrition: Proceedings of a symposium held in Arlington, Virginia, June 28-July 1, 1992, ed. P. K. Johnston. *American Journal of Clinical Nutrition* 59 (Supplement): 1255s-62s.

Ferro-Luzzi, A., and F. Branca. 1995. The Mediterranean diet, Italian style: Prototype of a healthy diet. *American Journal of Clinical Nutrition* 61 (Supplement): 1338s-45s.

Ferro-Luzzi, A., and S. Sette. 1989. The Mediterranean diet: An attempt to define its present and past composition. *European Journal of Clinical Nutrition* 43: 13-30.

Fidanza, F. 1979. Diets and dietary recommendations in ancient Greece and Rome and the school of Salerno. *Progress in Food and Nutrition Science* 3: 79-99.

FAO (Food and Agriculture Organization of the United Nations). 1991. *Food balance sheets, 1984-1986 average.* Rome.

Gerrior, S. A., and C. Zizza. 1994. *Nutrition content of the U.S. food supply, 1909-1990.* U.S. Department of Agriculture Home Economic Research Report No. 52. Hyattsville, Md.

Giacco, R., and G. Riccardi. 1991. Comparison of current eating habits in various Mediterranean countries. In *The Mediterranean diets in health and disease,* ed. G. A. Spiller, 3-9. New York.

Giacosa, A., and M. J. Hill, eds. 1993. *The Mediterranean diet and cancer prevention: Proceedings of a workshop organized by the European Cancer Prevention Organization and the Italian League Against Cancer, Cosenza, Italy, June 28-30, 1991.* Andover, England.

Giacosa, A., F. Merlo, P. Visconti, et al. 1993. Mediterranean diet: An attempt at a clear definition. In *The Mediterranean diet and cancer prevention: Proceedings of a workshop organized by the European Cancer Prevention Organization and the Italian League Against Cancer, Cosenza, Italy, June 28-30, 1991,* ed. A. Giacosa and M. J. Hill, 1-14. Andover, England.

Gifford, K. D., G. Drescher, and N. H. Jenkins, eds. 1993. *Diets of the Mediterranean: A summary report of the 1993 International Conference on the Diets of the Mediterranean, Cambridge, Massachusetts, January 20-23, 1993.* Boston, Mass.

Goldstein, J. 1994. *Mediterranean the beautiful: Authentic recipes from the Mediterranean lands.* New York.

Grieco, A. J. 1993. Olive tree cultivation and the alimentary use of olive oil in late medieval Italy (ca. 1300-1500). In *Oil and wine production in the Mediterranean area,* ed. M.-C. Amouretti and J.-P. Brun. *Bulletin de Correspondance Hellénique* (Supplement 26). Paris.

Gussow, J. D. 1994. Ecology and vegetarian considerations: Does environmental responsibility demand the elimination of livestock? In Second International Congress on Vegetarian Nutrition: Proceedings of a symposium held in Arlington, Virginia, June 28-July 1, 1992. *American Journal of Clinical Nutrition* 59 (Supplement): 1110s-16s.

1995. Mediterranean diets: Are they environmentally responsible? *American Journal of Clinical Nutrition* 61 (Supplement): 1383s-9s.

Haddad, E. H. 1994. Development of a vegetarian food guide. In Second International Congress on Vegetarian Nutrition: Proceedings of a symposium held in Arlington, Virginia, June 28-July 1, 1992. *American Journal of Clinical Nutrition* 59 (Supplement): 1248s-54s.

Hamlin, S. 1994. Mediterranean madness. *The Washington Post*, June 8, pp. E1, E10.

Heimendinger, J., and M. A. S. Van Duyn. 1995. Dietary behavior change: The challenge of recasting the role of fruits and vegetables in the American diet. *American Journal of Clinical Nutrition* 61 (Supplement): 1397s-1401s.

Helsing, E. 1995. Traditional diets and disease patterns of the Mediterranean circa 1960. *American Journal of Clinical Nutrition* 61 (Supplement): 1329s-37s.

Helsing, E., and A. Trichopoulou, eds. 1989. The Mediterranean diet and food culture - a symposium. *European Journal of Clinical Nutrition* 43: 1-92.

Hurley, J., and B. Liebman. 1994. When in Rome. . . . *Nutrition Action Healthletter* 21: 1, 5-7.

James, W. P. T. 1988. *Healthy nutrition: Preventing nutrition-related diseases in Europe.* Copenhagen.

Jamison, D. T., and W. H. Mosley. 1991. Disease control priorities in developing countries: Health policy responses to epidemiological change. *American Journal of Public Health* 81: 15-22.

Jenkins, N. H. 1994. *The Mediterranean diet cookbook: A delicious alternative for lifelong health.* New York.

Johnston, P. K., ed. 1994. Second International Congress on Vegetarian Nutrition: Proceedings of a symposium held in Arlington, Virginia, June 28-July 1, 1992. *American Journal of Clinical Nutrition* 59 (Supplement): 1099s-1262s.

Kafatos, A., I. Kouroumalis, I. Vlachonikolis, et al. 1991. Coronary-heart-disease risk-factor status of the Cretan urban population in the 1980s. *American Journal of Clinical Nutrition* 54: 591-8.

Keys, A. 1995. The Mediterranean diet and public health: Reflections. *American Journal of Clinical Nutrition* 61 (Supplement): 1321s-24s.

ed. 1970. Coronary heart disease in seven countries. *Circulation* 41 (Supplement): 9-13 and 1186-95.

Keys, A., C. Aravanis, H. Blackburn, et al. 1980. *Seven countries: A multivariate analysis of death and coronary heart disease.* Cambridge, Mass.

Keys, A., F. Fidanza, V. Scardi, et al. 1954. Studies on serum cholesterol and other characteristics on clinically healthy men in Naples. *Archives of Internal Medicine* 93: 328-35.

Keys, A., and M. Keys. 1959. *Eat well and stay well.* New York.

1975. *How to eat well and stay well the Mediterranean way.* New York.

Kromhout, D., A. Keys, C. Aravanis, et al. 1989. Food consumption patterns in the 1960s in the seven countries. *American Journal of Clinical Nutrition* 49: 809-94.

Kromhout, D., A. Menotti, and H. Blackburn, eds. 1994. *The Seven Countries Study: A scientific adventure in cardiovascular disease epidemiology.* Utrecht, the Netherlands.

Kummer, C. 1993. The Mediterranean diet. *Self* (July): 75-9, 129.

Kushi, L. E., E. B. Lenart, and W. C. Willett. 1995a. Health implications of Mediterranean diets in the light of contemporary knowledge. 1. Plant foods and dairy products. *American Journal of Clinical Nutrition* 61 (Supplement): 1407s-15s.

1995b. Health implications of Mediterranean diets in the light of contemporary knowledge. 2. Meat, wine, fats, and oil. *American Journal of Clinical Nutrition* 61 (Supplement): 1416s-27s.

LaVecchia, C., F. Lucchini, E. Negri, et al. 1993. Patterns and trends in mortality from selected cancers in Mediterranean countries. In *The Mediterranean diet and cancer prevention: Proceedings of a workshop organized by the European Cancer Prevention Organization and the Italian League Against Cancer, Cosenza, Italy, June 28-30, 1991*, ed. A. Giacosa and M. J. Hill, 81-103. Andover, England.

Levenstein, H. 1985. The American response to Italian food, 1880- 1930. *Food and Foodways* 1: 1-24.

Levenstein, H. A., and J. R. Conlin. 1990. The food habits of Italian immigrants to America: An examination of the persistence of a food culture and the rise of "fast food" in America. In *Dominant symbols in popular culture*, ed. R. B. Browne, M. W. Fishwick, and K. O. Browne, 231-46. Bowling Green, Ohio.

Mertz, W. 1992. Food intake measurements: Is there a "gold standard"? *Journal of the American Dietetic Association* 92: 1463-5.

National Research Council. 1948. *Recommended dietary allowances.* Revised edition. Washington, D.C.

1989. *Diet and health: Implications for reducing chronic disease risk.* Washington, D.C.

Nestle, M. 1993. Food lobbies, the food pyramid, and U.S. nutrition policy. *International Journal of Health Services* 23: 483-96.

Traditional models of healthy eating: Alternatives to "technofood." *Journal of Nutrition Education* 26: 241-5.

1995a. Dietary guidance for the 21st century: New approaches. *Journal of Nutrition Education* 27: 272-5.

Nestle, M. 1995b. Mediterranean diets: Historical and research overview. *American Journal of Clinical Nutrition* 61 (Supplement): 1313s-20s.

1995. Mediterranean diets: Science and policy implications. *American Journal of Clinical Nutrition* 61 (Supplement): 1313s-1427s.

O'Brien, P. 1995. Dietary shifts and implications for U.S. agriculture. *American Journal of Clinical Nutrition* 61 (Supplement): 1390s-96s.

OECD (Organization of Economic Cooperation and Development). 1991. *Food consumption statistics, 1979-88.* Paris.

Serra-Majem, L., and E. Helsing, eds. 1993. Changing patterns of fat in Mediterranean countries. *European Journal of Clinical Nutrition* 47 (Supplement).

Seymour, T. D. 1907. *Life in the Homeric age.* New York.

Shulman, M. R. 1989. *Mediterranean light: Delicious recipes from the world's healthiest cuisines.* New York.

Simopoulos, A. P. 1995. The Mediterranean food guide: Greek column rather than an Egyptian pyramid. *Nutrition Today* 30: 54-61.

Spiller, G. A., ed. 1991. *The Mediterranean diets in health and disease.* New York.

Trichopoulou, A., K. Katsouyanni, and C. Cnardellis. 1993. The traditional Greek diet. *European Journal of Clinical Nutrition* 47 (Supplement 1): 76s-81s.

Trichopoulou, A., K. Katsouyanni, S. Stuver, et al. 1995. Consumption of olive oil and specific food groups in relation to breast cancer risk in Greece. *Journal of the National Cancer Institute* 87: 110-16.

Trichopoulou, A., N. Toupadaki, A. Tzonou, et al. 1992. The macronutrient composition of the Greek diet: Estimates derived from six case-control studies. *European Journal of Clinical Nutrition* 47: 549-58.

USDA (U.S. Department of Agriculture). 1968. *Food consumption, prices, and expenditures.* Agriculture Economic Report No. 138. Washington, D.C.

    1992. *The food guide pyramid.* Home and Garden Bulletin No. 252. Hyattsville, Md.

USDA/USDHHS (U.S. Department of Agriculture and U.S. Department of Health and Human Services). 1995. *Nutrition and your health: Dietary guidelines for Americans.* Fourth edition. Washington, D.C.

USDHHS (U.S. Department of Health and Human Services). 1988. *The surgeon general's report on nutrition and health.* Washington, D.C.

Varela, G., and O. Moreiras. 1991. Mediterranean diet. *Cardiovascular Risk Factors* 1: 313-21.

Vermeule, E. 1964. *Greece in the Bronze age.* Chicago.

Verschuren, M., D. R. Jacobs, Bennie P. M. Bloemberg, et al. 1995. Serum total cholesterol and long-term coronary heart disease mortality in different cultures: Twenty-five-year follow-up of the Seven Countries Study. *Journal of the American Medical Association* 274: 131-6.

Vickery, K. F. 1936. Food in early Greece. *Illinois Studies in Social Sciences* 20: 1-97.

Wells, C. 1975. Prehistoric and historical changes in nutritional diseases and associated conditions. *Progress in Food and Nutrition Science* 1: 729-79.

Willett, W. C. 1994. Diet and health. What should we eat? *Science* 264: 532-7.

Willett, W. C., F. Sacks, A. Trichopoulou, et al. 1995. Mediterranean diet pyramid: A cultural model for healthy eating. *American Journal of Clinical Nutrition* 61 (Supplement): 1402s-6s.

Wolfert, P. 1994. *The cooking of the Eastern Mediterranean: 215 healthy, vibrant, and inspired recipes.* New York.

World Bank. 1993. *World development report: Investment in health.* Washington, D.C.

WHO (World Health Organization of the United Nations). 1994. *World health statistics annual, 1993.* Geneva.

WHO/FAO (World Health Organization and Food and Agriculture Organization). 1993. *Food and health indicators in Europe: Nutrition and health, 1961-1990.* Computer program. Copenhagen.

Yonge, C. D., trans. 1909. *The Deipnosophists or banquet of the learned of Athenaeus.* 3 vols. London.

Young, L., and M. Nestle. 1995. Portion sizes in dietary assessment: Issues and policy implications. *Nutrition Reviews* 53: 149-58.

V.C.2   Southern Europe

The basic ingredients that have historically comprised the southern European diet are well known and have recently received much attention for their health-promoting benefits: These are bread, wine, olive oil, and a wide variety of fruits and vegetables supplemented by fish, dairy products, and a relatively small amount of animal flesh.

Less known, however, are the historical forces that shaped how southern Europeans think about food. Essentially, three rival systems have influenced the culture of food in southern Europe since late antiquity, and in various combinations these systems have informed eating patterns at all levels of society.

The most pervasive of these food systems might be called "Christian," although its roots are not necessarily found in the teachings of Jesus and his disciples. It encompasses monastic asceticism as well as the calendar of fasts and feasts that have historically regulated food consumption. In all its manifestations, the ideal goal of Christian foodways has been spiritual purity through the control of bodily urges, though this can easily be lost sight of when rules are bent and holidays become occasions for excess.

The second major system is medical in origin and has gained and lost popularity in the past two millennia depending on the state of nutritional science, though it continues to influence common beliefs to this day. The object of this system of "humoral physiology," of course, is the maintenance or recovery of health by means of dietary regimen.

Lastly, the "courtly" or gastronomic food culture has also profoundly influenced southern Europe, radiating from urban centers of power such as Rome, Naples, Venice, and the courts of Aragon, Castile, and Provence. Its goal is ostensibly pleasure, but this is usually mixed with motives of conscious ostentation in order to impress guests.

Whereas religious, medical, and gastronomic considerations shape the foodways of most cultures, it is their unique and often surprising combinations that make those of southern Europe especially fascinating. The gourmand monk, the duke surrounded by swarms of physicians, the parvenu townsman indulging his taste for spices – all reveal glimpses into the dynamics of society and the ways that individuals express themselves through food preferences, which in southern Europe are to a great extent informed by one or more of these fundamental systems.

Christianity

Although "Quadragesima," or Lent, was instituted in remembrance of Christ's 40-day fast in the desert, there is little in the biblical account of Christ and his followers that would warrant either regular fasting or placing restrictions on which foods can be consumed. In fact, the Gospels consciously reject the dietary legalism of the Old Testament and assert that all foods are clean: "Not that which goeth into the mouth defileth a man" (Matt. 15: 11). Furthermore, Christ celebrated numerous feasts – the marriage at Cana, supper at Emmaus, the "Last Supper."

Fasting, or a denial of bodily urges to achieve spiritual purity, seems to be more directly rooted in

Greek and Eastern ideas about the dualism of body and soul. If the body is merely a temporary corruptible prison for the eternal soul, then suppressing its sinful demands will cleanse the spirit in anticipation of its release from bodily constraint. Rejecting the appetites for food, sex, and sleep becomes a path to righteousness.

St. Anthony (c. 250–350) was the most popular of the early ascetics, and the example of his austerities in the Egyptian desert would inspire many future Christians. The church fathers also adopted a favorable stance toward fasting and abstinence. St. Augustine (354–430) recommended abstinence from meat and drink in an epistle to his sister's nunnery, and both St. Ambrose (340?–397) and St. Jerome (340?–420) were influential in advocating an abstemious diet for monastics in Italy.

It was St. Benedict of Nursia (c. 480–547) who would be most influential in framing a rule that would form the foundation for European monasticism. However, before we examine this specific institution, the more general topic of public fasts demands attention.

In the fourth and fifth centuries, the Christian church gradually defined the fast as an abstention from meat and animal products such as milk and eggs and a limitation of meals to one a day. The 40 days between Ash Wednesday and Easter, as well as the 30 days of Advent preceding Christmas, were set aside as the most important fasts. Wednesdays and Fridays, and sometimes a third day of the week, were also designated as fast days, as were the evenings preceding holidays. Although originally proscribed, fish increasingly became the ideal food for these periods.

In principle, fasts were intended to be public expressions of self-denial in atonement for sins. Minor mortifications would presumably quell the passions and turn the mind to spiritual exercise in preparation for major holy celebrations. Depending on their budgets, people could, in practice, consume rare and expensive fish, dried fruits, and spiced confections, so Lent did not necessarily involve a sacrifice of luxury. Rather in wealthy households it could become the occasion for the ingenious invention of meatless dishes incorporating almond milk to replace cream. But for the majority of people a normally meager diet would now be limited to bread, legumes, and the often reviled stockfish.

The cyclical seasons of want were bracketed by festivals of plenty, and numerous saint's days and local celebrations punctuated the medieval calendar. The festival of St. Iago in Spain and that of St. Joseph in Italy are two examples. Many of these feasts originated in pagan agricultural rites that were absorbed into the early church and transformed into holy days. Each town across southern Europe would also celebrate the feast of its own patron saint with specially prepared foods.

The most universal feast was held on the day before Ash Wednesday, Martedi Grasso or Mardi Gras, when all meat and eggs had to be consumed before Lent. This day of meat eating or "Carnevale" often became the occasion for gross indulgence. Drunkenness, flesh eating, violence, and sexual license were all associated with this binge preceding the rigors of abstinence.

By the late Middle Ages, mock battles would be held between personifications of Carnival and Lent, and the natural order of society would be subverted in mock trials, mock weddings, and even mock prayers. Indeed, the world was said to be turned upside down in this brief catharsis of revelry (Burke 1978). Gluttony was still considered among the seven deadly sins, though this rule, too, was momentarily suspended.

The most important "feast" in the Christian calendar, however, was of a more sacred nature. The sacrament of the Eucharist, in which bread or a thin wafer consecrated by a priest is placed in the mouth of each communicant, offers a form of spiritual nourishment. After the Fourth Lateran Council in 1215, the official doctrine of transubstantiation held that the substance of the bread is transformed into the actual body of Christ while its "accidents" or shape still appear to be bread. Through this miracle, and the act of eating the bread, one receives merit, which aids in salvation. Drinking wine is also central to the sacrament, although it was customarily reserved only for priests. The wine becomes the blood of Christ in the same way that the bread becomes the body. Thus, the everyday acts of eating and drinking were transformed into one of the central mysteries of the Christian church.

Also central to the culture of food as influenced by Christianity was the development of monasticism. In his "Rule" for monks at Monte Cassino in the sixth century, St. Benedict laid down specific regulations for food consumption that spread across Europe. Two cooked dishes were to be offered at either the noontime (prandium) or late afternoon (cena) meal and a third dish of fresh fruit or vegetables when available. Each monk was to be given a pound of bread daily as well as a "hemina" of wine, which was roughly two glasses (St. Benedict 1981: chap. 40, n. 40.3).

St. Benedict noted that wine was hardly a proper drink for monks, but few could be convinced of that in his day. Benedict also carefully fit meals into the daily schedule of prayers, though over the years his original provisions were supplemented by snacks such as the "collation," eaten while hearing readings from St. Cassian's Collations. There might also have been extra portions of food, the "pittance" provided by pious benefactors, though this may not have amounted to much, considering what this word has come to mean.

Most important, in addition to the regular cycles of fasting, monks were expected to abstain entirely from meat, except perhaps on rare occasions, as when dining in private with the abbot or when ill. These rules were often observed only in the breach, especially as monasteries grew more wealthy and lax in the tenth and eleventh centuries. Cheese was eventually allowed, following the logic that it is no more flesh than olive oil is wood (Moulin 1978: 87). Other prohibitions were also avoided: St. Benedict cannot have been referring to fowl when demanding that monks abstain from the meat of quadrupeds (St. Benedict 1981: chap. 39).

Rather than models of austerity, many monasteries became gastronomic enclaves, and there is, no doubt, some truth to the complaints of St. Peter Damian and Dante Alighieri about portly Benedictines (Dante 1939: 130). In addition to preserving and spreading viticulture throughout Europe, the monks originated many renowned cheeses, pastries, and confections. From their medicinal gardens they also concocted many celebrated cordials, chartreuse, and vermouth – not to mention champagne (Dom Perignon in the seventeenth century).

It was precisely in reaction to this gastronomic luxury and laxity that many new and more rigorous orders were founded in successive waves of religious revival. In contrast to lavish Cluniac monasteries, Cistercian simplicity began to flourish in the late twelfth century, influenced by St. Bernard of Clairvaux. Later came new austere mendicant orders such as the Franciscans, and following the advent of bubonic plague, a number of intensely penitential and flagellant orders flourished, such as the Gesuati. At any rate, the ascetic attitude toward food remained active in spite of the luxury of wealthier orders.

Many holy men and women so successfully mortified their flesh through abstinence that we can only conclude they deliberately starved themselves to death. This was precisely the goal of some Cathars in the South of France, who believed (heretically) that the world was created by the devil and that everything in it, the body as well as food, was evil. For the Cathars, starvation was a way to attain spiritual perfection. The Carthusians, an entirely different vegetarian order, had to go out of their way to assert the goodness of food to avoid being suspected of the Cathar heresy.

Self-starvation itself, however, was not necessarily considered heretical or demoniacal. St. Catherine of Siena, it has been suggested, suffered from a form of anorexia and subsequently became a model consciously imitated for centuries (Bell 1985). For many young women, conquering the self and hunger may have been the only outlet for expressing their pious urges in an entirely male-dominated society, the ideal of holiness being achieved only with the destruction of appetites and often the body itself.

Following the Counter Reformation, asceticism was gradually supplanted by activism as the ideal fruit of devotion. The Lenten fast, however, remained in force up until Vatican II, and to this day many Catholics continue the practice as an integral part of their food heritage.

Humoral Physiology

Physicians promulgated another theoretical food system, humoral physiology, which had a profound impact on the culture of food in southern Europe. As a legacy of Greek science, nutritional theory survived in more or less threadbare form through the early Middle Ages. Among the Moors of Spain it did undergo a rich development, but its first major revival in the Latin West was within the walls of the earliest universities, most notably at Salerno, Montpellier, Bologna, and, later, at Padua and Valladolid.

Translating Galen and Hippocrates via Arabic sources and commentaries, Gerard of Cremona (1140–1187) and Arnald of Villanova (1235–1312) provided Europe with its first guides to nutrition. The popular *Regimen Sanitatis* (c. 1160) of Salerno was the most widely known of the early diet books, and works continued to be written through the Middle Ages by individuals such as Magninus of Milan and Ugo Benzo.

During the Renaissance, dozens of new works were printed throughout southern Europe, the most popular by Marsilio Ficino, Platina, and Girolamo Savonarola. A second major revival followed in the sixteenth century, as complete and accurate translations of ancient Greek texts became available. Despite extensive scientific research in the seventeenth and eighteenth centuries, the old humoral system was fully abandoned only in the nineteenth century, and it still survives in the popular consciousness, most notably in Latin America.

Humoral physiology is based on the idea that four major fluids dominate the human body: blood, phlegm, choler, and black bile (or melancholy). Each "humor" is composed of two basic elements: Heat and moisture are the elements that make up blood; cold and moisture constitute phlegm; heat and dryness combine to form choler; and cold and dryness make up melancholy. When the body is in a state of health, the four humors were said to be balanced, or in the correct proportion of 16 parts to 4 parts to 1 part to 1/4 part. An imbalance of humors was seen as the origin of sickness and disease. Each individual, however, was also said to have his or her own natural "complexion" or constitution in which one humor dominated, and this distinctive makeup determined the nature of bodily functions, character, and intelligence.

That this system was well known is confirmed by frequent references to it in southern European art and literature from the High Middle Ages onward. But the system was not merely a philosophical abstraction or literary conceit. People did try to judge the state of their bodies' vital signs and tried to correct imbalances through regulation of the "nonnaturals" or external influences, such as sleep, exercise, air quality, sexual activity, and – most important for this discussion – diet.

Essential to this system was the belief that each food also had its own complexion or dominant humor and would thus interact with the humoral balance of the individual who consumed it. Several signs revealed the qualities of a food: color, aroma, and, most notably, taste. Sweetness was evidence of heat and moisture. Spicy, salty, and bitter foods were all considered hot and dry in varying degrees; we still describe foods like chilli peppers as "hot." Cold and dry foods tasted sour, styptic, or tannic (hence a "dry" wine). Lastly, insipid and watery foods were composed of cold and moist elements. Foods in each of these categories also promoted their own specific humor in the body when eaten. Cool and moist cucumbers supposedly converted into phlegm; hot and dry cinnamon became choler; and sugar made good blood.

As a rule, healthy individuals were advised to consume foods similar to their own natural complexions. When "distempered" or ill, one should consume the opposite foods to correct the imbalance. Medicines were prescribed following the same logic. A "cold" or phlegmatic imbalance might be corrected with hot and dry spices, or a more potent medicine if more serious. Tobacco was first taken for such conditions. When a person was overheated, a cold acidic drink was viewed as a good corrective.

By the mid-sixteenth century, physicians most frequently recommended nourishment opposite to the natural complexion, but such advice merely assumed that the patient was usually somewhat distempered, and the recommendation did not constitute a change in theory (Flandrin 1982, 1987: 295-6).

The complexion of each food also determined how it would best combine with other foods. An excessively cold and moist food, such as melon, was best corrected with salt or prosciutto. Fatty phlegmatic meats were more digestible with hot and dry spices. A food whose substance was difficult to "concoct" in the stomach, such as crass and gluey fish, would be improved by a cutting lemon juice or vinegar.

Indeed, humoral physiology is at the very heart of many culinary traditions that persist in southern Europe to this day. Salads are a perfect example. Cold and moist lettuce is combined with hot and dry herbs, both of whose humoral natures are counteracted by hot and dry salt and cold and dry vinegar, given further balance by hot and moist oil. Consider quail with grapes, strawberries with balsamic vinegar, or pork with mustard. All these combinations have their origin in humoral dietary theory.

According to dietary theorists, however, deciding exactly what to eat was a far more complicated affair than simply balancing flavors. Each meal also required consideration of the season, because the body was thought to respond to atmospheric conditions and air quality. The age and gender of the diner was also essential; young people were thought to have hotter systems, as were all males. This is why wine was considered harmful for boys but excellent for the aged *(Vinum lac senum est)*. The amount of physical exer-

cise people performed also helped determine the most healthful diet for them. According to the theory, laborers had hotter stomachs and could digest tougher, denser, and darker foods such as beans, sausages, coarse whole grain breads, and porridge, but the leisured required more subtle and rarefied foods such as chicken, eggs, white bread, light wines, and refined sweets. Clearly, social prejudice was built right into the system.

The amount of sexual activity also had to be taken into account, for this heated and dried the body, using up nutrients as blood was supposedly converted into semen. Hot foods could overheat the sexually active or actually incite lust. Conversely, a less nutritious diet was seen as an aid to celibacy; less blood, and ultimately less semen, would be produced. Cold foods, such as lettuce, became effective anaphrodisiacs recommended for priests and others with a need for them.

Mood was also directly related to diet. A diet of cold and dry foods, such as beef, could lead to depression, as could crass, indigestible foods, which clogged the body and permitted humors to accidentally corrupt. Laziness could be triggered by a debilitating "phlegmatic" humor, just as overly hot foods could provoke wrath. Equally, the emotional state of the individual determined which foods were corrective. Melancholic people, for example, were cheered up with aromatics, borage, hot (and moist) wines, and sweets.

Many popular dietary recommendations, however, appear to have derived from a source other than standard humoral physiology. Frequently, physicians mentioned that the character traits of a particular animal would produce similar traits in the person who ate it. Thus, the flesh of rabbits would make one timid, and it was often described as a melancholic food. But highly strung birds could make one nervous and edgy, even causing insomnia. The same elements that materially caused these characteristics in the animal were transferred into the consumer. In similar fashion, a light and subtle wine was thought to produce, in a process not unlike distillation, light "spirits" that flowed easily through the brain and instilled subtlety of thought. This process of direct transference was also applied to specific animal parts: Testicles promoted virility, brains gave rise to wit, blood (or milk, which was believed to be produced from blood in the mammary glands) fortified the weak and blood-deficient.

Direct transference began to be criticized in the mid-sixteenth century and was eventually banished from nutritional theory along with the doctrine of signatures, which posited that foods good for specific ailments would bear the marks of their potency in their outward form. That is, brain-shaped walnuts were good for the intellect; red wine was an analogue for blood. But by the mid-seventeenth century the entire system of humoral physiology had been called into question, particularly after systematic research had been conducted into the process of digestion. An entirely new system to replace humoral theory appeared in the nineteenth century with Justus von Liebig and the discovery of the role of proteins, carbohydrates, and fats, and in the twentieth century with the discovery of vitamins.

The Courtly Aesthetic

The third major influence on the foodways of southern Europe derives from the social connotations of particular foods and methods of preparation. Historically, it was usually the court that set culinary trends, which then spread to lower ranks of society. But this was not simply a process of invention and imitation. Specific items could be devalued or revived, depending on which social class they were currently associated with.

In southern Europe it is particularly the proliferation of social strata and the specialization of the economy that have generated a wealth of food prejudices (Goody 1982). In a relatively unstratified society, where the majority of the population is involved in food production and eats essentially the same diet, few foods will be associated with particular classes. This was most likely the case in the early Middle Ages. But in many parts of southern Europe, particularly in trading and manufacturing centers, where there always have been both noble and impoverished classes, food prejudices become central, and this has been increasingly true from the High Middle Ages to the present.

Specific foods also rise and fall in popularity. For example, in the Middle Ages and early Renaissance, saffron was a symbol of wealth and privilege because it was expensive and because it lent a dazzling effect to foods. The way to impress a guest was to present a saffron-daubed dish, sparkling like gold. Indeed, saffron became a symbol for gold, and to eat it represented a literal incorporation of wealth. However, enthusiasm for saffron abated during the sixteenth century, when for the first time it was cultivated on a large scale (Toussaint-Samat 1992: 522). As a consequence, it became far more affordable, less potent as a symbol of wealth, and at court it went out of fashion. Sugar had much the same history, beginning when it was first processed in Portuguese and Spanish colonies (Mintz 1985).

Economic factors can also influence the association of a particular food with a certain class. For example, in the sixteenth century, as populations grew and the living standard of the majority dropped, the price of meat rose considerably faster than that of grains. Thus, a greater proportion of expendable income had to be spent on the former, a process described as "depecoration." Poorer people were forced to purchase less fresh meat, and what meat products they could afford would necessarily be long-

lasting or preservable. Examples include sausages and smoked meats, as well as herring and salted codfish. As these items became identifiable as peasant food, they were increasingly reviled at court - and, it is interesting to note, condemned by dieticians.

Other foods readily identified with the peasantry - beans and onions and porridges of barley and millet (and later maize, as in polenta) - were stigmatized as southern European society was increasingly stratified. Particular foods became more obvious symbols of class. To consume something beyond one's budget was an act of social climbing, just as eating "common" foods showed a lack of taste and breeding.

Oddly enough, though, peasant foods came back into fashion, particularly during periods of nostalgia for simplicity and earthiness, as in the Romantic movement or in recent decades. The most interesting and subtly malleable food prejudices always have and still do center around bread. Because it has been the staple of the West, bread preferences are almost always an encapsulation of social climate. In fact, at times, the whiteness and texture of bread have been arranged hierarchically and have matched precisely the structure of society.

Illustrative is fifteenth-century Ferrara, where an essentially two-tiered society was reflected in the distinction between fine white bread and all other types (Camporesi 1989). Seventeenth-century works depict each social level with its own proper type of bread, but in other periods, brown, whole wheat, and multigrained breads have gained popularity. When ethnic awareness is valued, rustic, homemade loaves reappear.

If we specifically examine courtly food fashions, a number of interesting patterns emerge. The oldest and most obvious symbols of nobility were large game animals, such as roast boar or venison, presented whole to a large hall of retainers. Such viands would be carved and apportioned according to rank, and naturally the most honored (and favored) guests would be seated closest to the lord (Visser 1991). This type of meal perfectly matched the feudal warrior society in which prowess on the hunt was valued as much as it was in battle.

Gradually, however, this rustic sort of meal was replaced on noble tables with meals of magnificence and sophistication. Perhaps originating in the Burgundian court, dishes including peacocks (resewn into their feathers), swans, baked porpoises, and sturgeons became fashionable and quickly spread to Italy and the rest of southern Europe. Exotic spices and sugar, liberally strewn over each dish, also became requisite symbols of wealth; even pearls, amber, and gold might be incorporated into elaborately prepared confections. Disguised foods and hybrid creations, such as half-pig and half-chicken, also became popular. These new foods signified aesthetically new symbols of power and new values of wealth, as well as new far-flung connections.

An entire literary genre flourished that described the proper way to throw a banquet, and by the time of the Renaissance, precise rules for carving and using newly introduced cutlery were elaborated (Rosselli 1516; Romoli 1560). This new "civilized" behavior at the table reflected a pacification of society as governments claimed a monopoly on violence (Elias 1982). A profusion of tastes and textures became the hallmark of sophistication. Cristophoro di Messisbugo described a Ferrarese banquet for 54 guests held during Lent in 1529. It included over a dozen courses that consisted of 15 to 54 individual servings of 140 separate foods and required over 2,500 plates. It is interesting to note that each course also contained savories, sweets, soups, and salads in no discernible order (Messisbugo 1549).

When lower social classes (such as wealthy merchants) began to imitate such ostentatious meals, however, once again courtly fashion shifted – this time toward simplicity and refinement. New American products made their appearance. Chocolate drinking spread quickly from Spain as the ideal drink for indolent aristocrats (Schivelbusch 1992). Italian chefs were lured to northern courts, and the French entirely transformed haute cuisine in the seventeenth century by increasingly abandoning spices and the juxtaposition of flavor and texture. The new culinary aesthetic became one of simple ingredients, delicacy of preparation, and careful ordering of courses (Revel 1982; Mennell 1985: 71). French classicism in art, absolutism in government, and courtly cuisine thereafter dominated in southern Europe, though regional variations did not disappear. The tomato, for example, caught on in the south much more than elsewhere in Europe.

The influence of the courtly aesthetic declined in nineteenth-century Europe in the wake of popular revolutions, and the democratization of governments ushered in a similarly leveling tendency in taste. A "bourgeois" cuisine introduced a greater simplicity that was, in part, a reaction against aristocratic refinement, and there eventually arose a new awareness and appreciation of folk recipes and traditional foodways, especially with the growth of nationalism.

In the modern era in southern Europe an even greater splintering of society into various groups has resulted in further proliferation of eating styles and a greater need of individuals to be associated with a distinctive group on the basis of taste. Today, vegetarianism, fast food, health food, ethnic food, and nouvelle cuisine all vie for adherents with their own distinctive ideologies and approaches. The modern era in southern Europe can also be sharply contrasted with preceding centuries because of the advance of food technologies in areas such as scientific methods of farming, canning, refrigeration, and factory processing. Food industries are now entirely geared toward a consumer society and are firmly linked to global markets. Not only have subsistence crises and hunger become things of the past for most in the developed world, but they have been replaced with the problem of overeating.

To conclude, three ideologies of food – Christian, dietetic, and courtly – reveal some of the ways southern Europeans have thought about food and indicate the kinds of considerations that entered into their food choices. But little, thus far, has been mentioned of what they actually had to choose from, and thus, in closing, a very brief catalog of the most common ingredients and their particular social or medical associations is offered.

Wheat has always been southern Europe's dominant grain, used primarily in leavened breads. Until recently, the whitest and most finely bolted flour was considered the most prestigious as well as the most healthful; flours containing bran were thought to be crass and fit only for laborers. Various pastries and cookies were praised by physicians for their restorative power and were certainly indulged in at court as well as within monasteries throughout the Middle Ages. Only in the early modern period were they judged to be unhealthy enticements, precisely at the time when sugar and spices became available to ordinary people.

Pasta made its appearance in the late Middle Ages, and from the start was condemned by physicians as difficult to digest. Although pasta was usually associated with common kitchens, courts did not entirely reject it, as is evidenced by Bartolomeo Scappi's references to macaroni (Scappi 1570). Extruded pasta, usually made with semolina flour, has come in dozens of sizes and shapes since the late nineteenth century.

Barley has also been popular since ancient times and was most frequently used in porridges and polenta, as were millets, although these were replaced entirely by maize, introduced in the sixteenth century. Rice had been an expensive luxury, usually served with milk and sweetened. It was first cultivated widely in the fifteenth century in Lombardy, and later in Spain, after which a stout variety (*arborio*) became the basis of risotto and paella.

Legumes, particularly fava beans, peas, and chickpeas, have flourished since Roman times. None were considered suitable for delicate constitutions, and since the late Renaissance were increasingly stigmatized as peasant food. Nonetheless, beans were perhaps the quintessential Lenten fare for those with modest budgets, and new varieties of beans introduced from the Americas have also been popular.

As for vegetables, few were considered especially nutritious, but watery cucumbers, zucchini, and squashes, although frowned upon by physicians, were nonetheless cultivated and enjoyed at all levels of society. The vegetables particularly associated with southern Europe have been salad greens: lettuce, sorrel, endive, purslane, orache, radicchio, dandelion, spinach, and beet and turnip greens. In addition, all varieties of the Brassica family were consumed: cabbages, broccoli, cauliflower, and kale, as well as such others as artichokes, cardoons, asparagus, and fennel. Eggplants were probably introduced by the Arabs, but they were considered very dangerous, along with other members of the Solanaceae. Tomatoes have been a staple of southern European cuisine for only the past few centuries; along with capsicum peppers, they were widely used after their introduction from the New World in the sixteenth century.

Onions and garlic, traditionally, have been indispensable flavorings, though the latter, in the past as now, has strong peasant associations. Truffles, particularly the white variety from Piedmont and the black from Perigord, have always been highly prized luxuries. But as with mushrooms, physicians usually considered them dangerous "excrements of the earth."

The most distinctively southern European herbs are parsley, oregano, rosemary, thyme, sage, fennel, aniseed (the fruit of the anise plant), and mint - all praised as hot and dry "correctives." Also widely used are bay laurel, myrtle, juniper, lovage, lemon balm, saffron, wormwood, borage, rue, savory, lavender, and, finally, basil, which had a mixed reception among physicians. Spices most frequently imported into Venice, Genoa, Marseilles, and, later, Lisbon and Seville include pepper, cinnamon and cassia, cloves, nutmeg and mace, grains of paradise (malagueta pepper), coriander and cumin, ginger, and galanga - although these have all waxed and waned in popularity on aristocratic tables.

Olives and olive oil have been traditional staple commodities, along with grapes, citrus fruits (since late antiquity), figs, and imported dates. Peaches and melons were wildly popular in early modern courts but were strongly denounced by dietary theorists as excessively cold, moist, and corruptible. Cherries, plums, strawberries, pomegranates, quinces, apples, and pears have also been popular - especially in art - as symbols for the Nativity. Among nuts, almonds, pistachios, pine nuts, walnuts, and hazelnuts take first place, and chestnuts, too, have been important, particularly in the Cévennes Mountains and around Rome. Chestnuts, however, were often described as peasant food.

Cheese from Piacenza seems to have been the first cheese to be universally praised in southern Europe. It was superseded, however, by *parmigiano-reggiano* and *pecorino romano*. *Mozarella di bufala* and *ricotta* are also renowned. The south of France boasts many incomparable cheeses as well, and Spain and Portugal both produce especially good cheeses made from the milk of goats and ewes.

Fowl, both domestic and wild, were credited by physicians with being the most tempered of foods and were lauded at court. They included chickens, pheasants, pigeons and partridges, and later guinea fowl and turkeys, as well as numerous tiny birds or "ucelli" (larks, thrushes, and sparrows). Ducks and geese were quite often associated with Jews, who salted and cured them. Eggs were esteemed as the ideal food for convalescents and as symbols of Christ's resurrection.

With the coming of Lent, fish appeared on most tables, although for the poor it was usually dried cod. Sardines and anchovies, squid and octopus, crustaceans, and shellfish were all consumed, along with a wide variety of fresh fish from the Atlantic, the Mediterranean, the Adriatic, and from lakes and rivers. Among these were tuna, mackerel, mullet, bass, trout, perch, pike, carp, sole, and turbot - to name but a few. At court, mammoth sturgeons, newly born eels, turtles, snails, and even tender young frogs (eaten whole) were all fashionable at one time or another.

Among the meats consumed, veal and kid were considered the most healthful and the easiest to digest. Beef was to be reserved for robust laborers, as were innumerable varieties of pork sausage, blood sausage, organ meats, and other "salume" - though prosciutto was served on wealthy tables as well as poor. Lamb and rabbits generated a good deal of medical controversy, as did those game meats most readily associated with rural nobility.

Lastly, to do justice to the topic of wine would be impossible in this chapter. But in short, it is indispensable to Christianity, has been viewed as essential to a healthful diet in both past and very recent nutritional theories, and remains a principal object of gastronomic snobbery. Perhaps coffee has been its only serious rival in recent times.

Kenneth Albala

Bibliography

Bell, Rudolph M. 1985. *Holy anorexia.* Chicago and London.

Benedict of Nursia, St. 1981. *The rule of St. Benedict,* ed. Timothy Fry. Collegeville, Minn.

Burke, Peter. 1978. *Popular culture in early modern Europe.* New York.

Camporesi, Piero. 1989. *Bread of dreams* (Il pane salvaggio), trans. David Gentilcore. Cambridge.

Dante Alighieri. 1939. *Paradiso,* trans. John Sinclair. New York.

Elias, Norbert. 1982. *The history of manners,* trans. Edmund Jephcott. New York.

Flandrin, Jean-Louis. 1982. Médecine et habitudes alimentaire anciennes. In *Pratique et discours alimentaires à la Renaissance,* ed. Jean Claude Margolin and Robert Sauzet, 85-97. Paris.

  1987. Distinction through taste. In *A history of private life,* Vol. 3, ed. Phillipe Aries and George Duby, 295-6. Cambridge, Mass.

Goody, Jack. 1982. *Cooking, cuisine and class.* Cambridge.

Henisch, Bridget Ann. 1976. *Fast and feast: Food in medieval society.* University Park, Pa., and London.

Mennell, Stephen. 1985. *All manners of food.* Oxford.

Messisbugo, Christophoro di. 1549. *Banchetti.* Ferrara, Italy.

Mintz, Sidney W. 1985. *Sweetness and power: The place of sugar in modern history.* Harmondsworth, England.

Moulin, Leo. 1978. *La Vie Quotidienne des Religieux au Moyen Age*. Paris.

Revel, Jean-Francois. 1982. *Culture and cuisine* (Un festin en paroles), trans. Helen R. Lane. New York.

Romoli, Domenico. 1560. *La singolar dottrina*. Venice.

Rosselli, Giovanni. 1516. *Opera nuova chiamata epulario*. Venice.

Scappi, Bartolomeo. 1570. *Opera*. Rome.

Schivelbusch, Wolfgang. 1992. *Tastes of paradise* (Das Paradies, Geschmack und die Vernunft), trans. David Jacobson. New York.

Toussaint-Samat, Maguelonne. 1992. *History of food* (Histoire naturelle et morale de la nourriture), trans. Anthea Bell. Oxford.

Visser, Margaret. 1991. *The rituals of dinner*. New York.

V.C.3 ⁘ France

The Dominance of the French *Grande Cuisine*

Many in Western societies as well as upper-class members of non-Western societies consider French cookery to be the world's most refined method of food preparation. This reputation has mainly to do with the *grande cuisine,* a style of cooking offered by high-class restaurants and generally regarded as the national cuisine of France. The *grande cuisine* attained its status because it emphasizes the pleasure of eating rather than its purely nutritional aspects. Whereas all cuisines embody notions of eating for pleasure, it was only in France, specifically in Paris at the beginning of the nineteenth century, that a cuisine that focused on the pleasure of eating became socially institutionalized. Moreover, it was the bourgeois class of the period that used this emphasis on eating for pleasure for their cultural development. Previously, the aristocracy had determined the styles and fashions of the times, including the haute cuisine, but this privilege was temporarily lost with the French Revolution.

The middle class also used the *grande cuisine* to demonstrate a cultural superiority over other social groups with growing economic power and, thus, the potential to rise on the social ladder. At the same time, restaurants – new and special places created for the *grande cuisine* – came into being. Spatially institutionalized, the *grande cuisine* was transformed into a matter of public concern and considerable debate (Aron 1973).

The institutionalization of a cuisine that emphasized the pleasure of eating had many effects, not the least of which was that in France, more than in other European societies, eating and drinking well came to symbolize the "good life" (Zeldin 1973-7). As such, the *grande cuisine* became culturally important for all French classes, not only for the middle class that had created it, with the result that cooking and discussions about food and the qualities of wines came

to be of paramount moment. Indeed, this self-conscious stylization of eating and drinking by all classes of France led to the description of the French by other Europeans as pleasure-oriented, and the characterization of the French style of living as *savoir vivre.*

Within French society, the manner of eating became an important indication of an entire lifestyle because eating habits represented a part of culture in which social differences and dissimilarities were expressed more intensely and more subtly than in any other area. Pierre Bourdieu's study, *La Distinction,* impressively showed this phenomenon in relation to French society (1979).

Another effect of the institutionalization of the *grande cuisine* went beyond French society: The *grande cuisine* became the model and the basis for an internationally renowned cuisine and one that is culturally and socially more highly valued than other regional and national cuisines. Prices reflect this valuation most clearly. French restaurants not only are associated with gourmet food but are also the most expensive restaurants in practically any country. This internationalization of the *grande cuisine* has led to the adoption and variation, in other nations, of French recipes, French food decoration, and French ideas of service, such as the order that dinner courses should follow. The international dominance of the *grande cuisine* can be most clearly seen by the fact that the menu, the cooking language, the organization of the kitchen, and the training of the cooks are all to a large extent based on French models.

Outside of France, the *grande cuisine* holds the reputation of being a national cuisine, with people forgetting perhaps that there also exist a number of different French regional cuisines. These are bound to each other not so much by common cooking traditions as by a complicated cultural rating scheme that determines the cultural superiority or inferiority of cuisines of similar regional and social origin. This cultural judgment is also applied to those who cook and eat these regional dishes, which means that foods can be used to establish symbolic boundaries and to produce social inequality (cf. Gusfield 1992).

We can illustrate this social process with the *grande cuisine* and the regional cuisines. The former originated in an urban, aristocratic, and bourgeois environment; the latter represent rural and lower-middle-class cooking. They are not variations, one on the other, but opposites, each with different "cultural capital" (Bourdieu 1979). The *grande cuisine* is considered to be well developed, refined, and luxurious; rural cooking is described as simple, plain, and modest (Bonnain-Moerdyk 1972). Not only do these descriptions standardize the styles of cooking, they also express the meaning and function of eating and drinking in those social classes that have a special cuisine. The cultural meanings that can be derived from the *grande cuisine* suggest that members of the bourgeois and aristocratic classes are elevated beyond the mere physical need of nourishment, whereas characterizations of the styles of cooking of the lower, middle, and rural classes emphasize the physical aspect of eating. It is said that these classes do not possess the "cultural capital" necessary to go beyond the physical need to eat and drink. Thus, different cuisines are used for cultural and social differentiation and establish (as well as reflect) social inequality.

The History of the French Cuisine

One might think that there are no better resources than recipe collections and cookbooks to reconstruct what in former centuries was considered delicious cooking. Such sources, however, are inherently biased because only the wealthy classes could read and write, and there are no written reports about the cooking customs of the majority of the population. Moreover, it is doubtful that we can deduce from those recipe collections and cookbooks we do have what foodstuffs were even eaten by the upper classes. Most of the time recipes were not written by cooks because the majority of them could not read and, consequently, could not always have strictly followed recipes. Most cookbooks, then, presumably served more to idealize the aristocratic style of eating than to give cooking instructions, and we can only hope to learn from them something about the cooking notions of a certain class of literate people at a particular time.

In general, cookbooks and recipe collections are examined historically for two reasons (Barlösius 1992). One of them is to discover tendencies in the regionalization of cookery. In France this is apparent only from the nineteenth century onward because it was then that "the upper classes began to take interest in regional folklore," and, of course, this included an interest in regional cookery as well (Flandrin and Hyman 1986: 4). A second reason is to reconstruct long-term changes in cooking customs in order to discern processes of cultivation and civilization (see, for example, the works of Jean-Louis Flandrin [1983, 1984, 1986]).

The Fourteenth to the Eighteenth Century

The earliest known French recipe collection is the "Ménagier de Paris" from the fourteenth century. The oldest known French cookbook is the *Viandier de Taillevant*, published by Pierre Gaudol between 1514 and 1534. In both, we can find only a few clues to the regional origins of the recipes and other instructions (Stouff 1982; Bonnet 1983; Laurioux 1986), and in fact, it can be shown that some recipes were taken from previously published collections. Some were entirely plagiarized, others only partly changed.

Another resource, very famous and popular in Europe at that time, was the cookbook *De Honesta Voluptate* (c. 1475) by Platina (Bartolomeo Sacchi). Taken together these cookbooks give the impression that there was no regional or rural differentiation in cooking in Europe during the Middle Ages. "Cookbooks, regardless of who their readers might have been, diffused culinary models inspired more by aristocratic practices than by those of the common people, and were more cosmopolitan than regional" (Flandrin and Hyman 1986: 4). The European aristocracy had, then, a common culture in eating and drinking that was not restricted by state borders. The later development and proclamation of national cuisines is closely connected to the process of state formation, which was reinforced by the assertion of independent cultures in support of national identities (Barlösius in press).

Common European cooking traditions endured until the seventeenth century, when national cuisines began to develop. It was only when French cookery became culturally stylized and was used to mark social differences that it also became a model for the courtly and aristocratic cuisines of Europe. This conscious cultural creation of cookery and table manners shows itself most clearly in the fact that before the seventeenth century, cookbooks and recipe collections were rarely published. Then, suddenly, in the seventeenth and eighteenth centuries, many cookbooks appeared. The first of this series was *Cuisinier François* by François Pierre de la Varenne, published again and again from 1651 until 1738. Other very influential cookbooks were the 1656 *Le Cuisinier* by Pierre de Lune, the 1674 *L'Art de Bien Traiter* by L. S. R., François Massialot's *Le Cuisinier Royal et Bourgeois* (published 1691–1750), and Menon's *Nouveau Traité de la Cuisine* (1739).

In these books, changes in cooking were described with terms like *ancien* and *moderne*, which were also used to indicate changes in other arts (Barlösius 1988). The cookery of the Middle Ages was criticized as being rude, even ridiculous (whereas the new cookery was considered to be refined and cultivated). Culinary tastes had obviously changed. The cooks of the seventeenth century, especially, complained about the medieval customs of cooking food too long and overseasoning it. One result was that Asian spices, like saffron, ginger, cinnamon, passion fruit seeds, and mace, were hardly used in the new cuisine, although native herbs, such as chervil, tarragon, basil, thyme, bay leaves, and chives, became popular (Flandrin 1986).

The new culinary taste was also apparent in meat choices. During the Middle Ages, the menu of the aristocracy consisted mainly of dishes with chicken and venison (Revel 1979). Beef and pork were scarcely ever eaten, although beef was an ingredient in broths and soups. Other meats that were consumed seem exotic even today, as for example, swans, storks, cranes, peacocks, herons, and large sea mammals.

During the first decades of the seventeenth century, recipes for big birds and sea mammals like whales, dolphins, and seals disappeared from the cookbooks. It was not just that such meats were believed to have no gastronomical value; they were no longer considered edible, and attempts to prepare them marked one as uncultivated, to say the least. In fact, all animals were scratched from the menu that were not especially raised or chased for food. Also out of fashion was the medieval penchant for realistic presentation, in which, for example, cooked birds might be redecorated with their feathers before being served. At this point, then, beef dishes and some pork dishes came into fashion, but only those that used the most valuable and exquisite meat parts, such as fillets, loins, legs, and hams (cf. Flandrin 1986).

Such changes give the impression that cooking was natural and bland in the seventeenth and eighteenth centuries, but this is the case only when measured against medieval cookery. In comparison with today's food preparation, however, the courtly eighteenth-century aristocratic cuisine was heavy, excessive, and complicated. Original flavors were altered, even overwhelmed, with excessive seasoning and the mixing of different kinds of foods. The aristocratic love of splendor demanded as many dishes as possible on the table, and flavor and taste were subordinated to food decoration. Until the nineteenth century, it was common to serve food *à la française,* which signified that many different kinds of dishes were offered at the same time. There were no strict rules concerning the number of dishes, but often, depending on the number of guests, there might be as many different dishes per course as there were guests, and there was a minimum of three courses. Thus, this could mean that a meal with 25 persons in attendance required 25 different dishes per course, meaning that 75 dishes were served altogether (Malortié 1881). It is true that the guests had a much greater choice than today, but inevitably many of the dishes were cold by the time they were finally served and people had the opportunity to eat them.

Table manners also changed with culinary tastes to become standardized and strictly regulated. During the Middle Ages, everybody shared the same plate and cutlery. But in the seventeenth and eighteenth centuries, each person had his or her own plate, glass, cutlery, and napkin. People were embarrassed to eat from the same plate as others or to use the same knife or glass, and with the new regulations, the distance between guests became wider (Elias 1981). Table manners were constantly cultivated and regulated down to the tiniest details. Some of the rules even changed to their opposites. In the sixteenth and seventeenth centuries, for example, it was proper to cut one's bread with a knife, but in the eighteenth century, this was considered bad form. Instead, one broke bread with the hands.

Thus, medieval notions (albeit aristocratic ones) of how to organize eating, drinking, meals, and cooking were culturally devalued, and new (but also aristocratic) ones were put in their place. Most likely much of the reason for this change was that the aristocrats were interested in creating greater social distance between themselves and the growing masses, and contributing to this desire was an increased emphasis on cultural characteristics, such as refined culinary taste and distinguished table manners. Certainly it is the case that social differentiation processes were at work at the dinner table as well as in other areas of everyday life. Thus, the aristocracy developed a lifestyle in which culinary and other cultural attitudes became an important means of establishing as well as reflecting social distances and defining social units. This new development was the haute cuisine.

The Emergence of the Grande Cuisine in the Nineteenth Century

In the seventeenth and eighteenth centuries, like music, painting, and literature, the haute cuisine served to express courtly aristocratic lifestyles. Only cooking and eating that demonstrated wealth, luxury, and pomp could accomplish this goal and distinguish the aristocracy in no uncertain terms from the rising middle class.

Haute cuisine was institutionalized in the *salle à manger* (dining room) of the aristocracy. Alexandre Dumas once complained that in the salons, commoners like Montesquieu (Charles Louis de Secondat), Voltaire (François-Marie Arouet), and Denis Diderot discussed important social issues in a serious and enlightened fashion, but sophisticated cookery was available only to the aristocrats (Dumas 1873: 30). Middle-class notions about cookery were excluded from the *salle à manger.* It is noteworthy that in the second half of the eighteenth century, haute cuisine was one of the last cultural areas in which the aristocratic taste still dominated (Barlösius 1988).

The aristocratic host (amphitryon) was called, after the verse by Molière [Jean-Baptiste Pocquelin]), *le véritable Amphitryon est l'Amphitryon où on mange.* He invited his guests, selected the menu, and made sure that the *salle à manger* looked splendid. At the beginning of the nineteenth century, Alexandre L. B. Grimod de la Reynière, in his book *Manuel des Amphitryon,* described standards of behavior for aristocratic hosts (Grimod 1808). Indispensable characteristics were wealth, good taste, an innate sensitivity, the desire to eat well, generosity, gracefulness, vividness, and a predilection for order. That money alone was not enough to run an excellent household could be observed again and again among the nouveaux riches (the "new rich") of the French Revolution (Grimod 1808).

The cooks who provided the haute cuisine were craftsmen who had an excellent knowledge of their craft. No aesthetic creativity was needed, however, and because of social position, they could not pursue their artistic inclinations, which were frequently directed toward the simplification of food presentation and spicing as well as a refined design of taste and flavor.

The aristocracy demanded a visible stylization that was in contrast to the cook's focus on the taste of the food rather than its appearance. The *salle à manger* as well as the amphitryon (host) were symbols of the ancien régime, so that the bourgeois *grande cuisine* was, to a great extent, developed in the restaurants. In fact, as already noted, it was at the time of the French Revolution that restaurants were established in Paris in great number (Andrieu 1955; Guy 1971; Mennell 1985). Before 1789, there were fewer than 50 restaurants in Paris; by 1820, the number had climbed to 3,000 (Zeldin 1973–77: Vol. 1, 739). It was in these restaurants that a bourgeois eating culture was established and the *salle à manger* disparaged, although its example was followed in standards of service, tableware, crystal, and cutlery.

The founding of the restaurants was the most important step in the process of changing aristocratic haute cuisine to bourgeois *grande cuisine*. Everybody who had enough money could eat in restaurants, where cookery was no longer the privilege solely of the aristocrats (Aron 1973; Barlösius and Manz 1988), and a cuisine that placed emphasis on the pleasure of eating was no longer influenced by aristocratic taste. In short, restaurants and their cooks succeeded in making cooking an aesthetic, taste-oriented art, which did not focus on a certain class (Barlösius and Manz 1988).

Indeed, the cooks helped to institutionalize the *grande cuisine* (Barlösius 1988). Many who had previously worked for the aristocracy now became cooks in the restaurants. They were responsible for menu planning, food design, and the financial aspects of meal production and began a process of professionalizing themselves as they assumed total responsibility for the design of the cuisine. Not only did they regard their cookery as an art, they defined themselves as artists whose task it was to make cooking equal to already established arts such as music and painting. Like other arts, that of cooking constantly changed because the cooks were competitive and strove for social recognition. But in calling themselves artists, they overlooked the fact that many of them were not working independently, and thus, it is not surprising that their working conditions and wages were often below those of other skilled workers.

Another factor in the institutionalization of the *grande cuisine* was the gourmand. Gourmands, who were supposed to be well informed in food matters and to have well-developed tastes, began to educate the public with an outpouring of gastronomic literature. Important works were Grimod de la Reynière's *Almanach des Gourmands* and Anthèlme Brillat-Savarin's *La Physiologie du Goût* (Grimod 1803–12; Brillat-Savarin 1833).

In fact, the gourmand took the place of the traditional aristocratic amphitryon, who did not fit into the sophisticated bourgeois culture of eating. Whereas an amphitryon was considered to be a gourmand because of his social position, social background was not important for a gourmand, who represented the bourgeois idea of a connoisseur. The following characteristics necessary to a gourmand were listed: a sensitive and well-developed sense of flavor, a distinctive aesthetic taste, and the ability to put the pleasure of eating into words. Finally, the gourmand was supposed to know in theory what the cook knew and did in practice, because only with that knowledge would the gourmand be able to make a sound judgment about food and drink (Brillat-Savarin 1833).

From the gourmand, professional gastronomic critics evolved. They ranked the restaurants according to a rating scheme and also published gastronomic guides. One of the first institutions of gastronomic criticism was the Société des Mercredis, founded in 1781 or 1782 by Grimod de la Reynière and some 17 gourmand friends, with Grimod as its chairman until 1810. This jury examined the quality of restaurants, with the members meeting once a week to jointly determine their expert opinions. Grimod was the first to have the idea of forming a jury whose only task was to taste and rate food. Inevitably, his jury was also the first to be accused of partiality in its judgments and, thus, of jeopardizing those restaurants that got low marks. With only a few exceptions, the jury's judgments were published from 1803 until 1812 in the *Almanach des Gourmands* (Guy 1971; Revel 1979).

The Société des Mercredis and the *Almanach des Gourmands* were forerunners of all those institutions of gastronomic criticism that followed, such as the various restaurant guides. Early in the twentieth century, the most influential gastronomic critic was Curnonsky (pseudonym Maurice-Edmond Sailland), who in 1928 founded the *Académie de Gastronome* on the model of the *Académie Française* (Curnonsky and Rouff 1921–8). In France, the best-known restaurant guides are those by Michelin and Kléber-Colombes.

Journals can also be indirect instruments of gastronomic criticism. For example, they give obligatory descriptions of the kinds of food to eat and how to enjoy eating them, and superficially, one cannot detect any traditional regulations and standardizations in these publications, such as, for example, rules of behavior. But such publications, nevertheless, belong to a genre in which questions of taste and table manners are dealt with, even if in subtle ways and not in the form of regulations. As in the past, today's media that focus on gastronomic criticism and the development of taste constitute a means of potentially producing social distance, as well as other distinctions, and setting a certain standard of cooking and taste.

The Change of the Grande Cuisine

At the beginning of the nineteenth century, the bourgeois *grande cuisine* was still detached from the traditions of the aristocratic haute cuisine, although not completely so, as is shown by recipes and food decoration. During this phase, the *grande cuisine* was influenced by Antonin Carême, said to be its founder, and by Antoine Beauvilliers, one of the first of the restaurant cooks (Beauvilliers 1814–16; Carême 1821, 1843–8). In his three-volume work *L'Art Culinaire de la Cuisine Française au Dix-neuvième Siècle,* first published in 1830, Carême described this cuisine extensively and depicted it in very detailed and exact drawings. He claimed the Italian architect Andrea Palladio (1508–80) as his model and adapted classical architectural forms to food presentation. No wonder the *grande cuisine* of this period, with its preference for regulated forms and symmetrical arrangement, can be called *cuisine classique.*

Carême concentrated on the visual aspect of cookery and not so much on food flavor. He also held to the *service à la française,* viewing as much less elegant the *service à la russe,* which was becoming more and more popular in restaurants. The latter corresponds mainly to today's style of service: The food is put on plates in the kitchen and served immediately to guests instead of being arranged aesthetically on the table beforehand.

Two cookbooks published later in the nineteenth century became very famous: These were Felix Urbain Dubois and Émile Bernard's *La Cuisine Classique* and Jules Gouffé's *Le Livre de la Cuisine.* In these volumes the tension between artful food decoration and the development of flavor and taste was discussed, but no unanimous decision was arrived at (Gouffé 1867; Dubois and Bernard 1874). Dubois and Bernard did not favor the *service à la russe* because, for them, cookery had to appeal to all of the senses. They did, however, simplify food decoration.

The contradiction between style and flavor became a point of dispute among Parisian chefs in the 1880s: Should food presentation be simplified in order to enhance the pleasure of eating? And if so, did that mean that cooks had to give up their claim to be artists? This debate, carried on in the cooks' clubs and journals, was a reaction to the criticisms that cookery was in crisis and had become decadent because it had neither adapted to alterations in taste nor paid attention to social changes in the clientele of the restaurants. The discussion was led by cook Prosper Montagné, who slowly succeeded in establishing that cookery had to focus primarily on food flavor and taste (Montagné and Salles 1900). At this juncture, the *cuisine classique* was developing into a cuisine that was aimed at an integration into new social realities – a *cuisine moderne.*

The cooks of the *cuisine moderne* reacted to alterations in taste as well as to social changes. Among these was the fact that people increasingly had limited time when eating in a restaurant. Another had to do with a change in the mixture of restaurant customers by the late nineteenth and early twentieth centuries. Auguste Escoffier, the most famous cook of that period, recommended that his colleagues study the tastes and habits of their guests and adapt their cookery to them, with special attention to those tastes that had changed over the years (Escoffier 1921). The cooks went into action. They simplified their recipes, shortened cooking times, left out superfluous decoration, and tried to speed up service in order to satisfy their new kinds of customers. Their artistry now focused fully on the composition of the food's flavor and taste (Barlösius 1988).

Yet the *cuisine moderne* was itself soon due for modification. Formerly it was thought that there existed universally valid rules for cooking; these determined which foods went well together and how they were to be prepared and decorated. In other words, people believed that recipes were independent of the cook. Cookery was regarded as an art, but not as an individual art whereby each cook had his own particular style that distinguished him from all others. In the 1930s, however, the obligatory cooking rules of the *cuisine moderne* were relaxed. Now cooks were asked to improvise when cooking. Traditional notions of matching foods were not taught anymore. Cooking came to be treated as an experiment, and this cookery was called *cuisine de liberté,* or the nouvelle cuisine.

Fernand Point, its most famous practitioner, placed emphasis on the arrangement of side dishes while simplifying existing recipes and developing new ones (Point 1969). The *cuisine de liberté* stressed the food's own taste and aimed at the perfection of cookery so as to create the best-quality dishes. In order to achieve this effect, new cooking methods were developed to retain the natural flavors, tastes, and colors of food. Although Point had not yet thought in terms of the nutritional and physiological aspects of his cookery, the nouvelle cuisine did integrate modern knowledge about nutrition that appealed to a new health consciousness.

The *grande cuisine* had scarcely been concerned with the health aspects of food, but now cooks attempted to link the pleasures of eating with foods that were healthful. It became very important to cook foods that were light and easily digestible. Moreover, the cooks of the nouvelle cuisine distanced themselves from industrialized food production. They disapproved of canned and prefabricated foods on the grounds of poor quality and demanded a return to small-farm food production.

The nouvelle cuisine also accepted regional cooking traditions to an unprecedented extent, and with this development, the dominance of Parisian cuisine, which had existed since the emergence of haute cuisine, was diminished. Nonetheless, in restaurants the nouvelle cuisine was expensive, and relatively few were able to afford it. For its part, the *grande cuisine* had begun to influence private cooking. Through television shows and mass-produced cookbooks, chefs were able to introduce their cookery to large segments of the population. Whereas original haute cuisine cookbooks had been written only for aristocratic and bourgeois households, and those in the first phase of the *grande cuisine* had addressed cooks in restaurants, now many cookbooks focused on family and household cooking. Thus, on one hand, the cooks opened up new sources of revenue with their books and shows, and on the other hand, the public became more interested in the art of cooking.

French Regional Cuisines

The term "regional cuisines" refers to the cookery and foodways of specific geographic areas whose borders frequently correspond with ethnic boundaries. The emergence of regional cuisines is often explained in climatic, biological, and geographic terms, and certainly these naturally caused differences help explain the more or less distinct division between northern and southern French cookery. The cuisines of southern France are marked by Mediterranean culture and more resemble Italian and Spanish regional cuisines than those of northern France. The latter are similar to cuisines found in Belgium and in the region of Baden, in Germany. The natural differences between the Mediterranean and northern French cuisines are certainly demonstrated by their use of fats. Southern cookery is based on cooking oils, such as nut and olive oils, whereas northern cookery uses butter and lard. There is also a difference in beverage preference, with those in southern France preferring wine and those in northern France beer or cider (Hémardinquer 1961; Mandrou 1961).

Such differences are not sufficient, however, to explain the emergence of small regional differences in cookery (Flandrin 1983). The concept of regional cookery presupposes that common ways of preparing food are cultural specialties that are further developed to become objects of cultural identity. Through these processes, demarcation from other cuisines occurs because of different methods of food preparation. Cooking, then, is a sociocultural phenomenon, and different recipes and foodways are the products of this phenomenon. And when certain recipes become cultural characteristics, the cuisines are distinguishable and can be regarded as independent cultural products. Therefore, cuisines can establish cultural differences as well as common grounds.

These social contexts explain why cooking traditions, which frequently differ from region to region, are stylized as regional cuisines only if the region as a whole is perceived as a cultural, ethnic, or political unity. Most of the time, the process of regionalization has been a reaction against the centralizing tendencies of the state. Thus, the first explicitly regional cookbooks published in France, appearing during the course of the nineteenth century, can be looked upon as evidence of a conscious cultural upgrading of typically regional ways of cooking (Capatti 1989). But they can also be seen as constituting a reaction against the increasing cultural dominance of the *grande cuisine,* which emanated, of course, from Paris.

Rural traditions, however, were not included in such regional cookbooks. They described urban bourgeois cookery only because the increasing centralizing tendency of Paris meant that the urban bourgeoisie in the rest of the country were not only spatially but also socially and culturally pushed into a peripheral border position. In short, the formation of independent regional cultural identities, even if only in terms of eating and drinking, can be interpreted as cultural self-assertion in the face of the emergence of a "national" cuisine.

The conscious development of regional cuisines led to popular dishes, beverages, and often cheeses that are frequently pointed to as typical and characteristic of particular regions. Wines, dishes featuring sausages with sauerkraut, the now-famous quiche, and Muenster cheese, for example, are culinary features of the Alsace-Lorraine region. Typical of the cuisine of Normandy are seafood, cider, and Calvados and the cheeses Camembert, Brie, and Pont l'Évêque. The cuisine of Provence is based on garlic, tomatoes, and olive oil. Bouillabaisse is often noted as one of its typical dishes; it consists of fish and crustaceans from the Mediterranean. The most famous dishes of the cuisine of Brittany are thin, sweet, or salty pancakes called crepes and galettes. Some areas are more famous for their wines than their cookery, especially Bordeaux, Bourgogne, Touraine, and Champagne. But in these regions, even though the wines are deemed more important than food, they nonetheless symbolize true eating enjoyment (Fischer 1983).

Although certain dishes and beverages have been pointed to as characteristic of specific regional cuisines, it is not always safe to conclude that they are consumed very heavily in their region, and in fact, statistics bear this out. One reason is that many typically regional dishes are traditionally prepared for festive occasions but not for everyday consumption. Another is that these dishes may be quantitatively a small part of the diet when compared to basic foods like bread. The main reason, however, is that regional cuisines tend to reflect the national cuisine in the sense that they assign to some foods a special historical status that is not deserved. To take Provence as an example, it can be demonstrated that foods that are supposed to be native and indispensable to its cuisine do not necessarily originate in that region. Tomatoes, beans, potatoes, and artichokes are the basic elements of the cuisine of Provence. But none of these foods originated there; rather, they reached southern France only following the fifteenth century (cf. Stouff 1982; Flandrin and Hyman 1986).

French Cuisine – Today and the Future

In recent years, it has become apparent that for many in the West, French cookery is no longer seen as the culinary standard, or even as the most refined cuisine. Other cuisines, such as those of Italy or Japan, are regarded as on an equal level, even though, both nationally and internationally, the French government and lobbies for the country's gastronomic arts attempt to forestall this loss of predominance by means of advertising, awards, "taste-training" events, and even great state dinners.

Why is the French style of cuisine (which was, after all, something of a standard for more than 300 years) losing its dominant position now? Two important reasons, among many, are directly connected with each other. One is that the European aristocracy and the established middle classes, for whom France served for so long as the culturally guiding nation, in language and cuisine as well as in civilization generally, no longer hold a culture-forming position, and the new cultural elites have oriented themselves to other lifestyles. The second reason reflects the shifting of political, economic, and cultural positions of power within the global society. Although French cuisine, in particular, maintained a European dominance in the past, the increasing acceptance and popularity of, say, Japanese cuisine illustrates something of the cultural competition internationally at the turn of the twenty-first century. In other words, both within Europe and in other parts of the world, French culture and, therefore, French cuisine have become devalued in terms of prestige.

The future will show if another cuisine will replace that of France in a position of prominence. It is more likely, however, that several different national styles of cookery will achieve acceptance as equally delightful and ideal. One thing is already certain: The French cuisine (and French wines as well) are no longer matchless in quality.

Eva Barlösius

Bibliography

Andrieu, Pierre. 1955. *Histoire du restaurant*. Paris.

Aron, Jean-Paul. 1973. *Le mangeur du 19ième siècle*. Paris.

Barlösius, Eva. 1988. Eßgenuß als eigenlogisches soziales Gestaltungsprinzip. Zur Soziologie des Essens und Trinkens, dargestellt am Beispiel der grande cuisine Frankreichs. Ph.D. thesis, Universität Hannover.

1992. The history of diet as a part of the *vie matérielle* in France. In *European food history,* ed. H. J. Teuteberg, 90–108. Leicester, England.

In press. Cucina. In *Enciclopedia del corpo*. Rome.

Barlösius, Eva, and Wolfgang Manz. 1988. Der Wandel der Kochkunst als genußorientierte Speisengestaltung. Webers Theorie der Ausdifferenzierung und Rationalisierung als Grundlage einer Ernährungssoziologie. *Kölner Zeitschrift für Soziologie und Sozialforschung* 4: 728–46.

Beauvilliers, Antoine. 1814–16. *L'art du cuisinier*. Paris.

Bonnain-Moerdyk, Rolande. 1972. Sur la cuisine traditionelle comme culte culinaire du passé. *Revue de la Société d'Ethnologie Française* 3–4: 287–94.

Bonnet, Jean-Claude. 1983. Les manuels de cuisine. *18ième Siècle* 15: 53–64.

Bourdieu, Pierre. 1979. *La distinction. Critique sociale du jugement*. Paris.

Brillat-Savarin, Anthèlme. 1833. *La physiologie du goût*. Paris.

Capatti, Alberto. 1989. *Le goût du nouveau. Origines de la modernité alimentaire*. Paris.

Carême, Antonin. 1821. *Projets d'architecture dédiés à Alexandre Ier*. Paris.

1843–8. *L'art culinaire de la cuisine française au dix-neuvième siècle. Traité alimentaire et practique*. Paris.

Curnonsky [Maurice-Edmond Sailland] and Marcel Rouff. 1921–8. *La France gastronomique. Guide des merveilleuses culinaires et des bonnes auberges françaises*. Paris.

Dubois, Felix Urbain, and Émile Bernand. 1874. *La cuisine classique*. Paris.

Dumas, Alexandre. 1873. *Le grand dictionnaire de la cuisine*. Paris.

Elias, Norbert. 1981. *Über den Prozeß der Zivilisation*. 2 vols. Frankfurt.

Escoffier, Auguste. 1921. *Guide culinaire*. Paris.

Fischer, M. F. K., trans. 1983. *Die Küche in Frankreichs Provinzen*. Stuttgart.

Flandrin, Jean-Louis. 1983. Le goût et la nécessité: Sur l'usage des graisses dans les cuisines d'Europe occidentale (XIVe–XVIIIe siècle). *Annales* E.S.C. 369–401.

1984. Internationalisme, nationalisme, et régionalisme dans la cuisine du 14e et 15e siècles: Le témoignage des livres de cuisine. In *Manger et boire au Moyen Age*. 2 vols. 75–91.

1986. La distinction par le goût. In *Histoire de la vie privée,* Vol. 3, ed. Philippe Ariès and Georges Duby, 266–309. Paris.

Flandrin, Jean-Louis, and Philip Hyman. 1986. Regional tastes and cuisines: Problems, documents and discourses on food in southern France in the sixteenth and seventeenth centuries. *Food and Foodways* 2: 1–31.

Gouffé, Jules. 1867. *Le livre de la cuisine*. Paris.

Grimod de la Reynière, Alexandre L. B. 1803–12. *Almanach des gourmands*. Paris.

1808. *Manuel des amphitryon*. Paris.

Gusfield, Joseph R. 1992. Nature's body and the metaphors of food. In *Cultivating differences. Symbolic boundaries and the making of inequality,* ed. Michèle Lamont and Marcel Fournier, 75–104. Chicago.

Guy, Christian. 1971. *La vie quotidienne de la société gourmande en France au XIXe siècle*. Paris.

Hémardinquer, Jean-Jacques. 1961. Essai de cartes de graisses en France. *Annales* E.S.C. 747–9.

Laurioux, Bruno. 1986. Les premiers livres de cuisine. *Histoire* 3: 51–7.

Malortié, Karl Ernst von. 1881. *Das Menü*. Second edition. Hannover.

Mandrou, Robert. 1961. Les consommations des villes françaises (viandes et boissons) au milieu du XIXième siècle. *Annales* E.S.C. 740–4.

Mennell, Stephen. 1985. *All manners of food: Eating and taste in England and France from the Middle Ages to the present*. Oxford.

Montagné, Prosper, and Prosper Salles. 1900. *La grande cuisine illustrée*. Paris.

Point, Fernand. 1969. *Ma gastronomie*. Paris.

Revel, Jean-Francois. 1979. *Un festin en paroles*. Paris.

Stouff, L. 1982. Y avait-il à la fin du moyen-age une alimentation et une cuisine provençale originale? *Manger et boire au moyen age,* Vol. 2. Paris.

Zeldin, Theodore. 1973–77. *France, 1848–1945*. 2 vols. Oxford.

V.C.4 ⮿ The British Isles

Prehistory (6000 B.C. to 54 B.C.)

Until very recently, all settled communities have eaten the foods that their geographic contexts offered. Once Britain was cut off from the mainland of the Continent (by 6500 B.C.) and fishing was feasible in the clement weather of the summer, fish became as integral a part of the local diet as meat was in the winter. Yet the bulk of the diet (about 85 percent) was made up of plant foods, as it always had been. Humankind has relied on wild foods for 99.8 percent of its time on the planet. There are over 3,000 species of plants that can be eaten for food, but only 150 of these have ever been cultivated, and today the peoples of the world sustain themselves on just 20 main crops. We underestimate the harvest from the wild that humankind gathered and the detailed knowledge, passed on from generation to generation, about which plants were toxic, which were healing, and which were sharp, bitter, sweet, and sour; such knowledge must have been encyclopedic.

The women and children gathered roots, leaves, fungi, berries, nuts, and seeds. Early in the spring the new shoots of sea kale, sea holly, hogweed, bracken, "Good King Henry," and asparagus could be picked. Then there were bulbs to be dug up that had stored their energy during the winter. These included the bulbs of lilies and of the *Alliums* (including wild garlic), the rhizomes of "Solomon's Seal," and the tubers of water plants that were dried and then ground to make a flour. Baby pinecones and the buds of trees were also springtime foods, not to mention the cambium, the inner live skin beneath the outside bark of the tree, which in the spring was full of sweet sap and yielded syrup. The new leaves of wild cabbage, sea spinach, chard, and sea purslane could be picked, as could fat hen, orache, nettle, purslane, mallow, and much else. Other edible leaves were those of yellow rocket, ivy-leaved toadflax, lamb's lettuce, wood sorrel, dandelion, red clover, wild marjoram, and salad burnet (Colin Renfrew, in Black 1993). The flavoring herbs, like wild mustard, coriander, poppies, corn mint, juniper, and tansy, would have been gathered with pleasure. Wild birds' eggs were also eaten in the spring, with a small hole made in an egg's shell and the egg sucked out raw. The bigger eggs, however, would have been cooked in their shells in the warm embers of a fire.

In the autumn, there were fruits to be gathered, like crabapples that were sliced and dried for the winter, along with berries (sloes, elderberries, strawberries, and blackberries), mushrooms, large tree fungi (like *Fistulina hepatica*), and nuts. Hazelnuts, walnuts, sweet chestnuts, pine nuts, beechnuts, acorns, and different kinds of seeds were also stored. In addition, lichens and algae (both very nutritious) were gathered and dried, and cakes were made out of them.

Fishing communities grew up at the mouths of estuaries and along coasts where there were sheltered coves and inlets that could harbor boats and fishing equipment. Dragnets of nettle fiber were held between boats, woven basketlike traps caught crabs and lobsters, and fresh fish (trout, salmon, and pike) were speared with tridents of sharpened bone lashed to a stick. Fish were wind-dried and smoked over peat or wood fires.

Seabirds, killed with clay pellets flung by slings or with arrows having blunt wooden heads, were another source of food (Wilson 1973). Unplucked birds were covered with a thick layer of smeared clay and cooked in the embers of a fire. Large seabirds – oily and strong in flavor – could also have been smoked over a fire and stored for the winter. Smaller game birds in the forest were more difficult to catch, though traps made of nets might have been used. In the late Upper Paleolithic site at Kent's Cavern, Torquay, the bones of grouse, ptarmigan, greylag goose, and whooper swan were found (Renfrew, in Black 1993).

In the winter, red deer, roe deer, elk, wild oxen, and wild boar were hunted, whereas smaller game like wildcats, foxes, otters, beavers, and hares were frequently caught in traps. Nooses, hung from trees, served as one form of trap. Hounding animals into gullies was another method of capture. Deer-antler mattocks were wielded to hack meat off the carcass, whereas flint knives were employed for skinning. Nothing was wasted: The gut and stomach were used as casing for the soft offal, cut up small and mixed with fat and herbs, then slowly roasted.

The first domestic animals were brought to Britain around 3500 B.C. by the islands' first farmers, Neolithic immigrants from the coasts of western and northwestern Europe. Following their introduction, herds of sheep, goats, cattle, and pigs grazed in forest clearings. Unwanted male cattle were poleaxed, and many of the bones were split to extract the marrow. That a large number of calves were killed suggests that there would also have been a generous supply of milk with which to make butter and cheese.

The Celts, who began to settle in Britain from the eighth century B.C., added hens, ducks, and geese to the list of Britain's domesticated animals. They refused to eat the wild horses and instead tamed them for riding and for drawing wagons and chariots. The Celts were the first to recognize that the soil of Britain is more fertile than that of continental Europe, and they cleared forests to plant cereals and to allow pasture to grow for grazing. They preserved meat, fish, and butter in salt and exported British beef to the Continent. The Celts also tilled the soil so successfully that they exported grain to many parts of Europe. In Britain, they built underground grain storage silos.

The Celts processed wheat by setting ears alight,

then extinguishing the fire when the husks were burnt. The wheat was then winnowed and baked, and saddle querns were used to grind it into flour. These industrious farmers also began beekeeping, with conical hives made from wickerwork daubed with mud or dung. They employed shallow earthenware pots as drinking vessels, whereas deeper pots were made for cooking pottages (mixtures of meat, grains, leaves, roots, and herbs) slowly over a fire.

Honey and water, left together in a pot, will ferment, and this drink – mead – was often flavored with wild herbs and fruits. Some cow, ewe, and goat milk might have been drunk fresh, but most of it would have been made into cheese and only the whey drunk. The Celts made an unhopped beer from barley and wheat, first allowing the grain to germinate, then stopping this process with heat and allowing it to ferment. Finally, they also imported wine and, later, began to grow vines themselves.

The Roman Period (54 B.C. to A.D. 407)

The Romans raised vines in southern England and grew peaches, apricots, figs, and almonds in sheltered gardens. Beef and mutton were consumed in large quantities by Roman soldiers, as was pork where it was plentiful in the south and east of England.

The Romans introduced animal farming by enclosing large tracts of land, where they kept red, roe, and fallow deer, and wild boar, as well as bears captured in Wales and Scotland. Moreover, their villas had *leporaria* for keeping hares and rabbits in estate gardens, along with pheasants, peacocks, guinea fowl, partridges, and wild pigeons – the latter kept in columbaria (dovecotes). The Romans' pigs were confined in sties in order to fatten them. Snails were confined upon islands, so that they could not escape, and were fattened on milk, wine must, and spelt; when they became so fat that they could not get back into their shells, they were fried in oil. The Romans tamed barnacle geese and mallards and, of course, also raised chickens and capons (castrated male chicks), which (like other food animals) they kept in confinement and fattened.

They considered all kinds of shellfish to be great delicacies, and many of the oyster beds that still exist today were started by the Romans. They also brought into Britain many new spices, as well as the traditions of Greek and Roman cuisine that were as refined and sophisticated as a civilization could demand. Columella (Lucius Junius Moderatus), the Roman poet and agronomist, mentioned the use of lamb or kid rennet for making cheese. Previously, plant rennet – wild thistle, nettle, or lady's bedstraw – may have been used, perhaps discovered by accident when stirring warm milk with a stem or twig of one of these plants.

The Romans also introduced the cultivation of oat and rye, though barley was the predominant crop.

They brought their bread ovens and even the *cilabus* (a portable oven) to Britain and used eggs in cooking, a practice unknown to the Celts. Eggs and milk were heated together to make a custard; eggs were fried in oil and eaten with a sauce poured over them; eggs were mixed with pounded meat or fish to make rissoles, sausages, and stuffings. With Roman rule came imported pepper, ginger, cinnamon, cassia, and other spices from the East, and white mustard cultivation was introduced. The grains of the white mustard were pounded and mixed with white vinegar to preserve vegetables. For table use, the mustard was mixed with almonds, honey, and oil.

The Romans were obsessed with two flavorings. One was the powdered root of *silphium,* which no longer exists but is thought to have been a little like asafetida. The other was *liquamen,* a sauce made from rotting small fish, which was a cross between anchovy essence and the clear fish sauce of the Orient. There were *liquamen* factories all over the Roman Empire. Honey was also a favorite flavoring, and several writers devoted pages to the craft of beekeeping in their farming manuals. In addition, cheese was much used in cooking, quite often with fish.

The Romans introduced lentils into Britain and, for the first time, cultivated globe artichokes, asparagus, shallots, and endive. They also popularized wild plants like "Good King Henry," corn salad, nettles, and pennycress. In addition, they brought new herbs to Britain, among them borage, chervil, dill, fennel, lovage, sage, and thyme.

There is an assumption that Roman banquets were an excuse for gluttony and vulgarity, even though many of their writers reveal both fine taste and moderation in their selection of foods. Notorious gluttons like the emperor Vitellius Aulus might eat four huge meals a day, but many others, like Pliny the Younger (Gaius Plinius Caecilius Secundas), would partake only of meals that were simple and informal. Pliny (1748) condemned a dinner of oysters, sow's innards, and sea urchins while listing his own notion of an evening meal: lettuce, snails, eggs, barley cake, and snow-chilled wine with honey. A dinner described by Martial (Marcus Valerius Martialis) (1993) was rather more elaborate, though he called it modest, and it was served in a single course: a kid with meatballs, chicken, ham, beans, lettuce, and leek, flavored with mint and rocket. Such a sense of a modest, well-balanced meal, with plenty of fresh green vegetables and fruits, would not be found in Britain for another 2,000 years.

The Romans encouraged wine making. They had wines flavored with salt water, resinated wines flavored with myrtle or juniper, and medicated wines mixed with herbs and taken for various ailments. Sweet wines were made by adding honey, rose petals, or citron leaves; spiced wine was made by adding wormwood. By contrast, the Britons continued to drink unhopped beer.

The Early Medieval Period (407 to 1066)

After the Romans departed, sheep, pigs, and goats were the main livestock kept, and cattle were raised as plough and draft beasts. Sheep supplied wool and milk; pigs were economical, as they ate waste and foraged in the woodlands. The rabbits escaped from the *leporaria* and died out in the wild, as did the guinea fowl and the peacocks. But hens and geese were still kept by some for their eggs and flesh, although wild birds were the only kinds available to the majority of people. Fowlers hunted birds with nets, snares, birdlime, traps, and hawks, and falconry became the sport of kings.

Germanic tribesmen added ale to the alcoholic beverages of Britain. Ale is a drink made from fermented barley or wheat, and alehouses sprang up in every village and hamlet. The beer of Britain tended to be sweeter and darker, whereas ale could be both light and mild. Mead, however, remained the drink of the elite.

After the rites of the Catholic church had taken hold in Britain (by the sixth century A.D.), fast days numbered half of the year and, later on, even more than half. This encouraged fishing, which had declined under the Germanic settlers, who were mainly farmers. But now fishermen had larger boats and longer lines and could venture farther out to sea. Drift nets grew larger, so that shoals of herrings might be caught, and the herring industry on the east coast of Britain had become important to the economy by the time of the Norman conquest in 1066. Stranded whales belonged to the Crown, but except for the tongue (thought to be a delicacy), they were generally granted to the tenant who owned that piece of shoreline. Whale meat was salted and preserved for Lenten food.

The use of olive oil disappeared with the Romans to be replaced with butter (much of it made from ewes' milk), which found its way into all cooking. The majority of the population lived, as they always had, on daily pottage, which was a stew of cereal grains with green leaves and herbs (generally orache, cabbage, or wild beet) flavored with thyme, rosemary, and onion. The starches in the cereal thickened the stew, but a richer meal was made by adding fat from a carcass or animal bones. Plants with seeds that have a high oil content were particularly treasured, and linseed was eaten extensively in rural communities from prehistory until very recently.

The seasons dramatically influenced what people could eat. Winter was a time of scarcity. From November to April there was no pasture, and the little hay that could be cut had to be saved for the draft animals, the warhorses, and the breeding stock. Thus, most of the animals were slaughtered before the winter began. The slaughter of hogs began in September, whereas cows were killed for the Feast of St. Martin (November 11). On this day all the offal was cooked and eaten, for it could not be preserved (like the carcass meat) by salting, drying, or smoking. Chitterlings, tripe, black puddings, pasties of liver, and dishes of kidneys were all eaten during this feast that was called Yule. Later, the offal was also pickled in spiced ale for a short time to make "'umble pie" for Christmas.

Beginning in the sixth century, the Slavs introduced a new type of plow in Europe, which made it possible to bring new expanses of land under cultivation. It needed six to eight oxen to pull it, but it cut deeply into the soil and turned the furrow over at the same time. One result was that a three-field system of crop rotation came into being; one field was planted with wheat or rye, the second with peas, lentils, or beans, and the third was left fallow. The countryside fed the towns, where people also kept hens, cows, and pigs. The latter are excellent scavengers. They frequented the dark, narrow alleys where the refuse from the houses was discharged; without pigs, the people of medieval towns would have been practically buried under their own sewage and rubbish, especially after those towns began to grow in population. Certainly, epidemics like the plague would have decimated towns and their peoples long before they did.

The Medieval Period (1066 to 1485)

In the thirteenth century, herrings were gutted, salted, then smoked. The industry grew, and a century later, the fish were also salted and packed into barrels. Smoked and pickled herring became a major source of protein for the poor throughout the winter.

Fish played a large role in medieval banquets as well. They were baked in pies, made into shapes or jellies, and large creatures like the porpoise were cooked whole and carved as if they were big roasts. But because of the great number of fast days, the nobles ate three courses of meat - beef or mutton, fowl, and game - on those days when meat was permitted.

The invading Normans brought with them new varieties of apples and pears and other fruits such as peaches, cherries, gooseberries, plums, medlars, and quinces. Returning Crusaders introduced citrus fruits and pomegranates to Britain from the Middle East, though these remained rare and expensive. Dried fruits were imported from the Mediterranean and were considered medicinally better for the body than fresh fruits.

The medieval garden was well stocked with a great variety of herbs and salad plants that appeared in herbals with instructions on what ailments they would cure. Salads were eaten with oil, vinegar, and salt. The earliest salad recipe, from around 1390, called for such plants as parsley, sage, onions, leek, borage, fennel, cress, rosemary, rue, and purslane to be mixed together. Over a hundred herbs are listed as necessary to the garden in a fifteenth-century list.

The Crusaders also brought back with them a great range of spices, along with many ideas about the dishes that they were used in. Meat and fish dishes were flavored with such things as ginger, cinnamon, nutmeg, cloves, and grains of paradise. Indeed, in the thirteenth century, ginger, cinnamon, cloves, galingale, mace, nutmeg, cubebs, coriander, and cumin were listed as occupants of at least one English cupboard. The old Roman trade routes, which began in southern China, the Moluccas, Malaya, and India, and extended to the ports of the eastern Mediterranean, were flourishing again. The Crusaders had discovered sugarcane growing on the plains of Tripoli, and by the end of the eleventh century, sugar had begun creeping into British recipes. Even then, sugar came in the same hard, pyramid-shaped loaves (which had to be scraped or hacked at) that were still around at the beginning of the nineteenth century.

Cider making was introduced to Britain from Normandy in the middle of the twelfth century and, at first, was confined to Kent and Sussex in the southeast. But it soon spread to East Anglia and Yorkshire. If cider was made from pears, it was called "perry." Whey and buttermilk were drunk by peasants. Sweet wines, which became immensely popular, were imported from southern Europe and the eastern Mediterranean, another result of the Crusades. Wines from Crete, southern Italy, Tuscany, Spain, and Provence were also highly valued. Madeira malmsey was exported by the Portuguese after 1421, following the planting of malvasia grapes from Crete.

Wheat was cultivated for the fine white bread of the nobility, whereas barley was grown for brewing. Oats (that withstood both cold and rain) were raised in northern Britain to be used in pottages, porridges, and thick soups. Rye was grown to make bread for the majority, who lived off their daily pottages, supplemented by curd cheese, eggs, and whey. Poaching was a capital offense, as the forests belonged to the king. Nonetheless, much netting of game birds and trapping of deer and boar continued because, for the people, starvation was never far away. If the weather destroyed a harvest, then famine was likely that winter. Beginning around 1315, at the start of the Little Ice Age (caused by an advance of polar and alpine glaciers that lasted until 1700), Britain suffered years of famine that brought on revolts and rebellion (Tuchman 1978).

Cheese was made from the milk of goats, ewes, and cows, sometimes mixed together, at other times separated to make particular cheeses. Milk was seldom drunk fresh; the nobility thought it was unhealthy as it curdled in the stomach. Besides, the popularity of butter, cheese, whey, curds, cream, and buttermilk was such that fresh milk was thought too valuable to be used simply for drinking. In the summer, strawberries and cream constituted a rural banquet. Drinks called possets were fashioned with milk curdled by ale. Often flavored with fruits and honey, possets could also be drained and made into a dessert to be cut into slices.

Fast days provoked much ingenuity (among the rich) in replacing forbidden foods with alternative concoctions. Almond milk, an expensive substitute for cows' milk, was curdled, pressed, drained, and transformed into cream cheese. Eggs were modeled from fish roe, and ham and bacon were made from salmon masquerading as lean meat, with pike as the fat (Wheaton 1985). St. Thomas Aquinas, at one point, stipulated that chickens were aquatic in origin; therefore, because they counted as fish, they could be eaten on fast days. At rich monasteries, rabbits were bred for their embryos, as these did not count as meat either.

Those who could afford it ate from "trenchers," which were thick slices of coarse rye and wheat bread with a little of the center scooped out. "After the meal, these were collected and given to the poor. During a meal, the nobility used several trenchers, made from a better class of bread. Much of the meat consumed by the rich came from hunting, and so a great variety of fresh game could be eaten throughout the winter. In addition to wild boar and deer, there were also birds, ranging from herons, swans, and peacocks to curlews, partridges, pigeons, quail, snipe, and woodcocks.

Medieval feasts could be as elaborate as those of Roman times. Illustrative is the banquet of three courses given upon the coronation of Henry IV in 1399. The first course had 10 different dishes: slices of meat, cooked in a spiced sweet-and-sour sauce; a puree of rice and mulberries, sweetened with honey and flavored with wine and spices; a boar's head; baby swans; a capon; pheasants; herons; and a pie made from cream, eggs, dates, prunes, and sugar. Then the "subtlety," a highly decorated dish of pastry, jelly, almond paste, and sugar, was brought in to indicate the end of the first course.

A second course, of nine dishes, comprised venison, calf's-foot jelly, stuffed suckling pigs, peacocks, cranes, rabbits, pies, chickens, and fritters. Another subtlety was followed by the third course of 16 dishes, which included a lot of small game birds as well as jellied eggs and custard tarts. What is interesting about medieval menus is the similarity of the courses. There was no sense of a first course being an appetizer to whet the palate or of the last course being something to refresh or pacify the diner. Those ideas were lost with the Romans, and it was many centuries before they returned. Meanwhile, simple gluttony and gorging prevailed.

Pie makers were familiar figures in medieval England. The pie was a development of the Roman idea of using a flour and water paste to seal the cooked juices of a piece of meat. But because in England butter and lard were mixed in with the flour, it was possible to make a free-standing paste container that could be packed full of a mixture of meat, game, fish, and vegetables. In 1378, a special ordinance of Richard II regulated the prices cooks and pie bakers in London could charge for their roasted and baked meats (Wilson 1973).

Except for the peasants, who still gathered much wild food, people did not eat many vegetables, which were believed to be sources of disease, especially when raw. *The Book of Keruynge* (1508), for example, warned its readers to "beware of green sallettes." But onions, leeks, garlic, and cabbage were thought not to be harmful so long as they were cooked thoroughly. This was usually the case after stewing for long hours with meat or carcass bones to make soup.

Craftsmen and workers in the towns enjoyed a better diet than peasants in the countryside. An act passed in 1363 ordered that servants of noblemen, as well as artisans and tradesmen, were to have meat or fish once a day, as well as milk and cheese. Breakfast was bread and ale, with possibly some pickled herrings or cheese. A midday meal bought at a tavern or cookshop could be roast meat, stew or soup, bread, cheese, and ale. Supper was bread and cheese again, perhaps with cold meats, and ale or wine. The law's concern with the welfare of servants was a direct result of the Black Death, which had severely pruned the population, making the survivors substantially more valuable.

In the few decades that came before the onset of the plague, however, a rise in population outpaced agricultural production, which meant overpopulation, undernutrition, and a people more vulnerable to disease. Agricultural methods and tools had not advanced for 800 years; the clearing of productive land had been pushed to its limits, and poor soils could not be made more productive nor crop yields raised. When the plague appeared, in 1348, people starved by the thousands, and the peasantry bore the brunt. The chronicler Henry Knighton, canon of Leicester Abbey, reported 5,000 dead in one field alone, "their bodies so corrupted by the plague that neither beast nor bird would touch them" (Tuchman 1978: 103). Fields went uncultivated, seeds were unsown, dikes crumbled, and salt water soured the land. "So few servants and labourers were left," wrote Knighton, "that no one knew where to turn for help."

The plague killed 40 percent of Europe's population by 1380 and halved it by the end of the century. Yet as with servants, the catastrophic event improved the lives of those peasants who survived. Landowners reduced rents and sometimes even forgave them altogether. The acreage sowed in grain 30 years after the onset of the plague was only half what it had been before the calamity. But the plague did mean that some peasants became tenant farmers, and the size of their holdings continued to grow in ensuing centuries.

Tudor, Elizabethan, and Stuart England (1485 to 1688)

Many of the foods and dishes eaten during the Middle Ages remained popular into the sixteenth and seventeenth centuries. Although new and exotic American foodstuffs could be obtained, many of these took centuries to become part of the diet. An exception was the turkey, which had found its place upon English tables by the 1540s. However, potatoes, tomatoes, peppers, and haricot beans took 200 years or more before they were ever eaten, except as rare, exotic ingredients on the tables of the wealthy.

As Iberian sugar production on islands off Africa and in the Americas increased, the national consumption of sugar rose. Queen Elizabeth was inordinately fond of sweetmeats, and the wealthy all suffered from tooth decay. Sugar was used to make the most intricate shapes and sculptures for banquets. Birds, beasts, and fruits were contrived from spun sugar, placed in baskets of marzipan, and sometimes made even more lifelike by painting and gilding.

Hunting – still the most popular pastime of the nobility – also provided occasions for ornate al fresco breakfast banquets. The gentry ate dinner at 11:00 in the morning and supper between 5:00 and 6:00 in the evening. Meals were now served on plates, and trenchers were unknown, although they lived on in the practice of serving cubes of bread beneath boiled or stewed meats. Potteries producing tin-glazed earthenware were established in Norwich and London at the end of the sixteenth century by Andries and Jacob Jansen from Antwerp (Peter Brears, in Black 1993), and glass became fashionable for drinking vessels, although silver and gold cups remained popular with the nobility.

An act of Parliament in 1548 made Saturday a fish day so as to encourage both shipbuilding and fishing. The English fishing fleet on the east coast was in constant competition with the Dutch, who fished openly in England's coastal waters and sold their catch in English ports. Salted fish was never very popular in Britain, and more effort was made to bring in fresh fish for sale. Shellfish remained the most popular seafoods; lobsters, crabs, shrimps, and prawns were boiled and eaten cold, and sometimes lobsters were boiled, then wrapped in brine-soaked rags and kept for a few months buried in sand. Oysters were eaten both fresh and pickled in vinegar. Anchovies from the Mediterranean became increasingly popular; pickled in brine, they served as appetizers before meals and were added to meat and fish dishes for flavor. Fish pies were a common dish in Lenten fare. These were filled with a mixture of herrings, salmon, eels, and sturgeon and made with butter, egg yolks, spices, and dried fruits. There were various recipes for an Elizabethan fish-day salad that usually included herbs and periwinkles, along with white endive and alexander buds, with whelks to garnish the whole.

Local cheeses became widely known through the popularity of cheese fairs that were visited by merchants, factors, and peddlers, who bought cheeses for resale elsewhere. The best were selected for the rich. Highly thought of were Banbury and Cheshire cheeses, in which, it was said, neither the rennet nor the salt could be tasted. Cheeses were also imported from abroad; Parmesan was the most popular, although Dutch cheeses were also appreciated.

In the seventeenth century, a much greater range of salad plants were grown in the walled gardens of the great estates. John Evelyn (1620–1706), in his *Acetaria, a Discourse on Sallets,* enthused over the health-giving properties of the "Herby-Diet." Yet vegetables were still frowned upon by the majority of people, with the lack of fresh vegetables in the diet evidenced by the prominence of scurvy. Gideon Harvey, physician to Charles II, spoke of it in 1675 as the "Disease of London" (Spencer 1993: 214).

Distillation of plant juices became a public activity following the dissolution of the monasteries, as monks found new vocations as apothecaries and distillers, and English soldiers, returning from the Dutch wars, spread the popularity of strong liquors. Nonetheless, beer and ale remained the most popular beverages.

Early Modern England: The Agricultural Revolution (1688–1750)

Farming technology had progressed little between the sixth and eighteenth centuries. Because there was no winter pasture, the animals were still killed at the beginning of winter. But new ways of feeding cattle began to change this situation. It was discovered that cattle could be fattened very nicely on turnips, and a manual, *The Practical Farmer* by William Ellis (1732), advised giving cattle rapeseed cakes and turnips for winter provision, as was done in Holland. There, it had been discovered that cattle would thrive on the residue left after the oil (used for lighting) had been pressed from crushed rapeseed. Later, other vegetables, such as swedes, mangelwurzels, clover, and cabbages, were also used for winter cattle feeding.

At the same time, more efficient farm tools were being invented. Jethro Tull devised the first horse-drawn hoe and field drill, which wasted less seed and allowed more grain to be harvested. Farm tools were now made of cast iron and could be mass produced; the Rotherham plow was invented, and the first threshing machine appeared before 1800. Other machines were designed that could prepare animal feed, chop turnips, and cut chaff. Because animals could at last be maintained throughout the winter, those with the most valuable traits could be retained and used to breed in the spring. Robert Blackwell (1725–95), a Derbyshire breeder, introduced the longhorn, a cow that gave a high milk yield, and John Ellman (1755–1832) introduced a new breed of sheep, the Southdown, that fattened in half the time of other breeds. The growing size of animals not only increased yields of carcass meat and milk but also ensured finer-quality fleece from sheep and more hide from cows.

At the end of the seventeenth century came the creation of the Norfolk four-course system, whereby wheat was grown in the first year, turnips in the second, then barley with clover and ryegrass undersown in the third. In the fourth year the clover and ryegrass were either cut or used for grazing.

With this new farming technology came a need for larger fields, unimpeded by hedges. Gradually, the common land, where farmworkers traditionally had kept a cow, a pig, and a few hens, and where they gathered wood for cooking fires, was removed from public use by a series of Enclosures Acts. In the reign of George III (1760–1820) alone, 3 million acres of common land were added to private farming estates, hindering the ability of thousands of farmworkers to feed their families. Many emigrated to America, whereas others went into the factories in the new and burgeoning industrial cities.

The effect of the Enclosures Acts was far-reaching. Rural life was radically altered and partially destroyed, and whole villages were abandoned. Within a generation, cooking skills and traditional recipes were lost forever, as the creative interrelationship between soil and table (the source of all good cuisine) had been severed.

From then on, the diet of the workers rapidly declined, although in the north of England the potato had, at last, been accepted. In the south, wheat, the source of fashionable white bread, had taken over the land. A farm laborer with a wife and four children averaged £46 in annual earnings, but the cost of the same family's food amounted to £52 a year. Each week, such a family typically consumed 8 loaves of bread, 2 pounds of cheese, 2 pounds of butter, 2 ounces of tea, a half-pound of boiled bacon, and 2 pints of milk. By contrast, dinner for a late-eighteenth-century middle-class family of six has been depicted as consisting of three boiled chickens, a haunch of venison, a ham, a flour-and-suet pudding, and beans, followed by gooseberries and apricots (Drummond and Wilbraham 1959). Jonas Hanway, the reformer, said of the poor in Stevenage in 1767: "The food of the poor is good bread, cheese, pease and turnips in winter with a little pork or other meat, when they can afford it; but from the high price of meat, it has not lately been within their reach. As to milk, they have hardly sufficient for their use" (Drummond and Wilbraham 1959: 208).

The eighteenth century, however, was one in which vast amounts of meat were eaten by those who could afford it. Sydney Smith, canon of St. Paul's Cathedral, calculated that during his 77 years, he had consumed 44 wagonloads of meat and drink, which had starved to death fully 100 persons. In Smith's letters, and in Parson James Woodforde's diaries, accounts of meals are laden with meats: game, fowl, cold tongue and hams, roasted sweetbreads, giblet soup, pigeons, veal, and marrow sauces. Obesity was caricatured by artists like William Hogarth and Thomas Rowlandson, and huge weights, up to 40 stone (about 560 pounds), were attained by some people. Among meat eaters, meat consumption averaged about 147 pounds per person annually, about the per capita amount eaten today in the United States.

Throughout the century, market gardens had been started around growing cities and towns. London had gardens at Lewisham, Blackheath, Wanstead, and Ilford. A vegetable market at Liverpool arose because an influx of French Canadians wanted cheap vegetables for their soups. Most vegetables, however, were of poor quality and little variety (cabbages, carrots, spinach, sprouts, and turnips), although special vegetables were still grown in the walled gardens of great estates. Unfortunately, eighteenth-century practices of hygiene were not very advanced, and many of the barges that brought fruit and vegetables to the city of London took away the contents of the city's cesspits on their return journey.

Not only did overeating typify the times, so did an excess of fats used in cooking. Hannah Glasse (1971: 5) commented in her cookery book: "I have heard of a cook that used six pounds of butter to fry twelve eggs, when everybody knows (that understands cooking) that half a pound is full enough." Fashionable food centered around huge pies made from turkey and swan, or mixtures of game with veal, sweetbreads, mushrooms, and potatoes. Dr. Samuel Johnson's favorite dinner was "a leg of pork boiled till it dropped from the bone, a veal pie with plums and sugar and the outside cut of a salt buttock of beef" (Pullar 1970: 170).

Beer and ale remained the most popular drinks in Britain until the beginning of the eighteenth century, when home-brewed distilled spirits took over. Dutch *genever*, or gin, had begun to appear in England as early as Stuart times, and ginlike liquors, flavored with juniper berries, were made from beer dregs, lees of wine or cider, and soaked dried fruits. With the addition of extra yeast, large quantities of spirit could be distilled from any of these mixtures. Molasses fermented with barm (the yeasty froth on fermenting malt liquors) made a crude rum, and "grains of paradise" made the spirits hot and fiery in the mouth. British brandy was a spirit drawn from newly fermented barley malt.

Dutch-cultivated coffee beans spread from East Indian colonies to the West Indies and then to England. Coffeehouses became fashionable places to meet and gossip, and coffee was taken up by the nobility. It grew in popularity until the Georgian era, when tea began to compete with it. Drinking chocolate was perhaps not quite as popular, as the manner of making it was a chore. Cocoa beans were exported to England, where they were dried, peeled, and powdered. Next, sugar, cinnamon, vanilla, nutmeg, and ambergris were added, and then the mixture was rolled, made into cakes, and cast into molds. It was these cakes that had to be scraped and grated for use in drinks and puddings.

The foods eaten by the majority (the working and lower-middle classes) were all either grown locally or preserved by pickling and smoking. Jane Austen's father – a modest country clergyman – farmed a smallholding where he kept cows, pigs, and sheep and grew wheat for making bread. His wife kept fowl and looked after the vegetables, herb garden, and orchard. She taught her daughters how to supervise the making of butter, cheese, preserves, pickles, and homemade wines, as well as how to brew beer and cure bacon and hams (Black 1993). But such a life and its lessons were lost as the century grew older, the towns larger, and the world smaller.

Later Modern England: The Industrial Revolution (1700 to 1900)

As more and more factories were built for the mass production of goods, so towns and cities grew to serve the factories. The population of London quadrupled in the nineteenth century. In 1800, Manchester had 75,000 inhabitants; some 50 years later, there were 400,000. Social reformers were astonished that although riches grew and a new bourgeoisie of affluence appeared, the most abject poverty afflicted the majority of workers. Potatoes, bread, and tea constituted the main diet of the poor; about once a week there was some milk and sugar and, perhaps once a year, a piece of bacon. Almost half of the children born in towns died before they were 5 years old, whereas those who survived were severely undernourished, low in stature, physically weak, and frequently grew up deformed by rickets.

Nearly all food was adulterated with illegal additions to make it stretch further. Alum was added to bleach flour for white bread; various drugs and flavorings, even sulfuric acid, were put into hops. The leaves of ash, sloe, and elder were mixed into tea. Copper was used to color pickles green, red lead colored the rind of Gloucester cheese, and coffee contained roasted corn and red ocher.

The growing, well-off middle class in the towns and cities did not possess large estates, as the old landed gentry still did, which meant that the middle classes owned no source of natural foods. Thus, the nineteenth century produced the modern grocer, and railroads made it possible for milk and produce from the country to be delivered to the center of any great metropolis. Steam trawlers replaced sailing boats, and the railways also carried fresh fish, well-chilled in ice, to inland areas. Cod became commonplace, and the first fish-and-chips shops opened. The invention of bottling and canning methods of food preservation put many cheaper items onto grocers' shelves, where bottled sauces, along with canned foods – vegetables, meats, fish, and fruits – were now essential provisions. Aberdeen, although 515 miles away, became the abattoir of London because of the ability to send carcasses overnight by rail. The world had become one huge food market. After 1880, Australian beef could be sent by sea in refrigerated ships. Tea from India was no longer expensive, nor was wheat from America; hence, not only was a greater range of cheaper food now available, but much of it was packaged beguilingly, with certain brand names becoming household words.

The middle-class Victorian housewife had most of her fresh foods delivered. The baker, muffin man, and milkman made their rounds daily. The fishmonger brought cod, hake, salmon, skate, eels, herring, and shellfish; the greengrocer called with a wide range of seasonal vegetables delivered to him early from the market gardens. If a housewife left her basement kitchen to shop, it was only to buy from the butcher and the poulterer. Veal was the cheapest meat; calf's-feet jelly and a pig's-head brawn would both be appreciated by the family. Capons and pheasants were thought of as party dishes, and small game birds were kept to be served as savories (Black 1993).

A German chemist, Justus von Liebig, helped increase food production with his advocacy of artificial fertilizers at the same time that his research in nutrition attempted to classify foods scientifically. His main discovery in this endeavor was that of the food chain – the interdependence of plants and animals – and his research into plant nutrients led to his identification of protein, which resulted, during the next century, in fundamental changes in the ways that food was thought of, grown, and eaten.

The diet of the poor, however, did not improve; their wages were still low and malnutrition was widespread. In 1847, the Vegetarian Society was founded in the midst of industrial Britain. It was very much a social reforming movement, dedicated to temperance and the improvement of the working classes. Vegetarianism also flourished for a time among members of the affluent middle classes, who saw themselves as social reformers. They were shocked at the inadequacy of the diets of working people. Bread and jam (with the jam made from colored, sweetened fruit or vegetable pulp) was all that some children ate throughout the day. This scandal was at last drawn to the government's attention when cannon fodder was needed; in the enlistment for the Boer War (1899–1902), it was discovered that 37 percent of the volunteers were so unfit for service that they had to be invalided out.

The Twentieth Century

British society and its food did not change until after the end of World War I (1914–18). The postwar period was one of intense trading and competition in the world market. For the first time, people could eat tropical fruits (imported from the East) in winter; shipments of chilled apples and pears came all the way from New Zealand. Canada, Australia, and the Argentine grew wheat and exported it to Britain, and

in addition to fruits, butter and lamb from New Zealand competed with Danish butter, eggs, and bacon. But the British farmer, too, had to compete with these cheaper imports.

More foods were now packaged under brand names that soon became familiar, and consumers grew to expect an improved quality of service from retailers and food producers. Many of the household cooking chores had already been eliminated, as much of the food – custard, blancmange, jellies, gravy, and porridge – now came out of packages. Breakfast revolved around corn flakes or other cereal products, and the range of canned foods included not only soups but salmon, corned beef, vegetables, fruits like pineapple, and even game birds and condensed milk. Many of the favorite dishes for special occasions might come from a variety of containers, which was a boon for many, as servants were rapidly becoming nonexistent, except in extremely wealthy households. Food retailing in Britain in the 1930s absorbed nearly one-third of the national income.

What consumers failed to realize was that many additives entered these new foods. Food manufacturers added preservatives and improvers – anticaking agents to stop flour, milk, salt, and sugar from forming lumps; emulsifying agents, to blend substances that tended to separate; sequestrants, to keep fats from going rancid – none of which were disclosed on the labels.

Evidence of vitamins and how they contribute to health was published in 1911, and the subject, from then on, was never far from the public eye. It was gradually realized that afflictions like pellagra, rickets, scurvy, and beriberi, once believed to be contagious, were actually the result of deficiencies in vital elements of the diet. Of course, some of the new knowledge required generations to take hold. For example, the idea that brown flour, which contained all the bran and minerals, was more healthful than white flour was first mooted in the last quarter of the nineteenth century but required a full hundred years to be accepted.

In 1914, as in the Boer War, it was once more noted that volunteers for the armed services were grossly undernourished, and at last, the government took action by stressing the importance of the health of munitions workers and the importance of adequate nutrition to the workforce as a whole. By the end of World War I, a thousand industrial canteens were supplying a million meals a day, and workers in British industry, now for the first time had hot, well-cooked meals at reasonable prices (Burnett 1966).

By the time of World War II (1939–45), the government was far better prepared than before to ration food while increasing its production. A Food (Defence Plans) Department had been set up in 1936, but in 1939 Britain was only 30 percent self-sufficient in food compared with 86 percent for Germany. Rationing, however, was begun immediately because all the details had been worked out and the ration books printed. The science of nutrition was now so advanced that the nation's diet could be planned informatively and wisely. Food technology, it was also seen, could play a vital part in economizing on shipping space by dehydrating vegetables, drying eggs and bananas, importing boneless meat, and compressing carcasses. A good example is "Spam" – the bane of the wartime kitchen. A Food Advice Division was set up to give nutrition information to the public through radio and newspapers.

Britain rationed meat, bacon, cheese, fats, sugar, and preserves on a per person basis. Bread was brown, and vitamins A and D were added to margarine. Additional proteins, vitamins, and minerals were given to small children and to pregnant or nursing mothers. Communal feeding grew in importance; firms employing more than 250 people were required to provide a canteen service, and school canteens began to ensure that all children had at least one well-balanced meal a day. British restaurants in the blitzed areas provided hot, cheap, nutritious meals to the general public and grew to number 2,000 in 1943.

Millions of people "dug for victory." Flower beds and lawns gave way to vegetable gardens. A great amount of potatoes was eaten, and the consumption of green vegetables and fresh fruit also increased. Throughout the war, there was a decline in infant mortality, and the general health of children improved. On average, they were taller and heavier, and for the first time in British history, the poorest third of the population was eating an adequate and balanced diet. In fact, the British diet has never been more healthful, before or since the war, however much the people complained. They were then consuming a great deal more fiber, much less sugar and refined flours, little meat, and more fresh fruit and vegetables. The war encouraged people to go into the woods and hedgerows to harvest wild foods, to make jams out of sloes and rose hips, and to gather fungi, wild herbs, and greens for flavoring.

Rationing continued until 1953, and for a time there was even less food available than during the war. Women had tasted independence during the war years, and they were not always prepared to return to full-time domesticity. There was a move for women to go out to work, and to encourage this, there was a growth in domestic technology. From the mid-1950s onward, certain trends are noticeable. Less food was bought for home consumption, meals were smaller and lighter, and there was a growing demand for "convenience foods." This was a new concept: processed foods that are labor-saving because they can be prepared and brought to the table in only a few minutes. In this category, the greatest rise in consumption has been in quick-frozen foods (Burnett 1966), followed by precooked chilled dishes and microwave meals.

Such a change in diet would not have been possible had it not been for a postwar revolution in farming methods throughout the world, occurring on a scale far greater than that of the previous agricultural revolution in the eighteenth century. Intensive factory farming was an idea explored because of the rigors of wartime rationing and the fear that there would not be enough protein for a growing world population. Various factors coming together in the 1950s allowed for new methods. First, there was research in cellular growth and DNA, so that natural hormones could be extracted from livestock, then used to stimulate desired characteristics. Second, the ability was enhanced for chemical companies to research and produce a varied range of drugs, including antibiotics, that allowed farmers to keep greater numbers of animals than ever envisioned before. And third, new building technology could provide cheap housing units for animals, with concrete stalls and automatic feeders and timers that made controlled feeding, watering, and lighting feasible. One result was that fewer and fewer stockmen were needed on the farm to watch over and care for the animals.

Also in the 1950s, agriculture began to spawn a vast number of different but interdependent industries engaged in the development of new equipment, fertilizers, and seeds, as well as new techniques and products for the storage, processing, and preservation of foods. As a consequence, heavily mechanized farms with computer technology made farmers more and more dependent on a host of suppliers. A farmer might often be unable to make a choice on the way he reared his livestock because of the rules laid down by a particular supplier. Large companies, such as those of the pharmaceutical industry, were financing farming with millions of pounds of capital, which meant that the farmer was controlled from a remote city office. Agriculture had become a highly sophisticated energy-intensive system for transforming one series of industrial products into another series of industrial products that just happened to be edible (George 1986).

Selective breeding of livestock also became a new skill, and improvements in the control of selective breeding are certain to continue in the future. But this development also means that we lose genetic diversity (21 British cattle breeds have become extinct since the beginning of the twentieth century). When one bull can sire over a quarter of a million offspring, it allows for enormous inbreeding, which can reveal hitherto unsuspected defects (Johnson 1991). One of the drawbacks for the consumer with these new methods of rearing livestock is that a lack of exercise, combined with a rich protein diet, produces a carcass high in saturated fats. There is also a wide belief that food produced in such a way has less flavor than when natural rearing and feeding is employed. Fully 63 percent of housewives in Britain in the 1980s felt that food had less flavor than it did 20 years earlier (Johnson 1991).

This sense that basic English foods have become

blander (Johnson 1991) may partly explain the great popularity of ethnic foods and restaurants. Since the 1950s, Chinese, Indian, Cypriot, Thai, and Mexican restaurants have grown up throughout the towns and cities of Britain. No doubt, the willingness to try new foods was encouraged by postwar travel, although packaged holidays in the popular cheaper resorts of Europe now cater to the most conservative of British tastes with fish and chips, roast beef, and Yorkshire pudding. Popular food is also controlled by American companies that produce hamburgers, fried chicken, and the like. This is poor food nutritionally, with a high amount of saturated fat; nonetheless, it symbolizes the American way of life, and by consuming fast food, the eater becomes a part of that way of life. Indeed, this demonstrates how atavistic food consumption still is and how little it has changed from the days of prehistory, when to eat the meat of an ox meant that one was hoping to attain the strength of oxen.

In reaction to factory farming, to the widespread exploitation of animals, and to the high amount of saturated fat in the British diet, the vegetarian movement has grown in the last 40 years. In 1945, there were 100,000 vegetarians in Britain; by the 1990s there were 3 million, the number having doubled during the 1980s. Moreover, 40 percent of British people have reduced their consumption of red meat or entirely eliminated it from their diets (Spencer 1993).

Because of the worldwide market, there is now a far greater range of food available to more people than ever before in history. Yet the diet of the majority tends to be high in refined carbohydrates, sugars, and salt and relies on convenience foods, which lack the fiber and essential vitamins and minerals provided by fresh vegetables and fruits. Food has become blander and more stereotyped over the last 30 years, and the divide between rich and poor has not gotten any smaller. In fact, with a doubling of the population predicted within the next 40 years, it can only grow wider.

Colin Spencer

Bibliography

Ayrton, Elizabeth. 1974. *The cookery of England.* Harmondsworth, England.
Black, Maggie. 1993. *A taste of history.* London.
Burnett, John. 1966. *Plenty and want.* London.
Drummond, J. C., and Anne Wilbraham. 1959, new edition 1991. *The Englishman's food.* London.
George, Susan. 1986. *How the other half dies.* London.
Glasse, Hannah. [1796] 1971. *The art of cookery made plain and easy.* Hamden, Conn.
Johnson, Andrew. 1991. *Factory farming.* Oxford U.K., and Cambridge, Mass.
Martial. 1993. *Epigrams,* ed. and trans. D. R. Shackleton. 3 vols. Cambridge, Mass.

Pliny the Younger. 1748. *Correspondence,* trans. William Melmoth. 2 vols. Dublin.
Pullar, Phillipa. 1970. *Consuming passions: A history of English food and appetite.* London.
Spencer, Colin. 1993. *The heretic's feast: A history of vegetarianism.* London.
Tannahill, Reay. 1973. *Food in history.* New York.
Tuchman, Barbara W. 1978. *A distant mirror: The calamitous 14th century.* New York.
Wheaton, Barbara Ketcham. 1983. *Savouring the past.* London.
Wilson, C. Anne. 1973. *Food and drink in Britain.* Harmondsworth, England.

V.C.5 Northern Europe – Germany and Surrounding Regions

The majority of foods found in modern northern Europe – which includes the lands around the North Sea and the Baltic Sea and those of northern Alpine region – are not indigenous to the area. It is here, however, that one of the most stable of humankind's agricultural systems was established, and one that has proved capable of providing densely populated areas with a high standard of living. Such an agricultural bounty has helped northern Europe to become one of the most prosperous areas of the world.

The Paleolithic Period

The northern European environment underwent drastic change several times during the Pleistocene. Glaciers coming from Scandinavia and the Alps covered a large part of the landscape with glacigenic sediment several times during the Ice Age. Forests retreated from northern Europe and were replaced by a type of vegetation that can be regarded as a mixture of those of tundra and steppe. In this environment, forest-adapted herbivores were replaced by large grazing species such as caribou *(Rangifer tarandus),* wild horse *(Equus* sp.), and mammoth *(Mammonteus primigenius).* These species, associated in small or bigger herds, migrated from the north to the south and vice versa in a yearly cycle. In summer they fled north from the multitude of biting insects (to Jutland, for example), and in winter they were attracted by the somewhat higher temperatures in areas of the south, such as that just north of the Alps.

Reindeer herds proved to be a very good source of food for Paleolithic reindeer hunters, whose widespread presence in northern Europe is well established by excavations. The hunters migrated with the herds from the south to the north and back again. Prehistoric humans located their temporary dwelling places so as to achieve a maximum vantage point – usually so they could hunt downhill using their lances and bows or a kind of harpoon made of stone and bone material (Bandi 1968: 107–12; Kuhn-Schnyder 1968: 43–68; Rust 1972: 19–20, 65–9).

Although the archaeological evidence for hunting is very clear, hunters doubtless also gathered wild plants. The latter, however, is very difficult to demonstrate, as it is rarely possible to find plant material, such as fruits and seeds, preserved in the layers of Paleolithic camp excavations.

During the late glacial period, trees from the south colonized northern Europe so thoroughly that the landscape was nearly totally forested. Unfortunately, we know little about human nutrition following the return of forested conditions to northern Europe. Reindeer and other steppe-tundra fauna became locally extinct in the newly forested regions.

The Mesolithic Period

There is clearer evidence for human nutrition at the beginning of the postglacial period (the interglacial hiatus in which we live), approximately 11,000 years ago. Following the retreat of the Würmian glaciers, forests again established themselves in most parts of northern Europe to the extent that these landscapes became unsuitable for reindeer and other large herd herbivores. The reindeer herds retreated to those parts where tundra was established: northern Scandinavia, northern Finland, and northern Russia. It is only in these regions that a "Paleolithic way of life" has remained possible up to the present day, because the relationship between reindeer herds and hunters has remained as in millennia before. In the unforested region of the extreme north it is also still possible to practice Paleolithic hunting methods, as exemplified by the Laplanders and Inuit.

In most landscapes of northern Europe, however, hunting methods and nutrition changed, reflecting the changing environment. The forests were invaded by smaller and less frequent solitary woodland fauna, such as red deer *(Cervus elaphus)*, boar *(Sus scrofa)*, and badger *(Meles)*. These species are difficult to hunt in dense forests, and they do not provide a large meat yield. Changes in the vegetational environment were reflected in the hunter's tool kit. Long-range projectile weapons, for example, cannot be used in a wooded landscape. Smaller hunting tools constructed from "microliths" (typical archaeological remnants of the Mesolithic period) were better suited to the vegetation and woodland prey (Wyss 1968–71, 3: 123–44).

Life during the Mesolithic was perhaps harder than during the Paleolithic. It was more difficult to hunt an animal in a wooded landscape, and thus meat was certainly not available all the time. Possibly the plant component of the diet became more important during the Mesolithic. For example, at the very few Mesolithic dwelling places that have been examined by environmental archaeologists, there is evidence of the use of hazelnuts *(Corylus avellana)* (Vaughan 1987: 233–8).

During the Mesolithic, hazelnut bushes spread rapidly to many parts of Europe, as evidenced by pollen diagrams. This is in contrast to the vegetation development of the earlier interglacials. Hazelnuts are heavy, with low dispersal rates, so that it is very unlikely that the plant diffused unaided to all parts of northern Europe at the same time. Instead, it has often been assumed that hazelnuts were culturally dispersed by Mesolithic peoples (Firbas 1949: 149; Smith 1970: 81–96). Indeed, the distribution of these nuts is recorded by pollen analysis in the Mesolithic layer of Hohen Viecheln at the border of Lake Schwerin in northern Germany (Schmitz 1961: 29).

Most likely the expansion of hazelnut distribution was due to the nuts' chance spread during the preparation of "hazelnut meals" by migratory Mesolithic people. Most of the other wild fruits available in the present-day northern European woodlands are not archaeologically recorded for the Mesolithic, nor for the Neolithic period, which has been much more intensively examined by environmental archaeologists. Thus, it is unlikely that strawberries, wild apples, and pears, for example, contributed to human nutrition during the Mesolithic (Küster 1986: 437).

The Neolithic Period

The transition from the Mesolithic to the Neolithic has often been regarded as a revolution by northern European archaeologists (Childe 1956: 66–104). But the Mesolithic–Neolithic transition, with its change from a hunter–gatherer community to a sedentary food-producing farming community, was not a revolution in other parts of the world such as the Near East. In these areas a gradual evolution can be traced from the one stage to the other. In contrast, the transition from hunting and gathering to farming in northern Europe seems to have indeed been a revolutionary process, in which none of the nutritional mainstays of the Mesolithic was incorporated into the Neolithic food-production system.

Rather, all wild elements of the new farming system had been previously cultivated or domesticated elsewhere, mainly in the Near East. Both domesticated animals and cultivated crops were introduced into northern Europe, primarily from the Near East, and were, therefore, exotic elements at the beginning of the Neolithic. Near East domesticates, such as cattle *(Bos primigenius f. taurus)*, goats *(Capra aegagrus f. hircus)*, sheep *(Ovis ammon f. aries)*, and pigs *(Sus scrofa f. domestica)* were introduced into many parts of northern Europe during the Neolithic.

Although most had been introduced in the Balkans, only some of the ancient Near Eastern crops became important in Neolithic northern Europe. It is very likely, however, that each component of a well-balanced vegetarian regime (starch from cereal crops, proteins from pulses, and fat from oil plants) was available to all Neolithic settlements in the region.

In most parts of northern Europe, einkorn *(Triticum monococcum)* and emmer *(Triticum dicoccon)* were the predominant cereals during the Neolithic. Both traveled upstream on the Danube River and downstream on the Rhine River from the Balkans to northern Europe. The same expansion route can be traced for peas *(Pisum sativum)* and lentils *(Lens culinaris),* the major pulses of the Neolithic, although at that time lentils had a more extensive distribution. Today, lentil production is restricted by climatic conditions in many parts of northern Europe. Linseed *(Linum usitatissimum)* was the major oil (and also fiber) crop (Knörzer 1991: 190-3; Küster 1991: 180-2). Only in the extreme west - in southwestern Germany, along the Rhine, in the Netherlands, and in some parts of Scandinavia - were different crops apparently grown. Wheat *(Triticum aestivum* and/or *Triticum durum)* and naked barley *(Hordeum vulgare)* cultivation is evidenced in southwestern Germany and Switzerland (Jacomet and Schlichtherle 1984: 153-76; Küster 1991: 180-2), in the Netherlands, and in southwestern Scandinavia. These plants had their origins in the Near East but likely expanded via the Mediterranean and western Europe (Bakels 1982: 11-3). The only crop not of Near Eastern origin found in the Neolithic of northern Europe, the opium poppy *(Papaver somniferum),* most likely arrived from the western Mediterranean. Inside northern Europe, regional differences in agriculture and nutrition are traceable from the early Neolithic onward, making clear the borders between "economic provinces." For example, barley was important from the very beginning in southwestern Germany and the Netherlands but not in Bavaria and the Rhineland. Yet barley did become important later on in areas where it had not been grown during the early Neolithic.

Through agriculture, the northern European landscape was totally changed by humans. The clearing of the earlier wooded landscape caused environmental changes that are not completely understood today. Hunting, fishing, and the gathering of plants were activities still practiced by the early farmers, but the bulk of human nutrition was certainly derived from agricultural products.

Yet the variety of nutriments available in the Neolithic was severely limited. Because there were very few crops, no herbs and spices, and no cultivated fruits, all meals must have tasted very nearly the same, day in and day out, save on those rare occasions when a meat dish was available.

Toward the end of the Neolithic, some Mediterranean flavorings were introduced in northern Europe, but only in those parts that had cultural and economic contacts with Mediterranean areas. Among the imports were parsley *(Petroselinum crispum),* celery *(Apium graveolens* var. *juice),* and dill *(Anethum graveolens),* which reached some areas of southwestern Germany and northern Switzerland to enliven drab fare (Küster 1985; Jacomet 1988). Other spices were employed in the preservation and storage of meats. This importation of Mediterranean spices is the earliest indication we have of some sophistication in food preparation, as well as a gardening culture, in the southern parts of northern Europe. Following the end of the Neolithic, herbs and spices disappear from the record, and there are no remains of such plants in northern Europe in Bronze Age and even Iron Age settlements.

The Bronze Age and Iron Age

After the Neolithic Revolution, the development of northern European agriculture was influenced more by evolutionary than revolutionary processes. Although the people still did not personally participate in the process of domesticating animals and plants, they did continue to import new cultigens and domesticates. The basic diet, however, does not seem to have undergone any dramatic shifts.

Through trial and error, Bronze Age and Iron Age farmers discovered those crops that were best adapted to the environmental conditions of northern Europe. As they did so, einkorn, which provides only a small yield, became less common, whereas emmer, barley, and (from the early Bronze Age onward) spelt *(Triticum spelta)* were increasingly cultivated. Spelt, however, was common only in some regions: at the northern border of the Alps, in Jutland, and in southern Sweden, where it possibly was grown as a winter crop.

As a rule, only two different crops were grown in a settlement, which left such agricultural communities susceptible to crises when one or the other cereal had poor yields. Indeed, it seems likely that at times famine may have been the result of the ecological instability that a farming community relying on the cultivation of just two different crop species can create. And, of course, the crops were not just for human consumption; they also helped to feed the livestock.

During the Bronze Age, the horse *(Equus przewalskii f. caballus)* was domesticated. This probably took place in eastern Europe, but horses were subsequently introduced into northern Europe, where they not only were used for riding, transport, and agriculture but also became an important component of the human diet (Wyss 1971). Unlike other livestock, horses cannot subsist solely on leaf hay; they require special supplemental feed. Thus, it is striking that the introduction of domesticated horses coincided with the expansion of the millets *(Panicum miliaceum* and *Setaria italica)* and the horsebean *(Vicia faba)* into northern Europe. But whereas the impetus for the adoption of these plants may have been the feeding of horses, during the late Bronze and Iron Ages millets and beans doubtless also contributed to human nutrition.

Over time, agricultural methods became more sophisticated, with better ploughs (as metals were increasingly available), bigger fields, the use of better-adapted plants, and concomitant greater yields. But the basic elements of human nutrition remained more or less the same. Cereal crops, pulses, and oil plants still provided the bulk of the daily fare, and milk was plentiful. But meat was eaten only on special occasions, as reflected in hoary rules concerning the consumption of meat that have persisted until today.

Since animals were not hunted every day and only seasonally slaughtered, meat, as a scarce item, became regarded as an important component of banquets. In fact, from ancient times onward a good reason for inviting numerous guests to a banquet was so that the bulk of any meat served was consumed before it became rancid. Because slaughtering was commonly done in autumn, banquets were (and often still are) given in late autumn and around the time of Christmas. By contrast, meat was normally not consumed during the winter and spring months, when people maintained only as many cattle as were necessary for breeding. This period corresponds to the fasting season (Lent) of the Catholic church between Shrove Tuesday and Easter. Lamb was and remains a traditional dish at an Easter banquet, for this was the time of year when an abundance of newborn sheep could be culled from the flock.

The Roman Age

Around the time of the birth of Christ, parts of northern Europe situated southwest of the Rhine and south of the Danube became colonies of the Roman Empire. Within this area, foodstuffs took on an increasingly important role in Roman commerce, with the Rhine serving as an important trading route. Wheat, rice *(Oryza sativa),* and exotic spices were transported downstream to Roman garrisons and to towns in northwestern Germany and the Netherlands. However, colonies not situated near the Rhine, although involved in the trade of spices and wine, did not trade in bulky items such as grain. Thus, in these regions, the Romans had to force the subdued peoples to deliver crops to the towns and settlements where their soldiers and civilians lived.

There were great efforts during Roman times to increase crop yields, which can be seen in the construction of the villa system. Sophisticated agricultural methods were practiced. But ultimately, difficulties in transporting enough food to the Roman soldiers in those parts of the Imperium not accessible by river routes may be one of the reasons for the decline of the Roman Empire in the Danube provinces. By contrast, the area between Cologne and the Netherlands was one of the economically most powerful parts of the Imperium even in the late Roman age.

Outside of the Roman Empire, some improvement of agricultural methods also took place. Rye *(Secale cereale)* and oats *(Avena sativa)* were grown as additional crops, certainly enlarging and stabilizing of the food supply and possibly enabling the local farmers to export crops to Roman towns. Yet despite the influence of Roman commerce and the presence of trade routes in the area, the peasant diet, at least, seems to have been similar to that of prehistoric times.

The inhabitants of towns and garrisons, by contrast, enjoyed considerably more variety in viands. Those who had the ability bought many different spices at market, and cultivated fruits became available. In fact, the oldest fruit-tree groves and vineyards in northern Europe date from the Roman Age. The basic requirement for these was the stability that Roman rule brought to settlements. Prehistoric settlements had lasted for only a few decades at the most – not long enough for the fruits of groves and vines to appear in any abundance.

The Middle Ages

Many of the Roman trade routes were still used after the Romans departed. For example, the trade route along the Rhine remained important, and its commerce was extended by Viking merchants to the coasts, to northwestern Germany, and to the islands and peninsulas around the North Sea: England, Ireland, Iceland, Norway, and Jutland. Artifacts that represent importations into Viking settlements, such as wine and wine vessels in Haithabu (Behre 1983), serve to document the existence and extensiveness of these routes.

The Hanse merchants added the areas around the Baltic Sea to their economic empire, bringing exotic food to the towns along the Baltic coast. Indeed, at times there was more imported food inside the towns than local products. As an example, during a period of grain shortage in Lubeck, marzipan, a bread that is baked not of ordinary flour but of almond "flour" and sugar, is said to have been invented (Küster 1987).

The food trade in northern Europe experienced yet another shift when the exchange began of meat (or livestock) and crops between the agricultural and grassland areas. In the Netherlands, oxen were taken from Frisia westward to the big towns, whereas crops were transported from the dry, sandy areas to the fen landscapes where cattle farms came into existence (Bieleman 1989). The trade of oxen, in turn, led to the development of "oxen routes" inside northern Europe. In the late Middle Ages, as food transport and trade became more important, these activities were no longer confined to waterways but were also carried out over such overland routes.

All parts of northern Europe that were distant from the trade routes had remained rural, and the diets of their residents continued to be restricted to the few elements of food (cereals, pulses, oil plants) that had been exploited since prehistoric times. Only the species of plants had changed. Rye, oats, and, in some areas, wheat had become more important, whereas emmer was only rarely cultivated.

Urban growth meant a continuing demand for as much food as possible, which led to intensive agricultural production. Nearly all woods were cleared, and a sophisticated rotation system – winter crop, summer crop, and fallow – came into existence. The settlements became stable and were usually arranged around a church. As during Roman times, such stability (in towns, monasteries, and castles) promoted the cultivation of fruit trees and vines, the produce of which was available in the markets. Yet the demands of rapidly growing urban populations frequently led to shortages in basic foodstuffs like flour, which in turn led to conflict and even civil war between city peoples and peasants. The *Bauernkrieg* ("Peasants' War") of 1525 was perhaps the most famous of these conflicts, signaling the end of the Middle Ages and its accompanying social system in northern Europe.

Modern Times

During the following centuries, it became even more difficult for rural farmers to supply enough food for urban populations that continued to swell (Abel 1978). There was one crisis after another, which brought periods of famine in northern Europe and periods of migration to North America. But at the same time, American food plants were taking root in Europe.

In the period of mercantilism, just prior to the Age of Industrialization, factories were founded in many parts of northern Europe. People began working for wages, and thus many more became dependent on the food market, which had difficulty meeting demand, especially in years with low crop yields. In response, northern European landowners forced peasants to cultivate the American potato *(Solanum tuberosum),* which delivered a high yield of food per unit of land cultivated.

In principle, such cultivation made it possible for ordinary workers to buy sufficient food in the form of potatoes to sustain themselves. But the expanded food supply caused rapid population growth and a concomitant growth of towns. Indeed, the industrialization of northern Europe would not have been possible without the introduction of the potato (Küster 1992a).

It was not, however, until the nineteenth and twentieth centuries that the peasants' diet began to include imported food items, such as spices, long enjoyed by town dwellers. This change was precipitated by an extensive construction of railways that linked the countryside with the cities. With the new foodstuffs came grocers to the villages. They were called "Kolonialwarenhändler" in the German language, which means "colonial produce merchants." Yet only exotic food imports were sold in the grocery shops, whereas the most important constituents of the diet were provided by the farmers themselves.

During the nineteenth and twentieth centuries, the construction of railways has also led to further spatial concentration of cattle raising and crop production.

With the invention of mineral fertilizers that were transported by rail, crop production was abandoned in mountainous areas but intensified in the plains. In addition, the great increase in yield on fertilized fields led to the abandonment of remote acres where spruce forests could be planted.

Another agrarian and nutritional revolution was caused by the beginning of extensive maize *(Zea mays)* cultivation during the past few decades. Maize silage provides enough food for large cattle and chicken producers, causing meat and eggs to become relatively cheap to northern European consumers. Since World War II there has been a marked shift toward increased meat consumption. The protein-rich diet causes health problems, and dietitians recommend eating more grains and vegetables and less meat and eggs. In northern Europe today, food shortages are not a problem, and the price of food plays less of a role in determining an individual's nutrition than it did in the past. It is interesting that despite the great variety of foods available on the shelves in the supermarket, dietitians are recommending a return to the dietary staples of prehistoric times (Haenel 1986).

Nonetheless, a huge variety of foods is now produced in northern Europe, and other foods produced outside of that region can be purchased by almost everyone. Some of the crops produced, such as wheat, barley, oats, and rye, have been grown and consumed for millennia. Others, such as potatoes and maize from the Americas, are relatively new but very important. Also important are certain foods brought in from abroad. Rice, which is imported in large quantities from South Asia, is one of these. Coffee and tea are others. The northern Europeans have long been fond of hot beverages, and today Dutch and Saxonian coffees are famous the world over.

In a remarkable turnaround compared with the past, today more crops and meat are produced in northern Europe than can be consumed by the people of the region, and such abundance has created great political and economic problems. Oversupply of such items as pork, butter, wine, and apples has prompted the common market of the European Union to insist on less production, and farmers have been forced to destroy a portion of their harvests and cut back on the amount of meat produced. Because areas where long-established crops can be cultivated have become increasingly restricted, farmers are turning to alternative crops such as spelt, flax, and sunflowers. Many products from these new crops are available in health-food stores as well as supermarkets, as northern Europeans, like people in other developed countries, are giving more thought to improving their nutrition.

Another important nutritional development in the region began in the 1950s, when labor shortages there opened the way for southern European workers to move north. With them came their national cuisines and specialty restaurants; Italian and Greek foods are very popular in northern Europe today. Pizza restaurants can be found even in small villages, and frozen pizza is one of the most common fast-food dishes in the home.

In addition to the influence of southern Europeans, there has been a substantial culinary contribution made by the people of now-independent overseas colonies to their former mother countries. Just as Indian food and restaurants are common in England, and North African cookery is widespread in France, there are many Indonesian restaurants in the Netherlands.

As the northern European countries have become more prosperous, they have also attracted the peoples (and thus the foods) of most of the rest of the world. Chinese restaurants, for example, are ubiquitous, and spring rolls and other Chinese dishes are available in all the supermarkets.

Indeed, because of prosperity on the one hand and all of these culinary choices on the other, cooking at home has come to an end in many households. It is easy and inexpensive to purchase already prepared dishes from the supermarket in cans, or frozen, or dried. Moreover, it has become very common to eat in what might be termed "neighborhood" restaurants where one encounters friends and can relax. Fast-food restaurants from America have been introduced but are still not all that popular because they are too hurried.

Clearly, then, the history of food and drink in northern Europe has entered into a unique chapter. There is an abundant variety of both native and exotic foods available, and famine is unknown. More and more customers are demanding higher-quality foodstuffs, and it has become fashionable, for example, to use the very best olive oils and spiced vinegars in the preparation of salads. Factories that turn out convenience foods, such as mashed potato powder and instant soups and sauces, are supplemented by a market network that supplies frozen and fresh fruits, vegetables, meats, and fish, all of which combine to supply a high – perhaps too high – level of nutrition for the northern European.

This situation stands in stark contrast to nutritional levels in the poorer regions of the world. For economic and political as well as logistical reasons, it is a complicated matter to ship foods from northern European countries to the underdeveloped nations. But some, especially the Scandinavians, have done much to help improve the standard of living, including the level of nutrition, of developing-world peoples. Moreover, there are regular airlifts from northern Europe to famine-ravaged regions of the world, although, of course, balanced diets are hardly provided in such bulk shipments.

In conclusion, it is worth stressing that the sheer amount of nutrients available to northern Europeans today also stands in stark contrast to their own long past of undernutrition and even famine. One hopes that one day soon, like the northern Europeans, the people in today's developing countries will be confronting the problem of overnutrition.

Hansjörg Küster

Bibliography

Abel, W. 1978. *Agrarkrisen und Agrarkonjunktur.* Third edition. Hamburg and Berlin.

Bakels, C. C. 1982. Der Mohn, die Linearbandkeramik und das westliche Mittelmeergebiet. *Archäologisches Korrespondenzblatt* 12: 11–13.

Bandi, H.-G. 1968. Das Jungpaläolithikum. In *Archäologie der Schweiz,* ed. Schweizerische Gesellschaft für Archäologie, Vol. 1, 107–22. Basel.

Behre, K.-E. 1983. *Ernährung und Umwelt der wikingerzeitlichen Siedlung Haithabu. Die Ergebnisse der Untersuchungen der Pflanzenreste.* Neumünster, Germany.

Bieleman, J. 1989. Die Verschiedenartigkeit der Landwirtschaftssysteme in den Sandgebieten der Niederlande in der frühen Neuzeit. *Siedlungsforschung* 7: 119–30.

Childe, V. G. 1956. *Man makes himself.* Third edition. London.

Firbas, F. 1949. *Waldgeschichte Mitteleuropas,* Vol. 1. Jena, Germany.

Haenel, H. 1986. Ernährung in der Steinzeit – Ernährung heute. *Wissenschaft und Fortschritt* 36: 287–90.

Jacomet, S. 1988. *Planzen mediterraner Herkunft in neolithischen Seeufersiedlungen der Schweiz.* In *Der prähistorische Mensch und seine Umwelt,* ed. H. Küster. *Forschungen und Berichte zur Vor- und Frühgeschichte in Baden-Württemberg* 31: 205–12. Stuttgart, Germany.

Jacomet, S., and H. Schlichtherle. 1984. Der kleine Pfahlbauweizen Oswald Heers. Neue Untersuchungen zur Morphologie neolithischer Nacktweizen-Ähren. In *Plants and ancient man,* ed. W. van Zeist and W. A. Casparie, 153–76. Rotterdam.

Knörzer, K.-H. 1970. *Römerzeitliche Pflanzenfunde aus Neuss.* Berlin.

1981. *Römerzeitliche Pflanzenfunde aus Xanten.* Cologne, Germany.

1991. Deutschland nördlich der Donau. In *Progress in Old World palaeoethnobotany,* ed. W. van Zeist, K. Wasylikowa, and K.-E. Behre, 189–206. Rotterdam.

Kuhn-Schnyder, E. 1968. Die Geschichte der Tierwelt des Pleistozäns und Alt-Holozäns. In *Archäologie der Schweiz,* ed. Schweizerische Gesellschaft für Archäologie, Vol. 1, 43–68. Basel.

Küster, H. 1985. Neolithische Pflanzenreste aus Hochdorf, Gemeinde Eberdingen (Kreis Ludwigsburg). In *Forschungen und Berichte zur Vor- und Frühgeschichte in Baden-Württemberg* 19: 13–83. Stuttgart, Germany.

1986. Sammelfrüchte des Neolithikums. *Abhandlungen aus dem Westfälischen Museum für Naturkunde* 48 (2/3): 433–40.

1987. *Wo der Pfeffer wächst. Ein Lexikon zur Kulturgeschichte der Gewürze.* Munich.

1991. Mitteleuropa südlich der Donau, einschliesslich Alpenraum. In *Progress in Old World palaeoethno-*

botany, ed. W. van Zeist, K. Wasylikowa, and K.-E. Behre, 179-87. Rotterdam.

1992a. Neue Pflanzen für die Alte Welt. Kartoffel und Mais als Kärrner der Industriellen Revolution. *Kultur und Technik* 16: 30-5.

1992b. Römerzeitliche Pflanzenreste. In *Ein Geschirrdepot des 3. Jahrhunderts. Grabungen im Lagerdorf des Kastells Langenhain,* ed. H.-G. Simon and H.-J. Köhler, 184-8. Bonn, Germany.

Rust, A. 1972. *Vor 20000 Jahren. Rentierjäger der Eiszeit.* Third edition. Neumünster, Germany.

Schmitz, H. 1961. Pollenanalytische Untersuchungen in Hohen Viecheln am Schweriner See. In *Hohen Viecheln. Ein mittelsteinzeitlicher Wohnplatz in Mecklenburg,* ed. E. Schuldt, 14-38. Berlin.

Smith, A. G. 1970. The influence of Mesolithic and Neolithic man on British vegetation: A discussion. In *Studies in the vegetational history of the British Isles,* ed. D. Walker and R. G. West, 81-96. London.

Vaughan, D. 1987. The plant macrofossils. In *Prehistoric and Romano-British sites at Westward Ho!, Devon. Archaeological and palaeoenvironmental surveys 1983 and 1984. Studies in palaeoeconomy and environment in South West England,* ed. N. D. Balaam et al., 233-8. Oxford.

Wyss, R. 1968-1971. Technik, Wirtschaft und Handel. In *Archäologie der Schweiz,* ed. Schweizerische Gesellschaft für Archäologie, 3 vols. 3: 123-44. Basel.

V.C.6 ❧ The Low Countries

The term "Low Countries" is used here to mean the Netherlands. Belgium, known in the past as the southern Netherlands, has been independent since the 1830s. Situated between France to the south and the Netherlands to the north, Belgium has had a different history and has developed different cultural characteristics since the seventeenth century. Thus, in this chapter, Belgian culinary culture is employed for comparative purposes only.

A general overview of the history and culinary culture of the Netherlands should, perhaps, start with the observation that the Dutch have never succeeded in being proud of their cuisine. This seems to be a reflection of a lack of national pride that sometimes borders on indifference. If asked, most would probably not be able to identify important, genuinely national, dishes. Moreover, if such a dish were named, it might well be *rijsttafel,* which is not Dutch in origin but Indonesian and is a product of the Dutch East Indian colonies. Such a lack of concern with indigenous culinary culture forms a more or less sharp contrast to the attitudes of the inhabitants of neighboring Western European countries like Belgium, France, and, to some degree, Germany.

Over the centuries, foreign visitors have repeatedly expressed amazement at the Dutch lack of exaltation of the table. But since the late Middle Ages, daily food has always been prepared according to the general rule that it must be simple, nourishing, and cheap. Only after World War II did this undemanding attitude begin to change.

Contrasts and Similarities: The Late Middle Ages (1300 to 1500)

Little evidence is available about food and drink in the late medieval Low Countries. Cookery books in this era were exclusively aimed at the secular and ecclesiastical upper classes. The recipes, nevertheless, give some indication of the extremely wide range of possible dishes at the tables of the elite. The first Dutch-language cookbook, printed in Brussels by Thomas van der Noot in 1510 and titled *Een notabel boecxken van cokeryen* ("A notable book of cookery"), offers medieval recipes for festivities such as weddings and banquets that deal with the preparation of sauces, jellies, fish, meat, fowl and game, pies, tarts and other pastries, eggs, dairy products, various sugars, wine, and, finally, candied quinces and ginger.

The recipes come from various sources, many of them French, which underlines the observations of Stephen Mennell (1985) about the essential similarity of the tables of the medieval rich everywhere in western Europe, with the elite following culinary standards that were mostly Italian and French. It was especially at such festivals that princes, nobles, and church dignitaries ate and drank lavishly. The festive banquets of the Burgundian dukes, at that time rulers in northern France and the southern Netherlands (Flanders), initiated a luxurious and flamboyant civilization that served as a model all over Europe, as did the ceremonies of their peripatetic courts.

Prodigious consumption at the courts, particularly of meat (from pigs, calves, sheep, various fowl, and game) and wine, contributed to the maintenance of the high social position of the nobility. So, too, did the lavish use of precious spices and sugar in the preparation of a large number of dishes to be presented all at once. A refined taste, however, still had to be acquired, and social standards in eating, appetite, and table manners evolved only over the course of a lengthy civilizing process (Elias 1994). In the Middle Ages, quantity prevailed over quality, in no small part because of the irregularity of the food supply. It was a time when harvests failed, diseases killed domestic animals, and life was made even more insecure by pestilence and war (Mennell 1985: 20-39).

Religious restrictions on the consumption of meat and dairy produce also exerted a profound influence on cooking and eating. Prescribed days of abstinence were not confined to the period of Lent but (in addition to special days of fasting) were in force twice each week, which made for a total of about 150 days of food proscriptions every year. These religious rules of abstinence and fasting raised impediments to, and at the same time opened possibilities for, the culinary creativity of the cooks at the courts as well as those in ordinary kitchens. Fish – a preferred Lenten food – was abundantly available from the sea as well as from the many rivers and lakes in the Low Countries. Thus, meals at the court of the Bishop of Utrecht in the fourteenth century included about 20 different fish dishes, such as haddock, plaice, whiting, eel, herring (in various preparations), sturgeon, pike, perch, and carp. But Lenten abstinence may also have hindered the use of certain cooking methods – such as frying in northern Europe, where butter was the principal edible fat – and in such areas hampered the development of culinary variety in general. By contrast, in southern Europe, where olive oil – not proscribed during Lent – was the major fat, the days of abstinence may have encouraged the inventiveness of cooks, especially in the competition for prestige at noble and royal courts (Jobse-van Putten 1995).

Thus, sharp contrasts existed between festive and daily eating, between feasting and fasting, and between years of plenty and those of scarcity. Other contrasts and variations were related to the rhythm of the seasons, to the church calendar, to the regional agricultural produce, and, above all, to the social strata. To this might be added the contrast between fresh and preserved foods. Except for the short periods during harvest and slaughter, no possibility existed of eating one's fill of fresh vegetables and meat. Rather, because of the rapid deterioration of foodstuffs, they were generally consumed as salted and dried products.

The ecological and geographic conditions typical of a northwestern European delta, with its rivers, lakes, sea inlets, and clay soils, applied especially to the western and northern parts of the Netherlands – Holland, Zeeland, and Friesland – that were to assume a dominant position in the Dutch Republic. The eastern and southern parts of the territory were higher and more sandy, with vegetation different from the lower regions. Such a division between the northwest and the southeast was for centuries an important factor in the economic and agricultural structure, influencing the products available for consumption. The cultivation of grains, for instance, was a matter largely defined by climate and soil.

In fourteenth-century Europe, famines and epidemics, most notably the Black Death, caused a considerable reduction of the population that in turn led to a transformation in the production and distribution of food. The grazing of cattle increased relative to the growing of crops, and for a time, meat was available in larger quantities, even for the poor. Later on, however, the cultivation of grains increased in the Low Countries as elsewhere in Europe, transforming them into staple foods.

A moderate maritime climate in the Low Countries allowed the growing of several types of cereals, including barley, oats, and rye. At least initially, wheat could be cultivated only in the southwest, and rye became the prominent grain in the Netherlands, even

though wheat was the more appreciated of the two (Jobse-van Putten 1995: 83). Unfortunately, the quantity of grain produced was not sufficient for the population and had to be supplemented by imports from eastern Europe. In the thirteenth and fourteenth centuries, this took place within the flourishing trade network of the Hanse – towns of the Hanseatic League – through which substantial parts of northern Europe were commercially interrelated, forming a line from the Baltic Sea and the river Danube in the east to Bruges (Flanders) and London in the west. In the fifteenth century, the position of the Hanse deteriorated, and the grain trade shifted to Amsterdam, which became the most important grain center, not only for the Low Countries but for Europe as a whole.

From the fourteenth century onward (although in Flanders much earlier), economic differentiation began to take place. The importance of money and trade increased; means of transport were improved; and cities came into being. Consequently, some farmers began to produce for the market. Butter and cheese, for example, were made in the low-lying grasslands of Holland and Friesland (where animal husbandry was important) and later became very famous delicacies. Despite such surplus production, however, subsistence agriculture remained the dominant economic pattern, especially on the small and isolated mixed farms in the eastern and southern parts of the Low Countries (Burema 1953: 29).

This type of economy substantially influenced attitudes toward preserving, cooking, and eating home-produced foods, an influence that endured, in part at least, until the second half of the twentieth century (Jobse-van Putten 1995: 379-84). Meals everywhere in the Low Countries were prepared in roughly similar fashion, although local and regional differences in agricultural products and technical conditions of cookery caused variations from place to place in the composition and taste of dishes and drinks. Grain was cooked as porridge (often the poorer qualities), baked as pancakes or bread, and brewed for beer. Porridge could be made in a pot over an open fire, but bread required an oven and, thus, tended to be found in the households of those in more fortunate circumstances. Beer was the common drink, as water was of poor quality and milk was mainly used for making butter and cheese. Vegetables and fruits – thought to be unhealthy – were not much appreciated. Nonetheless, tubers, beetroots, turnips, and peas were often daily foods by necessity. Green leafy vegetables were little known and eaten only among the upper strata. The number of meals per day depended on social position. The elite preferred two meals, but those performing physical labor often ate three or more times daily. In rural areas, frequent hot meals were common.

The ordinary medieval hot meal among country people and townsfolk consisted of a half-liquid pottage, which was a mush made of water, milk, or beer, root vegetables, and pulses (various types of peas) or grain, sometimes enriched with a piece of meat or lard. This dish, prepared over an open fire, like porridge, underwent changes as different ingredients became available throughout the seasons. If an oven was available, bread went with each of the day's hot and cold meals.

In the consumption of pottage, the Low Countries were not very different from other western European countries during the Middle Ages. The records of two hospitals in the cities of Leiden and Utrecht between 1367 and 1500 indicate that pottages were an important dish in both institutions. Meat and fish (salted herring was a preferred Lenten food) were served with bread once or twice a day, and smaller meals consisted of bread, butter, cheese, eggs, and milk, buttermilk, or beer (Jobse-van Putten 1995: 145-50). Every part of an animal (head, brain, eyes, and entrails) was utilized in meat dishes, and the frequency with which such dishes were served by the two hospitals in question is an indication of both the relative prosperity of the cities and the abundance of meat in this period.

Is it possible to discern some traits of an emerging national cuisine in the Low Countries during the late Middle Ages? And is there any indication of a continuity with later developments in Dutch foodways? The little available evidence suggests a negative answer to both questions. The similarities in foodways with other western European countries seem to have been substantially greater than the differences. National states were later inventions, and local and regional networks were dominant in determining the production, distribution, and preparation of foods. The contrasts between common and festive fare, and between meal preparation among the elite, on one hand, and the masses, on the other, were everywhere alike.

There were, of course, some contrasts. One was the Dutch dependency on butter and meat fat for cooking instead of olive oil. That Dutch butter and cheese were famous products at an early stage, and continued to be so for centuries, was another. A final difference was the Dutch expertise in horticulture, which had gained a widespread reputation.

Gardening was initially practiced in the monasteries, but castles and country houses also began to develop cabbage patches and orchards for pears and apples. In addition, commercial gardens were cultivated near cities. Like butter and cheese, horticultural produce was later promoted for export. Foreigners came to regard it as "typically Dutch," and it also achieved fame. Catherine of Aragon, for example, had salad vegetables brought to the English court from Holland by a special courier (Burema 1953: 16).

Rise and Fall of the Dutch Republic (1500 to 1800)

As already noted, strangers visiting the Netherlands over the centuries have often noted a simplicity in cuisine and lack of refinement in the eating and drink-

ing habits of its citizens. The latter were frequently portrayed as people with little discrimination but fond of large quantities of food, which they swallowed quickly. By the late Middle Ages, the Dutch were also well known for their exorbitant drinking habits (Burema 1953: 53). Seventeenth-century paintings by Rembrandt and others show overloaded tables and bacchanalian parties of guilds and fraternities. Yet other paintings show families praying before a simple meal of nothing but bread and cheese. Although some of the latter may carry moral and religious messages, the same simplicity is also mentioned in foreigners' descriptions (Schama 1987: 159-75). Together, these images give an impression of both the exception and the rule in Dutch eating and drinking in the sixteenth and seventeenth centuries. Feasting was characterized by excessive indulgence, reminiscent of the late medieval Burgundian court. Yet daily meals were frugal and consisted, more often than not, of only one or two courses, even among the well-to-do and the aristocracy. As both types of meals lack refinement, how does one interpret the combination of excess and simplicity that has become a distinguishing mark of Dutch culinary culture?

Popular wisdom has it that Dutch culinary mediocrity was caused by Calvinism, which frowned on mundane pleasures. Indeed, the economic and social influence of religion, especially of Calvinism, has been a much-discussed topic among historians and sociologists, who have pondered, among other things, the extent to which it was a force in the sociogenesis of the Dutch Republic and in subsequent public and private spheres of life. Culinary attitudes and preferences, of course, belong to both spheres and are part of the lifestyles and mentalities of the social groups in power. Thus, to understand the culinary culture of the Netherlands, a look at the process of state formation and related economic development is indispensable.

Certainly, the shift of the commercial and industrial center of gravity in Europe from the south to the northwest was an important marker in the beginning of the modern age, and the Low Countries were at the heart of this process. But the forces that led to the flourishing economic position of the Republic of the Seven United Provinces from 1588 to 1795 had already been set in motion by the end of the fifteenth century. At that time, the Low Countries were under the rule of the Habsburg monarchs, who were able, through fortuitous marriages, to enlarge their domains to include Austrian, Burgundian, and Spanish territories.

Situated as they were around the estuaries of the rivers Scheldt, Maas, and Rhine, the inhabitants of the Low Countries knew how to take advantage of the new economic opportunities this expansion provided. The development of new technologies to master floodwaters, the reclamation of land, and the construction of an early infrastructure of navigable canals and windmills were an important Dutch contribution to modern European economic growth. In addition, there were well-known Dutch advances in shipping and commerce, and development also occurred in other important fields such as agriculture, fisheries (especially herring), and industry (principally textiles and timber). It is important to note that all of this economic upsurge had already taken place before the Reformation, with its various brands of Protestantism (especially Calvinism), could have had any influence (De Vries and Van der Woude 1995: 23–67, 205–13).

Moreover, even the Calvinist influence was often moderated by a liberal and humanistic Christian faith in the tradition of Desiderius Erasmus. Consequently, Calvinism never succeeded in achieving a religious monopoly; indeed, many citizens clung to the old Roman Catholic church. This is not to say, however, that Calvinism was not an important force in Dutch history. It helped sustain the country during its revolt against the Spanish Habsburgs, and the great merchants who emerged as the Dutch Republic came into existence were supporters of the Reformation. These men found their rising influence in the affairs of the state legitimized by the new Protestant faith, and they, along with the patricians, did impress a cultural style on the public and private spheres of daily life that was typical of the urban bourgeois from Holland and Zeeland.

This meant that the exceptionally broad, but differentiated, middle classes in the cities were at the heart of the republican society (Huizinga 1984: 39–59; Van Deursen 1992) – a situation that was fundamentally different from other European countries such as England and France. In England, both the royal court and the rural gentry left their mark on cultural life, whereas in France, new cultural models, in foodways as in other areas, were pioneered at the urban court where the king and nobility resided (Mennell 1985: 102–34). But in the Netherlands, during the sixteenth and seventeenth centuries, the dominance of bourgeois influence, legitimized by the characteristic Christian lay religiosity of either the orthodox Calvinist or the liberal humanist, resulted in a frugal and simple culinary style.

This simplicity was not the case on festive occasions, however, despite the complaints of some Calvinist ministers about the collapse of tables under the weight of too many dishes, and despite the decrees issued by Doctor Nicolaas Tulp (the mayor of Amsterdam around 1660) against excessive expenditures for eating and drinking at weddings, christenings, and funerals. Indeed, such festivals were occasions when considerations of social status and competition overcame the ever-present virtue of thriftiness (Van Otterloo 1986: 39–43).

From 1500 to 1800, as in the late Middle Ages, the main foods remained grain, tubers, meat, lard, fish, cheese, and butter. The central importance of the grain market in Amsterdam meant an increasing abundance of wheat, and wheat bread became the most popular farinaceous food among the urban well-to-do, as well as among the patricians in their country houses. In addition, spices, for those who could afford them, were increasingly available from 1602 onward because of the trading efforts of the Dutch East India Company.

The diets of artisans and farmers centered mainly on a daily porridge, sometimes interchanged with or complemented by pancakes and rye bread. Bread might be accompanied by butter or cheese, but not both. The two together were viewed as a needless luxury, even as "devil's work." If possible, bread was eaten at breakfast with fish, porridge, or another hot dish, and perhaps at a third or even fourth meal in the early evening with a pottage. Many varieties of bread were used, depending on social position and the type, rhythm, and place of work.

In distinguished circles, the salad, an invention diffused from the south, often accompanied the early evening meal or was used as an entrée at the beginning of a hot meal. Initially, beer was the beverage of choice at meals, but later on it was largely replaced by milk, buttermilk, or whey, although the poor generally drank water. After 1680, coffee began to be used; in the eighteenth century, it became a popular drink, and there were many coffeehouses in the cities and towns. Tea – called "women's tobacco" – also came into use and long remained a high-status beverage, partly because of the costly tea set required by social custom. Tea was drunk by the wives of patricians and bourgeois regents and diffused very slowly among the lower social strata during the eighteenth and nineteenth centuries (Jobse-van Putten 1995: 151–226).

For many, the day's two hot meals generally consisted of one to three courses: a starter, a main course, and possibly a dessert. The starter might have been a salad or a *sop* (pottage) from groats or bread soaked in milk or broth. Other possibilities were a dish of pulses with butter and onions, braised root vegetables, or cabbage. Dessert was usually buttermilk porridge in rural areas; among the urban merchants, however, pastry (for example, "shoemaker's tart," made from apples, bread, and eggs) and fruits were common. The main course was a dish of fish or meat, served, if possible, with green herbs, prunes, or currants. In wealthy households, this course might be followed by oysters or lobster with sweet sauces (Burema 1953: 96).

The relative simplicity of the bourgeois kitchen was reflected in the unique cookbook of Dutch origin *De verstandige Kock of Sorghvuldige Huyshoudster* ("The Prudent Cook or Careful Housekeeper"), published in Amsterdam in 1667. This frequently reprinted book was intended for wealthy merchants who owned country houses and had access to produce from their own gardens (gardening was a relatively new pursuit of the urban elite). The book opens with instructions for building a kitchen range that permitted the simultaneous preparation of separate dishes. Next, the book deals with the preparation of salads (both cooked and raw); vegetables (braised in sauces thickened with bread crumbs); meat, game, and fowl; salted fish, fish from the sea, and freshwater fish (the three separate chapters on fish indicate the importance of this food); and cakes, tarts, and pastry. The traditional Dutch pottage of meat and vegetables is present in the cookbook as a "Spanish hodge-podge," and a few recipes are given for a festive mixed-meat dish, *olipodrigo,* that was widely known in Europe (Van't Veer: 1966: 69–93).

In the eighteenth century, there was a growing French cultural influence among the elite, and a modest refinement can be discerned in cookery, table manners, table coverings, and tableware. The fork increasingly became an obligatory instrument after the 1750s, and pewter and silver, as decorative materials, were now preferred over copper or iron. For the upper classes, ambivalence about luxury at the table now belonged to the past. But at the same time, the gulf between rich and poor increased considerably, and the potato would soon become crucial to the survival of the latter.

That gulf was also manifested in poems and plays that ridiculed bourgeois virtues, such as, for example, the preference of aristocrats and their bourgeois imitators for game and white bread (*Heerenbroot* or "lord's bread") instead of rye bread and cheese (Schama 1987: 172; Zahn 1989: 48–52, 272). Indeed, a widespread contempt for the upper classes and their ostentation helped bring about a society without a steep social hierarchy or an influential central court. This situation, however, as suggested by Jack Goody (1982: 97–134) and Stephen Mennell (1985: 103–34), may have discouraged the rise of a uniquely Dutch haute cuisine.

Modernization and Industrialization: The Modern World (1800 to 1960)

In 1795, the Low Countries became a part of Napoleonic France. The administration by regents and merchants came to an end, and Amsterdam's trade monopoly shifted to England. These developments increased the general impoverishment of many in the population that had already begun with economic deterioration during the late eighteenth century. Following the period of French control, the Low Countries became a kingdom ruled by the princes of Orange. William I (1813–40), the "king-merchant," tried to restore the old Dutch commercial position and to give the country new economic life by the founding of trading companies, the construction of roads and canals, the reclamation of land, and other modernizing measures. But his efforts were more or less unsuccessful. Moreover, during his reign, there was the 1830 separation of Flanders and the Walloon provinces in the south from the rest of the nation; these united to become the country of Belgium.

The 1840s are well known in western European history as a decade of turbulence and revolution, caused in part by recurring shortages of food. This was certainly the case in the Netherlands, where the decade represents a low point in Dutch history. A dearth of grain put even bread and porridge out of reach of both the masses in the cities and many in the countryside. Meat and lard virtually disappeared from the diet, and countless people ate potatoes, carrots, and turnips, or perhaps only potatoes, morning, noon, and evening.

Indeed, from the end of the eighteenth century onward, potatoes increasingly became a staple food for the nation and a substitute for unaffordable bread. In 1847 and 1848 this near-exclusive dependence on potatoes had disastrous consequences, as the potato blight during these years triggered crop failures and famine. Food shortages were joined by epidemics – as was often the case in the preindustrial period – to produce high death rates, primarily in the strongly urbanized province of North Holland. Fortunately, many of the urban poor were helped by local administrations or by charitable institutions. Soup kitchens and eatinghouses provided portions of cheap or free food, and the thin soup (invented by Count Benjamin Rumford and composed of bone-jelly, beans, potatoes, and sometimes turnips or carrots) that became famous all over Europe was also popular in the Netherlands.

Slight improvements in the food supply were made intermittently during the decades that followed, but in the 1880s, a deep agricultural crisis, caused by a sudden profusion of overseas grain, again brought widespread shortages and misery, this time mainly in the countryside, as local grain prices tumbled. After 1890, however, substantial economic growth took place in the Netherlands, and industrialization, improved transportation, and an ensuing rise in income brought an expansion of the distribution and affordability of foodstuffs.

In the twentieth century, two World Wars and the economic crisis of the 1930s again caused shortages, but after the 1950s, food scarcity and hunger became things of the past, and a new age of plenty was under way. Paralleling these developments was the modernization of Dutch foodways that took place between 1880 and 1960. This modernization involved the diffusion of food and drink innovations, new dishes, and new sequences of meals that passed, in general, from the upper to the lower classes, from town to country, and from the western market-oriented regions to the eastern and southern provinces, hitherto geared to subsistence agriculture. At the start of this period, contrasts were sharp, but by the end, similarities were the norm, brought about by increasing education, democratization, and uniformity (Van Otterloo 1990: 127–84; Jobse-van Putten 1995: 499–506).

These were long-term processes that involved, among other things, what might be called the replacement of foods of necessity with foods of luxury, as qualitatively better and more expensive foods gradually became more accessible to more people. In other words, potatoes, pulses, root vegetables, and grains such as buckwheat and rye were little by little replaced by wheat, meat, butter, cheese, other dairy produce, and sugar. The change began with the replacement of rye (cheaper but nutritious) with wheat, most preferred but more expensive. The next phase, after World War II, saw a decline in the consumption of wheat (bread) but steep increases in the per capita intake of meat, cheese, and sugar. The position of potatoes as a staple food, strong during the entire nineteenth century, began to deteriorate after 1900, and after 1920, potato consumption declined at an accelerated pace (Van Otterloo 1990: 45–8).

Industrialization also had revolutionizing effects on food and meals in the production of foodstuffs and in the organization of work and the family. The shifting of food production to the factory was made possible by rapidly increasing scientific knowledge in relation to the mechanization and "chemicalization" of food. Industrially processed ingredients, like corn flour, *fécule* (custard powder), "Oxo" (bouilion cubes), margarine, canned vegetables, meat, and fish, had become available at the end of the nineteenth century and were readily so during the interwar years. The food industry promoted its products through advertisements and educational campaigns, sometimes enlisting cookery teachers, even doctors, to inspire public trust in the new time- and energy-saving processed foods.

As elsewhere, the level of education in the Low Countries increased considerably after 1900. Women benefited from cooking classes and schools of home economics that taught the principles of hygiene and nutrition and, not incidentally, how to prepare tasty and healthy meals. (Although similar institutions were known elsewhere in western Europe, cookery books used in Dutch schools were distinguished by meticulous calculations of the prices of ingredients.) After 1930, radio and women's magazines helped to diffuse such knowledge, and in this way, the culinary cultures of Europe, especially that of France, trickled down to the middle and lower classes in the cities and, finally, to the country people in the eastern and southern provinces of the Netherlands. Also crucial to such a democratization of taste was the metamorphosis of the kitchen range, along with an increasing ease of securing water, gas, and electricity.

The modern industrial organization of work and the family also brought about several important changes in the dishes of Dutch people and in their meal system as a whole. The number, type, and composition of meals one consumed had for centuries reflected social, regional, and rural–urban differences. But now there was a movement toward uniformity (Jobse-van Putten 1995: 275–498). The number of meals in a day became three – generally a cold break-fast, a cold lunch, and a hot dinner at about 6:00 in the evening. Coffee and tea, popular among the urban middle classes since the end of the eighteenth century, now diffused (coffee in particular) to the whole Dutch populace and were drunk throughout the day, both with and between meals; these drinks replaced to a great extent other beverages like beer, milk, and buttermilk. Tea, at first a prestigious middle-class beverage drunk in the afternoon with a biscuit or a sweet, began somewhat later than coffee to accompany breakfast or lunch.

At breakfast, potatoes, porridge, and pancakes gave way to just bread and tea or coffee. A cold lunch around noon was an invention of the industrial age, suited to the new rhythm of work. Initially, hot potato meals were taken to the factory, but these were soon replaced with packets of bread brought from home. Much later, canteens supplied foods for employees, as they did elsewhere in Europe. Dinner in the Netherlands evolved into a three-course hot meal, ideally with a starter, preferably (vegetable) soup based on a meat stock, a French custom that between 1900 and 1940 was gradually adopted in the Low Countries (where pork or chicken was used as a stock instead of beef). The main course (again ideally) consisted of potatoes and gravy, cooked vegetables with a sauce, and a meat dish. Following this was a sweet dessert of (partly industrially processed) pudding, custard, or fresh or preserved fruits.

At first, this highly prestigious bourgeois meal was consumed exclusively on Sundays and festive occasions in the countryside, but it was later adopted in the cities as well. Thus, the centuries-old regional diversity of meals, comprising pancakes, porridges, stews, and thick soups based on pulses, grain, rice, and turnips, largely disappeared.

We might pause to ask and answer the question of whether any aspect of culinary culture in the Netherlands during this period was typically Dutch and thus unique in Europe. This was certainly not the case with breakfast, which seems to have followed the common Continental evolutionary path. At most, it was different only because of particular bread fillings, like chocolate sprinkles. The singular addiction of the Dutch to coffee and tea breaks at work is perhaps a national sin, not elsewhere indulged to the same extent.

Lunch took on a very simple form; it was mainly served cold and without frills. Except for an occasional salad, it continued the Dutch tradition of simplicity and frugality. This was also generally true of dinner, which had a simple and straightforward character, in which quantity (but also nutritiousness) continued to be preferred above quality and refinement. Another illustration of simplicity and frugality was the late development of habitually eating out in the Netherlands. In Belgium, restaurants had become popular as early as 1840, but restaurants in the Netherlands were only hesitantly visited beginning in about the 1890s, and eating out did not become a socially acceptable habit until the 1960s and later (Scholliers 1993: 71).

Globalization and Civilization: The Low Countries since the 1960s

World War II shook the Netherlands much more violently than World War I, and the populace experienced the distress of occupation and a scarcity of goods, even the pangs of hunger. Following the war, reconstruction of the economy and the country's infrastructure were priorities for the government and goals that required the utmost efforts of the entire population. Consumption was therefore postponed, and frugality continued.

The eating and drinking habits in the Netherlands were also patterned on the prewar model. No fundamental developments occurred except for a limited upsurge of interest in Indonesian food. This arose because of the tens of thousands of soldiers and people of mixed Dutch-Indonesian descent who flooded into the Netherlands during the years following the independence of this former Dutch colony.

Dutch postwar industriousness ultimately resulted in economic prosperity, and with it came a climate of widespread opposition to old ways and established authority. This was, of course, not unique to the Netherlands. In other Western countries, such as the United States, France, and Germany, similar developments took place, particularly at universities, where forces of change were aimed at questions of power and dependency in relationships between authorities and citizens, younger and older generations, and men and women. Institutional practices in the spheres of government, education, work, family life, and leisure were fundamentally altered by a cultural revolution in which the young formed the vanguard.

Frugality and hard work yielded to the drive for enjoyment, and pleasures such as popular music, sports, and travel became paramount. Consumption in the private sphere arose as a respected goal; certain brands of clothes became status symbols; homes were equipped with new furniture, televisions, washing machines, refrigerators, and other appliances. With Saturday as well as Sunday decreed days of leisure, weekends underwent a complete metamorphosis in family activities that encouraged the more convenient preparation of foods. As incomes rose and leisure hours increased, sociability became more important. Visits and parties were – as always – accompanied by food and drink, and traveling abroad led to exposure to the foodways of other cultures. Mediterranean countries such as France, Spain, Italy, and the former Yugoslavia became preferred holiday destinations for wide segments of the population.

At the same time, migrant workers came from areas of southern Europe to take jobs in the Netherlands. In the 1970s and 1980s, many foreigners, along with nonwhite citizens of the Caribbean, especially Suriname, were attracted by the high levels of welfare and social security, all of which transformed the Netherlands into a multicultural and, in some respects, a multiethnic society.

Other important transformations took place in the private sphere. These had to do with changing relationships among family members, now that people increasingly worked outside of the home. A growing divorce rate, an earlier independence of the young, and a rise in the number of old people combined to stimulate a substantial growth in the number of one- and two-person households. Such new and distinct conditions of life in the Netherlands led, among other things, to a fundamental alteration of the Dutch attitude toward food, which started among the middle classes but reached into innovative groups in the lower strata.

As elsewhere in the West, eating became less associated with a physical need to fill the stomach and more with a fashion of dining well, even elegantly, and the status that this conveyed. A flood of cookbooks, glossy cookery magazines, even serious treatises on culinary culture, swept into the bookshops and newsstands; cooking classes and culinary demonstrations on television became popular, and the media increasingly devoted columns and programs to the pleasures of the table.

Exotic herbs, spices, and other ingredients became available, and the figure of the gourmet was no longer one likely to be scorned or ridiculed. This does not mean that a genuine high culinary culture developed in the Netherlands, as it did in Belgium (Scholliers 1993), but it was the case that a "civilizing" of eating and taste spread throughout the various social strata. Eating out in restaurants and inviting nonfamilial guests for dinner at home – practices that formerly had never been common – gradually became the norm, and the per capita use of alcoholic beverages and soft drinks rose to heights never seen before. Between 1965 and 1990, the consumption of beer multiplied by two and a half times, wine by four, and soft drinks by slightly more than two and a half (CBS 1994).

The new and discriminating Dutch taste was not characterized by uniformity. Rather, there were various (and sometimes contradictory) trends, as international foodstuffs were increasingly distributed across the globe. A demand for exotic food was first apparent in the success of Chinese and Indonesian restaurants, which appealed to the Dutch because the food was cheap and large quantities were provided. Asian food was followed by Mediterranean cuisine from the various countries visited by vacationing Dutch, and from this point, culinary inquisitiveness spread to include foods from more distant parts of the world, like Mexico and Japan.

Indeed, the Dutch developed a world cuisine of their own, although the exotic dishes that comprised it were often not relished in their original forms and strong flavors but were shaped and moderated to meet the Dutch preference for bland tastes. Another international eating trend was adopted in the form of fast food from the United States, which had, in many respects, replaced France as a postwar cultural model for the Netherlands.

Like others in the West, the Dutch have embraced the tendency to make cooking in the home as easy as possible, which has meant a greater use of convenience food in preparing meals, and the use of snack foods has become marked. Many working housewives and mothers (whose numbers have increased substantially) now regularly escape their previously important duty of cooking for the family, and in fact, the rhythms of work and leisure of individual household members no longer coincide, which has changed the pattern of meals. Nowadays, the hot family meal in the evening might be the only one shared; yet even then, individual members of the household frequently have other commitments that oblige them to use the microwave to heat their share of the meal at a later time.

The consumption of snacks (described as grazing) in between, instead of, or in combination with regular meals has increased considerably. In addition, many restaurants, ranging from very exclusive to very simple, have come into existence to meet the new needs of the different strata of the population. Between 1965 and 1990, the number of restaurants multiplied five times (CBS 1994). Typically, these establishments borrow from cuisines the world over: snack bars and take-out restaurants feature American hamburgers, Indonesian *nasi*, Belgian *patates frites*, and Italian pizza.

As elsewhere, such changes in eating habits have brought anxiety about extremely processed food and concomitant concerns about obesity, food allergies, eating disorders, and food additives and contaminants. Vegetarianism and other movements supporting specific dietary principles have grown in popularity and in acceptance. In short, various trends and countertrends emphasizing the enjoyment, but also the dangers, inherent in food developed in contradiction with one another. This is, indeed, a remarkable change in a country that has never been characterized by a pronounced culinary culture! Both developments may be interpreted as aspects of the globalization of eating and drinking in the Netherlands (Elias 1994).

Summary

In this chapter, it has been suggested that the development of Dutch eating habits over the centuries has been influenced by a complex set of interrelated economic, political, and sociocultural forces. Processes of state formation and nation building, civilization, and democratization have marked the culinary culture of the Low Countries since the Middle Ages.

Until the last few decades, the Dutch maintained a preference for cheap, simple, and nourishing food, even though their cooks had obtained ideas and inspiration from foreigners, particularly the French, since the Middle Ages. That a high culinary culture was never created in the Netherlands differs greatly from the experience of Belgium, where, in the last 150 years, one has developed that is much appreciated abroad as well as at home.

The lack, however, of a haute cuisine in the Netherlands does not mean that the Dutch retained their seventeenth-century habits of binge eating and drinking at festivals. Rather, the French influence on daily life among the elite increased substantially in the eighteenth century, with Dutch patricians losing their bourgeois mentality and coming to resemble aristocrats in the usual sense. This change increasingly shaped their preferences and manners according to French (courtly) ways, particularly in dress and in the choice of dishes and recipes. The growing "civilizing of appetite" (Mennell 1985: 20–40) impeded immoderate "guzzling" among broader strata of the urban middle classes and encouraged them at the same time to permit themselves the luxury of refinement in eating, tableware, and table manners. Later rounds of democratization and civilization took place during the nineteenth and twentieth centuries and ultimately reached farmers and other country people and urban workers.

In the aftermath of World War II, new culinary models from America, the Mediterranean, and the (postcolonial) Far East became available. Subsequently, a decrease in the consumption of bread and potatoes, backbones of the earlier Dutch meal, bore witness to fundamental changes at the Dutch table. The movement from potatoes to pasta has meant a fading both of the traditional composition of meals and of national boundaries. To eat in a typically Dutch way seems to mean "going global" in the Netherlands at the turn of the twenty-first century.

Anneke H. van Otterloo

Many thanks to Dr. Jozien Jobse-van Putten and to Prof. Dr. Stephen Mennell for their fruitful comments on an earlier version of this chapter.

Bibliography

Burema, L. 1953. *De voeding in Nederland van de Middeleeuwen tot de twintigste eeuw* (Food in the Netherlands from the Middle Ages to the twentieth century). Assen, the Netherlands.

CBS (Centraal Bureau voor de Statistiek) (Central Bureau of Statistics). 1994. *Vijfennegentig jaren statistiek in tijdreeksen, 1899-1994*. The Hague.

De Vries, Jan, and Ad van der Woude. 1995. *Nederland 1500-1815. De eerste ronde van moderne economische groei* (The Netherlands 1500-1815: The first round of modern economic growth). Amsterdam.

Elias, Norbert. [1939] 1994. *The civilizing process.* Oxford.

Goody, Jack. 1982. *Cooking, cuisine and class. A study in comparative sociology.* Cambridge.

Huizinga, Johan. [1941] 1984. *Nederlands beschaving in dezeventiende eeuw. Een schets* (Dutch civilization in the seventeenth century: A sketch). Groningen, the Netherlands.

Jobse-van Putten, Jozien. 1995. *Eenvoudig maar voedzaam. Cultuurgeschiedenis van de dagelijkse maaltijd in Nederland* (Simple, but nutritious: A cultural history of the daily meal in the Netherlands). Nijmegen, the Netherlands.

Mennell, Stephen. 1985. *All manners of food. Eating and taste in England and France from the Middle Ages to the present.* Oxford.

　　1988. Voorspel: Eten in de Lage Landen. In his *Smaken verschillen. Eetcultuur in Engeland en Frankrijk van de Middeleeuwen tot nu*, 15–29. Amsterdam.

Mennell, Stephen, Anne Murcott, and Anneke H. van Otterloo. 1992. *The sociology of food: Eating, diet and culture.* London and Delhi.

Romein, Jan, and Annie Romein. 1979. *De Lage Landen bij de zee. Een geschiedenis van het Nederlandse volk* (The Low Countries: A history of the Dutch nation). Utrecht.

Schama, Simon. 1987. *Overvloed en onbehagen* (The embarrassment of riches). Amsterdam and London.

Scholliers, Peter. 1993. *Arm en rijk aan tafel. Tweehonderd jaar eetcultuur in België* (Rich and poor at table: Two hundred years of culinary culture in Belgium). Berchem and Brussels, Belgium.

Van Deursen, A. Th. [1978] 1992. *Mensen van klein vermogen: Het 'kopergeld' van de Gouden Eeyw* (People of little riches: The small coins of the Golden Age). Amsterdam.

Van Otterloo, Anneke H. 1986. Over de culinaire culturen in Noord en Zuid. Enkele opmerkingen bij de sociogenese van nationale stijl en regionale variaties (About culinary cultures in the north and south). *Groniek* 95: 36–55.

　　1990. *Eten en eetlust in Nederland (1840-1990). Een historisch-sociologische studie* (Eating and appetite in The Netherlands (1840-1990): A historical and sociological study). Amsterdam.

Van 't Veer, Annie. 1966. *Oud-Hollands kookboek* (Old Dutch cookbook). Utrecht and Antwerp.

Zahn, Ernest. 1989. *Regenten, rebellen en reformatoren. Een visie op Nederland en de Nederlanders* (Regents, rebels and reformers: A view on the Netherlands and the Dutch). Amsterdam.

V.C.7 ❧ Russia

Dietary patterns in Russia display marked continuities over most of the past millennium or so. Staple foodstuffs have remained remarkably constant, and despite the introduction of new foods and beverages in later centuries and the gradual eclipse of a few items, the diets of the vast majority of the population underwent little qualitative change until well into the nineteenth century. Russia, relatively isolated from the West until the reigns of Peter I and Catherine in the eighteenth century, was as conservative in its cuisine as it was in politics and society, and the sharp gap between rich and poor was reflected in what they ate and drank.

Russia is defined for the purposes of this study as the lands inhabited by the modern eastern Slavic peoples, the Belorussians in the west, the Ukrainians in the south, and the Russians in the north and center of "European Russia." Brief mention is made of the Baltic, Transcaucasian, Siberian, and central Asian peoples, primarily as their foods influenced the diets of their Slavic rulers in the Russian Empire and the Soviet Union. Imperial Russia also controlled Finland and much of Poland during the nineteenth century, but these areas are not considered here.

Peoples ancestral to the modern eastern Slavs apparently began spreading out from their homeland in the territory near the modern borders of Poland, Belarus, and Ukraine around the seventh century. They moved into the forests of central and northern Russia at the expense of scattered Finnic peoples, most of whom were eventually absorbed or displaced. Expansion into the grasslands of the Ukraine and beyond was much slower because the steppes were dominated by pastoral peoples of Turkic and Mongol stock. The medieval Kievan state was able to hold the horsemen at bay for a while, but by the twelfth century the Slavs began to retreat northward under nomad pressure. Not until the sixteenth century was the new Muscovite state strong enough to begin the reconquest of the Ukraine and extend Russian power down the Volga. Traditional Russian cuisine developed in the forest zone but was profoundly influenced by expansion into the grasslands and along trade routes.

Early Russian Diets

Archaeological evidence indicates that the early Slavic inhabitants of the forest, like their Finnic neighbors, were farmers who used slash-and-burn techniques to make clearings for their villages and farms. Their primary grain was rye; oats, buckwheat, and barley played secondary roles, and wheat was always uncommon in the north. Grain was consumed primarily as bread, including the famous Russian black rye bread, but gruels (kasha) and porridges were common as well. Noodles were borrowed from the Tatars in the thirteenth or fourteenth century. Grain was also converted into beverages ranging from the virtually nonalcoholic *kvas* to light beer *(braga)* and beer.

A variety of fruits and vegetables were also grown. Turnips, hardy enough to thrive in the harsh northern climate, were an important root crop; carrots, beets, and radishes were also significant. Garlic and onions were common seasonings. Cabbages and cucumbers were important in diets, both fresh or preserved by pickling or in salt. Such preparations provided the main supply of vegetables during the long winter and were essential as antiscorbutics. Cabbage soup *(shchi)* was and remains a dietary staple. There was at least limited cultivation of apple and cherry orchards from very early times.

The long winters created severe forage problems that precluded large-scale stock raising, but limited numbers of cows, horses, pigs, chickens, and ducks were kept. Possession of livestock was a measure of family wealth. Slaughtering was usually done in the fall. Milk, meat, and eggs were scarce and expensive and generally appeared in meals on feast days and festivals. Hard cheeses were not important, but cottage cheese was fairly common.

The forests also supplied many foods. Game animals provided welcome meat, especially in areas with sparse populations. Ducks, geese, and other birds were widely hunted and traded. Fish, fresh from local streams and ponds, or traded in salted or dried form, were the major source of animal protein. Wild nuts and berries provided seasonal variety, and mushroom gathering was and remains a popular activity. The forest was also a habitat for bees, whose hives were raided for wax and honey. The latter was a prized sweetener and was often fermented into mead. Beekeeping eventually became a lucrative sideline for some farmers.

Salt, crucial for preserving fish, meat, and vegetables, was mined in rock form in a few places and was later obtained from the sea in the Crimea and salt lakes near Astrakhan at the mouth of the Volga. The major sources of salt, however, were well north of Moscow. Boiling seawater to crystalline salt was being done on the White Sea by the twelfth century, and salt production developed into an important industry in this remote region. By the fourteenth century wells were being drilled to tap underground brine pools at many sites between Moscow and the White Sea. Salt was an essential commodity and its production and trade were lucrative and heavily taxed enterprises.

In the tundra zone of the far north, from the Lapps (Saami) of the Kola Peninsula to the Chuckchi in extreme northeastern Siberia, Russian fur traders and pioneers encountered peoples who survived by hunting land and sea mammals, fishing, and herding reindeer. Further south, in the Siberian taiga forest, aboriginal peoples like the Yakuts supplemented hunting and fishing with stock raising. Russians venturing into such environments had, of course, to adapt to local conditions, but they traded with their countrymen for grain and introduced bread and other grain products, including fermented and distilled beverages, to their northern neighbors.

Daily diets were strongly influenced by religious requirements and the seasons. Conversion to Christianity, traditionally dated to 988, had a profound impact on food consumption patterns. The Orthodox calendar included a large number of feast and fast days which, to the amazement of some foreign observers, were widely observed. Church fasts included Lent, the 40 days before Christmas, and the Saints Peter and Paul fast. This fast, which ended on June 28 and could last from one to six weeks, depending on when Easter fell, came at a time when stored food was running low and caloric demands for agricultural work were very high.

Meat was forbidden during all fasts; fish and all foods of animal origin were forbidden during Lent. Wealthy Russians, however, frequently enjoyed elaborate fish dishes and fine wines during fast periods. Feast days, including Christmas, Easter, weddings, harvest celebrations, and, sometimes, funerals, were the major occasions for eating meat, pastries, and other rarities and for hearty drinking bouts. Binge drinking, and to some extent, binge eating, were regular features of Russian life, reflecting both the agricultural cycle and religious observances.

Peasants ate best in the fall, when the new harvest was gathered and animals were slaughtered. Mushrooms were hunted all over Russia and the Ukraine. They were both a prized food and an excuse for convivial excursions. The autumn was a common time for weddings and associated feasts. Fresh fruits and vegetables were available during the warmer months, but stored grain, pickled cabbage, and salted cucumbers were the winter staples. Food supplies often ran low in the spring; diminished stores and religious fasts meant lean meals during plowing and planting time in the late spring.

The conquest of the entire Volga River to its mouth on the Caspian Sea, completed by 1569, placed Russia in an advantageous position to trade for spices, notably pepper, saffron, and cinnamon. Melons and fruits from central Asia became more accessible, and the empire gained new sources of salt. The Volga and its tributaries provided a rich variety of fish, including sturgeon and its caviar and the sterlets, a variety of small sturgeon that delighted both Russian and visiting foreign gourmands. Fish were sold dried or salted and even transported live in special boats for the tables of the Tsar and other notables. Frozen fish were widely distributed during the winter. *Pirogi* (sing. *pirog*), pastries filled with meat, fish, or other delicacies, and *pel'meni,* small Siberian dumplings, probably entered the Russian diet during the sixteenth century. They may have been borrowed from Finnic or Tatar peoples of the Volga valley.

Russia slowly and erratically expanded into the Ukraine and southern Russia during the sixteenth, seventeenth, and eighteenth centuries. The conquest of these rich black-earth grasslands provided the basis for extensive wheat cultivation and a growing export of grain. Ukrainians and Russian colonists were able to raise more fruit and vegetables in these milder climes and to keep more livestock. Meat, though not milk, played a larger role in diets. Beets were a popular crop, and beet soup *(borshch)* held the place of cabbage soup *(shchi)* in the Ukrainian cuisine. Beets were also made into *kvas,* which was not only a beverage but a common stock for Ukrainian soups and stews. Large quantities of watermelons and eggplants were grown in some districts for local consumption and for trade.

The Eighteenth Century

The eighteenth century was a period of change in Russian diets, particularly among the elite, as many new foodstuffs were introduced. Peter the Great's opening to the West, symbolized by his construction of a new capital on the recently conquered shores of the Baltic, and complemented by the modernizing policies of Catherine at the end of the century, exposed the growing Russian Empire to an array of new foods and drinks from Europe, Asia, and the Americas. European, especially French, chefs appeared in many noble homes, and gourmet cooking spread among courtiers and other members of the elite. The first Russian cookbook appeared in 1779; it was followed by many translations of German and French cookbooks, sometimes adapted to local ingredients and tastes.

A few Russians learned to eat salads, an innovation dismissed by others as the equivalent of eating grass. The Dutch had introduced asparagus in the 1600s; at the end of the century a French visitor was treated to "dates from Egypt" by a clergyman in the far north. Tea, coffee, sugar, and the tomato were introduced among the upper classes. Elegant finger foods for hors d'oeuvres *(zakuski)* provided refreshment at receptions.

Wine had always been imported in small quantities by the church for communion and had occasionally graced the tables of the elite, but in the eighteenth century wines from Europe, and later from Armenia, Georgia, and parts of the southern Ukraine, gained popularity in gentry homes. Distilled spirits, first introduced from the Baltic and Poland in the 1500s, began to displace mead and beer, even in some poor households. Tea, known as a curiosity from the seventeenth century, was brewed in ornate samovars in the homes of the rich and in new urban cafés during the 1700s, and tea drinking began to percolate down the social scale. Tea was often served with cane sugar from the West Indies. Sugar, a major import by the late 1700s, gradually replaced honey as a sweetener, first in the homes of the wealthy, and then, like tea and vodka, it spread to more humble abodes.

Two other New World cultigens reached Russia during the eighteenth century. The potato, as in Ireland and Hungary (and like cassava in western Africa), was introduced to prevent famines. Catherine issued an edict recommending its cultivation after a dearth in food production in 1765, but this directive garnered little response except in the Baltic provinces dominated by German nobles, who took more interest in the tuber and made sure that their Baltic peasants did, too. For decades, however, the potato was scorned by the Slavic peasantry, remaining only a curiosity on the tables of sophisticates. Maize, introduced into eastern Europe in the eighteenth century and a staple crop in Hungary, Serbia, and Romania by the nineteenth century, remained insignificant in Russia, except in Bessarabia (Moldova) in the far southwest.

The tradition of keeping foreign dignitaries busy with lengthy banquets, featuring numerous rich dishes served in a seemingly endless sequence and even more numerous alcoholic toasts, reached a high stage of development during this period. Such ostentatious hospitality, already given mixed notice by sixteenth-century English and Dutch visitors, has continued until the present. The foreigners were well treated, kept in a haze during their visit, and distracted from seeing or hearing things that their hosts preferred they not know about.

The Nineteenth Century

Dietary innovations began to reach the peasantry, the vast majority of the population, only in the nineteenth century. The gradual spread of sugar beets and tomatoes in the Ukraine and southern Russia, and potatoes, especially in northern and central regions, did make something of a difference in the nutritional regimen. Still, dietary surveys and travelers' reports indicate strong continuity in the consumption patterns of most Russians. Tastes in beverages underwent more significant change as tea and vodka became widely used at all levels of society.

Bread, generally the familiar dark rye loaf, remained the staff of life. Wheat bread became a little more common, especially in the Black Earth areas of the Ukraine and in the Volga provinces, but most wheat was produced for export. A working man commonly ate 3 to 5 pounds of bread daily. Kasha was also a frequent dish. On feast days, and sometimes more often in prosperous households, dough was used to make *pirogi* filled with meat, cottage cheese, cabbage, or berries; or *blini,* thin yeast-leavened pancakes rolled up and filled with sweets or smothered in butter and sour cream; or *knyshi,* pastry puffs filled with cream.

Cabbage and cucumbers were the most important vegetables, but serf and free-peasant gardens generated a variety of produce. Onions and garlic continued to be popular seasonings, and peas, melons, berries, turnips, and other garden produce were appreciated during the summer. Oils from hemp, flax, and sunflower seeds (another American introduction) were used in cooking. Mushrooms, nuts, and berries were collected in the forest and could be salted or dried for the winter. Apiaries, providing honey, were common, and many peasants kept pigs, sheep, and/or poultry. The diet was monotonous and often lacked protein, especially for the poor. A rural doctor in the 1860s blamed the bad health of peasants in Pskov Province largely on their diet, which was mostly rye bread and cabbage. However, a study of villages in Tambov Province suggested that serfs in the early nineteenth century had better diets than contemporary French or Belgian peasants. In particular, these rural Russians enjoyed more meat.

The most important addition to the diets of most nineteenth-century Russians was the potato. Except in the Baltic and Polish provinces, potato cultivation was negligible until the 1830s. The peasants saw no need for them, especially since land and labor would have to be diverted from rye, and some even opposed potatoes on religious grounds. But government interest in and encouragement of potato cultivation grew after famines in the 1830s to the extent that heavy-handed official pressure produced several potato riots. By 1843, however, a German traveler, Baron von Haxthausen, noted that potatoes were being introduced into parts of Yaroslavl Province. Some peasants were interested in the tubers, others were coerced into planting them, and potato cultivation spread slowly. Nobles sometimes used them to feed livestock. In general, the potato spread into Belorussia and the northwestern provinces during the 1840s and 1850s, and thence into most of northern and central Russia and the Ukraine. By 1900 it had become a staple in most areas, often eaten in soup.

Meat and dairy products remained too expensive for most peasants, but the growing towns provided a market for cattle and milk. Milk and butter were most extensively consumed in the Baltics and in the north; peasants in the south and in the Ukraine generally had more meat. Even in areas of the south and southeast with large cattle herds, few peasants ate beef. Cattle were destined for urban markets. Peasants were more likely to eat pork, mutton, or poultry, the frequency of such meals being directly correlated with household wealth. Fish remained an important food during the numerous fasts, especially for those living near rivers and lakes or wealthy enough to purchase dried or salted fish.

Diets of the gentry were obviously richer and more diversified than those of the peasantry, but they varied greatly according to wealth and individual preference. City dwellers, including the merchant and artisan groups, had access to more imported foods and items from distant parts of the empire than all but the most opulent country residents. Many nobles spent the summers on their estates, where fresh foods were readily available, and wintered in the city. Even the petty rural landowner tended to take afternoon tea with pastries, biscuits, cheeses, caviar, jellies, jams, and other snacks, and have a heavy evening meal.

Hospitality was generous on country estates, and guests could expect to be well fed. Picnics were popular on pleasant days. In the evening, diners enjoyed *zakuski*, followed by a soup course with *pirogi*, a fish or poultry course often served cold, and a meat course with potatoes and vegetables. Salads remained unusual. Beef was especially popular with those who could afford it. Appropriate wines and champagnes might be served with each course. A meal would be capped by sweets and cognac or a dessert wine. Wealthy nobles sometimes maintained fishponds and built hothouses to provide fruits and vegetables off-season and icehouses to preserve them. Rich and even middle-class Russians employed skilled cooks, sometimes specially trained serfs, in their kitchens. A French- or Paris-trained chef was a mark of distinction. Conspicuous food consumption, the use of luxury foods and beverages from abroad, and elaborate meals for guests were marks of high status and gentility.

Servants in great houses ate less grandly, though they did have access to leftovers and could sometimes appropriate items meant for the master's table. Still, if the recommendations of the leading nineteenth-century cookbook are any indication, household servants ate better than the peasants. For breakfast they might have had potatoes with fried eggs or porridge; dinner menus included *shchi* with buckwheat kasha, or *borshch* with dumplings, or barley soup and roast beef with mashed potatoes, or vegetable soup with a meat and barley kasha. On feast days servants were to have meat or poultry and assorted *pirogi.*

Alcoholic Beverages

Patterns of beverage consumption showed some dramatic changes in the nineteenth century. *Kvas,* a barely alcoholic product of bread or grain fermentation over a few days, was the basic daily drink and an important part of the diet. It was widely made and consumed in the home and dispensed by peddlers in towns and markets. *Kvas* could be produced from barley, oats, rye, and wheat, or, in the Ukraine, from beets, and was sometimes flavored with berries or fruit. It was most popular in central Russia and Siberia. There were numerous regional varieties.

Light beer *(braga)* and beer were popular, especially in the Baltics, Belorussia, and the Ukraine, but were less widely consumed in Russia and Siberia. Much was home-brewed, but taverns selling commercial beers appeared in the villages and towns. The state levied heavy taxes on commercial beer. Mead continued to decline and became a rarity by midcentury. Tea drinking, accompanied by sugar, spread slowly but became widespread in the villages by the 1880s.

The drink that became most popular, most destructive, most controversial, and most profitable for the government was vodka. According to legend, Vladimir of Kiev, the ruler who chose Orthodox Christianity as the new religion in 988, rejected Islam because strong drink was "the joy of the Rus." Small-scale distilleries began operating in the late sixteenth century in the Baltic region and along the trade routes between Moscow and the White Sea port of Archangelsk, but vodka, "little water," did not begin to make inroads in the general population until the second half of the eighteenth century.

Distillation of grain was a monopoly of the state and privileged nobles and was heavily taxed. As early as the 1720s, liquor taxes made up 11 percent of government revenues; the percentage had almost doubled by midcentury. In 1767 liquor monopolies in central Russia were sold to contractors and, except for a brief period of state monopoly in the 1820s, liquor farmers controlled the trade in central Russia until 1863. The farmers operated small drinking places scattered in the villages and towns. Their profits, although extensive, were reduced by the sums they paid the government for their local monopolies and by bribes paid to officials of all ranks.

From 1863 until the 1890s the state again assumed a monopoly to raise additional revenues, after which free trade and an excise tax system were introduced. During the period from 1805 to 1913, receipts from alcohol sales, primarily vodka, averaged 31.4 percent of all state revenues. Free trade prevailed in the western provinces, keeping prices lower and, thus, consumption higher. In the early twentieth century, state production of a uniform product at relatively low cost also encouraged greater consumption.

Social commentators, doctors, church leaders, and sometimes even government officials displayed growing concern over alcoholism during the nineteenth and early twentieth centuries. Vodka was the problem, not *kvas* or beer. Russians consumed 40 times more alcohol in the form of spirits than as beer or ale. Indeed, per capita beer consumption in the 1850s was less than 2 liters a year, far below the roughly 20 liters in the Polish provinces or 50 liters in Britain. Yet per capita vodka consumption was no higher than the use of distilled spirits in other European countries. As in early-nineteenth-century America, the problem was binge drinking; drinking simply to get drunk.

Drinking remained, as in previous centuries, partially linked to social and religious rituals and to mutual-aid activities like barn raisings or group harvest efforts. Cultural restraints on alcohol consumption, however, tended to weaken in the countryside and were especially weak in the cities. Contemporary observers decried the impact of the taverns on family and economic life and on the health of heavy drinkers. Reform efforts were hampered by the crucial role that vodka played in state finance. But concern was clearly rising, and in 1914 Russia embarked on a widely ignored experiment in prohibition.

The Soviet Period

The revolutions of 1917 inaugurated several years of severe food shortages. The new Bolshevik regime inherited food production and distribution difficulties as well as the alcohol problem from its Tsarist predecessor. These were compounded by World War I, the bloody Civil War, and the flounderings of the new regime. Despite many drastic policy changes, Russian patterns of eating and drinking showed substantial continuity with the past.

The industrial north continued to be a grain-deficit region with cities and rural dwellers that had to be supplied from the south and, increasingly, from Kazakhstan and Siberia. Improvements in internal transportation facilitated grain flows and allowed fruits and vegetables to reach European Russia from the Transcaucasian and central Asian republics. Much of central Asia, especially Uzbekistan, became a food deficit area with an economy based on cotton monoculture. Collectivization of agriculture, conducted during the 1930s at great human cost, did not solve the grain production problem, nor did the plowing of "virgin lands" or massive attempts to grow maize during the post-Stalin period.

Grain imports from the West have been necessary almost annually since the 1960s. Livestock production and meat consumption increased but continued to lag far behind Western norms, although in the years after World War II, efficient Russian fishing fleets roamed distant seas, providing more fish for Soviet consumption. Government policies kept food prices artificially low, with rationing and inflation masked by periodic shortages and long lines in shops.

Collective farmers were allowed to work small plots for their own profit. These intensively worked gardens produced a large proportion of the meat, eggs, milk, and fresh fruits and vegetables that appeared in urban markets. Armenian, Georgian, and central Asian entrepreneurs even found it profitable to bring melons and other produce from their sunny climes to the cold cities of northern Russia.

Rural diets did not begin to show major changes until after 1953, and even by 1960 there was remarkable continuity with prerevolutionary times. Table V.C.7.1, calculated from data presented by Basile Kerblay, demonstrates that (except for legumes, which are not shown), rural consumption levels in 1940 were still a little below averages prevailing at the end of the Tzarist rule. Cereals, potatoes, vegetable oils, sugar, meat, and fish were consumed in lower quantities in 1940 than before the revolution; people ate only marginally more vegetables, dairy products, and eggs.

In 1913, vegetable foods provided 84.2 percent of calories consumed by peasants, and 62.8 percent of the total came from cereals (Table V.C.7.2). In 1960 the comparable figures were 80 percent from plant sources, with 56 percent from grains. The most important change from 1940 to 1960 was the greater share of calories provided by vegetable oils and sugar. Consumption of foods of animal origin, especially fish and eggs, had increased significantly in the postwar years.

Official consumption data averaged for the entire population of the Soviet Union are shown for 1913, 1965, 1970, and 1976 in Table V.C.7.2. Quantities of meat, eggs, fish, dairy products, vegetables, fruits and berries, and sugar rose dramatically, with major gains in eggs and dairy products in the decade after 1965. Grains contributed less, with most of the decline coming before 1965. Government data paint a picture very much like those of Kerblay.

Table V.C.7.1. *Indexes of food consumption by collective farmworkers (1896-1915 = 100)*

	1940	1960
Cereals	63-71	58-66
Potatoes	85-91	104-12
Vegetables and fruit	96-114	132-58
Vegetable oils	76	214
Sugar	69	510
Meat, fat, and poultry	75-84	139-56
Fish	47-57	148-82
Milk and dairy products	110	149
Eggs	108	310

Source: Data from Kerblay (1962), p. 894.

Table V.C.7.2. *Consumption of major foods, 1913-1976 (kg/person/yr; except eggs)*

	1913	1965	1970	1976
Meat and meat products	29	41	48	55
Milk and dairy products	154	251	307	315
Eggs (units)	48	124	159	206
Fish and fish products	6.7	12.6	15.4	18.5
Sugar	8.1	34.2	38.8	40.4
Vegetable oils	–	7.1	6.8	7.7
Potatoes	114	142	130	119
Vegetables and melons	40	72	82	85
Fruits and berries	11	28	35	37
Bread and pasta	200	156	149	142

Source: Data from *Narodnoe khozyaistvo SSSR za 60 let* (1977), p. 511.

As in Tsarist Russia, members of the elite in the Soviet Union enjoyed a far greater variety and higher quality of foods and beverages than the bulk of the population. Ranking party officials and favored athletes, dancers, scientists, musicians, and other prominent persons had access to the finest domestic and foreign goods in special stores that were off-limits to workers and peasants. Such privileges marked a new elite and gave them excellent reasons to conform to the system.

Although food prices were heavily subsidized for most of the Soviet period, Russians continued to devote a substantial, though declining percentage of their incomes to food. Data for urban workers and employees of collective farms, presented for the period from 1940 to 1990 in Table V.C.7.3, show steady declines for both groups. It is interesting to note that the poorly paid farmers had to spend a higher proportion of their incomes for food than did urban contemporaries. Many toiled on farms that specialized in grain or cotton production, but even those who raised crops for themselves on private plots still had to buy much of their food.

Urbanization has been a major theme in the twentieth-century history of Russia, and urban diets have undergone somewhat more change than those of rural areas. Most of the improvements have come since the late 1940s, following the horrors of collectivization, forced industrialization, and World War II. City dwellers do consume a wider variety of foodstuffs than in the past, and the amount of foods of animal origin has increased significantly. Indeed, greater livestock production became a major goal

with Stalin's successors. Still, travelers and medical observers continue to describe a diet heavy in starches and low in fresh vegetables and fruits. Throughout the post-1945 period, production problems and a primitive distribution system have meant periodic shortages and long lines in shops. Meat and poultry remain expensive and of low quality. Sausage is a major component of meat consumption. Fat intake has risen and is, along with alcohol, implicated in rising rates of cardiovascular morbidity and mortality.

The Soviet regime never solved the alcohol problem it inherited from Tsarist times. Prohibition collapsed during the war, and with the establishment of stability in the early 1920s, old drinking habits reappeared. During the 1920s and 1930s there were intensive efforts to reduce drinking both in cities and in the countryside, but these had little impact. Officials decried the adverse effects of excess drinking on production and health, but the state continued to reap huge revenues from liquor sales. For example, during the 1960s and 1970s, taxes on alcohol produced about 10 percent of the state's income. Home distillation began in earnest during the Soviet period, as people coped with high prices and poor-quality state production and evaded periodic temperance campaigns by making *samogon*. Normal vodka had an average alcohol content of 40 percent; the alcohol content in *samogon* ranged from 25 to 75 percent. In the late 1950s and early 1960s, however, ethanol shortages led many to consume stolen wood alcohol, with sometimes fatal results. Cheap sugar, available from Cuba from the early 1960s, was a boon to *samogon* producers.

Table V.C.7.3. *Food as a percentage of family expenditure, 1940-90*

	1940	1965	1970	1975	1980	1985	1990
Industrial workers and employees	53.8	37.9	35.7	32.9	35.9	33.7	29.9
Collective farmworkers	67.3	45.2	40.4	37.1	39.6	36.3	32.4

Sources: Data from *Narodnoe khozyaistvo SSSR za 60 let* (1977), pp. 490-1, and *Narodnoe khozyaistvo SSSR v 1990 q* (1991), pp. 113-4.

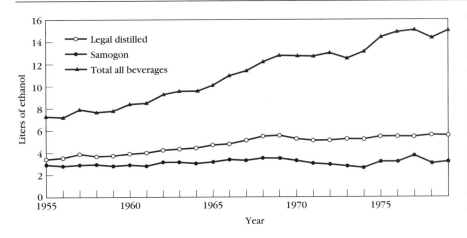

Figure V.C.7.1.1. Pure alcohol consumption per person over 15 years old, 1955–79. Total includes *samogon*, state-produced "strong" drinks, and state-produced wines and beers. Totals do not include home-brewed beer, *braga*, or wine, estimated by Treml as the equivalent of at least one additional liter of pure alcohol per person over 15 per year. Also excluded is consumption of stolen industrial alcohol. (Data from Treml, 1982, p. 68.)

Fig V : C : 7 : 1

Officials continued to decry the costs of alcohol abuse, and in the 1980s both Yuri Andropov and Mikhail Gorbachev attempted to control sales and enforce moderation in drinking habits, but their campaigns had little success. Indeed, as Figure V.C.7.1 shows, per capita alcohol consumption rose steadily and alarmingly in the years from 1955 to 1979, and it has remained high since then. Beer, *braga,* and wine consumption were clearly eclipsed by "strong" distilled beverages, although use of the former also rose. The heaviest drinkers were males in the Baltic and Slavic republics, especially Russia, Estonia, and Latvia. Per capita consumption was less in the traditional Islamic regions and in the wine-producing republics of Armenia and Georgia.

In 1970 it was estimated that Soviet citizens over the age of 15 spent an average of 13 percent of their incomes on state-produced alcoholic beverages. For Russia, the figure was 15.8 percent. These estimates do not include *samogon* or home-produced beer or wine. It is not surprising that health officials have placed much of the blame for high death rates among middle-aged and elderly Slavic males on alcohol abuse. Acute alcohol poisoning killed almost 40,000 people in 1976, a rate almost 90 times that of the United States. The impact of alcoholism on diseases of the liver and the cardiovascular system was also much greater than in the United States.

Famines

A final aspect of food history in Russia must be mentioned: famine. In Russia, as in most other preindustrial societies, bad weather and war often resulted in serious food shortages, sometimes over large regions. In contrast to the Western experience, however, famines continued to ravage Russia until the mid–twentieth century. Major famines have been recorded from the tenth century until 1946-7; even in the nineteenth century there were famines or serious, widespread food shortages in roughly one year out of five. Bad weather, primarily cold in the north and drought in the south and in the Volga provinces, triggered many famines, but war and government policies frequently compounded or, sometimes, even created them.

Other factors made Russia particularly vulnerable to dearths. The deep poverty of most Russians meant that personal food reserves were usually inadequate to carry families over bad years. Many of the central provinces suffered serious rural overpopulation by the nineteenth century; seasonal labor migration to cities or richer agricultural areas and permanent migration to the Volga region and Siberia were inadequate safety valves. The Tsarist government made some efforts to monitor agricultural conditions and store grain for emergencies, yet lack of revenue and bureaucratic ineptitude hampered relief efforts. The government was usually too weak to control hoarding and speculation, even when it tried. But fortunately Russia was so large that the whole country could not be affected by the same adverse weather conditions or, usually, the same war or disorders, so there were always food surplus regions that could supply suffering provinces.

Large-scale movement of foodstuffs was, however, hindered by huge distances and a backward transportation system. Even the development of a national rail network in the late nineteenth century, although certainly helpful, was inadequate to meet needs. When frosts came too early or too late, or when the rains failed, peasants tightened their belts. They adulterated bread with a variety of wild plants and weeds, collected what they could from woods and fields as famine foods, and slaughtered their animals. Frequent dearths and the vagaries of the annual dietary cycle gave the peasants ample opportunity to learn to cope with food shortages.

Despite folk wisdom, peasant toughness, and relief efforts, the death tolls from famine were sometimes enormous. The 1891-2 famine killed roughly 400,000 people, despite government relief measures that were far more successful than critics of the regime would admit. Millions perished in 1921-2 when famine, caused by drought, the devastation of the Civil War, and ideologically driven state policies, swept the Volga provinces and part of the Ukraine. Only massive aid from the United States and Europe prevented a much greater catastrophe. The horrible famine of 1933–4, which ravaged most of the Ukraine and parts of the Volga basin and the northern Caucasus, was the direct result of Joseph Stalin's drive to collectivize agriculture and destroy the more prosperous stratum of the peasantry. Death tolls are currently being debated, but it is clear that several million perished. Similarly, the postwar famine of 1946–7, which killed at least several hundred thousand people, owed more to recollectivization of zones liberated from the Germans and government reconstruction priorities than to dry weather.

Conclusion

It would be wrong to conclude this survey on such a bleak note, especially as the Russian, Belarussian, and Ukrainian peoples are attempting to create new economic and political orders. Privatization of agriculture and free retail trade should bring better quality and more variety to grocery shelves. Russia is once again open to new dietary influences, ranging from McDonald's, Pepsi, and pizza to haute cuisine from France. By the same token, Russian foods, from caviar and beef Stroganoff to pirogi and borshch, have enriched the cuisines of many countries as Russian, Ukrainian, and Jewish migrants have brought them to Europe and North America.

K. David Patterson

Bibliography

Conquest, Robert. 1986. *The harvest of sorrow: Soviet collectivization and the terror-famine*. New York.

Dando, W. A. 1976. Man-made famines: Some geographic insights from an exploratory study of a millennium of Russian famines. *Ecology of Food and Nutrition* 4: 219–34.

Farley, Marta Pisetska. 1990. *Festive Ukrainian cooking*. Pittsburgh, Pa.

Herlihy, Patricia. 1991. Joy of the Rus: Rites and rituals of Russian drinking. *The Russian Review* 50: 131–47.

Hoch, Steven L. 1986. *Serfdom and social control in Russia: Petrovskoe, a village in Tambov*. Chicago.

Kerblay, Basile. 1962. L'évolution de l'alimentation rurale en russie (1896-1960). *Annales: Économies, Sociétés, Civilisations* 17: 885–913.

Matossian, Mary. 1968. The peasant way of life. In *The peasant in nineteenth-century Russia*, ed. Wayne S. Vucinich, 1–40. Stanford, Calif.

Narodnoe khozyaistvo SSSR v 1990 q. 1991. Finansy i statistika. Moscow.

Narodnoe khozyaistvo SSSR za 60 let. 1977. Tsentral'noe statisticheskoe upravlenie. Moscow.

Rabinovich, Michail G. 1992. Ethnological studies in the traditional food of the Russians, Ukrainians and Byelorussians between the 16th and 19th centuries: State of research and basic problems. In *European food history: A research review*, ed. Hans J. Teuteberg, 224–35. Leicester, England.

Smith, R. E. F., and David Christian. 1984. *Bread and salt: A social and economic history of food and drink in Russia*. Cambridge.

Toomre, Joyce. 1992. *Classic Russian cooking: Elena Molokhovets' A gift to young housewives*. Bloomington, Ind.

Treml, Vladimir G. 1982. *Alcohol in the USSR: A statistical study*. Durham, N.C.

The History and Culture
of Food and Drink in the Americas

V.D.1 ☙ Mexico and Highland Central America

The diversity of the natural environment in Mexico and highland Central America has influenced the development of food and dietary patterns. From the aridity of the great Sonoran Desert in the north, through the temperate basins of the Valley of Anahuac, to the tropical forests of the south, different climates and soils have conditioned what and how people ate. Within the larger regions, hundreds of microregions have had their own environmental and dietary characteristics, and for millennia cultures have modified these environments to suit their food needs. Three especially profound events that have influenced environment and diet are the emergence of agriculture, the arrival of Europeans (1519), and the technological and organizational changes of the twentieth century.

Early Diet

Before the advent of agriculture, hunting, fishing, and gathering provided the nutrients for Mexican diets. Most large mammals had become extinct by about 7200 B.C., and four plants in particular - mesquite, nopal, maguey, and wild maize (teozinte) - increasingly complemented a diminishing amount of animal protein provided by fishing and hunting. Even after the rise of sedentary societies dependent on agriculture, food gathering continued to provide essential nutrients for most indigenous groups. Densely populated communities in the central highland valleys and seminomadic peoples in the arid north enriched their food supply by collecting larvae, insects, and grubs, in addition to small mammals and reptiles.

As food production became more abundant, the quantity of collected foods declined, and it was on the base of domesticated crops that Mexican civilization rested. Maize, squash, beans, tomatoes, chillies, amaranth, several cactus varieties, and many fruits (among them avocado and guava) constituted the diet of the vast majority of Mexicans.

Maize was the main food of the sedentary peoples of all of highland Middle America. In the highlands of Guatemala one Quiché Maya word for maize is *kana,* which means "our mother." Maize was so important to some cultures that without it there was a cultural sense of hunger, even if other foods were available (Herrera Tejada 1987: 230-3). Maize is a particularly fertile and nutritious plant, capable of providing abundant calories and nutrients. When it is eaten with beans, another staple of the highland diet, the lysine, isoleucine, and tryptophan deficiencies in maize are overcome, and provides a pattern of amino acids similar to that of animal protein. Moreover, the traditional preparation of maize, which involves soaking the kernels in a lime (CaO) solution, releases niacin for the consumer and provides significant amounts of calcium.

Maize's centrality to the diet can be seen in the diverse ways that it was prepared. First eaten raw for its juices or toasted over a fire, its preparation as a food gradually took many shapes and forms. When ground finely and added to liquid, it formed the gruel known variously as *atole, pozole,* or *pinole.* As a *masa,* or dough, it was a food for the most versatile of cooks. In addition to diverse tortillas (thin griddle cakes) and tamales (dumplings steamed in corn husks), maize was cooked in myriad other shapes with such names as *peneques, pellizcadas, sopes,* and tostadas. In addition, it could be popcorn, a preparation now well known the world over. Maize has served as a plate to support other foods (as in a taco), as the base for complicated dishes (for example, an enchilada), and as a napkin.

Another important food for the sedentary people of Mexico was squash, by which we mean a number of plants belonging to the genus *Cucurbita,* which includes pumpkins, squash, and zucchini, among others. All were fully employed as food sources. Their stems constituted an ingredient of a soup now called *sopa de guias;* the tasty yellow flowers have also long been a part of soups, stews, and quesadillas, and the fruit itself can be boiled. In recent times, brown sugar and cinnamon have been added to form a thick syrup that transforms the boiled fruit into *calabaza en tacha,* the classical dessert for the *Día de los Muertos.* Pumpkin seeds are usually left to dry in the sun and then are toasted and eaten with a dash of salt. By weight, they have a higher content of isoleucine, leucine, lysine, methionine, phenylalanine, threonine, tryptophan, and valine than maize, beans, amaranth, and even egg whites. These seeds are also known as a medicine to get rid of tapeworms.

As already mentioned, many wild foods, some of them peculiar to Mexico's Central Valley region, were essential to the diet. *Tecuitlatl (Spirulina geitleri),* an algae collected from the surface of lakes in the valley, was particularly important as a source of protein, vitamins, and minerals. According to sixteenth-century reports, sufficient amounts of the algae were available to make it nutritionally significant.

Animal foods complemented the many plants that were the basis of the highland diet. Along with domesticated rabbits, dogs, and turkeys, the Aztecs enjoyed a variety of wild animals, birds, fish, reptiles, amphibians, and insects. Many of these food sources have remained parts of nutritional regimes into the twentieth century. Indeed, the turkey has subsequently gained greater importance in the cuisine. Despite the availability of wild fowl and then of domesticated ducks and chickens introduced by the Spaniards, the turkey survived as a culturally important food in Mexico. In contrast, Mexican hairless dogs *(xoloitzcuintli)* are no longer eaten.

The pre-Columbian diet of Middle America was also complex. The region dominated by the Maya had as much diversity as the central highlands. Along the coast and river estuaries, fish and shellfish provided essential nutrients. Cultivated maize was supplemented by plants such as *chaya (Cnidoscolus chayamansa)* and *ramón (Brosimum alicastrum). Ramón* may have been an especially significant foodstuff. Under cultivation, this tree produced large quantities of edible seeds that had a protein content between 11.4 and 13.4 percent, substantially higher than local grains (Puleston and Puleston 1979). Several root crops provided carbohydrates for the diet: *jícamas (Pachyrhizus erosus), camotes (Ipomoea batatas), yuca (Manihot esculenta),* and *malanga (Xanthosoma sp.)* (Vargas 1984: 278).

The quantity and quality of food in early diets remain open to interpretation. Anthropological evidence provides insights into specific sites during narrow time periods, but it does not help in the problem of generalizing for the region. One approach to the question of diet has been to analyze the carrying capacity of the land (population density versus potential food resources) on the eve of the arrival of Europeans. But even if it were possible to determine the precise carrying capacity of any region, it would not necessarily reveal how much people ate. Based on carrying capacity, estimates for the central region of Mexico range from 1,400 to 2,629 calories per person per day (Ortiz de Montellano 1990: 80).

One line of investigation that has revealed new insights into the quality of the diet has focused on Aztec cannibalism. The investigation took its modern form when Michael Harner published a widely cited article that emphasized protein deficiency as a reason for Aztec cannibalism (Harner 1977). According to his reasoning, the dense population of central Mexico, so dependent on a maize diet, lacked adequate numbers of domesticated animals, and hunting and gathering could not have supplied sufficient whole protein to compensate for its lack in the diet. Climatic uncertainties and recurring droughts in the late fifteenth century further contributed to deficiencies in the Aztec food supply.

Debate over such issues has led to different conclusions. One, which counters the protein-deficiency argument, stresses that the Aztec diet delivered plenty of good-quality protein. In addition, there is evidence showing that Aztecs suffered from gout, a condition associated with too much protein (Ortiz de Montellano 1990: 86, 121). Also useful in the debate is recognition of the success of Mesoamerican agricultural practices. Systems of terracing, irrigating, fertilizing, and the justly famous *chinampas* (artificial islands that could yield as many as four harvests a year), all combined to produce abundant quantities of food. Intercropping, or the growing of several crops together, was also beneficial. Intercropping was particularly useful when beans were planted with maize because the nitrogen-fixing beans helped increase maize yields (Ortiz de Montellano 1990: 94-7). In addition, the traditional *milpa* practice of planting squash and maize and letting edible wild herbs grow next to the latter served both to deter pests and to provide additional foods before the corn harvest, a time when there could have been scarcity.

Food preparation and consumption practices also contributed to good nutrition. As mentioned, maize, when prepared as a *masa* and eaten with beans and amaranth, delivers proteins comparable to those from animal sources. Other culinary staples added to the nutritional well-being of indigenous peoples as well. Chillies, full of vitamin C, were commonplace in the Aztec diet. So were tomatoes, as significant sources of minerals and vitamin C, and *quelites* (wild edible herbs), rich in vitamin A.

Far from being a monotonous and boring series of dishes, Mexican cuisine had great culinary variety, the result of an imaginative mixture of ingredients and methods of preparing them. Sauces or moles were common, and different combinations of chillies gave them different flavors. One such sauce is *pipián,* a thick mixture with a special texture made from ground squash seeds. A well-chosen combination of sauces could add different flavors to vegetables and meats while also providing more protein.

Mesoamericans also knew how to ferment several vegetable products, the best known of which is the sap of maguey *(agave),* used to produce the mildly alcoholic beverage *pulque.* They also fermented several maize products. *Pozol* was and is a popular preparation made with a combination of several varieties of corn, whereby the *masa* is made into small balls, which are covered with leaves and left to ferment. The balls are then dissolved in water to make the *pozol.* Mexican biologists and chemists (Cañas et al. 1993) have found that this kind of fermentation enhances the amount of protein the drink contains because of the growth of microorganisms.

Contact and Dietary Change

The arrival of the Spaniards in Middle America initiated dietary and cultural changes that have continued until today. The precise extent and pace of such changes remain subjects for research and interpretation, but the broad outlines of the process can be addressed.

Although the Spaniards expected to replicate their traditional food patterns in the New World, the extent to which they fulfilled this expectation depended on local geographic and cultural forces and on policies of trade and commerce. In the Caribbean, climate and culture hindered the establishment of Spanish alimentary regimes. There, Spanish culture survived through adaptation to local conditions and through an elaborate system of trade that supplied the islands. Wheat, the staple of the Spanish diet, was central to the trade.

In Mexico and the highlands of Central America, soil and climatic conditions encouraged the establishment of wheat production. The quantity and flavor of wheat grown in the valleys of the central highlands and in the broad plain of the *Bajío* became renowned throughout Middle America. Production of wheat often exceeded demand, and in the eighteenth century wheat exports fed soldiers and sailors garrisoned in Havana. As wars increased in frequency, the demand for wheat grew, and Mexico lost the Caribbean market to the United States, not because of insufficient grain for export but because of the higher cost of transporting Mexican grain.

Wheat was always a political issue in Mexico following the Conquest. In the late 1520s in Mexico City, legislation mentioned the importance of a supply of "white, clean, well-cooked and seasoned bread, free of barley and sand" (*Actas del Cabildo* 1889-1916, 1: 146-7). By the eighteenth century, when the capital city may have been consuming over 40 million pounds of bread a year, the problem of sufficient wheat bread had become considerably more complex. The quantity and quality of bread available was the result of the interaction among *hacendados* (wheat farmers), *molineros* (millers), *panaderos* (bakers), *pulperos* (small shopkeepers), and harried

public officials who tried to regulate prices and quality (Super 1982; García Acosta 1989).

Other grains, barley and rye in particular, were introduced to Mexico but assumed only regional importance. After wheat, rice probably had the most success of any of the imported grains among all ethnic and social groups in Middle America. By the middle of the seventeenth century, Panama was already producing enough of a surplus to support a small export trade to Peru (Castillero-Calvo 1987: 428). In Mexico, Indians came to depend on rice as a complement to or substitute for maize. External influences on the preparation of rice continued into the twentieth century. *Morisqueta,* rice prepared by a technique supposedly introduced by the Japanese, became common in the rural Mexican diet in the 1940s, and rice achieved even more fame as the basis for a drink known as *horchata,* prepared with rice flour, sugar, cinnamon, and ice (Horcasitas 1951: 162-3).

Even before they planted these grains, Spaniards introduced new sources of animal protein to Middle America. Pigs in particular were the animals of conquest – they were mobile, adaptable, and efficient producers of fat and protein. Their rapid proliferation presaged a century in which animal foods were more abundant than ever before or since. Sheep multiplied almost as rapidly. By the end of the sixteenth century, the Tlaxcala-Puebla region counted 418,000 head of sheep; Zimatlán-Jilotepec 360,000; and the Mixteca Alta 238,000 (Dusenberry 1948; Miranda 1958; Matesanz 1965).

Cattle followed pigs and sheep, transforming dietary patterns wherever they went. Enormous herds dominated the central and north-central regions of Mexico, where the landed estate system began to take shape in the late sixteenth century. Cattle were valuable for their hides; meat was of secondary importance, as reflected by the very low price of beef.

Meat-based diets were widespread throughout Mexico and Middle America, extending south to Panama. Indeed, meat may have been more abundant in the Panamanian diet than in that of the Mexican (Castillero-Calvo 1987: 432-4; Super 1988: 28-32). The period of abundant meat in the central areas, however, came to an end as the great herds exhausted the grasslands. But the period itself left a dietary legacy that continued through succeeding centuries. Fat from cattle had become the substitute for the European's olive oil and butter. Ignaz Pfefferkorn, a Jesuit very concerned with his stomach, summarized the situation in the eighteenth century: "The art of butter-making is as unfamiliar in Sonora as it is in all of America" (Pfefferkorn 1949).

Wheat and meat were the staples of the diet, providing the energy necessary for the establishment of Spanish society in Mexico. Along with the staples came scores of other foods, most of them basic to the Spanish diet at home. Among the vegetables common in the sixteenth century were onions, garlic, carrots, turnips, eggplants, and lentils; common fruits included peaches, melons, figs, cherries, oranges, lemons, limes, and grapefruit. Most of these foods had become regular items in the diet by the end of the sixteenth century and remain so today.

Olives and grapes did not follow this pattern. Both were essential to the Spanish diet, but neither had lasting success in Mexico. After an auspicious start, the cultivation of both was deliberately limited to ensure that southern Spain had a captive export market. Much olive oil and wine was still being imported at the end of the eighteenth century, but their dietary importance had declined because of Spanish mercantilist regulation and changing food preferences.

Sugar has a special place among the foods that came to the New World. In Mexico, Hernando Cortés was the first landholder to devote large areas to the cultivation of sugarcane. Production soon increased and sugar was exported; at the same time it became widely appreciated by the Mexican people. Its availability and price made it a good substitute for the relatively more expensive honey and the syrup fabricated by boiling the sap of the maguey plant. With a cheap and readily available sweetener, Mexicans were soon experts in preparing a wide variety of desserts and sweets that became characteristics of the cuisine (Zolla 1988).

Formation of the Creole Diet

The blending of indigenous and European foods and food techniques began immediately after the Conquest. The result was the emergence of a *comida novohispana,* which in turn became the basis of Mexican regional cuisines. Some elaborate dishes are elegant testimony to the fusion of the two food traditions. *Mole poblano* is one of the most highly regarded, with its chocolate base seasoned with different types of chillies and nuts. To this dish Europeans contributed foods and spices that they brought with them from the Old World: onions, garlic, cloves, cinnamon, and nutmeg. The fowl in the dish, almost secondary to its flavor, was either turkey (native to Mexico) or chicken (introduced into Mexico after the Conquest). Although dishes such as mole and *chiles en nogada* (chillies stuffed with minced meat and fruits, covered with a thick nut sauce) rightly deserve notice, an even more basic fusion was taking place. As mentioned, European livestock began providing the fat that native cuisine lacked, and fat from pigs, and then from cattle, was quickly absorbed into the Indian diet. Even dishes that might have seemed to be pure reflections of pre-Hispanic dietary regimes came quickly to depend for flavor on fat from Old World animals. *Frijoles refritos, gorditas,* quesadillas, and other traditional Mexican dishes were not prepared before the Conquest. The technique of frying itself was introduced only in the sixteenth century. Indeed,

most of the dishes so closely associated with Mexican cuisine – *carnitas, tortas,* tacos, and *tamales* – are prepared with animal fats, cheeses, onions, garlic, and bread, all of which were introduced by Europeans.

The diffusion of these foods among different indigenous groups has been a matter of some discussion. Chickens, pigs, and goats quickly became familiar parts of Indian economic activity and regular items in the diet. When prices were low enough, meat from cattle and bread from wheat were also eaten. But there are questions of how rapidly and to what extent beef and wheat were integrated into the diet of indigenous groups. A traditional interpretation is that there was little fusion of the different food traditions and that the "Indians continued their almost exclusively vegetarian diet: corn in liquid and solid form, beans, vegetables and chile; for bread, meat, and other foods were far too expensive for them" (Gamio 1926: 116). Recent research on the colonial period, however, suggests that fusion was much more extensive and that Native American diets did include wheat and meat, foods traditionally associated with a European diet (Castillero-Calvo 1987; Super 1988).

The development of a new diet did not necessarily require the addition of new foods. For example, *pulque,* already mentioned as the fermented juice of the maguey plant, emerged as the most widely consumed beverage of the central highlands because traditions that had limited its intake before the Conquest weakened in the sixteenth century. The resulting widespread consumption continued into the twentieth century. Although *pulque* provided needed carbohydrates, minerals, and vitamins to the diet, it also contributed to the image of widespread alcohol abuse among Indians and mestizos in Mexico.

Commercial production of this beverage spread with Spanish society and the emergence of the hacienda. The technology of *pulque* production remained essentially the same as before the Conquest, but new storage vessels of leather and wood made it possible to produce larger amounts of *pulque* more easily. Drinks from sugarcane (many different types of *aguardiente* were popular by the eighteenth century) were also accepted by indigenous cultures but did not replace *pulque* as a daily beverage. Of all the foods and beverages of indigenous cultures in Mexico, *pulque* remained the most politicized, sparking medical, moral, and economic controversy into the twentieth century (Calderón Narváez 1968; Leal, Rountee, and Martini 1978; Corcuera de Mancera 1990).

It is impossible to reduce the complex changes that took place in the diet during the colonial period to a series of statistics measuring calories and other nutrients. Nevertheless, the weight of the evidence suggests that the collision of cultures in the sixteenth century resulted in an initial improvement in nutrition among the poorer classes. The gains made were difficult to sustain as the colonial period drew to a close, and by the end of the eighteenth century the nutritional status of the individual was probably lower than it had been two centuries earlier (Borah 1979–89; Castillero-Calvo 1987; Super 1988). It is also important to note that until the late nineteenth century, Mexican regionalism was very pronounced, which encouraged the continued independent evolution of local cuisines.

The Nineteenth Century

Patterns of food production and distribution were disrupted by the struggle for independence and subsequent economic dislocations. But independence did not lead to the development of new alimentary regimes. Despite new influences affecting food preparation techniques for the wealthy (French food fashions, for example), most Mexicans continued to rely on diets that had changed very little from the colonial period.

The emergence of new agricultural and land-tenure patterns in the second half of the century may have reduced dietary quantity, but it is difficult to generalize for the entire region. Some of the prices for basic foods – maize, beans, rice, and chillies – did increase sharply, especially during the final years of the nineteenth century and the first few years of the twentieth. But such prices usually reflected trends in central Mexico that were not representative of the country as a whole. During the nineteenth century, regional variation continued to characterize food availability, prices, and consumption in rural Mexico.

As during earlier periods, the complex labor relationships of the haciendas influenced the availability of food. These in turn had regional variations. For example, in the Puebla-Tlaxcala region of central Mexico, although the *peones alquilados* (daily, weekly, or seasonal laborers) might have had high wages, they seldom received food rations. In contrast, the *peones acasillados* who lived on the haciendas often received fixed amounts of food and had the right to work a small amount of land, called a *pegujal,* for their own benefit. An interesting dimension of rural labor arrangements was the obligation of the *servicio de tezquiz,* whereby daughters and wives of rural workers prepared *atole* and tortillas for hacienda personnel. This, as with fieldwork, was paid for both in specie and in kind. In the latter case, the women received up to one *almud* (4.625 liters) of maize for performing this service (Coatsworth 1976; Cross 1978; Borah 1979–89; Nickel 1982: 125–48).

The traditional view is that a marked decline in nutrition occurred in the late nineteenth century. There is, however, some evidence to counter this view, which is based on wage and price data that can be misleading when local labor relationships are not understood. In many areas of rural Mexico, peasants continued to hold on to their land, producing for subsistence and then for the market. Workers who were entirely dependent on their employers often had access to rations that provided for their own – and their families' – basic caloric needs. Salaries, although low, were sufficient to buy some meat and nonessential foods. This is not to suggest that diets were good, or perhaps even adequate. But they were, it seems, not as bad as traditionally described.

The Twentieth Century

Like the struggle for independence that began the nineteenth century, the Mexican Revolution (1910-17) created disruptions in the production and distribution of food. As severe as these were in some areas, they were essentially transitory and had little lasting impact on food and diet.

More important were two gradual processes that would shape the history of food in the twentieth century. First was the continuing commercialization of food production, a process with origins in the advent of sixteenth-century European agricultural practices. It gained momentum during the colonial period and then surged under the rule of Porfirio Díaz (1876-1911) in the late nineteenth century as more and more land was devoted to agricultural products for an export market, particularly cattle, sugar, coffee, and two nonfood crops – cotton and henequen.

The latest step in this process has been the increase in the production of fruits, vegetables, and meats for the U.S. market, beginning in the 1960s. Related to this was the leap in the production of sorghum (used for cattle feed), which has become a leading crop in Mexico (Barkin 1987: 281). Similar to soya in Brazil, sorghum emerged to satisfy the demands of the export market rather than internal needs. One consequence has been increasing pressure on resources traditionally used to produce foods for local consumption.

The second process has been the industrialization of food production and distribution. The *molino de nixtamal,* a mill for maize flour, has had particularly far-reaching impact. Making tortillas by hand is a time-consuming process, once performed daily by homemakers, but with the introduction of the *molinos* in the early years of the twentieth century, and then of new methods of packaging and distributing tortillas, the traditional social roles of women changed. Freed from a daily four to six hours of labor with tortillas, women have had to adjust to new social and economic relationships. Cultural attitudes toward maize, still a sacred food among some highland Guatemala peoples, also changed as maize production was subjected to mechanization (Keremitis 1983; Herrera Tejada 1987; Vargas 1987).

The establishment of the *molino de nixtamal* is only one example of the growing consolidation of the processing and distribution of food. As in other societies experiencing rapid urbanization and industrialization, Mexico has seen its food systems undergo a profound alteration. National and transnational corporations influence everything about food from price to fashion, with the result that traditional foods and methods of preparation are giving way to national and global food processing and distribution systems. Such changes have also accentuated the loss of Mexican self-sufficiency in food production (Barkin 1987; Vargas 1987).

All of these changes have meant a new era in the history of Middle American food habits. Unfortunately, the new era has not yet shown the capacity to eliminate the nutritional problems that still plague many people, especially the poor in rural areas. Although malnutrition seldom reaches the level of starvation, high rates of infant mortality, low birth weights, and chronic illness and development problems afflict the poor. Average caloric intakes, some 2,600 per person per day in Mexico in the 1970s, obscure the regional inequalities in diet. People in rural zones of the south might consume less than 2,000 calories – an intake comparable to the poor of India, Kenya, or Vietnam (Pineda Gómez 1982: 104–7).

The Mexican government has created several programs to counter problems of malnutrition and the negative effects of the globalization of food production and distribution. It first directed its efforts toward the creation of a national marketing system, the *Compañia de Subsistencias Populares* (CONASUPO), whose mission has been to regulate the price and availability of food by intervening in national and international markets. A much heralded governmental effort was the *Sistema Alimentario Mexicano* (SAM), a program launched in 1980. SAM aimed to improve national nutritional well-being by focusing resources on the increased production and distribution of domestic foods. This was accomplished by providing technology, credit, and price supports to small producers, thereby encouraging them to contribute more effectively to satisfying national nutritional needs. On the heels of SAM came the *Programa Nacional de Alimentación* (PRONAL), an even more comprehensive effort that focused on creating an integrated national food system. New governmental policies that have favored free enterprise and international commerce have hindered public programs intended to increase food availability to the poor.

One solution to the problem of malnutrition is a reliance on the natural diversity and traditional foods of a region. The significance of traditional foods, such as *quelites* (cultivated and wild herbs), for example, has been increasingly recognized as a result of a classic 1946 study of the very poor Otomi Indians of the Mezquital valley. Despite the almost total absence of foods common to middle-class urban diets, especially meat, wheat bread, dairy products, and processed foods, the Otomi, who consumed *quelites,* showed few signs of malnutrition (Anderson et al. 1946).

Conclusion

Mexico's food system has suffered a long and complicated evolution. Elements of the past combine every day with those of the present on Mexican tables. Old Mesoamerican foods such as chillies, squash, beans, avocados, and all kinds of maize derivatives are considered necessary in a meal. These are enriched with foods from the Old World such as pork, beef, lettuce, rice, oranges, and coffee. Some of the old foods still have a special place in social gatherings. For instance, a traditional wedding deserves a *mole de guajolote* just as the typical breakfast on the day of a child's first communion is unthinkable without hot chocolate and *tamales.* Families going out at night patronize restaurants specializing in *pozole,* a stew with grains of corn, meat, and old and new spices. New foods appear continually: Coca-Cola is already a staple; hamburgers and hot dogs are everywhere; new Chinese restaurants and pizza parlors open every day. It is interesting to note that many of these foods become "Mexicanized." For example, the large hamburger restaurants offer chillies and Mexican sauces, and one can order a *pizza poblana* with long strands of green chilli and mole on it.

The increased modernization and internationalization of Mexican food and cuisine is clearly not without negative consequences. The variety of foods that characterized nutritional regimes in the past is declining; vast areas of land that once carried edible wild plants and animals have been cleared for agriculture, cattle raising, and expanding towns and cities. Packaged and processed foods, often less nutritious than their natural counterparts, are becoming more widespread, and there is still acute and chronic malnutrition in several parts of Mexico, even as obesity is a growing problem in affluent sectors of cities. Despite these problems, Mexico has a wide range of natural and cultural resources that may be called upon to help ensure a future where good diets are available to all.

John C. Super
Luis Alberto Vargas

Bibliography

Actas de cabildo de la ciudad de Mexico. 1889–1916. Mexico City.

Anderson, Richmond K., José Calvo, Gloria Serrano, and George C. Payne. 1946. A study of the nutritional status and food habits of Otomi Indians in the Mezquital valley of Mexico. *American Journal of Public Health* 36: 883–903.

Barkin, David. 1987. The end to food self-sufficiency in Mexico. *Latin American Perspectives* 14: 271–97.

Borah, Woodrow. 1979–89. Cinco siglos de producción y consumo de alimentos en el México central. *Memorias de la Academia Mexicana de la Historia, correspondiente de la Real de Madrid* 31: 117–44.

Calderón Narváez, Guillermo. 1968. Reflections on alcoholism among the pre-Hispanic peoples of Mexico. *Revista del Instituto Nacional de Neurología* 2: 5-13.

Cañas Urbina, Ana Olivia, Eduardo Bárzana García, et al. 1993. La elaboración del pozol en los Altos de Chiapas. *Ciencia* 44: 219-29.

Casillas, Leticia E., and Luis Alberto Vargas. 1984. La alimentación entre los Mexicas. In *Historia general de la medicina en Mexico*, Vol. 1, *Mexico antiguo*, ed. Fernando Martínez Cortés, 133-56. Mexico City.

Castillero-Calvo, Alfredo. 1987. Niveles de vida y cambios de dieta a fines del periodo colonial en América. *Anuario de Estudios Americanos* 44: 427-77.

Coatsworth, John H. 1976. Anotaciones sobre la producción de alimentos durante el Porfiriato. *Historia Mexicana* 26: 167-87.

Corcuera de Mancera, Sonia. 1990. *Entre gula y templanza. Un aspecto de la historia Mexicana.* Mexico City.

Cross, Harry. 1978. Living standards in rural nineteenth-century Mexico: Zacatecas, 1820-1880. *Journal of Latin American Studies* 10: 1-19.

Dusenberry, William H. 1948. The regulation of meat supply in sixteenth-century Mexico City. *Hispanic American Historical Review* 28: 38-52.

Gamio, Manuel. 1926. The Indian basis of Mexican civilization. In *Aspects of Mexican civilization*, ed. José Vasconcelos and Manuel Gamio. Chicago.

García Acosta, Virginia. 1989. *Las panaderías, sus dueños y trabajadores. Ciudad de México. Siglo XVIII.* Mexico City.

Harner, Michael. 1977. The ecological basis for Aztec sacrifice. *American Ethnologist* 4: 117-35.

Herrera Tejada, Clara. 1987. Cuando el maíz llora. *Revista de Indias* 47: 225-49.

Horcasitas de Pozas, Isabel. 1951. Estudio sobre la alimentación en el poblado de Acacoyahua. *Anales del Instituto Nacional de Antropologia e Historia* 5: 153-77.

Keremitis, Dawn. 1983. Del metate al molino: La mujer mexicana de 1910 a 1940. *Historia Mexicana* 33: 285-302.

Leal, Juan Felipe, Mario Huacuja Rountee, and Mario Bellingeri Martini. 1978. La compañía expendedora de pulques y la monopolización del mercado urbano: 1909-1914. *Revista Mexicana de Ciencias Políticas y Sociales* 24: 177-241.

Matesanz, José. 1965. Introducción de la ganadería en Nueva España. *Historia Mexicana* 14: 533-65.

Miranda, José. 1958. Origenes de la ganadería indígena en la Mixteca. In *Miscellanea Paul Rivet. Octogenario dicata,* 787-96. Mexico City.

Nickel, Herbert J. 1982. The food supply of hacienda labourers in Puebla-Tlaxcala during the Porfiriato: A first approximation. In *Haciendas in central Mexico from late colonial times to the revolution,* ed. Raymond Buve, 113-59. Amsterdam.

Ortiz de Montellano, Bernard R. 1990. *Aztec medicine, health, and nutrition.* New Brunswick, N.J., and London.

Pfefferkorn, Ignaz. 1949. *Descripción de la provincia de Sonora,* trans. Theodore E. Trautlein. Albuquerque, N. Mex.

Pineda Gómez, Virginia. 1982. Estudio comparativo de la alimentación en México con la de otros paises. *Anuario de Geografía* 22: 103-39.

Puleston, Dennis E., and Peter Oliver Puleston. 1979. El ramón como base de la dieta alimenticia de los antiguos mayas de Tikal. *Antropología e Historia de Guatemala* 1: 55-69.

Super, John C. 1982. Bread and the provisioning of Mexico City in the late eighteenth century. *Jahrbuch für Geschichte von Staat, Wirtschaft und Gesellschaft Lateinamerikas* 19: 159-82.

1988. *Food, conquest, and colonization in sixteenth-century Spanish America.* Albuquerque, N. Mex.

Vargas, Luis Alberto. 1984. La alimentación de los Mayas antiguos. In *Historia general de la medicina en Mexico,* Vol. 1, *Mexico antiguo,* ed. Fernando Martínez Cortés, 273-82. Mexico City.

1987. Mexico's food supply: Past, present and future. In *Food deficiency: Studies and perspectives,* 194-206. Bangkok.

Vargas, Luis Alberto, and Leticia E. Casillas. 1990. La alimentación en México durante los primeros años de la colonia. In *Historia general de la medicina en México,* Vol. 2, ed. Fernando Martínez Cortés, 78-90. Mexico City.

1992. Diet and foodways in Mexico City. *Ecology of Food and Nutrition* 27: 235-47.

Vasconcelos, José, and Manuel Gamio. 1926. *Aspects of Mexican civilization.* Chicago.

Zolla, Carlos. 1988. *Elogio del dulce. Ensayo sobre la dulcería mexicana.* Mexico City.

V.D.2 ❧ South America

The continent of South America has been a place of origin of many important food plants. Moreover, plant and animal introductions to the Americas made both before and after Columbus have provided an extraordinary diversity of food sources. Culinary traditions based on diverse foodstuffs show the imprint of indigenous, European, and African cultures. This is because food production and consumption in these lands stem from an environmental duality of both temperate and tropical possibilities. Moreover, throughout the twentieth century in South America, the binary distinction between food produced for commercial purposes and for subsistence needs has continued in a way that is unknown in North America. Contrasting nutritional standards and perturbations in supply add to the complexity of the total food situation in South America.

Domesticated Food Sources

The pre-Columbian peoples of South America domesticated more than 50 edible plants, several of which were such efficient sources of food that they subsequently have served as nutritional anchors for much of the rest of the world. The potato, manioc, and sweet potato, each belonging to different plant families, are among the top 10 food sources in the world today. The potato (*Solanum tuberosum* and related species) clearly originated in South America, where prior to European contact it was cultivated in the Andes through a range of 50 degrees of latitude. Archaeological remains of these tubers are scanty, but there is little doubt that Andean peoples have been eating potatoes for at least 5,000 years. The center of greatest morphological and genetic variability of potatoes is in southern Peru and northern Bolivia where they fall into five chromosome (ploidy) levels. That the potato is an efficient source of carbohydrates is well known, but it also provides not insignificant amounts of protein (in some varieties more than 5 percent), vitamins, and minerals. In the Andes, the tuber is traditionally boiled, but now it is also fried. *Chuño,* a dehydrated form of the fresh tuber, may have been the world's first freeze-dried food. Working at high elevation, Indians still go through the laborious process of exposing fresh potatoes to both above- and below-freezing temperatures before stepping on them with bare feet in order to make this easily stored form of food.

Manioc *(Manihot esculenta)* is another root crop from South America; it is grown and eaten in one form or another as far south as Corrientes Province, Argentina, and in the Andean valleys as high as about 2,000 meters above sea level. It is the top-ranking staple in the Amazon Basin where more uses and forms of processing are known than elsewhere. Its ability to grow in infertile soils, resistance to insect pests, and high caloric yield make it an attractive crop. The low protein (average of 2.5 percent) and the high levels of toxicity in certain varieties that force elaborate processing are its major disadvantages as human food.

The sweet potato *(Ipomoea batatas)* was known among early farming people of South America as far back as 4,000 years ago, but its origin is less understood than that of the potato because of the lack of plausible wild ancestors. The enlarged roots contain 25 to 28 percent carbohydrates, as well as about 5 percent sugar. In South America it is normally less of a staple than one might expect. Eaten usually in boiled form, it is also baked.

The rich array of South American root crops includes many scarcely known outside the continent. Probably domesticated before the potato in the Andes were *ullucu (Ullucus tuberosus), oca (Oxalis tuberosa),* and *añu (Tropaeolum tuberosum),* all three starchy additions to the stew pot. *Arracacha (Arracacia esculenta)* grows at lower elevations, primarily in Andean valleys from Venezuela to Bolivia. Its taste is reminiscent of parsnips. The tubers of jícama *(Pachyrhizus tuberosus)* and *ajipa (Pachyrhizus ahipa)* are typically eaten raw for their sweet flesh with a crunchy texture. *Achira (Canna edulis)* is a very starchy addition to the diet of some people in the Andean valleys. There are also several other tubers with very local distributions that are relics of a prior time and can be expected to become extinct.

Several "pseudo-cereals" survive as crops in the Andes, the most important being quinoa *(Chenopodium quinoa),* which is planted from Colombia to Chile and Argentina. Its average protein content of 13 percent is higher than that of wheat, and its high concentration of essential amino acids, especially lysine, has helped make it a staple for Andean people for at least two millennia.

The hardiest chenopod crop is *cañihua (Chenopodium pallidicaule),* now localized on the Altiplano of southern Peru and Bolivia. The tiny seeds are toasted or cooked in porridge, and the protein content is at least as high as that of quinoa. Growing in warm and dry valleys of the Andes as a relict crop is *kiwicha (Amaranthus caudatus).* Its nutritious seeds, sometimes popped, are usually eaten as a gruel.

Two leguminous seed plants are also among South America's contributions to the world's food inventory. The peanut *(Arachis hypogaea),* a major crop in Asia and Africa today, was probably domesticated in the zone circumscribed by Paraguay and southern Brazil. At least this is the region where the world's center of peanut diversity is found. This crop has both large amounts (25 to 35 percent) of protein and a high fat content (43 to 54 percent). The seeds have been eaten raw, boiled, and toasted, but the major use of the peanut today is for its oil. The other leguminous seed plant is the kidney bean *(Phaseolus vulgaris),* which may be of South American origin, although a wild relative is found as far north as Mexico. There is considerable diversity in the size, shape, and color of the kidney beans in South America, which are basic sources of vegetable protein for millions of people in South America and elsewhere in the world.

Several kinds of domesticated cucurbits are South American in origin. Crookneck squash *(Cucurbita moschata),* winter squash or *zapallo (Cucurbita maxima),* and *achokcha (Cyclanthera pedata)* are used in soups and stews.

Valuable fruit-bearing plants were domesticated in South America and in some cases have spread elsewhere in the tropics. The pineapple *(Ananas comosus)* had spread throughout the New World tropics by the time Columbus arrived, but it is certainly of South American origin. However, which one of the numerous wild-growing species of *Ananas* is the direct ancestor of this noble fruit has not yet been resolved. The fruit of this perennial, herbaceous plant is highly regarded around the world for the distinctive flavor of its sweet flesh and juice.

Papaya *(Carica papaya)* yields a more fragile fruit with a soft, sweet pulp around an inner mass of small round seeds. Its place of origin appears to be in warm eastern Andean valleys, but its earliest recorded use was in Central America.

Three South American members of the Solanaceae yield an edible fruit. One of these is the *pepino dulce* or melon pear *(Solanum muricatum),* with a sweet and juicy yellowish flesh reminiscent of cantaloupe. A second fruit in this family is the tree tomato *(Cyphomandra betacea),* yielding a red fruit the size and shape of an egg that tastes like an acid tomato. The third member is *naranjilla* or *lulo (Solanum quitoensis);* it comes from a bushy herb with seedy fruits that are the size of a small orange. Its vitamin-rich juice is greatly appreciated in Ecuador. Although no mention of this fruit appears in the historical record before the seventeenth century, much about it suggests that it was domesticated earlier.

Passiflora is a genus of edible fruits that grows on climbing herbaceous vines. The two major species, *Passiflora edulis (granadilla)* and *Passiflora quadrangularis (maracuja),* are grown for their sweet-tart juice containing 8 to 10 percent sugar. Cold fruit drinks and an ice cream flavor are made with the juice.

Colonial Transfer: Wheat and Olive Oil

The pre-Columbian inventory of crops and animals sustained the people who consumed it just as well as the late medieval food sources provided for Europeans. Nevertheless, when the potential of Spanish agriculture was added to the indigenous inventory, the nutritional possibilities were enhanced. Some of the European plants and animals fit into one or another ecological niche better than the native domesticates and gradually became indispensable.

Among Europeans in South America, the most desired of Old World foods was wheat. In addition to its flavor and texture, wheat bread had a strong symbolic identification with Spanish culture, whereas maize, after reaching Iberia, had a much lower standing as a food suitable to and for the Spanish palate. But within South America, wheat could not be successfully grown in warm, wet zones, thus eliminating the Amazon Basin, the Llanos, most of the Brazilian Planalto, the Guianas coast, and most other coastal plains in the tropical parts of the continent.

Hardtack *(bizcocho),* the earliest wheat food in South America, was imported from Spain. Wheat production was important in the Andes from Venezuela to Bolivia, and by the 1550s and 1560s, fresh bread was widely available. The grain was ground on gristmills turned by a horizontal waterwheel. In fact, wheat production, once important in the region, could become important again if imports were cut off. In the early 1980s, for example, Brazil imported almost as much wheat as it produced. But in 1988, this country achieved self-sufficiency in wheat, the result of paying Brazilian farmers three times the world price.

Another basic staple among the Iberians was olive oil, which was shipped to South America for more than a century in the early colonial period. Although other vegetable oils could readily substitute for olive oil, the latter had a particular flavor that Spaniards much appreciated. Starting an olive grove in the New World required patience; the trees did not begin to bear fruit profitably for 30 years, and they could only be grown in certain places. Olive trees require a climatic regime of winter rains and summer drought, and they tolerate no (or only very light) frost. These conditions could be found only in central Chile, although on the desert coast of Peru and in rain-shy western Argentina, olive trees would grow and yield

fruit under irrigation. Elsewhere, olive growing was out of the question.

Common Prepared Foods

All of South America except Patagonia has granted to maize a place in the diet. In Colombia and Venezuela, corn is commonly ground into meal or flour to make an *arepa,* a bland undercooked ball of grilled corn dough. Wrapped in banana leaves and steamed, maize dough is made into tamales called *hallacas* in Colombia and Venezuela, and *humintas* in Ecuador, Peru, Bolivia, and Argentina. As in North America, boiled green corn on the cob is also eaten, especially in the Andean countries.

Wheat in the form of bread has continued to be much favored throughout South America, even in places where the grain cannot be successfully grown and supplies must be imported. Other ways of using it are in turnovers; filled with meat or cheese, they are much loved especially in Chile, Argentina, Bolivia, and Uruguay. Another wheat product, pasta, is now an important food in South America, and every country has semolina factories set up by Italian immigrants.

Unlike in Africa or Asia, no cultural barriers in South America have inhibited the consumption of meat, except that of the horse and the donkey. Beef, pork, and chicken are most widely consumed, though production of the latter has been industrialized only in this century. As in North America, the flesh of cattle is the preferred meat, with the difference being that South Americans willingly consume a wider range of the edible parts of the animal. The kidney, brain, and tripe that are processed into pet food in the United States are considered delicacies by many South Americans. Peruvians have such a special affinity for cubed, marinated, and skewered beef hearts *(anticuchos)* that they import substantial quantities of this organ from Argentina. Meat in South American butcher shops is sold mostly in slabs or chunks, not the particular cuts familiar to North American or European cooks. The four native domesticates – llama, alpaca, guinea pig, and Muscovy duck – are not major food sources. Wild game and land turtles, sold in markets, are still a source of meat in the Amazon Basin, although river fish supply most of the animal protein in this region. Saltwater fish form a basic element of diet in coastal towns and cities around the continent, somewhat more so on the Pacific side than on the Atlantic. Unlike in Europe, inland locales depend little on fish in the diet, a legacy in part of the poor transportation that has hindered its shipment.

Introduced fruit-bearing plants add to the wide range of produce that overflows markets from Bucaramanga to Brasília. But they have not necessarily turned adults into high per capita fruit eaters. Not infrequently, fruit production exceeds consumption, and much is left to rot. Bananas, including plantains, are nutritionally the most important fruit, and especially in tropical lowland locales, various kinds of bananas and plantains are a staple carbohydrate. Citrus is abundant in all countries, primarily as fresh fruit; a daily dose of orange juice is not yet part of Latin American custom. Mangoes are especially plentiful in hot, tropical areas with a pronounced wet and dry season. Avocados, native to Central America, are not as popular as one might expect, given a fat content (up to 30 percent) that is quite extraordinary for a fruit. The southern cone countries grow high-quality pome fruits; apples and pears from the Argentine valley of Rio Negro have long been exported to the tropical countries to the north.

Condiment use cannot be easily generalized. Most South Americans do not follow the Mexican pattern of the lavish use of chilli peppers. Yet, some local cuisines in western South America, for example those of Arequipa, Peru, make abundant use of capsicum, and are quite different from, say, the bland food that characterizes Florianopólis, Brazil, or Mendoza, Argentina. Generally, the more one goes into a diet focused on meat, the lower the seasoning profile. Heavy doses of onions and garlic often flavor food, and a good squirt from a lemon or lime cuts the grease in fried meats. Fresh coriander is a favorite cooking herb used in the Andean countries.

After the sixteenth-century introduction of sugarcane, honey was pushed into the background as a sweetener. Sweet desserts and liquids were one of the dietary outcomes of expansive sugar production and consumption. Brazilians prefer a sugary paste of guava or quince or a coconut-based sweet. In Hispanic countries, caramelized milk custard (flan) is the customary way to end a meal, clearly a transfer from Spain. Most people eat no cakes or pastries. As in Iberia, confections made with eggs, nuts, and sugar have been a specialty of convents. The nuns sell them to the public at designated times of the year. Beginning in this century, commercially manufactured candies featuring chocolate have satisfied the urban craving for sweets.

Forms of Preparation

Except for fruit, little food is eaten raw in South America. Salads of uncooked greens were rarely eaten before the twentieth century and still are not common in most diets. In Brazil, Japanese immigrants were the first people to commercialize salad vegetables seriously. Especially in São Paulo, Japanese-Brazilians grow and market fresh produce, an outgrowth of what was initially a desire to satisfy their own ethnic preferences.

Cooking methods vary regionally to some extent. Boiling is the traditional method of preparing many foods, and pre-Columbian peoples used ceramic pots for cooking. The Spaniards and Portuguese also had this tradition. Hearty soups and stews that combine meat, fat, and vegetables are found in different countries

under local names – *puchero* in Argentina, *cazuela* in Chile, *chupe* in Peru, and *ajiaco* in Colombia. Their warmth is especially welcome in the high-altitude chill or during the winter months in the south. Stew was first on the list of dishes in nineteenth-century Lima, Peru. Common ingredients marked a European tradition: beef, mutton, salt pork, sausage, pig's feet, cabbage, banana, rice, and peas; the native contribution was sweet potato, manioc, annatto and chilli pepper (Squier 1877). Because no major source of cooking oil existed in the pre-Columbian period, frying was introduced to South America by Europeans. Both frying and boiling are fuel-efficient ways to cook in fuel-deficient areas. Zones of high meat consumption feature roasting and barbecue.

Regional Dietary Traditions

Each national society and some areas within countries have their own dietary peculiarities. Brazil is especially characterized by the widespread acceptance of manioc, even among people of European origin. Wheat flour was often not available, and this alternative carbohydrate was close at hand and cheap. Brazilians consume much manioc in the form of a toasted flour *(farinha)*. Rice is another basic carbohydrate in Brazil because it grows well in tropical environments; when it is combined with black beans, whole protein is added to the diet. Thin slabs of meat, typically barbecued, form an element of the Brazilian diet, except among the very poor. *Feijoada,* a grand totemic dish of peasant origin, cuts across socioeconomic and ethnic boundaries. Although not recorded before the nineteenth century, *feijoada* has now come to symbolize Brazilian identity. This hearty concoction consists of rice, black beans, dried meats, sausage, and toasted manioc flour, and is garnished with kale and orange slices. Within Brazil, the northeast has the most original cookery. *Vatapá,* a famous dish of Bahia, combines shrimp and peanuts served with highly spiced coconut milk and palm oil. *Cuscuz paulista,* derived from the couscous of North Africa, uses cornmeal, not seminola, as the principal farinaceous ingredient.

The diets of the peoples of highland South America from Andean Venezuela through Bolivia are heavy in carbohydrates. The potato is a major element of the diet; maize is another staple food in this region. Meat is eaten much less in the highlands than in other parts of South America.

Carnivory has given the two Rio de la Plata countries a special nutritional cachet. With a developing-world income profile, Argentina and Uruguay have nevertheless a per capita meat consumption of more than 100 kilograms (kg) per year. Internal beef consumption has been so high at times that foreign demand has not always been adequately supplied. Fish resources are curiously underutilized. White bread is a staple food for this zone, the prime wheat-growing area of all of Latin America. The Mediterranean origin of the great majority of Argentines and Uruguayans partly explains the high-per capita wine consumption.

Chilean diets depend on seafood to a far greater extent than do diets elsewhere in Latin America. Markets are full of swordfish, oysters, mussels, shrimp, scallops, abalone *(locas),* and sea urchins. Fishing is rewarding in Chile's productive cold waters and is reinforced by the country's maritime orientation and limited extent of good livestock pasture. Within South America, the artichoke is a common vegetable only in Chile. Chileans are avid bread eaters and also have developed creative ways to use fruit.

The Guianas have non-Iberian food traditions. The complex ethnic patterns there range from African, East Indian, Amerindian, Javanese, Dutch, and British to French, making it difficult to generalize about cuisine in this zone of northern South America. The one dietary constant among most people in this region is an emphasis on rice.

Food specializations also give rise to a critical attitude and an inclination to make quality judgments. Argentines are cognoscenti in such questions as what quality of beef constitutes prime sirloin. Coastal-dwelling Chileans know the precise balance of ingredients that makes the most savory *chupe de mariscos.* Peruvians of all classes are knowledgeable about the culinary virtues of different varieties of potatoes. Paraguayans pass easy judgment on the right texture for *chipá,* a baked product made with manioc flour.

Nutritional Standards

Caloric intake within South America varies widely from more than 3,000 calories per day in Argentina to between 2,000 and 2,200 calories per day in Bolivia, Peru, and Ecuador. Throughout the 1980s, Argentina's animal protein consumption was more than three times that of Bolivia and Peru. Even in Venezuela, where per capita income is somewhat higher than in Argentina, the people enjoy less than half the protein intake. In spite of the country's developing-world economy, Argentina's has been one of the best-fed populations in the world. However, Argentina's cornucopian reputation has suffered as economic stagnation and hyperinflation have sharply reduced the purchasing power of the majority. In 1989, supermarkets in Rosario and elsewhere were mobbed by people who could not pay the inflated prices for staple items.

In analyzing South America as a whole in the late twentieth century, one must conclude that, despite the richness of the region's dietary patterns, many poor people have diets that can only be termed bad. Infants and children of poor families get insufficient protein for proper development. Milk consumption is low in South America, a result of various factors: nonavailability in remote areas, the high cost of canned milk, and/or lack of education about its nutritional importance. Lactose intolerance, especially among people of native and African origin, is also probably a very important factor in explaining low levels of milk intake.

Protein deficiencies seem especially incongruous in countries that have fishing industries. After World War II, for example, Peru exported fish meal to Europe largely as chicken feed. It was only with the revolutionary military regime of Juan Velasco, who came to power in 1969, that there was a serious attempt to get fish beyond the coastal ports to the highlands. By 1973, refrigerated fish depots began operating in several highland towns. Yet a decade later, these government-managed marketing channels were gone and fish consumption correspondingly dropped there. Peasants do not always eat the protein they produce themselves. Eggs and poultry in the Andes are often sold on the market rather than consumed at home, in part perhaps a legacy of the Spanish colonial period when eggs and live hens were a tribute item to government officials and payment in kind *(camarico)* to the local priest.

Food-Related Customs

South Americans have given special importance to the family-centered midday meal, a custom transferred from Mediterranean civilization. But in recent decades, the North American pattern of a quick, light lunch has made inroads in large South American cities where some business people have adopted a hectic "time is money" attitude. Evening meals in urban settings are typically late, especially in places where a collation is taken in the late afternoon. Snacking is common, fostered by food vending in public places. In most South American towns and cities, many poor people eke out a precarious living by preparing and selling foods on the street. Some rural folk in the Andean highlands follow a two-meal pattern that permits uninterrupted agricultural labor throughout the day. Among people with little formal education, food is often categorized as being either "hot" or "cold," referring not to its actual temperature but other, often ineffable, qualities. The result is a complicated etiquette determining which foods or drinks should accompany or follow others.

The eclecticism of food intake that characterizes present-day North America is less elaborated in South America where, because of a lack of many wide choices, monotony of diet is scarcely an issue. Only large cities offer exposure to foreign cuisines; moreover, many people are cautious about experimenting with new foods or food formats. The tradition of having domestic help and daily marketing reduces demand for canned and frozen foods in the diets of many people who could afford to buy them. The middle-class practice of hiring cooks of peasant origin reinforces culinary conservatism within families.

No national cuisine in Latin America completely

exploits the subtleties of flavor offered by its nutriments. Emile Daireaux, a Frenchman who traveled in Argentina in the 1880s, noted the splendid array of inexpensive food available, but the absence of epicurean discrimination. His explanation evoked the lack of a refined culinary tradition in southern Spain whence early Argentine settlers came (Daireaux 1888). Much more so than in Europe, large food portions became a measure of proper hospitality. Among the Latin American underprivileged, overweight has been a sign of well-being. Ideas about the links between diet and health are less developed than in the Puritan colossus to the north where cholesterol counting and vitamin content preoccupy consumers. Nonetheless, food movements such as vegetarianism and a preference for organic foods do exist in South America among small circles of urban people open to foreign influence.

Beverages and Drinks

Although coffee was hardly known in Latin America before the nineteenth century, it has subsequently become the outstanding hot beverage of the continent. Its preparation in the various countries meets very different standards (high in Brazil, low in Peru, for example). Many people in Uruguay, Paraguay, Argentina, and southern Brazil still prefer yerba maté, which in the late colonial period was also consumed in Bolivia and Peru.

Bottled beer, produced in commercial breweries started mostly by Germans, has become the preferred alcoholic beverage in South America. In hot climates such as Brazil, cold beer is especially popular, but even in the gelid Andes, bottled beer, imbibed at room temperature, is now the preferred vehicle for sociability. Partly due to intense propaganda *(beber cerveza es beber salud)* in this region, bottled beer has made deep inroads even in zones of traditional *chicha* consumption. The latter is a local fermented corn beverage of the Andes, often made under unsanitary conditions. Its popularity has waned in much the same way as has *pulque* in Mexico. Wine competes seriously with beer only in Argentina and Chile, doubtlessly because these countries both have major viticultural production. Carbonated, sweetened, and flavored soft drinks are wildly popular in South America and serve as a double foil for water loss in hot climates and impure water supplies. Much is bottled under license from multinational firms, such as Coca-Cola. In Brazil, native fruit flavors, such as the highly popular guaraná, expand the range of soft drinks.

Distilled beverages, led by rum, have been an important social lubricant among Latin Americans since the nineteenth century. A colonial reserve toward the popular consumption of these spirits broke down after independence was achieved in most countries. Much sugarcane is grown for rum; in some countries its only competitor is grape brandy, called *pisco* in Peru and Chile, *singani* in Bolivia, and *aguardiente* in Argentina. Unlike the high value placed on sobriety in Mediterranean Europe, inebriation is a regular and rather shameless outcome of social drinking in South America.

Food Exports and Imports

Food sent to international markets has been a critical source of foreign exchange in South America, but it is no longer as central a trade item as it once was. In Venezuela, food exports are insignificant compared to the income generated by petroleum products. In Colombia, coffee is important, but less so than cocaine, which does not enter into trade statistics. Ecuador is still a leading banana exporter, but petroleum has relieved that country's dependency on that one fruit. Sugar production has greatly declined in Peru since the government turned the big estates into cooperatives. Bolivia cultivates less than one percent of its territory and exports hardly any foodstuffs.

Chile, on the other hand, has found an export niche in fresh fruit: Table grapes, peaches, nectarines, pears, plums, and kiwifruit now fill American supermarket produce displays from December to May at a time when domestic sources of these items are not normally available. By the late 1980s, the Chilean fruit industry employed some 250,000 people, earning 12 percent of the country's export income. Chile is also the world's leading exporter of fish meal and has enjoyed a large growth in fish farming in the south. Brazil exports soybeans, coffee, and sugar in large quantities and a number of specialty items, such as hearts of palm. Of all the South American nations, Argentina and Uruguay have depended most heavily on food export. Meat and wheat from these two countries helped to feed Europe during much of the twentieth century. Throughout the 1980s, food comprised more than half of all Argentine exports, far more in percentage terms than that of any other country of the continent. Nevertheless, in Argentina only 11 percent of the population was engaged in agriculture in 1987, compared to 43 percent in Bolivia and 38 percent in Peru.

Several South Americans countries have imported staples to cover food deficits. In Venezuela, processed foods, especially from the United States, dominated the middle- and upper-class market basket until the 1960s. But then Venezuela increasingly restricted these imports, favoring the Venezuelan subsidiaries of the North American–based firms (Wright 1985). Poor countries have been recipients of food aid, also largely from the United States. Under U.S. Public Law 480 ("Food for Peace"), passed in 1954, large quantities of wheat, powdered milk, and cheese were subsequently distributed, some sold for local currency ("Title 1") and some donated ("Title 2"). Brazil and Colombia formerly received this kind of food aid; Peru and Bolivia still do.

In 1990 the United States provided $85 million in food aid to Peru, which reached 13 percent of the population. But serious structural problems arise when city dwellers are able to buy imported food that is often sold cheaper than local farmers can produce it. Agriculture is undermined, exacerbating dependency on foreign food and intensifying the pattern of rural-to-urban migration. Regional self-sufficiency correspondingly declines. In the Peruvian and Bolivian Andes, the rice, sugar, wheat flour, noodles, and cooking oil brought from the coast or abroad have partially replaced the traditional staples, which used to be acquired by barter among peoples in different environmental zones.

Food Supply Problems

In most South American countries, food production has not kept pace with the growth of population. The slow rise or even decline in per capita agricultural output on the continent has several causes. Misuse of land resources is one such cause; many areas are seriously eroded, and this is reflected in declining yields. Ill-conceived agrarian reform programs have reduced the ability of countries to feed themselves. The breakup of large estates in Bolivia in the 1950s, Chile in the 1960s, and Peru in the 1970s each had this effect. At the same time, state and private investment in rural development has been sparse compared with investments that go to urban areas. The number of food producers in South America falls every year, a phenomenon that, however, is not matched by increases in productive efficiency. The meager return for unremitting hard work has accelerated rural-to-urban migration.

Natural hazards have periodically caused food shortages in South America. Droughts at distressingly frequent intervals in northeastern Brazil have shriveled standing crops, killed livestock, and brought mass starvation. During the "grande sêca" of 1877–9 in Ceará, between 200,000 and 500,000 people died, and most survivors were forced to migrate out of the region. The long history of famine in the Brazilian northeast prompted Josue de Castro to aim a Marxist critique at the problem in his book translated into several languages, including English as *The Geography of Hunger*. In 1955–6, a famine brought on by drought scourged the highlands of southern Peru. Food relief was not well timed or organized, with the result that some peasants starved, others were dispossessed, and some resorted to selling their children. The ability of modern South American governments to bring food relief to needy people has generally improved throughout the decades. But parts of the continent are still vulnerable to starvation if crops fail. In some ways, food production and distribution in South America reached its acme during the Inca Empire (A.D. 1200 to 1531). Surpluses of grains and chuño, moved by llama trains to specially constructed storehouses, were redistributed when regional or local food shortages occurred.

As one of the offshoots of Western civilization, South America shares some food characteristics and customs with Europe and North America. But tropical conditions, a strong indigenous presence, and weakly developed economies have greatly influenced the content of its food inventory, traditions, and nutritional profiles.

Daniel W. Gade

Bibliography

Brücher, Heinz. 1989. *Useful plants of neotropical origin and their wild relatives.* Berlin.

Cascudo, Luis de Câmara. 1967. *História da alimentação no Brasil.* 2 vols. São Paulo.

Daireaux, Emile. 1888. *La vie et les moeurs á La Plata.* 2 vols. Paris.

Estrella, Eduardo. 1986. *El pan de América: Etnohistoria de los alimentos aborígenes en el Ecuador.* Madrid.

Leonard, Jonathan Norton. 1968. *Latin American cooking.* New York.

Squier, Ephraim. 1877. *Peru: Incidents of travel and exploration in the land of the Incas.* London.

Super, John C. 1988. *Food, conquest, and colonization in sixteenth-century Spanish America.* Albuquerque, N. Mex.

Super, John C., and Thomas Wright, eds. 1985. *Food, politics, and scarcity in Latin America.* Lincoln, Nebr.

Weismantel, Mary J. 1988. *Food, gender, and poverty in the Ecuadorian Andes.* Philadelphia, Pa.

Wright, Eleanor Witte. 1985. Food dependency and malnutrition in Venezuela, 1958–74. In *Food, politics and society in Latin America,* ed. John C. Super and Thomas Wright, 150–73. Lincoln, Nebr.

V.D.3 ᭛ The Caribbean, Including Northern South America and Lowland Central America: Early History

In writing the history of culinary practices, there is a tendency to emphasize the ethnic character of diets (González 1988). Yet nowhere are historical entanglements more apparent than in the international character of modern cuisine, even if explicit ethnic territories are strongly defended. Foods are often defined with apparent regard to national origin: Indian corn, Irish potatoes, Italian tomatoes, Dutch chocolate, and Hawaiian pineapple, to name but a few. However, the plants that form the basis of many European cuisines in fact originated in the Americas (Keegan 1992), and American diets were transformed in what Alfred Crosby (1986) has described as the creation of the neo-Europes.

"You call it corn, we call it maize." Contrary to the American television commercial in which a very Navaho-looking women makes that statement, the word is actually of Taino origin. Peter Martyr was among the first Europeans to describe this plant that the native West Indians called *maíz (Zea mays)* (Sauer 1966: 55). Other Taino words for plants and animals have also entered the English lexicon, including *cazabi* and *yuca (Manihot esculenta* Crantz), *guayaba (Psidium guajava* L.), *bixa (Bixa orellana* L.), *iguana,* and *manati (Trichechus manatus)* (Oviedo [1526] 1959: 13–16; Taylor 1977: 20–1).

Cultigens from the circum-Caribbean lowlands have also been of significant effect (Keegan et al. 1992). Tomatoes (*Lycopersicon esculentum* Mill.) were first encountered in coastal Mexico, where the Spanish were also treated to a drink called *chocolatl,* a blend of cacao (*Theobroma cacao* L.), peppers (*Capsicum* spp.), and other spices (including *Bixa orellana* L.). Cacao won immediate acceptance; together, it and vanilla (*Vanilla* spp.), a semidomesticated lowland orchid, have become the most important flavorings in the world. In contrast, the *tomatl* (tomato) languished under the specter of its membership in the "deadly" nightshade family of plants. First grown as an ornamental, and only much later as food, the tomato eventually reshaped Italian cuisine.

American foods have been reinterpreted in ever-changing dietary contexts since their "discovery" by Europeans. Maize, in particular, has been manipulated for use as a building material, lubricant, automobile fuel, and universal hardening additive. The objective of this review is to introduce a well-structured methodology for examining past diets, while at the same time providing comprehensive empirical coverage of the regions first reached by the Spaniards after 1492.

We begin with the native Tainos who occupied the Greater Antilles and Bahama Islands at the time of European contact (see Figure V.D.3.1). Their culinary practices are traced through the Saladoid expansion to their mainland South American origins. The earlier "preagricultural" Caribbean peoples, called Archaic in the regional parlance (Rouse 1986, 1992), are then briefly considered. Although little is known of Archaic diets, it has been suggested that the Tainos developed from the synergy of Archaic and Saladoid cultures (Chanlatte Baik and Narganes Storde 1990). The scope is then expanded to include pre-Columbian plant migrations into the circum-Caribbean.

Taino Diet and Nutrition

The study of prehistoric diet and nutrition in the Caribbean is a relatively recent phenomenon. Moreover, the investigators who have concerned themselves with these issues have approached the subject in a variety of ways. The earliest efforts involved the enumeration of plants and animals described in the contact-period chronicles (Fewkes 1907; Rouse 1948; Sturtevant 1961, 1969; Sauer 1966). More recently,

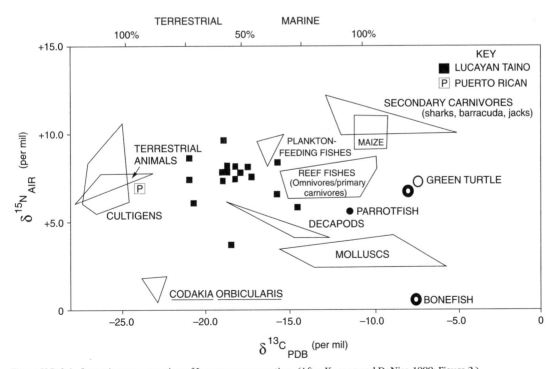

Figure V.D.3.1. Isotopic reconstruction of Lucayan consumption. (After Keegan and DeNiro 1988: Figure 2.)

attention has been drawn to the importance of diet and nutrition (Wing and Brown 1979). The analysis of animal remains in archaeological sites has been underway for some time (Wing and Reitz 1982; Wing and Scudder 1983). The investigation of archaeological plant remains has also been initiated. Although most of these studies are not yet published, they are investigating pollen, phytoliths, wood charcoal, and carbonized structures for the purposes of identifying cultigens, firewood, and modifications of the landscape (for example, Fortuna 1978; Pearsall 1985; Piperno, Bush, and Colinvaux 1990; Newsom 1993). Stable-isotope analysis has been used to investigate prehistoric diets (Keegan and DeNiro 1988; Klinken 1991), and studies of human skeletal remains have uncovered evidence of diet-related pathologies (Budinoff 1987).

Because different investigators approach questions of diet and nutrition from different perspectives, there has been a problem with the integration of their results. The author of this chapter has argued that diverse empirical studies need to be integrated in a well-structured research methodology (Keegan 1987; Keegan and DeNiro 1988). Such a methodology must include explanations for why people ate what they did, must predict what people should have eaten, and must incorporate techniques for determining the variety of foods people consumed.

The study of West Indian diets described here uses models developed in evolutionary biology under the title "Optimal Foraging Theory" (Winterhalder and Smith 1981; Smith 1983; Keegan 1986a; Smith and Winterhalder 1992). It was hypothesized that Caribbean diets would reflect the efficient capture of the aggregate nutritional currencies – calories and protein. The theory was examined with data derived from ethnological, ethnohistorical, zooarchaeological, paleobotanical, and other techniques, which specified what foods were eaten and the relative costs of obtaining these foods (Keegan 1985). Finally, osteochemical techniques were used to evaluate what food items were consumed from the record they left in the human skeleton (Keegan and DeNiro 1988). This three-tier approach provides a robust solution to questions of prehistoric diet and nutrition (see Bell 1992).

West Indian Food Items

The first task in reconstructing prehistoric diets involves compiling a list of the plants and animals that were consumed. Ethno-historic reports described the Taino in the Greater Antilles as practicing a mixed economy of root-crop horticulture and hunting-fishing-collecting (Fewkes 1907; Rouse 1948; Sauer 1966; Wing 1969; Wing and Reitz 1982).

The Spanish chroniclers reported that the Tainos cultivated manioc (*Manihot esculenta* Crantz),[1] sweet potatoes (*Ipomoea batatas* [L.] Lam.), yautía or cocoyam (*Xanthosoma sagittifolium* Schott), llerén

(*Calathea allouia* [Aubl.] Lindl.), peanuts (*Arachis hypogaea* L.), maize (*Zea mays* L.), beans (*Phaseolus* spp.), cucurbits (*Cucurbita* spp.), chilli peppers (*Capsicum frutescens* L. or *Capsicum annuum* L.), and fruit trees, including mamey (*Mammea americana* L.), jagua or genipop (*Genipa americana* L.), hicaco or cocoplum (*Chrysobalanus icaco* L.), guanábana or soursop (*Annona muricata* L.), bixa or annatto (*Bixa orellana* L.), guava (*Psidium guajava* L.), and cupey (*Clusea rosea*) (Fewkes 1907; Rouse 1948; Sturtevant 1961, 1969; Sauer 1966; Guarch 1974; Nadal 1981). Most of these cultigens were carried into the Antilles by the Island Arawak (see Ford 1984; Schultes 1984). A variety of wild or quasi-domesticated plants were also in use, including the stems of the cycad *Zamia,* primrose (*Oenothera* sp.), purslane (*Portulaca* sp.), masticbully (*Mastichodendron foetidissimum*), sapodilla (*Manilkara* sp.), cockspur (*Celtis iguanaea*), palm fruits, sea grapes (*Coccoloba uvifera*), pigeon plum (*Coccoloba diversifolia*), and panicoid grasses (*Setaria* spp.) (Sturtevant 1969; Fortuna 1978; Newsom 1993). The carbonized remains of maize, chilli peppers, palm fruits, and at least two unidentified tubers (probably manioc and sweet potato) are among the plant remains identified in West Indian sites (Newsom 1993).

As is the case with modern tropical horticulturalists, life revolved around garden cycles (Malinowski 1978; Johnson 1983). Garden plots (called *conucos* by the Tainos) of about one to two hectares per household were cleared at regular, possibly annual, intervals. Clearing involved the use of stone axes or shell tools to slash brush, fell trees, and girdle large trees so that they would drop their leaves. After clearing, the brush was left to dry and was then burned, releasing the nutrients stored in the vegetation.

Planting came next and was done with a sharpened digging stick. Manioc was planted in small mounds of loose earth, called *montones.* After planting, the gardens were weeded and the mature crops harvested; replantings were made on a continuous basis until the garden was abandoned. (Unlike temperate gardens that die in the winter, tropical gardens can be maintained for years.) After a few years, garden production was reduced to certain tree crops, and new gardens had to be prepared. The old garden was then left fallow until covered by at least secondary forest growth, at which time it might again have been cleared. The importance of the agricultural cycle is reflected in stone alignments, which were used to chart the summer solstice and the rising and setting of stars that were important in Native American agricultural calendars. The most notable examples are site MC-6 on Middle Caicos in the Turks and Caicos Islands and La Plaza de Chacuey in the Dominican Republic (Castellanos 1981; Aveni and Urton 1982; Alegría 1983).

Taino cultigens grew and matured at different rates. Consequently, the diet of the inhabitants changed continuously with the seasons. Nonbitter maniocs and other root crops would have been available throughout the year. Boiling was the usual method of cooking. Bitter maniocs, so-called because they contain toxic levels of cyanogenic glucosides, must be grated and squeezed before consumption (Roosevelt 1980: 129). The juice releases its toxins when exposed to air or cooked; the boiled juice, called *cassirepe,* is a base for pepper pots and manioc beer. The pulp is dried for use as starch (flour); it is also toasted to make farina or for use as an ingredient in tapioca. The reward for so much additional processing effort is indefinite storability (Roosevelt 1980: 129). Water is added to the starch to make pancakelike cassava bread that is baked on large, round, pottery griddles called *burénes.*

Manioc was the staple crop intensively cultivated on mounds at the time of European contact (Sturtevant 1969). Maize is reported to have been grown for roasting ears and, to some extent, for bread grain, but it was not a major foodstuff (Sturtevant 1961; Sauer 1966). Maize was apparently a late introduction and may have been the focus of agricultural intensification in the Greater Antilles at the time of Spanish contact (Keegan 1987; compare Lathrap 1987).

In addition to "outfield" garden plots, there were house gardens closer to and around the dwellings. House gardens contained new varieties of cultigens, herbs and spices, medicinal and narcotic plants, vegetable dyes, fruit trees, and other cultigens that required special attention or were needed frequently in small quantities (Lathrap 1977, 1987). A list of possible house-garden plants is given in Table V.D.3.1.

A meal without meat would not have been considered complete. As is typical of most islands, the West Indies have a depauperate terrestrial fauna (Keegan and Diamond 1987). Indigenous land mammals are limited to bats, rodents of the tribe Oryzomyini, spiny rat (Echimyidae), and small rodents (*Geocapromys* sp., *Isolobodon portoricensis, Plagiodontia* sp.). Opossum (*Didelphis virginiana*), agouti (*Dasyprocta aguti* L.), and armadillo (*Dasypus novemcinctus*) were introduced from the South American mainland (Eisenberg 1989). In addition, a type of small deer called brocket (*Mazama americana*) was known in Trinidad, which was connected to the mainland until the end of the Pleistocene (Wing and Reitz 1982). Other land animals include iguanas (*Iguana* sp., *Cyclura* spp.), crocodiles (*Crocodylus* sp.), a variety of small reptiles (e.g., *Anolis* sp.), land crabs (*Cardisoma guanhumi, Gecarchinus* sp.), numerous birds, and a land snail (*Caracolus* sp.) (Wing 1969; Wing and Reitz 1982; Wing and Scudder 1983; Steadman et al. 1984; Watters et al. 1984; Morgan and Woods 1986; deFrance 1988, 1989; Fandrich 1990). The Tainos kept domesticated Muscovy ducks (*Cairina moschata*) and dogs (*Canis familiaris*) (Sauer 1966; Wing and Scudder 1983). It is also likely that a variety of grubs and insects were consumed (see Johnson and Baksh 1987).

A number of these animals, such as *Isolobodon* (Reitz 1986), crocodile (McKinnen 1804; deFrance

1991), and iguana (Iverson 1979), suffered local extinctions after the arrival of Europeans (Olsen 1982; Morgan and Woods 1986).

The main component of prehistoric Antillean vertebrate faunal assemblages is marine fishes (Wing and Reitz 1982). In the Bahamas, marine fishes account for more than 80 percent of the estimated maximum vertebrate biomass in the sites with analyzed assemblages (Wing 1969; Wing and Scudder 1983; Keegan 1986b; deFrance 1991). A representative list of fish species identified in Lucayan sites is presented in Table V.D.3.2.

In addition to fishes, several large aquatic animals have also been identified in Antillean sites. These include marine turtles (mostly Chelonidae), porpoises (Delphinidae), West Indian monk seals (*Monachus tropicalis*), and manatees (*Trichechus manatus*) (Wing and Reitz 1982; Watters et al. 1984). These large reptiles and mammals have been emphasized in the subsistence activities of peoples throughout the circum-Caribbean (Nietschmann 1973; Davidson 1974; Campbell 1978; Wing and Reitz 1982; McKillop 1985).

The final category of subsistence remains is marine mollusks. Molluscan shell is the most abundant type of refuse in prehistoric sites in terms of both volume and mass. Despite this abundance, molluscan shell represents relatively small edible packages. The most important mollusks were queen conch (*Strombus gigas*), West Indian top shell (*Cittarium pica*), tiger lucine clams (*Codakia orbicularis*), chitons (*Chiton* spp.), and nerites (Keegan 1985; deFrance 1988).

Meats were roasted over a fire or barbecued ("barbecue" is derived from a Taino word). It has been suggested that the Lucayans may have used another traditional form of tropical-forest cooking called the "pepper pot." Pepper pots are stews, kept simmering over a low fire, to which meats and vegetables are added to replenish the pot. The large, thick clay pots made in the Bahamas and in the Lesser Antilles were well suited to this type of food preparation (Allaire 1984).

When viewed with regard to the number of different ways in which individuals could satisfy their hunger, the West Indies are noteworthy for the surfeit of options. It is difficult to imagine that anyone ever went hungry. Yet the fact that these people were selective in their food choices provides an important challenge. It is not sufficient simply to list the items that were, or may have been, eaten; rather, the criteria upon which dietary selections were based must be identified.

Because there is too much local variability to treat all West Indian diets as equivalent (deFrance 1988), the following study focuses on the subsistence decisions of the Lucayans. The Lucayans are of Taino ancestry. They occupied the Bahama archipelago between A.D. 600 and 1500 (Keegan 1992). Lucayan diet breadth is evaluated by comparison with an economic model of the diet that would result from the cost-efficient capture of nutritional currencies.

Table V.D.3.1. *Comparison of house-garden cultigens in native Amazonian and prehistoric West Indian gardens*

House garden plants	Native Amazonian house gardens		Prehistoric Antilles
	General	Machiguenga	
Agave sp. (sisal fiber)	–	–	St
Anacardium occidentale (cashew bush)	X	–	–
Anadenanthera peregrina (leguminous tree)	X	–	–
Ananas sp. (pineapple)	X	X	–
Annona sp. (soursop fruit)	–	X	St
Arachis hypogaea (peanut)	–	X	S, St
Bixa orellana (red dye)	X	X	S
Bocconia sp. (plume poppy)	–	–	F
Bromelia sp.	–	X	F
Bursera simaruba (gum elemi)	–	–	F
Capsicum sp. (pepper)	X	X	S, St
Carica papaya (papaya fruit)	X	X	F
Cassia sp.	–	–	X F
Cecropia peltata (mulberry)	–	–	F
Chenopodium ambrosoides (lamb's-quarters)	–	–	F
Chrysobalanus icaco (cocoplum fruit)	–	–	St
Chtysophyllum caimito (caimito fruit)	X	–	F
Crescentia cujete (calabash tree)	X	X	F, S
Cucurbita sp. (squash)	–	X	St
Cyperus sp. (sedge)	–	X	F
Datura sp. (moonflower, fish poison)	–	X	–
Digetaria sp. (grass)	–	–	F
Genipa americana (genipe, black dye)	X	–	S
Gossypium sp. (cotton)	X	X	S
Guazuma ulmifolia (chocolate)	–	–	F
Guilielma gasipaës (peach palm)	X	–	–
Helecho sp. (tree fern, fire box)	–	–	F
Inga sp. (guaba fruit)	X	X	F
Jacquemontia petantha (chainnindo)	–	–	F
Jatropha cura (psychic nut)	–	–	St
Lagenaria sp. (bottle gourd)	X	X	St
Mammea americana (fruit tree)	–	–	S
Nicotiana sp. (tobacco)	X	X	F, S
Peperonia sp.	–	–	F
Piptadenia peregrina (cahoba, narcotic)	–	–	S
Psydium guajava (guava fruit)	X	X	F
Puosopis juliglora	–	–	F
Ricinus comunis (castor bean)	–	–	F
Roystonea hispaniolana (palm)	–	–	F
Sapindus saponatia (soapberry)	–	–	F
Solanum sp.	X	X	F
Spondias mombin (cashew bush)	–	–	F
Syzysium jambas (jambolan plum)	–	–	F
Theobroma sp. (cacao)	X	X	–
Thrychilia hirta	–	–	F
Vetiveria alliacea	–	–	F
Wallenia sp.	–	–	F
Zamia debilis (cycad, starchy bread root)	–	–	F

Note: Native Amazonian lists are based on Lathrap's (1977) general list (column 1), and Johnson's (1983) list of minor cultigens in Machiguenga gardens (column 2). Prehistoric Antillean cultigens (column 3) are identifed in ethnohistoric reports (*S* = Sauer 1966; *St* = Sturtevant 1961) and in Fortuna's (1978) analysis (denoted by *F*) of pollen samples from Sanate Abajo, Dominican Republic (A.D. 1020). Many of these "cultigens" are actually managed, tended, and transplanted non- or quasi-domesticated species. (Johnson's [1983] longer list of 80 cultigens was shortened by deleting major cultigens [manioc, maize, beans], historic introductions [sugarcane], and plants that were not identified by their taxonomic name.)

Source: After Keegan (1987), Table 15–1.

Table V.D.3.2. *Fishes identified in Lucayan sites*

Fish genera (most common = >90% of genera)
Haemulon (grunt)
Sparisoma (parrot fish)
Lutjanus (snapper)
Acanthurus (surgeonfish)
Scarus (parrot fish)
Epinephelus (grouper)
Mulloidichthys (goatfish)
Pomacanthus (angelfish)
Calamus (porgy)
Albula vulpes (bonefish)

Other fish genera (<10% of genera)
Inshore-estuarine habitat
   Lactophrys (trunkfish)
   Gerreidae (mojarro)
   Eucinostomus (mojarro)
   Diodon (porcupinefish)
   Sphoeroides (puffer)
   Lachnolaimus (hogfish)
   Stronbylura (needlefish)
   Belonidae (needlefishes)
   Centropomus (snook)
   Sciaenidae (drums)
   Selene (lookdown)
Banks and reef habitats
   Halichoeres (wrasse)
   Elegatis (wrasse)
   Holocentrus (squirrelfish)
   Holocanthus (angelfish)
   Flammeo (squirrelfish)
   Chaetodon (butterfly fish)
   Serranidae (groupers)
   Ocyurus (yellowtail snapper)
   Gymnothorax (moray eel)
Two or more habitats
   Scorpaena (scorpion fish)
   Balistidae (triggerfish)
   Carangidae (jacks)
   Sphyraena (barracuda)
   Sharks and rays

Source: After Keegan (1986b).

Lucayan Diet Breadth

Lucayan diet can be described as consisting of inputs from five general sources: cultivated roots and tubers, maize, terrestrial animals, marine fishes, and marine mollusks (Sears and Sullivan 1978; Keegan 1992). These foods were obtained from the forest, the coastal strip, and the sea. To evaluate the Lucayan's behavior as cost-efficient foragers, the capture of foods in the three habitats is reviewed first. After identifying the foods and their associated costs, their return rates are compared by using a model derived from Optimal Foraging Theory. Finally, the diets predicted with the model are compared to the isotopic signatures in the bones of 17 individuals. The isotopic signatures reflect the foods that these individuals consumed.

Lucayan Food Procurement

The main component of the forest habitat was gardens. These were probably prepared in coastal accumulations of humic enriched sandy soil and would have followed the pattern of other tropical gardens (Ruddle 1974; Johnson 1983). Gardens were stable patches where output could be modified in response to changing needs. Root-crop horticulture provides high total and marginal rates of return. Average yields of manioc in Brazil are reported as 14.2 million calories per hectare (Roosevelt 1980: Table V.D.3.1). Using a generous estimate of human caloric needs (2,700 calories per day), 14 adults could have been supported on one hectare of land for an entire year. The availability of calories in other foods, which have higher net return rates, would have precluded the need for complete reliance on manioc production.

Because manioc does not require fertile soils for efficient tuber production, a single plot can be cultivated for many years. Long-term land use is not practiced in the tropical forest today because total human protein requirements also are met through garden production. The characteristics of maize make long-term, cost-efficient production on a single plot of land impossible (Keegan 1986a). Furthermore, yields from long-term manioc gardens can be increased by intercropping other cultigens (for example, sweet potatoes, cocoyams, fruit trees). These crops do not interfere with the growth of the manioc plants; rather, they increase yields per hectare for the additional investment of planting and harvesting, they aid in preventing weed growth, and they fill areas that would otherwise go unused (Ruddle 1974; Brierley 1985; Keegan 1986a). It is likely that the initial colonists planted small gardens with a diversity of crops, with garden size set by the caloric returns from manioc in relation to the caloric needs of the group. As population increased, garden size would have increased and other cultigens would have been added to the gardens.

The principal shortcoming of manioc is its low protein content (Roosevelt 1980). Since human nutritional requirements cannot be satisfied with manioc alone, other sources of protein had to be sought. In addition to animal protein sources, such cultigens as maize, beans, or ground nuts could have been added to the garden as protein supplements. These cultigens are more expensive in terms of harvesting and processing, contribute to a more rapid exhaustion of garden soils, and are available only during specific seasons.

Maize is the most cost-efficient of the high-protein cultigens. From Allen Johnson's (1983) studies it was estimated that maize has a marginal return rate of 20 grams of protein per hour of labor (Keegan 1986a). This return rate is higher than that for many other Lucayan foods. This would have promoted its acceptance when it became available after about A.D. 1100 (Keegan 1987). The disadvantages of maize production are the plant's need for fertile soils, its availability during only one season of the year, and the high cost of storing and processing maize when it is grown for use throughout the year. Thus, maize constituted only a partial solution to the problem of protein production.

Marginal return rates for animal species that inhabit the forest favor their use over horticulture. These animals (that is, hutia, iguana, and land crabs) could not, however, satisfy total needs. Their combined densities are equivalent to 1,861,950 calories per hectare, which could support only two individuals for a year if every animal was captured. But (in economic terms) intensive use would have rapidly reduced the frequency of encounters (that is, animals would not be seen very often), with the result a decline in the average return rate to a level below the marginal rate for other food sources (including horticulture). When this decline reached that level, those other foods would be added to the diet (Winterhalder and Smith 1981; Smith 1983). For the Lucayans, this other source of protein was the sea.

The inference from the economic model is that terrestrial animals were pursued whenever they were encountered. It is probable that game was taken in or near gardens (Linares 1976) and during visits to the coast. The forest is a difficult patch to traverse, and hunting trips in the forest were probably infrequent, especially after the decline of initially high prey densities. Since all of these small game were regular visitors to the coastal strip, the most efficient strategy would be to forage in this area. Travel along the coast is also less difficult, and other food sources would doubtless have been encountered (for example, wild plants, littoral mollusks).

The one exception to the forest-hunting proscription is land crabs, which congregate in the low areas that provide for moist burrows. These locations could be identified, and hunting could be accomplished with guaranteed results. But even land crabs can be taken on the coastal strip, especially when they congregate for mating (Gifford 1962; deFrance 1988).

The coastal strip is comprised of the beach patch and the rocky intertidal patch, and it provides access to marine habitats. The beach patch was the site of seasonal monk seal aggregations, turtle nesting grounds, and the accidental beaching of whales. In addition, terrestrial animals frequent this patch. Because settlements were located on the coast, the Lucayans were in a position to monitor activities on the beach.

The highest average return rate was available in the beach patch, although the highest return species were not available in all locations at all times (for instance, green turtles, monk seals, and whales). Turtles would have been available from April to July, and monk seals for about six weeks centered on December. Both would have been the focus of procurement efforts during their seasonal abundances.

The rocky intertidal patch supports dense aggregations of West Indian top shells, nerites, and chitons.

Top shells have a relatively high net return rate, and of the three they are the only ones used today with any frequency. However, the use of top shells is limited by two factors. Rocky intertidal zones are small, averaging less than three meters wide, and they are irregularly distributed. These snails also are easily exploited and would have rapidly disappeared following the start of human predation. The other common littoral mollusks have lower return rates. These low values suggest that they were exploited during periods of food shortage. In any case, chitons and nerites should have been among the last items added to the diet.

The marine environment is comprised of a tidal-flat patch and a reef patch. The tidal-flat patch can be further divided by procurement strategies into infaunal mollusk collecting (that is, in the mud–sand substrate), epifaunal mollusk collecting (that is, on the substrate), and fishing. These strategies are discussed in turn.

The tiger lucine clam, *Codakia orbicularis,* is the most commonly used infaunal mollusk species. They occur at high densities beneath shallow grass flats and would have provided a stable resource supply (Jackson 1972, 1973). In terms of weight, tiger lucine clams provided a more significant source of food than intertidal mollusks (Rose 1982). Yet, tiger lucine has low net return rates of both calories and protein. It is, however, possible that these rates have been underestimated in the present study. A study of pelecypod collecting in Australia indicated a caloric return rate that is twice that estimated for *Codakia orbicularis* (Meehan 1977). Historical evidence suggests that even if the return rates were underestimated, the ranking relative to other food items is accurate. Tiger lucine clams should therefore have also been one of the last items added to the diet.

The epifaunal gastropod *Strombus gigas* is the highest ranked marine resource. It is available at high densities on shallow grass flats (Doran 1958; Hesse and Hesse 1977) and was a significant component of the diet. The high return rates place *Strombus gigas* in the initial optimal diet. Foraging trips over the shallow grass flats would also have led to encounters with marine fishes, such as bonefish *(Albula vulpes).*

The net return rate for fishes has been calculated as an average for all fishing strategies. Higher returns could have been obtained by pursuing particular strategies, such as the capture of fishes encountered during *Strombus gigas* collecting trips, but present evidence is not sufficient to discriminate the return rates for alternative strategies (Johannes 1981; Kirch 1982; Keegan 1986a). The average values for all fishing strategies places fishing just below rock iguana in the ranking of protein returns.

Optimal Horticulturalists

Having discussed the major habitats and their patches, attention is next focused on the food quest. In which patch should food be sought first? How much time should be devoted to the food quest in each patch? When should new foods be added to the diet? More complete information on time allocation and predation rates are needed before a quantitative solution for patch selection decisions can be calculated.

A qualitative solution can be proposed in the Lucayan case because the net return rates for the second through eighth ranked resources are sufficiently similar to analyze dietary change in a diet-breadth framework (Table V.D.3.3). This approach is based on the identification of horticultural production as part of the original subsistence endowment, and by the distribution of higher ranked resources in forest, coastal, and marine patches. Furthermore, the location of permanent settlements on the coast would eliminate significant differences in the time invested in traveling between patches.

The logic behind the use of the diet-breadth model, rather than the patch-selection model, is as follows. Although the patch-selection model compares average returns from different patches (including transportation time), while the diet-breadth model compares marginal returns to the overall foraging efficiency, the marginal return rates calculated for Lucayan food sources include some time investments that are better considered as search time. (Search time is a component of average return calculations.) This conflation of average and marginal returns results from the character of the information available to calculate those rates.

A second factor is that foraging from a central place should require similar investments in the time required to travel between patches. The high-ranked items in the Lucayan diet all have population densities that would have been rapidly depleted after the start of human predation. This reduction of animal densities would produce a reduction in the average return rates. Since the marginal rates for high-ranked items are similar, as is the time invested in traveling between patches, the marginal return rates should approximate the long-term decision-making problem. In other words, foraging decisions can be modeled as reflecting habitat selection based solely on short-term differences in resource distributions in each of the patches. This type of patch selection is so "fine-grained" (homogeneous) that it closely resembles and even operates like the diet-breadth model.

The diet-breadth model predicts that diet breadth will be expanded (in other words, items will be added to the diet) when the marginal return rate for a resource is equal to the average return rate for all higher-ranked resources. Because manioc cultivation was practiced when the Bahama archipelago was colonized, the higher-ranked resources would also have been in the original optimal set. These high-ranked resources are hutia, land crabs, queen conch, and rock iguana. This analysis suggests that despite their current absence in archaeological samples, green turtles and monk seals would have been captured during their seasonal availabilities. The food items mentioned

Table V.D.3.3. *Return rates and resource rankings of Lucayan foods*

Food Sources	Average weight/ individual (kg)	Kcal/ kg	Grams protein (kg)	Handling time (hr/kg)	Pop. density (kg/ha)	E/h	gP/h	Rank E/h	Rank gP/h
Green turtles (*Chelonia mydas*)	19.0	1300	2.2	0.026	2609	50,000	84	1	1
Hutia (*Geocapromys* sp.)	1.4	1500	1.5	0.12	21	12,500	13	2	5
Land crab (*Cardisoma* sp.)	0.2	900	1.7	0.10	2000	9,000	17	3	3
Queen conch (*Strombus gigas*)	0.17	800	1.3	0.09	850	8,889	14	4	4
Rock iguana (*Cyclura carinata*)	0.7	2000	2.4	0.24	15	8,333	10	5	6
Horticulture									
root crops	–	–	–	–	–	5,000	–	6	–
maize	–	–	–	–	–	–	20	–	2
All fishes	0.25	1000	1.9	0.22	–	4,545	9	7	7
West Indian top shell (*Cittarium pica*)	0.035	800	1.3	0.25	1750	3,200	5	8	8
Chiton sp.	0.005	800	1.3	0.5	500	1,600	3	9	9
Codakia orbicularis	0.01	800	1.3	1.39	4000	576	1	10	10
Nerites (*Nerita* sp.)	0.002	800	1.3	1.4	400	471	<1	11	11

Note: E/h is calories per handling hour; gP/h is grams of protein per handling hour.

Source: After Keegan (1985).

should have provided a diet sufficient to preclude the need to eat any other foods. One qualification to this is that high-ranked fishes, such as bonefish, were probably pursued when encountered during foraging on the tidal flats.

Terrestrial animals in the Bahamas are susceptible to overexploitation. Their availability would have rapidly declined after a short period of intense predation and as human population growth increased the demand for these foods (Iverson 1979; Jordan 1989). In addition, land clearance and other changes to the landscape would effect the survival of other species (Olsen 1982). The first response to a decline in high-ranked resources would be to migrate to previously unexploited habitats. Thus, the rapid decline in high-ranked terrestrial animals would have encouraged the rapid migration of people to unoccupied islands. When new areas were no longer available, then the intensification of foraging in the marine habitat should have occurred.

The redistribution of the human population was no longer a cost-efficient option when the presence of other settlements prevented people from moving into pristine areas. When such social circumscription occurred, the currency demands had to be satisfied in the vicinity of the village over a longer period of time. In response to the combined effects of increased demand due to population growth and declining returns due to long-term exploitation, the intensification of production could only focus on two options. These options were increased use of marine habitats and changes in garden breadth. The total contribution of land animals would have continued to decline as human population numbers increased. In marine habitats, sea turtles, *Strombus gigas,* and certain species of fish would have been the initial focus, with other fishes added to the diet as other fishing techniques were introduced, and ending with the highest-ranked littoral mollusk, *Cittarium pica,* the West Indian top shells. But this species would also have been rapidly exhausted in areas of human settlement.

During the final phase, the lowest-ranked foods (that is, nerites, chitons, and tiger lucine) would have been added in turn. *Strombus gigas* would have been sought at more distant locations, and a variety of more intensive fishing strategies would have been introduced. It is likely that fish traps were introduced early in this phase as the availability of such visible diurnal species as bonefish declined and as fishes had to be sought at more distant locations, such as along the barrier coral reef. Horticultural production would have been intensified with the addition of beans, groundnuts, and maize, all of which are high carbohydrate- and protein-producing cultigens. Fields might have been fallowed for shorter lengths of time, although the sandy soils may have supported production for longer periods than was possible on other tropical soils (as in the Yucatan Peninsula, Mexico; Roosevelt 1980). Nitrogen-fixing legumes could have

helped to maintain soil fertility. In the final phase, agriculture was intensified by the terracing of hillsides, the irrigating of fields, and the building of raised and drained fields (Zucchi and Denevan 1979).

The preceding discussion has served to identify three discrete diets. An initial diet was composed of root crops, land animals, and a few high-ranked marine species. This was followed by a second diet that included the consumption of more marine foods, a continuing contribution from root crops, and a precipitous decline in the contribution from land animals. In the third diet, land animals were reduced to a very minor level of use, marine production was further intensified, and horticulture was expanded to include higher-cost cultigens, such as maize and beans, which increased total protein and carbohydrate returns from the garden. It is this final pattern that is evident in the Lucayan faunal samples that have been analyzed to date (Wing and Reitz 1982; Wing and Scudder 1983; deFrance 1991).

Stable Isotope Analysis

The three diets just described were proposed on the basis of data gathered from ethnographic analogy, ethnohistoric reports, ethnobiological analyses, and formal economic models. To determine how well these diets reflect the actual subsistence practices of the Lucayans, a different analytical technique must be used to avoid circular reasoning. Stable-isotope analysis provides such a technique (Schoeninger and DeNiro 1984; Sealey 1986; Ambrose 1987, 1993; Keegan 1989c; Schoeninger et al. 1989; Sillen et al. 1989; see Stokes 1995 and de France et al. 1996 for new perspectives on this question.)

The Lucayan diet was evaluated by first measuring or estimating the carbon- and nitrogen-isotope compositions of food items and then measuring these in bone collagen extracted from 17 Lucayan skeletons. The results were then compared in order to determine the most likely components of the Lucayan diet.

An immediate division into marine and terrestrial food groups was observed in the carbon-isotope ratios. The marine group has an average delta^{13}C of –11 per mil, whereas the terrestrial group has an average delta^{13}C value of –25 per mil. Using these averages, the diet delta^{13}C values calculated for the Lucayan individuals can be interpreted. For instance, a diet delta^{13}C value of –11 per mil would suggest complete reliance on marine foods, a diet delta^{13}C of –25 per mil would suggest complete reliance on terrestrial foods, and a diet delta^{13}C value of –18 per mil would suggest equal contributions from both. Based on an estimated ±1 per mil uncertainty in the fractionation factor between diet and bone collagen, the diets of Lucayan individuals range from an estimated 71 ± 7 percent reliance on terrestrial foods (–21 per mil) to an estimated maximum of 74 ± 7 percent reliance on marine foods (–14.6 per mil).

If this interpretation is correct, the range in

delta[13]C values estimated for the diets of Lucayan individuals can be interpreted as reflecting a shift in consumption practices through time. The three most negative delta[13]C values (all around −20 per mil) match the first of the proposed diets in which land animals were abundant and only the highest-ranked marine organisms were consumed. The second dietary pattern would account for the majority of Lucayan individuals (n = 11), whose diet delta[13]C values of −18 ± 1 per mil reflects almost equal contributions from marine and terrestrial sources. The remaining three individuals exhibit ideal consumption patterns in the 66 to 74 ± 7 percent marine range (diet delta[13]C values of −15.2 ± .6 per mil). Such a strong reliance on marine foods is unlikely due to the relatively higher costs of marine fishing and collecting in relation to horticulture. An alternative interpretation is that the higher delta[13]C values indicate that maize was being consumed in substantial quantities during at least part of the year.

The carbon isotopes confirm the presence of three distinct diets. One explanation for these differences is that they represent changes in diet breadth through time. Unfortunately, the skeletons came from burials in caves and were not associated with materials that could be used to date them (Keegan 1982; Keegan and DeNiro 1988). Other explanations, such as the influence of more localized factors, must be entertained. Further investigations are needed to relate the isotopic study to expectations based on empirical studies and theoretical projections.

A second part of the isotopic study examined nitrogen-isotope distributions. Nitrogen-isotope values for marine and terrestrial food sources overlap, and so they cannot be used to distinguish among the contributions of land animals, cultivated roots and tubers, maize, and reef fishes in the Lucayan diet (Keegan and DeNiro 1988). When the isotopic signatures of Lucayan individuals are compared to this average, 76 percent of the individuals (n = 13) fall within ±1 per mil of this range.

Deviations from that average diet can be explained with reference to the lower values of mollusks and the higher values of pelagic fishes and marine mammals relative to other dietary components. One individual from Crooked Island had a higher dietary value, which suggests that pelagic fishes and/or marine mammals comprised a larger component of his diet and that mollusks made a relatively minor contribution. The location of this burial in an area where the barrier coral reef approaches the shore and the reef flat has a restricted range places this individual in the vicinity of marine habitats that are the most likely sources of such a dietary combination (Keegan 1982, 1986b).

The three individuals' diet values that are lower than the average probably reflect a stronger reliance on mollusks and perhaps a corresponding reduction in the consumption of higher-order carnivorous fishes. All three of these individuals are from islands with extensive *Thalassia* seagrass meadows (Grand Bahama Island and Great Abaco on the Little Bahama Bank, and Providenciales on the Caicos Bank). These shallow banks provide access to extensive mollusk populations while restricting access to reef-associated fishes (Wing and Reitz 1982; Wing and Scudder 1983; Keegan 1986b). Two of the individuals are less than 0.6 per mil below the average range, which reflects an increase in mollusk consumption to a level of less than 10 percent of total consumption. The other is 2.4 per mil below the average range, which suggests a reliance on mollusks and possibly other marine invertebrates approaching 40 percent of the diet.

The carbon- and nitrogen-isotope ratios are significant in their unequivocal rejection of commonsense interpretations of archaeological deposits. These deposits are largely composed of marine mollusk shells, the size and durability of which have led some investigators to propose that mollusks comprised as much as 95 percent of the meat protein in Lucayan diets. It is clear in the isotopic signatures of the 17 Lucayans that mollusks played a much more modest role in the diet. The same is true for the slave populations that followed them (Armstrong 1983).

The physical examination of the skeletons from the Bahamas indicates that the Lucayans enjoyed good health and nutrition (Keegan 1982). They certainly did not suffer from the nutritional and diet-related disorders of other prehistoric horticulturalists (Cohen and Armelagos 1984). They also lack the dental pathologies observed in Saladoid and Ostionoid burials at the Maisabel site, Puerto Rico. Linda Budinoff (1987), who analyzed the Maisabel skeletons, concluded that sand adhering to foods, exoskeleton and shell adhering to invertebrates, and a high percentage of carbohydrates in the diet conspired to destroy the teeth. One result was that middle-aged people had mouths more typical of old people.

In sum, the preceding examination of Lucayan diet has drawn together evidence from a variety of sources. On a general level, the empirical findings are consistent with the expectations derived from the formal model. There is every reason to believe that the Lucayans, and by extension other Tainos, were efficient, even optimal, horticulturalists.

Culinary Origins of the Tainos

The origins of the Tainos are conveniently traced to the banks of the Orinoco River in Venezuela (Rouse 1989a). As early as 2100 B.C., villages of horticulturalists who used pottery vessels to cook their food had been established along the Middle Orinoco. During the ensuing two millennia, their population increased in numbers, and they expanded downriver and outward along the Orinoco's tributaries (Lathrap 1977, 1987; Roosevelt 1980; Sanoja Obediente and Vargas 1983). One path of expansion led these people to the coast of the Guianas (Rouse 1992). From the Guianas, the opening of the West Indies awaited only the discovery of Grenada, which is separated from Trinidad by the widest gap in the chain of islands leading to Puerto Rico.

The movement of these people down the Orinoco River and through the Lesser Antilles to Puerto Rico is well documented (Roosevelt 1980; Sanoja Obediente and Vargas 1983; Zucchi, Tarble, and Vaz 1984; Rouse 1986). It is easily traced because these people manufactured a characteristic type of pottery known as Saladoid after the archaeological site of Saladero, Venezuela, at which it was first described (Rouse and Allaire 1978). In particular, the use of white-on-red painted decorations has facilitated the identification of the path along which this population expanded. Another indicator of migration is the presence of certain animals in the island archaeological remains.

The Saladoid expansion into the Antilles occurred at a rapid pace. The earliest Ceramic-Age settlements in the West Indies date to about 400 B.C. (Rouse 1989b; Haviser 1991; Siegel 1991). Saladoid settlements appear simultaneously on Puerto Rico and the islands of the Lesser Antilles (Rouse 1992). Given what is known of human reproductive potentials and the time that elapsed between departure from the mainland and colonization of Puerto Rico, the inescapable conclusion is that only the very best locations on a few of the Lesser Antilles were settled at this time. The most likely scenario is that most islands were settled temporarily and were then abandoned in favor of more abundant food resources on other islands. Only those few locations with superior resource concentrations were settled for a period that could be considered permanent (Watters 1982; Keegan and Diamond 1987; Haviser 1991). This practice of establishing temporary settlements that were moved in response to resource availability is typical of extensive horticulturalists, which the Saladoid peoples are believed to have been (Conklin 1968; Ruddle 1974; Johnson 1983).

Since paleobotanical studies have only recently been attempted, the composition of the Saladoids peoples' gardens has been hypothesized from ethnohistoric and ethnological descriptions of cultivations (Sturtevant 1961; Roosevelt 1980), and from the presence of certain food-processing artifacts. It has been proposed that manioc was the staple, but that a variety of other cultigens were also grown. The hypothesized importance of root crops is consistent with the results obtained from stable isotope analysis.

The earliest known villages in the Lesser Antilles follow the riverine settlement pattern of the mainland. On Grenada, Antigua, St. Martin, Vieques, St. Croix, and St. Kitts, the villages were located inland on river terraces, which provided access to the best setting for gardens (Haviser 1991; compare Siegel 1991). The shifting, extensive character of gardening practices is evident from the absence of deeply stratified sites and from settlement patterns in which different components are arranged in horizontal and sometimes overlapping relationships (Watters 1982).

Shortly after the initial colonization of the Antilles, there was a rapid and almost complete shift from inland to coastal settlement locations. Although horticulture continued as the primary source of foodstuffs, the change in settlement patterns was accompanied by a shift in midden deposits from terrestrial to marine animal remains. At the earliest sites, the remains of land crabs predominate in archaeological deposits. However, following the shift to coastal villages, the shells of marine mollusks and bones of marine fishes are the main components of archaeological deposits (Carbone 1980a; Goodwin 1980; Jones 1985; deFrance 1988, 1989; Keegan 1989b; Fandrich 1990). Stable isotope analysis has confirmed this strong initial reliance on terrestrial foods. One individual from the Hacienda Grande site (Rouse and Alegría 1990), an initial-period Saladoid settlement on Puerto Rico (around A.D. 100), has been analyzed. This individual exhibits a 93 ± 7 percent reliance on terrestrial foods (Keegan and DeNiro 1988).

Two explanations have been suggested to account for this shift from an emphasis on land resources to one on marine resources. The first proposed that a growing human population soon depleted the availability of terrestrial resources, which resulted in the shift to marine resources (Goodwin 1979). The second explanation proposed that changes in climate resulted in drier conditions, which acted to reduce population densities of the humidity-sensitive land crabs (Carbone 1980a, 1980b). Both are possible, but the first seems to have had the larger effect.

The examination of subsistence change on the mainland is instructive. In her study of Saladoid peoples on the Orinoco River of Venezuela, Anna Roosevelt (1980: 230–3) projected a population growth rate in Parmana that is exactly the same as the rate estimated for St. Kitts (Goodwin 1979). This coincidence suggested the question: As a shift in protein sources occurred when the population density doubled from about 1.5 to 3.0 persons per square kilometer in Parmana, did anything similar happen on St. Kitts? In Parmana, there was a shift in protein sources to an emphasis on maize in the diet (Roosevelt 1980; Merwe, Roosevelt and Vogel 1981); on St. Kitts, it has been estimated that the shift from land crabs to marine mollusks occurred at an equivalent population doubling point (Keegan 1989b).

In sum, Saladoid peoples expanded from northeastern Venezuela and the coast of the Guianas through the Lesser Antilles and Puerto Rico to establish a frontier in eastern Hispaniola. The initial migration through the Lesser Antilles to Puerto Rico took place in less than one century (Keegan 1995), a period that was insufficient for the establishment of permanent communities on every island in the Lesser Antilles. One stimulus to this rapid expansion was the small size of these islands and their limited terrestrial resource bases (Harris 1965). These constraints are apparent in the rapid and almost complete shift from terrestrial to marine sources of animal protein at the same time that the shift to coastal settlement locations provided ready access to the marine environment. The completion of this transformation of a riverine people to an island people was the economic foundation on which Taino societies developed.

Archaic West Indians

Archaeological investigations have documented the presence of human groups in the Greater Antilles by 4000 B.C. (Rouse and Allaire 1978; Veloz Maggiolo 1971–72). By most accounts, these groups were aceramic, preagricultural hunter-fisher-gatherers whose lifeways emphasized the gathering of wild plants and the exploitation of marine resources (Rouse 1948; Veloz Maggiolo and Vega 1982; Sanoja Obediente and Vargas 1983; Keegan 1994). G. J. van Klinken's (1991) stable-isotope study of 24 individuals from Aruba, Bonaire, and Curaçao, in the Netherlands Antilles, indicated a diet of C_4 grasses and marine animals from seagrass and coral-reef habitats. Dave Davis (1988: 181) has pointed out that the assumed lack of cultigens is based on the weakest of evidence. Lee Ann Newsom's (1993) study of plant remains from archaeological sites has led her to propose that "preagricultural" West Indians (Archaic peoples) were managing, and possibly cultivating, a suite of indigenous seed-bearing plants. Such incipient cultivation is now well documented among foragers (Ford 1985; Vaquer et al. 1986).

In reconstructing Archaic subsistence, it is usually assumed that a population of hunter-gatherers called Guanahatabey (or erroneously, Ciboney) survived in western Cuba until European contact (Rouse 1948). The author of this chapter has recently shown that there is not sufficient evidence to support that belief (Keegan 1989a; compare Rouse 1992). Therefore, ethnohistoric reports of Guanahatabey subsistence cannot be used to illuminate Archaic diets.

Paleobotanical evidence for the Archaic is limited. Only the starchy stem of the wild cycad Zamia and a fruit known as cupey (Clusea rosea) have been recovered in excavations (Nadal 1981; Veloz Maggiolo and Vega 1982). Both of these plants were cultivated by the Tainos, and it is possible that other Taino cultigens (for example, soursop, sweetsop, hogplum, guava, pineapple) were also eaten (Davis 1988: 181). The most common fauna in Archaic sites

are mollusks and reef fishes from shallow offshore habitats.

Marcio Veloz Maggiolo and Bernardo Vega (1982) propose an initial "adaptation" model of archaic subsistence in the Caribbean commencing around 9000 B.C. on the western coast of the United States and extending through Panama around to Trinidad. Trinidad was connected to the mainland until about 6000 B.C., with the Banwari-type occupation dating between 5500 to 3500 B.C. The diet was based on gathered plants and mollusks, with an emphasis on mangrove swamps, along with the hunting of small-to-middle-size game. Archaeological sites in the Dominican Republic date from between 2000 and 1500 B.C. Zamia and cupey were already present by this time, and land snails (Polydontes sp., Caracolus sp.), oyster (Crassostrea rizhoporae), intertidal gastropods (Cittarium pica), land crabs (Geocarcinus lateralis), marine cockroach (Acanthopleura sp.), parrot fishes (Scaridae), iguana (Cyclura sp.), and medium-size rodents (Heteropsomys sp., Isolobodon sp., and Nesophontes sp.) were also eaten.

The second adaptation, called Barrera-Mordan, dates to around 3000 B.C. in Cuba, Puerto Rico, and the Dominican Republic, and shows affinities with sites in the Colombian lowlands and Venezuela. This occupation was characterized by a more specialized emphasis on mollusks from sandy beaches (for instance, Arca spp., Codakia orbicularis), and the disappearance of mortars and pestles, suggesting a decline in the use of seeds, roots, and berries.

The third adaptation was based on fishing and mollusk gathering from beaches and mangrove swamps. It is distinguished by the high frequency of shell tools and occurs in Sambaqui-type shell mounds in northern Venezuela, including the offshore islands of Cubagua and Manicuare, Trinidad, Cuba, and the Dominican Republic (Sanoja Obediente and Vargas 1983). These sites date to around 4000 B.C. in Venezuela and 2000 to 1200 B.C. in Cuba and the Dominican Republic.

These relationships among the peoples whose material remains have been used to characterize these adaptations await further specification. It is interesting to note that in contrast to the horticultural Saladoid peoples, whose earliest adaptation seems to have emphasized terrestrial resources, the Archaic peoples had a more pronounced emphasis on the marine environment. Davis (1988) has commented on the absence of land crabs in Archaic sites, given the importance of land crabs in early Saladoid sites. It is likely that the availability of an efficient calorie producer (manioc) allowed the early Saladoids to pursue the higher-ranked but less abundant animals of the interior, whereas the Archaic peoples had to emphasize calorie capture in coastal habitats. The shift to marine resources by Saladoid peoples shows a convergence in diet with regard to protein capture that would reflect the decline in terrestrial animals.

When Old Met New

The arrival of the Spanish brought dramatic changes to the circum-Caribbean (Keegan 1996). The most notable change was the rapid decline in the native population due to warfare, disease, and abuse. Prior to their demise, the native peoples were the major suppliers of food for the European colonists. By 1497 the five major *cacicazgos* (regions ruled by a paramount *cacique* or chief) were providing tribute in the form of food and labor, a practice that mirrored tribute made to Taino caciques (Moscoso 1986). Manuel García-Arevalo (1990: 272) has noted that "dietary patterns and foodways were among the most important of the Taino contributions to be integrated into colonial culture" and that "cassava bread came to be known as the 'bread of the conquest.'"

The Spanish also introduced a variety of animals into these depauperate islands. Cattle *(Bos taurus)*, which were brought from the Canary Islands multiplied in unprecedented fashion on Hispaniola (Reitz 1986: 319, 1988), where cattle ranching became a significant occupation (Ewen 1990). In addition, pigs *(Sus scrofa)*, goats and sheep, horses *(Equus* sp.), chickens *(Gallus gallus)*, and rats and mice *(Rattus norvegicus, R. rattus, Mus musculus)* were introduced, the latter as unintended stowaways (Crosby 1972, 1986; Reitz 1986). It is interesting to note that the Spanish presence in early contact-period sites is more often identified by the occurrence of pig and rat bones than by European objects (Deagan 1988). Cattle, pigs, goats, and chickens adjusted to the climate. Pigs were so well adjusted that they were released on islands to form feral herds that could be hunted when needed. As Charles Ewen (1991: 108–9) expressed it, "[T]he diet of the colonists [showed] a mixture of the Iberian barnyard complex of peninsular Spain and the mixed hunting-fishing strategies of the indigenous peoples."

In colonizing the circum-Caribbean, the initial Spanish objective was to recreate their Iberian homeland (Crosby 1972, 1986). The colonists who founded St. Augustine in Florida brought seed stock for planting wheat and other cereals, cuttings for vineyards, and animals for breeding stock. They soon learned that the climate and soils were unsuited to this economy. Cereals withered on the stock, olives and grapes failed to grow, and their preferred meat source, sheep, did not thrive (Scarry and Reitz 1990: 344). In addition to raising cattle, the Spaniards introduced sugarcane as a cash crop. By 1545, there were 29 sugar mills belonging to prominent people on Hispaniola (García-Arevalo 1990: 275). Sugar was the magnet for the next invasion (Mintz 1985).

Subsistence practices in the sixteenth-century Spanish colonies mirrored those of the native economies that preceded them. The major change was the use of domesticated animals as a meat source, comprising from 20 to 50 percent of the vertebrate taxa (Reitz 1986: 319). In addition, peaches, melons, and watermelons produced well (Scarry and Reitz 1990: 350). Lastly, the Spanish continued to import Old World foodstuffs that would not grow in the colonies, including wheat, olives, and wine, but these supplies were rare and unreliable (Sauer 1966). According to Margaret Scarry and Elizabeth Reitz (1990: 344–5): "One soldier testified [in 1573] that rations were often short and that 'when there was nothing they ate herbs, fish and other scum and vermin.'"

British and African Arrivals

The British colonies pursued two very different types of plantation economies. In Jamaica and the Lesser Antilles, sugarcane was grown by slave labor for export, whereas in the Bahamas, cotton, utilizing far fewer slaves, was the main commodity (Craton 1978; Riley 1983; Saunders 1985; Craton and Saunders 1992). In both areas the vegetable portion of the meal was grown largely on provision grounds, although wheat flour and locally unavailable foodstuffs were imported. Indian corn *(Zea mays)* was the staple. In addition, true yams *(Dioscorea* sp.), sweet potatoes, eddoes *(Colocasia* sp.), okras *(Hibiscus esculentus)*, pigeon peas *(Cajanus cajan)*, red peas or cowpeas, black-eyed peas, snap beans, cabbage, pumpkins, castor oil, and Guinea corn (sorghum) were also grown (Farquharson 1831–2; Handler and Lange 1978). The new additions to this list were imported from Africa and Asia in the course of the slave trade. Kimber (1988) provides a remarkable discussion of plant introductions and use on the island of Martinique.

Some livestock and fowl were raised on the plantations, but most of the meats that were consumed were imported. Imports included salt beef and salt pork. It is ironic that salt fish, imported from North America, was a staple. In the study of faunal remains at Drax Hall, Jamaica, Douglas Armstrong (1983) detected little in the way of fresh fish, mollusks, or other sorts of wild game. However, following emancipation, there was a strong reliance on rocky intertidal mollusks.

Although foodstuffs were usually distributed to slaves for cooking, a main meal was sometimes served from a central kitchen on Barbadian plantations in the nineteenth century (Handler and Lange 1978). Slaves prepared their meals on an open fire by roasting or boiling. Jerome Handler and F. W. Lange suggest that meals were nutritious and monotonous, and that food allowances were often of insufficient quantity. As a result, the theft of food was common, and it was not considered wrong to steal from the master.

Slaves were also given allowances of rum, one effect of which was a condition called "dry bellyache." Handler and colleagues (1986) have shown that dry bellyache was caused by lead poisoning. Lead was the "demon" in rum; it was used in the equipment in which rum was distilled.

D. Gail Saunders (1985: 166) and others have noted that African foods such as accara, foo-foo, agedi, and my-my are remembered and still cooked in the Bahamas today. She describes accara as being a patty made with black-eyed peas, okras, onion, red peppers, flour, thyme leaves, tomato, and salt. With emancipation, what was remembered of African foodways was mapped onto the local environment.

Garifuna Diet

All of the preceding examples find their ultimate expression in the Garifuna. The Garifuna, often referred to as Black Caribs, presently occupy the coast of Central America from Belize to Nicaragua. They developed from intermixture of the Island Caribs and Africans in a social environment that was manipulated by white Europeans. By 1700, a new society that was racially and culturally distinct from the Island Caribs had developed on St. Vincent (Kirby and Martin 1972). What is striking about the Garifuna is that their diet reflects "the various exotic cultural influences experienced over the past 400 years" (González 1988: 98).

The best-known item in the Island Carib diet is human flesh. It was in reference to the Island Caribs that the term "cannibal" originated. More recently, investigators have questioned whether the Island Caribs did, in fact, consume human flesh or whether this practice was ascribed to them in order to permit their capture as slaves under Spanish law (Myers 1984; Davis and Goodwin 1990; Wilson 1990). The present consensus is that anthropophagy was practiced in ritual settings, perhaps even as a display of fierceness, but that it never served as a source of dietary protein as has been suggested for the Aztecs (Harner 1977; compare Garn 1979).

It is likely that many of the cultigens attributed to the Tainos were also cultivated by the Island Caribs. The staples of their diet were cassava bread made from bitter manioc, and fish. They also cultivated sweet potatoes, chilli peppers, peanuts, beans, guava, soursop, and mamey. Pineapple (*Ananas comosus* [L.] Merr.) is described as having been fermented into wine (Rouse 1948; Sturtevant 1969), an activity still practiced by the Garifuna.

Oranges, citrons, grapefruits, figs, rice, bananas, and plantains were introduced from the Mediterranean by the Spanish (González 1988: 101). Cacao was introduced from the mainland because of its importance as a European trade item, an importance it maintains today. The introduction of coconut, the most important source of oil for the Caribs, is not recorded. The Spanish also introduced fowl and pigs. Feral pig herds achieved substantial numbers following their release. Okra, akee (*Blighia sapida* Konig), pigeon peas, marijuana, senna (*Cassia italica*), yams (*Dioscorea* sp.), sorghum, and plantains accompanied slaves from Africa (Sturtevant 1961; Grimé 1979; González 1988: 101). Finally, mangoes, sugarcane, coffee, and arrowroot (*Maranta arundinacea*) were introduced at an early date, the latter by the Tainos (Sturtevant 1969; Handler 1971; González 1988: 101; Newsom 1993). Nancie González's (1988: Table 5.1) summary of modern ceremonial foods by probable date of introduction neatly summarizes the successive waves of culinary influence (Table V.D.3.4).

Table V.D.3.4. *Garifuna ceremonial foods and the probable time of their introduction*

	Prehistoric	Sixteenth century	Nineteenth century	Twentieth century
Uwi	Fish Iguana Crab Fish roe	Chicken Eggs Pork	Lobster White cheese	Bologna
Breadkind	*Areba* Malanga Cassava gruel Sweet potato pudding Sweet manioc	–	Plantains Tamales Green bananas Rice and beans Banana fritters Tomato slices Rice gruel	Spaghetti White bread Cabbage
Sweets	–	Mangoes Watermelon	Coconut candy Cashew fruit	Cookies Hard candy
Beverages	*Hui*	–	Rum Coconut water	Kool-Aid Coca-Cola Orange pop Beer

Source: After González (1988), Table 5.1.

Through the eyes of the Garifuna, Nancie González (1988) describes the progressive homogenization of tropical diets among peoples of African ancestry. The pepper pot of the Island Caribs has today been replaced by *falmou,* a concoction of fish, tubers, and coconut milk. Both *Capsicum* (chilli peppers) and *cassirepe* (boiled juice of bitter manioc) have fallen out of favor. Fish stews similar to *falmou* are also popular with the Miskitos and other Belizean creoles (Nietschmann 1973: 37). Bitter manioc continues as an important source of food, and it joins maize, rice, and wheat as ubiquitous starches, along with mango, papaya, and watermelon as ubiquitous fruits on both sides of the Atlantic (González 1988: 105–6). Yet despite this convergence in food items, the menus maintain their separate ethnic dimensions.

Summary

Caribbean diets were strongly influenced by the diffusion of domesticated plants and animals. The initial conditions were established more than 10,000 years ago as biogeographic processes shaped the indigenous vegetation and fauna (Watts 1987). With the arrival of humans, this landscape was irrevocably modified to serve human needs. It is possible that the earliest immigrants did not bring new plants or animals with them, and that their procurement strategies had little impact on the islands. They were, however, followed by extensive horticulturalists who slashed and burned the forests and introduced a suite of new plants. Every wave of immigrants brought new cultigens and new ways to process or prepare those that were already present. In the end, the more than 40 different cultigens have been mentioned in this review.

Animals were also introduced. The earliest introduction was the dog, and others, such as hutia, agouti, and guinea pig, had their insular distributions enlarged. The Spanish made the biggest impact, bringing cattle, chickens, goats, rats, sheep, horses, and donkeys. These animals helped transform luxuriant tropical vegetation into scrub forage. As some animals were introduced, others became extinct (Olsen 1982; Morgan and Woods 1986). Manatee, monk seal, and sea turtles are either extinct or nearly so, and even the ubiquitous queen conch is now in short supply (Hesse and Hesse 1977).

Today, most West Indians have forsaken agriculture and instead rely on imported foods. For instance, Ifill noted in his study of Grenada that "in 1974 the estimated daily calorie intake per capita was 1,958.4 of which 1,535.9 [was imported].... With respect to protein per capita, daily intake was 46.03g, of which imported food supplied 31.72g" (quoted in Brierley 1985: 52). Despite this national reliance on imported foods, rural peoples remain dependent on local production on both provision grounds and kitchen gardens.

This infield (kitchen garden)–outfield (provision grounds) division finds its recent origins in the slave plantation economy, but it mirrors practices that can be traced to South America and Africa. Present-day kitchen gardens reflect both continuity with and a synthesis of the past. For example, J. S. Brierley's (1985: Table 2) list of 20 common plants in Grenadian kitchen gardens includes crops from South America, Africa, Asia, Europe, and Oceania, as well as the Caribbean (1985: Table 5). As Brierley (1985: 55) points out, these are not simply a random selection of available cultigens; rather, the "nutritional balance of [the] crops must be attributed ... to traditional knowledge and a process of selection governed by the dietary needs and ecological potential of the region."

Despite repeated waves of new peoples and new dietary items, the climate and ecology have shaped culinary practices. Until the very recent reliance on a cash economy, diets have been shaped by the low-cost caloric productivity of root crops (manioc, sweet potato, yams, dasheen), the paucity or expense of terrestrial animals (hutias, iguanas, cattle, sheep, and goats), and abundant but labor-intensive marine organisms (fishes, turtles, queen conch). In some ways, the more things changed, the more they remained the same. One result is a convergence of diets throughout the tropics as cultigens and animals are shared around the world.

William F. Keegan

Notes

1. Manioc occurs in both bitter and nonbitter ("sweet") varieties, although these varieties are members of the same species.

Bibliography

Alegría, R. E. 1983. *Ball courts and ceremonial plazas in the West Indies.* New Haven, Conn.

Allaire, L. 1984. A reconstruction of early historical Island Carib pottery. *Southeastern Archaeology* 3: 121–33.

Ambrose, S. H. 1987. Chemical and isotopic techniques of diet reconstruction in eastern North America. In *Emergent horticultural economies of the eastern woodlands,* ed. W. F. Keegan, 87–107. Carbondale, Ill.

1993. Isotopic analysis: Methodological and interpretive considerations. In *Elemental and isotopic analyses: Understanding diet and diseases in past populations,* ed. M. K. Sanford, 59–130. London.

Ambrose, S. H., and L. Norr. 1993. Relationship of carbon isotope ratios of dietary protein and energy to those of bone collagen and apatite. Paper presented at the 58th annual meeting of the Society for American Archaeology, St. Louis, Mo.

Armstrong, Douglas V. 1983. *The "old village" at Drax Hall plantation: An archaeological examination of an Afro-Jamaican settlement.* Ph.D. thesis, University of California, Los Angeles.

Aveni, A. F., and G. Urton, eds. 1982. *Ethnoastronomy and archaeoastronomy in the American tropics.* New York.

Bell, J. A. 1992. Universalization in archaeological explanation. In *Metaarchaeology: Reflections by archaeologists and philosophers*, ed. L. Embree, 143-64. Boston, Mass.

Boucher, P. P. 1992. *Cannibal encounters: Europeans and Island Caribs, 1492-1763*. Baltimore, Md.

Brierley, J. S. 1985. West Indian kitchen gardens: A historical perspective with current insights from Grenada. *Food and Nutrition Bulletin* 7: 52-60.

Budinoff, Linda C. 1987. An osteological analysis of the human burials recovered from Maisabel: An early ceramic site on the north coast of Puerto Rico. Paper presented at the Twelfth International Congress for Caribbean Archaeology, Cayenne, French Guyana.

Butt, Audrey J. 1977. Land use and social organization of tropical forest peoples of the Guianas. In *Human ecology in the tropics*, ed. J. P. Garlick and R. W. J. Keay, 1-17. London.

Campbell. David G. 1978. *The ephemeral islands*. London.

Carbone, V. A. 1980a. Some problems in cultural paleoecology in the Caribbean Area. *Proceedings of the Eighth International Congress for the Study of the Pre-Columbian Cultures of the Lesser Antilles*, 98-126. Tempe, Ariz.

1980b. The paleoecology of the Caribbean area. *Florida Anthropologist* 33: 99-119.

Castellanos, R. 1981. La plaza de Chacuey, un instrumento astronomico megalitico. *Boletin del Museo del Hombre Dominicano* 16: 31-40.

Chanlatte Baik, L. A., and Y. M. Narganes Storde. 1990. *La nueva arqueologia de Puerto Rico (su proyección en las Antillas)*. Santo Domingo.

Clough, Garrett C. 1972. Biology of the Bahamian hutia, *Geocapromys ingrahami. Journal of Mammology* 53: 807-23.

Cohen, Mark Nathan, and George Armelagos. 1984. *Paleopathology at the origins of agriculture*. New York.

Conklin, Harold S. 1968. An ethnoecological approach to shifting agriculture. In *Man in adaptation: The cultural present*, ed. Y. A. Cohen, 126-31. Chicago.

Craton, Michael. 1978. *Searching for the invisible man*. Cambridge.

Craton, M., and G. Saunders. 1992. *Islanders in the stream*. Athens.

Crosby, Alfred W. 1972. *The Columbian exchange*. Westport, Conn.

1986. *Ecological imperialism*. Cambridge.

Davidson, William V. 1974. *Historical geography of the Bay Islands, Honduras*. Birmingham, Ala.

Davis, Dave D. 1974. Some notes concerning the Archaic occupation of Antigua. *Proceedings of the Fifth International Congress for the study of the Pre-Columbian Cultures of the Lesser Antilles*, 65-71. Antigua.

1988. Coastal biogeography and human subsistence: Examples from the West Indies. *Archaeology of Eastern North America* 16: 177-85.

Davis, D. D., and R. C. Goodwin. 1990. Island Carib origins: Evidence and non-evidence. *American Antiquity* 54: 37-48.

Deagan, Kathleen. 1988. The archaeology of the Spanish contact period in the Caribbean. *Journal of World Prehistory* 2: 187-233.

deFrance, Susan D. 1988. *Zooarchaeological investigations of subsistence strategies at the Maisabel site, Puerto Rico*. M.A. thesis, University of Florida, Gainesville.

1989. Saladoid and Ostinoid subsistence adaptions: Zooarchaeological data from coastal occupation on Puerto Rico. In *Early ceramic population lifeways and adaptive strategies in the Caribbean*, ed. P. Siegel, BAR International Series 506, 57-78. Oxford.

1991. *Zooarchaeological research on Lucayan Taino subsistence: Crooked Island, Bahamas*. Florida Museum of Natural History. Gainesville.

deFrance, S. D., W. F. Keegan, and L. A. Newsom. 1996. The archaeobotanical, bone isotope, and zooarchaeological records from Caribbean sites in comparative perspective. In *Case studies in environmental archaeology*, ed. E. J. Reitz, L. A. Newsom, and S. J. Scudder, 289-304. New York.

Doran, Edwin, Jr. 1958. The Caicos conch trade. *The Geographical Review* 48: 388-401.

Eisenberg, John F. 1989. *Mammals of the neotropics: The northern neotropics, Vol. 1: Panama, Colombia, Venezuela, Guyana, Suriname, French Guiana*. Chicago.

Ewen, Charles R. 1990. The rise and fall of Puerto Real. In *Columbian consequences, Vol. 2: Archaeological and historical perspectives on the Spanish borderlands east*, ed. D. H. Thomas, 261-8. Washington, D.C.

1991. *From Spaniard to Creole: The archaeology of cultural formation at Puerto Real, Haiti*. Tuscaloosa, Ala.

Fandrich, Judith. 1990. Subsistence at Pearls, Grenada, W.I. (A.D. 200). In *Miscellaneous project report number 44*, Florida Museum of Natural History, 14-47. Gainesville.

Farquharson, Charles. 1831-2. *A relic of slavery: Farquharson's journal for 1831-32*. Copied from the original by O. J. McDonald, 1957. Nassau, Bahamas.

Fewkes, J. W. 1907. The aborigines of Puerto Rico and neighboring islands. *Twenty-fifth annual report of the U.S. Bureau of American Ethnology, 1903-1904*, 35-281. Washington, D.C.

Ford, Richard I. 1984. Prehistoric phytogeography of economic plants in Latin America. In *Pre-Columbian plant migration*, ed. D. Stone, Papers of the Peabody Museum of Archaeology and Ethnology, Vol. 76, 175-83. Cambridge, Mass.

1985. *Prehistoric food production in North America*. Ann Arbor, Mich.

Fortuna, Luis. 1978. Analisis polinico de Sanate Abajo. *Boletin del Museo del Hombre Dominicano* 10: 125-30.

García-Arevalo, Manuel. 1990. Transculturation in contact period and contemporary Hispaniola. In *Columbian consequences, Vol. 2: Archaeological and historical perspectives on the Spanish borderlands east*, ed. D. H. Thomas, 269-80. Washington, D.C.

Garn, Stanley M. 1979. The noneconomic nature of eating people. *American Anthropologist* 81: 902-3.

Gifford, Charles A. 1962. Some observations on the general biology of the land crab, *Cardisoma guanhumi* (Latreille) in South Florida. *Biological Bulletin* 123: 207-23.

González, Nancie L. 1988. *Sojourners of the Caribbean: Ethnogenesis and ethnohistory of the Garifuna*. Urbana, Ill.

Goodwin, R. C. 1978. The Lesser Antilles archaic: New data from St. Kitts. *Journal of the Virgin Islands Archaeological Society* 5: 6-16.

1979. *The prehistoric cultural ecology of St. Kitts, West Indies: A case study in island archaeology*. Ph.D. Thesis, Arizona State University, Tempe, Ariz.

1980. Demographic change and the crab-shell dichotomy. *Proceedings of the Eighth International Congress for the study of the Pre-Columbian cultures of the Lesser Antilles*, 45-68. Tempe, Ariz.

Grimé, William E. 1979. *Ethno-botany of the Black Americans*. Algonac, Mich.

Guarch, J. M. 1974. *Ensayo de reconstrucción ethno-histórica del Taino de Cuba*. Havana.

Handler, J. S. 1971. The history of arrowroot and the origin of peasantries in the British West Indies. *Journal of Caribbean History* 2: 46-93.

Handler, J. S., A. C. Aufderheide, R. S. Corruccini, et al. 1986. Lead contact and poisoning in Barbados slaves: Historical, chemical, and biological evidence. *Social Science History* 10: 399-425.

Handler, J. S., and F. W. Lange. 1978. *Plantation slavery in Barbados.* Cambridge.

Harner, Michael. 1977. The ecological basis for Aztec sacrifice. *American Ethnologist* 4: 117-35.

Harris, David R. 1965. *Plants, animals and man in the outer Leeward Island, West Indies: An ecological study of Antigua, Barbuda, and Anguilla.* Berkeley, Calif.

Haviser, J. B., Jr. 1989. Preliminary results of test excavations at the Hope Estate Site (SM-026), St. Martin. *Proceedings of the Eleventh International Congress for Caribbean Archaeology,* eds. E. N. Ayubi and J. B. Haviser, 647-66, Curaçao.

1991. Development of a prehistoric interaction sphere in the northern Lesser Antilles. *New West Indian Guide* 65: 129-51.

Hesse, R. C., and K. O. Hesse. 1977. The conch industry in the Turks and Caicos Islands. *Underwater Naturalist* 10.

Hulme, P., and N. L. Whitehead. 1992. *Wild majesty: Encounters with Caribs from Columbus to the present day.* Oxford.

Iverson, J. B. 1979. Behavior and ecology of the rock iguana, *Cyclura carinata. Bulletin of the Florida State Museum* 24.

Jackson, J. B. C. 1972. The ecology of the mollusks of *Thalassia* communities, Jamaica, West Indies. II. Molluscan population variability along an environmental stress gradient. *Marine Biology* 14: 304-37.

1973. The ecology of the mollusks of *Thalassia* communities, Jamaica, West Indies. I. Distribution, environmental physiology, and ecology of common shallow-water species. *Bulletin of Marine Science* 23: 313-50.

Johannes, R. E. 1981. *Words of the lagoon.* Berkeley, Calif.

Johnson, Allen. 1983. Machiguenga gardens. In *Adaptive responses of Native Amazonians,* ed. R. B. Hames and W. T. Vickers, 29-63. New York.

Johnson, A., and M. Baksh. 1987. Ecological and structural influences on the proportions of wild foods in the diets of two Machiguenga communities. In *Food and evolution,* ed. M. Harris and E. B. Ross, 387-406. Philadelphia, Pa.

Jones, Alick R. 1985. Diet change and human population at Indian Creek, Antigua. *American Antiquity* 50: 518-36.

Jordan, Kevin. 1989. *The ecology of the Bahamian hutia (Geocapromys ingrahami).* Ph.D. Thesis, University of Florida, Gainesville.

Keegan, W. F. 1982. Lucayan cave burials from the Bahamas. *Journal of New World Archaeology* 5: 57-65.

1985. *Dynamic horticulturalists: Population expansion in the prehistoric Bahamas.* Ph.D. thesis, University of California, Los Angeles.

1986a. The optimal foraging analysis of horticultural production. *American Anthropologist* 88: 92-107.

1986b. The ecology of Lucayan Arawak fishing practices. *American Antiquity* 51: 816-25.

1987. Diffusion of maize from South America: The Antillean connection reconstructed. In *Emergent horticultural economies of the eastern woodlands,* ed. W. F. Keegan, 329-44. Carbondale, Ill.

1989a. Creating the Guanahatabey (Ciboney): The modern genesis of an extinct culture. *Antiquity* 63: 373-9.

1989b. Transition from a terrestrial to a maritime economy: A new view of the crab/shell dichotomy. In *Early ceramic population lifeways and adaptive strategies in the Caribbean,* ed. P. Siegel, BAR International Series 506, 119-28. Oxford.

1989c. Stable isotope analysis of prehistoric diet. In *Reconstruction of life from the skeleton,* ed. M. Y. Iscan and K. A. R. Kennedy, 223-36. New York.

1992. *The people who discovered Columbus: An introduction to the prehistory of the Bahamas.* Gainesville, Fla.

1994. West Indian archaeology. 1. Overview and foragers. *Journal of Archaeological Research* 2: 255-84.

1995. Modeling dispersal in the prehistoric West Indies. *World Archaeology* 26: 400-20.

1996. West Indian archaeology. 2. After Columbus. *Journal of Archaeological Research* 4: 265-94.

Keegan, W. F., and M. J. DeNiro. 1988. Stable carbon- and nitrogen-isotope ratios of bone collagen used to study coral-reef and terrestrial components of prehistoric Bahamian diet. *American Antiquity* 53: 320-36.

Keegan, W. F., and J. M. Diamond. 1987. Colonization of islands by humans: A biogeographical perspective. In *Advances in archaeological method and theory,* Vol. 10, ed. M. B. Schiffer, 49-92. San Diego.

Keegan, W., C. M. Porter, N. Silk, W. L. Stern, et al. 1992. *New World harvest: A teacher's manual.* Gainesville, Fla.

Kimber, C. T. 1988. *Martinique revisited: The changing plant geographies of a West Indian island.* College Station, Tex.

Kirby, I. E., and C. I. Martin. 1972. *The rise and fall of the Black Caribs of St. Vincent.* St. Vincent.

Kirch, P. V. 1982. The ecology of marine exploitation in prehistoric Hawaii. *Human Ecology* 10: 455-76.

Klinken, G. J. van. 1991. *Dating and dietary reconstruction by isotopic analysis of amino acids in fossil bone collagen - with special reference to the Caribbean.* Publications of the Foundation for Scientific Research in the Caribbean Region No. 128. Amsterdam.

Lathrap, D. W. 1977. Our father the cayman, our mother the gourd: Spinden revisited, or a unitary model for the emergence of agriculture in the New World. In *Origins of agriculture,* ed. C. A. Reed, 713-51. The Hague.

1987. The introduction of maize in prehistoric eastern North America: The view from Amazonia and the Santa Elena Peninsula. In *Emergent horticultural economies of the eastern woodlands,* ed. W. F. Keegan, 345-71. Carbondale, Ill.

Linares, Olga. 1976. "Garden hunting" in the American tropics. *Human Ecology* 4: 331-49.

Loven, S. 1935. *Origins of the Tainan culture, West Indies.* Göteborg, Sweden.

Malinowski, Bronislaw. [1935] 1978. *Coral gardens and their magic.* New York.

McKillop, Heather I. 1985. Prehistoric exploitation of the manatee in the Maya and circum-Caribbean areas. *World Archaeology* 16: 337-53.

McKinnen, Daniel. 1804. *Tour through the British West Indies, in the years 1802 and 1803 giving a particular account of the Bahama Islands.* London.

Meehan, Betty. 1977. Man does not live by calories alone: The role of shellfish in a coastal cuisine. In *Sunda and Sahul,* ed. J. Allen, J. Golsen and R. Jones. New York.

Merwe, Nikolaas J. van der, Anna Cartenius Roosevelt, and J. C. Vogel. 1981. Isotopic evidence for prehistoric subsistence change at Parmana, Venezuela. *Nature* 292: 536-8.

Mintz, Sidney W. 1985. *Sweetness and power.* New York.

Morgan, Gary S., and Charles A. Woods. 1986. Extinction and the zoogeography of West Indian land mammals. *Biological Journal of the Linnean Society* 28: 167-203.

Moscoso, Francisco. 1986. *Tribu y Clase en el Caribe Antiquo.* Dominican Republic.

Myers, Robert A. 1984. Island Carib cannibalism. *Nieuwe West-Indische Gids* 158: 147-84.

Nadal, Joaquin E. 1981. El caimito, el copey y los chronistas. *Boletin del Museo del Hombre Dominicano* 16: 75-81.

Newsom, Lee Ann. 1993. *Native West Indian plant use.* Ph.D. thesis, University of Florida, Gainesville.

Nietschmann, Bernard. 1973. *Between land and water: The subsistence ecology of the Miskito Indians, eastern Nicaragua.* London.

Olsen, Storrs. 1982. Biological archaeology in the West Indies. *The Florida Anthropologist* 35: 162-8.

Oviedo, Gonzalo Fernández de. [1526] 1959. *Natural history of the West Indies,* ed. and trans. S. A. Stoudemire. Chapel Hill, N.C.

Pearsall, D. M. 1985. Analysis of soil phytoliths and botanical macroremains from El Bronce archaeological site, Ponce, Puerto Rico. Appendix B in *Archaeological data recovery at El Bronce, Puerto Rico. Final report, phase 2,* ed. L. S. Robinson, E. R. Lundberg, and J. B. Walker. Jacksonville, Fla.

Piperno, D. R., M. B. Bush, and P. A. Colinvaux. 1990. Paleoenvironments and human occupation in late-glacial Panama. *Quaternary Research* 33: 108-16.

Reitz, Elizabeth J. 1986. Vertebrate fauna from locus 39, Puerto Real, Haiti. *Journal of Field Archaeology* 13: 317-28.

1988. Impact of animals introduced to the New World: The case of Puerto Real, Haiti. Paper presented at Rethinking the Encounter: New Perspectives on the Conquest and Colonization, 1450-1550. Gainesville, Fla.

Riley, Sandra. 1983. *Homeward bound.* Miami.

Roosevelt, Anna C. 1980. *Parmana: Prehistoric maize and manioc subsistence along the Amazon and Orinoco.* New York.

Rose, Richard. 1982. The Pigeon Creek site, San Salvador, Bahamas. *The Florida Anthropologist* 35: 129-45.

Rouse, Irving. 1948. The West Indies. In *Handbook of South American Indians, Vol. 4, The circum-Caribbean tribes,* ed. J. H. Steward, 497-503. Washington, D.C.

1986. *Migrations in prehistory: Inferring population movements from cultural remains.* New Haven, Conn.

1989a. Peopling and repeopling of the West Indies. In *Biogeography of the West Indies, past, present and future,* ed. C. A. Woods, 119-35. Gainesville, Fla.

1989b. Peoples and cultures of the Saladoid frontier in the Greater Antilles. In *Early ceramic population lifeways and adaptive strategies in the Caribbean,* ed. P. E. Siegel, BAR International Series No. 506, 283-403. Oxford.

1992. *The Tainos.* New Haven, Conn.

Rouse, I., and R. E. Alegría. 1990. *Excavations at Maria de la Cruz Cave and Hacienda Grande Village site, Loiza, Puerto Rico.* Yale University Publications in Anthropology No. 80. New Haven, Conn.

Rouse, I., and L. Allaire. 1978. Caribbean. In *Chronologies in new world archaeology,* ed. R. E. Taylor and C. Meighan, 431-81. New York.

Ruddle, Kenneth. 1974. The Yupka cultivation system: A study of shifting cultivation in Colombia and Venezuela. *Ibero-Americana* No. 52. Los Angeles.

Sanoja Obediente, Mario and Iraida Vargas. 1983. New light on the prehistory of eastern Venezuela. *Advances in World Archaeology* 2: 205-44.

Sauer, Carl O. 1966. *The early Spanish main.* Berkeley, Calif.

Saunders, D. Gail. 1985. *Slavery in the Bahamas, 1648-1838.* Nassau.

Scarry, C. Margaret, and Elizabeth J. Reitz. 1990. Herbs, fish, scum, and vermin: Subsistence strategies in sixteenth-century Spanish Florida. In *Columbian consequences, Vol. 2, Archaeological and historical perspectives on the Spanish borderlands east,* ed. D. H. Thomas, 343-54. Washington, D.C.

Schoeninger, M. J., and M. J. DeNiro. 1984. Nitrogen and carbon isotopic composition of bone collagen from marine and terrestrial animals. *Geochimica et Cosmochimica Acta* 48: 625-39.

Schoeninger, M. J., M. J. DeNiro, and H. Tauber. 1983. Stable nitrogen isotope ratios of bone collagen reflect marine and terrestrial components of prehistoric human diet. *Science* 220: 1381-3.

Schoeninger, M. J., K. M. Noore, M. L. Murray, and J. D. Kingston. 1989. Detection of bone preservation in archaeological and fossil samples. *Applied Geochemistry* 4: 281-92.

Schultes, R. E. 1984. Amazonian cultigens and their northward and westward migration in pre-Columbian times. In *Pre-Columbian plant migration,* ed. D. Stone, Papers of the Peabody Museum of Archaeology and Ethnology, Vol. 76, 19-37.

Sealey, J. C. 1986. *Stable carbon isotopes and prehistoric diets in the south-western Cape Province, South Africa.* Cambridge Monographs in African Prehistory. Cambridge.

Sears, William H., and Shaun D. Sullivan. 1978. *American Antiquity* 43: 3-25.

Siegel, Peter E. 1991. Migration research in Saladoid archaeology: A review. *The Florida Anthropologist* 44: 79-91.

Sillen, A., J. C. Sealey, and N. J. van der Merwe. 1989. Chemistry and paleodietary research: No more easy answers. *American Antiquity* 54: 504-12.

Smith, Eric Alden. 1983. Anthropological applications of optimal foraging theory: A critical review. *Current Anthropology* 24: 625-51.

Smith, Eric Alden, and Bruce Winterhalder. 1992. *Evolutionary ecology and human behavior.* New York.

Steadman, D. W., D. R. Watters, E. J. Reitz, and G. K. Pregill. 1984. Vertebrates from archaeological sites on Montserrat, West Indies. *Annals of the Carnegie Museum* 53: 1-29.

Stokes, A. V. 1995. Understanding prehistoric subsistence in the West Indies using stable isotope analysis. In *Proceedings of the 15th International Congress for Caribbean Archaeology,* ed. R. Alegría and M. Rodríguez, 191-200. San Juan.

Sturtevant, William C. 1961. Taino agriculture. *Anthropologica* Supplement No. 2: 69-82.

1969. History and ethnography of some West Indian starches. In *The domestication and exploitation of plants and animals,* ed. P. J. Ucko and G. W. Dimbleby, 177-9. Chicago.

Taylor, Douglas. 1977. *Languages of the West Indies.* Baltimore, Md.

Vaquer, Jean et al. 1986. Gisement chasséen de la fosse de La Toronde à Cavanac (Aude). *Gallia préhistoire* 29: 173-92. Paris.

Veloz Maggiolo, Marcio. 1976. *Medioambiente y adaptacion humana en la prehistoria de Santo Domingo.* Santo Domingo.

Veloz Maggiolo, Marcio, and Bernardo Vega. 1982. The Antillean preceramic: A new approximation. *Journal of New World Archaeology* 5: 33-44.

Veloz Maggiolo, Marcio. 1971-72. Las Antillas precolombinas ecología y población. *Revista dominicana de arqueología y antropología* 2: 165-69. Santo Domingo.

Watters, David R. 1982. Relating oceanography to Antillean archaeology: Implications from Oceania. *Journal of New World Archaeology* 5: 3-12.

Watters, D. R., E. J. Reitz, D. W. Steadman, and G. K. Pregill. 1984. Vertebrates from archaeological sites on Barbuda, West Indies. *Annals of the Carnegie Museum* 53: 383-412.

Watts, David. 1987. *The West Indies: Patterns of development, culture and environmental change since 1492.* Cambridge.

Wilson, Samuel M. 1990. *Hispaniola: The chiefdoms of the Caribbean in the early years of European contact.* Tuscaloosa, Ala.

Wing, Elizabeth S. 1969. Vertebrate remains excavated from San Salvador Island, Bahamas. *Journal of Caribbean Science* 9: 25-9.

  1989. Human exploitation of animal resources in the Caribbean. In *Biogeography of the West Indies,* ed. C. A. Woods, 137-52. Gainesville, Fla.

Wing, Elizabeth S., and A. B. Brown. 1979. *Paleonutrition.* New York.

Wing, Elizabeth S., and Elizabeth J. Reitz. 1982. Prehistoric fishing communities of the Caribbean. *Journal of New World Archaeology* 5: 13-32.

Wing, Elizabeth S., and Sylvia J. Scudder. 1980. Use of animals by prehistoric inhabitants of St. Kitts, West Indies. *Proceedings of the Eighth International Congress for the Study of the Pre-Columbian cultures of the Lesser Antilles,* 237-45. Tempe, Ariz.

  1983. Animal exploitation by prehistoric people living on a tropical marine edge. In *Animals and archaeology. 2. Shell middens, fishes and birds,* eds. C. Grigson and J. Clutton-Brock, BAR International Series No. 183, 197-210. Oxford.

Winterhalder, B., and E. A. Smith, eds. 1981. *Hunter-gatherer foraging strategies.* Chicago.

Zucchi, A., and W. M. Denevan. 1979. *Campos elevados a historia cultural prehispanica en los llanos occidentales de Venzuela.* Caracas.

Zucchi, A., K. Tarble, and J. E. Vaz. 1984. The ceramic sequence and new TL and C^{14} dates for the Aguerito site of the Middle Orinoco. *Journal of Field Archaeology* 11: 155-80.

V.D.4 ⮌ The Caribbean from 1492 to the Present

Following 1492, the Caribbean basin became a cultural meeting ground that remains unsurpassed for the variety of influences: European, Asian, African, and American. At times, the clash of cultures led to tragedy, such as the destruction of pre-Columbian Indians by European diseases or the centuries of African enslavement on sugar plantations. But the Caribbean people have also produced cultural triumphs, not the least of which are the tropical dishes of island cooking.

Cuisine can provide important insights into the process of cultural change. Each new group of immigrants to the Caribbean, from Taino "natives" (originally from South America) to Spanish conquistadors and from African slaves to Asian laborers, brought with them their knowledge of foods and how to prepare them. Island cuisine drew together maize and manioc from America, domesticated pigs and cattle from Europe, garden plants, such as okra and akee, from Africa, and citrus fruits and rice from Asia. Unfortunately, notwithstanding this rich variety of foods, poverty has made malnutrition a recurring problem in the region. Slaves (and many whites) suffered from a frightful variety of nutrition-related diseases, many of which have returned to haunt the impoverished masses of the twentieth century. Modernization has, meanwhile, threatened to replace traditional dishes with a processed and packaged uniformity of industrial foods. But island cooks have adapted to pressures, both economic and ecological, to create a genuinely global cuisine with a uniquely local taste.

The Columbian Exchange

The arrival of Europeans transformed the ecology of the Caribbean basin, but it did so in an uneven manner. Sixteenth-century Spaniards concentrated their colonizing efforts on the Greater Antilles, comprising Cuba, Hispaniola, Jamaica, and Puerto Rico. The newcomers brought with them the staples of Mediterranean life, including plants, animals, and diseases (the latter having a disastrous impact on the native population), but they made little effort to consolidate their hold over the region. The Lesser Antilles, stretching from the Virgin Islands just east of Puerto Rico to the Venezuelan coast, did not attract European attention until the seventeenth century, when British, French, Dutch, and Danish colonists began challenging the Iberian New World monopoly. These new settlers, although left with only smaller islands unsettled by the Spanish, soon built wealthy plantations based on sugar harvested by African slaves. By the eighteenth century, the sugar economy had spread to encompass virtually the entire Caribbean.

Culinary Encounters

Spanish settlers, having exhausted the Caribbean's scant gold deposits within a few decades, recognized that a different approach was necessary in order to make their fortunes in the New World. For a model, they looked to the Canary Islands, off the coast of Africa, which had fallen to Spaniards in the last two decades of the fifteenth century. The natives there had quickly disappeared, either through death from European diseases or through intermarriage with European settlers, and the conquerors had reshaped the islands' ecology by introducing Mediterranean plants and animals. Spanish settlers hoped to create still more of these island replicas of Europe in the Caribbean (Crosby 1986: 80-100).

The Taino inhabitants of the Caribbean consumed foods that were quite different from those of Europe.

Their staple crops were not grains but rather roots, such as manioc (*Manihot esculenta*), sweet potato (*Ipomoea batatas*), and tania (*Xanmthosoma* spp.). Maize (*Zea mays*) was also cultivated although it did not add significantly to the native diet. Islanders prepared cassava "bread" from the poisonous manioc by grating the root, squeezing out its toxic juice, pressing the meat into a flat bread, and baking it on a griddle. Native fruits and vegetables included pineapple (*Ananas comosus*), guava (*Psidium guajava*), mamey (*Mammea americana*), pawpaw (*Carica papaya*), cashews (*Anacardium occidentale*), common beans (*Phaseolus vulgaris*), and lima beans (*Phaseolus lunatis*). These plants occasioned different reactions from the Europeans, who ate some eagerly and fed others to pigs. The conquistadors marveled at the game eaten by the Indians – "all sorts of wild and poisonous beasts" – including dogs, snakes, rodents, raccoons, armadillos, lizards, tapirs, opossums, and spiders. Seafood was more to the Spaniards' taste, with such items as bagre (a catfish of Caribbean and South American waters), mullet, herring, mackerel, tunny, shark, rayfish, dogfish, crayfish, shrimp, mussels, clams, oysters, crab, conches, and turtles (Morison 1963: 216–19; Sauer 1966: 53–9; Newson 1976: 41–57).

Notwithstanding the bountiful native foods, European settlers yearned for more familiar fare. Their habitual Mediterranean cuisine consisted of three staple items: wheat bread, olive oil, and vinifera wine. Spaniards considered wheat (*Triticum aestivum*) essential for both body and soul. According to an eleventh-century papal edict, it was the only grain that could serve as the Holy Eucharist (Ross 1977: 61–9). Wine from grapes (*Vitis vinifera*) fulfilled an equally important role in the Catholic Mass as the blood of Christ. And although priests could proceed in their work without olives (*Oleo europea*), Spanish cooks certainly could not. Christopher Columbus brought wheat seeds on his second voyage in 1493, but the grain refused to grow in the tropical climate, and transplanted vine cuttings and olive seedlings fared no better. Even imported Communion wafers "did bend like to wet paper, by reason of the extreme humidity and heat" (Crosby 1972: 65; Newson 1976: 84–6).

European livestock, by contrast, multiplied rapidly in the islands. In 1493 Columbus introduced horses, cattle, pigs, goats, and sheep to the New World. The goats and sheep proved ill adapted to the humid Caribbean air, but the other animals prospered. Diego Velázquez claimed that by 1514, the pig population of Cuba had increased to 30,000. Puerto Rico became an important center of cattle raising and exported large quantities of jerked beef and prepared hides during the seventeenth century. Spanish sailors purposely turned breeding stock loose on islands so that future visitors would have access to pork and beef. Unfortunately, rats and other vermin, inadvertently carried by the Europeans, likewise became firmly established on the islands (Crosby 1972: 75–9; Newson 1976: 88–90; Dietz 1986: 8).

Caribbean gardens and orchards became much more diverse as a result of the Columbian exchange. Colonists planted cabbages (*Brassica* sp.), onions (*Allium cepa*), carrots (*Daucus carota*), lettuce (*Lactuca sativa*), radishes (*Raphanus sativus*), garlic (*Allium sativum*), and chickpeas (*Cicer arietinum*). Large numbers of Asian plants arrived in the New World during the sixteenth century. In some cases, they had previously been introduced to Spain by the Muslims; in other instances, they reached the Caribbean via the slave trade. Citrus fruits included lemons (*Citrus limon*), limes (*C. aurantifolia*), and sour oranges (*C. aurantium*), as well as the European sweet orange (*C. sinensis*). Other Asian plants that thrived in the Caribbean were muskmelons (*Cucumis melo*), pomegranates (*Punica granatum*), plantains and bananas (*Musa paradisiaca sapientium*), eggplants (*Solanum melongena*), ginger (*Zingiber officinale*), cinnamon (*Cinnamomum zeylanicum*), and rice (*Oryza sativa*). Coconuts (*Cocos nucifera*), of undetermined origin, were present on the Pacific Coast in pre-Columbian times, but Spaniards probably introduced them to the Caribbean. The most significant of the new arrivals, however, was sugarcane (*Saccharum officinarum*), which ultimately dictated the social structure of most of the region (Watson 1974: 8–35; Newson 1976: 46, 84–7).

These new crops gave little compensation to the natives for the destruction caused by European diseases and labor drafts. Conquistadors received grants of Tainos entrusted to their care (*encomienda*), ostensibly for conversion to Christianity, but certainly as a source of labor as well. Moreover, the Spanish crown condoned outright slavery in the case of Carib tribes because of their "warlike nature" and supposed cannibalistic practices. The harsh working conditions for both Tainos and Caribs alike would have precipitated high death and low birth rates. But epidemics, such as that of smallpox, which began in 1518, also joined in the slaughter because the Indians had little resistance to European diseases. Indeed, it was with only small exaggeration that Bartolomé de las Casas claimed in 1542 that the Caribbean natives had virtually disappeared. By 1570, Indians in the Spanish Antilles numbered 22,000, a fourth of the entire population of those islands. And having resisted enslavement for centuries, a handful of Caribs survive to the present on Dominica (Sauer 1966: 203–5; Newson 1976: 149, 170; Knight 1990: 41–3; Hulme and Whitehead 1992: 345).

Following the conquests of Mexico in 1521 and Peru in 1532, the majority of colonists proceeded to the mainland, hoping to make their fortunes from Indian labor and silver mines, and the Greater Antilles were left with only a few small settlements of people who subsisted on corn and cassava. Havana became the leading port because of its strategic location on the route of silver fleets returning to Spain. For the next two and a half centuries, Spain's Caribbean colonies served mainly as defensive outposts, guarding against incursions by rival European powers.

The Tyranny of Sugar

Spaniards established sugar mills on Hispaniola as early as 1515 and operated a thriving business in the mid-1500s, but by the end of the century production had stagnated. Portuguese plantations in Brazil then dominated New World sugar production until 1630, when the Dutch West India Company invaded the South American colony. After the Dutch were finally driven out, they carried the Brazilian techniques to French and English planters in their newly founded colonies in the Lesser Antilles.

Sugar monoculture first took root in Barbados and then spread to other British and (later) French islands. The initial settlers of Barbados had made a meager living growing low-quality tobacco and cotton on small estates. But the introduction of sugar by Dutch merchants, beginning in the 1630s, transformed the island. Thanks to Europe's developing sweet tooth, the new industry proved enormously profitable, causing land values to rise astronomically. Smallholders sold out to an emerging planter elite, who, in their hunger for land, cleared much of the remaining forests until most of the island's acreage was planted in cane or food crops to feed whites and their slaves. But Europeans on the islands soon became a minority as tens of thousands of African slaves were imported to work the plantations. By 1680, sugar estates had gained similar domination over the rest of the British Antilles. The French were slower to make the transition from small farms, where they grew tobacco and cotton, to large plantations devoted to sugarcane grown by slaves. Nevertheless, by the mid-eighteenth century, Saint-Domingue, Guadaloupe, and Martinique had become major centers of sugar production, and by the latter part of the century, Caribbean sugar production amounted to nearly a quarter of a million tons (Dunn 1972: 46-62; Mintz 1985: 32-5; Watts 1987: 296-300; Tomich 1990: 15).

Sugar exports from the Spanish Antilles did not revive until the mid-eighteenth century. Royal trade regulations prevented colonial producers from selling sugar to northern European markets and limited the supplies of African slaves. Tax reforms undertaken in the 1740s reversed this situation, and exports to Spain increased massively. This trend accelerated in 1762 after British forces had captured Havana and imported thousands of additional slaves. When the Spanish regained control of the island the following year, they allowed Britain to continue trading with the port, and delighted by the additional tax revenues, officials encouraged cane production on Puerto Rico and Hispaniola as well. By the mid-nineteenth century, following the revolution on Saint-Domingue, Cuba had become one of the most profitable colonies in the world (Hall 1971: 98-100; McNeill 1985: 162-70; Dietz 1986: 19-20; Watts 1987: 301-4).

One final element of the Columbian exchange that resulted directly from the labor demands of sugar plantations was the transportation to the New World of huge numbers of African slaves. Philip Curtin (1969: 265-9; 1976: 595-605) estimated that Caribbean planters imported almost 5 million slaves, fully half the total brought to the Americas. And with them came African foods. Plants introduced to the Americas via the slave trade included watermelons *(Colocynthis citrullus),* okra *(Hibiscus esculentus),* taro *(Colocasia esculenta* – called eddo in the West Indies), oil palms *(Elaeis guineensis),* pigeon peas *(Cajanus cajan),* and yams *(Dioscorea* spp.) (Harris 1965: 92-3, 115; Newson 1976: 161). But familiar foods notwithstanding, the journey to America made significant changes in the diets of enslaved Africans.

Plantation Nutrition

The food aboard slave ships provided an ominous portent of life in the New World. The standard fare consisted of a dreary soup of rice, yams, horsebeans, palm oil, and red peppers. Illness followed the slaves throughout the voyage, from the initial shock of sea-sickness to lingering bouts of dysentery and, finally, the bleeding gums of scurvy (Kiple 1984: 57-64). A slave who survived the trip could expect little improvement on the plantation because, as J. Harry Bennett (1958: 37) explained, "he ate from his master's purse, and every mouthful was measured in cash." Virtually every nutritional deficiency disease was experienced by slaves somewhere in the West Indies. But although the African population ate poorly, Europeans spared no expense on their own, often imported foods.

Slave Subsistence

Sidney Mintz (1985: 55-61) has demonstrated that Caribbean sugar plantations, although worked by slave labor, were managed as capitalist enterprises. Planters faced enormous risks in the fluctuating world sugar market and sought to minimize their operating expenses whenever possible. Although buying slaves represented a substantial fixed investment, feeding them offered endless opportunities for cost cutting. Thus, in the early years when sugar prices were high, many estate managers planted every available acre in cane and fed their slaves with imported grain and dried meat. But as competition drove prices down, planters economized by reducing rations and allowing slaves to cultivate subsistence crops, especially on mountain slopes unfit for sugar cultivation. But despite marginal lands and limited free time, slaves with their own fields consumed a better diet than those who worked exclusively in the cane fields.

In practice, plantation diets fell between the two extremes of entirely ration-fed slaves and those who had to be self-sufficient. But even on the most heavily planted sugar islands, such as Barbados, Antigua, and St. Kitts, slaves kept small kitchen gardens with herbs, squash, peppers, and okra, and certain fields called "Negro fields" or "Negro ground" were set aside for slave use. Conversely, on islands with large areas of mountainous terrain, such as Jamaica and Martinique, plantation managers often bought staples, including corn, rice, manioc, yams, plantains, and bananas, rather than allocating provision grounds and free time to the slaves. Moreover, slaves on virtually all of the islands depended for animal protein on imports of dried meat and salted fish (Kiple 1984: 67; Morrissey 1989: 51–7; Tomich 1990: 271).

Mercantile policies dictated that provisions for the Caribbean sugar islands come from within each empire. Thus, British merchants supplied their plantations with salt cod and corn from New England, jerked beef from Ireland, herring from the North Sea, and rice from South Carolina. Many smaller Jamaican estates with less-favorable lands also produced staple crops for sale to the sugar plantations (Milling 1951: 82; Dunn 1972: 210, 276; Kiple 1984: 69). The French settlements of Guadeloupe, Martinique, and Saint-Domingue, meanwhile, imported a significant portion of the codfish harvested off Newfoundland (McNeill 1985: 112). And as Spanish sugar production expanded in the nineteenth century, planters on Cuba and, to a lesser extent, Puerto Rico began importing large quantities of rice and jerked beef (Humboldt 1969: 305; Dietz 1986: 19–20). Yet despite the intentions of colonial officials, smugglers cut across imperial lines on a regular basis (Liss 1983: 77; Pérotin-Dumon 1991: 65).

Imperial regulations also attempted to assure that slaves received adequate rations. The French *Code Noir*, promulgated in 1685 by Finance Minister Jean-Baptiste Colbert, required masters to issue each adult slave two pounds of salted beef or three pounds of fish and six pounds of cassava bread or the equivalent of manioc flour. British slave codes were more concerned with preserving order than protecting slaves, and it was not until the late eighteenth and early nineteenth centuries that a standard ration of about three pounds of meat or fish per week began to be prescribed. Eighteenth-century Spanish authorities, likewise, made belated calls for a weekly meat ration of three pounds. But once again, plantation reality differed sharply from imperial regulations, and many managers admitted feeding their slaves half of the required amounts, and they were often in such a rancid state that most of the nutrients were gone. Although slaves responded by stealing food whenever possible, this expedient was no substitute for adequate rations (Dunn 1972: 239; Friedman 1982: 507; Kiple 1984: 68, 77; Dirks 1987: 61–7, 100; Stein 1988: 52).

Slaves prepared their rations using simple cooking techniques taken from their African homelands or borrowed from native Indians. Cassava bread was made by means of pre-Columbian procedures for removing the toxic juice and then baking the grated flesh into a flat bread. Slaves who grew their own maize on provision grounds preferred to roast whole ears and eat them on the cob. But as a ration, they typically received corn in the form of meal, which was made into a thin gruel called "loblolly" or "coo-coo." Other foodstuffs, including salted meat or fish, yams, plantains, and vegetables, were boiled together in an iron pot. The ingredients of these stews varied among the islands according to availability. For example, slaves on Antigua reportedly ate a breakfast of eddo (taro), okra, yams, and other vegetables. On Jamaica, the pepper pot contained greens, such as callaloo, starch from yams or plantains, red pepper, and bits of fish (Harris 1965: 115; Dunn 1972: 278–9; Kiple and Kiple 1980: 202; Dirks 1987: 53–4).

Even this simple fare was threatened in the late eighteenth century, however, when imperial warfare and natural disaster led to a major subsistence crisis. Trouble began in 1774 when the American Continental Congress resolved to stop exporting goods to British dominions, including the West Indies. By 1776, the revolutionaries succeeded in rendering the British sugar industry unprofitable, and famine appeared on Barbados, Antigua, and St. Kitts. At first, Jamaican slaves fared better because of the availability of provision grounds. But beginning in 1780, the islands were struck by a series of hurricanes that killed thousands and destroyed provisions. Even after the final storms of 1786, thousands more died from malnutrition, dysentery, and other epidemic diseases. The British government compounded the disaster by refusing to allow a resumption of trade with the newly independent United States (Sheridan 1976: 615–41; Dirks 1987: 80).

The decade-long crisis demonstrated the need to make the islands more self-sufficient. One response of the British government was to import new food crops to the islands. In 1778, slave ships brought the akee fruit (*Blighia sapida*) to Jamaica from West Africa. An Asian domesticate, the mango (*Mangifera indica*), arrived a few years later, and both fruits became important for slave subsistence. In 1787, the Royal Navy dispatched HMS *Bounty* under William Bligh to bring the breadfruit (*Artocarpus incisa*) from Tahiti. Thwarted at first by a notorious mutiny, in 1793 Bligh succeeded in his mission with the HMS *Providence*, earning a handsome reward from the Jamaican assembly. Unfortunately, the Jamaican slaves refused to eat the unfamiliar fruit, and for the next fifty years it was fed to pigs (Parry 1955: 1–20).

A more important change came from the expansion of slave provision grounds and slave markets. Slaves in Jamaica and Saint-Domingue had long produced staple crops on their provision grounds, and they even dominated the island markets. Amelioration laws, issued in the British Antilles late in the eighteenth century, encouraged more slaves on other islands to grow their own provisions. French officials on Martinique likewise allowed provision grounds and free time to grow substitutes for the rations handed out by masters (Mintz 1974: 180–213; Kiple

1984: 67–71; Tomich 1990: 262–5). And slaves who produced their own foods ate substantially better diets. According to Barry Higman (1979: 373–86), better nutrition was the reason that American-born slaves grew taller in the Bahamas than on islands where sugar was the primary crop. But despite attempts at amelioration, slave diets contained grave deficiencies.

Diet and Disease

One of the most notable aspects of the West Indian sugar industry was the failure to develop a self-sustaining slave population. Caribbean planters, unlike their North American counterparts, had to import tens of thousands of workers each year to replace those who had died. This policy may have developed in the seventeenth century from the cold calculation that it was more expensive to maintain slaves in good health than to work them to death and import replacements. But planters did not see their work force reproduce even after the abolition of the slave trade in the nineteenth century. One of the primary reasons for the slaves' failure to reproduce was the inadequate levels of nutrition. Diet-related diseases ran the gamut from protein and vitamin deficiencies to hypertension and lead poisoning.

Kenneth Kiple (1984: 77–81) has shown that slave diets were nutritionally deficient even if slaves actually received the provisions specified by legal requirements. For example, prescribed rations of dried beef and fish would appear to have exceeded the modern recommended dietary allowance of protein, but in fact, the slaves received these foods in a less-than-ideal state. One observer described the fish as "little better than a mass of foetid matter, containing as little nutrition as the brine in which they lie" (Kiple 1984: 80). Beef likewise lost much of its protein from the curing process. Protein deficiency weakened the slaves' immune systems and led in turn to widespread outbreaks of tuberculosis, dysentery, and other infectious diseases. Poor sanitary conditions unquestionably contributed to these epidemics, but slaves could have resisted many of these diseases with adequate supplies of protein (Kiple 1984: 142–3; Dirks 1987: 85).

Kiple has also documented shortages of most important vitamins, as well as calcium and iron. The most serious problems resulted from deficiencies of vitamin B_1 (thiamine) and B_3 (niacin). Slaves subsisting on white rice were at risk of developing beriberi, a thiamine-deficiency disease that takes two distinct forms. Both wet beriberi, with symptoms including swelling of the limbs and cardiac failure, and dry beriberi, characterized by muscular deterioration and paraplegia, were common to the Caribbean under the names "dropsy" and *mal d'estomach*. Corn rations, meanwhile, led to pellagra, a niacin-deficiency disease that caused dermatitis, dysentery, dementia, and death. Requirements for other vitamins, such as A and C, might have been satisfied by tropical fruits and chilli peppers. Unfortunately, low quantities of dietary

fat prevented full utilization of vitamin A, and as a result, night blindness often reached epidemic proportions. The incidence of scurvy symptoms, including bleeding gums, festering wounds, and frequent bruises, implies a similar deterioration of vitamin C, probably due to excessive cooking. Deficiencies of A and C also slowed the absorption of calcium and iron, leading in turn to rheumatism, periodontal disease, dental caries, and anemia, although iron cooking pots would have helped offset the latter problem (Kiple 1984: 76–103).

Nutritional diseases took their worst toll among young children. Malnourished mothers often gave birth prematurely, and even full-term infants were often significantly underweight. The mother's poor health continued to have an adverse effect on her children throughout nursing. Neonatal tetany, caused by calcium shortages in the mother's milk, killed large numbers of infants in the first few weeks of life. Thiamine deficiencies were also passed on to children in the form of infantile beriberi because slave mothers, who did not themselves display symptoms of beriberi, were often unable to provide sufficient quantities of thiamine to their children. Youngsters, even after surviving the critical first year, still faced great risk at the time of weaning. The gruel given to replace a mother's milk contained little protein, and physicians frequently reported the swollen bellies symptomatic of kwashiorkor. Infant mortality rates on Caribbean plantations were higher even than among slaves in the United States, which helps explain the much greater number of Africans imported to the islands (Kiple 1984: 113–34; Dirks 1987: 85).

With the numerous deficiencies in the slave diet, it is ironic that one potentially serious health problem may have resulted from excessive consumption of sodium. West Africa was a particularly salt-poor region, and the inhabitants apparently adapted to this shortage by naturally retaining sodium. Experiments, for example, have shown that the perspiration of Africans contains much less sodium than that of whites. But once in the Caribbean, African slaves frequently found themselves confronted with sodium in the form of salted beef and fish, and especially with a substantial ration of salt itself. Thomas Wilson (1987: 257–68) has estimated that slaves may have received 20 times the modern recommended amount of salt. The resulting hypertension, although difficult to diagnose without a blood pressure cuff, probably contributed to the incidence of death by "dropsy." To relieve this chemical imbalance along with other nutritional deficiencies, many slaves engaged in "dirt-eating" (pica). Planters often believed this practice to be a method of committing suicide, and they muzzled slaves suspected of it (Kiple 1984: 46; Dirks 1987: 86–7).

Some Caribbean slaves also suffered from acute lead poisoning from a wide variety of sources. Water channeled by lead gutters, and foods exposed to the lead glaze of earthenware pottery, were potential sources of lead, as were lead-lined boilers and gutters used in sugar refining. Worst of all, slaves who drank cheap rum could have taken in large amounts of lead in alcohol, which was distilled in equipment with lead pipes and fittings. The body retains this excess lead in soft tissue, such as the brain, producing disastrous effects, including headaches, paralysis, coma, and death. One prominent symptom of lead poisoning was the "dry bellyache" – extremely painful intestinal cramps accompanied by severe constipation – which a contemporary described as an "excruciating torture of the bowels" (Handler et al. 1987: 140–66). Sailors, soldiers, and other poor whites also experienced this malady.

Malnourished slaves seldom challenged the society that held them in bondage; what planters feared most was the sudden burst of energy that came with the harvest around Christmas. Robert Dirks (1987: 167–84) has described the effects of relief-induced agonism, a condition of extremely aggressive behavior exhibited by people allowed to eat plentifully after a long period of semistarvation. Slaves in the British West Indies consumed little during the fall months as both sugarcane and provision crops matured. In December, when the end of the hurricane season brought merchant ships and planters handed out special bonuses of sugar, rum, and fish, the slaves suddenly had an overabundance of food. They responded by indulging in orgiastic revels of drinking, dancing, and occasional rebellion. This "Black Saturnalia" provided a temporary reversal of roles in which planters cringed as slaves approached, but after a few days of release, the slaves' world returned to its grim normality.

Dining in the Great House

Some plantation owners, while limiting slave rations to save a few pennies, often spent outlandish sums to maintain their own extravagant lifestyles. For example, the governor of Barbados celebrated a 1688 holiday by setting a 250-foot table for the island's leading citizens and opening wine casks in the streets for less distinguished souls. Richard Dunn (1972: 263–4, 280) has speculated that this penchant for conspicuous consumption derived from the hierarchical significance attached to food and clothing in early modern Europe. Each social class had a distinctive style of diet and dress, and nouveaux riches planters adhered to these standards, regardless of the discomforts involved in eating heavy roasts on a humid afternoon or wearing woolen coats and trousers under the tropical sun. But notwithstanding the determination of sweaty, constipated settlers, the islands demanded some adaptation or creolization of European cuisine.

The essentials of proper British dining comprised beef, bread, and beer, but reproducing this diet proved difficult in the tropics. Fresh meat spoiled virtually overnight, and so planters had to rely on salted beef, pork, and fish, although the fish was mackerel and salmon rather than the cheap cod fed to slaves. Wheat, likewise, tended to go bad on the long voyages from Bristol and Philadelphia; thus, planters consumed hard biscuits rather than the soft bread favored in England. Finally, beer proved highly perishable in the tropical climate, and so settlers slaked their thirst with rum, punch, fruit juices, and imported wines and brandy. But what the meals lacked in quality was made up for in quantity; dinner parties with heavily piled tables constituted the sine qua non of planter affluence. A guest at one such party was so impressed by a table with massive piles of meats, fruits, and cakes that she "kept her feet out from under the table for fear it would collapse" (Dunn 1972: 272–81; quotation from Dirks 1987: 45).

The Creole inhabitants of Cuba and Puerto Rico similarly sought to recreate traditional Spanish life in the tropics. Havana cooks used olive oil and garlic with a Mediterranean generosity that overwhelmed Fanny Calderón de la Barca (1966: 28), the Scottish wife of a Spanish minister, on her visit to the island in 1839. She did, however, take great pleasure from the custards, ices, meringues, and other Spanish sweets available on the island. Berta Cabanillas de Rodríguez (1973: 336) likewise emphasized the Spanish character of recipes in the anonymous 1849 volume *El Cocinero Puertorriqueño*. To satisfy the demand for Iberian foods, the islands imported large amounts of Mexican wheat flour and Spanish wines and liquors (Humboldt 1969: 300; Lipsett-Rivera 1990: 463).

Frenchmen living on Guadeloupe, Martinique, and Saint-Domingue were no less eager to enjoy the foods of their homeland. Dominican priest and bon vivant Père Jean-Baptiste Labat imported French wine to the Caribbean as early as 1693 and insisted on drinking a glass with dinner, even after he had been captured by the Spanish. A nineteenth-century visitor observed that French cooking in the Antilles was done in the style of Provence rather than Paris, with olive oil instead of cream, perhaps as a concession to the environment. But French bread remained an invariable staple, and bakeries on Martinique employed women to carry fresh loaves to country estates on a daily basis so that planters did not have to forgo this national treasure (Hearn 1970: 112, 350; Labat 1970: 57, 186).

Despite these links with metropolitan capitals, Europeans never escaped their dependence on African slaves. On the islands of Jamaica and Saint-Domingue, slaves dominated local markets with produce from their provision grounds. They reportedly drove very hard bargains, and even merchants complained that they could not afford fresh eggs, poultry, and produce. If having to buy groceries from slaves caused consternation among whites, the fear that the food might be poisoned provoked genuine terror. Mass hysteria swept Saint-Domingue in the 1780s, and a number of slaves suspected of using poison were put to death. A fear of the slaves was not unfounded, as demonstrated by a slave rebellion in the 1790s that destroyed the colony's sugar economy and threatened the entire Caribbean plantation society (Hall 1971: 68–72; Geggus 1991: 100).

Modern Diet and Nutrition

In 1789 the French declared liberty to be one of the "rights of man," and a short time later the slaves of Saint-Domingue launched their own revolution to attain this goal. After more than a decade of fighting, in 1804 Haiti finally gained independence; to preserve it, the former slaves systematically destroyed the island's sugar economy. Terrified of the Haitian revolution, Caribbean planters fought hard to prevent its spread. Emancipation came slowly to the region. It began in the British colonies in 1834 (followed by a so-called apprentice period) and culminated in Cuba in 1886. However, as emancipation proceeded, planters replaced the slaves with indentured servants from the Far East. Independence, likewise, remained elusive. As European empires retreated, the United States came to dominate the region. Cuban and Puerto Rican sugar plantations passed into the hands of companies like the American Sugar Refining Company, while the cane workers remained destitute. So, although the citizens of the islands long ago escaped slavery, they have subsequently gained only limited control over their destinies.

Asian Transplants

Even as European legislators debated slave emancipation in the early 1800s, Caribbean planters began searching for an alternate source of labor. Imperial expansion into the Far East offered the prospect of endless supplies of indentured Asians to replace the liberated African slaves. In 1838, the year in which slavery ended in the British Antilles, the first boatload of indentured servants arrived from India. Cuba, likewise feeling the pinch of British abolitionism because of the Royal Navy's war on the slave trade, began to encourage Chinese migration from ports opened after the first Opium War (1839–42). Indentured Asians suffered working conditions little better than those of African slaves, but fortunately, the period of servitude ended much more quickly. By 1920, when the last indenture contract was canceled, Asians had made a significant impact on Caribbean culture and cuisine.

The number of Asian workers who migrated to the West Indies, although fluctuating with the sugar market, totaled more than 500,000 by the end of the nineteenth century. The typical contract specified five- to seven-year terms of indenture and offered minuscule wages, but agents stationed in the ports of Calcutta and Madras had no trouble attracting workers from the impoverished Indian countryside. British Guiana and Trinidad received the majority of the Indian migrants, about 380,000 in all, while some 45,000 went to Jamaica and other British islands. In 1860 the British government allowed French agents to recruit 6,000 Indians annually to work in the West Indies, and a decade later the Dutch received a similar conces-

sion. Only about 18,000 Chinese migrants went to the British Antilles. Cuba was their preferred destination, and between 1847 and 1874, nearly 125,000 Chinese came to work on Spanish sugar plantations (Tinker 1974: 52–4, 99, 112; Look Lai 1993: 292).

Indenture contracts usually required workers to return to their homeland at the end of the term, but Asians nevertheless established permanent communities on a number of islands. East Indians in Trinidad took advantage of slumps in the sugar market to entrench themselves in the local economy by growing rice. Chinese immigrants, meanwhile, sought to establish a niche in the Caribbean grocery trade. Competition from these newcomers was often resented, and Chinese people living in Jamaica sometimes became the targets of racial violence. Another barrier to the formation of Asian communities in the Caribbean was the shortage of women. Planters contracted far greater numbers of East Indian men than women; nevertheless, by the end of World War I, additional migration had evened out the sex ratio among East Indians in Trinidad and Martinique. Chinese men faced an even greater imbalance, for Cuba accepted only 62 Chinese women in the nineteenth century. As a result, men tended to marry Creoles and became assimilated more thoroughly than did the East Indians (Tinker 1974: 34, 364, 372; Johnson 1987: 82–95; Look Lai 1993: 188–216).

Asians made significant contributions to the cuisine of the islands. Rice had already been established by Spaniards and Africans centuries before the first Asians arrived. But East Indians carried *massala,* the unique spice combinations that form the basis for curry. They also introduced ghee, the clarified butter essential for traditional Hindu cooking, and roti, a form of flat wheat bread often served with curry. Foods have fulfilled an important role as part of the Hindu *yagna* celebrations that propagate religious and ethnic values in Trinidad. Chinese immigrants were more generally assimilated along with their foods, such as steamed fish and stir-fried vegetables, which became an important part of Cuban cuisine (Lambert Ortiz 1986: 7, 352; Vertovec 1990: 89–111; Mackie 1991: 144).

New Peasants, Old Problems

Caribbean slaves, once freed from the plantations, proceeded to form what Mintz (1974: 132) has called a "reconstituted" peasantry. Across the Caribbean, tens of thousands of freedmen and their families abandoned the lowland estates to build new villages in the highlands where sugarcane did not grow. The new yeoman farmers enlarged their provision grounds and expanded the production of export crops, such as allspice (*Pimenta officinalis*), coffee (*Coffea arabica*), bananas, cotton, ginger, and arrowroot, which had been grown for the first time during the later slave period. Improved nutrition led to a dramatic fall in the infant mortality rate, and African-Americans in the Caribbean finally began to reproduce their numbers naturally. The population of Jamaica, for example, nearly doubled in the half century after emancipation.

And despite political turmoil, Haiti likewise recorded demographic growth in the nineteenth century, a clear indication that the revolution improved conditions for the island's black majority (Kiple 1984: 118; Watts 1987: 456–64, 507–15).

In the twentieth century, population growth accelerated to dangerous levels, however, as a result of government programs to control disease and improve nutrition. Mosquito eradication campaigns finally began to bring yellow fever and malaria under control around the turn of the century. Authorities acted more slowly to alleviate the problems of malnutrition; nevertheless, by the 1970s, most of the islands had begun educational campaigns aimed at promoting adequate childhood nutrition. After 1959, Fidel Castro brought Cuba to the forefront of the movement to improve the health of rural children. Unfortunately, these reforms stimulated Caribbean population growth at rates in excess of 3 percent annually from 1950 to 1970 – some of the highest rates in the world. And ever-increasing populations have placed enormous pressure on island ecology. For example, Haitian peasants now cultivate subsistence crops on mountain slopes so steep that they need ropes to support themselves. The resulting erosion makes it even more difficult to sustain agriculture on the island (May and McLellan 1973: 145, 174, 220; Kiple 1984: 175–87; Watts 1987: 518).

Dietary deficiency diseases continue to afflict children throughout the Caribbean. Statistics from the United Nations Food and Agriculture Organization (FAO) reveal that the inhabitants of several islands, particularly Hispaniola, consume significantly below the recommended dietary allowances of vitamins and minerals. And because these figures represent nationwide averages, the poorest segments of Caribbean society suffer serious malnutrition. In the 1970s, the FAO estimated that protein-calorie deficiency strikes 30,000 to 50,000 Jamaican children, with the most serious cases exhibiting symptoms of kwashiorkor and marasmus. Moreover, studies of childhood deaths on the island indicate that a majority are nutrition related, and fully a third may have resulted directly from malnutrition. A survey of children in the Dominican Republic found only 25 percent with adequate nutrition levels, and of those admitted to hospitals, 39 percent suffered from kwashiorkor and 90 percent from anemia. Haiti recorded one of the highest infant mortality rates in the world, with 146.5 deaths per 1,000 live births in the 1970s. And village surveys found Haitian children to be as seriously malnourished as those of the neighboring Dominican Republic (May and McLellan 1973: 125, 177, 225; Kiple 1984: 184–6).

The problems of food shortages have been exacerbated by government attempts to implement crash industrialization programs and reliance on imported food. Such a lack of self-sufficiency was not unusual; as early as the 1880s, the small island of St. Pierre had become so dependent on canned foods from the United States that an American steamer was called a "food ship." Nevertheless, industrialization programs further reduced the region's capacity to support itself, as Puerto Rico's "Operation Bootstrap" demonstrated, beginning in 1949. Although aggregate incomes rose dramatically, the problem of unemployment remained, and in 1974 the United States government was forced to extend the food stamp program to the island. This, in turn, distorted the local economy, creating black markets in goods and labor and ruining the island's small farmers. It meant not only that people bought rice from California instead of the countryside but also that they discarded traditional dishes in favor of sugar-laden processed foods. Elsewhere in the region, the urban poor could not afford expensive imports, leading to widespread malnutrition and, at times, political unrest, such as the 1984 food riots in the Dominican Republic (Hearn 1970: 294; Weisskoff 1985: 60–4; Dietz 1986: 27, 63, 122; Knight 1990: 323).

Socialist Cuba attempted to balance modernization with equality, but despite some initial success, by the 1990s hunger had become widespread. Prior to Castro's revolution, malnutrition had been a serious problem in the Cuban countryside, with the daily diet deficient by 1,000 calories. Although Castro created a successful rural health-care system, initial mistakes in agricultural development led to a reliance on subsidies from the Soviet Union. By the mid-1980s imports had fallen from one-third of total food consumption to below 20 percent, at the same time that per capita intake of calories and proteins increased. But just a few years later, the collapse of communism in Eastern Europe closed markets for Cuban sugar and ended the subsidized petroleum supplies. While ration cards had long been a fact of life, in the early 1990s hunger, again, became a serious problem (Zimbalist and Brundenius 1989: 103–9; Miller 1992: 130–3).

The failure of Caribbean industrialization has driven millions to flee the region in search of a better life. Puerto Ricans, taking advantage of their United States citizenship, have flooded into New York, particularly the South Bronx. New York has also become home to large numbers of Jamaicans, Haitians, and Dominicans, while Cuban refugees have turned Miami into the second largest Cuban city. Shortly before Dutch Guiana became the independent state of Suriname in 1975, nearly 40 percent of the population had migrated to the Netherlands. The human tragedy of such an exodus from the Caribbean is best illustrated by the boatloads of Haitians braving the sea to escape the successive dictatorships and intense poverty of their homeland (Richardson 1989: 203–28).

Transnational Cuisine

The Caribbean people have been relatively slow to adopt the concept of nationalism, either within individual island states or as a pan-Caribbean phenomenon. This has resulted, in part, from the lingering colonial presence of the United States and European powers. Most of the British Antilles did not gain their independence until the 1970s, and foreign rule persisted until recently in the Netherlands Antilles. The Virgin Islands and Puerto Rico are part of the United States, just as Guiana, Guadeloupe, and Martinique are French departments. None of these has achieved the status of an independent nation. The diversity of ethnic origins has likewise impeded the formation of Caribbean nationalism, as even basic definitions of "race" within the region defy easy explanation (Mintz 1974: 315–24). Finally, massive migration, both from the islands to former colonial capitals and among different islands, has diffused the pressure for unifying nationalist ideologies. Yet, for all the regional and ethnic diversity, it is nevertheless possible, as Mintz (1974) has shown, to identify a uniquely Caribbean culture and cuisine.

Of course, the Caribbean traveler could find many different styles of cooking, perhaps the least representative being that served in tourist hotels. A typical menu might include fresh grilled fish, garnished with tropical fruits and washed down with a rum cocktail. But for the majority of the people in the Greater Antilles, seafood has meant salt cod rather than fresh fish. Moreover, hotel restaurants import the majority of their foods; even the tropical fruits often come from Florida. And those "authentic" island recipes, generally, have little real connection with the foods of the common people. Bonham Richardson (1992: 109) noted that visitors "find the mock authenticity of tourist-oriented dinner menus appealing, but they probably would not tolerate the fare consumed by Caribbean working classes."

While tourists seek sanitized versions of local cuisine, the natives have turned in ever-greater numbers to processed foods from the United States and Europe. Each new import, from spaghetti and canned soups to Nescafé and Johnny Walker, gains gourmet status because of its high cost, and poor islanders suffer acute embarrassment if they cannot offer guests a can of Spam (Wilson 1973: 22, 107). The adoption of Western consumption patterns led one Bahamian housewife to declare that she had given up preparing meals because her family "snacks outside continuously" (May and McLellan 1973: 13). Big Macs and Kentucky Fried Chicken have become common on the islands, and even socialist Cuba has succumbed to the lure of pizza parlors. The 1989 opening of the first McDonald's in Barbados saw serious traffic jams as cars lined up to enter the drive-through lane (Kurlansky 1992: 98).

Despite the encroachment of processed foods, however, it is still possible to recognize a peasant-based, pan-Caribbean cuisine. The simultaneous diversity and continuity of this food can be seen in the ubiquitous meal of rice and beans. This combination appears in Spanish-speaking islands as *moros y cristianos* (Moors and Christians), among French dominions as *pois et riz* (beans and rice), and in Jamaica as rice and peas (although it is generally made with dried red beans instead of fresh pigeon peas). Regional variations exist, even within the larger islands. In Cuba, for example, the residents of Havana eat the small black beans of neighboring Yucatán, whereas people in Oriente Province prefer the red beans common to Jamaica and Puerto Rico. Many other methods exist for preparing the staple, rice, among the most extravagant of which are the Haitian favorite *riz au djon-djon* (rice with black mushrooms) and Venezuela's rich, caramel *arroz con coco* (rice with coconut milk). Nevertheless, rice with beans remains the basis of regional cooking (Lambert Ortiz 1986: 258–82; Mintz 1974: 227; Sokolov 1991: 64).

Although relatively expensive compared to such root crops as cassava and yams, beans and rice provide a source of protein that is much cheaper than that from animal products. Neither beans nor rice alone yields a high-quality protein because the former lacks the essential amino acids methionine and cystine, while the latter is deficient in lysine. But together, each offsets the deficiency in the other, creating a complete amino acid chain that allows the body to build tissue efficiently. This nutritional synergism seems all the more fortuitous given that the American bean did not encounter Asian rice until after 1492 (Sanjur 1970: 26).

Similar eclectic combinations abound throughout the Caribbean. Codfish and akee, the national dish of Jamaica, originated with slaves who mixed the salt fish rations provided by planters with the akee fruit, an African domesticate that did not arrive in the island until 1778. Another common dish dating back to the period of slavery is callaloo soup, which takes its name from the leaves of the taro, and also includes okra and salt pork. Tamales, corn confections originally from Mexico, are widely prepared in Cuba, Martinique, and Venezuela. The dish most commonly associated with the French islands of Martinique and Guadeloupe is, ironically, a curry, *le colombo*. Elizabeth Lambert Ortiz (1986: 2) has observed that the identification of a food with a particular island has little to do with the dish's origins because of the wide travels of gifted cooks. It is this constant migration of diverse peoples that has defined the culture and cuisine of the Caribbean.

Jeffrey M. Pilcher

Bibliography

Armstrong, Douglas V. 1990. *The old village and the great house: An archaeological and historical examination of Drax Hall Plantation St. Ann's Bay, Jamaica.* Urbana, Ill.

Bennett, J. Harry. 1958. *Bondsmen and bishops.* Berkeley, Calif.

Cabanillas de Rodríguez, Berta. 1973. *El puertorriqueño y su alimentación a través de su historia (siglos XVI al XIX).* San Juan.

Calderón de la Barca, Fanny. 1966. *Life in Mexico: The letters of Fanny Calderón de la Barca,* ed. Howard T. Fisher and Marion Hall Fisher. Garden City, N.Y.

Crosby, Alfred W., Jr. 1972. *The Columbian exchange: Biological and cultural consequences of 1492.* Westport, Conn.

1986. *Ecological imperialism: The biological expansion of Europe, 900-1900.* Cambridge.

Curtin, Philip D. 1969. *The Atlantic slave trade: A census.* Madison, Wis.

1976. Measuring the African slave trade once again: A comment. *Journal of African History* 17: 595-605.

Dietz, James L. 1986. *Economic history of Puerto Rico: Institutional change and capitalist development.* Princeton, N.J.

Dirks, Robert. 1987. *The Black Saturnalia: Conflict and its ritual expression on British West Indian slave plantations.* Gainesville, Fla.

Dunn, Richard S. 1972. *Sugar and slaves: The rise of the planter class in the English West Indies, 1624-1713.* Chapel Hill, N.C.

Friedman, Gerald C. 1982. The heights of slaves in Trinidad. *Social Science History* 6: 482-515.

Geggus, David. 1991. The major port towns of Saint Domingue in the later eighteenth century. In *Atlantic port cities: Economy, culture, and society in the Atlantic world, 1650-1850,* ed. Franklin W. Knight and Peggy K. Liss, 87-116. Knoxville, Tenn.

González, Nancie L. 1988. *Sojourners of the Caribbean: Ethnogenesis and ethnohistory of the Garifuna.* Urbana, Ill.

Goslinga, Cornelis Ch. 1971. *The Dutch in the Caribbean and on the wild coast, 1580-1680.* Gainesville, Fla.

1985. *The Dutch in the Caribbean and in the Guianas, 1680-1791.* Assen, the Netherlands.

Hall, Gwendolyn Midlo. 1971. *Social control in slave plantation societies: A comparison of St. Domingue and Cuba.* Baltimore, Md.

Handler, Jerome S., Arthur C. Aufderheide, Robert S. Corruccini, et al. 1987. Lead contact and poisoning in Barbados slaves: Historical, chemical, and biological evidence. In *The African exchange: Toward a biological history of black people,* ed. Kenneth F. Kiple, 140-66. Durham, N.C.

Harris, David R. 1965. *Plants, animals, and man in the Outer Leeward Islands, West Indies: An ecological study of Antigua, Barbuda, and Anguilla.* Berkeley, Calif.

Hearn, Lafacadio. 1970. *Two years in the French West Indies.* Upper Saddle River, N.J.

Higman, Barry W. 1976. *Slave population and economy in Jamaica, 1807-1834.* Cambridge.

1979. Growth in Afro-Caribbean slave populations. *American Journal of Physical Anthropology* 50: 373-86.

Hulme, Peter, and Neil L. Whitehead. 1992. *Wild majesty: Encounters with Caribs from Columbus to the present day.* Oxford.

Humboldt, Alexander. 1969. *The island of Cuba.* New York.

Johnson, Howard. 1987. The Chinese in Trinidad in the late nineteenth century. *Ethnic and Racial Studies* 10: 82-95.

Kiple, Kenneth F. 1984. *The Caribbean slave: A biological history.* Cambridge.

Kiple, Kenneth F. ed., 1988. *The African exchange: Toward a biological history.* Durham, N.C.

Kiple, Kenneth F., and Virginia H. Kiple. 1980. Deficiency diseases in the Caribbean. *Journal of Interdisciplinary History* 11: 197-215.

Knight, Franklin W. 1990. *The Caribbean: The genesis of a fragmented nationalism.* Second edition. New York.

Kurlansky, Mark. 1992. *A continent of islands: Searching for the Caribbean destiny.* Reading, Mass.

Labat, Jean Baptiste. 1970. *The memoirs of Père Labat, 1693-1705,* trans. John Eaden. London.

Laguerre, Michel S. 1990. *Urban poverty in the Caribbean: French Martinique as a social laboratory.* New York.

Lambert Ortiz, Elizabeth. 1986. *The complete book of Caribbean cooking.* New York.

Lewicki, Tadeusz. 1974. *West African food in the Middle Ages: According to Arabic sources.* London.

Lipsett-Rivera, Sonya. 1990. Puebla's eighteenth-century agrarian decline: A new perspective. *Hispanic American Historical Review* 70: 463-81.

Liss, Peggy K. 1983. *Atlantic empires: The network of trade and revolution, 1713-1826.* Baltimore, Md.

Look Lai, Walton. 1993. *Indentured labor, Caribbean sugar: Chinese and Indian migrants to the British West Indies, 1838-1918.* Baltimore, Md.

Mackie, Cristine. 1991. *Life and food in the Caribbean.* New York.

May, Jacques M., and Donna L. McLellan. 1973. *The ecology of malnutrition in the Caribbean.* New York.

McNeill, John R. 1985. *Atlantic empires of France and Spain: Louisbourg and Havana, 1700-1763.* Chapel Hill, N.C.

Miller, Tom. 1992. *Trading with the enemy: A yankee travels through Castro's Cuba.* New York.

Milling, Chapman J., ed. 1951. *Colonial South Carolina: Two contemporary descriptions.* Columbia, S.C.

Mintz, Sidney W. 1974. *Caribbean transformations.* Chicago.

1983. Caribbean marketplaces and Caribbean history. *Radical History Review* 27: 110-20.

1985. *Sweetness and power: The place of sugar in modern history.* New York.

Morison, Samuel Eliot. 1942. *Admiral of the Ocean Sea: A life of Christopher Columbus.* Boston, Mass.

1963. *Journals and other documents on the life and voyages of Christopher Columbus.* New York.

Morrissey, Marietta. 1989. *Slave women in the New World: Gender stratification in the Caribbean.* Lawrence, Kans.

Newson, Linda A. 1976. *Aboriginal and Spanish colonial Trinidad: A study in culture contact.* London.

Parry, John H. 1955. Plantation and provision ground: An historical sketch of the introduction of food crops in Jamaica. *Revista de Historia de America* 39: 1-20.

Pérotin-Dumon, Anne. 1991. Cabotage, contraband, and corsairs: The port cities of Guadeloupe and their inhabitants, 1650-1800. In *Atlantic port cities: Economy, culture, and society in the Atlantic world, 1650-1850,* ed. Franklin W. Knight and Peggy K. Liss, 58-86. Knoxville, Tenn.

Quintana, Epaminondas. 1942. El problema dietético del Caribe. *América Indígena* 2: 25-8.

Richardson, Bonham C. 1989. Caribbean migrations, 1838-1985. In *The modern Caribbean,* ed. Franklin W. Knight and Colin A. Palmer, 203-28. Chapel Hill, N.C.

1992. *The Caribbean in the wider world, 1492-1992: A regional geography.* Cambridge.

Ross, Oliver D. 1977. Wheat growing in northern Spain. *North Dakota Quarterly* 45: 61-9.

Sanjur, Diva. 1970. *Puerto Rican food habits: A socio-cultural approach.* Ithaca, N.Y.

Sauer, Carl O. 1966. *The early Spanish Main.* Berkeley, Calif.

Sheridan, Richard B. 1976. The crisis of slave subsistence in the British West Indies during and after the American Revolution. *William and Mary Quarterly* 33: 615-41.

Sokolov, Raymond. 1991. *Why we eat what we eat: How the encounter between the New World and the Old changed the way everyone on the planet eats.* New York.

Stein, Robert L. 1988. *The French sugar business in the eighteenth century.* Baton Rouge, La.

Super, John C. 1988. *Food, conquest, and colonization in sixteenth-century Spanish America.* Albuquerque, N. Mex.

Tinker, Hugh. 1974. *A new system of slavery: The export of Indian labour overseas, 1830-1920.* London.

Tomich, Dale W. 1990. *Slavery in the circuit of sugar: Martinique and the world economy, 1830-1848.* Baltimore, Md.

Vertovec, Steven. 1990. Oil boom and recession in Trinidad Indian villages. In *South Asias overseas: Migration and ethnicity,* ed. Colin Clarke, Colin Peach, and Steven Verotvec, 89-111. Cambridge.

Watson, Andrew M. 1974. The Arab agricultural revolution and its diffusion, 700-1100. *Journal of Economic History* 34: 8-35.

Watts, David. 1987. *The West Indies: Patterns of development, culture and environmental change since 1492.* Cambridge.

Weisskoff, Richard. 1985. *Factories and food stamps: The Puerto Rico model of development.* Baltimore, Md.

Wilson, Peter J. 1973. *Crab antics: The social anthropology of English-speaking Negro societies of the Caribbean.* New Haven, Conn.

Wilson, Thomas W. 1987. Africa, Afro-Americans, and hypertension: An hypothesis. In *The African exchange: Toward a biological history of black people,* ed. Kenneth F. Kiple, 257-68. Durham, N.C.

Zimbalist, Andrew, and Claes Brundenius. 1989. *The Cuban economy: Measurement and analysis of socialist performance.* Baltimore, Md.

V.D.5   Temperate and Arctic North America to 1492

In writing about the history of food and drink in pre-Columbian North America, one is reminded that for the temperate part of the continent, we are describing cultures primarily known only through archaeological and archival research. Very few native populations survived the events of the past five centuries, and those that did endured considerable cultural modifications. Nonetheless, many of the foods and drinks they used became important legacies to the new North American and global foodways that emerged after 1492, and certainly such foods were critical to the survival of the first European colonists who established permanent communities there.

Perhaps the most important of these were pumpkins, squash, beans, and maize (corn), and although few of these crops were originally domesticated in temperate North America, today they, as well as indigenous cultivation and preparation techniques, continue to be valued.

The practice of mixing maize, beans, and squash in gardens was developed by Native Americans, who also contributed many maize dishes, including hominy, grits and other gruels, breads made with corn flour, corn on the cob, and succotash (Hudson 1976: 498-9). Early North Americans gave sunflowers to the world's economy and contributed to the development of modern strawberry, blackberry, raspberry, blueberry, cranberry, hickory, and pecan varieties (Trager 1970: 278-80; Hedrick 1972). Finally, such preservation techniques as drying fruits or vegetables and curing meat by smoking over hickory coals have Native American antecedents (Hudson 1976: 499).

Native North American cuisine is important to scholars for its contribution to knowledge about adaptations to tropical, temperate, and arctic environments. In the sixteenth century, the continent was not occupied by a single people making use of a limited suite of plants and animals. Instead, many different peoples wove the resources of their regions into complex and specialized strategies that were finely adapted to local environmental features.

Subsistence patterns in the northern portion of the continent may be broadly generalized into subarctic and arctic hunting traditions and temperate seed-gathering traditions (Spencer and Jennings 1965: 2). The latter were widespread, forming the basis for farming lifestyles that developed in many areas. A farming tradition was being widely practiced in the temperate eastern sector of the continent and in the Southwest when the first European explorers arrived. The farming traditions of the temperate Eastern Woodlands had a profound impact on the earliest European colonists; indeed, those who survived did so only because they adapted to North American conditions, melding their own foodways with native North American dietary traditions (Reitz and Scarry 1985). In the sixteenth century, the "transplanted Spaniard" either adapted, left the colony, or died.

Because of the importance of Eastern Woodlands farming traditions to sixteenth-century European colonization, this chapter focuses on that region and, for historical depth, traces Mississippian dietary practices from their antecedents in the nonhorticultural Paleo-Indian and Archaic cultures into the horticultural traditions of the Late Archaic and Woodland periods (Table V.D.5.1). It concludes with an examination of the impact of native foodways on sixteenth-century Spanish colonies. Common names are used throughout the text; however, scientific names of plants and animals frequently found in Eastern Woodlands sites are provided in Tables V.D.5.2 and V.D.5.3.

Table V.D.5.1. *General chronological sequence*

Period	Age
Contact	A.D. 1520-1700
Mississippian	A.D. 1000-1520
Late Woodland	A.D. 600-A.D. 1000
Middle Woodland	A.D. 1-A.D. 600
Early Woodland	700 B.C.-A.D. 1
Late Archaic	4000-700 B.C.
Early and Middle Archaic	8000 B.C.-4000 B.C.
Paleo-Indian	?-8000 B.C.

Source: Modified from Steponaitis (1986).

Table V.D.5.2. *List of scientific and common names for plants*

Scientific name	Common name	Scientific name	Common name
Wild fruits and berries		**Roots and tubers**	
Amelanchier spp.	Serviceberry	*Acorus calamus*	Sweet flag
Asimina triloba	Papaw	*Allium cernuum*	Wild onion
Celtis occidentalis	Hackberry	*Allium canadense*	Wild garlic
Crataegus spp.	Hawthorn	*Amphicarpa bracteata*	Hog peanut
Diospyros virginiana	Persimmon	*Apios americana*	Groundnut
Fragaria virginiana	Wild strawberry	*Camassia esculenta*	Wild hyacinth
Gaylussacia spp.	Huckleberry	*Dentaria* spp.	Toothwort
Gleditsia aquatica	Honey locust	*Helianthus tuberosus*	Jerusalem artichoke
Ilex verticilliata	Winterberry	*Ipomoea pandurata*	Wild sweet potato
Malus coronaria	Crabapple	*Medeola virginiana*	Indian cucumber
Morus rubra	Red mulberry	*Nelumbo lutea*	American lotus
Nyssa spp.	Black gum	*Orontium aquaticum*	Golden club
Opuntia spp.	Prickly pear	*Peltandra virginica*	Arrow arum
Passiflora incarnata	Maypop	*Sagittaria* spp.	Arrowhead
Physalis spp.	Groundcherry	*Scirpus validus*	Bulrush
Prunus americana	Plum	*Smilax* spp.	Greenbrier
Prunus serotina	Wild black cherry	*Typha* spp.	Cattail
Rhus spp.	Sumac	*Zamia* spp.	Coontie
Ribes spp.	Gooseberry		
Rubus spp.	Blackberry-raspberry	**Beverages and condiments**	
Sambucus spp.	Elderberry	*Acer* spp.	Maple
Solanum americanum	Black nightshade	*Ilex vomitoria*	Yaupon, black drink
Vaccinium spp.	Blueberry	*Ilex cassine*	Dahoon holly
Viburnum spp.	Blackhaw	*Lindera* spp.	Spicebush
Vitis spp.	Wild grape	*Liquidamber styraciflua*	Sweet gum
Yucca spp.	Common yucca	*Persea borbonia*	Sweet bay
		Sassafras albidum	Sassafras
Nuts			
Carya glabra	Pignut hickory	**Eastern Woodland cultivated or domesticated plants**	
Carya illinoensis	Pecan	*Chenopodium berlandieri* ssp. *jonesianum*	Domestic chenopod
Carya laciniosa	Shellbark hickory		
Carya ovata	Shagbark hickory	*Cucurbita pepo* ssp. *ovifera* v. *ovifera*	Gourd-squash
Carya tomentosa	Mockernut hickory		
Castanea dentata	American chestnut	*Helianthus annuus* v. *macrocarpus*	Domestic sunflower
Castanea pumila	Chinquapin		
Corylus spp.	Hazelnut	*Hordeum pusillum*	Little barley
Fagus spp.	Beechnut	*Iva annua* v. *macrocarpa*	Domestic sumpweed
Juglans cinerea	Butternut	*Lagenaria siceraria*	Bottle gourd
Juglans nigra	Black walnut	*Phalaris caroliniana*	Maygrass
Quercus alba	White oak	*Polygonum erectum*	Erect knotweed
Quercus coccinea	Scarlet oak		
Quercus macrocarpa	Burr oak	**Introduced tropical domesticated plants**	
Quercus prinus	Chestnut oak	*Amaranthus hypochondriacus*	Pale-seeded amaranth
Quercus rubra	Red oak	*Capsicum* sp.	Chilli pepper
Quercus velutina	Black oak	*Cucurbita argyrosperma* (formerly *C. mixta*)	Cushaw squash
Edible seeds and greens		*Cucurbita pepo* ssp. *pepo*	Pumpkin-marrows
Amaranthus spp.	Pigweed	*Cucurbita moschata*	Moschata squash
Ambrosia trifida	Giant ragweed	*Phaseolus lunatus*	Lima bean
Ambrosia cf. *artemisiifolia*	Common ragweed	*Phaseolus vulgaris*	Common bean
Arundinaria gigantea	Large cane	*Zea mays*	Maize
Arundinaria tecta	Small cane	**Introduced Old World cultigens**	
Chenopodium album	Lamb's quarter	*Citrullus vulgaris*	Watermelon
Chenopodium berlandieri	Goosefoot	*Corylus avellana*	Domestic hazelnut
Echinochloa spp.	Cockspurgrass	*Cucumis melo*	Melon
Euphorbia maculata	Spruge	*Ficus carica*	Fig
Impatiens spp.	Jewelweed	*Pisum sativum*	Common pea
Iva ciliata	Marshelder	*Prunus persica*	Peach
Leersia oryzoides	Rice cutgrass	*Triticum* spp.	Wheat
Lepidium virginicum	Peppergrass	*Vigna unguiculata*	Cowpea
Phaseolus polystachios	Wild bean	*Vitis vinifera*	Wine grape
Phytolacca americana	Pokeweed	**Wild progenitors**	
Plantago rugelii	Plantain	*Cucurbita pepo* ssp. *ovifera* v. *texana*	Texas wild gourd
Portulaca oleracea	Purslane	*Chenopodium berlandieri*	Wild goosefoot
Rumex spp.	Dock	*Iva annua* v. *annua*	Wild sumpweed
Sabal palmetto	Cabbage palm	**Fish poisons**	
Serenoa repens	Saw palmetto	*Aesculus* spp.	Buckeye
Strophostyles helvola	Wild bean	*Tephrosia virginiana*	Devil's shoestring
Vicia spp.	Vetch		

Table V.D.5.3. *List of scientific and common names for animals*

Scientific name	Common name	Scientific name	Common name
Crustacea		**Freshwater fishes**	
Penaeus spp.	Shrimp	*Acipenser* spp.	Sturgeon
Callinectes sapidus	Blue crab	*Lepisosteus* spp.	Gar
Menippe mercenaria	Stone crab	*Amia calva*	Bowfin
		Notemigonus crysoleucas	Golden shiner
Freshwater bivalves		*Carpiodes cyprinus*	Quillback
Actinonaias spp.	Mucket	*Catostomus* spp.	Sucker
Amblema spp.	Threeridge	*Ictiobus* spp.	Buffalo
Anodonta spp.	Floater	*Hypentelium* spp.	Hog sucker
Cyclonaias tuberculata	Purple wartyback	*Minytrema melanops*	Spotted sucker
Elliptio spp.	Spike	*Moxostoma* spp.	Redhorse
Fusconaia spp.	Pigtoe	*Ameiurus* spp.	Bullhead catfish
Lampsilis spp.	Mucket	*Ictalurus* spp.	Freshwater catfish
Lasmigona spp.	Heelsplitter	*Noturus* spp.	Madtom
Obovaria spp.	Hickorynut	*Pylodictis olivaris*	Flathead catfish
Pleurobmea spp.	Pigtoe	*Esox* spp.	Pike
Quadrula spp.	Pimpleback	*Exox masquinongy*	Muskellunge
Tritogonia verrucosa	Pistolgrip	*Lepomis* spp.	Sunfish
Uniomerus tetralasmus	Pondhorn	*Micropterus* spp.	Bass
		Pomoxis spp.	Crappie
Marine bivalves		*Perca flavescens*	Yellow perch
Brachidontes spp.	Mussel	*Aplodinotus grunniens*	Freshwater drum
Geukensia demissa	Ribbed mussel		
Anadara spp.	Ark	**Marine fishes**	
Glycymeris spp.	Bittersweet	*Acipenser* spp.	Sturgeon
Agropecten spp.	Scallop	*Albula vulpes*	Bonefish
Crassostrea virginica	Oyster	Clupeidae	Herring
Mactra fragilis	Eastern mactra	*Arius felis*	Hardhead catfish
Donax spp.	Coquina	*Bagre marinus*	Gafftopsail
Tagelus spp.	Tagelus	*Opsanus tau*	Oyster toadfish
Polymesoda carolinana	Marsh clam	*Centropomus* spp.	Snook
Chione spp.	Venus shell	*Morone* spp.	Temperate bass
Mercenaria spp.	Hard clam	*Centropristis* spp.	Sea bass
Protothaca spp.	Venus	*Pomatomus saltatrix*	Bluefish
		Caranx spp.	Jack
Freshwater gastropods		*Chloroscombrus chrysurus*	Atlantic bumper
Campeloma spp.	Campeloma	*Archosargus probatocephalus*	Sheepshead
Pomacea spp.	Applesnail	*Bairdiella chrysoura*	Silver perch
		Cynoscion spp.	Sea trout
Marine gastropods		*Leiostomus xanthurus*	Spot
Littorina irrorata	Periwinkle	*Menticirrhus* spp.	Kingfish
Strombus spp.	Queen conch	*Micropogonias undulatus*	Atlantic croaker
Crepidula spp.	Slipper-shell	*Pogonias cromis*	Black drum
Polinices duplicatus	Shark eye	*Sciaenops ocellatus*	Red drum
Busycon spp.	Whelk	*Mugil* spp.	Mullet
Melongena spp.	Crown conch	*Paralichthys* spp.	Flounder
Ilynassa obsoleta	Mud nassa	*Chilomycterus*	Burrfish
Nassarius spp.	Nassa	*Diodon histrix*	Porcupine fish
Fasciolaria spp.	Tulip shell		
Pleuroploca spp.	Horse conch	**Amphibians**	
		Siren lacertina	Greater siren
Sharks and rays		*Amphiuma means*	Two-toed amphiuma
Ginglymostoma cirratum	Nurse shark	*Rana catesbeiana*	Frog
Odontaspis taurus	Sand tiger shark		
Carcharhinus leucas	Bull shark	**Reptiles**	
Carcharhinus plumbeus	Sandbar shark	*Alligator mississippiensis*	Alligator
Galeocerdo cuvier	Tiger shark	*Chelydra serpentina*	Snapping turtle
Rhizoprionodon terraenovae	Sharpnose shark	*Macroclemys temmincki*	Alligator snapping turtle
Sphyrna mokorran	Great hammerhead shark	*Kinosternon* spp.	Mud turtle
Sphyrna tiburo	Bonnethead shark	*Sternotherus* spp.	Musk turtle
Sphyrna zygaena	Smooth hammerhead	*Chrysemys picta*	Painted turtle
Pristis pectinata	Smalltooth sawfish	*Deirochelys reticularia*	Chicken turtle
Dasyatis spp.	Stingray	*Graptemys* spp.	Map turtle
Aetobatis narinari	Spotted eagle ray	*Pseudemys* spp.	Cooter
Myliobatis spp.	Eagle ray	*Malaclemys terrapin*	Diamondback terrapin
Rhinoptera bonasus	Cownose ray	*Terrapene carolina*	Box turtle

Table V.D.5.3. *(continued)*

Scientific name	Common name	Scientific name	Common name
Trachemys spp.	Slider	*Strix varia*	Barred owl
Gopherus polyphemus	Gopher tortoise	Picidae	Woodpecker
Apalone spp.	Softshell turtle	Corvidae	Crow
Chelonidae	Sea turtle	Muscicapidae	Thrush
Colubridae	Nonpoisonous snake	Mimidae	Thrasher
Viperidae	Poisonous snake		
		Mammals	
Birds		*Didelphis virginiana*	Opossum
Gavia immer	Common loon	*Sylvilagus* spp.	Rabbit
Podilymbus podiceps	Pied-billed grebe	*Sciurus* spp.	Squirrel
Phalacrocorax auritus	Cormorant	*Tamias striatus*	Chipmunk
Ardea herodias	Great blue heron	*Marmota monax*	Woodchuck (groundhog)
Botaurus lentiginosus	American bittern	*Geomys* spp.	Pocket gopher
Casmerodius albus	Great egret	*Spermophilus* spp.	Ground squirrel
Egretta tricolor	Tricolored heron	*Ondatra zibethicus*	Muskrat
Aix sponsa	Wood duck	*Castor canadensis*	Beaver
Anas spp.	Dabbling duck	*Erethizon dorsatum*	Porcupine
Aythya spp.	Diving duck	*Tursiops truncatus*	Bottle-nosed dolphin
Branta canadensis	Canada goose	*Canis familiaris*	Dog
Chen caerulescens	Snow goose	*Canis latrens*	Coyote
Cygnus spp.	Swan	*Canis lupus*	Gray wolf
Lophodytes cucullatus	Hooded merganser	*Urocyon cineroargenteus*	Gray fox
Oxyura jamaicensis	Ruddy duck	*Ursus americanus*	Black bear
Mergus spp.	Merganser	*Ursus arctos*	Brown bear
Spatula clypeata	Shoveler	*Procyon lotor*	Raccoon
Coragyps atratus	Black vulture	*Lontra canadensis*	Otter
Buteo platypterus	Broad-winged hawk	*Mephitis mephitis*	Striped skunk
Colinus virginianus	Quail	*Mustela frenata*	Long-tailed weasel
Meleagris gallopavo	Wild turkey	*Mustela vision*	Mink
Rallus elegans	King rail	*Spilogale putorius*	Spotted skunk
Porzana carolina	Sora	*Taxidea taxus*	Badger
Fulica americana	Coot	*Felis rufus*	Bobcat
Grus canadensis	Sandhill crane	*Felis concolor*	Cougar
Charadrius vociferus	Killdeer	*Alces alces*	Moose
Catoptrophorus semipalmatus	Willet	*Cervus elaphus*	Elk or wapiti
Galinago gallinago	Common snipe	*Odocoileus virginianus*	White-tailed deer
Laridae	Gull	*Rangifer tarandus*	Caribou
Ectopistes migratorius	Passenger pigeon	*Bison bison*	Bison or buffalo
Zenaida macroura	Mourning dove		

Cultivation, Domestication, and Horticulture

Evidence of horticulture is lacking for some areas of the Eastern Woodlands, which may signify either that horticulture was not practiced everywhere or that plant use in some locations is still poorly studied. Likewise, evidence of a domesticated plant variety in one area does not mean that this variety was grown throughout the region at the same time or that it was grown universally at any time.

As Richard Ford (1985a) has observed, the paths from wild to domesticated plants and from foraging to farming were not direct. A continuum exists between the wild and domesticated states, and doubtless plants passed through stages when they were intentionally tended, tilled, transplanted, or sown, but were not fully domesticated (Ford 1985a). Domestication is difficult to demonstrate with archaeological materials unless a phenotypic change can be spied that corresponds with genetic changes reflecting human intervention. Changes in color, for example, are often associated with domestication in both plants and animals, but are not normally found in the archaeological record. "Cultivated" plants are found in the archaeological record – often in large numbers in some deposits – indicating that they were probably intentionally propagated. But morphological changes providing evidence of the domesticated state are not observed (Ford 1985a; Fritz 1990). Plants are considered "domesticated" when archaeological remains reveal those signs of phenotypic alteration that indicate that domestication did take place. A domesticated plant would not normally be found unassociated with humans and, in fact, they often cannot survive without human intervention.

In North America, both cultivated and domesticated plants were grown under horticultural rather than agricultural conditions. Entirely different energy inputs are required by these systems because agriculture involves domestic animals and horticulture does not (Kottak 1987: 269-71). Agricultural techniques must produce adequate calories not only for humans but also for a complex of domestic animals, whereas horticultural production only meets human nutritional needs.

Although domestic crops in the Eastern Woodlands were grown under horticultural conditions, this does not mean that farming was limited to temporary fields or small garden plots. Rather, plants were grown in many large fields (Riley 1987; Woods 1987) that were permanently maintained with digging sticks and hoes, classic horticultural implements, and not with the agricultural plow.

Because cultivation and domestication of plants is achieved gradually, it is unlikely that North American farmers completely abandoned the use of wild foods. Certainly this would have been the case in the Eastern Woodlands, where those proteins, fats, vitamins, and minerals derived from animals could only be obtained through foraging, trapping, hunting, and fishing.

The Eastern Woodlands

Most of temperate North America from the Gulf of Mexico and Atlantic seaboards westward beyond the Great Lakes region is characterized by extensive, mixed-deciduous forests (Map V.D.5.1). The northern boundary of the Eastern Woodlands is defined by a mean annual January temperature of -10° C and the western boundary by a line marking rainfall equal to 80 percent evaporation (Shelford 1974: 17). It is the southern half of the Eastern Woodlands that is most closely associated with the Mississippian tradition of the sixteenth century (Smith 1986). The northern border of the Southeastern Woodlands is around 38° north latitude, roughly corresponding with the farthest glacial advance, which occurred around 16,000 B.C.

Map V.D.5.1. The Eastern Woodlands.

(Shelford 1974: 19; Delcourt and Delcourt 1981). Winters are relatively short and the growing season long. Annual rainfall varies from 100 to 150 centimeters (cm) and is greatest in the spring and summer, especially along the coasts and in the mountains (Shelford 1974: 56). The Southeastern Woodlands are well watered, with numerous rivers, floodplains, marshes, swamps, and lakes. Systems, such as that associated with the Mississippi River, drain vast portions of the continent. There are many smaller drainage systems throughout the region, particularly along the Atlantic and Gulf coasts.

Climate and vegetation in the Southeast were dynamic in the late Pleistocene and early Holocene (King and Lindsay 1976; Wright 1976; Delcourt and Delcourt 1981, 1983). During the late Pleistocene, the northern portion of the continent was covered by glaciers. At the peak of continental glaciation, about 16,000 B.C., boreal forests of spruce, jack pine, fir, and some deciduous trees covered much of the unglaciated interior plateau, whereas deciduous oaks and hickories mixed with southern pines were found on the coastal plain (Delcourt and Delcourt 1981, 1983; Smith 1986). At the same time, Gulf and Atlantic sea levels were 60 to 130 meters lower than today, and so the coastal plain was considerably broader (Blackwelder, Pilkey, and Howard 1979).

Temperate conditions began to replace boreal ones about 12,000 B.C., and by roughly 8000 B.C., temperate deciduous vegetation dominated most of the region between 34° and 43° north latitude (Delcourt and Delcourt 1981, 1983). South of this area there had generally been little change in vegetation since about 18,000 B.C. About 7000 B.C. the postglacial trend of rising temperatures culminated in a warm, dry period known as the Hypsithermal Interval (Deevey and Flint 1957; Wright 1976). Temperatures began to cool again after about 5000 B.C., and by 3000 B.C., an essentially modern climate prevailed, with forests achieving distributions similar to those of the sixteenth century (Wright 1976; Delcourt and Delcourt 1981). Important additional events at this time were a rise in sea level (with modern sea levels reached about 3000 B.C.) and changes in regional hydrology (Wright 1976: 586; Delcourt et al. 1980; Brooks and Sassaman 1990).

Origins of Mississippian Foodways

Humans probably came to the Eastern Woodlands sometime between 40,000 and 15,000 years ago, first crossing from Asia to North America while the floor of the Bering Strait was exposed by low Pleistocene sea levels (Dincauze 1985; Steponaitis 1986). Prey species important to humans, such as brown bear, moose, elk, white-tailed deer, and bison, had made a similar crossing somewhat earlier (Kurtén and Anderson 1980: 410, 416–17). Caribou probably originated on Beringia itself (Kurtén and Anderson 1980: 315).

Late Pleistocene conditions are associated with what is known in human terms as the Paleo-Indian period (Table V.D.5.1; Smith 1986; Steponaitis 1986). Information about subsistence in the Eastern Woodlands during this time is limited. Most people probably lived in small hunting and gathering bands using an impermanent residential pattern to take advantage of seasonal fluctuations in resources. From the limited evidence available, the foods commonly consumed by Paleo-Indians appear to have included hackberry, blackberry–raspberry, blueberry, hickory, walnut, goosefoot, bivalves, gastropods, fish, turtle, wild turkey, rabbit, squirrel, elk, and white-tailed deer (Adovasio et al. 1978). Although a number of now-extinct Pleistocene animals, such as giant land tortoise, ground sloth, mastodon, mammoth, horse, and tapir, lived in the Eastern Woodlands at this time, few remains have been found in contexts that conclusively prove that extinct animals were hunted by Paleo-Indians (Bullen, Webb, and Waller 1970; Wood and McMillan 1976; Clausen et al. 1979; Graham et al. 1981; Dincauze 1985; Grayson 1991).

Modern geological, climatic, and biological conditions are associated with the Archaic period, which began about 8000 B.C. (Table V.D.5.1). The Early and Middle Archaic periods were characterized by the use of modern animal species by peoples who employed a combination of gathering, hunting, and fishing techniques (Neusius 1986). The *atlatl*, or spear thrower, was used in hunting, whereas netsinkers and fishhooks indicate that fishing was part of the subsistence strategy. Nets could also have been used to capture reptiles, birds, and mammals. Grinding stones suggest that some foods were ground or pulverized.

Evidence for plant use in the Early and Middle Archaic is limited (Byrd and Neuman 1978; Yarnell and Black 1985; Neusius 1986). Seeds of fleshy fruits, such as papaw, hackberry, persimmon, plum, wild black cherry, elderberry, and wild grape, are abundant relative to other seeds throughout the Archaic period. Although walnut and acorn were commonly used in the Archaic, hickory is the most abundant nut found in archaeological deposits (Yarnell and Black 1985). However, Richard Yarnell and Jean Black (1985: 97) argue that in terms of nut food consumed, acorns were the most important plant food in the Southeast until the Mississippian period, at which time they were replaced by maize. Their estimates of dietary contribution suggest that acorns contributed 75 percent of the nut food consumed, whereas hickory nut comprised 20 percent (Yarnell and Black 1985). American chestnut, hazelnut, and beechnut were used in small amounts. Seeds of plants used for greens, such as pokeweed and purslane, are relatively abundant in some Early and Middle Archaic deposits (Yarnell and Black 1985). Some of the starchy-seed plants that later became important as cultivated and domesticated plants, such as goosefoot, may have been used for their leaves rather than for seeds during much of the Archaic period. This would account for their low numbers in Early and Middle Archaic deposits (Bye 1981; Yarnell and Black 1985).

The Late Archaic period is characterized by signs of demographic growth and sedentism in many parts of the Southeast (Steponaitis 1986). Large Late Archaic shell middens are characteristically found along streams and estuaries. There is evidence that residences in some aquatic and estuarine settings may have been multiseasonal, if not year-round (Reitz 1988). Elsewhere, dense midden deposits suggest increased and/or long-term use of specific locations. Large middens, as well as storage pits, indicate a higher degree of sedentism than earlier, although it has been suggested that subterranean storage facilities may indicate concealment of storable foods during periods when villages were abandoned (DeBoer 1988).

Cooking techniques such as stone boiling in baskets and stone bowls had probably been utilized throughout the Archaic period, but clay vessels reflect widespread adoption of food-preparation methods requiring containers that could be placed directly in or over fires and left to simmer unattended for long periods of time. Late Archaic fiber-tempered ceramics from the southeastern Atlantic coast are among the earliest known in the hemisphere (Smith 1986; Steponaitis 1986).

The Late Archaic is marked by changes in the use of plant resources. Nuts continued to be relied upon extensively, but starchy and oily seed use increased (Yarnell and Black 1985; Fritz 1990). Seeds found in large numbers in Late Archaic deposits include ragweed, goosefoot, wild beans, hog peanut, maygrass, and erect knotweed. The relative abundance of seeds from plants used for greens but not for seeds, such as pokeweed and purslane, declined from earlier Archaic levels and remained low until the Mississippian period (Yarnell and Black 1985). Yarnell and Black interpret this as evidence that starchy seeds contributing both greens and seeds, such as goosefoot, may have replaced plants that provided only greens, such as pokeweed and purslane (Yarnell and Black 1985). Seeds from such fruits as hackberry, persimmon, plum, blackberry-raspberry, elderberry, blackhaw, and wild grape are commonly identified in Late Archaic deposits, although the degree to which specific fruits and berries were used varied regionally (Kay, King, and Robinson 1980; Johannessen 1984; Watson 1985). Remains of American lotus at some sites indicate use of aquatic plants.

The Late Archaic is characterized by evidence for plant cultivation and domestication in some midlatitude, interior locations (Asch and Asch 1985; Cowan 1985; King 1985; Watson 1985, 1989; Smith 1989; Fritz 1990). Maygrass was probably a cultivated plant by 2000 B.C. (Cowan 1978; Yarnell and Black 1985). Domestication is first clearly demonstrated for the Eastern Woodlands with the identification of domestic chenopod, sunflower, and sumpweed at some Late

Archaic sites (Yarnell 1969, 1972, 1978; Marquardt 1974; Asch and Asch 1978; Conard et al. 1984; Heiser 1985; Smith 1985b, 1989; Yarnell and Black 1985; Fritz 1990). Important indigenous cultivated and domesticated plants suggest that the development of horticultural traditions in the Eastern Woodlands was not dependent upon introductions from tropical America (Yarnell and Black 1985). The increase in cultivated and domesticated plants is associated with an increase in pollen of species commonly found in disturbed habitats, such as garden plots (Delcourt 1987).

Occasional identifications of gourd-squash indicate the presence of this plant after 5000 B.C. at a few eastern locations, although its status is currently being debated (Ford 1981; Conard et al. 1984; Asch and Asch 1985; King 1985; Decker 1988; Decker and Newsom 1988; Watson 1989; Fritz 1990; Decker-Walters 1993). There is, however, growing evidence for domestication of some varieties of gourd-squash in the Late Archaic Eastern Woodlands (Kay et al. 1980; Ford 1981; Conard et al. 1984; King 1985; Yarnell and Black 1985; Smith 1987b, 1989; Decker 1988; Fritz 1990). Recent work suggests that a native wild plant closely related to the gourd-squash, the Texas wild gourd, was present in North America and might have been the source of domestic gourd-squash found in the Eastern Woodlands (Decker 1988; Smith 1989; Fritz 1990; Decker-Walters 1993). Gourd-squash includes acorn squash, scallop squash, fordhook, crookneck, and most of the ornamental gourds (King 1985), although the gourd-squash found in deposits about 2000 B.C. were probably woody varieties used for containers and oily seeds, rather than the fleshy vegetable found in the sixteenth century (Yarnell and Black 1985; King 1985).

The origin of bottle gourd is also in doubt (Heiser 1989; Smith 1989; Fritz 1990). Very small seeds and thin-walled fragments of bottle gourds found at two Eastern Woodlands deposits, dated between 5350 and 2300 B.C., suggest that they may have been used very early. Remains of bottle gourds that were clearly domesticated are found in contexts that date from around 1300 B.C. or a little before (Smith 1985b; Yarnell and Black 1985; Fritz 1990; Yarnell 1993). It is probable that the recovery of bottle gourd remains from contexts with early dates indicates that this plant reached the Eastern Woodlands serendipitously (Heiser 1989; Fritz 1990), perhaps by floating to the eastern seaboard from tropical America or Africa (Smith 1985b, 1989; Yarnell and Black 1985; Heiser 1989; Fritz 1990). It seems likely that bottle gourds were valued as containers, rather than as food (King 1985).

Although plant use was highly dynamic at the end of the Archaic period, use of animal resources seems to have remained stable at those few locations for which stratigraphic sequences are available. Archaic peoples consumed a broad range of animals, which suggests subsistence strategies making use of the most efficient resources available in a particular setting. In general, animal remains indicate strategies that combined white-tailed deer and a wide range of other species. Other taxa included bivalves and gastropods, gar, bowfin, sucker, catfish, sunfish, freshwater drum, snapping turtle, mud–musk turtle, box turtle, pond turtle, softshell turtle, snakes, opossum, rabbit, squirrel, woodchuck, pocket gopher, muskrat, beaver, black bear, raccoon, badger, and elk (Curren 1974; Stoltman 1974; Parmalee, McMillan, and King 1976; Neusius 1986). In some areas, migratory waterfowl were taken in season, but usually birds other than quail, wild turkey, and passenger pigeon were not a major part of Archaic diets. In coastal settings, this list becomes even more complex, with estuarine mollusks and fishes dominating the diet, whereas mammals, including white-tailed deer, were rarely consumed (Reitz 1988).

The Archaic is followed by the Woodland period, which began about 700 B.C. (Table V.D.5.1). In the Eastern Woodlands, extensive earthworks were constructed during this period; some of these assumed large geometric patterns, although many were conical earthen burial mounds. There were numerous villages of various sizes, of which some were occupied throughout the year. Villages were particularly common at coastal and aquatic settings, from which a complex of wetland, aquatic, and estuarine resources were used. Evidence for regional variation in diets is much stronger for the Woodland period than for the Archaic period, perhaps because more data are available.

During the Woodland period, there was an increase in the cultivation of starchy and oily seed crops and a corresponding decrease in reliance on nuts, although hickory and acorn continued to be important resources (Yarnell and Black 1985). Pawpaw, persimmon, wild strawberry, honey locust, maypop, plum, sumac, blueberry, wild grape, wild beans, and American lotus were also used (Watson 1969: 53; Munson, Parmalee, and Yarnell 1971; Byrd and Neuman 1978; Johannessen 1984; Yarnell and Black 1985; Gardner 1987). Seeds from greens are recovered from archaeological sites in low numbers, and remains of starchy seeds are notably more abundant in Woodland deposits than in Archaic ones (Yarnell and Black 1985).

The energy base for increased sedentism and mound construction in the interior upland areas of the Eastern Woodlands probably came from cultivated and domesticated plants (Yarnell and Black 1985; Fritz 1993). Little barley, maygrass, and erect knotweed were probably cultivated at this time, joining chenopod, sunflower, and sumpweed that had been domesticated in the Late Archaic (Ford 1981; Smith 1985b; Yarnell and Black 1985; Steponaitis 1986). This group of indigenous cultivated and domesticated grains comprises what is known as a starchy seed complex. Little barley and maygrass were summer-maturing starchy seeds, whereas erect knotweed and chenopod

were fall-maturing seeds (Smith 1985a), as were the oily seeds of sunflower and sumpweed. Yarnell (1993) estimates that at one site, starchy and oily seeds contributed as much as 76 percent of the plant foods in the diet, and starchy seeds may comprise as much as 90 percent of the seeds recovered from a Middle Woodland deposit (Yarnell and Black 1985). Domestic gourd–squash and bottle gourd were grown along with food crops in small gardens (Smith 1985b; Yarnell and Black 1985).

Maize is the only domesticated food plant of clearly tropical origin found in Middle Woodland deposits (Fritz 1990). It was introduced to the Eastern Woodlands from Mesoamerica sometime around A.D. 200 (Conard et al. 1984; Chapman and Crites 1987), although isotopic and other studies of human skeletal systems do not show that it was more than a minor component in the diet until many centuries later (Merwe and Vogel 1978; Bender, Baerreis, and Steventon 1981; Boutton et al. 1984; Ambrose 1987). A domesticated tropical pumpkin–marrow variety was introduced from Mesoamerica at the very end of the Woodland period, probably about A.D. 1000 (Smith 1989).

The increase in horticultural activities during the Woodland period is reflected in wood-charcoal and pollen studies in several locations. Late Archaic wood-charcoal assemblages at several sites are dominated by plants associated with floodplains, but in Middle Woodland samples, floodplain species drop to 10 percent of the wood spectrum (Johannessen 1984; Fritz 1990). Trees associated with disturbed habitats, such as pine, red cedar, tulip tree, and giant cane, increase during this same period (Fritz 1993). This evidence indicates that stream-terrace vegetation was cleared for planting (Chapman et al. 1982; Delcourt 1987; Smith 1987a; Fritz 1990). Many of the plant species used in the Eastern Woodlands also thrive in open or disturbed habitats, demonstrating this preference by living as commensal plants around human habitations (Yarnell 1982; Gremillion 1989).

Not all of these plants were grown throughout the Eastern Woodlands, although there is evidence for a Late Archaic–Woodland tradition that featured small starchy seeds in some portions of the region (Smith 1985a; Fritz 1993). One of the intriguing problems is that the starchy seed complex appears to have been of minor importance on the coastal plain. This may be because appropriate recovery techniques have not been used at archaeological sites below the fall line, or it might indicate that an entirely different complex of resources supported communities on the coastal plain and in the lower Mississippi River valley.

Evidence for Woodland animal use is much more abundant than for the Archaic period. It suggests, however, continuity rather than discontinuity in the animals harvested (Munson et al. 1971; Parmalee, Paloumpis, and Wilson 1972; Byrd and Neuman 1978; Springer 1980; Styles 1981; Kelly and Cross 1984;

Reitz, Marrinan, and Scott 1987; Reitz 1988; Reitz and Quitmyer 1988; Styles and Purdue 1991). This is surprising for two reasons. Sometime in the Woodland period, bows and arrows began to be used to hunt animals, augmenting the earlier spears. Additionally, the increased use of cultivated and domesticated plants might have called for an alteration of the strategies used to capture animals due to schedule conflicts or different opportunities to capture garden-raiding species. With more data we may find that subtle, site-specific changes did occur, but at present it would appear that there were no dramatic changes. All of the animals listed in Table V.D.5.3 have been found in most Woodland samples. The Archaic tradition of combining white-tailed deer with many other species continued into the Woodland period. Often those other species were aquatic or estuarine animals, which sometimes were used more frequently than land mammals, including white-tailed deer (Styles 1981; Reitz 1988; Reitz and Quitmyer 1988).

Mississippian Cuisine

Mississippian societies were among the most complex north of Mexico (Table V.D.5.1). The area associated with the Mississippian tradition includes most, although not all, of the Southeastern Woodlands (Smith 1986). It was densely populated in the sixteenth century by farmers who lived in villages organized into complex, hierarchical chiefdoms. The chief was a governing figure who inherited the role (Steponaitis 1986; Welch 1991). Many Mississippian communities had at least one flat-topped pyramidal earthen mound, and some of the larger towns had smaller subsidiary villages affiliated with them.

Chiefs who commanded large numbers of warriors collected tribute from vassal communities. This often took the form of goods, such as ceramic or copper objects, but it included maize, shell beads, bear canines, and deer hides as well (Welch 1991). Mississippian societies were not found universally throughout the Eastern Woodlands, but they had become widespread in the region after A.D. 1000, and in the sixteenth century, it was this lifestyle that was most frequently encountered by European explorers of the Southeast.

Mississippian cuisine included three types of resources: wild plants, wild animals, and cultivated and/or domesticated crops. A representative but incomplete list of some food resources and their scientific names is presented in Tables V.D.5.2 and V.D.5.3.

Wild Plants

Wild fruits, berries, and nuts were widely used in the Southeast (Medsger 1976; Byrd and Neuman 1978; Yarnell and Black 1985). Perhaps the most widely used fruit was persimmon, but many fruits and berries were included in Mississippian diets. In the sixteenth century, Old World watermelons, figs, and

peaches were added to the list. These fruits achieved such rapid acceptance by Native Americans that they preceded European explorers, who often thought them to be indigenous (Hudson 1976: 295). Such nuts as hickory, pecan, black walnut, and a wide variety of acorns were also frequent components of Mississippian meals.

Wild plants added a variety of greens, roots, tubers, and grains to the Mississippian diet. Large cane, wild beans, and vetch were often eaten by Mississippian peoples, depending on availability. Unfortunately, archaeological evidence for greens is limited unless seeds accompanied the leaves to be eaten, as in the case of ragweed. In addition, jewelweed, peppergrass, pokeweed, and purslane provided greens. Many of these plants are now considered weeds and are often found around human habitations, whereas others are abundant in low-lying damp locations, such as river valleys (Medsger 1976). Fungi may have been consumed, but little archaeological evidence survives for their use (Swanton 1946: 244).

Roots and tubers were an important wild resource for Mississippian peoples, although archaeological evidence is extremely rare due to preservation biases. From ethnographic evidence we know that sweet flag, wild onion, wild garlic, hog peanut, groundnut, wild hyacinth, toothwort, Jerusalem artichoke, wild sweet potato, Indian cucumber, greenbrier, and coontie were all used. Many of these plants are found in swamps, on marshy ground, and along lakes and streams (Medsger 1976). Some of the tubers and roots used are actually found in water, including American lotus, golden club, arrow arum, arrowhead, bulrush, and cattail.

Some plants provided condiments, beverages, and oil. Honey locust, maypop, sumac, maple, spicebush, sweet gum, and sweet bay were made into sweeteners and beverages (Hudson 1976: 309; Medsger 1976). Sassafras was used not only as a drink but also to thicken soups (Hudson 1976: 309). One of the most remarked upon drinks was cassina, made from yaupon holly. Yaupon could be made into a simple caffeinated beverage or into "black drink." Black drink had an emetic effect and was important in rituals on the coastal plain (Medsger 1976: 215-16; Hudson 1979; Welch 1991: 113-14). Plants, particularly the nuts, provided oil. Salt was obtained from salt licks as well as through trade with coastal peoples (Swanton 1946: 242, 268, 300-4; Hudson 1976: 316; Muller 1984), and some plants offered salt substitutes (Swanton 1946: 270, 303).

Wild Animals

Although many nutrients associated with plants could be obtained from either wild or cultivated-domesticated plants, sources of meat and animal-derived proteins, fats, minerals, and vitamins were almost entirely wild, with the possible exception of the dog, which may have been consumed in some locations (Hudson

1976: 289-90). Animals may be roughly divided into forest and aquatic–estuarine categories. In some respects this division is an artificial one because many animals that do not actually live in water are found in close proximity to it.

A wide range of forest animals were consumed by Mississippian peoples (Reitz 1982; Kelly and Cross 1984; Reitz et al. 1987; Carder 1989). Land resources often overlooked in discussions of Mississippian diets include box turtle, gopher tortoise, and snake. Quail, wild turkey, passenger pigeon, mourning dove, and a variety of small song birds were also sometimes included in Mississippian diets. Likewise, such mammals as opossum, rabbit, squirrel, woodchuck, black bear, raccoon, elk, and white-tailed deer were widely consumed.

Many Mississippian sites are found on river floodplains and bottomlands, and so it is not surprising that numerous aquatic animals were used by Mississippian peoples (Springer 1980; Hale 1984; Carder 1989). Where freshwater bivalves and gastropods were eaten, they accumulated into very large middens. However, the nutritional contribution of mollusks is uncertain (Parmalee and Klippel 1974).

Remains of fish are abundant in many deposits. In freshwater settings, fish may include gar, bowfin, sucker, catfish, pike, sunfish, and drum. Amphibians are not frequently found in Mississippian deposits, but sirens, amphiuma, and frogs were clearly eaten in some communities. A wide range of reptiles, including alligator, snapping turtle, mud turtle, musk turtle, map turtle, cooter, slider, softshell turtle, and snakes, were used. Wetland birds were used in large numbers only at sites located along important migration routes. At such sites heron, duck, and geese were consumed. In addition to these resources, such aquatic mammals as muskrat, beaver, and otter were eaten.

Coastal sites with access to estuarine settings form a special case. Archaeological evidence for use of a wide range of animal resources is abundant. This array includes crustacea, bivalves, gastropods, sharks, rays, and bony fish. Turtles were commonly consumed, particularly those found only in estuarine settings, such as diamondback terrapin. Evidence for use of sea turtle meat or eggs is very limited, as is evidence for widespread use of birds and land mammals. Remains of white-tailed deer, for example, are often nonexistent at coastal Mississippian sites (Reitz 1985, 1988; Reitz and Quitmyer 1988). Mammals restricted to marine settings, such as dolphins and manatees, were occasionally eaten, but at most villages they were probably not commonly used.

Cultivated and Domesticated Crops

Farming was a key Mississippian subsistence activity. Cultivated crops included little barley, maygrass, and erect knotweed, whereas domesticated ones included chenopod, gourd–squash, sunflower, sumpweed, and bottle gourd (Yarnell and Black 1985;

Steponaitis 1986; Fritz 1990). All were indigenous to the Eastern Woodlands, and in some communities starchy seeds contributed an average of 78 percent of the total identifiable seeds (Johannessen 1984). Although none of these plants individually constituted a complete protein source, their nutritional value was quite high and, when combined with other plants, would have provided a complete protein (Asch and Asch 1978; Cowan 1978; Crites and Terry 1984; King 1985). Maygrass is higher in protein than the other starchy seeds and is similar in protein density to fish (Crites and Terry 1984), although like all plants, it is inadequate in at least one essential amino acid (Asch and Asch 1978; Crites and Terry 1984). Sumpweed and sunflower seeds have a high oil content, with sunflower seeds yielding 20 percent oil (Medsger 1976). Chenopod, little barley, maygrass, and erect knotweed are high in carbohydrates (Crites and Terry 1984).

The domestic plants considered most characteristic of Mississippian diets, however, were introduced from tropical America. These included pale-seeded amaranth, pumpkin–marrow, the common bean, and maize (Fritz 1984; Yarnell and Black 1985). Tropical plants were introduced to the Eastern Woodlands just prior to or during the Early Mississippian period, but as already mentioned, maize was a minor crop throughout the Southeast for several centuries and only became important in most areas sometime between A.D. 800 and 1100 (Fritz 1990). At some sixteenth-century Mississippian sites, maize was clearly the most significant domesticated plant and had already become far more important than indigenous cultivated or domesticated plants. But at other sites, starchy seeds continued to be more abundant than maize (Scarry 1993a). The tropical common bean may have been added to the Mississippian diet as late as the 1400s (Fritz 1990).

Very little is known about either wild or domestic plant use by Mississippian peoples living in coastal settings. Although there have been lengthy discussions about the role of maize in coastal Mississippian economies, there has been little archaeological evidence of its importance (Yarnell and Black 1985; Reitz 1988, 1990).

Food Procurement Technology

The combination of wild fruits, nuts, tubers, seeds, and animals with maize and other crops provided a solid subsistence base characteristic of the Mississippian period. Such a base could have been exploited in a number of different ways to produce a surplus for storage and exchange. Many cultivated and domesticated crops were grown together in large, permanent fields, as well as in smaller gardens on river terraces (Swanton 1946: 304-10; Hudson 1976: 290-1; Smith 1985b; Riley 1987; Woods 1987).

Mississippian peoples living near large population centers appear not to have engaged in slash-and-burn or swidden cultivation, although people living in smaller communities may have done so. In some places, raised fields were constructed to improve drainage (Riley 1987; Woods 1987). The primary horticultural implements used were stone and bone hoes, stone axes, and digging sticks. Horticultural activities were largely the domain of women, although men participated in the initial clearing of the fields (Hudson 1976: 295).

Numerous techniques were used to acquire wild resources (Swanton 1946: 265–304, 310–44; Hudson 1976: 272–88), with many of these so sufficiently generalized that they could be applied to the acquisition of more than one resource. Wild berries, nuts, seeds, and tubers were gathered with the aid of beaters, skin bags, baskets, and digging sticks. Similar techniques and tools could have been used to collect most of the mollusks. Fish may have been captured using trotlines, gorges, spears, nets, weirs, and traps, and there is some evidence for the use of fish poisons (Swanton 1946: 246–7, 332–44; Rostlund 1952: 127–33). The latter are most effective in quiet waters, and many of the fish found in Mississippian sites are common in calm aquatic locations.

Fish were also caught with handlines or speared (Rostlund 1952: 113–26), and trotlines and traps would have been ideal for capturing aquatic turtles and mammals. Sirens, frogs, and snakes might also have been caught with such devices, and traps of various kinds, decoys, and snares would also have been useful for capturing most land animals (Swanton 1946: 328–32). Indeed, although larger animals, such as elk and white-tailed deer, could be hunted using spears, clubs, blowguns, and bows and arrows, traps and snares would have been considerably more efficient.

A particularly useful hunting strategy would have involved the careful visiting of gardens and fields each morning and evening in order to surprise garden-raiding animals (Linares 1976). Many of the birds and mammals commonly consumed by Mississippian peoples are attracted to crops, so that traps set in or near fields should have been productive. Hunting at night with torches would also have been effective, and communal surround drives were employed in some areas in the Southeast (Swanton 1946: 313; Hudson 1976: 275–6). Mississippian peoples may have burned forest underbrush in order to improve the growth of vegetation preferred by white-tailed deer. At the same time, this would have made more abundant the nuts and other plants that prefer open habitat (Yarnell 1982).

Foods were prepared in a number of ways (Swanton 1946: 351–72; Hudson 1976: 300). In addition to being consumed fresh, fruits, nuts, seeds, greens, roots, tubers, and meats were preserved by drying either through simple exposure to sun and air or by smoking. Mortar and pestle were employed to pulverize or grind foods to ready them for preservation, as

well as for immediate consumption (Hudson 1976: 301, 307).

Maize was consumed in many forms. In addition to use as a vegetable (such as roasted "corn-on-the-cob"), it was treated with wood-ash lye and made into hominy. The lye treatment increases the amounts of the amino acid lysine and of the vitamin niacin available from maize (Katz, Hediger, and Valleroy 1974). From hominy, a number of maize dishes were made (Hudson 1976: 305). Hominy might be eaten whole or ground into flour for breads that were fried, boiled, or baked. In addition, maize was often combined with other foods, such as nuts and beans. Combinations of beans and maize were particularly common and are nutritionally interesting because each plant complements the limiting amino acids in the other, so that together they provide a complete protein source (Katz, Hediger, and Valleroy 1974).

Elsewhere in North America

Not all of the peoples living in North America in the sixteenth century were farmers. Two of the most distinct examples of nonhorticultural foodways were to be found on the Northwest Coast and in the Arctic. Although both of these areas had early contact with Europeans, it is probably significant that this contact was largely intermittent and did not lead to permanent sixteenth-century European settlements, such as those that developed on the Atlantic coast.

The Northwest Coast is a long, narrow area stretching along the Pacific coast of North America from, roughly, 60° to 42° north latitude. It has a relatively mild climate but a rugged topography and a temperate rain forest that is broken at frequent intervals by streams used by anadromous fish, especially members of the salmon family. The area is well known for its large sedentary villages, elaborate woodworking skills, and complex social organization supported without horticultural input (Stewart 1977; Isaac 1988; Suttles 1990b).

In large part, the reason for the lack of horticulture was a well-developed marine fishery, especially one associated with the vast, but highly seasonal, salmon runs into coastal rivers. Salmon, surf perch, rockfish, greenling, lingcod, sculpin, red Irish lord, and many other fish were the source of most of the meat in the diet (Mitchell 1988; Wessen 1988; Wigen and Stucki 1988; Suttles 1990b). But whales, porpoises, harbor and fur seals, sea lions, and sea otters were also consumed. Many of these mammals were high in fat, and a smelt, known as eulachon, provided an edible oil. Mussels and clams were taken from the marine environment, as was a wide range of ducks and other birds.

Freshwater fish and mammals, such as beaver and otter, were frequently eaten, although gastropods and bivalves were apparently seldom used in most areas. Land mammals, such as bear, raccoon, elk, deer, and caribou, were consumed, but not as commonly as marine resources. Inasmuch as many of these animals were only abundant seasonally, preservation techniques, including drying and smoking and the liberal use of oil as a preservative, were well developed.

Such an elaborate marine fishery has often obscured the fact that plants gathered but not cultivated played an important role in the diet (Spencer and Jennings 1965; Suttles 1990a). Many species of fruits and berries were consumed, including salmonberry, gooseberry, currant, red elderberry, huckleberry, salal, and cranberry (Suttles 1990a). These were dried and combined with oil and fish to form pemmican. Rhizomes, such as bracken, sword fern, lady fern, spiny wood fern, male fern, and licorice fern, were consumed, and rice-root lily, chocolate lily, camas, tiger lily, wild onion, fawn lily, wild hyacinth, and a tuber known as wapato were also eaten. Several marine algae were part of the diet, as was the edible cambium of spruce, pine, hemlock, alder, and cottonwood bark; tree lichen; and, in some locations, mushrooms (Suttles 1990a). Nuts were also consumed, but seeds were not widely used (Suttles 1990a).

In sharp contrast to the foodways of the Northwest Coast and the Eastern Woodlands were the Arctic hunting traditions developed in the far north of the continent by Eskimos, or Inuits (Damas 1984b). The southern boundary of the Arctic roughly corresponds with the tree line, where the boreal forest ends and the northern treeless region, or tundra, begins. This also marks the distribution of prey species significant in the hunting strategies practiced in the Arctic region (Damas 1984a: 1).

Both plant and animal resources have been limited in the Arctic, and prior to the sixteenth century, most peoples there specialized in a maritime strategy that focused on whales, walrus, and seals. But many also hunted hares, ground squirrels, and especially caribou, along with the flesh and the eggs of ducks, geese, sea birds, and ptarmigans. Fishing and mollusk gathering were also important activities. Since many of these resources were highly mobile, as well as markedly seasonal, Arctic peoples adapted their settlement patterns to correspond with the seasonal cycle of animals important to their diets. This unique inventory of animals was hunted with a highly complex technology (Balikci 1984).

Until recently, the Arctic diet was distinctive for its low content of plant resources, which meant little in the way of carbohydrates. In the absence of plant carbohydrates, humans can utilize protein only in the presence of fat; and an important characteristic of many of the animals consumed in the Arctic region was their high fat content (Freeman 1984: 45). Nonetheless, several plant foods were consumed in season. These included salmonberry, cranberry, crowberry, blueberry, cow parsnip, a lily bulb, licorice root, willow leaves, sourdock, cowslip, anemone greens,

parsnip, and kelp and other algae (Lantis 1984: 176; Ray 1984: 289).

Native Foodways and European Colonies

The first Europeans to maintain a permanent presence in temperate North America were the Spaniards. The Spanish colony of La Florida, which encompassed a portion of the Atlantic coastal plain and the Florida peninsula, was established in 1565 and lasted for 200 years. Unfortunately, very little archival evidence is available for Spanish diets in the Southeast during the sixteenth century. We do know that supply lines to La Florida were unsatisfactory and subject to interruptions. Natural disasters and attacks by a variety of human foes contributed to the unreliability of imported staples, munitions, and other supplies. Disease and other natural disasters further hampered efforts to develop the colony. In the records that are available, Spanish governors complained bitterly of starvation and of eating unwholesome foods. If we are to believe the official correspondence, sixteenth-century St. Augustinians, at the least, had very little to eat, and sometimes subsisted on extremely unpalatable foods, or even nonfoods.

Data on plant and animal use recovered from archaeological sites in Florida indicate, however, that complaints of food shortages in the colony were probably exaggerated (Reitz and Scarry 1985). This is not to deny that food might have been scarce occasionally. But there is nothing in the archaeological record to suggest that starvation of the sort reported by some Spanish governors was a common phenomenon or that inedible, nonnutritious resources were consumed often enough to become noteworthy.

Rather, what we have is evidence that the colonists adapted to North American conditions and blended their own foodways with native North American dietary traditions (Reitz and Scarry 1985). During the first few years of colonization, the plant and animal foods consumed by Spaniards and Native Americans were very similar (Reitz 1985; Scarry and Reitz 1990).

Domesticated and wild plants employed by indigenous Native Americans dominated the list of plants consumed by Spaniards in the sixteenth century (Reitz and Scarry 1985; Scarry and Reitz 1990). Squash, sunflower, beans, and maize comprised about half of the vegetable part of the diet, with nuts and wild fruits making up an additional third. The primary Old World domesticated crops in the diet were watermelon, melon, and peach (Reitz and Scarry 1985: 56). Efforts to grow wheat were generally unsuccessful. It is interesting to note that indigenous New World domesticated crops, such as chilli peppers, moschata squash, and lima beans, previously unknown in La Florida, were apparently imported from Mesoamerica by the Spaniards.

Sea and land animals used by Spaniards in the sixteenth century were mostly wild (Reitz and Scarry

1985; Scarry and Reitz 1990). Over a third of their meat came from sharks, rays, and bony fishes, with the most common the hardhead and gafftopsail catfish, sheepshead, Atlantic croaker, black drum, red drum, and mullet. A wide range of reptiles, including sea turtles, entered the diet, but predominating were the estuarine diamondback terrapin and freshwater turtles, such as the cooter and slider. Ducks, Canada geese, and turkeys were the most important of the wild birds that were harvested. Although opossum, rabbit, squirrel, and raccoon found their way to Spanish tables, deer and gopher tortoise were generally the most prevalent wild land animals. Domestic animals contributed less than half of the meat consumed by Spaniards: Beef was probably more common in the diet than either pork or chicken (the only domesticated bird); sheep and goats were very rare.

Archaeological data indicate that the Spaniards combined Eurasian and American foods into a locally viable cuisine, but like the Native Americans, Spaniards were heavily dependent upon indigenous crops and wild animals. To this complex of local resources they brought some Eurasian plants and animals that could do well on the coastal plain. In terms of animal resources, this strategy continued with little modification until the end of Spanish governance in the eighteenth century (Reitz and Cumbaa 1983).

Conclusion

A study of native North American subsistence strategies is important for the contribution it can make to our knowledge of foodways in temperate environments and for an understanding of the importance that such strategies had for European colonists. A survey of food and drink in North America shows that Native Americans employed the resources available to them in complex and specialized ways. The foodways of the Eastern Woodlands combined a wide range of wild, cultivated, and domesticated plants and many different wild animals into a mixed subsistence strategy. The resources used were primarily low-cost, calorically productive ones acquired from nearby fields, forests, and waterways. The archaeological record of the Eastern Woodlands suggests that patterns established in the Archaic continued with subtle modifications into the Mississippian period and even into the early years of European expansion. Over time, however, subsistence strategies came to include an increasingly diverse complex of crops and wild resources. The most significant changes that took place in foodways in the Eastern Woodlands were the development of indigenous cultivated and domesticated crops and the eventual addition of tropical cultigens to local farming traditions. These changes resulted in a cuisine that supported large numbers of people with complex political and economic systems.

The native foodways of the Eastern Woodlands had a profound impact on sixteenth-century Spanish colonists, who benefited from the well-established mixed economy practiced in the region. They altered indigenous practices primarily through the introduction of domestic animals and by adding a few of their plants to augment a diet based on American crops. Not only did this interchange enable European colonial efforts to succeed but it also ensured that many of the foods and drinks used by native North Americans would survive to be included in North American and global foodways in the twentieth century.

Elizabeth J. Reitz

I am grateful to Gayle J. Fritz, David R. Huelsbeck, and C. Margaret Scarry for their assistance in the preparation of this chapter. I am particularly pleased that Dr. Scarry was willing to share with me the text of the book she was editing while it was still in manuscript form. Errors in interpretation, however, are my own.

Bibliography

Adovasio, J. M., J. D. Gunn, J. Donahue, and R. Stuckenrath. 1978. Meadowcroft rockshelter, 1977: An overview. _American Antiquity_ 43: 632-51.

Ambrose, Stanley H. 1987. Chemical and isotopic techniques of diet reconstruction in eastern North America. In _Emergent horticultural economies of the Eastern Woodlands,_ ed. W. Keegan, Southern Illinois University, Center for Archaeological Investigations, Occasional Papers No. 7, 87-107. Carbondale.

Asch, David L., and Nancy B. Asch. 1978. The economic potential of _Iva annua_ and its prehistoric importance in the lower Illinois Valley. In _The nature and status of ethnobotany,_ ed. R. I. Ford, University of Michigan, Museum of Anthropology, Anthropological Papers No. 67, 300-41. Ann Arbor, Mich.

1985. Prehistoric plant cultivation in west-central Illinois. In _Prehistoric food production in North America,_ ed. R. I. Ford, University of Michigan, Museum of Anthropology, Anthropological Papers No. 75, 149-203. Ann Arbor, Mich.

Balikci, Asen. 1984. Netsilik. In _Handbook of North American Indians: Arctic,_ Vol. 5, ed. D. Damas, 415-30. Washington, D.C.

Bender, Margaret M., D. A. Baerreis, and R. L. Steventon. 1981. Further light on carbon isotopes and Hopewell agriculture. _American Antiquity_ 46: 346-53.

Blackwelder, Blake W., Orrin H. Pilkey, and James D. Howard. 1979. Late Wisconsinan sea levels on the southeast U.S. Atlantic shelf based on in-place shoreline indicators. _Science_ 204: 618-20.

Boutton, T. W., P. D. Klein, M. J. Lynott, et al. 1984. Stable carbon isotope ratios as indicators of prehistoric human diet. In _Stable isotopes in nutrition,_ ed. J. R. Turnland and P. E. Johnson, _American Chemical Society Symposium Series_ No. 258, 191-204.

Boyd, Donna C., and C. Clifford Boyd. 1989. A comparison of Tennessee Archaic and Mississippian maximum femoral lengths and midshaft diameters: Subsistence change and postcranial variability. _Southeastern Archaeology_ 8: 107-16.

Bridges, Patricia. 1989. Changes in activities with the shift in agriculture in the southeastern United States. _Current Anthropology_ 30: 385-94.

Brooks, Mark J., and Kenneth E. Sassaman. 1990. Point bar geoarchaeology in the upper coastal plain of the Savannah River Valley, South Carolina: A case study. In *Archaeological geology of North America,* ed. N. P. Lasca and J. Donahue, Geological Society of America Centennial Special Vol. 4, 183-97. Boulder, Colo.

Buikstra, Jane E., J. Bullington, D. K. Charles, et al. 1987. Diet, demography, and the development of horticulture. In *Emergent horticultural economies of the Eastern Woodlands,* ed. W. Keegan, Southern Illinois University, Center for Archaeological Investigations, Occasional Papers No. 7, 67-85. Carbondale.

Bullen, Ripley P., S. D. Webb, and B. I. Waller. 1970. A worked mammoth bone from Florida. *American Antiquity* 35: 203-5.

Bye, Robert A., Jr. 1981. Quelites - ethnoecology of edible greens - past, present, and future. *Journal of Ethnobiology* 1: 109-23.

Byrd, Kathleen M., and Robert W. Neuman. 1978. Archaeological data relative to prehistoric subsistence in the lower Mississippi River alluvial valley. *Geoscience and Man* 19: 9-21.

Carder, Nanny. 1989. Faunal remains from Mixon's Hammock, Okefenokee Swamp. *Southeastern Archaeology* 8: 19-30.

Chapman, Jefferson, and Gary Crites. 1987. Evidence for early maize *(Zea mays)* from the Icehouse Bottom site, Tennessee. *American Antiquity* 52: 352-4.

Chapman, Jefferson, Paul A. Delcourt, Patricia A. Cridlebaugh, et al. 1982. Man-land interaction: 10,000 years of American Indian impact on native ecosystems in the lower Little Tennessee River Valley, eastern Tennessee. *Southeastern Archaeology* 1: 115-21.

Clausen, Carl J., A. D. Cohen, C. Emiliani, et al. 1979. Little Salt Spring, Florida: A unique underwater site. *Science* 203: 609-14.

Conard, N., D. L. Asch, N. B. Asch, et al. 1984. Accelerator radiocarbon dating of evidence for prehistoric horticulture in Illinois. *Nature* 308: 443-6.

Cowan, C. Wesley. 1978. The prehistoric use and distribution of maygrass in eastern North America: Cultural and phytogeographical implications. In *The nature and status of ethnobotany,* ed. R. I. Ford, University of Michigan, Museum of Anthropology, Anthropological Papers No. 67, 263-88. Ann Arbor.

1985. Understanding the evolution of plant husbandry in eastern North America: Lessons from botany, ethnography, and archaeology. In *Prehistoric food production in North America,* ed. R. I. Ford, University of Michigan, Museum of Anthropology, Anthropological Papers No. 75, 205-43. Ann Arbor.

Crites, Gary D., and R. Dale Terry. 1984. Nutritive value of maygrass, *Phalaris caroliniana. Economic Botany* 38: 114-20.

Crosby, Alfred W., Jr. 1972. *The Columbian exchange: Biological and cultural consequences of 1492.* Westport, Conn.

Curren, Cailup B. 1974. An ethnozoological analysis of the vertebrate remains of the Little Bear Creek site (1 Ct° 8). *Journal of Alabama Archaeology* 20: 127-82.

Damas, David. 1984a. Introduction. In *Handbook of North American Indians: Arctic,* Vol. 5, ed. D. Damas, 1-7. Washington, D.C.

Damas, David, ed. 1984b. *Handbook of North American Indians: Arctic,* Vol. 5. Washington, D.C.

DeBoer, Warren R. 1988. Subterranean storage and the organization of surplus: The view from eastern North America. *Southeastern Archaeology* 7: 1-20.

Decker, Deena S. 1988. Origin(s), evolution, and systematics of *Cucurbita pepo* (Cucurbitaceae). *Economic Botany* 42: 3-15.

Decker, Deena S., and Lee A. Newsom. 1988. Numerical analysis of archaeological *Cucurbita pepo* seeds from Hontoon Island, Florida. *Journal of Ethnobiology* 8: 35-44.

Decker-Walters, Deena S. 1993. New methods for studying the origins of New World domesticates: The squash example. In *Foraging and farming in the Eastern Woodlands,* ed. C. M. Scarry, 91-7. Gainesville, Fla.

Deevey, Edward S., Jr., and R. F. Flint. 1957. Postglacial hypsithermal interval. *Science* 125: 182-4.

Delcourt, Helen R. 1987. The impact of prehistoric agriculture and land occupation on natural vegetation. *Trends in Ecology and Evolution* 2: 39-44.

Delcourt, Paul A., and H. R. Delcourt. 1981. Vegetation maps for eastern North America, 40,000 Yr B.P. to the present. In *Geobotany II,* ed. R. C. Romans, 123-65. New York.

1983. Late Quaternary vegetational dynamics and community stability reconsidered. *Quaternary Research* 19: 265-71.

Delcourt, Paul A., H. R. Delcourt, R. C. Brister, and L. E. Lackey. 1980. Quaternary vegetation history of the Mississippi embayment. *Quaternary Research* 13: 111-32.

Dincauze, Dena F. 1985. An archaeological evaluation of the case for pre-Clovis occupations. *Advances in World Archaeology* 3: 275-323.

Ford, Richard I. 1981. Gardening and farming before A.D. 1000: Patterns of prehistoric cultivation north of Mexico. *Journal of Ethnobiology* 1: 6-27.

1985a. The processes of plant food production in prehistoric North America. In *The nature and status of ethnobotany,* ed. R. I. Ford, Museum of Anthropology, University of Michigan, Anthropological Papers No. 67, 1-18. Ann Arbor.

Ford, Richard I., ed. 1978. *The nature and status of ethnobotany.* Museum of Anthropology, University of Michigan, Anthropological Papers No. 67. Ann Arbor.

1985b. *Prehistoric food production in North America.* Museum of Anthropology, University of Michigan, Anthropological Papers No. 75. Ann Arbor.

Freeman, Milton M. R. 1984. Arctic ecosystems. In *Handbook of North American Indians: Arctic,* Vol. 5, ed. D. Damas, 36-48. Washington, D.C.

Fritz, Gayle J. 1984. Identification of cultigen amaranth and chenopod from rockshelter sites in northwest Arkansas. *American Antiquity* 49: 558-72.

1990. Multiple pathways to farming in precontact eastern North America. *Journal of World Prehistory* 4: 387-435.

1993. Early and Middle Woodland period paleoethnobotany. In *Foraging and farming in the Eastern Woodlands,* ed. C. M. Scarry, 39-56. Gainesville, Fla.

Gardner, Paul S. 1987. New evidence concerning the chronology and paleoethnobotany of Salts Cave, Kentucky. *American Antiquity* 52: 358-67.

Gilbert, Robert I., Jr., and James H. Mielke, eds. 1985. *The analysis of prehistoric diets.* Orlando, Fla.

Gill, Steven J. 1983. *Plant utilization by the Makah and Ozette people, Olympic Peninsula, Washington.* Pullman, Wash.

Graham, R. W., C. V. Haynes, D. L. Johnson, and M. Kay. 1981. Kimmswick: A Clovis-Mastodon association in eastern Missouri. *Science* 213: 1115-17.

Grayson, Donald K. 1984. *Quantitative zooarchaeology: Top-*

ics in the analysis of archaeological faunas. Orlando, Fla.

1991. Late Pleistocene mammalian extinctions in North America: Taxonomy, chronology, and explanations. *Journal of World Prehistory* 5: 193-231.

Gremillion, Kristen Johnson. 1989. The development of a mutualistic relationship between humans and maypops (*Passiflora incarnata* L.) in the southeastern United States. *Journal of Ethnobiology* 9: 135-55.

Hale, H. Stephen. 1984. Prehistoric environmental exploitation around Lake Okeechobee. *Southeastern Archaeology* 3: 173-87.

Hastorf, Christine, and Virginia S. Popper, eds. 1988. *Current paleoethnobotany: Analytical methods and cultural interpretations of archaeological plant remains.* Chicago.

Hedrick, U. P., ed. 1972. *Sturtevant's edible plants of the world.* Reprint, New York.

Heiser, Charles B., Jr. 1985. Some botanical considerations of the early domesticated plants north of Mexico. In *Prehistoric food production in North America,* ed. R. I. Ford, University of Michigan, Museum of Anthropology, Anthropological Papers No. 75, 57-72. Ann Arbor, Mich.

1989. Domestication of Cucurbitaceae: *Cucurbita* and *Lagenaria.* In *Foraging and farming: The evolution of plant exploitation,* ed. D. Harris and G. Hillman, 471-80. London.

Hudson, Charles M. 1976. *The southeastern Indians.* Knoxville, Tenn.

Hudson, Charles M., ed. 1979. *Black drink: A Native American tea.* Athens, Ga.

Isaac, Barry L., ed. 1988. *Research in economic anthropology: Prehistoric economies of the Pacific Northwest Coast.* Greenwich, Conn.

Johannessen, Sissel. 1984. Paleoethnobotany. In *American Bottom archaeology,* ed. C. Bareis and N. Porter, 197-214. Urbana, Ill.

Johnson, A. Sidney, H. O. Hillestad, S. F. Shanholtzer, and G. F. Shanholtzer. 1974. *An ecological survey of the coastal region of Georgia.* National Park Service, Scientific Monograph Series No. 3. Washington, D.C.

Katz, S. H., M. L. Hediger, and L. A. Valleroy. 1974. Traditional maize processing techniques in the New World. *Science* 184: 765-73.

Kay, J., F. B. King, and C. K. Robinson. 1980. Cucurbits from Phillips Spring: New evidence and interpretations. *American Antiquity* 45: 806-22.

Keegan, William F., ed. 1987. *Emergent horticultural economies of the Eastern Woodlands.* Southern Illinois University, Center for Archaeological Investigations, Occasional Papers No. 7. Carbondale.

Kelly, Lucretia S., and Paula G. Cross. 1984. Zooarchaeology. In *American Bottom archaeology,* ed. C. J. Bareis and J. W. Porter, 215-32. Urbana, Ill.

King, Frances B. 1985. Early cultivated cucurbits in eastern North America. In *Prehistoric food production in North America,* ed. R. I. Ford, University of Michigan, Museum of Anthropology, Anthropological Papers No. 75, 73-97. Ann Arbor.

King, James E., and Everett H. Lindsay. 1976. Late Quaternary biotic records from spring deposits in western Missouri. In *Prehistoric man and his environments: A case study in the Ozark highland,* ed. W. R. Wood and R. B. McMillan, 63-78. New York.

Kottak, Conrad Phillip. 1987. *Anthropology: The exploration of human diversity.* New York.

Kurtén, Bjorn, and Elaine Anderson. 1980. *Pleistocene mammals of North America.* New York.

Kusmer, Karla D., Elizabeth K. Leach, and Michael J. Jackson. 1987. Reconstruction of precolonial vegetation in Livingston County, Kentucky, and prehistoric cultural implications. *Southeastern Archaeology* 6: 107-15.

Lantis, Margaret. 1984. Nunivak Eskimo. In *Handbook of North American Indians: Arctic,* Vol. 5, ed. D. Damas, 209-23. Washington, D.C.

Larsen, Clark Spencer. 1981. Skeletal and dental adaptations to the shift to agriculture on the Georgia coast. *Current Anthropology* 22: 422-3.

1982. The anthropology of St. Catherine's Island. III. Prehistoric human biological adaptation. *Anthropological Papers of the American Museum of Natural History* 57: 157-276.

1984. Health and disease in prehistoric Georgia: The transition to agriculture. In *Paleopathology at the origins of agriculture,* ed. M. N. Cohen and G. J. Armelagos, 367-92. Orlando, Fla.

Larsen, Clark Spencer, and D. H. Thomas. 1982. The anthropology of St. Catherine's Island. IV. The St. Catherine's period mortuary complex. *Anthropological Papers of the American Museum of Natural History* Part 4, 57.

Larson, Lewis H. 1980. *Aboriginal subsistence technology on the southeastern coastal plain during the late prehistoric period.* Gainesville, Fla.

Linares, Olga. 1976. "Garden hunting" in the American tropics. *Human Ecology* 4: 331-49.

Marquardt, William H. 1974. A statistical analysis of constituents in human paleofecal specimens from Mammoth Cave. In *Archeology of the Mammoth Cave area,* ed. P. J. Watson, 193-202. New York.

McMillan, R. Bruce. 1976. The Pomme de Terre study locality: Its setting. In *Prehistoric man and his environments: A case study in the Ozark highland,* ed. W. R. Wood and R. B. McMillan, 13-44. New York.

Medsger, Oliver Perry. 1976. *Edible wild plants.* New York.

Merwe, N. J. van der, and J. D. Vogel. 1978. ^{13}C content of human collagen as a measure of prehistoric diet in Woodland North America. *Nature* 276: 815-16.

Mitchell, Donald. 1988. Changing patterns of resource use in the prehistory of Queen Charlotte Strait, British Columbia. In *Research in economic anthropology: Prehistoric economies of the Pacific Northwest Coast,* ed. B. L. Isaac, 245-90. Greenwich, Conn.

Muller, Jon. 1984. Mississippian specialization and salt. *American Antiquity* 49: 489-507.

Munson, Patrick J., Paul W. Parmalee, and Richard A. Yarnell. 1971. Subsistence ecology of Scovill, A terminal Middle Woodland village. *American Antiquity* 36: 415-20.

Neusius, Sarah W., ed. 1986. *Foraging, collecting, and harvesting: Archaic period subsistence and settlement in the Eastern Woodlands.* Southern Illinois University, Center for Archaeological Investigations, Occasional Papers No. 6. Carbondale, Ill.

Parmalee, Paul W., and W. E. Klippel. 1974. Freshwater mussels as a prehistoric food resource. *American Antiquity* 39: 421-34.

Parmalee, Paul W., R. B. McMillan, and F. B. King. 1976. Changing subsistence patterns at Rodgers Shelter. In *Prehistoric man and his environments: A case study in the Ozark highlands,* ed. W. R. Wood and R. B. McMillan, 141-62. New York.

Parmalee, Paul W., Andreas A. Paloumpis, and Nancy Wilson. 1972. *Animals utilized by Woodland peoples occupying the Apple Creek site, Illinois.* Illinois State Museum, Reports of Investigations No. 23. Springfield.

Pearsall, Deborah M. 1989. *Paleoethnobotany.* San Diego, Calif.

Powell, Mary Lucas, P. S. Bridges, and A. M. W. Mires, eds. 1991. *What mean these bones?: Studies in southeastern bioarchaeology.* Tuscaloosa, Ala.

Ray, Dorothy Jean. 1984. Bering Strait Eskimo. In *Handbook of North American Indians: Arctic,* Vol. 5, ed. D. Damas, 285-302. Washington, D.C.

Reitz, Elizabeth J. 1982. Vertebrate fauna from four coastal Mississippian sites. *Journal of Ethnobiology* 2: 39-61.

  1985. A comparison of Spanish and aboriginal subsistence on the Atlantic coastal plain. *Southeastern Archaeology* 4: 41-50.

  1988. Evidence for coastal adaptations in Georgia and South Carolina. *Archaeology of Eastern North America* 16: 137-58.

  1990. Zooarchaeological evidence for subsistence at La Florida missions. In *Columbian consequences: Archaeological and historical perspectives on the Spanish borderlands east,* ed. D. H. Thomas, 543-54. Washington, D.C.

  1992. Zooarchaeological method and theory and their role in southeastern archaeological studies. In *The development of southeastern archaeology,* ed. J. Johnson, 230-50. Tuscaloosa, Ala.

Reitz, Elizabeth J., and Stephen L. Cumbaa. 1983. Diet and foodways of eighteenth-century Spanish St. Augustine. In *Spanish St. Augustine: The archaeology of a colonial Creole community,* ed. K. A. Deagan, 152-85. New York.

Reitz, Elizabeth J., Rochelle Marrinan, and Susan L. Scott. 1987. Survey of vertebrate remains from prehistoric sites in the Savannah River Valley. *Journal of Ethnobiology* 7: 195-221.

Reitz, Elizabeth J., and Irvy R. Quitmyer. 1988. Faunal remains from two coastal Georgia Swift Creek sites. *Southeastern Archaeology* 7: 95-108.

Reitz, Elizabeth J., and C. Margaret Scarry. 1985. *Reconstructing historic subsistence with an example from sixteenth-century Spanish Florida.* Society for Historical Archaeology, Special Publication No. 3. Tucson, Ariz.

Riley, Thomas J. 1987. Ridged-field agriculture and the Mississippian economic pattern. In *Emergent horticultural economies of the Eastern Woodlands,* ed. W. Keegan, Southern Illinois University, Center for Archaeological Investigations, Occasional Papers No. 7, 295-304. Carbondale.

Rostlund, Erhard. 1952. *Freshwater fish and fishing in native North America.* University of California, Publications in Geography, Vol. 9. Berkeley, Calif.

Ruff, Christopher B., Clark Spencer Larsen, and Wilson C. Hayes. 1984. Structural changes in the femur with the transition to agriculture on the Georgia coast. *American Journal of Physical Anthropology* 64: 125-36.

Scarry, C. Margaret. 1993a. Variability in Mississippian crop production strategies. In *Foraging and farming in the Eastern Woodlands,* ed. C. M. Scarry, 78-90. Gainesville, Fla.

Scarry, C. Margaret, ed. 1993b. *Foraging and farming in the Eastern Woodlands.* Gainesville, Fla.

Scarry, C. Margaret, and Elizabeth J. Reitz. 1990. Herbs, fish, scum, and vermin: Subsistence strategies in sixteenth-century Spanish Florida. In *Columbian consequences: Archaeological and historical perspectives on the Spanish borderlands east,* ed. D. H. Thomas, 343-54. Washington, D.C.

Shelford, Victor E. 1974. *The ecology of North America.* Urbana, Ill.

Smith, Bruce D. 1984. *Chenopodium* as a prehistoric domesticate in eastern North America: Evidence from Russell Cave, Alabama. *Science* 226: 165-7.

  1985a. *Chenopodium berlandieri* ssp. *jonesianum:* Evidence for a Hopewellian domesticate from Ash Cave, Ohio. *Southeastern Archaeology* 4: 107-33.

  1985b. The role of *Chenopodium* as a domesticate in pre-maize garden systems of the eastern United States. *Southeastern Archaeology* 4: 51-72.

  1986. The archaeology of the southeastern United States from Dalton to DeSoto (10,500 B.P.-500 B.P.). In *Advances in world archaeology,* Vol. 5, ed. F. Wendorf and A. E. Close, 1-92. Orlando, Fla.

  1987a. The economic potential of *Chenopodium berlandieri* in prehistoric eastern North America. *Journal of Ethnobiology* 7: 29-54.

  1987b. The independent domestication of indigenous seed-bearing plants in eastern North America. In *Emergent horticultural economies of the Eastern Woodlands,* ed. W. F. Keegan, Southern Illinois University, Center for Archaeological Investigations, Occasional Papers No. 7, 3-47. Carbondale.

  1989. Origins of agriculture in eastern North America. *Science* 246: 1566-71.

Smith, Bruce D., ed. 1990. *The Mississippian emergence.* Washington, D.C.

Spencer, Robert R., and Jesse D. Jennings, eds. 1965. *The Native Americans.* New York.

Springer, James Warren. 1980. An analysis of prehistoric food remains from the Bruly St. Martin Site, Louisiana, with a comparative discussion of Mississippi Valley faunal studies. *Mid-Continental Journal of Archaeology* 5: 193-223.

Steponaitis, Vincas P. 1986. Prehistoric archaeology in the southeastern United States, 1970-1985. *Annual Review of Anthropology* 15: 363-404.

Stewart, Hilary. 1977. *Indian fishing: Early methods on the northwest coast.* Seattle, Wash.

Stoltman, James B. 1974. *Groton plantation: An archaeological study of a South Carolina locality.* Harvard University, Peabody Museum, Monograph No. 1. Cambridge, Mass.

Styles, Bonnie Whatley. 1981. *Faunal exploitation and resource selection: Early Late Woodland subsistence in the lower Illinois Valley.* Evanston, Ill.

Styles, Bonnie Whatley, and James R. Purdue. 1991. Ritual and secular use of fauna by Middle Woodland peoples in western Illinois. In *Beamers, bobwhites, and bluepoints: Tributes to the career of Paul W. Parmalee,* ed. J. R. Purdue, W. E. Klippel, and B. W. Styles, Illinois State Museum, Scientific Papers No. 23, 421-36. Springfield.

Suttles, Wayne. 1990a. Environment. In *Handbook of North American Indians: Northwest Coast,* Vol. 7, ed. W. Suttles, 16-29. Washington, D.C.

Suttles, Wayne, ed. 1990b. *Handbook of North American Indians: Northwest coast,* Vol. 7. Washington, D.C.

Swanton, John R. 1946. *The Indians of the southeastern United States.* Smithsonian Institution, Bureau of American Ethnology, Bulletin No. 137. Washington, D.C.

Tannahill, Reay. 1973. *Food in history.* New York.

Taylor, Walter W., ed. 1957. *The identification of non-artifactual archaeological materials.* Washington, D.C. 1-64.

Trager, James. 1970. *The food book.* New York.

Watson, Patty Jo. 1985. The impact of early horticulture in the upland drainages of the Midwest and Midsouth. In *Prehistoric food production in North America,* ed. R. I. Ford, University of Michigan, Museum of Anthropology, Anthropological Papers No. 75, 99-147. Ann Arbor.

  1989. Early plant cultivation in the eastern woodlands of North America. In *Foraging and farming: The evolution of plant exploitation,* ed. D. Harris and G. Hillman, 555-71. London.

Watson, Patty Jo, ed. 1969. *The prehistory of Salts Cave, Kentucky*. Illinois State Museum, Reports of Investigations No. 16. Springfield, Ill.

Welch, Paul D. 1991. *Moundville's economy*. Tuscaloosa, Ala.

Wessen, Gary C. 1988. The use of shellfish resources on the Northwest Coast: The view from Ozette. In *Research in economic anthropology: Prehistoric economies of the Pacific Northwest Coast*, ed. B. L. Isaac, 179-207. Greenwich, Conn.

Wigen, Rebecca J., and Barbara Stucki. 1988. Taphonomy and stratigraphy in the interpretation of economic patterns at Hoko River rockshelter. In *Research in economic anthropology: Prehistoric economies of the Pacific Northwest Coast*, ed. B. L. Isaac, 87-146. Greenwich, Conn.

Wing, Elizabeth S., and Antoinette B. Brown. 1979. *Paleonutrition: Method and theory in prehistoric foodways*. Orlando, Fla.

Wood, W. Raymond, and R. Bruce McMillan, eds. 1976. *Prehistoric man and his environments: A case study in the Ozark highland*. New York.

Woods, William I. 1987. Maize agriculture and the late prehistoric: A characterization of settlement location strategies. In *Emergent horticultural economies of the Eastern Woodlands*, ed. W. F. Keegan, Southern Illinois University, Center for Archaeological Investigations, Occasional Papers No. 7, 275-94. Carbondale.

Wright, H. E. 1976. The dynamic nature of Holocene vegetation, a problem in paleoclimatology, biogeography, and stratigraphic nomenclature. *Quaternary Research* 6: 581-96.

Yarnell, Richard A. 1969. Contents of human paleofeces. In *The prehistory of Salts Cave, Kentucky*, ed. P. J. Watson, Illinois State Museum, Reports of Investigations No. 16, 41-54. Springfield.

1972. *Iva annua* var. *macrocarpa*: Extinct American cultigen? *American Anthropologist* 74: 335-41.

1978. Domestication of sunflower and sumpweed in eastern North America. In *The nature and status of ethnobotany*, ed. R. I. Ford, Museum of Anthropology, University of Michigan, Anthropological Papers No. 67, 289-99. Ann Arbor.

1982. Problems of interpretation of archaeological plant remains of the Eastern Woodlands. *Southeastern Archaeology* 1: 1-7.

1993. The importance of native crops during the Late Archaic and Woodland periods. In *Foraging and farming in the Eastern Woodlands*, ed. C. M. Scarry, 13-26. Gainesville, Fla.

Yarnell, Richard A., and M. Jean Black. 1985. Temporal trends indicated by a survey of Archaic and Woodland plant food remains from southeastern North America. *Southeastern Archaeology* 4: 93-106.

V.D.6 ❧ North America from 1492 to the Present

The food history of Native Americans before the time of Columbus involved ways of life ranging from big-game hunting to (in many cases) sophisticated agriculture. The history of foodways in North America since Columbus has been the story of five centuries of introduced foodstuffs, preparation methods, and equipment that accompanied peoples from Europe, Asia, and Africa, with the food culture of North America having been enriched by each addition.

The Sixteenth Century

Most narrative histories of North America give little attention to the sixteenth century, even though two earthshaking events took place during this time that were to alter the continent's history fundamentally. One was the demographic collapse of the native populations in the face of Eurasian diseases, such as smallpox. This made possible the second, which was the establishment of European settlements along the eastern seaboard without substantial native resistance.

The Native Americans

The peoples of North America, who numbered perhaps 20 million in 1492, dwelled in societies of many different types, with their cultures shaped by their foodways. Thus, those who depended on hunting and gathering usually lived in roaming bands, whereas maize agriculture normally implied settled life in villages or towns. In the north and west of the continent, the hunter–gatherer lifestyle still predominated in 1492. Game varied from bison on the Great Plains to rats in the deserts of the Southwest. Men hunted and women gathered in these usually nomadic, band-level societies. Some bands, like the Mi'kmaq of Nova Scotia, grew one crop, such as tobacco, and hunted and gathered the remainder of their food supply (Prins 1996). It is important to note that the European picture of Indians as primitives did not allow for such sophistication. The Mi'kmaq knew perfectly well what agriculture was but chose to obtain their food from the wild and to plant only tobacco, which the wild could not provide. Where a staple food could be collected easily, such as in parts of California (where acorns were the daily fare) or in northern Minnesota (where wild rice was the staple), the natives frequently formed settlements (Linsenmeyer 1976).

An agricultural complex had been developing for centuries in eastern North America when Ponce de León stepped ashore in 1513. Older staples, such as Jerusalem artichoke and sumpweed, had given way to Mexican maize, beans, and squash. Varieties of maize adapted to extreme conditions permitted horticulture to flourish as far north as the Dakotas.

In the Southeast and the Mississippi Valley, the area of the Mississippian culture, intensive agriculture supported cities resembling those of Mexico and Peru, with thousands of inhabitants, elaborate social systems, and multiple castes (Duncan 1995). Maize, beans, and squash, along with fish and game, fed the masses. A ceremonial beverage made from yaupon holly, called "black drink," was a caffeine-containing stimulant similar to tea or coffee (Hudson 1979). (It is strange that alcohol was almost unknown among North American natives, although some made a sort of ale from maize or maple sap; after European contact, however, alcoholism would become a serious problem for them.) The "Gentleman of Elvas," chronicler of Hernando De Soto's expedition (1539–42), described one Mississippian city – near the future site of Augusta, Georgia – that was ruled by a queen he called the "Lady of Cofachiqui" from a pyramidal mound topped by her large wooden house (Duncan 1995). Fields of maize stretched as far as the horizon. The surplus from the fields went into granaries to feed people in need – a mark of true civil society (Crosby 1986). Clearly, these people and others, like those who built the mounds at Cahokia in Illinois (Middle Mississippian ancestors of the Siouan-speaking Indians), had sophisticated state-level societies with governmental systems, long-distance trade, and complex religions.

Cofachiqui also had four huge barns wherein the dead from a smallpox epidemic were mummified, and by 1650, her elaborate society had vanished, likely because of further outbreaks of disease (Duncan 1995). Perhaps 90 percent of North America's native population died in a series of "virgin-soil" epidemics, and much knowledge of foodstuffs and other cultural traditions was lost forever in this immense demographic disaster (Crosby 1986).

In addition to their deadliness, the epidemics were demoralizing, as traditional religious and medical practices proved useless. Some Native Americans believed that the end of the world had come, and needless to say, diseases precipitated a great deal of migration: Tribes moved to escape the pathogens, to flee from enemies that they were too weak to resist, or to invade the territory of decimated foes. The map of aboriginal America was altered beyond the scholar's power to reconstruct. The Mississippian peoples vanished, and tribes having no knowledge of the origin of the great mounds took their places.

The Spanish Borderland Settlements

During the sixteenth century, Spanish priests and soldiers established several missions in the Southeast. St. Augustine was the most important, but others came into being along the coasts of Georgia, Carolina, and (briefly) Virginia. Both literary and archaeological evidence indicate that the Spanish imported a large amount of food, including wine and wheat flour (Milanich 1995). But more important for day-to-day survival were native foodstuffs, such as maize, yaupon, and wild game, provided by Indians living at the missions.

Spanish explorers also distributed wheat flour to native rulers and passed out European seeds as gifts to natives, with translated instructions for growing them; the peach orchards of the Mississippi Natchez stand as testimony to how far these plants spread (Farb 1968; Milanich 1995). In the warm climate, mis-sion gardens yielded favorites brought from Europe, such as melons, figs, hazelnuts, oranges, chickpeas, greens, herbs, peas, garlic, barley, pomegranates, cucumbers, wine grapes, cabbage, lettuce, and even sugarcane. In addition, the Spanish carried the sweet potato of the Caribbean to Florida, where it was previously unknown (Milanich 1995).

Such plant transfers – not only from the Old World to the New but also from one area of the New World to another – resulted in confused, albeit enriched, foodways. Moreover, as Alfred Crosby (1986) has pointed out, Old World species exhibited an ability to edge out their New World counterparts, with "ecological imperialism" the result. Large numbers of wild horses, cattle, and hogs multiplied in an environment free of accustomed predators, and even the honeybee (native to Eurasia) thrived, while the pollen it spread about fertilized imported European plants that depended upon it. The result was an abundance of food in virtually all the neo-European societies of the New World – a situation that has continued to the present (Crosby 1986).

The Seventeenth Century

The Chesapeake Region

The seventeenth century saw the planting of permanent English colonies in North America, including the beginning of European settlement of the Chesapeake. Colonists usually brought provisions reflecting the diet of contemporary Britain, which was based on grains, meat, and milk products. Bread, the daily staple, ranged from the mixed-grain bread of the poor to the "white" bread of the wealthy. Luxurious meals for the upper classes included elaborate spicing, many pastries, and complex cooking methods reminiscent of those of the Near East, with copious use of rose water, almonds, and currants (Hess 1992). *Martha Washington's Booke of Cookery* (Hess 1981), a seventeenth-century manuscript recipe book (although some recipes in it are a good deal older) passed down in the Custis family of Virginia, provides a glimpse of this cuisine, with its profusion of custard curd dishes, rose water, garlic (later to be virtually forbidden), almond-scented meats, and practical hints on preserving foodstuffs (cherries, peas, turnips, and even oysters pickled in barrels) and distilling homemade medicines. Among other recipes is one for apple pie, foreshadowing its status as an American icon; oat "greats" (groats), soon to be replaced by American "grits" of corn (maize), are mentioned as well.

In the mid–1580s, English settlers landed on Roanoke Island in present-day North Carolina, but the first permanent British colony was Jamestown, Virginia, established in 1607 by 105 Englishmen, among whom there was but a single farmer. In an ensuing period of starvation, poisonous "Jimson" weeds, oysters, maize (stolen from the local Powhatan Indians), and even, apparently, human flesh kept the colonists from dying out completely (Smallzreid 1956). Thereafter, much more attention was paid to crops. British wheat did poorly in the climate of the Chesapeake, and the settlers came to depend on cornbread, grits, and pork. Their hogs ate maize, along with acorns and peanuts. "Ashcake" and "hoecake," baked in ashes on the blade of a hoe, were the staples of poor whites and, later, of black slaves, some of whom had known maize in Africa because of the slave traders, who imported the plant to feed slaves awaiting transport to the Americas. Bread was baked on coals or fried in pork fat, and meat was roasted, fried, or boiled (Fischer 1989). Cornbread was the food of the poor because of the ease with which maize could be grown, but the wealthy enjoyed its taste as well (Horry 1984). However, an overreliance on maize was to lead to malnutrition and vitamin deficiencies in the South, with poor health a consequence (Kiple and King 1981).

It is worth noting that some food historians attribute numerous American dishes, ranging from strawberry shortcake to Brunswick stew, and their means of preparation to the native peoples (Root and de Rochemont 1976). However, although the native origin of such foodstuffs as maize and venison is obvious, a survey of the foodways of the Powhatans of Virginia reveals that they contributed little that was exotic to the English settlers. For example, a feast prepared in 1607 at Arrohateck, Virginia, included mulberries and strawberries boiled with beans, cornbread, "meale," and a "land turtle" – hardly sophisticated fare (Rountree 1989). The truth of the matter was that the Indians of the Eastern Woodlands lacked salt and spices (even the hot peppers of Mexico and Peru), as well as frying pans and other iron utensils, ovens, wheat, sugar, dairy products, and all domestic animals save the dog. Thus, to assert that strawberry shortcake derives from an Indian dish that was nothing more than berries and maize or beans boiled together is, perhaps, something of an exaggeration. It is important not to confuse the Indians of North America with those of Central or South America: Although many have written that the native peoples of North America had, for example, the potato and the chilli pepper, as did, respectively, the Inca and the Aztecs, this was simply not the case.

New England

The Massachusetts area received its first white settlers with the *Mayflower* in late 1620. Following a harsh winter during which many of them died, the colonists learned from the Native American Wampanoags how to hunt and fish in the new land and how to plant crops. The following November established a landmark in American culinary history: the first "thanksgiving dinner," prepared by the Pilgrims and their Wampanoag hosts. In truth, the modern Thanksgiving holiday dates back only to Civil War times, and as for the Pilgrims' thanksgiving, there is no mention of the famous turkey.

In 1630, 1,000 colonists arrived on the 17 ships of the Winthrop fleet to found the Massachusetts Bay colony. Their provisions included cheese, salt fish, pork and beef, oatmeal, hard biscuit, bread and butter, peas, onions, raisins, prunes, and dates, with cider, beer, water, sweet wine, and small amounts of brandy, called "aqua vitae" (Smallzreid 1956). Because a virgin-soil epidemic had reportedly annihilated the local Indians in 1617, the landing of the settlers went unchallenged, and they proceeded to found a colony of self-sufficient farmers. They ate well, if somewhat monotonously; an average of 3,200 to 5,000 calories a day was the norm in New England (Derven 1984). As did their neighbors to the south, these settlers also consumed maize meal, both as porridge and as bread or "johnnycake," but the diet did not focus on "hog and hominy," as it did in Virginia.

The use of land for small farms meant that both rich people and poor were rare in New England (Lockridge 1985). The cold climate enabled rye to grow successfully, resulting in "rye'n'injun" ("rye and Indian," a bread baked with rye and maize meal) and "Boston brown bread," made from rye, wheat, and maize that was steamed over a kettle of beans cooking with pork and molasses. (The careful cook allowed the residual heat of the oven to keep beans warm for Sundays, when – for religious reasons – no cooking or other work was permitted.) Although yeast will not act well on any grain but wheat, the rye and maize breads of colonial America could be raised with "pearl ash" (potassium bicarbonate, made from wood ashes) or with beaten eggs (Hess 1992). The most ubiquitous dishes were pies, baked (like bread and beans) in wood-fired brick ovens modeled after those used in England. Indeed, a "Yankee" was to be defined as someone who ate pie for breakfast. The types of pies reflected the seasonal availability of fruits; and because the pie makers made use of first one fruit and then another throughout the year, there was a virtual calendar of pies (Fischer 1989).

Molasses was the usual sweetener (white sugar was expensive), and it was also employed in making rum. Drinking in New England centered on alcoholic beverages, with hard cider and some beer competing with rum. Although wine grapes would not grow, bees thrived, and a few settlers managed to make honey mead, which they had known in England (Wolcott 1971). Bread, cookies, and even beer could be made from pumpkins, which were a staple for New Englanders. In fact, the ease of growing pumpkins meant that "old Pompion was a saint," and "pumpkin sause [pumpkin stewed with butter, spices, and vinegar] and pumpkin bread" were on every table (Crawford 1914: 382; Wolcott 1971).

The Middle Region: Pennsylvania and New York

The New Amsterdam colony, which became New York, and the Quaker settlement in Pennsylvania were two other sites of seventeenth-century colonization, both settled by peoples whose foodways reflected diverse origins. In New Amsterdam, the Dutch relished heavy meals of meat and bread, washed down with tea (a Dutch favorite before it became popular in England) and followed by large amounts of rich pastry. Perhaps one-fourth of the houses in New Amsterdam sold beer, tobacco, or spirits (Booth 1971).

In seventeenth-century Pennsylvania, the colonists were a mixture of Quakers, other English settlers, and some Swedes (Nash 1968). David Hackett Fischer (1989) has claimed that the northern British origin of the Quakers encouraged a distinctive pattern of foodways, of which the consumption of apple butter and dried beef was typical. By contrast, Karen Hess (1992), who has examined the Penn family cookbook and other early American sources, found nothing unique about Quaker cookery, and it has also been pointed out that the distinctive cuisine of the north of England (including Yorkshire), based on grain porridge, oatcake, and ale, did not resemble Pennsylvania cooking (Brears 1987). Thus, there is little consensus about the cuisine of the Pennsylvania Quakers (Lea 1982), although perhaps its distinctiveness could be argued because of what was *not* consumed. The Quakers' wish to isolate themselves from the sinful world led to abstinence from many foodstuffs. Some, for example, refused to use sugar because it was made by slaves. Others rejected spices, saying that they altered the taste of food (Fischer 1989).

The Spanish Borderlands

By the 1600s, the Spanish settlements along the Carolina and Virginia coasts had been abandoned, although St. Augustine in Florida continued as home to a small Spanish colony that imported much of its food. Aside from game, the local foodstuffs consumed were maize and yaupon holly, from which was made the Indians' "black drink," containing caffeine. A priest explained that yaupon was drunk "every day in the morning and evening" and that "any day that a Spaniard does not drink it, he feels that he is going to die" (Sturtevant 1979: 150)

In the Southwest, which had been settled from Mexico during the sixteenth century, the traditional cookery of Native Americans came to include Spanish imports, such as domesticated food animals, sugar, tea, and coffee. As the hunter–gatherer Navaho and many other tribes became pastoralists, they adopted a diet of mutton, bread, and coffee (Driver 1961). Perhaps ironically, many Indian groups in the Southwest learned maize agriculture from the Spaniards, and beef and maize became the staples for many in this ranching land. Food was plentiful, if judged by a book on early California cooking that lists five daily meals. For dinner, a well-off family in Spanish California might have a selection of foods that mixed Iberian fruit preserves and wine, a salad of local pigweed, Mexican tortillas, beans, and succotash, and such European-influenced dishes as fried rice and coffee (Smallzreid 1956).

The Eighteenth Century

In America, the eighteenth century brought a "golden age" for the planters of the Chesapeake region. Cultural amalgamation among the several colonies meant the end of religious uniqueness for the New England Puritans and Pennsylvania Quakers. The Indians were forced beyond the Appalachian Mountains, and the colonies' political consolidation that began with the Albany Plan of Union ended with American independence and the Constitution of the United States. This political union meant that, in the long run, neither the Native Americans nor the Spaniards would retain their lands. The field of cookery also became "independent," as English cookbooks were succeeded by the first American cookbooks.

In all American societies, food availability depended on the seasons. Autumn saw an abundance, but late winter and early spring meant the "six weeks' want" (Farrington 1976). It was a time when greens and roots were used to relieve the monotony of stale meal and beans before the first garden vegetables came in. The southern colonies had longer growing seasons and thus less of an annual time of "want." However their warmer climate encouraged a hostile disease environment, with the result that New England families were larger and life spans longer (Fischer 1989).

It has been claimed that, in general, early Americans disliked, or at least seldom consumed, vegetables, and it was certainly the case that – in an age without refrigeration – green vegetables kept poorly. Moreover, without a marketing and transportation system, availability was limited; once the season for a particular food had passed, there would be no more of it until the following year. Perhaps most importantly, modern varieties of vegetables did not exist: There was no tomato designed to ripen slowly off the vine, nor a maize cultivar that stayed sweet. To obtain and cook vegetables required a certain tenacity, and in an age ignorant of vitamins and fiber, some people simply did not bother with them.

In spite of these factors, however, many Americans seem to have enjoyed vegetables and fruits. Amelia Simmons, in compiling her 1796 cookbook, evidently assumed that any good meal included vegetables (Simmons 1965). Vegetables were cooked for longer periods than they are today (in order to ensure their safety and edibility by those with few or no teeth) but were not necessarily boiled into mush, as is sometimes asserted. The eighteenth-century South Carolina housewife Sarah Rutledge, for example, boiled her cauliflower for only 15 minutes (Rutledge 1979).

Many people raised fruits and vegetables in abundance. An example comes from an 1806 gardening calendar kept by a Charleston lady who grew fruit trees, strawberries, gooseberries, currants, raspberries, thyme, savory, hyssop, peas, beans, cabbage, lettuce, endive, potatoes, artichokes, and Jerusalem artichokes (Tucker 1993). Thomas Jefferson and his Paris-trained slave-chef James Hemings kept a huge garden of peas, cauliflower, cabbage, lettuce, parsley, kale, tarragon, broccoli, spinach, "corn salad," endive, savory, turnips, carrots, beets, salsify, parsnips, radishes, onions, eggplant, melons, and beans (Tucker 1993). They even sprouted endive in the cellar to provide salads in wintertime.

New England

In the eighteenth century, the people of Massachusetts were suppliers of rum for slavers and ships for whaling and fishing. The colony was a hub of trade: Spices and foodstuffs from all corners of the globe passed through New England markets. However, its own cooking centered mostly, as before, on bread, beans, fish, and salt meat. The British habits of overcooking meat and greens persisted, as did such customs as brewing special beers for special occasions (Crawford 1914). Quilting bees ended with tea served in the English style, featuring sweets, "sage cheese" (flavored with that herb), and pastries (Crawford 1914). A favorite meal was the "boiled dinner" comprised of boiled meats and vegetables and, perhaps, boiled "bag pudding" for dessert (Farrington 1976).

Substantial meals were the rule, and pie for breakfast meant plenty of calories to start the day. A visitor to Boston in 1740 remarked on the abundance of poultry, fish, venison, and butcher's meat available. The ordination of a minister called for a celebratory meal of turkeys, pumpkins, cakes, and rum. Harvard students, however, ate meager meals of cold bread and hot chocolate (Crawford 1914). There was little opposition to alcohol consumption in early America, and pastor and congregation alike drank it before Sunday church services, as well as at every meal (Rorabaugh 1979). In addition to huge amounts of bread, porridge, and cheese, the average New Englander annually consumed some 32 gallons of hard cider, 15 pounds of butter, 40 gallons of milk, between 2 and 3 pounds of tea, more than 150 pounds of meat, 10 pounds of sugar, and 1 gallon of molasses (Derven 1984).

Trade made the merchant class wealthy in what had once been an egalitarian colony, and the menus of the wealthy could be elaborate. John Adams, certainly well-to-do, served a dinner of Indian pudding with molasses and butter, veal, bacon, neck of mutton (a dish also featured in Martha Washington's cookbook), and vegetables (Fritz, 1969). A Quaker friend outdid Adams with "ducks, hams, chickens, beef, pig, tarts, creams, custards, jellies, fowls, trifles, floating islands [a custard dish], beer, porter, punch, and wine" (Smallzreid 1956: 61). Nonetheless, despite such heavy eating habits, the old Puritan ideals died hard: Jokes had it that a New England family made the same roast gander serve as a main course for seven days in a row (Crawford 1914)!

The Middle Region

In the eighteenth century, Pennsylvania became home for large numbers of German settlers (later known as the "Pennsylvania Dutch"). Deemed not assimilable by many, they colonized the back country and prospered. Many joined the great migration southward along the Appalachian Mountains and ended up in Virginia and the Carolinas. Along with the iron cookstove, these Germans contributed waffles, "shoofly pie," scrapple, new kinds of sausage, vinegar, and more pastries – including doughnuts (Farrington 1976).

Technological innovations spread from the middle colonies. By 1750, a cast-iron pot – with a rim on the lid to hold coals – was in common use. Called a "Dutch oven," it was used to bake bread, roast meats, and make stews and other dishes; in modified form, it has remained in use to this day (Ragsdale 1991). The famous stove of inventor and ambassador Benjamin Franklin improved on German models. Franklin was perhaps the most famous vegetarian of his time, having been inspired by English vegetarian and pacifist Thomas Tryon (Spencer 1995). Franklin eschewed meat and beer in order to improve his health and drew up lists of vegetarian dishes for his landlady to prepare. Toward the end of his life, however, he returned to eating some meat.

As the century came to a close, the cosmopolitan city of Philadelphia had 248 taverns and 203 boardinghouses (Pillsbury 1990). Its diverse population of English, Germans, Swedes, and Africans contributed to a varied cuisine, including the famous "Philadelphia pepper pot," which, although attributed to George Washington's cook, is similar to a Caribbean dish of the same name.

Like Pennsylvania, New York contained a mixture of cultures. Foods in this port city included so much fish and fowl that servants (who apparently wanted more meat) complained if salmon was served more than once a week or heath hen (a bird now extinct) more than three times (Farrington 1976). Such an abundance of animal food on the table was unlike Old World cuisines, which relied on porridge, bread, and potatoes. Each year, two crops of peas and one of buckwheat came from the rich soil, which also produced rye, barley, maize, potatoes, and turnips (Tucker 1993). Food for the city of New York also arrived from the "garden colony" of New Jersey (Farrington 1976) and from what is now upstate New York, where Dutch and German settlers had introduced new kinds of plows and wagons to make their farms more productive. The "Dutch plow" or "Rotherham plow" (in fact, it originally derived from China) had a share and moldboard cast in one continuous piece (Temple 1986), and its advanced design greatly eased the task of plowing. The crops on Dutch farms were diverse, with those farms reflecting the intensive use of space typical of the Netherlands.

European fruits did well; farmers planted great orchards of apples to make cider, a favorite alcoholic beverage, which was often distilled into "Jersey lightning" by means of freezing it until a core of alcohol remained within the ice. But apples were also used in numerous other ways. For example, apple pie and milk were the nightly fare for "Hector St. John" (Michel G. J. de Crèvecoeur, author of *Letters from an American Farmer*) in the late eighteenth century (Sokoloff 1991). Long before the American Revolution, eating shops and taverns provided places to dine out in New York (Pillsbury 1990). One of these was the Queen's Head (soon known as Fraunces Tavern), which opened in 1770 and was still in business over a century later (Root and de Rochemont 1976). By the end of the eighteenth century, New York had 121 taverns and 42 boardinghouses that served food and drink (Pillsbury 1990).

The Chesapeake Region and the South

As mentioned, the eighteenth century was a "golden age" for some in the Virginia tidewater. The period saw a shift from tobacco monoculture to the mixed growing of tobacco and grain, although the former continued to dominate the region. Plantations worked by African slaves yielded an abundance of maize and other foodstuffs, and maize remained the staple for the slaves, as well as for poor whites. For others, there was either bread (made from dough that rose by the addition of beaten egg) or "beaten biscuit" (made with wheat flour) that was laid on a stump and struck repeatedly with an ax handle until it began to rise (Farrington 1976).

The predominance of maize in baking meant much cornbread, almost always eaten hot; when cornmeal was fried, the result was "hushpuppies." Maize was also fed to hogs, the principal source of meat in the South until the twentieth century. In addition, the mash made from maize was distilled into corn whiskey, which was popular even before the Revolution. Later, with rum from the British West Indies more difficult to obtain, corn whiskey became the liquid staple of what has been termed the "alcoholic republic" (Rorabaugh 1979). Rum or whiskey was mixed with water and sugar to become toddy; with fruit and sugar, it was punch (Farrington 1976). Some beer was drunk, including "Roger's best Virginia ale," brewed in Williamsburg (Hume 1970). But English beer yeasts spoiled in the American summer heat, and winter killed them, making beer brewing a difficult proposition (Rorabaugh 1979). Although Virginians also made cider and some wines in the colonial period, distilled spirits kept the best (Hume 1970).

Some of the gentry were voracious consumers of alcohol. When the governor of Virginia, Lord Norborne Berkeley Botetourt, died in 1770, he left behind more than 2,000 bottles of wine, brandy, and ale and many kegs of spirits (Hume 1970). Three years later, his successor, Lord John Murray Dunmore, ordered 15 dozen bottles of both ale and strong beer from England, as well as wine glasses, cloves, and 20 dozen packs of cards (Smallzreid 1956).

Wine, tea, coffee, and the spicy dishes of the early modern period figured prominently as the kitchens of the planters began to turn out the first high cuisine in British America (Fischer 1989). Much of this has been attributed to African cooks, who knew how to use flavorings and spices. Most plantations maintained kitchens in buildings separated from the main house (because of a fear of fire), as well as icehouses (where winter ice was stored in layers of straw), barns for grain and animals, springhouses (for storage of dairy products in cold water), and smokehouses (for preserving meat, such as the famous Virginia hams, by smoking).

Plantation dinners could be elaborate, multicourse affairs with abundant meats, hot breads, seasonal vegetables and fruits, and large amounts of alcohol. At Westover Plantation on the James River, blue-winged teal (duck), venison, asparagus, and garden peas were common on William Byrd's table (Fischer 1989). Other favorite dishes were "spoonbread" (a maize casserole), ham cooked in any of a dozen ways, oysters ("cooked any way"), fried chicken, fricassee of chicken, lamb, game, pies filled with meat or fowl, and the region's own peanut soup and peanut pie.

Foods in the South were preserved by drying, salting, and smoking, and although English cookbooks had long advised preserving fruits in brandy, this was a costly treat, available only for the rich. In general, for most in colonial Virginia, winter meant monotonous meals of cornbread, beans, and ham; variety in off-season meals had to await canning, which came with the Industrial Revolution.

English colonization spread farther south in the late seventeenth and early eighteenth centuries. In 1670, settlers and slaves from the crowded sugar island of Barbados had landed on the coast named "Carolana" for Charles I, with its capital city of Charleston, named for Charles II. By the early eighteenth century, Carolina was thriving, its semitropical economy based on the growing of indigo, hemp, sugar, and rice. The whites of Charleston drank beer and whiskey, both made from maize, and ate cornbread, but they also became – in that time, at least – the only society of English-speaking people to eat rice as a dietary staple (Rutledge 1979). They retained wheat for bread making, but meals were centered on rice, which even today is more prominent on Charleston tables than on many others in America.

Slaves, some of whom had known rice in Africa, provided much of the knowledge for planting, harvesting, and cooking it, although some innovations, such as the use of tidal flows to drive water into the rice paddies, were conceived by the whites (Dethloff 1988). Rice was generally prepared in the "Indian" or "African" manner, in which boiling was followed by steaming. Among the favorite rice dishes were "pilau," made with pork, "hoppin' John," made with black-eyed peas and ham hocks, and breads made with rice and wheat flour (Hess 1992). This rice-eating plantation society spread to coastal Georgia, and in both colonies, the isolation of African slaves on rice-growing sea islands led to the distinctive culture, language, and cookery of the African-American "Gullahs." Abundant seafood, rice, maize meal, and hot peppers were combined in such Gullah dishes as "down'ya stew" and shrimp-and-grits (Junior League of Charleston 1950).

Harriott Pinckney Horry, daughter of a prominent South Carolina Huguenot family, left a recipe book written at the end of the eighteenth century that provides some insight into the local cuisine. Her "journey cake" was made from either rice or maize; she also cooked with tomatoes, fresh ginger, and chilli peppers (Horry 1984). Clearly, her kitchen was the scene of good, and sometimes spicy, cooking.

Canada and American Independence

To the north, there was another society as different from Massachusetts as Massachusetts was from Virginia. In Quebec and Acadia, settlers from Normandy brought with them ways of cooking and bread making that persisted into the twentieth century. The center of their diets was the *pain de campagne*, or "bread of the countryside," made from a mixture of grains and baked in a wood-fired oven of clay or brick (Nightingale 1971). This bread – made in large loaves, four pounds being usual – was also the common bread of France during this period (so-called French bread was not made until the nineteenth century) (Boily-Blanchette 1979). Such dishes as meat pie (spiced with cinnamon or cloves) and yellow pea soup still survive in Quebec and Acadia (Gotlieb 1972).

Local ingredients modified the French-derived cookery of Quebec. Maple syrup found its way into everything from meat glazes to dessert pies, sometimes with disconcerting results, and hams were boiled in maple sap at sugar-making time (Benoäit 1970; Gotlieb 1972). The famous Oka cheese (similar to cheddar) also originated in this era (Gotlieb 1972), and American chillies were used to season pickled onions (Benoäit 1970).

British Canada's cooking was English in derivation, and plain dishes, such as boiled mutton and calf's head, as well as sweet custards, were common (Nightingale 1971). As in Massachusetts, entire meals were boiled in one iron pot; bacon, cod, and eggs, cooked together with potatoes and turnips, was one such sturdy meal (Nightingale 1971). Boiled "bag puddings," made with flour, eggs, and fruit, were often served for dessert (Benoäit 1970). As with other European colonies in North America, there was an abundance of foods. Oats grew well in Canada and went into oatmeal and bread; there were even "pilafs" made from oat groats instead of rice. "Grits" (Martha Washington's "greats") meant oat groats instead of corn, although "corn cake" did grace some Canadian tables (Benoäit 1970).

On the coast, oysters were a poor man's dish, and lobsters were so common as to be practically value-less, making people ashamed to eat them (Gotlieb 1972). Clams and cod went into pies, which in Canada were as popular as in New (and old) England (Benoäit 1970). Salt pork was so universal that it was even used in sweet cakes (Nightingale 1971). To accompany these dishes, Canadians made a variety of "wines" from all sorts of foodstuffs. Their "port wine," for example, was a concoction of whole wheat, currants, raisins, and potatoes that contained no grape juice. "Parsnip wine" and "beet wine" were other drinkables (Nightingale 1971). These country wines, like rum, owed their fermentation to sugar that Maritime settlers obtained from the sugar islands. Rum is still a preferred beverage in New Brunswick, where a "black rum" unknown in the United States is a favorite (Personal communication from Charles Morrisey 1996).

Canada and the colonies to the south were to be separated politically as well as in culinary matters. The American Revolution led to significant changes both on and off the table. American corn whiskey became more popular than rum, and it has been claimed that many drank coffee instead of tea as a show of loyalty to the new republic. But although tea was no longer available through British channels (as it had been before the Revolution), American traders began to obtain it directly from China. The switch from tea to coffee began in the early nineteenth century as Brazil began shipping more coffee to North America. This dramatically reduced prices and thus encouraged more widespread use of the beverage (Cummings 1940).

The Revolution affected the cooking of Canada, as thousands of loyalists fled the thirteen colonies to settle there. Some refugees from Virginia baked cornbread on the hearth or in a skillet (Nightingale 1971), although their "johnnycake" became decidedly Canadian with the addition of maple syrup. Fried chicken and "spoonbread," suggestive of a southern influence, were also enjoyed in Canada, and the chicken curry that came north was, as in South Carolina, called "country captain" and attributed to sea trade with India (to conform to local tastes, the Nova Scotian version of the dish called for only a single teaspoon of curry powder for a four-pound chicken) (Nightingale 1971). Yankee influence, in the form of Boston baked beans, was apparent in Nova Scotia as well (Benoäit 1970). Tea remained the preferred hot beverage, and teahouses were opened there as well as in other regions of Canada.

A Canadian cookbook of this period dealt apologetically with chilli peppers because they were a part of recipes from "Old Country people" and "Western dishes" for "a man's world" (Benoäit 1970: 86, 175, 182). On the other hand, "green tomato chow," a version of "chowchow" (a relish common in the American South), contained red peppers, and its apples and cucumbers link it, like chowchow, with the mixed fruit-and-vegetable pickles of medieval

England (Benoäit 1970). Perhaps Canada's most eccentric contribution to American cooking resulted from the resettlement of the Acadians, or Cajuns, in Louisiana. These exiled French-Canadians adopted the hot spices, rice, and seafoods of their new home and created a cuisine unlike any other (Root and de Rochemont 1976).

Cookbooks and Cooking

The first cookbook published in America was E. Smith's *The Compleat Housewife,* a 1742 reprint of a 1727 British volume (Smallzreid 1956). Other English cookbooks, such as Hannah Glasse's *The Art of Cookery,* were also printed in America but reached few readers in a land where many were illiterate and any kind of book ownership was rare. In 1796, Amelia Simmons, styling herself "an American orphan," published *American Cookery* in Hartford, Connecticut (1965). It was the first cookbook to include recipes employing such American staples as maize and pumpkins. For "johnnycake" or "hoecake" (the first recipe for cornbread in English), she instructed the reader to "scald 1 pint of milk and put to 3 pints of indian meal, and half pint of flour – bake before the fire" (Simmons 1965: 57). The author also included numerous recipes for vegetables and mentioned five kinds of cabbage and nine different beans. Kitchen gardens were apparently common in her world, as she supplied information on how to plant and harvest.

Simmons's book indicates how tastes had changed in Anglo-America since colonial times (for one thing, spicy dishes were no longer in favor) and also reveals several continuing trends in the food history of North America. First, there was still the immense abundance of food available that has already been noted. Second, cookery retained its English character, with minimal seasoning and meat as the center of the meal. Third, the authorities on cookery were not (as, for example, in France) a restaurant-trained elite but rather housewives and home cooks. Although Simmons herself was careful about cooking, the attention to quality of ingredients and cooking methods that later distinguished the *grande cuisine* of France were, on the whole, lacking in American cooking. It was apparent that, in cooking, America had inherited both the good and the bad from England.

The Nineteenth Century

During the nineteenth century, Native American populations continued to decline as European, African, and some Asian peoples filled the North American continent. Wild game, although still common, had been hunted to the point that several species, such as the passenger pigeon, beame as extinct as some of the Indian peoples who had once preyed on them (Root and de Rochemont 1976).

Three nineteenth-century trends combined to revolutionize the American diet. One was immigra-

tion, involving a mass of Europeans, as well as the arrival of the first Chinese immigrants in the west of the continent. The second (which created the first) was the Industrial Revolution. The third (made both possible and necessary by the first two) was the use of industrial technology to provide the growing population of European-Americans with a quantity and variety of foods undreamed of in previous ages. The quality of that food, however, was – and remains – questionable.

Regional Foodways of America

The North and urban squalor. Urban workers seldom enjoyed well-balanced meals. Americans who had migrated from rural regions crowded together with immigrants in the "slum" areas of northern cities, where fresh foods were largely unavailable, and hunting, fishing, and gardening were difficult, if not impossible. Consequently, as a rule, the diet of urban workers was inadequate in all but calories; fresh vegetables and fruit were almost absent from their tables, save for a few weeks in the summer and fall. Throughout the United States, the favorite vegetables were potatoes and cabbage, and the favorite fruit remained apples in their hundreds of local varieties (Levenstein 1988).

Southern and African-American foodways. The nineteenth century's antebellum epoch brought with it increasing polarization between North and South. As the nation lurched toward the Civil War, northern religious reformers and abolitionists attacked the institution of slavery, while southerners from the Chesapeake region, the "Rice Coast," the back country, and the western states of the newer South defended it. These disparate regions of the South became united, first by the slaveholding ideology, and then by the Confederate "Cause."

Southern cooking at this time was still marked by a preponderance of locally produced staples, such as maize, salt pork, and garden greens. Beef was little known and fresh milk almost nonexistent (Hilliard 1988). Whether or not the diet of black slaves was adequate has long been debated, but one conclusion is that although adequate in calories, it lacked sufficient protein and vitamins. Protein-calorie malnutrition and vitamin deficiencies are attested to by contemporary evidence (Kiple and King 1981). Some slaves kept garden plots or animals – a source of economic independence – but although a few could hunt or fish, most relied almost solely on rations. These provided a relatively monotonous diet of salt pork, maize meal, and, sometimes, molasses or sweet potatoes, although most slaves were given vegetables in season (Hilliard 1988). The use of fatty rather than lean pork for slaves was justified by the conviction that fat provided the energy needed for hard labor. The slaves' diet was the basis for modern "soul food."

For the planter class, excess was frequently the

rule. One of the most astounding of many extravagant dishes was the "Carolina wedding cake" made in 1850, which called for, among other things, 20 pounds each of butter, sugar, flour, and raisins, as well as 20 nutmegs and 20 glasses of brandy (Junior League of Charleston 1950). One author has estimated that it would have required 1,500 eggs and weighed a total of 900 pounds (Smallzreid 1956). Similar excesses were evident among cooks who deep-fried entire turkeys and garnished tables with great bowls of turtle steaks, merely to whet appetites (Hilliard 1988). One dinner on record featured ham, turkey, chicken, duck, corned beef, fish, sweet potatoes, "Irish" potatoes, cabbage, rice, beets, 8 pies, syllabub, jelly, "floating islands," and preserves (Rutledge 1979). Peach brandy and corn whiskey washed all of this down.

Virginians were as proud as South Carolinians of their reputation for gracious living. Tomatoes figured prominently in Mary Randolph's *The Virginia House-Wife*, originally published in 1828 but actually based on plantation cookery from the colonial era. Randolph, a relative of Thomas Jefferson, presented such recipes as hot-pepper vinegar, buttered okra, and stewed tomatoes, along with plenty of others for pork dishes and cornbread. Other writers, such as Letitia Burwell (1895), reveled in the colonial and antebellum past with exuberant nostalgia. Among her memories was afternoon tea with Robert E. Lee, who displayed the Custis silver of Mount Vernon at his table amid a truly English array of cakes and pastries. But such fondly recalled luxuries were not typical of Southern living, with its sharp polarization of the culture by class and race, at the table as well as in church and home.

Emancipation from slavery brought no freedom from a restricted diet, and after the Civil War, the poor – both black and white – lived on a regimen of cornbread, beans, grits, biscuits, and salt pork. Cornbread predominated over wheat bread even among those who could afford the latter: Southerners had come to prefer its distinctive taste (Hilliard 1988). The poorest chewed dirt, apparently to relieve the symptoms of hookworms, and frequently suffered from pellagra. This nutritional deficiency disease was the result of a diet lacking in niacin (one of the B vitamins) and progressed from diarrhea and dermatitis to dementia and death. Ingestion of any niacin source, such as fresh meat, was the cure (Cummings 1940). Poverty shaped the diet of the South in other ways. The poor used sorghum syrup to sweeten their coffee, pastries, and cornbread (because store-bought sugar was too expensive), and sorghum, an African plant, is still grown in the South to provide a flavorful sweetener (Cummings 1940). Similarly, the southern poor used cayenne *(Capsicum annuum)*, which could be homegrown, instead of store-bought black pepper (Hess 1992).

The West and Hispanic foods. The foods of the Southwest added still another culinary experience for the American palate. During the second quarter of the nineteenth century, the United States expanded, by conquest and by land purchase, into this large area with its predominantly Hispanic population. The region's culinary heritage was rooted in part in the chilli-laced tamales and tortillas of the Aztecs and their predecessors and in part in the culture of Iberia. Shipments of olive oil, hams, wine, and even saffron arrived regularly from Spain (Linsenmeyer 1976). The last Spanish governor of California was inaugurated in 1816 with a gala affair featuring poultry, game birds, cordials, wine, fresh fruit, breads, and cakes (Linsenmeyer 1976). Salmon, crab, and pork were cheap in this new land, and the vines left by the Spanish friars formed part of the foundation for today's California wine industry (Lichine et al. 1982).

Cultures and foodways blended as time passed. A Texas landowner took stock of his garden in 1839. The fruits alone comprised peach, fig, raspberry, quince, plum, "sour orange," melon, pomegranate, and strawberry; in addition, there were 13 herbs and 22 kinds of vegetables (Tucker 1993). That he grew such Spanish favorites as quince and chilli peppers is worth noting, and clearly a blending of cultures took place at his table. By contrast, the early Anglo settlers of Arizona stuck to such familiar favorites as roast beef, sourdough bread, and rhubarb pie (DeWitt and Gerlach 1990).

Also in the nineteenth century, a spicy stew of meat, beans, and chillies received its name, *chile con carne*. In 1828, a writer mentioned it as the staple of the poor, and although no recipe was given, it is clear that the dish was prepared with ingredients similar to those that go into it today. Linked to cowboys (for whom beef and beans were staples), to Mexico (where similar dishes had been served for some time), and to the "chili queens" who served it from market stalls, *chile* soon became a regional favorite (DeWitt and Gerlach 1990). By 1896, an Army cookbook included "Spanish" recipes that were actually Mexican, such as tamales, tortillas, *chiles rellenos,* and refried beans with cheese (Levenstein 1988).

Before the Civil War, white settlers had moved into Oregon and Washington, where they found a potential culinary paradise. The Indians of the area had scorned agriculture because game and fish were so abundant. The salmon, abalone, and wild berries of the Northwest were supplemented by the white settlers with grain, meat animals, and fruit trees, all of which prospered in that climate (Root and de Rochemont 1976).

The Plains. The slaughter of the American bison (and of the Indians who depended on them) opened the Great Plains to white settlement. The artifact that increased the area's attractiveness was the steel plow, which enabled farmers to turn the tough sod of the plains and, thus, to grow wheat, with the result that wheat bread became available throughout the entire country (Root and de Rochemont 1976). A staple of these plains pioneers and others was sourdough bread, leavened by a yeast starter that was kept active by periodic feedings of water and flour. Known from California to the Canadian wilderness, it formed the basis of loaves of bread, pancakes, and even sweet desserts, and "sourdough" became the nickname of inhabitants of Alaska (Gotlieb 1972).

Pioneers also ate all kinds of game. Imaginative cooks made such dishes as stuffed moose heart and smoked gopher; others improvised French-style soups with fish from Canadian lakes (Gotlieb 1972). German and Czech pioneers brought one-pot casseroles to the region. A favorite on the trail was dried-apple pie: A cook rolled the crust out on the wagon seat, reconstituted the dried fruit by soaking, and had a pie ready to bake in the Dutch oven at day's end (Tannahill 1988).

No such treats characterized the foodways of the rapidly disappearing Indian population. Equipped with guns and horses, the Plains tribes had hunted the buffalo, using every part of it for food, implements, and shelter. But the wars against the whites ended with the natives confined on reservations and dependent for food on government handouts. Ruth Little Bear of the Blackfoot tribe recalled her grandmother's tales of food in a previous time, when buffalo tripe was stuffed with tenderloin, and neither spices nor utensils were used. She also provided recipes for fried bread, yeasted bread, and "bannock," the Scottish name for pan-baked bread, a staple among Indians subsisting on government-issued salt pork, flour, and rice (Hungry Wolf 1982). Other Indian dishes, dating from a time before the reservations, included a soup made from berries, "prairie turnip" (a wild root gathered by the tribes), and many kinds of smoked and boiled meat (Laubin and Laubin 1957).

Immigration

With the advent of steamships, the second half of the nineteenth century became a period when, for the first time, large numbers of non-English-speaking peoples poured into the United States to challenge the cultural dominance of the Anglo-Saxon "Old Americans." Of these, perhaps the most prominent in bringing new tastes were the Italians and the Chinese. Although immigrants from other areas also contributed ethnic dishes to the American repertoire, the Italians and Chinese founded the first "ethnic restaurants" and brought in new foods that Americans accepted, albeit after some initial misgivings.

European immigration. Irish settlers, fleeing the potato famine of the late 1840s, comprised the first wave of nineteenth-century immigrants. Like the English, the Irish had little tradition of refined cuisine, and those who were immigrants to hardscrabble Newfoundland continued to make such peasant dishes as "colcannon," a mixture of mashed potatoes, kale, and butter (Gotlieb 1972). In New York, Irish immigrants relied on bread, fried meats, pastries, and tea (Shapiro

1986). The Irish also brought Catholicism, with its insistence on Lenten fasts and meatless Fridays. However, despite their centuries-long experience in brewing and distilling, the Irish had little influence on American alcoholic beverages. American beer takes after German beer, and American whiskey was a unique maize product unknown in the British Isles until relatively recently.

Italians arrived toward the end of the century. Their traditions of cuisine, which stretch far back into history, were sophisticated, shaped in part by the variety of foods in sunny Italy and in part by the chronic scarcity in that country of fuel for fires, meaning that quickly cooked foods were cheaper to prepare. Their many contributions to American cuisine include pasta, olive oil, the versatile tomato, and wine. It is the case that as early as the time of Jefferson, some Americans were growing tomatoes and cooking pasta; indeed, Jefferson bought a pasta-making machine in Italy. But it was in the late nineteenth century that Italian immigrants inundated the Northeast, bringing with them a desire for fresh vegetables (especially tomatoes) and other staples of their Mediterranean homeland. During the depression of the early 1890s, the city of Detroit offered gardeners the use of vacant lots, and by 1896, this practice had spread to some 20 other cities, including New York. Reporters remarked on the lavish plots of tomatoes, peppers, and eggplant grown by Italians (Tucker 1993).

Immigration from Eastern Europe brought large numbers of Poles and Jews to America. Their culinary contributions included the dark rye breads of their homelands and the complex kosher dishes that were the stock-in-trade of the original Jewish delicatessens. Highly seasoned cold meats made the prohibition of cooking on the Sabbath more tolerable, and still do, although today such delicatessens, which are everywhere, are frequented by Jews and Gentiles alike.

The Jewish dietary laws that were cherished in the Old World, however, were frequently disregarded in the New. Jewish writers, such as Harry Golden (1958), have commented wryly that Chinese dishes, which nearly always included pork, were simply too much of a temptation for Jewish people. In fact, the Reform denomination of Jews set aside kosher dietary laws.

Other Eastern Europeans also came to America, in many cases settling in ethnic enclaves within large cities. Food festivals and church events helped to preserve the customs and dishes of such lands as Serbia, Lithuania, and Slovakia.

Chinese immigration. Far more exotic to Americans than the Eastern Europeans were the Chinese immigrants. The first Chinese came to America around 1820, and significant numbers followed during the California gold rush. Mostly Cantonese, they grew Asian vegetables in their garden plots and introduced stir-frying, the use of new seasonings, and above all, the Chinese restaurant (Linsenmeyer 1976; Tucker

1993). Preserved ginger, Chinese oranges, dried seafoods, and bean curd were imported, and each immigrant was allowed to carry in two jars of ginger for personal use (Linsenmeyer 1976). Shipping records show imports of foodstuffs as mundane as rice and as exotic as sharks' fins (Linsenmeyer 1976). Because of the southern Chinese origin of these immigrants, however, they did not bring with them the potted dishes and wheat breads of northern China, which remained unknown in America for another century and a half (Tropp 1982).

Restaurants

In the early decades of the nineteenth century, virtually no restaurants existed outside of the eastern cities with their grand hotels, although, of course, inns and taverns offered food (Root and de Rochemont 1976). But soon the excellent fare and low prices of Chinese restaurants made them a success despite an American apprehensiveness born of rumors that accused the Chinese of eating cats and dogs. Such "Chinese" dishes as "chop suey" and "chow mein" were actually invented in America and became American favorites; chop suey even made its way along with the Canadian Pacific railroad into the depths of that northern land (Smallzreid 1956; Benoäit 1970).

The most famous restaurant in the Northeast was Delmonico's in New York; first opened in 1825, it offered a menu and cooking style that were largely French, with some American concessions, such as "hamburger steak" (Pillsbury 1990). Eleven restaurants and three generations later, Prohibition caused the last Delmonico's to close in 1923 (Root and de Rochemont 1976), having served every president of the United States from 1825 to 1900; other clientele had ranged from Mark Twain to the Prince of Wales.

Toward the end of the century, Italians had also begun opening restaurants, and these joined other restaurants and saloons as welcome additions to the urban landscape of industrial America. In addition, industry and capitalism brought forth the first national chain restaurant, the Harvey House, founded in 1876 (Pillsbury 1990), which served standardized fare in locations along railway lines.

Food and Technology in the Nineteenth Century

The Industrial Revolution, which introduced mechanical power to produce consumer goods in quantity, brought widespread dietary changes, not least among them the advent of processed foods. By 1876, America was exporting yearly to Britain a million pounds of margarine, or "butterine," made from waste animal fat (Tannahill 1988). "Crisco," a mixture of fats, became a popular product that freed the housewife from having to render or strain hot grease, and powdered gelatin eliminated the labor of boiling calves' feet (Nightingale 1971). Roller mills manufactured white flour, which – despite its cheapness – kept longer, made loaves that rose higher, and was easier to digest

than brown flour (Tannahill 1988). In addition, it made much better sauces and pastries.

The Industrial Revolution also ushered new technology into the kitchen. The cast-iron stove meant that women no longer needed open fires for cooking, and the age-old risk of serious burns or even death for women who cooked at open hearths began to disappear (Smallzreid 1956). Refrigerated railcars and ships made fresh foods available far from their points of origin, and canning enabled the storage of large amounts of these and other foods for consumption out of season.

Fruits and vegetables had been preserved since Roman times by pickling or cooking with honey. With the 1809 development in France of "bottled" foods, and the later invention of the screw-top Mason and Ball jars in 1858, home "canning" became reliable and safe, and factory canning a multimillion-dollar industry (Root and de Rochemont 1976). The first tin cans were handmade, but the invention in 1849 of a machine that could produce them meant substantially lower prices for the food that they contained. The invention came just in time for the California gold rush, and by 1850 the miners were already eating large amounts of canned fish, shellfish, tomatoes, and peas (Root and de Rochemont 1976). The most significant food to be canned was milk, a process pioneered by Gail Borden and patented in 1856. His firm supplied large amounts of sugared, canned milk and juice to the Union army during the Civil War (Cummings 1940) and was still in business, although struggling, at the end of the twentieth century.

Recipe books provided instructions on canning for American housewives, who might each put up hundreds of jars of preserves each year, in addition to numerous crocks of pickles, relishes, "piccalilli," homemade catsup, and sauerkraut (Smallzreid 1956). Vegetables from the home garden and fruit from nearby orchards and farmers' markets were combined with spices in family recipes, and women often worked together to can as much as possible while a fruit or vegetable was in season.

Another method of keeping food was the icebox whose invention seems to have taken place in Maryland at the beginning of the nineteenth century – the broiling summers there doubtless the "mother" of this invention. But the ice had to be changed frequently, which would ultimately be remedied by home refrigeration. The discovery of the vapor-refrigeration principle and the invention of various compression machines were initial steps in this direction, and by the end of the Civil War, ice-making machines existed. By 1880 some 3,000 patents had addressed the topic of refrigeration – and some of these in turn led to a revolution in the meat industry.

The dominance of pork began to wane – even in the South – as southwestern cattle drives and the Chicago stockyards made available an enormous amount of beef (Levenstein 1993). Industrial workers' families, who had eaten only small amounts of fresh meat in the 1830s, consumed two pounds daily in 1851, and fresh meat was much more nutritious than the salted and preserved meats of colonial days. Milk consumption doubled, and the use of vegetables increased greatly (Cummings 1940).

Chicago's stockyards were modernized in the 1860s, and by 1875, manufacturers such as Swift and Armour, boasting of the cleanliness of their production facilities, had established their brands as leaders in the meat-packing industry, positions they still hold. In the 1870s and 1880s, railcars and ships, now equipped with refrigerators, carried meat to all parts of America (Root and de Rochemont 1976), and as Kathleen Ann Smallzreid (1956: 103) has noted, "refrigeration probably did more to change the flavor of the American meal than any other invention, and in doing so brought health as well as enjoyment to the table."

The newly mechanized stockyards used all parts of the animals they processed, including bone for china and glycerin for explosives (Smallzreid 1956). Unfortunately, federal inspection was negligible in the era of "robber barons"; sanitation was nonexistent, and by the turn of the century, conditions in Chicago meatpacking plants were horrific. When, in 1906, socialist writer Upton Sinclair published his eyewitness account of this situation, entitled *The Jungle*, the public was outraged. Meat sales dropped by half as people read of diseased animals, dirt, and excrement – as well as human body parts severed in accidents – being canned and sold along with the meat (Sinclair 1984). In reaction, President Theodore Roosevelt urged passage of the country's first Pure Food and Drug Law, mandating (among other things) inspection of meats sold in interstate commerce (Root and de Rochemont 1976). Despite this action, however, even as late as the 1970s, such foods as chicken pie were still being made under conditions considerably less than sanitary.

In addition to meat, trains carried fresh vegetables and fruits. Navel oranges from Bahia, Brazil, were planted in Florida in 1870 and in California in 1873. In 1887, California shipped 2,212 railcar loads of citrus fruit, mostly navel oranges. Five years later, that number had swollen to 5,871 carloads of oranges and 65 of lemons (Smallzreid 1956). Grapefruits were popular as well; in 1889, Florida shipped 400 tons of them. Bananas from Costa Rica were already arriving in quantity when in 1899 the United Fruit Company was founded. Thus began a monopoly of banana production in Central America and the Caribbean as well as a monopoly of distribution in the United States that would last throughout most of the twentieth century (Smallzreid 1956).

Sales of sugar doubled between 1880 and 1915 (Cummings 1940), and new sweets began to appear. Chocolate, once known to the Aztecs as a bitter spice and to the Spaniards as a beverage, was first made into candy in the second quarter of the nineteenth century. In 1876, "milk chocolate" was invented (Root and de Rochemont 1976). Cake making became easier – a result of improved baking powder – and ice cream, a rare treat before the invention of refrigeration, became available to all (Cummings 1940; Smallzreid 1956). In Canada, however, many rural areas saw almost no store-bought candy; even in the 1870s, candy was still made at home from maple syrup (Nightingale 1971).

The purchase of staples at stores was more typical as the century passed. The "New Woman" of the late nineteenth century was ready to give thought and action to such problems as women's rights, suffrage, and education because many household tasks had been eliminated. (It has recently been argued that mechanization increased housewives' workloads, but anyone who has cleaned clothes using lye soap and a boiler, or cooked a four-course meal over an open hearth, may appreciate why so many felt the immense appeal of the new technology.) As a rule, women no longer made soap, pickles, cheese, and cloth; nor grew vegetables, fruits, and medicinal herbs; nor butchered nor made beer at home (Smallzreid 1956).

Until the 1890s, the main meal ("dinner") was still eaten at noon, as it continued to be in much of rural America well into the twentieth century (Plante 1995). Typical meals in the late nineteenth-century Northeast might include a breakfast of corn muffins, fried potatoes, and fish, and a dinner might begin with macaroni soup and move on to duck salmi, baked potatoes, oyster salad, canned peas, and celery sauce, finishing with pumpkin pie. Supper, much lighter, could be muffins, dried beef, tea rusks, and baked apples (Smallzreid 1956).

Drinking in the Nineteenth Century

Drinking also changed drastically in the nineteenth century. The massive consumption of hard liquor in the early years peaked around 1840 at perhaps five gallons of alcohol annually per adult (Rorabaugh 1979). It subsequently declined for two reasons. The first was the rise of the American beer industry. German immigrants brought with them the knowledge of brewing lager, a much lighter beer than had previously been available to Americans, and the end result was the German-American beer of the twentieth century. The second reason had to do with the temperance movement. Its advocates railed against "Demon Rum" and urged its replacement by tea, coffee, or pure water (available for the first time in American cities).

Until the last decades of the century, coffee was usually made in the old way, by roasting beans over a fire or on the stove and grinding them at home; eggs and salt were used to get the coffee to settle (Smallzreid 1956). Inventors, however, had turned their attention to the improvement of coffee processing, and, in 1880, Joel Cheek of the Atlantic and Pacific Tea

Company developed a coffee roaster that allowed less flavor to escape during the roasting process. He marketed the coffee produced by this new method through his company's stores, naming the brand after the Maxwell House hotel in Nashville, where it was first served (Smallzreid 1956).

Ladies still met in the afternoon for tea, but this practice had nowhere near the popularity that it possessed in Canada and Australia, which had retained ties of tea and government with Great Britain. As late as 1834 in New York, tea (and coffee) was served in bowls as well as in cups, and into the twentieth century, some tea and coffee drinkers kept to the Chinese practice of pouring their drink from the cup into the saucer, from which they could sip it as it cooled (Pillsbury 1990).

Health, Nutrition, and Food Fads

The increase in the consumption of fruits and vegetables as well as meat and dairy products meant significant changes in the health of Americans. By the 1860s, life expectancy had lengthened, and Union soldiers during the Civil War (1861 to 1865) were, on the average, a half inch taller than soldiers had been in the period from 1839 to 1855 (Cummings 1940). Some researchers have claimed that average American stature subsequently decreased with the immigration of shorter peoples from southern and eastern Europe. In the 1880s, however, clothiers had to work from a scale of sizes larger than that previously in use, and a modern *corsetière* lamented that patterns from the nineteenth century were useless in the twentieth, indicating further increases in height and changes in body shape.

That nutritional improvements were taking place in America is borne out by the fact that health and stature did continue to increase as the turn of the twentieth century approached and passed. Harvard undergraduates in 1926, for example, were an inch taller than their fathers had been; the women of Vassar and Mount Holyoke were more than an inch taller than their mothers, and the width of their hips had decreased. In the same year, Boston schoolboys were three inches taller than boys of 1876 (Cummings 1940). Increasingly larger sizes of clothing at the end of the twentieth century suggested that, for better or for worse, Americans are continuing to get larger.

To return to the trend of the nineteenth century, however, it would seem that the presumed deleterious effects of using canned food, white flour, and too much sugar were more than offset by the abundance of fresh foods that Americans ate (Cummings 1940). Moreover, nutritional health was improving not only in spite of the increase in industrial food processing but also in the face of a number of faddish nutritional theories that, despite their shortcomings, enjoyed wide popularity.

The nineteenth century saw some strange food practices, with "Grahamism" perhaps the best-known example. Sylvester Graham combined a romantic admiration for "nature" with a fear of processed foods – especially roller-milled, white, bread flour – and preached that poor health could be remedied by regular bathing, drinking water instead of alcoholic beverages, exercise, vegetarianism, and avoidance of sexual activity.

Indeed, Graham took vegetarianism to a new extreme by rejecting sugar, mustard, catsup, pepper, and white bread, as well as meat (Root and de Rochemont 1976), and along with others of his ilk, he imagined that the classical Greeks and Romans had also been vegetarian, or at least partly so (Green 1986). "Grahamists" ate whole-wheat bread, dairy products, fruits, vegetables, and "Graham crackers," made with whole-wheat flour and molasses and invented by Graham, who claimed that such a diet would prevent illness and insanity and lessen sexual desire. Graham made many converts – despite hostility from butchers and bakers – and special boardinghouses opened to provide the food he recommended. Called "the prophet of brown bread and pumpkins," he counted among his disciples Sojourner Truth, Horace Greeley, and the entire sect of Shakers, who were vegetarians for about 10 years (Green 1986), although their rules later permitted some meat consumption.

Other nutritional theorists also linked religion, sex, and food. Mrs. Horace Mann, author in 1861 of a stern work on food and righteousness entitled *Christianity in the Kitchen,* argued that rich concoctions, such as wedding cake, suet-laced plum pudding, and thick turtle soup, were masses of indigestible material, which should never find their way to any Christian table, and that "there is no more common cause of bad morals than abuses of diet" (Shapiro 1986: 130; Tannahill 1988).

Another reformer, the Reverend Henry Ward Beecher (brother of Catherine Beecher and Harriet Beecher Stowe), feared processed flour as much as Graham did. Beecher argued that "the staff of life . . . has become a weak crutch," and his daughters held that store-bought white bread was "so much cottonwool" (Root and de Rochemont 1976: 22).

New "health foods" were another legacy of Grahamism, with cold breakfast cereal the most prominent. The Seventh Day Adventists, members of a church founded in 1863, held that meat, spices, tea, coffee, tobacco, and alcohol were both unhealthy and immoral and that "foods of vegetable origin" paved the way to salvation and to "God-given health and happiness" (Smallzreid 1956: 150; Root and de Rochemont 1976). They therefore began to manufacture healthy and "moral" foods in Battle Creek, Michigan, where, in 1876, Dr. John H. Kellogg invented breakfast flakes made from wheat. C. W. Post, a client, joined the quest for "moral" foods. He began to sell "Postum" (a coffee substitute) in 1895 and "Grape Nuts" cereal in 1898 (Smallzreid 1956). "Shredded Wheat," another health-food favorite, was invented in 1891 by Henry Perkey, a non-Adventist entrepreneur (Smallzreid 1956). In all cases, commercial versions of these products, which incorporated a great deal of sugar, bore little resemblance to the ascetic foods envisioned by their inventors.

An even stranger fad than Grahamism was "mastication," the brainchild of Horace Fletcher. Fletcher believed that a "filtering organ" in the back of the mouth performed most digestion and that an inordinate amount of chewing was necessary to stimulate it. Chewing each bite of food 32 times was recommended, and college students were recruited to practice it. But because excessive chewing interfered with the pleasure of eating, the mastication theory was soon abandoned (Levenstein 1988).

A more important influence on American foodways in the late nineteenth and early twentieth centuries was that of "domestic science." Beginning in the last quarter of the nineteenth century, increasing numbers of women learned about cooking through classes centered on the application of science to the kitchen. Such women as Catherine Beecher, author of a book on "frugal housewifery," urged women to take control of the household economy in order to save money on food and other expenses (Shapiro 1986). But although the ideas that they learned (such as balancing protein and carbohydrates so as to provide nutritious and inexpensive meals) were good ones, the results of their application were not necessarily so. Breakfasts of fruit, stewed corn, baked potatoes, and hot water won approval, whereas hot bread and griddlecakes were abhorred (Shapiro 1986). "Manly" meals of beans, potatoes, and beef alternated with "ladies' luncheons" of salads, marshmallows stuffed with raisins, and "Dainty Desserts for Dainty People," which allegedly appealed to "delicate" feminine tastes (Shapiro 1986: 99).

Another product of the period's obsession with "science" was the work of Fannie Farmer. A teacher at the Boston Cooking School, she originated the concept of "level measurement," which was probably the first challenge in all of history to the slapdash practice of using a pinch of this and a smidgen of that. Farmer's 1896 *Boston Cooking-School Cook Book* incorporated cooking-school methods and level measures in the belief that anyone who read it could learn to cook. Every cookbook that gives exact measurements is a tribute to the tremendous impact of this woman (Farmer 1896). The use of cookbooks and level measurements and the influence of cooking schools and nutritional theories would come to predominate in American kitchens of the twentieth century.

The Twentieth Century

The twentieth century saw far-reaching changes in the foodways of America. The development of hybrid maize and other crops, the application of high technology to food processing and cooking, and the growth of such commercial interests as fast-food restaurant chains and supermarkets all contributed to these changes.

Although most Americans entered the century with their near-Puritanical distaste for "fancy cooking" well intact, this attitude coexisted alongside the allure of the exotic. "Theme restaurants," looking like Arabian tents or Southern mansions, arose to serve the same steak and lobster as more mundane establishments. The most popular place for lunch in the early twentieth century – as before – was the saloon, with its free food for customers who purchased alcoholic beverages.

The early part of the twentieth century saw a continuation of the gorging of the previous century. In 1913, a New York dinner hosted by Frank Woolworth (founder of the "five-and-ten" store chain) featured caviar, oysters, turtle soup, pompano with potatoes, guinea hen, terrapin, punch, squab, grapefruit-walnut salad, ice cream, cake, coffee, and wine (Levenstein 1988). But change was in the air, occasioned by an ever-growing interest in home economics and nutrition and an awareness of the lighter meals served in other parts of the world.

The diets of ordinary people were improved, as more and more could afford to take advantage of new technologies, such as refrigeration and canning. Certainly there was a greater abundance of vegetables consumed, as farmers' markets made them readily available during the season; preservation and storage for consumption later in the year had also become easier. Thus, in the early part of the century, steelworkers in Pennsylvania, for example, ate typical American suppers of meat, beans, potatoes, fruit, beets, and pickles. Other meals served by their wives included spinach, tomatoes, and eggplant (Levenstein 1988). Towns famous for particular fruits or vegetables began to hold festivals to celebrate their abundance of such crops as artichokes, or apples, or pumpkins, or pecans, or garlic (Levenstein 1993).

Like their eastern counterparts, midwestern farm families ate much meat, milk, vegetables, and fresh fruit in the early twentieth century (Cummings 1940). However, this was not true for many in the South. Kentuckians in 1919 and 1920 were relying on pork and maize meal augmented with white flour, and many in the Blue Ridge mountains had similarly restricted diets, with coffee and flour the only store-bought foods (Cummings 1940). When federal relief came to the South during the Great Depression, such foods as whole-wheat flour and grapefruit juice were as alien as coconuts to those in rural areas, who often ignored these introduced foods because they were unfamiliar (Cummings 1940).

The nutritionists of the early twentieth century failed on several counts. One problem was their belief that "mixed foods" were hard to digest. Thus, immigrants were pressured to give up nourishing ethnic dishes, such as Hungarian goulash, for pork chops and applesauce. Another problem was the contemporary enthusiasm for canned foods, even in preference to local, fresh ones, which meant that vitamins and minerals were often inadequate. A third problem was the continued hostility of the nutritionists toward spices and flavorings as well as "fancy cooking" (Shapiro 1986; Levenstein 1988). This often resulted in bland and insipid dishes that made it difficult to interest anyone in this "new nutrition." Even fresh, hot bread was frowned upon as indigestible by the experts, who advised immigrant families to buy their breakfast bread and pastries during the evening before they were to be eaten so as not to endanger their family's health (Shapiro 1986).

These same experts told black migrants from the South to abandon "corn pone" and pork in favor of codfish balls and Boston brown bread, although few of them actually did so (Shapiro 1986). Some immigrants also resisted the pressure to conform, most notably the Italians (Shapiro 1986), although the restaurants they established served Italians and others with Americanized versions of spaghetti, garlic bread, and more (Levenstein 1993).

A final problem with the new nutrition was the inconvenience of lengthy food preparation, such as the making of stews, which the nutritionists favored. But greater changes in working-class foodways were afoot. The same era that saw the failed efforts of the nutritionists also witnessed the birth of an American tradition when, in 1916, the nineteenth century's "hamburger steak" was made into a sandwich by the founders of the White Castle restaurant chain, Billy Ingram and Walter Anderson (Pillsbury 1990).

The Era of Prohibition

In 1919, the United States adopted Prohibition. The Volstead Act – a constitutional amendment outlawing the commercial manufacture and sale of alcoholic beverages – had its roots in the temperance movement that had arisen in reaction to the endemic drunkenness of the late eighteenth and early nineteenth centuries. Long unsuccessful at the national level, the movement had gained momentum during World War I, and suddenly the saloons and free lunches were no more. Prohibition also encouraged the conversion of bars to sandwich counters and hamburger "joints," while chains of "family restaurants," such as White Tower, its rival White Castle, and Howard Johnson's, spread across the nation (Pillsbury 1990).

Once Prohibition laws were in place, organized criminal syndicates and smugglers began providing illegal liquor and beer to those thirsty Americans who were not already making their own. But concern over the rise of crime and violence associated with Prohibition, as well as the onset of the Great Depression, ultimately combined to ensure the repeal of the Volstead Act.

The Great Depression and World War II

The crash of the stock market in late 1929 signaled the start of a decade of severe economic difficulties for the United States, as well as for the rest of the world's developed nations. Oral history and folklore recount stories of "making do," and the outright hunger and dietary changes brought about by the depression are reflected in national statistics of the time. Meat consumption dropped from an average of 130 pounds per person per year to 110 pounds. Americans ate an average of just under 10 pounds of dried beans to fill up; the average in 1920 had been just under 6 pounds (Brewster and Jacobson 1978).

The Great Depression was followed by World War II, which shaped the course of world history for the next 50 years. Both world wars had stimulated vigorous drives to persuade the public to eat perishables so that such staples as wheat and beef could be sent overseas to the troops. However, this was not necessarily a hardship. "Meatless days," the aim of a program established to restrict meat consumption, were bearable when Americans could eat salmon, lobster, or tuna instead (Levenstein 1988). Likewise, because candy companies received large rations of sugar, candy consumption went from 13 pounds per person in the 1930s to 21 pounds in 1944 (Brewster and Jacobson 1978). "Victory gardens" helped to ease the shortage of rationed foods, although, in terms of rationing, Americans were scarcely as deprived as their European counterparts (Tucker 1993). Campaigns prompted people to can foods, and pressure cookers were made available (often on loan from the government), with the average family putting up 165 jars of canned goods annually (Levenstein 1993). In 1941, wartime nutritionists drew up the first table of recommended dietary allowances (RDAs) for the chief nutrients. Flour and milk were quickly "fortified" with them (Levenstein 1993), with the augmentation viewed as an inexpensive way to attract consumers (Brewster and Jacobson 1978).

Changes in agricultural technology also began to affect the American diet. In the 1940s, the use of hybrid strains of maize had increased the U.S. maize yield from 30 bushels per acre to 40; by 1980, yields of 100 bushels per acre were the norm. Because hybrid seeds were produced by crossing parent strains, however, farmers who wanted the greater yields that hybrids made possible had to buy seed each year, instead of saving it, as had been the case in the past. Immense profits followed for seed companies as hybrid tomatoes, cotton, and other crops were developed (Kloppenburg 1988). One result has been that older, open-pollinated strains of maize and vegetables have been neglected and, in some cases, pushed to extinction. Another result, in the eyes of critics, is that because much of the increased maize yield has served as animal fodder and only reaches consumers secondhand in the meat they purchase, much energy and land is devoted to (and pollutants created by) what might be seen by some as waste on a massive scale.

"Convenience" Foods and
the Homogenization of Tastes

With the 1950s, the new "consumer society" began to demand convenience in food preparation and consumption. Sales of fresh fruit dropped from 140 pounds per person in the 1940s to 90 pounds in the 1960s, whereas those of preserved fruit – loaded with sugar – increased (Brewster and Jacobson 1978). Intensive marketing of soft drinks (the amount consumed went from 90 servings per person per year in 1939 to 500 in 1969) led to a drop in coffee drinking, although the consumption of tea (mostly iced tea) increased very slightly (Brewster and Jacobson 1978). With the promise of more leisure time for cooks and their families, the proliferation of packaged foods put on the table such dishes as a so-called Welsh rarebit, made easier to prepare with Kraft's "Cheese Whiz" – a processed, foamy "cheese" product sprayed from an aerosol can – introduced in 1953 (Levenstein 1993). Another new food for many 1950s Americans was pizza, made by Italians in local restaurants, and a treat for Mom on her "night off" (Levenstein 1993). Pizza, as is true of many other Americanized foods, soon bore little resemblance to that made in the nation associated with it.

Local menus became more homogeneous in the twentieth century as canned and frozen foods, along with air-shipped fresh foods, increasingly meant that the same foods were available everywhere. As a result, it was (and is) easier for Virginians to buy kiwifruit (imported from New Zealand) than papaws (grown in their own state). Another consequence of the mass movement of staples was the establishment of fast-food restaurant chains. These differed from the chain restaurants of the nineteenth and earlier twentieth centuries in that the standardization of food preparation produced procedures that could be performed by low-paid, unskilled workers. McDonald's, perhaps the best known of the fast-food chains, began its rise in 1954, when Ray Kroc bought the McDonald brothers' restaurant and began to expand its hamburger business (Kroc 1977). By 1990, McDonald's had 8,000 outlets in the United States alone. Each served standardized foods, such as french fries made from Russet Burbank potatoes of uniform size, which were aged for a predetermined period to ensure that uniformity. The mid–1950s also saw the beginnings of Kentucky Fried Chicken, Burger King, Lums, and a number of other chains that soon followed (Pillsbury 1990).

These restaurants owed their success to several factors. First, identical portions of food could be refrigerated or frozen and shipped to any restaurant in the chain, ensuring that food that tasted the same could always be found under a familiar sign. Second, fried chicken and grilled hamburgers could easily be turned out in assembly-line style, with prices so low that local restaurants had great difficulty in competing. Third, diners generally served and cleaned up after themselves.

Fast food is almost always high in sugar and fat, and the nature of the business, until recently, made fresh fruit and vegetables unlikely offerings. However, in view of the health and environmental concerns of the 1990s, some chains have made salads and pasta available and have added lowfat products.

Revolutions in Food Technology
and Distribution

Over the course of the twentieth century, American grocery shopping increasingly centered on large chain stores, which offered a vast variety of foods, ranging from fresh meats and fish to canned and baked goods to an ever-increasing array of frozen foods. Credit for the latter belongs to Clarence Birdseye, originator in the late 1920s of the brand of frozen foods that bears his name. He developed the "quick-frozen" method, along with cardboard packages that allowed food to freeze and thaw while maintaining an attractive appearance (Levenstein 1993). General Foods purchased his company and prospered, as many American households – even during the depression years – acquired refrigerators with freezing compartments. Others prospered as well; as early as 1941, there were already some 250 firms marketing frozen foods. Refrigerators in the home brought about a reduction in the consumption of canned condensed milk and a concomitant increase in the use of fresh milk (Brewster and Jacobson 1978).

The use of twentieth-century high technology in mass-production food processing was matched by technological advances in the kitchen at home. In general, however, the latter was more an adaptation of traditional cooking strategies to new technologies than the development of a truly new style of cooking. Thus, although the wood-fired ovens of the early nineteenth century were replaced by gas and electric ovens, the cook still put food inside and shut the door to bake, roast, or warm it. Pots were placed on gas or electric burners, just as they had been on wood stoves. Even "new" cooking methods that came into widespread use, such as stir-frying, were rooted in much older cooking techniques (Tropp 1982), while boiling, broiling, frying, and other methods of great antiquity continued to be basic.

Technology, however, has resulted in better and more convenient stoves, cooking "islands" in the kitchen, and a whole array of food processors, choppers, blenders, and toasters. One product of recent technology is the microwave oven, which was common by the 1980s despite widespread misconceptions that it emitted dangerous radiation and made food radioactive. The main advantage of the microwave oven is that it can heat food faster and with less energy than a conventional stove.

Advances in food technology and distribution, however, have not resolved the problems faced by those of low socioeconomic status. Since World War II, government food programs have aimed at not only promoting good nutrition but providing it. Food stamps feed a large number of needy Americans, and the Women, Infants, and Children Program (WIC) distributes nutritious foodstuffs to pregnant and nursing mothers and to children under age 5. This effort has resulted in measurably higher birth weights and a lower percentage of birth defects (Levenstein 1993). There is opposition to these and other aid programs, but they do provide even the poorest Americans with access to supermarket foodstuffs.

Health Concerns

The large amounts of meat in the American diet has increasingly become a matter of concern in a country whose people consume one-third of all the meat available in the world (Root and de Rochemont 1976). The same is true of sugar. In the 1970s, American sugar consumption reached 99 pounds per person per year, or more than 4 ounces per day (Root and de Rochemont 1976; Mintz 1985), while the consumption of carbonated beverages totaled 107 billion bottles per year. The American "sweet tooth" doubtless has much to do with such health problems as weight gain, rotten teeth, indigestion, and heart and pancreatic troubles, including hypoglycemia and diabetes. It is also arguable that the replacement of more nourishing vegetable foods by sugar is a cause of iron and calcium deficiency (Root and de Rochemont 1976). The fact that Americans in 1976 took in 125 percent of the fat, yet only 75 percent of the carbohydrates, that had been consumed in 1910 has also become a cause for worry, as heart disease, cancer, and hypertension are all believed to be linked to a fatty diet (Brewster and Jacobson 1978; Robertson, Flinders, and Godfrey 1976).

The nutritionists of the 1970s began to shift the emphasis to holistic health and lifestyle, as it seemed clear that cancer and heart disease involved factors other than diet, such as smoking, lack of exercise, and stress. Cholesterol, a fatty substance that accumulates in arteries, began to receive blame for heart attacks with the meat and milk consumption of the previous century viewed as the reason for high cholesterol levels (Levenstein 1993), and in 1977, alarmed by this news, many Americans started to alter their eating habits by consuming more chicken, fish, and vegetables and less red meat and butter (Levenstein 1993). In something of a contradiction, however, overall beef consumption actually increased, largely because of an increasing reliance on fast foods. Food companies have responded to health concerns by marketing lowfat dishes in frozen and fresh forms (Levenstein 1993), but, of course, lowfat and diet foods often contain a plethora of chemical additives (Belasco 1989).

Alcohol is often seen as posing another health problem. Drinking has had an uncertain status in America since the repeal of Prohibition, and liquor, in particular, has come under attack for its empty calories. On the other hand, since the advantages of moderate wine consumption in the prevention of heart disease were discovered in studies of the "Mediterranean diet," it has become clear that moderate consumption of any alcohol can be preventive.

Alcoholic beverages from America's past have been resurrected. The hard cider enjoyed by colonists returned in the 1990s, and two brands share popularity with a variety of "microbrewed" beers (some of which are reminiscent of the beers of yesteryear that were brewed in taverns and private houses) and their mass-produced competitors. Even colonial pumpkin beer has returned. In addition, regional wineries as far north as British Columbia have begun to flourish, using hybrid grape strains capable of producing wine of varying quality. It is unfortunate that many of these, and other, alcoholic beverages often depend for their flavor and consistent quality on chemical additives.

Suspicion has been focused on additives since the late 1950s, when scientists found that the hormones used to fatten chicken and cattle were carcinogenic. Such concerns have resulted in tougher labeling laws and in the banning of dangerous chemicals, such as DDT (Levenstein 1993). Because such bans are generally based on studies involving rats and mice, there are also jokes about how everything gives cancer to mice. Less humorous, however, is the possibility of risks they pose for humans, who consume unknown (but apparently considerable) amounts of additives and chemicals every year. In the eyes of some, food companies argued for years to their discredit that all their ingredients were "natural" before they bowed to consumer pressure for change (Belasco 1989).

Recent Developments in Foodways

The "counterculture" movement of the 1960s brought about an idealistic renewal of interest in vegetarian diets, gardening, and subsistence agriculture. In addition, rural, agricultural communes were formed to pursue "alternative" or "spiritual" ways of life, although most of them were not vegetarian, and many raised animals for consumption. Commune recipes collected in 1970 and 1971 exhibited a heavy use of soybeans and whole grains (Horton 1972).

Food cooperatives, begun in the 1960s, provided members with access to unusual, foreign, and organic foods in exchange for labor. The most famous of these, Berkeley's "Food Conspiracy," gave rise to others. A 1990s form of collective food buying was community-supported agriculture (CSA). Thirty or more members belonged to a collective and paid large annual fees (perhaps as much as $1,000) to support a family farm, the produce from which was then divided among its supporters (Iggers 1996). Another new and different way of acquiring food has involved delivery companies that send shipments of meat and other foods (usually frozen) to fill members' home freezers. Such a service could save substantial amounts of money for members who buy in bulk, as well as ensuring that, as a rule, the meat they consume is of better quality than that offered to the general public.

The emphasis on healthy eating begun in the 1960s continues, as do attempts at self-sufficiency. In the 1990s, about 29 million Americans kept gardens, 26 million fished, and 14 million hunted game (Tucker 1993). Surveys in 1994 and 1997 indicated that at least 2 million Americans were vegetarians; many more, perhaps 10 million, avoided red meat. An estimated 500,000 of these went beyond vegetarianism to become "vegans," those who eat no foods of animal origin, such as milk, eggs, or honey (Personal communication from the Vegetarian Resource Group 1997). Inspired by "reverence for life" and "animal rights" ideals, vegans hope to create a lifestyle devoid of cruelty to animals. There is a large and growing body of information and misinformation available for vegetarians. The most famous vegetarian cookbook, *Laurel's Kitchen,* a volume replete with nutritional information, vegetarian and vegan recipes, and moral exhortations, was compiled by members of a vegetarian collective in Berkeley, California (Robertson, Flinders, and Godfrey 1976). Like Sylvester Graham before them, the authors of *Laurel's Kitchen* abhor spices, white flour, and meat.

Laurel Robertson and her colleagues drew heavily on the influential work of Adelle Davis and Frances Moore Lappé. Davis was a key figure in Rodale Press's network of organic gardening cooks and writers. Accused in the late 1950s and early 1960s of providing readers with potentially harmful information on vitamins and minerals, as well as disquieting cooking and eating practices, she was labeled "potentially dangerous" long before her death from cancer – a disease that she believed her pattern of mineral and vitamin consumption would prevent. She also thought that it would prevent heart disease, yet her editor, J. I. Rodale, died of a heart attack (Levenstein 1993).

Lappé, author of *Diet for a Small Planet,* advocated replacing meat protein with "complementary" proteins found in grains and beans in order to lessen the stress placed on the world's environment by the feeding of grain to meat animals. Lappé's inspiration had been another fad diet, "macrobiotics," invented by George Ohsawa in Paris and allegedly based on Zen monastic cooking from Japan. This regime consisted of a series of diets, each more restrictive than the last. At first, converts partook of fish, noodles, clam sauce, and vegetables, according to the season (round food was eaten in winter, for example). But at the most restrictive level of macrobiotics, no food was permitted save brown

rice and 8 ounces of liquid per day. The American Medical Association condemned macrobiotics, but this has only made it more attractive to "cranks" and conspiracy-minded "brown-ricers" (Levenstein 1993).

Then there have been fads, normally involving relatively small numbers of people, concerning cooking utensils. An example was the German *Römertopf* ("pot of the Romans"), an unglazed clay vessel used to bake meat and vegetables without the use of oil. Although capable of producing interesting results, the pot was difficult to use with many traditional recipes and proved to be a commercial failure in the United States (Tropp 1982). Another fad, backyard grilling, represents a considerable expansion of men's role in home cooking, which early in the twentieth century was limited to carving the meat (Levenstein 1993).

In a wider and somewhat contrasting development, the increase in career options for women has brought about a partial eclipse of regional and ethnic cooking traditions, as fewer families cook traditional meals "from scratch" at home. Although such meals were never fads, the often laborious preparation of such ethnic foods as tamales or raviolis is now generally confined to holidays. At the turn of the 1990s, only about 15 percent of American households regularly cooked and ate three meals a day at home (Belasco 1989).

Nonetheless, the appeal of the exotic is stronger than ever, with fads for ethnic cuisine coming and going much like technological fads such as home bread- and pasta-making machines. One important result has been to make exotic ingredients increasingly more available. Native American foods, such as Jerusalem artichokes and wild mushrooms, can be found in giant chain stores side by side with Thai lemongrass, fresh habanero peppers, Italian mushrooms, and sun-dried tomatoes. Honey mead, nowadays little known in the Western world, can generally be found in Ethiopian restaurants; "chicken Kiev" and fried rice, once rare treats, are now available in grocery stores in both frozen and unfrozen forms (Levenstein 1993).

Another exotic influence has to do with the latest influx of Spanish-speaking peoples to the United States during the latter half of the twentieth century, along with an increase in the number of Americans who speak Spanish. This trend has led to a nationwide acceptance of "Mexican" or "Tex-Mex" (meaning a combination of Texan and Mexican) foods. Chi-Chi's, Taco Bell, and other restaurant chains serve various versions of "Tex-Mex" cuisine to millions of customers, and burritos, tacos, and salsa are available in restaurants and supermarkets everywhere. Indeed, sales of salsa surpassed those of catsup in the 1990s.

The chilli pepper became a trend in itself in the 1990s. Catalogs listed hundreds of varieties of hot sauce, and representations of peppers decorated everything from china to underwear (DeWitt and Gerlach 1990). Monthly magazines and Internet Web sites listed enormous numbers of hot and hotter dishes; some incorporated explosive amounts of capsaicin (the chemical that produces the chilli's characteristic burning sensation), which is derived from specially bred varieties of peppers. Just one Red Savina, the hottest chilli pepper marketed in 1996, was alleged to be capable of producing spicy "heat" in 200 pounds of sauce!

Chilli peppers also figure prominently in the new cooking of Asian-Americans. The presence of Chinese people in California since the days of the gold rush has introduced the sophisticated culture and cookery of China to consumers. Changes in immigration laws in 1965 permitted a new wave of Asian immigrants, many of them Chinese, who found a tradition of Chinese-American cooking already in place. The 1980s fad for stir-frying induced supermarkets to carry Oriental vegetables, bean sprouts, soy sauce, and other Chinese sauces. Woks and Chinese steamers appeared in gourmet food stores, and earlier Cantonese restaurants were joined by Sichuan, Hunan, and "Peking"-style eateries. Ordinary Americans discussed and ate "pot-stickers" and other dim sum (a series of small portions of a variety of foods), and the availability of Asian foods – including Korean, Vietnamese, and Thai, among others – continues to grow.

Food writers and chefs, such as Julia Child, Craig Claiborne, James Beard, and Martin Yan also helped to introduce exotic cooking techniques and ingredients in their television programs and cookbooks. Child was perhaps the most influential in a drive to bring French cuisine to the American table; Yan's "Yan Can Cook" combined Chinese-American food with comedy and culture; and Beard's cookbooks are valuable resources for anyone studying gourmet cooking. The popularity of such books and programs has encouraged in Americans both a receptiveness to new ingredients and a demand for produce, meats, and seasonings that are absolutely fresh.

The Future

It is not easy to predict the future of foodways in America. Such major trends as preservation by freezing, dehydration, irradiation, and the use of additives will doubtless continue. The near future may bring "tissue culture," a technology that can produce coffee, spices, and drugs without growing entire plants (Kloppenburg 1988). The accelerating demand for speed and convenience in the 1990s that resulted in so many new time-saving products will probably also stay with us. Examples of really "fast" foods are packaged salads, sold with dressing so that the consumer simply opens the package and eats; microwave brownies, "baked" in a microwave oven; caramel topping that requires only pouring onto baked apples; "no-bake" cheesecake in machine-made pie crusts; and even ready-made omelettes that can be microwaved.

It seems clear that more and more processed foods of every kind, including those altered by biotechnology, will confront the consumers of the future. Probably we will also continue to witness the phenomenon of one ethnic food fad succeeding another, this accompanied by the marketing of ethnic foodstuffs in "Americanized" forms to satisfy desires for foods that are exotic but nevertheless familiar. Health and environmental concerns will doubtless lead to an increasing consumer insistence on accurate labeling and honest marketing procedures. As the planet becomes increasingly crowded in the twenty-first century, more efficient strategies will be required to feed growing numbers of people. America's vast bounty will likely be called upon, and it is to be hoped that the response will be both thoughtful and caring.

James Comer

Bibliography

Belasco, Warren J. 1989. *Appetite for change: How the counterculture took on the food industry.* Ithaca, N.Y.

Benoäit, Jehane. 1970. *The Canadiana cookbook: A complete heritage of Canadian cooking.* Toronto.

Boily-Blanchette, Lise. 1979. *The bread ovens of Quebec.* Ottawa.

Booth, Sally Smith. 1971. *Hung, strung & potted: A history of eating in colonial America.* New York.

Brears, Peter C. D. 1987. *Traditional food in Yorkshire.* Edinburgh.

Brewster, Letitia, and Michael F. Jacobson. 1978. *The changing American diet.* Washington, D.C.

Burwell, Letitia M. 1895. *A girl's life in Virginia before the war.* New York.

Crawford, Mary. 1914. *Social life in old New England.* New York.

Crosby, Alfred W. 1986. *Ecological imperialism: The biological expansion of Europe, 900–1900.* Cambridge.

Cummings, Richard Osborn. 1940. *The American and his food: A history of food habits in the United States.* Chicago.

Derven, Daphne. 1984. Deerfield foodways. In *Foodways in the northeast,* ed. Peter Benes and Jane Montague Benes, 47–63. Boston, Mass.

Dethloff, Henry C. 1988. *A history of the American rice industry, 1685–1985.* College Station, Tex.

DeWitt, David, and Nancy Gerlach. 1990. *The whole chili pepper book.* London.

Driver, Harold Edson. 1961. *Indians of North America.* Chicago.

Duncan, David Ewing. 1995. *Hernando de Soto: A savage quest in the Americas.* New York.

Farb, Peter. 1968. *Man's rise to civilization as shown by the Indians of North America from primeval times to the coming of the industrial state.* New York.

Farmer, Fannie Merritt. 1896. *The Boston Cooking-School cook book.* New York.

Farrington, Doris. 1976. *Fireside cooks and black kettle recipes.* Indianapolis, Ind.

Fischer, David Hackett. 1989. *Albion's seed: Four British folkways in America.* New York.

Fritz, Jean. 1969. *George Washington's Breakfast.* New York.

Golden, Harry. 1958. *Only in America.* Cleveland, Ohio.

Gotlieb, Sandra. 1972. *The gourmet's Canada.* Toronto.

Green, Harvey. 1986. *Fit for America: Health, fitness, sport, and American society.* New York.

Hess, Karen. 1992. *The Carolina rice kitchen: The African connection.* Columbia, S.C.

Hess, Karen, transcr. and annot. 1981. *Martha Washington's booke of cookery.* New York.

Hilliard, Sam. 1988. Hog meat and corn pone: Foodways in the antebellum South. In *Material life in America 1600-1860,* ed. Robert Blair St. George, 311-32. Boston, Mass.

Horry, Harriott Pinckney. 1984. *A colonial plantation cookbook: The receipt book of Harriott Pinckney Horry, 1770,* ed. Richard J. Hooker. Columbia, S.C.

Horton, Lucy. 1972. *The country commune cookbook.* New York.

Hudson, Charles M. 1979. Introduction. In *Black drink,* ed. Charles M. Hudson. Athens, Ga.

Hume, Rosemary. 1970. *Cordon bleu book of jams, preserves and pickles.* Chicago.

Hungry Wolf, Beverly. 1982. *The ways of my grandmothers.* New York.

Iggers, Jeremy. 1996. *The garden of eating: Food, sex, and the hunger for meaning.* New York.

Junior League of Charleston. 1950. *Charleston receipts collected by the Junior League of Charleston,* ed. Mary Vereen Huguenin and Anne Montague Stoney. Charleston, S.C.

Kiple, Kenneth, and Virginia Himmelsteib King. 1981. *Another dimension to the black diaspora: Diet, disease, and racism.* Cambridge.

Kloppenburg, Jack. 1988. *First the seed.* New York.

Kroc, Ray, with Robert Anderson. 1977. *Grinding it out: The making of McDonald's.* Chicago.

Laubin, Reginald, and Gladys Laubin. 1957. *The Indian tipi; its history, construction, and use.* Norman, Okla.

Lea, Elizabeth E. 1982. *A Quaker woman's cookbook: The domestic cookery of Elizabeth Ellicot Lea,* ed. William Woys Weaver. Philadelphia, Pa.

Levenstein, Harvey A. 1988. *Revolution at the table: The transformation of the American diet.* New York.

1993. *Paradox of plenty: A social history of eating in modern America.* New York.

Lichine, Alexis, et al. 1982. *New encyclopedia of wines & spirits.* 3d edition. New York.

Linsenmeyer, Helen Walker. 1976. *From fingers to finger bowls.* San Diego, Calif.

Lockridge, Kenneth A. 1985. *A New England town: The first hundred years: Dedham, Massachusetts, 1636-1736.* Expanded edition. New York.

Milanich, Jerald T. 1995. *Florida Indians and the invasion from Europe.* Gainesville, Fla.

Mintz, Sidney W. 1985. *Sweetness and power: The place of sugar in modern history.* New York.

Nash, Gary B. 1968. *Quakers and politics: Pennsylvania, 1681-1726.* Princeton, N.J.

Nightingale, Marie. 1971. *Out of old Nova Scotia kitchens.* New York.

Pillsbury, Richard. 1990. *From boarding house to bistro: The American restaurant then and now.* Boston, Mass.

Plante, Ellen. 1995. *The history of the American kitchen.* New York.

Prins, Harald E. L. 1996. *The Mi'kmaq: Resistance, accommodation, and cultural survival.* Fort Worth, Tex.

Ragsdale, John. 1991. *Dutch ovens chronicled.* Fayetteville, Ark.

Randolph, Mary. [1828] 1984. *The Virginia house-wife.* Columbia, S.C.

Robertson, Laurel, Carol Flinders, and Bronwen Godfrey. 1976. *Laurel's kitchen: A handbook for vegetarian cookery & nutrition.* Berkeley, Calif.

Root, Waverley Lewis, and Richard de Rochemont. 1976. *Eating in America: A history.* New York.

Rorabaugh, W. J. 1979. *The alcoholic republic: An American tradition.* New York.

Rountree, Helen C. 1989. *The Powhatan Indians of Virginia: Their traditional culture.* Norman, Okla.

Rutledge, Sarah. [1847] 1979. *The Carolina housewife.* Facsimile edition. Columbia, S.C.

Shapiro, Laura. 1986. *Perfection salad: Women and cooking at the turn of the century.* New York.

Simmons, Amelia. [1796] 1965. *American cookery.* Grand Rapids, Mich.

Sinclair, Upton. [1906] 1984. *The jungle.* Cutchogue, N.Y.

Smallzreid, Kathleen Ann. 1956. *The everlasting pleasure: Influences on America's kitchens, cooks, and cookery, from 1565 to the year 2000.* New York.

Sokoloff, Raymond A. 1991. *Why we eat what we eat: How the encounter between the New World and the Old changed the way everyone on the planet eats.* New York.

Spencer, Colin. 1995. *The heretic's feast: A history of vegetarianism.* Hanover, N.H.

Sturtevant, William. 1979. Black drink and other caffeine-containing beverages among non-Indians. In *Black drink,* ed. Charles M. Hudson, 151-83. Athens, Ga.

Tannahill, Reay. 1988. *Food in history.* Revised edition. New York.

Temple, Robert K. G. 1986. *The genius of China: 3,000 years of science, discovery, and invention.* New York.

Tropp, Barbara. 1982. *The modern art of Chinese cooking.* New York.

Tucker, David. 1993. *Kitchen gardens in America.* Ames, Iowa.

Wolcott, Imogene, ed. 1971. *The Yankee cookbook: An anthology of incomparable recipes from the six New England states, and a little something about the people whose tradition for good eating is herein permanently recorded.* Revised edition. New York.

V.D.7 ❧ The Arctic and Subarctic Regions

Traditional foodways have played an intrinsic part in the daily lives of the Native American peoples in the Arctic and Subarctic. Unlike other Americans, whose visits to their local grocery stores for food are seldom memorable, the people of Minto could look at a piece of dried fish and remember where they caught it, the activity on the river, and congratulations received from family members. The point is that food is more intimate for those who catch, grow, or gather it than for those who simply drop it into a shopping cart. The procurement, processing, preparation, and serving of food unites such people with their history, their future, and each other. The use of local resources serves as a direct emotional and spiritual link to the environment on which they depend.

This chapter explores the prehistoric, historic, and current dietary patterns of Native Americans in Alaska, Canada, and Greenland. Because of the wide variety of cultures in the Subarctic and Arctic, this is necessarily a general discussion.

The People

The Native American groups of the Arctic and Subarctic consist of two major genetic and linguistic populations – the Northern Athapaskan Indians and the Eskimo. In Alaska and Canada, the Eskimo are generally coastal people who are believed to have entered North America some 9,000 years ago. The older denizens are the Northern Athapaskans, located for the most part in the interior of Alaska and Canada, who are thought to have crossed the Bering Strait about 15,000 years ago.

Environment

Subarctic

The Tanana people are Athapaskans who reside in the area of Minto Flats on the Alaska Plateau, which is dissected by the Yukon, Tanana, and Kuskokwim rivers. The landscape includes mountain ranges of 3,000 to 4,000 feet, rivers, streams, marshes, grassy fields, and islands.

There are four seasons in this Subarctic region. The winter – long, dark, windy, and very cold – is a time when minimal light and extreme cold limit travel. Spring is associated with the thawing of the rivers and boat travel, but frequent stops to warm up with tea and snacks are necessary to combat the cold. Spring weather is variable from day to day, with warm days and cold nights. Summer is short, warm, and without darkness, with rainy days often bringing concern about flooding rivers. These are the months that are associated with travel on the rivers and roads and, of course, with fishing and gathering. Autumn is marked by the gradual darkening of the night and colder days. By late autumn, the leaves have changed color or fallen, the snow has returned, and the focus is on moose and duck hunting.

A wide variety of flora are present in the Subarctic. Tree types include aspen, white spruce, birch, poplar, and willow. The spruce, birch, and willow are used for medicine, building materials, and fuel. Edible plants include wild rhubarb, Indian potato, wild onion, lowbush cranberry, highbush cranberry, blueberry, wild rose, and raspberry.

Animal populations that are hunted and trapped are mountain sheep, moose, bear, muskrat, rabbit, beaver, porcupine, and duck. A variety of fish are avail-

able, including salmon, burbot, grayling, whitefish, pike, and sucker.

All Northern Athapaskan populations practice a subsistence strategy of hunting, gathering, and fishing, which varies with location. It is a seminomadic subsistence strategy which, for some, involves moving from their villages to winter, summer, fall, and spring camps in order to take advantage of the local resources of each, although many now reside permanently in the winter camp.

There are, of course, regional variations. For example, the Tanaina, who reside in a lush coastal and riverine environment around the Cook Inlet in southern Alaska, have access to a wide variety of marine and inland resources. They are primarily hunters and fishers who procure mussels, crabs, seals, beluga, moose, caribou, and groundhogs. But their diet also incorporates a wide variety of plant resources during the spring, summer, and fall.

By contrast, more northerly populations, such as the Koyukon, live in a riverine environment considerably more mountainous. Like the Tanaina, these people also depend on hunting and fishing but rely more heavily on the latter throughout the year because of their access to the Yukon River. Salmon (chinook, chum, coho, and sockeye) has long been a primary resource for the Koyukon.

Arctic

The Arctic is designated as a high-altitude region, usually lying above the tree line. It includes a broad expanse of land stretching from western Alaska through Canada as well as Greenland. The ground is frozen year-round (permafrost), and minimal precipitation occurs.

The diversity of food sources in the Arctic is low compared to the Subarctic region. Eskimo populations throughout the Arctic depend mostly on marine species, including seals, whales, walrus, and fish (Freeman 1984). But inland fish are also procured, including char, trout, pike, grayling, and salmon (Freeman 1984). The most important land mammals that provide food are the caribou, arctic hare, and musk ox.

Precontact Subsistence

The majority of precontact Northern Athapaskan groups were interior populations of hunters, fishers, and gatherers, whose seasonal rounds were similar to the pattern seen today.

In winter – a time of minimal subsistence activity – large groups congregated at winter camps, where local resources were processed for food and clothing, and some celebrations were held. When the weather improved, from spring through fall, the larger groups divided into individual family groups that traveled to smaller camps, permitting greater access to food resources. Each family group tended to visit the same camp sites – loosely considered the group's own "territory" – every year. Some, such as the Upper Tanana people, were more dependent on large game, but they nonetheless fished the inland lakes and tributaries and the Tanana River. Spears, bows and arrows, fish traps, gill nets, dip nets, lures, and hooks were all employed in this seasonal harvest of protein, the storage of which was, obviously, important for the coming winter months (Sullivan 1942; VanStone 1974).

Throughout the spring, summer, and fall, the Northern Athapaskans dried, froze, and stored food in birchbark baskets above and below ground. The caches aboveground were small boxlike shelters on stilts with cutout openings or doors. Belowground the caches were dug into the permafrost and covered with wood to seal in the cold air and to protect against animals.

The mobility of the Northern Athapaskans allowed consistent access to food sources, yet their small groups were able to avoid depletion of such sources in any one subsistence area by having a variety of sites. The Tanana Valley people, for example, still continue to use a number of different sites during the year, moving from one to another by birchbark canoe or by snowshoe (Sullivan 1942; VanStone 1974).

In the spring and summer, the major foods obtained included whitefish, salmon, duck, and birds' eggs. Gathered products, such as blueberries and cranberries, were also stored during the late summer and fall months. The important foods during autumn were moose, caribou, duck, grouse, and rabbits. In the winter, stored foods were supplemented by trapping small game and by ice fishing.

Throughout the year, families spent considerable time exploiting other resources as well. Ducks were hunted in the spring as soon as the weather warmed and people could safely travel by boat. In the summer, berries and small animals were sought, in addition to fish, whereas larger mammals were hunted or trapped mostly during the fall. Such a pattern of seasonal subsistence was common for Indian populations, such as the Kutchin, Koyukon, Ingalik, Kolchan, Tanaina, and Ahtna (Clark 1981; De Laguna and McClellan 1981; Hosley 1981a; Slobodin 1981; Snow 1981; Townsend 1981).

In addition, some populations, such as the Ahtna and the Tanaina, who resided close to mountainous regions, could hunt Dall sheep (De Laguna and McClellan 1981; Townsend 1981). The Koyukon, who are northwest of the Tanana, actively traded with the Eskimo, which increased their subsistence region (Slobodin 1981), and some populations in the Subarctic, such as the Tanaina, hunted sea mammals along the coast of southern and western Alaska (Townsend 1981).

Almost all native Alaskan populations continued their seminomadic lifestyle until the turn of the twentieth century, when increased mining and fur-trading activities eventually brought about the development of permanent villages. But even today there are still many hunting and gathering populations that carry on in a traditional manner (Hosley 1981a; Berger 1985). Older members pass on subsistence knowledge to the rest of the population, which links the generations together (Berger 1985).

Contact and Chance in Subsistence and Diet

Prolonged contact with Western culture brought a dependence on trade goods, such as guns, iron chisels, knives, and axes and gradually led to the development of sedentary camps around the trading posts, which disrupted traditional subsistence activities (VanStone 1974; Martin 1978; McClellan 1981; Frank 1983; Newman 1985, 1987; Yerbury 1986).

In Canada, reliance on trade goods brought an increasing interdependence between Indians and trading-post inhabitants, as many of the former entered into economic relationships with traders. They hunted and fished for them, receiving trade items, such as guns, for their efforts.

One need only consider the disruption brought about when the Canadian Iroquois began, in the mid–seventeenth century, to hunt for furs instead of food. After depleting their own traditional hunting grounds of both food and fur-bearing animals, they began to encroach on the territories of neighboring groups. And as food resources continued to decline, they became increasingly more dependent on the trading posts. By the early 1800s, the moose and caribou had been overhunted and a dietary change had taken place, forcing the Indians to rely on hares, fish, and purchased food (Martin 1978). Yet even as food resources declined, sedentary life fostered Iroquois population growth, which considerably enhanced the risk of severe food shortages (Ray 1974).

To obtain goods to trade for food, many Alaskan natives turned to trapping in the late 1800s (McClellan 1981; Schneider 1986). The steel trap gained importance around 1900 and accelerated the pace of trapping animals for economic rather than subsistence reasons. Cash and trade relationships with the Alaska Commercial Company and the Western Fur and Trading Company, in particular, enabled Alaskan natives to purchase Western foods and products from trading posts and from Europeans moving through the region.

Animal populations declined as trapping increased and native human populations became more sedentary. Native trappers traveled ever farther away from these settlements in search of quality pelts, and it became necessary to leave family members behind, often for days. Moreover, as native populations continued to nucleate into fewer, and larger, settlements on the main rivers, the decrease in nomadic patterns led to a summer–winter dualism. By the middle to late 1930s, many families had established a pattern of occupying fishing camps during the summer and trapping and hunting from more permanent villages in the winter (Hosley 1981a). Finally, and obviously, an exchange of the traditional subsistence lifestyle for a kind of Western economic mode of living meant that increased sedentism also disrupted traditional dietary patterns.

Trade goods offered unique tastes in compact forms that were intriguing to the native populations. Foods high in carbohydrates, such as the white potato or crackers, infrequently found in the traditional diet, seemed attractive because they added variety. Other items, such as coffee, tea, flour, and sugar, quickly became staples to be purchased in bulk, and they are still bought in large quantities today. Coffee and tea quickly replaced the beverages decocted from local plants because they were easier to acquire than the traditional items.

The seductive appeal of trade goods reached out even as far as to the Greenland Eskimo (Freuchen 1935). Their participation in European whaling activities was rewarded with a variety of Western foods, such as tea, coffee, crackers, oatmeal, and chocolate (Freuchen 1935). The growing dependence on such foods was well documented by Peter Freuchen: "[T]he coffee beans they purchase raw and roast them to a crisp. To make them go a long way, the Eskimos mix the beans with rice or barley.... This form of coffee turns them into near-addicts. When they are without coffee, they say they feel worse than when they are starving" (1935: 109).

Disruption of traditional life by the fur trade was further exacerbated by the gold rush (1884 to 1920). Alaskan natives who had become dependent on Western products now encountered much difficulty in obtaining them. Competition for scarce food resources pushed the price of Western foods beyond their purchasing ability, and as a consequence, natives took jobs for wages in mining towns and on riverboats to increase their purchasing power. The trend toward sedentism that had begun with the fur trade accelerated, with some people abandoning all of their traditional subsistence activities as a result of the high wages to be obtained in the towns and on the rivers. And, as highways and roads were built in Alaska, the natives sought jobs associated with their construction.

Although such activity was generally destructive of old ways, such goods as firearms and dogsleds did help some people to adhere to traditional subsistence activities and diets. Certainly the rhythm of subsistence hunting was altered dramatically with the introduction of firearms, as hunting changed from a communal to an individual activity. It was the use of the rifle that ensured that moose and caribou would continue to be overhunted. Indeed, the caribou were ultimately decimated because they traveled in large herds, and with decreasing caribou, native populations focused their hunting strategies on the moose. Along with the greater access to food resources permitted by the rifle, hunters also increased their harvest of fur-bearing animals.

The adoption of sleds pulled by dogs was yet another factor that affected Indian lifestyle. Dogsleds permitted travel in the winter months, which extended the trapping season. In addition, as Robert A. McKennan (1981) points out, the introduction of the dog team increased both the need and the market for dried fish, an easily transportable dog food.

With an increased demand for fish, the Lower Tanana Indians adopted the use of the fishwheel, which meant larger quantities of fish for both human and animal populations. But because the fishwheel required deep and fast-moving water in order to be functional, Indian populations began moving away from the smaller rivers to the larger Tanana River.

Other dramatic changes came with the introduction of transportation based on fossil fuels (Cohen 1974), such as gasoline-powered boats, snowmobiles, and automobiles. Boats greatly increased access to local resources, especially during the fowl- and moose-hunting seasons. Water travel thus became more efficient, and winter and summer villages were able to be more widely separated (Hosley 1981a: 551).

Other gasoline-powered vehicles also allowed native people to move within their subsistence area faster and more frequently. In the 1960s, the Canadian Netsilik used snowmobiles to chase caribou. Unfortunately, it was this combined use of gasoline-powered vehicles and firearms that brought about the near total destruction of caribou in Canada (Neatby 1984). Another technological factor that encouraged this sort of overhunting was the home freezer, which led to the taking of more game and fish than could be immediately used.

Current Dietary Patterns

The Mix of Western and Traditional Foods

Current diets in the Subarctic and Arctic contain a mixture of traditional and Western foods. Many native populations eat such a combination because they are unable to obtain adequate foodstuffs by reliance on either traditional subsistence activities or Western resources alone. Traditional activities are frequently limited by participation in wage labor, yet many people are unable to afford the cost of Western foods on a daily basis.

This reliance on both subsistence foods and trade goods is aptly described by Kristin Borre (1991: 49) for an Inuit population of North Baffin Island, Canada. In this Arctic region, traditional hunting activities are of great importance, with children ages 7 to 15 contributing 40 percent, men 37 percent, and women 23 percent of the effort to capture most of the protein consumed. But despite a high level of traditional subsistence pursuits, the Inuit are also incorporating Western foods, purchased for immediate consumption, into their diet. Among other things, Western foods are increasingly attractive to younger members of the community.

A similar pattern can be observed among the Inupiat of Alaska's North Slope. Although many of the adult men work as wage laborers in the oil development at Prudhoe Bay, the Inupiat still need to rely on traditional food hunting and gathering for about 45 percent of foods consumed. Their increased income has resulted in the consumption of junk foods, especially soda pop and candy by the children (Kruse, Kleinfeld, and Travis 1982).

The uneasy juxtaposition of Western foods and traditional foods in the diet is evident in Richard K. Nelson's description of Athapaskan Alaskan life: "Sitting down for an evening meal, members of an Athapaskan family might find moose meat, bear grease, and wild berries on the table along with store-bought soup, bread and butter, and canned fruit. Before eating, someone may give a Christian blessing; and then a young daughter might be told not to eat a certain food because it is tabooed for a woman her age" (1986: 214).

Ceremonial Diet

Ceremonial food use, which also features a variety of traditional and Western foods, deserves consideration in any discussion of food and drink among current Subarctic and Arctic populations. Thus, the ensuing discussion highlights Alaskan Athapaskan potlatches observed by this author in 1987 and 1989, which illustrate the incorporation of both, along with comparative examples drawn from both Canada and Greenland.

Potlatches serve the important purpose of marking an event taking place or a stage of life. Such events include death, the memory of a person (and perhaps the making of a memorial song), a birthday, the first salmon catch of the season, a moose killed, a marriage, and important meetings. The largest potlatches are the funeral and memorial ceremonies. Family members give a memorial potlatch some one to five years after an individual's death. Memorial song potlatches are organizational ceremonies to create a song about the life of the person who died. Important meeting potlatches usually occur when a weighty decision has to be made concerning the village. The occasion may specifically involve an individual, or a family, but the holding of a potlatch often radiates out gradually to include the entire village, as well as other villages, due to the interrelationships existing within the population. The extensive quantity of food available during potlatches means that the Northern Athapaskan people understand them to be feasts as well.

Knowledge of an impending major potlatch, such as a birthday or a memorial, spreads quickly through villages in interior Alaska – especially the ones in proximity to Minto by river travel or to Fairbanks by air. People in different villages have developed close ties at potlatches, events that encourage them to reevaluate long-held traditions, relationships with friends, and village ties.

At another level, the potlatch is an occasion for distributing goods (Langdon and Worl 1981). During any type of potlatch, people who attend receive both food and gifts. The latter are given in respect and gratitude by the people hosting the potlatch. At a funeral potlatch, for example, some of the possessions of the deceased are given as presents, which makes them emotionally significant for the recipients.

Extensive quantities of food are common in ceremonies in the Subarctic and Arctic. One example is the Northern Alaskan Coast Eskimo Messenger Feast, which is a matter of competition among villages, with the village giving the feast attempting to "overwhelm a guest with food" (Spencer 1984).

A wide range of traditional foods, featuring both animal and plant items, is served at potlatches. Important animal dishes are moose, duck, salmon, beaver, and whitefish. Plant foods include a variety of berries, such as blueberries and highbush and lowbush cranberries, all boiled with water, flour, and sugar.

At a major potlatch, such as a funeral, the chiefs and other men receive the most highly desired portions of food, such as the large bones with moose meat still attached and the heads of salmon. Fish heads, considered a high-status food, are also served to the elder women.

Although moose meat is an important traditional food served at every potlatch, it obviously is of greatest importance at a first moose potlatch. After a family obtains its first moose of the season, its members hold a potlatch during which moose may be the only traditional food served.

The use of a traditional food as the primary dish also occurs at a first salmon potlatch, which is held in the village after someone catches the first salmon in the spring. Following the first catch, every effort is made to procure enough salmon for everyone. At the potlatch, the salmon is cooked in a variety of ways – boiled, in soup, and its eggs are also served.

Other protein foods, such as beluga, are important ceremonial foods for the MacKenzie Delta Eskimo. Marine animals are also used by the Iglulki to supplement "feasts of boiled meat . . . to which the whole camp was invited" (Mary-Rousseliere 1984: 440).

Western foods too are consumed at the potlatches, although these products are generally considered supplemental to traditional foods. Of all the village potlatches, the birthday ceremony contains the greatest variety of Western products, such as barbecued chicken, hot dogs, carrots, celery, green salad, fruit salad, white cake with frosting, deviled eggs, cauliflower, margarine, jam, and sweet soft drinks.

By contrast, at funeral potlatches mostly traditional foods are employed. Funeral potlatches have been a tradition of the Minto people for a long time, which explains the greater use of traditional foods, whereas birthday potlatches are relatively new (elders have indicated that they never used to celebrate the event). Thus, the presence of more Western foods corresponds with the newness of the birthday potlatch.

Current Dietary Patterns and Health

Traditional diets in both the Subarctic and Arctic provided much protein with a good ratio of unsaturated to saturated fats, and they were low in sugar and carbohydrates. But current Western foods incorporated into the diet do just the opposite in that they deliver high levels of saturated fats, sugar, and carbohydrates.

H. H. Draper (1977) discusses the contrasting health effects of traditional and Western foods in the diet of the Arctic Inuit. The traditional diet yielded much protein, and the consumption of the stomach contents of caribou, along with seasonal plant harvests, contributed important vitamins and minerals to the regimen. But the addition of dairy products, sugar, and carbohydrate-laden foods to the diet has created serious health problems. In the case of dairy products, Native American populations lack the ability to absorb lactose, and lactose malabsorption can produce cramping and diarrhea (Harrison 1975). There are other health difficulties that arise from the sugar and carbohydrates in the Western diet, ranging from tooth decay and obesity to diabetes and heart disease. In short, a departure from traditional diets to which they were well adapted has created a frequently life-threatening crisis of health for native peoples of the Subarctic and Arctic regions of the Americas. Alleviation of that crisis must begin with this realization.

Linda J. Reed

Bibliography

Ammitzboll, T., M. Bencard, J. Bodenhoff, et al. 1991. Clothing. In *The Greenland mummies,* ed. P. Jens, H. Hansen, Jorgen Meldgaard, and Jorgen Nordqvist, 116-49. Washington, D.C.

Berger, Thomas R. 1985. *Village journey: The report of the Alaska Native Review Commission.* New York.

Borre, Kristin. 1991. Seal blood, Inuit blood, and diet: A biocultural model of physiology and cultural identity. *Medical Anthropology Quarterly* 5: 48-62.

Bresciani, J., W. Dansgaard, B. Fredskild, et al. 1991. Living conditions. In *The Greenland mummies,* ed. P. Jens, H. Hansen, Jorgen Meldgaard, and Jorgen Nordqvist, 150-67. Washington, D.C.

Clark, A. McFadyen. 1981. Koyukon. In *Subarctic,* ed. J. Helm, 582-601. Washington, D.C.

Cohen, Yehudi A. 1974. Culture as adaptation. In *Man in adaptation: The cultural present,* ed. Y. A. Cohen, 45-68. Chicago.

Counter, S. Allen. 1991. *North pole legacy: Black, white and Eskimo.* Amherst, Mass.

De Laguna, Frederica. 1977. *Voyage to Greenland.* New York.

De Laguna, Frederica, and Catharine McClellan. 1981. Ahtna. In *Subarctic,* ed. J. Helm, 641-63. Washington, D.C.

Draper, H. H. 1977. The aboriginal Eskimo diet in modern perspective. *American Anthropologist* 79: 309-16.

Dumond, Don E. 1977. *The Eskimos and Aleuts.* London.

Ellestad-Sayed, J. J., J. C. Haworth, and J. A. Hildes. 1978. Disaccharide malabsorption and dietary patterns in two Canadian Eskimo communities. *American Journal of Clinical Nutrition* 31: 1473-8.

Frank, Ellen. 1983. *Moving around in the old days.* Fairbanks, Alaska.

Freeman, Milton M. R. 1984. Arctic ecosystems. In *Handbook of North American Indians,* Vol. 5, 36-48. Washington, D.C.

Freuchen, Peter. 1935. *Arctic adventure: My life in the frozen North.* New York.

Gullov, H. C., and Jorgen Meldgaard. 1991. Inuit and Norsemen. In *The Greenland mummies,* ed. P. Jens, H. Hansen, Jorgen Meldgaard, and Jorgen Nordqvist, 13-36. Washington, D.C.

Harrison, Gail G. 1975. Primary adult lactase deficiency: A problem in anthropological genetics. *American Anthropologist* 77: 812-35.

Hosley, Edward H. 1981a. Environment and culture in the Alaska plateau. In *Subarctic,* ed. J. Helm, 546-55. Washington, D.C.

    1981b. Intercultural relations and culture change in the Alaska plateau. In *Subarctic,* ed. J. Helm, 618-22. Washington, D.C.

Joos, Sandra K. 1985. Economic, social, and cultural factors in the analysis of disease: Dietary change and diabetes mellitus among the Florida Seminole Indians. In *Ethnic and regional foodways in the United States: The performance of group identity,* ed. Linda Brown and Kay Mussell, 217-37. Knoxville, Tenn.

Kruse, John A., Judith Kleinfeld, and Robert Travis. 1982. Energy development on Alaska's North Slope: Effects on the Inupiat population. *Human Organization* 41: 97-106.

Langdon, Steve, and Rosita Worl. 1981. *Distribution and exchange of subsistence resources in Alaska.* Technical paper No. 55, University of Alaska. Fairbanks, Alaska.

Lippe-Stokes, Susan. 1980. Eskimo story-knife tales: Reflections of change in food habits. In *Food, ecology and culture: Readings in the anthropology of dietary practices,* ed. J. R. K. Robson, 75-82. New York.

Martin, Calvin. 1978. *Keepers of the game: Indian-animal relationships and the fur trade.* Berkeley, Calif.

Mary-Rousseliere, Guy. 1984. *Handbook of North American Indians,* Vol. 5, 431-46. Washington, D.C.

Maxwell, Moreau S. 1985. *Prehistory of the Eastern Arctic.* Orlando, Fla.

McClellan, Catharine. 1981. Tagish. In *Subarctic,* ed. J. Helm, 35-42. Washington, D.C.

McClellan, Catharine, and Glenda Denniston. 1981. Environment and culture in the cordillera. In *Subarctic,* ed. J. Helm, 372-86. Washington, D.C.

McKennan, Robert A. 1981. Tanana. In *Subarctic,* ed. J. Helm, 562-76. Washington, D. C.

Neatby, Leslie H. 1984. *Handbook of North American Indians,* Vol. 5, 377-90. Washington, D.C.

Nelson, Richard K. 1986. *Hunters of the northern forest: Designs for survival among the Alaskan Kutchin.* Chicago.

Newman, Peter Charles. 1985. *Company of adventurers.* New York.

    1987. *The story of the Hudson's Bay Company.* New York.

Ray, Arthur J. 1974. *Indians in the fur trade. Their role as trappers, hunters and middlemen in the lands Southwest of Hudson Bay, 1660-1870.* Toronto.

Schaefer, Otto. 1971. When the Eskimo comes to town. *Nutrition Today* 8: 8-16.

Schneider, William S. 1986. On the back slough. In *Interior Alaska: A journey through time,* ed. Robert M. Thorson, Anchorage, Alaska.

Slobodin, Richard. 1981. Kutchin. In *Subarctic,* ed. J. Helm, 514-32. Washington, D.C.

Snow, Jeanne H. 1981. Ingalik. In *Subarctic,* ed. J. Helm, 602-17. Washington, D.C.

Spencer, Robert F. 1984. North Alaska Coast Eskimo. In *Handbook of North American Indians,* Vol. 5, 320-37. Washington, D.C.

Sullivan, R. J. 1942. *The Ten'A food quest.* Ph.D. thesis, Catholic University of America, Washington, D.C.

Townsend, Joan B. 1981. Tanaina. In *Subarctic,* ed. J. Helm, 623-40. Washington, D.C.

VanStone, James W. 1974. *Athapaskan adaptations: Hunters and fishermen of the Subarctic forests.* Chicago.

1984. Mainland Southwest Alaska Eskimo. In *Handbook of North American Indians,* Vol. 5, 224-42. Washington, D.C.

Vogt, Evon Z. 1972. The acculturation of American Indians. In *Perspectives on the North American Indians,* ed. M. Nagler, 2-13. Toronto.

Yerbury, J. C. 1986. *The Subarctic Indians and the fur trade, 1680-1860.* Vancouver, B.C.

V.E

The History and Culture of Food and Drink in Sub-Saharan Africa and Oceania

V.E.1   Africa South from the Sahara

Describing the principal sources of food for the inhabitants of Africa south from the Sahara is a relatively easy task. Most diets are dominated by products made from a single staple crop, and there are not all that many of them. Maize, sorghums, pearl or bulrush millet, and rice are the prominent grains, and cassava, yams, and bananas or plantains account for most of the vegetatively propagated varieties. Furthermore, their general geographies can be explained, for the most part, by annual totals and seasonality of rainfall. For example, near the dry margins of cropping, pearl millet makes its greatest dietary contribution, whereas the equatorial zone is where bananas and plantains come to the fore. Even adding in the role played by livestock, one that varies from insignificant to crucial, does not overly complicate the picture. Among farmers, fowl are fairly ubiquitous, while sheep, goats, and cattle are kept wherever diseases, especially sleeping sickness, do not prohibit them. When aridity intervenes to make crop cultivation too hazardous to rely upon, the herding of camels or cattle becomes the primary subsistence activity.

The problems come when attempting to go much beyond this level of generality. There is a plethora of other foods that are important to diets, including those from wild sources, and matters get even more difficult to sort out when issues of history, culture, and nutritional adequacy must be addressed. The region's human diversity is enormous, and most food systems display a complex interweaving of influences, ranging from the distant past to the present. Unfortunately, trying to understand what has happened through time is hindered by a dearth of information. The written record is sparse before the twentieth century, and archaeology, so far, has produced very few dates. As a result, temporal insights often must rely on somewhat less precise sources of information, such as paleobotany, historic and comparative linguistics, and cultural anthropology.

Our understanding of current diets and their adequacy is only slightly better informed. During recent decades, Africa south from the Sahara has replaced China and India as the "land of famine." Actual famine, however, has visited only restricted areas, such as portions of the Sahel, Somalia, and Mozambique. Elsewhere, people have not been starving, although only a few elites enjoy the luxuries of Western-like food abundance. Serious nutrition-related health problems clearly exist, especially among young children and reproductive-age women, and the food production data do point to an ever more precarious supply situation throughout much of the region. But surveys that allow for comparing diets and nutritional well-being are woefully inadequate.

As a result, the following presentation is offered in the spirit of being one best estimate. It begins with an overview of African "agricultural origins and dispersals," to borrow a title from Carl Sauer (1969), which, contrary to many earlier interpretations, were not all by-products of Egyptian influences. Other Africans engaged in their own domesticating processes, leading to the crops that provided the basic raw materials for the transition to food-producing ways of life. The most significant imports, the subjects of the next section, entered already existing agricultural systems. A brief discussion of food preparations and eating habits follows, and the final section is devoted to an assessment of what appear to be the most widespread diet-related disorders, excepting famine.

African Agricultural Origins

We can begin some 9,000 years ago when all Africans southward from the Sahara still gathered, hunted, and fished for their foods, with the particular dietary mix governed by what the local environment could provide. For example, on the vast savanna-covered plateaus, the abundance of game animals allowed meat to be eaten regularly, along with a variety of nuts, berries, roots, and tubers. Meat was harder to come by in more densely forested habitats, but freshwater fish were widely available as complements to vegetable foods, whereas along some coastal sections, extensive middens testify to the dietary importance of shellfish. Virtually all of the area appears to have been occupied, at least on a seasonal basis; exceptions were the higher elevations, the heart of the Sahara Desert (much less extensive then than now), the narrow strip of the Namib Desert, and the deeper recesses of the equatorial rain forest. For the most part, people lived in small, mobile bands exploiting territories that necessitated the use of tens of square kilometers to supply the subsistence needs of one adult.

By way of contrast, certain riparian habitats north and east of the equatorial rain forest supported higher population densities and more sedentary occupancy. They did so because of Late Stone Age technological advances that allowed people to use a diverse array of plants, including wild grass seeds, for foodstuffs, as well as to engage in an intensified exploitation of fish and waterfowl (Sutton 1977). The evidence to date points to such locales as these as having been at the forefront of domestication activities in Africa south from the Sahara, thus lending support to the agricultural origins models developed by D. Rindos (1984) and R. S. MacNeish (1992). Shortly thereafter, other movements in the direction of agriculture took place along the rain forest–savanna ecotone of western and central Africa and within what is now Ethiopia.

Whether there were broad zones or precise centers of domestication activity at the outset cannot be determined, but no matter which situation prevailed, the diffusion pattern evolved into one of multiple frontiers carrying a variety of crops and animals. And the pace of change varied considerably. In some instances, Stone Age economies seem to have given way quickly, but the norm was for agriculture to gain ascendancy over gathering, hunting, and fishing only very gradually.

Crops

The earliest signs of possible domestication come from two sites within the Sahara. One is at Nabta Playa in western Egypt, where a number of sorghum-type seeds have been found in deposits dated 8,100 years ago (Wasylikowa et al. 1993). Whether they were cultivated or gathered, however, cannot be determined. The other is in the Ahaggar and contains a seed, two pollen grains, and grain impressions, dated between 6,850 and 5,350 years ago, of what could be pearl millet *(Pennisetum glaucum)* (Muzzolini 1993). This is not much to go on, but the Ahaggar does fall within the biogeographical range of related wild varieties, while the timing corresponds to a moist episode that would have supported millet cultivation at favorable Saharan locales, such as in the highlands and along the shores of then fairly numerous lakes and rivers (Harlan 1989). Also dated to approximately the same time as the Nabta Playa and Ahaggar finds are Neolithic sites that have yielded

pottery, grindstones, and rubbers. Their presence by no means guarantees cultivation, but the large numbers of artifacts add extra fuel to the speculation that something of significance was indeed taking place (Camps 1982).

Farther south, events moved more slowly, although both botanical and linguistic research indicates that domestication processes were trending in the direction of agriculture within several different zones during the period from 5,000 to 4,000 years ago. One zone followed the Sahel–savanna country stretching from the upper Niger River valley, through the Lake Chad basin, to Dar Fur. Overall, the western half appears to have been more active, accounting for African rice *(Oryza glaberrima)*, fonio *(Digitaria exilis)*, guinea millet *(Brachiaria deflexa)*, watermelon *(Colocynthis citrullus)*, and Bambara groundnuts *(Voandzeia subterranea)*. The area east of Lake Chad was where the first sorghums *(Sorghum bicolor)* seem to have been cultivated. Later activities produced a variety of specialized sorghum races that would serve as the principle food source for peoples inhabiting the semiarid and subhumid regions of not only Africa but also India (Harlan 1989 and 1992).

So far, this vast zone to the south of the desert has yielded only two archaeological sites with substantiated evidence about the course of early crop cultivation. The oldest is Dhar Tichitt located in what is now south-central Mauritania, where P. J. Munson (1976) has documented a progression from an earlier riparian-type economy to a village-based one growing pearl millet by 3,100 years ago. No in-migration is indicated, thus pointing to diffusion from the Sahara as the likely source for the millet. The other site is Daima on the western side of Lake Chad. Here, excavations of earthen mounds have revealed the presence of a mixed economy involving fishing, hunting, gathering, herding, and crop cultivation centered on sorghums dating back to 2,500 years ago (Connah 1981). The agriculture practiced at Daima was advanced enough to support villages of more than 100 inhabitants and, therefore, must have been preceded by earlier developments that have not yet been unearthed.

Ever since the days of N. I. Vavilov (1926), the area within and around the Ethiopian highlands has been identified as a likely source of indigenous crop domestication. Now well established as coming from the cooler, seasonally rainy uplands of the center and east are teff *(Eragrostis tef)*, noog *(Guizotia abyssinica)*, and finger millet *(Eleusine coracana)*, whereas ensete *(Musa ensete)* and coffee *(Coffea arabica)* are ascribed to the warmer, wetter southwestern forests. Dates are unconfirmed, but opinion based on linguistic analyses favors something on the order of 5,000 years ago for the upland crops (Ehret 1979; Phillipson 1993). This date may be fairly accurate because when wheat and barley arrived from south Arabian sources, about 3,000 years ago, they seem to have been incorporated into already well established agricultural systems.

Finally, various African communities appear to have been experimenting with yam cultivation (primarily *Dioscorea rotundata* and *Dioscorea bulbifera*) along a wide front following the savanna–rain forest ecotone in western Africa (Alexander and Coursey 1969). How far back in time this goes cannot be determined, but it must have been by at least 5,000 years ago because of the association of yams with several major population migrations dated to around this time (Ehret 1982). Because of the workings of humid climates and acidic soils on a plant that is inherently perishable to begin with, archaeology is unlikely ever to shed much light on the origins of yam cultivation, and, thus, further insights will have to continue to be based primarily on advances in botanical and linguistic research.

Kersting's groundnuts *(Kerstingiella geocarpa),* cowpeas *(Vigna unguiculata),* and the oil palm *(Elaeis guineensis)* are other crops thought to derive from the same general ecotone environment (Harlan 1992), but so far only cowpeas have been archaeologically confirmed. These come from the several Kintampo sites focused on central Ghana, and are dated to around 3,800 years ago (Flight 1976). The inhabitants of Kintampo also made considerable use of oil palm kernels, but these probably came from the harvesting of stands of protected wild trees.

Livestock

Unlike its crops, Africa south from the Sahara has depended upon external sources for its most important livestock. No possible ancestors for sheep or goats existed on the continent. Instead they arrived in several waves, from southwestern and central Asian sources, and quickly became integral parts of agricultural systems developed in Egypt and the Maghreb. The first cattle also seem to have entered from the east, although it is possible that indigenous varieties of *Bos primigenius* were domesticated within the Sahara (Smith 1992). These were all humpless types from which the fully domesticated *Bos taurus* arose. Later, but at least by 2,500 years ago, came humped *Bos indicus* types that probably entered Africa both via Egypt and from seaborne contacts with India along the east coast. Eventually, *B. taurus* and *B. indicus* crosses produced several distinctive African breeds, such as the Fulani, Sanga, and Afrikander (Blench 1993; Clutton-Brock 1993).

One initial route of livestock diffusion went upstream along the Nile, as is evidenced at the archaeological sites of Kadero and Esh Shaheinab near the junction of the White and Blue Niles. Wheat and barley may have been grown here as well, but it was sheep, goats, and cattle that constituted the main additions to a preexisting riverine-based Stone Age economy by 7,000 years ago (MacNeish 1992). From here, livestock continued to spread inland, reaching the region of Ethiopia between 5,000 and 6,000 years ago (Ehret 1979).

Roughly contemporaneous with Kadero and Esh Shaheinab are signs of other emergent livestock-based economies within and around the Saharan highlands of Dar Fur, Tibesti, Air, and Ahaggar. The evidence includes animal skeletons, material cultural remains, and, most convincingly, rock art at the remarkable site of Tassili-n-Ajer (Lhote 1959). Preserved there since approximately 7,000 years ago are scenes of what clearly are domesticated, humpless, long-horn cattle, along with their herders (Camps 1982).

When camels first made their way to Africa remains unclear. The dromedary had been domesticated in the Arabian peninsula by at least 3,800 years ago, but it does not seem to have become important in Egypt and the Sahara until much later, perhaps not until Roman times. Rather than entering with caravans crossing via the Sinai, as most experts have tended to think, camels may have first reached Africa by being transported across the Red Sea, a route which would help to explain their seemingly greater antiquity among desert-dwelling nomads in this corner of the continent (Zeuner 1963).

Even more mystery surrounds the entry of the common fowl *(Gallus gallus)* into Africa. We know that they were present in Egypt over 3,000 years ago, but that is about all (Simoons 1961). The usual assumption is that they probably spread from here up the Nile Valley corridor, and it is possible that chickens could have been carried across the Sahara once they had reached the Maghreb. A still later introduction (about A.D. 500) may have been with Malayo-Polynesian voyagers, who touched at points along the Indian Ocean coast on their way to Madagascar. Today, chickens are kept by farmers virtually everywhere, although much of their popularity seems to be quite recent.

Africa can claim two animal domesticates, neither of which, however, became important sources of food. One is the ass *(Equus asinus),* for which the Nubian wild race seems to have provided most of the genetic material (Zeuner 1963). It was in use as a beast of burden in Egypt, and presumably in Nubia, by 5,000 years ago, and from there spread to Ethiopia, the Horn, and the Sahel/Sudanic zone of western Africa at uncertain dates. The other is the guinea fowl, derived largely from *Numidia meleagris galeata,* which appears to have been first raised in the savannas of western Africa. Appreciated more for its aesthetic qualities than anything else, it often cannot be easily differentiated from the wild varieties that are still found widely outside the rain forest zones (Donkin 1991).

These are the essential domesticates that supported the rise of food-producing economies in Africa south from the Sahara. Over a span of 4,000 to 5,000 years, they have been carried across the subcontinent's diverse environments by a complex mix of population migrations and technological diffusions.

Many of these, however, can only be speculated about.

Regional Agricultural Dispersals

Western Africa

The pace of agricultural development in the Sahelian and Sudanic zones of western Africa seems to have intensified under competition and population pressure from southward-drifting livestock herders seeking respite from the ever-worsening aridity that had set in by 4,000 years ago. The evidence points to their having been members of a rapidly diverging Nilosaharan language group, other members of which were also the likely first cultivators of pearl millet (Ehret 1993). The most attractive destinations would have been the water and grazing resources along the upper Niger River valley and its tributaries, the Senegal River valley, and Lake Chad, then much larger than it is now. The Lake Chad area seems to have been occupied by yet other Nilosaharans, in all probability growing sorghums. In the other two areas, however, the herders would have encountered members of the Mande and Atlantic branches of the Niger-Congo language group. It was among them that agricultural systems of production were developing around African rice, fonio, and guinea millet. From all appearances, the Nilosaharans were absorbed, but they did leave livestock as one of their legacies.

Eventually, pearl millet and sorghums spread throughout the Sahelian and Sudanic zones, cultivated either in the flood plain style known as *crue* and *decrue* or else on the interfluves as parts of land-extensive systems of shifting cultivation (Harris 1976). Cattle, sheep, and goats also spread throughout the region, although often herded by specialists, most notably the Fulbe or Fulani. Their origins are traceable to the Senegal River valley, where they may have arisen out of a synthesis of Nilosaharan herders and resident Atlantic-speaking cultivators (Smith 1992).

The Kintampo sites demonstrate that agriculture was on the fringes of the tropical forest zone of western Africa more than 3,000 years ago. Crops were probably still less important than gathered plant foods, but there is strong evidence that goats and sheep had achieved considerable economic importance (Stahl 1993). How long it took from the time of Kintampo for agriculture to reach into the forest itself cannot be determined, although it is unlikely that much of a move was made prior to 2,000 years ago. Then it arrived from two directions. In the west it accompanied the migrations of Atlantic- and Mande-speaking peoples who brought their African rice with them. Farther east, yams accompanied the expansion of other Niger-Congo speakers, this time affiliated with the Kwa and Ijoid families. Eventually, a line that still holds today at approximately the Bandama River in the Ivory Coast came to separate distinctive rice- and yam-eating zones.

A few domesticates from the tropical forest were added to the crop inventory as supplements to the staples. Those in most widespread use include okra *(Hibiscus esculentus)*, kola *(Cola sps.)*, akee *(Blighia sapida)*, and the melegueta pepper *(Aframomum melegueta)*. Also associated with the forest are dwarf varieties of humpless short-horn cattle that are somewhat tolerant of virtually ubiquitous sleeping sickness but yield very little milk. Most likely, they are adaptations of the types represented at Tassili (Blench 1993).

Ethiopia and the Horn

In general, the Ethiopian food crop domesticates remained rather narrowly confined to their original environments. The major exception is finger millet, which spread along with the migrations of Southern Cushites that began around 4,000 years ago. A branch of the Cushitic division of the Afroasiatic group that originated in Ethiopia, these people left their highland home for present-day Kenya and Tanzania (Ehret 1979). Taking with them livestock as well, the Southern Cushites were entering virgin agricultural country, but in such few numbers that most of it remained the province of hunter-gatherers until the arrival of later agriculturists.

Some other Cushites had become livestock specialists and claimed the semidesert and desert lands surrounding the Ethiopian highlands. The most ancient are the Beja (the Blemmeys of the Egyptians), who took possession of the lands astride the Red Sea coast. When their migrations first began is unclear, but they probably date to between 4,000 and 3,000 years ago. Camels were crucial to their advance through the desert, and if the time estimates are correct, they would have been Africa's original camel herders and the likely source for the animal's introduction into Egypt. Later, camels fueled the expansions of the Afar and Somali, who occupied the arid lands stretching from Djibouti to the Tana River in Kenya.

Equatorial Africa

The first agriculturists to approach the equatorial rain forest were proto–Central Sudanic (Nilosaharan group) speakers. They did not, however, enter the forest, remaining instead in the savanna and woodland country to the north, where they could cultivate sorghums and tend herds of cattle, sheep, and goats. Getting closer were Ubangian communities whose settlements reached the northern fringes of the forest (David 1982). Early yam–oil palm cultivators located in the Cameroon highlands, they had begun an expansion around 5,000 years ago that took them eastward through the lands straddling the watershed of the Nile and Congo rivers.

It was left to yet another group of yam-cultivating Niger-Congo speakers, the Bantu, to take food-producing economies into the rain forest proper. Originating in the vicinity of the Cross River valley of present-day Nigeria, they had entered the equatorial forest by

4,000 years ago (Ehret 1982). Avid fisher folk as well as farmers, the pioneers followed the Atlantic coast and river valleys west of the immense swamp along the lower reaches of the Ubangi River before it joins the Congo. Subsistence needs kept the frontier moving until advance communities eventually reached the forest's southern end. Some people then headed east and followed northward-flowing rivers back into the forest, completing a cycle by 2,000 years ago that created a linearlike pattern of Bantu-speaking fishing–farming villages surrounded by bands of pygmoid gatherer-hunters in the deeper forest recesses (Vansina 1990).

Eastern Africa

The transition of eastern Africa from a region of gatherer-hunters to agriculturists was linked to a complex interweaving of population migrations that spanned some 3,500 or more years. As noted, peoples of Southern Cushitic linguistic background introduced finger millet–based agriculture into parts of eastern Africa. Their migrations seem to have centered on better-watered upland areas, such as the slopes of mounts Kenya and Kilimanjaro (Nurse 1982).

At about the same time, or only slightly later, Central Sudanic agriculturists with sorghum and livestock entered the interlacustrine region of present-day Uganda, and may have eventually reached as far south as the Zambezi River valley. As with the Southern Cushites, their numbers were few, and they gave way between 3,000 and 2,000 years ago to Bantu migrants who had tracked through the equatorial forest following easterly rather than southerly routes. Adding Central Sudanic grain-farming and livestock-rearing technologies to their yam-based agriculture, the Bantu were set to claim most of eastern Africa's cultivable lands as their own (Ehret 1982). By 500 years ago, they had created a wide variety of agricultural systems, ranging from intensively irrigated ones to those using land-extensive methods of shifting cultivation.

The noncultivable lands of eastern Africa, ranging from semiarid to desert, fell to various herding peoples. The north of what is now Kenya was claimed by Cushitic-speaking Somali and Oromo, who (because of the aridity) emphasized camels, while cattle-oriented Nilotes (Nilosaharan group) took possession of the richer grassland and savanna habitats of the interior plateaus.

Southern Africa

As in equatorial and eastern Africa, food-producing economies reached the southern portions of the continent in the company of migrants. Some of them were Khoe-speakers, now called Khoikhoi (formerly Hottentot). They acquired (probably from Bantu sources) sheep and maybe goats, but not crops, somewhere in the vicinity of the middle portions of the Zambezi River valley about 2,000 years ago. From here they spread southward into the semiarid range lands bordering the Kalahari, and thence into the

summer rainfall country from the Orange River valley to the Cape of Good Hope, either displacing or intermingling with bands of San (formerly Bushman)-speaking hunter-gatherers (Elphick 1977).

Following the Khoikhoi, but entering different environmental zones, were various communities of Bantu. Some were related to those who had moved through the equatorial rain forest. Continuing on a southward course, they entered the vast expanses of drought-prone and soil-poor brachystegia or miombo woodlands that stretch beyond the Zambezi River. Poorly suited to yam cultivation, at the outset the migrants were forced to rely on gathering, hunting, and fishing for subsistence. But then, sometime just prior to 1,500 years ago, sorghums and millets were acquired from yet other Bantu groups that had begun moving south from eastern Africa. With these crops, much of the area could support at least land-extensive forms of shifting cultivation. Although livestock also were introduced, their roles were restricted by the widespread prevalence of sleeping sickness.

Much better habitats were encountered by the eastern stream of Bantu. One favored route led around lakes Tanganyika and Nyasa and onto the Zimbabwe plateau, and thence to the high veld of South Africa. By A.D. 500, these areas, free from sleeping sickness and comparatively well watered, had been reached by advance communities with grain-growing and livestock-herding economies, although cattle do not seem to have been important until the advent of the New Iron Age after A.D. 1,000. Yet another route followed by Bantu agriculturalists went along the coast through Mozambique and into Natal, which also seems to have been reached by around 1,500 years ago (Hall 1990).

It thus took about 6,000 years from the signs of its first appearance for agriculture to make its way to the extreme southern end of the continent. To an almost exclusive degree, the crops involved were of African origin. However, some of the more important later developments were hinged to imports, and it is to these that the discussion now turns.

Later Imports

Plantains and Bananas

The first of the later imports to have widespread agricultural repercussions in Africa south from the Sahara were plantains and bananas (*Musa sp.*). Two routes of entry from their southeast Asian source of origin seem possible. The first could have brought them to Egypt over 2,000 years ago via trade with India; from Egypt they spread along the Nile to its headwaters in the Great Lakes region of eastern Africa. The second possibility involves Malayo-Polynesian voyages to the east coast on the way to settling Madagascar. Cuttings could have survived the long sea voyages, and therefore joined other crops, such as cocoyam (*Colocasia antiquorum*) and sugarcane (*Saccharum offici-*

narum), sometime during the second half of the first millennium A.D.

By whatever route, the adoption of bananas and plantains became crucial to the spread of agriculture through the lowland equatorial rain forest. People now had a high-yielding crop that allowed for relatively permanent villages to be established away from the river valleys and deeper into the forest proper. Bananas and plantains also played an important role in augmenting agricultural productivity throughout the moister zones of the Great Lakes region and in the uplands of eastern Africa, such as around the lower slopes of mounts Kenya and Kilimanjaro, thus helping to create some of Africa's most densely settled areas outside Egypt.

Asiatic Yams

It is possible that Asiatic yams (principally *D. alata* and *D. esculenta*) also reached Africa with the Malayo-Polynesian voyages. Their rise to prominence, however, seems mainly to have followed their importation by the Portuguese during the sixteenth century. Because of higher yields, they have largely replaced the indigenously developed varieties throughout the yam belt of western Africa and elsewhere, to the point where the latter serve more for ritual than staple-food purposes (Coursey 1976; Harris 1976).

Maize

Reports continue to circulate about the cultivation of maize having been widespread prior to the Columbian voyages, but it was only after the introduction of American varieties *(Zea maize)* that the crop became an important component of many African food systems. Although the evidence is far from definitive, it does point to the Portuguese as, once again, the carriers, and if this is true, then maize probably had many points of entry along the Atlantic and Indian Ocean coasts. Indeed, there is really no other way to explain its seemingly sudden appearance by the seventeenth century in places as far apart as the Senegal River valley, the Congo basin, the Natal coast of South Africa, and Zanzibar (Miracle 1966).

The frontiers of maize have been moving ever since, to the point where today its now numerous varieties have become the predominant staple for many people in Africa south from the Sahara. Areas where it is particularly important include the highlands of Kenya, Rwanda and Burundi, Malawi, the coastal savanna gap from eastern Ghana to Benin, the Bie Plateau of Angola, and the well-watered areas from Zambia to South Africa. The attractions of maize have been its high yields and invulnerability to bird attacks in comparison with millets and sorghums. About the only places where it does not show up among the list of important crops are in the lowland equatorial zone, the Sahel, and highland Ethiopia, and among rice growers in western Africa. Maize is Africa's most researched food crop, and the development of varieties that are more drought resistant and that will grow in cooler highland climatic conditions has added to its attractions.

Cassava

There is little doubt about cassava *(Manihot utilissima* or *M. esculenta)* having been brought to Africa by the Portuguese. They found it growing in Brazil and, as with maize, seem to have taken it with them to many of their African landfalls. Initially, the most important of these was the Kongo Kingdom, located south from the Congo River below Malebo Pool. Cassava gained favor here early in the sixteenth century and rather quickly spread both north and south around the equatorial rain forest, apparently being welcomed as a high-yielding alternative to yams and sorghums (Jones 1959). As the slave trade intensified across this region, cassava became even more important. Harvesting could await the disappearance of the turbulence brought by slavers, and cassava flour could be made into cakes for storage and long-distance travel. As the demand grew, some peoples responded by forming their own slave-run plantations to grow cassava. Ironically, its appearance in central Africa probably kept populations growing sufficiently so that the slave trade and slavery could continue (Miller 1989).

A link to slavery may also partially explain cassava's importance in and around the Niger delta, although much of its spread there, and elsewhere in coastal West Africa, seems to have occurred after 1800 (Jones 1959). Commercial agriculture had begun to expand across the region from Ghana to Nigeria, and cassava's adoption may have been a response to a decline in other food crops as more land was given over to cacao *(Theobroma cacao),* another import from the Americas, and oil palm cultivation.

Cassava's tolerance to a wide range of soil types and moisture conditions, along with the ability to remain unharvested after ripening, made it a favorite of many colonial agricultural officials. They viewed cassava as an ideal famine-prevention food, and thus encouraged plantings in such areas as the upper Guinea Coast and interior eastern Africa where it had not found an earlier enthusiastic reception. Today cassava is tropical Africa's most widely planted crop, and the region has become the world's leading producer.

Two other American crop introductions need to mentioned. One is the groundnut *(Arachis hypogaea).* Groundnuts serve both as a food and cash crop for many Africans in the subhumid and semiarid parts of the continent, with the rural economies of Senegal and northern Nigeria particularly dependent on them. The second crop introduced from the Americas is the sweet potato *(Ipomoea batatas).* Although not really a staple anywhere in Africa, it is nevertheless an important secondary food source virtually everywhere it can be grown.

Food Preparation and Eating Habits

In Africa a staple food crop is just that – the principal item in the diet, eaten most days if not virtually every day. If a grain is used, most often it will be pounded into a flour, whereas root crops frequently are grated before being boiled. In either case, the end product is a stiff porridgelike substance that is normally formed into bite-size balls. These are then eaten with a variety of stews and soups. Greens of one kind or another will almost always be one of their ingredients, and onions are increasingly common. Otherwise, the additives will depend on local availability and preferences. Meat is always desired but is infrequent. Along coasts and rivers, small amounts of fish are commonly put into stews and soups, and oils, mostly from palms and groundnuts, are in regular use. Salt is a necessity, but the use of other spices varies considerably. In general, tastes tend to be on the bland side throughout most of eastern, central, and southern Africa, while in parts of western Africa and Ethiopia, the stews are often fired with chilli peppers.

Other kinds of preparations include roasting maize ears and steaming sliced cassava, plantains, and sweet potatoes in leaf wrappers. Rice is prepared in the usual boiled manner, and to an ever-increasing extent, imported varieties are preferred because of their higher quality. Such preferences are especially true of urban dwellers, who have created a demand for imported wheat flours to make leavened breads as well. Cassava flour is also used for bread, and in Ethiopia a flat bread made from teff or wheat is the staple source of carbohydrates for people living in the highlands.

All kinds of other foods, especially gathered ones, find their ways into African diets. By far the most common are greens of one kind or another; mushrooms are also widely eaten. Termites are popular, as are various caterpillars and mollusks. These days, game meats are increasingly uncommon, and the vast majority of people will never have occasion to eat them. In fact, game meats have fallen out of favor, even when made available as a part of government game-cropping schemes. Far preferred, if affordable, are beef, mutton, and goat. Vegetarianism by choice is not part of any African cultural tradition.

Contrary to what might be expected, pastoralists, such as the Fulbe and Maasai, also eat very little meat. They rely on fresh and soured milk, along with butter, as their staples, and slaughter animals only for special ceremonial occasions or when these become old and feeble. Milk products are uncommon for most other Africans, as is indicated by the high rates of lactose intolerance that exist, especially in western and equatorial Africa (Kretchmer 1977).

The normal pattern is for one large meal to be served each day. Both morning and evening meals tend to be more like snacks and often involve leftovers. Almost everywhere, men eat separately from women and young children and are served first. Individual plates are not used; rather, each person takes from common bowls and pots.

Meals are seldom accompanied by beverages, except if these are part of feasts. The drinking of alcoholic beverages, however, is virtually ubiquitous, except among Muslims. Traditional products are all basically variations of two themes. The most widespread is the fermentation of one of the crops into something beerlike. Finger millet is the grain generally employed by many eastern and central Africans, whereas maize is popular in South Africa. Also widely used are sorghums and bananas, with the higher sugars from the latter yielding greater alcohol content. A favored practice is to add honey to the fermentation to push the alcohol level even higher. The second theme is found mainly within the equatorial zone and along the coast. Here palm trees are topped to produce a sap that is turned into palm wine, which achieves greater strength than the beers.

In recent decades, commercially distilled spirits and brewed beers have become the alcoholic drinks of choice for many people. As a consequence, alcoholism is now a serious social and health problem, especially in Africa's rapidly growing cities.

Many food avoidances exist, the most widespread of which is attached to eggs. Some peoples, particularly in Kenya, eschew eggs altogether, equating them with excrement, but more often the restriction falls on girls and reproductive-age women. Reasons stated vary from eggs causing sterility or excessive sexuality to adversely affecting fetal development (Simoons 1961). Less widespread, but of considerable cultural and historical interest, is the avoidance of fish by peoples from Ethiopia southward through Kenya to Tanzania. They are all of Cushitic linguistic affiliation or others who have been heavily influenced by them (Murdock 1959). The reasons are lost in antiquity, but may relate to the low-caste status of fisher folk in the development of Cushitic society, one in which the vast majority of people are either farmers or herders.

Diet-Related Disorders

As a whole, Africa south from the Sahara has become characterized by a worsening food-supply crisis. This is illustrated by the sequence of famines, beginning with the Sahel and Ethiopia in the early 1970s and continuing to Somalia and Mozambique at the outset of the 1990s, and by a regionwide decline in per capita food production over roughly the same period of time. Only by the importation of more and more staple foodstuffs have famines and near famines been averted elsewhere.

Both because of their episodic nature and the coverage they have received, Africa's famines are not discussed here beyond a note of the complexity of their causes. Although natural events, particularly droughts, have often been involved, these have largely been triggers setting off deeper economic and political charges that initiate the famines. Attention is focused here, however, on more chronic diet-related disorders. These include the various syndromes of protein–energy malnutrition (PEM), vitamin A deficiency, anemias, and goiter.

Protein–Energy Malnutrition

There is very little doubt that, taken together, the syndromes of protein–energy malnutrition constitute the most widespread and serious diet-related disorders in Africa south from the Sahara. From the sketchy evidence available, it does seem that pure cases of kwashiorkor are rather rare today. Apparently, all of the earlier research on it has paid off, particularly with regard to recognizing kwashiorkor in its early stages and alerting parents to take children with symptoms to clinics and hospitals (Newman 1995). The current status of the other two clinical syndromes of marasmus and marasmic kwashiorkor is less certain. Early weaning onto inadequate breast-milk substitutes and exposure to bacterial contamination are still widespread, and in fact, the kinds of poverty, especially in urban areas, that favor this combination of health threats have been growing rather than declining. Unfortunately, the available medical and survey data are inadequate to the task of making any kind of reasonable statements about comparative frequencies.

Somewhat more can be said about the several growth measurements that are used to identify mild-to-moderate forms of PEM. Stunting, for example, is widespread, with rates for children under 5 years of age running from a low 16.6 percent in the Ivory Coast, to 47.8 percent in Burundi, to 53.7 percent in Malawi (Carlson and Wardlaw 1990). One can argue about the standards used for such determinations, but what we know from other sources about food availability in such places as Burundi and Malawi would confirm that many young children are suffering from chronic malnutrition that quickly can go from mild-to-moderate to clinical when infections strike.

Vitamin A Deficiency

Vitamin A deficiencies that lead to vision impairment are far more localized than PEM. They are almost completely absent from humid tropical regions, where sources of preformed vitamin A and beta-carotene are abundant. In contrast, these can be in short supply (especially seasonally) in drier environments, and this is where the problems are concentrated. Some fairly good studies of different time periods have come from Nigeria, and they document a north-to-south incidence gradient (Nicol 1949; Oke 1972). Similarly, the dry Luapula Valley is Zambia's trouble spot, with a recent study having recorded a deficiency rate of 75 percent among preschool children (Lubinga 1989).

The symptoms of severe vitamin A deficiency run a gamut from Bitot's spots, through night blindness, to keratomalacia. When the latter stage is reached, death usually follows within a short time because of the problems of caring for the blind in physically hazardous environments. Treatment of vitamin A deficiency is inexpensive and can easily prevent the occurrence of impaired vision, but sadly, access to treatment is still wanting in poorer, more remote areas (Sommer 1982).

Anemias

Two kinds of diet-related anemias seem to afflict many African women and are especially health threatening during their reproductive years. One is the megaloblastic variety, which develops from a severe deficiency of folic acid. The primary source for folic acid is green leafy vegetables, and most women do, in fact, ingest adequate quantities of these. However, seasonal shortages can occur, especially in more arid habitats, and during times of drought, greens may be almost totally unavailable.

A more widespread anemia stems from iron deficiency, although seldom is the cause dietary. Sometimes it results from metabolic malfunctioning that inhibits iron absorption, but much more common are cases associated with parasitic infestations, notably malaria, hookworm, and roundworm (Latham 1965).

Goiter

Goiters, resulting from a dietary deficiency of iodine, can be encountered in many parts of the continent where the ancient basement geological complex predominates as the bedrock. Because it lacks iodine, so, too, do the soils and, therefore, the plants. The center of endemicity seems to be Zaire, where incidences of up to 100 percent have been recorded within some communities (DeVisscher et al. 1961). Also possibly contributing to the high rates are goitrogenous agents in widely eaten cassava and cabbage. The majority of goiters occur to young women because of the thyroid stresses resulting from menstruation, pregnancy, and lactation. Most are temporary, having little or no health impact, although several studies have found a connection between community incidences of endemic goiter and cretinism (Bastinie et al. 1962; Delange and Ermans 1971).

James L. Newman

Bibliography

Adams, W. Y. 1977. *Nubia: Corridor to Africa.* Princeton, N.J.

Alexander, J., and D. G. Coursey. 1969. The domestication of yams. In *The domestication and exploitation of plants and animals,* ed. P. J. Ucko and G. W. Dimbley, 405-25. London.

Bastinie, P. A., A. M. Ermans, O. Thys et al. 1962. Endemic goiter in the Uele Region III. Endemic cretinism. *Journal of Clinical Endocrinology and Metabolism* 22: 187-94.

Blench, R. 1993. Ethnographic and linguistic evidence for the prehistory of African ruminant livestock, horses, and ponies. In *The archaeology of Africa: Food, metals, and towns,* ed. T. Shaw, P. Sinclair, B. Andah, and A. Okpoko, 71-103. London.

Butzer, K. W. 1976. *Early hydraulic civilization in Egypt: A study in cultural ecology.* Chicago.

Camps, G. 1982. The beginnings of pastoralism and cultivation in north-west Africa and the Sahara: Origins of the Berbers. In *The Cambridge history of Africa, Vol. 1: From earliest times to c. 500 B.C.,* ed. J. D. Clark, 548-623. Cambridge.

Carlson, B. A., and T. M. Wardlaw. 1990. *A global, regional and country assessment of child malnutrition.* New York.

Clutton-Brock, J. 1993. The spread of domestic animals in Africa. In *The archaeology of Africa: Food, metals, and towns,* ed. T. Shaw, P. Sinclair, B. Andah, and A. Okpoko, 61-70. London.

Connah, G. 1981. *Three thousand years in Africa.* Cambridge.

Coursey, D. G. 1976. The origins and domestication of yams in Africa. In *Origins of African plant domestication,* ed. J. R. Harlan, J. M. J. de Wet, and A. B. L. Stemler, 383-408. The Hague.

David, A. 1982. Prehistory and historical linguistics in central Africa: Points of contact. In *The archaeological and linguistic reconstruction of African history,* ed. C. Ehret and M. Posnansky, 78-103. Berkeley, Calif.

Delange, F., and A. A. Ermans. 1971. Role of a dietary goitrogen in the etiology of endemic goiter on Idjwi Island. *American Journal of Clinical Nutrition* 24: 1354-60.

DeVisscher, M., C. Beckers, H.-G. Van Den Schrieck et al. 1961. Endemic goiter in the Uele Region (Congo Republic) I. General aspects and functional studies. *Journal of Clinical Endocrinology and Metabolism* 21: 175-88.

Donkin, R. A. 1991. *Meleagrides: An historical and ethnographic study of the Guinea fowl.* London.

Ehret, C. 1979. On the antiquity of agriculture in Ethiopia. *Journal of African History* 20: 161-77.

1982. Linguistic inferences about early Bantu history. In *The archaeological and linguistic reconstruction of African history,* ed. C. Ehret and M. Posnansky, 57-65. Berkeley, Calif.

1993. Nilo-Saharans and the Saharo-Sudanese Neolithic. In *The archaeology of Africa: Food, metals, and towns,* ed. T. Shaw, P. Sinclair, B. Andah, and A. Okpoko, 104-25. London.

Elphick, R. 1977. *Kraal and castle: Khoikhoi and the founding of white South Africa.* New Haven, Conn.

Flight, C. 1976. The Kintampo culture and its place in the economic prehistory of West Africa. In *Origins of African plant domestication,* ed. J. Harlan, J. M. J. de Wet, and A. B. L. Stemmler, 211-21. The Hague.

Frend, W. H. C. 1978. The Christian period in Mediterranean Africa, c. A.D. 200 to 700. In *The Cambridge history of Africa, Vol. 2: from c. 500 B.C. to A.D. 1050,* ed. J. D. Fage, 410-89. Cambridge.

Hall, M. 1990. *Farmers, kings, and traders: The peopling of Southern Africa, 200-1860.* Chicago.

Harlan, J. R. 1989. The tropical African cereals. In *Foraging and farming: The evolution of plant exploitation,* ed. D. R. Harris and G. C. Hillman, 335-43. London.

1992. Indigenous African agriculture. In *The Origins of*

agriculture: An international perspective, ed. C. W. Cowan and P. J. Watson, 59-70. Washington, D.C.

Harris, D. R. 1976. Traditional systems of plant food production and the origins of agriculture in West Africa. In *Origins of African plant domestication,* ed. J. R. Harlan, J. M. J. de Wet, and A. B. L. Stemler, 311-56. The Hague.

Hillman, G. C. 1989. Late Palaeolithic plant foods from Wadi Kubbaniya in upper Egypt: Dietary diversity, infant weaning, and seasonality in a riverine environment. In *Foraging and farming: The evolution of plant exploitation,* ed. D. R. Harris and G. C. Hillman, 207-39. London.

Jones, W. O. 1959. *Manioc in Africa.* Stanford, Calif.

Kretchmer, N. 1977. The geography and biology of lactose digestion and malabsorption. *Postgraduate Medical Journal* 53: 65-72.

Latham, M. 1965. *Human nutrition in tropical Africa.* Rome.

Lhote, H. 1959. *The search for the Tassili frescoes.* London.

Lubinga, D. 1989. Valley of the blind. *IDRC Reports, n. 18.* Ottawa.

MacNeish, R. S. 1992. *The origins of agriculture and settled life.* Norman, Okla.

Miller, J. C. 1989. *Way of death: Merchant capitalism and the Angolan slave trade, 1730-1830.* Madison, Wis.

Miracle, M. P. 1966. *Maize in tropical Africa.* Madison, Wis.

Munson, P. J. 1976. Archaeological data on the origins of cultivation in the southwestern Sahara and the implications for West Africa. In *Origins of African plant domestication,* ed. J. R. Harlan, J. M. J. de Wet, and A. B. L. Stemler, 187-209. The Hague.

Murdock, G. P. 1959. *Africa: Its peoples and their culture history.* New York.

Muzzolini, A. 1993. The emergence of a food-producing economy in the Sahara. In *The archaeology of Africa: Food, metals, and towns,* ed. T. Shaw, P. Sinclair, B. Andah, and A. Okpoko, 227-39. London.

Newman, J. L. 1995. From definition, to geography, to action, to reaction: The case of protein-energy malnutrition. *Annals of the Association of American Geographers* 85:233-45.

Nicol, B. M. 1949. Nutrition of Nigerian peasant farmers with special reference to the effects of riboflavin and vitamin A deficiency. *British Journal of Nutrition* 3: 25-43.

Nurse, D. 1982. Bantu expansion into East Africa: Linguistic evidence. In *The archaeological and linguistic reconstruction of African history,* ed. C. Ehret and M. Posnansky, 199-222. Berkeley, Calif.

Oke, O. L. 1972. A nutrition policy for Nigeria. *World Review of Nutrition and Dietetics* 14: 1-47.

Phillipson, D. W. 1993. The antiquity of cultivation and herding in Ethiopia. In *The archaeology of Africa: Food, metals and towns,* ed. T. Shaw, P. Sinclair, B. Andah, and A. Okpoko, 344-57. London.

Rindos, D. 1984. *The origins of agriculture: An evolutionary perspective.* Princeton, N.J.

Sauer, C. O. 1969. *Agricultural origins and dispersals.* Second edition. Cambridge, Mass.

Simoons, F. J. 1961. *Eat not this flesh: Food avoidances in the old world.* Madison, Wis.

Smith, A. B. 1992. *Pastoralism in Africa: Origins and development ecology.* London.

Sommer, A. 1982. *Nutritional blindness: Xeropthalmia and keratomalacia.* New York.

Stahl, A. B. 1993. Intensification in the West African late stone age: A view from central Ghana. In *The archaeology of*

Africa: Food, metals and towns, ed. T. Shaw, P. Sinclair, B. Andah, and A. Okpoko, 261–73. London.

Sutton, J. E. G. 1977. The African Aqualithic. *Antiquity* 51: 25–34.

Vansina, J. 1990. *Paths in the rain forest.* Madison, Wis.

Vavilov, N. I. 1926. Studies on the origins of cultivated plants. *Bulletin of Applied Botany and Plant Breeding* 16: 1245.

Wasylikowa, K., J. R. Harlan, J. Evans, et al. 1993. Examination of botanical remains from early neolithic houses at Nabta Playa, Western Desert, Egypt, with special reference to sorghum grains. In *The archaeology of Africa: Food, metals and towns,* ed. T. Shaw, P. Sinclair, B. Andah, and A. Okpoko, 154–64. London.

Zeuner, F. E. 1963. *A history of domesticated animals.* London.

V.E.2 ❧ Australia and New Zealand

Australia and New Zealand are Pacific Rim countries situated on the southwestern edge of that vast ocean. But although Australia has been peopled for at least 50,000 years (some now say 70,000), and New Zealand for just over 1,000, the dominant foodways of both have been shaped over just the last 200 years – since the beginning of British settlement in Australia in 1788. The indigenous people, the Aborigine in Australia and the Maori in New Zealand, are now minorities in their own lands (Aborigines comprise less than 2 percent of Australia's population and Maori about 15 percent of New Zealand's), and the foods and beverages they consume have been markedly influenced by food and drink of British origin. Indeed, from a contemporary perspective, food and drink in Australia and New Zealand – the lands "down under" – predominantly derive from the strong British heritage.

In this chapter, the environments of Australia and New Zealand are briefly described, not only because they are notably unique but also because they were so amenable to "ecological imperialism" (Crosby 1978). The food systems of the indigenous peoples, although now vastly altered, are also outlined, but the bulk of the chapter is devoted to the processes that produced contemporary patterns of food and drink consumption among both the immigrants and the indigenous peoples.

Natural Environments

Australia

Because of its transitional position between the low and middle latitudes, about 40 percent of Australia is located within the tropics. However, the southwestern and southeastern littoral zones lie within the midlatitudes and have temperature and rainfall regimes somewhat similar to those of western and Mediterranean Europe and, consequently, have proven conducive to the naturalization of European flora and fauna. The continent is an ancient and stable one. Large parts of it have an aspect of sameness, with almost monotonous expanses of flat land and sweeping vistas (McKnight 1995), and only in the Eastern Highlands is there great topographical variety.

Climatically, two features stand out: aridity and tropicality. Central and western Australia are arid, and well over half of the continent receives less than 15 inches of rainfall a year. By contrast, northern Australia (away from the east coast) has a monsoonlike climate, which brings abundant moisture between November and March, followed by a seven- or eight-month dry season. The northeastern coast is humid and hot, but the southeast has true midlatitude conditions with adequate precipitation, although the summers are hotter than in comparable latitudes in the Northern Hemisphere. The southwest enjoys a subtropical dry-summer/wet-winter situation – a "Mediterranean-type" climate.

The flora and fauna that developed in Australia and provided the subsistence for its indigenous people are unique, primarily because of nearly 100 million years of isolation, during which the present biota evolved and diversified without interference from immigrant species. About 80 percent of Australia's 25,000 species of plants are endemic, with two genera, the eucalypts or "gums" (*Eucalypt* spp.) and the acacias or "wattles" (*Acacia* spp.) overwhelmingly dominant. Furthermore, much Australian flora exhibits pronounced xerophytic (drought-resistant) characteristics. Only over the last few million years has there been a limited exchange of biota between Australia and (the biotically rich) Southeast Asia. In the past 200 years, the introduction of new species, mostly of European origin, has dramatically impacted the landscapes, especially of temperate Australia.

Australia's assemblage of terrestrial animal life is also unique. The more familiar placental animal groups are absent, their place being taken by marsupials, the majority of which are herbivores, including the macropods (kangaroos and wallabies, rat kangaroos, wombats, phalangers, "possums," and koala). There are also a number of carnivorous marsupials ("mice," "moles," "cats," and "devils") and a group of numbats (anteaters), as well as omnivorous marsupials called bandicoots. Additionally, Australia has two monotremes (egg-laying mammals), the duck-billed platypus *(Ornithorhynchus anatinus)* and the spiny anteater *(Tachyglossus aculeatus)*. Placental mammals are recent arrivals, which until the introduction of European species after 1788 were mostly rats, mice, and bats from Southeast Asia. Australia also has a wide variety of reptilian fauna, an exceedingly varied and singular avifauna, and abundant insects and arthropods but limited amphibian and freshwater fish life.

New Zealand

In contrast to Australia, New Zealand is characterized by sloping land, true midlatitude climates, and dense vegetation. It is located along the "Pacific Rim of Fire," and vulcanism is evident in the North Island; alpine mountains dominate parts of the South Island. Everywhere else, hill country and small valley plains dominate, except in the eastern part of the South Island where the Canterbury Plain, New Zealand's largest lowland, is located.

Overall, the climate can be characterized as "marine west coast," dominated by air from the oceans, especially from the west. Some parts of the east (leeward) side of major mountains are relatively dry, but in most of the country, the precipitation averages between 30 and 60 inches annually, with mountain regions receiving more. Temperatures are moderate (50° F to 80° F in summer and 30° F to 70° F in winter), again except for the mountains.

Prior to human occupation, the islands were heavily forested, with more than 75 percent of the total area covered with what the early British settlers called "bush." Much of this was actually a sort of temperate rain forest, which had evolved in relative isolation under unstable (volcanic and glacial) environmental conditions. The fauna inhabiting this environment was conspicuous by the lack of land mammals (other than a species of bat) and was dominated by bird life, a distinctive feature of which was the relatively high degree of flightlessness. The kiwi, New Zealand's national emblem, shares this characteristic, along with a variety of rails, woodhens, and other species.

The most notable nonflying birds were the two dozen species of moa – ostrichlike birds, now extinct, some of which were very large. Various types of waterfowl, parrots, and innumerable "bush birds," large and small, were also present in abundance, along with some species of lizards, but there were no amphibians save for a few species of frogs. A rich marine-mammal population included fur seals, sea lions, leopard seals, elephant seals, dolphins, and many species of whales, as well as an abundance of fish and mollusks.

Indigenous Food Systems

Australia

The unique and remote Australian environment provided a home for the Australian Aborigines, who comprised a distinctive society of hunters, gatherers, and fishers. Arriving from what is now Southeast Asia possibly as many as 70,000 years ago, over the subsequent millennia they spread across and occupied all parts of the continent at varying densities, depending on local environmental conditions. Mostly they led a seminomadic existence, but their movements were not helter-skelter (Davis and Prescott 1992). It is thought that there may have been from 500 to 600 tribes or tribelets, with each recognizing the territoriality of others.

Within each tribe there were usually several clans of a few dozen people each. Although there is no evidence of formal agriculture, the gathering and distribution of seed, the management of natural vegetation by fire, and the rudimentary cultivation of yams (*Dioscorea* spp.) in certain areas indicate some degree of plant husbandry. There were no domesticated animals except the dog. The total population of Aborigines at the time of European contact is not known. The most widely accepted estimate is about 300,000, although some authorities place the number as high as 1.5 million (McKnight 1995). Geographic distribution, density, and mobility were closely related to the availability of food, water, and other resources (Berndt and Berndt 1988).

Most Aboriginal languages had special terms for vegetable foods, as distinct from terms for the flesh of animals, birds, reptiles, fish, mollusks, and insects. Generally, foods from vegetable sources fell into three main categories: roots and tubers, fruits, and seeds (although some plants produced more than one type of food item, and, in a few instances, it was the pith of the plant that was consumed). There were considerable differences in the importance of various types of plant foods between ecological zones. In the vast desert and semiarid areas, Aborigines utilized between 60 and 100 edible species of plants (Latz and Griffin 1978; Peterson 1978). However, this extensive list could be reduced to about a dozen staples. (A staple is a plant species that singly or in combination with another accounts for at least 50 percent of the diet during the period it is consumed.)

Principal staples were the roots of various species of *Ipomoea* (convolvulus), *Vigna lancelota*, and *Portulaca oleracea* ("pigweed"); the fruits of *Solanum* (for example, the "bush tomato"), *Ficus*, and *Santalum* (the "quandong") species; and *Leichardtia australis* (the "bush banana"). Other principal staples were the seeds of various *Acacia* species ("wattles"); grasses, such as those of the genus *Panicum;* and herbs, such as *Rhyncharrhena linearis* (the "bush bean") (Peterson 1978; Palmer and Brady 1991). It is estimated that plants provided some 70 to 80 percent of the diet (in terms of bulk) consumed by desert Aborigines (Gould 1969).

In the more humid southeast, about 140 species of plants were eaten (Flood 1980). These included the roots and tubers of various lilies (such as *Aguillaria minus,* the "vanilla lily"); at least 20 species of terrestrial orchids (for example, *Gastrodia sesamoides,* the "potato orchid"); bulrushes *(Typha orientalis* and *Typha domingensis);* and the bracken fern *(Pteridium esculentum).* Also consumed were the roots and tubers of various dandelionlike plants, including the "yam daisy" *(Micoseris scapigera),* the "native carrot" *(Geranium solanderi),* and the "Australian carrot" *(Daucus glochidiatus).* Seasonal fruits, such as the "native cherry" *(Exocarpus cuppressiformis),* "native raspberries" *(Rubus triphyllus),* currants *(Coprosma quadrifida),* and the "kangaroo apple" *(Solanum linearifolium)*, entered the diet. The pith of tree ferns (*Dicksonia antarctica* and *Cyathea* spp.) was also consumed. More plant foods were eaten in the coastal regions of the southeast than in the highlands, but on the plains of the eastern interior, grass seed, especially the native millet *(Panicum decompositum)*, was the staple plant food.

In the tropical north, there were also a large number of plant foods. One study has identified 47 species of root crops and 49 of fruit or seed used by Aborigines (Crawford 1982), although the staples varied between coastal regions and river valleys and the interior (Turner 1974; Levitt 1981). Among the roots and tubers eaten, various yam species (for example, *Dioscorea transversa*, the "long yam," and *Dioscorea bulbifera*, the "round yam") were the most important, but the tubers of various convolvulus species (*Ipomoea* spp.), lilies (for example, the "blue water lily," *Nymphaea gigantica*), the "swamp fern" *(Blechnum indicum)*, and the "wild kapok" *(Cochlospermum gregorii)* were also consumed.

Seeds from numerous trees, including various *Acacia* species (Levitt 1981), as well as seeds from some species of *Sorghum* were consumed in the north, along with a large number of nuts – from the Zamia palm *(Cycas angulata)*, the Pandanus *(Pandanus spiralis)*, and the "nut tree" *(Terminalia grandiflora)*. Fruits included several species of *Ficus*, the "jungle plum" *(Buchaninia arborescens)*, the "native gooseberry" *(Physalis minima)*, the "big green plum" *(Planchonella pohlmaniana)*, the red "wild apple" *(Syzygium suborbiculare)*, and the "wild prune" *(Pouteria sericea)* (Davis and Prescott 1992).

Considerable variation also existed in the types of flesh eaten. Snakes and lizards, especially two species of "monitor" lizard or goanna *(Varunus varius* and *Varunus giganteus)*, were commonly consumed, as were a number of small marsupials and rodents (Peterson 1978; Flood 1980). In wetter areas, "possums" (phalangers) were frequently a part of the diet (either the "brushtail possum," *Trichosurus vulpecula,* or the "mountain possum," *Trichosurus canicus)*, along with various gliders (for example, the "squirrel glider," *Petaurus norfolcensis,* and the "greater glider," *Schoinobates volans)*, the koala *(Phascolarctos cinereus)*, and various types of "flying foxes" *(Pteropus* spp.).

Bandicoots *(Perameles* spp.) and other marsupial "rats" and "mice" (for example, *Antechinus* spp. and *Sminthopsis* spp.) served as food, as did rodents of various types (for example, the "broad-toothed rat," *Mastocomys fuscus,* and the "bush rat," *Rattus fuscipes)*. In addition, larger marsupials contributed to the human diet, although in arid and semiarid areas they were relatively limited, and even in wetter areas were problematic to hunt, requiring cooperative ventures that involved considerable numbers of hunters. The latter generally used fire (Peterson 1978), but in the New England tablelands, large permanent nets

were employed (Flood 1980). The red kangaroo *(Macropus rufus)*, the "Euro" *(Macropus robustus)*, and the gray kangaroo *(Macropus fuliginosus)*, as well as numerous wallaby species (for example, the "red-necked wallaby," *Macropus rufogriseus)* were all hunted. In the wetter areas, wombats *(Vombatus ursinus)* became important dietary items.

It has been estimated that in coastal and riverine regions, fish, shellfish, and crustaceans made up perhaps as much as 40 percent of the diet (Flood 1980). In the southeast, fish – caught by line, net, trap, or spear – included mullet (mainly *Mugil cephalus)*, snapper *(Chrysophrys auratus* and *Trachichthodes affinus)*, and various types of wrasses (for example, parrot fish and red cod, *Pseudolabrus* spp.). Such shellfish as the pipi *(Paphies australis)*, cockles *(Chione stutchburyi)*, mussels *(Perna canaliculus* and *Mytilus edulis)*, the catseye *(Lunella smaragda)*, and the mudsnail *(Amphibda crenata)* were very important food items, as were crayfish *(Jassus* spp.), gathered along rocky shorelines.

In the coastal areas of the tropical north, a diversity of marine resources was enjoyed. Green sea turtles *(Chelonia mydas)* were hunted and their eggs gathered. The dugong *(Dugong dugon)*, a herbivorous marine mammal, was another valuable source of animal protein, especially in the Torres Strait region and off the coasts of Arnhem Land (Turner 1974). There is no question, however, that in the coastal regions of the north, where they were obtainable throughout the year, fish were the staple food.

Other marine resources that made important contributions to the diet in some areas included freshwater fish, shellfish, and crustaceans. In the watershed of the Murray-Murrumbidgee system (Flood 1980), the Murray cod *(Maccullochella macquariensis)*, the "trout cod" *(Maccullochella mitchelli)*, the silver perch *(Bidyanus bidyanus)*, crayfish, mussels, and the platypus *(Ornithorhynchus anatinus)* were captured and consumed. In the far north during the monsoon, the barramundi *(Lates calcarifer)*, a large, tasty fish, was hunted with spears across the inundated floodplains (Davis and Prescott 1992). Rivers flowing to the Tasman Sea throughout the southeast of the continent contained eels *(Anguilla* spp.).

Birds constituted an important source of food, although in very dry areas they were probably only substantial food items following the infrequent heavy rains (Frith 1978). On the more humid plains of the north, east, and southwest, emu *(Dromiceius novaehollandie)* were plentiful and available throughout the year, but they were difficult to catch (Flood 1980). Ducks, such as the "mountain duck" – *Tadorna tadornoides* – of the southeast, were abundant in swamps and lagoons and along the rivers, as were black swans *(Cygnis atratus)* and a variety of other waterfowl. Wild turkeys (the Australian bustard, *Eupodotis australis)* were another excellent source of food on the open plains, and smaller birds were probably an important source of protein because they could be hit with stones relatively easily (Flood 1980). Eggs also provided food and, in some places, were seasonally very important. For example, in the Daly River country, just south of Darwin, the goose-egg season could be counted on for an abundant harvest (Berndt and Berndt 1988).

Valuable contributions to the diet were made by various types of insects, with perhaps the most widely utilized the larvae of various moths, collectively called "witchetty grubs" (Peterson 1978). Among these, probably the most important were the larvae of the Cossidae family, especially *Xyleutes lencomochla,* which feed on the roots of certain acacias. In the southeast, especially in the granite peaks of the highlands, another moth, the bogong *(Agrotis infusa),* was important. During the spring and early summer, these moths migrated to the mountains, where they occupied fissures, clefts, and caves in summit rocks and could be collected and eaten in vast numbers (Flood 1980).

The primary beverage of the Aborigines appears to have been water. It does not seem that there were any intoxicating beverages, although in some areas, plants (for example, wild honeysuckle and pandanus fruit), honey, and such insects as crushed green ants were mixed with water (Massola 1971). In the more tropical parts of the continent, the Aborigines chewed the leaves of three plants *(Nicotiana gossei, Nicotiana excelsior,* and *Duboisia hopwoodi)* (Berndt and Berndt 1988), and on the north coast, tobacco was introduced by Makassan traders sometime after the sixteenth century (Berndt and Berndt 1988).

The seasonal distribution of edible plants and the movements of fish and animals imposed seasonal patterns of diet, as well as patterns of movement over territories (Crawford 1982). Any single Aborigine territory encompassed a variety of ecological systems and, thus, was capable of producing a variety of food supplies throughout the year.

In general, during the dry season (the winter in the north and the summer in the southwest), the Aborigines lived in the river valleys, and those in the Kimberleys, for example, started exploiting the first of the roots reaching maturity when the rains ceased around April or May (Crawford 1982). By June and July, they were digging up root plants in the alluvium along the banks of creeks and rivers, and at this time, they began burning spinifex and cane-grass to stimulate the regrowth that attracted kangaroos. Water lily tubers were harvested in August and September when water levels were low, and as the weather became hotter, ephemeral pools were poisoned for fish.

When the rains came in December, the camps were moved onto higher ground, although fruits and seeds were still gathered in the valleys. In the rich coastal areas of the southeast, seasonal movement was less than that elsewhere, but it did involve getting food from the bush during the winter and from the rivers and coasts during the summer (McBryde 1974). People in the highlands and tablelands had a more nomadic existence, moving away from the higher land in the winter. Tribal territories were generally much smaller in the humid areas than in semiarid and desert areas.

Apart from knowing the right season, the right times for certain foods, and the right places to find them, obtaining them involved the use of implements and tools (Berndt and Berndt 1988). For plant foods, gathered almost exclusively by women, the most important tool was the digging stick. Men knew how to interpret the spoors of various creatures and to decoy animals and birds, and they had to be adept at spear throwing. Fire was commonly used in both hunting and food gathering (Latz and Griffin 1978). People were conscious of the abundance of food plants after burning but attributed this phenomenon to associated ceremonies performed to increase rain and food. The effect of frequent burning was to produce a series of small patches – at different stages of recovery from fire – that sustained different plant and animal communities.

Culinary practices were fairly rudimentary. Some fruits and tubers required no preparation and were usually eaten when and where they were found. Most roots, however, were cooked for some minutes in hot ashes or sand. The more fibrous roots were pulverized, and bitter or poisonous tubers were sliced, soaked, and baked, often several times (Crawford 1982). Grass seed was crushed in a stone mortar and mixed with water, with the resultant "dough" baked in hot ashes (Massola 1971). Small animals were cooked in hot ashes, and larger ones in earth ovens. Sometimes foods were mixed to improve their flavors and to make them more palatable; additives included gums from acacia trees, water sweetened with honey, and crushed green ants (Crawford 1982).

New Zealand

The first humans to settle in New Zealand (who came to be called Maori in the early nineteenth century) were Polynesians who arrived between 1,000 and 2,000 years ago (Davidson 1984). The precise dates are unknown, but there is no hard evidence of settlement before A.D. 800, and recently, dates of A.D. 1000 to 1200 have been suggested (Anderson 1989). Like the eastern Polynesian societies from whence they came, Maori obtained their food by gardening, raising domestic animals, hunting (particularly fowling), fishing and shellfish gathering, and gathering uncultivated and semicultivated plants (see Nancy Davis Lewis, chapter V.E.3.). However, in this temperate, midlatitude land, gardening (as practiced elsewhere in Polynesia) was at best marginal and at worst impossible. Indeed, there is now considerable evidence to suggest that even in regions most amenable to horticulture, gardens may have contributed only about 50 percent of the means of subsistence (Jones 1995).

Thus, the food quest in some communities can truly be described as "hunting-and-gathering."

Two aspects of Maori foraging and farming have dominated discussions of prehistoric subsistence (Davidson 1984). Hunting for *moa* has captured both popular and scientific interest for more than a century. But more recently, scholars have been equally impressed by the Maori achievement of adapting the sweet potato or kumara *(Ipomoea batatas)* to an annual cycle in a temperate climate. Moreover, it has been recognized that Maori moa hunting was merely one aspect of more general hunting activities, and that the use of other plants, particularly the bracken-fern root, or *aruhe*, also constituted very important adaptations in some areas (Young 1992).

Of the range of tropical crops that the Polynesian settlers must have tried to introduce, only six species survived until early European times: the sweet potato, taro *(Colocasia esculenta),* yam or *uhi (Dioscorea alata* and *Dioscorea esculenta),* the "bottle gourd" or *hue (Lagenaria siceraria),* the "paper mulberry" or *aute (Broussonetia papyrifera),* and a species of "cabbage tree" or *ti (Cordyline terminalis).* In 1769, Captain James Cook and his companions identified all six, but soon thereafter the yam and the paper mulberry seem to have died out (Davidson 1984).

The three main cultivated food plants were sweet potatoes, taro, and the bottle gourd, of which sweet potatoes were by far the most important. Indeed, the whole question of the introduction of horticulture in New Zealand has been bedeviled by controversy, which has centered on the sweet potato, because to grow it in New Zealand required both its adaptation to new climatic conditions and the protection of the plant and its fruits from extremes of temperature and heavy winter rains. The Maori developed an array of pits in which to store tubers – a departure from methods used elsewhere in Polynesia, where the plants grew perennially and were planted from shoots, and the tubers remained in the ground until required. Exactly how the sweet potato – an American plant – reached New Zealand (and the rest of Oceania, for that matter), let alone how its cultivation and storage came to be, remains a subject of speculation. We do know that by the twelfth century, sweet potato cultivation seems to have expanded from the northern part of the North Island into the southern part and, soon thereafter, into the northern South Island.

The species of cabbage tree, *Cordyline terminalis,* was brought to New Zealand from the tropics, but other cabbage trees *(Cordyline pumilio, Cordyline australis,* and *Cordyline indivisa)* are natives and were also exploited for food. The white inner trunk of young trees and the fleshy taproot were both used. Roots, often a meter in length, were split in two and cooked in an earth oven, and the trunks were prepared in the same manner (Young 1992).

Like cabbage trees, the *karaka (Corynocarpus laevigatus)* was also "semicultivated," yielding bounti-

ful crops of plum-size, oval berries that turned orange when ripe. The outer flesh of this fruit is tasty, but the bulk of the food value is in the kernel, which is highly poisonous if eaten raw. Ripe berries were gathered from the ground and trod upon with bare feet to work off the outer flesh (Burton 1982). Next, the kernels were steamed in an earth oven for 24 hours, steeped in running water for a lengthy period to extract the bitter alkaloid poison, then preserved by drying in the sun; subsequently, they were stored in baskets.

Between the gardens and the bush lay areas where the bracken fern *(Pteridium aquilinum* var. *esculentum)* grew. The tips of the new fronds can be eaten raw or boiled, but the roots *(aruhe* in Maori) were the major parts of the plant that were consumed. This fern was usually dug up in the spring, at a time when the roots are about an inch thick and break crisply to reveal a white interior with a few black fibers. They were dried on shaded platforms by the wind, then roasted, scraped, the inner flesh pounded, and baked into small loaves.

Truly "wild" foods were secured from the forest. There are at least 190 edible native plants found in New Zealand (Crowe 1997), and Maori used most of them. A variety of roots were utilized, including those from two species of bindweed *(Calystegia* spp.); terrestrial orchid tubers (examples include those of the "potato orchid," *Gastrodia cunninghamii,* the "onion orchid," *Microtes unifolia,* and the "sun orchid," *Thelymitra longifolia);* the roots of the bulrush or *raupo (Typha orientalis);* and the rock lily *(Arthropodium cirratum).*

Shoots and leaves from a wide range of other species were used as greens. Important among these were the young fronds of a number of ferns, such as the curling buds of the hen-and-chicken fern, *Asplenium bulbiferum* (which taste like asparagus) and especially the "sow thistle" or *puha (Sonchus asper).* An introduced species, *Sonchus oleraceus,* is still eaten today. Like the pith of the cabbage tree, that of the black tree fern of the forest *(Cyathea medullus)* was baked for several hours on hot embers, then peeled and eaten, or, alternately, steamed in an earth oven, sliced, and dried on sticks.

The berries of numerous trees were consumed, but those of the *hinau (Elaeocarpus denatus),* the *tawa (Beilschmiedia tawa),* and the *tutu (Coriaria* spp.) underwent elaborate processing. *Hinau* berries, for example, were pounded and sifted to remove the hard kernels, and the meal was then kneaded into a paste and formed into dark brown, oily cakes that were cooked and could be stored. A somewhat simpler procedure subjected the kernels of *tawa* berries to roasting in hot ashes or steaming in an earth oven. Perhaps *tutu* berries underwent the most complex processing. The only part of these that was not deadly poisonous was the purple juice of the sepals enclosing the fruits. That juice was first sieved, with any vestiges of seeds, stalks, or leaves discarded, after which it was permitted to set until it became a relish, or it was boiled with the pith of tree fern or with pieces of bull kelp *(Durvillea antarctica)* to form jellies.

A large number of other trees supplied insignificant amounts of small berries, but these were not staple foods. They were often called "children's food," although many were regarded as delicacies. Sweeteners also were obtained from the bush, mainly from the nectar of flowers and from certain vines, such as the *rata (Metrosideros fulgens)*. A very important food item in some areas was the pollen of the *raupo (Typha orientalis)*, which was dried, stripped from the stems, sifted, mixed with water, then made into loaves and steamed.

Of the Polynesian domestic animals (the pig, *Sus scrofa,* the chicken, *Gallus gallus,* and the dog, *Canis canis*) described by Nancy David Lewis (chapter V.E.3.), only the dog seems to have survived the journey to New Zealand. Dogs were kept as food animals as well as for hunting birds, and their dietary importance varied from place to place. They were probably seldom a major source of protein but always a steady and reliable one (Davidson 1984). In addition, the small Polynesian rat *(Rattus exulans)* accompanied humans to New Zealand, and although it can hardly be viewed as a domesticated animal, it was a scavenger around settlements and a fruit-eating forest dweller that was esteemed as a delicacy. "Rat runs," where snares were laid, were so valuable that they were virtually "owned" by families, or by individuals.

There were also numerous hunted animals, particularly the fur seal *(Arctocephalus forsteri),* and a wide variety of birds to capture, including the large flightless moa, already mentioned. The importance of the fur seal in the pre-European diet has only recently been appreciated. When Polynesians first arrived, the fur seals bred prodigiously, and as one seal represents an enormous amount of meat, they were probably as important in the diet as moa. They were gradually reduced in number and driven from their northern breeding grounds before the arrival of the Europeans, but they remained important in the south. Other marine mammals, such as sea lions, leopard and elephant seals, dolphins, and whales, were eaten when they were occasionally captured or, in the case of whales, washed up on beaches.

Although moa may not have dominated the early human diet in New Zealand as once thought, they were an important food item everywhere. While the dates of the final disappearance of moa from different parts of the country are not established, the birds seem to have survived in some localities until about the fifteenth century. Apart from moa, the most important birds eaten were shags, penguins (especially the Little Blue), ducks (particularly the Grey, *Anas gibberifrons,* and the Paradise, *Tadorna variegata*), the sooty shearwater (the "mutton bird" of later times), and various rails.

A variety of "bush" birds were eaten as well. These included the *kaka (Nestor meridonalis),* the pigeon *(Hemiphaga novaeseelandiae),* the *tui (Prosthermadera novaeseelandiae),* the *kiwi (Apteryx* spp.), the *kakapo (Strigops habroptilus),* parakeets (*Cyanoramphus* spp.), wattled birds, albatrosses, mollyhawks, and various gulls.

Birds were captured or killed with nets, spears, and snares, and by hand collection of the young. Bush birds were most commonly snared and speared in the autumn and early winter when berries were ripe or when nectar was in the flowers early in the summer. Bird carcasses were preserved in fat in airtight containers made from either gourds or bull kelp (Belich 1996).

Shellfish formed a very important item of Maori diet, especially by the eighteenth century and in the northern part of the country, where the most productive shellfish beds were located (Davidson 1984). Shellfish gathering was largely women's work, as was the gathering of crabs, sea urchins, and *kina.* In contrast, the catching of fin fish was largely done by men (Young 1992). Hook-and-line fishing, as well as various types of nets and traps, were used to catch snapper, red cod, barracouta, trevally, yellow-eyed mullet, and various wrasses. Many other fish were also caught and consumed, but there was considerable regional variation in the most important species. In the north, snapper dominated, but in the south it was barracouta and red cod. A considerable quantity of the fish caught was baked and hung from poles and racks to dry for future use. Seaweed, especially a type called *karenga (Porphyra columbina),* was also consumed, as was bull kelp *(Durvillaea antarctica,* which served additionally to make storage containers for other foods) and sea lettuce *(Ulva lactuca).*

Inland dwellers utilized small freshwater fish, such as the *kokopu* (a native trout), grayling, postlarval young trout returning upstream (known as *inanga* or whitebait), and a species of lamprey. Freshwater crayfish and mussels were consumed, but the most important freshwater creatures were eels, taken in basketwork traps. In some locations, elaborate weirs were constructed to channel eels during their migrations.

Although methods of preserving and preparing food have been mentioned, the latter deserve further comment. The earth oven (a circular hole in the ground about 2 feet in diameter and about 1 foot deep), called either a *hangi* or an *umu,* was the principal method of cooking (Crowe 1997). A fire was made in the hole, and a layer of stones laid upon it; these, when heated, were removed, and the embers cleaned out. The heated stones were returned to the hole, covered with green leaves, and sprinkled with water; then more leaves were added, and food baskets or leaf-wrapped food placed on this layer. The food was covered with still more leaves, wet flax mats, old baskets, and the like, and the whole sprinkled liberally with water and covered with earth so that the steam could not escape. A family's food would normally cook in an hour or less, although larger amounts took longer. In addition, some food was doubtless roasted in hot ashes. Another technique, stone boiling, was also in common usage. Water and food were placed in a wooden trough, and red-hot stones added to bring the water to a boil.

Finally, a comment upon cannibalism is necessary. Human flesh did constitute part of the diet (at least of eighteenth-century males) (Davidson 1984), but the practice seems to have been a form of revenge *(utu)*, desecrating the victims beyond the grave by turning them into cooked food (Belich 1996). Although it fascinated and revolted early European observers, the preponderant evidence indicates that those cannibalized were enemies captured or killed in war, and cannibalism was primarily an ultimate way of subjugating adversaries (Hanson and Hanson 1983).

By way of summary then, broadly speaking, New Zealand in the eighteenth century was divided into three areas in terms of the mix of foods consumed (Cumberland 1949; Lewthwaite 1949). In the northern area, horticulture was most successful, and the many harbors and estuaries contained rich fish and shellfish resources. Along the coasts of the southern North Island and northern South Island, and in the interior of the North Island, horticulture was more marginal, and hunting and gathering much more significant. Apart from the northern fringe, people in the South Island depended on hunting, fishing, and the gathering of wild plants.

The period between A.D. 1350 and 1600 was one of transition. The early settlers had exploited the premium game animals, such as moa and seals, to the point of exhaustion, and this led people to move into areas suitable for gardening, particularly in the north; it also resulted in an increased reliance on fishing and gathering throughout the islands. Large-scale marine fishing seems to have increased in importance after 1600, but the hunting of smaller birds and the trapping of eels were also significant. Gardening certainly dominated in the north, but elsewhere the "semicultivated" plants also grew in importance in the diet.

After European contact, the Maori were quick to adopt a variety of European plants, in part to vary the diet in those areas where traditional horticulture had been practiced, and in part to create a new dimension in economics where traditional horticulture had been impossible. More vigorous varieties of sweet potatoes and taro were introduced, as was the white potato *(Solanum),* which probably dates from the early 1770s. Because it was easier to grow than the sweet potato and provided a higher yield, it rapidly gained popularity everywhere (Burton 1982; Belich 1996). Less popular European vegetables introduced in the eighteenth century were carrots, pumpkins, cabbages, turnips, and parsnips (Burton 1982) – although fruit trees, especially peaches, were welcomed. Maize was the first cereal to gain acceptance; wheat was adopted only during the 1840s and 1850s.

Of the European animals, the pig – well established and running wild by the early nineteenth century – was the earliest and most successful introduction. No other animal in New Zealand yielded such a large quantity of meat, and pork became an important source of protein. In fact, pork and white potatoes joined native *puha* (sow thistle) and sweet potatoes, foods from the sea, and birds from the forest as the Maori diet in the early decades of the nineteenth century. At first, all of these new introductions may have contributed to an improvement in nutrition, but once Maori began selling land and losing access to the resources of the bush and water, the quality of the diet diminished (Pool 1991).

From Colonies to Nations

The British Heritage

Although numerous Dutch, Portuguese, French, Spanish, and British explorers had touched the shores of Australia and New Zealand from the late sixteenth century onward, it was only in the late eighteenth century that European colonization of these lands commenced. The 1769 voyage of Captain Cook initiated this process, and the establishment by the British of a penal colony at Botany Bay in 1788 (soon moved to Sydney Harbour) marked the beginning of their (since then) permanent – and largely unchallenged – presence in these southern lands.

Several other penal colonies and one free-settler colony (South Australia) were established by 1840, but in the early years it was Sydney that dominated British affairs in the South Pacific. Among other things, Sydney was the base from which New Zealand's resources – enumerated as flax, timber, whales, seals, sex, and souls by James Belich (1996) – were exploited, and it was not until after 1840 that the direct settlement of New Zealand proceeded. Even then, Australian influences remained strong, especially with regard to food and beverage habits.

The free settlers (both working- and middle-to-upper class) who went to Australia and New Zealand after 1840 were from very similar socioeconomic backgrounds, and not surprisingly, the economies of the two countries developed in very similar ways. Australia was a little more Irish (and Catholic) than New Zealand because in Australia's formative years, more than one-third of the settlers (both convicts and assisted migrants) were from Ireland. In New Zealand, by contrast, approximately one-quarter of the settlers were Scots, and only 19 percent were Irish. Nonetheless, according to Michael Symons (1982), the Irish influence on antipodean food included a strong preference for potatoes, the method of cooking them (boiling in a cauldron), and a liking for strong drink consumed away from home at pubs.

English settlers comprised barely a half of those arriving in the colonies, and the overall mixed British – in contrast to purely English – character of the population also had considerable influence on eating and drinking in the region. Indeed, the food and beverage habits carried to Australia, and later to New Zealand, were basically those of Britain's burgeoning urban underclass: potatoes, bread, and tea, with a little sugar, milk, and occasionally bacon (see Colin Spencer, chapter V.C.4.).

On the other hand, some of the assisted migrants, from the working and lower-to-middle classes, were from rural backgrounds and accustomed to a bit more diversity in their diets (potatoes, bread, cheese, butter, bacon, milk, tea, sugar, peas, turnips, and a little meat). Moreover, the officers and officials of the Australian penal colonies and, later, the wealthier settlers in both Australia and New Zealand brought with them the food habits of a middle class, sometimes with upper-class aspirations. Colin Spencer (chapter V.C.4.) describes a late-eighteenth-century middle-class meal in England as consisting of three boiled chickens, a haunch of venison, a ham, flour-and-suet pudding, and beans, followed by gooseberries and apricots. As a rule, large amounts of meat were consumed by those who could afford it, and such vegetables as cabbages, carrots, spinach, Brussels sprouts, and turnips were common. Beer and ale were the most popular drinks until distilled spirits, such as gin and crude rums, took over during the eighteenth century.

Pastoral Economies

In both Australia and New Zealand, the early years of settlement were characterized by a failure to establish successful farms and achieve self-reliance in food production. The area around Sydney was poor farming country, and in the early nineteenth century, sheep farming for wool production became the lifeblood of Australia. Sheep reached New Zealand a bit later (1833), pastoralism expanded in the 1840s, and by the late 1850s, wool was also central to the New Zealand economy.

In Australia, a lasting dependence upon imported foodstuffs developed. New Zealand also depended on imports, but in addition, such settlements as Auckland, Wellington, New Plymouth, and Nelson came to rely on a flourishing Maori agriculture for their supplies of potatoes, maize, onions, cabbages, peaches, sweet potatoes, pumpkins, grapes, melons, apples, and quinces, as well as flour (milled in Maori mills), fish, chickens, geese, turkeys, and goats (Belich 1996). It was only in the late 1850s that settlers began to produce much of their own food and the role of the Maori as food providers began to decline.

The last half of the nineteenth century brought stunning transformations to Australia and New Zealand. The gold rushes that began in both countries during the 1850s precipitated rapid social and economic changes, including the growth of urban areas, so that by 1900, these areas encompassed about 50 percent of the population (Symons 1982). In addition, railway networks opened up areas for the production

of food of all types, not only for local consumption but also for export. After the 1870s, and especially after the inauguration of refrigerated shipping in 1882, both Australia and New Zealand became producers of meat (mutton, lamb, and beef), dairy products, and later fruit, for the British market. By the late nineteenth century, livestock ranching and the growing of both temperate and tropical cereals, fruits, and vegetables were all well established in areas suited to them, and in Australia, irrigated farming was developing along the Murray-Murrumbidgee river system. In well-watered, temperate New Zealand, the native vegetation was largely replaced by exotic pasture grasses to feed the introduced animals (Crosby 1978), and in southeastern Australia and along the northeastern coast (where the growing of sugar and tropical fruits came to dominate), the landscapes were transformed as well.

One outcome of the success of pastoralism was that Australia and New Zealand became nations of meat eaters. Up through the 1870s, there was no overseas market for meat, which, as a consequence, was inexpensive relative to people's incomes (Burton 1982). Meat in large amounts was eaten at every meal: beefsteaks or mutton chops at breakfast, cold beef at luncheon, and roast or boiled beef or mutton at dinner (Symons 1982; Walker and Roberts 1988).

"Rations" and "Crew Culture"

Convicts (under sentence of "transportation" to Australia) along with their guards, working-class settlers bound for New Zealand, and assisted migrants to both countries (not to mention the crews of the ships carrying them all) were all provided with "rations." The voyage from the British Isles was a long one, with three to six months the norm (the "First Fleet" to Australia in 1787 and 1788 took eight-and-a-half months), and although officers and cabin passengers enjoyed a satisfactory diet, the rations for the rest – which were not satisfactory – remained remarkably the same for more than 70 years.

By way of illustration, the weekly rations for each of the Royal Marines aboard during the First Fleet's voyage to Botany Bay were 7 pounds of bread, 2 pounds of salt pork, 4 pounds of salt beef, 2 pounds of peas, 3 pounds of oatmeal, 6 ounces of butter, three-quarters of a pound of cheese, and a half-pint of vinegar, along with 3 quarts of water a day (Symons 1982); the convicts' rations were two-thirds those of the marines. More than a half-century later, during the 1840s, New Zealand Company settlers were provided with 3.5 pounds of salt meat and 5.25 pounds of biscuit weekly, supplemented with rice, flour, oatmeal, dried peas, dried potatoes, raisins, butter, sugar, coffee, and tea.

Nor did the issuance of rations necessarily end when one stepped ashore. In Australia, the convicts and guards from the First Fleet had to subsist on rations for nearly three years, because agriculture had not yet developed (Walker and Roberts 1988). In the early settlements in New Zealand, ordinary migrants lived on New Zealand Company rations so long as the Company's money lasted (Belich 1996). But it was sheep farming that firmly entrenched the "ration mentality" in Australian and New Zealand food culture.

Sheep grazing required complements of shepherds as well as gangs to shear the sheep, usually made up of itinerant males, who were the founders of many working-class traditions in both countries. Shepherds were partially paid in rations; handed out on Saturday nights and supplemented with spirits and a paycheck, this food eventually earned the name "Ten, Ten, Two, and a Quarter" because it usually included 10 pounds of flour, 10 pounds of meat, 2 pounds of sugar, a quarter-pound of tea, and salt (Symons 1982).

"Ten, Ten, Two, and a Quarter" was the monotonous diet of the rural workforce until well into the twentieth century, and it was very characteristic of the diet of "crews" of coastal seamen, soldiers, sawyers, millworkers, construction workers, road and railway builders, miners, gum diggers, and farmhands. The "crew culture" was a factor in quite a few industries, and despite the many different kinds of work, involved a number of common characteristics: The work was dangerous; the crews lived in rough conditions; they used similar slang; most members were single; most spent their money on binges; and most ate a ration-style diet.

Basically, then, for the first half century, the majority of Australians were reared on what might be called prison rations – a practice that was transferred to New Zealand. In both countries, crew culture was reinforced by the dominant means of cooking: an open fire, whether at a campsite or in a hut or cottage. With the necessary implements – hatchet, knife, quart-pot (the "billy can"), and frying pan – the standard rations made a "damper," a fry of meats, and pots of tea. The "damper" was flour and water, cooked in the ashes of the fire; the meat was salt pork, corned beef, or freshly slaughtered mutton; the tea, although taken with plenty of sugar, usually lacked milk. Its abundance meant that meat was consumed at every meal.

More Genteel Food Habits

In contrast to the diets of the lower classes, the foodways carried to these new lands by the more genteel folk reflected the social differences of the Great Britain they had just left. Cabin passengers breakfasted on rolls, toast, cold meat, and hot chops. At luncheon, the fare was ham, tongue, beef, pickles, bread, and cheese, and in the evening they dined on preserved salmon, soup, goose, saddle of mutton, fowls, curry, ham, plum puddings, apple tarts, fruit, and nuts, all of this washed down with stout, champagne, sherry, and port (Belich 1996).

Once ashore, these elite few endeavored to maintain their notions of genteel dietary regimes. Thus, as early as 1789, it is recorded that the governor of New South Wales, the senior officers of the regiment guarding the convicts, and the senior officials of the civil administration sat down to several courses of fish, meat, and game (Clements 1986). Or again, in New Zealand of the 1850s, the meal served at an elegant dinner party might have included local fish, beef, sweet potatoes, Irish pork, Lancashire ham, and Cheshire cheese (Burton 1982). Indeed, just a few years later, an upper-class "colonial banquet" in Australia consisted of asparagus, turtle soup, trumpeter (a local fish) with butter sauce, lamb *à la poulette,* roast kangaroo, Australian blue cheese, wines, and liqueurs with coffee (Symons 1982). Later in the century, a suggested menu for a dinner party included oysters, turtle soup, baked barramundi, "beef olives" and chicken cream, roast fillet of beef, roast turkey and bread sauce, asparagus on toast, "angel food" cake, cherries in jelly, fruit, olives, and deviled almonds (Symons 1982).

Generally speaking, middle-class meals were enormous. Breakfast consisted of porridge, bacon and eggs or lamb cutlets, and perhaps curry or fish (Burton 1982). Luncheon might feature soup, a roast joint, vegetables, and cooked pudding or fruit. Four- or five-course family dinners were not uncommon, beginning with an "appetizer" of soup or fish, continuing with a roast, vegetables, and a pudding, and topped off with fruit and cheese.

Diet and Modernization

Food habits were considerably influenced by late-nineteenth-century technological developments, such as urbanization, railroads that rapidly transported products, and breakthroughs in food processing and preservation (including refrigeration). Australia and New Zealand were becoming modern, mass-consumption societies.

Giant roller mills producing refined white flour began to appear in the 1860s, and from this time on, workers, like their counterparts in Britain, began to enjoy a cornucopia of biscuits, macaroni, jams, confectionery, cordials, pickles, condiments, and snacks. These products, with their brand names, were advertised extensively and commonly sold in the emerging grocery shops. Also in the 1860s, beer (now "bottom fermented" and thus capable of longer-term storage and long-distance transportation) was brewed, and by 1900, today's major brewery corporations were already in existence.

Cooking technology also changed. At the beginning of the nineteenth century, cooking was mostly done over an open fire, where meats were roasted and stewpots suspended. One refinement at this time was the "Dutch oven" or "camp oven," a round pot with legs and a handle so that it could either stand or hang. By the middle of the nineteenth century, the "Colonial oven," a simple cast-iron box with a door in front that sat in the fireplace, had come into widespread use. Cast-iron ranges were imported beginning in the 1850s, and by the 1870s, locally manufactured stoves had entered the market (Burton 1982). This was at about the same time that the first gas stoves were introduced, permitting better control of the cooking process.

By the early twentieth century, a new array of processed and packaged foods – that supplemented the basic bread, mutton, beef, pork, milk, eggs, fruit, vegetables, and tea – were in common use. As Symons (1982) has noted, tea was the national beverage, and alcohol was not usually drunk with meals (other than by the upper classes), but rather was imbibed separately in hotel bars (Wood 1988). By the time of World War I, both Australia and New Zealand had seen the development of strong temperance movements, which proved powerful enough to persuade governments to hold referendums on the outright prohibition of alcoholic beverages, and some of the voting was very close. During the war, hotel bar hours were curtailed (Symons 1982), with closing time usually at 6:00 P.M., leading to the infamous "six o'clock swill."

During the 1920s, numerous developments further standardized eating habits. Fresh fruits and nuts were heavily promoted, as were pasteurized milk and ice cream (Symons 1982). Bread – a staple in urban areas since the time of early settlement – was baked mostly in mechanized bakeries, and to see it wrapped for sale in grocery stores was becoming common in Australia. Iceboxes were now widespread, and by the 1920s, wealthier housewives were looking forward to owning their own refrigerators.

The 1920s also saw an increased American influence on food, as sundae shops and soda fountains arrived and such big American food companies as Heinz, Kellogg, and Kraft moved in. These, along with such others as Nestlé (Switzerland) and Cadbury (England), came to dominate Australian and New Zealand eating and drinking habits. They pushed early "convenience" foods, defined as those that needed no cooking outside of the factory, which simplified breakfast and provided after-school and bedtime snacks. One product epitomizes this era. "Vegemite," made from brewery waste (spent yeast), became a runaway success after its alleged health attributes were extensively advertised during the 1930s and 1940s (Symons 1982). The post–World War II baby boom created a huge new market for "Vegemite, the family health food."

At this time, too, food companies and women's magazines promoted a more dainty cuisine aimed at the afternoon tea market: "Lamingtons" (chocolate-and-coconut-coated cubes of cake), "Anzac biscuits" (made of coconut, rolled oats, and golden syrup), and especially the "Pavlova" (made of whipped egg whites, corn flour, vinegar, sugar, a few drops of vanilla essence, and a pinch of cream of tartar, baked and topped with whipped cream and fruit – especially passionfruit and, today, kiwifruit). Pavlova, named after the famous ballerina ("It is as light as Pavlova"), is alternatively said to have originated in both Australia and New Zealand (Symons 1982).

World War II had much influence upon food and beverage habits. Rationing was introduced, which curtailed the use of sugar, tea, flour, and meat. However, the demand for more fruit and vegetables created by the presence of U.S. military forces in Australia and New Zealand brought about an increase in the acreage planted with both. Vegetables were also increasingly canned and, later, dehydrated to provide the military with preserved food. The meat-processing industry was compelled to upgrade its standards and put out new canned meats, such as *chile con carne,* luncheon meats, "Spam," and Vienna sausage (Symons 1982). Coca-Cola came with the American troops and stayed after they left.

Until the 1960s in both Australia and New Zealand, bread, milk, vegetables, groceries, and meat were all delivered. But with the advent of relatively inexpensive automobiles (first in Australia and quite a bit later in New Zealand) and universal ownership of refrigerators, supermarkets began to control food sales, all of which had the effect of furthering the trend toward nationally standardized and distributed food. Supermarket giants came to dominate food marketing with "prepackaging," bright labels, and an emphasis on low prices rather than on quality. These chain-store companies did not like dealing with small producers and growers. Because they preferred products with long shelf life, they tended to offer canned, dried, and frozen rather than fresh foods, processed by industrial-size producers who could guarantee regular supply, consistent quality, and steady prices.

By identifying gaps on the supermarket shelves, such producers brought forth a new array of food-stuffs, many of a "convenience" nature, such as "Muesli," reconstituted orange juice, teabags, pizza, frozen fruits and vegetables, and the like. Foods of this sort were marketed as "labor-saving," were usually aimed at target groups after extensive market research, and were given scientific credence through the endorsement of "home economists" and "nutrition experts" (Symons 1982). This was especially characteristic of the frozen-food industry, which included such internationally known brand names as Birdseye (owned by Unilever in Australia and New Zealand), as well as local processors (for example, Watties in New Zealand) that began freezing peas, corn, berry fruits, Brussels sprouts, beans, and asparagus during the 1950s and later expanded into fish products, "TV dinners," frozen chips, cakes, poultry, and meats.

As has been the case in developed countries elsewhere, recent decades have also witnessed the sacrifice of family farms to agribusiness, monoculture, the intensive use of fertilizers and pesticides, and the arrival of scientifically "engineered" fruits and vegetables, made possible by agricultural research and funded by both governments and private corporations (Symons 1982). Recently, however, new "alternative" farming ventures have also arisen that produce organic fruit and vegetables and market them directly to consumers through resurrected city markets. At the same time, the "back to the earth" movement has supplemented the limited information prevailing in industrial societies concerning the imitation of developing-world cuisine (Symons 1982). In Australia, the food items of the original inhabitants have begun to be noticed again, but as yet in New Zealand, there has not been the same level of interest in "Maori" food other than breads, seafoods *(kai moana)*, and foods cooked in the traditional earth oven (Osborne 1989; Paul 1996).

Eating Out

Eating establishments have existed since the beginnings of settlement in Australia, and in fact, in 1800 the Freemason's Arms in Sydney served excellent French-style food. More commonly, early eating houses and taverns dished out boiled mutton and broths, but both the Australian and New Zealand colonies had numerous eating houses with reputations for excellent "British cookery" (Symons 1982). The belle epoque for fine restaurants was between 1890 and World War I, when in all of the major cities, gourmet restaurants served a wide range of continental cuisines. Following the war, however, gourmets could lament that the two countries had only one diet: steaks, chops, beef, mutton, potatoes, and gravy, with suet pudding and slabs of cheese (Symons 1982).

For the less wealthy, "fourpenny" and "sixpenny" restaurants, serving basic meats and vegetables, had come into being at about the middle of the nineteenth century (Symons 1982). The fish-and-chip shop, a feature of Australian and New Zealand life that has remained, albeit modified, to the present day, arrived somewhat later. Another such feature is the ubiquitous meat pie brought by the British, which evolved over a long period to become the standardized dish common since the 1920s (Symons 1982). Men commonly ate meat pies at sporting events and as a counter lunch item in hotel bars. By World War II, the meat pie had become a "national dish" in both countries. The New Zealand Food and Drug Regulations of 1973 state that meat pies shall be encased in a pastry shell and contain not less than 25 percent cooked or manufactured meat (Burton 1982).

Until recently, "going out to dinner" for many Australians and New Zealanders meant the fish-and-chip shop or the "pie cart," a mobile, trailerlike café parked at a convenient location, which served meat pies with various accompaniments (for example, mashed potatoes and peas, known all together as "pea, pie, and pud"), as well as various other types of portable food to its customers (Burton 1982). Even as late as the 1960s, the only alternatives to the fish shop and the pie cart were the dining rooms of hotels and exclu-

sive private clubs, both of which served a very standard antipodean cuisine: steak and chips, roast meats and vegetables, bread and butter, tea, and ice cream with passion fruit (Symons 1982).

By the late 1960s, however, the pie carts and the fish-and-chip shops began receiving stiff competition from American-style fast-food outlets. Kentucky Fried Chicken was the first, in 1968, and McDonald's and Pizza Hut were not far behind. A decade later, such fast-food franchises were everywhere, although their products did not completely replace fish-and-chips and meat pies, and many of the traditional fish-and-chip shops have recently expanded their "takeaway" (carry-out) menus to include Chinese food as well as a variety of European fast foods, such as gyros and kebabs. Fast-food outlets of this type, often operated by recent immigrants, have contributed significantly to the diversification of foodways in Australia and New Zealand.

Of even more importance, however, has been the recent explosive growth of all types of restaurants. Some of this growth can be attributed to the influence of immigrants from Europe soon after World War II and, more recently, from Asia and the Pacific region. But as affluence grew in both Australia and New Zealand, more people began to visit Europe and other places around the world, and as they did so, they discovered that there was more to the "good life" than steak-and-eggs and chips.

Contemporary Food and Beverage Ways

Migrants, overseas travel, the window to the world opened by television, affluence, and the continuing globalization of food have all contributed to the diversification of Australian and New Zealand diets. Another significant change has been in drinking habits. An accompaniment to the growth of diversified, quality eating places has been the proliferation of locally produced wines, some of fine quality, some not. Although Australians and New Zealanders were and are beer drinkers, they have also historically drunk sweet wines, characteristically "screw-topped Riesling" (Symons 1982).

Grapes have long been grown, since 1791 in Australia and 1819 in New Zealand (de Blij 1985). Wine making developed early in Australia: By the 1820s, it was successful around Sydney and had expanded to the Hunter Valley. In the 1830s and 1840s, viticulture and wine making began in Victoria and South Australia, and a solid market for sweet and fortified wines developed. During the 1960s and the years that followed, the industry was transformed, with new, high-quality cultivars planted; technological and wine-making improvements led to a vastly expanded and diversified array of wines to meet developing consumer tastes.

Large-scale wine making is much more recent in New Zealand, which had only 200 acres planted with wine grapes in 1945. But the industry expanded enormously after 1960, with white varietals initially dominating. Today, red varietals have also come into their own, and there are more than 140 vineyards marketing wine in New Zealand. Some are owned by large corporations; yet there are also many small producers making excellent wines.

"One Continuous Picnic"?

Symons (1982) has characterized eating and drinking in Australia since 1788 as "one continuous picnic," and the contention here is that the same has been true in New Zealand. Both peoples were dispatched to the antipodes with packed provisions – "rations" – of salt pork and ship's biscuits. Pastoralists were paid in rations of flour (for damper), "billy tea," and slabs of meat, and the indigenous peoples learned their new foodways from the "crews" who were transforming their lands. The railways sent Australians and New Zealanders jaunting off with a litter of tins and bottles. More recently, semitrailer trucks have brought in Coca-Cola, frozen puff pastry, and "Big Macs." The concept of a picnic highlights the most essential character of Australian and New Zealand food right from the beginning: portability. Even the penchant for outdoor barbecuing (the "put-another-shrimp-on-the-barbie" syndrome) can be interpreted in this light. Broiling meat and seafood over hot coals harks back – nostalgically? – to an earlier age, when men (and women, when they were present) cooked their rations over open fires with a minimum of equipment.

Brian Murton

Bibliography

Altman, J. C. 1987. *Hunters and gatherers today. An aboriginal economy in North Australia.* Canberra.

Anderson, Atholl. 1989. *Prodigious birds: Moas and moa-hunting in prehistoric New Zealand.* Cambridge.

Belich, James. 1996. *Making people. A history of the New Zealanders from Polynesian settlement to the end of the nineteenth century.* Auckland.

Berndt, Ronald M., and Catherine H. Berndt. 1988. *The world of the first Australians. Aboriginal traditional life: Past and present.* Canberra.

Burton, David. 1982. *Two hundred years of New Zealand food and cookery.* Wellington.

Clements, Fredrick W. 1986. *A history of human nutrition in Australia.* Melbourne.

Crawford, I. M. 1982. *Traditional aboriginal plant resources in the Kalumburu area. Aspects of ethno-economics.* Perth.

Crosby, Alfred W. 1978. Ecological imperialism. *The Texas Quarterly* 21: 10-22.

Crowe, Andrew. 1997. *A field guide to the native edible plants of New Zealand.* Auckland.

Cumberland, Kenneth B. 1949. Aotearoa Maori: New Zealand about 1780. *Geographical Review* 39: 401-24.

Davidson, Janet. 1984. *The prehistory of New Zealand.* Auckland.

Davis, S. L., and J. R. V. Prescott. 1992. *Aboriginal frontiers and boundaries in Australia.* Melbourne.

de Blij, Harm. 1985. *Wine regions of the Southern Hemisphere.* Totowa, N.J.

Flood, Josephine. 1980. *The moth hunters. Aboriginal prehistory of the Australian Alps.* Canberra.

Frith, H. J. 1978. Wildlife resources in central Australia. In *The nutrition of Aborigines in relation to the ecosystem of central Australia,* ed. B. S. Hetzel and H. J. Frith, 87-93. Melbourne.

Gould, R. A. 1969. *Yiwara. Foragers of the Australian desert.* New York.

Hanson, F. Allan, and Louise Hanson. 1983. *Counterpoint in Maori culture.* London and Boston, Mass.

Jones, Kevin. 1995. *Archaeology of the eastern North Island, New Zealand.* Wellington.

Latz, P. K., and G. F. Griffin. 1978. Changes in aboriginal l and management in relation to fire and food plants in central Australia. In *The nutrition of the Aborigines in relation to the ecosystem of central Australia,* ed. B. S. Hetzel and H. J. Frith, 77-86. Melbourne.

Levitt, Dulcie. 1981. *Plants and people: Aboriginal uses of plants on Groote Eylandt.* Canberra.

Lewthwaite, Gordon R. 1949. Human geography of Aotearoa about 1790. Unpublished M.A. thesis, University of Auckland.

Massola, Aldo. 1971. *The Aborigines of south-eastern Australia as they were.* Melbourne.

McBryde, Isabel. 1974. *Aboriginal prehistory in New England. An archaeological survey of northeastern New South Wales.* Sydney.

McKnight, Tom. 1995. *Oceania. The geography of Australia, New Zealand, and the Pacific islands.* Englewood Cliffs, N.J.

Osborne, Christine. 1989. *Australian and New Zealand food and drink.* New York.

Palmer, Kingsley, and Maggie Brady. 1991. *Diet and dust in the desert. An aboriginal community, Maralinga Lands, South Australia.* Canberra.

Paul, Joanna. 1996. *The Maori cookbook.* Auckland.

Peterson, N. 1978. The traditional pattern of subsistence to 1975. In *The nutrition of Aborigines in relation to the ecosystem of central Australia,* ed. B. S. Hetzel and H. J. Frith. Melbourne.

Pool, Ian. 1991. *Te Iwi Maori. A New Zealand population past, present, and projected.* Auckland.

Symons, Michael. 1982. *One continuous picnic. A history of eating in Australia.* Adelaide.

Turner, David H. 1974. *Tradition and transformation. A study of Aborigines in the Groote Eylandt area, northern Australia.* Canberra.

Walker, R. B., and D. C. K. Roberts. 1988. Colonial food habits: 1788-1900. In *Food habits in Australia. Proceedings of the First Deakin/Sydney Universities Symposium on Australian Nutrition,* ed. A. Stewart Truswell and Mark L. Wahlqvist, 40-59. Richmond, Victoria.

Wood, Beverley. 1988. Food and alcohol in Australia: 1788-1938. In *Food habits in Australia. Proceedings of the First Deakin/Sydney Universities Symposium on Australian Nutrition,* ed. A. Stewart Truswell and Mark L. Wahlqvist, 157-77. Richmond, Victoria.

Young, Jeffrey M. 1992. A study of prehistoric Maori food. M.A. research essay, Department of Anthropology, University of Auckland.

V.E.3 ❧ The Pacific Islands

In the Pacific Islands (or Oceania) great distances, distinct island environments, and successive waves of peoples reaching island shores have all shaped foodways, including gathering, hunting, and fishing, agricultural practices and animal husbandry, and modern food distribution systems.

The peoples of Oceania (which was subdivided by Eurocentric cartographers into Melanesia, Polynesia, and Micronesia) arrived at their island homes over a span of many thousands of years. The various islands have substantial differences in natural resources, and the inhabitants have had different experiences with explorers, colonizers, and missionaries. But since the 1960s, many of the peoples and lands of Oceania have had in common their own decolonization and integration into the global economy. What follows is a description of the history and culture of food and nutrition in the Pacific Islands that recognizes diversity yet also attempts to leave the reader with an impression of the whole.

The Pacific Region

In the vastness of the Pacific Ocean are some of the world's smallest nations and territories. Politically there are 22 states, excluding both Hawaii and New Zealand. The region's giant is Papua New Guinea. With a total land area of 462,000 square kilometers, it is over five times larger than all the other Pacific states combined. This nation, inhabited for many thousands of years longer than the rest of the region, is also home to over 60 percent of the region's population of 6 million individuals, whose diversity is illustrated by the more than 800 languages spoken in Papua New Guinea alone. Fiji is the only other Oceanic territory with a population of more than 500,000. By contrast, Tokelau, a territory of New Zealand, is made up of three coral atolls with a combined land area of 10 square kilometers and a population of 1,600. Cultural definitions of the region, however, incorporate New Zealand as well as Hawaii. New Zealand is treated elsewhere in this work, but for comparative purposes, this chapter includes several references to its original inhabitants, the Maori.

The Environment

The island types of Oceania range from the large, mountainous eastern half of the island of New Guinea, which the nation of Papua New Guinea shares with Indonesian Irian Jaya, to tiny coral atolls dispersed across the central and eastern Pacific. The dominant tectonic feature of the region is the Pacific Plate, which is moving slowly to the northwest and underthrusting the Asian land mass. Its western boundary forms the Pacific "Rim of Fire," characterized by volcanism and earthquake activity. In broad outline, the region presents a continuum of environments, from larger continental islands, extensions of the Asian land mass, and andesitic volcanoes in the western Pacific to basaltic volcanic islands and coral atolls in the north and east.

There are three major island types: continental, volcanic, and coral atolls. The islands in the west, many of which are continental islands, tend to be larger and geologically complex. Typically they include intrusions of andesitic volcanic rock and are surrounded by fringing and barrier reefs. These islands have a varied topography, contain metal-bearing ores, and can develop diverse soil types, rendering large areas suitable for agricultural development. The volcanic islands, produced by andesitic, explosive volcanoes west of the Andesite line and basaltic shield volcanoes in the Pacific Basin, are much more homogeneous. Weathering produces islands with steep, rugged interiors. Fertile soils may develop on weathered slopes and in the rich alluvial deposits on valley floors.

Coral islands are the third major island type in the region. Some cultures of the Pacific are found exclusively on these resource-limited islands. Most islands in the tropical Pacific are surrounded by barrier or fringing reefs. As the final stage in the evolution of these islands, only the coral remnants remain, leaving either an atoll, a ring of coralline islets surrounding a central lagoon, or a raised coral reef. Several variations of these two main types exist. Coral islands have a more limited agricultural potential, although the upraised limestone islands may develop fertile soils under some conditions. Water is often a limiting factor because of a lack of orographic precipitation and limited storage capacity.

The Climate

Whereas almost all the islands fall within the tropics and have high year-round temperatures, these conditions are moderated by oceanic location and offshore winds. In the eastern Pacific, north of the equator, the dominant trade winds are from the northeast; south of the equator, they are from the southeast. But in the western Pacific, seasonal monsoons influence weather patterns. The northwest monsoon reaches as far east as Papua New Guinea, the Solomons, and the Carolines, bringing storms and rain in the winter. During the rest of year, the dry southwest monsoon often brings drought. Trobriand islanders refer to this as the *molu*, or hunger season.

Between the two trade-wind belts are the doldrum areas, the largest of which extends as far west as the Solomons. The doldrums are characterized by low wind velocities, high humidity, cloudiness, and high temperatures. There, atolls with no orographic precipitation, especially those close to the equator, such as the Northern Line Islands in the eastern Pacific, can be subject to extreme drought. On high islands in the trade-wind belts there is significant dissymmetry between wet windward and dry lee shores. Typhoons (hurricanes) are also a threat throughout the region.

In addition to influencing climate, the ocean currents of the Pacific have played a major role in determining flora and fauna of Oceania. Those currents, along with prevailing wind patterns, also set the parameters for long-distance sea voyaging. Oceanic peoples with sophisticated navigational techniques and maritime skills reached these remote islands in the Pacific to complete humankind's occupation of the globe about a thousand years ago.

Flora and Fauna

The flora and fauna of the island Pacific are products of their distance from Asia and, to a lesser degree, from Australia. They are also products of the great distance between islands in the eastern Pacific and North and South America. Other variables include rainfall, altitude, soil, soil salinity, groundwater, insolation, and human activity (Oliver 1989). Terrestrial plants had to have reproductive parts capable of being carried by wind or birds or humans, or of surviving immersion in salt water. Generic diversity drops significantly as one moves from west to east. As the water gaps become larger, this tendency is increased, producing a significantly more depauperate flora and fauna in the eastern Pacific.

D. Oliver (1989) has listed the natural vegetation complexes encountered in the region. Seacoast or strand vegetation, confined to narrow coastal areas, is found on most islands. Additional lowland vegetation types include mangrove forest, swamp, and rain forest found on both continental and volcanic mountainous islands. Lowland rain forest, the most widespread vegetation type in the Pacific, provides important resources for food, medicines, fiber, and building materials. But population pressure and the search for exploitable resources such as lumber have led to encroachment and environmental degradation.

Other vegetation types are more restricted in their distribution. With increasing altitude or distance from the equator, for example, at 3,000 feet in equatorial Papua New Guinea and at 900 feet in Fiji, high montane cloud forests are found. Alpine vegetation is encountered only on the highest islands – extensively only on Papua New Guinea and Hawaii and in patches on the Solomons. Finally, grasslands and savanna woodlands, resulting from either insufficient rain or anthropomorphic processes such as burning, occur on New Guinea and lee areas on some of the other islands of Melanesia (including Viti Levu), on Hawaii, and on Easter Island in Polynesia.

The fauna is equally depauperate. West to east, there is a severe attenuation of terrestrial vertebrate genera. When the Polynesians first reached Hawaii's shores, the only mammals they found were the hoary bat *(Lasiurus)* and the Hawaiian monk seal *(Monaachus)*. A similar attenuation can be seen with land birds. There are 869 species in Papua New Guinea and only 17 in Tahiti. This pattern is also evident in freshwater fauna. Marine species are more widely distrib-

uted; however, the marine biota is also less diverse in the eastern Pacific than in the west. For example, there are 60 species of cowries in the Marianas Islands in western Micronesia and only 35 in Hawaii.

Peoples of the Pacific

The complex history of the Oceanic peoples is less well understood than the region's natural environment, and it is a history that is continually being revised as archaeologists, linguists, ethnobotanists, and geneticists uncover new evidence.

In discussing the interplay of productive practices and social systems, the geographer B. Currey (1980) borrowed from earlier ethnographic depictions to characterize the Melanesians as gardeners, some of whom developed complex systems (revolving around the raising of pigs) in which status was more individually than communally derived, and leaders were seen as "Big Men." Polynesians were depicted as gardeners and fishermen, with societies built on group solidarity and relatively equal access to food (although some highly stratified societies developed, especially in Tahiti and Hawaii). The Micronesians were described as traders who developed interisland trading networks and various forms of class stratification. Although this is a gross generalization, for our purposes it is a useful one. But where did these people come from?

It is now evident that Pacific Island peoples, and most of their domesticated plants and animals, originated in Southeast Asia. Between 60,000 and 8,000 years ago, two distinct "races" of modern-type humans inhabited the islands to the west of New Guinea: Mongoloids in the north and west and Sundanoids (also known as Australoids or old Melanesians) in the south and east (Oliver 1989). By 40,000 years ago, during periods of lowered sea level, Sundanoids moved into New Guinea and the Sahul shelf of Australia (Bellwood 1979). The earliest occupation of New Guinea, however, was probably even earlier, although permanent sites were not established in the highlands until 25,000 years ago (Gorecki 1986).

Oliver (1989) has suggested that between 10,000 and 5,000 years ago, four important introductions reached the Pacific Islands: (1) genes carrying Mongoloid traits, (2) languages of the Austronesian family, (3) objects relating to animal domestication and plant cultivation, and (4) knowledge to improve seagoing craft and boat handling. The latter began an era in which the far reaches of the Pacific were discovered and inhabited.

By 5,000 years ago, most of the Sundanoid peoples of Southeast Asia had been replaced or absorbed by others with different traits, such as lighter skin, straighter hair, rounder crania, and flatter brow ridges. These pioneers began to move into the Pacific Islands, possibly from the region bordering the Celebes Sea. They reached western Micronesia (Palau and the Marianas Islands) about 3,600 years ago, having crossed open ocean distances of some 500 miles. At about the same time, another group that was more or less Mongoloid moved along the north coast of New Guinea to the Solomons, Vanuatu, and Fiji.

These eastward-moving peoples were farmers and fishermen, who kept dogs and pigs, developed sophisticated fishing techniques, and also hunted. Their cultivated crops included taro, yams, bananas, sugarcane, breadfruit, coconut, the aroids *(Cyrtosperma* and *Alocasia),* sago, and, probably, rice, although at the time of European contact rice was found only in the Marianas.

The absence of rice in most of the Pacific Islands is one of prehistory's most tantalizing questions. Works by Peter Bellwood (1979) and J. Clark and K. Kelly (1993) suggest that rice was somehow lost from the horticultural complex and that sagos and taros replaced it in swampy areas, whereas yams and tree crops were grown in dry fields and swamp-garden margins. But in another interpretation, M. Spriggs (1982), who posited a Southeast Asian origin for Pacific agriculture, has argued that the techniques used for irrigated taro reached the Pacific before rice was established as a staple in Southeast Asia.

Some 3,500 to 3,300 years ago, a wave of Mongoloid-featured, Austronesian-speaking migrants moved southeast across the Pacific and rapidly established settlements in Fiji, and then in Tonga and Samoa. Those who arrived in Samoa and Tonga were the ancestors of present-day Polynesians. They brought with them Lapita ware – a type of stamped and incised pottery that probably originated in the Admiralty Islands and the Bismarck archipelago. They had a well-developed maritime technology, were expert fishermen, and also were horticulturalists who raised pigs and chickens. They developed sophisticated exchange networks, transporting goods across long distances. Some 600 years later, another migratory group from the west, with different traits, reached Fiji to mix with the islanders and become ancestors of the Fijians (Oliver 1989).

From Tonga and Samoa, the rest of Polynesia was settled over time with differentiation in language and other aspects of culture. Spriggs and A. Anderson (1993) have argued for settlement dates of A.D. 300 to 600 for the Marquesas, sometime after A.D. 750 for the Society Islands, and A.D. 600 or later for Hawaii. Anderson (1991) has suggested dates of A.D. 1000 to 1200 for New Zealand and the end of the first millennium for Easter Island.

There has been less research for Micronesia, in part because it presents a more difficult environment for archaeological investigation. As mentioned previously, the Marianas were settled by Austronesian-speaking Mongoloids at least 3,600 years ago. Recent evidence suggests that descendants of the first inhabitants of Palau and the Marianas moved east into the Caroline Islands before Oceanic-speaking peoples migrated to Micronesia via the Solomons, Gilberts,

and Marshalls (Oliver 1989). Migrants had reached the southern Gilberts by 3,500 to 3,000 years ago.

Plant Foods of the Pacific

Because they share a tropical and subtropical climate, as well as a flora and fauna with common origins, it should be no surprise that there are many similarities in the history and culture of food and nutrition among the peoples of the Pacific. Some plants have been identified as specifically Pacific cultivars, notably the fruited pandanus, sugarcane, and the *Australimusa* banana. The coconut may have had multiple domestication sites (Sauer 1971). The major staple root crops, yams *(Dioscorea)* and taros *(Colocasia esculenta, Cyrtosperma chamissonis,* and *Alocasia macrorrhiza,* are from Southeast Asia, as is the *Areca catechu* palm (Lebot, Merlin, and Lindstrom 1992). Bellwood (1979) has discussed evidence of gardening and pig raising in the central highlands of New Guinea from 5,500 to 6,000, and possibly as many as 9,000, years ago. More recent evidence suggests that agricultural techniques appeared independently in Papua New Guinea 9,000 years ago, possibly predating their development in neighboring Southeast Asia. There is evidence of 9,000-year-old domestication and cultivation from the Kuk Swamp in Upper Wangi, New Guinea (Gorecki 1986), but it seems likely that intensive and continuing horticulture was not established in highland Papua New Guinea until about 4,000 years ago.

D. Yen (1991), the preeminent Pacific ethnobotanist, has recently proposed a model that attempts to explain the diffusion of agricultural crops across the Pacific: Agriculture began with the independent early domestication of endemic species in the New Guinea region about 10,000 years ago. It was accelerated by the introduction of species from Southeast Asia (about 6,000 years ago), and again by the advent of crop plants from the Americas, most notably the sweet potato. These arrived in Polynesia in prehistoric times but were not introduced into western Melanesia, including Papua New Guinea, until Western contact.

The timing of the introduction of the sweet potato and its role in the development of highland New Guinea's complex agricultural systems, which supported very large populations, has been the subject of considerable academic speculation. A parallel controversy surrounds the timing of the precontact introduction of the sweet potato into eastern Polynesia (see the discussion under "Root Crops").

Root Crops

Taro. Taro refers to four members of the Araceae family, *Alocasia macrorrhiza* (giant taro), *Cyrtosperma chamissonis* (giant taro or swamp taro, grown largely on atolls), *Xanthosoma* sp., (kong kong taro or American taro, a post-Columbian introduction from South

America), and *Colocasia esculenta* (true taro). The last is the most widely distributed, and in many places in Oceania, it was the favored staple. Ancient Hawaiians, perhaps Oceania's most sophisticated agriculturalists, recognized between 150 and 175 distinguishable varieties of taro (Murai, Pen, and Miller 1958). Taro was the main staple of Hawaiians and Samoans.

Colocasia taro is believed to have been among the first root crops to be domesticated (Pollock 1992). Traditionally, it was found from South Asia through Indonesia to the Pacific. Recent evidence suggests widely distributed multiple sites for the domestication of taro, with one of those sites being highland Papua New Guinea (Yen 1993). Polynesian taro, however, could be derived from a narrower genetic base that had its origins in Indonesia, although New Guinea may have been the immediate area of domestication (Yen 1991). Archaeologist Spriggs (1982), relying in part on similarities in the irrigation technologies of New Guinea and island Southeast Asia, argued that taro originated in Southeast Asia and diffused from there into the Pacific.

Recent evidence suggests human use of *Colocasia* 28,000 years ago in Kilu Cave, a Pleistocene site in the Solomon Islands. This discovery supports the hypothesis that the natural distribution area of *Colocasia*, and perhaps other aroids, included Australia, New Guinea, and the northern Solomons (Loy, Spriggs, and Wickler 1992). *Colocasia* (true taro), whose corm and leaves are both eaten, grows best in shady, well-watered settings, such as lowland and montane rain forests to about 7,000 feet (Oliver 1989). As was the case in Indonesia and Melanesia, *Colocasia* was also produced in sophisticated valley terrace systems in the Cook Islands, in eastern Polynesia, and with a system of aqueducts in Hawaii.

Cyrtosperma taro grows in coastal freshwater marshes. It is a much larger tuber that remains edible in the ground for several years and was an important crop in Micronesia because of its tolerance of stagnant, brackish water. Shoots of the rootstock are also planted, with compost and soil, in pits dug into coral to reach the freshwater lens. *Cyrtosperma* is labor-intensive, and some island peoples have surrounded its production with much secrecy while growing huge specimens for ceremonial exchange. *Alocasia* taro requires the least moisture and is the hardiest, but the edible starchy stem contains oxylate crystals and must therefore be processed prior to consumption. Usually a subsidiary food, it is highly valued in Samoa and Tonga.

Yams. *Dioscorea* are grown throughout the tropical world, and the relationship of those in the Pacific to those in Africa, tropical America, and Asia has not been fully established. *Dioscorea alata* and *Dioscorea esculenta,* the most common Pacific species, may well have been domesticated in Southeast Asia. In order to produce a large tuber, *D. alata* needs a prolonged dry season and, thus, in the Pacific tends to be an upland

rather than a lowland crop. Yams also need deep planting in light, well-drained soil; where good drainage is wanting, the technique of mounding is employed, with the vines trained to climb poles or trees.

The tubers, which can reach 9 feet in length and more than 100 pounds in weight, are often prized for size rather than food value, as the flesh of such large specimens is too coarse to eat. Their production, like that of *Cyrtosperma* taro, is often surrounded with much ritual and secrecy. Farmers gain prestige for their skill as gardeners, and yam production is at the center of a number of Melanesian societies. In Fiji, where yams were the focus of the diet, the calendar revolved around their growing season. The tubers can be left in the ground or stored for months. Traditional yam storage houses are sometimes very elaborate, as those in the Trobriand Islands.

Sweet potato. As already noted, the presence of the sweet potato *(Ipomoea batatas),* like the absence of rice, has been the subject of much speculation by those concerned with the history of Oceania. This is because at the time of European contact, the sweet potato (an American plant) was found in almost every high-island archipelago, and those who suggest a New World origin for Pacific human populations have made the plant a part of their argument.

Yen (1974), citing botanical and linguistic evidence, has suggested that the sweet potato reached the Pacific from South America in three separate introductions, all via human agency, because the sweet potato does not propagate after lengthy immersion in seawater. According to this hypothesis, the plant was first introduced into the Marquesas, in the eastern Pacific, between A.D. 400 and 800. This took place after the first settlement of the Marquesas and before the subsequent settlement of Hawaii and Easter Island. From there the sweet potato was carried to other parts of Polynesia and eastern Melanesia. What this implies for proponents of eastward or westward voyaging is one of the intriguing dilemmas of Oceanic prehistory. Another hypothesis posits a second post-Columbian Portuguese introduction, in which the sweet potato supposedly traveled (via Africa and India) through Indonesia to New Guinea and New Britain during the sixteenth century. Finally, it is believed that in the seventeenth century, still another introduction took place in the Manila Galleons from Mexico to the Philippines; after that, sweet potatoes were carried to the Marianas and East Asia.

Sweet potatoes grow in a wide range of conditions and can be cultivated at high elevations. They are fairly tolerant of dry, sandy soils and typically are grown in mounds. Sweet potatoes were part of the highly complex agricultural systems that evolved in Papua New Guinea and were also important in Hawaii and Easter Island. Because of the difficulty of production in cooler climates, they became a valued luxury in temperate New Zealand.

Tree Crops

A large array of fruit and nut crops are found in Melanesia, but they become fewer in the more restricted environments that occur as one moves to the east. Only the main food tree crops – coconut, sago, breadfruit, pandanus, and banana – are discussed here; *Areca catechu* (betel nut) is treated along with kava and toddy in a later section.

Coconut. Perhaps the Pacific region is associated more with the coconut palm, found along the littoral of most tropical islands, than with any other plant. *Cocos nucifera* is widespread, but because of temperature requirements, it is not found in New Zealand above about 1,000 feet, and it has been extinct on Easter Island for over 600 years. Although considerable debate has surrounded the role of humans in the distribution of the coconut palm, and although the plant can propagate itself, most stands have been planted by humans (Oliver 1989). It is a very important supplement to starchy staples throughout the region.

As a result of centuries of selection and propagation, Pacific Islanders recognize many horticultural varieties of the coconut. The immature nut is filled with liquid, which, over time, turns into a layer of hard, white meat. The meat is often eaten as a snack, and it is also scraped and pressed to produce coconut "cream," an important component of Pacific dishes. At full development, the center of the nut contains a spongy, jellylike mass of embryo known as "spoon meat," which is sometimes fed to infants or to those who are ill. The "milk" of immature nuts ("drinking nuts") is an important source of liquid when water is in short supply. Coconut oil can be extracted after grating the meat and exposing it to the sun for several days.

The production of copra (dried coconut meat) for export has been a mainstay of Pacific economies since the 1860s, as it can be stored on and transported from the most remote of island locations. Copra, however, is an intermediate commodity; the ultimate product is coconut oil for food and industrial purposes. Unfortunately, global economic changes, transportation costs, the increasing use of substitute oils, and alleged health risks associated with consuming coconut oil have rendered copra an increasingly marginal export commodity.

Sago. Metroxylon sp. is a pinnate-leafed palm that reaches 30 to 50 feet tall and grows in swampy areas as far east as Samoa and the Caroline Islands. The trunk is filled with a starch that the plant employs to nourish its inflorescence; thus, the tree is commonly harvested just before flowering (at about 8 to 15 years of age). Sago palms are high-yielding, producing about 300 pounds of starch per tree. The tree is felled, split, and the pulp pulverized. The starch is then washed out of the fiber and allowed to dry, producing sago "flour," which keeps for months. The flour is made into pancakes, cooked as a porridge, and can also be used as a thickener for other dishes. Sago has been a staple for many groups in Papua New Guinea and a dietary supplement for others there and in the Solomons and Vanuatu, although it is not now as widely exploited as it once was (Connell and Hamnett 1987). It was rarely used in Polynesia or Micronesia.

Breadfruit. Artocarpus sp., with origins in the Malay archipelago, is a handsome tree growing to 60 feet in height, with large, shiny, lobed leaves. It does especially well in the Marquesas Islands, where it provides the staple food. William Dampier, who found breadfruit on Guam in 1686, may have given it its English name (Murai et al. 1958). One hundred years later, Captain William Bligh's fateful voyage of the *Bounty* began as an effort to carry breadfruit from Tahiti to the West Indies. The plant was successfully transported there in 1792 but did not become a food for slaves as was originally intended. They refused to eat it.

Artocarpus altilis and *Artocarpus incisus* are both seedless, whereas *Artocarpus mariannensis,* the variety found in Papua New Guinea, contains seeds. The fruit, cultivated primarily in Micronesia and Polynesia, is round or elliptical and reaches up to 10 inches in diameter. Breadfruit tolerates less salt than both coconut and pandanus and, hence, is more restricted in its coastal distribution. It is also drought-intolerant. The fruit is eaten cooked, but the seeds may be consumed raw. Where it is an important staple, the fruit is traditionally preserved for months or years at a time in a covered pit, in which it ferments, producing a distinctive and, to Pacific Islanders, delicious flavor. Production is seasonal, with a large summer harvest and a smaller winter one.

Pandanus. Pandanus sp. (also called the "screw-pine") is an Indo-Pacific genus with several species. It has long, narrow, prickly leaves and aerial roots. Both edible and inedible varieties grow in the Pacific region. In some parts, cultivated and semicultivated plants are a primary food source, most notably among some groups in Papua New Guinea and on the coral islands of Micronesia and Polynesia. In the latter areas, a number of parts of *Pandanus tectoris* are eaten: the "heart" or terminal bud of the branch, young leaves, the tips of aerial roots, and the seeds and fleshy portion of the fruit (Oliver 1989). In cultivated varieties, the fruits can weigh as much as 30 pounds, with 50 or more phalanges or keys with seeds at the end.

Pandanus is high in sugar, carbohydrates, and vitamin A. It can be eaten raw, but it is also cooked and made into a flour or a paste, both of which can last for months. In some parts of the Pacific, the paste is wrapped in plaited pandanus leaves and tied with coconut cord. In former times, these bundles could reach up to 6 feet in length and 1 foot in diameter (Murai et al. 1958). Pandanus is a major staple on coral atolls and once provided an important food source for long-distance voyaging.

Banana. Before European contact, the bananas of Oceania were either "cooking bananas" or plantains, and not the sweet ones eaten raw, although *Musa paradisiaca* (sweet bananas) and *Musa troglodytarum* (cooking bananas) are both of Southeast Asian origin and have a number of cultivars. In most cases, bananas were a supplement to the diet rather than a staple. Today, some of the varieties introduced by Europeans are preferred in the green stage for cooking, as in Samoa. In Polynesia, bananas were grown both as part of shifting cultivation and as perennial herbs in gardens and around settlements. Western perceptions to the contrary, the traditional diets of Pacific Islanders were not complemented by an abundance of fresh fruits. Citrus fruits and pineapple were introduced to Oceania by Westerners. Pacific fruits like the papaya were typically given away or, in modern times, sold. Both papayas and mangoes are fed to pigs.

Other Crops

Sugarcane. Saccharum officinarum, which when chewed satisfies both hunger and thirst, and *ti (Cordyline fruticosa, Cordyline terminalis),* with a root very high in sugar, were among the plants that Polynesians carried with them on their voyages, and both became widely established species. The former is best known in Oceania as a plantation crop on Hawaii and Fiji.

Manioc (cassava). Manihot esculenta or *Manihot utilissima,* an American plant, was introduced early into the Pacific by the Spaniards, but it did not become widespread as a food until the middle of the twentieth century. Since then, it has become an important staple in the Pacific, as elsewhere in the developing world. In Fiji, manioc superseded taro decades ago in total area under cultivation (Thaman 1990). Sometimes perceived as a lazy man's crop because of its ease of cultivation, it has been planted in areas where cash crops have captured the most productive land. With long, thin, tuberous, edible roots, most varieties contain toxic hydrocyanic acid and must be processed before consumption. Manioc grows best in wet climates, but it can survive dry periods. Usually baked or boiled, it can be processed and stored like flour. It is high in starch but low in vitamins and minerals, and, hence, its widespread displacement of traditional staples is decried by some nutritionists.

Food Production Systems

Oliver (1989) has noted that a major generalization which could be made about food production in Oceania is that individual plants have been planted and tended there, in contrast to the sowing of large quantities of seed. Fire, adzes, and axes were used to clear the land, and digging sticks were employed for planting. Weeds and pigs were common problems, and islanders appealed to the supernatural for protection against crop pests and diseases. During recent research in Fiji, an Indian farmer suggested to me that it was still much better to pray than spray.

Agriculture

Agricultural production systems are closely tied to land tenure, which in most Pacific societies was, and to a large degree remains, communal. Land itself has a deep spiritual meaning in Pacific societies (Bonnemaison 1984). P. Cox and S. Banack (1991) have noted that in much of Polynesia, land and most equipment was the common property of descent groups and was allocated at the lowest unit of the group. This practice was modified in the most highly stratified societies, as in Hawaii, where at the time of Western contact, chiefs directly controlled the land. Many groups in Oceania had access to several microenvironments, such as strand and swamp. Typically, in Polynesia, the units of land tenure were pie-shaped wedges, from mountaintop to outer reef, that spanned four or five ecological zones. These lands were used both for production and for hunting and gathering (Oliver 1989).

Writing of Polynesia, P. Kirch (1991) has argued that the range of production systems reflected an adaptation not only to the wide range of environments that the islanders encountered but also to demographic and sociopolitical circumstances such as expansion and intensification. The agronomic complex of any location was also influenced by other factors. Not all food plants and animals made or survived voyages to new islands, and the voyagers themselves may not have been vested with all the agronomic lore of their home islands.

As already mentioned, there is a west-to-east decline in numbers of cultivated and husbanded species of plants and animals that mirrors, to a degree, the decline of indigenous flora and fauna but may also reflect the attrition wrought by long voyages. Moreover, as islanders moved from high to low islands, there were many adaptations in food production that reached their extreme in temperate New Zealand, where most tropical crops did not thrive. Taro could be grown in the north, but not very successfully, and other important crops, such as coconut, breadfruit, and banana, did not become established. The edible fern, *Pteridium esculentum,* became an important staple, and New Zealand Maori were highly dependent on both the rich avifauna and marine species.

In general, according to Oliver (1989), extended kin groups (those who slept together and ate together) constituted food-producing units, except in societies where gender segregation dictated eating and sleeping patterns. In Melanesia, males were primarily responsible for site preparation, climbing high trees, and felling sago palms. Females were usually, although not universally, responsible for weeding, planting, and harvesting. Kirch (1991) wrote that in

Polynesia most agricultural labor was done by males, with assistance from women in weeding, mulching, harvesting, and carrying crops. But in other societies, especially where dry-field cultivation was the norm (as on the islands of Hawaii and Maui), more female labor may have been required. Even in the 1990s, the role of women's labor in agricultural production was underestimated. Women's roles in gardening and pig rearing in Melanesian societies also had implications for women's roles in political and ritual life in these societies (Manderson 1986).

Types of production systems. Kirch (1991) described five types of agricultural systems in Polynesia, and these can be modified for Oceania as a whole. The initial phase in most high-island locations was shifting cultivation with aroids and yams. It was often succeeded by arboriculture and field rotation.

The second, dry-field cultivation, developed out of the intensification of shifting cultivation. Both shifting cultivation and dry-field cultivation are practiced today.

Water control, a third system, included inundated fields created by terracing, drained garden systems in swampy areas, and pit cultivation. The most highly developed forms include the miles of intricate drainage systems for sweet potato gardens on the marshy valley floors in highland New Guinea and the sophisticated taro drainage and irrigation systems found in New Caledonia, Fiji, Hawaii, and elsewhere in Polynesia. Yen (1991) has noted that irrigation has been the most commonly used method of raising *Colocasia* taro. Growing taro under irrigation is highly productive, resulting in considerable surplus, and Kirch (1984) has argued that such surpluses were important to the rise of Polynesian chiefdoms in late precontact Hawaii.

Arboriculture, the fourth system, was typical of lowland Melanesia with a mix of fruit- and nut-bearing species. Although arboriculture declines to the east, monocropping of breadfruit (*Artocarpus* sp.) did develop in Polynesia, especially in the Marquesas. Other important tree crops include the almost ubiquitous coconut, *Spondias dulcis -vi* or Kafika apple, and *Inocarpus fagifer,* the Tahitian chestnut.

Kirch identified animal husbandry as a fifth system in his classification and noted that pigs, dogs, and chickens (the Southeast Asian triad) were the three species raised in Polynesia, although one or more may have been absent in marginal eastern Polynesia and on some atolls. Most were found on Pacific islands at the time of Western contact, although chickens were absent in much if not most of Melanesia. In some New Guinea societies, wild cassowaries were captured and raised for food (Oliver 1989). Dogs were more marginal than pigs in most Pacific societies and usually survived by scavenging, except in Hawaii, where they were tended and fed. The chicken (*Gallus gallus)* was also a scavenger, although it was carefully husbanded on Easter Island (where the dog and the pig were absent), and there it served some of the ceremonial purposes that pigs did on other islands. Dogs were used in hunting where there were sufficient ground animals, as in Melanesia and New Zealand, but also served as food themselves in Hawaii and the Society Islands (Oliver 1989).

Pigs played a central role in many of the cultures of Oceania, especially in Melanesia. They were probably introduced to New Guinea from Indonesia as early as 5,000 years ago, but their range did not extend to Micronesia or, as noted, Easter Island, and they were not found in New Caledonia or New Zealand at the time of Western contact (Oliver 1989).

These pigs (*Sus scrofa*) were thin, long-legged "razorbacks," unlike today's much larger and fatter domestic pigs. Different husbandry strategies for pigs evolved, such as letting them forage exclusively, or feeding them occasionally, or constraining and feeding them all the time. In parts of Melanesia, much attention was lavished on pigs; their births were surrounded with ceremony, and they were suckled (as were dogs in some places), bathed, and fed premasticated food. They were a very important symbol of wealth and central to ritual, social relationships, and political power. In highland New Guinea, sweet potato gardens supported the production of large numbers of pigs, typically for ceremonial exchange (Megitt 1974), although many pigs were also slaughtered for ceremonial purposes (Oliver 1989) and consumed by kin and other social groups.

Hunting and Gathering

Hunting, gathering, and fishing in coastal and riverine locations were the only food-producing activities of humans in Oceania for the first 20 or so millennia (Oliver 1989). In most traditional societies (exceptions were a few in Papua New Guinea), hunting, although an important source of protein, did not provide the bulk of calories, which came from wild plants, grubs, insects, and, especially, marine foods.

Because of the paucity of mammals on the islands to the east, the hunting of avifauna, for both food and feathers, was well developed. In New Zealand, the arrival of the earliest inhabitants rapidly led to the extinction of 11 species of *moa* – giant flightless birds – and other species as well. In many parts of Oceania, the gathering of seabird and turtle eggs supplemented the diet, and fruit bats were hunted as far east as Samoa and Tonga.

It bears repeating, however, that the major constraint on hunting and gathering in the islands of the eastern Pacific was the severe attenuation of indigenous species of both plants and animals. E. S. C. Handy and E. G. Handy (1972) listed the wild species used in Hawaii as six species of ferns, six of roots or tubers, eight of nuts and berries, two of tree fruits, four of leaves, numerous species of seaweed, and many species of birds, but only one insect, the grasshopper.

Fishing

There is also an attenuation of both freshwater and marine fish species from west to east. Marine foods were a key to the peopling of the Pacific, and fishing was and remains a very important food-securing activity in the region, especially on the high islands and atolls of the central and eastern Pacific. Traditional fishing methods were many and varied. Relatively sessile marine creatures, such as mollusks and sea urchins and other slow-moving animals, were caught by hand in the inshore waters. Harvesting sea turtles was also common in many locations. On the reef and in the lagoon, stupefacients were used, as well as mesh nets, draft nets, spears, nooses (for eels and, in Hawaii, sharks), traps and snares, and lines for angling (Oliver 1989). The fishhooks of Oceania reveal a fascinating array of special-purpose applications.

The collection of *limu* (seaweed) has been particularly important in Polynesia, as was documented in the extensive work of I. Abbott (1991). There are 63 Hawaiian names for edible marine and freshwater plants, representing about 30 separate species. Hawaiians considered *limu* and *poi* a particularly satisfying dish. Elsewhere in Polynesia, *limu* was typically consumed with coconut cream or grated coconut, and the fact that *limu* was not eaten with coconut in Hawaii has been used to argue for a relatively late arrival of the coconut there (Handy and Handy 1972).

Culinary Practices

Beginning with the early explorers, discussions of the meaning of food and of meals in Oceania have been confused by Western preconceptions. For example, Nancy Pollock (1986, 1992), using evidence from Fiji, Hawaii, Tahiti, and elsewhere, has noted that the concept of a "meal" is less important than it is in Western societies (although the meaning of meals may be changing with the fast-food culture in the West). Typically, meals, as defined by Westerners, were consumed once or twice a day and consisted of a starch and an accompaniment, with perhaps a condiment, such as salt, mashed shellfish in brine, crushed insects, or seaweed.

Oliver (1989) has described the main meal, usually freshly cooked, as generally eaten in the late afternoon after the day's work was over. The first meal of the day might have been a light one consisting of leftovers from the previous day, and lunch was often foodstuffs collected and cooked during work, such as breadfruit roasted over an open fire. Oliver (1989) has also made some interesting generalizations about the various food habits of the region, which, although diverse, share many similarities. The peoples of Polynesia and Micronesia have tended to have more food recipes, even though they had fewer nonmarine food resources, than those of Melanesia, and oven baking has been more common in Polynesia and Micronesia. Polynesians and Micronesians also had more food-

preparation instruments – pounders, graters, spitters, and fire tongs. The implements used in eating included breadfruit or *ti*-leaf "plates," sharpened sticks, and sometimes wooden bowls, baskets, and seashells. Fingers also served as eating implements.

Food Preparation

Some Oceanic foods were eaten raw – small fish, marine invertebrates, pandanus "keys," coconut, and some fruits – although, as already noted, the adult diet typically did not include much fruit (Oliver 1989).

Cooking methods included broiling over fire or on hot ashes or stones, with the food either uncovered or leaf-wrapped, and sometimes hot stones were put in the body cavity of an animal. Where clay pots were part of the material culture, foods were sometimes boiled. In the early 1800s, whalers and missionaries introduced boiling pots and frying techniques.

The most distinctive cooking style, and one that is indigenous to Oceania, involves the use of the earth oven or *umu*. There are both household and communal ovens (Pollock 1992), with the latter a significantly larger version of the former. There were variations in the oven preparation, but generally a pit was dug and lined with stones upon which a fire was lit. Following this, the heated ash was brushed aside, some of the stones removed, and the remaining stones covered with green leaves. The foods to be cooked were placed on the stones, then covered with hot rocks and ash, leaves, fronds, perhaps earth, and, today, a burlap sack. Although such a slow-cooking technique is laborious, it persists in the region, particularly for feasts and Sunday meals.

No regionwide survey of cooking responsibilities has been carried out, but examples from 21 societies in Oceania revealed situations where women did all the cooking, others where women did the daily cooking and men cooked for feasts (which may be the most common), still others where both men and women cooked daily and for feasts, and the example of Truk, where men did most of the cooking on a daily basis as well as for festive occasions. In at least one society (Yap) each gender regularly cooked for itself, and in Tahiti there was some prohibition against women eating foods cooked by men (Oliver 1989).

Preservation

The storage of food, especially for times of natural disaster or human conflict, was well developed in parts of Oceania, perhaps especially so in the more environmentally sensitive areas. Pollock (1992) has argued that this practice developed not only for times of shortage but also because of a preference for the added taste of fermentation, as in *poi*, the taro dish of Hawaii, or in fermented breadfruit. In the famine-prone Marquesas, breadfruit was traditionally prepared by young men (it was believed that it would store longer if the men were virgins), fermented, and placed in *ti*-lined wooden vessels, and the *ma* was stored in underground pits for months or years. Similarly, taro and breadfruit paste were left to ferment and, sometimes, stored for 10 years or more.

Polynesian arrowroot and, more recently, manioc were preserved as flour. Sago starch was dried, fish were dried and/or salted, and bananas could also be dried or stored in tightly wrapped packets. Well-aired storage houses were used for yams, and food was also preserved by not harvesting it. As already noted, *Cyrtosperma* taro grown in pits can survive in swampy areas for a number of years, and both *Dioscorea* yams and manioc can be left in the ground.

Feasting and Ceremonies

Because they figure so predominantly in Pacific life, feasts have received a great deal of ethnographic attention. They were often dictated by political motives and defined by structured social relationships and religious considerations. They were also important mechanisms for exchange and had considerable economic significance.

Feasts, surrounded with rules and rituals, usually involved large numbers of individuals and a great amount and variety of food. In some societies, all food was prepared and eaten at the location where the feast took place; in others, cooked or uncooked food was given to guests for later consumption (Oliver 1989).

In Melanesia, feast preparations might have included the slaughter of hundreds of pigs. As mentioned previously, there and elsewhere, as in Pohnpei in Micronesia, gardeners would jealously and often secretly raise huge yams. No longer edible, these tubers nonetheless displayed the agriculturalist's prowess and earned credit in ceremonial exchange. Often an enormous amount of food was prepared – much more than could be consumed – and this also carried ceremonial and sociopolitical significance.

Food Taboos

Throughout Oceania, eating was governed by taboos based variously on age, sex, marital status, pregnancy, social grouping and rank, illness, and bereavement. According to Oliver (1989), the most widespread prohibitions were those based on totemism whereby groups would not eat food items (including many wild species) with which they were perceived to have a spiritual relationship. Food taboos for women in Oceania were common, and in ancient Tahiti, women were generally prevented from eating pig, dog, turtle, albacore, shark, dolphin, whale, and porpoise – all foods highly valued or in short supply (Manderson 1986).

Jocelyn Linnekin's book *Sacred Queens and Women of Consequence* (1990) has described a situation in Hawaii in which the dichotomies between chief and commoner or male and female defined social reality. Women were prohibited from eating with men, and cooking was men's work. The choicest foods were offered to chiefs and sacrificed to the gods. Such foods were prohibited to women, although female chiefs were exempt from punishment (which could be death) for infractions.

Further light is shed on food taboos for women in Polynesia by Pollock (1992), who cited J. Williams's (1838) comments about the Cook Islands:

> Females at Rarotonga were treated as inferiors. They were neither allowed to eat certain kinds of food which were reserved for the men and the gods, nor to dwell under the same roof with their tyrannical masters, but were compelled to take their scanty meal of inferior provisions at a distance while the "lords of creation" feasted upon the "fat of the land" and the "abundance of the sea." (Williams 1838: 180)

Women typically had even more restricted food choices during pregnancy, as the maternal diet and development of the fetus were directly associated (Manderson 1986). A woman might, for example, have avoided eating a fish with a displeasing appearance for fear that her child might resemble the fish. Taboos were not, however, exclusive to women. Pork, a highly valued food, was prohibited to women in a number of Pacific societies, but in a few others, for example among the Etoro of New Guinea, the situation was reversed. For men, pork consumption was believed to deplete strength (Rappaport 1968). In the stratified societies of Polynesia, chiefs also imposed prohibitions on certain foods (e.g., pork, specific fishes, or food crops) for sociopolitical reasons, to assure the supply or protect the resource. Feasts might accompany the lifting of such prohibitions.

Eating and Body Size

In most of the societies of Polynesia, and especially among the nobility, large stature and obesity were highly regarded in both men and women. Large size was associated with status and hospitality; thus, a fat chief signified a wealthy society. Moreover, in some societies, such as that of Tahiti, obesity meant increased sexual attractiveness (Oliver 1989). There are numerous accounts of individuals of chiefly rank consuming seemingly impossible quantities of food and achieving a size that rendered them largely immobile. But even ordinary individuals took great pleasure in gorging on huge quantities of food, especially in Polynesia. One explanation for this practice is that it was a response to the seasonal availability of food. Pollock (1992) has noted that if taro was plentiful, it was not unusual for an adult to eat 5 to 10 pounds of it at a sitting.

Oliver (1989), though, referring to the work of M. Young (1971), pointed out a contrasting example, the Kalauna people of Goodenough Island in southeastern New Guinea, whose goal was "full gardens and small bellies." The latter was associated with physical beauty and was attained by hunger-suppressing magic and willpower.

Cannibalism

The role that cannibalism played in the Pacific has probably been exaggerated, and in fact there is evidence to suggest that in some instances, tales of cannibalism were fabricated by islanders to shock naive Europeans. Labeling enemies as cannibals was probably also a popular strategy. There are, however, credible reports of the practice of cannibalism in New Guinea, the Bismarcks, the Solomons, the New Hebrides, New Caledonia, Fiji, New Zealand, the Marquesas, the Gambiers, and Easter Island (Oliver 1989).

The practice was most prevalent in Melanesia (although not all Melanesians were cannibals), to which the appellation "Cannibal Isles" was applied. Oliver (1989), with some reservations about attributing motive, distinguished three categories of cannibalism. In the first, the purpose was to obtain meat (or, specifically, human meat); the second involved punishment, usually of a foreigner or, less commonly, of a local offender, and the practice also was used as a gesture of extreme contempt toward the victim. The third category invoked the realm of magic: In this case, the eating of an enemy, friend, or relative was done to absorb one or more of his or her important attributes. In this latter case, only specific parts of the body, such as the brain, the eye, the heart, the liver, or the genitals, were consumed.

Cannibalism for the purpose of punishment seems to have been the most widely practiced form, and cannibalism for magic ends was more common in Polynesia than Melanesia. In Micronesia, the only evidence we have of cannibalism has been the consumption of token parts of deceased relatives in Truk. A similar practice in highland New Guinea, where parts of the brain were consumed, especially by women and children, led to the transmission of the slow viral disease *kuru.* Cannibalism in the region probably reached its height in Fiji and the western Solomons after firearms were introduced. In the Solomons, firearms rendered raiding and head-hunting more efficient, and in eastern Viti, Levu chiefs imposed a levy of human bodies for consumption. The material culture of Fiji included special wooden cannibal forks, which today are reproduced for sale as tourist "art."

To Drink and Chew

Kava

With a few localized exceptions in the western Pacific, Oceania has had only two traditional drug plants, kava and betel, but only kava, a narcotic infusion of the pulverized root of *Piper methysticum,* is indigenous to the region. V. Lebot, M. Merlin, and L. Lindstrom (1992) have argued that kava was domesticated in the northern islands of Vanuatu about 3,000 years ago. Although kava is not technically classified as a drug because it does not promote addiction or dependence, its active ingredients, kavalactones, have mild narcotic, soporific, and diuretic properties. It is also a muscle relaxant.

The origin of kava is a prominent theme in Oceanic mythology (Lebot et al. 1992). Uprooted after several years of growth, the roots are dried or, less frequently, prepared green. The preparation of kava is often surrounded by highly ritualized ceremonies, and it is an integral part of religious and social life, especially in Tonga, Fiji, Pohnpei, and Samoa.

Two traditional patterns of kava use can be distinguished. In Samoa, Tonga, Fiji, Rotuma, Futuna, Uvea, and Vanikoro, the primary use has been ceremonial and the effects mild. The dry roots are prepared with a substantial quantity of water. But in Hawaii, eastern Polynesia, Vanuatu, Choiseul, and parts of New Guinea, where drinking has tended to be a more individual activity, green roots were often employed with less water added. This mixture was more potent and often resulted in sleep and paresis of the lower limbs.

Whereas kava consumption has generally been and remains a male activity, some age and gender restrictions have been relaxed, and practices are not uniform throughout Oceania. In Fiji, it is believed that drinking moderate amounts of kava when pregnant is good for the fetus and that it will ease childbirth. The drinking of kava during breast feeding is thought to favor the production of milk. In other Pacific societies, infertility has been attributed to kava, and it was also used as an abortifacient. In addition to its ceremonial role, kava has a more general place in Pacific societies. Laborers in rural areas share kava after a hard day's work, and in the towns, others gather at bars for the same purpose (Lebot et al. 1992).

In recent years, kava has become a cash crop in several Pacific countries, and it is now exported from Vanuatu, Tonga, and Fiji to other island countries and nations with Pacific Island populations. There is also an increasing market to meet the demands of the European pharmaceutical industry.

Betel

Betel is the other traditional Pacific drug, although betel chewing is more restricted than the consumption of kava and is found primarily in parts of Melanesia and western Micronesia, notably Palau, the Marianas, and Yap. Betel is employed in exchange and has some ceremonial significance, but its use is not nearly as ritualized as that of kava. It is not usually prohibited to women, although it is more commonly chewed among men.

The shorthand term "betel" refers to a combination of the hot and acrid nut of the *Areca catechu* palm, the bean or stem of the *Piper betel* vine (of the same family as kava), and slaked lime (from either seashells, coral, or mountain lime). There are various methods of using betel, but typically the ingredients are made into a wad, chewed in the mouth, and pressed against the cheek, irritating the mucous membrane and producing a localized sensation. The red fibers and juices are expectorated. The alkaloid arecoline is a stimulant with nicotine-like properties, and betel chewers believe it increases work capacity. As a rule, users of betel have darkened teeth and red stains around the mouth.

Toddy

Another drug used in some Pacific societies, most notably in Micronesia, is palm wine or "toddy," made from the sap of the coconut palm. The practice of collecting the sap from incisions made in the bound spathe of the palm's inflorescence probably originated in the Philippines. The sweet, milky-white sap is high in vitamin B and is consumed fresh. It is considered an ideal food for infants, the sick, and the elderly; it is also used as a flavoring agent in cooking and is boiled as a confection. Processed, it was sometimes stored as a famine food, but left to ferment for several days, it becomes an alcoholic drink.

Alcohol

Alcohol use has become common in the Pacific, although patterns of consumption vary throughout the region. In places where ceremonial kava drinking was traditional, the use of alcohol (usually beer) tends to be a social rather than a solitary activity, and drinks are consumed quickly – an entire bottle of beer in one draft, akin to drinking the entire bowl of kava.

By contrast, in his studies in Papua New Guinea, M. Marshall (1982) found that beer drinking tended to be patterned more on the Australian "mateship" and egalitarian model. Although per capita consumption of alcohol is less than it is in developed nations, high levels of individual intake are common, with drunkenness the major goal, especially among young men.

The Contemporary Pacific

Dietary Colonialism?

In most Pacific Island societies, explorers, whalers, and ships' crews stopping for provisions provided the earliest contact with the West. Later, the economic history of the Pacific came to be dominated to varying degrees by colonization, missionary influences, land alienation, and the production of primary products for export. At first it was the production of copra that altered patterns of daily life and land use in much of the region. Following this it was sugar, bananas, cacao, coffee, oil palm, pineapple, and other tropical export crops.

In Fiji and Hawaii in particular, such activities also altered the ethnic composition of the population, which has influenced the cuisines that we find in those places today. For example, beginning in the 1880s, East Indians were brought to Fiji as indentured laborers for the sugar plantations, and today approximately half the population is East Indian. No wonder that curries are common there.

At the northeastern anchor of the Polynesian triangle, in Waikiki, one can, if so inclined, order rice and Portuguese sausage at McDonald's. This offering, how-

ever, is but a pale example of the diversity of cuisines available on almost any business street in Honolulu, largely a legacy of the successive waves of immigrants – Chinese, Japanese, Portuguese, and Filipino – who began arriving in the 1850s to labor on the sugar and pineapple plantations of Hawaii. Later immigrants, the largest numbers from Korea and Southeast Asia, have added to the rich tapestry of ethnic cuisines. In the 1990s, chefs of Hawaii blended the culinary techniques and flavors inherited from the Pacific, Asia, California, and Europe to create their own versions of the new regional cuisines (Henderson 1994).

The Political and Economic Context

Although the Pacific's most international cuisines are found in Hawaii, some foods and foodstuffs from distant places have long been available to those in the urban and port areas throughout Oceania. The salt beef, weevil-laden flour, stale cabin biscuits, and moldy apples that were the fare of the earliest missionaries have been supplanted by tinned fish, frozen meats (including lamb flaps and turkey tails – leftovers from the livestock and poultry industries of Australia and New Zealand), rice, soft drinks, and "cheese twists." In addition to Western food staples, elements of a simplified Chinese-style cuisine, such as dried fish imported from Asia, rice, and condiments, are found in the many parts of the Pacific with Chinese immigrants, and one can find "take-aways" selling "chop suey" in Apia, Western Samoa, whereas "chicken lon-grice" (rice noodles) and *lomi lomi* salmon (an adaptation from the salt salmon of sailing ships) have become part of the typical "traditional" Hawaiian luau.

Nonetheless, although by the 1990s the island states of the Pacific were, to a greater or lesser degree, integrated into the global economy, in many ways they continue to occupy its fringes, or, as a prominent geographer has suggested, "the Earth's Empty Quarter" (Ward 1989). Although the majority are politically independent or self-governing, true economic independence eludes most, and this marginal role in the global economy can (with remoteness and a continued dependence on agricultural exports) influence contemporary diets in complex ways. The agricultural mosaic that one finds in the Pacific has been strongly influenced by the colonial experience, when economic activities focused on the production and export of primary crops produced on plantations, either through myriad cooperative schemes or as cash crops. But despite the beginning of decolonization in the early 1960s, this pattern has continued, with development officials and international aid agencies strongly urging the production of export crops, hailing such activity as the "road to development."

Consequently, prime garden lands were often converted to the production of cash crops, and subsistence plots were moved to more distant and more marginal land. Especially in Melanesia (Hau'ofa and Ward 1980), where women are the primary subsistence gardeners, such events increased the workload of women, demanding more of their time and energy, which may in turn have had a negative nutritional impact on the entire family, or at least on the young children.

By the early 1980s, as the nutritional and economic fallacy of cash-crop dependence became increasingly apparent, a more balanced approach, stressing food self-sufficiency and the production of indigenous crops, was adopted. This new approach reflected general changes in development thinking, but it was also the result of the efforts of academics, nutritionists, and others (Parkinson 1982) who advocated changes in government policy. The shift took place at a time when Pacific nations began to gain their political independence, and advocating food self-sufficiency became an important symbolic component of the process.

The production of food and other agricultural products remains the dominant economic activity for most of the population of Oceania. Yen wrote in 1980 that a mix of subsistence production and cash-cropping was the most common form of agriculture in Oceania, and this was probably still true in the 1990s. Pollock (1992), using data from 1980 to 1985, noted that foodstuffs constituted approximately 25 percent of total imports by value, but thought that this proportion was beginning to drop, perhaps because of efforts at food self-sufficiency. Data from eight of the countries in the region in the mid-1970s indicated that from 15 to 26 percent of total import dollars was spent on food, with the average somewhat under 20 percent (Lewis 1981). More recent data have suggested rates closer to 15 percent, especially for the more populous countries like Papua New Guinea, Fiji, and the Solomon Islands. But there are exceptions such as American Samoa, whose people spend 62 percent of total import dollars on food (South Pacific Economic and Social Database 1993) and a few islands where virtually all food is imported.

Urban and Rural Diets

Approximately 30 percent of the population in the Pacific can be classified as "urban," although this is a relative concept in the region. Many families produce some garden crops in periurban and urban areas, and many also receive produce through members of their extended families who reside in rural areas. It is no surprise that there tends to be a continuum from traditional to Western (or modern) diet as one moves from rural to urban areas and, for that matter, from the less "developed" parts of the region, like highland Papua New Guinea, to the more developed, as for example, Guam.

Families in rural areas are more dependent on locally produced foodstuffs, both because less imported food is available and because they have less money with which to purchase it. But it would be a mistake to assume that today's rural diets are the same as precontact diets (Pollock 1992). Rural producers in periurban areas may also have diets dominated by imported staples. Employing a household strategy designed to meet an increasing need for cash, rural producers may sell a truckload of taro and other produce and then, at considerably lower cost, purchase enough rice and flour to feed their families. The diet may be less expensive and less nutritious, but cash will be available for other needs.

Moreover, although the situation is beginning to change, in part as a response to government policy and incentives, it is not uncommon, depending on the season in urban markets, to find traditional staples, such as yams, taro, or sweet potatoes, and fish priced beyond what many urban consumers can afford (except, perhaps, for special occasions).

What People Eat

Since their earliest encounters with the West, Pacific peoples have been introduced to new foods, and these have become part of both the regular diet and, in some cases, the status food employed for ceremonial exchange. It is thought that the first canned product encountered by the Samoans was canned pea soup *(pisupo)* – a term used today for another imported and highly valued product, corned beef. Not only is *pisupo* common fare in Samoa, but kegs of beef in brine and case upon case of canned fish make up part of the exchange that accompanies ceremonial occasions.

As already noted, a rough continuum with respect to diet exists in the region, although only rural peoples in Melanesia and, perhaps to a lesser degree, remote parts of Fiji, Polynesia, and Micronesia have diets similar to those eaten by their forebears. In urban areas, people eat a mélange of traditional and Western foods on a daily basis and also patronize "take-aways" and fast-food establishments. At one time, the McDonald's in Guam was the largest in the world, and although it has lost this distinction, there are now three McDonald's franchises on that island. But for ceremonial occasions, and perhaps on Sundays (particularly in Polynesia), urban dwellers, like their rural counterparts, prepare a traditional meal and share it with the extended family.

Although one might decry the dietary change, the reasons for it are not difficult to understand. Foremost among them are the cost, degree of availability, and preparation time required for many traditional foodstuffs, as well as the influences of advertising and changing tastes. Certainly the highly refined imports of flour and rice, sugar, soft drinks, frozen meats, and high-fat corned beef make up a large part of the urban diet. Probably the most likely to be malnourished are the poor, often recent migrants to the towns, who have the least access to garden produce and the least cash to buy nutritionally sound foodstuffs. They may also be living in circumstances that do not facilitate food preparation.

Pacific Markets

Urban markets have existed, often in the same location, since colonial times, as products of the introduced cash economy. In one section there will be mounds of root and tree crops – yams, taro, sweet potatoes, cassava, coconuts, bananas, breadfruit, and other traditional foodstuffs. In another section, tables are piled with market garden produce and vegetables – greens, cabbages, squash, onions, and pumpkins. Fish and marine products are displayed in yet another section, whereas in still another, partly in response to increasing tourism, handicrafts may be found – woven pandanus and coconut-frond mats, baskets, hats, and fans, tapa, shells, shell and tortoiseshell jewelry, and wooden carvings of varying quality. In a central market there may be booths that sell a limited assortment of grains and canned or processed food. In Suva or Lautoka, Fiji, there are stalls selling *yaqona* (both kava root and the powdered form), and others with burlap bags overflowing with tumeric, chillies, and garam masala, the colorful Indian spices. In addition, prepared food and drink is often available.

Larger urban centers have supermarkets that sell fresh, frozen, and canned imported products and, sometimes, a limited selection of local ones. Some of these stores are modern versions of the old Burns Philp's or Morris Headstrom outlets of the colonial Pacific. But there are also smaller, less well-stocked groceries.

Rural stores tend to be small and often precarious business operations. In remote areas, tinned meats or fish, flour, rice, cabin biscuits, cooking oil, and tea may or may not be available. More prosperous operations may have a freezer with fish and meat, but the frozen food is often of questionable quality given the vagaries of electricity and appliance repair.

Health and Nutrition

A great deal has been written about diet, health, and nutrition in the Pacific, with much of the focus on the nutritional and health consequences that have resulted from incorporation into the global economy. This transition has been accompanied by an "epidemiological transition" (Omran 1971), in which dietary change and concomitant obesity have emerged as causal factors (Taylor, Lewis, and Levy 1989), and chronic and noncommunicable diseases have taken the lead as causes of death in the more modernized or "Westernized" parts of the Pacific.

Early studies of hypertension, such as that of more than 30 years ago by I. Prior and F. Davidson (1966), found that blood pressure did not increase with age in some traditional Pacific societies. But more recent studies show increases in blood pressure with modernization: Examples include elevated blood pressure (above 160/95) in 36 percent of males in Nauru and 34 percent of male Chamorros in Guam. Elevated blood pressure is also found in 7 percent of urban Fijians, as compared with 2 percent of rural Fijians (Coyne 1984). Hypertension is more common in the more developed Polynesian and Micronesian societies than those of less developed Melanesia. That lifestyle appears to play a significant role was made clear by P. Baker and J. Hanna (1981), who found blood pressures among the lowest in the world in a traditional Western Samoan village and among the highest in the world among Samoans in Hawaii.

Researchers have also found some of the world's highest rates of diabetes mellitus II (DM) in the Pacific. Prevalence rates in the region ranged from none in highland Papua New Guinea to 30.3 percent in adults in Nauru and were generally higher among females than males, as is typical elsewhere (Taylor and Bach 1987). The DM rates in Nauru rival those of the Pima Indians of the United States, previously thought to have the highest rates in the world. Other studies found elevated rates (over 12 percent) in both urban and rural Fijian Indians, Western Samoans in San Francisco, urban dwellers in Papua New Guinea, and Wallasians living in New Caledonia (Lewis 1988). Recent data for Hawaii give age-adjusted DM rates of 46.2/1,000 for Hawaiians and 22.5/1,000 for non-Hawaiians (State of Hawaii 1992). In the over-65 population, rates for Hawaiians are almost three times those of non-Hawaiians. A number of risk factors have been identified, including genetic predisposition, obesity, diet, levels of activity, and more subtle effects of modernization.

Baker (1984) has elaborated on the "thrifty gene hypothesis" proposed by J. Neel (1962) to suggest that long-distance voyaging and bouts of acute short-term starvation following natural disasters (trials endured by those who settled the remote Polynesian and Micronesian islands) produced genotypes suited to such conditions. With the adoption of modern lifestyles, however, these genotypes may be predisposed to elevated blood pressure, obesity, and diabetes mellitus.

The role of diet in shaping contemporary health patterns in Oceania is complex and much remains to be discovered. Pollock (1992) calls researchers to task for equating "traditional diets" with modern rural diets in urban–rural studies. There are also important biological differences between populations, and such studies have employed a Western biomedical framework of analysis that largely ignores the meaning of food in Pacific societies.

Unfortunately, undernutrition as well as overnutrition is a problem (and an increasing one) in the Pacific, particularly, but not exclusively, in urban areas. As elsewhere, it is the nutritionally vulnerable young children and, sometimes, the elderly who suffer the most severe consequences. Throughout the region, the high cost of imported goods, a lack of knowledge about healthful diets, and a lack of gardening land in urban areas have served to undermine nutrition. In the Solomon Islands, a national survey found malnutrition affects 22 percent of children aged 0 to 4. In the Marshall Islands, 11 percent of urban children are underweight, and one-third of all deaths are of children under age 5. At the other end of the nutritional spectrum, 30 percent of the urban population over age 15 have diabetes (Republic of the Marshall Islands 1990, cited in Bryant 1993).

Summary

We have only an incomplete understanding of the role of diet in health and disease in the Pacific region. We have a somewhat better, but still incomplete, picture of what people are eating. It is a mix of foods that tends to more closely mirror traditional diets in the less developed and more rural parts of the region, although these diets are certainly not unmodified. But in other parts of the Pacific, especially in urban areas, diets are made up of imported foods, often of poor nutritional quality. However, traditional meals and feasts are still important in the Pacific.

There are cultural as well as economic and nutritional reasons for reexamining traditional diets within a framework that is relevant for the populations involved. Food remains an important cultural symbol and can be an important component of cultural identity. The Waianae Diet Program, a community-based program developed in response to high rates of obesity and chronic disease among native Hawaiians, is founded on traditional diets and cultural values and includes group support and a weight-loss protocol that is not calorie-restricted. Short-term results indicate significant reductions in weight, blood pressure, serum lipids, and serum glucose (Shintani et al. 1994). Although long-term research is needed and the positive results for individuals may be difficult to maintain over time, this culturally sensitive program is an example of the efforts being made to reassess and encourage traditional Pacific diets.

Holo i'a ka papa, kau 'ia e ka manu. This Hawaiian proverb, literally translated, means: "When the shoals are full of fish, birds gather over them" – a familiar and welcome sight to island fishermen. Its proverbial meaning is that where there is food, people gather (Puki 1983). The sharing of food – for ceremonial or merely social purposes – remains a dominant thread in the complex, rich fabric of culture in the Pacific. The thread and fabric will continue to evolve and change as they have done over the course of history, as the islands and islanders, increasingly less isolated, nonetheless continue to reassert their Pacific identities in a rapidly changing modern world.

Nancy Davis Lewis

Bibliography

Abbott, I. 1991. Polynesian uses of seaweed. In *Islands, plants and Polynesians: An introduction to Polynesian ethnobotany,* ed. P. Cox and S. Banack, 135–45. Portland, Ore.

Anderson, A. 1991. The chronology of colonization in New Zealand. *Antiquity* 65: 767–95.

Baker, P. 1984. Migration, genetics and the degenerative diseases of South Pacific islanders. In *Migration and mobility,* ed. A. Boyce, 209–39. London.

Baker, P., and J. Hanna. 1981. Modernization and the biological fitness of Samoans: A project report on a research program. In *Migration, adaptation and health in the Pacific,* ed. C. Fleming and I. Prior, 14–26. Wellington, New Zealand.

Baker, P., J. Hanna, and T. Baker, eds. 1986. *Changing Samoans: Behavior and health in transition.* New York.

Barrau, J. 1956. *Polynesian and Micronesian subsistence agriculture.* Noumea, New Caledonia.

     1958. Subsistence agriculture in Melanesia. *Bernice P. Bishop Museum Bulletin* 219: 1–111. Honolulu, Hawaii.

     1961. Subsistence agriculture in Polynesia and Melanesia. *Bernice P. Bishop Museum Bulletin* 223. Honolulu, Hawaii.

Bellwood, P. 1979. *Man's conquest of the Pacific: The prehistory of Southeast Asia and Oceania.* New York.

Blumer, R. 1968. The strategies of hunting in New Guinea. *Oceania* 38: 302–18.

Bonnemaison, Joel. 1984. The tree and the canoe: Roots and mobility in Vanuatu. *Pacific Viewpoint* 25: 117–51.

Brookfield, H. C. 1989. Global change and the Pacific: The coming half century. *The Contemporary Pacific* 1/2: 1–18.

Bryant, J. 1993. *Urban poverty and the environment in the South Pacific.* Armidale, New South Wales.

Casswell, S. 1986. *Alcohol in Oceania.* Auckland, New Zealand.

Clark, J., and K. Kelly. 1993. Human genetics, paleoenvironments and malaria: Relationships and implications for the settlement of Oceania. *American Anthropologist* 95: 612–30.

Clark, W. C. 1971. *Place and people: An ecology of a New Guinea community.* Berkeley, Calif.

Connell, J., and M. Hamnett. 1987. Famine or feast: Sago production in Bougainville. *Journal of Polynesian Society* 87: 231–41.

Cox, P., and S. Banack, eds. 1991. *Islands, plants, and Polynesians: An introduction to Polynesian ethnobotany.* Portland, Ore.

Coyne, T. 1984. *The effect of urbanization and Western diet on the health of Pacific island populations.* South Pacific Technical Paper 186. Noumea, New Caledonia.

Currey, B. 1980. Famine in the Pacific: Losing the chances for change. *Geojournal* 4: 447–66.

Doumenge, J. P., D. Villenave, and O. Chapuis. 1988. *Agriculture, food and nutrition in four South Pacific archipelagos.* Bogor, Indonesia.

Etkin, N., and M. Ross. 1982. Food as medicine and medicine as food: An adaptive framework for interpretation of plant utilization among the Hausa of northern Nigeria. *Social Science and Medicine* 16: 1559–73.

Firth, R. 1967. *The work of gods in Tikopia.* Melbourne.

Frenk, Julio. 1992. Balancing relevance and excellence: Organizational responses to link research with decision making. *Social Science and Medicine* 35: 1397–1404.

Gorecki, P. 1986. Human occupation and agricultural development in the Papua New Guinea highlands. *Mountain Research and Development* 2: 159–66.

Handy, E. S. C., and E. G. Handy, with M. Pukui. 1972. *Native planters in old Hawaii.* This manuscript was published as the *Bernice P. Bishop Museum Bulletin* 233 by the Bishop Museum Press. Honolulu, Hawaii.

Hau'ofa, E., and R. G. Ward. 1980. The social context. In *South Pacific agriculture: Choices and constraints*, ed. R. G. Ward and A. Proctor, 49-71. Canberra, Australia.

Henderson, B., L. Kolonel, R. Dworsky, et al. 1985. Cancer incidence in the islands of the Pacific. *National Cancer Institute Monograph* 69: 73-81.

Henderson, J. 1994. *The new cuisine of Hawaii*. New York.

Johannes, R. E. 1981. *Words of the lagoon: Fishing and marine lore in the Palau district of Micronesia*. Berkeley, Calif.

Kahn, M. 1986. *Always hungry, never greedy: Food and the expression of gender in a Melanesian society*. Cambridge and New York.

Kirch, P. 1984. *The evolution of Polynesian chiefdoms*. Cambridge.

　1986. Rethinking Polynesian prehistory. *Journal of Polynesian Society* 95: 9-40.

　1991. Polynesian agricultural systems. In *Islands. plants, and Polynesians*, ed. P. Cox and S. Banack, 113-34. Portland, Ore.

Kofe, S. 1990. *Household food security in selected Pacific island countries*. Noumea, New Caledonia.

Lebot, V. 1991. Kava. In *Islands, plants and Polynesians*, ed. P. Cox and S. Banack, 169-201. Portland, Ore.

Lebot, V., M. Merlin, and L. Lindstrom. 1992. *Kava: The Pacific drug*. New Haven, Conn.

Lewis, N. 1981. Ciguatera, health and human adaptation in the island Pacific. Ph.D. thesis, University of California, Berkeley, Calif.

　1986. Disease and development: Ciguatera fish poisoning. *Social Science and Medicine* 23: 983-93.

　1988. Modernization, morbidity and mortality: Noncommunicable diseases in the Pacific Islands. *Pacific Islands Development Program*. Honolulu, Hawaii.

Lindstrom, L. 1987. *Drugs in western Pacific societies*. Landham, Md.

Linnekin, Jocelyn. 1990. *Sacred queens and women of consequence: Rank, gender and colonialism in the Hawaiian islands*. Ann Arbor, Mich.

Loy, T., M. Spriggs, and S. Wickler. 1992. Direct evidence for human use of plants 28,000 years ago: Starch residues on stone artifacts. *Antiquity* 66: 898-912.

Malinowski, B. 1936. *Coral gardens and their magic*. 2 vols. London.

Manderson, L., ed. 1986. *Shared wealth and symbol: Food, culture and society in Oceania and Southeast Asia*. Cambridge and New York.

Marshall, M. 1991. The second fatal impact: Cigarette smoking, chronic disease, and the epidemiological transition in Oceania. *Social Science and Medicine* 33: 1327-42.

　ed. 1982. *Through a glass darkly: Beer and modernization in Papua New Guinea*. Monograph 18, Institute of Applied Social and Economic Research. Boroko, Papua New Guinea.

Marshall, M., and L. Marshall. 1975. Opening Pandora's bottle: Reconstructing Micronesians' early contacts with alcoholic beverages. *Journal of the Polynesian Society* 84: 441-65.

Megitt, M. J. 1974. "Pigs are our hearts!" The exchange cycle among the Mae Enga of New Guinea. *Oceania* 44: 165-203.

Murai, M., F. Pen, and C. Miller. 1958. *Some tropical South Pacific island foods*. Honolulu, Hawaii.

Neel, J. 1962. Diabetes mellitus: A thrifty genotype rendered detrimental by "progress." *American Journal of Human Genetics* 14: 353-62.

Oliver, D. 1974. *Ancient Tahitian society*. 3 vols. Honolulu, Hawaii.

　1989. *Oceania: The native cultures of Australia and the Pacific Islands*, Vols. 1 and 2. Honolulu, Hawaii.

Omran, A. R. 1971. The epidemiological transition: A theory of epidemiology and population change. *Milbank Memorial Fund Quarterly* 44: 509-38.

Parkinson, S. 1982. Nutrition in the South Pacific – past and present. *Journal of Food and Nutrition* 39: 121.

Pawley, A., ed. 1991. *Man and a half: Essays on Pacific anthropology and ethnobiology in honor of Ralph Bulmer*. Auckland.

Pirie, P. 1994. *Demographic transition in the Pacific Islands: The situation in the early 1990s*. East West Center Working Paper No. 5. Honolulu, Hawaii.

Pollock, N. 1974. Breadfruit or rice? Dietary choice on a Micronesian atoll. *Ecology of Food and Nutrition* 3: 107-15.

　1986. Food classification in three Pacific societies: Fiji, Hawaii and Tahiti. *Ethnology* 25: 107-17.

　1992. *These roots remain: Food habits in the islands of the central and eastern Pacific since Western contact*. Honolulu, Hawaii.

Prior, I., and F. Davidson. 1966. The epidemiology of diabetes in Polynesians and Europeans in New Zealand and the Pacific. *New Zealand Medical Journal* 65: 373-83.

Puki, M. K. 1983. *O' lelo no'eau Hawaiian: Proverbs and poetic sayings*. Honolulu, Hawaii.

Rappaport, R. 1968. *Pigs for the ancestors: Ritual ecology in a New Guinea people*. New Haven, Conn.

Ravuvu, A. 1991. A Fijian cultural perspective on food. In *Food and nutrition in Fiji*, ed. A. Janese, S. Parkinson, and A. Robertson, 622-36. Suva, Fiji.

Reinman, F. 1967. *Fishing; an aspect of oceanic economy: An archaeological approach*. Chicago.

Sahlins, M. 1976. *Culture and practical reason*. Chicago.

Sauer, D., in Yen, D. 1971. A reevaluation of the coconut as an indicator of human dispersal. In *Man across the sea*, ed. C. L. Riley, J. C. Riley, C. W. Pennington, and R. L. Rand, 309-13. Austin, Tex.

Shintani, T., S. Beckham, H. O'Connor, et al. 1994. The Waianae Diet Program: A culturally sensitive, community-based obesity and clinical intervention program for the native Hawaiian population. *Hawaii Medical Journal* 53: 134-5.

South Pacific Economic and Social Database. 1993. *Western Samoa statistical compendium*. Canberra, Australia.

Spriggs, M. 1982. Taro cropping systems in the Southeast Asian Pacific region. *Archeology in Oceania* 17: 7-15.

Spriggs, M., and A. Anderson. 1993. Late colonization of eastern Polynesia. *Antiquity* 67: 200-17.

State of Hawaii. 1992. *Native Hawaiian health data book*. Honolulu, Hawaii.

Taylor, R. 1985. Mortality patterns in the modernized Pacific island nation of Nauru. *American Journal of Public Health* 75: 149-55.

Taylor, R., and F. Bach. 1987. *Proportionate hospital morbidity in Pacific island countries circa 1980*. Noumea, New Caledonia.

Taylor, R., N. Lewis, and S. Levy. 1989. Societies in transition: Mortality patterns in Pacific island populations. *International Journal of Epidemiology* 18: 634-43.

Thaman, R. 1988. Health and nutrition in the Pacific Islands: Development or underdevelopment? *Geojournal* 16: 211.

　1990. The evolution of the Fiji food system. In *Food and nutrition in Fiji*, ed. A. Janese, S. Parkinson, and A. Robertson, 23-107. Suva, Fiji.

Ward, R. G. 1989. Earth's empty quarter? The Pacific Islands in a Pacific century. *The Geographical Journal* 155: 235-46.

Whistler, W. A. 1991. Polynesian plant introductions. In *Islands, plants, and Polynesians: An introduction to Polynesian ethnobotany,* ed. P. Cox and S. Banack, 41-66. Portland, Ore.

Williams, J. 1838. *A narrative of missionary enterprises in the South Sea Islands.* London.

Wilson, A., R. Taylor, G. Nugumi, et al. 1983. *Solomon Islands oral cancer study.* South Pacific Commission Technical Paper No. 183. Noumea, New Caledonia.

Yen, D. 1974. The sweet potato and Oceania. This monograph was published as the *Bernice P. Bishop Museum Bulletin* 236 by the Bishop Museum Press. Honolulu, Hawaii.

　　1980. Pacific production systems. In *Pacific production systems,* ed. R. G. Ward and A. Proctor, 74-106. Canberra, Australia.

　　1985. Wild plants and domestication in the Pacific Islands. In *Recent advances in Indo-Pacific prehistory,* ed. V. N. M. Misra and P. Bellwood, 315-26. New Delhi.

　　1991. Polynesian cultigens and cultivars: The question of origins. In *Islands, plants and Polynesians: An introduction to Polynesian ethnobotany,* ed. P. Cox and S. Banack, 67-98. Portland, Ore.

　　1993. The origins of subsistence agriculture in Oceania and the potentials for future tropical crops. *Economic Botany* 47: 3-14.

Young, M. 1971. *Fighting with food: Leadership, values, and social control in a Massim society.* Cambridge.

V.F

Culinary History

Since the 1970s, historical studies of food in particular cultures have emerged as a new field, "culinary history." Culinary history studies the origins and development of the foodstuffs, equipment, and techniques of cookery, the presentation and eating of meals, and the meanings of these activities to the societies that produce them. It looks at practices on both sides of the kitchen door, at the significance of the food to the cook and to those who consume it, and at how cooking is done and what the final product means. Consequently, culinary history is widely interdisciplinary. Studies make connections between the sciences – medical, biological, and social – and the humanities and draw heavily on anthropology, economics, psychology, folklore, literature, and the fine arts, as well as history. These multidisciplinary perspectives are integrated along geographic and temporal dimensions, and as a consequence, culinary history encompasses the whole process of procuring food from land or laboratory, moving it through processors and marketplaces, and finally placing it on the stove and onto the table. It emphasizes the role that food-related activities play in defining community, class, and social status – as epitomized in such fundamental human acts as the choice and consumption of one's daily bread.

Culinary history can also be defined by what it is not. It is not, for example, simply a narrative account of what was eaten by a particular people at a particular time. Nor is it a matter of rendering entertaining stories about food, or telling anecdotes of people cooking and eating, or surveying cookbooks. But it *is* informed analysis of how food expresses the character of a time, place, society, and culture. Put plainly, culinary history goes beyond anecdotal food folklore and descriptions of cuisine and cooking at a particular point in time to incorporate historical dimensions.

Times, Places, and Themes

Culinary history can (and should) be part of a number of avenues of investigation, such as social history, women's history, and anthropological analyses of food habits, systems, folklore, and material culture. There follows a brief examination of each of these.

Culinary History As Social History

In Europe, which has been the dominant geographic focus of culinary historians, there are basically three strands of investigation: First, there are the cuisines of the prosperous classes, including traditions of court and aristocracy; second, there is the food of middle and lower classes in urban settings; and third, there are the cuisines of rural societies of all classes. The presence or absence of haute (high) cuisine is itself a socially significant part of culinary history (Goody 1982).

Culinary history also plays an important role in regional and, later, national social histories, such as those of England, France, Spain, Germany, and Italy (Toussaint-Samat 1992; Brillat-Savarin 1995). French "*Annales* School" publications on food in social history (Braudel 1966), annual Oxford Food History Symposia, and historical analyses of European food folklorists are examples (Fenton 1986; Teuteberg 1993; Mennell 1996).

Thematic studies examine such topics as the historical significance of agricultural stresses in classical Greece (Garnsey 1990); the culinary impact of sugar and cooking ideas brought by North Africans to Spain and Italy (Peterson 1980); the insatiable demand for spices, which led Portuguese and Italian explorers – and, ultimately, Columbus – to search for new sources of supply (Laurioux 1985, 1989); the importance of the North Atlantic fisheries and their related salt fish industries; and the determinants and consequences of European demands for exotic food items, such as sugar, coffee, tea, and chocolate (Lippmann 1929; Mintz 1985; Coe and Coe 1996).

The impact of the "Columbian exchange" on both sides of the Atlantic has been told through the histories of food plants, their agricultural modes of production, and the techniques of food processing (Crosby 1972; Long 1996). The new foods and their impact on production, processing, and marketing - and on regional, national, and local cuisines – have been traced by European historians and food ethnologists, who follow evidence of introductions and diffusions through herbals, agricultural or botanical histories, food trade records, and other literary or documentary sources (Arnott 1976; Fenton and Owen 1981; Kaneva-Johnson 1995).

The diffusion and adoption of New World foods such as potatoes, maize, and chilli peppers – and the cultural, social, nutritional, and demographic changes occasioned by this – also created new food economies and cultures in Asia and Africa as these foods supplanted numerous older ones (Miracle 1966; Anderson 1988; Hess 1992). The shifts from traditional coarse grains (such as sorghums and millets) to maize in East Africa and from yams to cereal grains or cassava in Central and West Africa, as well as the commercialization of livestock, provide fine examples of the ways in which social history can be traced in terms of culinary history. Colonization and subsequent internationalization of food economies permanently affected gender and age relations in production, consumption, and cuisine.

Another significant watershed is the Industrial Revolution, which in Britain was driven in part by a widespread availability of sugar calories from the New World (consumed in relatively new beverages such as tea, coffee, and cacao) (Mintz 1985) and calories from the highly productive New World potato, which also fueled wars of nationalism in Germany (Salaman 1985). A history of caffeinated beverages from this period can tie together vastly changing food patterns all over the globe as well as economic issues of social history, like changing landholding and cropping patterns, slavery, and imperialism.

In the Western Hemisphere, European colonization resulted in the blending of foods of New and Old World origins. Later watersheds in the culinary history of the United States include the Civil War and its aftermath, with the growth of large industrial agribusinesses (Levenstein 1988); ethnic migrations from Europe in the nineteenth and twentieth centuries, and from Asia after the 1950s; and post–World War II migrations of African-Americans from the predominantly rural southern states to the urban northern states (Jerome 1980). The resulting cuisines have been analyzed in terms of "acculturation" or "changing food habits" of the ethnic populations (Mead 1964; National Research Council 1981) and in terms of their food components, formats, and cycles (see Goode 1989). In the case of Jewish-Americans, for example, their use of food is seen as a principal element in struggles either to maintain or reshape identities (Joselit, Kirshenblatt-Gimblett, and Howe 1990; Roden 1996).

All such phenomena, however, are presented within the larger context of a changing American culinary mosaic. Such national and regional analyses of culinary practices in relation to significant changes in the social order can also be found in the literature of the food habits of Europe (Fenton and Owen 1981; Rotenberg 1981), India (Katona-Apte 1976; Appadurai 1988), and China (Chang 1977; Anderson 1988; Simoons 1991). All interlink major temporal divides or points of transition with the construction of new cuisines.

Culinary History As Women's History

Culinary history, especially in the United States, has emerged, albeit slowly, out of women's history. In the past, feminist historians' analyses of women's domestic work (private sphere) – as contrasted with wage work (public sphere) – tended to focus more on child rearing and other household tasks (Strasser 1982; Cowan 1983). These scholars avoided looking at cooking, allegedly because the kitchen symbolized submission to the oppression of patriarchy, whereas their goal was to elucidate the historical sources and contexts of women's empowerment.

Important linkages of kitchen concerns to the public sphere, however, are found in Catharine Beecher's writings (and schools) of domestic science (Beecher 1869; Sklar 1973) and in the New England Kitchen, established by Ellen Richards and her Boston associates as a place where immigrants could learn to cook and enjoy Yankee cuisine as one dimension of their American assimilation (Levenstein 1988). In their eagerness to hasten the assimilation of immigrants, the New England Kitchen reformers overlooked the reluctance of groups to give up traditional foods in exchange for unfamiliar ones. As a result, this "noble experiment" was a failure.

Serious scholarly attention to domestic culinary arts has grown with the maturation and acceptance of women's history as an academic field and with the recognition that cookbooks, diary descriptions of food acquisition and eating events, and kitchen material culture are important dimensions of that history. Gender analysis, applied to the preparation and consumption of food, reveals cultural differences influencing what male and female cooks prepare, as well as changes over time and place. As a case in point, nineteenth- and twentieth-century cookbooks provide evidence that men and women were expected to eat differently. Such books make distinctions between "men's" (heavy meat dishes) and "women's" (lighter) foods. They also show that gender biases against domestic cooking by men have tended to lessen in later suburban contexts of backyard grilling. Moreover, connections made between meat and fat consumption and heart disease have significantly altered notions about the appropriateness of the "heavy" foods for males (Shapiro 1986).

Cookbooks published by women's voluntary associations often provide obvious links between women's history and culinary history. The tradition of these books began in the United States just after the Civil War, when women formed groups to aid veterans or their widows and orphans (e.g., Ladies Relief

Corps 1887). Since that time, thousands of such books have been published by groups of women all over the United States and sold to support churches, synagogues, schools, museums, and other community institutions, or to memorialize the favorite recipes of multigenerational families or groups of friends. In most cases, such books are the only records these groups left behind. They offer a unique resource for examining women's roles as community builders, especially where they contain chapters on the history of their communities, with particular attention given to the history and accomplishments of their own organizations (Brown and Brown 1961; Cook 1971; Wheaton 1984).

Culinary History As Nutritional Anthropology

Culinary history has also grown out of (but goes beyond) the study of cultural cuisines, defined as the culturally elaborated and transmitted body of food-related practices of any given culture. The latter includes descriptions of characteristic foods and their flavorings and textures, along with their symbolic combination in meals, menus, formats, and seasonal or lifetime cycles of ritual foods and eating (Rozin 1973; Messer 1984; Goode 1989). Nutritional anthropology, however, considers the distances and means by which food ingredients travel over time; the origins and diffusions of processing techniques; and the routes of commercial or customary distribution of foods from sites of production to final consumption destinations. The discipline adds to historical studies a biological dimension that probes the significant coevolution of cultural culinary components and cuisines and human populations. Evolutionary biocultural studies of the consumption of milk (McCracken 1971) and sugar (Messer 1986) are two examples of the types of anthropological studies of foodways that also fit the category of culinary history (Ritenbaugh 1978).

Biological anthropologists have tried to understand the evolution of favorable nutritional patterns – the mechanisms by which traditional peoples "unlock" potential nutritional values in their staple foods through cooking methods and dietary preferences. Studies have analyzed the significance of culinary techniques (such as the alkali processing of maize or the calcium/magnesium-salt processing of soy) in optimizing the nutritional quality of dietary food staples. Additionally, researchers have assessed the ways in which combinations of food components, such as maize with beans and squash seeds, or rice with soybeans, enhance nutritional values and have charted the distribution and diffusion of processing techniques, dietary combinations of foods, and dietary staple foods from their traditional areas to new locales (Katz 1987).

Moreover, anthropologists connect the history of diet with the history of disease. Their studies examine age- or gender-related dietary beliefs and practices, the impact of these practices on infant and child mor-

tality (as well as pregnancy outcomes), and the circumstances under which such beliefs and practices change. Nutritional anthropological studies also analyze the so-called diseases of civilization (diabetes, coronary heart disease, hypertension, and various types of cancers) that seem to have accompanied dietary "Westernization" (including increased fat consumption) in most places where it has occurred (reviewed in Messer 1984).

Comparisons of recent with earlier ethnographic data on food systems and diets in Latin American, Asian, and African localities provide excellent opportunities for tracking changing relationships between food and the social order and elucidating the range of forces – from local to global – that influence such changes. One current of change has been proposed by cultural materialists, who view diet as shaped mainly (or exclusively) by ecological and political–economic ("material") conditions (Harris 1979).

Another current has been illuminated by symbolic or structural anthropologists, who emphasize how food and cooking express ideological–structural dimensions of social groups and their interrelationships. Notions of "purity and pollution" dominate Hindu rules, regulations, and rites surrounding all aspects of food, its preparation and serving, and social behavior (e.g., Khare 1976). M. Douglas discerned a structural logic of "pure" versus "anomalous" categories operating as the basis of food avoidances among the African Lele and then extended that principle to "The Abominations of Leviticus" (Douglas 1966). She moved on to decipher the social meanings of meals in European society (Douglas 1972) and food and the social order across cultures (Douglas 1984).

Claude Levi-Strauss's three-volume analysis of indigenous South American mythologies demonstrates how food and the "cooking" idiom are key to understanding social organization and cosmology (Levi-Strauss 1969, 1973, 1978). All of these analyses demonstrate that eating, cooking, and thinking are essentially philosophical operations, although most culinary studies tend to focus on sensory, technical, or instrumental dimensions of nutrition (Curtin and Heldke 1992).

In summary, anthropologists analyzing changes in foodways or food systems (culinary history) employ a combination of mental and material dimensions and approaches (Messer 1984, 1989). Anthropological approaches to understanding traditional cuisines and dietary change range from the social-structural, cognitive, and symbolic to the psychological, ecological, economic, and political, and to the relationships between nutrition and health. Studies go far back in time to elucidate culinary techniques beginning with elementary hunting, digging, processing, and use of fire (Gordon 1987; Stahl 1989) and extend forward through the present to the food of the future (Messer 1996b). Ethnographers, in the course of fieldwork, may increase their understanding by actively engaging in culinary activities of the past. Archaeologists, too, use experimental ("hands-on" or experiential) approaches, especially to increase their understanding of stone-tool manufacture, the use of such tools, and food-related artifacts in the archaeological record.

"Hands-on" Approaches to Culinary History

Culinary historians share some of the same pleasures and problems experienced by art historians and musicologists. Theory is an important dimension of such studies, but historical discussion must be tempered with a thorough understanding of the craft in order to interpret sources accurately. For culinary historians and the curators of living-history museums, this means researching and producing period meals that employ traditional techniques and authentic ingredients (within the limits of availability) (Noel Hume and Noel Hume 1978; Oliver 1995; Scully and Scully 1995; Dalby and Grainger 1996). Sometimes, substitutions must be made for ingredients no longer known or available, such as the replacement of silphium by celery seed in recipes for a Roman banquet (Arndt 1993). But the ingredients used must be appropriate to the period rather than to modern culinary conventions; for example, mushrooms or walnuts – not tomatoes – go into a catsup recipe from eighteenth-century North America. As with the written mode, such active culinary research compares food-related activities at different times and places using truly interdisciplinary frameworks and methods of analysis.

Museums have joined the enterprise with increasingly well-informed displays of their collections. Among these are reconstructions of cooking and dining venues such as the exhibitions of tables set in the modes of historical eras at the Historical Museum in Stockholm, the Alimentarium at Vevy in Switzerland, the Musée de l'homme in Paris, and the royal tables at Versailles (Musées Nationaux 1993), along with reenactments of cooking and dining, all of which illuminate the uses of culinary space and materials (see, for example, Deetz 1996).

Sources and Venues

Culinary historical scholarship draws on conventional documentary sources, such as diaries, letters, and travelogues, and also on less conventional sources, such as cookbooks and anthropological data.

Manuscript Sources

Diaries, account books, and letters are rich in data that can provide culinary understanding of peoples and periods. Samuel Pepys's diaries abound in accounts of meals. Lady Mary Wortley Montague took note of what she ate. The letters of Voltaire (François-Marie Arouet), too, show his tastes in food (and friends): Inviting a friend to dinner, he offered "a truffled turkey as tender as a squab and as fat as the bishop of Geneva." Felix Platter, a sixteenth-century

Swiss medical student at Montpelier, described the pungent foods served him and how he, a Protestant, evaded the rigors of the Lenten fast by cooking eggs over a candle in his room (Wheaton 1983).

Diaries and letters can be accessed by first consulting annotated bibliographies, then turning to specific texts or collections of letters. Examples with numerous food references include *Jane Austen's Manuscript Letters in Facsimile* (Carbondale, Ill., 1990); *Boswell's Journal of a Tour to the Hebrides with Samuel Johnson, LL.D.* (New York, 1936); *Mary Chesnut's Civil War* (New Haven, Conn., 1981); and *The Diary of a Country Parson: The Reverend James Woodforde* (London, 1924–31).

In addition, unpublished correspondence and other personal papers of leading American culinary figures such as Julia Child, Irma Rombauer, and M. F. K. Fisher are available in the manuscript collections of the Schlesinger Library at Radcliffe College.

Printed Literature

Travel literature. Travelers often describe food acquisition, preservation, and preparation, as well as meals. Such descriptions, however, should be used cautiously, because national, religious, class, and personal prejudices all work against dispassionate reporting. Sentimentalism, naivete, and ignorance are additional problems, because travelers without linguistic competence must frequently depend on interpreters and native informants who, whether reliable or not, may not be completely understood. Moreover, travelers have been known to copy from one another's accounts and to exaggerate – if not lie about – what they have seen. To this we might add that the memories of travelers are not infallible, and they are sometimes very gullible. Marco Polo, for example, is credited with having introduced pasta into Italy because he speaks of eating noodles during his travels in China. However, vermicelli was being produced on a commercial scale in Sicily a full century before his birth (Perry 1981). Culinary legends, once started, are hard to eradicate.

The use of travelers' accounts and diaries as sources for culinary history is usually a two-stage process. Annotated bibliographies are useful for pointing to accounts that contain relevant material. For descriptions of Russia, for example, one might begin with H. W. Nerhood's *To Russia and Return: An Annotated Bibliography of Travelers' English-Language Accounts of Russia from the Ninth Century to the Present* (1968). This in turn can lead to individual accounts, such as *The Russian Journals of Martha and Catherine Wilmot* (not published until 1934) and *Russia . . . and the Interior of the Empire* by Johann G. Kohl (1842), which are replete with descriptions of Russia's nineteenth-century foods. Examples of such works for other locales are those by P. Gerbod (1991 edition) for eighteenth-century France; W. Mayer (1961 edition) for early European travel in Mexico;

A. Tinniswood (1989) and W. Matthews (1967) for England; L. Arksey, N. Pries, and M. Reed (1983–7) for the United States; and J. Robinson (1990) on the subject of women travelers. The periodical *La Vie Quotidienne* (published in Paris since the 1930s) draws on travel diaries kept in many times and places.

Science and medicine. Travel literature is also a useful entry point for exploring food and nutritional health beliefs and practices. From Herodotus and Pliny the Elder onward, classic travel or "natural history" accounts influenced medieval and later European "epitomizers" and "cosmographers," whose often fanciful anecdotes of food customs lived on in the herbals and materia medica of both the Renaissance and the early modern period. Herbals and bestiaries contain information about how different kinds of plants and animals were believed to affect the human mind and body; they were one of the principal venues through which the nutritional and medical theories of antiquity and of the Islamic world were conveyed to a larger audience (Arber 1953, 1990; Anderson 1977).

Medical histories and encyclopedias of materia medica trace the diffusion of humoral health and nutritional theory from the classical and Islamic worlds into Europe (Siraisi 1990). Excellent comprehensive histories of the technology of the Old World are the eight-volume *A History of Technology* (1954–8), by C. Singer and colleagues, and J. Needham's *Science and Civilization in China* (1954–88); both works include extensive information on agricultural sciences.

Agricultural and cooking technology. Farm books offer insights into household and commercial agriculture, food processing, and storage technologies and demonstrate how rural estates were managed (Serres 1804; Markham 1986). They provide one class of information on the larger topic of cooking technologies that controlled and varied the character of local cuisines over time (Toomre 1992). Cooking arrangements set limits on what could be cooked. Shifts from hearths to freestanding cookstoves and ovens, as well as changes in fuel types, provide historical indicators of social standing (Cowan 1983) and also show up as a nutritional constraint where the cost of fuel is a major cooking expense, as it continues to be in contemporary developing countries.

Cooks used the heat of both kitchen fires and the sun to dry fruits and vegetables for winter storage and, occasionally, to preserve fruit in sugar. The milder warmth of the kitchen dried herbs, and the steady temperature of the earth preserved foods where cellars provided the only refrigeration. Even in the nineteenth century, ice houses were a luxury for most people. The culinary history of developing countries includes efforts by food technologists to overcome constraints on the seasonal availability of vitamin- and mineral-rich fruits and to encourage more economical food purchases through improved storage and preservation methods (Riddervold and Ropeid 1988; see also occasional publications of the Program against Micronutrient Malnutrition, based in Atlanta, Georgia).

Watersheds in the history of technology, in addition to enclosed-firebox stoves and gas-powered stoves, include running water, electricity, refrigeration, home freezing, the food processor, and the microwave oven (Drummond and Wilbraham 1991). The works by Singer and colleagues (1954–8) and Needham (1954–88) offer a treasure trove for exploring culinary technology the world over (see also Forbes 1955–65 and the following citations). Changes in European cooking technologies can be gleaned through histories of domestic science instruction (McBride 1976; Davidson 1982; Attar 1987) and also through histories of the changing roles of domestic servants (Maza 1983; Fairchilds 1984).

Legal documents. Legal frameworks constitute another category of historical data revealing what were generally elite understandings of food qualities. From Roman times onward, governments usually attempted to supervise and control the quality and price of the principal staple – in the case of Europe, either flour or bread (McCance and Widdowson 1956; Kaplan 1976).

Governments also have regulated consumption of food and drink through control of the grain trade, sumptuary laws, and taxes on commodities such as salt, tea, and alcoholic beverages. Some regulations, such as the classical Athenian ban on speculation in grain, were intended to prevent hoarding of scarce food supplies. Others were meant to maintain class distinctions and to minimize trade deficits. Thus, in Renaissance Florence, wedding banquets of the bourgeois class were limited to three courses, and in eighteenth-century Sweden, coffee consumption was restricted to limit the importation of this expensive foreign product. Such efforts, however, were usually not very successful: The Florentine cooks invented delicacies that circumvented the course limit imposed, and the flavor of coffee became so desirable in Sweden that it was – and still is – used in making pot-roast gravy. In the 1560s, French sumptuary laws limiting the size of meals were simply ignored (Braudillart 1878–80).

Famine and food relief (or the history of hunger) is also a growing field of inquiry. The field includes global, regional, and period-specific studies (Newman 1990) that trace the ecological and political (trade and aid) causes of food shortages and analyze the motivations and relative effectiveness of emergency and other assistance. J. Drèze and A. Sen (1989) and R. Huss-Ashmore and S. Katz (1989, 1990) have produced analytical frameworks and case studies for the period during and following World War II. Although most emergency food aid is conceived to be humanitarian, M. Wallerstein (1980) has demonstrated how, during the Cold War, food aid was mostly political, intended to reward and to influence the behavior of friendly nations.

In developing countries, objectives of food aid have also included the development of tastes, and thereby markets, for the products of developed countries. This is a process connected to macroeconomic policies favoring the production of cash (export) over subsistence crops and the importation of cheap food (Lappe and Collins 1978). The recent history of food relief can be gleaned through the biannual *Hunger Report* of the Brown University World Hunger Program (Messer 1996b), the annual *Disasters Report* of the International Federation of Red Cross–Red Crescent Societies, and research publications of the Institute of Development Studies, Sussex (Maxwell and Buchanan-Smith 1994).

Dictionaries and encyclopedias. Dictionaries, lexica, and encyclopedias are rich sources for understanding food names, distributions, and associated lore. In both the New and Old Worlds, many contain entries on both individual ingredients and cuisines as a whole (see Brokgauz and Efron 1898; Rodinson 1949; Lewis, Pellat, and Schart 1965; Yule and Burnell 1968; *Kodansha Encyclopedia of Japan* 1983; Long 1996). New World "deadly nightshades" (tomato and potato) in Europe, for example, were labeled dangerous "apples" associated with lust, illness, or evil, which retarded their acceptance (Wheaton 1983). Word lists tend to highlight in special ways those foods that are most culturally important. For example, it was recorded – in sixteenth-century Spanish lists of words of the Aymara, a South American people – that the Aymara calculated time in terms of how long it took to boil a potato (Coe 1994).

Lexica also offer period-linked data on plant and animal food names, culturally recognized flavors and aromas, and other sensory or cultural qualities by which people in particular times and places ranked foods and food processing (see, e.g., Johns 1990). Word lists also document judgments of similarity and dimensions of difference between old and new foods; for example, New World "maize" was initially glossed "turkie wheat" (that is, foreign wheat) by the English (*Oxford English Dictionary*).

Folklore. Folklore, myth, and legend also tend to feature food and the quest for it (Darnton 1984). The European story of Hansel and Gretel, in which children deprived of food become prey to some wicked monster but then are able to overcome such evil by trickery or the help of some animal companion, has variants the world over. Children's literature instructs the young; cultural mythologies offer archetypes of how staple foods came to be and describe their cultural association with heroes or gods and their relationship with other cosmological elements, such as sun, wind, and rain.

Knowledge of fermentation and associated culinary techniques are also embedded in folklore. Indigenous Mexican folklore celebrates (and people imbibe) the effervescent products of fermented maguey in weddings and saints' rituals (see essays in Long 1996). In the Near East, wheat and barley – leavened into beer and bread – also leavened social life and carried their own mystique. The festival of the unleavened bread separated the new from the previous year's grain in ancient Middle Eastern cultures, a ritual later transmitted in modern times as the Jewish Passover. Unleavened bread (matzo) lately finds its greatest folkloric elaboration in factories in Brooklyn, New York (run by ultra-Orthodox Jewish sects), that squeeze operations for each cake of matzo into a magical 18 minutes to avoid any (unlucky and forbidden) fermentation (Jochnowitz 1996). Folklorists also record and analyze food ceremonies marking yearly and human life cycles and map distributions of food usages and terminologies (Hoefler 1908; Bächtold-Stäubli 1927–42; Gennep 1927; Wildhaber 1950).

Fiction, plays, and poetry. Since the time of Homer, descriptions of food have been used in literature to advance plot, characterize place or setting, and describe characters. Greek and Roman writings depict eating by both gods and humans and are mines of useful culinary information (Gowers 1993). Gastronomy appears as a major theme in Molière's comedy *Jean-Baptiste Poquelin* (Tobin 1990) and in *Dead Souls,* the work of Gogol. Careful descriptions of what people were eating are also part of the great literature of Charles Dickens and James Joyce (Armstrong 1992).

Visual Materials

Moving pictures. A modern media analogue to folklore, although more for entertainment than moral message, are films featuring food. Although many earlier films (such as *Gone with the Wind* and *Tom Jones*) featured blockbuster food-preparation and eating scenes, the 1980s and 1990s have witnessed an explosion of films principally devoted to the sensory and social dimensions of culinary arts. *Tampopo, Babette's Feast, Like Water for Chocolate,* and *Eat, Drink, Man, Woman* are four key examples. Even the violent satire *Pulp Fiction,* although principally a gangster story, interspersed some of its bloodier episodes with eating scenes that spoofed commercial food advertising and restaurant scenes from other films.

Food documentaries are the other major category of video that depict food culture. Special topics in the United States include the economic significance of restaurants and markets for immigrant groups (e.g., Cambodian-run donut shops) and documentaries about authentic preparation of ethnic foods (chicken soup, gefilte fish, Italian bread, Asian noodles). Food films increasingly are collected and shown at "ethnographic film" festivals, and food preparation is a growing theme for television. Public television stations around the country devote considerable airtime to cooking programs.

Still pictures. More conventionally, "still" pictures – drawings, paintings, photographs, and prints – provide period records, although, as with written sources, they must be used with care (Fare 1976; Henisch 1985; Bergstrom 1989). Sources include cookbooks and herbals, as well as more conventional art. Unfortunately, until the nineteenth century, most cookbooks did not include illustrations; exceptions are Bartolomeo de Scappi's *Cuoco Secrete di Papa Pio Quinto* (Cooking Secrets of Pope Pius V) (Venice, 1570), and Marx Rumpolt's *Ein Neu Kockbuch* (Frankfurt, 1581). From the seventeenth century, herbals offer increasingly naturalistic plant representations, and at all times there are eating scenes in ritual texts and paintings. Culinary historians who use works of art as source materials must be aware of the many conventions that dictate what is represented. For example, European still-life paintings focus in loving detail on foodstuffs both raw and prepared. Meats, fish, and the humbler vegetables appear in kitchen and market scenes. More luxurious vegetables, as well as fruit, confectionery, baked goods, and game, are shown in dining rooms and out-of-doors on terraces. Usually, readily recognizable foodstuffs are depicted, such as poultry roasting on a spit in eighteenth-century English genre scenes or pancakes being fried in the seventeenth-century Low Countries.

Some iconographical themes are especially good sources for pictures of food and food uses. Among Biblical topics, one finds everything from the miraculous fall of manna in the desert and the first Passover in the Old Testament to the wedding at Cana and the miraculous feeding of the five thousand in the New Testament. The "Seven Works of Mercy" (from Christ's Sermon on the Mount) include feeding the poor, caring for the sick, and giving drink to the thirsty. Secular subjects feature public rituals such as the Lord Mayor's banquet in London, coronation feasts, soup kitchens, and, by the nineteenth century, restaurants and genre paintings. Family portraits and conversation pieces often show gatherings around tables. Vincent Van Gogh's *Potato Eaters* (1885) is one of a number of household eating scenes by European oil painters that document the increasing significance of the humble tuber (Tilborgh 1993), and art criticism surrounding this and Jean-François Millet's earlier *Potato Planters* reveals much about the lingering snob appeal of bread versus potatoes in European diets and class structures (Murphy 1984).

Kitchen representations can be supplemented by works on architecture that offer ideas about how kitchens were laid out, as well as by examination of surviving cooking rooms, kitchens, and equipment (l'Orme 1567; Musée des Augustins 1992; Landesdenkmalamt Baden-Württemberg und der Stadt Zürich 1992). Archaeological and anthropological evidence also contributes useful findings that can amplify or modify evidence from visual and written sources.

Anthropological Evidence
Archaeological reports and dietary reconstructions detail histories and movements of food components and associated modes of preparation, storage, and distribution. Recent findings and analyses of the intestinal remains of well-preserved human "bog" specimens provide spectacular information about the diets and nutritional deficiencies of yesteryear. More routinely, skeletal and bone mineral analyses indicate seasonal or chronic malnutrition, particularly over periods of transition from foraging to farming (see essays in Harris and Hillman 1989). To determine culinary histories of particular sites and regions, archaeological reconstructions use the material remains of plants and animals, along with cooking and storage implements and architectural remains.

Ethnographic reports include descriptions of dietary life that become benchmarks for historical and cross-cultural comparison. Anthropological studies also draw on linguistic and literary sources, matching them to material remains and documentary evidence, which together allow the reconstruction of cuisines at particular points in and over time. Semiotic analyses of symbol, myth, and ritual, such as Levi-Strauss's *The Raw and the Cooked,* provide particularly rich metaphorical constructs for linking culinary practices to cultural transformations and patterns of migration, along with the ways in which the significance of particular food plants or animal species, or specific manners of preparation, are marked in myth and ritual and change over cultural time and space.

Ethnographic data also document changing food preferences and tastes and link them to major changes in food and political-economic systems and nutritional-health beliefs and practices. Anthropologists extend the dicta "tell me what you eat and I'll tell you who you are" (from the French) and "you are what you eat" (from the German) from the food itself to its preparation, distribution, and consumption, which are cultural and social markers as well. Recent studies explore how major transformations in agricultural technologies and available plant varieties, such as "Green Revolution" grains and the expansion of world agricultural trade and aid, can influence nutrition, health, and culture in developing areas. Among the results of such changes is increasing worldwide literacy and, consequently, the availability of written recipes from nonlocal sources (Appadurai 1988).

Cookbooks and Cooking Journals
Cookbooks provide specific information about ingredients, equipment, and techniques that cannot be found elsewhere. Some also contain information about daily life, gender roles, regional and economic

differences in diet and literacy, and the development of a culinary language. They must, however, be seen in the context of the time and place in which they were produced and in the context of their relationship to other cookbooks (Toomre 1992). For example, most cookbooks published in the United States in the early twentieth century were addressed to women cooking at home, whereas most published in France before the middle of the nineteenth century were addressed to men cooking for patrons from among the wealthiest segments of society.

Bibliographies of cookery books from Europe and the United States include Theodor Drexel, *Katalog der Kochbücher-Sammlung* (Frankfurt-am-Main, 1885); Georges Vicaire, *Bibliographie Gastronomique* (Paris, 1890); Katherine Golden Bitting, *Gastronomic Bibliography* (San Francisco, 1939); Arnold W. Oxford, *English Cookery Books to the Year 1850* (London, 1913); Elizabeth Driver, *A Bibliography of Cookery Books Published in Britain, 1875-1914* (London, 1989); Virginia Maclean, *A Short-Title Catalogue of Household and Cookery Books Published in the English Tongue, 1701-1800* (London, 1981); Dena Attar, *A Bibliography of Household Books Published in Britain, 1800-1914* (London, 1987); Eleanor Lowenstein, *Bibliography of American Cookery Books, 1742-1860* (Worcester, Mass., 1972); Richard M. T. Westbury, *Handlist of Italian Cookery Books* (Florence, 1963); and Jacqueline Newman, *Chinese Cookbooks: An Annotated English-Language Compendium Bibliography* (New York, 1987).

Scholarly Societies and Symposia

Culinary history is being pursued on a worldwide basis in many different venues – in museums, libraries, and universities, and by scholars working outside of any formal academic institutional framework. *Petits Propos Culinaires* (essays and notes on food, cookery, and cookery books) and *Food and Foodways* are publications dedicated to culinary history, as was (to a lesser extent) the *Journal of Gastronomy,* which was published for several years by the American Institute of Wine and Food. In addition, the Foodways Section of the American Folklore Society, with partial support from the Michigan Traditional Arts Program, publishes the biannual journal *Digest: An Interdisciplinary Study of Food and Foodways.* Scholars of culinary history meet at conferences, the most long-standing of which is the biannual or triannual International Ethnological Food Research Congress.

Oxford Symposia on Food and Cookery have been published by Prospect Books (London), and the proceedings of one-day conferences held at the Brotherton Library in Leeds were published in six volumes of *Food and Society* by Edinburgh University Press. The Schlesinger Library of Radcliffe College and the Culinary Historians of Boston (CHB) cosponsored and published proceedings from a conference, *Current*

Research in Culinary History: Sources, Topics, and Methods (Cambridge, Mass., 1985).

Madison, Wisconsin, was the site of the 1997 joint meeting of the Agriculture, Food, and Human Value Society (AFHVS) and the Association for the Study of Food and Society (ASFS) – the latter a 12-year-old international interdisciplinary organization dedicated to studying the complex relationship between food and society. The meeting attracted several hundred food scholars – organic farmers, sociologists, chefs, medical historians, anthropologists, and nutritionists. Occasional conferences on specialized food topics have multiplied in recent years. In 1982, the Dublin Seminar for New England Folklife chose "Foodways of the Northeast" as the topic of its annual conference and later published the papers as its *Annual Proceedings 1982.* The Russian Research Center at Harvard University sponsored a conference in 1993 entitled "Food in Russian History and Culture," the papers of which appeared in a book of the same name (Glants and Toomre 1997). The University of New Hampshire held an interdisciplinary conference on food and culture; Boston University sponsored its sequel in 1995.

Additional venues are "living-history" museums, pioneering examples of which are Skansen in Stockholm, Sweden, and the Netherlands Open-Air Museum in Arnhem. In the United States, Sturbridge Village, Plimoth Plantation, and Colonial Williamsburg regularly sponsor programs in culinary history that include both lectures and demonstrations of culinary implements and hearthstone cooking. In conjunction with the Quincentenary (1992), museums on both sides of the Atlantic sponsored exhibits and conferences on the "Columbian exchange," such as the Smithsonian Institution exhibit and conference "Seeds of Change" (Viola and Margolis 1991). In Texas, the George Ranch, outside of Houston, emphasizes the history of black cowboys and chuck-wagon cooking, whereas the Jordan-Bachmann farm in Austin focuses on nineteenth-century German influences in the area, including regional foodways.

Scholarly and professional societies publish various materials of interest. The London Classical Society hosted *Food in Antiquity: Studies in Ancient Society and Culture* (Wilkins, Harvey, and Dobson 1995). Food and nutrition panels are featured at the annual meetings of major academic professional societies such as the American Anthropological Association (Huss-Ashmore and Katz 1989, 1990; Sharman et al. 1991), the American Studies Association, and the American Sociological Association (Maurer and Sobal 1995; Whit 1995). Food history panels are also found at the Eighteenth Century Society, the French Language Association, the American Historical Association, the American Association for the Advancement of Slavic Studies, and the Society for French Historical Studies. The breadth of interest in the field is shown by the wide range of scholarly and trade journals that publish food articles emphasizing cultural, social, historical, or literary themes, with special issues devoted to food topics in history, art history, regional foodways, literature, or films.

Since 1980, Boston has become a center for the study of culinary history. The Schlesinger Library of Radcliffe College, which is devoted to women's history, houses a growing culinary collection of over 12,000 volumes on food and, since 1990, has hosted monthly meetings of the CHB and a professional chefs' forum. Other active groups of culinary historians in the United States are located in the cities of Ann Arbor, Michigan, New York, Houston, Texas, Honolulu, Hawaii, and Washington, D.C., as well as in various cities of California. Activities are also expanding in Mexico, where scholars from the fields of history, anthropology, and biology orchestrated a symposium marking 500 years of European–New World food encounters (Long 1996), and where ethnobiologists and food anthropologists sponsor lectures and publications predominantly on food history topics, including an "Antropologia y Alimentacion" section of *Antropologicas,* a periodical of the Instituto de Investigaciones Antropologicas of the National Autonomous University of Mexico (UNAM).

Conclusion

Culinary history is emerging as an academic specialty. Programs at Boston University's Metropolitan College, courses taught at the Radcliffe College Seminars, and courses within the New York University (NYU) Food Studies Program combine culinary history with cultural studies and, at NYU, nutrition. Apart from these more humanistic approaches, histories of crop plants, agricultural and food processing technologies, and food commerce offer a growing literature on food within the history and sociology of science and technology. Ingredients and technology play off each other to create change in cuisine. Illustrative are the modern varieties of grains and tubers that since the 1970s have been changing the basic foods people eat in developing countries. Another example is the new enzyme processing, which is leading to the replacement of cane sugar by corn syrup in processed foods and, consequently, is influencing sugar- and corn-based economies all over the world. Yet another example – about which much will be written in coming years – concerns the history of foods formulated and aggressively marketed by transnational corporations such as Coca Cola and McDonald's, along with the nutritional and cultural consequences for populations that consume these products rather than other foods. These are but three illustrations of the ever-expanding list of aspects of food and nutrition that culinary historical perspectives help elaborate.

In addition, we can expect growing interest in culinary history on at least four fronts. The first is a growing medical interest in the history of food, diet, and nutritional health, prompted by concern about the extent to which diets play an etiologic role in coronary heart disease, hypertension, cancers, and diabetes. This avenue of investigation seeks to understand the sources of dietary variation and the circumstances under which food habits have changed in the past. The second is a growing agricultural–biological interest in the diversity of food species (and varieties) and their histories. This interest forms part of a global effort to conserve biodiversity. The third is the growing interest in culinary arts in the humanities, both as a part of women's history and also as a special area of literature and the fine arts. Finally, many with political–economic and ethnic-studies perspectives within anthropology, political science, economics, sociology, and history are becoming increasingly interested in the history of food and cuisine for the ways these shape – and are shaped by – social forces. Culinary history will continue to have numerous disciplinary voices.

Ellen Messer
Barbara Haber
Joyce Toomre
Barbara Wheaton

Bibliography

Anderson, E. 1988. *The food of China.* New Haven, Conn.

Anderson, F. J. 1977. *An illustrated history of herbals.* New York.

Appadurai, A. 1988. Cookbooks and cultural change: The Indian case. *Comparative Studies in Society and History* 30: 3-24.

Arber, A. 1953. From medieval herbalism to the birth of modern botany. In *Science, medicine, and history: Essays in the evolution of scientific thought and medical practice written in honor of Charles Singer,* ed. E. A. Underwood, 317-26. London.

1990. *Herbals: Their origins and evolution. A chapter in the history of botany, 1470-1670.* Second edition. Cambridge.

Arksey, L., N. Pries, and M. Reed. 1983-7. *American diaries: An annotated bibliography of published American diaries and journals.* 2 vols. Detroit, Mich.

Armstrong, H. 1992. *The joyce of cooking.* Dublin.

Arndt, A. 1993. Silphium: Spicing up the palate. *Proceedings of the Oxford Symposium on Food and Cookery,* 28-35. London.

Arnott, M., ed. 1976. *Gastronomy: The anthropology of food habits.* The Hague.

Attar, D. 1987. *A bibliography of household books published in Britain, 1800-1914.* London.

Bächtold-Stäubli, Hanns, ed. 1927-42. *Handwörterbuch des deutschen Aberglaubens.* 10 vols. Berlin and Leipzig.

Beecher, C. E. 1869. *The American woman's home, or principles of domestic science.* New York.

Bergstrom, I. 1989. *Still life of the golden age. Northern European paintings from the Heinz family collection.* Washington, D.C.

Braudel, F. 1966. *La Méditerranée et le monde en l'époque de Philippe II.* Second edition. Paris.

Braudillart, H. 1878–80. *Histoire du luxe privée et public de l'antiquité jusqu'à nos jours.* 4 vols. Paris.

Brillat-Savarin, J. A. 1995. *The physiology of taste, or meditations on transcendental gastronomy,* trans. M. F. K. Fisher. Washington, D.C.

Brokgauz, F. A., and I. J. Efron, eds. 1898. *Entsiklopedicheski slovar'.* St. Petersburg.

Brown, E., and B. Brown. 1961. *Culinary Americana.* New York.

Chang, K. C., ed. 1977. *Food in Chinese culture: Anthropological and historical perspectives.* New Haven, Conn.

Coe, S. 1994. *America's first cuisines.* Austin, Tex.

Coe, S., and M. Coe. 1996. *The true history of chocolate.* New York.

Cook, M. 1971. *America's charitable cooks: A bibliography of fundraising cook books.* Kent, Ohio.

Cowan, R. S. 1983. *More work for mother. The ironies of household technology from the open hearth to the microwave.* New York.

Crosby, A. 1972. *The Columbian exchange. Biological and cultural consequences of 1492.* Westport, Conn.

Curtin, D. W., and L. M. Heldke, eds. 1992. *Cooking, eating, thinking. Transformative philosophies of food.* Bloomington, Ind.

Dalby, A., and S. Grainger. 1996. *The classical cookbook.* Los Angeles.

Darnton, R. 1984. *The great cat massacre and other episodes in French cultural history.* New York.

Davidson, C. 1982. *A woman's work is never done: A history of housework in the British Isles, 1650–1950.* London.

Deetz, J. 1996. *In small things forgotten: An archaeology of early American life.* Revised and expanded edition. New York.

Douglas, M. 1966. *Purity and danger.* Baltimore, Md.
  1972. Deciphering a meal. *Daedalus* 101: 61–81.
  ed. 1984. *Food and the social order.* New York.

Drèze, J., and A. Sen. 1989. *Hunger and public action.* New York.

Drummond, J. C., and A. Wilbraham. 1991. *The Englishman's food.* Second edition, rev. D. Hartley. London.

Fairchilds, C. 1984. *Domestic enemies: Servants and their masters in old regime France.* Baltimore, Md.

Fare, M. 1976. *La vie silencieuse en France: La nature morte au XVIIIe siècle.* Freiburg, Germany.

Fenton, A. 1986. *Food in change: Eating habits from the Middle Ages to the present.* Atlantic Highlands, N.J.

Fenton, A., and T. M. Owen, eds. 1981. *Food in perspective. Proceedings of the Third International Conference on Ethnological Food Research, in Cardiff, Wales, 1977.* Edinburgh.

Forbes, R. J. 1955–65. *Studies in ancient technology.* 9 vols. Leiden, the Netherlands.

Garnsey, P. 1990. Responses to food crisis in the ancient Mediterranean world. In *Hunger in history: Food shortage, poverty, and deprivation,* ed. L. Newman, 126–46. New York.

Gennep, A. van. 1927. *Manuel de folklore Français contemporain.* Paris.

Gerbod, P. 1991. *Voyages au pays des mangeurs de grenouilles: La France vue par les Britanniques du XVIIIe siècle à nos jours.* Paris.

Glants, M., and J. Toomre, eds. 1997. *Food in Russian history and culture.* Bloomington, Ind.

Goode, J. 1989. Cultural patterning and group-shared rules in the study of food intake. In *Research methods in nutritional anthropology,* ed. G. Pelto, P. Pelto, and E. Messer, 126–61. Tokyo.

Goody, J. 1982. *Cooking, cuisine, and class: A study in comparative sociology.* New York.

Gordon, K. 1987. Evolutionary perspectives on human diet. In *Nutritional anthropology,* ed. F. E. Johnston, 3–46. New York.

Gowers, E. 1993. *The loaded table: Representations of food in Roman literature.* New York.

Harris, D. R., and G. C. Hillman. 1989. *Foraging and farming. The evolution of plant exploitation.* London.

Harris, M. 1979. *Cultural materialism. The struggle for a science of culture.* New York.

Hemardinquer, J. J. 1970. *Pour une histoire de l'alimentation.* Paris.

Henisch, B. 1985. Unconsidered trifles: The search for cooking scenes in medieval sources. *Schlesinger Library-Culinary Historians of Boston proceedings: Current research in culinary history: Sources, topics, and methods,* 110–21. Cambridge, Mass.

Hess, K. 1992. *The Carolina rice kitchen: The African connection.* Columbia, S.C.

Hocquet, J. C. 1989. *Le sel de la terre.* Paris.

Hoefler, M. 1908. *Gebildbrote der Faschings-, Fastnachts- und Fastenzeit.* Vienna.

Huss-Ashmore, R., and S. Katz, eds. 1989, 1990. *African food systems in crisis. Part 1: Microperspectives. Part 2: Macroperspectives.* Langhorne, Pa.

Jerome, N. 1980. Diet and acculturation: The case of black American immigrants. In *Nutritional anthropology,* ed. N. W. Jerome, R. Kandel, and G. Pelto, 275–325. New York.

Jochnowitz, E. 1996. Making sense of matzoh: History, meanings, and message. Presentation to the Culinary Historians of Boston, December 12. Boston, Mass.

Johns, T. 1990. *With bitter herbs they shall eat it.* Tucson, Ariz.

Joselit, J. W., B. Kirshenblatt-Gimblett, and I. Howe. 1990. *Getting comfortable in New York: The American Jewish home, 1880–1950.* New York.

Kaneva-Johnson, M. 1995. *The melting pot: Balkan food and cookery.* London.

Kaplan, S. 1976. *Bread, politics, and political economy in the reign of Louis XV.* The Hague.

Katona-Apte, J. 1976. Dietary aspects of acculturation: Meals, feasts, and fasts in a minority community in South Asia. In *Gastronomy: The anthropology of food habits,* ed. M. Arnott, 315–26. The Hague.

Katz, S. 1987. Food and biocultural evolution: A model for the investigation of modern nutritional problems. In *Nutritional anthropology,* ed. F. E. Johnston, 47–66. New York.

Khare, R. 1976. *Hindu hearth and home.* Durham, N.C.

Kodansha encyclopedia of Japan. 1983. Tokyo.

Ladies Relief Corps of South Framingham. 1887. *Tested recipes for the inexperienced housewife.* Framingham, Mass.

Landesdenkmalamt Baden-Württemberg und der Stadt Zürich, ed. 1992. *Stadtluft, Hirsebrei, und Bettelmönch. Die Stadt um 1300.* Zurich and Stuttgart.

Lappe, F. M., and J. Collins. 1978. *Food first. Beyond the myth of scarcity.* New York.

Laurioux, B. 1985. Spices in the medieval diet: A new approach. *Food and Foodways* 1: 43–76.
  1989. *Le moyen age à table.* Paris.

Levenstein, H. 1988. *Revolution at the table. The transformation of the American diet.* New York.

Levi-Strauss, C. 1969, 1973, 1978. *The raw and the cooked; From honey to ashes; The origin of table manners,* trans. J. Weightman and D. Weightman. New York.

Lewis, B., Ch. Pellat, and J. Schart. 1965. *Encyclopedia of Islam*. Leiden, the Netherlands.

Lippmann, E. von. 1929. *Geschichte des Zuckers seit den ältesten Zeiten bis zum Beginn der Rübenzuckerfabrikation*. Second edition. Berlin.

Long, J., ed. 1996. *Conquista y comida: Consecuencias del encuentro de dos mundos*. Mexico City.

l'Orme, P. de. 1567. *Le premier tome de l'architecture*. Paris.

Markham, G. 1986. *The English housewife*, ed. M. Best. Kingston, Ontario.

Matthews, W. 1967. *British diaries: An annotated bibliography of British diaries written between 1442 and 1942*. Gloucester, Mass.

Maurer, D., and J. Sobal, eds. 1995. *Eating agendas. Food and nutrition as social problems*. Hawthorne, N.Y.

Maxwell, S., and M. Buchanan-Smith, eds. 1994. *Linking relief to development*. IDS Bulletin No. 25. Sussex.

Mayer, W. 1961. *Early travelers in Mexico, 1534-1816*. Mexico City.

Maza, Sarah C. 1983. *Servants and masters in eighteenth-century France: The uses of loyalty*. Princeton, N.J.

McBride, T. M. 1976. *The domestic revolution: The modernization of household service in England and France, 1820-1920*. New York.

McCance, R. A., and E. M. Widdowson. 1956. *Breads, white and brown: Their place in thought and social history*. Philadelphia, Pa.

McCracken, R. D. 1971. Lactase deficiency: An example of dietary evolution. *Current Anthropology* 12: 479-517.

Mead, M. 1964. *Food habits research: Problems of the 1960s*. National Academy of Sciences, National Research Council, Publication No. 1225. Washington, D.C.

Mennell, S. 1996. *All manners of food: Eating and taste in England and France*. Second edition. Urbana, Ill.

Messer, E. 1984. Anthropological perspectives on diet. *Annual Review of Anthropology* 13: 205-49.

  1986. Some like it sweet. Estimating sweetness preferences and sucrose intakes from ethnographic and experimental data. *American Anthropologist* 88: 637-47.

  1989. Methods for studying determinants of food intake. In *Research methods in nutritional anthropology*, ed. G. Pelto, P. Pelto, and E. Messer, 1-33. Tokyo.

  1996a. Food wars: The use of hunger as a weapon in 1994. In *The hunger report: 1995*, ed. E. Messer and P. Uvin, 19-48. The Netherlands.

  1996b. Visions of the future: Food, hunger, and nutrition. In *The hunger report: 1995*, ed. E. Messer and P. Uvin, 211-28. The Netherlands.

Mintz, S. 1985. *Sweetness and power*. New York.

Miracle, M. 1966. *Maize in tropical Africa*. Madison, Wis.

Murphy, K. 1984. *Millet*. Boston, Mass.

Musée des Augustins, Toulouse. 1992. *Plaisirs et manières de table aux XIVe et XVe siècles*. Toulouse, France.

Musées Nationaux. 1993. *Réunion des Musées Nationaux*. Paris.

National Research Council, Committee on Food Consumption Patterns. 1981. *Assessing changing food consumption patterns*. Food and Nutrition Board, U.S. National Research Council. Washington, D.C.

Needham, J. 1954-88. *Science and civilization in China*. 6 vols. Cambridge.

Nerhood, H. W. 1968. *To Russia and return: An annotated bibliography of travelers' English-language accounts of Russia from the ninth century to the present*. Columbus, Ohio.

Newman, L. F., ed. 1990. *Hunger in history: Food shortage, poverty, and deprivation*. Cambridge, Mass.

Noel Hume, A., and I. Noel Hume. 1978. *Food*. Colonial Williamsburg Archaeological Series No. 9. Williamsburg, Va.

Oliver, S. 1995. *Saltwater foodways: New Englanders and their food at sea and ashore*. Mystic, Conn.

Perry, C. 1981. The oldest Mediterranean noodle: A cautionary tale. *Petits Propos Culinaires* 9: 42-5.

Peterson, T. 1980. The Arab influence on western European cooking. *Journal of Medieval History* 6: 317-40.

Riddervold, A., and A. Ropeid. 1988. *Food conservation: Ethnological studies*. London.

Ritenbaugh, C. 1978. Human foodways: A window on evolution. In *The anthropology of health*, ed. E. E. Bauwens, 111-20. St. Louis, Mo.

Robinson, J. 1990. *Wayward women: A guide to women travelers*. New York.

Roden, C. 1996. *The book of Jewish food: An odyssey from Samarkand to New York*. New York.

Rodinson, M. 1949. Recherches sur les documents arabes relatifs la cuisine. *Revue des Études Islamiques*: 95-165.

Rotenberg, R. 1981. The impact of industrialization on meal patterns in Vienna, Austria. *Ecology of Food and Nutrition* 11: 25-35.

Rozin, E. 1973. *The flavor principle*. New York.

Salaman, R. [1949] 1985. *The history and social influence of the potato*, ed. J. Hawkes. Cambridge and New York.

Scully, D. E., and T. Scully. 1995. *Early French cookery: Sources, history, original recipes, and modern adaptations*. Ann Arbor, Mich.

Serres, O. de. [1600] 1804. *Le théâtre d'agriculture*. Paris.

Shapiro, L. 1986. *Perfection salad: Women and cooking at the turn of the century*. New York.

Sharman, A., J. Theophano, K. Curtis, and E. Messer, eds. 1991. *Diet and domestic life in society*. Philadelphia, Pa.

Simetti, M. T. 1989. *Pomp and sustenance. Twenty-five centuries of Sicilian food*. New York.

Simoons, F. 1991. *Food in China: A cultural and historical inquiry*. Boca Raton, Fla.

Singer, C., E. J. Holmyard, A. R. Hall, and T. I. Williams. 1954-8. *A history of technology*. 8 vols. Oxford.

Siraisi, N. G. 1990. *Medieval and early Renaissance medicine: An introduction to knowledge and practice*. Chicago.

Sklar, K. K. 1973. *Catharine Beecher: A study in American domesticity*. New Haven, Conn.

Stahl, A. B. 1989. Plant-food processing: Implications for dietary quality. In *Foraging and farming. The evolution of plant exploitation*, ed. D. R. Harris and G. C. Hillman, 171-94. London.

Strasser, S. 1982. *Never done. A history of American housework*. New York.

Teuteberg, H. J. 1993. *Kulturthema Essen: Ansichten und Problemfelder*. Berlin.

Tilborgh, L. van. 1993. *The potato eaters by Vincent Van Gogh*. Zwolle, the Netherlands.

Tinniswood, A. 1989. *A history of country house visiting: Five centuries of tourism and taste*. Oxford.

Tobin, R. W. 1990. *Tarte à la crème: Comedy and gastronomy in Molière's theater*. Columbus, Ohio.

Toomre, J. 1992. *Classic Russian cooking: Elena Molokhovets' "A gift to young housewives."* Bloomington, Ind.

Toussaint-Samat, M. 1992. *A history of food*, trans. A. Bell. Oxford.

Viola, H. J., and C. Margolis, eds. 1991. *Seeds of change: A quincentennial commemoration.* Washington, D.C.

Wallerstein, M. 1980. *Food for war - food for peace.* Cambridge, Mass.

Wheaton, B. 1983. *Savoring the past: The French kitchen and table from 1300 to 1789.* Philadelphia, Pa.

    1984. The cooks of Concord. *Journal of Gastronomy* 1: 5-24.

Whit, W. C. 1995. *Food and society: A sociological approach.* New York.

Wildhaber, R. 1950. *Schneckenzucht und Schneckenspeise.* Basel.

Wilkins, J., D. Harvey, and M. Dobson, eds. 1995. *Food in antiquity.* Exeter, England.

Yule, H., and A. C. Burnell. [1903] 1968. *Hobson-Jobson: A glossary of colloquial Anglo-Indian words and phrases, and of kindred terms, etymological, historical, geographical and discursive, by Henry Yule and A. C. Burnell,* ed. William Crooke. Second edition, reprint. New Delhi.

PART VI

History, Nutrition, and Health

Part VI takes up questions of food and nutrition that have historical as well as contemporary relevance. It begins with two chapters that continue a now decades-long debate over the extent to which improved nutrition may be responsible for reduced mortality within populations – a debate that has centered on, but certainly has not been limited to, the circumstances surrounding the population increases of the countries of Europe since the eighteenth century.

These are followed by a group of chapters that, although not specifically addressing matters of mortality decline, do help to illuminate some of its many aspects. An elaboration of the concept of synergy, for example, emphasizes the important role that pathogens (or their absence) play in the nutritional status of an individual, whereas the chapter on famine reveals the circumstances within which synergy does some of its deadliest work.

Stature, discussed next, is increasingly employed by historians as a proxy for nutritional status, and final adult height can frequently be a function of the nutrition of the mother before she gives birth and of the infant and child following that event – a subject treated in the following chapter. A chapter on adolescent nutrition and fertility, harking back to matters of population increase, is succeeded by another concerned with the linkage between the nutrition of a child and its mental development.

By way of a transition to a second group of chapters in Part VI focusing on culture and foods is a chapter on the biological and cultural aspects of human nutritional adaptation. This discussion is followed by chapters that scrutinize food choices, food fads, food prejudices and taboos, and social and cultural food uses. Probably since humans first set foot on earth, they have believed in the magical properties of some foods and the medicinal qualities of others; both of these aspects of eating are examined in chapters on foods as aphrodisiacs (and anaphrodisiacs) and as medicines.

Not necessarily unrelated is the subject of vegetarianism, both condemned and embraced as a way of life, not to mention as a dietary regimen. Because of the controversial nature of vegetarianism we have both pro and con chapters on the matter to close out Part VI.

VI.1 ✑ Nutrition and the Decline of Mortality

Together with economic growth and technological advances, improvements in health and longevity are the typical hallmarks of a population's transition to modern society. Among the earliest countries to undergo such experiences were England and France, where mortality rates began declining steadily during the eighteenth century. Elsewhere in western and northern Europe, health and longevity began to improve during the nineteenth century. In the twentieth century, this pattern has been replicated in developing countries throughout the world.

Understanding the causes that underlie this pattern of mortality decline is important not only as a matter of historical interest but also because of the practical implications for policies that aim to improve life in developing countries, and for forecasting changes in mortality in developed countries. Accordingly, there has been much interest in identifying the causes of patterns of mortality decline and measuring their impact. By the 1960s, a consensus had emerged that the factors underlying mortality trends could be delineated within four categories, as reported in a study by the United Nations (UN) (1953): (1) public-health reforms, (2) advances in medical knowledge, (3) improved personal hygiene, and (4) rising income and standards of living. A later UN study (1973) added as an additional category "natural causes," such as a decline in the virulence of pathogens.

McKeown's Nutrition Hypothesis

Against this consensus view, the British epidemiologist Thomas McKeown argued in a series of influential articles and books from 1955 to the mid-1980s that the contribution of medicine to the decline of mortality before the twentieth century had been relatively small. Rather, relying on a residual argument that rejected other factors as plausible explanations, he proposed that improvement in nutrition was the primary cause of the mortality decline.

McKeown's view was best set forth in his 1976 book, *The Modern Rise of Population*. In it, he argued that the modern growth of population was attributable to a decline of mortality rather than to changes in fertility, and he sought to identify what had brought about death-rate reductions since the eighteenth century. His investigation relied heavily – indeed, almost exclusively – on cause-of-death information, which had been nationally registered in England and Wales since 1837. McKeown himself was aware that his evidence was geographically limited and did not fully cover the time period during which mortality had declined. Nevertheless, he believed that his findings could be generalized to explain the modern mortality experience of other European countries.

McKeown's analysis of causes of death in England and Wales during the period from 1848–54 to 1971 led him to the conclusion that the reduction of the death rate was associated predominantly with infectious diseases. Of the decline in mortality during that period, 40 percent resulted from a reduction in airborne diseases, 21 percent from reduction in water- and foodborne diseases, and 13 percent from reduction in other types of infections. The remainder (26 percent) was attributable to a lesser incidence of noninfective conditions. Thus, McKeown found that three-quarters of the mortality decline since the mid–nineteenth century could be explained by the reduction in infectious diseases. He further reasoned that despite sketchy historical evidence from the period before the beginning of cause-of-death registration, this trend could be extrapolated backward to the start of the modern mortality decline around the beginning of the eighteenth century. By his reckoning, 86 percent of the reduction in death rates from then until 1971 had resulted from a decline in mortality from infectious diseases. For McKeown, then, this conclusion was the central feature of mortality decline and constituted evidence against which the merits of alternative explanations of mortality decline would be judged.

McKeown methodically classified possible reasons for the lesser incidence of mortality from infectious diseases into four categories: (1) changes in the character of the diseases themselves, (2) advances in medical treatment, or the prevention and treatment of diseases by immunization and therapy, (3) reduced general exposure to disease, and (4) increased general resistance to disease because of improved nutrition. Taking these categories one at a time, he systematically considered each of the major disease groups (airborne infections, water- and foodborne infections, and other infections) in turn, and concluded that the only category that satisfactorily explained the decline in mortality was increased disease resistance resulting from improved nutrition.

In examining changes in the character of diseases as a possible explanation of mortality decline, McKeown found little reason to believe that this had been responsible for a substantial reduction in deaths from infectious diseases. By changes in the character of diseases he meant changes in the interaction between the infectious microorganism and the human host and whether such changes meant a decline in the virulence of the pathogen or an increased resistance in the human host through natural selection.

Although he acknowledged that a change in the character of scarlet fever did result in a reduction of deaths from that disease in the latter half of the nineteenth century, McKeown thought it "frankly incredible" that the other major airborne diseases of the period, which included tuberculosis, influenza, and measles, had all undergone such fortuitous changes simultaneously. On the contrary, he pointed out that tuberculosis, for example, continues to have devastating effects on populations not previously exposed to it. Nor did he think it likely that natural selection could have increased people's resistance to such diseases, leading to a decline in mortality. For such genetic selection to have occurred, McKeown pointed out that certain deleterious effects of early industrialization and urbanization, such as crowding, should have produced high mortality in the eighteenth century. Through natural selection, that experience would have left a population with greater resistance to the airborne diseases, which would account for lower mortality rates later on. However, McKeown believed that death rates during the eighteenth century had simply been too low to support such a theory.

Water- and foodborne diseases warranted a similar conclusion. McKeown did not altogether rule out the possibility that changes in the character of those diseases could have played some role in the reduction of mortality associated with them. But he thought that improved hygiene, leading to reduced exposure, was a much more convincing explanation. As for vector-borne diseases, typhus was mentioned as one that might have been affected by a change in its character. However, the contribution of the decline of this disease to the fall of mortality over the past three centuries was small.

The next possible reason for a decline in mortality from infectious diseases that McKeown dealt with was medical advances, and it is here that his arguments impressively marshaled historical evidence. He built his case against a significant role for medical treatment by examining the temporal pattern of death rates of the most lethal diseases. He first took care to point up the distinction between the interests of the physician and those of the patient. Although since the eighteenth century many important advances have been made in medical knowledge and institutions, such advances were not always immediately effective against diseases; they often required considerable intervals before becoming of practical, demonstrable benefit to the patient. In making this distinction, McKeown contended that whether different preventive measures and treatments in history had been effective could not be judged reliably from contemporary assessments; instead, their efficacy would best be determined in light of critical present-day knowledge.

Tuberculosis, the largest single cause of death in the mid–nineteenth century and the decline of which was responsible for a fifth of the subsequent reduction in mortality, served as a case in point. The identification of the tubercle bacillus by Robert Koch in 1882 was an important event in the progress of medical knowledge, but its immediate contribution to reducing tuberculosis was minimal. In addition, of the numerous treatments that were tried in the nineteenth and early twentieth centuries, none could be judged by modern medical knowledge to have been effective against the disease. Rather, McKeown suggested that effective treatment actually began only with the introduction of streptomycin in 1947 and *bacille Calmette-Guérin* (BCG) vaccination on a large scale in England and Wales from 1954. By these dates, however, mortality from tuberculosis had already fallen substantially. Roughly 60 percent of the decline since 1848–54 had already taken place by the turn of the twentieth century, and this decline continued up to the introduction of effective chemotherapy around 1950. If the medical contribution was meaningful only after 1950, it was therefore impossible for medical advances against tuberculosis to have been a major factor in the mortality decline, most of which had taken place by then.

Similarly, when the temporal patterns of mortality decline from the other major airborne diseases of the nineteenth century were compared with the dates of introduction of effective treatment or immunization against them, McKeown found that most of the fall in the death rates they produced had also occurred before effective medical measures became available. An exception to this was smallpox, the decline of which since the mid–nineteenth century was thought to be the result of mass vaccination. But McKeown pointed out that the reduction in smallpox mortality was associated with only 1.6 percent of the reduction in the death rate from all causes. McKeown also doubted that the rapid decline of mortality from diseases spread by water and food since the late nineteenth century owed much to medical measures. He thought that, in many cases, immunization was relatively ineffective even at the time he wrote, and that therapy of some value was not employed until about 1950.

Finally, reduced exposure to infection was considered as a possible explanation of mortality decline. In the case of airborne diseases, McKeown once again found little reason to think that reduced exposure had been a major factor in their decline. Indeed, he thought that the fall in deaths from measles and scarlet fever owed very little to reduced exposure, and although he allowed that reduced exposure did play a role in the decline of other airborne diseases such as tuberculosis, whooping cough, diphtheria, and smallpox, he believed that this was only a secondary consequence of other influences that lowered the prevalence of disease in the community.

In the case of water- and foodborne diseases, McKeown conceded that reduced exposure had played a greater role in reducing mortality than it had with airborne diseases, especially during the second half of the nineteenth century. Purification of water, efficient disposal of sewage, provision of safe milk, and improved food hygiene all contributed to the decline of mortality. He also felt that personal hygiene, particularly regular bathing, may have encouraged the abatement of typhus in the eighteenth and nineteenth centuries.

In summary, McKeown dismissed the ability of both changes in the character of infectious diseases and advances in medical treatment to account for the modern mortality decline. He thought the contribution of sanitation and hygiene had been somewhat more significant but still of limited scope and primarily confined to the second half of the nineteenth century. Therefore, advances in general health based on improved nutrition constituted the only possibility left that could explain the mortality decline, and, in McKeown's view, it was also the most credible explanation.

In support of his circumstantial case for nutrition, which he had arrived at by a process of elimination, McKeown offered some pieces of positive evidence. First, he pointed out that the great expansion of the English and Welsh populations during the eighteenth and early nineteenth centuries had been accompanied by an important increase in domestic food production. However, as McKeown conceded, the central question for the nutritional argument was whether the amount of food per capita, rather than total food consumption, had increased during that period. He found that evidence to settle the matter directly was unavailable and chose instead to consider the relationship between malnutrition and infection. Thus, as the second piece of evidence in support of nutrition, he pointed to the situation in developing countries, where malnutrition contributes largely to the high level of infectious deaths. Malnourished populations are more susceptible to infections and suffer more seriously when they are infected. McKeown also emphasized the dynamic interaction that exists between nutrition and infection, frequently characterized as synergism. Since infections adversely affect nutritional status, a vicious cycle between disease and malnutrition often results – a cycle characteristic of poverty and underdevelopment.

Reaction to the McKeown Thesis

McKeown's thesis drew the attention of scholars from a wide spectrum of disciplines. As it provided a theoretical framework that wove together such themes as industrialization, urbanization, rising standards of living, changing health, and shifting demographic patterns, it could hardly have failed to attract the interest of social scientists, especially demographers and economic historians. A number of studies extended McKeown's argument to the history of mortality rates in the United States (Meeker 1972; Higgs 1973, 1979; McKinlay and McKinlay 1977). In all probability, the contemporary interest in McKeown's nutritional thesis was also in part a consequence of great public concern over the "population bomb" – the fear that the explosive worldwide population increase in the post–World War II period would eventually lead to catastrophic shortages of food and other natural resources. It is not difficult to understand that an audi-ence constantly reminded, and so vividly, of the Malthusian link between food supply and population growth would have been receptive to McKeown's argument giving primacy to nutrition as the factor explaining the decline of mortality.

Reaction to the McKeown thesis, however, was by no means uniformly favorable. Although acknowledging that nutrition had played a role in mortality decline, many scholars nevertheless felt that McKeown had greatly overstated its importance. Of particular concern to critics of the nutrition hypothesis were the gaps in historical evidence. McKeown himself had freely conceded that the basic data were inadequate, but he had still believed that enough pieces existed to "cover the canvas" with a sketch or a comprehensive interpretation, the details of which could be filled in later as data and methodology improved. Not surprisingly, much of the research that countered his viewpoint addressed this evidential gap: Some offered differing interpretations of the sparse existing data, whereas others unearthed new evidence. Whatever the merits of McKeown's own arguments, there is no question that the debate he ignited over the role of nutrition in the modern decline of mortality was productive in that it defined the issues to be researched and spurred the search for new evidence.

Some critics were skeptical that an insufficient supply of food had been responsible for the high mortality rates in preindustrial societies. P. E. Razzell (1974), for example, questioned the food-supply hypothesis, citing the absence of a significant mortality differential between social classes. If nutrition was the critical factor, one would expect the aristocracy to enjoy lower mortality levels than the poor. Yet, in what came to be known as the "peerage paradox," he found that there was little difference in the mortality rates among the peerage and those of the laboring classes in England before 1725, and although presumably the poorer classes should have benefited more from any overall improvement in diet, the reduction in mortality after 1725 was greater among the aristocracy. Moreover, M. Livi-Bacci (1991) noted that in several other European countries as well, the aristocracy had not enjoyed any advantage in mortality over the lower classes. Furthermore, his examination of the European experience from the time of the Black Death to the era of industrialization led him to doubt whether nutritional improvement had shown any long-term interrelationship with mortality rates.

Other criticisms of the McKeown thesis were mainly directed against his underestimation of the role of public health. S. H. Preston and E. van de Walle (1978) concluded that, at least in France, water and sewage improvements had played a major role in urban mortality decline during the nineteenth century. Similarly, S. Szreter (1988) and A. Hardy (1993) argued that in England, preventive public-health initiatives had made significant contributions to the decline in prevalence and severity of a number of diseases, including smallpox, typhoid fever, typhus, and tuberculosis. In addition, purification of milk was thought specifically to have contributed to the fall in infant mortality (Beaver 1973).

McKeown's heavy reliance on English and Welsh data may also have caused him to overstate the case for nutrition. In an analysis of changes in mortality patterns among 165 populations, Preston (1976) pointed out that the English and Welsh experience was exceptional. Between 1851-60 and 1891-1900, decreased mortality from respiratory tuberculosis accounted for 44 percent of the drop in age- and sex-standardized death rates in England and Wales, whereas the normal reduction in other countries had been 11 to 12 percent. Similarly, a decrease in deaths from other infectious and parasitic diseases accounted for 48 percent of the mortality decline in England, compared to the standard 14 percent elsewhere. Preston (1976: 20) concluded that "the country with the most satisfactory early data appears to offer an atypical account of mortality decline, a record that may be largely responsible for prevailing representations of mortality reduction that stress the role of specific and readily identified infectious diseases of childhood and early adulthood."

During several decades of often heated debate over the nutrition hypothesis, virtually all aspects of McKeown's argument have been examined in great detail by critics and supporters alike. The points on which there is agreement after such prolonged and extensive investigation are certainly worth noting. That nutrition did play a role in the mortality decline is not disputed; the disagreement is over the magnitude of its contribution. Although McKeown was generally not receptive to criticisms of his thesis, in a later work (1988) he did acknowledge that the contribution of public-health measures had been greater than he had originally concluded. One important point of McKeown's that has survived intact is that specific therapeutic medical treatments had little impact on mortality reduction.

Generalizing the last point, some critics have commented that no single factor by itself – including nutrition – appears able to account for the mortality decline. Preston (1976) found that nutrition, as proxied by income levels, accounted for only about 20 percent of the fall in mortality between the 1930s and the 1960s. In fairness to McKeown, however, it should be noted that the period covered by Preston's study coincides with the era of antibiotics, whereas McKeown's arguments relied on the trends of mortality patterns before that time.

Diet versus Nutritional Status

In the debate over the role of nutrition in mortality decline, a great deal of confusion has been caused by differences in the ways the term "nutrition" has been understood and used by different investigators. Some have interpreted nutrition to mean food supply or diet, whereas others have followed epidemiologists or nutritionists by taking it to mean nutritional status, or net nutrition, which is the balance between the intake of nutrients and the claims against it. McKeown, the original proponent of the nutrition hypothesis used the term in both senses, although his writings indicate that he was aware of the difference between the two concepts. Lately, R. W. Fogel (1986, 1993, 1994) has suggested that when nutrition is mentioned in connection with food, the terms "diet" or "gross nutrition" be used. He advocated that the term "nutrition" itself be reserved for use in the sense of net nutrition – the balance of nutrients that becomes available for cellular growth – to avoid any further confusion.

There are clear advantages to adopting such a definition, not least of which is that it clarifies and suggests new avenues of research (as discussed shortly). However, as this new definition of nutrition is still not completely free of some pitfalls that could lead to further misunderstanding, it is worth considering in some detail what it actually means. That is, what are the determinants of nutritional intake, and what factors count as claims against that intake?

In a broad sense, nutritional intake may be taken to mean food supply, as has often been assumed in the debate over the historical role of nutrition. But complications exist even in the quantification of this relatively simple measure. Leaving aside the difficulty of obtaining reliable figures for gross food production in the past, one must also face the tricky issue of how to estimate the losses in nutrients that occur because of different, and often inefficient, food-storage, preparation, and preservation technologies.

These considerations, in turn, immediately suggest that quality, as well as quantity, is an important aspect of nutrition, a fact that may go far in explaining the peerage paradox. McKeown (1976) maintained that the peerage must have been eating unhealthy, or even infected, food, in which case the larger quantities they consumed could hardly be taken as grounds for expecting better health than that found among the lower classes. Fogel (1986) has also pointed out that toxic substances in the diet of the aristocrats, such as large quantities of salt and alcohol, would have had negative effects on their health and mortality. He has emphasized that the impact on the overall mortality rate of the peerage would have been especially large if it showed up mainly as high infant mortality, possibly because of adverse effects on the fetuses of mothers who apparently imbibed huge quantities of wine and ale on a daily basis. Moreover, Fogel has noted that the decline in infant and child mortality among the peerage after 1725 was paralleled by a gradual elimination of the toxic substances from the aristocratic diet between 1700 and 1900.

Another important way in which nutritional intake can be significantly influenced is through the presence of diseases that affect the body's ability to absorb nutrients. This ability can be measured as Atwater factors – food-specific rates at which the energy value of a person's food intake is transformed into metabolizable energy. Atwater factors are usually in the 90 to 95 percent range for healthy populations, but they can be as low as 80 percent among undernourished populations in which recurrent episodes of acute diarrhea may impair the absorption of nutrients (Molla et al. 1983).

Against the nutritional intake, all claims on nutrients must be deducted in order to arrive at the figure for nutritional status, or the balance that can be metabolized for cellular growth. The claims on nutrients can be broadly classified into three categories of energy expenditures: the energy required for basic maintenance of the body, the energy for occupational and discretionary activities, and the energy to fight infections. The first of these categories, basic maintenance, accounts for most of the body's energy usage and consists mainly of the Basal Metabolic Rate (BMR). BMR is the energy required to maintain body temperature and to sustain the normal functioning of organs, including heart and respiratory action. Roughly speaking, it is equivalent to the energy expended during rest or sleep and can be considered the default cost of survival in terms of energy.

Although there is some variation among individuals, BMR varies mainly by age, sex, and body weight. In particular, the association with body weight is strong enough that within any age/sex category, BMR can be predicted by a linear equation in body weight alone (WHO 1985). The BMR for an adult male, aged 20 to 39 and living in a moderate climate, ranges between 1,350 and 2,000 kilocalories (kcal) a day, which would amount to somewhere between 45 and 65 percent of his total daily energy intake. It should be noted that BMR does not allow for such basic survival activities as eating, digestion, and minimal personal hygiene.

Occupational and discretionary activities account for most, if not all, of the energy requirements beyond basic maintenance. Discretionary activities include walking, recreation, optional household tasks, and exercise. The pattern of energy expenditure among these categories will necessarily vary with individual activity patterns, which are influenced greatly by age, sex, occupation, culture, and technology. A World Health Organization (WHO) report (1985) estimated the energy requirements of a young male office clerk to be 1,310 kcal for basic maintenance (51 percent), 710 kcal for work (28 percent), and 560 kcal for discretionary activities (22 percent). The energy usage of a young subsistence farmer with a moderate work level in Papua New Guinea was given as 1,060 (40 percent), 1,230 (46 percent), and 390 (15 percent) kcal over the same expenditure categories. In yet another pattern of energy usage, a young housewife in an affluent society requires 1,400 (70 percent), 150 (8 percent), and 440 (22 percent) kcal, respectively.

The adverse effects of infections on nutrition go far beyond their impact on the body's ability to absorb nutrients. Fever directly increases metabolic demands, and the excess energy expenditure so induced by an infection therefore constitutes a separate, additional claim on nutrients. Other effects of infections that are similarly harmful include the loss of nutrients resulting from vomiting, diarrhea, reduced appetite, or restrictions on diet. For instance, R. Martorell and colleagues (1980) estimated that during an episode of diarrhea, the loss of total energy intake from reduced food intake alone can be as much as 40 percent. Malnutrition also has the effect of weakening the immune system and, thus, making the body more susceptible to infections, which can have further negative effects on nutrition in a deteriorating cycle.

The preceding discussion shows that nutritional balance is jointly determined by nutritional intake and various claims on that intake. Both intake and claims comprise a great range of factors, which appears to be broad enough to include almost every determinant of health and mortality. There is obviously a great difference between nutrition in the sense of diet and such a broadly inclusive concept as that of net nutrition. For some, it may seem natural to question whether the precision in the definition of nutritional status actually masks a vagueness in practical usability.

As a hypothetical example, suppose a new medical therapy is introduced that effectively cures a certain infectious disease, and that this therapy has the effect of substantially improving nutritional status by saving nutrients that would formerly have been lost to prolonged infection. If the overall result is a reduction in mortality, credit ought to go to the new medical treatment, but by definition, it can also be said that the lower death rate is the result of improved nutrition. Similarly, an effective public-health measure that lowers the prevalence of some infectious disease could still be considered a case in which improved nutrition leads to mortality decline.

Evidently the different causes of mortality decline can no longer be considered mutually exclusive when nutrition is defined as net nutrition, and it is no longer clear what to make of statements that compare the contribution of nutrition to that of medical treatment or public-health measures. This ambiguity is perhaps especially noticeable and problematic to those who continue to think about the role of nutrition in the context of the debate initiated by McKeown.

A related difficulty that follows from the new definition is that, even today, nutrition as a net balance is quite difficult to measure accurately. Estimating how nutritional status has changed throughout the past several centuries is even harder. In order to calculate claims against the intake of nutrients, the determinants of those claims – such as a population's body weight distribution (from which BMR is derived), its members' activity levels in work and leisure, and the prevalence, severity, and duration of infections suffered by them – all must be taken into account. Once again, the new definition does not appear to be very helpful for those interested in applying it directly to resolve issues raised by the nutrition hypothesis of mortality decline.

It should be noted, however, that ambiguity and difficulty of measurement are not problems newly introduced by the adoption of a definition of nutrition as net nutritional balance. Instead, the new definition serves to highlight the fact that the debate over the role of nutrition has lacked agreement on the exact meaning of nutrition. The view of nutrition as the balance between nutrient intake and energy expenditure also suggests that influences on health and longevity cannot be easily or even meaningfully sorted into discrete, measurable categories. Rather, health and mortality outcomes are now viewed as the joint result of several different processes that continually interact to determine health and aging.

In recent years, such a reassessment of the relationship between nutrition, health, and mortality has led some researchers, notably Fogel and his colleagues, to shift their focus away from the original debate over McKeown's nutrition hypothesis to other aspects of nutrition and mortality. The balance of this chapter briefly considers these new developments.

Anthropometric Measures

The difficulty of measuring or estimating nutritional status – especially with regard to the potential data deficiencies in historical research or in studies of developing countries – has prompted investigators to search for other measures that can be used as proxies for nutrition. Fortunately, there exists a class of measures that are comparatively easily observed (often even far back into the past) and are also known to be sensitive to variations in nutritional status. These are anthropometric measures, especially those of body height and body weight. Since weight is positively correlated to height, a measurement of weight-for-height is usually used, the most popular being the Body Mass Index (BMI), also known as the Quetelet index. It is derived as body weight in kilograms (kg) divided by the square of height in meters (m), or kg/m^2.

Height and BMI reflect different aspects of a person's nutritional experience. Adult height is an index that represents past cumulative net nutritional experience during growth. Studies in developing countries have shown that nutrition in early childhood, from birth to about age 5, is especially important in determining final adult height (Martorell 1985). Malnutrition among children of this age causes growth retardation, which is known as stunting. Although it is possible for some "catch-up" growth to occur later, this is unlikely to happen in an impoverished environment that was probably responsible for the malnourishment and stunting in the first place. BMI, in contrast, primarily reflects a person's current nutritional status. It varies directly with nutritional balance; a positive balance increases body mass, and a negative balance indicates that the body is drawing on its store of nutrients.

Interest in height and BMI as proxy measures for nutrition has, in the context of research on nutrition and mortality, naturally been directed to their association with morbidity and mortality. Although anthropometric measures had previously been used as predictors of the risks of morbidity and mortality for young children, H. Th. Waaler's (1984) large-scale study of Norwegian adults was among the first to show that height and weight could be used to predict morbidity and mortality risks for adults as well. When Waaler analyzed age- and sex-specific risks of dying by height classes among 1.8 million Norwegian adults between 1963 and 1979, he found that there was a stable relationship between adult height and mortality risk that could be characterized as a J-shaped curve. Within each age/sex group, mortality risk was highest among the shortest group of people and declined at a decreasing rate as height increased. This negative association between height and mortality risk has received much attention in historical research, which has sought to tie the increasing secular trends in the mean heights of different populations to parallel improving trends in their health and life expectancies (Fogel 1986; Floud, Wachter, and Gregory 1990; Komlos 1994; Steckel 1995).

Waaler also found a stable relationship between BMI and mortality risk, which can be characterized as a U-shaped curve. Risk is unresponsive to weight over a wide range, from about 20 to 28 BMI, but it increases sharply at either tail beyond that range. As historical data on weight distribution are harder to come by than data on height, little research making use of this risk–BMI relationship has yet been done. However, in an interesting development, some attempts have been made to use height and BMI simultaneously to predict mortality risk, rather than using each anthropometric measure separately (Fogel 1993, 1994; Kim 1996).

As height represents an individual's early nutrition and BMI his current nutritional status, the resulting height-weight-risk surface makes better use of all nutritional information than the height-risk or BMI-risk curves. Fogel (1994) used such a surface to suggest that the combined effect of increases in body height and weight among the French population can explain about 90 percent of the French mortality decline between 1785 and 1870, but only about 50 percent of the actual mortality decline since then. Another study, using a similar surface to track secular changes in height, weight, and the risks of old-age morbidity in the United States, also has found that factors other than height or BMI explain a larger share of elderly health improvement from 1982 to 1992 than during the period from 1910 to the early 1980s (Kim 1996).

In closing this chapter, it seems appropriate to devote a bit more attention to recent methodologies that may help to shed more light on the relationship between nutrition and mortality decline. For example, in addition to height and BMI, waist-to-hip ratio (WHR) is another anthropometric measure that has gained acceptance as a predictor of chronic diseases, especially for coronary heart disease and non-insulin-dependent diabetes mellitus (Bjorntorp 1992; Hodge and Zimmet 1994; Baumgartner, Heymsfield, and Roche 1995). Although BMI and WHR are generally correlated and are therefore both linked to the risk of chronic diseases associated with obesity, a weakness of BMI is that it does not indicate body composition such as lean body mass versus total body fat, nor is it indicative of the distribution of fat within the body.

By contrast, WHR, as a measure of central adiposity, has been found in a number of studies to have predictive power independent of BMI. J. M. Sosenko and colleagues (1993) have reported that WHR was significantly higher among diabetic women and also among men (although not as markedly as among women), whereas BMI failed to differentiate between diabetics and nondiabetics. Similarly, A. R. Folsom and colleagues (1994) examined Chinese men and women aged 28 to 69 from both urban and rural areas and found that abdominal adiposity – represented by an elevated WHR – was independently associated with cardiovascular risk factors. Although BMI was also associated in a similar direction with most of these risk factors, the mean level of BMI in this study was relatively low, ranging from 20.1 to 21.9 among 4 sex- and age-groups, confirming that WHR is useful as a predictor of cardiovascular disease even among a lean Asian population. S. P. Walker and colleagues (1996) found in a five-year follow-up study of 28,643 U.S. male health professionals that BMI was only weakly associated with stroke risk, but that WHR was a much better predictor even when BMI, height, and other potential risk factors were taken into account. Yet although these studies suggest that there is a strong case for using WHR in conjunction with or perhaps as a substitute for BMI, it should be remembered that data on BMI are often more easily obtained or reasonably estimated, making BMI useful as a predictor or proxy for health or nutritional status in studies involving historical populations or in other situations in which detailed anthropometric data are lacking.

The preceding discussion on the role of adult height as a predictor of morbidity and mortality in middle or old age, combined with the theory that nutrition during the very early stages of life is a major determinant of adult height, suggests the possibility

that the roots of some later-in-life diseases can be found very early in life, and intriguing research carried out by D. J. P. Barker and others (Barker 1993, 1994) has made this possibility seem a probability. In focusing on events surrounding birth for explanations of diseases in later life, Barker and his colleagues located United Kingdom birth records from Hertfordshire, Sheffield, and Preston, all of which contained detailed information on the infants. The Hertfordshire records covered births between 1911 and 1930 and included birth weight, weight at 1 year of age, number of teeth, and other details. The records from Sheffield and Preston covered roughly the same period but were even more detailed, and their inclusion of length from crown to heel, head circumference, biparietal and other head diameters, placental weight, and (after 1922) chest and abdominal circumferences allowed the computation of various body proportions. Linking these birth records with those still surviving as adults and with the records of those who had since died made it possible to investigate any relationship between at-birth measurements and health events in later life.

This research, compactly summarized by Barker (1994), has uncovered numerous associations between various birth measurements and disease in later life, including hypertension, excessive levels of blood cholesterol, non-insulin-dependent diabetes, and death rates from cardiovascular disease. Among men, low birth weight and weight at 1 year of age were associated with premature death from cardiovascular disease. Females whose weight was low at birth but above average as adults also experienced increased death rates. Other measurements at birth that indicate slow fetal growth have also been found to predict higher death rates from cardiovascular disease. These include thinness (as measured by the ponderal index – birth weight/length^3), small head circumference, short length, low abdominal circumference relative to head size, and a high placental-weight-to-birth-weight ratio. As slow growth in utero is often followed by slow growth afterward, these findings suggest one pathway through which nutrition, adult height, and mortality in old age may be related (cf. Barker, Osmond, and Golding 1990).

From birth records linked to survivors rather than to death records, Barker and his colleagues were also able to analyze the connection between measurements at birth and chronic diseases or their risk factors among the survivors. Babies who were small for date or with a higher ratio of placental weight to birth weight, both of which indicate undernutrition in utero, were found to have higher systolic and diastolic blood pressure as children and as adults. These findings were independent of, or dominated, the effects of the later-life environment, including the current weight, alcohol consumption, and salt intake of the subjects. The blood pressure of the mother was also found to be a nonfactor. Reduced liver size, as measured by abdominal circumference, was associated with raised serum concentrations of total and LDL cholesterol levels in both men and women. Based on these findings, Barker has suggested that impaired liver growth in late gestation may permanently alter the body's LDL cholesterol metabolism, resulting in an increased risk of coronary heart disease later in life. In both men and women, low birth weight predicted higher rates of non-insulin-dependent diabetes and impaired glucose tolerance.

British birth records have also been useful in establishing a link between infectious disease in childhood and chronic disease in later life. A follow-up study of men from the Hertfordshire records, which recorded illnesses periodically throughout infancy and early childhood, showed that death rates from chronic bronchitis were higher among those who had low birth weights and low weights at 1 year of age (Barker et al. 1991). In addition, S. O. Shaheen and colleagues (1995) have reported that among survivors represented in the Hertfordshire and Derbyshire records, men who had suffered bronchitis or pneumonia in infancy had significantly impaired lung function as measured by mean FEV_1 (forced expiratory volume in one second). These findings support the hypothesis that lower-respiratory-tract infections in early childhood lead to chronic obstructive pulmonary disease in late adult life.

The relationship of maternal (and thus fetal) nutrition – and that of infants – with diseases of later life was one, of course, that McKeown did not examine. That such a relationship seems to exist is one more powerful example of the complex nature of nutrition on the one hand and mortality on the other.

John M. Kim

Bibliography

Barker, D. J. P. 1994. *Mothers, babies, and diseases in later life.* London.

 ed. 1993. *Fetal and infant origins of adult disease.* London.

Barker, D. J. P., K. M. Godfrey, C. Fall, et al. 1991. Relation of birthweight and childhood respiratory infection to adult lung function and death from chronic obstructive airways disease. *British Medical Journal* 303: 671–5.

Barker, D. J. P., and C. Osmond. 1986. Infant mortality, child nutrition, and ischaemic heart disease in England and Wales. *Lancet* 1986i: 1077–81.

Barker, D. J. P., C. Osmond, and J. Golding. 1990. Height and mortality in the counties of England and Wales. *Annals of Human Biology* 17: 1–6.

Baumgartner, R. N., S. B. Heymsfield, and A. F. Roche. 1995. Human body composition and the epidemiology of chronic disease. *Obesity Research* 3: 73–95.

Beaver, M. W. 1973. Population, infant mortality, and milk. *Population Studies* 27: 243–54.

Bjorntorp, P. 1992. Abdominal fat distribution and disease: An overview of epidemiological data. *Annals of Medicine* 24: 15–18.

Floud, R., K. Wachter, and A. Gregory. 1990. *Height, health, and history.* Cambridge.

Fogel, R. W. 1986. Nutrition and the decline in mortality since 1700. In *Long-term factors in American economic growth,* ed. S. L. Engerman and R. E. Gallman, 439–555. Chicago.

 1993. New sources and new techniques for the study of secular trends in nutritional status, health, mortality, and the process of aging. *Historical Methods* 26: 5–43.

 1994. Economic growth, population theory, and physiology: The bearing of long-term processes on the making of economic policy. *American Economic Review* 84: 369–95.

Folsom, A. R., Y. Li, X. Rao, et al. 1994. Body mass, fat distribution and cardiovascular risk factors in a lean population of South China. *Journal of Clinical Epidemiology* 47: 173–81.

Hardy, A. 1993. *The epidemic streets: Infectious disease and the rise of preventive medicine, 1856–1900.* Oxford.

Higgs, R. 1973. Mortality in rural America, 1870–1920: Estimates and conjectures. *Explorations in Economic History* 10: 177–95.

 1979. Cycles and trends of mortality in eighteen large American cities, 1871–1900. *Explorations in Economic History* 16: 381–408.

Hodge, A. M., and P. Z. Zimmet. 1994. The epidemiology of obesity. *Baillieres Clinical Endocrinology and Metabolism* 8: 577–99.

Kim, J. M. 1996. The economics of nutrition, body build, and health: Waaler surfaces and physical human capital. Ph.D. dissertation, University of Chicago.

Komlos, J., ed. 1994. *Stature, living standards, and economic development: Essays in anthropometric history.* Chicago and London.

Livi-Bacci, M. 1991. *Population and nutrition: An essay on European demographic history,* trans. Tania Croft-Murray. Cambridge and New York.

Martorell, R. 1985. Child growth retardation: A discussion of its causes and its relationship to health. In *Nutritional adaptation in man,* ed. K. Blaxter and J. C. Waterlow, 13–30. London.

Martorell, R., C. Yarbrough, S. Yarbrough, and R. E. Klein. 1980. The impact of ordinary illnesses on the dietary intakes of malnourished children. *American Journal of Clinical Nutrition* 33: 345–50.

McKeown, T. 1976. *The modern rise of population.* New York.

 1979. *The role of medicine.* Princeton, N.J.

 1988. *The origins of human disease.* Oxford.

McKeown, T., and R. G. Brown. 1955. Medical evidence related to English population changes in the eighteenth century. *Population Studies* 9: 119–41.

McKeown, T., R. G. Brown, and R. Record. 1972. An interpretation of the modern rise of population in Europe. *Population Studies* 26: 345–82.

McKinlay, J., and S. McKinlay. 1977. The questionable contribution of medical measures to the decline of mortality in the twentieth century. *Milbank Memorial Fund Quarterly* 55: 405–28.

Meeker, E. 1972. The improving health of the United States, 1850–1915. *Explorations in Economic History* 9: 353–73.

Molla, A., A. M. Molla, S. A. Sarker, and M. Khatun. 1983. Whole-gut transit time and its relationship to absorption of macronutrients during diarrhoea and after recovery. *Scandinavian Journal of Gastroenterology* 18: 537–43.

Preston, S. H. 1976. *Mortality patterns in national populations.* New York.

Preston, S. H., and E. van de Walle. 1978. Urban French mortality in the nineteenth century. *Population Studies* 32: 275-97.

Razzell, P. E. 1974. An interpretation of the modern rise of population in Europe: A critique. *Population Studies* 28: 5-17.

Shaheen, S. O., D. J. P. Barker, and S. T. Holgate. 1995. Do lower respiratory tract infections in early childhood cause chronic obstructive pulmonary disease? *American Journal of Respiratory and Critical Care Medicine* 151: 1649-51.

Sosenko, J. M., M. Kato, R. Soto, and R. B. Goldberg. 1993. A comparison of adiposity measures for screening non-insulin dependent diabetes mellitus. *International Journal of Obesity and Related Metabolic Disorders* 17: 441-4.

Steckel, R. H. 1995. Stature and the standard of living. *Journal of Economic Literature* 33: 1903-40.

Szreter, S. 1988. The importance of social intervention in Britain's mortality decline, c. 1850-1914. A reinterpretation of the role of public health. *Social History of Medicine* 1: 1-37.

UN (United Nations). 1953. *The determinants and consequences of population trends.* New York.

　　1973. *The determinants and causes of population trends.* New York.

Waaler, H. Th. 1984. Height, weight, and mortality: The Norwegian experience. *Acta Medica Scandinavica* 679 (Supplement): 1-51.

Walker, S. P., E. B. Rimm, A. Ascherio, et al. 1996. Body size and fat distribution as predictors of stroke among US men. *American Journal of Epidemiology* 144: 1143-50.

WHO (World Health Organization). 1985. *Energy and protein requirements.* Technical Report Series, No. 724. Geneva.

VI.2 ❧ Nutrition and Mortality Decline: Another View

The importance of nutrition to the preservation of human health cannot be reasonably denied. However, the extent of its power may have been overstated in recent years. For millions of Americans, "natural foods and vitamins" are seen as almost magical preservers of health, beauty, and longevity. Indeed, claims for the healing properties of nutrients have become an integral part of the post–World War II "baby-boomer" generation's vision of the world. For many, "faith" in the power of proper nutrition is part of a secular religion that comes close to denying the inevitability of aging and death. Vitamin C is considered a panacea one day and beta-carotene the next, as are such foods as broccoli and garlic. With such a cornucopia of natural "medicines," who would ever think that the history of humankind would reveal so much disease and ill health?

Although such popular exaggerations of the benefits of various nutriments are easily dismissed by serious scholars, other more scholarly claims are not. One suggestion dealing with the historical importance of nutrition has received remarkably widespread support in academic circles and, among historians, has become the orthodox explanation for understanding a key aspect of the modern world: increased longevity.

The McKeown Thesis

The classic formulation of this explanation was provided by the medical historian Thomas McKeown (1976, 1979), who argued that the reasons for the decline of mortality in the Western world over the last three hundred years have been largely the result of rising living standards, especially increased and improved nutrition. Equally important, the decline was not the result, as so many had rather vaguely believed, of any purposeful medical or public-health interventions.

Such a theory, of course, was not long confined to historical debates because of its clear policy implications for the allocation of resources in the developing (and the developed) world today. If the historical decline of mortality in the West occurred independently of science and medicine, then the high death rates in the developing world could best be combated by vigorously pursuing higher living and nutritional standards. Not only was money expended on high-technology hospitals and doctors ill spent, but even funds for immunization campaigns were a waste of limited resources. As McKeown put it: "If a choice must be made, free school meals are more important for the health of poor children than immunization programmes, and both are more effective than hospital beds" (McKeown 1979).

This revolutionary theory has a number of emotional and intellectual attractions. First, it constitutes a devastating attack on the legitimacy and claims of societal "authority," represented in this case by the medical profession and, to a lesser extent, the public-health and scientific establishments. The "experts" who claim the right to guide and control society and its inhabitants, based upon their past accomplishments, are revealed as self-deluded, if not as outright frauds. Such a critical position resonates very well in an era characterized by relentless attacks on all types of authority and one in which the delegitimization of social institutions is a daily affair.

What radical social critic could have better put what many regard as an imperious medical profession in its place than McKeown, who wrote (in an attempt to dispel the "erroneous belief" that he was hostile to the medical profession): ". . . if medical intervention is often less effective than most people, including doctors, believe, there is also a need . . . for greater emphasis on personal care of the sick (the pastoral role of the doctor) . . ." (McKeown 1979: ix). (Later in the same work [p. 112], he stated that the key advance in personal medical interventions in the past was the control of cavities by the dental profession.)

Second, McKeown's view of the nature of health is also very congenial to the post–World War II generation's view of life, death, and aging: "Most diseases, including the common ones, are not inevitable. . . . [Modern medicine is based on a different idea.] It assumes we are ill and must be made well, whereas it is nearer to the truth to say that we are well and are made ill" (McKeown 1979: 117–18). In addition, his work has an appeal to earlier generations, especially his claim that persons in their 70s who lived a healthy life would be as vigorous and capable as they were in their 30s! What the thesis seems to promise is eternal youth, if not eternal life, completely under the control of the careful and concerned individual without the messy intervention of doctors and other self-proclaimed experts. Such a view, when coupled with impressive scholarship, is very persuasive by itself, and the fact that the medical profession had indeed severely exaggerated its performance historically has also made it easier for many to embrace the argument.

Third, the McKeown thesis can be and has been profitably used by people representing a wide variety of political and ideological positions. In the West, it can be aimed at established authority figures in attempts to delegitimize basic Western institutions. The supposed accomplishments of science, medicine, and the public-health service, which bolster the West's claims to superiority as a civilization, can be denied.

For leftists in the developing world, the McKeown thesis could free their countries from dependence on Western medical and scientific expertise and technology. Better a homegrown political upheaval with land redistribution than a measles shot or a CAT scan machine. Since good health is promised as a natural by-product of a rising standard of living and better nutrition, its eventuality depends on radical politics, not on "imperialistic" science or medicine (Muraskin 1995).

But the Right also has had reasons to be attracted to the McKeown thesis, which lends support to deemphasizing expensive medical care for the "masses," both at home and abroad. If medicine and technology are not the key to lower mortality, why waste money on them in a time of escalating, and certainly threatening, medical costs? If the poor are underserved by doctors, maybe they are better off than their richer neighbors who are plagued by ineffective medical personnel and their iatrogenic interventions.

Despite the appeal of the McKeown thesis to so many political sectors, there are a number of reasons for criticism, not the least among them that McKeown reached his conclusion about the importance of nutrition in the mortality decline through the process of elimination of possible alternatives. If all the other possibilities are false, then the last standing explanation is the correct one.

Almost all of those who have questioned McKeown's argument have been struck by this methodology. For such a procedure to be effective, it is mandatory that all possible alternatives be presented and adequately explored. But this is impossible because history, science, and medicine are full of unknowns. Thus, although such a procedure may be suggestive and help generate a useful hypothesis, strong direct evidence must be presented to make an adequate case.

McKeown postulated that there were only five possible reasons for the decline of mortality in the West:

1. Medical intervention (including immunizations).
2. Public-health measures (for example, better sanitation, water purification, and food hygiene).
3. Changes in the nature and virulence of microorganisms.
4. Reduced contact with microorganisms.
5. Increased and improved nutrition.

He then proceeded to argue that until recently, it was assumed that "medical" interventions were the primary cause of increased life expectancy. This term, however, tended to include both personal medical care and public-health policies – two types of activities that must be separated for purposes of analysis.

The main thrust of his argument was aimed at the claims of personal medical care. He demonstrated that the decline in mortality was well advanced long before medical science developed effective forms of disease therapy or prevention. His proofs were elaborate and rather convincing. Unquestionably, McKeown has clearly, and probably permanently, deflated the claim that personal medical care played a major role in increasing longevity in the West. But such a claim could exist only because of the ahistorical nature of most public discourse in the West.

If most laypeople and doctors felt that modern medicine had performed miracles, very few of them, if challenged, would have insisted that medicine's effectiveness went back much before the advent of antibiotics in the 1940s or sulphonamides in the 1930s. Although there were great scientific minds, like Robert Koch or Louis Pasteur, in the late nineteenth century, there was no adequate control over infectious diseases. For most, modern medicine was probably viewed as so miraculous specifically because the nineteenth century (and the first third of the twentieth century) was seen as so bleak and unhealthy. Thus, McKeown's debunking of a tendency to view earlier medicine with lenses of the present was, in fact, an easy victory.

His larger thesis, however, required similar attacks on other possible causes of mortality decline. He disposed of the importance of immunizations (which he grouped with personal medical care rather than public-health activities) by arguing, on the one hand, that they occurred significantly later than the decline in mortality for the various diseases they were created to treat[1] and, on the other hand, that vaccinations did little or no good in the absence of better nutrition.

He gave considerably more credit for the lowering of mortality to public-health measures, especially clean water and safe food, than he gave to personal medical care, but as with immunizations, he argued that these measures were put in place long after mortality had already significantly declined.

McKeown next considered the possibility that a decline in the natural virulence of microorganisms or a decrease in exposure of the general population to dangerous pathogens led to the decline of mortality in the West. His discussion of these possibilities, however, was far more cursory than his argument about the ineffectiveness of personal medical care. In short, his convincing argument against much of a role for clinical medicine in the improvement of life expectancy did not carry over into an analysis of the other possibilities he set forth. Thus, one could argue that McKeown presented a fascinating and stimulating hypothesis that somehow came to be understood as an established truth.

Attacks on the McKeown Thesis

One of the most interesting assaults on the credibility of the McKeown thesis originated with a Danish anthropologist, Dr. Peter Aaby. His extensive research on measles mortality in Guinea-Bissau, West Africa, provided a unique opportunity for such an attack because McKeown used the World Health Organization's (WHO) position on measles to support his argument for the importance of nutrition over immunization in the decline of mortality. McKeown (citing WHO) claimed that vaccination of an underfed child is not protective, whereas a well-nourished child does not need vaccination to survive the disease. In other words, another bowl of rice is preferable to a measles shot.

Aaby claimed to have shared such a view until his discoveries in Guinea-Bissau no longer supported it. He wrote that there are three general ways of looking at measles mortality:

1. Emphasizing "host factors" (malnutrition, age of infection, genetics).
2. Emphasizing "transmission factors" (greater exposure, more virulent strains, synergism between infections).
3. Emphasizing "treatment and medical care factors" (ineffective treatment or neglect of effective treatments). (Aaby 1992: 155–6)

Certainly, most of the emphasis has been on host factors. In the case of measles, which kills about one and half million children a year in the developing world, "[t]hose who die are seen as somehow weaker than other individuals," and "severe measles has been explained particularly with reference to [host factors such as] malnutrition, the age at infection, genetic susceptibility and underlying disease" (Aaby 1992: 156).

Such an interpretation, Aaby maintained, easily leads to the implication that severe measles is a disease of the weak who are on the road to death, if not from this disease then from another. The implication for policy is that little is accomplished by immunization because of the phenomenon of "replacement mortality." Thus, the solution to preventing death from measles is not to fight the disease but to fight general malnutrition. Clearly, this is a position strongly supportive of McKeown's own view.

Aaby, however, found that the situation in Guinea-Bissau was not so supportive. The children who died were not noticeably different in nutritional level from those who survived. Moreover, the general level of nutrition in the country was quite adequate – better, in fact, than in countries (such as Bangladesh) with much lower rates of mortality from measles. Instead of nutrition, according to Aaby, the factor differentiating those who died and those who did not was whether the child was an "index case" or a "secondary case" in a family.

Index cases (the first persons infected) were usually exposed outside the home. By contrast, secondary cases were usually the siblings of those index cases who had brought the infection into the home. The difference in mortality risk between the two groups was striking, with secondary cases much more likely to succumb to the illness. The apparent reason for the disparity was that the index cases had experienced much less exposure to the virus (contracted in social interactions outside the home) than the secondary cases – who were continuously exposed by actually living with an infected sibling. The key, according to Aaby, was not nutritional status in the face of measles, but rather the degree of exposure to the illness.

Aaby also compared rates of measles mortality between different countries. He found that Bangladesh had significantly lower rates than Guinea-Bissau despite poorer levels of nutrition. But in Guinea-Bissau, fully 61 percent of the children under 3 years old were secondary cases (with the case fatality rate [CFR] a horrifying 25 percent), whereas in Bangladesh, secondary cases were only 14 percent, and the CFR was 3 percent.

The reason proposed for the extreme variance was that "[l]arger families and a high incidence of polygamy mean[t] that children in West Africa h[ad] a much greater risk of becoming secondary cases . . ." because there were large numbers of young, susceptible siblings living at home (Aaby 1992: 160). This factor also seemed to account for the lower mortality rates Aaby found among East Africans when compared to West Africans – that is to say there were fewer wives and fewer children in East Africa.

In addition, Aaby observed that the severity or mildness of the disease in the index case correlated with the likelihood of mortality and secondary cases. In other words, the more severe the index case, the higher the rate of death in secondary cases; and the milder the index case, the lower the death rate of subsequent cases. There also seemed to be an "amplification phenomenon" in which severe cases brought into a household (or institution or military camp) created waves of infection, each more severe than the last.

The Guinea-Bissau research also uncovered other unexpected transmission factors that correlated with significantly higher levels of measles mortality. The most surprising finding was that infection by a member of the opposite sex produced a noticeably greater chance of death than infection by someone of the same gender. Studies in other developing countries have found a similar cross-gender transmission factor, and Aaby, doing historical research, discovered that such a situation existed in Copenhagen at the turn of the twentieth century (Aaby 1992: 162).

In addition, this concentration on transmission factors, rather than host factors, brought to light a "delayed impact," which constitutes a long-term measles effect. Most studies deal with acute measles death (that is to say within one month of the appearance of the rash). But in Guinea-Bissau, "children who had been exposed to measles at home during the first six months of their lives had a mortality [rate] between ages six months and five years which was three times higher than community controls (34 percent vs. 11 percent)" (Aaby 1992: 164).

When background factors were taken into account, "the mortality hazards ratio was 5.7 times higher . . . among the exposed children than the controls" (Aaby 1992: 164). The "delayed excess mortality" existed both among children who had measles and among those without clinical symptoms. In light of this finding, it seems possible that the total mortality from measles infection is far higher in the developing world than is assumed.

Aaby has speculated on the possible meanings of this delayed mortality. One is "some form of persistent infection and immuno-suppression" at work. In addition, community studies in Nigeria, Guinea-Bissau, Senegal, Zaire, Bangladesh, and Haiti have shown that children immunized against measles have experienced major drops in overall mortality in the years after vaccination:

> In all studies the reduction in mortality was greater than expected from the direct contribution of measles death to over all mortality. For example, in Bangladesh, the reduction in mortality between 10 and 60 months of age was 36% although measles accounted only for 4% of all deaths among the controls . . . Thus measles immunization seems to be highly effective in preventing both acute and delayed mortality from the disease. (Aaby 1992: 167)

Aaby believed that what he learned from Guinea-Bissau and other developing countries sheds light on the historical decline of mortality in the West. He suggested that transmission factors, rather than improved nutrition (or age of infection), can best account for the decline of measles mortality in the developed world. In summing up his detailed argument he wrote:

> It seems likely that the most important causes of measles mortality decline were social changes which diminished the risk of intensive exposure within the family. Chief among these were the fall in family size [that is to say fewer susceptible siblings at home to infect] and greater social contact among young children which increased the risk [and benefits] of infection outside the home. Furthermore, the continual reduction in the numbers of fatal cases has reduced the risk of transmission of measles in a severe form [and thus eliminated the amplification effect]. (Aaby 1992: 170–1)

This conceptualization of the decline of measles mortality in terms of transmission rather than nutrition, Aaby believed, provides a model that can be used for other diseases as well. For example, he maintained that McKeown severely underestimated the importance of smallpox vaccination to the decline of mortality in the West, and he suggested that smallpox (which struck the well nourished and malnourished alike) may have had the same kind of delayed mortality effect as measles. Thus, people weakened by smallpox may have been more vulnerable to tuberculosis (TB) or other diseases. He speculated that the decline of smallpox may have led the way to the decline of TB, and the latter, McKeown maintained, was the key to the decline of mortality in the developed world (Aaby 1992: 178).

The significance for us of Aaby's work is that transmission factors such as severity of exposure, size of family, cross-sex infection, and delayed mortality were not discussed and then successfully eliminated by McKeown's analysis. Thus, it would seem that whether Aaby is right or wrong about other diseases, or even about the decline of measles in the West, he has made the point that McKeown's nutrition thesis is vulnerable and, perhaps, has been embraced too readily.

A second attack was made by Simon Szreter, a specialist in British history, who challenged McKeown's work not simply on its relevance to other countries but even on its accuracy for Great Britain. He stated his thesis very succinctly:

> It will be urged that the public health movement working through local government, rather than nutritional improvements through rising living standards, should be seen as the true moving force behind the decline of mortality in [the late nineteenth century]. (Szreter 1988: 2)

Szreter pointed out that although McKeown explicitly recognized the positive role that hygiene improvements in public-health measures involving municipal sanitation played in saving lives, he nevertheless maintained that "their impact and effects were . . . very much of a secondary and merely reinforcing kind" (Szreter 1988: 3) compared to better nutrition. It is interesting to note that Szreter believed that the effect of McKeown's emphasis on nutrition and his "devastating case against the pretension of the 'technocratic' section of the post-war medical profession" has led to the belief that "organized human agency in general had remarkably little to do with the historical decline of mortality in Britain . . ."(Szreter 1988: 3).[2]

This belief, in turn, led Szreter to criticize McKeown for his failure to carefully assess "the *independent* role of those socio-political developments which were responsible for such hard-won improvements as those in working conditions, housing, education, and various health services" (Szreter 1988: 11). Moreover, given McKeown's emphasis on the role of food it might have been expected that he would look closely at the history of the fight against food adulteration, but he did not. Rather, McKeown treated political, social, and cultural changes that were also arguably important in the mortality decline as a simple "automatic corollary of changes in a country's per capita real income" (Szreter 1988: 11).

According to Szreter, though, in the last third of the nineteenth century, after the "heroic age" of public-health activism in Britain had ended without much success on the national level, countless underpaid and overworked officials fought bitterly but successfully for better sanitation and increased disease prevention at the local level. There was nothing automatic about either their struggles or their victories – though historians, said Szreter, have missed the importance of such activities by focusing on the apparent ineffectiveness of the *national* sanitation reform movement during the middle decades of the nineteenth century and the decline of that movement after 1871 (Szreter 1988: 21–5).

McKeown, however, contended that the key to the decline of mortality in Britain was the decline of TB, which is caused by an airborne pathogen that does not respond to public-health measures but does respond to improved nutrition, and that, in any event, the decline of the disease predated effective medical or public-health measures. In addition, he alleged that TB was in decline before most other major diseases. This chronology is important, because if TB declined after public-health interventions, or if other diseases declined first, then those previous events, rather than improved nutrition, might account for the fall in TB mortality.

McKeown claimed that TB declined in Britain from 1838 onward (that is to say quite early). However, Szreter contended that there was actually a fluctuation in TB mortality, which rose once more after 1850 and did not decline again until after 1866–7. Moreover, Szreter, like Aaby, pointed out that smallpox mortality had declined considerably earlier than TB; thus,

even if tuberculosis had started to decline as early as 1838, McKeown would still have underestimated the possible effects of that prior decline on tuberculosis mortality (Szreter 1988: 15).

In addition, McKeown placed his emphasis on the decline in airborne diseases (as opposed to water- and foodborne diseases) because airborne diseases were not amenable to public-health interventions. Thus, their decline would seem to indicate an alternative source of amelioration. However, the airborne disease category that McKeown highlighted included not only TB, which did decline, but also a composite group – bronchitis, pneumonia, and influenza – that constituted the second most important cause of death in the mid–nineteenth century. That group of airborne diseases *increased* until after 1901, becoming the single most common cause of death and a greater killer than TB had been in 1850 (Szreter 1988: 13).

According to Szreter, one of the major effects of dividing the airborne diseases into two categories – TB and bronchitis/pneumonia/influenza – is that when the increased mortality of the latter group is set against the lower mortality of the former, it leaves the decline in food- and waterborne diseases as the most important reason for the decline of mortality, which does not support McKeown's argument. Yet Szreter pointed out that the almost complete elimination of smallpox, cholera, and typhoid during the late nineteenth century is proof of the effectiveness of public-health interventions, and that the rise of mortality for the bronchitis/pneumonia/influenza group "may well be evidence that in those areas . . . where preventive legislation and action was *not* forthcoming," problems occurred (Szreter 1988: 27). It is significant that clean air was an issue neglected by Victorian reformers, and the resulting urban smog probably goes far to help explain the high incidence of respiratory disease.

Szreter also indicated that infants did not benefit from the late-nineteenth-century decline of mortality in Britain; yet, after 1901, infant mortality fell rapidly. This reduction of infant mortality required the intervention of social services and the willingness of families to allow middle-class social workers to enter homes to instruct in hygienic food preparation (Szreter 1988: 28–31).

Thus, for Szreter, "[t]he invisible hand of rising living standards, conceived as an impersonal and ultimately inevitable by-product of general economic development, no longer takes the leading role as historical guarantor of the nation's mortality decline" (Szreter 1988: 34–5).

A third attack on the McKeown thesis comes from Leonard Wilson, an American historian. If Szreter argued that McKeown exaggerated the significance of the decline in TB mortality, Wilson directly challenged McKeown on the reason for TB's decline, which Wilson attributed not to improved nutrition but rather to segregation of those who had the disease.

In support of his position, Wilson highlighted a fact

that exposes one of the more glaring weaknesses in McKeown's argument: Tuberculosis was widespread among persons of the upper classes, who were, of course, the most likely to be well nourished. McKeown, however, claimed that despite adequate nutrition, their defenses were overwhelmed by constant contact with the lower classes – among whom the bacteria was ubiquitous. Wilson pointed out that the problem with this line of reasoning is that it acknowledges that the key to infection for the upper classes was their degree of exposure, which is one of the possible alternatives to the theory of improving nutrition (Wilson 1990). Thus, at the very least, the McKeown thesis turns out to be a dual theory of the decline of TB: a nutrition theory for the poor and an exposure theory for the rich, which seems to render the nutrition thesis considerably less persuasive.

The thesis that Wilson advanced is that the decline of TB mortality was closely linked to the degree to which individuals with TB were segregated during the periods they were most infectious. He argued that in Great Britain the provision of poor relief in workhouses (rather than at home) and the establishment of sanatoria led to a decline in the TB death rate compared to other societies that allowed infectious individuals to live freely in the community in close contact with their families. He contended that McKeown underestimated the importance of these segregating institutions because most individuals spent only limited time in them, and they did not cure individuals with the disease. But Wilson suggested that some segregation, although less helpful than a lot of separation, was still better than none and was sufficient to account for the declining mortality rate. The failure to cure tubercular individuals, although a tragedy for them, was less important than preventing transmission to others.

To test this thesis, Wilson compared the experience of a number of countries and ethnic groups. He found, for example, that Ireland experienced both declining food prices and rising incomes in the years after 1870, but experienced no significant decline in TB mortality.

Yet during the same period, Ireland did enjoy a decline in the typhus death rate, which no one claims was nutritionally related. Typhus-infected individuals were segregated and the contagion was controlled. By contrast, tuberculosis victims, after being reduced to poverty, as were almost all TB victims, were given home relief, which allowed them to live surrounded by family members whom they continued to infect. But in England, in contrast to Ireland, relief was restricted to poor-law infirmaries and workhouses, which kept infectious individuals out of the community and away from their families during the period when they were most intensively infectious. Those segregating institutions also taught the infected how to dispose of their sputum and lower the danger of spreading the infection when they were again free to go home (Wilson 1990: 384).

According to Wilson, before the advent of antibiotics, the segregation of contagious individuals was a necessity if diseases like TB or typhus were to be controlled. He pointed out that leprosy also declined, in both England and continental Europe, with the isolation of lepers. An exception, however, was Norway, where lepers were not segregated, and there the disease not only failed to decline but actually increased during the nineteenth century (Wilson 1990: 384–5).

Wilson accused McKeown of dismissing the importance of the discoveries of Koch and others in the decline of tuberculosis mortality because no therapies came out of those scientific breakthroughs for generations. Such a view, he asserted, ignores the fact that many nations and municipalities instituted segregation and isolation procedures soon after the cause of TB was discovered. For example, in New York City after 1889, the Health Department emphasized the danger of contagion and pushed for sanitary disposal of sputum, disinfection of rooms, and the opening of special hospitals for TB patients. Vigorous policing helped maintain the long and steady decline of tuberculosis in the city from 1882 to 1918, at which point three large TB hospitals were built.

Thus, Wilson argued that the decline in tuberculosis was not the result of a rising standard of living but rather of reduced opportunities for patients to spread the infection, and he pointed out that the recognition of the importance of segregation came directly from Koch's discoveries (Wilson 1990: 381).

In another study by Wilson, this time of tuberculosis in Minnesota, he was able to look directly at the effect of standard of living on the decline of the disease and to test the relationship between nutrition (or at least standard of living) and TB in a kind of "natural laboratory" which existed in that state.

For many decades, Minnesota had the reputation of having a remarkably healthy climate – with a very low tuberculosis rate. This changed as European immigrants reached the state, many of them suffering from the disease. The Irish immigrants had the highest rate – in keeping with conditions in their native land, where home relief allowed ill individuals to remain with their families. In Minnesota, the Irish still continued to live at home if infected and, consequently, infected their relatives. Scandinavian immigrants also had high rates of tuberculosis, as did the countries from which they came. However, German immigrants had a low rate of TB, similar to conditions in their homeland.

These different groups settled in Minneapolis, where their social and economic conditions were remarkably uniform. There was no major difference in their standard of living, only in their TB rates, which reflected their countries of origin, not their current conditions. What ultimately brought those rates down for the Irish and Scandinavians was not better food and housing but the decision to build sanatoria and segregate infectious individuals (Wilson 1992).

Thus, Wilson argued, McKeown ignored the key role played by public-health measures in lowering the TB death rate by finding the source of infection and working to prevent its transmission. Going beyond Szreter, Wilson suggested that medical men, from Koch down to doctors in the sanatoria, were vital elements in this process.[3]

The scholarly articles of Wilson, Szreter, and Aaby go a long way toward a successful undermining of the claims that McKeown has made about the pivotal role of nutrition in the decline of mortality in the West. Their arguments have been significantly advanced by the publication of Anne Hardy's book, *The Epidemic Streets: Infectious Disease and the Rise of Preventive Medicine, 1856–1900* (1993), a detailed study of disease in London during the last half of the nineteenth century. Hardy looked intensively at the history of eight major infectious diseases of the period (whooping cough, measles, scarlet fever, diphtheria, smallpox, typhoid, typhus, and tuberculosis) but did not restrict herself to the relatively superficial level of citywide sources. She focused instead on the district level, and on many occasions provided elaborate quantitative analyses of disease incidence street by street in particularly unhealthy areas. What she illustrated is the incredible complexity of the disease situation that broad-based national and city sources obscure. Hardy skillfully integrated quantitative and qualitative materials, and by doing so, enabled the reader to appreciate the immense amount of ambiguity and confusion involved in questions of disease etiology.

Hardy's discussion required her to investigate the myriad social, cultural, economic, political, and biological factors that influenced the morbidity and mortality rate for each disease. For example, tuberculosis rates were determined by the nature and location of housing, the extent of overcrowding, culturally shaped fears of fresh air, medical and folk-nursing practices, occupational hazards, class-based food preferences, and the synergistic effects of simultaneous infections – to name just a few.

Hardy also discussed "high risk" occupations in which workers were exposed to filth and foul air in closed and unventilated rooms. These included not only tailors and furriers but also such well-paid (and well-fed) workers as printers and clerks. The growth, decline, and geographic concentration of different trades directly influenced the local TB rates. Popular fears of fresh air and night chills led to nursing practices that kept the sick in closed rooms where family members were exposed to concentrated doses of pathogens. Ethnic groups in London (Jewish, Irish, Italian) differed in their cleanliness and general hygienic practices, and in methods of child rearing; this differentially affected their disease rates – independent of their generally inadequate incomes.

Hardy made it quite clear that before investigators can generalize about infectious disease in broad fashion, they must have a firm knowledge of the complex-

ities and subtleties of the ways in which people actually live. In her work, Hardy did what professional historians are best at doing: puncturing those grand theories that social scientists and historical amateurs sometimes produce.

Of course, the confusion and ambiguity of real history is less intellectually satisfying than sweeping theories of cause and effect. Hardy's detailed discussions often make the reader cry out for simplicity and certainty, but neither history nor Hardy is able to oblige. Nevertheless, Hardy was willing to present some broad conclusions from her study. In looking at the major infectious diseases that afflicted the people of London, she commented:

> The epidemiological record clearly suggests . . . that it was not better nutrition that broke the spiral of deaths from infectious disease after 1870, but intervention by the preventive authorities, together with natural modifications in disease virulence, which reduced exposure to several of the most deadly infections. . . . McKeown was a scientist speculating on historical phenomena, . . . and [he was] unfamiliar . . . with historical realities. (Hardy 1993: 292–3)

Like Szreter, Hardy found that the power of preventive medicine did not derive from national governmental policy but was rooted "in the persevering implementation of local measures based on local observation by a body of professional men whose sole responsibility was to their local community" (Hardy 1993: 292). As England's population was "above the critical threshold of under-nutrition below which resistance to infection is affected," it was consciously planned human intervention, not improved nutrition, that was the key to lower mortality rates (Hardy 1993: 292).

In summing up her survey of the eight major diseases she studied, Hardy pointed out the significant difference between those that affected children and those that affected adults. The latter were responsive to preventive actions, whereas the former were not. And it was among the adult diseases that the major drop in mortality in the late nineteenth century actually occurred:

> The impact of smallpox, typhoid and typhus, and (more arguably) of tuberculosis, was significantly reduced through the activities of the preventive administration . . . The reduction in deaths from both typhoid and typhus through diligent local activity and public-health education was a major achievement of the Victorian preventive administration. And for tuberculosis, similarly, general sanitary improvements, in the sense of slum-clearances, new housing, constant water supplies, and the growing emphasis on domestic cleanliness, were probably important.

Environmental and occupational factors were clearly of considerable importance . . . and the Victorian evidence suggests that these were more potent . . . than . . . nutritionally satisfactory diet. (Hardy 1993: 290-1)

Hardy did not claim that her work ends the historical discussion of the role of nutrition in the decline of infectious disease in the West, but she has clearly moved the debate to a higher level by demonstrating, as did Szreter, that accurate knowledge of infectious disease requires intensive study of local materials.

Investigators of the modern developing world have also contributed to the search for explanations of mortality declines other than that of a rising standard of living and improved nutrition. John Caldwell, for example, has argued for the importance of "cultural, social and behavioral determinants of health" in the developing world (Caldwell 1993: 125). He reported on a major 1985 conference that looked closely at a group of health "success stories," in which poor countries achieved high life expectancy rates despite severely limited resources (for example, the Indian state of Kerala [66 years; per capita income $160–270], Sri Lanka [69 years; $320], Costa Rica [74 years; $1,430], China [67 years; $310]). The conference organizers concluded that "the exercise of 'political will' " by China, and of both "political and social will" by Kerala, Sri Lanka, and Costa Rica were keys to their success. They placed their "emphasis on comprehensive and accessible health programmes with community involvement and the importance of education, especially female schooling" (Caldwell 1993: 126).

Caldwell carried out additional analysis of the conference material, combined it with other data from high-achieving/low-income countries, and found that the strongest correlation with reduced mortality was the educational level of women of maternal age. He contended that the most efficacious of the noncommunist countries have benefited from a historical "demand for health services and education, especially the all-important schooling of girls, arising from the long-existing nature of the societies, particularly the independence of their women, [and] an egalitarian-radical-democratic tradition . . ." (Caldwell 1993: 126). These positive factors, however, although ultimately vital, could not bear fruit until modern health services became available: "When health services arrived here and elsewhere mortality fell steeply because of a symbiotic relationship between an educated independent population determined to use them and make them work, and readily available health services" (Caldwell 1993: 126).

Caldwell concluded from his research that mortality levels similar to those of industrial societies could be reached in the developing world within two decades if all children were educated through elementary school. Education and modern medicine interact as a potent combination. Thus, if Caldwell and

his colleagues provided no direct evidence to undermine McKeown's claim that the standard of living and nutrition was the key to the decline of mortality in the West, they nevertheless undercut his argument for the relevance of such a notion for the developing world today.[4]

Clearly, Szreter, Caldwell, Wilson, and Aaby were not in agreement as to the reasons for either past or present declines in mortality. But they did agree on the conclusion that the importance of nutrition and rising standards of living has been substantially overstated. Each one of them provided a provocative and plausible alternative explanation that was either unknown to McKeown and his supporters or given insufficient attention. The work of these researchers and others (Christopher Murray and Lincoln Chen 1993) has kept alive the debate over the role of improving nutrition in the decline of mortality in the West.

William Muraskin

Notes

1. McKeown made a number of exceptions, such as smallpox, polio, and diphtheria antitoxin. However, he claimed that most of the decline in mortality resulted from lower rates of other diseases, especially tuberculosis, which did not have a vaccine or drug therapy until comparatively late.

2. Szreter said that the belief that the public-health movement in Britain had little effect on mortality is even accepted by British historians of public health. Interestingly enough, he believed that the McKeown thesis is clearly not relevant to other countries but only to Britain, and, thus, he does not discuss the "grander" McKeown thesis. He based his view on the work of Samuel H. Preston, whose work, dealing with countries other than Britain, he considered definitive (see, for example, Preston 1975). Szreter characterized Preston's position by saying that "it has been upward shifts in the level of medical technology and services available and the successful introduction of public health measures which has been markedly more significant than rising per capita incomes [i.e., general standard of living] . . . in accounting for their falling levels of mortality" (Szreter 1988: 4).
Preston's views have not had as far-reaching an effect on the general view of the issue as Szreter believed. In fact, his key research was published in the 1970s, *before* the McKeown thesis became the established view. This is not to say that it is not useful for a critique of McKeown, but only that it has not been as successfully used for that purpose as Szreter believed.

3. Wilson's argument flies in the face of much of the new research on tuberculosis presented in such studies as Linda Bryder's *Below the Magic Mountain: A Social History of Tuberculosis in Twentieth-Century Britain* (1988) and Francis Smith's *The Retreat of Tuberculosis, 1850-1950* (1988). However, most of that work was written under the influence of the McKeown thesis and has a strong antimedicine and anti-public-health (at least insofar as it was represented by sanatoria) emphasis. Interestingly enough, however, Smith saw segregation of infectious individuals in English workhouses as important in the decline of tubercu-

losis – just as Wilson did. Nancy Tomes, in her excellent review of the new tuberculosis literature, commented on the tendency to ignore the importance of the new bacteriological research in creating the concept of disease communicability and preventability. It was, she said, also medical science that created the tuberculin test, a tool that made the tracking of TB possible, thus permitting contemporaries to discover the social and economic conditions that favored the spread of the disease (see Tomes 1989).

4. Whereas Caldwell suspected that maternal education would also explain the decline of mortality in the West during the early twentieth century, he accepted the work of Preston as proving that to be untrue. For Caldwell, the reason for the difference between the West and the developing world was that sufficient effective health knowledge and practical applications to counteract the effects of broad economic forces were simply not available to educated mothers. Fortunately, such knowledge was available for the developing world after World War II. Caldwell was especially impressed with the power of education to convince people that they can and should collaborate to reduce mortality. Such education is "essentially Western education, and it carries a powerful Western pro-science message" that overcomes many of the indigenous beliefs that prevent effective action by parents.

Bibliography

Aaby, Peter. 1992. Lessons for the past: Third World evidence and the re-interpretation of developed world mortality decline. *Health Transition Review* 2 (Supplementary issue): 155-83.

Bryder, Linda. 1988. *Below the magic mountain: A social history of tuberculosis in twentieth-century Britain.* New York.

Caldwell, John. 1993. Health transition: The cultural, social and behavior determinants of health in the Third World. *Social Science and Medicine* 36: 125-35.

Hardy, Ann. 1993. *The epidemic streets: Infectious disease and the rise of preventive medicine, 1856-1900.* Oxford.

McKeown, Thomas. 1976. *The modern rise of population.* New York.

1979. *The role of medicine: Dream, mirage or nemesis.* Princeton, N.J.

Muraskin, William. 1995. *The war against hepatitis B: A history of the International Task Force on Hepatitis B Immunization.* Philadelphia, Pa.

Murray, Christopher, and Lincoln Chen. 1993. In search of a contemporary theory for understanding mortality change. *Social Science and Medicine* 36: 143-55.

Preston, Samuel. 1975. The changing relation between mortality and level of economic development. *Population Studies* 29: 231-48.

Smith, Francis. 1988. *The retreat of tuberculosis, 1850-1950.* New York.

Szreter, Simon. 1988. The importance of social intervention in Britain's mortality decline c. 1850-1914: A re-interpretation of the role of public health. *Social History of Medicine* 1: 1-37.

Tomes, Nancy. 1989. The white plague revisited. *Bulletin of the History of Medicine* 63: 467-80.

Wilson, Leonard. 1990. The historical decline of tuberculosis in Europe and America: Its causes and significance. *Journal of the History of Medicine and Allied Sciences* 43: 366-96.

1992. The rise and fall of tuberculosis in Minnesota: The role of infection. *Bulletin of the History of Medicine* 66: 16-52.

VI.3 ❧ Infection and Nutrition: Synergistic Interactions

The interactions of malnutrition and infection are synergistic, with each modifying the other in ways that cannot be predicted from studying just one condition or the other (Scrimshaw, Taylor, and Gordon 1968). The superimposed infection is more likely to be responsible for nutritional disease than a shortage of food alone. During recovery from infectious disease, however, the quantity and quality of food available is usually the limiting factor. Moreover, the frequency and severity of infections is increased for individuals whose nutritional status is poor. Although this increase depends in part on the social and environmental circumstances frequently associated with malnutrition, more important is the reduced resistance to infection directly associated with nutrient deficiency. This chapter examines the reasons why diseases are often more common and severe in the malnourished and discusses the metabolic and other functional consequences of infections.

Nutrition and Disease Morbidity and Mortality

The high frequency of diarrheal and respiratory diseases among young children in developing countries is both a major contributor to malnutrition and a consequence of lowered immunity in a poor sanitary environment combined with unsatisfactory personal hygiene (Mata 1978; Guerrant et al. 1983; Black, Brown, and Becker 1984). Furthermore, in both developing and industrialized countries, nosocomial infections (those originating in hospitals) are responsible for worsening the nutritional status of patients and thereby increasing overall morbidity and case fatality rates (Gorse, Messner, and Stephens 1989; Scrimshaw 1989).

In children whose nutritional status is poor, episodes of any of the common communicable diseases of childhood tend to be more severe and to have more secondary complications. In Guatemala, 50 percent of children with whooping cough require more than 12 weeks, and 25 percent more than 25 weeks, to recover the weight lost because of the disease (Mata 1978). In addition, there is recent evidence for a striking reduction of mortality after vitamin A supplementation was given to populations of underprivileged children in Indonesia (Sommer, Tarwotjo,

Table V1.3.1. *108 Acute infections among 32 children ages 2 to 9 years observed in a "model" convalescent home in Guatemala City for 90 days*

Disease	Total no. of episodes
Infectious hepatitis	2
Measles	2
Bronchopneumonia	3
Bronchial asthma and asthmatic bronchitis	15
Gastroenteritis	5
Amebiasis	9
Parotitis	4
Chicken pox	3
Gonococcal vaginitis	11
Purulent otitis media	4
Acute tonsillitis	7
Upper respiratory infection	15
Fever of unknown origin	9
Urinary infection	1
Impetigo and cellulitis	13
Skin allergy	5

Source: Unpublished INCAP data.

Hussaini et al. 1983, Sommer, Tarwotjo, Djunaedi et al. 1986) and India (Rahmathullah et al. 1990) and, in general, to poorly nourished children who acquire measles (Barclay, Foster, and Sommer 1987; Hussey and Klein 1990; Coutsoudis et al. 1992).

Even under relatively favorable institutional conditions, morbidity rates for children or the elderly can be very high. Table VI.3.1 lists 108 infections over a 90-day period among 32 well-fed children 2 to 9 years old in late recovery from malnutrition in a model convalescent home in Guatemala City (unpublished data from the Institute of Nutrition of Central America and Panama [INCAP], Guatemala City, Guatemala). Similar reports have come from orphanages in other countries. Under the less favorable conditions of open pediatric wards in developing countries, cross-infections among children are increased by low resistance and add to the duration of morbidity and to mortality rates.

Malnutrition, Infection, and Growth

Many studies confirm a reciprocal relationship between morbidity from diarrhea and other infectious diseases and growth (e.g., in the Gambia, Rowland, Cole, and Whitehead 1977; in Uganda, Cole and Parkin 1977; in Mexico, Condon-Paloloni et al. 1977; in Bangladesh, Black et al. 1984; in Sudan, Zumrawi, Dimond, and Waterlow 1987). Significant negative correlation of young child growth with diarrheal and other infections is a constant finding (e.g., Kielman, Taylor, and Parker 1978; Lutter et al. 1989; Martorell, Rivera, and Lutter 1990). In children whose nutritional status is marginal, measles will strongly reduce growth in ensuing weeks (in India, Reddy et al. 1986;

in Kenya, Duggan and Milner 1986; in Guatemala, Mata 1978). Even immunizations can affect the growth of poorly nourished children (Kielman et al. 1978). However, in the Guatemalan, Colombian, and Mexican studies, the negative effect of diarrhea on growth was prevented by a nutritious supplement. Thus, when the diet is adequate, the impact of acute infections on growth is usually transient (Lutter et al. 1989).

The Impact of Malnutrition on Resistance to Infection

It appears that every known nutrient deficiency can affect disease resistance if it is sufficiently severe, and this is also true for many nutrient excesses. A review of the logarithmic increase in research on nutrition and immunity clearly reveals that the same common mechanisms are affected by many different nutrients. The main mechanisms are still those identified in the 1968 World Health Organization (WHO) monograph, *Interaction of Nutrition and Infection* (Scrimshaw et al. 1968). These include physical barriers that depend on epithelial and other tissue integrity; phagocytosis; cell-mediated immunity; some forms of nonspecific resistance; and antibody formation. Recent advances in immunologic research and understanding have greatly enhanced knowledge of the mechanism of nutritional effects on both humoral and cell-mediated immunity.

One class of lymphocytes, the B cells, develop immunoglobulins or antibodies as integral proteins on their surface. The immunoglobulins are divided into five classes, A, D, E, G, and M, which vary in their susceptibility to nutritional deficiencies. Some lymphocytes function as memory cells for the production of large numbers of specific antibody-containing cells when the host is exposed to subsequent challenge or infection of the same kind. There is evidence that large numbers of these memory cells are attracted by the mammary gland when the mother develops an infection and contribute appropriate antibodies to breast milk (Hansen 1992).

Cell-mediated immunity offers a number of different stages in T-cell differentiation and function that can be affected by nutrient deficiencies. Both B cells and T cells recognize antigens and other mitogens, but the latter do not secrete antibodies. Some T cells have helper or suppressor cell functions through membrane surface receptors. Another subpopulation is that of the natural killer (NK) cells that function even before the other T cells respond and that can lyse particular cells without being previously sensitized. NK cells may be activated by interferon and influenced by eicosanoid-derived essential fatty acids (Byham 1991). The proliferation of both T and B cells in response to mitogens is impaired with various deficiencies that may include that of vitamin B_6 in the elderly (Meydani et al. 1990).

Humoral Immunity

Humoral immunity is lost in kwashiorkor (Olarte, Cravioto, and Campos 1956; Budiansky and da Silva 1957; Reddy and Srikantia 1964; Brown and Katz 1966), but once dietary treatment is initiated, antibody formation is restored (Pretorius and de Villiers 1962). M. G. Wohl, J. G. Reinhold, and S. B. Rose (1949) studied the antibody response to typhoid immunization in a Philadelphia hospital and found a markedly slower response in adult patients with albumin levels below 4.0 grams (g) per 100 milliliters (ml) and an improvement when those patients were given a protein supplement. R. E. Hodges and colleagues demonstrated conclusively that severe pantothenic acid and pyridoxine deficiency can interfere with antibody response to typhoid antigen, but it required a combination of deficient diets and metabolic antagonists to each of the vitamins (Hodges et al. 1962a, 1962b). Correcting the deficiencies returned the responses to normal. In experimental animals, it has been shown that sufficiently severe deficiencies of almost any essential nutrient can interfere with antibody formation (Scrimshaw et al. 1968). Although few of these experimental studies have public-health significance in human populations, they may be relevant to patients with metabolic and neoplastic disease and to some therapeutic regimens.

Phagocytosis

Phagocytic cells include both circulating leukocytes and the fixed macrophages in the reticuloendothelial system. A reduced phagocytic response with severe protein malnutrition was documented in the previously mentioned WHO monograph (Scrimshaw et al. 1968), but no other nutrients were mentioned in this regard. The phagocytic response in marasmus was reported to be normal, presumably because in marasmus (but not in kwashiorkor) amino acids are mobilized from skeletal muscle and are available for protein synthesis. Since 1968, much has been learned about nutritional interference with phagocyte function. Table VI.3.2 lists the

Table VI.3.2. *Antimicrobial systems in the neutrophil*

Oxygen dependent	Oxygen independent
Myeloperoxidase dependent	Acid environment
MPO plus halide plus H_2O_2	Cationic proteins
Myeloperoxidase independent	Lactoferrin
Hydrogen peroxide (H_2O_2)	Lysosomal hydrolases
Hydroxyl radical (OH·)	Lysozyme proteases
Singlet oxygen ($^1O_2$)	Neutral proteases
Superoxide anoin (O_2·)	Sequestration of phagocytic vacuole

Source: Stinnet (1983).

antimicrobial systems that have been identified in the neutrophil (Stinnett 1983). Phagocytes contain a collection of neutral proteases and lysozyme, an enzyme that hydrolyzes bacterial walls, as well as lactoferrin. Most of these mechanisms for killing infectious agents have been found susceptible to deficiency of one or more specific nutrients.

Delayed Cutaneous Hypersensitivity

The delayed cutaneous hypersensitivity response is a sensitive indicator of poor nutritional status. It is based on a combination of sequential processes involving sensitization of T lymphocytes against a macrophage-processed antigen, the production of soluble mediators (lymphokines), and an inflammatory response when sensitized T cells recognize and interact with an intradermally injected antigen. Lymphokines released at the local site produce the dermal induration characteristic of the response.

Children with a subnormal rate of growth due to protein deficiency show an impaired delayed hypersensitivity response to tuberculin (Jayalakshmi and Gopalan 1958; Harland 1965; Chandra 1972, 1977; Neumann, Stiehm, and Swenseid 1977). This is illustrated in Figure VI.3.1, in which serum transferrin serves as an indicator of protein depletion (Chandra and Newberne

Figure VI.3.1. Cutaneous delayed hypersensitivity to 5 t.u. tuberculin related to serum transferrin concentration in patients with pulmonary tuberculosis. A positive Mantoux test, induration 10 mm, was generally observed in individuals with serum transferrin level of ≥ 162 mg. Patients studied through the courtesy of Dr. H. B. Dingley, Tuberculosis Hospital, New Delhi. (From Chandra and Newberne 1977.)

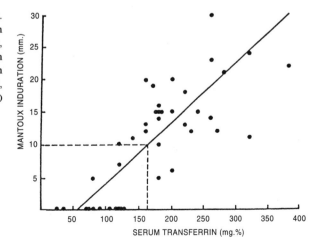

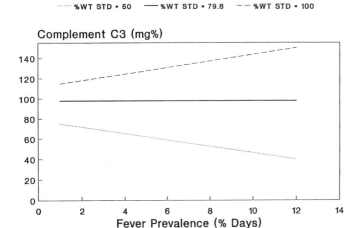

Figure VI.3.2. Serum C3 levels correlated with infection-morbidity indicated by the number of days of fever. Three weight categories in reference to the standard are shown. In well-nourished children, C3 concentration increases with infection. In the undernourished, C3 levels generally decrease. (From Kielman et al. 1976.)

1977). The failure to produce a response in malnourished children with the strong sensitizing agents 2,4-dinitrochlorobenzene and 2,4-dinitroflurobenzene has been reported by many authors (e.g., Smythe et al. 1971; Feldman and Gianantonio 1972; Chandra 1974; Schlesinger and Stekel 1974; Dutz et al. 1976; Smith et al. 1977). The case is similar with malnourished adults (Law, Dudrick, and Abdou 1973). Patients with iron-deficiency anemia also have a reduced delayed cutaneous hypersensitivity (Joynson et al. 1972).

Complement

Complement is a heat-labile opsonin in normal serum that can promote the lysis of other cells. It is a system of 17 protein compounds in two different pathways that sequentially activate specific proteases that deposit complement-3 on a particle to make it capable of being phagocytositized or lysed (Stinnett 1983). Complement-3 is susceptible to protein–energy deficiency (Sirisinha et al. 1973; Chandra 1975; Suskind et al. 1976; Neumann et al. 1977). Figure VI.3.2 presents data from India relating complement response to percentage of standard weight (Kielman et al. 1976).

Iron Withholding

Although, as indicated previously, iron deficiency is associated with increased morbidity and mortality from infections, it is a paradox that biological mechanisms for withholding iron from infectious agents appear to be an important means of inhibiting their replication. Both circulating transferrin and lactoferrin released by macrophages have an affinity for iron that is greater than that of bacterial sideophores. With infection, a rapid transfer of circulating iron to an intracellular compartment is mediated by the cytokine interleukin (Keusch 1990).

Other Mechanisms

Although included for completeness, nutritionally induced changes in tissue integrity are least important in explaining increased susceptibility to infection.

Nevertheless, epithelial tissues and mucous membranes are barriers to the direct penetration of infectious agents. Examples are the dermatosis associated with kwashiorkor and pellagra, the spongy gums of scurvy, and the epithelial lesions of vitamin A deficiency. When the skin is affected, the epithelial layers of the respiratory and intestinal tracts are usually also affected. Wound healing, fibroblast response, and collagen formation are other processes affected.

The clearest evidence that intestinal flora play a role in resistance to some infections is the decrease of Escherichia coli infections among breast-fed infants (Ross and Dawes 1954; Gyllenberg et al. 1957; György, Dhanamitta, and Steers 1962). Endocrine changes, whether the result of nutritional or other causes, can also affect any of the aforementioned resistance mechanisms.

Antagonisms between Nutrient Deficiencies and Infections

The 1968 WHO monograph (Scrimshaw et al.) reported 40 studies in experimental animals in which diets that were severely deficient in one or more B vitamins inhibited infections, compared with 70 in which similar diets worsened them. In 14 studies examining low-protein diets, antagonism was observed and compared with 94 in which synergism was the outcome. The 3 studies that involved iron deficiency reported a synergism between iron deficiency and hookworm in rats, dogs, and cats. Because the degree of deficiency in human populations always seemed to be associated with synergism, these reports of antagonism between malnutrition and infection in some experimental studies were not deemed to be important to public health.

There have, however, been studies that reported giving large doses of iron to severely iron-deficient children with kwashiorkor (McFarlane et al. 1970; Murray et al. 1978b) and to severely anemic refugees in Somalia (Bullen 1976; Murray et al. 1978a), which resulted in overwhelming infections. Moreover, the principle of withholding an essential nutrient from an infectious agent or a tumor cell underlies modern antibiotic therapy and chemotherapy.

How Infections Worsen Nutritional Status

Anorexia

Even when efforts are made to maintain a constant food intake during illness, anorexia will generally lead to a consistent decrease in food consumption even with infections as mild as that produced by immunization against yellow fever (Gandra and Scrimshaw 1961). Anorexia reduces the intake not only of protein and calories but also of most other nutrients. This effect contributes to precipitating clinically evident deficiencies of any nutrients that are already limiting.

Cultural and Therapeutic Practices

When young children experience febrile infections and diarrhea there is a strong tendency of the caregiver to withdraw solid food. Commonly, a thin starchy or sugary gruel that is low in protein and energy density is substituted (Hoyle, Yunus, and Chen 1980; Khan and Ahmad 1986). In field studies it is not possible to separate the effects of anorexia from those of deliberate withdrawal of food for cultural reasons. R. Martorell and C. Yarborough (1983) described an average reduction of 19 percent in dietary energy intake with various infections in Guatemalan children. Intakes were consistently less in children with diarrhea than in those without at all periods from 15 to 60 weeks (Mata et al. 1977; Martorell, Yarborough, et al. 1980; Martorell, Rivera, et al. 1990). Energy intakes in children under 5 years of age in Bangladesh were more than 40 percent less during acute diarrhea than after recovery (Hoyle et al. 1980). In Peru they decreased from 10 to 86 percent among breast-fed children with diarrhea (Bentley et al. 1991).

Despite a decrease in both intake and absorption of nutrients due to anorexia accompanying an infection, these losses are very much less than when food is withheld (Chung 1948; Chung and Viscorova 1948). Although consumption of food is reduced by anorexia, purposeful withholding of food may have a much greater impact. The clinical and public-health lesson is that food should not be withdrawn during diarrheal and other infections.

Malabsorption

In addition to the decrease in food intake with diarrhea, protein absorption is commonly reduced by 10 to 30 percent and occasionally by as much as 40 percent. A. W. Chung and B. Viscorova (1948) reported that the absorption of nitrogen in four children with diarrhea varied from 40 to 74 percent, and absorption of fat varied from 39 to 67 percent. Data from the International Center for Diarrheal Disease Research, Bangladesh (ICDDRB), on patients with diarrhea due to rotavirus show average absorption rates of 43 percent for nitrogen, 42 percent for fat, 74 percent for carbohydrate, and 55 percent for total energy. Slightly higher averages are managed by patients with diarrhea due to enteropathogenic E. coli and Shigella (Molla et al. 1982). E. D. Moyer and M. C. Powanda (1983) have summarized additional literature indicating a range of malabsorption for subjects with diarrhea of about 40 percent for proteins, 23 to 50 percent for fats, and 73 to 77 percent for carbohydrates. The high incidence of diarrheal disease in young children makes this malabsorption especially important for them.

Bacterial, viral, and protozoan enteritides cause similar malabsorption, as do intestinal parasites such as hookworm, fish tapeworm, ascaris, and Strongyloides, and it is also observed in systemic disorders such as measles, tuberculosis, malaria, and streptococcal infections. The mechanisms of malabsorption with these infections include shortened intestinal transit time, physical blocking of mucosal surfaces, and mesenteric blood flow.

Some children with acute diarrheal disease of nonspecific origin develop a persistent carbohydrate intolerance and experience a much more severe and prolonged nutritional deficit (Rosenberg and Scrimshaw 1972). In addition, between 30 percent and 50 percent of individuals living in an unsanitary environment in warm climates develop tropical jejunitis with chronic changes in the intestinal epithelium that include flattening of the villi and loss of microvilli (Klipstein and Falaiye 1969; Keusch, Plaut, and Troncale 1970; Bayless, Swanson, and Wheby 1971; Lindenbaum, Harmon, and Gerson 1972). This phenomenon undoubtedly occurs in most developing countries, which include Haiti (Klipstein et al. 1968), India (Gorbach et al. 1970; Baker 1972), Thailand (Sprinz et al. 1962; Keusch 1972), Bangladesh (Lindenbaum, Gerson, and Kent 1971), Colombia (Ghitis, Tripathy, and Mayoral 1967; Mayoral et al. 1967), and Puerto Rico (Lugo-de-Rivera, Rodriguez, and Torres-Pinedo 1972). In addition, I. Rosenberg, N. W. Solomons, and R. E. Schneider showed in 1977 that most rural Guatemalans had reduced absorption of protein and carbohydrates.

Catabolic Losses

A catabolic response occurs with all infections, even when they are subclinical (Beisel 1972, 1975, 1977; Beisel and Wannemacher 1980; Keusch and Farthing 1986). This is true even for yellow fever immunizations (Gandra and Scrimshaw 1961) and asymptomatic Q-fever infections (Beisel 1977). Once an infection is established, the breakdown of skeletal muscle protein begins and alanine and glutamine are synthesized and transported to the liver, where they are used for gluconeogenesis. This process occurs whether or not the infection causes fever. Increased losses of vitamin A, B-vitamins, ascorbic acid, and iron are also observed.

The stimulus for these changes comes from the release of interleukin-1 when macrophages break down, and from the resulting endocrine changes (Wannemacher 1977). More than two-thirds of the negative nitrogen balance of a young man with tularemia was due to this metabolic response, and the remainder to a spontaneous decrease in food intake (Beisel et al. 1967). Even an individual with completely asymptomatic Q fever can have an increasingly negative cumulative nitrogen balance for as long as 21 days (Beisel 1977).

Anabolic Losses

There is a marked increase in nitrogen retention following chicken pox, despite only a modest decrease in retention during the period of the rash (Wilson, Bressani, and Scrimshaw 1961). During an infection, amino acids are diverted from normal pathways for the synthesis of immunoglobulins, lymphokines, C-reactive proteins, and a variety of other proteins, including key liver enzymes (Wannemacher 1977). This diversion accounts for the finding that the extra nitrogen retained during the recovery period in metabolic balance studies exceeds that accounted for by the magnitude of the negative balance measured during the acute phase of an infection.

Fever

Whatever its benefits in increasing resistance to infection-induced disease, fever has a metabolic cost. The regulation of normal body temperature within a narrow range is a complex phenomenon. It is modified by the endogenous pyrogenic activity of interleukin-1 released by mononuclear leukocytes in response to infection. The resulting fever increases the basal metabolic rate 13 percent for each rise in temperature of 1 degree Celsius (DuBois 1937). During a period of high fever, metabolism may increase by nearly one-third. There is a relationship between basal metabolic rate and temperature measured in various infections. The increase varies between 30 and 60 percent for a 3-degree rise.

Additional Intestinal Losses

Although difficult to measure separately from malabsorption, a significant contributor to malnutrition in some infections is the direct loss of nutrients into the gut. Protein-losing enteropathy has been described for measles (Axton 1975; Dosseter and Whittle 1975; Sarker et al. 1986), diarrhea (Waldman 1970; WHO 1980; Rahaman and Wahed 1983), and especially shigellosis (Rahaman, Alam, and Islam 1974). Alpha 1-antitrypsin is a simple and useful quantitative marker for estimating the loss of protein into the gut in diarrheal disease (Rahaman and Wahed 1983), and it should be used for this purpose in studying the effects of other kinds of infections.

In ICDDRB studies, nearly two-thirds of patients with enterotoxigenic E. coli (ETEC) and 40 percent of those with rotavirus diarrhea were also found to have an excessive loss of protein in the feces (Molla et al. 1983). Between 100 and 500 ml of serum was lost in the feces each day by shigellosis patients due to protein-losing enteropathy. Bleeding into the intestine from Schistosoma mansoni (hookworm) also represents a loss of energy, iron, and other nutrients.

Reduced Growth and Weight Loss

As described earlier, children subjected to frequent infections and borderline diets show reduced growth. The result is a decrease in nutrient requirements that is proportionately larger for protein than for dietary energy. This loss is because the requirement for average daily growth of a 2-year-old child is about 12 percent of the total protein requirement, only about 2 percent of total energy needs. The savings from growth impairment are generally not sufficient to avoid actual weight loss, an almost inevitable consequence of infection.

Infectious Diseases and Nutrient Requirements

Bacterial, Viral, and Protozoal Infections

As already emphasized, the metabolic consequences of systemic infections depend not on the specific causative organism but rather on a common sequence of metabolic events.

Parasitic Infections

As an acute febrile illness, malaria has the same consequences as other acute systemic infections (Barr and DuBois 1918; McGregor 1982; Tomkins et al. 1983). This is also true for febrile episodes associated with toxoplasmosis, onchocerciasis, leishmaniasis, and trypanosomiasis. However, there may be additional local effects from parasitic infections. Reduced intestinal absorption of nitrogen can occur in malaria as a consequence of reduced mesenteric blood flow (Migasena and MaeGraith 1969). Anemia is a common sequel to Plasmodium falciparum infection and to a lesser extent in the other malaria types (McGregor et al. 1966), which is due in part to an increased iron loss because of hemolysis. Immunologic destruction of unparasitized erythrocytes may also occur (Zuckerman 1966).

Giardia lamblia has been well documented as a common cause of chronic malabsorption, including wasting, hypoalbuminemia, diarrhea, steatorrhea (Chauduri 1943; Amini 1963; Solomons 1982), and malabsorption of fats and carbohydrates (Veghelyi 1938; Palumbo, Scudmore, and Thompson 1962; Kluska 1972; Riis 1975; Khosla, Sharma, and Srivastava 1978). Poor absorption of vitamin A is seen in giardiasis (Chesney and McCoord 1934; Katsampes, McCowd, and Phillips 1944; Mahalanabis et al. 1979). Several investigators have reported evidence of ileal malabsorption of vitamin B_{12} as a result of this infection (Peterson 1957; Antia et al. 1966; Notis 1972). Low serum folate levels in patients with Giardia infections have also been described.

Intestinal helminths, such as ascaris (Venkatachalam and Patwardhan 1953; Tripathy et al. 1972; Gupta et al. 1977; Brown et al. 1980; Taren et al. 1987), hookworm (Layrisse et al. 1964), *Strongyloides* (Milner et al. 1965; O'Brien 1975; Carvalho Filho 1978), *Trichuris* (Jung and Beaver 1951; Layrisse et al. 1967), and heavy infections of *Trichocephalus*, may also reduce intestinal absorption of protein and other nutrients (Crompton 1986). Careful metabolic balance studies generally fail to detect a significant effect of mild to moderate worm burdens on intestinal absorption, although appetite may be reduced (Bray 1953; Kotcher et al. 1966; El-Mawla, Abdallah, and Galil 1966). Vitamin A malabsorption has been described with ascariasis (Sivakumar and Reddy 1972). *Ascaris* and *Chlonorichis* can also cause biliary and pancreatic obstruction (Rosenberg and Bowman 1982).

Of the hookworms, *Necator americanus* causes a loss of about 0.03 ml of blood per worm per day (Roche et al. 1957a, 1957b; Roche and Perez-Gimenez 1959), whereas *Ancylostoma duodenale* causes a 5 to 10 times greater blood loss per worm (Farid et al. 1965). Although approximately half of the iron is reabsorbed (Roche and Perez-Gimenez 1959; Giles, Watson Williams, and Ball 1964), the loss in heavily infected patients ranged from 14 to 45 ml of blood per day. Surprisingly, even with severe hookworm anemia, adequate dietary iron can fully compensate for these losses without removal of the worms. L. S. Stephenson, D. W. T. Crompton, M. C. Latham, and colleagues (1980) described growth impairment with *Ascaris* infection, and, later, Stephenson, Latham, K. M. Kurz, and colleagues (1989) showed that active antihelminth treatment improved the growth of Kenyan schoolchildren with combined hookworm, trichuris, and ascaris infection.

The massive bleeding from the intestinal tract, sometimes seen in *Schistosoma mansoni*, may require surgical intervention. This parasite can also obstruct lymphatic return and thereby interfere with fat absorption. Other reported nutritional consequences of heavy *S. mansoni* infections in human clinical studies include daily loss of albumin, zinc, and vitamin A; elevated fecal fat and glucose intolerance; and subnormal levels of serum carotene (Waslien, Farid, and Darby 1973). Most of the protein in the blood entering the gut due to intestinal bleeding in hookworm infection is reabsorbed, but in heavily infected patients, increased fecal protein loss may occur (Blackman et al. 1965). Individuals with *Schistosoma hematobium* lose blood in the urine and are also at increased risk of iron deficiency.

Because of their aggregate bulk, some parasites compete with the host for some of the nutrients essential to both. Where the Scandinavian custom of consuming marinated raw freshwater fish persists, massive infection of the fish tapeworm *Diphyllobothrium latum* is associated with megaloblastic anemia due to competition for vitamin B_{12} (Von Bonsdorff 1948, 1956, 1964). This effect (and that of *G. lamblia*) may also partially be caused by hypochlorhydria or achlorhydria in the stomach (Hoskins et al. 1967), which interferes with vitamin B_{12} absorption.

Effects of Infections on Specific Nutrients

Protein

All of the mechanisms for the impact of infection worsen protein status, and as a result, clinical protein deficiency is often precipitated in individuals whose nutritional status is borderline. Powanda (1977) has summarized data for a wide variety of acute infectious diseases in adults by adding the total nitrogen losses and dividing them by the number of days over which these losses occurred. For all infections, the average loss of 0.6 grams of protein per kilogram per day (g/kg/day) is equal to the mean estimated protein requirement for adults. Diseases associated with diarrhea or dysentery produced an average protein loss of 0.9 g/kg/day. Higher losses were observed with typhoid fever and other severe infections, reaching 1.2 g/kg/day.

Measurements of the catabolic response in infection using urinary 3-methylhistidine as a measure of muscle protein catabolism in the septic patient suggest an average additional protein loss in the urine during sepsis to be the equivalent of 1.14 g/kg/day (Long et al. 1977). None of these calculations include energy expended for the multiple anabolic responses or make allowances for dietary change or for nutrient malabsorption.

Both metabolic and field observations suggest that even with an optimum diet, it may take two to three times longer to replete than to deplete an individual. If the diet is not sufficient for a maximum rate of recovery, daily improvement is correspondingly reduced and the time required for complete recovery increased. The more severe and closely spaced the episodes of infection, the more likely that full recovery will not occur and that the adverse effects will become cumulative.

Infections are likely to precipitate clinical protein deficiency in children whose nutritional status is borderline. Diarrhea is reported from many countries to be the most common contributory cause of kwashiorkor (Scrimshaw et al. 1968). This is the case even when the episode is not necessarily severe, because it may be only the latest in a long series of diarrheal, respiratory, and other infections that are progressively depleting, when there is neither sufficient food nor time for complete recovery between episodes. Kwashiorkor has been reported to follow measles, chicken pox, German measles, whooping cough, and other common communicable diseases of childhood. Measles has a particularly strong impact on nutritional status, causing a sharp drop in serum albumin (Dosseter and Whittle 1975), lean body mass (unpublished data from Fernando Viteri, Institute of Nutrition of Central America and Panama [INCAP], Guatemala City, Guatemala), and growth rates (Mata 1978).

Table VI.3.3. *Intake of calories in acute state (A), and 2 weeks (R₁) and 8 weeks (R₂) after recovery (mean ± SD)*

Etiology	A	R_1	R_2
Cholera	74.9 ± 36.20	111.1 ± 35.4	109.59 ± 31.7
Rotavirus	68.5 ± 22.6	87.2 ± 26.2	115.0 ± 20.2
ETEC	70.7 ± 37.9	90.97 ± 28.4	114.9 ± 19.0
Shigella	70.0 ± 28.2	100.5 ± 27.8	109.3 ± 18.8

Source: Molla et al. (1983).

Energy

Obviously, the severity of an energy deficit is related to the duration and magnitude of malabsorption in each individual situation; rarely does such a condition pose a major threat to nutrition unless infection is chronic or recurrent. For most respiratory diseases the energy cost is minimal, but for diarrheal diseases and the common communicable diseases of childhood, it can add significantly to a chronic energy deficit. Food intake is observed to drop during acute infection and then to increase during recovery to above normal levels if the diet is sufficient. Table VI.3.3 shows the large increase in caloric intake during convalescence from diarrhea in Bangladesh when a good diet is available ad libitum (Molla et al. 1983).

Vitamin A

Vitamin A blood levels are appreciably reduced in pneumonia, rheumatoid arthritis, acute tonsillitis, and infectious hepatitis (May et al. 1940; Shank et al. 1944; Harris and Moore 1947; Jacobs et al. 1954). Vitamin A is not normally found in the urine but does appear there in at least some infectious diseases (Moore 1957; Goldsmith 1959). Lower serum carotene and vitamin A levels have been reported with hookworm disease (Rodgers, Dhir, and Hosain 1960).

The capacity of infections to precipitate xerophthalmia and keratomalacia in individuals already marginally deficient in vitamin A is well established (Oomen 1959; McLaren 1963; Sommer 1982; Sommer et al. 1983; Sommer, Katz, and Tarwotjo 1984; Stanton et al. 1986; Tielsch et al. 1986; De Sole, Belay, and Zegeye 1987). The effect is particularly severe with measles (Sommer et al. 1984). A significant drop in serum vitamin A levels has been observed in children with acute respiratory infection, gastroenteritis, and measles; levels return to normal after recovery (National Institute of Nutrition 1980).

The adverse effect of intestinal parasitic infections on vitamin A absorption has already been described. Enteric infections of bacterial and viral origin also have this effect (Nalin et al. 1980; West and Sommer 1985), as do systemic febrile illnesses (Heymann 1936; Shank et al. 1944; Lala and Reddy 1970; Sivakumar and Reddy 1975). B. Sivakumar and V. Reddy (1972) reported that only 30 to 70 percent of ingested vitamin A is absorbed by children with acute diarrhea and respiratory infections. Although infec-

tion clearly impairs both dietary carotene and vitamin A absorption (West, Howard, and Sommer 1989), sufficient amounts of supplementary vitamin A can still be absorbed orally for effective treatment of corneal xerophthalmia.

Ascorbic Acid

Ascorbic acid levels decrease in plasma and increase in the urine of infected individuals compared to noninfected persons living under comparable conditions. This is seen even with the common cold and with immunization against smallpox and measles (Scrimshaw et al. 1968; Hume and Weyers 1973). Historically, infections are associated with the onset of florid scurvy in individuals already on a borderline diet (Scrimshaw et al. 1968).

B-Vitamins

The classic nutritional diseases of beriberi and pellagra, caused respectively by deficiencies of thiamine and niacin, were known to be precipitated in vulnerable individuals by a variety of infections. This finding is of more than historical interest because alcoholics frequently consume diets low in B-vitamins, and infections increase the likelihood of clinically significant deficiencies of the B complex. Given the frequency with which infections occur in indigent alcoholics, physicians treating them should be aware of this connection. W. R. Beisel and colleagues (1972) have reported a marked increase in riboflavin excretion with infection.

Minerals

Iron. When anemia is present at the time of an infection (or even moderate iron deficiency without anemia) a number of normal resistance mechanisms are compromised. Impaired processes include phagocytic killing power; delayed cutaneous hypersensitivity, T-cell proliferation, and T-killer cell activity; and if the anemia is sufficiently severe, impaired antibody formation.

Yet when individuals compromised in this way are given parenteral iron or large doses of oral iron the result may be an overwhelming infection, as described for children with kwashiorkor (Baker et al. 1981; Lynch et al. 1984; Picciano, Weingartner, and Erdman 1984; Beard et al. 1988) and for severely malnourished adults (Murray et al. 1975, 1978a, 1978b; Barry and Reeve 1977; Bercroft, Dix, and Farmer 1977; Weinberg 1978, 1984). This occurs because the infective agent is supplied with iron before the host immune system has had time to recover. However, field studies have shown that iron fortification (supplementation of poorly nourished adults with up to 100 milligrams [mg] of iron daily, and proportionately less for children) always results in *decreased* morbidity from infectious disease (Scrimshaw 1990b).

Copper and zinc. Careful metabolic studies by C. Castillo-Duran, P. Vial, and R. Uauy (1988) have documented the impact of diarrhea on zinc and copper status. Metabolic balances of the minerals were strongly negative during the period of acute diarrhea, compared with strongly positive balances in the control subjects. During the recovery period, zinc balances became positive (405.3 ± 20.4 mg/kg/day), but copper balance remained negative, although less so (-21.5 ± 46.7 mg/kg/day).

The mechanism for the loss is wastage from the gastrointestinal tract through malabsorption and excessive endogenous losses. Since the normal state for the growing infant is net retention of these minerals, the true magnitude of such losses is somewhat greater. Clearly, the inevitable combination of reduced oral intake and increased fecal losses of minerals should be taken into account in the management of prolonged diarrhea. These losses cannot be predicted from serum levels because copper levels often increase during infections as a result of stimulation of the hepatic production of cerruloplasm (Kampschmidt et al. 1973).

It is noteworthy that in a study by R. F. Kampschmidt and colleagues (1973) serum copper levels were significantly lower in diarrhea cases than in control cases. Conversely, plasma zinc levels often decline during acute infections because of an internal redistribution of the metal to the liver. The reduced retention of zinc during diarrhea thus interacts with the redistributional influence of the infection. On the basis of this study, it is reasonable to suggest that treatment regimens for diarrhea should contain supplemental amounts of copper and zinc, but whether this addition would make a detectable difference in therapeutic results remains to be demonstrated.

Nutrient Allowances for Infectious Disease Morbidity

Although it is important to provide a nutritious diet and encourage adequate nutrient intakes during an acute infection, some decrease resulting from anorexia is almost inevitable, and it is generally useless to attempt to increase food intake *during* illness. For the multiple reasons discussed in this chapter, persons are normally depleted to a greater or lesser degree during an infection. However, during the *recovery* period, there is a metabolic window in which appetite is increased and the rate of retention, at least for protein, may be as much as nine times the average daily requirement.

A 1979 United Nations University report calculated that a malnourished 1-year-old child depleted by an infectious episode lasting 7 days would need approximately 136 kilocalories (kcals) (569 kilojoules [kjoules]) per kilogram per day, and 2.56 grams of protein per kilogram per day, for repletion in 30 days. It should be noted that the same weight deficit without infection would have required less than one-third the amount of protein per kilogram per day but approximately the same amount of energy. Despite

clear evidence of the heavy burden of infection on the populations of developing countries, and the increased nutrient needs above normal requirement levels during convalescence from episodes of infectious disease, this issue is not dealt with quantitatively in national and international recommended nutrient allowances. The comment of a "Consultation on Energy and Protein Requirements" (FAO/WHO/UNU 1985) is illustrative of such vagueness: "[T]he increased requirement average of a population of school children would not be large." The report goes on to emphasize the need for preventing infections, rather than simply meeting increased requirements for recovery resulting from them. This emphasis is important but not helpful to the hundreds of thousands of children in developing countries whose diets are already deficient or borderline.

R. G. Whitehead (1977) recommended a 30 percent increase in energy and a 100 percent increase in protein to optimize nutritional repletion of young children depleted by infection. This recommendation is consistent with data summarized by Powanda (1977) and N. S. Scrimshaw (1977). Moyer and Powanda (1983) discuss the basis for significantly increased nutrient requirements during convalescence without arriving at quantitative recommendations. However, a task force report (Rhode et al. 1983) utilizing this and other information concluded that children should be offered 50 percent more than their usual diet for two to four times the duration of the illness *or* fed extra food daily until the weight prior to illness is regained or exceeded. Unfortunately, the diet of most infants and young children (and some adults) in developing countries is commonly too marginal to permit repletion before another episode of infection further depletes the individual.

The *energy* cost of depositing a gram of protein is estimated to be 24 kcal (100 kjoules), or about 6 kcal (25 kjoules) of total weight gain (United Nations University 1979). If this figure is applied to the observed protein losses previously summarized, average energy losses suggest a loss from this source alone of between 4 and 5 kcals (17 to 21 kjoules) per kilogram per day. This would correspond to 14, 22, and 29 kcal (59, 92, and 121 kjoules) per kilogram in children or adults. This loss appears to be minor, but it represents from 14 to 29 percent of the requirements of a 1-year-old child.

The energy cost of growth of children recovering from protein–energy malnutrition was found to be in the range of 4 to 5 kcal (17 to 21 kjoules) per gram of weight gain, with 40 percent of this amount considered to be fat tissue and 60 percent protein tissue (Jackson, Picou, and Reeds 1977). The energy cost of synthesizing a gram of lost protein is 7.5 kcal (31 kjoules) per gram and for replacing a gram of fat 11.6 kcal (49 kjoules). During the recovery period, this loss must be made up, together with deficits arising from malabsorption, infection-stimulated catabolism, and internal synthesis in reaction to infection. Such an increase in energy requirement during the convalescent period is difficult to quantify, however, because it is so variable.

Summary

The interactions of malnutrition and infection in human populations are almost always synergistic in the sense that each worsens the other. Deficiencies of protein, iron, and vitamin A are particularly likely to be responsible for an increase in morbidity and mortality from infectious diseases in underprivileged young children. In hospitalized patients, malnutrition often contributes to the severity of nosocomial infections. Mechanisms for increased susceptibility to infection with malnutrition include altered tissue integrity, impaired antibody formation, and many aspects of cell-mediated and nonspecific immunity. These include T-cell proliferation, killer T cells, helper T cells, complement C-3, phagocytic killing power, immunoglobulins G and E, delayed cutaneous hypersensitivity, and other parameters of cell-mediated immunity. Although iron deficiency interferes with several of these parameters of cell-mediated immunity, it can impair replication of some infectious agents. Severely iron-deficient individuals should receive supplementary iron to restore immunity, but never in high doses.

The mechanisms whereby systemic infections worsen nutritional status include anorexia, cultural withdrawal of solid food, increased metabolic losses, decreased intestinal absorption, and internal diversion of nutrients for immune proteins. The practical significance of these effects depends on the prior nutritional status of the individual, the diet during the infection, and the adequacy of the diet for prompt recovery. Intestinal parasitic infections, when sufficiently heavy, interfere with absorption of nutrients and have a variety of additional adverse effects that depend on their specific nature. Individuals who live in environments with frequent enteric infections develop chronic intestinal mucosal changes that impair nutrient absorption. Food intake should be maintained to the extent possible during an infection despite anorexia, and then increased during the convalescent period.

Nevin S. Scrimshaw

Bibliography

Amini, F. 1963. Giardiasis and steatorrhoea. *Journal of Tropical Medicine and Hygiene* 66: 190-2.

Antia, F. P., H. G. Desai, K. N. Jeejeebhoy, et al. 1966. Giardiasis in adults. Incidence symptomatology and absorption studies. *Indian Journal of Medical Sciences* 20: 471-7.

Axton, J. H. M. 1975. Measles: A protein-losing enteropathy. *British Medical Journal* 3: 79-80.

Baker, E. C., G. C. Mustakas, J. W. Erdman, Jr., and L. T. Black. 1981. The preparation of soy products with different levels of native phytate for zinc availability studies. *Journal of the American Oil Chemists Society* 58: 541-3.

Baker, S. J. 1972. Tropical sprue. *British Medical Bulletin* 28: 87-91.

Barclay, A. J. G., A. Foster, and A. Sommer. 1987. Vitamin A supplements and mortality related to measles: A randomised clinical trial. *British Medical Journal* 1: 1067-8.

Barr, D. P., and E. F. DuBois. 1918. Clinical calorimetry XXVII: The metabolism in malarial fever. *Archives of Internal Medicine* 21: 627-58.

Barry, D. M. J., and A. W. Reeve. 1977. Increased incidence of gram-negative neonatal sepsis with intramuscular iron administration. *Pediatrics* 60: 908-12.

Bayless, T. M., V. L. Swanson, and M. S. Wheby. 1971. Jejunal histology and clinical status in tropical sprue and other chronic diarrheal disorders. *American Journal of Clinical Nutrition* 24: 112-16.

Beard, J. L., C. M. Weaver, S. R. Lynch, et al. 1988. The effect of soybean phosphate and phytate content on iron availability. *Nutrition Research* 8: 345-52.

Beisel, W. R. 1972. Interrelated changes in host metabolism during generalized infectious illness. In *Malabsorption and nutrition,* ed. I. Rosenberg and N. S. Scrimshaw, 1254-60. Bethesda, Md.

1975. Metabolic response to infection. *Annual Review of Medicine* 26: 9-20.

1976. The influence of infection or injury on nutritional requirements during adolescence. In *Nutritional requirements in adolescence,* ed. J. McKigney and H. N. Munro. Cambridge, Mass.

1977. Magnitude of the host nutritional response to infection. *American Journal of Clinical Nutrition* 30: 1236-47.

Beisel, W. R., Y. F. Herman, H. E. Sauberlich, et al. 1972. Experimentally induced sandfly fever and vitamin metabolism in man. *American Journal of Clinical Nutrition* 25: 1165.

Beisel, W. R., W. D. Sawyer, E. D. Ryll, and D. Crozier. 1967. Metabolic effects of intracellular infections in man. *Annals of Internal Medicine* 67: 744-79.

Beisel, W. R., and R. W. Wannemacher. 1980. Gluconeogenesis, ureagenesis, and ketogenesis during sepsis. *Journal of Parenteral and Enteral Nutrition* 4: 277-85.

Bentley, M. E., R. Y. Stallings, M. Fukumoto, and J. A. Elder. 1991. Maternal feeding behavior and child acceptance of food during diarrhea, convalescence, and health in the Central Sierra of Peru. *American Journal of Public Health* 81: 43-7.

Bercroft, D. M. O., M. R. Dix, and K. Farmer. 1977. Intramuscular iron-dextran and susceptibility of neonates to bacterial infections. *Archives in Diseases of Childhood* 52: 778-81.

Black, R. E., K. H. Brown, and S. Becker. 1984. Effects of diarrhea associated with specific enteropathogens on the growth of children in rural Bangladesh. *Pediatrics* 73: 799-805.

Blackman, V., R. D. Marsden, J. Banwell, and M. H. Cragg. 1965. Albumin metabolism in hookworm anaemias. *Transactions of the Royal Society of Tropical Medicine and Hygiene* 59: 472-82.

Bray, B. 1953. Nitrogen metabolism in West African children. *Proceedings of the Nutrition Society* 7: 3-13.

Brown, K. H., R. H. Gilman, M. Khatum, and M. G. Ahmed. 1980. Absorption of macronutrients from a rice-vegetable diet before and after treatment of ascariasis in children. *American Journal of Clinical Nutrition* 33: 1975-82.

Brown, R. E., and M. Katz. 1966. Failure of antibody production to yellow fever vaccine in children with kwashiorkor. *Tropical and Geographic Medicine* 18: 125-8.

Budiansky, E., and N. N. da Silva. 1957. Formação de anticorpos na distrofia pluricarencial hidropigenica. *Hospital* 52: 251.

Bullen, J. J. 1976. Acute diarrhoea in childhood. In *Ciba Foundation Symposium*, 149-62. Amsterdam.

Byham, L. D. 1991. Dietary fat and natural killer cell function, *Nutrition Today* 1: 31-6.

Carvalho Filho, E. 1978. Strongyloidiasis. *Clinics in Gastroenterology* 7: 179-200.

Castillo-Duran, C., P. Vial, and R. Uauy. 1988. Trace mineral balance during acute diarrhea in infants. *Journal of Pediatrics* 113: 452-7.

Chandra, R. K. 1972. Immunocompetence in undernutrition. *Journal of Pediatrics* 81: 1194-200.

1974. Rosette-froming T lymphocytes and cell-mediated immunity in malnutrition. *British Medical Journal* 3: 608-9.

1975. Serum complement and immunoconglutin in malnutrition. *Archives in Diseases of Childhood* 50: 225-9.

1977. Cell-mediated immunity in fetally and postnatally malnourished children from India and Newfoundland. In *Malnutrition and the immune response*, ed. R. Suskind, 111-15. New York.

Chandra, R. K., and P. M. Newberne. 1977. *Nutrition, immunity and infection: Mechanisms of interactions*. New York.

Chauduri, R. N. 1943. A note on giardiasis with steatorrhea. *Indian Medical Gazette* 78: 284-5.

Chesney, J., and A. B. McCoord. 1934. Vitamin A of serum following administration of Haliver oil in normal children and in chronic steatorrhea. *Proceedings of the Society of Experimental Biology* 31: 87.

Chung, A. W. 1948. The effect of oral feeding at different levels on the absorption of food stuffs in infantile diarrhea. *Journal of Pediatrics* 33: 1-13.

Chung, A. W., and B. Viscorova. 1948. The effect of early oral feeding versus early oral starvation on the course of infantile diarrhea. *Journal of Pediatrics* 33: 14-22.

Cole, T. J., and J. M. Parkin. 1977. Infection and its effect on the growth of young children: A comparison of the Gambia and Uganda. *Transactions of the Royal Society of Tropical Medicine and Hygiene* 71: 196-8.

Condon-Paloloni, D., J. Cravioto, F. E. Johnston, et al. 1977. Morbidity and growth of infants and young children in a rural Mexican village. *American Journal of Public Health* 67: 651-6.

Coutsoudis, A., P. Kiepiela, M. Broughton, and H. M. Coovadia. 1992. Nutritional and immunological consequences of measles treated with vitamin A or placebo in young African children. In *Nutrition and immunology*, ed. R. K. Chandra, 143-62. St. John's, Newfoundland, Canada.

Crompton, D. W. 1986. Nutritional aspects of infection. *Transactions of the Royal Society of Tropical Medicine and Hygiene* 80: 697-705.

De Sole, G., Y. Belay, and B. Zegeye. 1987. Vitamin A deficiency in southern Ethiopia. *American Journal of Clinical Nutrition* 45: 780-4.

Dinarello, C. A. 1984. Interleukin-1 and the pathogenesis of the acute-phase response. *New England Journal of Medicine* 311: 1413-18.

Dosseter, J. F. B., and H. C. Whittle. 1975. Protein-losing enteropathy and malabsorption in acute measles enteritis. *British Medical Journal* 2: 592-3.

DuBois, E. F. 1936. *Basal metabolism in health and disease.* Philadelphia, Pa.

1937. *The mechanism of heat loss and temperature regulation.* Stanford, Calif.

Duggan, M. B., and R. D. G. Milner. 1986. Composition of weight gain by Kenyan children during recovery from measles. *Human Nutrition, Clinical Nutrition* 40C: 173-83.

Dutz, W., E. Rossipal, H. Ghavami, et al. 1976. Persistent cell mediated immune deficiency following infantile stress during the first 6 months of life. *European Journal of Pediatrics* 122: 117.

El-Mawla, N. G., A. Abdallah, and N. Galil. 1966. Studies on the malabsorption syndrome among Egyptians. 5. Faecal fat and D-xylose absorption tests in patients with ascariasis and taeniasis. *Journal of the Egyptian Medical Association* 49: 473.

FAO/WHO/UNU. 1985. *Energy and protein requirements.* Technical Report Series 724. Geneva.

Farid, Z., J. H. Nichols, S. Bassily, and A. R. Schulert. 1965. Blood loss in pure *Ancylostoma duodenale* infection in Egyptian farmers. *American Journal of Tropical Medicine and Hygiene* 14: 375.

Feldman, G., and C. A. Gianantonio. 1972. Aspectos immunologicos de la desnutrición en el niño. *Medicina* 32: 1-9.

Gandra, Y. R., and N. S. Scrimshaw. 1961. Infection and nutritional status. II. Effect of mild virus infection induced by 17-D yellow fever vaccine on nitrogen metabolism in children. *American Journal of Clinical Nutrition* 9: 159-63.

Ghitis, J., K. Tripathy, and G. Mayoral. 1967. Malabsorption in the tropics. II. Tropical sprue versus primary protein malnutrition: Vitamin B$_{12}$ and folic acid studies. *American Journal of Clinical Nutrition* 20: 1206-11.

Giles, H. M., E. J. Watson Williams, and P. A. J. Ball. 1964. Hookworm infection and anaemia. *Quarterly Journal of Medicine* 33: 1-24.

Goldsmith, G. A. 1959. *Nutritional diagnosis.* Springfield, Ill.

Gorbach, S. L., J. G. Banwell, B. Jacobs, et al. 1970. Tropical sprue and malnutrition in West Bengal. I. Intestinal microflora and absorption. *American Journal of Clinical Nutrition* 23: 1545-58.

Gorse, G. J., R. L. Messner, and N. D. Stephens. 1989. Association of malnutrition with nosocomial infections. *Infection Control and Hospital Epidemiology* 10: 194-203.

Guerrant, R. L., L. V. Kirchoff, D. S. Shields, et al. 1983. Prospective studies on diarrheal illness in northeastern Brazil: Patterns of disease, nutritional impact, etiologies, and risk factors. *Journal of Infectious Diseases* 148: 986-97.

Gupta, M. C., S. Mithal, K. L. Arora, and B. N. Tandon. 1977. Effect of periodic deworming on nutritional status of ascaris infected pre-school children receiving supplementary food. *Lancet* 2: 108-10.

Gyllenberg, H., and P. Roine (with H. Unkila and M. Rossander). 1957. The value of colony counts in evaluating the abundance of '*Lactobacillus' bifidus* in infant feces. *Acta Pathology Microbiology Scandinavica* 41: 146.

György, P., S. Dhanamitta, and E. Steers. 1962. Protective

effects of human milk in experimental staphylococcus infection. *Science* 137: 338.

Hansen, L. A. 1992. Immunity of breast feeding. In *Nutrition and immunology,* ed. R. K. Chandra, 45–62. St. John's, Newfoundland, Canada.

Harland, P. S. E. G. 1965. Tuberculin reactions in malnourished children. *Lancet* 1: 719–21.

Harris, A. D., and T. Moore. 1947. Vitamin A in infective hepatitis. *British Medical Journal* 1: 553.

Heymann, W. 1936. Absorption of carotene. *American Journal of Diseases in Childhood* 51: 273–83.

Hodges, R. E., W. B. Bean, M. A. Ohlson, and R. E. Bleiler. 1962a. Factors affecting human antibody response. III. Immunologic responses of men deficient in pantothenic acid. *American Journal of Clinical Nutrition* 11: 85.

　　1962b. Factors affecting human antibody response. IV. Pyridoxine deficiency. *American Journal of Clinical Nutrition* 11: 180.

Hoskins, L. C., S. J. Winawer, S. A. Broitman, et al. 1967. Clinical giardiasis and intestinal malabsorption. *Gastroenterology* 53: 265–79.

Hoyle, B., M. Yunus, and L. C. Chen. 1980. Breast feeding and food intake among children with acute diarrhoeal disease. *American Journal of Clinical Nutrition* 33: 2365–71.

Hume, R., and E. Weyers. 1973. Changes in leucocyte ascorbic acid during the common cold. *Scottish Medical Journal* 18: 3.

Hussey, G. D., and M. Klein. 1990. A randomized, controlled trial of vitamin A in children with severe measles. *New England Journal of Medicine* 323: 160–4.

Jackson, A. A., D. Picou, and P. J. Reeds. 1977. The energy cost of relating tissue deficits during recovery from a protein energy malnutrition. *American Journal of Clinical Nutrition* 30: 1514–17.

Jacobs, A. L., Z. A. Leitner, T. Moore, and I. M. Sharman. 1954. Vitamin A in rheumatic fever. *Journal of Clinical Nutrition* 2: 155.

Jayalakshmi, V. T., and C. Gopalan. 1958. Nutrition and tuberculosis. I. An epidemiological study. *Indian Journal of Medical Research* 46: 87–92.

Joynson, D. H. M., A. Jacobs, D. M. Walker, and A. E. Dolby. 1972. Defect of cell-mediated immunity in patients with iron-deficiency anaemia. *Lancet* 2: 1058–9.

Jung, R. C., and P. C. Beaver. 1951. Clinical observations on *Tricocephalus trichiurus* (whipworm) infestation in children. *Pediatrics* 8: 548–57.

Kampschmidt, R. F., H. F. Upchurch, C. L. Eddington, and L. A. Pulliam. 1973. Multiple biological activities of partially purified leukocytic endogenous mediator. *American Journal of Physiology* 224: 530–3.

Katsampes, C. P., A. B. McCowd, and W. A. Phillips. 1944. Vitamin A absorption test in cases of giardiasis. *American Journal of Diseases of Children* 67: 189–93.

Keusch, G. T. 1972. Subclinical malabsorption in Thailand. I. Intestinal absorption in Thai children. *American Journal of Clinical Nutrition* 25: 1062–6.

　　1990. Immunity and infection in iron deficiency. In *Functional significance of iron deficiency,* ed. C. O. Enwonwu, 81–92. Nashville, Tenn.

Keusch, G. T., and M. J. G. Farthing. 1986. Nutrition and infection. *Annual Review of Nutrition* 6: 131–54.

Keusch, G. T., A. G. Plaut, and F. J. Troncale. 1970. The interpretation and significance of the xylose tolerance test in the tropics. *Journal of Laboratory and Clinical Medicine* 75: 558.

Khan, M. U., and K. Ahmad. 1986. Withdrawal of food during diarrhoea; major mechanisms of malnutrition following diarrhoea in Bangladesh children. *Journal of Tropical Pediatrics* 32: 57–61.

Khosla, S. N., S. V. Sharma, and S. C. Srivastava. 1978. Malabsorption in giardiasis. *American Journal of Gastroenterology* 69: 694–700.

Kielman, A. A., C. E. Taylor, and R. L. Parker. 1978. The Narangwal nutrition study: A summary review. *American Journal of Clinical Nutrition* 31: 2040–52.

Kielman, A. A., I. S. Uberoi, R. K. Chandra, and V. L. Mehra. 1976. The effect of nutritional status on immune capacity and immune responses in preschool children in a rural community in India. *WHO Bulletin* 54: 477–83.

Klipstein, F. A., and J. M. Falaiye. 1969. Tropical sprue in expatriates from the tropics living in the continental United States. *Medicine* 48: 475–91.

Klipstein, F. A., I. M. Samloff, G. Smarth, and E. A. Schenk. 1968. Malabsorption and malnutrition in rural Haiti. *American Journal of Clinical Nutrition* 21: 1042.

Kluska, J. 1972. Carbohydrate absorption disorders in the course of lambliosis. *Wiadomosci Parazytologiczne* 18: 43–55.

Kotcher, E., M. Miranda, R. Esquivel, et al. 1966. Intestinal malabsorption and helminthic and protozoan infections in the small intestine. *Gastroenterology* 50: 366.

Lala, V. R., and V. Reddy. 1970. Absorption of beta-carotene from green leafy vegetables in undernourished children. *American Journal of Clinical Nutrition* 23: 110–13.

Law, D. K., S. J. Dudrick, and N. I. Abdou. 1973. Immunocompetence of patients with protein-caloric malnutrition. *Annals of Internal Medicine* 79: 545–50.

Layrisse, M., L. Aparcedo, C. Martinez-Torres, and M. Roche. 1967. Blood loss due to infection with *Trichuris trichura. American Journal of Tropical Medicine and Hygiene* 16: 613–19.

Layrisse, M., N. Blumenfeld, L. Carbonell, et al. 1964. Intestinal absorption tests and biopsy of the jejunum in subjects with heavy hookworm infection. *American Journal of Tropical Medicine and Hygiene* 13: 2.

Lindenbaum, J., C. D. Gerson, and T. H. Kent. 1971. The recovery of small intestinal structure and function after residence in the tropics. I. Studies in Peace Corps volunteers. *Annals of Internal Medicine* 74: 218.

Lindenbaum, J., J. W. Harmon, and C. D. Gerson. 1972. Subclinical malabsorption in developing countries. *American Journal of Clinical Nutrition* 25: 1056–61.

Long, C. L., W. R. Schiller, W. S. Blakemore, et al. 1977. Muscle protein ataboism in the septic patient as measured by 3-methylhistidine excretion. *American Journal of Clinical Nutrition* 30: 1349–52.

Lugo-de-Rivera, C., H. Rodriguez, and R. Torres-Pinedo. 1972. Studies on the mechanism of sugar malabsorption in infantile infectious diarrhea. *American Journal of Clinical Nutrition* 25: 1248–53.

Lutter, C. K., J. O. Mora, J. P. Habicht, et al. 1989. Nutritional supplementation: Effects on child stunting because of diarrhea. *American Journal of Clinical Nutrition* 50: 1–8.

Lynch, S. R., J. L. Beard, S. A. Dassenko, and J. D. Cook. 1984. Iron absorption from legumes in humans. *American Journal of Clinical Nutrition* 40: 42–7.

Mahalanabis, D., T. W. Simpson, M. L. Chakraborty, et al. 1979. Malabsorption of water miscible vitamin A in children with giardiasis and ascariasis. *American Journal of Clinical Nutrition* 32: 313–18.

Martorell, R., J. Rivera, and C. K. Lutter. 1990. Interaction of diet and disease in child growth. In *Breastfeeding, nutrition, infection, and infant growth in developing and emerging countries,* ed. S. A. Atkinson, L. A. Hanson, and R. K. Chandra, 307-21. St. John's, Newfoundland, Canada.

Martorell, R., and C. Yarborough. 1983. The energy cost of diarrheal diseases and other common illnesses in children. In *Diarrhea and malnutrition: Interactions, mechanisms, and interventions,* ed. L. D. Chen and N. S. Scrimshaw, 125-42. New York.

Martorell, R., C. Yarborough, S. Yarborough, and R. E. Klein. 1980. The impact of ordinary illnesses on the dietary intakes of malnourished children. *American Journal of Clinical Nutrition* 33: 345-50.

Mata, L. J. 1978. *The children of Santa Maria Cauque: A prospective field study of health and growth.* Cambridge, Mass.

Mata, L. J., R. A. Kromal, J. J. Urrutia, and B. Garcia. 1977. Effect of infection on food intake and the nutritional state: Perspectives as viewed from the village. *American Journal of Clinical Nutrition* 30: 1215-27.

May, C. D., K. D. Blackfan, J. F. McCreary, and F. H. Allen, Jr. 1940. Clinical studies of vitamin A level. *Journal of the American Medical Association* 123: 1108.

Mayoral, L. G., K. Tripathy, F. T. Garcia, et al. 1967. Malabsorption in the tropics: A second look. I. The role of protein malnutrition. *American Journal of Clinical Nutrition* 20: 866-83.

McFarlane, H., S. Reddy, K. J. Adcock, et al. 1970. Immunity, transferring and survival in kwashiorkor. *British Medical Journal* 4: 268-70.

McGregor, I. A. 1982. Malaria: Nutritional implications. *Review of Infectious Disease* 4: 798-803.

McGregor, I. A., K. Williams, W. Z. Billewicz, and A. M. Thomson. 1966. Hemoglobin concentration and anaemia in young West African (Gambian) children. *Transactions of the Royal Society for Tropical Medicine and Hygiene* 60: 650-67.

McLaren, D. S. 1963. *Malnutrition and the eye.* New York.

Meydani, S. N., J. D. Ribaya-Mercado, R. Russell, et al. 1990. The effect of vitamin B-6 on the immune response of healthy elderly. In *Micronutrients and immune functions,* ed. A. Bendich and R. J. Chandra. *Annals of the New York Academy of Science* 587: 303-6. New York.

Migasena, P., and B. G. MaeGraith. 1969. Intestinal absorption in malaria. I. The absorption of an amino acid (AIB-1-¹⁴C) across the gut membrane in normal and plasmodium knowlesi-infected monkeys. *Annals of Tropical Medical Parasitology* 63: 439.

Milner, P. F., R. A. Irvine, C. J. Barton, et al. 1965. Intestinal malabsorption in *Strongyloides stercoralis* infestation. *Gut* 6: 574.

Molla, A., A. M. Molla, A. Rahim, et al. 1982. Intake and absorption of nutrients in children with cholera and rotavirus reinfection during diarrhoea and after recovery. *Nutrition Research* 2: 232-42.

Molla, A. M., A. Molla, S. A. Sarker, and M. M. Rahaman. 1983. Food intake during and after recovery from diarrhea in children. In *Diarrhea and malnutrition: Interactions, mechanisms, and interventions,* ed. L. D. Chen and N. S. Scrimshaw, 113-23. New York.

Moore, T. 1957. *Vitamin A.* London.

Moyer, E. D., and M. C. Powanda. 1983. Diarrhea and nutrient requirements. In *Diarrhea and malnutrition: Interactions, mechanisms, and interventions,* ed. L. C. Chen and N. S. Scrimshaw, 161-76. New York.

Murray, M. J., A. B. Murray, C. J. Murray, and M. B. Murray. 1975. Refeeding-malaria and hyperferraemia. *Lancet* 1: 653-4.

1978a. The certain adverse effect of iron repletion on the course of certain infections. *British Medical Journal* 2: 1113-15.

1978b. Diet and cerebral malaria: The effect of famine and refeeding. *American Journal of Clinical Nutrition* 31: 57-61.

Nalin, D. R., R. Russell, H. Greenberg, and M. M. Levine. 1980. Reduced vitamin A absorption after enteric infections. In *Current chemotherapy and infectious disease.* Proc. 11th CC 19th ICAAC American Society of Microbiology, 947-8. Washington, D.C.

National Institute of Nutrition. 1980. Effect of infection on serum vitamin A levels. In *Annual report,* 79-82. Hyderabad, India.

Neumann, C. G., E. R. Stiehm, and M. Swenseid. 1977. Complement levels in Ghanaian children with protein–calorie malnutrition. In *Malnutrition and the immune response,* ed. R. M. Suskind, 191-4. New York.

Notis, W. M. 1972. Giardiasis and vitamin B₁₂ malabsorption. *Gastroenterology* 63: 1085.

O'Brien, W. 1975. Intestinal malabsorption in acute infection with *Strongyloides stercoralis. Transcript of the Royal Society for Tropical Medicine and Hygiene* 69: 69-77.

Olarte, J., J. Cravioto, and B. Campos. 1956. Inmunidad en el niño desnutrido. I. Producción de antitoxina diftérica. *Boletin Médico Hospital Infanta* 13: 467.

Oomen, H. A. P. C. 1959. Nutrition and some disorders of the eye in the tropics. *Tropical and Geographical Medicine* 11: 66.

Palumbo, P. J., H. H. Scudmore, and J. H. Thompson, Jr. 1962. Relationship of infestation with *Giardia lamblia* to intestinal-malabsorption syndromes. *Proceedings of the Mayo Clinic* 37: 589.

Peterson, G. M. 1957. Intestinal changes in *Giardia lamblia* infestation. *American Journal of Rontgenerentology* 77: 670-7.

Picciano, M. F., K. E. Weingartner, and J. W. Erdman, Jr. 1984. Relative bioavailability of dietary iron from three processed soy products. *Journal of Food Science* 49: 1558-61.

Powanda, M. C. 1977. Changes in body balances of nitrogen and other key nutrients: Description and underlying mechanisms. *American Journal of Clinical Nutrition* 30: 1254-68.

Pretorius, P. J., and L. S. de Villiers. 1962. Antibody response in children with protein malnutrition. *American Journal of Clinical Nutrition* 10: 379-83.

Rahaman, M. M., A. K. M. J. Alam, and M. R. Islam. 1974. Leukemoid reaction, hemolytic anaemia, and hypoproteinaemia in severe *Shigella dysenteriae* type-1 infection. *Lancet* 1: 1004.

Rahaman, M. M., and M. A. Wahed. 1983. Direct nutrient loss and diarrhea. In *Diarrhea and malnutrition: Interactions, mechanisms, and interventions,* ed. L. C. Chen and N. S. Scrimshaw, 155-60. New York.

Rahmathullah, L., B. A. Underwood, R. D. Thulasiraj, et al. 1990. Reduced mortality among children in southern India receiving a small weekly dose of vitamin A. *New England Journal of Medicine* 323: 929-87.

Reddy, V., P. Bhaskaran, N. Raghuramulu, et al. 1986. Relationship between measles, malnutrition, and blindness: A prospective study in Indian children. *American Journal of Clinical Nutrition* 44: 924-30.

Reddy, V., and S. G. Srikantia. 1964. Antibody response in

kwashiorkor. *Indian Journal of Medical Research* 52: 1154-8.

Rhode, J. E., R. A. Cash, R. L. Guerrant, et al. 1983. Therapeutic interventions in diarrhea. In *Diarrhea and malnutrition: Interactions, mechanisms, and interventions,* ed. L. C. Chen and N. S. Scrimshaw, 287-98. New York.

Riis, P. 1975. Giardiasis: A cause of intestinal malabsorption. *Journal of the Royal College of Physicians* 10: 61-6.

Roche, M., and M. E. Perez-Gimenez. 1959. Intestinal loss and reabsorption of iron in hookworm infection. *Journal of Laboratory and Clinical Medicine* 54: 49.

Roche, M., M. E. Perez-Gimenez, M. Layrisse, and E. D. Prisco. 1957a. Gastrointestinal bleeding in hookworm infection. Studies with radioactive Cr^{51}; report of 5 cases. *American Journal of Digestive Diseases* 2: 265.

1957b. Study of urinary and fecal excretion of radioactive chromium Cr^{51} in man, its use in the measurement of intestinal blood loss associated with hookworm infection. *Journal of Clinical Investigation* 36: 1183.

Rodgers, F. C., P. K. Dhir, and A. T. M. Hosain. 1960. Night blindness in the tropics. *Archives of Opthalmology* 63: 927.

Rosenberg, I. H., and B. B. Bowman. 1982. Impact of intestinal parasites on digestive function in humans. *Federation Proceedings* 43: 246-50.

Rosenberg, I., and N. S. Scrimshaw. 1972. Workshop on malabsorption and nutrition. *American Journal of Clinical Nutrition* 25: 1045-1289.

Rosenberg, I., N. W. Solomons, and R. E. Schneider. 1977. Malabsorption associated with diarrhea and intestinal infections. *American Journal of Clinical Nutrition* 30: 1248-53.

Ross, C. A. C., and E. A. Dawes. 1954. Resistance of the breast-fed infant to gastro-enteritis. *Lancet* 1: 994.

Rowland, M. G. M., T. J. Cole, and R. G. Whitehead. 1977. A quantitative study into the role of infection in determining nutritional status in Gambian village children. *British Journal of Nutrition* 37: 441-50.

Sarker, S. A., M. A. Wahed, M. M. Rahaman, et al. 1986. Persistent protein losing enteropathy in post measles diarrhoea. *Archives of Diseases of Children* 61: 739-43.

Schlesinger, L., and A. Stekel. 1974. Impaired cellular immunity in marasmic infants. *American Journal of Clinical Nutrition* 27: 615.

Scrimshaw, N. S. 1977. Effect of infection on nutrient requirement. *American Journal of Clinical Nutrition* 30: 1536-44.

1989. Malnutrition and nosocomial infection (Editorial). *Infection Control Hospital Epidemiology* 10: 192-3.

1990a. Energy cost of communicable diseases in infancy and childhood. In *Activity, energy expenditure and energy requirements of infants and children,* ed. B. Schurch and N. S. Scrimshaw, 215-38. Lausanne.

1990b. Functional significance of iron deficiency: An overview. In *Functional significance of iron deficiency,* ed. C. O. Enwonwu, 1-14. Nashville, Tenn.

In press. Effect of infection, including parasitic diseases, on nutrient requirements. In *International nutrition,* ed. O. Galal.

Scrimshaw, N. S., C. E. Taylor, and J. E. Gordon. 1968. *Interactions of nutrition and infection.* Geneva.

Shank, R. E., A. F. Coburn, L. V. Moore, and C. L. Hoagland. 1944. The level of vitamin A and carotene in the plasma of rheumatic subjects. *Journal of Clinical Investigation* 23: 289-95.

Sirisinha, S., R. Suskind, R. Edelman, et al. 1973. Complement and C3 proactivator levels in children with protein-calorie malnutrition and effect of dietary treatment. *Lancet* 1: 1016-20.

Sivakumar, B., and V. Reddy. 1972. Absorption of labelled vitamin A in children during infection. *British Journal of Nutrition* 27: 299-304.

1975. Absorption of vitamin A in children with ascariasis. *American Journal of Tropical Medicine and Hygiene* 78: 114-15.

Smith, N. J., S. Khadroui, V. Lopez, and B. Hamza. 1977. Cellular immune response in Tunisian children with severe infantile malnutrition. In *Malnutrition and the immune response,* ed. R. M. Suskind, 105-9. New York.

Smythe, P. M., G. G. Breton-Stiles, H. J. Grace, et al. 1971. Thymolymphatic deficiency and depression of cell-mediated immunity in protein-calorie malnutrition. *Lancet* 2: 939-43.

Solomons, N. W. 1982. Giardiasis: Nutritional implications. *Review of Infectious Diseases* 4: 859-69.

Sommer, A. 1982. *Nutritional blindness: Xerophthalmia and keratomalacia.* London.

Sommer, A., J. Katz, and I. Tarwotjo. 1984. Increased risk of respiratory disease and diarrhoea in children with pre-existing mild vitamin A deficiency. *American Journal of Clinical Nutrition* 40: 1090-5.

Sommer, A., I. Tarwotjo, E. Djunaedi, et al. 1986. Impact of vitamin A supplementation on childhood mortality: A randomized controlled community trial. *Lancet* 1: 1169-73.

Sommer, A., I. Tarwotjo, D. Hussaini, and D. Susanto. 1983. Increased mortality in children with severe vitamin A deficiency. *Lancet* 2: 582-8.

Sprinz, H., R. Sribhibhadh, E. J. Gangarosa, et al. 1962. Biopsy of the small bowel of Thai people. *American Journal of Clinical Pathology* 38: 43.

Stanton, B. F., J. D. Clemens, B. Wojtyniak, and T. Khair. 1986. Risk factors for developing mild nutritional blindness in urban Bangladesh. *American Journal of Diseases of Children* 140: 584-8.

Stephenson, L. S., D. W. T. Crompton, M. C. Latham, et al. 1980. Relationships between *Ascaris* infection and growth of malnourished preschool children in Kenya. *American Journal of Clinical Pathology* 33: 1165-72.

Stephenson, L. S., M. C. Latham, K. M. Kurz, et al. 1989. Treatment with a single dose of Albendazole improves growth of Kenyan schoolchildren with hookworm *Trichuris trichiura* and *Ascaris lumbricoides* infections. *American Journal of Tropical Medicine and Hygiene* 41: 78-87.

Stinnett, J. D. 1983. *Nutrition and the immune response.* Boca Raton, Fla.

Suskind, R., R. Edelman, P. Kulapongs, et al. 1976. Complement activity in children with protein-calorie malnutrition. *American Journal of Clinical Nutrition* 103: 226.

Taren, D. L., M. C. Neshiem, D. W. T. Crompton, et al. 1987. Contribution of ascariasis to poor nutritional status of children from Chiriqui Province, Republic of Panama. *Parasitology* 45: 1466-91.

Tielsch, J. M., K. P. West, Jr., J. Katz, et al. 1986. Prevalence and severity of xerophthalmia in southern Malawi. *American Journal of Epidemiology* 124: 561-8.

Tomkins, A. M., P. J. Garlick, W. N. Schofield, and J. C. Waterlow. 1983. The combined effects of infection and malnutrition on protein metabolism in children. *Clinical Science* 65: 313-24.

Tripathy, K., E. Duque, O. Bolanos, et al. 1972. Malabsorption syndrome in ascariasis. *American Journal of Clinical Nutrition* 25: 1276.

United Nations University. 1979. Protein-energy requirements under conditions prevailing in developing countries: Current knowledge and research needs. *Food and Nutrition Bulletin*. Supplement 1, Tokyo.

Veghelyi, P. V. 1938. Giardiasis in children. *American Journal of Diseases of Children* 56: 1213-41.

Venkatachalam, P. S., and V. N. Patwardhan. 1953. The role of *Ascaris lumbricoides* in the nutrition host: Effects of ascariasis on digestion of protein. *Transactions of the Royal Society of Tropical Medicine and Hygiene* 47: 169.

Von Bonsdorff, B. 1948. Pernicious anemia caused by *Diphyllobothrium latum* in the light of recent investigations. *Blood* 3: 91-102.

  1956. Parasitological reviews: *Diphyllobothrium latum* as a cause of pernicious anemia. *Experimental Parasitology* 5: 207.

  1964. The fish tapeworm, *Diphyllobothrium latum*; a major health problem in Finland. *World Journal of Medicine* 11: 170.

Waldman, T. A. 1970. Protein-losing enteropathy. In *Modern trends in gastroenterology*, ed. W. I. Card and B. Creamer, 125-42. London.

Wannemacher, R. W. 1977. Key role of various individual amino acids in host response to infection. *American Journal of Clinical Nutrition* 30: 1269-80.

Waslien, C. I., Z. Farid, and W. J. Darby. 1973. The malnutrition of parasitism in Egypt. *Southern Medical Journal* 66: 47-50.

Weinberg, E. D. 1978. Iron and infection. *Microbiology Review* 42: 45-66.

  1984. Iron withholding: A defense against infection and neoplasia. *Physiology Review* 64: 65-102.

West, K. P., G. R. Howard, and A. Sommer. 1989. Vitamin A and infection: Public health implications. In *Annual Review of Nutrition*, ed. R. E. Olson, E. Beutler, and H. P. Broquist, 63-86. Palo Alto, Calif.

West, K. P., Jr., and A. Sommer. 1985. Delivery of oral doses of vitamin A to prevent vitamin A deficiency and nutritional blindness. *Food Review International* 1: 355-418.

Whitehead, R. G. 1977. Protein and energy requirements of young children living in the developing countries to allow for catch-up growth after infections. *American Journal of Clinical Nutrition* 30: 1536.

Wilson, D., R. Bressani, and N. S. Scrimshaw. 1961. Infection and nutritional status. I. The effect of chicken pox on nitrogen metabolism in children. *American Journal of Clinical Nutrition* 9: 154-8.

Wohl, M. G., J. G. Reinhold, and S. B. Rose. 1949. Antibody response in patients with hypoproteinemia – with special reference to the effect of supplementation with protein or protein hydrolysate. *Archives of Internal Medicine* 83: 402.

WHO (World Health Organization). 1980. Parasite related diarrhoeas. *WHO Scientific Working Group, WHO Bulletin* 58: 819-30.

Zuckerman, A. 1966. Recent studies on factors involved in malarial anemia. *Military Medicine* 131: 1201-16.

Zumrawi, F. Y., H. Dimond, and J. C. Waterlow. 1987. Effects of infection on growth in Sudanese children. *Human Nutrition, Clinical Nutrition* 41C: 453-61.

VI.4   Famine

Despite swelling populations around much of the globe, the enormous expansion of agricultural productivity, the rapid development of transport facilities, and the establishment of globally interlinked market networks have made it theoretically possible to provide adequate food for all. Yet famine and hunger still persist and, indeed, proliferate in some parts of the world. Their durable character represents a perplexing and wholly unnecessary tragedy (Drèze and Sen 1989; Watts and Bohle 1993b). Although the extent of hunger in the world will never be known with precision (Millman 1990), it has been estimated that in the early 1990s, more than 500 million adults and children experienced continuous hunger and even more people were deemed vulnerable to hunger, with over 1 billion facing nutritional deficiencies (WIHD 1992).

The community concerned with world hunger is far from unanimous in its understanding of the situation. S. Millman (1990) likens the situation to the parable of the elephant and the blind men, whereby hunger is perceived differently by those encountering different aspects of it. It is significant that these varying perceptions correspond to particular disciplinary or professional orientations, leading to different diagnoses of the nature of the problem and its underlying causes and implying distinct foci for policy interventions.

Problems of food supply, then, are among the most bewildering, diffuse, and frustrating of humankind's contemporary dilemmas. Within the lifetime of each of us, official views of the world food situation have oscillated from dire predictions of starving hordes to expectations of a nirvana of plentiful food, then back to impending doom. One expert states that famine is imminent, whereas another declares that our ability to adequately feed the world's people is finally within reach.

The term "famine" is one of the most powerful, pervasive, and (arguably) emotive words in our historical vocabulary. This in itself makes it all the more difficult to isolate its meaning and wider significance. But to this end, the ensuing chapter addresses the following topics: A brief review of famine in history; a definition of famine and its various dimensions; the identification and description of a range of cultural and social famine coping practices in traditional societies; an examination of the literature on the causes of famine, along with some of the recent attempts to model famine vulnerability and the famine process; and, finally, a focus on past and present attempts to develop famine policies.

Famine in History

Famines are woven into the fabric of history; indeed, as D. Arnold (1988) has pointed out, they are important historical markers, often used by chroniclers and historians in search of points in time when the normal rhythms of human life were interrupted, or when momentous developments appeared to have a discernible beginning or end. In singling out famines in this way, historians have done rather more than just seize upon convenient dates by which to slice up history into manageable portions. They have also followed the perceptions and traditions of the people themselves. In preliterate societies, particular famines, along with other collective catastrophes, served as a common means of recording and recovering the experience of the past.

We know that famines have led to untimely deaths for at least 6,000 years, which makes it necessary to simplify the enormously complex array of data and sources concerning them. W. A. Dando (1980) has identified a system of world famine regions for the period from 4000 B.C. to A.D. 1980. The first region, for the period from 4000 to 500 B.C., is Northeast Africa and West Asia, where the earliest authentic records of famine have been found, including several from the Nile Valley dated as early as 4247 B.C. The famine in Egypt of Joseph's day (1708 B.C.), recorded in the Old Testament, appears to have been part of a much more widespread scarcity throughout West Asia. Until 500 B.C., the literature of this area continued to be studded with accounts of famines.

In the thousand years after 500 B.C., the heaviest concentration of accounts mentioning famine are found in the region that became the Roman Empire. Imperial Rome may have brought order and organization to subjugated peoples, but Mediterranean Europe still experienced at least 25 major famines during this period. After A.D. 500, western Europe emerged as the region to which the extant accounts of famine most frequently refer. Up to A.D. 1500, the British Isles suffered from at least 95 famines, France suffered 75, and other famines or severe food shortages were recorded throughout these territories as well.

Indeed, famines are a much discussed part of the European experience until the nineteenth century. However, both the incidence and extent of major European famines seem to have begun to decline in the seventeenth and eighteenth centuries (Grigg 1985). Thus, the last major famine in England occurred in A.D. 1620, in Scotland in the 1690s, in Germany, Switzerland, and Scandinavia in 1732, and in France in 1795. During the nineteenth century, many parts of Europe were afflicted with harvest failure and high prices in 1816, and the 1840s were also a period of acute food shortage, including the "Great Famine" in Ireland (1846–51). But in general, even localized food crises diminished in Europe after the eighteenth century, and although until the mid-1800s most Europeans remained in a chronic state of undernourishment (Cipolla 1976), at least western Europe had shaken off the specter of famine.

The fourth famine region was eastern Europe, whose various sectors experienced more than 150 recorded famines between A.D. 1500 and 1700. Expanding the time frame a little, in Russia at least 100 hunger years and 121 famine years were recorded between A.D. 971 and 1974 (Dando 1980). Famine occurrence in imperial Russia reached its high point in the nineteenth century, but even after the revolution of 1917, the scourge of famine could not be eliminated. In 1921 and 1922, approximately 9 million people starved to death; in 1933 and 1934, the number was between 4 and 7 million, and in 1946 and 1947, it was nearly 2 million. The famines of 1921 and 1922 resulted from the breakdown of order associated with civil war, and those of the 1930s reflect Stalin's forced collectivization of agriculture. The famine of 1946–7 was also man-made. A decision to rigorously restore the provisions of the collective farm charter, which had been relaxed during World War II, coupled with a drought and the use of scarce grain in other segments of the world to promote communist goals, produced this famine (Dando 1980).

From A.D. 1700 to 1970, Asia emerged as the world's foremost famine area. In South Asia, legends and records document more than 90 major famines over the last 2,500 years, two-thirds of them after 1700, but most were localized (Kulkarni 1990), with only an occasional one (like the *Durga Devi* famine of the late fourteenth century in the Deccan) that covered a large area. Although all of India suffered to some extent in the early eighteenth century, without question the late eighteenth and nineteenth centuries were that country's time of famines. They devastated Bengal in 1770, the Ganges Valley, western India, the Deccan, and Madras in 1783, and almost all of the peninsula in 1790. In the first half of the nineteenth century, major famines took place from 1802 to 1804, in 1806 and 1807, in 1812, 1824, and 1825 and 1826, from 1832 to 1834, in 1837 and 1838, and in 1854. Most of these, however, were limited in their extent, although they did cause intense suffering and death regionally.

But the period between 1860 and 1880 in India was one in which five major famines and three local scarcities followed each other in rapid succession (Kulkarni 1990). The famines were widespread, but after 1880 there was a period when only local scarcities occurred and no famines. Then, in 1895, perhaps the most disastrous famine of the century began in the middle and upper Ganges Valley and spread, in 1896, to the whole South Asian region. This was followed by the famine of 1899 and 1900, which devastated a large area of the peninsula and the northwest as well.

There have also been a number of famines in the twentieth century in South Asia. In 1907 and 1908, one descended on the middle and upper Ganges Valley, but thereafter, although there were scarcities, no famine occurred until that of Bengal in 1943. Nor did scarcity and famine cease after India gained its independence in 1947. There was widespread scarcity (and probably starvation, despite denials of this by the

Indian central government and various state governments) in 1952 and 1953, and again between 1965 and 1967, 1970 and 1973, and in 1986 and 1987. In addition, Bangladesh was severely affected by famine in 1974.

Over the past 2,000 years, China has recorded perhaps as many as 90 famines per century. But, as in South Asia, the nineteenth century saw China's most devastating famines. Droughts, floods, locusts, hurricanes, and earthquakes were natural disasters that induced crop failures, but the breakdown of civil society and warfare also were important factors. Four of these famines alone (in 1810, 1811, 1846, and 1849) are reported to have claimed 45 million lives. Nine million died in the famine from 1875 to 1878 in northern China. Other severe famines were recorded in 1920 and 1929, and there was a particularly harsh one between 1958 and 1961, when it is estimated that between 14 and 26 million (and perhaps even as many as 40 million) people died (Kane 1988; Article Nineteen 1990).

Elsewhere in Asia there have been localized famines in many places over the past 200 years or so, and of late, areas such as Timor and Kampuchea have been afflicted. In the latter country, the decade of the 1970s was one of continuous food crisis, deepening into famine in 1975 and 1979; the latter has been described as the "most catastrophic famine in the history of the Khmer people" (Ea 1984).

Even North and South America, as well as the Pacific, have not escaped unscathed from famine. For example, in the middle of the fifteenth century, a four-year sequence of frosts and droughts produced a terrible famine in central Mexico (Townsend 1992), and famines, caused by a combination of drought and lack of political and economic cohesion, have been frequent in northeast Brazil (Cunniff 1996). Even in the lush, tropical Caribbean islands, famines were common during the seventeenth and eighteenth centuries, through a combination of physicoenvironmental, biological, and socioeconomic circumstances (Watts 1984). In the Pacific, small islands, vulnerable to environmental and societal perturbations, have always been susceptible to food shortages and famine (Currey 1980). Indeed, even in Hawaii, since European contact, famines have occurred on average every 21 years (Schmitt 1970).

Although famines have struck many parts of the world in the past two decades, sub-Saharan Africa has been especially hard hit and has afforded the contemporary world some extremely powerful and distressing visions of famine. However, famine in Africa is not a new phenomenon. Oral traditions from many areas mention numerous occurrences in precolonial times (Arnold 1988b), and colonial records document many more (Hill 1977; Watts 1983). Yet, as late twentieth-century events in Bosnia-Herzegovina reminded us, no place is free from famine, and one of its contemporary faces is worn by victims of war.

Nevertheless, although nearly 200 million people each year continue to be plagued by hunger, the trend in famines since the end of World War II has clearly been a downward one (Kates et al. 1988). This trend reflects both a lessening of famine generally and a major shift in incidence from populous Asia to less populous Africa. The Alan Shawn Feinstein World Hunger Program at Brown University, using data averaged for 7-year periods beginning in 1950, has found that the average number of people residing in countries in which *The New York Times* reported famine was 790 million annually from 1957 to 1963, but declined to an average of 265 million in the period from 1978 to 1984. Since that time, the average has dropped below 200 million.

Definitions and Dimensions of Famines

Millman (1990) has identified three hunger-related situations in the world today: food shortage, food poverty, and food deprivation. These situations are distinguished from one another primarily by the level of human organization (from an entire population to households to the individual) at which scarcity is manifested. "Food shortage" indicates a situation in which total food supplies within a bounded region are insufficient to meet the needs of its population. "Food poverty" refers to the situation in which a household cannot obtain enough food to meet the needs of all of its members. "Food deprivation" refers to insufficient food availability for an individual. At each level, the commonly used term "food security" can be taken to mean an ability to avoid the corresponding hunger situation. Food shortage is among the causes of food poverty, which in turn is among the causes of food deprivation. However, other factors may operate to cause food poverty when there is no food shortage, and food deprivation where there is no food poverty.

Thus, hunger is not a single, uniform experience. Its manifestations range from vulnerability resulting from dietary traditions that mesh imperfectly with variations in need over the life cycle, to household food insecurity rooted in poverty, to aggregate food-supply shortfalls, which, when they worsen, can become the massive hunger crises affecting large numbers within specified regions and generating substantial increases in mortality. The latter, in popular thinking, are called "famines." Certainly, the most poignant manifestations of hunger are famines, which we have become accustomed to thinking of as "disasters" of a particularly horrific kind, replete with human misery on a massive, almost unimaginable, scale.

Famine: A Subjective Window on Poverty and Hunger

One of the debates over famine that has emerged involves the question of whether it is a discrete event or merely the tip of an iceberg of underlying social, economic, and political processes (Currey 1992). Many writers (e.g., Mellor and Gavian 1987) have defined famine as a discrete event, separate from chronic hunger. Furthermore, the World Bank (1986) has separated transitory food insecurity from chronic food insecurity, and the World Food Programme has focused most of its attention on nutrition in times of disaster. B. Currey (1992), however, has questioned whether such crisis management is the most cost-effective means of reducing world hunger and has suggested that more efforts be directed toward building resilient agricultural systems and long-term monitoring of rural development.

Such differences in approach highlight one of the problems with famine, which, as a concept and as a historical phenomenon, presents us with a fundamental paradox: It is both event and structure (Arnold 1988). On one hand, it is clearly an "event." There may be widely different opinions as to exactly when a particular famine begins or ends, but there is common agreement that it occupies a finite span of historical time and human experience. Basically, famine signifies an exceptional (if periodically recurring) event – a collective catastrophe of such magnitude as to cause social and economic dislocation. It generally results in abnormal levels of destitution, hunger, and death. It can lead to the complete disintegration of customary patterns of work and subsistence and can greatly disrupt customary norms of social behavior, not to mention levels of mortality.

And yet, at the same time, famine cannot be meaningfully considered in isolation from the economic, social, and political structures of a specific society. Occasionally, we document a specific disaster, resulting in a famine, in a society that is otherwise relatively secure in its provisioning. More commonly, however, famine acts as a revealing commentary upon a society's deeper and more enduring difficulties. In other words, famine can be viewed as a subjective window on poverty and hunger. The proximate cause of a famine may lie in some apparently unpredictable "natural disaster," like a flood or drought, or in a human calamity like a civil war or invasion (Arnold 1988). But these are often no more than "triggering" events, intensifying or bringing to the fore a society's already extant vulnerability to food shortages and famine. Any historical understanding of famine must, therefore, be alert to its structural causes and to its social and cultural parameters, as well as to what happened during the crisis itself.

This approach to famine, as a meeting and intermingling of event and structure, partially derives from a perspective that sees history not as simply a narrative sequence of great events and personalities but as a search for underlying structures and recurrent patterns, famines among them (Arnold 1988). In a similar manner, it has been recognized among social scientists that individual action or agency is constrained by the relationship between agency and structure, and this dialectic takes place not only locally but on a world scale (Wisner 1993). Thus, although a famine can arise locally, the constraints on humans that create their vulnerability to it can originate in the influence of structures located on other continents.

Famines As History

Famines form an integral part of formal attempts to record and recall the past in many parts of the world. Among other things, they act as an aid to recall, as a reminder of their terrifying consequences, and, sometimes, as a key to their putative meanings. The practice of naming famines is one indication that in the popular memory at least, all famines were far from identical, whatever similarities they might bear for outside observers. For example, India's famines commonly bore the title of the Hindu calendar year in which they occurred. Others were named after vengeful deities or were seen as marking the onset of the *Kali Yuga,* the Hindu age of suffering, corruption, and human misery. In Africa, rural people have often named famines after what they exchanged or sold to get food, or after what people ate.

Such examples highlight the fact that famines are "hitching posts" of history (Shipton 1990) and the poles around which experiences and impressions are organized and collected. Thus, famine forms a link between the world of personal memory and the broader domain of collective consciousness, despite the fact that many academic historians have been skeptical about the authenticity of famine accounts found in folklore, oral history, and even chronicles.

In the past, as famines touched the lives of millions deeply and directly, they lived on in collective memory, and terror of their return kept them alive in that memory. We should remember that it has only been in the last century or so that people in Western societies have felt themselves immune to famine and discarded such cumulative folk experience as redundant. Perhaps it is this lack of fear of famine that most critically divides us from our own past and from the lives of a large part of the world's peoples today (Arnold 1988).

Famine As Demographic Crisis

One of the ways in which famines impress themselves upon collective memory and experience is through the colossal and devastating mortality involved. However, mortality statistics can give only a rough impression of a famine's magnitude, and it would be unrealistic to credit such data with any real precision. Until the last century or two, few governments kept reliable and detailed records of vital data. Historians who have attempted to reconstruct famine mortality in the remote past have tried to compensate for this deficiency by using parish records, tax returns, and similar sources. But these records seldom provide a dependable picture of mortality trends over a wider area, and even where there was some form of birth and death registration, famine mortality was often grossly underreported. Local officials themselves fell ill, died, or deserted their posts. The deaths of villagers who wandered off elsewhere in search of food passed unrecorded. Thus, it is not surprising that our understanding of the relationships between demographic processes and famine is extremely limited (Hugo 1984).

Indeed, although mortality is viewed as one of famine's major effects and is, in fact, an integral part of many of its definitions, there is surprisingly little data to precisely quantify the impact of famine on mortality rates, even in modern times; the famines of the 1970s and 1980s stand out as examples (Hugo 1984). Accounts of famines in preindustrial societies usually paint pictures of death on a massive scale. P. A. Sorokin (1942, 1975), one of the earliest writers to systematically summarize the demographic impacts of famine on mortality, has suggested that in affected areas, death rates sometimes reached 200, 500, or even 800 for every 1,000 people, as compared with normal rates of 10 to 30. He maintains that in the Soviet famine of 1921, for example, regional death rates reached 600 per 1,000.

The concept of "excess deaths" has been found to be useful in examining the impact of contemporary famines on mortality. "Excess deaths" refers to the "number of deaths over and above those that would have occurred if previous nutritional conditions had prevailed" (Bongaarts and Cain 1981). Very few studies have employed this concept. One of these, by A. K. Sen (1980), makes several reasonable corrections to the existing mortality data for the 1943 Bengal Famine and concludes that the total figure for excess mortality associated with that famine was 3 million. Another, by J. C. Caldwell (1975), estimates that the excess mortality for the entire Sahelian region during the famines of 1970 to 1974 was no more than 250,000, despite massive publicity that insisted that many more people were dying, and M. Alamgir (1980), in a third study, estimates the excess mortality for Bangladesh in 1974 and 1975 as 1,500,000.

Famines also seem to have distinct phases of mortality response (Ruzicka and Chowdhury 1978; Bongaarts and Cain 1981). There appears to be an initial phase during which mortality rates respond immediately to the food crisis. This is followed by a second phase that sees mortality rates at least twice as high as normal, and a third involving a gradual rate decline. Finally, there is a phase in which mortality rates are actually lower than "normal" because the most vulnerable groups in the population have already been severely pruned.

Demographers have also tended to neglect the differential mortality within subgroups in populations during famines. Best documented are excess death rates among infants and children. Illustrative is the Bangladesh Famine of 1974 and 1975, during which there was a 70 percent increase in the infant mortality rate in a sample of 228 villages containing 120,000 people, which meant 529 deaths per 1,000 live births (Ruzicka and Chowdhury 1978). A study of the 1980 famine in Daramoja, Uganda, measured an infant mortality rate of 607 per 1,000 live births.

The elderly also are especially vulnerable to excess mortality in times of famine (Chen and Chowdhury 1977), as are pregnant and lactating women (Bongaarts and Cain 1981). In addition, there is no doubt that famine mortality disproportionately affects poor and landless people. For example, in Bangladesh, the 1975 crude death rate among landless families was three times higher than among those with at least three acres of land (Chen and Chowdhury 1977). It also is clear that in the 1943 Bengal Famine, the most affected group in terms of excess mortality was that of agricultural laborers (Mukherji 1965).

Although discussion of the demographic impact of famine has concentrated on assessments of mortality, another important dimension is its impact on fertility (the demonstrated capacity of women for reproducing) and fecundity (a predisposition or latent capacity for reproducing). There is considerable evidence to suggest that fertility, as demonstrated by birth rates, follows a distinctive pattern during famines (Bongaarts and Cain 1981). Birth rates initially remain at prefamine levels, then rapidly decline, some nine months after the famine's onset, to rates only 30 to 75 percent of those that are normal (depending on the severity of the famine). The low point in birth rates usually occurs nine months after the end of the crisis. But following this point, the conception rate recovers quickly, and the famine-induced period of depressed fertility is followed by one in which the birth rate exceeds prefamine levels for up to three years. Reasons for this pattern are varied. Fecundity is decreased by minimal nutrition and psychological stress. Hunger also tends to diminish the frequency of intercourse, and spouses are often separated by temporary migration during famines. In addition, there is an increase in voluntary birth control, sexual abstinence, abortion, and, historically at least, infanticide (Sorokin 1942; Connell 1955; Ruzicka and Chowdhury 1978).

As yet, there is little information on socioeconomic differentiation in the pattern of fertility response to famine, but the scattered evidence suggests that it is the poor and landless who most reduce their rate of conception during such a crisis (Stein et al. 1975; Ruzicka and Chowdhury 1978).

A third important demographic feature of famine is migration, which in traditional societies has historically been one of the most important ways that people have coped with famine. Although migration should be studied in relationship to mortality and fertility, in this chapter it will be considered with other coping strategies.

Famine and Disease

Assessments of the demographic impact of famine are greatly complicated by the disease factor because, in most famines, mortality from epidemic disease has greatly exceeded that from actual starvation. For example, during the course of the Bengal Famine of 1943, starvation was identified as the cause of death in only about 5 percent of cases; cholera, malaria, and smallpox accounted for the great majority of the 3 million deaths. Moreover, in the 1940s, just as in the nineteenth century, the colonial administration in India was loath to acknowledge starvation as a cause of death. This situation has continued since 1947 because famine mortality in India has remained a political matter.

The reasons for the intertwining of epidemics and famine appear to be both physiological and social. Malnutrition can weaken the body's immune responses, creating a diminished resistance to infection and a reduced capacity to recover from it. Further, migration has the effect of spreading disease to areas not directly affected by hunger. During times of famine, personal hygiene also tends to be neglected. Debilitated people may fail to wash, and they may drink filthy or contaminated water. They may consume "famine foods" (unripe grain, grass, or roots) in an attempt to suppress hunger; this sometimes causes diarrhea and vomiting, which results in a further weakening of the body and a greater risk of spreading disease. The high level of famine mortality, in other words, is partially a consequence of the nature of the expedients people adopt to try to escape from hunger and partly one of the disruption created by famine in customary patterns of social behavior.

Famine Chronology

All famines have their own internal chronology. Because hunger seldom kills outright and immediately, the symptoms of growing hunger may not be apparent to outsiders until destitution and debilitation have already reached an advanced stage. Thus, the duration of famine can be reckoned according to a variety of different criteria, and definitions made by those actually subject to the famine may differ greatly from those made by officials. Those experiencing a famine might date its onset from the first warning signs of approaching calamity, such as the delayed arrival of the rains and the first withering of standing crops. Officials, by contrast, might see a famine as beginning only when food prices climb to abnormal heights or when the signs of distress among the starving poor are given governmental recognition. Equally, an official definition of famine might end with the closing of state-managed relief work, though this may occur well before survivors of the famine feel themselves free of its grip.

Traditional Cultural and Social Coping Practices

"Coping" is the manner in which people act, within the constraints of existing resources and the range of expectations of a situation, to achieve various ends (Blaikie et al. 1994). In general, such action involves no more than "managing resources," but more specifically, it usually means how this management is accomplished under unusual and adverse circumstances. Thus, coping can include defense mechanisms, active ways of solving problems, and methods for handling stress. Resources for coping with famine include labor power, land, tools, seed for crops, livestock, draft animals, cash, jewelry, other items of value that can be sold, and, of course, storable food stocks, as well as skills and specialized knowledge. In order for tangible resources to be mobilized, people must be entitled to command them, which may be achieved in many ways. Among them are using the market, exercising rights, calling upon obligations (of household members, kin, patrons, friends, and the general public, by appeals to moral duty as in alms and charitable giving), stealing, or even committing violence. In many cases, specialized knowledge is required with certain resources, for instance, in locating wild foods, determining the moisture capacity of certain soils, discovering water sources, or finding wage labor in distant cities or plantations.

Although the range of strategies to prevent or minimize the risk of famine is enormous, two generalizations can be made. First, the objective of many of these strategies is to secure necessities, such as access to a minimum level of food, shelter, and physical security, rather than to increase income. Second, maintaining command of these basic needs in a risky environment usually implies employing multiple, varied methods of access to resources. These include diversifying production strategies, setting up nonagricultural income sources, strengthening or multiplying social support networks, and developing a demographic strategy aimed at the creation, maintenance, and mobilization of human labor.

Diversification is one strategy, and the production of farming people is usually diversified, involving mixed cropping, intercropping, the cultivation of non-staple crops, and the use of kitchen gardens. The result is often a "normal surplus" in good years because it is planned on the basis of meeting subsistence needs even in bad (but not the worst conceivable) years. Because planting a greater variety of crops provides the best chance of an optimum yield under all variations of weather, plant disease, and pest attack, it represents one of the most important precautionary strategies for coping with food shortages (Klee 1980; Wilken 1988).

Another important preventive/mitigating strategy involves the development of social support networks. These include a wide variety of rights and obligations among members of the same household (for example, wives and husbands, parents and children), within the extended family, and within other groups with a shared identity, such as clan, tribe, and caste. Parents may try to make strategic choices of marriage for children into comparatively wealthy families, which might increase their ability to call on resources in difficult times (Caldwell, Reddy, and Caldwell 1986). Within the household and family, successfully securing resources in potentially disastrous times depends upon the implicit bargaining strength of its members and on their "fallback" positions (Agarwal 1990) or "breakdown" positions, if cooperation in this bargaining position should fail (Sen 1988, 1990).

It has also been argued that in societies where people habitually live in the shadow of hunger, those people develop, or are the beneficiaries of, social and cultural practices that ensure that even the poorest will not starve to death. Such practices are based on ideas of "shared poverty" and "mutual assistance," which some writers term the "moral economy of the poor" (Scott 1976). Under circumstances of famine, those who have food share it with destitute kinsmen and needy neighbors. These noneconomic relations in times of hardship include those between patrons and clients and between rich and poor. They offer a minimum subsistence and a margin of security, and they constitute a "subsistence ethic" based on reciprocity. There are many examples of this type of relationship (see Bhatia 1963 on India and Scott 1976 on Southeast Asia).

Although most examples are drawn from the past, it would seem that this "moral economy" has not completely broken down in the contemporary world. For example, reports indicate that during the drought and period of extreme food shortage from 1980 to 1983 in southern India, the support system worked well, at least for the aged (Caldwell et al. 1986). Further, A. Gupta (1988) goes so far as to say that the continued existence of such support in present-day India is responsible for the retention of people in the countryside. In Nepal, it has been found that the wealthy are encouraged to avoid reducing daily wages for agricultural work in difficult times and to refrain from selling grain outside the village (Prindle 1979).

In general, it seems that when the outcome of a season is still uncertain, landlords and patrons make some provision for laborers and the poor. But once signs of a famine are evident, landowners respond by reducing their number of field hands. As the crisis deepens, workers in other sectors of an agrarian society, such as fishermen, artisans, and a range of rural dependents, become affected by the lack of patronage and support from the wealthy as well, a situation that has been documented in many parts of the world (Arnold 1988).

Rural households try to build up stores of food and salable assets. However, the first is difficult to achieve for people who are involved in a web of impoverishment and exploitation that is a normal and continuing part of life. In many parts of Africa, Asia, and Latin America (and in Europe in the past), even in "normal years," most households experience shortfalls in production for their own consumption. Furthermore, some staples, like potatoes (which simply cannot be kept for as long as a year – or until the next harvest),

rot and become inedible. Hence the historical attractiveness of cereal crops, because they can be stored for long periods. However, most people do have a range of salable assets (e.g., furniture, cooking utensils, jewelry, farm implements, livestock, and land) that can be converted to food as necessary.

Another strategy to mitigate the potential impact of famine is that of having a large number of children, thus improving security by increasing possible future family income. This strategy is an important one in places like Bangladesh, where children are considered to be a less risky investment than land (Cain 1978).

Once famine has begun, precautionary mechanisms are put into practice. There are others, which cannot be developed in advance but which also come into play as the famine unfolds. When there is a potential food shortage and possible famine, the period during which stress develops can be long, allowing for a succession of strategies. A review of a number of major studies of coping mechanisms in the face of famine (Watts 1983b; Corbett 1988; Rahmoto 1988; Waal 1989; Agarwal 1990; Brown 1991; O'Brien and Gruenbaum 1991) clearly identifies a sequence of activities. These include religious rituals and ceremonies, identification of scapegoats, reduction of the amount of food consumed and a longer spacing out of meals, substitution of lower-quality and wild foods, and calling for resources from others (especially family and kin), along with generating household income by wage labor, petty commodity production, and the sale of easily disposable items (as long as such sales do not undermine future productive capacity). But as the food crisis deepens, loans from moneylenders and the sale of important items, such as draft animals, agricultural implements, and livestock, become common. Finally, if all preceding strategies have failed to maintain minimum food levels, migration often ensues. But let us now examine some of these coping mechanisms in more detail.

The cultural context of famine has everywhere been reflected in religion, and one of the first responses to famine in any society has likely been an intensification of ritual. Prayers offered up in churches, mosques, and temples are supplemented by special rituals and ceremonies in streets, fields, and public places. Deities, saints, even plants and animals, are invoked.

When rituals fail to bring relief, more divisive or desperate responses can follow. Sometimes, scapegoats are sought out. Other times, the physical and spiritual anguish brought on by famine and pestilence has bred religious fanaticism. In some instances, the persistence of famine has caused doubts about the gods of the established pantheon. For example, in the famines of the late 1870s in India and China, Western missionaries won converts by pointing to the apparent failure of local deities to protect worshipers from want. In some societies, however, the people place great faith in divine will and believe it blasphemous to question their gods' purposes and intentions.

As a famine marches remorselessly onward, societies respond more materially. For example, the planting of a crop might be delayed, crop varieties with shorter growing seasons or lower water requirements might be planted, parts of farms might be abandoned and effort focused on better locations, or seed grain might be consumed rather than sown. While this is happening, households might reduce the amount of food consumed at each meal and space meals out over longer and longer intervals (just as they do during the "hungry gap," a period of seasonal food shortage that is a part of normal life; during this time, people know that they will lose some weight and then recover) (see Garine 1991).

In order to eke out food supplies, adulteration of staples often occurs. As a crisis deepens further, wild, "famine" foods replace staples. Different items fall into this category in different parts of the world. In Niger, for example, the pith of palm trees and lily roots are used, and in nineteenth-century Ireland, it was nettles, berries, fungi, seaweed, frogs, and rats. In China, people have eaten grass, bark, and even earth to quell hunger. As "famine" foods were often found on communal lands, continuing access to such lands today can be especially significant in densely populated regions (Blaikie, Harriss, and Pain 1985; Agarwal 1990; Chambers, Saxena, and Shah 1990).

At this stage, people usually sell the few assets they have to buy food, especially once food resources available from family and kin have been exhausted, along with other sources of family income such as wage labor, petty commodity production, and artisanal work. Houses are stripped of their furniture, doors, and window frames. Women sell cooking utensils and jewelry, and finally, farm animals and implements are sold, thus jeopardizing prospects of agricultural recovery after the famine ends. People may try to borrow money, but often moneylenders and even banks are loath to give credit in years when there is no harvest to lay claim to. As a last resort, land might be sold, which (along with migration) is one of the unmistakable signs of acute and deepening crisis. In Bengal in 1943, for example, over 250,000 households sold all their land, and 600,000 more sold part of their holdings. Considering the importance of land, such sales are a sign of desperation. As in the past, losing land as a result of famine is still one way in which property holders sink into the residual class of landless laborers. The sale brings short-term relief from starvation but has the net effect of increasing vulnerability.

While all of this is happening, those in the worst-hit portion of the population frequently begin to contest their deprivation. Laborers and tenants petition landlords, patrons, and governments, demanding to be fed. In the past, and in some places today, a lack of response to such pleas for relief has led to the looting of grain stores, market stalls, warehouses, carts, trucks, and barges. It is at such moments of mounting tension, anger, and fear that the idea of the poor having a right to food is most forcefully evinced (Thompson 1971). But food riots in most places and times have not lasted indefinitely; rather, they died away once provision was made for the basic needs of the hungry or, more often, the situation deteriorated further until no food was to be had by any means.

One common alternative has been recourse to what officialdom and the propertied elites have seen as "crime"; like food riots and looting, this measure has been a characteristic and almost universal way of coping with famine. Famine crime has assumed many forms, ranging from an intensification of normal banditry, sheep stealing, and petty theft, to murder. Usually, as society fractures under famine's pressure, crimes against property and persons soar.

When all attempted strategies have failed to maintain minimum food levels, migration occurs. Although this can be considered a demographic response to famine, it is also an important coping strategy. Much famine migration has been short-term and over relatively short distances, and once conditions have improved, people return to their homes and farms. This was true in Europe in the past (Sorokin 1942), and it certainly has been the case in a variety of other places in the world. During the Indian famines of the nineteenth century, there were many such movements to unaffected areas, and to the cities, in search of relief. In Brazil, the northeast has witnessed temporary flights to the towns in 1878, in 1915, from 1930 to 1932, in 1942, and in 1958. The Sahelian crisis from 1970 to 1974 also produced large-scale population movement (Caldwell 1975), much of which focused on refugee camps. There was also much short-distance local migration, some of it to the cities.

But famine-induced migration also has a permanent dimension, which is one of the more enduring demographic consequences of famine. It can be documented from preindustrial Europe, where this type of "forced" migration resulted in the colonization of new agricultural areas. Perhaps the most spectacular famine-induced migration out of any area in Europe was associated with the Irish famine from 1846 to 1851, when about 1 million people migrated to the United States and England. Between 1852 and 1916, another nearly 5 million Irish left, three-quarters of them bound for the United States. During the Sahelian crisis, much of the famine-induced urbanization, especially of pastoralists, was permanent (Colvin 1981). The sequence of famines in the Brazilian northeast has produced a permanent migration of peasants to the tropical rain forests of Amazonia and to São Paulo and Rio de Janeiro. In the nineteenth century, famine was one of the impelling forces behind the Indian diaspora to Natal, Mauritius, Malaya, Fiji, Guyana, and nearby Sri Lanka (then Ceylon). The exodus from southern India to the tea and coffee plantations of Sri Lanka reached its peak during the 1870s, a time when a high level of labor demand was matched by famine in Madras.

Women and Famine

The burden of famine has fallen, and in many developing-world societies continues to fall, with exceptional severity on women. One reason for this is that, in many parts of the world, women traditionally either have been the main agricultural producers or have constituted a substantial part of the agrarian workforce. Colonial regimes often had no practical interest in developing opportunities for women. Education and new employment opportunities were directed toward men, who took up work in the mines, on the plantations, and in the cities, often far from their home villages, weakening their commitment to subsistence labor, which, more often than not, was left to the women. Thus, the onset of a famine hits women directly. Their food production dwindles, and when field laborers are dismissed or left without employment, they lose cash and in-kind income as well.

The burden of famine also has fallen heavily on women because of their customarily low status in patriarchal societies. In many societies there is a cultural expectation that women will sacrifice their food and, ultimately, their lives to enable their husbands and sons to survive. Women normally eat after the men, and when food is in short supply, female children tend to be neglected and resources concentrated on male children. There is a great deal of historical and contemporary evidence to show that part of the burden of hunger and suffering has been transferred to women through neglect, starvation, abandonment, and sale into prostitution. Women, in short, have been victimized in the interests of male survival.

Famines, therefore, impose enormous physical and emotional suffering upon women. Women have often killed their children; marital relationships can be strained to the point of divorce and abandonment; and hunger can drive women into prostitution and slavery. They have been sold by landowners, moneylenders, and other males with authority over them, for money and for food. Further, in many parts of the world, even today, one of the commonest responses to famine has been the sale of children, especially girls. Thus, the devaluing of life that occurs in a famine has often further favored male power and ascendancy.

Conflicting Ideas about Famine Causation

An enormous literature has grown up to explain why famines occur. Once, "acts of God" and "freaks of nature" were seen as self-sufficient explanations for why people hungered and died. Warfare, blockades, and deliberate hoarding of grain have also been commonly used to explain why famine happened. Today, writers on the causes of famine are more disposed to see these as only precipitating or contributory factors, and, increasingly, famine has come to be regarded as a complex phenomenon, more a symptom than a cause.

One of the main sources of confusion about the subject arises from the multiple causes of famines and their great variety in space and time. Some of the literature makes a distinction between "general and predetermining factors," or the time–geographic dimensions of famine (long-term, intermediate, and immediate), and the trigger mechanism of the actual famine (Currey 1979, 1980; Murton 1980). W. I. Torry (1986) uses similarly distinct "ultimate" and "proximate" causes of famine, and P. M. Blaikie and colleagues (1994) employ the terms "root causes" and "underlying pressures," which create "unsafe conditions." It is also important to acknowledge that if there are many combinations of factors and mechanisms that bring about famine, then each famine is unique. Indeed, the task of building theories of famines is particularly difficult because of the complexity of each specific case. Any theory will involve an understanding not only of the existing systems of production but also the distribution of food in terms of access to land and inputs, as well as the operation of the market, the determination of prices, and the behavior of traders in food staples (Canon 1991). Government policies with regard to food production and distribution (and famine relief) may also play a profound role. Then there is always a series of contextual events peculiar to each famine, a "sequence of events" (Alamgir 1981), or in Currey's (1984) parlance, a "concatenation."

Two main (and largely competing) types of famine explanation, based on differing sets of causal mechanisms, can be identified. Many commentators have assumed that a famine arises out of an actual shortfall in the means of subsistence, or as it is commonly labeled, a food availability decline (often abbreviated to FAD). Either some natural disaster occurs, causing a crop failure to reduce the aggregate amount of food available, or population in the long term outstrips the quantity of food available. The other mechanism involves the decline in some people's entitlements to food (abbreviated to food entitlement decline, or FED). According to this explanation, first articulated by Sen (1981), famine is a result of the ways in which access to food is reduced because of the operation of social and political processes that deny or lessen "entitlement" to food.

These processes may involve a deterioration in the ability of people to grow their own food or to buy it through various forms of exchange. To this context should be added the impact of various hazards that may not reduce the overall amount of food but instead affect the success of different groups of people in fulfilling their entitlements. This type of explanation focuses much more firmly on relations of power within a society that may account for the distribution of assets and income (unequal in "normal" times) that become a matter of life and death in times of famine. This model tends to reduce the causal importance of natural events, which although they may be limited to a decline in the aggregate supply of food (with the impact of drought, flood, or pest attack), are analyzed in the context of the political economy of root causes and predetermining factors. In other words, people are made vulnerable to the impact of a natural hazard by their place in the economic, political, and social processes that affect their exchange entitlements.

Food Availability Decline (FAD)

The school of thought that attributes famine to an aggregate decline in the supply of food is clearly linked to explanations of famine in terms of natural events. In particular, drought has been identified as a major immediate cause of crop failure and, therefore, of a decline in food supply. It is difficult to find pure supply-side explanations of famine in the recent literature, but between the decline in aggregate food supplies and its immediate causes (such as drought) on one side, and the detailed mechanisms that actually precipitate famines on the other, the emphasis is usually on the former (Blaikie et al. 1994).

In addition to analyses of recent famines, the historical literature contains considerable discussion of the long-term shifts of climate that have appeared to gradually undermine a society's apparently secure subsistence base. Generally, whereas most historians have been wary of embracing the type of "climatic determinism" posited by Ellsworth Huntington (1915, 1919) and have tended to see climatic variations as too short-term and peripheral to provoke major subsistence crises, others have acknowledged that a substantial number of historical famines in many parts of the world were preceded by partial or complete failure of the rains (Arnold 1988).

Unfortunately, much of the writing also tends to subtly argue that if famines could be attributed to natural causes, they could be explained in terms of exceptional events and not by continuing and normal social processes (Hewitt 1983b). K. Hewitt (1983a) even argues that a previous generation of academics and practitioners virtually ostracized those who sought explanations that went deeper than the impact of the natural hazard. Given the dominance of science and technology in the modern era, the publication of any analysis of causes that failed to suggest that hazards could be modified and responded to by technology resulted in the exile of its authors from the mainstream social explanation.

Another important element in the food availability decline approach has been the "overpopulation" thesis. Deeply rooted in Western thought, the thesis is most commonly identified with the writings of Thomas Malthus (Turner 1986), who believed that the food supply was relatively inelastic, increasing at best by arithmetical progression, whereas population rose in geometrical leaps and bounds. In periodically sweeping away the excess population, famines maintained a rough equilibrium between population and subsistence. However, this thesis was to prove unten-

able for Britain (and Europe generally), where a transformation of industry and commerce improved agricultural productivity and transportation and led to the increased importation of foodstuffs. Not only did rapid population growth fail to trigger famine, but standards of living rose. Increasing prosperity and material security, however, were also accompanied by a growing practice of birth control through various means.

Although Malthus's thesis seemed to square with nineteenth- and early-twentieth-century reality only in places like India and China, since the 1950s, famines and food crises in Africa and Asia have led to a strong revival of interest in his ideas. Population in the developing world has risen sharply, largely as the result of improved medical services and sanitation. Food production is frequently, but not altogether accurately, assumed to have not kept up, and with too little food to go around and too many mouths to feed, famine has been predicted on a global scale by numerous "prophets of doom," as for example, Paul Erlich (1968), and W. and P. Paddock (1967). But very often these dire predictions are based on simple measurements of global food supply stocks versus rising population rates, without taking into account high levels of wasteful food consumption in the West, the nature of foodstuffs produced, and the unequal nature of food distribution (between nations, and within states, classes, and even families).

Food Entitlement Decline (FED)

In *Poverty and Famines* (1981), the Indian economist Amartya Sen challenges the view that famines are caused by food availability decline. As already noted, he views famine as the result of the many and complex ways in which people's access to food is reduced because of the operation of social and political processes that deny or lessen their "entitlement" to food. Such an approach distinguishes between aggregate availability or supply of food and an individual access to, or ownership of, food. People obtain food through five different types of "entitlement relationships" in private-ownership market economies (Sen 1981; Drèze and Sen 1989, 1990): (1) There is production-based entitlement, which is the right to own food that one produces with one's own or hired resources; (2) there is trade-based entitlement, which describes the rights associated with ownership when they are transferred through commodity exchange; (3) there is own labor entitlement, which is the trade-based and production-based entitlement when one sells one's own labor power; (4) there is inheritance and transfer entitlement, which is the right to own what is given by others (gifts) and what is transferred by the state, such as pensions; (5) there are extended entitlements, which are entitlements that exist outside legal rights (for example, ownership) and are based on legitimacy and expectations of access to resources.

Such entitlements are not fixed and equal but vary according to an individual's position within a wider system of production, exchange, control, and distribution. Entitlements are either owned by a person or can be exchanged by that person for other commodities. People are vulnerable to starvation if their endowment does not contain adequate food or resources to produce food and their capacity to exchange labor or other goods and services cannot be translated into enough food. This situation can occur without a decline in aggregate food supply and without any disruption or malfunction of the market.

The food entitlements decline approach just discussed recognizes the relations of power within a society that may account for the distribution of assets and income and that become a matter of life and death in times of famine. It also acknowledges the importance of changes in purchasing power. Further, it disaggregates regional food production and availability and follows through how food is distributed to individuals (it permits analysis of intrahousehold food allocation and explains why the rich never die in famines and why some classes benefit from them). This approach involves the regional, national, and world economy in the analysis and draws attention to the possible prevention of famines by food imports.

There have, of course, been criticisms of the food entitlement decline approach. First, there is a scale and boundary problem: If the analysis is stretched to include a big enough area, there is always enough food to avert a famine. Second, some famines clearly have had their origins in food availability decline, and although it may be incorrect to identify this as an ultimate or even most important cause, it is inescapable that a fall in the amount of locally produced food (because of war, drought, or longer-term environmental decline) hinders the ability of people to find alternative sources of food. Third, initially, entitlements, as well as resources (endowments), were conceived of as static and given. But recent research (Watts 1991) has pointed out that they are fought over and constitute the terrain of struggle within societies in which group interests (defined by class, caste, gender, age, ethnicity) are in contradiction.

In conclusion, the entitlements approach to the analysis of famine has released famine study from theoretical constraints. However, this pursuit of a single theory of the mechanisms of famine has diverted attention from multiple causality and the possibility of famines at different times in the same place being caused by a mix of factors. This concern has led to the further development of the concept of famine vulnerability, to which the food entitlements decline approach alludes but fails to pursue in depth.

Famine Vulnerability Models

Two models have recently been proposed that attempt to take into account the multiplicity of factors that make people vulnerable to famine. The first,

developed by M. Watts and H. G. Bohle (1993a, 1993b), argues that the locally and historically specific configuration of poverty and hunger defines what they call a "space of vulnerability." These researchers set out to provide a theoretical means by which this space can be "mapped" with respect to its social, political, economic, and structural–historical coordinates. They endeavor to radically extend the concept of entitlements, not simply in a social or class sense but in a political and structural sense, to take account of (1) the particular distribution of entitlements and how they are reproduced in specific circumstances; (2) the larger arena of rights in which entitlements are defined, fought over, contested, and won and lost (that is, empowerment or enfranchisement); and (3) the structural properties (what they call "crisis proneness") of the political economy that precipitate entitlement crises.

Watts and Bohle review the extensive literature relating to "entitlement and capability," "empowerment and enfranchisement," and "class and crisis." They emphasize that these processes can be grasped only relationally (as congeries of social relations), and they develop a tripartite structure that defines the space of vulnerability through the intersection of the three causal powers: command over food (entitlement); state–civil society relations seen in political and institutional terms (enfranchisement/empowerment); and the structural–historical form of class relations within a specific political economy (surplus appropriation/crisis proneness).

The intersection of these causal powers produces three parallel analytical concepts; economic capability, property relations, and class power. Economic capability emerges from particular configurations of entitlement and empowerment, property relations from the intersection of entitlement and political economy, and class power from specific forms of political economy and empowerment. The three causal powers or processes (entitlement, empowerment, political economy) are conceived of as accounting for mass poverty associated with specific long-term (structural) changes. Famine results from violent short-term changes in these same mechanisms.

The space of vulnerability also has an internal structure in which it is possible to locate vulnerable groups and regions. Because the concept of vulnerability is relational, the space and shape of vulnerability is given by its social relations. For example, if famine is described as a food entitlement problem, vulnerability is located in the realm of economic, and especially market, relations. If, conversely, famine resides in the powerlessness of individuals, classes, and groups to claim and enforce food entitlements, then vulnerability is determined by the power and institutional relations within civil society. Finally, if famine is driven by processes of exploitation and surplus appropriation, it accordingly occupies a location within the space of vulnerability that lies in the realm of class relations.

It is also possible to place both vulnerable groups (social) and vulnerable regions (spatial) within the space of vulnerability. In the former, vulnerable individuals, groups, and classes can be located according to the causal processes that present possibilities and constraints in the sphere of subsistence. Individuals and groups vulnerable to market perturbations and unable to cope with food entitlement decline because they are resource and/or asset poor, may be located in the "economic space" of vulnerability. If the likelihood of deprivation is rooted in politics that can be inscribed in gender (patriarchal politics), work (production politics), and the public sphere (state politics) – all of which may render individuals and groups powerless – their location in the "political space" of vulnerability is determined by power and institutional relations. Finally, if deprivation arises from processes of surplus extraction and appropriation, individuals and groups are located in the "structural–historical" space of vulnerability given by specific configurations of class relations. All these spaces obviously exist simultaneously. Determining the precise weighting becomes important in assessing the ways in which famine differs between Somalia, Kampuchea, or Bangladesh.

This social map of vulnerability has a geographic or spatial counterpart. Vulnerable regions can be located in relationship to the tripartite structure of causal processes. Economically marginal regions that regularly or sporadically experience fluctuation in productivity and prices are most liable to food entitlement crises (they occupy the "economic space" of vulnerability). Peripheral regions experience vulnerability through relations of dependency to a regional core that drains surpluses and resources away (they occupy the "political space" of vulnerability). Finally, regions shaped by endemic crises and conflicts (both economic and ecological) due to processes of commercialization, proletarianization, and marginalization are logically situated in the "structural–historical" space produced by class relations.

In summary, this modeling of the "spaces of vulnerability" integrates many of the factors identified by previous research on famine into a more logical and causal structure. It provides a way to integrate the intersections of structures, tendencies, and conjunctures as they impinge on the famine process. The specific content of the social space of vulnerability, the actual concatenation of events that might trigger famine, and the specific structural forces at work, although deriving from the abstract causal structure, will naturally be time- and place-specific.

Blaikie and colleagues (1994) also have produced a comprehensive dynamic framework, which they call an "access model." They focus on the way unsafe conditions arise in relation to the economic and political processes that allocate assets, income, and other resources in a society. Natural events are integrated into the model through a focus on how resources are allocated by social processes. "Access" involves the ability of an individual, family, group, class, or community to use resources that are directly required to secure a livelihood.

Access to those resources is always based on social and economic relations, usually including the social relations of production, gender, ethnicity, status, and age. Rights and obligations obviously are not equally distributed among all people, and it is argued that less access to resources leads to increased vulnerability. The model incorporates the notion of "trigger events": war, as in the case of Ethiopia (1984 and 1990), Angola, Chad, Sudan, and Mozambique (1984); or natural hazards, as in the case of the Sahel (1970-6), Sudan (1985), and Ethiopia (1973). The model analyzes the structures and processes of famine in relation to making a living in normal times. It is an iterative approach in which "external" shocks and triggers have their impact upon the structures and processes of political economy.

Famine Policy

Although an enormous literature has grown up to explain why famines occur and what to do about them, it is clear today that there is disjuncture between explanation and policy. Explanation is largely a product of the academic world. Policies for dealing with famine are a product of famine relief agencies, governmental advisers, and governments. The lack of affinity between the two types of literature is surprising. In an ideal world there should be a progressive and interacting relationship between theories of famine avoidance and relief and policy, but instead they are widely apart. The two sides are separated almost by a different language and are pervaded by different constraints and concerns.

Policy in the Past

Certainly, the fortunes of the state, whether in Europe, Africa, or Asia, have long been bound up with the containment or prevention of famine and, more generally, with provisioning the populace. Protecting its subjects from starvation and extreme want has for centuries been one of the primary functions of government and one of the principal expectations of the public. If we look for pre-twentieth-century evidence of the state as an agency of famine control and as a provider of famine relief, we can find it in places as far apart as China and Europe. In China, state paternalism, fostered by the ideology of the Confucian state, led to the protection of peasants from the worst effects of natural disasters, as well as measures for famine prevention and relief. But this system began to break down in the nineteenth century, and the situation remained chaotic until after 1949. Famine control was one of the first priorities of the new Communist state and, seemingly, one of its great successes, until the famine from 1958 to 1961 cruelly exposed the limitations of China's agrarian revolution.

In medieval times, European states did what little they could to avert the threat of famine. As Europe crossed the threshold from medieval to modern times, problems of provisioning (especially of the growing cities) increased, as did the problems of maintaining order in food-shortage situations. One response in England in the late sixteenth century was the issuing of orders, which became the bases for the English Poor Law, to counter the problem of vagrancy and destitution. In France, the provisioning of Paris received special attention from the government, and alarm over basic subsistence needs helped to make the revolution of 1789.

In Europe, however, as agriculture became more productive and increasingly market-oriented, governments sought to free themselves from the obligation to feed people and regulate markets. In France, attempts to make subsistence a matter of individual rather than state concern was short-lived, but in England, ideas of "free trade" gained increasing momentum in the late eighteenth century and the early years of the nineteenth. In 1814 and 1815 the Corn Laws, the last bastion of old protectionists and paternalists, were eroded, and in 1846, under Sir Robert Peel, they were finally swept away. By this time in Britain, policy-makers were imbued with the belief that market forces should not be tampered with and that self-reliance must not be weakened or local effort superseded by the activities of the government. This commitment to laissez-faire, and the notion that the state should not intervene in famines, was immediately tested in Ireland, where initially the state's role was seen as being strictly confined to providing employment on public works. Only in 1847 was emergency relief belatedly instituted.

The Indian Famine Codes
In India, the East India Company administration also strongly supported the new orthodoxy. Even during the famines and shortages of the early nineteenth century, the presidency and provincial governments adhered firmly to the principles of noninterference in the operation of the market and trade. But it became evident, particularly during the heavy mortality of the 1860s and 1870s, that a policy of laissez-faire alone would not meet the extreme recurrent crises of famine. A number of reports demonstrated that the government had lost enormous amounts of revenue by not investing in irrigation, other preventive works, and railways to stimulate production and to move food to food-shortage areas. Although the general principle of nonintervention in the grain trade remained inviolate until World War II, by the late 1870s there were moves, however hesitant, toward greater state responsibility for the Indian economy and for the welfare of the Indian people.

This change in policy resulted in the first coherently written explanation of famine, linked to policy recommendation. From the 1860s extensive reports were written on famine, and in 1878 the First Famine Commission was appointed (Brennan 1984). Its reports of 1880 led to the drafting of the Famine Codes of the mid-1880s by each of the provinces of India. The reports also contained much speculation about the causes of famine. The reports are especially instructive on the relation between the theories of famine causation and policies of prevention, relief, and rehabilitation.

Reasonably effective policies were formulated from these efforts. The Famine Codes reveal a professed dislike of interference in the operation of the market through price controls, and contain the belief that free trade is the best guarantee of satisfying effective demand. There is also an aversion to charity and free handouts and a strong ethic of "self-help." Thus, the backbone of famine relief was massive public works generating guaranteed employment, plus free assistance for those unable to work. That the latter breached ideology was accepted as necessary to prevent people from dying. Tests were established to ensure that only the deserving received relief. There were detailed instructions in the Codes about early warning signs of impending famine; the duties of the police, medical officers, and other local officials; wages and rations; famine relief works; and many other practical instructions. The codes were used by the British until 1947. Their effectiveness is still the subject of heated debate, with an overstated radical and nationalist critique on one extreme and an imperialist apologist defense on the other, but since 1947, the Codes have continued to form the basis of famine prevention and relief. Thus, the Maharashtra drought of 1970 to 1973 was effectively prevented from triggering a famine by an employment guarantee scheme similar to that found in the earlier Codes.

Contemporary Policy Directions
Contemporary policymaking recognizes that for each link in any explanation of a famine there are a range of policy measures. A key issue that must be addressed is the relationship of policy action to the level of a problem where it can be effectively altered. Although an integrated explanation of famine may be intellectually fulfilling, a policy has to be located at a level at which it can make a significant impact: There must be a short-run effectiveness, as human lives often depend on it. However, often a focus on the short term can lead to a loss of any sense of the real causes of vulnerability. This is the contradiction that faces the makers of famine policy: They are restricted by temporal and spatial scales at which they must work and to which they must fit their policies.

Food Security
At the international and national level, achieving aggregate food security has been an important policy goal. In particular, national food self-reliance is frequently seen as a defense against famine. However,

with global increases in flows of goods and information, localized and even national production failures have become increasingly remediable by imports of food, whether as trade or aid. At the global level, food supplies over the last couple of decades have been sufficient to provide an adequate (although near-vegetarian) diet to all, if distributed equitably. However, global food supplies are still not distributed according to need, and shortages at regional, national, and even subcontinental levels have continued.

During the 1980s and early 1990s, some shortages have been caused by the continuing difficulty that international humanitarian relief efforts have had in gaining access to affected populations caught up in civil wars. This has led to the discussion in a number of countries of when and how national sovereignty should yield to humanitarian care for people in disastrous situations. This problem is more than a relief policy issue, and it raises geopolitical and, above all, ethical concerns about the human right to food, shelter, and health care (Waal 1991).

The theoretical advances that Sen's entitlement theory has afforded have led to some reevaluation of the importance of food security at the national and international levels. The insights that form the theory also suggest that a disaggregated approach to food security is required, which has led to a growing policy concern for vulnerable groups at the local level and the promotion of the idea that entitlements should be strengthened. However, at the level of large regions and nations, concerns over food availability remain important, especially where agreements among countries to exchange grain are involved, as in the case of southern Africa.

Any discussion of food security must also consider the political and economic significance of food aid since World War II. The United States, as a major food surplus state, has used food aid as an important political tool. Food assistance has been withheld from Marxist-run governments but ensured to reliable and dependent allies. Yet, in addition to these political objectives, continuing food aid abroad has helped to save grain farmers from bankruptcy at home. Overseas aid has been vital to the U.S. economy as a safety valve for its domestic overproduction. In 1961 the Kennedy administration was faced with the greatest American food surplus in history, and it was this domestic situation, rather than humanitarian concern, that prompted massive grain shipments overseas in the following years, notably in 1966 when one-fifth of the entire U.S. wheat crop was sent to India to relieve the effects of famine in Bihar.

Food aid has accounted for 28 percent of U.S. overseas development assistance since 1946. The Agricultural Trade Development and Assistance Act of 1954 (Public Law 480) was debated and approved by Congress not for humanitarian reasons or for development ends, but in order to promote trade and dispose of existing surpluses. Food aid has served to open new markets for American farm products, especially in Africa and Asia, often to the detriment of local agriculture, and the threat of food withdrawal or denial has been used to put pressure on countries to accept other forms of American economic intervention and political control.

Relief and Development

The issue of food aid raises another very important question: Should famine prevention efforts be short-term, basically the giving of food relief, or long-term, and more of a developmental nature in scope? In many ways this is something of an academic question, because so long as there are food shortages and famines in the contemporary world and there are donors willing to provide food aid and cash, short-term relief assistance will continue to be important.

Today, in addition to relief provided by national governments in times of crisis, there are a number of United Nations agencies and numerous nongovernmental organizations involved in famine relief (see Busetto 1993; Cullinan 1993; Katona-Apte 1993; Longford 1993; Singer 1993). The earliest United Nations agency established to provide humanitarian relief was the United Nations International Children's Emergency Fund (UNICEF), set up in 1946 to help children in the aftermath of World War II. Various other agencies, such as the United Nations High Commission for Refugees, established in 1951, and the United Nations Relief and Works Agency, established in 1950, have been active in the provision of relief, but since 1963 the World Food Programme has been the primary international agency involved in food aid.

Over the past three decades, the World Food Programme has invested approximately $13 billion and has provided more than 40 million tons of food aid to combat world hunger and to promote economic and social development. Food aid has been used to assist more than 1,600 development projects and 1,200 emergency operations. Within the United Nations system, the World Food Programme is now the largest source of grant assistance to developing countries, the largest source of assistance for poor women, and the largest provider of grant assistance for environmental activities in developing countries. The agency is headquartered in Rome, and although it has employees in 85 countries, it spends less than 6 percent of its budget on administration.

From the outset, the agency aimed to serve as more than a mechanism for surplus disposal or a means of providing charity for the poor. Indeed, by the late 1980s, two-thirds of its resources were being spent on development activities. However, numerous emergencies since that time have channeled 60 percent of its current resources into relief operations, and in 1993, new development commitments received only $250 million, in contrast to $778 million in 1988. At present, the agency has at any one time about 5 million tons of food in transit on 50 chartered ships, but it is hoped that once present emergencies end it will again be able to emphasize development.

Throughout the world, there are also a very large number of nongovernmental organizations, such as Save the Children, Oxfam Lutheran World Federation, Red Cross, Africare, Food for the Hungry, and Catholic Relief, involved in relief activities. Although many have other objectives, because they operate at local levels they are well placed to provide famine relief, sometimes parallel to large-scale governmental and international aid and sometimes as a conduit for that aid. Many also endeavor to administer food relief in ways that strengthen local livelihoods in the long run. Basically, these groups are involved in both relief and development, as they realize that relief alone can create dependency. But the great number of such organizations can occasionally create the problem of "swamping" affected areas by official and nongovernmental organizations who frequently do not coordinate their activities and who often collectively provide excessive relief assistance but not enough help for long-term mitigation.

Longer-term mitigation involves less direct measures for preventing famine, and the most important policy requirement is the strengthening of rural livelihoods. Of course, these measures can have objectives other than famine prevention and have development goals that are justifiable as ends in themselves. For example, in India, the government has attempted land reform, improved agricultural production technology, encouraged better processing and storage, operated a fairly effective system of public distribution of food, and developed a well-tried decentralized emergency response mechanism. All of this means that a reasonably effective famine prevention strategy has emerged, although malnutrition is still widespread. Nevertheless, as we have seen, it is difficult anywhere to demonstrate the level of impact of general rural development policies in famine prevention because the causes of famine are conjunctional and always involve a complexity of factors.

Early Warning Systems

The Indian Famine Codes established the idea of warning indicators that could be used to predict the onset of famine. For long, they were the only "early warning system" in operation, but since the Sahelian famine of the early 1970s, a number of famine early warning systems have been established (Blaikie et al. 1994). There are many different approaches to such systems. Some involve the use of sophisticated technology, such as the Food and Agricultural Organization's Global Information and Early Warning System, developed in the 1970s, which predicts crop yields by establishing biomass from satellite imagery. Another comparable approach is the United States–funded Famine Early Warning System. Approaches like this are all based on the assumption that famines are primarily caused by natural events and that technological solutions will be important mitigating elements. However, other early warning systems are much less complex and involve the collection and collation of local-level information on food stocks, prices, and such things as the sale of household assets.

Summary and Conclusion

Although there is considerable uncertainty regarding the nature and extent of the world's food problems, hunger is a contemporary reality, even within rich countries. Everyone must eat, and because of this simplest of all imperatives, famine is a subject of urgent contemporary concern. It casts a harsh but clear light on the nature and problems of the societies it afflicts and the world in which it exists. However, "famine" is a rather imprecise term normally used to describe events associated with natural hazards such as drought, floods, and pest infestations, and with political events such as war, malicious or inappropriate state policies, and ethnic prejudice. Famine is often (though not always) preceded by prolonged malnutrition and hunger, and part of the difficulty in defining it arises from the need to make a distinction between "ordinary" hunger and the phenomenon of famine. The latter term is generally reserved for situations in which starvation affects large numbers of people in a distinct area, which has been influenced by a natural or political event, leading to a larger number of deaths from starvation and illness than would normally be expected. By contrast, ordinary hunger is conventionally explained as a result of the imperfections of economic systems. Clearly, then, famine remains in danger of being explained as something caused by an exceptional political or natural factor – one that is abnormal and outside the responsibility of the usual operation of economic and political systems.

Fortunately, of late it has been recognized that natural hazards or political events are no more than immediate "triggers" or proximate causes. The "ultimate causes" must be sought out and understood in the normal economic and political sphere. Basically, a proper understanding of famine and all its dimensions requires an approach that does not merely deal with shortages of food but focuses instead on the inability of people to consume enough food. Thus, instead of treating famine as a shortage of food, it is preferable to analyze the different ways in which people are prevented (by natural or human events) from getting enough to eat. Using this alternative approach, it can be asked why certain groups of people are predisposed to famine before the impact of any trigger event, natural or political. Such a predisposition has been termed vulnerability, and the ultimate causes of famine can then be analyzed as those that create the conditions in which certain trigger events lead to the collapse in people's ability to acquire adequate nutrition.

This issue is not merely theoretical because the policy implications of understanding famine as inadequate consumption rather than inadequate availability are likely to be very different. When famine occurs even though food is available, or when famine affects some groups but not others, then food aid may be irrelevant. This issue is now at the core of the interpretation of famine and associated policy directions. It is one not of food security but of entitlement security and its corollary, the reduction of vulnerability among those who are the most vulnerable.

Brian Murton

Bibliography

Agarwal, B. 1990. Social security and the family: Coping with seasonality and calamity in rural India. *Journal of Peasant Studies* 17: 341-412.

Alamgir, M. 1980. *Famine in South Asia: Political economy of mass starvation.* Cambridge, Mass.

    1981. An approach towards a theory of famine. In *Famine: Its causes, effects, and management,* ed. J. Robson, 19-44. New York.

Arnold, D. 1988. *Famine: Social crisis and historical change.* Oxford.

Article Nineteen (International Centre on Censorship), ed. 1990. *Starving in silence: A report on famine and censorship.* London.

Bhatia, B. M. 1963. *Famines in India.* Bombay.

Blaikie, P. M., T. Cannon, I. Davis, and B. Wisner. 1994. *At risk; natural hazards, people's vulnerability, and disasters.* London.

Blaikie, P. M., J. C. Harriss, and A. Pain. 1985. *Public policy and the utilization of common property resources in Tamilnadu, India.* Report to Overseas Development Administrators, Research Scheme R3988. London.

Bongaarts, J., and M. Cain. 1981. *Demographic responses to famine.* The Population Council, Center for Policy Studies Working Paper. New York.

Brennan, L. 1984. The development of the Indian Famine Code. In *Famine as a geographical phenomenon,* ed. B. Currey and G. Hugo, 91-111. Dordrecht, the Netherlands.

Brown, E. P. 1991. Sex and starvation: Famine and three Chadian societies. In *The political economy of African famine,* ed. R. Downs, D. Kerner, and S. Reyna, 293-321. Philadelphia, Pa.

Busetto, B. J. 1993. WFP and UNICEF. Relying on each other's strengths. *World Food Programme Journal* 26: 17-19.

Cain, M. 1978. *The household life cycles and economic mobility in Bangladesh.* The Population Council, Center for Policy Studies Working Paper. New York.

Caldwell, J. C. 1975. *The Sahelian drought and its demographic implications.* Overseas Liaison Committee, American Council of Education, Paper No. 8. Washington, D.C.

Caldwell, J. C., P. H. Reddy, and P. Caldwell. 1986. Period high risk as a cause of fertility decline in a changing rural environment: Survival strategies in the 1980-1983 South Indian drought. *Economic Development and Cultural Change* 34: 667-701.

Canon, T. 1991. Hunger and famine: Using a food systems model to analyse vulnerability. In *Famine and food*

scarcity in Africa and Asia: Indigenous responses and external intervention to avoid hunger,* ed. H. G. Bohle, T. Canon, G. Hugo, and F. N. Ibrahim, 291-312. Bayreuth, Germany.

Chambers, R., N. Saxena, and T. Shah. 1990. *To the hands of the poor: Water and trees.* Boulder, Colo.

Chen, L. C., and A. K. M. A. Chowdhury. 1977. The dynamics of contemporary famine. In *Proceedings of Internal Union for the Scientific Study of Population,* Population Conference, Mexico, 1977. Liège, Belgium.

Cipolla, C. M. 1976. *Before the Industrial Revolution: European society and economy, 1000-1700.* New York.

Colvin, L. G., C. Ba, B. Barry, et al. 1981. *The uprooted of the western Sahel.* New York.

Connell, K. H. 1955. Marriage in Ireland after the famine: The diffusion of the match. *Journal of the Statistical and Social Inquiry Society of Ireland* 19: 82-103.

Corbett, J. 1988. Famine and household coping strategies. *World Development* 16: 1099-112.

Cullinan, S. 1993. The growth of WFP. *World Food Programme Journal* 25: 13-20.

Cunniff, Roger Lee. 1996. Drought region (Brazil). In *Encyclopedia of Latin American history and culture,* ed. Barbara A. Tenenbaum. New York.

Currey, B. 1979. Mapping areas liable to famine in Bangladesh. Ph.D. dissertation, University of Hawaii.

    1980. Famines in the Pacific: Losing the chances for change. *Geojournal* 4: 447-66.

    1984. Coping with complexity in food crisis management. In *Famine as geographical phenomenon,* ed. B. Currey and G. Hugo, 183-202. Dordrecht, the Netherlands.

    1992. Is famine a discrete event? *Disasters* 16: 138-44.

Cutler, P. 1984. Famine forecasting: Prices and peasant behaviour in northern Ethiopia. *Disasters* 8: 48-55.

Dando, W. A. 1980. *The geography of famine.* London.

Downs, R. E., D. O. Kerner, and S. P. Reyna, eds. 1991. *The political economy of African famine.* Philadelphia, Pa.

Drèze, J., and A. Sen. 1989. *Hunger and public action.* Oxford.

    eds. 1990. *The political economy of hunger.* 3 vols. Oxford.

Ea, M. 1984. War and famine: The example of Kampuchea. In *Famine as geographical phenomenon,* ed. B. Currey and G. Hugo, 33-47. Dordrecht, the Netherlands.

Erlich, Paul. 1968. *The population bomb.* New York.

Garine, I. de. 1991. Seasonal food shortage, famine and socioeconomic change among the Massa and Mussey of northern Cameroon. In *Famine and food security in Africa and Asia: Indigenous responses and external intervention to avoid hunger,* ed. H. G. Bohle, T. Canon, G. Hugo, and F. N. Ibrahim, 83-99. Bayreuth, Germany.

Greenough, P. R. 1982. *Prosperity and misery in modern Bengal: The famine of 1943-44.* Oxford.

Grigg, D. 1985. *The world food problem 1950-1980.* Oxford.

Gupta, A. 1988. *Ecology and development in the Third World.* London.

Hewitt, K. 1983a. The idea of calamity in a technocratic age. In *Interpretations of calamity,* ed. K. Hewitt, 3-32. Boston, Mass.

    ed. 1983b. *Interpretations of calamity.* Boston, Mass.

Hill, P. 1977. *Population, prosperity and poverty. Rural Kano 1900 and 1970.* Cambridge and New York.

Hugo, G. 1984. The demographic impact of famine. In *Famine as geographical phenomenon,* ed. B. Currey and G. Hugo, 7-31. Dordrecht, the Netherlands.

Huntington, E. 1915. *Civilization and climate.* New Haven, Conn.

1919. *The pulse of Asia. A journey in central Asia illustrating the geographical history.* New York.

Kane, P. 1988. *Famine in China: Demographic and social implications.* London.

Kates, R. W., R. S. Chen, T. E. Downing, et al. 1988. *The hunger report 1988.* The Alan Shawn Feinstein World Hunger Program, Brown University. Providence, R.I.

Katona-Apte, J. 1993. Food aid fights malnutrition. *World Food Programme Journal* 25: 2-6.

Klee, G., ed. 1980. *World systems of traditional resource management.* New York.

Kulkarni, S. N. 1990. *Famines, droughts and scarcities in India.* Allahabad, India.

Longford, S. 1993. Delivering the food. *World Food Programme Journal* 25: 27-31.

Mellor, J. W., and S. Gavian. 1987. Famine: Causes, prevention and relief. *Science* 235: 539-45.

Millman, S. 1990. Hunger in the 1980s. Backdrop for policy in the 1990s. *Food Policy* 15: 277-85.

Mukherji, K. 1965. *Agriculture, famine and rehabilitation in South Asia.* Calcutta.

Murton, B. 1980. The temporal dimensions of famine vulnerability in Ganjam District in the mid-nineteenth century. *The Indian Geographical Journal* 55: 1-11.

O'Brien, J., and E. Gruenbaum. 1991. A social history of food, famine, and gender in twentieth-century Sudan. In *The political economy of African famine,* ed. R. Downs, D. Kerner, and S. Reyna, 177-203. Philadelphia, Pa.

Paddock, W., and P. Paddock. 1967. *Famine - 1975! America's decision: Who will survive.* Boston, Mass.

Prindle, P. H. 1979. Peasant society and famines: A Nepalese example. *Ethnology* 1: 49-60.

Rahmoto, D. 1988. *Peasant survival strategies.* Geneva.

Ruzicka, L. T., and A. K. M. A. Chowdhury. 1978. *Demographic surveillance system - Matlab.* Vol. 4, *Vital events and migration, 1975.* Dacca, Bangladesh.

Schmitt, R. C. 1970. Famine mortality in Hawaii. *Journal of Pacific History* 5: 109-15.

Schoepf, B. G. 1992. Gender relations and development: Political economy and culture. In *Twenty-first-century Africa: Toward a new vision of self-sustainable development,* ed. A. Seidman and A. Anong, 203-41. Trenton, N.J., and Atlanta, Ga.

Scott, J. C. 1976. *The moral economy of the peasant: Rebellion and subsistence in Southeast Asia.* New Haven, Conn.

Sen, Amartya K. 1980. Famine mortality: A study of the Bengal Famine of 1943. In *Peasants in history: Essays in honour of Daniel Turner,* ed. E. J. Hobsbawm, 144-220. Calcutta.

1981. *Poverty and famines: An essay on entitlement and deprivation.* Oxford.

1988. Family and food: Sex bias in poverty. In *Rural poverty in South Asia,* ed. T. N. Srinivasan and P. K. Bardhan, 453-72. New York.

1990. Gender and cooperative conflict. In *Persistent inequalities: Women and world development,* ed. I. Tinker, 123-49. Oxford.

Shipton, P. 1990. African famines and food scarcity: Anthropological perspectives. *Annual Review of Anthropology* 19: 353-94.

Singer, H. W. 1993. Food aid. A historical perspective. *World Food Programme Journal* 25: 7-10.

Sorokin, P. A. 1942. *Man and society in calamity.* New York.

1975. *Hunger as a factor in human affairs.* Gainesville, Fla.

Stein, Z., M. Lusser, G. Saenger, and F. Marolla. 1975. *Famine and human development: The Dutch hunger winter of 1944/45.* New York.

Thompson, E. P. 1971. Moral economy of the English crowd in the eighteenth century. *Past and Present* 50: 76-136.

Torry, W. I. 1986. Economic development, drought and famine. Some limitations of dependency explanations. *Geojournal* 12: 5-18.

Townsend, Richard F. 1992. *The Aztecs.* New York.

Turner, M., ed. 1986. *Malthus and his time.* Basingstoke, England.

Vaughan, M. 1987. *The story of an African famine: Gender and famine in twentieth-century Malawi.* Cambridge and New York.

Waal, A. de. 1989. *Famine that kills. Darfur, Sudan, 1984-1985.* Oxford.

1991. Famine and human rights. *Development in Practice: An Oxfam Journal* 1: 77-83.

Watts, D. 1984. Cycles of famine in islands of plenty: The case of the colonial West Indies in the pre-emancipation period. In *Famine as a geographical phenomenon,* ed. B. Currey and G. Hugo, 49-70. Dordrecht, the Netherlands.

Watts, M. 1983a. On the poverty of theory: Natural hazards research in context. In *Interpretations of calamity,* ed. K. Hewitt, 231-62. Boston, Mass.

1983b. *Silent violence: Food, famine and peasantry in northern Nigeria.* Berkeley, Calif.

1991. Entitlements or empowerment? Famine and starvation in Africa. *Review of African Political Economy* 51: 9-26.

Watts, M., and H. G. Bohle. 1993a. Hunger, famine and the space of vulnerability. *Geojournal* 30: 117-26.

1993b. The space of vulnerability. The causal structure of hunger. *Progress in Human Geography* 17: 43-67.

Wilken, G. 1988. *Good farmers. Traditional agricultural resource management in Mexico and Central America.* Boulder, Colo.

Wisner, B. 1993. Disaster vulnerability: Scale, power, and daily life. *Geojournal* 30: 127-40.

World Bank. 1986. *Hunger and poverty.* Washington, D.C.

WIHD (World Institute on Hunger and Development). 1992. *Second annual report on the state of world hunger.* Washington, D.C.

VI.5 ❧ Height and Nutrition

Scientists have long recognized that there is a close association between the height of a population and its nutritional status, and by the end of the nineteenth century governments were coming under increasing pressure to measure their citizens as a means of determining that status.[1] Many have done so in the twentieth century, as height and weight statistics have played an ever increasing role in health assessment programs (Tanner 1981). This chapter employs the data generated thus far to construct a general picture of changes in height and nutritional status in various countries during the course of the twentieth century.

The studies on which this chapter is based have taken a variety of forms. Most of the information about changes in average heights has been derived from school surveys, but a great deal of data on adult heights is also available. Many of these data have been derived from military recruiting records and are primarily concerned with the heights of adult men (Floud, Wachter, and Gregory 1990).

In addition, a number of investigations have focused on changes in the timing of growth spurts and in overall rates of growth. These investigations have tended to focus on the age of peak-height-velocity (PHV) in both males and females and the onset of menarche in girls (e.g., Matsumoto et al. 1980; Matsumoto 1982; Danker-Hopfe 1986). Some observers have also examined changes in the relative dimensions of different parts of the body, such as leg length and sitting height (Himes 1979; Tanner et al. 1982).

The relationship between social and economic changes and changes in height is both simple and complex. On the one hand, there is a clear association between the average height of a population and its standard of living. This is reflected in the unprecedented improvements in average height that have occurred in many parts of the world during the past one hundred years, and in the differences that continue to exist between the average heights of people from different socioeconomic backgrounds (e.g., Rea 1971; Rona, Swan, and Altman 1978; Jones, Nesheim, and Habicht 1985).

On the other hand, it is much more difficult to define the precise significance of different components of the "standard of living." Most observers, for example, would agree that the two most important environmental determinants of height are diet and disease, but it has proven extremely difficult to establish their relative importance (Roche 1979). Some have suggested that "health care may be more important than nutrition in the first year of life" and that "nutrition may be more important than health care" after the first year, but the evidence on which these suggestions are based is far from conclusive (Floud et al. 1990: 249).

Another area of difficulty concerns the relationship between environmental and genetic influences. There are evident differences among the heights and rates of growth of different ethnic groups, but the extent to which these differences are genetic or environmental in origin is not clear (Eveleth 1979: 388; Eveleth and Tanner 1991). However, it is reasonable to argue that changes in the average height of members of the same ethnic group over time reflect environmental and nutritional changes rather than changes in genetic potential (Floud et al. 1990). We can also seek to isolate the genetic determinants of growth by comparing the heights and weights of members of the same ethnic group in different circumstances and in different parts of the world (e.g.,

Moore 1970; Greulich 1976; Bindon and Zansky 1986).

It is important to remember that changes in social and economic conditions can affect heights and rates of growth in a number of different ways. In general, undernourished children who are subjected to repeated bouts of infection grow more slowly than children who are well nourished and live in a largely disease-free environment. Undernourished children experience the adolescent growth spurt at a later age, and although they continue to grow for a longer period, their final height is shorter. These differences mean that the gap between the heights of the two populations is at its greatest when the more favored children reach adolescence. The increase in the average value of children's heights has, therefore, been considerably greater than the increase in the average heights of adults (Floud et al. 1990; Eveleth and Tanner 1991).

The structure of this chapter follows that laid down in P. Eveleth and James Tanner's invaluable surveys of *Worldwide Variation in Human Growth* (1976, 1991). The first two parts examine the main trends in the average height of Europeans in Europe and the heights of Europeans outside Europe. This is followed by sections on the heights of Africans in Africa and the Americas; the heights of Asiatics in Asia and the Americas; the heights of Indo-Mediterraneans in the Near East; the heights of peoples in North Africa and India; and finally the heights of Australian Aborigines and Pacific Island peoples. The last section summarizes the evidence and considers some of the implications of that evidence for future health policy.

Europeans in Europe

Europeans living in Europe have been the subject of a particularly large number of anthropometric surveys. Many of the earlier investigations were concerned with the heights of adult male army recruits, but the present century has seen a growing concentration on the heights of schoolchildren. We also possess a considerable amount of data on the age at which European girls reach menarche, and there is some information about changes in European birth weights. The long history of anthropometric monitoring in Europe, combined with the availability of large amounts of data, has encouraged a number of investigators to use the heights of Europeans as "standards" against which to assess the growth of other population groups (e.g., Eveleth and Tanner 1976, 1991).

Studies of European heights provide some of the clearest evidence of the increase in average height that has occurred in most parts of the world during the course of the twentieth century. In 1991, for example, Eveleth and Tanner reported evidence of a secular trend toward increased adult height in

Table VI.5.1. *Changes in the heights of European army recruits circa 1900–1975*

Country	Period	Change in height (cm)
Belgium	1902/4–69	8.1
Denmark	1904/5–66/75	8.4
France	1900–60	7.5
Germany (Bavaria)	1900–58	4.2
Italy	1900–52	3.6
Netherlands	1907–75	11.1
Norway	1900-60	6.7
Spain	1903/6–55	3.1
Sweden	1900–74	8.1
Switzerland	1908/10–57	6.2

Source: Floud (1984).

Sweden, Finland, Norway, France, the United Kingdom, Italy, Germany, Czechoslovakia, Poland, Hungary, the Soviet Union, the Netherlands, Belgium, Switzerland, and Austria (Eveleth and Tanner 1991).[2] Similarly, in 1984 Roderick Floud showed that the average height of army recruits in 10 European countries increased by between 3.1 and 11.1 centimeters (cm) during the years 1900 and 1975 (Table VI.5.1).

Some investigators have attempted to infer changes in average height by comparing the average height of men and women of different ages at the same point in time. Thus in 1971 Erik Bjelke demonstrated that Norwegians who were born between 1920 and 1929 were between 1.7 and 1.8 centimeters taller than Norwegians who had been born a decade earlier (Bjelke 1971). In 1988, Mary Walker, A. Shaper, and G. Wannamethee compared the heights of 7,735 British men who were born between 1919 and 1939 and concluded that the average heights of successive birth cohorts had risen by approximately 1.3 centimeters per decade (Walker, Shaper, and Wannamethee 1988).

There have also been a large number of investigations into the heights of children. The average height of 5-year-old boys in London increased by 7.4 cm between 1905–12 and 1966, whereas the average height of 5-year-old girls increased by 7.5 cm (Cameron 1979). Even more dramatic was the average height increase of 12-year-olds in Oslo, which was 12 cm for boys and 12.5 cm for girls between 1920 and 1975 (Brundtland, Liestøl, and Walløe 1980). In Sweden, the average height of 12-year-old children increased by a similar amount between 1883 and 1965–71 (Ljung, Bergsten-Brucefors, and Lindgren 1974), and the average height of 13- to 14-year-old children in Holland increased by more than 20 cm between the mid–nineteenth century and 1965 (van Wieringen 1979).

In addition, there have been striking changes in the heights of children in central and eastern Europe.

For example, the average height of Czechoslovakian 12-year-olds increased by between 12.8 and 15.5 cm between 1895 and 1968-70 (Suchy 1972), whereas the average height of 14- to 18-year-olds in Moscow increased by between 3.6 and 5.7 cm between 1925 and 1965 (Vlastovsky 1966). Moreover, the average heights of 12-year-old girls and 14- to 15-year-old boys in Zagreb increased by 10 cm and 13 cm, respectively, between 1951 and 1982 (Prebeg 1984).

Secular changes in birth weights and rates of physical maturation have also been examined by a number of authors. Of the two, the history of birth weights has received rather less attention, but new data are slowly becoming available (e.g., Ward 1988, 1990). In 1966, V. Vlastovsky demonstrated that the average length of newborn boys in Kursk City rose between 1930 and 1939 and rose again after the end of the Second World War. However, babies born in 1959 were only 0.1 cm longer than boys born 20 years earlier. The average weight of newborn boys increased from 3.43 kilograms (kg) in 1930 to 3.49 kg at the end of the 1950s. In 1988 Margit Rosenberg revealed that the average birth weight of children in Oslo, Bergen, and Trondheim increased by approximately 0.2 kg between 1860 and 1980. However, these increases are much smaller than the increases in the heights (and weights) of older children and adults (Malina 1979a). In 1981 Tanner estimated that the average birth weight of full-term males born at the end of the nineteenth century was only 0.1 kg less than that of European children today.[3]

By contrast, changes in the rate of maturation and in age of menarche have been much more dramatic. In 1962 Tanner suggested that mean menarcheal age had declined by 4 years in Norway between 1840 and 1950; by 1.7 years in Sweden between 1890 and 1950; by 2.3 years in Finland between 1860 and 1940; and by 3.0 years in Germany over the same period (Tanner 1962, 1966; Steendijk 1966).[4] There is also evidence after the Second World War of a continuation in this secular trend in Austria, Belgium, Bulgaria, Denmark, Finland, France, Germany, Greece, Hungary, Italy, the Netherlands, Poland, Romania, Spain, Sweden, the United Kingdom, Yugoslavia, and the former Soviet Union (Danker-Hopfe 1986; see also Venrooij-Ijsselmuiden, Smeets, and van der Werff Ten Bosch 1976; Laska-Mierzejewska, Milicer, and Piachaczek 1982; Helm and Helm 1984, 1987).

Some writers have suggested that the trend toward earlier maturation may be slowing down and that in some areas it may have ceased or even been reversed (Eveleth and Tanner 1976, 1991; Vercauteren and Susanne 1985). However, in 1986 Heidi Danker-Hopfe compared the median menarcheal ages of girls in eight countries in the 1950s and 1960s with the median menarcheal ages of girls in the same areas in the 1970s and 1980s and found an average decline in menarcheal age of approximately three and a half months (Table VI.5.2).

Table VI.5.2. *Median menarcheal age of girls in various European countries, 1950s-60s and 1970s-80s*

Country	Period	Change in median age at menarche (yrs)
Belgium	1965–80/1	−0.10
Croatia (Zagreb)	1964–82	−0.45
France (Paris)	1965/6–74	−0.22
Hungary (Szeged)	1958/9–81/2	−0.43
Italy (Florence)	1955/7–77	−0.58
Netherlands	1965–80	−0.15
Poland (Warsaw)	1965–76	−0.28
United Kingdom (N.E. England and Newcastle-on-Tyne)	1967–71/9	−0.06

Source: Danker-Hopfe (1986).

Europeans Outside Europe

Despite a wealth of information about the heights of Europeans in Europe, we know much less about the secular trend in the heights of European descendants in other parts of the world. The one obvious exception to this rule is the history of changes in the heights of European descendants in the United States. But there is also some information about long-term trends in the heights of European descendants in Australia, the Caribbean, and parts of South America. There have, however, been very few studies of the heights of European descendants in southern Africa.

The main trends in the heights of white Americans in the United States have been summarized on many occasions, including the work of Thomas Cone (1961), Howard Meredith (1963, 1976), Robert Fogel (1986), and Richard Steckel (1989, 1992). In 1986, Fogel revealed that the average heights of native-born white Americans rose steadily from the beginning of the eighteenth century up until the middle of the nineteenth century. This was, however, followed by a sharp decline in the heights of those born during the second half of the nineteenth century, although there was a resumption of the general upward trend in the first third of the twentieth century. Some writers have suggested that the secular trend ceased after World War II, but this suggestion was subsequently contradicted (Bakwin and McLaughlin 1964; Damon 1968). In 1989 R. Bock and R. Sykes demonstrated that the heights of people attending the Fels Institute in Ohio continued to increase after 1945, and T. Greiner and C. Gordon (1992) claimed that the average height of successive birth cohorts of white Americans increased by 0.7 cm per decade between 1910–14 and 1970–4 (Bock and Sykes 1989; Greiner and Gordon 1992).

In addition to studying the heights of adult Americans, a number of authors have also attempted to examine the heights of children. Cone, for example, showed that the average height of Boston children increased by between 3 and 7 centimeters between 1877 and 1930–56, and Harry Bakwin suggested that this trend continued into the early 1960s (Cone 1961; Bakwin 1964). The most comprehensive survey of heights in the United States was carried out by Meredith in 1963, who found that there had been very little change in either the length or weight of newborn infants since the end of the nineteenth century, but that there had been substantial increases in the heights of children from the age of 1 onward.

It is unclear whether these increases have continued toward the present. Eveleth and Tanner found no evidence of any increase in the heights of children in the United States between 1963–70 and 1976–80, but D. Jones, M. Neshiem, and J.-P. Habicht claimed that there was an increase in the heights of poor children over the same period (Jones et al. 1985; Eveleth and Tanner 1991).

There have also been a number of investigations into changes in the age of menarche among U.S. girls. In 1962 Tanner suggested that the mean age of menarche in the United States fell from 14.2 to 13.0 years between 1900 and 1950. These results have been confirmed by Grace Wyshak and Madeline Goodman. In 1983 Wyshak demonstrated that the mean menarcheal age among women born before 1920 was 0.86 years greater than the mean menarcheal age of women born after 1940 (Wyshak 1983). Goodman studied the mean age of menarche of 3,205 Caucasian, Japanese, and Chinese women in Hawaii who had been born between 1900 and 1940. The menarcheal age of the Caucasian women declined by 2.28 months per decade, whereas that of the Japanese and Chinese women declined by 6.36 months and 5.24 months, respectively (Goodman 1983).[5]

In view of the available data, it is probably inevitable that the anthropometric history of European descendants outside Europe should tend to concentrate on the history of those in the United States. There is, however, some evidence of secular changes in the heights of European descendants in Australia, Cuba, Argentina, and Venezuela. In 1983, for example, Antonio Gordon found that the average height of Cuban men had increased by between 5 and 6 cm since the start of the century, although he denied that the nutritional condition of the Cuban population had improved during the course of this period.

In Argentina, H. Lejarraga and colleagues (1989) showed that the average height of 15-year-old children in Buenos Aires had increased by between 6.5 and 8.2 cm during the interval between 1938 and 1981, and that the average height of 15-year-olds in Entre Rios had increased by between 4.5 and 6 cm between 1950 and 1981. In 1981 N. Farid-Coupal, M. Contreas, and H. Castellano discovered that the mean menarcheal age of girls in the Carabobo district of Venezuela fell by 1.7 years between 1937 and 1969. Moreover, the average height of children in Carabobo increased by 1.6 cm between 1978 and 1987 (Blanco, Landaeta-Jiménez, and Castellano 1989).

We also possess a limited amount of information about the heights of European descendants in Australia and Mozambique. The average height of children in western Australia increased by between 2 and 6 cm between 1940 and 1971, and that of children in Sydney increased by between 2 and 4 cm between 1937 and 1965 (Blanksby et al. 1974). These increases are somewhat greater than those recorded among white children in Mozambique. The average height of 7-year-old children in Lourenço Marques increased by only 0.5 cm (boys) and 1.5 cm (girls) between 1930 and 1965 (Martins 1971).

Africans at Home and Abroad

There have been a number of investigations into the heights of African populations in recent years, but very few of these provide any clear opportunity for chronological comparison. The main source of information about secular trends in the heights of Africans and people of African ancestry has been the United States. The lack of information about secular changes in the heights of Africans in Africa, combined with the poor social and economic circumstances of most of the continent's countries, has made it difficult to construct normal standards for assessing the growth of African children. However, studies of well-off Africans and black populations in the United States have shown that black children grow more quickly than white children between the ages of circa 8 and 14 years and experience puberty at an earlier age. These studies also suggest that Africans and African-Americans are more long-limbed than Europeans and white Americans, but that there is little difference in their final heights (Eveleth and Tanner 1991).

In view of the long history of anthropometric measuring in the United States, it is not surprising that we should possess quite a lot of information about the heights of black Americans. In 1963 Meredith suggested that the average height of 1-year-old boys rose by 5.7 cm between 1918-19 and 1944-56, and that the average height of 6-year-old boys rose by 6.3 cm between 1896-8 and 1957-8. In a separate study, William Moore discovered that the average height of 12-year-old boys increased by 17.41 cm between 1890 and 1968, whereas that of 12-year-old girls increased by 19.57 cm over the same period (Moore 1970). It is not clear whether the heights of black Americans continued to increase after this date. In 1979 Eveleth, E. Bowers, and J. Schall claimed that the average height of black adolescents in Philadelphia had increased by approximately 3.3 cm between 1956-65 and 1977, but the most recent national survey suggests that there was no increase in the heights of black children between 1963-70 and 1976-80 (Eveleth and Tanner 1976, 1991; Jones et al. 1985).

The availability of separate information about the heights of blacks and whites in the United States provides a valuable opportunity to study the secular trend in the heights of different population groups in the same national environment, but it must be admitted that the overall results are somewhat unclear. In his 1963 paper, Meredith argued that black males experienced greater increases in average height between the ages of 0 and 3, whereas white children experienced greater rates of increase between the ages of 6 and 17 (Meredith 1963). Yet Meredith also argued that black men experienced a greater increase in average height during early adulthood, and Moore has claimed that the average height of 14-year-old black boys increased by 2.88 cm per decade between 1890 and 1968. Previous estimates, however, had placed the rate of increase among black and white boys at 1.95 cm and 1.92 cm, respectively (Moore 1970). By contrast, Greiner and Gordon's study of the heights of successive birth cohorts of U.S. army recruits contradicted both studies. They argued that the average height of black Americans born between 1910-14 and 1970-4 increased at less than half the rate achieved by white Americans during the same period (Greiner and Gordon 1992).

Despite such an abundance of information about the heights of African-Americans, we know rather less about secular changes in the heights of Africans in other parts of the world – including Africa itself. The most detailed information comes from southern Africa, where there have been a number of studies of the heights of South African blacks and Kalahari Bushmen. P. Tobias (1962, 1974) found that the average height of adult Bushmen (San) had increased by approximately 3.5 cm since the start of the century, and in 1985 A. Hausman and E. Wilmsen revealed that the heights of San children continued to increase between 1967-8 and 1979-80 (Tobias 1962, 1974; Hausman and Wilmsen 1985).

The situation regarding black populations in other parts of southern Africa is more unclear. Tobias (1975) has argued that most southern African populations "show either the absence of the secular trend . . . or a frankly reversed secular trend" (145), but A. Walker and B. Walker have claimed that the average heights of black children in South Africa rose by up to 6.9 cm between 1938 and 1976 (Tobias 1975; Tobias and Netscher 1976; Walker and Walker 1977).[6]

A number of other studies have focused on the secular trend in the heights of Africans and people of African ancestry in Gambia, Mali, Nigeria, and the Caribbean island of Aruba. In 1981 Elisabeth van Wering demonstrated that the average height of children aged 5 to 14 on Aruba had increased by between 0.7 and 5.8 cm between 1954 and 1974. In a 1979 study suggesting improving nutrition in Nigeria, G. Ucho and A. Okorafor found that the mean menarcheal age of girls had fallen by approximately four months per decade since the early 1960s. However, no evidence of a secular trend toward greater height has been found in either Mali or Gambia. In Mali, the average height of adult men increased by only 0.2 cm between 1902 and 1985 (Prazuck et al. 1988). A longitudinal study of the heights of adult men and women in Gambia between 1951 and 1975 indicated that there was a slight tendency for height to decrease with age, but this was attributed to improvements in measuring techniques rather than to any real improvement in the heights of later-born subjects (Billewicz and Macgregor 1982).

Asiatics in Asia and the Americas

The term "Asiatic" describes a wide range of peoples who are believed to have originated in what is now known as the "Far East." Thus present-day Asiatic populations include Mongols, Arctic Eskimos, American Indians, and Indonesian-Malays. The latter group alone includes the indigenous populations of Japan, China, Thailand, and the Philippines (Eveleth and Tanner 1976, 1991). So far as the secular trend in height is concerned, we have much information about the heights of Japanese people in Japan and the United States and about Chinese people in China and Hong Kong. There is a smaller amount of information about the heights of other Asiatic populations in the United States, South America, and Indonesia.

The Japanese are arguably the most-measured population group in the world. This is largely because Japanese authorities instituted a national program of anthropometric monitoring at the start of the twentieth century and have continued to publish the results ever since (Tanner 1986). In 1966 Eiji Takahashi showed that the average height of Japanese adolescents increased slowly but steadily between 1900 and 1937. Then there was a sharp fall in average heights during World War II, followed by an even sharper increase between 1945 and 1960. The average heights of Japanese adolescents continued to increase after 1960, and in 1982 Tanner and his colleagues found that the average heights of 12-year-old girls and 13-year-old boys had increased by 7.9 cm and 9.7 cm, respectively, between 1957 and 1977. The average height of Japanese adults increased by 4.3 cm (men) and 2.7 cm (women) over the same period (Takahashi 1966; Tanner et al. 1982; see also Meredith 1976).

Students of the growth of Japanese children have also examined changes in the rates of their ages of peak-height-velocity. In 1982 Kenji Matsumoto demonstrated that the age at which Japanese children achieved their peak-height-velocity had fallen steadily over the course of the twentieth century (Matsumoto 1982; see also Nagai et al. 1980). Matsumoto also noted that the age at which girls achieved their peak-height-velocity had fallen particularly rapidly since the end of World War II, and he attributed this change to the dramatic improvement in the nutritional status of Japanese women during that period (Matsumoto et al. 1980). These conclusions correspond closely to those reached by students of the age of menarche. The mean menarcheal age of Japanese girls fell from

15.0 years for those born between 1896 and 1900 to 12.5 years for those born between 1966 and 1970 (Hoshi and Kouchi 1981; Nakamura et al. 1986).

In addition to the Japanese data, there is also a growing body of information about the height of Chinese people in both China and Hong Kong. In 1984 Alan Piazza found that the average height of Chinese boys remained roughly constant between 1915–25 and 1951–8, but rose very sharply between 1951–8 and 1979. He was unable to locate representative data for Chinese girls in the earlier period, but he was able to show that their heights rose equally sharply from 1951 onward.[7] There have also been significant changes in the heights of Chinese children in Hong Kong. J. Ling and N. King found that the average heights of 12-year-old boys increased by 6.7 cm and those of 12-year-old girls increased by 4.2 cm between 1961–3 and 1982–4 (Ling and King 1987: 187; see also Leung et al. 1987). The mean menarcheal age of South Chinese children in Hong Kong fell from 12.85 years in 1961–3 to 12.59 years 16 years later (Low, Kung, and Leong 1982).

We also have some information about the heights of Asiatic peoples in the southern United States, South America, and Indonesia. Pierre van der Eng has argued that the average heights of Indonesian and Indo-European children probably increased between 1911 and the late 1930s, but he was unable to find evidence of any further change between the late 1930s and 1973 (Eng 1995). Robert Malina and A. Zavaleta (1980) have indicated that the average heights of Mexican-American children aged 6 to 8 in the southern United States remained unchanged between 1929–31 and 1968–72, but small increases were recorded in the heights of those aged 8 to 15. The average height of Mexican-American children increased at all ages and at a greater rate between 1968–72 and 1982, but the overall rate of increase still lagged behind that of other U.S. groups. Malina, R. Martorell, and F. Mendoza (1986) concluded that the low rate of secular increase among Mexican-Americans reflected their failure to benefit from social and economic improvements, but their data may have been distorted by the inclusion of an influx of new migrants from Mexico and other South American countries.[8]

It is interesting to compare the heights of Mexican-Americans in the United States with those of Asiatic peoples in South America. In 1974, Eveleth, F. Salzano, and P. de Lima studied the heights of 363 Xingo Indians in Brazil between the ages of 20 and 50 and found no evidence of any increase in the average height of successive birth cohorts (Eveleth, Salzano, and de Lima 1974). In 1982 G. Gonzales, I. Crespo-Retes, and R. Guerra-Garcia claimed that the average height of Puno Indians between the ages of 7 and 20 had increased substantially between 1945 and 1980, but they could find no evidence of any increase in adult heights (Gonzales, Crespo-Retes, and Guerra-Garcia 1982). The findings for adults, but not for children, were echoed by John McCullough in his study of the heights of Yucatec Maya between 1895 and 1968. McCullough concluded that the majority of Mesoamerican populations had failed to experience the secular increase in height that had been observed in most parts of the world since the beginning of the twentieth century (McCullough 1982).

Indo-Mediterraneans of the Near East, North Africa, and India

The term "Indo-Mediterraneans" is used to describe the indigenous populations of the "Near East," North Africa, and India. It includes a wide range of diverse groups, including Hamites, Indo-Dravidians, Egyptians, Kuwaitis, and Libyans, but we know comparatively little about the secular trend in their growth or development. The majority of the relevant published studies concentrate on the populations of different parts of India, but it is possible to supplement these with some observations about possible trends in the heights of people in Ethiopia, Egypt, and Turkey.

Although there have been a number of studies focusing on different aspects of growth and stature in various parts of India, no consistent picture has emerged. It would appear that the pattern of change has varied considerably both between periods and between regions. In 1976 P. Ganguly examined secular changes in the height of 60 population groups and concluded that the dominant trend was toward a diminution of height rather than an increase (Ganguly 1977). This conclusion was reinforced by a study carried out in Hyderabad in 1977, but other investigations contradict it (Shatrugna and Rao 1987). In 1982 L. Sidhu, L. Bhatraga, and A. Dubey argued that the average height of well-off boys attending the Yadvindera Public School in Patiala increased by 7.5 cm between 1948–52 and 1973–7, and S. Singh and P. Malhotra contended that the mean menarcheal age of girls in Patiala fell by 0.65 years between 1974 and 1986 (Sidhu, Bhatraga, and Dubey 1982; Singh and Malhotra 1988). In 1981 D. P. Kaur and R. Singh compared the heights of Gujarati parents with those of their adult offspring and found that the children's heights exceeded their parents' by an average of 2.2 cm (Kaur and Singh 1981).

In view of the uncertainty surrounding the secular trend in the heights of Indians, it is interesting to compare the results of a number of different surveys carried out at different points in time between 1938 and 1982–3. In 1938 A. Chatterjee examined the average heights of more than 33,000 Bengali schoolboys, and the results were republished by W. M. Krogman in *Growth of Man* in 1941. These figures can be compared with the heights of the Indian boys whose measurements were reproduced in Eveleth and Tanner's two volumes in 1976 and 1991. The results suggest that the average height of Indian boys may have declined between 1938 and 1956–65 and then increased sharply between 1956–65 and 1982–3 (Table VI.5.3). However, it is important to note that

these surveys were carried out in different (although partly overlapping) areas and that they may have included different social groups.

One should also be mindful of such caveats when examining the secular trend in the height of other Indo-European populations. In the case of Egypt, information is available about the heights of 10- to 12-year-old boys in the whole of Egypt from 1956 to 1965 and about 10- to 12-year-old boys in East Cairo in circa 1981. The data show that the second group of children were between 3 and 4 cm taller than the first group, but this does not necessarily mean that the East Cairo children were taller than children from the same area or social background in the earlier study.

There is a similar problem with the data for Ethiopia, which show that "Ethiopian and Eritrean" children were between 5.2 and 6.7 cm shorter in 1958 than children in Addis Ababa and other urban areas 7 years later. In the case of Turkey, we can see that 13-year-old girls and 15-year-old boys in Ankara in 1950 were between 3.4 and 14.3 cm shorter than "poor" and "well-off" children in Istanbul in 1970. The figures suggest that average heights may have increased over time, but the difference between Ankara children in 1950 and poor children in Istanbul in 1970 is much less than the difference between the poor children and their well-off contemporaries.

Australian Aborigines and Pacific Island Peoples

This section reviews the available evidence regarding secular changes in the heights of the indigenous inhabitants of Australia, New Zealand, and the Pacific Islands. There have been a number of such studies of Aboriginal children, and in addition, a comparative study has been conducted of the heights of different groups of Samoan children. Insights can also be gained into the pattern of secular change by comparing the results of various surveys of the heights of people in Papua New Guinea.

The most detailed published effort examining Australian Aborigines in order to investigate the extent and nature of secular changes was that carried out by M. Barrett and T. Brown in 1961–9. They found that the adult heights of Aborigines in the central-western part of the Northern Territory were about 5.5 cm greater than the heights of comparable groups of Aborigines 30 years earlier (Barrett and Brown 1971). It is not clear, however, whether the experience of this group was typical of that of other Aborigines or whether the trend toward increased height has continued up to the present day.

In 1991 Eveleth and Tanner compared the heights of children in Barrett and Brown's survey with those of Aboriginal children in western Australia in 1983, and they found that the heights were almost identical. But, as they themselves pointed out, it was impossible to say whether this meant that the secular trend had been halted or merely obscured by cross-sectional

Table VI.5.3. *Average heights of selected groups of Indo-Mediterranean children at different periods*

Country	People or place	Period of study	Source	Height at age 13 (cm)
1. Males				
India	Bengal	<1938	Krogman 1941	147.9
India	India	1956–65	Eveleth & Tanner 1976	141.5
India	Calcutta	1982–3	Eveleth & Tanner 1991	151.5
Egypt	Egypt	1962–3	Eveleth & Tanner 1976	146.3
Egypt	East Cairo	<1981	Eveleth & Tanner 1991	149.0
2. Females				
Ethiopia	Ethiopia & Eritrea	1958	Meredith 1969	142.8
Ethiopia	Urban	1965	Eveleth & Tanner 1976	148.0
Ethiopia	Addis-Ababa	1965	Eveleth & Tanner 1976	147.1
Turkey	Ankara (urban)	1950	Meredith 1969	144.5
Turkey	Istanbul (well-off)	<1973	Eveleth & Tanner 1976	155.6
Turkey	Istanbul (poor)	<1973	Eveleth & Tanner 1976	147.9

Country	People or place	Period of study	Source	Height at age 15 (cm)
1. Males				
India	Bengal	<1938	Krogman 1941	161.3
India	India	1956–65	Eveleth & Tanner 1976	153.0
India	Calcutta	1982–3	Eveleth & Tanner 1991	162.4
Egypt	Egypt	1962–3	Eveleth & Tanner 1976	159.7
Egypt	East Cairo	<1981	Eveleth & Tanner 1991	167.5
Ethiopia	Ethiopia & Eritrea	1958	Meredith 1969	152.2
Ethiopia	Urban	1965	Eveleth & Tanner 1976	158.5
Turkey	Ankara (urban)	1950	Meredith 1969	152.7
Turkey	Istanbul	<1973	Eveleth & Tanner 1976	167.0
Turkey	Istanbul (poor)	<1973	Eveleth & Tanner 1976	159.9

regional variations (Eveleth and Tanner 1976, 1991; see also Abbie 1967, 1968).[9]

In addition to these investigations, we can also examine a more recent inquiry into the heights of three different groups of Samoans. In 1975–7 J. Bindon and S. Zansky compared the heights of children in a "traditional" community of Western Samoa with those of children in two more "modern" communities in American Samoa and Hawaii. They found that there was little difference between the American Samoan children and the Samoan children on Hawaii, but both were consistently taller than the "traditional" children in Western Samoa (Bindon and Zansky 1986). The heights of the Hawaiian Samoans were also considerably greater than those of native Hawaiian children who were measured almost half a century earlier. The average height of native Hawaiian children who were measured before 1930 was approximately 7 cm less than that of Hawaiian Samoan children in the mid-1970s (Krogman 1941).

Insights into the pattern of secular change among Pacific Island peoples can also be gained by comparing the results of a number of recent surveys of the heights of the Bundi and Manus peoples of Papua New Guinea. The Bundi, for example, were among the smallest people in the world when they were first measured by L. A. Malcolm in 1958–60, but their heights had increased considerably by the time a second survey was carried out in 1983–4 (Malcolm 1970; Zemel and Jenkins 1989).

There is also some evidence of an increase in the heights of Manus girls between 1966–8 and 1982, although the heights of Manus boys remained virtually unchanged (Heath and Carter 1971; Schall 1989). In view of the discrepancy between the data for boys and girls and the small number of children involved, it would probably be unwise to reach any firm conclusions about trends in the height of this population at the present time (Eveleth and Tanner 1976, 1991).

Conclusions

This chapter has shown that the average height of people in most parts of the world has increased since the beginning of the twentieth century and that most population groups are probably taller now than at any time in the recent past (Kates and Millman 1990). However, the secular trend toward greater height has been neither universal nor rectilinear (Roche 1979). The average height of populations has increased much more rapidly in Europe and the United States than in many parts of Africa, Asia, and South America, and even those countries that have registered the greatest increases in height have also experienced periods in which the secular trend has either been arrested or reversed (Takahashi 1966; van Wieringen

1979). Moreover, the distribution of heights in virtually all parts of the world continues to be marked by social and economic inequalities (Eveleth and Tanner 1991). This finding suggests that even within the "developed" world large numbers of children do not experience the nutritional and environmental conditions necessary for the achievement of their full height potential (Jones et al. 1985; Whincup, Cook, and Shaper 1988).

A number of writers have attempted to account for the secular trend and for the variations within it. Malina (1979b) attributed the trend to improvements in nutrition and sanitation, urbanization, industrialization, reduced family size, genetic selection, and heterosis. Eveleth and Tanner (1991) have credited improvements in nutrition, the control of infectious diseases, reduced family size, better health care, and population mobility. Other scholars who have examined the consequences of the secular trend have associated it with the reduction of mortality, the lengthening of the female reproductive span, changes in the relationship between children and adults, and increases in physical performance and efficiency (Himes 1979; Malina 1979a, 1979b; Waaler 1984; Eveleth and Tanner 1991).

Several writers have examined the relationship between changes in height (and other anthropometric indicators) and economic growth. In 1984 Floud concluded that variations in Gross Domestic Product (GDP) per head and in infant mortality rates explained "about 96 per cent of the observed variation in heights between and within western European populations since 1880," and that "an increase of one U.S. dollar (at constant 1970 prices) in GDP per capita has been accompanied by an increase in the average height of the population of 0.003 centimeters" (Floud 1984: 18). In 1988 H. Brinkmann, J. Drukker, and B. Slot argued that there was a close association between changes in GDP and the height of Army conscripts in Holland, and K. Liestøl found evidence of a similar relationship between changes of GDP and mean age of menarche in Norway (Liestøl 1982; Brinkmann, Drukker, and Slot 1988; but see also Mandemakers and van Zanden 1993). In 1988 L. A. Schmitt and G. A. Harrison concluded that "affluence" was the most important single cause of the differences that they observed in the average heights of 58 populations whose heights had been recorded in *Human Biology* and *Annals of Human Biology* over the previous 20 years (Schmitt and Harrison 1988).

Although economic growth is probably a necessary precondition for the long-term improvement of health and nutrition, it is not the only factor that has influenced trends in average height over the past 200 years. Both John Komlos and Floud have demonstrated that it is possible for the average height of a population to decline even when its GDP is increasing. In 1989 Komlos showed that soldiers who grew up in the economically more developed regions of the Hapsburg Empire during the second half of the eighteenth century were shorter than soldiers who grew up in the less developed regions, and Floud revealed that the average height of successive birth cohorts of British soldiers declined during the middle years of the nineteenth century (Komlos 1989; Floud et al. 1990). In 1983 Steckel concluded that differences between the average heights of 22 contemporary populations were attributable to variations in national income, income inequality, and welfare provision (Steckel 1983). These findings are reinforced by the dramatic increases in average height in China and those that have been achieved in some parts of India and Sri Lanka since the end of World War II (Drèze and Sen 1989; Kates and Millman 1990).

Bernard Harris

Notes

1. For example, in 1904 the British Interdepartmental Committee on Physical Deterioration urged the government to institute a national program of anthropometric monitoring as a means of providing accurate information about the health and physique of the British population (see Harris 1989).
2. There is also evidence of a secular trend toward greater adult height among the Skolt Lapps of northern Finland (see Lewin, Jürgens, and Louekari 1970).
3. Bakwin (1964) has demonstrated that the weight of Scottish newborns increased by several hundred grams in the 85-year period between 1850-60 and 1935-45. But this appears to be the exception rather than the rule so far as European studies are concerned.
4. It is likely that Tanner overestimated the decline in mean menarcheal age in Norway. More recent estimates suggest that the actual age of menarche in 1840 was between 15.6 and 16.0 years. This would mean that the decline in mean menarcheal age between 1840 and 1950 was between 2.4 and 2.8 years (see Bruntland and Wallø 1976; Brudevoll, Liestøl, and Wallø 1979, 1980).
5. Goodman interviewed 1,291 Caucasian women, 1,519 Japanese women, and 395 Chinese women. Results were based on personal recall (Goodman 1983).
6. It is important to note that the average height of black South Africans remained well below that of more affluent black populations elsewhere in the world, as well as that of white children in the same country (Walker and Walker 1977).
7. The average height of Chinese children between the ages of 7 and 14 increased by approximately 8.04 cm between 1951-8 and 1979. The rate of increase was greater than that of any European population and roughly equal to that of Japanese children in this period (Piazza 1984).
8. These findings contrast with those of Greiner and Gordon (1992), who claim that the increase in the average height of successive birth cohorts of Hispanic-Americans was greater than that of any other ethnic group. However, they also claim that the overall rate of increase for Hispanic-Americans, for a range of 22 bodily dimensions, was generally below that of the white population.
9. W. J. Fysh and colleagues (1977) compared the birth weights of infants at Cherborg and Palm Island Aboriginal settlements in 1953, 1963, and 1972. There was a small increase in the birth weights of male infants at Cherborg set-

tlement between 1953 and 1963 but a sharp decline between 1963 and 1972. By contrast, the birth weights of male infants at Palm Island settlement increased between 1963 and 1972. The birth weights of female infants remained unchanged in both settlements.

Bibliography

Abbie, A. 1967. Skinfold thickness in Australian Aborigines. *Archaeology and Physical Anthropology in Oceania* 2: 207-19.

1968. The homogeneity of Australian Aborigines. *Archaeology and Physical Anthropology in Oceania* 3: 223-31.

Bakwin, H. 1964. The secular change in growth and development. *Acta Paediatrica* 53: 79-89.

Bakwin, H., and S. McLaughlin. 1964. Secular increase in height: Is the end in sight? *Lancet* 2: 1195-6.

Barrett, M., and T. Brown. 1971. Increase in average height of Australian Aborigines. *Medical Journal of Australia* 2: 1169-72.

Billewicz, W., and I. Macgregor. 1982. A birth-to-maturity longitudinal study of heights and weights in two West African Gambian villages, 1951-75. *Annals of Human Biology* 9: 309-20.

Bindon, J., and S. Zansky. 1986. Growth patterns of height and weight among three groups of Samoan preadolescents. *Annals of Human Biology* 13: 171-8.

Bjelke, E. 1971. Variation in height and weight in the Norwegian population. *British Journal of Preventive and Social Medicine* 25: 192-202.

Blanco, M., M. Landaeta-Jiménez, and H. Castellano. 1989. Secular trend in height and weight: Carabobo, Venezuela. In *Auxology '88: Perspectives in the science of growth and development*, ed. J. Tanner, 207-10. London.

Blanksby, B., L. Freedman, P. Barrett, and J. Bloomfield. 1974. Secular change in the heights and weights of Western Australian primary schoolchildren. *Annals of Human Biology* 1: 301-9.

Bock, R., and R. Sykes. 1989. Evidence for continuing secular increase in height within families in the United States. *American Journal of Human Biology* 1: 143-8.

Brinkman, H., J. Drukker, and B. Slot. 1988. Height and income: A new method for the estimation of historical national income series. *Explorations in Economic History* 25: 227-64.

Brudevoll, J., K. Liestøl, and L. Walløe. 1979. Menarcheal age in Oslo during the last 140 years. *Annals of Human Biology* 6: 407-16.

Brundtland, G., K. Liestøl, and L. Walløe. 1980. Height, weight and menarcheal age of Oslo schoolchildren during the last sixty years. *Annals of Human Biology* 7: 307-22.

Brundtland, G., and L. Walløe. 1976. Menarcheal age in Norway in the nineteenth century: A reevaluation of the historical sources. *Annals of Human Biology* 3: 363-74.

Cameron, N. 1979. The growth of London schoolchildren 1904-66: An analysis of secular trend and intra-county variation. *Annals of Human Biology* 6: 505-25.

Cone, T. 1961. Secular acceleration of height and biologic maturation in children during the past century. *Journal of Pediatrics* 59: 736-40.

Damon, A. 1968. Secular trend in height and weight within old-American families at Harvard 1870-1965. *American Journal of Physical Anthropology* 29: 45-50.

Danker-Hopfe, H. 1986. Menarcheal age in Europe. *Yearbook of Physical Anthropology* 29: 81-112.

Drèze, J., and A. Sen. 1989. *Hunger and public action.* Oxford.

Eng, P. van der. 1995. An inventory of secular changes in human growth in Indonesia. In *The biological standard of living on three continents: Further explorations in anthropometric history*, ed. J. Komlos, 175-90. Boulder, Colo.

Eveleth, P. 1979. Population differences in growth: Environmental and genetic factors. In *Human growth*, Vol. 3, ed. F. Falkner and J. Tanner, 373-94. London.

Eveleth, P., E. Bowers, and J. Schall. 1979. Secular change in growth of Philadelphia black adolescents. *Human Biology* 51: 213-28.

Eveleth, P., F. Salzano, and P. de Lima. 1974. Child growth and adult physique in Brazilian Xingu Indians. *American Journal of Physical Anthropology* 41: 95-102.

Eveleth, P., and J. Tanner. 1976. *Worldwide variation in human growth.* First edition. Cambridge and New York.

1991. *Worldwide variation in human growth.* Second edition. Cambridge and New York.

Farid-Coupal, N., M. Contreras, and H. Castellano. 1981. The age at menarche in Carabobo, Venezuela, with a note on the secular trend. *Annals of Human Biology* 8: 283-8.

Floud, R. 1984. The heights of Europeans since 1750: A new source for European economic history. *National Bureau of Economic Research Working Papers*, No. 1318, Cambridge, Mass.

Floud, R., K. Wachter, and A. Gregory. 1990. *Height, health and history: Nutritional status in the United Kingdom 1750-1980.* Cambridge.

Fogel, R. 1986. Nutrition and the decline in mortality since 1700: Some preliminary findings. In *Long-term factors in American economic growth*, ed. S. Engerman and R. Gallman, 439-555. Chicago.

Fysh, W., R. Davidson, D. Chandler, and A. Dugdale. 1977. The weights of Aboriginal infants: A comparison over twenty years. *Medical Journal of Australia Special Supplement* 1: 13-15.

Ganguly, P. 1977. The problem of human adaptation: An overview. *Man in India* 57: 1-22.

Gonzales, G., I. Crespo-Retes, and R. Guerra-Garcia. 1982. Secular change in growth of native children and adolescents at high altitude: I. Puno, Peru 3,800 metres. *American Journal of Physical Anthropology* 58: 191-5.

Goodman, M. 1983. Letter to the editor – Secular changes in recalled age at menarche. *Annals of Human Biology* 10: 585.

Gordon, A. 1983. The nutriture of Cubans: Historical perspective and nutritional analysis. *Cuban Studies* 13: 1-38.

Greiner, T., and C. Gordon. 1992. Secular trends of 22 body dimensions in four racial/cultural groups of American males. *American Journal of Human Biology* 4: 235-46.

Greulich, W. 1976. Some secular changes in the growth of American-born and native Japanese children. *American Journal of Physical Anthropology* 45: 553-68.

Harris, B. 1989. Medical inspection and the nutrition of

schoolchildren in Britain, 1900-50. Ph.D. thesis, University of London.

Hausman, A., and E. Wilmsen. 1985. Economic change and secular trends in the growth of San children. *Human Biology* 57: 563-71.

Heath, B., and J. Carter. 1971. Growth and somatotype patterns of Manus children, Territory of Papua and New Guinea: Application of a modified somatotype method to the study of growth patterns. *American Journal of Physical Anthropology* 35: 49-67.

Helm, P., and S. Helm. 1984. Decrease in menarcheal age from 1966 to 1983 in Denmark. *Acta Obstetricia Gynecologica Scandinavica* 63: 633-5.

  1987. Uncertainties in designation of age at menarche in the nineteenth century: Revised means for Denmark, 1835. *Annals of Human Biology* 14: 371-4.

Himes, J. 1979. Secular changes in body proportions and composition. In *Secular trends in human growth, maturation and development*. Monographs of the Society for Research in Child Development 44 (Serial no. 179, nos. 3-4): 28-58.

Hoshi, H., and M. Kouchi. 1981. Secular trend of the age at menarche of Japanese girls with special regard to the secular acceleration of the age at peak height velocity. *Human Biology* 53: 593-8.

Jones, D., M. Nesheim, and J.-P. Habicht. 1985. Influences in child growth associated with poverty in the 1970s: An examination of HANESI and HANESII cross-sectional US national surveys. *American Journal of Clinical Nutrition* 42: 714-24.

Kates, R., and S. Millman. 1990. On ending hunger: The lessons of history. In *Hunger in history: Food shortage, poverty and deprivation*, ed. L. Newman, W. Crossgrove, R. Kates, et al., 389-407. Oxford.

Kaur, D., and R. Singh. 1981. Parent–adult offspring correlations and heritability of body measurements in a rural Indian population. *Annals of Human Biology* 8: 333-9.

Komlos, J. 1989. *Nutrition and economic development in the eighteenth-century Habsburg monarchy.* Princeton, N.J.

  ed. 1995. *The biological standard of living on three continents: Further explorations in anthropometric history.* Boulder, Colo.

Krogman, W. M. 1941. *Growth of man.* The Hague, the Netherlands.

Laska-Mierzejewska, T., H. Milicer, and H. Piechaczek. 1982. Age at menarche and its secular trend in urban and rural girls in Poland. *Annals of Human Biology* 9: 227-34.

Lejarraga, H., I. Meletti, S. Brocca, and V. Alonso. 1989. Secular trend and environmental influences on growth at adolescence in Argentina. In *Auxology '88: Perspectives in the science of growth and development,* ed. J. Tanner, 211-19. London.

Leung, S., Y. Lam, S. Lui, et al. 1987. Height, weight and head circumference in Shatin children 3-7 years of age: Further evidence for secular changes. *Hong Kong Journal of Paediatrics* 4: 43-51.

Lewin, T., H. Jürgens, and L. Louekari. 1970. Secular trend in the adult height of Skolt Lapps: Studies in 1915, 1934 and 1968 of stature changes at population and familial level in a genetic isolate. *Arctic Anthropology* 7: 53-62.

Liestøl, K. 1982. Social conditions and menarcheal age: The importance of early years of life. *Annals of Human Biology* 9: 521-37.

Ling, J., and N. King. 1987. Secular trends in stature and weight in southern Chinese children in Hong Kong. *Annals of Human Biology* 14: 187-90.

Ljung, B., A. Bergsten-Brucefors, and G. Lindgren. 1974. The secular trend in physical growth in Sweden. *Annals of Human Biology* 1: 245-56.

Low, W., L. Kung, and J. Leong. 1982. Secular trend in the sexual maturation of Chinese girls. *Human Biology* 54: 539-51.

Malcolm, L. 1970. Growth and development of the Bundi children of the New Guinea highlands. *Human Biology* 42: 293-328.

Malina, R. 1979a. Secular changes in growth, maturation and physical performance. *Exercise and Sports Sciences Review* 6: 203-55.

  1979b. Secular changes in size and maturity: Causes and effects. In *Secular trends in human growth, maturation and development.* Monographs of the Society for Research in Child Development 44 (serial no. 179, nos. 3-4): 59-102.

Malina, R., R. Martorell, and F. Mendoza. 1986. Growth status of Mexican-American children and youths: Historical trends and contemporary issues. *Yearbook of Physical Anthropology* 29: 45-79.

Malina, R., and A. Zavaleta. 1980. Secular trend in the stature and weight of Mexican-American children in Texas between 1930 and 1970. *American Journal of Physical Anthropology* 52: 453-61.

Mandemakers, C., and J. L. van Zanden. 1993. The height of conscripts and national income: Apparent relations and misconceptions. *Explorations in Economic History* 30: 81-97.

Martins, D. da Costa. 1971. Height, weight and chest circumference of children of different ethnic groups in Lourenço Marques, Moçambique, in 1965, with a note on the secular trend. *Human Biology* 43: 253-64.

Matsumoto, K. 1982. Secular acceleration of growth in height in Japanese [children] and its social background. *Annals of Human Biology* 9: 399-410.

Matsumoto, K., Y. Kudo, H. Takeuchi, and S. Takeda. 1980. Secular trend in age of maximum increment in mean height of Japanese children born from 1887 to 1965. *Wakayama Medical Reports* 23: 99-106.

McCullough, J. 1982. Secular trend for stature in adult male Yucatec Maya to 1968. *American Journal of Physical Anthropology* 58: 221-5.

Meredith, H. 1963. Change in the stature and body weight of North American boys during the last eighty years. *Advances in Child Development and Behaviour* 6: 69-114.

  1969. *Body size of contemporary youth in different parts of the world.* Monographs of the Society for Research in Child Development 34 (serial no. 131, no. 7).

  1976. Findings from Asia, Australia, Europe and North America on secular changes in mean height of children, youths and adults. *American Journal of Physical Anthropology* 44: 315-26.

Moore, W. 1970. The secular trend in physical growth of North American Negro schoolchildren. *Monographs of the Society for Research in Child Development* 35: 62-73.

Nagai, N., K. Matsumoto, T. Mino, et al. 1980. The secular trends in the menarcheal age and the maximum growth age in height for Japanese schoolgirls. *Wakayama Medical Reports* 23: 41-5.

Nakamura, I., M. Shimura, K. Nonaka, and T. Miura. 1986. Changes of recollected menarcheal age and month among women in Tokyo over a period of ninety years. *Annals of Human Biology* 13: 547-54.

Piazza, A. 1984. *Food consumption and nutritional status in the People's Republic of China.* Boulder, Colo.

Prazuck, T., A. Fisch, E. Pichard, and Y. Sidibe. 1988. Lack of secular change in male adult stature in rural Mali West Africa. *American Journal of Physical Anthropology* 75: 471-5.

Prebeg, Z. 1984. Secular trend in growth of Zagreb schoolchildren. In *Human growth and development*, ed. J. Borms, R. Hauspie, C. Sand, et al., 201-7. New York.

Rea, J. 1971. Social and economic influences on the growth of pre-school children in Lagos. *Human Biology* 43: 46-63.

Roche, A. 1979. Introduction. In *Secular trends in human growth, maturation and development*. Monographs of the Society for Research in Child Development 44 (serial no. 179, nos. 3-4): 1-2.

Rona, R., A. Swan, and D. Altman. 1978. Social factors and height of primary schoolchildren in England and Scotland. *Journal of Epidemiology and Community Health* 32: 147-54.

Rosenberg, M. 1988. Birth weight in three Norwegian cities, 1860-1984: Secular trends and influencing factors. *Annals of Human Biology* 15: 275-88.

Schall, J. 1989. Fat patterns and blood pressure among the Manus of Papua New Guinea: A migrant study. *American Journal of Physical Anthropology* 78: 296.

Schmitt, L., and G. Harrison. 1988. Patterns in the within-population variability of stature and weight. *Annals of Human Biology* 15: 353-64.

Shatrugna, V., and K. Rao. 1987. Secular trends in the height of women from the urban poor community of Hyderabad. *Annals of Human Biology* 14: 275-7.

Sidhu, L., B. Bhatraga, and A. Dubey. 1982. Secular trends in height and weight of Punjabi boys. *Anthropologischer Anzeiger* 40: 187-92.

Singh, S., and P. Malhotra. 1988. Secular shift in menarcheal age of Patiala India schoolgirls between 1974 and 1986. *Annals of Human Biology* 15: 77-80.

Steckel, R. 1983. Height and per capita income. *Historical Methods* 16: 1-7.

1989. Heights and health in the United States 1710-1950. In *Auxology '88: Perspectives in the science of growth and development*, ed. J. Tanner, 175-85. London.

1992. Stature and living standards in the United States. In *American economic growth and standards of living before the Civil War*, ed. R. Gallman and J. Wallis, 265-308. Chicago.

Steendijk, R. 1966. The secular trend in growth and maturation. *Tijdschrift voor sociale Geneeskunde* 44: 518-23.

Suchy, J. 1972. Trend of physical development of Czech youth in the twentieth century. *Review of Czechoslovak Medicine* 18: 18-27.

Takahashi, E. 1966. Growth and environmental factors in Japan. *Human Biology* 38: 112-30.

Tanner, J. 1962. *Growth at adolescence, with a general consideration of the effects of hereditary and environmental factors upon growth and maturation from birth to maturity.* Second edition. Oxford.

1966. The secular trend towards earlier physical maturation. *Tijdschrift voor sociale Geneeskunde* 44: 524-38.

1981. *A history of the study of human growth.* Cambridge and New York.

1986. Growth as a mirror of the condition of society: Secular trends and class distinctions. In *Human growth: A multidisciplinary review*, ed. A. Demirjian, 3-34. London and Philadelphia, Pa.

Tanner, J., T. Hayashi, M. Preece, and N. Cameron. 1982. Increase in length of leg relative to trunk size in Japanese children and adults from 1957 to 1977: Comparison with British and with Japanese Americans. *Annals of Human Biology* 9: 411-23.

Tobias, P. 1962. On the increasing stature of the Bushmen. *Anthropos* 57: 801-10.

1974. Growth and stature in southern African populations. In *The human biology of environmental change: Proceedings of a conference held in Blantyre, Malawi, April 5-12, 1971*, ed. D. Vorster, 96-104. London.

1975. Stature and secular trend among South African Negroes and San Bushmen. *South African Journal of Medical Sciences* 40: 145-64.

Tobias, P., and D. Netscher. 1976. Evidence from African Negro skeletons for a reversal of the usual secular trend. *Journal of Anatomy* 121: 435-6.

Ucho, G., and A. Okorafor. 1979. The age at menarche in Nigerian urban schoolgirls. *Annals of Human Biology* 6: 395-8.

van Venrooij-Ijsselmuiden, M., H. Smeets, and J. van der Werff Ten Bosch. 1976. The secular trend in age at menarche in the Netherlands. *Annals of Human Biology* 3: 283-4.

Vercauteren, M., and C. Susanne. 1985. The secular trend of height and menarche in Belgium: Are there any signs of a future stop? *European Journal of Pediatrics* 144: 306-9.

Vlastovsky, V. 1966. The secular trend in the growth and development of children and young persons in the Soviet Union. *Human Biology* 38: 219-30.

Waaler, H. 1984. Height, weight and mortality: The Norwegian experience. *Acta Medica Scandinavica*, Supplementum 679: 1-51.

Walker, A., and B. Walker. 1977. Studies on increases in growth rate of South African black schoolchildren and their significance to health. *South African Medical Journal* 51: 707-12.

Walker, M., A. Shaper, and G. Wannamethee. 1988. Height and social class in middle-aged British men. *Journal of Epidemiology and Community Health* 42: 299-303.

Ward, J. 1990. Weight and length at birth in Edinburgh, 1847-1920. Paper presented to the Tenth International Economic History Congress, University of Leuven, August.

Ward, W. 1988. Birth weight and standards of living in Vienna, 1865-1930. *Journal of Interdisciplinary History* 19: 203-29.

Wering, E. van. 1981. The secular growth trend on Aruba between 1954 and 1974. *Human Biology* 53: 105-15.

Whincup, P., A. Cook, and A. Shaper. 1988. Social class and height. *British Medical Journal* 297: 980-1.

Wieringen, J. van. 1979. Secular growth changes. In *Human growth*, Vol. 2, ed. F. Falkner and J. Tanner, 445-73. London.

Wyshak, G. 1983. Secular changes in age at menarche in a sample of United States women. *Annals of Human Biology* 10: 75-7.

Zemel, B., and C. Jenkins. 1989. Dietary change and adolescent growth among the Bundi (Gende-speaking) people of Papua New Guinea. *American Journal of Human Biology* 1: 709-18.

VI.6 ❧ The Nutrition of Women in the Developing World

There are at least two reasons why the nutritional status of women should be distinguished from that of men. The first is that a woman's nutritional status has a direct impact on her children. Better-nourished mothers lead to better-nourished infants by virtue of prepregnancy nutritional status, weight gain during pregnancy, and diet during lactation. This approach to women's nutritional status encapsulates the traditional "breeder and feeder" view.

The second reason is that women exhibit certain nurturing and allocative behaviors, reflecting societal roles, that enhance the food and nutrition security of the entire household and of children in particular. This behavior is most commonly demonstrated in the way women allocate their time and their own income and is particularly visible in certain types of female-headed households. Through both the direct and indirect links, women are the "gatekeepers" of the food and nutritional status of their household's members.

The objective of this chapter is to summarize the literature underlying such links between gender and nutrition within a conceptual framework. Eight main links are identified and discussed in turn, although it should be recognized that this organization is merely a convenient representation of the issues, and that there is considerable overlap across links.

Link 1. Mother's Nutritional Status, Infant and Child Health, and Supplementary Feeding

Birth weight is the single most important determinant of neonatal and infant mortality and of child growth to the age of 7. A number of maternal factors have been shown to be significant determinants of birth weight; most important is the mother's progravid weight and weight gain during pregnancy. Women entering pregnancy with a low preconception weight are several times more likely to produce a low-birth-weight baby (one less than 2,500 grams). Mean birth weight increases, and the incidence of low birth weight decreases, as the preconception weight of the mother increases (Lechtig et al. 1975).

Birth weight and maternal weight gain during pregnancy are also highly correlated, in part, because prenatal weight gain is associated with a decrease in the incidence of prematurity (gestational age less than 37 weeks). If nutritional status before pregnancy, as judged by low progravid weight, is less than adequate, weight gain during pregnancy becomes even more important in influencing neonatal outcomes.

Unfortunately, data indicate that weight gain during pregnancy in developing countries is typically suboptimal. In developed countries the average weight gain during pregnancy is 10 to 12 kilograms, but in developing countries it is 2 to 7 kilograms (Ghassemi 1990). Moreover, for many women in developing countries, negative weight gains are common during pregnancy. Part of the reason for this is a tendency to either not increase food intake or, in some cases, to decrease the amount of food consumed – a phenomenon labeled "eating down" during pregnancy (Brems and Berg 1988).

Although limiting calorie consumption during pregnancy is practiced by some women, in many areas a high level of physical activity, uncompensated by additional calories, is the more common reason for low weight gain during pregnancy. For example, a study in Gambia showed that birth weights were decreased only after the peak period of agricultural labor; during nonpeak seasons, birth weights were close to international norms (Lawrence and Whitehead 1988). Such data indicate that when agricultural labor demands are high, women are unable to cope with pregnancy solely by increasing caloric consumption.

Certain types of illness patterns during pregnancy can also have an adverse effect on the development of the fetus and the neonate. The incidence of low birth weight is known to increase following rubella, and the early onset of labor is common for women with hepatitis and measles. Some maternal infections can cause intrauterine growth retardation, and these infections are more common where poor hygiene is prevalent, as is the case in many low-income areas of developing countries. Thus, a study in four villages in Guatemala indicated high rates of maternal infections during pregnancy and consequently intrauterine exposure of the fetus to infectious agents (Lechtig et al. 1974).

In more general terms, the morbidity of mothers also correlates with a higher incidence of low birth weight. Classification of women in the four Guatemalan villages into high or low morbidity groups found that 33 percent of infants born to those in the high morbidity group were low birth weight compared to 10.5 percent of infants from women of low morbidity (Lechtig et al. 1974). The authors also found that those in the high morbidity group tended to come from homes with low calorie availability; they interpreted this to mean that morbidity during pregnancy is likely to be associated with a low energy consumption.

These maternal characteristics often occur in combination with each other. In other words, women who begin pregnancy with a low progravid weight often gain inadequate weight and have a high incidence of infection during pregnancy.

Dietary supplementation schemes targeted to high-risk women have been one type of intervention aimed at reducing adverse outcomes of pregnancy. A number of investigations in developing countries have indicated that calorie supplementation during pregnancy results in improved birth weight, decreases rates of prematurity, increases weight gain of the mother, and decreases incidence of anemia and toxemia in program participants (Iyenger 1967; Lechtig et al. 1975; Kielmann, Taylor, and Parker 1978). However, not all programs have been successful, and some researchers have criticized supplementation schemes as being too expensive for the benefits produced (Beaton and Ghassemi 1982). Those deemed successful have certain characteristics in common; typically a large ration is targeted to nutritionally vulnerable women, usually in combination with prenatal health services (Kennedy and Knudsen 1985).

Now, however, maternal dietary supplementation schemes are a less popular type of nutrition intervention. Irregular participation because of little time for such an activity was a major factor limiting effectiveness. A more promising approach to improving women's nutritional status, including that of pregnant women, is to decrease their physical activity – particularly during the last trimester of pregnancy. This approach appears more culturally acceptable than promoting maternal weight gain in many developing countries.

Link 2: Women's Nutritional Status, Time Allocation, and Energy Expenditure: Output Effects

The general assumption is that better-nourished individuals will be more productive. However, the empirical literature that deals with the effects of improved nutritional status on physical and cognitive productivity in developing countries is relatively thin. The evidence is strongest for men, because male labor force data are most readily available. An example of the short-term impact of calorie intake on productivity and capacity may be found in E. Kennedy's 1989 study of women in the south Nyanza district of rural Kenya. There, increases in household income (in both female- and male-headed households), due to agricultural commercialization, raised female calorie intake but did not improve female nutritional status (according to anthropometric measures) or health status. Female body mass index actually declined during a time of rising calorie intake, suggesting that the energy intensity of female activities was increasing disproportionately.

Short-run income-enhancing attempts to alleviate the time constraint of women may not succeed, even if a woman is prepared to place her nutritional needs above those of her family. A 1988 study by S. Kumar and D. Hotchkiss of Nepalese hill districts found that because of low agricultural productivity, new land needed to be cleared to maintain household basic needs. However, the subsequent deforestation increased the time allocated by women to collect fuel. This meant less time for female agricultural labor input, which led to fewer calories from this income source, which, in turn, increased the need for deforestation, and so on, in a downward spiral.

Link 3: Women's Share of Household Income and Household Food Security: Roles, Preferences, and Constraints

Household food security has been defined as the access of all people at all times to sufficient food for an active and healthy life (World Bank 1986). Two of the biggest determinants of household food consumption are income and prices. Rising income and falling food prices increase a household's ability to obtain an adequate diet. However, an accumulating body of evidence now suggests that it is not simply the *level* of household income but *who earns* that income that is important in improving a household's food intake.

Income controlled by women, particularly in Africa, is more likely to be spent on food than is male-controlled income (Braun and Kennedy 1994). At similar levels of income, households with more women-controlled income are more likely to be food secure. Evidence for the positive influence of female control of income on household food expenditure (Haddad and Hoddinott 1991), calorie intake (Garcia 1991), and anthropometric indicators (Thomas 1990) is increasing in both Africa and Asia.

This influence may be explained by a number of factors: (1) societal gender roles that cast women in the role of "gatekeepers"; (2) different preferences (women may prefer to spend more on children's food because they spend more time with them); (3) different constraints (women may spend more on food when more income is earned because of a need to purchase more expensive calories that take less time to prepare); or (4) different transaction costs (women earn money in flows that are more easily spent on food). Whatever the reason, getting income into the hands of women seems to be one way of enhancing the household's food security.

Link 4: Women's Time Allocation, Energy Expenditure, and Household Food Security: The Value of Women's Time

During times of economic hardship, women tend to act as "shock absorbers" for the welfare of the household, reflecting the undervalued nature of their time. There is a certain invisibility to the economic contribution of women outside the home as measured by censuses and International Labor Organization (ILO) statistics. R. B. Dixon (1982) documented this invisibility for a number of countries by comparing data from ILO, the Food and Agricultural Organization of the United Nations (FAO), and national agricultural census estimates of the percentage of the agricultural labor force that is female. For many North African and South Asian states, these three sets of statistics are widely divergent, and the formal censuses tend to cloak secondary and tertiary female economic activities.

An example of this shock-absorber behavior has been characterized in Latin America as the "feminization" of poverty (Buvinic 1990). During economic crises that result in less male employment, women enter the labor force to bolster household income and food security. But because women are less well educated, they tend to accept jobs that men would not and are paid very low wages for those jobs because the supply of female labor outweighs the demand for it.

Link 5: Household Food Security and Preschooler Food Security: Intrahousehold Allocation of Food

The identification of pockets of malnutrition and poverty within otherwise "better-off" households is one indication that household resources are not always allocated equitably or according to need. A survey of 45 developing countries found that in all but two of these girls die at a higher rate than boys between the ages of 1 and 4 (MacCormack 1988).

Part of this gender disparity in mortality is because of intrahousehold resource allocation. There are strong indications that female children are discriminated against in the allocation of food and other resources in South Asia (Carloni 1981; Chen, Huq, and d'Souza 1981; Harriss 1986). In sub-Saharan Africa, however, evidence for the maldistribution of food and other resources away from girls is not as clear. A recent review of nutrition studies in Africa by P. Svedberg (1990) did not find girls disfavored relative to boys in terms of anthropometric indicators. One interpretation of these findings is that the economic value of girls to households is more explicit and obvious in Africa than in Asia.

Another point, however, is that young children – whether boys or girls – seem to be generally disfavored in the allocation of family food. In recent studies from Kenya and the Philippines, preschool-aged children had a lower level of dietary energy adequacy than the household as a whole. In Kenya, average household calorie adequacy was 94 percent of requirements, but the energy adequacy of the child's diet was only between 60 and 70 percent, depending on age. Similarly, in the Philippines, although household calorie adequacy was in the 85 to 95 percent range, it was only 70 percent for preschoolers (Kennedy and Haddad 1992).

It is important to note, however, that the allocation bias of food tends to disappear for boys as they get older, but not for girls. Females tend to meet a smaller percentage of their energy requirements than do males in the same households (McGuire and Popkin 1990), in part because of a biased allocation of food away from women, and in part because of the energy intensity of women's activities.

This combination of women's reproductive role, heavy workload, and inadequate diet contributes to a series of nutritional problems for developing-country females, not least among them that they live shorter lives by about 10 years when compared to women in the industrialized world (Ghassemi 1990). A majority of the world's women are anemic; nonpregnant women are 2 to 3 times more likely to be anemic than men, whereas pregnant women are 20 times more likely to be anemic (McGuire and Popkin 1990).

To some extent, the poor nutritional status of women is due to differences in bargaining power and productivity across household members. For instance, if one individual in a household has better nutritional status than the remaining household members, is this attributable to his or her superior bargaining power, or is it simply an efficient allocation of resources to the individual best able (now or later) to raise household income? The primary determinants of bargaining power and productivity are cultural phenomena on the one hand (discrimination in, for example, education, time burdens, health care) and randomly distributed initial endowments of physical and cognitive abilities on the other hand.

Link 6: Women's Time Allocation and Preschooler Nutritional Status: Female-Headed Households

In many countries, the pattern of bias in the allocation of food to young children is influenced by the gender of the head of household. Recent studies in Kenya, Malawi, and the Dominican Republic, for example, find that at very low levels of income, some types of female-headed households – those in which the male head of household is absent for more than 50 percent of the time – have lower levels of preschooler malnutrition than male-headed households at comparable income levels (Kennedy and Peters 1992). This finding tends to buttress our earlier assertion that women may allocate proportionately more of their incomes to food and more of the household calories to children.

Other types of time-intensive nurturing behavior, such as feeding children more frequently, are also more common in some types of female-headed households. Such behavior is important to understand, because interventions that can promote appropriate nurturing behavior for children may be quite effective in enhancing nutritional status.

The successful food security and nutrition coping mechanisms exhibited in some types of female-headed households have limits, however. The growing number of female-headed households in developing countries is of concern because these households tend to be more vulnerable to poverty, and in Latin America, a growing number of women and children are living in poverty because of the increase of such households (Buvinic 1990). Women in female-headed households tend to be poorer because they have less access to labor, land, credit, and government resources (Rosenhouse 1989). In addition, as already mentioned, where women can participate in the labor force, they tend to do so with low-paying jobs (Buvinic 1990).

Link 7: Preschooler Nutritional Status and Women's Time Allocation: Intergenerational Effects

The nutritional status and morbidity levels of preschoolers will help determine the transmission of nutritional status across generations. Studies cited under Link 4 demonstrate the importance of early nutrition on later physical and cognitive performance. An additional pathway is through role-model formation and expectation setting. Better-educated parents, who promote better nutritional status for their children, will tend to expect enhanced school performance, which, in turn, will promote enhanced adult productivity. This is one way of breaking the intergenerational cycle of poverty and poor nutritional status.

Evidence of intergenerational transmission effects is provided by M. Buvinic (1990): Abandoned mothers in Santiago, Chile, tend to come from female-headed households. Moreover, D. Thomas (1991) has shown, with data from Ghana, the United States, and Brazil, that the intergenerational effects tend to run along gender lines: The father's education has a stronger effect on the son's anthropometric status, and the mother's education has a stronger effect on the daughter's anthropometric status.

Other intergenerational effects include (1) the impact healthier infants have on reduced health expenditures later in life and (2) the improved provision of old-age security for parents from healthier children.

Link 8: Women's Nutritional Status and Their Time Allocation and Energy Expenditure: A Zero-Sum Game?

Non-income-mediated pathways may be as important, or in some cases more important, than income alone in improving or maintaining child nutritional status. Almost all the non-income links to nutritional status are time-intensive. Links 2, 4, and 6 discuss the impact of women's time allocation decisions on household income, household food security, and preschooler nutritional status. Link 8 suggests that these relationships are not without cost (and are, therefore, unsustainable) in terms of women's nutritional status.

Time allocation studies indicate that, on average, women in developing countries put more hours per day into nonleisure activities than do men (Juster and Stafford 1991). Not only are women actively engaged in agriculture and wage-generating activities, but a substantial amount of their day is devoted to home production activities such as getting water and fuel wood, preparing meals, and child care. In many rural areas, domestic activities account for the largest proportion of women's time in any given day. Unfortu-

nately, low-income women have even longer working days than their higher-income counterparts, further exacerbating the poverty–malnutrition cycle.

In addition, many of the health-promoting strategies advocated as part of the child survival revolution – breast feeding, growth monitoring, oral rehydration therapy – add to the time constraints of women. Indeed, the low level of utilization of these child survival strategies may be related to the lack of time of the mother (Leslie 1989).

Women's time constraints have a negative effect on their own nutritional status. As already indicated in the previous section, biased allocation of food away from women in many countries, particularly in South Asia, combine with long hours of labor to work a decidedly negative impact on women's nutritional status. Thus, the few studies on women's nutritional status that exist indicate that malnutrition is more common in women than in men (McGuire and Popkin 1990).

Conclusions

The major links between women's nutritional status, household food security, and infant–child nutritional status have been discussed. In the past great attention has been focused on the effect of nutritional status during pregnancy and lactation on neonatal and perinatal nutritional status. Yet the prepregnant weight of the mother influences birth weight more than weight gain during pregnancy. Unfortunately, few interventions have addressed nutritional status issues related to nonpregnant women. A potentially cost-effective nutrition intervention, however, would be one aimed at improving the nutritional status of high-risk female adolescents.

Any intervention designed to improve the nutrition of women must take their time constraints into consideration. Failure to ensure regular participation of women was one reason for the lack of any robust effects of prior dietary supplementation schemes. Time-saving, and thus energy-saving, programs offer a greater potential than other types of interventions for improving women's nutrition. Since the greatest portion of the day for rural women is devoted to home production activities – getting water and fuel, housework, cooking, and so forth – any program that can decrease this time may have a significant nutrition benefit.

Much of the discussion in the literature stresses the improvement of women's nutrition as an equity issue. However, there are strong efficiency reasons why policy makers would want to improve women's nutrition. Better-nourished women are more economically productive. Thus, because women are major actors in developing-country agriculture – particularly in Africa – interventions that improve their nutritional status also offer the potential of ensuring a more productive agricultural sector.

Eileen Kennedy
Lawrence Haddad

Bibliography

Alba, M. 1991. Early childhood factors as determinants of education and earnings: The case of four rural villages in Guatemala. Ph.D. dissertation, Food Research Institute, Stanford University.

Beaton, G., and H. Ghassemi. 1982. Supplementary feeding programs for young children in developing countries. *American Journal of Clinical Nutrition* 34 (Supplement 1982): 864-916.

Braun, J. von, and E. Kennedy, eds. 1994. *Commercialization of agriculture: Poverty and nutritional effects.* Baltimore, Md.

Brems, S., and Alan Berg. 1988. *"Eating down" during pregnancy: Nutrition, obstetric, and cultural considerations in the Third World.* Washington, D.C.

Buvinic, M. 1990. The feminization of poverty. In *Women and nutrition,* United Nations Administrative Committee on Coordination/Subcommittee on Nutrition Symposium Report, Nutrition Policy Discussion Paper No. 6. Geneva.

Carloni, A. S. 1981. Sex disparities in the distribution of food within rural households. *Food and Nutrition Bulletin* 7: 3-12.

Chen, L., E. Huq, and S. d'Souza. 1981. Sex bias in the family allocation of food and health care in rural Bangladesh. *Population and Development Review* 7: 55-70.

Chung, K. 1991. Nutritional status and work productivity. Ph.D. dissertation, Food Research Institute, Stanford University.

Deolalikar, A. 1988. Nutrition and labor productivity in agriculture: Estimates for rural South India. *Review of Economics and Statistics* 703: 406-13.

Dixon, R. B. 1982. Women in agriculture: Counting the labor force in developing countries. *Population and Development Review* 8: 539-66.

Garcia, M. 1990. Resource allocation and household welfare. Ph.D. dissertation, Institute of Social Studies, The Hague.

1991. Impact of female sources of income on food demand among rural households in the Philippines. *Quarterly Journal of International Agriculture* 30: 109-24.

Ghassemi, H. 1990. Women, food, and nutrition – issues in need of a global focus. In *Women and nutrition,* United Nations Administrative Committee on Coordination/Subcommittee on Nutrition Symposium Report, Nutrition Policy Discussion Paper No. 6. Geneva.

Haddad, L., and H. Bouis. 1991. The impact of nutritional status on agricultural productivity: Wage evidence from the Philippines. *Oxford Bulletin of Economics and Statistics* 531: 45-68.

Haddad, L., and J. Hoddinott. 1991. Gender aspects of household expenditures and resource allocation in the Côte d'Ivoire. Applied Economics Discussion Paper 112. Institute of Economic Studies Working Paper, Oxford University.

Harriss, B. 1986. The intrafamily distribution of hunger in South Asia. In *Hunger and public policy,* ed. J. Drèze and A. K. Sen. Oxford.

Iyenger, L. 1967. Effect of dietary supplementation late in pregnancy on the expectant mother and her newborn. *Indian Journal of Medical Research* 55: 85-9.

Juster, F. T., and F. P. Stafford. 1991. The allocation of time: Empirical findings, behavioral models, and problems of measurement. *Journal of Economic Literature* 24: 471-522.

Kennedy, E. 1989. *The effects of sugarcane production on food security, health and nutrition in Kenya: A longitudinal analysis.* International Food Policy Research Institute Research Report 78. Washington, D.C.

Kennedy, E., and L. Haddad. 1992. Food security and nutrition 1971-1991: Lessons learned and future priorities. *Food Policy* 17: 2-6.

Kennedy, E., and O. Knudsen. 1985. A review of supplementary feeding programmes and recommendations on their design. In *Nutrition and Development,* ed. Margaret Biswas and Per Pinstrup-Andersen, 77-96. New York.

Kennedy, E., and P. Peters. 1992. Household food security and child nutrition: The interaction of income and gender of household need. *World Development* 20: 1077-85.

Kielmann, A., C. E. Taylor, and R. L. Parker. 1978. The Narangwal nutrition study: A summary review. *American Journal of Clinical Nutrition* 31: 2040-52.

Kumar, S., and D. Hotchkiss. 1988. *Consequences of deforestation for women's time allocation, agricultural production, and nutrition in hill areas of Nepal.* International Food Policy Research Institute Research Report 69. Washington, D.C.

Lawrence, M., and R. G. Whitehead. 1988. Physical activity and total energy expenditure of child-bearing Gambian village women. *European Journal of Clinical Nutrition* 42: 145-60.

Lechtig, A., L. J. Mata, J.-P. Habicht, et al. 1974. Levels of immunoglobulin M (Igm) in cord blood of Latin American newborns of low socioeconomic status. *Ecology of Food Nutrition* 3: 171-8.

Lechtig, A., C. Yarbrough, H. Delgado, et al. 1975. Influence of maternal nutrition on birth weight. *American Journal of Clinical Nutrition* 28: 1223-33.

Leslie, J. 1988. Women's work and child nutrition in the Third World. *World Development* 16: 1341-70.

1989. Women's time: A factor in the use of child survival technologies? *Health Policy and Planning* 4: 1-16.

MacCormack, C. 1988. Health and the social power of women. *Social Science and Medicine* 26: 678.

Mayatech. 1991. *Gender and adjustment.* Silver Spring, Md.

McGuire, J., and B. Popkin. 1988. The zero-sum game: A framework for examining women and nutrition. *Food and Nutrition Bulletin* 10: 27-32.

1990. Beating the zero-sum game: Women and nutrition in the Third World. In *Women and nutrition,* United Nations Administrative Committee on Coordination/Subcommittee on Nutrition Symposium Report, Nutrition Policy Discussion Paper No. 6, 11-65. Geneva.

Rosenhouse, S. 1989. Identifying the poor: Is headship a useful concept? Living Standards Measurement Study Working Paper 58. Washington, D.C.

Svedberg, P. 1990. Undernutrition in sub-Saharan Africa: Is there a gender bias? *Journal of Development Studies* 26: 469-86.

Thomas, D. 1990. Intrahousehold resource allocation: An inferential approach. *Journal of Human Resources* 25: 635-64.

1991. *Gender differences in household resource allocations.* Living Standards Measurement Survey Working Paper 79. Washington, D.C.

World Bank. 1986. *Poverty and hunger: Issues and options for food security in developing countries.* A World Bank Policy Study. Washington, D.C.

VI.7 ✍ Infant and Child Nutrition

Infant Feeding in Prehistory

Prehistoric patterns of human infant feeding are important for understanding the forces that have shaped the nutritional requirements of today's infants and the biological capacities of their mothers to satisfy these requirements through lactation. The primary sources of data to reconstruct such patterns are observational studies of nonhuman primates in the wild, particularly the great apes, and ethnographic studies of contemporary peoples whose nomadic lifestyle and level of material culture probably approximate those of the first humans.

As a mammalian class, virtually all primates – prosimians, monkeys, and apes, as well as humans – follow a k-strategy of reproduction. That is, they have a small number of infants, most born as singletons, in whom considerable parental attention and effort are invested. The consequence is that a relatively high number of offspring live to adulthood, with the success of such a strategy depending on close physical contact for protection. Thus, nonhuman primate parents carry, rather than cache, their infants – a constant contact that is reinforced by primate milks. These are uniformly high in sugar and low in satiety-producing fat – a milk composition more suited to a frequent-snacking pattern of eating than to one of large, isolated meals. Frequent nursing episodes enhance the amount and, possibly, the energy density of milk (Quandt 1984a). They also delay the return of ovulation, leading to longer birth intervals. Such a biobehavioral complex involving infant feeding, infant care, and birth spacing was doubtless encouraged by the selection process in primate evolution, and consequently, infant feeding became an integral part of the reproductive process, as is demonstrated by studies of human foragers.

The infants of the latter are normally kept in skin-to-skin contact with the mother, and nursing takes place frequently upon demand. Observational studies of the !Kung San of the Kalahari Desert, for example, show that mothers nurse their infants only briefly, but as often as four times per hour during the daytime for an average of two minutes per feeding. Cosleeping of mothers and infants is the rule, and infants also nurse at will during the night (Konner and Worthman 1980). Birth intervals in this noncontracepting group average 44 months (Lee 1979). Weaning among hunter-gatherers is generally gradual, with complete severance not occurring until the next child is born. Premasticated foods are gradually added to the diet, because there are few available foods that can be otherwise managed by very small children.

Infant Feeding in the Historical Period

From the Neolithic to the Renaissance

The Neolithic Revolution brought significant alterations in infant- and child-feeding practices. This transition from a foraging subsistence base to one that incorporated a variety of food production techniques began some 8,000 to 10,000 years ago and was first accomplished in at least six places, including Egypt, Mesopotamia, highland Peru, Mesoamerica, the Indus Valley, and China. Accompanying these changes in food sources were the origins of urbanism, stratified social organization, and writing and record-keeping, along with a host of other cultural traits that joined to comprise what we regard as civilization.

Data on infant-feeding practices come from a variety of artifacts of these civilizations. In addition to archaeological data, there are documentary sources, including art, inscriptions, and early writings. Interpretation of these data is aided by ethnographic analogy with contemporary nonindustrialized societies.

Food production, as opposed to foraging, brought two major changes in the feeding of young children. One of these was the addition of starchy, semisoft foods to the infant diet as a complement to breast milk. Food production meant that the grains or tubers from which such foods could be made were now dependable staples. Cooked into gruels of varying consistency, these foods offered infants and young children relatively innocuous flavor, readily digestible carbohydrate composition, and concentrated energy. Such foods, however, could lead to infectious diseases when contaminated and to equally serious undernutrition, as vegetable foods are deficient in essential amino acids. Consequently, if they were given in place of breast milk, they made for a protein-deficient diet.

With the second change, which came with the domestication of such animals as cows, sheep, goats, and camels, nonhuman milks became available to supplement or even to replace breast milk and to serve as nutrient rich foods for children after weaning. Although there is no record of such milks in the New World or in the civilizations of eastern Asia, their use is well documented elsewhere.

Together these changes in feeding were closely linked to the population explosion that accompanied the Neolithic. The newly available infant foods could shorten the period of intensive breast feeding, leading to shorter periods of postpartum infecundability and, thus, shorter intervals between births. The latter requires substitute foods for infants abruptly displaced from the breast by subsequent newborns, and the milks and cereals were such substitutes.

This does not, of course, mean that breast feeding was abandoned. Early civilizations of the Near East (c. 3000 B.C.) left abundant evidence of their infant-feeding attitudes and practices. Sculptures, paintings, and inscriptions all indicate that mothers were highly regarded and that breast feeding was practiced. For

Egypt, medical papyri from about 1550 B.C. contain remedies and recommendations for a variety of nursing problems still addressed today. These include ways to increase milk supply, to ease breast pain, and to evaluate milk quality. Ointments, incantations, and magico-religious spells are also included.

Wet nursing seems to have been a well-accepted practice in Egypt and Mesopotamia. Among the ancient Egyptian royalty, wet nursing was apparently the usual method of feeding highborn infants, with the nurses accorded high status in the royal court (Robins 1993). During periods of Greek and Roman rule in Egypt, the practice changed so that wet nursing became even more widespread and was frequently performed by slave women. In addition to wet nursing, there is pictorial evidence of infants being fed animal milks from horn-shaped and decorated vessels. We cannot know how frequently such artificial feeding was practiced, but it seems likely that most infants were breast-fed. In the case of wet nursing, there were contracts that specified how long a wet nurse should suckle a child and how the child should be weaned before being returned to the parents (Fildes 1986).

Near Eastern texts also prescribed the weaning diet of young children. After several months of exclusive breast feeding, it was recommended that animal milks and eggs be added to the diet and that animal milks become the principal food after weaning, which occurred at 2 to 3 years of age. Other foods were not introduced until teeth were cut, and these were primarily fruits and vegetables. The feeding of corn and pulses to weaning infants is described in the Old Testament.

There is limited mention of infant feeding in the writings of the philosophers of ancient Greece. These make it clear that infants were breast-fed, usually from the first day after birth, but there is no indication if this initial feeding was done by the mother or another woman. (In this connection, Aristotle noted that the early milk is salty.) Wet nurses were used by the wealthy, but there was regional and temporal variation in whether they resided with the family and whether they were slaves. We have little evidence to indicate when children nursed by their own mothers were weaned or how, although it is probable that animal milks, cereals, and honey were employed in the task. Pottery feeding vessels of various designs have been found that were probably used during and after weaning to feed animal milks to children.

Roman physicians from the first and second centuries A.D. were the first to focus significant attention on the health of infants. The most influential of these, Soranus of Ephesus, wrote on gynecology in the second century, and his works were translated and circulated throughout Europe during medieval times (Atkinson 1991). The writings of Soranus and his contemporaries indicate some controversy over whether new arrivals should be given the mother's breast immediately, or whether a wet nurse should substitute until the mother's mature milk came in. There was also disagreement about whether or not newborns should be given purgatives to help remove the meconium.

Physicians discussed the personal qualities of wet nurses in their writings because there was widespread belief that those qualities could be transmitted via the nurses' milk. Thus, Spartan nurses were highly valued for their ability to transmit stamina and good physical and mental health (Fildes 1986). Despite the recommendation of physicians that other foods be withheld until teeth were cut, their writings indicate that women were feeding cereals to infants as young as 40 days. Writers disagreed over giving wine to infants, as well as over the value of prechewed foods. Although the literary sources do not mention their use, feeding vessels are common artifacts from Roman times. Ages recommended for weaning ranged from 2 to 3 years (deMause 1974).

Ancient Ayurvedic medical texts from the second millennium B.C. through the seventh century A.D. contain clear and consistent discussions of pediatrics and infant feeding in India. Practices in the first few days of life were ritualized and quite similar to those still employed in India and among those of Indian heritage elsewhere. These included the feeding of ghee (clarified butter) and honey mixed with other substances in a specific order and at regular intervals over three days. On the fourth day, milk was expressed from the mother's breasts, and then the infant was put to nurse. As in other civilizations, a wet nurse was employed if the mother was unable to nurse, and there is mention in the texts of the use of cow's and goat's milk if breast milk was insufficient. However, no feeding vessels are mentioned in the literature or have been found as artifacts from ancient India, so the extent (and method) of artificial feeding is unknown.

The concept of balance is found throughout the Ayurvedic writings on infant feeding. A wet nurse, for example, was to be neither fat nor thin, neither fickle nor greedy (Fildes 1986). The quality of milk could be disturbed by extreme emotions and could be brought back into balance with a specific diet. The first non-milk baby food in India was rice. The timing of this feeding varied, but in many cases coincided with the eruption of teeth. Weaning from the breast occurred in the third year.

Although the texts from ancient civilizations do not link feeding practices to infant health, some of those mentioned, such as giving infants cereals or animal milks within the early weeks of life, must have led to illnesses. Contamination of these foods probably occurred with some frequency, as climates were hot and sanitary practices for food storage were not well developed. Preference for spring weaning in some places, for example, was probably based on seasonal patterns of disease and the known association of weaning and disease.

Careful study of populations undergoing the change from foraging to food production elsewhere indicate that an epidemiological transition also took place. The skeletal sequence from the Dickson Mounds, Illinois (A.D. 950 to 1300), for example, shows evidence of lower life expectancy at birth with the shift to food production (Goodman et al. 1984). Skeletons and dentition of adults bear evidence of infectious disease episodes and some deficiency diseases (Cassidy 1980). These same nutrition-related health difficulties probably characterized many populations of settled horticulturalists, with greater problems present among those who were most crowded and whose resources were seasonally strained.

From the Renaissance to the Eve of Industrialization

Most data bearing on infant and child nutrition during the centuries spanning the Renaissance and the beginning of industrialization are from Europe and its colonies. During this period, Europe was characterized by changing medical knowledge, social divisions, and cultural patterns. At the same time, great portions of the rest of the world were changed by the diffusion of European customs, much of this occurring within the context of slavery and colonial domination. In Europe and in the colonies, most infants of the sixteenth century were breast-fed by their mothers, and when mothers could not or did not nurse, wet nurses were employed. There were class differences in feeding practices throughout the period, with change coming sometimes from the upper and sometimes from the lower classes. There were regional differences as well, which make generalizations difficult and trends hard to describe in a simple fashion.

Neonatal feeding focused on the use of purgatives to help remove the fetal meconium from the intestines. It was believed that the consumption of milk before purging the meconium could lead to a dangerous coagulation in the bowels. The use of substances for purges such as almond oil, butter, and honey was continued from ancient times, and wine, pharmaceutical purges (such as castor oil), and others, like salt water or soap, became popular in the late seventeenth century. These were administered at regular intervals over the first few days of life, a period during which women were advised not to breast-feed their infants.

In fact, the period of withholding breast milk could range from a few days up to a month. This was in part because a mother was believed to need time to recover from the delivery and, also, to become "clean" after the vaginal discharge had stopped. But in addition, the infant was thought to be at risk of harm from the mother's impure colostrum and, as already mentioned, from the coagulation of colostrum and

meconium (Fildes 1986). The effect of this delay in breast feeding was to deprive the infant of the immune properties of the colostrum and to cause dehydration and weight loss. In addition, it disrupted the supply and demand nature of lactation, so that mothers might lack sufficient milk to feed their babies properly.

But such ideas began to change in the mid–seventeenth century following the publication of a number of medical and midwifery texts that advocated the feeding of colostrum, although it doubtless took some time for such new notions to be put into practice. A major impetus for such change came from English lying-in hospitals, where, by 1750, purgative use was discouraged and breast feeding of infants within 24 hours was advocated to reduce the incidence of breast abscesses and infections, both of which were major causes of maternal mortality. However, an important by-product of this practice was a marked decline in infant mortality as well (Fildes 1980).

These lying-in hospitals were used by poor women for delivery and were the site of medical training for both physicians and midwives who became advocates of early breast feeding. At the same time, upperclass women were beginning to read and to be influenced by treatises on infant care that incorporated the new medical ideas about early feeding. These changes in neonatal feeding were probably more responsible for the decline in infant mortality observed in England from the late preindustrial to the industrial period than any other factor (Fildes 1980).

During the preindustrial era, maternal breast feeding was practiced by most mothers after the neonatal period. They nursed infants with no supplemental foods for at least one year and usually continued breast feeding well into the second year of life until the infant was capable of consuming the family diet. Weaning from the breast was sometimes gradual and sometimes abrupt, with bitter substances smeared on the breast to deter the child; or the child was sent to stay with friends until weaning was accomplished (Treckel 1989).

The actual timing of weaning was dictated by the seasons and by the dental development of the child. The fall and spring were believed to be the best seasons for severance from the breast, and weaning in the summer and winter months was discouraged. This was because of presumed dangers of summer infections and the perils of winter cold. Children were also believed to be at risk of illness and death until most of their teeth had erupted, and so weaning was postponed until this had occurred. Nipple shields were sometimes used to reduce discomfort for mothers.

Until the late seventeenth century, upper-class women were more likely to employ wet nurses than to breast-feed children themselves. Although this practice was rationalized by women as avoiding a delay in feeding the infant because of the avoidance of colostrum, it was probably mostly the result of ideas about sexuality and gender roles held by upper-class women. Because sexual intercourse was believed to hasten the resumption of menstruation and to impair both the quality and quantity of breast milk, sexual abstinence until weaning was encouraged by medical authorities. The employment of a wet nurse avoided this issue, and husbands were normally responsible for the decision to seek a wet nurse. In so deciding, husbands were able to assert patriarchal authority and establish "ownership" of the child. In other words, having a wet nurse rather than the mother feed the child (especially when the child was sent away to be nursed) focused attention on the woman as wife and diminished her identity as mother (Klapisch-Zuber 1985).

If wet nursing solved some problems, however, it brought with it others. Because breast milk was believed to transmit the characteristics of the woman who produced it, care had to be taken in choosing and supervising a wet nurse. The possibilities for the transmission of influences ranged from temperament to physical attributes such as hair color and complexion. It was best if a boy's wet nurse had herself borne a boy, and a girl's borne a girl, so that appropriate gender demeanor would be transmitted.

Earlier in this period, there was general acceptance throughout Europe of women who employed wet nurses, although many physicians and moralists condemned the practice. But after the Reformation, there was considerably more sentiment against wet nursing. Indeed, mothers who did not breast-feed were portrayed as evil and self-indulgent in both popular tracts and in sermons (Lindemann 1981), and there was concern that the practices of upper-class women might spread to the lower classes. In the American colonies, wet nursing was deplored because of the Puritan ethic, which encouraged women to devote themselves to motherhood and not indulge their sensual urges. Women who placed their infants with wet nurses were criticized for being vain and sinful (Treckel 1989).

Such sentiments apparently also resulted in a reduced use of wet nurses among members of the stricter Protestant sects in England and in some countries on the Continent (Lindemann 1981; Fildes 1986). However, in other places, most notably France, wet nursing continued at all levels of society. Elsewhere, by the late eighteenth century, upper-class women had begun to nurse their own infants. But in France, the use of wet nurses began to spread from the upper to the lower social strata, resulting in an increasing reliance on rural wet nurses by the lower and working classes of growing urban populations (Sussman 1982; Fildes 1988). Infants were sometimes sent a considerable distance into the countryside to live with a wet nurse, not returning until the prescribed age of weaning, which could be several years of age. This brought with it considerable infant mortality, as there was little supervision of wet nurses to ensure that infants were fed and cared for.

It is the case, however, that perhaps because of its prevalence wet nursing was more regulated in France than elsewhere. Starting in the seventeenth century, a number of *recommandaresses* were authorized in Paris by local judiciaries to require registration of those wet nurses who took infants home with them to rural parishes. These *recommandaresses* were later consolidated and regulations added to protect the lives of the children in question. For example, nurses were forbidden to take on more than two infants at a time, and still later, additional regulations set the prices for wet nursing. In 1769, the *recommandaresses* were abolished and replaced with a single authority that was designed to enhance communication between parents and nurses and to enforce the payment of the wages to the nurse. Although the intentions of these regulations may have been good, the wet-nursing business was, in fact, highly entrepreneurial, with individuals contracting to bring infants to nurses in the countryside, competing against one another to do so, and more concerned with profits than with the welfare of parents, nurses, or infants. Infant mortality rates were extremely high.

One of the reasons wet nursing flourished in France was the doctrine of the Catholic Church, which solved the problem of the taboo on sexual intercourse during breast feeding by recommending that infants be placed with a wet nurse so that husbands could enjoy the conjugal relations they felt were owed to them. Other factors also contributed to the extensiveness of wet nursing. As we just noted, by the eighteenth century, large numbers of urban Frenchwomen had entered the workforce, and their work as artisans, shopkeepers, and domestics for upper-class families provided little opportunity to care for a baby. The crowded nature of living and working conditions in cities also made nursing a baby difficult, and a lack of safe breast milk substitutes left wet nursing as the only alternative.

The decline in wet nursing in France and elsewhere has been attributed to a number of factors. The foremost cultural theory – that of the "discovery of childhood" – has been the subject of considerable debate (Bellingham 1988). Philippe Aries (1962) has argued that in the past, child mortality was so high that adults invested little money or interest in children, who were frequently neglected or abused; wet nursing was, according to Aries, one form of such neglect. However, Edward Shorter (1976) has viewed the maternal investment in children less than 2 years of age as a product of modernization. As Enlightenment philosophers and physicians began to attack wet nursing and other child-care practices, upper-class mothers began to devote themselves to feeding, rearing, and caring for their own children. Such concerns for the welfare of the child gradually trickled down to the lower classes.

Infant Feeding in the Industrial Era

The Industrial Revolution of the nineteenth century brought dramatic changes in lifestyle that had drastic effects on infant-feeding practices. People flowed from traditional towns and villages to large urban communities, and with the concentration of the population in cities came overcrowding, contaminated water and milk supplies, and infectious diseases spawned by poor sanitation and crowded living conditions. Women entered the labor force in large numbers and, for both men and women, work was no longer based at home.

Enhanced access to education increased the literacy level of the population, and magazines, newspapers, and books became widely available. Included among these were infant-care manuals and numerous advertisements for infant foods, all of which heightened public demand for new products and services that would benefit their children (Fildes 1991). Moreover, improvements in the recording of vital statistics in the second half of the nineteenth century increased awareness of high infant-mortality rates, and – as inadequate nutrition was seen as a cause of disease and death – this also stimulated interest in infant feeding.

Research-oriented physicians and scientists developed theories of infant nutrition, and both practitioners dealing with breast-fed infants who were not thriving and mothers having problems with breast feeding sought nutritional solutions (Apple 1987). Although mothers' milk was recognized as the best food for infants, that milk had to be of optimal quality, and this, both physicians and mothers believed, was not always the case. Breast milk quality might be compromised by the mother's health, her behavior, even her disposition. Factors alleged necessary to the production of adequate milk ranged from consuming a good diet and getting sufficient rest to avoiding strong emotions and physical labor. Because these factors were thought to compromise the milk of wet nurses as well as mothers, wet nursing increasingly fell into disfavor.

Because wet nurses were used less, and women were working outside the home in large numbers, infants were fed foods other than breast milk by their caretakers (often, young girls) during the working day. Paps and porridges were made, frequently with bread and water flavored with a little milk and sugar, and kept warm all day on the stove to be fed as needed. When this food failed to soothe an infant, commercial baby tonics were given. Containing laudanum, these were probably very successful at quieting a hungry or fretful baby.

The infant-feeding practices of working-class Europe spread to other parts of the world as populations came under the economic domination of England and the other colonizing countries. Plantation systems and other labor-intensive industries needed a constant supply of workers, and returning mothers to work as soon as possible after giving birth was in the interest of the dominating powers. In the English-speaking Caribbean, for example, the African practice of prolonged breast feeding was discouraged among slaves. After returning to work, mothers left their infants in creches where they were fed paps and panadas by elderly caretakers in between nursing breaks (King and Ashworth 1987). These early supplemental foods were very similar to those fed in England at the time (Fildes 1986).

Such economic and social changes in the last half of the nineteenth century, as well as research into the chemical composition of milk in Europe and the United States, paved the way for the use of artificial milks or formula milks. Certainly, women were ready to adopt such milks. Most middle-class households could not afford a servant to breast-feed infants while the mother was engaged in activities outside the home, and working-class women had to wean their infants at a very young age to enter the labor force.

The earliest scientists to make a substantial impact on feeding practices through the development of formulas were Philip Biedert in Germany and Arthur Meigs in Philadelphia (Wood 1955). Biedert was the first to suggest modification of cow's milk, noting its high protein content and hard-curd consistency relative to human milk. He recommended the addition of cream, whey, and sugar to make cow's milk more digestible for human infants. Meigs published nutrient analyses of human and cow's milk in 1884, which showed the higher carbohydrate and lower protein and fat content of human milk. He was able to demonstrate that the protein of human milk formed a softer curd than cow's milk and thought that the addition of lime water was important to make cow's milk more alkaline. In combining the work of Biedert with his own, Meigs was able to produce what was to be one of the most popular formulas for the transformation of cow's milk into an approximation of human milk.

The problem of infant diarrhea provided the research impetus for therapeutic artificial milks, and two schools of thought developed. In the United States, that thought was complex, as Thomas Morgan Rotch (a professor of pediatrics at Harvard University) and his followers developed the "percentage method," based on Meigs's recommendations. Rotch advocated individualized infant-formula prescriptions that required considerable mathematical calculation and a hospital laboratory to produce.

In Europe at the same time a "caloric method" was developed by Heinrich Finkelstein, who hypothesized that infant diarrhea resulted from the fermentation of carbohydrates in the intestine. This theory led to the invention of "Eiweissmilch," a low-carbohydrate, high-protein milk produced by a process of sieving curdled casein back into artificially soured milk. In contrast to Finkelstein, Adalbert Czerny concluded that infant diarrhea resulted from an intolerance of milk fat. Almost simultaneously, he developed a mixture of butter and flour that was added to milk.

By 1910, the percentage method had fallen into disfavor, and pediatricians were noting a disturbing number of occurrences of deficiency diseases, such as scurvy, among infants fed the artificial milks. These infants also suffered high rates of mortality (Levenstein 1983). Reformers advocated a series of different measures, ranging from educating the poor to breastfeed to regulating the milk supply so as to guarantee its cleanliness. But while physician-scientists were developing formulas that could be prescribed to mothers for home preparation, chemists were devising other alternatives to breast milk, and the success of these products indicated the existence of a previously unrecognized market. The subsequent commercial marketing of formulas, in contrast to their prescription by physicians, once again gave control of infant-feeding decisions to mothers, as in the past when they had decided between breast-feeding or employing wet nurses. By the end of the nineteenth century, mothers could choose from viable alternatives to breast feeding, and in the twentieth, their preferences made artificial feeding a cultural norm.

Such changes in infant feeding were part of the transformation of medicine into a scientific profession, and at the turn of the century, science was highly valued and viewed as the key to resolving numerous important problems (Rosenberg 1976). As physicians obtained more and more scientific knowledge, they became increasingly regarded as experts with privileged information (Apple 1987).

The "Scientific" Era

Infant feeding in the 1930s and 1940s differed somewhat from earlier practices; there was a general acceptance of simpler infant formulas, and researchers themselves were involved in the commercialization of formulas. Thereafter, as the dangers and difficulties of artificial feeding lessened, the flurry of research on infant nutrition declined as well (Apple 1987). By the middle of the twentieth century, most babies in the United States were bottle-fed with artificial milks, as were a high percentage of babies in the industrialized countries of Europe and in those under European influence. The belief was that artificial feeding, with its scientific basis and medical direction, was equal or superior to breast feeding.

No wonder then that survey data from the United States, Europe, and European-influenced countries showed a consistent decline in breast feeding during the twentieth century. The number of breast-fed infants born in the United States dropped from 77 percent between 1936 and 1940 to 25 percent by 1970. Duration of breast feeding also declined from a 1930s average of 4.2 months to 2.2 months in the late 1950s (Meyer 1958, 1968; Hirschman and Hendershot 1979; Hendershot 1980, 1981).

There were striking demographic patterns of

Table VI.7.1. *Percentage of first-born infants ever breast-fed between 1951 and 1970 in the United States, by ethnic group and education*

Category	1951–5	1956–60	1961–5	1966–70
Ethnic group				
White	49	43	39	29
Black	59	42	24	14
Hispanic	58	55	39	35
Education				
< 9 yrs	62	53	40	32
9–11 yrs	50	40	29	17
12 yrs	45	40	32	23
13–15 yrs	57	48	50	35
>15 yrs	46	50	69	57

Source: From Hirschman and Hendershot (1979).

breast feeding during this period (Table VI.7.1). Although breast feeding was more common among blacks than whites earlier in the twentieth century, its subsequent decline was greater among blacks so that only 14 percent breast-fed by 1970, compared with 29 percent of whites and 35 percent of Hispanics. The relationship of education to breast feeding changed as well. In the early 1950s, the practice was most common among women with lower educational levels; better-educated mothers were less likely to breast-feed. But this trend was reversed by the 1970s – a phenomenon interpreted as a "trickling down" of values and behaviors from upper- to lower-class women (Salber, Stitt, and Babbott 1958; Meyer 1968). The incidence of breast feeding in the United States reached a low of 22 percent in 1972 – a downward trend paralleled in England (Newson and Newson 1963) and elsewhere.

Although recommendations from professional medical groups stressed breast feeding throughout this period, a variety of factors worked against it. One was the continued high value placed on science and technology and their applications to medicine (Apple 1987), as physicians and nurses learned more and more about artificial feeding and less and less about breast feeding. Moreover, birth became more of a medical event, and mothers who delivered in hospitals frequently stayed as long as two weeks. During that time, infants were often artificially fed because they were separated from their mothers and only brought to them to be nursed at fixed intervals. Mothers were instructed to wear face masks while breastfeeding, their nipples were washed before feeding, and they were not allowed to hold their babies afterward. All these practices virtually guaranteed that mothers' milk supplies would be inadequate and that their babies would require formula to supplement or replace breast milk.

That such hospital practices contributed to breastfeeding problems was recognized by some physicians (for example, Aldrich 1942). However, professional medical journals included recommendations from other practitioners who advised mothers to feed thickened cereal and other foods from an early age (Clein 1943; Stewart 1943). Others advocated feeding schedules, and some even recommended reducing the number of feedings to match family mealtimes (Clein 1943), reflecting cultural themes of regimentation and discipline applied to the infant (Millard 1990).

As already noted, by the 1970s the downward trend in breast feeding was reversed in the United States. More mothers initiated breast feeding, and they breast-fed for longer periods of time (Martinez and Nalezienski 1979; Hendershot 1981). This return to breast feeding paralleled the earlier decline, although now it was women of higher socioeconomic status who rediscovered the practice. As with the development of formula in the first half of the century, popular books and pamphlets stressed the scientific aspects of the "new" feeding method, which with breast feeding focused on greater disease resistance, prevention of allergies, and enhanced mother–infant bonding.

The return to breast feeding in Western countries in the 1970s was fueled by growing health activism and advocacy by women. As women discovered that they knew relatively little about their bodies and that they were dependent on the largely male medical community, lay efforts of women educating women grew (Boston Women's Health Book Collective 1976). La Leche League had been founded in 1956 as an organization focused on providing mothers with practical knowledge of breast feeding (La Leche League International 1963). The league filled a void. Few physicians had received any training in breast feeding, and lay breast-feeding knowledge had been lost as women turned to bottle feeding.

Breast feeding as promoted by La Leche League clashed sharply with other aspects of American culture. The League's promotion of extended breast feeding until a child weaned itself, often at 2 or 3 years of age, was at odds with cultural values of fostering independence. Infant-centered feeding patterns, with frequent nursing during the day and nighttime nursing, contrasted with the prevailing norm of scheduled feedings and use of the clock (Millard 1990). Comparing studies of League and non-League mothers shows the sharp contrast in feeding styles. Whereas League mothers nursed an average of 15 times per day (Cable and Rothenberger 1984), non-League mothers averaged only 7 (Quandt 1986).

The upward trend in breast feeding reached a peak in 1982 with 61 percent of newborns breast-fed and two-thirds of those still breast-feeding at 3 months of age (Martinez and Krieger 1985). But as the decade wore on, interest in breast feeding once again eroded, and by its end only 52 percent of newborns and 18 percent of 6-month-olds were breast-fed. The decline in initiation and duration was greatest among nonwhite mothers, younger mothers, and those with less

education (Ryan et al. 1991). A similar decline in breast feeding was recorded in Great Britain for the same period (Emery, Scholey, and Taylor 1990).

There are several possible explanations. Alan S. Ryan and colleagues (1991) suggest that there was a decline in attention given breast feeding in the public press at the same time that manufacturers of formula began to aggressively market their products through television and direct mailings to new parents. Economic pressures may also have contributed, because mothers in the labor force breast-fed less (Ryan and Martinez 1989). Indeed, even those not working outside the home expressed the need to be unencumbered by breast feeding if the need or opportunity to work arose (Wright, Clark, and Bauer 1993).

In addition to this cultural explanation of a decline in breast feeding, other scientists combined biological and behavioral perspectives into explanatory models that drew on rapid advances (during the 1980s) in knowledge of the hormonal control of milk production and milk volume (Stuart-Macadam and Dettwyler 1995). They pointed to the need for frequent stimulation of the nipple to maintain milk production (Quandt 1984b) and for baby-led feeding schedules to allow infants to regulate their own hunger and satiety levels through fat intake (Woolridge 1995). Sara A. Quandt (1984b) demonstrated that the introduction of beikost (nonmilk foods) to the diet of infants in the first 3 months of life resulted in declines in the number of breast feeds per day and, ultimately, in the duration of breast feeding. Thus, shorter durations of nursing at the population level appear to have a biobehavioral basis and are not simply the result of marketing of formula or women working outside the home.

Twentieth-Century Infant Feeding in the Developing World

In the second half of the twentieth century, considerable concern arose over changes in infant-feeding patterns occurring in developing countries. This was especially the case with changes thought to be the result of the marketing malpractice of multinational corporations (Chetley 1986). Scores of reports documented the promotion and sale of infant formula in developing countries, often to mothers who could not afford formula and who lived in circumstances where it could not be hygienically prepared. As a result, it was charged, low-income families were spending a large proportion of their incomes on products that were actually dangerous to the health of infants and also, because of the availability of breast milk, unnecessary. Indeed, dependence on formula meant erosion of breast-feeding knowledge and practices and increased poverty and infant mortality. Horror stories of "bottle babies" fed contaminated and overdiluted formula drew international attention, and pictures of infant graves marked by nursing bottles aroused anger toward the companies promoting the products.

After the publication, in 1974, of *The Baby Killer* (Muller 1974) and its German translation, Nestlé filed a libel suit against the Third World Action Group responsible for the translation. Although the group was found guilty of misrepresenting the formula manufacturer, it was assessed only a nominal fine, whereas the conduct of the formula manufacturer drew considerable public outcry. A number of public action groups joined to form the Infant Formula Action Coalition (INFACT), and in 1977, INFACT began to promote a consumer boycott of all Nestlé products. The boycott was extremely successful, with participation by large numbers of citizens as well as governmental agencies in the United States and Canada (Van Esterik 1989). In 1981, the World Health Organization (WHO) and the United Nations International Children's Emergency Fund (UNICEF) adopted a code of marketing with which Nestlé agreed to abide. INFACT called off the boycott in 1984.

Scientific research on infant-feeding patterns in developing countries, however, provides a more complex picture than that conveyed by the problems arising from the simple substitution of bottled formula for breast feeding. In some areas, new feeding modalities and products were added to existing breast-feeding practices. The contents of infant-feeding bottles were highly varied. There was inter- and intracultural variation in how breast feeding was practiced before the promotion of formula by multinational corporations. For example, mixed breast and artificial feeding had been common in the Caribbean for centuries, whereas extended breast-feeding had been the norm in Africa and Asia (King and Ashworth 1987).

Data gathered around 1980 from large, nationally representative samples for the World Fertility Survey in 17 countries make possible some tentative generalizations about the state of breast-feeding practices in the second half of the twentieth century (Popkin et al. 1983). In Asia and the Pacific Islands, the practice continued to be very common, with virtually all mothers initiating breast feeding. Over 90 percent of infants were still breast-fed at 3 months of age and between 60 and 90 percent at 12 months. Breast feeding was slightly more common and of longer duration in rural than in urban areas. Supplementation of breast feeding was often delayed until after 12 months.

In Latin America, by contrast, as many as 20 percent of infants were never breast-fed, and by 6 months of age, less than 60 percent were breast-fed. The vast majority were weaned by 12 months. Rural–urban differences were pronounced, with more and longer duration of breast feeding in rural areas.

African breast-feeding rates were intermediate between those of Asia and Latin America. Overall, these findings indicate that a general decline in breast-feeding duration, but not breast-feeding incidence, had occurred. This change is probably tied to overall patterns of modernization (for example, changes in women's participation in the labor force and changes in postpartum sex taboos) and not exclusively to the promotional effects of formula manufacturers.

International interest in infant-feeding practices in developing countries stems from a broader and long-standing concern about child survival and the effects of malnutrition on the long-term functional development of children (Mosley and Chen 1984). The link of breast feeding of short duration and abrupt weaning to kwashiorkor and extended, unsupplemented breast feeding to marasmus was established by the 1960s (Williams 1955; McLaren 1966; Cravioto et al. 1967) and attributed to a variety of adverse biological and social factors. Both human and animal studies demonstrated that the long-term consequences of these severe forms of protein–energy malnutrition included impaired mental development (Pollitt 1969; Winick 1969). More recently, a series of intervention and observational studies has shown that even marginal malnutrition results in growth stunting in early life and continued functional impairments later in life (Allen 1995). The results of such studies make it clear that achieving adequate nutrition for infants is the foundation for optimal health in whole populations.

Sara A. Quandt

Bibliography

Aldrich, C. Anderson. 1942. Progress in pediatrics: Ancient practices in a scientific age – feeding aspects. *American Journal of Diseases of Childhood* 64: 714–22.

Allen, Lindsay H. 1995. Malnutrition and human function: A comparison of conclusions from the INCAP and nutrition CRSP studies. *Journal of Nutrition* 125 (Supplement 4): 1119S–1126S.

Apple, Rima D. 1987. *Mothers and medicine: A social history of infant feeding, 1890–1950.* Madison, Wis.

Aries, Philippe. 1962. *Centuries of childhood. A social history of family life,* trans. Robert Baldick. New York.

Atkinson, Clarissa W. 1991. *The oldest vocation. Christian motherhood in the Middle Ages.* Ithaca, N.Y.

Bellingham, Bruce. 1988. The history of childhood since the "invention of childhood": Some issues in the eighties. *Journal of Family History* 13: 347–58.

Bostock, John. 1962. Evolutional approach to infant care. *Lancet* 1 (7238): 1033–5.

Boston Women's Health Book Collective. 1976. *Our bodies, ourselves.* Second edition. New York.

Cable, T. A., and L. A. Rothenberger. 1984. Breastfeeding behavioral patterns among La Leche League mothers: A descriptive survey. *Pediatrics* 73: 830–5.

Cassidy, C. M. 1980. Nutrition and health in agriculturalists and hunter-gatherers. In *Nutritional anthropology: Contemporary approaches to diet and culture,* ed. Norge W. Jerome, Randy F. Kandel, and Gretel H. Pelto, 117–45. Pleasantville, N.Y.

Chetley, A. 1986. *The politics of baby food.* London.

Clein, Norman W. 1943. Streamlined infant feeding: A feeding routine utilizing earlier addition of solid foods and fewer feedings. *Journal of Pediatrics* 23: 224-8.

Cravioto, J., H. G. Birch, E. R. DeLicardie, and L. Rosales. 1967. The ecology of infant weight gain in a preindustrial society. *Acta Paediatrica Scandinavica* 56: 71-84.

deMause, Lloyd. 1974. The evolution of childhood. In *The history of childhood,* ed. Lloyd deMause, 1-73. New York.

Emery, J. L., S. Scholey, and E. M. Taylor. 1990. Decline in breast feeding. *Archives of Diseases of Childhood* 65: 369-72.

Fildes, Valerie. 1980. Neonatal feeding practices and infant mortality during the 18th century. *Journal of Biosocial Science* 12: 313-24.

　1986. *Breasts, bottles and babies. A history of infant feeding.* Edinburgh.

　1988. *Wet nursing from antiquity to the present.* New York.

　1991. Breast-feeding practices during industrialisation, 1800-1919. In *Infant and child nutrition worldwide: Issues and perspectives,* ed. Frank Falkner, 1-20. Boca Raton, Fla.

Goodman, A. H., J. Lallo, G. J. Armelagos, and J. C. Rose. 1984. Health changes at Dickson Mounds, Illinois (A.D. 950-1300). In *Paleopathology at the origins of agriculture,* ed. Mark N. Cohen and George J. Armelagos, 271-306. New York.

Hendershot, G. E. 1980. *Trends in breast feeding.* National Center for Health Statistics, Public Health Service. U.S. Department of Health, Education, and Welfare Publication No. 80-1250. Hyattsville, Md.

　1981. *Trends and differentials in breast feeding in the United States, 1970-75.* Working Paper Series No. 5, Family Growth Survey Branch, National Center for Health Statistics, Public Health Service, U.S. Department of Health, Education, and Welfare. Hyattsville, Md.

Hirschman, C., and G. E. Hendershot. 1979. *Trends in breast feeding among American mothers.* Vital and Health Statistics, Series 23, No. 3. DHEW Publication No. (PHS) 79-1979. National Center for Health Statistics, Public Health Service, U.S. Department of Health, Education, and Welfare. Hyattsville, Md.

Hopkins, Eric. 1994. *Childhood transformed: Working-class children in nineteenth century England.* Manchester, England.

King, Jean, and Ann Ashworth. 1987. Historical review of the changing pattern of infant feeding in developing countries: The case of Malaysia, the Caribbean, Nigeria, and Zaire. *Social Science and Medicine* 25: 1307-20.

Klapisch-Zuber, Christiane. 1985. *Women, family and ritual in Renaissance Italy.* Chicago.

Konner, Melvin, and Carol Worthman. 1980. Nursing frequency, gonadal function, and birth-spacing among !Kung hunter-gatherers. *Science* 207: 788-91.

La Leche League International. 1963. *The womanly art of breastfeeding.* Franklin Park, Ill.

Lee, Richard B. 1979. *!Kung San: Men, women, and work in a foraging society.* New York.

Levenstein, Harvey. 1983. "Best for babies" or "preventable infanticide"? The controversy over artificial feeding of infants in America, 1880-1920. *Journal of American History* 70: 75-94.

Lindemann, M. 1981. "Love for hire": The regulation of wet nursing business in 18th century Hamburg. *Journal of Family History* 6: 379-95.

Martinez, Gilbert A., and Fritz W. Krieger. 1985. Milk-feeding patterns in the United States. *Pediatrics* 76: 1004-8.

Martinez, Gilbert A., and John P. Nalezienski. 1979. The recent trend in breast-feeding. *Pediatrics* 64: 686-92.

McLaren, S. D. 1966. A fresh look at protein-calorie malnutrition. *Lancet* 2: 485-8.

Meyer, Herman F. 1958. Breast feeding in the United States: Extent and possible trends. *Pediatrics* 22: 116-21.

　1968. Breast feeding in the United States; report of a 1966 national survey with comparable 1946 and 1956 data. *Clinical Pediatrics* 7: 708-15.

Millard, Ann V. 1990. The place of the clock in pediatric advice: Rationales, cultural themes, and impediments to breastfeeding. *Social Science and Medicine* 31: 211-21.

Mosley, W. Henry, and Lincoln C. Chen, eds. 1984. *Child survival - strategies for research.* Cambridge and New York.

Muller, M. 1974. *The baby killer.* London.

Newson, John, and Elizabeth Newson. 1963. *Infant care in an urban community.* New York.

Pollitt, Ernesto. 1969. Ecology, malnutrition, and mental development. *Psychosomatic Medicine* 31: 193-200.

Popkin, Barry M., Richard E. Bilsborrow, John S. Akin, and Monica E. Yamamoto. 1983. Breast-feeding determinants in low-income countries. *Medical Anthropology* 7: 1-31.

Quandt, Sara A. 1984a. Nutritional thriftiness and human reproduction: Beyond the critical body composition hypothesis. *Social Science and Medicine* 19: 177-82.

　1984b. The effect of beikost on the diet of breast-fed infants. *Journal of the American Dietetic Association* 84: 47-51.

　1986. Patterns of variation in breast feeding behaviors. *Social Science and Medicine* 23: 445-53.

Robins, Gay. 1993. *Women in ancient Egypt.* Cambridge, Mass.

Rosenberg, C. E. 1976. *No other gods: On science and American social thought.* Baltimore, Md.

Rotch, Thomas Morgan. 1907. An historical sketch of the development of percentage feeding. *New York Medical Journal* 85: 532-7.

Ryan, Alan S., and Gilbert A. Martinez. 1989. Breast-feeding and the working mother: A profile. *Pediatrics* 83: 524-31.

Ryan, Alan S., David Rush, Fritz W. Krieger, and Gregory E. Lewandowski. 1991. Recent declines in breast-feeding in the United States, 1984 through 1989. *Pediatrics* 88: 719-27.

Salber, E. J., P. G. Stitt, and J. C. Babbott. 1958. Patterns of breast feeding: Factors affecting the frequency of breast feeding. *New England Journal of Medicine* 259: 707-13.

Shorter, Edward. 1976. *The making of the modern family.* New York.

Stewart, Chester A. 1943. The use of cereal-thickened formulas to promote maternal nursing. *Journal of Pediatrics* 23: 310-14.

Stuart-Macadam, Patricia, and Katherine A. Dettwyler, eds. 1995. *Breastfeeding: Biocultural perspectives.* Chicago.

Sussman, George D. 1982. *Selling mothers' milk. The wet-nursing business in France 1715-1914.* Urbana, Ill.

Treckel, Paula A. 1989. Breastfeeding and maternal sexuality in colonial America. *Journal of Interdisciplinary History* 20: 25-51.

Van Esterik, Penny. 1989. *Beyond the breast-bottle controversy.* New Brunswick, N.J.

Williams, Cicely D. 1955. Factors in the ecology of malnutrition. In *Proceedings of the Western Hemisphere Nutrition Congress.* American Medical Association. Chicago.

Winick, Myron M. 1969. Malnutrition and brain development. *Journal of Pediatrics* 74: 667-79.

Wood, Alice L. 1955. The history of artificial feeding of infants. *Journal of the American Dietetic Association* 31: 474-82.

Woolridge, Michael W. 1995. Baby-controlled breastfeeding: Biocultural implications. In *Breastfeeding: Biocultural perspectives,* ed. Patricia Stuart-Macadam and Katherine A. Dettwyler, 217-42. Chicago.

Wright, Anne L., Clarina Clark, and Mark Bauer. 1993. Maternal employment and infant feeding practices among the Navaho. *Medical Anthropology Quarterly* 7: 260-80.

VI.8 ❧ Adolescent Nutrition and Fertility

The relationship between nutrition and adolescent fertility has been a topic of much discussion in recent research on human biology. The apparent increase in the incidence of teenage pregnancy in Western societies has led some researchers to wonder whether there are biological as well as cultural factors that influence this phenomenon (Vinovskis 1988). Studies of adolescents in different geographic and socioeconomic settings have demonstrated that the age at which sexual maturity is reached is not fixed but is heavily shaped by numerous influences, such as fatness at adolescence, physique, health status, genetics, degree of physical activity, and socioeconomic status (Maresh 1972; Johnson 1974; Short 1976; Zacharias, Rand, and Wurtman 1976; Frisch 1978; Meyer et al. 1990; Moisan, Meyer, and Gingras 1990; Wellens et al. 1990).

Since the reproductive process requires energy, reproductive ability is curtailed in times of food scarcity or when calories burned through physical exertion or exercise exceed the amount provided by food intake. Undernourished women, for example, reach menarche later and experience menopause earlier than do well-nourished ones. Poorly nourished women also have higher frequencies of irregular menstruation and anovulatory menstrual cycles, with menstruation and ovulation disappearing entirely if malnutrition is severe. During pregnancy, malnourished women have a greater likelihood of miscarriage, and if they do carry the infant to term, they experience a longer period of lactational amenorrhea. In men, severe malnutrition leads to loss of libido, a decrease in prostate fluid and in sperm count and mobility, and, eventually, the loss of sperm production altogether. For children and adolescents, undernutrition delays the onset of puberty in both boys and girls, and

limits the fecundity of those who have achieved sexual maturity (Frisch 1978).

Researchers disagree, however, on the precise way to measure adequate nutritional status. Some, most notably Rose Frisch (1978), argue that achievement of a critical weight is the major factor in achievement of sexual maturity. Others argue that body composition, particularly the percentage of body fat, is the most important determinant of sexual maturity (Crawford 1975).

Much more is known about the effects of nutrition on adolescent fertility in girls than in boys (Boyd 1980). Fertility in girls is usually based on age at menarche, although even this event is not a foolproof measure because adolescent girls experience a number of anovulatory cycles before establishing regular menstruation (Short 1976). Nevertheless, researchers have clearly established that poorly nourished girls, female athletes, and girls with anorexia nervosa and other eating disorders reach menarche at later ages, have higher incidences of amenorrhea, and have a greater frequency of anovulatory cycles than do girls who have adequate dietary intake relative to calories expended (Frisch 1978; Wyshak and Frisch 1982).

Fertility in boys, however, is much harder to determine. The main indicator of male fertility is spermatogenesis, determined by measuring the amount of sperm contained in the seminal fluid. But data on the beginning of spermatogenesis is more difficult to obtain because there is no clearly visible sign, as is the case in menarche. Moreover, it is not clear whether the appearance of spermatozoa in the urine is a reliable measure of fertility in adolescent boys (Baldwin 1928; Short 1976). Some researchers have attempted to use age of first ejaculation (Kinsey 1948) as an indicator of male fertility, but this, too, is unreliable (Brown 1966; Short 1976). Consequently, less is known about the factors that influence adolescent male fertility.

The Secular Trend in Sexual Maturity

One of the more controversial issues in the history of adolescent sexuality is whether the age of sexual maturity has declined over time. Nearly all of the discussion in this area centers around the apparent declining age of menarche, particularly among young women in Europe and the United States. G. von Backman (1948) and J. M. Tanner (1962) were among the first to suggest that the age of menarche has declined precipitously over the past several hundred years, from a high of 17 or 18 in early modern times to an average age of 12 in contemporary Western societies.

Most historians and researchers in human biology have accepted this model of a secular trend in age at menarche (Zacharias et al. 1976; Frisch 1978; Shorter 1981). Some scholars, however, have questioned the methodology employed in determining the age of menarche in the past. It has been argued that the evidence for Tanner's secular trend is based on extremely small samples of young women, and some have questioned whether these findings can be applied to larger populations (Brown 1966; Bullough 1981). In addition, others have pointed out that the way in which age at menarche is usually determined is flawed, for it relies on the recollected memory of women who were interviewed much later in life. It has been suggested that during the nineteenth century, an early age of menarche was often associated with sexual promiscuity and/or working-class status. Therefore, some women may have stated a higher age of menarche than they actually experienced, in order to maintain an image of middle-class respectability (Brown 1966; Bojlén and Bentzon 1968; Diers 1974; Bullough 1981). Even Tanner admitted that "the early studies of age of menarche suffered from disadvantages of both sampling and technique" (Tanner 1968, 1973, 1981b).

Another troubling aspect of historical research on the secular trend is the fact that age of menarche appears to be younger in both ancient and medieval times than in the nineteenth century. Reviews of Greek and Roman textbooks, for example, indicate that the average age of menarche in the ancient world was about 13.5 years (Amundsen and Diers 1969; Diers 1974), and evidence from medieval textbooks indicates that the age of menarche varied from 13 to 15 years (Post 1971; Amundsen and Diers 1973; Diers 1974). Researchers are cautious about this evidence, however, because it comes from medical textbooks, rather than from direct observations of young women (Diers 1974).

Some historians have even suggested that there might be ideological reasons for placing so much faith in a secular trend in age at menarche. Both Vern L. Bullough (1981) and Maris A. Vinovskis (1988), for example, have argued that the secular trend is often linked with the increasing problem of teenage pregnancy in contemporary American society and is used to justify very stringent policies regarding teenage sexuality.

Despite these criticisms, however, most researchers do agree that there has been some decrease in the age of menarche over time. Even Bullough states: "Undoubtedly there has been some drop in menarcheal age in the United States since the 19th century, to under 13 in the 1980s" (Bullough 1981: 366). The consensus in recent research on the secular trend is that there has been a statistically significant decline in age at menarche, but the drop has been much less precipitous than that suggested by Tanner and Backman (Frisch 1978; Wyshak and Frisch 1982; Golub 1983).

The History and Geography of Studies on Adolescents

Scientific interest in the fertility and growth of young men and women dates back to at least ancient Greece. Aristotle was among the first to observe the negative effect of excessive training and undernutrition on young boys. He also warned of the dangers of precocious sexuality, claiming that "the physique of men is also supposed to be stunted when intercourse is begun before the seed has finished its growth" (quoted in Tanner 1981a: 8).

During Roman imperial times, Soranus noted that vigorous exercise could inhibit menstruation, but he stated that this was normal and did not require intervention. Like Aristotle, Soranus noted that precocious "excretion of seed is harmful in females as well as males," and that "men who remain chaste are stronger and bigger than others" (quoted in Tanner 1981a: 10). As a result of these warnings about precocious sexuality, Roman law linked the age of marriage with the age of puberty, which was believed to be 14 for boys and 12 for girls (Amundsen and Diers 1969; Tanner 1981a).

In the Middle Ages, the Renaissance, and the early modern period, medical texts tended to echo the writings of ancient authors on the subject of adolescent growth and development. Among them, as among the ancient authors, there seems to have been at least some understanding that the onset of puberty, and particularly the onset of menarche, was linked with nutritional status. G. Marinello, for example, observed in the sixteenth century that some girls menstruated earlier than others. He stated that "the cause of variation is [differences in] the natural composition of the body, or complexion or habits; thin and long girls [menstruate] later[,] fat and strong ones earlier" (Marinello 1574, quoted in Tanner 1981a: 21). Similarly, Hippolytus Guarionius (1571–1654), a contemporary of Francis Bacon, noted that peasant girls in seventeenth-century Germany menstruated later than the daughters of townsfolk or aristocracy. Guarionius noted that "the cause seems to be that the inhabitants of the town consume more fat (moist) foods and drink and so their bodies become soft, weak, and fat and come early to menstruation, in the same way as a tree which one waters too early produces earlier but less well-formed fruit than another" (quoted in Tanner 1981a: 29).

During the eighteenth and nineteenth centuries, ideas about adolescent growth and development shifted as a result of contemporary debates about the place of so-called inferior races in the natural order. The egalitarian rhetoric of the Enlightenment called into question earlier ideas of racial inferiority, implying that the "natural rights of man" applied to men and women of all races, classes, and ethnic origins. But many scientists at this time endorsed racist ideas about human difference and looked for physical traits that would demonstrate that working-class Europeans, Africans, Asians, and Native Americans were inferior to white, middle-class Europeans (Stepan 1982; Schiebinger 1993). One of the physical signs that was used to "prove" the inferiority of nonwhite and working-class individuals was early age of menstruation and physical maturity, because such traits seemed to place these groups closer to animals.

Scientists attributed the allegedly early age of puberty in nonwhite and lower-class individuals to two causes: precocious sexual activity and warm climate. Both of these factors, it was argued, caused a buildup of heat in the body. Because many believed that heat was the engine of growth, anything that caused an accumulation of heat would lead to an early age of puberty. Albrecht von Haller (1775), for example, claimed that girls in the southerly regions of Asia, where the climate was warm, were marriageable in their eighth year and gave birth in their ninth or tenth year; conversely, women in Arctic regions did not menstruate until age 23 or 24. This view was shared by other eighteenth-century writers, most notably J. F. Freind (1738), Herman Boerhaave (1744), and Montesquieu (1751). Similarly, Martin Schurig (1729), a Dresden physician, noted that bodily maturation in girls could be accelerated by indulging in conversations with men, kissing, and other sorts of sexual encounters. Schurig claimed that indulgence in sexual activity was why prostitutes and lower-class women had an earlier age of menarche than did gentlewomen (Tanner 1981a).

To be sure, some authors, most notably George-Louis Leclerc de Buffon (1749–1804) and John Roberton (1832, 1845), continued to argue that nutritional status was the most important factor in determining age of puberty. During the middle-to-late nineteenth century, Charles Darwin (1868) also tried to postulate a relationship between food supply and fertility, observing that domestic animals with a regular, plentiful food supply were more fertile than corresponding wild animals. Moreover, reformers who were interested in improving the plight of the laboring classes argued strongly against the idea that lax morals caused an early age of puberty among working-class girls. On the contrary, they argued that difficult living conditions delayed puberty in the working classes (Whitehead 1847).

Climatic theories about puberty persisted well into the twentieth century. As late as the 1950s, some medical writers were still claiming that women from the tropics matured much earlier than those from temperate or cold climates (Peters and Shirkande 1957; Shaw 1959).

As a result of the views described above, middle-class parents in Europe and the United States viewed precocious puberty with a certain degree of alarm. Nineteenth-century medical-advice literature cautioned mothers to prevent all children, but especially daughters, from masturbating, reading romantic novels, and indulging in any activity that might excite the sexual passions (Neuman 1975). Many physicians also believed that too much consumption of meat contributed to precocious sexual longings and sexual development in young girls and could even cause insanity and nymphomania. Doctors, therefore, advised mothers to restrict their daughters' intake of meat in order to prevent such disasters (Brumberg 1988). In retrospect, this advice may have contributed to the perceived secular trend in the age of menarche.

During the mid–twentieth century, a number of developmental studies uncovered the methodological flaws in earlier studies of the effect of sexual activity and climate on age of puberty. Tanner (1962), for example, demonstrated that many of the studies of adolescents from tropical regions were performed on girls and boys from wealthy families who had access to abundant sources of protein-rich foods and, therefore, did not represent the average age of puberty in these societies. Moreover, researchers noted that the age of menarche in Eskimo girls was actually earlier than that of western European girls, a phenomenon that resulted from the Eskimos' meat-rich diet (Bojlén and Bentzon 1968).

The most definitive studies on the relationship between nutrition and adolescent fertility were performed during and after World War II. Studies of children who had experienced famine, illness, and other harsh conditions during the war years showed a definite link between poor nutrition and age of physical maturity (Ellis 1945; Markowitz 1955; Krali-Cercek 1956; Maresh 1972; Wellens et al. 1990; Murata and Hibi 1992). Likewise, cross-cultural studies of women in both Western and non-Western countries have demonstrated that socioeconomic status and, hence, nutrition, are much more important than climate in determining age of puberty (Kolata 1974; McBarnette 1988; Brink 1989; Riley, Huffman, and Chowdhury 1989). These discoveries have completely undermined earlier notions about the effect of climate or sexual activity on age of puberty and have established once and for all that nutritional status is the determining factor in age of sexual maturation.

Heather Munro Prescott

Bibliography

Amundsen, D. W., and C. J. Diers. 1969. The age of menarche in classical Greece and Rome. *Human Biology* 41: 125–32.

    1973. The age of menarche in medieval Europe. *Human Biology* 45: 363–9.

Aristotle. 1948. *Politics,* trans. E. Barker. Oxford.

Backman, G. von. 1948. Die beschleunigte Entwicklung der Jugend. *Acta Anatomica* 4: 421–80.

Baldwin, B. T. 1928. The determination of sex maturation in boys by a laboratory method. *Journal of Comparative Psychology* 8: 39–43.

Boerhaave, Herman. 1744. *Praelectiones academicae in proprias institutiones rei medicae,* with notes by Albrecht von Haller. 3 vols. Göttingen.

Bojlén, K., and M. W. Bentzon. 1968. The influence of climate and nutrition on age at menarche: A historical review and modern hypothesis. *Human Biology* 40: 69–85.

Boyd, Edith. 1980. *Origins of the study of human growth,*

based on unfinished work left by Richard E. Scammon, ed. Bhim Sen Savara and John Frederick Schilke. Portland, Ore.

Brink, Pamela J. 1989. The fattening room among the Annang of Nigeria. *Medical Anthropology* 12: 131–43.

Brown, P. E. 1966. The age at menarche. *British Journal of Preventive Social Medicine* 20: 9–14.

Brumberg, Joan Jacobs. 1988. *Fasting girls: The emergence of anorexia nervosa as a modern disease.* Cambridge, Mass.

1993. "Something happens to girls": Menarche and the emergence of the modern hygienic imperative. *Journal of the History of Sexuality* 4: 99–127.

Buffon, Georges-Louis Leclerc de. 1749–1804. *Histoire naturelle, générale et particulière avec la description du Cabinet du Roi.* Paris.

Bullough, Vern L. 1981. Age at menarche: A misunderstanding. *Science* 213: 365–6.

Crawford, John D. 1975. Body composition and menarche: The Frisch-Revelle hypothesis revisited. *Pediatrics* 56: 449–58.

Darwin, C. 1868. *The variation of plants and animals under domestication.* New York.

Diers, Carol Jean. 1974. Historical trends in the age at menarche and menopause. *Psychological Reports* 34: 931–7.

Duncan, J. M. 1884. *On sterility in women.* Philadelphia, Pa.

Ellis, Richard W. B. 1945. Growth and health of Belgian children during and after the German occupation (1940–44). *Archives of Diseases in Childhood* 20: 97–109.

Freind, J. F. 1738. *Emmenologia,* trans. M. Devaux (first published Oxford 1703). Paris.

Frisch, Rose E. 1978. Population, food intake, and fertility. *Science* 199: 22–30.

Golub, Sharon. 1983. *Menarche: The transition from girl to woman.* Lexington, Mass.

Guarionius, Hippolytus. 1610. *Die Greuel der Verwüstung menschlichen Geschlechts.* Ingolstadt, Germany.

Haller, Albrecht von. 1775. *Herrn Albrecht von Hallers Anfangsgründe der Phisiologie des menschlichen Körpers.* Berlin.

Johnson, F. E. 1974. Control of age at menarche. *Human Biology* 46: 159–71.

Kinsey, A. C. 1948. *Sexual behavior in the human male.* Philadelphia, Pa.

Kolata, G. B. 1974. !Kung hunter-gatherers: Feminism, diet and birth control. *Science* 185: 932–24.

Krali-Cercek, Lea. 1956. The influence of food, body build, and social origin on the age at menarche. *Human Biology* 28: 393–406.

Maresh, Marion M. 1972. A forty-five year investigation for secular changes in physical maturation. *American Journal of Physical Anthropology* 36: 103–10.

Marinello, G. 1574. *Le medicine partenenti alle infermita delle donne.* Venice.

Markowitz, Stephen D. 1955. Retardation in growth of children in Europe and Asia during World War II. *Human Biology* 27: 258–73.

McBarnette, Lorna. 1988. Women and poverty: The effects on reproductive status. *Women and Health* 12: 55–81.

Meyer, François, Jocelyne Moisan, Diane Marcoux, and Claude Bouchard. 1990. Dietary and physical determinants of menarche. *Epidemiology* 1: 377–81.

Moisan, Jocelyne, François Meyer, and Suzanne Gingras. 1990. Diet and age at menarche. *Cancer Causes and Control* 1: 149–54.

Montesquieu, C. L. de Sede. 1751. De l'esprit des lois. *Oeuvres complètes* (Bibliothèque de la Pléiade), Vol. 7, Book 16. Dijon.

Murata, Mitsunori, and Itsuro Hibi. 1992. Nutrition and the secular trend of growth. *Hormone Research* 38 (Supplement 1): 89–96.

Neuman, R. P. 1975. Masturbation, madness, and the modern concepts of childhood and adolescence. *Journal of Social History* 8: 1–27.

Osler, David C., and John D. Crawford. 1973. Examination of the hypothesis of critical weight at menarche in ambulatory and bedridden mentally retarded girls. *Pediatrics* 51: 675–9.

Peters, H., and S. M. Shirkande. 1957. Age at menarche in Indian women. *Fertility and Sterility* 8: 355.

Post, J. B. 1971. Age at menarche and menopause: Some medieval authorities. *Population Studies* 25: 83–7.

Potter, Robert G. 1975. Changes of natural fertility and contraceptive equivalents. *Social Forces* 54: 36–51.

Richardson, Barbara D., and Linda Pieters. 1977. Menarche and growth. *American Journal of Clinical Nutrition* 30: 2088–91.

Riley, A. P., S. L. Huffman, and A. K. M. Chowdhury. 1989. Age at menarche and postmenarcheal growth in rural Bangladeshi females. *Annals of Human Biology* 16: 347–59.

Roberton, John. 1832. An inquiry into the natural history of the menstrual function. *Edinburgh Medical and Surgical Journal* 38: 227.

1845. On the period of puberty in Hindu women. *Edinburgh Medical and Surgical Journal* 64: 156.

Schiebinger, Londa. 1993. *Nature's body: Gender and the making of modern science.* Boston, Mass.

Schurig, Martin. 1729. *Parthenologia historico-medica, hoc est viginitatis consideratio, qua ad eam pertinens pubertates et menstruatio, item varia de insolitis mensium viis, nec non de partium genitalium miliebrium pro virginitatis custodia.* Dresden.

Shaw, W. 1959. *Textbook of Gynecology.* Seventh edition. London.

Short, R. V. 1976. The evolution of human reproduction. *Proceedings of the Royal Society of London* 195: 3–24.

Shorter, Edward. 1981. L'age des Premières Règles en France, 1750–1950. *Annales: Économies, Sociétés, Civilisations* 36: 495–511.

Smith, W. T. 1855. *On the causes and treatment of abortion and sterility.* London.

Soranus. 1950. *Gynecology,* trans. O. Temkin. Baltimore, Md.

Stepan, Nancy. 1982. *The idea of race in science: Great Britain 1800–1960.* Hamden, Conn.

Tanner, J. M. 1962. *Growth at adolescence.* London.

1968. Earlier maturation in man. *Scientific American* 218: 2–8.

1973. Growing up. *Scientific American* 229: 34–43.

1981a. *A history of the study of human growth.* London.

1981b. Menarcheal age. *Science* 214: 604–5.

Vinovskis, Maris A. 1988. *An "epidemic" of adolescent pregnancy? Some historical and policy considerations.* New York.

Wellens, Rita, Robert M. Malina, Gaston Beunen, and Johan Lefevre. 1990. Age at menarche in Flemish girls: Current status and secular change in the 20th century. *Annals of Human Biology* 17: 145–52.

Whitehead, J. 1847. *On the causes and treatment of abortion and sterility. . . .* London.

Wyshak, Grace, and Rose E. Frisch. 1982. Evidence for a secular trend in age of menarche. *New England Journal of Medicine* 306: 1033–5.

Zacharias, Leona, William M. Rand, and Richard J. Wurtman. 1976. A prospective study of sexual development and growth in American girls: The statistics of menarche. *Obstetrical and Gynecological Survey* 31: 325–37.

VI.9 ❧ Nutrition and Mental Development

Most research on nutrition and human mental development has focused on protein–energy malnutrition (PEM), which consists of deficits in energy and protein as well as other nutrients (Golden 1988). But there is also an extensive literature on the importance to mental development of trace elements and vitamins, as well as the impact of short-term food deprivation. Thus, although the bulk of this essay focuses on PEM and mental development, we begin with an examination of these other areas of concern.

Vitamins and Trace Elements

General Vitamin and Mineral Deficiencies

It is well understood that severe vitamin deficiencies may have drastic effects on mental development. Serious thiamine and niacin deficiencies, for example, as well as those of folic acid and vitamin B_{12}, can cause neuropathy (Carney 1984). But milder, subclinical vitamin deficiencies are much more common, and thus their influence on mental development is presumably of much greater importance. Unfortunately, the extent to which multivitamin and mineral supplements influence intelligence in schoolchildren remains unknown, although this question has been the subject of at least five clinical trials (Schoenthaler 1991).

One study of 90 Welsh children using a multivitamin–mineral supplement over a nine-month period indicated that supplementation produced an increase in nonverbal IQs (Benton and Roberts 1988). A similar study of 410 children in the United States over 13 weeks also revealed an overall increase in nonverbal IQs (Schoenthaler 1991). However, in a Belgian study of 167 children who were supplemented for five months, only boys whose diets had previously been nutritionally deficient showed an increase in verbal IQs (Benton and Buts 1990). Other studies, one in London and the other in Scotland, reported no significant effects of supplementation (Naismith et al. 1988; Crombie et al. 1990).

Reasons for inconsistent findings may have to do with differences in the duration of the programs or may lie in the nature of the children's normal diets. Because supplementation is most likely to benefit children whose diets are deficient in one or more of the chief nutrients, more consistent results might have been obtained if the subjects had been restricted to children with deficient diets. Another problem with these studies is that a variety of vitamins and trace elements were administered in the supplements. Thus, it is not possible to single out those nutrients that may have played key roles in raising nonverbal IQs.

Trace Elements

Among the trace elements there are two that have been the subject of much research and are known to have a substantial influence on mental development.

Iodine. One is iodine, which is required for the production of thyroxine. Iodine deficiency during pregnancy can cause deficits in fetal brain maturation, resulting in cretinism. There are two types of cretinism, neurological and myxedematous; mental retardation is a symptom of both. Other symptoms of neurological cretinism include spastic diplegia and deaf-mutism, whereas dwarfism is symptomatic of myxedematous cretinism.

Cretinism, however, is not the only manifestation of iodine deficiency, and a number of others have been identified. These are referred to as iodine-deficiency disorders (IDD) (Hetzel 1983) and include goiter, neuromotor delays, deaf-mutism, and an increase in both pre- and postnatal mortality rates (Stanbury 1987).

Cretinism seems to be the extreme in a spectrum of cognitive and psychomotor deficits caused by iodine deficiency. Studies in Indonesia and Spain have indicated that village children living in iodine-deficient regions had poorer levels of mental and motor development than other village children who did not live in such areas (Bleichrodt et al. 1987). It may be that other disparities between the villages played a role in the differences. But, in a village in Ecuador, iodine supplementation of pregnant mothers reportedly led to improved motor development of the children, in comparison with children in a nonsupplemented village (Fierro-Benitez et al. 1986). Similar results were derived from a clinical trial conducted in Zaire (Thilly et al. 1980).

Yet in other studies, iodine supplementation seems to have been less effective. One of these, conducted in Peru, reported no effect on the development of the infants of mothers supplemented during pregnancy (Pretell et al. 1972). Two other studies involved schoolchildren. One, carried out in Bolivia, revealed no changes in school achievement and development despite iodine supplementation (Bautista et al. 1982), and a Spanish study discovered no effect on the mental or psychomotor development of supplemented children (Bleichrodt et al. 1989).

Clearly, more research of a conclusive nature is needed. There are some 800 million persons at risk of iodine deficiency in Asia, Africa, and Latin America;

close to 200 million persons in the world suffer from goiter, and more than 3 million are cretins (Hetzel 1987). This is especially tragic because iodine deficiency is so easily prevented by the consumption of iodized salt or iodized oil, or by iodine injection.

Iron. Iron is the second of the trace minerals that play a decided role in mental development. Its deficiency is the main cause of anemia, an important nutritional problem in both developed and developing countries. Because anemia symptoms include listlessness and lassitude, iron deficiency can and does negatively affect the cognitive processes.

Early investigations indicated associations between iron-deficiency anemia and poor levels of cognition in children. However, there were problems in eliminating social factors that could also be causal (see, for example, Webb and Oski 1973). Subsequent studies on iron-deficient children suggest, among other things, that the adverse effects of iron deficiency on the cognitive processes are most apparent when the deficiency is severe enough to cause anemia.

Age has much to do with such findings, as does the duration of the periods of iron supplementation. For example, in five studies, supplementation was given for periods of less than two weeks, and developmental levels assessed on infant scales were used as outcome measures. No significant gains from supplementation were discovered in four of the studies, which were conducted in Guatemala (Lozoff et al. 1982), Costa Rica (Lozoff et al. 1987), Chile (Walter et al. 1989), and North America (Oski and Honig 1978). A fifth study, in Chile, did find an improvement in developmental levels, although the absence of a placebo group compromised the results (Walter, Kovalskys, and Stekel 1983).

In another group of studies, however, children under two years of age were supplemented for longer periods. Two such studies were preventive trials in which high-risk children were supplemented from the age of 2 to 3 months and then tested at 12 months. In Chile, such supplementation produced better development (Walter et al. 1989), and in Papua New Guinea, supplemented children had longer fixation times than the controls (Heywood et al. 1989). On the other hand, in the United Kingdom, a group that underwent two months of supplementation did not produce better development scores than a placebo group, although a greater number of treated children achieved normal rates of development (Aukett et al. 1986). In Costa Rica, after three months of supplementation, children who experienced complete recovery of their iron status clearly benefited from the supplements (Lozoff et al. 1987). However, a study in Chile found no effect after three months of supplementation (Walter et al. 1989).

It appears that, as a rule, the longer the duration of treatment, the more likely there will be benefits in developmental levels. It has been suggested that iron deficiency affects such development because it reduces a child's span of attention (Pollitt et al. 1982). But children under two years of age are difficult to assess, and only one study thus far has attempted to look at the matter (Heywood et al. 1989).

Results seem to be more positive in children over two years of age. Indeed, 10 studies have reported improvement in mental functions after iron supplementation. Three of these were conducted in Indonesia, and improvements in both cognitive functions and school achievement levels were reported after two or three months' treatment (Soemantri, Pollitt, and Kim 1985; Soemantri 1989; Soewondo, Husaini, and Pollitt 1989).

In India, two studies found improved cognitive functions after three months of supplementation (Seshadri and Gopaldas 1989); another, in Egypt, reported the same after four months of treatment (Pollitt et al. 1985). In India, two additional clinical trials showed improvements in IQ scores after three months of supplementation with both iron and folic acid (Seshadri and Gopaldas 1989). In the United States, the results of two studies, which were not true clinical trials, indicated that supplementation produced improvements in the cognitive functions of anemic children (Pollitt, Leibel, and Greenfield 1983a), and similar conclusions were reached in Guatemala (Pollitt et al. 1986). But two other studies, in the United States and Thailand, showed no apparent improvements with iron supplementation (Deinard et al. 1986; Pollitt et al. 1989).

From the foregoing, then, it would seem that there is good evidence to indicate that iron-deficiency anemia has detrimental effects on the mental development of children over the age of two, and that supplementation will erase those effects. In younger children, however, the evidence is less conclusive. In fact, there is little or no evidence of benefits with supplementation lasting less than two weeks, and although investigations with longer-term treatment have yielded more positive findings, such findings are inconsistent.

Nonetheless, the evidence generated by such investigations is of vital importance because about 51 percent of preschool-age and 38 percent of school-age children in developing countries, and 10 percent of preschool-age and 12 percent of school-age children in developed countries, are anemic (DeMaeyer and Adiels-Tegman 1985).

Short-Term Food Deprivation

Although improvement in school achievement is one of the goals of school feeding programs, there have been few well-designed evaluations of their effectiveness (Pollitt, Gersovitz, and Gargicilo 1978). The best results are most likely to be derived from such programs in developing countries where the prevalence of undernutrition is greater. But, unfortunately, most investigations conducted in these countries have tended to be poorly designed (Levinger 1986).

One exception was a small Jamaican study using a matched control group. It related improvements in school achievement to the school feeding plan, but not to improvements in nutritional status as such (Powell, Grantham-McGregor, and Eston 1983). It was speculated that the mere alleviation of hunger during school hours produced improvements in cognitive functions and behavior.

The most sensitive method of examining the effects of short-term food deprivation on mental functions involves studies in which children are used as their own controls and in which their performance is compared with and without breakfast. Four such studies (including three from the United States) have reported detrimental effects on mental functions when breakfast was omitted. In one of these, the omission of breakfast showed a deterioration in cognitive functions only in children with low IQs (Pollitt, Leibel, and Greenfield 1981). When the investigation was replicated, deterioration was found in the cognitive functions of all children (Pollitt et al. 1983b). Another study indicated that the detrimental effect on cognitive functions became worse as the period of deprivation increased (Conners and Blouin 1983).

In Jamaica, an investigation into the effects of missing breakfast among both undernourished and adequately nourished children discovered that the cognitive functions of undernourished children deteriorated with the omission of breakfast, whereas those of adequately nourished children did not (Simeon and Grantham-McGregor 1989).

The reason for the impact of short-term food deprivation on cognitive functions is not clear. However, it likely has a metabolic basis, which may result in changes in arousal levels (Pollitt et al. 1981) or in neurotransmitter levels (Wurtman 1986). The relationship between arousal levels and performance is complex (Kahneman 1973) and varies with the nature of the task (Hebb 1972) and the subjects (Eysenck 1976).

It does seem clear that undernourished children are more susceptible to cognitive function impairment resulting from short-term food deprivation than are adequately nourished children. It is possible that malnutrition may serve to sensitize the children to the stress of the omission of food. In other words, they may appraise the situation as being more threatening than do better-nourished children (Barnes et al. 1968; Smart and Dobbing 1977). But the response of malnourished children may also be due to abnormalities in carbohydrate metabolism. Illustrative is the fact that, during severe PEM, children have low fasting glucose and insulin levels (James and Coore 1970; Alleyne et al. 1972).

In concluding this discussion of short-term food deprivation and cognitive functions, we should note that although the impact of such deprivation appears to be small, there may be important consequences. If, for example, food deprivation occurs frequently over a long period, the effects may be cumulative and lead to poor levels of development and school achievement. Indeed, food deprivation, which is hardly uncommon in malnourished children, may play a significant role in the low levels of mental development generally found in such children.

Protein–Energy Malnutrition

There have been three major classifications of PEM, with the Gomez classification being the first (Gomez et al. 1955): Children suffering from PEM were described as being mildly, moderately, or severely malnourished, depending on their deficits in weight compared to reference values for their sex and age. However, a second classification – the Wellcome classification – takes into account the presence of edema as well as weight deficits (Wellcome Trust Working Party 1970).

These two classifications are generally used in the identification of children with severe PEM. But the use of weight and age alone is not very useful in discriminating between different types of mild-to-moderate PEM. For example, a child with a low weight-for-age may be tall and thin or short and fat. To address this problem, J. Waterlow (1976) introduced a third classification, which employs height expressed as a percentage of the expected value for age and sex, and employs weight as a percentage of the expected value for the height and sex of an afflicted child. Low height-for-age, or stunting, is thought to reflect long-term PEM, whereas low weight-for-height, or wasting, is believed to reflect recent nutritional experiences.

The prevalence of mild-to-moderate PEM in developing countries ranges from 7 to 60 percent, whereas that of severe PEM is between 1 and 10 percent (Grant 1990). PEM has a decided impact on mental development, and with an estimated 150 million children suffering from the affliction worldwide, its potential cost in human, as well as social and economic, terms is staggering.

Mild-to-Moderate PEM

A number of observational studies have associated mild-to-moderate PEM with poor mental development. Yet PEM tends to occur amid economic deprivation that has its own deleterious effects on development. Because it is not possible to control for many of these factors, the most effective way to determine the impact of PEM lies in the use of experimental study designs.

Unfortunately, there have been only a few experiments in which at-risk children have been supplemented and their mental development compared with that of controls. What follows is a brief summary of the findings of observational studies and experimental studies, although only those in which there was statistical control of confounding background variables are mentioned.

Observational studies. Investigations examining associations between mild-to-moderate PEM and the mental development of preschool-age children have been conducted in Colombia (Christiansen et al. 1977), Guatemala (Lasky et al. 1981), and Jamaica (Powell and Grantham-McGregor 1985). The results of the three studies indicated that PEM was associated with poor development.

Another seven studies involved school-age children. Undernutrition in children was associated with poor school achievement levels in the Philippines (Popkin and Lim-Ybanez 1982; Florencio 1988), Nepal (Moock and Leslie 1986), and India (Agarwal et al. 1987), and with low IQs in Jamaica (Clarke et al. 1991). In Guatemala, a study showed a close association between undernutrition and low IQs, whereas in Kenya, malnutrition was correlated with poor levels of cognitive functions (Johnston et al. 1987; Sigman et al. 1989).

Experimental studies. There are two types of supplementation investigations: preventive and remedial. The former focuses on high-risk mothers who are supplemented during pregnancy, and on their offspring who are supplemented in early childhood to prevent them from becoming undernourished. By contrast, in remedial studies, the focus is on already undernourished children who are supplemented to improve their nutritional status.

The findings of experimental studies in developed countries are especially likely to be inconsistent. In one preventive investigation, carried out in North America, supplementation during pregnancy provided the infant with only small advantages in play, and none in development, during its first year of life (Rush, Stein, and Susser 1980). Two other trials revealed no apparent benefits for the infants whose mothers had received supplements (Osofsky 1975; Pencharz et al. 1983). In a fourth study in which supplementation began during pregnancy and continued during the first year of life, children experienced large gains in development, compared with their older siblings (Hicks, Langham, and Takenaka 1982).

One reason for the inconsistency in the findings of these four studies is that in a developed region like North America, the children under scrutiny would probably not have become malnourished, regardless of whether they had supplemented mothers.

A fifth supplementation study in the developed world was remedial. Carried out as a clinical trial in England (Lucas et al. 1990), it investigated the effects of an enriched formula on the development of small preterm children. Marked benefits were shown at 18 months, especially in motor development.

It is the case, however, that studies conducted in developing countries where malnutrition is endemic are much more useful in determining whether the association between PEM and mental development is causal. One from Colombia, in which the supplementation was preventive, produced evidence of beneficial effects, first in motor development (Mora et al. 1979) and later in language (Waber et al. 1981). In Taiwan, supplementation of pregnant mothers, but not of children, led to benefits in motor development when the children were eight months old, although there was no effect on mental development (Joos et al. 1983). Supplementation of both mothers and children, however, resulted in gains in mental and motor development in Mexico (Chavez and Martinez 1982), and in cognitive functions in Guatemala (Freeman et al. 1980).

As for remedial studies, in one conducted in Colombia, both malnourished and adequately nourished children were supplemented for one year. Only those who had been malnourished improved in their development (Mora et al. 1974). In a second such investigation in Colombia, a supplementation–stimulation program was found to encourage mental development and a subsequent improvement in school performance. Moreover, such positive effects increased with the duration of the program. However, supplementation alone had no effect on development (McKay et al. 1978).

Jamaica was the site of a third remedial study, in which children ages 9 to 24 months, with low heights-for-age, were given nutritional supplementation for two years. There was a beneficial effect on development. Locomotor development was affected first, followed by mental functions. This clinical trial also had a stimulation component, and the effects of supplementation and stimulation were additive and not interactive (Grantham-McGregor et al. 1991).

To sum up, in developing-world countries, improvement in mental development was found in studies in which supplementation was preventive. This was also the case in two of the three remedial investigations. There were design flaws in some of the investigations, but considering the consistency of the findings across developing countries, the evidence indicates that both remedial and preventive supplementation encourage development. In general, however, the benefits are small, perhaps because the gains in growth were also small in the supplemented children. Indeed, the actual levels of supplementation were less than intended because of the problems of food sharing and substitution that occur in supplementation studies (Beaton and Ghassemi 1982).

Finally, the importance of the cumulative effect of mild-to-moderate undernutrition (or its absence) throughout childhood cannot be accurately assessed in supplementation programs lasting a relatively short period of time and producing only small improvements in growth.

Severe PEM

The most common method of defining severe PEM in children is the Wellcome classification, which includes those suffering from marasmus, kwashiorkor, or marasmic-kwashiorkor.

Because it is not ethical to conduct experimental studies with severely malnourished children, investigations have been observational, and most of the children studied were treated in hospital in the acute stage. Early studies reported poor levels of mental development in children with severe PEM (see, for example, Gerber and Dean 1956). There followed a series of cohort studies of school-age children who survived severe PEM in early childhood.

As in examinations of mild-to-moderate PEM, a main problem was that the poor socioeconomic environment in which the victims lived tended to confuse the relationship between PEM and poor mental development. The use of well-matched controls was therefore essential and improved over time. Two strategies were employed to control for social background. The first was the use of siblings of the index children as controls, and the second included the use of children from similar socioeconomic backgrounds.

These strategies, of course, have inherent problems. Although it is reasonable to assume that both the index child and the sibling have lived under similar socioeconomic conditions, there are unavoidable biases when siblings are used as controls. It is not possible, for example, to control for age and birth order, both of which affect development. In addition, it is possible that a child who has become severely malnourished has not been treated the same way as a sibling who was not malnourished. Most importantly, it is probable that the siblings were also malnourished and, consequently, had lowered levels of mental development themselves. Finally, there is evidence that long-term PEM may have greater negative effects on mental development than an episode of severe PEM (Grantham-McGregor, Powell, and Fletcher 1989). Therefore, the true effects of severe PEM are likely to be worse than those determined from studies using sibling comparisons.

The use of nonsibling controls from the same socioeconomic class also presents problems. Families of children with severe PEM tend to be poorer (Richardson 1974) and to have less stimulating home environments (Cravioto and DeLicardie 1972) than their control comparisons, and both of these factors can affect mental development. In the following discussion, research on the effects of severe PEM on mental development during its acute phase will be discussed first, followed by a look at investigations of its long-term sequelae. Finally, the effects of severe PEM, as demonstrated by studies conducted in developed countries, will be reviewed.

Acute stage. In early reports, children suffering from severe PEM were described as apathetic (Williams 1933) and having poor levels of mental development (Cravioto and Robles 1965; Yatkin and McLaren 1970; Monckeberg 1979). Although there was some evidence of improvement after clinical recovery, these studies had no controls. But, in a controlled study in Jamaica, severely malnourished children were found to have lower levels of mental development when compared with controls hospitalized for other illnesses. The developmental levels of both groups improved during their hospital stay. However, the malnourished group failed to reduce their deficit relative to the controls. The children who had suffered from PEM were also less active, more apathetic, and less exploring than the controls (Grantham-McGregor et al. 1990).

Long-term effects with nonsibling controls. In examining the long-term effects of PEM, eight studies were identified in which school-age children who had previously suffered from the illness were compared with nonsibling controls. In seven of these efforts, the malnourished children had lower levels of mental development than the controls. One, conducted in India, indicated that the index children had lower scores in perceptual, abstract, and verbal abilities, as well as in memory and sensory integration (Champakam, Srikantia, and Gopalan 1968).

Two other studies were conducted in Jamaica. In the first, the index children were found to have lower IQs (Hertzig et al. 1972) and lower school achievement levels (Richardson, Birch, and Hertzig 1973) than controls. The second Jamaican study also found deficits in IQs (Grantham-McGregor, Schofield, and Powell 1987) and school achievement (Powell and Grantham-McGregor 1990). In Barbados, children who had previously been severely malnourished were found to have lower IQs than controls (Galler et al. 1983b), and more behavior problems (Galler et al. 1983a), learning disabilities (Galler, Ramsey, and Solimano 1984a), and motor delays (Galler et al. 1984b).

In Uganda, severe PEM was also found to be associated with deficits in mental and motor development (Hoorweg and Stanfield 1976), and in Nigeria, children who had been severely malnourished had lower scores in a number of tests of cognitive functions (Nwuga 1977). Similarly, in South Africa, children who had previously suffered from severe malnutrition had lower IQs, lower levels of school achievement, and more behavior problems than controls (Stoch and Smythe 1976). Another South African study, however, was the only one of the eight under discussion that reported no difference in development between survivors of severe PEM and controls (Bartel et al. 1978).

Long-term effects and sibling controls. The long-term effects of PEM have also been examined in eight studies in which the development of school-age children who had previously been severely malnourished was compared with that of their siblings. Five of these studies revealed deficits in development. In Nigeria, index children were found to have lower IQs than their siblings (Nwuga 1977), whereas in India they had poorer levels of school achievement (Pereira, Sundaraj, and Begum 1979). In Mexico, boys who were previously severely malnourished had lower IQs than their siblings, although no difference was found with girls (Birch et al. 1971). In Jamaica, index children had lower verbal IQs (Hertzig et al. 1972) and more behavior problems (Richardson et al. 1973) than siblings, but there was no difference in school achievement levels. In South Africa, there was no difference in IQs between previously severely malnourished children and their siblings. However, the index children showed lower school achievement and produced lower scores on a drawing test (Evans, Moodie, and Hansen 1971).

Yet, severe PEM was found to have no effect on children's school achievement in Peru (Graham and Adrianzen 1979), and none on motor development in South Africa (Bartel et al. 1978). Another South African study examined the impact, on young adults, of severe PEM in early childhood. No difference was found in school attainment or in social adjustment when compared with their siblings (Moodie et al. 1980).

Developing countries. As we have mentioned, in studies conducted in developing countries, it is difficult to separate the effects on mental development of severe PEM from those of poor environment. Therefore, investigations using subjects from developed countries can be helpful. Unlike the situation in developing countries, where poverty is the primary cause of malnutrition, children in developed countries generally become malnourished because of diseases, such as cystic fibrosis. Since the children's developmental state tends not to be associated with deprived social conditions, such cases present an opportunity to view the long-term effects of severe PEM from a fresh angle.

The results of these studies have been inconsistent. Small deficits in children's development were demonstrated in some instances (Klein, Forbes, and Nader 1975; Winick, Meyer, and Harris 1975; Carmona da Mota et al. 1990), but no deficits were found in others (Lloyd-Still et al. 1974; Valman 1974; Ellis and Hill 1975). It is possible that the findings in developed countries have not been as consistent as those in developing countries because the children in the former tended to have less severe episodes of PEM that continued for shorter periods.

It is also possible that the environments in which the children were raised after the episode of PEM had a modifying effect. Psychosocial stimulation can improve the development of severely malnourished children. Such improvements were only transient in the wake of short-term programs (McLaren et al. 1973; Cravioto and Arrieta 1979) but lasted for several years following a three-year program (Grantham-

McGregor et al. 1987). This effect is consistent with animal studies in which stimulation has decreased the adverse effects of severe PEM on development (Levitsky 1979).

Clearly, then, there are problems with inferring a causal relationship between severe PEM and poor mental development on the basis of nonexperimental studies. Nonetheless, the results of the studies reviewed indicate that children who are severely malnourished in early childhood and are raised in deprived conditions usually have lower levels of mental development than similarly deprived children who are not severely malnourished. The effects have been more consistent in studies in which malnourished children were compared with nonsibling controls rather than with siblings. This may be because of overmatching in the latter studies.

The mechanism linking PEM to poor mental development is not clearly established, but there are several hypotheses that assume a causal relationship. Children who died from severe PEM have been found to have smaller brains than comparison children (Winick and Rosso 1969; Rosso, Hormazabal, and Winick 1970; Dickerson, Merat, and Yusuf 1982), and it is certainly possible that impairments in brain growth may have adverse effects on mental development. Although findings from animal studies indicate that the anatomical changes due to PEM are persistent (Bedi 1987), it is not clear if this is the case in humans. In addition, it is not known if children with mild-to-moderate PEM also experience impaired brain growth.

The brain function of severely malnourished children has also been investigated by using evoked brain potentials. However, here the findings have proven inconsistent. In Mexico, abnormal auditory evoked potentials were found in severely malnourished children when compared with matched controls, and the abnormality persisted after clinical recovery (Barnet et al. 1978). In South Africa, the results of electroencephalograph (EEG) measurements indicated that children who had previously been severely malnourished had delays in brain development when compared with their siblings, but there was no difference when compared with nonsibling controls (Bartel et al. 1979). On the other hand, two other South African studies found no difference in EEGs when previously severely malnourished children were compared either with their siblings (Evans et al. 1971) or with nonsibling controls (Stoch and Smythe 1976).

It has been speculated that malnourished children are less active, explore their environments less, and thus acquire skills more slowly than adequately nourished ones. It may well be that in addition, their caretakers become less responsive to them, thus exacerbating poor development. Yet, although malnourished children have been shown to have lower activity levels and poorer developmental levels than adequately nourished children (Chavez and Martinez 1982; Meeks Gardner et al. 1990), there is no evidence showing that reduced activity precedes poor development (Grantham-McGregor et al. 1990).

In conclusion, it seems clear that various nutritional deficiencies have adverse effects on mental development. There are concurrent deficits in development in the face of mild-to-moderate PEM, severe PEM, short-term food deprivation, and iron-deficiency anemia. Maternal iodine deficiency has long-term effects on development, and severe PEM, usually, has long-term effects on mental development, if the children live in poor environments. But it has not yet been established that less severe PEM has long-term sequelae.

Donald T. Simeon
Sally M. Grantham-McGregor

Bibliography

Agarwal, D., S. Upadhyay, A. Tripathi, and K. Agarwad. 1987. Nutritional status, physical work capacity and mental functions in schoolchildren. *Nutrition Foundation of India, Scientific Report No. 6.*

Alleyne, G., P. Trust, H. Flores, and H. Robinson. 1972. Glucose tolerance and insulin sensitivity in malnourished children. *British Journal of Nutrition* 27: 585-92.

Aukett, M., Y. Parks, P. Scott, and B. Wharton. 1986. Treatment with iron increases weight gain and psychomotor development. *Archives of Disease in Childhood* 61: 849-57.

Barnes, R., C. Neeling, E. Kwong, et al. 1968. Post-natal nutritional deprivations as determinants of adult rat behavior toward feed, its consumption and utilization. *Journal of Nutrition* 96: 467-76.

Barnet, A., I. Weiss, M. Sotillo, and E. Ohlrich. 1978. Abnormal auditory evoked potentials in early infancy malnutrition. *Science* 201: 450-1.

Bartel, P., R. Griesel, L. Burnett, et al. 1978. Long-term effects of kwashiorkor on psychomotor development. *South African Medical Journal* 53: 360-2.

Bartel, P., R. Griesel, I. Freiman, et al. 1979. Long-term effects of kwashiorkor on the electroencephalogram. *American Journal of Clinical Nutrition* 32: 753-7.

Bautista, A., P. Barker, J. Dunn, et al. 1982. The effects of iodized oil on intelligence, thyroid status and somatic growth in school-age children from an area of endemic goiter. *American Journal of Clinical Nutrition* 35: 127-34.

Beaton, G., and H. Ghassemi. 1982. Supplementary feeding programs for young children in developing countries. *American Journal of Clinical Nutrition* 35 (Supplement): 863-916.

Bedi, K. 1987. Lasting neuroanatomical changes following undernutrition. In *Early nutrition and later achievement,* ed. J. Dobbing, 1-49. London.

Benton, D., and J.-P. Buts. 1990. Vitamin/mineral supplementation and intelligence. *Lancet* 335: 1158-60.

Benton, D., and G. Roberts. 1988. Effect of vitamin and supplementation on intelligence of a sample of schoolchildren. *Lancet* 1: 140-3.

Birch, H., L. Pineiro, E. Alcalde, et al. 1971. Relation of kwash-iorkor in early childhood and intelligence at school age. *Pediatric Research* 5: 579-85.

Bleichrodt, N., F. Escobar del Rey, G. Morreale, et al. 1989. Iodine deficiency, implications for mental and psychomotor development in children. In *Iodine and the brain,* ed. G. Delong, J. Robbins, and P. Condliffe, 269-87. New York.

Bleichrodt, N., I. Garcia, C. Rubio, et al. 1987. Developmental disorders associated with severe iodine deficiency. In *The prevention and control of iodine deficiency disorders,* ed. B. Hetzel, J. Dunn, and J. Stanbury, 65-84. Amsterdam.

Carmona da Mota, H., A. Antonio, G. Leitao, and M. Porto. 1990. Late effects of early malnutrition. *Lancet* 335: 1158.

Carney, M. 1984. Vitamin deficiencies and excesses: Behavioral consequences in adults. In *Nutrition and behavior,* ed. J. Galler, 193-222. New York.

Champakam, S., S. Srikantia, and C. Gopalan. 1968. Kwashiorkor and mental development. *American Journal of Clinical Nutrition* 21: 844-52.

Chavez, A., and C. Martinez. 1982. *Growing up in a developing community.* Guatemala City.

Christiansen, N., L. Vuori, J. Clement, et al. 1977. Malnutrition, social environment and cognitive development of Colombian infants and preschoolers. *Nutrition Reports International* 16: 93-102.

Clarke, N., S. Grantham-McGregor, and C. Powell. 1991. Nutrition and health predictors of school failure in Jamaican children. *Ecology of Food and Nutrition* 26: 47-57.

Conners, C., and A. Blouin. 1983. Nutritional effects on behavior of children. *Journal of Psychiatric Research* 17: 193-201.

Connolly, K., P. Pharoah, and B. Hetzel. 1979. Fetal iodine deficiency and motor performance during childhood. *Lancet* 1: 1149-51.

Cravioto, J., and R. Arrieta. 1979. Stimulation and mental development of malnourished infants. *Lancet* 2: 899.

Cravioto, J., and E. DeLicardie. 1972. Environmental correlates of severe clinical malnutrition and language development in survivors from kwashiorkor or marasmus. In *Nutrition, the nervous system and behavior,* Scientific Publication No. 251, 73-94. Washington, D.C.

Cravioto, J., and B. Robles. 1965. Evolution of adaptive and motor behavior during rehabilitation from kwashiorkor. *American Journal of Ortho-Psychiatry* 35: 449-64.

Crombie, I., J. Todman, G. McNeil, et al. 1990. Effect of vitamin and mineral supplementation on verbal and nonverbal reasoning of schoolchildren. *Lancet* 335: 744-7.

Deinard, A., A. List, B. Lindgren, et al. 1986. Cognitive deficits in iron-deficient and iron-deficient anaemic children. *Journal of Pediatrics* 108: 681-89.

DeMaeyer, E., and M. Adiels-Tegman. 1985. The prevalence of anemia in the world. *World Health Statistics Quarterly* 38: 302-16.

Dickerson, J., A. Merat, and H. Yusuf. 1982. Effects of malnutrition on brain growth and development. In *Brain and behavioral development,* ed. J. Dickerson and H. McGurr, 73-108. Glasgow.

Dickie, N., and A. Bender. 1982. Breakfast and performance. *Human Nutrition: Applied Nutrition* 36A: 46-56.

Dwyer, T., M. Elias, J. Warram, and F. Stare. 1972. Effects of a school snack program on certain aspects of school performance. *Federal Proceedings* 31: 718.

Ellis, C., and D. Hill. 1975. Growth, intelligence and school performance in children with cystic fibrosis who have had an episode of malnutrition during infancy. *Journal of Pediatrics* 87: 565-8.

Evans, D., A. Moodie, and J. Hansen. 1971. Kwashiorkor and intellectual development. *South African Medical Journal* 45: 1413-26.

Eysenck, M. 1976. Arousal, learning and memory. *Psychological Bulletin* 83: 389-404.

Fierro-Benitez, R., R. Casar, J. Stanbury, et al. 1986. Long-term effects of correction of iodine deficiency on psychomotor development and intellectual development. In *Towards the eradication of endemic goiter, cretinism and iodine deficiency*, ed. J. Dunn, E. Pretell, C. Daza, and F. Viteri, 182-200. Washington, D.C.

Florencio, C. 1988. *Nutrition, health and other determinants of academic achievement and school-related behavior.* Quezon City, Philippines.

Freeman, H., R. Klein, J. Townsend, and A. Lechtig. 1980. Nutrition and cognitive development among rural Guatemalan children. *American Journal of Public Health* 70: 1277-85.

Galler, J., F. Ramsey, and G. Solimano. 1984a. The influence of early malnutrition on subsequent behavioral development. III. Learning disabilities as a sequel to malnutrition. *Pediatric Research* 18: 309-13.

Galler, J., F. Ramsey, G. Solimano, and W. Lowell. 1983a. The influence of early malnutrition on subsequent behavioral development. II. Classroom behavior. *Journal of the American Academy of Childhood Psychiatry* 22: 16-22.

Galler, J., F. Ramsey, G. Solimano, et al. 1983b. The influence of early malnutrition on subsequent behavioral development. I. Degree of impairment of intellectual performance. *Journal of the American Academy of Childhood Psychiatry* 22: 8-15.

1984b. The influence of early malnutrition on subsequent behavioral development. IV. Soft neurologic signs. *Pediatric Research* 18: 826-32.

Gerber, M., and R. Dean. 1956. The psychological changes accompanying kwashiorkor. *Courier* 6: 6-15.

Golden, M. 1988. The role of individual nutrient deficiencies in growth retardation of children as exemplified by zinc and protein. In *Linear growth retardation in less developed countries*, ed. J. Waterlow, 143-64. New York.

Gomez, F., R. Galvan, J. Cravioto, and S. Frenk. 1955. Malnutrition in infancy and childhood with special reference to kwashiorkor. *Advances in Pediatrics* 7: 131-69.

Graham, G., and B. Adrianzen. 1979. Status at school of Peruvian children severely malnourished in infancy. In *Behavioral effects of energy and protein deficits*, ed. J. Brozek, 185-94. Washington, D.C.

Grant, J. 1990. *The state of the world's children.* New York.

Grantham-McGregor, S., J. Meeks Gardner, S. Walker, and C. Powell. 1990. The relationship between undernutrition, activity levels and development in young children. In *Activity, energy expenditure and energy requirements of infants and children*, ed. B. Schurch and N. Scrimshaw, 361-83. Geneva.

Grantham-McGregor, S., C. Powell, and P. Fletcher. 1989. Stunting, an episode of severe malnutrition and mental development in young children. *European Journal of Clinical Nutrition* 43: 403-9.

Grantham-McGregor, S., C. Powell, S. Walker, and J. Himes. 1991. Nutritional supplementation, psychosocial stimulation, and mental development of stunted children: The Jamaican study. *Lancet* 338: 1-5.

Grantham-McGregor, S., W. Schofield, and C. Powell. 1987.

Development of severely malnourished children who received psychosocial stimulation: Six year follow-up. *Pediatrics* 79: 247-54.

Hebb, D. 1972. *Textbook of psychology.* Philadelphia, Pa.

Hertzig, M., H. Birch, S. Richardson, and J. Tizard. 1972. Intellectual levels of school children severely malnourished during the first two years of life. *Pediatrics* 49: 814-24.

Hetzel, B. 1983. Iodine deficiency disorders (IDD) and their eradication. *Lancet* 2: 1126-9.

1987. An overview of the prevention and control of iodine deficiency disorders. In *The prevention and control of iodine deficiency disorders*, ed. B. Hetzel, J. Dunn, and J. Stanbury, 7-31. Amsterdam.

Heywood, A., S. Oppenheimer, P. Heywood, and D. Jolley. 1989. Behavioral effects of iron supplementation in infants in Madang, Papua New Guinea. *American Journal of Clinical Nutrition* 50: 630-40.

Hicks, L., R. Langham, and J. Takenaka. 1982. Cognitive and health measures following early nutritional supplementation. *American Journal of Public Health* 72: 1110-8.

Hoorweg, J., and J. Stanfield. 1976. The effects of protein-energy malnutrition in early childhood on intellectual and motor abilities in later childhood and adolescence. *Developmental Medicine and Child Neurology* 18: 330-50.

James, W., and H. Coore. 1970. Persistent impairment of insulin secretion and glucose tolerance after malnutrition. *American Journal of Clinical Nutrition* 23: 386-9.

Johnston, F., S. Low, Y. de Baessa, and R. McVean. 1987. Interaction of nutrition and socio-economic status as determinants of cognitive development in disadvantaged urban Guatemalan children. *American Journal of Physical Anthropology* 73: 501-6.

Joos, S., E. Pollitt, W. Mueller, and D. Albright. 1983. The Bacon Chow study: Maternal nutritional supplementation and infant behavioral development. *Child Development* 54: 669-76.

Kahneman, D. 1973. *Attention and effort.* Englewood Cliffs, N.J.

Keister, M. 1950. Relation of mid-morning feeding to behavior of nursery school children. *Journal of the American Dietetic Association* 26: 25-9.

Klein, P., G. Forbes, and P. Nader. 1975. Effects of starvation in infancy (pyloric stenosis) on subsequent learning abilities. *Journal of Pediatrics* 87: 8-15.

Laird, D., M. Levitan, and V. Wilson. 1931. Nervousness in school children as related to hunger and diet. *Medical Journal Records* 134: 494-9.

Lasky, R., R. Klein, C. Yarbrough, et al. 1981. The relationship between physical growth and infant behavioral development in rural Guatemala. *Child Development* 52: 219-26.

Levinger, B. 1986. *School feeding programs in developing countries: An analysis of actual and potential impact.* AID Evaluation Special Study No. 30. Washington, D.C.

Levitsky, D. 1979. Malnutrition and the hunger to learn. In *Malnutrition, environment and behaviour: New perspectives*, ed. D. Levitsky, 161-79. Ithaca, N.Y.

Lloyd-Still, J., I. Hurtwitz, P. Wolf, and H. Shwachman. 1974. Intellectual development after severe malnutrition in infancy. *Pediatrics* 54: 306-11.

Lozoff, B., G. Brittenham, F. Viteri, et al. 1982. The effects of short-term oral iron therapy on developmental deficits in iron-deficient anaemic infants. *Journal of Pediatrics* 100: 351-7.

Lozoff, B., G. Brittenham, A. Wolf, et al. 1987. Iron deficiency anemia and iron therapy effects on infant developmental test performance. *Pediatrics* 79: 981-95.

Lucas, A., R. Morley, T. Cole, et al. 1990. Early diet in preterm babies and developmental status at 18 months. *Lancet* 335: 1477-81.

McKay, H., L. Sinisterra, A. McKay, et al. 1978. Improving cognitive ability in chronically deprived children. *Science* 200: 270-8.

McLaren, D., U. Yatkin, A. Kanawati, et al. 1973. The subsequent mental and physical development of rehabilitated marasmic infants. *Journal of Mental Deficiency Research* 17: 273-81.

Meeks Gardner, J., S. Grantham-McGregor, S. Chang, and C. Powell. 1990. Dietary intake and observed activity of stunted and non-stunted children in Kingston, Jamaica. Part II: Observed activity. *European Journal of Clinical Nutrition* 44: 585-93.

Meyers, A., A. Sampson, M. Weitzman, et al. 1989. School breakfast program and school performance. *American Journal of Disease of Children* 143: 1234-9.

Monckeberg, F. 1979. Recovery of severely malnourished infants: Effect of early sensory-affective stimulation. In *Behavioral effects of energy and protein deficits,* ed. J. Brozek and B. Schurch, U.S. Department of Health, Education, and Welfare Publication No. 79-1906, 121-230. Washington, D.C.

Moock, P., and J. Leslie. 1986. Childhood malnutrition and schooling in the Terai region of Nepal. *Journal of Development Economics* 20: 33-52.

Moodie, A., M. Bowie, M. Mann, and J. Hansen. 1980. A prospective 15-year follow-up study of kwashiorkor patients. Part II. Social circumstances, educational attainment and social adjustment. *South African Medical Journal* 58: 677-81.

Mora, J., A. Amezquita, L. Castrol, et al. 1974. Nutrition, health and social factors related to intellectual performance. *World Review of Nutrition and Dietetics* 19: 205-36.

Mora, J., J. Clement, N. Christiansen, et al. 1979. Nutritional supplementation, early stimulation and child development. In *Behavioral effects of energy and protein deficits,* ed. J. Brozek and B. Schurch, U.S. Department of Health, Education, and Welfare Publication No. 79-1906, 225-69. Washington, D.C.

Naismith, D., M. Nelson, V. Burley, and S. Gatenby. 1988. Can children's intelligence be increased by vitamin and mineral supplements? *Lancet* 2: 335.

Nwuga, V. 1977. Effect of severe kwashiorkor on intellectual development among Nigerian children. *American Journal of Clinical Nutrition* 30: 1423-30.

Oski, F., and A. Honig. 1978. The effects of therapy on the developmental scores of iron-deficient infants. *Journal of Pediatrics* 92: 21-5.

Osofsky, H. 1975. Relationships between pre-natal medical and nutritional measures, pregnancy outcome, and early infant development in an urban poverty setting. I. The role of nutritional intake. *American Journal of Obstetrics and Gynaecology* 123: 632-90.

Pencharz, P., A. Heller, A. Higgins, et al. 1983. Effects of nutritional services to pregnant mothers on the school performance of treated and untreated children. *Nutrition Research* 3: 795-803.

Pereira, S., R. Sundaraj, and A. Begum. 1979. Physical growth and neuro-integrative performance of survivors of pro-tein-energy malnutrition. *British Journal of Nutrition* 212: 165-71.

Pharoah, P., K. Connolly, B. Hetzel, and R. Ekins. 1981. Maternal thyroid function and motor competence in the child. *Developmental Medicine and Child Neurology* 23: 76-82.

Pollitt, E., M. Gersovitz, and M. Gargicilo. 1978. Educational benefits of the United States school feeding program: A critical review of the literature. *American Journal of Public Health* 68: 477-81.

Pollitt, E., P. Hathirat, N. Kotchabhakdi, et al. 1989. Iron deficiency and educational achievement in Thailand. *American Journal of Clinical Nutrition* 50: 687-97.

Pollitt, E., R. Leibel, and D. Greenfield. 1981. Brief fasting, stress and cognition in children. *American Journal of Clinical Nutrition* 34: 1526-33.

1983a. Iron deficiency and cognitive test performance in preschool children. *Nutrition and Behaviour* 1: 137-46.

Pollitt, E., N. Lewis, C. Garcia, and R. Shulman. 1983b. Fasting and cognitive function. *Journal of Psychiatric Research* 17: 169-74.

Pollitt, E., C. Saco-Pollitt, R. Leibel, and F. Viteri. 1986. Iron deficiency and behavioral development in infants and pre-school children. *American Journal of Clinical Nutrition* 43: 555-65.

Pollitt, E., A. Soemantri, F. Yunis, and N. Scrimshaw. 1985. Cognitive effects of iron-deficiency anemia. *Lancet* 1: 158.

Pollitt, E., F. Viteri, C. Saco-Pollitt, and R. Leibel. 1982. Behavioral effects of iron deficiency anemia in children. In *Iron deficiency: Brain biochemistry and behavior,* ed E. Pollitt and R. Leibel, 195-208. New York.

Popkin, B., and M. Lim-Ybanez. 1982. Nutrition and school achievement. *Social Science and Medicine* 16: 53-61.

Powell, C., and S. Grantham-McGregor. 1985. The ecology of nutritional status and development in young children in Kingston, Jamaica. *American Journal of Clinical Nutrition* 41: 1322-31.

1990. Selective review of studies on the behavioral effects of childhood malnutrition. In *Child nutrition in south-east Asia,* ed H. Visser and J. Bindels, 125-40. Dortrecht, the Netherlands.

Powell, C., S. Grantham-McGregor, and M. Elston. 1983. An evaluation of giving the Jamaican government schoolmeal to a class of children. *Human Nutrition: Clinical Nutrition* 37C: 381-8.

Pretell, E., T. Torres, V. Zenteno, and M. Cornejo. 1972. Prophylaxis of endemic goiter with iodized oil in rural Peru. *Advances in Experimental Medicine and Biology* 30: 249-65.

Richardson, S. 1974. The background histories of schoolchildren severely malnourished in infancy. *Advances in Pediatrics* 21: 167-95.

Richardson, S., H. Birch, and M. Hertzig. 1973. School performance of children who were severely malnourished in infancy. *American Journal of Mental Deficiency* 77: 623-32.

Rosso, P., J. Hormazabal, and M. Winick. 1970. Changes in brain weight, cholesterol, phospholipid and DNA content in marasmic children. *American Journal of Clinical Nutrition* 23: 1275-9.

Rush, D., Z. Stein, and M. Susser. 1980. A randomized controlled trial of pre-natal nutritional supplementation in New York City. *Pediatrics* 65: 683-97.

Schoenthaler, S. 1991. Brains and vitamins. *Lancet* 337: 587-8.

Seshadri, S., and T. Gopaldas. 1989. Impact of iron supplementation on cognitive functions in pre-school and school aged children: The Indian experience. *American Journal of Clinical Nutrition* 50: 675-86.

Sigman, M., C. Neumann, and A. Jansen. 1989. Cognitive abilities of Kenyan children in relation to nutrition, family characteristics and education. *Child Development* 60: 1463-74.

Simeon, D., and S. Grantham-McGregor. 1989. Effects of missing breakfast on the cognitive functions of schoolchildren of differing nutritional status. *American Journal of Clinical Nutrition* 49: 646-53.

Smart, J., and J. Dobbing. 1977. Increased thirst and hunger in adult rats undernourished in infancy: An alternative explanation. *British Journal of Nutrition* 37: 421-30.

Soemantri, A. 1989. Preliminary findings on iron supplementation and learning achievement of rural Indonesian children. *American Journal of Clinical Nutrition* 50: 698-702.

Soemantri, A., E. Pollitt, and I. Kim. 1985. Iron deficiency anemia and educational achievement. *American Journal of Clinical Nutrition* 42: 1221-8.

Soewondo, S., M. Husaini, and E. Pollitt. 1989. Effects of iron deficiency on attention and learning process in preschool children: Bandung, Indonesia. *American Journal of Clinical Nutrition* 50: 667-74.

Stanbury, J. 1987. Iodine deficiency disorders: Introduction and general aspects. In *The prevention and control of iodine deficiency disorders,* ed. B. Hetzel, J. Dunn, and J. Stanbury, 35-47. Amsterdam.

Stoch, M., and P. Smythe. 1976. 15-year developmental study on the effects of severe undernutrition during infancy on subsequent physical growth and intellectual functioning. *Archives of Disease in Childhood* 51: 327-36.

Thilly, C., G. Roger, R. Lagase, et al. 1980. Fetomaternal relationship, fetal hypothyroidism, and psychomotor retardation. In *Role of cassava in the etiology of endemic goiter and cretinism,* ed A. Ermans, N. Mbulamoko, F. Delange, and R. Ahluwalia, 111-20. Ottawa.

Upadhyay, S., D. Agarwal, K. Agarwal, et al. 1988. Brief fasting and cognitive functions in rural school children. *Indian Pediatrics* 25: 288-9.

Valman, H. 1974. Intelligence after malnutrition caused by neonatal resection of ileum. *Lancet* 1: 425-7.

Waber, D., L. Vuori-Christiansen, N. Ortiz, et al. 1981. Nutritional supplementation, maternal education and cognitive development of infants at risk of malnutrition. *American Journal of Clinical Nutrition* 34: 807-13.

Walter, T., I. de Andraca, P. Chadud, and C. Perales. 1989. Iron deficiency anemia: Adverse effects on infant psychomotor development. *Pediatrics* 84: 7-17.

Walter, T., J. Kovalskys, and A. Stekel. 1983. Effect of mild iron deficiency on infant mental development scores. *Journal of Pediatrics* 102: 519-22.

Waterlow, J. 1976. Classification and definition of protein energy malnutrition. In *Nutrition in preventative medicine,* ed. G. Beaton and J. Bengoa, World Health Organization Monograph Series, No. 62, 530-55, Geneva.

Webb, T., and F. Oski. 1973. Iron deficiency anemia and scholastic achievement in young adolescents. *Journal of Pediatrics* 82: 827-30.

Wellcome Trust Working Party. 1970. Classification of infantile malnutrition. *Lancet* 2: 302.

Williams, C. 1933. A nutrition disease of childhood associated with a maize diet. *Archives of Disease in Childhood* 8: 423-33.

Winick, M., K. Meyer, and R. Harris. 1975. Malnutrition and environmental enrichment by early adoption. *Science* 190: 1173-5.

Winick, M., and P. Rosso. 1969. Head circumference and cellular growth of the brain in normal and marasmic children. *Science* 190: 1173-5.

Wurtman, R. 1986. Ways that food can affect the brain. *Nutrition Reviews* 44 (Supplement): 2-6.

Yatkin, V., and D. McLaren. 1970. The behavioral development of infants recovering from severe malnutrition. *Journal of Mental Deficiency Research* 14: 25-32.

VI.10 ❧ Human Nutritional Adaptation: Biological and Cultural Aspects

The extraordinary diversity of aboriginal food cultures testifies to the capacity of many combinations of foodstuffs to sustain human health and reproduction. From this diversity it is apparent that humans have no requirement for specific foods (with the qualified exception of breast milk, which can be replaced by the milk of other mammals but with less satisfactory results). Modern nutritional science has demonstrated that good health is dependent upon the consumption of a discrete number of biochemical compounds that are essential for normal metabolism but cannot be synthesized de novo in the body. These compounds or their metabolic precursors can be obtained from many different combinations of foods.

It is possible that there are still unidentified trace elements required in such small amounts that it has not yet been possible to demonstrate their essentiality, although it is unlikely that they are of any clinical importance in human nutrition. It is probable that current perceptions of the amounts of some nutrients required for optimal health – such as the relative amounts of various fatty acids necessary for the prevention of cardiovascular disease – will undergo further change, but the present state of nutritional knowledge is adequate as a basis for evaluating the quality of different food cultures in terms of their ability to provide the nutrients required for nutritional health.

This chapter evaluates two contrasting food cultures: the carnivorous aboriginal diets of the Arctic Inuit and the traditional cereal-based diets consumed by the inhabitants of Southeast Asia and of Central and South America. Also, the current nutritional health of these populations is evaluated in terms of their adaptation to a modern diet and lifestyle.

Biological Adaptation to the Intuit Diet

Although nutritional anthropologists have concluded that the diets of most hunting and gathering societies were more varied than those of early agricultural societies, this clearly was not true of the aboriginal diet of the Inuit inhabitants of the high Arctic. Although berries and the leafy parts of edible plants were available in the Subarctic region, the diet of the Inuit residing 300 miles above the Arctic Circle was, for all practical purposes, carnivorous (that is, they were hunters but not gatherers).

Current diet recommendations in industrial societies promote the consumption of a mixture of foods belonging to four or more food groups: cereals, fruits and vegetables, meat and fish, and dairy products. The native diet of the Arctic Inuit – caribou, seal, and whale meat, augmented with lesser amounts of fish, birds, eggs, and the meat of other land mammals – is composed of foods belonging to only one of these groups.

Meat consumption in modern societies is being discouraged because of its propensity to cause cardiovascular disease. Yet, when the Inuit were first examined by ships' doctors, they were found to be virtually free not only of vascular disease but of renal disease, hypertension, and diabetes as well (Thomas 1927; Robinhold and Rice 1970; Mouratoff and Scott 1973). These conditions are the main manifestations of malnutrition in modern societies. The factors underlying the successful adaptation of the Inuit to their extraordinarily narrow food base have been discussed elsewhere (Draper 1977) and are further examined in the context of current knowledge in the following sections.

Sources of Metabolic Fuel
The Inuit native diet frequently is characterized as being high in protein or high in fat, but from the standpoint of metabolic adaptation, its most important feature is its low content of carbohydrate. In the absence of plant sources of starch and sugars, carbohydrates in the diet were limited to small amounts of glycogen and the sugar moieties of the glycoproteins and glycolipids present in animal tissues.

The postprandial energy state following consumption of the modern mixed diet, in which carbohydrates constitute the main source of energy, is marked by the conversion of excess glucose to fat for energy storage. The postprandial state following consumption of a carnivorous diet is marked by the obligatory synthesis of glucose, which is essential for brain function and other metabolic processes. Inasmuch as fatty acids, the main source of energy in the diet, cannot be converted to glucose, most of the glucose required must be obtained from gluconeogenic amino acids. Glycerol, the backbone of dietary triglycerides (fat) and of phospholipids, is an additional but minor metabolic source of glucose.

Because of its low carbohydrate content, the native Inuit diet had to be sufficiently high in protein, not only to supply the amino acids required for the synthesis of body proteins but to maintain normoglycemia as well. In some Inuit food subcultures, such as that of the caribou eaters of the Arctic tundra, pro-

tein (rather than fat) probably constituted the main source of energy in the diet, because caribou is much lower in fat than is modern beef.

The high rate of gluconeogenesis in the Inuit requires large amounts of enzymes (which consist mainly of proteins) for the conversion of amino acids to glucose and for the conversion of waste amino acid nitrogen to urea. These processes, respectively, account for the large livers and urine volumes long associated with Arctic Inuit. Increased enzyme synthesis in response to an increase in substrate concentration (so-called feed forward regulation of enzyme reactions) is a major form of metabolic adaptation to changes in diet composition.

Sources of Vitamins
The vitamins of the large B-complex group function as cofactors for enzymes involved in the metabolism of many biochemical compounds, including amino acids, fatty acids, and glucose. Consequently, there is a natural association between the amounts of these vitamins and the amounts of enzyme proteins present in the tissues of animals. Most of the protein in the liver, where many of these transactions occur, consists of enzyme proteins. This association is most apparent in the case of vitamin B_6, which functions exclusively in enzymatic transformations of amino acids, such as the aminotransferase reactions required to remove their nitrogen groups before their conversion to glucose.

As a result, the requirement for this vitamin is proportional to protein intake. Although the high-protein Inuit diet generates a high B_6 requirement, the risk of B_6 deficiency fails to increase with protein intake because of the strong association between this vitamin and protein in the diet. There is a similar, though less strong, association between other B vitamins and dietary protein. In contrast to cereal-based food cultures, there is no history of deficiencies of the B-complex vitamins among carnivores. The adequacy of the aboriginal Inuit diet in these nutrients was further ensured by their custom of eating food in the fresh, frozen, or lightly cooked state.

The nutriture of the Inuit with respect to vitamin C, a vitamin generally associated with fruits and vegetables, has long held a fascination for nutritionists. As for other apparent mysteries about Inuit nutrition, however, their freedom from vitamin C deficiency is readily explicable in terms of current knowledge relative to the amount of vitamin C required for the prevention of scurvy, its concentration and stability in the diet, and the capacity for storage. Prevention of scurvy requires 10 milligrams (mg) or less per day, an amount available from the fresh or frozen raw tissues of animals that synthesize it. The liver of land and sea mammals, often eaten fresh while still warm, is a good source of vitamin C. Seal liver, an Inuit delicacy, contains about 35 mg per 100 grams (g), an amount sufficient to provide for significant storage (Geraci and Smith 1979).

The epidemics of scurvy among Europeans in the eighteenth and nineteenth centuries were caused by the oxidation of vitamin C in grains and salt meats during long sea and land voyages and by its leaching from foods during cooking in water. Further, it is not necessary, as a recent advertisement claims, "to get your vitamin C every day." The amount of vitamin C stored by a typical adult in the United States or Canada is sufficient to prevent a deficiency, in the absence of any intake, for about 30 days (Baker et al. 1971).

The need to envelop the body in heavy clothing against the cold during the long winter night deprives the Arctic Inuit of solar radiation, the main source of vitamin D in temperate and tropical climates. The Inuit experience demonstrates that at least in some environments, there is an absolute dietary requirement for vitamin D, a nutrient that some have proposed be reclassified as a hormone because it can be synthesized in adequate amounts in the skin with sufficient exposure to sunlight. The high concentrations of vitamin D in the oils of fish and fish-eating sea mammals make up for limited synthesis of vitamin D in the skin during the Arctic winter, as demonstrated by the lack of historical evidence of rickets in Inuit children and of osteomalacia in adults consuming the native diet. These oils also provide an abundance of vitamin A. The occurrence of toxic amounts of vitamin A in polar bear liver, accumulated through the fish and seal food chain of this species, forms the basis of one of the strongest Inuit food taboos.

The vitamin E nutriture of the Inuit is unusual because their carnivorous diet contains no cereal oils, the main source of vitamin E in the modern mixed diet. Further, the high concentration of polyunsaturated fatty acids from fish and marine mammals in this diet generates a high requirement for vitamin E to maintain their oxidative stability in the tissues. Nonetheless, analysis of the blood plasma of Northern Alaskan Inuit has revealed concentrations of vitamin E similar to those of the general U.S. population (Wo and Draper 1975).

The explanation for this finding lies in a difference in the forms of vitamin E present in carnivorous and mixed diets. Although the total amount of vitamin E present in the mixed diet is substantially higher than in the carnivorous diet, only about one-quarter of the total occurs in the form of alpha-tocopherol; the rest is present mainly as gamma-tocopherol, which has only about 10 percent as much biological activity. In contrast, animal tissues contain almost exclusively alpha-tocopherol. Consequently, the amount of vitamin E in the Inuit native diet, expressed as biological activity, is comparable to that in the mixed diet.

As is evident from the pungent odor of volatile products of lipid peroxidation that permeates Inuit villages in summer, the concentration of vitamin E in the highly unsaturated oils of aquatic species is inadequate to protect them from oxidative rancidity when they are exposed to an air environment, even though it is sufficient at the reduced oxygen tension and temperature of their natural aquatic environment. In general, the concentration of vitamin E in plant oils and animal fats is proportional to the amount necessary to stabilize the unsaturated fatty acids they contain. For example, the inheritance of vitamin E and polyunsaturated fatty acids in maize is genetically linked, so that varieties high in polyunsaturated fatty acids are also high in vitamin E (Levy 1973). Fish, seal, and whale oils, on the other hand, impose a burden on the vitamin E requirement that must be borne by other food sources of the vitamin. Although Canadian Indians consuming a diet high in fish have been found to have a plasma vitamin E level below that of the general population (Desai and Lee 1974), dietary vitamin E deficiency has not been documented.

Sources of Inorganic Nutrients

Human requirements for inorganic nutrients (often loosely referred to as minerals) are qualitatively similar to those of other mammalian species. Hence, the carcasses of animals are a good source of these nutrients in human diets, provided they are eaten in their entirety, as they were (less the skin and compact bone) by the Arctic Inuit. The inorganic elements most frequently at risk of deficiency in human diets are iron and iodine. Iron deficiency, often precipitated by intestinal infections and diarrhea, is most prevalent among malnourished consumers of low-protein vegetarian diets. Iron is accumulated in animal tissues in the iron-binding liver proteins hemosiderin and ferritin, which, together with hemoglobin and other iron-containing proteins, provide an abundance of bioavailable iron in a carnivorous diet. Risk of iron deficiency is reduced by an adaptive feedback mechanism that increases the efficiency of iron absorption on a low-iron diet. This mechanism also serves to prevent iron toxicity on the high-meat Inuit diet by suppressing the absorption of excess dietary iron.

Iodine deficiency is a prevalent problem in various human populations, arising in some cases from its deficiency in the soil (for example, the "goiter belt" around Hudson's Bay) and in other cases from the ingestion of plant goitrogens. Neither of these circumstances applies to the Inuit native diet, which is devoid of goitrogens and is high in iodine from foods of aquatic origin. This diet also contains an abundance of zinc, which is present in marginal amounts in cereal diets high in phytin, a component of fiber that inhibits zinc absorption.

Meat has a very low calcium content, and in the absence of dairy foods, which supply about 75 percent of the calcium in the food supply of most industrialized societies, the spongy trabecular bone of land and sea mammals and the soft bones of fish are an essential source of this element in the native Inuit diet. Bone chewing, a nutritional as well as a social custom, is now nearly extinct, and a low consumption of dairy products has resulted in a calcium intake among the Inuit that is both below the historic level and below intake level currently recommended in the United States for optimal development of the skeleton during growth and for its stability during aging. However, the intake is comparable to the amount delivered by cereal-based diets, and there is no clear evidence that the lowered intake results in a state of calcium deficiency.

The body has an ability to adapt to a range of calcium intakes by modulating the efficiency of calcium absorption from the intestine. This ability, which serves to protect against both calcium deficiency and toxicity, is one of the best understood of metabolic adaptations to a change in nutrient intake. It involves an increase in the synthesis of parathyroid hormone in response to a small decline in serum calcium concentration caused by a decrease in calcium intake. This hormone effects an increase in the renal synthesis of 1,25-dihydroxycholecalciferol, the active form of vitamin D, which, in turn, enhances the synthesis of a calcium transport protein in the intestinal epithelium that is required for the active absorption of calcium.

The result is an increase in the efficiency of calcium absorption following a reduction in intake that restores serum calcium homeostasis. Whether this mechanism is fully successful in enabling adequate amounts of calcium to be absorbed to maximize skeletal development during growth and minimize bone loss during aging is a question of current interest with respect to the relationship between calcium intake and the incidence of osteoporosis.

The Inuit of Northern Alaska and Canada undergo a more rapid rate of aging bone loss, a risk factor for osteoporosis, than Caucasians consuming the mixed diet (Mazess and Mathur 1974, 1975). The high-protein, high-phosphorus, low-calcium content of the native diet has been implicated in this phenomenon. However, the high rate of aging bone loss in the Inuit does not appear to be associated with a high incidence of osteoporotic bone fractures.

This may be explained by a difference in bone morphology between the Inuit and Caucasians; the shorter, thicker bones of the Inuit may have a greater weight-bearing capacity than the longer, thinner bones of Caucasians. The rapid bone loss in the Inuit, nevertheless, may have relevance for the high incidence of fractures among elderly consumers of the "Western diet," which contains about twice as much protein as necessary to meet the protein requirement and an excess of phosphorus arising from a natural association of this element with protein and from the widespread use of phosphate food additives.

Oxidation of excess sulfur amino acids present in high-protein diets generates hydrogen ions and sulfate (sulfuric acid) that is excreted in the urine. On a high-protein (usually high-meat) diet the urine consequently is acid, whereas on a low-protein (usually high-cereal) diet it is near neutrality or slightly alkaline. Unopposed acidification of the renal filtrate decreases the reabsorption of calcium and increases its loss in the urine.

In experiments on adults fed purified proteins, this loss was found to amount to 300 mg per day, indicative of rapid bone loss, at a daily protein intake of 95 g, an amount well within the range of intakes on the mixed diet and low by Inuit standards (Linkswiler, Joyce, and Anand 1974). The protein intake of aboriginal Inuit adults in northwest Greenland has been estimated at nearly 400 g per day (Bang, Dyerberg, and Sinclair 1980). On a high-protein diet composed of normal foodstuffs, however, the decrease in calcium reabsorption by the proximal renal tubules caused by urine acidification is not unopposed.

The increased intake of phosphorus on high-protein diets results in a depression of serum calcium and a consequent increase in the synthesis of parathyroid hormone, which stimulates calcium reabsorption from the renal tubules and thereby counteracts the calciuretic action of excess dietary protein. Whether these opposing effects of dietary protein and phosphorus on urinary calcium excretion are always fully offsetting is not clear. However, it has become apparent that the most important nutrient ratio, from the standpoint of bone homeostasis, is not the ratio of calcium to phosphorus, which has received most attention, but the ratio of protein to phosphorus, which is fundamental to the maintenance of calcium balance on a high-protein diet. Whether the increased rate of bone resorption associated with excess dietary phosphate and protein observed on the Inuit diet and on the high-protein modern diet (Calvo, Kumar, and Heath 1988) results in increased bone loss and risk for osteoporosis is still controversial.

Metabolic Adaptation to Dietary Lipids

Danish studies on nutritional adaptation among the Inuit of northeast Greenland undertaken in the late 1960s and early 1970s led to an explanation for their low incidence of cardiovascular disease and to important innovations in methods for its prevention and treatment in modern societies. These studies revealed a protective effect of the unusual fatty acids present in the fish and marine mammal oils consumed in large quantities by the Inuit. Such oils contain polyunsaturated fatty acids with extremely long carbon chains (up to 22 carbon atoms) and unusually large numbers of double bonds (up to 6), characteristics that confer on them a low melting point that enables aquatic species to maintain membrane fluidity at the temperature of their environment. In contrast, the polyunsaturated fatty acids of cereal oils, the main source of fat in the modern mixed diet, contain up to 18 carbon atoms and up to 3 double bonds.

Another important difference is that the first double bond in most of the highly unsaturated fatty acids in the Inuit diet occurs between the third and fourth carbon atoms (n-3 fatty acids), whereas the first double bond in most of the fatty acids in cereals occurs between the sixth and seventh carbon atoms (n-6 fatty acids). The metabolic significance of this distinction is that the n-3 and n-6 fatty acids are precursors of two distinct groups of hormones, the prostacyclins and the prostaglandins, that have significantly different effects on the metabolism of blood lipids. They therefore also differently affect the risk of heart attack. Prostacyclins reduce the plasma triglyceride (fat) level, as well as the propensity of the blood to clot (and hence the risk of an embolism). A negative effect of the high n-3 fatty acid content of the Inuit diet is its tendency to cause nosebleeds (Fortuine 1971).

As a result of these findings, increased consumption of fish has been recommended as part of the Western diet, and concentrates of n-3 fatty acids prepared from fish oil are used in the clinical management of cardiovascular disease. The n-3 fatty acids have become recognized as dietary essentials for both children and adults, and official recommendations have been issued relative to their desirable level of intake (National Research Council, U.S. Academy of Sciences 1989; Health and Welfare Canada 1990). This series of events serves as an example of the value of cross-cultural research as a source of information relevant to the nutritional health of all human societies.

There is little doubt that hypercholesterolemia is a risk factor for heart attacks, and a plasma cholesterol level of 200 mg per deciliter or less has been selected as a desirable goal. Diet recommendations for the prevention of heart disease in modern societies call for a reduction in cholesterol intake to 300 mg per day or less (National Research Council, U.S. Academy of Sciences 1989; Health and Welfare Canada 1990). In light of these recommendations, the rarity of cardiovascular disease among the Inuit (Thomas 1927), whose traditional diet is extraordinarily high in cholesterol, seems anomalous.

Electrocardiographic recordings made on Northern Alaskan Inuit adults in the 1970s (by which time only about 50 percent of their calories were derived from native foods) revealed an incidence of abnormalities only half that recorded in a reference population of U.S. Caucasian adults (Colbert, Mann, and Hursh 1978). Indigenous foods in the partially acculturated diet of a cohort of adult Inuit living in the northwest Alaskan village of Point Hope in 1970 averaged 918 mg per day (range 420 to 1650 mg) (Feldman et al. 1978).

Studies on the epidemiology of hypercholesterolemia carried out between 1937 and 1961 showed "a strong tendency towards normocholesterolemia . . . among the unacculturated Eskimo groups but increased rates of elevated serum cholesterol among modernized Eskimos" (Feldman et al. 1978: 174). It is noteworthy that the plasma cholesterol levels of the Inuit during that period were similar to those of adults in the general population of the

United States, despite a twofold difference or more in cholesterol intake.

The explanation for this discrepancy has been provided by epidemiological and laboratory research on the relationship between the intake of cholesterol in the diet and the level of cholesterol in the plasma. The Inuit experience is consistent with the conclusion of A. Keys, J. T. Anderson, and F. Grande (1965), the originators of the connection between dietary fat and heart disease, and with the observations of subsequent investigators: In the normal, healthy, adult population, the level of cholesterol in the diet has only a minor influence on blood cholesterol.

The current public preoccupation with dietary cholesterol and the promotion of "cholesterol-free" foods is attributable to a seemingly logical assumption that lowering cholesterol intake should lower plasma cholesterol. This is often true in patients with clinical hypercholesterolemia, a condition associated with genetic and various metabolic disorders, including diabetes and obesity, in which the metabolic control mechanism that normally downregulates the synthesis of cholesterol in the body in response to a high intake in the diet is impaired.

This is, however, weak justification for imposing a limit of 300 mg per day on the intake of cholesterol by "the generally healthy population" for whom diet recommendations are issued (National Research Council, U.S. Academy of Sciences 1989; Health and Welfare Canada 1990). The "cholesterol free" label on foods has been used as a "red herring" to attract attention away from the more important characteristics of foods from the standpoint of their effect on plasma cholesterol, namely the amount and composition of the fat they contain.

Current nutrition recommendations in industrialized countries include a call for a reduced consumption of "red meat" as a means of lowering the risk of cardiovascular disease. This edict seems paradoxical in view of the reported absence of this disease among Inuit consumers of the native meat diet. It is aimed at the consumption of beef, which bears the stigma (no longer fully justified) that it is high in fat and saturated fatty acids and low in polyunsaturated fatty acids. (The term "red meat" itself seems anomalous, since the redder meat is, the lower it is in fat.)

Contrary to the general impression that all animal tissues are high in saturated and low in polyunsaturated fatty acids, the tissues of the fish and of the land and sea mammals that constituted most of the Inuit diet are the reverse. The lipids of seal, whale, walrus, and polar bear meat contain 15 to 25 percent polyunsaturated fatty acids, consisting mostly of fatty acids of the n-3 type (Wo and Draper 1975). In contrast to beef, caribou meat is so low in fat that the Inuit dip it in seal oil to improve its palatability. The lipids of caribou muscle have been found to contain 5.6 percent arachidonic acid and 15.4 percent linoleic acid of the n-6 polyunsaturated fatty acid series.

In contrast, values of 0.5 percent arachidonic acid and 2.5 percent linoleic acid have been reported for beef muscle (Link et al. 1970). Most of the polyunsaturated fatty acids in both caribou and beef muscle are located in the phospholipids of cell membranes. The phospholipids of beef muscle have a level of polyunsaturates comparable to that in caribou muscle (Link et al. 1970), but have been swamped by saturated fatty acids as a result of selection of beef animals for "marbling" with intramuscular fat to increase the palatability of their meat.

Current diet recommendations in the United States and Canada also call for a reduction in fat intake to 30 percent of calories or less as a further means of reducing the risk of cardiovascular disease (National Research Council, U.S. Academy of Sciences 1989; Health and Welfare Canada 1990). The experience of the Inuit, however, indicates that it is the composition of dietary fat, rather than its level in the diet, that is of primary importance in the prevention of heart disease.

This view is supported by the low incidence of cardiovascular disease among consumers of the "Mediterranean diet," which contains a preponderance of monounsaturated fatty acids derived mainly from olive oil used in cooking. These acids replace more saturated than polyunsaturated fatty acids in the diet, thereby shifting the ratio in favor of polyunsaturates. The role of this ratio is also indicated by an analysis of changes in the composition of dietary fat in the United States from the 1960s through the 1980s, an interval during which the death rate from heart disease declined by about 25 percent (Stephen and Wald 1990).

The data show that there was an increase in the ratio of polyunsaturated to saturated fatty acids in the diet over this period from about 0.25 to 0.50. This increase was due mainly to a decrease in the intake of total fat, which entailed a discrimination against "visible fat" (such as the peripheral fat around the outside of steak) that consists mostly of saturated fatty acids. These observations further indicate that it is the composition of dietary fat, rather than the amount of fat consumed, that is of prime importance in the prevention of cardiovascular disease. Reducing total fat intake, however, is the only practical means of increasing the ratio of polyunsaturated to saturated fatty acids in the modern diet of industrialized countries.

The ratio of polyunsaturates to saturates in the native Inuit diet is difficult to estimate with accuracy and is highly variable, but it clearly exceeds the ratio of 0.50 calculated for the U.S. diet in the 1980s (Stephen and Wald 1990) and probably exceeds the 1.0 ratio proposed in modern diet recommendations. Inuit diets in northwestern Greenland in 1976 were estimated to have a ratio of 0.84, compared to a ratio of 0.24 in the diet of Danes (Bang et al. 1980). In addition to a reduction in total fat consumption to 30 percent of energy intake, current recommendations call

for a 1:1:1 ratio of polyunsaturates to saturates to monounsaturates (Health and Welfare Canada 1990). The protection from cardiovascular disease afforded by the profile of fatty acids in the native Inuit diet is encouragement that implementation of these recommendations will confer a similar benefit on modern societies.

Adaptation to Dietary Sugars

The Inuit of western Greenland and northwestern Alaska are uniquely susceptible to congenital primary sucrase-isomaltase deficiency, a condition presumably related to the absence of sucrose in their traditional diet over many centuries (McNair et al. 1972; Raines, Draper, and Bergan 1973). Its epidemiology is familial, and studies on Greenland Inuit have indicated that it is due to a deficiency of an autosomal recessive gene. Its incidence was estimated to be about 3 percent in northwestern Alaska and 10 percent in a sample of hospital patients and staff in northeast Greenland.

This deficiency has a major effect on the capacity of those Inuit affected to deal with the modern diet. For example, children are unable to eat an ice-cream cone or drink a bottle of carbonated beverage unless it contains a synthetic sweetener in place of sucrose. In this respect, sucrase deficiency differs from lactase deficiency, in which lactase production declines during growth but persists at a reduced level in adulthood. Sucrase deficiency, a recently recognized cause of diarrhea in Inuit children, is present in acute form from birth.

The options available for dealing with it include replacing sucrose with other sugars (such as invert sugar in honey), using synthetic sweeteners, or taking oral sucrase preparations made from the intestinal juices of animals. Sucrase-isomaltase deficiency appears to be absent among Alaskan Inuit residents of the Subarctic, where the traditional diet has contained sucrose present in fruits and berries.

As in most societies (excepting mainly those of northern European origin), Inuit children undergo a progressive decrease in the intestinal synthesis of lactase during growth to a level that limits the amount of milk and milk products that can be digested in adulthood (Kretchmer 1972). Based on the results of a standard lactose tolerance test – which involves administering 50 g of lactose (the amount present in a liter of cow's milk), measuring the subsequent rise in plasma glucose, if any, and recording any adverse clinical reactions, such as abdominal cramps or diarrhea – about 70 percent of Inuit adults have been characterized as "lactose intolerant" (Gudmand-Hoyer and Jarnum 1969). However, if given a dose of 10 g of lactose (the amount present in a cup of milk), a large majority of Inuit adults experience no adverse symptoms and, therefore, from a nutritional standpoint, may be regarded as "lactose tolerant."

With respect to their ability to digest lactose, the Inuit resemble a majority of the world's population.

Alaskan Inuit children routinely consume milk or other dairy products as part of a school lunch program. The breakpoint in lactose tolerance in adults typically falls between 10 and 20 g (Raines et al. 1973); intakes in this range can be repeated after an interval of several hours. Hence, for most individuals, lactose intolerance is not a serious impediment to the acquisition of the calcium and other nutrients present in dairy foods.

Adaptation to the Modern Diet

Historically, the greatest threat to the nutritional status of the Arctic Inuit was famine, triggered by failure to catch a bowhead whale or by the failure of the caribou to run. In such exigencies, seals were the most reliable dietary staple. The Inuit population was kept in balance with its food supply by periodic famines, by a high infant mortality, by an extremely high rate of fatal accidents among adults pursuing the hunting culture, and if necessary, by infanticide. They had no nutrition education and no need for it. Their custom of eating animals almost in their entirety provided them with all the nutrients necessary for nutritional health, assuming their foods were available in sufficient amounts. There were no "junk foods" in their diet. Food not eaten fresh was preserved in the frozen state in the ice cellars that are still prevalent in Arctic Inuit villages. The central nutritional imperative was simply to get enough to eat.

For the first time since they migrated across the Bering Strait several thousand years ago, the Inuit in the twentieth century have been confronted with the necessity of making significant food choices in order to be well fed. Fractionation of primary foodstuffs by the modern food-manufacturing industry has generated multitudes of products of highly variable nutritional quality that must be reassembled in specific combinations to ensure a balanced diet. This necessity has led to the development of a set of rules for selecting proper combinations of foods that are inculcated into children by their parents and teachers and communicated to the public through nutrition education programs. To assist consumers in following these rules, a list of the nutrients that processed foods contain must be put on their labels, including the contribution of one serving to the recommended daily intake of each nutrient. A large government bureaucracy is devoted to ensuring that foods actually contain the amounts of nutrients listed on the label, and another agency is responsible for determining whether claims made for their efficacy in the prevention of disease are valid.

To primitive peoples whose only previous nutritional imperative was to get enough to eat, dealing with the complexities of the modern diet presents serious problems of nutritional adaptation. These problems are reflected in the poor nutritional status of Inuit and Amerindian inhabitants of the urban centers of Alaska and Canada. The nutritional health of urban Inuits is inferior to that of their forebears, as

well as to that of their Arctic contemporaries who still maintain a semblance of the traditional diet and lifestyle (Colbert et al. 1978).

The younger generation of Inuit, like younger generations of most other native minorities, has abandoned the traditional diet almost entirely. The incidence of obesity, hypertension, and cardiovascular disease among Alaskan Inuit follows an increasing gradient from the high Arctic to the Subarctic to the modern cities of the south (Colbert et al. 1978). The incidence of diabetes is also increasing, but is still substantially lower than in Caucasians (Thouez et al. 1990; Young et al. 1990).

The decline in the nutritional status of the Inuit in the second half of the twentieth century has more to do with psychosocial factors than with a lack of nutritious foods. Educational and technical deficiencies, loss of social status in the community, deterioration of cultural values, lack of a sense of community, and discrimination in employment are factors in their poor nutritional status. The modern Inuit are at a watershed in social acculturation, unwilling to revert to their traditional lifestyle, yet unable to cope successfully with the complexities of an industrialized society.

Metabolic Adaptation to Cereal-Based Diets

The cereal-based diets consumed by the inhabitants of Southeast Asia and of Central and South America are in direct contrast to those consumed by the Inuit; that is, they are high in carbohydrates and low in protein and fat, rather than vice versa. Consequently, the bioenergetic transformations imposed by this diet, are also reversed. Fat stored in the adipose tissues is formed primarily by lipogenesis from glucose released in carbohydrate digestion, rather than by the fatty acids released by fat digestion. As polyunsaturated fatty acids cannot be synthesized in the body, fat formed from glucose consists mainly of saturated and monounsaturated fatty acids. In contrast to the massive conversion of excess amino acids to glucose on the Inuit diet, most of the limited amounts of amino acids in cereal diets are used for the synthesis of tissue proteins.

In addition to food shortages caused by crop failures, cereal-based food cultures have been subject to epidemic deficiencies of specific nutrients, notably beriberi caused by thiamine deficiency in the case of rice diets and pellagra caused by niacin deficiency in the case of maize diets. These diseases have created a prevalent impression that cereal diets are low in nutritional quality, but, in fact, these afflictions were the result of a disruption of native food cultures by foreign influences or the failure of foreigners to adopt the native culture.

Replacement of brown rice with more prestigious polished rice, a minor food in Europe but the staple food in Southeast Asia, removed most of the thiamine from the diet and resulted in a classic example of so-called cultural malnutrition. The traditional method of preparing maize practiced by the Mexican Indians, which entailed grinding it in lime water, was not followed by the black and "poor white" populations of African and European origin who inhabited the southern United States.

Their maize diet had several nutritional liabilities. The niacin in maize is present in complex forms from which it must be released by some type of hydrolysis, which in the native Indian culture took the form of alkaline hydrolysis effected by grinding with lime water. Further, maize protein is low in tryptophan, an amino acid that can be converted to niacin in the body. Although pellagrins consumed substantial amounts of pork, it consisted mostly of fat ("sowbelly") that contained little niacin, protein, or tryptophan. The Indian practice of grinding maize in lime water presumably arose out of experience. Not only was it instrumental in protecting them from the ravages of pellagra but it also contributed substantially to their intake of calcium, which is low in cereal grains.

Cereal diets are lower in protein than modern mixed diets and tend to be associated with protein-deficiency diseases, such as kwashiorkor, a severe condition affecting impoverished children during the postweaning period. It is marked by an edema that wrongly gives the impression that the children are of normal weight. When their serum protein level is restored by providing enough dietary protein, the edema dissipates, revealing severe emaciation (marasmus) caused by inadequate energy intake. This condition of protein–calorie malnutrition can be prevented by providing an adequate cereal-based weaning diet, indicating that the main etiological factor is a lack of food, rather than a lack of protein specifically.

When sufficient calories are supplied to prevent the utilization of dietary amino acids for energy production, these acids become available for the synthesis of tissue proteins. Most cereal-based diets, particularly if they contain (as they usually do) small amounts of animal products, such as fish, chicken, eggs, or meat, provide enough protein to satisfy the requirement for this nutrient. Diets based on cassava, a root vegetable with no redeeming nutritional qualities other than as a source of calories, are an exception to this generalization.

Vitamin B_{12} occurs only in foods of animal origin, which, therefore, must be included in all so-called vegetarian food cultures. Strict vegetarian diets, such as that of the "vegans," can result in macrocytic anemia and irreversible neurological damage caused by a deficiency of this vitamin. On the other hand, most of the B-complex vitamins and vitamin E are plentiful in the bran and germ of cereal grains. The vegetables and fruits that normally constitute a major part of vegetarian diets provide folic acid, vitamin C, and vitamin K and are good sources of beta-carotene, a precursor of vitamin A in the body. Yet, until programs of vitamin A supplementation were instituted in the mid–twentieth century, vitamin A deficiency was the main cause of blindness among children in Indonesia and other Southeast Asian localities, despite the fact that edible plants capable of preventing it were readily available.

Cereal diets have been of particular interest from the standpoint of mineral nutrition. Phytin, a component of the fiber of cereals (particularly wheat), binds dietary zinc, preventing its absorption and, at high intakes, precipitating a zinc deficiency. Dwarfism among poor Middle Eastern children, long presumed to be of congenital origin, was found to be due to chronic zinc deficiency caused by the consumption of large quantities of unleavened wheat bread (Prasad et al. 1963). Yeast fermentation degrades phytin and, thereby, prevents zinc deficiency, a relationship that evidently escaped recognition in this food culture for generations, even though the relationship between fermentation and the production of alcohol (presumably a higher priority) was known and exploited. Phytin also binds calcium, but to a lesser extent, and the capacity to adapt to a low intake of this element aids in the prevention of calcium deficiency.

Unlike carnivorous diets, which in general contain adequate amounts of essential trace elements to meet human requirements (because these elements are also essential in the diet of food animals), the trace element content of plants often reflects the content of the soil on which they were grown. Keshan disease, an acute cardiomyopathy among children in the Keshan district of China, is caused by an extremely low concentration of selenium in local soils and, consequently, in the cereals grown on these soils. Locally grown plant foods constitute the bulk of the diet in this area. Such deficiencies are less likely to occur on mixed diets, which contain plant foods grown on a variety of soils, as well as foods of animal origin.

The low calcium content of cereal diets is of current interest with respect to the role of this element in the prevention of osteoporotic bone fractures in elderly adults. Paradoxically, the incidence of hip fractures associated with the cereal-based food cultures of Japan and other Asian countries appears to be lower than it is in Western countries where calcium intake, derived mainly from dairy foods, is substantially higher (Fujita 1992). Whether this apparent anomaly reflects a minor role of calcium in the prevention of hip fractures, a high calcium requirement generated by the high-protein Western diet, a difference in lifestyle, a difference in the incidence of falls, a genetic involvement, or the effect of some unidentified factor is a question raised by cross-cultural studies on the epidemiology of osteoporotic bone disease.

Adaptation to Dietary Toxins

Plants did not evolve with the idea that they should be good to eat. In fact, the synthesis by plants of substances toxic to their predators (humans, animals, insects, and microbes) has been a major factor in survival to the present day. Humans and animals have eaten them at their own peril, sorting out those that, based on experience, could be safely added to their diet. A. C. Leopold and R. Ardrey (1972) have developed the thesis that the presence of toxins in plants was an important determinant of the dietary habits of primitive societies.

In addition to natural insecticides and substances poisonous to animals, plants contain a multitude of compounds that make them unsafe for human consumption: hemagglutinins, enzyme inhibitors, cyanogens, antivitamins, carcinogens, neurotoxins, and allergens, among others. Accounts of their occurrence have been given elsewhere (Ory 1981; Lampe 1986). L. S. Gold and colleagues (1992) have argued that nearly all the carcinogens in the diet are of natural rather than – as widely perceived – industrial origin. Although rigorous toxicological testing of food additives on laboratory animals is required before they are approved for human consumption, no such tests have been applied to the natural toxins present in the diet. Broadening of testing for carcinogenicity to include these compounds recently has been recommended (Gold et al. 1992).

Compounds toxic to humans are more likely to be encountered in foods of plant origin because they have not been subjected to toxicological screening by first having been consumed by animals. Many toxins that are not overtly toxic to animals are at least partially catabolized by enzymatic detoxification systems present in animal tissues, notably the microsomal mixed-function oxidase system in the liver. Some toxins in plants are destroyed by cooking, but this method of food preparation appears to have been practiced only during the last 20 percent of human existence (Grivetti 1981).

Removal of toxins from plants by selective breeding and food processing has made it possible to add many new foods to the modern mixed diet. In addition, commerce in foodstuffs has diluted the high concentrations of toxins present in plants grown in specific localities. For example, the soil in some areas of the western United States contains high levels of selenium, an element that is accumulated in the seed of wheat and other cereals. When these locally grown grains constitute the bulk of the diet fed to farm animals, they can cause severe symptoms of selenium toxicity and even death. It must be presumed that they also caused at least mild toxicity among the early settlers in the same areas, for whom locally grown grains made up a major part of the diet. Modern commerce in foodstuffs has resulted in dilution of high-selenium foods and removed the risk of toxicity among consumers of the mixed diet.

Numerous substances have been added to the modern diet to improve its nutritional quality and safety. The required listing of these supplementary nutrients and additives on the label of processed foods has created a prevalent impression among consumers that some products consist mainly of synthetic industrial chemicals of questionable safety. In fact, nearly all food supplements and additives are either natural substances or exact replicas of natural substances already present in the diet or in the body (Branen, Davidson, and Salminen 1989). Most cases of food poisoning in modern societies are caused by microbial toxins formed as a result of careless handling and preservation in the home.

The few additives of purely synthetic origin have been subjected to the exhaustive life-cycle testing on laboratory animals required by food safety laws. Two such substances are the lipid antioxidants, BHA and BHT, used to prevent the oxidation of polyunsaturated fatty acids in foods, a widespread problem in the food industry resulting in flavor deterioration and the formation of products that pose a possible health risk. The synthetic sweeteners used in low-calorie beverages were approved only after years, or even decades, of safety evaluation. As indicated, there are several grounds upon which the modern diet can be criticized, but the common impression that it is less safe, in toxicological terms, than so-called natural diets is without foundation. Indeed, the reverse is the case.

The epidemiology of cancer in modern societies shows correlations of uncertain interpretation with diets high in fat and protein, but none with the use of food additives (Doll 1992; Lutz and Schlatter 1992). There are correlations, probably signifying causation, between the presence of certain substances in the diet and a high incidence of specific cancers. These include stomach cancer among Japanese and other Asians who consume large quantities of heavily salted foods, and liver cancer in Madagascans who consume moldy peanuts containing the potent carcinogen aflatoxin B_1. There is no current information as to the possible role of natural chemicals in the estimated 35 percent of cancers in industrialized societies that are "diet related" (Doll 1992). W. K. Lutz and J. Schlatter (1992) have pointed out that this figure is "provocatively close" to the prevalence of overnutrition (that is, obesity) in these societies.

There remain a number of toxicological risks associated with the modern diet that are preventable or avoidable: formation of microbial toxins in poorly preserved foods; overdosing or accidental poisoning with synthetic vitamins; ingestion of harmful bacteria, residual plant enzymes, and antinutrients resulting from inadequate cooking; consumption of carcinogenic amino acid derivatives produced by overcooking meats; and ingestion of natural toxicants in such foods as mushrooms. There are also numerous allergens present in foods that seriously affect food selection by individuals but which do not have an important influence on general food cultures. The occurrence of immunological toxicants in foods has been discussed by L. W. Mayron (1981).

Cultural Factors in Nutritional Adaptation

There are many dietary practices that are not explicable in terms of environmental, nutritional, or toxicological (that is, biological) determinants. They are attributable to traditions (religious, societal, and familial) that often distinguish one food culture from another, even when their practitioners share other common influences on food choices, such as food economics, social class, and occupational status. Traditional ceremonies surrounding the procurement of food are still in evidence among some hunting cultures, as exemplified in the ceremony held by the Arctic Inuit on the eve of the annual whale hunt, even though this hazardous undertaking is no longer necessary to meet their nutritional needs.

Religious prohibitions affect the consumption of beef, pork, dairy products, and fish, as well as processed foods that contain substances of animal origin. Adherents to some food cultures would rather starve than consume foods that are a common item in other cultures (for example, dog meat and insects). Food fads, prevalent in modern societies, have a major, but usually short-term, influence on food practices. The role of cultural factors as determinants of traditional and modern food habits is discussed in several reviews and books (Wing and Brown 1979; Grivetti 1981; Axelson 1986; Gordon 1987; Kittler and Sucher 1989).

Notwithstanding the strength of cultural traditions, studies on intersocietal migrants and aboriginal societies undergoing acculturation have shown that changes in food habits can occur relatively rapidly, particularly among the young. A diet survey conducted on the inhabitants of an Arctic Inuit village in the early 1970s showed that about 50 percent of calories were still derived from native foods in the diet of adults, compared to only about 25 percent in the diet of children, even though all foods were eaten at home (Raines and Heller 1978). A similar generation gap in the acceptance of new foods has been observed among Chinese immigrants to the United States (Axelson 1986).

Adaptation to a new food culture often begins with the preparation of new foods by traditional methods and by selection of commercially prepared facsimiles of traditional foods, such as prepared tortillas by Mexican Americans (Axelson 1986). P. G. Kittler and K. Sucher (1989) compared the traditional food cultures of Native Americans, that of the original European settlers, and that of recent immigrants from other countries. Further, they traced the changes in native and foreign food cultures that have taken place to the present time. They concluded that the modern mixed diet reflects a strong influence of European food traditions on the dietary habits of all segments of the population, but that there is also clear evidence of an influence of all the major food cultures brought to America, except those brought by blacks. Consumption of traditional Native American foods is confined mainly to Indian reservations. The decimation of the Amerindian food culture is reflected in an extraordinarily high incidence of diseases that are the modern hallmarks of malnutrition in America.

Paradoxically, overnutrition in industrialized societies is more prevalent among the poor than among the affluent. Analysis of the disposal of family income in the United States indicates that expenditures for food are not closely related to income (Popkin and Haines 1981). This finding is attributable to the low cost of food, which makes it possible for even the poor to conserve family income by buying inexpensive food items.

The relationship between the cost of food and its nutritional quality is also weak. The poor nutritional status of blacks and Native Americans is not due in any major degree to an inability to buy nutritious food. It is, more importantly, a reflection of a lack of education that precludes understanding the health risks associated with obesity, a low social status lacking the peer pressure to maintain normal body weight that prevails among the middle and upper classes of society, and incomplete emergence from the agrarian culture of the nineteenth and early twentieth centuries. It was only some 50 years ago that obesity was regarded as a sign of good health and a source of energy that could be called upon in times of ill health. Popular figures in Western social culture (Shakespeare's Falstaff and Santa Claus, for example) are portrayed as jolly, fat men. It is understandable, therefore, that the opposite perception of obesity has not yet permeated all levels of American society.

H. H. Draper

Bibliography

Axelson, M. L. 1986. The impact of culture on behavior. *Annual Reviews in Nutrition* 6: 345-63.

Baker, E. M., R. E. Hodges, J. Hood, et al. 1971. Metabolism of ^{14}C- and ^{3}H-labelled L-ascorbic acid in human scurvy. *American Journal of Clinical Nutrition* 24: 444-54.

Bang, H. O., J. Dyerberg, and H. M. Sinclair. 1980. The composition of the Eskimo food in northwestern Greenland. *American Journal of Clinical Nutrition* 33: 2657-61.

Branen, A. L., P. M. Davidson, and S. Salminen, eds. 1989. *Food additives.* New York.

Calvo, M. S., R. Kumar, and H. Heath. 1988. Elevated secretion and action of serum parathyroid hormone in young adults consuming high phosphorus, low calcium diets assembled from common foods. *Journal of Clinical Endocrinology and Metabolism* 66: 823-9.

Colbert, M. J., G. V. Mann, and L. M. Hursh. 1978. Clinical observations on nutritional health. In *Eskimos of northwest Alaska. A biological perspective,* ed. P. L. Jamison, S. L. Zegura, and F. A. Milan, 162-73. Stroudsburg, Pa.

Desai, I. D., and M. Lee. 1974. Plasma vitamin E and cholesterol relationship in western Canadian Indians. *American Journal of Clinical Nutrition* 27: 334-8.

Doll, R. 1992. The lessons of life: Keynote address to the Nutrition and Cancer Conference. *Cancer Research* (Supplement) 52: 2024s-9s.

Draper, H. H. 1977. The aboriginal Eskimo diet in modern perspective. *American Anthropologist* 79: 309-16.

Feldman, S. A., A. Rubinstein, C. B. Taylor, et al. 1978. Aspects of cholesterol, lipid, and carbohydrate metabolism. In *Eskimos of northwestern Alaska. A biological perspective*, ed. P. L. Jamison, S. L. Zegura, and F. A. Milan, 174-83. Stroudsburg, Pa.

Fortuine, R. 1971. The health of the Eskimos, as portrayed in the earliest written accounts. *Bulletin of the History of Medicine* 45: 97-114.

Fujita, T. 1992. Comparison of osteoporosis and calcium intake between Japan and the United States. *Proceedings of the Society for Experimental Biology and Medicine* 200: 149-52.

Geraci, J. R., and T. G. Smith. 1979. Vitamin C in the diet of Inuit hunters from Holman, Northwest Territories. *Arctic* 32: 135-9.

Gold, L. S., T. H. Slone, B. R. Stern, et al. 1992. Rodent carcinogens: Setting profiles. *Science* 258: 261-5.

Gordon, K. D. 1987. Evolutionary perspectives on human diet. In *Nutritional anthropology,* ed. F. E. Johnston, 3-40, New York.

Grivetti, L. E. 1981. Cultural nutrition: Anthropological and geographical themes. *Annual Reviews in Nutrition* 1: 47-68.

Gudmand-Hoyer, E., and S. Jarnum. 1969. Lactose malabsorption in Greenland Eskimos. *Acta Medica Scandinavica* 186: 235-7.

Health and Welfare Canada. 1990. *Nutrition recommendations.* Ottawa.

Keys, A., J. T. Anderson, and F. Grande. 1965. Serum cholesterol responses to changes in diet. II. The effect of cholesterol in the diet. *Metabolism* 14: 759-65.

Kittler, P. G., and K. Sucher. 1989. *Food and culture in America.* Florence, Ky.

Kretchmer, N. 1972. Lactose and lactase. *Scientific American* 227: 70-8.

Lampe, K. F. 1986. Toxic effects of plant toxins. In *Toxicology.* Third edition, ed. C. D. Klassen, M. O. Amdur, and J. Doull, 757-67. New York.

Leopold, A. C., and R. Ardrey. 1972. Toxic substances in plants and food habits of early man. *Science* 176: 512-14.

Levy, R. D. 1973. Genetics of the vitamin E content of corn grain. Ph.D. thesis, University of Illinois at Urbana-Champaign.

Link, B. A., R. W. Bray, R. G. Cassens, and R. G. Kaufman. 1970. Fatty acid composition of bovine skeletal muscle during growth. *Journal of Animal Science* 30: 726-31.

Linkswiler, H. M., C. L. Joyce, and C. R. Anand. 1974. Calcium retention of adult males as affected by level of protein and calcium intake. *Transactions of the New York Academy of Sciences,* Series II 36: 333-40.

Lutz, W. K., and J. Schlatter. 1992. Chemical carcinogens and overnutrition in diet-related cancer. *Carcinogenesis* 13: 2211-16.

Mayron, L. W. 1981. Food and chemicals as immunologic toxicants. In *Antinutrients and toxicants in foods,* ed. R. L. Ory, 117-41, Westport, Conn.

Mazess, R. B., and W. Mathur. 1974. Bone mineral content of northern Alaskan Eskimos. *American Journal of Clinical Nutrition* 27: 916-25.

1975. Bone mineral content of Canadian Eskimos. *Human Biology* 47: 45-63.

McNair, A., E. Gudmand-Hoyer, S. Jarnum, and L. Orrild. 1972. Sucrose malabsorption in Greenland. *British Medical Journal* 2: 19-21.

Mouratoff, G. J., and E. M. Scott. 1973. Diabetes mellitus in Eskimos after a decade. *Journal of the American Medical Association* 226: 1345-6.

National Research Council, U. S. Academy of Sciences. 1989. *Recommended dietary allowances.* Washington, D.C.

Ory, R. L., ed. 1981. *Antinutrients and natural toxicants in foods.* Westport, Conn.

Popkin, B. M., and P. S. Haines. 1981. Factors affecting food selection: The role of economics. *Journal of the American Dietetic Association* 79: 419-25.

Prasad, A. S., A. Miale, Jr., Z. Farid, et al. 1963. Zinc metabolism in patients with syndrome of iron deficiency anemia, hepatosplenomegaly, dwarfism and hypogonadism. *Journal of Laboratory and Clinical Medicine* 61: 537-49.

Raines, R. R., H. H. Draper, and J. G. Bergan. 1973. Sucrose, lactose, and glucose tolerance in northern Alaskan Eskimos. *American Journal of Clinical Nutrition* 26: 1185-90.

Raines, R. R., and C. A. Heller. 1978. An appraisal of the modern north Alaskan diet. In *Eskimos of north Alaska. A biological perspective,* ed. P. L. Jamison, S. L. Zegura, and F. A. Milan, 145-56. Stroudsburg, Pa.

Robinhold, D., and D. Rice. 1970. Cardiovascular health of Wainwright Eskimos. *Arctic Anthropology* 7: 83-5.

Stephansson, V. 1936. Adventures in diet. Reprinted from *Harper's Magazine* by the Institute of Meat Packers. Chicago.

Stephen, A. M., and N. J. Wald. 1990. Trends in individual consumption of dietary fat in the United States, 1920-1984. *American Journal of Clinical Nutrition* 52: 457-69.

Thomas, W. A. 1927. Health of a carnivorous race. *Journal of the American Medical Association* 88: 1559-60.

Thouez, J-P., J. M. Ekoe, P. M. Foggin, et al. 1990. Obesity, hypertension, hyperuricemia and diabetes mellitus among the Cree and Inuit of northern Quebec. *Arctic Medical Research* 49: 180-8.

Wing, E. S., and A. B. Brown. 1979. *Paleo-nutrition.* New York.

Wo, C. K. W., and H. H. Draper. 1975. Vitamin E status of Alaskan Eskimos. *American Journal of Clinical Nutrition* 28: 808-13.

Young, T. K., E. J. E. Szathmary, S. Evers, and B. Wheatley. 1990. Geographic distribution of diabetes mellitus among the native population of Canada: A national survey. *Social Science and Medicine* 31: 129-39.

VI.11 ❧ The Psychology of Food and Food Choice

We can think of the world, for any person, as divided into the self and everything else. The principal material breach of this fundamental dichotomy occurs in the act of ingestion, when something from the world (other) enters the body (self). The mouth is the guardian of the body, a final checkpoint, at which the decision is made to expel or ingest a food.

There is a widespread belief in traditional cultures that "you are what you eat." That is, people take on the properties of what they eat: Eating a brave animal makes one brave, or eating an animal with good eyesight improves one's own eyesight (reviewed in Nemeroff and Rozin 1989). "You are what you eat" seems to be "believed" at an implicit level, even among educated people in Western culture (Nemeroff and Rozin 1989). It is an eminently reasonable belief, since combinations of two entities (in this case, person and food) usually display properties of both. Thus, from the psychological side, the act of eating is fraught with affect; one is rarely neutral about what goes in one's mouth. Some of our greatest pleasures and our greatest fears have to do with what we eat.

The powerful effect associated with eating has a strong biological basis.[1] Humans, like rats, cockroaches, raccoons, herring gulls, and other broadly omnivorous species, can thrive in a wide range of environments because they discover nutrients in many sources. But although the world is filled with sources of nutrition, there are two problems facing the omnivore (or generalist). One is that many potential foods contain toxins. A second is that most available (nonanimal) foods are nutritionally incomplete. An apt selection of a variety of different plant foods is required for the survival of omnivorous animals to the extent that they cannot find sufficient animal foods. Animal foods tend to be complete sources of nutrition, but they are harder to come by because they are less prevalent and because they are often hard to procure (for example, they move). Hence, the omnivore must make a careful selection of foods, avoiding high levels of toxins and ingesting a full range of nutrients. Any act of ingestion, especially of a new potential food, is laden with ambivalence: It could be a good source of nutrition, but it might also be toxic.

Specialist species, such as those that eat only insects, can identify food as small moving things; specialists that eat only one species or group of plants may identify food by some common chemical property of these plants. There is no simple, genetic way to program an omnivorous animal to identify food by its sensory properties, because anything might be food and anything might contain toxins (or harmful microorganisms). Hence, omnivores must basically learn what is edible and what is not and what constitutes a good combination of edibles. This learning is facilitated by a few biologically (genetically) based biases:

1. An innate tendency in many species (including rats and humans) to ingest things that taste sweet (correlated with the presence of calories in nature) and to avoid things that taste bitter (correlated with the presence of toxins in nature [Garcia and Hankins 1975]).
2. Conflicting tendencies to be interested in new foods and a variety of foodstuffs but to fear anything new. This results from what I have called the generalist's (omnivore's) dilemma; the importance of exploring new foods to obtain adequate nutri-

tion across different areas and seasons and, yet, the dangers of ingesting toxins in doing so. The conflicting tendencies are manifested as a cautious sampling of new foods and a tendency to eat a number of different foods in any day.
3. Special abilities to learn about the consequences of ingestion. Here omnivores face a difficult challenge, because both the positive and negative effects of foods occur many minutes to hours or even days after ingestion. But omnivores, like rats and humans, can learn to associate a food with the consequences of ingestion even if they occur some hours later (Garcia, Hankins, and Rusiniak 1974; Rozin 1976).
4. A few special preprogrammed food selection systems. These include systems that signal to an animal that it is in need of energy (what we loosely call "hunger"), water ("thirst"), and sodium ("sodium appetite"). The sodium system, at least for the rat, is linked to an innate recognition of the taste of the needed nutrient. As shown originally by the great food selection psychologist, Curt Richter, rats deprived of sodium for the first time in their lives show an immediate preference for the taste of sodium (salt) (Richter 1956; Denton 1982; Schulkin 1991). There is some evidence for something that may resemble an innate sodium-specific hunger in humans (Beauchamp, Bartino, and Engelman 1983; Shepherd 1988).

The psychology of human food-related behavior falls naturally into two areas. One is concerned with how much is eaten (the starting and stopping of eating, defining the meal). Almost all psychological research is devoted to understanding what determines how much people and animals eat and the disorders of this process (such as obesity and anorexia). These issues are discussed elsewhere in this work. But this chapter focuses on the second area, what is eaten, that is, on food selection.[2]

The Human Omnivore

Food selection can be accomplished by genetic programming (for example, the avoidance of bitter tastes), by individual experience with foods (for example, learning that a certain food causes adverse symptoms), or by social transmission. Social transmission obviously has the virtue of sparing an organism the efforts and risks of discovering what is edible and what is not. In nonhuman animals, there is social transmission that can be called inadvertent; that is, animals may learn to eat what their parents or conspecifics eat by some sort of exposure to the conspecifics when eating (see Galef 1988, for a review). Humans, however, have two other powerful modes of transmission of food preferences and information (see Rozin 1988, for a review). One is an indirect social effect: social institutions, cuisines, and technological advances that make certain varieties of nutritious foods easily available (for instance, by agriculture or importation) and reduce the likelihood of contact with harmful potential foods (such as poisonous mushrooms). The second effect is explicit teaching about food preferences by example or by transmission of information (for example, "don't eat wild-growing mushrooms"). There is no firm evidence for any nonhuman species of explicit (intentional) teaching about appropriate foods (Galef 1988).

Humans share with animals both the nutritive need for food and the derivation of pleasure from ingestion. However, humans supplement these two functions of food with others as well (Rozin 1990b). Food and eating can serve a social function by providing an occasion for the gathering of kin at mealtimes. Food also acts as a vehicle for making social distinctions (as in serving certain foods to indicate high regard for a guest) and as culture-wide social markers (as when cuisines serve as distinctive characteristics of different groups). In the form of cuisine, food also produces an aesthetic response that extends well beyond animal pleasure. And finally, for many people in the world, most particularly Hindu Indians, food is a moral substance; eating certain foods and avoiding others is a means of preserving purity, avoiding pollution, and leading a proper life (Appadurai 1981). The multiple functions of food for humans make the understanding of human uses of food and attitudes to food an extremely complex task.

The Psychological Categorization of Food

We are accustomed to biological/taxonomic (species) and nutritional classifications of foods. But for a psychology of food, the important distinctions are those made in the human mind, and these are only weakly related to scientific classifications of foods.

The simplest approach to human food choice is to determine, for any group of people, the types and amounts of foods consumed (or more easily, purchased). We can call this measure food *use*. It is of special significance from the point of view of economics, but it has a major shortcoming as a measure of human food selection, since much food use is determined by its cost and availability. It would certainly be inaccurate to assume that because a group consumes more of X than Y, that they prefer X, when it may be that X is simply more available or less costly.

A more appropriate psychological measure is *preference,* which indicates, with price and availability controlled, which foods a person or group chooses. Yet it would be a mistake to assume that preference is a direct and infallible measure of liking for particular foods. A dieter, for example, might like ice cream better than cottage cheese but prefer (choose) cottage cheese. *Liking,* then, is a third way of describing food selection. It usually refers to attitudes about the sensory properties of foods, most particularly the oral sensations (tastes, aromas [flavors], "mouth feel"). Thus, a psychology of human food choice must address the question of why particular humans or groups of humans use, prefer, and like particular foods.

Further analysis suggests that there is a richer psychological categorization of foods for humans. Of all the potential edibles in the world (which essentially means anything that can be gotten into the mouth), a first simple division is between items that are accepted and those that are rejected by any individual or group. However, acceptance or rejection can be motivated by any of three reasons (or any combination of these) (see Table VI.11.1; Rozin and Fallon 1980; Fallon and Rozin 1983).

One reason is "sensory-affective." This has to do with liking or disliking the sensory properties of a food. Foods that are accepted or rejected primarily on sensory-affective grounds can be called "good tastes" or "distastes," respectively. If X likes lima beans and Y does not, the reason is almost certainly sensory-affective. Most of the differences in food likes within a well-defined cultural group have to do with differences in sensory-affective responses.

A second reason for rejecting a food is anticipated consequences. One may reject a food (which we call

Table VI.11.1 *Psychological categorization of acceptance and rejection*

Dimensions	Rejections				Acceptances			
	Distaste	Danger	Inappropriate	Disgust	Good taste	Beneficial	Appropriate	Transvalued
Sensory-affective	–			–	+			+
Anticipated consequences		–				+		
Ideational		?	–	–	?		+	+
Contaminant		–		–				+
Examples	Beer Chilli Spinach	Allergy foods Carcinogens	Grass Sand	Feces Insects	Saccharin Favorite foods	Medicines Healthy foods	Ritual foods	Leavings of heroes, loved ones, or deities

Source: From Fallon and Rozin (1983).

a dangerous food) because one believes ingestion will be harmful (it may be high in fats, or may contain carcinogens). Or one may accept a food (which we call a beneficial food) because it is highly nutritive or curative (perhaps a vitamin pill or a particular vegetable).

A third, uniquely human reason for food acceptance or rejection is what we call ideational; it is the nature of the food and/or its origin that primarily determines our response. Thus, we reject a very large number of potential foods because we have learned simply that they are not food: paper, tree bark, stones. These (inappropriate) entities may not be harmful and may not taste bad; they simply are not food. This inappropriate category is very large, yet there is a much smaller (appropriate) category on the positive side: foods that we eat just because they are food. Certain ritual foods might fall into this category.

We have now used three reasons to generate three categories of acceptance (good tastes, beneficial, and appropriate) and three of rejection (distaste, danger, and inappropriate). There remains one more major category of rejection that represents, like inappropriate, a fundamentally ideational rejection. We call this category disgust: Although it is primarily an ideational rejection, disgusting items are usually believed to taste bad and are often believed to be harmful. Feces seems to be disgusting universally; in American and many other Western cultures, insects fall within this category as well.

Disgusting items have the unique property that if they touch an otherwise acceptable food, they render that food unacceptable; we call this psychological contamination (Rozin and Fallon 1987). The category of disgusts is large. The opposite positive category, which we call transvalued foods, is very small. These are foods that are uplifting for ideational reasons and which are often thought to be beneficial and tasty. A good example is "prasad" in Hindu culture. Food that has been offered to the gods, and is subsequently distributed to worshippers who believe it to have been partly consumed by the gods, is considered especially desirable (Breckenridge 1986).

A psychological account of food choice would have to explain how foods come to be in any of the eight categories we have generated.

Accounting for Food Preferences and Likes

It must be true that human food attitudes result from some combination of three sources of information or experience: biological heritage (that is, our genes), cultural environment, and unique individual experience. I shall examine each of these contributing causes, with emphasis on the last, most psychological of the three. Of course, the distinction among genetic, cultural, and individual-psychological origins of human preferences is somewhat arbitrary, and there is a great deal of interaction among these forces. Nonetheless, the distinction is very useful.

Genetic Aspects of Food Selection

By their nature, omnivores carry into the world little specific information about what is edible and what is not. I noted taste biases, suspicion of new foods with an opposing tendency to seek variety, and some special abilities to learn about the consequences of food. However, there are individual differences among people that have genetic bases and that influence food selection. The small minority of these directly affect the nervous system and food choice. The best-investigated example is an inherited tendency to taste (or not to taste) a certain class of bitter compounds (identified by one member of this category, phenylthiocarbamide or PTC). This ability is inherited as a simple, single-locus, Mendelian recessive trait (Fischer 1967) and probably has some modest effect on preferences for certain bitter substances, such as coffee. The incidence of PTC tasting differs in different cultural groups.

More commonly, genetic differences in metabolism affect the consequences that different foods have and, hence, whether they might enter the beneficial or harmful category for any individual. A well-investigated example is lactose intolerance, but others include a sensitivity to wheat protein (gluten) and sensitivity to a potential toxin in fava beans (see Katz 1982; Simoons 1982, for reviews). In the case of lactose intolerance, the inability of most human beings to digest milk sugar (lactose) as adults (a genetically determined trait) accounts for the absence or minimal presence of raw milk and other uncultured milk products in the majority of the world's cuisines. Those who are lactose intolerant can develop lower gastrointestinal symptoms (cramps, diarrhea) upon ingestion of even relatively moderate amounts of uncultured milk.

The fact remains that although there are genetic influences on food choice, they are rather minor, at least at the individual level. An indication of this is that the food preferences of identical twins are not much (if at all) more similar than are the preferences of fraternal twins (Rozin and Millman 1987).

Culture and Food Selection: Cuisine

Although it has never been directly demonstrated, it seems obvious that the major determinant of any individual's food preferences is his or her native cuisine. Put another way, if one wanted to guess as much as one could about a person's food attitudes and preferences, the best question to ask would be: What is your native culture or ethnic group? Not only would this response be very informative but there is also no other question one could ask that would be remotely as informative. In terms of the taxonomy of food acceptances and rejections (Table VI.11.1), cultural forces generally determine the ideational categories and strongly influence the good tastes–distastes and danger–beneficial categories.

This influence, obviously acquired in childhood, can be generally described as a body of rules and practices that defines what is appropriate and desirable food and how it is to be eaten. The most systematic description of the food itself comes from Elisabeth Rozin's (1982, 1992) analysis of cuisine. She posits three components that give a characteristic ethnic quality to any dish: The staple ingredients, the flavor principles (for example, the recurrent soy sauce, ginger root, rice wine combination in Chinese food), and the method of processing (for example, stir-frying for many Chinese foods).

Furthermore, cuisines specify the appropriate ordering of dishes within a meal (Douglas and Nicod 1974) and the appropriate combinations and occasions on which particular foods are consumed (Schutz 1988). All of these factors, along with rules about the manner and social arrangement of eating and the importance and function of food in life, are major parts of the human food experience and are basically part of the transmission of culture. That these cultural forces are strong is indicated by the persistence of native food habits, sometimes called the conservatism of cuisine in immigrant groups. Generations after almost all traces of original-culture practices are gone, the basic food of the family often remains the native cuisine (see, for example, Goode, Curtis, and Theophano 1984).

Psychological Determinants of Food Selection

Within the minimal constraints of biology and the substantial constraints and predispositions imposed by culture, any individual develops a set of culture-appropriate, but also somewhat unique, food preferences. I shall now address what little we know about how this happens.

Early Childhood: Milk and Weaning

Humans and other mammals begin life with one food: milk. It is both nutritive and associated with maternal nurturance. A first trauma in life is weaning away from this "superfood," which is accomplished in culturally variable ways. There is no evidence for special attachments that humans develop to this earliest food, although such a permanent attachment (liking) has been documented with respect to species recognition in a number of species: Exposure to a member of the species (usually a parent) at a critical period in development leads to a permanent attachment to and preferential recognition of that object. But this process of imprinting would be highly maladaptive for early food for mammals because they would then spend their lives seeking an unattainable food. Milk, for example, only became available as a food for some humans after infancy with the development of

dairying, which occurred relatively recently in human history (see Rozin and Pelchat 1988, for further discussion).

Neophilia and Neophobia

As omnivores, humans show both a tendency to be interested in new foods and a fear of new foods. Both tendencies have benefits and risks. The neophilic (attraction to new food) tendency manifests itself not only in an interest in genuinely new foods but also in a desire for variety in the diet. Thus, humans (and other animals) tend to come to like a food less if they eat it almost exclusively (boredom effect) and tend to eat more when confronted with a variety of foods. This general phenomenon has been called sensory specific satiety and has been subjected to systematic analysis by B. J. Rolls and her colleagues (Rolls et al. 1985).

Below the age of about 2 years, children seem to have little neophobia and, quite willingly, put almost anything into their mouths (reviewed in Rozin, 1990c). Presumably, parental monitoring of their food access controls this otherwise dangerous tendency. After 2 years of age, at least in American culture, children sometimes enter a neophobic phase, in which they refuse all but a few types of food. We do not know the origin or adaptive value (if any) of this pattern. In American culture, some adults also find an extremely limited range of foods acceptable, though most children with this extreme neophobia recover from it. Neophobia varies greatly across individuals in North America, and a scale has been developed to measure this tendency in both children and adults (Pliner and Hobden 1992).

Food Preferences and the Adult Taxonomy

We know very little about how, within any culture and individual, specific foods become categorized in accordance with the taxonomy presented in Table VI.11.1. I review here what is known.

Acquired dislikes. Best understood is the origin of the distinction between the danger and distaste categories. Generally, if a relatively new food is consumed, and this is followed within hours by unpleasant symptoms that include nausea, the food comes to be a distaste. However, if nausea is not a part of the symptoms, the result is usually that the food enters the danger category; that is, it is avoided because of anticipated harm, but is not distasteful (Pelchat and Rozin 1982). The taste-aversion learning originally described in rats by J. Garcia and his colleagues (1974) seems to be an example of acquired distaste mediated by nausea. Hence, nausea appears to be a magic bullet, producing distastes. This is not, however, to say that this is the only way in which distastes can be produced. There is evidence, for example, that when a food is accompanied by a bad taste (for example, when a bitter taste is added to a food), the food itself becomes distasteful, even when the originally unpleasant taste is removed (Baeyens et al. 1990).

Acquired likes. So far as we know, there is no magic bullet like nausea on the negative side that makes a potential food into a good taste (a liked food). However, this happens very frequently. There is evidence for three processes that contribute to acquired likes.

One of these is mere exposure. That is, simple exposure to a food (meaning its ingestion) is usually accompanied by an increased liking for the food (Pliner 1982). The mechanism for this may be nothing other than mere exposure. The effects of mere exposure on liking have been shown in many domains other than food (Zajonc 1968).

A second process that accounts for acquired likes is classical (Pavlovian) conditioning. That is, if an already liked entity (called an unconditioned stimulus) is paired with (that is, is contingent with) a relatively neutral potential food, the potential food tends to become more liked. This process of change in liking for a stimulus as a result of contingent pairing in humans has been called evaluative conditioning (Martin and Levey 1978; Baeyens et al. 1990). One example involves pairing of a flavor (conditioned stimulus) with the pleasant experience of satisfaction of hunger (unconditioned stimulus). In a laboratory setting, humans have been shown to increase liking for a food the ingestion of which is followed by satiety (Booth, Mather, and Fuller 1982).

Another example involves presentation (contingent pairing) of one flavor of herbal tea (conditioned stimulus) with sugar (unconditioned stimulus) and another flavor of tea without sugar. After a number of presentations, subjects tend to prefer the flavor of the tea that was paired with sweetness, even when that flavor is presented without sugar (Zellner et al. 1983).

Within the context of evaluative conditioning, it is likely that the major class of potent (unconditioned) stimuli that influence food likes is social. In particular, the perception (often, perhaps, by facial expression) of positive affect in another (respected) person in conjunction with consumption of a particular food probably makes that food more liked by the "observer." Recently, a first study has shown such an effect in the laboratory. Subjects who observe a person indicating pleasure in drinking a beverage from a glass of a particular shape (as opposed to other shapes) come to prefer that particular glass shape (Baeyens et al. 1994).

A third process that influences liking is also social, but it does not operate through conditioning. Rather, the perception of liking or value in a respected other operates more directly to influence one's own attitudes. For example, when a respected other uses a food as a reward (indicating that he/she values the food), a child tends to come to prefer (like) that food more (Birch, Zimmerman, and Hind 1980). Furthermore, there is evidence, both from the general litera-

ture in social psychology (Lepper 1983) and the development of food preferences (Birch et al. 1982), that the perception that the self or others consume a food for clear personal gain (nutrition, social advantage) is destructive to the development of liking. That is, when children perceive that a food preference (in themselves or others) is "instrumentally" motivated, that is, connected to a specific reward, they tend not to shift their liking for the food in question.

Reversal of Innate Aversions

Humans are almost unique among mammalian (if not all) generalists in developing strong likes for foods that are innately unpalatable. These include such common favorites as the oral or nasal irritants in chilli peppers, black pepper, ginger, horseradish, and alcoholic beverages or tobacco, and the bitter tastes in certain fruits, tobacco, most alcoholic beverages, coffee, chocolate, burnt foods, and so forth. Reversals of innate aversions seem to occur in all cultures (cuisines). They might well be accounted for in terms of the operation of the factors (mere exposure, evaluative conditioning, social influence) that have already been identified. But there are also some special mechanisms of acquired liking that require an initially negative response. Two have been identified, with particular reference to the acquisition of a liking for the innately negative oral burn of chilli pepper (Rozin 1990a).

In the service of maintaining the body at an optimum level of function, humans and other species seem to have compensatory mechanisms, which neutralize disturbances by producing, internally, events that oppose the original event. These internally generated events are called opponent processes (Solomon 1980). For example, it is widely believed that endorphins, natural opiatelike substances, are released in the brain to reduce a chronic pain experience. R. L. Solomon (1980) and others have suggested that opponent processes become more potent as they are repeatedly stimulated and have used this feature to account for the basic process of addiction. Normally, when one experiences something painful, one withdraws and avoids the situation in the future. However, in the case of the chilli pepper and other culturally supported innately negative entities, there is a strong cultural force that reintroduces the aversive experience. Thus, children end up repeatedly sampling the unpleasant burn of chilli pepper, permitting the development of a strong opponent process, which may grow to the extent that it overcompensates for the pain and produces net pleasure (perhaps by oversecretion of endogenous opiates) (Rozin 1990a). Hence, the negativity of an innately aversive substance may provide the conditions for an acquired liking.

A more cognitive account of the reversal of innate aversions engages a uniquely human interest in mastering nature. The signals sent to the brain from innately unpalatable substances impel the organism to reject them; they are adaptively linked to a system that rids the organism of harmful entities. But many innately unpalatable substances are not harmful, at least in modest doses (chilli pepper, ginger, coffee). Though chilli pepper makes the novice feel as if his palate will peel away, it is, in fact, harmless. It is possible that the realization that a substance–experience elicits bodily defensive mechanisms, but is actually safe, is a source of pleasure. We call this pleasure that comes from mastery over nature benign masochism (Rozin 1990a). A more striking instance is the unique human activity of enjoying bodily manifestations of fright (as opposed to pain): People presumably enjoy roller coasters because their body is frightened, but they know that they are actually safe.

Disgust: The Food-Related Emotion

The strongest reaction to a potential food is surely the revulsion associated with disgusting entities (Table VI.11.1). The emotion of disgust elicited in these situations is characterized by withdrawal, a sense of nausea, and a characteristic facial expression. According to our analyses (Rozin and Fallon 1987; Rozin, Haidt, and McCauley 1993), following on the seminal contributions of Charles Darwin (1872) and A. Angyal (1941), disgust is originally a food-related emotion, expressing "revulsion at the prospect of oral incorporation of offensive substances. The offensive substances are contaminants, that is, if they contact an otherwise acceptable food, they tend to render that food unacceptable" (Rozin and Fallon 1987: 23). Our analysis holds that disgust originates from distaste (and shares, to some extent, a facial expression with distaste), but is in fact quite distinct from distaste in adults. For example, the idea of a distasteful entity in one's stomach is not upsetting, but the idea of a disgusting entity in one's stomach is very upsetting.

The intensity of the disgust experience derives, in part, from the "you are what you eat" principle, since, by this principle, one who ingests something offensive becomes offensive. Virtually all food-related disgust entities are of animal origin. We have proposed that the core disgust category is all animals and their products (Rozin and Fallon 1987). In line with Angyal's suggestion (1941), we agree that feces is the universal disgust substance, and almost certainly the first disgust, developmentally. The potency of disgust elicitors is evidenced by the contamination property, a feature that seems to characterize disgust cross-culturally.

Disgust provides an excellent example of how a food system becomes a template or model for more elaborated systems. The emotion of disgust seems, through cultural evolution, to have become a general expression of anything offensive, including nonfoods. Our analysis suggests that principal elicitors of disgust cross-culturally include reminders of our animal origin (such as gore, death), a wide range of interpersonal contacts (such as wearing the clothing of undesirable persons), and certain moral offenses often involving purity violations or animality (Rozin et al. 1993).

Transmission of Food Preferences and Attitudes

Most available models for the acquisition of food preferences would predict a rather high correlation between the food preferences of parents and those of their children. For the first years of life, parents are the primary teachers and exemplars of eating and food choice for children. In addition, to the extent that there are individual differences in preferences that have genetic contributions, one would expect parent–child resemblances. Yet, the literature (reviewed in Rozin, 1991) indicates very low correlations between the food preferences of parents and their children (in the range of 0 to 0.3), whether the younger generation in the studies is one of preschoolers or of college age. There is no reasonable account for these low correlations; they do not result from the fact that the parents have different preferences for the foods under study, so that the child gets "mixed messages." Parent–child correlations remain low even when the parents are very similar in their preferences for the foods under study (Rozin 1991). Alternative sources of influence on children include peers and siblings (for whom there is evidence of some substantial resemblance [Pliner and Pelchat 1986]), and the media. The effectiveness and mode of operation of these and other influences has yet to be evaluated.

The low parent–child correlation for food preferences is part of what has been called the family paradox (Rozin 1991). The paradox is extended by the fact that there is no consistent evidence that mothers (as principal feeders and food purveyors) show higher child resemblance than do fathers, nor that same-sex parents have greater influence than opposite-sex parents – as views about identification might suggest (Pliner 1983; Rozin 1991).

The puzzling lack of parent–child resemblance for food (and other) preferences contrasts with much higher parent–child resemblance for values (Cavalli-Sforza et al. 1982; Rozin 1991). Apparently, values (such as religious or political attitudes) are more subject to parental influence. In this regard, it is of interest that food preferences may, under some circumstances, become values. Food is intimately related to moral issues in Hindu India, such that a leading scholar of this area has described food in Hindu India as a "biomoral substance" (Appadurai 1981). But even in Western cultures, specific foods may enter the moral domain. For example, vegetarianism for some has moral significance. It would be interesting to see if parental influence is greater on children for whom a preference has been moralized than for those for whom the preference is not moralized.

Attitudes and Choice: An Alternative Approach

The framework I have provided for examination of human food selection emphasizes the psychological categorization of foods and the combined influences of biological, psychological, and cultural factors on food selection. The emphasis has also been on the developmental history of food preferences. There are alternative formulations from within both psychology and marketing. A particularly prominent approach, based on the study of attitudes and their relation to behavior, examines the factors currently influencing selection of a particular food, independent of the ultimate origin of these causes. In other words, this approach models what would be going on in the head of a person in a supermarket faced with a choice between two products. For convenience, the forces acting on a person at a time of choice can be categorized as those attributable to the food and its properties, the person, and socioeconomic factors (Shepherd 1988).

The theory of reasoned action (Ajzen and Fishbein 1980) has probably been the most successful framework for analysis of choices in terms of the action of contemporary forces. According to this approach, the principal cause of a behavior (for instance, selecting a particular food) is the intention to behave in such a manner, and the principal predictors of the intention are personal attitudes to the behavior (for instance, whether it is seen as good or bad) and subjective norms (the perceived opinions of significant others about whether the behavior should be performed). Personal attitudes are themselves a function of a set of beliefs about the outcome of the behavior (food choice) in question (will it promote overweight, will it produce a pleasant taste?) and the evaluation of that outcome (is it good or bad?). A set of salient beliefs is determined, and the sum of the product of each belief and its evaluation composes the attitude score. The subjective norm is predicted in the same manner by the sum of normative beliefs about whether specific relevant people or groups think that the target person should perform the behavior, each norm multiplied by the motivation to comply with it.

A number of studies (see Tuorila and Pangborn 1988; Towler and Shepherd 1992) have applied the Ajzen-Fishbein model to food choices, with some success, in terms of prediction of consumption from (usually) questionnaire data on beliefs, evaluations of beliefs, subjective norms, and motivation to comply with those norms. Target foods have included a variety of dairy products, meats, and other high-fat foods. The results, on subjects from the Western-developed world, show a tendency for personal attitudes to be better predictors of choice than subjective norms. They also suggest that taste of food is the most important predictor of attitudes, with health effects often the second-best predictor (see Shepherd 1989b for a general discussion).

Food Selection Pathology in America

Throughout history, food has been viewed as not only the principal source of sustenance but also a major source of pleasure. In the United States, a surfeit of food, a developing concern about long-term harmful effects of certain foods, and a standard of beauty for women (at least among the white middle class in the United States) that is much thinner than the average woman have all contributed to an ambivalent, sometimes negative attitude to food (Polivy and Herman 1983; Rodin et al. 1985; Becker 1986; Rozin 1989; Rodin 1992).

Consumption of foods, especially those that are highly tasty and fattening, becomes for many a source of fear and guilt, rather than pleasure. The focal group for this (what I will call) pathology of food is white middle-class American women, among whom there is considerable concern about obesity and, consequently, considerable efforts aimed at dieting (Rodin 1992). One consequence of this is that eating disorders, such as anorexia nervosa and various forms of bulimia, are increasing in American women, whereas such disorders are at much lower levels in American males and virtually absent in developing countries (McCarthy 1990).

One cause of this hyperconcern about food, as mentioned, is the standard of thinness accepted by American women; unlike American men, American women see themselves as substantially overweight (Rozin and Fallon, 1988). Furthermore, white middle-class American women are more worried about being above ideal weight than are men; that is, even when men recognize that they are overweight, food is less likely to become a source of fear and guilt for them.

Although food is obviously a necessity for survival, potentially harmful effects on health of certain foods have come to be a matter of concern for many Americans. This recent concern results from a number of factors:

1. The reduction in death from infectious diseases has produced a corresponding increased incidence of death from degenerative diseases. This changes the focus of food risk from acute to chronic effects.
2. Epidemiological evidence on harmful effects of food, which is accumulating at a rapid rate, is conveyed to a public fascinated with such information in a salient – even sensational – way by the media.
3. Americans have become obsessed with longevity, or perhaps, immortality.
4. Americans (and others) are unprepared to deal with and evaluate the constant wave of food (and other) risk information to which they are exposed. They have never been taught cost–benefit analysis or interpretations of very low probabilities and have beliefs about food that are often incorrect. For example, many believe that if something is thought to be harmful at high levels, then it is also

harmful at trace levels. Such dose insensitivity causes some to shun even traces of salt, fats, or sugars (Rozin, Ashmore, and Markwith 1996). In addition, many Americans falsely believe that "natural" foods are invariably healthy, and processed foods are likely to be harmful. In fact, over the short term, the opposite is clearly true (that is, acute illness is more likely to be caused by natural foods), and there is reason to believe that in many cases, the long-term risks posed by the consumption of natural foods are higher than those posed by processed versions of the same foods (Ames et al. 1987). The centrality of food in life and the great concern about putting things in the mouth and body probably causes people to overestimate long-term food risks in contrast to other risks, such as driving.

The result is that eating, which is one of the greatest sources of pleasure and health that humans can experience, has become a nightmare for some and, in fact, threatens to become an American cultural nightmare. We can only hope that this obsessive concern does not, like so many other attitudes and beliefs of Americans, spread around the world.

Paul Rozin

Notes

1. See Rozin (1976) and Rozin and Schulkin (1990) for more detailed discussions of the biological and psychological frameworks for human food selection.
2. More extended reviews of the area covered in this chapter can be found in the volumes of collected papers by Barker (1982), Dobbing (1988), Shepherd (1989a and 1989b), and Thomson (1988); in books by Fischler (1990) and Logue (1991); and in specific review articles by Birch (1986), Blundell (1983), Booth (1982), Krondl and Lau (1982), Meiselman (1988), Pangborn (1980), P. Rozin (1982), Rozin and Schulkin (1990), Rozin and Vollmecke (1986), and Schutz and Judge (1984). Major historical summaries of basic points of view on food selection include those by Mead (1943), Richter (1943), and Young (1948).

Bibliography

Ajzen, I., and M. Fishbein. 1980. *Understanding attitudes and predicting social behavior.* Englewood Cliffs, N.J.

Ames, B. N., R. Magaw, and L. S. Gold. 1987. Ranking possible carcinogenic hazards. *Science* 236: 271-80.

Angyal, A. 1941. Disgust and related aversions. *Journal of Abnormal and Social Psychology* 36: 393-412.

Appadurai, A. 1981. Gastro-politics in Hindu South Asia. *American Ethnologist* 8: 494-511.

Baeyens, F., P. Eelen, O. Van den Bergh, and G. Crombez. 1990. Flavor-flavor and color-flavor conditioning in humans. *Learning and Motivation* 21: 434-55.

Baeyens, F., B. Kaes, P. Eelen, and P. Silverans. 1994. Observational evaluative conditioning of an embedded stimulus element. *European Journal of Social Psychology* 26: 15-28.

Bakwin, H., and R. M. Bakwin. 1972. *Behavior disorders in children.* Philadelphia, Pa.

Barker, L. M., ed. 1982. *The psychobiology of human food selection.* Bridgeport, Conn.

Beauchamp, G. K., M. Bertino, and K. Engelman. 1983. Modification of salt taste. *Annals of Internal Medicine* 98: 763-9.

Becker, M. H. 1986. The tyranny of health promotion. *Public Health Review.* 14: 15-25.

Birch, L. L. 1986. Children's food preferences: Developmental patterns and environmental influences. In *Annals of child development,* Vol. 4., ed. G. Whitehurst and R. Vasta. Greenwich, Conn.

Birch, L. L., D. Birch, D. W. Marlin, and L. Kramer. 1982. Effects of instrumental eating on children's food preferences. *Appetite* 3: 125-34.

Birch, L. L., S. I. Zimmerman, and H. Hind. 1980. The influence of social-affective context on the formation of children's food preferences. *Child Development* 51: 856-61.

Blundell, J. E. 1983. Problems and processes underlying the control of food selection and nutrient intake. In *Nutrition and the brain,* Vol. 6, ed. R. J. Wurtman and J. J. Wurtman, 163-231. New York.

Booth, D. A. 1982. Normal control of omnivore intake by taste and smell. In *The determination of behavior by chemical stimuli. ECRO symposium,* ed. J. Steiner and J. Ganchrow, 233-43. London.

Booth, D. A., P. Mather, and J. Fuller. 1982. Starch content of ordinary foods associatively conditions human appetite and satiation, indexed by intake and eating pleasantness of starch-paired flavors. *Appetite* 3: 163-84.

Breckenridge, C. 1986. Food, politics and pilgrimage in South India, A.D. 1350-1650. In *Food, society, and culture: Aspects of South Asian food systems,* ed. R. S. Khare and M. S. A. Rao. Durham, N.C.

Cavalli-Sforza, L. L., M. W. Feldman, K. H Chen, and S. M. Dornbusch. 1982. Theory and observation in cultural transmission. *Science* 218: 19-27.

Darwin, C. R. 1872. *The expression of emotions in man and animals.* London.

Denton, D. 1982. *The hunger for salt.* Berlin.

Dobbing, J., ed. 1988. *Sweetness.* London.

Douglas, M., and M. Nicod. 1974. Taking the biscuit: The structure of British meals. *New Society* (December 19): 744-7.

Fallon, A. E., and P. Rozin. 1983. The psychological bases of food rejections by humans. *Ecology of Food and Nutrition* 13: 15-26.

Fischer, R. 1967. Genetics and gustatory chemoreception in man and other primates. In *The chemical senses and nutrition,* ed. M. Kare and O. Maller, 61-71. Baltimore, Md.

Fischler, C. 1990. *L'Homnivore.* Paris.

Galef, B. G., Jr. 1988. Communication of information concerning distant diets in a social central-place foraging species: Rattus norvegicus. In *Social learning: A comparative approach,* ed. T. Zentall and B. G. Galef, Jr., 119-40. Hillsdale, N.J.

Garcia, J., and W. G. Hankins. 1975. The evolution of bitter and the acquisition of toxiphobia. In *Fifth international symposium on olfaction and taste,* ed. D. Denton and J. P. Coghlan, 1-12. New York.

Garcia, J., W. G. Hankins, and K. W. Rusiniak. 1974. Behavioral regulation of the milieu interne in man and rat. *Science* 185: 824-31.

Goode, J., K. Curtis, and J. Theophano. 1984. Meal formats, meal cycles and menu negotiation in the maintenance of an Italian-American community. In *Food in the social order,* ed. M. Douglas, 143–218. New York.

Katz, S. H. 1982. Food, behavior and biocultural evolution. In *The psychobiology of human food selection,* ed. L. M. Barker, 171–88. Westport, Conn.

Krondl, M., and D. Lau. 1982. Social determinants in human food selection. In *The psychobiology of human food selection,* ed., L. M. Barker, 139–51. Westport, Conn.

Lepper, M. R. 1983. Social control processes and the internalization of social values: An attributional perspective. In *Social cognition and social development,* ed. E. T. Higgins, D. N. Ruble, and W. W. Hartup, 294–330. New York.

Logue, A. W. 1991. *The psychology of eating and drinking.* Second edition. New York.

Marriott, M. 1968. Caste ranking and food transactions: A matrix analysis. In *Structure and change in Indian society,* ed. M. Singer and B. S. Cohn, 133–71. Chicago.

Martin, I., and A. B. Levey. 1978. Evaluative conditioning. *Advances in Behavior Research and Therapy* 1: 57–102.

McCarthy, M. 1990. The thin ideal; depression and eating disorders in women. *Behavior Research and Therapy* 28: 205–15.

Mead, M. 1943. The problem of changing food habits. *Bulletin of the National Research Council* 108: 20–31.

Meiselman, H. L. 1988. Consumer studies of food habits. In *Sensory analysis of foods,* ed. J. R. Piggott, 267–334. London.

Nemeroff, C., and P. Rozin. 1989. An unacknowledged belief in "you are what you eat" among college students in the United States: An application of the demand-free "impressions" technique. *Ethos. The Journal of Psychological Anthropology* 17: 50–69.

Pangborn, R. M. 1980. A critical analysis of sensory responses to sweetness. In *Carbohydrate sweeteners in foods and nutrition,* ed. P. Koivistoinen and L. Hyvonen, 87–110. London.

Pelchat, M. L., and P. Rozin. 1982. The special role of nausea in the acquisition of food dislikes by humans. *Appetite* 3: 341–51.

Pliner, P. 1982. The effects of mere exposure on liking for edible substances. *Appetite* 3: 283–90.

1983. Family resemblance in food preferences. *Journal of Nutrition Education* 15: 137–40.

Pliner, P., and K. Hobden. 1992. Development of a scale to measure the trait of food neophobia in humans. *Appetite* 19: 105–20.

Pliner, P., and M. L. Pelchat. 1986. Similarities in food preferences between children and their siblings and parents. *Appetite* 7: 333–42.

Polivy, J., and C. P. Herman. 1983. *Breaking the diet habit.* New York.

Richter, C. P. 1943. Total self regulatory functions in animals and human beings. *Harvey Lecture Series* 38: 63–103.

1956. Salt appetite of mammals: Its dependence on instinct and metabolism. In *L'instinct dans le comportement des animaux et de l'homme,* 577–629. Paris.

Ritson, C., L. Gofton, and J. McKenzie, ed. 1986. *The food consumer.* Chichester, England.

Rodin, J. 1992. *Body traps.* New York.

Rodin, J., L. Silberstein, and R. Striegel-Moore. 1985. Women and weight: A normative discontent. In *Psychology and gender. Nebraska Symposium on Motivation,* ed. T. B. Sonderegger. Lincoln, Neb.

Rolls, B. J., M. Hetherington, V. J. Burley and P. M. van Duijvenvoorde. 1985. Changing hedonic responses to foods during and after a meal. In *Interaction of the chemical senses with nutrition,* ed. M. R. Kare and J. G. Brand, 247–68. New York.

Rozin, E. 1982. The structure of cuisine. In *The psychobiology of human food selection,* ed. L. M. Barker, 189–203. Westport, Conn.

1992. *Ethnic cuisine* (original 1983 title: *The flavor principle cookbook*). New York.

Rozin, P. 1976. The selection of foods by rats, humans, and other animals. In *Advances in the study of behavior,* Vol. 6, ed. J. Rosenblatt, R. A. Hinde, C. Beer, and E. Shaw, 21–76. New York.

1982. Human food selection: The interaction of biology, culture and individual experience. In *The psychobiology of human food selection,* ed. L. M. Barker, 225–54. Westport, Conn.

1988. Social learning about foods by humans. In *Social learning: A comparative approach,* ed. T. Zentall and B. G. Galef, Jr., 165–87. Hillsdale, N.J.

1989. Disorders of food selection: The compromise of pleasure. *Annals of the New York Academy of Sciences Series* 38: 63–103.

1990a. Getting to like the burn of chili pepper: Biological, psychological and cultural perspectives. In *Chemical irritation in the nose and mouth,* ed. B. G. Green, J. R. Mason, and M. L. Kare, 231–69. Potomac, Md.

1990b. Social and moral aspects of food and eating. In *Cognition and social psychology: Essays in honor of Solomon E. Asch,* ed. I. Rock, 97–110. Potomac, Md.

1990c. Development in the food domain. *Developmental Psychology* 26: 555–62.

1991. Family resemblance in food and other domains: The family paradox and the role of parental congruence. *Appetite* 16: 93–102.

Rozin, P., M. B. Ashmore, and M. Markwith. 1996. Lay American conceptions of nutrition: Dose insensitivity, categorical thinking, contagion, and the monotonic mind. *Health Psychology* 15: 438–47.

Rozin, P., and A. E. Fallon. 1980. Psychological categorization of foods and non-foods: A preliminary taxonomy of food rejections. *Appetite* 1: 193–201.

1987. A perspective on disgust. *Psychological Review* 94: 23–41.

1988. Body image, attitudes to weight, and misperceptions of figure preferences of the opposite sex: A comparison of males and females in two generations. *Journal of Abnormal Psychology* 97: 342–5.

Rozin, P., J. Haidt, and C. R. McCauley. 1993. Disgust. In *Handbook of emotions,* ed. M. Lewis and J. Haviland, 575–94. New York.

Rozin, P., and L. Millman. 1987. Family environment, not heredity, accounts for family resemblances in food preferences and attitudes. *Appetite* 8: 125–34.

Rozin, P., and M. L. Pelchat. 1988. Memories of mammaries: Adaptations to weaning from milk in mammals. In *Advances in psychobiology,* Vol. 13, ed. A. N. Epstein and A. Morrison, 1–29. New York.

Rozin, P., and J. Schulkin. 1990. Food selection. In *Handbook of behavioral neurobiology,* Vol. 10: *Food and water intake,* ed. E. M. Stricker, 297–328. New York.

Rozin, P., and T. A. Vollmecke. 1986. Food likes and dislikes. *Annual Review of Nutrition* 6: 433–56.

Schulkin, J. 1991. *Sodium hunger. The search for a salty taste.* New York.

Schutz, H. G. 1988. Beyond preference: Appropriateness as a measure of contextual acceptance of food. In *Food acceptability,* ed. D. M. H. Thomson, 115–34. London.

Schutz, H. G., and D. S. Judge. 1984. Consumer perceptions of food quality. In *Research in food science and nutrition*. Vol. 4: *Food science and human welfare*, ed. J. V. McLoughlin and B. M. McKenna, 229–42. Dublin.

Shepherd, R. 1988. Sensory influence on salt, sugar and fat intake. *Nutrition Research Reviews* 1: 125–44.

1989a. Factors influencing food preferences and choice. In *Handbook of the psychophysiology of human eating*, ed. R., Shepherd, 3–24. Chichester, England.

Shepherd, R., ed. 1989b. *Handbook of the psychophysiology of human eating*. Chichester, England.

Simoons, F. J. 1982. Geography and genetics as factors in the psychobiology of human food selection. In *The psychobiology of human food selection*, ed. L. M. Barker, 205–24. Westport, Conn.

Solomon, R. L. 1980. The opponent process theory of acquired motivation. *American Psychologist* 35: 691–712.

Steiner, J. E. 1979. Human facial expressions in response to taste and smell stimulation. In *Advances in child development and behavior*, Vol. 13, ed. H. W. Reese and L. P. Lipsitt, 257–95. New York.

Thomson, D. M. H., ed. 1988. *Food acceptability*. London.

Towler, G., and R. Shepherd. 1992. Application of Fishbein and Ajzen's expectancy-value model to understanding fat intake. *Appetite* 18: 15–27.

Tuorila, H., and R. M. Pangborn. 1988. Behavioural models in the prediction and consumption of selected sweet, salty and fatty foods. In *Food acceptability*, ed. D. M. H. Thomson, 267–79. London.

Young, P. T. 1948. Appetite, palatability and feeding habit: A critical review. *Psychological Bulletin* 45: 289–320.

Zajonc, R. B. 1968. Attitudinal effects of mere exposure. *Journal of Personality and Social Psychology* 9 (Part 2): 1–27.

Zellner, D. A., P. Rozin, M. Aron, and C. Kulish. 1983. Conditioned enhancement of human's liking for flavors by pairing with sweetness. *Learning and Motivation* 14: 338–50.

VI.12 ❧ Food Fads

The term "food fad" often refers to socially deviant, cultlike eating behavior. Examples include diets that contain massive amounts of supposedly healthy foods, such as garlic; those that prohibit the consumption of allegedly hazardous products, such as sugar or white bread; and those that emphasize natural foods and question the purity of goods available in supermarkets (Fieldhouse 1986). Charlatans claiming to have discovered nutritional fountains of youth and cures for cancer become best-selling authors overnight, only to disappear shortly afterward. But they are not the only promoters of culinary fads. The *Webster's Third New International Dictionary* defines *fad* as "a pursuit or interest followed usu. widely but briefly with exaggerated zeal. . . ." Sophisticated diners who flock to Ethiopian restaurants one month and to Thai restaurants the next thus qualify as faddists but not necessarily as deviants.

That a food or group of foods is especially health promoting serves as the most characteristic claim of food faddists, both wild-eyed cult leaders and bottom-line business executives. Nevertheless, profit and power often provide unspoken motivations behind the crusades of both groups. Moreover, the nutritional science used to back assertions of healthfulness has developed in a halting, incomplete, and often contradictory manner. This chapter evaluates the validity of many of these nutritional claims while it examines a wide range of food fads that have appeared throughout the world, particularly in the last two centuries, in the contexts of the spread of industrial capitalism, the concern for moral standards, and the creation of social identity.

Food and Industry

Prior to the age of industrial capitalism, fads of any sort were limited to a small elite. Peasants living at the edge of subsistence simply could not afford to experiment with fashions that were soon discarded. With the rise of mass production, however, disposable goods became not only a possibility but almost a necessity: Planned obsolescence, for example, allowed auto makers to continue producing cars although virtually everyone already owned one. The imperatives of food marketing led to product differentiation as manufacturers sought to market ever greater quantities of food, and culinary fashions changed with startling speed in the restaurant industry's fiercely competitive environment. Food fads have also spread throughout the world in recent decades as multinational corporations have cultivated markets in developing countries.

Cuisine and Capitalism

The rise of European industrial capitalism depended on a surplus of workers, which required a corresponding surplus of food. Quantitative increases in the food supply resulted from an eighteenth-century agricultural revolution, but at the same time, European diets underwent qualitative changes as well. Anthropologist Sidney Mintz (1985) has shown that refined sugar from Caribbean colonies became an essential part of British working-class diets. Whether drunk with tea or eaten in jam, sugar provided the cheapest possible source of energy for workers and thus helped hold down industrial wages. The role of sugar continued to grow as food manufacturers expanded their control over world markets. In ongoing efforts to increase sales, advertisers have launched countless new food fads in the hope that they would become cultural icons.

Sociologist Jack Goody (1982) has identified four basic components in the industrial transformation of food: improvements in preservation, mechanization, transportation, and retailing. Salt, sugar, and vinegar had long been used to preserve food, but modern canning dates only to 1795, when French chef Nicolas Appert combined pressure cookers with glass bottles to help supply Napoleon's armies. Nineteenth-century technological improvements allowed the substitution of cheaper tin cans for bottles and permitted the mass marketing of canned fish, meat, vegetables, condensed milk, and prepared foods. At the same time, artificial freezing of meats became widespread, although frozen vegetables remained impractical until the early-twentieth-century development of moisture-proof cellophane wrapping.

Mechanization, in turn, allowed the mass production of canned and frozen foods, which the steadily improving transportation methods, such as steamships and railroads, carried to distant markets. Finally, these foods were distributed to consumers through a nineteenth-century revolution in retailing. Grocers, who formerly had specialized in small-scale, nonperishable luxury goods, such as spices, tea, and sugar, took over the trade in canned goods. As this market grew, such grocers as Thomas Lipton built chains of stores and, ultimately, incorporated butchers, bakers, and other traditional food suppliers into new supermarkets.

The food-processing industry made its most dramatic advances in the 1950s, a decade when food scientists seemed to have discovered the legendary philosopher's stone. These modern alchemists could grant virtual immortality to foods, and if they failed to create gold, Twinkies came pretty close. With chemical preservatives, breads lasted longer, vegetables maintained their color, and fats did not go rancid. At the same time, vitamins, hormones, and antibiotics increased livestock productivity. Artificial flavors and colors even made it seem possible to do away with plants and animals entirely: A General Foods researcher claimed that there were not enough strawberries grown in the world to meet the demand for Jell-O (Levenstein 1993).

Demand for industrial food products, such as strawberry Jell-O, derived largely from modern marketing techniques, including branding, packaging, and advertising. An early pioneer in this field was the National Biscuit Company, which came to dominate the soda-cracker industry at the turn of the twentieth century. Nabisco packaged its crackers in waxed-paper wrapping to convey a sanitary image quite different from that of the crushed and moldy crackers available in general stores' cracker barrels. In 1899, the company adopted a distinctive, if rather corny, brand name, the "Uneeda" cracker, and with heavy advertising, it captured 70 percent of the American cracker market. Imitators came up with similar names, such as "I wanta cracker" and "Hava cracker," but lacking Nabisco's enormous advertising budget, they proved commercial failures (Levenstein 1988).

Marketing techniques have become more sophisticated with the growth of mass media. Children in particular are the targets of television advertisements for junk foods, such as Chocolate Frosted Sugar Bombs. A recent study found that the odds of a child's being overweight go up by 2 percent for every hour per day spent watching television (O'Neil 1994). Although obesity is not solely a function of watching television, modern marketing techniques can be enormously successful in creating a demand for new foods. For example, Pringles "newfangled" potato chips, made by Procter and Gamble in a Tennessee factory from dehydrated potato mash and shipped across the country in tennis ball cans, seemed a particularly unlikely commercial venture. Nevertheless, with the assistance of a $15 million advertising campaign, the product captured 10 percent of the national market despite the fact that it tasted, as a company executive admitted, "more like a tennis ball than a potato chip" (Levenstein 1993: 197).

Retailers, likewise, contributed to the proliferation of new products. Supermarket chains, in their ongoing effort to maximize sales, stocked ever greater numbers of manufactured foods. Trendy new items were displayed in conspicuous places – at eye level on shelves and at the ends of aisles – where they were more likely to be purchased. Marketing research also found that simply having a superabundance of foods on hand encouraged people to buy more. This "virtuous circle" has seemed to fulfill the capitalist dream of production feeding consumption in never-ending succession. Perhaps the greatest threat to supermarket sales has come not from declining consumption of processed foods but, rather, from the ever-greater convenience offered by fast-food restaurants (MacClancy 1992).

The Rise of Restaurants

Culinary legend credits the French Revolution with having launched the modern restaurant industry. With noblemen fleeing the country or facing the guillotine, great chefs supposedly offered their services to the newly ascendant bourgeoisie by opening restaurants. But in fact, restaurants had already existed for centuries in England and had even begun to spread to the Continent before 1789 (Mennell 1985). Given the French stereotype of being a nation of cooks, it is not surprising that they have claimed the restaurant as their own invention. With more recent trends in fast-food chains, however, it seems only just that history returns the birthplace of the restaurant to its native "nation of shopkeepers."

There may be some truth in the French claim, however, for French haute cuisine reached its highest peaks in nineteenth-century Paris. Chef Antonin Carême (1784–1833) developed an architectural approach to cuisine, not only in the sculpting of elaborate centerpieces but also in the harmonious blending of multiple flavors. He constructed his dishes meticulously from the *fonds* up, adding, extracting, reducing, and garnishing, yet arriving in the end at a simple and unified whole. His successor, Auguste

Escoffier (1846–1935), codified these techniques in the 1902 *Guide Culinaire,* which provided a standard reference work for future chefs.

The consumers of this haute cuisine consisted exclusively of the rich, for no one else could afford its costly ingredients and rarefied preparations. Carême spent his final years working for the Baron James de Rothschild, whereas Escoffier and his partner, César Ritz, founded some of Europe's finest hotels. Their wealthy clients demanded more than refined cuisine; they also wanted constant novelty, preferably in the form of new dishes named in their honor, such as Escoffier's melba toast, named for Austrian opera singer Nellie Melba. Constantly searching for new recipes, chefs often turned for inspiration to traditional peasant dishes, which they transformed by substituting expensive truffles and caviar for more rustic ingredients. The results of this faddish search for novelty are cataloged in Escoffier's *Guide Culinaire,* with its almost 3,000 recipes (Mennell 1985).

It is no oxymoron to speak of a haute cuisine fad, for although few could afford to eat at the great hotels, their cooking styles were followed widely by lesser restaurants in late–nineteenth–century Paris. Jean-Paul Aron (1979) has shown that expensive cuisine became affordable to the masses through the creative use of leftovers. Paris supported thriving networks for distributing secondhand foods, and as the meats and vegetables got older, the sauces covering them got thicker. Fraudulent restaurants displayed counters full of fresh fruits, meats, and vegetables, but these foods were only rented, and clients actually received nothing but leftovers. Even the wine was bad, pressed as it was from the bloated grapes of over-fertilized vines, blended with grain alcohol for added bite, then adulterated with plaster to deepen the color (Loubère 1978).

Concern about impure food in the United States led to perhaps the most important development in the modern restaurant industry, the franchise system. Chains, such as the Fred Harvey System, had long catered to traveling Americans, but although they offered reliable service, the corporate owners often had difficulty finding managers who could turn a profit. Howard Johnson, a Massachusetts business-man, solved this problem in the 1930s by creating a franchise system in which individual owner-operators managed the restaurants and paid royalties to the parent company. Gleaming orange porcelain tile not only advertised the restaurants' cleanliness but was also visible to motorists miles away. Franchising truly came of age in the 1950s, when "Ronald McDonald" became surrogate uncle to the baby-boom generation. McDon-ald's appealed to suburban families by offering immediate service, made possible by assembly-line grills and drive-through windows. But competing chains soon appeared, and just as the great chefs of Europe struggled to create new dishes, McDonald's, Burger King, and Kentucky Fried Chicken marketed count-less food fads, from the now-extinct Hulaburger to the seemingly immortal Egg McMuffin (Love 1986; Levenstein 1993).

While fast-food chains sprouted across the landscape, and even gourmet restaurants began using frozen vegetables, a new trend appeared at the highest levels of the restaurant universe. The *nouvelle cuisine* of the 1970s insisted on the use of only the freshest ingredients in the kitchen. Inspired by the great Fernand Point (1897–1955), who shunned Paris to operate a small restaurant in Vienne, the *nouvelle cuisiniers* became chef proprietors in provincial towns. What made their style unique was not the artful decoration of plates borrowed from the Japanese, or the minuscule portions, which led to confusion with the haute dieting of Michel Guérard's *cuisine minceur.* Instead, as Raymond Sokolov (1991) notes, the new recipes parodied rules laid down at the turn of the century by Escoffier. The salmon scaloppine with sorel sauce of Jean and Pierre Troisgros followed the procedure for pounding veal into thin scallops but resulted in a different, more delicate taste. Such chefs as Paul Bocuse eventually rose to become globe-trotting show-business stars, although from that status it was a quick tumble to obscurity.

The nouvelle cuisine attracted perhaps its most devoted following in California, which has always been a natural location for restaurant fads. Trendy chefs wore the spokes off their exotic-ingredient wheels of fortune in the 1980s, and enterprising restaurateurs were willing to invest in any theme, no matter how bizarre. Such places as the Bombay Bicycle Club, Orville Bean's Flying Machine, and Thank God It's Friday each had appropriate wall decor, if not menus. Meanwhile, Ed Debevic's, an upscale version of greasy-spoon diners, demonstrated the powerful appeal of restaurant nostalgia. Owned by Chicago's Lettuce-Entertain-You Restaurant Corporation, Debe-vic's attempted to recreate the "Happy Days" of the 1950s, but at least one skeptical patron had to ask her gum-smacking waitress: "Is this place fun, or is it just pretending to be?" (Belasco 1993: 241; Gutman 1993; Levenstein 1993).

Coca-Colonization

Critics might question the ambience of restaurants like Debevic's, but no one could doubt the profitability. With annual revenues of more than $4 million per restaurant, the only question for executives was how to grow further, and the answer seemed to lie in global expansion. Food manufacturers had been building international networks for more than a century. Kellogg's shipped breakfast cereals to Europe, Hormel marketed Spam in Latin America, Nestlé sold baby formula in Africa, and Coca-Cola distributed its bottles just about everywhere. But it was not until the 1970s that McDonald's led fast-food franchises into a search for global markets. Once the process had begun, golden arches sprang up in large cities everywhere, and the Big Mac seemed destined to become the culinary standard for middle-class consumers across the planet.

The success of international food marketing derived largely from the prestige value of its Western origins. In peasant societies around the world, the high cost of canned spaghetti and Spam gave these products status appeal far beyond their intrinsic culinary value (Kalčik 1984). Fast-food chains purposely resisted adapting to foreign tastes, calculating that their American origins would maximize sales. Kentucky Fried Chicken, for example, boosted sales in Japan with clever advertisements showing Americans eating the Colonel's chicken for Thanksgiving dinner. One Japanese executive even claimed that "if we eat McDonald's hamburgers and potatoes for a thousand years, we will become taller, our skin will become white, and our hair blonde" (Love 1986: 426).

Not all Japanese wanted white skin and blond hair, however. Many people rejected the foreign products and assumed ultranationalistic attachments to domestic foods, such as rice. More commonly, non-Western nations created industrialized versions of their own native cuisines. Japanese children ate tuna-fish crackers, while their Mexican counterparts munched pork-rind–flavored chips. Coke and Pepsi competed in Asia against local brands of ginseng cola. Unlike McDonald's, they increased sales by reformulating their syrup to suit indigenous tastes, typically by making them even sweeter than the American versions. So even as international capitalism worked to create a homogeneous world cuisine, it also contributed to ethnic diversity.

Food and Morality

Connections between diet and morality are common throughout world history. Jewish and Moslem dietary laws, for example, defined pork as unclean and prohibited its consumption. Many followers of Buddha went further and, out of a belief in reincarnation, abstained from all animal products. Confucius laid down social rather than religious rules for the correct preparation and consumption of foods. Because of their ancient heritage, none of these beliefs qualify as fads. Yet modern advocates of dietary restrictions – branded charlatans, and often with good reason – make similar claims that certain foods must be avoided as either polluted or sacred.

Victorian Movements

Sylvester Graham (1794–1851) originated modern food fads in the United States. About 1830, this Presbyterian minister from Connecticut developed a theory of health and morality he called "the Science of Human Life." He claimed that "natural" living was the secret to happiness and was the only way to avoid the menace of "dyspepsia" or indigestion, at the time a widely feared affliction. The two greatest dangers to a

natural life were an improper diet and sexuality. Graham warned his followers to avoid highly seasoned food, rich pastries, and, especially, meat. These foods stimulated the body, provoked sexual activity, and led to irritation, inflammation, and debility. Physical excitement, in turn, impaired spiritual health; vegetarianism, thus, became vital to personal salvation. Graham lectured up and down the Atlantic coast, building a loyal following and providing a model for future food faddists.

Historian Stephen Nissenbaum (1980) has found the key to Graham's crusade in his namesake bread. Graham decried the widespread consumption of commercially baked white bread and called for a return to coarse, homemade, whole wheat "Graham" bread (very different, despite its name, from the modern "Graham cracker"). The problem lay not in the loss of nutrients from removing the bran; instead, he concluded, white bread was too nutritious for the human body to digest. The additional bulk of whole wheat helped to balance the diet and prevent the alarming excesses caused by the consumption of white bread. According to Nissenbaum, the true concern was not the type of flour but, instead, the rising commercialization of production and the imminent breakdown of family life in Jacksonian America. Graham bread represented a return to a simpler subsistence lifestyle, sheltered by family values from the vagaries of the market economy.

The future of Graham's bread lay, ironically, in the breakfast cereal industry. Dr. James C. Jackson (1811–95), a recovered dyspepsia patient, created the first of these breakfast foods in 1863. "Granula," as he called it, consisted of Graham flour and water, formed into thin sheets and baked, then ground and baked again. The product proved a commercial failure, however, because it had to be reconstituted overnight in milk to provide an edible consistency. This drawback was later overcome by Dr. John Harvey Kellogg (1852–1943), a member of the Seventh-Day Adventist Church, who had adopted Sylvester Graham's dietary doctrines. Kellogg served "Granola" at the Adventist's sanitarium in Battle Creek, Michigan, to patients who included John D. Rockefeller, Theodore Roosevelt, and Amelia Earhart. However, a copyright infringement suit by Jackson prevented him from marketing the product. In 1895, Kellogg and his younger brother Will Keith (1860–1951), who actually founded the eponymous corporation, perfected a ready-to-eat breakfast cereal of wheat flakes, then proceeded to develop corn and rice flakes. But what ultimately made Battle Creek's breakfast cereal industry successful was not the convenience of Kellogg's corn flakes but rather the advertising genius of rival Charles W. Post (1854–1914), who made millions selling his own brand of wheat flakes with outlandish patent medicine claims (Carson 1957).

The Reverend Graham and Dr. Kellogg shared their vegetarian doctrines with European counterparts, such as the German clergyman Eduard Baltzer (1814–87). Influenced by Christoph Wilhelm Hufeland's 1796 work, *Makrobiotik,* which described magical forces for prolonging life, Baltzer published his four-volume *Die natürliche Lebensweise* (The natural way of life), a treatise on vegetarianism, from 1868 to 1872, and also founded Germany's first vegetarian club (Kühnau 1970).

The Victorian preoccupation with dyspepsia gave health advocates an enormous concern for regular bowel movements. Kellogg and others considered three trips to the lavatory a daily minimum. To assure this routine, young boys, in particular, received enemas and mineral oil, for cleansing the body was believed to be the only way of preventing less healthy outlets, such as masturbation. British Prime Minister William E. Gladstone himself stated that to assure proper digestion (and, presumably, regularity), he chewed each bite of food 32 times, once for each tooth. American businessman Horace Fletcher (1852–1919) took this advice to the extreme and chewed food until it dissolved in his mouth. He considered 32 chews sufficient for a piece of bread but claimed that a shallot had once required 720 chews. Although mistaken in his belief that digestion took place in the back of the throat, Fletcher produced remarkably odor-free stools, which he distributed freely by mail. Despite such promotional efforts, the chewing fad quickly passed, but the dream of healthy bowels lives on with the popularity of high-fiber bran cereals (Levenstein 1988; MacClancy 1992).

Nineteenth-century food faddists, although they seem absurd to modern science, nevertheless made a number of sound points. Vegetarian diets with large quantities of whole grains contrasted favorably with the carnivorous appetites of wealthy Victorians. Frequent complaints of indigestion and constipation seem quite understandable among people who consumed beefsteak, mutton chops, corned beef hash, scrambled eggs, fried potatoes, and hot cakes for breakfast (Levenstein 1988).

Science, Reform, and Fads

Elite banquet tables attracted the criticism of scientists as well as faddists. Harvey Levenstein, in a pathbreaking, two-volume social history of food in the United States (1988, 1993), examined how nutritional science affected American diets. Beginning in the late nineteenth century, home economists, the extension agents of this new science, attempted to transform the nation's eating habits. They particularly deplored the diets of newly arrived immigrants, such as Italians, Slavs, and Jews, but immigrant cooks clung tenaciously to their Old World recipes. And contrary to the reformers' expectations, popular awareness of nutrition opened fertile ground for a new generation of food faddists.

Chemists Wilbur Atwater and Ellen Richards initiated the study of domestic science in the United States in the 1880s. Using nutritional methods developed several decades earlier by German researcher Justus von Liebig, they attempted to determine the most efficient way to feed people the required proteins, carbohydrates, and minerals. The ideal diet, they concluded predictably, consisted of New England dishes, such as pressed meat, creamed codfish, boiled hominy, baked beans, and Indian pudding. The only acceptable seasoning was a bland white sauce. Home economists, seeking to gain scientific respectability, distanced themselves from mere cooking teachers, a field in which they perhaps recognized their own incompetence. As a result, they emphasized accuracy over taste, giving students scientifically precise recipes and warning them never to improvise in the kitchen (Shapiro 1986; Levenstein 1988).

Although middle-class housewives dutifully followed their textbook recipes for white sauce, no amount of coaching sufficed to persuade immigrants to give up their ethnic foods. Social workers tried in vain to convince Italian women of the inefficiency of paying high prices for imported pasta and cheeses. They had greater luck in changing the eating habits of children eager to fit in with their peers, even though the milk in school lunches often caused problems for lactose-intolerant ethnic groups. But these children counted as triumphs for the dietary reformers, who were more concerned about assimilating foreigners than improving their diets. Not until World War I, when Italy allied with the United States, did home economists concede that pastas offered an economical source of nutrition at a time of meat shortages (Levenstein 1988).

Dietary reform also became an important program for Mexican leaders around the turn of the twentieth century. They accepted the Victorian idea that spicy foods provoked immorality, and they blamed the disorderly behavior of the working classes on the consumption of chilli peppers. Mexican reformers, like their North American counterparts, established schools of domestic science to inculcate bourgeois family values among poor women. Educational kitchens took as their model diet the bland food of Britain, a drastic change indeed, and one that never caught on among Mexican cooks (Pilcher 1993).

The language of science appealed not only to elite reformers attempting to transform popular behavior but also to food faddists seeking to justify their outlandish claims. Dr. William Howard Hay, for example, used the difference between carbohydrates and proteins to explain eating disorders. This City University of New York medical school graduate developed a theory for the proper combination of foods. He believed that carbohydrates and proteins should never be eaten at the same meal because the body uses alkaline enzymes to digest carbohydrates whereas acids work on proteins. Thus, if a person ate both types of foods together, the alkalines and acids would neutralize one another, the stomach would be unable to digest anything, and the food would simply rot in the intestines. This posed a dilemma, for most foods contain both proteins and carbohydrates. Fortunately, although Hay's combining rules gained great popularity in the 1920s and 1930s, his theory was exposed as flawed because the alkaline enzymes operate in one part of the intestine and the acids in another (Pyke 1970; Deutsch 1977).

Hay's ideas about acids and alkalines, however, were carried to even greater extremes by Alfred W. McCann (1879–1931). A journalist in the muckraking tradition, McCann crusaded against food-processing firms with dramatic headlines that attracted both a wide popular following and numerous libel suits. He also predicted the imminent depletion of world food supplies and advocated the slaughter of all cattle to make grain cheaper. But his most outlandish claim was that Americans suffered from an epidemic of "acidosis." The causes of this supposed acid overdose ranged from improperly combined carbohydrates and proteins to eating meat and processed foods. The deadly effects, as McCann preached tirelessly in the press and on the radio, included "kidneycide" and heart attacks. In 1931, following a radio broadcast warning the public of the dangers of acidosis, McCann himself died of a heart attack (Deutsch 1977).

As with Graham, the food industry ultimately had the last laugh by turning McCann's crusades into advertising copy. The California Fruit Growers, for example, asserted that Sunkist brand citrus fruits actually had a beneficial alkaline effect despite their apparent acidity (Levenstein 1993). By the 1950s, food manufacturers had seemingly conquered American supermarkets with their myriad frozen, condensed, dehydrated, preserved, and otherwise processed products. But a backlash soon developed that revived many of the food fads of the nineteenth century.

The Counterculture Strikes Back

Like Upton Sinclair, who intended his 1906 book *The Jungle* as a radical call for socialism and instead contributed to a middle-class crusade for pure food, the late-1960s counterculture's attempt to overthrow industrial capitalism left one of its deepest imprints on the American diet. Food made an appealing medium of protest, both for its basic role in human life and because of the enormous changes effected by the food-processing industry. The radicals denounced such technological marvels as Wonder Bread, Minute Rice, and instant mashed potatoes, and echoing Sylvester Graham, they called for a return to natural foods, including whole wheat bread, brown rice, and wildflower honey. And although the majority of hippies ultimately abandoned their communes and reincorporated themselves into the society they had condemned, they did bring health foods and herb teas back with them into the mainstream (Belasco 1993).

The counterculture's pure-food protests grew out of news stories concerning the health hazards of pesticides and additives. In her 1962 book *The Silent Spring,* Rachel Carson warned that the pesticide DDT accumulated in the fatty tissue of both humans and animals with potentially fatal results. The U.S. Department of Agriculture insisted that the pesticide posed no danger; nevertheless, within a decade additional studies had confirmed Carson's claim, and the government banned DDT. And this was only the first wave in a flood of media revelations proclaiming the hazards of mercury in tuna, hormones in beef, arsenic in chickens, and carcinogens in bacon (Belasco 1993; Levenstein 1993).

Food-industry spokesmen, with the support of the U.S. Food and Drug Administration (FDA), responded by denying all charges against additives. Working on the theory that anything carbon was natural, they defended the use of petrochemicals as preservatives. They also observed that all foods contained carcinogens, which was true but begged the question of whether additives were in fact harmful in the quantities found in processed foods. Food lobbies' credibility suffered when the public learned of ties between scientific experts and the food industry. Frederick Stare, for example, founder of Harvard's Department of Nutrition and a leading crusader against food fads, testified in support of Kellogg's, Carnation, and other food corporations that donated large sums to his school (Levenstein 1993).

To avoid potential hazards in foods, the counterculture turned for guidance to organic gardening and to health-food experts, such as Jerome Irving (J. I.) Rodale (1899–1971). Rodale had founded the magazine *Organic Gardening and Farming,* in 1940, but had made little money because of the limited interest in compost fertilizers and natural insecticides. Another of his magazines, *Prevention,* was constantly accused of quackery by the medical establishment. By about 1969, however, such abuse by the medical establishment actually benefited Rodale; although by this time his son Robert had taken over editorial duties, hippies who rejected conventional authorities began to follow the Rodale gospel. Wilderness survivalist Euell Gibbons (1911–75) and vitamin supplement advocate Adelle Davis (1904–74) also enjoyed revivals. Perhaps the most persuasive arguments for the vegetarian cause came from Frances Lappé's bestselling *Diet for a Small Planet* in 1971. She relied on science, not mysticism, and based her diet on protein complementarity, those combinations of grains and legumes that supply the full range of amino acids needed for protein utilization. At the same time, her observations about beef cattle displacing peasants resonated with the moral outrage then being expressed by Vietnam War protesters (Deutsch 1977; Belasco 1993; Levenstein 1993).

Counterculture members, in search of social revitalization and alternate methods of health maintenance, often joined groups that were following natural and even mystical lifestyles. The most dedicated withdrew to agrarian communes, but the goal of independence proved elusive, and many survived poor harvests with the help of food stamps. Health-food stores and co-ops boomed during the early 1970s by offering more convenient sources of organically grown products. At the same time, large numbers of people formed communal kitchens, many of which grew into health-food restaurants. Mystical religious groups, such as the Hare Krishna and Divine Light, also contributed to the spread of health foods (Kandel and Pelto 1980; Belasco 1993).

Zen macrobiotics became one of the most controversial of the mystical health-food movements. Created by Japanese philosopher George Ohsawa (early in the twentieth century), macrobiotics applied the principles of yin and yang to food. Animal foods, such as meats and eggs, stood at the yang end of the spectrum while sugar and chemicals tended toward yin. The center included vegetables, fruits, and whole-grain cereals, and a diet of these foods represented the path to harmony with nature. Brown rice formed the exact midpoint, and this alone constituted the ideal macrobiotic diet. Unfortunately, nutritional-deficiency diseases began appearing in the Berkeley area, and in 1965, a young woman starved to death while seeking enlightenment. Nevertheless, macrobiotic restaurants attracted large audiences even among nonbelievers (Fieldhouse 1986; Levenstein 1993).

Other fads, such as the vitamin craze, penetrated deep into mainstream society. Megavitamin advocates claimed that when taken in sufficient quantities, vitamin C cured colds and other infections, whereas vitamin E improved sexual performance. Faddists even invented new vitamins, such as B_{15}, supposedly found in apricot kernels and capable of curing cancer. Scientific support for vitamins came from Nobel Prize–winning scientists Albert Schweitzer and Linus Pauling, and by 1969, half of all Americans regularly took vitamin supplements. Nevertheless, megavitamins provided questionable benefits. Excessive quantities – and some people advocated consuming hundreds of times the recommended daily allowances – of vitamins were simply eliminated by the body (Deutsch 1977; Levenstein 1993).

The health-food movement, considered a fad in the late 1960s and early 1970s, had become an important part of nutritional orthodoxy by the 1990s. Breakfast cereal manufacturers, some of the worst abusers of consumers' nutritional health, reformulated such products as Fruit Loops, Sugar Pops, and Cocoa Krispies to give them nutritional respectability. Meanwhile, artisanal bakers of crusty whole grain breads, although still no threat to the makers of Wonder Bread, have appeared throughout the country. And Alice Waters parlayed a communal kitchen for Berkeley radicals into Chez Panisse – one of the country's most innovative and respected restaurants (Thorne 1992; Belasco 1993; Levenstein 1993).

Food and Identity

Jean-Anthelme Brillat-Savarin (1755–1826), one of the pontiffs of French cuisine, affirmed the connection between cuisine and identity in his often abbreviated phrase, "Tell me what you eat, and I'll tell you who you are." One wonders how the venerable French gourmet would respond to modern food faddists recounting their gastronomic experiences. Certainly, he would find kindred souls among the new generation of globe-trotting gourmets, constantly seeking out variety among diverse ethnic cuisines. The legions of dieters starving themselves to attain fashion-model figures might be more difficult for him to comprehend. But most baffling of all would be the culinary changes wrought by modern technology and mass advertising.

The Obsession with Weight

Historian Hillel Schwartz (1986) dates the origins of the modern obsession with weight to the turn of the twentieth century. Although Victorian dyspepsia cures often resembled contemporary reducing diets, adherents hoped to gain a *feeling* of lightness, rather than to transform their outward appearance. But with the *fin de siècle*, fat went out of fashion. The husky men of Gilded Age banquets were condemned for their conspicuous consumption, while the voluptuous women portrayed in impressionist paintings turned to diets and exercise. Once the general trend toward slimness had begun, it proved difficult to stop. Feminine ideals fluctuated – the boyish flappers of the 1920s gave way to more rounded figures in the 1930s – but the overall trend headed ever downward, and by the 1960s, many considered film stars Marilyn Monroe and Jayne Mansfield to be overweight. The increasingly impossible standards of physical beauty encouraged countless fad diets.

Patent-medicine hucksters quickly saw the potential profits from dieting. Some were relatively benign, such as Jean Down's "Get Slim," which was simply pink lemonade, and Dr. W. W. Baxter's "phytolacca," a purgative found in the pokeberry, and supposedly eaten by overweight migratory birds. Other formulations proved more hazardous, such as "Helen's Liquid Reducer Compound," which promised in the 1930s that you could "Gargle your fat away!" with a compound of peppermint, bleach, and hydrogen peroxide. One of the most dangerous patent medicines of all was an obesity tablet marketed about 1910 that contained strychnine and arsenic (Deutsch 1977; Schwartz 1986).

As scientific knowledge advanced and the FDA's enforcement powers increased, patent medicines were replaced by liquid diets and prescription drugs. The former consisted of food powders mixed with water and taken in place of breakfast and lunch. Beginning in the 1930s with Dr. Stoll's Diet Aid, these milkshake-like concoctions have returned regularly to later generations under the names "Metrecal," "Natur-slim," "Herbalife," and "Slimfast." The 1930s also marked the discovery of amphetamines as appetite suppressants. Although widely prescribed since the 1950s, often with barbiturates to offset the jitters, amphetamines lose their effectiveness after six to ten weeks. Pharmaceutical companies have nevertheless continued to search for dieting drugs, one of the latest being a fat-blocking pill that attempts to prevent the body from absorbing dietary fats (Schwartz 1986).

The diet industry has offered seemingly endless opportunities for market growth and product differentiation. In the 1950s and 1960s, dieters could turn for help to group therapy in TOPS (Take Off Pounds Sensibly), Overeaters Anonymous, and Weight Watchers. The latter company, founded in 1964 by Brooklyn housewife Jean Nidetch, had built revenues of $39 million in little more than a decade. By the 1980s, food manufacturers had focused much of their chemical wizardry on producing an amazing array of "lite" foods, including diet colas, low-calorie "spreads," low-fat cheese foods, light beers and wines, and diet frozen dinners (Schwartz 1986; Belasco 1993).

Self-proclaimed diet experts also kept a constant eye out for new gimmicks, in the process reviving many food fads from the past. Harvey and Marilyn Diamond, for example, in the 1985 best-seller *Fit for Life,* advocated a "natural" life of vegetarianism and Fletcher-style chewing and warned against the mixing of proteins and carbohydrates. Dr. Robert Atkins, meanwhile, had rediscovered the high-protein, low-carbohydrate diet first made famous by Englishman William Banting (1798–1878). *Dr. Atkin's Diet Revolution,* published in 1972, not only sold millions of copies but also served as advertising for his extremely lucrative weight-loss clinic. Susan Powter, author of the 1992 *Stop the Insanity,* reversed this plan and called for a high-carbohydrate, low-fat diet. Best known for her white, crew-cut hair, Powter also marketed highly successful aerobic exercise videos.

The dieting mania dramatizes the continued importance of food in the social construction of identity. Diet and exercise fanatics considered a fashionable body image, rather than health, the ultimate goal. And as the anorexia nervosa epidemic of the 1970s demonstrated, the pursuit of such a fashionable body can ultimately prove hazardous to the health. Actress Jane Fonda admitted that she had suffered from bulimia, making her both advocate and victim of the culture of slimness. It seems appropriate that such a culture first appeared in advanced capitalist countries because the contradictions inherent in this search for perfection have alienated large numbers of people from their own sources of nourishment.

The Ethnic Revival

Food helps define the identity not only of individuals but also of groups. Just as progressive dietary reformers used cooking classes as a means of assimilating immigrants in turn-of-the-century America, people in the postcolonial world have sought to counter Western capitalist hegemony by forging national cuisines. This culinary ethnic revival eventually began to colonize the United States through the combined efforts of talented immigrant cooks and adventuresome American eaters. The resulting mixtures have enriched the diets and tastes of both groups.

Cookbooks defining national cuisines have recently emerged throughout the postcolonial, postindustrial world, and in some places, middle-class women, searching for a national identity to replace colonial ideologies, have often turned to indigenous folk traditions. In Mexico, such traditions have revived the popularity of peasant foods (for example, maize tortillas and tamales), which had formerly been snubbed as Indian foods by both Spanish and Creole elites. Following the revolution of 1910 and the resulting search for Mexico's indigenous roots, an emerging middle class embraced tamales as national symbols. In much the same way, Egyptians proclaimed their patriotism by eating *ful medames,* a peasant bean dish, while Brazilians honored *feijoada,* a combination of meats, beans, and rice similar to African-American "soul food" (Roden 1972; Oliven 1984; Pilcher 1993). In India, the national revival did not seek out lower-class traditions because of strict caste laws about purity. Instead, as Arjun Appadurai (1988) notes, cookbooks allowed middle-class women to experiment with regional recipes and thus eliminate ethnic barriers to Indian nationalism.

As national cuisines appeared in many countries, gastronomic pluralism gained new acceptance in the United States. Historian Donna Gabaccia (1998) shows how ethnic businesses packaged Chinese, Mexican, Italian, and other foreign foods for mainstream American consumers. These enterprises often began as neighborhood restaurants and grocery stores, and although catering at first to immigrant communities, they had to adapt to produce available in the United States. Chow mein, for example, was invented in San Francisco by an immigrant Chinese cook. Recipes often needed further alterations to attract wider audiences, as Italians found when they sold more tomato sauce by limiting the garlic, which most Americans found distasteful. Such modified ethnic foods often gained great popularity; salsa sales recently surpassed those of catsup in the United States. Ethnic identities themselves became blurred by constant mixing as the culinary melting pot produced such hybrids as taco pizza.

Many consumers rejected this trend and sought out more authentic versions of foreign cuisines. Sophisticated diners in the 1960s and 1970s, led by Craig Claiborne of the *New York Times* and Gael Greene of *New York Magazine,* discovered new dialects of French, Italian, and Chinese in the regional cuisines of Provence, Lombardy, and Sichuan. From there it was a small step to the foods of Thailand,

Turkey, Ethiopia, and Argentina. In the 1980s, residents of New York City, Washington, D.C., and San Francisco had to work full time just to keep up with the latest fads in Afghan, Moroccan, and Peruvian restaurants. And those bold enough to seek out ethnic grocers could reproduce exotic dishes at home with the help of cookbooks by Diana Kennedy, Claudia Roden, Ken Hom, and Paula Wolfert or the excellent series by Time-Life Books. Alternately, cooks could follow Jane and Michael Stern across the interstate highway system to sample the regional foods of the United States (Barr and Levy 1984; Levenstein 1993).

The search for ethnic and regional variety eventually percolated down to that culinary lowest common denominator, the fast-food franchise. Taco Bell, the most successful example, mass-marketed a bowdlerized version of border cuisine, while the Golden Wok and Teriyaki Express served up Asian-style fast foods, and Wienerschnitzel claimed German ancestry for its hot dogs. Meanwhile, the drive-through menus of major chains featured regional American dishes, such as McDonald's southern-barbecue–inspired McRib sandwich, and Arby's Philadelphia steak and cheese sandwich. Perhaps the greatest variety in ethnic fast food can be found, appropriately, in the food court of any neighborhood shopping mall. Adolescents searching out new styles in clothes or the latest in music can now take a break for the most recent food fad.

The Meal Is the Message

The pursuit of fashion, whether in food, dress, music, or automobiles, preoccupies many in modern society. People spend enormous sums keeping up with the latest trends, investing not only their money but also their personal identity in constantly changing commodities. For fashionable elites, being seen in the newest restaurant is more important than the meal itself, while the success of a dinner party depends on serving food that the guests have never before tasted. Fashion's arbitrary whims, likewise, facilitate contradictions, such as "lite" foods that are low in fat but high in sodium. As fads come and go, social norms seem increasingly arbitrary, and moral behavior, ultimately, loses all meaning (Finkelstein 1989).

Roland Barthes (1979) notes further that mass-marketed food has expanded far beyond the dining room, invading all aspects of modern life. Snack foods and TV dinners have made eating a part of the media experience; drive-through windows have transformed dashboards into lunch counters (Levenstein 1993). At the same time, the social implications of eating have changed as fast-food combo meals and individually packaged frozen dinners have replaced the traditional family dinner pot. Each person seemingly has greater freedom of choice, yet choices are actually often determined by marketing executives in corporate offices (Mintz 1985).

Important changes have occurred in the production as well as the consumption of food. The alienation of cook from food had already become apparent by the 1950s when cake-mix manufacturers changed the recipe on the boxes to include eggs and oil – at first they required only water – so that people would feel they were actually doing something (Levenstein 1993). But more fundamentally, as John Thorne (1992) has pointed out, the oral culture of the kitchen is being replaced by the written word, and with it an artisanal approach to cooking is giving way to science. Microwave ovens and food processors have taken over the demanding skills needed at the cutting board and over the stove, while cookbooks with fixed recipes, exact measures, and precise times have obviated tasting, smelling, or even watching what is going on in the kitchen. Ironically, a rapid growth in cookbook sales has coincided with a sharp decline in the number of meals eaten at home (Shapiro 1994). Cookbooks have gone from utilitarian kitchen manuals to glossy coffee-table books, travel guides, and parodies, such as the 1989 *Manifold Destiny: The Only Guide to Cooking on Your Car Engine* and *The Bubba Gump Shrimp Co. Cookbook,* which appeared in 1994.

These changes do not necessarily herald the culture of annihilation predicted by Umberto Eco (1968). Mass culture, according to Eco, relies on simple, repetitive formulas, such as commercial jingles, that deny consumers any form of participation in producing and interpreting the message. Yet even, or perhaps especially, small children are far from the defenseless consumers assumed by Eco. Recall the oft-repeated tale of Pop Rocks, a candy that fizzes in the stomach like carbonated water. Some nameless youth of urban legend supposedly ate a bag of Pop Rocks, washed them down with a cola, and then exploded. This story, in its very childishness, reveals a world far different from that of television's Pepsi Generation.

Food has long provided rich material for anthropologists seeking to interpret societies, and in the modern world this symbolic wealth is particularly great in the recent fad of food movies. The darkest fears of Barthes and Eco are played out in the film *Age of Innocence* (1993), where lavish depictions of Delmonico's haute cuisine have more appeal than do the repressed members of Gilded Age high society. Nevertheless, food can also serve as a means to personal fulfillment, both spiritual, in *Babette's Feast* (1987), and sexual, in *Like Water for Chocolate* (1992); both in the workplace, as in *Tampopo* (1987), and at home, as in *Eat, Drink, Man, Woman* (1994). The meaning of food fads, whether they annihilate individual judgment or facilitate culinary expression, must ultimately be decided anew as each philosopher gazes into his or her Cuisinart.

Jeffrey M. Pilcher

Bibliography

Appadurai, Arjun. 1988. How to make a national cuisine: Cookbooks in contemporary India. *Comparative Studies in Society and History* 23: 3-24.

Aron, Jean-Paul. 1979. The art of using leftovers: Paris, 1850-1900. In *Food and drink in history: Selections from the Annales: Économies, Sociétés, Civilisations,* Vol. 5, ed. Robert Forster and Orest Ranum, trans. Elborg Forster and Patricia M. Ranum, 98-108. Baltimore, Md.

Barr, Ann, and Paul Levy. 1984. *The official foodie handbook: Be modern - worship food.* New York.

Barthes, Roland. 1979. Toward a psychosociology of contemporary food consumption. In *Food and drink in history: Selections from the Annales, économies, sociétés, civilisations,* ed. Robert Forster and Orest Ranum, 166-73. Baltimore, Md.

Belasco, Warren J. 1993. *Appetite for change: How the counterculture took on the food industry.* Ithaca, N.Y.

Carson, Gerald. 1957. *Cornflake crusade.* New York.

Deutsch, Ronald M. 1977. *The new nuts among the berries.* Palo Alto, Calif.

Eco, Umberto. 1968. *Apocalipticos e integrados ante la cultura de masas.* Barcelona.

Fieldhouse, Paul. 1986. *Food and nutrition: Customs and culture.* London.

Finkelstein, Joanne. 1989. *Dining out: A sociology of modern manners.* Washington Square, N.Y.

Gabaccia, Donna R. 1998. *We are what we eat: Ethnic food and the making of Americans.* Cambridge, Mass.

Goody, Jack. 1982. *Cooking, cuisine and class: A study in contemporary sociology.* Cambridge.

Gutman, Richard J. S. 1993. *American diner: Then and now.* New York.

Herbert, Victor. 1980. *Nutrition cultism: Facts and fictions.* Philadelphia, Pa.

Kalčik, Susan. 1984. Ethnic foodways in America: Symbol and performance of identity. In *Ethnic regional foodways in the United States: The performance of group identity,* ed. Linda Keller Brown and Kay Mussell, 39-65. Knoxville, Tenn.

Kandel, Randy F., and Gretel H. Pelto. 1980. The health food movement: Social revitalization or alternative health maintenance system? In *Nutritional anthropology: Contemporary approaches to diet and culture,* ed. Norge W. Jerome, Randy F. Kandel, and Gretel H. Pelto, 327-63. Pleasantville, N.Y.

Kühnau, Joachim. 1970. Food cultism and nutrition quackery in Germany. In *Food cultism and nutrition quackery,* ed. Gunnar Blix, 59-68. Uppsala.

Levenstein, Harvey A. 1988. *Revolution at the table: The transformation of the American diet.* New York.

1993. *Paradox of plenty: A social history of eating in modern America.* New York.

Loubère, Leo. 1978. *The red and the white: A history of wine in France and Italy in the nineteenth century.* Albany, N.Y.

Love, John F. 1986. *McDonald's: Behind the arches.* New York.

MacClancy, Jeremy. 1992. *Consuming culture: Why you eat what you eat.* New York.

Mennell, Stephen. 1985. *All manners of food: Eating and taste in England and France from the Middle Ages to the present.* Oxford.

Mintz, Sidney. 1985. *Sweetness and power: The place of sugar in modern history.* New York.

Nissenbaum, Stephen. 1980. *Sex, diet, and debility in Jacksonian America: Sylvester Graham and health reform.* Chicago.

Oliven, Ruben George. 1984. The production and consumption of popular culture in Brazil. *Latin American Perspectives* 11: 103-15.

O'Neil, Patrick M. 1994. Saturday morning commercials short on veggies, long on sugar. *Charleston Post and Courier.* December 18.

Pilcher, Jeffrey M. 1993. ¡Vivan tamales! The creation of a Mexican national cuisine. Ph.D. thesis, Texas Christian University, Fort Worth.

Pyke, Magnus. 1970. The development of food myths. In *Food cultism and nutrition quackery,* ed. Gunnar Blix, 22-9. Uppsala.

Roden, Claudia. 1972. *A book of Middle Eastern food.* New York.

Schwartz, Hillel. 1986. *Never satisfied: A cultural history of diets, fantasies, and fat.* New York.

Shapiro, Eben. 1994. Thousands of cookbooks in search of some cooks. *Wall Street Journal.* March 2, Sec. B, p. 1.

Shapiro, Laura. 1986. *Perfection salad: Women and cooking at the turn of the century.* New York.

Sokolov, Raymond. 1991. *Why we eat what we eat: How the encounter between the New World and the Old changed the way everyone on the planet eats.* New York.

Tannahill, Reay. 1988. *Food in history.* New York.

Thorne, John. 1992. *Outlaw cook.* New York.

Young, James Harvey. 1989. *Pure food: Securing the Federal Food and Drugs Act of 1906.* Princeton, N.J.

VI.13 ❧ Food Prejudices and Taboos

Over the past 2,000 years, scholars have produced a vast literature on food prejudices and taboos. This literature, however, is complicated by confusing etymology and indiscriminate or inconsistent application of several terms, such as food aversions, avoidances, dislikes, prejudices, prohibitions, rejections, and taboos/tabus.

The term *aversion* is used by food-habit researchers primarily in the context of disliked or inappropriate foods, whereby individuals elect not to consume items because of specific, defined, biological or cultural criteria. Some human food aversions, for example, are immediate as when foods are tasted and disliked because of sensory properties of odor, taste, and texture. Other foods are avoided because of biological-physiological conditions posed by nausea and vomiting, "heartburn" or "acid stomach," intestinal distress associated with flatulence, or acute diarrhea. Still other food aversions are cultural or psychological in origin, as evidenced when individuals report that they dislike specific foods even though the items have never been consumed by them. In such instances, anticipation triggers avoidance or aversive behavior, and merely the color, shape, or images of the food source itself are enough to elicit aversion and the individual decision not to eat.

The word *taboo* or *tabu,* in contrast, implies a moral or religious context of foods or food-related behavior. Taboo, the Polynesian concept to "set apart," includes the suggestion that some human activities, and eating behavior specifically, may be either protective or deleterious to the environment, to the consumer, or to society at large. Food-related taboos in this context are identical to dietary prohibitions, whereby foods and food-related behaviors are forbidden for specific positive or negative reasons.

Attached to food prohibitions and taboos are a broad range of ecological, economic, religious, and social attributes that define intake restriction. Thus, consumption of prohibited foods may produce serious consequences for individuals, groups, and societies at large, and as a result, violators may face personal and social condemnation. Some taboos may be imposed to protect food crops at specific periods of the growth cycle, whereas other food-related practices may be instituted to distribute economic gain more effectively among individuals or groups in society. Most food-related taboos, however, are religious in nature and are imposed to provide structure and to regulate individual and social behavior.

Although individual food dislikes may lead to food rejection and, ultimately, to food prejudice, food dislikes are not dietary prohibitions or taboos. Nor are food aversions. Taboos, in essence, have their basis in behavioral, ecological, and religious strictures. Accordingly, all food-related taboos result in avoidance behavior – but food-related avoidance patterns may not result in taboos.

Approaches, Paradigms, and Themes

Scholars interested in the origins, development, and evolution of food prejudices and taboos range from professionals in the humanities to researchers in the biological and medical sciences (Frazer 1935; Gaster 1955; Simoons 1961, 1978; Douglass 1977; Grivetti 1978a, 1981a). The literature presented within this broad spectrum poses a basic conflict. Anchored at one end are representative descriptive studies where explanations for food-avoidance behavior and dietary taboos are set within concepts of folklore and mythology and where magic and superstition play important interpretive roles.

In opposition to this approach are studies by researchers who reject such empiricism and seek scientific understanding of and validation for human food-related behavior. Some scholars argue that there is logic in the so-called protective magic of food taboos, whereas others seek the rationale for dietary prohibitions in causal relationships between ingestion and manifestation of disease.

A review of food-habit literature from antiquity to the twentieth century reveals that scholars have advanced at least 11 hypotheses to explain the origins of dietary codes (Grivetti and Pangborn 1974; Grivetti 1980):

1. Aesthetics: Prohibitions are instituted because the appearance, behavior, source, or origin of certain foods is aesthetically revolting, contaminating, or polluting to humans (Douglas 1966).
2. Compassion: Prohibitions are intended to demonstrate human compassion toward specific animals that might otherwise serve as food resources (Scott 1866; Chadwick, 1890).
3. Divine commandment: Prohibitions have their origins in instructions directly to humans by a god, priestly intermediaries, or other cultural authorities. Adherents reject twentieth-century attempts at scientific enquiry and explanation (Singer 1907).
4. Ecology: Prohibitions evolve because of logical interrelations between human economic systems and the environment that ultimately determine which foods will be favored or rejected (Harris 1972, 1973).
5. Ethnic identity: Prohibitions are instituted to strengthen ethnic bonds that reinforce cultural identification by setting practitioners apart from food-related practices of other societies (Mays 1963).
6. Health and sanitation: Prohibitions reflect religious or medical insights on causal associations between ingestion and disease or illness (Arrington 1959).
7. Literary allegory: Prohibitions are not directed toward food, per se, but serve instead as oblique references to other behavioral, cultural, or political nonfood practices (Novatian 1957; Ginzberg 1961).
8. Natural law: Food-related behaviors and prohibitions are instituted to reinforce concepts of compassion and to identify abominations and define "unnatural" appetite gratification (Mackintosh 1959; Cook 1969).
9. Self-restraint/denial: Prohibited foods, once highly desired, are forbidden by priests or other cultural authorities to reduce gastronomic pleasure and to teach and reinforce moral discipline (Kellogg 1899).
10. Staple conservation: Prohibitions and taboos are established to conserve and extend the food supply, thereby improving human survival potential during periods of environmental crisis or conflict (Thompson 1949).
11. Sympathetic magic: Food prohibitions are related to specific behavioral or physical characteristics of animals and qualities that humans wish to avoid (Frazer 1935; Gaster 1955).

Although there have been thousands of descriptions of food and food-related taboos from antiquity into the twentieth century, contemporary analysis of how and why dietary prohibitions have evolved and how taboos and practices stabilize social and ethnic groups stems from the classic studies of food patterns and human food-related behavior in southern African societies (Richards 1932, 1939; Willoughby 1932).

Regarding thematic approaches taken by researchers on food prejudices and taboos, the most attractive and recognized theme has been religion, given the extensive literature on the dietary taboos of the major world faiths as exemplified by (1) Judaism (Kaufman 1957; Korff 1966; Cohn 1973; Dresser 1979; Regenstein and Regenstein 1979, 1988, 1991); by (2) Christianity (Hehn, 1885; Simoons 1961; Knutsson and Selinus 1970; Bosley and Hardinge 1992; Pike 1992); by (3) Islam (Roberts 1925; Sakr 1971, 1975; Grivetti 1975; Rahman 1987; Twaigery and Spillman 1989; Chaudry, 1992); and by (4) Hinduism (Harding 1931; Prakash 1961; Grivetti 1991a; Kilara and Iya 1992).

Gender and age are perhaps the second most common theme, and especially the question of how dietary prohibitions or taboos reinforce sex roles in society and characterize rites of passage, such as birth, coming of age, marriage, and death (Frazer 1935; Gaster 1955; Douglas 1966, 1977; Garine 1972).

A third common theme involves protection and takes two directions. One of these focuses on the question of whether dietary prohibitions are protective medically or nutritionally to humans (Bolton 1972; Jelliffe and Jelliffe 1978). The second has to do with whether dietary taboos protect the cultural-ecological setting of different societies and provide a balance to human use of environmental resources (Heun 1962; McDonald 1977).

Religion

Many religious practices that developed in antiquity and still regulate human behavior and social activities are known from accounts written in ancient Egypt and also stem from the religious practices and dietary codes of Judaism, Christianity, Islam, and Hinduism.

Ancient Egypt

The Nile Valley civilizations present a rich archaeological record and literature that reveal food-related practices, cooking, dining, and food patterns, and dietary prohibitions (Loret, 1892; Keimer 1924; Emery 1962; Darby, Ghalioungui, and Grivetti 1977). Although numerous dietary taboos are known from ancient Egypt, only two are reviewed here.

Cattle and beef. Herodotus (*The Histories* 11:41), writing in the fifth century B.C., stated that local Egyptian priests abstained from beef, especially the flesh of cows, and that this dietary pattern extended beyond the geographical limits of Egypt westward into Libya. Such a taboo attached to beef was also described in the fourth century B.C. by Philochorus

of Athens, who attempted to explain the practice when he wrote that

> at one time, also when there was a dearth of cows, a law was passed, on account of the scarcity, that they [the Egyptians] should abstain from these animals since they wished to amass them and fill up their numbers not be slaughtering them (Philochorus, cited in Athenaeus 1927-41, 9:375:C).

Porphyry (1965, 2:11), writing in the third century A.D., provided a relatively late glimpse of what might be taken as the impact of the beef prohibition in ancient Egypt when he stated that: "[w]ith the Egyptians . . . any one would sooner taste human flesh than the flesh of a cow."

Greek and Roman texts notwithstanding, the archaeological evidence emphatically disputes the presence of a sweeping beef taboo throughout ancient Egypt. Tomb and temple art throughout the dynastic period, 3200-341 B.C., provides abundant pictorial evidence of bovine slaughter and butchering. Indeed, thousands of carvings and paintings depict the capture and killing of cattle, butchers at work cutting up the carcasses, the display of beef haunches and organ meats in shops, and boiling and roasting beef (Darby et al. 1977).

It is true that specific types of bulls were worshiped at the urban sites of Heliopolis, Hermonthis, and Memphis, and that cows were worshiped throughout the Nile Valley as the incarnation of the goddesses Hathor and Isis. But such deification did not inhibit beef consumption throughout the Nile Valley of ancient Egypt at all geographical localities (Monet 1958).

Other writers, however, have readily accepted the Greek texts, ignored the archaeological data, and attempted explanations for Egyptian beef avoidance. J. G. Wilkinson, for example, wrote that "by a prudent foresight, in a country possessing neither extensive pasture lands, nor great abundance of cattle, the cow was held sacred and consequently was forbidden to be eaten" (Wilkinson 1854).

Yet deification of bulls and cows in ancient Egypt was not related to available pasture land or threatened extinction but to specific physical characteristics of individual bulls and cows (Darby et al. 1977). Furthermore, given the wide range of texts that clearly identify offerings of meat from bulls, bullocks, calves, and cows, it is erroneous to conclude that there was a sweeping beef prohibition associated with Egyptians of all periods. It may be that a more limited beef prohibition was intact during late- and postdynastic times, but it is not possible to state, categorically, whether the prohibition applied to all varieties of beef, or specifically to cows, or perhaps to female calves, or to other bovine categories (Darby et al. 1977).

Another aspect of the late dynastic beef prohibition deserves attention since it relates not to meat, per se, but to the Egyptian manner of butchering. Herodotus (*The Histories* 4:1) commented that "[n]o native of Egypt, whether man or woman . . . will use the knife of a Greek . . . or taste the flesh of an ox, known to be pure, if it has been cut with a Greek knife." Because the ancient Egyptian standard method of butchering was to cut the throat, then drain and collect the blood for food, it may be that this passage indicates some significant differences in butchering techniques between Egyptians and Greeks. It could also, of course, be taken as evidence of (or it possibly reflected) an Egyptian aloofness and sense of superiority over the Greeks (Darby et al. 1977).

Fish. Fish held a dual position throughout the dynastic period of ancient Egyptian history. Texts and tomb art document geographical locations where (and historical periods when) fishing was an accepted occupation and eating fish was acceptable. Indeed, Egyptian kings regularly supplied beef, fish, and vegetables to soldiers as military rations and sometimes presented fresh and dried fish as temple offerings. But other passages and depictions indicate that priests abstained from fish, that fishing as a profession was abhorrent, and that fish eaters were ceremonially impure (Darby et al. 1977).

Five specific varieties of Nile fish figured prominently in Egyptian religion and were widely rejected as food: the latus *(Lates niloticus;* perhaps *Tilapia nilotica),* the lepidotus *(Barbus bynni),* the maeotes (possibly a siluride), the oxyrhynchus *(Mormyrus* spp.), and the phagrus (identification uncertain; possibly *Hydrocyon forskalii).* The latus was worshiped at the site of Esna where thousands of mummified examples have been discovered, but reverence and dietary avoidance of this species at Esna did not preclude its widespread consumption elsewhere along the Nile.

The lepidotus was revered throughout the Nile Valley and thus widely rejected as food. The maeotes was worshiped near Aswan where it was rejected as food because it was considered a harbinger of the Nile flood. The oxyrhynchus was universally avoided as food for two distinctive reasons: The fish was associated with the god Seth, whose followers rejected it out of respect, whereas the followers of Osiris avoided oxyrhynchus because this species reportedly fed upon the phallus of their deity and, therefore, was an abomination. The phagrus was rejected for two reasons: (1) because its appearance also signaled the Nile flood, and (2) because it, too, had fed upon the phallus of Osiris (Darby et al. 1977).

Judaism

Two central texts present the Jewish dietary traditions and laws. The Torah stems from ancient oral traditions and was codified in its present literary form by, perhaps, the sixth century B.C. The Talmud, pro-

duced in Babylon and Jerusalem in the sixth century A.D., provides guidelines for Jewish moral conduct and incorporates numerous discussions and critical assessments of food and food-related issues.

Study of the Torah and Talmud suggests the development and evolution of Jewish dietary codes through seven stages:

Stage One: In Genesis 1:29-31, all products on earth are clean.

Stage Two: In Genesis 1:29-31, plant food constituted the initial diet of humans.

Stage Three: At the time of the flood, in Genesis 7:1-2, clean and unclean animals are differentiated, but not identified or specified.

Stage Four: In Genesis 7:1-2, both clean and unclean animals are saved and brought into the ark.

Stage Five: In Genesis 9:3-4, Noah and his descendants are permitted all food except blood after the biblical flood. An appropriate human diet is defined as a combination of plant and flesh foods.

Stage Six: Clean and unclean flesh foods are identified and specified, other forbidden foods and food-related behaviors are codified:

A. Clean meats were specified in Leviticus 11:2-3, 9, 21-2; and Deuteronomy 14:4-6, 9, 11, 20.

B. Unclean meats are discussed in Leviticus 11:4-8, 10-20, 23-31, 41-4; and Deuteronomy 14:7-8, 10, 12-19.

C. Blood was prohibited in Genesis 9:3-4; Deuteronomy 12:16, 23-4, and 15:23; 1 Samuel 14:32-4; and Ezekiel 44:7, 15.

D. Carrion was prohibited in Exodus 22:31; Leviticus 11:39-40, 17:15-16, 22:8; Deuteronomy 14:21; and Ezekiel 4:14.

E. Fat was prohibited in Exodus 29:13, 22; Leviticus 3:3-4, 9-10, 17, 23-5, and 9:19-20; 1 Samuel 2:15-16; and 2 Chronicles 7:7.

F. Meat offerings to idols were prohibited in Exodus 34:15.

G. Sinew was prohibited in Genesis 32:32.

H. Food contaminated by dead animals was prohibited in Leviticus 11:37-8.

I. Seed contaminated by dead animals was prohibited in Leviticus 11:37-8.

J. Food from the inside of a house where a person has died was prohibited in Numbers 19:14-15.

Stage Seven: Regulations forbidding mixing meat and milk products (Epstein 1948) are believed to stem from the commandment not to seeth a kid in its mother's milk in Exodus 23:19, 34:26; and Deuteronomy 14:21.

Clean-unclean food lists. The form, structure, and content of the clean and unclean food lists of Leviticus and Deuteronomy have remained the subject of considerable interest and debate since the early years of the Christian era (Barnabas 1961). If the clean and unclean food lists are examined in light of twentieth-century archaeological data and linguistic advances, two basic questions emerge. These concern translation accuracy and assignment rationale.

Taking up the question of translation accuracy first, an examination of Table VI.13.1 reveals linguistic consistency throughout the centuries for a number of specific forbidden foods, among them *arnevet* (hare), *gamal* (camel), and *hazir* (pig). The translations of other terms for forbidden foods, however, have not been consistent, and through the years some have been quite variable. The term *a'nakah,* for example, has been translated variously as ferret or gecko; *'aiyah* as crow, falcon, hawk, kite, and vulture; *homet* as lacerta, lizard, sand lizard, snail, and winding lizard; and *tinshemet* has been rendered variously as barn owl, chameleon, maldewerp, and mole.

Most identification and translation problems concern amphibians, birds, and reptiles. The difficulty lies with honest attempts at zoological identification based upon incomplete linguistic evidence, set within a wide range of possible eastern Mediterranean faunal representatives. Such linguistic difficulties were compounded in recent centuries when Christian missionaries translated the Old Testament into languages far removed from the origins of Judaism, where Mediterranean animals did not exist.

In the area of assignment rationale, the question of why foods became listed as clean or unclean has also been the subject of considerable debate. Seven of the eleven hypotheses discussed in the section "Approaches, Paradigms, and Themes" have been employed by various authors to support the origins of the Jewish dietary codes. Only three, however, can be critically examined: health or sanitation, ethnic identity, and ecological arguments (Grivetti and Pangborn 1974).

Table VI.13.1. *Selected forbidden foods: Leviticus (Hebrew source with English translations)*

English source	Chapter–verse with Hebrew term								
	Selected consistent translations				Selected inconsistent translations				
	11:4 gamal	11:5 shofan	11:6 arnevet	11:7 hazir	11:14 'aiyah	11:18 ka'at	11:30 a'nakah	11:30 homet	11:30 tinshemet
Lexicons									
Alcalay, 1962	Camel	Rock badger	Hare	Swine	Hawk	Pelican	Ferret	Lizard	Chameleon
Einspahr, 1977	Camel	Coney	Coney	Pig	Falcon	Night bird	Ferret	Lizard	Barn owl
		Dassie	Hare	Swine	Hawk	Pelican			Chameleon
		Rabbit	Rabbit		Vulture				
Torah									
1962	Camel	Rock badger	Hare	Swine	Falcon	Pelican	Gecko	Sand lizard	Chameleon
Bibles									
1530	Camel	Coney	Hare	Swine	Vulture	Pelican	Hedgehog	Snail	Mole
1560	Camel	Coney	Hare	Swine	Kite	Pelican	Rat	Stellio	Mole
1609	Camel	Cherogrillus	Hare	Swine	Vulture	Bittern	Shrew	Lizard	Mole
1611	Camel	Coney	Hare	Swine	Kite	Pelican	Ferret	Snail	Mole
1782	Camel	Coney	Hare	Swine	Kite	Pelican	Ferret	Snail	Mole
1805	Camel	Coney	Hare	Swine	Kite	Pelican	Hedgehog	Snail	Mole
1850	Camel	Cirogrille	Hare	Swine	Crow	Swan	Mygal	Lacerta	Maldewerp
1897	Camel	Coney	Hare	Swine	Falcon	Swan	Ferret	Winding lizard	Mole
1950	Camel	Rock badger	Hare	Pig	Falcon	Water hen	Ferret	Sand lizard	Chameleon
1953	Camel	Coney	Hare	Swine	Kite	Pelican	Ferret	Snail	Mole
1965	Camel	Coney	Hare	Swine	Falcon	Swan	Gecko	Sand lizard	Chameleon
1966	Camel	Hyrax	Hare	Pig	Buzzard	Ibis	Gecko	Chameleon	Tinshemet
1970	Camel	Rock badger	Hare	Pig	Black kite	Pelican	Fanfoot gecko	Sand lizard	Chameleon
1970	Camel	Rock badger	Hare	Pig	Falcon	Desert owl	Gecko	Skink	Mole
1973	Camel	Rock badger	Hare	Hog	Buzzard	Pelican	Ferret	Snail	Mole
1973	Camel	Rock badger	Hare	Swine	Falcon	Pelican	Gecko	Sand lizard	Chameleon
1976	Camel	Rock badger	Hare	Pig	Falcon	Horned owl	Gecko	Great lizard	Chameleon
1978	Camel	Coney	Rabbit	Pig	Black kite	Desert owl	Gecko	Skink	Chameleon
1981	Camel	Coney	Hare	Swine	Kite	Pelican	Gecko	Snail	Chameleon
1981	Camel	Coney	Rabbit	Pig	Black kite	Desert owl	Gecko	Skink	Chameleon
1989	Camel	Rock badger	Hare	Pig	Kite	Desert owl	Gecko	Sand lizard	Chameleon
1990	Camel	Rock badger	Hare	Pig	Kite	Desert owl	Gecko	Sand lizard	Chameleon

In the matter of *health and sanitation,* however, it is not logical to presume that the ancients were more observant and astute medically than nineteenth- and twentieth-century scientific physicians. Furthermore, few foods on the forbidden or unclean list pose direct health threats to consumers, whereas some foods on the clean list are vectors for anthrax, brucellosis, and various parasitic diseases.

Explanations based on *ethnic identity* presume that foods on the unclean list were once the dietary prerogatives of the ancient Egyptians, Canaanites, or other societies among whom the ancient Israelites lived or whom they had as geographical neighbors. Such explanations also hold that foods on the Jewish clean list once were prohibited or forbidden to non-Jews in the Mediterranean region. Analysis reveals that the ancient Egyptians in certain geographical areas and during certain historical periods ate pork, and they also consumed bustard, hare, locust, and ostrich. Moreover, several other animals on the Jewish unclean food list were worshiped by the ancient Egyptians, among them egret, hawk, heron, and vulture. But some meats on the clean list, such as beef, goat, and lamb, were also consumed, and cattle, goats, and sheep were worshiped by the ancient Egyptians (Darby et al. 1977).

The *ecological* hypothesis applied to pork avoidance suggests that pigs in the Mediterranean region could not compete economically with sheep and goats because they offered no hair products or milk, posed herding difficulties, and were ill suited to Middle Eastern heat. Supporters also state that as swine were in direct competition for scarce water and food resources, forbidding pork as food would not have been likely to cause sociocultural difficulties (Harris 1972, 1973). Archaeological evidence, however, can be used to counter these arguments because pigs were raised in Egypt for more than 5,000 years and, thus, were hardly ill suited to the region (Darby et al. 1977).

Ritual slaughter. The Judaic preparation of meat is characterized by a highly structured ritual that regulates slaughter, butchering, meat preparation, and cooking. Common explanations for the religious laws governing these practices suggest that compliance assures that meat products will be religiously suitable, that ritual requirements for human consumption will be met, and that meats prepared in such a manner will be safe for consumption (Levin and Boyden 1940; Maimonides 1956, 1967).

Within Judaism, meats are divided into two categories: *kosher,* or fit and suitable for human consumption, and *terephah,* or forbidden and unsuitable. Both kinds of meats are found in the food lists of Leviticus and Deuteronomy. In essence, terephah animals and meat products always are forbidden and never suitable as human food, whereas kosher meats and products may become terephah if ritual law is not followed.

The butcher must be an Orthodox Jew and in normal practice is a rabbi or a trained rabbinical designate. The butcher is responsible for inspecting animals prior to slaughter and declaring whether or not all accepted religious criteria are met. Thus, animals selected must be certified alive just before slaughter; a knife and no other instrument must be used. The cut must be made without hesitation or pause, in a straight line directly across the throat, with a motion that severs both gullet and windpipe.

Once the throat has been cut, the animal is suspended and bled. The cut is inspected carefully by the butcher, and if any minor lacerations are detected along the cut line, the meat is declared terephah. Similarly, after the carcass is skinned and muscle tissues inspected, there must be no ruptured blood vessels. Next, the lungs are inflated, placed under water, and inspected for any bubbles that might appear; if detected, the meat is declared terephah. Internal organs, including gall bladder, heart, kidney, liver, intestines, spleen, and stomach, are also examined for a wide range of critical signs that determine whether or not meat from the carcass will be classified as fit or unfit (Levin and Boyden 1940).

After inspection and certification, only the forequarters of the animal can be used as food; hindquarters are terephah. Rejection of the hindquarters is symbolic and linked with the account in Genesis 32:32 of Jacob's wrestling with an angel who touched Jacob on the ischiatic nerve.

In modern times, if the carcass meat must be held in a cooler for more than 72 hours, or if transportation of the carcass will exceed 72 hours, the meat must be ritually washed, otherwise kosher status is lost and the meat is reclassified terephah (Lipschutz 1988).

Because the eating of blood is prohibited, several food preparation and cooking techniques have been devised through the centuries that separate Orthodox Jews from others. Kosher meats are soaked in tap water, salted on all surfaces, then placed on a slanted drain board. They are rinsed twice to remove the salt. Rare meat is terephah and so all meats must be cooked thoroughly. As a consequence, cooking techniques, such as broiling and boiling, became institutionalized in order to meet the religious law and maintain kosher designation (Grunfeld 1972; Lipschutz 1988).

Meat and milk. Within the Jewish food tradition, kosher foods are assigned one of three categories: *fleishig* (meat and meat products), *milchig* (milk and dairy products), and *parveh* (neutral foods, defined as all other permitted foods). A wide range of laws govern the cooking and blending of these three categories: Fleishig and milchig foods can never be blended or combined, whereas parveh items, because of their neutral status, may be mixed with either meat or milk and dairy items. This strict observance of not mixing meat with milk is called *basar be halab.*

Yet the Jewish injunction against mixing meat and milk is not specifically defined in the Torah. Scholars searching for the basis of the *basar be halab* law consider three oblique Torah references with the common admonition found in Exodus 23:19, 34:26; and Deuteronomy 14:21: "Thou shall not seeth a kid in its mother's milk." But examination of the Torah also reveals that Jews once readily consumed meat and milk together at the same meal. And in Genesis (18:7-8) it is written that "Abraham ran unto the herd, and fetcht a calf tender and good, and gave it unto a young man; and he hastened to dress it. And he took butter, and milk, and the calf which he had dressed, and set it before them; and he stood by them under the tree, and they did eat."

Nonetheless, the laws and regulations that govern the dietary separation of meat and milk products are outlined in a wide range of Talmud texts, as noted by Akiba ben Joseph (A.D. 50-132), who stated that every kind of flesh is forbidden to be cooked in milk (Epstein 1948, 8:104a).

Talmud discussions define that which constitutes meat and milk, along with the concept of mixing (Grivetti 1980). The ancient rabbis agreed that beef certainly was meat but differed as to the definitions of poultry and fish. Most Orthodox Jews, both historically and in modern times, have considered poultry to be fleishig, but a minority view, championed by Rabbi Jose of Galilee (first to second century A.D.), held that poultry should be designated parveh and, thus, permitted to be mixed with either milchig or fleishig foods. Jose's semantical and biological argument was based on the premise that it was impossible to seeth poultry in "mother's milk"; although fowl could be mothers, they were incapable of producing milk (Mishayoth 8:4 in Blackman 1964).

What constitutes milk was easily answered in the ancient Mediterranean world: Permitted milks could come only from mammals on the clean-food lists. The definition of milk, however, has become less clear during the twentieth century with the use of nondairy cream substitutes prepared from soy-based products. Some nondairy creamers, for example, contain the milk protein sodium caseinate, which would make the product milchig; soy-based milks, however, would be parveh and permitted to be mixed with fleishig products (Freedman 1970).

Definitions for mixing involve less obvious considerations. It seems clear that foods blended during the preparation or cooking process would be classified as mixed, but Orthodox Jewish tradition presents expanded, broader definitions that allude to concepts of proximity and touching.

Consider, for example, that two people, not related to each other, sit at the same table but dine separately: One wishes to consume roast beef, the other cheese. If both persons sitting at the table are Orthodox Jews, the law governing mixing of meat and milk is broken. But if one is Orthodox and the other gentile, the law

is maintained and differentiation is based upon proximity and the probability of social exchange: If the two were Orthodox they would experience the temptation to share food because of ethnic affiliation or because of friendship (Epstein 1948, 8:107b).

Mixing presents other difficulties as well. Suppose that an Orthodox Jew wishes to purchase meat and cheese from different sections of the same store. When purchased, the products are wrapped separately, then placed inside a shopping bag. In this case, the law is not broken because fleishig and milchig products cannot touch physically (Epstein 1948, 8:107b). But when both categories of wrapped food are carried into the consumer's house, and then unwrapped, the law is precise: Fleishig and milchig products must be placed inside separate pantries. Furthermore, in the modern era of electricity, both categories of food must be kept inside separate refrigerators, and specific parveh foods must not be interchanged with the other refrigerator; otherwise all such items become terephah. Food preparation and cooking of meat or milk products must be done independently, using separate sets of utensils and appliances for fleishig and milchig products. Similarly, meat and milk dishes must be baked, broiled, or otherwise cooked inside separate ovens (Korff 1966; Grunfeld 1972).

Mixing meat and milk also includes the question of time. How long, for example, should consumers wait before dining on the other food class so that the two food categories do not mix inside the human body? Rabbi Hisda (third century A.D.) stated that the order of consumption determined the law: Meat could be eaten immediately after cheese, but one day had to pass if the order was reversed. In contrast, Rabbi Ukba (third to fourth century A.D.) argued that the order of consumption was unimportant and that one day must pass before consuming any food from the other category (Epstein 1948, 8:105a). By the twelfth century A.D., however, a compromise had been reached: a wait of six hours between meals of either food class (Kaufman 1957; Maimonides 1967).

Cultural-religious manifestation of the dietary separation of meat and milk are readily observable in Orthodox Jewish homes, less so in Conservative Jewish homes, and not usually apparent in Reform Jewish homes. Among the Orthodox, the following conditions are required when keeping the law: separate sets of table linen, separate pantries for food storage, separate electrical appliances and food preparation utensils, separate ovens (and microwave ovens) for cooking fleishig and milchig meals, separate condiment containers for meat and dairy dishes, and separate dishwashers (Frazer 1919; Gaster 1955; Natow, Iteslin, and Raven 1975).

Basar be halab. A wide range of arguments have been advanced to explain the law of *basar be halab*. Several have argued that the Torah passages are mistranslated, or that the law originally did not forbid boiling or preparing meat and milk together, but was intended to apply to cooking or mixing meat with blood (Cheyne 1907; Smith 1969). Others feel that the basis was one of "Natural Law and Divine Order," that cooking a kid in the milk of its mother would be an abomination and contrary to nature (Scott 1866; Mackintosh 1959; Cook 1969). Still others have explained the law using the argument that the ancient Jews were a compassionate people, not prone to acts that would lead to a baby goat's being boiled in the fluid intended for its own nourishment (Chadwick 1890).

Early writers such as Philo (1954, 4:16:97, 4:17:111, 4:24:124) offered still another explanation when he wrote that the meat–milk codes were instituted because the two foods in combination were stimulating and pleasure giving to the consumer and, therefore, should be denied to demonstrate self-restraint.

Other commentators have suggested that the reason might have to do with sympathetic magic, specifically the belief that animals could control their milk after humans had obtained it. In this case, the boiling or heating of milk would have been tantamount to applying fire to cattle udders. These writers suggest that the code was a part of widespread cultural practices adopted to protect herds, lest the cattle be damaged (Frazer 1907a, 1907b, 1919; Schmidt 1926).

Still other writers conclude that the basis for the dietary separation of meat and milk was based upon considerations of food spoilage and bacterial contamination. They have argued that given the hot, desert conditions found throughout the Middle East, although both meat and dairy products spoil, they spoil more quickly if blended. This view, however, may be easily rejected since blended foods, in fact, do not spoil more rapidly than meat or milk products served alone (van den Heever 1967).

Within Judaism, meat and milk are forbidden in combination – yet meat and milk dishes are highly esteemed within Islam. Middle Eastern Muslims, in turn, reject dietary combinations of fish and milk – yet fish and milk dishes are desirable within Judaism. These acceptable and forbidden patterns of mixing foods clearly have separated Jews and Muslims in the Middle East since at least the seventh century A.D. when Muslim forces invaded and occupied the lands of ancient Palestine. Since that time, the meat–milk and fish–milk prohibitions have served as ethnic markers and as a clear means of religious and cultural separation (Grivetti 1975, 1980).

Other food-related issues. A wide range of Jewish dietetic rules codified in the Torah and Talmud have been reviewed and summarized by modern scholars (Preuss 1978). One important Talmud directive encourages eating in moderation with the saying, "More people have died at the cooking pot, than have been victims of starvation" (Shabbach 33a). Salt and yeast are identified as harmful to consumers if eaten in large quantities (Berachoth 34a).

Numerous rabbis cited in the Talmud present arguments well beyond those governing the clean and unclean food lists of Leviticus and Deuteronomy. Rabbi Abaye (A.D. 280–339) argued that Jews should abstain from fish, fowl, and salted meat, and argued further that consumption of fish was detrimental to human eyesight (Nedarim 54b). Rabbi Mar bar Rav Ashi (fifth century A.D.) suggested that fish and meat, in combination, should not be salted and that the consumption of this mixture resulted in leprosy (Pesachim 112a). Rabbi Rab (second century A.D.) considered fish that had been chewed upon by other sea creatures; he concluded that in such cases where the fish already were dead, the dietary law could be kept by merely cutting away the chewed-upon portions (Jerushalmi Terumoth 8:46a).

Other Talmud passages discuss foods thought to be life threatening. Among them were peeled garlic, peeled onions, peeled eggs, and any diluted liquid kept overnight and exposed to the air (Niddah 17a). The Talmud also ponders the problem of honey and the law: Since the bee is an insect not on the clean list, how could honey be allowed as a food fit for human consumption? Various rabbis argued that bee honey should be permitted since the insect "expels unchanged that which it sucketh out of blossoms." By contrast, the rabbis viewed honey obtained from hornets or wasps as a type of saliva (ri'r), and thus a product expressly forbidden as food (Bechoroth 7b; Tosefta Bechoroth 1:8).

Further evolution of Jewish dietary codes is seen in the sixteenth-to-eighteenth–century health and dietary compendium called *The Book of God's Deeds* or *Sefer Mif'alot Elokim*. This text is important because it bridges the period between ancient and modern health-related issues and diet and contains several specific food and food-related prohibitions. It forbids almonds, hazelnuts, and walnuts (unless eaten after meals), enjoins the faithful from reading or studying while eating, and provides the strict instruction never to eat bread unless the loaf has been well baked (Ba'al Shem and Katz 1936).

Christianity

Early food taboos. Dietary prohibitions and taboos associated with Christianity developed in response to a classic philosophical schism: Should all foods be allowed, or should portions of the dietary codes of Judaism be incorporated by Christians? The early position regarding dietary taboos was Christian repudiation of earlier Jewish food laws and the concept that all foods were acceptable (Mark 7:18–21; Acts 10:8–16, 11:5–10; 1 Corinthians 6:12–13, 10:23, 25–7; 1 Timothy 4:3–5; Titus 1:14–15).

Subsequent debate, however, resulted in Christian reevaluation that permitted converts to maintain their earlier dietary restrictions. This, ultimately, led to the development of three Christian dietary taboos that have not been enforced throughout the centuries: blood (Acts 15:20, 29; 21:25), carrion and "things strangled" (Acts 15:20, 29 and 21:25), and foods previously offered or dedicated to idols (Acts 15:20, 29; 21:25; 1 Corinthians 8:1, 10, 28). Subsequent New Testament texts, however, advise only: "Whether, therefore ye eat, or drink, or whatsoever ye do, do all to the glory of God" (1 Corinthians 10:31).

Subsequent food taboos and concerns. Such a laissez-faire attitude regarding dietary matters within the church continued toward the present. One notable flurry of debate erupted in the second century concerning marine species of fish. Although fish were widely consumed by Mediterranean Christians at this time, concern was expressed that marine species might feed upon the bodies of mariners and soldiers buried at sea. In this case, was the human consumption of such fish tantamount to cannibalism? A second concern had to do with the "essence" of the human body incorporated into fish tissue, which was viewed as an impediment to the reconstitution of the deceased for resurrection, and from this concern flowed another. If the soul of a sailor became part of fish tissue, it would pass directly into the consumer's body. Yet two souls could not occupy the same human body. Clearly, argued the opponents of marine fish consumption, such a food should be avoided.

Fortunately for fish lovers, however, Athenagoras, an Athenian Christian apologist, ably presented a number of positive counterarguments that succeeded in ensuring that the Christian faithful could continue dining on Mediterranean fish.

If there was little proscribing of foods in the history of early Christianity, there was much concern over foodstuffs that centered on physical, in contrast to spiritual, health. For example, John Chrysostom (later Saint John, 345?–407), an important fourth-century Christian leader and author of numerous religious tracts, also wrote extensively on diet. One of his major themes was that reduced food intake and regular fasting were important for Christians. In his words (Homily 22):

> frugality and a simple table are the mother of health. . . . Now if abstinence is the mother of health, it is plain that eating to repletion is the mother of sickness and ill health, and brings forth diseases . . . caused by gluttony and satiety. . . . Abstinence [from food], in truth, as it is the mother of health, is also the mother of pleasure.

In like fashion, the fifth-century Greek physician Anthimus, in his work on *The Dietetics,* advised Christians to be moderate in their eating and drinking habits. In addition, he cautioned that foods consumed should be readily digestible, and he warned against

eight items: bacon rind, aged cheese, hard-boiled eggs, fish that were not fresh, mushrooms, oysters, pickled meats, and pigeons (Gordon 1959).

Such warnings may also be found in the thirteenth-century text *Regimen Santitatas Salernitatum,* which is a blend of Christian and Muslim dietary traditions. Foods specifically identified to be avoided were those supposed to engender the formation of black bile. Other foods, described as "enemies of the sick," were also to be avoided by Christians. These offenders were: apples, cheese, goats, hares, salted meats, milk, peaches, pears, veal, and venison (Temkin 1953; Harrington 1957; Arano 1976).

Absolute food prohibitions within Christianity, however, are a relatively recent phenomenon, initiated by newly formed denominations. The Seventh-Day Adventists, for example, maintain the dietary prohibitions of the Jews against foods on the unclean lists found in Leviticus and Deuteronomy. They also abstain from alcohol consumption and frown upon "hot" spices and condiments, specifically, chilli pepper and black pepper. Aged cheeses (Limburger and Roquefort) are also discouraged. Moreover, the faithful are cautioned:

> Those who indulge in meat eating, tea drinking, and gluttony are sowing seeds for a harvest of pain and death. . . . A diet of flesh meat tends to develop animalism. . . . Flesh meats will deprecate the blood. Cook meat with spices, and eat it with rich cakes and pies, and you have a bad quality of blood. . . . Tea is poisonous to the system. Christians should let it alone. The influence of coffee is in a degree the same as tea, but the effect on the system is still worse. . . . Never take tea, coffee, beer, wine, or any spirituous liquors (Counsels on Diet and Foods 1938).

Members of the Church of Jesus Christ of Latter-day Saints, the Mormons, also reject alcohol and so-called hot drinks, defined as coffee and tea (Word of Wisdom in Smith 1833). In fact, many Mormons have extended this "hot drink" prohibition to any food or beverage that contains caffeine (Pike 1992).

Islam

Muslim dietary prohibitions are documented in two sources, the Koran and the Hadith. The Koran, the divine word of God revealed to the Prophet Mohammed, divides food into two basic categories: halal, or permitted, and haram, or forbidden. The Koran specifically forbids six foods or food categories: blood, carrion, pork, intoxicating beverages prepared from grapes *(khmr),* intoxicating drugs, and foods previously dedicated or offered to idols (Roberts 1925; Sakr 1971). The Hadith, or the collected traditions and sayings attributed to the Prophet Mohammed, contains a broad range of food-related passages.

A wide assortment of human behaviors relating to

food and the food quest are carefully coded in both the Koran and the Hadith. Muslims, for example, may not hunt when on religious pilgrimage to Mecca (Koran 99). At the time of slaughter of permitted animals, the name of God must be mentioned, specifically the phrase: "In the Name of God, the Compassionate, and the Merciful," or *Bisimallah er Rahman er Rahim*. The throat of the animal must be cut in front with a knife, with the exception of two allowed foods: fish, because their throat already is cut (that is, gills), and locusts, because they spring upward and aspire to heaven. If the butcher is distracted and the name of another person or deity is mentioned during slaughter or while butchering the carcass, the flesh of that animal is designated haram, forbidden. If meat is slaughtered correctly, but not permitted to bleed out, the flesh also is designated haram. Meat slaughtered by Christians and Jews may or may not be permitted; meat from animals slaughtered by atheists is always forbidden (Sakr 1971).

Because conservative Muslims living beyond the boundaries of the Middle East frequently do not know the religious orientation of butchers who prepare meat for sale in markets, some turn to vegetarianism during their time abroad or butcher their own animals on specific feast dates (Grivetti, unpublished data).

Local traditions also dictate food prohibitions. In Egypt, for example, some birds consumed elsewhere in the Middle East and Mediterranean region by Muslims are not killed because the bird call resembles pious, religious phrases. The dove (*Streptopelia* spp.) may be avoided as food in Egypt because its call is said to imitate the words: "Oh, all merciful; Oh, all merciful," or *Ya Rahman; Ya Rahman*. Other prohibited birds include the hoopoe (*Upupa epops*), who produces the sound: "Oh, all pitiful; Oh, all pitiful," or *Ya Raouf; Ya Raouf*, and the stone curlew (*Burhinus oedicnemus*), whose cry is said to mimic: "The Universe is Yours, Yours, Yours, Oh, master of the Universe," or *Al-Moluk lak lak lak Ya Sahib al- Moluk* (Darby et al. 1977).

The Hadith also delineates specific kinds of animals to be avoided as food. Among them are all quadrupeds that seize their prey with their teeth. Expressly identified are hyenas, foxes, and elephants. All birds with talons are prohibited. Specifically forbidden (without talons) is the pelican (Guillaume 1924).

The prominent medieval Persian physician Ibn Sina wrote, regarding prohibited foods, that fish should not be taken after laborious work or exercise because it undergoes decomposition and then decomposes the humors (*The Canon* No. 767). Elsewhere, he wrote on prohibited combinations of food:

> Certain rules must be noted in regard to combinations of food: milk must not be taken with sour foods; fish must not be taken with milk for in that case chronic ailments such as leprosy

(*juzam*) may develop; pulses must not be taken with cheese or radishes or with the flesh of flying birds; barley-meal should not follow a dish of rice and sour milk (Ibn Sina 1930).

Other texts by Ibn Sina document still more inappropriate food combinations: milk with acid food, Indian peas with cheese, and fine flour with rice and milk ("Advice on Foods," cited in Kamal 1975).

Hinduism

The most ancient known Hindu document that considers food and dietary prohibitions is the Caraka-Samhita, written about 1500 B.C. and attributed to the physician Caraka. Specific passages in this important text (Caraka 1981) identify dietary principles, permitted and prohibited foods, and regimens for various diseases. Ancient Hindu diet was perceived as consisting of two types: immobile (plants) and mobile (animals). Diet patterns were classified according to four manners of intake: beverages, eatables, chewables, and lickables. Each of these intake categories was further based upon six types of taste: astringent, bitter, pungent, salty, sour, and sweet. Innumerable variations of diet resulted that were based upon 12 categories of food and factors of abundance, combination, and preparation (Grivetti 1991a).

The Caraka-Samhita (Caraka 1981) identifies food items designated as unwholesome and to be avoided by the majority of people. Among them are black gram bean (pulse category); rainy season river water (water category); beef (animal meats category); young dove (bird and fowl category); frog (animals living in holes category); sheep milk (animal milks category); and elephant fat (fats of plant-eating animals category).

Included elsewhere in the Caraka-Samhita (Caraka 1981) are other foods to be avoided:

> Meat from animals who die natural deaths, are emaciated, too fatty, too old, too young, any animal killed by poison, not maintained on pasture [land], and meat from all animals bitten by snakes or tigers. . . . Vegetables affected by insects, wind, or sun; vegetables that are dried, old, unseasonable or not cooked with fat. . . . Fruits that are old, unripe, damaged by insects, animals, by snow, or sun, [all vegetables that] grow in unnatural places or [at] unnatural times, or are rotted.

A further development and expansion of Hindu food-related codes is embodied later in texts collectively called the Dharma-Sutra. These law codes, derived from oral tradition that date perhaps to 1500 B.C., had been collected, edited, and presented in written form by the sixth century B.C. The texts are divided into separate tracts: Apastamba (Müller 1896a), Baudhayana (Müller 1882a), Gautama (Müller 1896b), and Vasishtha (Müller 1882b). The document called Manu (1896c), or Laws of Manu, is a subsequent summary and synthesis that probably dates from the third century A.D.

The Hindu dietary prejudices and taboos presented in the Dharma-Sutra are subsumed under five broad rubrics that reflect aspects of human occupation, food location, human and animal behavior, and animal morphology. The fifth category identifies specific proscribed items (Apastamba 1896, 1:5.16:1–1:6:19:15; Baudhayana 1896, 1:5:9:1–2:7:12:12; Gautama 1896, 17:1–38; Manu 1896, 4:205–25; 5:5–56; Vasishtha 1896, 14:2–48; Grivetti 1991a):

Prohibitions associated with human professional and physiological status: All foods offered by an actor, artisan, basket maker, blacksmith, carpenter, cobbler, dyer, eunuch, goldsmith, harlot, hermaphrodite, hunter, hypocrite, informer, jailer, leaser of land, manager of a lodging, menstruating woman, miser, musician, paramour of a married woman, person who is ill, physician, police officer, prisoner, ruler of a town, seller of intoxicating beverages, spy, tailor, thief, trainer of hunting dogs, usurer, weapons dealer, or woman with no male relative.

Prohibitions associated with food location: All foods stored inside the house where a relative has died, all foods served from a wooden platform or table, items eaten while standing, and all foods prepared out of sight and sold by street vendors.

Prohibitions associated with human behavior and contact: All foods received directly from the hand of another person, any food sneezed upon or touched accidentally by a human garment or human foot, any item that contains a hair or insect, all foods specifically prepared for another person, and any consumables that have remained overnight in contact with air that subsequently have soured.

Prohibitions associated with animal behavior and contact: All foods sniffed at by a cat or smelled by a cow, meat from any animal that died after being worried by dogs, meat from any animal that behaved in a solitary manner, and all birds that scratch with their feet or thrust forward with their beak.

Prohibitions associated with animal morphology: All meats or milk products from animals with a single hoof, five toes, double rows of teeth, excessive hair, or no hair; any mammal with young that has recently died, milk or meat from any cow that has suckled a strange calf, and any permitted animal that has delivered twins.

Prohibitions associated with specific foods: Specifically identified prohibited foods fit three broad categories:

1. Plants and plant products: garlic, leek, mushroom, onion, turnip, young sprouts, tree resin, and red juice or sap extracted from any plant.
2. Animals: alligator, crab, crocodile, fish with misshapen heads; cormorant, crow, dove, duck, egret, falcon, flamingo, heron, ibis, osprey, parrot, black partridge, pigeon, raven, sparrow, starling, swan, vulture, and woodpecker; village pig and other tame village animals; black antelope, flying fox, and porpoise.
3. Beverages: milk from any buffalo, cow, or goat within 10 days after calving; any milk from camels, sheep, or wild deer; and water that accumulates at the bottom of a boat.

Prohibitions by Gender and Age

Numerous dietary prohibitions within a society are universal, applying to males and females of all ages. In other instances, however, taboos may be instituted at specific ages or associated with one gender. Dietary taboos practiced in the Republic of Botswana by the baTlokwa ba Moshaweng, a Tswana agro-pastoral cattle-keeping society of the eastern Kalahari Desert, offer examples of both.

General Prohibitions

Female and male baTlokwa of all ages reject antbear or aardvark (*Orvcheropus afer afer*) as food because they consider it inappropriate to kill and eat their tribal totem animal (see Table VI.13.2 for a list of

Table VI.13.2. *BaTlokwa ba Moshaweng: Foods restricted by gender and age*

	Females		Males	
	Characteristic or permitted	Prohibited or restricted	Characteristic or permitted	Prohibited or restricted
Death				
–	Eggs	Antbear	Eggs	Antbear
–	Meat: chin	Insects	Honey	Insects
Elderly	Meat: nose	–	Francolin	Small birds
Adults	Meat: placenta	–	Kidney	Small mammals
			Meat: stillborn calf	
			Tortoise	
Menopause or activity decline				
–	Liver	Antbear	Eggs, heat	Antbear
Active	–	–	Lung, rumen	Insects
Adults	–	–	Meat: forelegs & hindlegs	Small birds
				Small mammals
				Stillborn calf
Puberty				
–	Fish	Antbear	Eggs	Antbear
–	Insects	Eggs	Fish	Francolin
Childhood	–	Francolin	Insects	Honey
		Honey	Small birds	Tortoise
		Tortoise	Small mammals	
Weaning/off breast				
–	Breast milk	Beans	Breast milk	Beans
–	Donkey milk	Eggs	Donkey milk	Meat
Infancy	–	Solid food	–	Solid food
Birth				

foods restricted by age and gender). Pork is also not consumed by males and females of all ages for other reasons. Many state that pork is a disgusting food and offer explanations, such as that pigs are dirty, smelly, and disgusting in appearance and that they consume feces and even their own young. Still others reject pork because they say that the meat is too fatty for human consumption. BaTlokwa who break their universal taboo and eat pork, however, still may reject specific portions of the carcass: In contrast with the bones of acceptable animals, those of pigs are never cracked and chewed to extract marrow, lest the consumer become deaf (Grivetti 1976).

Several agro-pastoral Tswana societies living in the eastern Kalahari Desert do not eat locally grown oranges in the belief that the first maturing fruit is poisonous. Respondents state that it is impossible to determine precisely which orange ripens first. Therefore, locally grown oranges are all rejected, and oranges that are consumed are imported from South Africa.

Some baTlokwa, however, believe that planting orange trees is unnatural and possibly dangerous because this tree is not native to the eastern Kalahari. Other baTlokwa explain their prohibition using an analogy with another local Kalahari tree, *Melia azsedarach*: Although baTlokwa men and women readily dig up wild plants from surrounding bushlands and transplant them into their household gardens, they never experiment with *Melia azsedarach* in the belief that transplanting it will cause the death of all family members except the gardener, who then must suffer a life of loneliness (Grivetti 1976).

The baKwena, linguistic and cultural relatives of the baTlokwa who occupy territory southwest of the baTlokwa homelands, also reject oranges as food for still another reason. Documentation exists that the nineteenth-century missionary David Livingstone was the first to import orange trees into the Kalahari Desert in baKwena territory, and he is suspected of initiating the orange taboo to curtail theft from his orchard (Grivetti 1978b).

Age-Gender Matrix

The baTlokwa ba Moshaweng exhibit a well-structured pattern of food prohibitions reflecting dual themes of age and gender. But those dietary taboos and prohibitions that reinforce gender identification at specific periods of the human physiological cycle are balanced by other foods that are characteristically associated with the consumer's age and gender.

Infancy. Certain baTlokwa food-related behaviors regulate infant feeding practices. Parents must eat before feeding their infants, as it is forbidden to hold or allow the infant to sit on the parent's lap while the adult is eating. They believe that to do so makes the infant greedy. Furthermore, widows and widowers are discouraged from feeding infants. But if they do, the infant must be held facing away from the adult to avoid eye contact (Grivetti 1978b).

Childhood. Seven foods expressly taboo to baTlokwa children are dietary prerogatives of elderly men. These foods include two types of honey, tortoise, and five birds: dikkop *(Burhinus capensis),* francolin *(Francolinus* spp.), guinea fowl *(Numida meleagris),* horn-bill *(Tockus* spp.), and red-crested korhaan *(Lophotis ruficrista).* The baTlokwa associate these seven items with memory and believe that their consumption exacerbates forgetfulness: Because elderly men are perceived as forgetful anyway, and memory should be developed in children, these seven foods are critical markers for age (Grivetti 1978b).

Other food taboos of childhood are associated with food remnants, especially sorghum porridge that sticks to wooden serving spoons. Boys are told that if they lick porridge from such utensils, they will develop breasts and resemble women (cultural reference to gynecomastia). Girls, on the other hand, are cautioned that such behavior will delay breast development (Grivetti 1976).

The actions of children at mealtime are also regulated. BaTlokwa children are forbidden to touch the floor with the left hand while eating as this is interpreted as a sign of laziness. Furthermore, children are not allowed to speak during mealtime because of a widely held conviction that "a talking child becomes lean" (Grivetti 1976).

When baTlokwa children are ill, mothers prepare a special sorghum beer called *bojalwa jwa tlhogwana,* to be drunk by all family members in the belief that this practice hastens recovery. While the tlhogwana is being prepared, no one in the family is allowed to sample it at any stage of the brewing process or to taste the sediment at the bottom of the clay or iron beer pot. To do so, reportedly, will make the child's illness acute (Grivetti 1976).

Adolescence. After baTlokwa children mature sexually and enter their reproductive years, other food-related prohibitions and taboos become operative. Teenage girls are prohibited from consuming eggs, a restriction that differentiates them sharply from male counterparts, who may eat eggs with impunity. The adolescent female egg prohibition is explained at several levels. Some respondents state that the prohibition is linked to the undesirable condition of adolescent pregnancy. It is thought that girls who eat eggs will become sexually overactive, possibly promiscuous, and, consequently, might conceive at an age when they would be unable to care properly for their babies. Others think that adolescent girls who eat eggs will experience difficult labor, and should the mother and child survive, the neonate will likely die soon after delivery because of impaired breathing. Adolescent women should also avoid eggs because even if they deliver healthy children, the latter will cry regularly and wake the family in the early morning in silly attempts to mimic roosters (Grivetti 1976).

Adult/mature years. Three cuts of beef are prohibited to baTlokwa pregnant women in the belief that they cause difficult labor and delivery. These are the fourth stomach *(ngati)*; the large intestine *(mongopo)*; and both meat and marrow extracted from lower leg bones *(ditlhako tsa kgomo).* Also forbidden during pregnancy are the meat, fat, and skin located under the belly of an ox *(mofufu wa kgomo),* thought to make the child greedy, or to promote the development of a large stomach (Grivetti 1976).

Commercial candy, available to the baTlokwa since the late nineteenth century, is proscribed during pregnancy. Its consumption is thought to cause the ensuing newborn to drool and spit up saliva. Similarly, sour milk *(madila)* is forbidden to the mother during pregnancy in the belief that it will later cause the newborn to vomit copiously (Grivetti 1978b).

After delivery, baTlokwa mothers enter a period of confinement for 3 to 6 months. During this period the mother is not permitted to eat with her bare hands. All foods must be cut, then transferred to the mouth with a utensil; otherwise it is believed that the mother's supply of breast milk will be adversely affected (Grivetti 1978b).

Elderly pattern. Elderly baTlokwa men and women are released from all previous culturally imposed dietary prohibitions and may eat any available food.

Gender, Pregnancy, and Allopathy

Throughout the Old and New Worlds, millions of people follow allopathic practices that specifically encourage or prohibit various foods during illness and during changes in physiological status, such as pregnancy and lactation. Allopathic systems emerged initially in India and subsequently spread to China and westward into the Mediterranean basin to influence Greek, Roman, Byzantine, and Jewish, Christian, and Muslim medical practices. Such practices became global during the fifteenth- and sixteenth-century era of exploration, and influenced the development of medicine in North, Central, and South America, as well as those portions of Africa and Asia colonized by Europeans (Grivetti 1991a).

At the core of allopathic medicine is the concept that illness and disease may be classified as hot or cold, and wet or dry, and that foods available to consumers are, likewise, hot (heating) or cold (cooling). Health in this system is perceived as a state of balance, whereby healthy individuals are neither too hot nor too cold; illness, accordingly, is perceived as a state of imbalance, and cures aim at restoring balance by treating with opposites. Thus, hot diseases are treated with cold foods, dry diseases with wet foods, and so forth (Grivetti 1991a, 1991b, 1991c, 1992).

Chinese Yang–Yin

Of specific interest to the study and evaluation of food prohibitions and taboos is the question of how concepts of hot or cold remain constant or shift, depending upon the consumer's gender and, in the case of women, whether or not they are pregnant or lactating. Traditional Chinese allopathic practitioners explain that pregnancy produces a physiological state of extreme heat (yang), which requires a cooling (yin) diet in order to restore balance. Dietary management during pregnancy has been considered in a wide range of works by ancient and medieval Chinese physicians.

Among them are texts on diet and food prohibitions by Chang Chi (A.D. 142-220), Hsü Chih-Ts'asi (A.D. 510-90), Sun Ssu-Mo (A.D. 581-682), Chen Tzu Ming (perhaps A.D. 960-1027), and Chu Chen-Heng (A.D. 1281-1358). In addition to these classical Chinese texts, numerous social scientists and physicians of the past 50 years also have written on hot-cold foods, and especially foods that are encouraged or prohibited during pregnancy and lactation (Platt and Gin 1938; Read 1976, 1977a-e; Pillsbury 1978; Anderson 1980, 1984; Tan and Wheeler 1983; Wheeler and Tan 1983; Hsu et al. 1986).

A review of both ancient and modern sources reveals that Chinese dietary prohibitions during pregnancy generally fit eight food categories (Grivetti 1991c).

1. The first and largest category is that of *meats and eggs.* Here prohibited items include: beef, bullfrog, carp, carp roe, chicken, crab, deer fat, dog, donkey, duck (wild and domesticated types), eel, eggs, elk, frog, gecko, goat (both meat and liver), horse, mule, pheasant, rabbit, sheep (mutton and liver), shellfish, sparrow brain, toad, and turtle.
2. Under the category of *cereals,* only barley is prohibited.
3. In the *legumes and seeds* group, almonds, amaranth, beans, and soybeans are prohibited.
4. Prohibitions on *vegetables* include bean leaf and mushrooms.
5. Among the *fruits,* banana, litchi, pear, pineapple, and watermelon are taboo.
6. In the category of *spices and flavorings,* garlic and ginger are forbidden.
7. Proscribed *beverages* include beer, soda pop, tea, and wine.
8. Among the *miscellaneous foods,* all frozen items are prohibited, along with malt, seaweed, and sloughed snake skin (used medicinally).

Set within the hot-cold paradigm, which encourages cooling foods, there seem to be three primary categories of explanation for these food prohibitions (Grivetti 1991c): Some of the foods are viewed as likely to cause *potential miscarriage or spontaneous abortion.* Among these are almonds, amaranth, banana, barley, beans, beer, eggs and salt, frozen foods, horse meat, pineapple, seaweed, and soybeans. Another group of foods is implicated in *transverse presentation, difficult delivery,* and *postpartum bleeding.* These are alcoholic beverages, crabs, donkey meat, duck, horse meat, mule meat, pheasant, sheep liver, shellfish, and tiger bones.

A final group of foods is believed to have a *negative impact on the neonate.* Birthmarks, for example, can be the work of beef, sparrows, or soybean paste, whereas deer fat, elk meat, or sparrow brain can cause blindness or other eye diseases. Boils, sores, and other skin lesions are associated with carp, carp roe, and shellfish, a deformed neck with turtles, and an early death (or during childhood) with frogs. Epilepsy in the child can be caused by either mushrooms or sheep (mutton). The latter is also held responsible for fever. A hoarse voice is linked to toads, jaundice to bananas, muteness or a hare lip to bullfrogs, chickens, dogs, ducks, eels, goats, rabbits, and turtles, whereas fresh ginger can trigger polydactyly (an extra digit).

Still other dietary prohibitions during pregnancy are related to the notion that the foods in question will produce specific undesirable behaviors once the child has grown to maturity. Chinese traditionalists believe, for example, that should women consume sparrow cooked in alcohol or wine during pregnancy, the child will exhibit lewd, licentious behavior as an adult (Grivetti 1991c).

The focus is upon cooling foods (yin) during pregnancy, and yin foods are commonly low in protein and energy. Consequently, dietary reliance upon these items during pregnancy often results in a low-birth-weight baby – but an easier delivery for the mother.

After delivery, the Chinese allopathic system classifies lactating women as strongest yin. Consequently, diet at this time is based upon hot (yang) foods that are high in protein and energy, thus providing a sound nutritional basis for postpartum recovery and breast milk production (Pillsbury 1978).

Taboos as Protective for Society and the Individual

Dietary taboos and prohibitions have also been considered from the viewpoint of protection. In some instances, such practices protect local and regional ecology or agricultural crops during various phases of their growth cycle; in other cases, they have to do with human health and disease.

Crop Protection
As residents of the arid Kalahari Desert of eastern Botswana, the baTlokwa face uncertainties of unseasonable weather, specifically uneven rainfall and drought, hail, and desiccating winds. The baTlokwa attempt to minimize these uncertainties by instituting a range of taboos and prohibitions in a cultural attempt to regulate weather.

The appearance and timing of rainfall in the Kalahari is critical to growing crops, and three specific taboos are instituted in the conviction that enforcement will assure rain. If the following taboos are broken, however, traditionalists believe that the rain clouds will be driven away:

1. Salt must never be thrown into a cooking fire or accidentally spilled onto flames or embers.
2. During their one-year mourning period, widows and widowers cannot wash their body during daylight and are forbidden to walk about the village during the heat of midday.
3. Pregnant or menstruating women are not allowed to walk across agricultural fields, or to touch agricultural equipment, such as plow blades, harnesses, and yokes, lest the heat of their bodies burn the earth or render the ground sterile (Grivetti 1981b).

Health Protection
There is also much in the way of literature that suggests that the origin and development of many dietary taboos may lie in attempts to maintain human health and reduce disease.

Pigs and pork. In ancient Egypt, swine played a role in both religious and dietary practices. In some historical eras, at specific geographical localities, pork was a highly favored food, but during other periods and at other locations pork was forbidden.

Before 3200 B.C., Egypt consisted of two distinctive geographical-cultural entities: a pork-consuming north or Lower Egypt, and a pork-avoiding south or Upper Egypt (Menghin and Amer 1932). Shortly after 3200 B.C., however, both regions were united politically when the South conquered the North. One result of this conquest was a broadly based pork avoidance throughout the Egyptian Nile Valley and Delta that predates the Jewish pork prohibition by more than 2,000 years.

Pigs in the ancient Egyptian pantheon were associated with Seth, the evil brother of Osiris. During political periods when Osiris worship dominated, pork was avoided, but when Seth gained ascendancy, pork was widely consumed. Certainly pork was an important food during the reign of Amenhotep III (about 1405–1370 B.C.), who offered pigs to the temple of Ptah at Memphis. Seti I, father of Ramses II (about 1318–1298 B.C.), allowed pigs to be raised inside the temple of Osiris at Abydos (Newberry 1928: 211). That swine were eaten by Egyptians during the Ramessid Period is confirmed by the large numbers of pig bones found in refuse-trash heaps associated with the workman's village of Deir-el-Medina at Thebes (Kees 1961).

By late dynastic times and during the subsequent Greek and Roman periods, however, literary and pictorial evidence for pork consumption or avoidance in

Egypt reveals the same kind of curious dichotomy that was noted previously for beef. On the one hand, a wide range of sources document pork consumption. One description, dating from the third century B.C., indicates that Egyptian priests at the city of Naucratis in the Egyptian delta were served pork (Hermeias, cited by Athenaeus *Deipnosophists* 4, 149:F). Moreover, numerous Greek and Roman writers commented on the widespread presence of pigs throughout Egypt. Pliny (*Natural History,* 13:50) reported that swineherds fed their animals dates and lotus stems, and Polynaeus (*Stratagems of War* 4:19) noted that herds of swine were raised near Memphis. Heliodorus's Ethiopian history (1587: 130) described herds of pigs at Aswan.

There are also, however, Greek and Roman writers who indicate that there was a strong dietary avoidance of pork in Egypt. Indeed, both Plutarch (*Isis and Osiris* 353: 5) and Aelian (*Characteristics of Animals* 10: 16) stated that pork was forbidden as food throughout Egyptian territory, and Sextus Empiricus (*Outlines of Pyrrhonism* 3: 233) wrote that Egyptian priests would sooner die than eat swine's flesh.

This ancient Egyptian pork avoidance, which dates from about 3200 B.C., predates the Mosaic codes against pork by more than 200 years. Yet, as we have seen in Egypt, pork avoidance was not associated with any relationship between ingestion and disease, but rather was instituted by the followers of Osiris because the pig was the cult animal of Seth (Darby et al. 1977).

It is true that one frequently mentioned reason for pork avoidance links pork consumption with trichinosis (Sakr 1991; Chaudry 1992). But although pork taboos have been instituted in Africa and the Middle East for at least 5,200 years, the relationship between eating pork and contracting trichinosis was not established until the nineteenth century (Hilton 1833; Owen 1835; Zenker 1860; Paget 1866).

Moreover, although associations between parasitism and disease would have been readily apparent in cattle, goats, sheep, and a wide range of fish and fowl, dietary taboos in Judaism, Christianity, and Islam do not exist for these animals. Further, there are no formalized, coded taboos in these three faiths for toxic mushrooms, or such plants as aconite or datura, which are lethal and clearly more deadly than eating pork infected with *Trichina (Trichinella) spiralis.*

Carrion. Meat from an animal that "dies of itself" is proscribed by each of the monotheistic faiths that developed in the Mediterranean region. For Jews, the injunction is repeated six times (Exodus 22:31; Leviticus 11:39–40, 17:15–16, and 22:8; Deuteronomy 14:21; and Ezekiel 4:14); for Christians, three times (Acts 15:20, 29, 21:25); and for Muslims, four times (Koran: The Cow, 168; Koran: The Table, 4; Koran: Cattle, 145; Koran: The Bee, 115).

The rejection of carrion as human food is hardly universal, however. Many societies readily consume carrion and "rancid meat" as dietary staples. Indeed, dietary use of carrion by circumpolar Arctic societies has been reviewed extensively (Borgoras 1909; Eidlitz 1969), and consumption of carrion by European Gypsies has been well documented, especially the use of animals burned to death by brush and forest fires (Petrovic 1939).

All of this brings up the question of whether religious prohibitions against carrion are in fact protective. Clearly, the potential for disease transmission exists if humans consume infected carrion, but to reject carrion as human food merely upon the *potential* for disease transmission is illogical, given that humans consume fish, fowl, meats, and plant foods that can and do create serious health problems after consumption.

In fact, it could be argued that eating carrion is protective in that it has helped millions of people survive periods of food shortages, wartime famines, and climatic stress. Indeed, droughts of recent decades in the southern African Kalahari Desert region severely challenged regional agro-pastoralists, who suffered loss of their herds but maintained their dietary and nutritional status by consuming carrion. When cattle and other livestock died of thirst or environmental stress, the baTlokwa butchered the carcasses and the carrion was steamed, with leaves of *Croton gratissimus* used to remove "off" odors. Such meat then was sun-dried and jerked and could be readily stored as a suitable famine food (Grivetti 1976, 1978b).

It is interesting to note that most baTlokwa agro-pastoralists are animists or moderate Christians; in contrast, most agro-pastoralists of the drought-stricken Sahel are Muslim. Both Christianity and Islam prohibit carrion consumption, but there are distinctive regional and cultural differences in keeping "the law."

Harmful foods not prohibited. Returning to a question posed earlier, if health considerations lie at the root of the carrion (and other food) prohibitions, then it might be asked why there are no codified prohibitions in Buddhism, Christianity, Hinduism, Islam, or Judaism for moldy grain (manifest as the human disease ergotism), or for fava beans (favism), or for field vetch (lathyrism).

To employ another example, human poisoning from eating European migratory quail (*Coturnix coturnix*) is manifest as the human illness coturnism. This food-related problem, documented since biblical times (Numbers 11:31–4), was known to Greek and Roman naturalists, among them Aristotle (*On Plants* 820: 6–7), Lucretius (*On the Nature of Things* 4: 639–40) and Pliny (*Natural History* 10: 33). However, no dietary codes were instituted to protect consumers. Furthermore, subsequent medieval Jewish and Muslim physicians described human poisoning from quail, among them Maimonides (*Commentary*

Epidemiarum 6: 5), Ibn Sina (*The Canon* 2:2:2:5), Qazwiny (*Kitab Aga'il* 2: 250), and al-Demiri (*Hayat al-Hayawan al Kubra* 1: 505). Nonetheless, not only were potentially toxic quail not proscribed but they have also remained a favorite food of Middle Eastern Jews, Christians, and Muslims throughout the centuries (Kennedy and Grivetti 1980).

Concluding Comments

The literature on food prohibitions and taboos is ancient and voluminous, and most certainly reflects human interest in understanding how and why specific foods have been proscribed throughout the ages. More than 10 hypotheses have been advanced to explain the origins and development of food-related taboos, and evidence in support of them and against them can be marshaled for each.

Some who study food-related taboos have worked for decades to identify unifying concepts that would explain ancient as well as contemporary human behavior toward food. Some have attempted scientific explanations; others have sought meaning in nonscientific descriptions. Most accounts have stressed the cultural-religious aspects of food prejudices in Christianity, Hinduism, Islam, or Judaism. Beyond religion, however, lie still other categories of food prohibitions associated with the consumer's age and gender, ecological protection, and medical-nutritional themes. But within this enormous body of literature, there remains a single concept that has been expressed in two ways: *Food for one is not food for all,* and *One man's meat is another's poison.*

Louis E. Grivetti

Bibliography

Aelian. 1958-9. *On the characteristics of animals,* trans. A. F. Scholfield. 3 vols. Cambridge, Mass.

Alcalay, R. 1962. *The complete English-Hebrew dictionary.* Hartford, Conn.

al-Demiry [Kamal ed-Din Mohammad Ibn Moussa]. 1957. *Hayat al-Hayawan al Kubra.* Third edition. Cairo.

Anderson, E. N. 1980. "Heating" and "cooling" foods in Hong Kong and Taiwan. *Social Science Information* 19: 237-68.

      1984. "Heating" and "cooling" foods re-examined. *Social Science Information* 23: 755-73.

Arano, L. C. 1976. *Tacuinum sanitatis: The medieval health handbook,* trans. L. C. Arano. New York.

Arberry, A. J., trans. 1955. *The Koran interpreted.* London.

Aristotle. 1955. On plants. In *Aristotle: Minor works,* trans. W. S. Hett. London.

Arrington, L. R. 1959. Foods of the Bible. *Journal of the American Dietetic Association* 35: 816-20.

Athenaeus, of Naucratis. 1927-41. *The Deipnosophists,* trans. C. B. Gulick. 7 vols. New York.

Athenagoras. 1956. The resurrection of the dead. In *The ante-Nicene fathers: Translations of the writings of the fathers down to A.D. 325,* Vol 2. *Fathers of the second century: Hermas, Tatian, Athenagoras, Theophilus, and Clement of Alexandria,* ed. A. Roberts and J. Donaldson. Grand Rapids, Mich.

Ba'al Shem, J., and N. Katz. 1936. Medical excerpts from Sefer mif'alot elokim [The book of God's deeds]. *Bulletin of the History of Medicine* 4: 299-331.

Bible. [1530] 1992. *Tyndale's Old Testament.* New Haven, Conn.

      [1560] 1969. *The Geneva Bible.* Madison, Wis.

      [1609] 1963. *The Holy Bible: Translated from the Latin Vulgate and diligently compared with Hebrew, Greek, and other editions in diverse languages and first published at the English College at Douay, Anno 1609.* Edinburgh.

      [1611] 1968. *The Holy Bible: The authorized or King James version of 1611 now reprinted with apocrypha.* New York.

      [1782] 1968. *The Holy Bible as printed by Robert Aiken and approved and recommended by the Congress of the United States of America in 1782.* New York.

      1805. *The Holy Scriptures, faithfully and truly translated by Myles Cloverdale, Bishop of Exeter.* Second edition. London.

      1850. *The Holy Bible containing the Old and New Testaments . . . in the earliest English version made from the Latin Vulgate by John Wycliffe and his followers.* Oxford.

      1897. *The Emphasised Bible: A new translation by J. B. Rotherham,* Vol. 1. Genesis-Ruth. Cincinnati, Ohio.

      1950. *The Basic Bible: Containing the Old and New Testaments in basic English.* New York.

      1953. *King James edition.* London.

      1965. *The amplified Bible.* Grand Rapids, Mich.

      1966. *The Jerusalem Bible,* ed. A. Jones. Garden City, N.Y.

      1970a. *The New American Bible: Translated from the original languages, with critical use of all the ancient sources by members of the Catholic Biblical Association of America.* New York.

      1970b. *New World translation of the Holy Scriptures.* Brooklyn, N.Y.

      1970c. *The New English Bible with apocrypha.* New York.

      1973. *The Holy Bible: Revised Standard Version consisting of the Old and New Testaments. . . . Being the version set forth A.D. 1611, revised A.D. 1881-1885 and A.D. 1901.* New York.

      1978. *New International Version.* Grand Rapids, Mich.

      1981a. *The New Layman's Parallel Bible (King James Version, New International Version, Living Bible, Revised Standard Version).* Second edition. Grand Rapids, Mich.

      1981b. *The NIV Triglot Old Testament.* Grand Rapids, Mich.

      1989. *The Holy Bible: New Revised Standard Version.* New York.

      1990. *Life Application Bible.* Iowa Falls, Iowa.

Blackman, P., trans. 1964. Mishayoth. In *Order kodashum: Chullin.* Second edition. New York.

Bolton, J. M. 1972. Food taboos among the Orang Asli in west Malaysia: A potential nutritional hazard. *American Journal of Clinical Nutrition* 25: 789-99.

Borgoras, W. 1909. The Chuckchee. Material Culture. *Memoirs of the American Museum of Natural History* 11: 193-208.

Bosley, G. C., and M. G. Hardinge. 1992. Seventh-Day Adventists: Dietary standard and concerns. *Food Technology* 46: 112-13.

Bush, L. E. 1990. The word of wisdom in early nineteenth-century perspective. In *The Word of God: Essays on Mormon Scripture*, ed. D. Vogel, 161–85. Salt Lake City, Utah.

Caraka. 1981. *Caraka-Sambita: Agnivesa's treatise refined and annotated by Caraka and redacted by Drdhabala*, Vol. 1. *Sutrasthana to Indriyasthana.* ed. and trans. Priyavrat Sharma. Delhi.

Chadwick, G. A. 1890. *The book of Exodus: The Expositor's Bible*, ed. W. Robertson Nicoll. London.

Chang Chi. 1990. *Chin kuei yuao lueh* [Important principles from the golden treasure chest], redacted by Ching Chun. Taipei.

Chaudry, M. M. 1992. Islamic food laws: Philosophical basis and practical implications. *Food Technology* 46: 92–3, 104f.

Chen Tzu Ming. 1977. *Fu jen liang fang* [Excellent formulas for women]. Taipei, Taiwan.

Cheyne, T. K. 1907. *Traditions and beliefs of Ancient Israel.* London.

Chu Chen-Heng. 1984. *Tan chi hsin fa* [Methods from tan chi]. Taipei, Taiwan.

Cohn, J. 1973. *The royal table: An outline of the dietary laws of Israel.* New York.

Cook, S. A. 1969. Notes to the third edition. In *Lectures on the religion of the Semites: The fundamental institutions.* ed. W. R. Smith, 576–7. New York.

Counsels on Diet and Foods. 1938. *Counsels on diets and foods: A compilation from the writings of Ellen G. White.* Washington, D.C.

Crysostum (See John Chrysostom)

Darby, W. J., P. Ghalioungui, and L. E. Grivetti. 1977. *Food: The gift of Osiris.* 2 vols. London.

Douglas, M. 1966. *Purity and danger: An analysis of concepts of pollution and taboo.* London.

1977. Structure of gastronomy. In *Russell Sage Foundation annual report for the year 1976–1977*, 41–57. New York.

Dresser, M. 1979. Kosher catering: How and why. *Cornell Hotel Restaurant Administration Quarterly* 20: 83–91.

Ehrman, A., ed. 1965. *The Talmud with an English translation and commentary.* Jerusalem.

Eidlitz, K. 1969. Food and emergency food in the circumpolar area. *Studia Ethnographica Uppsaliensia* 32: 108–62.

Einspahr, B. 1977. *Index to Brown, Driver, and Briggs: Hebrew lexicon.* Chicago.

Emery, W. B. 1962. *A funerary repast in an Egyptian tomb of the archaic period.* Leiden, the Netherlands.

Epstein, I., ed. 1948. *Seder Kodashim: II (Hullin)*, trans. E. Cashdan. London.

Frazer, J. G. 1907a. Folklore in the Old Testament. In *Anthropological essays presented to Edward Burnett Tylor*, 101–74. Oxford.

1907b. Not to seethe a kid in its mother's milk. *Man* 7: 166.

1918–19. *Folklore in the Old Testament: Studies in comparative religion, legend, and law.* 3 vols. London.

1935. *The golden bough: A study in magic and religion.* Third edition. 12 vols. New York.

Freedman, S. E. 1970. *The book of Kashruth: A treasury of Kosher facts and frauds.* New York.

Garine, I. de. 1972. The socio-cultural aspects of nutrition. *Ecology of Food and Nutrition* 1: 143–63.

Gaster, T. H. 1955. *Customs and folkways of Jewish life.* New York.

Ginzberg, L. 1961. *The legends of the Jews*, Vol. 1. trans. H. Szold. Philadelphia, Pa.

Gordon, B. L. 1959. *Medieval and Renaissance medicine.* New York.

Grivetti, L. E. 1975. Flavor and culture: The importance of flavors in the Middle East. *Food Technology* 29: 38–40.

1976. Dietary resources and social aspects of food use in a Tswana tribe. Ph.D. dissertation, University of California, Davis.

1978a. Culture, diet and nutrition: Selected themes and topics. *BioScience* 28: 171–7.

1978b. Nutritional success in a semi-arid land: Examination of Tswana agro-pastoralists of the eastern Kalahari, Botswana. *American Journal of Clinical Nutrition* 31: 1204–20.

1980. Dietary separation of meat and milk: A cultural-geographical inquiry. *Ecology of Food and Nutrition* 9: 203–17.

1981a. Cultural nutrition: Anthropological and geographical themes. *Annual Review of Nutrition* 1: 47–68.

1981b. Geographical location, climate and weather, and magic: Aspects of agricultural success in the eastern Kalahari, Botswana. *Social Science Information: Human Societies and Ecosystems* 20: 509–36.

1991a. Nutrition past – nutrition today: Prescientific origins of nutrition and dietetics. Part 1. Legacy of India. *Nutrition Today* 26: 13–24.

1991b. Nutrition past – nutrition today: Prescientific origins of nutrition and dietetics. Part 2. Legacy of the Mediterranean. *Nutrition Today* 26: 18–29.

1991c. Nutrition past – nutrition today: Prescientific origins of nutrition and dietetics. Part 3. Legacy of China. *Nutrition Today* 26: 6–17.

1992. Nutrition past – nutrition today: Prescientific origins of nutrition and dietetics. Part 4. Aztec patterns and Spanish legacy. *Nutrition Today* 27: 13–25.

Grivetti, L. E., S. J. Lamprecht, H. J. Rocke, and A. Waterman. 1987. Threads of cultural nutrition: Arts and humanities. *Progress in Food and Nutrition Science* 11: 249–306.

Grivetti, L. E., and R. M. Pangborn. 1974. Origin of selected Old Testament dietary prohibitions. *Journal of the American Dietetic Association* 65: 634–8.

Grunfeld, D. I. 1972. *Dietary laws regarding forbidden and permitted foods, with particular reference to meat and meat products*, Vol. 1, *The Jewish dietary laws.* New York.

1972. *Dietary laws regarding plants and vegetables, with particular reference to the produce of the Holy land*, Vol. 2, *The Jewish dietary laws.* New York.

Guillaume, A. 1924. *The traditions of Islam. An introduction to the study of Hadith by A. Guillaume.* Oxford.

Harding, T. S. 1931. Food prejudices. *Medical Journal and Record* 133: 67–70.

Harrington, J. 1957. *The School of Salernum: Regimen Sanitatis Salerni.* Rome.

Harris, M. 1972. Riddle of the pig. *Natural History* 81: 32–6.

1973. Riddle of the pig II. *Natural History* 82: 20–5.

Hehn, V. 1885. *The wanderings of plants and animals from their first home*, ed. J. S. Stallybrass. London.

Heliodorus. 1587. *An Aethopian historie written in Greek by Heliodorus no less wittie than pleasaunt*, trans. T. Underdowne. London.

Heun, E. 1962. Nutrition and abstention in primitive peoples. *Medical Mirror* 1: 1–4.

Hilton, J. 1833. Notes on a peculiar appearance observed in human muscle, probably depending upon the formation of very small cysticerci. *London Medical Gazette* 11: 605.

Hsu, H-Y., Y-P. Chen, S-U Shen, et al. 1986. *Oriental materia medica: A concise guide.* Long Beach, Calif.

Ibn Sina [Abu Husayn Ibn Abdullah Ibn Sina]. 1930. *A treatise on the canon of medicine of Avicenna: Incorporating a translation of the first book,* trans. O. C. Gruner. London.

Jelliffe, D. B., and E. F. P. Jelliffe. 1978. Food habits and taboos: How have they protected man in his evolution? *Progress in Human Nutrition* 2: 67-76.

John Chrysostom. 1957. Homily 22 on John 2:4-10. In *Saint John Chrysostom: Commentary on Saint John the Apostle and Evangelist,* Vol. 33, *The Fathers of the Church: A New Translation,* trans. T. A. Goggin, 212-21. New York.

Kamal, H. 1975. *Encyclopedia of Islamic medicine: With a Greco-Roman background.* Cairo.

Kaufman, M. 1957. Adapting therapeutic diets to Jewish food customs. *American Journal of Clinical Nutrition* 5: 676-81.

Kees, H. 1961. *Ancient Egypt: A cultural topography,* ed. T. G. H. James, trans. I. F. E. Morrow. London.

Keimer, L. 1924. *Die Gartenpflanzen im alten Aegypten.* Hamburg.

Kellogg, S. H. 1899. The book of Leviticus. In *The Expositor's Bible,* ed. W. R. Nicholl, 277-304. London.

Kennedy, B. W., and L. E. Grivetti. 1980. Toxic quail: A cultural-ecological investigation of coturnism. *Ecology of Food and Nutrition* 9: 15-42.

Kilara, A., and K. K. Iya. 1992. Food and dietary habits of the Hindu. *Food Technology* 46: 94-104.

Kleist, J. A., trans. 1961. The epistle of Barnabas. In *Ancient Christian Writers,* Vol 6. London.

Knutsson, K. E., and R. Selinus. 1970. Fasting in Ethopia: An anthropological and nutritional study. *American Journal of Clinical Nutrition* 23: 956-69.

Korff, S. L. 1966. The Jewish dietary code. *Food Technology* 20: 76-8.

Levin, S. I., and E. A. Boyden. 1940. *The Kosher code of the orthodox Jew: Being a literal translation of that portion of the sixteenth-century codification of the Babylonian Talmud which describes such deficiencies as render animals unfit for food (Hilkot Terefor Shulhan 'Aruk); To which is appended a discussion of Talmudic anatomy in the light of science of its day and of the present time.* New York.

Lipschutz, Y. 1988. *Kashruth: A comprehensive background and reference guide to the principles of Kashruth.* Brooklyn, N.Y.

Loret, V. 1892. *La flore pharonique d'après les documents hiéroglyphiques et les spécimens découverts dans les tombes.* Paris.

Lucretius. 1910. *On the nature of things,* trans. C. Bailey. Oxford.

Mackintosh, C. H. 1959. *Notes on the Pentateuch.* New York.

Maimonides. 1956. *The guide for the perplexed.* Second edition, trans. M. Friedländer. London.

　1967. *Sefer ha-mitzvoth,* trans. C. B. Chavel. 2 vols. London.

　1970-1. *The medical aphorisms of Moses Maimonides,* ed. S. Munter, trans. F. Rosner. New York.

　1987. *Maimonides' commentary on the aphorism of Hippocrates,* trans. F. Rosner. Haifa, Israel.

Mays, J. L. 1963. The book of Leviticus; The book of Numbers. In *The Layman's Bible Commentary,* Vol. 4, ed. D. H. Kelly, D. G. Miller, A. B. Rhodes, and D. M. Chalmers, 49. Richmond, Va.

McDonald, D. R. 1977. Food taboos: A primitive environmental protection agency (South America). *Anthropos* 72: 734-48.

Menghin, O., and M. Amer. 1932. *The excavations of the Egyptian University in the neolithic site of the Maadi: First preliminary report.* Cairo.

Monet, P. 1958. *Everyday life in Egypt in the days of Ramses the Great,* trans. A. R. Maxwell-Hyslop and M. S. Drower. London.

Müller, F. M., ed. 1882a. Baudhayana. In *The Sacred Laws of the Aryas: As taught in the schools of Apastamba, Gautama, Vasishtha, and Baudhayana,* Part 2. Vasishtha and Baudhayana, Vol. 14, *The Sacred Books of the East,* trans. G. Buhler. Second edition. Oxford.

　1882b. Vasishtha. In *The Sacred Laws of the Aryas: As taught in the schools of Apastamba, Gautama, Vasishtha, and Baudhayana,* Part 2. Vasishtha and Baudhayana, Vol. 14, *The Sacred Books of the East,* trans. G. Buhler. Second edition. Oxford.

　1896a. Apastamba. In *The sacred laws of the Aryas: As taught in the schools of Apastamba, Gautama, Vasishtha, and Baudhayana,* Part 1. Apastamba and Gautama, Vol. 2, *The Sacred Books of the East,* trans. G. Buhler. Second edition. Oxford.

　1896b. Gautama. In *The Sacred Laws of the Aryas: As taught in the schools of Apastamba, Gautama, Vasishtha, and Baudhayana,* Part 1. Apastamba and Gautama, Vol. 2, *The Sacred Books of the East,* trans. G. Buhler. Second edition. Oxford.

　1896c. Manu. In *The laws of Manu: Translated with extracts from seven commentaries,* Vol 25, *The sacred books of the East,* trans. G. Buhler. Oxford.

Natow, A. B., J. Iteslin, and B. C. Raven. 1975. Integrating the Jewish dietary laws into a dietetics program. *Journal of the American Dietetic Association* 67: 13-16.

Newberry, P. 1928. The pig and the cult animal of Set. *Journal of Egyptian Archaeology* 14: 211-25.

Novatian. 1957. On the Jewish meats. In *The Ante-Nicene Fathers,* Vol. 5, ed. A. Roberts and J. Donaldson. trans. R. E. Wallis, 645-50. Grand Rapids, Mich.

Owen, R. 1835. Description of a microscopic entozoon infesting the muscles of the human body. *Transactions of the Zoological Society of London* 1: 315-24.

Paget, J. 1866. On the discovery of Trichina. *Lancet* 1: 269-70.

Petrovic, A. 1939. Contributions to the study of the Serbian Gypsies. Part 2: The eating of carrion. *Journal, Gypsy Lore Society* (3rd Series) 18: 24-34.

Philo. 1954. On the special laws. In *The collected works of Philo,* Vol. 8, trans. E. H. Colson, 7-155. London.

Pike, O. A. 1992. The church of Jesus Christ of Latter-Day Saints: Dietary practices and health. *Food Technology* 46: 118-21.

Pillsbury, B. L. K. 1978. "Doing the month": Confinement and convalescence of Chinese women after childbirth. *Social Science and Medicine* 12: 11-22.

Platt, B. S., and S. Y. Gin. 1938. Chinese methods of infant feeding and nursing. *Archives, Diseases of Childhood* 18: 343-54.

Pliny. 1919-1956. *Natural history,* trans. H. Rackham and W. H. S. Jones. 8 vols. Cambridge, Mass.

Plutarch. 1936. Isis and Osiris. In *Moralia,* Vol. 5, trans. F. C. Babbitt. Cambridge, Mass.

Polynaeus. 1793. *Stratagems of War,* trans. R. Shepherd. London.

Porphyry. 1965. *On abstinence from animal food,* trans. Thomas Taylor. London.

Prakash, O. 1961. *Food and drinks in ancient India: From earliest times to c. 1200 A.D.* Delhi.

Preuss, Julius. 1978. *Julius Preuss' Biblical and Talmudic medicine,* ed. and trans. F. Rosner. New York.

Qazwiny [Zakaria ibn Mohammed ibn Mahmoud]. 1957. *Kitab aga'il el-makhlouquat wa ghara'ib el-mawgoudat.* 2 vols. Cairo.

Rahman, F. 1987. *Health and medicine in the Islamic tradition: Change and identity.* New York.

Read, B. E. 1976. *Chinese materia medica: Animal drugs.* Taipei.

    1977a. *Chinese materia medica: Avian drugs.* Taipei.

    1977b. *Chinese materia medica: Dragon and snake drugs.* Taipei.

    1977c. *Chinese materia medica: Fish drugs.* Taipei.

    1977d. *Chinese materia medica: Insect drugs.* Taipei.

    1977e. *Chinese materia medica: Turtle and shellfish drugs.* Taipei.

Regenstein, J. M., and C. E. Regenstein. 1979. An introduction to the kosher dietary laws for food scientists and food processors. *Food Technology* 33: 89-99.

    1988. The kosher dietary laws and their implementation in the food industry. *Food Technology* 42: 86, 88-94.

    1991. Current issues in kosher foods. *Trends in Food Science and Technology* 2: 50-4.

Richards, A. I. 1932. *Hunger and work in a savage tribe: A functional study of nutrition among the southern Bantu.* London.

    1939. *Land, labor and diet in northern Rhodesia: An economic study of the Bemba tribe.* Oxford.

Roberts, R. 1925. *The social laws of the Qorân: Considered and compared with those of Hebrew and other ancient codes.* London.

Sakr, A. H. 1971. Fasting in Islam. *Journal of the American Dietetic Association* 67: 17-21.

    1975. Dietary regulation and food habits of Muslims. *Journal of the American Dietetic Association* 58: 123-6.

    1991. *Pork: Possible reasons for its prohibition.* Lombard, Ill.

Schmidt, N. 1926. The numen of Penuel. *Journal of Biblical Literature* 45: 260-79.

Scott, T. 1866. *The Holy Bible containing the Old and New Testaments according to the authorized version with explanatory notes, practical observations, and copious marginal references.* New edition. 2 vols. London.

Sextus Empiricus. 1933. *Outlines of Pyrrhonism,* Vol 1, *Sextus Empiricus,* trans R. G. Bury. New York.

Simoons, F. J. 1961. *Eat not this flesh: Food avoidance in the Old World.* Madison, Wis.

    1966. The geographic approach to food prejudices. *Food Technology* 20: 274-6.

    1978. Traditional use and avoidance of foods of animal origin: A cultural historical review. *BioScience* 28: 178-84.

Singer, I. 1907. *The Jewish encyclopedia,* Vol 4. New York.

Smith, Joseph. [1833] 1869. A word of wisdom, for the benefit of the council of high priests, assembled in Kirtland, and church, and also the saints in Zion. In *The book of doctrine and covenants of the Church of Jesus Christ of Latter-Day Saints; Selected from the revelations of God by Joseph Smith, president.* Sixth European edition, 240-1. London.

Smith, W. R. 1969. *Lectures on the religion of the Semites: The fundamental institutions.* Third edition. New York.

Sun Ssu-Mo. 1980. *Ch'ien-chin i-fang [Formulas worth a thousand thals of gold].* Third edition. Taipei, Taiwan.

Tan, S. P., and E. Wheeler. 1983. Concepts relating to health and food held by Chinese women in London. *Ecology of Food and Nutrition* 13: 37-49.

Temkin, O. 1953. Greek medicine as science and kraft. *Isis* 44: 213-26.

Thompson, L. 1949. The relations of men, animals and plants in an island community. *American Anthropologist* 51: 253-76.

Torah. 1962. *The Torah: The five books of Moses.* Philadelphia, Pa.

Twaigery, S., and D. Spillman. 1989. An introduction to Moslem dietary laws. *Food Technology* 43: 88-90.

van den Heever, L. W. 1967. Some public health aspects of meat and milk. *South African Medical Journal* 41: 1240-43.

Wheeler, E., and S. P. Tan. 1983. From concept to practice: Food behavior of Chinese immigrants in London. *Ecology of Food and Nutrition* 13: 51-7.

Wilkinson, J. G. 1854. *A popular account of the ancient Egyptians.* 2 vols. New York.

Willoughby, W. C. 1932. *Nature-worship and taboo: Further studies in "The soul of the Bantu."* Hartford, Conn.

Zenker, F. A. 1860. Ueber die Trichinen-Krankheit des Menschen. *Virchows Archiv für pathologische Anatomie und Physiologie und für klinische Medizin* 18: 561-72.

VI.14   The Social and Cultural Uses of Food

Food is what Marcel Mauss (1967) called a "total social fact." It is a part of culture that is central, connected to many kinds of behavior, and infinitely meaningful. Food is a prism that absorbs a host of assorted cultural phenomena and unites them into one coherent domain while simultaneously speaking through that domain about everything that is important. For example, for Sardinians, bread is world (Counihan 1984). In the production, distribution, and consumption of bread are manifest Sardinian economic realities, social relations, and cultural ideals. An examination of foodways in all cultures reveals much about power relations, the shaping of community and personality, the construction of the family, systems of meaning and communication, and conceptions of sex, sexuality, and gender. The study of foodways has contributed to the understanding of personhood across cultures and historical periods (see Messer 1984).

Every coherent social group has its own unique alimentary system. Even cultures in the process of disintegration reveal their plight in the ways they deal with and think about eating.[1] Cultures articulate and recognize their distinctiveness through the medium of food. The English call the French "Frogs" because of their habit (wildly barbarian to the English) of eating the legs of that creature (Leach 1964: 31). In the Amazon region, Indian tribes that appear alike in the eyes of an outsider nonetheless distinguish themselves from one another in part through their different habits, manners, and conceptions of eating. Maligned other groups are defined as those who eat people and animals thought disgusting, as for example, "frogs and snakes and mice" (Gregor

1985: 14). Food systems are, of course, intimately related to the local environment, but in most cultures "only a small part of this edible environment will actually be classified as potential food. Such classification is a matter of language and culture, not of nature" (Leach 1964: 31). The study of foodways enables a holistic and coherent look at how humans mediate their relationships with nature and with one another across cultures and throughout history.

Food and Power

David Arnold (1988: 3) suggests that "food was, and continues to be, power in a most basic, tangible and inescapable form." Frances Moore Lappé and Joseph Collins (1986) make a strong argument that there is no more absolute sign of powerlessness than hunger, since hunger means that one lacks the control to satisfy the most basic subsistence need. Food is a central concern in the politics of nation states. Whereas Piero Camporesi (1989: 137) argues that chronic hunger and malnutrition were part of a calculated strategy of early modern political elites to maintain their power by keeping the poor debilitated and dazed, Arnold (1988) and others[2] point out that extreme hunger can bring about popular protest that may seriously weaken a government's stability. According to Arnold (1988: 96), "The fortunes of the state, whether in Europe or in Africa or Asia, have long been closely bound up with the containment or prevention of famine and, more generally, with provisioning the populace."

In stratified societies, hunger – like poverty – is far more likely to strike people in disadvantaged and devalued social categories: small children, the mentally ill, the handicapped, women, people of color, and the elderly (Physicians Task Force on Hunger in America 1985; Brown 1987; Brown and Pizer 1987; Arnold 1988; Glasser 1988). Food scarcity mirrors and exacerbates social distinctions; famine relief goes first to groups with power, and in times of economic crisis, the rich get richer by buying the land and other resources of the poor as the latter give them up in the struggle to eat.

A person's place in the social system can be revealed by what, how much, and with whom one eats. As Jack Goody (1982: 113) says, "the hierarchy between ranks and classes takes a culinary form." In India, caste is marked quite conspicuously by different food habits and rules prohibiting eating with those of lower caste (Goody 1982: 116 ff.; Khare and Rao 1986). Different consumption patterns are one of the ways the rich distinguish themselves from the poor (Bennett 1943; Fitchen 1988; Weismantel 1988). For example, according to Carol J. Adams (1990: 30), the consumption of meat protein reveals "the white Western world's enactment of racism. . . . The hierarchy of meat protein reinforces a hierarchy of race, class, and sex." Sugar was at first only a food of the rich, who used it to (among other things) create fabulous, ostentatious sculptures that proclaimed their wealth and power through extravagance with the precious and desirable commodity (Mintz 1985).

As sugar became more plentiful, however, the poor were increasingly able to eat it, which they did, in part, in an effect to emulate the rich and achieve a like status. Sugar consumption conveyed "the complex idea that one could *become* different by *consuming* differently" (Mintz 1985: 185). But to eat sugar, the poor sacrificed other foods, and their diet suffered, whereas the rich who could eat sugar *and* other foods simply chose new ways of proclaiming their difference. According to Stephen Mennell:

> Likes and dislikes are never socially neutral, but always entangled with people's affiliations to class and other social groups. Higher social circles have repeatedly used food as one of many means of distinguishing themselves from lower rising classes. This has been manifested in a succession of styles and attitudes towards food and eating (Mennell 1985: 331–2).

Class distinctions are also manifest through rules about eating and through the ability to impose rules on others (Counihan 1992). For example, we live in a culture that values thinness.[3] The dominant culture – manifest in advertising, fashion, and the media – projects a belief that thinness connotes control, power, wealth, competence, and success (Dyrenforth, Wooley, and Wooley 1980). Research has revealed that obesity for women varies directly with class status and ethnicity. Greater wealth and whiteness go along with thinness; poor Puerto Rican, black, and Native American women have lower status and greater obesity rates than well-off Euro-American women (Garb, Garb, and Stunkard 1975; Beller 1977; Stunkard 1977; Massara and Stunkard 1979; Massara 1989; Sobal and Stunkard 1989). The standard of thinness upholds a class structure where men, whites, and the rich are superior to women, people of color, and the poor.

Food and Community

Manners and habits of eating not only display the complex intricacies of the social hierarchy but also are crucial to the very definition of community, the relationships between people, interactions between humans and their gods, and communication between the living and the dead. In many societies, communal feasts involve a periodic reaffirmation of community "based upon primal conceptions of the meaning of eating and drinking in common. To eat and drink with someone was at the same time a symbol and a confirmation of social community and of the assumption of mutual obligations" (Freud 1918: 174).

Sharing food ensures the survival of the group both socially and materially. A companion is literally a person one eats bread with (Farb and Armelagos 1980: 4). Refusal to share food is a sign of enmity and hostility; as Marcel Mauss (1967: 58) reports of Brahmans, "A man does not eat with his enemy." For eating together is a sign of kinship, trust, friendship, and in some cultures, sexual intimacy, as we shall discuss further.

On a day-to-day basis, food exchanges are crucial in maintaining good relations between individuals. The message of the following Sardinian proverb (Gallini 1973: 60) is relevant in many cultures:

> Si cheres chi s'amore si
>   mantenzat
> prattu chi andet, prattu
> chi benzat.

> If you want love to be
>   maintained
> for a plate that goes,
> let a plate come back.

Mauss (1967) has shown the pervasive cultural power of the gift that keeps individuals constantly indebted to each other and continuously engaged in positive interaction through giving. In his interpretation of Mauss, Marshall Sahlins has said, "The gift is alliance, solidarity, communion, in brief, peace" (1972: 169). Food is an extremely important component of reciprocal exchanges, more so than any other object or substance (Mauss 1967). As Sahlins says: "By comparison with other stuff, food is more readily, or more necessarily shared" (1972: 215).

Bronislaw Malinowski (1961: 168–72), Miriam Kahn (1986, 1988), and Michael Young (1971) have explicitly demonstrated how in Melanesia, feasting both joins people in community and establishes power relations. Kahn (1986, 1988) describes two different kinds of feasts held by the Wamirans of Papua New Guinea, the T-mode (transaction) feast that serves to reinforce power ranks and the I-mode (incorporation) feast that strengthens community solidarity; "both types of exchanges are equally necessary" (Kahn 1986: 125). Similarly, in the Sardinian community of Tresnuraghes (Counihan 1984), the annual St. Mark celebration involves a collective feasting on mutton, donated by wealthy shepherds, and bread, donated by villagers seeking or repaying divine assistance. This redistributive feast serves simultaneously to bring the community together, to make abundant food available to the poor, and to display the wealth and prestige of those able to sponsor the feast. Similar redistributive celebrations occur in a wide range of peasant and tribal societies and are central to the maintenance of community and political organization.[4]

In many cultures, food is instrumental in maintaining good relations between humans and their gods. In Christianity, a central symbol is the consumption of bread, both by Christ and his disciples at the Last Supper, and regularly by the faithful in the Communion ritual (Feeley-Harnik 1981; Bynum 1987). The bread, or host, is the body of Christ; it stands for redemption, holiness, and salvation. The faithful literally eat their God, and, in so doing, incorporate the values and messages of their religion. Ancient Greeks, and many other peoples, use food sacrifices as a means of propitiating their gods (Mauss 1967; Detienne and Vernant 1989). Tibetan Buddhist Sherpas consciously cajole their gods with food offerings and say, "I am offering you the things which you eat, now you must do whatever I demand" (Ortner 1975: 147). By consciously employing the mechanisms of hospitality with the gods that facilitate human interaction, Sherpas hope that "aroused, pleased, and gratified, the gods, like one's neighbors, will feel 'happy' and kindly disposed toward the worshippers/hosts and any requests they might make" (Ortner 1975: 146–7).

Offerings of food to the deceased are a common cultural means of ensuring good relations with them (Frazer 1951; Goody 1962; Huntington and Metcalf 1979; Nutini 1988). On All Souls' Day or Eve, throughout the Christian world, people make food offerings and sometimes prepare entire meals for the dead. Some Sicilians eat fava beans; others consume cooked cereals (De Simone and Rossi 1977: 53–4). In Bosa, on All Souls' Day, Sardinians prepare *sa mesa,* literally, "the table," which is a meal for the deceased that they lay out as they are going to bed (Counihan 1981: 276–9). They always include spaghetti and *pabassini,* a special cookie made for All Souls' Day, as well as many other foods, including bread, nuts, fruit, and sometimes wine, beer, Coca-Cola, juice, coffee, snuffing tobacco, or cigarettes. The meal is destined specifically for one's own dead relatives, and often the optional food items reflect a specific deceased person's preferences in life. The meal serves to communicate and maintain good relations with the dead, just as food exchanges regularly do with the living.

In some cultures, the living actually eat the dead to honor them and gain some of their powers (Arens 1979; Walens 1981; Sanday 1986). Sigmund Freud argued that consumption of the deceased is based on the belief that "by absorbing parts of the body of a person through the act of eating we also come to possess the properties which belonged to that person" (1918: 107). The Yanomamo Indians of the Venezuelan Amazon eat the ashes of their deceased loved ones to ensure a successful afterlife. When ethnographer Kenneth Good was deathly sick with malaria, his informants expressed their affection by assuring him, "Don't worry, older brother. Don't worry at all. We will drink your ashes" (Good and Chanoff 1991: 133). Consumption establishes connection between the living and the dead, between humans and their gods, among neighbors and kin, and, in particular, among family members.

Food and Family

Feeding is one of the most important channels of infant and child socialization and personality formation.[5] In fact, the Pacific Atimelangers studied by Cora Du Bois believe that the original creation of human beings was from food; they were "created from molded rice and corn meal" (1941: 278-9). Food and the manner of giving it make the child. As Margaret Mead said, "It seems probable that as he is fed every child learns something about the willingness of the world to give or withhold food, to give lavishly or deal out parsimoniously" (1967: 70).

According to Freud, the child's earliest experiences of eating are the stage for important developmental processes and shape his or her lifelong personality: "The first and most important activity in the child's life, the sucking from the mother's breast," introduces the child to sexual pleasure and prefigures later adult sexuality (Freud 1962: 43; see also Malinowski 1927). Furthermore, breast feeding becomes part of the process of individuation for the child. As it recognizes gradually that the mother is other, and that its source of food is outside of itself, the child begins to establish an autonomous and bounded identity.

In some cultures, the family may be most effectively conceptualized as those people who share a common hearth (Weismantel 1988: 169). As Janet Siskind says of the Sharanahua Indians of the Peruvian Amazon, "Eating with people is an affirmation of kinship" (1973: 9). So important is feeding to the establishment of parent–child relations in Kalauna, Goodenough Island, that "fosterage . . . is wholly conceived in terms of feeding" (Young 1971: 41). Young goes on to note that this same "identification is buried in our own language: Old English 'foster' means 'food'" (1971: 41). In Kalauna, the father establishes his paternity by providing food for his pregnant wife. Young says:

> While the role of the mother in producing the child is self-evident, the father must reinforce his own role by feeding his wife during pregnancy. This is explicitly seen as nurturing the foetus, and it is a principal element in the ideology of agnatic descent (1971: 40).

Problematic feeding can lead to personality disturbances in children, and dysfunctional families may have members who suffer from eating problems (Palazzoli 1971; Bruch 1973). Anna Freud suggests that disturbed eating patterns may be "symbolic of a struggle between mother and child, in which the child can find an outlet for its passive or active, sadistic or masochistic tendencies towards the mother" (1946: 121).

Dorothy N. Shack (1969) and William A. Shack (1971) attribute a host of personality characteristics of the Gurage of Ethiopia to their inconsistent early-childhood feeding habits and later patterns of want and glut that reveal severe "dependency-frustration" (W. Shack 1971: 34). Gurage children are often neglected when hungry and then finally fed to excess after crying for hours (D. Shack 1969). Adults eat sparingly and quickly on normal occasions, but occasionally find themselves forced to eat when not hungry at feasts or as guests (W. Shack 1971). D. Shack argues that such eating patterns contribute to the development of personality traits that include "selfishness," "emotional detachment," "unrelatedness," "passivity," "dependency," and feelings of worthlessness (1969: 298).

W. Shack suggests that because the food supply is particularly unreliable for low-status men, they are susceptible to *awre* (spirit possession), marked by "loss of appetite, nausea and intermittent attacks of severe stomach pains" (1971: 35). The affliction is cured through a collective ritual in which the victim is covered by a white shawl, seated in a smoky room, and given special food called *bra-brat*. With this, he "begins greedily and ravenously stuffing his mouth" and continues to do so until the spirit, "speaking through the possessed person, utters with a sigh, several times – *'tafwahum'* – 'I am satisfied'" (W. Shack 1971: 36). The rite of *awre*-spirit exorcism allows a low-status man deprived of both food and prestige to gain both. It is a temporary overcoming of the dependency frustration embedded in the cultural foodways that produces a chronic anxiety in those most often hungry. The Gurage exemplify how feeding patterns can influence personality formation and show how different cultures have distinct ways of ensuring that people get fed.

Food as Meaning, Symbol, and Language

In every culture, foodways constitute an organized system, a language, which – through its structure and components – conveys meaning and contributes to the organization of the natural and social world. According to Roland Barthes (1975: 49-50), "Food . . . is not only a collection of products that can be used for statistical or nutritional studies. It is also a system of communication, a body of images, a protocol of usages, situations and behavior." Foodways are a prime domain for conveying meaning because eating is an essential and continuously repeated activity; foods are many; there are different characteristics of texture, taste, color, and modes of preparation of food that are easy labels for meaning; food constitutes a language accessible to all; and eating is extremely pleasurable.

In examining the meaning of food, social scientists have studied *cuisine,* the food elements used and rules for their combination and preparation; *etiquette and food rules,* the customs governing what, with whom, when, and where one eats; *taboos,* the prohibitions of and restrictions on the consumption of certain foods by certain people under certain conditions; and *symbolism,* the specific meanings attributed to foods in specific contexts.[6] There is of course much overlap between these four domains. For example, the study of Jewish dietary law[7] involves examination of foods eaten and not eaten and the legitimate bases of their combination (cuisine). But it also concerns the study of meals, the arrangement and sequence of foods, peoples' roles in the preparation and serving of food, and their placement at the table (etiquette). In addition, it includes the study of foods not eaten and why (taboo). And finally, to make sense out of all this, it involves the study of the complex and multivocal meanings of the foods and the behaviors centered around them (symbolism).

Food functions effectively as a system of communication because human beings organize their foodways into an ordered system parallel to other cultural systems and infuse them with meaning: "The cuisine of a people and their understanding of the world are linked" (Soler 1973: 943, my translation). It is to this cultural association between food and meaning that Claude Lévi-Strauss (1963a: 89) was referring in his oft-quoted statement that certain animal species are chosen as totems "not because they are 'good to eat' but because they are 'good to think.'" Foods have and convey meanings because they are part of complex systems; "food categories . . . encode social events" (Douglas 1974: 61). Jean Soler suggests that a food taboo "cannot be understood in isolation. It must be placed in the center of the signs of its level, with which it forms a system, and this system must itself be connected to systems of other levels, with which it articulates to form the socio-cultural system of a people" (1973: 946, my translation).

Structuralists (for example, Lévi-Strauss 1966; Verdier 1969) emphasize the dual nature of food and cuisine, which both stand between and mediate nature and culture. The process of naming a wild product as food and transforming it into something edible involves the "culturizing" of nature. And cuisine, because it is a "means of transformation, must facilitate at least metaphorically all transformation" (Verdier 1969: 54). Hence, foods are very often used in rites of passage (see Goody 1982: 79–81).

Among the Mehinaku, initiation ceremonies for girls involve the ritual of first menses, for boys the ear-piercing ceremony. These rituals and the related blood flow are seen as parallel and involve the same restrictions on eating:

Both boys and girls must follow certain food taboos to ensure the rapid cessation of the flow of blood and a favorable dream. Initially, the children are subject to a fast; they are allowed to drink water after twenty-four hours. . . . Following the fast, they may eat all foods but fish, which would prolong the blood flow. "Fish," it is said, "eat other fish and therefore are filled with blood." Monkeys and birds eat only fruit and have a "different kind of blood" and are there-

fore acceptable to "menstruating" boys and girls. . . . With the total cessation of the flow of blood, a ceremony reintroduces fish to the diet. The boys are led outside, taste a small amount of fish, and spit it onto a fiber mat. The girls follow the same ritual inside the house. . . . Fish are now permissible . . . (Gregor 1985: 189).

Here food is used to signify the transformation of boys to men and girls to women while it simultaneously marks the similarity of the maturation of boys and girls (see also S. Hugh-Jones 1979 and C. Hugh-Jones 1979, especially chapter 5).

Food can be used metaphorically to convey just about any imaginable condition, thought, or emotion. American college students, for example, express feelings of love, anger, anxiety, depression, sorrow, and joy through their eating habits (Counihan 1992). After a satisfying meal, Sardinians say, "*consolada(o) soe*" – "I am consoled" – and imply the metaphorical and physical overlap between good food and good feelings (Counihan 1981). Because of the strong visceral pleasure of eating and pain of hunger, food readily adopts powerful connotations and is a rich symbol in written and oral literature.

Food in Folklore and Literature

Food meanings are paramount in Lévi-Strauss's (1963b, 1966, and 1969) monumental study of mythology. He is concerned with understanding, through mythology, the structure of the human mind. According to Lévi-Strauss, binary oppositions are embodied in our brains and appear in many levels of our thinking. The oppositions in the human relationship to nature mediated through food (for example, "the raw and the cooked," nature and culture, or animal and human) reveal universals in human thinking.

In stories told to children, proper eating represents humanness and effective socialization, whereas out-of-control eating and cannibalism stand for wildness and incomplete socialization. The widely known European folktale "Hansel and Gretel" is a good example of these themes; it "is about conflicting family loyalties expressed in terms of sharing and hoarding food" (Taggart 1986: 435). Bruno Bettelheim interprets the food themes of the story as being about children's struggle to outgrow oral dependency and symbiosis with the mother (1975: 159–66). Hansel and Gretel are forced from home due to food scarcity and they, subsequently, gobble up the candy house without thought or restraint.

This regression to "primitive incorporative and hence destructive desires" only leads to trouble, as they are trapped by the wicked witch, "a personification of the destructive aspects of orality" (Bettelheim 1975: 160, 162). Eventually, the children use reason to dominate their oral urges and refuse food so as to be able to kill the witch. Then they inherit her jewels and become reunited with their family in a new status: "As the children transcend their oral anxiety, and free themselves of relying on oral satisfaction for security, they can also free themselves of the image of the threatening mother - the witch - and rediscover the good parents, whose greater wisdom - the shared jewels - then benefit all" (Bettelheim 1975: 162). Their struggle with food, in essence, represents stages in their maturation.

The same theme about the power of food in family relations is beautifully depicted in Maurice Sendak's Caldecott Medal–winning children's story *Where the Wild Things Are* (1963). The tale, which many have placed in the category of superb children's literature, goes something like this: Once upon a time there was an energetic little boy, Max, who put on his wolf costume and pretended to be a ferocious animal. He annoyed his mother so much with his rambunctious behavior that she called him a "wild thing." When in response he threatened to eat her up, she made him go to bed without his supper.

While Max was lying in the dark, his room turned into a dense forest, and a boat arrived. He boarded it and it took him to the land where the wild things lived. He "tamed" them, and they liked him so much that they crowned him their king, which began a boisterous and rowdy time for all.

After a while Max became annoyed by all the commotion and wanted it to stop. As their king he called an end to the rumpus and sent everyone to bed without supper. By now he missed his family and their love for him, and he detected a wonderful aroma that could only be the good food at his house. Very homesick now, he decided to give up his crown and leave the kingdom. He told the wild things that he wanted to go home.

His unruly subjects, however, were not willing to let him leave. They first claimed to love him too much to let him go; in fact, they said that they loved him so much they would rather eat him up than see him leave. But when he insisted, they acted ferociously toward him, making horrible sounds and showing their fangs, and their eyes were evil and menacing. The boy relinquished his kingdom nonetheless and boarded the boat from which he waved good-bye. The way home was a very long journey. It seemed to the little boy to take over a year - but when he finally arrived back in his room, a meal was laid out to greet him. It was still warm.

Sendak's story shows how food is a source of love, power, socialization, and connection between parents and children. In the story, Max is a "wild thing," an incompletely socialized child. His wildness is shown by the wolf suit and his desire to eat his mother up, a desire that simultaneously expresses the incomplete separation of the child from the mother. This theme of eating as incorporation is recreated later in the story when the wild things want to eat Max up, to keep

him from leaving them. But Max does not stay with the wild things; he feels the pull of love in the smells of "good things to eat" that come from the place "where someone loved him best of all." He follows a long journey home where love awaits him in the form of the supper that was previously denied him because of his bad behavior. The fact that "it was still hot" symbolizes the mother's love that persists and is there to facilitate his socialization.

Food, Gender, Sex, and Sexuality

One of the most significant domains of meaning embodied in food centers on the relation between the sexes, their gender definitions, and their sexuality:

> Wives are like mothers. When we were small our mothers fed us. When we are grown our wives cook for us. If there is something good, they keep it in the pot until we come home. When we were small we slept with our mothers; when we are grown we sleep with our wives. Sometimes when we are grown we wake in the night and call our wives 'mothers' (Du Bois 1944: 96).

Eating is a sexual and gendered activity throughout life. Food may stand for sex; as Thomas Gregor says of the Mehinaku Indians, "A literal rendering of the verb to have sex might thus be 'to eat to the fullest extent.' . . . The essential idea is that the genitals of one sex are the 'food' of the other's" (1985: 70). Food and sex are metaphorically overlapping: Eating may represent copulation; foods may stand for sexual acts. The poet George Herbert captured this relation in the early seventeenth century: " 'You must sit down,' says Love, 'and taste my Meat.' / So I did sit and Eat" (quoted in Starn 1990: 78). In many cultures, particularly those with food scarcity, food gifts may be an important path to sexual liaisons (Holmberg 1969: 126; Siskind 1973).

In all cultures there are associations between eating, intercourse, and reproduction.[8] These activities share certain biopsychological attributes - particularly their contributions to life and growth, their passing in and out of the body, and their mingling of discrete individuals - that endow them with metaphorical and symbolic identity. Food and sex are analogous instinctive needs (Freud 1962: 1), and there is a lifelong connection between oral pleasure and sexual pleasure (Freud 1962: 43). Eating together connotes intimacy, often sexual intimacy or kinship (Freud 1918: 175; Siskind 1973: 9). Hence, both eating and copulation could be seen as effecting social merging.

Precisely because eating and intercourse both involve intimacy, they can be dangerous when carried out with the wrong person or under the wrong conditions. Hence, food consumption and sexual activity are surrounded with rules and taboos that regulate them and also reinforce beliefs about gender basic to the social order (see especially Meigs 1984). Food and sex both have associated etiquette about their appropriate times, places, and persons; often people with whom one can eat are those with whom one can have sex and vice versa (see, for example, Tambiah 1969). Among the Trobriand Islanders, a man and woman announce their marriage by eating yams together in public; before this they must never share a meal (Weiner 1988: 77).

Maleness and femaleness in all cultures are associated with specific foods, and rules exist to control their consumption (see Frese 1991 and Brumberg 1988: 176–8). For example, the Hua of New Guinea have elaborate conceptions about *koroko* and *hakeri'a* foods. The former are cold, wet, soft, fertile, fast-growing foods associated with females; the latter are hot, dry, hard, infertile, and slow-growing foods associated with males. Women can become more like men by consuming *hakeri'a* foods, which, it is believed, help minimize menstrual flow. Men, on the other hand, proclaim publicly that female foods and substances are "not only disgusting but also dangerous to the development and maintenance of masculinity." Secretly, however, they eat foods associated with females to gain vitality and power (Meigs 1984).

In general, the association between food and sex is deeper, more extensive, and more intimate for women than it is for men (see, for example, Bynum 1987: xiv). In all cultures, women's primary responsibilities involve food provisioning and the bearing and rearing of children (D'Andrade 1974; Moore 1988). Although these activities are undertaken with widely ranging amounts of autonomy, prestige, and control, they are nonetheless universally linked to womanhood. Women *are* food to the fetus and infant: The breasts can be sources of both sexual pleasure and food. As Mead noted, for women but not for men, both food and sex involve a posture of inception: "[T]he girl finds that the reinterpretation of impregnation and conception and birth fits easily into her early experience with the intake of food" (1967: 143). Where women are valued, their parallel experiences of eating, intercourse, and birth are likely to be positive, but where women are devalued, these activities can be a source of shame and subordination.

In the United States, for example, female college students report that they feel ashamed to eat in front of men with whom they have a romantic involvement (Counihan 1992). They fear fat with obsession and terror (Orbach 1978; Millman 1980; Chernin 1981), and report that men denigrate and gain power over them by saying they eat too much or are too fat (Millman 1980; Counihan 1992). In gender-stratified cultures as diverse as England (Charles and Kerr 1988), Italy (Counihan 1988), and Andean Ecuador (Weismantel 1988), men control women by claiming the authority to judge the meal the latter have cooked for them.

The power relations around food mirror the power of the sexes in general.[9] Whereas men gain power in some cultures by controlling money, and hence food purchasing power (Charles and Kerr 1988), women exert considerable power in all cultures by their control of food preparation and consumption. Adams (1990) argues that patriarchal power in Western society is embodied in the practice of eating meat, which involves the linking of women and animals and their objectification and subordination. Women can rebel through vegetarianism, which from this perspective is a political statement: a rejection of patriarchal power and values, an expression of feminism, and a claiming of female power over self and nature.

Among the Zumbaguan Indians of Andean Ecuador, the senior female is in charge of preparing and serving meals (Weismantel 1988: 28–9). This gives her the ability to determine hierarchies by the order in which she serves people and the contents of the plate she gives them (Weismantel 1988: 182). A woman can even punish an errant husband who finally returns from a drinking spree by serving him massive quantities of rich food that the husband, by force of etiquette, eats, with extremely unpleasant physical results.

In Western societies, for at least eight centuries, some women have used food in symbolic ways as a path to power.[10] Today, modern anorexics starve themselves, sometimes to death, to achieve physical and spiritual perfection. Their behavior is strikingly similar to that of medieval holy women in the fourteenth, fifteenth, and sixteenth centuries, although the cultural contexts of their behaviors are rather different (Bell 1985; Bynum 1987; Brumberg 1988; Counihan 1989). Medieval holy women fasted for religious and spiritual perfection (that is, holiness): They used eating or fasting as a path to reach God and to circumvent patriarchal, familial, religious, and civil authority. Some women achieved sainthood by virtue of the spirituality they revealed, primarily through fasting and other food-centered behaviors, such as multiplying food in miracles, exuding holy oils or milk from their own bodies, and giving food to the poor (Bynum 1987). Contemporary anorexics attempt to achieve perfection through self-control and thinness. They receive pitying recognition from family, friends, and medical professionals, and may die unless they find a path to the self-esteem, sense of control, and autonomy they so desperately seek through fasting (Bruch 1973, 1978; Lawrence 1984; Brumberg 1988).

Between men and women, food is a means of differentiation, as well as a channel of connection. By claiming different roles in regard to food and distinct attributes through identification with specific foods, men and women define their masculinity and femininity, their similarities and differences. They use food and food metaphors to achieve the most intimate union, as witnessed through language that equates eating with sexual relations and through practices that equate the exchange of food – whether with candlelight dinners in four-star restaurants or with baked taro on Trobriand verandas (Weiner 1988) – with sexual intimacy.

Conclusion

Food, although essential to biological survival, takes on myriad meanings and roles in contributing to "the social construction of reality" (Berger and Luckmann 1966). As humans construct their relationship to nature through their foodways, they simultaneously define themselves and their social world (Berger and Luckmann 1966: 180–3). Through the production, distribution, and consumption of food, they act out their most important relationships: with their family, with their own and the opposite sex, with the community, with the dead, with the gods, and with the cosmos. Food orders the world and expresses multiplex meanings about the nature of reality. The social and cultural uses of food are many and they provide much insight into the human condition.

Carole M. Counihan

Notes

1. The following sources treat social responses to food shortages and famine: Richards 1932, 1939; Firth 1959; Holmberg 1969; Turnbull 1972, 1978; Laughlin and Brady 1978; Colson 1979; Prindle 1979; Dirks 1980; Young 1986; Vaughan 1987; Messer 1989; Newman 1990.
2. See, for example, Tilly 1971; Hilton 1973; Kaplan 1976, 1984, 1990; Barry 1987; Mackintosh 1989.
3. Some works that explore the U.S. value on thinness are the following: Powdermaker 1960; Bruch 1973, 1978; Boskind-Lodahl 1976; Stunkard 1977; Orbach 1978; J. R. Kaplan 1980; Millman 1980; Styles 1980; Boskind-White and White 1983; Counihan 1985, 1989; Schwartz 1986; Sobal and Stunkard 1989.
4. Perhaps the most well-known redistributive ritual is the potlatch of the Northwest coast Indians, a feast that involves enormous conspicuous consumption in a competition between tribes to establish prestige and power relations, debts, social congress, and communion with the gods. See Benedict 1934; Codere 1950; Mauss 1967: 31–7; Piddocke 1969; and Harris 1974.
5. Some sources on feeding as a form of socialization and personality formation are the following: Du Bois 1941, 1944; Bossard 1943; A. Freud 1946; S. Freud 1962; Mead 1963, 1967; Holmberg 1969; D. Shack 1969; W. Shack 1971; Bruch 1973; Farb and Armelagos 1980.
6. The following sources have material on the meaning of food through the study of symbolism, taboo, etiquette, and/or cuisine: Lévi-Strauss 1966; Holmberg 1969: 78–81, 173–5; Lehrer 1969, 1972; Verdier 1969; Firth 1973; Murphy and Murphy 1974: 162–3; Ortner 1975; C. Hugh-Jones 1979, especially chapters 5 and 6; S. Hugh-Jones 1979; Farb and Armelagos 1980; Goody 1982; Laderman 1983; Mennell 1985; Manderson 1986.
7. On Jewish dietary law see Douglas 1966; Soler 1973; Alter 1979; Feeley-Harnik 1981; Fredman 1981; Harris 1985.
8. Works that have abundant material on the overlap between food, sex, and sexuality are Tambiah 1969; Verdier 1969; Murphy and Murphy 1974; Farb and Armela-

gos 1980; Meigs 1984; Gregor 1985; Pollock 1985; Kahn 1986; Herdt 1987; Frese 1991.
9. Some sources that focus explicitly on food and the power relations between men and women are the following: Charles and Kerr 1988; Counihan 1988; Weismantel 1988; Babb 1989; McIntosh and Zey 1989.
10. There is an enormous literature on what Jane R. Kaplan (1980) has called "the special relationship between women and food." In Western culture, women have variously used compulsive eating, obesity, fasting, or the symbolic value of food as a means of expressing themselves and coping with the problems of achieving a meaningful place in a world where they are defined as subordinate. Some sources dealing with women's complicated relationship to food are the following, in alphabetical order: Bell 1985; Beller 1977; Boskind-Lodahl 1976; Boskind-White and White 1983; Bruch 1973, 1978; Brumberg 1988; Bynum 1987; Charles and Kerr 1988; Chernin 1981, 1985; Counihan 1985, 1988, 1989, 1992; Gordon 1988, 1990; J. Kaplan 1980; Lawrence 1984; Massara 1989; Millman 1980; Orbach 1978; Palazzoli 1971; Schwartz 1986; Styles 1980; Thoma 1977; Waller, Kaufman and Deutsch 1940.

Bibliography

Adams, Carol J. 1990. *The sexual politics of meat: A feminist-vegetarian critical theory*. New York.

Alter, L. 1979. A new theory of *Kashrut. Commentary* 68: 46–52.

Arens, William. 1979. *The man-eating myth*. New York.

Arnold, David. 1988. *Famine: Social crisis and historical change*. New York.

Babb, Florence E. 1989. *Between field and cooking pot: The political economy of marketwomen in Peru*. Austin, Tex.

Barry, Tom. 1987. *Roots of rebellion: Land and hunger in Central America*. Boston, Mass.

Barthes, Roland. 1975. Toward a psychosociology of contemporary food consumption. In *European diet from pre-industrial to modern times*, ed. Elborg Forster and Robert Forster, 47–59. New York.

Bell, Rudolph. 1985. *Holy anorexia*. Chicago.

Beller, Anne Scott. 1977. *Fat and thin: A natural history of obesity*. New York.

Benedict, Ruth. 1934. *Patterns of culture*. Boston, Mass.

Bennett, John. 1943. Food and social status in a rural society. *American Sociological Review* 8: 561–9.

Berger, Peter, and Thomas Luckmann. 1966. *The social construction of reality: A treatise in the sociology of knowledge*. New York.

Bettelheim, Bruno. 1975. *The uses of enchantment: The meaning and importance of fairy tales*. New York.

Boskind-Lodahl, Marlene. 1976. Cinderella's stepsisters: A feminist perspective on anorexia nervosa and bulimarexia. *Signs* 2: 342–56.

Boskind-White, Marlene, and William C. White. 1983. *Bulimarexia: The binge/purge cycle*. New York.

Bossard, James H. S. 1943. Family table talk: An area for sociological study. *American Sociological Review* 8: 295–301.

Brown, J. Larry. 1987. Hunger in the U.S. *Scientific American* 256: 37–41.

Brown, J. Larry, and H. F. Pizer. 1987. *Living hungry in America*. New York.

Bruch, Hilde. 1973. *Eating disorders: Obesity, anorexia nervosa and the person within*. New York.

1978. *The golden cage: The enigma of anorexia nervosa.* New York.

Brumberg, Joan Jacobs. 1988. *Fasting girls: The emergence of anorexia nervosa as a modern disease.* Cambridge, Mass.

Bynum, Caroline Walker. 1987. *Holy feast and holy fast: The religious significance of food to medieval women.* Berkeley, Calif.

Camporesi, Piero. 1989. *Bread of dreams: Food and fantasy in early modern Europe,* trans. David Gentilcore. Chicago.

Charles, Nickie, and Marion Kerr. 1988. *Women, food and families.* Manchester, England.

Chernin, Kim. 1981. *The obsession: Reflections on the tyranny of slenderness.* New York.

1985. *The hungry self.* New York.

Codere, Helen. 1950. *Fighting with property: A study of Kwakiutl potlatches and warfare 1792-1930.* Monographs of the American Ethnological Society, 18. New York.

Colson, Elizabeth. 1979. In good years and bad: Food strategies of self-reliant societies. *Journal of Anthropological Research* 35: 18-29.

Counihan, Carole. 1981. Food, culture and political economy: Changing lifestyles in the Sardinian town of Bosa. Ph.D. dissertation, University of Massachusetts.

1984. Bread as world: Food habits and social relations in modernizing Sardinia. *Anthropological Quarterly* 57: 47-59.

1985. What does it mean to be fat, thin, and female in the United States? *Food and Foodways* 1: 77-94.

1988. Female identity, food, and power in contemporary Florence. *Anthropological Quarterly* 61: 51-62.

1989. An anthropological view of Western women's prodigious fasting. *Food and Foodways* 3: 357-75.

1992. Food rules in the U.S.: Individualism, control and hierarchy. *Anthropological Quarterly* 65: 55-66.

D'Andrade, Roy G. 1974. Sex differences and cultural institutions. In *Culture and personality, contemporary readings,* ed. Robert A. Le Vine, 16-39. New York.

De Simone, Roberto, and Annabella Rossi. 1977. *Carnevale si chiamava vincenzo.* Rome.

Detienne, Marcel, and Jean-Pierre Vernant. 1989. *The cuisine of sacrifice among the Greeks,* trans. Paula Wissing. Chicago.

Dirks, Robert. 1980. Social responses during severe food shortages and famine. *Current Anthropology* 21: 21-44.

Douglas, Mary. 1966. *Purity and danger.* London.

1974. Deciphering a meal. In *Myth, symbol and culture,* ed. Clifford Geertz, 61-81. New York.

Du Bois, Cora. 1941. Attitudes towards food and hunger in Alor. In *Language, culture, and personality: Essays in memory of Edward Sapir,* ed. L. Spier, A. I. Hallowell, and S. S. Newman, 271-81. Menasha, Wis.

1944. *The people of Alor.* 2 vols. New York.

Dyrenforth, Sue R., Orland W. Wooley, and Susan C. Wooley. 1980. A woman's body in a man's world: A review of findings on body image and weight control. In *A woman's conflict: The special relationship between women and food,* ed. J. R. Kaplan, 29-57. Englewood Cliffs, N.J.

Farb, Peter, and George Armelagos. 1980. *Consuming passions: The anthropology of eating.* New York.

Feeley-Harnik, Gillian. 1981. *The Lord's table: Eucharist and Passover in early Christianity.* Philadelphia, Pa.

Firth, Raymond. 1959. *Social change in Tikopia: Restudy of a Polynesian community after a generation.* New York.

1973. Food symbolism in a pre-industrial society. In *Symbols: Public and private,* ed. Raymond Firth, 243-61. Ithaca, N.Y.

Fitchen, Janet M. 1988. Hunger, malnutrition and poverty in the contemporary United States: Some observations on their social and cultural context. *Food and Foodways* 2: 309-33.

Frazer, James G. 1951. *The golden bough: A study in magic and religion.* New York.

Fredman, Ruth Gruber. 1981. *The Passover seder: Afikoman in exile.* Philadelphia, Pa.

Frese, Pamela. 1991. The union of nature and culture: Gender symbolism in the American wedding ritual. In *Transcending boundaries: Multi-disciplinary approaches to the study of gender,* ed. P. R. Frese and J. M. Coggeshall, 97-112. New York.

Freud, Anna. 1946. The psychoanalytic study of infantile feeding disturbances. *The psychoanalytic study of the child. An annual,* 2: 119-32.

Freud, Sigmund. 1918. *Totem and taboo.* New York.

1962. *Three contributions to the theory of sex,* trans. A. A. Brill. New York.

Gallini, Clara. 1973. *Dono e Malocchio.* Palermo.

Garb, Jane L., J. R. Garb, and A. J. Stunkard. 1975. Social factors and obesity in Navajo children. *Proceedings of the First International Congress on Obesity,* 37-9. London.

Glasser, Irene. 1988. *More than bread: Ethnography of a soup kitchen.* Tuscaloosa, Ala.

Good, Kenneth, and David Chanoff. 1991. *Into the heart: One man's pursuit of love and knowledge among Yanomama.* New York.

Goody, Jack. 1962. *Death, property and the ancestors: A study of the mortuary customs of the Lodagaa of West Africa.* London.

1982. *Cooking, cuisine, and class: A study in comparative sociology.* Cambridge.

Gordon, Richard A. 1988. A sociocultural interpretation of the current epidemic of eating disorders. In *The eating disorders,* ed. B. J. Blinder, B. F. Chaiting, and R. Goldstein, 151-63. Great Neck, N.Y.

1990. *Anorexia and bulimia: Anatomy of a social epidemic.* Cambridge.

Gregor, Thomas. 1985. *Anxious pleasures: The sexual lives of an Amazonian people.* Chicago.

Harris, Marvin. 1974. Potlatch. In *Cows, pigs, wars and witches,* ed. Marvin Harris, 111-30. New York.

1985. The abominable pig. In *Good to eat: Riddles of food and culture,* ed. Marvin Harris, 67-87. New York.

Herdt, Gilbert. 1987. *The Sambia: Ritual and gender in New Guinea.* New York.

Hilton, Rodney. 1973. *Bond men made free: Medieval peasant movements and the English rising of 1381.* New York.

Holmberg, Allan R. 1969. *Nomads of the long bow: The Siriono of Eastern Bolivia.* Prospect Heights, Ill.

Hugh-Jones, Christine. 1979. *From the Milk River: Spatial and temporal processes in northwest Amazonia.* Cambridge.

Hugh-Jones, Stephen. 1979. *The palm and the Pleiades: Initiation and cosmology in northwest Amazonia.* Cambridge.

Huntington, Richard, and Peter Metcalf. 1979. *Celebrations of death. The anthropology of mortuary ritual.* Cambridge.

Kahn, Miriam. 1986. *Always hungry, never greedy: Food and the expression of gender in a Melanesian society.* Cambridge.

1988. "Men are taro" (They cannot be rice): Political aspects of food choices. *Food and Foodways* 3: 41-58.

Kaplan, Jane Rachel, ed. 1980. *A woman's conflict: The special relationship between women and food.* Englewood Cliffs, N.J.

Kaplan, Steven L. 1976. *Bread, politics and political economy in the reign of Louis XV.* The Hague.

1984. *Provisioning Paris: Merchants and millers in the grain and flour trade during the eighteenth century.* Ithaca, N.Y.

1990. The state and the problem of dearth in eighteenth-century France: The crisis of 1738-41 in Paris. *Food and Foodways* 4: 111-41.

Khare, R. S., and M. S. A. Rao. 1986. *Food, society and culture: Aspects in South Asian food systems.* Durham, N.C.

Laderman, Carol. 1983. *Wives and midwives: Childbirth and nutrition in rural Malaysia.* Berkeley, Calif.

Lappé, Frances Moore, and Joseph Collins. 1986. *World hunger: Twelve myths.* New York.

Laughlin, Charles, and Ivan Brady, eds. 1978. *Extinction and survival in human populations.* New York.

Lawrence, Marilyn. 1984. *The anorexic experience.* London

Leach, Edmund. 1964. Anthropological aspects of language: Animal categories and verbal abuse. In *New directions in the study of language,* ed. E. H. Lenneberg, 23-63. Cambridge, Mass.

Lehrer, Adrienne. 1969. Semantic cuisine. *Journal of Linguistics* 5: 39-56.

1972. Cooking vocabularies and the culinary triangle of Lévi-Strauss. *Anthropological Linguistics* 14: 155-71.

Lévi-Strauss, Claude. 1963a. *Totemism.* Boston, Mass.

1963b. The structural study of myth. In *Structural anthropology,* ed. Claude Lévi-Strauss, 202-28. New York.

1966. The culinary triangle. *Partisan Review* 33: 586-95.

1969. *The raw and the cooked: Introduction to a science of mythology,* trans. John Weightman and Doreen Weightman. New York.

1973. *From honey to ashes: Introduction to a science of mythology,* trans. John Weightman and Doreen Weightman. New York.

Mackintosh, Maureen. 1989. *Gender, class and rural transition: Agribusiness and the food crisis in Senegal.* London.

Malinowski, Bronislaw. 1927. *Sex and repression in savage society.* Chicago.

1961. *Argonauts of the western Pacific.* New York.

Manderson, Lenore, ed. 1986. *Shared wealth and symbol: Food, culture and society in Oceania and Southeast Asia.* Cambridge.

Massara, Emily B., and Albert J. Stunkard. 1979. A method of quantifying cultural ideals of beauty and the obese. *International Journal of Obesity* 3: 149-52.

Massara, Emily Bradley. 1989. *Que Gordita. A study of weight among women in a Puerto Rican community.* New York.

Mauss, Marcel. 1967. *The gift: Forms and functions of exchange in archaic societies.* New York.

McIntosh, William Alex, and Mary Zey. 1989. Women as gatekeepers of food consumption: A sociological critique. *Food and Foodways* 3: 317-22.

Mead, Margaret. 1963. *Sex and temperament in three primitive societies.* New York.

1967. *Male and female: A study of the sexes in a changing world.* New York.

Meigs, Anna S. 1984. *Food, sex, and pollution: A New Guinea religion.* New Brunswick, N.J.

Mennell, Stephen. 1985. *All manners of food: Eating and taste in England and France from the Middle Ages to the present.* Oxford.

Messer, Ellen. 1984. Anthropological perspectives on diet. *Annual Review of Anthropology* 13: 205-49.

1989. Small but healthy? Some cultural considerations. *Human Organization* 48: 39-52.

Millman, Marcia. 1980. *Such a pretty face: Being fat in America.* New York.

Mintz, Sidney. 1985. *Sweetness and power: The place of sugar in modern history.* New York.

Moore, Henrietta. 1988. *Feminism and anthropology.* Minneapolis, Minn.

Murphy, Yolanda, and Robert Murphy. 1974. *Women of the forest.* New York.

Newman, Lucile, ed. 1990. *Hunger in history: Food shortage, poverty, and deprivation.* New York.

Nutini, Hugo. 1988. *Todos Santos in rural Tlaxcala: A syncretic, expressive, and symbolic analysis of the cult of the dead.* Princeton, N.J.

Orbach, Susie. 1978. *Fat is a feminist issue: The anti-diet guide to permanent weight loss.* New York.

Ortner, Sherry B. 1975. Gods' bodies, gods' food: A symbolic analysis of a Sherpa ritual. In *The interpretation of symbolism,* ed. R. Willis 133-69. New York.

Palazzoli, Maria Selvini. 1971. Anorexia nervosa. In *The world biennial of psychiatry and psychotherapy,* Vol. 1, ed. Silvano Arietti, 197-218. New York.

Physicians Task Force on Hunger in America. 1985. *Hunger in America: The growing epidemic.* Middletown, Conn.

Piddocke, Stuart. 1969. The potlatch system of the southern Kwakiutl: A new perspective. In *Environment and cultural behavior,* ed. Andrew P. Vayda, 130-56. Garden City, N.J.

Pollock, Donald K. 1985. Food and sexual identity among the Culina. *Food and Foodways* 1: 25-42.

Powdermaker, Hortense. 1960. An anthropological approach to the problem of obesity. *Bulletin of the New York Academy of Medicine* 36: 286-95.

Prindle, Peter H. 1979. Peasant society and famine: A Nepalese example. *Ethnology* 18: 49-60.

Richards, Audrey I. 1932. *Hunger and work in a savage tribe: A functional study of nutrition among the southern Bantu.* London.

1939. *Land, labour and diet in northern Rhodesia: An economic study of the Bemba tribe.* London.

Sahlins, Marshall. 1972. *Stone Age economics.* New York.

Sanday, Peggy. 1986. *Divine hunger: Cannibalism as a cultural system.* Cambridge.

Schwartz, Hillel. 1986. *Never satisfied: A cultural history of diets, fantasies and fat.* New York.

Sendak, Maurice. 1963. *Where the wild things are.* New York.

Shack, Dorothy N. 1969. Nutritional processes and personality development among the Gurage of Ethiopia. *Ethnology* 8: 292-300.

Shack, William A. 1971. Hunger, anxiety, and ritual: Deprivation and spirit possession among the Gurage of Ethiopia. *Man* 6: 30-45.

Siskind, Janet. 1973. *To hunt in the morning.* Oxford and New York.

Sobal, Jeffrey, and Albert J. Stunkard. 1989. Socioeconomic status and obesity: A review of the literature. *Psychological Bulletin* 105: 260-75.

Soler, Jean. 1973. Sémiotique de la nourriture dans la Bible. *Annales: Économies, Sociétés, Civilisations* 28: 943-55.

Starn, Frances. 1990. *Soup of the day: A novel.* New York.

Stunkard, Albert J. 1977. Obesity and the social environment: Current status, future prospects. *Annals of the New York Academy of Sciences* 300: 298-320.

Styles, Marvalene. 1980. Soul, black women and food. In *A woman's conflict: The special relationship between women and food,* ed. J. R. Kaplan, 161-76. Englewood Cliffs, N.J.

Taggart, James M. 1986. "Hansel and Gretel" in Spain and Mexico. *Journal of American Folklore* 933: 435–60.

Tambiah, S. J. 1969. Animals are good to think and good to prohibit. *Ethnology* 8: 423–59.

Thoma, Helmut. 1977. On the psychotherapy of patients with anorexia nervosa. *Bulletin of the Menninger Clinic* 41: 437–52.

Tilly, Louise. 1971. The food riot as a form of political conflict in France. *Journal of Interdisciplinary History* 2: 23–57.

Turnbull, Colin. 1972. *The mountain people.* New York.

1978. Rethinking the Ik: A functional non-social system. In *Extinction and survival in human populations,* ed. C. Laughlin and I. Brady, 49–75. New York.

Vaughan, Megan. 1987. *The story of an African famine: Gender and famine in twentieth-century Malawi.* Cambridge.

Verdier, Yvonne. 1969. Pour une ethnologie culinaire. *L'Homme* 9: 49–57.

Walens, Stanley. 1981. *Feasting with cannibals: An essay on Kwakiutl cosmology.* Princeton, N.J.

Waller, J. V., R. Kaufman, and F. Deutsch. 1940. Anorexia nervosa: A psychosomatic entity. *Psychosomatic Medicine* 2: 3–16.

Weiner, Annette B. 1988. *The Trobrianders of Papua New Guinea.* New York.

Weismantel, M. J. 1988. *Food, gender, and poverty in the Ecuadorian Andes.* Philadelphia, Pa.

Young, Michael. 1971. *Fighting with food: Leadership, values and social control in a Massim society.* Cambridge.

1986. "The Worst Disease": The cultural definition of hunger in Kalauna. In *Shared wealth and symbol: Food, culture and society in Oceania and Southeast Asia,* ed. L. Manderson, 111–26. New York.

VI.15 ❧ Food as Aphrodisiacs and Anaphrodisiacs?

According to the first edition of the *Encyclopaedia Britannica* (1771), aphrodisiacs are "medicines which increase the quantity of seed, and create an inclination for venery." Since the twentieth-century advent of sexual endocrinology, the definition of an aphrodisiac has become restricted to "a substance which excites sexual desire" (*Steadman's Medical Dictionary,* 25th edition, 1990). The search for aphrodisiacs is rooted in universal anxieties about sexual performance and fertility. In many instances since ancient times, a distinction has been made between substances that were alleged to improve fertility (quantity of seed) and those that only stimulate the sex drive (inclination to venery). Some authorities held that the latter could only be achieved by achieving the former.

The scope of this essay is limited geographically to Europe and the Near East and, so far as possible, to foods and their preparation. Adequate nourishment has always been recognized as a requirement for health and a normal level of sexual activity, although the norm for the latter undoubtedly varies somewhat among cultures.

In ancient medical practices, when and by what indications nutritive and medicinal qualities of foods were differentiated is uncertain. A rather clear distinction, however, was made by Heracleides of Tarentum, a Greek physician in the first century B.C. In writing about aphrodisiacs, he said that "bulbs, snails, eggs and the like are supposed to produce semen, *not because they are filling,* but because their very nature in the first instance has powers related in kind to semen" (Athenaeus 1951: 275).

Another nagging question had to do with whether plant and animal products that ordinarily are not foods should be considered medicines or just special foods. Andrew Boorde (died 1549), a London physician, exemplified the vagueness of dietary–medicinal distinctions: "[A] good cook is half a physician. For the chief physic (the counsel of a physician excepted) does come from the kitchen: wherefore the physician and the cook for sick men must consult together for the preparation of meate [foods] for sick men" (1870: 227).

According to ancient literature, aphrodisiacs and their opposite, anaphrodisiacs, were generally simple rather than multi-ingredient prescriptions. This pattern gradually changed, and the most elaborate prescriptions were written in sixteenth- and seventeenth-century Europe (and much earlier in the Near East). Table VI.15.1

Table VI.15.1. *Ancient sexual stimulants and depressants*

Aegina	Pliny	Dioscorides	Paul
Aphrodisiacs			
Anise	–	+	–
Basil	+	–	–
Carrot	–	+	–
Clary (Salvia)	–	+	–
Gladiolus root	+	*	–
Orchid bulbs			
Major orchis bulb	+	+	+
Erythraicon bulb	+	–	–
Satyrion bulb	+	+	+
Pistachio nuts	+	+	–
Rocket	+	+	+
Sage	–	+	–
Sea fennel	+	–	+
Turnip	+	–	+
Skink flesh	+	+	+
River snails	+	–	–
Anaphrodisiacs			
Agnus castus	x	x	x
Dill	–	x	–
Gladiolus root	–	**	–
Lentil	–	x	–
Lettuce	–	x	–
Nasturtium (cress)	x		
Minor orchis bulb	x	x	–
Rue	x	x	x
Water lily	x	x	–

*Upper gladiolus root.

**Lower gladiolus root.

Sources: Pliny (1963); Gunther (1959); Adams (1847).

lists the substances that were cited as aphrodisiacs and anaphrodisiacs by three ancient authorities, Pliny and Dioscorides from the first century A.D. and Paul of Aegina from the seventh century. The former two listed more substances than did Paul because they, and especially Pliny, sought to record every one they encountered and did not necessarily vouch for each. All three concurred about only three aphrodisiacs: varieties of orchid bulbs, leaves and seeds of rocket *(Eruca sativa),* and the flesh of the skink (a North African lizard). They agreed on only two anaphrodisiacs: the seed and, presumably, leaf decoction (tea) of *Vitex agnus castus* (also called the chaste tree), and parts of rue *(Ruta graveolens),* an evergreen shrub (Adams 1847, 3; Gunther 1959; Pliny 1963: Vols. 7 and 8).

A Western philosophical association between dietary gratification and sexual stimulation was enunciated most clearly by St. Thomas Aquinas (died 1274) in his *Summa Theologica.* The biological aspects of the explanation were those of Galen, and they remained unchallenged for almost three more centuries. According to Thomas, the most urgent of the carnal vices was lust, with gluttony the second. Both were viewed as vices because they distracted from intellectual pursuits that brought men close to God. Moreover, certain foods both provided sensual gratification and created great incentive to lust. Such potentially lust-inducing foods and the qualities by which they could be identified should be learned so as to avoid them.

Procreation, according to Thomas, who did not distinguish this from "lust," required the participation of three components: heat, vital spirit, and humor. Whatever enhanced the production of any of the three might be sexually stimulating. Substances that heated the body, such as wine, would stimulate the production of more heat. Flatulent foods, in turn, were part of the production of the vital spirit. Meat, the most nutritious food, was needed to produce humor. Lust, however, was kindled more by drinking wine than by eating meat. The more an animal resembled humans, the greater pleasure and nutrition it offered as food: "Animals which rest on the earth and breathe air and also their products, such as milk. Because of these resemblances to mankind, when they are eaten they produce a greater surplus of the seminal matter which is the immediate inciter of lust" (Aquinas 1932, 9: 189; 13: 71–2).

This definition, however, fails to explain the selection of one particular lizard and is inconsistent with the aphrodisiacal properties that, by the Middle Ages, were attributed to birds' eggs, roe, and fowl. A final peculiarity shown in Table VI.15.1 is that different parts or combinations of the same sources were accorded opposite effects. A bifid root might have stimulant properties assigned to one segment and inhibitory effects to another. The small quantity of flesh adjacent to the skink's kidneys was deemed especially stimulating because of its proximity to an excretory organ. However, if this was mixed with lentils or lettuce seed, the opposite effect was achieved (Gunther 1959: 108).

The reputation of several ancient remedies can be attributed to their alleged physical resemblance to genitalia. Illustrative is the association of double orchid bulbs with testes, with the very names of these bulbs revealing their perceived application: *Orchis* means testicle, and a single bulb variety was called *satyrion* (the mythological sexually aggressive satyr) (Brondegaard 1971). But orchid bulbs, along with carrots, turnips, and the like (which possibly bear some genital resemblances), were not ordinarily considered aphrodisiacal. Rather, the quality nearest to a common denominator that ancient aphrodisiacs supposedly possessed was that they presumably stimulated urine flow.

Some ancient aphrodisiacal attributions were based on mythology. Aphrodite, the goddess of love, for example, was said to consider sparrows sacred because of their "amorous nature" and, thus, they were included in some love potions. Although both bird and fish eggs were prescribed, among birds a predilection for the eggs and (especially) the brains of sparrows persisted at least through the Middle Ages. Geoffrey Chaucer in 1390 in *The Canterbury Tales* described the Summoner to be "as hot and lecherous as a sparrow" (1952: 42). Sparrows also were distinguished from other small birds by allegedly being "hard of digestion" (Chaucer 1952: 270). Yet this quality would, for most authors, have disqualified sparrows as aphrodisiacs.

Because the anatomic and physiological ideas expounded by Galen (A.D. 129–210) reigned unchallenged from the third to at least the sixteenth century, their relationship to the identification of supposed aphrodisiacs requires some scrutiny. According to Galenic humoral principles, the effects of nutrients on sexual function, most clearly that of the male, were governed both by their inherent humoral qualities and by the responses they elicited when consumed. To be effective as an aphrodisiac, a nutrient had to be "warm and moist." Substances that were "cold and dry" had the opposite effect. The production of semen and erectile potency were differentiated. Although both required warm and moist nutrients for nonspecific stimulation, semen production needed particularly nourishing foods. Improvement of erectile potency demanded foods that generate "windiness" because "the penis is tensed . . . when the hollow nerve [corpus cavernosus] is filled with pneuma" (Galen 1968: 656–60). Thus, the English anatomist Thomas Vicary (died 1562) could write: "This member has three holes. Through one passeth insensible pollution and wind that causes the penis to rise. The other two holes . . . are for the sperm and . . . for urine" (1888: 81–2). "Insensible pollution" was the pneuma, which in this location was viewed as an inflator. "Wind" provided the expulsive force for semen and other excreta. Consequently, foods reputed to be flatulent were also thought to stimulate the emission of semen, provided the diet was sufficiently nutritious for an adequate amount to have been produced.

Earlier, the influential medical translator and commentator Constantinus Africanus (Constantine of Carthage, 1015-87) had concurred that the ideal aphrodisiac is nutritious, warm, and moist and that it generates windiness. And it was because few substances were reputed to contain all of the required humoral qualities that later prescriptions tended to become much more complex than they had been in the more ancient, particularly pre-Galenic, writings. Constantine, for example, prescribed "a tested electuary which increases lust" containing 19 ingredients. One of these, which remained popular for several centuries, was *linguae avis* (Delany 1970: 55-65), which in this case did not mean birds' tongues, but rather was the name for ash seeds. It is interesting to note that in *The Merchant's Tale,* Constantine was cursed because his "book" *De Coitu* apparently revealed aphrodisiacal recipes (Chaucer 1952: 36-7).

The Spice Trade

Spices were vital ingredients in the formulation of aphrodisiacs, rendering many such recipes dependent on imported materials. While the Roman Empire was in existence, spices doubtless reached Europe from Asia Minor via Roman legions, and probably supply was never interrupted entirely after its collapse. By the ninth century or so, Arab traders were supplying parts of Europe with spices from as far away as India and China. However, a great increase in the quantity and variety of spices for Europe was initiated in 1499 when the Portuguese navigator, Vasco da Gama (died 1524), rounded the Cape of Good Hope to reach India and returned to Lisbon with a cargo of pepper. A round-trip between Lisbon and the west coast of India in the late sixteenth century took about 18 months but could produce great profits. One hundred pounds of pepper, purchased in Calicut for 3 ducats, wholesaled in Lisbon for 25 ducats, and then retailed for 80 ducats in Venice.

Spices were the predominant Asiatic import, and pepper, used also as a food preservative, was the most important. Illustrative is the inventory of four ships that returned to Lisbon from India in 1580. It revealed a total cargo weighing 2,695,100 pounds, of which 97.6 percent was spices (Guerra 1965). Spain, the other Iberian nation, also got into the spice business following its conquest of Mexico in 1521. The Americas not only had indigenous spices to offer but also provided locations to cultivate spices previously grown only in Asia. Thus, ginger (the first transplanted spice crop) was introduced into Mexico in 1530; by 1587 Spain was importing 2¼ million pounds of ginger, ten times that carried by the Portuguese from India.

All of this activity in spices made a big business out of spice retailing, the practitioners of which since the Middle Ages had not only filled prescriptions but also supplied cooks with spices. Indeed, guilds of "pepperers" and "spicers" had been formed from the twelfth to the fourteenth centuries, and in England in 1617, a separate guild of apothecaries that distinguished them from grocers was created by royal edict (Kremers and Urdang 1951: 83-4, 136-40).

Semitic Influences

One of the tales from *The Book of the Thousand Nights and One Night* [The Arabian Nights], which probably is at least a thousand years old, contains an early example of the complexity that aphrodisiacal prescriptions achieved quite early in the Near East. The story of "Beautyspot" pertains to a merchant whose marriage has been childless for 40 years. This was cured by a prescription that consisted of spices and foods. Different translations vary in some of the ingredients, but two versions agree on six of the spices. Richard Burton's version also includes opium, skink meat, frankincense, and coriander (1885: 30-2). These were to be mixed in honey and consumed after a meal of hotly spiced mutton and pigeon. In another text, musk and roe are added as final ingredients. But before consuming this prescription, a special aphrodisiacal diet had to be adhered to for three days; it was limited to hotly spiced roasted pigeons, male fish with intact genitalia, and fried rams' testicles.

Another ancient ingredient that found its way into some European prescriptions was mandragora, or mandrake. Dioscorides said obscurely that "the root seems to be a maker of love medicines" (Gunther 1959: 473-4). Pliny, on the other hand, made no claim for a sexual effect (Pliny 1963, 7: 241-3). Both referred to a white male and a black female variety, but neither suggested that the plant might resemble human form as did later writers. They agreed that ingesting it induced sleep, that it could be used for surgical anesthesia, and that an overdose was fatal.

It is interesting that mandrake differs from most plants alleged to affect sexual function in that it actually has demonstrable physiological effects. It is related to deadly nightshade, or belladonna, and its content of hyoscyamine makes it potentially lethal. Yet it had a long-standing reputation in the Near East for encouraging female fertility. In Genesis 30:14-21, for example, Leah, who had become infertile, was given mandrake (manner unspecified), after which she conceived three more children.

Although most claims that mandrake corrects female infertility derived from this biblical reference, in the seventeenth century decoctions of the "white male" variety were alleged to overcome impotence as well (Thorndyke 1958: 10-13). Yet in 1771, the medicinal demise of mandrake was announced in an entry of the first edition of the *Encyclopaedia Britannica:*

"Authors have spoken very largely and idly of the virtues of this plant. The most common quality attributed to it, is that of rendering barren women fruitful: but we have no tolerable foundation for this: what we certainly know of it is, that is has a soporific virtue like that of opium."

A leading medieval writer who expounded the aphrodisiacal qualities of various foods was Rabbi Moses ben Maimon, or Maimonides (1135-1204). A Talmudic scholar who became physician to Sultan Saladin of Egypt, Maimonides was medically a follower of Galen and of Avicenna. He differed from others of the period in regard to aphrodisiacs mainly in placing greater emphasis on meats and organs, although not ignoring vegetables and spices. Maimonides was blunt about the relative aphrodisiacal merits of foods and medicines, insisting that nutriments were of much greater value than medications. However, one needed to be selective. Foods (and medications) that moistened and warmed the body (that is, had the Galenic qualities of heat and humidity) were deemed to some degree aphrodisiacal, whereas those that were cooling and drying were to be avoided because of their anaphrodisiacal effects.

In addition to the guidance provided by Galenic qualities, symbolism also played a role in identifying other substances (Rosner 1974: 18-29). For example, one of Maimonides's "very special" prescriptions required one to: "[t]ake the penis of an ox, dry it and grind it. Sprinkle some of this on a soft-boiled egg, and drink in sips" (Rosner 1974: 29).

The desired stimulation was sometimes transmitted through an intermediate. According to an Indian recipe some two centuries after the foregoing: "Boil the penis of an ass together with onions and a large quantity of corn. With this dish feed fowl, which you then eat" (Burton 1964: 242).

During the late sixteenth century in Europe, the compounding of ingestible phallic symbols varied only slightly from some of the prescriptions of Maimonides. For example:

A man whose conjugal ardor has cooled should take the penis of a stag that has been killed while in rut, dry it and grind it into a powder. He should take 5 gm. of this and a dram of black pepper, mix these together in a drink of malmsey, and take it in the morning. Taken several days in a row it will make him right again (Mattioli 1590: 447b).

The Doctrine of Signatures

It is clear that symbolism has been used in the assignment of aphrodisiacal properties to plants and animal parts since pre-Christian times. But the delineation of a philosophy based on analogizing the appearance of natural objects with their perceived utility was delayed until the sixteenth century. It sprang from the ideas of the anti-Galenic itinerant Swiss physician

Paracelsus (1493-1541) and was popularized by some of his followers. One of the best known of the latter was German physician Oswald Croll (about 1560-1609). In the introduction to his *Basilica Chymica* (original 1609, English 1670) he stated the belief most clearly:

If he so desireth to be an expert physician, and to have knowledge of those things which point to Medicine, by that Art, which Nature externally proposeth by Signes, he may understand that those internally signify: for every thing that is intrinsical, bares the external figure of its occult property, as well in insensible as sensible Creatures. Nature as it were by certain silent notes speakes to us, and reveals the ingenuity and manners of every Individual. ... As our intimate manners from external figures of the Body may be found out, so from the exteriour Signatures of Plants, Man may be admonished of their interiour Vertues. For Plants do as it were in occult words, manifest their excellency, and open the Treasures of hidden things to sickly Mortalls; that Man, of all Creatures the most miserable, may learn in grievous Diseases, where to find relief (Croll 1670: 3).

Herbals in the Sixteenth and Seventeenth Centuries

The complexity of European aphrodisiacal prescriptions in the sixteenth century is particularly well illustrated by concoctions called *diasatyrion* (so named because although they were based on an orchid bulb, they had additional ingredients as well). The following directions for the preparation of a diasatyrion were published in 1536:

Take male orchid bulb, satyrion bulb, parsnip, sea holly, nutmeg, pistacio nuts, and pine nuts, 12 drams each, carnation, ginger, anise, ash seed, and rocket seed, each 5 drams, and musk 7 grains. Compound with a sufficient amount of honey.
Grate orchid bulbs and parsnip and cook for a short time while stirring with a spatula. Then add the pine nuts and pistacios, also grated. After brief cooking, remove from the fire and add the other ingredients, except for the musk. The latter is added the very last, [diluted] in rosewater (Schumacher 1936: 98-9).

Judging by the contents of herbals, which were the principal textbooks of materia medica of the time, the number of botanicals to which aphrodisiacal properties were attributed reached their peak between the late sixteenth and the late seventeenth centuries. The 1554 herbal of Pietro Mattioli (1500-77), in its expanded German edition of 1590, contained 39 such entries, about two-thirds of which would ordinarily be considered vegetables, spices, or edible nuts

Table VI.15.2. *Most commonly cited aphrodisiacs, 1546–1710*

Orchis, cynosorchis, dog-stones	8
Carrot	8
Mustard	7
Anise	6
Asparagus	6
Nettles	6
Claire, scarlet sage (Salvia)	5
Ladies bedstraw (Galium verum)	5
Ash seed (Lingua avis)	4
Rampion	4
Rocket	4
Sweet pea	4
Terebinth seed (Pistacia terebinthus)	4

(1590: 28). Yet most of the time the various herbalists failed to agree on the foods that had aphrodisiacal qualities, and even in comparing the 1597 and 1636 editions of the herbal of John Gerarde (1545–1612), one discovers numerous changes. For example, 35 substances in the earlier edition but only 30 in the later are said to be sexual stimulants. Moreover, only 24 were endowed with such a virtue according to both texts (Gerarde 1597; 1636).

A survey of eight herbals published between 1546 and 1710 found 13 substances (see Table VI.15.2) with alleged aphrodisiacal properties that are identified in at least four of them (Bock 1546; Dodoens 1578; Mattioli 1590; Gerarde 1597, 1636; Parkinson 1640; Theodorus 1664; Salmon 1710). The list was led by the double orchid bulb (8) and the carrot (8) (now gaining in aphrodisiacal reputation), followed by mustard seed (7), and anise, asparagus, and nettles (6 each).

It is difficult to explain the aphrodisiacal reputation of some foods in terms other than those having to do with their remote origin or their initial scarcity. The reception of the American potato in Europe serves as a good example.

The English word "potato" is derived from the generic term for the sweet potato, *Ipomoea batatas.* The sweet potato was a staple food in the West Indies and was among the plants that Columbus brought back from his first voyage. It was planted in Spain, but because it requires a warm climate, it did not do well in northern Europe, where it became a scarce, imported item. The white potato probably reached Spain no later than 1570 and it may have been introduced in England by Francis Drake in 1586. During the first half of the seventeenth century, the "common potato" and the "Virginia potato" were the names of the sweet and the white potato, respectively (Salaman 1949: 130–2, 142–8, 424–33).

The sweet potato, at least in sixteenth- and seventeenth-century England, was eaten mainly as a candied delicacy. But in a late sixteenth-century description of English dietary customs, it was referred to as a "venereous root" (Harrison 1577: 129), and it repeat-edly appears on the seventeenth-century stage as an aphrodisiac, by itself and in complex recipes. In *The Merry Wives of Windsor* (Shakespeare 1971) Shakespeare has Sir John Falstaff tell a lady before embracing her: "Let the sky rain potatoes; let it thunder to the tune of Green Sleeves; hail kissing comfits, and snow eringoes; let there come a tempest of provocation, I will shelter me here" (Act 5, Scene 4).

In modern terms, Falstaff fantasized being inundated with sweet potatoes and candied fruit or vegetables (which could be a reference to the preferred preparation of the sweet potato), and candied sea holly, which was also recognized as an aphrodisiac. According to Gerarde's herbal:

> The roots [of eringoes, which is the same as sea holly] preserved with sugar . . . are exceeding good to be given unto old and aged people that are consumed and withered with age. . . . It is also good for other sorts of people that have no delight or appetite to venery, nourishing and restoring the aged, and amending the defects of nature in the younger (1597: 1000).

In the mid–seventeenth century, as potatoes became more available (although still expensive), it is probably this tuber that was now being referred to in various recipes and theatrical comments. The entry on the potato in the 1710 herbal by the English physician William Salmon (1644–1712) combines its nutritive quality with its alleged effect on libido and fertility:

> They stop fluxes of the bowels [diarrhea], nourish much, and restore a pining Consumption [tuberculosis]. Being boiled, baked, or rosted [sic], they are eaten with good Butter, Salt, Juice of *Oranges* or *Limons,* and double refined Sugar, as common Food: they encrease Seed and provoke Lust, causing Fruitfulness in both sexes, and stop all sorts of Fluxes of the Belly. (1710:)

In 1805, however, Sir Joseph Banks (1743–1820), then president of the Royal Society of London, called quasi-official attention to the fallacious use of these vegetables:

> [T]he sweet potatoe was used in England as a delicacy long before the introduction of our potatoes; it was imported in considerable quantities from Spain and the Canaries, and was supposed to possess the power of restoring decayed vigor. The kissing comfits of *Falstaff,* and other confections of similar imaginary qualities, with which our ancestors were duped, were principally made of these, and of eringo roots.

The potatoes themselves were sold by itinerant dealers, chiefly in the neighborhood of the Royal Exchange, and purchased when scarce at no inconsiderable cost, by those who had faith in their alleged properties (Banks 1805, 1: 8-12).

Although potatoes and sweet potatoes are examples of foods that lost their aphrodisiacal reputation quite early, that of the oyster has persisted from ancient times into the twentieth century. The Roman author Juvenal (second century A.D.), in a satire on the unrestrained behavior of contemporary women, associated loss of sexual decorum with alcoholic intoxication and the eating of "giant oysters at midnight" (Ramsay 1940: 107). Oysters, however, appeared infrequently among the aphrodisiacs in medical texts, and their folkloric popularity has been better reflected in literature. For example, in a comedy staged in 1611 by the London playwright George Chapman (died 1634), a "lover" in preparation for seduction is to be strengthened with "a banquet of Oyster-pies, Potatoes, Skirret rootes, Eringoes, and divers other whetstones of venery" (Act 2: 31). And it is interesting that in the nineteenth century, Jonathan Pereira (1804-53), professor of materia medica in London, in his authoritative textbook on medications merely commented: "An aphrodisiac property is usually ascribed to oysters" (1846: 47).

A hypothesis for the stimulatory reputation of oysters harkens back to the doctrine of signatures with their influence due to a resemblance to the female pudenda. But even if correct, it does not explain why, as therapeutics gradually became more rational, oysters maintained their aphrodisiacal reputation.

In the twentieth century, Havelock Ellis (1859-1939), the pioneer English sexologist, returned to the ancient principle that an aphrodisiac must foremost be nutritious. He speculated that "oysters and other shellfish . . . in so far as they have an action whatsoever on the sexual appetite, only possess it by virtue of their generally nutritious and stimulating qualities." He therefore concluded that because it is nutritious and easily digestible, "[a] beefsteak is probably as powerful a sexual stimulant as any food." Since it required relatively little energy to digest, more energy was available for other activities, including those that were sexual (Ellis 1906: 174). This is reminiscent of Galen's concept that to effect spermatogenesis, foods must be particularly nutritious.

Beverages and Anaphrodisiacs

A glimpse of the ancient ambivalence about the role of wine in sexual matters can be found in the Old Testament story of Lot's daughters, who each intoxicated their aged father with wine in order to be impregnated by him (Genesis 19:32-6). Perhaps the role of wine in this case was not that of an aphrodisiac but rather a sedative to overcome the taboo against incest. In the ancient world wine was consumed extensively, in part as medicine, but seemingly not as a sexual stimulant.

By the time of the Middle Ages this had changed. Maimonides, for one, strongly advocated wine as a sexual stimulant:

> Drinking honey water promotes erections, but even more effective in this regard than all medicines and foods is wine. . . . [I]t arouses the erections all the more when one enjoys the wine with desire, and after the meal and after the bath, because then its effect is far greater than that of anything else (Rosner 1974: 20-1).

About two centuries later, the Catalan physician Arnaldus de Villanova (1236-1311) wrote a manuscript on wine that, in 1478, became the first book on the subject to be printed. He believed that many specific varieties of wine exerted a restorative effect in the face of certain ailments. Thus "[w]ine made from fennel seeds stimulates sexual urge, consumes dropsy and leprosy. . . . It increases milk and the natural sperm" (1943: 39).

Later in the fourteenth century, Chaucer had one of his female characters voice the understanding that wine may affect both sexes similarly:

> Whenever I take wine I have to
> think of Venus, for as cold engenders hail
> A lecherous mouth begets a lecherous tail.
> A woman in her cups has no defense,
> As lechers know from long experience (1952: 295).

Yet if inebriation could leave a woman defenseless, it could also render a male incapable of taking advantage of her. This was expressed especially well by the French physician-novelist, François Rabelais (died 1553):

> When I say that wine abateth lust, my meaning is wine immoderately taken; for by intemperance, proceeding from the excessive drinking of strong liquor, there is brought upon the body . . . a chillness in the blood, a slackening in the sinews, a dissipation with a pervasive wryness and convulsion of the muscles, all which are great lets and impediments to the act of generation. . . . Wine nevertheless, taken moderately, worketh quite contrary effects, as is implied in the old proverb which saith: Venus taketh cold when not accompanied by Ceres and Bacchus. [Love is suppressed when it is not accompanied by food and drink] (1931, Book 3: 540).

The best-known literary comment on such contradictory effects of alcohol emanates from Shakespeare (Macbeth, Shakespeare 1971): "Lechery, sir, it provokes, and unprovokes; it provokes the desire, but it takes away the performance. Therefore much drink may be said to be an equivocator of lechery" (Act 2, Scene 3).

Most discussions of the sexual effects of alcohol have pertained to wines and, more recently, to liqueurs.

An exception is found in the herbal of Jacobus Theodorus (died 1590), a southern German physician who was enthusiastic about another beverage:

Beer brewed from wheat, above all as a beverage, but also when used in food: on soups, sauces, and porridge, increases the natural seed, straightens the drooping phallus up again, and helps feeble men who are incapable of conjugal acts back into the saddle (1664: 641).

Nothing substantial has been added to an understanding of the behavioral effects of alcohol in the twentieth century. Clinicians who wrote extensively on sexual matters, such as the Swiss psychiatrist August H. Forel (1848-1931) and the German venereologist Iwan Bloch (1872-1922), both expounded on the pseudoaphrodisiacal effects that may occur when inhibitions are suppressed by small amounts of alcohol and the increasing anesthetic effect of gross intoxication.

Bloch speculated that moderate quantities of alcohol exert a dual effect, as "general psychic stimulant" and as a specifically sexual stimulant. But with a more protracted consumption of alcohol, the "psychic stimulation" deteriorates into "psychic paralysis" (loss of inhibition or judgment) before sexual excitement also wanes, leaving a gap of unrestrained sexual excitation. He concluded: "For the normal individual alcohol is not a means for the increase of sexual potency, but the reverse" (1919: 293, 444).

Other writers, biased by the temperance movement, were more outspoken. Thus, according to Forel:

The drink habit corrupts the whole of sexual life. . . . Most narcotics, especially alcohol (either fermented or distilled) have the peculiarity of exciting the sexual appetite in a bestial manner, thereby leading to the most absurd and disgusting excesses, although at the same time they weaken the sexual power (1926: 332, 503).

Moving to nonalcoholic beverages, cacao (or cocoa), imported to Spain from the Caribbean islands, became a popular drink by 1580, after it had been modified into chocolate by the addition of sugar and milk. Although it was designated as "cold and dry," chocolate gained some reputation as an aphrodisiac. The reasons for this are uncertain. One mid-eighteenth-century French author implied that chocolate "promotes Venery" due to its nutritive quality. Because it is also a stimulant, its consumption is desirable as a restorative for old and phlegmatic people, while it should be avoided by "young people of a hot and bilious Constitution" (Lemery 1745: 364, 366).

Another reference work of the period states that cacao is cooling and yet "stimulates to Venery causing Procreation and Conception, facilitates Delivery, preserves Health, helps Digestion, makes people inclinable to seed" (Pomet 1748: 131-2). Yet in the seventeenth century, it had also become customary to mix various traditionally aphrodisiacal spices, such as pepper and cinnamon, with cacao. Proportions were adjusted to taste or according to the medicinal purpose. Hence, cacao may have been used by some to modify the potency of more traditional aphrodisiacs, and not actually accorded much potency of its own.

Although introduced to Europe toward the end of the sixteenth century, coffee did not become a popular beverage until about the middle of the seventeenth century - somewhat later than chocolate. As the popularity of coffee spread, so too did a rumor from its source in the Near East that, at least when consumed in excess, it suppressed sexual desires. Yet coffee was (correctly) recognized as having the ability to stimulate urine production, and since there had been an association between diuretics and aphrodisiacal properties since ancient times, any easy acceptance of the rumor seems inconsistent. Indeed, an English author felt the need to point out (published posthumously, 1746) that it is "an egregious Mistake, not only among the Persians, but also among most other Nations, to think that the Seed which when toasted is called Coffee . . . is of so cooling a Quality as to produce Impotence, even in those who use it frequently; for it dries them (Paulli 1746: 138-9).

In the nineteenth century, some settled for the same explanation that had been offered for the dual effects of alcohol. For example, M. Lallemand, a member of the Montpellier medical faculty, declared that coffee "augments the venereal desires, favors erections, and accelerates ejaculations; taken in excess, however . . . they are diminished and even completely extinguished." His explanation was that "what passed in the urinary organs is a good index of what is going on in the spermatic; the secretion of semen was increased as well as that of urine" (1866: 199-200). The implication was that although coffee is primarily an aphrodisiac, impotence eventually results from gonadal exhaustion caused by the protracted spermatorrhea-inducing stimulus.

Half a century later, Bloch continued to insist that coffee in sufficient volume induced impotence, which persisted as long as excessive coffee consumption continued (1919: 444). And an author in 1928, who still accepted that coffee ordinarily was an anaphrodisiac, recommended that in cases of impotence due to depression, it could act as a sexual stimulant by counteracting the symptom of fatigue (Loewe 1928: 184-6).

Anaphrodisiacs

As indicated in the discussion of coffee, save for alcohol consumed in excess, the list of dietary anaphrodisiacs is rather short and ambiguous. Among generally accepted foodstuffs, however, lettuce has had the most durable reputation - one probably originating in Greek mythology. The beautiful youth Adonis, killed by a wild boar, was laid out on a bed of lettuce by his lover, Venus (*Larousse Encyclopedia of Mythology* 1959: 81-2). Alternatively, he was killed in a field of wild lettuce (Athenaeus 1951: 301-3), or Venus threw herself on a bed of lettuce to lull her grief and repress her desires (Paris 1828: 9). In any event, the transient survival of a mortal, even when loved by a deity, became equated with the rapid withering of lettuce, which, in turn, became associated with impotence. Thus, according to Dioscorides, lettuce "is somewhat in virtue like unto Poppy.... [I]t is in generall soporiferous and easing of Paine" (Gunther 1959: 177). Such a notion is readily associated with the obviously anaphrodisiacal effect of sedation. According to Boorde, who wrote in the sixteenth century, lettuce "doth extynct veneryous actes, yet it doth increase mylke in a womans breste" (1870: 281).

One of the simpler seventeenth-century anaphrodisiacal recipes was a salad of lettuce, purslane, and mint with vinegar (Plater, Cole, and Culpeper 1662: 172). A contemporaneous prescription combined the alleged chemical and mineral anaphrodisiacal magic of many plants. Its ingredients were conserves of water lilies and of mint, candied lettuce and coolwort, seeds of Agnus castus (chaste tree), rue, coral, crystal, and camphor, made into an electuary with syrup of purslane.

Complex prescriptions were in demand, in part, at least, because of the paradoxical response of some persons to any one ingredient. In this regard, Nicolas Venette (1633-98), a French physician, informed his readers:

> Lettice and Succory, for Example, prevents the Generation of seed in most Men. But I know that in some it produces such a Plenty, especially if they eat it at Nights, as to subject them to Nocturnal Pollutions. This same experience teaches us, that Pepper and Ginger [usually aphrodisiacal] diminish the Seed, and dissipate Winds that are necessary to the action of Love (1906: 174-5).

Although most sexually inhibiting advice pertained to men, in the seventeenth century anaphrodisiacs were also prescribed to control "womb-furie." This was a manifestation of an "immoderate desire for carnal copulation [which] is able to master the Rational faculty [resulting in] Love-melancholy." The ailment was attributed mainly to virgins, young widows, and wives of impotent husbands. Thus a diagnosis of "immoderate desire" was doubtless based, at times, on some quite overt symptoms (Riverius 1655: 417-18).

Relevant prescriptions resemble those for the control of male lust, which were "cooling and sedating." Foodstuffs made up a minority of the ingredients, but among them, the leaves, stalks, and seeds of lettuce were the most common. Their alleged sedative effect was fortified by the inclusion of poppy seeds among the dozen or so ingredients (Riverius 1655: 417-8).

Disbelievers

Over the centuries, doubts about the effectiveness, mechanism of action, and the very existence of aphrodisiacs were occasionally raised, although most were limited or ambiguous. The Roman poet Ovid (43 B.C.-A.D. 18), who may have been the first recorded doubter, wrote in his *Ars Amatoria* (The Art of Love):

> There are, that strong provoking potions praise
> and nature with pernicious med'cines raise:
> Nor drugs nor herbs will what you fancy prove,
> And I pronounce them pois'nous all in love.
> Some pepper bruis'd, with seeds of nettles join,
> And clary steep in bowls of mellow wine:
> *Venus* is most adverse to forc'd delights
> Extorted flames pollute her genial rites.
> With fishes spawn thy feeble nerves recruit,
> And with eringo's hot salacious root.
> The goddess worship'd by th' *Erycian* swains,
> *Megara's* white shallot, so faint, disdains.
> New eggs they take, and honey's liquid juice,
> And leaves and apples of the pine infuse.
> Prescribe no more my muse, nor med'cines
>   give,
> Beauty and youth need no provocative
> (1776, Book 2: 55-6).

Clearly, Ovid has provided a fine list of aphrodisiacal ingredients. But he warns that youth and beauty are sufficiently strong attractants that artificial stimulants are not only superfluous but counterproductive because artificially induced passion ("extorted flames") destroys true love.

Disagreement had always existed about the substances that affect sexual function and in which ways, but because the concept of objective therapeutic evaluation had yet to be devised, authors tended to ignore, rather than attack, claims with which they disagreed. But this situation gradually began to change at the end of the sixteenth century, with mandrake the first target. Gerarde, who acknowledged numerous botanical aphrodisiacs, disparaged anyone who would prescribe this root:

> Mandrake is called of the Graecians *Circea* of Circe the Witch, who by Art could procure love: for it hath beene thought that the roote heere of serveth to winne love.... There have been many ridiculous tales brought up of this plant, whether of olde wives or some runnegate surgeons or phisickmongers, I know not ..., but sure some one or moe *[sic]* that sought to make themselves famous in skillful above others were first brochers of that errour I spake of (1597: 280-2).

Mandrake also came under attack in a larger effort aimed at the demolition of the doctrine of signatures by Sir Thomas Browne (1605-82). Although he did not mention aphrodisiacs as such in his *Pseudodoxia epidemica* (1646), his argument is relevant because "signatures of nature" were so important in the identification of these substances. Browne denounced as a "false conception" the notion that bifurcated root resembled human thighs. He pointed out that mandrake did not necessarily have a bifid root, and when it did, the two were often interwoven, destroying any human resemblance. Furthermore, bifid roots were not unique to this plant, and thus it made no sense to ascribe powers to mandrake because of a natural signature and not ascribe the same to a bifid carrot or a parsnip. In addition, such a notion gave rise to fraud because roots of other plants were carved to imitate bifid mandrake "to deceive unfruitful women" (1927: 285–99).

The waning of the conviction that the physical appearance of a natural object offered clues to its medicinal value did not, however, foster skepticism about substances believed to have a genital effect. But it did shift the focus to their intrinsic qualities. According to *A Golden Practice of Physick,* a well-known English medical text of 1662:

> [I]t is our opinion that such medicines [aphrodisiacs] work by a manifest quality, rather than by stretching the Yard [penis] with Wind as some say (which cannot be) besides their secret hidden quality which was observed by the first teachers of such things, from the whiteness of the flesh, fruits, and roots, resembling seed: Or because Taken from Leacherous Creatures; or from their shape resembling Stones [testicles] as the Satyrions or plants called Dogstones; or like a rough wrinkled Cod [scrotum], as Toad-stools or Mushrooms (Plater, Cole, and Culpeper 1662: 172).

Having disposed of both the pneuma mechanism of erection and a doctrine of signatures, the authors proceeded to provide a lengthy list of animals, animal products, vegetables, and seeds that would serve as sexual stimulants. Meats were best because they nourish well and produce much blood. Species to be selected should have white tissue, such as brain, testicles, and much marrow, particularly when these were obtained from "the most lecherous Beasts." The latter were cocks, quail, and the ever-present sparrow, along with beaver flesh and, in the case of the fox, just his testicles.

The sea creatures on the list were exclusively invertebrate, and were followed by nuts, grains, and vegetables. But at this point, without explanation, the authors veer away to conclude that the preparation of sexual stimulants was more important than the ingredients. All of these foods had the same effect, but "especially if they be peppered and salted: for Pepper stimulateth and provoketh Venery, and we suppose that when such things are so eaten it comes rather from the sauce than the meat" (Plater, Cole, and Culpeper 1662: 172).

Hermann Boerhaave (1668–1738), a famous professor of medicine at Leiden, wrote somewhat hesitantly regarding "generators of seed." These were the various botanicals, mammalian and rooster testicles and brains that "are commended by the Ancients; but these are doubtful, and perhaps vain" (1740: 152).

Later in the eighteenth century, however, the very existence of aphrodisiacs was clearly denied for the first time, with the credit going to William Cullen (1710–90), a leading physician of Edinburgh. Among the terms he defined in his *Treatise on the Materia Medica* (1789) we find:

> *Aphrodisiaca.* Medicines supposed to be suited to excite the venereal appetite, or to increase the venereal powers. I do not know that there are any medicines of specific power for these purposes; and therefore the term seems to have been for the most part improperly employed (1808: 107).

Nevertheless, despite Cullen's influential reputation, and the increasing skepticism of science, the popularity of aphrodisiacal prescriptions and recipes did not lose their popularity.

Lay Literature

Until recently, physicians saw only a minority of medical problems and were not consulted at all by large segments of the population. Medical advice, however, still reached many through a genre of "domestic medicine" books that began to appear in the vernacular in the seventeenth century. They became particularly popular toward the end of the eighteenth century and continue to be published today. And until the middle third of the twentieth century, far more people were likely to have been influenced by the recommendations in these popular books than by any personal contact with physicians.

Because these publications focused on actions that could be taken without the intervention of a physician, dietary advice was prominent, and as late as the nineteenth century, the problems that diets were intended to correct were "acidity" and "wind" (gas formation). Acids were deemed to irritate the urinary passages, thereby stimulating sexual sensations, and gaseousness stimulated the urge to expulsion, that is, ejaculation. Substances that induced either were generally considered aphrodisiacal, and those that counteracted them were anaphrodisiacal.

Thus, a domestic-advice book from 1800 recommended that to increase seminal fluid, the diet should emphasize milk, eggs, and tender and nutritious meats, as well as herbs and roots that were mild, spicy, and diuretic. Conversely, to inhibit passion, one was advised to resort to a diet that was less nutritious, to avoid spices, and to abstain from alcoholic beverages. "Cooling" nourishment, such as lettuce and cucumbers, was seen to be beneficial (Willich 1800: 557–61).

A similar volume in the latter part of the nineteenth century relied more on medicines than on diet to counteract impotence. In regard to nutrition, the reader was told only to rely on "plain, simple, easily digested, and nourishing food." Much greater attention, however, was paid to "spermatorrhea" (involuntary seminal emissions), as well as, implicitly, those voluntary emissions resulting from the sin of masturbation. The dietetic component of this therapy for spermatorrhea consisted of the avoidance of carbohydrates because they were thought to readily ferment, producing gas in the stomach and acid in the intestines. Such acids were then absorbed, and they acidified the urine, "causing great irritation of the lining surface of the bladder and urinary passages, greatly increasing and perpetuating the disease." More specifically, fruits and vegetables were to be eaten sparingly and milk was to be avoided. Distilled spirits were preferable to beer, wine, and other fermented liquors, although water and black tea were viewed as the safest beverages. Coarse, well-baked wheat bread, fresh eggs, and various meats, stewed or boiled to tenderness, formed the most curative diet. The author conceded that it did not afford much variety, but "it offers the most abundant nutrition, and aids materially in the cure of this ailment" (Gleason 1873: 454–60).

In a book written in 1894, Dr. J. Harvey Kellogg (1852–1943), the inventor of corn flakes, taught that the sole cause of almost all impotence was sexual excess of some kind. Consequently, controlling spermatorrhea prevented impotence. Such control required avoidance of all stimulation, dietetically including "tea and coffee, spices and other condiments, and animal food [because they] have a special tendency in this direction" (1894: 267–77, 319, 613). Other (and earlier) widely used books, such as those by S. A. Tissot (1769) and H. Buchan (1778), had avoided sexual matters other than pregnancy.

The Early Twentieth Century

The observation of Havelock Ellis (1906) that high nutritive value and ease of digestion are the only criteria for a dietary aphrodisiac coincided with a shift, at least in the medical literature, away from the notion that some foods could exert a specifically sexual effect. In texts of materia medica published between 1891 and 1911, the only real food item to which aphrodisiacal powers were attributed was in a work by the American physiologist Roberts Bartholow (1831–1904). He wrote: "Carrot seems . . . to produce diuresis, augment menstrual flux, and cause aphrodisiac effects in the male" (1903: 791). Some newer herbs, such as *damiana,* were recommended, as were metals reminiscent of Paracelsian teachings, among them gold chloride, iron arsenite, and zinc phosphide (Bartholow 1903: 297, 175, 135).

With the disappearance of aphrodisiacal foods from (at least) *scientific* discussion in the twentieth century, however, there remains only the question of vitamins to be dealt with, and of these the only ones shown to be specifically relevant to any aspect of sexual function are vitamins A and E. The American biochemist Herbert M. Evans (1882–1971), who discovered vitamin E in 1922 (Evans and Bishop 1922), subsequently found with collaborators that a lack of this substance from the diet of male rats resulted in sterility due to deterioration of the seminiferous tubules, but not to a loss of the sex drive. Females did not become sterile, but they did abort their fetuses. Vitamin A deficiency also resulted in male sterility (Evans 1932a, 1932b).

Rodent experiments such as these were misunderstood or distorted by the lay press and by charlatans touting the "anti-sterility vitamin" as a cure for all sorts of sexual dysfunctions of men and women. Some published case reports suggested that vitamin E might assist those women who have had spontaneous abortions to carry a pregnancy to term (American Medical Association Council on Pharmacy and Chemistry 1940: 2214–18). However, habitual abortion is not the result of vitamin E deficiency, and the reliability of vitamin E administration for such a problem has not been proven. Vitamin deficiencies, unless they are a part of starvation, seem to have no effect on human sexual activity.

Conclusion

According to modern science, the only substances in the realm of food and drink that can be considered to have a potentially aphrodisiacal effect are alcoholic beverages in quantities sufficiently small to reduce inhibitions without overtly sedating. There are no positive sexual stimulants and no inhibitors other than sedating amounts of alcoholic beverages. Circumstances surrounding the consumption of food or drink may, of course, exert a positive or negative psychological influence on sexual desire, which is another way of saying that the alleged sexual effects of foods are culturally determined, psychological factors. And the desire of the public for aphrodisiacal foods to exist continues to support the publication of books with titles such as *Aphrodisiac Culinary Manual* (Heartman 1942), *Venus in the Kitchen* (Douglas 1952), *The Virility Diet* (Belham 1965), and *Lewd Food* (Hendrickson 1974).

Thomas G. Benedek

Bibliography

Adams, Francis, trans. 1847. *The seven books of Paulus Aegineta,* Vol. 3. London.
American Medical Association Council on Pharmacy and Chemistry. 1940. The treatment of habitual abortion with vitamin E. *Journal of the American Medical Association* 114: 2214–18.
Aquinas, St. Thomas. 1932. The *"Summa Theologica" of*

St. Thomas Aquinas, Vols. 9, 13, trans. Fathers of the English Dominican Province. London.

Arnaldus de Villanova. 1943. *The earliest printed book on wine,* trans. Henry E. Sigerist. New York.

Athenaeus. 1951. *The Deipnosophists,* trans. C. B. Gulick. Cambridge, Mass.

Banks, J. 1805. An attempt to ascertain the time when the potato (Solanum tuberosum) was first introduced into the United Kingdom. *Transactions of the Horticultural Society* 1: 8-12.

Bartholow, R. 1903. *A practical treatise on materia medica and therapeutics.* Eleventh edition. New York.

Belham, G. 1965. *The virility diet.* London.

Bloch, I. 1919. *The sexual life of our time.* London.

Bock, H. 1546. *Kreuter Buch.* . . . Strasbourg.

Boerhaave, H. 1740. *A treatise on the powers of medicines,* trans. J. Martin. London.

Boorde, A. 1870. Compendyous regyment or a dyetary of helth. In *Andrew Boorde's introduction and dyetary,* ed. F. J. Furnivall. London.

Brondegaard, V. J. 1971. Orchideen als Aphrodisiaca. *Sudhoff's Archiv für Geschichte der Medizin* 55: 22-57.

Browne, T. 1927. *The works of Sir Thomas Browne,* ed. C. Sayle. Edinburgh.

Buchan, W. 1778. *Domestic medicine, or, the family physician.* Norwich, England.

Burton, R. F. 1885. *The book of the thousand nights and one night,* Vol. 4. London.

Burton, R. F. trans. 1964. *The perfumed garden of the Shayk Nefzawi.* New York.

Chapman, G. 1611. *May-day, a witty comedie.* London.

Chaucer, G. 1952. *The Canterbury tales,* trans. N. Coghill. Baltimore, Md.

Croll, O. 1670. *Treatise of signature of internal things.* London.

Cullen, W. 1808. *Treatise on the materia medica.* Third American edition. Philadelphia, Pa.

Delany, P. trans. 1970. Constantinus Africanus' *De coitu. Chaucer Review.* 4: 55-65.

Dodoens, R. 1578. *A niewe herball; or histories of plantes,* . . . trans. H. Lyte. London.

Douglas, Norman. 1952. *Venus in the Kitchen or, Love's Cookery Book.* London.

Ellis, H. 1906. *Studies in the psychology of sex,* Vol. 3. Philadelphia, Pa.

Evans, H. M. 1932a. Testicular degeneration due to inadequate vitamin A in cases where E is adequate. *American Journal of Physiology* 99: 477-86.

1932b. Vitamin E. *Journal of the American Medical Association* 99: 469-75.

Evans, H. M., and K. S. Bishop. 1922. Existence of a hitherto unknown dietary factor essential for reproduction. *Journal of the American Medical Association* 81: 889-92.

Forel, A. 1926. *The sexual question,* trans. C. F. Marshall. Brooklyn, N.Y.

Galen. 1968. *On the usefulness of the parts of the body,* trans. M. T. May. Ithaca, N.Y.

Gerarde, J. 1597. *The herball; or, generall historie of plantes.* London.

1636. *The herball; or, general historie of plantes,* amended by T. Johnson. London.

Gleason, C. W. 1873. *Everybody's own physician.* Philadelphia, Pa.

Guerra, F. 1965. Drugs from the Indies and the political economy of the sixteenth century. In *Analecta Medico-Historica,* ed. M. Florkin, 29-54. New York.

Gunther, R. T. 1959. *The Greek herball of Dioscorides,* trans. John Goodyear. New York.

Halban, J., and L. Seitz. 1924. *Biologie und Pathologie des Weibes,* Vol. 2. Berlin.

Harrison, W. 1577. *The description of England,* ed. G. Edelen. Ithaca, N.Y.

Heartman, C. F. 1942. *Aphrodisiac culinary manual.* New Orleans, La.

Hendrickson, R. 1974. *Lewd food.* Radnor, Pa.

Kellogg, J. H. 1894. *Plain facts for old and young: Embracing the natural history hygiene of organic life.* Burlington, Iowa.

Kremers, E., and G. Urdang. 1951. *History of pharmacy.* Second edition. Philadelphia, Pa.

Lallemand, M. 1866. *A practical treatise on the causes, symptoms, and treatment of spermatorrhoea,* trans. H. J. McDougall. Fifth American edition. Philadelphia, Pa.

Larousse encyclopedia of mythology. 1959. New York.

Lemery, M. L. 1745. *A treatise of all sorts of foods,* trans. D. Hay. London.

Loewe, S. 1928. Praktische Therapie mit Aphrodisiaka. *Deutsche Medizinische Wochenschrift* 54: 184-6.

MacDougald, D. 1961. Aphrodisiacs and anaphrodisiacs. In *The encyclopedia of sexual behavior,* Vol.1, ed. A. Ellis and A. Abarbanel. New York.

Mattioli, P. 1590. *Kreuterbuch,* . . . trans. and enlarged J. Camerarium. Frankfurt am Main.

Ovid. 1776. *The art of love,* trans. anon. London.

Paris, J. A. 1828. *Pharmacologia.* American edition. New York.

Parkinson, J. 1640. *Theatrum botanicum: The theater of plants, or a universal and compleate herball.* London.

Paulli, S. 1746. *A treatise on tobacco, tea, coffee, and chocolate,* trans. Dr. James. London.

Pereira, J. 1846. *The elements of materia medica and therapeutics,* Vol. 1. Second American edition. Philadelphia, Pa.

Plater, F., A. Cole, and N. Culpeper. 1662. *A golden practice of physick.* London.

Pliny. 1963. *Natural history,* Vols. 7, 8, trans. W. H. S. Jones. Cambridge, Mass.

Pomet, P. 1748. *A complete history of drugs.* Fourth edition. London.

Rabelais, F. 1931. *The works of Francis Rabelais,* ed. A. J. Nock and C. R. Wilson. New York.

Ramsay, G. G., trans. 1940. *Juvenal and Persius.* Cambridge, Mass.

Riverius, L. 1655. *The compleat practice of physick,* trans. N. Culpeper, A. Cole, and W. Rowland. London.

Rosner, F. 1974. *Sex ethics in the writings of Moses Maimonides.* New York.

Salaman, R. 1949. *The history and social influence of the potato.* Cambridge.

Salmon, W. 1710. *The English herbal or history of plants.* London.

Schumacher, B., trans. 1936. *Das Luminare majus von Joannes Jacobus Manlius de Bosco, 1536.* Mittenwald, Bavaria.

Shakespeare, W. 1971. *William Shakespeare: The Complete Works.* London.

Steadman's medical dictionary. 1990. Twenty-fifth edition. Baltimore, Md.

Theodorus, Iacobus (Tabernaemontani) 1664. *Neuw Vollkommentlich Kreuterbuch.* . . . Basel.

Thorndyke, L. 1958. *A history of magic and experimental science,* Vol. 7. New York.

Tissot, S. A. 1769. *Advice to people in general with respect to health.* Fifth edition. Dublin.

Venette, N. 1906. *The mysteries of conjugal love reveal'd.* Paris.

Vicary, T. 1888. *A profitable treatise of the anatomie of man's body,* . . . ed. F. J. Furnival and P. Furnivall. London.

Willich, A. F. 1800. *Lectures on diet and regimen . . . for the use of families.* London.

VI.16 ✑ Food as Medicine

Definitions

The eminent medical historian Henry E. Sigerist once noted that "[t]here is no sharp borderline between food and drug," and that both dietetic and pharmacological therapies were "born of instinct" (Sigerist 1951: 114-15). Today we tend to focus our studies of food on its nutritive values in promoting growth and health and in preventing disease, but for many centuries past, food had an additional, specifically medical role – as a remedy for illness.

The United States Food, Drug, and Cosmetic Act, signed into law June 27, 1938, provides no clearer differentiation between "food" and "drug" than Sigerist could. According to the current wording of that legislation, which updated the Pure Food and Drug Act of 1906, "the term 'food' means (1) articles used for food or drink for man or other animals, (2) chewing gum, and (3) articles used for components for any other such article," whereas "the term 'drug' means (A) articles recognized in the official United States Pharmacopoeias [and several other compendia]; and (B) articles intended for use in the diagnosis, cure, mitigation, treatment, or prevention of disease in man or other animals; and (C) articles (other than food) intended to affect the structure or any function of the body of man or other animals; and (D) articles intended for use as a component of any articles specified in clause (A), (B), or (C)." Under clause (B) above, many items that have traditionally been considered foods might also be regarded as drugs under federal law, although they seldom are. The Food and Drug Administration (FDA) can intervene in cases involving food only when it judges an item to be misleadingly labeled as a "food"; it specifically excludes vitamins from the category "drugs."

The Foundation for Innovation in Medicine recently coined the word "nutraceutical" to signify "any substance that can be considered a food and provides medical and health benefits, including the prevention and treatment of disease. Such products include traditional foods, isolated nutrients, dietary supplements, genetically engineered 'designer' foods, herbal products and processed foods" (*Tufts Journal* 1992: 10). However, the very concept of nutraceuticals seems to sidestep even the vague definitions with which the FDA is tethered. Indeed, it is probably not possible to differentiate foods from drugs with mutually exclusive definitions. The ambiguity, troublesome as it may be in some contexts, has deep historical roots. Until the early twentieth century, physicians routinely prescribed specific foods and diets for their medical – that is, curative or preventive – value. The reader should also keep in mind that nonprofessional healers, such as wives and mothers, have employed the same food remedies for similar purposes.

Rarely is it possible to pinpoint the putative healing roles of specific components of traditional foods, such as the oils that confer distinctive tastes on several botanical flavors and spices, or extracts with known pharmacological properties, such as the active principles of coffee, tea, and cocoa. Similarly, we are not concerned with toxins or biological contaminants of foods, such as the ergot alkaloids produced by a fungus that sometimes infects bread made with rye (Hofmann 1972) or the anticoagulant found in spoiled sweet-clover fodder for domestic cattle. Nor does this chapter deal with foodstuffs that only incidentally provide raw starting materials for synthesizing what are unmistakably drugs – for example, the yams from which are extracted the diosgenins that are used as starting material in the manufacture of steroids.

Medical Dietetics

Its Roots in the Ancient World

Beginning with the premise that "[m]an knew only too well that he could not live without food, that food sustained life," Sigerist postulated: "Physiology began when man . . . tried to . . . correlate the actions of food, air, and blood" (Sigerist 1951: 348-9). Ancient Egyptians, for instance, developed an ingenious theory to account for the transformation of food and air into the substance of the human body and to explain disease. Not only did they recognize the hazards of an inadequate food supply but they also knew when to prescribe a normal diet for the sick or injured, and their physicians used many items in the ordinary diet as remedies that would become common in later European cultures (Estes 1989; Manniche 1989).

The Egyptians' major sweetening agent, honey, was perhaps the most effective of all their medicines. Its efficacy as a wound dressing, attributable chiefly to the desiccating effect on bacteria of its 80 percent sugar content, probably led to its further use in many oral remedies because of its ability to prevent infection; Egyptian medical theory associated even superficial infections with internal disturbances. Modern laboratory studies have shown that honey could, indeed, have inhibited the growth of the bacteria that often contaminate wounds until normal immunological and tissue repair processes had been completed (Estes

1989: 68-71). Because it has the same effect on bacteria as honey, a thick paste of ordinary granulated sugar is sometimes applied to infected wounds today (Seal and Middleton 1991), but honey is unlikely to have been selectively effective as an antimicrobial agent when taken internally.

Although some of the Egyptians' speculative pathophysiological concepts can be recognized among the Greeks' explanations of health and disease, it was the latter that directly shaped many aspects of the relationship between food and health that survived for the next 2,500 years. As early as the sixth century B.C., the philosopher-physician Alcmaeon of Croton recognized that the body's growth depends on its food intake. A century later, the Hippocratic school of physicians described food as one source of the body's energy and its heat (Winslow and Bellinger 1945). Other sixth-century Greek thinkers tried to explain the conversion of food to parts of the body. Thales of Miletus, for example, in Asia Minor, thought that its primary substance was water, whereas Anaximenes, also of Miletus, argued that it was air. In the fifth century, the Sicilian philosopher Empedocles said that the four irreducible elements – fire, water, earth, and air – were the basic components of both food and body. He and his contemporary Anaxagoras, the first major philosopher to live in Athens, agreed with Alcmaeon that each foodstuff contains particles that are assimilated to specific parts of the body; Empedocles said that each assimilated particle fits exactly into the body part that takes it up (King 1963: 56-68; Leicester 1974: 9).

In the fourth century B.C., Aristotle followed Empedocles and Anaxagoras when he postulated that the four elements are blended from four "qualities" – hot, cold, moist, and dry – that are reciprocally paired in each element. He also held that the primary "chemical" reaction of the body is *pepsis,* a word that has historically been translated into English as "coction," from the Latin *coquere,* to cook. In both Latin and English forms, coction implies heating and ripening (of both fruit and morbific matter), and it was associated in English medical texts with perfecting something via natural processes. Aristotle used pepsis in the same way, describing it as the changes a foodstuff undergoes as it is prepared in the gastrointestinal tract for assimilation into the body. In short, both the Greek "pepsis" and the English "coction" were taken to mean "digestion." Hence, the diagnosis of dyspepsia was a synonym for indigestion. According to Aristotle, normal coction of foods, fueled by the body's innate heat, thickens the body's fluids. By contrast, coction is incomplete in the sick, resulting in abnormally thin, or watery, fluids (Leicester 1974: 15-18, 33-5).

In the second century A.D., the physician whose teachings came to dominate Western medical thought for seventeen centuries, Galen of Pergamum, in Asia Minor, reemphasized the teachings of Hippocrates, and postulated that all physiological activity depends on balances described by Aristotle (Winslow and Bellinger 1945; King 1963: 56-68; Leicester 1974: 9). According to Galen's medical configuration of Aristotle's physiological model, blood is associated with heat and moisture, phlegm is associated with moisture and cold, black bile is associated with cold and dryness, and yellow bile with dryness and heat.

Moreover, each humor was associated with one of the seasons, just as Posidonius of Rhodes, in about 100 B.C., had associated each with a corresponding temperament (Leicester 1974: 30-2). Blood was now associated with spring and the sanguine temperament, water with winter and the phlegmatic temperament, black bile with autumn and melancholy, and yellow bile with summer and the choleric or bilious temperament. (These terms for the temperaments, however, were not introduced until the twelfth century A.D., by Honorius of Autun.) The humoral theory satisfactorily explained the physiological clues to the balances that had to be rectified in order to restore health and stability to the sick body. At the same time, it permitted the construction of a pragmatic approach to the principles of medical therapy, including dietetics.

These principles were based on the premise that imbalances among the humors could be corrected by administering drugs – or foods – with appropriately opposite properties. Thus, because bilious fevers were associated with dryness and increased body heat, they should be treated with moist, cool remedies in order to rebalance the blood and yellow bile – the humors most disturbed in such patients. Similarly, dropsy, the accumulation of water in the tissues, should be treated with remedies that dried them, such as diuretics. Obviously, many foods could correct imbalances as well as doctors' drugs could. Cool, moist vegetables, for example, like cucumbers, were well suited to the needs of bilious fever patients.

The Hippocratic texts show that physicians of the fifth century B.C. recognized the influence of nourishment on human health. This was almost certainly not a new idea even then, but these are the earliest such writings to have survived. The *Regimen for Health* focuses on the therapeutic value of food, whereas the first section of the *Aphorisms* describes diet with special reference to illness. It teaches that proper nourishment, because of its influence on digestion, is more important to the sick patient than drugs (Lloyd 1978: 206-10, 272-6). Other authorities added that a carefully chosen diet can rectify disturbances in the balances of heat, cold, dryness, and moisture caused by exhaustion of the energy normally derived from the diet, or by changes in one's external circumstances, such as sudden wealth or poverty. Remedies were classified medically by the proportions of the same four qualities in each, and foods were further categorized as to whether they were wild or domesticated (Edelstein 1987, orig. 1931). In short, foods, like drugs, were prescribed in order to correct imbalances among the humors or to modify digestive processes that would themselves influence the humors, as far as ancient physicians could tell.

Dietetic instructions were designed to ensure optimum digestion, in order to minimize the amount of undigestible residues that could accumulate in the alimentary tract. Hence, in a physiological echo from the banks of the Nile, Diocles of Carystus, an Athenian physician of the fourth century B.C., cautioned: "The chief meal is to be taken when the body is empty and does not contain any badly digested residues of food" (Sigerist 1987: 238–40, orig. 1961), which, in the Egyptian tradition, were major causes of illness (Estes 1989: 80–91).

Hellenistic medical writers went beyond the Hippocratics when they asserted that a healthy diet is more important than post hoc healing of the sick. But emphasis on merely maintaining a healthy lifestyle receded when it became less feasible in the rapidly changing world of the Roman Empire. And by then, physicians were giving increased attention to diet as a coequal branch of their practice along with drugs and manual operations, such as bleeding – a differentiation that dominated the structure of professional medicine well past the Middle Ages (Siraisi 1981: 252; Edelstein 1987).

Early in the first century A.D., the Roman encyclopedist Celsus again echoed the Egyptian preoccupation with the intestines when he wrote that "digestion has to do with all sorts of troubles." His dietary guide, in the time-honored Aristotelian tradition, included lists of drugs that heat or cool; those that are least and most readily digested; those that move the bowels or constrict them; those that increase urine output, induce sleep, and draw out noxious materials that cause disease; and those that suppress illness with or without simultaneously cooling the patient. Celsus, however, concluded his pages on dietetics on a note of skepticism: "But as regards all these medicaments, . . . it is clear that each man follows his own ideas rather than what he has found to be true by actual fact" (Celsus 1935, 1: 77, 207–15).

A century later, Galen taught that most illnesses are caused by "errors of regimen [including diet], and hence avoidable." He went on to explain how appropriate attention to food, drink, and air can preserve and restore health (Temkin 1973: 40, 154–6). Indeed, his *Therapeutic Method* required that the physician understand precisely how the four basic physiological qualities of life were mixed in every foodstuff, as well as in every drug (Smith 1979: 103).

The complexities involved are evident in the *Materia Medica* by Celsus's near contemporary Dioscorides, a peripatetic Greek physician from Asia Minor (Dioscorides 1934). His book remained the fountainhead of European therapeutics – and dietetics – for 15 centuries, and traces of its influence can be detected even today. Over the years, but especially in the Middle Ages, Dioscorides's descriptions were altered and expanded by commentators who, as Celsus had feared, relied as much on what they thought was true as on what was evident to the senses. An anonymous sixth-century author cited Hippocrates and Dioscorides in his book on the nutritional medical uses of plant foods, but he, too, found it difficult to differentiate clearly between "foods" and "drugs" (Riddle 1992, orig. 1984).

Dietetics in Medieval Europe

Diet retained its position as one of the three major modes of therapy, along with medicine and surgery, throughout the Middle Ages (Siraisi 1990: 121, 137). Although emphasis on the healthful properties of diet was first systematized by Greek writers, much of it was transmitted back to Europe in Arabic texts of the ninth to eleventh centuries that preserved Hippocratic and Galenic principles (Levey 1973: 33–5).

For instance, the *Canon of Medicine,* written about A.D. 1000 by the Persian physician Avicenna, made its initial impact on Europe when it was translated into Latin in the twelfth century at Toledo, by Gerard of Cremona. It had become a medical text at Montpellier by at least 1340, which helped to ensure the diffusion of Avicenna's ideas throughout Europe.

Avicenna perpetuated the Egyptian notion that excess food tends to putrefy, and its Greek corollary that it promotes indigestion and alimentary obstruction. He expanded the teachings of Greek, Roman, and Indian writers with his assertion that foods have medicinal properties that are unrelated to their hot, cold, moist, or dry qualities, while recognizing that some foods have therapeutic properties even when they have no nutritional value. His *Canon* classifies foods as of rich or poor quality, light or heavy, and wholesome or unwholesome, and includes dietary rules applicable to both health and disease, as well as a diet for the aged (Shah 1966: ix–x, 182–7, 309–20, 338–40, 359–61).

Avicenna simplified Galen's description when he explained how food is subjected to its first coction in the stomach, resulting in chyle, which passes, via the portal veins, to the liver. There a second coction turns it into yellow bile, black bile, and blood, while its aqueous residue is carried to the kidneys for eventual release from the body. At the same time, the residue of the first, gastric, coction is discharged, partly as phlegm, into the lower intestinal tract. The blood alone is subjected to a third coction, when the heart converts it to what Aristotle had called the vital spirit, and a fourth, in the brain, where it is further transformed into a psychic spirit (Leicester 1974: 59). This satisfying explanation facilitated the physician's choice of appropriately therapeutic drugs – or foods.

Constantinus Africanus, who died 50 years after Avicenna, translated many Arabic texts at Salerno (site of the first major medical school in Europe) and

Monte Cassino. His *Book of Degrees* complicated therapeutic procedures when he described gradations in the heat, cold, dryness, and moisture of foods and medicines: A food is hot in the first degree if its heating power is less than that of the human body; it is hot in the second degree if its heating power equals that of the body; in the third degree if its heat exceeds that of the body; and in the fourth degree if it is simply unbearably hot. In his translation of a commentary on a book by Galen, Constantinus summarized current thinking about the dietary approach to therapy: "Good food is that which brings about a good humor and bad food is that which brings about an evil humor. And that which produces a good humor is that which generates good blood" (Thorndike 1923, 1: 751; Leicester 1974: 62-5).

By the thirteenth century, Latin translations of Galen's specifically dietary works, such as *De Alimentorum Facultatibus* and *De Subtiliante Dieta,* along with translations of pseudo-Galenic works on the same subjects, such as *De Nutrimento* and *De Virtutibus Cibariorum,* had joined the works of Avicenna and other Arabic writers, and the dietary works of a ninth-century Egyptian writer, Isaac Judaeus, in many medical curricula. One of the most widely consulted late medieval medical manuals was by Peter the Spaniard, or Petrus Hispanus, of Paris (later Pope John XXI, for a year until his accidental death in 1277). His scholastic commentaries on Isaac's *Universal Diets* and *Particular Diets* led him to pose such questions as: "Why does nature sustain a multitude of medicines, but not of foods? . . . Is fruit wholesome? . . . Are eggs or meat better for convalescents? . . . Should paralytics eat fried fish? Are apples good in fevers? . . . Why do we employ foods hot in the fourth degree and not those cold in the same degree?"

Peter answered such queries with syllogisms premised on gradations in the four basic qualities of foods. At the same time, he disputed the ancient idea that foods could be fully assimilated into the structure of the body (Thorndike 1923, 2: 488–507). However, Peter was not alone in rationalizing medical dietetics. As late as the 1570s, medical faculty and students at Montpellier debated such theses as "[w]hether barley bread should be eaten with fruit," "whether it was safe for persons with kidney trouble or fever to eat eggs," and "whether dinner or supper should be the more frugal meal" (Thorndike 1941, 6: 222–3).

The prominent attention given to diet in the fourteenth century is exemplified by the physician among the tale spinners who accompanied Chaucer's pilgrimage to Canterbury:

He was well-versed in the ancient authorities;
In his own diet he observed some measure;
There were no superfluities for pleasure,
Only digestives, nutritives and such (Chaucer
   1960: 31).

It was not only physicians who were concerned with the relationship of diet to health in the Middle Ages, however. Medical authorities from Hippocrates to Avicenna were cited in many manuscripts designed for lay use (Thorndike 1940; Bullough 1957), such as several late medieval *Tacuina Sanitatis* (Handbooks of Health) based on the works of the eleventh-century Arabic physician Ibn Botlân. These manuscripts aimed, among their medical goals, to teach "the right use of food and drink," the "correct use of elimination and retention of humors," and how to moderate the emotions associated with each humor (Arano 1976: 6-10).

By the late Middle Ages, the therapeutic benefits of food had entered into the everyday planning of at least the grand households, the only ones for which evidence has survived. Spices, for example, were regarded as both aids to digestion and evidence of a host's wealth. Medieval herbals and dietaries listed the health-giving properties of foods in the classical humoral tradition. They classified foods and medicines by their degrees of heat, cold, moisture, and dryness. Thus, melons, obviously cold and moist, were suitable for treating patients with fevers. But it may be that this new order resulted from a misreading of the original texts, inasmuch as later writers did not retain it.

Largely under the influence of the *Regimen of Health,* which codified the prescripts for healthy living taught at Salerno in the eleventh century, physicians devised diets appropriate to both Aristotelian physiology and specific illnesses. Thus, Taddeo Alderotti, professor of medicine at Bologna in the late thirteenth century, recommended to many patients (probably chiefly those with fevers) that they avoid hot bread, cheese, fruits, beef, and pork, in favor of less-stimulating foods. However, in many instances, it is difficult to differentiate between his culinary and medical directions (Siraisi 1981: 293).

The patient's age was another determinant of therapeutic diets. In 1539, for example, a moderately moist and warm diet was still being recommended for young children, who were viewed as phlegmatic (that is, as very moist and cold). As they grew older, they were thought to become more sanguine or choleric, which meant that they would now benefit from much moister and colder foods. And as their strength declined in old age, they needed foods that were only as moderately moist and warm as those that had benefited them in childhood. Indeed, many foods were more closely associated, in medieval thinking, with illness than with their gustatory effects, although taste was a major clue to the presumed Galenic properties of any drug or food (Drummond and Wilbraham 1958: 65–77; Teigen 1987). In short, the medical correlates of food permeated many aspects of medieval life, from the preparation of patients for surgery to the choice of menus for banquets and bathing establishments (Cosman 1978).

Dietetics during the Scientific Revolution

The rudiments of modern chemistry were beginning to influence medical ideas in the late Middle Ages through the writings of alchemical physicians. In the late fifteenth century, for example, Conrad Heingartner of Zurich cautioned his readers to chew food thoroughly, in order to maximize its digestibility, and not to eat too many courses at one meal, because some foods are more readily digested than others. He also urged that the principal meal be taken at night, because the cold night air aids digestion by forcing the body heat necessary for its completion to stay deep inside the body (Thorndike 1934, 4: 377–8).

It is clear that Heingartner's concept of the physiology of digestion owed much to Hippocratic–Galenic medical concepts, but the latter were about to disappear in favor of more explicitly chemical explanations. The experimental science that began emerging in the late sixteenth century began, however slowly, to replace the classical Greek and Islamic traditions that had heretofore dominated European thought.

By the late seventeenth century, a major new hypothesis was beginning to hold sway over medical thinking. It postulated that illness represents imbalances not only in the classical four humors but also in the tone – the innate strength and elasticity – of the solid fibrous components of blood vessels and nerves. Both organs were considered to be hollow tubes that propelled their respective contents through the body with forces proportional to the tone of their constituent fibers. That is, the body was healthy when blood or "nerve fluids" could circulate freely, or when sweat, urine, and feces could be expelled freely, and so forth.

Thus, a fast pulse was the distinguishing hallmark of fever, which was interpreted as the result of excessive arterial tone, requiring depletive therapy to bring it under control. Conversely, a slow pulse was interpreted as evidence of a weakness that required stimulant therapy (Estes 1991a). Historians have labeled the new hypothesis as the "solidist theory," to distinguish it from the older humoral theory. The two concepts were by no means mutually exclusive, however, and most therapeutic effects were interpreted within the frameworks of both. Nevertheless, the older Hippocratic–Galenic focus became progressively less prominent in medical texts.

Dietetics fitted into the new theory as well as into humoralism. By the time solidism had taken hold in medical thinking, the specifically therapeutic role of diet had been clarified by categorizing daily menus as full, moderate (or middle), or low (or thin). As Thomas Muffett wrote in 1655: "The first increaseth flesh, spirits, and humors, the second repaireth only them that were lost, and the third lessenth them all for a time to preserve life" (Drummond and Wilbraham 1958: 121–2). That is, full diets are appropriate, if not necessary, for maintaining growth and strength in vigorous younger people, whereas moderate diets are more suitable for middle age, and low diets for old age or during illness at any age. Muffett's description would surely have been recognizable to Aristotle, but within the solidist framework, the low diet was said to be depletive, "sedative," or antiphlogistic (that is, antifebrile), suitable for reducing excessive tone of the arteries and nerves, whereas the stronger diets were said to be stimulating.

Although the discovery of the Americas put new foods on European tables, medical properties were initially ascribed only to sassafras, sarsaparilla, and the pleasurable stimulating beverages – coffee and chocolate. When John Josselyn returned to London from New England, he reported that American watermelons were suitable for people with fevers, and cranberries for those with scurvy and "to allay the fervour of hot Diseases" (Josselyn 1672: 57, 65–6). Yet such foods could not survive the transatlantic crossing to European markets. Immigrants to colonial New England harvested both "meate and medicine" in their gardens, sometimes from the same plant, in the tradition they had learned before leaving home. Many relied on herbals for descriptions of each plant's medical properties, which closely followed those of Dioscorides (Leighton 1970: 134–7).

Early in the eighteenth century, Ippolito Francesco Albertini, professor of medicine at Bologna, echoed Avicenna when he wrote that his mother should not eat a food, such as meat, "that is easily converted into blood." At about the same time, Albertini's brother-in-law, Vincenzo Antonio Pigozzi, also a physician, directed a correspondent to strengthen his patient's stomach with food and medicine because, as Celsus had said, it was "apt to be weak in students and other diligent and well-behaved persons," so that "their daily food, on account of its coldness, is poorly purified and digested" (Jarcho 1989: 99, 177).

Eighteenth-century British hospitals developed standard diets based on humoral and solidist precepts. A 1782 London hospital dietary mandated the same breakfast for patients on both low and full diets: water-gruel or milk porridge (made of 1.25 ounces of oatmeal, and raisins, in a pint of water or milk). The supper menu was the same, supplemented by the addition of a pint of broth (made by boiling a leg of lamb or other meat for 1.5 hours) four times a week, or a quarter pound of cheese or butter during the week. The full and low diets differed chiefly in their midday dinner menus.

Febrile patients on the low diet received rice milk twice a week. Also twice a week they were served bread pudding (made by soaking a half pound of bread crumbs in one pint of milk overnight and then adding two or three eggs before the mixture was boiled in a bag for a hour or so). Lamb or other meat broth was also on the menu twice a week, or plumb broth (made by boiling six ounces of meat or bone with a half pint of peas and a half ounce of oats in water). A quarter pound of boiled beef or mutton, or roast veal, was added to the menu twice a week, and a 14-ounce loaf of bread was served every day.

By contrast, patients on a full diet received rice milk once a week. A half pound of boiled pudding appeared weekly (made by boiling a mixture of one pound of flour, a quarter pound of suet or meat or eels, and fruits, in 13 ounces of water, for one to two hours). A half pound of beef or mutton was served with greens four times weekly, and a loaf of bread daily. In addition, patients on the low diet received one pint of small beer daily, while those on the full diet were allowed four times as much. The presumed medical qualities of the two diets differed chiefly with respect to the stimulating property of red meat; their total mass was nearly the same (Estes 1990: 66-7). Such diets perpetuated the ancient admonition to "feed a cold and starve a fever," whose origins are in the Hippocratic texts, and it has remained a guiding therapeutic principle down to our own time.

In 1772, Dr. William Cullen of Edinburgh lamented that although dietetic prescriptions were among the most valuable of all therapies, they had fallen out of regular medical use in recent years (Risse 1986: 220). He might have been surprised when, a few years afterward, his colleague, Dr. Andrew Duncan, Jr., increased the proportions of stimulating foods served to his febrile or otherwise debilitated patients, chiefly by increasing their meat allowances (Estes 1990: 65-8). In fact, by the end of the century, Dr. William Heberden of London was complaining that "[m]any physicians appear to be too strict and particular in the roles of diet and regimen," and he urged that the sick be allowed to choose their own diets, according to their own tastes (Heberden 1802: 1-5).

In the meantime, experimental chemistry had begun to shed new light on the physiology of digestion and on the respiratory processes involved in the conversion of food into energy, carbon dioxide, and the tissues of the body. Early in the seventeenth century, Jan Baptista Van Helmont, who lived near Brussels, showed that gastric juice is acid, and that it is necessary for the digestion of food. He may even have identified hydrochloric acid as its chief component, but it was not until 1752 that this was proved by René Antoine Ferchault, Sieur de Réamur, in France. Although Van Helmont's concept of digestion contained some Aristotelian elements, he did show that the acid in gastric juice is neutralized in the duodenum by bile from the liver. However, it was in 1736 that Albrecht von Haller, at Göttingen, established that bile emulsifies fats. Haller's teacher, Hermann Boerhaave of Leiden, had already laid the groundwork for differentiating what were later named proteins (in 1838) and carbohydrates (in

1844). Haller added the last major food class, fats. But Boerhaave and Georg Ernst Stahl, professor of medicine at Halle, both leading proponents of solidism, denied that gastric juice was acid. Instead, they favored the ancient concept that digestion was a putrefactive or fermentative process, which eventually was abandoned in the face of Réamur's proof that digestion represents the dissolution of foodstuffs in gastric acid (Drummond and Wilbraham 1958: 232-55; Leicester 1974: 96-7, 118-27; Estes 1991a).

Between 1700 and 1850, when modern experimental pharmacology began to be applied to the study of drug effects on living organisms, physicians trained in the European medical tradition used as drugs about 500 botanical remedies, and 170 chemical compounds and other materials. Any given eighteenth-century physician employed some 125 different botanical remedies in his standard repertoire, depending on his training and experience. Save for the few botanical remedies that had been introduced from the New World by then, the majority of plants prescribed in the eighteenth century had also been used by healers in the ancient Mediterranean world, including most of the medically important foodstuffs shown in the seven tables that follow (Estes 1990). They illustrate the specifically therapeutic roles of familiar culinary ingredients, while reemphasizing the difficulty of discriminating between foods and drugs. These tabulations may not be all-inclusive, and several items could have been included in more than one list. Most of these foods are more fully described elsewhere in this work.

Comments on Table VI.16.1

Many of these foodstuffs, familiar in both the kitchens and apothecary shops of the eighteenth and nineteenth centuries, had been used as medicines for at least 2,000 years. As in the Middle Ages, their tastes were the most valuable clues as to how they could benefit the sick. Although some had clear-cut effects, especially the stronger cathartics, others were more speculative, as dictated by humoral and solidist theory, than verifiable.

One need not wonder that physicians prescribed these or any other time-tested remedies for as long as they did. Because 90 to 95 percent of adult patients recovered following treatment, whatever it was, their physicians had no reason not to conclude that their prescriptions benefited their patients. The double-blind controlled clinical trials on which we rely today to *prove* the therapeutic efficacy of putative remedies were not developed until the mid–twentieth century (Estes 1991a). Thus, although a few items listed above might have moved the bowels to a modest extent, most of their other effects, such as those on body tone, digestion, or uterine function, were only presumed to occur, in accord with prevalent pathophysiologic theories.

Table VI.16.1 *Past and present medicinal uses of flavorings and spices*

Angelica: Weak cathartic, tonic, carminative.
Anise: Tonic, pectoral, carminative; lactagogue.
Assafoetida: Antispasmodic, expectorant, emmenagogue, diuretic, diaphoretic, mild cathartic, anthelmintic.
Canella: Stomachic, gentle tonic.
Capers: Weak cathartic, diuretic, deobstruent.
Caraway: Stomachic, carminative, diuretic.
Cardamom: Carminative, diaphoretic.
Chocolate: Stomachic, antidysenteric.
Cinnamon: Tonic, stomachic, carminative, astringent.
Cloves: Tonic, mild styptic.
Coriander: Carminative.
Cumin: For plasters.
Dill: Carminative.
Fenugreek: Aphrodisiac; for emollient plasters.
Garlic: Tonic, diaphoretic, expectorant, diuretic, carminative, emmenagogue, rubefacient.
Ginger: Tonic; rubefacient.
Horse radish: Tonic, diuretic, diaphoretic.
Hyssop: Expectorant, antitussive, pectoral, carminative.
Juniper: Carminative, stomachic, diuretic, diaphoretic, emmenagogue.
Licorice: Cathartic, expectorant.
Marjoram: Tonic, cephalic, expectorant, errhine.
Mustard: Stomachic, digestive, diuretic, diaphoretic, emetic, mild cathartic, antiscorbutic; blistering agent.
Nutmeg–mace: Tonic, narcotic, stomachic, antiemetic, astringent.
Parsley: Carminative, aperient, diuretic, emmenagogue.
Peppermint: Tonic, carminative, antispasmodic.
Peppers: Stimulant, digestive, antispasmodic.
Pimento: Tonic, carminative.
Rosemary: Antispasmodic, sedative, cephalic, emmenagogue.
Saffron: Cordial, narcotic, antispasmodic, emmenagogue.
Sage: Astringent, carminative, stomachic, nerve tonic.
Sarsaparilla: Antirheumatic, antivenereal, demulcent, diaphoretic.
Sassafras: Weak cathartic, tonic, blood purifier, diuretic, diaphoretic, antirheumatic, antisyphilitic.
Sesame: Mild cathartic.
Spearmint: Carminative, stomachic, antispasmodic, antiemetic, anti-icteric.
Thyme: Analgesic for toothache.
Tumeric: Tonic, weak cathartic, emmenagogue, anti-icteric.
Wintergreen: Astringent, antidiarrheal, emmenagogue, lactagogue.

Interesting and odoriferous compounds, some of which have biological effects in animals or man, have been extracted from several of these flavorings and spices, but most cannot be related to the clinical effects listed. The few extracts that might have modest pharmacological activity include the gingerols isolated from ginger (they can stimulate cardiac action); the terpinem-4-ol in juniper (which can increase renal glomerular filtration and irritate the uterus); the mildly cathartic glycerrhizin in licorice; the apiol in parsley (which may promote diuresis and stimulate the uterus); the weak smooth-muscle relaxant menthol in the mints; and the extremely potent irritant capsicin in peppers. Safrole, which is responsible for the taste of sassafras, has been banned in the United States because it is carcinogenic to animals when administered in high doses; like nutmeg, it has mild stimulating effects in man (*Lawrence Review* 1987-91). Still, many of these items can be found in modern grocery stores and among over-the-counter remedies.

Comments on Table VI.16.2
It is difficult to discover how these fruits and nuts entered common medical usage, although it seems likely that their adoption followed the discovery of their gustatory merits. A few have a mild cathartic effect, oranges and strawberries might well appear cool to the taste, and the slightly bitter taste of others might make them seem astringent, but no consistent pattern seems to associate these foods medically.

Comments on Table VI.16.3
Lettuce and endive produce a cooling sensation, but the other alleged properties of lettuce probably owe more to its confusion with another lettuce species that was rarely prescribed by physicians. Several compounds have been extracted from chicory, including its aromatic principle, acetophenone, but none has any ascertainable role in the effects listed for it in this table. The oxalic acid in the sorrels might have contributed to their reputations as refrigerants and antiscorbutics at a time when acids were deemed appropriate for the treatment of scurvy (Estes 1979), but the irritating (and potentially dangerous) acid is unlikely to have had any true therapeutic effect (*Lawrence Review* 1987-91).

Table VI.16.2. *Past and present medicinal uses of fruits and nuts*

Almond milk: Diluent; mild cathartic; counteracts blisters.
Blackberries: Slightly astringent.
Cherries: Tonic, slightly narcotic, anthelmintic, antiseptic.
Currants: For sore throat.
Damsons: Tonic, astringent, cathartic, emetic.
Dates: Emollient, slightly astringent.
Elderberries: Cathartic, deobstruent, diuretic, diaphoretic.
Figs: Mild cathartic.
Lemons: Stomachic, antiseptic; antiscorbutic (after the 1790s).
Olive [oil]: Demulcent cathartic; antidote to rattlesnake venom.
Oranges: Tonic, refrigerant, antispasmodic, stomachic, carminative, antiseptic, antiscorbutic (after the 1790s).
Peaches: Cathartic, sedative, anthelmintic.
Pokeberries: Emetic, cathartic, mild narcotic.
Pomegranate: Cathartic, astringent, antidiarrheal, anthelmintic.
Raspberries: Refrigerant, stomachic, diuretic, diaphoretic.
Strawberries: Refrigerant, tonic, diuretic, cathartic.
Tamarinds: Cathartic, refrigerant.
White walnut: Anti-inflammatory, cathartic.

Table VI.16.3. *Past and present medicinal uses of vegetables*

Asparagus: Diuretic, weak cathartic, deobstruent.
Cabbage: Cathartic, emollient (Sauerkraut: antiscorbutic).
Celery: Weak cathartic, carminative.
Chicory: Cathartic, gastrointestinal tonic, stomachic, refrigerant.
Endive: Cooling weak cathartic.
Lettuce: Cooling sedative narcotic, antidiarrheal, antitussive.
Onion: Stomachic, diuretic, diaphoretic, expectorant.
Sorrel: Refrigerant, diuretic, weak cathartic, antidiarrheal, antiscorbutic.
Watercress: Weak cathartic, antiscorbutic.

Table VI.16.4. *Past and present medicinal uses of beverages*

Alcohol: Tonic, carminative, digestive; rubefacient.
Chocolate: See under flavorings and spices in Table VI.16.1
Coffee: Astringent, antiseptic, strong tonic, digestive; to stay awake.
Milk: To stimulate natural secretions; antiscorbutic.
Tea: Diluent, diuretic, diaphoretic.
Wine: Stomachic, diaphoretic, tonic, digestive, astringent.

Comments on Table VI.16.4

Alcohol and wine were among the first remedies subjected to quantitative experimental studies which, in the end, merely validated their age-old use as tonics. The major active ingredients in chocolate, coffee, and tea are, respectively, theobromine, caffeine, and theophylline, which share several pharmacological properties, such as diuresis and central nervous system stimulation, although to varying degrees. Theophylline is a mainstay of bronchodilator therapy for patients with asthma and related diseases, whereas caffeine still has a minor role as a stimulant, chiefly in a few over-the-counter painkillers (Estes 1991a).

Comments on Table VI.16.5

Barley water had been a common drink for the sick since antiquity, especially in low diets for fever patients. Barley, bread crumbs, and wheat or wheat flour contributed their soothing and gluten-based binding and stiffening qualities to plasters and wound dressings. The bran in oatmeal does increase stool bulk, but before the twentieth century, no medical use could have been made of oat bran's ability to bind cholesterol in the intestinal tract, which can help lower cholesterol concentrations in the blood. Ergot first entered medical usage as a result of its contamination of bread

Table VI.16.5. *Past and present medicinal uses of grains*

Barley: Refrigerant, demulcent.
Bread crumbs: For gastrointestinal symptoms; in plasters, to stimulate suppuration.
Ergot, on rye: For postpartum care.
Oats: Cathartic.
Wheat: Visceral tonic; paste for plasters.

Table VI.16.6. *Past and present medicinal uses of gums and roots*

Jujubes: Deobstruent, decongestant.
Manna: Cathartic, expectorant, carminative.
Marshmallow: Emollient, demulcent.
Slippery elm: Emollient, expectorant, antidiarrheal; demulcent dressing.

made from its agricultural host, rye. It was recommended for obstetrical use in Germany in 1582, and reintroduced for that purpose in 1787. In 1807, Dr. John Stearns of New York promoted its use for hastening birth, and in 1824 Dr. David Hosack of the same city recommended it for the control of postpartum bleeding (Estes 1990: 175), but such use remained controversial (Berman 1992). It is now well established that the alkaloids extracted from ergot are potent constrictors of blood vessels; they have been used to control postpartum bleeding in the twentieth century.

Comments on Table VI.16.6

None of these gummy plant extracts is known to contain pharmacologically active principles. They probably owe their roles in medicine to their soothing qualities. The slippery, or red, elm entered medical usage largely through the works of Samuel Thomson, the botanical physician who stimulated the practice of do-it-yourself medicine in the United States early in the nineteenth century (Estes 1992). Later in the century, New England Shakers, who had adopted Thomson's medical system, made and promoted a flour derived from the tree's bark (Estes 1991b).

Comments on Table VI.16.7

Although burned eggshells might well be presumed to neutralize acids, it is doubtful that they would have provided an efficient remedy for the hyperacidity that was frequently diagnosed after Réamur's discovery of hydrochloric acid in the stomach. It was probably a remedy that evolved out of the discovery that the calcium oxide produced by burning eggshells was chemically equivalent to the alkaline quicklime made by similar techniques. Egg whites, on the other hand, can help neutralize toxic metal ions in the stomach. The cathartic effect of yolks is arguable, but their reputation as a cure for jaundice most likely stems simply from the fact that they are yellow. The properties associated with honey in the eighteenth century were

Table VI.16.7. *Past and present medicinal uses of miscellaneous foodstuffs*

Eggs: Burned shells, as antacid; whites, as an antidote for copper and mercury poisoning; yolks, as cathartic or anti-icteric.
Honey: Weak cathartic, detergent, expectorant.
Rapeseed: Attenuating, detergent, antiseptic, diaphoretic.

probably speculative, and we do not know if it was used in ways similar to those of the Egyptian physicians. Rapeseed oil, now called canola oil, contains nothing that might have led physicians to deduce the properties with which they credited it.

Dietetics and Modern Food Sciences

By about 1900, medical dietetics assumed new forms and goals in the wake of experimental laboratory investigations that permitted physicians to incorporate the concept of metabolic needs into their professional thinking. Although the identification and isolation of vitamins over the following three decades nearly completed that story, daily requirements for carbohydrates, fats, proteins, minerals, and vitamins are still being debated and modified. Many of today's medical concerns about foods are related to their statistical associations with specific illnesses. While such topics are explored elsewhere in this work, consideration of the transition from old to new concepts of medical dietetics is pertinent here.

The first foods to provide a true cure of any disease were citrus fruits, but the ready response they elicited in scurvy patients was not, at first, recognized as the result of replacing a substance that was missing from their diet. Indeed, James Lind's celebrated experiment with oranges and lemons on HMS *Salisbury* in 1747 was not the negatively controlled clinical trial it is often said to have been: He was only comparing six acids, including the fruits, because scurvy was thought to be a kind of fever and, therefore, treatable with almost any cooling acid. Some thought that excess alkalinity caused scorbutic fever, which led to the same therapeutic conclusion. Moreover, Lind did not argue that citrus fruits were the best protection against scurvy; indeed, he continued to recommend several other acids. Marine surgeons had recognized the antiscorbutic value of lemons by at least 1617, but not until 1795 did the British navy adopt limes as standard protection against scurvy (the U.S. Navy followed suit in 1812), as evidence of their efficacy continued to accumulate. Even so, navy surgeons knew only that lemons, limes, and oranges could prevent or cure the disease, not that they replenished the body's stores of a vital principle. When, in 1784, the Swedish chemist Karl Wilhelm Scheele discovered citric acid in lemons, he erroneously assumed that it was the active therapeutic principle, and it was not until the 1920s that the true antiscorbutic principle, ascorbic acid, was isolated and identified as essential to life (Estes 1979, 1985, 1990: 49, 116).

Studies of the physiology of digestion provided essential stepping-stones to the development of modern dietetic therapeutics early in the nineteenth century. In England, William Prout classified foods into the three major groups that are, in retrospect, recognizable as carbohydrate, protein, and fat. Friedrich Tiedemann and Leopold Gmelin reported from Heidelberg,

in 1826, that the ingestion of any kind of food increased the amount of acid in the stomach, and that the acid could dissolve all foods. Some investigators continued to argue that lactic acid was the active principle of digestion, but in 1852 Friedrich Bidder and Carl Schmidt of the German university at Dorpat, Estonia – then emerging as the first academic center for the study of pharmacology – showed that the free hydrochloric acid discovered by Réamur was the only acid in gastric juice (Leicester 1974: 147, 161–3).

The experiments on gastric function performed by U.S. Army surgeon William Beaumont led him to conclude, in 1833, that although animal and grain products are easier to digest than most vegetable foods, the differences are attributable only to the relative sizes of their constituent fibers, not to their other properties. He emphasized this by pointing out that the action of the hydrochloric acid in gastric juice is the same on all foodstuffs (Beaumont 1833: 275–8), as Tiedemann and Gmelin had shown.

By the 1840s, digestive enzymes had been found in saliva, gastric juice, and pancreatic juice, and by 1857 Claude Bernard had demonstrated that the glucose that provides the body's energy is released from glycogen that has been synthesized and stored in the liver (Leicester 1974: 165–9). It was probably these discoveries that permitted the eventual abandonment of dietetic therapies that had originated in the ancient world, especially when it became apparent that food itself does not alter normal gastric acid or digestive enzyme secretion, although both were eventually shown to be altered in specific diseases.

In 1816, François Magendie of Bordeaux found that dietary sources of nitrogen, especially meat, are essential for health in dogs, and that all the nitrogen necessary to sustain life comes from food, not air (Leicester 1974: 146). His work prompted the studies of Justus von Liebig, of Giessen, in Germany, which by 1840 had laid the foundations for the study of metabolism and other aspects of human nutrition. He showed, for instance, that the nitrogenous substances present in meat and some vegetable foods are assimilated into animal tissues, while carbohydrates like starch and sugar are consumed during oxidative respiration. Liebig's work began to elucidate the complex chemical interactions of foodstuffs with the fabric of the body (Drummond and Wilbraham 1958: 285–6, 345; Holmes 1973). In 1866, his pupil Carl von Voit showed that carbohydrates and fats supply all the energy used by the body, while its chief nitrogenous components, the proteins, are derived from dietary protein of both plant and animal origin (Leicester 1974: 192).

Perhaps with these discoveries in mind, in 1865 Liebig began to promote an "Extract of Meat" he had devised as a medicine for specific illnesses, such as typhoid fever and inflammation of the ovaries. He marketed it both as a proprietary remedy and, in Germany (but not Britain or the United States), as a prescription drug. Although it was shown almost immediately to lack meat's nutritive elements, the extract was a success in European, British, and American kitchens for many years afterward, especially when Liebig redirected its advertising toward over-the-counter consumers instead of physicians and pharmacists, who were unconvinced of its therapeutic value. The extract also prompted development of the first commercial formulations of infant foods, which were advertised as promoting growth and preventing disease (Apple 1986; Finlay 1992).

Like Liebig's Meat Extract and many botanical drugs, several foods were medically important in the eyes of nineteenth-century laymen, even if not in those of contemporary physicians. Some dietary lore was pure mythology, such as the aphrodisiacal properties imputed to nutmegs, tomatoes, quinces, and artichokes (Taberner 1985: 204-6, 60-3). However, many over-the-counter remedies or their ingredients had the imprimatur of regular medicine, as is evident in British and American home-medicine texts.

Such books evaluated not only the nutritive value of foods but also their specific physiological effects in health and disease. By way of example, when J. S. Forsyth prepared the twenty-second edition of William Buchan's *Domestic Medicine,* he moved the chapter on diet from near the end to the very beginning, and incorporated into it ideas he had developed in his own *Natural and Medical Dieteticon* (Buchan 1809: 413-31, 1828: 19-40). Forsyth began by explaining that the "constant use of bread and animal substances excites an unnatural thirst, and leads to the immoderate use of beer and other stimulating liquors, which generate disease, and reduce the lower orders of the people to a state of indigence" (Buchan 1828: 19). Moreover, he said: "The plethoric . . . should eat sparingly of animal food. It yields far more blood than vegetables taken in the same quantity, and, of course, may induce inflammatory disorders. It acts as a stimulus to the whole system, by which means the circulation of the blood is greatly accelerated" (Buchan 1828: 20). In other words, although a meat diet is best suited to the physiological needs of laborers, it predisposes them to intemperance and poverty.

Forsyth differentiated vegetables and meat in terms of their acidity and alkalinity. He said that plant foods are more acidic and lighter in the stomach; in addition, they mix more readily in the stomach with other foods, and are more constipating, than meat. By contrast, he thought that animal foods display the "greater tendency to alkalescency and putrefaction," which meant that they might cause diarrhea and dysentery, even if only rarely. Although in Forsyth's opinion they mixed less well with other foods during digestion, they did help keep the bowels regular. He concluded by pointing out that meat produces "a more dense stimulating elastic blood" than does a vegetable diet, because animal food "stretches and causes a greater degree of resistance in the solids, as well as excites them to stronger action" (Buchan 1828: 39-40). This explained the value of meat to the health of the workingman within the contexts of contemporary chemical knowledge and of the humoral and solidist medical traditions.

Although Buchan and his posthumous editor wrote for British readers in the first instance, their work found receptive audiences in the United States, where do-it-yourself medicine flourished more than in England. In 1830, John Gunn of Knoxville, Tennessee, explained to the people of America (he dedicated his book to President Andrew Jackson) that "[f]ood . . . is intended to support nature" (Gunn 1830: 124). According to Gunn, because the most nourishing food is of animal origin, it can overheat and exhaust the body, unlike vegetable foods. In this respect he went beyond Forsyth's caveats. Inasmuch as plant foods cause stomach acidity, flatulence, and debility if they are the only items in the diet, Gunn recommended a diet with balanced amounts of meat and vegetables.

Guides to diet as a way to health proliferated throughout the nineteenth century. Some were mixed with exhortations against alcohol or doctors' drugs, while others promoted the benefits of physical culture. Gymnastics enthusiast Dio Lewis, for example, published books specifically related to gastrointestinal health, including *Talks about People's Stomachs* (Boston, 1870) and *Our Digestion; or My Jolly Friend's Secret* (Philadelphia, 1874). The latter title alone suggests that the book focuses on how to avoid the unpleasant sour feeling that characterizes dyspepsia. Similar titles appeared in England, such as W. T. Fernie's *Meals Medicinal: . . . Curative Foods From the Cook; In Place of Drugs From the Chemist* (Bristol, 1905).

Some British writers had been promoting meatless diets for a century before Dr. William Lambe claimed, in 1806, that such diets are not hazardous, and could even cure tuberculosis. His work seems to have prompted Percy Bysshe Shelley, at the age of 21, to write a vegetarian tract that was republished many times between 1813 and 1884. But most physicians, a conservative lot, argued that plant foods are hard to digest, and would have agreed with Forsyth that meat is essential for maintaining strength and vitality (Green 1986: 46-7; Nissenbaum 1988: 45-9).

Thus, by the end of the nineteenth century, scientific studies of the chemistry of foods were being translated into professional texts and domestic health guides written by physicians. Most of the foodstuffs used as medicines during the 25 centuries between the era of Hippocrates and the discovery of pathogenic microbes in the 1870s quietly disappeared from pharmacopoeias in the early twentieth century, as did the vast majority of historic drugs. From then on, until the recent emergence of medical nutrition as a clinical subspecialty, regular medicine nearly abandoned the therapeutic application of diet to disease, save for patients with specific biochemical defects of intermediary metabolism or those with vitamin deficiencies.

In the meantime, however, some of the newly emerging information about foods (and distortions of it) was being exploited by promoters who functioned outside the mainstream of regular medicine, but who well understood the needs of mainstream Americans. They and their followers liked to think of themselves as innovators or "reformers."

Alternative Dietetics

A number of nineteenth-century American health reformers – many of them energetic entrepreneurs – mounted effective populist attacks on both traditional and modern medical ideas simultaneously. Their chief selling point was that their ideas were more prophylactic than curative, a highly liberal position in a proud new republic in which regular medicine was dominated by political conservatives.

The allure of do-it-yourself medicine for the traditionally self-reliant American public was quickened by Samuel Thomson, an itinerant New England healer who, beginning in 1805, found that his system of botanical medicine was more profitable than farming. Although the curative focus of his system revolved around a relatively small number of remedies made from indigenous plants, Thomson also emphasized the importance of proper diet for health. His own version of the Hippocratic concept of the humors presumed that all disease arises from disordered digestion, resulting in insufficient heat for maintaining normal body function (Estes 1992).

Regular physicians were privately incensed at the economic competition inherent in Thomson's system – one of his marketing slogans was "Every man be his own physician" – but in public they could only charge him with unscientific reliance on a single dogma, his insistence that all disease was caused by cold. Such notions were not entirely new. In 1682 an anonymous French writer who thought the large intestine was the primary seat of all disease had urged his readers to be their own physicians, and to use botanical remedies that grew in their own country (Thorndike 1958, 8: 409). But in the 1680s, such suggestions must have been seen as only adding to the surfeit of emerging medical ideas and not as heresy or competition.

The true fountainhead of the healthy diet in America was Sylvester Graham, a Presbyterian clergyman who preached the physiological benefits of abstinence from alcohol and sex, as well as dietary reliance on homegrown and homemade whole wheat bread. His medical notions were not entirely original, however. They stemmed largely from those of François-Joseph-Victor Broussais, a physician in Napoleonic France who had taught that all disease was caused by an irritation in the gastrointestinal tract. Therefore, said Broussais, almost any illness can be cured by removing the responsible stimulating irritation with bleeding and his version of a low diet.

Because of the historical association of meat eating with potentially pathogenic stimulation, vegetarian writers such as Graham associated avoidance of animal foods, alcohol, and sexual arousal with physical, moral, and spiritual health. The ideal diet he began advocating in the 1830s consisted of two small meatless meals daily that included whole wheat bread and cold water. Graham said that his regimen would preclude the exhaustion and debility that usually follow excessive stimulation (Nissenbaum 1988: 20, 39–49, 57–9, 126–7, 142–3).

His influence has persisted to the present in several guises. Graham certainly fostered the notion that a meat diet was the major cause of dyspepsia (Green 1986: 164). The self-sufficient Shakers, who farmed and sold medicinal herbs, adopted his teachings along with those of Thomson, and sold flour made to Graham's specifications. However, although the Shakers believed that dyspepsia was the quintessential disease of postwar America, they were not vegetarians themselves (Green 1986: 30–1; Estes 1991b).

The Grahamite proselytizing of Dr. Russell T. Trall has had the most lasting impact of all. He emerged in the 1840s as an energetic and prolific promoter of hydropathy, the water-cure techniques introduced in Austria by Vincenz Preissnitz, who, like Thomson, found healing more lucrative than farming (Armstrong and Armstrong 1991: 81–2). Preissnitz did not preach vegetarianism, but his American disciple did. Trall rationalized his therapeutic methods by updating the ancient four temperaments in what he said was a more "practical" classification.

He associated the nervous temperament with the nervous system, and the sanguine temperament with the arteries and lungs. He explained that these two temperaments were more active, or irritable, than the bilious temperament, which he paired with the veins and musculoskeletal system, or the lymphatic temperament, paired with the abdominal viscera. Thus, Trall described the gastrointestinal tract as torpid and incapable of irritation in persons with a lymphatic temperament (Trall 1852: 287–90).

Although he cited Liebig's differentiation of nitrogenous from non-nitrogenous foods, Trall based much of his dietary argument on his own reading of Genesis 1:29: "Behold, I have given you every herb bearing seed, which is upon the face of all the earth, and every tree in which is the fruit of a tree yielding seed; to you it shall be for meat." From this, Trall concluded that "the vegetable kingdom is the ordained source of man's sustenance" (Trall 1852: 399).

He went on to adduce anatomical, physiological, and "experimental" (actually, testimonial) evidence for the medical efficacy of a vegetable diet. He stated that the secretions of vegetable eaters are "more pure, bland, and copious, and the excretions . . . are less offensive to the senses," and that their blood is "less prone to the inflammatory and putrid diatheses." As a result, their "mental passions are more governable and better balanced," a conclusion that Graham would have seconded, although he might not have accepted Trall's association of any temperament with a nonirritable intestinal tract (Trall 1852: 410–12). Neither would Graham have tolerated Trall's opinion that certain boiled or broiled meats, white fish, and an occasional egg were acceptable. Still, the major item on the menu at Trall's water-cure establishments was unleavened bread made of coarse-ground, unsifted meal like Graham's (Trall 1852: 421–4).

Ellen G. White, who began the Seventh-Day Adventist movement in the late 1840s, at the time Graham and Trall were achieving fame, was interested in the teachings of both. The Adventists' continuing adherence to a vegetable diet today is presumed to be responsible, in large measure, for their lesser risk of major degenerative diseases (Webster and Rawson 1979).

In 1866, Mrs. White opened the Western Health Reform Institute in Battle Creek, Michigan, as an Adventist retreat that served its guests two vegetarian meals a day, modeled on those advocated by Russell Trall, along with the full range of water cures. Ten years later, Dr. John Harvey Kellogg became the Institute's medical director. There he invented and prescribed the original versions of "Granola" and peanut butter, and the rolled breakfast cereals that he developed in collaboration with his younger brother, Will Keith Kellogg. Not only were cereals nutritious, said the brothers, but they would also counteract the autointoxicants then being accused of causing many illnesses, and facilitate bowel movements.

Charles W. Post, a former patient at the Battle Creek Sanitarium (as J. H. Kellogg renamed it), followed suit with his own "Postum" (1895), "Grape-Nuts" (1898), and "Post Toasties" (1908). The Kelloggs had set up a company to manufacture their products, but it was after the brothers had parted ways that W. K. Kellogg in 1906 introduced "Corn Flakes." Although the Kelloggs and Post had many competitors among health-food manufacturers in the Battle Creek area alone, their products still dominate the marketplace for breakfast cereals. Their initial success was attributable largely to their advertised medical uses. Like other bran foods, W. K. Kellogg's "All-Bran" was first marketed as a relief from constipation. In 1931 Nabisco's "Shredded Wheat," a competing product, was proclaimed to offer "Strength in Every Shred" (Green 1986: 305–12; Whorton 1988; Armstrong and Armstrong 1991: 99–119).

A few other foods entered the realm of medical usage outside the framework established by Sylvester Graham. The most visible was probably the tomato, one of the most fleeting therapeutic discoveries in the history of medicine. Many Europeans had regarded it as inedible or poisonous after it was brought from the New World in the 1540s, because it belongs to the same family as the deadly nightshade. Its therapeutic value was reported in London as early as 1731, but when sent to North America soon afterward, it was only as an ornamental plant (Smith 1991).

In 1825, Dr. Thomas Sewall reported, in Washington, D.C., that tomatoes could cure bilious disease, probably because they have particles that are yellow, as is jaundice, produced by the accumulation of yellowish bile pigments in the skin as a result of liver or gall bladder disease. Then, in 1835, a brazen medical entrepreneur, John Cook Bennett, began telling Americans that tomatoes could cure diarrhea and dyspepsia. He claimed that Indians used them to promote diuresis, while others said they were good for fevers. The agricultural press spread Bennett's enthusiasm, and within five years several extracts of tomato had been marketed as typical panaceas (Smith 1991).

An 1865 advertisement claimed that "Tomato pills, will cure all your ills." However, reports of the hazards of tomatoes, as well as their lack of therapeutic efficacy, had already begun to resurface. Although the merits of tomatoes were being debated as late as the 1896 annual meeting of the American Medical Association, they had long since lost their medical appeal – but by then they had become firmly established in American cookery (Smith 1991).

The role of food as therapy is still central to several modern alternative-healing systems. Naturopathic healers (also known as naturists) cite Samuel Thomson as their chief source of authority, declaring that the "Naturist will be both dietician and herbalist." They, too, look on the stomach as "in almost every instance the seat of disease," and like Russell Trall, they cite Genesis 1:29 (Clymer 1960: 12, 33, orig. 1902). Some naturopathic regimens include coffee enemas, administered at two-hour intervals, to cleanse the intestines.

Occasionally, a small number of people will use a food for medical reasons despite evidence of the dangers of such usage. For example, unpasteurized milk has been promoted neither by advertising nor by any organization – its use seems to be inspired chiefly by folklore, supported by its consumers' supposition that it is a matter of freedom of choice. Those who persist in using raw milk, sometimes illegally, claim that it has more nutritive value than pasteurized milk, that it increases their resistance to disease and enhances their fertility, and that it contains unidentified substances, such as an "antistiffness factor" that helps prevent rheumatism (Potter et al. 1984).

When the word "macrobiotic" entered English usage in the early eighteenth century, it signified a diet or other rules of conduct that would prolong life. Its modern usage appeared in the early 1960s, when a Japanese, Georges Ohsawa, introduced a new concept in dietary therapy. He began with the premise that there is "no disease that cannot be cured by 'proper' therapy." His idea of "proper" therapy, which originated in ancient Chinese ideas of the balance between the complementary forces of yin and yang, was based on white grain cereals and on avoiding fluids. As much as 30 percent of the diet could be meat when the patient began the prescribed regimen, but by the time he or she had progressed through the entire ten-step sequence, which Ohsawa called the "Zen macrobiotic diet," the patient would be eating only grain products. In the 1970s, Michio Kushi revised Ohsawa's diet after its inventor had died, but without its meatless extremes. In addition, Kushi developed a cadre of "counselors" whose special training permits them alone to make diagnoses within the system. Many do so by iridology, which associates segments of the iris with specific parts of the body (iridology has also been practiced by chiropractors, among others). Because Ohsawa had said that the macrobiotic diet could cure any disease, it is sometimes resorted to by victims of cancer, who are instructed to chew each mouthful 150 times, to enhance the food's strengthening yang properties and to preclude overeating; healthy people need chew only 50 times (Macrobiotic diets 1959; AMA Council 1971; Simon, Wortham, and Mitas 1979; Cassileth and Brown 1988).

In the 1920s, a German physician, Max Gerson, developed a dietary cure for cancer based on his belief (which accorded with the pioneering studies of intermediary metabolism by Otto Warburg) that the rate of cancer cell growth depends on imbalances in the aerobic and anaerobic metabolic reactions of the malignant cells. Gerson said his diet would restore those balances to normal by, among other things, increasing potassium intake. It resembles the diet served at Russell Trall's water-cure establishments, with the addition of calves' liver, a mixture of special fruit juices, and coffee enemas. Gerson refined his regimen after emigrating to the United States, and it is still available from his heirs in Tijuana, Mexico (American Cancer Society 1990; Green 1992).

Other clinics in Tijuana offer diets that are said to cure cancer by strengthening the immune system and minimizing the intake of potential toxins. Such programs are often accompanied by vitamins, minerals, enzymes, and gland extracts and by stimuli to moral and religious health that are reminiscent of the activities provided at the Battle Creek Sanitarium (American Cancer Society 1991). Several diets and dietary supplements have been marketed without any medicalized rationalization beyond that used to promote five products sold by United Sciences of America, Inc.: "to provide all Americans with the potential of optimum health and vital energy" (Stare 1986).

Modern foods that originated in nineteenth-century efforts to improve the American diet are as healthful as their nutritional content allows. Nevertheless, today many of them - especially breakfast cereals - are fortified with vitamins and minerals, often to enhance their presumed acceptability to consumers. But no one has yet discovered a food or devised a diet that can be proved to cure diseases, such as arthritis, cancer, or any other illness that is not the result of a specific nutritional deficit.

Dietetics in Other Cultures

Important discoveries in the biochemistry of food began to appear in the twentieth century, many of them soon after the discovery of vitamins. Eventually they led to the somewhat contentious discussions of the influence of specific foods on human illness that are a recurrent feature of American culture today. We have few written records that permit detailed comparisons of the dietary medicine practiced in cultures other than those whose roots were in ancient Egypt, Greece, and Rome. But the broad outlines of medical dietetics in a few other cultures can be ascertained.

Among North American Indians

There is evidence that at least some Indian groups of North America had specific ideas of what constituted a proper diet, and that they took dietary precautions when they were sick, such as starving a fever. Colonists reported that New England Indians remained healthy so long as they continued to eat their usual foods, and that they rejected some English foods even when, as hunter-gatherers, they were at the mercy of an uncertain food supply (Vogel 1970: 251-3).

Several Indian societies put plant foods to differing therapeutic uses. Pumpkins were used by the Zunis to treat the skin wounds made by cactus spines, but by the Menominees as a diuretic. New England Indians thought that sarsaparilla was useful as food when they were on the move, whereas the Iroquois used it to treat wounds. The Penobscots of the East Coast and the Kwakiutls of the West Coast used sarsaparilla as a cough remedy, and the Ojibwas applied it to boils and carbuncles (Vogel 1970: 356-61). It seems clear that such uses were as much based on the *post hoc ergo propter hoc* fallacy as were those in the Hippocratic–Galenic tradition. The Aztecs found some uses for the indigenous flora of Mexico that resembled those of their unrelated neighbors north of the Rio Grande. Thus, both Aztecs and the Indians who lived in Texas used the pods and seeds of edible mesquite as a remedy for diseased eyes (Ortiz de Montellano 1990).

In the Far East

The Chinese diet was even more rigidly associated with physiological concepts than that of the Graeco-Roman tradition. Balance between the classical complementary forces of yin and yang dominated the structure and function of the body, and was as important to health as were balances among the Hippocratic humors. The basic digestive processes described in Chinese texts resemble those postulated by Aristotle, although only the latter based some of his conclusions on dissections. The Chinese assumed that food passes from the stomach to the liver, where it yields its vital forces to the muscles, and its gases to the heart (the origin of both blood and animal heat), while its liquid components move to the spleen, then the lungs, and finally the bladder (Leicester 1974: 45–9).

According to the teachings of Huang Ti, the mythical Yellow Emperor said to have reigned about 2600 B.C., but probably not written down before 206 B.C., proper medical treatment includes foods that can correct the patient's "mode of life." Because the Chinese recognized five elements – water, fire, wood, metal, and earth – the number five recurs throughout Chinese thought: They associated each of the five major organs – liver, heart, lungs, spleen, and kidneys – with one of the "five grains," the "five tree-fruits," the "five domesticated [meat] animals," and the "five vegetables," in terms of any organ's nourishment. In ancient China, as in the medieval European tradition, taste was correlated with a food's action, but within a different framework: Sweet foods were appropriate to the health of the liver, sour foods to the heart, bitter foods to the lungs, salty foods to the spleen, and pungent foods to the kidneys (Veith 1949: 1–9, 55–8).

The canonical sweet foods of Chinese dietetics (rice, dates, beef, and mallows) were believed to enter the body through the spleen, to produce a slowing effect. Sour foods (small peas, plums, dog meat, and leeks) enter via the liver, and produce an astringent, or binding, effect. Bitter foods (wheat, almonds, mutton, and scallions) enter via the heart, and strengthen, or dry, the body. Salty foods (large beans, chestnuts, pork, and coarse greens) enter through the kidneys, with a softening effect. And, finally, pungent foods (millet, peaches, chicken meat, and onions) disperse the smallest particles of the body after entering it via the lungs. One important precept that followed from these complex relationships was that a patient should avoid foods of the correlative taste whenever he or she had a disease in the organ through which that taste enters the body (Veith 1949: 199–207). The traditional Ayurvedic medical practices of India share many concepts with those of China, although their professional literatures differ in their underlying cosmological premises (Leicester 1974: 51–2).

Chinese medical dietetics loosened its adherence to strict rules as the centuries passed. For instance, although Ko Hung (under the nom de plume Pao-p'u Tzu) described basic principles for constructing healthy diets in about A.D. 326, he did not prescribe specific foods as cures, even if he did maintain that a patient's blood supply can be increased simply by eating more food (Huard and Wong 1968: 19–23). Yet eventually, as European dietary and medical notions penetrated the Far East, many traditional Chinese remedies disappeared – but not all of them.

By contrast, the medical lore of neighboring Tibet did not succumb to external influence. Along lines that Galen might have approved, Tibetan healers classified patients, in the first instance, as wind-types, bile-types, or phlegm-types, and, secondarily, by habitus, complexion, powers of endurance, amount of sleep, personality, and life span. For each patient type and subtype – they were all mutually exclusive – doctors prescribed specific medicines and foods, although their prescriptions show that they recognized more mixtures of the basic types than might have been supposed from their texts alone (Finckh 1988: 68–73).

Food or Drug? The Example of Garlic

Therapeutic descriptions by medical authorities since Dioscorides are still being cited in order to market some foods that were used as medicine in the ancient world. Such foods are not advertised as remedies; if they were in the United States, at least, they would be subject to the proofs of efficacy and safety required by the Food and Drug Administration. Nevertheless, they illustrate the continuing difficulty of devising mutually exclusive definitions of foods and drugs. The long history of garlic as a medical remedy is not only a case in point; it also exemplifies historical changes in medical theory.

Garlic in Ancient and Medieval Medicine

Garlic is the bulb of *Allium sativum,* a member of the lily family; the Romans derived the Latin genus name from a Celtic word for pungent bitterness. Ancient Egyptians did not use garlic as a remedy, but they did include it in a foul-smelling amulet designed to keep illness away from children (Sigerist 1951: 283). It was also found among Tutankhamen's burial goods – as a seasoning (Block 1985; Manniche 1989: 70–1). Modern Sudanese villagers, like some ancient Egyptians, place garlic in a woman's vagina to determine if she is pregnant; if she is, the characteristic odor will appear in her breath the next day (Estes 1989: 117). Ancient Mesopotamians prescribed garlic for toothache and painful urination and incorporated it in amulets against disease, as did the Egyptians (Levey 1966: 251). Traditional Chinese medicine associated garlic with the spleen, kidneys, and stomach, while Ayurvedic practitioners in India considered it a panacea, even if its specific actions were understood in the humoral and solidist traditions (Hobbs 1992).

The first-century testimonies of Dioscorides and Pliny the Elder provide similar pictures of the use of garlic in Graeco-Roman practice. The nearly complete text of its description by Dioscorides is given here because his book was the bedrock of virtually all herbal lore and prescription writing for the next 15 centuries. The translation is from the first – and still only – English version (1655) of his *Materia Medica:*

It hath a sharp, warming biting qualitie, expelling of flatulencies, and disturbing of the belly, and drying of the stomach causing of thirst, & of puffing up, breeding of boyles in ye outsyde of the body, dulling the sight of the eyes. . . . Being eaten, it drives out the broade wormes, and drawes away the urine. It is good, as none other thing, for such as are bitten of vipers, or of the Haemorrhous [hemorrhoids], wine being taken presently after, or else that being beaten small in wine, & soe dranck. It is applyed also by ye way of Cataplasme [a watery poultice] both for the same purposes profitably, as also layd upon such as are bitten of a mad dogge. Being aten, it is good against the chaunge of waters. . . . It doth cleare the arteries, & being eaten either raw or [boiled], it doth assuage old coughes. Being dranck with decoction of [oregano], it doth kill lice and nitts. But being burnt, and tempered with hon[e]y it doth cure the sugillationes oculorum [black eyes], and Alopeciae [bald spots] being anointed [with it], but for the Alopeciae (it must be applyed) with unguentum Nardinum [an extract of *Nardostachys jatamansi*]. And with salt & oyle it doth heale [papular eruptions]. It doth take away also the Vitiligenes, & the Lichenes, & the Lentigenes, and the running ulcers of the head, and the furfures [purpural spots], & ye Lepras [other spots, not leprosy], with hon[e]y. Being boiled with Taeda [pine tar] and franckincense, & kept in the mouth it doth assuage the paine of ye teeth. And with figge leaves & [cumin] it is a Cataplasme for such as are bitten of the Mygale [shrew-mouse]. But the leafes decoction is an insession [insertion into the vagina] that brings downe the Menstrua & the Secundas. It is also taken by way of suffumigation [fumigation, in which the patient stands over the burning medicine so that its fumes rise into her vagina] for ye same purpose. But the stamping that is made of it and ye black olive together, called Myrton, doth move the urine & open ye mouths of ye veines & it is good also for the Hydropicall [edematous] (Dioscorides 1934: 188–91).

In short, Dioscorides says that garlic expels intestinal worms and skin parasites, protects against venomous animals, neutralizes internal and external inflammations of many kinds, relieves toothaches and coughs, reduces hemorrhoids, and stimulates menstruation. Most important of all for later writers, garlic removes excess fluid from the body by dilating blood vessels and stimulating the kidneys.

Pliny, on the other hand, was an inquisitive encyclopedist, not a physician. In his *Natural History* he lists many of the same uses for garlic. But whereas only Dioscorides says that it can move the urine, Pliny adds that garlic can cure epilepsy, cause sleep, stimulate the libido, and neutralize the poisonous effects of

aconite and henbane (although such antidotal effects are unlikely) (Manniche 1989: 70–1; Hobbs 1992). Together, he and Dioscorides dictated the therapeutic uses of garlic for centuries.

Thus, al-Kindi, a royal tutor in ninth-century Baghdad, transmitted lessons he had learned from Greek and Roman sources when he said that garlic was good for inflamed ears (Levey 1966: 251). As Arabic works became available in European languages, ancient remedies were systematized within an increasingly rigid humoral framework. Consequently, the entry for garlic in a late–fourteenth-century *Tacuinum Sanitatis* says: "*Nature:* Warm in the second degree, dry in the third. *Optimum:* The kind that does not have too pungent a smell. *Usefulness:* Against poisons. *Dangers:* For the faculty of expulsion, and the brain. *Neutralization of the Dangers:* With vinegar and oil" (Arano 1976, plates 96–7). Such information changed from time to time, perhaps as doctors changed their minds, but also perhaps because of errors in transcribing manuscripts: A slightly later version of the same health handbook says exactly the same things about garlic, but describes it as warm in the fourth degree.

The most famous surgeon in sixteenth-century Europe, Ambroise Paré, based his therapeutic assessments on his own observations, perhaps because he had not learned his profession by scholastic disputation in a university. He thought garlic's major value was as a preventive against serious contagions:

Such as by the use of garlick have not their heads troubled, nor their inward parts inflamed, as Countrey people, and such as are used to it, to such there can bee no more certain preservative and antidote against the pestiferous fogs or mists, and the nocturnal obscurity, than to take it in the morning with a draught of good wine; for it being abundantly diffused presently over all the body, fils up the passages thereof, and strengtheneth it in a moment (Paré 1634: 823–4, 1031).

Paré's therapeutic reasoning is obscure; he seems to have presumed an analogy between garlic and onions, both of which he classified among the hottest of all remedies, those warm in the fourth degree. Surgeons who agreed with his Galenic assumptions quickly adopted an onion poultice Paré had invented on the premise that onions "attract, draw forth, and dissipate the imprinted heate" (Sigerist 1944).

Throughout the seventeenth century, physicians and laymen alike employed garlic as a diuretic and for virtually all the other uses listed by Pliny and Dioscorides, as well as for its ability to protect against contagious diseases (Leighton 1970: 306–7; Hobbs 1992). It was the major ingredient in one of more than 50 prescriptions recommended by the eminent London physician Thomas Willis for treating serious respiratory disease, especially consumption (Willis

1692: 86). As late as the early nineteenth century, physicians still relied on the properties that Dioscorides had ascribed to garlic, as revealed by its description in an influential 1794 compendium of medical practice:

The root applied to the skin inflames. . . . Its smell is extremely penetrating and diffusive; when the root is applied to the feet, its scent is soon discovered in the breath; and taken internally, its smell is communicated to the urine, or the matter of an issue, and perspires through the pores of the skin. This pungent root stimulates the whole body. Hence, in cold leucophlegmatic habits, it proves a powerful expectorant, diuretic, and if the patient be kept warm, sudorific; it has also been supposed to be emmenagogue. In catarrhous disorders of the breast, flatulent cholics, hysterical, and other diseases proceeding from laxity of the solids, it has generally good effects: it has likewise been found serviceable in some hydropic cases. . . . The liberal use of garlick is apt to occasion headachs, flatulencies, febrile heats, inflammatory distempers, and sometimes discharges of blood from the haemorrhoidal vessels. In hot bilious constitutions, where there is already a degree of irritation, and where there is reason to suspect an unsound state of the viscera, this stimulating medicine is manifestly improper [contraindicated], and never fails to aggravate the distemper. Garlick made into an ointment with oils, &c. and applied externally, is said to resolve . . . cold tumors, and has been greatly esteemed in cutaneous diseases. It has likewise been sometimes employed as a repellent. When applied in the form of a poultice to the pubis, it has sometimes proved effectual in producing a discharge of urine, when retention has arisen from a want of due action of the bladder; and some authors have recommended, in certain cases of deafness, the introduction of a single clove, wrapt in thin muslin or gauze, into the meatus auditorius [ear canal] (*Edinburgh New Dispensatory* 1794: 87–8).

The *Dispensatory,* which reflects contemporary therapeutic practices at the Royal Infirmary of Edinburgh, also points out that garlic has been reported to be an effective treatment for malaria and smallpox. William Buchan of Edinburgh described a garlic ointment for whooping cough that could be prepared at home:

by beating [it] in a mortar . . . with an equal quantity of hog's lard. With this the soles of the feet may be rubbed twice or thrice a day; but the best method is to spread it upon a rag, and apply it in the form of a plaster. It should be

renewed every night and morning at least, as the garlic soon loses its virtue (Buchan 1809: 212).

James Thacher presented selected aspects of the Edinburgh professors' views of garlic in his influential *American New Dispensatory* (Thacher 1813: 135–6). The first U.S. *Pharmacopoeia* (1820), which owed much of its content to its Edinburgh counterpart, included garlic among the remedies accepted by the American medical profession. Its 1905 edition listed it for the last time, but garlic as a recommended remedy remained in the United States as late as the 1936 edition of the *National Formulary* (Vogel 1970: 306–7).

Garlic during the Scientific Revolution

Solidist theories of pathophysiology melded well with the emergence of experimental chemistry in the eighteenth century. In 1822, Jacob Bigelow, a professor of medicine at Harvard, based much of his brief description of garlic's effects on those of its active principle, recently isolated as an oil:

Garlic and other plants of its genus have a well known offensive odour and taste, which, however, in a weakened state, render them an agreeable condiment with food. These qualities depend on a thick, acrid, yellowish, volatile oil, which may be separated by distillation, leaving the bulbs nearly inert. Garlic is stimulant, expectorant and diuretic. It is given in the form of syrup in chronic coughs, and the secondary stages of pneumonia; also, in combination with other medicines, in dropsy. Externally the bruised bulbs, in the form of a poultice, act as rubefacients (Bigelow 1822: 58).

An important reference text published 50 years later describes the effects of garlic much as both Dioscorides and Bigelow had, but within the more explicit context of solidist physiology:

Its effects on the system are those of a general stimulant. It quickens the circulation, excites the nervous system, promotes expectoration in debility of the lungs, produces diaphoresis or diuresis according as the patient is kept warm or cool, and acts upon the stomach as a tonic and carminative. It is also said to be emmenagogue. . . . Moderately employed, it is beneficial in enfeebled digestion and flatulence. . . . It has been given with advantage in chronic catarrh, and other pectoral affections in which the symptoms of inflammation have been subdued, and a relaxed state of the vessels remains. . . . If taken too largely, or in excited states of the system, garlic is apt to occasion gastric irritation, flatulence, hemorrhoids, headache, and fever. As a medicine, it is at present more used externally than inwardly. Bruised, and applied to the feet, it acts very beneficially, . . . in disorders of the head; and is especially useful in the febrile complaints of children, by quieting restlessness and producing sleep. Its juice ... is frequently used as a liniment in infantile convulsions, and other spasmodic or nervous affections in children (Wood and Bache 1874: 87-9).

Although garlic was not among the materia medica of Thomson (Estes 1992), one of his followers, the prominent eclectic physician John King, described its efficacy as a gastric tonic, as an anthelmintic, and in respiratory illnesses, especially those of children (Hobbs 1992). Despite the Shakers' unreserved reliance on Thomson's teachings, they recommended garlic as a stimulating tonic to promote expectoration in upper respiratory conditions, and to promote both diuresis and bowel movements. They also applied it externally to relieve pulmonary symptoms, just as Willis and the doctors of Edinburgh had done (Miller 1976: 177).

Modern herbalists preserve some indications for garlic inherited from the ancient world, including its use in love potions and prophylactic amulets. Others also prescribe it for effects not recognizable among those mentioned in medical works of the past, such as for "life-prolonging powers," and improved memory and mental capacity (Huson 1974: 32-3, 53-4, 252, 279, 312).

Garlic in the Modern Laboratory

In 1844, Theodor Wertheim, a German chemist, distilled a strongly pungent substance from garlic oil. He called the chemical group associated with the characteristic odor "allyl," from the plant's scientific name. Exactly 100 years later, Chester J. Cavillito and his colleagues at Sterling-Winthrop Company laboratories in Rensselaer, New York, discovered the chemical structure of allicin, the compound in garlic that produces its odor.

Four years later, in 1948, Arthur Stoll and Ewald Seebeck, at Sandoz Company laboratories in Basel, isolated alliin (0.9 percent of fresh garlic), the molecule that is biotransformed to allicin (0.1-0.5 percent of fresh garlic, up to 0.9 percent of garlic powder), which represents a doubling of the alliin molecule. The reaction is mediated by the enzyme allinase (in association with the coenzyme pyridoxal phosphate, or vitamin B_6). Garlic does not emit its typical odor until it is crushed. Stoll and Seebeck found that crushing releases allinase from the bulb's cells, permitting it to act on alliin to produce the odoriferous allicin (as well as ammonia and pyruvate ion).

Finally, in 1983, Eric Block of New York and workers at the University of Delaware and at the Venezuelan Institute of Scientific Investigations in Caracas established the structure of ajoene (*ajo* is the Spanish word for garlic), formed by the condensation of two molecules of allicin in garlic cloves. Ajoene cannot be detected in proprietary preparations of garlic, only in fresh cloves (Block 1985; *International Garlic Symposium* 1991: 10-11).

Several potentially therapeutic effects have been attributed to garlic oil and its chemical constituents since the early 1980s. Some preparations reduce plasma concentrations of cholesterol, triglycerides, and low-density lipoproteins to a modest extent, while increasing high-density lipoproteins. These effects seem to be secondary to inhibition of an enzyme necessary for cholesterol synthesis (hydroxy methyl glutaryl coenzyme A reductase), and may be associated with the ability of the same preparations to reduce blood pressure in hypertensive animals and men. An aqueous extract of garlic has been reported to inhibit angiotensin converting enzyme; modern drugs that selectively inhibit that enzyme are highly effective as antihypertensive medicines. Garlic and its extracts also inhibit thrombosis by inhibiting platelet aggregation, decreasing blood viscosity, dilating capillaries, and triggering fibrinolysis (clot breakdown). Ajoene, which is about as potent as aspirin as an antithrombotic compound, blocks platelet fibrinogen receptors. Indeed, it is probably the major antithrombotic factor in garlic juice (Block 1985; *Lawrence Review* 1988; Auer et al. 1990; Kiesewetter et al. 1990; Mader 1990; Vorberg and Schneider 1990; *International Garlic Symposium* 1991: 9, 19-44).

In 1858 Louis Pasteur found that garlic has antibacterial properties. Later studies have shown that a highly diluted solution of its juice can inhibit the growth of several important pathogenic bacteria, including *Staphylococcus, Streptococcus, Bacillus,* and *Vibrio cholerae,* as well as pathogenic yeasts and other fungi. Since then, garlic has been reported to inhibit the in vitro growth of several species of fungi, gram-positive and gram-negative bacteria, and the tuberculosis bacillus, and to reduce the infectivity of viruses, such as influenza B. Because it is the malodorous allicin that is responsible for garlic's antimicrobial effects, it is no surprise that the Sandoz Company decided not to develop it as an anti-infective drug following the discoveries of Stoll and Seebeck.

Other studies have demonstrated garlic's antineoplastic activity in rodents, but this effect may be associated with the trace elements germanium and selenium, rather than with allicin or its metabolites. Finally, recent evidence suggests that garlic decreases plasma concentrations of thyroxine, thyroid stimulating hormone, and glucose (and increases the concentration of insulin) (Block 1985; *Lawrence Review* 1988; Horowitz 1991; *International Garlic Symposium* 1991: 28-39; Farbman et al. 1993).

Several preparations of garlic are available in the United States as "health foods," although no clinical indication other than "goodness" is advertised for them – thus exacerbating the problem inherent in the coined word "nutraceutical." Most research on the therapeutic effects of garlic has been carried out in Great Britain and Europe, where garlic's medical value is more widely proclaimed. Some commercial garlic preparations are said to lack the characteristic odor, which means they are probably incapable of the potentially beneficial effects that have been attributed to alliin, allicin, and ajoene. Moreover, even though garlic has been used for culinary purposes for many centuries with no known toxic effects, it is possible that concentrated preparations might have deleterious effects in patients with diabetes or those taking anticoagulant drugs, but no reports of such effects seem to have been published (*Lawrence Review* 1988). Several sulfur-containing compounds found in fresh garlic have been held responsible for the acute gastroenteritis that ingestion of large amounts of its buds may induce in young children, while chronic ingestion of garlic has been reported to produce goiter by inhibiting iodine uptake by the thyroid gland (Lampe and McCann 1985: 28-9).

Whatever the eventual fate of garlic in pharmacological therapeutics, its history well illustrates how medical concepts have often been adapted to fit newly emerging ideas, even in the absence of any validation of the revised medical notions – other than the evidence implicit in the average adult patient's 95 percent chance of recovering from any nondevastating illness. Until the twentieth century, physicians had no better evidence on which to base dietetic prescriptions and recommendations. As Marie-François-Xavier Bichat said about two centuries ago: "The same drugs were successively used by humoralists and solidists. Theories changed, but the drugs remained the same. They were applied and acted in the same way, which proves that their action is independent of the opinion of doctors" (Estes 1990: ix). Clearly, Bichat would have included foods – even garlic – within the meaning of his word "drugs."

J. Worth Estes

Appendix: Definitions of Drug Properties

Anthelmintic: A drug that expels worms from the intestines.

Antidysenteric: Relieves dysentery.

Antihysteric: A form of antispasmodic used to treat several conditions regarded as "hysteric."

Anti-icteric: For treatment of jaundice *(icterus).*

Antiseptic: To prevent putrefaction *(sepsis).*

Antispasmodic: Reduces spasms (including fast heart rate), but without inducing insensibility (as narcotics do).

Antitussive: Cough suppressant.

Aperient: A weak cathartic.

Astringent: Strengthens a body that is too relaxed, or reduces excessive evacuations; also see *Styptic.*

Attenuating: Thins and divides the humors into smaller particles.

Carminative: Expels gas from the intestines, especially in dyspepsia.

Cathartic: A drug that promotes defecation, or increases fluid secretion from the intestinal lining.

Cephalic: For disorders of the head.

Demulcent: Lubricates organ surfaces (especially of intestines).

Deobstruent: Removes obstructions to the free flow of urine, sweat, feces, phlegm, bile, and blood.

Detergent: Cleanses or purges.

Diaphoretic: A drug that increases sweating, by stimulating blood vessels in the skin.

Digestive: Improves digestion and, therefore, nutrition.

Diluent: Dilutes blood, facilitating diuresis and diaphoresis.

Diuretic: A drug that promotes urine by stimulating the kidneys.

Emetic: A drug that induces vomiting.

Emmenagogue: Promotes menstruation.

Emollient: Reduces tension in rigid or distended organs, and warms and moistens them.

Errhine: Increases discharge from the nose; induces sneezing.

Expectorant: Promotes secretion and ejection of mucus from the lungs and trachea.

Lactatogue: Stimulates lactation.

Laxative: A gentle cathartic.

Narcotic: Affects the brain, by sedating *or* stimulating it.

Nervine: In seventeenth century, an emollient unguent for the sinews; from the eighteenth century, a stimulating tonic for weak nerves.

Pectoral: For disorders of the chest and lungs; often an antitussive and/or expectorant.

Rubefacient: Reddens or irritates the skin.

Stomachic: Warms and strengthens the stomach.

Styptic: An astringent for external use.

Tonic: Strengthens the body by increasing the force of the circulation, animal heat, secretions, digestion, or muscular activity, especially in debilitating illness.

Bibliography

American Cancer Society. 1990. Gerson method. *Ca* 40: 252-6.

1991. Questionable cancer practices in Tijuana and other Mexican border clinics. *Ca* 41: 310-19.

AMA (American Medical Association). Council on Foods and Nutrition. 1971. Zen macrobiotic diets. *Journal of the American Medical Association* 218: 397.

Apple, Rima D. 1986. "Advertised by our loving friends": The infant formula industry and the creation of new pharmaceutical markets. *Journal of the History of Medicine and Allied Sciences* 41: 3-23.

Arano, Luisa Cogliati. 1976. *The medieval health handbook "Tacuinum Sanitatis."* New York.

Armstrong, David, and Elizabeth Metzger Armstrong. 1991. *The great American medicine show.* New York.

Auer, W., A. Eiber, E. Hertkorn, et al. 1990. Hypertension and hyperlipidaemia: Garlic helps in mild cases. *British Journal of Clinical Practice* 44, no. 8, supplement 69: 3-6.

Beaumont, William. 1833. *Experiments and observations on the gastric juice and the physiology of digestion.* Plattsburgh, N.Y.

Berman, Paul. 1992. Obstetrical practice in south central Massachusetts from 1834 to 1845. *Proceedings of the Dublin Seminar for New England Folklife* 15: 185-90.

Bigelow, Jacob. 1822. *A treatise on the Materia Medica.* Boston, Mass.

Block, Eric. 1985. The chemistry of garlic and onions. *Scientific American* 252 (March): 114-19.

Buchan, William. 1809. *Domestic medicine.* Edinburgh.
       1828. *Domestic medicine.* Exeter, N.H.

Bullough, Vern L. 1957. The medieval medical university at Paris. *Bulletin of the History of Medicine* 31: 197-211.

Cassileth, Barrie R., and Helene Brown. 1988. Unorthodox cancer medicine. *Ca* 38: 176-86.

Celsus. 1935-38. *De medicina,* trans. W. G. Spencer. 3 vols. Cambridge, Mass.

Chaucer, Geoffrey. 1960. *The Canterbury tales,* trans. Nevill Coghill. Harmondsworth, England.

Clymer, R. Swinburne. [1902] 1960. *The medicine of nature.* Quakertown, Pa.

Cosman, Madeleine Pelner. 1976. *Fabulous feasts: Medieval cookery and ceremony.* New York.
       1978. Machaut's medical world. *Annals of the New York Academy of Science* 314: 1-36.

Dioscorides. 1934. *The Greek herbal,* trans. John Goodyer, ed. Robert T. Gunther. Oxford.

Drummond, J. C., and Anne Wilbraham. 1958. *The Englishman's food. A history of five centuries of English diet.* Revised edition. London.

Edelstein, Ludwig. 1987. The dietetics of antiquity. In *Ancient medicine: Selected papers of Ludwig Edelstein,* ed. Owsei Temkin and C. Lilian Temkin, 303-16. Baltimore, Md.

Edinburgh new dispensatory. 1794. Fourth edition. Edinburgh.

Estes, J. Worth. 1979. Making therapeutic decisions with protopharmacologic evidence. *Transactions and studies of the college of physicians of Philadelphia* n.s. 1: 116-37.
       1985. A naval surgeon in the Barbary Wars: Dr. Peter St. Medard on *New York* 1802-3. In *New aspects of naval history,* ed. Department of History, U.S. Naval Academy. Baltimore, Md.
       1989. *The medical skills of ancient Egypt.* Canton, Mass.
       1990. *Dictionary of protopharmacology. Therapeutic practices, 1700-1850.* Canton, Mass.
       1991a. Quantitative observations of fever and its treatment before the advent of short clinical thermometers. *Medical History* 35: 189-216.
       1991b. The Shakers and their proprietary medicines. *Bulletin of the History of Medicine* 65: 162-84.
       1992. Samuel Thomson rewrites Hippocrates. *Proceedings of the Dublin Seminar for New England Folklife* 15: 113-32.

Farbman, Karen S., Elizabeth D. Barnett, Gilles R. Bolduc, and Jerome O. Klein. 1993. Antibacterial activity of garlic and onions: A historical perspective. *Pediatric Infectious Disease Journal* 12: 613-14.

Finckh, Elisabeth. 1988. *Studies in Tibetan medicine.* Ithaca, N.Y.

Finlay, Mark R. 1992. Quackery and cookery: Justus von Liebig's extract of meat and the theory of nutrition in the Victorian age. *Bulletin of the History of Medicine* 66: 404-18.

Green, Harvey. 1986. *Fit for America: Health, fitness, sport, and American society.* New York.

Green, Saul. 1992. A critique of the rationale for cancer treatment with coffee enemas and diet. *Journal of the American Medical Association* 268: 3224-7.

Gunn, John. 1830. *Gunn's domestic medicine, or poor man's friend.* Knoxville, Tenn.

Heberden, William. 1802. *Commentaries on the history and cure of diseases.* London.

Hobbs, Christopher. 1992. Garlic – the pungent panacea. *Pharmacy in History* 34: 152-7.

Hofmann, Albert. 1972. Ergot – a rich source of pharmacologically active substances. In *Plants in the development of modern medicine,* ed. Tony Swain, 235-60. Cambridge, Mass.

Holmes, F. L. 1973. Justus von Liebig. In *Dictionary of scientific biography,* Vol. 8, ed. Charles Coulston Gillispie, 329-50. New York.

Horowitz, Janice M. 1991. Wonders of the vegetable bin. *Time,* September 2: 66.

Huard, Pierre, and Ming Wong. 1968. *Chinese medicine,* trans. Bernard Fielding. New York.

Huson, Paul. 1974. *Mastering herbalism.* New York.

International garlic symposium: Pharmacy, pharmacology and clinical application of Allium sativum. 1991. Berlin.

Jarcho, Saul. 1989. *Clinical consultations and letters by Ippolito Francesco Albertini, Francesco Torti, and other physicians.* Boston, Mass.

Josselyn, John. 1672. *New-England's rarities discovered.* London.

Kiesewetter, H., F. Jung, C. Mrowietz, et al. 1990. Effects of garlic on blood fluidity and fibrinolytic activity: A randomised, placebo-controlled, double-blind study. *British Journal of Clinical Practice* 44, no. 8, supplement 69: 24-9.

King, Lester S. 1963. *The growth of medical thought.* Chicago.

Lampe, Kenneth F., and Mary Ann McCann. 1985. *AMA handbook of poisonous and injurious plants.* Chicago.

Lawrence review of natural products. 1987-91. St. Louis, Mo.

Leicester, Henry M. 1974. *Development of biochemical concepts from ancient to modern times.* Cambridge, Mass.

Leighton, Ann. 1970. *Early American gardens: "For meate or medicine."* Boston, Mass.

Levey, Martin. 1973. *Early Arabic pharmacology: An introduction based on ancient and medieval sources.* Leiden.

Levey, Martin, trans. 1966. *The medical formulary or aqrabadhin of al-Kindi.* Madison, Wis.

Lloyd, G. E. R., ed. 1978. *Hippocratic writings.* Harmondsworth, England.

Macrobiotic diets for the treatment of cancer. 1959. *Ca* 39: 248-51.

Mader, F. H. 1990. Treatment of hyperlipidaemia with garlic-powder tablets. *Arzneimittelforschung/Drug Research* 40: 3-8.

Manniche, Lise. 1989. *An ancient Egyptian herbal.* London.

Miller, Amy Bess. 1976. *Shaker herbs, a history and compendium.* New York.

Nissenbaum, Stephen. 1988. *Sex, diet, and debility in Jacksonian America.* Westport, Conn.

Ortiz de Montellano, Bernard. 1990. *Aztec medicine, health, and nutrition.* New Brunswick, N.J.

Paré, Ambroise. 1634. *The workes of that famous chirurgion Ambrose Parey,* trans. Thomas Johnson. London.

Potter, Morris E., Arnold F. Kaufmann, Paul A. Blake, and Roger A. Feldman. 1984. Unpasteurized milk. The hazards of a health fetish. *Journal of the American Medical Association* 252: 2048-52.

Riddle, John M. 1992. The pseudo-Hippocratic *Dynamidia*

No. 11 in *Quid pro quo: Studies in the history of drugs.* Hampshire, England.

Risse, Guenter B. 1986. *Hospital life in enlightenment Scotland. Care and teaching at the Royal Infirmary of Edinburgh.* Cambridge.

Seal, D. V., and K. Middleton. 1991. Healing of cavity wounds with sugar. *Lancet* 338: 571-2.

Shah, Mazhar J., trans. 1966. *The general principles of Avicenna's Canon of Medicine.* Karachi.

Sigerist, Henry E. 1944. Ambroise Paré's onion treatment of burns. *Bulletin of the History of Medicine* 15: 143-9.

1951. *A history of medicine. I. Primitive and archaic medicine.* New York.

1987. *A history of medicine. II. Early Greek, Hindu, and Persian medicine.* New York.

Simon, Allie, David M. Wortham, and John A. Mitas II. 1979. An evaluation of iridology. *Journal of the American Medical Association* 242: 1385-9.

Siraisi, Nancy G. 1981. *Taddeo Alderotti and his pupils. Two generations of Italian medical learning.* Princeton, N.J.

1990. *Medieval and early renaissance medicine: An introduction to knowledge and practice.* Chicago.

Smith, Andrew F. 1991. Tomato pills will cure all your ills. *Pharmacy in History* 33: 169-77.

Smith, Wesley D. 1979. *The Hippocratic tradition.* Ithaca, N.Y.

Stare, Frederick J. 1986. Marketing a nutritional revolutionary "breakthrough": Trading on names. *New England Journal of Medicine* 315: 971-3.

Taberner, Peter V. 1985. *Aphrodisiacs: The science and the myth.* Philadelphia, Pa.

Teigen, Philip M. 1987. Taste and quality in 15th- and 16th-century Galenic pharmacology. *Pharmacy in History* 29: 60-8.

Temkin, Owsei. 1973. *Galenism: Rise and decline of a medical philosophy.* Ithaca, N.Y.

Thacher, James. 1813. *The American new dispensatory.* Boston, Mass.

Thorndike, Lynn. 1923-58. *A history of magic and experimental science.* 8 vols. New York.

1940. Three tracts on food in Basel manuscripts. *Bulletin of the History of Medicine* 8: 355-69.

Trall, R. T. 1852. *The hydropathic encyclopedia.* New York.

Tufts Journal. 1992. Editors' Commentary. December: 10.

Veith, Ilza, trans. and ed. 1949. *Huang ti nei ching su wen: The yellow emperor's classic of internal medicine.* Baltimore, Md.

Vogel, Virgil J.. 1970. *American Indian medicine.* Norman, Okla.

Vorberg, G., and B. Schneider. 1990. Therapy with garlic: Results of a placebo-controlled, double-blind study. *British Journal of Clinical Practice* 44, no. 8, supplement 69: 7-11.

Webster, Ian W., and Graeme K. Rawson. 1979. Health status of Seventh-Day Adventists. *Medical Journal of Australia* 1: 417-20.

Whorton, James C. 1988. Patient, heal thyself: Popular health reform movements as unorthodox medicine. In *Other healers: Unorthodox medicine in America,* ed. Norman Gevitz, 52-81. Baltimore, Md.

Willis, Thomas. 1692. *The London practice of physick.* London.

Winslow, C.-E. A., and R. R. Bellinger. 1945. Hippocratic and Galenic concepts of metabolism. *Bulletin of the History of Medicine* 17: 127-37.

Wood, George B., and Franklin Bache. 1874. *Dispensatory of the United States of America.* Thirteenth edition. Philadelphia, Pa.

VI.17 ♋ Vegetarianism

Human populations often have been obliged to subsist on an all-vegetable diet because of a poverty or scarcity of animal foods. The term "vegetarianism," nevertheless, is usually reserved for the practice of voluntary abstention from flesh on the basis of religious, spiritual, ethical, hygienic, or environmental considerations. These in turn have led to still finer distinctions regarding exactly what nonmeat articles of diet are permissible, resulting in the fragmentation of vegetarians into several groups. The great majority of adherents are "lacto-ovo" vegetarians, who reject flesh but find dairy products and eggs acceptable. Smaller groups include "vegans," who admit no animal products whatsoever into their diet; "lacto-vegetarians," who consume milk but not eggs; "ovo-vegetarians," who allow eggs but not milk; "fruitarians," who eat only fruits and nuts; "raw foodists"; and "natural hygienists," who scorn even vegetable foods if these have been processed or refined. And because – for all those classes – vegetarianism implies a concern to persuade others to adopt meatless diets, the history of vegetarianism is, at core, the history of the development of arguments used to justify and to proselytize for a vegetable diet.

Vegetarianism in Eastern Religion

The most notable examples of a religious basis for vegetarianism are to be found in Asian culture. Hinduism, though not requiring a strictly vegetable diet, has fostered a significant tradition of vegetarianism among certain believers for more than two millennia. The practice is still more widespread in Buddhism, where the doctrine of ahimsa, or nonviolent treatment of all beings, forbids adherents to kill animals for food. Many Buddhists do, nevertheless, eat meat, supporting the indulgence with the argument that the animal was killed by others. Jainism, likewise, espouses ahimsa and specifically denies meat to any practitioners of the faith (Barkas 1975; Akers 1983: 157-64).

Vegetarianism has continued as a common practice down to the present in Asia, especially in India. In Western societies, religion has also been a factor in the history of vegetarianism, but there it has played a relatively minor role compared to philosophical and scientific influences. The Western rationale for a vegetable diet is, in truth, the result of a considerably more complicated evolution shaped by a variety of cultural forces, which are outlined in this chapter (Whorton 1994).

Vegetarianism in Antiquity

The term "vegetarianism" was coined relatively recently, in the mid–nineteenth century, as the consumption of a flesh-free regimen began to assume the form of an organized movement. As a practice, however, it dates to much earlier times. No later than the third century A.D., in fact, Porphyry could describe the doctrine as already "ancient," as well as characterize the self-image vegetarianism had long embraced and would retain: It was "a dogma . . . dear to the Gods" (Porphyry 1965: 22).

The antiquity of the dogma can be traced to Pythagoras, the Greek natural philosopher of the sixth century B.C., who founded a religious community in southern Italy in which vegetarianism is reputed to have been part of the rule of life. Pythagoras scorned the eating of meat because of his belief in the Orphic concept of the transmigration of souls: If human spirits were reborn in other creatures, animal souls must be of the same quality as human souls, and animals must be as deserving of moral treatment as people. The killing of an animal was equivalent to murder, and the eating of it akin to cannibalism (Dombrowski 1984; Spencer 1993).

Additional justifications of vegetarianism with arguments dear to the gods were forwarded by several authors in later antiquity. During the first two centuries of the Christian era, Ovid and Plutarch both denounced slaughter as vicious treatment of innocent animals: "O horrible cruelty!" the latter remonstrated, that "for the sake of some little mouthful of flesh, we deprive a soul of the sun and light, and of that proportion of life and time it had been born into the world to enjoy" (Plutarch 1898: 6). Plutarch's essay "Of Eating of Flesh," in fact, provided the most comprehensive yet concise statement against conventional diet to be penned before the Renaissance and offered several objections that would become stock components of the vegetarian rationale on to the present day. These included physical arguments to complement the spiritual ones.

Flesh foods, Plutarch asserted, "by clogging and cloying" the body, "render [men's] very minds and intellects gross" (Plutarch 1898: 9). People, furthermore, could not have been intended by nature to be meat eaters, "for a human body no ways resembles those that were born for ravenousness" (Plutarch 1898: 7); it lacks fangs, claws, and all the other predatory equipment of carnivores. Finally, meat was prejudicial to health, causing "grievous oppressions and qualmy indigestions," and bringing "sickness and heaviness upon the body" (Plutarch 1898: 14).

The last vegetarian treatise from antiquity was the third-century work of the neo-Platonist Porphyry, *On Abstinence from Animal Food,* an elaboration of earlier authors' objections to meat, with particular emphasis on vegetable diet for spiritual purification: "The eye of the soul will become free, and will be established as in a port beyond the smoke and the waves of the corporeal nature" (Porphyry 1965: 53). Nevertheless, as Plutarch had recognized, "it is indeed a hard and difficult task . . . to dispute with men's bellies, that have no ears" (Plutarch 1898: 10).

The despair of vegetarians throughout the centuries has been that, in most people, the stomach speaks more loudly than the conscience, and it demands flesh. Nor did the rise of Christianity to cultural dominance strengthen the voice of conscience in support of animal welfare. Although the medieval church harbored vegetarian sects such as the Manichees, the orthodox position was that presented by Aquinas, that humankind had been granted dominion over the animal creation to use to suit their needs. Aquinas's insistence on rationality as a requirement for the extension of moral consideration to a being overrode the notion of kinship between people and animals that had been put forward by ancient vegetarians (Aquinas 1989: 146, 188). To be sure, individual church luminaries – Saints John Chrysostom and Benedict, for example – forswore the consumption of meat; but their motivation was primarily the wish to suppress their own carnal appetites rather than to extend compassion to the animal creation (Dombrowski 1984).

The Seventeenth and Eighteenth Centuries

Not until the seventeenth century was there to be any expansion of the brief against meat eating, but then one encounters, in the works of Thomas Tryon, the most broad-based argument yet for the virtues of a vegetable diet (that an Englishman should revive vegetarianism was prophetic, for England would serve as the fountainhead of vegetarian thought well into the nineteenth century). In *The Way to Health, Long Life and Happiness* (1683: 447), this dissenting religionist-cum-health-reformer and sometime poet begged readers to consider,

> How shall they but Bestial grow,
> That thus to feed on Beasts are willing?
> Or why should they a long Life know,
> Who daily practice KILLING?

In those two couplets is expressed much of the modern rationale for a vegetarian diet. The killing of animals must be discountenanced both because it inflicts pain and death on "fellow creatures" and because scripture indicates that the original diet appointed by God for humankind was meatless (Gen. 1:29). Those who feed on meat will grow bestial in both mind and spirit, whereas those who actually carry out the slaughter of animals for food will become so hardened to suffering as to lose compassion for fellow humans as well, and even to commit crimes against them.

But Tryon's case against flesh food is most significant for raising the issue of physical health to a new level of emphasis. He did not merely declare that meat eaters would not know a long life or would in other ways suffer infirmity. Tryon proposed a distinct physical mechanism for flesh food's mischief, observing that "nothing so soon turns to Putrifaction" as meat, then adding that "'tis certain, such sorts of food as are subject to putrifie before they are eaten, are also liable to the same afterwards" (Tryon 1683: 376).

Meat, in other words, because it is highly putrescible even after ingestion, must "breed great store of noxious Humours" (Tryon 1683: 377). There was the pathological justification for Tryon's charge that had it not been for the adoption of a carnivorous diet, "Man had not contracted so many Diseases in his Body" (Tryon 1683: 446). Indeed, flesh eating produced so much sickness, and vice as well, that if it were abandoned, he suggested, society would have no need for physicians or lawyers (Tryon 1683; Ryder 1979).

Both the medical and the moral strains would remain central to vegetarian philosophy throughout the 1700s. Toward the end of that century, moreover, each would take on additional import. Greater attention to the moral implications of diet was encouraged by developments in two areas of inquiry in particular: physiology and religion. The former discipline had been dragged into the arena of philosophical dispute in the mid–seventeenth century by the physiological theories of René Descartes.

The Cartesian proposal that beasts were mere automata, utterly lacking in consciousness and sensation, had focused scientists' and philosophers' attention on the question of animal pain and provoked extensive debate over the morality of slaughter, vivisection experiments, and other uses of animals for human benefit (Cottingham 1978). It was generally agreed that Descartes had erred, that animals truly do experience pain; but it was also suggested that their pain is not felt as keenly as that of humans, and that, in any event, people are justified in using lower creatures to realize their own desires.

During the eighteenth century, however, studies of the nervous system demonstrated close structural similarities between humans and higher animals, sharply increasing the probability that brutes suffered pain as severely as people: "Answer me, mechanist," Voltaire sneered at the Cartesian physiologists, "Has nature arranged all the springs of feeling in this animal in order that he should not feel? Has he nerves in order to be unmoved?" (Voltaire 1962: 113). At the same time, and in England especially, several intellectual currents were fostering a stronger feeling of relationship to animals. The Enlightenment's promotion of natural rights and humanitarian sympathy for the less fortunate encouraged a heightened sensitivity to physical pain and abhorrence of cruelty that was being occasionally extended to lower creatures by the later 1700s.

Jeremy Bentham, the founder of utilitarianism, expressed the new solicitude for animal welfare in his refutation (1789) of the argument that brutes do not deserve kindness because they are not rational beings. "The question," he insisted, "is not, Can they *reason?* nor, Can they *talk?* but, Can they *suffer?*" (Bentham 1961: 380-1). That point was not necessarily an endorsement of vegetarianism; as Bentham observed, a butcher might give an animal a quicker and less painful death than it could expect from nature (implying that meat eating was actually the more humane diet) (Bentham 1961).

Nevertheless, every animal had a right – the word is Bentham's – not to be tormented. This concept of animal rights was, meanwhile, being advanced by several other Enlightenment authors, some of whom included the right not to be used as food. Simultaneously, English religious thought was entertaining the supposition that animals have souls and even a heaven, thereby at least suggesting a neo-Pythagorean condemnation of flesh eating (Stevenson 1956; Turner 1980: 1-14).

The Nineteenth Century

Regard for animal welfare was intensified still further at the beginning of the nineteenth century by a more politically directed religious movement. Evangelicalism, the outgrowth of John Wesley's determination to make Christianity a "social gospel," was dedicated through aggressive political action to relieving the miseries of society's downtrodden and exploited. Evangelicals succeeded in moving Parliament to legislate against the slave trade, child labor, Britain's barbaric penal code, and numerous other injustices. Among Evangelical good works was an animal protection campaign that attacked the mistreatment of animals used for labor or sport and resulted in Western society's first animal welfare legislation, a law passed in 1822 to protect work animals from abuse (Turner 1980: 15-38).

The new climate of distaste for animal cruelty gave vegetarianism added appeal, of course; and though it would remain the doctrine of a small fringe group, membership in the fold did increase significantly around the turn of the nineteenth century. Vegetarian literature grew apace, no longer just an occasional volume from an isolated eccentric but now a steady flow of treatises voicing outrage at the cruel ravages visited upon defenseless creatures. The title of the first major work in this new genre captures its prevailing sentiment perfectly: *The Cry of Nature,* as John Oswald named his book, *Or, an Appeal to Mercy and to Justice, on Behalf of the Persecuted Animals* (1791). Romantic sensitivity to the beauty and innocence of nature gushed through such volumes; Oswald's frontispiece, for example, portrayed a slaughtered fawn spilling its blood upon the earth while its mother tearfully called on it to rise. Nearby, an unclothed child of nature hid her face in shame. "Come," Oswald invited, "approach and examine with attention this dead body. It was late a playful fawn, which, skipping and bounding . . . awoke, in the soul of the feeling observer, a thousand tender emotions. But the butcher's knife hath laid low the delight of a fond dam, and the darling of nature is now stretched in gore upon the ground" (Oswald 1791: 22-3).

If the moral hideousness of slaying animals for food was the dominant theme of early-century vegetarianism, the physical repulsiveness of flesh food was hardly overlooked. Oswald requested readers to gaze upon the scene of carnage a second time: "Approach, I say, ... and tell me, tell me, does this ghastly spectacle whet your appetite? Delights your eyes the sight of blood? Is the steam of gore grateful to your nostrils, or pleasing to the touch, the icy ribs of death? ... or with a species of rhetoric, pitiful as it is perverse, will you still persist in your endeavour to persuade us, that to murder an innocent animal, is not cruel nor unjust; and that to feed upon a corpse, is neither filthy nor unfit?" (Oswald 1791: 22–3).

Filthy and unfit are moral terms, of course, but they have physiological connotations as well. What one sees here, and can find expressed still more overtly in subsequent vegetarian literature, is the suggestion that the revulsion produced by the sight of blood and the smell of gore is not simply an aesthetic reaction; it is also a physiological response to physical filth and physical unfitness, an indication that the human body is not designed to receive such food as nutriment.

Vegetarianism, Science, and Medicine

The physiological superiority of a vegetable diet was an especially critical point to demonstrate by the beginning of the nineteenth century. Enlightenment philosophy had elevated science to the position of an indispensable method of investigation and proof. Therefore, if the newly energized vegetarianism of the early 1800s was to legitimate itself in society's eyes, it had to prove itself nutritionally as well as spiritually.

It had to be demonstrated, first of all, that one could survive in reasonable health without flesh foods. It was generally assumed that meat, being most closely akin chemically to human muscle, must be more easily digested and assimilated than plants and provide greater strength and endurance. An all-vegetable diet, this reasoning supposed, must be debilitating, and surely self-preservation carried greater moral weight than kindness to other species.

Two English physicians were especially influential for presenting evidence that vegetarianism was not, after all, a form of slow suicide. The first was George Cheyne, one of the most widely read health writers of the eighteenth century. A high liver in his younger days, Cheyne turned to lacto-vegetarianism in the 1720s in order to reduce his now bloated and unwieldy 32-stone frame. But not only did he manage to shed considerable weight on his diet of milk and vegetables; various other complaints that had nagged him for years (headache and depression, for example) disappeared as well. Through subsequent observations of "my own crazy Carcase" (1734: xvi), as well as of numerous patients, Cheyne became convinced that flesh food "inflames the Passions, and shortens Life, begets chronical Distempers, and a decrepid Age"

(Cheyne 1734: 94). His several guidebooks to health were the first to recommend vegetarianism almost exclusively for reasons of physical well-being and to back claims of health with clinical cases.

Still more clinical evidence of the healthfulness of a vegetable diet was presented in 1809 by another London practitioner, William Lambe. Lambe had relieved himself of long-standing illness three years earlier by removing meat from his table. He had then applied that diet to the care of his patients and succeeded in curing, he believed, numerous cases of asthma, tuberculosis, and other chronic complaints, including cancer. Although he insisted that "a strict vegetable regimen" was an "absolute necessity" in the management of chronic illness, he was less forceful in his advocacy of vegetarianism for the healthy. He proposed only that meat was unnecessary, and that "what is unnecessary cannot be natural, [and] what is not natural cannot be useful" (Lambe 1815: 172).

Lambe's branding of meat as unnatural food for humans did sway several individuals well known in English society to convert to vegetarianism. Most prominent of all among these was the Romantic poet Percy Shelley, who in 1813 produced an emotionally charged pamphlet titled *A Vindication of Natural Diet*. In this work, logic was subjected to a fair amount of violence, yet the *Vindication* did achieve a certain balance by assigning roughly equal weight to both the moral and the physical objections to a flesh diet.

On the one side, the bloody excesses of the French Revolution and the tyranny of Napoleon were credited to the Gallic appetite for rare meat. But on the other, there was the assurance that "the bile-suffused cheek of Buonoparte, his wrinkled brow, and yellow eye, the ceaseless inquietude of his nervous system" were incontrovertible proof that he had not "descended from a race of vegetable feeders" (Shelley 1884: 17). Meat, Shelley declared bluntly, is "demonstrably pernicious" (20), as clear a demonstration as any being the "easiness of breathing" (24) acquired by vegetarians, granting them "a remarkable exemption from that powerful and difficult panting now felt by almost everyone after hastily climbing an ordinary mountain" (24).

Realistically, of course, the uphill battle had to be fought by vegetarians. Not only was the weight of medical opinion still on the side of meat, so was public opinion and, even more important, popular taste: "The forbidding of animal food," Lambe had despaired, is "an injunction that sounds more unwelcome to English ears than any perhaps that could be given" (Lambe 1815: 130). For such prejudice to be overcome, meat had to be transformed into a positive menace by the construction of physical arguments that were more sophisticated than were warnings that flesh eaters make poor alpinists. The elevation of physiology to primacy in the ongoing formulation of a rationale for vegetarianism, however, was the work of American theorists rather than English or other European ones.

Vegetarianism in America

Vegetarianism was brought to the United States toward the end of the 1810s by William Metcalfe, an envoy of the Bible Christian Church. The first organization in modern times to make vegetarianism one of the requirements of membership, the Church had been founded in Manchester, England, in 1807 by the Swedenborgian minister William Cowherd (there is a Dickensian irony in the names of the vegetarian leaders of the early 1800s – Cowherd, Metcalfe, and Lambe all conjuring up visions of chops and roasts). Though motivated in part by humanitarian sentiment, Cowherd had been equally impressed by the writings of Cheyne, and he forbade his congregation meat (and alcohol too), largely for reasons of health (Forward 1898: 7).

The Bible Christian sect would continue in existence in England until the 1880s at least, but its greatest impact came early in the century and on American soil. About 1830, in the process of organizing a New World branch of his church in Philadelphia, Metcalfe caught the attention of Sylvester Graham, a Presbyterian minister turned temperance lecturer. Graham, at that time, was in the process of expanding temperance into an all-inclusive program of physical and moral reform, and Metcalfe's understanding of the virtues of a vegetable diet was in perfect philosophical harmony with the American's own view of health behavior generally.

Graham's popular health reform movement, the first stage of what would become an enduring tradition of hygienic extremism in America, operated on the assumption that the laws of health were as much the dictates of God as the Ten Commandments, and, therefore, the two sets of rules could not conflict: Physiology must be congruent with morality. Acting from this certainty, that any behavior that tarnished the soul must also injure the body, Graham and his health reform comrades bombarded the public of the 1830s to 1850s with health injunctions against alcohol, extramarital sex, late-night entertainments, and sundry other practices both hateful and hurtful; included among these, by necessity, was the consumption of meat (Whorton 1977, 1982).

Graham hardly labored alone in erecting more extensive physiological supports for vegetarianism. Numerous health reformers participated, most notably William Andrus Alcott, who in the late 1830s supplanted Graham as commander of the forces of health reform. One of the most prolific self-help writers of the entire nineteenth century, Alcott contributed an 1838 volume under the title *Vegetable Diet*, specifying in his subtitle that vegetarianism was *Sanctioned by Medical Men and by Experience in All Ages*. The book was intended, in short, to show that science corroborated Christian moral principles

(or at least his interpretation of the spirit of compassion of the New Testament). Comparative anatomy was one of the sciences applied to the task, though the similarity of human teeth and intestines to those of herbivores had been pointed out by any number of earlier authors. Rather it was the still emerging science of nutrition that seemed to offer the most up-to-date demonstration that meat was a poison, and Alcott, Graham, and other health reformers mobilized an impressive array of entirely new nutrition-based arguments to prove their point.

The arguments were impressive, that is, for their quantity. Qualitatively, however, they were completely inadequate and scientifically invalid, both because of the period's severely limited understanding of nutrition and biochemistry and because of health reformers' determination to force science into the straitjacket of their moral preconceptions. The latter was facilitated by the adoption of the theory of pathology that had recently been formulated by French physician François Broussais, a theory that attributed all illness to overstimulation of body tissues, especially those of the digestive tract.

As stimulation was already a loaded word morally – to the Victorian mind, arousal of carnal appetites and animal passions was the root of all evil – Broussais's pathology offered an ideal foundation for the construction of a health reform version of vegetarianism. Consequently, stimulation arguments too numerous to recount were advanced by health reform apologists for vegetable diets throughout the antebellum period.

One effort, for example, interpreted the famous in vivo digestion experiments performed in the 1820s by William Beaumont on a man with a gastric fistula. Beaumont's studies included measurement of the digestion times required by various foods, accomplished by tying food samples to a string, introducing them into the stomach, and retrieving them hourly for inspection. Beaumont's conclusion was that, "generally speaking, vegetable aliment requires more time, and probably greater powers of the gastric organs, than animal" (Beaumont 1833: 36).

Graham objected, maintaining that greater speed of digestion is clearly an indication of a more intense response by the vital powers to the stimulus of food. The more intense a response, he reminded, the more intense the stimulus must be, so meat must be more stimulating – pathologically stimulating – than vegetables. There was additional evidence in the feeling of warmth experienced after a meal rich in meat. A later generation would attribute this to the specific dynamic action of protein, but for health reformers it was a "digestive fever" in which, according to Alcott, "the system ... is inevitably worn into a premature dissolution, by the violent and unnatural heat of an over-stimulated and precipitate circulation" (Alcott 1840: 221).

Meat even stimulated itself, decomposing (as Tryon had noted two centuries earlier) in much less time than vegetables. It followed that human flesh constructed from the excessively stimulated molecules of meat must also be less stable and more subject to decay. That explained, in Alcott's opinion, why vegetarians smelled better. "The very exhalations of the lungs," he asserted, "are purer, as is obvious from the breath. That of a vegetable-eater," he had determined, "is perfectly sweet, while that of a flesheater is often as offensive as the smell of a charnel-house. This distinction is discernible even among the brute animals. Those which feed on grass . . . have a breath incomparably sweeter than those which prey on animals. Compare the camel, and horse, and cow, and sheep, and rabbit, with the tiger (if you choose to approach him), the wolf, the dog, the cat and the hawk. One comparison will be sufficient; you will never forget it" (Alcott 1838: 233–4).

Still more to the point, however, was that the unstable atoms of a carnivore's muscles must be subject to more rapid molecular turnover than a vegetarian's tissues and, hence, subject to accelerated aging and premature death. The mechanics of life could be summed up simply: "A man may not inaptly be compared with a watch – the faster it goes the sooner it will run down" (Cambell 1837: 291).

The condemnation of fast living was a double entendre, for try as they might to present their ideas as concrete science, health reform vegetarians could never stop moralizing. Alcott, for instance, immediately followed his alarm over the "violent and unnatural heat" of a flesh eater's digestive fever with the observation that a vegetable diet is cooling, and "has a tendency to temper the passions" (Alcott 1840: 221). Colleague Russell Trall was even more uneasy about untempered passions, warning that "no delusion on earth [is] so widespread [as] this, which confuses stimulation with nutrition. It is the very parent source of that awful . . . multitude of errors, which are leading the nations of the earth into all manner of riotous living, and urging them on in the road to swift destruction" (Trall 1860: 10).

To their credit, health reform vegetarians balanced their thrilling flights of theory with down-to-earth demonstrations by cases. The proof of the theory, after all, was in the state of health of those who practiced it, and history could offer robust vegetarians aplenty in evidence. The first to be recognized, predictably, were the antediluvians, those original folk whose simple diet kept them vigorous all the way to the end of their 900 years. But pagans could serve the cause as well, though, surprisingly, it was pagan soldiers, especially those of the Roman army, who were held up as paragons of hygiene, as they had marched to their greatest victories on plain vegetable rations.

The incongruity of the diet of gentleness and benevolence providing the strength for battlefield slaughter was missed by the health reformers in their excitement over the physical glory of the vegetarians of antiquity. Subsistence on vegetable food, according

to an agitated Graham, was "true of all those ancient armies whose success depended more on bodily strength and personal prowess, in wielding warclubs and grappling man with man in the fierce exercise of muscular power, and dashing each other furiously to the earth, mangled and crushed and killed" (Graham 1839: 188).

More recent, and less brutal, examples were more convincing and suitable. Alcott allotted nearly 200 pages of his book on vegetable diet to the presentation of testimonials, including such samples of prodigious vitality as Amos Townsend, a graminivorous bank cashier, who could "dictate a letter, count money, and hold conversation with an individual, all at the same time, with no embarrassment" (Alcott 1838: 75–6).

The Establishment of Vegetarian Societies

That American vegetarians' more pronounced orientation toward health impressed European counterparts is evident from the deliberations associated with the founding of the first national vegetarian organization. On September 30, 1847, meat abstainers from all parts of England gathered in Ramsgate, Kent, to form the Vegetarian Society. It was at this organizational meeting that the term "vegetarian" was coined, being taken from the Latin "vegetus": lively or vigorous. The founding members then pledged themselves "to induce habits of abstinence from the flesh of animals as food, by the dissemination of information upon the subject, by means of tracts, essays, and lectures" (Forward 1898, 22).

When they next enumerated the "many advantages" of vegetable diet that would be presented through literature and lecture, the traditionally favored advantage, morality, was pushed to a subsidiary position; again, vigor was the emphasis, their list beginning with "physical" improvements. The Society's monthly, The Vegetarian Messenger, was launched two years later and granted the same prominence to the physical in its messages; by 1853, 20 physicians and surgeons were included among the organization's membership of more than 800 (Forward 1898: 22, 33).

The new group's unorthodox philosophy immediately attracted ridicule. Punch, for instance, reported that "a prize is to be given [by the Society] for the quickest demolition of the largest quantity of turnips; and a silver medal will be awarded to the vegetarian who will dispose of one hundred heads of celery with the utmost celerity" ("Vegetarian Movement" 1848: 182). An organized movement of vegetarianism did spread with celerity. American vegetarians quickly followed the English lead, forming the American Vegetarian Society in 1850. As with its predecessor, the very first resolution adopted by this society recognized the value of a vegetable diet for health, declaring "that comparative anatomy, human physiology, and . . . chemical analysis . . . unitedly proclaim the position, that not only the human race may, but *should* subsist upon the products of the vegetable kingdom" ("Proceedings" 1851: 6). Morality did nevertheless follow close behind, with the next three resolutions adopted claiming biblical and ethical sanctions for vegetarianism.

In the meantime, vegetarianism was undergoing a similar development on the European continent. There, treatises such as *Thalysie: ou La Nouvelle Existence (Thalysie: Or the New Existence)* by Jean Antoine Gleizes (1840), and *Pflanzenkost, die Grundlage einer neuen Weltanschauung (Vegetable Diet, the Foundation of a New Worldview)* by Gustav von Struve (1861), slowly raised public awareness of the dietary alternative and attracted followers.

The first national organization of vegetarianism on the continent was established in Germany in 1866, under the leadership of Eduard Baltzer. Vegetarian journals and magazines appeared during the midcentury, beginning in England with the *Vegetarian Advocate* (1848) and the *Vegetarian Messenger* (1849) and continuing in the United States with the *American Vegetarian* (1851), published by the American Vegetarian Society. During the decade of the 1870s, vegetarian restaurants were established in major European and American cities; London could boast of a dozen by the end of the century (Forward 1898: 102). Finally, the first international organization was launched in 1908: The International Vegetarian Union.

Henry Salt

Britain and the United States remained the centers of vegetarian philosophy and practice into the twentieth century. In the former, the cause of vegetable diets was advanced with particular eloquence by Henry Salt (Mohandas Gandhi, among others, credited Salt for his conversion to vegetarianism). Author of numerous books calling for reform of social injustices, Salt was nevertheless best known (or most notorious) for his advocacy of *Animals' Rights Considered in Relation to Social Progress,* the title of an 1892 volume that attacked every form of exploitation of the brute creation. There, and in his later *The Logic of Vegetarianism* (1899), Salt employed a thoroughly unsentimental approach to argue that philosophy and science, alike, required abstention from meat.

Philosophy, his *logic* of vegetable diet posited, could not support the common assumptions that human beings have no moral relationship or obligation to other creatures and that the killing of animals for food is a law of nature. The latter idea had become an especially popular justification for meat eating in the wake of Charles Darwin's explanation of nature's rule of survival of the fittest. The response of Salt, and other late-century vegetarians, was that cooperation among animals was as common a strategy for survival as competition, and that human cooperation with other species was positively enjoined by Darwin's theory that people had descended from animal ancestors: How could one justify the slaughter of creatures with whom humans shared a "bond of consanguinity" (Salt 1892, 1899: 50)? Just such a bond had, in fact, been suggested by Darwin himself in *The Descent of Man;* there he presented a sizable body of evidence to demonstrate that "there is no fundamental difference between man and the higher mammals in their mental faculties. . . . The difference in mind between man and the higher animals, great as it is, certainly is one of degree and not of kind" (Darwin 1874: 74, 143).

The Twentieth Century

John Harvey Kellogg

Evolutionary kinship with livestock was also a significant element in the case constructed by America's most influential spokesman for vegetarianism in the early twentieth century. John Harvey Kellogg, however, gave greater emphasis to medical than to biological theory and propounded what was clearly the period's most persuasive argument against the consumption of meat. Kellogg was bred, if not born, a Grahamite by virtue of his family's membership in the Seventh-Day Adventist Church, an institution that gave allegiance to Graham's hygienic system on the basis of the divine, health-related visions experienced by spiritual leader Ellen White (Numbers 1976).

Kellogg also received training in hydropathy, an alternative system of medical practice that treated all conditions with applications of water and exhorted all patients to abide by Graham's rules of health. (Kellogg's mentor, and the leading figure in American hydropathy, Russell Trall, was a founding member and officer of the American Vegetarian Society, and the author of a volume titled *The Scientific Basis of Vegetarianism* [1860]).

Kellogg also completed a program of orthodox medical training and then, in 1875, returned to his native Battle Creek, Michigan, to assume the directorship of a struggling hospital and health-education facility operated by the Adventist Church. Not only did he quickly transform the Battle Creek Sanitarium into a thriving business, he built it into the most famous health institution in the country from the 1880s until World War II. As part of the Sanitarium's dietary program, Kellogg, along with his brother Will, created an assortment of meat substitutes and other vegetarian health foods, including the breakfast cereals that have immortalized the family's name (Schwartz 1970; Whorton 1982: 201–38).

Kellogg also lectured tirelessly, from coast to coast, and wrote voluminously. In addition to editing the popular periodical *Good Health,* he authored several dozen books, addressing every aspect of personal health behavior from *The Evils of Fashionable Dress,* to *Plain Facts about Sexual Life,* to *Colon Hygiene.* The last topic, the health of the large bowel, represented Kellogg's most significant contribution to the updating of the nutritional argument for vegetarianism. Here, he elaborated the dietary implications of one of the grand pathology fads of the turn of the twentieth century – intestinal autointoxication.

In the 1880s, laboratory scientists had isolated several substances produced in the intestinal tract through the bacterial putrefaction of undigested protein. The compounds were determined to be toxic when injected directly into the bloodstream in animals, and it was quickly supposed they might be absorbed from the colon into the human bloodstream and then circulated to play havoc throughout the body. Since these agents of self-poisoning were products of bacterial activity, the theory of autointoxication could be seen as an extension of medical bacteriology. Thus clutching the coattails of the germ theory, autointoxication swept into professional and popular awareness at the end of the nineteenth century (Chen and Chen 1989; Whorton 1991).

For Kellogg, autointoxication theory provided enough ammunition to support several book-length attacks on meat eating. In such works as *Autointoxication or Intestinal Toxemia* (1918), *The Itinerary of a Breakfast* (1919), and *The Crippled Colon* (1931), he expounded time and again on how the common diet contained so much protein from its flesh components as to encourage the growth and activity of proteolytic bacteria in the colon. As the microbes operated on undigested flesh food, the body would be "flooded with the most horrible and loathsome poisons" (Kellogg 1918: 131) and brought to suffer headache, depression, skin problems, chronic fatigue, damage to the liver, kidneys, and blood vessels, and other injuries totaling up to "enormous mischief." Anyone who read to the end of Kellogg's baleful list must have been ready to agree that "the marvel is not that human life is so short and so full of miseries, mental, moral, and physical, but that civilized human beings are able to live at all" (Kellogg 1918: 131).

"Civilized" referred to the fiber content of the ordinary diet, too. Modern people, Kellogg chided, ate too concentrated a diet, with insufficient bulk to stimulate the bowels to action. A vegetarian diet, he added for the unaware, was high in roughage. Its other advantage was that it was low in protein. The high-protein diet common to flesh eaters was ideal fodder for the putrefactive microorganisms of the colon, whereas its low-fiber content reduced its rate of movement to a crawl that gave the microbes time to convert all unabsorbed protein to poisons. In the meat eater's sluggish bowels, Kellogg believed, lay "the secret of nine-tenths of all the chronic ills from which civilized human beings suffer" (1919: 87), including "national inefficiency and physical unpreparedness," as well as "not a small part of our moral and social maladies" (Kellogg 1919: 93).

Morality could be merged with medicine in other ways. In *Shall We Slay to Eat*, Kellogg applied a bacteriologic gloss to the age-old objection to the cruelty of slaughter. Reminding readers of the gentleness of unoffending cows and pigs (animals with whom humans were bound by evolution), Kellogg then forced them, Oswald-like, to look upon the "tide of gore," the "quivering flesh," the "writhing entrails" of the butchered animals, and to listen to their squealing and bleating as they died (Kellogg 1905: 145–67). What he counted upon ultimately to move his readers, though, was the abominable filth through which the tide of gore flowed. The Augean nastiness of the typical abattoir (here nauseatingly detailed a year before the publication of Upton Sinclair's much more famous *The Jungle*) ensured that meat must be infested with every germ known: "Each juicy morsel," Kellogg revealed, "is fairly alive and swarming with the identical micro-organisms found in a dead rat in a closet or the putrefying carcass of a cow" (Kellogg 1923: 107).

Alexander Haig

Even biochemistry, just then blossoming as a laboratory science, was recruited to the vegetarian campaign. The other major pathology fad of the early twentieth century was uricacidemia, a disease-inducing state discovered by London physician Alexander Haig. Through a process too involved to be recounted here, Haig convinced himself during the 1880s that his migraine attacks were due to excess uric acid in his blood. As so often happens when an enthusiast discovers the source of his own health problems, Haig was soon blaming uric acid for everybody's problems. Through selective use of biochemical data and oversimplification of biochemical theory, Haig was able to propose mechanisms by which uric acid could cause every complaint from flatulence to cancer. His presentation of that thesis, a 900-page opus called *Uric Acid As a Factor in the Causation of Disease*, passed through seven editions in the 1890s and early 1900s. Haig's notions were soon disowned by his medical brethren, but the public's fear of uric acid carried into the 1920s and brought greater popular attention to bear on vegetarianism.

It was not necessarily approving attention, for the uric-acid-free diet Haig recommended was a highly restrictive system of eating. It required, after all, the elimination of every food containing either uric acid or purines that could be metabolized into uric acid. That rule eliminated not only all meat but many vegetables as well – beans, peas, asparagus, mushrooms, and whole-grain cereal products. Haig was thus left with milk, cheese, some vegetables, fruit, nuts, and – a unique position for a food reformer – white bread. Additional blandness was imposed by the prohibition of coffee and tea on the grounds that they contained methyl xanthines (it was later determined that caffeine and similar compounds are not metabolized into uric acid). And any rejoicing that at least alcoholic beverages were free of uric acid–producing substances was quickly squelched by Haig's assurance that his diet removed any need for stimulation and thus destroyed the taste for strong drink (Haig 1892).

The physical advantage of Haig's diet was demonstrated by the extraordinary success of several athletes who adopted it. Indeed, as early-twentieth-century society became captivated by competitive sports, vegetarians of every persuasion turned to athletic conquest for practical proof of the nutritional superiority of their regimen. As a result, a remarkable record of vegetarian victories in all sports was compiled in the 1890s and early 1900s, from the cycling records established by England's aptly named James Parsley to the championships won by the tug-of-war team of the unfortunately named West Ham Vegetarian Society. (Among the flesh-abstaining champions was Haig's son Kenneth, who won prizes as an Oxford rower but eventually was removed from his boat for fear that "his diet would demoralize . . . the rest of the crew.") Carnivorus competitors refused to acknowledge the vegetarians' athleticism, however, crediting their triumphs not to diet but to the dedication and competitiveness bred by fanaticism (Whorton 1981).

The "Newer Nutrition"

If full-fledged vegetarianism was still being taken lightly, the early twentieth century did foster a new respect for the nutritional value of vegetables; though few accepted vegetable foods as wholly sufficient for a healthful diet, all did come to see the consumption of vegetables as necessary to health. The critical development was the growth of understanding of vitamins over the first two decades of the century, accompanied by the realization that vitamin-rich fruits and vegetables were badly neglected at most tables. The most prominent representative of the so-called newer nutrition, vitamin discoverer Elmer McCollum, estimated in 1923 that "at least 90 per cent" of the food eaten by most American families was restricted to the old standards of white bread and butter, meat, potatoes, sugar, and coffee. His call for nationwide dietary reform aimed at educating and converting the public to replace much of the traditional diet with what he called the "protective foods."

The resultant dietary education campaign made the 1920s as truly the decade of newer nutrition as of bathtub gin and jazz. Food educators bombarded the public through lectures, newspapers, magazines, textbooks, and comic strips and were gratified to see the national consumption of fruits and vegetables increase markedly. To note one of the more extraordinary examples, between 1925 and 1927, the spinach intake of schoolchildren in Fargo, North Dakota, grew tenfold (Whorton 1989).

Public consciousness of the nutritional virtues of plant foods was not limited to vitamin awareness. Another dominant health theme of the 1920s was the lack of bulk in modern society's diet of refined and processed foods. Bulk foods were needed, of course, to prevent constipation, and ultimately autointoxication, still an unsettling threat in the public mind. The Kelloggs, Charles W. Post, and other manufacturers of bran-containing breakfast cereals fostered popular anxiety over torpid intestines with grossly exaggerated advertising warnings, giving the 1920s as pronounced a fiber consciousness as any more recent decade. But there was also the disinterested promotion of a higher-fiber diet by altruistic health reformers, some of them physicians and scientists.

At the head of this group was Britain's archenemy of autointoxication, the renowned surgeon Sir William Arbuthnot Lane. Convinced that the upright posture and soft lifestyle of civilized people weakened the colon and produced "chronic intestinal stasis," Lane surgically removed the colons of hundreds of patients during the 1910s in order to save them from autointoxication. The risks of surgery, as well as criticism from his professional colleagues, forced Lane to stop doing colectomies in the 1920s. But he remained convinced that constipation was the fundamental disease of civilization and was responsible for a host of illnesses, including colon cancer and other neoplasms. Consequently, in 1926, he organized the New Health Society in London and dedicated the last 17 years of his life to lecturing and writing on the dangers of intestinal stasis. Through Lane, the New Health Society, and the magazine *New Health,* British and American consumers were repeatedly harangued about the importance of fruits and vegetables for maintaining bowel regularity and preventing more serious diseases (Whorton 1991).

Vegetarianism and Health

Frequently included in Lane's presentations were anecdotal reports of the relative freedom from autointoxication diseases enjoyed by the vegetarian populations of less-developed nations. But it was not until the late 1940s, after Lane had died and autointoxication had disappeared from orthodox medical theory, that epidemiological studies of so-called developing-world cultures began to verify Lane's anecdotes by demonstrating statistical correlations between a high intake of dietary fiber and low incidences of hemorrhoids, gallstones, colon cancer, and various other "Western diseases" (Trowell 1981). Although some of the specific conclusions associated with the dietary fiber hypothesis have sparked debate, not to say controversy, among nutritionists and other health scientists, fiber has been officially recognized as an essential dietary component, and the general public has clearly been impressed with the health benefits of a diet high in unrefined vegetable foods.

Highly publicized studies linking cholesterol and saturated fats with cardiovascular disease have similarly conditioned society to associate vegetarianism with health and have motivated physicians and nutritionists to study heart disease and longevity in vegetarian groups such as Seventh-Day Adventists and Trappist monks. Those studies, conducted from the 1950s onward and too numerous to cite specifically, have largely confirmed what early-nineteenth-century vegetarians initially proposed, that a vegetable diet not only is capable of sustaining health but may actually improve it as well (Hardinge and Crooks 1963; Amato and Partridge 1989: 10-15).

Vegetarianism and Ethics

Running parallel with the twentieth-century growth of medical support for vegetarianism has been the expansion of the diet's moral rationale. Until recently, this argument has been aimed almost exclusively at the pain inflicted on animals at the time of slaughter and the injustice of depriving them of life. Some attention has also been directed to the discomforts endured by livestock being driven or transported to market; this issue was introduced into deliberations in the mid-nineteenth century, as animals began to be shipped in crowded boxcars and ship holds. Although both types of objections continue, discussion has widened since the middle of the twentieth century to take in the treatment of meat animals throughout their lives.

The transformation of farming into agribusiness, including the adoption of economies of scale in stock raising, fostered a system of more intensive rearing methods – "factory farming" – that confined animals in unnatural environments from birth. Ruth Harrison's 1964 *Animal Machines* first directed public attention to the raising of chickens in overcrowded coops and the packing of pigs into "Bacon Bin" fattening houses. Photographs of veal calves penned in narrow wooden cages all the days of their short lives soon became a common feature in vegetarian appeals (outdone in emotional impact only by the pictures of bludgeoned baby seals used in anti-fur advertisements). The maintenance of hens under similar conditions has encouraged lacto-ovo vegetarians to give up eggs; some have abandoned milk products as well in protest of the dairy industry's practice of separating calves from their mothers soon after birth (and the subsequent transformation of those calves into veal). Thus, the ranks of vegans have grown considerably in the later twentieth century (vegans are sometimes referred to as "pure" vegetarians, but there is some question about the applicability of the term, since the word "vegetarian" was minted to refer to a diet that includes eggs and milk). Even meat eaters have been affected by the critique of factory farming, a sizable number now selecting "free range" animal products whenever they are available.

The Animal Rights Movement

Bentham's proposal that slaughtering an animal for food saves it from a more painful and protracted death in the wild has lost its cogency in the age of the factory farm; now an animal's entire existence might be seen as one long death. The morality of imposing such an existence on any creature has been raised to a higher level of discussion, moreover, by the animal rights movement of the last quarter century. Peter Singer's 1975 work, *Animal Liberation,* the chief catalyst of the movement, is a work in which the heavily sentimental tone of traditional vegetarian moralism is set aside in favor of a rigidly philosophical analysis that recognizes animals as sentient beings, capable of experiencing pain and pleasure, and concludes that they should, therefore, be accorded the same respect as humans in areas where their interests are affected. Various violations of those interests are attacked by Singer (and they are much the same as the ones assailed by Salt nearly a century before) – for example, the use of animals in experimental research and the raising of animals for fur.

Because of the sheer numbers involved, however, the worst example of "speciesism" – the practice of moral discrimination purely on the basis of biological species – is the raising and killing of animals for food: "the most extensive exploitation of other species that has ever existed" (Singer 1975: 92; Regan 1975). The most significant element in such exploitation, however, is regarded not as the unnatural conditions of life imposed upon livestock or even their physical suffering. Fundamental to the animals' rights analysis is the affirmation of a right to life for every creature. Thus, even if the animal is allowed a free-range existence and is slaughtered painlessly, the simple act of killing it for food constitutes an unjustifiable moral offense.

The arguments of Singer, Tom Regan, and other advocates of equal moral consideration for animals have elicited a serious response from the philosophy community. Over the past two decades, professional journals and conferences have given an extraordinary amount of attention to the issue of animal rights and its practical applications, including vegetarianism. To be sure, much of the reaction among philosophers has been critical. The Singer analysis has been faulted on grounds of logic and even attacked as a trivialization of civil rights, women's rights, and other movements promoting more moral treatment of fellow human beings (Francis and Norman 1978).

Yet a good bit of the discussion has supported the animal rights arguments, endorsing both the abstract proposition of an animal's right to life and older sentiments such as an intuitive appreciation that eating animals with whom people sense a bond of kinship is wrong (Diamond 1978). Speciesism has acquired an odious taint as well from the human exploitation of wild animals that has pushed many species to the brink of extinction, and by studies of communication in other mammals that have strengthened our feeling of relation to the rest of the animal kingdom.

Vegetarianism and the Environment

Not only have the moral and medical defenses of a vegetable diet grown stronger individually over the twentieth century, they have been buttressed in recent decades by environmental arguments. This is not an entirely new approach – eighteenth- and nineteenth-century vegetarians occasionally pointed out that less land would be needed for agriculture if people were fed on grain rather than meat – and it is a frequently cited truism in vegetarian literature today that 16 pounds of grain are required to produce 1 pound of meat. But with the twentieth century's rapid increase of human population, the ceaseless conversion of arable land into housing developments and shopping malls, and the dramatic expansion of industry and the spread of industrial pollution, the degradation of the environment has become an object of grave scientific and public concern. As attention has been focused ever more sharply on the multitudinous threats to the fragile environment of our shrinking globe, a flesh diet has been recognized as a significant contributor to environmental decline.

The ecology of meat eating was first explored thoroughly by Frances Moore Lappé, whose 1971 best-seller *Diet for a Small Planet* examined livestock farming's toll on the land, water, and air. Since Lappé, it has become commonplace for vegetarian literature to detail the soil erosion associated with the cultivation of livestock food crops; the excessive demands on water supplies to irrigate those crops; the pollution of waterways by field and feedlot runoff; the large amounts of fossil fuel energy expended in raising meat animals; even the contribution to global warming made by the methane released in cattle flatulence. Lately, the destruction of the tropical rain forest to provide more grazing land for beef cattle has been singled out as flesh diet's greatest threat to the viability of "spaceship earth." And in the end, ecology has returned to ethics. In the twentieth-anniversary edition of *Diet for a Small Planet* (1991), Lappé concentrated her criticisms on the immorality of growing grain for the fattening of cattle while millions of people worldwide starve.

A final characteristic of contemporary vegetarianism is its accomplishment of a joining of East and West. The Western counterculture's fascination with Asian religious traditions has been an important contributor to the growth of vegetarianism over the past quarter century, with vegetarian religious sects such as the International Society for Krishna Consciousness now widely distributed through North America and Europe. Voluntary vegetarianism remains the practice of a small minority of the world's population, of course; the number of practitioners, nevertheless, has risen to a historic high due to the combination of spiritual, ethical, medical, and environmental preoccupations resident in the mentality of the late twentieth century. In the United States, there are now approximately 9 million people identifying themselves as vegetarians, whereas another 40 million claim to have decreased their flesh food intake for reasons of health, morals, or ecological concern (Amato and Partridge 1989).

James C. Whorton

Bibliography

Akers, Keith. 1983. *A vegetarian sourcebook.* New York.

Alcott, William. 1838. *Vegetable diet: As sanctioned by medical men, and by experience in all ages.* Boston, Mass.

1840. Animal and vegetable food. *Library of Health* 4: 220-2.

Amato, Paul, and Sonia Partridge. 1989. *The new vegetarians.* New York.

Aquinas, Thomas. 1989. *Summa theologiae: A concise translation,* ed. Timothy McDermott. London.

Barkas, Janet. 1975. *The vegetable passion.* New York.

Beaumont, William. 1833. *Experiments and observations on the gastric juice, and the physiology of digestion.* Plattsburgh, N.Y.

Bentham, Jeremy. 1961. *An introduction to the principles of morals and legislation.* Garden City, N.Y.

Cambell, David. 1837. Stimulation. *Graham Journal of Health and Longevity* 1: 290-1.

Chen, Thomas, and Peter Chen. 1989. Intestinal autointoxication: A medical leitmotif. *Journal of Clinical Gastroenterology* 11: 434-41.

Cheyne, George. 1734. *An essay of health and long life.* London.

Cottingham, John. 1978. "A brute to the brutes?": Descartes' treatment of animals. *Philosophy* 53: 551-9.

Darwin, Charles. 1874. *The descent of man.* New York.

Diamond, Cora. 1978. Eating meat and eating people. *Philosophy* 53: 465-79.

Dombrowski, David. 1984. *The philosophy of vegetarianism.* Amherst, Mass.

Forward, Charles. 1898. *Fifty years of food reform.* London.

Francis, Leslie, and Richard Norman. 1978. Some animals are more equal than others. *Philosophy* 53: 507-27.

Graham, Sylvester. 1839. *Lectures on the science of human life.* Boston, Mass.

Haig, Alexander. 1892. *Uric acid as a factor in the causation of disease.* London.

Hardinge, Mervyn, and Hulda Crooks. 1963. Non-flesh dietaries. *Journal of the American Dietetic Association* 43: 545-9.

Harrison, Ruth. 1964. *Animal machines.* London.

Kellogg, John Harvey. 1905. *Shall we slay to eat?* Battle Creek, Mich.

1918. *Autointoxication or intestinal toxemia.* Battle Creek, Mich.

1919. *The itinerary of a breakfast.* Battle Creek, Mich.

1923. *The natural diet of man.* Battle Creek, Mich.

Lambe, William. 1815. *Additional reports on the effects of a peculiar regimen.* London.

Lappé, Frances Moore. 1971. *Diet for a small planet.* New York.

Numbers, Ronald. 1976. *Prophetess of health: A study of Ellen G. White.* New York.

Oswald, John. 1791. *The cry of nature.* London.

Plutarch. 1898. Of eating of flesh. In *Plutarch's miscellanies and essays,* Vol. 5, trans. William Goodwin, 3-16. Boston, Mass.

Porphyry. 1965. *Porphyry on abstinence from animal food*, trans. Thomas Taylor. London.

Proceedings. 1851. *American Vegetarian* 1: 6.

Regan, Tom. 1975. The moral basis of vegetarianism. *Canadian Journal of Philosophy* 5: 181–214.

Ryder, Richard. 1979. The struggle against speciesism. In *Animals' rights - a symposium*, ed. David Patterson and Richard Ryder, 3–14. Fontwell, England.

Salt, Henry. 1892. *Animals' rights considered in relation to social progress.* London.

  1899. *The logic of vegetarianism.* London.

Schwartz, Richard. 1970. *John Harvey Kellogg, M.D.* Nashville, Tenn.

Shelley, Percy Bysshe. [1813] 1884. *A vindication of natural diet.* London.

Singer, Peter. 1975. *Animal liberation: A new ethics for our treatment of animals.* New York.

Spencer, Colin. 1993. *The heretic's feast.* London.

Stevenson, Lloyd. 1956. Religious elements in the background of the British anti-vivisection movement. *Yale Journal of Biology and Medicine* 29: 125–57.

Trall, Russell. 1860. *The scientific basis of vegetarianism.* Philadelphia, Pa.

Trowell, Hugh. 1981. *Western diseases, their emergence and prevention.* Cambridge, Mass.

Tryon, Thomas. 1683. *The way to health, long life and happiness.* London.

Turner, James. 1980. *Reckoning with the beast.* Baltimore, Md.

The vegetarian movement. 1848. *Punch* 15: 182.

Voltaire. 1962. *Philosophical dictionary*, Vol. 1, trans. Peter Gay. New York.

Whorton, James. 1977. "Tempest in a flesh-pot": The formulation of a physiological rationale for vegetarianism. *Journal of the History of Medicine and Allied Sciences* 32: 115–39.

  1981. Muscular vegetarianism: The debate over diet and athletic performance in the progressive era. *Journal of Sport History* 8: 58–75.

  1982. *Crusaders for fitness: The history of American health reformers.* Princeton, N.J.

  1989. Eating to win: Popular concepts of diet, strength, and energy in the early twentieth century. In *Fitness in American culture: Images of health, sport, and the body, 1830–1940*, ed. Kathryn Grover, 86–122. Amherst, Mass.

  1991. Inner hygiene: The philosophy and practice of intestinal purity in Western civilization. In *History of hygiene. Proceedings of the 12th international symposium on the comparative history of medicine - east and west*, ed. Y. Kawakita, S. Sakai, and Y. Otsuka. Tokyo.

  1994. Historical development of vegetarianism. *American Journal of Clinical Nutrition* 60 (Supplement): 1103–9.

VI.18 ❧ Vegetarianism: Another View

Early Humankind

Vegetarianism is a cultural and social, rather than a biological, phenomenon. Anatomically and physiologically, the digestive organs of the human species are designed for both animal and plant foods. Moreover, a global cross-cultural survey demonstrates the fact that all cultures, past and present, have revealed a preference for at least some form of animal fat and protein and that none have ever been totally vegetarian (Abrams 1987b: 207–23).

Current paleoanthropological research indicates that humans have been on this earth for some 3 to 4 million years. For over 99 percent of that time, humans were hunters and gatherers (Cohen 1977: 15; Johanson and White 1979: 321–30). From the Australopithecines to the inception of agriculture, humans gradually developed more efficient tools to obtain food, especially for hunting game. *Homo erectus* pursued large game, and early *Homo sapiens,* the late Paleolithic humans, were even more dedicated in this regard.

Indeed, the availability of game may well have dictated human settlement patterns. As population pressure mounted in Africa, the original home of humankind, herds of game dwindled, forcing people further afield to follow other herds. This ultimately led to human settlements in Asia, Europe, the Americas, and Australia - in all of the continents except Antarctica.

About 10,000 years ago, beginning in the Middle East, people finally started to raise plant foods because of their own growing number, on the one hand, and because so many game animals were scarce or had been hunted to extinction, on the other. And with sedentary agriculture came political organization and formal religions.

Religion and Diet

As people settled into sedentary agriculture, meat-eating prohibitions gradually became part of the tenets of some of their religions, such as Hinduism. Ultra-orthodox Hindus and Jains, for example, are strict vegetarians, but as anthropologist Marvin Harris points out, in earlier times the Hindus were beef eaters. Later, beef eating was restricted, primarily, to the Brahman caste; and finally, the practice became prohibited for all Hindus.

Harris has argued that such a prohibition was the result of human population growth. Because cows were valuable as draft animals and as providers of milk and dung (as fuel for cooking), it was wasteful to use them for meat. In fact, Harris argues that the consumption of certain animals is prohibited in many cultures for pragmatic reasons (Harris 1977: 129–52) and that compliance is more likely when such prohibitions are codified as tenets of religion (Dwyer et al. 1973: 856–65; Mayer 1973: 32; Todhunter 1973: 286).

Other religious groups that today adhere to some type of vegetarianism include Buddhists, Seventh-Day Adventists, and orders such as the Roman Catholic Trappist monks. Justification of vegetarianism on religious grounds may be because it is more spiritual, or because it is more in harmony with nature, or because of the conviction that all animal life is sacred (Abrams 1980: 53–87).

Modern-Day Vegetarianism

A phenomenal escalation of vegetarianism, which began in the 1960s, has occurred in the Western world and has had little to do with religion (Erhard 1973: 4–12; Sonnenberg and Zolber 1973). The new vegetarians include a wide variety of individuals with concerns ranging from what animals are fed and injected with to environmental problems and world hunger to the indictment of cholesterol and animal fats as causative factors in the development of vascular diseases, cancers, and premature deaths.

There is also considerable variation in the practice of vegetarianism. At one extreme are the vegans, who exclude all types of animal protein from their diet and subsist solely on vegetables, seeds, nuts, and fruits. Moreover, their dietary beliefs are extended to other daily activities. Vegans shun clothing made of animal products such as wool, silk, leather, fur, or pearl (Erhard 1974: 20–7). They abstain from using consumer goods, such as soap or cosmetics made with animal fat or brushes of animal hair, and they refuse immunization from animal-derived sera or drugs, or toiletries whose safety has been determined by animal testing.

Vegetarians toward the middle of the continuum choose a wider variety of foods and include certain animal protein foods in their diets. Lacto-vegetarians, for example, use dairy products; ovo-vegetarians, eggs; pollo-vegetarians, poultry; and pesco-vegetarians, fish. Some will use more than one type of animal protein foods, such as lacto-ovo vegetarians, who consume dairy products and eggs along with other foods.

Opposite to the vegans on the vegetarian continuum are the red-meat abstainers, who consume all animal protein foods except beef, lamb, and pork (Fleck 1976: 408–27).

Extreme Vegetarianism and Health

One form of extreme vegetarianism is the final stage of the Zen macrobiotic diet. This vegetarian phenomenon attained some popularity in the Western world during the 1960s but has declined since its founder's death. The diet encompasses a life philosophy based on a loose reading of Buddhist symbolism and the ancient Chinese dualistic concept of yin and yang (Dwyer 1979: 1–2). Allegedly, humans achieve harmony in all of life's manifestations by reaching a balance between the cosmic forces of yin and yang, which oppose while they complement one another (Keen 1978), such as male/female; contraction/expansion; and fire/water. In terms of food, such dualities are manifested in complements such as animal versus vegetable; mineral versus protein and fat; bitter and salty versus sweet.

According to the philosophy behind the macrobiotic persuasion, disease results from yin/yang imbalances, which can be restored by an ideal diet. The individual must follow 10 stages of an elaborate dietary regimen, with the final stage consisting solely of brown rice, salt, and fluids such as herbal teas. Reaching this final stage, presumably, assures attainment of perfect health, freedom from all disease, and spiritual enlightenment. In this latter connection, macrobiotics has been especially popular. Some individuals have embraced it in a search for an alternative to drug experimentation in order to experience a "natural high" (Keen 1978).

Yet one account, *The Death Diet* (Christagu 1967: 43–7), has described the tragedy suffered by a young couple upon reaching the tenth stage of the macrobiotic diet. The health of the male was impaired severely, and the woman died. Her death certificate read, "Multiple vitamin and protein deficiencies precipitated the chain of events leading to her death" (Mayer 1975).

Total vegetarians are likely to suffer deficiencies of many of the chief nutrients, among them vitamin B_{12}. All foods of animal origin contain vitamin B_{12}, yet plant sources for this vitamin are unreliable. The human body stores at least a thousand times the Recommended Dietary Allowance (RDA) of vitamin B_{12}, which is an amount sufficient to maintain serum levels in some people for up to five years, although there are a wide range of serum levels associated with the deficiency. Thus, deficiency may not be apparent for some time while reserves of the vitamin are gradually being tapped (Ellis and Mumford 1967: 205; Ellis and Montegriffo 1970: 249). It can be difficult to detect vitamin B_{12} deficiency because of the high folic acid intake of vegetarians, which frequently masks symptoms of the condition (Brown 1990: 175). All of this is particularly unfortunate because early detection of the deficiency is vital to avoid irreversible neurological impairment.

Some vegetarians, although aware of the risk of vitamin B_{12} deficiency, depend nonetheless on plants for this vitamin, despite the unreliability of such foods as a source. When found in plants, vitamin B_{12} is present only because of bacteria growing on the plant or because the plant has been contaminated by bacteria, especially from fecal matter. Spirulina and tempeh, used frequently by vegetarians as vitamin B_{12} sources, have virtually none and in fact provide B_{12} analogues that actually block the metabolism of functional vitamin B_{12} (Bailie 1987: 98–105).

Vitamin B_{12} deficiency can result in megaloblastic anemia, a grave condition. In the mid-1970s, a high incidence of megaloblastic anemia was reported among orthodox Hindus who had emigrated from India to England. The phenomenon was puzzling. The orthodox Hindus did not have vitamin B_{12} deficiency while they lived in India, nor after they first emigrated, but developed the deficiency during their residence in England. Their diet was similar in both countries. But investigations revealed that the cause stemmed from differences in growing, processing, and packaging foods in the two countries.

In India, where crops had minimal applications of costly pesticides, many plants were insect-contaminated, and the insects, or their eggs and larvae, contributed a supply of vitamin B_{12} to the diet. Additional opportunities for insect contamination were provided by minimally processed or packaged food. Thus, in India, the orthodox Hindus had adventitiously obtained sufficient vitamin B_{12} to prevent deficiency, a finding that helps to explain why extreme vegetarians in other developing countries may escape it as well. But ironically, the privileged in those countries, who can afford to purchase imported foods that are highly processed and protectively packaged, may suffer from an inadequate vitamin B_{12} intake (Rose 1976: 87).

In addition to lacking vitamin B_{12}, extreme vegetarian diets are often deficient in adequate proteins and even calories. Moreover, total vegetarian diets tend to be low in calcium and riboflavin (Raper and Hill 1973). Certain coarse, green leafy vegetables may be high in calcium, but the calcium is not well absorbed because of the high fiber content of the diet, and other minerals, including zinc, phosphorus, and iron, may also be poorly absorbed (Haviland 1967: 316–25; Reinhold et al. 1976: 163–80; Bodzy et al. 1977: 1139; Freeland, Ebangit, and Johnson 1978: 253).

Calcium absorption is also impaired by certain green leafy vegetables, such as spinach and Swiss chard, that contain oxalates. These compounds bind with calcium during digestion to form insoluble calcium oxalate, which is not utilized, and the calcium is excreted in the feces (Albanese 1980). Moreover, whole grains, frequently consumed in large quantities by many vegetarians, are high in phytates, and these substances, like the oxalates, interfere with calcium absorption (Hegsted 1976: 509). Similarly, vegetarians may have low zinc levels due to phytates and oxalates in their diets. In contrast, foods from animal sources provide dietary zinc, but they do not contain the inhibiting phytate and oxalate compounds (Prasad 1966: 225–38).

Zinc insufficiency is one of the greatest but least-known dangers of vegetarianism, according to the late Carl C. Pfeiffer, who commented wryly that "the light headed feeling of detachment that enshrouds some vegetarians can be caused by hidden zinc hunger, rather than by some mystical quality of the brown rice or other food consumed" (Pfeiffer 1975: 103). Among other things, low zinc levels are related to male infertility. In one study, mild zinc depletion in nine male volunteers resulted in decreased fertility, and the sperm count of the men fell to an infertility level after the men intentionally ate a zinc-deficient diet for about six months (Prasad 1982).

Obtaining sufficient iron can also be a problem for vegetarians, and women on strict vegetarian diets, especially during child-bearing years, may have real difficulties in this regard (Mayer 1973: 32). As with zinc, foods of animal origin are reliable iron sources, whereas foods of plant origin are not. Moreover, heme iron from foods of animal origin is absorbed and utilized far more efficiently than nonheme iron from plant foods: 10 to 30 percent can be absorbed from animal foods, compared with only 2 to 10 percent from plant foods; and finally, phytates and oxalates interfere with iron absorption (Finch 1969: 3).

Normal plasma estrogen levels are necessary for women's menstrual regularity. Because nutrition can affect hormone levels, dietary differences may affect menstrual patterns, as was shown in a study of evenly matched nonvegetarian and vegetarian premenopausal women at the Milton S. Hershey Medical Center in Hershey, Pennsylvania: Only 4.9 percent of the nonvegetarians experienced menstrual irregularities, whereas 26.5 percent of the vegetarians had difficulties. The probability of menstrual regularity was associated positively with protein and cholesterol intake and negatively with dietary fiber and magnesium intake (Pedersen, Bartholomew, and Dolence 1991: 879–85). Such results are consistent with the hypothesis that premenopausal vegetarian women have circulating estrogen concentrations (Lloyd, Schaeffer, and Walter 1991: 1005–10) and that these women may also have decreased reproductive capacity (Pedersen et al. 1991: 879–85). Another study at the Hershey Medical Center reveals that the frequency of menstrual irregularity was significantly higher in a lacto-ovo vegetarian group of women than in a matched group of nonvegetarian women (Lloyd et al. 1991: 1005–10).

Infants and children may suffer the most from extreme vegetarian diets. Commenting on this issue, the pediatrician George Kerr observed that "history has many examples of parents abusing children for the very best intention.... Specifically, should we start considering reporting these cases of growth failure on vegan diets to the authorities involved with child abuse?" (Kerr 1974: 675–6).

Infants breast-fed by women who are strict vegetarians have been found to be deficient in vitamin B_{12}, and such lactating women are advised both to take a vitamin B_{12} supplement and to include soybean milk or fermented soybean foods in their diets (Dwyer 1979: 1–2). Vegetarian infants and children tend to be smaller and to grow at a slower rate than do children from the general meat-eating population. One factor may be the high-bulk/low-calorie content characteristic of vegetarian diets (Erhard 1973: 11).

Pediatricians have expressed concerns about the vulnerability of infants and growing children who are especially at risk from extreme vegetarianism. "Kokoh," a special macrobiotic infant-feeding formula, was found to be capable of inducing kwashiorkor, one form of protein–energy malnutrition. Moreover, the

American Academy of Pediatrics (ACP) has reported that infants fed solely on this formula from birth usually are underweight within a few months and below average in total body length (Abrams 1980: 57).

Other research and clinical observations have also shown that infants fed no animal protein fail to grow at a normal rate and may develop kwashiorkor. Infants who are breast-fed and then placed on vegan diets do not grow or develop as normal infants, nor do they do as well as infants fed vegetarian diets supplemented with cow's milk (Erhard 1973: 10–12).

Vegetarianism and Chronic Diseases

Ancel Keys's seminal reports (Keys 1956: 364; Keys, Anderson, and Grande 1957: 959), followed by others, suggested a direct relationship between diet, especially animal fats, heart disease (Connor, Stone, and Hodges 1964: 1691–1705; West and Hayes 1968: 853; Anderson, Grande, and Keys 1976: 1184), and colon cancer (Burkitt 1971: 3, 1973: 274; Berg, Howell, and Silverman 1973: 915; Reiser 1973: 524, 1978: 865; Hill 1975: 31; Howell 1975; Nichols et al. 1976: 1384; Truswell 1978: 977–89). Conclusions drawn from these studies, however, remain controversial, and many other studies take issue with them (Mann et al. 1961: 31; Mann 1977: 644; Enstrom 1975: 432; Lyon, Klauber, and Gardner 1976: 129; Enig, Munn, and Keeney 1978: 2215; Glueck and Connor 1978: 727).

Nonetheless, the public has been led to believe that foods that contain saturated fat and cholesterol, such as eggs and red meats, are related to heart disease and colon cancer. In fact, some alarmed individuals have embraced a limited or total vegetarian diet in the belief that such measures will ward off these illnesses (Hardinge and Stare 1954: 83; West and Hayes 1968: 853; Ruys and Hickie 1976: 87; Sanders, Ellis, and Dickerson 1978: 805).

In truth, however, research has produced contradictory and puzzling findings. Seventh-Day Adventists, for example, have an educational health program for their members that advocates a well-balanced diet, including milk and eggs, along with other foods. In other words, these lacto-ovo vegetarians eat adequate amounts of animal protein foods, although they exclude red meats. Additionally, Seventh-Day Adventists have been found to have lower rates of cancer and coronary artery disease than the general American population (Wynder, Lemon, and Bross 1959: 1016–28). For cancer, they experience a 50 to 70 percent lower mortality incidence than the general population (Phillips 1975: 3513). For coronary heart disease, mortality was lower in males under 65 years of age than in the general population but not in males over 65, nor in females of any age (Phillips et al. 1978: S191).

Because Seventh-Day Adventists are red-meat abstainers, it was assumed that such abstention accounted for their lower incidence of heart disease than that of the general public. But other confounding factors may play important roles in preventing these diseases. For example, Seventh-Day Adventists abstain from tobacco, alcohol, and caffeinated beverages (Dwyer 1979: 1–2).

Members of the Church of Jesus Christ of Latter Day Saints (Mormons) provide another homogeneous group for study. Mormons are not red-meat abstainers, but the church urges moderation in lifestyle. Compared to the American average, Utahan Mormons were found to have a 22 percent lower incidence of cancer in general and a 34 percent lower incidence of colon cancer (Lyon et al. 1976: 129). However, Puerto Ricans, who eat large amounts of animal fats, especially pork, have very low rates of colon and breast cancers (Enig et al. 1978: 2215). Such contradictions practically leap off the pages of a comparative study of the incidence of breast and colon cancers conducted in Finland and the Netherlands. People in these two countries eat similar levels of animal fats per person per day, but despite this similarity, the incidence of breast and colon cancer in the Netherlands was nearly double that of Finland (Enig et al. 1978: 2215).

Nor are such contradictions confined to cancer. A study in western Australia has contradicted the notion that a high serum cholesterol level increases the risk of heart attack. Three groups of mothers and children were studied: those with high, those with medium, and those with low cholesterol levels. The groups had no significant differences in their daily dietary intake of proteins, fats, and carbohydrates, and obesity was ruled out as a factor, because cholesterol levels did not differ between the obese and the nonobese.

The conclusion reached was that diet did not appear to account for differences in cholesterol levels in a culturally homogeneous group. Furthermore, the "correlation between habitual diet and the average serum cholesterol level is good between contrasting populations (for example, people of Japan and Finland)" but "within a given culture, people eating the same kind of food can have different serum lipids. Those who develop coronary heart disease do not necessarily eat differently from those who do not" (Hitchcock and Gracey 1977: 790).

More recently, additional confounding evidence has been contributed by the so-called French Paradox. The eating habits of people in Gascony, in the southwest of France, were studied for 10 years. This area is noted as the world's leading producer of cholesterol-laden foie gras. People in Gascony consume goose and duck fat liberally, snack on dried duck skin, and eat more than twice as much foie gras as other French people and 50 times as much as Americans. Yet they were found to have the lowest incidence of death from cardiovascular disease in all of France. In Gascony, of 100,000 middle-aged men, about 80 die annually of heart attack, compared with 145 elsewhere in France and 315 in the United States (O'Neill 1991: 1, 22).

Fats

Because of the negative publicity that fats have received of late, we sometimes tend to forget that fat is essential for proper growth and development, even for life itself. Fat provides essential fatty acids necessary for cell membrane structure and for prostaglandins; it also acts as a carrier for the fat-soluble vitamins. Humans require different types of fats for different purposes, both structural and storage. Structural fats make possible the growth of the brain and the central nervous system and maintain cell membrane integrity. Structural fats are found inside the cell. Cell membranes are not mere envelopes but active parts of the cell, arranged as an orderly production line, creating some things, breaking down others, and transferring raw materials (nutrients) as needed from one place to another. Storage fats, no less important, are used for energy (Crawford and Marsh 1989: 120).

Vegetable Oils

It may be unfortunate that millions of people have been persuaded to change their choices of fat in the belief that oils from plants containing predominantly polyunsaturated or monounsaturated fatty acids are good, and fats from animals are bad. There is an argument that large amounts of polyunsaturated oils in the diet may be detrimental to health (Lyon 1977: 28–31). Although vegetable oils have been offered with promises of risk reductions for cardiovascular diseases, some authorities find these claims to be misleading and inaccurate (Pinckney and Pinckney 1973: 31–8; Moore 1989: 40–95).

Eggs and Cholesterol

Cholesterol has also gotten a bad press, which tends to obscure its vital roles in human health. It is needed for the transmission of nerve impulses throughout the body, and, in fact, the nervous system cannot function properly with insufficient cholesterol. In addition, cholesterol is needed to produce sex hormones. Indeed, it may well be because cholesterol is so crucial that the human body does not depend solely on dietary sources but also manufactures cholesterol. If dietary cholesterol is insufficiently supplied, then the body manufactures more to meet its requirements. Thus, Roger J. Williams turned current wisdom on its head when he observed that "anyone who deliberately avoids cholesterol in his diet may be inadvertently courting heart disease" (Williams 1971: 73).

In response to public concern about eggs and their cholesterol content, food processors have countered by concocting products that contain egg white (the noncholesterol component) but no yolk (the cholesterol-containing component). These products were intended for omelets and scrambled egg dishes. M. K. Navidi and F. A. Kummerow of the Burnsides Research Laboratory, University of Illinois, undertook an experiment to determine the nutritional value of such replacer eggs. They fed one group of lactating rats exclusively on fresh eggs and another group on Egg Beaters. They intended to run the experiment for 40 days, but all the rats on the egg substitute were dead in 17 days. They were underweight, were severely stunted in growth, and had mottled hair. All the rats on fresh whole eggs were healthy and normally sized (Navidi and Kummerow 1974: 565).

Diet and Primitive Societies

In using the term "primitive," we would note at the outset that there are no primitive peoples. The term, when used by anthropologists, denotes the development of technology used by cultures.

Not many hunting and gathering societies have survived to the present, and those that have are rapidly becoming acculturated. Yet the few still in existence have been extensively studied, with such efforts contributing considerably to our knowledge of the diet and health of past peoples.

Among other things, such knowledge disputes vegetarians who defend their practice with the claim that individuals in primitive societies (and presumably our ancestors) were herbivores who lived primarily on plant foods. The evidence is that most hunting-and-gathering peoples consume large amounts of meat and other types of animal protein whenever it is available.

The Eskimos constitute a classic example. They lived almost entirely on a traditional diet of raw sea and land mammals, fish, and birds, and so long as the traditional diet was followed, Eskimos remained in excellent health. Indeed, the raw meat and organs of these animals, including the liver and the adrenal glands, even provided an ample supply of vitamin C, so long as the meat was raw or cooked only a little. Being heat-sensitive, vitamin C is destroyed in meats by normal cooking (Stefansson 1960: 58).

Although it was obvious that Eskimos could thrive on a diet of raw meat (Stefansson 1937), the notion persisted that such a diet would probably harm Europeans, which led to an interesting experiment. Under the auspices of the Russell Sage Institute of Pathology at Bellevue Hospital (an affiliate of the Cornell University Medical College of New York), the anthropologist Vilhjalmur Stefansson and his colleague Karsten Anderson volunteered to eat a ratio of 2 pounds of raw lean meat to a half pound of raw fat and nothing else daily for a year. Both men thrived. After the year was up, Stefansson, who had previously lived for years on the Eskimo diet, continued on it for decades more and enjoyed sound health until his death at age 83. Similarly, Anderson was found to be in better physical condition after eating the traditional Eskimo diet for the year than when he began the experiment (Stefansson 1957: 60–89).

The Eskimo diet, then, also tends to confound the notion that meat and fats undermine human health. Paul Martin, for example, who spent years in the Arctic, discovered that although Eskimos consumed large amounts of animal fats, whale blubber, and seal oil, they did not have problems with cholesterol and, in fact, were remarkably free of degenerative diseases, especially those related to heart and to blood pressure (Martin 1977: 25-8).

Another observer of indigenous Eskimo culture concluded that the native diet of raw land and sea mammals and fish provided all the nutrients needed for excellent health (Schaefer 1971: 8-16). Unfortunately, with their adoption of industrialized foods since World War II, consisting mainly of refined carbohydrates (sugar and white flour), chemically altered fats, and other highly processed foods, the Eskimos began to suffer from those degenerative diseases common to the modern industrialized world (Schaefer 1971: 8-16).

George V. Mann, of Vanderbilt University Medical College, who challenged Keys's fat hypothesis, initiated several studies with the few available primitive societies still living largely on animal foods. He reasoned that if a high fat and cholesterol intake really did cause heart disease, then hypercholesteremia and coronary heart disease ought to characterize the health of groups of people living on high fat and cholesterol diets.

Mann first studied the Pygmies in the African rain forest. Almost untouched by civilization, these people have continued on a traditional diet of large amounts of meat, supplemented with plant foods. But Mann discovered that despite a high level of meat consumption, adult male Pygmies had the lowest cholesterol levels yet recorded (Mann et al. 1961).

Next, Mann observed the Masai of Tanganyika, a nomadic pastoral people living almost exclusively on meat, cow's blood, and milk. His examination of 400 Masai adult males revealed very little cardiovascular disease and no signs of arteriosclerotic disease. As a result of his investigation, Mann concluded that the widely held notion that meat and milk cause coronary heart disease is unsupported by the evidence (Mann 1963: 104).

Modern Nutrition and Tooth Decay

Tooth decay has been known throughout human history, but only in relatively modern times has it become endemic. The evidence shows that tooth decay was rare throughout the Paleolithic period, which spanned some 3 to 4 million years.

When the hunting-and-gathering way of life gave way to stable agriculture, though, the switch led, among other things, to increased tooth decay. And it would seem that dependence on high-carbohydrate foods, such as grains and other plant foods, began to seriously undermine the health of those who did not find a way to maintain a favorable dietary balance between high-quality animal protein foods and lower-quality plant protein foods (Page and Abrams 1974: 188-203, 214-26; Abrams 1976: 102-12, 1978: 41-55).

Skeletal remains of European populations reveal a slow, steady increase in tooth decay from the Neolithic period when agriculture first began until the present, when it escalated (Wells 1964; Abrams 1976: 102-12, 1978: 41-55). Such a deterioration in teeth is also vividly portrayed in the experience of the Lapps (Sami) of northern Europe, who until recently had hunted in a manner similar to that of the late Paleolithic age and lived mainly on reindeer meat. They consumed about a pound of meat per person each day and were renowned for their healthy teeth. Eighteenth-century skeletal remains show a cavity rate of only 1.5 percent in Lapp teeth. But gradually, Lapps adopted the industrialized diet, with the result that their cavity rate has soared to 85 percent (Pelto and Pelto 1979: 292-301).

Examination of the skulls of the ancient Norse, who subsisted almost entirely on fish, seafood, and animals, also showed that dental decay was rare (Page and Abrams 1974: 188-203, 214-26). But skeletal remains of prehistoric Indians in the California area, whose diet was primarily vegetarian, revealed that 25 percent of the population had some tooth decay (Pelto and Pelto 1979: 292-301). Substantially worse were the teeth of prehistoric Indians in New Mexico, whose diet was based on corn (maize), supplemented with a few other plant foods and small amounts of animal protein. Tooth decay was a problem for 75 percent of that population (Pelto and Pelto 1979: 292-301).

Such relationships between diet and dental decay, as well as other degenerative diseases, has also been well documented by Weston A. Price's pioneering efforts around the globe. He found, for example, that so long as the Australian Aborigine, Polynesian, Eskimo, and other peoples followed their traditional diets, consisting of animal foods and unrefined, unprocessed plant foods, they had an exceptionally low incidence of caries and other health problems. But after adopting an industrialized diet these same peoples developed rampant tooth decay and other degenerative diseases, as well as malformations in offspring (Price 1989: 59-72).

Animal experiments have yielded similar results that underscore observations on human populations. Protein-malnourished rat pups developed more caries than when protein was amply supplied. Rats fed adequate calories but no protein also had a high incidence of tooth decay (DiOrio, Miller, and Navia 1973: 856-65; Menaker and Navia 1973: 680-7; Navia 1979: 1-4). Clearly, such findings suggest that humans, especially infants and children, are more susceptible to tooth decay if deprived of adequate animal protein foods.

Diet and the Lower Primates

It is sometimes argued that the basic human diet should be plant food because closely related species of primates such as monkeys and apes are vegetarian. Yet, since World War II, ethological studies on primates in the wild have shown that monkeys and apes, despite a predominantly vegetarian diet, nonetheless seek out small animals, insects, insect eggs, and larvae as food (Abrams 1980: 75).

Marmosets and squirrel monkeys are especially fond of crickets and flies (Abrams 1980: 75). Baboons actively hunt, kill, and eat a variety of wild animals, and zoo marmosets have failed to mate until animal foods were added to their diets (Abrams 1978: 42–50). Jane Goodall has witnessed chimpanzees in the wild fashioning crude tools to gather termites as food and has observed them killing and eating arboreal monkeys, baby baboons, and other small animals (Goodall 1971).

Gibbons often eat rodents, birds, and small antelopes. Orangutans feed on larvae, beetles, nesting birds, and squirrels. And in captivity, gorillas show a preference for meat over vegetarian fare (Perry 1976: 165–85). In this connection, it should be noted that the desire of chimpanzees to eat meat does not stem from a lack of plant foods, which are abundant and constitute most of their diet (Eimerl and De Vore 1968: 142–52; Goodall 1971).

Such findings have made it necessary to reclassify monkeys and apes. Rather than being herbivores, these animals are now recognized as omnivores, and the reason that they do not eat more animal food than they do may be the result of a limited ability to provide it in great abundance. But in seeking the animal foods that they do consume, monkeys and apes are most likely driven by a basic need to meet nutritional requirements that are available only from animal protein (Abrams 1980: 76).

The tree shrew, the most primitive of all the living primates, is closest in structure to the fossil ancestors of the first primates, who date from about 70 million years ago. The tree shrew is almost exclusively an insectivore (Berg et al. 1973: 915). Such findings about the primate progenitors of humans strongly suggest that all primates, including humans, have a basic need for some animal protein in the diet (Abrams 1980: 76).

In moving away from lower primates to humans, we find that available paleontological and archaeological data can tell us much about the diet of humans for most of their time on earth.

Humans as Hunters

Fossil remains of *Australopithecus,* the first humans (Dart 1969: 42–189; Leakey 1971: 215–90), have been found over the savannas of South and East Africa (Leakey 1971: 215–90). They ate their food raw, but unlike other primates, they made and utilized crude stone tools to collect more food per unit of time. Their diet consisted of insects and small animals and plant foods that could be eaten raw as found in nature (Biegert 1975: 717–27). They scavenged, eating the remains of any large carcass they found, and apparently were able to obtain surprisingly large amounts of meat (Schaller and Lowther 1969: 307–34).

Through mutations and natural selections, about a million years ago a more advanced human, *Homo erectus,* evolved. These people developed far more efficient tools and techniques for hunting large animals and spread from Africa into Asia and southern Europe (Constable 1973: 29–37, 70).

Between 35,000 and 70,000 years ago, modern *Homo sapiens* evolved. The late Paleolithic *Homo sapiens* is exemplified by Cro-Magnon man (Prideaux 1973). *Homo sapiens* continued to improve hunting techniques and followed game from Africa to the far north of Europe and, finally, to Siberia, the Americas, and Australia. Cro-Magnon's religion and magic, reflected in extraordinary cave art, centered around the theme of the hunt for large game.

Both archaeological excavations and cave art reveal the variety of meat available. In Europe and Asia, for example, Cro-Magnon hunted for bear, cave lion, hyena, wild horse, bison, woolly rhinoceros, reindeer, chamois, ibex, woolly mammoth, and deer. In the Americas, the quarry became the dire wolf, mammoth, giant beaver, giant sloth, American camel, and more than 100 other species (Prideaux 1973: 12, 14, 42–78). But beginning about 40,000 years ago, many of the large animal species began to die out worldwide, and by approximately 10,000 years ago, numerous animals had been hunted to extinction (Martin 1967: 32–8). Anthropologist Sherwood L. Washburn has postulated that the quest for game was a significant factor in the evolution and intellectual development of humans. Beginning with the *Australopithecines* and continuing over eons until the domestication of plants and animals, humans increasingly learned to be ever more efficient hunters, to devise better and better strategies, and to invent and improve better and more effective tools as well as techniques for using them. That humans were forced to shift from hunting and gathering to sedentary agriculture because of a decreasing supply of large animals suggests that they were too successful in perfecting their hunting techniques (Washburn 1961: 299).

Nutrients in Plants and Animals

It should be clear by now that our ancestors, both of the lower primates and of humans, consumed much in the way of animal food and with good reason, for nutrients in meat are much more highly concentrated and are utilized more efficiently than those from plant foods. For example, venison provides 572 calories/100 grams of weight, compared with only 100 calories from a similar amount of fruits and vegetables (White and Brown 1973: 68–94). Humans, then, developed an ability not only to hunt an animal efficiently but also to digest it efficiently. Through natural selection both of these abilities afforded humans an adaptive advantage for survival in a changing environment (Bronowski 1972: 42–56).

A full day of foraging is required to obtain the amount of food value from plants that is found in one small animal. By eating animals that lived on grasses and leaves, humans could obtain a highly concentrated and complete food, converted from plants into meat. When humans moved into the cold regions of northern Europe and Asia, they had to rely on meat even more. Edible plant foods were available only seasonally, whereas game was available throughout the year (Campbell 1976: 253–302). Moreover, game did not need to be cooked, whereas many plant foods had to be prepared in this fashion to be edible. *Homo erectus* may have used fire to a very limited extent some 300,000 years ago, but the evidence is sparse and questionable. Fire's general use, according to both paleontological and archaeological records, began only about 40,000 to 50,000 years ago (Abrams 1976: 102–12).

The use of fire, extended to food preparation, resulted in a great increase and variety of plant food supply. All of the major basic domesticated plant foods, such as wheat, barley, rice, millet, rye, and potatoes, require cooking before they are suitable for human consumption. In fact, in a raw state, many plants contain toxic or indigestible substances or antinutrients. But after cooking, many of these undesirable substances are deactivated, neutralized, reduced, or released; and starch and other nutrients in the plants are rendered absorbable by the digestive tract. Thus, the use of fire to cook plant foods doubtless encouraged the domestication of these foods and, thus, was a vitally important factor in human cultural advancement (Abrams 1986: 24–9).

In summary, it seems clear that the natural diet of humans is an omnivorous one and that proteins from animal sources are vital to health and well-being. This is because proteins differ in quality, depending on the amino acids from which they are built. Some amino acids ("nonessential" or "dispensable") can be synthesized in the human body; others ("essential" or "indispensable") must be supplied by food. For optimal protein quality, all amino acids must be present and in optimal ratios with one another. No individual plant meets these requirements, whereas all foods of animal origin do.

The egg represents the ideal quality protein against which all other proteins are measured in terms of its protein efficiency ratio (PER). At the top of the PER scale, the egg is followed closely by proteins from other animal sources, both organ and muscle meats. The PERs for plant foods such as legumes, grains, and seeds are much lower on the scale because all are limited by a low level of one or more of the amino acids, which are not in good balance with each other. To obtain an amount sufficient to meet human requirements, one would need to consume enormous quantities of a plant food, and the total diet would become imbalanced.

Perhaps in the future, with genetic engineering and other scientific and technological advances, it will become possible to develop plant foods that will supply, in ideal balance, all the amino acids and other nutrients required for optimal health. Meanwhile, it seems prudent to keep the traditional dietary wisdom of our predecessors and apply it, insofar as possible, to modern life, meaning that humans should eat a varied, balanced diet consisting of both animal and plant foods, all in moderation.

H. Leon Abrams, Jr.

Bibliography

Abrams, H. Leon. 1976. *Inquiry into anthropology.* New York.
  1978. A diachronic preview of wheat in hominid nutrition. *Journal of Applied Nutrition* 30: 41–55.
  1980. Vegetarianism: An anthropological/nutritional evaluation. *Journal of Applied Nutrition* 32: 53–87.
  1986. Fire and cooking as a major influence on human cultural advancement: An anthropological/botanical/nutritional perspective. *Journal of Applied Nutrition* 38: 24–9.
  1987a. Hominid proclivity for sweetness: An anthropological view. *Journal of Applied Nutrition* 39: 35–41.
  1987b. The preference for animal protein and fat: A cross-cultural survey. In *Food and evolution: Toward a theory of human food habits,* ed. Marvin Harris and Eric B. Ross, 207–23. Philadelphia, Pa.
  1989. The relevance of Paleolithic diets in determining contemporary nutritional needs. *Journal of Applied Nutrition* 31: 43–59.
Albanese, A. A. 1980. *Nutrition for the elderly.* New York.
Anderson, Joseph T., Francisco Grande, and Ancel Keys. 1976. Independence of the effects of cholesterol and degree of saturation of the fat in the diet on serum cholesterol in man. *American Journal of Clinical Nutrition* 29: 1184–9.
Bailie, I. E. 1987. The first international congress on vegetarian nutrition. *Journal of Applied Nutrition* 39: 97–105.
Berg, J. W., M. A. Howell, and S. J. Silverman. 1973. Dietary hypotheses and diet-related research in the etiology of colon cancer. *Health Services Reports* 88: 915–24.
Biegert, J. 1975. Human evolution and nutrition. *Progress in Food and Nutrition Science* 1: 717–27.
Bodzy, Pamela W., Jeanne N. Freeland, Margaret A. Eppright, and Ann Tyree. 1977. Zinc status in the vegetarian. *Federation Proceedings* 36: 1139.
Bronowski, Jacob. 1972. *The ascent of man.* Boston, Mass.
Brown, Myrtle L., ed. 1990. *Present knowledge in nutrition.* Sixth edition. Washington, D.C.
Burkitt, Denis P. 1971. Epidemiology of cancer of the colon and rectum. *Cancer* 28: 3–13.
  1973. Some diseases characteristic of modern Western civilization. *British Medical Journal* 1: 274–8.
Campbell, Bernard G. 1976. *Humankind emerging.* Boston.

Campbell, Sheldon. 1978. Noah's ark in tomorrow's zoo: Animals are a'comin' two by two. *Smithsonian* 8: 42-50.

Christagu, R. 1967. The death diet. *Fact* 4: 43-7.

Cohen, Mark Nathan. 1977. *The food crisis in prehistory.* New Haven, Conn.

1989. *Health and the rise of civilization.* New Haven, Conn.

Connor, William E., Daniel B. Stone, and Robert E. Hodges. 1964. The interrelated effects of dietary cholesterol and fat upon human serum lipid levels. *Journal of Clinical Investigation* 41: 1691-1706.

Constable, G. 1973. *The Neanderthals.* New York.

Crawford, Michael, and David Marsh. 1989. *The driving force: Food, evolution, and the future.* New York.

Dart, R. 1969. *Adventures with the missing link.* New York.

DiOrio, Louis P., Sanford A. Miller, and Juan M. Navia. 1973. The separate effects of protein and calorie malnutrition on the development and growth of rat bones and teeth. *Journal of Nutrition* 103: 856-65.

Dwyer, Joanna. 1979. Vegetarianism. *Contemporary Nutrition* 4: 1-2.

Dwyer, Joanna, Laura D. V. H. Mayer, Randy Frances Kandel, and Jean Mayer. 1973. The new vegetarians. *Journal of the American Dietetic Association* 62: 503-9.

Eimerl, S., and Irven De Vore, eds. 1968. *The primates.* New York.

Ellis, Frey R., and V. M. E. Montegriffo. 1970. Veganism, clinical findings and investigations. *American Journal of Clinical Nutrition* 23: 249-55.

Ellis, Frey R., and P. Mumford. 1967. The nutritional status of vegans and vegetarians. *Proceedings of the Nutrition Society* 26: 205-12.

Enig, Mary G., Robert J. Munn, and Mark Keeney. 1978. Dietary fat and cancer trends – a critique. *Federation Proceedings* 37: 2215-20.

Enstrom, J. E. 1975. Colorectal cancer and consumption of beef and fat. *British Journal of Cancer* 32: 432-9.

Erhard, Darla. 1973. The new vegetarians. Part I. *Nutrition Today* 8: 4-12.

1974. The new vegetarians. Part II. *Nutrition Today* 9: 20-7.

Finch, Clement A. 1969. Iron metabolism. *Nutrition Today* 4: 3.

Fleck, H. 1976. *Introduction to nutrition.* Third edition. New York.

Freeland, Jeanne H., M. Lavone Ebangit, and Pamela Johnson. 1978. Changes in zinc absorption following a vegetarian diet. *Federation Proceedings* 37: 253.

Glueck, Charles J., and William E. Connor. 1978. Diet-coronary heart disease relationships reconnoitered. *American Journal of Clinical Nutrition* 31: 757-37.

Goodall, Jane V. L. 1971. *In the shadow of man.* Boston.

Hardinge, Mervyn G., and Fredrick J. Stare. 1954. Nutritional studies of vegetarians: 2. Dietary and serum levels of cholesterol. *Journal of Clinical Nutrition* 2: 83-8.

Harner, Michael J. 1977a. The ecological basis of Aztec sacrifice. *American Ethnology* 4: 117-35.

1977b. The enigma of Aztec sacrifice. *Natural History* 86: 46-51.

Harris, Marvin. 1977. *Cannibals and kings, the origins of cultures.* New York.

Haviland, W. A. 1967. Stature at Tikal, Guatemala: Implications for ancient Maya demography and social organization. *American Antiquity* 32: 316-25.

Hegsted, D. Mark. 1976. Energy needs and energy utilization. Reprinted in *Nutrition Reviews' present knowledge in nutrition.* Fourth edition. New York.

Hill, M. J. 1975. The etiology of colon cancer. *Critical Reviews in Toxicology* 4: 31-82.

Hitchcock, Nancy E., and Michael Gracey. 1977. Diet and serum cholesterol. An Australian family study. *Archives of Disease in Childhood* 52: 790-3.

Howell, M. A. 1975. Diet as an etiological factor in the development of cancers of the colon and rectum. *Journal of Chronic Diseases* 28: 67.

Hunter, Beatrice Trum. 1978. *The great nutrition robbery.* New York.

Johanson, D. C., and T. D. White. 1979. A systematic assessment of early African hominids. *Science* 203: 321-30.

Keen, S. 1978. The pure, the impure, and the paranoid. *Psychology Today* 12: 67-8, 73-4, 76-7, 123.

Kerr, G. 1974. Babies who eat no animal protein fail to grow at normal rate. *Journal of the American Medical Association* 228: 675-6.

Keys, Ancel. 1956. Diet and development of coronary heart disease. *Journal of Chronic Diseases* 4: 364.

Keys, Ancel, Joseph T. Anderson, and Francisco Grande. 1957. Prediction of serum-cholesterol responses of man to changes in fats in the diet. *Lancet* 2: 959-66.

Laughlin, W. S. 1968. Huntington: An integrative biobehavior system and its evolutionary importance. In *Man the hunter,* ed. R. B. Lee and I. Devore, 304-20. Chicago.

Leakey M. D. 1971. *Olduvai gorge,* Vol. 3. Oxford.

Lloyd, T., J. M. Schaeffer, and M. A. Walter. 1991. Urinary hormonal concentrations and spinal bone densities of premenopausal vegetarian and nonvegetarian women. *American Journal of Clinical Nutrition* 54: 1005-10.

Lyon, J. L., M. R. Klauber, and J. W. Gardner. 1976. Cancer incidence in Mormons and non-Mormons in Utah, 1966-1970. *New England Journal of Medicine* 294: 129-33.

Lyon, N. 1977. Cholesterol – is just one heart threat. *Science Digest* 81: 28-31.

Mann, George V. 1963. Diet and disease among the milk and meat eating Masai warriors of Tanganyika. *Food and Nutrition* 34: 104.

1977. Diet-heart: End of an era. *New England Journal of Medicine* 297: 644-50.

Mann, George V., O. L. Roeis, D. L. Price, and J. M. Merrill. 1961. Cardiovascular diseases in African Pygmies. *Journal of Chronic Diseases* 15: 341.

Mann, George V., E. M. Scott, and L. M. Hursh. 1962. The health and nutritional status of Alaskan Eskimos, a survey of the interdepartmental committee on nutrition for national defense – 1958. *American Journal of Clinical Nutrition* 11: 31-76.

Martin, P. S. 1967. Pleistocene overkill. *Natural History* 76: 32-8.

1977. Eskimos, shocking example to us all, primitive diet vs. junk food. *Let's Live* 45: 25-8.

Mayer, Jean. 1973. Can man live by vegetables alone? *Family Health* 5: 32-4.

1975. An extreme case of self starvation. *Daily News* August 27.

Menaker, Lewis, and Juan M. Navia. 1973. Effect of undernutrition during the perinatal period on caries development in the rat: II. Caries susceptibility in underfed rats supplemented with protein or caloric additions during the suckling period. *Journal of Dental Research* 52: 680-7.

Moore, Thomas J. 1989. *Heart failure.* New York.

Navia, Juan M. 1979. Nutrition, diet and oral health. *Food and Nutrition News* 50: 1-4.

Navidi, Meena Kasmall, and Fred A. Kummerow. 1974. Nutritional value of Egg Beaters™ compared with "farm fresh eggs." *Pediatrics* 53: 565-6.

Nichols, Allen B., Catherine Ravenscroft, Donald E. Lamphiear, and Leon D. Ostrander, Jr. 1976. Daily nutritional intake and serum lipid levels: The Tecumseh study. *American Journal of Clinical Nutrition* 29: 1384–92.

O'Neill, Molly. 1991. Can foie gras aid the heart? A French scientist says yes. *New York Times,* November 17, pp. 1, 22.

Page, Melvin E., and H. Leon Abrams. 1974. *Your body is your best doctor.* New Canaan, Conn.

Pedersen, Ann B., M. J. Bartholomew, and L. A. Dolence. 1991. Menstrual differences due to vegetarian and nonvegetarian diets. *American Journal of Clinical Nutrition* 53: 879–85.

Pelto, G. H., and P. J. Pelto. 1979. *The cultural dimensions of the human adventure.* New York.

Perry, R. 1976. *Life in forest and jungle.* New York.

Pfeiffer, Carl C. 1975. *Mental and elemental nutrients.* New Canaan, Conn.

Phillips, Roland L. 1975. Role of life-style and dietary habits in risk of cancer among Seventh-Day Adventists. *Cancer Research* 35: 3513–22.

Phillips, Roland L., Frank R. Lemon, Lawrence Beeson, and Jan W. Kusma. 1978. Coronary Heart Disease mortality among Seventh-Day Adventists with differing dietary habits: A preliminary report. *American Journal of Clinical Nutrition* 31: S191–8.

Pinckney, Edward R., and Cathy Pinckney. 1973. *The cholesterol controversy.* Los Angeles.

Prasad, Amanda, ed. 1982. *Clinical, biochemical, and nutritional aspects of trace elements.* New York.

1966. *Zinc metabolism.* Springfield, Ill.

Price, Weston A. 1989. *Nutrition and physical degeneration.* Seventh edition. New Canaan, Conn.

Prideaux, T. 1973. *Cro-Magnon man.* New York.

Raper, N. R., and M. M. Hill. 1973. *Nutrition Program News* n.v.: 4.

Reinhold, J. G., B. Faradji, P. Abadi, and F. Ismail-Beigi. 1976. Decreased absorption of calcium, magnesium, zinc and phosphorus by humans due to increased fiber and phosphorus consumption as wheat bread. *Journal of Nutrition* 106: 493–503.

Reiser, Raymond. 1973. Saturated fat in the diet and serum cholesterol concentration: A critical examination of the literature. *American Journal of Clinical Nutrition* 26: 524.

1978. Oversimplification of diet: Coronary heart disease relationships and exaggerated diet recommendations. *American Journal of Clinical Nutrition* 31: 865–75.

Rose, M. 1976. Serum cholesterol and triglyceride levels in Australian adolescent vegetarians. *Lancet* 2: 87.

Ruys, J. J., and B. Hickie. 1976. *British Medical Journal* 2: 87.

Sanders, T. A. B., Frey R. Ellis, and J. W. T. Dickerson. 1978. Studies of vegans: The fatty acid composition of plasma choline phosphoglycerides, erythrocytes, adipose tissue, and breast milk, and some indicators of susceptibility to ischemic heart disease in vegans and omnivore controls. *American Journal of Clinical Nutrition* 31: 805–13.

Schaefer, Otto. 1971. When the Eskimo comes to town. *Nutrition Today* 6: 8–16.

Schaller, G. B., and G. Lowther. 1969. The relevance of carnivore behavior to the study of early hominids. *Southwest Journal of Anthropology* 25: 307–41.

Shaper, A. G. 1962. Cardiovascular studies in the Samburu tribe of Northern Kenya. *American Heart Journal* 63: 437–42.

Shaper, A. G., Mary Jones, and John Kyobe. 1961. Plasma-lipids in an African tribe living on a diet of milk and meat. *Lancet* 2: 1324–7.

Sonnenberg, L. C., and V. D. Zolber. 1973. Food for us all, the vegetarian study kit. *Journal of the American Dietetic Association* 62: 93.

Stefansson, Vilhjalmur. 1937. Food of the ancient and modern Stone Age man. *Journal of the American Dietetic Association* 13: 102–29.

1957. *The fat of the land.* New York.

1960. *Cancer: Disease of civilization?* New York.

Todhunter, E. Neige. 1973. Food habits, food faddism, and nutrition. *World Review of Nutrition and Diet* 16: 286–317.

Truswell, A. S. 1978. Diet and plasma lipids – a reappraisal. *American Journal of Clinical Nutrition* 31: 977–89.

Washburn, S. L. 1961. *Social life of early man.* New York.

Wells, C. 1964. Bones, bodies, and disease: Evidence of disease and abnormality in early man. New York.

West, Raymond O., and Olive B. Hayes. 1968. Diet and serum cholesterol levels; a comparison between vegetarians and nonvegetarians in a Seventh-Day Adventist group. *American Journal of Clinical Nutrition* 2: 853–62.

White, E., and D. Brown. 1973. *The first men.* Waltham, Mass.

Williams, Roger J. 1971. *Nutrition against disease.* New York.

Wynder, Ernest L., Frank R. Lemon, and Irwin J. Bross. 1959. Cancer and coronary artery disease among Seventh-Day Adventists. *Cancer* 12: 1016–28.

PART VII

Contemporary
Food-Related Policy Issues

The concern of Part VII is with the impact of economics, governments, politics, and special interest groups on diet in the twentieth century. It begins with the attention that nationalistic governments in the West belatedly paid to the nutritional health of their citizens at the turn of the twentieth century – the health of women, who provided offspring to strengthen the state demographically, and the health of men, who were called upon to fight for it. Mostly, however, Western governments have stopped short of active intervention in ensuring the food supply of individuals, and as the chapters on food entitlements and subsidies for infants and children make clear, such intervention – save for helping the very young – continues to be viewed with sufficient hostility that it is only grudgingly (and only partially) undertaken.

If governments are reluctant to underwrite food entitlements, however, they are much more willing to ensure the dissemination of nutritional guidelines, such as those discussed in the chapter dealing with recommended daily allowances of the chief nutrients and another treating recent food labeling requirements. Yet governments do not act in a vacuum, and the chapter on food lobbies in the United States (and elsewhere by implication) demonstrates the enormous ability of special interests to influence food policy, including the content of much of the nutritional information aimed at informing the public.

The question of the desirability of more or less government involvement in food matters runs deeply through the next few chapters. That food biotechnology may turn out to be a blessing, a curse, or both is a concern of considerable magnitude, and rightfully so, as the chapter on its politics and implications for policy makes evident. However, in what is becoming a roller-coaster look at new food technology, the chapter that follows on biotechnology and food safety seems more reassuring.

The chapter on food additives, which opens a window on the past and present of this fascinating world, is succeeded by another that portrays substitute foods and ingredients, such as margarine and artificial sweeteners, as superfluous at best and health hazards at worst. The author of the chapter on nonfoods as dietary supplements critically evaluates them by describing the history of three – bioflavonoids, dietary fiber, and carnitine – whereas the question of food safety is revisited one last time in the penultimate chapter with a look at the food toxins and poisons imparted by microorganisms.

The last chapter in Part VII takes us full circle by discussing a hypothesis much in the news from time to time – namely, that we modern humans need to be more mindful of the diets consumed by our Paleolithic predecessors so as to reduce our risk of cancer, coronary problems, and other chronic diseases. After all, so the message reads, in the short span of the 10,000 or so years that separates us from them, we have not had much of an opportunity to make biological adjustments so as to utilize foods obtained by farming as well as those secured by foraging.

VII.1 ❧ The State, Health, and Nutrition

Overview

The science of nutrition has influenced consumers in their choices about the kinds and optimal amounts of food to eat, but there are other influences as well, such as prosperity levels within a given population, the efficiency of transportation and distribution systems, and the standards of hygiene maintained by food producers, processors, and retailers.

One factor, however, that has not received much scholarly attention is the increased role of the state, either through direct or indirect means, in the production, distribution, and consumption of food. Only recently have historians addressed the development of food policies (mostly those in Europe) in order to understand the state's role in controlling and monitoring food supplies.

In early modern European societies, the maintenance of public order and the control of food supply were intimately related; religious and secular authorities alike had a vested interest in ensuring that production met the demands of consumption. The actions of these authorities (the distribution of food or price-fixing, for example) were largely responses to localized crises. What distinguishes modern food policies from their early modern antecedents are the intended goals of these policies, as well as the scientific nature of their implementation.

The rise of industrialization and urbanization in the nineteenth century prompted new concerns about food supplies. The competitive nature of an industrialized, capitalist food market increased popular anxieties about adulteration; one of the more important roles of the state was to regulate the hygienic quality of food supplies. The economic conditions of the nineteenth century provoked greater concern with population's risking dietary deficiencies and, therefore, poor health. Social reformers and scientific experts took a more active and deliberate interest in monitoring the health of the laboring classes through the measurement of food consumption levels.

It is not mere coincidence that the rise of modern European food policies paralleled the development of the science of nutrition. As physiologists and social scientists explored both the content of foods and the uses which consumers made of them, state policies utilized this information to safeguard public health, thereby increasing the productivity and longevity of the population. This chapter provides a schematic, comparative overview of state intervention in popular diet throughout the nineteenth and early twentieth centuries, a period when there was an increased recognition of the extent and effects of dietary deficiencies but no cohesive state programs to guarantee proper nutrition for all.

It was often for the sake of military strength that European governments showed interest in the nutritional status of their populations, but even then much of the burden for improving diets was placed on the nutritional education of housewives. World War I, as a contest of industrial and military strength, made necessary the efficient management of resources, including food. Governments were thrown into the roles of suppliers and distributors of foodstuffs, and much of food policy formation was piecemeal, at times chaotic, in nature.

Then, after the states had assumed new regulatory powers over food supplies, the question of whether continued intervention was necessary, or even desirable, formed the basis for interwar debates over the link between food policies, civilian health, and greater economic productivity. Although military and economic competition between nations continued to make civilian health important to national well-being, questions of degrees of state intervention to safeguard health were never adequately resolved. What was clear by the time of World War II, however, was that European states had become increasingly interested parties in matters of food consumption as they related to public health.

The Nineteenth Century

Throughout the nineteenth century, the twin processes of industrialization and urbanization brought dramatic changes to European food consumption habits. Decreased opportunity for domestic agricultural production placed populations, particularly urban ones, at the mercy of price fluctuations. Public discontent over food issues shifted away from riots and disturbances over food availability and toward forms of protest over wages, prices, and standards of living. The division of labor and the monetary economy in industrial capitalist societies brought the rise of commercial middlemen concerned with profits rather than increasing food supplies. This new business ethic spread fears of food adulteration and unscrupulous business practices for the sake of greater profits. Social scientists and reformers observed that in industrialized areas, the poorer segments of the laboring classes suffered from malnutrition, staving off their hunger with cheap carbohydrates such as those provided by bread, potatoes, liquor, and sugar.

Nonetheless, the nineteenth century can be characterized as one in which the quality and variety of diet slowly improved. In addition to sugar, new foodstuffs like wheaten flour, margarine, coffee, and chocolate became urban dietary staples as industrializing nations experienced what Hans Teuteberg has termed "the democratization of dietary gratification" (Teuteberg 1975: 79). By the latter half of the nineteenth century, the rationalization of agriculture, decreasing transport costs, and the industrial mass production of foodstuffs reduced food prices. In Germany, as household incomes rose, families consumed a richer diet and shifted their preferences from potatoes and grain to dairy products and meat, allotting less income for subsistence in relation to other expenditures (Offer 1989: 40).

This is not to say, of course, that meat was regularly consumed by everyone. Rural consumers might have eaten meat only once a week or on holidays. It is interesting to note, however, such changes in consumption patterns signaled new criteria for evaluating diet. In Great Britain, for example, the increase in meat and sugar consumption was seen as a shift to more energy-producing foods and therefore as more desirable for the average worker (Burnett 1966; Mennell 1985; Shammas 1990).

It was in the late nineteenth century that members of scientific communities began to shape dietary evaluation criteria. The science of physiology broke foods down into the essential components of carbohydrates, proteins, and fats. Social scientists, charitable organizations, and parliamentary committees documented the consumption habits of the laboring classes while evaluating standards of living and health. The scientific community also scrutinized some of the troubling effects of industrialization on dietary patterns. Levels of concern and scientific conclusions depended, of course, on national context. Italian physiologists, observing the effects of late-nineteenth-century industrialization on the population, noted that at the same time consumers could afford more nutritious foods, they could also afford alcohol, tobacco, sugar, and coffee, all of which could cancel out the beneficial effects of an improved diet (Helstosky 1996).

The term "diet," distinct from food or food consumption, indicated that there were new criteria for evaluating the place of food in everyday life. Diet implied a certain level of adequacy in food consumption patterns, whether measured by the emerging body of scientific knowledge about calories and nutrients or evaluated in terms of food's capacity to fuel laborers. Therefore, diet was simultaneously a prescriptive and descriptive term, denoting both current habits and a nutritional goal set by members of the scientific community. Statistical knowledge about actual dietary practice relied largely upon concrete records of consumption habits in the form of family budget studies. These studies ranged from government-funded inquests of large populations to studies of smaller groups, sometimes a single family, funded by universities and charitable concerns.

Generally, the period between 1850 and 1910 in western Europe was characterized by a broad range of state and private investigations into the living standards of agricultural and industrial workers (Porter 1986; Hacking 1990). One of the most influential of these, Frederic Le Play's *Enquete agricole* – commissioned by the French Ministry of Agriculture, Commerce, and Public Works – was published in 36 volumes between 1869 and 1870. In Le Play's analysis, dietary habits constituted only a small part of the standard of living; other factors such as literacy, wage rates, housing conditions, and delinquency, for example, also were given analytic leverage.

The European social scientific community followed Le Play's lead in structuring their own monographs; food consumption habits and spending were only parts of detailed works encompassing a wide array of social problems. Data on working-class family budgets from Belgium became the basis upon which the German statistician Ernst Engel formulated his famous law: The proportion of outgo used for food, other things being equal, is the best measure of the material standard of living of a population; the poorer the individual, family, or people, the greater must be the percentage of the income necessary for the maintenance of physical sustenance (Engel 1895).

Nineteenth-century determinations of living standards underscored the centrality of experts and the use of scientific criteria to define social problems. Such determinations also had the effect of emphasizing the importance of the relationship between dietary practice and the physical and social condition of a given population.

By the turn of the century, concrete budget studies of the laboring classes became the basis from which physiologists made nutritional recommendations for dietary intake. There was, however, little agreement over such recommendations. German physiologists like Carl von Voit and Jacob Moleschott defended high levels of dietary protein (between 100 and 130 grams per day), whereas American physiologist Russell Chittenden claimed the body could function adequately on only 60 grams of protein per day (Offer 1989: 39–44). There is no question that scientific recommendations reflected prevailing habits and consumption levels that varied from nation to nation. Uniform nutritional standards were not formulated until the Interallied Scientific Commission met in 1917 and recommended a daily intake of 145 grams of protein, 75 grams of fat, 490 grams of carbohydrates, and 3,300 calories for the average man of 154 pounds working at least an eight-hour day ("Scientists and the world's food problems" 1918: 493).

Debates over what did constitute an adequate intake of nutrients and calories, combined with tabulations of consumption habit by class and region, naturally led to questions of how to improve the nutritional quality of diet and who was to be responsible for such improvements. To some extent, European social scientists and physiologists looked to their governments to take a more active role in guaranteeing better nutrition for all. National governments sponsored investigations into living standards, and on the municipal and national levels, social welfare policies ameliorated poor living conditions through housing reform, consumer cooperatives, and health education programs.

There were no national food policies in the nineteenth century. There were, however, governmental actions that had the effect of improving nutritional standards, such as the adoption of standardized supervision against food falsifications and fraud, as well as assistance for specific populations at risk of dietary deficiencies. The first of these interventions, the regulation of the food market, was arguably one of the most important means of protecting public health. Yet most European governments were reluctant to intervene in the food market, even though in Great Britain, for example, works detailing fraudulent practices ranged from chemist Frederick Accum's *Treatise on the Adulterations of Food* (1820) to Henry Mayhew's *London Labour and the London Poor* (1861).

Such works provoked vigorous political and scientific debates over regulation, but in England there was no governmental attempt to intervene between producer, retailer, and consumer until the enactment of adulteration legislation in 1870 (Burnett 1966). Similarly, in Germany, controls for milk, one of the most commonly adulterated foods, were slow to develop, and it was not until 1879 that uniform food controls and punishments for adulteration were passed (Teuteberg 1994).

In Italy, regulations governing fraudulent retail practices were instituted in 1890 only to be judged ineffectual by the scientific community. As physiologist Adolfo Zerboglio noted in 1897, "[I]t is common knowledge that the poor are obliged to stave off their hunger with spoilt food . . . everyone knows how certain merchants will push poor quality food onto the poor, so as not to keep it in stock" (Zerboglio 1897: 12).

Similarly, governmental interventions to assist populations at risk, such as infants and children, were not fully organized and implemented until the turn of the twentieth century. Diet had improved for many as a result of the increased consumption of fresh fruits and vegetables, butter, and eggs. This was particularly true for Italy and Germany, where the effects of later industrialization were making themselves felt.

In Britain, the inadequate height of military recruits for the Boer War spawned a national debate focused on civilian health and fears of racial degeneration. The minimum height requirement for infantry recruits was lowered from 5 feet 6 inches to 5 feet 3 inches in 1883, and to 5 feet in 1902 (Drummond and Wilbraham 1939: 484–5). Although the stunted growth and malnourished physiques of urban dwellers was of considerable concern, more attention

in the ensuing scientific and political debates was given to housing and sanitary conditions than to the influence of inadequate nutrition on public health. The Royal College of Surgeons and Royal College of Physicians were both reluctant to undertake an inquiry into the nutritional status of the population. However, an interdepartmental Committee on Physical Deterioration finally concluded that poor nutrition was in fact playing a role in the continued physical degeneration of the British people. The committee's findings, issued in 1904, focused considerable attention on the preference for refined, white bread among the working classes, but also concentrated on the feeding of infants and children; working-class mothers were found to be poorly nourished and therefore unable to breast-feed properly (Drummond and Wilbraham 1939: 485–7; Winter 1980).

Mercantilist demographic pressures, coupled with the growing fear of national degeneration, led to a more focused educational campaign to raise the nutritional status of the family. Both charitable organizations and eugenics societies undertook to instruct British women on infant nutrition. These efforts, however, generated feelings of anxiety and inadequacy among working-class mothers faced with the task of juggling household budgets to procure better-quality foods when the formidable appetites of their families demanded quantity (Davin 1978). Social scientists and reformers frequently noted that working-class mothers sacrificed their own health in order to feed their families properly, and pregnant women, younger mothers, and children often subsisted on a diet of bread with margarine and tea (Ross 1993).

Similarly, European-wide campaigns to increase infant birth weight (and reduce infant mortality) focused on the health of the mother without making positive contributions toward maternal nutrition. By the late 1870s, doctors had come to recognize that poor maternal health (including nutrition), as well as short intervals between pregnancies, contributed to low birth weights and consequently to low levels of infant health, and by the end of the century the practice of weighing and measuring newborns in hospitals had become common. Policy suggestions in Switzerland, Germany, the Netherlands, and France, however, focused not on improving maternal nutrition but rather on the importance of a period of rest for mothers before giving birth to increase birth weight and reduce infant mortality (Ward 1993: 24–5).

In Britain, concern for the physical health of the population continued through World War I because of the size and health of military recruits and resurfaced once again during the "hungry thirties" (Winter 1980; Mayhew 1988). During this period, scientific documentation of poor physical stature associated individual health with living conditions, whereas public debates over state intervention linked standards of living to national economic health and military strength.

Great Britain was by no means the exception; across Europe in the early twentieth century, solutions to the problem of popular welfare were debated at national and international conferences on population, eugenics, hygiene, infant mortality, and social work.

Such concerns may be understood as characteristic of modernity (Horn 1994: 3–5) and must be seen within a broader context of national and local governmental efforts to "regulate the social" (Steinmetz 1993). But state intervention to improve housing conditions and sanitation was less controversial than efforts to improve diets. European governments were fundamentally uneasy with direct interventions in the everyday life of the family, and any policy that sought to redress nutritional deficiencies for entire populations was not easily reconciled with either liberal democratic governments or capitalist markets.

Even nutritional assistance to populations at risk – infants, schoolchildren, and the poor – was fraught with tension. At the municipal level, assistance was meted out with few problems. In the northern regions of Italy, where pellagra was prevalent, municipal governments worked in conjunction with charitable societies to organize and extend soup kitchens to those consuming the monotonous, maize-based diet that caused the disease (Porisini 1979). And in Germany, socialist and women's organizations pressured municipal governments to experiment with consumer cooperatives and other means of making food more affordable for the working classes (Steinmetz 1993: 4).

On the national level, however, intervention to provide more nutritious foods for those in need was limited to the provision of school meals and milk. School feedings were justified on both economic and eugenic grounds: to guarantee proper nutrition to the neediest so as to ensure the health of future generations.

Under pressure from school boards, school feedings were incorporated into national education acts on the grounds that improperly nourished children could not perform well. In France, free and subsidized meals for children were considered to be an integral part of the school system, and in Norway, breakfast was offered to all children, rich or poor. In the Netherlands, however, the School Act of 1900 contained provisions that food and clothing be supplied to needy children – a policy judged less successful precisely because school feeding was linked to poverty and therefore tainted by paternalism and charity (den Hartog 1994: 71).

In Great Britain, school-feeding policies grew out of charitable initiatives like the Destitute Children's Dinner Society (1864), but the government was long reluctant to act on a national level for fear that the poor would become dependent on the state for sustenance and other material needs. National intervention, however, was finally justified by the turn-of-the-century debate over health, efficiency, and empire triggered by the small stature of many who served in the Boer War (1899–1902).

In twentieth-century Europe, such an extension of state responsibility for assuring nutritional adequacy has often resulted from military (rather than economic or social) considerations. School meals were no exception. As John Burnett recently observed, "War, the fear of it and the retreat of the danger of it, has been a major influence throughout the history of school meals" (Burnett 1994: 55). But although the state increasingly justified intervention on the grounds of national survival, local officials and others continued to view the provision of free or cheap meals and milk as an act of charity.

World War I

The circumstances of World War I dramatically altered the attitude of European governments toward promoting civilian health through food policies. They literally were forced by wartime conditions to provide enough food to keep their populations fit for military and civilian service. If the war was a watershed in the history of modern food policy, it was not because governments were able to promote scientific principles of nutrition. Although scientific knowledge about vitamins and other nutrients in food was developing, it was difficult to incorporate this into wartime policies based on expediency.

Within both belligerent and occupied nations, the consumption of proteins and fats declined, and food shortages developed even in the postwar period. In western Europe, malnutrition aggravated mortality from tuberculosis, nephritis, and pulmonary diseases, especially in Germany and Belgium.

Within the Allied nations, World War I further spread the "democratization of dietary gratification" by narrowing dietary distinctions between socioeconomic classes. The homogenization of consumption patterns has been an overall trend in the twentieth century; however, "the principal agency in narrowing the gap between the rich and the poor was the social effect of the war" (Oddy 1990: 262). Full employment provided regular as well as increased incomes, and the extension of state control over food modified the division of food on the basis of price. To some extent, food consumption levels improved in the Allied nations because military provisioning made more nutritious foods available to soldiers. In the case of Great Britain, "the nation which went to war in 1914 was still so chronically undernourished that for millions of soldiers and civilians wartime rations represented a higher standard of feeding than they had ever known before" (Burnett 1966: 217). There is little doubt that this was the case for soldiers, but to make a similar argument for civilians would be a more complicated matter.

Indeed, a comparison between Great Britain and Italy during the war demonstrates that food policies aimed at civilians had a complex effect on living standards and consumption habits. In both nations, histories of popular diet published after the war claimed that living standards had been so miserable that wartime rationing actually improved the nutrition of many (Bachi 1926; Drummond and Wilbraham 1939). But if these assertions were true, it was for different reasons: The malnourished in Britain comprised the urban poor and the industrial working class, whereas in Italy it was the rural "backwards" peasantry that was in the worst dietary shape. In both nations, full employment and higher wages were the most significant factors in improving living standards. Rationing policies sought to make more food available to all. However, as price was still the limiting factor in working-class consumption, allowances for more expensive goods like meat did not make much difference if consumers could not afford a full ration. And as one history of British food policy points out, scientific experts still used calories to judge the adequacy of diet, so it was entirely possible that experts would not detect an actual decline in nutritional standards based on food substitution (Barnett 1985: 180–1).

In Great Britain and Italy, bread was never rationed but made available in varying weights and consistencies at different, sometimes subsidized, prices. Yet ensuring the availability of cheap bread, as a matter of wartime food policy, made a significant difference in working-class consumption habits. Not only were consumers able to stave off hunger with as much bread (barring occasional shortages) as they could eat, but subsidized bread freed up more of the household budget to purchase other necessity and non-necessity items. Non-necessity items in these cases were often modest: a few extra eggs, dairy products, coffee, or alcohol.

Moreover, even after the war had ended, the public furor ignited by the termination of the Italian bread subsidy in 1919 demonstrates that consumers had come to view cheap staple foods as an entitlement. The postwar bread riots and disturbances in Italy differed from those of earlier times; consumers still clamored for cheap bread, but they did so now in order to afford more coffee, tobacco, and wine (Helstosky 1996). Thus, food policies in Britain and Italy did not transform consumption habits among the lower classes all that dramatically, although there were subtle dietary changes that were significant for those who experienced them. The increased consumption of eggs and dairy products and of refined wheat-flour bread were critical indicators of an improved living standard.

Although the war's duration called for tightly organized systems of food controls, food policies in Europe progressed on a piecemeal basis, were sometimes chaotic in organization, and mixed private voluntarism with state bureaucracy. The aim was to ensure the health of the labor and military forces, and even in the absence of legal governments, as in the case of Belgium, a national committee (the *Comité national de secours et d'alimentation*) attempted to coordinate food aid at different levels to guard the welfare of Belgian labor and thus assure future economic security (Scholliers 1994: 40–1).

Whereas national governments coordinated food imports, requisitioning, and shipments of food out to military forces, municipal governments were usually the first to institute policies important for consumers. In Italy, the national government responded to, and coordinated, prefectural initiatives on price ceilings, rationing, and domestic trade controls. In wartime Berlin, the municipal government acted to control commercial practice in the interests of consumers and preserving domestic order (Davis 1993).

If the implementation of consumer-oriented policies had its origins in local politics, however, such policies branched out into national politics after 1917, when war weariness on both sides demanded a greater equalization of experience within populations, especially in terms of resource sharing and sacrifice. The most commonly discussed example of the shift from producer-oriented, paternalistic policies to consumer-oriented ones has been that of Germany (Kocka 1984; Offer 1989; Davis 1993). Increasing civil annoyance with the uneven distribution of food led to bitter criticism of food policies and mechanisms of distribution. Consumers chafed at the Reich's calls for a domestic truce (*Burgfrieden*) when they perceived disparities in the distribution and acquisition of food between regions and classes. The hardships experienced during the "turnip winters" of 1917 and 1918 led to civil unrest and attacks on commercial middlemen and contributed to a more generalized criticism of governmental war aims and military policy (Kocka 1984: 53–4).

As the war dragged on, Allied governments paid increased attention to consumption issues, primarily to keep civilian workers content and productive. Moreover, because the Allies borrowed both money and food from the United States, some consideration had to be given to managing consumption in order to extend food supplies. Voluntary measures urging austerity were common; wartime ministries resorted to rationing only as a last resort. Austerity campaigns forged a new bond between citizens, particularly women, and government. Budget management and providing the family with a more nutritious diet were tasks that fell upon the housewife, whether or not she worked. During the war, "economy could now be urged upon the housewife all the more strongly because it was justified on social rather than private grounds" (Mennell 1984: 249). It is likely that propaganda slogans like "food wasted is another ship lost" publicly reinforced women's intermediary roles as food preparers and paved the way for future negotiations between state and housewife for provisioning responsibilities.

The amount of food that Allied nations were able

to conserve was never enough in the eyes of Herbert Hoover, U.S. Food Administrator after August 1917 (and later the director of U.S. relief efforts). Following the advice of his "diet squad" of American physiologists, Hoover suggested that Europeans do more to curtail consumption by reducing their intake and substituting foods (Offer 1989: 377). It was during the negotiations between U.S. food administrators and European officials that the idea of transforming scientific findings directly into food policies was debated.

The nutritional studies of American scientists claimed that a general reduction in calories lowered individual body weight and basal metabolism, leading to a more economical working of the body. Hoover and others urged a general reduction in food consumption in order to reduce Allied wheat consumption by one-fourth, thereby easing the wartime strain on U.S. grain stocks (Offer 1989: 378). The British Royal Society soundly rejected such a proposal, noting that any such policy of forced reduction would risk both industrial efficiency and political stability.

Wartime conditions brought about a contradictory situation with respect to popular diet. Although the salaries of workers rose to allow for increased consumption, shortages of supplies and pressure from the United States acted to deny it, and whether consumers were able to purchase more nutritious foods with their additional money is open to question. After the war, the Carnegie Foundation sponsored research that examined changes in living standards and food supplies that had occurred during the war. Authors of these books – mostly economists and agricultural experts – observed mixed results. Economist Riccardo Bachi's study of wartime Italy, for example, concluded that the war improved the nutritional quality of diet primarily because prewar consumption levels were so low (Bachi 1926). Italian physiologists, however, contradicted Bachi's findings, asserting that consumers used higher wages to purchase non-nutritive goods like tobacco, coffee, and wine, thus succumbing to what one scientist termed "alimentary sensualism" (D'Alfonso 1918: 28).

Dr. M. Demoor of Belgium's *Académie Royale de Médecine* rejected the possibility of any objective and scientific study of alimentation during the war: The incomplete documentation of living standards meant that nothing but speculation was possible (Henry 1924: 195). In France, the continuation of subsidized prices for special groups like pregnant women, families with more than two children, and the aged indicated that rations were still not adequate for all segments of the population (Augé-Laribé and Pinot 1927: 258–9). It is difficult, then, to generalize about the nutritional content of diet during and immediately after the war. There were few detailed monographs written on living standards, and those that were usually addressed the situation of workers in industrialized areas.

It is also difficult to generalize about the impact of state policy on food consumption habits, given the wide variation in national experience. Assessments of policy have as much to do with social scientific observations of living standards (which are sorely lacking in many cases) as they do with public perceptions of policy efficacy. Consumers in Germany, where essential foods were rationed and often unavailable, interpreted the effects of food policies far differently from the way that consumers did in Britain, where only sugar and meat were rationed and most goods were continuously available for purchase.

Despite the sometimes chaotic nature of food policy development, what seems clear is that European governments assumed a greater responsibility for civilian health over the course of the war. Whereas state intervention prior to the war was limited to the regulation of food distribution and assistance for the few, wartime policies sought to control the mechanisms of production, distribution, and consumption. The few scientific observations of changing living standards during the war, combined with the standardized nutritional recommendations of the Interallied Scientific Commission, led to an even greater awareness of dietary "averages" to be met as policy goals for the interwar period. There was no question that European governments had become more involved in matters of food consumption as a result of the war; the questions open for debate during the interwar period were whether intervention should continue and for what purposes.

The Interwar Years into World War II

Wartime consumption patterns – more dairy products, meat, fruits, and vegetables, as well as further increases in wheat consumption – were consolidated during the prosperous 1920s and reversed in the following decade of economic crisis. Generally, with the continued development of food processing and retailing in the interwar period, all social classes were enjoying a greater variety of foods. These included industrially created foods like margarine, breakfast cereals, preserves, and meat or fish pastes, along with canned fruits and vegetables. Scientific knowledge about food continued to advance, and vitamins as well as minerals were pronounced essential components of diet. Recommendations for caloric intake, however, fell slightly during this period because greater numbers of people were living more sedentary lifestyles.

Feeding populations at risk became more closely related to the promotion of commercial concerns. The "Milk for Schoolchildren" program in Britain, for example, was sponsored by the National Milk Publicity Council. Similarly, nutritional education programs for housewives and mothers, as well as domestic economy literature, counseled women to buy only standardized, commercial products they could trust (such as foods from Nestlé and Leibig or brand-name products such as Bovril or Kellogg's Corn Flakes). This was probably useful advice for many housewives, especially wherever consumers patronized local shops with less than ideal hygienic practices.

In terms of broader food policies, the most interesting changes in the interwar period reflected the wide-ranging turbulence created by competing systems of political economy. This was the era when both liberal democracies and authoritarian regimes alike took a greater interest in popular health, although their concerns manifested themselves differently. In Great Britain, dietary standards were debated in an effort to address chronic poverty, although, typically, the state ultimately balked at the idea of assuming broader powers of intervention. In Fascist Italy and Nazi Germany, by contrast, food production and consumption were more carefully controlled so that the dictatorships could successfully implement policies of greater economic self-sufficiency. The economic crisis of the 1930s sharpened both the impulse toward autarky and the debate over state responsibility for minimal versus optimal health.

In Great Britain, the publication of John Boyd-Orr's *Food, Health and Income* in 1936 and B. Seebohm Rowntree's *Poverty and Progress* in 1941 pushed the issues of dietary standards and civilian health into the political forefront. Boyd-Orr's study found that 10 percent of the working population during these depression years earned wages that were insufficient to purchase a nutritionally adequate regime. Moreover, he determined that half of the general population consumed a diet that satisfied hunger but was deficient in the nutrients that would maintain what he called optimal health (Boyd-Orr 1937: 8). Lower than optimal dietary standards, he believed, were a financial drain on the state, and he argued for greater state intervention in nutritional matters. Both the findings and the conclusions of Boyd-Orr, however, were roundly criticized in both political and scientific circles for having greatly exaggerated dietary deficiencies in the general population.

Politically, the debate focused on whether the state should work to ensure dietary improvements for all or simply continue protecting populations at risk, such as children. Fear of creeping socialism prevented drastic intervention, but both sides of the political spectrum agreed to focus on improving child nutrition, the left in the hopes of extending state welfare and the right because of eugenic concerns with degeneration (Oddy 1990: 276). The scientific debate over popular nutrition centered upon whether income or food preparation played a more important role in determining the nutritional quality of diet. Scientists were divided on whether malnutrition was a product of ignorance or insufficient income (Mayhew 1988: 450). Despite Boyd-Orr's calls for greater state involvement, responsibility for proper nutrition ultimately was shifted to consumers; as physiologist E. P. Cathcart of the University of Glasgow stated, "It has been our experience, as a result of repeated dietary studies, that one of the most prominent contributory factors toward defective and deficient dietaries is not so much the inadequacy of income as its faulty expenditure" (Pike 1985: 36).

Thus, Britain did not undertake more drastic measures to improve the overall quality of diet. Governmental involvement remained limited to the continued nutritional education of mothers, school feedings, and interventions to meet the needs of the economic crisis.

With economic and agricultural crisis also came more action from European governments to protect domestic agriculture. These interventions assumed the primary form of tariffs, and when tariffs alone were insufficient, the second line of defense consisted of import quotas and milling requirements for domestic grains. Great Britain abandoned laissez-faire agricultural policies by adopting import duties and creating marketing boards. France organized marketing boards for agricultural staples like wheat and wine; Denmark introduced domestic market supports; Nazi Germany instituted a comprehensive organization of production, marketing, and trade; Italy intensified domestic grain production and tightened controls over imports (Tracy 1989).

Such protectionist policies had indirect effects on food consumption habits in the sense that they made domestic staples like wheat more expensive. If staple goods came to occupy a greater portion of the household food budget, this meant that less money was available for the non-necessity items consumers had become accustomed to purchasing during and after the war.

The effect of economic policies on food consumption habits seems particularly important in light of the fact that an adequate standard of living was tied intimately to the promotion of economic and political systems. In Fascist Italy, for example, the regime founded the Committee to Study the Problem of Alimentation in 1928. One of the Committee's responsibilities was to organize, conduct, and publicize grand inquests into the living standard, in order to prove to the rest of the world that fascism as an economic system was leading the nation out of its backward status.

By contrast, sociologists in Belgium worked to measure the nutritional standard of the working classes and, as Peter Scholliers has observed, "[t]heir writings had ideological aims, stressing the fact that the capitalist system was, in the long run, capable of ensuring a decent standard of living for all people" (Scholliers 1992: 73). Although authoritarian regimes in Italy and Germany worked to exert tighter controls over food production, distribution, and consumption, the primary goal of such policies was not to improve nutritional standards. Rather, the motive was to ensure that populations could survive on less food, should there be another war or invasion.

The experience of World War II threw European governments back into the roles of providers and coordinators of food supplies. Rationing was implemented earlier and, because of the duration and severity of the conflict, was imposed on more food items than during the previous war. The struggle for adequate sustenance was a more difficult one in many areas, as exemplified by the extension of the black market in foodstuffs and the use of goods as viable currency throughout the continent. As in the case of World War I, European governments again acted out of expediency, making it difficult to ensure proper nutrition through a rationalized program of food controls. It would not be until after the war and well into the economic miracle Europeans experienced in the 1950s and 1960s that consumers in some nations would experience the culture of superabundance and confront for the first time the health problems associated with overconsumption.

Summary

State intervention in matters of nutrition during the nineteenth and early twentieth centuries in Europe can be characterized by a hesitancy and a reluctance to assume greater responsibilities for the overall health of the population. Governmental concern over popular diet had as much to do with mercantilist and militarist anxieties as it did with a growing public awareness about the importance of nutrition in building and maintaining health. Even when limited interventions - such as the feeding of schoolchildren - sought to safeguard the economic and military future of European nations, these actions were rooted in the voluntaristic paternalism that characterized charity in earlier periods. Pressure to guarantee optimal health for entire populations came mostly from the scientific and social-scientific communities, but it was only under wartime conditions that states acted with such broad measures to guarantee a minimal subsistence for all.

This is not to say, however, that state activities did not influence patterns of food consumption. Direct and indirect intervention in food markets affected the allocation of household budgets and therefore the nutritional composition of diets. Over the course of the nineteenth and early twentieth centuries, European governments demonstrated an increasing interest in safeguarding the health of populations through food consumption; but their limited range of activities demonstrates the political and economic constraints under which they functioned. Prior to the formation of the post-1945 welfare state, which ideally regarded optimal health as a right of citizenship, decisions to implement food policies as a means of building labor productivity, reducing mortality, or satisfying eugenic concerns depended upon economic and political circumstances as much as they did on the scientific knowledge of nutrition.

Carol F. Helstosky

Bibliography

Augé-Laribé, Michel, and Pierre Pinot. 1927. *Agriculture and food supply in France during the war*. New Haven, Conn.

Bachi, Riccardo. 1926. *L'alimentaztione e la politica annonaria in Italia*. Bari, Italy.

Barnett, L. Margaret. 1985. *British food policy*. Boston, Mass.

Boyd-Orr, John. 1937. *Food, health and income: Report on a survey of adequacy of diet in relation to income*. Second edition. London.

Burnett, John. 1966. *Plenty and want: A social history of diet in England from 1815 to the present day*. London.

1994. The rise and decline of school meals in Britain, 1860-1990. In *The origins and development of food policies in Europe*, ed. J. Burnett and D. Oddy, 55-69. Leicester, England.

D'Alfonso, N. R. 1918. *Il problema dell'alimentazione come problema educativo*. Milan.

Davin, Anna. 1978. Imperialism and motherhood. *History Workshop Journal* 5: 222-49.

Davis, Belinda. 1993. Home fires burning: Politics, identity and food in World War I Berlin. Ph.D. thesis, University of Michigan.

den Hartog, Adel P. 1994. Feeding schoolchildren in the Netherlands: Conflict between state and family responsibilities. In *The origins and development of food policies in Europe*, ed. J. Burnett and D. Oddy, 70-89. Leicester, England.

Drummond, J. C., and Anne Wilbraham. 1939. *The Englishman's food: A history of five centuries of English diet*. London.

Engel, Ernst. 1895. *Die Lebenskosten belgischer Arbeiter-Familien früher und jetzt*. Dresden.

Hacking, Ian. 1990. *The taming of chance*. Cambridge and New York.

Helstosky, Carol. 1996. The politics of food in Italy from liberalism to fascism. Ph.D. thesis, Rutgers University.

Henry, Albert. 1924. *Le Ravitaillement de la Belgique pendant l'occupation Allemande*. Paris.

Horn, David G. 1994. *Social bodies: Science, reproduction and Italian modernity*. Princeton, N.J.

Hurt, John. 1985. Feeding the hungry schoolchild: The first half of the twentieth century. In *Diet and health in modern Britain*, ed. D. Oddy and D. Miller, 178-206. London.

Kocka, Jürgen. 1984. *Facing total war: German society, 1914-1918*, trans. B. Weinberger. Cambridge, Mass.

Mayhew, Madeleine. 1988. The 1930s nutrition controversy. *Journal of Contemporary History* 23:445-64.

Mennell, Stephen. 1985. *All manners of food: Eating and taste in England and France from the Middle Ages to the present*. London.

Oddy, Derek J. 1990. Food, drink and nutrition. In *The Cambridge social history of Britain, 1750-1950*, ed. F. M. L. Thompson, Vol. 2, 251-78. Cambridge and New York.

Offer, Avner. 1989. *The First World War. An agrarian interpretation*. Oxford.

Pike, Magnus. 1985. The impact of modern food technology

on nutrition in the twentieth century. In *Diet and health in modern Britain,* ed. D. Oddy and D. Miller, 32–45. London.

Porisini, Giorgio. 1979. *Agricoltura, alimentazione e condizioni sanitarie. Prime ricerche sulla pellagra in Italia dal 1880 al 1940.* Geneva.

Porter, Theodore M. 1986. *The rise of statistical thinking, 1820–1900.* Princeton, N.J.

Ross, Ellen. 1993. *Love and toil: Motherhood in outcast London, 1870–1918.* Oxford.

Scholliers, Peter. 1992. Historical food research in Belgium: Development, problems and results in the 19th and 20th centuries. In *European food history: A research review,* ed. H. J. Teuteberg, 71–89. Leicester, England.

　　1994. The policy of survival: Food, the state and social relations in Belgium, 1914–1921. In *The origins and development of food policies in Europe,* ed. J. Burnett and D. Oddy, 39–53. Leicester, England.

Scientists and the world's food problems. 1918. *National Food Journal* 1: 492–4.

Shammas, Carol. 1990. *The pre-industrial consumer in England and America.* Oxford.

Steinmetz, George. 1993. *Regulating the social. The welfare state and local politics in imperial Germany.* Princeton, N.J.

Teuteberg, Hans J. 1975. The general relationship between diet and industrialization. In *European diet from pre-industry to modern times,* ed. E. Forster and R. Forster. New York.

　　1994. Food adulteration and the beginnings of uniform food legislation in late nineteenth-century Germany. In *The origins and development of food policies in Europe,* ed. J. Burnett and D. Oddy, 146–60. Leicester, England.

Tracy, Michael. 1989. *Government and agriculture in western Europe, 1880–1988.* Third edition. New York.

Ward, Peter M. 1993. *Birth weight and economic growth. Women's living standards in the industrializing West.* Chicago.

Winter, J. M. 1980. Military fitness and civilian health in Britain during the First World War. *Journal of Contemporary History* 15: 211–44.

Zerboglio, Adolfo. 1897. *Le basi economiche della salute.* Alessandria, Italy.

Zimmerman, Carle C. 1936. *Consumption and standards of living.* New York.

VII.2 ❧ Food Entitlements

Throughout the world there is enough food to feed every human being. Yet hunger and malnutrition persist. "Food security" – that is, access to culturally acceptable nutriments, through normal channels, in quantities sufficient for daily life and work – should be among the most basic of universal human rights. Hunger, poverty, and marginalization are caused by political and economic forces and decisions, which result in entitlement failures that undermine food security at the household level.

Having enough to eat depends upon access to at least a minimum "floor" level of the means of subsistence. In one sense, human history may be viewed as a gradual expansion of a sense of responsibility for others, which helps to secure that minimum "floor" for ever-increasing numbers of people. The concept of an entitlement to subsistence for households within one's own clan has been accepted for ages. Such "food security" became available to citizens of Greece and Rome thousands of years ago and was extended to most Europeans beginning about 200 years ago (Kates and Millman 1990: 398–9).

In spite of this record of progress, however, hundreds of millions of people throughout the world suffer unnecessarily from hunger and malnutrition, and, although the proportion of hungry people is diminishing, their total number continues to grow. Between 1990 and 2000, the absolute number of hungry people was projected to continue to increase and then gradually decline to a level of about 3 percent of the world's population in 2050. "In the meantime, half of the world's women who carry the seeds of our future may be anemic, a third of the world's children may be wasted or stunted in body or mind, and perhaps a fifth of the world's people can never be sure of their daily bread, chapati, rice, tortilla, or ugali" (Kates and Millman 1990: 405). Today, some 1 billion children, women, and men daily confront chronic hunger and, consequently, the specters of starvation, undernutrition, deficiencies of iron, iodine, and vitamin A, and nutrient-depleting diseases (Kates 1996: 4–6).

Among the shades of hunger, starvation is the most arresting to the observer and receives major, if often belated, coverage by news media when it occurs. In the latter twentieth century, the plight of refugees in central Africa has been a current and recurrent example. Famine-related food shortages threaten roughly 1 percent of the world's population with starvation every year.

Undernutrition, the most widespread form of hunger, is especially dangerous for children. It affects their ability to grow, their cognitive development, and their susceptibility to illness. Even relatively mild "chronic undernutrition," the typical form of hunger in the United States, can permanently retard physical growth and brain development and can reduce the ability of children to concentrate and perform complex tasks.

Nutritional anemia (a condition in which a lack of dietary iron causes a shortage of red blood cells) can cause an impaired capacity for work and intellectual performance as well as a decreased resistance to disease and an increased susceptibility to lead poisoning. Nearly one-fifth of pregnant women in the United States suffer from this condition.

A lack of vitamin A in the diet permanently blinds 250,000 children throughout the world each year and increases the chances that millions more will suffer from the three leading child killers – diarrheal disease, measles, and pneumonia. Iodine deficiency results in the birth of 120,000 brain-damaged children annually; millions more grow up stunted, listless, mentally retarded, or incapable of normal speech, hearing, or both. In addition, nutrient-depleting diseases such as diarrhea, measles, malaria, and parasitic infestations prevent millions of people from fully benefiting from the nutrients contained in the nutriments they do manage to take in.

Rights, Entitlements, and the Right to Food

Virtually every society develops a social compact – a set of values and behavior standards – that defines the rights and responsibilities of its members. From the sixteenth through the early nineteenth centuries, survival was considered in European societies to be largely an individual or family-based responsibility, with food and other necessities procured through work. But assistance was available for some of those not able to achieve self-reliance through work, and the various European nations enacted strikingly similar laws that separated needy people into two distinct categories – those who were deemed worthy and those considered unworthy of public aid.

In England, for example, only children, the blind, the disabled, and those elderly persons who could not work were thought worthy of relief under the Poor Laws. Destitute but able-bodied unemployed persons risked savage treatment at the hands of local authorities. They could be consigned indefinitely to workhouses or prisons. Adults and children were severely punished, sometimes even executed, for stealing food (Dobbert 1978: 187).

Today, in the United States and other industrialized countries, able-bodied persons are expected to earn their livelihoods. Often, there is debate over the extent to which the state should meet the needs of those who cannot work – whether because of age, or physical or mental infirmity, or because jobs paying a livable wage are unavailable. For some who cannot attain self-reliance through work, the condition is temporary, and only transitional support is needed. For others, age or infirmity makes the attainment of self-reliance unrealistic; these persons require lasting support.

Human Rights

Human rights are "enforceable claims on the delivery of goods, services, or protection by others" – meaning that people in need can insist upon the delivery of assistance, with recourse, if necessary, to legal or moral enforcement of their demand (Eide, Oshaug, and Eide 1991: 426). Such rights are based on social obligations that are accepted by all persons without reference to distinctions of race, gender, nationality, language, religion, or socioeconomic class. Human rights may be promulgated globally but must be implemented locally within nationally determined limits (Barker 1991: 105, 203; Eide et al. 1991: 415).

Some analysts separate such rights into two categories: civil/political rights and social/economic/cultural rights. Civil and political rights are basic "rights recognized in democratic constitutions, such as life, liberty, and personal security; freedom from arbitrary arrest, detention, or exile; the right to fair and public hearings by impartial tribunals; freedom of thought, conscience, and religion; and freedom of peaceful association" (Barker 1991: 105). Social, economic, and cultural rights include "the right to work, education, and social security; to participate in the cultural life of the community; . . . to share in the benefits of scientific advancement and the arts" (Barker 1991: 105), *and the right to eat.*

The protection of vulnerable groups, such as the poor, those with handicaps, and endangered indigenous peoples, is a major aim of social, economic, and cultural rights. Taking these rights seriously requires grappling with issues of social integration, solidarity, equality, and distribution of wealth. Perhaps as a consequence, although civil and political rights have received considerable attention, social, economic, and cultural rights have been relatively neglected at both the international and national levels (Eide and Rosas 1995: 17).

Those who separate human rights into two distinct categories argue that civil and political rights emphasize "freedom from" state interference; they are absolute, are immediately realizable at little financial cost to governments, and are capable of being adjudicated in court. In contrast, social, economic, and cultural rights are seen as claims on the state for protection and assistance; these are relative to the circumstances of one's society, are only gradually realizable at substantial financial cost to governments, and are dependent upon politics rather than the courts for such realization. Other analysts, however, view the two categories of rights as interrelated and as addressing "different aspects of the same three basic concerns: integrity, freedom, and equality of all human beings" (Eide 1995a: 21–2; Eide and Rosas 1995: 17).

Humans require basic necessities such as food, clothing, and housing (depending on the cultural conditions in which they live) to enable them to participate fully – without shame or unreasonable obstacles – in the everyday life of their communities. The right to a standard of living that supports such participation is, therefore, a basic social right (Eide 1995b: 90).

The three major components of such a standard of living are adequate food, care, and the prevention and control of disease. As a basic social right, this standard of living is a necessary foundation for an effective social compact, but it is not a solely sufficient one, as the compact must also provide for other social, economic, and cultural rights, as well as for civil and political rights. Thus, the right to adequate food is an essential – and perhaps the most important – building block in the foundation of a satisfactory social compact.

"Adequate food" means that every household can depend upon the availability of a stable supply of culturally acceptable, uncontaminated, good-quality food, which provides all necessary energy, nutrients, and micronutrients (such as vitamins and iodine). Food adequacy implies economic and social (as well as environmental) sustainability, which entails access to food through a combination of fair wealth distribution and effective markets, together with various forms (public and private, formal and informal) of supports and "safety nets" (Eide 1995b: 90–1).

According to the United Nations Administrative Committee on Co-ordination, Subcommittee on Nutrition, "care is the provision in the household and the community of time, attention and support to meet the physical, mental and social needs of the growing child and other family members" (Eide 1995b: 91). Such care implies, among other things, access to primary health care, protection from infection, medical assistance during illness, and assistance to meet the needs of disability and old age. Adequate care is necessary for everyone but is especially important for vulnerable groups such as young children, pregnant and lactating women, and the elderly (Eide 1995b: 91–3).

Adequate prevention and control of disease is essential to a satisfactory standard of living because of the close connection between disease and malnutrition. Therefore, immunization and breast-feeding campaigns, oral rehydration child survival programs, nutrition education, sanitation programs, and the like are important contributions to living standards (Eide 1995b: 93).

Entitlements and "Entitlement Failure"

An entitlement is a societal obligation to provide support as a right when people have insufficient resources to live in conditions of health and decency (Melnick 1994: 54–6). Entitlement to food is the ability to command food through the various forms of exchange relationships to which one has access (Sen 1981). Amartya Sen describes three basic forms of food entitlement: "(a) access to resources to collect or to produce food, (b) the exchange of resources (property, money, labor power) for food, and (c) the receipt of gifts or grants of food or the resources to procure food" (Sen 1981; Kates and Millman 1990: 397). An entitlement approach to food security "requires a shift in thinking from *what exists?* to *who can command what?*" (Eide 1995b: 95).

Many other rights interact with and affect the entitlement to food. The right to property supports the right to food both because ownership of land makes it possible to grow food and because ownership of assets makes it possible to produce items that can be exchanged for food. As property is often unevenly distributed, the right to work at a living wage is directly related to the right to the income necessary to purchase food, and, of course, the right to work is in turn affected by the right to an education. If a person lacks property and is unable to work because of age, disability, illness, lack of skill or training, scarcity of appropriate jobs, or because available work does not pay a living wage, a right to social security becomes necessary to secure access to food (Eide 1995b: 95–6).

Sen's three basic forms of entitlement have not changed over time. What has changed "is the mix: from a primary emphasis on household self-provision, to slave, servant, or serf status where labor is appropriated in return for minimal entitlement, to market exchange of labor and production, and most recently to the development of extensive safety-nets of food security" (Kates and Millman 1990: 398).

Sen's conceptualization of "entitlement failure" (Sen 1981; Drèze and Sen 1990a, 1990b, 1990c, 1991) has provided a powerful analytical tool with which to understand and intervene in the political economy of hunger. Most important, the concept helps avoid the pitfall of assuming that per capita food supplies that on average seem adequate will result in universal food security. Just as it is possible to drown in a stream that averages only an inch deep, it is possible to starve in a world, nation-state, region, or even household in which there is a seemingly sufficient average food supply.

When some people thrive but others do not – whether in the presence of food or faced with food shortages – one must ask *why* some have access to sufficient food and thrive, whereas others, lacking access, sicken or die. For Sen, "entitlement failure" is the central cause of hunger, starvation, and famine. People suffer malnutrition and die of starvation because of an inability to claim access to sufficient food resources to meet their nutritional needs. Such entitlement failure is a consequence of choices made publicly and privately at the international, national, state, community, and household levels.

Household Food Security

For a right to food to have meaning, it must be implemented where food is actually consumed, by individuals at the household level. The presence of food supplies in a nation or region is no guarantee of food security if households lack access to them. Household food security depends upon a household's "access to a basket of food which is nutritionally adequate, safe, and culturally acceptable, procured in a manner consistent with the satisfaction also of other basic human needs, and obtained from supplies, and in ways, which are sustainable over time" (Eide et al. 1991: 455).

Even if a household has access to a supply of food that, if equitably shared, could meet the needs of all of its members, that food may or may not be available according to individual needs. In many societies, for example, men and boys eat first, and women and girls wait to eat whatever the males leave.

Strategies for Food Security

Jean Drèze and Sen (1990a: 22–6) describe two contemporary strategies for replacing persistent want and hunger with food security: "growth-mediated security" and "support-led security." Growth-mediated security is based upon rapid economic expansion, with benefits shared through new jobs and higher wages, and use of growth-generated resources "to expand public support of health, nutrition, education, and economic security for the more deprived and vulnerable" (Drèze and Sen 1990a: 22). The "trickle-down" economics promoted by some politicians in the United States and the structural adjustment policies promulgated by the World Bank and the International Monetary Fund both assume the creation of growth-mediated benefits, but whether such benefits are shared with poor and marginalized people is a matter of public policy choices.

By contrast, support-led security involves providing "public support measures without waiting for the country to become rich through economic growth" (Drèze and Sen 1990a: 24). China, Sri Lanka, Costa Rica, Cuba, Chile, Jamaica, and the state of Kerala in India are all examples of governments that have followed the support-led strategy with considerable benefit to marginalized citizens.

Although there is a significant difference between the two approaches, public support plays an important role in each. "Indeed, in the absence of public involvement to guarantee that the fruits of growth are widely shared, rapid economic growth" can have a negative impact on the entitlements that secure sufficient food and other necessities of life. It is, according to Drèze and Sen (1990a: 26), essential to replace "unaimed opulence" with growth benefits targeted to the needs of the marginalized.

Moreover, Asbjørn Eide has argued that it is a mistake to assume that governments must have the primary responsibility to provide food to needy people through costly, potentially overgrown state bureaucracies. Instead, governments should work to maximize the capability of individuals to provide food for themselves and their households through their own resources and efforts (Eide 1995a: 36–8). This goal involves three levels of obligation. First, governments must respect individual freedoms and resources; for example, government actions to ensure the land rights of endangered indigenous peoples and to clarify smallholders' titles to their land enable such people to maximize self-reliance and their ability to earn an adequate living. Second, governments must protect the rights of less-powerful people against more powerful interests that may exploit them and reduce their ability to be self-reliant. Third, when no other possibilities exist, governments must fulfill rights by direct action, such as providing for basic needs through programs of food aid or social security (Eide 1995a: 36–8).

The Evolution of an International Entitlement to Food

The development of a right to food is the culmination of several centuries of struggle to affirm human rights and then extend them to people without property,

such as former slaves, and women. The human rights from which the right to food has emerged are grounded in the philosophy of John Locke and Jean-Jacques Rousseau, in the 1690–1 British Bill of Rights, in the 1776 U.S. Declaration of Independence, and in the 1779 French Declaration on the Rights of Man and the Citizen (Dobbert 1978).

Until World War II, international law provided no basis for a right to food. The right could be claimed only by groups such as members of the armed forces (entitled to food in exchange for their willingness to fight) or the inmates of penitentiaries, almshouses, and similar public institutions, who were prevented from self-provision. Attitudes toward human rights, however, were fundamentally altered by the events surrounding World War II. The acute food shortages experienced by war-torn countries in Europe and elsewhere led to the emergence of the concept of a right to food as a universal right (Dobbert 1978: 188–9).

In 1941, in his well-known "Four Freedoms" State of the Union address, U.S. President Franklin D. Roosevelt introduced the concept of "freedom from want" into modern political discourse. Later that year, the Atlantic Charter – framed by Roosevelt and British Prime Minister Winston Churchill – called for international economic collaboration to secure "improved labor standards, economic advancement and social security" for all. Finally, in his 1944 State of the Union message, Roosevelt proposed an international "Economic Bill of Rights" recognizing that "true individual freedom cannot exist without economic security and independence." "People," he said, "who are hungry and out of a job are the stuff of which dictatorships are made" (Eide 1995a: 29).

International Conventions and Covenants

The Universal Declaration of Human Rights (UDHR), adopted by the General Assembly of the United Nations (UN) on December 10, 1948, is the foundation upon which efforts to realize an international right to food are based. In order to foster global freedom and democracy, the UDHR envisions worldwide human rights – to be monitored internationally and implemented nationally – for all people. Article 25(1) anticipates the right to food: "Everyone has the right to a standard of living adequate for the health and well-being of himself and his family, including food, clothing, housing and medical care and necessary social services" (Dobbert 1978: 192).

The UN Commission on Human Rights, which drafted the declaration, could not obtain the agreement of the United States and other nations of the industrial West to include both civil/political and social/economic/cultural rights in a single, legally binding convention. But subsequently, in 1966, 18 years after the promulgation of the UDHR, separate international covenants on civil/political rights and social/economic/cultural rights were adopted by the

UN General Assembly (Eide and Rosas 1995: 15). By 1995, 120 nations had ratified the international Covenant on Civil and Political Rights (CCPR).

The evolution of the international Covenant on Economic, Social and Cultural Rights (CESCR) has been more controversial. Article 11 contains the language most relevant to a right to food. By 1957, when most of the substantive language of the CESCR had been accepted, Article 11 stated simply that the nations party to the covenant "recognize the right of everyone to adequate food, clothing and housing" (Dobbert 1978: 191). In 1964, following a call by Dr. B. R. Sen, Director-General of the Food and Agriculture Organization of the United Nations, for a strengthening of the covenant, compromise language was adopted providing for a right to an adequate standard of living based on universal subsistence rights to adequate food and nutrition, clothing, housing, and necessary conditions of care (Dobbert 1978: 191–4). By 1995, the CESCR had been ratified by 118 nations. But although the U.S. government signed the covenant in 1976, it had still not been ratified by the U.S. Senate some 20 years later.

The actual enjoyment of these theoretically universal social, economic, and cultural rights still eludes many people throughout the world. Nevertheless, paying at least "lip service" to them provides an opportunity for advocates in all countries to press for their extension and implementation.

The Role of Intergovernmental Organizations

Several intergovernmental organizations (IGOs) have played important roles related to food security and contributed significantly to the conceptual evolution of a right to food but have been less successful in ensuring its realization. These include the Food and Agriculture Organization of the UN (FAO), the World Food Programme (WFP), the World Food Council (WFC), the International Fund for Agricultural Development (IFAD), the United Nations International Children's Emergency Fund (UNICEF), and the UN's World Health Organization (WHO) (Eide et al. 1991: 437–8).

The Food and Agriculture Organization was conceived during World War II and established in 1945, before the war ended. After the war, FAO made its headquarters in Rome, housed in the offices from which Italian dictator Benito Mussolini had hoped to rule an empire. The organization functions as a clearinghouse for scientific information on food and agriculture, but when it addresses structural causes of hunger, such as regulation of the world grain trade or issues of land reform, FAO risks conflict with its sponsoring governments.

FAO's role in promoting the right to food has varied from virtual inactivity to strong support, depending upon the bent of its directors. Although it was not until 1965 that the preamble to the FAO Constitution was amended to include "humanity's freedom from hunger," FAO played an important role in strengthening the CESCR. It was instrumental, too, in founding the World Food Programme and in initiating the 1974 International Undertaking on World Food Security, which recognized (paragraph I.1) "that the assurance of world food security is a common responsibility of the entire international community." In addition, the FAO worked to create the 1975 Food Security Assistance program to help developing countries implement national food-stock and reserve programs and was important in negotiating the nonbinding World Food Security Compact in 1985 (Tomasevski 1987; Eide et al. 1991). In 1996, FAO sponsored the International Food Summit in Rome.

The World Food Programme was founded by FAO and the United Nations in 1961. The WFP administers the food aid pledged by members of the United Nations for emergencies and development projects. When administered with careful attention to its effects on exchange entitlements, food aid can be very successful; by contrast, poorly targeted food aid can wreak havoc on entitlement relationships. The WFP has stressed the right to food "as the most fundamental of human rights, and a precondition to development" (Eide et al. 1995: 442–3).

The World Food Conference in Rome (held from November 5 to 16, 1974) focused global attention on the idea that hunger and malnutrition are solvable problems. It adopted the Universal Declaration on the Eradication of Hunger and Malnutrition, which proclaimed: "Every man, woman, and child has the inalienable right to be free from hunger and malnutrition in order to fully develop and maintain their physical and mental facilities" (Tomasevski 1987: 343). The declaration set a goal of eliminating hunger worldwide within 10 years and was subsequently endorsed by the UN General Assembly. Further activities intended to implement the declaration and the 22 resolutions of the conference included the establishment of the World Food Council, the FAO Committee on World Food Security, the International Fund for Agricultural Development, and the United Nations Administrative Committee on Co-ordination, Sub-Committee on Nutrition (ACC/SCN) (Tomasevski 1987).

The World Food Council was established by the UN General Assembly in December 1974 to coordinate the work of UN agencies related to "food production, nutrition, food security, food trade and food aid" (Tomasevski 1987: 346–7). In 1977, the WFC adopted the Manila Communiqué, an action program to eliminate hunger and malnutrition, and in 1979, it adopted the Mexico Declaration, which proposed, among other things, that countries "consider practical ways and means to achieve a more equitable distribution of income and economic resources so as to ensure that food production increases result in a more equitable pattern of food consumption" (Tomasevski 1987: 39–40). The ability of the WFC to serve as the UN's conscience on food security is, however, limited by its practice of operating on consensus, which precludes serious consideration of the more radical structural analyses offered by various country-groups. The WFC Secretariat has shown only moderate interest in promoting legal approaches to the right to food (Eide et al. 1991: 415).

The International Fund for Agricultural Development was established in 1976 with initial funding of $1 billion for programs to increase food production, reduce rural poverty, and improve nutrition in developing countries. IFAD gives priority to the poorest food-deficient countries and attempts to strengthen the entitlements of small and landless farmers. IFAD, then, is the IGO that works directly to reduce poverty among the most severely marginalized groups. Food security is now a major focus of its work.

The United Nations International Children's Emergency Fund was established in 1946 to promote health, education, and social services for children in developing countries and is actively employing in its work the Convention on the Rights of the Child (CRC), which was adopted by the UN General Assembly in November 1989. The CRC addresses rights to health (Article 24) and to social security (Article 25), whereas Article 27 recognizes "the right of every child to a standard of living adequate for the child's physical, mental, spiritual, moral and social development." The 1990 World Summit for Children sponsored by UNICEF to promote the CRC was attended by more than 70 heads of state, and by 1995, the convention had been ratified by 150 nations (Eide 1995a and 1985b). Until then, the United States was the sole major nonsignatory of the convention, and although the U.S. government at last signed the CRC (as a memorial to UNICEF executive director James Grant), it had not yet ratified the document by the end of the following year.

The World Health Organization, in response to worldwide activism against the irresponsible marketing of infant formulas, has worked to create awareness of infants' right to adequate nutrition. Its Code of Marketing of Breast Milk Substitutes was adopted by the World Health Assembly in 1981.

U.S.-Based Nongovernmental Organizations

During the 1970s and 1980s, a growing public awareness of the problem of hunger resulted in the establishment of a large number of antihunger nongovernmental organizations (NGOs). National and international NGOs based in the United States that have played substantial roles in the struggle to develop food security or the right to food include Oxfam America, Food for the Hungry, and the Campaign for Human Development (founded in 1970); Bread for the World (1974); Food First and World Hunger Year (1975); World Hunger Education Service (1976); the Hunger Project (1977); and Results (1980).

By 1985, the more economically developed countries supported an estimated 2,000 NGOs - mostly focused on development and self-help – throughout the world. Some were quite large; World Vision, for example, had 750,000 subscribers and raised an international budget of $300 million annually. Catholic Relief Services had a 1990 budget of $220 million, CARE $294 million, Lutheran World Relief $49 million, and Church World Service $43 million (Beckman and Hoehn 1992: 20–1).

Millions of U.S. residents have participated in episodic, short-term, hunger-relief activities in response to famines – such as aid concerts, "Hands across America," and the like (Millman et al. 1990: 326). In 1991, for example, "334,580 people participated in Church World Service 'CROP Walks' to raise money for anti-hunger efforts" (Beckman and Hoehn 1992: 15–18).

Development aid from the governments of developed countries increased from $7 billion to $48.1 billion between 1970 and 1988. "But most of this 'aid' is tied to political and commercial interests of the Northern governments, and often hurts rather than helps poor people in Southern hemisphere countries" (Beckman and Hoehn 1992: 22). Although the majority of U.S.-based NGOs focus on relief or development activities, Bread for the World and Results have mobilized substantial grass-roots constituencies lobbying for changes in U.S. public policy that will support food security.

Bread for the World (BFW) is an interdenominational Christian organization in the United States with about 40,000 members. BFW members lobby the U.S. Congress on policies that affect domestic and global hunger. In 1974, BFW mobilized its members to pressure the U.S. Congress to enact a "Right-to-Food Resolution." (H.R. 737 was passed in the U.S. House of Representatives with a vote of 340 to 61; S.R. 138 was passed in the U.S. Senate by voice vote.) The resolution by the House stated the sense of Congress as follows:

(1) the United States reaffirms the right of every person at home and abroad to food and a nutritionally adequate diet;

(2) the need to combat hunger shall be a fundamental point of reference in the formulation and implementation of United States policy in all areas that bear on hunger;

(3) the United States should seek to improve domestic food assistance programs for Americans in need, to ensure that all eligible recipients have the chance to obtain a nutritionally adequate diet;

(4) the United States should increase substantially its assistance for self-help development among the poorest people of the world with particular emphasis on increasing food production and encouraging improved food distribution and more equitable patterns of economic growth; this

assistance should be coordinated with expanded efforts by international organizations, donor nations, and recipient countries to provide a nutritionally adequate diet for all. (U.S. House of Representatives 1976b)

Among its lobbying efforts, BFW has led successful attempts to increase U.S. allocations for intergovernmental child survival programs that save millions of lives annually. Through its Transforming the Politics of Hunger project, BFW is encouraging those in the voluntary feeding movement to take a more active role in affecting governmental antihunger policy (Beckman and Hoehn 1992).

The Results organization is a hard-headed, policy-focused spin-off of the Hunger Project begun in 1977, which seeks "to empower people to take actions against hunger" (Millman et al. 1990: 327). By 1987, the Hunger Project claimed to have enrolled more than 5 million members in 152 countries (Millman et al. 1990: 327). Mobilization efforts by Results have included generating support in the United States and several other countries for the World Summit for Children and the Convention on the Rights of the Child.

International Nongovernmental Efforts

There are several international efforts to strengthen and implement the right to food that should be mentioned. An October 1981 meeting – organized in Gran, Norway, by the United Nations University – resulted in the 1984 publication of *Food As a Human Right* (Eide et al. 1984). The book emphasized (p. ix) that human food supplies are "filtered through socioeconomic processes which deny an adequate supply of food to many while delivering a large over-dose to a 'lucky' few" and that meaningful intervention "will probably require deep structural changes" that will generate conflict.

The World Institute for Development Economics Research (WIDER) was established by the United Nations University in 1984. The following year, it began its program, "Hunger and Poverty: The Poorest Billion," and in 1986, it sponsored (in Helsinki) a Food Strategies Conference to identify feasible opportunities for affecting world hunger. The conference pursued an entitlement approach emphasizing public intervention to improve literacy rates, life expectancy, and infant mortality in low-income nations. Follow-up activities to the WIDER conference included publication of the three-volume work *The Political Economy of Hunger* (Drèze and Sen 1990a, 1990b, 1990c).

In June 1984, the Right to Food Project of the Netherlands Institute for Human Rights (SIM), with cosponsorship by the Norwegian Human Rights Project, brought together "42 lawyers, nutritionists, and development experts, from all parts of the world, and from both nongovernmental and intergovernmental organizations" (Alston and Tomasevski 1984:

215). Participants in the conference, "The Right to Food: From Soft to Hard Law," criticized discussions of world hunger as frequently oversimplified. Instead of being defined simply in terms of calorie/protein requirements, hunger, they contended, should be analyzed "in terms of economic, social, political, cultural, and other structural factors, which deprive some people of access to land, work and food" (Alston and Tomasevski 1984: 217). A wide range of discussions focused on causes (for example, land tenure and access to work and food), rather than on manifestations, of hunger. The conference proceedings were published as *The Right to Food*, which attempted, "for the first time, to make hunger a prominent issue on the human rights agenda and to put the right to food on the agenda of national and international human rights agencies" (Alston and Tomasevski 1984: 7).

The SIM conference called for a translation of the "soft law" norms of human rights into "hard law" capable of adjudication. Conferees proposed monitoring the implementation of the right to food through (1) an international system based on cooperation among the relevant UN agencies, (2) a redesign of the CESCR reporting system, and (3) an NGO network using an Amnesty International–style "mobilization of shame" approach (Alston and Tomasevski 1984: 220). The greatest need, according to the SIM conferees, was for:

> a network of support by and among NGOs which would include the mobilization of other private sector groups such as professional organizations of lawyers and doctors and churches in the fight against hunger. This network could strengthen existing NGOs, building and using human rights law and developing a concrete, realistic program of action on the right to food. (Alston and Tomasevski 1984: 220)

Five years later, in 1989, "a group of 24 planners, practitioners, opinion leaders, and scientists," brought to Bellagio, Italy, by the World Hunger Program of Brown University, adopted "The Bellagio Declaration: Overcoming Hunger in the 1990s." Its signers represented national or international agencies, organizations, universities, and research institutes in 14 countries, both northern and southern.

Whereas some advocates approach ending hunger incrementally, and others envision more fundamental structural changes, the Bellagio Declaration sought a "common middle ground" in which half of the world's hunger could be ended in a decade by appropriately applying the "better and the best" of current programs throughout the world. The Bellagio strategy included: (1) eliminating deaths from famine, (2) ending hunger in half of the poorest households, (3) cutting malnutrition in half for mothers and small children, and (4) eradicating iodine and vitamin A deficiencies (Kates and Millman 1990).

In December 1992, preceding the International Conference on Nutrition in Rome, a Task Force on Children's Nutrition Rights was established under the aegis of the World Alliance on Nutrition and Human Rights. The task force encouraged national workshops "designed to launch locally-based long-term campaigns to strengthen children's nutrition rights, giving attention to both their articulation in the law and the effective implementation of that law." Workshops were held in Guatemala and Mexico in 1993 and are being planned in several additional countries (Kent 1993a).

The Task Force on Children's Nutrition Rights is collaborating with the Foodfirst Information and Action Network (FIAN), an "international human rights organization for the right to feed oneself" (Kent 1993b: 10), which has chapters in several countries. At the June 1993 World Conference on Human Rights in Vienna, FIAN took the lead in advocating an optional protocol for the CESCR that would empower individuals to bring human rights complaints to the UN Committee on Economic, Social, and Cultural Rights (Kent 1993b).

In the 1990s, poor weather conditions reduced world grain reserves to a perilously low level and caused the price of grain to rise. Although this was a boon to farmers in grain-exporting countries like the United States, it played havoc with the economies of grain-importing countries throughout the developing world. Concurrently, total annual commitments of external assistance to agriculture in developing countries fell from about $16 billion in 1988 to about $10.7 billion in 1993.

Prompted by widespread food insecurity, the FAO made plans for the World Food Summit in Rome in 1996 to deal with problems of hunger and malnutrition. The summit, the first global conversation in 22 years that was focused specifically on food and hunger adopted the Declaration on World Food Security and Plan of Action, which reaffirmed the right to be free from hunger through universal access to safe and nutritious food and pledged to reduce the number of hungry people to 400 million by the year 2015.

The retreat from the 1974 World Food Conference goal of ending hunger worldwide in 10 years to the 1996 World Food Summit goal of reducing hunger by half in 20 years reflected diminished support by the United States and other developed countries for a legal right to food. During the two years of negotiations on the 1996 summit documents, U.S. representatives repeatedly expressed concern that a right to food could expose producing countries to lawsuits and trade complaints from the developing world. In opposition to the 1996 declaration, the U.S. delegation to the summit contended that the right to food is only an "aspiration" that creates no international obligation for governments.

Entitlement Failure: And the Right to Food

In light of this chapter's recitation of the resolutions, conventions, declarations, protocols, visions, and down-to-earth efforts of IGOs and NGOs to nurture recognition of the right to food and to implement food security, one might be tempted to ask why hunger and malnutrition persisted as the twentieth century came to a close. Is there any reason for hope that the right to food will become as commonly accepted as, say, entitlement to public education, and that the global right to food will become as commonly accepted as civil and political rights? Where must we go from here in order to attain the basic social justice reflected in a universal, implementable right to food security?

To speak only about the United States, the challenge seems especially daunting during a time in which public programs are under attack. Even with the present food-security safety net relatively intact, 4 million U.S. children under age 12 experience hunger, and every year another 9.6 million are at risk of hunger. In fact, 29 percent of U.S. children live in families that experience food shortage problems year after year (FRAC 1995: v–vi), and poor children in the United States have less access to food than poor children in 15 other industrial nations (Bradsher 1995). The U.S. welfare "reform" legislation of 1996, which replaced the entitlement to public assistance of families with dependent children with a time-limited, work-based program, might well push more than 1 million additional children below the U.S. poverty threshold.

The human costs of slow progress are great. The demise of hunger is not guaranteed. But hunger can be ended, if we choose. R. W. Kates and Sara Millman (1990: 404) describe the progress that has been made and the challenges we still face:

> In global terms, there is enough food to go around. In the 1960s the earth passed the first threshold of theoretical food sufficiency (enough to provide a near-vegetarian diet for all if distributed according to need) and [is] approaching a second threshold of improved diet sufficiency (enough to provide 10 percent animal products). But we are still a long way from a third threshold of a full but healthy diet with the choices available in industrialized nations. Projecting world food demand, under alternative assumptions of both diet and population growth, indicates that nearly three times the present level of production might be required for an improved diet and almost five times for a full, but healthy, diet, some 60 years from now.

In other words, there is cause for hope. Reduced contributions for development aid will harm, yet not cripple, development efforts. The dramatic strengthening of civil society in some developing countries is one of the major causes for hope.

Moreover, there is a deep-seated tradition in a number of the industrialized nations of caring for one's poorer neighbors. Widespread public opinion in the United States holds that no one should go hungry. Perhaps BFW and its antihunger-movement allies will succeed in transforming the politics of hunger and in energizing the feeding movement to affect the direction of national aid policies. A reenergized, populist, antihunger movement throughout the world, armed with appreciation of entitlement failure as the key to understanding the political economy of hunger, may yet succeed in transforming "soft" concern about hunger into the "hard law" of an enforceable, adjudicatory right to food.

William H. Whitaker

An earlier version of this chapter was presented at the Fourth International Convention in Social Work, "Redesigning the Future: New Answers in Response to Current Challenges," Universidad Nacional Autónoma de México, Escuela Nacional de Trabajo Social, October 2–4, 1996, Mexico City.

Bibliography

Alston, P., and Katarina Tomasevski. 1984. *The right to food.* The Hague.

Barker, R. L. 1991. *The social work dictionary.* Second edition. Washington, D.C.

Beckman, D., and Richard Hoehn. 1992. *Transforming the politics of hunger.* Washington, D.C.

Bradsher, Keith. 1995. Low ranking for poor American children: U.S. youth among worst off in study of 18 industrialized nations. *The New York Times,* August 14, p. A9.

Dobbert, J. P. 1978. Right to food. In *The right to health as a human right,* ed. René-Jean Dupuy, 184–213. The Hague.

Drèze, Jean, and Amartya Sen. 1990a. *The political economy of hunger.* Vol. 1, *Entitlement and well-being.* Oxford.

1990b. *The political economy of hunger.* Vol. 2, *Famine prevention.* Oxford.

1990c. *The political economy of hunger.* Vol. 3, *Endemic hunger.* Oxford.

1991. Public action for social security: Foundations and strategies. In *Social security in developing countries,* ed. E. Ahmad, J. Drèze, J. Hills, and A. Sen, 1–40. Oxford.

Eide, Asbjørn. 1995a. Economic, social and cultural rights as human rights. In *Economic, social, and cultural rights: A textbook,* ed. A. Eide, C. Krause, and A. Rosas, 21–40. Boston, Mass.

1995b. The right to an adequate standard of living including the right to food. In *Economic, social, and cultural rights: A textbook,* ed. A. Eide, C. Krause, and A. Rosas, 89–105. Boston, Mass.

Eide, A., W. B. Eide, S. Goonatilake, et al., eds. 1984. *Food as a human right.* Tokyo.

Eide, A., A. Oshaug, and W. B. Eide. 1991. Food security and the right to food in international law and development. *Transnational Law and Contemporary Problems* 1: 415–67.

Eide, A., and Allan Rosas. 1995. Economic, social, and cultural rights: A universal challenge. In *Economic, social, and cultural rights: A textbook,* ed. A. Eide, C. Krause, and A. Rosas, 15–19. Boston, Mass.

Food Research and Action Center (FRAC). 1995. *Community childhood hunger identification project: A survey of childhood hunger in the United States.* Washington, D.C.

Hellman, J. A. 1994. *Mexican lives.* New York.

Kates, R. W. 1996. Ending hunger: Current status and future prospects. *Consequences* 2: 3–11.

Kates, R. W., and Sara Millman. 1990. On ending hunger: The lessons of history. In *Hunger in history: Food shortage, poverty, and deprivation,* ed. L. F. Newman, 389–407. Cambridge, Mass.

Kent, George. 1993a. Children's right to adequate nutrition. *International Journal of Children's Rights* 1: 133–54.

1993b. Nutrition and human rights (United Nations Administrative Committee on Coordination, Subcommittee on Nutrition [SCN]). *SCN News* 10: 9–12.

Melnick, R. Shep. 1994. *Between the lines: Interpreting welfare rights.* Washington, D.C.

Messer, Ellen. 1996. The human right to food (1989–1994). In *The hunger report: 1995,* ed. E. Messer and P. Uvin, 65–82. Amsterdam.

Millman, S., S. M. Aronson, L. M. Fruzzetti, et al. 1990. Organization, information, and entitlement in the emerging global food system. In *Hunger in history: Food shortage, poverty, and deprivation,* ed. L. F. Newman, 307–30. Cambridge, Mass.

Sen, A. 1981. *Poverty and famines: An essay on entitlement and deprivation.* Oxford.

Tomasevski, K., ed. 1987. *The right to food: A guide through applicable international law.* Boston, Mass.

U.S. House of Representatives, Committee on International Relations, Subcommittee on International Resources, Food, and Energy. 1976a. *Hearings on H. Con. Res. 393, the right-to-food resolution.* Washington, D.C.

1976b. *Right to food resolution.* Report 94-1543, Part 1. Washington, D.C.

VII.3 ❧ Food Subsidies and Interventions for Infant and Child Nutrition

One hundred and fifty million children, or one in three, in the developing world are seriously malnourished (United Nations Development Program 1990). This includes 38 million children underweight, 13 million wasted, and 42 million stunted. In addition, 42 million children are vitamin A–deficient (West and Sommer 1987), 1 billion people, including children, are at risk of iodine-deficiency disease (Dunn and van Der Haar 1990), and 1.3 billion have iron-deficiency anemia (United Nations 1991).

Malnutrition, whether undernutrition per se or a specific micronutrient deficiency, is usually the result of an inadequate intake of food because households do not have sufficient resources. In a review of the income sources of malnourished people in rural areas, J. von Braun and R. Pandya-Lorch (1991) found that among households with a per capita income below $600 (U.S.), there was a close relationship between household food security and the nutritional status of children.

The problems associated with nutritional deprivation are compounded when access to sanitation is limited, because poor sanitation and hygiene results in increased morbidity. This condition is often accompanied by a reduction in food intake at the very time when energy and nutrient requirements are high. About one-third of the populations of developing countries has access to sanitation, and just over half have access to safe water, but there are large urban–rural differences. Ease of access to water is 48 percent lower in rural areas than urban areas, and overall access to sanitation is 77 percent lower in rural areas (United Nations Development Program 1990).

Although urban populations may appear better off than rural ones, the plight of the urban poor is getting worse. The average annual growth rate of urban populations in developing countries is 3.7 percent, whereas that of rural ones is 0.9 percent (Hussain and Lunven 1987). However, in urban slums and squatter settlements, the population of which represents one-quarter of the world's "absolute poor," the growth rate may exceed 7 percent per annum. This rapidly expanding population comprises people who often lack the resources to obtain an adequate diet for either themselves or their children.

There are also gender, social, and cultural inequalities in addition to urban–rural disparities. In the rural areas of Africa and the urban slums of Latin America, women commonly head the household. In many cases, these women are compelled to be employed, but in general their remuneration is low because they tend to work in subsistence agriculture or in the informal sector, where women's wages are lower than those of men. Social and cultural inequalities also often favor males over females, which is manifested in, for example, better health care and nutrition for males and neglect of female education. Irrespective of the environmental and political situation, social, economic, and cultural interactions exist that make improving the nutritional status of the poor a formidable task.

Targeting interventions so that those most nutritionally vulnerable, especially children, can benefit is important not only from an economic perspective but also in terms of the nutritional impact of the intervention program. Thus, although policy makers may be interested in improving the nutritional status of preschoolers, to focus solely on this age group is neither realistic nor practical (Berg 1986; Beaton and Ghassemi 1987). Indeed, in order to improve the nutritional status of infants and young children, it is more cost-effective to use programs that would bene-

fit the entire household. The objective of a food-policy program aimed at the poor should be to improve their nutritional status by improving their access to food. However, unless nutritional considerations are explicitly stated in a food policy, it cannot be considered a food policy (Berg 1986).

Food policies can be based on *economic* and *nutrition* interventions. Specific economic interventions, which aim to stabilize food prices, may include those to increase agricultural and livestock production, to commercialize agriculture, to hold buffer stocks, and to subsidize consumer food prices. In addition to food policies, there are also other macro-economic policies that influence the availability and consumption of food. An overvalued foreign exchange rate, for example, may discourage farmers from producing food because imported food can be cheaper. Similarly, food production can decline when industrial development is carried out at the expense of agricultural development.

Nutrition interventions, however, include food fortification, the use of formula foods, supplementary feeding programs, food-for-work and food-for-cash programs, and nutrition education. The boundaries between economic and nutrition interventions are not always distinct. Supplementary feeding and food-for-work programs, for example, can be considered as consumer food-price subsidies or as income transfers.

This chapter reviews the different economic and nutrition interventions that are used as policy tools to increase the energy and nutrient intakes of the poor, thereby increasing their household food security and the nutritional status of their infants and young children.

Economic Interventions

Agricultural and Livestock Production

Increased agricultural and livestock production are often prerequisites for food security because they generate additional amounts of both food and income. Increasing productivity, however, entails changing or modifying an existing production system to make it more cost-effective. This may be achieved in a number of ways: first, by increasing yields per unit of land area or worker; second, by ensuring the availability of sufficient inputs – fertilizer, pesticides, and so forth; and last, by establishing price relationships that can act as an incentive to both innovation and the mobilization of resources (Mellor undated).

Improved technology. The Green Revolution, through the use of improved technology, was instrumental in expanding world food production during the 1970s – in particular that of rice and wheat in Asia. Similar approaches are needed for the staple food crops grown in other parts of the world, especially in Africa. Specifically, attention needs to be given to root crops as well as to the more drought-tolerant cereals, such as sorghum and millet.

Expanding the area under cultivation and increasing cropping intensity are the means of increasing agricultural production, be it for home consumption or for sale. Outside of Africa, there is little scope to expand the area under cultivation. However, through the wider use of those improved crop varieties that are more resistant to pests and diseases, farm yields could be stabilized. The greater use of early-maturing varieties, which shorten the growing season, would also allow for multiple cropping. Intercropping, too, increases overall yields, stabilizes production, and allows food to be grown throughout a longer season. Management issues such as pest and disease control, the use of crop residues and animal manure as fertilizer, and soil conservation also help to augment yields and at the same time to lower the costs of production. Livestock productivity can be increased through better disease and parasite control. This not only results in farmers' getting a better yield of milk and a better price for their dairy products or meat but also improves the work performance of draft animals and thus the asset value of the animals themselves. An increase in agricultural and livestock production can result in an improvement in the nutritional status of households through increasing household food security, which can in turn reduce the risk of infants and young children from becoming undernourished.

Land reform. There is a great deal of evidence to show that small farmers are more productive per unit of land than are large farmers (Lipton 1985). This is because small farmers depend on family labor to grow high-value or double crops, to improve land in the slack season, to reduce fallow lands in area and duration, and to enhance yields through better cultivation practices. Large farmers tend to use imported machinery as a labor-displacing strategy, and such machinery depends on imported fuel and spare parts (Norse 1985; Longhurst 1987).

The inequality in both land ownership and tenure systems is the primary cause of poverty in the rural areas of Asia, Latin America, and, to a lesser extent, Africa (Norse 1985). Access to land clearly determines access to food and income (Braun and Pandya-Lorch 1991). Landless households that depend on the sale of their labor for survival are nutritionally the most vulnerable group. Sharecroppers and tenant farmers, who give part of their crop or work at peak agricultural times in lieu of rent, and very small farmers, are also extremely vulnerable nutritionally.

Availability of inputs and services. Unless soils are replenished, the production potential of land slowly declines as soil nutrients are depleted. Inputs, particularly fertilizer and water, are needed in order to maintain production levels. The money needed to finance these inputs, generated through credit, as well as an advisory service in the form of agricultural extension services, must be available. Both inputs and services should be available to women as well as to men because a great number of women are already involved in agriculture and dependence upon women's earnings increases as employment for men falls (Mencher 1986).

In addition to inputs and services, it is essential that the reliability and efficiency of the marketing infrastructure for both food and nonfood commodities be improved if farm income levels are to be raised. Distortions in policies that adversely affect the availability of agricultural inputs and services to the small farmer will limit any improvement in agricultural production and, ultimately, influence income and the nutritional status of young children.

Commercialization of Agriculture

The integration of small farmers into a market economy entails a shift from subsistence food crop to cash crop production. However, increasing the production of cash crops at the expense of domestic food crops can disrupt traditional economic and social relationships. This, in turn, may have an adverse impact on the income, food consumption, and nutritional status of the poor (Senauer 1990). The evidence to support this theory, however, is mixed, with some studies showing commercialization having a positive effect on nutritional status (Braun and Kennedy 1986; Braun 1989) and others showing either no effect (Kennedy and Cogill 1987) or a negative one (Pinstrup-Anderson 1985; Kennedy and Alderman 1987).

Commercialization of agriculture need not necessarily be detrimental to nutritional status for two reasons. First, even though the promotion of cash crop production may decrease domestic food production, the foreign exchange generated from agricultural exports can more than offset the cost of importing food for the domestic market. Second, nutritional problems are not necessarily the result of a lack of food, but may be caused by a lack of access to sufficient food, which in itself is determined by income levels and food prices. Thus, increasing the income of poor farmers, whether from food or nonfood crops, rather than simply increasing production, should be a priority for agricultural production programs.

In general, part of any increase in income is spent on food. Among the poor, the additional proportion spent on food may be quite high. This does not, however, necessarily mean that more energy will be consumed, because families may diversify their diet rather than increase the absolute quantity of the foods they already eat (Braun and Kennedy 1986). Thus, an increase in income alone will not necessarily result in better nutrition, and other interventions, such as nutrition education, are also needed.

Another aspect of commercialization is that income flow, as opposed to total income, is important in determining the impact of income on nutritional status. A lump sum of money, such as that generated from growing cash crops, is more likely to be spent on nonfood items such as school fees or housing, whereas continuous income is more likely to be spent on food (Kennedy and Alderman 1987).

The status of the person who controls the household's money may also be important. In many developing countries, the income generated from commercial crops is viewed as belonging to men, whereas that from food crops goes to women (FAO 1987). When women have some decision-making power, they are more likely than men to purchase food and health care (Kennedy and Cogill 1987). In some countries, such as India, the money earned by mothers has been found to have a greater impact on child nutrition than that from other income sources (Kumar 1979). Braun and Pandya-Lorch (1991) have claimed that women spend more of their income on food, whereas men spend their income according to personal taste on either food or nonfood items. This observation has important implications for programs that encourage expanding the cultivation of a particular crop that can change the way in which a household's land is allocated for food and nonfood crops. Any program that reduces the amount of land available for food production without altering the control and use of income can adversely affect nutritional status.

Type of income can also influence consumption patterns. In India, S. Kumar (1979) found that payment in kind, rather than in cash, was used for consumption. Likewise, J. Greer and E. Thorbecke (1983) noted that in Kenya, income from food production rather than from off-farm work was associated with increased food intake. E. Kennedy and H. Alderman (1987) suggested that income from home gardens and home production was more likely to increase household food intake than was an equivalent amount of cash income. This interpretation emphasizes the importance of the role of women in agricultural programs, given that, in general, they control the food produced for household consumption and the income generated from the sale of food crops. Obviously, their position has important implications for child nutrition.

Buffer Stocks

Buffer stocks are strategic food stores that are used to meet fluctuations in demand, or to accommodate fluctuations in supply, when there are no alternative sources of food. Buffer stocks are primarily used to stabilize prices – for example, at times of harvest failure or just prior to the harvest season when supplies are low.

In order to stabilize prices, buffer stocks should be released onto the market and sold at a controlled, or intervention, price once a predetermined consumer "ceiling price" has been reached. Over time, the intervention price, paid by the consumer, needs to fall, as does the producer price. In order to avoid a decline in production associated with the use of buffer stocks, grain has to be bought up when the producer price on the free market falls below a predetermined "floor price."

The margin between the floor price paid to farmers and the ceiling price paid by consumers is crucial to the stabilization desired from the use of the buffer stock. If the range is wide, so that the floor price is low and the ceiling price high, then net flows of food will be small and infrequent. This situation will allow stock levels to be relatively small, but the effect on the market will also be small. In contrast, if the margin is too narrow, then the floor price may rise above the producer price or the ceiling price below the consumer price. This will cause stock levels to fluctuate wildly. Thus, the narrower the margin the larger the food stock required to maintain it, but the greater the stability in prices.

Political pressure – from farmers (to increase producer prices) and from urban consumers (to keep consumer prices low) – can undermine a buffer-stock scheme, as can private commodity dealers. For buffer stocks to be effective in stabilizing prices, the operators must have foresight and knowledge about the different types of price fluctuations (regional, seasonal, annual, inflationary, and so forth). In addition, the administration of buffer stocks should be independent so as to resist political pressure. Finally, storage costs of the buffer stock should be low (Streeten 1987).

Buffer stocks are both difficult to administer and expensive to maintain. For example, 1 ton of buffer-stock wheat held in the Sahel can cost $500 (U.S.), as compared with a price of $200 (U.S.) per ton (including freight) for wheat purchased on the world market (Streeten 1987). Aside from capital costs (such as warehouses, staff training, and the initial cost of the grain) and recurrent costs (wages, pesticides, building maintenance, and so forth), buffer stocks incur such additional costs as the interest on the funds tied up in the stock, the value of losses caused by pests, and losses resulting from deterioration in quality. S. Maxwell (1988) suggests that these additional costs may be larger than the capital or maintenance costs, although they are rarely included in estimates of buffer-stock costs. In Sudan, for example, these additional costs were equivalent to 40 percent of the purchase price of sorghum.

Buffer stocks have been used as a means to get grain to food-deficient areas in Indonesia (Levinson 1982) and as a famine reserve in Ethiopia (Maxwell 1988). These programs were implemented with the assumption that the poor, who are the most nutritionally vulnerable, would not suffer from any further deterioration in nutritional status.

Consumer Food-Price Subsidies

Consumer food-price subsidies are essentially income transfer policies that enable consumers to buy food at a lower price. They exist because cheap food is often regarded as a nutritional as well as a political necessity (Pinstrup-Anderson 1985, 1988).

Food subsidies have been found to have a positive impact on nutritional status in a number of countries (Pinstrup-Anderson 1987). This impact has been achieved in three ways. First, food subsidies increase the purchasing power of households because their members can buy more food for the same price. Second, they may reduce the price of food relative to the price of other goods, thus encouraging households to buy more food. Third, they may make certain foods cheaper relative to others and thereby change the composition of the diet.

Food subsidies, however, are not necessarily the most economic means of increasing the food intake of the poor. This is because they benefit all income levels: The rich, who do not need the subsidy, gain more than the poor because the rich can afford to buy more of the subsidized food. In addition, households do not necessarily increase their intake of the subsidized food; they may instead use the savings from its availability to buy other food or nonfood items that may be of limited nutritional benefit.

There is evidence, however, that food subsidies do increase the real income of the poor. In one study, food subsidies represented the equivalent of 15 to 25 percent of total incomes of poor people (Pinstrup-Anderson 1987). Because poor households spend between 60 and 80 percent of their income on food, the economic benefit of subsidized food as a proportion of current income is larger for the poor than for the rich, even if the absolute value of the subsidy is greater for the rich.

Food-subsidy programs have also been found to increase energy intakes at the household level, although the effect at the individual level is not always apparent. In Kerala, India, Kumar (1979) found that the subsidized ration resulted in an increase in energy intake by the lowest income group of 20 to 30 percent.

Food subsidies are often considered more beneficial to urban than to rural populations. Alderman and Braun (1986) learned that the Egyptian subsidies on bread benefited the urban population more than did subsidies on wheat flour. However, the opposite was true in rural areas where there were fewer bakeries to sell subsidized bread. R. Ahmed (1979), in Bangladesh, found that although only 9 percent of the population lived in urban areas, two-thirds of the subsidized cereal went to urban consumers. In Pakistan, B. Rogers and colleagues (1981) discovered that ration shops, which sold rationed subsidized wheat flour, had no significant effect on the energy intake of the rural population, whereas that of the urban population was increased by 114 calories per capita. Clearly, the transportation and administrative costs involved in serving a scattered rural population may limit the extent of a subsidy network. In addition, the threat of political unrest in urban areas is often a reason for governments to pursue food-price subsidies.

The political and economic climate invariably determines who benefits from a food subsidy program and how the program is implemented. The effect of food subsidies on household food consumption and, ultimately, on the nutritional status of children will depend, in part, on whether there is a *general* food subsidy, a *rationed* food subsidy, or a *targeted* food subsidy. In addition, the choice of the food to be subsidized is important.

General food subsidy. A general food subsidy is one in which the subsidized price of a specified food (or foods), in the market is below that of supply. Although politically very popular, such programs may not be the most efficient or effective way to improve the nutritional status of the poor. General price subsidies are costly and may divert financial resources from other programs, such as employment creation and wage increases, that would increase the purchasing power of the poor (Reutlinger 1988). In addition, in order to help pay for the subsidy, the programs themselves may cause increases in the prices of other foods that are important in the diet of the poor.

Yet a number of countries have implemented general food subsidy programs, which, in spite of their costs, have benefited the poor. For example, wheat flour and bread are subsidized throughout Egypt at ration shops, with no restrictions on the amount that may be purchased. Oil, sugar, and rice are also subsidized, but the supply of these is rationed. In addition, there are government-controlled cooperatives that sell subsidized frozen meat, poultry, and fish. Alderman and Braun (1984) have reviewed the Egyptian program, in which over 90 percent of the population derived benefits. In 1980, the subsidies cost the government some $1.6 billion, which was equivalent to 20 percent of concurrent government expenditure. But along with the cost burden of the general subsidy, there were noticeable nutritional gains, as shown in the fact that per capita energy intake in Egypt was greater than that in any of the countries having a per capita gross national product (GNP) up to double that of Egypt.

Access to subsidized food, however, was biased toward the rich in Egypt for a number of reasons (Alderman, Braun, and Sakr 1982). First, the lack of refrigeration facilities in rural areas precluded cooperatives from operating there, although ration shops were omnipresent. Second, the wealthier neighborhoods of Cairo appeared to have better supplies of the subsidized commodities, such as rice, than did the poor areas. In addition, although subsidized rationed commodities, such as oil, were not always rationed in the rich neighborhoods, oil was not even always available in the poor areas. Third, in addition to the regular cooperatives, civil servants and workers had their own workplace cooperative shops (in locations where more than 200 people were employed), which received extra allocations of subsidized meat and poultry. Fourth, wealthier households could afford to employ servants to fetch and queue for the subsidized food. Last, wealthier households could afford to pay bribes to ensure preferential access to subsidized food.

The Egyptian study found that although there were large variations in access to the subsidized food and also inequalities in the distribution system, the poor did benefit from an effective increase in purchasing power as a result of access to cheap food. Indeed, food subsidies accounted for 12.7 percent of expenditures for the lowest income quartile in urban areas and 18 percent of total expenditures of the poorest households in rural areas.

Rationed food subsidies: Dual prices. A dual price system is one in which certain quantities of food are rationed at a subsidized fixed price, and unlimited quantities are available at the prevailing market price. Typically, a household's quota for a rationed food is less than the total amount required by the household, and the difference is made up from purchases in the open market, where prices are higher. This arrangement effectively allows households to increase their expenditure on food.

Dual price systems, utilizing ration shops, have been implemented in India for wheat, rice, and small amounts of coarse grains (Scandizzo and Tsakok 1985) and in Pakistan for the wheat flour known as "atta" (Alderman, Chaudhry, and Garcia 1988). The ration price in India was 60 percent, and that in Pakistan 51 percent, of the open market price.

Targeted food subsidies: Food stamps. A food-stamp program is one in which coupons are sold to a selected target group who may then buy specific foods of a stated value in authorized stores. The store cashes in the coupons at a bank and the bank is reimbursed by the government. The rationale behind food stamps, in contrast to cash transfers, is that households are more likely to increase food intake with transfers in kind rather than in cash (Kumar 1979). In other words, "leakage," meaning the purchase of non-food items or more expensive "prestigious" food, is lower. Kennedy and Alderman (1987) noted that unless the value of the food stamps is more than that which a household would normally spend on food, there is no reason to expect the nutritional effect to be greater than that of giving a direct cash transfer. If, however, the cost of the coupons is close to that which the household would normally spend on food but the quantity of food that can be purchased with the coupons is higher, then the nutritional effect would be larger than that of a cash transfer. This is because, in addition to the income effect, food is cheaper at the margin. An example frequently cited is that of the U.S. food-stamp program, which until 1979 enabled a household to spend, say, $100 (U.S.) to receive $150 (U.S.) worth of food stamps.

Although it has been argued that food-stamp programs are costly to implement, S. Reutlinger (1988) has pointed out that the direct costs of administering a food-stamp program could be small because it brings in customers, so there would be no need for shops or banks to charge for processing the coupons. In addition, marketing costs may fall, which could lead to lower food prices because of an increased volume of shop sales. Thus, the only administrative costs are for printing the coupons, handling the distribution, and regulating against abuses.

As with all food-distribution programs, identifying the target group is not easy. Colombia, for example, has had a program in which only households in low-income regions with young children and pregnant or lactating women were eligible to participate. Coupons were distributed through health centers, where growth monitoring and nutrition education were carried out concurrently. The value of the food stamps was 2 percent of average income, but there was no evidence that the nutritional status of the target group improved (Pinstrup-Anderson 1987). In Sri Lanka, only households whose "declared" incomes were below a specified level could receive food stamps. However, this restriction meant that wage-earning workers on the tea estates where hunger was present did not qualify for food stamps even though they were one of the nutritionally most needy groups (Edirisinghe 1987).

In order to increase food intake and, thus, the nutritional status of the poor, the value of the food stamps must be indexed to inflation. This was not done in Sri Lanka, and so, over a four-year period, the value of the food stamps declined to 56 percent of their original value. The net result was that the already low total energy intake of the poorest 20 percent of the population declined by 8 percent.

Like other food-price subsidy programs, coupons do not necessarily result in increased consumption if the food issued does not meet the perceived needs of the household. The latter will depend on a household's composition and food preferences. In Colombia, for example, the foods that could be purchased with food stamps included highly processed foods not normally consumed by the poor.

In addition, the need for cash to buy the coupons often discriminates against the neediest households, which do not always have a regular source of cash. Moreover, even when a household does have income, it may not be sufficient to cover the cost of the coupons. But unfortunately, setting up a progressive program in which the price of the coupons is based on what a household can pay is not feasible in many societies (Pinstrup-Anderson 1987).

Choice of subsidized food. Most programs subsidize a staple cereal, and when the entire population consumes significant quantities of that staple, the cost can become prohibitive. In order to cover the costs and ensure that the poorest sections of the population benefit, the selection of the food to be subsidized is critical, particularly where more than one food is considered a staple. In Brazil, for example, C. Williamson-Gray (1982) found that subsidizing wheat bread resulted in a decrease in the energy intake of the poor. This was because the poor substituted the still more expensive subsidized bread for rice and other foods, thus decreasing their total intake of food. Williamson-Gray suggested that subsidizing cassava, rather than wheat, would have been better. Such a subsidy would have effectively increased the income of the poor because cassava is not prominent in the diet of the rich.

It has been pointed out that where "inferior" foods are subsidized, the subsidy program becomes self-targeting toward the group that consumes the "inferior" food. For this to happen, however, the "inferior" food must be consumed by a large proportion of the targeted population. Various studies cited by P. Pinstrup-Anderson (1988) indicate that subsidizing highly extracted wheat flour benefits the poor more than the rich largely because the latter perceive such flour as lower in quality because of its physical appearance.

As can be seen, a range of economic policies have been used, directly or indirectly, to improve food security among the poor. Undernutrition is inexorably linked with poverty, and unless poor households have the ability and resources to feed themselves, their infants and young children will suffer. For this reason, the focus of food-related economic policies has been at the household level.

Nutrition Interventions

Like economic interventions, nutrition interventions can be targeted or nontargeted. Once implemented, nontargeted interventions, such as food fortification, protect the entire population against a specific nutrient deficiency from an early age. Targeted interventions, such as the use of formula foods, feeding programs, and nutrition education, attempt to focus specifically on infants and young children, although many also include pregnant and lactating women. This section reviews the most commonly used nutrition interventions: food fortification, formula foods, supplementary feeding programs, and nutrition education.

Food Fortification

Food fortification is the addition of specific nutrients to foods. It can be used to restore nutrients lost in processing or to increase the level of a specific nutrient in a food. Examples of fortified food commonly consumed in developing countries include milk containing vitamin D (originally introduced to prevent infantile rickets) and salt to which iodine is added (to prevent goiter).

To ensure that the most vulnerable members of the population benefit from food fortification, the vehicle for fortification must be a staple food consumed throughout the year by a large proportion of people with relatively little inter- and intraindividual variation. Intake levels must be self-limiting to minimize the possibility of toxicity. The level of fortification must be such that it contributes significantly to nutritional requirements without altering the taste, smell, look, physical structure, or shelf life of the food vehicle. Because control and monitoring procedures must be adopted at the manufacturing level to ensure that fortification levels are adequate, legislation may be necessary (International Nutritional Anaemia Consultative Group 1977, 1981; Bauernfeind and Arroyave 1986; Arroyave 1987).

The advantages of food fortification are many. Such a procedure is socially acceptable; it does not require the active participation of the consumer; it requires no changes in food purchasing, cooking, or eating habits; and the fortified food remains the same in terms of taste, smell, and appearance. Because the product to be fortified should already be marketed and have a widespread distribution system, fortified food can be introduced quickly; its benefits are readily visible; legislation for compliance is possible; its use is relatively easy to monitor; it is the cheapest intervention for a government; and it is the most effective sustainable method of eliminating a micronutrient deficiency (International Nutritional Anaemia Consultative Group 1977, 1981; Bauernfeind and Arroyave 1986; Venkatesh Mannar 1986; Arroyave 1987).

The main disadvantage of food fortification is that although it is applied to a food that is processed and marketed throughout a society, only those who consume that food will benefit. Fortification, for example, will not benefit people who use only locally produced or unprocessed foods. Other disadvantages are that fortified food reaches nontargeted as well as targeted individuals and may not be the most economical way to reach the target group. Moreover, when the cost of fortification is passed on to the consumer, purchasing patterns may change adversely among those most intended to benefit. Fortification also involves recurring costs. Finally, political will, legislation, and mechanisms to enforce decisions to fortify foods are necessary to ensure the success of such programs (Bauernfeind and Arroyave 1986; Arroyave 1987).

Among the nutritional deficiencies of children for which the use of fortified foods has been advocated in the developing world are the control of xerophthalmia, or night blindness (International Vitamin A Consultative Group 1977), goiter (Dunn and van der Haar 1990), and nutritional anemia (International Nutritional Anaemia Consultative Group 1977, 1981; United Nations 1991). One example of the use of a specific commodity as a vehicle for vitamin A fortification to control xerophthalmia is sugar in Guatemala (Arroyave 1986, 1987). Another is the use of vitamin A–fortified monosodium glutamate in the Philippines (Latham and Solon 1986) and Indonesia (Muhilal et al. 1988), although large-scale programs have not been implemented. Iodization of salt to control goiter has been successfully introduced in China, India, and 18 countries in Central and South America, although in the latter case, some countries have had a recurrence of iodine deficiency due to a lack of continuous monitoring and control measures (Venkatesh Mannar 1986). Fortification of wheat flour with an iron salt to control nutritional anemia is being implemented in Grenada. Trials on other nonfortified foods have been implemented in a number of developing countries. In Thailand, for example, fish sauce, a widely used condiment, is fortified with an iron salt (WHO 1972). In South Africa, curry powder has been fortified with iron EDTA (ethylenediaminetetraacetic acid) (Lamparelli et al. 1987), and in Chile, reconstituted lowfat milk is fortified with an iron salt, whereas wheat biscuits have been fortified with bovine hemoglobin (Walter 1990).

Formula Foods

Formula foods are premixed foods made from unconventional sources. They may be made by combining a local cereal grain with a vegetable/pulse protein rich in the amino acids deficient in the cereal. Originally, formula foods were developed as low-cost milk substitutes to be fed to weaning children. Two classic examples are a milk substitute made from corn and cottonseed flour (INCAPARINA), and corn-soya-milk (CSM). CSM is an important food-aid commodity and a major staple of many ongoing supplementary feeding programs.

The advantages of formula foods are that they are cheaper than conventional sources of animal protein, vitamins, and minerals and can be formulated to meet the specific nutritional needs of a target group while providing energy at the same time. In addition, they do not require cold storage.

The disadvantages are that although the costs are less than those of animal protein supplements, they are higher than those of cereal staples because of manufacturing and distribution costs. The main beneficiaries of formula foods tend to be urban populations because the formula foods are generally sold through commercial channels and can become prohibitively expensive in rural areas. B. Popkin and M. C. Latham (1973) estimated that formula foods were priced at between 8 and 40 times the cost of homemade traditional foods on a nutrient-per-dollar basis. In addition, a lack of familiarity with formula foods may result in low levels of acceptability. Thus, on balance, the use and potential of such foods appear to be somewhat limited in terms of developing countries, particularly in rural areas.

Supplementary Feeding Programs

Supplementary feeding programs are conducted at health centers, schools, or community facilities, which have the advantage of keeping capital outlays low by using existing institutional infrastructures. They also facilitate decisions on intrahousehold food distribution in situations when food and income are limited. Politically, such programs are acceptable because they often generate support among the recipients.

There are, however, disadvantages involved in feeding programs. First and foremost is their cost. Apart from the possible cost of the food (which may or may not be donated food aid), there are the administrative and operational expenses of the program. These include those of transport, storage, wages, overhead, physical plant, fuel, and cooking utensils. In addition, the operation of feeding programs in health centers or schools imposes extra work on the staff, which may be detrimental to the institution's core concerns and thus is itself a hidden cost. Further questions include whether the intended beneficiaries actually participate in and benefit from the program, whether a feeding program based on imported food aid encourages black marketeering, whether the food is used for political ends, and whether feeding programs create psychological, nutritional, and political dependence.

Participation in any feeding program depends upon a number of factors, which ultimately determine the success of the program when that success is measured in terms of an improvement in nutritional status. Criteria for success include the quality and quantity of food reaching the recipients, the regularity of supply, the timing of meals, the nutritional status of the participants, and the degree of targeting.

The quality of foods served in a feeding program is important in enhancing the overall quality of the diet provided. For example, powdered milk fortified with vitamins A and D is preferable to unfortified milk. Where premixes are employed, the addition of sugar to an oil/cereal base or oil to a sugar/cereal base not only increases the energy density of the food but also renders it more palatable and, thus, increases the likelihood of its being eaten. The use of premixes has both advantages and disadvantages. On the positive side, leakage of one of the commodities (sharing or selling the commodity) is restricted, especially if a high value is put on a particular food. On the other hand, although premixes may be made up of foods that are consumed locally, the appearance and consistency of a cooked premix may be alien to the intended beneficiaries.

The quantity of food each participant receives is critical to the success of any feeding program. In general, "average" rations are based on the extent to which the general diet is deficient in both energy and specific nutrients. But no allowances are made for individual variation or for leakage. Thus, Kennedy and Alderman (1987), for example, cite a CARE review finding that in four feeding programs, 62 to 83 percent of the total energy gap was the fault of the supplementary foods. In yet another feeding program in India, sharing reduced the amount of the ration consumed by child beneficiaries by 50 percent.

Minimizing leakage through the use of increased rations, or by having on-site feeding programs, will inevitably add to costs, but these measures are more likely to encourage attendance and produce viable results (Kennedy and Knudsen 1985). One difficulty encountered in all supplementary feeding programs, regardless of leakage, is ensuring that children actually eat an adequate amount of food. Undernourished children are often anorexic. Their total intake is likely to be greater if they are fed on a "little and often" basis rather than at set meals. This means that on-site feeding centers need to operate beyond conventional working hours and may require additional staff.

The regularity of supply of supplementary food is essential for it to have an impact. Regularity, however, can be impaired by transportation and bureaucratic constraints. Any uncertainty in supply can result in a reluctance on the part of local administrators to invest either time, personnel, or resources in a supplementary feeding program. Uncertainty in supply may also jeopardize existing programs by generating ill will among the recipients, especially if they have to travel or wait for food that fails to arrive.

The timing of the issuance of supplementary meals is also important for two reasons. First, it influences how much food a child will eat, and second, it may determine the extent to which the supplementary meal is considered as a substitute for the home meal. A meal served early in the morning is unlikely to be fully eaten by a participant if the individual has already eaten at home. At the same time, it may deter a mother from giving her child an adequate meal first thing in the morning if she knows there will be one at the feeding center. The same consideration applies to other supplementary meals given near the times that meals would normally be eaten in the home. To overcome this effect, feeding programs in some countries (for example, Guatemala) changed the time at which the food was distributed so that it was perceived as a "snack" rather than a meal (Anderson et al. 1981; Balderston et al. 1981).

The initial nutritional status of the participants in a feeding program influences the success of the program. Indeed, the greatest benefit from a supplementary feeding program ought to be seen among the most undernourished children (Beaton and Ghassemi 1987). For this reason the "targeting" of feeding programs becomes very important (Kennedy and Knudsen 1985; Kennedy and Alderman 1987).

Yet targeted programs are often politically difficult to implement because they involve singling out one group of people, which may not be socially or culturally acceptable. Conversely, groups not in nutritional danger, who want to benefit from what is perceived

as a "free handout," should be excluded. In order to target successfully, there must be some criteria with which to identify the intended beneficiaries (Anderson 1986). All too often, the data for doing this are limited (Cornia 1987).

Where undernutrition is widespread, feeding programs that are well targeted geographically can be effective in reaching the nutritionally disadvantaged population. This type of targeting is generally used in drought situations – for example, in Sudan and Ethiopia between 1984 and 1986. Geographic targeting is appropriate for areas in which there is a concentration of intended beneficiaries. Kennedy and Alderman (1987) have suggested that if less than 20 percent of households or children in an area are nutritionally needy, then geographic targeting on its own is unlikely to be an effective tool.

Once vulnerable individuals have been identified, targeting at the community level can be directed at households or individuals. This will largely depend on whether the program aims to improve the energy intake of vulnerable households or only that of vulnerable children and women. At the community level, targeting often relies on some arbitrary cutoff point using nutritional criteria such as weight-for-height, weight-for-age, and in some cases, middle-upper-arm circumference. Children are enrolled in and discharged from feeding programs based on nutritional status criteria. Once a child reaches and maintains an acceptable level of nutrition for a specified time period (at least one month), he or she can be discharged from the program.

Because undernutrition often involves not only a simple food deficit but also problems of sanitation and hygiene, it is important to address these factors as well so as to reduce the likelihood of children being caught in the undernutrition–morbidity cycle that inevitably ends in their being readmitted into a feeding program.

A feeding program must not overlook the importance of maintaining an improved nutritional status once it has met its objectives, and the causes of undernutrition have been removed (Pinstrup-Anderson 1987). G. H. Beaton and H. Ghassemi (1987) have suggested that although the implementation of a feeding program may improve nutritional status, it may also disrupt the equilibrium between a community and its environment. Because of this, when a feeding program is terminated, it is essential that it be phased out over a period of time in order to ensure that the positive results of the program are not lost and that the circumstances that led to the establishment of the program in the first place do not occur again.

Supplementary feeding programs fall into four categories: on-site, take-home, school, and community programs. Each of these can also be used as a vehicle for nutrition education, which is an essential component of any feeding program that hopes to modify nutritional behavior.

On-site and take-home feeding programs. On-site and take-home feeding programs are generally aimed at children 6 months to 5 years old, women in the last trimester of pregnancy, and women in the first six months of lactation. On-site programs involve the beneficiaries' attendance at a feeding center once or twice a day to receive food rations, whereas take-home programs distribute rations at regular intervals.

As previously mentioned, on-site programs tend to cost more than take-home programs, and although the beneficiaries of the former are more likely to consume the food themselves, the coverage of such programs is usually limited in both area and numbers. In addition, there is some evidence that the supplementary food is more likely to serve as a substitute (rather than a supplement) for the food that would otherwise be eaten at home (Beaton and Ghassemi 1987). Kennedy and Alderman (1987) point out that because a household operates as an economic unit, it attempts to promote the well-being of all its members. A child who receives food at a feeding center may be considered to have been fed already and is thus given less food at home, with a resulting net energy intake that is considerably lower than intended by the planners of supplementation. There is also the danger that when the responsibility for feeding a child is removed (albeit temporarily) from the mother, undernutrition may come to be regarded as a disease to be cured through outside interventions, rather than through a reallocation of resources within the household.

Take-home programs have more scope for leakage than do on-site programs because the food may be shared among the whole household or sold. M. Anderson and colleagues (1981) compared supplementary feeding programs in five countries and found that 79 to 86 percent of children attending on-site feeding centers ate their ration, whereas only 50 percent of children receiving a take-home ration did so.

Distributed food is more likely to be shared if it is a food that is widely accepted by the local population as appropriate for consumption. Indeed, Beaton and Ghassemi (1987), in their review of over 200 reports on feeding programs, found that sharing accounted for 30 to 60 percent of the food distributed, and the overall net increase in food intake of the target population was only 45 to 70 percent. The investigators concluded that on-site and take-home programs are not effective in reaching children less than 2 years of age, although such children are nutritionally a very vulnerable group. The reasons cited for failing to enroll children younger than 2 years included the use of unfamiliar weaning foods that are considered inappropriate by mothers, as well as the mothers' lack of knowledge about feeding children of this age.

Because of the time often required for travel to a feeding center, feeding programs may suffer from low participation and low attendance and have difficulties in reaching the most vulnerable groups. In their review of feeding programs, Beaton and Ghassemi (1987) found that participation rates were 25 to 80 percent of the intended level of distribution. Low participation and attendance result in part from the fact that mothers are often working, either domestically (collecting water or firewood, preparing food, looking after a large family, and so forth), or on their land, or in the informal sector. Participating children left with older siblings do not always benefit from the feeding program because the older children may not know how to prepare the supplementary food or not understand its importance. Indeed, experience in Sudan showed that older children were more interested in playing than in bringing an undernourished child to a feeding center on time or in attempting to feed a child who was anorexic.

School feeding programs. School feeding programs have been widely adopted in many countries. Such programs encourage school enrollment and attendance and improve school performance and cognitive development (Freeman et al. 1980; Jamison 1986; Moock and Leslie 1986). Many, however, operate only during the school year. School meals may replace, rather than supplement, meals eaten at home, although in situations when the mother is not at home during the day, it is questionable whether the child would get a midday meal anyway. In the latter situation, the advantage of the school meal outweighs the disadvantage of its possibly being a replacement meal. In India, school feeding programs were found to influence household expenditure patterns because school meals were cereal-based, which allowed households to spend less money on cereals and more on milk, vegetables, fruits, and nonvegetarian foods (Babu and Hallam 1989).

Among the poor, however, school-age children are often required to work to augment the household's meager income or to look after younger siblings while the adults work. Indeed, in many situations, children from the most vulnerable households are the least likely to be at school and, thus, the least likely to benefit from a school feeding program.

Community feeding programs. Strictly speaking, community feeding programs provide replacement or substitute rather than supplementary meals. Community-organized mass feeding programs, known as *comedores,* have been implemented in Lima, Peru (Katona-Apte 1987). There, members of a group of women take turns preparing morning and midday meals. Standardized portions are sold at set prices to participants, whose entitlement depends on household size. The money collected is used to purchase foods additional to those contributed by donor agencies. Households pay for meals depending upon their circumstances, although the *comedor* does limit the number of free meals it issues each day.

The advantage of community feeding programs is that they benefit from economies of scale. Thus, not only the quantity but the quality of the meals will most likely be nutritionally superior to that of meals that would have been prepared at home. Communal kitchens also afford participating mothers more time for other activities, and yet one more benefit of a community-based program is that it gives women the opportunity to interact with and help each other.

The disadvantages of community-based feeding programs are that they do not allow for individual food preferences and that they take the control and responsibility of feeding the family away from the household. This runs the risk of child undernutrition coming to be perceived as a problem that the household cannot solve.

Food-for-Work and Food-for-Cash Programs

Food-for-work (FFW) and food-for-cash (FFC) programs are indirect nutrition interventions involving labor-intensive employment programs. Such programs effectively subsidize labor through the provision of either food or wages as remuneration, thereby improving a household's access to food and reducing the risk of child undernutrition. The short-term outcome of such programs is the creation of employment for the poor, whereas the long-term one is income generation for both poor and nonpoor through the development of an asset base (Biswas 1985; Stewart 1987; Braun, Teklu, and Webb 1991; Ravallion 1991).

The participation and involvement of both the local community and government in the design and implementation of the program is essential if the poorest people, who generally have no power base, are to participate in and benefit from it. Payment, whether in cash or as food, must be determined by the prevailing food-market conditions (Braun et al. 1991). Poor people already spend a large proportion of their income on food, and any increase in income is generally translated into further food purchases (Alderman 1986; Braun and Kennedy 1986). In order to ensure that this change takes place, the existing food market must be such that it can cope with the increased demand without price increases that will negate some positive effects of the program.

There are numerous advantages to FFW or FFC programs in terms of improving household food security and, thus, nutritional status. First, because of their relatively low level of remuneration, they do tend to reach the poor and are, consequently, self-targeting. Second, they are relatively low-cost in relation to the jobs they create. Third, they develop and improve a much needed infrastructure. Fourth, they increase local purchasing power. Fifth, they increase food demand through the generation of income for the poor, which will stimulate the local market. Sixth, there is no notion of charity. Seventh, they enable communities to be involved in their own asset creation, including that of environmental sanitation,

thereby reducing the morbidity–undernutrition risk. Eighth, they can be implemented in the slack agricultural season, thereby reducing seasonal fluctuations in income and, thus, dependency on moneylenders in rural areas (Biswas 1985; Stewart 1987; Braun et al. 1991).

The constraints of FFC and FFW programs are that many developing countries – particularly in Africa – do not have the institutional capabilities to set up, monitor, and maintain them. In many situations, it is not easy to determine the wage rate or to identify suitable small-scale infrastructural projects. In addition, the quality of the work carried out may be poor because of insufficient funds or inadequate work performance. Finally, the programs depend not only on the existence of surplus labor but also on the willingness of the laborers to be mobilized (Braun et al. 1991; Ravallion 1991).

Funds for FFW or FFC programs are generated through food aid, which can be used directly or indirectly, with the latter meaning that the food is sold and the proceeds are used to subsidize the program. As a result of administrative costs, food aid has been estimated to cost between 25 and 50 percent more than purely financial aid (Thomas et al. 1975; World Bank 1976), and food aid is not appropriate in rural areas with surplus agricultural production because it can depress local prices and incomes.

Nutrition Education

The main purpose of nutrition education is to change behavior patterns that determine the distribution of food within a household so as to reduce any intra-household inequality in nutritional status. However, without a proper understanding of the problems and constraints that households face, nutrition education on its own will have little impact. For example, if income is the most limiting factor, then education to reallocate income or food within the household is unlikely to be effective (Pinstrup-Anderson 1987). Indeed, nutrition education is likely to be useful only when households are capable of responding – for example, when a large proportion of the budget is spent on nonessential goods.

The most widely used themes in nutrition education are the encouragement of breast feeding; the introduction of appropriate food supplements for breast-fed infants between the ages of 4 and 6 months; the best use of scarce money to purchase the cheapest combination of nutritious food; the minimization of food wastage through improved food preparation and preservation; safer food preservation procedures; and ways to cook more efficiently, thereby saving on fuel costs (Manoff 1987). However, each theme cannot be treated as a discrete educational entity. For example, the promotion of breast feeding is related to the nutrition of both pregnant and lactating women, the introduction of weaning foods, the prevention and control of diarrheal disease, the adverse marketing practices of commercial breast milk substitutes, changes in hospital practices, and changes in policies such as paid maternity leave and provision of nurseries at the workplace.

Nutrition education techniques have relied largely on mass media campaigns and face-to-face communication through maternal-child-health clinics, women's groups, agricultural extension agents, and so forth. Few, however, involve the community, although R. C. Hornik (1987) and R. K. Manoff (1987) have suggested that unless communities develop the messages and undertake the administrative and financial responsibility for nutrition education programs on their own, it is unlikely that nutrition education will be effective on a large scale. If people pay for a service, however, they will use it and change their behavior.

Although the mass media has the potential to inform a large number of people, the number of people who can be reached in the lowest economic strata – nutritionally the most vulnerable – is generally not large. Irrespective of literacy levels, the majority of people in developing countries do not have access to newspapers, and there are only about 170 radios and 40 televisions per 1,000 people in the entire developing world (United Nations Development Program 1990). Moreover, in many developing countries there are multiple languages and dialects, as well as differing religious beliefs, ethnic groups, and cultural practices. Nationalized mass media messages may, therefore, not be very appropriate.

Women comprise the majority of the 870 million illiterate adults in the developing world (United Nations Development Program 1990). But mothers are not the only ones to whom messages need to be directed in order to effect a change in behavior. The medical profession, too, could play a much larger role than it currently does. In addition, schoolchildren, religious leaders, and the members of any institutionalized program have a role to play in nutrition education. If behavior is to be truly changed, however, the focus must be on ways to educate and communicate both relevant and appropriate nutrition advice.

The preceding sections show the range of nutrition policies that may be used to improve the nutritional status of infants and young children. Each policy has been analyzed in terms of its benefits and constraints, but it is difficult to ensure that the most nutritionally vulnerable children do, indeed, benefit from an intervention. For this reason, it is more appropriate to identify the vulnerable groups – that is, poor households with specific characteristics – than the vulnerable children. In short, to improve the nutritional status of infants and young children, economic and nutrition interventions must be aimed at poor households.

Penelope Nestel

Bibliography

Ahmed, R. 1979. *Foodgrain supply, distribution, and consumption policies within a dual pricing mechanism: A case study of Bangladesh.* International Food Policy Research Institute Research Report No. 8. Washington, D.C.

Alderman, H. 1986. *The effect of food price and income changes on the acquisition of food by low-income households.* Washington, D.C.

Alderman, H., and J. von Braun. 1984. *The effects of the Egyptian food subsidy system on income distribution and consumption.* International Food Policy Research Institute Research Report No. 45. Washington, D.C.

    1986. Egypt's food subsidy policy: Lessons from the past and options for the future. *Food Policy* 11 (3): 223-7.

Alderman, H., J. von Braun, and S. A. Sakr. 1982. *Egypt's food subsidy and rationing system: A description.* International Food Policy Research Institute Research Report No. 34. Washington, D.C.

Alderman, H., G. Chaudhry, and M. Garcia. 1988. *Household food security in Pakistan: The ration shop system.* International Food Policy Research Institute Working Papers on Food Subsidies No. 4. Washington, D.C.

Anderson, M. 1986. Targeting food-aid from a field perspective. In *Nutritional aspects of project food-aid,* ed. M. Forman, A21-37. Rome.

Anderson, M., J. E. Austin, J. D. Wray, and M. F. Zeitlin. 1981. *Nutrition interventions in developing countries, study 1: Supplementary feeding.* Cambridge, Mass.

Arroyave, G. 1986. Vitamin A deficiency control in Central America. In *Vitamin A deficiency and its control,* ed. J. C. Bauernfeind, 405-23. Orlando, Fla.

    1987. Alternative strategies with emphasis on food fortification. In *Delivery of oral doses of vitamin A to prevent vitamin A deficiency and nutritional blindness: A state-of-the-art review,* ed. K. P. West and A. Sommer, 87-91. (United Nations Subcommittee on Nutrition, Administrative Committee on Co-ordination. Subcommittee on Nutrition); Nutrition policy discussion paper no. 2. Rome.

Babu, S. C., and J. A. Hallam. 1989. Socioeconomic impacts of school feeding programs: Empirical evidence from a South Indian village. *Food Policy* 14: 58-66.

Balderston, J., A. B. Wilson, M. E. Freire, and M. S. Simonen. 1981. *Malnourished children of the rural poor.* Boston, Mass.

Bauernfeind, J. C., and G. Arroyave. 1986. Control of vitamin A deficiency by the nutrification food approach. In *Vitamin A deficiency and its control,* ed. J. C. Bauernfeind, 359-84. Orlando, Fla.

Beaton, G. H., and H. Ghassemi. 1987. Supplementary feeding programs for young children in developing countries: A summary of lessons learnt. In *Food policy: Integrating supply, distribution, and consumption,* ed. J. P. Gittinger, J. Leslie, and C. Hoisington, 413-28. Baltimore, Md.

Berg, A. 1986. Integrating nutrition in food policy analysis. In *Food policy: Frameworks for analyses and action,* ed. C. K. Mann and B. Huddleston, 50-4. Bloomington, Ind.

Biswas, M. 1985. Food-aid, nutrition, and development. In *Nutrition and development,* ed. M. Biswas and P. Pinstrup-Anderson, 97-119. Oxford.

Braun, J. von. 1989. *Commentary: Commercialization of smallholder agriculture - policy requirements for capturing gains for the malnourished poor.* International Food Policy Research Institute Report 11 (2): 1-4.

Braun, J. von, and E. Kennedy. 1986. *Commercialization of subsistence agriculture: Income and nutritional effects in developing countries.* International Food Policy Research Institute Working Papers on Commercialization of Agriculture and Nutrition No. 1. Washington, D.C.

Braun, J. von, and R. Pandya-Lorch. 1991. *Income sources of malnourished people in rural areas: Microlevel information and policy implications.* International Food Policy Research Institute Working Papers on Commercialization of Agriculture and Nutrition No. 5. Washington, D.C.

Braun, J. von, T. Teklu, and P. Webb. 1991. *Public works for food security: Concepts, policy issues, and review of experience in Africa.* International Food Policy Research Institute Working Papers on Food Subsidies No. 6. Washington, D.C.

Cornia, G. A. 1987. Social policymaking: Restructuring, targeting, efficiency. In *Adjustment with a human face: Protecting the vulnerable and promoting growth,* ed. G. A. Cornia, R. Jolly, and F. Stewart, 165–82. Oxford.

Dunn, J. T., and F. van der Haar. 1990. *A practical guide to the correction of iodine deficiency.* International Council for Control of Iodine Deficiency Disorders Technical Manual No. 3. Amsterdam.

Edirisinghe, N. 1987. *The food stamp scheme in Sri Lanka: Costs, benefits, and options for modification.* International Food Policy Research Institute Research Report No. 58. Washington, D.C.

FAO (Food and Agriculture Organization). 1987. Women in African food production and food security. In *Food policy: Integrating supply, distribution, and consumption,* ed. J. P. Gittinger, J. Leslie, and C. Hoisington, 133–40. Baltimore, Md.

Freeman, H. E., R. E. Klein, J. W. Townsend, and A. Lechtig. 1980. Nutrition and cognitive development among rural Guatemalan children. *American Journal of Public Health* 70: 1277–85.

Greer, J., and E. Thorbecke. 1983. *Pattern of food consumption and poverty in Kenya and effects of food prices.* Ithaca, N.Y.

Hornik, R. C. 1987. Nutrition education: An overview. In *Food policy: Integrating supply, distribution, and consumption,* ed. J. P. Gittinger, J. Leslie, and C. Hoisington, 429–35. Baltimore, Md.

Hussain, A. M., and P. Lunven. 1987. Urbanization and hunger in the cities. *Food and Nutrition Bulletin* 9: 50–61.

International Nutritional Anaemia Consultative Group. 1977. *Guidelines for the eradication of iron deficiency anaemia.* Washington, D.C.

  1981. *Iron deficiency in women.* Washington, D.C.

International Vitamin A Consultative Group. 1977. *Guidelines for the eradication of vitamin A deficiency and xerophthalmia.* Washington, D.C.

Jamison, D. T. 1986. Child malnutrition and school performance in China. *Journal of Development Economics* 20: 299–309.

Katona-Apte, J. 1987. Food-aid as communal meals for the urban poor: The *comedor* program in Peru. *Food and Nutrition Bulletin* 9: 245–8.

Kennedy, E., and H. Alderman. 1987. *Comparative analyses of nutritional effectiveness of food subsidies and other food-related interventions.* Washington, D.C.

Kennedy, E., and B. Cogill. 1987. *Income and nutritional effects of the commercialization of agriculture in southwestern Kenya.* International Food Policy Research Institute Research Report No. 63. Washington, D.C.

Kennedy, E., and O. Knudsen. 1985. A review of supplementary feeding programs and recommendations on their design. In *Nutrition and development,* ed. M. Biswas and P. Pinstrup-Anderson, 77–96. Oxford.

Kennedy, E., and P. Pinstrup-Anderson. 1983. *Nutrition-related policies and programs: Past performances and research needs.* Washington, D.C.

Kumar, S. 1979. *Impact of subsidized rice on food consumption and nutrition in Kerala.* International Food Policy Research Institute Research Report No. 5. Washington, D.C.

Lamparelli, R. D., A. P. MacPhail, T. H. Bothwell, et al. 1987. Curry powder as a vehicle for iron fortification: Effects on iron absorption. *American Journal of Clinical Nutrition* 46: 335–40.

Latham, M. C., and F. S. Solon. 1986. Vitamin A deficiency in the Philippines. In *Vitamin A deficiency and its control,* ed. J. C. Bauernfeind, 425–43. Orlando, Fla.

Levinson, F. 1982. Towards success in combating malnutrition: An assessment of what works. *Food and Nutrition Bulletin* 4: 23–44.

Lipton, M. 1985. *Land assets and rural poverty.* World Bank Staff Working Paper No. 616. Washington, D.C.

Longhurst, R. 1987. Policy approaches towards small farmers. In *Adjustment with a human face: Protecting the vulnerable and promoting growth,* ed. G. A. Cornia, R. Jolly, and F. Stewart, 183–96. Oxford.

Manoff, R. K. 1987. Nutrition education: Lessons learned. In *Food policy: Integrating supply, distribution, and consumption,* ed. J. P. Gittinger, J. Leslie, and C. Hoisington, 436–42. Baltimore, Md.

Maxwell, S. 1988. *Food security study: Phase 1.* Brighton.

Mellor, J. W. Undated. *The emerging world food situation and challenges for development policy.* International Food Policy Research Briefs No. 1. Washington, D.C.

Mencher, J. 1986. Women and agriculture. In *Food policy: Frameworks for analyses and action,* ed. C. K. Mann and B. Huddleston, 39–49. Bloomington, Ind.

Moock, P. R., and J. Leslie. 1986. Childhood malnutrition and schooling in Terai region of Nepal. *Journal of Development Economics* 20: 35–52.

Muhilal, D. Permeisih, Y. R. Idjradinata, Muherdiyantiningsih, and D. Karyadi. 1988. Vitamin A-fortified monosodium glutamate and health, growth, and survival of children: A controlled field trial. *American Journal of Clinical Nutrition* 48: 1271–6.

Norse, D. 1985. Nutritional implications of resource policies and technological change. In *Nutrition and development,* ed. M. Biswas and P. Pinstrup-Anderson, 20–42. Oxford.

Pinstrup-Anderson, P. 1985. The impact of export crop production on human nutrition. In *Nutrition and development,* ed. M. Biswas and P. Pinstrup-Anderson, 43–59. Oxford.

  1987. Nutrition interventions. In *Adjustment with a human face: Protecting the vulnerable and promoting growth,* ed. G. A. Cornia, R. Jolly, and F. Stewart, 241–56. Oxford.

  1988. The social and economic effects of consumer oriented food subsidies: A summary of current evidence. In *Food subsidies in developing countries,* ed. P. Pinstrup-Anderson, 3–20. Baltimore, Md.

Popkin, B., and M. C. Latham. 1973. The limitations and dangers of commerciogenic nutritious foods. *American Journal of Clinical Nutrition* 26: 1015–23.

Ravallion, M. 1991. On the coverage of public employment schemes for poverty alleviation. *Journal of Development Economics* 34: 57–79.

Reutlinger, S. 1988. Urban malnutrition and food interventions. *Food Policy* 10: 24–8.

Rogers, B., et al. 1981. *Consumer foodprice subsidies.* Cambridge, Mass.

Scandizzo, P. L., and I. Tsakok. 1985. Food price policies and nutrition in developing countries. In *Nutrition and development,* ed. M. Biswas and P. Pinstrup-Anderson, 60–76. Oxford.

Senauer, B. 1990. Household behavior and nutrition in developing countries. *Food Policy* 15: 408–17.

Stewart, F. 1987. Supporting productive employment among vulnerable groups. In *Adjustment with a human face: Protecting the vulnerable and promoting growth,* ed. G. A. Cornia, R. Jolly, and F. Stewart, 197–217. Oxford.

Streeten, P. 1987. *What price food? Agricultural price policies in developing countries.* Ithaca, N.Y.

Thomas, J. W., S. J. Burki, P. C. Davies, and R. M. Hook. 1975. *Employment and development: A comparative analysis of the role of public works programs.* Cambridge, Mass.

United Nations. 1991. Controlling iron deficiency. United Nations Administrative Committee, Coordination-Subcommittee on Nutrition Policy Discussion Paper No. 9. Geneva.

United Nations Development Program. 1990. *United Nations development report.* Oxford.

Venkatesh Mannar, M. G. 1986. Control of iodine deficiency disorders by iodination of salt: Strategy for developing countries. In *The prevention and control of iodine deficiency disorders,* ed. B. S. Hetzel, J. T. Dunn, and J. B. Stanbury, 111–26. Amsterdam.

Walter, T. 1990. Combating iron deficiency in Chile: A case study. In *Combating iron deficiency anemia through food fortification technology.* International Nutritional Anemia Consultative Group. Washington, D.C.

West, K. P., and A. Sommer. 1987. *Delivery of oral doses of vitamin A to prevent vitamin A deficiency and nutritional blindness: A state-of-the-art review.* (United Nations Administrative Committee on Co-ordination. Subcommittee on Nutrition). Policy discussion paper no. 2. Rome.

Williamson-Gray, C. 1982. *Food consumption parameters for Brazil and their application to food policy.* International Food Policy Research Institute Research Report No. 32. Washington, D.C.

World Bank. 1976. *Public works programs in developing countries: A comparative analysis.* Staff Working Paper No. 224. Washington, D.C.

WHO (World Health Organization). 1972. *Nutritional anaemias.* Technical Report Series No. 503. Geneva.

VII.4 ❧ Recommended Dietary Allowances and Dietary Guidance

To view this topic in perspective, we need answers at the outset to two questions: "What are Recommended Dietary Allowances (RDA)?" and "What purpose do they serve?" RDA are a set of *dietary standards;* they are *reference values* for the amounts of essential nutrients and food sources of energy that should be present in human diets. Standards of this type, based on the best available scientific knowledge, are needed by policy administrators, public-health officials, physicians, dietitians, and educators who have responsibility for establishing food and health policy; for providing the public with reliable dietary advice; for planning nutritionally adequate food supplies for large groups of people; and for assessing the adequacy of diets consumed by individuals or populations.

Definition of RDA

RDA for essential nutrients are defined differently from RDA for food sources of energy. For essential nutrients, the RDA values are amounts judged to be high enough to meet the known physiological needs of practically any healthy person in a group that has been specified by age and sex. They exceed average requirements to ensure that few, if any, individuals who are consuming amounts of nutrients equivalent to the RDA will have inadequate intakes. In contrast, RDA values for food sources of energy are the *average* amounts needed by the members of each group. RDA are not, in themselves, general dietary recommendations, but as standards, they serve as the scientific basis for many aspects of practical nutrition and food and health policy (FNB 1989b).

Nomenclature

The name "Recommended Dietary Allowances" for these reference values was proposed by the Food and Nutrition Board (FNB) of the U.S. National Research Council (NRC) in 1941 when it first established a dietary standard (ADA 1941). As the term "RDA" was more and more widely used, it became evident that its meaning was not well understood. It was frequently used as a synonym for requirements or with the implication that RDA were dietary recommendations for use directly by the public. The response of the FNB was to increase the specificity of the definition in subsequent RDA reports and to include an introductory section explaining the uses of RDA (FNB 1974).

In an effort to distinguish more clearly between reference values and general dietary recommendations, some national and international committees have used other names for their dietary standards. A Canadian committee called its values simply a "Dietary Standard" (CCN 1940). The Food and Agriculture and World Health Organizations of the United Nations (FAO/WHO) have usually entitled their reports "Nutrient Requirements," with the dietary standards derived from the average requirements being designated as "Recommended Daily Intakes" (FAO/WHO 1970) or "Safe Levels of Intake" (FAO/WHO 1985). The United Kingdom adopted the term "Recommended Daily Amounts of Nutrients" (DHSS 1985). Canada (HWC 1983) and Australia (NHMRC 1990) have used "Recommended Nutrient Intakes." Recently, the United Kingdom adopted the terms "Dietary Reference Values for Food Energy and Nutrients" and "Reference Nutrient Intakes" (DHSS 1991). These are the clearest and most specific terms proposed. It is hoped that they will be widely accepted and thereby reduce misunderstanding about the meaning of dietary standards.

About 40 countries have established national dietary standards; at least 10 national committees have adopted the term "RDA," and several others the FAO/WHO standards (Truswell 1987, 1990). Although definitions of dietary standards differ slightly from one organization to another, and values for some nutrients differ from one national standard to another, the various sets of reference values (regardless of the names used for them) have all been designed for the same purposes. The term "RDA" is used for the most part in this chapter, but the equivalence of this and other terms for dietary standards should be kept in mind.

Historical Perspective

Prehistoric Knowledge of Food and Health

The essentiality of specific constituents of foods for human health and survival was discovered only during the nineteenth and early twentieth centuries. The concept of dietary standards and programs of dietary guidance based on knowledge of human needs for individual nutrients are, thus, of recent origin. However, as food is a basic biological necessity, our early ancestors undoubtedly learned through observation and much trial and error how to identify safe sources of nutriment from among the vast array of natural products available to them.

They discovered that some of these products were toxic and caused illness and even death. At the same time, they learned how to cope with several potentially dangerous foods and other dietary problems. For example, the indigenous peoples of the Amazon Basin found that the poisonous cassava root could be converted into a wholesome, edible product by steeping it in water, and peoples in the Arctic region discovered that scurvy, the debilitating and often fatal disease caused by a lack of ascorbic acid (vitamin C), was prevented or cured if they consumed extracts of evergreen needles (Clark 1968). Thus, the human species learned early to distinguish among natural products that were valuable sources of food, those that had medicinal properties, and those that contained poisons (Harper 1988). Oral transmission of such information can be viewed as the earliest form of dietary guidance.

In recent prehistoric times (12,000 to 5000 B.C.), the domestication of certain plants (especially cereal grains and legumes) and animals (sheep, goats, pigs, cattle) to provide safe and dependable sources of food (Cowan and Watson 1992) was undoubtedly based on this knowledge. Also, observations about the effects of certain foods and other natural products in

treating diseases expanded and, by early historic times (3000 to 500 B.C.) in Egypt, Babylonia, India, and China, had become intimately associated with an organized practice of medicine. In all of these civilizations, extensive lists of prescriptions (pharmacopoeias) were compiled, and an immense number of natural materials, especially herbs (some of which have since been shown to contain effective medicinal components) but also some traditional foods, were used as remedies for a variety of ailments.

In Egypt, for example, the onion, a good source of ascorbic acid, was recommended as a cure for a disease resembling scurvy. At the same time, much of the accumulated knowledge about the use of natural products for the treatment of illnesses was subjective and unreliable and was intertwined with mythical and magical beliefs. Major diseases were attributed mainly to supernatural causes and restoration of health to the magical or supernatural powers of the remedy or the healer (Ackerknecht 1982). Apart from improved methods of obtaining a dependable supply of food and increased knowledge of the medicinal properties of natural products, concepts of foods and nutriture during the early historic period differed little from those of the prehistoric period.

Medical Dietetics –
Hippocrates to the Renaissance

In Greece, a new attitude toward food and health began to emerge between 600 and 400 B.C. Physicians of the Hippocratic school of medicine in Cos rejected the belief that magical and supernatural influences determined human well-being. They accepted the viewpoint of the Ionian philosophers that the only reliable way to learn about the natural world was through direct observation and logical reasoning. Those physicians described the symptoms of their patients and the course of diseases in great detail with remarkable accuracy, and they recognized the recuperative powers of the body and the importance of food in maintaining or restoring health. They observed: "Growing bodies have the most innate heat; they therefore require the most food for otherwise their bodies are wasted. . . . In old persons the heat is feeble and they therefore require little fuel" (Adams 1952: 131).

Diet loomed large in both their diagnosis and treatment of diseases. The Greek physicians were concerned with what to feed, along with when, how much, and how often, and developed a complex system of dietetic medicine (Fidanza 1979). Despite their many astute observations, however, they believed that health depended upon the appropriate balance of four mystical humors – blood, phlegm, black bile, and yellow bile – and their associated qualities: warm, cold, moist, and dry. They believed that imbalances among these humors caused diseases (Ackerknecht 1982). They further believed that the basic elements of matter were fire, water, earth, and air – a concept proposed by Empedocles (490 to 430 B.C.) that remained the basis of theoretical chemistry until the eighteenth century (Brock 1993) – and that foods contained only a single source of nutriment: "aliment" (McCollum 1957: 63). These erroneous concepts of chemistry and human biology and reliance on subjective observations without controlled experimental studies prevented the early Greek physicians from achieving an understanding of the chemical nature of foods, the process of nutrition, and objective knowledge of relationships between diet and disease.

The Greek era of medicine culminated with Galen, who in the second century A.D. compiled an extensive record of Greek medical knowledge and his own contributions to it. He used the experimental method to establish that urine was formed in the kidney, not in the bladder, and recognized that food must undergo transformation in the body before it can be used to form tissues. But he, too, was limited by the chemical and biological concepts of the times. Of pertinence to the present topic, however, he codified rules of personal hygiene, of healthful living. He identified health-influencing factors over which the individual could exert some control – air, food and drink, activity, rest, sleep, evacuation, and passions of the mind – and he recommended moderation in all things (Whorton 1982).

Hippocratic and Galenic concepts dominated medicine in Europe until the seventeenth century, but they were gradually discarded as science progressed. The rules for healthful living, however, persisted and were a stimulus for many health movements in the eighteenth and nineteenth centuries (Burnham 1987), probably because they were compatible with the theology of the times in providing a moralistic solution for the sins of gluttony, sloth, and intemperance to which illness was attributed. Present-day dietary guidelines are a modern version of some of these rules. The objective remains the same – guidance for healthful living with moralistic overtones – but is now bolstered by scientific observations.

Knowledge of foods, nutrition, and relationships between diet and health advanced little for over 1,500 years following the death of Galen. With the decline of the Roman Empire and the rise of Christianity, interest shifted from the body to the soul; the social and religious environment was no longer conducive to investigations of natural phenomena. The concepts and teachings of the Greek philosophers and physicians became ossified, and it was only toward the end of the Renaissance that resistance to authoritarian doctrines and a rebirth of the scientific attitude opened the way for a new era of critical inquiry.

The nature of the transition is illustrated by the career of Paracelsus (1493–1541), a Swiss physician, alchemist, magician, and necromancer (Pachter 1951). He rejected the Galenic belief that diseases were caused by an imbalance of humors and proposed that they were caused by improper diet or defective body function. He taught that foods were sources of aliment, medicine, and poison, and asserted: It is the dose that makes the poison. Despite his enlightened approach, however, he accepted the magical "doctrine of signatures," the belief that potential remedies exhibited signs of the conditions for which they were effective – the shape of the leaves of the liverwort, for example, indicated its value for treating diseases of the liver. Thus, reading the efforts of Paracelsus to express his concepts of biological processes without knowledge of basic chemistry is reminiscent of viewing Michelangelo's unfinished statues, in which the partially formed figures appear to be struggling to break out of the blocks of marble.

The Enlightenment: The Impact of Science on Nutrition

By the beginning of the eighteenth century, the power of the scientific method to expand knowledge of natural phenomena had been demonstrated in the physical sciences through the investigations of Galileo Galilei (1564–1642) and Isaac Newton (1642–1727). The essentiality of a component of air for respiration had been established by Robert Boyle (1627–91) and his colleagues. The mystical elements assumed by the Greeks – Empedocles and Aristotle – and by the alchemists to be the basis of matter were being questioned. The anatomical observations of Andreas Vesalius (1514–64) had begun to undermine the authority of Galen, and William Harvey (1578–1657) made discoveries about the nature of blood circulation that opened up new approaches to the study of respiration (Wightman 1953). Yet knowledge of food and nutrition had advanced little. The Hippocratic belief that the state of health was determined by the balance of humors was still dominant in medicine, as was the concept that foods contained only a single source of nutriment.

There were, however, a few observations of links between foods, diet, health, and disease made during the seventeenth and eighteenth centuries that may be taken as harbingers of progress to come in nutrition (McCollum 1957; Guggenheim 1981). The effectiveness of citrus fruits and fresh vegetables as cures for scurvy was reported on several occasions during the seventeenth century (Carpenter 1988). Investigations of this disease by James Lind (1716–94) in 1753 led some 40 years later to the inclusion of citrus juice in the rations of sailors in the British Navy. Earlier Thomas Sydenham (1624–89), a prestigious London physician, had observed (in the 1670s) that a tonic of iron filings in wine produced clinical responses in anemic patients. Pellagra was noted by Gaspar Casal (1679–1759) to be associated with consumption of a poor diet, and in Germany, C. A. von Bergen noted in 1754 that liver, later found to be a good source of vitamin A, had been recommended in several places as a treatment for night blindness. But although Sydenham's observations could be taken as early evidence of the essentiality of iron (McCollum 1957), and the formal action of requiring citrus juice in the rations of British sailors as the initial example of a dietary standard (Leitch 1942), they were not recognized as such at the time, probably because success in treating diseases with foodstuffs was attributed to their content of medicinal substances.

The scientific contributions of Antoine-Laurent Lavoisier (1743-94) to our knowledge of the nature of gases, the process of oxidation, and the chemical structure of matter, which built on the discoveries of many of his predecessors and colleagues (Brock 1993), finally opened the way for an understanding of the composition of foods and the functions of individual food constituents in nutrition. After Lavoisier had shown that during combustion, various metals and carbon combined with oxygen and released heat, he and Pierre Simon de Laplace demonstrated (between 1770 and 1790) that respiration by guinea pigs and human subjects was an analogous process and that oxidation of carbon compounds by the body was accompanied by the release of heat (Lusk 1964). Foods, it was now evident, were not just a source of building materials for body substance but were also a source of energy for physical activity and other body functions.

In 1816, Françoise Magendie (1783-1855) concluded, from the results of experiments on dogs fed on diets that contained only carbohydrate or fat, that food was the source of nitrogen for the body. Although his experiments were less definitive than is often assumed (Carpenter 1994), his work led to the recognition that protein was an essential dietary constituent. During this time, the major constituents of foods had been separated and identified and, in 1827, William Prout (1785-1850), a London physician and scientist, proposed that the nutrition of higher animals was to be understood through consideration of the three major food components – carbohydrates, fats, and proteins. By 1850, largely through animal-feeding studies in Europe, particularly those conducted by Jean Baptiste Boussingault (1802-87) in France, five mineral elements – calcium, phosphorus, sodium, chloride, and iron – were known to be required in the diets of animals (McCollum 1957; Guggenheim 1981). The foundation for a science of nutrition had now been laid.

Nutrients As the Basis for Dietary Advice

After these advances, making dietary recommendations based on the chemical composition of foods was a concept finally approaching reality. During the 1830s, Boussingault in France, Gerrit Mulder (1802-80) in Holland, and Justus von Liebig (1803-73) in Germany had all proposed that the nitrogen content of a food could serve as an indicator of its nutritive value. Liebig began to teach that the "plastic" (nitrogen or protein) and "fuel" (carbohydrate plus fat) constituents of foods, together with a few minerals, represented the essentials of a nutritionally adequate diet. During the 1840s, Liebig and his colleagues in Giessen prepared extensive tables for predicting relative nutritive values of foods from their content of protein and energy-yielding constituents.

Mulder probably deserves credit for proposing the first dietary recommendations for a specific nutrient. In 1847, based on studies of Dutch army rations, he recommended 100 grams of protein daily for a laborer and 60 grams for a sedentary person (Todhunter 1954). In selecting a higher value for laborers, he was conforming with Liebig's erroneous belief that muscle protein was degraded during physical activity and was replaced by proteins from foods. During the 1850s, Lyon Playfair (1818-98), a professor of chemistry at Edinburgh who also accepted Liebig's hypothesis that muscular work involved breakdown of muscle protein, undertook extensive surveys of the protein consumed by men doing different types of work as a way of assessing protein needs. He took the results of his surveys (that laborers doing heavy physical work consumed much more protein than those who were less active) as support for Liebig's hypothesis. His results were not surprising. If food is readily available, individuals doing hard work will eat more than those working less vigorously and will therefore consume more protein whether or not they need it. Nonetheless, in 1865 he concluded that healthy adults should consume 119 grams of protein daily in a diet providing about 3,000 kilocalories of energy (Munro 1964).

This approach of basing dietary recommendations on estimates of the amounts and types of foods consumed by a generally healthy segment of the population was continued throughout the century. In Germany, Carl von Voit, a colleague of Liebig, on the basis of surveys of the diets of German workers in different occupations, reached essentially the same conclusions as Playfair, as did Wilbur Atwater (1844-1907), who had worked with Voit and later studied the diets of workers in the United States. But these recommendations were not actually dietary standards; all were based only on observed intakes of active healthy people, not on measured needs.

An exception was one set of recommendations by Edward Smith (1819-74), a British physician and scientist who had done extensive experimental studies of energy expenditure and nitrogen excretion by human subjects. During the depression of the 1860s, he was requested by the medical officer of the British Privy Council to determine the quantity and quality of food that would avoid "starvation-diseases" among the unemployed (Leitch 1942). He concluded from his experimental observations that a nutritionally adequate diet for working men should provide about 80 grams of protein and about 3,000 kilocalories of energy and recommended about 10 percent less for women. His recommendations were the first true dietary standards based on experimental evidence of human requirements (Todhunter 1961).

Throughout the nineteenth century, dietary recommendations were directed exclusively toward meeting needs for protein and energy, in large measure because of the prestige of Liebig, who had asserted strongly that protein and energy-yielding nutrients (fats and carbohydrates), together with a few minerals, were the essentials of a nutritionally adequate diet. This concept was the basis for dietary advice provided to the public by the U.S. Department of Agriculture (USDA) between 1890 and 1905. Yet, as early as 1849, J. Pereira (1804–53), a British physician and Fellow of the Royal Society, had questioned the validity of Liebig's views on the grounds that diets providing adequate quantities of protein and energy, but lacking variety, were associated with the occurrence of scurvy. Subsequently, several investigators in France, Britain, and Switzerland provided strong circumstantial evidence that foods contained many other unidentified substances essential for health (McCollum 1957; Guggenheim 1981). But it was only in the second decade of the twentieth century that Liebig's concept of a nutritionally adequate diet was generally acknowledged to be untenable. This came after experiments had demonstrated that modifications of diet or provision of dietary supplements could cure diseases such as beriberi in humans and scurvy in guinea pigs, and that supplements of small amounts of milk or egg could prevent growth failure in rodents fed a diet consisting of purified proteins, carbohydrates, fats, and minerals.

Evidence that several diseases associated with the consumption of poor diets were caused by nutritional deficiencies (MRC 1932) began to affect dietary recommendations toward the end of World War I. A Food Committee of the British Royal Society, besides recommending 70 to 80 grams of protein and 3,000 kilocalories of food energy for the "average man," stated that every diet should include "a certain proportion" of fresh fruits or green vegetables and that diets of all children should contain "a considerable proportion of milk" to protect against unknown dietary deficiencies (Leitch 1942). In response to this "newer knowledge of nutrition," the USDA in 1916 developed a food guide based on five food groups and recommended that diets be selected from a wide variety of foods to ensure that both known and unknown nutrients would be consumed in adequate amounts (Hertzler and Anderson 1974).

Between 1925 and 1935, the importance of consuming protective foods was also emphasized in reports of the British Medical Association (BMA) (1933) and a League of Nations committee on nutrition-related policy issues (1937). The objective of dietary recommendations prior to this time had been, first, to prevent starvation and malnutrition during periods of economic depression and, second, to maintain the working capacity of those in the labor force

and the army (Leitch 1942). The new recommendations were designed to improve the health of the entire population but were framed only in general terms because knowledge of human requirements for specific nutrients was sparse.

Dietary Standards – A New Concept

During the depression years from 1929 to 1935, E. Burnet and W. R. Aykroyd (1935) prepared a report on diet and health for the League of Nations. In it they emphasized the inadequate state of knowledge of human nutrition and the importance of investigating human needs for nutrients to provide a reliable base for dietary recommendations. An important outcome of the discussion of their report by the Assembly of the League was a statement calling attention to the need for, among other things, public education about the principles and practice of nutrition and the need to establish dietary standards (Harper 1985). This was the first time that a clear distinction was made between recommendations that represented food and nutrition policy and standards to establish that policy.

Between 1920 and 1940, rapid progress was made in advancing knowledge of the newly discovered essential nutrients. Chemical structures of some of the vitamins were determined, the effects of several vitamin and mineral deficiencies were described, and human needs for essential nutrients were investigated (McCollum, Orent-Keiles, and Day 1939; Rosenberg 1945). The knowledge needed for establishing dietary standards was becoming available.

Hazel Stiebling of the USDA, who had been a U.S. representative at meetings of League of Nations committees on food and nutrition problems, proposed the first set of standards for ensuring that diets used in feeding programs during the depression of the 1930s would be nutritionally adequate (Stiebling 1933). This standard for several essential nutrients – vitamins A and C, calcium, phosphorus, and iron – was subsequently expanded to include values for the vitamins thiamine and riboflavin (Stiebling and Phipard 1939). The values were derived from estimates of human requirements (USDA 1939). It is noteworthy that Stiebling and E. F. Phipard made separate recommendations for children of various ages and that they set their recommended intakes 50 percent above the average requirement to allow for variability among the requirements of individuals.

During this time, the League of Nations Technical Commission on Nutrition (1938) published recommended intakes for calcium and iron in addition to energy and protein. The commission did not make quantitative recommendations for vitamins but emphasized consumption of "protective foods" – meat, milk, leafy vegetables, fruits, eggs, organ meats, and fish – as important sources of vitamins and minerals and included specific recommendations for pregnant and lactating women. In 1939, the Canadian Council on Nutrition (CCN) (1940) proposed a "Canadian Dietary Standard" that included reference values for energy, protein, fat, calcium, iron, iodine, and vitamins C and D. Thus, by 1940 the principles for developing dietary standards had been established.

In 1940, at the request of the U.S. government, the NRC established a Committee on Food and Nutrition, which, a year later, was given permanent status as the Food and Nutrition Board (FNB). One of the first actions of the FNB in fulfilling its obligation of advising the federal government on problems relating to national defense was to prepare a set of dietary standards for adequate intakes of essential nutrients. The process by which this was done has been described by Lydia Roberts (1944, 1958), chair of the committee that was assigned this task. The set of values for nine essential nutrients adopted by the FNB, and designated as Recommended Dietary Allowances, was approved by the American Institute of Nutrition (the professional nutrition society of the United States) and subsequently accepted at a national conference on nutrition convened at the request of President Franklin Roosevelt in 1941. The reference values for seven of the nine essential nutrients included in this standard did not differ appreciably from those proposed by Stiebling and Phipard; the other two nutrients, niacin and vitamin D, were new additions.

The RDA publication has been revised nine times since 1941; the tenth edition was published in 1989. The number of nutrients for which RDA or safe and adequate intakes are established has expanded from 9 (ADA 1941) to 26 (FNB 1989b). Changes in the first seven editions have been summarized by Donald Miller and Leroy Voris (1969). The International Union of Nutritional Sciences has compiled detailed information on many national and international dietary standards (Truswell 1983).

The Process for Establishing Dietary Reference Values

The process by which dietary standards are established is described in the various RDA reports and has been discussed by Gordon Young (1964), Alfred Harper (1987a, 1994), Stewart Truswell (1990), Roger Whitehead (1992), and others cited by these authors. It involves appointment of a committee that assumes responsibility for selecting age-sex groups for which RDA are needed, evaluating information about human requirements for nutrients, and then establishing procedures for deriving appropriate recommended intakes from knowledge of the requirements for, and utilization of, nutrients.

Committees on Dietary Standards

In the United States, a committee appointed by the NRC and reporting to the FNB is assigned the task of setting RDA. In most other countries, committees to establish Recommended Nutrient Intakes are appointed by departments of health. The committees usually consist of 8 to 12 scientists with both a broad general knowledge of nutrition and expertise in one or more special areas. In brief, in the United States, individual members or subcommittees prepare background papers on one or more nutrients based on a critical evaluation of the scientific literature on human requirements. These papers are reviewed by the entire RDA committee at several meetings over a period of three years, and problems are identified and resolved, sometimes with the aid of consultants or workshops. After revisions, the final draft of the report is submitted to the NRC for further review and revision before the final version is published.

The international agencies – FAO and WHO – follow a different procedure. Their reports deal with only a few nutrients at a time. One report, for example, may be on energy and protein (FAO/WHO 1985), whereas another may discuss vitamin A, iron, folate, and vitamin B_{12} (FAO/WHO 1988). The two organizations jointly appoint a committee of from 12 to as many as 20 scientists from various nations and a secretariat, consisting mainly, but not exclusively, of members of their staffs, to coordinate and facilitate the work of the committee. Its members (and those of the secretariat) prepare background papers on different aspects of requirements for the nutrients under consideration; they then meet together for about 10 days to discuss and resolve problems and prepare a draft report. This is circulated to the members for comment, after which a subgroup of the committee and the secretariat prepare the final report for publication.

Age-Sex Groups

The first step in setting RDA is to select age ranges and age-sex groups for which separate RDA values are needed and to specify body weights appropriate for each group. Most RDA reports currently include values for some 15 age-sex groups and for gestation and lactation. This number of groups is necessary for two reasons – first, because requirements for nutrients per unit of body weight decline as the growth rate declines and, second, because RDA for essential nutrients are expressed as amounts recommended daily per person in the specified group rather than as amount per unit of body weight. The range of ages included within a group must, therefore, be narrow during early life, when requirements per unit of body weight are high, and during adolescence, when body size is increasing rapidly. Also, requirements per person for females differ from those for males, mainly, but not exclusively, because of differences in body size, so that, except at young ages, separate groups are also employed for the two sexes. The age ranges and weights for groups frequently differ from one country to another, making exact comparisons among values from different reports difficult.

For individuals or groups whose weights deviate considerably from the specified weights, RDA should be adjusted on the assumption that they are proportional to body weight. For those judged to be substantially overweight, adjustment on the basis of lean body mass is thought to be more appropriate. Body weights for the age-sex groups are currently based on information obtained in national health surveys. They are not "ideal" or "desirable" weights. In the United States, the values are the median weights observed for the population (FNB 1989b); in Britain they correspond with the fiftieth percentile for body weight (DHSS 1991).

Establishing RDA for Essential Nutrients

The objective in establishing RDA for essential nutrients is to identify a level of intake high enough to ensure that the tissues of virtually all individuals in the population will contain enough of the nutrient to prevent impairment of health even if intake is inadequate for some period of time. The time differs from one nutrient to another, owing to differences in the ability of the body to store and conserve them. To accomplish this objective, the usual procedure is, first, to assemble and evaluate the information on human requirements for the different age-groups that have been studied; second, to estimate the variability among requirements of individuals; and, third, to assess the effects of various factors that influence nutrient needs, such as efficiency of absorption and utilization in the body, the bioavailability of the nutrient from major foodstuffs, and the contributions of precursors of nutrients in the food supply. The extent to which the last group of factors influences RDA differs from nutrient to nutrient and depends upon the nature of the foods consumed.

Estimation of Requirements

Methods that can be used for estimating requirements differ from one nutrient to another, and there is not always agreement as to the most appropriate criteria for establishing when a requirement has been met. Maintenance of a satisfactory rate of growth is accepted generally as an appropriate criterion for establishing that the requirements of infants and young children have been met. The amounts of nutrients consumed by infants growing well on a diet of human milk or a formula of proven quality are generally viewed as satisfactory, but not necessarily minimal, estimates of infant requirements.

With adults, several approaches have been used. In the case of nutrients for which naturally occurring dietary deficiencies have been encountered, the amounts needed to prevent or cure deficiency signs have been estimated both in practical studies and experimentally. These include thiamine, niacin, vitamins A and C, iron, and iodine. Experimental studies in which human subjects have been depleted of a nutrient until they develop signs of deficiency and then are replenished with different amounts until the signs disappear have been used to estimate require-

ments for ascorbic acid, vitamins A, E, and B_6, riboflavin, and folic acid. These methods are based on the assumption that body reserves are adequately restored when deficiency signs disappear. Balance studies have been used to estimate requirements for protein, calcium, magnesium, and zinc. In these the minimal amount of nutrient required to just prevent loss from the body is estimated from measurements of intake of the nutrient and excretion of the nutrient or its metabolites by human subjects whose intakes are increased incrementally.

The body content (usually called the body pool) of a few nutrients, for example, vitamin B_{12}, ascorbic acid, and iron, can be measured directly by isotopic methods; then, relationships among intake, rate of loss, and the development of signs of deficiency can be established. For several others, an indirect measure of the state of body reserves can be estimated from measurements made while intake is varied, of the rate of excretion of the nutrient or one of its metabolites in urine (niacin, vitamin B_6), the concentration in blood (vitamin A), or the activity of an enzyme or other protein of which the nutrient is a component (thiamine, selenium).

Confidence in estimates of requirements is increased when there is reasonable agreement between values obtained by two or more methods. With all of these methods, however, an element of judgment is required in selecting the point at which the requirement is met. What, for example, is the appropriate body pool size, blood level, or enzyme activity to equate with an adequate intake, especially when the responses to increasing or decreasing intakes of nutrients are characteristically curvilinear and do not have clear inflection points?

Appearance of deficiency signs is clear evidence of an inadequate intake and, thus, prevention of these signs provides a guide to the minimal amount required. But it is a matter of judgment when it comes to how much the body pool, blood level, or metabolic indicator should be above the value associated with the prevention of signs. As intake of most nutrients is increased, excretion of the nutrient or of its metabolic products increases, and a sharp rise in body losses serves as an indicator that intake is in excess of needs. But as intake of some nutrients (vitamins A and D, for example) is increased, they continue to accumulate to a point at which toxic reactions can occur.

The total numbers of subjects studied in experiments on requirements, and the total amount of information available, is less than desirable. For many nutrients, values for intermediate age-groups must be obtained by interpolation from what is known about the requirements of infants and young adults; this is because few subjects at other ages have been studied. Differences in the judgments of various national committees lead to differences in estimates of the requirement. For a few nutrients, such as ascorbic acid and calcium, such differences in judgment are wide. But as a rule, the similarity of the values determined by different committees is impressive.

Individual Variability of Requirements

Individuals differ considerably in their requirements for essential nutrients owing to genetic differences among them. Stiebling and Phipard (1939) originally suggested that an intake of 50 percent above the average requirement should meet the needs of those with the highest requirements. L. B. Pett, C. A. Morrell, and F. W. Hanley (1945) assumed that requirements follow a Gaussian distribution, so RDA values would have to exceed average requirements by about three times the standard deviation of the mean in order to meet the needs of all individuals in the population. M. H. Lorstad (1971) subsequently proposed that a value two standard deviations above the average requirements (which would cover 97 to 98 percent of the population) would be an appropriate practical dietary standard. His proposal was adopted by FAO/WHO and has since been accepted generally. In view of the tendency of RDA committees to be generous rather than parsimonious in the selection of values for requirements, and of the ability of the body to conserve nutrients if intake is somewhat below the requirement without impairment of health, this would seem to be an acceptable approach.

In practice, for many nutrients there are not enough individual values to permit reliable estimates of the variability of requirements. In the case of nutrients for which the procedure has been applied, requirements follow a Gaussian distribution with coefficients of variation (the standard deviation expressed as a percentage of the mean) of about 15 (10 to 20) percent (Beaton 1994). If it is assumed that requirements for other nutrients follow a similar pattern, increasing the average requirement by about 30 percent should give an acceptable estimate for setting RDA generally (FAO/WHO 1988; Beaton 1991). Iron requirements of menstruating women, which are skewed toward the upper end of the range, are an exception.

Other Considerations in Setting RDA

RDA are the amounts of nutrients that should be present in foods as they are eaten. Losses of nutrients that occur during processing and preparation are not taken into account in setting RDA, but factors that influence the utilization of nutrients in the food ingested are. These include the digestibility of the foods, the biological availability of the nutrient from the food, absorption, and the presence in foods of precursors of certain nutrients. The requirement for protein, for example, is a composite requirement for nine essential amino acids and for a nonspecific source of nitrogen. The requirement for protein, thus, depends upon the digestibility of the protein and the proportions of amino acids it contains. RDA for protein are based on requirements for protein of the highest quality.

Many plant foods contain carotenoids, precursors of vitamin A (retinol) that differ in vitamin A value. To take this into account, RDA for vitamin A are expressed as retinol equivalents. The contributions from the vitamin and its precursors will depend upon the nature of the food supply. The amino acid tryptophan is a precursor of the vitamin niacin, so the need for this vitamin will depend upon the tryptophan content of the protein consumed. Thus, the RDA is expressed as niacin-equivalents.

The biological availability of iron may range from as low as 3 percent for foods of plant origin to 20 percent for foods of animal origin; hence, RDA for this nutrient will depend upon the proportions of plant and animal products in the food supply. Differences in the biological availability of nutrients in national food supplies account for some of the differences in RDA for essential nutrients among countries. There is no evidence to suggest that physiological requirements for different racial groups differ significantly.

RDA for Food Sources of Energy

The RDA for energy, expressed as kilocalories or megajoules per day (1,000 kilocalories equal 4.184 megajoules), are actually requirements for the components of the diet that, upon oxidation in the body, yield energy – carbohydrates, fats, and proteins. Ordinarily the amount of food consumed by most healthy individuals is controlled spontaneously by the body, over time, to an amount that will provide just enough energy to balance the amount expended and maintain body weight relatively constant – often for a period of years. If the RDA for energy were set, as for essential nutrients, at the upper end of the requirement range, it would be a recommendation for overconsumption and, hence, overweight for most people, because intakes in excess of the amount needed are not excreted but stored. The RDA values for energy are, therefore, average requirements for each group, not reference values for each individual in the group.

Energy requirements of individuals can be estimated from knowledge of their resting (basal) energy expenditure, energy expended for physical activity, and energy lost as heat from the stimulation of metabolism after a meal (thermogenesis). Resting energy expenditure varies with body weight, age, and sex. It can be estimated from equations derived empirically from relationships among basal metabolic rate, body weight, age, sex, and height, which are based on measurements of energy expenditures determined directly by calorimetry. Energy required for activity is estimated using factors that are multiples of the resting expenditure appropriate for each activity, and then multiplying these by the amounts of time spent in different activities (HWC 1990; Warwick 1990). The total of energy required for activity and resting energy expenditure, with an allowance for thermogenesis, yields the final value. The amount of food energy consumed daily, averaged over a period of several days,

provides a reasonable estimate of the energy requirements of adults who are maintaining a stable body
weight.

Uses of RDA

The original purpose of RDA was to "serve as a goal
for good nutrition" – to act as reference values for
planning nutritionally adequate food supplies and
diets for large groups of people, and for devising
dietary guidance systems based on sound scientific
principles for the public. They have since been used in
many other ways, some of which they were not
designed for and for which they have limitations that
are not always recognized. The uses can be separated
into two general categories: (1) "standards for dealing
with practical applications of nutrition," and (2) "guidelines for food and nutrition regulations and policies."
This distinction is somewhat arbitrary because practical applications may arise from, or even be the basis
for, policy decisions. Uses of RDA have also been
grouped in another, more technical, way. Those related
to planning food supplies and diets, offering dietary
guidance, and serving as standards for food regulations
and economic assistance programs have been categorized as *prescriptive* uses. Those related to assessment
of the adequacy of nutrient intake, diets, and food supplies have been termed *diagnostic* (Beaton 1994). The
former classification seems more appropriate for the
present purpose, even though the separation between
the categories is less distinct.

In using RDA as reference values for different purposes a question arises as to whether they apply
equally well to individuals and groups. For energy, the
situation is clear. RDA for energy are average values
for groups; for applications involving individuals,
energy needs of each person must be estimated separately. For essential nutrients the situation is more
complex. RDA for essential nutrients exceed the
requirements of nearly all persons in the specified
groups, so a food supply that meets the RDA should
be adequate for an individual and, provided it is distributed equitably, for all members of a group as well.
But when RDA are employed as standards for assessing the adequacy of essential nutrient intakes, the
answer is less clear. The problems that arise are considered in the following sections.

Uses Related to Practical Applications of Nutrition

Planning food supplies and diets. The RDA are used
to estimate the amounts of foods needed to provide
large groups of people, such as the armed forces or
populations of institutions, with nutritionally adequate diets. For this purpose, information is needed
about the proportions of the population in various
age-sex categories and about the composition of the
available foods. The RDA for energy, being average
requirements for each age-sex group, can be used to
calculate directly the total amount of energy sources
needed, as about half of the individuals in the group
should consume more and half less than the RDA. The
RDA for essential nutrients are then used as reference
values to assure that foods selected and diets formulated provide the requisite amounts of essential nutrients. Allowance must also be made for losses that
occur during food preparation. A similar procedure is
used by international agencies to estimate the adequacy of both the quantity and quality of food supplies of nations in meeting the nutritional needs of
their populations (FAO/WHO 1985).

It should be emphasized that the objective in planning food supplies and diets is not merely to provide
amounts of essential nutrients needed to meet RDA.
Diets should be composed of a wide variety of palatable and acceptable foods so that they will meet psychological and social needs and be eaten in the
required amounts over long periods of time. In trying
to accomplish this, the amount of vitamin A provided,
for example, will ordinarily vary greatly from one day
to another because relatively few foods are rich
sources of this vitamin. Although RDA are specified as
daily amounts, this kind of day-to-day variability in the
provision of individual nutrients need not be of concern as long as the total amount of each nutrient,
averaged over several days, meets the RDA.

Nutrition education. RDA are employed effectively by
health professionals for planning nutritionally adequate diets, but they are not designed for use by the
public. For people with limited knowledge of nutrition, RDA for nutrients must be translated in terms of
foods. A common way of doing this is by first separating familiar foods into a few groups on the basis of the
essential nutrients of which they are good sources,
and then, using the RDA as reference values, estimating the number of servings from each food group that
must be eaten daily to meet essential nutrient needs.

This has been the basis for a food guide, developed
by Louise Page and Esther Phipard (USDA 1957),
designed to explain how to obtain the required
amounts of essential nutrients from a specified number of servings selected from four familiar groups of
foods. The number of servings required by adults to
obtain the foundation for a nutritionally adequate diet
provided only 1,200 to 1,600 kilocalories daily and
allowed for obtaining the needed extra energy from
additional servings of any of a variety of foods.

The number and selection of servings were modified for children. Estimates of the nutrient content of
model diets based on this food guidance system
demonstrated that the principles underlying it are
sound. The system has been widely used in nutrition
education programs for teaching the principles of a
nutritionally adequate diet. Many modifications have
been proposed in order to adapt it for groups with
different cultural backgrounds, lifestyles, and incomes
(King et al. 1978). More recently, a modified version

based on five food groups – the "food pyramid" (USDA 1992) – was designed as a guide for the total diet and for limiting fat consumption.

Therapeutic nutrition. Although RDA are standards for nutrient intakes of healthy people, they serve equally well as a guide to the nutritional needs of persons with medical problems that do not affect food consumption or nutrient utilization. They also provide a baseline for modifying diets to meet the special nutritional needs of individuals who are ill. Loss of appetite, associated with many types of illness, can result in the wasting of tissues and depletion of body stores of nutrients that must be replenished. Infections of the gastrointestinal tract, disorders that cause malabsorption, systemic infections, injuries, renal failure, certain inborn errors of the metabolism, and many other health problems alter nutritional needs in different ways and to different degrees, owing to the impairment of absorption or excretion or to increased metabolic wastage of nutrients. Dealing with the specific nutritional needs resulting from these conditions requires specific clinical and dietary management.

Designing new or modified foods. RDA are employed in formulating new food products composed of highly purified constituents, foods for special dietary purposes, or products designed as meal replacements, such as special diets for weight reduction, so as to ensure that these will provide appropriate amounts of essential nutrients. When RDA are used for this purpose, it is essential to remember that they are standards for amounts of nutrients to be consumed daily. In the case of products that are total diet replacements, especially those for weight reduction that provide restricted amounts of energy sources, the daily allotment should contain amounts of nutrients that meet the entire RDA.

Foods for general use should contain essential nutrients in reasonable proportion to the amount of energy derived from the product. The concept of "nutrient density" – the amounts of nutrients in the product expressed per 1,000 kilocalories – provides the basis of a method for accomplishing this goal (Hansen, Wyse, and Sorenson 1979). To provide a set of standards, RDA are expressed as units of nutrient required per 1,000 kilocalories of energy sources required. The quantities of nutrients in the product can then be adjusted to correspond with the standard.

Some shortcomings of this procedure should be recognized. In establishing standards for nutrient density, only a single RDA value is used for each nutrient – usually the value for the age-sex group with the highest requirement. For other groups, the standards therefore deviate in varying degrees from the RDA. Nutrient density values have also been proposed as guides to the relative nutritive values of foods. Caution should be exercised, however, in employing the nutrient density concept to compare the nutritive values of foods. The contributions of foods to meeting nutritional needs depend not just on differences in their nutrient content but also on differences in the amounts consumed. Two foods may have the same nutrient density, but if one is eaten in an amount only 10 percent that of the other, their contributions to meeting nutrient needs will differ by tenfold.

Assessing the adequacy of nutrient intakes – individuals. The amounts of essential nutrients consumed by individuals can be estimated from records of the quantities of different foods they eat and tables of food composition. The amounts of nutrients consumed can then be compared with the RDA. Unfortunately, comparisons of this type permit few firm conclusions about the adequacy of intakes. Because RDA exceed the requirements of most people, the probability of nutritional inadequacy is obviously remote for those whose intakes equal or exceed the RDA. But because requirements of individuals differ widely, it is not valid to conclude that an intake below the RDA is inadequate. All that can be said is that the further the intake falls below the RDA, the greater is the probability that the intake is inadequate. This is not a shortcoming of the RDA; dietary standards generally are not meant to be used for this purpose. The adequacy of essential nutrient intakes of individuals can be evaluated accurately only by clinical and biochemical assessment, not by comparing intakes with the RDA or with any other standard.

Inability to quantify the degree of nutrient inadequacy from knowledge of intakes below the RDA has, however, stimulated efforts to apply statistical methods (and the risk concept) as an alternative procedure for assessing the adequacy of essential nutrient intakes. Application of probability analysis, using information about *requirements* (not RDA) and intakes of essential nutrients, has been proposed as a way of obtaining a quantitative estimate of the *risk* of nutritional inadequacy (FNB 1986; FAO/WHO 1988; Beaton 1991, 1994).

From plots of the cumulative percentage distribution of *requirements* (assuming they are normally distributed) against intake, the probability that an intake below the highest requirement is inadequate can be estimated; for example, the probability that an intake equal to the average requirement is inadequate is 50 percent. Although a quantitative estimate of the probability (risk) of a particular intake being inadequate is obtained through this type of analysis, it does not establish whether the intake actually is inadequate. But it can help in deciding if an individual should be referred for specific biochemical tests.

Uses Related to Food and Nutrition Policy

Nutritional standards are needed both for many food and nutrition programs and regulations and to provide a reliable scientific basis for interpreting the nutrient intake information that is employed to establish food and nutrition policy. For some of these uses, RDA are appropriate standards, but for others they are too complex and must be modified, or they are too limited in scope and must be used in conjunction with other standards.

Assessment of nutritional adequacy – populations. Information about the adequacy of essential nutrient intakes in a population is used to identify potential health problems. In assessing the adequacy of intakes in a population, one must take into account not only the variability of requirements but also the variability of intakes. Food and, hence, nutrient intakes of individuals vary widely. Even in developed countries, where the average nutritional intake of the population exceeds the RDA, those of many individuals are found to be less – and some much less – than the RDA (USDHHS/USDA 1986). This may occur for many reasons, such as poverty, illness, and ignorance, but the point is that even if the average intake of a population is in excess of the RDA, there is no assurance that all individuals within that population are meeting their requirements. Moreover, the problem of estimating the proportion of persons who have inadequate intakes remains unresolved.

From the results of dietary surveys of representative samples of large populations, the proportions of the population with different intakes can be determined. Then, with this information about the distribution of intakes, the same type of analysis that is used to assess the risk of inadequacy for an individual can be employed to assess the probable incidence (risk) of inadequate intakes in the population (FNB 1986; FAO/WHO 1988). This problem has been analyzed in detail by G. H. Beaton (1994), who concluded that only if the average intake of a population exceeds the *average requirement* by more than twice the coefficient of variation of the *average intake* will the probability of inadequate intakes in the group be low. This raises a question as to whether RDA for groups should be higher than those for individuals. The answer is not clear, but because the problem is important in relation to policy decisions, it is important to be aware of it. The actual prevalence of nutritional inadequacy in a population, as in an individual, can be assessed accurately only through clinical and biochemical observations, not by comparing the average population intake with a standard.

It seems not to be sufficiently appreciated, as Beaton (1994) has emphasized, that estimates of the probability of intake being inadequate are based on the observed distribution of individual *requirements* around the mean. Inclusion of a table of average requirements in RDA reports would be more useful than the table of RDA for assessing the adequacy of nutrient intakes by probability analysis. As all committees use essentially the same information for establishing requirements, a higher degree of agreement might be anticipated in establishing average requirements than in establishing RDA. Having both sets of values published together would also draw attention to the need for a critical assessment of criteria, both for establishing when a requirement has been met and for evaluating the process used to derive RDA from requirements.

Difficulties in trying to assess the adequacy of nutrient intakes using RDA as standards have also stimulated interest in alternative standards. Separate standards that represent the lower limits of acceptable nutrient intake have been developed in New Zealand, Norway, and Australia. These are to be used only for evaluating the adequacy of nutrient intakes (Truswell 1990). The FAO and WHO (1988) have published separate reference values for "basal requirements" and "safe levels of intake" (essentially RDA) for iron and for vitamin A.

The major problems in evaluating the adequacy of nutrient intakes from dietary information are not resolved by establishing new standards. Conclusions about inadequacy can still be drawn only in terms of probability or risk. Moreover, individuals cannot be identified as having inadequate intakes from dietary assessment alone, but as Truswell (1990) notes, intakes below the lower standard are more likely to be associated with deficiency than are intakes at some arbitrary level below the RDA.

Food labeling. To provide consumers with information about nutrient contributions of foods, the U.S. Food and Drug Administration (FDA) established a standard based on the RDA. To use the RDA directly for this purpose would be unwieldy and complicated; in order to devise a standard with a single set of values for food labeling, the FDA selected the highest values from among the RDA for 20 nutrients and called these U.S. Recommended *Daily* Allowances (NNC 1975). Nutrient contributions of products have been listed on labels as percentages of the U.S. RDA per serving. (The different meanings of the terms "U.S. RDA" and "RDA" had created a measure of confusion.)

There are differing views about the purpose of food labels: According to one, the label should provide information that can readily be related to nutritional needs, and thereby serve as a tool for nutrition education; according to another, the main purpose of having nutrition information on the label is to enable the purchaser easily to compare the nutrient contributions of different products. The U.S. RDA are not useful guides to nutrient needs of the various age-sex groups for which RDA are set other than for the adult male. They do serve effectively, however, for the primary purpose for which they were designed – to provide an easy and simple standard for comparing products as to the per-serving percentages of the U.S. RDA that they contain. U.S. RDA are also appropriate standards for programs that fortify foods with nutrients judged to be low in the food supply.

The FDA has recently established new standards for food labeling and regulations. The basic standard for essential nutrients – Reference Daily Intake – is a population-weighted average of the 1989 RDA values for age-sex groups beyond 4 years of age. The amount of nutrient provided by a food product may be included on the label as a percentage of the Daily Reference Value – the amount of the nutrient that should be provided by a diet that yields 2,000 kilocalories. This system will permit simple comparisons of the nutrient contributions of different foods just as the earlier system did, but the values will not relate closely to the RDA. It is essentially a modified form of the nutrient density concept and, as such, may eventually find a niche in nutrition education programs.

Food assistance and welfare programs. Most economic assistance programs of government agencies in the United States are direct or indirect food assistance programs. They include programs such as school lunches, supplementary food for women, infants, and children, and nutrition for the elderly. RDA are used as reference values for many of these programs. To assure that foods or meals supplied through these programs will be of high nutritional quality, it is required that they contain specified proportions of the RDA for certain nutrients. RDA are appropriate standards for meeting needs for essential nutrients, but they are not appropriate as the sole standards for planning meals or diets. As mentioned in relation to diet planning generally, planning meals requires, in addition, consideration of palatability, acceptability, and variety of the food supply, so that diets will be eaten and enjoyed over prolonged periods of time.

Meeting RDA has been an important consideration in developing the food plan that has served as the basis for allotting coupons in the food-stamp program, for licensing and certifying nursing homes and day-care centers, and for establishing the poverty level of income. RDA are appropriate standards for meeting needs for essential nutrients, but even though they are employed in conjunction with other standards, their use in this way has resulted in economic assistance programs being viewed as nutrition programs. It may make such programs more politically acceptable, but it also diverts attention from the need for broader and more comprehensive standards for them. It also has led to efforts to include use of RDA for economic assistance programs as part of the basis for setting RDA values, a procedure that, if accepted, would undermine their scientific validity as dietary standards.

Dietary guidance for the public. The RDA-based food guide system, employed in teaching the principles of a nutritionally adequate diet in nutrition education programs, was developed originally by the USDA as part of that agency's response to the policy of providing dietary guidance for the public. Many aspects of such guidance, however, extend beyond the scope of RDA, such as desirable proportions in the diet of carbohydrates, fats, and other sources of food energy; maintaining a healthful body weight; and associations between diet and disease. These topics ordinarily are discussed in only broad terms in RDA publications, and some are addressed in dietary guidelines adopted jointly (as part of current health policy) by the USDA and the U.S. Department of Health and Human Services (USDHHS) (1990), by Canada (HWC 1992), and by many other countries (Truswell 1987).

To comply with current health policy, a modified food guide system for selecting the *entire* diet from five food groups and emphasizing food selections that will reduce fat and cholesterol consumption (USDA 1992) has been substituted for the earlier one, which provided *partial* guidance in selecting only 1,200 to 1,800 kilocalories from four food groups as a basic diet – to be supplemented with other selections. This new system represents a shift in public dietary guidance in the United States, whereas in Canada, the four-food-group system, with an emphasis on meeting essential nutrient needs, has been retained (albeit with new guidelines for reduced fat consumption) (HWC 1992). RDA continue, nonetheless, to serve as the scientific basis for selecting a nutritionally adequate diet in programs of dietary guidance.

RDA and Changing Health Policy

During the past 30 years, emphasis in health policy in the United States and many other developed nations has shifted toward the prevention of chronic and degenerative diseases. This shift has been accompanied by changes in dietary guidance that require a different base of knowledge from that for guidance based on the RDA. When the nature of the changes is examined, it is evident that this has implications for the concepts of RDA.

Changing Emphasis in Food and Nutrition Policy

Changing health status. Health has improved dramatically in the United States during the twentieth century while dietary advice has been based on the RDA (USDHEW 1979). Nutritional deficiency diseases have been virtually eliminated; mortality from infectious diseases has declined sharply; the proportion of infants born who live to age 65 or older has increased from less than 40 percent to 80 percent or more; height at maturity has increased; and life expectancy has risen from less than 50 to about 75 years. These improvements have occurred in association with improved sanitation, diet, and medical care and a higher standard of living. The extent to which they are attributable to better diets cannot be established, but increased infant and childhood survival and increased growth rates and height at maturity could not have occurred unless diets had been nutritionally adequate (Harper 1987b).

A consequence of the high rate of survival of the young to old age, with a stable, then declining, birth rate, is that the proportion of people 65 years of age or older in the population has increased from 4 to 12 percent. Such aging of the population has been accompanied in most developed countries by an increase in the proportion of deaths from cardiovascular diseases and cancer, from about 20 percent of total deaths during the early 1900s to about 70 percent today.

New directions in dietary advice. The emergence of chronic and degenerative diseases as the major causes of death, coupled with the perception that alterations in diet may increase life expectancy by delaying the onset of such diseases (the causes of which are poorly understood), has brought about a striking change in food, nutrition, and health policy. Much greater attention is now being given to dietary guidance for the "prevention" of diseases associated with aging than to advice on how to select a nutritionally adequate diet (USDHHS 1988; USDA/USDHHS 1990).

This change in policy evolved over a period of more than two decades (Truswell 1987), mainly in response to reports of associations between the type and quantity of fat in the diet and mortality from heart disease. Conclusions drawn from these associations and accepted as the bases for changes in health policy have, nonetheless, been controversial (FNB 1980), and skeptical views have been expressed by numerous experts.[1] Later observations that high intakes of vegetables and fruits are associated with lower mortality from certain cancers expanded interest in diet modification as a disease prevention measure (USDHHS 1988; FNB 1989a). The underlying bases for these associations have not been established, and claims that certain known plant constituents (such as carotenoids) may be among the effective agents have led to further controversy. Despite this, however, the recommendation for increased consumption of vegetables and fruits is accepted generally, on several grounds, as appropriate nutrition policy.

In 1980, as the culmination of an effort to achieve consensus among conflicting views over the role of diet in delaying the onset of chronic and degenerative diseases, the USDA and USDHHS jointly adopted (and later revised) a set of "Dietary Guidelines for Americans" (USDA/USDHHS 1990). Two of the seven guidelines – "Eat a variety of foods" (a nutritionally adequate diet), and "Maintain healthy body weight" – are the essence of the RDA-based dietary guidance initiated decades ago for variety and moderation in food consumption. The others, recommending a diet low in fat (and especially in saturated fat and cholesterol), with plenty of vegetables, fruits, and grains (providing fiber) and only moderate use of sugars, salt, and alcohol, were proposed as guidelines for reducing the risk of developing chronic and degenerative diseases, as is emphasized in the text of the publication.

The purpose of these guidelines is distinctly different from those based on the RDA. They are uniform dietary recommendations for the entire population, adopted to institute a health policy for the control of diseases that are not products of nutritional deficiencies and to which individuals differ greatly in susceptibility. They deal mainly with foods and food constituents that are not essential nutrients (energy sources, fiber, cholesterol) and are based on information that is beyond the scope of the RDA – indirect evidence of associations that cannot be accurately quantified. RDA, in contrast to these guidelines, are quantitative reference values for intakes of essential nutrients. They are part of the information base employed in developing programs to institute a policy of encouraging consumption of diets containing adequate amounts of nutrients, deficits of which will cause diseases in all individuals in the population. In a recently published revision of *Dietary Guidelines for Americans* (USDA/USDHHS 1995), although the guidelines themselves remain essentially the same, the text has been modified considerably. Much more emphasis has been placed on dietary guidance for maintaining health and much less on diet as a disease prevention measure. This change has improved the balance between dietary guidance based on well-established knowledge of the effects of essential nutrients (the RDA) and guidance based on evidence, much of it indirect, of probable health benefits from other components of foods (including unidentified substances).

The adoption of a policy that emphasizes dietary modification as a means of disease prevention has led to proposals that the RDA concept be modified to conform with the new direction in health policy (Hegsted 1993; Lachance 1993; IM 1994). To accomplish this, the RDA would be expanded to include all dietary constituents shown to influence susceptibility to chronic and degenerative diseases; some examples are carotenoids (plant pigments, some of which are precursors of vitamin A), cholesterol, and fiber (Lachance 1993, 1994). Moreover, observations that high intakes of certain vitamins (especially those that can function as antioxidants, such as vitamins E and C) may reduce the risk of heart disease and some cancers have given rise to proposals that such information be used in setting values for the RDA (IM 1994). Controversy over issues of this type delayed revision of the tenth RDA report for several years (Pellett 1988).

If the basis for setting RDA is modified to include consideration of the effects of substances (such as fiber) that cannot be quantified accurately, and of medicinal or pharmacological effects of vitamins or other nutrients (which require amounts well in excess of those that can be obtained from diet), the RDA will cease to be reliable reference values for meeting basic physiological needs (Truswell 1990; Harper 1994; Rosenberg 1994). Such a change would represent modification of a standard (the RDA) to conform with policy. The RDA, which are set on the basis of critical scientific evaluation, would become a vehicle for dietary guidance comparable to dietary guidelines, which are established by consensus. To maintain the independence and integrity of sources of information employed in making policy decisions, it is essential that the process of evaluating information used in setting policy be separated clearly from the process used to develop programs to institute policy. Continuing the approach used in most countries of maintaining a clear separation between the process for establishing dietary guidelines and that for setting dietary standards (Reference Nutrient Intakes; RDA) will accomplish this. Separate publication of dietary guidelines also provides an appropriate mechanism for presenting information about the potential health benefits (even tentative ones) of foods and food constituents independently of the RDA. Adoption of the British approach of calling the dietary standards "reference values" would be a further contribution toward maintaining such separation.

Alfred E. Harper

Note

1. These experts include E. H. Ahrens, Jr. (1985); G. J. Brissom (1981); Harper (1987b); S. B. Hulley, J. M. B. Walsh, and T. B. Newman (1992); D. Kritchevsky (1992); J. McCormick and P. Skrabanek (1988); M. F. Muldoon, S. B. Manuck, and K. E. Matthews (1990); M. F. Oliver (1986); R. E. Olson (1986); R. L. Smith and E. R. Pinckney (1988, 1991); W. E. Stehbens (1989); and W. C. Taylor and colleagues (1987).

Bibliography

Ackerknecht, E. H. 1982. *A short history of medicine.* Baltimore, Md.

Adams, F., trans. 1952. Hippocratic writings. In *Great books of the Western world,* Vol. 10, ed. R. M. Hutchins. Chicago.

Ahrens, E. H., Jr. 1985. The diet-heart question in 1985: Has it really been settled? *Lancet* 1: 1085-7.

American Dietetic Association (ADA). 1941. Recommended allowances for the various dietary essentials. *Journal of the American Dietetic Association* 17: 565-7.

Beaton, G. H. 1991. Human nutrient requirement estimates. *Food Nutrition and Agriculture* 1: 3-15.

1994. Criteria of an adequate diet. In *Modern nutrition in health and disease.* Eighth edition, ed. M. E. Shils, J. A. Olson, and M. Shike, 1491-1505. Philadelphia, Pa.

Brissom, G. J. 1981. *Lipids in human nutrition.* Englewood, N.J.

British Medical Association (BMA). 1933. Committee on nutrition. *British Medical Journal,* Supplement 25.

Brock, W. H. 1993. *The Norton history of chemistry.* New York.

Burnet, E. T., and W. R. Aykroyd. 1935. Nutrition and public health. *Quarterly Bulletin of the Health Organization of the League of Nations* 4: 1-52.

Burnham, J. C. 1987. *How superstition won and science lost.* New Brunswick, N.J.

Carpenter, K. J. 1988. *The history of scurvy and vitamin C.* New York and Cambridge.

1994. *Protein and energy.* New York and Cambridge.

CCN (Canadian Council on Nutrition). 1940. The Canadian dietary standard. *National Health Review* 8: 1-9.

Clark, F. Le G. 1968. Food habits as a practical nutrition problem. *World Review of Nutrition and Dietetics* 9: 56-84.

Cowan, C. W., and P. J. Watson, eds. 1992. *The origins of agriculture.* Washington, D.C.

DHSS (Department of Health and Social Security) (U.K.). 1985. *Recommended daily amounts of food energy and nutrients for groups of people in the United Kingdom.* London.

1991. *Dietary reference values for food energy and nutrients for the United Kingdom.* London.

FAO/WHO (Food and Agriculture Organization and World Health Organization of the United Nations). 1970. *Requirements of ascorbic acid, vitamin D, vitamin B12, folate and iron.* WHO Technical Report Series No. 452. Geneva.

1985. *Energy and protein requirements.* WHO Technical Report Series No. 724. Geneva.

1988. *Requirements of vitamin A, iron, folate and vitamin B12.* FAO Food and Nutrition Series No. 23. Rome.

Fidanza, F. 1979. Diets and dietary recommendations in ancient Greece and Rome and the school of Salerno. *Progress in Food and Nutritional Sciences* 3: 79-99.

FNB (Food and Nutrition Board). 1974. *Recommended dietary allowances.* Eighth edition. Washington, D.C.

1980. *Toward healthful diets.* Washington, D.C.

1986. *Nutrient adequacy: Assessment using food consumption surveys.* Washington, D.C.

1989a. *Diet and health.* Washington, D.C.

1989b. *Recommended dietary allowances.* Tenth edition. Washington, D.C.

Guggenheim, K. Y. 1981. *Nutrition and nutritional diseases.* Lexington, Mass.

Hansen, R. G., B. W. Wyse, and A. W. Sorenson. 1979. *Nutritional quality index of foods.* Westport, Conn.

Harper, A. E. 1985. Origin of the recommended dietary allowances – an historic overview. *American Journal of Clinical Nutrition* 41: 140-8.

1987a. Evolution of recommended dietary allowances – new directions. *Annual Review of Nutrition* 7: 509-37.

1987b. Transitions in health status: Implications for dietary recommendations. *American Journal of Clinical Nutrition* 45: 1094-1107.

1988. Nutrition: From myth and magic to science. *Nutrition Today* 23 (January/February): 8-17.

1994. Recommended dietary intakes: Current and future approaches. In *Modern nutrition in health and disease.* Eighth edition, ed. M. E. Shils, J. A. Olson, and M. Shike, 1475-90. Philadelphia, Pa.

Hegsted, D. M. 1993. Nutrition standards for today. *Nutrition Today* 28: 34-6.

Hertzler, A. A., and H. L. Anderson. 1974. Food guides in the United States. *Journal of the American Dietetic Association* 64: 19-28.

Hulley, S. B., J. M. B. Walsh, and T. B. Newman. 1992. Health policy on blood cholesterol. *Circulation* 86: 1026-9.

HWC (Health and Welfare Canada). 1983. *Recommended nutrient intakes for Canadians.* Ottawa.

1990. *Nutrition recommendations.* Ottawa.

1992. *Food guide.* Ottawa.

IM (Institute of Medicine). 1994. *How should the recommended dietary allowances be revised?* Washington, D.C.

King, J. C., C. G. Cohenour, C. G. Corruccini, and P. Schneeman. 1978. Evaluation and modification of the basic four food guide. *Journal of Nutrition Education* 10: 27-9.

Kritchevsky, D. 1992. Unobserved publications. In *Human nutrition: A continuing debate*, ed. M. Eastwood, C. Edwards, and D. Parry, 51-60. London.

Lachance, P. 1993. *Proceedings of a workshop on future recommended dietary allowances.* New Brunswick, N.J.

  1994. The RDA concept: Time for a change. *Nutrition Reviews* 52: 266-70.

League of Nations. 1937. *Final report of the Mixed Committee of the League of Nations on the relation of nutrition to health, agriculture and economic policy.* League of Nations Official No. 13, II, A.

  1938. Report by the Technical Commission on Nutrition on the work of its third session. *Bulletin of the League of Nations Health Organization* 7: 461-82.

Leitch, I. 1942. The evolution of dietary standards. *Nutrition Abstracts and Reviews* 11: 509-21.

Lorstad, M. H. 1971. Recommended intake and its relation to nutrient deficiency. *FAO Nutrition Newsletter* 9: 18-24.

Lusk, G. 1964. Early history of nutrition. In *Milestones in nutrition,* ed. S. A. Goldblith and M. A. Joslyn, 19-94. Westport, Conn.

McCollum, E. V. 1957. *A history of nutrition.* Baltimore, Md.

McCollum, E. V., E. Orent-Keiles, and H. G. Day. 1939. *The newer knowledge of nutrition.* New York.

McCormick, J., and P. Skrabanek. 1988. Coronary heart disease is not preventable by population interventions. *Lancet* 2: 839-41.

Miller, Donald F., and Leroy Voris. 1969. Chronological changes in recommended dietary allowances. *Journal of the American Dietetic Association* 54: 109-17.

MRC (Medical Research Council) (U.K.). 1932. *Vitamins: A survey of present knowledge.* London.

Muldoon, M. F., S. B. Manuck, and K. E. Matthews. 1990. Lowering cholesterol concentrations and mortality: A quantitative review of primary prevention trials. *British Medical Journal* 301: 309-14.

Munro, H. N. 1964. Historical introduction: The origin and growth of our present concepts of protein metabolism. In *Mammalian protein metabolism,* ed. H. N. Munro and J. B. Allison, 1-29. New York.

NHMRC (National Health and Medical Research Council) (Australia). 1990. *Recommended nutrient intakes: Australian papers,* ed. A. S. Truswell. Sydney.

NNC (National Nutrition Consortium). 1975. *Nutrition labeling.* Bethesda, Md.

Oliver, M. F. 1986. Prevention of coronary heart disease - propaganda, promises, problems, and prospects. *Circulation* 73: 1-9.

Olson, R. E. 1986. Mass intervention versus screening and selective intervention for prevention of coronary heart disease. *Journal of the American Medical Association* 255: 204-7.

Pachter, H. M. 1951. *Magic into science.* New York.

Pellett, P. L. 1988. Commentary: The R.D.A. controversy revisited. *Ecology of Food and Nutrition* 21: 315-20.

Pett, L. B., C. A. Morrell, and F. W. Hanley. 1945. The development of dietary standards. *Canadian Journal of Public Health* 36: 232-9.

Roberts, Lydia J. 1944. Scientific basis for the recommended dietary allowances. *New York State Journal of Medicine* 44: 59-66.

  1958. Beginnings of the recommended dietary allowances. *Journal of the American Dietetic Association* 34: 903-8.

Rosenberg, H. R. 1945. *Chemistry and physiology of the vitamins.* New York.

Rosenberg, I. H. 1994. Nutrient requirements for optimal health: What does that mean? *Journal of Nutrition* 124 (Supplement): 1777-9.

Smith, R. L., and E. R. Pinckney. 1988. *Diet, blood cholesterol, and coronary heart disease.* Vol. 1, *A relationship in search of evidence.* Santa Monica, Calif.

  1991. *Diet, blood cholesterol, and coronary heart disease.* Vol. 2, *A critical review of the literature.* Santa Monica, Calif.

Stehbens, W. E. 1989. The controversial role of dietary cholesterol and hypercholesterolemia in coronary heart disease and atherogenesis. *Pathology* 21: 213-21.

Stiebling, H. K. 1933. *Food budgets for nutrition and production programs.* USDA Miscellaneous Publication No. 183. Washington, D.C.

Stiebling, H. K., and E. F. Phipard. 1939. *Diets of families of employed wage earners and clerical workers in cities.* USDA Circular No. 507. Washington, D.C.

Taylor, W. C., T. M. Pas, D. S. Shepard, and A. L. Komaroff. 1987. Cholesterol reduction and life expectancy: A model incorporating model risk factors. *Annals of Internal Medicine* 106: 605-14.

Todhunter, E. N. 1954. Biographical notes on the history of nutrition - Gerrit Jan Mulder. *Journal of the American Dietetic Association* 30: 1253.

  1961. Biographical notes on the history of nutrition - Edward Smith. *Journal of the American Dietetic Association* 39: 475.

Truswell, A. Stewart. 1983. Recommended dietary intakes around the world. *Nutrition Abstracts and Reviews* 53: 939-1015, 1075-1119.

  1987. Evolution of dietary recommendations, goals, and guidelines. *American Journal of Clinical Nutrition* 45: 1060-72.

  1990. The philosophy behind recommended dietary intakes: Can they be harmonized? *European Journal of Clinical Nutrition* 44 (Supplement 2): 3-11.

USDA (U.S. Department of Agriculture). 1939. *Food and life. Yearbook of agriculture.* Washington, D.C.

  1957. *Essentials of an adequate diet.* USDA Home Economics Research Report No. 3. Washington, D.C.

  1992. *Food guide pyramid.* Home and Garden Bulletin No. 249. Washington, D.C.

USDA/USDHHS (U.S. Department of Agriculture and U.S. Department of Health and Human Services). 1990. *Nutrition and your health: Dietary guidelines for Americans.* Home and Garden Bulletin No. 232, Third edition. Washington, D.C.

  1995. *Dietary Guidelines for Americans.* Washington, D.C.

USDHEW (U.S. Department of Health, Education, and Welfare). 1979. *Healthy people - the Surgeon General's report on health promotion and disease prevention.* USDHEW Publication No. 79-55071. Washington, D.C.

USDHHS (U.S. Department of Health and Human Services). 1988. *The Surgeon General's report on nutrition and health.* USDHHS (PHS) Publication No. 88-50210. Washington, D.C.

USDHHS/USDA (U.S. Department of Health and Human Services and U.S. Department of Agriculture). 1986. *Nutri-*

tion monitoring in the United States. USDHHS (PHS) Publication No. 86-1255. Washington, D.C.

Warwick, P. M. 1990. Predicting food energy requirements from estimates of energy expenditure. In *Recommended nutrient intakes: Australian papers,* ed. A. S. Truswell, 295-320. Sydney.

Whitehead, Roger G. 1992. Dietary reference values. *Proceedings of the Nutrition Society* 51: 29-34.

Whorton, J. C. 1982. *Crusaders for fitness.* Princeton, N.J.

Wightman, W. P. D. 1953. *The growth of scientific ideas.* New Haven, Conn.

Young, E. Gordon. 1964. Dietary standards. In *Nutrition: A comprehensive treatise.* Vol. 2, *Vitamins, nutrient requirements, and food selection,* ed. G. H. Beaton and E. W. McHenry, 299-325. New York.

VII.5 ❧ Food Labeling

In the United States, the past three decades have witnessed tremendous changes in the way the public views the foods it buys. Unlike counterparts in the developing world, where problems of food availability and food quantities still dominate, consumers in the United States (and the West in general) have become increasingly interested in the nutritional quality of the foodstuffs they are offered. As a consequence, nutrition labeling has emerged to play a key role in government regulation of the food supply, in informing consumers about the constituents of the foods they eat, and in the formulation and marketing of food products by the manufacturers.

The importance of food labels has come about in spite of the fact that during the last 20 years or so, policy decisions regarding the implementation of nutrition labeling have been made in a political environment that emphasizes nonintervention in the operation of market economies. Recent legislation in industrialized countries has taken, for the most part, a minimalist approach to the regulation of nutritional quality. But although still controversial, labeling is seen as an acceptable "information remedy" that requires relatively little market intervention, and most Western nations have established some form of legislative guidelines for the regulation of nutrition labeling. With the adoption of the Nutrition Labeling and Education Act (NLEA) in 1994 (Caswell and Mojduszka 1996), the United States is currently in the forefront of establishing a mandatory and comprehensive national nutrition labeling policy.

The growing interest in nutrition policy reflects the understanding that foods represent major potential risks to public health because of such factors as foodborne organisms, heavy metals, pesticide residues, food additives, veterinary residues, and naturally occurring toxins. But although these are very real health hazards, scientists believe that the risks associated with nutritional imbalances in the composition of the diet as a whole are the most significant in the longer run, particularly in industrialized countries, where the high percentage of fat in daily diets seems to significantly threaten public health (Henson and Traill 1993). The recognition of nutritional quality as a value in itself has led to a separation of the nutritional from other food safety issues and a growing tendency to develop legislation targeted specifically at nutrition.

The latter, along with a perceived need for nutrition labels, is a reflection of the social changes that are influencing how, where, and when, as well as what, people eat (Wilkins 1994). Perhaps the most important change is the growing number of households that consist of two working parents or a single parent. With such a change in family structure, more meals are consumed in restaurants, more foods are eaten at home that have been prepared elsewhere, and convenience items predominate among foods prepared at home. In addition, the traditional three meals per day are often replaced with ad hoc meals as consumers employ an even greater variety of "heat and eat" foods. As a result, the consumption of traditional staple foods, such as cereals and potatoes, has decreased, and in most industrialized countries, the consumption of meat, milk, and milk products has markedly risen. The percentage of fat in the diets of citizens in industrialized countries has thus grown substantially in the last half century. Whereas regional variations persist, these current trends in eating patterns have generally meant a much greater intake of fats as a percentage of calories, which many view as a major factor in increasing morbidity and mortality from so-called chronic diseases such as cancer and coronary artery disease (Helsing 1991).

Such linkages between diet and health, and the communication of this knowledge to the general public, have led to an increased demand for higher quality, to which producers and retailers have responded by extending the variety of foods offered for sale. The nutritional composition of many foods has improved as well as their labeling; this, in turn, has stimulated an even more intensive marketing of the nutritional attributes of food products, as producers have recognized that an informed public will pay for better nutrition. Thus, as growing numbers of scholarly studies show, nutrition labels have become vital to public knowledge about food and, consequently, to improving public health (Caswell 1991).

The Evolution of Labeling Regulation

Despite the recent importance that labeling has achieved, concerns with labeling food products according to safety and purity have a long history. For example, throughout the medieval and early modern periods, foods of all kinds were identified by origin and grade, and regulatory "marks" on bread go back at least to the reign of Henry III in thirteenth-century

Britain. Indeed, they were one of the most common forms of control imposed on food producers in the Middle Ages. Manufacturers also recognized the profitability of such regulation; the German "Brewing Purity Law" of 1516, imposed by the Bavarian court but readily adopted by German brewers, stands as an example that continues to this day as a marketing tool for beer.

The history of food regulation in its current form has its roots in aspects of late-nineteenth-century modernization and industrialization. Scientific chemical experimentation in the early 1800s made possible the sophisticated adulteration of food as well as tests of its quality. The later growth of international markets and transportation networks contributed to a decline of reliance on fresh food and advanced the increasingly impersonal aspects of food markets. The key to such markets was food durability, and as processing capabilities evolved through packaging, bottling, and canning in the nineteenth, and freezing in the twentieth century, so interests in marking and labeling food products by brand name and contents became increasingly important.

Because they presumably carried assurances of quality and consistency in an impersonal market, brand names substituted to some degree for the lack of face-to-face contact in modern retailing, and by 1900 food labels showing brand names were well established in the industrialized Western nations. In the United States, major brands dating from the late nineteenth century include those created by Joseph Campbell, H. J. Heinz, and P. D. Armour. By 1920, producers recognized that brand names were a significant factor in trade and worth protecting legally as the important "public face" of a company's product line (Wilkins 1994). Beyond displaying brand names that promoted company reputation and increased consumer recognition, food labels sometimes included frequently specious claims about the content, quality, and healthfulness of their products.

During the late nineteenth century, there was a growing government interest in regulating the food supply through inspection and control of such deceptive labeling. To some extent this was a response to varying national standards for the import of meat products, but it was also because of an increasing public recognition of the potential health hazard of processed food. In the United States, public and government concerns with food purity helped propel the outspoken Dr. Harvey Wiley, a chemist from Purdue University, into work on food safety with the Department of Agriculture in 1883. As leader of the Bureau of Chemistry, the forerunner of the U.S. Food and Drug Administration (FDA), Wiley worked on a variety of food- and health-related issues.

The Pure Food and Drug Act of 1906 for which he had labored long and hard (FDA 1993) marked a major step toward labeling regulation and offers a classic example of how interactions between consumers, government, and industry shape the food regulatory environment. Various attempts to pass food and drug legislation had languished in Congress for over 15 years, while food poisoning scandals and investigative reports appearing in the scientific and popular press called growing attention to abuses in the food industry. And public outcry against the unsanitary conditions in the meat-packing industry in Chicago was inspired by the publication of Upton Sinclair's 1905 novel, *The Jungle.*

All of this activity encouraged President Theodore Roosevelt to back legislation authorizing federal oversight of the food industry. The provisions of Wiley's Pure Food and Drug Act, along with an accompanying Beef Inspection Act, authorized the federal inspection of meat-processing plants, established controls on food additives and preservatives, and tightened controls on food labels (FDA 1993). The latter, in a major step forward, were now required to correctly identify the producer so as to facilitate consumer complaints. Food labels were also to honestly list package contents; descriptive superlatives, such as "best" or "superfine," had to be removed if the manufacturer could not prove the claim. If producers had products tested and registered by the Department of Agriculture, an official label could be used on these packages.

This provision, however, was weakened by the lack of postregistration oversight: Unless a consumer complained, producers could use official labels with impunity, even though product composition might have changed since initial registration. Thus, in a progression that became typical of industry reception of new food regulations, the powerful Chicago "Beef Trust" at first resisted the new legislation but then publicly adopted the federal stamp of approval in an effort to revive public confidence and increase flagging demand for its meat products (FDA 1993).

Other important regulatory measures were adopted in the United States during the following decades. In 1938 a new U.S. Food, Drug, and Cosmetic Act updated the 1906 Pure Food and Drug Act and tightened labeling regulations considerably. In addition to prohibiting statements that were false or misleading, the law prescribed that labels on all processed and packaged foods had to include the name of the food, its net weight, and the name and address of its manufacturer or distributor. A detailed list of ingredients was also required on certain products. The Food, Drug, and Cosmetic Act was subsequently updated, and in 1950, an Oleomargarine Act required clear labels on margarine spreads to distinguish them from butter. In 1957, the Poultry Act authorized the labeling of poultry products.

In 1969, the White House Conference on Food, Nutrition, and Health (FDA 1993) investigated dietary deficiencies in the United States and recommended that the federal government take a more active role in identifying the nutritional qualities of food, which set the stage for the differentiation of food safety from nutrition regulation. The 1970s saw an explosion of public interest in healthful foods, as fears of pesticides, food radiation, and mercury poisoning in fish, on the one side, and the rise of "health food," organic farming, and consumer watchdog groups, on the other, encouraged a more activist approach to nutrition policy and food labeling.

Recent Labeling Regulation in the United States

The United States, as the world leader in the regulation of nutrition labeling, moved from partial controls in the 1970s and 1980s on voluntary provision of nutrition information (on product labels) to mandatory nutrition labeling in the 1990s. No other Western nation has similar mandatory labeling regulations. This move was, in part, a response to heightened public awareness of nutrition-related health issues in the United States. But it represented, as well, an acknowledgment on the part of federal health agencies that a significant portion of the population had poor diets. At the same time, manufacturers discovered that nutritional claims on packaging labels could be powerful marketing tools.

In 1973 the FDA had issued rules requiring nutrition labeling on all packaged foods to which one or more nutrients had been added or on foods whose advertising included claims about their nutritional qualities and/or their importance in the daily diet. But for almost all other foods, nutrition labeling was voluntary. Voluntary nutrition labeling went into effect in 1975; if producers wished to include nutritional information on their packaging they could, but they were required to use a standardized, federally designed label, which remained in use until 1994.

From 1975 to 1984, food health claims for marketing purposes were prohibited; after 1984, however, some claims were allowed, following case-by-case review by the FDA for nutrient content and health claims (FDA 1993). However, this review process was lax, and little enforcement against deceptive claims took place, virtually inviting industry abuses. Examples included Salisbury steaks that were labeled "lowfat," even though the meat product derived 45 percent of its total calories from fat, and labels on potato chips that concealed high levels of cholesterol-elevating saturated fat.

In 1988, Surgeon General C. Everett Coop released a report on nutrition and health in which, for the first time, the federal government formally recognized the role of diet in the etiology of certain chronic diseases and proposed labeling policies. And after 1989, growing public interest in nutrition, and several publicized cases of label disinformation, led to stricter state and federal scrutiny of nutrient content and health claims on food labels. In 1990, negotiation between the FDA and the United States Department of Agriculture (USDA), often made tense by lobbying on the part of special-interest groups, led to the enactment by Congress of the Nutrition Labeling and Education Act (NLEA) (Gorman 1991). This legislation, which went into effect in 1994, makes nutrition labeling mandatory and strictly regulates nutrient content and health claims. Nutrition labeling, however, remained voluntary for raw foodstuffs (primarily fruits, vegetables, and meats), though grocery stores were allowed to post general nutrition information at the point of sale. Other exempted products from labeling included those destined for consumption away from home, as, for example, in restaurants, hospitals, and other institutions. Small producers, with annual gross sales under $500,000 or food sales under $50,000, were also exempt.

NLEA regulations changed the nutrients that must be listed on the redesigned "Nutrition Facts" panel, which appears on the back side of product packaging. The new list emphasizes fats, sodium, and cholesterol – nutrients that most consumers worry about having too much of rather than too little – and requires that manufacturers indicate percentages of the following macro- and micronutrients on food labels: total calories, calories derived from fat, total fat, saturated fat, cholesterol, total carbohydrates, sugars, dietary fiber, protein, sodium, vitamins A and C, calcium, and iron. Information on the content of these nutrients is presented in quantitative amounts and as percentages of standardized dietary reference values, stated as "Percent of Daily Value." Other nutrition labeling is permitted on a voluntary basis, including information on calories derived from saturated fat and polyunsaturated fat and listings on soluble fiber, insoluble fiber, potassium, and other essential vitamins and minerals.

The percentages given in the "Nutrition Facts" panel are based on standardized serving sizes to help consumers understand and compare the nutritional values of different foods. In fact, according to the NLEA, serving sizes are supposed to be consistent across product lines and close to the amounts people actually consume; the number and amounts of nutrients labeled is based on the serving or portion size supposedly eaten by an "average person" over the age of 4 and must be given in common household and metric measures. Packages that contain less than two servings are considered single-serving containers, and their nutrient contents have to be declared on the basis of the contents of the entire package.

In order to control the manipulation of food descriptors, the FDA has developed consistent and uniform definitions of nine nutrient content claims that expressly or implicitly characterize the level of a nutrient present in a product (such as the Quick Quaker Oats front label, which claims, in eye-catching yellow, that the product is a "lowfat food," a "good source of fiber," a "sodium-free food, and a "cholesterol-free food"). These nutrient content claims are allowed on a voluntary basis, but manufacturers can use them only when a food meets particular nutritional standards.

The nine descriptor terms include: free, low, high, source of, reduced, light (or lite), less, more, and fresh. Because these are key advertising terms and typically appear in marketing tag lines on product front labels, NLEA has encouraged producers to either reformulate their products or drop deceptive nutrient descriptors.

Until 1984, a food product making a claim about the relationship between a nutrient and a disease on its label was treated as a drug (FDA 1993). But in a major shift in nutrition regulatory policy, the NLEA, for the first time, allowed food labels to include voluntary health claims, linking a nutrient or food to the risk of specific diseases or health conditions. For example, within carefully defined limits, food labels are allowed to cite links between calcium and osteoporosis, sodium and hypertension, fat and cardiovascular disease, and fat and cancer (thus, the Quick Quaker Oats back label states in part that "[t]his product is consistent with the American Heart Association dietary guidelines" and that "diets low in saturated fat and cholesterol and high in fiber-containing grains ... may reduce risk of heart disease").

Recognizing that labels were of limited value without an informed and educated consumer who could understand them, the FDA has also begun a multiyear food labeling education campaign that involves participation by consumer advocates, industry groups and corporations, and other government agencies. Its purpose is to increase consumers' knowledge and to assist them in making sound dietary choices in accordance with the USDA-designed "Dietary Guidelines for Americans." The latter promotes a diet balanced between basic food groups and is usually represented in the form of a food pyramid.

The FDA estimates that in the United States the new food label will cost food processors between $1.4 and $2.3 billion over the next 20 years. But measured in monetary terms, the potential benefits to the public may well exceed the costs; health benefits potentially include decreased rates of coronary heart disease, cancer, osteoporosis, obesity, high blood pressure, and allergic reactions to food (FDA 1993).

Thus, the effects of nutrition labeling go far beyond serving as a shopping aid for consumers. The NLEA is also expected to have a significant impact on the functioning and performance of the food industry because manufacturers will redesign food nutritional profiles to meet changing consumer demands. In other words, for food companies the implementation of mandatory labeling requirements is likely to have important effects on both consumer demand and the marketing of foods (Caswell and Mojduszka 1996).

Nutrition Labeling in Europe

In post–World War II Europe, agricultural and food industry policies were mainly shaped by criteria such as the welfare of industrial workers, economic implications for farmers, national employment, and military security. So long as nutrition experts advised Ministry of Agriculture officials in various European countries on the best crops to cultivate to overcome food shortages in the immediate postwar years, health and nutrition issues were rarely central considerations in agricultural planning but instead were seen as primarily relevant to developing countries.

In 1974, however, the World Food Conference stressed the need for all countries to adopt food safety and nutrition policies, regardless of their stage of development. In Europe, Norway was the first industrialized country to adopt such a policy. By the mid-1980s, a number of health departments in European nations, including West Germany, France, and Great Britain, had issued reports on nutrition and diet, and international organizations such as the World Health Organization (WHO) and the Food and Agriculture Organization (FAO) – both offices of the United Nations – also called attention to the role of nutrients in human health in industrialized societies, citing dietary problems associated with oils and fats.

By 1990, seven countries in Western Europe had established food safety and nutrition policies similar to those in the United States before NLEA (Helsing 1991). But although the majority of these programs recognized that information and public education were key components of a national nutrition policy, they stopped short of requiring labeling on all processed food products.

The regulation of food and nutrition labeling in Europe has taken place within the context of attempts to establish a common European market. In 1979, the European Community (EC) issued rules on food safety and consumer protection based on the "Principle of Mutual Recognition," intended to standardize food health regulations to facilitate international trade. Under this rule, no EC country was to prevent the importation of a food product legally produced and sold in another country, even though the product might not be legally produced according to standards established by the importing country's own laws. Such a rule eased trade restrictions in the EC but presented risks of lowered food quality and safety in countries with more stringent quality standards.

To address these concerns, the EC expanded regulation in the 1980s with new rules on product definition, quality differentiation, and labeling. Under these directives food labels were required to display information on product characteristics, including quality, quantity, and origin of ingredients. Producers are prohibited from making health claims that link their product to the prevention or treatment of diseases. EC labeling policy was intended to supply European consumers with adequate information on nutrition and food quality to help them make informed choices in the grocery store without setting up rigid labeling regulations that might place burdens on individual national economies (Worley et al. 1994).

The variety of nutrition policies in Europe underscores the way variations in regional dietary patterns and differing political environments affect governments' willingness to establish nutrition regulations and is illustrated by a brief examination of food policy in Norway, Denmark, and Poland. In Norway, government planners chose a carefully activist nutrition policy, unique in the extent to which it relied on government intervention. Norway's readiness to adopt interventionist policies reflects in part the relative limits of the country's domestic agricultural sector, based heavily on dairy and beef production, and its dependence on foreign imports of sugar and grains.

Adopted in 1975, Norway's "Food Supply and Nutrition Policy" acknowledged the relationship between public-health objectives and food supply planning. The stated aims of the policy included encouraging healthy eating habits in the population, implementing the recommendations of the World Food Conference of 1974, and maximizing the domestic production of food to ensure the stability, security, and quality of the national food supply. Specific dietary changes recommended for the population – to reduce fat intake to 35 percent of total dietary energy, to increase the consumption of cereal and potatoes, to increase the proportion of polyunsaturated fat in the diet, and to increase the consumption of fish – reflected concerns over the dietary level of fat but also posed a potential threat to Norway's domestic agriculture.

Acting with support from a coalition of industry, consumer, and government representatives, the Norwegian government used a variety of consumer food subsidies (many were already in place) together with agricultural policies intended to slowly raise domestic production of grains while lowering consumer consumption of saturated fats, so as to protect both consumer and industry interests. Information controls forbade misleading advertising, particularly for foods with poor nutritional profiles such as ice cream, chocolate, and soft drinks. Educational programs were also launched and special attention was given to the nutritional content of school courses at the nursery, primary, secondary, and higher levels. Voluntary nutrition labeling of processed foods aimed to better inform the population on the nutritional content of food products. By 1990 fat consumption had dropped to the 35 percent target level and overall agricultural production rose as planned, demonstrating the success of Norway's combination of interventionist and information policies (Gormley, Downey, and O'Beirne 1987; Helsing 1991).

In Denmark, by contrast, food and nutrition policy came relatively late, and was poorly promulgated and coordinated. Acting in response to consumer interest in diet and health, the government adopted a formal nutrition policy in 1984. Unlike Norway, Denmark's policy did not formulate specific nutrition policy goals or assign responsibility for coordination of policy activities. Although the government helped estab-lish several research institutes focused on nutrition issues, little attention was given to providing nutrition information to the public. In 1990, Denmark's nutrient pattern failed to show the same dramatic improvements that had been seen in Norway (Helsing 1991).

Poland's experience with nutrition policy offers an exemplary case of the problems countries on the geographical and economic periphery of the European Union (EU) face in achieving standards deemed important by the Union. In Poland, as in other Eastern European countries with command economies before 1989, nutrition policy lags behind and creates problems for public health and international trade. Though the right of Polish consumers to truthful disclosure of information about the quality of food products was presumably guaranteed when the Polish government accepted United Nations Organization directives in 1985, advertising became the main – and not very satisfactory – source of information about food quality for most Polish people after 1989.

In April 1995, the Federation of Polish Consumers issued a report on "The State of Realization of Consumer Rights in the Polish Food Market" that called attention to shortcomings in the Polish regulatory system. The report made it clear that despite growing public awareness of nutrition issues, laws then in place that dealt with the nutritional composition of foods and their advertising were not effective because the Polish government lacked the power to enforce them. Thus, for example, it became impossible to fine manufacturers that used deceptive advertising because there was no government office to evaluate the nutritional claims made by advertisements.

An ineffective nutrition policy also affects foreign markets for Poland's agricultural products, and it would seem that food labeling policy is necessary to make Polish food acceptable and competitive in international markets as well as competitive with imports reaching Poland. The regulation of nutrition labeling would give Polish manufacturers incentives to quickly come into compliance with higher standards. Such a step would also provide Polish consumers with knowledge to protect themselves from risks posed by foods and save them from buying costly products whose quality is misrepresented. Like other central and Eastern European nations where agriculture and food production are key sectors of the national as well as the export economy, Poland faces the need to put in place effective regulations and enforcement policies that ensure the quality of food products and the reliability and usefulness of information provided on food labels.

An international comparison of nutrition regulation can also underline the importance of food labeling, not only for its value in public education and for encouraging better health but also as an increasingly important component of international trade. The stiffer regulatory environment in the United States poses potential barriers to the import of food from other countries, even those in Western Europe, where regulations are less strict (Worley et al. 1994). As countries in both Eastern and Western Europe and North America transform their regulatory requirements to comply with international trade agreements, informational approaches to food regulation will play a more significant role and will likely lead toward the gradual convergence of international regulatory policies.

This is a slow-moving process, largely because labeling policies evolve in different political climates and in response to different regional diets, but also because food manufacturers typically oppose mandatory nutrition labeling of foods. Changes in national nutrition-labeling regulation have to be carefully negotiated between consumer, government, and industry representatives and involve important policy issues.

Nutrition Labeling and Policy Issues

Since a better awareness of linkages between diet and health has been achieved, governments of many countries have been forced to confront the issue of market intervention in order to regulate food quality. There are two main approaches to the implementation of nutrition policies by central governments. The first, called the minimalist approach, stresses the responsibility of the individual in the attainment of a healthful diet. The role of government is limited to the development and advocacy of dietary guidelines and to the provision and monitoring of information available to the consumer on the nutritional composition of foods. The planned interventionist approach, in contrast, maintains that government should actively intervene in many sectors of the economy to achieve optimum nutrition for all citizens.

With the exception of Norway, however, developed nations have thus far adopted minimalist approaches to nutrition regulation that rely on market forces to ensure the nutritional quality of food products and the nutritious diets of their populations. Governments have many reasons for hesitating to adopt planned interventionist programs. The most common can be grouped under the headings "scientific/philosophical" and "political." Scientific/philosophical reasons include a lack of confidence in the scientific basis of most nutrition theories and thus a hesitation to intervene in nutrition-related health issues without "absolute" scientific proof. When combined with philosophical beliefs in the sufficiency of the market and a reluctance to interfere with the individual's freedom of choice, these reasons join to make a compelling argument for a minimalist approach.

Political reasons for the unwillingness of governments to adopt interventionist policies center primarily on the relative importance of the agricultural and food processing industry sectors in different countries. For example, in nations with economically highly ranked agriculture and food processing industries, like Denmark, the Netherlands, Ireland, and Belgium, politicians may be unwilling to interfere with food availability and choice because of resistance from powerful producers and various lobbies and a lack of a clear support from the public. Public demands for action, however, may encourage elected officials to address such issues (Gormley et al. 1987).

As already noted, though, even the implementation of a minimalist government nutrition policy has been politically controversial, especially in the United States and Great Britain, where the agricultural and the food processing industries were concerned that government efforts to implement dietary guidelines could threaten their survival. In fact, a successful implementation of the ideal dietary guidelines would imply reduced demand for meat, dairy products (two well-organized producer groups in the United States), eggs, fats, and sweets and increased demand for vegetables, fruits, cereals, and vegetable oils. This would represent a major shift in the diets of the populations and could potentially disrupt the food production sector. Not surprisingly, the regulation of nutrition has often been resisted by meat and dairy producers and other agricultural interests.

Nevertheless, despite the potential economic dislocation feared by advocates of a "hands-off" approach, there are compelling arguments for government intervention in nutrition regulation. Even though a degree of scientific uncertainty exists, most researchers agree that public health is well served by increased knowledge of nutrition and by the availability of nutritionally sound foods. Yet although it is true that producers will readily supply food with a positive nutrition profile if it is profitable for them to do so, the cost is a likely deterrent. Consequently, without some form of regulation to control the truthfulness of label claims, producers who do market higher-quality food face unfair competition from others offering less expensive, lower-quality products.

Following the philosophical assumptions surrounding belief in the "free market," some economists, policy makers, and food manufacturers have argued that relatively unregulated markets provide adequate information to consumers on the nutritional quality of foods, making government regulation of information disclosure unnecessary. In a perfectly operating market, product price will, theoretically, transmit all the information the consumer needs to make a rational, informed choice. A variety of products with different levels of quality and risks would be offered for sale at a variety of prices; higher nutritional quality would be signaled by higher prices. In a theoretically "free market," consumers would choose among a variety of foods based on their preferences for products and the attributes of those products (Caswell and Mojduszka 1996).

The actual marketplace, however, is rarely free or perfect in the theoretical sense and typically fails to provide either accurate nutritional information or foods with good nutritional profiles. Manufacturers are better informed about the content and nutritional profiles of their products than consumers. Consequently, if information on the nutritional quality of food is inaccurate, or if public perceptions about the risks or hazards associated with certain food products are incorrect, then consumers are exposed to health risks far greater than they would have been willing to face if they were able to make informed decisions. These factors imply that government should intervene in the marketplace to ensure the provision of nutritious food and, thus, enhance consumer health.

Governments in market economies have three basic instruments that can be used to influence the nutritional quality of the food supply: providing the public with more reliable information about nutrition, enhancing production standards at processing plants, and confronting manufacturers with pecuniary measures, including taxes, subsidies, and fines (Kramer 1990). Because the political and philosophical climate of the last two decades has favored minimalist approaches to market intervention, government agencies have focused mostly on the first of these. Information remedies can take a variety of forms: the mandatory disclosure of information about the nature of products by manufacturers; controls on claims made for product promotion; provision of public information and education; government subsidies for the provision of information; and control of product names. Such measures are undertaken in an attempt to encourage people to demand foods with a high nutritional profile and, as we have already noted, to inspire manufacturers to produce higher-quality foods. As we have seen, the NLEA, as promulgated by the FDA, leans heavily on information remedies.

Policy experts consider information regulation appropriate, and particularly valuable, in the case of nutrition because without it, it is generally impossible for consumers to determine either the health safety or the nutritional quality of food, even after the product has been bought and consumed. Advocates of the minimalist approach also assume that the regulation of information will encourage consumers to purchase more healthful food bundles, in turn compelling producers to improve the nutritional formulation of their products without direct legislative intervention in the production process.

Though the FDA contends that food prices will show little change as a result of mandatory nutrition labeling, reliance on information remedies to regulate food nutrition does impose other costs on consumers by forcing them to spend time reading labels and, of course, learning about nutrition. This can be something of a problem because minimalist information remedies do little to control food advertising beyond limiting false or misleading claims, and even under the relatively stringent NLEA rules, producers and marketers are able to sometimes use vague nutrition-related claims to powerfully influence consumer food choice. Finally, critics of the minimalist approach maintain that its intent is often severely weakened by a lack of formal government commitment to action. For example, educational or enforcement programs may have inadequate funding.

The effects of labeling regulation are difficult to measure. A 1996 survey in the United States showed mixed results: Whereas 58 percent of consumers polled said that they always read the nutrition label before buying a product for the first time (up from 52 percent in 1991), and more than half said they were trying to eat less fat, 46 percent agreed with the statement that "there is so much conflicting information about which foods are good for me that I'm not sure what to eat anymore" (Howe 1996).

Information remedies clearly have limits, and interventionist approaches, despite their current unpopularity, may ultimately offer consumers greater health protection by directly requiring producers to improve the quality of their foods. In a political climate that favors a minimalist approach, however, government adoption of nutrition regulation focused on information remedies can influence product design, advertising, consumer confidence in food quality, and consumer education about diet and health. The implementation of nutrition labeling regulation thus offers real health benefits to the general population and potentially improves both economic efficiency and public welfare (Caswell and Padberg 1992).

Conclusion

Before World War II, rules for information disclosure on food labels were generally understood as one component of more general food safety policies. After the war, nutrition was increasingly seen as an important factor in its own right, and by the 1970s, most developed countries had established nutrition policies that included provisions for consumer information and food labeling. Perhaps ironically, concerns with nutrition are greater in countries where there is abundant food for most citizens and malnutrition is a result of poor dietary habits rather than food shortages. In less developed countries, where nutrition deficits are often the result of a lack of food, regulation of nutrition through labeling may appear superfluous or unnecessary until supply problems are solved; in addition, neither consumers nor governments can afford the relatively high costs associated with labeling programs.

Nutrition labeling is only one of the possible policy tools available to governments as part of a modern program of nutrition and food safety regulation, but in an economic environment stressing free trade and nonintervention, it has become increasingly important. Product labeling and information disclosure requirements act as an interface between government requirements, manufacturer response, and consumer demand that encourages nonpunitive market incentives with relatively limited government interference. Nutrition labeling policies continue to evolve in an increasingly international environment and are now seen as possible nontariff barriers to the flow of international trade. Among the strongest incentives to modify nutrition labeling policy in the twenty-first century will be concerns with the compatibility of regulatory regimes across national boundaries.

Nutrition labels can provide an important benefit to the health of certain groups of consumers, but they also impose costs on consumers, producers, and government. The use of labels can require expensive monitoring programs in regulating industry and educational programs to encourage public awareness; producers may also be forced to invest in product reformulation and new label design. Labels are also something of a double-edged sword and, at times, have been used by manufacturers to misrepresent the nutrition profiles of certain foods in marketing campaigns. In the end, the success of nutrition labeling depends on a number of interacting factors, making effectiveness difficult to measure without broad studies that focus on changes in consumer awareness and dietary patterns, as well as on the introduction of new foods with more healthful nutrition profiles and improvements in the nutritional quality of existing food products.

Eliza M. Mojduszka

Henson, Spencer, and Bruce Traill. 1993. The demand for food safety: Market imperfections and the role of government. *Food Policy* 18: 152-62.

Howe, Peter J. 1996. American's dilemma: What's for dinner? *Boston Globe,* June 27, p. 3.

Kennedy, E., and L. Haddad. 1992. Food security and nutrition, 1971-91. Lessons learned and future priorities. *Food Policy* 17: 2-6.

Kinsey, Jean. 1993. GATT and the economics of food safety. *Food Policy* 18: 163-76.

Kramer, Carol S. 1990. Food safety: Consumer preferences, policy options, research needs. In *Consumer demands in the market place: Public policies related to food safety, quality, and human health,* ed. K. L. Clancy, 74-87. Washington, D.C.

Swinbank, Alan. 1993. Industry note: Completion of the EC's internal market, mutual recognition, and the food industries. *Agribusiness* 9: 509-22.

Wilkins, Mira. 1994. When and why brand names in food and drink? In *Adding value: Brands and marketing in food and drink,* ed. G. J. Jones and N. J. Morgan, 15-40. London and New York.

Worley, C. T., R. J. Folwell, V. A. McCracken, and G. L. Bagnara. 1994. Changing labeling regulations: Implications for international food marketing. *Journal of Food Distribution Research* 25 (February): 21-5.

  1995. Food label regulations in the United States and the European Community: International trade facilitators or non tariff barriers. *Journal of International Food and Agribusiness Marketing* 7: 91-103.

Zarkin, G. A., and D. W. Anderson. 1992. Consumer and producer responses to nutrition label changes. *American Journal of Agricultural Economics* 74: 1202-7.

Bibliography

Avery, F. 1984. Diet for a corporate planet: Industry sets world food standards. *Multinational Monitor* 14: 12-15.

Burton, Scott, and A. Biswas. 1993. Preliminary assessment of changes in labels required by the NLEA of 1990. *The Journal of Consumer Affairs* 27: 127-44.

Caswell, Julie A., ed. 1991. *Economics of food safety.* New York.

  1995. *Valuing food safety and nutrition.* Boulder, Colo.

Caswell, Julie A., and Eliza M. Mojduszka. 1996. Using informational labeling to influence the market for quality in food products. *American Journal of Agricultural Economics* 78: 1248-53, 1261-2.

Caswell, Julie A., and Daniel I. Padberg. 1992. Toward a more comprehensive theory of food labels. *American Journal of Agricultural Economics* 74: 460-8.

FDA (Food and Drug Administration). 1993. FDA consumer special report: Focus on food labeling. *FDA Consumer* 27 (May): 7-56.

Gorman, Christine. 1991. The fight over food labels. *Time* (July 15): 52-9.

Gormley, T. R., G. Downey, and D. O'Beirne. 1987. *Food, health, and the consumer.* London and New York.

Helsing, Elisabet. 1991. Nutrition policies in Europe: Background and organization. *Food Policy* 16: 371-83.

Henson, Spencer, and Wlodzimierz Sekula. 1994. Market reform in the Polish food sector: Impact upon food consumption and nutrition. *Food Policy* 19: 419-42.

VII.6 🔊 Food Lobbies and U.S. Dietary Guidance Policy

In April 1991, the United States Department of Agriculture (USDA) withdrew from publication its *Eating Right Pyramid,* a new food guide for the general public. Despite official explanations that the guide required further research, its withdrawal was widely believed to have been prompted by pressure from meat and dairy lobbying groups who objected to the way the *Pyramid* displayed their products (Burros 1991b; Combs 1991; Sugarman and Gladwell 1991; Nestle 1993a).

This incident focused attention on a continuing political and ethical dilemma in American government: The rights of individuals guaranteed by the First Amendment to the Constitution versus the social good. In this case, the dilemma involved the inherent right of private industries to act in their own economic self-interests versus the best judgments of health authorities as to what constitutes good nutrition for the public. The *Pyramid* controversy also focused attention on the dual and potentially conflicting USDA mandates to protect U.S. agricultural interests and to issue dietary recommendations to the public (Nestle 1993b).

To address such dilemmas, this chapter reviews the history of dietary guidance and lobbying policies in the United States, describes the principal food lobbies, and presents examples of ways in which they have influenced - or have attempted to influence - federal dietary advice to the public. Finally, it discusses options for correcting improper, sometimes unconscionable, food lobby influence on U.S. nutrition policies.

U.S. Dietary Guidance

From its inception in 1862, the USDA was assigned two roles that have led to the current conflict of interest: to ensure a sufficient and reliable food supply, and to "diffuse among the people of the United States useful information on subjects connected with agriculture in the most general and comprehensive sense of that word" (USDA 1862). In the early 1890s, the USDA began to sponsor research on the relationship between agriculture and human nutrition and to translate new discoveries into advice for consumers. By 1917, the agency had produced at least 30 pamphlets that informed homemakers about the role of specific foods in the diet of children and adults.

The USDA's first dietary recommendations established principles that govern its policies to this day. The agency recommended no specific foods or combinations of foods. Instead, it grouped foods of similar nutrient content into five general categories - fruits and vegetables, meats, cereals, sugar, and fat (Hunt and Atwater 1917). Such a recommendation was intended to encourage the purchase of foods from the full range of American farm products, for by 1921, improvements in agriculture had led to greater availability of many different kinds of foods, any one of which was said to contribute to wholesome and attractive diets (Hunt 1921).

Thus, the recommendation was supported by food and agricultural producers who suspected that the market for their products was becoming limited as the U.S. food supply was already sufficient to provide adequate food to all of its citizens; consequently, any increase in use of one food commodity would have to occur at the expense of others (Levenstein 1988). During the next 35 years, the USDA produced many pamphlets based on the food group approach, all emphasizing the need to consume foods from certain "protective" groups in order to prevent deficiencies of essential nutrients (Haughton, Gussow, and Dodds 1987). The number of recommended food groups, however, varied over the years in no consistent pattern (Nestle and Porter 1990).

At least some of the variation in the number of food groups reflected concerns about the impact of dietary advice on consumer purchases. A Great Depression-era food guide, noting that producers want "to know how much of different foods may well appear in the diets of different consumer groups, and

to what extent consumption may rise or fall as the economic situation changes," increased the number of food groups to 12 and included, for the first time, milk as a separate category (Stiebeling and Ward 1933).

In the 1950s, national nutrition surveys indicated that the diets of many Americans were below standard for several nutrients. To help the public choose foods more wisely, USDA nutritionists proposed a simplified guide based on four groups - milk, meats, vegetables and fruits, and breads and cereals - which, for the first time, would specify the number and size of servings.

Prior to its release, the USDA invited leading nutrition authorities to review the guide. Food industry representatives were also sent drafts because "it was felt that food industry groups would have a vital interest in any food guide sponsored by the government" (Hill and Cleveland 1970). Dairy organizations were pleased with the treatment given to milk and milk products, but "meat industry groups were unhappy about the serving size indicated for meat . . . [t]hey pointed out that this size is smaller than average" (Hill and Cleveland 1970). Despite these complaints, the controversial serving sizes (two daily portions of 2 to 3 ounces cooked meat) were incorporated unchanged into the final version of what became known as the *Basic Four* (USDA 1958). This guide remained the basis of USDA nutrition policies for the next 20 years (Figure VII.6.1). Except for the minor concern about portion size, food producer groups supported USDA efforts to promote consumption of more - and more varied - food products.

This relationship changed when policymakers became aware that nutritional deficiencies had declined in prevalence and had been replaced by chronic diseases related to dietary excesses and imbalances. Early reports on the role of dietary fat in atherosclerosis were published in the mid-1950s (Page, Stare, Corcoran et al. 1957), advice to reduce caloric intake from fat in 1961 (American Heart Association 1961), and recommendations for dietary changes and public policies to reduce coronary heart disease risk factors in 1970 (Inter-Society Commission 1970). These last recommendations called for significant reductions in overall consumption of fat (to 35 percent of calories or less), saturated fat (to 10 percent), and cholesterol (to 300 milligrams per day).

The 1977 Farm Bill (Public Law 95-113) specified that the USDA was to be responsible for a wide range of nutrition research and education activities, including dietary advice to the public. In 1988, in an effort to ensure that the federal government speak with "one voice" when it issues dietary recommendations, the House Appropriations Committee reaffirmed USDA's lead agency responsibility for this activity (U.S. House of Representatives 1988). As dietary recommendations shifted from "eat more" to "eat less," the USDA's dual responsibilities for protecting agricultural producers and advising the public about diet created increasing levels of conflict.

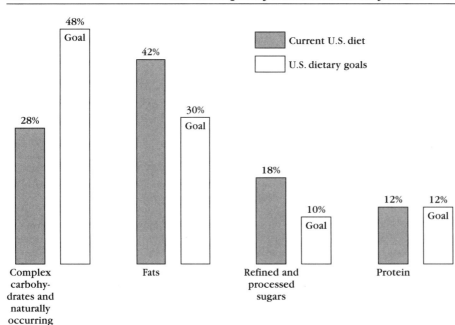

Figure VII.6.1. Meat and dairy groups approved as the 1958 *Basic Four*, as it emphasized the importance of their products in the U.S. diet. Meat producers complained, however, that the suggested portion sizes were too small. (From Hill and Cleveland 1970; USDA 1958.)

Although this conflict was often expressed in terms of the scientific validity of diet–disease relationships, it derived from the profound economic implications of dietary recommendations (Timmer and Nesheim 1979). Foods of animal origin – meat, dairy products, and eggs – have provided much of the total fat and saturated fat, and all of the cholesterol, in the U.S. food supply. In 1990, for example, meat provided 32 percent of the total fat and 40 percent of the saturated fat, and dairy products 12 and 20 percent, for a combined total of 44 and 60 percent, respectively (Raper 1991). Thus, advice to consume less fat and cholesterol necessarily translated into reduced intake of meat, dairy products, and eggs. By 1977, this message was well understood by nutrition scientists, dietitians, and consumer activists (U.S. Senate Select Committee 1977c) and was reflected in declining sales of whole milk and eggs (Putnam 1991). As these trends continued and as beef sales also began to decline, food producer lobbies became much more actively involved in attempts to discredit, weaken, or eliminate dietary recommendations that suggested using less of their products.

Lobbies and Lobbyists

In tribute to their level of influence, lobbies and lobbyists have been viewed as constituting a third house of Congress (Schriftgiesser 1951) or fourth branch of government (Berry 1984). But its members are appointed rather than elected, paid to represent private (and thus not always public) interests and to pursue those interests through activities that are often not in full view of the general public. Thus the actions of lobbies can and do raise concerns about their potential to corrupt democratic political processes (American Enterprise Institute 1980).

Definition of Lobbying

In the broadest possible sense, lobbying includes any legal attempt by individuals or groups to influence government policy or action; this definition specifically excludes bribery. All lobbying efforts involve three common elements: an attempt to influence governmental decisions, representation of the views of special interest groups, and communication with government officials or their representatives. Therefore, a lobbyist is an individual who communicates with a government official on behalf of a third party in the hope of influencing federal decisions. When surveyed, lobbyists have stated that their one common characteristic is similar to that of most others connected with the political process: They try to influence governmental decisions in some way (Milbrath 1963).

Lobbying in the United States

The history of attempts to control lobbying reflects basic tensions in the American political system. From its beginnings, this system has granted individuals the right to express political views publicly, to petition government regarding such views, and to organize on behalf of them. Elected officials of representative governments must listen to constituents, yet special interest groups constantly pressure the government to enact policies that may benefit relatively few constituents. Attempts to control such pressures, however, have been viewed as infringements of constitutionally guaranteed civil rights, and Congress has found it difficult to draft acceptable laws to curb lobbying abuses (Milbrath 1963). Despite substantial public and congressional concern about many lobbying activities, there is little consensus as to how such activities might be controlled (Berry 1984).

This dilemma appeared early in U.S. history. James Madison, writing of the "dangerous vice" of factions (the term he used for lobby groups), observed that they arise from causes inherent in human nature and in the unequal distribution of property. Relief from the "mischiefs of faction," according to Madison, would derive from the principles of majority rule proposed for the federal republic. A faction "may clog the administration, it may convulse the society," but under the terms of the Constitution, "it will be unable to execute and mask its violence" (Madison 1787: 45).

Indeed, from the earliest years of the new republic, public exposures of excessive and dishonest lobbying were followed by investigations and demands for regulation of interest groups. In response, Congress made sporadic attempts to control lobbying abuses. Proposed legislation typically passed in one house or the other but failed to become law. Congressional leaders were unable to agree on legislation that would curb dishonest lobbying yet permit individual rights to free speech and petition (Congressional Quarterly 1968).

Table VII.6.1 summarizes selected landmarks in the history of U.S. lobbying. As early as 1829, individuals who frequented the lobby of the state capitol in Albany in order to seek favors from New York legislators were called "lobby-agents." By 1832, Washington journalists were using the term "lobbyists" in the current meaning of the term. In 1877, frequent abuses led the state legislature of Georgia to declare lobbying to be a crime, and Massachusetts, Maryland, Wisconsin, and New York passed antilobby legislation between 1890 and 1905. Beginning in 1911, nearly every Congress attempted to probe and control lobbying and related activities. Between 1935 and the early 1940s, Congress enacted laws requiring employees of public utilities, the merchant marine, and foreign governments to register and report political contributions, and it prohibited labor unions from making such contributions. Such actions, however, failed to make any real progress in controlling lobbying abuses (U.S. Senate Special Committee 1957; Congressional Quarterly 1965).

Legislative Mandate

When Congress finally did address interest group practices, it made lobbying legal. The 1946 Federal Regulation of Lobbying Act protected lobbyists' rights and required only that persons paid to lobby, or the organizations paying them, disclose their identities and sources of funds. The act, which is still in force, requires lobbyists to register and to file with Congress sworn quarterly reports disclosing the amounts of

Table VII.6.1. *Selected landmarks in the history of U.S. lobbying*

1787	James Madison, in Federalist Paper No. 10, warns of the dangers of self-interested "factions" to government processes.
1792	First Amendment to Constitution guarantees right to free speech, assembly, and petition to Congress.
1829	The term "lobby-agent" is used to describe a person who frequents the lobby of the state capitol in Albany in order to seek special favors.
1832	Washington journalists first use the term "lobbyists."
1877	Georgia's constitution declares lobbying to be a crime.
1890–1900	Massachusetts, Maryland, Wisconsin, and New York pass anti-lobby legislation.
1907	Congress forbids corporations to make political campaign contributions in federal elections.
1919	Internal Revenue Service rules lobbying expenditures are not deductible from federal income taxes by businesses or individuals.
1935	Public Utilities Holding Company Act prohibits political contributions by utility companies and requires individuals who do make contributions to register and report.
1936	Merchant Marine Act requires similar registration and reporting.
1938	Foreign Agents Registration Act imposes registration and reporting requirements for political contributions.
1943	Smith-Connolly War Labor Disputes Act bars political campaign contributions in federal elections by labor unions during war emergency.
1946	Federal Regulation of Lobbying Act, adopted as Title III of the Legislative Reorganization Act of 1946 (P.L. 79-601), requires paid lobbyists to register and file financial reports.
1947	Taft-Hartley Act prohibits political campaign contributions by labor unions and corporations.
1954	Supreme Court upholds constitutionality of 1946 act in *U.S. v. Harriss;* limits law to individuals paid by a third party to communicate directly with members of Congress to influence legislation.
1956	In connection with a bribery attempt, Superior Oil Company attorneys become the first – and only – individuals to be convicted for failure to register under the 1946 act.
1957	Senate investigating committee finds 1946 act failing to achieve the disclosure aims that it was designed to accomplish.
1968	*Congressional Quarterly* lists 23 former senators and 90 former congressmen who have registered as lobbyists since 1946.
1974	Amendments to the Federal Election Campaign Act authorize the formation of Political Action Committees (PACs) to fund congressional campaigns.
1980	Congress attempts to revise the lobbying act.
1991	More than 7,000 individuals register as lobbyists.

Sources: Schriftgiesser (1951), U.S. Senate Special Committee (1957), Congressional Quarterly (1965, 1968), American Enterprise Institute (1980), and "Registered Lobbyists" (1991).

money they receive or spend, the individuals to whom they pay funds, the purposes of these payments, and the specific legislation that they are supporting or opposing (Schriftgiesser 1951; Congressional Quarterly 1965). This law, considered vague by virtually all authorities (U.S. Senate Committee 1991), was reduced further in coverage by challenges in federal courts. In a 1954 case, *U.S. v. Harriss,* the Supreme Court upheld the constitutionality of the act, albeit through a narrow interpretation; it limited the law's applicability only to individuals who solicited or received money for the purpose of lobbying members of Congress (Congressional Quarterly 1965).

These decisions leave much room for ambiguity; they can be interpreted as permitting interest groups to lobby congressional staff or officials and staff of cabinet departments and their agencies, and to decide for themselves whether and how much they need to report. The act defines no special enforcement procedures, even though it specifies criminal penalties for noncompliance. In its entire history, the act has resulted in only one conviction (Congressional Quarterly 1968). Despite repeated attempts to strengthen its provisions (American Enterprise Institute 1980), the 1946 act remains in force only as modified by *U.S. v. Harriss.* Thus, the view that lobbying legislation is unenforced, unenforceable, and widely ignored continues to prevail (U.S. Senate Committee 1991).

Registered Lobbyists
The extent to which the lobbying act may be ignored is uncertain. During the 20 years following its passage, an average of 400 lobbyists registered and reported contributions that amounted to $4 to $5 million annually, but these figures were considered low because of the many loopholes in reporting requirements (Congressional Quarterly 1968). The number of registrations grew rapidly from 1960 to 1980, partly in response to expansion in the size and complexity of government. In 1963, the government included 10 major cabinet departments and 70 major agencies, and Congress employed 7,700 aides. By 1991, these numbers had increased to 14, 140, and 20,062, respectively. The number of registered lobbyists doubled between 1976 and 1986 (Browne 1988). At the beginning of the 1990s, 7,000 to 8,000 individuals registered as lobbyists, many representing multiple organizations or causes (Registered lobbyists 1991; U.S. Senate Committee 1991).

The interests represented by lobbyists encompass every conceivable aspect of American corporate and private enterprise: banks; corporations; legal, public relations, and life insurance firms; educational institutions; professional societies; advocacy groups; city, state, and national governments; defense, health, computer, energy, drug, chemical, paper, tobacco, transportation, travel, and, of course, food industries. They all pay individuals to represent their interests to Congress. There is no industry too small, no group too isolated, and no opinion too extreme to lack a professional lobbyist. Lobbying is a multimillion-dollar industry with enormous impact on government decisions (U.S. Senate Committee 1991).

Food Lobbies
The Agricultural Establishment
By the end of World War II, farmers and food producers had come to view the USDA as their department and its secretary as their spokesman. Producers, together with USDA officials and members of the House and Senate Agricultural Committees, constituted the "agricultural establishment" and ensured that federal policies in such areas as land use, commodity distribution, and prices promoted their interests (Paarlberg 1964). The control exercised by producer groups over USDA and congressional actions was so complete that both the secretary of agriculture and the president were said to be excluded from any significant role in policy decisions (Kramer 1979).

The perpetuation of this system was guaranteed by the congressional seniority system and the strong representation on agriculture committees of members from farm states. Committee membership rarely changed hands. Allen Ellender (D-La), for example, chaired the Senate Agriculture Committee for a total of 18 years, and his successor, Herman Talmadge (D-Ga), held the chair for 10 more. Jamie Whitten (D-Miss), first elected to Congress when Franklin Roosevelt was president, chaired the House Agricultural Appropriations Subcommittee for so long that he was referred to as "the permanent secretary of agriculture" (Morgan 1978b); he was elected to his twenty-seventh term of office in 1992 and resigned the committee chair he had held since 1949 when he finally left office in 1994 (Binder 1995).

By the early 1970s, this system weakened as new constituencies demanded influence on agriculture policies. A combination of bad weather, poor harvests in foreign countries, and massive purchases of U.S. grain by the Soviet Union had led to increased food costs and consumer complaints (Kramer 1979). Agriculture was gaining in importance in the U.S. economy, and the food industry was expanding to include processors and marketers as well as producers (Morgan 1978b). Responsibility for providing food assistance to the poor was assigned to the USDA (Morgan 1978a). In response to demands from these constituencies, the House expanded the membership of its Agriculture Committee to include representatives from urban areas in 1974, and, in 1977, the agriculture committees of both houses were assigned jurisdiction for policies and programs related not only to agricultural production, marketing, research, and development, but also to rural development, forestry, domestic food assistance, and some aspects of foreign trade, international relations, market regulation, and tax policies (Knutson, Penn, and Boehm 1983).

Food Lobbyists

The number of food lobbying groups reflected the expansion in constituencies. In the 1950s, 25 groups of food producers dominated agricultural lobbying, but by the mid-1980s, 84 groups lobbied on food issues (Browne 1988). In the early 1990s, food lobbies included a multiplicity of groups, businesses, and individuals attempting to influence federal decisions. They represent producers, growers, marketers, processors, and distributors of every imaginable fruit, vegetable, cereal, baby food, diet aid, nutritional supplement, sweetener, and product grown or manufactured at the local, state, or national level. They also represent manufacturers of pesticides, feeds, and fertilizers; professional and health organizations; and food, nutrition, antihunger, and welfare activists (Registered lobbyists 1991). Table VII.6.2 lists specific examples of such groups. The number of active food lobbyists is uncertain. A 1977 study identified 612 individuals and 460 groups lobbying on food and agriculture issues (Guither 1980). A cursory review of current lobbyist registrations suggests that 5 to 10 percent of lobbyists are concerned with such issues.

Lobbying Methods

Personal Contacts

No matter whom they represent, all lobbyists use similar strategies to gain access and influence. Of these methods, lobbyists rank personal contacts as the most effective means of gaining access to government officials. These contacts are established through office visits, meetings, participation on advisory boards, testimony at hearings, social occasions, fundraising sessions, and performance of favors, as well as through the engagement of other individuals and groups to perform such favors. Lobbyists also organize meetings, provide technical advice, contribute to election campaigns, stage media events, employ public relations firms, organize public demonstrations, and encourage lawsuits (U.S. Senate Special Committee 1957; Milbrath 1963; Browne 1988).

Technical Expertise

Virtually all blueprints for successful lobbying emphasize the importance of knowledge and credibility (deKieffer 1981; Berry 1984). These attributes establish lobbyists as technical experts who provide Congress with well-researched advice on issues related to proposed legislation. The value of this expertise is, in part, responsible for a congressional reluctance to control lobbying activities.

Financial Contributions

Individual and corporate contributions and gifts to members of Congress are strictly regulated by the Federal Election Campaign Act. Small items such as lunches, books, awards, liquor, samples, and theater tickets are considered acceptable (deKieffer 1981). Also considered legal are very large payments for administrative costs, fundraising events, travel expenses, and honoraria. Thus in 1991 several food and agriculture corporations legally donated $100,000 or more each to the Republican Party (Babcock 1991).

An analysis of privately funded travel among members of the House of Representatives in 1989–90 identified nearly 4,000 trips sponsored by lobby groups, two-thirds of them corporations or trade associations.

Table VII.6.2. *Selected examples of food lobbying groups*

Commodity producer organizations
American Soybean Association
American Sugar Beet Growers Association
Florida Sugar Cane League
National Association of Wheat Growers
National Broiler Council
National Cattlemen's Association
National Corn Growers' Association
National Fisheries Institute
National Milk Producers' Federation
National Peanut Growers Group
National Pork Producers Council
Rice Millers' Association
United Egg Producers
United Fresh Fruit and Vegetable Association

Processing, manufacturing, and marketing organizations
American Frozen Food Institute
American Meat Institute
Chocolate Manufacturers' Association of the U.S.A.
Corn Refiners Association
Food Marketing Institute
Grocery Manufacturers of America
National Food Processors Association
National Frozen Food Association
National Soft Drink Association
Peanut Butter and Nut Processors' Association

Public interest groups and professional societies
American Cancer Society
American Dietetic Association
American Heart Association
American School Food Service Association
Center for Science in the Public Interest
Food Research and Action Center
Public Voice for Food and Health Policy
Society for Nutrition Education

Private food producers
Cargill
ConAgra
Archer-Daniels-Midland
Mars
Pizza Hut
Safeway Stores
Ralston-Purina

Sources: Guither (1980) and Browne (1988).

In particular, agriculture lobbies sponsored 390 trips and paid more than $500,000 in honoraria to House members during the 101st Congress; of these trips, 239 went to members of the House Agriculture and Appropriations Committees. The most frequent corporate-sponsored traveler was Charles Stenholm (D-Tex), a senior member of the Agriculture Committee. Of his 50 paid trips, agricultural interest groups sponsored 37; they also provided $38,250 in honoraria (McCauley and Cohen 1991).

Election Campaign Contributions
In 1974, amendments to the Federal Election Campaign Act authorized formation of Political Action Committees (PACs) by corporations and other groups to collect and disburse voluntary campaign contributions. Although the law limits the amount of money that can be contributed to any one candidate, it does not restrict the number of candidates to whom contributions can be made or the number of PACs that can contribute to any one candidate. In 1974-5, 608 PACs contributed $12.5 million to election campaigns; by 1982, 3,371 PACs, nearly half of them corporate, were contributing $83 million (Berry 1984); and by the election of 1989-90, nearly 4,700 PACs were contributing more than $370 million to candidates (Federal Election Commission 1991b).

The size of the contribution to any one candidate typically varied from $500 to $2,000; however, such contributions could add up to substantial amounts. In 1989-90, Senators Robert Dole (R-Kan), Jesse Helms (R-NC), and Tom Harkin (D-Iowa), all members of the Committee on Agriculture, Nutrition, and Forestry, received respectively $308,000, $790,000, and $1.5 million in PAC contributions. These amounts all derived from contributions of $5,000 or less (Federal Election Commission 1991a).

Relatively few PACs represent food and agriculture interests. In 1978, 82 such PACs were identified, 46 of them producer groups contributing a total of $1.4 million. The largest contributor was the Associated Milk Producers PAC, which distributed a total of $456,000 among 37 candidates for the Senate and 185 candidates for the House (Guither 1980). PACs representing the dairy industry remain relatively large contributors; an analysis by Common Cause of Federal Election Commission data found that dairy groups contributed nearly $1.8 million to candidates in 1989-90. In comparison, beef PACs contributed just over $326,000 in that election. In the period from 1985 to 1990, dairy PACs contributed a total of $5.5 million and beef PACs $864,000 to election campaigns, but these amounts were greatly exceeded by the $25, $23, and $12 million donated by the real estate and construction, insurance, and banking industries, respectively (Common Cause, personal communication).

In the 1989-90 election campaign, food and agriculture PACs, though still in the minority, were well represented. Contributions came from the sugar, meat, dairy,

egg, soft-drink, wine and liquor, rice, fruit, vegetable, seed, and snack food industries, as well as from PACs representing growers, distributors, manufacturers, and promoters. As an example, Table VII.6.3 provides a partial listing of food and agriculture PACs that contributed to the 1989-90 campaign of Senator Harkin. PACs representing consumer, health, or public interest groups are rare. As noted by Senator Dole in an earlier context, "there aren't any Poor PACs or Food Stamp PACs or Nutrition PACs or Medicare PACs" (Berry 1984).

Nevertheless, experts differ on whether the small amount of money contributed by any one PAC is sufficient to buy influence. Some political commentators believe that the power of PACs is overrated (Bowers 1991), whereas others view it as insidious, largely because members of the House and Senate who hold important positions on powerful committees become "... more beholden to the economic interests of their committee constituents than to the interests of their district residents or to the President or party" (Califano 1992).

Table VII.6.3. *A partial list of food and agriculture Political Action Committees (PACs) contributing to the 1989-90 election campaign of Senator Tom Harkin (D-IA), a member of the Appropriations and Agriculture, Nutrition and Forestry Committees*

Amalgamated Sugar Company
American Agriculture Movement
American Crystal Sugar Association
American Dietetic Association
American Meat Institute
American Sheep Industry
American Sugar Cane League
American Sugarbeet Growers
Archer-Daniels-Midland
Bakery, Confectionary, and Tobacco Workers
Dairymen Inc.
Diamond Walnut Growers
Florida Sugar Cane League
Food Marketing Institute
General Mills
Hawaiian Sugar Planters
Land O' Lakes, Inc.
Mid-America Dairymen
Milk Marketing Inc.
National Broiler Council
National Cattlemen's Association
National Farmers Union
National Pork Producers Council
National Restaurant Association
National Turkey Federation
Ocean Spray Cranberries
Peanut PAC of Alabama
Southern Wine and Spirits
Sunkist Growers
United Egg Association
United Fresh Fruit and Vegetable Association
Wheat for Congress
Wine Institute

Source: Federal Election Commission (1991b).

One study found that members of the House of Representatives who received dairy PAC funds were almost twice as likely to vote for legislation to maintain price supports as those who did not; that supporters of maintenance received 2.5 times more PAC funds than opponents; and that the more PAC money members received, the more likely they were to support such legislation (Public Citizens' Congress Watch 1982). Most experts agree that PACs give the appearance of purchasing influence, whether or not they actually do so.

Revolving Door

The transformation of government officials into lobbyists and of lobbyists into government officials is commonly known as the "revolving door." By 1968, at least 23 former Senators and 90 former Congressmen had registered as lobbyists for private organizations (Congressional Quarterly 1968). Job substitutions between food producer lobbies and the USDA have been especially frequent and noticeable. At the USDA, as many as 500 agency heads and their staff members are chosen on the basis of political party, support from key politicians, and other political criteria rather than expertise. Such appointments are strongly influenced by special interest groups (Knutson et al. 1983).

In 1971, for example, USDA secretary Clifford Hardin traded places with Earl Butz, who was director of the Ralston Purina Company; Butz became USDA secretary and Hardin went to Ralston Purina. One report identified several assistant secretaries, administrators, and advisers who joined the USDA from positions with meat, grain, and marketing firms or who left the agency to take positions with food producers (Jacobson 1974). The chief USDA negotiator arranging for private companies to sell grain to the Soviet Union in 1972 soon resigned to work for the very company that gained the most from the transaction (Solkoff 1985). More recently, the appointment of JoAnn Smith, a former president of the National Cattlemen's Association, as chief of the USDA's food marketing and inspection division raised questions about apparent conflicts of interest when she approved the designation "fat-reduced beef" for bits of meat processed from slaughtering by-products and opposed an American Heart Association proposal to put a seal of approval on certain meat products low in fat (McGraw 1991).

Generic Advertising (Checkoff Programs)

In an effort to counteract declining consumption trends, Congress passed a series of food promotion and research acts that require producers of 15 specific commodities – among them beef, pork, dairy products, milk, and eggs – to deduct or "checkoff" a fee from sales. These strictly enforced fees are then used to promote the commodities (Becker 1991). Through these and more than 300 state programs, about 90 percent of all U.S. producers contributed more than $530 million to promote about 80 farm commodities in 1986 (Blisard and Blaylock 1989).

The two largest national checkoff funds are dairy and meat; they generated $194 and $84 million, respectively, in 1986 (Blisard and Blaylock 1989). About half the funds are distributed to state commodity boards and the other half to national promotion and research boards. The beef checkoff began as a voluntary program generating $31,000 in 1922. In the 1970s, as beef consumption began to decline, the National Cattlemen's Association started lobbying for a compulsory program through a campaign that involved PACs, letter writing, and personal visits to members of Congress by hundreds of cattle farmers. The legislation passed in 1985; beef lobbies are especially effective because cattlemen are distributed among a great many states, and beef sales amount to nearly $22 billion annually (Wilde 1992). The beef checkoff generated nearly $90 million in 1991 (Cattlemen's Beef 1991).

The various checkoff boards collect and spend the funds, award contracts, and sponsor advertising, research, and education programs. Although the legislation prohibits use of the funds for lobbying, the distinction between promoting a product to consumers and to lawmakers can be subtle. The boards are closely affiliated with lobbying groups (Becker 1991), some even sharing office space. The Cattlemen's Beef Promotion and Research Board, for example, shared an address with the National Cattlemen's Association, and the National Pork Board shared offices, staff, and telephone services with the National Pork Producers Council. The legislation actually specifies that a certain percentage of checkoff funds must be allocated to the commodity groups who nominate members of the promotion boards to be appointed by the USDA (Cloud 1989).

Although checkoff funds are supposed to be used for research as well as advertising, only a small fraction is used for that purpose. Between 1986 and 1989, the Beef Board spent nearly $106 million, of which only about 5 percent went toward research and only 1.4 percent toward development of leaner products. At the same time, the board paid more than $1 million each to movie stars Cybill Shepherd and James Garner for participating in a beef advertising campaign (Parrish and Silverglade 1990).

Checkoff programs attempt to convince consumers to choose one type of food product over another (Becker 1991). The Meat and Beef Boards, for example, aim to build demand for red meats and meat products (National Live Stock and Meat Board 1987); encourage consumers to view beef as wholesome, versatile, and ever lower in cholesterol; and educate doctors, nurses, dietitians, teachers, and the media about the nutritional benefits of beef (Cattlemen's Beef 1990). Similarly, the Dairy Boards promote consumption of cheese, milk, butter, and ice cream as the best sources of calcium and other nutrients (Westwater 1988). For the most part, studies have shown a positive relationship between such campaigns and sales for a wide range of commodities. From 1984 to 1990, for example, generic advertising was associated with significant increases in consumption of milk and cheeses (Blisard, Sun, and Blaylock 1991). The Beef Board has attributed the industry's increased relative strength to the checkoff program (Cattlemen's Beef 1991).

Checkoff supporters maintain that these programs benefit farmers at little cost to the USDA and provide useful information to consumers. Of concern, however, is the potential of checkoff programs to increase food costs and competition between commodity groups and to promote products high in fat, saturated fat, and cholesterol. Of even greater concern is the ability of lobbying groups to use the millions of dollars available from check-off funds to influence food and nutrition policies (Becker 1991).

Brand Advertising

In 1991, the annual cost of all food product advertising was $8 billion (Becker 1991). In that year, food companies that were among the top 100 U.S. advertisers spent $3.9 billion to promote their products. Three billion dollars of this amount was spent on television commercials, one-third of them for snacks and soft drinks. The leading national advertiser, Procter and Gamble, which sells food products, among others, spent nearly $2.3 billion on advertising, and McDonald's, eighth in rank, spent more than $764 million ("The 100 Leading National Advertisers" 1991).

Academic and Professional Support

Food companies routinely fund academic departments, research programs, individual investigators, and meetings, conferences, journals, and other activities of professional societies. For example, at least 16 food or nutritional supplement companies provide funding for the *Journal of Nutrition Education;* 22 support educational activities of the American Society for Clinical Nutrition; and Kraft General Foods supports a consumer hot line staffed by the American Dietetic Association.

One survey of university nutrition and food science departments identified frequent food industry payments to faculty for consulting services, lectures, membership on advisory boards, and representation at congressional hearings. This same study noted several departments receiving significant portions of their research budgets from food company grants. These faculty and departments may disclose corporate connections willingly but are rarely required to do so; they are usually grateful for the support and deny that it affects their views in any way (Rosenthal, Jacobson, and Bohm 1976).

Such conflicts of interest are not confined to the United States; a British study found that 158 of 246 members of national committees on nutrition and

food policy consulted for, or received funding from, food companies (Cannon 1987). Such relationships naturally raise questions about the ability of academic experts to provide independent opinions on policy matters that might affect their sources of funding.

Food Lobbies in Action

Dietary Goals for the United States

Aware of evidence that diets high in fat, saturated fat, cholesterol, sugar, and salt were associated with chronic diseases, the staff of the Senate Select Committee on Nutrition and Human Needs, chaired by George McGovern (D-SD), held hearings on dietary determinants of obesity, diabetes, and heart diseases in 1973, and produced a report on nutrition and chronic disease in 1974. In July 1976, the committee held further hearings on the role of American food consumption patterns in cancer, cardiovascular disease, and obesity (U.S. Senate Select Committee 1977e).

On the basis of evidence presented at these hearings, the staff produced the February 1977 report *Dietary Goals for the United States.* Consistent with American Heart Association recommendations, the report established six goals for dietary change: Increase carbohydrate intake to 55–60 percent of calories; decrease fat to 30 percent, saturated fat to 10 percent, and sugar to 15 percent of calories; reduce cholesterol to 300 milligrams per day and salt to 3 grams per day. To achieve these goals, the committee advised consumption of more fruits, vegetables, whole grains, poultry, and fish, but less meat, eggs, butterfat, whole milk, and foods high in fat (U.S. Senate Select Committee 1977a).

Many groups objected to one or another of these recommendations, but the advice to "eat less" brought immediate protest from the groups most affected – cattlemen, the dairy industry, and egg producers. The cattle industry, especially in McGovern's home state, pressured the committee to withdraw the report. "Here, after all, was the Congress of the United States telling the public not to eat their products" (Broad 1979). Meat and egg producers demanded and obtained additional hearings to express their views. In these hearings, a pointed exchange between Senator Robert Dole and Mr. Wray Finney, president of the National Cattlemen's Association, established the basis for compromise on the key recommendation (No. 2) to eat less meat:

> *Senator Dole:* I wonder if you could amend No. 2 and say "increase consumption of lean meat"? Would that taste better to you?
> *Mr. Finney:* "Decrease is a bad word, Senator." (U.S. Senate Select Committee 1977d).

Committee members who represented states with large producer constituencies demanded changes in the report. McGovern "said he did not want to disrupt the economic situation of the meat industry and engage in a battle with that industry that we could not win" (Mottern 1978). The report was revised to state, "choose meats, poultry, and fish which will reduce saturated fat intake" (U.S. Senate Select Committee 1977b). These statements and later versions of recommendations concerning meat intake are listed in Table VII.6.4.

When Nick Mottern, the staff member who wrote the original report, objected to the changes, he was asked to leave his position (Mottern 1978). Shortly thereafter, McGovern was quoted as saying about McDonald's and other fast-food companies that "on the whole, quick foods are a nutritious addition to a balanced diet," leading one reporter to suggest that "still another industry has thrown its weight around" (Broad 1979).

Despite such compromises, the *Dietary Goals* report established the basis of all subsequent dietary recommendations and altered the course of nutrition education in the United States. This contribution, however, was the Select Committee's last. Shortly after release of the report, the Senate abolished the committee and transferred its functions to the Nutrition Subcommittee of the newly constituted Committee on Agriculture, Nutrition, and Forestry as of the end of the year (Hadwiger and Browne 1978). In 1980, McGovern lost his bid for reelection.

Table VII.6.4. *Evolution of federal recommendations to reduce dietary fat through changes in meat consumption*

Year	Report, Agency	Recommendation
1977	*Dietary Goals*, U.S. Senate	Decrease consumption of meat
1977	*Dietary Goals*, 2d ed., U.S. Senate	Choose meats . . . which will reduce saturated fat intake
1979	*Healthy People*, DHEW	Relatively . . . less red meat
1979	*Food*, USDA	Cut down on fatty meats (2 servings of 2–3 ounces each)
1980	*Dietary Guidelines*, USDA and DHEW	Choose lean meat
1985	*Dietary Guidelines*, 2d ed., USDA and DHHS	Choose lean meat
1988	*Surgeon General's Report*, DHHS	Choose lean meats
1990	*Dietary Guidelines*, 3d ed., USDA and DHHS	Have 2 or 3 servings, with a daily total of about 6 ounces
1991	*Eating Right Pyramid*, USDA	Choose lean meat (2–3 servings or 5–7 ounces)

Healthy People

In 1979, reflecting the emerging consensus among scientists and health authorities that national health strategies should be "dramatically recast" to emphasize disease prevention, the Department of Health, Education, and Welfare (DHEW) issued *Healthy People*. This report announced goals for a 10-year plan to improve the health status of Americans. Its nutrition section recommended diets with fewer calories; less saturated fat, cholesterol, salt, and sugar; relatively more complex carbohydrates, fish, and poultry; and less red meat. The report, noting that more than half the U.S. diet consisted of processed foods rather than fresh agricultural produce, suggested that consumers pay closer attention to the nutritional qualities of such foods (USDHEW 1979).

Because dietary advice to restrict red meat and be wary of processed foods was certain to attract notice, *Healthy People* was released in July without a press conference as one of the final official acts of Joseph Califano, who had been fired from his position as DHEW secretary by President Carter the month before. Nevertheless, the report elicited a "storm" of protest from the meat industry. The president of the National Live Stock and Meat Board was quoted as saying, "The report begins with 'the health of the American people has never been better,' and we think it should have ended right there" (Monte 1979: 4).

Healthy People became the last federal publication ever to suggest that Americans eat less red meat. When later asked about this issue, Surgeon General Julius Richmond speculated that subsequent editions of this report might advise a switch to lean meat rather than a decrease in intake of red meat in general (USDA and USDHEW 1980).

USDA's Food Books

Because USDA nutritionists found diets that met the *Dietary Goals* to be "so disruptive to usual food patterns," they developed a series of publications under the generic title *Food* to inform the public about ways to modify the calorie, fat, sugar, and salt content of diets (Wolf and Peterkin 1984). This first USDA publication to address diet and chronic disease, *Food: The Hassle-Free Guide to a Better Diet*, was notable for its caution:

> Many scientists say the American diet is contributing to some of the chronic diseases that hit people in later life. . . . Other scientists believe just as strongly that the evidence doesn't support such conclusions. So the choice is yours. (USDA 1979)

USDA staff revised the Basic Four to display the food groups in a vertical format with the vegetable/fruit and bread/cereal groups located above the dairy and meat groups. At the bottom, they added a fifth group of foods - fats/sweets/alcohol - that keep bad "nutritional company" and are high in calories but low in essential nutrients and fiber. To reduce fat intake, they suggested, "cut down on fatty meats."

Food was the most requested USDA publication in 1979 (Carol Tucker Foreman, personal communication). After the 1980 election, however, under pressure from representatives of the meat, dairy, and egg industries who objected to the negative advice about fat and cholesterol and the placement of their products below fruits, vegetables, and grains, *Food* was not reprinted and all action on subsequent publications in the series was suspended. Eventually, the USDA gave its completed page boards for *Food II* to the American Dietetic Association, which published them as two separate booklets in 1982 ("ADA to Publish" 1982). *Food* became the last federal publication to use the phrase "cut down" in reference to meat (see Table VII.6.4).

1980 Dietary Guidelines

In February 1980, the USDA and DHEW announced joint publication of *Nutrition and Your Health: Dietary Guidelines for Americans.* The recommendations were to eat a variety of foods; maintain ideal weight; avoid too much fat, saturated fat, and cholesterol; eat foods with adequate starch and fiber; avoid too much sugar and too much sodium. Those who consume alcohol should do so in moderation (USDA and USDHEW 1980). Because these guidelines had replaced the unacceptable "eat less" phrases with the vague "avoid too much," agency officials did not expect objections from food producers. As stated by USDA secretary Bob Bergland during the press conference: "They feared we might issue edicts like eat no meat, or eggs, and drink less whole milk. They have been waiting for the other shoe to fall. There is no shoe" (Greenberg 1980).

Indeed, the Food Marketing Institute (FMI) commented that the *Guidelines* are "simple, reasonable and offer great freedom of choice," and the American Meat Institute (AMI) called them "helpful," noting that they provide "a continuing and central role for meat" (USDA and USDHEW 1980). But for certain food producers, especially the meat industry, even these mild recommendations went too far; they lobbied Congress to end funding for the publication (Broad 1981). One commentator observed that the purpose of the USDA is to make it easier for farmers to make money, a goal that is not well served by permitting federal agencies "to run loose on such politically sensitive matters as red meat, butter, and eggs" (Greenberg 1980).

On the eve of Appropriation Committee hearings on the *Guidelines,* called in July by Senator Thomas Eagleton (D-MO), a coalition of 104 consumer and health organizations criticized producer efforts to suspend distribution of the publication (Haas 1980). In part, this coalition had been created in response to an attack from the quasi-federal National Research Council (NRC). In May 1980, just three months after release of the *Dietary Guidelines,* the NRC issued its belated response to the *Dietary Goals.* This report, called *Toward Healthful Diets,* immediately became notorious for its conclusion that advice to restrict intake of fat or cholesterol was unwarranted (NRC 1980). One explanation for this conclusion was that the report had been financed by food industry donations, and that at least 4 of the 15 Food and Nutrition Board scientists responsible for its development had been funded by egg, meat, or other food producers (Wade 1980). Shortly after the election, but before the Reagan administration assumed office, Congress established a committee to revise the *Guidelines.*

At this point, the demise of the *Guidelines* seemed virtually assured. The new USDA secretary, John Block, was an Illinois hog farmer who during his confirmation hearings had remarked that he was "not so sure government should get into telling people what they should or shouldn't eat" (Maugh 1982). Through the revolving door, two high-level USDA positions had been filled by a former executive director of the American Meat Institute and a lobbyist for the National Cattlemen's Association. In addition, one of Block's first acts had been to close USDA's Human Nutrition Center, a research unit remarkable for its promotion of consumer rather than producer interests and its linking of research to policies, such as the *Dietary Guidelines* (Broad 1981).

Further attacks on dietary recommendations followed the release of *Diet, Nutrition, and Cancer,* an NRC report that had been commissioned by the National Cancer Institute during the last year of the Carter administration (NRC 1982). Food producers objected to the recommendation to reduce fat to 30 percent of calories by decreasing intake of high-fat meats. Livestock prices had dropped following release of the report, leading one food industry representative to observe that advice on diet and cancer "could be very harmful long term to the meat industry" ("Livestock Prices Fall" 1982: 44). In response to a request from the National Pork Producers Council, seven members of Congress called for an investigation of the cancer report (U.S. General Accounting Office 1984), and USDA political appointees drafted a report rejecting the 30 percent fat recommendation (Zuckerman 1984).

1985 Dietary Guidelines

When the committee to revise the *Dietary Guidelines* was finally appointed, five of the six USDA nominees appeared to be closely connected to the food industry ("USDA Readies" 1983). When informed of the committee's composition, a prospective Department of Health and Human Services (DHHS) appointee threatened to resign, stating that he had "no intention of being part of a process that guts the guidelines" ("Dietary Guidelines Review" 1982: 6). To the surprise of critics, however, the committee eventually made only minor changes in the text (USDA and USDHHS 1985), and USDA secretary Block, joined by the National Cattlemen's Association, endorsed the *Guidelines,* admitting that "all of us have changed in our thinking" ("Reagan Administration" 1985: 2).

This change in views was principally the result of an increasing consensus on the scientific basis of diet and disease relationships, as expressed in three groundbreaking reports released in 1988 and 1989. The first was the NRC's *Designing Foods,* which recommended reducing fat intake to 30 percent of calories and challenged the meat industry to develop methods to raise leaner beef; remarkably, this report had been requested by the USDA and issued with the full cooperation of meat producers (NRC 1988). It was followed by the 1988 *Surgeon General's Report on Nutrition and Health* (USDHHS 1988) and the 1989 NRC *Diet and Health* study (NRC 1989). All three of these reports identified reduction of fat – particularly saturated fat – as the primary dietary priority. Because none of these reports elicited much critical comment, consensus on dietary recommendations appeared to have been achieved (Nestle and Porter 1990).

1990 Dietary Guidelines

Despite the apparent consensus among medical and scientific authorities, USDA political appointees argued that recent research had established a need to reexamine the *Dietary Guidelines.* Invoking the lead agency mandate, they pressed for and obtained appointment of a committee to write a third edition. As appointed, the new committee consisted of nine nutrition scientists and physicians with few apparent ties to the food industry. Of 13 groups who submitted written comments during committee deliberations, however, 10 represented food producers, trade associations, or organizations allied with industry (USDA 1990).

This process revealed that the current consensus on dietary recommendations had been achieved at the expense of clarity. To address concerns that certain foods are increasingly perceived as "bad" and unfit for inclusion in healthful diets, the committee altered the phrasing of the *Guidelines* to make their tone more positive. For the phrase, "avoid too much," it substituted, "choose a diet low in." For the phrase "choose lean meat . . . ," it substituted, "have two or three servings of meat . . . with a daily total of about 6 ounces." Its one significant achievement was to suggest upper limits of 30 percent of calories from fat and 10 percent from saturated fat – precisely those recommended by the 1977 *Dietary Goals.* Lest these figures appear too restrictive, however, the new edition emphasized:

> [T]hese goals for fats apply to the diet over several days, not to a single meal or food. Some foods that contain fat, saturated fat, and cholesterol, such as meats, milk, cheese, and eggs, also contain high-quality protein and are our best sources of certain vitamins and minerals. (USDA and USDHHS 1990)

Unlike the previous two editions, the 1990 *Dietary Guidelines* elicited no noticeable complaints from food producers.

The Food Guide Pyramid

In 1991, the interference of food lobbies in dietary guidance policy again came to public attention, this time over a food guide with a simple, pyramid-shaped graphic. This project had originated a decade earlier in response to criticisms that consumers would have difficulty planning menus that met dietary recommendations (Peterkin, Kerr, and Shore 1978). In the heat of the controversy over the 1980 *Dietary Guidelines,* USDA nutritionists had rushed a menu guide into print just prior to President Reagan's inauguration (USDA 1981).

With the *Guidelines* under revision, the nutritionists began to develop a new guide that would specify the numbers and sizes of food servings needed to meet its recommendations. They presented this guide in a wheel format for use in an American Red Cross course in 1984 (Cronin, Shaw, Krebs-Smith et al. 1987). Food industry experts objected to the study guides prepared for the course and requested extensive changes in the text (Zuckerman 1984); the wheel also proved difficult for the public to understand. Thus, USDA staff initiated a consumer research study to identify a more useful format; they continued to use the portion sizes and numbers presented in the wheel in subsequent publications such as the 1990 *Dietary Guidelines.*

The research demonstrated that consumers preferred the *Pyramid* over many other designs. Its graphic displays grains and cereals at the wide base, vegetables and fruits in the band above, meats and dairy foods in the narrow upper band, and fats and sweets in the narrow peak. The band width represents the number of portions of each food group recommended by USDA. But unlike earlier graphics, the *Pyramid* format indicates that the daily diet should include more servings of grains, fruits, and vegetables than of meats, dairy products, and fats and sweets.

Preparation of the *Pyramid* graphic and accompanying brochure began in 1988. During the next two years, these materials were reviewed extensively, publicized widely, and fully cleared for publication; they were sent to the printer in February 1991 ("A Pyramid Topples" 1991). In April, representatives of the National Cattlemen's Association saw a *Washington Post* report on the *Pyramid* (Gladwell 1991) and joined other producer groups to protest that it "stigmatized" their products and should be withdrawn immediately (Burros 1991b; Combs 1991; Sugarman and Gladwell 1991). Two weeks later, the newly appointed USDA secretary, Edward Madigan, a former

Republican congressman from Illinois, announced that the *Pyramid* required further testing on children and poorly educated adults and postponed its publication. His explanation for this decision, however, was widely disbelieved ("A Pyramid Topples" 1991). Instead, observers attributed his actions to a direct response to pressures from meat producer lobby groups.

During the following year, the USDA issued a new and far more expensive contract to retest alternative designs on children and low-income adults. While this research was in progress, newspaper and magazine reporters wrote repeatedly of the *Pyramid* incident as an example of the conflict of interest created by the dual mandates of the USDA to protect American agricultural interests and to advise the public about food choices; they also used the incident as an illustration of the excessive and heavy-handed influence of lobbyists in federal policy decisions (Nestle 1993a).

The research tested the impact of alternative designs – particularly bowl shapes – that were preferred by most food industry representatives. When the messages conveyed by bowl designs were tested against those conveyed by pyramid designs, the results were nearly indistinguishable. At that point, the USDA was faced with a dilemma; the agency could choose the original *Pyramid* and risk embarrassment over the delay, additional costs, and continued opposition from food producers, or it could choose the bowl design for what might be interpreted as political rather than scientific reasons. Eventually, the USDA chose the pyramid design, perhaps because press reports kept public attention focused on the issue.

In April 1992, USDA released its *Food Guide Pyramid*. This publication seemed quite similar to the previous version. Its most significant difference concerned the numbers of recommended servings. These were relocated outside the triangle and reset in boldface type that two to three daily servings of meat and dairy foods were still recommended (USDA 1992). This change, which gave no indication that the servings were meant to be small and an upper limit, pleased food producers who made no further complaints about this publication (Nestle 1993a).

1995 Dietary Guidelines

Lobbying from meat and dairy groups was noticeably absent during preparation of the fourth edition of the *Dietary Guidelines* (USDA and USDHHS 1995). The recommendation for meat was similar to that offered in previous editions – "Choose two to three servings of lean . . . meats" – and the accompanying text suggested the benefits of eating moderately from the meat and beans group and avoiding sources of saturated fat in the diet. For the first time, the *Dietary Guidelines* recommended meals with rice, pasta, potatoes, or bread at the center of the plate and included a section on vegetarian diets. Nevertheless, release of this report elicited no comments from meat

producers, perhaps because the meat serving was defined as 2 to 3 ounces, in effect extending the recommended intake range to 9 ounces per day.

Concluding Comments

Classic studies have viewed lobbying as a healthy influence within the political system that keeps Congress informed about issues, stimulates public debate, and encourages participation in the political process. These views find undue lobby influence unlikely, as "it is virtually impossible to steal or buy a public policy decision of any consequence in Washington" (Milbrath 1963).

Nonetheless, the history of dietary guidance policy records the increasing involvement of food lobbies – and the incorporation of their views – into federal recommendations for chronic disease prevention. In 1956, USDA staff drafted the *Basic Four* and, as a courtesy, permitted industry representatives to review it. But since 1980, food industry representatives increasingly have participated in the design of dietary guidance materials as well as in their review. This change in role occurred as the goal of dietary recommendations shifted from prevention of nutrient deficiencies to prevention of chronic diseases and from "eat more" advice to "eat less," and as food lobbies more vigorously defended their products against such advice.

Through their connections in Congress and the USDA, and use of their strong financial base, food lobbies successfully convinced government policymakers to alter advice about meat, a principal source of dietary fat, from "eat less" to "choose lean" to "have 2-3 portions." Yet this policy shift occurred concurrently with increasing scientific consensus that reduced fat intake would improve the health of the public, that the 30 percent target level has been a political compromise, and that evidence all along has supported a level of 20 to 25 percent or less (Burros 1991a; Wynder, Weisburger, and Ng 1992). To some extent, it seems likely that contradiction between scientific consensus and federal advice is responsible for Americans' failing to reduce their fat intake (McGinnis and Nestle 1989; Putnam 1991; Nestle 1995).

It must be emphasized that lobbying strategies are entirely legal and available to consumer groups as well as to food producers. What should be clear from this discussion, however, is that producer groups possess far greater resources for lobbying activities than do either consumer groups or the federal government. The hundreds of millions of dollars available to the meat and dairy lobbies through checkoff programs, and the billions of dollars spent on food advertising, far exceed the $1.3 million spent by the USDA on dietary guidance and research in 1991 (USDA 1991). As one commentator stated, it is unfortunate that "good advice about nutrition conflicts with the interests of many big industries, each of which has more lobbying power than all the public-interest groups combined" (Jacobson 1974).

The controversy over the *Eating Right Pyramid* demonstrates that the connections between members of Congress, USDA officials, and food lobbies must continue to raise questions about the ability of federal officials to make independent policy decisions. Individuals concerned about such issues might consider whether the USDA's conflicts of interest have so impaired its ability to educate the public about diet and health that such functions should be transferred to an agency less tied to food industry groups. Also worth consideration is more forceful advocacy of consumer perspectives to Congress, reform of lobbying laws, reduced dependence on PAC expenditures, tighter restrictions on the revolving door, disclosure of funding sources by members of advisory committees, and education of the public on the extent of lobbying influence.

Marion Nestle

Bibliography

ADA to publish Food II magazine as separate booklets. 1982. *CNI Weekly Report* 12: 1-2.

American Enterprise Institute. 1980. *Proposals to revise the lobbying law.* Washington, D.C.

American Heart Association. 1961. Dietary fat and its relation to heart attacks and strokes. *Circulation* 23: 133-6.

Babcock, C. R. 1991. $100,000 political donations on the rise again. *The Washington Post,* September 30, pp. A1, A4.

Becker, G. S. 1991. Farm commodity promotion programs. *Congressional Research Service Report for Congress,* 91-151 ENR. Washington, D.C.

Berry, J. M. 1984. *The interest group society.* Boston, Mass.

Binder, D. 1995. Jamie Whitten, who served 53 years in House, dies at 85. *The New York Times,* September 10, p. 53.

Blisard, W. N., and J. R. Blaylock. 1989. *Generic promotion of agricultural products.* USDA Economic Research Service Agricultural Information Bulletin No. 565. Washington, D.C.

Blisard, W. N., T. Sun, and J. R. Blaylock. 1991. *Effects of advertising on the demand for cheese and fluid milk.* USDA Economic Research Service Staff Report No. AGES 9154. Washington, D.C.

Bowers, J. 1991. *Political action committees: Selected references, 1989-1991.* Congressional Research Service report for Congress 91-382 L. Washington, D.C.

Broad, W. J. 1979. The ever-shifting dietary goals. *Science* 204: 1177.

1981. Nutrition research: End of an empire. *Science* 213: 518-20.

Browne, W. P. 1988. *Private interests, public policy, and American agriculture.* Lawrence, Kan.

Burros, M. 1991a. Eating well. Experts agree on one thing at least: Even less fat is better. *The New York Times,* July 31, p. C4.

1991b. U.S. delays issuing nutrition chart. *The New York Times,* April 27, p. 9.

Califano, J. A. 1992. Throw the rascals out sooner. *The New York Times Book Review,* September 27, p. 7.

Cannon, G. 1987. *The politics of food.* London.

Cattlemen's Beef Promotion and Research Board. 1990. *The beef board annual report.* Englewood, Colo.

1991. *The beef board annual report: A new direction.* Englewood, Colo.

Cloud, D. S. 1989. When Madison Avenue talks, farm-belt members listen. *Congressional Quarterly* 3047-51, November 11.

Combs, G. F. 1991. What's happening at USDA. *AIN Nutrition Notes* 27: 6.

Congressional Quarterly Service. 1965. *Legislators and the lobbyists.* Washington, D.C.

1968. *Legislators and the lobbyists.* Second edition. Washington, D.C.

Cronin, F. J., A. M. Shaw, S. M. Krebs-Smith, et al. 1987. Developing a food guidance system to implement the dietary guidelines. *Journal of Nutrition Education* 19: 281-302.

deKieffer, D. E. 1981. *How to lobby Congress: A guide for the citizen lobbyist.* New York.

Dietary guidelines review. 1982. *CNI Weekly Report* 12 (48): 6.

Federal Election Commission. 1991a. *Candidate index of supporting documents.* September 26. Washington, D.C.

1991b. *PAC activity falls in 1990 election.* Press release, March 31. Washington D.C.

Gladwell, M. 1991. U.S. rethinks, redraws the food groups. *The Washington Post,* April 13, pp. A1, A7.

Greenberg, D. S. 1980. Nutrition: A long wait for a little advice. *Science* 302: 535-6.

Guither, H. D. 1980. *The food lobbyists: Behind the scenes of food and agri-politics.* Lexington, Mass.

Haas, E. 1980. *Community Nutrition Institute press release: Over 100 organizations protest industry efforts to suppress national dietary guidelines.* July 15. Washington, D.C.

Hadwiger, D. G., and W. P. Browne, eds. 1978. *The new politics of food.* Lexington, Mass.

Haughton, B., J. D. Gussow, and J. M. Dodds. 1987. An historical study of the underlying assumptions for United States food guides from 1917 through the basic four food group guide. *Journal of Nutrition Education* 19: 169-75.

Hill, M. M., and L. E. Cleveland. 1970. Food guides – their development and use. *USDA Nutrition Program News* July/October: 1-6.

Hunt, C. L. 1921. *A week's food for an average family.* USDA Farmers' Bulletin No. 1228. Washington, D.C.

Hunt, C. L., and H. W. Atwater. 1917. *How to select foods. I. What the body needs.* USDA Farmers' Bulletin 808. Washington, D.C.

Inter-Society Commission for Heart Disease Resources. 1970. Primary prevention of the atherosclerotic diseases. *Circulation* 42: A55-98.

Jacobson, M. 1974. *Nutrition scoreboard,* 197-8. New York.

Knutson, R. D., J. B. Penn, and W. T. Boehm. 1983. *Agricultural and food policy.* Englewood Cliffs, N.J.

Kramer, J. 1979. Agriculture's role in government decisions. In *Consensus and conflict in U.S. agriculture,* ed. B. L. Gardner and J. W. Richardson, 204-41. College Station, Tex.

Levenstein, H. 1988. *Revolution at the table: The transformation of the American diet.* New York.

Livestock prices fall after report ties fat in diet to cancer. 1982. *The Wall Street Journal,* June 17, p. 44.

Madison, J. 1787. The federalist no. 10. In *The federalist papers,* by A. Hamilton, J. Madison, and J. Jay, ed. G. Wills, 42–9. New York.

Maugh, T. H. 1982. Cancer is not inevitable. *Science* 217: 36–7.

McCauley, M., and A. Cohen. 1991. *They love to fly . . . and it shows: An analysis of privately-funded travel by members of the U.S. House of Representatives 101st Congress (1989-1990).* Washington, D.C.

McGinnis, J. M., and M. Nestle. 1989. The Surgeon General's report on nutrition and health: Policy implications and implementation strategies. *American Journal of Clinical Nutrition* 49: 23–8.

McGraw, M. 1991. A case of "very vested interest." *Kansas City Star,* December 10, p. A6.

Milbrath, L. W. 1963. *The Washington lobbyists.* Chicago.

Monte, T. 1979. The U.S. finally takes a stand on diet. *Nutrition Action* 6: 4.

Morgan, D. 1978a. "Plain, poor sister" is newly alluring. *The Washington Post,* July 4, pp. A1, A8.

1978b. Trying to lead the USDA through a thicket of politics. *The Washington Post,* July 5, p. A8.

Mottern, N. 1978. Dietary goals. *Food Monitor.* March/April: 8–10.

National Live Stock and Meat Board. 1987. *The meat board: Who? What? Why?* Chicago.

NRC (National Research Council). 1980. *Toward Healthful Diets.* Washington, D.C.

1982. *Diet, nutrition, and cancer.* Washington, D.C.

1988. *Designing foods: Animal product options in the marketplace.* Washington, D.C.

1989. *Diet and health: Implications for reducing chronic disease risk.* Washington, D.C.

Nestle, M. 1993a. Dietary advice for the 1990s: The political history of the Food Guide Pyramid. *Caduceus* 9: 136–53.

1993b. Food lobbies, the food pyramid, and U.S. nutrition policy. *International Journal of Health Services* 23: 483–96.

1995. Dietary guidance for the 21st century: New approaches. *Journal of Nutrition Education* 27: 272–5.

Nestle, M., and D. V. Porter. 1990. Evolution of federal dietary guidance policy: From food adequacy to chronic disease prevention. *Caduceus* 6: 43–67.

The 100 leading national advertisers. 1991. *Advertising Age* (September 25).

Paarlberg, D. 1964. *American farm policy: A case study of centralized decision-making.* New York.

Page, I. H., F. J. Stare, A. C. Corcoran, et al. 1957. Atherosclerosis and the fat content of the diet. *Circulation* 16: 163–78.

Parrish, R. D., and B. Silverglade. 1990. *Testimony on the beef and pork promotion and research programs before the Committee on Agriculture, Subcommittee on Livestock, Dairy, and Poultry, U.S. House of Representatives.* Washington, D.C.

Peterkin, B. B., R. L. Kerr, and C. J. Shore. 1978. Diets that meet the dietary goals. *Journal of Nutrition Education* 10: 15–18.

Public Citizens' Congress Watch. 1982. *An ocean of milk, a mountain of cheese, and a ton of money: Contributions from the dairy PAC to members of Congress.* Washington, D.C.

Putnam, J. J. 1991. Food consumption, 1970–90. *FoodReview* 14: 2–11.

A pyramid topples at the USDA. 1991. *Consumer Reports* 56: 663–6.

Raper, N. 1991. Nutrient content of the U.S. food supply. *FoodReview* 14: 13–17.

Reagan administration OK's dietary guidelines. 1985. *CNI Weekly Report,* September 26, p. 2.

Registered lobbyists. 1991. *Congressional Record* 137 (122): HL 287–372, August 15.

Rosenthal, B., M. Jacobson, and M. Bohm. 1976. Feeding at the company trough. *Congressional Record* H8974–8977, August 26.

Schriftgiesser, K. 1951. *The lobbyists.* Boston, Mass.

Solkoff, J. 1985. *The politics of food.* San Francisco.

Stiebeling, H. K., and M. M. Ward. 1933. *Diets at four levels of nutritive content and cost.* USDA Circular No. 296. Washington, D.C.

Sugarman, C., and M. Gladwell. 1991. Revised food chart killed. *The Washington Post,* April 17, p. A1.

Timmer, C. P., and M. C. Nesheim. 1979. Nutrition, product quality, and safety. In *Consensus and conflict in U.S. agriculture,* ed. B. L. Gardner and J. W. Richardson, 155–92. College Station, Tex.

USDA and HEW unveil guidelines for healthy eating. 1980. *CNI Weekly Report* 10 (6): 1–2.

USDA readies to carve up the dietary guidelines. 1983. *Nutrition Action* 10: 3–4.

USDA (U.S. Department of Agriculture). 1862. *Department of Agriculture Organic Act* 12 Stat. 317, May 15.

1958. *Food for fitness: A daily food guide.* Leaflet No. 424. Washington, D.C.

1979. *Food: The hassle-free guide to a better diet.* Home and Garden Bulletin No. 228. Washington, D.C.

1981. *Ideas for better eating: Menus and recipes to make use of the dietary guidelines.* Washington, D.C.

1990. *Report of the Dietary Guidelines Advisory Committee on the dietary guidelines for Americans.* No. 261–463/20444. Washington, D.C.

1991. *1990 report on USDA human nutrition research and education activities: A report to Congress.* Washington, D.C.

1992. *The Food Guide Pyramid.* HG-249. Hyattsville, Md.

USDA and USDHEW (U.S. Department of Agriculture and U.S. Department of Health, Education, and Welfare). 1980. *Nutrition and your health: Dietary guidelines for Americans.* Washington, D.C.

USDA and USDHHS (U.S. Department of Agriculture and U.S. Department of Health and Human Services). 1985. *Nutrition and your health: Dietary guidelines for Americans.* Second edition. Washington, D.C.

1990. *Nutrition and your health: Dietary guidelines for Americans.* Third edition. Washington, D.C.

1995. *Nutrition and your health: Dietary guidelines for Americans.* Fourth edition. Washington, D.C.

USDHEW (U.S. Department of Health, Education, and Welfare). 1979. *Healthy people: The Surgeon General's report on health promotion and disease prevention.* DHEW (PHS) 79-55071. Washington, D.C.

USDHHS (U.S. Department of Health and Human Services). 1988. *The Surgeon General's report on nutrition and health.* Washington, D.C.

U.S. General Accounting Office. 1984. *National Academy of Sciences' reports on diet and health – Are they credible and consistent?* GAO/RCED-84-109. Washington, D.C.

U.S. House of Representatives. 1988. *Rural development, agriculture, and related agencies appropriations bill, 1989: Report No 100-690.* June 10, p. 107. Washington, D.C.

U.S. Senate Committee on Governmental Affairs. 1991. *The federal lobbying disclosure laws: Hearings before the*

Subcommittee on Oversight of Government Management, S-Hrg. June 20, July 16, September 25, pp. 102–377.

U.S. Senate Select Committee on Nutrition and Human Needs. 1977a. *Dietary goals for the United States.* February. Washington, D.C.

　1977b. *Dietary goals for the United States.* Second edition. December. Washington, D.C.

　1977c. *Dietary goals for the United States - Supplemental views.* November. Washington, D.C.

　1977d. *Diet related to killer diseases. III. Hearings in response to dietary goals for the United States: re meat.* March 24. Washington, D.C.

　1977e. *Final report.* December. Washington, D.C.

U.S. Senate Special Committee to Investigate Political Activities, Lobbying, and Campaign Contributions. 1957. *Final Report.* Washington, D.C.

Wade, N. 1980. Food Board's fat report hits fire. *Science* 209: 248–50.

We feel compelled to break relations. 1980. *CNI Weekly Report* 10 (24): 4–5.

Westwater, J. J. 1988. Dairy farmers are pioneers in promotion. In Marketing U.S. agriculture, ed. Deborah Takiff Smith. *The . . . Yearbook of Agriculture,* 271–5. Washington, D.C.

Wilde, P. 1992. No "meating" of minds: Are federal agriculture and health departments heading for a showdown? *Vegetarian Times* 174 (February): 58–62, 97.

Wolf, I. D., and B. B. Peterkin. 1984. Dietary guidelines: The USDA perspective. *Food Technology* 38: 80–6.

Wynder, E. L., J. H. Weisburger, and S. K. Ng. 1992. Nutrition: The need to define "optimal" intake as a basis for public policy decisions. *American Journal of Public Health* 82: 346–50.

Zuckerman, S. 1984. Killing it softly. *Nutrition Action* (January–February): 6–10.

VII.7 ❧ Food Biotechnology: Politics and Policy Implications

Food biotechnology – the use of recombinant deoxyribonucleic acid (rDNA) and cell fusion techniques to confer selected characteristics upon food plants, animals, and microorganisms (Mittal 1992; Carrol 1993) – is well understood as a means to increase agricultural productivity, especially in the developing world. The great promise of biotechnology is that it will help solve world food problems by creating a more abundant, more nutritious, and less expensive food supply. This theoretical promise is widely appreciated and beyond dispute (Rogers and Fleet 1989; U.S. Congress 1992).

Nonetheless, food biotechnology has elicited extraordinary levels of controversy. In the United States and in Europe, the first commercial food products of genetic engineering were greeted with suspicion by the public, vilified by the press, and threatened with boycotts and legislative prohibitions. Such reactions reflect widespread concerns about the safety and

environmental impact of these products, as well as about their regulatory status, ethical implications, and social value. The reactions also reflect public fears about the unknown dangers of genetic engineering and deep distrust of the biotechnology industry and its governmental regulators (Davis 1991; Hoban 1995).

Biotechnology industry leaders and their supporters, however, dismiss these public concerns, fears, and suspicions as irrational. They characterize individuals raising such concerns as ignorant, hysterical, irresponsible, antiscientific, and "troglodyte," and they describe "biotechnophobia" as the single most serious threat to the development, growth, and commercialization of the food biotechnology industry (Gaull and Goldberg 1991: 6). They view antibiotechnology advocates as highly motivated and well funded and believe them to be deliberately "interweaving political, societal and emotional issues . . . to delay commercialization and increase costs by supporting political, non-science-based regulation, unnecessary testing, and labelling of foods" (Fraley 1992: 43).

In the face of this controversy, industry leaders have concluded that their most important challenge is to find ways to allay public fears (U.S. Congress 1991a) and to "assure the public that the new food technologies are not only beneficial to society, but safe" (Gaull and Goldberg 1991: 9).

This divergence in industry and public viewpoints can be traced to the conflict inherent in the two basic goals of the food biotechnology industry: (1) to benefit the public by developing agricultural products that will solve important food problems, and (2) to benefit the industry itself through the successful commercial marketing of these products. Although development of genetically engineered food products might well be expected to meet both goals, such is not always the case. One problem is the lack of a viable market, which experts view as a major barrier to research on food problems of the developing world (Hodgson 1992). Another centers on industry needs for rapid returns on investment; such needs constitute a driving force in decisions about research and development and cause industry leaders to view legitimate public questions about the use, safety, or social consequences of particular food products as threats to the entire biotechnology enterprise.

This chapter examines the reasons why so potentially useful an application of molecular techniques to food product development has elicited so great a level of controversy in the United States and elsewhere. Using the situation in the United States as a case study, it reviews key issues of economics, marketing, and risk that have affected the development and implementation of regulatory policies for the commercial products of food biotechnology, particularly those that affect food safety, allergenicity, environmental impact, and intellectual property rights. It also addresses issues that have influenced public perceptions of these products and describes how these issues have affected industry and public responses to the first genetically engineered food products released in the United States. Finally, it suggests implications of the present controversy for future product development, industry actions, and public policies.

The Promise

There seems little doubt that biotechnology holds great promise for addressing world food problems, most notably the overall shortfall in food production now expected early in the twenty-first century (Fraley 1992). No theoretical barriers impede the use of the techniques of molecular and cellular genetics to improve the quantity and quality of the food supply, to increase food safety, and to reduce food costs (Reilly 1989; U.S. Congress 1992; Hayenga 1993). Table VII.7.1 lists the wide range of potential applications of food biotechnology that as of the mid-1990s were under investigation or are theoretically possible. Such applications could greatly increase world food production, especially given the conditions of poor climate and soil typical of many developing countries (Swaminathan 1982).

Table VII.7.1. *Theoretical and current applications of food biotechnology*

Improve the flavor, texture, freshness, or nutrient content of fruit and vegetables.
Modify seed storage proteins to increase their concentration of limiting amino acids such as lysine or tryptophan.
Alter the chain length and degree of saturation of plant seed oils.
Increase plant production of specialty chemicals such as sugars, waxes, phytooxidants, or pharmaceutically active chemicals.
Increase levels of vitamins and other nutrients in plant food crops.
Decrease levels of caffeine or other undesirable substances in plant food crops.
Increase resistance of crops to damage by insect or microbial pests.
Increase resistance of crops to "stress" by frost, heat, salt, or heavy metals.
Develop herbicide-resistant plants to improve weed control.
Enable crop plants to be grown under conditions of low input of fertilizers, pesticides, or water.
Enable major crop plants to fix atmospheric nitrogen.
Develop plant foods containing antigens that can vaccinate humans against disease.
Increase the efficiency of growth and reproduction of food-producing animals.
Create disease-resistant animals.
Develop animal veterinary vaccines and diagnostic tests.
Allow cows to produce milk containing recombinant human milk proteins that can be used in infant formulas.
Create microorganisms, enzymes, and other biological products useful in food processing.
Develop microorganisms capable of converting environmental waste products – plastics, oil, pesticides, or PCBs – into usable animal feeds.

The potential for such improvements in the food supply constitute the principal basis for industry and government conclusions that "biotechnology is the most important scientific tool to affect the food economy in the history of mankind" (Gaull and Goldberg 1991: 150), that "biotechnology promises consumers better, cheaper, safer foods" ("Biotechnology Promises" 1990: 1), and that "genetic engineering and biotechnology will create miracles to help us feed a hungry world efficiently and economically" (Sullivan 1991: 97).

Such promises, however, have not yet been fulfilled, nor are they likely to be realized in the immediate future (Messer and Heywood 1990), principally because many of the applications listed in Table VII.7.1 pose biological and technical problems of formidable complexity (Barton and Brill 1983; American Medical Association 1991). For example, many hundreds of as yet uncharacterized genes appear to be involved in the reproduction of corn (Kilman 1994b), and the more than 350 varieties of cassava (manioc) grown throughout the world seem especially resistant to transgenic transformations (Beachy 1993). But the slow progress of biotechnology in addressing world food problems should not imply that such problems cannot be solved. Given sufficient time, commitment, and funding support, the technical barriers almost certainly can be overcome.

Economic Issues

Costs and Benefits

Technical problems, however, are not the most important barriers to the application of food biotechnology to world agricultural productivity. Instead, the greatest barrier derives from the need of the industry to recover the costs of research and development and to maximize return on investment (Harlander 1989). Research costs are not trivial: The average genetically modified plant requires about $10 million (U.S.) to develop and about six years to become marketable (Ollinger and Pope 1995). Thus, the expected returns on such an investment need to be substantial (U.S. Congress 1991a). Although no products had as yet been brought to market, food biotechnology was considered in the early 1990s to have "a huge potential to make money" (Kim 1992a: B1). At that time some experts suggested that the value of the industry would increase to at least $50 billion by the year 2000 (Leary 1992a) and that the prices of biotechnology stocks would rise by 25 percent annually well into the 1990s (Somerville 1993).

To date, however, stock market returns have not reflected such projections. Although the biotechnology industry increased in sales, revenues, and numbers of companies and employees from 1989 to 1993, net losses also increased steadily during that period (Waldholz 1994). One notable exception has been the Monsanto Company; its stock prices gained 75 percent in 1995 (Fritsch and Kilman 1996) and another 70 percent in 1996 (Wadman 1996). Monsanto officials estimated that their products of plant biotechnology would earn $2 billion by the year 2000 and that sales would grow to $6 or $7 billion by 2005 and to $20 billion by 2010 (Feder 1996).

The generally poor performance of other food biotechnology stocks has been attributed to uneven management, corporate shortsightedness, and product failures (Hamilton 1994). It also has been attributed to lack of government investment. Although overall federal investment in biotechnology research exceeded $4 billion in 1994, only 5 percent of these funds supported agricultural projects; in contrast, 41 percent were applied to drug development (Caswell, Fuglie, and Klotz 1994). By the mid-1990s, only a few products had come to market, and their degree of acceptability was as yet unknown. The resulting uncertainties in profitability explain industry preoccupation with issues of federal regulation, intellectual property, and public perception (Fraley 1992).

The need for return on investment has encouraged the industry to focus on the development of products that are most technically feasible, rather than those that might be most useful to the public or to developing countries. To date, food biotechnology research has tended to concentrate on agronomic traits that most benefit agricultural producers and processors. These include control of insects, weeds, plant diseases, and ripening, and production of crops that will resist insects and tolerate herbicides (Office of Planning 1988; Olempska-Beer et al. 1993). Research also has focused on the development of foods that will last longer on the shelf and cost less to process (U.S. Congress 1991a; Barnum 1992). A 1988 survey of 74 food processing firms that used biotechnology methods found that of their research projects, 27 percent were devoted to enzymes (such as those used in cheese manufacture), 15 percent to sweeteners, 11 percent to flavors, fragrances, and colors for prepared food products, and 10 percent to better detection of contaminants; the remaining 37 percent were concentrated on product development and processing methods (Reilly 1989). A more recent study reported that chemical and pesticide companies have obtained 41 percent of all permits for field testing of genetically engineered plants (Ollinger and Pope 1995).

In 1990, the leading 36 agrochemical and agricultural biotechnology companies together spent nearly $400 million on such research and development, but an order of magnitude less ("puny" by comparison) on projects designed to address agricultural problems of the developing world (Hodgson 1992: 49). Such problems – and their biotechnological solutions – are well defined (Bokanga 1995; Knorr 1995). Although many sources of private and public funding are available to support biotechnology projects in developing countries (Chambers 1995), these are fragmented, poorly coordinated, and often promote donors' priorities rather than those of the recipients (Messer 1992). One well-established research institute dedicated to improving crops in developing countries reports little success in obtaining industry financing or support beyond the permission to use patent-protected techniques "for specific crops under certain circumstances" (Beachy 1993: 61). Such observations have led commentators to conclude: "Nearly 20 years into the gene-splicing revolution, the industry has ballooned to well over 1,000 public or private companies that have raised about $20 billion. Yet no one has cured cancer or produced a bioengineered miracle of loaves and fishes for a hungry Third World. The industry is still peddling dreams . . ." (Hamilton 1990: 43).

Marketing Barriers

To assure adequate returns on investment, the biotechnology industry must create and sell new products. These products, however, compete with other products in a market that is already highly competitive because the United States vastly overproduces food (Stillings 1994). In 1990, for example, the U.S. food supply made available an average of 3,700 kcal/day for every man, woman, and child in the country (Putnam and Allshouse 1996), even though adult men require two-thirds that amount, women about half, and children even less (National Research Council 1989). Because the amount of energy that any one person can consume is finite, such overproduction implies that a choice of any one food product will preclude choice of another.

Food marketers compete for consumer purchases through two principal means: advertising and new product development. Retail sales of food generated $791 billion in 1994. In the same year, food marketers spent $9.8 billion on direct consumer advertising and about twice that amount on retail promotion in trade shows, product placements, point-of-purchase campaigns, and other incentives. From 1984 to 1994, food companies introduced 125,000 new products into U.S. markets, more than 15,000 of them in 1994 alone (Economic Research Service 1994; Gallo 1995). Nevertheless, such efforts have failed to improve overall growth in the food processing sector, which has increased at less than 1 percent per year since the late 1940s, a rate considered stagnant by comparison to other industries. In so competitive an environment, biotechnology is seen as a crucial force for development of new products that will increase the country's overall economic productivity (Reilly 1989).

Risk Issues

Tryptophan Supplements

From the standpoint of the biotechnology industry and its supporters, genetically engineered foods are no different from foods produced by conventional genetic crosses. Therefore, industry supporters argue that any risks associated with these foods are extremely small and greatly outweighed by their benefits (Gaull and Goldberg 1991; Miller 1991; Falk and Bruening 1994). Critics, however, insist that food biotechnology raises safety concerns that in the absence of prior experience are difficult to define, predict, or quantify. They point, as an example, to the case of tryptophan supplements to illustrate the unknown hazards of commercial biotechnology.

In 1989, health officials linked tryptophan supplements from a single manufacturer to an unusual syndrome of muscle pain, weakness, and increased blood levels of certain white cells (eosinophils), a constellation of symptoms termed eosinophilia-myalgia syndrome (Centers for Disease Control 1989). Eventually, more than 1,500 cases of illness and nearly 40 deaths were attributed to the use of such supplements as a self-medication for insomnia and other conditions (Roufs 1992; Mayeno and Gleich 1994). Because tryptophan is a normal amino acid component of all proteins, investigators believed that toxic contaminants must have developed during the manufacturing process. This process involved the creation of a strain of bacteria genetically manipulated to produce high levels of tryptophan and extraction of this amino acid through a series of purification steps (Fox 1990).

To date, characterization of the toxic components remains incomplete (Mayeno and Gleich 1994). Although it appears unlikely that the genetic engineering methods were directly at fault (Philin et al. 1993), their use to modify a bacterial strain created a situation in which toxic products were formed, albeit inadvertently (Aldhous 1991). This example suggests that concerns about the unknown hazards of biotechnology have some basis in experience.

Allergenicity

Because genes encode proteins, and proteins are allergenic, the introduction of allergenic proteins into previously nonallergenic foods could be another unintended consequence of plant biotechnology. In a finding described as "Another shadow . . . cast over the agricultural biotechnology industry . . ." (Winslow 1996: B6), researchers have now demonstrated that an allergenic protein from Brazil nuts can be transferred to soybeans, and that people with demonstrable allergies to Brazil nuts react similarly to soybeans that contain the Brazil-nut protein (Nordlees et al. 1996).

The Brazil-nut soybeans were developed as a means to increase the content of the amino acid methionine in animal feeds, which must otherwise be supplemented with methionine to promote optimal growth. The Brazil-nut protein is especially rich in methionine and its gene was a logical choice as a donor. Nuts, however, are often allergenic, and the investigators happened to have collected serum samples from people known to be allergic to Brazil nuts. Thus, they had in place all the components necessary to test for allergies to Brazil-nut proteins. Such compo-

nents are rarely available for testing other potentially allergenic proteins, however.

Adverse reactions to food proteins can be documented in just 2 percent of adults and 8 percent of children (Sampson and Metcalfe 1992), but many more people are expected to develop food sensitivities as proteins are increasingly added to commercially prepared foods. Soy proteins, for example, already are very widely used in infant formulas, meat extenders, baked goods, and dairy replacements. Most biotechnology companies are using microorganisms rather than food plants as gene donors. Although these microbial proteins do not appear to share sequence similarities with known food allergens (Fuchs and Astwood 1996), few of them have as yet entered the food supply. At the present time, their allergenic potential is uncertain, unpredictable, and untestable (Nestle 1996).

As discussed in the following section, allergenicity raises complicated regulatory issues. Under a Food and Drug Administration (FDA) policy established in 1992, the manufacturer of the Brazil-nut soybeans was required to – and did – consult the FDA about the need for premarket testing. Because testing proved that the allergenic protein had been transmitted, the company would have been required to label its transgenic soybeans. Because the company had no simple method in place to separate soybeans intended for animal feed from those intended for human consumption, it withdrew its transgenic soybeans from the market. This action was interpreted by supporters of the FDA policy as evidence of its effectiveness.

Others, however, viewed this event as further evidence that the FDA policy could not protect consumers against lesser-known transgenic allergens to which they might be sensitive and, therefore, favored industry. The lack of a requirement for labeling was of particular concern, as avoidance is often the only effective way to prevent allergic reactions. In 1993, the FDA requested public comment on whether and how to label food allergens in transgenic foods (FDA 1993). Then, in 1994, the FDA drafted a rule that would require companies to inform the agency when developing new transgenic foods, in part to help resolve safety issues related to allergenicity. Implementation of such a rule seemed unlikely, however, especially because the biotechnology industry demanded that any such requirement be limited in scope and "sunset" after three years ("Bio Favors" 1994). To date, the FDA has not reported or acted on the public comments related to labeling of transgenic allergens.

Policy Issues

Regulation

Current debates about the regulation of food biotechnology center on a conflict between issues of safety on the one hand and a broad range of ecological, societal, and ethical issues on the other. For the industry and its supporters, safety is the only issue of relevance. Because the safety of most genetically engineered products is well supported by science, regulations appear to create unnecessary barriers to further research and economic growth (Gaull and Goldberg 1991; Miller 1991). For critics, however, regulations must be designed to protect the public not only against known safety risks but also against those that cannot yet be anticipated (Mellon 1991). In addition, as discussed in the next sections, critics view safety as only one component of a far broader range of concerns about the impact of biotechnology on individuals, society, and the environment – issues that might also demand regulatory intervention. For government officials, regulation of food biotechnology must find the proper balance between oversight of the industry and encouragement of its efforts to develop and market new food products (U.S. General Accounting Office 1993). Thus far, the balance achieved by existing regulatory policies has satisfied neither the industry nor consumer groups.

Table VII.7.2 outlines key historical events in the development of policies for regulation of food biotechnology. This history has resulted in current regulatory policies that affect three key areas of concern: food safety, environmental protection, and intellectual property rights.

Table VII.7.2. *Key events in the history of the commercialization of food products of biotechnology in the United States*

1930	Congress passes Plant Patent Act, extending protection to distinct, asexually propagated varieties.
1970	Plant Variety Protection Act extends patent rights to new sexually propagated plant varieties.
1973	Cohn and Boyer clone insulin gene using rDNA technology.
1975	Asilomar Conference suggests guidelines for rDNA research.
1976	Genentech established as the first company dedicated to exploitation of rDNA technology. NIH publishes safety guidelines for rDNA research.
1980	U.S. Supreme Court rules that microorganisms may be patented (*Diamond v. Chakrabarty*); first patent issued for rDNA construction to Cohn and Boyer. Genentech stock sets Wall Street record (share price rises from $35 to $89 in 20 minutes). Congress passes amendments to Patent Acts allowing nonprofit institutions and small businesses to retain titles to patents developed with federal funds.
1982	Recombinant insulin approved for use. Transgenic plant prodcued using *agrobacterium* transformation system.
1983	A plant gene is transferred from one species to another. Executive order permits large businesses to hold title to patents developed with federal funds.
1985	The Environmental Protection Agency (EPA) issues use permit to Advanced Genetic Sciences for release of organisms genetically engineered to lack ice-nucleation proteins. Patent Office extends protection to corn with increased levels of tryptophan (*ex parte* Hibberd). FDA authorizes sales of meat and milk from cows treated with recombinant bovine somatotropin (rbST); reaffirms safety of these foods in 1988, 1989, and 1990.
1986	Office of Science and Technology Policy issues Coordinated Framework for the Regulation of Bio-Technology, partitioning regulatory responsibility among USDA, EPA, FDA, and, to a lesser extent, NIH (51 FR 23302, June 26).
	Congress passes Technology Transfer Act permitting companies to commercialize government-sponsored research. USDA develops transgenic pigs carrying the gene for human growth hormone.
1987	Tomatoes with a gene for insect resistance are field-tested. USDA requires field-testing permits only for genetically engineered organisms that present risks to plants (52 FR 22892, July 16).
1988	Patent Office extends patent protection to genetically engineered animals.
1990	Food and Drug Administration (FDA) approves recombinant chymosin (rennet) as generally recognized as safe (GRAS). NIH issues statement that rbST is safe.
1992	FDA announces policy on foods derived from new plant varieties (57 FR 22984, May 29). USDA grants Calgene, Inc. permission to field-test the Flavr Savr tomato.
1993	FDA requests data and information on labeling issues related to foods derived from biotechnology (58 FR 25837, April 28); approves rbST for commercial use (58 FR 59946, November 12); requests public comment on whether and how to label food allergens in transgenic foods. Congress issues moratorium on use of rbST. Patent Office resumes granting patents on genetically engineered animals.
1994	Congressional moratorium on rbST expires.
	USDA reaffirms policies that genetically engineered livestock and poultry are subject to existing regulations for slaughter, research, and inspection (59 FR 12582, March 17).
	FDA publishes interim guidance on voluntary labeling of milk from cows treated with rbST and forbids statements such as "rbST-free" (59 FR 6279, February 10); concludes consultation with Calgene, Inc., finding no significant difference between the Flavr Savr and other tomatoes with a history of safe use (59 FR 26647, May 23); approves use of aminoglycoside 3'-phosphotransferase II (the kanamycin-resistance gene) for use in developing new varieties of tomatoes, oilseed rape, and cotton (59 FR 26700, May 23); concludes consultation approving seven other genetically altered plants, including tomatoes, squash, potato, cotton, and soybeans.
	EPA announces that federal pesticide laws will apply to toxins and other substances introduced into crop plants through genetic engineering (59 FR 60496, November 23).
1996	Congress requires USDA to discontinue its advisory committee on food biotechnology and close its Office of Agricultural Biotechnology.
	Allergen from Brazil nuts is transmitted to transgenic soybeans; transgenic herbicide resistance is transmitted to weeds, raising environmentalist concerns.
	Monsanto plants Bt cotton, herbicide (Roundup)-resistant soybeans. Ciba-Geigy plants herbicide-resistant corn. Both encounter consumer resistance in Europe. The European Union approves the soybeans, requires committee discussion of the corn, approves the corn but requires labeling of transgenic crops.

Table VII.7.3. *Safety issues raised by food biotechnology*

Unanticipated health effects resulting from genetic manipulations.
Increase in levels of naturally occurring toxins or allergens.
Activation of dormant toxins or allergens.
Introduction of known or new toxins, allergens, or antinutrients.
Adverse changes in the composition, absorption, or metabolism of key nutrients.
Increase in antibiotic-resistant microorganisms through use of antibiotic marker genes.
Transmission of herbicide resistance to weeds.
Adverse changes in the nutrient content of animal feed.
Increased levels of toxins in plant by-products fed to animals.

Food Safety

From the first, gene cloning experiments elicited safety concerns, mainly focused on the potential hazards of releasing new organisms with unknown properties into the environment. At a conference in 1975, scientists suggested stringent guidelines for research studies employing recombinant DNA techniques. The following year, the National Institutes of Health required researchers to follow similar guidelines. In subsequent years, as understanding of the techniques improved, concerns about safety diminished and the guidelines were modified accordingly. Nevertheless, common genetic methods for food modification involving, for example, bacteria that cause crown gall (a plant disease), marker genes for

antibiotic resistance, and insertion of genes from one living species into another, continued to elicit debate about the known and unknown hazards of such techniques (International Food Biotechnology Council 1990). Table VII.7.3 summarizes the principal safety issues that have been raised by the use of food biotechnology.

In 1986, the White House Office of Science and Technology Policy (OSTP) developed a "Coordinated Framework" for regulating biotechnology based on the premise that its products were no different from those developed through conventional techniques, and that existing laws and agencies were sufficient for their regulation. OSTP specified the distribution of regulatory responsibility among the various federal agencies. Under laws then in effect, responsibility for the regulation of food biotechnology involved no less than three offices reporting directly to the president; four major federal agencies; eight centers, services, offices, or programs within agencies; and five federal committees – all operating under the authority of 10 distinct acts of Congress (U.S. Congress 1992).

As might be expected, critics immediately identified a substantial lack of coordination, duplication of effort, overlapping responsibility, and gaps in oversight in this regulatory framework (Mellon 1988; Fox 1992). Because the principal laws affecting food safety were written before biotechnology became an

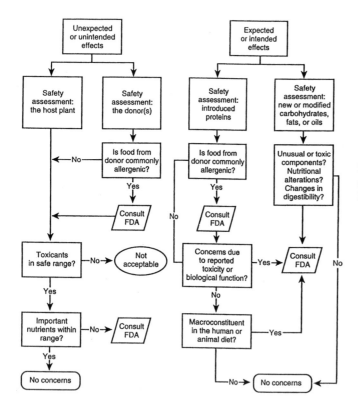

Figure VII.7.1. Food and Drug Administration Policy guidelines for regulation of foods developed through biotechnology. (From Food and Drug Administration 1992.)

issue, they did not necessarily apply to the new methods (Browning 1992). Thus, the confusing and uncertain regulatory status of recombinant products stimulated the food biotechnology industry to demand more precise guidance from the FDA. The President's Council on Competitiveness, a group dedicated to reducing regulations that impede industry, strongly supported such demands (Leary 1992b).

In response, the FDA developed a formal policy for the regulation of plant foods produced through biotechnology (FDA 1992). The agency designed this policy to be "scientifically and legally sound and . . . adequate to fully protect public health while not inhibiting innovation" (Kessler et al. 1992: 1832). This policy framework is summarized in Figure VII.7.1. The policy presumed that foods produced through rDNA techniques raised no new safety issues and could be regulated by the FDA's postmarket authority for foods "Generally Recognized as Safe" (GRAS). Therefore, safety evaluation would focus on changes in the "objective characteristics" of foods – new substances, toxins, allergens, or nutrients – and not on the techniques used to produce them. Under this policy, the FDA would invoke its testing requirements for new food additives, and would require industry consultation, only if the transgenic foods contained unusual or potentially toxic components (e.g., allergens). This new biotechnology policy required no premarket safety evaluation, premarket approval by the FDA, or special labeling of the new foods.

The response of the industry to these "election-year efforts by the White House to provide . . . as much regulatory relief as possible," was enthusiastic and viewed as "a very strong incentive for investment in the agricultural/food biotechnology area" (Ingersoll 1992: B1). One investment analyst summarized the new policy as an "assurance that after all a company's planning for a picnic, the government won't rain on it" (Kim 1992b: B3).

By contrast, consumer groups criticized the policy as inadequate to protect public safety and threatened to respond with mail campaigns and legal challenges (Hoyle 1992). A group of leading chefs in New York City called for an international boycott of genetically engineered foods, with one quoted as saying:

> I don't want a biotechnician in a lab coat telling me it's a better tomato . . . I think mother nature does a great job on her own. These people are tampering with the ecosystem and will cause problems. But what is most disturbing to me is the idea of selling the food without a label. ("Chefs Urge Boycotting" 1992: C6)

Critics of the policy were especially concerned about the lack of requirements for premarket testing and labeling (Hopkins, Goldburg, and Hirsch 1991). Commentators wondered whether this policy of "least regulatory resistance" actually might increase public suspicion of genetically engineered foodstuffs

(Hoyle 1992), especially in light of increasing press attention to "Frankenfoods" (O'Neill 1992). In response to such concerns, a federal study recommended formal review of the entire federal regulatory framework for food biotechnology in order to establish a better regulatory balance between promotion of the industry and protection of the public (U.S. General Accounting Office 1993).

Despite the controversy, the FDA implemented its policy. By late 1994, the agency had approved the marketing of tomatoes genetically engineered to reach optimal ripening after they were picked, milk from cows treated with a recombinant growth hormone, a virus-resistant squash, an insect-resistant potato, an herbicide-resistant cotton (used to make seed oil for animal feed), and herbicide-resistant soybeans (Associated Press 1994).

Environmental Impact

The "Coordinated Framework" affirmed that the U.S. Department of Agriculture (USDA) and the Environmental Protection Agency (EPA) were the primary agencies responsible for regulating agricultural biotechnology (see Table VII.7.2). Under the authority of two laws – the Federal Insecticide, Fungicide, and Rodenticide Act (FIFRA) and the Toxic Substances Control Act (TSCA) – the EPA was authorized to regulate genetically engineered organisms used to control insects and other pests, including those viral and bacterial, as well as any genetically engineered chemicals that might be hazardous to humans or to the environment. The EPA classified rDNA as such a substance and began to require biotechnology companies to obtain permits prior to the manufacture or release of their agricultural products (Caswell et al. 1994).

EPA policies were designed to address concerns that widespread agricultural use of new kinds of living species might present direct risks to human health. Such risks, however, are seen as minimal by environmentalists as well as by experts sympathetic to the industry (Mellon 1988; Miller 1994). Instead, the chief concern of environmental advocates is that agricultural biotechnology poses uncertain – but potentially grave – ecological risks. They offer considerable evidence to support the possibility that biotechnological organisms might displace existing plants and animals, create new plant pathogens, disrupt ecosystems, reduce crop diversity, and change climate patterns (Mellon 1988; Rissler and Mellon 1993). In addition, environmentalists are even more concerned about the impact of biotechnology on ongoing efforts to promote more widespread use of sustainable agricultural practices. They note, for example, that a large proportion of agricultural biotechnology research is dedicated to the development of herbicide-resistant crops, and that such research stimulates reliance on chemical herbicides to manage pests (Goldburg et al. 1990).

Thus, the EPA's 1994 decision to apply federal pesticide laws to toxins and other pesticidal substances introduced into crop plants through rDNA techniques was especially controversial. The biotechnology industry opposed it as an anachronistic and scientifically indefensible decision and noted that the EPA should instead have considered a risk-based regulatory system focusing on the organisms themselves rather than on the processes by which they were created. For the industry, the EPA decision would undoubtedly "exert a profoundly negative effect" on research into biological pest management strategies, particularly those unlikely to provide a sufficient financial return (Miller 1994: 1817).

Environmental advocates, although "pleased that EPA plans to regulate such crops the way it regulates traditional chemical pesticides," were also dissatisfied; they noted that the EPA rules focused "too narrowly on the development of genetically engineered, toxin-producing crops," and were insufficiently attentive to the potential hazards of herbicide-resistant crops that were virtually certain to bring about increases in the use of potentially damaging herbicides (Environmental Defense Fund 1994: 1). The marketing by the Monsanto Company of soybeans genetically engineered to be resistant to Roundup, a widely used herbicide also produced by that company, has only heightened such concerns (Feder 1996; Fritsch and Kilman 1996).

Environmentalist doubts about the adequacy of EPA regulatory policies were further stimulated by two events in 1996. That year, farmers planted 2 million acres with cotton engineered by the Monsanto Company to contain Bt *(Bacillus thuringiensis)*, a soil bacterium that produces a compound toxic to cotton bollworms and other common insect pests. Bt has long been a key component of pest management in sustainable agricultural systems. When the Bt crop failed to protect thousands of acres of cotton against bollworms, observers feared that so large a planting had induced selection for insects resistant to Bt, thereby rendering the toxin useless for sustainable or any other type of agriculture (Kaiser 1996). EPA officials were reported to have asked Monsanto to test the surviving bollworms for Bt resistance, but to have admitted ". . . that further evaluation of the crop is entirely dependent on Monsanto's own reporting" (Benson, Arax, and Burstein 1997: 68).

Also in 1996, researchers reported that oilseed rape (canola) plants genetically engineered to resist herbicides readily transmitted herbicide resistance to related weed plants – plants that could reproduce rapidly (Mikkelsen, Anderson, and Jorgensen 1996). This report led critics to charge that transgenic crops could lead to the creation of "superweeds" and, therefore, to "ecological catastrophe." Despite this charge, federal officials continued to argue that monitoring of herbicide resistance should not be their responsibility: ". . . it is the developer of the product that has the interest in assuring that resistance does not build up"

(Kling 1996: 181). Well before the time this statement was published, however, Congress had removed the USDA from involvement in biotechnology policy by eliminating funding for its advisory committee on biotechnology research and its Office of Agricultural Biotechnology (Fox 1996).

Intellectual Property Rights

United States intellectual property laws grant rights to patent owners to exclude everyone else from making, using, or selling the protected product for at least 17 years. Patents were first granted to plant varieties developed through asexual propagation in 1930. In 1970, Congress extended these rights to new varieties of plants developed through traditional genetic methods of sexual propagation. In 1980, the Supreme Court granted patent rights to microorganisms developed through rDNA techniques, and the Patent Office issued the first patent for such an organism. Patent rights were further extended to genetically engineered plants in 1985 and to animals in 1988 (U.S. Congress 1989, 1991a).

The patenting of biotechnological microorganisms and plants provided a major incentive for the growth of the food biotechnology industry, and patent rights are believed to have greatly stimulated such growth during the 1980s. Within just a few years, however, patent awards were challenged by industry and government officials in the United States, Canada, and Europe. By 1995, the U.S. Patent Office had issued 112 patents for genetically engineered plants. Among these were exclusive patent rights to one company for all forms of bioengineered cotton and to another for all uses of the "antisense" genes that were used to create the Calgene tomato (see later section on the "Flavr Savr" tomato). The breadth of such patents ". . . stunned the agricultural biotechnology community . . . It was as if the inventor of the assembly line had won property rights to all mass-produced goods . . . ," and numerous lawsuits were soon filed (Stone 1995: 656).

The patenting of animals has generated even greater debate, particularly from animal-rights organizations and other groups concerned that the genetic engineering of farm animals might adversely affect family farmers, be cruel to animals, and endanger other living species (U.S. Congress 1989). The principal arguments for and against the patenting of transgenic animals are summarized in Table VII.7.4 (U.S. Congress 1991a).

Perhaps in response to concerns about such issues, the Patent Office ceased issuing patents for transgenic animals in 1988. In 1993, it resumed processing of the 180 animal patent applications that had accumulated during this "self-imposed moratorium" (Andrews 1993). By that time, far fewer companies were attempting to patent farm animals, largely because persistent technical problems and concerns about costs had encouraged them to shift to more

Table VII.7.4. *The principal arguments for and against the patenting of transgenic animals*

Arguments for patenting transgenic animals

Patent laws regulate inventiveness, not commercial uses.
Patenting is an incentive to research and development.
Patenting enables the biotechnology industry to compete in international markets.
Patenting is preferable to trade secrets.
Patenting rewards innovation and entrepreneurship.

Arguments against patenting transgenic animals

Metaphysical and theological considerations make patenting untenable.
Patenting involves inappropriate treatment of animals.
Patenting reflects inappropriate human control over animal life.
Patenting disturbs the sanctity and dignity of life.
Most other countries do not permit patenting of animals.
Patenting could cause adverse economic effects on developing countries.
Patenting promotes environmentally unsound policies.
Animal patents will increase costs to consumers and producers.
Animal patents will result in further concentration in agricultural production.
Patent holders will derive unfair benefits from royalties on succeeding generations of patented animals.

Sources: U.S. Congress (1989) and Fox (1992).

profitable areas of research. But lobbyists against animal patents, such as Jeremy Rifkin, a leading antibiotechnology advocate, continued to protest Patent Office policies on both philosophical and economic grounds:

> We believe the gene pool should be maintained as an open commons, and should not be the private preserve of multinational companies . . . this is the Government giving its imprimatur to the idea that there is no difference between a living thing and any inert object . . . it's the final assault on the sacred meaning of life and life process. (Andrews 1993)

International Trade

Soybeans are used in more than 60 percent of all the processed foods sold in European markets (Wolf 1997). Transgenic, herbicide-resistant soybeans constituted 2 percent of the 59 million tons grown in the United States in 1996, their first year of production (Ibrahim 1996). Corn exports to Europe were valued at $500 million in 1995 (Wadman 1996). Transgenic Bt corn, also herbicide-resistant, was expected to account for half of the nearly $25 billion in annual sales in the United States within just a few years (Wolf 1997). Clearly, any action interfering with acceptance of transgenic crops would have grave economic consequences.

But European consumers were highly resistant to the idea of transgenic foods. This resistance has been attributed in part to memories of Nazi eugenics during World War II (Dickman 1996), in part to concerns that the antibiotic-resistance marker gene used in constructing the corn might spread to animals and to people, and in part to fears generated by the 1996 food-safety crisis over "mad cow" disease in England. The transmission of antibiotic-resistant bacteria from animals and milk to people had been demonstrated some years earlier (Holmberg et al. 1984; Tacket et al. 1985) but did not involve plants. The transmission of "mad cow" disease, although poorly understood, also did not appear to involve plants (Smith and Cousens 1996). European consumers, however, also were reacting to broader issues related to what they viewed as the arrogance of American officials who were claiming the superiority of their food safety criteria and were attempting to control trading policies through sanctions against European countries conducting business with Iran, Libya, or Cuba.

The transgenic soybeans and corn were approved as safe by the governments of the United States, Canada, and Japan. The European Union (EU) approved the import and processing of transgenic soybeans in April 1996. It referred the approval of the transgenic corn to scientific committees in June, thus raising the possibility that Europe might refuse corn from the United States and thereby cause a "corn war" (Wadman 1996). In October, Jeremy Rifkin announced the initiation of a worldwide boycott of genetically engineered crops produced in the United States. Rifkin was joined in this effort by an official of EuroCommerce, a trade association representing a large number of retail and commerce groups in 20 European countries, who called for separation and labeling of products using these grains so that European consumers could decide whether to buy them (Jones 1996). As the official later explained:

> Our message from our customers is that for whatever reason they would prefer not to have it in their foodstuffs . . . I am telling the American exporters to please, in this season, if you are wise, don't ship those soybeans to Europe because you may trigger a lasting reaction. And, if you must, separate and label them. (Ibrahim 1996: D1)

Surveys reported that 85 to 90 percent of European consumers wanted genetically engineered foods to be labeled as such (Ibrahim 1996: D24). Labeling, however, would require strict separation of genetically engineered from the usual varieties of corn or soybeans. Producers considered such separation impractical. If consumers refused to buy transgenic corn, or the European Union banned its import, U.S. producers would lose more than half a billion dollars in corn sales alone. This situation generated "tremendous interest" in a small company in Iowa that was marketing a test that could identify soybeans, corn, and other plants that had been genetically engineered (Wadman 1996). In December, the EU approved the genetically modified corn, leading the biotechnology industry to be "... optimistic that Europeans will come around to the benefits of genetically engineered crops" (Wolf 1997: 8). The EU ruling required labeling of genetically modified foods, however: "We must not miss this opportunity to repeat our clear signal that better labeling is one of the ways forward in this area" ("EU Approves" 1997: 1).

In Canada, a proposal to establish a central biotechnology regulatory agency met with opposition from farm, consumer, and industry groups, all of which viewed the current system of joint regulation by the departments of health and agriculture as satisfactory. Industry groups were especially concerned that government policies provide explicit regulations for the development and introduction of new plant varieties. Consumer proposals for labeling were opposed by the Canadian Federation of Agriculture:

> Canada must be in step with our major partners to ensure that Canada's labeling policy does not conflict ... and thereby reduce the competitiveness of Canadian producers ... The development of labeling regulations must recognize that the imposition of a labeling regime that is not based on science would have a negative trade implication for Canada. (Elliott 1996: 3)

Public Perceptions

Because food is overproduced in the United States and the West generally, and because the food industry is so competitive, biotechnology industry leaders view consumer acceptance of their products as an issue of critical importance: "Both the industrial and scientific communities have lagged in their understanding of the importance of the public's attitude toward biotechnology ... It is the consumer – the poorly informed and uninitiated average individual – who holds the key to our future" (Walter 1995: 216).

Consumer surveys do indeed document a fundamental public misunderstanding of basic food safety issues. Many surveys have reported a large proportion of respondents to be deeply concerned about the hazards of pesticides or irradiation, whether or not they believe these hazards to be more important (Food Marketing Institute 1994) or less important (Lynch and Lin 1994) than the far greater dangers of microbial contamination.

Because of the importance of consumer attitudes to the future of the industry and to federal regulatory efforts, various agencies in the United States and Canada have conducted surveys designed specifically to reveal consumer perceptions of food biotechnology. The methods used to obtain this information have varied among the surveys, and their results are not strictly comparable. Nevertheless, the results of such surveys have proven remarkably consistent over time, and they reveal an internally consistent logic of considerable predictive value.

At least three surveys have examined public attitudes toward agricultural biotechnology in the United States. In 1986, the Office of Technology Assessment commissioned the Harris organization to conduct focus groups and to administer a telephone survey of a national probability sample of 1,273 adults on perceptions of science, genetic engineering, and biotechnology (U.S. Congress 1987). In 1992, the USDA commissioned a telephone study of the attitudes of 1,228 consumers, along with a series of focus groups (Hoban and Kendall 1993; Zimmerman et al. 1994). In addition, Rutgers University researchers conducted a telephone survey of 604 New Jersey residents in May of 1993 (Hallman and Metcalfe 1993).

The results of these surveys are summarized in Table VII.7.5. Despite differences in method, population, and year, they yielded virtually identical responses that provide a consistent picture of public attitudes toward food biotechnology. Although respondents to all three surveys displayed a limited understanding of science and technology, they expressed high levels of interest in those fields, as well as high expectations that food biotechnology would produce benefits for them and for society as a whole. The respondents were concerned about the potential and unknown dangers of genetically engineered foods, but they believed that the benefits of biotechnology outweighed any risks, and they strongly supported continued federal funding of food biotechnology research.

It is especially noteworthy that the survey participants preferred some genetically engineered food products to others. They were most likely to accept products that appeared to be beneficial to health or society, to save money or time, to be safe, or to improve the environment.

Safety considerations, although often the focus of biotechnology debates (Hopkins et al. 1991), did not emerge in these surveys as the most important public concern. Instead, survey respondents appeared most troubled by ethical issues related to food biotechnology. Thus, they were more willing to accept genetically engineered foods that involved plants rather than animals, that did not harm animals, and that did not involve the transfer of animal genes into plants. These views derived from value systems that encompassed issues extending far beyond food safety (see Table VII.7.4), and the importance of such value systems to consumer perceptions of biotechnology cannot be overestimated:

> Whatever the actual saliency of these ethical charges and critiques, obviously fundamental social, cultural, and religious values are at stake, arising out of broad cultural traditions and interests. Animal biotechnology, coupled to the engines of corporate economics, is felt to threaten fundamental and traditional moral, religious, and cultural orientations (Donnelley, McCarthy, and Singleton 1994: S21).

Table VII.7.5. *Public perceptions of food biotechnology*

Respondents express	U.S. Congress (1987)	Hoban and Kendall (1993)	Hallman and Metcalfe (1993)
Great interest in food biotechnology	✓	✓	✓
Limited understanding of science and techniques	✓	✓	✓
Expectations that food biotechnology will benefit them and society	✓	✓	✓
Concerns about unknown risks	✓	✓	✓
Expectations that benefits will outweigh risks	✓	✓	✓
Belief that government should continue to fund food-biotechnology research	✓	✓	✓
Greater willingness to accept products that			
Directly benefit health, consumers, or society	✓	✓	✓
Save money or time	–	✓	✓
Are safe	✓	✓	✓
Help improve the environment	✓	✓	✓
Involve plants rather than animals	✓	✓	✓
Do not harm animals	✓	–	✓
Do not involve transfer of animal genes into plants	–	✓	–
Distrust of government credibility related to science and technology	✓	✓	✓
Distrust of government regulatory ability	✓	✓	✓
Distrust of the biotechnology industry	✓	✓	✓
Belief that food biotechnology should be regulated	✓	✓	✓
Belief that biotechnology-derived food products should be labeled	✓	✓	✓

All three surveys confirmed substantial public distrust of government credibility in scientific and technical safety matters and in the ability of government to regulate food biotechnology appropriately. Respondents were equally skeptical of the ability of the biotechnology industry to make decisions in the public interest. For these reasons, all three surveys indicated that the large majority of respondents wanted genetically engineered food products to be labeled as such. A 1993 survey conducted in Canada reported similar results (Walter 1995).

Industry leaders have tended to interpret such results – scientific misunderstanding, fear of unknown dangers, concern about animal welfare, distaste for transgenic experiments, and demand for regulation and food labeling – as evidence for public irrationality (Gaull and Goldberg 1991; Walter 1995). They and others further interpret these survey results as strongly supporting the need for comprehensive education campaigns to inform consumers about the safety and benefits of biotechnology (Bruhn 1992; Hoban and Kendall 1993; Walter 1995).

Such interpretations miss the most strikingly useful conclusion to be drawn from these surveys: Consumer acceptance of food biotechnology is entirely product-specific. The survey results clearly demonstrate that the public will readily accept genetically engineered products that are perceived as filling important needs: "People appear to be far more focused on the characteristics of products than the process used to create those products. People may be willing to overlook their objections to genetic engi-

neering if its products produce specific benefits" (Hallman and Metcalfe 1993: 3).

The results of the Canadian survey further support this conclusion:

> The Canadian public tends to consider biotechnology products individually, based mainly on their potential benefits. For example, the general concept of transferring genetic material from one plant to another was accepted by 51% of the respondents. This support jumped to 70% if the transfer improved plant nutritional value, though it slid to only 36% if the transfer only improved plant color ... Products with laudable goals were strongly supported, while those with dubious benefit were rejected. (Walter 1995: 216)

Such results demonstrate that the key issue in consumer acceptance of genetically engineered foods is the value of the specific product to public health and welfare. The implication of these results is equally clear: If the food biotechnology industry wants consumers to accept its products without protest, it must market products worthwhile to the public as well as to the industry.

Predictive Implications: U.S. Case Studies

The survey results also suggest an analytical framework for predicting the degree of difficulty with which a given genetically engineered food is likely to achieve public acceptance in the United States. This

Table VII.7.6. *Analytical framework for predicting public acceptance of a food product of biotechnology*

1. Is the food valuable? Will it
   Increase nutrient content?
   Increase food availability?
   Decrease food cost?
   Improve food taste?
   Grow better under difficult conditions?
   Reduce use of herbicides and pesticides?
2. Is the food safe for people and for the environment?
3. Is the food ethical? Does it avoid
   Harm to animals?
   Insertion of animal genes into plants?

analysis presumes that consumer acceptance is predicated on the importance of a product, its safety, and its ethical value. To predict whether a product will be acceptable, one need only ask the questions listed in Table VII.7.6. If the answers to all three questions are affirmative, the product is highly likely to be accepted by the great majority of consumers. To the extent that the answers are negative or equivocal, consumer resistance is likely to increase. Consumer responses to the genetically engineered products that have been approved for marketing in the United States constitute case studies that illustrate the predictive value of such questions.

Pharmaceuticals

By the early 1990s, the FDA had approved at least 15 recombinant drugs for use in human subjects. Recombinant insulin, for example, was the first to receive approval, in 1982. This drug is of unquestioned utility (U.S. Congress 1991a). It solves problems of scarcity and quality, as it can be produced in unlimited quantities. Its amino acid structure is identical to that of human insulin, and it is, therefore, superior to insulin obtained from the pancreas of pigs or cows. It is safe and raises no ethical issues. Recombinant insulin readily meets all three criteria for consumer acceptance, and it is neither surprising nor inconsistent that activists against biotechnology in the United States have never protested its use.

Chymosin

Recombinant enzymes used in food manufacture also have been accepted readily. Chymosin, an enzyme used to coagulate milk to make cheese, was traditionally extracted from the stomachs of calves and sold as part of a mixture called rennet. The enzyme was difficult to extract, varied in quality, and was scarce and expensive. Through rDNA techniques, the gene for chymosin was transferred to bacteria that can be grown in large quantities. Chymosin derived from this process was approved for food use in 1990 (U.S. Congress 1991a). This action elicited no noticeable complaints from biotechnology critics, not only because the manufacturer saw "little to gain from waving the

biotech flag," but also "because the alternative is slaughtering baby calves" (Kilman 1994b: R7). This product also meets the three criteria for consumer acceptance: It is more useful, more ethical, and just as safe as the product it replaced.

The "Flavr Savr" Tomato

Americans have come to expect tomatoes to be available on a year-round basis. The market for fresh tomatoes was estimated at between $3 and $5 billion annually in the early 1990s (Fisher 1994; Hilts 1994). In 1993, American farmers produced nearly 16 pounds of fresh tomatoes per capita and another 77 pounds per capita for processing (Putnam and Allshouse 1994). But supermarket tomatoes, bred for disease resistance, appearance, and durability, have long been the bane of consumers longing for "backyard" taste and freshness (Mather 1995).

Beginning in the mid-1980s, Calgene, a California-based biotechnology company, invested $25 million and eight years of effort to develop a tomato with a reversed (and, therefore, blocked) gene for ripening. This process was designed to permit it to be picked and marketed at a more mature stage of ripeness and taste (U.S. Congress 1991a). Calgene expected this "Flavr Savr" tomato to capture at least 15 percent of the market for fresh tomatoes as soon as it became available (Kim 1992b). The company planned to market – and label – the tomato as genetically engineered to taste better.

As the first company to develop such a food, Calgene voluntarily sought FDA guidance on the tomato's regulatory status in 1989, long before it was ready to market. In 1990, Calgene requested an FDA advisory opinion as to whether the gene for resistance to the antibiotic kanamycin, used as part of the genetic engineering process, could be used as a marker in producing tomatoes and other crops. The following year, Calgene requested a more formal FDA "consultation" on whether the Flavr Savr would be subject to the same regulations as conventional tomatoes, and, in 1992, the company published a comprehensive report on the tomato's safety and nutrient content (Redenbaugh et al. 1992).

The following year, Calgene filed a petition with the FDA to approve the kanamycin-resistant gene as a food additive. The FDA reviewed this request under its 1992 policy and also requested an opinion from its Food Advisory Committee (FDA 1994a; Hilts 1994). In its review, and during the committee hearings, the FDA insisted that the discussion focus exclusively on safety questions. Consumer and other representatives on the committee said they were ". . . frustrated by a debate that, to them, ignores other key issues that affect consumers' preferences for foods, such as religious, ethical, or aesthetic criteria . . . They also say that such foods should carry labels" (Fox 1994: 439).

The FDA decision, in 1994, that "all relevant safety questions about the new tomato had been resolved"

(FDA 1994a) was greeted as "terrific news for the industry," and the price of Calgene stock increased slightly (Fisher 1994: B7). Consumer groups, however, charged that the FDA review of the tomato had been an anomaly because the approval system had been entirely voluntary. Certain antibiotechnology advocacy groups threatened picket lines, "tomato dumpings," boycotts, and legal challenges (Leary 1994). Most analysts, however, believed that consumers would accept the tomato if they perceived its improved taste to be worth what it would cost (O'Neill 1994). Although the price was originally expected to be twice that of conventional varieties (Sugawara 1992), the cost of the tomato was reduced in test markets to compete with locally grown products (Biotech 1994). By the summer of 1996, however, supplies of the tomato were still too limited to determine its level of acceptance.

From the answers to the questions in Table VII.7.6, some consumer resistance should be expected. Although the Flavr Savr is demonstrably safe, it raises issues related to its impact on small tomato growers. Its benefit to the public is restricted to taste. Perhaps most important, its higher costs identify the Flavr Savr as a luxury product targeted to an upscale market.

To Calgene, however, the tomato was well worth the huge investment of time, money, and effort; indeed, it was said that part of the effort involved providing members of Congress with bacon, lettuce, and Flavr Savr sandwiches (Stix 1995). FDA approval of the tomato paved the way for subsequent approval of the company's seed oils, herbicide-resistant cotton, and other genetically engineered crops, raising hopes that Calgene would at last obtain a return on its investment. The company was reported to have lost more than $80 million since its formation in the early 1980s (McMurray 1993), and it continued to report losses during 1994. In June 1995, Monsanto, the manufacturer of recombinant bovine somatotropin (see next section), purchased 49.9 percent of Calgene, thus becoming the leading supplier of fresh tomatoes in the nation (Fisher 1995).

Bovine Somatotropin

The story of recombinant bovine somatotropin (rbST), the first food product to be approved by the FDA under its 1992 policy, best illustrates how issues of societal benefit, safety, and ethics contribute to consumer resistance to biotechnology. The product, a growth hormone that increases milk production in cows by at least 10 to 20 percent (Pell et al. 1992), has elicited an extraordinary level of debate. Its very name is controversial: Most proponents use its scientific name, rbST, whereas critics tend to use its more readily understandable common name, Beef (or Bovine) Growth Hormone, abbreviated rBGH (Daughaday and Barbano 1990). For purposes of consistency, this chapter employs the term rbST.

The Monsanto Company developed rbST in the mid-1980s and promoted it as a means to make dairy farming more efficient. Although such efficiency would seem to be of great benefit to consumers, critics soon raised questions about the product's effects on human health, animal welfare, and the economic viability of small dairy farms (U.S. Congress 1992). They also raised issues related to consumers' freedom of choice in the marketplace: When the FDA ruled that milk from cows treated with rbST cannot be so labeled.

For the industry and its supporters, concerns about factors other than safety were seen as irrelevant and highly threatening to the future of agricultural biotechnology; if rbST failed in the marketplace, the entire industry would be in jeopardy (Schneider 1990). Accordingly, this hormone and an equivalent product for pigs were extolled as:

> Biotechnological miracles that would give consumers more for their money at less cost to the environment. Yet these and other long-tested products . . . are likely to be mired in continuing controversies instigated more by ignorance, nostalgia and a Luddite view of technology than by understanding and actual fact . . . whether such improvements will ever reach the marketplace will depend largely on how well consumers accept BST (Brody 1993: C17).

Yet rbST was controversial almost from its inception. By 1989, during periods of testing on commercial farms and research centers in nearly every major dairy state (Schneider 1989, 1990), rbST had become the target of groups concerned about family farms as well as of those suspicious of genetic engineering (Sun 1989). As a result, supermarket chains announced that they would not carry milk from rbST-treated cows, and dairy companies such as Ben and Jerry's stated that their products would carry label statements that opposed the use of rbST (Schneider 1989). The state legislatures of Wisconsin and Minnesota temporarily banned the sale of rbST, an action considered extraordinary in the case of a product not yet approved for commercial use (Schneider 1990). By 1992, four major supermarket chains, two large manufacturers of dairy products, and the nation's largest dairy cooperative had joined the boycott (Miller 1992), as had many small farmers, dairy cooperatives, and groceries (Day 1994). Such a level of protest might easily have been anticipated, as rbST raised many of the issues suggested by the questions in Table VII.7.6.

Safety issues. Bovine somatotropin stimulates milk production, and the natural hormone is always present in cow's milk in low concentrations. Milk from rbST-treated cows contains both the natural hormone and rbST; these are almost identical and cannot easily be distinguished, complicating efforts to require labeling. The hormone is unlikely to be harmful to humans, even though its concentration is higher in milk from treated cows. Its protein structure differs from that of the human hormone and it is biologically inactive in humans. Moreover, like all proteins, the cow hormone is largely broken down in the human intestinal tract. The hormone had been tested on 21,000 cows, and described in more than 900 research papers by 1992, with no indication of untoward effects on human health (Miller 1992).

Despite this evidence, critics continued to raise doubts about safety because of concerns about two factors that might be present in rbST milk: insulin-like growth factor-I (IGF-I) and antibiotics (Blayney 1994). Treatment with rbST increases concentrations of IGF-I in cows' milk, raising concerns that this factor might stimulate premature growth in infants and cancers in adults. Proponents of rbST argue that the factor appears to be relatively inactive in rats, is denatured in infant formulas, and seems unlikely to be absorbed by the human digestive tract in sufficient amounts to be harmful (Juskevich and Guyer 1990). A federal study has confirmed that IGF-I concentrations are indeed higher in rbST-treated cows but concluded that more research would be needed to determine whether the higher levels posed any risk (U.S. General Accounting Office 1992b).

The second concern arose because cows treated with rbST develop udder infections (mastitis) more frequently than untreated cows. Such infections are treated with antibiotics that can appear in milk and meat and, theoretically, contribute to human antibiotic resistance. Although federal regulations require testing for antibiotic residues in milk, the FDA tests for only a small fraction of animal drugs in common use – just 4 out of 82 in one study – leading to charges that the agency lacks a comprehensive strategy for monitoring animal drugs (U.S. General Accounting Office 1992a). These concerns led yet another federal committee to recommend discontinuation of rbST marketing until antibiotic risks could be evaluated; at the same time, the committee called for development of a feasibility study of rbST labeling to provide information to the public (U.S. General Accounting Office 1992b). As discussed here, these recommendations were not implemented.

In 1990, Monsanto-sponsored scientists reported in a leading medical journal that rbST milk was safe for human consumption and that FDA studies had answered all safety questions (Daughaday and Barbano 1990). That same year, FDA scientists reviewed more than 130 studies of the effects of rbST on cows, rats, and humans and concurred in the conclusion that the hormone did not affect human health (Juskevich and Guyer 1990). The publication of this last report in a prestigious scientific journal was judged "unprecedented," as it gave the appearance of a conflict of interest: The FDA seemed to be acting as a proponent of a drug that it had not yet approved (Gibbons 1990). Critics viewed the report as "part of a

campaign by the four companies developing the drug and portions of the dairy industry to calm the public's concern. . . . The review could not have been conducted without the permission of the manufacturers to disclose their own confidential studies on the safety of the drug" (Schneider 1990: A18). Nevertheless, a panel of experts recruited by the National Institutes of Health (NIH) also concluded that milk from rbST-treated cows was essentially the same – and as safe – as milk from untreated cows (Office of Medical Applications 1991).

Animal welfare. Because treatment of cows with rbST increases milk production, concerns have also been expressed about the effect of the drug on the health and reproductive ability of the animals. In addition to increasing cases of mastitis, injections of rbST have been reported to produce localized reactions at the injection sites in some cows (Pell et al. 1992; U.S. General Accounting Office 1992b). Despite FDA and industry assertions that appropriate herd-management practices can minimize such problems, they are nonetheless regularly reported. Between March 1994 and February 1995, for example, more than 800 farmers filed complaints with the FDA about animal health problems related to the use of rbST. Yet, according to the FDA, such reports "raise no new animal health concerns" ("Over 800 Farmers" 1995: 6).

Dairy farming. In the opinion of many, arguments about the safety of rbST have tended to obscure "the real issue – the economic impact of BGH once it hits the market" (Sun 1989: 877). For years, dairy production has exceeded demand, resulting in large surpluses of milk, butter, and other dairy products; such surpluses are purchased by the government to maintain prices (Schneider 1989). Common use of rbST will almost certainly increase milk production, but the effects of this increase on prices to farmers and costs to consumers and the government are difficult to predict. One estimate has suggested that the use of rbST will lead to a 2 percent decrease in prices paid to farmers and, therefore, to a 1 percent decline in farm income by 1999 (U.S. Congress 1991b). Any decline in milk consumption, coupled with increasing supplies, might be expected to accelerate trends toward the elimination of small dairy farms (Schneider 1994b). Federal spending on dairy price supports might also increase, although such an increase could be offset by the lower costs of federal commodity distribution programs (Blayney 1994).

Whether rbST milk will cost less is uncertain. The industry contends that the use of the hormone will reduce farm production costs because equivalent amounts of milk can be produced by fewer cows. Although it might seem logical that creation of milk surpluses would lead to lower prices, any price decline stimulates higher levels of federal spending to protect farm incomes (Kilman 1994b). Most commentators – but not all (U.S. Congress 1991b) – believe that at least some dairy farmers will be forced out of business.

Regulation. In 1985, the FDA permitted Monsanto to use the drug on an experimental basis (Schneider 1989). The agency reaffirmed the safety of rbST milk and meat in 1988, 1989, and again in 1990 (Miller 1992), as did the NIH in 1990 (Office of Medical Applications 1991) and the Office of Technology Assessment in 1991 (U.S. Congress 1991b). FDA approval of rbST as a new animal drug product appeared imminent (Miller 1992), but in August 1993, Congress enacted a 90-day moratorium on rbST sales. In fact, the Senate, concerned about the fate of small dairy farms, had approved a moratorium lasting an entire year, but House opposition forced this compromise ("BGH Moratorium" 1993).

After lengthy deliberations, advisory committee consultations, and public hearings, the FDA approved Monsanto's rbST as a new animal drug in November 1993. In announcing the decision, the FDA commissioner stated: "There is virtually no difference in milk from treated and untreated cows . . . in fact, it's not possible using current scientific techniques to tell them apart . . . we are confident this product is safe for consumers, for cows and for the environment" (Schneider 1993: 1).

FDA approval applied only to the Monsanto product, although approval of products from other companies was expected to follow ("FDA Approves" 1993). Industry representatives hailed the FDA decision as a strong signal that the administration intended to reduce regulatory barriers, as a victory for Monsanto, and as a "banner day for agricultural biotechnology" (Schneider 1993: 9). The actual effect of the ruling, however, would not be seen until the moratorium on sales ended. In the meantime, Monsanto was reported to be giving the product to farmers at no cost ("FDA Approves" 1993).

Because dairy companies, concerned about consumer reactions to rbST, had been labeling their products as "BGH-free," industry groups requested FDA guidance on the labeling of dairy products derived from untreated cows. In February 1994, the FDA stated that it did not have the authority to require special labeling and ruled that companies might voluntarily inform customers that they were not using rbST, provided "that any statements made [we]re truthful and not misleading." Because all milk contains some bST, milk could not be labeled as "BGH-free." Because bST and rbST are indistinguishable, milk also could not be labeled as "rBGH-free." However, these designations could be used if accompanied by a statement that put them in proper context: "[N]o significant difference has been shown between milk derived from rbST-treated and non-rbST-treated cows" (1994b: 6280).

Nevertheless, the state of Vermont passed legislation requiring the labeling of milk from rbST-treated cows, in conflict with FDA rulings: "Vermonters have the right to know what is in the food they eat . . . In particular, there is a strong public interest in knowing whether or not rbST has been used in the production of milk and milk products" (Schneider 1994d: A16). By 1996, however, industry groups had successfully challenged this law in the courts ("Court Strikes Down" 1996).

Moreover, two major milk marketers launched new brands certified as coming from untreated cows. In response, Monsanto warned dairy companies that such labels were misleading and "might create the impression that something is wrong with milk from treated cows" (Kilman 1994a: B7). By May 1994, Monsanto had sued at least two dairy companies to force them to comply with the FDA ruling. Because the dairies lacked resources as extensive as Monsanto's, they seemed certain to lose the suits. As one report stated, "Everyone is terrified of Monsanto . . . it is quite ominous" (Burros 1994: C4).

International implications. The European Community (EC) has long been skeptical about the use of growth hormones in cattle. This is the result of 1980 incidents in which consumption of baby foods containing veal from cows treated with diethylstilbestrol was associated with cases of premature sexual development in infants. Despite such skepticism, in 1987 Monsanto Europe requested approval of rbST from the EC's Committee for Veterinary Medicinal Products (Vandaele 1992). The following year, however, the EC banned nontherapeutic use of hormones in the domestic livestock industry and soon extended the ban to countries that exported meat to the EC.

This action raised trade issues related to the use of rbST (Krissoff 1989). In 1991, the Veterinary Products Committee decided that rbST met requirements for quality, efficacy, and safety and posed no risk to consumers or cows. But this decision was overruled by the EC Directorates General, an action seen as a "blow to agricultural biotechnology" (Vandaele 1992: 148). Indeed, the EC executive committee proposed a seven-year ban on rbST use because it feared that the hormone might undermine efforts to reduce farm surpluses.

Thus, rbST became caught in a "policy paradox"; it would be manufactured by Monsanto in Europe, where it could not be sold, and then exported to the United States, where its use was permitted (Aldhous 1993). In 1995, the United States successfully persuaded the EC to declare that all Codex Alimentarius international standards for food additives, including animal drugs, should be based on science (i.e., biological safety). This was clearly an effort to force the EC to permit the use of rbST-derived milk and meat. But a straightforward motion by the United States for EC approval of rbST as posing no health risk fared less well; it was postponed until the Codex meeting scheduled for 1997 (Leonard 1995).

Industry actions. As early as 1987, rbST was expected to become agricultural biotechnology's first billion-dollar product (Sun 1989). In 1989, the market for rbST was estimated at $100 to $500 million annually (Schneider 1989); more recent estimates have been somewhat higher (Millstone, Brunner, and White 1994; Schneider 1994a). The potential for such a large return on investment helps to explain Monsanto's unusually aggressive sales tactics (Feder 1995) and heavy-handed political actions to protect and promote this and its other products (Benson et al. 1997). Certainly the company took full advantage of its connections in government. FDA employees with ties to Monsanto played key roles in the agency's review of rbST (Schneider 1994e; U.S. General Accounting Office 1994), and Monsanto enlisted an influential former congressman, to whom the secretary of agriculture owed his appointment, to encourage the USDA to prevent Congress from studying the economic effects of rbST (Engelberg 1994).

Monsanto leveled charges of plagiarism against independent researchers who had used company data to analyze counts of white blood cells ("pus," according to critics) in rbST-treated milk, thereby preventing publication of their report (Millstone et al. 1994). The company used legal and political strategies to resist demands for labeling and recruited dairy industry executives to help persuade the FDA to establish favorable labeling guidelines. In addition, Monsanto was reported to have recruited at least two Washington law firms to monitor dairies for advertising and labeling violations and to instigate legal action against milk processors who had "inappropriately" misled customers (Schneider 1994c).

To some extent, these efforts succeeded. By March 1995, Monsanto claimed to have sold 14.5 million doses of rbST during the previous year and stated that 13,000 dairy farmers, or 11 percent of the potential market, were customers (Feder 1995). Sales were said to be especially strong in the state of New York, with 10 percent of dairy farmers reported to be using rbST. But in Wisconsin, where milk is the foundation of a $10 billion dairy industry, only 5 percent of the state's 29,000 dairy farmers were said to be using the hormone (Schneider 1994c), and 90 percent were reported as hoping that the drug would never be widely adopted. Overall sales for the first year were estimated at $70 million, far short of what had been anticipated (Feder 1995).

Consumer responses. The degree of consumer acceptance of rbST was also uncertain in 1995. A telephone survey of 1,004 adults suggested that use of rbST would have no impact on milk consumption, as most respondents had never heard of the drug. However, the phrasing of the survey questions, which used the term somatotropin rather than "growth hormone," and emphasized safety rather than issues of ethics and values, may have led respondents to more favorable answers. For example, respondents answered positively (scoring 6.18 on a scale where 10 is strongly positive) to this question:

> The National Institutes of Health, the American Medical Association, and several other independent medical groups have found milk from cows that receive BST is unchanged, safe, and nutritionally the same as milk currently on grocery store shelves. Given this information, how acceptable do you find the use of BST. . . ? (Hoban 1994: 8)

The lack of labeling of rbST dairy products complicates understanding of consumer acceptance. Despite FDA rulings, surveys demonstrate overwhelming consumer support for special labeling of rbST products (Blayney 1994). Supporters of rbST have argued that the marketplace should be allowed to decide the commercial fate of the hormone (Sun 1989), but without labeling, consumers cannot easily make their opinions known.

Implications. Public skepticism about rbST relates to nearly all of the areas of concern listed in Table VII.7.6. Given the strength of these concerns, this product seems an unfortunate first choice for commercialization. United States farmers already overproduce milk, and rbST offers no clear benefit to consumers in availability, price, or quality. It will not even create more manufacturing jobs, as most rbST will be made and packaged in Europe (Hansen and Halloran 1994). That the product affects milk itself is also unfortunate: "Is there any product in the world that has tried harder to sell itself as wholesome and pure than milk? . . . It is a food for innocent, trusting children, culturally laden with symbolism. Any adulteration of milk . . . is seen as taboo" (Kolata 1994: E13).

The primary gainers from rbST, therefore, appear to be its manufacturers and the large dairy farmers who can best exploit its use. As summarized by the head of a dairy company that refuses to use rbST:

> We do know that the use of BGH will increase the supply of milk at a time when we already have a tremendous surplus. It does not make any sense to exacerbate this problem with a product about which there are so many legitimate doubts, a product whose principal beneficiaries will be chemical companies and corporate agribusiness. (Cohen 1993: 1)

Policy Implications

This history indicates that the controversy over food biotechnology derives from the conflict between the industry's need to be profitable and the desire of consumers for products that are economically and socially valuable, as well as safe. Therefore, to frame the debate about food biotechnology in terms of rational science versus an irrational public is to do a disservice to both.

Biotechnology is not inherently dangerous, and it is capable of doing much good. The public is not inherently irrational and is quite capable of judging whether genetically engineered products are worth buying. Few consumers demand that biotechnology "pack up its test tubes"; they support industry efforts to impart to food plants desirable qualities such as resistance to diseases and pests to food plants. At the moment, however, many view the great promise of biotechnology as having been betrayed (Hamilton 1990: 43).

Thus, the open contempt of policymakers and industry leaders for public misunderstanding of science and technology misses an important point. As this analysis has indicated, public views of biotechnology in the United States are product-specific and, as such, are logical, consistent, and predictable. Analysts of biotechnology policy who are aware of this logic recommend that regulators and the public decide the risks and benefits of each new product on a case-by-case basis (Davis 1991). They agree with industry that the marketplace should be allowed to determine the success of these products. They suggest that the products be labeled so that the public can make informed decisions in that marketplace and believe that if industry is producing valuable products, the label will encourage the public to purchase them.

Although it is always useful to educate the public about the benefits of science and technology, education alone will not solve problems of consumer acceptance. The analysis presented here suggests that it will continue to be difficult to convince the public that genetically engineered food products are necessary or safe as long as the principal beneficiary of food biotechnology is the industry itself. If the food biotechnology industry wants to convince the public that its products are beneficial, it will need to place far greater emphasis on the development of truly useful products, those that foster sustainable agriculture, drought- and pest-resistance, and improved nutrient quality.

This analysis also argues in favor of the development of federal regulatory mechanisms capable of addressing a much broader range of issues than just food safety. As noted by one commentator, regulations should be based on a comprehensive analysis of policy and assessment of technology that examines the full range of social and environmental consequences of technological change (Brown 1991).

That the agricultural biotechnology industry would benefit from such an analysis is evident from recent events. Developing-world countries are moving quickly to develop recombinant crops that will solve their local food problems. These efforts, which derive directly from the need to produce more food, are focusing on improvements in disease resistance and nutritional quality, especially among native plant species (Moffat 1994; Bokanga 1995). Such efforts deserve much support and should encourage food biotechnology companies in industrialized nations to focus research and development efforts on products that will benefit individuals and societies as well as the companies' investors.

Marion Nestle

Bibliography

Aldhous, P. 1991. Yellow light on L-tryptophan. *Nature* 353: 490.

1993. Thumbs down for cattle hormone. *Science* 261: 418.

American Medical Association, Council on Scientific Affairs. 1991. Biotechnology and the American agricultural industry. *Journal of the American Medical Association* 265: 1429-36.

Andrews, E. L. 1993. U.S. resumes granting patents on genetically altered animals. *The New York Times,* February 3, pp. A1, D5.

Associated Press. 1994. Seven engineered foods declared safe by FDA: Some scientists question biotech standard. *The Washington Post,* November 3, p. A11.

Barnum, A. 1992. Brave new foods: Bioengineered crops could meet consumer resistance. *San Francisco Chronicle,* June 15, pp. B1, B6.

Barton, K. A., and W. J. Brill. 1983. Prospects in plant genetic engineering. *Science* 219: 671-6.

Beachy, R. 1993. Transferring genes. In *Symbol, substance, science: The societal issues of food biotechnology, conference proceedings,* ed. W. S. Burke, 45-51, 61-2. Research Triangle Park, N.C.

Benson, S., M. Arax, and R. Burstein. 1997. A growing concern: As biotech crops come to market, neither scientists – who take industry money – nor federal regulators are adequately protecting consumers and farmers. *Mother Jones* 21: (January/February): 36-43, 66, 68, 71.

BGH moratorium. 1993. *Nutrition Week* (August 6): 5.

BIO favors limited notification on biotech food 3-year sunset. 1994. *Food Chemical News* (May 16): 7-8.

Biotech. 1994. *Nutrition Week* (August 26): 7.

Biotechnology promises consumers better, cheaper, safer foods. 1990. *Food Insight Reports* (March/April): 1.

Blayney, D. P. 1994. Milk and biotechnology: Maintaining safe, adequate milk supplies. *FoodReview* 17: 27-31.

Blayney, D. P., R. G. Fallert, and S. D. Shagam. 1991. Controversy over livestock growth hormones continues. *FoodReview* 14: 6-9.

Bokanga, M. 1995. Biotechnology and cassava processing in Africa. *Food Technology* 49: 86-90.

Brody, J. E. 1993. Of Luddites, cows, and biotechnology miracles. *The New York Times,* November 17, p. C17.

Brown, G. 1991. Recent American agricultural history. In *New technologies and the future of food and nutrition,* ed. G. E. Gaull and R. A. Goldberg, 25-36. New York.

Browning, Graeme. 1992. Biotech politics. *National Journal* (February 29): 511-14.

Bruhn, C. M. 1992. Consumer concerns and educational strategies: Focus on biotechnology. *Food Technology* 45: 80, 95, 97.

Burros, M. 1994. More milk, more confusion: What should the label say? *The New York Times,* May 18, pp. C1, C4.

Carrol, W. L. 1993. Introduction to recombinant-DNA technology. *American Journal of Clinical Nutrition* 58 (Supplement): 249s–258s.

Caswell, M. F., K. O. Fuglie, and C. A. Klotz. 1994. *Agricultural biotechnology: An economic perspective.* USDA Agricultural Economic Report No. 687. Washington, D.C.

Centers for Disease Control. 1989. Eosinophilia-myalgia syndrome - New Mexico. *Journal of the American Medical Association* 262: 3116.

Chambers, J. A. 1995. Creating new partnerships in global biotechnology. *Food Technology* 49: 94–6.

Chefs urge boycotting new foods. 1992. *The New York Times* (June 3): C6.

Cohen, B. 1993. *Ben & Jerry's testifies before FDA in favor of BGH labeling.* Press Release. Waterbury, Vt.

Court strikes down Vermont BGH dairy labeling law. 1996. *Nutrition Week* 26: 2.

Daughaday, W. H., and D. M. Barbano. 1990. Bovine somatotropin supplementation of dairy cows: Is the milk safe? *Journal of the American Medical Association* 264: 1003–5.

Davis, B. D., ed. 1991. *The genetic revolution: Scientific prospects and public perceptions.* Baltimore, Md.

Day, K. 1994. Where did the milk come from? Tracking dairy hormone may prove impossible. *The Washington Post,* February 13, pp. A1, A22.

Dickman, S. 1996. Germany joins the biotech race. *Science* 274: 1454–5.

Donnelley, S., C. R. McCarthy, and R. Singleton, Jr. 1994. *The brave new world of animal biotechnology.* Special supplement to the *Hastings Center Report* 24: S1–31.

Economic Research Service. 1994. *Food marketing review, 1992–93.* USDA Agricultural Economic Report No. 678. Washington, D.C.

Elliott, I. 1996. Proposed Canadian biotech agency opposed. *Feedstuffs* (November 11): 3, 6.

Engelberg, S. 1994. Democrats' new overseer is everybody's Mr. Inside. *The New York Times,* August 19, pp. A1, A16.

Environmental Defense Fund. 1994. *EDF cautiously praises EPA's proposed genetic engineering rule.* Press Release. New York.

EU approves Bt corn, but it must be labeled. 1997. *Genetically Modified Foods Market Intelligence* (January 8): 1–2.

Falk, B. W., and G. Bruening. 1994. Will transgenic crops generate new viruses and new diseases? *Science* 263: 1395–6.

FDA approves biotech milk hormone, will not require BGH labeling. 1993. *Nutrition Week* (November 12): 1–2.

Feder, B. J. 1995. Monsanto has its wonder hormone. Can it sell it? *The New York Times,* March 12, p. 8.

1996. Out of the lab, a revolution on the farm: New genetic weapons to battle bugs and weeds. *The New York Times,* March 3, Sect. 3, pp. 1, 11.

Fisher, L. M. 1994. Developer of the new tomato expects a financial bonanza. *The New York Times,* May 19, p. B7.

1995. Monsanto to acquire 49.9% of biotechnology company. *The New York Times,* June 29, p. D3.

FDA (Food and Drug Administration). 1992. Statement of policy: Foods derived from new plant varieties; notice. *Federal Register* 57: 22984–23005.

1993. Food labeling: Food derived from new plant varieties. *Federal Register* 58: 25837–41.

1994a. *Biotechnology of food.* Washington, D.C.

1994b. Interim guidance on the voluntary labeling of milk and milk products from cows that have not been treated with recombinant bovine somatotropin. *Federal Register* 59: 6279–80.

Food Marketing Institute. 1994. *Trends in the United States: Consumer attitudes and the supermarket, 1994.* Washington, D.C.

Fox, J. L. 1990. Tryptophan production questions raised. *Bio/Technology* 8: 992.

1994. FDA nears approval of Calgene's Flavr Savr. *Bio/Technology* 12: 439.

1996. USDA downplays closing of biotech advisory programs. *Nature Biotechnology* 14: 261.

Fox, M. W. 1992. *Superpigs and wondercorn.* New York.

Fraley, R. 1992. Sustaining the food supply. *Bio/Technology* 10: 40–3.

Fritsch, P., and S. Kilman. 1996. Huge biotech harvest is a boon for farmers - and for Monsanto. *The Wall Street Journal,* October 24, pp. A1, A10.

Fuchs, R. L., and J. S. Astwood. 1996. Allergenicity assessment of foods derived from genetically modified plants. *Food Technology* 50: 83–8.

Gallo, A. E. 1995. *The food marketing system in 1994.* USDA Agricultural Information Bulletin No. 717. Washington, D.C.

Gaull, G. E., and R. A. Goldberg, eds. 1991. *New technologies and the future of food and nutrition.* New York.

Gibbons, A. 1990. FDA published bovine growth hormone data. *Science* 249: 852–3.

Goldburg, R., J. Rissler, H. Shand, and C. Hassebrook. 1990. *Biotechnology's bitter harvest: Herbicide-tolerant crops and the threat to sustainable agriculture.* Biotechnology Working Group. Washington, D.C.

Hallman, W. K., and J. Metcalfe. 1993. *Public perceptions of agricultural biotechnology: A survey of New Jersey residents.* Ecosystem Policy Research Center, Rutgers University, and New Jersey Agricultural Experiment Station, Cook College. New Brunswick, N.J.

Hamilton, J. O'C. 1990. A tempest in a cottonfield: Are Calgene's herbicide-resistant seeds a boon or a biohazard? *Business Week* (April 9): 43.

1994. Biotech: An industry crowded with players faces an ugly reckoning. *Business Week* (September 26): 84–92.

Hansen, M. K., and J. M. Halloran. 1994. Make them label it. Letter to the Editor. *The New York Times,* February 21, p. A16.

Harlander, S. K. 1989. Biotechnology opportunities for the food industry. In *Biotechnology and the food industry,* ed. P. L. Rogers and G. H. Fleet, 1–16. New York.

Hayenga, M. L. 1993. Food and agricultural biotechnology: Economic implications. *American Journal of Clinical Nutrition* 58 (Supplement): 313s–316s.

Hilts, P. J. 1994. Genetically altered tomato moves toward U.S. approval. *The New York Times,* April 9, p. 7.

Hoban, T. J. 1994. *Consumer awareness and acceptance of bovine somatotropin (BST).* Unpublished survey conducted for the Grocery Manufacturers of America.

1995. The construction of food biotechnology as a social issue. In *Eating agendas: Food and nutrition as social problems,* ed. D. Maurer and J. Sobal, 189–212. New York.

Hoban, T. J., and P. A. Kendall. 1993. *Consumer attitudes about food biotechnology: Project summary.* Raleigh, N.C.

Hodgson, J. 1992. Biotechnology: Feeding the world? *Bio/Technology* 10: 47–50.

Holmberg, S. D., M. T. Osterholm, K. A. Senger, and M. L. Cohen. 1984. Drug-resistant *Salmonella* from animals fed antimicrobials. *New England Journal of Medicine* 311: 617-22.

Hopkins, D. D., R. J. Goldburg, and S. A. Hirsch. 1991. *A mutable feast: Assuring food safety in the era of genetic engineering.* New York.

Hoyle, R. 1992. FDA's slippery food policy. *Bio/Technology* 10: 956-9.

Ibrahim, Y. M. 1996. Genetic soybeans alarm Europeans. *The New York Times,* November 7, pp. D1, D24.

Ingersoll, B. 1992. New policy eases market path for bioengineered foods. *The Wall Street Journal,* May 26, pp. B1, B6.

International Food Biotechnology Council. 1990. Biotechnologies and food: Assuring the safety of foods produced by genetic modification. *Regulatory Toxicology and Pharmacology* 12 (Supplement): S1-196.

Jones, H. C. 1996. Rifkin launches latest boycott. *Feedstuffs* (October 14): 3.

Juskevich, D. C., and C. G. Guyer. 1990. Bovine growth hormone: Human food safety evaluation. *Science* 249: 875-84.

Kaiser, J. 1996. Pests overwhelm Bt cotton crop. *Science* 273: 423.

Kessler, D. A., M. R. Taylor, J. H. Maryanski, et al. 1992. The safety of foods developed by biotechnology. *Science* 256: 1747-9, 1832.

Kilman, S. 1994a. Dairy-food concerns launch products from cows not treated with hormone. *The Wall Street Journal,* May 2, p. XX. Sec B, p. 7.

1994b. Growing pains: Genetic engineering's biggest impact may eventually be in agriculture. The key word: eventually. *The Wall Street Journal,* May 30, p. R7.

Kim, J. 1992a. Biotech firms design food for thought. *USA Today,* April 28.

1992b. Genetic agriculture gets go-ahead. *USA Today,* May 27, p. B3.

Kling, J. 1996. Could transgenic supercrops one day breed superweeds? *Science* 274: 180-1.

Knorr, D. 1995. Improving food biotechnology resources and strategies in developing countries. *Food Technology* 49: 91-3.

Kolata, G. 1994. When the geneticists' fingers get in the food. *The New York Times,* February 20, p. E13.

Krissoff, B. 1989. The European ban on livestock hormones and implications for international trade. *National Food Review* 12: 34-6.

Leary, W. 1992a. Cornucopia of new foods is seen as policy on engineering is eased. *The New York Times,* May 27, p. A1.

1992b. Gene-altered food held by the F.D.A. to pose little risk. *The New York Times,* May 26, pp. A1, C9.

1994. F.D.A. approves altered tomato that will remain fresh longer. *The New York Times,* May 19, pp. A1, B7.

Leonard, R. E. 1995. Codex at the crossroads: Conflict on trade, health. *Nutrition Week* 25 (July 14): 5-6.

Lynch, S., and C.-T. J. Lin. 1994. Food safety: Meal planners express their concerns. *FoodReview* 17: 14-18.

Mather, R. 1995. *A garden of unearthly delights: Bioengineering and the future of food.* New York.

Mayeno, A. N., and G. J. Gleich. 1994. Eosinophilia-myalgia syndrome and tryptophan production: A cautionary tale. *Trends in Biotechnology* 12: 346-52.

McMurray, S. 1993. New Calgene tomato might have tasted just as good without genetic alteration. *The Wall Street Journal,* January 12, p. B1.

Mellon, M. 1988. *Biotechnology and the environment.* Washington, D.C.

1991. An environmentalist perspective. In *The genetic revolution: Scientific prospects and public perceptions,* ed. B. D. Davis, 60-76. Baltimore, Md.

Messer, E. 1992. Sources of institutional funding for agro-biotechnology for developing countries. *Advanced Technology Assessment Systems* 9: 371-8.

Messer, E., and P. Heywood. 1990. Trying technology: Neither sure nor soon. *Food Policy* 15: 336-45.

Mikkelsen, T. R., B. Anderson, and R. B. Jorgensen. 1996. The risk of crop transgene spread. *Nature* 380: 31.

Miller, H. 1991. Regulation. In *The genetic revolution: Scientific prospects and public perceptions,* ed. B. D. Davis, 196-211. Baltimore, Md.

1992. Putting the bST human-health controversy to rest. *Bio/Technology* 10: 147.

1994. A need to reinvent biotechnology regulation at the EPA. *Science* 266: 1815-18.

Millstone, E., E. Brunner, and I. White. 1994. Plagiarism or protecting public health? *Nature* 371: 647-8.

Mittal, G. S. 1992. *Food biotechnology.* Lancaster, Pa.

Moffat, A. S. 1994. Developing nations adapt biotech for own needs. *Science* 265: 186-7.

National Research Council. 1989. Recommended Dietary Allowances. 10th edition. Washington, D.C.

Nestle, M. 1996. Allergies to transgenic foods – questions of policy. *New England Journal of Medicine* 334: 726-8.

Nordlee, J. A., S. L. Taylor, J. A. Townsend, et al. 1996. Identification of a Brazil-nut allergen in transgenic soybeans. *New England Journal of Medicine* 334: 688-92.

Office of Medical Applications of Research. 1991. *Bovine somatotropin: National Institutes of Health Technology Assessment Conference statement, December 5-7, 1990.* Washington, D.C.

Office of Planning and Evaluation and Center for Food Safety and Applied Nutrition. 1988. *Food biotechnology: Present and future.* 2 vols. Washington, D.C.

Olempska-Beer, Z. S., P. M. Kuznesof, M. DiNovi, and M. J. Smith. 1993. Plant biotechnology and food safety. *Food Technology* 47: 64-72.

Ollinger, M., and L. Pope. 1995. *Plant biotechnology: Out of the laboratory and into the field.* USDA Agricultural Economic Report No. 697. Washington, D.C.

O'Neill, M. 1992. Geneticists' latest discovery: Public fear of "Frankenfood." *The New York Times,* June 28, pp. A1, A14.

1994. Tomato review: No substitute for summer. *The New York Times,* May 19, p. B7.

Over 800 farmers report problems related to rBGH. 1995. *Nutrition Week* (June 2): 6.

Pell, A. N., D. S. Tsang, B. A. Howlett, et al. 1992. Effects of a prolonged-release formulation of Sometribove (n-methionyl bovine somatotropin) on Jersey cows. *Journal of Dairy Science* 75: 3416-31.

Philin, R. M., R. H. Hill, W. D. Flanders, et al. 1993. Tryptophan contaminants associated with eosinophilia-myalgia syndrome. *American Journal of Epidemiology* 138: 154-9.

Putnam, J. J., and J. E. Allshouse. 1996. *Food consumption, prices and expenditures, 1970-95.* USDA Statistical Bulletin No. 928. Washington, D.C.

1994. *Food Consumption, Prices and Expenditures 1970-95.* USDA *Statistical Bulletin.* Washington, D.C.

Redenbaugh, K., W. Hiatt, B. Martineau, et al. 1992. *Safety assessment of genetically engineered fruits and vegetables: A case study of the Flavr Savr tomato.* Boca Raton, Fla.

Reilly, J. M. 1989. *Consumer effects of biotechnology.* USDA

Agricultural Information Bulletin No. 581. Washington, D.C.

Rissler, J., and M. Mellon. 1993. *Perils amidst the promise: Ecological risks of transgenic crops in a global market.* Washington, D.C.

Rogers, P. L., and G. H. Fleet, eds. 1989. *Biotechnology and the food industry.* New York.

Roufs, J. B. 1992. Review of L-tryptophan and eosinophilia-myalgia syndrome. *Journal of the American Dietetic Association* 92: 844–50.

Sampson, H. A., and D. D. Metcalfe. 1992. Food allergies. *Journal of the American Medical Association* 268: 2840–4.

Schneider, K. 1989. Stores bar milk produced by drug: Five big chains take action – U.S. calls process safe. *The New York Times,* August 24, pp. A1, A18.

     1990. F.D.A. defends milk-producing drug in study. *The New York Times,* August 24, p. A18.

     1993. U.S. approves use of drug to raise milk production: Gain for biotechnology. *The New York Times,* November 6, pp. 1, 9.

     1994a. Farmers eager to test drug to get more milk. *The New York Times,* February 5, p. 6.

     1994b. Grocers challenge use of new drug for milk output. *The New York Times,* February 4, pp. A1, A14.

     1994c. Lines drawn in a war over a milk hormone. *The New York Times,* March 9, p. A12.

     1994d. Maine and Vermont restrict dairies' use of a growth hormone. *The New York Times,* April 15, p. A16.

     1994e. Question is raised on hormone maker's ties to F.D.A. aides. *The New York Times,* April 18, p. A9.

Smith, P. G., and S. N. Cousens. 1996. Is the new variant of Creutzfeldt-Jakob disease from mad cows? *Science* 273: 748.

Somerville, C. R. 1993. Future prospects for genetic modification of the composition of edible oils from higher plants. *American Journal of Clinical Nutrition* 58 (Supplement): 270s–275s.

Stillings, B. R. 1994. Trends in foods. *Nutrition Today* 29: 6–13.

Stix, G. 1995. A recombinant feast: New bioengineered crops move toward market. *Scientific American* 273: 38–9.

Stone, R. 1995. Sweeping patents put biotech companies on the warpath. *Science* 268: 656–8.

Sugawara, S. 1992. For the next course, "engineered" entrees? "Genetic" tomato may launch an industry. *The Washington Post,* June 10, p. F1.

Sullivan, L. W. 1991. The link between nutrition and health. In *New technologies and the future of food and nutrition,* ed. G. E. Gaull and R. A. Goldberg, 97. New York.

Sun, M. 1989. Market sours on milk hormone. *Science* 246: 876–7.

Swaminathan, M. S. 1982. Biotechnology research and Third World agriculture. *Science* 218: 967–72.

Tacket, C. O., L. B. Dominguez, H. J. Fisher, and M. L. Cohen. 1985. An outbreak of multiple-drug-resistant *Salmonella* enteritis from raw milk. *Journal of the American Medical Association* 253: 2058–60.

U.S. Congress, Office of Technology Assessment. 1987. *New developments in biotechnology – background paper: Public perceptions of biotechnology.* OTA-BP-BA-45. Washington, D.C.

     1989. *New developments in biotechnology: Patenting life – special report.* OTA-BA-370. Washington, D.C.

     1991a. *Biotechnology in a global economy.* OTA-BA-494. Washington, D.C.

     1991b. *U.S. dairy industry at a crossroad: Biotechnology and policy choices – special report.* OTA-F-470. Washington, D.C.

     1992. *A new technological era for American agriculture.* OTA-F-475. Washington, D.C.

U.S. General Accounting Office. 1992a. *Food safety and quality: FDA strategy needed to address animal drug residues in milk.* GAO/RCED-92-209. Washington, D.C.

     1992b. *Recombinant bovine growth hormone: FDA approval should be withheld until the mastitis issue is resolved.* GAO/PEMD-92-26. Washington, D.C.

     1993. *Food safety and quality: Innovative strategies may be needed to regulate new food technologies.* GAO/RCED-93-142. Washington, D.C.

     1994. *Letter from Acting General Counsel Robert P. Murphy to the Honorables George E. Brown, Jr., David Obey, and Bernard Sanders.* B257122. Washington, D.C.

Vandaele, W. 1992. bST and the EEC: Politics vs. science. *Bio/Technology* 10: 148–9.

Wadman, M. 1996. Genetic resistance spreads to consumers. *Nature* 383: 564.

Waldholz, M. 1994. An industry in adolescence. Think of biotechnology as a teenager: Lots of promise, lots of headaches. *The Wall Street Journal,* May 20, p. R4.

Walter, R. 1995. We must boost public acceptance of biotech. *Bio/Technology* 13: 216–17.

Winslow, R. 1996. Allergen is inadvertently transferred to soybean in bioengineering test. *The Wall Street Journal,* March 14, p. B6.

Wolf, J. 1997. Europe turns up nose at biotech food: Lacking EU rules for modified crops, farm sector could suffer. *The Wall Street Journal,* January 2, p. 8.

Zimmerman, L., P. Kendall, M. Stone, and T. Hoban. 1994. Consumer knowledge and concern about biotechnology and food safety. *Food Technology* 48: 71–7.

VII.8   Food Safety and Biotechnology

The ready availability of safe, wholesome food is often taken for granted by citizens of modern societies. However, maintaining the safety of a large, diverse food supply is a challenging undertaking that requires coordinated effort at many levels. In this chapter, the principles of food safety are discussed first with regard to traditional foods and then again as they concern novel foods developed through genetic modification.

Definitions and Priorities

The term "food safety," as used today, encompasses many diverse areas, including protection against food poisoning and assurance that food does not contain additives or contaminants that would render it unsafe to eat. The term evolved mainly in the context of preventing intoxication by microbial poisons that act quickly (within hours to a day or two of exposure) and often induce such serious symptoms as convulsive vomiting and severe diarrhea, or respiratory failure and death (Cliver 1990). An example of the former is staphylococcal food poisoning, caused by the proteinaceous enterotoxins of the pathogenic bacterium *Staphylococcus aureus* (Cliver 1990). Botulism is an example of the latter, caused by the neurotoxins synthesized by *Clostridium botulinum* (Cliver 1990).

Both staphylococcal food poisoning and botulism result from ingesting toxins that are preformed in the implicated foods. For illness to ensue, it is necessary only to ingest the toxin, not the microbe itself. Food poisoning may also follow the ingestion of certain pathogenic bacteria, such as *Salmonella,* which produce gastrointestinal (GI) infections, and *Escherichia coli* 0157:H7, which produces an infection and a potent toxin within the GI tract (Cliver 1990). The infection results in bloody diarrhea, while the toxin enters the bloodstream and induces kidney damage.

Given the foregoing, it should come as no surprise that the Food and Drug Administration (FDA), the lead federal agency charged with ensuring the safety of the food supply in the United States, considers foodborne microbial pathogens and the toxins they produce to be the most important of the various food safety risks (Table VII.8.1). Unfortunately, evidence indicates that the public often tends to focus too much on pesticide residues and food additives, wrongly believing that the risk from these materials is as great as that from pathogenic microorganisms (Pariza 1992c).

Table VII.8.1. *Ranking food safety risks*

1. Food-borne disease.
2. Environmental contaminants.
3. Naturally occurring toxins.
4. Food additives.
5. Pesticide residues.

Source: Young (1989).

Table VII.8.2. *Summary of reported food-borne disease outbreaks in the United States, 1983-7*[a]

Etiologic agent	Percentage of cases	Percentage of outbreaks[b]
Pathogenic bacteria[c]	92	66
Viruses[c]	5	5
Parasites[c]	<1	4
Chemical agents[d]	2	26

[a]During this time period, 91,678 cases and 2,397 outbreaks of foodborne illness were reported to the Centers for Disease Control (CDC). The etiologic agent was identified in 38 percent of the outbreaks. These data are summarize in this table.

[b]An outbreak is the occurrence of two or more cases of illness transmitted by a single food.

[c]Pathogenic bacteria, viruses, and parasites are all classified as microorganisms.

[d]Some instances of chemical poisoning were actually due to chemical toxins produced by microorganisms. No instances of illness traced to synthetic chemicals were identified in the report.

Source: Bean et al. (1990).

Microbial Foodborne Illness

Table VII.8.2 shows a summary of foodborne illness in the United States, compiled by the Centers for Disease Control (CDC), from 1983 to 1987 (Bean et al. 1990). But according to both the CDC and the FDA, the reported cases and outbreaks account for only a tiny fraction of the total foodborne illnesses that occurred during that period. It is estimated that several million cases of microbial food poisoning actually occur in the United States each year (Archer and Kvenberg 1985).

Foodborne illness is caused by a relatively small number of bacterial species. All raw foods contain microorganisms, some of which may be pathogens. Whether or not this becomes a problem is determined largely by how the food is handled prior to consumption. Pathogen growth depends on a number of factors. The most important of these are (1) the levels of salt and other electrolytes present in the food; (2) the types and amount of acid in the food; (3) the amount of available water; (4) the presence of microbial inhibitors (both naturally occurring and synthetic); (5) storage conditions; and (6) cooking conditions. Safe food processing depends on understanding these factors and effectively utilizing the basic principles of microbiology as they apply to foods.

In addition to precipitating illness and soaring medical costs, foodborne illness can also bring economic devastation for producers of an implicated product (Todd 1985). A dramatic example occurred in 1982, when two Belgians developed botulism after sharing a can of Alaskan salmon. One of them subsequently died of the illness.

The problem was traced to a can press that was used at the processing plant to form the can in question. The press was defective and had produced a tiny rupture in the wall of the implicated can. The rupture, which was virtually invisible, nonetheless permitted a small amount of nonsterile water to be drawn into the can during the cooling step that followed heat processing. The water was contaminated with spores of *Clostridium botulinum* which, once inside the can, germinated and produced the toxin that induced the illness. Fears that other cans might have been similarly damaged prompted voluntary recalls of much of the canned Alaskan salmon produced that year. In all, 60 million cans were recalled and discarded (Hayes 1983).

Foods provide a medium for the growth of specific pathogens, but they can also be passive carriers for virtually any pathogen capable of producing infection via the oral route. In this case the pathogens do not actually have to grow in the food. They need only to survive. Good examples are the foodborne viruses, such as the virus that causes hepatitis A. These cannot grow in the foods that carry them, yet illness follows ingestion of the contaminated food.

It should be noted that food spoilage and food safety are not related in a direct manner. A food may be spoiled but nonetheless safe. Alternatively, however, a food can contain bacterial toxins at deadly levels yet appear perfectly "normal." And finally, it is important to recognize that not all microbes in food are bad. Rather, harmless microorganisms are an integral part of many traditional foods. One could not produce bread, cheese, yoghurt, soy sauce, sauerkraut, beer, or wine without specific yeasts, bacteria, and molds. Such microorganisms are needed to induce desirable changes in the food through a process called "fermentation." Besides providing characteristic flavors, fermentation is also an important, effective method of food preservation. The harmless fermentation microorganisms produce microbial inhibitors and otherwise change the ecology of the food in ways that discourage subsequent pathogen growth.

Risks from Synthetic Chemicals

The data summarized in Table VII.8.2 indicate that the risk of developing foodborne microbial illness is far higher than the risk of becoming ill because of exposure to toxic chemicals in food. The instances of chemical poisoning reported in Table VII.8.2 represent almost exclusively naturally occurring toxins or contaminants. Only one approved food additive (monosodium glutamate) was reported as possibly causing illness in two outbreaks that occurred in 1984, involving a total of seven persons. In no instance was a synthetic chemical identified in the CDC report as a cause of illness (Bean et al. 1990). The data summarized in Table VII.8.2 refer to clinical illness, almost all of which is acute (that is, there is only a short time interval between exposure and onset of symptoms). Of course, questions about risks from "chemicals" in food often center on chronic effects, such as cancer, which in humans takes many years to develop.

The causes of chronic illness are much more difficult to determine because of the long time intervals between initial exposure and the onset of symptoms. Nonetheless, there is an extensive toxicology data base against which hypotheses can be tested. For example, based on these data, one may conclude that it is highly unlikely that synthetic pesticide residues or food additives pose a cancer risk to consumers (Ames, Profet, and Gold 1990; Pariza 1992a, 1992b).

Risks of Naturally Occurring Pesticides

Plants lack the defenses that animals possess (mobility, claws, and teeth), and so they must rely on passive defenses that are effective in situ. Accordingly, evolution has provided plants with the ability to synthesize naturally occurring toxins. In a very real sense, plants are practitioners of chemical warfare against potential predators.

The natural toxins that plants produce are usually nonspecific in nature; that is, they act against a variety of potential pests, including mammals as well as insects. The pathways regulating the synthesis and expression of these toxins tend to be under general control, meaning that any number of stresses, from insect infestation to drought, can "turn on" the entire spectrum of chemical and biological defenses that a plant possesses.

In this context, crop breeding can be seen as a means of controlling unwanted wild traits, such as toxin production, in plants destined for the table. Experience has shown that this is a relatively easy matter, even without any knowledge of the underlying science, doubtless because toxin production is not an inherent part of the growth and reproductive processes. Humans select and artificially propagate variants that would not otherwise survive but that nonetheless exhibit desirable traits. Because of the genetic linkage within the generalized protective mechanism pathways, increased expression of traits that humans deem desirable will usually be accompanied by decreased toxin expression (International Food Biotechnology Council 1990).

Unfortunately, selected traits that make a plant desirable as human food also make it desirable to insects. This, in fact, is why synthetic pesticides are used: They replace the naturally occurring pesticides and related survival traits that have been bred out of food plants.

Yet, although the natural pesticide levels of food plants have been lowered considerably through breeding, they have not been totally eliminated. Rather, the data in Table VII.8.3 show that many commonly consumed food plants and plant products contain naturally occurring pesticidal carcinogens. Moreover, unlike synthetic chemicals, which must be rigorously tested before regulatory agencies will approve them for food-related use, the toxins made naturally by plants are not ordinarily subjected to any sort of testing (Ames et al. 1990). For some individuals, however, it is unsettling to learn that many of those substances that have been tested have proved to be carcinogenic in rat or mouse feeding studies.

Yet it is important to put these findings into perspective by a consideration of (1) the relative exposure of the public to natural versus synthetic carcinogenic pesticide residues, and (2) the relative risk of cancer from these exposures.

With regard to exposure, FDA data indicate that the average daily intake of synthetic pesticides per person in the United States is 0.09 milligrams (mg) (Ames et al. 1990). About half of this intake (0.04 mg) comes from four chemicals that were not carcinogenic in high-dose rodent feeding studies. Thus, assuming that all of the remaining exposure is to carcinogenic pesticides (an unlikely assumption), the maximum exposure to synthetic carcinogenic pesticide residues is 0.05 mg per person per day.

Table VII.8.3. *Some natural pesticidal carcinogens in food*

Rodent carcinogen	Plant food	Concentration, ppm
5-/8-methoxypsoralen	Parsley	14
	Parsnip, cooked	32
	Celery	0.8
	Celery, new cultivar	6.2
	Celery, stressed	25
ρ-hydrazinobenzoate	Mushrooms	11
Glutamyl r-hydrazinobenzoate	Mushrooms	42
Sinigrin (allyl isothiocyanate)	Cabbage	35–590
	Collard greens	250–788
	Cauliflower	12–66
	Brussels sprouts	110–1560
	Mustard (brown)	16000–72000
	Horseradish	4500
Estragole	Basil	3800
	Fennel	3000
Safrole	Nutmeg	3000
	Mace	10,000
	Pepper, black	100
Ethyl acrylate	Pineapple	0.07
Sesamol	Sesame seeds (heated oil)	75
α-methylbenzyl alcohol	Cocoa	1.3
Benzyl acetate	Basil	82
	Jasmine tea	230
	Honey	15
Catechol	Coffee (roasted beans)	100
Caffeic acid	Apple, carrot, celery, cherry, eggplant, endive, grapes, lettuce, pear, plum, potato	50–200
	Absinthe, anise, basil, caraway, dill, marjoram, rosemary, sage, savory, tarragon, thyme	>1000
	Coffee (roasted beans)	1800
Chlorogenic acid (caffeic acid)	Apricot, cherry, peach, plum	50–500
	Coffee (roasted beans)	21600
Neochlorogenic acid (caffeic acid)	Apple, apricot, broccoli, brussels sprouts, cabbage, cherry, kale, peach, pear, plum	50–500
	Coffee (roasted beans)	11600

Source: Ames, Profet, and Gold (1990).

By comparison, it is estimated that Americans consume 1.5 grams of natural pesticides per person per day, or about 15,000 times more than the amount of synthetic pesticides. Moreover, many of these natural pesticides are also carcinogenic in high-dose rodent feeding studies (Table VII.8.3). Clearly, the public is exposed to far higher levels of naturally occurring pesticides, and, in fact, when compared to naturally occurring pesticides, synthetic pesticide exposure is trivial (Ames et al. 1990).

Moreover, toxicology is not just about exposure levels to toxic substances, because animals, including humans, have numerous biochemical and physiological resources to defend against such exposure. These defenses include enzymes that detoxify toxins and repair toxin-induced damage to DNA and other important biological structures, as well as the continual shedding of cells at epithelial surfaces that are most exposed to toxic insult (that is, cells at the surface of skin, eyes, and gastrointestinal tract). In short, humans have layer on layer of protection against the toxic dangers of "natural" environments.

Because of the immense number and variety of potential toxins, the defense systems must by necessity be general in nature. In this regard, there is nothing unique about synthetic pesticides. The protective mechanisms that act against naturally occurring toxins also act against synthetic toxins. These protective mechanisms are, of course, even more effective when the dose is exceedingly low as is the case with exposure to synthetic pesticide residues on produce. Moreover, it is important to note that the biological effects produced in animals by naturally occurring pesticides and other potential toxins are not always adverse. Rather, paradoxically, many of the substances shown in Table VII.8.3 that cause cancer when fed to rodents at excessively high levels seem to protect against cancer when fed at the lower, more realistic levels encountered in a normal diet (Pariza 1993).

One implication of this paradox is that unrealistically high dose cancer tests have been responsible for indicting the naturally occurring substances shown in Table VII.8.3. In fact, this consideration has led many experts to reexamine the entire framework through which we detect and regulate "carcinogens" (Ames et al. 1990; Pariza 1992c; National Research Council 1993).

The Safety of Novel Foods

There are many kinds of novel foods. In the simplest sense, a food may be novel in one locale and a dietary staple in another. Examples include the many foods that crossed the Atlantic Ocean between Europe and the Americas in the years following Columbus's voyages (Goldblith 1992). Corn, potatoes, tomatoes, and cacao (chocolate), which today are common throughout the world, were novelties for everyone on earth, save the Native Americans, just 500 years ago.

At the other end of the spectrum are novel foods developed by using recombinant DNA technology (for example, Calgene's flavr savr tomato). The recombinant DNA process is defined as "cutting and recombining DNA molecules to remove segments from or otherwise modify an organism's genetic material, or to combine segments of DNA from different types of organisms" (International Food Biotechnology Council 1990:).

Discovered and refined only since the 1970s, recombinant DNA methods represent a revolutionary means of controlling the introduction of new traits into plants, animals, and microorganisms. It should be stressed, however, that the "revolution" is not the process itself. There is ample evidence that gene transfer between different species has occurred throughout the history of life on this planet (International Food Biotechnology Council 1990). Rather, the revolution is that humans are able to control the process. For the first time in history, it is possible to direct the transfer of DNA from one species to another. It is also possible to create entirely new genes that, seemingly, have not existed before and transfer them into living hosts where the new genes will then replicate along with the host's genetic material.

The incredible power of this technology has led some to conclude that to prevent misuse, the process itself must be carefully regulated. Others argue that the process is simply a scientific tool and that the focus of regulation should be on the products of biotechnology, not on the process.

With specific regard to food, most experts agree that the focus of safety evaluation should be on the novel foods themselves, and not on the process whereby novel foods are developed (International Food Biotechnology Council 1990; Kessler et al. 1992). The rationale for this reasoning is that recombinant DNA technology is no less safe than plant breed-

ing or any other traditional means of genetic manipulation. In all cases, one is (or should be) concerned with the expression of genetic information.

For example, in traditional plant breeding, one should determine if unexpected traits that bear on safety are expressed by the new cultivar. Such unexpected traits may arise directly from the genetic material itself that has been transferred in the cross may result because the transferred genetic material affected a regulatory element, thereby inducing the expression of an undesirable new trait (for example, the expression of a toxin).

In any attempt to establish the safety of a novel food, the same procedures should be followed to assure that the gene being transferred produces a safe product and that the gene does not induce changes in the recipient that bear on health and safety issues.

Addressing the first concern (whether the gene that is being transferred produces a safe product) is a relatively straightforward matter. This is because the gene can be completely defined. If the gene codes for a protein, it, too, can be completely defined and studied directly for toxigenic potential.

The second concern (whether the transferred gene induces changes in the recipient that bear on health and safety issues) is somewhat more problematic, as it is with traditional methods of genetic modification.

For example, the data of Table VII.8.3 indicate that many food plants naturally produce potentially carcinogenic compounds. As already discussed, the expression of such natural pesticides does not occur at a constant rate irrespective of other considerations. Rather, these substances are under genetic control, which in turn is influenced by environmental factors, such as insect infestation and drought. A pertinent example shown in Table VII.8.3 concerns celery.

Celery produces a class of natural pesticides called psoralins, which are light-activated mutagenic carcinogens. Ordinarily, the concentration of psoralins in celery is about 0.8 parts per million, which is too low to produce evidence of adverse effects in persons who consume the vegetable. However, through the use of traditional breeding methodology, an insect-resistant celery cultivar was developed that contained about 10 times the concentration of psoralin typically found (Table VII.8.3). This level was sufficiently high to produce skin irritations in consumers (Ames et al. 1990). Ordinary celery, subjected to stress, contains still higher levels of psoralin.

The increased psoralin content of the new celery cultivar was the result of genetic manipulation via traditional crop breeding techniques. It represents a reversal of the more commonly observed trend of decreased levels of naturally occurring toxicants in plants as they are "domesticated" through crop breeding (International Food Biotechnology Council 1990). In this particular case, however, the breeder's goal was to select for enhanced insect resistance so as to minimize the need for synthetic pesticides. Hence, the outcome of increased levels of psoralin (celery's natural insecticide) is not surprising. It should be noted that when the excessive psoralin problem was discovered, the cultivar was quickly withdrawn from the market (Ames et al. 1990).

This example offers insight into the evaluation of the safety of novel foods. The issue is whether introducing the new gene into the recipient triggers a response by the recipient that bears on health and safety. One of the main considerations is the possibility of increased synthesis of a toxicant synthesized naturally by the recipient plant (such as psoralin in a hypothetical novel celery).

There is considerable information on naturally occurring toxicants that are produced by food plants (International Food Biotechnology Council 1990). Such information can provide the framework for comparing the natural toxin levels in a novel food with those in its traditional (unmodified) counterpart - for instance, the psoralins in the hypothetical novel celery versus those in ordinary celery. A given plant species produces only a limited number of the known naturally occurring toxicants (usually restricted to a specific chemical class). Hence, it is not necessary to analyze each plant for every known, naturally occurring toxin. Rather, effort can be concentrated on the potential toxicants with which the plants in question are known to be associated. Such assays can take the form of specific chemical analyses, possibly coupled with judicious, limited animal testing (International Food Biotechnology Council 1990; Kessler et al. 1992).

The concept of comparative toxicology - assessing safety of a novel food by comparing it with its traditional counterpart - is central to the food safety assessment schemes developed by the International Food Biotechnology Council, a food and biotechnology industry-sponsored group (International Food Biotechnology Council 1990) and the FDA (Kessler et al 1992). In addition to assays for specific toxins, one should also consider changes in composition that might affect pathogen growth (Pariza 1992b).

Conclusion

With the advent of biotechnology, the production and availability of food is entering a new era of great promise for improved human welfare. Procedures and methodologies are available to ensure the safety of the novel foods that have been and will be developed through biotechnology (International Food Biotechnology Council 1990; Kessler et al. 1992). These procedures and methodologies are not fundamentally different from those used now to assure the safety of traditional foods developed though traditional means of breeding and improvement.

Michael W. Pariza

Bibliography

Ames, B. N., M. Profet, and L. S. Gold. 1990. Dietary pesticides (99.99% all natural). *Proceedings of the National Academy of Science* 87: 7777-81.

Archer, D. L., and J. E. Kvenberg. 1985. Incidence and cost of foodborne diarrheal disease in the United States. *Journal of Food Protection* 48: 887-94.

Bean, N. H., P. M. Griffin, J. S. Goulding, and C. B. Ivey. 1990. Foodborne disease outbreaks, 5-year summary, 1983-1987. *Morbidity Mortality Weekly Report* 39(SS-1): 1-23.

Cliver, D. O., ed. 1990. *Foodborne Diseases.* New York.

Goldblith, S. A. 1992. The legacy of Columbus, with particular reference to foods. *Food Technology* 46: 62-85.

Hayes, A. H., Jr. 1983. The Food and Drug Administration's role in the canned salmon recalls of 1982. *Public Health Report* 98: 412-15.

International Food Biotechnology Council. 1990. Biotechnologies and food: Assuring the safety of foods produced by genetic modification. *Regulatory Toxicology and Pharmacology* 12: S1-196.

Kessler, D.A., M. R. Taylor, J. H. Maryanski, et al. 1992. The safety of foods developed by biotechnology. *Science* 256: 1747-9, 1832.

National Research Council. 1993. *Issues in Risk Assessment.* Washington, D.C.

Pariza, M. W. 1992a. A new approach to evaluating carcinogenic risk. *Proceedings of the National Academy of Science* 89: 860-1.

  1992b. Foods of new biotechnology vs traditional products: Microbiological aspects. *Food Technology* 46: 100-2.

  1992c. Risk assessment. *Critical Reviews in Food Science Nutrition* 31: 205-9.

  1993. Diet and Cancer: Where do matters stand? *Archives of Internal Medicine* 153: 50-6.

Todd, E. C. D. 1985. Economic loss from foodborne disease and non-illness related recalls because of mishandling by food processors. *Journal of Food Protection* 48: 621-33.

Young, F. E. 1989. Weighing food safety risks. *FDA Consumer* September: 8-13.

VII.9 ❧ Food Additives

Foods are biological products and, therefore, incorporate complex physical and biochemical systems. Many vegetables, fruits, and (sometimes) meat and fish are eaten raw, but in general they are cooked. And cooking induces profound chemical and physical changes. Some changes, such as the denaturation of protein and the gelation of starch, render food more digestible and are beneficial; others, by improving appearance, color, flavor, and texture, are also desirable. But some that cause heat damage to proteins, the loss of vitamins, or the formation of carcinogens on the surfaces of roast and barbecued meats are deleterious. Cooking leads to the use of one system, or a component of it, in the establishment of another. An example would be the role of egg yolks in emulsifying oil and water (vinegar) to make mayonnaise and to color it. Cooking also permits the use of major and minor ingredients and, thus, infinite variation in the final dish, but it also opens the way for the entry into food of nonfood substances derived from utensils and containers, and from the kitchen itself.

Food processors operate highly organized and sophisticated kitchens, and they apply detailed scientific knowledge of the raw materials to the production and packaging of products in response to market demands for variety, safety, wholesomeness, nutrition, and reasonable price. In effect, food processors are "super-cooks," but if in making mayonnaise they use lecithin (emulsifier) and beta-carotene (color) instead of egg yolk, or if they add acetic or citric acids instead of vinegar, then they are using additives.

Put simply, a food additive is a substance deliberately added to food by the processor to facilitate processing or to improve appearance, texture, flavor, keeping quality, or nutritional value. By contrast, any unwanted substance that finds its way into food is a contaminant. This may be defined even more widely as a substance that is not normally present in that food in its natural form; or is present in concentrations not normally found; or is not permitted under the food regulations to be present; or, being an additive as defined under the regulations, exceeds the concentration permitted.

Unfortunately, practice denies such simplicity, and the Codex Alimentarius Commission uses the following definition:

> "Food additive" means any substance not normally consumed as food by itself or not normally used as a typical ingredient of the food, whether or not it has nutritive value, the intentional addition of which to food for a technological (including organoleptic) purpose in the manufacture, processing, preparation, treatment, packing, packaging, transport or holding of such food results, or may be reasonably expected to result, (directly or indirectly) in it or its by-products becoming a component of or otherwise affecting the characteristics of such foods. The term does not include "contaminants" or substances added to food for maintaining or improving nutritional qualities (Codex Alimentarius Commission 1979).

There are gaps and uncertainties in such a definition. The key word in the Codex definition is "intentional." This excludes substances in which residues are inevitably present that are legitimately used in the production and processing of food. Strictly speaking, these residues are contaminants, but they are variously described as adventitious, indirect, incidental, or unintentional additives and are treated by most regulatory authorities in the same way as substances added for functional purposes to the food itself. They include pesticide residues, processing aids, sanitizers,

boiler water additives, and packaging migrants and are quite different in kind, and often in concentration, from industrial contaminants, such as the notorious mercury contamination of the fish in Minimata Bay, Japan, and polychlorinated biphenyls (PCBs). For the purposes of this discussion, then, substances permitted by the Codex definition, together with such nutrients as vitamins and minerals, will be considered to be additives.

Food Additives in History

There is nothing new about the concept of food additives. The ancient Chinese unknowingly used traces of ethylene and propylene from burning paraffin to ripen fruit, although additives were probably used originally simply to preserve food. Smoking is an ancient method of food preservation, usually for meat or fish, which relies partly on drying and partly on the preserving chemicals in the smoke.

Similarly, the resins added to Greek wine act as mild preservatives, and in classical times, the pitch linings of amphorae contributed substances that helped to preserve the wine carried in them. More recently, the practice of burning sulfur in empty wine barrels not only fumigated the barrel but also adventitiously ensured that the wine filling the barrel would be treated with sulfur dioxide, still the preservative of choice in the industry.

It is possible, however, that the first additive deliberately used to preserve foods was salt. Salted foods, especially fish, were known in antiquity. Salt was used lavishly as a preservative; the Romans made a fish sauce, liquamen, in which the fermentation, as well as the keeping quality, was controlled by adding salt. Salt is, however, so familiar and is used so much in such proportions that we now think of it as an ingredient, in contrast to an additive.

The same could be said of sugar, which emerged much later, possibly from India. Salt, however, is a simple inorganic chemical, whereas cane (or beet) sugar is a rather more complex organic molecule. White granulated sugar is a very pure chemical of great value in food preparation, whether in the home or factory. In honey and dried fruits, the sugar present acts as a preservative as does cane sugar in jams – the value of sugar as a flavoring is obvious. Sugar is a functional additive, but today, like salt, it too is thought of as an ingredient. However, saltpeter (sodium nitrate), which has been used from ancient times as a preservative, is *not* considered an ingredient but is firmly classified as an additive and is subject to continuing scrutiny.

Fermentation was long used as an empirical method of preservation. Alcoholic fermentation is itself a kind of preservation, and alcohol, in the form of brandy, was used in brandied wines as an additive. The production of lactic acid by fermentation, as in cheese, yoghurt, certain cured sausages, and sauerkraut, is another historical example of the formation of a preservative in situ by fermentation. And the acetic acid of vinegar was used by the Romans as a preservative for fruits and vegetables. A modern parallel is the surface treatment of meat with acetic acid to prolong shelf life.

The use of spices as flavorings is very old, as is the Western spice trade with the East. Even if the popularity of spices in Europe was really the result of an efficacy in masking the flavors of salted and tainted meats, the demand for them was established, and it is now known that they also act as mild preservatives. Some 600 years ago, hops were added to beer as a flavoring, which was not at first appreciated; but it was then noted that hopped beer kept better than unhopped ale. Hop resins, too, function as preservatives, but both spices and hops also are today classified as ingredients.

Before the factory production of food, preservation and flavor seem to have been more important than color. Nonetheless, saffron was used as a food color in ancient Egypt, and upper-class Romans had a preference for white bread, which was produced for them by sieving the flour and then adding alum, a practice that persisted until the end of the nineteenth century. Food coloring became popular in medieval times but was confined to the kitchens of the castles and great houses whose chefs used many colors of plant origin. These included indigo, alkanet from the root of borage, sanders from sandalwood, saffron from crocuses, marigold, and turmeric; greens came from the chlorophyll of sage and spinach, and pinks, blues, mauves, and violets from petal extracts.

In the seventeenth century, cochineal (from the dried insect *Coccus cacti*) and annatto (from the seeds of the shrub *Bixa orellana*) reached Europe from the New World. The latter was used to color butter and cheese, although in the eighteenth century butter was colored with saffron. In addition, the greening of vegetables by cooking in copper vessels was well known. No food-processing industry existed, however, and additives were confined to the kitchen and to farmhouse and village technology – that is, to butter, cheese, wine, and cider making, and to brewing, baking, and milling. Because there was no food industry, there were no processing aids, sanitizers, boiler water additives, or packaging migrants; nor were there any agricultural chemicals. But there was lead, an outright contaminant that came from the pipes of water systems; from cooking, eating, and drinking utensils; and from ingredients.

The Romans employed lead for collecting and distributing water, and their methods persisted. Even today lead pipes are used for water reticulation in many old houses and buildings in Britain and Europe. In the ancient world, food was cooked and stored in vessels of lead, leaded bronze and brass, and pewter and was served on lead and pewter plates and dishes. The Romans lacked sugar and, for a sweetener, used grape juice concentrated by boiling in lead vessels, because of the extra sweetness derived from the lead salts (Nriagu 1983).

So high was the lead content of the food and drink (especially wine) consumed by the upper-class Romans that lead poisoning has been confidently proposed as one of the major causes of the decline of the Roman Empire (Gilfillan 1965; Nriagu 1983).

Lead acetate ("sugar of lead") itself, and other lead compounds, were used as sweeteners in wine well into the nineteenth century (Christison 1835; Johnson 1989). In 1767 the disease "Devonshire colic" was identified as lead poisoning and traced to lead fittings on cider presses and lead-lined tanks to hold the apple juice, which, because of the malic acid content, readily picks up lead (Baker 1767, cited in Smith 1986; MAFF 1983). Also during this period, warnings were issued about the danger of the solution of lead from the glazes on earthenware (Drummond and Wilbraham 1957), but as late as the 1870s, lead salts, especially chromate, were being added as colors to confectionery (Dunn 1878). Thus, by 1905, when the Australian state of Victoria introduced food regulations, the first of those regulations included the prohibition of lead in or in contact with food.

The attempts of governments, however, to regulate food additives had a long history. In the late Middle Ages, for example, saffron was used by pastry cooks to simulate eggs, and by the seventeenth century, butter was being colored with annatto. But in 1574 the authorities in the French city of Bourges acted to prohibit egg simulation, and in 1641 Amsterdam prohibited annatto coloring in order to protect May butter, which, because of its color, enjoyed a premium (Meijer 1961; Truhaut and Souverain 1963).

In England in the eighteenth century, claims that chalk and ground bones were added to bread to whiten it were successfully refuted (Drummond and Wilbraham 1957). But there is no doubt that alum was used in this capacity. Calcium carbonate in the form of marble, chalk, or shells was added to beer and cider to counteract acidity; bean flour and isinglass were used as clarifiers; and copperas (iron sulfate) was added to produce a "head" (Drummond and Wilbraham 1957).

With the emergence of factories during the Industrial Revolution, adulteration increased dramatically. Most of this had to do with cheaper substitutes, but some of it involved what would now be called additives: colors, flavors, thickeners, and so forth. In 1820, F. Accum, for example, reported among other things the whitening of bread with alum, the greening of pickles with copper salts, the coloring of Gloucester cheese with red lead, and the flavoring of beer with *Cocculus indicus*. By midcentury, alum, black lead, Prussian blue, lead chromate, copper carbonate, red lead, vermilion, and copper arsenite were all being used in food and confectionery (Mitchell 1848; Hassall 1855; Campbell 1990). One example of such usage involved spent tea leaves that were "faced" with a mixture of Prussian blue and turmeric to permit their resale as green tea (Cochran 1870).

At least as early as the 1840s, sodium nitrate was employed to preserve butter (Anon. 1843). From the 1830s to the 1870s, attempts were made in Australia to preserve meat with sulfites, phosphoric and lactic acids, acetates, nitrates, and nitrites for shipment to Britain (Farrer 1980). Boric and salicylic acids emerged later in the century as flavored preservatives for sausages, milk, and cordials, and in the United States, this led eventually to the "Poison Squad" of volunteers set up by H. H. Wiley, Chief Food Chemist of the U.S. Department of Agriculture, to test the safety of preservatives then in use.

Similar concerns had surfaced elsewhere. In Canada, a report to a meeting of the British Medical Association in Toronto in 1905 resulted in the Adulteration Act, under which the first list of additives prohibited for use in food was published (Pugsley 1959). In Australia, a report by the Victorian Government Analyst covered (among other things) colors, preservatives, flavors, saccharin, and alum. This led at the end of 1905 to the aforementioned Pure Food Act (Farrer 1980).

In 1856 William Perkin's accidental discovery of mauveine initiated the dyestuffs industry, which by the beginning of the twentieth century made available a large number of synthetic colors, some 80 of which were being used in food (Noonan and Meggos 1980). Their tinctorial properties were such as to require only very small concentrations to obtain the desired result, and thus they were perceived to be, and were, much safer than the lead, copper, and even arsenic salts that had been used for so long. In 1906, the United States listed 7 colors permitted to be used in foods, and in the interests of commercial rationalization, the number of dyes of "food grade" were soon limited elsewhere by manufacturers. In the period up to World War II, the American list was extended, and lists of colors permitted to be used in foods were adopted by various other countries.

Also in the early years of the twentieth century, borates and salicylates fell into disuse as preservatives and were largely replaced with sulfites and benzoates. For thickening and stabilizing, regular flour was employed (that is, the starch in it), along with corn flour, gelatin, and gums, and the natural lecithin of egg yolk was a common emulsifier. Changes came only after the World War II, when the carcinogenicity of additives and even of ingredients became an issue, and when large numbers of new functional additives became available.

Food Additives in Processing

The appearance, flavor, texture, and keeping quality of foods have always been important, and as noted, additives have long been used to improve them all.

By enabling food to be presented in new, attractive, stable, and convenient ways, modern food additives have raised consumers' expectations to the extent that the demand for the advantages that food additives confer may be said to be sociological rather than technological.

Some may argue that it is the food technologist who has created such a demand, but at best this would be only half true. Colors, flavors, and preservatives have been used for centuries. Gelatin for jelly making, for example, was laboriously prepared in medieval times, and no doubt earlier, from calves' feet and hartshorn. Chemical aerators for baked goods have been dated from 1842 when Abel Conant obtained a patent for a baking powder. The role of the food technologist has been to simplify the preparation of many of the traditional additives and to offer better, more reliable, and safer alternatives to other older additives, while simultaneously providing and responding to the demand for greater variety, more convenience, and better keeping quality in the food products themselves.

Functional Additives

Table VII.9.1 is by no means a complete summary of food additives and the functions they perform, and it is readily apparent that some of them serve more than one purpose. The discussion that follows will concentrate not so much on the additives themselves as on the properties modified by them.

Organoleptic properties: Color and flavor. Color has a great deal to do with food selection and appreciation, and thus the argument in favor of the addition of food colors to processed foods is primarily aesthetic. Nonetheless, there are three technological justifications: (1) to intensify natural colors considered by manufacturer and consumer to be too weak; (2) to smooth over color variations in the raw material and thus to ensure standardization of the product in the marketplace; and (3) to replace color lost during processing by heating, chemical reaction (for example, bleaching with sulfur dioxide used as a preservative), or light.

Although all three justifications could be considered extensions of the aesthetic argument, they are part of the fulfillment of consumer expectations and therefore of importance to both manufacturer and consumer. Many natural colors are included in the various permitted lists; some are synthetic but their number is slowly diminishing.

No matter how tempting a food may look, however, if its flavor is found to be unacceptable it will not be bought a second time. Apart from confectionery and beverages (specifically, soft drinks), which are special cases, the arguments for the addition of flavors to foods are the same as those for adding colors. In addition, there is a fourth justification, which is (4) to make flavorful and attractive an otherwise unin-

Table VII.9.1. *Food additives and their functions*

Additives	Appearance	Texture	Keeping quality	Flavor	Nutritive value
Acidulants, alkalis & buffers	–	–	x	x	–
Aerators	x	x	–	–	–
Anticaking & free-running agents	x	x	–	–	–
Antioxidants	–	–	x	–	–
Colors	x	–	–	–	–
Emulsifiers, gums & stabilizers	x	x	–	–	–
Enzymes	–	x	–	x	–
Flavors	–	–	–	x	–
Humectants	–	x	x	–	–
Minerals	–	–	–	–	x
Preservatives	–	–	x	–	–
Sequestrants	--	x	–	–	
Sweeteners	–	–	–	x	–
Vitamins	–	–	–	–	x

Source: Farrer (1987).

teresting formulated product, such as a meat analogue from spun vegetable protein.

Natural flavorings have always been used, and by far the largest proportion of food flavors employed today are of natural origin. Because of the chemical complexity of flavors and the low concentrations normally required, it has been difficult to classify and control them, but they are generally recognized as falling into a few categories: (1) aromatic, but natural, raw materials of vegetable or animal origin, such as spices and meat extract; (2) natural flavors that are concentrates of materials in the first category; and (3) natural flavoring substances isolated from them. Then there are (4) flavoring substances that are synthesized or isolated; and finally, (5) artificial flavoring substances that simulate natural flavors but are not found in them. All flavors in the first three categories contain dozens, sometimes hundreds, of separate, naturally present, and identifiable chemical compounds.

Flavorings are sold in solution, and the *solvents* used, very often alcohol, are subject to the same scrutiny as the flavors themselves. *Flavor enhancers* are compounds that, apart from salt, have little flavor of their own but have the property of intensifying other flavors. Monosodium glutamate (MSG), possibly the best known of these, was identified early this century from a seaweed preparation known in antiquity for its property of intensifying other flavors.

Some *enzymes* are very useful in establishing flavor profiles. These substances are of natural origin and are able, among many other things, to split fats, proteins, and carbohydrates. Those associated with flavor development are usually lipases ("fat splitters") and proteinases ("protein splitters"). They are, perhaps, most obviously active in cheese. Some, in purified form, may be used to develop flavor in other products. Food acids, *acidulants,* have long been known in the form of vinegar (acetic acid), lemon juice (citric acid), and the juices of other fruits, such as verjuice from grapes and the malic acid of apples.

Their influence on flavor is well known, and many products are flavored with, say, citric or acetic acids.

Nonnutritive sweeteners (as distinct from sugars) are a special group of flavors. The oldest is saccharin, which is hundreds of times sweeter than cane sugar but leaves a slightly bitter aftertaste. More recently, the cyclamates and aspartame were introduced, but the former, probably unfairly, fell under a cloud of suspicion. The latter is now well established, and although these compounds cannot exactly duplicate the taste of sugar, they are valuable in making a useful range of products available to diabetics and people on weight-reduction diets.

Pouring and slicing: Texture. Many different substances are variously classified as *modifiers and conditioners.* Between them they contribute to all the qualities of food except nutritive value – especially to appearance and texture. They ensure that emulsions do not break, that salad dressings pour satisfactorily, that baked products do not collapse in crumbs, that crystals of ice, salt, or phosphate, do not form where they are not wanted, and so forth.

Emulsifiers facilitate the dispersion of water and oil in each other to form the emulsions of such things as cake batters, salad dressings, ice cream, processed cheese, and some meat products. Gums of vegetable origin and thickeners and stabilizers, such as gelatin, starches, and modified starches, are then used to stabilize the systems. *Humectants* maintain the texture of such items as fruitcake and Christmas puddings, by preventing them from drying out, and *anticaking agents* ensure that salt, milk powders, and the like will run freely when poured.

Aerators have been used traditionally in baked goods to establish the desired texture, in this case, crumb structure, and in so doing have contributed to appearance. Yeasts, as well as yeast food to stimulate fermentation, make up a biological system of aeration, but chemical aerators also are common. They consist of slow-acting acidulants and baking soda and are designed to liberate carbon dioxide slowly enough to enable the desired texture to develop. *Enzymes* are used to modify texture in many products, and the oldest application may well be the use of rennet to set the curd for cheese making. Other applications are the tenderizing of meat, modification of gluten in dough making, digestion of pectin in fruit products to reduce gelling, and reduction of haze in beer.

Shelf life: Preservatives and antioxidants. Food, by its very nature, is perishable because it supports the growth of microorganisms, such as molds, yeasts, and bacteria. As they grow, these organisms can destroy food and render it unfit for human consumption. Yet sometimes, before its unfitness is apparent, such food can be positively dangerous to health. The empirical *preservatives* of history – salt, sugar, wood smoke, burning sulfur, and the alcohol and acid of fermentation – have been discussed, as have the chemical preservatives that came into use during the nineteenth century.

Modern methods of food processing, especially heat processing and refrigeration, have greatly reduced the need for chemical preservatives, although it is sometimes necessary to include one to protect a product once the container has been opened. This is particularly the case in tropical countries where many do not have home refrigeration. In addition, some modern packaging techniques rely on preservatives. For example, the flexible packaging material used for cheese frequently carries the antimycotic, sorbic acid, to inhibit the growth of the mold spores that are inevitably present on cheese surfaces.

Preservatives are also important in some processes. When meat, for example, is comminuted (as in the making of sausage), heat is generated in it, and the inclusion of a preservative, usually a sulfite, is necessary to stop the growth of microorganisms. Wine making is more difficult without the help of sulfur dioxide to control unwanted microbial growth, and for the same reason this preservative is used frequently in fruit juices.

Nitrates have long been associated with the preservation of meat, and it is now understood that nitrate reduces readily to nitrite, which inhibits the growth of *Clostridium botulinum,* the most deadly of all food-poisoning organisms. It is also the case that nitrates, via the nitrites, may give rise to nitrosamines that have proved carcinogenic in rats. Yet the benefit of the inhibition of *Cl. botulinum* outweighs the very low risk associated with nitrosamine formation.

That oils and fats develop rancidity is well known. This is a common flavor defect caused by oxidation that can also produce unacceptable colors and textures. These oxidation defects may be delayed (but not corrected or ultimately prevented) by the addition of *antioxidants,* and these compounds can, thus,

be regarded as a special class of preservatives. In addition, because rancidity is promoted by traces of copper and iron, it is sometimes beneficial to add a *sequestrant* to an oil, which locks up such trace metals and eliminates their catalytic effect.

Some antioxidants, such as ascorbic acid (vitamin C), the tocopherols (vitamin E), and natural phospholipids (lecithin, for example), occur naturally in fruit and vegetables, whereas others, like the gallates, are synthetic compounds. Antioxidants may be used in oils and fats, as well as in other food products where their use has been shown to prolong shelf life. Also it has been suggested that some antioxidants in food may offer protection against certain forms of cancer of the alimentary tract.

The acidity (or alkalinity) of a biological system is an extremely important property, usually expressed as pH within a range from 1 (very acid) through 7 (neutral) to 14 (very alkaline). *Acids,* such as the vinegar used in salad dressings, send the pH down, whereas *alkalis* move it up. If it is necessary to hold the pH steady, a *buffer* is added. This is a substance that has the ability to "soak up" the acidity or alkalinity. Phosphates are the most common buffers used in food systems. The pH of most phosphates ranges from about 3 (some salad dressings) to about 8. Low pH (high acidity) inhibits microbial growth; conversely, higher pH, either slightly acid or on the alkaline side of neutral, favors such growth, meaning that meats and some cheeses are more vulnerable to microbial spoilage than, say, tomato products. Clearly then, the keeping quality of food products may frequently be improved by lowering the pH.

Nutritive value. Vitamins and minerals are added to foods for a number of reasons, the most important being to protect or improve nutritive value. The invention of margarine in 1870 introduced a new product that lacked the vitamins A and D of butter. This deficiency was not, of course, discerned until after the discovery of vitamins early in the twentieth century, and when eventually sources of A and D were commercially available, it became obligatory for the margarine manufacturers to add them to their products. This is a good example of the addition of a nutrient to a substitute (or analogue) in order to match the concentration found in the natural product.

A fine example of the rectifying of processing losses that could otherwise endanger the health of whole communities is found in the addition of B vitamins (especially thiamine) to rice after it is stripped of a vitamin-rich husk in a polishing process intended to improve keeping quality. Similar examples include the addition of calcium to the British national loaf in wartime; the addition of vitamin D to milk; the addition of iodine to salt or to bread for the prevention of goiter; and the addition of fluoride to water for the prevention of dental caries. All are illustrative of government additive programs in the interests of their constituents.

Rather different, however, was the addition of nutrients for purely commercial reasons – an initiative that dated from the late 1940s, when vitamins became freely available as ordinary items of commerce. A rash of advertising claims were made to the effect that the addition of large "unnatural" concentrations of vitamins, and some minerals, made products more "healthy." As a result of such exagerated claims, some countries now limit the addition of vitamins and minerals to specific products and in specific concentrations.

During the processing of food, it is inevitable that (as in the kitchen) vitamins and minerals will be lost to a greater or lesser extent. The example of polishing rice is a special case, but in both kitchen and factory, losses resulting from leaching and heat are common, which is the reason for the addition of sufficient quantities of vitamins to replace these losses. Similarly, the concentrations of some vitamins will fall during storage, and additions ensure that at the end of the stated shelf life of the product the vitamin activity claimed or expected will still be present. There might also be reason to standardize a product made from variable raw material, so that it contains the level of a vitamin or a mineral that would normally be expected of it.

Indirect Additives

Additives from the field. Many chemicals are used in agriculture, horticulture, and animal husbandry, and it is inevitable that traces of them will find their way into foods. Because of this result, some regulatory authorities subject such chemicals to the same close scrutiny as is given to additives proper. Of these substances, the most important are pesticides, which are used directly on food products. Traces large or small, usually depending on the way in which instructions for harvesting are observed, will be found on almost all raw food materials, and regulations governing the concentrations of pesticides permitted in food offered for sale have been introduced throughout the world since the 1950s. It is fortunate that the development of the wide range of chemical pesticides available today coincided quite closely with the discovery and application of modern methods of chemical analysis, which permit the measurement and detection of pesticides in very low concentrations.

Additives from the factory. Many substances are legitimately used in the food factory to facilitate processing and to clean and sanitize both plant and equipment, and these may be found in foods in minute amounts. For example, traces of boiler water additives to prevent the buildup of scale in steam boilers can be transferred in droplets of water in wet steam. Processing aids that may enter foods include flocculants and clarifying agents, enzymes, lubricants (such as medicinal paraffin on packaging machinery), and talc (on certain types of confectionery), along with quick-release agents in the baking industry. In addition, because cleanliness and the highest hygienic standards are essential, detergents (which sometimes must be quite specialized) and sanitizers used daily in food factories, can also enter foods.

Additives from the package. The first packages in modern food technology were Nicolas Appert's glass jars of the 1780s, which were followed by tin cans in 1810. The former contribute little to the food packed in them. But the latter may transfer tin, iron, and (in the past) even lead from the solder used to seal the can, although recent concern over lead in food has resulted in the development of the welded can (to eliminate the soldered side seam). Canned foods inevitably pick up some tin. This metal has not been a cause of significant concern, but the amount that might reach the consumer has been reduced, even though it occasionally imparts a desirable flavor, as with canned asparagus.

The wide use of plastics, both rigid and flexible, in the packaging of food products has focused attention on traces of residual monomers, plasticizers, colors, and so forth that may find their way from the package into the food, especially oily and fatty products. Some of these substances are potentially dangerous, and industry worldwide has collaborated with regulators to develop strict guidelines for plastics that come into contact with foods.

Control of Food Additives

The English "Assize of Bread," which remained in force from 1266 until the Bread Act of 1822, controlled weight and price but not additives. The French "Livres des Métiers" of 1268 sought to protect both the pocket and the health of the consumer and touched upon additives by forbidding the flavoring of beer. The appointment of German wine inspectors for Swabia and Alsace dates from 1488, and measures were taken at about this time by companies in England, the Netherlands, and France to protect their good names by controlling the misuse of certain additives.

In 1701, the government of Denmark issued an order against food that was tainted or unwholesome or that could cause sickness. This was a vague regulation with only the faintest implication of additive control, but a list of colors permitted for use in food was issued in Denmark in 1836, well before the first dye was synthesized. In 1887 the use of harmful colors in foods was forbidden by the German "Color Act" (Hinton 1960; Uhl and Hansen 1961; Hamann 1963; Truhaut and Souverain 1963).

In England, additive control was inextricably linked with the control of adulteration. Accum's 1820 treatise dealt primarily with adulteration, and only with modern eyes can it be seen as an indictment of the abuse of additives. Similarly, the search for pure food in the United Kingdom, which has been well documented by I. Paulus (1974), was only incidentally related to additive control. Regulations under the Victoria (Australia) Pure Food Act of 1905 and those flowing from the American Pure Food and Drug Act of 1906 were not primarily directed at additives, although as noted, concern over lead incidentally finding its way into food was a factor. The French, too, early in the twentieth century, accepted the possibility of dangerous metals (lead, zinc, arsenic, antimony) entering the food from utensils or kitchen equipment (Truhaut and Souverain 1963), and up to World War II many countries placed limitations of one kind or another on colors, preservatives, and heavy metals in foodstuffs.

Concern over food additives, first by governments and then by consumers, began to intensify in the 1950s. There were four reasons:

1. Results from animal tests in the late 1930s strongly suggested that a so-called coal tar dye used to color butter and margarine was carcinogenic; this finding converged in the late 1940s with a growing awareness of environmental links with some forms of cancer, and a 1952 lecture by A. F. J. Butenandt on the carcinogenicity of some food colors was taken up by the press (Hamann 1963).
2. Food technology had emerged during the war as an important new subject of study, and industry was offering a range of substances that could simplify the preparation of many existing products and permit the formulation and manufacture of new ones.
3. Analytic chemistry was on the threshold of enormous advances, and the detection and measurement of additives and the like was fast becoming easier.
4. There were new needs and, through United Nations agencies, new opportunities for the international regulation of food.

Governments in a number of countries appointed committees and developed mechanisms to study and propose regulations for food additives. In 1956, the United Nations Food and Agriculture and World Health Organizations set up a Joint Expert Committee on Food Additives (JECFA) for the same purpose. JECFA adopted a set of principles as follows:

- Food additives should not be used to disguise faulty processing or handling techniques, nor to deceive the consumer with regard to the nature or quality of the food.
- Special care should be exercised in the use of additives in foods that may form a major part of the diet of some sections of the community, or that may be consumed in especially large quantities at certain seasons.

- The choice of food additives should be related to the prevailing dietary patterns within a community. The availability of essential nutrients and their distribution in the various foods consumed should be taken into account before the true significance of making a further addition of a particular nutrient (e.g., calcium or phosphorus) or of using an additive that may change the pattern of nutrients in a food (e.g., an oxidizing agent) can be assessed.
- The specifications needed for each food additive have been compiled with three main objectives in mind: to identify the substance that has been subjected to biological testing; to ensure that the substance is of the quality required for safe use in food; to reflect and encourage good manufacturing practice (JECFA 1957).

In 1953, Australia had adopted similar principles (Farrer 1990). In Canada, the Adulteration Act of 1884 had included four general principles related to food additives, and in 1906 a report to the Canadian government made six recommendations, which, though directed specifically at preservatives, were the first related to the use of food additives (McGill 1906). The four general principles called for toxicological safety, technological need, labeling, and, where there is no provision for their use, exclusion. In effect, these are the principles that govern the use of food additives today.

Expert committees in many developed countries and the Scientific Committee for Food (SCF) of the European Community (EC) gather and assess information from many sources before deciding whether to recommend a specific additive for use in food and, if so, under what conditions. In some countries the technological need for a given additive in a given product must be demonstrated. But the SCF makes the questionable assumption that a request for permission to use an additive is prima facie evidence of technological need and concerns itself only with toxicological safety. In both cases, if there is any doubt about the toxicological safety of the additive in the way it is to be used, it will not be recommended. JECFA has a key role in establishing toxicological safety, and the information it seeks is detailed and stringent. Full details of the substance are required: how it is made, likely impurities, its method and rate of use, what happens to it in food, its effect on nutrients, and the substitute additives available.

Much detailed toxicological and pharmacological information about the additive also is sought: the no-observable-effect level (NOEL) of additives – that is, the concentration in the diet expressed as mg/kg of body weight that may be consumed over several generations without producing any discernible effect;

acute and chronic toxicity; the results of studies on carcinogenicity, mutagenicity, and teratogenicity, and of changes induced in cells and the nervous system; and whether the additive triggers or exacerbates an effect caused by another substance or alters the balance between naturally occurring substances. The 1980s saw a heightened awareness of the allergenic properties of some additives, and it is possible that in the future, more questions will be asked about neurotoxicity. The results obtained from all these studies are important, but equally important are the methodologies, which also must be reported.

From all the information generated by these investigations and using a safety factor of, usually, 100, JECFA calculates an Acceptable Daily Intake (ADI). This is "the amount of a chemical which may be ingested daily, even over a lifetime, without appreciable risk to the consumer in the light of all the information available at the time of the evaluation" (JECFA 1957). *Without appreciable risk* is taken to mean the practical certainty that injury will not result after a lifetime exposure (Vettorazzi 1975). If the data are insufficient to satisfy the committee, a "Temporary ADI" may be adopted, or it may be a case of "No ADI Allocated." Substances of very low toxicity are classified as "ADI not Specified," and the designations "Not to be used" and "Decision postponed" speak for themselves. JECFA assessments are very thorough, and its recommendations count for a great deal with both national and international regulatory authorities. They are reflected in the International Standards of Codex Alimentarius, which are of increasing importance in the world trade of food products.

In some countries, permitted additives have been listed for use in all foods, as, for example, substances classified in the United States as GRAS (Generally Recognized as Safe). In others, such as the United Kingdom, the tendency has been to let the courts decide what is "harmful," although the Public Health Regulations 1925 (Preservatives etc. in Food) limited preservatives to sulfur dioxide, sulfites, benzoic acid, and benzoates, and their use to 20 categories of food (nitrates were excluded from the definition of "preservative").

The trend now is to limit additives to specified products and limit them up to specified concentrations. These limitations combine the concepts of technological need and toxicological safety-in-use. In addition, former blanket labeling provisions (for example, the general statement "Artificially Colored") are being replaced by explicit requirements for the naming of each additive, or at least inclusion on the label of identifiable codes, such as the numbering system used in Europe and elsewhere. These requirements make it possible for persons who show idiosyncratic responses to avoid substances that are safe-in-use for the vast majority of people.

Because the evidence relating to substances proposed for use as food additives is freely available all over the world, lists of permitted additives and their concentrations are very similar. Nevertheless, there are differences, most of which reflect likes, prejudices, cultural differences, and politics. In the latter case, the range is from the influence of pressure groups (those of both consumers and industry) to the widespread effect of the American "Delaney Clause." Enacted by the U.S. Congress in 1958, this clause prohibits the use in food of any substance that has been shown to cause cancer when ingested by humans or any animal.

Ostensibly unchallengeable, this clause has caused untold difficulty in America and in many other countries as well. It takes into account no qualifying circumstance, such as dose levels (that is, amount of substance in a serving), variations in the responses of different animal species, the size of the animal, the frequency of consumption of the substance, and so on. Moreover, in the words of one commentator, "this clause has generated much controversy because of recognition by most scientists that the continued existence of mankind is silent witness to the fact that low levels of carcinogens can be tolerated" (Wodicka 1980). Fortunately, no other country is so legally constrained as the United States. There was recourse to the principle of *de minimis non curat lex* ("the law is not concerned with trifles"), which enabled some scientific evaluations to be made (Middlekauf 1985), but only for a few years. In 1992 a court decision in the United States ruled that the Delaney Clause meant *no* levels of carcinogens were permissible (Winter 1993). Because of the extreme sensitivity of modern methods, this definition has created a difficult (some would say, impossible) situation.

Food Additives in Popular Culture

Late–twentieth-century food-additive usage has a foundation of scientific evaluation that is not readily apparent to the casual observer. Newspaper articles, radio and television programs, books, even school teachers, inveigh against food additives as "chemicals added to our food." Some individuals class as contaminants certain substances that add quality to processed food products, and reject additives without any understanding of their functions. Nor is it generally understood that more fearsome substances occur naturally in foods than are ever added by humans.

Some food manufacturers have sought to profit from public uneasiness by advertising their products as free from all, or at least free from stipulated classes of, additives. One result has been to reinforce many consumers' uncertainties while creating unjustified suspicion of other products.

For many people, the most damning thing about food additives is that they are "chemicals," and chemicals are perceived as something to be avoided. Unfortunately, the chemical nature of food and of life itself is generally unappreciated. The body contains thousands of chemicals from the simple, such as water and salt (sodium chloride), to the complex, such as hemoglobin and cholesterol, and all are necessary for life itself. Water, salt, and many others must be supplied in the food, whereas hemoglobin and thousands more such compounds are made by the body as required. In addition, there are substances such as cholesterol, which is both manufactured in vivo and supplied in foods, such as eggs. And then, there is monosodium glutamate (MSG), which is naturally present in some foods, manufactured in the body from others, *and* also used as an additive.

For generations, cooks have used potassium hydrogen tartrate and sodium hydrogen carbonate. Better known as cream of tartar and baking soda, respectively, both are chemicals and both are food additives. There are many such examples of additives with familiar names; but there are others, known only by intimidating chemical names, that are no less safe. Similarly, many examples could be given of chemical reactions that occur in food during cooking and processing and of others that go on continuously in the body to permit such simple operations as breathing or typing these words.

Late-twentieth-century opponents of food additives cite several concerns. A major one relates to possible long-term and cumulative effects of their consumption, and the further possibility of interactions in vivo of additives with each other, with other food constituents, and with body components. Another concern is that toxicologically innocuous substances may cause nutritional imbalance or the physical obstruction of some biological process. Certainly, none of these possibilities should be unequivocally dismissed, but the detailed and exhaustive testing of substances proposed as food additives is intended to ensure that in the circumstances in which they are eventually permitted to be used, they will be safe; that is, they will be "safe-in-use."

Early in the sixteenth century, the Renaissance physician Paracelsus wrote that all substances are poisons and it was the right dose that differentiated a poison from a remedy. This truth is the clue to the understanding and acceptance of food additives. It is a statement of what is now called dose–response, of which probably the most familiar modern example is the effect of alcohol. For each person there is a limited number of drinks ("units" of alcohol) that produce no visible response in his or her behavior, but once that limit is passed there is a clearly visible response.

Put another way, given time, it is conceivable that the body can cope with any dose, but some substances can quickly swamp the body's capability to deal with them. Cyanide is well known as a deadly poison, but marzipan contains cyanide. It is, however, in such a small concentration that the body can deal

with it without visible response, and in some countries, cyanide is specifically permitted by regulation to be present in marzipan up to a specified (very low) level. Dose–response, knowingly or not, is considered by everyone who drinks fermented liquids, and it is at the heart of food-additive usage. So, too, is risk–benefit analysis.

Certainly there is risk in food consumption, but the greatest risk is not that of food additives but, rather, that of food poisoning. This is a microbial risk, and it is increasing as people eat out more often and as an increasing number of housewives work and find themselves taking shortcuts in the kitchen. It has been calculated that the risk of food poisoning is 100,000 times greater than any risk from food additives (Truswell et al. 1978).

Nonetheless, the community has the right to expect that food-additive usage is fully explained and is as safe as it can be. And government, industry, and food technologists have the responsibility to see that it is.

K. T. H. Farrer

Bibliography

Accum, F. 1820. *Treatise on the adulteration of foods and culinary poisons.* London.

Anonymous. 1843. *Belfast News Letter.* April 14.

Baker, G. 1767. *Medical tracts read at the College of Physicians between 1767 and 1785.* London.

Begley, S. 1991. The contrarian press. *Food Technology* 45: 245–6.

Campbell, W. A. 1990. Vermilion and verdigris – not just pretty colours. *Chemistry in Britain* 26: 558–60.

Christison, R. 1835. *A Treatise on poisons in relation to medical jurisprudence, physiology and the practice of physic.* Third edition. Edinburgh.

Cochran, W. 1870. Exhausted tea leaves. *The Food Journal* 1: 161.

Codex Alimentarius Commission (1979). *Guide to the safe use of food additives.* Rome.

Drummond, J. C., and Anne Wilbraham. 1957. *The Englishman's food: A history of five centuries of English diet.* London.

Dunn, F. 1878. Confectionery analysis. *Industrial and Technological Museum Laboratory Notes and Museum Record* 1: 5–9.

Farrer, K. T. H. 1979. Adulterations of all descriptions. *Food Technology in Australia* 31: 340–9.

  1980. *A settlement amply supplied: Food technology in nineteenth century Australia.* Melbourne.

  1987. *A guide to food additives and contaminants.* Carnforth, Lancashire, England.

  1990. The Australian Food Additives Committee 1953–1963. 1. Cutting the pattern with colours. *Food Australia* 42: 146–50.

Feingold, B. F. 1975. *Why your child is hyperactive.* New York.

Gilfillan, S. C. 1965. Lead poisoning and the fall of Rome. *Journal of Occupational Medicine* 7: 53–60.

Hamann, V. 1963. *Food additive control in the Federal*

Republic of Germany. FAO Food Additive Control Series No. 7. Rome.

Hassall, A. H. 1855. *Food and its adulterations*. Reports of the *Lancet* Analytical Sanitary Commission. London.

Hinton, C. L. 1960. *Food additive control in the United Kingdom*. FAO Food Additive Control Series No. 2. Rome.

ILSI Australia. 1991. The scientific facts about MSG. Papers and discussion of a symposium held in Sydney, 31 July under the auspices of the International Life Sciences Institite, Australian Chapter. *Food Australia* 43 (Supplement): S2–19.

Johnson, H. 1989. *The story of wine*. London.

JECFA (Joint Expert Committee on Food Additives) 1957. *First Report: General principles governing the use of food additives*. Geneva.

Loblay, R. H., and A. R. Swain. 1985. Adverse reactions to tartrazine. *Food Technology in Australia* 37: 508–10.

Lockey, S. D. 1959. Allergic reactions due to F. D. and C. Yellow No. 5 tartrazine, an aniline dye used as a coloring and identifying agent in various steroids. *Annals of Allergy* 17: 719–21.

MAFF. 1983. U.K. Ministry of Agriculture, Fisheries and Food. *Food additives and contaminants committee report on the review of metals in canned foods*. FAC/REP/38. London.

McGill, A. 1906. Legislation regarding food preservatives. *British Medical Journal* 2: 858–86.

Meijer, W. 1961. *Food additive control in the Netherlands*. FAO Food Additive Control Series No. 3. Rome.

Middlekauf, R. D. 1985. Delaney meets de minimis. *Food Technology* 39: 62–9.

Miller, K. 1982. Sensitivity to tartrazine. *British Medical Journal* 285: 1597–8.

Mitchell, J. 1848. *Treatise on the falsification of food and the chemical means used to detect them*. London.

National Advisory Committee on Hyperkinesis and Food Additives. 1980. *Final report to the Nutrition Foundation*. New York.

Noonan, J. E., and H. Meggos. 1980. Synthetic food colors. In *Handbook of food additives,* Vol. 2, second edition, ed. T. E. Furia, 339–83. Boca Raton, Fla.

Nriagu, J. O. 1983. *Lead and lead poisoning in antiquity*. New York.

Paulus, I. 1974. *The search for pure food: A sociology of legislation in Britain*. London.

Pugsley, L. I. 1959. *Food additive control in Canada*. FAO Food Additive Control Series No. 1. Rome.

Smith, M. 1986. Lead in history. In *The lead debate*, ed. R. Lansdown and W. Yule, 7–24. London.

Truhaut, R., and R. Souverain. 1963. *Food additive control in France*. FAO Food Additive Control Series No. 6. Rome.

Truswell, A. S., N.-G. Asp, W. P. T. James, and B. MacMahon. 1978. Food and cancer: Special report. *Nutrition Reviews* 36: 313–14.

Uhl, E., and S. C. Hansen. 1961. *Food additive control in Denmark*. FAO Food Additive Control Series. No. 5. Rome.

Vettorazzi, G. 1975. The safety evaluation of food additives: The dynamics of toxicological decision. *Lebensmittelwissenschaft und Technologie* 8: 195–201.

Winter, C. K. 1993. Pesticide residues and the Delaney Clause. *Food Technology* 57: 81–6.

Wodicka, V. O. 1980. Legal considerations on food additives. In *Handbook of food additives,* Vol. 2. Second edition, ed. T. E. Furia, 1–12. Boca Raton, Fla.

VII.10 ✌ Substitute Foods and Ingredients

Substitute Foods

Substitute foods mimic their traditional counterparts: margarine as butter; nondairy products as milk, cream, and cheese; or extruded soybean mixes as bacon, beef, poultry, or fish. But although substitute food products may resemble their traditional counterparts, they are also likely to be composed of substances from totally different sources. The substitutes are partitioned and restructured, whereas the traditional foods are intact.

In the past, substitute foods were frequently developed as inexpensive replacements for more costly primary foods. An example is a cheese replacer. However, in recent years, substitute foods have been introduced and promoted for health reasons associated with reducing the intake of saturated fat, cholesterol, and calories. Examples are nonfat frozen desserts, egg replacers, and reduced-calorie baked goods.

On occasion, a substitute food, first launched as an inexpensive replacer, has become more expensive than its traditional counterpart. An example is margarine, originally offered as an inexpensive substitute for butter. But later it was promoted as more healthful than butter, and some special margarines became more expensive than butter (Sanford 1968).

Margarine as a Paradigm

Margarine was the first successful substitute food. A search for a butter substitute began in the early 1800s, and commercial production of margarine was launched in 1873.

Normally, the predominantly unsaturated oils used in margarine manufacture would soon oxidize and turn rancid when exposed to air. But the process of hydrogenation employed in its manufacture modifies the oils and makes them more saturated and durable. The raised melting point improves the fat's consistency and color for the deep-frying of foods, and it protects both the fats and the foods made with them from developing off-flavors. These qualities made hydrogenated oils suitable for the manufacture of margarine and other solid shortenings and for use in numerous processed foods.

Although hydrogenation serves a technological purpose, there are biological and nutritional consequences. Hydrogenation converts the *cis* form of fatty acids, naturally present in oils, to a trans form. The original molecular pattern is rearranged, and the biological quality has become nutritionally inferior. Normally, trans isomers are not present in human tissues. If present, they are less well utilized in the human body. They do not circulate in the blood, nor do they move through the tissues as liquids. They may disrupt the permeability characteristics of the membranes of the body's cells and prevent normal transport of nutrients into and out of cells (Emken 1984).

By the mid-1950s, warnings were sounded about the health risks of consuming hydrogenated fats and oils. A leading article in the *Lancet* predicted that "[t]he hydrogenation plants of our modern food industry may turn out to have contributed to the causation of a major disease" (Fats and Disease 1956: 55).

Shortly thereafter, Dr. Hugh Sinclair, at Oxford University's Laboratory of Human Nutrition, reported that hydrogenation of fats produced a deficiency of essential fatty acids (EFAs) by destroying them, or resulted in abnormal toxic fatty acids with an antiEFA effect both in animal experiments and with clinical human studies. Sinclair demonstrated that a deficiency of EFAs is "a contributory cause in neurological diseases, heart disease, arteriosclerosis, skin disease, various degenerative conditions such as cataracts and arthritis, and cancer" (Sinclair 1957: 33).

Additional reports and critical assessments of trans fatty acids in margarine and processed foods containing hydrogenated fats and oils were made by others (Bicknell 1960; Kummerow et al. 1974; Enig, Munn, and Keeney 1978; Enig et al. 1983; Keeney 1981; Enig, Budowski, and Blondheim 1984).

By the 1980s, a Canadian government task force had noted the apparent cholesterol-raising effects of trans fatty acids (Beardsley 1991). The group recommended that margarine manufacturers should reduce the amounts by modifying the hydrogenation process.

A turning point was reached in 1990, when a study directed attention to the hypercholesterolemic effect of trans fatty acids in margarine (Mensink and Katan 1990). The researchers found that these isomers raised levels of unfavorable low-density lipoproteins (LDLs) and lowered levels of favorable high-density lipoproteins (HDLs) to an even greater extent than did saturated fat. Trans fatty acids increased the lipoprotein risk profile. The researchers recommended avoidance of trans fatty acids by those at risk of atherosclerosis.

Additional incriminating evidence was revealed. At an epidemiology conference in 1993 sponsored by the American Heart Association, a team of Harvard University researchers reported the results of a survey of 239 heart attack patients and 282 healthy controls. After having analyzed the eating patterns of their subjects, the investigators had calculated the trans fatty acid intake. Even after adjustments for numerous factors, the association of trans fatty acids with heart attacks remained highly significant. Individuals who consumed more than two and a half pats of margarine daily had a nearly two and a half times greater risk of heart attack than did those who never used margarine (Ascherio 1993).

Release of the Nurses Health Study in 1993 corrob-orated these findings (Willett et al. 1993). For eight years, 85,000 nurses had been monitored for margarine intake. Women who ate products that contained hydrogenated fats and oils had increased their risks of heart attack by 70 percent. Those who ate more than four teaspoons of margarine daily in all products, and especially in white breads and cookies, were at far greater risk of coronary heart disease (CHD) than those who consumed margarine less than once a month. The researchers noted that as a result of pressure from well-intentioned but unenlightened activists, fast-food restaurants had switched from beef tallow to partially hydrogenated vegetable oils for deep-fat frying. The quantity of trans isomers in beef tallow is 3 to 5 percent; in hydrogenated vegetable oils, it is 30 percent.

The history of margarine can serve as a paradigm for the risk inherent in the use of all substitute foods. Indeed, the European Community Commission has proposed that novel foods and ingredients be regulated. At a toxicology forum, members described the need to evaluate them as a "burning and timely issue. . . . We need to look at them from both toxicological and nutritional viewpoints. It's a whole new era" (Somogyi 1993: 18).

Substitute Ingredients

Similar to substitute foods, ingredients, too, have been developed as inexpensive replacements for more costly or scarce ingredients. Examples are imitation vanillin, substituted for vanilla flavoring; inexpensive trash fish used in making surimi "sea legs" to simulate lobster; or the simulated maple taste in pancake blend syrup, in lieu of maple syrup.

In recent years, many substitute ingredients, like substitute foods, have been developed in response to concerns regarding certain health risks inherent in the industrialized diet, such as undesirable high levels of calories, fat, cholesterol, and sodium, or undesirable low levels of dietary fibers. One such effort has been to find a substitute for sugar.

Sugar Substitutes

The search for sugar substitutes has been driven by forces that involve health considerations. At first, the search was to meet a medical need: an acceptable sweetener that was tolerated by diabetics. Later, the driving forces were for sugar substitutes that were noncariogenic (to avoid tooth decay) and noncaloric or low caloric (to control weight).

Gradually, these specific health considerations became more generalized. A recent survey found that the main incentive for consumers to choose low-caloric products was to maintain overall health, rather than merely to reduce weight (Wilkes 1992).

In 1978, some 42 million Americans consumed low-calorie foods and beverages. By 1986, the number had more than doubled, to 93 million; and in 1991, it reached 101 million. In 1993, a national survey disclosed that the number had risen to 136 million, and low-calorie foods and beverages were being consumed by 73 percent of the total U.S. adult population (Fat Reduction in Foods 1993). The most popular low-calorie foods and beverages are soft drinks, consumed by 42 percent of all adults; sugar substitutes in other beverages and foods, consumed by 31 percent; sugar-free gums and candies, used by 28 percent; and sugar-free gelatins and puddings, eaten by 18 percent (Wilkes 1992).

Saccharin: An early substitute. Saccharin, an early sugar substitute, has been in continuous use as a noncaloric sweetener since the turn of the twentieth century. At present, however, it competes against more recently introduced noncaloric and low-caloric sweeteners. In fact, it was saccharin's beleaguered history of use in the United States that gave impetus to the development of alternatives (National Academy of Sciences 1975). In 1977, saccharin was found to be carcinogenic in rats, and the Food and Drug Administration (FDA) attempted to ban its use under the Delaney Clause in the 1958 Food Additives Amendment to the 1938 Food, Drug, and Cosmetic Act (U.S. House of Representatives 1977). However, the U.S. Congress enacted a moratorium on the ban, and the moratorium was renewed several times. Then, in 1991, the FDA announced its decision to withdraw the proposed 1977 ban. Thus, saccharin continues to be used in the United States food supply, and currently, it is also employed in more than 90 other countries (Wilkes 1992; Dillon 1993; Giese 1993).

Aspartame: A low-caloric substitute. Aspartame, approved by the FDA in 1981 for table use, represented the first sugar substitute approved in America in more than 25 years. Aspartame consists of two amino acids, L-phenylalanine and L-aspartic acid, and is 180 to 200 times sweeter than sucrose. Hence, it can be used at such a low level that it contributes only 4 calories per gram, and is regarded as a low-caloric sweetener (also known as a high-intensity sweetener).

Soft drinks account for 80 percent of aspartame's use in the United States. However, since aspartame's original approval, its use has been extended to thousands of food and beverage products, including carbonated soft drinks, refrigerated fruit juices, milk beverages, ready-to-drink teas, and frozen desserts, puddings, fillings, and yoghurt products, in addition to its use as a table sweetener (Wilkes 1992; Dillon 1993; Giese 1993).

The United States now accounts for approximately 80 percent of the global market for aspartame, although it is predicted that worldwide consumption will more than double by the end of the twentieth century. Aspartame is approved for use in more than 90 countries and is available, worldwide, in more than 5,000 products (Wilkes 1992).

Like saccharin, aspartame has been indicted for producing various adverse health effects, especially among heavy users (U.S. Senate 1987). These include numerous central nervous system and digestive system disturbances (Centers for Disease Control 1984; Monte 1984; Yokogoshi et al. 1984; Wurtman 1985; Drake 1986; Walton 1986; Koehler and Glaros 1988; Lipton et al. 1989; Potenza and El-Mallakh 1989; McCauliffe and Poitras 1991).

In 1984, the Centers for Disease Control conducted a four-month review of 517 consumer complaints relating to aspartame usage. The conclusions were that the complaints "do not provide evidence of the existence of serious widespread adverse health consequences attendant to the use of aspartame." However, further monitoring was advised (Centers for Disease Control 1984: 607).

Acesulfame K: A low-caloric substitute. The most recently introduced low-caloric sugar substitute is acesulfame K. Presently, it is used in about 600 food products in more than 50 countries. In 1988, the FDA approved its use for tabletop sweeteners, chewing gums, dry beverage bases, and dry dessert bases. Future approvals may be extended for confectionery products, baked goods, soft drinks, and other liquid beverages (Giese 1993).

Glycyrrhizin: Flavorant and sweetener. Glycyrrhizin, in the root of the licorice plant, is an intensely sweet triterpenoid saponin. It is from 50 to 100 times sweeter than sucrose. Extracts are used to flavor and sweeten confectionery products (Cook 1970). Glycyrrhizin is on the FDA list of GRAS (Generally Recognized as Safe) substances as a flavorant but not as a sweetening agent. However, food manufacturers have increasingly been using glycyrrhizin for its sweetening quality.

Metabolic studies have shown that glycyrrhizin can be hydrolyzed by human intestinal microflora to release glucuronic acid, a sugar that is almost completely metabolized. Moreover, glycyrrhizin has corticoid activity, influencing steroid metabolism to maintain blood pressure and volume and regulate glucose–glycogen balance. At high levels, glycyrrhizin is capable of producing a variety of health problems, including hypokalemia, high blood pressure, and muscular weakness (Chamberlain 1970; Robinson, Harrison, and Nicholson 1971; Blachley and Knochel 1980; Edwards 1991; Farese et al. 1991).

Other available sugar substitutes. Numerous low- or noncaloric sugar substitutes are in use elsewhere in the world but await approval in the United States. Sucralose, for example, was approved in 1991 for use in Canada, and shortly thereafter in Australia, Mexico, and Russia. Sucralose is 600 times sweeter than sucrose, and it does not break down in the body. It is manufactured by a multistep process that involves the selective chlorination of sucrose. Although a food-additive petition for sucralose use in 15 food and beverage categories was submitted to the FDA as early as 1987, the data are still under review. Applications are pending also in the United Kingdom and the European Community (Lite Sweeteners Maneuver 1989; Canada First Country 1991; Canada Clears Sucralose 1991; U.S. Department of Agriculture 1991).

Alitame, a low-caloric sugar substitute awaiting FDA approval, is 2,000 times sweeter than sucrose. It is formed by two amino acids, L-aspartic acid and D-alanine, and 2,2,4,4-tetramethylthietanyl, a novel amine. The aspartic acid component is metabolized normally; the alanine amide goes through the body with minimal metabolic changes. In the United States, a petition was filed for use of alitame in a broad spectrum of food products as early as 1986. But although alitame has been approved for use in Australia, New Zealand, and Mexico, the FDA is still reviewing the data (Alitame 1990; U.S. Department of Agriculture 1991).

Oligofructosaccharides (FOS) are natural sugar polymers that are potential sugar replacers. They contribute only 1.5 calories per gram and can be manufactured from sucrose by means of a fungal enzyme. They are reported to stimulate the growth of healthy bifidobacteria in the human intestine. At present, they are used in Japan (Mitsuoka 1990; Modler, McKellar, and Yaguchi 1990; Fat Reduction in Foods 1993). In the United States, interest in FOS is focused more on their value as dietary sweeteners than on their therapeutic benefits.

Potential botanical substitutes. Numerous substitute sweeteners can be derived from botanicals. Many have had a long history of use elsewhere but lack regulatory approval in the United States.

Dihydrochalcones are derived from two flavones, naringin and neohesperidin, found in citrus peels, and are several hundred times sweeter than sucrose. Many studies have confirmed their safety. The Scientific Committee for Food of the Commission of the European Community has allocated for dihydrochalcones an Acceptable Daily Intake (ADI) of 5 milligrams per kilogram of body weight. Currently, this sugar substitute is approved for use in Belgium and Argentina. The FDA has requested additional toxicological tests (New 'Super Sweeteners' 1970; McElheny 1977).

Stevia *rebaudiana* is a South American plant that yields several sweet compounds. Purified glycoside components of this plant have been employed for many years in South America. Currently, the main consumers of steviosides are the Japanese. Dental research suggests that *S. rebaudiana* may suppress the growth of oral microorganisms (Shock 1982).

The red serendipity berry (*Dioscoroephyllum cuminsii* Diels) from Africa contains a sweet component, monellin. A sweet herb from Mexico (*Lippia dulcis*) has hernandulcin, an intensely sweet sesquiterpene. Some plants commonly grown in the United States also have sweet constituents. Leaves of the herb, sweet cicely (*Myrrhis odorata),* known as the candy plant, have been used as a sweetener and flavor enhancer in conserves and to sweeten tart foods. The dried leaves of the big-leafed hydrangea (*Hydrangea macrophylla* var. Thunbergii) and the rhizomes of the common fern (*Polypodium vulgare* L.) also contain sweet constituents.

A final sweetener from botanicals is *Lo Han Kao* (*Momordica grosvenori* Swingle), a fruit from southern China. The purified sweetener from the dried fruit is about 400 times sweeter than sucrose (Inglett 1981).

Alternative approaches for substitutes. One innovation in the search for sugar substitutes is the utilization of molecules that are mirror images. Natural sugars usually occur in the so-called D-form, which is metabolized. The mirror image, which rarely occurs in nature, is in the L-form and is not metabolized. This feature makes L-sugars attractive candidates as noncaloric sugar substitutes. Currently, 3 of the 10 known L-sugars have been selected for safety testing and scale-up production studies (Process Yields No-Cal 1981; The Use of Sucrose 1982; L Sugars 1989; Giese 1993).

Another approach is to attach small molecules of sweeteners that are normally absorbed to much larger polymer molecules that are not absorbed. The sweetening agent leached to the polymer passes intact through the intestinal tract and is excreted unabsorbed (In the 1980s 1979).

The introduction of noncaloric and low-caloric sugar substitutes has not lessened the consumption of caloric sweeteners. On the contrary, there has been a steady increase in the use of *all* types of sweeteners – caloric, noncaloric, and low caloric (U.S. Department of Agriculture 1988). By 1993, the annual consumption of caloric sweeteners had reached 144.8 pounds per person in the United States (U.S. Department of Agriculture 1993).

Concomitantly, obesity continues as one of the most common and important medical conditions in the United States. More than one-third of all adults in the population are significantly overweight (Najjar and Rowland 1987; Sichieri, Everhart, and Hubbard 1992). The prevalence of obesity in some minority groups, especially Native Americans, African-Americans, and Hispanic women, reaches as high as 50 percent of these populations (Williamson et al. 1990). Although the problem of obesity is multifactorial, caloric intake is an important aspect. Clearly, the sweetening substitutes have not alleviated this problem; rather, they offer increased possibilities for food technologists to create a range of highly processed foods and beverages that further encourage poor food choices.

Fat Substitutes

The growing interest in fat and cholesterol reduction gained impetus in the 1980s and led to a multiplicity of developments for partial and total fat substitutes. In 1989 some 450 new food products introduced in the U.S. marketplace were labeled "low fat" or "nonfat." By 1992, 519 new low-fat or low-cholesterol products had been launched. Fully one-third of these products were dairy foods. Others included baked goods, condiments, meats, and snacks (Mancini 1993).

By 1993, more than two-thirds of all American adults were consuming low- or reduced-fat foods and beverages, and they expressed the desire to have still others available. It was predicted that, eventually, a low-fat version of virtually every type of food would become available (Mancini 1993).

Hydrocolloid-based fat substitutes. Many partial fat substitutes are made from cellulosics. Some are hydrocolloid stabilizers, such as cellulose gel from microcrystalline cellulose (MCC) isolated from plants (Cellulose Gel Helps 1990); powdered cellulose, a by-product of the pulp paper industry (Powdered Cellulose Reduces 1990); and semi- or totally synthetic celluloses that are nonabsorbable (Klose and Glicksman 1968).

Carbohydrate-based hydrocolloid fat substitutes consist of water-soluble polymers from vegetable gums, such as carrageenan and guar (Starches Replace Fat 1989; Fat Substitutes 1990). The polymers are also derived from plant starches, such as those from potato and corn (Potato Starch Replaces 1989); from dextrins, such as those in tapioca (Potato Starch Replaces 1989); and from maltodextrins, such as those in hydrolyzed cornstarch (Get Rid of Unwanted Fat 1989). Some of these complex carbohydrates are absorbable, whereas others are not (Klose and Glicksman 1968).

One cereal-based fat substitute, "oatrim," has notable characteristics as a fat substitute. It is derived from soluble oat fiber and from beta-glucans – complex carbohydrates contained in oat and other cereal grains – that have been found useful in lowering cholesterol. Thus, oatrim not only serves as a fat substitute but also as a cholesterol reducer.

Oatrim is made by treating oat bran and oat flour with alpha amylases. The starches are converted to amylodextrins, which, along with the beta-glucans, go into solution. The process yields a smooth, bland, white gel that can be used in numerous types of foods, such as extra-lean ground-beef mixtures, luncheon meats, cookies, muffins, and nonfat cheeses.

Consumption of oat bran had been promoted because of its ability to reduce cholesterol. However, it was found that the amounts needed were too great

and could lead to gastrointestinal problems. In contrast, oatrim retains the cholesterol-reducing properties of oats and can be useful for this purpose at realistic levels of consumption (McBride 1993; American Chemical Society 1990).

Oatrim has been honored as being among the hundred most significant new technologies of 1993 (Hardin 1993). George E. Inglett and his associates at the U.S. Department of Agriculture's National Center for Agricultural Research at Peoria, Illinois, patented Oatrim in 1991. Several national and multinational food companies have obtained licenses to manufacture and use oatrim in food products.

Microparticulated protein. Several protein-based low-fat substitutes have been developed. The first to win FDA approval (1990) was Simplesse, developed by NutraSweet, a subsidiary of Monsanto. Simplesse contains only 1.3 calories per gram of food, compared to 9 calories in traditional fats. It is composed primarily of milk and egg white proteins, with added vegetable gum, lecithin, sugar, acid, and water. The molecules of the proteins are rearranged in a process called microparticulation. The resulting proteins consist of extremely small spherical particles, about one-thousandth of a millimeter in diameter. In this shape and size, the particles roll over one another, are perceived as being fluid, and mimic the mouthfeel and appearance of real fat (Fat Substitutes on the Horizon 1988).

Although the FDA concluded that Simplesse is safe because it consists of common food components, such an assumption has been challenged. The decreased particle size and homogenization of milk and egg white proteins may influence free cholesterol absorption. The technique creates stereochemical changes of amino acids and peptides, which could alter ratios of neurotransmitters and induce hyperinsulinemic responses (Roberts 1989).

In addition, concerns have been expressed about the potential sensitizing properties of Simplesse for individuals who have egg and/or milk intolerance. Dr. Ronald A. Simon, a member of FDA's Ad Hoc Advisory Committee on Hypersensitivity, warned of the possibility of unique antigens in Simplesse that might be sensitizing and induce allergenicity. He urged that careful studies be conducted prior to sanctioning Simplesse for general use to determine what reactivity-sensitivity there might be, and encouraged allergenicity tests for both the product and any metabolic breakdown products (Allergy Specialist Expresses Concern 1988; see also Zikakis 1974 and Roberts 1989).

Another fat substitute based on egg and milk is under FDA review. Kraft General Foods has petitioned for approval of its product Trailblazer, which is a modified protein texturizer. It consists of a mixture of dried egg white and whey protein concentrate or skim milk, changed in form, and combined with xanthan gum and food-grade acid. Vitamin A, normally present in milk fat, is absent from this mixture, and Kraft announced that it would add vitamin A to any frozen dessert products made with Trailblazer (Dziezak 1989).

Emulsifier-based fat substitutes. Emulsifiers to reduce fat levels were introduced as early as the 1930s, in "superglycerated" shortenings. In recent years, the application of emulsifier technology, in conjunction with other functional ingredients, has made it possible to achieve greater fat reduction (Fat Reduction in Foods 1993).

Emulsifiers themselves may be fat derivatives, with mono- and diglycerides constituting a major category. By changing the positions on the glyceride molecule, emulsifiers can be made to function differently in the body (Richard 1990). Every emulsifier has both hydrophilic and lipophilic portions, which makes the characteristic oil-and-water interface possible. The hydrophilic-lipophilic–based emulsifiers have a fat-derived component, usually one or more fatty acids attached to the hydrophilic portion of such substances as glycerine, sorbitol, sucrose, or propylene glycol. These emulsifiers, usually combined with water, can replace fat in food products. Some, such as the polyglycerol esters (PGEs), with or without added fat, offer the mouthfeel of fat. The PGEs have been used to provide about one-third fewer calories than traditional fats in food products (Richard 1990).

Due to their chemical composition or molecular weight, some of the emulsifiers (although fat derived), are poorly metabolized and absorbed. Similarly, some PGEs, which are complex molecules of glycerine and fatty acids, may be so large that they are hydrolyzed only partially in normal fat metabolism. Thus, they are not absorbed fully by the body (Richard 1990). Medium-chain triglycerides (MCTs) are metabolized by a different pathway, and normally are not stored in the body. Rather, they are burned as energy (Richard 1990).

Future synthetic fat substitutes. Sucrose polyester (SPE) functions and tastes like fat. Its molecules are too large to be broken down by the body's enzymes, and so it is neither digested nor absorbed. SPE is a mixture of hexa-, hepta-, and octa-esters that form when sucrose is esterified with long-chain fatty acid molecules derived from a fat, such as soy oil (Inglett 1981). Under development for several decades, SPE was accidentally discovered by researchers at Procter and Gamble (P&G) who were searching for fatty acids more easily digestible by premature infants than were those found in milk. It was patented by P&G in 1971 (The Use of Sucrose 1982).

In 1987, P&G petitioned the FDA to approve its SPE product (Olestra) for use as a fat substitute to replace up to 35 percent of traditional oils and shortenings for home and commercial uses, such as grilling; seasoning of vegetables, meats, and fish; and making doughnuts, sauces, and salad oils. It also replaces up to 75 percent of traditional oils and shortenings used in deep-fat frying in food-service outlets. Another use is in the commercial manufacture of snack foods, such as potato chips (McCormick 1988).

Researchers have suggested that in addition to such SPE features as its escape from digestion and absorption, other characteristics may also prove beneficial. By interfering with cholesterol absorption, SPE might lower blood cholesterol and prevent or retard the development of atherosclerosis and bowel cancer. Moreover, it was thought that SPE might help block absorption of such toxins as DDT (dichlorodiphenyltrichloroethane) and other harmful compounds that remain in the body's fatty tissues for long periods, and might also help to expedite the excretion of such toxins from the body (Glueck, Mattson, and Jandecek 1979; Progress with Sucrose Polyester 1980; The Use of Sucrose 1982; Mellies et al. 1983; Sucrose Polyester 1983).

In human tests, however, SPE produced some adverse effects, such as gastrointestinal distress, including bloating, flatulence, nausea, diarrhea, soft oily stools, anal leakage, and increased urgency or frequency of bowel movements (Mellies et al. 1983). To avoid these problems, researchers modified the product's chemical structure. Another problem was that SPE blocked absorption of vital fat-soluble vitamins, especially A and E. Thus SPE could produce serious vitamin deficiencies (Mattson, Hollenbach, and Kuehlthau 1979).

The FDA classified Olestra as a food additive, and, legally, this classification required P&G to demonstrate that the substance was safe under conditions of its intended use (Definition of the Term 1985). After this classification, safety questions were raised by a panel of a dozen scientists organized by the Medatlantic Research Foundation, a private research group. The panel requested the FDA to require additional studies on the long-term health effects of Olestra and its possible absorption by humans (Swasy 1989). In 1989, P&G initiated additional safety tests to avoid having the FDA delay any further review by several years and secured approval for Olestra in 1996.

Meanwhile, other fatty acid–based fat substitutes are being developed. Among them is phenylmethylpolysiloxane (PS), a polymeric liquid oil that is chemically inert and nonabsorbable (Braco, Baba, and Hashim 1987). Another is dialkyl dihexadecylmalonate (DDM), a synthetic fat substitute with potential applications for high-temperature use with fried snack foods. DDM is reported to be minimally digested and absorbed (Fat Substitute Menu 1990; Spearman 1990).

In addition, work is proceeding on an esterified propoxylated glycerol (EPG) nonabsorbable fat substitute intended for cooked and uncooked food products (Dziezak 1989). Under investigation are alkyl glycoside fatty acid polyester (AGFAP) (Schiller, Ellis, and Rhein 1988); raffinate polyesters (trisaccharide fatty esters) (Schiller et al. 1988); and trialkoxytricarballylate (TATCA) (Fat Substitute Menu 1990), a nonhydrolyzable noncaloric oil-like compound.

Fat substitutes and safety concerns. The prospect of many food products with fat substitutes raises safety concerns. Many of the fat substitutes, such as SPE, are regarded by the FDA as food additives, and, as a rule, a food additive represents only a very small percentage of a food product, at most only 1 or 2 percent. But with synthetic fat substitutes, the percentage is far higher. As replacers of fat – a macronutrient in the diet – these substances might replace up to 40 percent of calories consumed daily.

In this event, it seems clear that present safety tests are inadequate, and new ones need to be devised that go beyond the traditional guidelines, which in this instance would mean guidelines that address more than 100 percent of the test diet. For widely used fat substitutes, the traditional margins of safety – between no effect levels in animals and estimated exposure levels in many humans – may need to be reduced. The FDA needs to find ways of modifying the traditional safety factor and, at the same time, to assure that food additives are safe (Scarbrough 1989).

Fat substitutes and nutritional concerns. It has been suggested that low-fat diets might compromise the intake of adequate amounts of certain nutrients, including essential fatty acids, calcium, iron, and zinc (Rizek, Raper, and Tippett 1988). Unfortunately, few feeding studies have been conducted with fat substitutes. Some trials suggest that they are ineffective for weight control, because individuals fed a meal that contained a lower than usual amount of caloric fat tended to compensate by eating more food at the next meal (Stark 1988).

Similarly, in animal studies, decreased carbohydrate intake made the subjects more hungry and resulted in an increased total food intake (Gladwell 1990). All of this, of course, raises the question of whether a decreased fat intake will result in a similar compensatory mechanism if fat substitutes gain widespread use.

Many health professionals are wary about the trend toward extensive use of fat substitutes. For years, public health programs have attempted to modify dietary habits. Americans have been encouraged, repeatedly, to increase consumption of nutrient-rich vegetables, fruits, whole-grain products, and lean foods of animal origin, while decreasing consumption of high-fat and high-sugar foods.

Thus, some health professionals are concerned that the availability of numerous low-fat and nonfat products (as well as those with low-caloric and noncaloric sweeteners) will lure consumers away from healthful nutrient-dense foods to poorer selections. A spokesperson for the American Heart Association cautioned that Simplesse, the first of the newly approved fat substitutes, "may do little but reinforce the country's taste for high-fat foods" (Fat Substitute Rolled Out 1990: 39).

Food products made with fat substitutes may follow a consumption pattern similar to that of the sugar substitutes. The latter originally were hailed as the great hope for banishing obesity. However, this condition is more of a problem than ever. Will the fat substitutes, which offer a similar promise, also prove ineffective?

Beatrice Trum Hunter

Bibliography

Alitame. 1990. *Chilton's Food Engineering* 62: 31.
Allergy specialist expresses concern about Simplesse sensitivities. 1988. *Food Chemical News* 30: 36.
Alper, Joseph. 1982. Finding a sugar replacement. *What's Happening in Chemistry?*, Vol. 31.
American Chemical Society. 1990. *Oat gel replaces fat, lets frozen desserts reduce your cholesterol.* Press release, April 24.
Ascherio, A. 1993. Epidemiology conference, American Heart Association (Poster Session). Santa Fe, New Mexico. March 19, 1993. *Food Chemical News* 35: 22–3.
Aspartame critics persist, recommend avoidance during pregnancy. 1984. *Medical World News,* Psychiatry edition. February 29, pp. 11–12.
Beardsley, T. 1991. *Trans* fat: Does margarine really lower cholesterol? *Scientific American* 264: 34.
Best, D. 1987. Conference unveils new ingredient technologies. *Prepared Foods* 156: 165.
Bicknell, F. 1960. *Chemicals in food and in farm produce: Their harmful effects.* London.
Blachley, J. D., and J. P. Knochel. 1980. Tobacco chewer's hypokalemia: Licorice revisited. *The New England Journal of Medicine* 302: 784–5.
Blakeslee, S. 1990. New light being shed on early mechanisms of coronary heart disease. *The New York Times.* March 27, p. C3.
Braco, E. F., N. Baba, and S. A. Hashim. 1987. Polysiloxane: Potential noncaloric fat substitute; effects on body composition of obese Zucker rats. *American Journal of Clinical Nutrition* 46: 784–9.
Calorie Control Council. 1993. *Fat reduction in foods.* Technical Report of the Calorie Control Council. Atlanta.
Canada clears sucralose use in a range of foods, beverages. 1991. *Food Chemical News* 33: 35–6.
Canada first country to approve sucralose. 1991. *Calorie Control Commentary* 13: 1.
Cellulose gel helps trim the fat. 1990. *Dairy Foods* 91: 76.
Centers for Disease Control. 1984. Evaluation of consumer complaints related to aspartame use. *Morbidity and Mortality Weekly Report* 33: 605–7.
Chamberlain, T. J. 1970. Licorice poisoning, pseudoaldosteronism and heart failure. *Journal of the American Medical Association* 213: 1342.
Cook, M. K. 1970. Ammoniated glycyrrhizin: A useful natural

sweetener and flavour potentiator. *The Flavour Industry* 1: 831-2.

Definition of the term "food additive." 1985. Item 201(a) in *Federal Food, Drug and Cosmetic Act, as Amended, and Related Laws, 4.* Washington, D.C.

Dillon, P. M. 1993. Sweet options. *Chilton's Food Engineering* 65: 101-4.

Drake, M. E. 1986. Panic attacks and excessive aspartame ingestion. *Lancet* 328: 631.

Dziezak, J. D. 1989. Fat substitutes. *Food Technology* 43: 66-74.

Edwards, C. R. W. 1991. Lessons from licorice. *The New England Journal of Medicine* 325: 1242-3.

Emken, E. A. 1984. Nutrition and biochemistry of *trans* and positional fatty acid isomers in hydrogenated oils. *American Review of Nutrition* 4: 339-76.

Enig, M. G., P. Budowski, and S. H. Blondheim. 1984. Trans-unsaturated fatty acids in margarines and human subcutaneous fat in Israel. *Human Nutrition: Clinical Nutrition* 38C: 223-30.

Enig, M. G., R. J. Munn, and M. Keeney. 1978. Dietary fat and cancer trends - a critique. *Federation Proceedings* 2215-20. Federation of American Societies for Experimental Biology (FASEB). Bethesda, Md.

Enig, M. G., L. A. Pallansch, J. Sampugna, and M. Keeney. 1983. Fatty acid composition of the fat in selected food items with emphasis on *trans* components. *Journal of the American Oil Chemists' Society* 60: 1788-95.

Enig, M. G., L. A. Pallansch, H. E. Walker, et al. 1979. Trans fatty acids: Concerns regarding increasing levels in the American diet and possible health implications. *Proceedings: Maryland Nutrition Conference for Feed Manufacturers* 9-17. Baltimore, Md.

Farese, R. V., E. G. Biglieri, C. H. L. Shackleton, et al. 1991. Licorice-induced hypermineralocorticoidism. *The New England Journal of Medicine* 325: 1223-7.

Fats and disease. 1956. *Lancet* 270: 55.

Fat substitute menu: Under development and review. 1990. *Calorie Control Commentary* 12: 5.

Fat substitute rolled out. 1990. *American Medical News* 33: 39.

Fat substitutes. 1990. *Chilton's Food Engineering* 62:69.

Fat substitutes on the horizon. 1988. *Calorie Control Commentary* 10: 3.

Get rid of unwanted fat with GPC's maltrin/Maltodextrins. 1989. Advertisement in *Dairy Foods* 90: 27.

Giese, J. H. 1993. Alternative sweeteners and bulking agents. *Food Technology* 47: 114-26.

Gladwell, M. 1990. Does fake fat pose diet risk? *The Washington Post.* April 15: A18.

Glueck, C. J., F. H. Mattson, and R. J. Jandecek. 1979. The lowering of plasma cholesterol by sucrose polyester in subjects consuming diets with 800, 300, or less than 50 mg of cholesterol per day. *American Journal of Clinical Nutrition* 32: 1636-44.

Hardin, B. 1993. *Oatrim wins new technology award.* U.S. Department of Agriculture, Office of Public Affairs, Press Release. Washington, D.C.

Inglett, G. E. 1981. Sweeteners - a review. *Food Technology* 35: 37-8, 40-1.

Ingredient notes. 1993. *Prepared Foods* 162: 46.

In the 1980s: Nonabsorbable polymer-leached additives. 1979. (In special section "Foods of Tomorrow.") *Food Processing* 12(F): 22-3.

Keeney, M. 1981. Comments on the effects of dietary trans-fatty acids in humans. *Cancer Research* 41: 3743-4.

Klose, R. E., and M. Glicksman. 1968. Sodium carboxymethyl-

cellulose. In *Handbook of food additives,* ed. T. E. Furia, 338-41. Cleveland, Ohio.

Koehler, S. M., and A. Glaros. 1988. The effect of aspartame on migraine headache. *Headache* 28: 10-14.

Kummerow, F. A., T. Mizuguchi, T. Arima, et al. 1974. Swine as an animal model in studies on atherosclerosis. *Federation Proceedings* 33: 235. Federation of American Societies for Experimental Biology (FASEB). Bethesda, Md.

Lipton, R. B., L. C. Newman, J. S. Cohen, and S. Solomon. 1989. Aspartame as a dietary trigger of headache. *Headache* 29: 90-2.

Lite sweeteners maneuver for heavyweight title. 1989. *Prepared Foods* 158: 92.

L sugars under development. 1989. *Food Technology* 43: 138.

Mancini, L. 1993. Low fat comes of age. *Chilton's Food Engineering* 65: 149-58.

Mattson, F. H., E. J. Hollenbach, and C. M. Kuehlthau. 1979. The effects of a non-absorbable fat, sucrose polyester, on the metabolism of vitamin A by the rat. *Journal of Nutrition* 109: 1688-93.

McBride, J. 1993. Two thumbs up for Oatrim. *Agricultural Research* 41: 4-7.

McCauliffe, D. P., and K. Poitras. 1991. Aspartame induced lobular panniculitis. *Journal of the American Academy of Dermatitis* 24: 298-300.

McCormick, R. 1988. Sucrose esters. *Prepared Foods* 4: 120-1.

McElheny, V. K. 1977. An alternative sweetener in focus. *The New York Times.* March 16: 42.

Mellies, M. J., R. J. Jandacek, J. D. Taulbee, et al. 1983. A double-blind placebo-controlled study of sucrose polyester in hypercholesterolemic outpatients. *American Journal of Clinical Nutrition* 37: 339-46.

Mensink, R. P., and M. B. Katan. 1990. Effects of dietary *trans* fatty acids on high-density and low-density lipoprotein cholesterol levels in healthy subjects. *The New England Journal of Medicine* 323: 439-44.

Mitsuoka, T. 1990. Bifidobacteria and their role in human health. *Journal of Industrial Microbiology* 6: 263-8.

Modler, H. W., R. C. McKellar, and M. Yaguchi. 1990. Bifidobacteria and bifidogenic factors. *Journal of the Canadian Institute of Food Science and Technology* 21: 29-41.

Moffat, A. 1990. Fiber fracas at FASEB. *Science* 3: 1442.

Monte, W. C. 1984. Aspartame: Methanol and the public health. *Journal of Applied Nutrition* 36: 42-54.

Najjar, M. F., and M. Rowland. 1987. Anthropometric reference data and prevalence of overweight. *Vital Health Statistics* 2. No. 238. National Center for Health Statistics. Hyattsville, Md.

National Academy of Sciences. 1975. *Sweeteners: Issues and uncertainties,* 127-74. Washington, D.C.

New "super sweeteners" made from citrus peel. 1970. (In special section "Foods of Tomorrow.") *Food Processing* 3 (Summer F): 4-6.

Pfizer moves in a new direction. 1991. (In section "Industry Report.") *Chilton's Food Engineering* 63: 17.

Potato starch replaces fats and oils. 1989. *Prepared Foods* 158: 91.

Potenza, D. P., and R. S. El-Mallakh. 1989. Aspartame: Clinical update. *Connecticut Medicine* 53: 395-400.

Powdered cellulose reduces fat content in fried foods. 1990. *Chilton's Food Engineering* 61: 40.

Process yields no-cal "left-handed" sugars. 1981. *Food Development* 15: 10.

Progress with sucrose polyester. 1980. *Research Resources Reporter* 4: 8-9.

Richard, W. D. 1990. Lower calorie food formulations using lipid-based ingredients. Symposium in *Fat and Fiber*. Calorie Control Council/George Washington University School of Medicine. Washington, D.C.

Rizek, R. L., N. R. Raper, and K. S. Tippett. 1988. Trends in U.S. fat and oil consumption. *Journal of the American Oil Chemists' Society* 65: 722-3.

Roberts, H. J. 1989. The licensing of Simplesse. An open letter to the FDA. *Journal of Applied Nutrition* 41: 42-3.

Robinson, H. J., F. S. Harrison, and J. T. L. Nicholson. 1971. Cardiac abnormalities due to licorice intoxication. *Pennsylvania Medicine* 74: 51-4.

Sanford, D. 1968. Unmilk, cowing the consumer. *New Republic*. August 10, pp. 11-3.

Scarbrough, F. E. 1989. Safety and testing of fat substitutes and replacements. Annual Meeting, American Dietetic Association. In *Fats, Nutrients or Nuisance?*, 72. Kansas City, Mo.

Schiller, Z., J. E. Ellis, and R. Rhein. 1988. NutraSweet sets out for fat-substitute city. *Business Week*. February 15, pp. 100-3.

Shock, C. C. 1982. Rebaudi's stevia: Natural noncaloric sweeteners. *California Agriculture* 37: 4-5.

Sichieri, R., J. E. Everhart, and V. S. Hubbard. 1992. Relative weight classifications in the assessment of underweight and overweight in the United States. *International Journal of Obesity* 16: 303-12.

Sinclair, H. 1957. Sees essential fatty acid lack causing degenerative disease. *Drug Trade News* 32: 33, 50.

Somogyi, A. 1993. Dietary effects in toxicity testing: When do physiological effects become toxic manifestations? Panel Discussion, Toxicology Forum, Aspen, Colorado. *Food Chemical News* 35: 16-18.

Spearman, M. E. 1990. Malonate esters: Thermally stable nonnutritive oil for snack food use. Symposium in *Fat and Fiber*. Calorie Control Council/George Washington University School of Medicine. Washington, D.C.

Specialty starches function as fat and oil replacements. 1990. *Chilton's Food Engineering* 62: 30.

Starches replace fat. 1989. *Prepared Foods* 158: 102.

Stark, C. 1988. Fake fats raise real issues. *Professional Perspectives* 4: 4. Nutritional Science, Cornell University, Ithaca, New York.

Sucrose polyester for hypercholesterolemia. 1983. *Anabolism, Journal of Preventive Medicine* 2: 1-2.

Swasy, A. 1989. P&G fat substitute moves sluggishly toward market. *Wall Street Journal*. April 24, p. 1.

U.S. Department of Agriculture, Economic Research Service. 1988. *Sugar and sweetener, situation and outlook yearbook*, Table 25: 57. Washington, D.C.

U.S. Department of Agriculture, Economic Research Service. 1991. World and U.S. high intensity sweeteners. *Sugar and sweetener, situation and outlook report* 16: 25. Washington, D.C.

U.S. Department of Agriculture, Economic Research Service. 1993. *Sugar and sweetener, situation and outlook yearbook*, Table 44: 79. Washington, D.C.

The use of sucrose polyester in weight reduction therapy. 1982. *Journal of the American Medical Association* 248: 2963-4.

U.S. House of Representatives. 1977. *Proposed saccharin ban: Hearings before the Subcommittee on Health and the Environment of the Committee on Interstate and Foreign Commerce*. Washington, D.C.

U.S. Senate. 1987. *"NutraSweet" - health and safety concerns: Hearings before the Subcommittee on Labor and Human Resources*. Washington, D.C.

Walton, R. G. 1986. Seizure and mania after high intake of aspartame. *Psychosomatics* 27: 218-20.

Wilkes, A. P. 1992. Expanded options for sweetening low-calorie foods. *Food Product Design* 2: 58-69.

Willett, W. C., M. J. Stampfer, J. E. Manson, et al. 1993. Intake of *trans* fatty acids and risk of coronary heart disease among women. *The Lancet* 341: 581-5.

Williamson, D. F., H. S. Kahn, P. L. Remington, and R. F. Anda. 1990. The 10-year incidence of overweight and major weight gains in U.S. adults. *Archives of Internal Medicine* 150: 665-72.

Wurtman, R. J. 1985. Aspartame: Possible effects on seizure susceptibility. *Lancet* 326: 201.

Yokogoshi, H., C. H. Roberts, B. Callabero, and R. J. Wurtman. 1984. Effects of aspartame and glucose administration on brain and plasma levels of large neutral amino acids and brain S-hydroxyindoles. *American Journal of Clinical Nutrition* 40: 1-7.

Zikakis, J. P. 1974. Homogenized milk and atherosclerosis. Letter in *Science* 183: 472-3.

VII.11 ❧ Nonfoods as Dietary Supplements

Food: A substance (of natural origin) ingested to maintain life and growth.

Diet: The habitual pattern of consumption of food and drink.

Supplement: That which supplies a deficiency or fulfills a need.

The semantically inclined will, no doubt, perceive an element of inconsistency in the title of this contribution. Any food(stuff) ingested for a nutritional purpose is, it could be argued, ipso facto a dietary component. To refer to "nonfood dietary supplements" would, therefore, be meaningless.

On the other hand, foods are often defined in traditional- historical terms, and it is apparent that there are a substantial number of "nutritionally significant" substances which, although not ordinarily components of a diet, may nevertheless be ingested in special circumstances. Whether such "foreign" substances are then described as food(stuffs) or as dietary nonfood(stuffs) is very much a matter of opinion.

The issue is further clouded by a tendency to regard foods as being of natural origin, whereas certain dietary supplements, although having a clearly definable nutritional role, may nevertheless have a "nonnatural" (synthetic) origin. And whereas "true" foods are rarely challenged in terms of potential toxicity, this is not the case with supplements - as evidenced, for example, by the American report on the safety of amino acids used as dietary supplements (Anderson, Fisher, and Raiten 1993).

Again, one must distinguish between nonfoods as dietary supplements and nonfoods as dietary components. Geophagists, picaists, and drug addicts may, in certain circumstances, ingest large amounts of nonfood materials, but these fall outside the scope of this discussion. Supplementation implies that the additional material is introduced intentionally for an avowedly dietary reason and is a substance that could not, in normal circumstances, be supplied by realistic dietary manipulation.

Since the purpose of dietary supplementation is to improve the nutritional status of the subject (thus distinguishing dietary supplements from pharmacological treatments), its practice must be congruous with generally accepted nutritional thought – which, in turn, implies that the intentional use of dietary supplements is a development of fairly recent origin. Consequently, the significance attributed to many nonfood supplements has, in recent years, ebbed and flowed, thereby reflecting the kaleidoscopic nature of orthodox nutritional thought itself.

By the same token, it is equally apparent that the concept of nonfood dietary supplements is a relative one, with the lines of categorization shifting from community to community. Thus dietary fiber, a widely advocated nonfood dietary supplement in the Western European diet, would have no such status in many African communities. Equally difficult to define is the distinction between the use of a supplement in a dietary capacity and its use as a pharmacological agent. Megadoses of ascorbic acid (vitamin C) may, in this respect, be contrasted with the more moderate levels used for orthodox dietary supplementation; and the use of arginine to modify immunity and intestinal carrier systems could, it may be argued, reflect a pharmacological, rather than a nutritional, role for supplementation (Hirst 1993; Park 1993).

By the late nineteenth century, the categorization of foods in functional terms had progressed considerably. Foods were described as "body-building" (nitrogenous) or "energy-forming" (nonnitrogenous), and there was, consequently, a tendency to simplify dietary concepts and to limit precepts to recognizably bona fide members of these two groups. However, by the turn of the century, the recognition of the role of vitamins – nonfoods in a quantitative sense – and the blurring of the lines of demarcation between "energy" and "growth" foods provided a more flexible conceptual framework for the proliferation of ideas about the usefulness of nonfood supplementation.

This chapter therefore deals with substances that, without falling into the conventional categories of dietary components (protein, energy sources, vitamins, and minerals), are nevertheless believed to enhance dietary effectiveness. They would not, in normal circumstances, be supplied by customary dietary components – either because the foods containing them are ingested in supposedly inadequate amounts (as in the case of dietary fiber in certain communities) or because the substance in question is not readily available from food(stuff) sources. This latter category is, in evolutionary terms, less likely to exist and, it could be argued, implies more of a pharmacological relationship than a nutritional one. Perhaps with this in mind, Michele Sadler, in a recent discussion of dietary supplements, has referred to them as "Functional Foods" and has defined them as lying between foods and pharmaceuticals (1993).

Three examples of "nonfood" dietary supplements are discussed below. All have achieved, at different times, some significance as supplements during the last 40 years or so, and they represent three "etiologically" different categories.

Bioflavonoids

The term "bioflavonoids" has been widely used to refer to those flavonoids that are believed to have pharmacological or nutritional properties. They have no apparently essential role in nutrition and, consequently, no daily requirement can be specified. Nevertheless, for a period of some 30 years they were held to have an "adjuvant" role in maintaining good health – possibly by enhancing the activity of vitamin C.

The flavonoids are a large group of plant compounds based on a $C_6C_3C_6$ skeleton. They are of widespread distribution in the plant kingdom, being virtually ubiquitous in angiosperms and also existing in more primitive groups, such as green algae, and Bryophyta, including Hepaticae. It has been estimated that in the West, the average per capita daily intake of bioflavonoids is approximately 1 gram (g) (Middleton 1988). Higher animals have, perforce, evolved in an environment in which, of necessity, their feeding habits exposed them to a wide range of flavonoid material, ingested as "secondary" components of foodstuffs. It is, therefore, quite conceivable that this evolutionary exposure to a wide range of flavonoids has elicited physiological and biochemical responses in higher animals. Certainly some bioflavonoid features, such as their ability to chelate with metals and the antioxidant activity associated with hydroxyl groups, indicate a considerable potential for biochemical involvements.

Bioflavonoids first attracted the attention of nutritionists in the 1930s when Hungarian workers reported that certain vegetables and fruits (notably citrus) contained substances capable of enhancing the antiscorbutic properties of ascorbic acid (vitamin C) and even of partially substituting for it. It was claimed that "the age-old beneficial effect of fruit juice is partly due to its vitamin P *[sic]* content" (Bentsáth, Rusznyák, and Szent-Györgyi 1937: 327); it was also suggested that "citrin," a flavonoid preparation, could prolong the survival period of scorbutic guinea pigs and that extracts of *Citrus limon* and *Capsicum annuum* could correct capillary fragility – a condition characteristic of ascorbic acid deficiency (Bentsáth, Rusznyák, and Szent-Györgyi 1936). The new factor(s) was regarded as separate from vitamin

C and was designated "vitamin P" (Rusznyák and Szent-Györgyi 1936), and sometimes was named, primarily by French workers, the "C_2" factor. However, the true nature of the relationship (if any) between the bioflavonoids and vitamin C was unclear, and later work indicated that some of the earlier results were probably attributable to traces of vitamin C in the flavonoid preparations. Nevertheless, by the late 1930s the bioflavonoids had acquired a niche, albeit a minor one, in the annals of vitaminology. But considerable reservations remained about their real nutritional significance (Harris 1938: 28).

In 1949 Harold Scarborough and A. L. Bacharach published an important review article summarizing the work done between 1935 and 1949, and dismissing any suggestion that vitamin P could generally substitute for vitamin C. They centered their attention on the influence of bioflavonoids on capillary resistance and quoted with approval an earlier statement that "guinea pigs placed on a scorbutic diet supplemented with adequate amounts of ascorbic acid show a decline in capillary strength . . . restorable by vitamin P" (Scarborough and Bacharach 1949: 11).

The consensus of opinion in 1950 was that flavonoids were of physiological significance and that their main influence (on capillary resistance) was mediated independently of vitamin C. Nevertheless, the Joint Committee on Biochemical Nomenclature (United States) recommended in 1950 that the term "vitamin P" be replaced by the designation "bioflavonoids"; and in 1980 the (U.K.) Committee on Dietary Allowances of the Food and Nutrition Board (COMA) indicated that the bioflavonoids should be regarded as pharmacological, rather than as nutritional, agents.

Interest in the possible nutritional significance of bioflavonoids forged ahead during the 1950s (see Table VII.11.1), with a continuing emphasis upon their possible adjuvant relationship with vitamin C. It is interesting to note that almost half of the bioflavonoid papers published during the period from 1948 to 1957 dealt with the specific bioflavonoid rutin (quercetin-3-rutinoside).

Table VII.11.1. *Publications during 1930-90 relating to the nutritional significance of (a) bioflavonoids and (b) carnitine*

	Bioflavonoids	Carnitine
1930-9	29 [53]	0
1940-9	51 [102]	0
1950-9	60 [172]	9 [25]
1960-9	35 [132]	9 [35]
1970-9	19 [85]	23 [104]
1980-9	7 [30]	93 [384]

Source: Based on papers abstracted in *Nutrition Abstracts and Reviews* and expressed per 20,000 total nutrition papers; the figures in brackets refer to the "uncorrected" total number of publications on bioflavonoids and carnitine, respectively.

Rutin was widely used at the time in model experimental systems and is still sold as a dietary supplement, sometimes in the form of extracts of buckwheat *(Fagopyrum esculentum),* one of its principal natural sources. Other specific compounds to receive attention by nutritionists were quercetin and hesperidin.

Work on bioflavonoids was extended in the 1950s and 1960s to include a wide range of supposed physiological and biochemical involvements. Possibly for historical reasons, workers in Eastern European countries were particularly active in this respect. K. Böhm, in his 1968 monograph, cited some 40 definable influences of flavonoids in humans – although the evidence for many of these was weak and sometimes contradictory. M. Gabor, in his 1972 monograph, dealt almost exclusively with one of these suggested areas, namely the supposed anti-inflammatory effect of flavonoids. Other, and more overtly nutritional, areas where bioflavonoids were believed to have a role were hepatic detoxication and lipid utilization (Hughes 1978).

Nonetheless, by the 1960s, interest in a nutritional role for bioflavonoids had peaked, along with their associated use as dietary supplements (see Table VII.11.1). Thereafter the main nutritional interest in bioflavonoids centered on their supposed synergistic relationship with vitamin C and their possible role as antioxidants. There was substantial evidence that bioflavonoids could "enhance" the ascorbic acid status of hypovitaminotic C guinea pigs, and much work in the 1960s and 1970s was aimed at elucidating the nature of this relationship. Discussions centered on whether bioflavonoids could actually substitute for (or synergistically assist) vitamin C in some of its roles, or whether they increased the availability of vitamin C either by protecting it from oxidative breakdown in the tissues or by enhancing its absorption from the gastrointestinal tract (Hughes and Wilson 1977).

Two aspects of flavonoid metabolism attracted some attention – their antioxidant capacity and, in some cases, an apparent mutagenicity. But studies of the nutritional significance of these features gave inconsistent and difficult-to-interpret results. For example, one study dealing with mice indicated that, whereas a dietary supplement of quercetin shortened life span, a flavonoid-rich extract of black currants (containing quercetin together with other flavonoids) extended it (Jones and Hughes 1982). Moreover, none of these studies provided any incontrovertible evidence of an essential role for bioflavonoids in nutrition, and a recent reviewer opined that their function in health and disease as natural biological response modifiers still needed to be determined (Middleton 1988). M. M. Cody, in a contribution to the *Handbook of Vitamins,* dealt with bioflavonoids under the heading "Substances without vitamin status" (Cody 1984: 578-85).

Nonetheless, there remains a certain amount of residual evidence favoring the use of bioflavonoids as a dietary supplement to enhance the absorption of vitamin C from the gastrointestinal tract and, possibly, its subsequent retention by the tissues (Hughes and Wilson 1977). As a consequence, to advocate the ingestion of "natural" vitamin C (as, for example, in the form of bioflavonoid-rich black currant juice) – rather than the synthetic "tablet" form of the vitamin – by persons otherwise recalcitrant to vitamin C absorption (such as the elderly) is not entirely without experimental basis.

For the decade 1980–9, however, only 30 "nutritionally orientated" bioflavonoid publications could be identified, and general interest in the erstwhile suspected nutritional role of bioflavonoids and in their consequent use in dietary supplementation would now appear to be waning.

The recent COMA report dismissed them as an "unnecessary substance" and made no recommendation for their use as a supplement.

Dietary Fiber

There were many "latent" references to dietary fiber before it was identified and characterized as a specific dietary component. Early writers on diet, such as Thomas Elyot (*The Castel of Helth* ... [1541]), Ludovicus Nonnius (*De Re Cibaria* [1645]), and Thomas Moffet (*Health's Improvements* [1655]), who referred to the laxative property of whole-meal bread (when compared with lower-extraction-rate breads), were in reality commenting on the fiber content.

Thomas Cogan, the Elizabethan dietitian, wrote in his *The Haven of Health:* "Browne bread made of the coursest of wheate floure, having in it much branne . . . shortly descendeth from the stomacke [and] . . . such as have beene used to fine bread, when they have beene costive, by eating browne bread and butter have been made soluble" (1612: 25).

Similarly, Thomas Venner, the Bath physician, wrote of whole-meal bread in his *Via Recta ad Vitam Longam* that

> by reason of some part of the bran which is contained in it, it doth sooner descend and move the belly, for there is a kind of abstersive [laxative] faculty in the bran: wherefore for those that are healthy, and yet subject to costiveness, and also for such as would not wax grosse, it is most profitable (1638: 25).

This comment is curiously congruous with the standpoint adopted by present-day fibrophiles.

Hugh Trowell, in his extensive bibliography *Dietary Fibre in Human Nutrition* (1979), mentions a paper written in 1919 as the earliest to deal with definable fiber (cellulose) per se. Arthur Rendle-Short, a British surgeon, argued in the 1920s that epidemiological evidence suggested a relationship between lack of dietary cellulose and the incidence of appendicitis. The earliest title in Trowell's bibliography to contain the term "fibre" was one by M. A. Bloom, published in 1930.

It was not until the 1970s, however, that a wide interest emerged in the nutritional significance of what had been regarded, until then, merely as dietary "roughage," or waste material. Three names are usually associated with this phase in the history of fiber. One is that of T. L. Cleave, a British naval doctor, who argued (1974) that a number of pathological conditions were probably attributable to an increased intake of refined sugar and starch. Although Cleave did not emphasize the mirror image of his thesis – namely, that an increasingly refined diet was in reality a low-fiber one – he has, nevertheless, been widely, and somewhat incorrectly, hailed as a pioneer of current dietary fiber hypotheses.

A more overt and direct link between fiber lack and disease was promulgated in the 1970s by Hugh Trowell (1979; see also 1985) and by Denis Burkitt (1971), and the genesis of modern fiber studies has become almost synonymous with their names. Burkitt himself, in tracing the early history of thought on fiber, has included a fourth name, that of A. R. Walker of South Africa. The number of identifiable publications on the subject of dietary fiber rose from an annual average of 10 in the late 1960s to 125 in the early 1970s; 10 years later (in 1983), the average had risen to well over 500. Trowell's original thesis (1960) stemmed from his observation that a number of diseases that appeared to be characteristic of affluent Western technological communities were rare or absent in the more "primitive" parts of Africa with which he was familiar. He drew particular attention to the differential incidence of diseases of the gastrointestinal tract and suggested that a high consumption of fiber-rich foods was protective against noninfective diseases of the large bowel. Similarly, and independently, Burkitt (in 1971) published his evidence that dietary fiber might be protective against colorectal cancer.

At that time, however, there was no generally accepted definition of dietary fiber, and much confusion stemmed from the use of values for "crude" fiber (the residue left after serial extraction with acid and alkali). This was a measure that excluded the bulk of the cellulose and hemicellulose material, both important components of dietary fiber. The problem of definition was, of course, inextricably linked to difficulties in the development of a method for the accurate determination of fiber (Englyst and Cummings 1990). Trowell, in 1971, defined dietary fiber as the plant cell material that was resistant to digestion by the gastrointestinal enzymes, and this became the accepted definition. More recently the term "dietary fiber" has been displaced by the resurrected form "nonstarch polysaccharide material," which reflects current analytic procedures.

The original "dietary fiber hypothesis" was soon extended by other workers to embrace suggested relationships between dietary fiber and nongastrointestinal diseases, particularly cardiovascular disorders (for example, Judd 1985; Kritchevsky 1988). Epidemiological studies indicated a negative correlation between fiber intake and the incidence of cardiovascular disease, and experimental studies showed that certain types of dietary fiber were potent hypocholesterolemic agents. However, relationships of this type posed a problem. By definition, dietary fiber was a substance that did not leave the gastrointestinal tract. How then could one explain its supposed "extragastrointestinal" effects?

Nor was it always easy to distinguish between a direct protective effect of fiber and a displacement effect on "harmful" dietary components. Mechanisms based on a fiber-mediated inhibition of cholesterol absorption or an increased bile acid excretion were among those mooted. But much of the epidemiological work related to fruit and vegetable intake and not to intake of fiber per se. M. L. Burr and P. M. Sweetnam (1982), however, found that in Wales, a vegetarian lifestyle could be correlated with a reduced incidence of heart disease, but fiber intake could not.

The picture was further complicated by the interrelationships now known to exist between dietary fiber and the intestinal flora. This is a complex two-way relationship. Not only are certain types of fiber subject to degradation by colonic bacteria, but there is also increasing evidence that fiber itself may, in turn, modify the nature and metabolic activity of the colonic flora, with consequent modifications to the formation and absorption of a wide range of metabolites. Considerations of this type have led to suggestions that dietary fiber may modify the estrogen status in females, with consequent implications for a protective role for fiber in breast cancer and, possibly, other cancers (Hughes 1990; Adlercreutz 1991).

The current consensus would appear to favor an increased fiber intake in the Western-type diet, but an optimal intake has yet to be clearly delineated. Appeals to primitive dietary patterns are of little help in this respect, as the fiber intake of humans has fluctuated substantially during their stay on earth. Estimates based on coprolite analysis have indicated substantially higher ingestion of dietary fiber by primitive peoples than by their present-day descendants, with daily intakes of 100 to 200 grams occurring at certain periods. In addition, there have been significant changes in fiber intake at critical points in the socioeconomic development of humanity, such as during the "neolithic transition" (Eaton 1990).

Fifteen years after the birth of the fiber hypothesis, Rodney H. Taylor, in a leading article in the *British Medical Journal* (1984), questioned the prophylactic usefulness of high-fiber diets except for improving colonic function and alleviating constipation. Recent dietary precepts are almost equally noncommittal in their advocacy of dietary fiber. The most recent COMA recommendation (1991) echoed Taylor's doubts. Although advocating an increase in NSP (nonstarch polysaccharides) from the current average intake of 13 g/day to 18 g/day to improve bowel function, the committee was unable to find sufficient evidence for a direct mediating influence of fiber in other suggested areas, such as diabetes and cardiovascular disease. Moreover, the increased intake, it was suggested, should be attained by dietary manipulation, rather than by overt supplementation. It is possible that after a quarter of a century of often frenzied investigative activity, the dietary fiber movement is beginning to disintegrate.

Carnitine

Carnitine was discovered at the beginning of this century when its presence in Liebig's meat extract – at the time a popular dietary supplement – was reported. Twenty years later its structure was elucidated, and it was shown to be (beta-hydroxy-gamma-(trimethylamino)-butyric acid. But it attracted little biochemical or nutritional attention until the late 1950s when its role in the metabolism of fats was described. Reviewing the situation at that time, G. Fraenkel and S. Friedman wrote that "a small amount of evidence has been pieced together indicating that carnitine may be active in the metabolism of fats or their derivatives" (1957: 104).

Subsequent, in vivo studies with labeled fatty acids confirmed this conclusion, and within a few years the role of carnitine in stimulating the mitochondrial oxidation of fatty acids was generally accepted (Olson 1966). Subsequent investigations revealed the nature of the mechanism of this stimulation when it was shown that carnitine acts as a transport molecule for the movement of long-chain fatty acid molecules into the mitochondrial matrix. A number of situations in which carnitine has a derived or secondary role as a buffering agent for acyl groups have also been described (Cerretelli and Marconi 1990).

A lack of carnitine, or a reduced or defective activity of one or more of the transport enzymes, would therefore reduce the availability of fat as a source of energy. This could be significant in cases where it is believed that a substantial proportion of the energy metabolism is derived from fat – as in the newly born infant or in cardiac muscle metabolism. It would appear, however, that in the short term, substantial falls in carnitine are required before an impairment of fatty acid oxidation becomes apparent (Carroll, Carter, and Perlman 1987).

The body is able to biosynthesize carnitine, and by the 1980s the biosynthetic pathway had been elucidated. It was shown that the precursor molecules were lysine and methionine, two essential dietary amino acids. The lysine is methylated by the methionine to form the protein-bound trimethyllysine, which is then hydroxylated to form beta-hydroxy-N-trimethyllysine. This is converted, first to gamma-butyrobetaine and then to carnitine (Rebouche and Paulson 1986).

Carnitine deficiency diseases, resulting from a defect in the biosynthetic pathway, have been described. Such a condition was first reported by A. G. Engel and C. Angelini in 1973, and since then a number of apparently different types of carnitine deficiency have been noted and discussed in the literature. Two basic types are sometimes recognized – systemic carnitine deficiency (characterized by a general reduction of carnitine in the tissues, including the liver) and muscle or myopathic deficiency, in which the reduction in carnitine occurs in the muscles. In such cases, carnitine replacement therapy is a recognized mode of treatment; supplementation must take the form of L-carnitine, the DL/D form being ineffective and, in some cases, further exacerbating the condition.

There are also a number of secondary or noncongenital syndromes that respond to treatment with carnitine, some of which are side effects of other clinical conditions (Rebouche and Paulson 1986; Smith and Dippenaar 1990). Carnitine levels are, in general, lower at birth than in adulthood, and there is evidence that some newly born infants may have a reduced capacity for carnitine biosynthesis. At birth, too, fatty acids become increasingly important as an energy source (Smith and Dippenaar 1990), and it has been suggested that all infants should receive carnitine supplements at least until the end of their first year of life (Olson, Nelson, and Rebouche 1989; Giovannini, Agostoni, and Salari 1991). A recent COMA report accepted that carnitine supplements could be necessary "for low birth weight or preterm infants" (Committee on Medical Aspects of Food Policy 1991: 135). Barbara Bowman, in a recent review, has pointed out that carnitine "appears to be a conditionally essential nutrient in malnutrition and in newborns, pregnant and lactating women, patients receiving dialysis or total parenteral nutrition, and patients with liver disease" (1992: 142).

Many of these examples of carnitine supplementation presumably stem from the correction of an abnormal feature of carnitine metabolism or by restoring a defective carnitine status to normal. Others are more overtly pharmacological than nutritional in nature. A striking example of the pharmacological use of [acetyl]carnitine was the report of a double-blind, randomized, controlled clinical trial in which the progression of Alzheimer's disease was significantly delayed by the ingestion of 2 grams of acetyl-carnitine daily for a year (Spagnoli et al. 1991).

Whether carnitine supplementation has a role in normal or "nonclinical" nutrition is more debatable. Much of the discussion in this respect has centered on the possibility of using carnitine supplements to enhance aerobic power and the capacity for physical exercise (Cerretelli and Marconi 1990). Theoretically, such supplementation could be advantageous in a situation characterized by an increased demand for "physical energy" and, more specifically, in circumstances characterized by (1) an increased use of fatty acids as an energy source, and (2) a depression in the biosynthetic capacity of the body.

A depressed biosynthetic capacity might, in turn, result from a reduced availability of the essential nutrients involved in the biosynthetic pathway. This latter consideration – the influence of other dietary factors on carnitine status – could be of some significance and is central to the concept of carnitine as a conditionally essential nutrient.

The hydroxylation reactions in the formation of carnitine from lysine and methionine require ascorbic acid (vitamin C) as a cofactor; in addition, two members of the vitamin B complex (niacin and pyridoxine) are involved, as is iron. The endogenous formation of carnitine, therefore, involves the participation of six obligatory dietary components – a requirement that places it in a "high risk" category with respect to inadequate supporting diets. A review has underlined this point:

> If the exogenous supply of carnitine is temporarily cut off, and provided the subject is not suffering from protein hypo- or malnutrition (as may happen in vegetarianism) plasma carnitine concentrations do not shift . . . [but] however, drop sharply if the co-factors essential for carnitine synthesis are lacking (Giovannini, Agostoni, and Salari 1991: 88).

Of the essential cofactors, lysine (often the limiting amino acid in poor-quality diets and frequently present in a physiologically unavailable form [Helmut 1989]) and ascorbic acid (vitamin C) are probably the most critically important ones. There is evidence, both experimental and circumstantial, that a reduced availability of one or both of these essential nutrients results in a fall of carnitine and possibly a reduction of carnitine-mediated energy release. Thus, the intake of three compounds – preformed carnitine, lysine, and vitamin C (the three forming the "carnitine base") – will determine the carnitine status of an individual, and one can point to a number of historically significant situations where a reduced carnitine base has resulted in the emergence of a stage consistent with what we now know to be the physiological consequences of carnitine deficiency: primarily a reduced capacity for sustained muscular exercise (Hughes 1993).

Thus, there are grounds for believing that the fatigue and lassitude, invariably present in the early stages of scurvy, could have resulted from the impairment of carnitine synthesis, which in turn would have resulted from a deficiency of vitamin C (Hughes 1981, 1993; see also Figures VII.11.1 and VII.11.2). It is tempting to speculate that the lowered aptitude for physical

2   DE SCORBUTO.

merare conabor; ejufque veftigia prementi, morbum in tria ftadia dividere liceat.

STADIUM PRIMUM.

Incipit infolita laffitudine, pigritia, fedendi et decumbendi amore; moeftitia maeroreque frangitur animus. Ægri facies pallefcit, tumefcit, et quae partes antea rubicundo colore nitebant, ut oculorum anguli, jam colore obfcure flavefcente fordefcunt. Magna eft debilitas, nifu leviffimo fpirandi difficultas adeft, cor celerrime palpitat; doloribus variis vagifque pectoris praefertim et articulorum torquetur aeger; adeo debilia fiunt genua, ut corpus vix fuftentare queant. Tumefcunt gingivae, pruriunt, et leviffima caufa fanguine fluunt, deinde quafi lividae, fpongiofae et fungofae evadunt, (quod morbi fignum certiffimum eft), et halitus graviffime olet. Cutis initio plerumque ficca afperaque fit, in eaque maculas diverfi coloris et magnitudinis videre eft, a fubrubro in lividum colorem plerumque

Figure VII.11.1.   Eighteenth-century description of scurvy which includes fatigue and lassitude. (From Kiernan 1783.)

394   OF THE SCURVY.

fome food; or any difeafe which greatly weakens the body, or vitiates the humours.

SYMPTOMS.——This difeafe may be known by unufual wearinefs, heavinefs, and difficulty of breathing, efpecially after motion; rottennefs of the gums, which are apt to bleed on the flighteft touch; a ftinking breath; frequent bleeding at the nofe; crackling of the joints; difficulty of walking; fometimes a fwelling and fometimes a falling away of the legs, on which there are livid, yellow, or violet-coloured fpots; the face is generally of a pale or leaden colour. As the difeafe advances, other fymptoms come on; as rottennefs of the teeth, hæmorrhages, or difcharges of blood from different parts of the body, foul obftinate ulcers, pains in various parts, efpecially about the breaft, dry fcaly eruptions all over the body, &c. At laft a wafting or hectic fever comes on, and the miferable patient is often carried off by a dyfentery, a diarrhœa, a dropfy, the palfy, fainting fits, or a mortification of fome of the bowels.

Figure VII.11.2.   Another eighteenth-century description of scurvy suggestive of carnitine deficiency. (From Buchan 1791.)

labor displayed by potato-eating Irish and by vegetable-eating French peoples and commented on by a number of observers in the last century was, at least in part, attributable to a reduced carnitine base (Young 1780; Lewes 1859; Bennet 1877; Williams 1885). A diet that centered almost exclusively on potatoes (as was eaten in Ireland during the nineteenth century) would contain virtually no preformed carnitine. Moreover, 20 pounds of potatoes would have to be eaten to obtain the amount of lysine present in half a pound of meat.

The remarks of George Henry Lewes in 1859 are interestingly pertinent in this respect. Describing the relative capacities of the French and the English for physical work he wrote:

> It is worth noting that the popular idea of one Englishman being equal to three Frenchmen, was found by contractors to be tolerably accurate, one Englishman really doing the work of two and a half men; and M. Payen remarks that the consumption of mutton in England is three times as much as that in France. . . . [B]y giving the Frenchmen as ample a ration of meat as that eaten by the Englishman, the difference was soon reduced to a mere nothing (1859, 1: 174).

Lewes's reference to mutton was, in this respect, a strikingly apt one, for of all meats and fishes analyzed to date, mutton has by far the highest carnitine concentration (Smith and Dippenaar 1990).

The belief in a positive correlation between animal protein intake and capacity for physical work was a central feature of dietary thought until disproved by the biochemical reductionism of the post-Liebigean era. H. Letheby summarized some of this anecdotal evidence in his Cantor Lectures in 1868:

> [T]here is always a relation between the amount of nitrogen contained [in] the food and the labor value of it. Carnivorous animals, for

example, are . . . stronger and more capable of prolonged exertion than herbivores. . . . The bears of India and America, says Playfair, which feed on acorns, are mild and tractable whilst those of the polar regions, which consume flesh, are savage and untameable. The Peruvians whom Pizarro found in the country at its conquest were gentle and inoffensive in their habits, and they subsisted chiefly on vegetable food; whilst their brethren in Mexico, when found by Cortes, were a warlike and fierce race, feeding for the most part on animal diet. . . . The Hindoo navvies also who were employed in making the tunnel of the Bhore Ghat Railway, and who had very laborious work to perform, found it impossible to sustain their health on a vegetable diet; and being left at liberty by their caste to eat as they pleased they took the common food of the English navigators, and were then able to work as vigorously (1870: 79).

About seventy years later, Robert McCarrison (also in a series of Cantor Lectures) made almost the same point by comparing the diets and physical capabilities of different Indian races (McCarrison 1944). In general, however, by the beginning of the twentieth century, advances in our knowledge of muscle biochemistry were beginning to undermine the belief in a necessary relationship between animal protein intake and physical activity (Hutchinson 1902: 38).

It is interesting to note that the same biochemical reductionism that dismissed the supposed relationship between activity and a "strong" (animal protein) diet now prompts us to reconsider this anecdotal evidence from the standpoint of "carnitine base" status. Many of the "weak" or "poor" diets referred in this section would almost certainly be found wanting in this respect. By the same token, it has been suggested that certain significant socioeconomic changes could imply a change in carnitine base availability. Thus the "Neolithic transition," although leading to an improved supply and availability of food, almost certainly resulted in a reduction in dietary quality and, particularly, in that of the "carnitine base" (Cohen 1990; Hughes 1993).

Such considerations are of direct interest vis-à-vis carnitine supplementation. In more general terms, they underline the importance in supplementation studies of considering each situation on its own merits. Any reduction in one or more of the components of the dietary carnitine base could indicate a need for carnitine supplementation. A sudden fall in the animal protein intake or in the availability of the lysine component or in vitamin C intake (as would appear to occur in the institutionalized elderly where the tissue concentrations of vitamin C are significantly below those believed to be functionally desirable in younger subjects) could result in a reduction in endogenously formed carnitine (Hughes 1993).

General Observations

The entire issue of dietary supplementation is clouded by adventitious circumstances and considerations. Thus it will be apparent that certain intellectual environments or passing paradigms of scientific thought can be particularly favorable to the concept of dietary supplementation. The burgeoning interest in bioflavonoids in the late 1940s and 1950s (and in fiber in the 1970s) was probably not unassociated with two acceptable features of nutritional thought at the time: (1) the belief in "subclinical" manifestations of deficiency diseases (which, in some undefined way, were believed to exist despite a normal intake of accepted nutrients); and (2) the conviction that supplementation of foodstuffs with micronutrients was nutritionally appropriate – a belief that, in cases such as the supplementation of low-extraction flour, carried the seal of government approval.

It is true that there have always been those who advocated supplementation for scientifically inadequate reasons. Such persons belong to the same category as those who, also for nonscientific reasons (such as folklore or romantic naturalism), favored brown (whole-meal) bread rather than low-extraction breads (McCance and Widdowson 1956). Where arguments for supplementation stem from external sources of this nature and are, consequently, difficult to accommodate within the current framework of scientific thought, they should always be treated with proper scientific skepticism and subjected to the appropriate scientific scrutiny. If it turns out that the advocacy of a supplement is consonant with current biochemical thought, then the arguments for its use can be that much more convincing.

The three examples outlined in this essay represent, in this respect, cases of dietary supplementation with three quite different origins. The suggested use of bioflavonoids stemmed, in essence, from a mixture of folklore and weak anecdotal evidence, supported originally by unconfirmed laboratory reports, and was enthusiastically embraced by believers in the value of natural foods as contrasted with manufactured ones. There are many other erstwhile dietary supplements that belong to this category – "vitamin B_{15}" (pangamic acid), "vitamin B_{17}" (laetrile), sea salt, and a host of herbal preparations. These supplements, for the most part, entered the nutritional field, as it were, from "outside" and for nonscientific reasons. Their alleged efficacy was, consequently, more easily disproved by accepted experimental and statistical techniques, and their use was frequently subjected to criticism and, sometimes, ridicule by scientifically orientated "establishment" nutritionists (see, for example, Bender 1985).

Fiber belongs to a somewhat different category of nonfood supplements, as its appearance as a candidate for dietary status was the consequence of epidemiological studies, although it must be admitted that in a nutritional context, it is not always easy to distinguish between "strong anecdotal evidence" (as presented, for example, by Trowell in his early studies) and statistically acceptable epidemiological evidence. Unlike the bioflavonoids, however, dietary fiber has achieved a foothold in current nutritional thought mainly because of strong correlative evidence coupled with the results of some experimental studies. Dietary intervention studies with fiber have been somewhat less successful, and accommodating the purported advantages of fiber supplementation within the current ambit of biochemical thought still poses considerable problems.

Carnitine represents a third etiologic category of potential dietary supplements. Its emergence as a factor of possible nutritional significance, in contrast to the two other examples discussed, was an "internal" event; it was not thrust upon nutritional thought, as it were, from the outside. Arguments for its acceptance in certain circumstances as a dietary supplement placed no conceptual strain on contemporary nutritional thought. In scientific terms it belongs, therefore, to a more acceptable category than the other two examples discussed. Other putative supplements whose emergence has reflected the current state of the art, rather than external and unrelated circumstances are taurine (which, alongside carnitine, receives conditional acceptance as a supplement in the current COMA report), inositol, para-amino benzoic acid, and specific amino acids. In all such cases of putative dietary supplements, the final verdict must await extensive experimental work and intervention studies.

This brief survey of the recent history of three "nonfood" dietary supplements should serve to illustrate three important and cautionary facts. First, it is useful, as far as possible, to distinguish between a pharmacological role and a nutritional role for supplements. Second, one should exercise caution before accepting claims based on anecdotal evidence or derived from statements or arguments external to (and sometimes in open contradiction to) current scientific thought. Third, and most importantly, dietary supplementation must be defined in terms of lacunae and imbalances in the existing dietary pattern, rather than in terms of absolute requirements – the concept of "conditional essentiality."

Classical nutrition derived much of its strength (and lately, some of its weaknesses) from generalizations based on an essentially reductionist and unitary approach to dietary components. A necessary condition for its success was the virtual exclusion of any conceptually extraneous matter, such as the possible importance of nonobligatory dietary components, the significance of dietary interactions, and the importance of the changing balance between tissue demands and nutrient availability. There are signs that current nutritional thought is shedding at least some of its traditional absolutism (Hughes 1993: 40-1). Future studies will presumably be designed not so much to prove in absolute terms the usefulness of specific supplements but to define the nutritional circumstances in which such conditionally essential nutrients as carnitine and fiber would be deemed to be necessary.

R. E. Hughes

Bibliography

Because of the wide range of topics covered, the references cited in this article are, for the most part, restricted to (1) historically important ones and (2) general review articles wherein references to more specific papers may be located.

Adlercreutz, H. 1991. Diet and sex hormone metabolism. In *Nutrition, toxicity and cancer,* ed. I. R. Rowland, 137-195. Boca Raton, Fla.

Anderson, S. A., K. D. Fisher, and D. J. Raiten. 1993. Safety of amino acids used as dietary supplements. *American Journal of Clinical Nutrition* 57: 945-6.

Bender, A. E. 1985. *Health or hoax.* Goring-on-Thames, England.

Bennet, J. H. 1877. *Nutrition in health and disease.* London.

Bentsáth, A., S. Rusznyák, and A. Szent-Györgyi. 1936. Vitamin nature of flavones. *Nature* 138: 798.

1937. Vitamin P. *Nature* 139: 326-7.

Bloom, M. A. 1930. Effect of crude fibre on calcium and phosphorous retention. *Journal of Biological Chemistry* 89: 221-33.

Böhm, K. 1968. *The flavonoids.* Aulendorf, Germany.

Bowman, Barbara A. B. 1992. Acetyl-carnitine and Alzheimer's disease. *Nutrition Reviews* 50: 141-4.

Buchan, William. 1791. *Domestic medicine.* Twelfth edition. London.

Burkitt, D. P. 1971. Possible relationships between bowel cancer and dietary habits. *Proceedings of the Royal Society of Medicine* 64: 964-5

Burr, M. L., and P. M. Sweetnam. 1982. Vegetarianism, dietary fibre and mortality. *American Journal of Clinical Nutrition* 36: 873-7.

Carroll, J. E., A. L. Carter, and S. Perlman. 1987. Carnitine deficiency revisited. *Journal of Nutrition* 117: 1501-3.

Cerretelli, P., and C. Marconi. 1990. L-carnitine supplementation in humans. The effects on physical performance. *International Journal of Sports Medicine* 11: 1-14.

Cleave, T. L. 1974. *The saccharine disease.* Bristol, England.

Cody, M. M. 1984. *Handbook of vitamins,* ed. L. J. Machlin, 578-85. New York.

Cogan, Thomas. 1612. *The haven of health . . .* London.

Cohen, M. N. 1990. *Hunger in history,* ed. Lucile F. Newman, 56-97. Oxford.

Committee on Medical Aspects of Food Policy. 1991. *Dietary reference values for food energy and nutrients for the United Kingdom.* London.

Eaton, S. B. 1990. Fibre intake in prehistoric times. *Dietary Fibre Perspectives* 2: 27-40

Engel, A. G., and C. Angelini. 1973. Carnitine deficiency of human skeletal muscle with associated lipid storage myopathy; a new syndrome. *Science* 179: 899-902

Englyst, H., and J. Cummings. 1990. Dietary fibre and starch; definition, classification and measurement. *Dietary Fibre Perspectives 2,* 3-26.

Fraenkel, G., and S. Friedman. 1957. Carnitine. *Vitamins and Hormones* 15: 73-118

Gabor, M. 1972. *The anti-inflammatory action of flavonoids.* Budapest.

Giovannini, M., C. Agostoni, and P. C. Salari. 1991. Is carnitine essential in children? *Journal of International Medical Research* 19: 88-102

Harris, L. J. 1938. *Vitamins and vitamin deficiencies.* London.

Helmut, F. E. 1989. Factors influencing uptake and utilisation of macronutrients. In *Nutrient availability,* ed. D. A. T. Southgate et al., 330-9. London.

Hirst, B. H. 1993. Dietary regulation of intestinal nutrient carriers. *Proceedings of the Nutrition Society* 52: 315-24.

Hughes, R. E . 1978. Fruit flavonoids: Some nutritional implications. *Journal of Human Nutrition* 32: 47-52.

1981. Recommended daily amounts and biochemical roles – the vitamin C, carnitine, fatigue relationship. In *Vitamin C,* ed. J. N. Counsell and D. H. Hornig, 75-86. London.

1990. Dietary fibre and female reproductive physiology. *Dietary Fibre Perspectives* 2: 76-86.

1993. *L-carnitine: Some nutritional and historical perspectives.* Basel.

Hughes, R. E., and H. K. Wilson. 1977. Flavonoids: Some physiological and nutritional consequences. *Progress in Medicinal Chemistry* 14: 285-301.

Hutchinson, R. 1902. *Food and the principles of dietetics.* London.

Jones, E., and R.E. Hughes. 1982. Quercetin, flavonoids and the life-span of mice. *Experimental Gerontology* 17: 213-17.

Judd, P. A. 1985. Dietary fibre and gallstones. *Dietary Fibre Perspectives* 1: 40-6.

Kiernan, Richard. 1783. *De scorbuto.* Edinburgh.

Kritchevsky, D. 1988. Dietary fibre. *Annual Review of Nutrition* 8: 301-28.

Letheby, H. 1870. *On food.* London.

Lewes, George Henry. 1859. *The physiology of common life.* 2 vols. Edinburgh and London.

McCance, R. A., and E. M. Widdowson. 1956. *Breads white and brown.* London.

McCarrison, R. 1944. *Nutrition and national health.* London.

Middleton, E. 1988. Some biological properties of plant flavonoids. *Annals of Allergy* 61: 53-7.

Olson, J. A. 1966. Lipid metabolism. *Annual Review of Biochemistry* 35: 559-98.

Olson, A. L, S. E. Nelson, and C. J. Rebouche. 1989. Low carnitine intake and altered lipid metabolism in infants. *American Journal of Clinical Nutrition* 49: 624-8.

Park, K. G. M. 1993. The immunological and metabolic effects of L-arginine in human cancer. *Proceedings of the Nutrition Society* 52: 387-401.

Rebouche, C. J., and D. J. Paulson. 1986. Carnitine metabolism and function in humans. *Annual Review of Nutrition* 6: 41-66.

Rusznyák, S., and A. Szent-Gyorgyi. 1936. Vitamin P: Flavonols as vitamins. *Nature* 138: 27.

Sadler, Michele. 1993. Functional foods: Foods of the future. *Nutrition and Food Science* 4: 11-13.

Scarborough, Harold, and A. L. Bacharach. 1949. Vitamin P. *Vitamins and Hormones* 7: 1-55.

Smith, K. A., and N. G. Dippenaar. 1990. Carnitine: A review. *South African Journal of Food Science and Nutrition* 2: 28-34.

Spagnoli, A., U. Lucca, G. Nenasce, et al. 1991. Long-term acetyl-L-carnitine treatment in Alzheimer's disease. *Neurology* 41: 1726-32.

Taylor, Rodney H. 1984. Bran yesterday . . . bran tomorrow? *British Medical Journal* 289: 69-70.

Trowell, Hugh C. 1960. *Non-infective disease in Africa.* London.

1979. *Dietary fibre in human nutrition: A bibliography.* Bristol.

1985. Dietary fibre: A paradigm. *Dietary fibre, fibre-depleted foods and disease.* London.

Venner, Tobias. 1638. *Via recta ad vitam longam, or A Plain Philosophical Demonnstration of the Nature . . . of all things as by way of nourishment. . . .* London.

Williams, W. M. 1885. *The chemistry of cookery.* London.

Young, A. 1780. *A tour in Ireland,* Vol 2. London.

VII.12 ❧ Food Toxins and Poisons from Microorganisms

The Processes Affecting Toxicity

Rather than undertaking a categoric examination of the myriad toxins in food, this essay highlights various considerations that should provide a sense of perspective in viewing toxins as a whole. It is important to realize that toxic substances must negotiate the various degradation and propulsive properties of a gastrointestinal tract in order to be absorbed and exert a harmful effect on the body. The ability of the toxin to be absorbed helps determine the amount of a substance that must be ingested before toxic effects become manifest. Moreover, the handling of ingested toxins by an immature gastrointestinal tract of a premature or term newborn infant may be different from that of the fully developed gastrointestinal tract.

Development of the tract begins during the first 12 weeks of gestation as it matures from a straight tube to one that is progressively convoluted, and the surface area for absorption increases. Over the next six months, the gut acquires a sophisticated immune system and the capacity to digest complex carbohydrates, fats, and proteins. Not all of these mechanisms, however, are fully functional until several months after birth.

The extent to which ingested substances, including food and toxins, are absorbed by the intestine is dependent on the capabilities it has developed to deal with carbohydrates, fats, proteins, water, and ions. These are highly complex issues about which varying amounts of information are understood. Nevertheless, a general concept of how absorption occurs may help put the discussion of food toxins in context.

Carbohydrates constitute the nutrients that provide the largest proportion of calories in the Western diet. Carbohydrate intake, in an adult diet, is approximately 400 grams per day. The major ingested carbohydrates are starch, sucrose (table sugar), and lactose (milk sugar) as 60 percent, 30 percent, and 10 percent, respectively, of the total digestible carbohydrates.

Starch is broken down by enzymes acting within the lumen or tube of the small intestine. The smaller molecules of sugar are digested (broken down) to molecules consisting of one to a few linked sugar molecules, and most are transported across the intestinal wall and into the blood by an energy-requiring "pump" enzyme system in the cell membrane (Van Dyke 1989).

Proteins undergo initial digestion in the stomach and are broken down further by pancreatic enzymes in the small intestinal lumen until they become either individual amino acids or small multiamino acid units called oligopeptides. The intestine has evolved separate transport mechanisms for absorption of different types of amino acids as well as oligopeptides.

Digestion of fat begins in the mouth but is primarily accomplished in the upper small intestine where bile acids from the gallbladder emulsify the fat, permitting the efficient action of the pancreatic enzyme lipase to break down the fats into free fatty acids. Because fats are poorly soluble in water, they are transported by micelles, made of bile acids and fat, to the surface of the upper small intestinal wall where they are absorbed as free fatty acids across the intestinal wall. There they enter either the blood, bound to proteins, or the lymphatic system. Many of the toxic substances in food are absorbed by the protein or fat digestion mechanism (Van Dyke 1989).

Other than the processes of digestion and absorption, intestinal factors that may affect the toxicity of substances in foods include the rapid turnover and sloughing of the intestinal epithelial cells in direct contact with toxins. Persons with intestines in which cell turnover has been slowed, as with those in developing countries suffering from protein–energy malnutrition, may be at greater risk of absorbing toxins from dietary staples.

Another factor is the motility of the gastrointestinal tract. Rapid transit, such as in diarrhea, may minimize the contact of foreign substances with the small intestine and thus reduce the opportunities for absorption (Silverman and Roy 1983). An additional consideration that has not been well studied is the presence of a variety of ingested substances in the intestinal lumen that may interfere with the ability of a toxic substance to come into contact with the intestinal absorptive surface. Thus, for example, the ingestion of phytates from various crops may interfere with the absorption of metals, such as zinc and calcium (Alpers 1989; Wallwork and Sandstead 1990).

Sometimes the ingestion of large quantities of one metal can inhibit the absorption of another. Such an inverse relationship exists between copper and zinc (Li and Vallee 1980). Furthermore, the porosity of the gastrointestinal tract is greater in young infants than in older children and adults (Silverman and Roy 1983). This allows the direct passage of intact proteins, and perhaps other substances as well, from the intestinal lumen into the blood, which could make infants more vulnerable to various toxins than older individuals.

The Concept of Bioavailability

Collectively, those factors that regulate intestinal absorption of toxic substances in foods, as well as of required nutrients, determine the *bioavailability* of the toxin. Although the bioavailability of many of the food toxins has not been clearly defined, it is important to consider this aspect of food toxins, because bioavailability will influence the amount of a substance that must be ingested before its toxicity becomes manifest. It is also a consideration in devising specific therapies for the ingestion of known toxins, such as the use of activated charcoal to bind a toxin in the intestinal lumen or the induction of vomiting to empty the stomach of a potential toxin.

An example of how bioavailability influences the degree to which toxic substances can produce harm is that of aluminum. Aluminum is the third most abundant element on earth and is a contaminant of many foods and medicinal products (Alfrey 1983). When it enters patients as a contaminant of solutions used for hemodialysis or intravenous feeding (total parenteral nutrition), it accumulates in bones, causing reduced bone formation and mineralization (Klein 1990). In addition, it interferes with hemoglobin synthesis, producing anemia, and in patients with kidney failure, it can accumulate in the brain causing progressive dementia and convulsions (Alfrey 1983). By contrast, oral intake of aluminum in normal individuals without damaged kidneys is well tolerated.

Excessive aluminum ingestion, as with long-term consumption of aluminum-containing antacids, may bind phosphate in the intestine and produce phosphate deficiency (Klein 1990). However, ingestion of aluminum in quantities present in normal Western diets (Alfrey 1983) or in currently manufactured infant formulas (Sedman et al. 1985) poses no threat to health so long as the kidneys function normally. The reason for this appears to be that the intestinal absorption of aluminum is very poor, probably less than 0.5 percent of intake, and the kidneys are efficient in eliminating that which is absorbed, leaving very little to accumulate in tissues (Klein 1990). Thus, oral intake of even large quantities of aluminum is not generally harmful because the bioavailability of aluminum in food is very low.

Metabolism

Once ingested, toxins that are absorbed are metabolized. The substances in question undergo biochemical transformation, largely in the liver, by a series of enzymes known as microsomal mixed function oxidases. Some of the reactions involving processes such as oxidation, reduction, or hydrolysis may increase or decrease the activity of the substances.

Other reactions, termed conjugation, involve coupling between the toxin and an endogenous molecule, such as a carbohydrate or an amino acid. These conjugation reactions often result in inactivation (Goodman and Gilman 1980). The fate of the particular toxin in the body will be determined by the relative rates of increased activation and inactivation. The enzymes involved in these reactions are subject to a wide range of individual variability in which genetics, age, body temperature, and nutritional status play important roles.

In general, very young children have a reduced quantity of microsomal enzymes, compared to older individuals. An increase in body temperature produces an increase in all aspects of metabolism, including microsomal enzyme activity, and protein–energy malnutrition depresses the activity of microsomal enzymes (Goodman and Gilman 1980).

The substances themselves may alter the activity of selected microsomal enzymes. Thus, such metals as aluminum, cadmium, and lead have been reported to reduce selectively some microsomal enzyme activity, although these same metals may increase the activity of some conjugating enzymes (Bidlack et al. 1987). Therefore, the variability resulting from the interaction of all the factors influencing metabolism of ingested toxins makes it extraordinarily difficult to predict the fate of any individual substance once absorbed.

It should be evident that both the bioavailability and metabolism of food toxins are very poorly understood variables, and the ensuing discussion of the nature of food toxins must be viewed in light of the highly complex response of the body to these substances, either alone or in combination.

Food Toxins

Food toxins can be generally categorized as plant pesticides (natural and synthetic), mycotoxins, metals, and animal toxins, as well as toxins present in foods as the result of industrial contamination. Each category is considered in turn in this section.

Plant Pesticides

Plant pesticides may be synthetic or natural. In recent years, synthetic pesticides have aroused public concern about possible health effects, especially carcinogenicity. Data gathered by the U.S. Food and Drug Administration (FDA) and reported by B. Ames, M. Profet, and L. Gold (1990a) showed that the average dietary intake of synthetic pesticide residues was 0.09 milligrams (mg) per person per day, compared to 1.5 grams per person per day of natural pesticides. Of the 0.09 mg, four chemicals not carcinogenic in rodents – ethylhexyl diphenyl phosphate, chloroprophan, malathion, and dicloran – constitute approximately half the intake, leaving 0.05 mg synthetics, primarily polychlorinated biphenyls (PCBs), as the only possible carcinogens consumed.

FDA monitoring for pesticides in food samples for a one-year period between 1986 and 1987 revealed that exposure of the American population to PCBs and other synthetic pesticides was consistently less than limits set by the U.S. Environmental Protection Agency (EPA), with less than 1 percent of samples containing pesticide residues exceeding the regulatory limits imposed by the FDA (Ames, Profet, and Gold 1990a).

In 1981, R. Doll and R. Peto estimated that approximately 35 percent of cancer cases could be attributed to the human diet. If true, and if synthetic pesticides account for such a small quantity of dietary intake, it is reasonable to cast suspicion, as do Ames, Profet, and Gold (1990b) and R. Beier (1990), on the natural pesticides.

These phytotoxins, as they are called, constitute a wide variety of chemical compounds produced by plants in response to injury from insects, fungi, climate, animal predators and physical damage. Although synthetic pesticide residues may be present in plants in the parts per billion range, natural pesticides may be present in plants in the parts per million or even parts per thousand range. Thus, they are present in much greater concentration than are the synthetic residues.

As an example, glucobrassicin, a polycyclic hydrocarbon, has a breakdown product called indole carbinol. Glucobrassicin is found in large quantities in vegetables, such as broccoli and Brussels sprouts. When these vegetables are chewed (cooked or raw), they release an enzyme that breaks down the glucobrassicin to indole carbinol. This substance acts biochemically in a manner similar to dioxins, some of which may be a carcinogenic synthetic residue. However, although the EPA has set an acceptable human dose limit for dioxin of 6 mg per kilogram (kg) per day, 100 mg of broccoli is estimated to contain 5 mg of indole carbinol (0.1 mg/kg/day) (Ames et al. 1990a).

Despite the large number of natural pesticides, relatively few have been tested for toxicity. Ames and colleagues (1990a, 1990b) estimate that they abound in the tens of thousands, existing in every edible vegetable and fruit to varying degrees. Yet it has also been estimated that only about 2,800 chemicals have been tested in laboratory animals, mainly rodents, for toxicity (Ames et al. 1990b).

The main categories of toxicity include (1) the potential to cause chromosome breakage in vitro, (clastogenicity); (2) the potential to cause genetic mutations (mutagenicity); (3) the potential to produce birth defects (teratogenicity); and (4) the potential to produce tumors (carcinogenicity). The vast majority of tests done using laboratory animals are carried out in rodents and at "maximum tolerated" (near-toxic) doses given chronically. B. N. Ames and colleagues (1990a) cite data showing that of 340 natural pesticides administered to rodents in conventional chronic high-dose protocols, approximately 70 percent were either carcinogens, mutagens, or both. Yet data on toxicity of these natural pesticides for humans are sparse. In addition, some of these natural pesticides (phytoalexins) have other properties that cause more acute toxicity in humans and animals without necessarily being carcinogenic.

Examples of natural chemicals that are harmful to humans include those found in a variety of Asian herbs containing pyrrolizidine alkaloids, which can be toxic to the liver. Thus, Indian herbal teas are known to cause hepatic veno-occlusive disease. Similarly, comfrey tea, made of the leaves and roots of the Japanese comfrey herb, are hepatocarcinogenic in rats, although insufficient data are available for humans. However, as much as 26 mg of pyrrolizidine alkaloids could be consumed in a cup of comfrey tea (Beier 1990).

Another instance of natural pesticides being harmful to human beings is the case of the white potato. Introduced into the Western diet as a result of the Spanish conquest of Peru, the white potato contains two major glycosteroid alkaloids, alpha solanine and alpha chaconine. Both are cholinesterase inhibitors, and thus have the potential to interfere with autonomic nervous system function.

Several outbreaks of a syndrome resembling gastroenteritis with a headache have been attributed to these alkaloids when the concentration of alpha solanine ranged from 100 to 400 micrograms per gram (μg/g) potato. Since not only the consumption of potatoes but also that of their skins (the site of peak alkaloid concentration) is increasing in restaurants, and at least one company is manufacturing a potato chip made from skins, it is possible that further outbreaks of alpha solanine poisoning will be seen. This is of special concern because these alkaloids appear to be resistant to cooking and frying. Some snack foods contain more than 7 times the safe limit of glycoalkaloids (limit of 200 μg/g potato) (Beier 1990).

Potatoes also contain nitrates with an average level of 119 μg/g fresh weight. Nitrates can react with various amine compounds to form N-nitroso compounds, which are carcinogenic and mutagenic in rodents. Potatoes supply 14 percent of the per capita ingestion of nitrates in the United States (Beier 1990).

In addition, there is epidemiological evidence suggesting that the glycoalkaloids in potatoes may be teratogenic in human beings. Attempts to breed strains more resistant to the potato blight fungus have led to an increase in the amount of natural pesticides produced by new strains of potato. L. Penrose (1957) has pointed out that Ireland has weather conducive to the growth of the blight fungus and also the world's highest incidence of anencephaly (congenital absence of the cranial vault) and spina bifida. Other areas of the world that have developed varieties of potato more resistant to blight have undergone as much as a doubling of the frequency of anencephaly (Beier 1990).

The risk of anencephaly is not eliminated by avoiding the consumption of potato during pregnancy. That the theoretical risk remains is suggested in the report by R. Beier (1990) that solanium, the aglycone derivative of alpha solanine, is stored in the body for a long time and could possibly be released during periods of increased metabolic demand, such as pregnancy. Although evidence supporting a role of the potato glycoalkaloids in the pathogenesis of anencephaly is only circumstantial, a case can surely be made for the need to determine more definitively the relationships of these natural pesticides to human birth defects.

The example of celery being harmful to humankind is more clearly established than that of the potato. The parsley plant group, most prominently celery, contains phytoalexins known as furanocoumarins. These are photosensitizing toxins that will cause both contact dermatitis and photodermatitis. Grocery workers subject to repeated handling of apparently healthy celery have experienced photodermatitis.

The problem stems from attempts to breed a more naturally pest-resistant form of the plant that have produced an elevation in its furanocoumarin content (Beier and Oertli 1983). In the epidemic of photodermatitis in grocery store workers, the linear furanocoumarin content was 14 times higher in the celery in question than in other celery varieties; psoralen, the most photosensitizing of the linear furanocoumarins, was 19 times higher than in other varieties of celery (Beier 1990).

Other evidence of harm to humans done by photosensitizing furanocoumarins are anecdotal. Psoralen ingestion followed by ultraviolet light exposure can produce cataracts in animals and humans (Lerman 1986). Severe, even fatal burns may occur in individuals ingesting psoralen and then visiting tanning parlors (Beier 1990).

These same linear furanocoumarins also are found in citrus and fig plants, which contain furanocoumarin in the peels that are used as flavorings for candies, soft drinks, and baked goods. D-limonene, a psoralen and coumarin derivative, is sold as an insecticide to control pests on household pets (Beier 1990). Fig photodermatitis is seen in fig handlers: In Turkey, 10 percent of fig handlers reportedly contract it (Beier 1990).

In addition, some crops are cultivated in developing countries because they are hardy and do not need the protection of expensive synthetic pesticides. However, they do require extensive processing to detoxify them. For example, much of the cassava root in South America and Africa contains cyanide in high concentrations and is edible only following washing, grinding, scraping, and heating (Beier 1990). Ataxia, or neuromuscular incoordination, due to chronic cyanide poisoning is prevalent in many of the areas of

Africa where cassava is consumed (Cooke and Cock 1989). Similarly, in India the pest-resistant grain *lathyrius sativas* is grown with its seeds containing a potent neurotoxin, B-N-oxalyl-amino alanine, the cause of a crippling nervous system disorder, neurolathyrism (Jayaraman 1989).

As an alternative to plant breeding and use of synthetic pesticides, "organic" farmers claim to use only natural pesticides from one plant species against pests that attack a different species. Thus, phytoalexins, such as rotenone, employed in India as a fish poison, or pyrethrins from chrysanthemum are used. These naturally derived pesticides have not been studied in sufficient detail to determine carcinogenicity in rodents (Ames et al. 1990a, 1990b).

Inasmuch as there are so many natural pesticides in virtually all our edible produce, one might wonder how it is that we are protected against them. Given the complexities in evaluating the effects of bioavailability and tissue metabolism of these toxins, this becomes a very difficult question. But it does seem that what is true for rodents may not be true for humans. Thus, species differences in the bioavailability and metabolism of naturally occurring toxins may account for differences not only in the minimum ingested quantity but also in the time course necessary to produce toxicity in humans. It is possible that humans rapidly metabolize natural pesticides to nontoxic metabolites or are not so susceptible to their toxic actions as laboratory rodents.

Secondly, even within the scope of rodent testing, doses of phytoalexins lower than the maximum tolerated dose may be protective or anticarcinogenic. Examples of this include limonene, caffeic acid found in coffee bean and potatoes, and indole carbinol (Ames et al 1990a). Often, feeding rodents large quantities of cruciferous vegetables, such as broccoli, cabbage, and Brussels sprouts, before their exposure to known carcinogens, such as aflatoxin, decreases the incidence of tumors and increases the rate of survival (Ames et al. 1990b). In contrast, if the experiment is performed in reverse and rodents are given the carcinogen prior to feeding on cruciferous vegetables, the incidence of tumors is increased.

Thus, in summary, the naturally occurring phytoalexins in our foods and medicinal herbs have not been subject to the same intensive scientific scrutiny as have the synthetic pesticides. But the public's current health concerns, the United States government recommendations that more fiber and starch be included in the American diet, and the popularity of "natural" foods and remedies sold in health-food stores combine to make mandatory an increasing amount of scientific study of the safety of such chemicals in the Western diet.

Furthermore, the continued prescription of herbal remedies without scientific basis, on the one hand, and consumption of agricultural staples high in natural pesticides by people in developing countries, on the other hand, pose both real and potential hazards of global dimensions.

Mycotoxins

Perhaps the reverse of the production of natural pesticides by plants responding to infestations and physical damage is the manufacture of toxic metabolic products by the invaders of the plants (that is, fungi). One example is the production of fungal toxins or mycotoxins. Mycotoxin poisoning was noted in ancient times in China and Egypt, and an epidemic identified by some as ergotism (one form of such poisoning) was recorded in Sparta in 430 B.C. (Beier 1990).

The mycotoxin thought to be most responsible for human disease is aflatoxin. Some others also implicated in human toxicity are ochratoxin A, trichothecenes, zearalenone, deoxynivalenol, citrinin, stergmatocytin, and ergot. These mycotoxins are relatively small molecules, with which humans most likely come in contact through contaminated foods.

The Food and Agriculture Organization of the United Nations (FAO) has estimated that 25 percent of the world's food crops are contaminated by mycotoxins, including 10 to 50 percent of the grain crops in Africa and the Far East (Mannon and Johnson 1985). Aflatoxins are primarily found in corn, peanuts, cottonseed, and tree nuts; ergot alkaloids, in rye and wheat; ochratoxin and T-2 toxin, in a variety of grains including barley, oats, corn, soybeans, wheat, and rice; penicillic acid, in corn and dried beans; and zearlenone, in corn and wheat (Beier 1990). Of all the fungi producing mycotoxins, only *aspergillus flavus* and *aspergillus parasiticus* produce aflatoxin, which is the most highly publicized fungal toxin affecting human health (Beier 1990).

Acute aflatoxicosis in humans has been reported from Taiwan and Uganda (U.S. Council for Agricultural Science and Technology 1989). The syndrome is manifested by abdominal pain, vomiting, liver necrosis, and fatty infiltration, as well as the accumulation of fluid in the lungs (pulmonary edema).

In 1974 in western India, unseasonal rains and food scarcity were responsible in over 200 villages for the consumption of corn contaminated with aflatoxin as high as 16 parts per million. Of 994 patients examined there were 97 fatalities (mostly due to gastrointestinal bleeding). However, the presence of other mycotoxins in the corn could not be ruled out, and consequently the epidemic may have been the work of multiple mycotoxins.

This example, along with other reported cases among children in Thailand, combine to suggest a serious risk of acute aflatoxicosis in developing countries where contaminated grain is more likely to be marketed for human consumption than in developed countries. A report by the U.S. Council for Agricultural Science and Technology (1989) suggests that acute aflatoxicosis poses a low risk in Western diets due to the apparent rarity of heavily contaminated grain in the food supply.

Conversely, aflatoxin B_1 has produced liver tumors in several species of experimental animals and is listed as a probable human carcinogen by the International Agency for Research on Cancer (U.S. Council for Agricultural Science and Technology 1989). Thus, there is concern about chronic low-level exposure of humans to aflatoxin despite the low risk of massive doses. The 1989 report by the U.S. Council for Agricultural Science and Technology has reviewed epidemiological studies from both Asia and Africa and concluded that the incidence of liver cell cancer is higher in regions where there is high chronic exposure to aflatoxin. However, there is no evidence that this correlation represents cause and effect.

In fact, a study of rural white males from different sections of the United States (Stoloff 1983) found that despite an estimated 1,000-fold difference in the intake of aflatoxin among men in different regions, the risk of death from liver cell cancer was only 6 to 10 percent higher in the most exposed population. Moreover, Chinese males living in the United States have a high incidence of liver cell carcinoma despite a low likelihood of exposure to aflatoxin (Stoloff 1983). Therefore, the risk of aflatoxin B_1 to humans as a probable carcinogen is still uncertain, at least with consumption of Western diets.

In addition to the encouragement of proper harvesting, drying, and storing methods, attempts are currently being made with a variety of techniques to degrade or otherwise chemically alter aflatoxin in grains (Beier 1990). Thus, as with aflatoxins, other mycotoxins probably pose a greater threat to human health in developing countries than in the more developed countries. In the former, the scarcity of food and the increased likelihood of grain contamination combine to magnify the likelihood of human consumption of tainted food products. Nevertheless, contaminated grains that may, from time to time, enter Western markets constitute at least a theoretical risk and mandate continued vigilance by governmental regulating agencies over national food supplies.

Fish Toxins

Endogenous toxins produced by fish may be less of a public health problem than industrial contaminants entering the food chain via fish or other foods. However, ciguatoxin, saxitoxin, and tetrodotoxin are acknowledged food hazards, and mention of them should be made. Ciguatera poisoning was described as early as the 1600s in the New Hebrides (now Vanuatu), and in 1774, the British navigator Captain James Cook reported an outbreak of apparent ciguatera poisoning in New Caledonia (Hokama and Miyahara 1986).

Ciguatoxin is of low molecular weight and belongs to a class of organic compounds called polyethers. It is one of the most potent toxins known, yet associated with few fatalities because its concentration in fish flesh is very low (Tachibana et al. 1987). The toxin is synthesized by a species of flagellate called *Gambierdiscus toxicus* and is passed through the aquatic food chain from herbivorous to carnivorous fish and then to humans, usually by consumption of certain reef fishes encountered around islands in the Caribbean and in the Pacific (Hokama and Miyahara 1986).

The onset of toxic symptoms may begin 10 minutes to 24 hours after consumption with gastrointestinal symptoms, such as diarrhea, vomiting, and abdominal pain. Neurological symptoms are caused by ciguatoxin's disruption of ion transport mechanisms that aid in the transmission of impulses along nerve axons (Hokama and Miyahara 1986). The symptoms include increased sensitivity to cold, which produces a painful tingling sensation, dilatation of the pupils, weakness, unsteady gait (ataxia), and abnormalities in deep tendon reflexes. With a large dose of ciguatoxin, respiratory depression may occur, and neurological symptoms can persist for months. Cardiovascular effects of ciguatoxin include abnormalities in blood pressure and heart rate, initially low, then sometimes too high, with an occasional irregular heart rhythm. These effects usually disappear within 48 to 72 hours. Of interest and concern, however, is that multiple poisonings of an individual generally increase his or her sensitivity to the toxin, resulting in more severe clinical effects with repeated ingestion.

Saxitoxin, like ciguatoxin, is produced by one or more species of flagellates (Valenti, Pasquini, and Andreucci 1979). These toxins, however, are often found in mollusks, which concentrate them. Saxitoxin is found, for the most part, in the Alaska butter clam and in mussels and scallops, especially during the warm months of the year. An epidemic of saxitoxin poisoning that occurred in Italy in October 1976 was attributable to the consumption of contaminated shellfish (Valenti et al. 1979).

Like ciguatoxin, saxitoxin is an organic compound of low molecular weight that acts as a neurotoxin by blocking the channels for sodium ion to cross the membranes of excitable nerve cells, thus blocking transmission of neuromuscular impulses. Symptoms usually appear within 30 minutes of ingestion. These include numbness around the mouth, lips, face, and extremities; a broad-based gait with neuromuscular incoordination, accompanied by nausea and vomiting and diarrhea; loss of voice; impaired swallowing; and respiratory impairment, which can lead to death within 12 hours.

A lethal dose of saxitoxin is reported to be 1 to 2 milligrams, whereas the concentration for saxitoxin in affected mollusks consumed in Italy ranged from 556 to 1479 micrograms per 100 grams pulp. Thus, there must be individual variation in the susceptibility to the effects of saxitoxin, because very large quantities of pulp are normally consumed.

Tetrodotoxin was first isolated in 1894 from the fugu (also called puffer) fish. It is found primarily in fish inhabiting the waters of Japan, China, and Polynesia and is one of the most potent toxins known. Ingestion of 2 grams of fish eggs can kill a person (Valenti et al. 1979). Female fish appear to produce greater amounts of toxin than males. Balloon fish, shellfish, toad fish, and globe fish also are known to produce tetrodotoxin. Like saxitoxin, tetrodotoxin is a rapid-acting sodium-ion channel poison that blocks neuromuscular conduction (Valenti et al. 1979).

The onset of symptoms occurs between 10 and 50 minutes following ingestion, with vomiting, spreading numbness, voice loss, swallowing difficulty, and respiratory depression. In Japan, more than half the victims die within an hour of ingestion, and 100 percent of those that die do so within 24 hours. Those ingesting only a minimal amount of tetrodotoxin recover without residual problems (Valenti et al. 1979).

The fugu fish is considered a delicacy by the Japanese, and restaurant chefs must have a special license from the government to prepare it in such a way that tetrodotoxin is inactivated. There are some anecdotal reports in the medical literature claiming that rapid administration of anticholinesterase drugs, such as edrophonium, can immediately reverse the paralytic effects of tetrodotoxin (Torda, Sinclair, and Ulyatt 1973; Chew et al. 1984).

Food Poisoning from Microorganisms and Their Toxins

Food poisoning is, regrettably, more than an occasional public health problem, usually resulting from either unhygienic food preparation or food storage or both. Spoiled food is contaminated primarily by toxins produced by strains of clostridium and staphylococcus. Salmonella may itself contaminate certain foods, but it does not produce a toxin, according to present knowledge. The causative organism for anthrax is among a group of other microorganisms found in spoiled food. The disease results from the ingestion of contaminated undercooked meat and is manifested by bloody diarrhea, pain, and occasionally shock. Anthrax is seldom a problem in the West and is more often encountered in underdeveloped countries (American Academy of Pediatrics 1991).

Bacillus cereus, a spore-forming gram-positive rod, may be present in a variety of foods. In fried rice (where it frequently occurs) it causes vomiting, and in meat and vegetables it causes diarrhea. The spores are relatively heat resistant, and the organism can grow and produce toxins in the intestine. The course is usually mild and resolves spontaneously within 24 hours (American Academy of Pediatrics 1991).

Two forms of clostridial food poisoning are noteworthy, that originating from *Clostridium botulinum* (botulism) and that generated by *Clostridium perfringens.* Botulism is a neurological disorder pro-

duced by neurotoxins A, B, E, and F of *Clostridium botulinum.* The toxins create a flaccid paralysis of the muscles of swallowing and phonation, as well as double vision, blurred vision, and slurred speech. Infant botulism, which occurs primarily in those less than 6 months old, is manifested by constipation, loss of muscle tone, a weak cry, poor feeding, a diminished gag reflex, and ocular palsies.

The neurotoxins are found in improperly preserved foods, especially those that are home processed and canned (American Academy of Pediatrics 1991). Illness occurs when the neurotoxins in unheated food are consumed. Most cases of infant botulism do not have a known source for the clostridial spores. However, honey is one identified source, corn syrup another. The American Academy of Pediatrics (1991) recommends withholding honey and, perhaps, corn syrup from an infant's diet for the first 6 months of life.

The cramping abdominal pain and watery diarrhea that develop 8 to 24 hours following ingestion of beef, poultry, gravy, and, notoriously, Mexican food usually result from a heat-labile enterotoxin produced by type A *C. perfringens.* The infection is generally acquired at places where food is prepared in large quantities and kept warm for long periods. Thus schools, camps, caterers, restaurants, and public markets where cooking is done would be typical sources of the infection. As in the case of infection by *B. cereus,* the symptoms usually resolve spontaneously within 24 hours (American Academy of Pediatrics 1991).

Caliciviruses are RNA viruses that can cause gastroenteritis-like symptoms lasting approximately four days. Outbreaks have been reported in children in institutional settings in Japan and the United Kingdom. Contaminated shellfish and cold foods are thought to be vehicles of transmission (American Academy of Pediatrics 1991).

Campylobacter jejuni, one of the most common organisms causing bloody diarrhea, has been isolated from the feces of turkeys and chickens. Transmission occurs by intake of contaminated food, including unpasteurized milk and improperly cooked poultry (American Academy of Pediatrics 1991).

Vibrio cholerae and its toxin can be acquired from ingestion of contaminated shellfish. The recent cholera epidemic in Peru and other parts of South America was originally attributable to "ceviche" (raw fish treated with lime juice) that was contaminated by *V. cholerae.* Adequate cooking eradicates the organism from foodstuffs.

Listeria monocytogenes is a cause of neonatal and perinatal infection. During outbreaks it has been traced to maternal intake of unpasteurized cheese or contaminated cole slaw, and milk has also been implicated.

Norwalk viruses can produce a gastroenteritis along with muscle aches, fever, and crampy abdominal pain. These RNA viruses are implicated in epidemics of gastroenteritis, and outbreaks are associated with eating contaminated shellfish and salads (American Academy of Pediatrics 1991).

Salmonellosis, or gastroenteritis produced by non-typhoid strains of salmonella, can be contracted from improperly processed meat or unpasteurized milk. Food handlers who carry salmonella are additional sources of outbreaks (American Academy of Pediatrics 1991).

Staphylococcus aureus and, occasionally, staphylococcus epidermitis can produce a variety of heat-stable enterotoxins: A, B, C_{1-3}, D, E, and F. The enterotoxins, if present in such foods as egg and potato salads, cream-filled pastries, poultry, and ham can produce abdominal cramping pain, nausea, vomiting, and diarrhea from 30 minutes to 7 hours after ingestion. The symptoms are severe but self-limited (American Academy of Pediatrics 1991).

Yersinia enterocolitica, an infection that may mimic other gastrointestinal diseases, including Crohn's disease (a chronic inflammatory bowel disease) and lymphoma, may be contracted by the consumption of contaminated food, especially uncooked pork and unpasteurized milk (American Academy of Pediatrics 1991).

Finally, one of the routes of transmission of toxoplasmosis, caused by a multi-organ protozoan pathogen with multiple disease manifestations, is by the consumption of poorly cooked meat. The same is true for trichinosis, caused by the nematode *Trichinella spiralis*. It too can cause anything from mild gastroenteritis to severe multiorgan disease and death.

Contamination of Food by Industrial Products

Industrial human-made toxins that contaminate foods include the heavy metals, such as lead, cadmium, and mercury, as well as lighter metals such as aluminum, dealt with in the section "The Concept of Bioavailability." Other industrial contaminants include halogenated hydrocarbons used as pesticides. The following section cites several examples of these contaminants as industrial disasters, as well as potential hazards.

Metal Contamination
Cadmium. In the Japanese prefecture of Toyama in the Jinzu River basin, postmenopausal women became ill after eating cadmium-contaminated rice. The illness, known as "itai-itai disease" was characterized by bone pain, osteoporosis, X-ray appearance of bone thickening overlying an incomplete fracture, and kidney disease as manifested by protein and sugar in the urine. Cadmium ingestion has also been the result of leaching from cadmium-plated containers by acidic drinks, such as fruit juices. These types of containers are now prohibited by law in many parts of the United States (Klein and Snodgrass 1993).

Cadmium may be deposited in soil and water near industrial plants that utilize it in metallurgy, plastics stabilizers, nuclear reactor rods, battery plants, and semiconductors. Because cadmium concentration in the soil can be high in these areas, crops grown in such soil may have high cadmium levels (Klein and Snodgrass 1993). Such may have been the case with itai-itai disease. Cadmium can also enter the aquatic food chain, especially through plankton, mollusks, and shellfish.

Mercury. Two major disasters have been reported as a result of epidemic mercury ingestion. One of these, in Japan, involved two episodes of methyl mercury ingestion as a result of waste dumping by an acetaldehyde manufacturing plant that discarded mercury into Minimata Bay. In 1956 and again in 1965, many infants of mothers from the cities surrounding the bay were born with brain malformations. They, and older individuals, developed irreversible neurological disease known in the literature as "Minimata disease."

In Iraq, a similar set of neurological problems developed following the 1971 consumption of bread made from wheat contaminated by a mercury-containing fungicide. The neuropathies resulted from degeneration of the nervous tissue caused by the mercury. Symptoms in exposed infants included cerebral palsy, psychomotor retardation microcephaly, spastic or flaccid paralysis, visual disorders, and convulsions. In older individuals, muscle weakness and visual and hearing impairment were prominent (Klein and Snodgrass 1993).

Lead. Although there are no recent major disasters on record for lead such as those reported for cadmium and mercury, it is now recognized that ingestion of even small quantities of lead, especially by children, may result in both behavioral and learning disorders. This finding is the work primarily of H. L. Needleman and colleagues (1990). The main source of lead ingestion by children has been lead-based paint that chips off the walls in run-down inner-city housing. However, it is apparent that other sources of lead ingestion include foods. In many cases, this is because agricultural vehicles, which are not required to use unleaded gasoline, release lead-containing exhaust onto crops, and lead accumulates most prominently in green, leafy vegetables. In addition, acidic foods can leach lead from the lead solder in cans (Klein and Snodgrass 1993).

Aluminum. Aluminum contaminates many foods in our diet, with the average adult consuming from 2 to 5 milligrams per day (Alfrey 1983). The Joint Food and Agriculture Organization/World Health Organization Expert Committee (1989) has indicated that a provisional tolerable weekly intake is around 7 mg per kilogram body weight.

Aluminum accumulation in bone has been associated with reduced bone formation and mineralization, in some cases leading to fractures and severe skeletal pain (Alfrey 1983, Klein 1990). It has also been implicated in a progressive dementia affecting uremic patients (Alfrey 1983). As we mentioned, the intestinal absorption of dietary aluminum is very low, about 0.5 percent (Klein 1990).

In recent years, the detection of large quantities of aluminum in some infant formulas has caused concern (Sedman et al. 1985). This has prompted the American Academy of Pediatrics to caution against the use of soy-based formulas (which have a high content of aluminum) for premature infants because of their immature kidney function (American Academy of Pediatrics Committee 1986). The source of the aluminum contamination in these soy formulas is the calcium and phosphate salts added to them, as well as the soy-protein isolate itself. The calcium and phosphate salts make up the chief sources of aluminum contamination of intravenous feeding solutions in use in hospitals (Sedman et al. 1985).

Chlorinated Hydrocarbons

There are numerous reports of halogenated, primarily chlorinated hydrocarbons contaminating the food chain, either via intake by fish or contamination of livestock feed. According to several reports, fish have been contaminated with DDT (dichlorodiphenyltrichloroethane) and other organic compounds, such as PCB (polychlorinated biphenyls), resulting in high human adipose tissue concentration of these chemicals (Kreiss et al. 1981; Ansari et al. 1986). It is also clear that these chlorinated hydrocarbons can concentrate in human breast milk to levels that may reach 20 times their concentration in cow's milk, with large dosing of infants a potential result (Fytianos et al. 1985).

Although all of the health implications (including carcinogenicity) of these ingestions are not understood, there is a report of more than 3,000 patients who developed porphyria in southeast Turkey following ingestion of hexachlorobezene fungicide added to wheat seedlings. Many of the breast-fed infants in this exposure under 1 year of age died as a result (Cripps et al. 1984).

In Michigan in 1973–4, there was a large environmental exposure because of the erroneous mixing of approximately one ton of polybrominated biphenyls (PBBs), a commercial flame retardant, into livestock feed. By mid-1974 virtually every Michigan resident had been exposed to these polybrominated biphenyls by consuming contaminated meat, milk, eggs, and other dairy products. Approximately 300 farm family members who consumed contaminated products from their own farms were followed for study (Anderson et al. 1979; Meester 1979).

Although no specific disease was identified, many of the exposed individuals complained of fatigue, visual problems, skin rashes, reduced resistance to infection, reduced tolerance of alcoholic beverages, and reduced libido. Several individuals complained of migratory arthritis, and one patient had aplastic anemia. The amount of polybrominated biphenyls in the subcutaneous fat did not correlate with symptoms, nor was there any kind of a dose–response relationship. The potential for carcinogenicity is uncertain although animal data suggest this is a risk in high-dose, long-term exposure (Groce and Kimbrough 1984). Furthermore, G. Lambert and colleagues (1990) have found that the hepatic microsomal enzymes of individuals exposed to PBBs remain activated up to 10 years following exposures. These activated enzymes are capable of producing carcinogenic metabolites from drugs and other organic compounds.

Conclusion

This chapter is intended to point out the variability of human defenses against the toxic substances we ingest; to illustrate the scope of our dietary exposure to toxins and putative toxins; to suggest our relative ignorance of the potential for harm caused by the myriad chemicals we consume with our food; to indicate that the majority of these are natural and not synthetic; and to show that industrial mishaps can indeed affect our food supply.

Although the public generally has confidence in the food with which it is supplied, there is a need for further scientific study of the effects of natural chemicals on our health, as well as a need for vigilance on the part of both industry and government to ensure that our food supply is neither needlessly nor irresponsibly contaminated.

Finally, in less-developed areas of the world, where the food available for human consumption is scarce and less subject to official scrutiny, the problem of toxic ingestion is magnified and its true extent probably unknown at the present time.

Gordon L. Klein
Wayne R. Snodgrass

The authors would like to express appreciation to Douglas E. Goeger, assistant professor of preventive medicine and community health at the University of Texas Medical Branch at Galveston, for the provision of key references as well as helpful comments. They would also like to thank Wilma L. Nance for manuscript preparation.

Bibliography

Alfrey, A. C. 1983. Aluminum. *Advances in Clinical Chemistry* 23: 69–91.

Alpers, D. H. 1989. Absorption of vitamins and divalent minerals. In *Gastrointestinal disease: Pathophysiology, diagnosis, management,* ed. M. H. Sleisinger and J. S. Fordtran, 1057–8. Philadelphia, Pa.

American Academy of Pediatrics. 1991. *Report of the Committee on Infectious Diseases,* 1-670. Elk Grove Village, Ill.

American Academy of Pediatrics, Committee on Nutrition. 1986. Aluminum toxicity. *Pediatrics* 78: 1150-4.

Ames, B. N., M. Profet, and L. S. Gold. 1990a. Dietary pesticides (99.99% all natural). *Proceedings of the National Academy of Sciences of the United States of America* 87: 7777-81.

1990b. Nature's chemicals and synthetic chemicals: Comparative toxicology. *Proceedings of the National Academy of Sciences of the United States of America* 87: 7782-6.

Anderson, H. A., A. S. Wolff, R. Lilis, et al. 1979. Symptoms and clinical abnormalities following ingestion of polybrominated biphenyl-contaminated food products. *Annals of the New York Academy of Sciences* 320: 684-702. New York.

Ansari, G. A. S., G. P. James, L. A. Hu, and E. J. Reynolds. 1986. Organochlorine residues in adipose tissue of residents of the Texas Gulf Coast. *Bulletin of Environmental Contamination and Toxicology* 36: 311-16.

Beier, R. 1990. Natural pesticides and bioactive components in food. *Reviews of Environmental Contamination and Toxicology* 113: 47-137.

Beier, R. L., and E. H. Oertli. 1983. Psoralen and other linear furocoumarins as phytoalexins in celery. *Phytochemistry* 22: 2595-7.

Bidlack, W. R., R. C. Brown, M. S. Meskin, et al. 1987. Effect of aluminum on the hepatic mixed function oxidase and drug metabolism. *Drug-Nutrient Interactions* 5: 33-42.

Chew, S. K., L. S. Chew, K. W. Wang, et al. 1984. Anticholinesterase drugs in the treatment of tetrodotoxin poisoning. *Lancet* 2: 108.

Cooke, R., and J. Cock. 1989. Cassara crops up again. *New Scientist* 122: 63-8.

Cripps, D. J., H. A. Peters, A. Grocner, and I. Dogranaci. 1984. Porphyria turcica due to hexachlorobenzene: A 20 to 30 year follow-up study on 204 patients. *British Journal of Dermatology* 111: 413-22.

Doll, R., and R. Peto. 1981. The causes of cancer: Quantitative estimates of avoidable risks of cancer in the United States today. *Journal of the National Cancer Institute* 66: 1171-1308.

Fytianos, K., G. Vasilikotis, L. Weil, and N. Laskaridis. 1985. Preliminary study of organochlorine compounds in milk products, human milk and vegetables. *Bulletin of Environmental Contamination and Toxicology* 34: 504-8.

Gilman, Alfred Goodman, Louis S. Goodman, Alfred Gilmar, et al. 1980. *The pharmacological basis of therapeutics.* Sixth edition. New York.

Groce, D. F., and R. D. Kimbrough. 1984. Stunted growth, increased mortality, and liver tumors in offspring of polybrominated biphenyl (PBB) dosed Sherman rats. *Journal of Toxicology and Environmental Health* 14: 695-706.

Hokama, Y., and J. T. Miyahara. 1986. Ciguatera poisoning: Clinical and immunological aspects. *Journal of Toxicology and Toxin Reviews* 5: 25-53.

Jayaraman, K. S. 1989. Neurolathyrism remains a threat in India. *Nature* (London) 339: 495.

Joint Food and Agriculture Organization/World Health Organization Expert Committee on Food Additives. 1989: 33rd Report. *Evaluation of certain food additives and contaminants.* World Health Organization Technical Report No. 776, 1-64. Geneva.

Klein, G. L. 1990. Nutritional aspects of aluminum toxicity. *Nutrition Research Reviews* 3: 117-41.

Klein, G. L., and W. R. Snodgrass. 1993. The toxicology of heavy metals. In *Encyclopedia of food science, food technology and nutrition,* ed. R. Macrae, R. Robinson, and M. Sadler. London.

Kreiss, K., M. M. Zack, R. D. Kimbrough, et al. 1981. Cross-sectional study of a community with exceptional exposure to DDT. *Journal of the American Medical Association* 245: 1926-30.

Krishnamachari, K. A., R. V. Bhal, V. Nagaraja, and T. B. G. Tilak. 1975. Hepatitis due to aflatoxicosis. An outbreak in Western India. *Lancet* 1: 1061-3.

Lambert, G. H., D. A. Schoeller, H. E. B. Humphrey, et al. 1990. The caffeine breath test and caffeine urinary metabolite ratios in the Michigan cohort exposed to polybrominated biphenyls: A preliminary study. *Environmental Health Perspectives* 89: 175-81.

Lerman, S. 1986. Photosensitizing drugs and their possible role in enhancing ocular toxicity. *Ophthalmology* 93: 304-18.

Li, T.-K., and B. L. Vallee. 1980. The biochemical and nutritional roles of other trace elements. In *Modern nutrition in health and disease,* ed. R. S. Goodhart and M. E. Shils, 408-41. Philadelphia, Pa.

Mannon, J., and E. Johnson. 1985. Fungi down in the farm. *New Scientist* 105: 12-16.

Meester, W. D. 1979. The effects of polybrominated biphenyls on man: The Michigan PBB disaster. *Veterinary and Human Toxicology* 21 (Supplement): 131-5.

Needleman, H. L., A. Schell, D. Bellinger, et al. 1990. The long-term effects of exposure to low doses of lead in childhood. An 11-year follow-up report. *New England Journal of Medicine* 322: 83-8.

Penrose, L. S. 1957. Genetics of anencephaly. *Journal of Mental Deficiency Research* 1: 4-15.

Sedman, A. B., G. L. Klein, R. J. Merritt, et al. 1985. Evidence of aluminum loading in infants receiving intravenous therapy. *New England Journal of Medicine* 312: 1337-43.

Silverman, Arnold, and Claude C. Roy. 1983. *Pediatric clinical gastroenterology.* Third edition. St. Louis, Mo.

Stoloff, L. 1983. Aflatoxin as a cause of primary liver cell cancer in the United States: A probability study. *Nutrition and Cancer* 5: 165-86.

Tachibana, K., M. Nukina, Y.-G. Joh, and P. J. Scheuer. 1987. Recent developments in the molecular structure of ciguatoxin. *Biological Bulletin* 172: 122-7.

Torda, T., E. Sinclair, and D. B. Ulyatt. 1973. Puffer fish (tetrodotoxin) poisoning: Clinical record and suggested management. *Medical Journal of Australia* 1: 599-602.

U.S. Council for Agricultural Science and Technology. 1989. *Mycotoxins: Economic and health risks.* Task Force Report No. 116. Ames, Iowa.

Valenti, M., P. Pasquini, and G. Andreucci. 1979. Saxitoxin and tetrodotoxin intoxication: Report of 16 cases. *Veterinary and Human Toxicology* 21 (Supplement): 107-10.

Van Dyke, R. W. 1989. Mechanisms of digestion and absorption of food. In *Gastrointestinal disease: Pathophysiology, diagnosis, management,* ed. M. H. Sleisinger and J. S. Fordtran, 1062-88. Philadelphia, Pa.

Wallwork, J. C., and H. H. Sandstead. 1990. Zinc. In *Nutrition and bone development,* ed D. J. Simmons, 316-39. Oxford.

VII.13 ⊷ The Question of Paleolithic Nutrition and Modern Health: From the End to the Beginning

A conviction has been growing among some observers that contemporary human health could be substantially improved if we would just emulate our hunter–gatherer ancestors in dietary matters. A look at this contention seems an appropriate way to bring this work to a close because the subject takes us full circle – linking contemporary issues of food and nutrition with our Paleolithic past. In addition, it offers an opportunity for some summary, and, finally, it provides a chance to remind ourselves of how ephemeral food and nutritional dogma can be.

In fact, in retrospect we call such fleeting tenets "Food Fads" (see the treatment by Jeffrey M. Pilcher, this work chapter VI.12), and in the United States at least, it was not very long ago that vitamin E capsules were being wistfully washed down in the hope of jump-starting sluggish libidos (Benedek, this work chapter VI.15). Not long before that, the egg was enshrined as the "perfect" food, with milk in second place, and cholesterol, now an apparently significant ingredient in the gooey deposits that plug heart arteries, was not a word in everyday vocabularies (Tannahill 1989).

In those "B.C." (before cholesterol) days, meat was in, and the starchy foods (potatoes, breads, and pastas), although full of fiber, were out – considered bad for a person's waistline and health, not to mention social standing. Garlic had a similarly dismal reputation – only foreigners ate it – and only winos drank wine. Who could have foreseen then that we would soon toss all of that nutritional lore that guided us into the ash heap of history and embrace its polar opposite – the "Mediterranean Diet" (Keys and Keys 1975; Spiller 1991; see also Marion Nestle, chapter V.C.1).

This, however, leads us back to the just-mentioned "growing conviction" among some students of current science and distant history that a fundamental flaw in our present approach to nutrition is a failure (or refusal) to realize that our diets were programmed at least 40,000 years ago and thus we are, to a very important extent, what our ancestors ate. Moreover, these same students believe that it is our obliviousness to the obvious that will prove most baffling of all to future observers of our nurture and nature (Eaton, Shostak, and Konner 1988a, 1988b; Nesse and Williams 1994; Profet 1995).

The purveyors of *The Paleolithic Prescription* (Eaton et al. 1988a; see also their "Stone Agers in the Fast Lane" [1988b]) belong to a group that subscribes to what has been labeled "Darwinian medicine" – a school of thought that has called into question many

of the notions we have about nutriments and nutrients, as well as many practices in the practice of medicine.

Illustrative is the medical treatment of fever, routinely but perhaps mistakenly lowered with pain relievers. Fever, it is argued, is a part of a highly evolved defense system for combating pathogens. When fever is artificially lowered, that system is impaired, and recovery may take longer and be less perfect (Kluger 1979).

Another example is "morning sickness," said to arise from a mechanism evolved in the distant past to produce sufficient queasiness in newly pregnant women that they avoid foods – like slightly overripe meat, or cruciferous vegetables – that could be mildly toxic and, therefore, harmful to fetuses, which are especially vulnerable during the first trimester of pregnancy. If such ideas are correct, then it is possible that treating this Stone Age condition with modern nausea-preventing drugs increases the risk of birth defects (Profet 1995).

A final example from the medical side of the Darwinian thinkers' agenda has to do with what have become alarmingly high rates of breast and ovarian cancer. The Darwinians suggest that contemporary women endure an estimated three times more days with menstrual cycles than their hunter–gatherer ancestors because the latter averaged more children and breast-fed each for about three years – all of which suppressed menstrual cycles. The condition of modern women means three times the exposure to surges of estrogen that occur during those cycles – and estrogen has been implicated in the generation of female cancers (Nesse and Williams 1994).

No less disturbing are the nutritional implications that emerge from similar lines of reasoning that reach back into Paleolithic times. As we saw in Part I of this work, written by bioanthropologists, our hunter-gatherer forebears may have enjoyed such variety in viands that they fared better nutritionally than any of their descendants who settled down to invent agriculture; indeed, in terms of stature, it would seem that they did better than practically everyone who has lived ever since (see Mark Nathan Cohen 1989 and this work chapter I.6; Clark Spencer Larsen, this work chapter I.1).

Data on both stature and nutrition indicate that human height began to diminish with the transition from collecting to growing food, finally reaching a nadir in the nineteenth century. It has only been in the twentieth century that humankind, at least in the West, has started to measure up once again to our ancestors of at least some 25,000 to 10,000 years ago (Eaton et al. 1988a; Harris, this work chapter VI.5).

Proof of the early decline in stature and health, along with soaring rates of anemia and infant and child mortality, lies mostly in the skeletal remains of those who settled into sedentary agriculture. Such remains also bear witness to deteriorating health through bone and tooth lesions – caused on the one hand by an ever-more-circumscribed diet and on the other by the increased parasitism that invariably accompanied sedentism (Larsen 1995).

Paradoxically, then, enhanced food production, made possible by the switch to herding and growing, resulted in circumscribed diets and nutritional deficiencies. Thus it would seem that the various Neolithic revolutions of the world, which invented and reinvented agriculture and are collectively regarded as the most important stride forward in human history, were actually backward tumbles as far as human health was concerned. Moreover, when we remember that the superior nutritional status of the hunter-gatherers over that of their sedentary successors was achieved and maintained without two of the food groups – grains and dairy products – that we now call "basic" but which only came with the Neolithic Revolution, the hunter-gatherers' superiority seems downright heretical in the face of current nutritional dogma.

In longitudinal terms, humans have been on the earth in one form or another for a few million years, during which time they seem to have perpetuated themselves with some efficiency. About 1.5 million years ago, they shifted from a diet of primarily unprocessed plant foods to one comprised of increasing amounts of meat, some of which was scavenged. Approximately 700,000 years ago, humans began the deliberate hunting of animals, and Homo sapiens, who some 100,000 years ago had brains as large as ours today, became expert at it, judging from the frequent discoveries of abundant large-mammal remains at ancient sites (Larsen, this work chapter I.1). Meat may have constituted as much as 80 percent of the diet of those proficient at hunting, but they also ate wild vegetables and fruits; and certainly, as the Darwinists point out, it was these foods – meat, vegetables, and fruits – that constituted the diet from 25,000 to roughly 10,000 years ago (Eaton et al. 1988a).

In light of this nutritious past, it can be argued that humans are best adapted to these "old" food groups. Certainly, one piece of evidence in such an argument seems to be that humans are among the very few animal species that cannot synthesize their own vitamin C – an ability made superfluous by the great amounts forthcoming from the fruits and vegetables in the diet, and apparently lost along the evolutionary trail (Carpenter 1986; see also R. E. Hughes, this work chapter IV.A.3).

The other side of that coin, however, is that humans may not be well adapted to the "new" foods – dairy products and grains – and it is worth noting that from a nutritional standpoint, hunter-gatherers seem to have gotten along better nutritionally without these two food groups than the sedentary folk who created them and have used them ever since.

Recently, of course, meat – one of the old food groups – has become a primary suspect in the etiol-

ogy of chronic illnesses, especially that of coronary artery disease, and it has been pointed out that modern-day hunter-gatherers (for example, the !Kung San in and around Africa's Kalahari desert) take in much more meat and, thus, more cholesterol than medicine today recommends. The traditional !Kung San and other modern-day hunter-gatherers, however, have very low blood-cholesterol levels and virtually no heart disease. Similarly, the Inuit of the Arctic and Subarctic, until recently at least, consumed mostly animal foods with the same lack of deleterious effects. It has only been with their switch to the foods the rest of us eat that their health has begun to deteriorate (Eaton et al. 1988a; see also Harold H. Draper, this work chapter VI.10; Linda Reed, this work chapter V.D.7).

It is true that hunted animals as a rule have only a fraction (about one-seventh to one-tenth) of the fat of their domesticated counterparts, along with a better ratio of polyunsaturated to saturated fats. Consequently, it has been estimated that our hunter-gatherer ancestors got only about 20 percent of their calories from fats, whereas fats deliver about 40 percent of the total calories in modern diets. But because the amount of cholesterol in meat is little affected by fat content, it would seem that our ancestors, like the !Kung San, also consumed more cholesterol than we do today and more than is recommended by nearly all medical authorities (Eaton et al. 1988a; see also Stephen Beckerman, this work chapter II.G.10).

It is interesting that a group of researchers in the United Kingdom has argued that cholesterol may not be the culprit – or at least not the only culprit – in bringing about coronary artery disease. Their search for its causes entailed the systematic and painstaking gathering, in all of Europe, of data on diets and deaths from heart disease, and analysis of this data has revealed one positive correlation: People living in the four European countries with the highest rates of heart disease (all in northern Europe) take in far more calcium than people in the four countries with the lowest rates (all in southern Europe) (see Stephen Seely, this work chapter IV.F.4).

Of course, that which is a significant correlation to some is merely an interesting speculation to others. But it may be the case that calcium can be harmful, depending on its source. During hunting-and-gathering times, calcium came mostly from plant foods, and bone remains indicate that our ancestors got plenty of it. Since the Neolithic, however, dietary calcium has increasingly been derived from dairy products, such as cheese and yoghurt – and milk, for those who can tolerate it.

Indeed, "tolerate" is the key word as far as milk is concerned, and, presumably, much of the reason for the difference in calcium intake between northern and southern Europeans is that the latter are less likely to consume milk after weaning because they are more likely to be lactose intolerant (cheese and yoghurt are less of a problem because when milk is fermented, lactose is converted to lactic acid) (Kretchmer 1993; see also K. David Patterson, chapter IV.E.6). Northern Europeans, by contrast, collectively constitute a lactose-tolerant enclave in a largely lactose-intolerant world, and, not incidentally, the point is made that white North Americans, whose ancestral homeland was northern Europe, are also able to tolerate milk and also suffer high rates of coronary artery disease (Seely, this work chapter IV.F.4).

One might then argue that in an evolutionary scheme of things, dairy products are newfangled: Allergies to cow's milk are common among children, and milk-based formulas can be deadly for infants (Fauve-Chamoux, this work chapter III.2). It may be true that lactose intolerance is Nature's way of preventing the consumption of much in the way of dairy foods that can calcify the arteries, and the heart attacks suffered by adult northern Europeans and their progeny in other parts of the world are the price of overcoming this trait. It is interesting to note that areas in Europe where oats are consumed are also those with the highest rates of coronary disease, and oats contain a great deal of calcium (Seely, this work chapter IV.F.4), which moves us to grains – the other "new" food group.

As with dairy products, it may be that humans are not well adapted to grains either. People with celiac disease – caused by the proteins in wheat and some other grains – most certainly are not. And perhaps significantly, this relatively rare genetic condition has its highest frequency in those regions that spawned the most recent major wheat-producing societies (see Donald D. Kasarda, this work chapter IV.E.2). Is it, therefore, possible that celiac disease is a holdover from earlier times, when the body evolved a mechanism to prevent the consumption of toxic wild grains? One trouble with such an argument, of course, is the need to explain how it was that the Neolithic Revolution ever got off the ground in the first place if people were genetically incapable – at least initially – of digesting the crops they grew.

One answer that has been proposed is that grains were not originally grown because of a need for food but, rather, because of a taste for alcohol (Katz and Voigt 1986; see also Phillip A. Cantrell, this work chapter III.1). It appears that barley-ale was being produced at least 7,500 years ago, and the records of the ancient Sumerians, for example, show that a staggering (no pun intended) 40 percent of their grain production went into brewing (Tannahill 1989). And ale making did precede bread making, so perhaps there was a time when grains were mostly for drinking, and only later was there a shift toward eating them.

The rise to prominence of grains that tended to narrow the diet – wheat in temperate Asia and Europe, rice in tropical and semitropical Asia, millet and sorghums in Africa, and maize in the Americas – was perhaps the most important factor in the previously mentioned decrease in human stature and significant deterioration of dental and skeletal tissues. This is because these so-called "super" foods are super only in the sense that they have sustained great numbers of people; they are far from super nutritionally. Almost all are poor sources of calcium and iron; each is deficient in essential amino acids, and each tends to inhibit the activities of other important nutrients (Larsen, this work chapter I.1, upon which the following paragraph also is based).

Rice, for example, inhibits the activity of vitamin A, and if its thiamine-rich hulls are pounded or otherwise stripped away, beriberi can be the result. The phytic acid in wheat bran chemically binds with zinc to inhibit its absorption, which, in turn, can inhibit growth in children. Zein – the protein in maize – is deficient in three essential amino acids, which, if not supplemented, can also lead to growth retardation; moreover, because the niacin contained in maize is in bound form, many of its consumers have suffered the ravages of pellagra. In addition, maize (along with some other cereals) contains phytates that act against iron absorption and also has sucrose, which – we are continually reminded – exerts its own negative impact on human health (significantly, dental caries were exceedingly rare in preagricultural societies). In short, it is arguable that humans may not be programmed for the newfangled grains either.

Much firmer ground, however, is reached with the assertion that humans are definitely not programmed for the quantities of sodium chloride many now take in. Even the most carnivorous of our ancestors, on an 80 percent meat diet, would have ingested less than half of the average per capita daily salt intake in the United States, and of course, excessive dietary salt has been linked with stomach cancer and hypertension, the latter disease a major contributor to heart attacks, kidney failure, and especially strokes. Modern-day hunting-and-gathering populations that consume little sodium (meaning amounts comparable to those of our hunter–gatherer forebears) suffer no hypertension – not even, it is interesting to note, the age-related increase in blood pressure that medicine has come to believe is "normal" (Cohen, this work chapter I.6).

In the case of sodium chloride, as in that of lactose absorption, western Europeans, once again, pioneered in the attempt to reprogram the Stone Age metabolism, although in this case they were joined by East Asians. All mammals normally consume less sodium than potassium, which complements bodily mechanisms that strive to conserve sodium, because the mineral is, after all, crucial to life itself. But not the Europeans – at least not after salt became an inexpensive commodity some 1,000 years ago. They preserved foods with salt, cooked them in salt, then added more salt at the table, with the result that over the ages, their bodies seem to have learned to some extent to rid themselves of sodium with brisk efficiency through urine and perspiration (Kiple 1984;

Eaton et al. 1988a; see also Thomas W. Wilson and Clarence E. Grim, this work chapter IV.B.7).

By contrast, it has been argued that those not of western European (and probably eastern Asian) ancestry and, thus, without a long history of heavy salt consumption, such as African-Americans (whose ancestral lands were poor in salt, whose ancestral cooking habits did not call for it anyway, and whose bodies seem still to treat the mineral as something precious to be conserved), are in considerable peril in cultures where sodium is routinely added at almost every step in food preservation, processing, preparation, and consumption (Wilson 1987; Wilson and Grim, this work chapter IV.B.7). Moreover, because potassium is progressively leached out during these procedures, people in affluent countries have now turned the Stone Age potassium-to-sodium ratio upside down and are consuming some 1.5 times as much sodium as potassium (see David S. Newman, this work chapter IV.B.6). Modern-day hunter-gatherers, by contrast, are said to have potassium intakes that exceed sodium by 10 times or more (Eaton et al. 1988a).

Another controversial, but fascinating, avenue of investigation traveled by some of the Darwinian thinkers has to do with iron, an essential mineral found in all cells in the body and a key component of hemoglobin, wherein can be found about 70 percent of all our iron. The remaining 30 percent is stored in the spleen, the liver, and especially in bone marrow, where it can be called upon as needed. Iron-deficiency anemia is the most common form of anemia worldwide and is especially prevalent in developing countries, where the diet is likely to contain little meat (from which iron is most efficiently absorbed) but much vegetable food (from which iron is poorly absorbed). Moreover, some dietary substances in vegetable foods, such as oxalic acid and tannic acid, actually interfere with iron absorption (Eaton et al. 1988a; Bollet and Brown 1993).

As a few of the authors in the present work point out, however, the presence of pathogens also affects iron levels, and the impact of this presence is more profound than that of dietary imbalance. Helminthic parasites, such as the hookworm, make their living on human blood and the iron it contains, and they frequently cause anemia when they prosper to the point that they become too many, taking too much advantage of a good thing (see Susan Kent, this work chapter IV.D.2; Kent and Patricia Stuart-Macadam, this work chapter IV.B.3; Nevin S. Scrimshaw, this work chapter VI.3).

What is of interest in addition to helminthic parasites, however, is a recently demonstrated and much more subtle interaction of iron and smaller parasites. Bacteria and viruses also need iron to multiply. To forestall such multiplication, or at least to slow it down, our bodies have developed the knack of reacting to pathogenic presence by drawing down the iron supply in the blood and putting it in storage – in

effect, starving the pathogens – until the danger has passed, whereupon iron levels in the blood are permitted to rise again (Kent, this work chapter IV.D.2). But it would seem that only a small percentage of physicians are aware of this phenomenon, with the result that they may mistake bodily defenses for anemia and issue prescriptions for iron that can hurt the patients while helping the pathogens (Kent, this work chapter IV.D.2; see also Nesse and Williams 1994).

Moreover, studies in Polynesia, New Guinea, and West Africa have demonstrated that infants given iron have a much higher incidence of serious infectious diseases than those who are not given iron, and that discontinuing the administration of iron in itself lowers the incidence of infections. Thus, it is urged that health workers be reeducated to understand that, in many instances, the high incidence of anemia in the developing world does not mean a dietary failure that requires iron administration; rather, it means that an important bodily defense is at work, combatting high rates of parasitism (Nesse and Williams 1994; Kent, this work chapter IV.D.2).

In the developed world, the argument continues, the extent to which iron may be a threat to health is compounded, and the body confounded, by the indiscriminate and massive iron fortification of many cereal products and the regular use of iron supplements. This may be especially serious in countries like the United States, where elderly men and postmenopausal women have the highest incidence of anemia – which, it is contended, is really anemia defending against the chronic diseases to which these groups are most vulnerable, including neoplastic cells that, like pathogens, also need iron for multiplication. In addition, evidence is accumulating that high iron levels play a significant role in coronary artery disease (Kent, this work chapter IV.D.2).

Another recently recognized bodily mechanism that evolved with humans has to do with an unfortunately tenacious ability of the body to maintain a certain level of fat, even if it is an unhealthy level. A recent Rockefeller study (Leibel, Rosenbaum, and Hirsch 1995) indicates that the body has a preset level of fat that it strives to maintain by changing the efficiency with which it metabolizes food, so that it can either reduce or increase the amount of fat going into storage. What this means – to put the Rockefeller study together with the so-called thrifty-gene theory first advanced by the geneticist James Neel (1962) – is that those who try to lose weight seem to be up against Stone Age "thrifty genes" that probably evolved during the glacial epochs. Then, nutrition under harsh climatic conditions often would have been a matter of feast and famine, and individuals who, during times of feasting, could most efficiently store excess calories as fat to ride out famines would have enjoyed a considerable survival advantage over those lacking this ability (see Leslie Sue Lieberman 1993 and this work chapter IV.E.7).

Today, however, these thrifty genes are blamed

directly for diabetes and gallstones and indirectly for all conditions in which obesity is a contributing factor. Apparently, here is another Stone Age mechanism that is troubling modern humans, particularly when today's diets give us calories in such compact forms that we can easily get more than we need before ever feeling comfortably full. It has been estimated that, in hunter–gatherer days, 5 pounds of food were required to provide 3,000 calories; today, 5 pounds of food may deliver upwards of 9,000 calories – some 3 times as many (Eaton et al. 1988a; Lieberman 1993).

Such a caloric conundrum presents an especially serious hazard to some groups of humans in transition. Studies of Native Americans, Australian Aborigines, Pacific islanders, and Alaskan Eskimos all have reported precipitous declines in health, suffered upon the abandonment of traditional diets and patterns of exercise (Lieberman 1993; Kunitz 1994). North American Indians, along with Polynesians, Micronesians, and native Hawaiians, have some of the highest rates of diabetes mellitus in the world. In sub-Saharan Africa, hypertension rates are rising alarmingly in the cities, where salt-laden prepared foods are replacing the foods of the villages. And coronary artery disease and hypertension are becoming commonplace in the Pacific, where just decades ago they were unknown (Wilson 1987; Lieberman 1993; Kunitz 1994; Draper, this work chapter VI.10; see also Nancy Davis Lewis, this work chapter V.E.3).

By way of concluding, it remains to be seen how much blame for current chronic diseases can be laid on Paleolithic nutritional adaptations. Another factor, of course, is that to some extent, humans have also been shaped by the requirements of more recent ancestors. Those who settled into cold and damp places, for example, chose diets that were rich and fatty and that helped build fat to insulate against the weather. In warm climates, where evaporating perspiration served to cool the body, strong herbs and spices that encouraged sweating were consumed; and much liquid was drunk to replace lost fluids. Today, central heating obviates the need for a fatty diet, and air conditioning reduces the need to sweat. But there are many dietary holdovers from those old days, too, that do humans no good and, in tandem with Stone Age genetic mechanisms, perhaps a great deal of harm. For example, it was not all that long ago that the author of a late-eighteenth-century cookbook picked a quarrel with a competing writer who called for 6 pounds of butter to fry 12 eggs. One-half that amount of butter was plenty, she primly assured her readers (Tannahill 1989).

Yet, hardly anybody wants to return to a hunting-and-gathering lifestyle. And although history sheds no light on an ideal diet, it does, in a way, defend those grains and dairy products that have just been examined and which, it can be argued, at least have been consumer tested for the past 8,000 to 10,000 years.

Nonetheless, what our authors and others have had to say on matters of Paleolithic nutrition has been well researched, well reasoned, and well received in many quarters. In other words, their work is not wild speculation, and their point, namely that natural selection has not had time to revise our bodies to cope with modern diets, is a good one. But about all Darwinian nutrition can actually do for us at this point is to remind us of the wisdom of moderation in food consumption and nutritional supplementation from yet one more perspective.

Kenneth F. Kiple

Bibliography

Beckerman, Stephen. Game. This work chapter II.G.10.
Benedek, Thomas. Food as aphrodisiacs and anaphrodisiacs? This work chapter VI.15.
Bollet, Alfred J., and Audrey K. Brown. 1993. Anemia. In *The Cambridge world history of human disease*, ed. Kenneth F. Kiple, 571–7. Cambridge and New York.
Cantrell, Phillip A., II. Beer and ale. This work chapter III.1.
Carpenter, Kenneth J. 1986. *The history of scurvy and vitamin C*. Cambridge and New York.
Cohen, Mark Nathan. 1989. *Health and the rise of civilization*. New Haven, Conn.
    History, diet, and hunter-gatherers. This work chapter I.6.
Draper, Harold H. Human nutritional adaptation: Biological and cultural aspects. This work chapter VI.10.
Eaton, S. Boyd, Marjorie Shostak, and Melvin Konner. 1988a. *The Paleolithic prescription*. New York.
    1988b. Stone Agers in the fast lane: Chronic degenerative diseases in evolutionary perspective. *American Journal of Medicine* 84: 739–49.
Fauve-Chamoux, Antoinette. Human breast milk and artificial infant feeding. This work chapter III.2.
Harris, Bernard. Height and nutrition. This work chapter VI.5.
Hughes, R. E. Vitamin C. This work chapter IV.A.3.
Kasarda, D. Celiac disease. This work chapter IV.E.2.
Katz, Solomon H., and Mary Voigt. 1986. Beer and bread: The early use of cereals in the human diet. *Expedition* 28: 23–34.
Kent, Susan. Iron-deficiency and anemia of chronic disease. This work chapter IV.D.2.
Kent, Susan, and Patricia Stuart-Macadam. Iron. This work chapter IV.B.3.
Keys, A., and M. Keys. 1975. *How to eat well and stay well, the Mediterranean way*. New York.
Kiple, Kenneth F. 1984. *The Caribbean slave: A biological history*. Cambridge and New York.
Kluger, Matthew J. 1979. *Fever; its biology, evolution, and function*. Princeton, N.J.
Kretchmer, Norman. 1993. Lactose intolerance and malabsorption. In *The Cambridge world history of human disease*, ed. Kenneth F. Kiple, 813–17. Cambridge and New York.
Kunitz, Stephen. 1994. *Disease and social diversity: The European impact on the health of non-Europeans*. New York.
Larsen, Clark Spencer. 1995. Biological changes in human populations with agriculture. *Annual Review of Anthropology* 24: 185–213.
    Dietary reconstruction and nutritional assessment of past peoples: The bioanthropological record. This work chapter I.1.

Leibel, R. L., M. Rosenbaum, and J. Hirsch. 1995. Changes in energy expenditure resulting from altered body weight. *New England Journal of Medicine* 332: 621-8.

Lewis, Nancy Davis. The Pacific islands. This work chapter V.E.3.

Lieberman, Leslie Sue. 1993. Diabetes. In *The Cambridge world history of human disease,* ed. Kenneth F. Kiple, 665-76. Cambridge and New York.

  Obesity. This work chapter IV.E.7.

Matzen, Richard N., and Richard S. Lang, eds. 1993. *Clinical preventive medicine.* St. Louis, Mo.

Neel, J. V. 1962. Diabetes mellitus: A "thrifty" genotype rendered detrimental by "progress." *American Journal of Human Genetics* 14: 353-62.

Nesse, Randolph M., and George C. Williams. 1994. *Why we get sick: The new science of Darwinian medicine.* New York.

Nestle, Marion. The Mediterranean (diets and disease prevention). This work chapter V.C.1.

Newman, David S. Potassium. This work chapter IV.B.6.

Patterson, K. David. Lactose intolerance. This work chapter IV.E.6.

Pilcher, Jeffrey M. Food fads. This work chapter VI.12.

Profet, Margie. 1995. *Protecting your baby-to-be: Preventing birth defects in the first trimester.* New York.

Reed, Linda. The Arctic and Subarctic regions. This work chapter V.D.7.

Sandford, Mary K., ed. 1993. *Investigations of ancient human tissue.* Amsterdam.

Scrimshaw, Nevin S. Infection and nutrition: Synergistic interactions. This work chapter VI.3.

Seely, S. The cardiovascular system, coronary artery disease, and calcium: An hypothesis. This work chapter IV.F.4.

Spiller, Gene A., ed. 1991. *The Mediterranean diets in health and disease.* New York.

Tannahill, Reay. 1989. *Food in history.* New York.

Wilson, Thomas W. 1987. Africa, Afro-Americans, and hypertension: An hypothesis. In *The African exchange: Toward a biological history of black people,* ed. K. F. Kiple, 257-68. Durham, N.C., and London.

Wilson, Thomas W., and Clarence E. Grim. Sodium. This work chapter IV.B.7.

PART VIII

A Historical Dictionary
of the World's Plant Foods

This final portion of the book is perhaps the most ambitious. It was initially conceived of as a dictionary of the exotic plants mentioned in the text, which our authors would otherwise be called upon to identify in their chapters and, in so doing, interrupt their narratives.

The expansion of Part VIII began when it was decided to include entries on *all* plant foods mentioned in the text and continued when it became apparent that the various fruits of the world do not lend themselves to generalized essays, because many have been mostly seasonal items in the diets of relatively few – and often unrelated – people. For example, the ancient Malaysians ate the "Java apple" (*Eugenia javanica*) when it was ripe, whereas, on the other side of the world, Native Americans of Brazil did the same with their "pitanga" (*Eugenia uniflora*). The plants that produce these two fruits are both in the same genus of the family Myrtaceae, but there is little that historically connects their human consumers (unlike the consumers of maize or wheat or potatoes). Thus, save for a few staples (bananas and plantains, for example), fruits really did not seem to belong in the earlier parts of the work dealing with staple foods, and when it was decided to treat fruits in individual dictionary entries – and not as botanical families, or even, as a rule, as genera – there seemed no question that these entries should be included in Part VIII.

More expansion ensued when our students, researching the gathered foods mentioned in a number of the chapters (such as those dealing with hunters and gatherers, early North America, the ancient Near and Middle East, and Australia and New Zealand), began making their own discoveries of gathered foods not covered in those chapters. These were subsequently included as entries in the dictionary, with the result

that Part VIII also offers a glimpse of the myriad wild foods that sustained our hunting-and-gathering ancestors during almost all of humankind's time on earth – a glimpse of especial interest to those of us whose diets are generally limited to a relatively few commercialized plant foods. Among other things, these dictionary entries might be viewed as collectively questioning the wisdom of the progressive limiting of viand variety in the human diet that began with the invention of agriculture.

A final effort, which also expanded the size of Part VIII, was an attempt to include as many as we could identify of the common names (and synonyms) for food plants in English (and some in other languages). We hope that this labor will help researchers in sorting out items mentioned in the world's various spice trades; others who might find it useful to know that words like "colewort" (in Old English texts) would today mean cabbage (with "coleslaw" a reminder of the earlier name); and still others who might be interested to learn, for example, that "pigweed" can mean amaranth, goosefoot, lamb's-quarter, purslane, *quelites,* and quinoa (which in turn is also "quinua" and begins another long list of common names).

We have, in addition, attempted to provide something of the history of the more than 1,000 plant foods treated in Part VIII whenever such information was available. However, much of such history remains speculative, because although individual species may have evolved in discrete locations, many plants were moving across continents and even oceans – on their own or with human help – long before the dawn of recorded history.

Plant names constitute perhaps the single most daunting obstacle to an enterprise like Part VIII. Obviously, different languages and cultures have assigned their own common names to plants, so that well-traveled plants will generally have a host of them, and much-used names may well refer to multiple plants – as the previously mentioned example of "pigweed" illustrates. Scientific names – generally Latinized botanical terms drawn from Greek and Latin – were intended to remedy this problem so that at least the scientific community concerned with plants could speak the same language despite differences in plants' common names. But languages change, and change can be vexing. Disagreements about classification mean that equivalents are frequently used in the realm of scientific names designating genus and species (we indicate this with an equals sign [=] whenever we have turned up the information). Illustrative are some plants of the genus *Eugenia* that have also been assigned to the genus *Syzygium,* so that, for example, the fruit with the common name "rose apple" is both *E. jambos* and *S. jambos.* In addition, new scientific names may have come into use

that were not employed by the sources we consulted. It was only at the last minute, for example, that we became aware that *Lens culinaris* was now an acceptable designation for lentils, previously called *Lens esculenta* (hence, *Lens esculenta = L. culinaris*). We have dealt as best we could with such taxonomic tribulation, but because we are not botanists, we have doubtless misunderstood, misinterpreted, and mistreated such information at various points, and for this we apologize.

Virtually all of the entries in Part VIII were written "in-house" by the editors, with plenty of research help from the members of our staff, led by Stephen V. Beck, all of whom are credited in the work's general acknowledgments. At this point, however, we would like to acknowledge and thank Charles B. Heiser, who contributed the entry on the "Jerusalem Artichoke," and Jeffrey M. Pilcher, who wrote some of our Mesoamerican entries. Both of these scholars also made contributions elsewhere in this work, and we are most grateful for their extra effort.

Abalong - *see* **COCOYAM**
Abata kola - *see* **KOLA NUT**
ABIU - A native of lowland South America, the abiu (*Pouteria cainito*) is a relative of the sapodilla, the mamey sapote, and the canistel. The abiu is a small yellow fruit, which grows on a tree that can reach upward of 30 feet in height. Like its better-known relatives, the abiu contains a sticky latex within its skin. Although the fruit is appreciated locally, it is generally not commercially exploited in its homeland; however, some varieties that have been introduced into South Asia and Australia reportedly have commercial possibilities.

Abóbora - *see* **CALABAZA (SQUASH)**
Abyssinian banana - *see* **ENSETE**
ACACIA - There are a number of species of (chiefly tropical) trees belonging to the genus *Acacia,* with some (especially *A. senegal*) exuding from their trunks a gum - called "gum arabic" - that has a wide variety of commercial uses, including many in food manufacturing and processing. In much of the tropical world, the gum as well as the leaves, pods, and seeds of acacia trees have food uses. The pods and seeds are dried and ground into a flour used for bread-making. In Mexico, the pods of the prairie acacia (*A. angustissima*) were consumed by Native Americans, as were those of the catclaw acacia (*A. greggii*) in what is now the southwestern United States. Acacia has a multitude of other names, including "wattle," "mimosa," and "Egyptian thorn."
Common names and synonyms: Catclaw acacia, Egyptian thorn, mimosa, prairie acacia, wattle(s).
ACEITUNA - Also called "olivo" and "paradise tree," the aceituna (*Simarouba glauca*) is a tree native to tropical America. It is prized for its oil seeds and for its edible fruit pulp, which is normally eaten raw. The aceituna is found in most produce markets of Central America, especially in El Salvador, where the trees are grown commercially. In addition to Central America and Mexico, the tree can be found throughout the Caribbean region, in Florida, and in Hawaii.
Common names and synonyms: Olivo, paradise tree.
ACEROLA (*see also* **CHERRY**) - Also known as the "Barbados cherry" and the "West Indian cherry," the acerola is so called because of its supposed resemblance to the Mediterranean azarole. The original habitat of the best-known species of acerola (*Malpighia glabra*) included the Caribbean region, southern Texas, Mexico, and Central America; today, however, it can be found in South America and throughout the southern United States. The fruit is borne on thick, quick-growing bushes and trees that reach from 6 to 25 feet in height. With its small size and bright red coloring, it bears a superficial resemblance to a cherry. Unlike a cherry, however, the acerola contains three seeds and has vertical grooves in its skin. Rich in vitamin C, the unripe

acerola far surpasses all other fruits as a source of this nutrient, containing an incredible 20 times the ascorbic acid of an orange. Too tart for consumption as a fresh fruit, it finds many uses in the preparation of jellies, jams, preserves, and baby foods (in combination with other fruits to increase the amount of vitamin C), as well as in the pharmaceutical industry.
Common names and synonyms: Barbados cherry, *huesito,* Surinam cherry, West Indian cherry.
Acha - *see* **FONIO**
Achee - *see* **ACKEE**
Achiote - *see* **ANNATTO**
ACHIRA - Plants of the genus *Canna* are most often cultivated for ornamental use. The fleshy rhizomes of the achira (*Canna edulis*), however, produce a yellow starch that has long been a foodstuff consumed in the Andean region. It probably originated in the area that is now Peru, where remains of the plant - dating back to 2500 B.C. - have been excavated. Today, *C. edulis* is grown and marketed for human consumption in an area ranging from Chile to Venezuela in South America, on some islands in the Caribbean, to a lesser extent in Java and northern Australia, and, finally but not least, in Vietnam, where, during the past three decades, large areas have been devoted to its cultivation in order to make the highly prized transparent noodles that are an indispensable part of that country's cuisine. The plant has also been cultivated in subtropical Hawaii as a feed for cattle and pigs.
Common names and synonyms: Australian arrowroot, canna, gruya, Queensland arrowroot, *tous-les-ois.*
Achis - *see* **AMARANTH**
Achita - *see* **AMARANTH**
Achokcha - *see* **KORILA**
Achotillo - *see* **SOUARI NUT**
ACKEE - A West African plant, the ackee (*Blighia sapida*) reached the West Indies during the latter part of the eighteenth century and spread from there to most of tropical America. Some have credited its introduction to Captain William Bligh (hence the genus name *Blighia*), but most agree that it reached the Caribbean aboard slave ships. In fact, the presence of ackee in Jamaica has been dated from 1778, when the first known ackee slips were purchased from the captain of a slave ship by a local physician/botanist. In any event, the plant's introduction was a welcome one, as it occurred during a period in which warfare and hurricanes had triggered a desperate search for new foodstuffs for the slaves on English plantations. The large, shrublike ackee tree grows almost anywhere in the tropics, bears red- or orange-colored fruits in its fourth year, and will then bear fruit twice a year for the next half century or so. Despite the tree's West African origin, the main focus of ackee cultivation, consumption, and exportation today is in the West Indies. When cooked, the fruit has an appearance and taste that have been

compared to those of a fine omelette - or brains (a nickname is "vegetable brains"), depending on the point of view. The classic use of ackee is in its famous gastronomical marriage with salted codfish. The fruit, which splits open when ripe, consists of pink pods, black seeds, and a fluffy yellow pulp. Only the yellow pulp is edible, however; the pink tissue contains a toxic peptide. All unopened (and thus unripe) ackees are toxic. Historically, this toxicity has been responsible for a number of deaths among Jamaican children, who ate fallen fruit picked up from the ground. Because of its potential danger to the unwary, ackee is generally only available in cans outside of the regions where it is grown. The fruit is a good source of beta-carotene and vitamin C.

Common names and synonyms: Achee, akee, vegetable brains.

ACORN - Technically, an acorn is the fruit of any oak tree (genus *Quercus,* of which there are some 400 to 500 species). The oak is native to all the continents except Australia, and edible acorns may be found in Europe and Asia as well as in North America. Yet even the so-called sweet acorns have a high content of tannic acid, meaning that all acorns are best leached and roasted before eating. In North America, sweet acorns from the white oak (*Q. alba*) have been the most popular. Today, acorns - which constitute an annual crop larger than all other nut crops put together - constitute a vastly underexploited resource that is utilized mostly as feed for hogs. In the past, however, acorns have been a staple food for many people (they were doubtless among the wild foods that humans gathered over many millennia), and they are still widely eaten in southern Europe. In North America, acorns sustained many Native American groups, who exploited some 20 species and ground the nuts to make breads and porridges, thereby supplementing diets composed largely of smoked fish and meat. Throughout the Middle Ages and since, acorns have been extensively used for meat production, and hogs were annually herded into forests during the oak mast. Acorns entered the diets of the first Europeans to reach North American shores, and during the Civil War, when blockades and wartime conditions in general made coffee scarce, ground acorns were discovered to be a serviceable substitute. Very sophisticated methods of employing acorns can be found in the areas around the Mediterranean from Turkey to Spain, as well as in Japan. The nuts have a high carbohydrate content and are relatively high in protein. It is interesting to note that some acorns are technically (and correctly) referred to as "beechnuts."

Common names and synonyms: Beechnut.

ACORN SQUASH (*see also* **SQUASH AND PUMP-KIN**) - An American native - and one of the most familiar squashes in North America - the acorn squash (*Cucurbita pepo*) is so called because it is shaped something like an acorn. It is a winter squash with a hard, ridged rind which makes it difficult to peel, but it is easily cut in half for stuffing and is excellent for baking. The acorn squash has a mild, nutty flavor and delivers a good deal of calcium but (in view of its orange-colored flesh) surprisingly little beta-carotene.

See in addition: "Squash," Part II, Section C, Chapter 8, and "Squash and Pumpkin" in this section.

Adam's-needle - *see* **YUCCA**
Adlay millet - *see* **JOB'S-TEARS**
Advance - *see* **LOQUAT**
Adzuki bean - *see* **AZUKI BEAN**
Aerial yam - *see* **AIR POTATO**
African bitter yam - *see* **BITTER YAM**
African horned cucumber - *see* **KIWANO**
African horned melon - *see* **KIWANO**

AFRICAN LOCUST - The genus *Parkia* - named for Mungo Park, the famous late-eighteenth-century explorer of West Africa - is comprised of a number of leguminous trees of tropical Africa. Among them is the African locust (*Parkia africana*), which has pods containing edible seeds that are generally roasted. A close relative is *P. biglandulosa,* which bears very rich seeds that are usually boiled and made into cakes.

AFRICAN LOCUST BEAN - A tall tree of the West African tropics, the African locust bean (*Parkia filicoidea*) has leaves that are cooked and used as a vegetable. When the seeds are ripe, they are considered by some to be an aphrodisiac. The seeds are also pressed for a cooking oil.

African pumpkin - *see* **OYSTERNUT**

AFRICAN RICE (*see also* **RICE**) - African rice (*Oryza glaberrima*) is one of the two cultigens of the genus *Oryza*. The other, of course, is common or Asian rice. Although the two are similar in many respects, the latter has been far more successful in terms of consumer appeal and as a market commodity of global proportions.

It has been theorized that *O. glaberrima* was domesticated from the wild annual *O. barthii,* which grew in the flood basin of the central Niger delta, and that cultivation of the crop was under way as early as 3,500 years ago. From the Niger delta, it was introduced into other parts of West Africa, where farmers further developed the grain into diverse cultivars that could thrive in deepwater basins, water holes in savannas, forest zones, swampy areas, or dry highlands.

African rice, like its better-known relative, is an outstanding source of energy and important vitamins and minerals. It surpasses whole wheat and maize in terms of protein, is devoid of cholesterol, and is low in sodium and fat. Most varieties have a reddish color, which is perhaps one of the reasons that the more polished, white, Asian types have largely replaced *O. glaberrima* - even in regions where for many centuries it was both an important component of cherished rituals and an essential food. Another reason is that the Asian types of rice are more easily produced, harvested, and milled. Those who continue the cultivation of African rice are generally small-scale farmers, frequently in remote areas, who prefer the grain's distinctive taste, aroma, and coloring; consequently, the crop is grown mostly for local use. Such cultivation occurs on the "floating fields" of the flood plains of Nigeria, in Mali on the Niger's inland delta, and, to a lesser extent, on the hills near the Ghana–Togo border and in Sierra Leone.

African rice is prepared in the same manner as Asian rice, but traditional African uses include fermenting the grain to make regionally popular beers, as well as converting it to flour to make a variety of baked goods. The rice also still figures prominently in a number of West African rituals.

See in addition: "Rice," Part II, Section A, Chapter 7.

African spinach - *see* **AMARANTH**

African tea - *see* **KHAT**

AFRICAN YAM BEAN - Also known as the "wild yam bean," the African yam bean (*Sphenostylis stenocarpa*) is cultivated in West Africa and equatorial Central Africa and grows wild in the African tropics. The pods, seeds, and tubers of the African yam bean are all eaten, and its leaves are cooked as a vegetable.

Common names and synonyms: Wild yam bean.

AGAR (*see also* **SEAWEED**) - Called "agar-agar" in the past, agar is a gelatin obtained from seaweed – especially seaweeds belonging to the genera *Euchema* and *Gelidium*. It has reportedly been used in China since A.D. 300, and perhaps somewhat later in Japan (where it is called *kanten*). Many kinds of jellied sweets that are sold in tropical Asia retain their firmness because of agar, which is employed to thicken other foods as well. Agar also finds its way into vegetable dishes and salads and, in addition, has a number of medical uses.

Common names and synonyms: Agar-agar, *kanten*.

See also: "Algae," Part II, Section C, Chapter 1.

Agar-agar - *see* **AGAR, LAVER, SEAWEED**

Agati - *see* **SESBAN**

AGAVE - Any of numerous American plants of the genus *Agave* go by this name as well as "maguey" or "century plant." The latter term implies longevity and is the name of one variety (*A. americana*) that is common in the deserts of northern Mexico and the southwestern United States. This plant flowers only after 20 to 30 years of life, and then dies. Agaves are evergreens with fleshy, lance-shaped leaves. They were used as food by Native American peoples, who roasted the leaves and grilled the "heart" of the plant. In fact, remains found in the caves of Tehuacán indicate that agave was already an important food source by 6500 B.C. The 2-meter-long leaves also served as shelter material and as fuel, but perhaps the most common use of the plant was the fermentation of the sweet liquid

that accumulates inside (up to 1,200 liters in a single plant) to make a thick alcoholic beverage called *pulque*. Later, the fermented juice was distilled by Spanish settlers to make *mescal* and tequila. Current Mexican law stipulates that tequila must be made from blue agave plants (*A. tequilana*) grown in the state of Jalisco, where the town of Tequila is located. The agave worm (also called the maguey worm or *gusano*) was formerly added to bottles of tequila to provide a measure of quality and potency – a weak alcohol content allowed the worm to rot. Nowadays, however, the outrageous prices offered for *gusanos* have forced small distillers to substitute slivers of maguey or sugarcane.

Common names and synonyms: Blue agave, century plant, maguey.

Agnus castus - *see* **CHASTE TREE**

Aguacate - *see* **AVOCADO**

Ague bark - *see* **HOPTREE**

Aguweed - *see* **BONESET**

Ahipa - *see* **AJIPA**

Ahuacatl - *see* **AVOCADO**

Ahuyama - *see* **CALABAZA (SQUASH)**

Aibika - *see* **SUNSET HIBISCUS**

Airelle de myrtille - *see* **CRANBERRY**

AIR POTATO (*see also* **YAMS**) - A native of South Asia that later spread to the South Pacific region and is now cultivated throughout the world's tropics and subtropics, the "air potato" (*Dioscorea bulbifera*) is also called the "potato yam" and the "aerial yam." Its name derives from the fact that its edible, potato-like tubers do not all form underground; instead, many are produced at the junction of the leaves and the stem of this tall, climbing herb.

Common names and synonyms: Aerial yam, potato yam.

See in addition: "Sweet Potatoes and Yams," Part II, Section B, Chapter 5.

Aiwain - *see* **AJOWAN**

AJÍ (*see also* **CHILLI PEPPERS**) - This chilli pepper (*Capsicum baccatum*) is of the Andes region of South America, where it is understandably known as *ají* because (in western South America and the West Indies) the word *ají* means chilli. The pepper called *ají* is - at least when fresh - a thin, tapered chilli, some 3 to 4 inches in length, with green or red flesh, which provides considerable heat for salsas and cooked dishes. When dried, the pepper is known as *ají mirasol* or *ají amarillo*, because its ripe red color turns yellowish. In this form, the pepper is used in a variety of sauces and also to make *ceviche* in Peru. Another pepper called *ají* is *ají panca*, a mild pepper that dries to a chocolate brown color and is used to make chilli sauces and various cooked dishes - generally featuring fish.

Common names and synonyms: Ají amarillo, ají mirasol, ají panca.

See in addition: "Chilli Peppers," Part II, Section C, Chapter 4.

Ají amarillo - *see* **AJÍ**

AJÍ DULCE (*see also* **CHILLI PEPPERS**) - In western South America and the Caribbean, the word *ají* frequently connotes all chilli peppers - and *dulce* would seem to suggest a sweet pepper. But this member of the genus *Capsicum* (*C. chinense* Jacq.) is not the mild-mannered chilli pepper its name implies. Rather, it is an aggressive Venezuelan relative of the fiery habanero pepper (also of the species *C. chinense*), which it resembles somewhat in shape, although it is quite a bit larger.

See in addition: "Chilli Peppers," Part II, Section C, Chapter 4.

Ají mirasol - *see* **AJÍ**

AJIPA (*see also* **LEGUMES**) - Like jícama, ajipa (*Pachyrhizus ahipa*) is a legume that develops swollen roots. Also called a "yam bean," it is unknown outside of South America, where it was grown by ancient Native Americans. The white tubers are often eaten raw in salads, to which they add a crispness and a sweet taste. The tubers are also boiled or steamed like potatoes.

Common names and synonyms: Ahipa, yam bean.

Ají panca - *see* **AJÍ**

AJOWAN - A native of southern India, ajowan (*Carum ajowan*) is also grown in an area that extends westward from Afghanistan, across Iran, and into Egypt - and doubtless has been for thousands of years. Although its whole or ground seeds have a taste similar to that of thyme, the plant is actually related to caraway and is used in much the same way as the latter in breads and pickles and with legumes.

Common names and synonyms: Aiwain, ajwain, bishop's-weed, *omam, omum*.

See also: "Spices and Flavorings," Part II, Section F, Chapter 1.

Ajwain - *see* **AJOWAN**

Aka-suguri - *see* **CURRANT(S)**

Akee - *see* **ACKEE**

Alcachofa - *see* **ARTICHOKE**

Alecost - *see* **COSTMARY**

ALEXANDER - There are a number of plants called alexander, alexanders, or alexander buds. One is *Smyrnium olusatrum* - a European plant with the name of "alexanders" that resembles celery and was cultivated in the past as a potherb. Alexanders is also a name that was applied in the past to various members of the parsley or carrot family (Umbelliferae). Finally, alexanders can mean any plant of the genus *Zizia*, especially golden alexanders (*Z. aurea*), a native of eastern North America. This plant has yellow flowers and can be found in moist woods and meadows. The young umbels of the flowers were eaten by Native Americans just as they began to bud.

Common names and synonyms: Alexander buds, alexanders, golden alexanders.

Alexander buds - *see* **ALEXANDER**

Alexanders - *see* **ALEXANDER**

ALFALFA - A native of Eurasia, alfalfa (*Medicago sativa*) is a tall, cloverlike plant belonging to the pea family. It is now grown in North America (frequently as a cover crop to reduce erosion) and used for fodder. Its other uses are also mostly non-culinary: The fiber is employed in the production of paper; the drying oil derived from the seeds goes into paints; and the plant is a commercial source of chlorophyll. After the introduction of alfalfa into the New World, its tiny seeds were consumed by some Native American groups and are still used for sprouting by many concerned with health foods. The seeds are high in the minerals calcium, magnesium, and potassium, and the leaves (also edible) are high in vitamins A, C, D, E, and K.

Common names and synonyms: Lucerne, sativa.

Algae - *see* **SEAWEED**

Algarroba - *see* **ALGARROBO, CAROB, MESQUITE**

ALGARROBO - A native of Peru and Ecuador, the algarrobo (*Prosopis pallida* - also called "algarroba") is a tree that has been naturalized in Puerto Rico and Hawaii (where it is called "kiawe"). Its sweet pods are made into a syrup used in various drinks. The algarrobo blanco (*Prosopis alba*), which is found in subtropical Argentina, Uruguay, Paraguay, and southern Brazil, has pods that have been toasted to make a coffee substitute and are also used to make other beverages as well as flour.

Common names and synonyms: Algarroba, algarrobo blanco, ibope, igope, kiawe, tacu, white algarrobo.

ALICANTE BOUSCHET (*see also* **GRAPES**) - A cross between Grenache and Petite Bouschet, the Alicante Bouschet grape (*Vitis vinifera*) is deep purple in color with a thick skin. The latter attribute made these grapes extremely popular during the days of Prohibition in the United States, because they could withstand rough handling when shipped to the homes of aspiring private wine makers. The Alicante Bouschet is used primarily for blending.

See in addition: "Wine," Part III, Chapter 13.

ALKANET - A European plant, alkanet (*Alkanna tinctoria*) yields a dye from its roots that is used to color some cheeses and improve the color of inferior ports and other wines.

Alligator pear - *see* **AVOCADO**

Allouya - *see* **GUINEA ARROWROOT**

ALLSPICE - Unlike most spices (which are indigenous to the tropics of southern China, southern India, and the East Indies), allspice (*Pimenta dioica*) is a berry of the New World, native to the West Indies and Central America. A member of the myrtle family, allspice was used by the Taino and Carib Indians (and quite possibly also by those of the Mesoamerican mainland) long before the Europeans reached the Americas. The small, aromatic, tropical tree and its berries were among the many early "discoveries" of Spanish explorers, who mistook the pea-sized berries for peppercorns. In fact, even today the Spanish word *pimenta* refers to allspice. The Spaniards introduced the spice into Europe in the sixteenth century, and in both whole and ground forms it has subsequently become a part of the cuisines of many peoples across the globe. Allspice, which begins as a purple berry but turns brown when sun-dried, acquired its English-language name because of its versatility: Its taste is like a combination of nutmeg, cinnamon, and clove. It is best in sweet and savory dishes and is used frequently in mulled wines and for pickling, not to mention in fruitcakes and spice cakes. Commercially, allspice is important in the production of catsup, sauces for meats, sausages, and cured meats. Today, allspice remains American – it is grown exclusively in the Western Hemisphere, especially in Jamaica (where it still thrives in the wild). That island, with its limestone soils, is the biggest allspice producer, and the Jamaicans also use the berries to make a kind of rum.

Common names and synonyms: Jamaica pepper, myrtle pepper, *pimenta,* pimento.

See also: "Spices and Flavorings," Part II, Section F, Chapter 1.

ALMOND (*see also* **CUDDAPAH ALMOND, JAVA ALMOND, MALABAR ALMOND**) – Almonds are the fruit seeds of *Prunus dulcis* (formerly *P. amygdalus*) = *Amygdalus communis,* a tree closely related to the peach and the plum, and are said to be native to the Mediterranean region and western Asia, where (like many other wild nuts) they doubtless helped to sustain our hunting-and-gathering forebears. Perhaps the oldest, as well as the most widely known, of the world's nut crops, almonds were first cultivated in Europe by the Greeks, are mentioned frequently in the Old Testament, and were a favorite of the Romans, whose sugared almonds may' have been among the first sweetmeats in history. Recipes incorporating almond "flour" date from the Middle Ages in Europe, a period when almond "milk" was also used – as a liquid substitute for milk and eggs on days of fasting. The Spaniards brought the almond to the New World, where it is now grown extensively in California, and that state has joined Spain and Italy as a leading producer of the most important nut in the world nut trade. There are two types of almonds: sweet and bitter. Nuts of the latter type contain prussic acid and thus are toxic when raw; these must be blanched and roasted before being processed into an oil, a paste, or an extract that is used to flavor liqueurs and some confections. Sweet almonds, by contrast, are eaten whole, as well as blanched, slivered, chopped, diced, and ground for pastries and for meat and vegetable dishes. Almond paste is the soul of macaroons and marzipan. An almond tree will bear nuts for a half century or more, producing between 25 and 40 pounds annually. Almonds contain more calcium

than any other kind of nut and are also a source of the B vitamins and vitamin E. They provide a small amount of protein and are high in fat.

ALOCASIA (*see also* **TARO**) – As members of a genus belonging to the family Araceae, *Alocasia* species are related to taro (*Colocasia esculenta*). These plants are cultivated in tropical areas throughout Asia, and their roots are starchy and nutritious. The "giant taro" or "giant alocasia" (*A. macrorrhiza*) and the "Chinese taro" (*A. cucullata*) have tubers that are eaten as cooked vegetables, whereas *A. indica* is used in Indian curries.

Common names and synonyms: Ape, Chinese taro, elephant-ear plant, giant alocasia, giant taro, *pai.*

See in addition: "Taro," Part II, Section B, Chapter 6.

Alpine strawberry – *see* **WILD STRAWBERRY**

Alverja – *see* **PIGEON PEA**

AMALAKA – Also known as "emblic," the amalaka (*Phyllanthus emblica*) is a large tree, native to Malaya but cultivated throughout South and Southeast Asia and now grown in Puerto Rico as well. It produces small, walnut-sized, green-to-yellow fruits, which are sour and are generally used for jams, pickles, and chutneys. The fruits are very high in vitamin C.

Common names and synonyms: Amalaki, emblic, Indian gooseberry, Malacca tree, myrobalan.

Amalaki – *see* **AMALAKA**

Amarante – *see* **AMARANTH**

AMARANTH (*see also* **CHENOPODIUM, CHINESE AMARANTH**) – Hernando Cortés, the Spanish conqueror of Mexico, prohibited the cultivation of the amaranth grown in Mesoamerica (*Amaranthus hypochondriacus* and *A. cruentus* – a third species, *A. caudatus,* was cultivated in the South American Andes) because it was used for religious as well as culinary purposes. The result is that this legendary plant of the Aztecs, which they called *huautli,* has only recently been rediscovered by the West, although it has long been grown in India and tropical Africa – in fact, in most of the world's tropical areas – and the Mexican descendants of the Aztecs have continued its cultivation on their *chinampas.* Because the tiny, usually yellowish (but sometimes red) amaranth grains do not come from a member of the grass family, they are technically not grains at all. Rather, the plant is a member of the chenopod family – related to lamb's-quarter and tumbleweed – and grows well (to about 6 feet in height) in hot and sunny locations. But whether it is a weed or not, the sesame-like amaranth seed, with its pleasant nutty flavor, is packed with calcium, magnesium, and iron, delivers a considerable amount of folacin and riboflavin, and has a high protein content. In addition to the seeds, the leaves are also eaten (much like spinach) wherever amaranth is extensively cultivated. Amaranth seeds are usually boiled and eaten as a porridge or used as an ingredient in soups and stews. In addition, they can be popped and used to make *alegría,* a popular sweet in Mexico. Amaranth sprouts are also good to eat.

Common names and synonyms: Achis, *achita,* African spinach, amarante, *bledos,* bondue, bush greens, *ckoito, coimi, coyo, cuime,* green leaf, *huautli,* Indian spinach, Joseph's-coat, kiwicha, livid amaranth, love-lies-bleeding, *millmi,* pale-seeded amaranth, pigweed, princess-feather, purple amaranth, quintonil, redroot, spinach-grass, Surinam spinach, wild beet, wild blite.

See in addition: "Amaranth," Part II, Section A, Chapter 1.

Amarelle - *see* **CHERRY**

Ambarella - *see* **GOLDEN APPLE**

Amber - *see* **AMBERSEED**

AMBERCANE (*see also* **SORGHUM**) - Grown especially in South Africa, ambercane (*Sorghum dochna* or *S. bicolor*) is a grain crop much like millet and is used in much the same manner.

See in addition: "Sorghum," Part II, Section A, Chapter 9.

AMBERSEED - Also called "ambrette" and "musk seed," amberseed is the seed of the abelmosk (*Hibiscus Moscheutos*), which is a bushy herb. Native to tropical Asia and the East Indies, amberseed has long been used as a flavoring in coffee and in perfumery.

Common names and synonyms: Amber, ambrette, musk seed.

See also: "Spices and Flavorings," Part II, Section F, Chapter 1.

Ambrette - *see* **AMBERSEED**

American angelica - *see* **PURPLESTEM ANGELICA**

American beech (tree) - *see* **BEECHNUT**

AMERICAN BITTERSWEET - Also known as "false bittersweet," "climbing bittersweet," and a host of other common names, American bittersweet (*Celastrus scandens*) is a woody vine that grows on trees and fences. It has clusters of greenish flowers and a yellow fruit in the form of a yellow capsule, neither of which is edible - in fact, the entire plant is toxic. But the twigs and inner bark were used as food by Native Americans, who discovered that boiling eliminated the poison.

Common names and synonyms: Bittersweet, climbing bittersweet, false bittersweet. American black walnut - *see* **WALNUT**

American horsemint - *see* **BEE BALM, BERGAMOT**

AMERICAN LINDEN - Also called "basswood" and other common names, the American linden (*Tilia americana*) is a forest tree that is especially common in mountainous terrain from Canada to Georgia. Native Americans harvested its sap for a beverage and ate its inner bark. The young leaves can be made into a salad, cooked as a vegetable, and added to soups and stews. The red berries of the tree are also edible, making it a year-round food source.

Common names and synonyms: Basswood, linden, whitewood.

American mandrake - *see* **MAYAPPLE**

American storax - *see* **SWEET GUM**

American styrax - *see* **SWEET GUM**

American taro - *see* **MALANGA**

American wormseed - *see* **EPAZOTE**

Amra - *see* **HOG PLUM**

ANAHEIM (*see also* **CHILLI PEPPERS**) - This member of the genus *Capsicum* (*C. annuum*) is named for the city of Anaheim, California, where the pepper was first grown at the beginning of the twentieth century. Another name, "California chilli," honors its home state. It is actually, however, a "New Mexican chilli," which is another of its aliases, along with "long green chilli" and "long red chilli." The Anaheim is a relatively mild pepper (although some can be hot), is frequently seen in produce markets, and is one of the most commonly used peppers in the United States. As its various names imply, the Anaheim pepper is green while still maturing and red after it has matured. It is eaten in both forms (the red is the sweeter of the two), is often roasted or pickled, and - when stuffed - is the star of the Mexican classic *chillis rellenos.* Anaheims are also dried and made into a powder called *chilli colorado.* A *pasado* is a red Anaheim that has been roasted, peeled, and dried.

Common names and synonyms: California chilli, Chile Colorado Anaheim, Chile Verde Anaheim, *chilli colorado,* long green chilli, long red chilli, New Mexican chilli, *pasado,* Red Chile Anaheim.

See in addition: "Chilli Peppers," Part II, Section C, Chapter 4.

Anana - *see* **PINEAPPLE**

Anana del monte - *see* **POSHTE**

Ananás - *see* **PINEAPPLE**

Ananas de Mexico - *see* **MONSTERA**

Anato - *see* **ANNATTO**

Ancho - *see* **POBLANO**

ANDEAN LUPIN (*see also* **BEANS, LEGUMES**) - Known also as the "South American lupin" and "lupino," as well as a number of other names such as *chocho* and *tarvi,* the Andean lupin (*Lupinus mutabilis*) is a leguminous plant with large seeds (as a rule, bigger than lima beans) that served as food for ancient, pre-Incan peoples of the central Andean region. The Andean lupin is still widely cultivated there, even though the seeds contain alkaloids that must be leached out by a complex procedure. As with so many other poisonous plants, one can only wonder how the Andean lupin ever came to be widely used - or even used at all. The seeds are rich in protein and oil, are used in soups and stews, and can be made into a flour.

Common names and synonyms: Chocho, lupino, South American lupin, *tarvi.*

ANEMONE GREENS - Some greens from plants of the genus *Anemone* are used for food and medicinal purposes. The leaves of *A. flaccida* are eaten in Japan and China, whereas Eskimos eat the leaves of *A. narcissiflora* raw, fermented, or in oil. The crushed leaves of *A. hepatica* yield anemone camphor, which is used as a tonic. × *A. hupehensis* Hort. Lemoine var. *japonica* is cultivated in China for its roots, which are believed to be useful in treating heart disease. When collected during flowering, the dried plant *A. patens* is used to increase appetite and restore digestion.

ANGELICA (*see also* **PURPLESTEM ANGELICA**) – One of the tallest growing of the herbs, angelica (*Angelica archangelica*) provides stems as well as roots and leaves that are boiled and eaten as a vegetable. Angelica has a long history of use for medicinal purposes – indeed, its name (Latin for "angel") was assigned because of its healing properties. Angelica was one of the so-called scurvy grasses that were thought either to drive the disease away or to keep it at bay, and (until well into the twentieth century) after long winters, Icelanders dug up the roots to cure their bleeding gums. Today, oil from the roots and seeds is used for flavoring liqueurs, and the herb is used mostly in candied form. The stems are crystallized with sugar and employed in fruitcakes, as a flavoring in jams, and as a decoration for pastries.

Common names and synonyms: European angelica, garden angelica, Japanese angelica, scurvy grass, wild angelica.

Angel's-trumpet - *see* **MOONFLOWER**

ANGLED LUFFA – Also called "Chinese okra" because it is shaped like okra, the angled luffa (*Luffa acutangula*) is a dark green cucurbit native to India and has been grown (often on trellises) for many thousands of years for its tasty young fruits (the mature fruits become bitter). It is used mostly in China as a vegetable. Another more fibrous species, *L. aegyptiaca,* is dried and its fibrous skeleton used as a sponge. The United States is a major consumer of luffas and imports millions each year. But although it is called the "sponge gourd," *L. aegyptiaca* is also a food, and its flowers, buds, leaves, and young fruits are all eaten.

Common names and synonyms: Chinese okra, loofah, smooth loofah, sponge gourd, vegetable sponge.

ANGOSTURA – The bitter and aromatic bark of either of two Brazilian trees (*Galipea officinalis* and *Cusparia trifoliata* = *C. febrifuga*) is used to make a tonic called "angostura," named after a river town in Venezuela that is now called Ciudad Bolívar. "Angostura" is also the name of a proprietary brand of bitters made in Trinidad.

Common names and synonyms: Bitters.

ANISE (*see also* **CICELY, FENNEL, STAR-ANISE, SICHUAN PEPPERCORN**) – Also called aniseed, anise (*Pimpinella anisum*) is a native of the Mediterranean region (it grows wild in Greece and Egypt) and is one of the oldest of the spices. Anise was used by the ancient Greeks, Romans, and Hebrews, who viewed it as a powerful medicine, and today is grown in an area extending from southern Russia across South Asia, as well as in Mexico. Anise is a relative of dill, chervil, coriander, and cumin and has a licorice-like taste (after the seeds are dried) that is used to flavor liqueurs such as the

Pernod of France, the ouzo of Greece, the anisette enjoyed in Spain, and the arrack of the eastern Mediterranean. Oil of anise has medicinal properties and is employed in cough syrups and lozenges. As a spice in the kitchen, anise is added to salads, pastries, fruit dishes, sauces, meat dishes, and fish and shellfish.

Common names and synonyms: Aniseed, *jintan,* sweet cumin.

See in addition: "Spices and Flavorings," Part II, Section F, Chapter 1.

Aniseed - *see* **ANISE**

Anise-pepper - *see* **SICHUAN PEPPERCORN**

Anise root - *see* **CICELY**

ANISILLO – A member of the New World genus *Tagetes* (which includes the garden marigold), anisillo (*T. minuta*) is an annual herb that grows to a height of from 3 to 6 feet. Throughout much of Latin America, it is dried and used to make a tealike beverage that is flavorful both hot and cold and is also thought of as a medicine. The dried plant is also added to rice dishes and stews for flavoring.

Common names and synonyms: Chilca, chinchilla, chiquilla, suico, wild marigold.

Anjou (pear) - *see* **PEAR**

ANNATTO – The bright red or yellow-brown fruits of the annatto plant (*Bixa orellana*), an American spice, have been employed more for their color than their flavor. Indeed, Native Americans of the Caribbean and Mesoamerica decorated their bodies with dyes made from the pulp that surrounds the seeds of this rough, berry-like fruit. The seeds are used – whole or ground – to color (and flavor) dishes such as Jamaica's famed ackee-fish-and-rice and the popular Mexican chilli powders. Annatto was carried by the Manila galleons to the Philippines, where the seeds have become important in many dishes. In Europe, annatto is used to color cheeses, butter, and oils.

Common names and synonyms: Achiote, anato, arnato, bija, bijol, *bixa,* lipstick tree, roucou.

See also: "Spices and Flavorings," Part II, Section F, Chapter 1.

Annual bunch grass - *see* **TEF**

Anon - *see* **SWEETSOP**

Anona - *see* **CHERIMOYA, CUSTARD APPLE**

Anona blanca - *see* **ILAMA**

Anu - *see* **MASHUA**

Ao-Togarashi (chilli pepper) - *see* **ASIAN CHILLIES**

Ape - *see* **ALOCASIA**

Apio - *see* **ARRACACHA**

APIOS – Also called "potato bean" and "groundnut" (but not to be confused with the peanut), apios (*Apios americana* or *A. tuberosa*) is a legume native to and found throughout eastern North America. Its edible underground tubers, roots, and seeds were gathered and widely consumed by Native Americans long before the Europeans arrived, but the plant was probably never cultivated. Apios is a twining vine with flowers ranging in color from pink to purple. It may have been taken to Europe as an ornamental as early as the end of the sixteenth century, and – later – there were thoughts of employing it as a potato substitute during the mid-nineteenth-century Irish potato famine. The idea was dropped, however, as disease-resistant lines of potatoes were developed. Among tubers, apios is very high in protein as well as carbohydrates, with a crude protein content about three times that of the potato. In addition, apios is unique among root and tuber crops for its ability to fix nitrogen. It nonetheless remains a neglected crop.

Common names and synonyms: Bog potato, groundnut, Indian potato, potato bean, Virginia potato, wild bean, wild potato.

Appalachian tea - *see* **WINTERBERRY**

APPLE (*see also* **CRAB APPLE**) – This fruit of legends – ranging from the tale of an apple as the cause of the Trojan War to the steady hand and eye of William Tell – is classified, along with the pear, as a pome fruit (meaning one with a compartmented core), and in fact "pome" means apple in Latin. Over 7,000 varieties of the apple (*Pyrus malus* or *Malus domestica*) are grown worldwide, and no wonder, for apple trees are valued not only for their fruit but also for their beauty in gardens and on lawns. Once the tree begins to bear fruit (after some 5 to 10 years for regular trees, but only 2 to 3 years for dwarf trees), it will continue to do so for upward of a century. Cultivated apples are descendants of wild or crab apples and are believed to have originated in Southwest Asia and the region around the Mediterranean. However, because crab apples still grow wild in Central Asia and Europe, some would widen the area of origin. Evidence indicates that this fruit, reputed to be the forbidden fruit of the Garden of Eden, was being cultivated and stored at least 5,000 years ago, and probably long before that. Apples were grown by the Etruscans, the Egyptians, the Greeks, and the Romans and, as with so many other food plants, were spread about Europe within the Roman Empire and thus have been cultivated there for at least 2,000 years. Apples reached the Americas in the seventeenth century with the early colonists, and today about 2,500 varieties are grown in the United States alone. Only 16, however, account for over 90 percent of the total U.S. production, about half of which goes into apple products such as cider, juice, applesauce, and the like. The leading 8 of the top 16, which account for 80 percent of U.S. production, are as follows:

- Golden Delicious, which when ripe is yellow and is the most widely consumed apple in the world. It was developed by accident in West Virginia toward the end of the nineteenth century.
- Granny Smith, a pale green apple, originated in Australia at about the middle of the nineteenth

century. It is good eaten raw, is used for juice, and is suitable for general baking, for stuffing, for chutneys, and for salsas.
- Jonathan, a dark red and juicy apple, is used for juice and applesauce as well as for baking and stuffings.
- McIntosh is a greenish red apple that is good eaten raw and is used for juice and applesauce.
- Red Delicious, a red apple with crisp, juicy flesh, is the most popular apple in the United States.
- Rome Beauty, a red or red-striped apple, is favored for baking but is a bit mealy for eating out of hand.
- Stayman is a purplish apple for all-purpose use.
- York, also called York Imperial, is another good baking apple. It has a pink skin.

Other apples have somewhat specific uses. The Gravenstein is used mostly for applesauce; the Northern Spy is good for pies; the Winesap is a favorite for making cider. The sour crab apple is used for making jellies.

Most apples have a high sugar content, are low in tannin, and are slightly acidic. They are only a fair source of minerals, but they provide some vitamin A and have a good measure of vitamin C in their peels. Because apples are high in sugar, they are also high in carbohydrates.

Common names and synonyms: Cider apple, cooking apple, crab (wild) apple, dessert apple, Golden Delicious, Granny Smith, Gravenstein, Jonathan, McIntosh, Northern Spy, pippin, pome(-fruit), Red Delicious, Rome Beauty, Rome Delicious, Russet, Stayman, Winesap, Yellow Delicious, York, York Imperial.

Apple banana - *see* **BANANA**
Apple cactus - *see* **CACTUS APPLE**
Apple mint - *see* **MINT**
Apple-of-love - *see* **EGGPLANT**
Apple pear - *see* **ASIAN PEAR**
Apricock - *see* **APRICOT**
APRICOT – A sweet-sour fruit, the apricot (*Prunus armeniaca*) was long viewed as a kind of plum – and one that came from Armenia. In truth, it is a stone fruit (a drupe) of the same family as the peach, plum, almond, nectarine, and cherry and apparently originated (despite its scientific name) in China, where it has been cultivated for some 5,000 years. From China, the apricot traveled by way of northern India, finally reaching the Near East. After this, both Alexander the Great (356–323 B.C.) and, later, Roman legionnaires are credited with carrying the fruit to Europe. From Greece and Rome, apricots spread throughout Europe, and the Spaniards introduced them to the New World, where today they grow from Chile to California, with the latter area accounting for most North American production. In Europe, Spain is the leading producer of apricots. These walnut-sized fruits, which resemble peaches with their copper-colored

flesh, are versatile in that they can be eaten fresh, dried, or canned and may be worked into rolls (apricot "sheets"), made into jelly, grilled, and poached. The kernels are a source of oil (although those of some varieties are poisonous), and the leaves can serve as fodder for sheep and goats. Apricots are an excellent source of beta-carotene, vitamin C, and potassium; when dried, they also are a good source of iron.

Common names and synonyms: Apricock.

Apricot vine - *see* **MAYPOP**

Arabian tea - *see* **KHAT**

ARAÇÁ-BOI - A fruit that is practically unknown outside of the Amazon Basin, the *acraçá-boi* (*Eugenia stipitata*) has a pleasant appearance. It is also sweet smelling but has such a fiercely sour taste that its juice must be sweetened before consumption.

ARAÇÁ-PERA (*see also* **GUAVA**) - A wild guava of the Amazon, the *araçá-pera* (*Psidium angulatum*) provides a sour juice that must be both diluted and sweetened to make it palatable.

Arbor-vitae - *see* **CEDAR**

Archiciocco - *see* **ARTICHOKE**

Areca nut palm - *see* **BETEL NUT**

ARGAN - An evergreen tree native to North Africa (probably Morocco), the argan (*Argania sideroxylon*) has fruits with a high oil content. About the size of plums, they are pressed for an oil much appreciated by the Moroccans for its aroma and as a cooking medium. The oil can be found in specialty stores in the United States, but at a considerable price.

ARMENIAN CUCUMBER (*see also* **CUCUMBER**) - With other common names like "snake melon" and "snake cucumber," the Armenian cucumber (*Cucumis melo*) is - not surprisingly - very long (up to 3 feet) and very narrow (up to 3 inches in diameter). But it is not a cucumber. Rather, it is a melon, like the muskmelon (also *C. melo*), and a native of the Old World tropics. The Armenian cucumber, however, is not eaten as a melon but is used mostly for preserves.

Common names and synonyms: Japanese cucumber, snake cucumber, snake melon.

See in addition: "Cucumbers, Melons, and Watermelons," Part II, Section C, Chapter 6.

Arnato - *see* **ANNATTO**

AROIDS (*see also* **COCOYAM, TARO**) - The inclusive common name for all plants belonging to the Araceae family, the term "aroids" denotes over 1,000 genera and approximately 2,000 species, 90 percent of which are tropical in origin and grown largely as ornamentals. The exceptions are staple crops such as cocoyam and taro (genus *Colocasia*), which are cultivated in Southeast Asia, Malaysia, and the Pacific Islands. *Poi,* a Hawaiian dish, is made from taro. Monstera fruits, also part of the Araceae family, are edible as well.

Arracach - *see* **ARRACACHA**

ARRACACHA - A root of the Andean region of South America, arracacha (*Arracacia xanthorrhiza* or *A. esculenta*) is a staple for many of the Native Americans living there and, indeed, may be one of the oldest of the cultivated plants in that region. It stands in place of the potato in the diet and, in fact, was domesticated prior to the potato. Also called the "Peruvian carrot," arracacha is related to celery and - aboveground - resembles it. But belowground it has carrotlike roots that are boiled. Their flavor, according to expert Noel Vietmeyer, combines the tastes of celery, roasted chestnuts, and cabbage. No longer confined to the Andean region, arracacha is consumed throughout much of Latin America.

Common names and synonyms: Apio, arracach, arracacia, fecula, Peruvian carrot, Peruvian parsnip, r'accacha, white carrot.

Arracacia - *see* **ARRACACHA**

ARROW ARUM - A hardy North American perennial marsh plant, arrow arum (*Peltandra virginica*) is also called "green arrow arum," "Virginian tukahoe," "Virginian wake-robin," and "tukahoe." Native Americans in what is now the eastern United States ate the roots, stems, and flowers as vegetables.

Common names and synonyms: Green arrow arum, tukahoe, Virginian tukahoe, Virginian wake-robin.

ARROWHEAD - Arrowhead plants (genus *Sagittaria*) are widespread in the shallow waters of ponds, streams, and marshes, and those that are edible have roots that are cooked like potatoes or dried for flour. Some Native Americans used *S. latifolia* extensively, often acquiring it by discovering caches of the plants stored away by muskrats. *Sagittaria sinensis* is cultivated extensively in parts of China and Japan. Its root is similar to a lily bulb in appearance, has a bland, sweet taste, and is used in the same way as a potato.

Common names and synonyms: Arrowleaf, duck potato, swamp potato, wapata, wapato, wapatoo.

Arrowleaf - *see* **ARROWHEAD**

ARROWROOT - A perennial plant of the American tropics, arrowroot (*Maranta arundinacea*) is native to South America and the Caribbean and has been naturalized in southern Florida. It is also cultivated in Southeast Asia, Australia, and South Africa. The plant grows to a height of 3 to 5 feet, has long, very pointed leaves and small white flowers, and is cultivated for its starchy roots, which yield an edible starch that makes both a flour and a very smooth jelly or paste. The flour is almost all starch, is easily digested, is often employed as a thickener, and is prized by many chefs for making sauces. Both flour and jelly are used in infant foods, puddings, ice cream, and arrowroot biscuits, as well as in the manufacture of cosmetics and glue. Because Native Americans believed that the root absorbed poison from arrow wounds (hence its name), the plant has long been thought to have medicinal properties.

Starchy products from other plants are often subsumed under the general rubric of the term "arrowroot," and some can substitute for arrowroot. *Tacca leontopetaloides,* for example, is known as "Polynesian arrowroot."

Common names and synonyms: Polynesian arrowroot, tapioca, yuquilla.

Arrugula - *see* **ARUGULA**

Artichaut - *see* **ARTICHOKE**

ARTICHOKE - Although at least three vegetables are called artichokes, the globe or French artichoke (*Cynara scolymus*) has little relationship to either the Jerusalem artichoke or the Chinese artichoke. This is fortunate, because there is confusion enough created by the numerous varieties of the globe artichoke grown around the world. In Europe, the leaves are often reddish in color, but in the United States the only variety normally encountered in produce departments is the Italian Green Globe, with most of these grown in California. The artichoke appears to have originated in North Africa (where it still exists in a wild state). It subsequently became a wild thistle in Sicily, where its bitter leaves as well as its flower heads were gathered for food. The Greeks and Romans began its cultivation, and the parts of the immature flower head – artichoke leaves (tender and fleshy at the base) and bottoms ("hearts") – have been enjoyed at least since Roman times. The artichoke became an important part of Italian gastronomy and was subsequently imported to France by Queen Catherine de Médicis. Artichokes did not reach the United States until the nineteenth century. Today, the Spaniards, French, and Italians are the most fervent artichoke enthusiasts on the European continent, and California, Belgium, France, and the Mediterranean countries are the vegetable's most prolific producers. Similar to a miniature cabbage in appearance, the artichoke has leaves that are steamed and eaten with a dipping sauce, and the "hearts" and "bottoms" are sautéed, steamed, pickled, and cut into salads. Artichokes may be purchased fresh, frozen, and canned, and "baby" artichokes are frequently available marinated in jars. Artichokes are a good source of vitamin C and dietary fiber.

Common names and synonyms: Alcachofa, archiciocco, artichaut, articiocco, baby artichoke, *carciofo,* French artichoke, globe artichoke, Italian Green Globe, *karzochy.*

Articiocco - *see* **ARTICHOKE**

ARUGULA - Also known as "rocket" and "garden rocket," this native of Europe and western Asia (*Eruca sativa*) is a cruciferous plant that has long provided tender, slightly bitter, mustard-flavored greens for the salad bowls of southern Europeans and Italian-Americans. Lately, it has become widely available in the United States, where it has been naturalized. Its leaves resemble those of the radish, which is a close relative. The seeds of arugula are also eaten, and they yield an oil that is used for culinary purposes, as a lubricant, and in medicines. Arugula is loaded with vitamins A and C and – like many greens – provides much iron and calcium as well.

Common names and synonyms: Arrugula, garden rocket, jamba oil, Mediterranean rocket, rocket, rocket salad, roka, roquette, rucola, rugala, rugela, rugula.

See also: "Cruciferous and Green Leafy Vegetables," Part II, Section C, Chapter 5.

Aruhe - *see* **BRACKEN FERN**

Arvi - *see* **COCOYAM**

ASAFETIDA - Asafetida (ass-uh-feh-TEE-da; *asa* from the Persian "gum" and *foetida* from the Latin "stinking") is a spice made from a notoriously bad-smelling plant (*Ferula assa-foetida*) of the carrot family, which can grow to 10 or even a dozen feet in height. The plant is a native of Iran and Afghanistan, is related to fennel, and is commonly used in Indian and – to a lesser extent – other Asian and Middle Eastern cuisines. Because of its fetid odor (some say it is like that of garlic), the Germans called it *Teufelsdreck,* which can be translated as "devil's-dung." But in the past asafetida was worn around the neck as an amulet to ward off disease and during medieval times to ward off witches. Asafetida was also prized in the ancient world for its alleged contraceptive powers, and the Romans regarded it as a substitute for silphium, an herb that became extinct about the time of Nero. Fortunately, the plant's odor, caused by sulfur compounds, disappears during cooking, and the leaves and stems are eaten as a vegetable. The spice, made from the milk-like juice of asafetida, usually comes in ground form and is added very sparingly to dishes such as meatballs and to pickles for its truffle-like flavor. It is also an ingredient in the venerable Lea & Perrins Worcestershire sauce.

Common names and synonyms: Asafoetida, assafetida, assafoetida, devil's-dung, food-of-the-gods, *hing,* stinking gum, *Teufelsdreck.*

See also: "Spices and Flavorings," Part II, Section F, Chapter 1.

Asafoetida - *see* **ASAFETIDA**

Assafetida - *see* **ASAFETIDA**

Assafoetida - *see* **ASAFETIDA**

ASAM GELUGUR - A fruit from a tall tree that is native to Burma and Malaya, *Garcinia atroviridis* is orangish to yellow when ripe, round, about 3 inches in circumference, and very tart. As a rule, the fruit is sun-dried and used in curries. Immature fruits are incorporated in chutneys.

ASIAN CHILLIES (*see also* **CHILLI PEPPERS**) - Although all members of the genus *Capsicum* are native to the Americas, Asian peoples have enthusiastically adopted chilli peppers (which first reached Asia via the trading empires of Spain and Portugal) and incorporated them into the respective cuisines of the region. Many of the chillies, such as jalapeños, serranos, and Anaheims, would be familiar to Westerners, but others, now associated firmly with Asian cooking, would not. Among these are the tiny, red or green "bird's-eye" or "bird" chillies, which (frequently in dried form) give Thai cuisine its well-deserved reputation for fiery tastes. Another chilli, called "Thai" (this one about an inch and a half in length, and pointed), is also often dried, comes in green and red, and delivers significant heat (that lingers). A close relative of the Thai pepper is the Korean chilli, which is employed to put a bit of bite in *kimchee*. *Togarashi* chillies (often called by the Spanish *Japonés* in markets) are the Japanese equivalent of the Thai bird's-eye and, like it, are intensely hot. By contrast, the small, green *Ao-Togarashi* chillies have a mild flavor, as do the long, deep red Kashmiri chillies, which are employed for their color.

Common names and synonyms: Ao-Togarashi, bird chilli, bird's-eye, *Japonés,* Kashmiri chilli, Korean chilli, Thai chilli, Tien-tsin, *Togarashi.*

See in addition: "Chilli Peppers," Part II, Section C, Chapter 4.

ASIAN PEAR (*see also* **PEAR**) – A wide variety of seemingly different fruits are called "Asian pears" (*Pyrus ussuriensis* or *Pyrus pyrifolia*). Many of these now grow in the western part of the United States – having been brought there by Chinese immigrants during the nineteenth century – but have been widely marketed only in the past few decades. Among these are "apple pears," "sand pears," "Chinese pears," and "Oriental pears" that range in size from very small to quite large. These fruits often resemble a cross between an apple and a pear and come in a wide variety of colors. But all are juicy and so crisp that they can be sliced very thinly. Like other pears, they are eaten raw as well as cooked. There are more than 25 varieties of Asian pears in U.S. markets (where the most popular one is the "Twentieth Century") and more than 100 varieties available in Japan. Asian pears are a good source of vitamin C and fiber.

Common names and synonyms: Apple pear, Chinese pear, Japanese pear, *nashi,* Oriental pear, salad pear, sand pear.

Asiatic aubergine – *see* **EGGPLANT**
Asiatic yam – *see* **LESSER YAM, WATER YAM**
ASPARAGUS – A member of the lily family (which includes leeks, garlic, onions, and other relatives of the grasses), this perennial (*Asparagus officinalis*) was doubtless an important gathered food for our Stone Age ancestors. There are about 300 species of asparagus native to a region that extends from Siberia to southern Africa (and possibly species native to South America as well). Some, mostly of African origin, are poisonous and are grown only for ornamental purposes; these include the ubiquitous "asparagus fern" or "florist's fern." Wild asparagus

grows like a weed on English seacoasts, in the southern parts of eastern Europe, and on the steppes of the tundra, where horses and cattle graze on the vegetable. Asparagus has long been praised for both its culinary merit and its alleged medicinal properties, especially in the case of the kidneys. It has been cultivated since at least the time of the ancient Greeks and was a favorite of the Romans.

Asparagus can be green or white; the latter is the product of a method whereby soil is heaped on the growing stalks so as to block the sunlight necessary for chlorophyll production. White asparagus, with a stronger and somewhat more bitter flavor, is much more appreciated in Europe (especially in Spain and certain parts of France) and Argentina than in the United States, where commercial growers are mostly concerned with green asparagus. Although asparagus has a fairly short growing season in the United States, fresh spears can be purchased year-round because of South American production. France and Italy are also large producers. Frozen and canned asparagus is available, with the frozen close to the fresh in taste and nutritional value. The fresh green spears and green spears with white butts are frequently braised but are also excellent when steamed. Most canned asparagus is blanched white. Fresh asparagus has a large amount of vitamin C, although much can be lost during storage and preparation as well as during canning procedures. Asparagus is also high in vitamins A and E. Asparagus seeds have served as a substitute for coffee.

Common names and synonyms: Asparagus fern, florist's fern, garden asparagus, green asparagus, special bean, white asparagus, wild asparagus.

Asparagus bean – *see* **COWPEA, WINGED BEAN**
Asparagus broccoli – *see* **CALABRESE, CAULIFLOWER**
Asparagus lettuce – *see* **LETTUCE**
ASPARAGUS PEA – A native of southern Europe, the asparagus pea (*Lotus tetragonolobus*) is frequently confused with Africa's winged bean (*Psophocarpus tetragonolobus*) because of its winged pod. Asparagus peas are enjoyed as young edible pods that have an asparagus-like flavor and are prepared and served much like asparagus.

ASSAM AUR AUR – A native of Malaysia, and a fruit that has long grown wild in Southeast Asia, assam aur aur (*Garcinia hombroniana* Pierre) is now regarded as a candidate for cultivation as a specialty fruit. It is a close relative of the mangosteen, and its major culinary use involves its dried, crimson-colored rind – used as a relish in curries. In the past, the pulp of assam aur aur was fermented into a vinegar.

Assam – *see* **TEA**
Assfoot – *see* **COLTSFOOT**
ATEMOYA – A delicious dessert fruit that was created in the American tropics and subtropics, the atemoya (genus *Annona*) is a hybrid resulting from a

cross between the cherimoya and the sweetsop. The fruit, which grows on small trees, is cultivated in southern Florida, the West Indies, and Central and South America in the New World. It has spread to Australia, New Zealand, and the Philippines in Oceania and to India, Israel, and South Africa in the Old World. The fruit looks somewhat like an artichoke on the outside; inside, it is pudding-like, creamy, and sweet. The taste of the atemoya resembles that of vanilla custard. It is a fine source of vitamins C and K as well as potassium.

Aubergine - *see* **EGGPLANT**

Auguweed - *see* **BONESET**

Australian arrowroot - *see* **ACHIRA**

AUSTRALIAN BLUE SQUASH (*see also* **SQUASH AND PUMPKIN**) - Although all squashes and pumpkins have an American origin, the Australian Blue squash (*Cucurbita maxima*) was developed in Australia. Also called the Australian Queensland pumpkin, it looks like a blue-gray-green pumpkin that is flat on both ends. Its soft flesh and mild flavor contribute to its frequent use in soup and bread making.

Common names and synonyms: Australian Queensland pumpkin.

See in addition: "Squash," Part II, Section C, Chapter 8.

AUSTRALIAN CARROT - A wild, dark-rooted carrot - native to Australia - the Australian carrot (*Daucus glochidiatus*) belongs to the same genus as the common carrot, which is domesticated in much of the rest of the world. The Australian version of the vegetable was one of the many foods gathered by the Aborigines.

AUSTRALIAN CHESTNUT - Also known as the "Moreton Bay chestnut" and the "bean tree" (because its fruits come in long pods), this big, evergreen, leguminous tree belongs to the pea family. The Australian chestnut (*Castanospermum australe*) produces large brown seeds that have long been an important food for the Aborigines. Like true chestnuts, these seeds are generally roasted before consumption.

Common names and synonyms: Bean tree, Moreton Bay chestnut.

Australian corkscrew tree - *see* **SESBAN**

AUSTRALIAN CURRANT - A small tree or shrub, *Leucopogon richei* is native to Australia and has white, edible fruits. These were among the many gathered fruits that sustained the Aboriginal population.

Australian desert kumquat - *see* **AUSTRALIAN DESERT LIME**

AUSTRALIAN DESERT LIME - Also known as the Australian desert kumquat, the Australian desert lime (*Eremocitrus glauca*) is a fruit - related to the orange - that grows on a shrub (an Australian native) about 8 to 10 feet in height. The pale yellow fruits are egg shaped and are made into beverages, jams, and preserves.

Common names and synonyms: Australian desert kumquat.

Australian nut - *see* **MACADAMIA NUT**

Australian Queensland pumpkin - *see* **AUSTRALIAN BLUE SQUASH**

Autumn olive - *see* **ELAEAGNUS**

Avens - *see* **HERB BENNET**

AVOCADO - The avocado (*Persea americana*) apparently originated in Central America, where it was cultivated as many as 7,000 years ago. It was grown some 5,000 years ago in Mexico and, by the time of Christopher Columbus, had become a food as far south as Peru, where it is called *palta*. Legend has it that Hernando Cortés found avocados flourishing around what is now Mexico City in 1519. The English word "avocado" is derived from the Aztec *ahuacatl,* which the Spaniards passed along transliterated as *aguacate*. Other names for the avocado are "alligator pear" and "butter pear," probably because of its green, leathery rind and buttery-, nutty-tasting flesh. Avocados are classified into three races, Guatemalan, Mexican, and West Indian, among which the Mexican is the least popular. Avocados have been grown in California and Florida since the middle of the nineteenth century, and – although there are more than 20 varieties of avocados on the market – for North Americans, they basically fall into two categories: those from California (a Guatemalan–Mexican hybrid and others of the Guatemalan race) and those from Florida (the West Indian race). Among those from California are Bacon, Zuttano, and Fuerte, and especially the Hass variety (by far the most abundant and, many say, the best tasting), a darker, bumpy-skinned, and considerably smaller fruit than the green, smooth-skinned Florida kinds (such as Lulu, Booth, and Waldin), which can look like pale green melons. The Florida avocados are lower in fat and calories than those grown in California but also have less texture and taste. Because avocados (along with olives and coconuts) contain high amounts of oil (avocado oil is similar to olive oil), their green, white, or yellow flesh doubtless played an important role in the otherwise lowfat diets of pre-Columbian peoples. Indeed, a recipe for guacamole – mashed avocados with spices – comes to us from the Aztecs. The Spaniards ate avocados with sugar, salt, or both, and introduced them into other parts of the Americas as well as other tropical parts of the world. But until the end of World War II, avocados were virtually unknown in Europe. This is no longer the case, however, as advertising has paved the way for their entrance into European produce markets everywhere. Today, avocados are considered a "fruit-vegetable," meaning that they go with both fruit and vegetable salads, are great with poultry and pasta, and make a nice sandwich as well. Avocado orchards stretch from California to Florida and from the Caribbean to Peru in the Americas. Avocados are grown in West Africa, in the countries surrounding the Indian Ocean, and in Israel, which supplies much of the European demand. In addition to its fat content, the avocado is fairly high in beta-carotene, is poor in vitamin C, is high in the B vitamins, and delivers a number of minerals.

Common names and synonyms: Aguacate, *ahuacatl*, alligator pear, avocado pear, *avocat*, Bacon, Booth, butter pear, Fuerte, Guatemalan avocado, Hass, Lulu, Mexican avocado, *palta*, Waldin, West Indian avocado, Zuttano.

Avocado pear - *see* **AVOCADO**

Avocat - *see* **AVOCADO**

AZAROLE - Native to North Africa and the Middle East, the azarole tree (*Crataegus azarolus*) is also known as the "Spanish pine," and its fruit as the "Neapolitan medlar" - both names suggesting its popularity in the Latin countries. By contrast, the fruit reached England in 1640 but never caught on there or in northern Europe. Azarole fruits range from red to yellow in color, are about the size of a crab apple, and make excellent preserves and marmalade as well as wine. The tree's flowers were once used to make a liquor, and its young buds and leaves are ingredients in salads. Azarole fruits are high in vitamin C and the B complex.

Common names and synonyms: Neapolitan medlar, Spanish pine.

AZUKI BEAN (*see also* **BEANS**) - This small, red bean (*Phaseolus angularis* - also known as the adzuki bean) is almost square in shape. It is native to China, where - as in Japan and Korea as well - it is grown extensively. Azuki beans are mostly dried and prepared by boiling, but they are also available canned in many countries around the world. The beans are generally used in dessert dishes. They are made into a paste for stuffing pastries, and pureed, they become a part of ice cream.

Common names and synonyms: Adzuki bean.

See in addition: "Beans, Peas, and Lentils," Part II, Section C, Chapter 3.

B

BABACO (*see also* **PAPAYA**) - A native of Ecuador, the babaco (*Carica pentagona*) - a close relative of the papaya (*Carica papaya*) - is a cross between the mountain papaya (*C. pubescens*) and the chamburo (*C. stipulata*). We have, however, no idea of the antiquity of the fruit, which was discovered in the 1920s by European botanists. It is oblong in shape and has a yellowish green edible skin and pale yellow flesh. In the early 1970s, the fruit was introduced into New Zealand, where it has become yet another South American adoptee. Babaco is very high in vitamin C.

Babricorn bean - *see* **SWORD BEAN**

Bachang - *see* **HORSE MANGO**

Bachelor's-button - *see* **CORNFLOWER**

Bacon - *see* **AVOCADO**

Bactrian typha - *see* **MAIZE**

BACURÍ - A South American native, the bacurí (*Platonia esculenta* or *P. insignis*) is a yellow fruit that grows on a tall timber tree. A relative of the mangosteen, the fruit has creamy, white, and sweet flesh. The bacurí is commercially grown - and rather intensively so - in the Amazon Basin.

Common names and synonyms: Bacury, bakuri.

BACURIPARI - A small tree, native to the Amazon region of South America, the bacuripari (*Rheedia macrophylla*) produces a fruit of the same name that is somewhat like the mangosteen, a close relative. Its flesh is white and creamy, with a fine flavor, quite similar to that of the bacurí.

Bacury - *see* **BACURÍ**

Badian anise - *see* **STAR-ANISE**

BAEL FRUIT - Also known as the "bel-fruit" and "Bengal quince," the bael fruit grows on the bael tree (*Aegle marmelos*), a native of India that is now grown throughout much of South and Southeast Asia. The tree reaches about 40 feet in height, and its fruits are generally about 2 to 5 inches across. The Portuguese called them *marmelos* because they have the flavor of marmalade and can be eaten raw. Bael fruits are also used to make a refreshing beverage.

Common names and synonyms: Bael tree, bel-fruit, Bengal quince, Indian bael, *marmelo*.

Bahama whitewood - *see* **WHITE CINNAMON**

Bajra - *see* **MILLET**

Bakeberry - *see* **CLOUDBERRY**

Baked-apple berry - *see* **CLOUDBERRY**

BAKUPARI - Also known as *pacura*, the bakupari (*Rheedia brasiliensis*) is a Brazilian tree that produces an edible, orange-colored fruit with snow-white flesh. The fruit is slightly acid and is eaten out of hand as well as made into jellies and jams.

Common names and synonyms: Pacura.

Bakuri - *see* **BACURÍ**

BALANITES - Members of *Balanites*, a small genus of Old World tropical trees that is part of the family Zygophyllaceae, are cultivated from Africa to Burma for the acorn-like drupes they produce. The nuts are sometimes used for food but are mostly employed for the production of an oil used in cooking.

Balata - *see* **MIMUSOPS**

Balazo - *see* **MONSTERA**

Balloonberry - *see* **STRAWBERRY-RASPBERRY**

Balm mint - *see* **LEMON BALM**

Balm-of-Gilead tree - *see* **BALSAM FIR**

BALSAM APPLE - A tropical vine, native to the Old World, the balsam apple (*Momordica balsamina*) has yellow flowers and a warty, orange fruit that is eaten raw, boiled, and fried. Also called the "wonder apple," it grows in the tropics of India, New Guinea, and the Philippine Islands.

Common names and synonyms: Wonder apple.

BALSAM FIR - A North American tree that provides an inner bark once used by Native Americans for food, the balsam fir (*Abies balsamea*) is also known as the "Canada balsam" and the "balm-of-Giliad tree." The balsam or pith was also eaten, but the bark - often used to make a kind of bread - was so important to some tribes that it could almost be called a staple.

Common names and synonyms: Balm-of-Giliad tree, Canada balsam.

Balsam herb - *see* **COSTMARY**

Balsam pear - *see* **BITTER MELON**

BAMBARA GROUNDNUT (*see also* **LEGUMES**) - This leguminous plant (*Voandzeia subterranea* or *Vigna subterranea*) develops underground, nutlike fruits. Similar to peanuts, the fruits are encased in pods and are rich in starch and protein. Grown in the arid lands of Africa, Asia, and South America, they are most popular in Zambia and Madagascar. Bambara groundnuts are eaten fresh or boiled and have a taste similar to peas. They are also dried, ground into flour, and used for baking.

Common names and synonyms: Bambarra, Bambarra nut, Congo goober, ground pea, voandzou.

Bambarra nut - *see* **BAMBARA GROUNDNUT**

Bamboo - *see* **BAMBOO SHOOT(S), WATER BAMBOO**

BAMBOO SHOOT(S) - Plants of the bamboo tribe (*Bambusaceae*) are among the tallest of the grass family, occasionally reaching heights of 100 feet. Bamboo "shoots" are their young stems. Bamboo plants and their shoots are native to the warmest parts of Africa, the Americas, and, of course, Asia. As any zoo aficionado knows, these are the favorite (and practically the only) food of China's pandas. Bamboo is also important in the cuisines of Asia's humans, who add the shoots to dishes for a crunchy texture and also pickle and candy them. Outside of Asia, the shoots are generally available only in canned form, although they can be found in some Asian-style markets. Fresh bamboo shoots deliver good amounts of thiamine, potassium, and vitamin B_6, but the canning process robs them of most of their nutrients.

Common names and synonyms: Takenoko, tung sun.

Bamia - *see* **OKRA**

BANANA (*see also* **BANANA FLOWER, ENSETE, PLANTAIN**) - The various forms of the banana (*Musa paradisiaca*) are probably native to South and Southeast Asia and doubtless helped feed hunter-gatherers for hundreds of thousands of years. The banana is among the oldest plants that humans have used, was one of the first to be cultivated, and today constitutes one of the most important food crops in the world. The identity of the exact homeland of the banana has been blurred by the plant's ability to spread rapidly throughout the tropics. By way of an example, when bananas reached the tropical New World (apparently with Spanish explorers), they propagated with such rapidity that some of the earliest chroniclers thought that the fruit was an American native. And bananas apparently reached tropical Africa and Polynesia much earlier (c. A.D. 500 and 1000, respectively) than they did the New World.

The banana "tree" is really a giant herb that can grow to 20 or more feet in height in only a year, even though it sprouts from a rhizome or corm. Suckers rise in clumps from the rhizome and, as they grow, form groups of flowers that can become bunches (called "hands") of bananas. One "hand" may consist of as many as 400 bananas, but that is all the plant will ever produce; after producing one bunch, it dies, although another sucker may grow from the rhizome to take its place. Bananas did not become commercially important for export until the nineteenth century (with the advent of refrigerated ships), and today Brazil is the biggest exporter and the United States the biggest importer of the fruit. But most bananas - about 80 percent - are consumed in their respective African, Asian, Caribbean, or Central and South American regions of production, where the fruit is often an important staple food.

Bananas - with some 200 varieties - come in different shapes, sizes, and colors. *Manzanos* (also called finger or apple bananas) are about the length of a finger and turn from yellow to black when ripe. Saba and Brazilian bananas are medium-sized, tart, and straight rather than curved, whereas red bananas are sweeter. The Cavendish, with its color ranging from green through yellow to black (indicating its degree of ripeness), is the banana most commonly encountered in the produce markets of North America. Other common varieties are the Martinique, the Jamaica, the Gros Michel, and the Bluefield. Bananas can be baked, fried, and grilled, although roughly one-half of those produced are simply peeled and eaten out of hand. Bananas are easily digestible, can be used at various stages of ripeness, and are an excellent source of carbohydrates, potassium, and vitamins A and C.

Common names and synonyms: Apple banana, Bluefield, Brazilian banana, Cavendish, dwarf banana, finger banana, Gros Michel, Jamaica, *manzano,* Martinique, *pisong jacki,* red banana, Saba, Silk Fig.

See in addition: "Bananas and Plantains," Part II, Section B, Chapter 1.

Banana chilli - *see* **WAX PEPPERS**

Banana de brejo - *see* **MONSTERA**

BANANA FLOWER (*see also* **BANANA**) - The banana fruit is not the only edible part of the banana plant (*Musa paradisiaca*). The male flowers - the compact, purple, pointed heads at the end of a forming bunch of bananas - are also eaten, often on the site where the bananas are grown. They are used as a vegetable and garnish in the countries of Southeast Asia, where they are available in local markets.

Common names and synonyms: Banana blossom, banana bract, banana bud, banana heart(s), *jantung pisang,* Silk Fig.

See in addition: "Bananas and Plantains," Part II, Section B, Chapter 1.

Banana heart(s) - *see* **BANANA FLOWER**

Banana pepper - *see* **WAX PEPPERS**

BANANA SQUASH (*see also* **SQUASH AND PUMPKIN**) - A sometimes huge squash, weighing upward of 30 pounds, the banana squash (*Cucurbita maxima*) is often sold in smaller pieces at produce counters. It is perhaps the most bland of this American species that was domesticated in South America. The banana squash has an orange flesh that is high in beta-carotene as well as vitamin C.

See in addition: "Squash," Part II, Section C, Chapter 8.

BAOBAB - A huge tree, native to tropical Africa, the baobob (*Adansonia digitata*) is famous for its trunk, which often reaches 30 feet in diameter. Also grown in India, the tree has an edible-fleshed fruit sometimes called "monkey-bread." The fruit is about 9 inches in length, oval, and hard-shelled, and has a fibrous, floury white pulp. Its juice is also consumed - after sweetening - and in the past was used to treat tropical fevers. The leaves of the tree are eaten as a vegetable.

Common names and synonyms: Monkey-bread.

Barbados cherry - *see* **ACEROLA**

Barbados eddoe - *see* **COCOYAM**

BARBADOS GOOSEBERRY (*see also* **BERRIES**) - A member of the large cactus family, the Barbados gooseberry (*Pereskia aculeata*) is native to the West Indies. Its edible yellow fruit resembles the gooseberry in appearance and has a fine taste. Also called the "lemon vine," this cactus has leaves that are edible as well; they are usually consumed raw.

Common names and synonyms: Leafy cactus, lemon vine.

Barbary fig - *see* **PRICKLY PEAR**

Barbe de capucin - *see* **CHICORY**

BARBERRY (*see also* **BERRIES**) - There are numerous different species of shrubs of the genus *Berberis* that bear small orange or red berries similar to currants. They can be found in Asia, Europe, North Africa, and North and South America, growing best where there is plenty of sunlight. A very popular barberry is *B. thunbergii,* a native of Japan, and there are other popular varieties native to Korea and Japan. In France, famous jams are made from the seedless barberry. The bright red berries ripen in the fall in North America and are especially abundant in New England. In the western United States, the barberry is called the "wild Oregon grape," or just "Oregon grape." The berries are generally very tart and are the basis of fine jellies and preserves. They were doubtless another food employed by hunting-and-gathering Native Americans, as were barberry leaves, which go nicely in salads and can be cooked as a vegetable.

Common names and synonyms: California barberry, holly-leaved barberry, Oregon grape, pepperidge, Rocky Mountain grape, seedless barberry, trailing mahonia, wild Oregon grape.

BARLEY (*see also* **WILD BARLEY**) - Barley (*Hordeum vulgare*) originated in western Asia, and, as our hunter–gatherer ancestors settled into sedentary agriculture during the Neolithic Revolution, it became one of the first grains to be cultivated. This grain has the advantage of a relatively short growing season and - because it matures quickly - has adapted to a considerable variety of environments. Barley was important in early Egypt and China but was displaced by wheat in ancient Rome. Like rye, it became a staple in northern Europe during the Middle Ages. Barley has also long been a source of drink as well as food. Malt is made from barley by soaking the seeds until they sprout. In the process, the proteins in the bran change into enzymes that convert starches - first into sugars and then into alcohol. As with other grains, barley is refined by milling to the point that many nutrients are stripped away. Pearl barley, for example, has had the entire outer husk removed. Pot or Scotch barley is much less refined and is good in soups. Barley flakes and grits are used in breakfast cereals. Barley has a nutlike flavor, is high in carbohydrates, and contains phosphorus, calcium, and some of the B-vitamin complex. In North America and Europe, most barley either is used for the production of beer, ale, and whiskey or becomes feed for animals. But in less-developed countries, such as many of those in Africa, barley is still an important part of the human diet, and it remains a staple in the Middle East.

Common names and synonyms: Barleycorn, barley flakes, barley grits, malt, naked barley, pearl barley, pot barley, Scotch barley, six-row barley, two-row barley.

See in addition: "Barley," Part II, Section A, Chapter 2; "Beer and Ale," Part III, Chapter 1.

BARREL CACTUS - There is some taxonomical dispute concerning the genera of these two cacti (*Ferocactus wislizenii* and *Echinocactus,* especially *E. grandis*) known as "barrel cactus." They are also called "visnaga." Both are natives of the southwestern United States. The barrel cacti provided stem pulp that served as food for Native Americans, as did their fruits.

Common names and synonyms: Fish-hook cactus, southwestern barrel cactus, visnaga.

Basil - An herb that is part of the mint family, is native to India (and possibly Africa as well), and is known as the tomato's best friend, basil (*Ocimum basilicum = O. americanum*) comes in many types - and more than a few colors - that are now distributed worldwide. Closing in on becoming the world's most popular herb, basil was virtually unknown outside of Europe 30 years ago. It is sometimes classified as either "sweet basil" or "bush basil." Sweet basil has a larger leaf that is more aromatic and flavorful. Bush basil (*Satureja vulgaris* or *Ocimum minimum* - also called "wild basil"), although native to the Old World, is widely naturalized in the Americas. Basil was used by the ancient Greeks, and the Greek word *basilikon,* meaning "royal," perhaps suggests that the herb was reserved for royalty. The Romans spread the herb around Europe, where basil's heart-shaped and aromatic leaves have long been a favorite of the Italians and the Provençals - indeed, in Italy the leaves are considered symbols of love. Basil is best fresh, is often used in soups and pâtés, is vital to Italian pesto, and is a natural companion for tomatoes in sauces and salads. Dried basil does not retain the same delicate flavor as the fresh leaves, but it is frequently added to sauces nonetheless. Many people preserve their fresh leaves in olive oil in a tightly sealed jar. Basil is also employed to flavor the liqueur Chartreuse.

Common names and synonyms: Basilic common, *basilico,* bush basil, sweet basil, wild basil.

See also: "Spices and Flavorings," Part II, Section F, Chapter 1.

Basilic common - *see* **BASIL**

Basilico - *see* **BASIL**

Basswood - *see* **AMERICAN LINDEN**

Batata dulce - *see* **SWEET POTATO**

Batavian endive - *see* **ENDIVE AND ESCAROLE**

BAYBERRY (*see also* **BERRIES**) - The shrubs *Myrica pensylvanica* and *M. cerifera* are North American plants that produce gray, waxy berries, which have historically been melted down into wax for candles. Bayberry leaves, however, have culinary applications. They are pickled and dried for use as a less pungent bay leaf in soups, stews, and the like.

Bay laurel - *see* **BAY LEAF**

BAY LEAF - The aromatic leaves of the bay laurel tree (*Laurus nobilis*) are regarded by many as an indispensable flavoring herb in the kitchen. The leaves come from a small evergreen that apparently was a native of Asia Minor but has been scenting the air of the Mediterranean region for so long that it is also thought of as native there. Indeed, the Romans used laurel leaves for fashioning garlands to honor soldiers, athletes, and poets - hence the term "laureate," which still persists to indicate preeminence. In earlier times, the laurel leaf also had a reputation for warding off evil. Aromatic bay leaves are among the most versatile herbs used in Mediterranean cooking and, in fact, are popular in most cuisines throughout the world. If used fresh, they are first crumbled; if dried, they can be used either whole, crumbled, or ground. Bay leaves are good (often with thyme) in almost any soup, stew, sauce, or meat dish (including pâtés) and are one of the principal ingredients in a bouquet garni. They are also important in pickling and are added to vinegars, marinades, and puddings. Laurel leaves are now produced in areas of North Africa and North America as well as in their traditional regions of cultivation.

Common names and synonyms: Bay laurel, Grecian laurel, laurel, sweet bay, sweet laurel.

See also: "Spices and Flavorings," Part II, Section F, Chapter 1.

BEACH PEA (*see also* **LEGUMES**) - A number of the fruits of the leguminous plants of the genus *Lathyrus* were used for food in the past by hunter-gatherers. Along the coasts of North America - including those of the Great Lakes - the immature seeds of the beach pea (*L. maritimus*) were eaten like sweet peas, and ripe ones were ground into a flour. The inflorescences of the sweet pea (*L. odoratus*), a popular garden flower originally from the Mediterranean region, may also have served as food in the past. Today, the plant is grown commercially for its flowers, which yield an essential oil used in perfumes. Other species have been used as food by Europeans and Asians over many millennia.

Common names and synonyms: Sweet pea.

See in addition: "Beans, Peas, and Lentils," Part II, Section C, Chapter 3.

BEACH PLUM (*see also* **PLUM**) - The beach plum (*Prunus maritima*) is a seacoast shrub that bears an edible plumlike fruit. This plant ranges along the east coast of North America from the province of New Brunswick in Canada to as far south as Virginia. It is a strange plant that frequents only seemingly infertile areas like sand dunes, and its fruit, which ranges from red and purple to yellow, can be sweet and delicious or so tart as to be inedible. The beach plum is used mostly for making a jelly that goes well with duck and venison.

Common names and synonyms: Shore plum.

Beaked hazel - *see* **HAZELNUT AND FILBERT**

Bean tree - *see* **AUSTRALIAN CHESTNUT**

BEANS (*see also* the various bean entries) - Beans were among the first (and most important) foods to be gathered. In Afghanistan, the Himalayan foothills, and central Asia, *Vicia faba* - the fava bean, broad bean, or Windsor bean - was food for hunter-gatherers tens of thousands of years ago, as was *Cicer arietinum* (the chickpea or garbanzo) - in western Asia. These were gradually brought under cultivation in an area encompassing much of Asia, the Middle East, and Egypt and had become staples in the diets of many long before the ancient Greeks employed them as counters for balloting. The Phoenicians are credited with carrying the chickpea to the western end of Europe, where "garbanzos" became entrenched in the diet of the Iberians and have continued as an important staple to this day. Moreover, in prehistoric times, three species of the genus *Lupinus* were brought under cultivation in the Mediterranean region and later embraced enthusiastically by the Greeks and Romans. These were the white lupine (*L. albus*), the blue lupine

(*L. angustifolius*), and the European yellow lupine (*L. luteus*). In addition to their splendid pink-and-blue flowers, lupines provide very nourishing seeds, but around the time of the Renaissance they began their disappearance from culinary use. To this day, however, large lupine seeds are preserved in brine by many peoples of the Mediterranean, who simultaneously strip them of their thick skins and pop them in the mouth, eating them as a snack.

Meanwhile, in the New World, a vast range of beans of the genus *Phaseolus* had, as in Europe, initially been gathered and later brought under cultivation. The first species to be domesticated was the common bean (*P. vulgaris*), which archaeological evidence from the Peruvian Andes suggests occurred about 8,000 years ago (findings from the Tehuacán Valley in central Mexico indicate domestication there about 1,000 years later). Varieties of the common bean were subsequently cultivated from southern South America to as far north as the St. Lawrence River. Among them were seeds we know today as turtle beans (black beans), kidney beans (including the white cannellini), Lamon beans, chili beans, cranberry beans, pinto beans, red beans, "great northern" beans, string (snap) beans, Romano (Italian green) beans, flageolets, and other round white beans ranging from the large marrow bean to the small pea or navy bean.

A second New World species is *P. lunatus,* comprised of the lima and sieva beans and so called because of the lunar – actually half-moon – shape of the seeds of some varieties. Archaeological evidence shows that, like common beans, lima beans (named after Peru's capital city) were in use in the Andean highlands some 8,000 years ago. However, they do not appear in the archaeological record of Mexico. The smaller sieva beans, by contrast, were apparently never in Peru but were grown in Mexico about 1,200 years ago, all of which has prompted the conclusion that the two varieties had a common ancestor but were domesticated independently by Andean and Mesoamerican farmers. In Peru, there is much evidence to indicate that lima beans were playing a major role in the diet 5,000 years ago. Today, the large lima beans are called "Fordhooks" or "butter beans," and the smaller sievas are called "baby limas." Other names for members of *P. lunatus* are "Madagascar bean" and "Towe bean."

The scarlet runner (*P. coccineus*), today often grown as an ornamental climber in the United States (but much appreciated at the table in Great Britain), is the third New World species. These beans were gathered about 9,000 years ago and were cultivated in Mexico at least 1,500 years ago (there is disagreement as to whether pods dating from about 4000 B.C. were gathered in the wild or were domesticated). Both the purple-seeded and white-seeded varieties are frequently cultivated

around poles (thus, "pole beans") to keep them from "running."

The fourth New World species of bean is the now obscure tepary bean (*P. acutifolius*). Of the four species, this one had the northernmost area of origin: Central Mexico, where teparies were cultivated about 5,000 years ago, and what is now the U.S. Southwest, which they reached by about 1,200 years ago. Apparently, the major use of teparies was to grind them into flour for more or less "instant" bean dishes.

The American beans began to travel after the arrival of the Iberians in the Americas. In the Far East, their reception was lukewarm because of local favorites such as the azuki bean (*P. angularis*), the mung bean (*P. aureus*), the cowpea (*Vigna unguiculata*), and, of course, the soybean (*Glycine max*) – today the most widely consumed bean in the world. Similarly, the West Africans had their own beans, such as the cowpea or black-eyed pea (actually a bean), and the winged bean (*Psophocarpus tetragonolobus*). But the American beans found ready acceptance in East Africa and in almost all of Europe.

Experimentation in bean breeding in Europe has produced considerable confusion. Native Americans probably consumed some beans as immature pods despite their stringiness, but the beans' major use was in the dried form, which was easily stored. The Europeans, however, sorted through the American beans and selected (and developed) many for use as snap beans. Thus, when the Europeans settled North America, they brought American beans back to their home hemisphere, but the green pods had become "French" beans – presumably because the French had given American beans the name *haricot*. In France, any bean of the genus *Phaseolus* is called an *haricot* whether fresh or dried, but in England "haricot" generally means a dried bean, whereas fresh pods are called French or green beans. Much breeding has finally removed the strings from string beans so that now they are known as "snap" beans, a category that includes green snap beans, green haricots, the Romano bean, the wax bean (the common name for the yellow snap bean), the purple wax bean, pole beans, scarlet runners, and even cowpeas when immature.

Some of the world's great dishes are based on beans. Among the first were the succotash of the Native Americans and the various "fabadas" (stews and soups made with fava beans) of Europe. Then there is the *cassoulet* of France, the *feijoada* of Brazil, the chile con carne of Texas, the "hoppin' John" of the U.S. South (and the three-bean salad of the United States in general), the hummus of the Middle East, the minestrone of Italy, the refried beans of Mexico, and, of course, Boston baked beans.

Beans are nitrogen-fixing, which means that when the plants are plowed under they become "green manure." Indeed, when beans are planted in rotation with wheat and barley, almost no fertilizer is required. Beans are cholesterol-free and high in vitamins, minerals, and soluble fiber. Long called "poor-man's-meat," they are also very high in protein.

Common names and synonyms: Azuki bean, baby lima, black bean, black-eyed bean, black-eyed pea, blue lupine, broad bean, butter bean, cannellini, chickpea, chile bean, chili bean, common bean, cowpea, cranberry bean, European yellow lupine, *faba,* fava, flageolet, Fordhook, French bean, *garbanzo,* great northern bean, green bean, green haricot, green snap bean, *haricot,* Italian green bean, kidney bean, Lamon bean, lima bean, lupine, Madagascar bean, marrow bean, mung bean, navy bean, pea bean, pinto bean, pole bean, poor-man's-meat, purple-seeded pole bean, purple-seeded scarlet runner, purple wax bean, red bean, Romano bean, scarlet runner, sieva bean, snap bean, string bean, tepary bean, Towe bean, turtle bean, wax bean, white bean, white cannellini, white lupine, white-seeded pole bean, white-seeded scarlet runner, Windsor bean, winged bean, yellow lupine, yellow snap bean.

See in addition: "Beans, Peas, and Lentils," Part II, Section C, Chapter 3; "Soybean," Part II, Section E, Chapter 5.

BEAN SPROUTS (*see also* **BEANS, MUNG BEAN, SOYBEAN**) - Typically from mung beans (*Phaseolus aureus*) or soybeans (*Glycine max*), the early shoots of these plants are widely used in Asian cooking. The 1- to 2-inch-long sprouts are tender and rich in vitamin C. They are usually eaten raw, although they can be lightly cooked and still retain their nutritive value.

See in addition: "Beans, Peas, and Lentils," Part II, Section C, Chapter 3; "Soybean," Part II, Section E, Chapter 5.

BEARBERRY (*see also* **BERRIES, HEATHER**) - Also known as "kinnikinnick" and "crowberry," the red bearberry comes from several North American shrubs (genus *Arctostaphylos*) that have small evergreen leaves and white or pink flowers. The eastern black bear is said to be fond of them, and they were among the many wild foods gathered by Native Americans.

Common names and synonyms: Crowberry, kinnikinnic, kinnikinnick.

Bearss - *see* **LEMON**

Bear's-weed - *see* **YERBA SANTA**

BEE BALM (*see also* **BERGAMOT**) - There is considerable confusion surrounding bee balm, balm, and melissa. Balm is a Eurasian native known as *Melissa officinalis* or melissa, from the Latin and Greek meaning "bee" and from "honey" or *meli* (consider the word "mellifluous") - the whole suggestive of the attraction that the flowers of this plant have for bees. Confusion began with one of the early Spaniards in the New World, Nicolas Monardes, a physician and naturalist, who seems to have been the first European to describe a close relative,

Monarda didyma, an American native that was subsequently named for him. This plant is called bergamot but is very commonly named bee balm and melissa as well - hence the confusion. Both plants are sweet, herbal members of the mint family. In the case of the American native (the Eurasian cousin is now naturalized in North America), the leaves were used by the Oswego Indians to make a kind of tea, and when rebellious North American colonists could no longer obtain tea through British channels, they copied the Indians in making what they called "Oswego tea." In the case of the Eurasian plant, it is still used today to flavor liqueurs such as Benedictine and Chartreuse. The leaves of both "bee balms" are also used fresh and dried to flavor pork dishes, cooked vegetables, salads, stews, and poultry.

Common names and synonyms: American horsemint, balm, bee herb, bergamot, garden balm, horsemint, melissa, Oswego tea, wild bee balm.

Beech mast - *see* **BEECHNUT**

BEECHNUT - Beech trees (genus *Fagus*) belong to the family that also includes oak and chestnut trees. Their bark is smooth, light colored, and easily scratched or carved upon; consequently, the European beech (*F. sylvatica*), in particular, served as a "bulletin board" for eons prior to the advent of paper. In Europe, beechnuts (referred to as "mast" or "beech mast") were employed - historically as well as today - in fattening hogs and for oil. During both of the twentieth-century world wars, however, beechnuts were used extensively by humans as a survival food. The American beech (*F. grandifolia*) is native to the eastern part of the United States, where many consider its nut to be among the best tasting of all. The flavor of this small nut is somewhere between that of chestnuts and hazelnuts. It can be eaten raw and is also often roasted, made into nut "butter," and pressed to yield a fine oil. It is interesting to note that the nuts produced by certain kinds of oak trees are technically known as beechnuts rather than acorns.

Common names and synonyms: American beech, beech mast, European beech, mast.

Beech wheat - *see* **BUCKWHEAT**

Beefsteak fungus - *see* **MUSHROOMS AND FUNGI**

BEEFSTEAK PLANT - Also called *shiso* by the Japanese, the beefsteak plant (*Perilla arguts*) - a member of the mint family - is native to Burma, China, and the Himalaya Mountains. Both the red and green varieties are cultivated for garnishes, sprouts, and use as a vegetable.

Common names and synonyms: Shiso.

Beef tongue - *see* **MUSHROOMS AND FUNGI**

Bee herb - *see* **BEE BALM, LEMON BALM**

BEET (*see also* **MANGELWURZEL, SWISS CHARD**) - All of today's beets are descended from a wild forebear whose green tops doubtless nourished our own prehistoric forebears. Indeed, the first cultivated beets were apparently tended only for their leaves (eaten like spinach), and it was not until the early Christian era that their roots became appreciated. The commercially most important descendant of the wild beet (*Beta maritima*) is the European sugar beet (*B. vulgaris* L. ssp.), which was developed to produce sugar and became a serious competitor of sugarcane in the nineteenth century. However, the red, yellow, and white edible roots of some of the other native European *B. vulgaris* varieties (beetroots as they are called in the United Kingdom) find their way to the dinner table. The red garden beet, essential to borscht, is also the ingredient of the famous Harvard beets dish (named and perhaps created because of the university's crimson colors) and is prominent as a pickled vegetable as well. In much of Europe, however, the yellow variety has historically been prized because of a sweeter taste and greater suitability for pickling. The white-rooted beet is important for its leaves and stalks, which can be put to use as substitutes for, respectively, spinach and asparagus. Still another beet, the mangelwurzel, with a very large bulb, is employed as animal fodder. Unfortunately, many (especially middle- and upper-class Europeans) feel that *all* beets are essentially animal food – or, at best, peasant food. Beet greens are a source of riboflavin, iron, and vitamins A and C. The roots are high in folacin and vitamin C. Beets are available fresh, pickled, and canned.

Common names and synonyms: Beetroot, chad, chard, European sugar beet, garden beet, Harvard beet, mangel, mangelwurzel, red beet, red-beet leaf, red garden beet, spinach beet, sugar beet, Swiss chard, white-rooted beet, wild beet, yellow beet.

Beetle-bung - *see* **BLACK GUM**
Beggar's-button(s) - *see* **BURDOCK**
Beldobes - *see* **QUELITES**
Bel-fruit - *see* **BAEL FRUIT**
BELGIAN ENDIVE (*see also* **CHICORY**) – Also called "French endive," Belgian endive (*Cichorium endivia*) is known in Europe as *witloof* and is a relative of both escarole and chicory. It is a smooth, pale, elongated, and slightly bitter vegetable, which has been forced from roots that have been covered with soil and kept in darkness – hence its pale color. Belgian endive is used in salads and is braised as a vegetable.

Common names and synonyms: French endive, red Belgian endive, white endive, *witloof.*

BELIMBING – A relative of carambola, the belimbing (*Averrhoa bilimbi*) is also known as the "sour finger carambola" and the "cucumber tree." The fruit is light green to yellow in color, about 3 inches in length, and is much like a small, unripe mango in appearance. It is much too sour to eat raw, and in Malaysia, Thailand, Indonesia, and the Philippines, it is stewed and added to curries to impart a sour taste. Belimbings are very high in vitamin C.

Common names and synonyms: Bilimbi, blimbling, cucumber tree, sour finger carambola.

Beli Pinot - *see* **PINOT BLANC**
Bellflower - *see* **CAMPANULA**
Bell pepper - *see* **SWEET PEPPERS**
Bendi - *see* **OKRA**
Bengal bean - *see* **PIGEON PEA**
Bengal gram - *see* **CHICKPEA**
Bengal grass - *see* **MILLET**
Bengal quince - *see* **BAEL FRUIT**
Benne - *see* **SESAME**
Ben(n)iseed - *see* **SESAME**
Benjamin bush - *see* **SPICEBUSH**
BENOIL TREE – Although originally native to the Indian subcontinent, benoil trees (*Moringa oleifera* and *M. pterygosperma*) are now found throughout the Old World tropics. The leaves and roots of this tree taste like horseradish and, chopped up and mixed with water or milk, are made into a sauce that is thought to aid digestion. The seeds yield an oil that is used for industrial purposes and also contain a sweetening substance. In short, virtually all parts of this tree are eaten or used in some way. The young seedpods – long and slender like drumsticks, and probably the source of the nickname "drumstick tree" – are eaten as a vegetable or used in curries. The roots may easily substitute for horseradish. The leaves – perhaps one of the richest sources of calcium in the plant world, and rich as well in vitamins, minerals, and proteins – are cooked and served as a vegetable and are also used as a flavoring and an animal feed.

Common names and synonyms: Drumstick tree, drumstick vegetable, horseradish tree, moringa nut.

Ber - *see* **DESERT APPLE**
BERGAMOT (*see also* **BEE BALM**) – The fruit called bergamot fruit comes from a small spiny tree (*Citrus bergamia*). It is called the bergamot orange, or mellarosa, and is halfway between an orange and a lemon. It is sour, and its leaves, flowers, and pear-shaped fruits are used mostly in perfumery. However, the oils from the rind are also employed in flavoring liqueurs, and the fruit goes into an Italian preserve, *mostarde di frutta.* The bergamot orange is grown mostly in the southern Italian province of Calabria.

Another plant called bergamot is wild bergamot, a name given to the leaves of any of several American plants of the genus *Monarda*. These are also known as "bee balm" and "American horsemint" and are made into tea.

Common names and synonyms: American horsemint, bee balm, bergamot herb, bergamot orange, horsemint, mellarosa, wild bergamot.

Bergamot lemon - *see* **LEMON**
Bergamot orange - *see* **ORANGE**
BERRIES (*see also* the various berry entries) – Berries were, arguably, among the very first human foods. Certainly they were a sweet seasonal staple

for our hunting-and-gathering ancestors for scores of millennia. And at some point in the past, humans learned to dry them and store them for use in the winter, to make them into various kinds of preserves, and to mix them with meats and fats to become pemmican, as did the Native Americans. Wild berry gathering remains a popular activity in Europe as well as North America, but most berries encountered in stores have been cultivated. There are several species of blackberries and raspberries (with segmented fruits) belonging to the genus *Rubus,* some of which have been cultivated since the seventeenth century or so. Smooth-skinned blueberries and cranberries are members of the genus *Vaccinium* that have been cultivated commercially for a century or more in the United States. Strawberries (*Fragaria* species), of course, are the most popular berries and are widely cultivated, as are currants (genus *Ribes*). Most berries are very rich in vitamin C and potassium. Berries come fresh, frozen, canned, and in some cases (for example, that of cranberries) as a juice.

BETEL NUT – The orange- to scarlet-colored fruit of a palm that is native to tropical Asia, betel nut (*Areca catechu*) is processed by boiling and drying, then mixed with betel leaves and lime and chewed by many people for its slight narcotic effect. Those who chew it believe that betel nut sweetens the breath, strengthens the gums, and promotes digestion.

Common names and synonyms: Areca, areca nut palm, betel(nut) palm, *catechu, pinang.*

Betel(nut) palm – *see* **BETEL NUT**
Bhindee – *see* **OKRA**
Bhindi – *see* **OKRA**
Bible leaf – *see* **COSTMARY**
Bible-leaf mace – *see* **COSTMARY**
Bigarade – *see* **ORANGE**
Bigarreau – *see* **CHERRY**
BIG GREEN PLUM (*see also* **PLUM**) – Known also as the wild plum, the big green plum (*Planchonella pohlmaniana*) is an edible fruit of Australia and one of the many that sustained its hunting-and-gathering Aboriginal population over millennia.

Common names and synonyms: Great green plum, wild plum.

BIG-LEAFED HYDRANGEA – A native of China, the deciduous shrub *Hydrangea macrophylla* is the ancestor of most of our garden hydrangeas. Its dried rhizomes and roots have been used as both a food and a medicine.

BIGNAY – Also called *buni,* "Chinese laurel," and "salamander tree," the bignay (*Antidesma bunius*) is a small tree – native to Australia and India – that is widely cultivated in Indonesia for its red and somewhat sour fruits (about half an inch in diameter) that grow in clusters. They are eaten raw as well as made into preserves, jellies, and syrups. They are also used to flavor brandies, and to make a sauce for fish.

Common names and synonyms: Buni, Chinese laurel, salamander tree.

Bija – *see* **ANNATTO**
Bijol – *see* **ANNATTO**
BILBERRY (*see also* **BERRIES**) – A European relative of the blueberry, the bilberry (*Vaccinium myrtillus* – also known as the whortleberry in Europe) seems its identical twin (the Australians call bilberries blueberries), save that they have differently shaped flowers and that the bilberry is a bit darker than the blueberry. Perhaps the result of a natural hybridization, the bilberry is the focus of northern European berry pickers as well as their counterparts in northern North America during the summer and fall months. But it also grows in California and the American Southwest, where it is wrongly called huckleberry as well as blueberry. Bilberries were an important food for many Native American tribes.

Common names and synonyms: Blueberry, huckleberry, *myrtille,* whortleberry, windberry.

Bilimbi – *see* **BELIMBING, CARAMBOLA**
Billion-dollar grass – *see* **JAPANESE MILLET**
Bilsted – *see* **SWEET GUM**
Bindi – *see* **OKRA**
Bindweed – *see* **ROUGH BINDWEED**
Bird chilli – *see* **ASIAN CHILLIES**
Bird pepper – *see* **BRAZILIAN MALAGUETA, TEPÍN CHILLIES AND RELATIVES**
Bird's-beak – *see* **CAYENNE PEPPER**
Bird's-eye – *see* **ASIAN CHILLIES**
Bird vetch – *see* **TUFTED VETCH**
BIRIBÁ – Native to northern South America and the West Indies, the biribá (*Rollinia deliciosa*) grows on a small tree and is most appreciated in northern Brazil, where it is grown commercially. It is a round, yellow, sweet, and juicy fruit that can weigh up to 3 pounds when mature. It is consumed fresh and made into juice.

Birthroot – *see* **TRILLIUM**
Bishop's-weed – *see* **AJOWAN**
Bistort – *see* **KNOTWEED AND SMARTWEED**
Bitter button(s) – *see* **TANSY**
Bitter cucumber – *see* **BITTER MELON**
Bitter gallberry – *see* **WINTERBERRY**
Bitter gourd – *see* **BITTER MELON**
BITTER MELON (*see also* **MELON**) – The fruit of a tropical vine, which is also known as "bitter cucumber," "balsam pear," and "bitter gourd," the bitter melon (*Momordica charantia*) originated in the Old World – possibly in Africa, but more likely in India – and was carried by the Portuguese to Brazil in the sixteenth or seventeenth century. Although now widespread in the tropical world from the Philippines to the Caribbean, the bitter melon is most highly regarded in much of Asia, where it is thought to have medicinal properties (it does contain quinine, which accounts for its bitter taste); it is believed to purify the blood and cool the body.

But the bitter melon is also cultivated as a food in China and South and Southeast Asia. The fruit has a skin that is light to bright green, wrinkled, and shiny, and it turns yellow as it ripens. Consumers look for the green skin because bitter melon is deemed best when it is immature. Like the cucumber, which it resembles, this fruit is usually prepared by halving it and scooping out the seeds. The Chinese braise or steam the bitter melon, whereas in India it is used in curries, pickled, frequently boiled and fried, and sometimes eaten raw after being steeped in water to remove the bitter taste.

Common names and synonyms: Balsam pear, bitter cucumber, bitter gourd, *kerela.*

See in addition: "Cucumbers, Melons, and Watermelons," Part II, Section C, Chapter 6.

Bitter oca - *see* OCA

Bitter orange - *see* ORANGE

BITTER POTATO (*see also* WHITE POTATO) - The bitter potato (*Solanum × juzepczukii* or *S. × curtilobum*) is an ancient food of the high Andean plateau spanning Peru and Bolivia, where its cultivation dates from at least 8,000 years ago. Early Spanish chroniclers mentioned potatoes that were processed by freezing, thawing, and drying to make *chuño* - a life-sustaining staple. Although bitter potatoes were not the only potatoes that were "freeze-dried" in this fashion, in their case such processing was essential to remove their glycoalkaloids. Both black and white versions of *chuño* are made; the former is a thoroughly dehydrated product that keeps well, and the more expensive white *chuño* is available in markets and consumed on festive occasions.

See in addition: "Potatoes (White)," Part II, Section B, Chapter 3.

Bitterroot - *see* VALERIAN

BITTER ROOT - A western North American plant, *Lewisia rediviva* was named for Meriwether Lewis of the Lewis and Clark expedition across the continent in 1806 and 1807. The plant has white flowers and fleshy, edible roots that were roasted or boiled and consumed by Native Americans in the western part of the country. They also dried and ground the roots into a meal.

Bitters - *see* ANGOSTURA

Bitter tomato - *see* LOCAL GARDEN EGG

BITTER VETCH (*see also* VETCH) - This Mediterranean herb (*Vicia ervilia* or *Ervum ervilia*) is widely cultivated as fodder for livestock. Care must be taken with bitter vetch, however, because its seeds are considered poisonous for pigs and dangerous when moist and mature. Occasionally, it is eaten in soups. Found in Europe, Asia, and the United States, bitter vetch is also known as ervil.

Common names and synonyms: Ervil.

Bitterweed - *see* RAGWEED

BITTER YAM (*see also* YAMS) - Also called "African bitter yam," the bitter yam (*Dioscorea dumetorum*) is a native of tropical Africa, where it has remained because of the bitter taste its name proclaims. The reason that it is cultivated at all (mostly in Nigeria) is that it apparently has a higher yield than most other African yams. It is usually boiled in soups and stews.

Common names and synonyms: African bitter yam, cluster yam, trifoliate yam.

See in addition: "Sweet Potatoes and Yams," Part II, Section B, Chapter 5.

Bixa - *see* ANNATTO

Black alder - *see* WINTERBERRY

BLACKBERRY (*see also* BERRIES) - There are numerous species of blackberries (genus *Rubus*), which are divided into those that grow on brambles and those that grow on trailing vines; the latter are often called "dewberries" in the southern United States. Together, the blackberry and the dewberry constitute the most important of the wild berry crops in the United States. As a rule, these berries are indeed black or purplish black and outwardly resemble raspberries (also of the genus *Rubus*) in that each berry looks like a cluster of very tiny berries. Blackberries are an autumn crop that was harvested far back in prehistoric times. Their remains have been found in excavations of the earliest European habitations. Blackberries were known to the ancient Greeks and were another of the many gathered foods that sustained Native Americans, who may also have used them medicinally. The berries are said to be good blood cleansers and useful in combating dysentery as well as colds, and the leaves have been employed against sore throats. Some hybrid varieties of the blackberry, such as boysenberries, loganberries, and olallieberries, have been developed. Like all berries, the blackberry is a fine source of vitamin C. It also provides a good deal of iron.

Common names and synonyms: Boysenberry, bramble(s), dewberry, loganberry, olallieberry.

Black-cap - *see* RASPBERRY

Black caraway (seed) - *see* NIGELLA

Black cumin - *see* NIGELLA

BLACK CURRANT (*see also* CURRANTS) - Called *cassis* by the French, the black currant (*Ribes nigrum*) is employed to make the cordial *crème de cassis* and an aperitif called "Kir"; it is also used as a garnish with ice cream.

Common names and synonyms: Cassis, European black currant.

Black dhal - *see* MUNG BEAN

Black diamond (truffle) - *see* TRUFFLE(S)

Black drink - *see* YAUPON

Black-eyed pea - *see* BEANS, COWPEA

Black gram - *see* MUNG BEAN

BLACK GUM - Also called "sour gum," "pepperidge," and "tupelo," the black gum (*Nyssa sylvatica*) is a tree of eastern, central, and southern North America. It produces small, blue-black, plumlike fruits that were among the many foods gathered by Native Americans.

Common names and synonyms: Beetle-bung, pep-peridge, sour gum, tupelo.

BLACK HAW (*see also* **BERRIES**) – Also known as "sweet haw," "sheepberry," "nannyberry," and "stag-bush," these trees have two different scientific names depending on where they are found. On the east coast of the United States, the black haw is known as *Viburnum prunifolium,* whereas in the Midwest and on the Pacific coast it is *Crataegus douglasii.* The trees are usually planted for ornamental purposes, although their small, blue-black fruits can be made into preserves; the leaves, too, are edible, as Native Americans well knew. The black haw is also known for the medicinal uses of its bark. Containing the bitter resin viburnin, it is used as a sedative, uterine relaxant, and diuretic.

Common names and synonyms: Hawthorn, nanny-berry, sheepberry, stagbush, sweet haw.

Black Indian hemp - *see* **HEMP DOGBANE**

BLACK MONKEY ORANGE – Native to southern Africa, *Strychnos madagascariensis* bears fruits that average a little over 3 inches in diameter and change from blue-green to yellow upon ripening. A thick shell protects the pulp, which is frequently made into a kind of jam by the Zulu people. In Zimbabwe, the pulp is dried in the sun or over a fire to serve as a nutriment during times of food short-age. The oil of the pulp is used as a medicine for dysentery.

Black nightshade - *see* **WONDERBERRY**

Black oyster-plant - *see* **SCORZONERA**

Black persimmon - *see* **BLACK SAPOTE**

Black salsify - *see* **SCORZONERA**

BLACK SAPOTE (*see also* **WHITE SAPOTE**) – A number of different fruits are called sapote (or sapota), which can produce considerable confusion. One might expect to find, for example, that the white sapote and the black sapote – both tropical American natives – are different-colored specimens of the same fruit. But they are not even of the same family: The white sapote belongs to the family Sapotaceae, and the black sapote to the family Ebenaceae. The black sapote (*Diospyros digyna* – a relative of the persimmon) does, how-ever, resemble the sapodilla in form, although it has a sweet, soft, dark brown flesh. It is a highly prolific tree, grown throughout the New World tropics and subtropics, as well as in Hawaii and California, and the fruit is principally used in desserts.

Common names and synonyms: Black persimmon, black sapota, chocolate-pudding fruit, *zapte negro.*

Black snakeroot - *see* **WILD GINGER**

Black tamarind - *see* **VELVET TAMARIND**

Blackthorn - *see* **HAW, SLOE**

BLADDER CAMPION – There are a number of plants of the genus *Silene* that are called "campion" – especially "bladder campion" (*S. cucubalus = S. vulgaris*). It is a European green gathered in the spring for use as a potherb, particularly in the south of France.

Bladder weed - *see* **KELP, SEAWEED**

Blanc Fumé - *see* **SAUVIGNON BLANC**

Blé de Turquie - *see* **MAIZE**

Bledos - *see* **AMARANTH**

Blessed herb - *see* **HERB BENNET**

Blimbling - *see* **BELIMBING**

BLOOD ORANGE (*see also* **CITRUS FRUITS, ORANGE**) – A very large variety of sweet orange, the blood orange (*Citrus sinensis*) has juice that is usually of a burgundy hue, which along with the red color of its flesh, accounts for its name. Blood oranges (also called pigmented oranges) are a favorite in Europe (especially in countries along the Mediterranean coastline) but have not really caught on in the United States, although the "Ruby Blood" and "Moro" varieties are grown in California and Florida. Blood oranges come mostly from Spain and Italy; important European varieties include the Span-ish *Sanguinella* and the "Maltese Blood." The Eng-lish call these fruits "Maltese oranges," the French "*Maltaise oranges,*" and it is from the latter people that a hollandaise sauce – with the addition of the grated rinds of blood oranges – received the name "maltaise sauce." Like other oranges, the blood orange is a good source of vitamin C and provides some fiber as well. Its red color, however, does not come from carotene, which is one of the many exceptions to the rule that red and orange coloring of fruits and vegetables is a promise of beta-carotene.

Common names and synonyms: Maltaise orange, Maltese Blood, Maltese orange, Moro, pigmented orange, Ruby Blood, *Sanguinella.*

BLUEBERRY (*see also* **BERRIES, BILBERRY**) – Blue-berries come from any of a number of shrubs of the genus *Vaccinium* that grow wild over much of the globe and can be found in the Western Hemi-sphere from Alaska to the jungles of South America. Those indigenous to North America are either high-bush (especially *V. corymbosum* - also called the swamp blueberry) or lowbush (*V. angustifolium* - sometimes called the sweet blueberry). The former type has been commercially cultivated in the United States throughout most of the twentieth century and is considerably larger than its wild counterparts. Blueberries, which look almost the same as huckleberries, keep longer in storage than other berries – in both fresh and frozen forms. Blue-berries were an important food for Native Ameri-cans, who used them in stews and dried and stored them for winter use. The Indians of Alaska have tra-ditionally preserved them in seal oil for consump-tion in the winter. Blueberries are frequently eaten alone as a fruit, but are also popular in muffins, pies, cobblers, jams, and jellies and are made into wine. They are an excellent source of vitamins A and C as well as fiber.

Common names and synonyms: Highbush blueberry, huckleberry, late sweet blueberry, late sweet bush, lowbush blueberry, low sweet bush, rabbit-eye blueberry, swamp blueberry, sweet blueberry, whortleberry.

Blueberry elder - *see* ELDERBERRY

Bluebottle - *see* CORNFLOWER

BLUE COHOSH - A plant with a number of common names, such as "papoose root," "squawroot," and "blue ginseng" or "yellow ginseng," the blue cohosh (*Caulophyllum thalictroides*) is found in eastern North America and is especially common in the Allegheny region. Its seeds have been roasted and used as a substitute for coffee, and its large leaves consumed after boiling, but its blue berries are said to be poisonous. Its rootstock, which contains an alkaloid, is used medicinally.

Common names and synonyms: Blue ginseng, papoose root, squawroot, yellow ginseng.

Blue ginseng - *see* BLUE COHOSH

Blue lupine - *see* BEANS

Blue mountain tea - *see* GOLDENROD

BLUE-STEM - A grass of the western United States, blue-stem (*Andropogon furcatus*) is also called "bluestem wheatgrass" and "western wheatgrass." Today it is used for hay; in the past both the stems and the seeds provided food for Native Americans; the plant also was used as a medicine for indigestion.

Common names and synonyms: Blue-stem wheatgrass, western wheatgrass.

Blue-stem wheatgrass - *see* BLUE-STEM

BLUE VERVAIN - A North American member of a genus that includes species scattered around the globe, blue vervain (*Verbena hastata*) grows as a weed throughout southern Canada and here and there in the United States – from Florida to Arizona. Native Americans processed the seeds of the plant by roasting and grinding them into a flour.

Common names and synonyms: False verbain, verbain, verbena, vervain, wild hyssop.

Blue water lily - *see* LOTUS

Bochweit - *see* BUCKWHEAT

Boechweite - *see* BUCKWHEAT

Bogbean - *see* BOG MYRTLE

BOG HEATHER - Also called cross-leaved heath and cross-leaf heath, bog heather (*Erica tetralix*) is a European shrub of bogs and marshes. Some varieties have dark, rose-red flowers with stems and petals that are said to be edible.

Common names and synonyms: Cross-leaf heath, cross-leaved heath.

BOG MYRTLE - Also called "Scotch gale" and "sweet gale," bog myrtle (*Myrica gale*) grows in bogs throughout the north temperate zone and has bitter-tasting leaves that are used as a potherb. In the

past, before the use of hops, bog myrtle was widely employed in western Europe for flavoring beer, and it is still used on occasion for this purpose in England, where hopped beer has always met with some consumer resistance. Another plant known as bog myrtle and similarly used is the buckbean (*Menyanthes trifoliata*).

Common names and synonyms: Bogbean, buckbean, marsh trefoil, Scotch gale, sweet gale.

Bog potato - *see* APIOS

Bog rhubarb - *see* COLTSFOOT

BOK CHOY (*see also* CABBAGE AND CHINESE CABBAGE) - This member of the cabbage family is an East Asian native and a mainstay in the diets of the region. But bok choy (*Brassica rapa*) is also available in the markets of Europe and North America. It is sometimes called Chinese cabbage or Chinese mustard cabbage, which leads to confusion with the real Chinese cabbage (napa). In appearance, its nonheading stalks and leaves (both are eaten) resemble Swiss chard, or celery without the ribs. The taste of the stalks is something like that of romaine lettuce, whereas the leaves have a definite cabbage-like flavor. Bok choy is a favorite among the stir-fry vegetables and, in addition to being a fine source of vitamins A and C, also provides some calcium.

Common names and synonyms: Celery cabbage, Chinese cabbage, Chinese mustard cabbage.

See in addition: "Cruciferous and Green Leafy Vegetables," Part II, Section C, Chapter 5.

BOLETE (*see also* MUSHROOMS AND FUNGI) - Several of the mushroom members of the genus *Boletus* are poisonous, but not *Boletus edulis,* also called *porcino,* cep, *cèpe de bolete,* and *cèpe de Bordeaux.* These are wild mushrooms – easily recognized by the presence of spongy tubes instead of gills under their brownish-colored caps - and are highly prized throughout much of Europe. Although this mushroom also grows in North America, it tends to be moldy and is often a prey of insects. But in the spring and again in the fall the Italians hunt and consume their *porcini* with gusto, as do the French their *cèpes,* and the Germans their *Steinpilze.* A delicious mushroom that is generally eaten fresh - but wonderful as well when dried - it is also powdered and preserved in oil. *Boletus edulis* provides some vitamin D and a little of the vitamin B complex. It is also a good source of fiber.

Common names and synonyms: Cep, *cèpe, cèpe de bolete, cèpe de Bordeaux,* king bolete, *porcini, porcino, Steinpilz.*

See in addition: "Fungi," Part II, Section C, Chapter 7.

Bonavist bean - *see* HORSE GRAM

Bondue - *see* AMARANTH

BONESET - Any of several plants of the genus *Eupatorium* - and especially *E. perfoliatum* - are called boneset, along with a host of other colorful names, such as "auguweed," "feverwort," and "sweating plant," all suggestive of past medicinal uses. Some species, like *E. dalea,* have been used as a vanilla substitute in the American tropics. The leaves and flowering tops of others are cooked as greens in Asia, and in North America, where *E. perfoliatum* is a common weed, these parts of the plant served Native Americans as a wild food. One North American species (*E. rugosum*) - called "white snake-root" - is toxic. This is the infamous weed that caused trematol poisoning in the cattle that grazed on it and "milk sickness" in the humans who drank their milk - a surprisingly frequent cause of death in the early decades of the nineteenth century.

Common names and synonyms: Aguweed, auguweed, feverwort, sweating plant, white snakeroot.

BONIATO (*see also* **SWEET POTATO**) - In Cuba, *boniato* (*Ipomoea batatas*) means sweet potato. This term is not to be confused with the Puerto Rican *boniata,* which means sweet yuca. Yet even the Cuban meaning is hazy, because white-fleshed sweet potatoes are preferred on that island, so that *boniato* has come to signify only the light-colored varieties that spread from their American homeland to Europe and throughout Asia - the latter region now grows some 90 percent of the world's production. A kind of cross between the orange sweet potato and a white potato, the *boniato* is a fair source of vitamin C and the B-vitamin complex. The whiter-fleshed varieties are not, however, good sources of beta-carotene, and some contain absolutely none.

Common names and synonyms: Cuban sweet potato, sweet potato, white sweet potato, yam (U.S.).

See in addition: "Sweet Potatoes and Yams," Part II, Section B, Chapter 5.

Bonnet pepper - *see* **HABANERO AND SCOTCH BONNET PEPPERS**

Booth - *see* **AVOCADO**

BORAGE (*see also* **INDIAN BORAGE**) - A native of the Middle East and Mediterranean regions, where it still grows wild, borage (*Borago officinalis*) has azure, nectar-filled flowers that bees love. The name derives from the Latin *burra* - meaning "rough hair" - and refers to the "hairs" that protrude from the stems and leaves of the plant, which taste something like unripened cucumbers. The Chinese stuff the leaves of borage in much the same way that Greeks stuff grape leaves. In France and Italy, the leaves are employed fresh in spring salads, are added to stews, and are used as a base for borage soup. In Germany, borage is often used in salads with dill, and in Britain and North America the leaves and flowers are sometimes added to cold drinks. Borage is also an ingredient in Pimm's No. 1, a gin drink of England. The flowers are added to salads and are frequently crystallized.

Borassus palm - *see* **WINE PALM**

Boreal vetch - *see* **TUFTED VETCH**

Borecole - *see* **COLLARDS, KALE**

Botoko plum - *see* **GOVERNOR'S PLUM**

BOTTLE GOURD (*see also* **CALABASH, SQUASH AND PUMPKIN**) - Although apparently a native of Africa, the bottle gourd (*Lagenaria siceraria*) spread to both Asia and the Americas in prehistoric times. In Mexico, bottle gourd remains dating from 7000 B.C. have been found, but how the Atlantic crossing was achieved is one of the mysteries surrounding the movements of plants in the distant past. The bottle gourd is so called because, when dried, it can be scooped out and employed as a container; such gourds were probably among the first utensils used by some human groups and, of course, are still in use as dipper gourds today. Although not well known as a food plant, bottle gourds are regularly consumed in India, China, and Japan and are similar in taste and texture to summer squashes. In India, the bottle gourd is called *doodhi,* and its flesh is added to stews and curries. In Japan, it becomes *kampyo* - the flesh is cut into ribbon-like strips that are dried and used as edible ties for packaging sushi. Bottle gourds are also employed as food in some of the countries of Latin America.

Common names and synonyms: Doodhi, hue, kampyo.

Bounce berry - *see* **CRANBERRY**

Box thorn - *see* **MATRIMONY VINE**

BOYSENBERRY (*see also* **BERRIES, BLACKBERRY**) - The boysenberry (*Rubus loganobaccus*) is the creation of twentieth-century American horticulturalist Rudolph Boysen, who in about 1920 created this huge blue-black hybrid berry by crossing the loganberry, the raspberry, and the blackberry. The boysenberry resembles the latter two in taste and has been assigned to the genus *Rubus.*

BRACKEN FERN - Also known simply as bracken or brake, this fern (*Pteridium aquilinum*) is well distributed throughout the world's temperate and tropical regions and has found use in such diverse corners of the globe as North America, Europe, Asia, the South Pacific, and the Canary Islands. The fronds are used for thatching and as fodder, but young ones are also cooked and eaten as a vegetable and made into soups. The rhizomes of the plant are roasted and ground into flour used in bread making. Native Americans steamed the fern in fire pits.

Common names and synonyms: Aruhe, bracken, brake.

Brake - *see* **BRACKEN FERN**

BRAMBLE(S) (*see also* **BERRIES, BLACKBERRY, BOYSENBERRY, CLOUDBERRY, DEWBERRY, JAPANESE WINEBERRY, LOGANBERRY, RASPBERRY, SALMONBERRY**) - An overarching name for any prickly plant or shrub of the genus *Rubus* is "bramble" or "brambles," which embraces blackberries, boysenberries, loganberries, and raspberries as well as other lesser-known species and varieties.

Brazilian cherry - *see* **PITANGA**

Brazilian grape tree - *see* **JABOTICABA**

BRAZILIAN MALAGUETA (*see also* **CHILLI PEPPERS**) - A small, greenish, tapered chilli pepper, the Brazilian malagueta (*Capsicum frutescens*) is not so narrowly confined as its name implies. It is actually a widely grown pepper, and its territory reaches north through Central America as far as Louisiana, where a variety called tabasco is grown.

Common names and synonyms: Bird pepper, tabasco pepper.

See in addition: "Chilli Peppers," Part II, Section C, Chapter 4.

BRAZIL NUT - This three-sided nut (*Bertholletia excelsa*) with a hard, dark shell grows in bunches of from one to more than two dozen nuts inside coconut-like shells (called *cocos* in Portuguese) on evergreens that tower over the Amazon rain forest. These nuts, which are native to Brazil and Guiana, take about 14 months to ripen after the flowers fade, and one tree can yield more than a half ton of fruit. There are some Brazil-nut plantations, but most are still harvested in the wild. And because the trees attain a height of upwards of 150 feet, and the *cocos* weigh about 5 pounds, and they are gathered only after they fall to the ground, harvesting these missiles can be hazardous work. It it interesting to note that Brazil nuts are not much consumed in Brazil, save for medicinal purposes. Rather, fairly early in the nineteenth century, the country began exporting almost the entire crop, and Europe and the United States became and remain the major importers. Because attempts have failed to cultivate the tree elsewhere, Brazil has a monopoly on more than the name. Brazil nuts have a high oil content and, consequently, are high in calories. But they are also a good source of calcium, thiamine, vitamin E, selenium, and sulfur-containing amino acids.

Common names and synonyms: Cream nut, para nut.

BREADFRUIT - The breadfruit tree (*Artocarpus altilis* = *A. communis* = *A. incisus*), which grows to about 40 feet in height, is native to the East Indies and the tropics of the South Pacific. It was carried eastward as far as the Hawaiian Islands by migrating Polynesians and is known to have been cultivated for more than 2,000 years as a staple food for Pacific peoples. Breadfruit was first described (for Europeans) by the English navigator William Dampier, who found it growing on Guam in 1688. About a century later, Captain James Cook observed the plant in Tahiti. This occurred in the aftermath of the American Revolution, which had resulted in much French interdiction of England's shipping to its colonies in the Caribbean and, consequently, much hardship for slaves on English

sugar plantations. In 1787, the British government dispatched HMS *Bounty,* commanded by Captain William Bligh (who had been Cook's lieutenant), to Tahiti to collect breadfruit and other plants that might be useful for feeding slaves. The notorious mutiny on the *Bounty* prevented Bligh from accomplishing this first attempt at his mission, but later - in 1793 - he succeeded in carrying to the West Indies a cargo that included young breadfruit trees. The slaves, however, refused to eat breadfruit, which resembled nothing they had known in either West Africa (the "breadfruit" there is *Treculia africana*) or the West Indies, and for a half century or so the fruits of *A. altilis* were a food mostly for hogs. Yet following the end of slavery, breadfruit finally found its way into human diets in the Caribbean. Not really a fruit, the breadfruit comes in many varieties, some with seeds and some without. The seeded varieties are known as "breadnuts" and can be roasted like chestnuts. Breadfruit is baked, boiled, roasted, fried, and dried to make flour. When utilized as a completely green vegetable, the breadfruit - which can attain the size of a cantaloupe - is hard like a raw potato; when a bit ripe (it does not keep well), it is more like a baked potato. Breadfruit absorbs the flavors of other foods and thus can stretch the taste of meats, fish, and fowl. Like cassava, however, it is lacking in most nutrients, save some calcium and vitamin C. Unfortunately, the latter is largely destroyed by the heat of cooking.

Common names and synonyms: Breadnut, *fruit à pain, pana de pepita, sukun.*

BREADNUT - Also called *ramón,* the breadnut is the fruit of *Brosimum alicastrum,* a tree native to the West Indies and Central America. The tree grows to some 75 feet in height and produces a heavy yield of edible fruit, either a large, somewhat flavorless, red variety or a smaller, better-tasting, yellow one. The Maya prepared the fruit in the same manner as maize - grinding it on a stone and patting it into a flat bread similar to a tortilla. The seeds were made into gruel after cooking in ash water to remove the bitterness of their latex outer coating. The Maya call the breadnut "food of the ancestors," and some experts believe it was the staple food of many Mesoamerican Indians before the Spanish conquest. Its English name came about because the fruit is round and nutlike and can be ground to make a substitute for wheat flour. But the word "breadnut" is also used to describe the seeded varieties of breadfruit (not a relative), and it is important not to confuse the two. Today, the breadnut remains a part of certain Mayan religious rituals, but on an everyday basis it is usually fed to pigs.

Common names and synonyms: Ramon, *ramón.*

BREADROOT (*see also* **INDIAN TURNIP**) - Also called "prairie turnip," *tipsin,* "Indian breadroot," and "breadroot scurf pea," breadroot (*Psoralea* *esculenta*) is a North American native that can be found on the plains from the Northwest Territories of Canada to Texas. Its thick, brown, edible starchy root was a staple for Native Americans and later sustained explorers and immigrants.

Common names and synonyms: Breadroot scurf pea, Indian breadroot, Indian potato, Indian turnip, prairie potato, prairie turnip, *tipsin.*

Breadroot scurf pea - *see* **BREADROOT**

Brinjal - *see* **EGGPLANT**

Bristle grass - *see* **MILLET**

Broad bellflower - *see* **CAMPANULA**

Broad-leaved tea-tree - *see* **CAJEPUT**

BROCCOLI (*see also* **BROCCOLI RAAB, CABBAGE, CALABRESE, CAULIFLOWER, CHINESE BROCCOLI**) - A member of the mustard family, and doubtless a descendant of the wild cabbage (*Brassica oleracea*), broccoli (*Brassica oleracea* var. *italica*) began as a wild-growing native of the Mediterranean region. Like all cabbages, broccoli was originally eaten for its stems, with the flowering heads a later development. Although broccoli is believed to be the forerunner of cauliflower - a vegetable known in Europe by the sixteenth century - it trailed behind cauliflower by about a century in culinary usage, save perhaps in Italy. The Italians claim broccoli as their own: The name comes from the Italian *brocco*, meaning "sprout" or "shoot," which, in turn came from the Latin *brachium*, meaning "arm" or "branch" - a succinct description of this plant with its many thick and fleshy stalks. Broccoli was introduced into England (where the term "broccoli" refers to cauliflower) around 1720 and was probably brought to North America soon thereafter, during colonial times. However, although much of the latter region offers the abundant moisture and cool climate that broccoli thrives within, the vegetable was not commonly grown in the United States until the twentieth century and only became popular after World War II - when returning GIs, who had eaten broccoli abroad, created a demand. It has subsequently become one of the most important frozen foods in the world. The green, unopened flower end is the part that is generally eaten, usually after steaming or boiling, although the leaves and tender parts of the stem can also be consumed. Broccoli is packed with vitamins and minerals, is an especially good source of vitamins A and C, and, as a cruciferous vegetable, is thought to be in the front line of foods that fight cancer.

Common names and synonyms: Asparagus broccoli, calabrese, Italian asparagus, sprouting broccoli.

See in addition: "Cruciferous and Green Leafy Vegetables," Part II, Section C, Chapter 5.

BROCCOLI RAAB (*see also* **BROCCOLI, CABBAGE**) - A favorite of the Italians (who call it *rapini*), broccoli raab (*Brassica napus*) is related to the turnip (some call broccoli raab "turnip broccoli") as well

as being a member of the family that includes cabbage, cauliflower, and broccoli. It has dark green leaves, and its stalks resemble thin broccoli stalks. It is cooked and eaten like broccoli or kale; its taste, which is pungent and somewhat bitter, seems to encompass all of the most zesty flavors of its relatives and can certainly enliven bland foods. Like most greens, this especially aggressive representative is a good source of vitamins A and C as well as calcium and iron.

Common names and synonyms: Broccoli rab, broccoli rabe, broccoli rape, *brocoletti di rape, brocoletto,* Italian turnip, rape, *rapini,* turnip broccoli.

See in addition: "Cruciferous and Green Leafy Vegetables," Part II, Section C, Chapter 5.

Broccoli rab - *see* **BROCCOLI RAAB**

Broccoli rabe - *see* **BROCCOLI RAAB**

Broccoli rape - *see* **BROCCOLI RAAB**

Brocoletti di rape - *see* **BROCCOLI RAAB**

Brocoletto - *see* **BROCCOLI RAAB**

Broken Orange Pekoe Fannings - *see* **TEA**

BROMELIA - *Bromelia* is the type genus of the family Bromeliaceae, which comprises plants often subsumed under the genus *Ananas,* such as the pineapple and the pinguin.

BROOKLIME - Also known as brooklyme, brooklime is any of several species of the genus *Veronica,* such as the Eurasian *V. beccabunga* and the American *V. americana,* which are edible aquatic or semi-aquatic plants similar to watercress.

Common names and synonyms: Brooklyme, speedwell.

Brooklyme - *see* **BROOKLIME**

Broomcorn - *see* **SORGHUM**

BRUSH CHERRY - An Australian shrub or tree, the brush cherry (*Eugenia myrtifolia* or *Syzygium paniculatum*) is also called native myrtle (in Australia) and rose apple. Its edible red fruit has a sweet-tasting white flesh that is sometimes made into jelly. The fruit has helped to feed the Aborigines over many millennia.

Common names and synonyms: Native myrtle, rose apple.

BRUSSELS SPROUT(S) (*see also* **CABBAGE**) - Members of the mustard family that descended from the cabbage (*Brassica oleracea*) and were named for the capital of Belgium, Brussels sprouts (*Brassica oleracea* var. *gemmifera*) are immature buds, shaped like tiny cabbages, that cluster on the main stem of the plant they grow on. Although the cabbage is native to the Mediterranean region (where it has been cultivated for some 2,500 years), Brussels sprouts were developed in northern Europe (the cabbage was carried there by the Romans) around the fifth century - or perhaps even later. One source claims that the plant was cultivated near Brussels in the thirteenth century; another places the first recorded description of Brussels sprouts in 1587; still another claims that they have been widely grown in Europe only since the seventeenth century; whereas at least one more source insists that they have become popular in Europe only since World War I. Of course, these claims are not necessarily contradictory. But surely, in view of its name, the plant must have been grown around Brussels at some time. Brussels sprouts reached North America with French settlers, who grew them in Louisiana, but they have been popular in the United States only during the twentieth century, with most grown in the states of New York and California. Brussels sprouts brim with vitamins. They are an especially good source of vitamins A and C and, like other members of the cabbage family, enjoy a reputation for lowering low-density lipoprotein and for preventing cancer.

See in addition: "Cruciferous and Green Leafy Vegetables," Part II, Section C, Chapter 5.

Buckbean - *see* **BOG MYRTLE**

BUCKEYE - Also called "horse chestnuts," buckeyes come from any of several trees of the genus *Aesculus*. Although poisonous when raw (because they are rich in saponin), buckeyes become edible when roasted and leached with water for a few days - a procedure with which Native Americans were familiar. They also used buckeyes raw as a fish poison. The seeds of local species are still consumed in Asia today.

Common names and synonyms: Horse chestnut.

BUCKTHORN - A number of shrubs and trees of the genus *Rhamnus* are called "buckthorn." They have berry-like fruits, and these - along with the bark and sap of the plants - have been mostly used as purgatives. However, the fruits of *R. crocea* in what is now southern California were eaten by Native Americans, as were those of *R. caroliniana* in the southeastern portion of North America.

Common names and synonyms: Redberry.

BUCKWHEAT - Grown extensively in China for millennia (although thought to be a native of Manchuria and Siberia), "buckwheat" is any plant of the genus *Fagopyrum*, especially *F. esculentum*. It is neither a true cereal nor a grass but constitutes a family of its own. Buckwheat was introduced into Europe toward the end of the Middle Ages. It does well in areas where the climate is cool and moist and became important in some northern and eastern European areas that had not only such a climate but also soils in which other grains did not thrive. In the Netherlands, the plant was called *boechweite* or "beech wheat," perhaps because the grains are shaped a bit like beechnuts. The Dutch, in turn, carried the grain to the New World, where the name became buckwheat. Another name, *kasha*, acquired from the Slavic mediators between Asia and Europe, is today applied to roasted and cracked buckwheat. Finely ground buckwheat is called buckwheat grits, whereas buckwheat groats are whole kernels that are either unroasted and white, or roasted and brown. In addition, the grain is turned into buck-

wheat flour for pancakes. The plant also serves as an animal feed, and its flowers and leaves yield a substance used in the treatment of hypertension. Today, the countries of the former Soviet Union (especially Russia) are collectively the main producers of buckwheat, of which there are three major varieties: Silverhull, Tartary, and Japanese.

Common names and synonyms: Beech wheat, *bochweit, boechweite,* buckwheat grits, buckwheat groats, Japanese buckwheat, *kasha,* Silverhull, Tartary.

See also: "Buckwheat," Part II, Section A, Chapter 3.

Buddha's-hand - *see* **CHAYOTE**

BUFFALO BERRY (*see also* **BERRIES**) - Two North American shrubs, *Shepherdia argentea* and *S. canadensis,* yield the silver buffalo berry and the russet buffalo berry respectively. Resembling currants (and sometimes called "Nebraska currants") as well as barberries, buffalo berries have long been a part of the Native American diet on the Great Plains and in western North America. The shrubs grow wild along streams and are one of the few plants that do well in a dry and rocky environment. *Sheperdia canadensis* (also known as the Canadian buffalo berry) produces the smaller of the two berries and is relatively tasteless. The berries of *S. argentea,* by contrast, are flavorful and used in jellies. Buffalo berries are a fine source of vitamin C.

Common names and synonyms: Canadian buffalo berry, Nebraska currant, russet buffalo berry, silver buffalo berry.

BUFFALO GOURD (*see also* **SQUASH AND PUMPKIN**) - A large plant with a bad smell, the buffalo gourd (*Cucurbita foetidissima*) grows wild in the south-central and southwestern United States as well as in northern Mexico. The fruits were sometimes used as rattles by Native Americans and reportedly were cooked and eaten at times, although today they are considered inedible. The seeds, however, were regularly consumed, generally after roasting and grinding them into a kind of mush. Oil was also obtained from the seeds. The pulp of the fruits and the huge root (which can weigh over 200 pounds) of the buffalo gourd contain saponin and were therefore employed as soap.

Common names and synonyms: Calabazilla, Missouri gourd.

See in addition: "Squash," Part II, Section C, Chapter 8.

Bulbine lily - *see* **YAM DAISY**

Bulghur - *see* **WHEAT**

Bullace grape - *see* **MUSCADINE**

Bullace plum - *see* **DAMSON PLUM**

Bullbrier - *see* **GREENBRIER**

Bull-dog - *see* **TURKEY FRUIT**

Bullock's heart - *see* **CUSTARD APPLE**

Bullrush - *see* **BULRUSH**

Bullsfoot - *see* **COLTSFOOT**

BULRUSH - A versatile food source in the wilderness, bulrushes (genus *Scirpus*) are grassy sedges that grow in wet places. These wild marsh plants have young shoots and juicy stem bases that can be boiled as greens or consumed raw in salads. In addition, the rhizomes are edible (they were often dried and ground), and the pollen was gathered by Native Americans to mix with flours for porridges and cakes. The seeds of some species are also edible. Most bulrushes are American natives, but Europe and Asia also have their own species – indeed, a bulrush constituted the Old Testament papyrus – and in East Asia the young stems of *S. fluviatilis* are still consumed today. Bulrush, broadly speaking, can also mean cattail, especially in Britain.

Common names and synonyms: Bullrush.

Bunchberry - *see* **CORNUS**

BUNCHOSIA - *Bunchosia argentea* is called the "peanut butter fruit" for the excellent reason that its flesh has both the consistency and the flavor of peanut butter. It is a native of tropical South America and is also grown in Florida, but it is uncommon almost anywhere else. The trees grow to more than 30 feet tall and bear flowers and fruit almost all year long. The small fruits are yellow or red, are oblong, and hang in clusters. Their flesh is the color of cream and, although sweet, is often too tart to be enjoyed fresh. The fruit may be made into preserves, but it is more frequently employed as a flavoring.

Common names and synonyms: Ciruela, peanut-butter fruit.

Buni - *see* **BIGNAY**

Burbank's spineless - *see* **PRICKLY PEAR**

BURDEKIN PLUM (*see also* **PLUM**) - The fruits of the Australian trees *Pleiogynium timoriense* and *P. solandri* are called "Burdekin plums." Both are plum-sized and edible, but the fruit of *P. timoriense* is purple, whereas that of *P. solandri* is red. They are not sweet and today are used mostly in jellies and jams. However, the fruits have long served as food for the Aborigines.

BURDOCK - Also known as "great burdock" and originally from Siberia, burdock (*Arctium lappa*) is cultivated for its long (up to 4 feet), slender, carrot-shaped taproot. The Japanese, who use burdock as others do carrots, are its foremost producers and consumers, although it can also be found in the markets of Taiwan and Hawaii. The roots are grated or cut into pieces and stir-fried or added to various dishes - especially soups - to which they contribute a somewhat earthy taste. The plant grows wild in North America and Europe, producing burrs that attach themselves to the clothing of those who cross meadows. Nutritionally, burdock offers mostly minerals, such as potassium and magnesium, although it is not a bad source of folacin.

Common names and synonyms: Beggar's-button(s), clotbur, edible burdock, *gobo*, great burdock, harlock.

BURMA MANGROVE - An evergreen tree of the Old World tropics, the Burma mangrove (*Bruguiera gymnorhiza*) produces edible, berry-like fruits. In some places, the bark is used as a flavoring; in others, the leaves are cooked as a vegetable.

BURNET - The name "burnet" comes from the Middle English and Old French *brunette,* which describes the brownish red flowers of the several species of this European native, now also commonly found in North America. One kind of burnet, *Poterium sanguisorba,* with cucumber-tasting leaves, was once a popular herb but is not much used anymore save in a few Italian and French dishes. In the past, however, especially in Elizabethan England, its leaves were frequently added to salads and sauces. There is confusion between this burnet and great burnet (*Sanguisorba officinalis*), also known mistakenly as bloodwort because of its reputation for stopping bleeding. Asian burnet and Japanese burnet are also different species.

Common names and synonyms: Garden burnet, lesser burnet, pimpinel, salad burnet, small burnet.

Burning bush - *see* **DITTANY**

BUSH CURRANT - A small tree or shrub that is also called the "currant bush," the bush currant (*Antidesma ghaesembilla*) is a wild plant of Australia that produces small edible purple or black berries.

Common names and synonyms: Currant bush, gucil.

Bush greens - *see* **AMARANTH**

Bush okra - *see* **JEW'S-MALLOW**

BUTTERCUP SQUASH (*see also* **SQUASH AND PUMPKIN**) - So called because of their turbanlike caps, the orange-fleshed and green-skinned buttercup squash and other moderate-sized varieties of *Cucurbita maxima* are also sometimes referred to as Kabocha-type squashes. These include the Black Forest, the Hokkaido (also Red Kuri), and Honey Delight varieties, all of which make good purees, soups, and pies.

Common names and synonyms: Black Forest, Hokkaido, Honey Delight, Kabocha, Red Kuri.

See in addition: "Squash," Part II, Section C, Chapter 8.

BUTTERFLY WEED - A plant mostly of eastern North America, the butterfly weed (*Asclepias tuberosa*) is the only one of the milkweeds that does not contain milky juice. Its roots were baked and eaten by Native Americans, as were its orange flowers, shoots, and leaves.

Common names and synonyms: Indian posy, orange milkweed, orange root, pleurisy root, tuberroot.

BUTTERNUT - *see also* **WALNUT**

BUTTERNUT SQUASH (*see also* **SQUASH AND PUMPKIN**) - Along with the acorn squash, the butternut (*Cucurbita moschata*) is the most common squash on the tables of North America. It is a winter squash that generally weighs from 2 to 4 pounds and has a tan skin, a long neck, and a swollen bottom. This squash is usually roasted, and its yellow flesh is high in beta-carotene.

See in addition: "Squash," Part II, Section C, Chapter 8.

Butter pear - *see* **AVOCADO**

Butterweed - *see* **HORSEWEED**

CABBAGE (*see also* the various *Brassica* entries) – Sources indicate that the cabbage (*Brassica oleracea*) is an ancient vegetable of the European Old World, but cabbages in China were mentioned by Confucius (d. 497 B.C.), which suggests that the plant traveled quite widely in the distant past. Certainly the wild cabbage must long ago have provided sustenance for those of our hunting-and-gathering ancestors who sought the vegetables out. The wild cabbage was a small plant that grew around European coastal areas (especially those of the Mediterranean) and – like broccoli – was first eaten for its stem. But by the time of the Romans, the head had become larger and more rounded, and the subsequent encouragement of various characteristics has resulted in some 400 varieties, such as numerous head cabbages, broccoli, Brussels sprouts, cauliflower, collards, kale, and kohlrabi, to name but a few. Moreover, the various Oriental species of the cabbage family include the Chinese cabbage (napa) and bok choy.

In general, cabbages have trouble with hot weather, although the ability of some (such as the frost-resistant green and red varieties) to thrive in cool climates made them important long ago in central and eastern Europe. Legend has it, however, that the technique of pickling cabbage to preserve it (as sauerkraut) reached Europe from China via the Tartars. In light of such widespread use, it is interesting to note that cabbages have never been uniformly accepted nor very highly regarded. They were not a part of the diet in the Neolithic Near East and, although apparently appreciated by the Greeks and Romans (at least for alleged medicinal qualities), were subsequently viewed in Europe as an unsophisticated food that gave off a bad smell when cooked and provoked flatulence when eaten.

Today, however, this remarkable group of vegetables is said to promote health by lowering cholesterol, preventing cancer, and providing the consumer with fiber and a number of important vitamins and minerals, especially vitamin C. Round cabbages have traditionally been boiled with meats and potatoes or beans in countless cultural versions of the "boiled dinner," and, because these vegetables were called cole cabbage and colewort in the past, we continue to refer to another means of cabbage preparation as "coleslaw," often without knowing why. Round cabbages include white, green, and red varieties with smooth leaves, as well as those with wrinkled leaves, such as the Savoy cabbage. European spring cabbages are one example of pointed cabbages, as is Chinese cabbage. Brussels sprouts are cabbages with hypertrophied buds. An example of a cabbage with dense flowering is the cauliflower, and a cabbage with its flowering in spears is broccoli.

Common names and synonyms: Cole cabbage, coleslaw, colewort, common cabbage, European spring cabbage, green cabbage, head cabbage, pointed cabbage, red cabbage, round cabbage, sauerkraut, Savoy cabbage, wild cabbage.
See in addition: "Cruciferous and Green Leafy Vegetables," Part II, Section C, Chapter 5.

Cabbage palm – *see* **HEART(S) OF PALM**

CABBAGE TREE – "Cabbage trees" (*Cordyline terminalis* and other species) are shrubs or small trees that are cultivated in India and the Pacific Islands, where the plant is also known as *ti,* ti palm, and palm lily. In Hawaii, the roots – high in sugar content – are fermented to make a beverage, and the long, sword-shaped leaves are exploited for making skirts and for other decorative purposes. The leaves are also used to wrap foods for baking in Polynesia, and in New Zealand fibers from the leaves are employed as a source of twine. Finally, the leaves are also used as plates, and young leaves are eaten as a potherb.
Common names and synonyms: Palm lily, *ti,* ti leaf, ti palm, ti root.

Cabbage turnip – *see* **KOHLRABI**

CABERNET (*see also* **GRAPES**) – There are two varieties of the cabernet grape (*Vitis vinifera*) – Cabernet Sauvignon and Cabernet Franc – both of which are red grapes employed in making the fine wines of Bordeaux and California. Indeed, Cabernet Sauvignon is the most important red wine grape in the world and is also grown in Australia, South Africa, and New Zealand, as well as in other European countries besides France.
Common names and synonyms: Cabernet Franc, Cabernet Sauvignon.
See in addition: "Wine," Part III, Chapter 13.

Cabernet Franc – *see* **CABERNET**
Cabernet Sauvignon – *see* **CABERNET**

CACAO – The cacao tree (*Theobroma cacao*) produces the pods that yield the oblong beans that are dried, pressed, and ground to produce cocoa butter and a reddish brown powder, cocoa. That it has been a well-appreciated substance is evident from the tree's scientific name, which in Greek means "food for the gods." A member of the same family as the kola nut of West Africa, cacao is native to the American tropics (and still grows wild in the Amazon rain forest as well as in the forests of Central America) but is now raised commercially in many other tropical regions of the world. It was apparently the Maya who first domesticated the cacao tree. Columbus encountered the plant in the West Indies and took it to Spain at the end of his second voyage. Hernando Cortés, however, has been credited with properly introducing cacao in Europe because he knew what to do with it (mix the powder with vanilla), having learned from the Aztecs whom he had just conquered. Beginning in Spain and then throughout the rest of Europe, cocoa preceded coffee and tea as a stimulating drink (it contains caffeine), and by the end of the seventeenth century there were chocolate houses all over the Continent. The chocolate industry was under way, and the Spaniards began to spread cacao cultivation around the world. Plants were taken to the island of Fernando Po off the west African coast, after which they entered Africa. Cacao traveled west from Mexico via the Manila galleons to take root in the Philippines, and its cultivation was subsequently extended throughout the East Indies by the Dutch. Chocolate (as opposed to cacao) production began in North America in 1765, and in 1779 Dr. James Baker (whose name is practically synonymous with chocolate in the United States) entered the business. In 1828, the Dutch invented a press that would remove much of the cocoa butter, and a bit later the techniques for making chocolate bars were developed. In 1876, the Swiss, by mixing cocoa powder and powdered milk, developed milk chocolate (which is still considered the best chocolate), and in 1900 Milton Hershey introduced the first "Hershey Bars" in the United States. Soon afterward, he began construction of a chocolate factory near Harrisburg, Pennsylvania, and there quickly grew up a town that was named Hershey, Pennsylvania, in 1903. In addition to the culinary uses of cacao, cocoa butter is employed in the manufacture of cosmetics and pharmaceuticals. The shells – left over after processing the cacao beans – serve as a source of theobromine (a mild stimulant) and vitamin D and are often used as animal feed.

Common names and synonyms: Chocolate, cocoa.

See also: "Cacao," Part III, Chapter 3; "Spices and Flavorings," Part II, Section F, Chapter 1.

Cachira - *see* **ICE-CREAM BEAN**

CACTUS APPLE - A large, treelike, thorny cactus native to South America, the cactus apple (*Cereus peruvianus*) produces edible fruits that are known as *pitaya* fruits to Latin Americans. *Pitayas* range in color from yellow to red and have a white flesh with small edible seeds.

Common names and synonyms: Apple cactus, *pitaya* (fruit).

Cactus fig - *see* **PRICKLY PEAR**
Cactus pad - *see* **NOPALES**
Cactus paddle - *see* **NOPALES**
Cactus pear - *see* **PRICKLY PEAR**
Cactus-spoon - *see* **SOTOL**
Caihua - *see* **KORILA**
Cail - *see* **KALE**
Caimito (fruit) - *see* **STAR-APPLE**
Cajá - *see* **TAPEREBÁ**

CAJEPUT - An East Indian tree, the cajeput (*Melaleuca quinquenervia* or *M. cajuputi*) has a bark that has long been used for sacred writing, and it yields a pungent oil that some call "tea-tree oil," which has had myriad nonfood uses - from a painkiller in dentistry, to a killer of fleas and lice, to

a mosquito repellent. But the oil is also used as a flavoring in foods ranging from baked goods through desserts to meat products and soft drinks.

Common names and synonyms: Broad-leaved tea-tree, punk tree, tea-tree oil.

CALABASH (*see also* **BOTTLE GOURD, XICALL**) - Also called the "tree gourd," this green fruit of the calabash tree (*Crescentia cujete*) has a hard outer rind that encloses a white pulp containing seeds. Probably both the sweetish fruit and the seeds have been eaten (and the pulp used medicinally), but the main use of the calabash has been as a container for food and beverages. In Africa, the name "calabash" has been applied to the bottle gourd (*Lagenaria siceraria*), which grows on a vine instead of a tree but has served many of the same functions as *C. cujete*.

Common names and synonyms: Bottle gourd, *calabaza, calebasse,* tree gourd.

CALABAZA (SQUASH) (*see also* **CALABASH, SQUASH AND PUMPKIN**) - *Calabaza* means "gourd" in Spanish, and the word is often intended to mean "calabash." But it has also come to mean a usually bright orange squash variety of the *Cucurbita moschata* species, which has flowers that – like its skin – range from creamy white to yellow to deep orange. This squash is a native American plant that can be found daily in the markets of the West Indies and Central and South America. Because it tends to grow to the size of a large pumpkin, it is often sold in pieces, but - like the pumpkin (a close relative) - the calabaza also comes in smaller sizes. Reportedly, this squash was an important food for the Indians of Florida when the Spaniards first reached that peninsula, and it has seemingly always been a favorite of Cubans and many other natives of the Caribbean islands. Calabaza goes well in stews, and pureed calabaza makes a fine soup. Many fry the raw squash in strips, and in Mexico pieces of young, green calabaza are sautéed with chicken. Calabaza is a fine source of vitamin A, folic acid, and potassium. Like pumpkin seeds, those of the calabaza are wonderful when toasted.

Common names and synonyms: Abóbora, ahuyama, crapaudback, Cuban squash, giraumon, toadback, West Indian pumpkin.

See in addition: "Squash," Part II, Section C, Chapter 8.

Calabazilla - *see* **BUFFALO GOURD, CABBAGE**

CALABRESE (*see also* **BROCCOLI**) - A variety of broccoli, calabrese (*Brassica oleracea* var. *italica*) is apparently named for Calabria, a region in the toe of Italy about to kick Sicily. Noted for its tightly packed green (or purple) flower heads, calabrese was introduced into France and England in the eighteenth century but was rare in the United States until after World War II. Today, however, California is a big producer of calabrese. The vegetable is high in vitamin C and some of the B vitamins as well as many of the trace minerals. Along with other members of the family Cruciferae, calabrese may be important in cancer prevention.

Common names and synonyms: Asparagus broccoli, sprouting broccoli.

See in addition: "Cruciferous and Green Leafy Vegetables," Part II, Section C, Chapter 5.

Calabur - *see* **CAPULIN**

Calalu - *see* **CALLALOO**

CALAMONDIN (*see also* **CITRUS FRUITS**) - Thought by many to be a naturally occurring hybrid between the Mandarin orange and the kumquat, the orange-hued calamondin grows on a small evergreen tree (now designated as × *Citrofortunella microcarpa,* although in the past it was called *Citrus mitis* or *Citrus reticulata*) and is also known as the "musk lime," "Panama orange," and "calamondin orange." The fruits are about 1.5 inches in diameter and look like tangerines. There is some debate as to whether the calamondin is a Philippine native or originated in China, but in any event it is today widely cultivated in the Philippines and also in Hawaii and Florida in the United States. Calamondins are made into marmalades, jellies, and beverages, are used to flavor teas, and are also eaten raw. They are a good source of vitamin C.

Common names and synonyms: Calamondin orange, China orange, musk lime, Panama orange, Philippine orange, to-kumquat.

Calamus - *see* **SWEET FLAG**

Calebasse - *see* **CALABASH**

California chilli - *see* **ANAHEIM**

CALLALOO (*see also* **COCOYAM, TARO**) - The name of a soup made in many islands of the Caribbean, callaloo is also the name of the large, wide, green leaves that go into it. One of these greens is amaranth (genus *Amaranthus*) - either "Surinam amaranth" (with an African origin) or "Chinese spinach" (which is probably native to the West Indies). The other kind of green is the leaves of dasheen or taro (*Colocasia esculenta*). Collectively called callaloo - and in some places "sagaloo" - the leaves resemble spinach or sorrel and are cooked as a vegetable dish. Fresh callaloo leaves can be found in West Indian markets in the summer months, and they are available canned throughout the year.

Common names and synonyms: Calalu, callalou greens, Chinese spinach, dasheen, sagaloo, Surinam amaranth, taro.

See in addition: "Amaranth," Part II, Section A, Chapter 1; "Taro," Part II, Section B, Chapter 6.

Caltrop - *see* **WATER CHESTNUT**

Calvance pea - *see* **CHICKPEA**

CAMAS - The bulbs of "camas" herbs (*Camassia scilloides* or *C. leichtlinii* and *C. quamash* or *C. esculenta*) constituted an important food for Native North Americans of the West and Northwest. Indeed, both were named by these peoples who originally roasted, baked, and boiled them. Their consumption required some caution, however, for camas bulbs can be confused with the "death camus" (*Zigadenus* spp.), which, as its common name suggests, is toxic and can be lethal. In fact, it frequently poisons grazing animals in the western United States. Camas is also called "wild hyacinth."

Common names and synonyms: Camash, camass, commas, common camass, quamash, sqamash, wild hyacinth.

Camash - *see* **CAMAS**

CAMBUCÁ - A rare fruit, the cambucá (*Marlierea edulis*) grows on a tree with a range that is mostly confined to the coastal forests of the Brazilian states of Rio de Janeiro and São Paulo. The cambucá is a relative of the guava and the jaboticaba, and its yellowish fruit has a good flavor. It is eaten raw and made into juice.

Camomile - *see* **CHAMOMILE**

Camote - *see* **SWEET POTATO**

CAMPANULA - The genus name for numerous species of plants known as "bellflowers" or "Canterbury bells" is *Campanula* (meaning "bell" and referring to the shape of the flowers). Found in temperate zones, especially in the Mediterranean and tropical mountains, three species have been used as food. In the past, the fleshy roots and leaves of *C. rapunculoides* were cultivated to be eaten in England, and the plant was carried to North America, where it is now naturalized. Rampion (*C. rapunculus*) - another European native - was also grown for its roots and leaves in centuries past. It has an edible root that is used in salads and shoots that are cooked like asparagus. In addition, the leaves of *C. versicolor* have been used in salads.

Common names and synonyms: Bellflower, broad bellflower, Canterbury bell(s), harebell, rampion.

Canada ginger - *see* **WILD GINGER**

Canada pea - *see* **TUFTED VETCH**

Canada snakeroot - *see* **WILD GINGER**

Canada sweetgale - *see* **SWEET FERN**

Canadian turnip - *see* **RUTABAGA**

Cañahua - *see* **CAÑIHUA**

Canary grass - *see* **MAYGRASS**

Candleberry - *see* **CANDLENUT**

CANDLENUT - Also called "candleberry" and "Indian walnut," the candlenut tree (*Aleurites moluccana*), native to tropical Southeast Asia, produces a seed kernel that is roasted and eaten. The seeds are more used, however, for their oil, which presumably at one time or another has been used for candle making.

Common names and synonyms: Candleberry, Indian walnut.

Candy plant - *see* **CICELY**

Canella - *see* **WHITE CINNAMON**

CAÑIHUA (*see also* **CHENOPODIUM, QUINOA**) - A native of the Andean regions of southern Peru and Bolivia, cañihua (*Chenopodium pallidicaule*) is a cold-resistant grain known also as "quañiwa" and "cañahua." It is used much like quinoa, but does better in high regions because it is tolerant of both frost and drier soils. In addition, it has a higher protein content. Cañihua was first cultivated by ancient settlers in the region and continues to be grown today, but botanists think that its domestication is not yet complete. The grain is used to make a flour called *cañihuaco* and to make soups, stews, and desserts. It is even employed to flavor drinks.

Common names and synonyms: Cañahua, quañiwa.

CANISTEL – The fruit of a tropical tree, canistel (*Pouteria campechiana*) probably originated in Central America (Costa Rica or Belize) but has now spread throughout the Caribbean. It is sold in Florida and is a favorite in the markets of Havana and Nassau. The fruit is oval, hard, and green, changing to soft, orange, and glossy when ripe. The flesh has the texture of a hard-boiled egg (another of its names is eggfruit) and a taste similar to that of a sweet potato. It is eaten raw with lemon juice, is good in salads, and is made into custards and ice cream. It is extremely rich in beta-carotene.

Common names and synonyms: Eggfruit (tree).

Cankerroot - *see* **GOLDTHREAD**

Canna - *see* **ACHIRA, BERRIES**

CANNELLINI BEAN (*see also* **BEANS**) – Much used in Italian soups and stews and often appearing as an antipasto dressed with olive oil, the cannellini bean (*Phaseolus vulgaris*) is a "common bean" of American origin. It is, in fact, a white kidney bean that may have been developed in Italy. Cannellini beans are generally sold in canned form.

See in addition: "Beans, Peas, and Lentils," Part II, Section C, Chapter 3.

Canola oil - *see* **RAPE**

CANTALOUPE AND MUSKMELON (*see also* **MELONS**) – A variety of muskmelon, the cantaloupe (*Cucumis melo*) belongs to the squash family and is a member of the genus that includes cucumbers. The places of origin of most melons are uncertain, but Africa (the home of the watermelon), the Near East, and India appear to be the most likely candidates. The muskmelon (*Cucumis melo*) probably entered Europe from the Muslim world via Spain, and during the Renaissance, monks developed the cantaloupe from muskmelons in the garden of the papal villa at Cantalupo, located close to Rome. It was muskmelon seeds, however, that were carried to the New World by Columbus and later planted by the Spaniards in California – so that today it is muskmelons that are generally consumed by North Americans, even if they mistakenly call the fruits "cantaloupes." The cantaloupe, also known as the "sugar melon," has remained mostly a European melon, is somewhat larger than the muskmelon, and has a warty or scaly rind, in contrast to the raised netting that characterizes the rind of the muskmelon. The orange flesh of both provides plenty of beta-carotene and vitamin C as well as potassium.

Common names and synonyms: Sugar melon.

See in addition: "Cucumbers, Melons, and Watermelons," Part II, Section C, Chapter 6.

Cantarela - *see* **OKRA**

Canterbury bell(s) - *see* **CAMPANULA**

CAPE GOOSEBERRY (*see also* **BERRIES**) – Also called the "Peruvian cherry" and the "Peruvian groundcherry," the cape gooseberry (*Physalis peruviana*), with pale-yellow blooms, is a native of tropical America and very closely related to the tomatillo (*Physalis ixocarpa*), also American in origin. Nonetheless, it is named the "cape gooseberry" because of a round-the-world journey that took it to, among other places, South Africa, where it was cultivated at the Cape of Good Hope. When first introduced in Australia, it was called the cape gooseberry, and the name stuck. Long before this, however, the berries grew wild and were important to many Native American groups, who ate them fresh and also dried them for winter use. The cape gooseberry has additional relatives, such as the Chinese lantern plant and the groundcherry (and, indeed, any of the plants of the genus *Physalis,* all of which have a parchment-like husk). Cape gooseberries are yellowish and juicy and a good source of beta-carotene, vitamin C, the B complex, phosphorus, and iron. They are frequently made into jams and jellies.

Common names and synonyms: Goldenberry, golden husk, groundcherry, Peruvian cherry, Peruvian groundcherry, strawberry tomato, winter cherry.

Cape periwinkle - *see* **PERIWINKLE**

CAPER(S) – A spiny trailing shrub, the caper bush (*Capparis spinosa*) grows to between 4 and 5 feet in height. It is native to the Mediterranean region and possibly to the Middle East as well. Its flower buds, which are picked and pickled in vinegar, are the capers that have been used since at least the time of the ancient Greeks as a condiment to add a salty-sour flavor to sauces, cheeses, salad dressings, stews, and various other meat and fish dishes. The caper bush grows wild and thrives in southern Europe, where Italy and Spain are the biggest caper producers.

Common names and synonyms: Caper berry, caper bud, caperbush, caper fruit, *cappero, kápari,* smooth caper, spiny caper, *tapèra.*

See also: "Spices and Flavorings," Part II, Section F, Chapter 1.

Cappero - *see* **CAPER(S)**

Capucine - *see* **MASHUA**

Capuli - *see* **CAPULIN, CHERRY**

CAPULIN (*see also* **CHERRY**) – Both the Mexican tree *Prunus capuli* and the Central and South American tree *P. salicifolia* are called "capulin" or "capuli." *Prunus capuli* is sometimes thought to be a form of the black cherry (*Prunus serotina*). Its edible cherries are consumed raw and in jellies, and their pits are ground to make flour. *P. salicifolia,* also known as the "tropical cherry," has edible purple cherries, which are also eaten out of hand or in preserves. Another fruit called "capulin" is the downy groundcherry (*Physalis pubescens*), which is also edible. Still another "capulin" is the Mexican wild plum (*Prunus capollin*), which is eaten both raw and cooked and turned into a juice that is combined with cornmeal and fried as cornmeal cakes. All of these fruits were important in the diet of Native Americans long before the arrival of Columbus. A final "capulin" is the small red fruit of *Muntingia calabura,* also called "calabur," "Panama berry," and "Jamaican cherry." This capulin has culinary applications like the others, but in addition, its leaves can be used to make a refreshing tea.

Common names and synonyms: Calabur, capuli, downy groundcherry, Jamaican cherry, Mexican wild plum, Panama berry, tropical cherry.

Carageen - *see* **CARRAGEENIN**

CARAMBOLA - The carambola (*Averrhoa carambola*) is also known as the "star fruit," and with good reason. It has an elongated yellow (sometimes white) body with five ribs that produce star shapes when it is sliced. Its native region was probably Malaysia, but the fruit now belongs to the world. Averrhoës, whose name it bears, was a twelfth-century Arab philosopher and physician who translated the works of Aristotle into Arabic. The word "carambola," however, is a Native American name for the fruit, and today it is cultivated in Asia, the West Indies, Florida, Hawaii, and Central and South America. The carambola has a fragrance reminiscent of quince and crisp, juicy flesh that can be either sweet or sour: Both tastes work well when applied to the appropriate salads, cooked dishes, and drinks. The carambola is also delicious eaten raw and provides the consumer with plenty of vitamin C.

Common names and synonyms: Belimbing, bilimbi, Chinese star fruit, five-angled fruit, star apple, star fruit.

CARAUNDA - Also known as "karanda," the caraunda (*Carissa carandas*) is an evergreen shrub or small tree of the East Indies that has a somewhat acidic fruit. In India, these reddish berries are eaten raw when ripe and pickled when not mature.

Common names and synonyms: Karanda.

CARAWAY - An herb native to Europe and Asia, caraway (*Carum carvi*) still grows wild on both continents. It is also a plant closely associated with the Arab world, where it is called *karawya,* and has traveled sufficiently widely to have become naturalized in the Americas. Its slightly sharp- and peppery-tasting seeds, which are ready for harvesting when they turn brown, have been used as a spice for at least 5,000 years, and there is reportedly evidence of their culinary use even prior to the Neolithic Revolution. Caraway seeds were an ancient item of importance in the spice trade and have been much in demand for the preservation of foods such as sauerkraut. Caraway was once enormously popular in English cookery. Shakespeare

mentions "a dish of caraways," and at Trinity College, Cambridge, the tradition of serving roasted apples with caraway continues. Today, caraway is most frequently used in northern European – especially German and Austrian – cooking. The seeds are a common ingredient in rye breads, sauerkraut, potato salads, cabbage dishes, goulashes, cheeses, cakes, and the German liqueur *Kümmel,* the name of which means caraway.

Common names and synonyms: Jintan, karawya, Kümmel.

See also: "Spices and Flavorings," Part II, Section F, Chapter 1.

Carciofo - *see* **ARTICHOKE**

CARDAMOM - A member of the ginger family, cardamom (*Elettaria cardamomum*) is a plant native to South Asia, and the Cardamom Hills in India were named for the cardamom growing there. The seeds of the plant, which come in triangular capsules, have been used as a spice since ancient times. They found their way to Europe along the caravan routes and were an important commodity in the Greek spice trade with the East as early as the fourth century B.C. Cardamom was a popular spice in Rome and presumably radiated out from there to those other inhabitants of Europe who could afford it. Today, there are cardamom plantations in much of the tropical world, including Central America, although southern India remains the largest producing region. The biggest consumers of cardamom are the diverse peoples of Scandinavia and India. Scandinavians use the sweetness of the seeds to flavor fruit dishes, gingerbread, and Swedish meatballs. The Indians use the dried and ground seeds as one of the essential ingredients of curry powder. In addition, cardamom is crucial to the flavored coffees of the Arab world, and an oil derived from the plant is employed in flavoring liqueurs. "Cardamom" is also the name of an East Indian plant (*Amomum cardamomum*) whose seeds are used as a bad substitute for true cardamom seeds.

Common names and synonyms: Cardamon, cardamum.

See also: "Spices and Flavorings," Part II, Section F, Chapter 1.

Cardamon - *see* **CARDAMOM**

Cardamum - *see* **CARDAMOM**

Cardi - *see* **CARDOON**

Cardoni - *see* **CARDOON**

CARDOON - One of the edible thistles, the cardoon (*Cynara cardunculus*) is a relative of the globe artichoke. It is celery-like in appearance, with silvery gray stalks. The plant is native to the Mediterranean region, where it has been cultivated since the days of the Romans and where it remains a popular vegetable in Spain, France, and Italy. Cardoons were cultivated for a time in the United States but were never much appreciated save by Italian-Americans, in whose markets the vegetables can still be found. It is unfortunate that cardoons are not more widely known because they have an excellent flavor. They are frequently eaten raw in a sauce of olive oil, anchovies, and garlic; when cooked (usually blanched), the stalks taste bitter-sweet – something like celery and something like artichokes. Cardoons are a good source of potassium, iron, and calcium.

Common names and synonyms: Cardi, cardoni, common cardoon, Paris cardoon, red-stemmed cardoon, Spanish cardoon, Tours cardoon.

CAROB – Carob pods grow on a leguminous tree (*Ceratonia siliqua*) of the pea family that can rise upward of 50 feet above the ground. Carobs are native to the eastern Mediterranean region (and possibly western Asia as well), where they were grown in ancient times by the Greeks, who also introduced their cultivation into Italy. The pods (which are sweet and are enjoyed by animals and humans alike) are probably the proverbial "locusts" eaten by John the Baptist during his stay in the wilderness and thus are called "Saint-John's-bread." They were also a staple in the diet of the Duke of Wellington's cavalry during the Peninsular War. The pods grow up to a foot in length, dry on the tree, and are harvested when they fall to the ground. They contain seeds whose weight is believed to have been used by early jewelers to determine the carat. Today, the seeds are utilized to make locust gum, which is employed in the food industry as a thickener, in the preparation of cheese and meat products, and to stabilize ice cream. A pulpy material from the pod is dried to become carob powder, a substance that is roasted and used as a substitute for cocoa and chocolate as well as coffee. Carob has far fewer calories than chocolate or cocoa and does not contain caffeine or cause allergies.

Common names and synonyms: Algarroba, locust, locust bean, Saint-John's-bread.

Carolina tea-tree – *see* **YAUPON**

CAROLINA VANILLA – An herb of the southeastern United States that reaches 2 to 3 feet in height, Carolina vanilla (*Trilisa odoratissima*) has leaves that are employed in large amounts to flavor tobacco. The leaves, which have a pleasing vanilla odor, are also used to make a fragrant tea.

Common names and synonyms: Deertongue, vanilla leaf, vanilla plant.

See also: "Spices and Flavorings," Part II, Section F, Chapter 1.

CARRAGEEN AND CARRAGEENIN (*see also* **SEAWEED**) – Also called "Irish moss" and "pearl moss," carrageen (*Chondrus crispus*) is a type of purple seaweed that frequents the coasts of the North Atlantic from the British Isles on the European side to the Maritime Provinces and New England on the American side. Most is harvested commercially for a gelatin used in food processing. It has also been used for clarifying beer, and some carrageen is employed in thickening soups and chowders and

making jelly. Carrageenin is an extractive of carrageen and other red algae (such as *Gigartina mammillosa*), used mostly as a suspending agent in foods. It is also called "Irish moss extractive."

Common names and synonyms: Carrageen, carragheen, Irish moss, pearl moss.

See in addition "Algae," Part II, Section C, Chapter 1.

CARROT – A root vegetable of the Umbelliferae family – and thus related to parsley, dill, and celery – the carrot (*Daucus carota* ssp. *carota* when wild and ssp. *sativus* when domesticated), although originally native to Afghanistan, is now found all over the world in many shapes, sizes, and colors. It grows best in moist soils and mild climates, and its taproot is the edible portion of the plant. Early varieties were red, black, or purple, and today carrots in Asia can look much like beets to Westerners, who would also probably approach with caution one carrot variety in the Far East that grows up to 3 feet long. Carrots were cultivated by the Greeks and the Romans but not used very widely in Europe until the Middle Ages. In the sixteenth century, a yellow strain began to develop, and, in Holland of the seventeenth century, the orange type now familiar in the West arose. After the carrot reached the Americas, it frequently escaped cultivation to become the wild carrot known as "Queen-Anne's-lace." Like so many other vegetables from Europe, carrots became popular in the New World only after Americans had occasion to visit the Continent in large numbers and become familiar with the foods there. In the case of this vegetable, the occasion was World War I, after which Michigan and California became the biggest carrot producers in the United States. Carrots are available fresh, canned, frozen, dehydrated, and as a juice. They are eaten raw and often added to salads, as well as becoming an important ingredient in dishes such as carrot cake. Cooked, they make an excellent ingredient in stews and soups. In addition, the seeds contain an oil that is expressed for flavorings and for perfumes. The carrot has a great reputation as a source of beta-carotene (the precursor of vitamin A) and vitamin C, and it joins other vegetables as an apparent cancer fighter, cholesterol lowerer, and fiber provider.

Common names and synonyms: Queen-Anne's-lace.

CASABA (MELON) (*see also* **MELONS**) – Also spelled "cassaba," the name casaba designates a variety of winter melon (*Cucumis melo*) named for Kassaba, itself a former name of Turgutlu, Turkey. The fruit has a yellow rind and sweet, whitish flesh that contains much vitamin C.

Common names and synonyms: Cassaba, winter melon.

See in addition: "Cucumbers, Melons, and Watermelons," Part II, Section C, Chapter 6.

CASCABEL (*see also* **CHILLI PEPPERS**) – In Spanish, *cascabel* means to jingle or rattle – and when this green or red pepper (about the size and shape of a small tomato) is dried and turns a brownish red, it becomes translucent and its seeds rattle about inside. Rarely used fresh, the dried *cascabel* (*Capsicum annuum*) is prized for the rich, smoky heat that it imparts to any dish or sauce in which it is simmered. Cascabel peppers are grown in Mexico but are available in the United States.

Common names and synonyms: Chilli bola.

See in addition: "Chilli Peppers," Part II, Section C, Chapter 4.

CASHEW – A kidney-shaped nut that grows in a double shell at the end of a strongly sweet-smelling, pear-shaped fruit, the cashew (*Anacardium occidentale*) is a very unusual nut. The largest part of the fruit is the juicy, pear-shaped fruit called the cashew "apple," which is eaten raw or fermented to become alcohol. The nut itself grows at the lower end of the "apple," but one never sees cashews sold in the shell for a very good reason. The cashew is related to poison ivy and poison sumac, and the shells contain an irritating oil that must be gotten rid of by heating before the nut can be extracted. The tree is a native of South America, but in the sixteenth century the Portuguese introduced it in the East African and Indian parts of their empire, and these areas are today the biggest exporters of cashews. Although lower in total fat than most nuts, cashews are high in saturated fat. They are a good source of folacin, iron, protein, and vitamin C. The cashew apple is also high in vitamin C and is used in beverages and to make jelly.

Common names and synonyms: Cashew apple, cashew fruit, cashew nut.

Cashew apple - *see* **CASHEW**
Cassaba - *see* **CASABA (MELON)**
Cassabanana - *see* **CUCUMBER**
Cassava - *see* **MANIOC**
Cassia - *see* **CINNAMON AND CASSIA, INDIAN BARK, SAIGON CINNAMON**
Cassina - *see* **YAUPON**
Cassine - *see* **DAHOON HOLLY**
Cassis - *see* **BLACK CURRANT**

CASTORBEAN – A native of Africa, the castor-oil plant (*Ricinus communis*) produces the castorbean – a poisonous seed – from which oil is extracted. The tree now grows throughout the tropical world, and its oil has many valuable industrial uses, but save for doses of the infamous castor oil, it is not consumed by humans.

Common names and synonyms: Castor-oil plant.

Castor-oil plant - *see* **CASTORBEAN**
Cat - *see* **KHAT**

CATARINA (*see also* **CHILLI PEPPERS**) – Grown in Texas and northern Mexico, the catarina chilli (*Capsicum annuum*) is red, some 1 to 2 inches in length, and can be either tapered or broad and oblong. Like its relative the cascabel, when the catarina is dried, its seeds rattle. Its moderate heat makes it an excellent ingredient in salsas.

See in addition: "Chilli Peppers," Part II, Section C, Chapter 4.

CATAWBA (GRAPE) (*see also* **GRAPES**) – The catawba is an American wine grape (*Vitis labrusca*) used to make Catawba wines. Called "one of the most celebrated of native American wines, at the beginning of the twentieth century, at century's end these heavy and somewhat sweet wines were virtually unknown. Most Catawba wines were white, and the highest priced were of the "sparkling" type. Some red Catawba was made, along with "sweet Catawba," which was a rich, fortified wine.

See in addition: "Wine," Part III, Chapter 13.

Catbrier - *see* **GREENBRIER**
Catchweed - *see* **GOOSEGRASS**
Catclaw acacia - *see* **ACACIA**
Catechu - *see* **BETEL NUT**

CATJANG (*see also* **COWPEA**) – One of the cowpeas of the genus *Vigna*, the catjang (*V. unguiculata*) is a relatively primitive form, cultivated mostly in Asia but also in Africa. Its main use is as animal feed, but people also use the seeds for food in both fresh and dried forms.

Common names and synonyms: Catjang pea.

See in addition: "Beans, Peas, and Lentils," Part II, Section C, Chapter 3.

Catjang pea - *see* **CATJANG**
Catmint - *see* **CATNIP**
Catnep - *see* **CATNIP**

CATNIP – A perennial herb native to Eurasia, catnip (*Nepeta cataria*) is now widely naturalized in North America. Usually regarded as a weed, it has flowering tops, grows to about 3 feet in height, and has long been associated with cats, which are attracted by its odor. But the leaves and roots of catnip have also been used medicinally and as food for millennia. Indeed, they are still regularly consumed in parts of East Asia.

Common names and synonyms: Catmint, catnep.

Cat's-eye - *see* **LONGAN**

CATTAIL – A familiar roadside sight along drainage ditches, cattails – of the genus *Typha* – are marsh-dwelling plants that are scattered about the world, and their various parts have been used as food by hunter-gatherers since time immemorial. Native Americans, for example, ate the tender shoots and leaf bases raw, dried and ground the rhizomes into flour, and even roasted and ate the tops like corn on the cob. The seeds are also edible, and the flowers provide a pollen that can be added to flour. Cattails and bulrushes are sometimes lumped together, but they belong to different genera.

Common names and synonyms: Reed-mace.

Cattley guava - *see* **STRAWBERRY GUAVA**

CAULIFLOWER (*see also* **CABBAGE**) – The cauliflower (*Brassica oleracea* var. *botrytis*), another – and many would say the most elegant – member of the sprawling cabbage family, is a direct descendant of the original wild cabbage and a close relative of broccoli. The kind of cauliflower usually found in vegetable hors d'oeuvres has a white head, achieved by growers who cover the flower head in its outer leaves so as to block sunlight and, thus, prevent the formation of chlorophyll. There is also a purple type, called cauliflower broccoli. The cauliflower (the name is probably from the Italian *caolifiori*, meaning "cabbage flowers") was apparently known in much of Europe during the Middle Ages, but then disappeared and had to be reintroduced to the rest of the Continent in the sixteenth century. This was accomplished by the Italians, probably from Cyprus, where the plant had reached from Asia. In Europe, where much cauliflower is consumed, Italy has long been the major producer. The vegetable could be found in U.S. markets from the turn of the twentieth century onward but consumption only became significant following World War II. Cauliflowers are very low in calories but rich in vitamin C, the B complex, and vitamin K (which helps to clot blood).

Common names and synonyms: Asparagus broccoli, broccoli (British), cauliflower broccoli.

See in addition: "Cruciferous and Green Leafy Vegetables," Part II, Section C, Chapter 5.

Caulorapa - *see* **KOHLRABI**

Cava - *see* **KAVA**

Cawesh - *see* **POSHTE**

Cayenne - *see* **CAYENNE PEPPER**

Cayenne cherry - *see* **PITANGA**

CAYENNE PEPPER (*see also* **CHILLI PEPPERS**) - Today, the term "cayenne" is synonymous with red pepper and can mean any of the ground, hot, red chilli peppers of the *Capsicum* species that are native to the Americas. And recipes from areas as diverse as Mexico and China, Louisiana and India, call for it. Originally, however, the pepper in question (*C. annuum*) was ground into powder in Cayenne in French Guiana (it is also called the ginnie pepper and guine pepper), and the term "cayenne" was meant to signify the hottest ground red pepper available. Cayennes are very hot, bright red when mature, long (some 4 to 6 inches) and slender, and generally are dried. These pointed red pods make an excellent addition to sauces, and when green they are incorporated in salsas. But their major use is in the production of powdered cayenne pepper (also designated hot red pepper). In addition, cayenne peppers have long been the primary ingredient in all of the Louisiana hot sauces except the Tabasco brand. The *de árbol* is a close relative of the cayenne pepper (and looks like it) and also is ground into powdered form. Another, smaller (about an inch long) close relative is the red *Pico de Pajaro* or "bird's-beak" - so named because of its beaklike shape. Today, cayenne peppers are grown in Mexico; Louisiana; South, Southeast, and East Asia; and West Africa.

Common names and synonyms: Bird's-beak, cayenne, *de árbol*, ginnie pepper, guine pepper, hot red pepper, *Pico de Pajaro*.

See in addition: "Chilli Peppers," Part II, Section C, Chapter 4.

Caygua - *see* **KORILA**

Caymito - *see* **STAR-APPLE**

Cayua - *see* **KORILA**

Ceci - *see* **CHICKPEA**

CEDAR - The name "cedar" embraces a number of trees of various genera, including those of the genus *Thuja*, which helped to feed Native Americans. In the northwestern portion of North America, the inner bark of the giant or western red cedar, *T. plicata*, provided food in much the same fashion as the inner bark of the slippery elm. In the Northeast, it was the white cedar (*T. occidentalis* - also known as northern white cedar, yellow cedar, featherleaf cedar, and arbor-vitae) that provided young shoots and leaves that were cooked like vegetables and made into tea.

Common names and synonyms: Arbor-vitae, featherleaf cedar, giant cedar, northern white cedar, western red cedar, white cedar, yellow cedar.

Ceiba - *see* **KAPOK TREE**

Celeriac - *see* **CELERY AND CELERY ROOT**

CELERY AND CELERY ROOT (*see also* **CELERY SEED**) - A member of the parsley family, and native to the Mediterranean region and the Middle East, wild celery (*Apium graveolens*) was one of the first vegetables to appear in recorded history. From the writings of Confucius, we know that celery (probably wild) was in use in China before 500 B.C. The ancient Egyptians gathered the plant for its seeds - used as seasoning - as well as for its stalks and leaves, whereas in ancient Greece celery had a medicinal as well as a culinary reputation.

Two types of celery have subsequently been developed. One is the so-called true celery (*Apium graveolens* var. *dulce*), with green or blanched stems that are eaten raw, sliced into salads, and cooked as a vegetable, and the seeds of which are still used as seasoning. The most common variety is the medium-green Pascal celery, which was first cultivated in Italy and, by the seventeenth century, in France. In the United States, commercial cultivation of Pascal celery dates from 1874, when Dutch farmers near Kalamazoo, Michigan, passed out free samples to train passengers to popularize the vegetable. Celery comes in both blanched form (celery hearts) and green with large, fleshy ribs, the difference being that the former is kept away from the sun to ensure whiteness. Celery leaves are sometimes cut up and dried to be added as an herb to stews, soups, and other dishes. Celery is reputed to lower blood pressure, is very low in calories, and provides a respectable amount of vitamin C and folacin.

The other type of celery (*Apium graveolens* var. *rapaceum*), cultivated for its starch-storing root rather than for stalks, is commonly called celery root or celeriac. It appears as an ugly sort of foodstuff – a gnarled, turnip-like form with dangling rootlets – ranging in size from an orange to a cantaloupe. But its zesty taste of celery and parsley intermingled has long been a part of French salads (often with a remoulade sauce) as well as an important ingredient of soups, stuffings, purees, and the like in Russia and the countries of northern Europe. Also called "knob celery" and "turnip-rooted celery," the root is a fair source of iron and calcium and makes a small contribution to the B-vitamin intake.

Common names and synonyms: Celeriac, *céleri rave,* celery heart(s), Hamburg celery, knob celery, Pascal celery, true celery, turnip-rooted celery, wild celery.

Celery cabbage - *see* **BOK CHOY, CHINESE CABBAGE**

Celery mustard - *see* **PAKCHOI AND KAI CHOY**

CELERY SEED - Celery (*Apium graveolens* var. *dulce*) was developed in seventeenth-century Europe from its wild predecessor and was first recorded as a plant in 1623 in France. The tiny brown seeds from celery impart a mild celery flavor to dishes in which the use of the stalks would not be appropriate, such as bread dough and sauces and some soups, salads, stews, and potato salads. Ground celery seeds also flavor celery salt, salad dressings, and the like.

See also: "Spices and Flavorings," Part II, Section F, Chapter 1.

Celtuce - *see* **LETTUCE**

Century plant - *see* **AGAVE**

Cep - *see* **BOLETE, MUSHROOMS AND FUNGI**

Cèpe - *see* **BOLETE, MUSHROOMS AND FUNGI**

Cèpe de bolete - *see* **BOLETE**

Cèpe de Bordeaux - *see* **BOLETE**

Ceriman - *see* **MONSTERA**

Ceriman de Mexico - *see* **MONSTERA**

CEYLON GOOSEBERRY (*see also* **BERRIES**) - Also known as *ketembilla,* and *quetembilla,* the Ceylon gooseberry (*Dovyalis hebecarpa*) is a fruit of tropical Asia that grows on a bushy shrub. The berries are maroon to purple in color and resemble gooseberries in appearance and taste. Today, the berries are cultivated throughout tropical Asia, and especially in India. Ceylon gooseberries are also commercially cultivated on a small scale in Florida and California. They are eaten fresh and made into preserves and jellies.

Common names and synonyms: Ketembilla, quetembila.

Ceylon spinach - *see* **MALABAR SPINACH, TALINUM**

Chaco - *see* **CHAYOTE**

Chad - *see* **BEET**

Chago - *see* **MAUKA**

CHAMBURO (*see also* **PAPAYA**) - A relative of the papaya, and papaya-like in appearance, the chamburo (*Carica pubescens*) is a native of northern South America that is now cultivated along the Andes as far south as Bolivia at altitudes of about 3,000 feet. The yellow fruit is tart, even when mature, and is generally made into juice or preserved instead of eaten raw.

CHAMOMILE - The dried flowers of chamomile (*Anthemis nobilis*) are used as an herbal infusion for baths and tisanes. They deliver a pungent, grassy flavor, and chamomile (also camomile) is said to be good for the digestive system. Chamomile teas were much consumed by Victorian ladies hoping to restore vitality. The herb was also employed historically as a gargle for sore throats.

Common names and synonyms: Camomile.

Champignon d'Paris - *see* **MUSHROOMS AND FUNGI**

Chan - *see* **HYPTIS**

CHANTERELLE (*see also* **MUSHROOMS AND FUNGI**) - The yellow or golden (although occasionally black or white) trumpets of the chanterelle (*Cantharellus cibarius*), a wild mushroom of the woodlands, are found in both Europe and North America. This edible fungus is gathered in abundance in the Pacific Northwest but has been especially appreciated in Europe, where it is known by many names, including *chanterelle* (French), *Pfifferling* (German), and *girolle* (Italian). The chanterelle has yet to be cultivated and thus is only gathered. Its taste varies widely – from delicate to fairly intense. The chanterelle is a good source of vitamins A and D and makes a contribution to the intake of the vitamin B complex.

Common names and synonyms: Chantarelle, forest mushroom, *girolle,* golden chanterelle, *Pfifferling.*

See in addition: "Fungi," Part II, Section C, Chapter 7.

Chard - *see* **BEET, SWISS CHARD**

CHARDONNAY (*see also* **GRAPES**) - The great white Burgundian wines of France, such as the light and dry Pouilly Fuissé, are made almost exclusively with Chardonnay grapes (*Vitis vinifera*), which are now grown all over the world. In the climate of Oregon, this grape grows so well that the state has become well known for its Burgundy-style wines. In California and Australia, Chardonnay is used to make dry wines as well as serving as a base for sparkling wines. It is a very expensive grape.

See in addition: "Wine," Part III, Chapter 13.

Charnushka - *see* **NIGELLA**

CHASTE TREE - Cultivated in both the New and the Old Worlds, this aromatic shrub or tree (*Vitex agnus-castus*) has a reputation for anaphrodisiac qualities – hence its name. But it is also called "wild pepper" and "monk's-pepper," and its seeds have served as a spice. The leaves of other *Vitex* species are used for tea, and some produce fruits that are consumed throughout the world's tropical zones.

Common names and synonyms: Agnus castus, hemp tree, Indian spice, monk's-pepper tree, sage tree, wild pepper.

Chawa - *see* **SWEET PEPPERS AND WAX PEPPERS**

CHAYA - Also called the "spinach tree," chaya (*Cnidoscolus chayamansa*) is found throughout Mesoamerica and the West Indies. In Mexico, this plant, which can attain the height of a human, has large leaves that are boiled and eaten as a vegetable and used to wrap tamales. The leaves must be boiled to render harmless a toxin they contain, and many varieties have stinging hairs on the leaves, which makes some cooks less than enthusiastic about their preparation.

Common names and synonyms: Spinach tree.

CHAYOTE (*see also* **SQUASH AND PUMPKIN**) - A member of the gourd family (Cucurbitaceae), this well-traveled, spiny vegetable (*Sechium edule*) originated in the American tropics. Called *chayotli* in Nahuatl, it was domesticated in what is now Mexico, was spread throughout South America after the Spanish conquest, and is now found in places as diverse and distant as North Africa and Indonesia. Such peregrinations doubtless account for its myriad names, a few of which are vegetable pear, mirliton, *pepinella, xuxu,* christophene, *chocho,* custard marrow, and *sousous.* The taste of this usually green, pear-shaped, vine-growing vegetable resembles that of other cucurbits such as zucchini and the summer squashes; unlike these, however, the chayote must usually have its skin removed before cooking. Most parts of the plant are edible, and the leaves and vine tips are eaten as vegetables. The tuberous roots, which are generally peeled and boiled and taste similar to a Jerusalem artichoke, are an important source of starch. The fruit is used like a squash. It is boiled, baked, fried, steamed, stuffed, pureed in soups, and made into desserts; many consider the seed a delicacy as well. Chayote is a fair source of vitamin C and potassium.

Common names and synonyms: Buddha's-hand, *chaco, chayotli, chinchayote, chocho, choko,* christophene, christophine, *chuchu,* custard marrow, *guispui,* mango squash, mirliton, *pepinella, sousous, tallon, tallote,* vegetable pear, *xuxu.*

Chayotli - *see* **CHAYOTE**

CHE (*see also* **BERRIES**) - A native of eastern Asia that was long ago naturalized in Japan and more recently introduced in Europe and the United States, che (*Cudrania tricuspidata*) is related to the mulberry and is sometimes called the "Chinese mulberry." Its fruits are relatively large, develop a bright, reddish color when ripe, and are reportedly delicious. In China, che leaves serve to feed silkworms when there is a shortage of mulberry leaves.

Common names and synonyms: Chinese mulberry, cudrang, mandarin melon-berry.

Checkerberry - *see* **WINTERGREEN**

Chekkurmanis - *see* **SWEET-SHOOT**

CHEMPEDAK - Probably native to Indochina, the chempedak tree (*Artocarpus integer*) is an ancient cultivar. Its yellowish to brown, oblong fruits are large - reaching a foot or more in length. The custard-like pulp is sweet and eaten raw, and the seeds are consumed after boiling.

CHENOPODIUM (*see also* various *Chenopodium* entries) - A large genus of herbs, *Chenopodium* includes the goosefoots and other plants that are found throughout the world's temperate regions - today mostly as weeds. Species raised in the pre-Columbian Americas that are still in cultivation include quinoa (*C. quinoa*), mostly grown in Ecuador, Peru, and Bolivia, and *cañihua* (*C. pallidicaule*), confined to the high Andes. In addition, *C. bushianum* appears to have been cultivated by Native Americans in eastern North America prior to the arrival of the Europeans, and *C. nuttalliae* was domesticated in Mexico. Since 1492, *C. huauzontle* has also been domesticated in Mexico, and both the Mexican grains are called *chia.* All of these plants were (and are) cultivated primarily for their seeds, which are ground to make breads, gruels, and - in the Andean regions - *chicha,* a beer. This does not mean, however, that the green, fleshy parts of the plants were not consumed, and other chenopods - for example, lamb's-quarter (*C. album*) and the wild spinach "Good-King-Henry" (*C. bonus-henricus*) - were gathered for their flower buds and greens. Still others, such as *epazote* (*C. ambrosioides*), called "Mexican tea" in Mexico and *paiko* in Peru, have served for thousands of years as seasonings.

Common names and synonyms: Chenopod, *chia, epazote,* goosefoot, lamb's-quarter, *paiko,* quinoa.

CHERIMOYA - No wonder the cherimoya (*Annona cherimola*) is sometimes called a "custard apple." When ripe, this heart-shaped, scaly, pulpy fruit has smooth, cream-colored flesh and tastes like a custard made from tropical fruit. Although much smaller than a watermelon, it has similar large, black seeds. The cherimoya's name comes from the ancient Quecha language, and the fruit is of American (specifically, the South American highlands) origin but has been grown for many centuries in Central America and the Caribbean region for local use. It has also moved as far as Iberia to the east and to Australia, New Zealand, and Malaysia in other parts of the globe. In the United States, the cherimoya is grown in California and Florida. But because it does not keep well in shipping, it is not generally available in produce markets, and those who cannot find this fruit must order it through specialty catalogs for an exotic treat. The cherimoya, of the same family as the sweetsop and the sugar apple, provides a good measure of vitamin C and some iron.

Common names and synonyms: Anona, chirimoya, custard apple, sherbet-fruit.

Chermai - *see* **OTAHEITE GOOSEBERRY**

CHERRY (*see also* **CAPULIN, CHERRY LAUREL, CHIMAJA, CHOKECHERRY, SAND CHERRY, SOUR CHERRY**) – Cherries come from any of several trees that belong to the genus *Prunus* and are part of the rose family. The small, rounded fruits are – along with apricots, peaches, and plums – "stone fruits," or "drupes." The cherry originated in temperate Europe and Asia, and doubtless wild cherries played a role in the human diet eons before the invention of agriculture and the beginning of recorded history. Our Neolithic ancestors extracted – and presumably fermented – cherry juice before it was discovered how to make wine from grapes.

The sweet cherry (*Prunus avium*) and the sour cherry (*P. cerasus*) are the two main cultivated types; such cultivation apparently stretches back at least to the ancient Greeks. Cherries were very popular in Germany, France, and England toward the end of the Middle Ages, and they reached the Americas with early immigrants. The bulk of the world's cherries is still produced in Europe. One important exception is the sour cherry, which is mostly cultivated in North America despite its historical background in the world of Rome (it is named for Cerasus in Pontus, the city where the Roman general Lucullus defeated Mithradates and Tigranes, after which he took their cherry trees back to Italy).

Various cultures have provided many names for the hundreds of varieties of cherries that are consumed fresh, canned, and frozen and used (among other things) for candies, jams, tarts, pie fillings, liqueurs (especially kirsch), and flavoring medicines. In parts of the Old World, the powder of ground cherrystones has been employed as a spice.

The bing cherry is perhaps the best known of the sweet varieties in the United States, and the Montmorency the best known of the sour. In addition, of course, there are wild red and black cherries. The wild black cherry, also known as the chokecherry (*Prunus virginiana*), was exploited by Native Americans in the eastern part of North America for both food and medicine long before the Europeans arrived. In fact, this cherry is still used in both capacities; it is a principal ingredient in cough medications, including the venerable "Smith Brothers'" cough drops. Wild black cherries also find their way into some rums. Cherries are high in potassium and, like all red fruits, contain vitamins A and C along with B vitamins.

Common names and synonyms: Amarelle, Bigarreau, bing cherry, bird cherry, black cherry, capuli, Capulin, chokecherry, Gean, Guigne, klarbar, Mazzard, Montmorency, pie cherry, red cherry, sour cherry, sweet cherry, tart cherry, wild black cherry, wild red cherry.

Cherry birch - *see* **SWEET BIRCH**

CHERRY LAUREL (*see also* **CHERRY**) – An evergreen plant of Europe, and now naturalized in North America, the cherry laurel (*Prunus laurocerasus*) bears small black fruits that have little taste. But its thick, glossy leaves have a flavor like bitter almond and are used in cooking - especially for flavoring dessert puddings.

Cherry pepper - *see* **HUNGARIAN CHERRY PEPPER**

CHERRY PLUM (*see also* **PLUM**) – Also known as the "myrobalan plum," the cherry plum (*Prunus cerasifera*) is an Asiatic fruit now used extensively in Europe for stock to bud domestic varieties. The European plum (*P. domestica*) is thought to be a hybrid of the cherry plum and the sloe. Cherry plums are yellow, red, or purple; they are juicy but not especially tasty.

Common names and synonyms: Myrobalan plum.

Cherry tomato - *see* **TOMATO**

CHERVIL – There is an annual chervil (*Anthriscus cerefolium*) and a biennial (*Chaerophyllum bulbosum*); the latter is also called "turnip-rooted chervil." Both are related to the carrot family and to parsley (which the annual variety resembles). The latter is native to western Asia and the Balkans (it grows wild in Iran and southwestern Russia) and derives its name from a Greek word meaning "cheer-leaf." The Romans used chervil for its aromatic, parsley-tasting, anise-smelling leaves and are credited with introducing it into western Europe and then spreading it about the continent. Chervil has parsley-like leaves, used for seasoning, that were long popular in England and today are especially appreciated in France. It is one of the fines herbes (along with parsley, chives, and tarragon) employed in salads and as potherbs. In addition, chervil is used much in the same way as parsley in fish and shellfish dishes, omelettes, soups, and sauces. The leaves are available both fresh and dried. The biennial, which is native to Europe, is grown for its carrot-like root.

Common names and synonyms: Garden chervil, leaf chervil, salad chervil, sweet cicely, turnip chervil, turnip-rooted chervil.

See also: "Spices and Flavorings," Part II, Section F, Chapter 1.

CHESTNUT – Members of the beech family, chestnut trees are native to the world's temperate regions, and there are several trees of the genus *Castanea* that bear nuts enclosed in a prickly burr. The name, said to derive from a town – Kastanéa – in Asia Minor, has been preserved in most of the countries of Europe where chestnuts are enjoyed (*Kastanie* in German and *châtaigne* in French, for example), and the aroma of roasting chestnuts during the holiday season has long been an indelible memory for most city dwellers of Europe and North America. In the early twentieth century in North America, the native chestnut (*Castanea dentata*) was almost totally destroyed by a blight - a destructive fungal bark disease that may have killed 3 billion or more chestnut trees between the turn of the century and

1940. Because Asiatic varieties of the chestnut tree proved resistant to the blight, an attempt has been made to substitute Chinese trees (and European varieties), but thus far practically all chestnuts that are roasted or boiled and chopped into dressings to accompany birds and game in America have been imported from Europe. They are not, however, European "horse chestnuts" (*Aesculus hippocastanum*), which are bitter and mildly toxic, unlike the American and other European varieties, which have a mild, sweet, nutty taste. Chestnuts have a mealy consistency reminiscent of roasted cassava or potatoes. They were mentioned and used by the ancient Greeks and Romans and have served some people very much as a staple crop. Indeed, dried chestnuts were historically ground into flour for making breads, and in some places chestnuts constituted the most important food for whole populations. The chestnut is the only nut high in vitamin C, and it is also a good source of the B vitamins. A bonus is that it is low in fat and calories.

Common names and synonyms: American chestnut, *châtaigne,* Chinese chestnut, dwarf chestnut, European chestnut, European horse chestnut, Japanese chestnut, *Kastanie,* Spanish chestnut, sweet chestnut.

See also: "Chestnuts," Part II, Section D, Chapter 1.

Chestnut bean - *see* **CHICKPEA**

CHIA - A species of sage that produces pods filled with tiny seeds, chia (*Salvia columbariae*) long provided Native Americans of southwestern North America with a grain substitute. In addition, the Aztecs, farther south, used these seeds and those of a Mexican chia (*Salvia hispanica*) to make a refreshing drink. The seeds are gathered much like grain and are then parched and ground into meal for baking flat breads and making porridges. Chia seeds were also often stored for future use.

Common names and synonyms: California chia, ghia, Mexican chia.

Chiccory - *see* **CHICORY**

Chich-pea - *see* **CHICKPEA**

Chickling grass - *see* **CHICKLING VETCH**

Chickling pea - *see* **CHICKLING VETCH**

CHICKLING VETCH (*see also* **LEGUMES**) - Also known as "grass pea" and "European grass pea," chickling vetch (*Lathyrus sativus*) is a pea cultivated in Europe for its seeds and for animal forage.

Common names and synonyms: Chickling grass, chickling pea, European grass pea, grass pea.

See in addition: "Beans, Peas, and Lentils," Part II, Section C, Chapter 3.

Chickory - *see* **CHICORY**

CHICKPEA (*see also* **BEANS**) - Known as *garbanzo* in Spanish, *ceci* in Italian, "gram" in India, and often as just plain "pulse" across the globe, the chickpea (*Cicer arietinum*) is an ancient pulse that originated in western Asia and was domesticated there some 7,000 years ago. The tan, hazelnut-sized seeds, with their wrinkled surfaces, nutty flavor, and crisp texture, soon became popular from the Mediterranean to India (as culinary traditions make clear) and today are practically universal. In the Near East, the chickpea is the basic ingredient for hummus and falafel and is frequently incorporated in couscous. In India, as the country's most important legume, the chickpea is roasted, boiled, and fried, is made into flour, and is part of a *dhal.* In the Mediterranean region, the chickpea figures prominently in the "poor cuisine" – as a staple in the diet of poor people, a substitute for meat (and sometimes for coffee as well), and an ingredient in the boiled dinners (*cocidos*) of Iberia.

Exactly when the chickpea reached Spain and Portugal is unclear – perhaps with the Phoenicians, certainly with the Romans. The Portuguese call the chickpea *grão do bico* ("grain with a beak") because of the little horn on the pea. From Iberia, chickpeas traveled to the Americas, where they achieved fame in Cuban bean soup and in menudo. The vegetable has also become a standard item on practically every salad bar in North America, a region where it can also be purchased dried or canned (but seldom fresh) in markets. Like almost all legumes, the chickpea is high in protein and the B-vitamin complex. Moreover, the chickpea and others of its relatives have recently come to be viewed as cholesterol fighters.

Common names and synonyms: Bengal gram, calvance pea, *ceci,* chestnut bean, chich, chich-pea, dwarf pea, garavance, garbanza, *garbanzo,* gram, gram pea, *grão do bico,* pulse, yellow gram.

See in addition: "Beans, Peas, and Lentils," Part II, Section C, Chapter 3.

CHICKWEED - So called because they are eaten by chickens, chickweeds (any of the various plants of the genus *Stellaria,* especially the common chickweed, *S. media*) have enjoyed something of a reputation for medicinal use. In fact, a synonym, "stitchwort," was assigned because of an alleged ability to cure pains in the side. Native to Europe, *Stellaria* species were given the Latin word for star as a name in view of the shape of their flowers. Several species of chickweed are eaten in Japan. In North America, *S. media* (introduced from Europe) has a reputation for making an excellent salad with its tender leaves and stems. The seeds are also edible. Today, chickweeds are used mostly as a potherb, but because they are so hardy, growing even throughout the winter months, and because they can be cooked as a green, they doubtless served for millennia as food for hunter-gatherers and also for those caught in famine circumstances, even in the colder seasons. The term chickweed can also refer to plants of the genus *Cerastium.*

Common names and synonyms: Common chickweed, stitchwort.

Chicle (tree) - *see* **SAPODILLA**

Chico - *see* **SAPODILLA**

CHICORY (*see also* **BELGIUM ENDIVE, ENDIVE AND ESCAROLE**) – Semantic problems abound with chicory (*Cichorium intybus*) – also called succory, radicchio, and red chicory), endive (*Cichorium endivia*), and escarole, which is the broadleafed variety of endive. All three are members of the dandelion family, but there the resemblance ends. *Cichorium endivia,* native to India, was the ancestor of endive and known to the Egyptians as well as to the ancient Greeks and Romans. By contrast, *C. intybus* is native to Europe, but the names nonetheless remain confused. In the United States, chicory is generally called Belgian endive, although this is also referred to simply as endive. The French, too, call it endive (and call endive *chicorée*), and radicchio is chicory's Italian name. The Flemish name for Belgian endive is *witloof* or "whiteleaf," because it was grown in cellars in dim light, which produced both the plant's whitish leaf color and its elongated leaves as they stretched out to seek light – indeed, modern methods of growing this pale, cigar-shaped vegetable follow the same principle. If part of the confusion is semantic, part also stems from the different uses of the plants. Chicory as well as endive roots are ground to become a natural coffee substitute (especially in France and French-influenced areas) or an addition to regular coffee for added flavor and reduced caffeine. However, the tight hearts of Belgian endive and radicchio are also attractive and slightly bitter ingredients in salads; in addition, their braised leaves can be a vegetable dish in their own right. Radicchio, although a relative newcomer to the U.S. culinary scene, is now grown domestically in New Jersey and California as well as in Italy and Mexico. Nonetheless, it remains a very expensive produce item.

Common names and synonyms: Asparagus chicory, *barbe de capucin,* Belgian endive, chiccory, chickory, endive, radicchio, *radicchio di castelfranco, radicchio di chiogga, radicchio di treviso, radicchio di Verona, radicchio rosso,* red chicory, redleafed chicory, red treviso chicory, red Verona chicory, *rosso di Verona,* succory, *witloef, witloof.*

Chico sapote - *see* **SAPODILLA**
Chico zapote - *see* **SAPODILLA**
Chihli cabbage - *see* **CHINESE CABBAGE**
Chiku - *see* **SAPODILLA**
Chilaca - *see* **PASILLA**
Chilca - *see* **ANISILLO**
Chilean cranberry - *see* **CHILEAN GUAVA MYRTLE**
CHILEAN GUAVA MYRTLE – Also called the Chilean cranberry, the Chilean guava myrtle (*Myrtus ugni*) is a small evergreen shrub with delicious mahogany red, sphere-shaped fruits that are an inch or more in diameter. The plant is a native of Chile; its fruits are used for jelly, and its fragrant leaves as well as the fruits are employed in flavoring water and making perfumes.

Common names and synonyms: Chilean cranberry, *ugni.*
CHILEAN PINE – Also known as the "monkey-puzzle," the Chilean pine (*Araucaria araucana*) is a South American native. It bears the name of Native Americans (the Araucana) who fought the Spanish conquistadors to a standstill in what is now Chile, and the tree also bears nuts that are eaten raw as well as boiled or roasted.

Common names and synonyms: Monkey-puzzle (tree).
Chile caballo - *see* **MANZANA**
CHILHUACLE PEPPERS (*see also* **CHILLI PEPPERS**) – The three *chilhuacle* chillies (*Capsicum annuum*) are all grown only in southern Mexico (Oaxaca and Chiapas). The *rojo* (colored a deep red), the *negro* (oxblood to almost black in tone), and the *amarillo* (with a reddish yellow hue) average some 2 to 3 inches in length and appear like miniature bell peppers (which are members of the same species), although the *chilhuacles* can also taper somewhat. The *chilhuacles* are moderately hot, are almost always dried, and generally are employed in mole sauces. Of the three, the *chilhuacle negro* is the most highly prized and thus the most expensive.

Common names and synonyms: Chilhuacle amarillo, chilhuacle negro, chilhuacle rojo.
See in addition: "Chilli Peppers," Part II, Section C, Chapter 4.
Chilhuacle rojo - *see* **CHILHUACLE PEPPERS**
Chili (pepper) - *see* **CHILLI PEPPERS**
Chilli bola - *see* **CASCABEL**
Chilli colorado - *see* **ANAHEIM, NEW MEXICO CHILLIES**
Chilli negro - *see* **PASILLA**
CHILLI PEPPERS (*see also* **SWEET PEPPERS**) – All chilli peppers belong to the genus *Capsicum* and are mostly varieties of two species – *C. annuum* and the generally smaller and hotter *C. frutescens.* Chilli peppers are native to the Americas, where they were cultivated for many thousands of years as they spread from South America north to Mesoamerica, the Caribbean, and the North American Southwest. When the Europeans reached the New World, chillies were the most common spice used by Native Americans. But after this they were no longer a secret from the rest of the world. Columbus called them *pimientos* after the *pimienta* or black pepper he had hoped to find and carried them to Iberia, whereupon they began to spread. Peppers also radiated to the East via the Spaniards' Manila galleons (trading between Mexico and the Philippines) and traveled with the Portuguese, who introduced the plants into West and East Africa, India, and the East Indies. The wildfire spread of chillies took place so quickly in the sixteenth century, and they became so well naturalized, that many in Africa, India, East and Southeast

Asia, and elsewhere began to think of the plants as native to their own regions of the world. The "fire" of chillies, which comes from the alkaloid capsaicin, is imparted in dozens of hot sauces throughout the world from Thailand (*nam prik*) to Mexico (*salsa*) to Tunisia (*barissa*), and chillies are vital in the cuisines of China, India, and Africa – south as well as north of the Equator. Chillies are green, yellow, red, or black in color and range in shape from long, skinny, hot, green chillies – or Anaheims – to the squat habaneros and jalapeños, to the plump, elongated serranos and banana chillies, to name but a few. All of these come dried as well as fresh and are crushed and ground. In addition to sauces, chillies are made into powders, pickled, smoked, roasted, and canned whole as well as chopped. Chillies are very high in vitamin C and also provide a good measure of vitamin A.

Common names and synonyms: Capsicum (pepper), *chile* (pepper), chili (pepper), chilli(es), Japanese mustard (Korean), pepper, pepper of Calicut (archaic), *pimiento,* red pepper.

See in addition: "Chilli Peppers," Part II, Section C, Chapter 4; "Spices and Flavorings," Part II, Section F, Chapter 1.

Chilli pequeño – *see* **TEPÍN CHILLIES AND RELATIVES**

Chilli pequín – *see* **TEPÍN CHILLIES AND RELATIVES**

Chilli rocoto – *see* **MANZANA**

Chilli seco – *see* **SERRANO**

CHIMAJA (*see also* **CHERRY**) – Also called the "holly-leaved cherry," this wild cherry plant (*Prunus ilicifolia*) has roots and leaves that are dried, ground, and added to the dishes of Mexico (where it originated) and those of the southwestern United States. The sweet fruit is also eaten, and in the past Native Americans processed the kernel of the stone to make a kind of meal.

Common names and synonyms: Holly-leaved cherry.

China bean – *see* **COWPEA**

CHINABERRY (*see also* **BERRIES**) – An Asiatic tree, the chinaberry (*Melia azedarach*) has smooth, yellow, edible berries. The tree has become naturalized in the southern United States. A soapberry (*Sapindus saponaria*) of the desert Southwest and Mexico is also called "chinaberry."

China orange – *see* **CALAMONDIN**

China sweet orange – *see* **ORANGE**

Chinchayote – *see* **CHAYOTE**

Chinchilla – *see* **ANISILLO**

CHINESE AMARANTH (*see also* **AMARANTH**) – There are several species of *Amaranthus* cultivated in southwestern Asia, with Chinese amaranth (*A. tricolor*) probably the most important. It is an ancient food that is mentioned in early Chinese records, but despite its scientific name, the plant seems to sport only two colors. The green kind resembles spinach and is used in much the same way in vegetable

dishes, salads, and the like. The other is known as "red-in-snow" in China, because it grows early in the spring when the ground still has something of a snow cover. This type is eaten fresh and also pickled. Chinese amaranth is grown to a limited extent for the Chinese market in the United States.

Common names and synonyms: Chinese spinach, red-in-snow, *tampala.*

See in addition: "Amaranth," Part II, Section A, Chapter 1.

Chinese anise – *see* **STAR-ANISE**

Chinese apple – *see* **POMEGRANATE**

CHINESE ARTICHOKE – The Chinese artichoke (*Stachys sieboldii* = *S. affinis*) has nothing to do with the globe artichoke. Rather, it is a crisp, edible tuber, which resembles the Jerusalem artichoke in taste and is native to and grown in China and Japan. Also called the Japanese artichoke, in Europe it goes by the name of *crosne,* which – according to legend – was also the name of a small town in France where the Chinese artichoke was introduced in 1822. Chinese artichokes are usually boiled for a few minutes and then eaten as a cooked vegetable; they may also serve as an ingredient in other dishes, especially soups.

Common names and synonyms: Crosne, Japanese artichoke, Japanese potato.

CHINESE BROCCOLI (*see also* **CABBAGE**) – Also known as *gai-larn,* "Chinese kale," and *kailan,* Chinese broccoli (*Brassica alboglabra*) resembles Chinese flowering cabbage but has a flavor similar to kale. As in the case of the flowering cabbage, the tender green stems are of more interest to consumers than the leaves. The stems are steamed or braised and often served with oyster sauce. They are also used in soups and noodle dishes.

Common names and synonyms: Chinese kale, *gai-larn, kailan.*

See in addition: "Cruciferous and Green Leafy Vegetables," Part II, Section C, Chapter 5.

CHINESE CABBAGE (*see also* **CABBAGE**) – Also called napa, nappa, celery cabbage, and *pe-tsai,* this vegetable (*Brassica pekinensis*) is often confused with bok choy (*Brassica chinensis*), which is also sometimes called "Chinese cabbage." They resemble one another in their oblong or pointed (as opposed to round) form. The leaves of the Chinese cabbage, which look something like those of pale romaine lettuce, are crisp, tender, mild tasting, and certainly more delicate than those of round cabbages. Chinese cabbage has been an important dietary item in China since ancient times and is also consumed in other parts of Asia – especially in Japan and Korea, where it is stir-fried, boiled, pickled, or braised for use in a number of different dishes (the well known Korean pickle, *kimchee,* is made with Chinese cabbage). Chinese cabbages were virtually unknown in the West until the Israelis began to grow them, after which growers in California followed suit (hence napa or nappa cabbage, after the Napa Valley). Chinese cabbage is high in folic acid, vitamin A, and potassium.

Common names and synonyms: Celery cabbage, *chihli* cabbage, Chinese broccoli, Chinese leaf, *chou de chine, gay lon, hakusai,* Michihli, Napa, napa cabbage, nappa cabbage, Peking cabbage, *pe-tsai,* pointed cabbage, Shantung cabbage, Tientsin, *wong bok.*

See in addition: "Cruciferous and Green Leafy Vegetables," Part II, Section C, Chapter 5.

Chinese chard - *see* **PAKCHOI AND KAI CHOY**

Chinese chestnut - *see* **CHESTNUT**

CHINESE CHIVE(S) - Other names for Chinese chives (*Allium tuberosum*) - such as "Oriental garlic," "Chinese leeks," "garlic chives," and "flowering chives" - indicate that not only are the leaves employed as chives but the bulbs are also used much like garlic. Flowering chives are Chinese chives that are allowed to mature and grow an edible pointed flower. The Chinese also grow these chives without exposure to sunlight, whereupon they become "yellow chives."

Common names and synonyms: Chinese leeks, flowering chives, garlic chives, Oriental garlic, yellow chives.

See also: "The *Allium* Species," Part II, Section C, Chapter 2.

Chinese cinnamon - *see* **CINNAMON AND CASSIA**

Chinese date - *see* **JUJUBE**

Chinese eddoe - *see* **COCOYAM**

Chinese fig - *see* **PERSIMMON**

CHINESE FLOWERING CABBAGE (*see also* **CABBAGE**) - Also called *choy sum* and "mock *pak choy,"* Chinese flowering cabbage (*Brassica parachinensis*) has long, white-to-green stems, with rounded green leaves. *Choy sum* means "vegetable hearts," and it is the stems rather than the leaves that are sought after. They are generally cooked without peeling and served with an oyster sauce.

Common names and synonyms: Choy sum, mock *pak choy.*

See in addition: "Cruciferous and Green Leafy Vegetables," Part II, Section C, Chapter 5.

Chinese garlic - *see* **CHIVE(S)**

Chinese gooseberry - *see* **KIWI FRUIT**

Chinese kale - *see* **CHINESE BROCCOLI, KALE**

Chinese lantern - *see* **TOMATILLO**

Chinese laurel - *see* **BIGNAY**

Chinese leaf - *see* **CHINESE CABBAGE**

Chinese leeks - *see* **CHINESE CHIVE(S)**

Chinese mulberry - *see* **CHE, MULBERRY**

Chinese mustard cabbage - *see* **BOK CHOY**

Chinese okra - *see* **ANGLED LUFFA**

Chinese olive - *see* **CHINESE WHITE OLIVE**

Chinese parsley - *see* **CILANTRO, CORIANDER**

Chinese pea - *see* **SUGAR PEA**

Chinese pear - *see* **ASIAN PEAR**

Chinese potato - *see* **CHINESE YAM**

Chinese radish - *see* **DAIKON**

Chinese raisin tree - *see* **JAPANESE RAISIN TREE**

Chinese red date - *see* **JUJUBE**

Chinese snow pea - *see* **SUGAR PEA**

Chinese spinach - *see* **CALLALOO, CHINESE AMARANTH**

Chinese squash - *see* **FUZZY MELON**

Chinese star fruit - *see* **CARAMBOLA**

CHINESE TALLOW TREE - Known also as "Chinese vegetable tallow" or simply "vegetable tallow," the Chinese tallow tree (*Sapium sebiferum*) is a native of China and Japan but is now grown in other countries of East and South Asia and the southern United States. Also called the "white wax-berry," the tree is cultivated for these fruits about the size of peas, the seeds of which yield an oil with numerous industrial applications. However, the oil is used for cooking in Asia.

Common names and synonyms: Chinese vegetable tallow, tallow tree, vegetable tallow, white wax-berry.

Chinese taro - *see* **ALOCASIA**

Chinese vegetable marrow - *see* **FUZZY MELON**

Chinese vegetable tallow - *see* **CHINESE TALLOW TREE**

CHINESE WHITE OLIVE - Often mistakenly called the "Java almond," the Chinese white olive (*Canarium album*) is a large tree of South and Southeast Asia that belongs to a large genus of tropical trees. Many of these bear nuts sometimes called pilai nuts. In the case of the Chinese white olive, it bears a fruit with pulp that is preserved for use as a condiment.

Common names and synonyms: Chinese olive.

Chinese winter melon - *see* **FUZZY MELON, MELONS**

CHINESE YAM (*see also* **LESSER YAM, YAMS**) - A yam that is a native of China and widely cultivated there, the Chinese yam (*Dioscorea batatas*) is also called "Chinese potato" and, sometimes, "cinnamon vine" because the flowers smell of cinnamon. The tubers, which are also grown in Japan and other parts of East Asia, are mainly employed in sliced and grated form to add substance to various dishes, but they can also be fried, baked, or boiled like potatoes. This yam, along with others, has served as food for the peoples of China since the days of the hunter-gatherers.

Common names and synonyms: Chinese potato, cinnamon vine.

See in addition: "Sweet Potatoes and Yams," Part II, Section B, Chapter 5.

Chipiles - *see* **QUELITES**

Chipotle (chilli) - *see* **JALAPEÑO**

Chipotle grande - *see* **JALAPEÑO**

Chiquilla - *see* **ANISILLO**

Chirauli nut - *see* **CUDDAPAH ALMOND**

Chirimen - *see* **KABOCHA (SQUASH)**

Chirimoya - *see* **CHERIMOYA, POSHTE**

CHIVE(S) - The chive (*Allium schoenoprasum*) is of the lily family, is related to the onion, leek, and garlic, and has the most delicate taste of all of its close relatives. Chives are grown for their long, thin, grasslike, hollow stalks, which are used in salads, cheeses, soups, omelettes, and other dishes. Chives are also among the fines herbes – a traditional French blend of chervil, chives, parsley, and tarragon used for seasoning soups, salads, omelettes, and cottage and cream cheeses. The chive is an ancient herb. It is said to be native to the Mediterranean, but it was known by the Chinese some 5,000 years ago (varieties are called "Chinese onion" and "Oriental garlic") and grew wild in North America as well. Chives were enjoyed by the ancient Greeks but only reached the gardens of much of the rest of Europe in the sixteenth century. Chives are rich in vitamins A and C.

Common names and synonyms: Chinese garlic, Chinese onion, Oriental garlic.

See also: "The *Allium* Species," Part II, Section C, Chapter 2; "Spices and Flavorings," Part II, Section F, Chapter 1.

Chocho - *see* ANDEAN LUPIN, CHAYOTE

Chocolate - *see* CACAO, MUTAMBA

Chocolate-pudding fruit - *see* BLACK SAPOTE

Choctaw-root - *see* HEMP DOGBANE

CHOKEBERRY (*see also* **BERRIES**) - The chokeberry (*Aronia melanocarpa* or *A. arbutifolia*), like its fellow family (Rosaceae) member, the chokecherry (*Prunus virginiana*), is a very astringent fruit. Nonetheless, in eastern North America, the red, purple, or black fruits were gathered by Native Americans, who dried them for winter use. Around 1700, the plant was imported into Europe, where it was desired more for the ornamental appeal of the shrub than for its bitter fruit. However, the berries also make a useful substitute for black currants in areas where these cannot be grown. Chokeberries are very rich in vitamin C.

CHOKECHERRY (*see also* **CHERRIES**) - A member of the Rosaceae family, the chokecherry (*Prunus virginiana*), also called the wild black cherry, is a wild North American cherry and should not be confused with another family member, the chokeberry. With a name like chokecherry, one can be certain that the dark red or blackish fruit is very astringent. Nonetheless, chokecherries were gathered by Native Americans, who dried them and combined them with other fruits for winter storage. Later foragers have used them for jams and jellies, and they were even cultivated for a time in the southern provinces of Canada. Chokecherries were also employed for decades in cough remedies and were the principal ingredient in "Smith Brothers'" cough drops. Like other sour cherries, chokecherries are high in vitamin C and beta-carotene.

Common names and synonyms: Black chokecherry, capulin, western chokecherry, wild black cherry, wild cherry.

Choko - *see* CHAYOTE

Chopsuey greens - *see* CHRYSANTHEMUM

Chou de chine - *see* CHINESE CABBAGE

Chou-rave - *see* KOHLRABI

Choy sum - *see* CHINESE FLOWERING CABBAGE, FLOWERING WHITE CABBAGE

Christmas Rose (grape) - *see* GRAPES

Christmas tea-bush - *see* YAUPON

Christophene - *see* CHAYOTE

Christophine - *see* CHAYOTE

CHRIST'S-THORN FRUIT - Several prickly or thorny bushes of Palestine and the Near East are called "Christ's-thorn," especially *Ziziphus* (= *Zizyphus*) *spina-christi* and *Paliurus spina-christi*. They bear a small, red, edible fruit (a jujube), which is dried and eaten locally. Also called "Jerusalem thorn," this bush is popularly believed to have been used to fashion Christ's crown of thorns.

Common names and synonyms: Christ-thorn berry, Jerusalem thorn.

Christ-thorn berry - *see* CHRIST'S-THORN FRUIT

CHRYSANTHEMUM - "Japanese greens" (*Chrysanthemum coronarium*), also called "chopsuey greens," and the crown daisy or garland chrysanthemum (*C. spatiosum*) both have aromatic leaves that are cooked much like spinach in East Asia and are also used raw as garnishes.

Common names and synonyms: Chopsuey greens, crown daisy, edible-leaved chrysanthemum, garland chrysanthemum, Japanese greens.

Chu chi - *see* MATRIMONY VINE

Chuchu - *see* CHAYOTE

CHUFA - The edible roots of the weed "chufa" (*Cyperus esculentus*) are tubers that look somewhat like peanuts and, in the past, have been called "earth almonds" and "rush nuts." They can be eaten raw or cooked by boiling or roasting. They are also dried for later use and made into a flour, and chufa seeds can substitute for coffee. In Europe and the Middle East, desserts and drinks are made from the tubers. The plant, which is widespread geographically, is also of some antiquity. It was used by native North Americans on one side of the world and by the ancient Egyptians on the other side. Another common (and confusing) name for chufa is galingale, which is actually *Alpinia galanga*.

Common names and synonyms: Earth almond, galingale, nut(-)grass, purple nutgrass, rush nut, sedge, tigernut, yellow nutsedge, zula nut.

CICELY - Also known as "sweet cicely" - and sometimes as "sweet chervil" and even "myrrh" and "garden myrrh" - cicely (*Myrrhis odorata*) is an herb native to the Savoy region of France. Its pale green leaves and especially its ripe, glossy brown seeds have a licorice-like flavor that goes well with fruits and in salads and desserts. Cicely is so sweet that it can be added to stewed fruit dishes (such as rhubarb) and thereby considerably reduce the amount of sugar that is normally called for. In the past, cicely roots were boiled and eaten as a vegetable, but the plant is much less popular than it once was.

Common names and synonyms: Anise root, candy plant, European sweet chervil, garden myrrh, myrrh, Spanish chervil, sweet chervil, sweet cicely.

Cilantrillo - *see* **CILANTRO**

CILANTRO (*see also* **CORIANDER**) - Cilantro is a term that indicates the fresh green leaves of coriander (*Coriandrum sativum*), a plant whose seeds are also used as a spice (treated separately - along with the history of the plant - under the entry **Coriander**). Also called Chinese parsley, the pungent leaves of cilantro were long ago thought by some to smell delightfully peppery and by others to carry the odor of bedbugs. Nonetheless, cilantro has been acclaimed today as the most common flavoring herb in the world. The word cilantro comes from Spanish, but in Caribbean Spanish the term is *cilantrillo,* which can lead to confusion. Cilantro is available in bunches in produce departments and looks much like flat-leafed parsley. But there is also "culantro," which tastes like cilantro (although stronger) but looks like blades of grass. Cilantro is most important to the cuisines of Iberia, the Middle East, China, India, and many of the South American countries, and it is absolutely crucial to Mexican cookery, in which it appears as a green in many dishes, especially in salsas, guacamole, and with fish. Until recently, however, when Mexican food became more popular and widespread, cilantro was little known in the United States. The leaves deliver some vitamin A as well as vitamin C.

Common names and synonyms: Chinese parsley, *cilantrillo,* coriander, culantro, Mexican parsley, *yuen sai.*

Cimaru - *see* **TONKA BEAN**

Cinderella pumpkin - *see* **ROUGE VIF D'ÉTAMPES (PUMPKIN)**

Cinnamon - *see* **CINNAMON AND CASSIA, INDIAN BARK, SAIGON CINNAMON, WHITE CINNAMON**

CINNAMON AND CASSIA (*see also* **SAIGON CINNAMON**) - These ancient spices - cinnamon (*Cinnamomum zeylanicum = C. verum*) and cassia (*Cinnamomum cassia*) - are both derived from the dried inner bark of two related evergreen trees that belong to the laurel family. The trees are native to different parts of Asia (Sri Lanka and Burma, respectively), and, thus, cinnamon was an early - as well as vital - item in the spice trade that moved from the East to the West. Evidence exists to suggest that cinnamon was valued by the ancient Egyptians for witchcraft and embalming and, perhaps, for culinary purposes as well. It is mentioned in the Old Testament (along with cassia) and in Sanskrit manuscripts. In the East, cassia was cultivated by the Chinese as early as 2500 B.C., and may have been in use well before that. Cinnamon has been credited with magical ("love potions") as well as medicinal properties, and a drink prescribed for colds by a Roman physician - hot liquor and stick cinnamon - is still in use today. At one time cinnamon was viewed as more precious than gold. Cinnamon has long been an essential ingredient in Moroccan and Greek chicken and beef dishes, and in the Middle East it is commonly used with meats, especially lamb. Europeans and North Americans tend to employ cinnamon mostly in sweets. Much of the cinnamon used in Europe is true cinnamon, whereas most of that reaching the United States is actually cassia. The difference is easy to spot: Cinnamon is tan, whereas cassia is reddish brown in color.

Common names and synonyms: Chinese cinnamon (cassia), cinnamon bark (both), false cinnamon (cassia), *kayu manis* (both), Seychelles cinnamon (cinnamon), sweet wood (both), true cinnamon (cinnamon).

See in addition: "Spices and Flavorings," Part II, Section F, Chapter 1.

Cinnamon bark - *see* **CINNAMON AND CASSIA**

Cinnamon vine - *see* **CHINESE YAM**

CINSAULT (*see also* **GRAPES**) - One of the important grapes of the southern Rhône Valley of France, the Cinsault (*Vitis vinifera*) is large, black, and used mostly to blend wines. A small amount is also produced in California.

See in addition: "Wine," Part III, Chapter 13.

Ciruela - *see* **BUNCHOSIA**

Citrange - *see* **CITRANGEQUAT**

CITRANGEQUAT (*see also* **CITRUS FRUITS, KUMQUAT, ORANGE**) - A cross between the orange relative *Poncirus trifoliata* and varieties of the sweet orange produced the hybrid known as a "citrange." Crossing the citrange with the kumquat has resulted in yet another hybrid, the "citrangequat" (involving three genera: *Citrus, Poncirus,* and *Fortunella*), which has a very sour fruit. Like the limequat and the orangequat, the citrangequat is the result of a breeding program - sponsored by the U.S. Department of Agriculture (USDA) - that is attempting to breed the cold-resistance of the kumquat into other plants.

CITRON (*see also* **CITRUS FRUITS, LEMON**) - A native of Southeast Asia, the citron (*Citrus medica*) was cultivated by the Chinese and Sumerians in very ancient times and in southern Italy, Corsica, and Sicily by around the fourth century B.C. It reached the Americas with the Europeans, and a small crop was finally grown in California at the beginning of the twentieth century. The citron is cultivated mostly for its thick, spongy rind, in appearance like the rind of a large lemon, which is candied and often chopped into fruitcakes. It is also used to make fruit syrups, liqueurs, and perfume. In the past, the citron was used medicinally, and it has enjoyed considerable religious significance. The unripe fruit is the "citron of the law" used by Jewish communities in ceremonies celebrating the harvest festival Succoth. The citron's principal areas of cultivation are Italy, Corsica, and Greece, and a variety came to be known as the "Leghorn citron" when the islands of Corsica and Sardinia shipped their crops to Leghorn, Italy, for processing.

Another fruit (*Citrullus lanatus* var. *citroides* – of the same species as the watermelon) is also called "citron" and, except for its bitter taste, resembles a small watermelon. That it is used somewhat in the same way as *C. medica* is suggested by another of its common names, "preserving melon." It is also called the "stock melon" because it is sometimes fed to hogs.

Common names and synonyms: Citron melon, Corsican citron, Diamante citron, esrog, ethrog, etrog, Leghorn citron, preserving melon, stock melon.

See in addition: "Cucumbers, Melons, and Watermelons," Part II, Section C, Chapter 6.

CITRUS FRUITS (*see also* the various citrus entries) – Save for recent hybrids (uglis, ortaniques, or tangelos, for example) and the grapefruit, all members of the citrus family (Rutaceae) originated in Southeast Asia (or – in the case of the sweet orange – China) and were first cultivated in China and India. Gradually they moved westward to Arabia and then to the countries surrounding the Mediterranean. The ancient Greeks apparently knew nothing of citrus fruits, and the Romans had only the citron. Oranges were recorded in Sicily at the beginning of the eleventh century and were reported as growing around Seville in Spain a couple of centuries later. The lemon was in the Near East by the tenth century or so and was being cultivated in Italy by the fifteenth century. Christopher Columbus and those explorers who followed in his wake scattered citrus seeds over much of the rest of the globe, discovering in the process the loose-skinned mandarin (tangerine) species that had long been cultivated in China and Japan. Grapefruits seem to have been born in the eighteenth century in the West Indies as a cross between the pomelo and the orange. The kumquat, a native of China and Japan, is not a citrus fruit but belongs to a similar genus.

Civet-cat fruit - *see* **DURIAN**

Ckoito - *see* **AMARANTH**

CLARY - An herb, clary (*Salvia sclarea*) is also called "clary sage." The taste of its flowering tops combines the flavors of sage and mint. In the past, clary was much employed in Europe as a seasoning for various foods and for wine. It is still used to enhance egg dishes and is one of the herbs that is used in making Italian vermouths.

Common names and synonyms: Clary sage.

See also: "Spices and Flavorings," Part II, Section F, Chapter 1.

Clear-up cactus - *see* **PITAHAYA**

Cleavers - *see* **GOOSEGRASS**

Clevner - *see* **PINOT BLANC**

Climbing bittersweet - *see* **AMERICAN BITTERSWEET**

Clotbur - *see* **BURDOCK**

CLOUDBERRY (*see also* **BERRIES**) - A creeping plant of northern climates, the cloudberry (*Rubus chamaemorus*) does best close to or even within the Arctic Circle, flourishing in the nearly 24-hour-long days of summer sunshine. The reddish orange to yellow fruit and white flowers of the cloudberry plant are found throughout the Scandinavian countries and Alaska. The Eskimos and Lapps collect the juicy, sweet berries in the fall and freeze them for winter consumption – the berries have doubtless done much over the centuries to provide vitamin C to peoples in a part of the world that is decidedly lacking in the usual fruits and vegetables. Cloudberries are also sold in northern Scandinavia for making preserves and baking pastries, and they are fermented to make vinegar. Like other berries, cloudberries are high in vitamin C.

Common names and synonyms: Bakeberry, baked-apple berry, *malka, Moltebeere,* salmonberry, *Torfbeere,* yellowberry.

CLOUD EAR (*see also* **MUSHROOMS AND FUNGI**) - The Tremellales, or the jelly fungi, are a group of gelatinous, edible wood fungi of which the cloud ears *Auricularia polytrica* and *A. auricula* are the species commonly eaten. They are brown to black gelatinous lobes that resemble human ears, are widely distributed in the world, and are found in the wild in clusters on logs. In China *A. polytrica* has been used in cooking for some 2,000 years. In the Pacific Northwest and Rocky Mountain regions of the United States they are often encountered near melting snow. Often consumed after being dried, cloud ears are most appreciated for their delicate flavor. In the Far East and in China, they are cultivated.

Common names and synonyms: Black (tree) fungus, Chinese mushroom, Jew's-ear, Judas('s) ear, *kikurage, mo-ehr, mook yee,* silver ear, tree ear, wood ear, *yun er.*

See in addition: "Fungi," Part II, Section C, Chapter 7.

CLOVE(S) - A pungent flavoring agent, the clove (*Syzygium aromaticum*) is another of those ancient spices that have an exotic past. Cloves are the dried buds of trees native to the Moluccas and provided one of the reasons those islands have long been called the Spice Islands. Centuries before the Christian era, cloves were used by the Chinese and became an important item in the spice trade with the West. The Egyptians, Greeks, and Romans were all familiar with cloves. Indeed, the name "clove" comes from the Latin word *clavus,* which means "nail" and aptly describes their appearance. The Portuguese were the first from the West to reach the Spice Islands and create a monopoly on the clove trade. At the beginning of the seventeenth century, they were succeeded by the Dutch, who established their own monopoly and limited production to just one of the islands. This monopoly was only broken at about the time of the American

Revolution, when a French diplomat managed to smuggle out some seedlings. Today, cloves are grown in Tanzania (which accounts for about half the world's production), Madagascar, Sri Lanka, and – in the New World – Grenada. Perhaps the first use of cloves was to freshen the breath, but it doubtless required little time to discover that their strong aroma and flavor went well with foods. Any meat dish, especially ham, can be enhanced with cloves. They are also called for in a multitude of recipes for spiced cakes, mincemeat, gingerbread, marinades, stewed-fruit dishes, any apple dish, and mulled-wine drinks. Cloves can be purchased dried, either whole or ground.

Common names and synonyms: Mother-of-clove(s).

See also: "Spices and Flavorings," Part II, Section F, Chapter 1.

CLOVER (*see also* **PRAIRIE CLOVER, SWEET CLOVER**) – Rarely used for human consumption except in times of famine, clover (genus *Trifolium*) is typically employed as fodder. Some exceptions are *T. repens, T. pratense,* and *T. campestre.* Icelanders boil *T. repens* (white Dutch clover, white clover) as a vegetable. In Europe, the young leaves of *T. pratense* (wild red clover) are eaten in salads and sandwiches, and the flowers are used to make a tea. A bitter variety, *T. campestre* (the "large hop clover") was used to flavor beer before the discovery of hops.

Common names and synonyms: Ladino clover, large hop clover, red clover, sweet clover, white clover, white Dutch clover, wild red clover.

Clusterbean - *see* **GUAR**

Cluster yam - *see* **BITTER YAM**

Cob - *see* **HAZELNUT AND FILBERT**

Cobnut - *see* **HAZELNUT AND FILBERT**

COCA - This shrub (*Erythroxylum coca*) is native to the Andean region of South America. The dried leaves yield a crystalline alkaloid substance known as cocaine. Taken internally, cocaine is a stimulant, whereas external use has the effect of a local anesthetic. The Indians of Peru and Bolivia chew the leaves to help them work long hours and ward off hunger, fatigue, and cold temperatures. This practice is comparable to the chewing of betel nut in Southeast Asia or kola nut in Africa. Some people make a coca "wine" from the leaves as well. Coca is also grown in Sri Lanka, Java, and Taiwan.

Common names and synonyms: Cocaine plant, spadic.

Cochineal plant - *see* **NOPALES**

COCKLEBUR - The seeds of the cocklebur (*Xanthium commune*) were used by Native Americans, who ground them into a meal. They may also have employed the shoots and leaves of *X. strumarium,* which others have reportedly boiled and eaten as a vegetable.

COCKSPUR (*see also* **BERRIES**) - A small tree of Colombia and Central America, *Celtis iguanaea* produces edible, berry-like fruits that are green when immature and yellowish when ripe. They are generally eaten raw and have an excellent taste.

Cockspur thorn - *see* **HAWTHORN BERRY**

Coco - *see* **COCONUT**

Cocoa - *see* **CACAO**

Cocoaplum - *see* **COCOPLUM**

COCONA (*see also* **BERRIES**) - A berry native to northern South America, cocona (*Solanum topiro = S. sessiliflorum*) is edible, although many other species of the genus *Solanum* are poisonous. The berry is cultivated today from Trinidad to Costa Rica and, although not known in the wild, also "voluntarily" plants itself in abandoned plots and clearings. The berries are yellowish to red when ripe and are covered with a kind of fuzz that can be brushed off.

Common names and synonyms: Topiro.

COCONUT - Hunter-gatherers doubtless learned hundreds of thousands of years ago to crack open these fruit seeds of the coconut palm (*Cocos nucifera*) for the "milk" and "meat" contained therein, not to mention the usefulness of the shell as a drinking and eating vessel and as a scraping utensil. Truly, the coconut is one of the oldest of food plants. It originated in the Malayan Archipelago but long ago distributed itself throughout the world's tropics because it easily floats and, hence, can cross oceans. The coconut is mentioned in Sanskrit manuscripts, but it is said that Marco Polo (in his narratives of his travels in Asia) was the first European to describe it. During the Portuguese expansion of the fifteenth and sixteenth centuries, coconuts were carried back to Europe, and the Portuguese gave us the name we know the fruit by today. They called it *coco,* which meant "head" or "noggin." The hairy shell that encloses the fruit is itself enclosed by a greenish, fibrous husk. As the fruit ripens within this double seal - full ripening requires a year - more and more of the thin white liquid within (coconut "water") is converted to meat (called copra when dried), which is pressed for oil and made into various coconut foods and cosmetic products. Coconut cream is a blending of the coconut water and flesh. For the moment, at least, the coconut - especially its oil - is somewhat in disrepute because of its heavy concentration of saturated fat.

Common names and synonyms: Coco, cokernut.

See also: "Coconut," Part II, Section E, Chapter 2; "An Overview of Oils and Fats," Part II, Section E, Chapter 1.

COCOPLUM - Also known as cocoaplum, hicaco, and icaco, the cocoplum (*Chrysobalanus icaco*) is the fruit of a small tree native to tropical America. The fruit's color can be either white, black, or a combination of the two, and cocoplums are generally used for preserves.

Common names and synonyms: Cocoaplum, hicaco, icaco, icaco plum.

COCOYAM (*see also* **TARO**) - Often - and understandably - confused with taro and with malanga, from both of which it is practically indistinguishable, the cocoyam (*Colocasia esculenta*) is a variety of taro that is probably native to India but also possibly to parts of Southeast Asia. The problem is that the taxonomy of the cultivars of *Colocasia* remains a subject of investigation. These plants have clearly traveled, moving from India to Egypt some 2,000 years ago and from there to southern Europe. From Iberia, the cocoyam was carried to the Americas and then probably introduced into West Africa from the New World. It was successfully established in East Africa as well and moved eastward out of India to the Pacific. In these travels, the cocoyam picked up many names. Like taro and malanga, the cocoyam is also called "dasheen," "eddoe," and a dozen other names, including "taro." Moreover, in West Africa malanga is also called cocoyam. The plant was especially important in the West Indies for feeding slaves, and it continues to be a common part of the diet in many islands. Its young shoots and leaves serve as a cooked vegetable (callaloo), and the tubers are fried, roasted, or boiled. The leaves are a good source of vitamin A, calcium, and potassium; the corms brim with starch and, thus, energy.

Common names and synonyms: Abalong, arvi, Barbados eddoe, Chinese eddoe, curcas, dagmay, dalo, dasheen, eddo, eddoe, *keladi,* koko, kolkas, malangay, malangu, taioba, taro, *taro de chine, ya, ya bené, yu-tao.*

See in addition: "Taro," Part II, Section B, Chapter 6.

Cocozelle - *see* **ZUCCHINI**

COFFEE - Also called *kaffe, kahve,* and *kahwa,* coffee (*Coffea arabica*) is surrounded by myths and legends, especially those dealing with the discovery of the plant, which seems to have originated in both Yemen and southern Ethiopia (in the province of Caffa). One of the most pervasive legends has an Arab goatherd around A.D. 850 becoming curious about the lively behavior of his goats and subsequently discovering that the animals were nibbling the coffee berries of nearby evergreen trees. Apparently, the first human use of coffee was to emulate the goats by also chewing the "beans" to get a lift, but by around A.D. 1000 (or even earlier) coffee beans were being roasted and crushed to make a beverage. From this point to the cultivation of coffee trees was a short step, and the beans came to be monopolized by Arab merchants, who shipped them from the Yemeni port of Mocha. Coffee quickly became an important beverage for the Muslims, who were prohibited alcohol (although many fanatically condemned the new drink), and coffeehouses of a sort were established in cities and towns throughout the Islamic world.

Constantinople (Istanbul) has been put forward as the location of the world's first real coffeehouse, established at about the end of the fifteenth century (the dates given vary from 1474 to 1554), and at about the same time coffeehouses were also opened in Medina, Mecca, Cairo, Damascus, and Baghdad - all of the capitals of the Islamic world. The new social centers were viewed with suspicion by various sultans worried about sedition, and coffeehouses were closed from time to time, but never for long. Coffee drinking had become an entrenched part of Arab life.

Europe soon had a similar experience. Venice, heavily involved in the spice trade, was exposed to coffee as early as the fifteenth century, and its first coffeehouse was established around the middle of the sixteenth century - about the same time that Vienna got its first one. Another century elapsed, however, before the new beverage moved northward and westward. Coffeehouses were opened at Oxford in 1650, at Marseilles in 1671, and at Paris the following year, but it was only in 1686 that the Café Procope, the first true café in Paris, opened its doors (it still exists although at a different location). It may be doubted that the first of the coffeehouses in England were inundated with patrons because - as late as 1657 in London - coffee was advertised as a medicine for ills such as gout and scurvy. But the coffeehouses clearly were doing a brisk business by 1675 when, like the Islamic sultans, King Charles II issued a proclamation to suppress them on the grounds that they were hotbeds of sedition. The proclamation, however, was rescinded the following year, and over time coffeehouses in England developed into gentlemen's clubs, whereas in France they continued to be cafés (albeit also clubs at times).

Both the British and the Dutch East India Companies bought coffee at Mocha for import into Europe, but as decades passed and overseas empires developed, the Arab monopoly on coffee became a major irritant. As the eighteenth century got under way, the Dutch began growing their own coffee in Java and later introduced it into Sri Lanka, whereas the English planted coffee in their West Indian colonies - especially Jamaica and Guiana. The Portuguese in Brazil were also in the coffee business (after the plant was introduced there from Guiana in 1727), and the French planted coffee, first in their colony of Martinique and a bit later in San Domingue - which, by the end of the eighteenth century (when the revolution began that would lead to the new nation of Haiti), was producing almost two-thirds of the world's supply. Later, coffee would also be a Cuban crop, and throughout the Americas coffee production became inextricably linked with slave labor, until abolition finally came to Brazil and Cuba in the last decades of the nineteenth century. Sugar was also cultivated with slave labor, and increasing sugar production, in turn, was inextricably linked with the soaring consumption of coffee – along with tea and chocolate – in Europe.

In 1774, in the soon-to-be United States, colonists were increasing their consumption of coffee as a protest against British taxes on tea, and this trend continued as a tea-drinking people were converted to coffee drinking. By 1850 or so, average per capita consumption exceeded 6 pounds annually. Americans were accustomed to buying their coffee beans green and doing their own roasting and grinding, but after the Civil War, Folger's Coffee (established in San Francisco) began to give people a choice. The Folger's brand was soon followed by Chase and Sanborn (which in 1878 became the first company to pack roasted coffee in sealed cans), Hills Brothers, and Maxwell House (named for a Nashville hotel). In 1901, the first "instant" coffee was invented in Chicago, and in 1964, General Foods introduced "Maxim" freeze-dried instant coffee.

Coffee is ground in different ways for different purposes: "Coarse" and "medium" for use in percolators, urns, and the like; "drip" (which is finer than medium) for use in electric drip coffee makers; and "fine" for cone filters and drip pots. There is also the very fine espresso, for espresso machines, and the even more finely ground Turkish, for use in Turkish brewers. Almost 90 percent of the world's coffee is *C. arabica*, but another species, *C. canephora = C. robusta* and generally known as *Robusta*, is cultivated in Africa and India and – because it is cheaper and contains substantially more caffeine – is often a component of supermarket blends. Brazil produces about half of the world's coffee and has been the major U.S. supplier since the early days of the republic. Jamaican Blue Mountain, Hawaiian Kona, Java, and Mocha coffees are relatively rare and highly prized, followed by the Andean-grown Colombian coffee (the top grade is *supremo*).

Common names and synonyms: Colombian coffee, espresso, Hawaiian Kona, Jamaican Blue Mountain, Java, joe, *kaffe, kahve, kahwa,* Mocha, *Robusta, supremo* coffee, Turkish coffee.

See also: "Coffee," Part III, Chapter 4.

Coffee weed - *see* SESBAN

COHUNE PALM - A native of Central America and Mexico, the cohune nut palm (*Orbignya cohune* and *Attalea cohune*) produces nuts that yield an oil that can substitute for coconut oil. In addition, the tree's young leaf buds are cooked and eaten as a vegetable.

Coimi - *see* AMARANTH
Coines - *see* QUINCE
Coing - *see* QUINCE
Coinworth - *see* PENNYWORT
Cokernut - *see* COCONUT
Cola nut - *see* KOLA NUT
Cole cabbage - *see* CABBAGE

Colewort - *see* CABBAGE
Colicroot - *see* WILD YAM
Colirrambano - *see* KOHLRABI
COLLARDS (*see also* CABBAGE, KALE) - Called *couve* in Brazil and often regarded as a form of kale (which they are, differing mostly in the smoothness of their leaves), collards (*Brassica oleracea* var. *acephala*) constitute one of the oldest members of the cabbage family and probably originated in the Mediterranean region. However, collard greens subsequently spread over much of the tropical and subtropical world and are cultivated today in Southeast Asia (including southern China), East and West Africa, the West Indies, South America, and the southern United States. Collards probably reached the Americas from Africa via the slave trade and are mostly consumed in those regions that formerly harbored slave societies. The flavor of the vegetable is milder than that of kale, and the large, dark green leaves, which are a component of southern "soul food," are traditionally boiled with pork or fatback. Collards supply folic acid and vitamin A and are a rich source of calcium, potassium, and iron. In addition, as a cruciferous vegetable, collards are said to act as a preventive against certain cancers.

Common names and synonyms: Borecole, collard greens, *couve,* kale.

See in addition: "Cruciferous and Green Leafy Vegetables," Part II, Section C, Chapter 5.

Colocynth - *see* EGUSI
Colombian coffee - *see* COFFEE
COLTSFOOT - The wide leaves of this plant (*Tussilago farfara*) resemble horses' hooves, hence the name "coltsfoot," along with a variety of similar names such as "assfoot," "foalfoot," "horsefoot," "sowfoot," and just plain "hoofs." Coltsfoot is a European plant with roots that have been used medicinally since the days of the ancient Greeks. The plant is now naturalized in eastern North America. When young, the leaves can be eaten raw, whereas older ones are cooked as greens, and ashes from the leaves have been used as a salt substitute. The plant also has a yellow flower head that opens only in sunny weather, and this, along with its stalk, is also edible when raw. Coltsfoot is grown and widely used in Japan, where the celery-like flavor of its green stalks is especially appreciated.

Common names and synonyms: Assfoot, bog rhubarb, bullsfoot, coughwort, foalfoot, hoofs, horsefoot, sowfoot.

Colza - *see* RAPE
COMFREY - A somewhat hairy herb that is native to Eurasia, comfrey (*Symphytum officinale,* among some 25 other comfrey species) has long been employed by humans, but more for healing than for sustenance. Its roots and leaves were used historically to treat wounds, and in fact, the name comes from ancient Greek and means to grow together – which in this case refers to the edges of wounds

and broken bones (accounting for one of the plant's old names, "knit-bones"). But comfrey is also edible. It is frequently used to make a tisane, can be added to salads, and is cooked like spinach as a vegetable.
Common names and synonyms: Knit-bones.

Comice - *see* **PEAR**

Comino - *see* **CUMIN**

Commas - *see* **CAMAS**

Common red ribes - *see* **CURRANT(S)**

COMMON REED - A plant widespread throughout the world, the common reed (*Phragmites communis* or *P. australis*) has rhizomes and roots that in Russia are harvested for their starch content. Native Americans also procured starch from the rootstock of the common reed and ate its young shoots. The stems - rich in sugar - have been ground into a sweet powder for use in baking. They also exude a gumlike substance that was highly regarded as a sweet by Native Americans.

Compass plant - *see* **SILPHIUM**

Concombre des Antilles - *see* **GHERKIN**

CONCORD GRAPE (*see also* **GRAPES**) - A variety of the fox grape, the North American Concord grape (*Vitis labrusca*) lacks sugar, which limits its use in wine making. But these grapes are much used for the production of grape juice and jellies. They come from a wild grape named after Concord, Massachusetts, by Ephraim Bull, who planted the vines there in 1843.

CONEFLOWER - Several plants are called coneflower. Those that are subsumed under the genus *Echinacea* are tall weeds with purple blossoms and grow throughout the prairie region of the United States. They have edible roots, leaves, and seeds that were used mostly for medicinal purposes by Native Americans. Another coneflower, *Ratibida columnifera*, is also a prairie plant, bearing leaves that Native Americans made into a tea. A final coneflower is *Rudbeckia laciniata*, of eastern North America, with leaves that were cooked as a vegetable.

Congo goober - *see* **BAMBARA GROUNDNUT**

Congo pea - *see* **PIGEON PEA**

Cook's-truffle - *see* **TRUFFLE(S)**

COOLWORT - An American plant also called false miterwort, toothwort, and foam flower, coolwort (*Tiarella cordifolia*) is a white-flowered herb of the woodlands and was reportedly used by Native Americans as a spice. The true miterwort (genus *Mitella*) is also called fairywort.
Common names and synonyms: Fairywort, false miterwort, foam flower, miterwort, toothwort.

Coontie - *see* **ZAMIA**

Coptis - *see* **GOLDTHREAD**

CORAL BEAN - Cultivated in Central America and Mexico, the coral bean trees - *Erythrina berteroana* (called *pito*) and *E. rubinervia* (called *gallito*) - all have young shoots, leaves, and buds that have long been consumed in salads, stews, and vari-

ous other dishes. Another species, *E. fusca,* is used in like fashion in India and the East Indies, whereas still another relative, *E. poeppigiana* (called *poro*), which serves as a shade tree for coffee bushes in Central and South America and the West Indies, has flowers that are used in salads and soups. The pretty (but poisonous) seeds of *pito* and *gallito* are used medicinally, as a toxin for rats and fish, and as beads that are strung together to make necklaces, bracelets, and the like.
Common names and synonyms: Gallito, macrette, pito, poro.

Corazon - *see* **CUSTARD APPLE**

CORDIA - A flowering shrub or small tree of Asia and Australia, cordia (*Cordia myxa*) belongs to a large genus of mostly tropical plants that bear fleshy, often edible fruits. In the case of cordia, it produces yellowish, nutlike fruits that helped to sustain aboriginal populations.

CORIANDER (*see also* **CILANTRO**) - Also known as cilantro, culantro, and Chinese parsley, coriander (*Coriandrum sativum*) is an herb that is cultivated for its aromatic seeds and leaves. It is a member of the parsley family and closely related to caraway. Coriander is apparently a native of the Mediterranean region, and its dried seeds have been in use for some 7,000 years. They have been found in the tombs of ancient Egypt and were widely used by the Hebrews, Greeks, and Romans (who flavored their bread with coriander) of antiquity. The seeds contain an aromatic oil and are used to flavor liquors (such as gin), to season soups and pastries, and to spice up marinades in Scandinavia and Greece. Dried coriander seeds are generally more appreciated in northern than in southern Europe, and coriander is vital to the cuisine of India because of its crucial role as an ingredient in curry powder.
Common names and synonyms: Chinese parsley, cilantro, culantro, *yuen sai.*
See in addition: "Spices and Flavorings," Part II, Section F, Chapter 1.

Corkwood tree - *see* **SESBAN**

Corn - *see* **MAIZE**

Cornel - *see* **CORNUS**

Cornelian cherry - *see* **CORNUS**

CORNFLOWER - A garden plant native to Eurasia, the cornflower (*Centaurea cyanus*) - like cornsalad - is so called because it is found in fields of corn. It is also known as "bachelor's-button" and "bluebottle" because of its bold blue blossoms. These flowers were used in the past by pastry chefs to provide a blue color for creamy desserts.
Common names and synonyms: Bachelor's-button, bluebottle.

CORN MINT - Found in temperate regions, this herb (*Mentha arvensis*) is cultivated commercially in China, Japan, and Brazil. The leaves yield an oil that is 60 percent menthol and is used to flavor pharmaceuticals, toothpaste, food products, cigarettes, and alcoholic beverages. The leaves can also be boiled and eaten or used as a condiment.

Common names and synonyms: Field mint, Japanese mint.

See also: "Spices and Flavorings," Part II, Section F, Chapter 1.

CORNSALAD – "Cornsalad," so named because these plants with small, bluish flowers grow in cornfields, actually refers to any of several plants of the genus *Valerianella,* especially *V. olitoria* and *V. locusta.* Also called "lamb's-lettuce," "field salad," "fat-hen," "lamb's-quarter," "marsh salad," "hog salad," and a variety of other names, these European natives – found throughout North America as well – provide slightly bitter-tasting leaves that are much appreciated in salads. The various types of cornsalad were considered weeds until the seventeenth century, when they began to be cultivated, and cultivation doubtless accounts for the different varieties now identified.

Common names and synonyms: European cornsalad, fat-hen, field salad, hog salad, lamb's-lettuce, lamb's-quarter, mache, *mâche,* marsh salad.

CORNUS – The genus *Cornus,* native to Europe, eastern Asia, and North America, includes a number of shrubs and trees that bear what is actually not a berry but a drupe. Among those in North America is *C. florida,* often called the "flowering dogwood," which is native to the eastern United States. This has edible fruits that (like the leaves) become scarlet-colored in the autumn. The "bunchberry" (*C. canadensis*) is a close relative, and Native Americans used this fruit for both food and medicine. The cornelian cherry (*C. mas*) is a European species, the fruit of which is eaten fresh and made into preserves and wine (*vin de corneulle*); at one time, it was widely cultivated.

Common names and synonyms: Bunchberry, cornel, cornelian cherry, dogberry, dog cherry, dogwood berry, dogwood cherry, dogwood tree, flowering dogwood, Siberian cherry, Tartar cherry.

Corsican citron – *see* **CITRON**

Cos – *see* **LETTUCE**

Coscushaw – *see* **CUSHAW (SQUASH)**

Costa Rican guava – *see* **WILD GUAVA**

Costeño – *see* **GUAJILLO AND PULLA CHILLIES**

COSTMARY – A plant that is native to Asia, was a popular herb in ancient Greece, and has seen both past and present use in England, costmary (*Chrysanthemum balsamita*) – with its leaves' hint of lemon and mint flavorings – is employed to season poultry as well as stuffings, soups, salads, and sauces. It was naturalized, and now grows wild, in North America, where it is known as "Bible leaf" because its long, narrow leaves were used in former times as page markers in Bibles. Costmary has also been known in the past as "alecost" because it was used in the production of home-brewed ale.

Common names and synonyms: Alecost, balsam herb, Bible leaf, Bible-leaf mace, mace, mint geranium.

See also: "Spices and Flavorings," Part II, Section F, Chapter 1.

COTTONSEED OIL – In 1887, Wesson Oil began as the Southern Cotton Oil Company in Philadelphia. The firm had cottonseed-crushing mills throughout the southern United States and quickly became the largest producer of cottonseed oil as well as the first U.S. manufacturer of vegetable shortening. Cottonseed oil (from cotton – genus *Gossypium*) was employed as an inexpensive substitute for olive oil in cooking and in salads prior to the advent of other oils, such as that from soybeans. Cottonseed oil has found continued use in the food-packing industry, as, for example, in the packing of sardines.

See also: "An Overview of Oils and Fats," Part II, Section E, Chapter 1.

Couch-couch – *see* **CUSH-CUSH YAM**

COUCH GRASS – Also known as "wheat grass" and a host of other names including "quack grass," couch grass (*Agropyron repens* = *Elytrigia repens*) is a Eurasian grass now naturalized in North America. It is generally used for grazing and hay production, but in medieval Europe the tender tips of its rhizomes were gathered in the spring to be eaten raw as a vegetable and the whole rhizome later dried to make a flour. Today, in England, the rhizomes are still gathered and dried (and sometimes exported to France and Italy) for making a tea and, when roasted, are used in Central Europe as a coffee substitute.

Common names and synonyms: Dogtooth, quack grass, quick grass, scutch, twitch grass, wheat grass.

Coughwort – *see* **COLTSFOOT**

Country almond – *see* **MALABAR ALMOND**

Courge – *see* **SQUASH AND PUMPKIN**

Courgette – *see* **SQUASH AND PUMPKIN, ZUCCHINI**

Cousee-cousee – *see* **CUSH-CUSH YAM**

COUVE (*see also* **CABBAGE, COLLARDS**) – Couve is a tall, dark green Portuguese cabbage that (like the 400-odd other cabbage varieties) is a member of the species *Brassica oleracea.* Couve has a taste that is something of a cross between turnip greens and kale, and it is the primary ingredient in *caldo verde,* the well-known soup of Portugal. Many Portuguese grow the cabbage in their yards; in Minho, it is often grown under trellised grape vines.

See in addition: Collards and "Cruciferous and Green Leafy Vegetables," Part II, Section C, Chapter 5.

Cowberry – *see* **LINGONBERRY**

Cow bitter(s) – *see* **TANSY**

COW PARSNIP – With a taste somewhat like that of asparagus, the leaves and stems of the European cow parsnip (*Heracleum sphondylium*), found in temperate areas of Europe and Asia, are cooked and consumed as a green vegetable, and its roots have been used as a condiment. In Lithuania and Poland, a home-brewed beer is made from the stems and seeds, and elsewhere in eastern Europe the cow parsnip was also employed to make borscht. The American cow parsnip (*H. lanatum*) has a much stronger taste and served Native Americans as a food. The roots were cooked, and the shoots and leaves were eaten both cooked and raw.

Common names and synonyms: American cow parsnip, European cow parsnip, Meadow parsnip.

COWPEA (*see also* **BEANS, LEGUMES**) - Also called "long bean," "asparagus bean," and "yard long bean" because of the length of its pods, the cowpea (*Vigna unguiculata* or *V. sesquipedalis* or *V. sinensis*) is, in fact, a bean. It has been cultivated since prehistoric times in tropical Asia (especially India) and is a relative of the mung bean and other Asian legumes, suggesting a South Asian origin for the plant. However, China has been proposed as another center of origin, and because the plant occurs in the wild in many parts of Africa, that continent may have been yet another cradle of the cowpea. It reached the New World via the slave trade and today is cultivated throughout the tropical and subtropical world.

The cowpea comes in a number of varieties. Black-eyed peas are perhaps the best known of these in the United States, where they are available fresh, dried, canned, and frozen. Crowder peas and field peas are other favorites, especially in the U.S. South. Prior to the Civil War, cowpeas were sometimes given to slaves but were used mostly for animal fodder. Today, they are one of the major constituents of "soul food."

Common names and synonyms: Asparagus bean, black-eyed bean, black-eyed pea, China bean, Crowder pea, field pea, long bean, red pea, southern pea, yard-long bean.

See in addition: "Beans, Peas, and Lentils," Part II, Section C, Chapter 3.

COWSLIP - Two plants are known by this name. The first is a European wildflower (*Primula veris*). Its sweet-smelling flowers are added to salads or used to make wine, vinegar, mead, and tea. The flower may also be candied. In the United States, however, "cowslip" refers to the marsh marigold, whose Latin name is *Caltha palustris*. This plant is found in the temperate regions of North America, Asia, and Europe. A hardy perennial herb, the entire plant is eaten as a vegetable. The leaves may also be used as a potherb, and the pickled flower buds can be substituted for capers.

Common names and synonyms: Kingcup, marsh marigold, may-bob, meadow-bright.

Cowtree - *see* **MIMUSOPS**
Cow vetch - *see* **TUFTED VETCH**
Coyo - *see* **AMARANTH**
Coyote melon - *see* **SQUASH AND PUMPKIN**
CRAB APPLE (*see also* **APPLE**) - There are several species of wild fruit trees of the genus *Malus* (espe-

cially *M. coronaria*) that produce small, brightly colored crab apples. The crab apple is the ancestor of cultivated apples and has been used as a food since prehistory, although the harsh, acidic taste of these fruits doubtless precluded eating them raw. Crab apples make excellent jellies and preserves.

Common names and synonyms: Sweet crabapple, wild apple.

Cramp bark - *see* **BERRIES, HIGHBUSH CRANBERRY**

CRANBERRY (*see also* **BERRIES, HIGHBUSH CRANBERRY, LINGONBERRY**) - Of the same genus as the blueberry, the cranberry (*Vaccinium macrocarpon*) is a North American shrub that is so named because its flower stamens resemble a beak – hence "crane berry," a name (which subsequently became "cranberry") assigned to it by the early European settlers in New England. The berries, which grew wild in New England, had long been used by Native Americans for pemmican (dried meats pounded into a paste and mixed with berries and fat). The early European settlers found cranberries too tart to eat by themselves but made them into pies, puddings, tarts, relishes, preserves, and cranberry sauce. Perhaps appropriately, it was in Massachusetts that commercial cranberry production was begun in the 1840s, and that state still supplies about half of the U.S. crop.

Cranberries are planted in sandy bogs that are irrigated, and harvesting entails loosening the berries so that they fall into the water, then sweeping the floating berries into processing machinery. Before being crushed, however, cranberries (also known as "bounce berries") are "bounced" to determine ripeness, meaning that they must clear a hurdle or are discarded.

Another, smaller cranberry (*V. oxycoccos*) is also native to North America as well as to northern Europe and Asia. It is seldom cultivated commercially, but the wild berries are picked for home consumption. The so-called lowbush cranberries are actually lingonberries. In addition, "highbush cranberries" are erroneously called cranberries. North American commercial cranberries have been introduced in the Scandinavian countries and Great Britain. Almost all of the commercial crop is made into juice or canned cranberry sauce. Cranberry juice is a recent (since 1959) development, representing a successful effort to diversify an industry that once did most of its business around the holidays, producing the indispensable accompaniment to turkey. Cranberries are very high in vitamin C and in the past have proven an effective cure for scurvy.

Common names and synonyms: Airelle de myrtille, American cranberry, bounce berry, crane berry, fen berry, large cranberry, small cranberry.

Cranberry bush - *see* **HIGHBUSH CRANBERRY**
Crane berry - *see* **CRANBERRY**

Crapaudback - *see* **CALABAZA (SQUASH)**
Cream nut - *see* **BRAZIL NUT**
Creeping myrtle - *see* **PERIWINKLE**
Creole mustard - *see* **HORSERADISH**
CREOSOTE BUSH - Also called the "little stinker" because of the resinous odor it gives off, the creosote bush (*Larrea tridentata* = *L. mexicana*) is a native of the desert Southwest of the United States and Mexico. It was used by Native Americans for medicinal purposes and as a wood for smoking foods. In addition, its flower buds have been consumed.
Common names and synonyms: Little stinker.
CRESS - "Cress" is a name applied to a number of greens belonging to the mustard family, especially garden cress (*Lepidium sativum*). The British are especially fond of cresses, which are grown in enormous quantities in market gardens around London. Young sprouts of garden cress are often mixed with mustard greens in salads. Another name for cress is "pepper-grass."
Common names and synonyms: Garden cress, pepper-grass.
See also: "Cruciferous and Green Leafy Vegetables," Part II, Section C, Chapter 5.
Crinkleroot - *see* **TOOTHWORT**
Crosne - *see* **CHINESE ARTICHOKE**
Cross-leaf heath - *see* **BOG HEATHER**
Crowberry - *see* **BEARBERRY**
Crowder pea - *see* **COWPEA**
Crown daisy - *see* **CHRYSANTHEMUM**
Cuachilote - *see* **CUAJILOTE**
CUAJILOTE - A tree native to Mexico and Central America, the cuajilote (*Parmentiera edulis* = *P. aculeata*) produces pointed, yellowish green fruits. They have a sweet taste and are eaten raw, cooked, and preserved (often as pickles).
Common names and synonyms: Cuachilote, guajilote.
Cubanelle pepper - *see* **SWEET PEPPERS**
Cuban spinach - *see* **PURSLANE**
Cuban squash - *see* **CALABAZA (SQUASH)**
Cuban sweet potato - *see* **BONIATO**
Cubeb - *see* **TAILED PEPPER**
Cuckoo flower - *see* **LADY'S SMOCK**
CUCUMBER (*see also* **GHERKIN, INDIAN CUCUMBER, SQUASH AND PUMPKIN**) - A native of southwestern Asia, the cucumber (*Cucumis sativus*) is a member of the squash family and has been cultivated since prehistoric times for its fruit. It is related to melons and, like melons, has a high water content, which means that it is always cool. The ancient Egyptians enjoyed cucumbers (and reputedly fed them to their Hebrew slaves), as did the Greeks and the Romans. The latter probably spread the cucumber about their empire (as was the case with so many foods), although at least one source states that the cucumber first reached France as late as the ninth century, and England only in the fourteenth century.

We know that the vegetable came to the Americas with the Spaniards, but a problem with keeping track of cucumbers historically is that there are so many related species. They range, for example, from the West Indian gherkin (*C. anguria*), a tropical American vine originally from Africa that reached the West Indies via the slave trade, to the snake or serpent cucumber (*C. melo* var. *flexuosus*), which is botanically a melon, to the African horned cucumber (*C. metuliferus*). Cucumbers are divided into three groups: the standard field-grown slicing cucumber, the new hothouse varieties (some of which are seedless), and the smaller pickling kinds.

The West Indian gherkin is perhaps the most widely used for this latter purpose, although, of course, all lend themselves well to pickling and to the relishes that are so prominent in Indian cookery. Cucumbers suffered a decline in popularity in Europe from the Middle Ages to the eighteenth century, as they fell under medical suspicion of being hard on the digestive system. They are low in calories but contain little in the way of important nutrients. Cucumbers can be baked, boiled, steamed, and braised as well as added to salads, and because of their high water content, they can also be used to make warm teas and cool drinks.
Common names and synonyms: American gherkin, cassabanana, cuke, gherkin, hothouse cucumber, lemon cucumber, Mandera cucumber, pickling cucumber, serpent cucumber, slicing cucumber, snake cucumber, West Indian gherkin.
See in addition: "Cucumbers, Melons, and Watermelons," Part II, Section C, Chapter 6.
Cucumber tree - *see* **BELIMBING**
Cucurutz - *see* **MAIZE**
CUDDAPAH ALMOND - Also called the "chirauli nut," the cuddapah almond (*Buchanania latifolia*) is a tree that provides food for the peoples of South and Southeast Asia and has also helped to feed the Aborigines of Australia. Moreover, the seeds, which are eaten, yield an edible oil used in cooking.
Common names and synonyms: Chirauli nut.
Cudrang - *see* **CHE**
Cuime - *see* **AMARANTH**
Cuke - *see* **CUCUMBER**
Culantro - *see* **CILANTRO, CORIANDER**
CUMIN - Known as *comino* in Spanish, cumin (*Cuminum cyminum*) seems to be a Mediterranean plant - as are most other members of the carrot family - although some think it originated in Asia, and it apparently has been cultivated in India, Egypt, and the Mediterranean region since time immemorial. Certainly cumin was prescribed in early Hindu medicine for a variety of ailments; it was also a popular spice in ancient Rome and is mentioned in both the Old and New Testaments of the Bible. Cumin seeds are aromatic and yield an oil used in the perfume industry. Whole or ground, they season many Mexican dishes and are a vital

ingredient in *chile* powders. Similarly, cumin is also crucial to curry powder and many dishes of India. In addition, North African recipes call for cumin in marinades, couscous, and lamb dishes. Finally, cumin is used in baking – especially in rye breads.

Common names and synonyms: Comino, cummin, jintan.

See also: "Spices and Flavorings," Part II, Section F, Chapter 1.

Cummin - *see* **CUMIN**

Cumquat - *see* **KUMQUAT**

Cup plant - *see* **SILPHIUM**

CUPUASSU - A relative of cacao, *cupuassu* (*Theobroma grandiflorum*) is a fruit of the Amazon Basin that is generally available in local markets. It is used for making sweetened juice and frozen desserts.

Curcas - *see* **COCOYAM**

Curcas oil - *see* **PHYSIC NUT**

Curcuma - *see* **TURMERIC**

CURLED DOCK - A European plant that has become naturalized as a weed in North America, curled dock (*Rumex crispus*) has long provided food for gatherers. Its leaves and seeds are edible, as is its large and fleshy root, which is dug up in the fall and dried.

Common names and synonyms: Curly dock, narrow dock, sour dock, yellow dock.

CURRANT(S) (*see also* **BERRIES, BLACK CURRANT**) - There are three kinds of European currants that come in the colors red, white, and black. These berries of the genus *Ribes* were cultivated in northern Europe prior to the seventeenth century and subsequently brought to North America. In addition, there is a native North American red currant – *Ribes sanguineum*. The European red currant (*R. rubrum*), a small, tart, red- or scarlet-colored berry, is much used in northern Europe for making juice, jellies, cakes and other desserts, compotes, and mixed drinks. The black currant (*R. nigrum*), which is of greater commercial importance, is the basis for jelly, juice, sweet must, and the liquor crème de cassis, as well as a clear, biting alcoholic beverage that is much like schnapps. White currants (*R. sativum*) are made into a white wine but are generally less used than red or black currants, which are very rich in vitamins A and C. Currants were extremely important in the diet of Native Americans, who cooked them, ate them raw, and made them into pemmican. In recent years, currants have been utilized less in the United States.

Common names and synonyms: Aka-suguri, black currant, common red ribes, European black currant, European red currant, garden currant, North American red currant, northern red currant, red currant, white currant.

Currant bush - *see* **BUSH CURRANT**

Curri - *see* **HAZELNUT AND FILBERT**

CURRY LEAF - The small, shiny, pungent leaves of this Asiatic shrub (*Murraya koenigii*) are used for flavoring. The curry leaf tree is best associated with Sri Lankan cuisine, but it grows in most tropical Southeast Asian countries. The leaves are employed fresh, dried, and powdered.

CUSHAW (SQUASH) (*see also* **SQUASH AND PUMPKIN**) - The designation of various squashes as cushaws has led to some semantic confusion. "Cushaw" is sometimes intended to be synonymous with "calabaza" squash. But one of the crooknecks of *Cucurbita moschata* that is widely grown in the United States received its name from the Algonquian *coscushaw*. In general, however, the cushaw squashes are understood to be of the species *C. mixta*, which grows in an area ranging from Costa Rica north to the southern United States. This "mixed" squash type was originally included in *C. moschata* but later came to be regarded as a separate species.

Common names and synonyms: Cashaw, *coscushaw*, crookneck.

See in addition: "Squash," Part II, Section C, Chapter 8.

CUSH-CUSH YAM (*see also* **YAMS**) - A native of northern South America and the Caribbean, the cush-cush yam (*Dioscorea trifida*) was an important food for resident Native Americans and is still widely cultivated in this region today; it is also now cultivated to a limited extent in the tropics of Asia and West Africa. The cush-cush is a climbing vine that produces subterranean, yellow-skinned tubers. These yams are small but have an excellent flavor and are frequently baked or boiled. The vegetable is called a *ñame* (e.g., *ñame vino, ñame de la India*) as well as *mapuey* in the Spanish-speaking Caribbean, whereas English speakers name it "couch-couch."

Common names and synonyms: Couch-couch, couche-couche, cousee-cousee, *ñame, ñame mapuey*, yampi.

See in addition: "Sweet Potatoes and Yams," Part II, Section B, Chapter 5.

CUSTARD APPLE (*see also* **CHERIMOYA, PAPAW, SWEETSOP, WHITE SAPOTE, WILD CUSTARD APPLE**) - The term "custard apple" is a nickname for the cherimoya but also refers to its close relative, the fruit known around the world as custard apple (*Annona reticulata*). Also called "bullock's-heart," it is a native of the American tropics, grows on a small tree with yellow flowers, is almost round and up to 4 or 5 inches in diameter, and has a tough skin, which protects a creamy white flesh of thick custard-like consistency. Its flavor is not especially appreciated by many (some find it insipidly sweet), but it is nonetheless widely cultivated in the West Indies, tropical Africa, and Southeast Asia. The custard apple, although generally eaten raw, is also used as a flavoring for milk shakes and the like.

Common names and synonyms: Anona, bullock's-heart, *corazon*, nona, pawpaw, sugar apple.

Custard marrow - *see* CHAYOTE
Cut-eye bean - *see* JACKBEAN
Cycad - *see* ZAMIA
Cydonian apple - *see* QUINCE
Cymling - *see* SQUASH AND PUMPKIN

Dagmay - *see* COCOYAM

DAHOON HOLLY - A native of southeastern North America, dahoon holly (*Ilex cassine*) has leaves that - like those of its close relatives, yaupon holly and yerba maté - contain a substantial amount of caffeine. Native Americans used them to brew an emetic tea, which was consumed in purification rituals.

Common names and synonyms: Cassine, dahoon.

DAIKON - A native of Asia and also called the "Oriental radish," the daikon (*Raphanus sativus* spp.) bears little resemblance to round, red-skinned radishes. It is a very long root that averages about a foot in length (although in Japan there are more oblate varieties) and is white in color. Daikon is the Japanese name for this type of radish, which is called *mooli* in India and the West Indies. The daikon is an ancient vegetable that is grown throughout Asia but is probably most appreciated in Japan, China, and Korea. It has a pungent flavor, which the Koreans utilize in a type of *kimchee*. In Japan, daikon is often grated and used as a condiment in numerous dishes including sushi, and in China it is worked into a pudding and served raw at dim sum restaurants.

Two relatives (also *R. sativus*) of the daikon are of interest as well. One is the red-fleshed radish called *sing li mei,* which means "the heart is beautiful." These are eaten as a snack food and add color to salads. Another is the "green Oriental radish," which can grow to a size approaching that of its giant cousin and which is generally used in soups and dishes that are simmered. In addition, spicy sprouts, called *kaiware,* can be grown from daikon seeds. *Kaiware* are most commonly used in salads or for garnish.

Common names and synonyms: Chinese radish, giant white radish, green Oriental radish, Japanese radish, Japanese white radish, *kaiware, mooli,* Oriental radish, red-fleshed radish, *sing li mei, tsumamina.*

See also: "Cruciferous and Green Leafy Vegetables," Part II, Section C, Chapter 5.

Dalima - *see* POMEGRANATE
Dalo - *see* COCOYAM

DAMIANA - The dried leaf of damiana (*Turnera diffusa* = *T. aphrodisiaca*) was consumed in the past for its alleged aphrodisiacal properties and as a tonic. It is a plant found in the American tropics and in Texas and California.

DAMSON PLUM (*see also* **PLUM**) - The Damson plum (*Prunus insititia*) is the classic small, dark blue plum that ripens in August and has been virtually unaltered for thousands of years. It is named for the city of Damascus, from which the fruit traveled to reach Italy and then spread out across the rest of Europe, where it grows today both in the wild and in home orchards. The Damson plum is notable for its ability to resist disease and cold and to thrive with little or no care. It is tart and used mostly in preserves and in the production of liqueurs such as slivovitz.

Common names and synonyms: Bullace plum, tart Damson plum.

Dancy tangerine - *see* MANDARIN ORANGE

DANDELION - Although regarded as a nuisance by many whose lawns become infested with these "weeds," dandelions (*Taraxacum officinale*) have served as a versatile wild food in the Old World since the days of the hunter-gatherers. This bright spring flower was reported in seventeenth-century Massachussetts, and dandelions had entrenched themselves in Australia by the mid-nineteenth century. Today the plants are cultivated commercially - by the French and the Italians in particular - for their bitter, chicory-like flavor. Dandelion leaves are eaten raw in salads or cooked as greens, whereas the roots are also edible and can be boiled or ground and used as a coffee substitute. The white crowns are cooked as a vegetable, the flower buds are frequently pickled, and the flower heads have been used to make wine. The leaves are very high in vitamin A and, like most other greens, provide an abundance of calcium and iron, some thiamine and riboflavin, and, if not cooked too thoroughly, vitamin C as well.

Darjeeling - *see* TEA
Darnel - *see* RYEGRASS
Dasheen - *see* CALLALOO, COCOYAM, MALANGA, TARO

DATE - Arabs say that there are as many culinary and pharmaceutical ways of using dates (*Phoenix dactylifera*) as there are days in the year, which serves to underscore the importance of dates to desert peoples. The date tree grows in hot and arid regions where most plants cannot, and at its top are clusters of dates packing a high-energy-giving sugar content of 54 percent. The date palm is thought to be native to North Africa and Arabia - three-quarters of the world's date crop is still produced in the Middle East - and its cultivation stretches back in time some 7,000 years, beyond even the time of the Sumerians and Babylonians, who made it their sacred tree. The name is from the Greek *daktulos* (meaning "finger," from the shape of the fruit). Dates were also known to Mediterranean peoples from early times, and the Spaniards introduced them into the New World. Spanish missionaries carried dates to California, which today - along with Arizona - produces most of the U.S. crop.

There are soft, semisoft, and dry dates, depending on moisture content. The semisoft Deglet Noor variety dominates U.S. production. Elsewhere the semisoft Zahidi and Medjool are popular, along with the Bahri, a soft date. Dates are eaten fresh, naturally preserved, or dried, and they are ground into meal to make cakes. In addition, dates are pressed for juice to make *shekar* and alcoholic beverages. They are an ingredient in many dishes of the Middle East and wherever else they have been cultivated for a long time. Most dates available outside of their growing areas are soft, partly dried ones. The sap of the date palm is also employed as a beverage. Aside from the Middle East and the United States, dates are grown in India, Pakistan, northern Africa, and the Canary Islands. Dates are high in calories but supply much potassium and a fair amount of vitamin B_6, niacin, iron, and magnesium.

Common names and synonyms: Bahri date, date palm, Deglet Noor date, dry date, Medjool date, red date, semisoft date, soft date, Zahidi date.

Date palm - *see* **DATE**
Date plum - *see* **PERSIMMON**
Datura - *see* **MOONFLOWER**
DAYLILY - Any of the plants of the genus *Hemerocallis* are called daylilies. These natives of Eurasia reached North America as garden plants but subsequently "went native" there as well. In China, the buds of *H. fulva* in particular are cooked in slow-simmering dishes. But any daylily buds are good boiled or stir-fried as a vegetable. Plants of the genus *Hosta* - called plantain lilies - are also referred to as "daylilies" but do not appear to be consumed as a food.

Common names and synonyms: Plantain lily.

DE AGUA (*see also* **CHILLI PEPPERS**) - A chilli pepper of the genus *Capsicum,* this medium-hot variety looks a lot like a larger but more slender version of the jalapeño. It is much used in parts of Mexico for stuffing and in salsas, but is seldom found north of the border.

See in addition: "Chilli Peppers," Part II, Section C, Chapter 4.

De árbol - *see* **CAYENNE PEPPER**
Deer's-ears - *see* **GENTIAN**
Deertongue - *see* **CAROLINA VANILLA**
Deglet Noor date - *see* **DATE**
Delica - *see* **KABOCHA (SQUASH)**
DELICATA (SQUASH) (*see also* **SQUASH AND PUMPKIN**) - A small squash, generally about 7 or 8 inches long with a diameter of 2 to 3 inches, the delicata (*Cucurbita pepo*) has a taste and smell of, alternatively, butternut squash, corn, or sweet potato - the latter the reason for another of its names, "sweet-potato squash." Of American parents, this is a delicious squash, "human-made" by squash breeding. It is a great source of vitamins A and C along with iron and potassium.

Common names and synonyms: Bohemian squash, Jack-Be-Little, Munchkin, sweet-potato squash.

See in addition: "Squash," Part II, Section C, Chapter 8.

Demon walnut - *see* **WALNUT**

Dent maize - *see* **MAIZE**
DESERT APPLE - Also known as "Indian jujube" and "ber" as well as "desert apple," the small thorny tree this fruit grows on (*Ziziphus mauritiana*) may be of either African or Indian origin. The fruits, which smell like carob, are round or oblong, about the size of plums, and have a taste that is sweet to slightly acidic and suggests that of an apple. They are eaten raw, preserved, or dried. The desert apple is cultivated as a desert crop in India but has spread throughout tropical Southeast Asia as well. It does best, however, where the climate is not continually moist. The name "jujube" comes from the French for a lozenge, which the fruit was supposedly reminiscent of.

Common names and synonyms: Ber, Indian jujube.

Desert blazing star - *see* **MOONFLOWER**
Desert holly - *see* **SALTBUSH**
Desert jointfir - *see* **MORMON TEA**
Desert lavender - *see* **HYPTIS**
Desert-spoon - *see* **SOTOL**
Desert thorn - *see* **MATRIMONY VINE**
Devil-in-the-bush - *see* **NIGELLA**
Devil's-bones - *see* **WILD YAM**
Devil's-claws - *see* **UNICORN PLANT**
Devil's-dung - *see* **ASAFETIDA**
Devilwood - *see* **OSMANTHUS**
DEWBERRY (*see also* **BERRIES, BLACKBERRY**) - Blackberries grow upright, whereas the several forms of the dewberry (such as *Rubus hispidus* and *R. caesius*) trail on the ground. Otherwise, dewberries (although sometimes a little smaller) are practically identical to blackberries, are used for the same purposes, and are rich in vitamin C.

Diamante citron - *see* **CITRON**
Dihé - *see* **TECUITLATL**
Dijon mustard(s) - *see* **MUSTARD SEED**
DILL - This herb (*Anethum graveolens*), a member of the parsley family and more aromatic than fennel (a relative), has been pronounced native to central Asia and to southeastern Europe. The name, however, comes from the Norse word *dilla,* meaning "lull," apparently because the seeds were believed to be good for insomnia. Confusion over the plant's origin is probably inevitable because it grows wild in most temperate regions. The ancient Greeks used dill as a remedy for hiccups as well as for culinary purposes, and it has been a part of Mediterranean cuisines ever since. The Romans credited the plant with fortifying qualities and made certain that gladiators were well fortified with it. As their empire receded, dill remained behind to become seminaturalized in much of northern Europe, although it has to be cultivated in the Scandinavian countries. Today, both dill seed and dill weed are used as seasonings. The aromatic seed heads flavor pickles (their best-known use for most Americans is in dill pickles), sauces, and other foods such as fish, cheeses, and yoghurt. The feathery green leaves

(dill weed) have a wonderful aroma when fresh and taste milder than the seeds. The fresh leaves go well in potato and tuna salads. Dried, the leaves lose all their aroma and most of their taste.

See also: "Spices and Flavorings," Part II, Section F, Chapter 1.

Dilly - *see* SAPODILLA

DITTANY - There are three herbs with the name dittany. One is an aromatic Old World plant called Crete dittany (*Origanum dictamnus*), a relative of marjoram and once believed to have the power to expel arrows from the body. The second is the so-called gas plant (*Dictamnus albus*), native to Eurasia and also named "burning bush" because it emits a vapor that can be ignited. The third is "stone mint" (*Cunila origanoides* – also known as Maryland dittany), an eastern North American plant that is a member of the mint family. True to its name, it grows in rocky places and was harvested by Native Americans to make a tea. Stone mint can also substitute for other herbs such as marjoram and thyme.

Common names and synonyms: Burning bush, Cretan dittany, Crete dittany, gas plant, Maryland dittany, stone mint.

Dock - *see* SORREL

Dogbane - *see* HEMP DOGBANE

Dogberry - *see* CORNUS, WINTERBERRY

Dog cherry - *see* CORNUS

Dog rose - *see* ROSE HIP(S)

Dogtooth - *see* COUCH GRASS

Dogwood berry - *see* CORNUS

Dogwood cherry - *see* CORNUS

Dogwood tree - *see* CORNUS

DOM PALM - Grown in Florida and the Nile region of Africa, the leaves of the plant *Hyphaene thebaica* are used for cordage, mats, and paper. The unripe seeds are eaten raw or made into sweetmeats or molasses. The outer husk or pulp is said to taste like gingerbread, thus encouraging its common names, "gingerbread palm" and "gingerbread tree."

Common names and synonyms: Doom palm, doum palm, Egyptian doum, gingerbread palm, gingerbread tree.

Doodhi - *see* BOTTLE GOURD

Doom palm - *see* DOM PALM

Douhé - *see* TECUITLATL

Doum palm - *see* DOM PALM

Downy groundcherry - *see* CAPULIN

Downy haw - *see* HAWTHORN BERRY

Dragon's-eye - *see* LONGAN

Dragon's-tongue - *see* PIPSISSEWA

Drumstick tree - *see* BENOIL TREE

Drumstick vegetable - *see* BENOIL TREE

DUAN SALAM - Also called "Indonesian bay" and "laurel leaf," duan salam (*Eugenia polyantha* or *Syzygium polyantha*) is a tall tree that seems to be a native of South Asia. Its aromatic leaves can be dried and used like bay leaves. When young, they are frequently cooked like greens, often with a bit of meat for flavoring.

Common names and synonyms: Indonesian bay, laurel leaf.

Duck potato - *see* ARROWHEAD

DUIKA - Called a wild mango - which it is not - the duika (*Irvingia gabonensis*) is a fruit that grows on trees of Central Africa. Its flavor is something like that of a mango but not very tasty. The seed, however, which is oily, provides cooking oil and is used to make Gabon chocolate.

Common names and synonyms: Wild mango.

Du jour - *see* KALE

Duku - *see* LANGSAT

DULSE (*see also* SEAWEED) - A coarse, reddish brown seaweed, dulse (especially *Rhodymenia palmata*) is found on North Atlantic coasts and is plentiful in New England waters and those of the British Isles. It is first dried in the sun, then used as a vegetable in salads and - in Scotland - as a condiment. Dulse is generally available in health-food stores.

Common names and synonyms: Dulce, sea moss.

See in addition: "Algae," Part II, Section C, Chapter 1.

DURIAN - A foul-smelling fruit with a spiked skin like that of a pineapple, the durian (*Durio zibethinus*) grows on a tall tree native to the Malaysian region but is now cultivated throughout Southeast Asia. When mature, the fruit is normally the size of a football and weighs about 5 pounds, although there have been reports of weights up to 100 pounds. The edible, cream-colored pulp has a delicious "figs-and-bananas" flavor - despite its obnoxious odor (some have likened it to that of Limburger cheese) - and is generally eaten raw, although unripe fruits can be boiled and eaten as a vegetable. The large seeds are roasted.

The fruit is also grown in East Africa, but, although introduced in the American tropics, did not become popular there. Because of their odor, durians are seldom available in fresh form. They are exported to Europe and the United States but few airlines will accept them for shipment. The fruit is also sold in cans and bottles, packed in sugar syrup. Durian is a fine source of potassium and fairly high in vitamin C.

Common names and synonyms: Civet-cat fruit, Lahong, Tutong.

Dutch durian - *see* SOURSOP

DUTCH RED PEPPER (*see also* CHILLI PEPPERS) - Understandably also known as the "Holland chilli," this member of the genus *Capsicum* is a fairly recently developed hybrid chilli pepper for the Dutch export trade in produce. It is red and hot and used in all the many ways - from stuffing to salsas to pickles - that other peppers have long been used.

Common names and synonyms: Holland chilli.

See in addition: "Chilli Peppers," Part II, Section C, Chapter 4.

Early Red - *see* LOQUAT

Earth almond - *see* CHUFA

EARTH NUT - In addition to serving as another synonym for peanut, the term "earth nut" can mean an Old World plant (*Conopodium denudatum* - also called "pignut") with small tubers that - in England at least - are often eaten raw. Another "earth nut," *Lathyrus tuberosus* (known as well as the "heath pea"), is also European in origin but is now naturalized in the United States. These tubers have been used as food and to flavor whiskey in Scotland and are now cultivated commercially in Holland. Both earth nuts reportedly have the flavor of chestnuts, and both have been mistakenly called chufa.

Common names and synonyms: Heath pea, pignut.

Ebisu - *see* KABOCHA (SQUASH)

Eboe yam - *see* WHITE YAM

Eddo - *see* COCOYAM, TARO

Eddoe - *see* COCOYAM, TARO

Eddy root - *see* TARO

Edible-pod pea - *see* PEA(S), SUGAR PEA

Eggfruit - *see* CANESTEL, LUCUMA

Eggfruit (tree) - *see* CANISTEL

EGGNUT - A little-known nut of the Amazon region, the eggnut (*Couepia longipendula*) has an extraordinarily hard shell that protects its oil-rich kernels. The nut is said to have an excellent flavor.

EGGPLANT - The size and color of the eggplant (*Solanum melongena*) range from the white, egg-shaped types of India (from whence the name derives) to a large, green or white variety of melon size, although the most common (in North America) remains the familiar dark purple, ovoid form sometimes called the "Japanese eggplant." In West Africa, eggplants - there called "garden eggs" - are small and round, with colors that run from white to yellow, whereas in the West Indies eggplants are often streaked with green and have a variety of names including "gully bean," "susumber," and "pea aubergine."

Known in much of the world as "aubergine" and in the Middle East as "poor-man's-caviar," the vegetable (technically a fruit) is native to southern and eastern Asia and was only introduced into Europe (by the Arabs via Spain) during the Middle Ages. It is a member of the nightshade family, which includes the potato, and has a reputation for bitterness, but is so versatile - it can be fried, grilled, boiled, baked, deep-fried, stuffed, or stewed - that its flavor changes with different methods of preparation, and in some cuisines (and diets) the eggplant, with its fleshy texture, takes the place of meat.

Eggplant is the star in many famous dishes, such as the moussaka of Greece and the eggplant parmigiana of Italy. Although not especially nutritious, the eggplant is a good source of folic acid.

Common names and synonyms: Apple-of-love, Asiatic aubergine, aubergine, baby eggplant, *brinjal,* garden egg, Guinea squash, gully bean, Italian eggplant, Japanese eggplant, melanzana, melongene, Oriental eggplant, pea apple, pea aubergine, poor-man's-caviar, susumber, *terong,* white eggplant.

EGUSI - The egusi (*Citrullus colocynthis*) is of the same genus as the watermelon and, like it, a native of tropical Africa. But the similarities end abruptly with taste, because the egusi is an extremely bitter fruit. Instead of the pulp, it is the seeds of the egusi that are utilized. Oil is extracted from them, and they are ground into powder for cooking purposes. They are also roasted for consumption.

Common names and synonyms: Colocynth.

See also: "Cucumbers, Melons, and Watermelons," Part II, Section C, Chapter 6.

Egyptian bean - *see* HYACINTH BEAN

Egyptian doum - *see* DOM PALM

Egyptian lotus flower - *see* LOTUS

Egyptian onion - *see* ONION TREE

Egyptian taro - *see* TARO

Egyptian thorn - *see* ACACIA

Egyptian tree onion - *see* ONION TREE

EINKORN (*see also* WHEAT) - This grain (*Triticum monococcum*) - a one-seeded wheat - is one (along with emmer) of the ancestral species of modern wheat and one of the founder grain crops of the Neolithic Revolution. Primitive varieties of einkorn such as *T. monococcum* spp. *boeoticum* originated in the Balkans, western Asia, and the eastern Mediterranean, and the transition to the cultivated variety (*T. monococcum*) probably took place in Anatolia. About 7,000 years ago, einkorn came to Europe, where it was grown until the nineteenth century, especially in barren regions where other crops were not successful. Primitive varieties still grow wild in the Balkans and West Asia. Although it is seldom cultivated as a cereal, einkorn is used as livestock feed and in the manufacture of beers and vinegars.

Common names and synonyms: One-grained wheat, wild einkorn, wild einkorn wheat.

See in addition: "Wheat," Part II, Section A, Chapter 10.

ELAEAGNUS (*see also* BERRIES) - There are a number of shrubs of the genus *Elaeagnus* that produce edible berries. *Elaeagnus umbellata,* the "autumn olive" of Asia, has small orange or red berries that are used like red currants or dried like raisins. *Elaeagnus angustifolia,* called the "Russian olive," "wild olive," or "oleaster," originated in Asia but is now a popular berry in southeastern Europe, its sweetness enjoyed raw or cooked. In the Philippines, the "lingaro" (*E. philippinensis*) - a large shrub - yields red berries that taste like cherries. Also in the East Asian neighborhood is the "silverthorn" (*E. pungens*), a spiny shrub or tree that has sweet red fruits. Finally, *E. commutata* - the "silverberry" - is a native of northwestern North

America with berries that helped to sustain Native Americans such as the Inuits.

Common names and synonyms: Autumn olive, lingaro, oleaster, Russian olive, silverberry, silverthorn, wild olive.

ELDERBERRY (*see also* **BERRIES**) – There are a number of shrubs and trees of the genus *Sambucus* (elder) that produce elderberries – some of the trees growing to upwards of 50 feet in height. A native of both the Americas (*S. canadensis* and *S. caerulea*) and the Old World (*S. nigra*), the elderberry has been gathered, dried, and cooked for millennia and its fragrant flowers added to salads and made into fritters. The berries vary considerably in color – ranging from blue to red to black – and also in taste. Popular wisdom holds that they should not be eaten raw in any quantity, and it is the case that the foliage and stems are slightly toxic. Native Americans employed elderberries as food and used the tree's vertical hollow stems for arrows and whistles and as taps for gathering maple sap. The ancient Greeks employed the stems for musical instruments called "sambuke." Elderberries are generally employed in tarts and pies and can be made into syrup, jelly, and wine. Although usually found in the wild, in Portugal elderberries are cultivated in large quantities and used to add a deep red color to port wine. Like all berries, elderberries are rich in vitamin C.

Common names and synonyms: American elder, American elderberry, blueberry elder, blue elderberry, eastern elderberry, red elderberry, western elderberry.

ELECAMPANE – A large herb of Eurasia, elecampane (*Inula helenium*) has been naturalized in North America. It has yellow flowers that are edible – as are its young leaves – but the major reason for the cultivation of elecampane, which has been going on since ancient times, is for its aromatic root, employed both medicinally and as a flavoring. The roots can be grated into a spice and added to any number of dishes. In the past they were candied; today their essential oil continues to flavor vermouth.

Elephant(-)apple – *see* **INDIAN WOOD-APPLE, QUINCE**

Elephant-ear plant – *see* **ALOCASIA**

Elephant's-ear – *see* **MALANGA, TARO**

Elk-weed – *see* **GENTIAN**

Emblic – *see* **AMALAKA**

EMMER (*see also* **WHEAT**) – A Eurasian wheat, and (along with einkorn) one of the ancestral species of modern wheat and a founder grain crop of the Neolithic Revolution, emmer (*Triticum dicoccum* = *T. dicoccon*) originated in the Middle East and western Asia at the dawn of the Neolithic Age. It is a winter or spring wheat and was used by the Babylonians and the Egyptians before it spread across Europe beginning about 5000 B.C., making

it one of the earliest grains to be cultivated there. But emmer, although hardy, was not suitable for bread making, and, slowly, crossbreeding with varieties of einkorn developed softer (and more productive) wheats that were suitable. Gradually, emmer gave way to these softer "bread wheats," although it is still grown in the United States for use as livestock feed and in breakfast cereals. Its starchy white flour is also favored for making fine pastries and cakes.

Common names and synonyms: Emmer wheat, German wheat, rice wheat, starch wheat, two-grained spelt, two-grained wheat, wild emmer wheat.

See in addition: "Wheat," Part II, Section A, Chapter 10.

Emu apple – *see* **SOUR PLUM**

ENDIVE AND ESCAROLE (*see also* **CHICKORY**) – This plant (*Cichorium endivia*) is a member of the daisy family and is cultivated for its crisp, succulent (if somewhat bitter) leaves that are used in salads and are also braised. It should not be confused with a relative – Belgian endive, called chickory in Europe. Its ancestor was wild chicory (probably native to India), but endive was domesticated early and grown in ancient Egypt, Greece, and Rome. It was introduced (or reintroduced) in Europe by the Dutch during the sixteenth century. The two principal types under cultivation are curly endive and broad-leafed or Batavian endive. The latter is also known as escarole (from the Old French *scariole* and Late Latin *escariola*) and has a bushy head with large, open, green and white leaves. The roots of this plant are ground, roasted, and added to coffee. Another variety, not bushy at all but rather blanched and spidery in appearance, is called *frisée*. Endive and escarole are fairly high in vitamin A and provide some vitamin C.

Common names and synonyms: Batavian endive, broad-leafed endive, *chicorée*, curly endive, *escariola, frisée, scariole.*

English tomato – *see* **KIWANO**

Enoki – *see* **ENOKITAKE, MUSHROOMS AND FUNGI**

ENOKITAKE (*see also* **MUSHROOMS AND FUNGI**) – Enokitake (*Flammulina velutipes* = *Collybia velutipes*) is a long-stemmed, tight-capped mushroom that is much appreciated in Japan, where it is cultivated. It grows wild in North America (where it is called the "winter mushroom"), but only the cultivated varieties are available in (usually Asian) markets. It is very white, has a somewhat sweet taste, and supplies a small quantity of the B-complex vitamins.

Common names and synonyms: Enoki, enok mushroom, golden mushroom, velvet stem, winter mushroom.

See in addition: "Fungi," Part II, Section C, Chapter 7.

Enok mushroom – *see* **ENOKITAKE**

ENSETE (*see also* **BANANA**) – Alternately called the "jungle banana," the "Abyssinian banana," and the "little red banana," this plant (*Musa ensete*) is now grown mostly as an ornamental because of its erect and bright green, broad leaves. Another fruit called "ensete" and closely related to the banana is *Ensete ventricosum,* which is grown as a staple in some of the higher altitudes of Ethiopia. The pulp is made into bread.

Common names and synonyms: Abyssinian banana, jungle banana, little red banana.

See in addition: "Bananas and Plantains," Part II, Section B, Chapter 1.

EPAZOTE (*see also* **CHENOPODIUM**) – Called *paiku* in Peru, this semicultivated green, epazote (*Chenopodium ambrosioides*) is traditional and necessary in Mexican and Central American cooking. The aromatic leaves (some would say the odor is foul, others find it pleasant) of this sweet and mild-flavored herb are found in markets on large green stalks as well as in chopped and dried forms. When added to dishes containing beans, epazote is believed to reduce gassiness, and it is also used to make "Mexican tea," which is another name for the plant. Epazote has a reputation for combating helminthic boarders in the body, and the leaves and tops of one variety (*C. ambrosioides* var. *anthelminticum*) are considered especially powerful in this regard. An essential oil is extracted from this plant for medicinal uses.

Common names and synonyms: American wormseed, Jerusalem oak, Mexican tea, wormseed.

Erigeron – *see* **HORSEWEED**
Eringo – *see* **SEA HOLLY**
Erosus yam bean – *see* **JÍCAMA**
Ervil – *see* **BITTER VETCH**
Eryngo – *see* **SEA HOLLY**
Escariola – *see* **ENDIVE AND ESCAROLE**
Escarole – *see* **ENDIVE AND ESCAROLE**
Espinaca acquatica – *see* **SWAMP CABBAGE**
Esrog – *see* **CITRON**
Ethrog – *see* **CITRON**
Etrog – *see* **CITRON**
European filbert – *see* **HAZELNUT AND FILBERT**
European grass pea – *see* **CHICKLING VETCH**
European sweet chervil – *see* **CICELY**

EVENING PRIMROSE – Native to North America, the various species of the genus *Oenothera* grow southward from British Columbia and Newfoundland and are found across most of the continental United States. The young shoots and leaves provided food for Native Americans, as did the boiled seeds and roots of some species. The evening primrose was one of the first American plants introduced as a food in Europe, where it was cultivated for both young shoots and roots. In France, *O. biennis* came to be known as *jambon du jardinier* or "gardener's ham."

Common names and synonyms: Gardener's ham, *jambon du jardinier.*

Evening star – *see* **MOONFLOWER**

EVERLASTING PEA – Any of several species of the genus *Lathyrus* – and especially *Lathyrus latifolius* – are called "everlasting pea." It is a native of southern Europe that is now consumed mostly in Asia, where the pods and shoots are boiled as a vegetable and the seeds are roasted.

Common names and synonyms: Perennial pea.

See also: "Beans, Peas, and Lentils," Part II, Section C, Chapter 3.

Exotic grape – *see* **GRAPES**

Faba – *see* **FAVA BEAN**
Fagara – *see* **SICHUAN PEPPERCORN**
Fairywort – *see* **COOLWORT**
False bittersweet – *see* **AMERICAN BITTERSWEET**
False coriander – *see* **LONG CORIANDER**
False miterwort – *see* **COOLWORT**
False sandalwood – *see* **TALLOW WOOD PLUM**
False verbain – *see* **BLUE VERVAIN**
Fameflower – *see* **TALINUM**
Fanweed – *see* **PENNYCRESS**
Fat(-)hen – *see* **CORNSALAD, GOOD-KING-HENRY**

FAVA BEAN (*see also* **BEANS, LEGUMES**) – Known to the English as the "broadbean" or the "horse bean," the fava (*Vicia faba* – from *faba,* which means "bean" in many of the Romance languages) has a very long history, figuring in Chinese cuisine at least 5,000 years ago. Today, favas are very prominent in the cuisines of Mediterranean countries, the Middle East, Africa, South America, and China, but not, for some reason, in that of North America – perhaps because of the need to skin them, which is time-consuming. A remote potential difficulty with ingesting the beans, or even inhaling the pollen from the flowers, is hemolytic anemia, brought on by a type of enzyme deficiency – glucose-6-phosphate-dehydrogenase (G6PD) deficiency – that has developed among some of the people of the world as a protection against malaria. Like most beans, favas deliver protein and iron and, in addition, are a good source of vitamin A and a good provider of the B-vitamin complex.

Common names and synonyms: Broadbean, horse bean, tickbean, Windsor bean.

See in addition: "Beans, Peas, and Lentils," Part II, Section C, Chapter 3.

Fecula – *see* **ARRACACHA**

Feijão-prêto – *see* **TURTLE BEAN**

FEIJOA – The feijoa, a fruit (*Feijoa sellowiana*), is a native of Brazil with a Portuguese name suggestive of a bean (in Portuguese, *feijão*). But although it is unlikely that the kiwi fruit–sized berry of this evergreen shrub would ever be confused with a bean, its common names – "pineapple guava" or even just "guava" – do tend to promote confusion. The feijoa has a green, bumpy skin and a jelly-like pulp surrounded by a whitish flesh with a delicious, tart taste that is something of a cross between the flavors of pineapple and strawberry and goes well in fresh fruit salads. Beginning at the end of the nineteenth century, the feijoa traveled from Brazil to be grown in and exported from southern Europe (1890) and California (1900) on one side of the in world and, more recently, New Zealand and Australia on the other. It is frequently eaten fresh or made into a jelly. When fresh, in particular, the feijoa is a good source of vitamin C.

Common names and synonyms: Guava, pineapple guava.

Felon herb - *see* **MUGWORT**

Fen berry - *see* **CRANBERRY**

FENNEL – Fennel (*Foeniculum vulgare*), a native of southern Europe, is often wrongly called "anise" or "sweet anise" because of its licorice flavor. However, that flavor is less pronounced in fennel than in anise, and the seeds (as well as the roots, leaves, and stalks) of fennel have been employed since ancient times as an ingredient in sauces, sausages, stews, and salads, as well as in breads and various meat, egg, and fruit dishes.

The herb was cultivated by the Egyptians and was popular with the ancient Greeks and Romans. According to Greek mythology, when humans received knowledge from Olympus, the gift came in the form of a fiery-hot coal within a fennel stalk. The name "fennel" derives from a Latin word that indicates a kind of sweet-smelling hay – a hay that was discovered to keep insects at bay. The use, as a vegetable, of the celery-like stalks and leaves of one variety, called "Florence fennel," is mostly seen in Italian cuisine (the root is especially vital in Sicilian cuisine), although fennel is also cultivated for its vegetable (in contrast to herbal) qualities in Greece, France, and the United States – in the latter case, largely because of an Italian-American demand.

Like the seed, the vegetable is licorice-like in taste and has long been associated in Europe with fish recipes. It is also employed raw in salads and appetizers and cooked in any number of dishes. The vegetable provides some vitamin A and niacin, and a little iron. The seed was called the "meetin' seed" by the early New England Puritans, who were accustomed to nibble them during church services. Fennel seeds are especially important in flavoring fish, shellfish, and fish sauces. They are also added to meat dishes, spaghetti sauces, and breads and pastries.

Common names and synonyms: Finocchio, Florence fennel, meetin' seed, Roman fennel, sweet anise, sweet fennel, wild fennel.

See also: "Spices and Flavorings," Part II, Section F, Chapter 1.

Fennel-flower - *see* **NIGELLA**

FENUGREEK – The leguminous seeds of fenugreek (*Trigonella foenum-graecum*), a Eurasian plant, are employed as a spice throughout the Mediterranean region, South Asia, and North Africa. Fenugreek was mentioned in the Ebers papyrus and was used by the ancient Egyptians to make a paste that, when applied to the body, was supposed to combat fevers. In Latin, the name means "Greek hay," presumably because the clover-like plant made good fodder for animals.

Fenugreek seeds have a bitter taste (which is removed by dry-roasting) and a yellow coloring, that they impart to other foods. Ground, they are an important ingredient in curry powders. In parts of Africa, the dried seeds are soaked and prepared like the legumes, which means they are rich in protein. The dried leaves (called *methi*) are mixed into vegetable dishes in Indian, Middle Eastern, and Asian cuisines. Other uses for fenugreek are as the most important flavoring in artificial maple syrup and in halvah, as well as an ingredient in some oral contraceptives. In addition to protein, fenugreek, like most other legumes, is high in the B-vitamins.

Common names and synonyms: Foenugreek, *methi.*

Fernbush - *see* **SWEET FERN**

Ferngale - *see* **SWEET FERN**

Fever bush - *see* **WINTERBERRY**

Feverwort - *see* **BONESET**

FIDDLEHEAD FERN – All ferns are "fiddleheads" when their new, tightly coiled, green shoots emerge from the earth – usually in the spring. After they uncoil into fronds, they are no longer edible, and as with certain mushrooms, there are questions about the edibility of some of the so-called fiddleheads which are suspected of being carcinogenic. However, the one usually marketed – the ostrich fern (*Matteuccia struthiopteris*) – is supposed to be safe. Fiddleheads grow in damp places and in North America are sought mostly in forests along the eastern seaboard, especially in New Brunswick, Maine, and Vermont. For some, their taste is akin to that of artichokes; for others, it is more like the flavor of asparagus. Although they are often added raw to salads, fiddleheads are best when (as with asparagus or artichoke hearts) they are lightly boiled and served with melted butter or some other appropriate dressing. The nutrients provided are vitamins A and C.

Common names and synonyms: Fiddlehead(s), fiddlehead greens, ostrich fern.

Fiddlehead greens - *see* **FIDDLEHEAD FERN**

Field horsetail - *see* **HORSETAIL PLANT**

Field mint - *see* **CORN MINT, MINT**

Field mushroom - *see* **MUSHROOMS AND FUNGI**

Field pea - *see* **COWPEA, PEA(S)**

Field pennycress - *see* **PENNYCRESS**

Field salad - *see* **CORNSALAD**

Field vetch - *see* **VETCH**

FIG - The common fig tree (*Ficus carica*) is a member of the mulberry family. Although a native of Southwest Asia, it long ago was growing wild around the Mediterranean basin, and its sweet, pear-shaped, and many-seeded fruit was picked up by hunter-gatherers. Figs have been cultivated for over 6,000 years, and nowadays practically every Mediterranean garden has its fig tree. When the fruits are ripe, the ground around becomes slippery with their pulp.

The fig was known to the Egyptians, the Greeks, and the Romans, who fed them to their gladiators for quick energy. The Greek word "sycophant," meaning "one who shows the fig," was first applied to the priests who declared that a fig crop was ripe and could be gathered. Later, it meant those who informed on individuals in the illegal fig trade from Greece. The common fig was brought to the Americas by the Spaniards around 1600 and was first planted in California by Franciscan friars around 1770. Commercial production there, however, only dates from about 1900. Today, California produces almost all of the U.S. crop. Other commercial producers are Italy, Turkey, Algeria, Greece, Spain, and Portugal.

In all, there are about 100 kinds of figs, such as the Smyrna fig; even the rubber and banyan trees are species of figs. Major varieties of the fruit are the Black Mission, with a black or purple skin; the Kadotta, with a yellow-green skin; a large fig, the Calimyrna, with a yellow-green skin; and the Brown Turkey, which has a somewhat purplish skin. The fruit is eaten fresh but is also stewed, canned, preserved, and dried. The latter form is the most nutritious, and for millennia dried figs have been a staple food in many parts of the world, where they were known as "poor-man's-food." Fig leaves are also eaten. Figs are a good source of carbohydrates, vitamin A, fiber, and potassium, as well as calcium, iron, and copper.

Common names and synonyms: Adriatic fig, Black Mission fig, Brown Turkey fig, Calimyrna fig, common fig, Kadotta fig, poor-man's-food, Smyrna fig, sycamore fig.

FIG-LEAFED GOURD (*see also* **SQUASH AND PUMPKIN**) - Unknown in the United States, although of American origin, the fig-leafed gourd (*Cucurbita ficifolia*) was cultivated at least 5,000 years ago in Peru. It is so called because the plant has leaves similar to those of the fig tree. Immature fruits are prepared and eaten like summer squashes, whereas the black seeds are roasted for consumption and are turned into a kind of gravy. In addition, the fruit of this versatile vegetable is candied for special occasions in Central American and Andean countries, and the flesh is also fermented to make beer.

Common names and synonyms: Malabar gourd.

See in addition: "Squash," Part II, Section C, Chapter 8.

Filbert - *see* **HAZELNUT AND FILBERT**

Filé - *see* **SASSAFRAS**

FINGER MILLET (*see also* **MILLET**) - Known as *ragi* in the dry areas of India and Sri Lanka, where it is a major grain, finger millet (*Eleusine coracana*) is generally made into flour, porridges, and flatbreads. It is also used for making beer. Higher in protein and fat than most other grains, finger millet is a very wholesome food.

Common names and synonyms: African millet, *ragi*.

See in addition: "Millets," Part II, Section A, Chapter 5.

Finocchio - *see* **FENNEL**

Fish-hook cactus - *see* **BARREL CACTUS**

Fitweed - *see* **LONG CORIANDER**

Five-angled fruit - *see* **CARAMBOLA**

Flag - *see* **IRIS**

Flageolet - *see* **BEANS**

Flag root - *see* **SWEET FLAG**

FLAX SEED - The fibers from a number of plants of the genus *Linum*, and especially the cultivated *L. usitatissimum*, have long been used to make fine linen, and for just as long the seeds of these plants have been crushed to make linseed oil. Indeed, flax is one of the oldest cultivated crops, dating back at least 7,000 years. The Egyptians raised it, and it was among the first crops in Syria and Turkey. Flax cultivation spread to Europe about 3,000 years ago. Although the oil is generally thought of as a drying oil - used in such products as paints and varnishes - one occasionally reads of it being employed as a cooking oil in the past. Flax seed has also been employed to make teas.

Common names and synonyms: Linseed (oil).

Florida arrowroot - *see* **ZAMIA**

Florida sago - *see* **ZAMIA**

Florist's fern - *see* **ASPARAGUS**

Flowering bean - *see* **MALOGA BEAN**

Flowering chives - *see* **CHINESE CHIVE(S)**

Flowering dogwood - *see* **CORNUS**

FLOWERING WHITE CABBAGE (*see also* **CABBAGE**) - A type of Chinese cabbage grown near Canton, the flowering white cabbage (*Brassica campestris*) is similar to broccoli and to bok choy, which seems to be a close relative. It is also called *choy sum* (which translates as "vegetable hearts"), and nearly all its parts are edible and highly nutritious.

Common names and synonyms: Choy sum.

See in addition: "Cruciferous and Green Leafy Vegetables," Part II, Section C, Chapter 5.

Flowery Orange Pekoe - *see* **TEA**

Fluted cucumber - *see* **OYSTERNUT**

FLUTED GOURD - Practically unknown in the United States, the fluted gourd (*Telfairia occidentalis*) is cultivated in West Africa, often on trellises. The fruit is not eaten, but the seeds are protein-rich and are roasted, boiled, and made into a powder for soups.

Common names and synonyms: Fluted pumpkin, oysternut.

Fluted pumpkin - *see* FLUTED GOURD
Foalfoot - *see* COLTSFOOT
Foam flower - *see* COOLWORT
Foenugreek - *see* FENUGREEK
FONIO - Fonio is perhaps the oldest of Africa's cereal crops. For thousands of years, fields of its barely knee-high stalks have stretched across the uplands of West Africa. White fonio (*Digitaria exilis*) is cultivated in an area that extends from the Atlantic coast to Chad. People on the central plateau in Nigeria call it *acha*. Black fonio (*Digitaria iburua*) is more likely found on the Jos-Bauchi Plateau of Nigeria and in northern Togo and Benin.

The history of the crop is little known, as scholars have yet to give it much attention. The seeds of both species are white, but black fonio (despite its lesser popularity) is nutritionally equal to its cousin. Their protein and fat contents are similar to those of wheat and fonio is very rich in several important amino acids.

Unlike some other ancient African cereals, fonio is still widely cultivated and serves as an important food for as many as 4 million people. No doubt one of the reasons for this is its excellent taste. Perhaps another reason is that the crop is particularly well suited to West Africa's semiarid savanna regions; it tolerates poor soil and often grows well where few other cultigens do. Moreover, a number of varieties mature very quickly, and hence provide food during normally lean times when other cereals are still far from being ready for harvest, giving rise to one of its many names – "hungry rice."

In many West African societies, fonio was (and still is) held in high esteem. At times, it was reserved for chiefs and royalty or saved for special festivities. In some cultures, it denoted part of the bride-price, and many feel that it is the best-tasting cereal of all. The kernels can be cooked as a porridge; they serve as a delicious base for couscous; and they are brewed into beer. Heated over a hot fire, they can be popped. Ground into flour, they are baked into breads or used as a substitute for semolina.

Common names and synonyms: Acha, black fonio, hungry rice, white fonio.

Food-of-the-gods - *see* ASAFETIDA
FOREST MILKBERRY - A tree of southern Africa, the forest milkberry (*Manilkara discolor*) ranges from 15 to over 50 feet in height and grows at many different altitudes. It bears flowers that are followed by tiny (less than a half inch in diameter) fruits that are fleshy and yellow to red in color.

Forest mushroom - *see* CHANTERELLE, MUSH-ROOMS AND FUNGI
Four-angled bean - *see* WINGED BEAN

Four-wing saltbush - *see* SALTBUSH
Foxberry - *see* LINGONBERRY
FOX GRAPE (*see also* GRAPES) - Originating in the New World, the fox grape (*Vitis labrusca*) was gathered by native peoples of eastern North America. Later, with the arrival of the Europeans, this purplish black fruit became the source of many cultivated grape varieties that were made into wine. These varieties are hardier and more disease resistant than grapes native to the Old World. Because the skin separates readily from the pulp, labrusca grapes are also called "slip-skin" grapes. The taste of these grapes made into wine has been defined as "foxy."

Common names and synonyms: Labrusca grape, slip-skin grape, wild grape.

See in addition: "Wine," Part III, Chapter 13.

Foxtail barley - *see* WILD BARLEY
Fremont screwbean - *see* MESQUITE
FRENCH COLOMBARD (*see also* GRAPES) - A high-yielding white grape, French Colombard (*Vitis vinifera*) is used in France mostly for making cognac. In California, it generally goes into bulk wines and is often marketed as chablis.

See in addition: "Wine," Part III, Chapter 13.

French endive - *see* BELGIAN ENDIVE
French peanut - *see* MALABAR NUT
French weed - *see* PENNYCRESS
Fresadilla - *see* TOMATILLO
FRESNO (*see also* CHILLI PEPPERS) - Another member of the genus *Capsicum,* the Fresno is a red pepper that resembles the jalapeño but is a bit wider (and hotter). It is grown in California and other places in the U.S. Southwest as well as in Mexico. In addition to their use in salsa, Fresnos are excellent when roasted.

See in addition: "Chilli Peppers," Part II, Section C, Chapter 4.

Frijol arroz - *see* RICE BEAN
Frijol negro - *see* TURTLE BEAN
Frisée - *see* ENDIVE AND ESCAROLE
Fruit à pain - *see* BREADFRUIT
Fruit-salad fruit - *see* MONSTERA
Fruta de Mexico - *see* MONSTERA
Frutillo - *see* MATRIMONY VINE
Fumé Blanc - *see* SAUVIGNON BLANC
Fuyu - *see* PERSIMMON
FUZZY MELON (*see also* MELONS) - Also called "hairy melon," "Chinese squash," "Chinese vegetable marrow," and "Chinese winter melon," the fuzzy melon (*Benincasa hispida = B. cerifera*) is a huge cucurbit that grows on a vine that spreads out over the ground like a pumpkin vine. Apparently native to southern China (and an ancient food of the Chinese), the fuzzy melon comes in two varieties; one is cylindrical in shape, whereas the other narrows at the middle like a dumbbell. Both have a splotchy green skin that is waxy (they are also called "wax gourds") and both are cov-

ered with white, fuzzy hairs. The flavor of their pale green flesh is reportedly delicious, and in addition to peeling them and eating them raw, fuzzy melons are braised, boiled, and used in stir-fries.

Common names and synonyms: Chinese squash, Chinese vegetable marrow, Chinese winter melon, hairy melon, *moqua*, wax gourd.

See in addition: "Cucumbers, Melons, and Watermelons," Part II, Section C, Chapter 6.

Gaai chow - *see* **PAKCHOI AND KAI CHOY**
Gaai choy - *see* **PAKCHOI AND KAI CHOY**
Gai chow - *see* **PAKCHOI AND KAI CHOY**
Gai choy - *see* **PAKCHOI AND KAI CHOY**
Gai-larn - *see* **CHINESE BROCCOLI**
Galanga - *see* **GALANGAL**
GALANGAL - Also called galingale, greater galangal (*Alpinia galanga*) is an aromatic root, native to Indonesia, that resembles ginger and is a close relative of the gingerroot family. It is joined in this relationship by both the lesser galangal (*A. officinarum*) and by galanga - *Kaempferia galanga*. In fact, greater galangal (also called laos) almost replaces gingerroot in much of the cooking of Southeast Asia. Lesser galangal and galanga are also eaten, but more as a cooked vegetable than a spice. At one time, galangal was widely used in Europe (for example, in England during the Middle Ages), where the root was sliced in both fresh and dried forms and added to dishes; it was also dried and ground. Now, however, galangal's principal use in the West is in making liqueurs and bitters.

Common names and synonyms: Galanga, galangale, galingale, greater galanga(l), laos, lesser galanga(l).

See also: "Spices and Flavorings," Part II, Section F, Chapter 1.

Galangale - *see* **GALANGAL**
Galega - *see* **GOAT'S-RUE**
Galingale - *see* **CHUFA, GALANGAL**
Gallberry - *see* **WINTERBERRY**
Gallito - *see* **CORAL BEAN**
GAMAY (*see also* **GRAPES**) - Grown in France, California, and elsewhere, Gamay grapes (*Vitis vinifera*) are used to produce the dry red table wines of the Beaujolais district of Burgundy. In California, two distinct types are grown: Napa Valley Gamay and Gamay Beaujolais. These names actually give a false impression. It seems that the Napa variety is the true Beaujolais grape, and the California Gamay Beaujolais is actually a variant of Pinot Noir - a famous grape of Burgundy.

Common names and synonyms: Gamay Beaujolais, Gamay Noir, Napa Valley Gamay.

See in addition: "Wine," Part III, Chapter 13.

Gamay Beaujolais - *see* **GAMAY**
Gamay Noir - *see* **GAMAY**
Gandul - *see* **PIGEON PEA**
Garavance - *see* **CHICKPEA**
Garbanzo - *see* **BEANS, CHICKPEA**
Garden balm - *see* **BEE BALM, LEMON BALM**
Garden egg - *see* **EGGPLANT, LOCAL GARDEN EGG**
Gardener's ham - *see* **EVENING PRIMROSE**
Garden huckleberry - *see* **WONDERBERRY**
Garden myrrh - *see* **CICELY**
GARLIC - A close relative of the onion, garlic (*Allium sativum*) is the common name for several small bulbous herbs of the lily family - among them British wild garlic (*A. oleraceum*), American wild garlic (*A. canadense*), and British and American field garlic (*A. vineale* - also known as "wild garlic"). *Allium sativum* is said by some to be a native of southern Europe; most, however, say central Asia.

Garlic was much appreciated by Egyptians, Hebrews, Greeks, and Romans, and by the time of the Middle Ages, was well entrenched in the cookery of southern Europe, where it remains to this day. Garlic may have somehow reached the Americas before the voyages of Christopher Columbus: The expedition of Hernando Cortés reportedly encountered it on its march into Mexico.

The term "garlic" comes from an old Anglo-Saxon word for "spear," after its spear-shaped leaves. Garlic is controversial - and not only because of "garlic breath." Throughout the ages, it has been regarded as a powerful medicine (even today it is viewed by some as protective against heart disease and cancer), an aphrodisiac, and a talisman for warding off demons and vampires. The bulb itself consists of bulblets or "cloves" grouped together between membranous scales and enclosed within a whitish or reddish skin. Recently, "elephant garlic," a hybrid of garlic and onion, has appeared in supermarkets - with its popularity the result of the current practice of garlic roasting. It is much larger than normal garlic bulbs (hence the name "elephant") and has a considerably milder flavor.

Common names and synonyms: American field garlic, American wild garlic, British field garlic, British wild garlic, elephant garlic, field garlic, *rocambole*, sand leek, wild garlic.

See also: "The *Allium* Species," Part II, Section C, Chapter 2; "Spices and Flavorings," Part II, Section F, Chapter 1.

Garlic chives - *see* **CHINESE CHIVE(S)**
GARLIC-MUSTARD - A tall weed that is native to Europe, garlic-mustard (*Alliaria officinalis = Sisymbrium alliarin*) has the odor of garlic (hence the scientific name, derived from "Allium"), tastes

something like mustard seed, and can be used in salads. Also called "hedge garlic," the plant was much used in the past by Europeans as an herb. It is now naturalized in North America.

Common names and synonyms: Hedge garlic.

Garnacha - *see* **GRENACHE**

Garnacha Blanc - *see* **GRENACHE**

Gas plant - *see* **DITTANY**

Gbanja kola - *see* **KOLA NUT**

Gean - *see* **CHERRY**

Genip - *see* **GENIPAP, SPANISH LIME**

GENIPAP - The greenish or russet-brown fruit of *Genipa americana* is the size of a small orange and grows in clusters. Its acidic taste militates against its consumption raw, and its common use is in marmalade-like preserves. However, a cool drink known as *genipapado* is also made from the fruits, and the plant yields an indelible blue dye used as body paint. Genipap is found in Mexico, the West Indies, and South America, where it is also known as the "marmalade box."

Common names and synonyms: Genip, genipe, genipop, jagua, marmalade box.

Genipe - *see* **GENIPAP, SPANISH LIME**

Genipop - *see* **GENIPAP**

GENTIAN - There are numerous plants of the type genus *Gentiana*, some with large blue flowers. The dried rhizome and roots of a yellow-flowered European variety, yellow gentian (*G. lutea*), are sometimes used to make a tonic. Another plant of the Gentianaceae family is called deer's-ears, elk-weed, or green gentian (*Frasera speciosa* or *Swertia radiata*). Its roots were consumed by Native Americans in the American West.

Common names and synonyms: Deer's-ears, elk-weed, gentian root, green gentian, yellow gentian.

Gentle balm - *see* **LEMON BALM**

Gerasole - *see* **JERUSALEM ARTICHOKE**

German mustard - *see* **HORSERADISH**

German wheat - *see* **EMMER**

Gerrard vetch - *see* **TUFTED VETCH**

GEWÜRZTRAMINER (*see also* **GRAPES**) - In German, Gewürz means "spice" or "herb," which serves to indicate the aroma of the wine made from these grapes (*Vitis vinifera*) of the Rhine valley type. The region of Alsace produces most of the dry white wine made from Gewürz (also called Traminer, which is actually a cousin) grapes in Europe. In the United States, the grapes are also employed to make very creditable California "Rhine" wines.

Common names and synonyms: Traminer.

See in addition: "Wine," Part III, Chapter 13.

GHERKIN (*see also* **CUCUMBER**) - There are several varieties of small, rough-skinned cucumbers called gherkins (an English name for cucumber), and there exists some confusion about their origin. It was long believed in the West that the original gherkin was the so-called Jamaican gherkin or West Indian gherkin (*Cucumis anguria*) - a trailing

herb also common in Brazil. But a kind of cucumber, which the English called "gherkin," has been eaten in India (where cucumbers are thought to have originated) for over 3,000 years and has been enjoyed in Europe since classical times. This was probably *C. melo* var. *conomon,* a native of India, commonly called the "Oriental pickling melon." The West Indian gherkin, by contrast, is a native of tropical Africa and thus must have reached the tropical New World from there, probably with the early-sixteenth-century slave trade. Soon afterward, it was carried back across the Atlantic and mentioned for the first time in Europe in a French publication of 1549. Immature gherkins are both cooked and eaten raw, but their general use is as pickles.

Common names and synonyms: Concombre des Antilles, Jamaican cucumber, Jamaican gherkin, Oriental pickling melon, *pepinito, pepino,* West Indian gherkin, West Indian gourd.

See in addition: "Cucumbers, Melons, and Watermelons," Part II, Section C, Chapter 6.

Ghia - *see* **CHIA**

Giant bladder weed - *see* **SEAWEED**

Giant cane - *see* **LARGE CANE**

GIANT GRANADILLA - A robust climbing vine that is a native of tropical South America, the giant granadilla (*Passiflora quadrangularis*) now grows throughout the tropical world. It has roundish, medium to dark green leaves that are 6 to 9 inches across, and pleasantly scented white flowers sometimes edged with pink. Its greenish yellow fruits can reach from 5 to 10 inches in length. Their shape is oblong, and their light-colored, firm flesh surrounds a cavity that is filled with numerous dark seeds embedded in a pink pulp. The juice is fragrant and slightly acidic and lends itself well to flavoring ice creams and other desserts and to making refreshing drinks. One such drink, known as a *marquesa* (or *markeesa*), is very popular in Indonesia. Unripe, the fruit may also be cooked and eaten as a vegetable. It contains considerable amounts of phosphorus and vitamin A.

GIANT HOLLY FERN - Known also as a "sword fern," which is the name given to several ferns of both the Old and the New Worlds, the giant holly fern (*Polystichum munitum*) is a plant of western North America. Native Americans ate the rhizome of this species, and those of other species are still consumed in Asia.

Common names and synonyms: Sword fern.

Giant sea kelp - *see* **KELP, SEAWEED**

Giant sunflower - *see* **INDIAN POTATO, SUNFLOWER OIL AND SEED**

Giant taro - *see* **ALOCASIA**

Giant white radish - *see* **DAIKON**

Gilliflower - *see* **GILLYFLOWER**

Gill-over-the-ground - *see* GROUND IVY

GILLYFLOWER - The term "gillyflower" (also spelled gilliflower) refers to any of several plants with fragrant flowers, generally of the genus *Dianthus,* an important Old World genus of herbs. Gillyflowers were used as herbs for flavoring food and especially beverages.
Common names and synonyms: Gilliflower.

Ginep - *see* SPANISH LIME

Gingelly - *see* SESAME

GINGER - The underground rhizome of a tropical flowering plant, gingerroot (*Zingiber officinale*) can be purchased fresh, dried, grated, ground, preserved in vinegar or syrup, and crystallized. If fresh, its tan skin must be removed before grating or slicing. The word *zingiber* means "horn-shaped" in Sanskrit and was applied to ginger because of the shape of its rhizomes. Ginger was used in China and India 7,000 years ago and was an important item in the spice trade that stretched overland and by sea from India to the ports of the eastern Mediterranean, and to Egypt via the Red Sea.

Although known to the Greeks and the Romans, ginger apparently only became popular in Europe during the Middle Ages. The Portuguese took it to Africa as they explored the western coast of that continent in the fifteenth century, and the Spaniards carried it to the New World in the following century. In fact, the latter encouraged the cultivation of ginger in the Americas as part of an effort to grow those exotic (and expensive) spices that usually were only available from the East.

Ginger requires fertile soil and a warm climate to grow properly, and Haiti and especially Jamaica became, and remain, major New World producers. In fact, it is said that the highest-quality ginger comes from the central mountain region of Jamaica. The sharp but sweet flavor of ginger goes well in Asian dishes, and the ground root is used extensively in baking - in gingerbread, spice cakes, and the like. It is also employed in making various alcoholic beverages.
Common names and synonyms: Gingerroot, Jamaica ginger.
See also: "Spices and Flavorings," Part II, Section F, Chapter 1.

Gingerbread palm - *see* DOM PALM

Gingerbread tree - *see* DOM PALM

Ginger bud - *see* MYOGA GINGER, TORCH GINGER

Ginip - *see* SPANISH LIME

GINKGO NUT - Also called the "maidenhair tree," the ginkgo nut (*Ginkgo biloba*) appears to be native to China. One says "appears" because the *Ginkgo* genus, with some of its representatives long extinct, includes members that are among the oldest plants on the planet. Their fanlike leaves basked in the same sunlight as the dinosaurs, and their fleshy, inedible, odoriferous, yellow fruit contains a plumlike, hard-shelled, cream-colored nut that must have provided food for humans since the beginning of their time on earth. Grown in China for thousands of years, the tree reached Japan about 1,000 years ago (presumably after first being introduced in Korea) and found its way to Europe during the early part of the eighteenth century. The tree is said to have first been planted in North America in 1784 in a garden outside of Philadelphia. The nuts are still widely used – after being roasted, grilled, steamed, or boiled – in Asian soups, appetizers, and desserts. Boiled and canned ginkgo kernels are imported from the Orient and are available in ethnic food stores.
Common names and synonyms: Ginkgo (tree), ginko nut (tree), maidenhair tree.

Ginnie pepper - *see* CAYENNE PEPPER

GINSENG (*see also* BLUE COHOSH) - There are a few plants of the genus *Panax* that are called ginseng (especially *P. quinquefolius* and *P. schinseng*) and are strongly associated with the Chinese, who credit their forked roots (which resemble the lower part of the human body) with health-giving and especially aphrodisiacal properties. Actually, however, *P. quinquefolius* is North American in origin, and its leaves were used by Native Americans to brew a kind of tea. They also consumed the roots of dwarf ginseng (*P. trifolius*) both raw and boiled. American ginseng is now cultivated in North America for export to China and for the health-food industry at home.
Common names and synonyms: American ginseng, dwarf ginseng.

Girasole - *see* JERUSALEM ARTICHOKE

Giraumon - *see* CALABAZA (SQUASH)

Girolle - *see* CHANTERELLE, MUSHROOMS AND FUNGI

Girsole - *see* JERUSALEM ARTICHOKE

GLASSWORT (*see also* SAMPHIRE) - Glasswort actually comprises a number of species, among them *Salicornia europaea* and *S. herbacea*, which are both edible and often called "samphire." A cousin, *S. stricta,* employed in the making of glass, may have provided the official name, although the crunching sound glasswort makes when stepped upon also sounds like glass being broken. The roots of these small plants grow wild along rocky seacoasts (even right through rocks) and have historically been much appreciated by the French and English, who pickled them. And today *S. europaea* is gathered commercially in France to be served raw with fish and pickled. Because the plant seems to flourish in the presence of salt, however, it also grows around salt marshes far away from the sea. The plant is crisp and salty tasting when young and can be used in salads as well as pickled. Glasswort is high in iron and vitamin C. In the United States, glasswort is generally but wrongly called samphire.
Common names and synonyms: Marsh samphire, *pousse-pied,* samphire, sea bean, seagrass, sea pickle.

Goa bean - *see* **WINGED BEAN**

GOAT CHILLI (*see also* **CHILLI PEPPERS**) - A cold-tolerant *Capsicum* variety, the goat pepper is said to belong to the species *C. pubescens* but cannot be crossed with any of its other members. It is grown in the high Andes, where its leaves as well as its dried fruit are used for seasoning.

Common names and synonyms: Goat pepper.

See in addition: "Chilli Peppers," Part II, Section C, Chapter 4.

Goat-nut - *see* **JOJOBA NUT**

Goat pepper - *see* **GOAT CHILLI**

GOAT'S-RUE - Also called "galega," goat's-rue (*Galega officinalis*) is a tall, bushy, blue-flowered European herb now cultivated as an ornamental but used in the past as a potherb.

Common names and synonyms: Galega.

Gobo - *see* **BURDOCK**

Golden alexanders - *see* **ALEXANDER**

GOLDEN APPLE - Not to be confused with the Golden Delicious apple, the golden apple (*Spondias cytherea = S. dulcis*) is not an apple at all, but rather a yellow fruit with a single large stone (something like the avocado) surrounded by flesh with a taste ranging from tart to sweet. It is a native of Polynesia but is widely grown in the West Indies. Golden apples are used for tall, sweet drinks and made into jam and chutneys. They are now available in many tropical markets.

Common names and synonyms: Ambarella, Jew plum, Otaheita-apple, vi-apple.

Goldenberry - *see* **CAPE GOOSEBERRY**

Golden button(s) - *see* **TANSY**

Golden chanterelle - *see* **CHANTERELLE, MUSHROOMS AND FUNGI**

GOLDEN CLUB - An aquatic plant native to the eastern United States, golden club (*Orontium aquaticum*) was exploited by Native Americans for food in a number of different ways. The roots were dried and made into flour, the seeds were also dried, and even the flowers were eaten.

Golden gram - *see* **MUNG BEAN**

Golden husk - *see* **CAPE GOOSEBERRY**

Golden mushroom - *see* **ENOKITAKE**

GOLDEN NUGGET (SQUASH) (*see also* **SQUASH AND PUMPKIN**) - The Golden Nugget (*Cucurbita maxima*) is a winter squash that - with its orange skin - looks like a miniature pumpkin. It is a product of plant breeding and has a pleasant squash taste. Generally baked or roasted, one Golden Nugget provides a single serving and delivers much in the way of vitamin A and iron.

Common names and synonyms: Gold Nugget.

See in addition: "Squash," Part II, Section C, Chapter 8.

Golden orange - *see* **KUMQUAT**

GOLDENROD - Native to central and eastern North America, one species of goldenrod (*Solidago odora*) is also known as "blue mountain tea" and "sweet goldenrod" because its fragrant leaves are made into a licorice- or anise-scented tea. The leaves of another species (*S. missouriensis*) were used as food by Native Americans, who ate them raw when young and cooked them as a vegetable.

Common names and synonyms: Blue mountain tea, sweet goldenrod.

Golden timothy (grass) - *see* **MILLET**

Gold Nugget - *see* **GOLDEN NUGGET (SQUASH)**

GOLDTHREAD - A small plant with shiny green leaves, native to both North America and northern Asia, goldthread (*Coptis trifolia*) is named for its long, slender, golden-colored roots. They are bitter but were apparently eaten by natives of the Northern Hemisphere. The roots have also been employed to flavor beer.

Common names and synonyms: Cankerroot, coptis, yellowroot.

Gombaut - *see* **OKRA**

Gombo - *see* **OKRA**

Goober (pea) - *see* **PEANUT**

GOOD-KING-HENRY (*see also* **CHENOPODIUM**) - A member of the goosefoot family, "Good-King-Henry" (*Chenopodium bonus-henricus*) is a Eurasian plant naturalized in North America and was said to be named for King Henry VII of England (reigned 1485-1509). But the truth seems to be that it was first named "Good-Henry" to distinguish it from a weed called "Bad-Henry," and "King" was added later. In England, the plant was also called "fat-hen" because chickens seemed to like it. Remains of the plant (a leafy green vegetable) have been found in Neolithic sites, but it was doubtless gathered by our Paleolithic forebears long before the dawn of agriculture. Good-King-Henry was cultivated as a potherb during the Middle Ages and the beginning of the modern period but afterward returned to the wild state in which it can be found (and gathered) today.

Common names and synonyms: Fat-hen, perennial goosefoot.

Goongoo pea - *see* **PIGEON PEA**

GOOSEBERRY (*see also* **BERRIES**) - The origin of the gooseberry (*Ribes grossularia = R. uva-crispa* - of the same genus as currants), and that of its name, is something of a mystery. The one that is cultivated is a Eurasian native that was apparently brought to France by the Normans in the tenth century. There - because it was made into a sauce to go with mackerel - the berry came to be known as *groseille à maquereau* ("currant for mackerel"). The English name is thought to have been the result of using the berry to stuff roasted goose and accompanying the dish with a relish of gooseberries as well. In Scandinavia, Hungary, and Russia, a soup is made with gooseberries. Over the past few centuries, the berry has been tinkered with by European farmers, so that now over 2,000 varieties exist that come in several shapes and sizes, almost all bigger and sweeter than the generally wild gooseberries that grow in the United States.

American gooseberries are apt to be rough and prickly. Although mostly greenish, they also come in shades of white and purple, and they vary in taste from sweet to sour, indicating the wide variety of species that provided Native Americans with food. Among the wild North American gooseberry species consumed by Native Americans were the "orange gooseberry" (*R. pinetorum*) and the "wolf currant" (*R. wolfii*); the latter is still in use in baking and making tart jellies. Where the gooseberry is cultivated in Europe – and now in New Zealand – the tree is often placed against brick or stone walls. In several areas of the United States and Canada, however, growing the fruit is prohibited because it is host to a disease called "white-pine blister-rust," which is deadly to white pine trees.

Common names and synonyms: English gooseberry, European gooseberry, *groseille à maquereau,* old gooseberry, orange gooseberry, wolf currant.

Gooseberry tree - *see* **OTAHEITE GOOSEBERRY**

GOOSEFOOT (*see also* **CHENOPODIUM, GOOD-KING-HENRY, QUINOA**) - The term "goosefoot" actually refers to a number of closely related plants of the genus *Chenopodium* that are also called "lamb's-quarter" and "pigweed." Some of these have arrived in the New World during the past few centuries from Europe, Asia, and elsewhere, but most are native to the Americas. Moreover, because "pigweed" is also a name for some members of genus *Amaranthus,* and "lamb's-quarter" another name for some members of genus *Valerianella,* we quickly sink into semantic quicksand. Goosefoot today is a weed with leaves that are sometimes gathered and eaten as a vegetable. In the pre-Columbian New World, goosefoot leaves were similarly gathered and used, but in Mesoamerica and the Andean region, the grains of another close relative, quinoa, were consumed as a cereal.

Common names and synonyms: Lamb's-quarter, pigweed.

GOOSEGRASS - A number of different grasses are named goosegrass, including several plants of the genus *Galium* (especially *G. aparine* - also called "cleavers" and "catchweed"), along with *Eleusine indica* and *Potentilla anserina,* among many others. The seeds of some were reportedly used for food by Native Americans.

Common names and synonyms: Catchweed, cleavers.

Gorget - *see* **POKEWEED**
Gota kola - *see* **PENNYWORT**
Gourd - *see* **PUMPKIN, SQUASH AND PUMPKIN**
GOVERNOR'S PLUM (*see also* **PLUM**) - Also called the "botoko plum" and "ramontochi," the governor's plum (*Flacourtia indica*) originated in South Asia and grows in tropical Africa but enjoys its greatest popularity in the West Indies. The plum is a small, purple fruit about the size of a large grape. High in vitamin C, governor's plums are regularly cooked and eaten with fish and make an excellent jelly.

Common names and synonyms: Botoko plum, ramontochi.

Gow kee - *see* **MATRIMONY VINE**
Goyave - *see* **GUAVA**
Grains-of-paradise - *see* **MELEGUETA PEPPER**
Gram - *see* **CHICKPEA**
Gram bean - *see* **MUNG BEAN**
Gram pea - *see* **CHICKPEA**
Granada - *see* **POMEGRANATE**
Granadilla - *see* **GIANT GRANADILLA, MAYPOP, PASSION FRUIT**
Granny's-bonnet - *see* **HABANERO AND SCOTCH BONNET PEPPERS**
Grão do bico - *see* **CHICKPEA**
GRAPEFRUIT (*see also* **CITRUS FRUITS**) - A large and tart member of the citrus family, the grapefruit (*Citrus* × *paradisi*) is so named because it grows in clusters like grapes. Its origins, however, are something of a mystery. All members of the citrus family (lemons, oranges, limes, etc.), save for the grapefruit, are native to Southeast Asia. The grapefruit, it seems, although of Southeast Asian parents, was born in the Americas. It is believed that one of its progenitors – the pomelo (*C. maxima*) – somehow crossed the Indian Ocean and moved about the Middle East, eventually reaching Europe and then sailing off to the West Indies. There, perhaps in the eighteenth century, it may be that either a mutation occurred or the pomelo was crossed with an orange, with the modern grapefruit the result.

But further confusing the picture was the arrival in the Americas around 1800 of a ship commanded by Captain James Shaddock, who brought a cargo of pomelos (or grapefruit), claiming that he had discovered them in the Fiji Islands. Consequently, the grapefruit was subsequently called "shaddock" in America. A variation on the story would have the captain taking the fruits to England, whereupon they were carried by the British to the Caribbean. A third version would have the pomelo reaching Florida, where it was hybridized with orange pollen for sweetness, and the grapefruit came into being. The Ruby Red grapefruit variety was definitely the result of a seed mutation in McAllen, Texas, in 1929. Certainly, the grapefruit has long been one of the most popular citrus fruits in North America, but it was only following World War II that it became a breakfast food in Europe - the result of American influence. Like all citrus fruits, the grapefruit is high in vitamin C.

Common names and synonyms: Marsh grapefruit, Ruby Red, shaddock, Thompson grapefruit, Webb grapefruit.

GRAPE LEAF - Greek and Middle Eastern recipes frequently call for young grape leaves (genus *Vitis*) to be wrapped around meat, rice, and other fillings, making little packages for poaching or steaming. The fresh leaves are generally first steamed or blanched. Grape leaves can also be purchased in cans.

GRAPES (*see also* RAISIN) - Botanically, the grape is a berry of any species of *Vitis,* the genus of the vine family that was growing wild over much of the earth long before there were humans about. In North America, the vines evolved toward the species *V. labrusca* - the fox grape, one variety of which is the Concord grape. But practically all of the world's wine comes from varieties of a single Old World species, *V. vinifera* - the vine that bears wine. It is thought to have originated in Asia Minor and, as people early discovered (to their delight) that grapes and their juice ferment, has been cultivated for some 6,000 years.

Perhaps the Egyptians initially exploited the grape on a large scale. New varieties were developed by the Greeks and, later, by the Romans, who first practiced grafting and who introduced the vines into the cooler regions of Europe, including what is now France. Over the centuries, human intervention has given rise to a great number of varieties, such as the Chardonnay, the Pinot Noir, and the Riesling, along with the many different grapes of Bordeaux, Burgundy, and the Rhineland, to name but a very few regions.

Although it is largely because of wine that the grape is one of the most heavily cultivated of all fruit crops, grapes are also eaten as fresh fruit. Until the beginning of the twentieth century, however, table grapes were not marketed but rather were consumed by those who grew them. (The grapes that make the best wine do not necessarily make the best dessert grapes.) Today, California table grapes include the Calmeria, the Christmas Rose, the Emperor, the Exotic, the Flame Seedless, the Perlette, the Red Globe (about the size of a small plum), the Ribier, the Ruby Seedless, the Superior, and the Thompson Seedless.

Table grapes that do not "measure up" to table-grape standards are made into juice and other nonalcoholic beverages. In 1869, "Welch's Grape Juice" was born in Vineland, New Jersey (but later moved to Watkin's Glen, New York), when prohibitionist Thomas Bramwell Welch developed a substitute for the wine used in his church's communion services. Grapes also become jellies and especially raisins, which have doubtless been eaten since humans discovered grapes. California is now the biggest producer of these wrinkly, sun-dried sweetmeats. In some cultures, the seeds of grapes have been consumed as well.

Common names and synonyms: Black grape, California grape, Calmeria, catawba, Christmas Rose, Concord grape, dessert grape, Emperor, European grape, Exotic, Flame Seedless, fox grape, green grape, muscadine, Perlette, Red Globe, Ribier, Ruby Seedless, scuppernong, southern fox grape, Superior grape, table grape, Thompson Seedless, wine grape.

See in addition: "Wine," Part III, Chapter 13.

Grass pea - *see* CHICKLING VETCH

Gravek-plant - *see* TRAILING ARBUTUS
Gray pea - *see* PIGEON PEA
Great angelica - *see* PURPLESTEM ANGELICA
Greater yam - *see* WATER YAM
Great green plum - *see* BIG GREEN PLUM
Grecian laurel - *see* BAY LEAF
Green bell pepper - *see* SWEET PEPPERS
Greenbriar - *see* GREENBRIER
GREENBRIER - A number of plants of the genus *Smilax* are called greenbrier, especially the prickly vine *S. rotundifolia,* found in the eastern United States. Its roots were used by Native Americans for starch, and the shoots were eaten both raw and cooked as a vegetable. Other species in Asia are still in use as food, including their berries. The roots of some American species, such as *S. aristolochiifolia,* provide sarsaparilla.

Common names and synonyms: Bullbrier, catbrier, greenbriar.

Greengage - *see* PLUM
Green gram - *see* MUNG BEAN
Green haricot - *see* BEANS
Green leaf - *see* AMARANTH
Green lemon - *see* LIME
Green mung bean - *see* LENTIL(S)
Green Oriental radish - *see* DAIKON
Green pepper - *see* SWEET PEPPERS
GREEN SAPOTE - Another of the sapotes, the green sapote (*Calocarpum viride = Pouteria viridis*) grows on a large, tropical, American evergreen tree. The fruits, each containing a single big seed, are ovoid and up to 6 inches long. The inner pulp of the fruit has a rich, sweet, creamy flavor.

Common names and synonyms: Injerto.

Green sloke - *see* SEAWEED
Green snap bean - *see* BEANS
Green Swiss chard - *see* SWISS CHARD
Green tea - *see* TEA
Green tomato - *see* TOMATILLO
GRENACHE (*see also* GRAPES) - There are both red and white Grenache grapes (*Vitis vinifera*), but unless white (Grenache Blanc or Garnacha Blanc) is specified, "Grenache" refers to the red version, Grenache Noir. The grape - the second most important in the world - is grown in Spain (there, it is called Garnacha) and California and is especially popular in the Rhône Valley of France. Grenache grapes have a high level of sugar and consequently can produce wines with a high percentage of alcohol.

Common names and synonyms: Garnacha, Garnacha Blanc, Grenache Blanc, Grenache Noir.

See in addition: "Wine," Part III, Chapter 13.

Grenache Blanc - *see* GRENACHE
Grenache Noir - *see* GRENACHE
Grenade - *see* POMEGRANATE
Grenadine - *see* POMEGRANATE
Groseille à maquereau - *see* GOOSEBERRY
Grosella - *see* OTAHEITE GOOSEBERRY
Ground bean - *see* HAUSA GROUNDNUT

Groundcherry - *see* **CAPE GOOSEBERRY**

GROUND IVY - Also called "gill-over-the-ground," ground ivy (*Glechoma hederacea*) is a Eurasian native. A creeping or trailing aromatic plant with small purple flowers, it has been used as a potherb and for making tisanes.

Common names and synonyms: Gill-over-the-ground.

Groundnut - *see* **APIOS, BAMBARA GROUNDNUT, HAUSA GROUNDNUT, PEANUT**

Ground pea - *see* **BAMBARA GROUNDNUT**

GRUMICHAMA - A Brazilian shrub, now grown in the West Indies and South Florida, the grumichama (*Eugenia dombeyi = E. brasiliensis*) has a very pleasant-tasting, purple-black fruit about the size and flavor of a cherry.

Gruya - *see* **ACHIRA**

Guaba - *see* **ICE-CREAM BEAN**

Guacimo - *see* **MUTAMBA**

Guaje - *see* **LEUCAENA**

GUAJILLO AND PULLA CHILLIES (*see also* **CHLLI PEPPERS**) - These two closely related chillies (*Capsicum annuum*) are very common in Mexico. Both grow to upward of 6 inches in length, are orange red in color, are tapered like an Anaheim, and are generally dried. The difference is mostly in the heat they produce. The *guajillo* is a relatively mild chilli that goes well in salsas and makes a fine chilli sauce. The *pulla* is used in the same ways but adds substantially more "fire" to dishes. Another relative, the *costeño,* is roughly the same color and also dried but is only about half as long and is even hotter than the *pulla.*

Common names and synonyms: Costeño.

See in addition: "Chilli Peppers," Part II, Section C, Chapter 4.

Guajilote - *see* **CUAJILOTE**

Guama - *see* **ICE-CREAM BEAN**

Guamochil - *see* **PITHECELLOBIUM**

Guanabana - *see* **SOURSOP**

GUAR (*see also* **LEGUMES**) - Also called "clusterbean" because of the way its pods cluster together, the guar (*Cyamopsis tetragonolobus*) is a native of India. This drought-tolerant legume has long been cultivated there for use in vegetarian cooking. Its small, hairy pods, which resemble soybeans, are picked when very young for human consumption. The rest are employed for fodder or for their seeds, which contain a gum used as a thickening agent.

Common names and synonyms: Clusterbean, *Gwaar ki phalli.*

GUARANÁ - A Brazilian climbing shrub that yields seeds from which a dried paste is made, guaraná (*Paullinia cupana*) contains much caffeine and tannin. The paste is employed medicinally, but the most important use of guaraná is as a base for the guaraná beverage, which is an enormously popular soft drink in Brazil.

Guasima - *see* **MUTAMBA**

GUAVA (*see also* **FEIJOA, ICE-CREAM BEAN, STRAWBERRY GUAVA, WILD GUAVA**) - Easily identified by an intense tropical aroma, the guava (*Psidium guajava*) is native to Brazil and possibly the Caribbean region. Today, however, its many varieties are commercially produced in Hawaii, Australia, India, Colombia, Venezuela, Mexico, South Africa, and Southeast Asia. There are also guava groves in Florida and California. The guava is highly vulnerable to fruit-fly infestation and therefore is rarely a welcome import. The fruit is usually pear shaped but sometimes round, ranges in size from that of a small egg to that of a large orange, and can taste either sweet or sour. The skin is almost always yellow green or pale yellow, and the meaty flesh runs from white to yellow or from pinkish to red. Guavas are eaten whole, sliced into salads, and made into guava paste or jelly for spreading on bread and crackers; they are also employed to make syrup and vinegar and are even boiled down to become "guava cheese." Guavas are rich in vitamin A, the B complex, and vitamin C.

Common names and synonyms: Brazilian guava, common guava, goyave, *guayaba,* Guinea guava, guyaba, lemon guava, montain guava, purple guava, *waiawi-'ula'ula.*

Guava machete - *see* **ICE-CREAM BEAN**

Guavo-bejuco - *see* **ICE-CREAM BEAN**

Guayaba - *see* **GUAVA**

Gucil - *see* **BUSH CURRANT**

Güero - *see* **WAX PEPPERS**

Guiana chestnut - *see* **MALABAR NUT**

Guigne - *see* **CHERRY**

GUINEA ARROWROOT - This perennial (*Calathea allouia*) has been cultivated by indigenous farmers in its tropical American habitat for more than a millennium. In Brazilian Amazonia, the plant held an important place in the diet and culture of native peoples until as recently as the 1950s. Increasingly, however, it has been abandoned by its traditional growers in favor of other crops or food products from industrialized regions. The Guinea arrowroot, also known as "sweet-cornroot" or "leren" (and *lerenes* in Puerto Rico), has several relatively large leaves (2 to 4 feet long) and white flowers aboveground, but it is cultivated for its tubers, which (like the potatoes they resemble) grow underground.

These roots are a rich source of many essential amino acids and are valued for their texture (which remains crisp even after cooking) and for their flavor (said to resemble that of green maize). Now grown throughout many parts of the world, including various countries in South America, Africa, and Asia, and particularly in Puerto Rico and other Caribbean islands, the Guinea arrowroot enhances numerous salads, stews, and fish dishes.

Common names and synonyms: Allouya, leren, *lerenes,*
llerén, lleren es, sweet-corm-root, *topee-tambu.*

Guinea corn - *see* **MAIZE, SORGHUM**

Guinea grains - *see* **MELEGUETA PEPPER**

Guinea squash - *see* **EGGPLANT**

Guinea yam - *see* **WHITE YAM, YELLOW YAM**

Guine pepper - *see* **CAYENNE PEPPER**

Güiro - *see* **XICALLI**

Guispui - *see* **CHAYOTE**

Gulfweed - *see* **SEAWEED**

Gully bean - *see* **EGGPLANT**

Gum arabic - *see* **ACACIA**

Gumbo - *see* **OKRA**

GUM PLANT (*see also* **YERBA SANTA**) - Also known
as "gumweed," the gum plant (*Grindelia robusta* or
G. squarrosa) is found in western North America. It
grows to about 18 inches in height, and its name
derives from a resinous substance that covers the
entire plant. Native Americans made tea from its
leaves, which they also chewed.

Common names and synonyms: Gumweed.

Gum tree - *see* **MANNA GUM**

Gumweed - *see* **GUM PLANT**

Gungo pea - *see* **PIGEON PEA**

Gunpowder - *see* **TEA**

Guyaba - *see* **GUAVA**

Guyana chestnut - *see* **MALABAR NUT**

Gwaar ki phalli - *see* **GUAR**

**HABANERO AND SCOTCH BON-
NET PEPPERS** (*see also* **CHILLI
PEPPERS**) - The name habanero
implies that the first of these small,
lantern-shaped chillies (they look like
miniature, collapsed bell peppers) is a
native of Havana, which seems to be
contradicted both by its scientific name *Capsicum
chinense* (most chilli peppers are *C. annuum*) and by
the fact that it is most extensively cultivated and consumed in Central America and the Yucatán. It is
slightly larger than its very close relative the Scotch
Bonnet (it does look a bit like one), which is grown
mostly on Jamaica and other Caribbean islands, and
with which it is regularly confused. The confusion is
eminently understandable because they do resemble
each other, in their colors (red, green, orange, and yellow) and because they hold the distinction of being
the hottest domesticated peppers in the world.

In a very close second place, however, are two
other relatives. One is the Jamaican hot pepper,
which is always a bright red but is similar in shape
to both the habanero and the Scotch Bonnet. The
other is the Rocotillo (sometimes called rocoto or
squash pepper because of a resemblance to pattypan squash), a South American chilli that ranges
from red to pale yellow in color and is a frequent
addition to ceviches.

A major use of these peppers (save for the
Rocotillo) is in commercially prepared hot sauces
(now available in astounding variety), with the
Scotch Bonnet prevailing in Jamaican jerk sauces
and the Jamaican hot pepper foremost in
Caribbean chutneys and curries. Habaneros and
Scotch Bonnets are also much used in the preparation of numerous dishes as well as sauces in Central and South America and in West Africa, where, as
in the Caribbean, they are greatly appreciated.

Common names and synonyms: Bonnet pepper,
Granny's-bonnet, Jamaican hot pepper, Jamaican
Red, Rocotillo, rocoto, squash pepper.

See in addition: "Chilli Peppers," Part II, Section C,
Chapter 4.

Habichuela - *see* **HYACINTH BEAN**

Hachiya - *see* **PERSIMMON**

HACKBERRY (*see also* **BERRIES**) - The genus *Celtis*
encompasses a number of trees and shrubs that
have a berry-like, often edible fruit that is sometimes called a "sugarberry." The hackberry was an
important food gathered in late fall and early winter by Native Americans for thousands of years. As
with the American persimmon, the berries are best
after the first frost. Hackberry seeds have also
served as a food.

Common names and synonyms: Sugarberry.

Hakusai - *see* **CHINESE CABBAGE**

HAMBURG PARSLEY (*see also* **PARSLEY**) - Popular
in central Europe, Hamburg parsley (*Petroselinum
crispum* var. *tuberosum*) is a variety of parsley cultivated not for its leaves but for its edible root,
which resembles a small parsnip. It has a strong
taste that is appreciated in stews.

HANOVER KALE (*see also* **CABBAGE, KALE**) -
Another member of the cabbage family, Hanover
kale (*Brassica napus*) has leaves similar to those of
spinach. They are used in salads and cooked as a
vegetable.

Common names and synonyms: Hanover salad,
spring kale.

See in addition: "Cruciferous and Green Leafy Vegetables," Part II, Section C, Chapter 5.

Harebell - *see* **CAMPANULA**

Haricot - *see* **BEANS**

Haricot riz - *see* **RICE BEAN**

Harlock - *see* **BURDOCK**

Haselnuss - *see* **HAZELNUT AND FILBERT**

Hass - *see* **AVOCADO**

HAUSA GROUNDNUT - Also called "ground bean"
and "Kersting's groundnut," the Hausa groundnut
(*Kerstingiella geocarpa* = *Macrotyloma geocarpa*) is an herb cultivated in the drier portions
of western Africa from Senegal to Nigeria. It produces pods that contain from 1 to 3 kidney-shaped
seeds. The seeds are high in protein, and the leaves
are also cooked as a vegetable. The Hausa groundnut is very similar to the more wide-ranging bambara groundnut.

Common names and synonyms: Ground bean, groundnut, Kersting's groundnut.

Hausa potato - *see* **KAFFIR POTATO, SUDAN POTATO**

Hautbois - *see* **WILD STRAWBERRY**

HAW (*see also* **BERRIES, BLACK HAW, HAWTHORN BERRY, SLOE**) - The reddish fruit of the hawthorn (genus *Crataegus*) is known as a haw. But in the United States the term has signified the bluish black, plumlike fruit of the blackthorn (*Prunus spinosa,* a Eurasian shrub) as well; this fruit is also called "sloe" and is used to flavor sloe gin. And the semantic confusion goes even further because the fruit of one of the hawthorns of southeastern North America (*C. uniflora*) is called both a "pear haw" and a "blackthorn." Haws were well utilized by Native Americans, who ate them raw and also dried them to make pemmican. The leaves of some species were eaten as well.

Common names and synonyms: Blackthorn, pear haw, sloe, stagbush.

Hawaiian Kona coffee - *see* **COFFEE**

HAWAIIAN PLANTAIN (*see also* **PLANTAIN**) - Perhaps better known as *hua moa,* the Hawaiian plantain (*Musa × sapientum*) is a common plantain of many Pacific Islands. In 1960, William F. Whitman brought the plant to the United States from Tahiti, and it has since found a comfortable niche in southern Florida and special favor with Cuban-Americans. The fruit is shorter but much thicker than the usual plantains and often looks as if two bananas were enveloped by the same skin. It is used like other plantains for frying and cooking in the unripe state but is also eaten out of hand when ripe.

Common names and synonyms: Hua moa.

See in addition: "Bananas and Plantains," Part II, Section B, Chapter 1.

Hawthorn - *see* **BLACK HAW, HAWTHORN BERRY**

HAWTHORN BERRY (*see also* **BERRIES**) - The genus *Crataegus* is comprised of a great number of thorny shrubs and trees that bear a reddish fruit called a haw. In England, the white to pink blossoms of the hawthorn, which appear in May, inspired the name of the ship *Mayflower.* The berry is actually a small pome fruit with a high sugar content. In the United States, those hawthorns that still have fruit in the winter help to sustain wildlife until spring. This "winter fruit" did the same for Native Americans.

Common names and synonyms: Cockspur thorn, downy haw, haw, hawthorn, haw tree (archaic), mayhaw, red haw, scarlet haw.

Haw tree - *see* **HAWTHORN BERRY**

HAZELNUT AND FILBERT - The term "hazelnut" has been used so interchangeably with "filbert" that the two are sometimes listed as synonymous in dictionaries - and no wonder, because they appear as practically identical, have the same sweet taste, and grow on shrubs or trees that are members of the birch family. But despite the German word *Haselnuss,* filberts come from Eurasian plants (*Corylus avellana,* the European filbert, and *C. maxima,* the giant filbert), whereas the hazelnut comes from an American shrub (*C. americana*). To add to the confusion, "hazelnut" (instead of "filbert") was apparently the name first given to this acorn-like nut in Europe because of its medium brown color (for example, the French word *noisette* means both the nut and the color). The name was later changed to filbert because St. Philbert's day falls on August 22, the day the nuts are supposedly finally ripe in France. The American hazelnut is found mostly in the eastern United States. In the Pacific states, imported filbert trees are cultivated. But, most of North America's hazelnuts are actually filberts imported from Turkey. For those who would dwell on the differences between hazelnuts and filberts, another has to do with the outer husks - those of hazelnuts are shorter, whereas the filbert husk extends beyond the nut. Like all nuts, hazelnuts and filberts alike provide some selenium, calcium, and iron, are rich in folacin, and supply vitamin E and the B complex.

Common names and synonyms: American hazelnut, beaked hazel, Chinese filbert, Chinese hazel, Chinese hazelnut, cob, cobnut, curri, European filbert, European hazel, giant filbert, *Haselnuss,* Himalayan hazel, Lambert's filbert, *noisette,* Siberian hazel, Tibetan filbert, Tibetan hazelnut, Turkish filbert, Turkish hazel.

Heartnut - *see* **WALNUT**

HEART(S) OF PALM - There are thousands of palm species in the world's tropics, all with edible "hearts," of which perhaps 100 have hearts large enough to be commercially valuable. In the United States the hearts have in the past often meant the terminal buds of the palmetto, a small palm (*Sabal palmetto* - called the "cabbage palm") that grows in Florida. More recently, the hearts have been the buds of South American (and especially Brazilian) members of the families Palmae and Arecaceae. The whole heart can weigh some 2 to 3 pounds and may be cut up and fried or boiled, as was the case in old Florida, where the vegetable was called "swamp cabbage." Most palm hearts today, however, are stripped of their tough husk, cut into small cylinders, and canned for use in salads or as a snack or appetizer served with a sauce. They have a delicate, asparagus-like flavor. Fortunately, the palms grow prolifically, because removing the heart kills the tree.

Common names and synonyms: Cabbage palm, palmetto, palm heart(s), swamp cabbage.

Heart snakeroot - *see* **WILD GINGER**

Heath - *see* **HEATHER**

HEATHER - Eurasian heather consists of *Calluna vulgaris* and several related plants of the genus *Erica.* Also called ling, heather grows in dense masses, with clusters of pink and purplish flowers. Heather ale – a traditional Scottish beverage – is made from the blossoms. In the southwest of North America, Native Americans have used the berries of the heather "manzanita" (*Arctostaphylos uva-ursi* – also called bearberry) for food and for making a beverage.

Common names and synonyms: Bearberry, heath, ling, pointleaf manzanita.

Heath pea - *see* **EARTH NUT**

Hedged gourd - *see* **KIWANO**

Hedge garlic - *see* **GARLIC-MUSTARD**

HEMLOCK - The soft inner bark of a few species of the evergreen trees of the genus *Tsuga* was used as food by Native Americans. That of western hemlock (*T. heterophylla*) and mountain hemlock (*T. mertensiana*) was shaped into loaves for baking. The bark of the eastern hemlock (*T. canadensis*) was also eaten, and its leaves were used to make a tea.

Common names and synonyms: Eastern hemlock, mountain hemlock, western hemlock.

HEMP DOGBANE - An American native that grows as a weed throughout the United States, hemp dogbane (*Apocynum cannabinum* - also known as Indian hemp) - has a rootstock that has long been used for medicinal purposes. The plant's leaves are poisonous, but its seeds were employed as food by Native Americans.

Common names and synonyms: Black hemp, black Indian hemp, Choctaw-root, dogbane, Indian hemp.

HEMP SEED - The seeds of hemp (*Cannabis sativa*), an Asiatic herb, yield a fatty oil that is used in cooking, mostly in Asia. The seeds have been cultivated for thousands of years and were often roasted for consumption. This plant that we know as marijuana has also long been a source of fiber for rope making.

Hemp tree - *see* **CHASTE TREE**

HERB BENNET - Also called the "blessed herb" and "avens," the herb bennet (*Geum urbanum*) is a European plant with yellow flowers and an odor of cloves. It has been grown or gathered as a potherb and has long been used to make a tea.

Common names and synonyms: Avens, blessed herb.

Herb-of-grace - *see* **RUE**

Hicaco - *see* **COCOPLUM**

HICKORY (*see also* **PECAN**) - Hickories (of the genus *Carya*) are American members of the walnut family that produce edible nuts. The only commercially important one of these nuts is the pecan (treated in a separate entry). Hickories are widespread throughout eastern and central North America and yield an incredible variety of nuts, the most abundant and popular of which come from the shagbark hickory (*C. ovata*).

Historically, these have been divided into thick-shell shagbarks and thin-shell shagbarks, with the latter nuts considered the most desirable because their meat is more easily obtainable. Native Americans of central and eastern North America made hickory nuts a regular part of their diet. Hickory nuts have a sweet flavor and are much used in baking. Chunks and chips of hickory wood are used to flavor barbecued and smoked meats. Hickory nuts provide calcium, potassium, iron, vitamin E, and the vitamins of the B complex.

Common names and synonyms: Shagbark, thick-shell shagbark, thin-shell shagbark.

HIGHBUSH CRANBERRY - A North American shrub, the highbush cranberry (*Viburnum trilobum*) has scarlet berries that are often mistakenly called "cranberries" and are used as a cranberry substitute in sauces. They were employed by Native Americans as a medicine and in stews, as well as for making teas and pemmican. The berries are low in calories and high in vitamin C and potassium.

Common names and synonyms: Cramp bark, cranberry bush, squaw bush, viburnum.

Higüero - *see* **XICALLI**

Hijiki - *see* **SEAWEED**

HINAU BERRY - The hinau (*Elaeocarpus dentatus*) is a New Zealand timber tree that produces an edible berry. The latter was one of the many gathered foods that sustained the Maori - the aboriginal people of New Zealand.

Hing - *see* **ASAFETIDA**

Hoarhound - *see* **HOREHOUND**

HOG PEANUT - Also called the wild peanut, the hog peanut (*Amphicarpaea bracteata*), a native of central North America, is a brown, edible seed. It comes in an underground pod, resembles a peanut, and is much appreciated by hogs. However, long before hogs arrived to root for these subterranean fruits, hog peanuts were being dug by Native Americans, for whom they were an important dietary item.

Common names and synonyms: Wild peanut.

HOG PLUM (*see also* **PLUM**) - Quite a few fruits go by the name of "hog plum." One is *Spondias pinnata*, a Malayan fruit also called *amra*. It is not much appreciated as it is said to smell of rotting apples. More popular in that part of the world is the "great hog plum" (*S. cytherea*), also known as *kĕdondong*, which has an oblong fruit that is yellow with whitish flesh when ripe. These fruits are eaten raw and stewed and also made into a jam or chutney. Other *Spondias* plants, such as *S. mombin* (the "yellow mombin") and *S. purpurea* (variously named "Spanish plum," "Jamaican plum," and "red mombin"), have edible fruits that resemble plum-sized mangoes and are called "hog plum" by some. In the United States, *Prunus americana* grows wild in its native Florida and South Carolina. Sometimes called a hog plum, it, too, is a small, oval-shaped fruit, which is generally made into jams and jellies.

Common names and synonyms: Amra, great hog plum, Jamaican plum, *kĕdondong*, red mombin, Spanish plum, yellow mombin.

Hog salad - *see* **CORNSALAD**

Hogweed - *see* **HORSEWEED**

Hoka - *see* **KABOCHA (SQUASH)**

Hokkaido - *see* **BUTTERCUP SQUASH**

Holland chilli - *see* **DUTCH RED PEPPER**

HOLLAND GREENS (*see also* **CABBAGE**) - Also known as "tyfon," Holland greens (*Brassica rapa* 'tyfon') are the greens of a new plant - a cross between the Chinese cabbage and the turnip. The new plant is tolerant of cold, grows vigorously, and is reluctant to bolt. Holland greens are used in the same fashion as turnip greens or mustard greens or collards - in salads and as a cooked vegetable.

Common names and synonyms: Tyfon.

See in addition: "Cruciferous and Green Leafy Vegetables," Part II, Section C, Chapter 5.

Holland pepper - *see* **SWEET PEPPERS**

Holly - *see* **DAHOON HOLLY, HOLLYBERRY, YAUPON, YERBA MATÉ**

HOLLYBERRY (*see also* **BERRIES**) - There are numerous trees and shrubs that we call holly, have bright red berries, and belong to the genus *Ilex*. Two are especially worthy of culinary comment. One is the American holly (*I. opaca*), native to the eastern United States, the berries of which yield an edible pulp that helped Native Americans with their vitamin C intake. The other is *I. paraguariensis,* native to Paraguay and Brazil in South America; its berries and leaves are employed to make yerba maté tea.

Common names and synonyms: American holly.

Holly-leaved barberry - *see* **BARBERRY**

Holly-leaved cherry - *see* **CHIMAJA**

Ho loan - *see* **SUGAR PEA**

HONEWORT - There are two related plants called honewort. One is *Cryptotaenia canadensis,* a native of North America; the other is a native of Japan - Japanese honewort (*C. japonica*), which is also called *mitsuba*. They are members of the carrot family, and the roots are often boiled and served with oil. The greens (which resemble flat Italian parsley) and stems have a distinctive flavor and are used as garnishes, eaten raw in salads, added to soups, and cooked as a vegetable. The Japanese variety is grown commercially in California for Japanese-Americans.

Common names and synonyms: Japanese honewort, Japanese parsley, *mitsuba*.

Honeyberry - *see* **SPANISH LIME**

HONEYDEW (MELON) (*see also* **MELONS**) - A winter melon (*Cucumis melo*), the honeydew has the advantage of keeping well for up to a month. As a consequence, these melons - about the size of large muskmelons, with a whitish rind and pale green flesh - are ubiquitous in produce markets.

Common names and synonyms: Winter melon.

See in addition: "Cucumbers, Melons, and Watermelons," Part II, Section C, Chapter 6.

HONEY LOCUST - A tall, usually spiny tree of eastern North America, the honey locust (*Gleditsia triacanthos*) bears long, twisted pods that resemble beans. These were cooked and eaten by Native Americans, even though they are reported to be mildly toxic. Because the pods have a sweetish pulp surrounding the seeds, the tree is also known as sweet bean, sweet locust, and honeyshuck.

Common names and synonyms: Honeyshuck, sweet bean, sweet locust.

Honey mushroom - *see* **MUSHROOMS AND FUNGI**

Honeyshuck - *see* **HONEY LOCUST**

HONEYSUCKLE - There are a number of species of the genus *Lonicera* - called honeysuckle - spread about the globe, and some are or have been used as food. Others, however, are toxic and can even cause death. Probably the edible ones have been consumed since the early days of the hunter-gatherers because they are sweet, whereas many (but not all) of the poisonous species are bitter. Native Americans enjoyed the sweetness of a few species, and in Japan, the young leaves of *L. japonica* (the Japanese honeysuckle) are still used as a vegetable.

Common names and synonyms: Japanese honeysuckle.

Honey tree - *see* **JAPANESE RAISIN TREE**

Hoofs - *see* **COLTSFOOT**

Hoogly - *see* **UGLI FRUIT**

HOP(S) - There are several twining vines of the genus *Humulus* - especially *H. lupulus*, a Eurasian-American vine - that have green, cone-like flowers. When dried, the flowers yield a bitter, aromatic oil used in brewing beer. Hop plants have been cultivated in Germany for about 1,000 years and were once used to prevent beer from spoiling. Hops also put out shoots in the spring that can be gathered and cooked and eaten like asparagus. Doubtless they were consumed by hunter-gatherers in Eurasia, as well as by Native Americans in the Western Hemisphere.

Common names and synonyms: Hop plant.

See also: "Beer and Ale," Part III, Chapter 1.

Hop plant - *see* **HOP(S)**

HOPTREE - A tall shrub of eastern North America, the hoptree (*Ptelea trifoliata*) is so called because its bitter fruits have been used as a substitute for hops in flavoring beer. Native Americans also ground them for use as a condiment, and after malaria was imported from Europe and Africa, the bark of the hoptree's roots was sometimes used like quinine against the disease.

Common names and synonyms: Ague bark, waferash.

HOREHOUND - The bitter extract of horehound (*Marrubium vulgare*) comes from an aromatic plant of the mint family. It is an Old World native now naturalized in North America. Horehound is used in candies, cordials, and cough medicines and has been cultivated since antiquity for other medicinal uses. It is also said to have been employed as a condiment.

Common names and synonyms: Hoarhound.

Horned melon – *see* **KIWANO**

Horse balm – *see* **HORSEWEED**

Horsebean – *see* **FAVA BEAN, JACKBEAN**

Horse chestnut – *see* **BUCKEYE**

Horsefoot – *see* **COLTSFOOT**

Horse grain – *see* **HORSE GRAM**

HORSE GRAM – Also called "horse grain" and "bonavist bean," the horse gram (*Dolichos biflorus*) is a native of the Old World tropics (probably India) that grows on a twining herb. The plant is generally cultivated for fodder in Asia, but its immature seeds are also used as food for humans.

Common names and synonyms: Bonavist bean, horse grain.

See also: "Beans, Peas, and Lentils," Part II, Section C, Chapter 3.

HORSE MANGO – Growing on a tree native to southern Asia that is some 70 feet in height, the horse mango (*Mangifera foetida*), reaches about 5 inches in length and about 3 inches in diameter. It is yellowish green when ripe and has a bright orange to yellow flesh. Unripe, the fruit contains a sap that irritates the skin and is not safe to eat. Even ripe the horse mango has a bad smell and consequently is seldom eaten raw. Instead, it is used in curries and made into chutney.

Common names and synonyms: Bachang.

Horsemint – *see* **BEE BALM, BERGAMOT**

HORSERADISH (*see also* **CABBAGE**) – A member of the cabbage family and a relative of the radish, horseradish (*Armoracia rusticana* = *A. lapathifolia*) is sometimes called "German mustard," perhaps because its strong, biting flavor derives from mustard oils that are released when the tissue of the root is cut. The latter is thick, white, and cylindrical, with a thin, brown skin, and is safe to eat even though the leaves and stems of the plant are said to contain a toxic substance.

Horseradish is native to southeastern Europe and western Asia (where it continues to grow wild) but is cultivated in most other parts of the world and has been naturalized in the northeastern United States and southern Canada. Traditionally, the root was peeled and grated in the home and served on the side with meats such as boiled beef. But grated horseradish became a commercial product in the first part of the nineteenth century. It was preserved in vinegar and bottled initially in brown bottles to disguise the turnip filler that was often included. In 1869, however, H. J. Heinz began his business at Sharpsburg, Pennsylvania, by packing processed horseradish in clear bottles.

Today, horseradish is generally bottled in combination with vinegar and salt, blended into a cream sauce, or mixed with mustard to become Creole mustard. Horseradish vinegar and horseradish powder are also horseradish products, as is red horseradish, which has had beet juice added to it. Horseradish is a good source of vitamin C.

Common names and synonyms: Creole mustard, German mustard, horse-reddish root (archaic), red horseradish.

See in addition: "Spices and Flavorings," Part II, Section F, Chapter 1.

Horseradish tree – *see* **BENOIL TREE**

HORSETAIL PLANT – Any of the various plants of the genus *Equisetum* are called horsetail. The field horsetail (*E. arvense*) of the United States and Canada produces brownish shoots that have been used medicinally, eaten as a vegetable, and made into tea. The plant also grows in Eurasia, where it long ago provided food for hunter-gatherers.

Common names and synonyms: Field horsetail.

HORSEWEED – Also called horse balm, butterweed, hogweed, mare's-tail, erigeron, and a host of other names, horseweed (*Erigeron canadensis* = *Conyza canadensis*) is a common herb found throughout North America. The boiled young seedlings served as food for Native Americans, and the plants were introduced in Japan, where they are still reportedly consumed. In addition, erigeron oil, which is used medicinally, is distilled from the plants.

Common names and synonyms: Butterweed, erigeron, hogweed, horse balm, mare's-tail.

Hot red pepper – *see* **CAYENNE PEPPER**

Huachinango – *see* **JALAPEÑO**

Hua moa – *see* **HAWAIIAN PLANTAIN**

Huautli – *see* **AMARANTH**

Huauzontle – *see* **QUINOA**

HUBBARD SQUASH (*see also* **SQUASH AND PUMPKIN**) – As old – as well as old-fashioned – squashes, the large Hubbards (*Cucurbita maxima*) are less popular today than in the past because they are indeed large, reaching 30 pounds or more, which frequently makes it necessary to sell them in pieces. The big Hubbards come in blue, orange, and green hues and generally have a wart-covered skin that can resist anything short of an axe in an attempt to carve them. Fortunately, there are now smaller Hubbards, such as the Baby Blue and Golden varieties, that come in a 5- to 15-pound range and are much easier to manage. Their flesh is a brilliant orange and has a superior taste.

Common names and synonyms: Baby Blue Hubbard, Golden Hubbard.

See in addition: "Squash," Part II, Section C, Chapter 8.

HUCKLEBERRY (*see also* **BERRIES**) – Any of a number of shrubs of the genus *Gaylussacia* bear huckleberries. They are American natives that traveled early to Europe. These blackish berries are often confused with blueberries (to which they are related) and are a great favorite of wildlife as well as humans, although they are not as sweet as blueberries. One of the many berries that were regular items in the diet of Native Americans, this berry also lent its name to the famous lad of literature, Huckleberry Finn. At one time, huckleberries were a staple food for Scottish Highlanders, who made them into – among other things – a wine. Huckleberries have become increasingly less popular with the commercial success of blueberries.

Common names and synonyms: Black huckleberry, common huckleberry, hurtleberry, whortleberry.

Hue - *see* **BOTTLE GOURD**

Huesito - *see* **ACEROLA**

HUITLACOCHE (*see also* **MUSHROOMS AND FUNGI**) - A maize-smut fungus, huitlacoche (*Ustilago maydis*) grows on cornstalks. It is a favorite in Mexico, where it can be found in restaurants and grocery stores, if only briefly during the summer. Huitlacoche is used in the same ways that mushrooms are used.

Common names and synonyms: Mexican corn fungus.

See in addition: "Fungi," Part II, Section C, Chapter 7.

HUNGARIAN CHERRY PEPPER (*see also* **CHILLI PEPPERS**) - A red and round pepper often encountered at salad bars, the Hungarian cherry pepper (*Capsicum annuum* L.) has numerous seeds and is generally sweet, although some can have a bit of a bite. The original area of domestication was probably Mexico, but these chillies are now distributed across the globe and are grown chiefly in California and eastern Europe, especially Hungary. Cherry peppers are often pickled and sold in jars. They are also dried to a mahogany color and used to flavor simmered dishes and to make sauces.

Common names and synonyms: Cherry pepper.

See in addition: "Chilli Peppers," Part II, Section C, Chapter 4.

Hungarian grass - *see* **MILLET**

Hungarian sweet chilli - *see* **SWEET PEPPERS**

Hungarian wax pepper - *see* **WAX PEPPERS**

Hungarian yellow wax pepper - *see* **WAX PEPPERS**

Hungry rice - *see* **FONIO**

Hurtleberry - *see* **HUCKLEBERRY**

Husk tomato - *see* **TOMATILLO**

HYACINTH BEAN (*see also* **BEANS**) - Also known as the "lablab bean," "Egyptian bean," and *habichuela*, the hyacinth bean (*Lablab niger* = *L. purpureus*) probably originated in tropical Asia but was introduced in tropical Africa about a thousand years ago and spread with the slave trade to the West Indies and Central and South America. The seeds are generally available in cans as well as fresh and dried forms. The immature pods, along with the young leaves, are cooked as a vegetable and contain much in the way of vitamin C.

Common names and synonyms: Egyptian bean, *habichuela*, lablab bean.

See in addition: "Beans, Peas, and Lentils," Part II, Section C, Chapter 3.

HYPTIS - There are several species of the genus *Hyptis,* the seeds of which were used as food by Native Americans and in some instances are still in use. One (*H. suaveolens*), a native of southern Mexico and Central America, is called "chan" or "wild spikenard"; its seeds, rich in linoleic acid, fed pre-Columbian peoples of the region. Two others, both called "desert lavender," are *H. albida* and *H. emoryi.* The former is a Mexican plant with leaves that are still used for flavoring foods. The latter, of the desert Southwest, provided seeds that were eaten whole, roasted, and ground into a meal. In addition, its minty leaves were used to make a tea.

Common names and synonyms: Chan, desert lavender.

Hyson - *see* **TEA**

HYSSOP - A venerable herb, native to the Mediterranean region and a member of the mint family, hyssop (*Hyssopus officinalis*) was employed by the ancient Greeks for medicinal purposes and is mentioned several times in the Bible (although some scholars believe that the "hyssop" of the Bible was not *H. officinalis*). The Arabs used it, and in the European Middle Ages hyssop was employed as a potherb. Its fresh leaves are aromatic, with a somewhat bitter taste, and are added to salads and pasta dishes. The dried leaves go well in soups and stews and are used in tisanes ("hyssop tea"). The purple hyssop flowers are also added to green salads, and hyssop oil flavors liqueurs such as the chartreuse and absinthe of France.

Common names and synonyms: Hyssop tea.

Hyssop tea - *see* **HYSSOP**

Hyuga - *see* **KABOCHA (SQUASH)**

Ibope - *see* **ALGARROBO**

Icaco - *see* **COCOPLUM**

Icaco plum - *see* **COCOPLUM**

ICE-CREAM BEAN - The ice-cream bean (*Inga vera*) apparently originated in Hispaniola, Jamaica, and Puerto Rico but has since joined *I. edulis* and other *Inga* species in Central and South America. The "beans" grow on evergreen trees that reach up to 60 feet in height and are widely used to shade coffee and cacao trees. The fruit is a hairy brown pod between 4 and 6 inches long that embraces a whitish pulp and several brown seeds. The pulp is eaten out of hand and used to flavor various desserts. In addition, Colombian Indians use the fruit to make *cachiri,* an alcoholic beverage. The blossoms are exceptionally rich in nectar and serve as a magnet for bees, thereby lending themselves to honey production.

Common names and synonyms: Cachira, guaba, guama, guava machete, guavo-bejuco.

Iceland lichen - *see* **ICELAND MOSS**

ICELAND MOSS - An edible lichen, Iceland moss (*Cetraria islandica*) is, as the name implies, found in northerly regions, frequently on heather moors. Its somewhat erect, reddish brown thallus lobes are boiled and dried before being ground into powder for use in baking.

Common names and synonyms: Iceland lichen, Island moss.

ICE PLANT - With a name like ice plant, it seems incongruous that this vegetable (*Mesembryanthemum crystallinum*) is a native of southern Africa and member of a family of some 600 species that are also mostly centered in that region. The name, however, has to do with its edible leaves, which are fleshy and seem to glint like ice crystals in the sunlight. They are cooked and eaten much like spinach.

Igope - *see* **ALGARROBO**

ILAMA - Another member of the family Annonaceae, the ilama (*Annona diversifolia*) is a fruit tree that grows on the Pacific slopes from Mexico to El Salvador but is most common in southwestern Guatemala. The fruit has a thin skin, which encloses flesh of a white to reddish color, and has the characteristically delicious, sweet flavor of the other "custard apples." Some find it better than the cherimoya; others think it inferior. The ilama is not, however, cultivated commercially on a large scale and is grown mostly by local peoples for their own consumption. Ilamas are eaten fresh and used as an ingredient in ice cream.

Common names and synonyms: Anona blanca.

IMBÉ - The trees of the imbé (*Garcinia livingstonei*) are grown mostly as ornamentals outside of their native habitat in East Africa. They are cultivated for fruit in Florida, but not commercially. The leaves are up to 6 inches in length and a glossy dark green; the fruits, which are yellow to orange in hue, are shaped somewhat like miniature apples and measure approximately 2 inches in diameter. They have a large seed covered by a small amount of juicy flesh and a thin, tender skin. The taste is pleasant but relatively tart, and imbé juice is noted for creating lasting stains. Most are eaten fresh, although some are employed in beverages.

Imbu - *see* **UMBÚ**

Imperial - *see* **TEA**

Inca wheat - *see* **QUINOA**

Indian almond - *see* **MALABAR ALMOND**

Indian bael - *see* **BAEL FRUIT**

Indian balm - *see* **TRILLIUM**

INDIAN BARK - Also known as "Indian cassia," Indian bark (*Cinnamomum tamala*) is a native of the Indian subcontinent and is grown extensively in northern India. Like its relatives, cassia and cinnamon, it is a tree cultivated for its bark, which is processed into a spice. In addition, its leaves are used as a flavoring in curries.

Common names and synonyms: Indian cassia.

See also: "Spices and Flavorings," Part II, Section F, Chapter 1.

INDIAN BORAGE - Probably a native of Indonesia (it grows wild in Malaysia), Indian borage (*Coleus amboinicus*) is grown in Southeast Asia and the West Indies for its aromatic leaves, which can substitute for sage. Indeed, the herb is used exactly like sage for seasoning stuffings, poultry, and other dishes.

Indian breadroot - *see* **BREADROOT**

Indian buchu - *see* **MYRTLE**

Indian cassia - *see* **INDIAN BARK**

Indian corn - *see* **MAIZE**

Indian cress - *see* **NASTURTIUM**

INDIAN CUCUMBER - Also known as "Indian cucumber root," this member of the lily family is a small herb (*Medeola virginica*) native to eastern North America. Native Americans enjoyed the plant's crisp and succulent white rhizomes, which have a texture and taste similar to that of cucumbers.

Common names and synonyms: Indian cucumber root.

Indian cucumber root - *see* **INDIAN CUCUMBER**

Indian date - *see* **TAMARIND**

Indian fig - *see* **PRICKLY PEAR**

Indian gooseberry - *see* **AMALAKA, OTAHEITE GOOSEBERRY**

Indian hemp - *see* **HEMP DOGBANE**

Indian jujube - *see* **DESERT APPLE, JUJUBE**

INDIAN LONG PEPPER - A native of South Asia, the Indian long pepper (*Piper longum*) is a member of the genus that includes the common black and white peppercorns. It is grown mostly in India and Indonesia for its berries, which are dried and used as a spice - generally by adding them whole to curries, pickles, and the like.

Indian mulberry - *see* **MORINDA**

Indian mustard - *see* **MUSTARD GREENS**

Indian nut - *see* **PINE NUT**

Indian pea - *see* **PIGEON PEA**

Indian pear - *see* **PRICKLY PEAR**

Indian posy - *see* **BUTTERFLY WEED**

INDIAN POTATO (*see also* **APIOS, BREADROOT**) - Any of several native American plants with edible tubers are called "Indian potatoes." One is the groundnut (apios; another is the breadroot; still another is the giant sunflower (*Helianthus giganteus*), which is a tall North American plant with edible tuberous roots. Finally, there is the "yamp" (or "yampa," or "yampah" - *Carum gairdneri* or *C. kelloggii*); also called the "squawroot," this plant, too, has fleshy, edible roots. Another "yampah" is "Parish's yampah" (*Perideridia parishii*), of the parsley or carrot family. Native to the southwestern United States, this plant provided roots that were an important food for Native Americans and pioneers, who frequently ground them into a flour.

Common names and synonyms: Giant sunflower, Parish's yampah, squawroot, yamp, yampa, yampah.

INDIAN PRUNE - Known as *rukam manis* in its native Malaysia, the Indian prune (*Flacourtia rukam*) belongs to a large family of mostly tropical trees. It produces a dark purplish red, plumlike fruit that is juicy and sweet when ripe. These fruits are generally eaten raw but are also used for jams and chutneys.

Common names and synonyms: Rukam, rukam manis.

Indian rice - *see* **WILD RICE**
Indian ricegrass - *see* **RICEGRASS**
Indian saffron - *see* **TURMERIC**
Indian soap - *see* **SOAPBERRY**
Indian sorrel - *see* **ROSELLE**
Indian spice - *see* **CHASTE TREE**
Indian spinach - *see* **AMARANTH, MALABAR SPINACH**

INDIAN TURNIP (*see also* **BREADROOT**) - There are quite a few plants with the name "Indian turnip." One, also called "jack-in-the-pulpit" (*Arisaema triphyllum*), has an acrid but edible tuber. Another is *Eriogonum longifolium,* the roots of which were consumed by Native Americans in the western United States. The tuberous roots of several species of the genus *Psoralea* (known collectively as "breadroots" as well as "Indian turnips") were also consumed, often after being dried and later ground into flour, but they could also be eaten raw. The leaves of some species were cooked and eaten as a vegetable.

Common names and synonyms: Breadroot, jack-in-the-pulpit.

Indian walnut - *see* **CANDLENUT**

INDIAN WOOD-APPLE - Also known as the "elephant-apple," the Indian wood-apple (*Feronia limonia = Limonia acidissima*) is probably a native of India but now grows throughout Southeast Asia. The fruit - borne on a medium-sized tree - has a woody shell, making it difficult to get at its pulp, which consists of many seeds surrounded by a red, gummy substance. The fruit can be eaten raw but is used mostly to make jelly, chutney, and a refreshing drink.

Common names and synonyms: Elephant-apple.

Indonesian bay - *see* **DUAN SALAM**
Injerto - *see* **GREEN SAPOTE**
Inkberry - *see* **POKEWEED, WINTERBERRY**
Intermediate wheatgrass - *see* **WILD TRIGA**

IRIS - Any of the various members of the *Iridaceae* genus are called "iris," which includes colorful, herbaceous plants that develop from rhizomes or bulbs. It is the rhizomes that serve as a food for humans, especially in East Asia. The roots of *I. germanica,* known as "orris root," are pulverized and used in perfumery, medicines, and as a flavoring in certain gins.

Common names and synonyms: Flag, orris root.

Irish moss - *see* **CARRAGEEN AND CARRAGEENIN, SEAWEED**
Irish potato - *see* **WHITE POTATO**
Irish shamrock - *see* **WOOD SORREL**
Island moss - *see* **ICELAND MOSS**
Italian asparagus - *see* **BROCCOLI**
Italian brown mushroom - *see* **MUSHROOMS AND FUNGI**
Italian parsley - *see* **LOVAGE, PARSLEY**
Italian squash - *see* **ZUCCHINI**
Italian turnip - *see* **BROCCOLI RAAB**

IVY GOURD (*see also* **TANDOORI**) - Not to be confused with the tandoori, which is also called "ivy gourd," this ivy gourd (*Coccinea cordifolia = C. grandis*) is a native of tropical Asia and Africa. Also called the "small gourd," the plant is cultivated today in India, Indonesia, and Sudan. Its leaves, roots, and immature fruits are cooked as vegetables.

Common names and synonyms: Small gourd.

JABOTICABA - A member of the Myrtaceae family, the jaboticaba (*Myrciaria cauliflora*) is a very popular fruit in Brazil. It is also an unusual tree, because the fruit and flowers are borne on the trunk and on older branches. In color, it is a dark purple or nearly black fruit and its size - about a half inch in diameter - is that of a grape. Indeed, its pulp has the taste of a sweet grape, but the skin is tough and generally not eaten. The jaboticaba is consumed raw, used in salads, and made into jellies and wine.

Common names and synonyms: Brazilian grape, Brazilian grape tree.

Jaca - *see* **JACKFRUIT**
Jack - *see* **JACKFRUIT**

JACKBEAN (*see also* **BEANS**) - Also called the "horsebean" and the "cut-eye bean" and sometimes confused with the sword bean (a close relative), the jackbean (*Canavalia ensiformis*) originated in Central America and the Caribbean area but now is grown throughout much of the tropical and subtropical world. The young pods and seeds are employed as a cooked vegetable, and the seeds can be dried for later use.

Common names and synonyms: Cut-eye bean, horsebean, sword bean.

See in addition: "Beans, Peas, and Lentils," Part II, Section C, Chapter 3.

Jack-Be-Little - *see* **DELICATA (SQUASH)**

JACKFRUIT - Also called "jakfruit," "jak," "nangka," and a half dozen other names mostly derived from the Portuguese *jaca,* the jackfruit (*Artocarpus heterophyllus = A. integrifolius*) is a tropical fruit closely related to the breadfruit. The consensus is that it is likely a native of India, but because it is of ancient cultivation and has spread so widely throughout tropical Asia, its original home will probably never be known with certainty. In more recent times, the jackfruit has also been grown in Africa and in tropical America, including Florida.

Like the breadfruit, the jackfruit can be large, with a length of up to 2 feet and a weight of up to 20 and, on occasion, even as much as 60 pounds. Layers of flesh around the seeds are sweet and can be eaten raw, but other parts of the fruit contain latex and must be cooked before eating. Often the seeds are roasted and eaten as well, either on their own or as an added seasoning in other dishes, especially curries. The jackfruit is rich in carbohydrates but offers little in the way of other nutrients.

Common names and synonyms: Jaca, jack, jack hirsutus Lam, jak, jakfruit, nangka.

Jack hirsutus Lam - *see* JACKFRUIT

Jack-in-the-pulpit - *see* INDIAN TURNIP

Jagua - *see* GENIPAP

Jak - *see* JACKFRUIT

Jakfruit - *see* JACKFRUIT

Jalapa hybrid - *see* JALAPEÑO

JALAPEÑO (*see also* **CHILLI PEPPERS**) - Named for the Mexican town of Jalapa, the jalapeño pepper (*Capsicum annuum*) is probably the best known of the hot chilli peppers and is believed to have been domesticated in Mexico long before the Spaniards arrived. Generally, jalapeños are purchased to be consumed while still green, but mature red fruits (with a sweeter flavor) are also readily available in most produce markets. The jalapeño is a fairly hot pepper and stars in many salsa preparations as well as in cooked dishes. Additionally, jalapeños are pickled and canned, stuffed as a snack, and roasted. Moreover, the ripe (red) form is dried and smoked (which imparts a chocolate-like flavor), after which it becomes a chipotle chilli, and the *huachinango,* a large and highly prized jalapeño, is similarly treated to become a chipotle grande.

The dried fruits are dark brown to black in color, are much gentler on the palate (with less heat) than the fresh peppers, and are available in cans in a red adobo sauce. Chipotles are vital to Mexican cuisine - as well as to that of the southwestern United States - and are used in stews, soups, and salsas. Other types of jalapeños that are smoked and dried include the *mora* or *mora rojo,* the *morita,* and the *mora grande* - the names indicating the relative sizes of these chillies, which range from about 3 inches to about 1 inch in length. And finally there is a new jalapeño - the Jalapa hybrid - which is more productive than its predecessors. Jalapeños are grown chiefly in Mexico (especially the *mora*), Texas, and New Mexico.

Common names and synonyms: Chipotle (chilli), chipotle grande, *huachinango,* Jalapa hybrid, *mora* chilli, *mora grande, mora rojo, morita.*

See in addition: "Chilli Peppers," Part II, Section C, Chapter 4.

Jamaican Blue Mountain - *see* COFFEE

Jamaican cherry - *see* CAPULIN

Jamaican cucumber - *see* GHERKIN

Jamaican hot pepper - *see* HABANERO AND SCOTCH BONNET PEPPERS

Jamaican plum - *see* HOG PLUM

Jamaican Red - *see* HABANERO AND SCOTCH BONNET PEPPERS

Jamaican sorrel - *see* ROSELLE

Jamaica pepper - *see* ALLSPICE

Jamba oil - *see* ARUGULA

Jamberry - *see* TOMATILLO

JAMBOLAN (*see also* **JAMBOLAN PLUM, PLUM**) - A native of India and Java, the jambolan tree (*Eugenia cumini* or *Syzygium cumini*) has now spread throughout much of the world's tropics. Its fruits, green at first, turn purple as they ripen. They are about the size of a Damson plum and are mostly eaten raw, although in India a wine is made from the ripe ones and a vinegar from those that are still green.

Jambolana - *see* JAMBOLAN PLUM

JAMBOLAN PLUM (*see also* **PLUM**) - Also called the jambolan, the jambolana, and the Java plum, the jambolan plum (*Eugenia jambolana*) is the fruit of a large tree found mostly in the East Indies and Australia. The fruits are disappointing when eaten raw, and the seeds are very astringent. The bark of the tree is used medicinally.

Common names and synonyms: Jambolan, jambolana, Java plum.

Jambon du jardinier - *see* EVENING PRIMROSE

Jambos - *see* JAVA APPLE, ROSE APPLE

Jambu - *see* JAVA APPLE, ROSE APPLE

Jambu merah (tree) - *see* MALAY APPLE

Jantung pisang - *see* BANANA FLOWER

Japanese artichoke - *see* CHINESE ARTICHOKE

Japanese brown mushroom - *see* MUSHROOMS AND FUNGI

Japanese bunching - *see* WELSH ONION

Japanese cucumber - *see* ARMENIAN CUCUMBER

Japanese greens - *see* CHRYSANTHEMUM

Japanese horseradish - *see* WASABI

Japanese medlar - *see* LOQUAT

JAPANESE MILLET (*see also* **MILLET**) - A quick-growing cereal, Japanese millet (*Echinochloa frumentacea*) can be ready for harvesting in about six weeks. It is also called "billion-dollar grass," and its light brown to purplish grains are used as a food in India and the Far East and serve as a quickly grown substitute if the rice crop fails.

Common names and synonyms: Billion-dollar grass.

See in addition: "Millets," Part II, Section A, Chapter 5.

Japanese mint - *see* CORN MINT

Japanese parsley - *see* **HONEWORT**

Japanese pear - *see* **ASIAN PEAR**

JAPANESE PLUM (*see also* **LOQUAT, PLUM**) - Thought to have originated in China - but domesticated in Japan - the Japanese plum (*Prunus salicina*) reached the United States around 1870 to become a popular fruit. It is relatively large for a plum (from 1.5 to 2 inches in diameter), reddish in color, and juicy when ripe. U.S. production is mostly in California.

Japanese potato - *see* **CHINESE ARTICHOKE**

Japanese pumpkin - *see* **KABOCHA (SQUASH)**

JAPANESE QUINCE - A native of China, the Japanese quince (*Chaenomeles speciosa*) is a small tree or shrub with scarlet flowers and widely grown as an ornamental. It produces a small fruit with a quince-like odor, which is generally made into jellies and jams.

Common names and synonyms: Japonica.

Japanese radish - *see* **DAIKON**

JAPANESE RAISIN TREE - Also called the "Chinese raisin tree," the Japanese raisin tree (*Hovenia dulcis*) is from both of these countries. A member of an Asiatic genus of trees and shrubs, it is a spicy-smelling plant that is grown for its sweet, swollen, reddish, edible flower stalks, which have a fruity taste.

Common names and synonyms: Chinese raisin tree, honey tree.

Japanese white celery mustard - *see* **PAKCHOI AND KAI CHOY**

Japanese white radish - *see* **DAIKON**

JAPANESE WINEBERRY (*see also* **BERRIES**) - Although the Japanese wineberry (*Rubus phoenicolasius*) is a native of Southeast Asia, it now grows wild in the southern Appalachian region of the United States. There it is called the "strawberry-raspberry" and resembles the latter of the two in appearance. Despite its designation as a "wineberry," the fruit is not, as a rule, made into wine, but it does yield a good-tasting juice.

Common names and synonyms: Strawberry-raspberry, wineberry.

Japonés - *see* **ASIAN CHILLIES, CHILLIES**

Japonica - *see* **JAPANESE QUINCE**

JASMINE - Any of a number of plants with extremely sweet-smelling flowers are called "jasmine" (genus *Jasminum*). The flowers are mostly prized for their essential oils that are used in perfumery, but they are also combined with black tea to make jasmine tea.

Java - *see* **COFFEE**

JAVA ALMOND - A member of an extensive genus of tropical plants, the Java almond (*Canarium commune*) is a large tree of the East Indies that produces rich, oily nuts of the same name. These are pressed for oil and used as food.

Common names and synonyms: Kanari.

JAVA APPLE - A native of Indonesia, the Java apple (*Eugenia javanica*) is one of the jambu fruits and, because of a similarity in both scientific and common names, often is confused with the rose apple. The Java apple, which is also known by the names "wax-apple" and "jambos," has fruits that are usually green, although some are pink or red, and they appear a little like miniature bell peppers. Called the wax-apple because of a skin that feels waxlike, the fruit is usually eaten raw but is also made into a sauce.

Common names and synonyms: Jambos, jambu, wax-apple.

Java jute - *see* **ROSELLE**

JAVANESE LONG PEPPER - Another member of the genus *Piper*, which includes common black and white peppercorns, the Javanese long pepper (*P. retrofractum* = *P. officinarum*) yields berries that are dried and added whole to curries and pickles. The Javanese long pepper is very much like its close relative, the Indian long pepper.

Java pepper - *see* **TAILED PEPPER**

Java plum - *see* **JAMBOLAN PLUM**

Jelly melon - *see* **KIWANO**

JELLY PALM - Also known as the pindo palm, the jelly palm (*Butia capitata*) is a native of South America and is now found throughout the West Indies and the U.S. South as far north as Georgia. It has white flowers that bloom in the spring, and the tree produces large bunches of yellow, orange, or pinkish fruits that are used to make jelly - hence the name. It might also have been called the "wine tree" after yet another use of the fruit.

Common names and synonyms: Pindo palm.

Jenny-stonecrop - *see* **STONECROP**

JERING - A native of tropical Asia, *Pithecellobium jiringa* has seeds that are boiled or roasted for food. The tree's young shoots and seed pods are also eaten.

JERUSALEM ARTICHOKE (*see also* **SUNFLOWER**) - Although widely cultivated around the world, Jerusalem artichokes (*Helianthus tuberosus*), which are the tubers of the American sunflower, are nowhere a major crop. In many places, however, these tubers serve as a minor source of food for humans and livestock. This vegetable is rather unusual among root and tuber crops in that the reserve food is inulin rather than starch. The plant is a hexaploid. Some have thought that *Helianthus annuus* (the wild sunflower) is involved as one of the parents in its origin, but it seems more likely that only perennial species figured in its ancestry.

The wild Jerusalem artichoke is widespread in eastern North America, and Native Americans adopted it as a cultivated plant in prehistoric times. The first written notice of the plant was provided in 1605 by Samuel de Champlain in his observations on the area that is now Massachusetts. Shortly after, the plant appeared in France and then spread throughout Europe. Its early reception as a food was favorable, one writer of the time stating that the tubers were "dainties for a Queene." Yet another was soon to state that they "caused the belly to be pained and [are] a meat more fit for swine, than man." But despite their flatulent properties, Jerusalem artichokes continue to be consumed, and in the United States in recent years they have enjoyed a renewed popularity. The tubers are generally eaten cooked, but they can be used raw in salads.

The name "Jerusalem artichoke" has generally been thought to be a corruption of the Italian *girasole articiocco*. The artichoke part is easily explained, for early writers found the taste to be similar to that of the more familiar globe (or French) artichoke. R. N. Salaman (1940), however, has suggested that Jerusalem is a corruption of Ter Neusen, a place in Holland from whence the tubers were imported into England.

Common names and synonyms: Gerasole, girasole, girsole, sunchoke.

See in addition: "Sunflower," Part II, Section E, Chapter 6.

Jerusalem oak - *see* EPAZOTE

JERUSALEM PEA (*see also* BEANS, LEGUMES) - A native of the East Indies but now cultivated mostly in West Africa, the Jerusalem pea (*Phaseolus trinervius*) is sometimes regarded as a variety of the mung bean. It grows wild in India, where it is considered a famine food. Each of the small pods of the Jerusalem pea contains about nine edible seeds.

See in addition: "Beans, Peas, and Lentils," Part II, Section C, Chapter 3.

Jerusalem thorn - *see* CHRIST'S-THORN FRUIT

Jesuit nut - *see* WATER CHESTNUT

JEWELWEED - Several American and Eurasian species of the genus *Impatiens* are known as jewelweed or "touch-me-not." Their leaves and stems are used as food in Asia, and the same parts of *I. capensis* were boiled and eaten by Native Americans in eastern and central North America.

Common names and synonyms: Touch-me-not.

Jew plum - *see* GOLDEN APPLE

Jew's-ear - *see* CLOUD EAR, MUSHROOMS AND FUNGI

JEW'S-MALLOW - Also known as "jute mallow," Jew's-mallow (*Corchorus olitorus*) is a native of India that now grows in most of the world's tropical and subtropical regions. This stout herb is cultivated in Egypt, Syria, South America, and the Caribbean as a potherb and in India for its jute fiber. The young, tender, green leaves of Jew's-mallow - which are edible (and palatable) raw as well as cooked - have been used for food since the days of the hunter-gatherers. In Egypt, they are used to make the country's national dish - a thick soup called *molokhia*. The greens are high in beta-carotene, calcium, and vitamin C.

Common names and synonyms: Bush okra, jute, jute mallow, long-fruited jute, Nalta jute, Spanish okra, tossa jute, tussa jute, West African sorrel.

JÍCAMA - A plant that provides both a root vegetable and beans, the jícama (*Pachyrhizus erosus* = *Dolichos erosus*) is also called "Mexican potato," "yam bean," and "potato bean." The jícama is an American native that - along with a closely related species, *P. tuberosus* (also called "yam bean" and ajipo) - was cultivated long ago by the Aztecs and the Maya. The young pods are eaten as a cooked vegetable. The root is cylindrical and has a rough, sandy-colored skin, the removal of which reveals a white interior. In the past, the roots were normally eaten raw and enjoyed for their cool crispness rather than their bland flavor. Today, jícama remains a popular snack food eaten with lime juice in Mexico as well as California, where it is also grown. It can be baked like a potato but is mostly pickled and included in salads and casseroles. Until recently, jícama was practically unknown in North America, but now it can be found in most produce departments. Asian-American cooks occasionally employ it as a substitute for water chestnuts.

Common names and synonyms: Erosus yam bean, *jícama de agua*, *jícama de leche*, Mexican potato, potato bean, yam bean.

Jícama de agua - *see* JÍCAMA

Jícama de leche - *see* JÍCAMA

Jicara - *see* XICALLI

Jimsonweed - *see* MOONFLOWER

Jintan - *see* ANISE, CARAWAY, CUMIN

JOB'S-TEARS (*see also* MILLET) - A grass probably native to Southeast Asia, "Job's-tears" (*Coix lacryma-jobi*) now grows throughout the world's tropics, where it is sometimes cultivated and sometimes regarded as a weed. At one time, it was a major cereal in India, where people pounded its large, nut-flavored grains into flour, cooked them in gruels and soups, ate them whole, and used them to make teas and fermented beverages. The grain remains a minor cereal in India and elsewhere, and the pearly white seeds of some ornamental varieties are often sold as beads and strung to make necklaces.

Common names and synonyms: Adlay, adlay millet, tear-grass.

See in addition: "Millets," Part II, Section A, Chapter 5.

Johannisberg Riesling - *see* RIESLING

Johnson grass - *see* SORGHUM

JOJOBA NUT - About the size of an acorn, the jojoba nut (*Simmondsia chinensis*) is - despite its scientific name - native to the North American Southwest and the Baja peninsula. The nuts grow on a bush, usually in a wild state, although today they are also cultivated for their oil, which is used in lubricants and medicines. In the past, however, Native Americans made a coffee-like beverage from the nuts.

Common names and synonyms: Goat-nut.

Joseph's-coat - *see* **AMARANTH**

Judas('s) ear - *see* **CLOUD EAR**

Juglans - *see* **WALNUT**

JUJUBE (*see also* **DESERT APPLE**) - A native of China with a French name meaning "lozenge," the jujube (*Ziziphus jujuba*) resembles a large, dark red cherry. The spiny tree that bears jujubes has been cultivated by the Chinese for more than 4,000 years and has been growing in the Mediterranean region for some 2,500 years. It has spread throughout East Asia and is also grown in parts of Africa. The jujube was introduced in the United States in 1837; better varieties were obtained from China in 1906, and they continue to thrive in the hot, dry climate of the U.S. Southwest, although they are not grown on a large commercial scale.

Also called "Chinese dates" and "Chinese red dates," jujubes were often cooked in traditional Chinese households with millet or rice to make a kind of sweet porridge, and the dried fruit has always been especially popular. There are other very similar and related fruits. One, called the Indian jujube (*Z. mauritiana*), produces a fruit with a color ranging from yellowish to orange and brown and is now grown in Florida. Another - a Mediterranean variety, *Z. lotus* - yields a fruit that is like a sweet olive. This is said to be the fruit of the lotus-eaters described by Homer in the *Odyssey*. The "Christ-thorn" berry (*Z. spina-christi*) is yet one more relative. Jujubes are eaten fresh but are also baked, boiled, stewed, and made into syrup. The juice of the fruit is employed in making the small candies that are called "jujubes." Jujubes (the fruit) are rich in vitamin C.

Common names and synonyms: Chinese date, Chinese jujube, Chinese red date, common jujube, cottony jujube, Indian jujube.

Jumbie bean - *see* **LEUCAENA**

Juneberry - *see* **SERVICEBERRY**

Jungle banana - *see* **ENSETE**

Jungle plum - *see* **LITTLE GOOSEBERRY TREE**

JUNIPER BERRY - The fruits of a small evergreen tree or shrub, juniper berries (*Juniperus communis*) are legendary in folklore for their supposed medicinal and magical properties. Their most important application, however, lies in the oil derived from the dried berries, which is added to the final distillation of gin for flavoring. The spicy taste of juniper is also added to other liquors and foods. In cooking, the dried and crushed (to release their full powerful flavor) berries work well with wild game and are added to sauerkraut, sausages, stuffings, and marinades as well. In Europe during the Middle Ages, juniper berries were used to flavor beef, pork, mutton, and especially venison. A bit later on, they were one of the ingredients employed to adulterate pepper.

Juniper berries grow wild in most of the world's temperate regions. In North America, they were used as food by some Native American groups, who ate them fresh and also dried and ground them to make a mush. Others have roasted juniper berries as a coffee substitute. But their flavor and especially their potency varies considerably. The best are said to come from southern Europe in general and the mountainous regions of Italy in particular.

Common names and synonyms: Common juniper.

See also: "Spices and Flavorings," Part II, Section F, Chapter 1.

JUNIPER MISTLETOE - A yellow-green mistletoe, juniper mistletoe (*Phoradendron juniperinum*) is parasitic to several species of juniper. It has translucent, globular berries that birds feed on, after which they carry the sticky seeds to other trees, thus spreading the parasite. At one time, the Navaho reportedly employed the berries for food, but today the juniper mistletoe is used only medicinally (by the Hopi Indians).

Common names and synonyms: Mistletoe.

Jute - *see* **JEW'S-MALLOW**

Jute mallow - *see* **JEW'S-MALLOW**

KABOCHA (SQUASH) (*see also* **SQUASH AND PUMPKIN**) - The name "kabocha" designates a group of squashes (*Cucurbita maxima* or *C. moschata*) that were developed in Japan and are exceptionally sweet and flavorful. Weighing an average of 3 to 4 pounds, they generally have thick, green skins with pale stripes and a yellow-orange flesh. The Japanese - who consume large amounts of squash on a per capita basis - are big importers of kabocha during the off-season, when they cannot grow it themselves. New Zealand and Mexico are major producers. Like other winter squashes, the kabocha contains much in the way of vitamins A and C.

Common names and synonyms: Chirimen, Delica, ebisu, hoka, Home Delite, hyuga, Japanese pumpkin, Sweet Mama.

See in addition: "Squash," Part II, Section C, Chapter 8.

Kachun - *see* **PEPINO**

Kaffir corn - *see* **SORGHUM**

Kaffir date - *see* **KAFFIR PLUM**

KAFFIR LIME (*see also* **CITRUS FRUITS**) - A species of *Citrus* grown in Southeast Asia, the Kaffir lime (*C. hystrix*) is cultivated more for its leaves than for its fruit, although its juice is used as a flavoring. The leaves are employed both fresh and dried (like bay leaves) in soups, curries, sauces, and gravies. Powdered leaves of the Kaffir lime can be found in Asian markets, but these are not totally satisfactory as a substitute for the whole leaves.

Common names and synonyms: Papeda, wild lime.

Kaffir orange - *see* **MONKEY ORANGE**

KAFFIR PLUM - A tree of South Africa, the Kaffir plum (*Harpephyllum caffrum*) produces a sweet, red fruit a bit smaller than a plum - in fact about the size of a date (and the fruit is also called a "Kaffir date"). The tree is now grown in California and Florida as an ornamental.

Common names and synonyms: Kaffir date.

KAFFIR POTATO - An apparently close relative of the Sudan potato, with which it shares the common name "Hausa potato," the Kaffir potato (*Plectranthus esculentus*) is a native of tropical West Africa that today is cultivated in an area extending throughout Central Africa and into East Africa. The tubers, which have been food for Africans since prehistoric times, are generally boiled and frequently added to the many vegetables in the always-simmering family soup.

Common names and synonyms: Hausa potato, Livingstone potato.

KAI APPLE - Also known as "kau apple" and "kei apple," the kai apple (*Aberia caffra* = *Dovyalis caffra*) is a South African native. The "apple" grows on a thorny tree or bush and is a very acidic, yellowish fruit with the general shape of an apple. It is usually employed to make preserves.

Common names and synonyms: Kau apple, kei apple.

Kai choy - *see* **PAKCHOI AND KAI CHOY**

Kail - *see* **KALE**

Kailan - *see* **CHINESE BROCCOLI**

Kaiware - *see* **DAIKON**

Kaki - *see* **PERSIMMON**

KALE (*see also* **CABBAGE, COLLARDS, HANOVER KALE**) - A variety of cabbage with ruffled, crinkled leaves that form no head, kale (*Brassica oleracea* var. *acephala*) is an ancient vegetable. It is descended from the wild cabbage, which was native to the Mediterranean region, doubtless was enjoyed by Stone Age hunter-gatherers, and may have been the first form of cultivated cabbage. It was one of the many plants consumed by the Romans, who spread its cultivation throughout their empire. Kale is a hardy plant that can be left in the ground over the winter and thus has been especially appreciated when other greens are scarce.

Curly kale is the variety most frequently consumed, although local forms have been developed in specific areas. Of these, Scotch kale (which is very curly and somewhat prickly) and blue kale (which is less curly and a blue-green in color) are probably the most common types. Kale has coarse leaves, which can become very wide, and grows best in cool weather.

It is used in several different ways, most typically in soups and salads or as a steamed vegetable. In Portugal, a special kind of kale - called *couve* - is grown to make the country's famed *caldo verde*. Colored varieties of kale - sometimes called "salad savory" - are grown as ornamentals; in Japan, for example, they are often employed to enhance flower gardens. Kale is rich in vitamins A and C and fairly high in calcium and iron.

Common names and synonyms: Blue kale, borecole, cail, Chinese kale, *couve*, curly greens, curly kale, du jour, green cabbage, kail, marrow stem, Nagoya kale, ornamental kale, peacock kale, red flowering kale, red-on-green flowering kale, red Russian kale, salad savory, Scotch kale, thousand-headed, white flowering kale.

See in addition: "Cruciferous and Green Leafy Vegetables," Part II, Section C, Chapter 5.

Kalonji - *see* **NIGELLA**

Kampyo - *see* **BOTTLE GOURD**

KAMUT (*see also* **WHEAT**) - Kamut (*Triticum turgidum*) is regarded by some to be the ancestor of grains and, at the very least, the oldest relative of modern durum wheats. This is reflected in the name "kamut," which was the ancient Egyptian word for wheat. There is disagreement over the plant's biological classification, and a number of different subspecies have been proposed.

About a half century ago, kamut reached America, and it is now produced commercially on a small scale in both the United States and Canada, mostly for the health-food market. It has never been hybridized, and its kernels are about three times the size of most wheat. They have a pleasant, nutlike flavor and are used - in conjunction with wheat flour - mostly for making pastas, puffed cereals, crackers, and bread. Kamut is high in dietary fiber and rich in the B-vitamin complex; it also delivers good quantities of folic acid and iron.

See in addition: "Wheat," Part II, Section A, Chapter 10.

Kana - *see* **MAIZE**

Kanari - *see* **JAVA ALMOND**

KANGAROO APPLE - A yellow, mealy fruit with the shape of an egg, the kangaroo apple (*Solanum aviculare*) grows on shrublike trees in New Zealand and Australia. It contributed to the diets of the aboriginal peoples of both countries.

Kang kong - *see* **SWAMP CABBAGE**

Kang(-)kung - *see* **SWAMP CABBAGE**

Kanten - *see* **AGAR**

Kápari - *see* **CAPER(S)**

KAPOK TREE - Also called the "silk-cotton tree" because of the cotton-like substance surrounding its seeds (which is used in life preservers), the kapok tree (*Ceiba pentandra*) is an East Indian native (now grown in Florida) and a close relative of Africa's famous baobab tree. The young leaves of the kapok tree are often cooked as a vegetable.

Common names and synonyms: Ceiba, silk-cotton tree.

KARAKA - *Karaka*, a Maori word, refers to an orange-colored fruit (*Corynocarpus laevigata*) of New Zealand, and the same word also means the tree on which the fruit grows. The fruit has an edible pulp and poisonous seeds, but – interestingly – the seeds are the most valuable part of this plant. When cooked and dried, they become edible, and they have long been an important item in the Maori diet.

Karamta - *see* **SWAMP CABBAGE**

Karanda - *see* **CARAUNDA**

Karaschi - *see* **MUSTARD SEED**

Karawya - *see* **CARAWAY**

Karenga - *see* **SEAWEED**

Karzochy - *see* **ARTICHOKE**

Kasha - *see* **BUCKWHEAT**

Kashmiri chilli (pepper) - *see* **ASIAN CHILLIES, CHILLI PEPPERS**

Kastanie - *see* **CHESTNUT**

Kat - *see* **KHAT**

Katook - *see* **SWEET-SHOOT**

Katuk - *see* **SWEET-SHOOT**

Kau apple - *see* **KAI APPLE**

KAVA - Also known as cava and kava-kava, kava (*Piper methysticum*) is a shrub of the tropical Pacific Islands. Its roots and rhizomes are dried and used to make an intoxicating beverage, which has long been used both in ceremonies and to promote friendships.

Common names and synonyms: Cava, kava-kava.

See also: "Kava," Part III, Chapter 6.

Kava-kava - *see* **KAVA**

Kayu manis - *see* **CINNAMON AND CASSIA**

Kechapi - *see* **SENTUL**

Kĕdondong - *see* **HOG PLUM**

Keemum - *see* **TEA**

Keemun - *see* **TEA**

Kei apple - *see* **KAI APPLE**

Keladi - *see* **COCOYAM**

KELP (*see also* **SEAWEED**) - Any of the brown and olive-green seaweeds of the orders Laminariales and Fucales are called "kelp," including several large Pacific plants known as "giant kelp," such as *Macrocystis pyrifera* and *Laminaria japonica*. The Japanese, in particular, are skilled in preparing kelp (called *kombu*) as a food product by drying and shredding it. Kelp is used in soups, is boiled as a vegetable, and is especially important in making stocks for savory dishes. It is also burned to produce iodine.

Common names and synonyms: Bladder weed, giant kelp, *kombu*, sea kelp, tangle kelp.

See in addition: "Algae," Part II, Section C, Chapter 1.

Kerela - *see* **BITTER MELON**

Kersting's groundnut - *see* **HAUSA GROUNDNUT**

Ketembilla - *see* **CEYLON GOOSEBERRY**

Key lime - *see* **LIME**

KHAT - Also called kat, cat, qat, qhat, and African or Arabian tea, khat (*Catha edulis*) is a shrub cultivated by the Arabs for its leaves. These are either chewed or made into a tea for the narcotic effect they produce.

Common names and synonyms: African tea, Arabian tea, cat, kat, qat, qhat.

See also: "Khat," Part III, Chapter 7.

Kiawe - *see* **ALGARROBO**

Kikurage - *see* **CLOUD EAR**

Kingcup - *see* **COWSLIP**

King-of-fruits - *see* **MANGOSTEEN**

King-of-trees - *see* **OLIVE**

King's-cure - *see* **PIPSISSEWA**

King's-nut - *see* **MARULA PLUM**

Kin-kan - *see* **KUMQUAT**

Kinnikinnic - *see* **BEARBERRY**

Kinnikinnick - *see* **BEARBERRY**

KIWANO - A member of the cucumber family, the kiwano (*Cucumis metuliferus*) was long known as the "African horned melon," but New Zealand growers had so much success marketing the Chinese gooseberry after they changed its name to "kiwifruit" that they have pursued a similar course with this fruit. It is a colorful one, about the size and shape of a small cucumber, with a bright orange (and inedible) skin covered with little horns, and bright green flesh. The kiwano is eaten raw and makes a fine ingredient in salads. It is, however, very expensive, and although now beginning to appear in produce markets, it has in the past been available only through mail-order businesses specializing in exotic fruits.

Common names and synonyms: African horned cucumber, African horned melon, English tomato, hedged gourd, horned melon, jelly melon, melano, *metulon*.

See also: "Cucumbers, Melons, and Watermelons," Part II, Section C, Chapter 6.

Kiwicha - *see* **AMARANTH**

KIWIFRUIT - The kiwifruit (*Actinidia chinensis*) was a small, hard berry growing wild in China at the beginning of the twentieth century. It was subsequently cultivated in New Zealand, where it was known as the "Chinese gooseberry." But later, when China became Communist China, the name "kiwifruit" was applied, thus disassociating it from its homeland. In part, this was to facilitate marketing in the West, and in part, it was because of the fruit's supposed resemblance to New Zealand's kiwi, a small, flightless bird with brown, hairlike plumage. The new name provoked a remarkable marketing success, and during the 1950s, New Zealand acreage devoted to the fruit increased rapidly to meet the sudden demand. The kiwifruit – about the size of a large egg – is very juicy and usually sweet, although sometimes it has a tart flavor. The thin skin is hairy and brown, and the flesh is a bright green with very small black seeds that surround a creamy white core. In addition to appearing in salads as a fresh fruit, the kiwifruit is also processed into juice, jams, and jellies and is canned and frozen. The fruit is grown on trellises and provides much in the way of vitamins A and C.

Common names and synonyms: Chinese gooseberry, *yang tao*.

Klarbar - *see* **CHERRY**

Knit-bones - *see* COMFREY

Knol-kohl - *see* KOHLRABI

KNOTTED WRACK (*see also* SEAWEED) - A perennial brown algae, knotted wrack of the genus *Ascophyllum* attaches itself to rocks in sheltered areas of temperate seas. In the United States, it is used mostly for fertilizers, soil conditioners, and fodder as well as packing material for shipping live lobsters and clams. However, this "sea vegetable" is also ground into a meal that is consumed by humans.

Common names and synonyms: Rockweed.

See in addition: "Algae," Part II, Section C, Chapter 1.

KNOTWEED AND SMARTWEED - A number of plants of the genus *Polygonum* are called "knotweed" or "smartweed." Many species, such as the Japanese knotweed (*P. cuspidatum* - also known as "Mexican bamboo"), have been introduced into the New World from Eurasia. Others, like *P. coccineum,* are natives of North America, and still others, like *P. viviparum,* are native to both North America and Eurasia.

In some cases, such as that of the "bistort" or "smokeweed" (*P. bistorta* or *P. bistortoides*), it was the rhizomes of the plant that were eaten by gatherers in the northern portions of the continents. But the young shoots and leaves of most knotweeds are also edible, and Japanese knotweed is cultivated for its immature stems, which are employed in salads and as a potherb. *Polygonum persicaria* may have been employed as food in the past; it was certainly used for medicinal purposes by Native Americans. The seeds of some species are edible as well. Native Americans, for example, ground the seeds of *P. douglasii* into a meal, whereas the seeds of *P. convolvulus* have long been made into a kind of porridge. And finally, the smartweed, "water pepper" (*P. hydropiper*), yields an acrid, peppery juice that has been used medicinally and as a condiment.

Common names and synonyms: Bistort, Japanese knotweed, lady's-thumb, Mexican bamboo, smokeweed, water pepper.

KOHLRABI (*see also* CABBAGE) - Native to northern Europe, kohlrabi (*Brassica oleracea* Gongylodes Group) is of the mustard family. It is a relative newcomer to *Brassica,* the cabbage genus, having been developed from marrow cabbages some 400 to 500 years ago. It was first described in the sixteenth century and by the end of that century was known in Germany, England, Italy, and Spain. But it was only cultivated in the United States at the beginning of the nineteenth century.

The name comes from the German words *Kohl* (meaning cabbage) and *Rabi* (meaning turnip), and in fact, it is a type of cabbage with stems that swell into turnip-like bulbs - hence, "turnip cabbage" is another of its names. Kohlrabi grows best in cool climates. It is sweet and crisp when the bulbs are small but tough and bitter when they grow large.

This vegetable can be eaten raw but is usually cooked and is commonly used in soups. Some kohlrabi varieties are "Prague Special," "Purple Vienna," "Triumph of Prague," and "White Vienna."

Common names and synonyms: Cabbage turnip, caulorapa, chou-rave, colirrambano, knol-kohl, koolrabi, Prague Special, Purple Vienna, Triumph of Prague, turnip cabbage, White Vienna.

See in addition: "Cruciferous and Green Leafy Vegetables," Part II, Section C, Chapter 5.

Koko - *see* COCOYAM

KOLA NUT - Native to West Africa, the kola nuts - *abata kola* (*Cola acuminata*) and *gbanja kola* (*C. nitida*) - have been an important trade commodity in sub-Saharan Africa for thousands of years. *Cola nitida* is indigenous to Ashanti, the Ivory Coast, and Sierra Leone but is now cultivated extensively in Nigeria as well. *Cola acuminata* is native to Nigeria, Gabon, and the Congo Basin but is less cultivated.

The kola nut is a brownish, bitter seed about the size of a chestnut. The nuts grow on small trees and are enclosed - beanlike - in green, wrinkled pods. Because they contain caffeine, kolatine, and theobromine, kola nuts have a stimulating effect when chewed or otherwise utilized, as, for example, in flavoring cola soft drinks. Kola nuts are also credited with allaying thirst and promoting energy. In addition to Africa, kola nuts are cultivated in the West Indies, South America, and Indonesia.

Common names and synonyms: Abata kola, cola, cola nut, *gbanja kola, owe kola.*

See also: "Kola Nut," Part III, Chapter 8.

Kolkas - *see* COCOYAM

Kombu - *see* KELP, SEAWEED

Kong(-)kong taro - *see* MALANGA

Koolrabi - *see* KOHLRABI

Korean chilli (pepper) - *see* ASIAN CHILLIES

KORILA (*see also* CUCUMBER) - A cucurbit that may have originated in the Caribbean region (but more likely South America or Mesoamerica), korila (*Cyclanthera pedata* - also known as the "wild cucumber") is now cultivated in all of these regions and in parts of Southeast Asia as well. The Incas ate the young fruits raw and stuffed the mature ones - often with meat - after which they were dried and stored in warehouses for future use. Today, the pale green fruits are still eaten raw and are frequently stuffed with meat or fish and baked. The shoots are also consumed, but the seeds generally are not.

Common names and synonyms: Achokcha, caihua, caygua, cayua, wild cucumber.

KUDZU - A vine native to Japan, kudzu (*Pueraria thunbergiana* = *P. lobata*) has starchy roots that can be boiled and eaten or are processed into a thickener for sauces. The plant has also been appreciated since ancient times for its medicinal properties, which supposedly become active when the roots are dried and ground into a powder. Kudzu has joined the group of Asian plants now growing in the southern United States.

KUINI - The kuini (*Mangifera odorata*) is a tall tree, probably native to Malaysia. It bears green, oval-shaped fruits about the size of large oranges. Their flesh is orange in color, quite juicy, and very sweet. The fruits have a strong smell when ripe, which tells their consumers they are safe. Immature fruits with little odor contain a poisonous sap. The kuini is eaten raw and used to make chutney.
Common names and synonyms: Kuwini.

Kumara - *see* **SWEET POTATO**

Kümmel - *see* **CARAWAY**

KUMQUAT (*see also* **LIMEQUAT**) - Native to East Asia, the several varieties of the kumquat tree (genus *Fortunella*) belong to the family Rutaceae - the same family as citrus fruits. Kumquats are cultivated throughout the subtropics, including places like California and Florida in the United States. The most common varieties are Nagami (*F. margarita*), Meiwa (*F. crassifolia*), and Marumi (*F. japonica*). The edible skin resembles that of an orange, and in fact, the kumquat was thought to be a citrus fruit until early in the twentieth century, when it was decided that it belongs to a different - but related - genus. The bright-colored, orange-yellow fruit is about the size of a large olive or a small plum, varies in shape between round and oval, and ranges in taste from sweet to mildly acidic. Availability is best during the winter. Kumquats are cooked, candied, canned, made into preserves, and used in salads, but most are popped into the mouth whole and eaten raw. Kumquats are an excellent source of vitamin C.
Common names and synonyms: Cumquat, golden orange, *kin-kan, limau pagar,* Marumi, Meiwa, Nagami.

KUNDANGAN - An Indochina native, the kundangan (*Bouea macrophylla*) is yellow, about the size of a small orange, and soft when ripe. The mature fruits are made into chutneys and jams, and the young green fruits are pickled for curries. This tree-growing fruit is also known as Setar and star.
Common names and synonyms: Setar, star.

Kusaie - *see* **RANGPUR AND KUSAIE**

Kuwini - *see* **KUINI**

Lablab bean - *see* **HYACINTH BEAN**

Labrusca grape - *see* **FOX GRAPE**

LADY APPLE -Also known as the "red wild-apple," the lady apple (*Syzygium suborbiculare*) is a relative of the clove. A wild, reddish fruit of Australia, it is mentioned as one of the gathered foods of the Australian Aborigines.
Common names and synonyms: Red wild-apple.

Lady('s)-finger(s) - *see* **OKRA**

LADY'S BEDSTRAW - Also known as "yellow bedstraw" and "yellow cleavers" (because the barbed stems cleave to fur and clothing), lady's bedstraw (*Galium verum*) shares the common name "bedstraw" with a few other species of the genus *Calium*. The name came about because the plants were used as mattress stuffing, but they also have some food value; the seeds, for example, have served as a coffee substitute.
Common names and synonyms: Yellow bedstraw, yellow cleavers.

LADY'S SMOCK - Also called "cuckoo flower," lady's smock (*Cardamine pratensis*) is a bitter cress of North America and Europe. It finds use mostly as a condiment.
Common names and synonyms: Cuckoo flower.

Lady's-thumb - *see* **KNOTWEED AND SMART-WEED**

Lahong - *see* **DURIAN**

Lambert's filbert - *see* **HAZELNUT AND FILBERT**

LAMBRUSCO (*see also* **GRAPES**) - The vines that produce the Lambrusco variety, an Italian wine grape (*Vitis vinifera*) that originated in the Emilia-Romagna wine region, are still heavily planted in the clay soils of the Po Valley. The Lambrusco grape makes a sweet, light- to medium-bodied, sparkling red wine that has been popular in the United States. Lambrusco grapes are also used to make dry red and white wines.
See in addition: "Wine," Part III, Chapter 13.

Lamb's lettuce - *see* **CORNSALAD**

LAMB'S-QUARTER (*see also* **CHENOPODIUM, CORNSALAD, GOOSEFOOT**) - The leaves of lamb's-quarter (*Chenopodium album*) - also known as pigweed - a wild plant common in Europe and now naturalized in North America, taste something like spinach when they are cooked. When young, they are delicious raw. The seeds are also edible after the saponin they contain is leached out.
Common names and synonyms: Goosefoot, pigweed.

Lampong (pepper) - *see* **PEPPER(CORNS)**

LANGSAT - Natives of western Malaysia, both the langsat and the duku are classified under the same botanical name - *Lansium domesticum*. Their pale yellowish, berry-like fruits have been grown since ancient times. In the fifteenth century, Chinese voyagers saw these fruit trees in Java and attempted without success to grow them in China. The trees will not tolerate even the slightest cold, nor will they endure long dry spells, all of which means that they have remained typically Malaysian. Aside from a milky juice present in the langsat, the major difference between the duku and the langsat seems to be that the duku is somewhat larger (about 2 inches long in contrast to about 1.5 inches for the langsat) but has fewer fruits in a bunch. The fruits, which are generally eaten raw, are not very sweet, and some are slightly bitter (the seeds are extremely bitter). Both fruits are difficult to find, even in Asian markets.

Common names and synonyms: Duku, lanzone.

Lanzone - *see* **LANGSAT**

Laos - *see* **GALANGAL**

Lapsung Souchong - *see* **TEA**

LARGE CANE - Also called "giant cane," large cane (*Arundinaria gigantea*) is the tall grass that constitutes the canebrakes of the southern United States. Its succulent young shoots were gathered by Native Americans to cook as a vegetable.

Common names and synonyms: Giant cane.

Laurel - *see* **BAY LEAF**

Laurel leaf - *see* **DUAN SALAM**

LAVENDER - An Old World plant now grown for its scent - from the essential oil of its flowers - lavender (*Lavandula officinalis* = *L. angustifolia*) was popular in the past as a potherb and was used for flavoring jellies as well. Its sole remaining culinary use is to make a tisane.

See also: "Spices and Flavorings," Part II, Section F, Chapter 1.

LAVER (*see also* **AGAR, SEAWEED**) - Any of several seaweeds - mostly of the genus *Porphyra* - are called laver, including such species as *P. laciniata* or *P. vulgaris* (red laver) and *P. tenera* or *P. umbilicalis* (green, purple, and sea laver). In Japan, laver is called *nori* and is employed principally to obtain a gelatin to make agar-agar, which are sheets of dried and compressed laver used as sushi wrappers. But laver is also shredded into soups and other dishes. In Scotland and Ireland, where this "sea vegetable" has been named *sloak* or *slook,* laver is boiled and served with butter, or perhaps fried in bacon fat after boiling. Laver is also pickled.

Common names and synonyms: Agar-agar, green laver, *nori,* purple laver, red laver, sea laver, *sloak, slook.*

See in addition: "Algae," Part II, Section C, Chapter 1.

Lead tree - *see* **LEUCAENA**

Leaf beet - *see* **SWISS CHARD**

Leafcup - *see* **YACÓN**

Leaf mustard - *see* **MUSTARD GREENS**

Leaf pekoe - *see* **TEA**

Leafy cactus - *see* **BARBADOS GOOSEBERRY**

LEAFY SPURGE - A tall perennial Eurasian herb that has been naturalized in the northern United States and Canada, leafy spurge (*Euphorbia esula*) has stems that contain a milky juice. Formerly, this plant and other species of the genus *Euphorbia* were used as purgatives - hence the name spurge - although some also have served as food.

LECHEGUILLA - With a name that is the diminutive of the Spanish *lechuga* (meaning "lettuce"), lecheguilla (*Agave lecheguilla*) is a wild lettuce that can be toxic to sheep and goats that feed on it.

Nonetheless, it was reportedly consumed by humans in the past.

Common names and synonyms: Lechuguilla.

Lechuguilla - *see* **LECHEGUILLA**

Leechee - *see* **LITCHI**

LEEK(S) - A plant related to the onion, the leek (*Allium porrum*) looks like a giant scallion. It is native to the Mediterranean region, where it was apparently cultivated in prehistory and later enjoyed by the ancient Greeks. The Roman emperor Nero ate leeks regularly, and the Romans carried leeks to much of the rest of Europe, where the vegetable was especially popular during the Middle Ages. In Wales, leeks are the national emblem and regarded as the national vegetable. Legend has it that seventh-century Welsh troops - in battle with the Saxons - wore leeks in their hats to distinguish themselves from the enemy.

Leeks are most appreciated in Europe, where they are a favorite; France, Belgium, and the Netherlands are the leading producers. California, New Jersey, and Florida satisfy much of the U.S. market. The vegetable - known as "poor-man's-asparagus" in France - is used to make soups, and is a vital ingredient in many of the French *potage* standards, including vichyssoise (which was actually invented in New York City). The Welsh and the Scots both have famous leek soups as well.

Leeks are also boiled, blanched, or braised, and served perhaps with cheese or a dressing. Despite its warm-climate origin, the leek is a hardy plant that can survive the ice and snow of the cold months in temperate climates and thus is a winter vegetable. Leeks are a rich source of folacin and a good source of vitamin C and vitamin B_6.

Common names and synonyms: Poor-man's-asparagus.

See also: "The *Allium* Species," Part II, Section C, Chapter 2.

Leghorn citron - *see* **CITRON**

LEGUMES (*see also* **BEANS, PEAS**) - The legumes (peas, beans, and lentils), also called pulses, are members of the second most important family of plants in the human diet (after the grasses that have given us our grains). It was the Romans who decided that a legume is the edible seed in a pod that splits into two valves with seeds attached to the lower edge of one of the valves, all of which means that peas as well as beans belong to the family Leguminosae (Fabaceae). The family name derives from the Latin verb *legendus* or *legere* and the Greek *legein,* meaning to gather or collect, and doubtless wild legumes were gathered by humans long before they got around to domesticating them. The first wave of the latter activity probably took place in the Near East, with the lentil, pea, chickpea, and broadbean all domesticated between 7000 and 3000 B.C.

Bean domestication in the Americas took place at about this same time, which saw four species of beans brought under human control beginning around 6000 B.C. These, all of the genus *Phaseolus* and called *haricots* by the French, added considerably to the world's stock of beans. The tepary bean developed in the area that became Mexico and the southeastern United States. The scarlet runner was domesticated farther south in Mexico, and the lima bean even farther south in the Andean region (a smaller sieva bean of the same species was developed in Mexico). However, by far the most familiar and most widespread of the American beans was the common bean (*P. vulgaris*), several varieties of which were cultivated from the Great Lakes to Argentina. These have since been further developed, so that today there are hundreds of varieties of the common bean, including the black bean, navy bean, kidney bean, pinto bean, white bean, and great northern bean.

Somewhat later in Asia, perhaps around 1000 B.C., the mung bean, the azuki bean, and the winged bean were domesticated, although all were apparently preceded a bit in China by the soybean. More complicated and less certain are the dates for the domestication of African legumes. The cowpea may have been cultivated as early as 3000 B.C. Domestication of the pigeon pea and the yam pea were presumably somewhat later, although too little is known with certainty about the development of legumes in Africa. In fact, in many instances, it is difficult if not impossible to determine which ones may have been Asian transients.

Without doubt, there are many species of legumes that have disappeared, and others may still await discovery. Some legumes, such as the peanut (which is eaten as a nut), the carob bean (made into a cocoa substitute), and alfalfa and jackbeans (used for animal fodder), are treated in separate entries.

See in addition: "Beans, Peas, and Lentils," Part II, Section C, Chapter 3; "Peanuts," Part II, Section D, Chapter 2; "Soybean," Part II, Section E, Chapter 5.

LEMON (*see also* **CITRUS FRUITS**) - A native of Southeast Asia, the lemon (*Citrus limon*) was slow to leave that region. Although it reached China about 1900 B.C., it was not until the Middle Ages that the fruit entered Europe via trade with the Arabs, who spread it around the Mediterranean basin from Greece to Spain. The word *citron* (or some variation of it) became the name given to the lemon by many of the various European peoples, although not by the Iberians. The Spaniards called it *limón*, and the Portuguese named it *limão* and carried both the fruit and the name to the New World. Indeed, lemons were reported growing in the Azores as early as 1494, and the men of Christopher Columbus and those who followed in their wake must have been quick to scatter lemon seeds around the West Indies, because lemon trees were recorded in the Greater Antilles

in 1557; 30 years later, lemon orchards were seen in South America.

The most common lemons are the "Lisbon" and the "Eureka" – both yellow ovoids with a blunt nipple at the flower end and a characteristic acid taste. The Eureka is distinguished by a short neck at the stem end and may have a few seeds, whereas the Lisbon is seedless. In the United States, Florida-grown lemons (of the Lisbon variety) are called "bearss." The Meyer lemon – a cross between a lemon and a tangerine – is golden in color and sweet. Yet another lemon, the bergamot, is grown largely for its aromatic leaves and skin. In terms of food use, lemons are employed in a number of ways. The taste of seafoods is frequently enhanced with a squeeze of lemon juice, and lemons are also used to flavor salads, vegetable and meat dishes, drinks (especially lemonade), sauces, and desserts. In addition, lemon peel yields an essential oil with a number of culinary and industrial applications. Lemons brim with vitamin C and, like limes, have long had a reputation as a scurvy preventive as well as a cure. During the California gold rush, scurvy was so prevalent that miners would pay up to a dollar for a lemon.

Common names and synonyms: Bearss, bergamot lemon, *citron* (archaic), Eureka lemon, *limão, limón, limou amarillo,* Lisbon lemon, Meyer lemon.

LEMON BALM - Probably a native of the Middle East and Asia, lemon balm (*Melissa officinalis*) has been cultivated in the Mediterranean at least since the time of the ancient Greeks. In fact, the name comes from the Greek *melissa,* meaning honeybee, which this lemon-scented plant attracts in abundance. The aromatic leaves with a distinct lemon odor are used fresh and dried to flavor fish and poultry dishes. They are also employed in stuffings, salads, and soups, and they go well in egg dishes. In addition, lemon balm is used as a flavoring in many liqueurs.

Common names and synonyms: Balm, balm mint, bee herb, garden balm, gentle balm, melissa, sweet balm.

Lemon cucumber - *see* **CUCUMBER, MANGO MELON**

LEMONGRASS - There are two grasses of the genus *Cymbopogon* that are cultivated for lemongrass oil. One is West Indian lemongrass (*Cymbopogon citratus*), which has long, spear-shaped leaves and is now grown in many tropical and subtropical parts of the world. The other is *C. flexuosus,* or East Indian lemongrass. In both instances, in addition to providing lemongrass oil for making perfumes, the whole stalk, with a strong, lemon-like flavor, is used in many dishes. Indeed, this herb is a most important ingredient in Asian cuisines, especially those of Vietnam and Thailand, where it provides both the base and added flavorings for numerous soups, including its namesake, "lemongrass soup." Lemongrass also goes well in curries, stews, and casseroles.

LEMON VERBENA – A plant originally native to Chile and Argentina, lemon verbena (*Lippia citriodora*) gives off a lemon-like scent when cut. It was long ago carried by the Spaniards to Europe, where an essential oil distilled from its leaves was employed in making soaps and cosmetics. The leaves of lemon verbena are used both fresh and dried in tisanes, salads, soups, stews, fruit drinks, and as a substitute for lemongrass in Asian recipes.
Common names and synonyms: Verbena.

Lemon vine – *see* **BARBADOS GOOSEBERRY**

LENTIL(S) (*see also* **BEANS, LEGUMES**) – Probably the oldest of the cultivated legumes (which also includes peas and beans), the lentil (*Lens esculenta*) – a native of Southwest Asia that had grown wild in the Middle East and central Asia – was brought under cultivation by the first Neolithic peoples of India, Egypt, and the Middle East some 9,000 years ago. They were heavily consumed by the ancient Greeks and Romans. The Egyptians were and remained the chief lentil exporter of those (and later) times and the Romans the chief importer. Since then, Europeans have continued to consume these little, flat, disk-shaped, dried seeds – mostly in soups, stews, and the like. The European variety is greenish or brownish in color, but others are often bright red, yellow, black, or green, and in South Asia they can be narrow in shape like rice grains. In India, lentils are usually served as *dahl* – a side dish that accompanies almost every meal – and they continue as a staple in the Middle East and Eastern Europe. Beans, peas, and lentils become intertwined in the Indian subcontinent. The black lentil (*Phaseolus mungo*) – used for *dahl* – is considered to have the best flavor. The red mung bean and the green mung bean or green lentil (*Phaseolus aureus*) are also used to make *dahl* in India and are sprouted throughout much of the rest of Asia. Yellow lentils (*Pisum sativum*) are closely related to the garden pea and, in addition to being used for *dahl*, are dry-roasted and seasoned to make a snack. Lentils are an important source of protein, are rich in folacin, iron, and phosphorus, and are a fair source of thiamine and vitamin B$_6$.
Common names and synonyms: Black lentil, brown lentil, green lentil, green mung bean, large-seeded lentil, red mung bean, small-seeded lentil, wild lentil, yellow lentil.
See in addition: "Beans, Peas, and Lentils," Part II, Section C, Chapter 3.

Lentisk – *see* **MASTIC TREE**
Leren – *see* **GUINEA ARROWROOT**
Lerenes – *see* **GUINEA ARROWROOT**
Lesser burnet – *see* **BURNET**
Lesser galanga(l) – *see* **GALANGAL**
LESSER YAM (*see also* **YAMS**) – An ancient cultivar that, although native to Southeast Asia, has been cul-

tivated in China for some 2,000 years, the lesser yam (*Dioscorea esculenta*) now grows throughout the world's tropics. These yams are used in soups and stews, are boiled as a vegetable, and are also roasted and fried.
Common names and synonyms: Asiatic yam, Chinese yam, potato yam.
See in addition: "Sweet Potatoes and Yams," Part II, Section B, Chapter 5.

LETTUCE – The various lettuces are plants of the genus *Lactuca* and – along with endive and dandelions – members of the daisy family. Wild lettuce was gathered for millennia by hunter-gatherers and was still being gathered by humans at the time of the ancient Greeks. The latter probably began its cultivation, which was continued by the Romans. The first cultivated lettuce was *L. serriola*, which is native to the Mediterranean region.

There are four major lettuce varieties. One, *L. sativa* var. *crispa*, consists of the red and green loose-leafed lettuces (also called garden lettuce), easily grown by gardeners and generally used in salads. A second, which is essentially confined to romaine (also called "cos" by the English after that once-Greek island), is *L. sativa* var. *longifolia* – the latter referring to the elongated head, the leaves of which are featured in Caesar salads. Butterhead lettuces (*L. sativa* var. *capitata*) include the Boston and Bibb lettuces with their "buttery" flavors. Boston lettuce is loosely headed and larger than the more compact Bibb lettuce (also called "limestone"), a recent (nineteenth-century) development. A fourth group consists of the iceberg lettuce (*L. sativa* var. *capitata*), more properly called "crisphead," which is actually classified with the butterheads but is a relatively new variety that emerged at the hands of growers in just the last century or so.

In addition to use in salads, lettuces are sometimes braised and creamed; in some cultures, lettuce seeds have been eaten as well as the leaves. Romaine and loose-leaf lettuces contain far more vitamin C and beta-carotene than iceberg, which provides relatively little in the way of nutrients. All, however, deliver some magnesium – perhaps the reason lettuce has been credited by some with soothing properties.
Common names and synonyms: Asparagus lettuce, Bibb lettuce, Boston lettuce, butterhead lettuce, celtuce, cos, crisphead lettuce, curled lettuce, garden lettuce, green oak-leaf lettuce, green romaine lettuce, head lettuce, iceberg lettuce, limestone lettuce, lolla rossa, loose-leaf lettuce, Perella Red, red oak-leaf lettuce, red romaine lettuce, romaine lettuce, Tango lettuce.

LEUCAENA – Known also as the "wild tamarind," "jumbie bean," and (in Spanish) *guaje*, the leucaena (*Leucaena leucocephala*) probably originated in Mexico and Central America but now grows throughout the world's tropics. It is a tree that produces flower buds, foliage, young pods, and seeds, all of which have been foods for humans since prehistoric times.

Common names and synonyms: Guaje, jumbie bean, lead tree, wild tamarind.

Libyan lotus - *see* **LOTUS**

Lichee - *see* **LITCHI**

Lichen(s) - *see* **ICELAND MOSS, MANNA**

Lichi - *see* **LITCHI**

LICORICE - The Greek word *glykyrrhiza,* meaning "sweet root," gave rise to the Latin name (*Glycyrrhiza glabra*) for licorice, which is the condensed juice from the roots of this Old World plant. A native of the Middle East, licorice was employed by the ancient Egyptians in medicinal preparations. Today, it is used in candy, to flavor liquors, and in the manufacture of tobacco. In addition, there is American licorice, *G. lepidota,* a wild licorice of North America with roots that were cooked by Native Americans, who also nibbled on the raw roots as a treat.

Common names and synonyms: American licorice, licorice root, liquorice, wild licorice.

See also: "Spices and Flavorings," Part II, Section F, Chapter 1.

Lily - *see* **DAYLILY, TIGER LILY**

Limão - *see* **LEMON**

Limau pagar - *see* **KUMQUAT**

LIME (*see also* **CITRUS FRUITS, LIMEQUAT**) - Like most of the other members of the citrus family, the lime (*Citrus aurantiifolia*) is native to Southeast Asia. It was first cultivated in China and India, then introduced in southern Europe (probably during the Crusades), and carried much later by the Spaniards to the West Indies. The original lime - small, round, and quite tart - is today called the "Mexican," "West Indian," or "Key" lime, with its juice deemed essential to Key lime pies. The limes generally encountered in the produce departments of U.S. supermarkets, however, are "Persian" (sometimes called "Tahiti") limes. These are larger and - save for the green skin - quite lemon-like in appearance. Persian limes are a fairly recent development, apparently the result of a cross between the Key lime and the citron early in the twentieth century. The lime and lemon industry of Florida (which provides close to 90 percent of the limes grown in North America) got its start in the 1880s, declined after freezes in the 1890s, and revived after World War I. Limes are very high in vitamin C and figured prominently in warding off scurvy, the dread disease of seamen from the sixteenth through the nineteenth centuries. In the eighteenth century, the British navy issued lime juice to all seamen to keep the disease at bay - hence the nickname "limeys."

Common names and synonyms: Green lemon, Key lime, Mexican lime, Persian lime, sour lemon, Tahiti lime, West Indian lime.

LIMEBERRY (*see also* **BERRIES**) - A spiny shrub of Southeast Asia, the limeberry (*Triphasia trifolia*) is now naturalized in Florida and Mexico, where it is often used for hedges. Its fruit is a small, red berry, called the "miracle fruit" because, after it is eaten, all subsequent foods eaten for hours to come will seem to have a sweet, lime-like taste.

Common names and synonyms: Miracle fruit.

LIMEQUAT (*see also* **KUMQUAT, LIME**) - A hybrid resulting from a cross between the Key lime and the kumquat, the limequat (genera *Citrus* and *Fortunella*) has a limelike flavor, and some varieties have an edible rind like the kumquat. Along with the orangequat and citrangequat, the limequat is the result of a U.S. Department of Agriculture breeding program to introduce the cold-hardiness of the kumquat into other plants.

LIMETTA (*see also* **CITRUS FRUITS**) - Also known as "sweet lemon" and "sweet lime" (with good reason), the limetta (*Citrus limetta*) looks like a lemon but is sufficiently lacking in citric acid that it is not sour. In fact, when eaten raw, the limetta tastes like lemonade, although it can be insipidly sweet when ripe. The best known of the limetta varieties is the Millsweet, which is grown in Italy and in California. Egypt and other tropical countries also cultivate limettas. Because they do not travel well, limettas are seldom seen in produce markets.

Common names and synonyms: Millsweet limetta, sweet lemon, sweet lime.

Limón - *see* **LEMON**

Limu - *see* **SEAWEED**

Ling - *see* **HEATHER**

Lingaro - *see* **ELAEAGNUS**

Lingen - *see* **LINGONBERRY**

LINGONBERRY (*see also* **BERRIES**) - The lingonberry (*Vaccinium vitis-idaea*) is the red and somewhat acidic fruit of a creeping evergreen shrub native to the northern regions of the world. Related to the cranberry, lingonberries are very popular in the Scandinavian countries, where they are made into preserves and pastries and served to accompany meat dishes. They are also mentioned with frequency as one of the foods of native North Americans.

Common names and synonyms: Cowberry, foxberry, lingen, mountain cranberry, rock cranberry.

Linseed (oil) - *see* **FLAX SEED**

Lipstick tree - *see* **ANNATTO**

Liquorice - *see* **LICORICE**

LITCHI - Also called lichee, lichi, and lychee, the litchi nut (*Litchi chinensis*) is actually a white, sweet berry with a rough, red or pink outer shell. A relative of the longan, litchis grow on tropical and subtropical evergreen trees that are members of the soapberry family and native to southern China, where they have been cultivated for at least 2,000 years. Only the pulp of the ripe fruit is eaten; the skin and seeds are inedible. Peeled, litchis look like large white grapes and have a sweet fragrance and flavor. Their appearance in the Western world began in 1775, when they were introduced in Jamaica, and now litchis are cultivated in Hawaii, California, and Florida (Florida's first crop was in 1916), as well as other tropical and subtropical areas of the world. Litchis are eaten raw, are also preserved and canned, and are high in vitamin C. In addition, dried litchis are consumed for their smoky flavor. Often called litchi nuts or litchis, these are not the central seeds – which are never eaten – but rather the raisinlike pulp.

Common names and synonyms: Leechee, lichee, lichi, litchi nut, lychee, lychi.

Litchi nut - *see* **LITCHI**

Little barley - *see* **WILD BARLEY**

LITTLE GOOSEBERRY TREE - Also called the "jungle plum," the little gooseberry tree (*Buchanania arborescens*) produces a wild, plumlike fruit that has served as food in the Australian bush for millennia.

Common names and synonyms: Jungle plum.

Little red banana - *see* **ENSETE**

Little stinker - *see* **CREOSOTE BUSH**

Liver fistulina - *see* **MUSHROOMS AND FUNGI**

Livingstone potato - *see* **KAFFIR POTATO**

Llerén - *see* **GUINEA ARROWROOT**

Llerenes - *see* **GUINEA ARROWROOT**

LOCAL GARDEN EGG - A close relative of the eggplant, the "local garden egg" (*Solanum incanum* and *S. macrocarpon*) comes in two forms. These are both cultivated in West Africa, even though the plants are generally regarded as wild forms of the eggplant. *Solanum incanum* is also known as the "bitter tomato" and is used in soups and stews to add flavor. *Solanum macrocarpon* is utilized more like the eggplant in that it is sliced and fried or cooked as a vegetable.

Common names and synonyms: Bitter tomato.

LOCUST (*see also* **AFRICAN LOCUST, AFRICAN LOCUST BEAN, CAROB, HONEY LOCUST, MESQUITE**) - A tall tree of eastern North America, also known as the "black locust," the locust tree (*Robinia pseudoacacia*) provided much in the way of food for Native Americans. Its edible flowers were sweet treats that were also used to make a tea; the young pods were cooked as a vegetable; and the seeds were boiled and eaten.

Common names and synonyms: Black locust, honey locust.

Locust bean - *see* **AFRICAN LOCUST BEAN, CAROB**

LOGANBERRY (*see also* **BERRIES, BLACKBERRY**) - The loganberry (*Rubus loganobaccus*) was produced in 1881 (it is a hybrid) by Judge James H. Logan (1841-1928) in Santa Cruz, California, and was introduced commercially in 1882. The red berry (similar to a blackberry) grows on a prickly bramble shrub, and although its parentage has been a matter of some debate, it would seem that it is a hybrid of the blackberry and the red raspberry. At one time it was grown commercially in California and the Pacific Northwest but proved overly susceptible to disease. Now loganberries generally are grown only in home gardens.

LONGAN - Sometimes called "dragon's-eyes," longans (*Euphoria longan* = *Dimocarpus longan*) are related to litchis. They are native to Southeast Asia and popular in southern China but are not a major crop outside of Asia, although a small one is raised in Florida. The fruit grows in clusters in the depths of thick evergreen trees that can reach up to 36 feet in height and 40 or more feet in circumference. This sweet fruit ranges in size from that of a grape to that of a plum. It is covered by a brown shell and has a whitish, jelly-like fruit with a single dark seed in the middle. Longans are usually eaten raw and are very high in vitamin C. They are also available canned.

Common names and synonyms: Cat's-eye, dragon's-eye, long an, longyen, lungan.

Long an - *see* **LONGAN**

Long bean - *see* **COWPEA, WINGED BEAN**

LONG CORIANDER - Also called "false coriander" and "fitweed," long coriander (*Eryngium foetidum*) is an herb with long, stiff, green leaves that have serrated edges and give off a strong smell when crushed. The plant is probably a native of China, where it has been used for thousands of years as a medicine as well as a substitute for coriander – both as a garnish and in cooking. The Chinese carried the long coriander throughout Asia, and it is now cultivated in Malaysia and India. It reached Europe in the seventeenth century and is also grown there.

Common names and synonyms: False coriander, fitweed.

See also: "Spices and Flavorings," Part II, Section F, Chapter 1.

Long-fruited jute - *see* **JEW'S-MALLOW**

Long green chilli - *see* **ANAHEIM, NEW MEXICO CHILLIES**

Longleaf ephedra - *see* **MORMON TEA**

Long pepper - *see* **PEPPER(CORNS)**

Long-podded cowpea - *see* **WINGED BEAN**

Long red chilli - *see* **ANAHEIM**

Longyen - *see* **LONGAN**

Lontar palm - *see* **WINE PALM**

Loose-leaf lettuce - *see* **LETTUCE**

LOQUAT - A native of eastern Asia, the loquat (*Eriobotrya japonica*) is a small tree of the rose family (Rosaceae), with fragrant white flowers and is often grown as an ornamental. It bears a popular Asian fruit - sometimes called the Japanese medlar or plum - that resembles an apricot in its yellow coloring, shape (like a pear), and tart flavor. The loquat originated in China and, after its introduction in Japan, was expanded into 10 or more species. Many uses have been found for this fruit in pies, jams, and salads, and in the production of liquors. It is also eaten fresh, stewed, candied, and preserved. Today, the fruit is grown in California, Florida, Hawaii, southern Europe, and Israel as well as East Asia. Loquats, however, are delicate fruits that are difficult to ship because they bruise easily. Canned loquats preserved in syrup are probably more widely available. Loquats are a fine source of beta-carotene.

Common names and synonyms: Advance, Champagne, Early Red, Japanese medlar, Japanese plum, nispero, Premier, tanaka, thales.

LOTUS - There are about 90 species of the water-lily family (Nymphaeaceae), many of which have served as food. The "sacred lotus" (*Nelumbo nucifera*), for example, is a perennial aquatic plant of India that was carried to China and to Egypt, where it was consumed at least 4,000 years ago. The poor in Egypt frequently have eaten the seeds and rhizome of the Egyptian lotus (*Nymphaea lotus*), boiled, dried, and ground into flour. Native Americans employed the yellow American marsh lotus (*Nelumbo lutea*) in much the same fashion, and the women would gather the roots of plants of the genus *Nuphar* from the lairs of beavers and muskrats that had collected them for their own use. The Chinese have eaten the rhizome of their pink lotus (*Nelumbo nucifera*) since ancient times and have used lotus leaves for wrapping food. In India, lotus is employed in curries, and all Asians appreciate its crunchy texture and its appearance. The tuberous roots have air tunnels, so that, when sliced, the crisp round looks like a piece of Swiss cheese or – perhaps a better description – a lacy-patterned snowflake. Lotus roots are sliced, chopped, and grated for soups, salads, and stir-frying.

Common names and synonyms: American marsh lotus, blue lotus, blue water lily, Chinese pink lotus, Egyptian lotus flower, Hindu sacred lotus, Libyan lotus, lotus root, water lily, water-lily tuber.

Lotus root - *see* **LOTUS**

LOVAGE - As is the case with numerous herbs employed at least since the time of the ancient Greeks and Romans, many uses for the seeds, leaves, and roots of lovage (*Levisticum officinale*) have been long forgotten. The plant, a native of Europe, looks like angelica, and in fact, its stems are candied like those of angelica. The leaves, however, are parsley-like, which has given rise to other names such as "Italian parsley," "love parsley," and "wild parsley." Yet lovage tastes very much like celery, and in parts of Italy the roots are peeled and cooked like celery root. Most uses, however, involve the leaves, which can be obtained fresh or dried (those that are dried retain their strong flavor), and sometimes the dried seeds, which are added to soups, salads, stuffings, and stews.

Common names and synonyms: Common lovage, garden lovage, Italian lovage, Italian parsley, love parsley, smallage, wild parsley.

Lovegrass - *see* **TEF**

Love-in-a-mist - *see* **NIGELLA**

Love-in-winter - *see* **PIPSISSEWA**

Love-lies-bleeding - *see* **AMARANTH**

Love parsley - *see* **LOVAGE**

Lovi-lovi - *see* **THORNLESS RUKAM**

Lucerne - *see* **ALFALFA**

LUCUMA - A native of South America that is partial to the coolness of highlands, the lucuma (*Pouteria obovata*) is, as its species name suggests, an egg-shaped fruit, also called eggfruit. It is yellow when mature and has a yellow flesh that is sometimes eaten raw but more often made into a drink. In Chile and Peru, where the lucuma is a commercial crop of some importance, the fruits are normally dried and ground into a powder that is stirred into milk.

Common names and synonyms: Eggfruit.

Lulo - *see* **NARANJILLA**

Lulu - *see* **AVOCADO**

Lungan - *see* **LONGAN**

Lupine(s) - *see* **ANDEAN LUPIN, BEANS**

Lupino - *see* **ANDEAN LUPIN, BEANS**

Lychee nut - *see* **LITCHI**

Lychi - *see* **LITCHI**

MABOLO - A relative of the persimmon and native to the Philippines but uncommon elsewhere, this fruit (*Diospyros discolor*) is also called the "velvet apple" from the reddish brown, peachlike hair that covers its thin skin. In fact, its shape is much like that of a peach. The skin may be pink or brown and turn a brilliant red in late summer when the fruit is ripe. Then it is eaten mostly fresh, skin and all, after the hairy covering has been rubbed off. But the mabolo is also made into desserts. Its flesh is creamy, its taste is sweet and slightly acidic, and its aroma is said to be reminiscent of cheese. For some, the taste may have to be an acquired one.

Common names and synonyms: Mabulo, velvet apple.

Mabulo - *see* **MABOLO**

MACA - A turnip-like plant of the mustard family, maca (*Lepidium meyenii*) was one of the root crops of the ancient Incas and has been cultivated for at least 2,000 years. Its small leaves are edible, and the small roots can be roasted or made into a gruel. Today, the plant is cultivated only on small plots at high altitudes in Peru, where strong winds and cold temperatures limit other crops. Peasants there believe that eating maca will help infertile couples to have children.

MACADAMIA NUT – Always in demand even though they contain more fat and calories than any of their counterparts, macadamia nuts are actually divided into two species, *Macadamia integrifolia* and *M. tetraphylla*. They represent one of Australia's few contributions to the food plants of the world (they were first called "Queensland nuts" by early white settlers). The nuts of *M. integrifolia* come from an evergreen tree native to the rain forests of southeastern Queensland, whereas *M. tetraphylla* is found farther south – in the rain forests of New South Wales.

Until 1858, they were enjoyed almost exclusively by the Aborigines, who had gathered them every autumn for millennia. But in that year a German botanist engaged in collecting Australian botanical specimens encountered and described a new genus of trees, which he named *Macadamia* in honor of an Australian friend, Dr. John Macadam (d. 1865).

Macadamia trees were introduced into Hawaii in 1881 and after 1930 became the basis of a major industry there. Indeed, at one time Hawaii produced some 90 percent of the world's supply, and macadamias remain one of that state's most important crops. However, Australian efforts over the past 30 years have begun to threaten the Hawaiian dominance of world production, and the nuts are grown in California as well. Impossible to open without some kind of nutcracker, macadamias have a superb crunch and taste has recommend them to the rarefied world of the gourmet – with a corresponding price. The nuts are a good source of protein and carbohydrates and are fairly high in magnesium and thiamine as well as iron.

Common names and synonyms: Australian nut, Queensland nut.

MACAW PALM – The macaw palm is also called "macaw tree" and *macaúba,* and these names are used for several species of the genus *Acrocomia,* which provide fruits that yield both pulp and kernel oil. Macaw palms grow throughout Central and South America in dry regions, where African oil palms do not do well. In some instances, the violet-scented oil is used only in perfumery, but in others the oils produced are edible and used in cooking.

Common names and synonyms: Macaúba, macaw tree.

MACE (*see also* **NUTMEG**) – This spice tastes like strong nutmeg, which is understandable, as mace is the lacy covering (aril) of the nutmeg berry. The berry fruits on an evergreen (*Myristica fragrans* = *M. officinalis*) that is a native of the Moluccas in the Spice Islands. After harvesting (several times a year), the berries are put in the sun to dry, and the mace is removed by hand and flattened into "blades" to dry separately from the nutmeg. Mace and nutmeg moved slowly westward, apparently reaching the Byzantine court in the sixth century. In the eleventh century, the famous Arab physician Avicenna described the two spices, and, in the following century, they seem to have reached Europe via Arab traders. Initially, however, they were used for perfumes or in medicines and only gradually found culinary applications.

After the Portuguese moved into the Spice Islands, they established a monopoly on mace and nutmeg as well as on cloves. The Dutch succeeded them as monopolists and worked zealously to prevent the export of any nutmeg trees. But during the wars of the eighteenth and nineteenth centuries, the islands were shuttled back and forth between Dutch and English domination, and – to be on the safe side – the latter took the opportunity to remove some of the trees to Singapore and to the West Indies. Today, the island of Grenada produces about 40 percent of the world's mace and nutmeg, although the trees are also grown in Brazil, Colombia, Central America, and Madagascar. Mace is available whole in "blades" and in ground form. It is used mostly in puddings, cakes, and sauces, and in poultry and fish dishes.

See in addition: "Spices and Flavorings," Part II, Section F, Chapter 1.

Mache – *see* **CORNSALAD**

Mâche – *see* **CORNSALAD**

Macho pepper – *see* **TEPÍN CHILLIES AND RELATIVES**

Macrette – *see* **CORAL BEAN**

Madeira – *see* **MALVASIA**

Maggistan – *see* **MANGOSTEEN**

Maguey – *see* **AGAVE**

MAHAWASOO – A South American tree, the mahawasoo (*Vaupesia cataractarum*) produces toxic oilseeds that are rendered edible by boiling. In the past, the seeds served as a famine food for Native Indians in the northwestern Amazon Basin, who also consumed them in connection with various ceremonial rites.

MAHUA – Native to the Indian subcontinent, mahua (*Madhuca longifolia*) is an evergreen tree, the seeds of which yield an oil that substitutes for butter and is used in cooking. The tree's flowers are also eaten and employed in the production of liqueurs. India is the major producer of mahua.

Maidenhair tree – *see* **GINKGO NUT**

MAIZE – Maize (*Zea mays*), native to the Americas and now the second-largest cereal crop in the world, has been one of the most versatile cultivated food plants in human history. Hundreds of varieties of maize (or "corn," as it is generally called in the United States) thrive in an astonishing assortment of geographic regions and environmental conditions, and the crop is employed in a number of ways, ranging from its increasing role as a staple food for humans in certain developing areas, to its principal present use as a feed for livestock animals (largely but not solely in industrialized countries), to its growing importance as a raw material in food processing and nonfood manufacturing.

It is usually accepted that maize was growing in Mesoamerica by between 8000 and 5000 B.C. Reliable archaeological evidence of domesticated maize dates from as long ago as 3600 B.C. in what is now central Mexico, and it is thought that domestication of the crop first took place - doubtless at a much earlier date - in this general area. To the south, a separate domestication of maize may have been accomplished at about the same time by South American Indians in the central Andes, or the crop may simply have traveled to that area from its point of origin. To the north, however, there seems to be no doubt that domesticated maize arrived much later, with locally adapted varieties appearing in the Eastern Woodlands of North America around A.D. 200 and in the central portion of the continent by about A.D. 600.

Indigenous American societies intensively cultivated maize, and it became a principal staple of the Aztecs, the Inca, the Maya, and many groups of North American Indians - especially those in what is now the southeastern United States - for several centuries before the arrival of Europeans. All parts of the plant were used for food and other purposes; the Inca even made maize "beers," known collectively as *chicha*. It is interesting that New World natives and their forebears - the original cultivators and consumers of maize - did not suffer from pellagra, the dangerous nutritional deficiency disease (caused by a lack of niacin, one of the B-vitamins) that has plagued most of the world's maize-eating peoples for centuries. This apparent immunity caused much puzzlement among medical researchers until it was realized that the Native American customs of preparing maize grain in alkali solutions and frequently consuming the grain in combination with leguminous vegetables tended to increase both the niacin availability and the protein quality of maize, thus greatly improving its nutritional value. But when maize was adopted as a staple food by Old World populations, and by non-natives (blacks and whites) in North America, these customs failed to accompany it, with pellagra the result.

Christopher Columbus carried maize to Spain, where by 1500 or so it was under cultivation. Before many years had passed, maize was being grown throughout the Iberian and Italian peninsulas and had appeared as a garden vegetable in England and central Europe; it had also entered eastern Europe via the Balkans and areas along the Danube River. By the seventeenth century, maize had become an important European field crop and staple food, especially in those areas that now comprise northern Italy, Romania, Slovenia, Serbia, and Bulgaria, in addition to Spain; perhaps a century

later, it was a principal dietary item in Austria-Hungary and southern France as well.

As the new crop spread across Europe, its New World origins were largely forgotten, but in each locality people at least knew that it came from somewhere else, and it was called "Barbary corn," "Egyptian corn," "Guinea corn," and a host of other names. "Corn" was a generic word meaning simply "grain" in a number of European languages, so that its many aliases actually identified maize as "foreign grain," and the American usage of "corn" for maize grows out of such terminology - in this case, "corn" is the shortened version of the English term "Indian corn," by which the colonists meant, of course, "Indian grain," or maize.

During the sixteenth century, Portuguese traders carried the plant to East Africa and Asia, whereas Arab merchants were probably responsible for its introduction into North Africa. Somewhat later, maize reached West Africa from the Caribbean and was used on both sides of the Atlantic as an inexpensive means of provisioning the human cargoes of the slave trade. The crop spread rapidly throughout the African continent, greatly augmenting the food supply, had become a major staple by the end of the nineteenth century, and even increased in importance by the late twentieth century. In Asia, maize spread along trade routes from the Indian subcontinent, reaching points in China and Southeast Asia by the mid-sixteenth century. It was established in the Philippines and Indonesia during the seventeenth century, and during the eighteenth was much expanded as a crop in China. From there, it spread to Korea and Japan.

Meanwhile, in North America, the early English colonists as well as later immigrants (unlike their Spanish predecessors) had adopted maize as a staple food, and the grain later became the foundation of the U.S. diet and the country's agricultural economy. Countless American dishes and recipes testify to the early pervasiveness of "corn" in direct human consumption, and beginning about the turn of the nineteenth century, U.S. farmers and gardeners began to develop a number of varieties of sweet corn for use as a vegetable (sweet varieties had, however, existed long before this in South America). Moreover, from the mid-nineteenth century onward, U.S. agricultural scientists took the lead in creating hybrid maize varieties with greatly increased grain yields and other desirable characteristics, and with the growth of American livestock industries, the value of "corn" for feeding animals destined to become food themselves surpassed even its importance as a human staple.

Today, maize provides the basis for a number of commercial and industrial products as well as human foods, including starches, sweeteners, corn "flakes" and other packaged breakfast cereals, corn "chips," corn oil, corn syrup, whiskeys, beers, ethanol, plastics, and – most important – animal feed.

Maize is a good source of carbohydrates, and thus of calories and energy, and is high in protein and certain essential fatty acids. But its protein quality is marginal, with low levels of the essential amino acids tryptophan and lysine. It is also low in calcium, and white maize is low in vitamin A.

Common names and synonyms: Bactrian typha, Barbary corn, *blé de Turquie,* corn, cornmeal, *cucurutz,* dent maize, Egyptian corn, flint maize, floury maize, Guinea corn, Indian corn, Indian meal, *kana,* mealies, *milho,* popcorn, Roman corn, *sara chulpi,* Sicilian corn, Spanish corn, sweet corn, Syrian dourra, Turkie corne, Turkish wheat, Virginia wheat, waxy maize, Welsch corn, yellow maize.

See also: "Maize," Part II, Section A, Chapter 4.

Maja pahit - *see* QUINCE

MALABAR ALMOND - Also called the "Indian almond," the "country almond," and the "tropical almond," the Malabar almond (*Terminalia catappa*) is an evergreen tree of tropical Asia – probably a native of the Malay Peninsula, although it is now planted in North America and elsewhere as an ornamental. The fruit is about 2 inches long and red to green in color, and its pulp is eaten for its sweet flavor. The almond-shaped kernel inside the fruit is also eaten both raw and roasted, but first it is necessary to break its very tough shell.

Common names and synonyms: Country almond, Indian almond, tropical almond.

Malabar chestnut - *see* MALABAR NUT

Malabar gourd - *see* FIG-LEAFED GOURD, SQUASH AND PUMPKIN

MALABAR NUT - A nut known by a number of common names such as "Guyana chestnut" and "French peanut," the malabar nut also has two scientific names – *Bombax glabra* and *Pachira aquatica.* A native of the tropical estuaries in a region that stretches from southern Mexico to Guyana and northern Brazil, the malabar nut grows on an attractive evergreen tree. The fruit is a relatively large green pod (4 to 12 inches long and 2 to 2.5 inches in diameter), which contains the nuts until it finally bursts to spill them on the ground. Consumed fresh, the nuts have a flavor reportedly like that of peanuts; when roasted or fried, the taste resembles that of chestnuts. The nuts are also ground into flour for bread, and the young leaves and flowers of the tree are cooked as a vegetable. Another Malabar nut, *Adhatoda vasica,* comes from an East Indian shrub and is used medicinally.

Common names and synonyms: French peanut, Guiana chestnut, Guyana chestnut, Malabar chestnut, provision tree, saba nut.

MALABAR SPINACH - Also called "red vine spinach," malabar spinach (*Basella rubra* = *B. alba*) is a plant of the Asian tropics that has now spread around the world to be cultivated in most tropical and temperate regions. In the Western Hemisphere, malabar spinach is grown in Mexico and parts of North America for its succulent leaves that are used in the same ways as spinach – as a potherb and raw in salads.

Common names and synonyms: Ceylon spinach, Indian spinach, red vine spinach, vine spinach.

Malacca tree - *see* AMALAKA

Malagueta (pepper) - *see* BRAZILIAN MALAGUETA, MELEGUETA PEPPER

MALANGA - When the Spaniards arrived in the West Indies, one of the first native American plants they described was *yautía* – still the Puerto Rican name for malanga. However, this leads us straight into a semantic jungle, because the plant is also called "tania," "elephant's-ear," and a score of other names, including "cocoyam" (which it is not) in Africa. Contributing to the confusion are some 40 species of malanga, many of which are mixed up with taro (*Colocasia esculenta*).

Perhaps the most important distinction to be made is that between white malanga (*Xanthosoma sagittifolium* = *X. violaceum*) and yellow (*X. atrovirens*). White malanga is tania and *yautía* and was also called "dasheen" historically in the West Indies – a name that also is used to refer to taro. However, white malanga is not cultivated for its tuber (as taro is) but rather for its stem and heart leaves, known in the West Indies as callaloo.

Yellow malanga, in contrast, is cultivated for a corm that is shaped like a big yam and is cooked in much the same ways, by boiling, steaming, baking, frying, or roasting. In Africa, the corms are sometimes ground to make "foo-foo." Malanga most probably originated in South America and was brought to the Caribbean Islands by migrating Taino and Carib Indians. It made another leap when it was introduced into West Africa – to feed slaves bound for the Americas – and took root there as one kind of cocoyam. Today, malanga is also cultivated in Central America, the Pacific Islands, and tropical Asia. Malanga provides mostly energy in the form of carbohydrates, although the yellow variety does contain a little vitamin A.

Common names and synonyms: American taro, callaloo, cocoyam, dasheen, elephant's-ear, kong(-)kong taro, spoonflower, tania, tannia, white malanga, *yautía,* yellow malanga.

See also: "Taro," Part II, Section B, Chapter 6.

Malangay - *see* COCOYAM

Malangu - *see* COCOYAM

MALAY APPLE - A native of Indonesia, the jambu merah tree has been cultivated for millennia. In the past few centuries, the Portuguese spread its fruit, the Malay apple (*Eugenia malaccensis* = *Syzygium malaccense*), throughout the tropical Old World, and the English brought it to the West Indies in the New World. Malay apples are oblong, about the size of a large orange, and red or crimson when ripe. They are generally eaten raw.

Common names and synonyms: Jambu merah (tree), Tahiti apple.

Malay gooseberry - *see* **OTAHEITE GOOSEBERRY**

Malka - *see* **CLOUDBERRY**

MALLOW - Native to Europe, several herbs of the Malvaceae family are called mallows and are employed to flavor cheese. In the United States, the best known of the mallows is the marsh mallow (*Althaea officinalis*). The plant was so called because it was found in and around marshes near the sea, and it has been naturalized in the marshes of eastern North America. In past centuries, the roots of the marsh mallow were used to flavor candy "marshmallows," which are now made with sugar, corn syrup, gelatin, and starch, then dusted with a little powdered sugar.

Common names and synonyms: Marsh mallow.

Malmsey - *see* **MALVASIA**

MALOGA BEAN - Also called the "flowering bean," the maloga bean (*Vigna lancelota*) is an Australian tree whose roots served as food for the Aborigines.

Common names and synonyms: Flowering bean.

Malt - *see* **BARLEY**

Maltaise orange - *see* **BLOOD ORANGE**

Maltese Blood (orange) - *see* **BLOOD ORANGE**

Maltese orange - *see* **BLOOD ORANGE**

MALVASIA (*see also* **GRAPES**) - An ancient fruit of Greece, Malvasia grapes (*Vitis vinifera*) were used during the Middle Ages to make sweet dessert wines that were frequently shipped from the Greek port of Monemvasia. The name Malvasia is an Italian corruption of that city's name, just as *malvoisie* is a French corruption and "malmsey" an English one. Actually, the name "Malvasia" refers today to a complex of varieties; these are among Italy's most widely planted grapes and constitute an important part of the grape crop of Spain as well. Those planted are mostly white, but there are also red grapes, and both sweet and dry wines are made from them. In addition, the Malvasia lives on in Madeira wine, which has traditionally been based on this grape.

Common names and synonyms: Madeira, malmsey, malvoisie.

See in addition: "Wine," Part III, Chapter 13.

Malvoisie - *see* **MALVASIA**

MAMEY SAPOTE - Little known outside the American tropics, the mamey (also mammey) sapote (*Calocarpum sapota = Pouteria sapota*) is related to the sapodilla and is found chiefly in Central America, Mexico, northern South America, Cuba, Hispaniola, and the state of Florida. The light, coffee-colored fruit grows on medium-sized trees. It is a large fruit, weighing up to a pound, with a rough, brown skin. The flesh is salmon colored and surrounds a large avocado-like pit. It has a rich and distinctive flavor, not appreciated by everyone. The mamey sapote is a good source of vitamins A and C.

Common names and synonyms: Mammey sapote, sapota.

MAMMEE - The tropical American mammee (*Mammea americana*) is native to the West Indies (and its fruits are common in markets there) but is now grown in the tropics and subtropics around the world, including Florida. Also known as the mammee apple and the San Domingo apricot, the fruit grows on trees that can reach 60 feet in height. It is about the size of a small grapefruit and tastes something like a tart apple while still green and something like an apricot when it is ripe and stewed. The fruit is sometimes eaten raw and in salads but is generally cooked. Mammee flowers are used to make an aromatic liqueur called *eau de Créole*. The mammee is not related to the mamey sapote.

Common names and synonyms: Mammee apple, mammy apple, San Domingo apricot, South American apricot.

Mammee apple - *see* **MAMMEE**

Mammee sapota - *see* **SAPODILLA**

Mammey sapote - *see* **MAMEY SAPOTE**

Mammy apple - *see* **MAMMEE**

Mamoncilla - *see* **SPANISH LIME**

Mamoncillo - *see* **SPANISH LIME**

Manchurian wild rice - *see* **WATER BAMBOO**

Mandarin melon-berry - *see* **CHE**

MANDARIN ORANGE (*see also* **CITRUS FRUITS**) - Other citrus fruits that are very similar (or identical) to the Mandarin orange include the tangerine, the *satsuma,* and the "Clementine," all of which are identified as members of *Citrus reticulata* and orange varieties. The Mandarin - developed in China, or possibly Cochin China (southern Vietnam) - probably took its name from the yellow robes of the Chinese civil servants called Mandarins. It worked its way toward the Near East at a leisurely pace and reached Europe directly from China only at the beginning of the nineteenth century. By midcentury, Mandarin oranges were being grown around the Mediterranean, and they entered the United States at about the same time. Believed to have originated in Tangier, they came to be known as tangerines in North America.

The Clementine - a cross between the Mandarin and the bitter orange - originated in Algiers, whereas the *satsuma* is a seedless Japanese Mandarin. In the early 1870s, Florida orange grower Col. George L. Dancy pioneered commercial tangerine cultivation, and the Dancy tangerine became the most popular of the Mandarin oranges. Florida remains the largest tangerine producer, although the fruits are also grown in California, Texas, and Louisiana. In 1898, U.S. Department of Agriculture botanist Walter Tennyson Swingle developed the tangelo, a cross between a tangerine and a grapefruit. All fruits belonging to *C. reticulata* are small, sweet, easily peeled, and segmented.

Common names and synonyms: Clementine, Dancy tangerine, *satsuma*, tangelo, tangerine.

Mandioc - *see* **MANIOC**

Mandioca - *see* **MANIOC**

MANDRAKE (*see also* **MAYAPPLE**) - An herb of southern Europe and North Africa, the mandrake (*Mandragora officinarum*) has spherical yellow fruits that in the past were believed to have aphrodisiacal properties. This was doubtless because the plant has a long forked root that was believed to resemble the human body from the waist down and was the subject of much sexual superstition. It was also a narcotic. The root was ground and used to encourage a sense of well-being, and possibly of enhanced sexuality.

Manga - *see* **MANGO**

MANGABA - An interesting vine (*Hancornia speciosa*) of Brazil called *mangabeira* produces the mangaba fruits, which are plum-sized and red and have a sweet taste. The same plant also produces a latex that yields a rubber.

Common names and synonyms: Mangabeira.

Mangabeira - *see* **MANGABA**

Man-gay - *see* **MANGO**

Mangel - *see* **BEET**

MANGELWURZEL (*see also* **BEET**) - From the German *Mangold-Wurzel,* meaning "beet root," the mangelwurzel is a variety of the common beet (*Beta vulgaris*) that is chiefly produced for cattle feed, although the young beets are sometimes consumed by humans.

Common names and synonyms: Mangle, mangold, mangold-wurzel.

Mangetout - *see* **PEAS, SUGAR PEA**

Mangga - *see* **MANGO**

Manggis - *see* **MANGOSTEEN**

Manggusta - *see* **MANGOSTEEN**

Mangle - *see* **MANGELWURZEL**

MANGO (*see also* **DUIKA, HORSE MANGO**) - The mango tree (*Mangifera indica*) is an Asian evergreen that can attain a height of 100 feet or more. It is cultivated throughout the tropics of the world, most abundantly in India (where it may have originated and where the mango is connected with both folklore and religious ceremonies) for its greenish yellow fruit, much of which is made into chutney. Mango flesh surrounds a flat but rounded seed or stone and is sweet and golden, even though the skin is tough and inedible. Mangoes are eaten ripe and pickled when green.

All of the 40-some species of *Mangifera* are Southeast Asian in origin, and some may have been domesticated as early as 4,000 to 6,000 years ago. Exactly how they were subsequently dispersed around the world is a matter of conjecture. The Portuguese (who named the fruit *manga*) doubtless had a hand in this in the sixteenth century, taking the mango to islands of the Pacific, throughout the Indian Ocean, and to the east and west coasts of Africa. Mangoes were planted in Brazil around 1700, were carried to the West Indies (where they remain extremely popular) at about the middle of the eighteenth century, and reached Florida (which now produces about 20 percent of the world's mangoes) in North America in the early nineteenth century.

Mangoes belong to the Anacardiaceae family, which includes poison ivy, and for those who are allergic, touching mango juice can cause the skin to swell and blister. For some reason, Midwesterners in the United States call sweet bell peppers "mangoes"; both are good sources of vitamin A and a great source of vitamin C and potassium, not to mention fiber. The mango kernel is also eaten after it is boiled or roasted.

Common names and synonyms: Manga, man-gay, mangga, man-kay.

Mangold - *see* **MANGELWURZEL**

Mangold-Wurzel - *see* **MANGELWURZEL**

MANGO MELON (*see also* **MELONS**) - The genus *Cucumis* embraces the different species of melons and cucumbers. The mango melon (*C. melo* var. *chito*) is a muskmelon that is mistakenly called a mango, and the fact that it is also known as a "lemon cucumber" further indicates a considerable popular ambivalence about this fruit's identity. It is a small melon - about the size of an orange, with a yellow skin and white flesh - and is cultivated primarily for making preserves and "mango pickles."

Common names and synonyms: Lemon cucumber.

See in addition: "Cucumbers, Melons, and Watermelons," Part II, Section C, Chapter 6.

Mango squash - *see* **CHAYOTE**

Mangostan - *see* **MANGOSTEEN**

MANGOSTEEN - This fruit, native to Malaya, enjoys a reputation among those who should know as the world's most delicious fruit. Actually a berry (and unrelated to the mango), the mangosteen (*Garcinia mangostana*) is the size of a small- to medium-sized orange, and at first glance with its purplish leathery skin looks something like a pomegranate. Its flesh is juicy, pink- or cream-colored, and somewhat tart; its taste blends the flavors of grape and strawberry by some accounts and those of peach and pineapple according to others.

The Portuguese called the fruit *manggusta* and later mangistão and *maggistan,* but by the seventeenth century it had become "mangostan" and eventually "mangosteen." It was described by Captain James Cook in 1770, was introduced in Ceylon (Sri Lanka) around 1800, and spread out from there. Today, the fruit is grown in parts of the southern United States, the West Indies, and Central America, as well as Southeast Asia, but nowhere on a commercial scale because it bruises too easily to ship well. A mangosteen is almost always eaten raw.

Common names and synonyms: King-of-fruits, *maggistan,* manggis, *manggusta,* mangostan, men-gu.

MANGROVE (*see also* **BURMA MANGROVE, TAGAL MANGROVE, NIPA PALM**) – The fruits and leaves of mangroves have long been used as food by indigenous peoples – especially during hard times. On the coasts of tropical America, West Africa, and the islands of Polynesia, the mangrove in question is the red mangrove (*Rhizophora mangle*), the fruit of which, with its starchy interior, can be eaten both fresh and preserved. Moreover, a light wine has been made from its fermented juice. In the Old World tropics (from South and East Africa to southern China, Australia, Melanesia, and Micronesia), the plant is the Asiatic mangrove (*R. mucronata*). This fruit would seem to be sweeter than its New World counterpart and, again, can be made into a light wine. Both plants have also long been a part of the pharmacopoeia of folk medicines.

Common names and synonyms: American mangrove, Asiatic mangrove, red mangrove.

Mani – *see* **PEANUT**

Manihot – *see* **MANIOC**

Manila bean – *see* **WINGED BEAN**

Manila tamarind – *see* **PITHECELLOBIUM**

Manilla bean – *see* **WINGED BEAN**

MANIOC – The name "manioc" (*Manihot esculenta*) comes from the Brazilian Indian word *mandioca,* but the plant is also known as cassava, yuca, and the tapioca-plant. A Brazilian native, it is a perennial shrub with long, narrow, starchy tubers. Manioc traveled in canoes with South American Indians migrating northward into the Caribbean and, later, in Portuguese ships from Brazil to Africa. Its advantages are that it requires little labor to cultivate yet produces more calories per acre than any other food plant, and it keeps in the ground until needed.

A disadvantage is that save for carbohydrates, it has little to offer in the way of nutrients. Another is that although sweet manioc varieties pose no threat, the roots of most varieties are bitter and can contain enough cyanide to be toxic. The poison must first be removed by pounding, scraping, and cooking. The vegetable is then boiled or baked like a potato, made into a flour for breads, and employed to thicken soup. The meal or flour is sprinkled onto most any dish. Tapioca is a kind of manioc flour.

Common names and synonyms: Cassava, mandioc, *mandioca,* manihot, tapioca-plant, yuca.

See also: "Manioc," Part II, Section B, Chapter 2.

Man-kay – *see* **MANGO**

MANNA – Some of the lichens of the genus *Lecanora* are called manna, presumably because one of them, *L. esculenta,* (a kind of moss containing a fungus that grows on trees, rocks, and stones and is blown about the desert), is reputed to be the manna that dropped out of heaven in ancient times to sustain the Israelites in their flight from Egypt. In the Mid-

dle East, lichen bread and manna jelly are made from it. Another "manna lichen" is *Gyrophora esculenta,* which is widely eaten in Japan.

Common names and synonyms: Manna lichen.

MANNA GUM – Also known as "manna eucalyptus" and "gum tree," the manna gum (*Eucalyptus viminalis*) is an Australian native (as are all eucalypts) that exudes a red gum or "manna" from punctures or cracks in the bark. This gum, along with the tree's aromatic leaves, was eaten by Australian Aborigines.

Common names and synonyms: Gum tree, manna eucalyptus.

Manna lichen – *see* **MANNA**

MANZANA (*see also* **CHILLI PEPPERS**) – Appearing very much like a small sweet bell pepper, the manzana, with black seeds that distinguish it as a member of *Capsicum pubescens,* has nothing sweet about it. Barely known to consumers in the United States, this pepper (like the other members of *C. pubescens*) originated in South America and migrated north, reaching Mexico and Central America, where it is now cultivated, perhaps as late as a century ago. This hot, deep yellow–colored pepper is frequently stuffed or used in salsas.

Common names and synonyms: Chile caballo, chilli rocoto, manzano.

See in addition: "Chilli Peppers," Part II, Section C, Chapter 4.

Manzanillo (olive) – *see* **OLIVE**

MAPLE SYRUP AND MAPLE SUGAR – Both maple syrup and maple sugar are made from the sap of several varieties of maple trees (*Acer* spp.) and especially from that of the sugar maple (*A. saccharum*). All of these trees are natives of the northern United States and Canada. The sap is collected by boring a tap-hole into the tree, then inserting a spout upon which a sap-bucket is hung. The collected sap is subsequently boiled down into syrup, and the granular residue left when all the liquid is gone is the sugar. Maple sugar (and syrup) was the only sweetener for Native Americans and continued to be the only one used in much of Canada and by some of those in the northeastern United States until fairly recently. The gathering season is in the early spring and ends when the trees begin to bud.

Common names and synonyms: Sugar maple (tree).

Mapuey – *see* **CUSH-CUSH YAM**

Maracuja – *see* **PASSION FRUIT**

Mare's-tail – *see* **HORSEWEED**

MARIGOLD – Although marigolds generally are thought of as members of the genus *Tagetes* and natives of tropical America, this familiar daisy-like flower (*Calendula officinalis*) – the "pot marigold" – is said to have originated in Europe. Its orange petals were used as one of the first coloring agents for cheeses and are sometimes employed as a substitute for saffron in rice dishes. Nowadays, the pot marigold is used much less frequently for seasoning foods than it was in the past, especially in the Middle Ages, when its cultivation began.

Common names and synonyms: Pot marigold, Scotch marigold.

MARJORAM AND OREGANO - Native to the Mediterranean region, oregano (*Origanum vulgare*) is actually a variety of wild marjoram. The name "oregano" comes from a Greek term meaning "joy of the mountains"; indeed, oregano thrives in mountainous terrain, and strongly flavored varieties of this herb - called *rigani* - grow in the mountains of Greece. Marjoram comes as pot marjoram (*O. onites*) and sweet marjoram (*O. majorana*). Both varieties have a flavor similar to, but more delicate than, that of oregano. Although marjoram and oregano have long played an important role in French, Greek, and especially Italian cuisines, it was only with the return of American GIs from Italy after World War II that the two spices became well known in the United States. They are available both fresh and dried and go well in tomato-based dishes. Oregano is the quintessential herb for pizza and is also an important ingredient in chilli powders.

Common names and synonyms: Knotted marjoram, pot marjoram, *rigani*, Spanish oregano, sweet marjoram, wild marjoram.

See also: "Spices and Flavorings," Part II, Section F, Chapter 1.

Marmalade box - *see* **GENIPAP**

Marmalade plum - *see* **SAPODILLA**

Marmelo - *see* **BAEL FRUIT**

MARROW - In the case of plant foods, the term "marrow" in its broadest sense can mean the pulp of any fruit. For the British in particular, "vegetable marrow" or "marrow squash" generally connotes summer squashes with white to green skins like the zucchini (*Cucurbita pepo*). In the eastern United States, however, "marrow" often indicates a huge orange winter squash (*C. maxima*) used in cooking.

Common names and synonyms: Marrow squash, vegetable marrow.

See also: "Squash," Part II, Section C, Chapter 8.

Marrow stem - *see* **KALE**

Marsh-elder - *see* **SUMPWEED**

Marsh mallow - *see* **MALLOW**

Marsh marigold - *see* **COWSLIP**

Marsh salad - *see* **CORNSALAD**

Marsh samphire - *see* **GLASSWORT**

Marsh trefoil - *see* **BOG MYRTLE**

Martynia - *see* **UNICORN PLANT**

MARULA PLUM - A large wild tree of southern Africa, the marula (*Sclerocarya caffra*) has plumlike fruits with a thick yellow peel and white, sweet-sour flesh. They are eaten raw, used to flavor alcoholic beverages, and made into juices and jams. In addition, the seeds of the fruits are eaten like nuts by aficionados, who are clearly enthusiastic about what they call the "king's-nut."

Common names and synonyms: King's-nut.

Marumi - *see* **KUMQUAT**

MASHUA - Also called *anu* (among other common names) and related to the ornamental nasturtium, the carrot- and potato-shaped tubers of mashua (*Tropaeolum tuberosum*) are an important staple in the Andean region, esprcially at altitudes where potatoes and other tubers cannot be grown successfully. The tubers of mashua are not eaten raw, but rather are cured in the sun, then freeze-dried and used like potatoes. The plant is also said to have medicinal properties.

Common names and synonyms: Anu, capucine, *ysaño*.

Mast - *see* **BEECHNUT**

Masterwort - *see* **PURPLESTEM ANGELICA**

MASTIC BULLY - *Sideroxylon mastichodendron* is a tree of South Florida and the West Indies with "ironlike" wood that in the past was useful for shipbuilding. The fruits of this and related species such as *S. foetidissimum* are edible although quite acidic.

MASTIC TREE - Also called "mastic shrub," the mastic tree (*Pistacia lentiscus*) is a small tree grown in southern Europe for mastic (also "lentisk") - a resin obtained by cutting into the tree. Mastic is used mostly for varnishes, paints, and the like, but the word "mastic" also designates an alcoholic beverage flavored with mastic. Another group of trees called mastic trees are South American "pepper trees" (genus *Schinus*), especially *S. molle*, a Peruvian evergreen that has small red drupes - the pink peppercorns that have recently been discovered to be potentially harmful. In the past, a good *chicha* (a beerlike drink) was made from the seeds of the tree they call *molle* in Peru.

Common names and synonyms: Lentisk, mastic shrub, *molle*, pepper tree.

Mat bean - *see* **MOTH BEAN**

Maté - *see* **YERBA MATÉ**

MATRIMONY VINE - Also called "box thorn," *gow kee,* and *chu chi,* the matrimony vine (of the genus *Lycium*) comprises *L. chinense* (originally from East Asia) and a number of species native to the southwestern United States and Mexico, such as *L. andersonii* - the "desert thorn." The tender leaves and shoots were eaten in the past by Native Americans and are still consumed in Asia. In addition, the plants produce red, juicy, oblong berries (known as *frutillos* in Mexico) that are edible but do not seem to excite much enthusiasm. They were put to use as a famine food by Native Americans.

Common names and synonyms: Box thorn, *chu chi,* desert thorn, *frutillo,* gow kee.

Matsutake (mushroom) - *see* **MUSHROOMS AND FUNGI**

Ma-tum - *see* **QUINCE**

MAUKA - Called *mauka* in Bolivia and *chago* (among other terms) in Peru, this plant (*Mirabilis expansa*) constitutes a seeming contradiction: It is a virtually unknown crop with a wide geographic distribution. Grown in the Andes region from Venezuela to Chile in small vegetable gardens, the cultivation of *mauka* was described for the first time only a quarter of a century ago. Both the tuberous roots and the leaves are consumed – the latter in salads and chilli sauces. The roots are used like manioc and are an ingredient in soups and stews.

Common names and synonyms: Chago.

MAVRODAPHNE (*see also* **GRAPES**) – Mavrodaphne is an eastern Mediterranean wine grape (*Vitis vinifera*), which the Greeks in particular have used to make sweet, portlike, dessert wines for many centuries. The name means "black laurel," and the grape is aromatic and powerful.

See in addition: "Wine," Part III, Chapter 13.

Maw seed - *see* **POPPY SEED**

Maya - *see* **PINGUIN**

MAYAPPLE (*see also* **MAYPOP**) – Because it was commonly known as the "American mandrake" or just plain "mandrake," many refrained from eating the mayapple (*Podophyllum peltatum*), fearing that like the mandrake of Europe, it too was poisonous. In fact, the roots, leaves, and seeds of this woodland plant of eastern North America *are* poisonous, but its lemon-shaped fruit is not and is often made into a marmalade. This wild-growing plant with its distinctive white flowers was surely also a food of Native Americans, who probably learned the hard way that only its fruit was edible.

Common names and synonyms: American mandrake, mandrake.

May-bob - *see* **COWSLIP**

Maycock - *see* **MAYPOP**

Mayflower - *see* **TRAILING ARBUTUS**

MAYGRASS – In North America, there are native species of maygrass (*Phalaris caroliniana*) as well as other species of the genus *Phalaris* that have been introduced from the Mediterranean region, from West Africa, and from the Canary Islands (the latter, *P. canariensis*, is called "canary grass"). Their seeds have been used as a grain and the young shoots eaten raw or cooked like a vegetable.

Common names and synonyms: Canary grass.

Mayhaw - *see* **HAWTHORN BERRY**

MAYPOP – A North American cousin to the South American passion fruit, the maypop (*Passiflora incarnata*) grows wild in the southeastern United States. Originally, the plant was called "maycock" after the Powhatan *machawq,* suggesting that Native Americans were familiar with it. The fruit is about the size of a small lemon, has a hint of a lemon taste, and has also been called "mayapple." In addition to the use of the fruit as a food, the leaves, stems, and yellow flowers of maypops have long been used medicinally.

Common names and synonyms: Apricot vine, granadilla, mayapple, maycock, wild passion-flower.

Mazzard - *see* **CHERRY**

Meadow-bright - *see* **COWSLIP**

Meadow fern - *see* **SWEET FERN**

Meadow mushroom - *see* **MUSHROOMS AND FUNGI**

Meadow parsnip - *see* **COW PARSNIP**

Meadow salsify - *see* **MOONFLOWER**

Mediterranean rocket - *see* **ARUGULA**

Medjool date - *see* **DATE**

MEDLAR – Originating in Persia (and possibly also in Europe), the medlar (*Mespilus germanica*) belongs to the apple family but is a small, round, brown fruit that looks like a plum. Medlars were known to the ancient Greeks, and Pliny wrote of the Romans having three kinds. Like so many fruits and vegetables, medlars were carried throughout the Roman Empire and afterward remained very popular in Europe. The fruit traveled with Europeans to North America, where medlar trees now grow from the southern United States to southern Canada. The medlar is interesting in that it is not edible until well after it has achieved ripeness – in fact when it has begun to decay. Its juice makes a fine cold drink, and although the pulp was once consumed raw, most medlars that are used nowadays go into jelly. Medlars are, in fact, becoming a forgotten fruit. This medlar should not be confused with the loquat, which is also called the Japanese medlar.

Meetin' seed - *see* **FENNEL**

Meiwa - *see* **KUMQUAT**

Melano - *see* **KIWANO**

Melanzana - *see* **EGGPLANT**

MELEGUETA PEPPER – Also known as "malagueta pepper" and "grains-of-paradise," melegueta pepper (*Aframomum melegueta*) is the pungent seed of a West African plant. Related to cardamom – and with a similar odor – the tiny grains have a hot and peppery taste and are used as a spice.

Common names and synonyms: Grains-of-paradise, Guinea grains, malagueta pepper.

See also: "Spices and Flavorings," Part II, Section F, Chapter 1.

Melilot - *see* **SWEET CLOVER**

Melissa - *see* **BEE BALM, LEMON BALM**

Melist - *see* **SWEET CLOVER**

Mellarosa - *see* **BERGAMOT**

Melloco - *see* **ULLUCO**

MELON CACTUS – Called "melon-thistle," "Turk's-cap," "Turk's-head," and *melon,* as well as melon cactus, about 35 species in the genus *Melocactus* in one form or another resemble melons and have a bristly crown filled with woolly fibrous matter. Many of these natives of the West Indies, Central America, and tropical South America (especially *M. communis* of Jamaica) bear small, pinkish, edible fruits.

Common names and synonyms: Melon, melon-thistle, Turk's-cap, Turk's-head.

Melon fruit - *see* **PAPAYA**

Melongene - *see* **EGGPLANT**

Melon pawpaw - *see* **PAPAYA**

Melon(-)pear - *see* **PEPINO**

MELONS (*see also* **PUMPKIN, SQUASH AND PUMPKIN,** and various melon entries) - Most melons are members of the extensive Cucurbitaceae or gourd family, along with such diverse relatives as the pumpkins and squashes of the New World and the cucumber of the Old World. Plant expert Charles B. Heiser, Jr., has pointed out that the Latin word *cucurbitare* means (or at least meant) "to commit adultery," and it is the case that melons have interbred so promiscuously that classification is difficult. What follows is a discussion of a few basic melon types.

Save for the watermelon, melons are like winter squashes in structure - with a thick rind and a seed-filled center. The watermelon, by contrast, resembles the cucumber in that its seeds are more evenly dispersed. Watermelons (*Citrullus lanatus = C. vulgaris*) are the first melons to show up in the historical record - about 6,000 years ago in Egyptian tomb art. However, it would appear from archaeological remains that they were in India much earlier - during prehistoric times - and unidentified melons were being cultivated in the Indus Valley about 4,000 years ago. This gives India a claim to be the cradle of melons, but Persia and tropical Africa have also been put forward as likely candidates. Most probably, tropical Africa was the home of the watermelon, and the other melons arose elsewhere - perhaps in both India and the Middle East. Certainly it was Africa that sent watermelons to the Americas via the slave trade, and now they are grown all around the globe.

The past of the other melons, all (along with the cucumber) closely related members of the genus *Cucumis,* is even more obscure. They seem to have been unknown to the ancients, and although Pliny in the first century A.D. apparently mentioned melons, it was not with much enthusiasm. Melons were still thought of as green vegetables - and not particularly good ones at that, unless they were cooked and eaten with plenty of spices. Nonetheless, melons were spread by the Romans throughout their empire; the Moors encouraged melon cultivation in Spain after their invasion in 711; and real enthusiasm for the fruits was expressed for the first time during the fifteenth century, when they became popular at the French court. Sweet melons seem finally to have been developed at this point - perhaps through the patience of Mediterranean gardeners in southern Europe, or perhaps in the Arab world - and were introduced into Europe via the Moors still holding Granada in Spain at the time.

And such development continued. The word for the melon known as cantaloupe (*Cucumis melo* var. *cantalupensis*) comes from Cantalupo, a papal garden near Rome where that variety of melon was born during the Renaissance. Christopher Columbus reached the West Indies with melon seeds, and melons were reported growing in New Mexico by 1540. Later, the Spaniards began cultivating muskmelons in California. In fact, what North Americans call cantaloupes are actually descendants of these muskmelons - the difference basically being that the muskmelon (*Cucumis melo* var. *reticulatus*) has a netted skin, whereas the true cantaloupe of Europe has a scaly or warty rind. Both have flesh ranging in color from orange to green, and both are aromatic. The Persian melon - also aromatic - is a variety of the muskmelon. The winter melons (*Cucumis melo* var. *inodorus*), by contrast, are not aromatic. These include the honeydew (the sweetest of the melons) and the casaba - a melon that has been crossed with the Persian melon to produce the Crenshaw.

Chief among the Asian melons is the bitter melon (*Momordica charantia*) - bitter, among other reasons, because it contains quinine, which has doubtless helped many to live with malaria in the Asian tropics. The bitter melon is braised or steamed and sometimes cut up and stir-fried. The Chinese winter melon or "fuzzy melon" (*Benincasa hispida*) - one of the largest vegetables grown - is also cooked as a vegetable.

All melons are rich in vitamin C and potassium. Those with orange flesh are also a good source of beta-carotene.

Common names and synonyms: Bitter melon, cantaloupe, casaba, Chinese winter melon, Crenshaw (melon), fuzzy melon, honeydew, muskmelon, Ogen melon, Oriental melon, Persian melon, sweet melon, watermelon, winter melon.

See in addition: "Cucumbers, Melons, and Watermelons," Part II, Section C, Chapter 6.

Melonshrub - *see* **PEPINO**

Melon-thistle - *see* **MELON CACTUS**

Men-gu - *see* **MANGOSTEEN**

Merkel - *see* **MOREL**

MERLOT (*see also* **GRAPES**) - A red grape, the Merlot (*Vitis vinifera*) produces a wine that has been used mostly to blend with other wines but is now achieving an identity of its own. Until 1970 or so, Merlot grapes were grown almost exclusively in Europe. Since that time, however, they have become increasingly popular in California, where initially they were used to blend with Cabernets. In the process it was discovered that Merlot grapes yield a wine that can stand on its own.

See in addition: "Wine," Part III, Chapter 13.

MERTAJAM - A tree native to Indonesia, the mertajam (*Erioglossum rubiginosum*) has small, purple fruits about the size of large grapes. They grow in clusters and have a somewhat astringent taste. Not a commercial fruit, the mertajam is made into jams and syrups.

MESQUITE - Also called "algarroba" and "honey locust," mesquite comprises several members of the genus *Prosopis* (especially *P. juliflora* var. *juliflora*), all of which are members of the pea family, Fabaceae. Mesquite plants are small trees or shrubs, native to the Americas and especially abundant throughout the southwestern United States and Mexico. The pods of *P. juliflora* var. *juliflora* are among the oldest known foods of humans in the New World and have long constituted a staple for Indians of the desert Southwest.

While still immature, the pods were eaten raw or cooked like a vegetable, and when ripe they yielded a sweetish pulp that was either eaten or fermented to make a mesquite wine. Generally, however, they were ground to make a meal called *pinole,* which was used to make a gruel, and today mesquite flour products are still popular. The branches also exude a sweet gum that can be eaten for dessert. The screwbean mesquite (*P. pubescens*), the western honey mesquite (*P. juniflora* var. *glandulosa*), and the velvet mesquite (*P. velutina*) were used in much the same fashion, with the latter also employed for medicinal purposes.

Common names and synonyms: Algarroba, Fremont screwbean, honey locust, screwbean, screwbean mesquite, screwpod mesquite, tornillo, velvet mesquite, western honey mesquite.

Mesta - *see* OKRA
Methi - *see* FENUGREEK
Metulon - *see* KIWANO
Mexi-Bell - *see* SWEET PEPPERS
Mexican apple - *see* WHITE SAPOTE
Mexican bamboo - *see* KNOTWEED AND SMART-WEED
Mexican breadfruit - *see* MONSTERA
Mexican corn fungus - *see* HUITLACOCHE
Mexican husk tomato - *see* TOMATILLO
Mexican parsley - *see* CILANTRO
Mexican potato - *see* JÍCAMA
Mexican strawberry - *see* PITAHAYA
Mexican tea - *see* EPAZOTE
Mexican wild plum - *see* CAPULIN
Michihli - *see* CHINESE CABBAGE
Mignonette pepper - *see* PEPPER(CORNS)
Milfoil - *see* YARROW
Milho - *see* MAIZE
Milkmaid - *see* YAM DAISY
MILKWEED - Most plants of the genus *Asclepias* have milky juice, especially *A. syriaca,* the "common milkweed" of eastern North America, which is also called "silkweed." It has clusters of purple blossoms and pointed pods that Native Americans dried and used to flavor foods.

Common names and synonyms: Common milkweed, silkweed.

MILLET (*see also* **FINGER MILLET, JAPANESE MILLET, JOB'S-TEARS, SORGHUM**) - Millet is a name applied to a variety of cultivated grasses (*Panicum* spp. and *Setaria* spp.) that are native to Asia and Africa. Millet was cultivated for food some 9,000

years ago at Thessaly in Greece (making it one of the oldest grains known to humans) and around 8,000 years ago in China (where it was considered one of the sacred plants). By the second century B.C. (and probably long before), millet was the most important cereal in Japan, and it was one of the first plants cultivated in Africa. It was an important crop in Europe during the Middle Ages and, much more recently, has been grown in the New World for hay.

Among the most important varieties are the "pearl," "finger," and "foxtail" millets. Despite the tiny size of millet grains (the smallest of all the grains), they have sustained huge numbers of people for millennia, and it is interesting to note that it was millet – not rice – that was first predominant in China. Early on, the significant centers of Chinese agriculture were in the north, where millet was an important staple. Because millets lack gluten, they are a particularly important food for those who must avoid that protein. However, the absence of gluten also means that millets cannot be used for making raised breads but only flatbreads. Pearl millet, the most important of the varieties grown for human consumption, is used for couscous and makes a fine hot cereal as well. Millet (available in health-food stores) provides the consumer with significant amounts of folacin, thiamine, and magnesium.

Common names and synonyms: Bajra, Bengal grass, bristle grass, bulrush millet, finger millet, foxtail millet, German millet, golden timothy (grass), guinea millet, Hungarian grass, Italian millet, *milho,* panic(oid) grass(es), pearl millet, *ragi,* Siberian millet.

See in addition: "Millets," Part II, Section A, Chapter 5.

Millmi - *see* AMARANTH
Millsweet limetta - *see* LIMETTA
Miltomate - *see* TOMATILLO
Mimosa - *see* ACACIA
MIMUSOPS - The *Mimusops* - within the family Sapotaceae - constitute a large genus (also called *Manilkara*) of tropical trees that are primarily used for timber but also yield a gum and bear edible fruits. Perhaps the best-known representative of the genus is the sapodilla (*Manilkara zapota*), but there are many others. One of these is *Mimusops parvifolia* of the Philippines and the southwestern Pacific area. Another is *Mimusops elengi,* a large East Asian tree called the "tanjong tree" (also the "Spanish cherry"), which has yellow berries that are eaten despite a floury consistency and also yield an oil from their seeds. The Brazilian cowtree (*Mimusops elata*) has fruits about the size of an apple, which yield a milky latex that is used in coffee. The naseberry (*Mimusops sieberii*) that grows in the southern United States and Mexico is eaten raw for its fine flavor. *Manilkara bidentata* (called "balata"), that grows in Trinidad and northern

South America, bears an oily, sweet fruit that is much appreciated by children. In addition, the young shoots of many of these trees are cooked and eaten with other vegetables, and the latex is chewed like gum.

Common names and synonyms: Balata, cowtree, naseberry, Spanish cherry, tanjong tree.

Miner's-lettuce - *see* **PURSLANE**

Miner's-salad - *see* **PURSLANE**

MINT (*see also* **CORN MINT**) - Some 600 perennial herbs of the genus *Mentha*, which are widely distributed throughout the world, fall under the rubric of mint - a name derived from the nymph Minthe, who was reputed to have turned into this plant. All apparently originated in the Mediterranean area and North Africa and have been used since ancient times for the flavor provide by the essential oils contained in their leaves. Perhaps the most ubiquitous of the mint plants is spearmint (*M. spicata*), which flavors a favorite tea in North Africa, mint juleps in the U.S. South (said to have been invented in 1809), and mint sauces or jellies to accompany lamb. A pungent offspring of spearmint is peppermint (*M. × piperita*), with its menthol-containing essential oil that adds flavor to many things from toothpaste to the liqueur crème de menthe and has dozens of pharmaceutical uses. Still another commonly grown variety is apple mint (*M. × rotundifolia*) - also called Bowles mint - which has the flavor of apples and is sweeter than other varieties. Mint is sold fresh or dried and goes well in herbal teas, salads, stews, and candies, and with fruit, poultry, meat, and fish dishes.

Common names and synonyms: Apple mint, Bowles mint, corn mint, field mint, pennyroyal, peppermint, red mint, Scotch spearmint, spearmint.

See in addition: "Spices and Flavorings," Part II, Section F, Chapter 1.

Mint geranium - *see* **COSTMARY**

MINTHOSTACHYS - The family Lamiaceae (Labiatae) comprises a great number of aromatic plants, many of which contain essential oils that are used for flavoring foods and teas. Among these are a dozen or so species of the genus *Minthostachys,* which are mintlike herbs native to a range in the Andean region stretching from Venezuela to Argentina. Piperina (*M. verticillata*), which grows in the latter country, is employed to make a popular tea called "Peperina." Tipo or poleo (*M. mollis*) and other species are also used to make beverages, and their minty flavor is employed as a condiment. Some of these herbs are added to potatoes in storage to inhibit sprouting.

Common names and synonyms: Piperina, poleo, tipo.

Mioga ginger - *see* **MYOGA GINGER**

Miracle berry - *see* **MIRACLE FRUIT**

MIRACLE FRUIT (*see also* **LIMEBERRY**) - Native to hot, tropical lowlands in West Africa, this fruit (*Synsepalum dulcificum*) is about the size and

shape of an olive and has a single seed surrounded by white flesh and a deep red skin. The fruit is eaten fresh but did not derive its name from an exceptional sweetness. Rather, "miracle fruit" comes from its ability to affect the palate in a way that makes subsequently consumed sour or acidic foods appear sweet. This "miraculous berry" grows on bushes or trees reaching up to 18 feet in height in their native habitat, but in other areas they rarely achieve 5 feet. The leaves are elongated and a lush green (in some varieties the leaves are hairy); the flowers are small and white.

Common names and synonyms: Miracle berry, miraculous berry.

Miraculous berry - *see* **MIRACLE FRUIT**

Mirliton - *see* **CHAYOTE**

Mississippi chicken corn - *see* **SORGHUM**

Missouri gourd - *see* **BUFFALO GOURD**

Mistletoe - *see* **JUNIPER MISTLETOE**

Miterwort - *see* **COOLWORT**

Mitsuba - *see* **HONEWORT**

Mizuna - *see* **MUSTARD GREENS**

MOCAMBO - Of the same genus as cacao (from which chocolate is made), the mocambo (*Theobroma bicolor*) is a tree that is native to Central and South America and reaches some 30 feet in height. Its fruit is cone shaped, with a chocolate-colored interior, and is used mostly for making a beverage.

Mocha - *see* **COFFEE**

Mock pak choy - *see* **CHINESE FLOWERING CABBAGE**

Mo-ehr - *see* **CLOUD EAR**

Molle - *see* **MASTIC TREE**

Moltebeere - *see* **CLOUDBERRY**

Mombin - *see* **HOG PLUM, YELLOW MOMBIN**

MONGONGO - This large, deciduous tree (*Ricinodendron rautanenii*), growing wild in the arid soils of southern Africa, belongs to the Euphorbiaceae, a generally poisonous family of plants. However, the fruit from this particular tree is not only edible but is said to provide over half of the daily calories consumed by the !Kung San, a hunting-and-gathering people of the Kalahari Desert. The fruit's flesh is edible, as is its kernel, which is protected by a hard-shelled stone. This nut is high in both fat and protein. Mongongo nuts do not mature on the tree but fall when still green. Only then do they start the ripening process, with the skin changing to brown, the flesh softening, and the flavor developing.

Monkey-bread - *see* **BAOBAB**

Monkey nut - *see* **PEANUT**

MONKEY ORANGE - This small, thorny shrub (*Strychnos spinosa*) can be found throughout tropical and subtropical eastern and southern Africa, particularly on arid savannas and the lower ranges of mountain slopes. The skin of its brilliantly green fruit changes to yellow when ripening. The gelatin-like flesh, too, is yellow, but of a darker shade. Sweet yet acidic in taste, the fruits are frequently mixed with milk. They are also used to make an alcoholic beverage. Unripe fruits and the roots of the shrub serve as the basis of a snakebite antidote for some native African peoples. The seeds of *Strychnos spinosa* are poisonous.

Common names and synonyms: Kaffir orange, Natal orange.

Monkey-puzzle (tree) - *see* CHILEAN PINE

Monk's pepper tree - *see* CHASTE TREE

MONSTERA - A peculiar-looking fruit, the monstera (*Monstera deliciosa*) is native to Mexico and Guatemala, where it is called *ceriman*. Also called the "Swiss-cheese plant" and "Mexican breadfruit," it is in fact the fruit of the split-leaf philodendron, which is (in smaller size), a familiar houseplant. The fruit grows on large vines with leaves up to 3 feet wide. In shape, it resembles an elongated pinecone, covered as it is with many small kernels. When ripe, these kernels split apart to reveal a pale yellow, sweet pulp with a delicious taste seemingly a cross between the flavors of banana and pineapple. If the fruit is not allowed to ripen fully, however, it can irritate the mouth and the throat. In the United States, the monstera is grown in Florida and California, and some gourmet shops carry the fruit.

Common names and synonyms: Ananas de Mexico, balazo, banana de brejo, ceriman, ceriman de Mexico, fruta de Mexico, fruit-salad fruit, Mexican breadfruit, pina anona, Swiss-cheese plant.

Montmorency - *see* CHERRY

Mook yee - *see* CLOUD EAR

Mooli - *see* DAIKON

MOONFLOWER - A number of plants are called "moonflower." One is *Mentzelia pumila*, the "desert blazing star" (also "evening star"), which, in addition to bright yellow, star-shaped flowers, has a bullet-shaped seed capsule. Native Americans ground these seeds for meal. Another moonflower is the yellow salsify (*Tragopogon dubius*), which is also called meadow salsify. It is a perennial herb that was introduced from Europe and is now naturalized in the Americas. Native Americans used this plant for both food and medicine. Two more moonflowers are comprised of South American plants of the genus *Datura* - called "angel's-trumpets" - that are cultivated for their large, trumpet-like flowers. In the United States, "sacred datura" (*Datura meteloides*), also called jimsonweed and moon lily, is a dangerous plant: All its parts are extremely poisonous if ingested. However, sacred datura was one of the most important medicinal plants for Native Americans.

Common names and synonyms: Angel's-trumpet, datura, desert blazing star, evening star, jimsonweed, meadow salsify, moon lily, sacred datura, yellow salsify.

Moon lily - *see* MOONFLOWER

Moqua - *see* FUZZY MELON

Mora - *see* JALAPEÑO

MOREL (*see also* **MUSHROOMS AND FUNGI**) - Perhaps the best-known and most sought-after type of fungus, morel mushrooms (genus *Morchella*) come in many varieties - all edible - and are distinguished by their hollow stems and the irregular pits and ridges in their cone-shaped caps. Of all the various morels, probably the two most common are the true or yellow morel (*M. esculenta*), which is 2 to 6 inches tall (3 to 4 inches making up the length of the cap), and the white morel (*M. deliciosa*), which is slightly longer and is thought to be the best-tasting morel. Morels grow wild, often in wooded areas that have been burned-over, but they cannot (at least to this point) be cultivated. They are used in several different dishes. Morels were doubtless viewed as a springtime delicacy by countless generations of Native Americans; moreover, there are European species of morels that have also been consumed for millennia.

Common names and synonyms: Black morel, golden morel, merkel, morille, narrow-capped morel, pinecone mushroom, sponge mushroom, true morel, white morel, yellow morel.

See in addition: "Fungi," Part II, Section C, Chapter 7; "Mushrooms and Fungi," Part VIII.

Morella - *see* WONDERBERRY

Moreton Bay chestnut - *see* AUSTRALIAN CHESTNUT

Morille - *see* MOREL

MORINDA - Members of a large genus of East Indian tropical trees and shrubs, many *Morinda* plants produce an edible, pulpy fruit that is eaten raw and often used in chutneys and curries. One of these, called the "Indian mulberry" (*M. citrifolia*), now grows in the Florida Keys.

Common names and synonyms: Indian mulberry.

Moringa nut (tree) - *see* BENOIL TREE

Morita - *see* JALAPEÑO

MORMON TEA - Also called the "desert jointfir" and "teposote" among other appellations, "Mormon tea" was sometimes the longleaf ephedra shrub (*Ephedra trifurca*), sometimes *E. nevadensis*, and sometimes *E. viridis*. It received the name "Mormon tea" after Mormon settlers in Utah made tea from the dried twigs and stems of these plants. However, Native Americans preceded the Mormons in using the various species of *Ephedra* for tea making and also for treating illnesses.

Common names and synonyms: Desert jointfir, longleaf ephedra, teposote.

Moro (orange) - *see* BLOOD ORANGE

Mostarda - *see* MUSTARD SEED

Mostaza - *see* MUSTARD SEED

MOTH BEAN - Native to tropical Asia and also called the "mat bean," the moth bean (*Phaseolus aconitifolius* = *Vigna aconitifolia*) is a small, yellowish brown seed in a cylindrical pod that grows on vines which provide a matlike cover for the soil. The bean is used, especially in India, for human food. It is made into dhal and bean paste, and the immature pods are cooked as a vegetable.

Common names and synonyms: Mat bean.

See also: "Beans, Peas, and Lentils," Part II, Section C, Chapter 3.

Mother-of-clove(s) – *see* **CLOVE(S)**

MOUNTAIN ASH – A native of northeastern North America and the Appalachian region, the mountain ash (*Sorbus americana*) produces clusters of orange red berries. Although these are much too bitter to eat out of hand, Native Americans in the past dried them and ground them into a meal. The berries are also made into syrup, jams, and the like.

Mountain balm – *see* **YERBA SANTA**

Mountain cranberry – *see* **LINGONBERRY**

Mountain hemlock – *see* **HEMLOCK**

Mountain hollyhock – *see* **WASABI**

MOUNTAIN PAPAYA – A hardy member of the papaya family, the mountain papaya (*Carica candamarcensis = C. pubescens*) constitutes an exception to the tropical nature of its relatives by growing at elevations of 8,000 to 9,000 feet in Ecuador and Colombia. The price of such cold-resistance, however, is a small, tart fruit. Too acidic to eat raw, it is always cooked, and then only eaten when better fruits are unavailable.

Mountain plum – *see* **TALLOW WOOD PLUM**

MOUNTAIN SORREL – Mountain sorrel (*Oxyria digyna*), with its long-stemmed leaves, grows in an area ranging from Alaska and Greenland through British Columbia to the mountains of New Hampshire. Eskimos gather mountain sorrel and ferment it like sauerkraut. Mountain sorrel is also eaten raw in salads when the plants are young, whereas mature plants are used as a potherb. The plant is a valuable source of vitamin C in the far north, accounting for its nickname "scurvy grass."

Common names and synonyms: Scurvy grass.

Mountain spinach – *see* **ORACH**

Mountain sumac – *see* **SMOOTH SUMAC**

Mousseron – *see* **MUSHROOMS AND FUNGI**

Mousseron d'automne – *see* **MUSHROOMS AND FUNGI**

Moutarde – *see* **MUSTARD SEED**

Moxa – *see* **MUGWORT**

MUGWORT – The dried leaves of the perennial Eurasian plants of the genus *Artemisia* – and particularly *A. vulgaris* – are called mugwort and have long been used as an herb to flavor various dishes, especially those containing fatty foods such as goose or pork. Mugwort's aromatic, slightly bitter taste is also good for seasoning stews, stuffings, sweets, and ale. Some make a tea from mugwort that is believed to relieve the symptoms of rheumatism, and it is employed to flavor absinthe. A related plant – *A. verlotorum,* called Chinese mugwort – is used in the Far East to flavor rice and as a tobacco

substitute, and its young leaves are boiled and eaten in Japan.

Common names and synonyms: Chinese mugwort, felon herb, *moxa.*

See also: "Spices and Flavorings," Part II, Section F, Chapter 1.

Mulato – *see* **POBLANO**

MULBERRY (*see also* **BERRIES**) – Several trees of the genus *Morus* have edible mulberries. The red mulberry (*M. rubra*), which is native to eastern and central North America, has fruits that resemble blackberries. The white – or "Chinese" – mulberry (*M. alba*) is the one that the Chinese use to feed silkworms. It has whitish or purplish fruit. The Russian mulberry (*M. nigra*), also called the black mulberry, was introduced in the United States during the last quarter of the nineteenth century. All mulberries are quite sweet, with the white mulberry being the sweetest. More popular in Europe than in the United States, mulberries are quite perishable and thus are not grown for market. They are eaten fresh and made into pies and jellies.

Common names and synonyms: Black mulberry, Chinese mulberry, red mulberry, Russian mulberry, white mulberry.

Munchkin – *see* **DELICATA (SQUASH)**

MUNG BEAN (*see also* **BEANS, LEGUMES**) – Small and frequently green, mung beans (*Phaseolus aureus*) are generally used for bean sprouts and are especially important in the cooking of both China and Japan, where they are frequently stir-fried. Also known as "black grams" and in India as "green grams," mung beans are also boiled and eaten as a vegetable, used in curries, and made into flour. The bean also finds its way into soups and is the base for cellophane noodles. In the past, consumers had to sprout mung beans themselves, but bean sprouts have been sold commercially on an ever-increasing scale since the 1950s.

Common names and synonyms: Black dhal, black gram, black mung, golden gram, gram bean, green gram, red mung, urd.

See in addition: "Beans, Peas, and Lentils," Part II, Section C, Chapter 3.

Muntok (pepper) – *see* **PEPPER(CORNS)**

Murnong – *see* **YAM DAISY**

MUSCADINE (*see also* **GRAPES**) – A purple grape of the southeastern United States, the muscadine (*Vitis rotundifolia* – also called the "bullace grape" and the "scuppernong") serves mostly as a grape for the table and for making jellies, jams, and juices. But some wine is made from muscadine grapes, especially dessert wines that taste something like muscat wines. There are several dozen cultivars of muscadines, grown mostly for use in the home and for local markets.

Common names and synonyms: Bullace grape, scuppernong, southern fox grape.

See in addition: "Wine," Part III, Chapter 13.

MUSCAT (*see also* **GRAPES**) – Several varieties of sweet white grapes are called muscats (*Vitis vinifera*) and are used for making wines such as muscatels and sauternes. They are also used as raisins and as table grapes.

See in addition: "Wine," Part III, Chapter 13.

MUSHROOMS AND FUNGI – Mushrooms are found in almost all temperate parts of the world. Although often viewed as the plant itself, they are actually the fruit of a network of stems that remain underground. The mushroom aboveground is there to propagate the organism by diffusing spores to extend the underground network. As plants that have neither leaves nor roots, mushrooms cannot photosynthesize sugars and instead live on the rotting remains of other organisms. That they are successful in such parasitic activity seems clear enough when one learns that (depending on the authority consulted) mushrooms and fungi comprise between 40,000 and 120,000 species around the world, of which some 1,800 are recognized as edible.

One cannot imagine our hunter–gatherer ancestors not eating mushrooms, which have been described as "vegetable meat." However, it is downright painful to imagine the trial-and-error process that eventually separated those that were edible from those that were poisonous. Perhaps early foragers concentrated on a few species that were fairly easy to identify, such as puffballs (of the family Lycoperdaceae) with their ball-shaped fruiting bodies. In fact, puffball remains have been found in Paleolithic settlements. Yet it may be that our Stone Age forebears had a substantially more sophisticated knowledge of fungi than this. Observation of contemporary hunter-gatherers indicates that they know a great deal about mushrooms both edible and poisonous, and they consume the former while employing the latter to bring down game and bring up fish.

Mushrooms of the *Agaricus* genus are among the relatively few fungi that can be grown commercially, and some of these have been propagated since classical times. The *Champignon d'Paris,* or Paris mushroom (*Agaricus bisporus* and *A. campestris*), is the most common mushroom in produce markets today. It is also called the common white mushroom, and if small, a "button" mushroom, or in France a *mousseron,* from which the English "mushroom" was derived. This mushroom has been cultivated since the seventeenth century in France. During Napoleonic times, they were grown on so-called farms located in caves in the many stone quarries close to Paris. There, the mushrooms were nurtured in the dark coolness, where humidity and temperature were both controlled, on beds of horse manure mixed with straw and soil – a method that is continued today both commercially and in the corners of family basements, with the important difference that the horse manure is now sterilized and pasteurized. Most mushrooms that come sliced or whole in cans, or marinating in jars, are "button" mushrooms.

By the late 1800s, mushrooms were being grown commercially in other countries. Italian growers also cultivated the common mushroom but preferring the brown-capped variety, which are often called cremini mushrooms (or Italian brown) and have an earthy flavor that is fine for soups and stews and for stuffing. The large and beefy Portabello (also Roma) is actually a fully grown cremini, with dense and meaty flesh that lends itself nicely to grilling or roasting. Originally, cremini mushrooms were imported from Italy, but now they are cultivated in the United States.

Although many swear by the hearty flavor of the cultivated Portabello, wild mushrooms are generally regarded as significantly more flavorful than their domesticated counterparts, and wild varieties are becoming increasingly available in produce markets, in both fresh and dried forms. One of these is the chanterelle (*Cantharellus cibarius*) – the golden chanterelle (*girolle*) of France, and the *Pfifferling* of Germany – which has long been highly regarded as a "forest" mushroom in Europe but is now becoming increasingly popular in the United States, where it grows in forests from coast to coast. It is orange in color, funnel shaped, and has firm, light, yellowish flesh. There are numerous other chanterelles that come in colors ranging from red, brown, and gray to orange-and-yellow, and almost all are also ranked as delicious, although they are much more difficult to locate.

Also in the delicious category is *Boletus edulis,* which goes by the name of *Steinpilz* in Germany, *porcini* in Italy, and *cèpe* (also cep) in France and the United States, where it grows as well. Indeed, many consider these stout-stemmed fungi with their large brown, dry caps to be the finest tasting of all the wild mushrooms. Their rich flavor and firm texture make them ideal for soups, sauces, and stuffings.

Morel (*Morchella esculenta*) fanciers, however, would give the "best-tasting" ranking to their favorite fungus. Nicknamed the "pinecone mushroom" because of the elongated, dome-like shape of its whitish to light brown head, which is composed of chambers that make it appear a network of ridges and pits, the true morel appears only in the spring and thus commands a very high price throughout the year.

Many mushrooms that are originally from the Far East are not only available dried and canned but can also be found fresh in produce markets the world over. Perhaps the best known of these – and certainly the most available – is the Japanese brown mushroom or shiitake (*Cortinellus shiitake*). Once grown only in Japan by introducing spores to a

local type of oak tree, this mushroom is now cultivated in the United States – on artificial logs. The
shiitake is umbrella-like in shape, brown to black in
color, and firmly textured; it has an assertive flavor
that goes well in sautés. Its cousin, the Chinese
black mushroom (*Lentinus edodes*), is actually
brown to pale buff in color. Known as the "winter
mushroom" in China (as is the shiitake, which is
also grown there), it is like most other mushrooms
in that its flavor intensifies with drying.

The enokitake (*Flammulina velutipes*), or sometimes just *enoki* (their home is on the stumps of
the Chinese hackberry tree called *enoki*), are slender mushroom stalks with small bulbs at the top,
which grow in clumps and reach upwards of 5
inches in length. Their delicate flavor is called for in
many Asian dishes, but they are best appreciated
when eaten raw in salads. Enokitake mushrooms
are now cultivated in California. Another cultivated
mushroom is the straw mushroom (*Volvariella
volvacea*) that is small, globe-shaped, and grown on
straw, from which it develops its distinctive earthy
taste. These are only occasionally found fresh, and
never dried, but are universally available in cans.

Rarely found outside of Japan is the matsutake
(*Armillaria edodes*), a thick, meaty, and delicious
mushroom that is very popular there and also very
expensive. A final Asian fungus is the cloud-ear fungus (*Auricularia auricula* and *A. polytrica*), better
known in the United States as "wood ear" but also
as "tree ear," "Jew's-ear," and "black tree fungus." The
cloud-ear fungus is highly regarded for supposed
medicinal properties (it does seem to thin the
blood) by the Chinese, who have also incorporated
it into their cuisine for at least 1,500 years. It is
found mostly in Asian markets in the United States.

Oyster mushrooms (*Pleurotus ostreatus*) are also
called "tree mushrooms" because they grow (in
clusters) on rotting trees in parts of every continent except Antarctica. Although a wild variety,
they are easily cultivated and thus widely available.
Of the same family is the most famous of the tree
fungi, the beefsteak fungus (*Fistulina hepatica*). It
is also known by a variety of other names, such as
"liver fistulina," "oak tongue," "vegetable beefsteak,"
and "beef tongue" because of its rough, reddish surface – which suggests a beef tongue or steak or
liver – and its reddish juice, not to mention a meaty
taste when cooked. A final mushroom that lives on
dead as well as living trees (in clusters) is the
honey mushroom (*Armillariella mellea*) – the
name describing the color of its cap rather than its
taste, which is delicious nonetheless.

The field mushroom (*Agaricus campestris* – also
"meadow mushroom" and "pink-bottom") is more
or less the same as the "common" mushroom (discussed first in this entry) except that it is a wild
version. Rodman's mushroom (*Agaricus rodmani*)
with its white to yellowish cap is another that is

very similar (and closely related) to the common
mushroom. Fairy-ring mushrooms (*Marasmius oreades*) are so called because of their tendency to
grow in rings or circles. They appear mostly in the
autumn and in France are called the *mousseron
d'automne* or the false *mousseron* because of the
resemblance of their caps to those of the button
mushroom.

Mushrooms are far more nutritious than many
people believe. In addition to a good deal of protein, they deliver essential minerals and substantial
amounts of the B complex. Moreover, they contain
various medicinal substances and some (such as
the common mushroom) may provide a cancer
preventive. Cooked fresh, mushrooms are considerably more nutritious than those that are available
marinated and canned. As a rule, dried mushrooms
have an intensely concentrated flavor (especially
after they are reconstituted by soaking in hot
water) and consequently are used more as a seasoning than as a vegetable. In the United States,
Pennsylvania is the leading mushroom-producing
state (accounting for about half the domestic
crop), and most of this activity is accomplished in
and around the little Pennsylvania town of Kennett
Square. Michigan, California, and Florida are also
important producers, and the countries of Italy,
France, China, Japan, and Thailand all export mushrooms in large quantities.

Common names and synonyms: Beefsteak fungus,
beef tongue, black tree fungus, brown-capped mushroom, button mushroom, cep, *cèpe, champignon
d'Paris,* chanterelle, Chinese black mushroom,
cloud-ear fungus, common mushroom, common
white mushroom, cremini mushroom, English mushroom, *enoki,* enokitake, fairy-ring mushroom, false
mousseron, field mushroom, forest mushroom,
girolle, golden chanterelle, honey mushroom, Italian
brown mushroom, Japanese brown mushroom,
Jew's-ear, liver fistulina, matsutake, meadow mushroom, morel, *mousseron, mousseron d'automne,*
oak tongue, oyster mushroom, Paris mushroom, *Pfifferling,* pinecone mushroom, pink-bottom, *porcini,*
Portabello, puffball, Rodman's mushroom, Roma, shiitake, *Steinpilz,* straw mushroom, tree ear, tree
mushroom, vegetable beefsteak, vegetable meat,
wild mushroom, winter mushroom, wood ear.

See also: "Fungi," Part II, Section C, Chapter 7.

Musk lime – *see* CALAMONDIN

Muskmelon – *see* CANTALOUPE AND MUSK-
MELON, MELONS

Musk seed – *see* AMBERSEED

Mustard cabbage – *see* PAKCHOI AND KAI CHOY

MUSTARD GREENS (*see also* **CABBAGE, MUSTARD
SEED**) – A vegetable belonging to the cabbage family (and also called "leaf mustard" and "leaf mustard
cabbage"), mustard greens (*Brassica juncea*) have
a more delicate flavor than kale, but one that is, at
the same time, more piquant. Most plants of the
genus *Brassica,* are of Eurasian origin. *Brassica*

juncea, however, is probably a native of Africa that spread into Asia, although the plant may have originated in China and spread outward from there. Mustard greens have an arching stalk and large green leaves, which grow in clusters. The leaves are generally eaten when young, because they become coarse with age. They can be cooked and eaten as a vegetable or used in salads. Mustard greens are fairly high in beta-carotene, vitamin C, and calcium.

Common names and synonyms: Brown mustard, Chinese mustard, curled mustard, Indian mustard, leaf mustard, leaf mustard cabbage, *mizuna,* Oriental mustard, rape(seed), red Asian mustard, southern curled mustard.

See in addition: "Cruciferous and Green Leafy Vegetables," Part II, Section C, Chapter 5.

MUSTARD SEED (*see also* **MUSTARD GREENS**) – There are three basic types of mustard that are all members of the cabbage family: black mustard (*Brassica nigra*); white mustard (*B. alba*); and brown mustard (*B. juncea*). The mustard plants were originally weeds, and some evidence suggests that our prehistoric ancestors may have utilized their seeds to chew with meat.

Mustard plants have been cultivated since ancient times and were highly valued for their oil content. The Greeks and Romans used mustard as a medicine and plaster for rheumatism and arthritis; it was also a part of the cuisine of the ancient Egyptians, Greeks, and Romans as a condiment; and mustard seed is mentioned several times in the New Testament.

Each country and region has subsequently developed mustards to accompany their own cuisines. Ground mustard seeds are mixed with a liquid medium (at which point a reaction of enzymes causes the seeds to become pungent), such as vinegar, wine, beer, or mayonnaise. One such medium was grape "must," hence the French *moutarde,* the Italian *mostarda,* the Spanish *mostaza,* and the English "mustard" – all from the Latin *mustum ardens,* meaning "burning must."

In China, white mustard seeds from the West (*B. alba* is a Mediterranean native) were being grown by the tenth century, but the hot Chinese mustard and the even hotter Japanese mustard (*karaschi*) are made from brown mustard seed. The English also have a preference for hot mustard, which goes well with sausages and rare roast beef. French mustards, such as those from Dijon, seem to go with French sausages, just as German mustards, such as Düsseldorf, are suited to the sausages of Germany. And what is a hot dog without the yellow (because of the turmeric added) mustard of the United States? In addition, mustard seeds and powder are used in cooking meats and vegetables, in pickling, and in the preparation of sauces, relishes, and salad dressings, and mustard seeds and oil are frequently added to dishes. Black mustard seeds, for example,

are vital to the cuisines (especially curries) of India, and many meats are dusted with mustard powder before cooking.

Common names and synonyms: Black mustard (seed), brown mustard (seed), Dijon mustard(s), Düsseldorf mustard, hot Chinese mustard, hot mustard, Japanese mustard, *karaschi, mostarda, mostaza, moutarde, mustum ardens,* white mustard (seed), yellow mustard.

See in addition: "Spices and Flavorings," Part II, Section F, Chapter 1.

Mustum ardens - *see* **MUSTARD SEED**

MUTAMBA – This native of both North and South America is a tall tree (*Guazuma ulmifolia*) with some 25 to 30 aliases ranging from "West Indian elm" and "mutambo" to "chocolate" and "guasima." The reason for the plethora of names is because it is known in many languages in a region stretching from Brazil to Peru to Mexico. The mutamba produces an edible fruit, but its major contribution has been to the herbal medicine practiced in all of the countries in which it is grown. The teas made from its bark, roots, and leaves have been used against everything from asthma to leprosy, often with such effectiveness that it has attracted the attention of medical science, and a number of studies have appeared on its usefulness against heart-related diseases and cancer.

Common names and synonyms: Chocolate, guacimo, guasima, mutambo, West Indian elm.

Mutambo - *see* **MUTAMBA**

MYOGA GINGER - A native of Japan, myoga (*Zingiber mioga*) is a member of the ginger family that is grown for its young shoots and buds. These are mostly used raw in salads and shredded as a garnish but are also added to soups and simmered dishes.

Common names and synonyms: Ginger bud, mioga ginger.

Myrobalan - *see* **AMALAKA**

Myrobalan plum - *see* **CHERRY PLUM**

Myrrh - *see* **CICELY**

Myrtille - *see* **BILBERRY**

MYRTLE (*see also* **CHILEAN GUAVA MYRTLE, PERIWINKLE**) - An evergreen aromatic shrub, native to the Mediterranean region and western Asia, myrtle (*Myrtus communis*) has blue-black berries that are sweet and pulpy and are dried for use as a condiment as well as eaten raw. Myrtle was enjoyed by the ancient Greeks, who also accorded it a role in their mythology (it was sacred to Aphrodite). Other myrtles are native to South America or New Zealand save for the North American native (*M. verrucosa*) called "stopper," which also has edible fruit.

Common names and synonyms: Indian buchu, "stopper."

MYRTLE APPLE - A wild shrub native to southern Africa, the myrtle apple (*Eugenia capensis*) provides both nourishment as a fruit and medicinal relief from diarrhea. It ranges in color from orange to red and looks like a tiny apple; on average, it reaches not quite 2 inches in diameter. Like the strawberries that they are said to resemble in taste, myrtle apples grow close to the ground and are ready for picking in summer. Their pulp is consumed as food, whereas the roots are used medicinally.

Myrtle flag - *see* SWEET FLAG
Myrtle-leafed orange - *see* ORANGE
Myrtle pepper - *see* ALLSPICE

Nagami - *see* KUMQUAT
Nalta jute - *see* JEW'S-MALLOW
Ñame - *see* CUSH-CUSH YAM
Ñame mapuey - *see* CUSH-CUSH YAM
Nana - *see* PINEAPPLE

NANCE - A relative of the acerola and native to the West Indies, Central America, and much of South America, the nance (*Byrsonima crassifolia*) is a small tree with yellow fruits ranging from the size of a walnut to that of a lemon. The fruit is sweet and generally eaten raw but is also turned into a juice that is sometimes fermented to make an alcoholic beverage.

Nangka - *see* JACKFRUIT
Nannyberry - *see* BLACK HAW
Napa - *see* CHINESE CABBAGE
Napa Valley Gamay - *see* GAMAY
Nappa - *see* CHINESE CABBAGE

NARANJILLA - Found in Ecuador, Peru, Colombia, and Costa Rica, this small shrub (*Solanum quitoense*) bears bright orange, tomato-shaped, edible fruit at altitudes of 3,000 to 5,800 feet. Also called *lulo*, it has a juicy pulp that is used to make drinks, sherbet, preserves, and pies. The juice is rich in proteins and mineral salts. It does not travel well, but the fruit's popularity in sherbets has led to its commercial cultivation in Ecuador.
Common names and synonyms: Lulo.

Narrow-capped morel - *see* MOREL
Narrow dock - *see* CURLED DOCK
Naseberry - *see* MIMUSOPS, SAPODILLA
Nashi - *see* ASIAN PEAR

NASTURTIUM - The west coast of South America is the homeland of this creeping or climbing plant (*Tropaeolum majus*) also known as "Indian cress," which has a surprising number of culinary uses. Its leaves and young shoots have a hot, peppery flavor that goes well in salads and with eggs. The buds are pickled and can substitute as capers, and the flowers are chopped and added to rice and pasta dishes. From time to time, the nasturtium has been cultivated in Europe for its culinary properties, and it is used as a food in Peru today, as it has been for thousands of years. The plant is rich in vitamin C.
Common names and synonyms: Garden nasturtium, Indian cress.

Natal orange - *see* MONKEY ORANGE
NATAL PLUM (*see also* SOUR PLUM) - This large, thorny, South African shrub (*Carissa grandiflora = C. macrocarpa*), which is used for hedges in Natal, bears a fruit called the Natal plum. It is purple and plumlike and has a taste of gooseberry that goes well in pies and preserves. The Natal plum now also grows in frost-free areas of the United States, including Hawaii.

NATIVE CHERRY - A shrubby tree of Australia, the "native cherry" (*Exocarpos cuppressiformis*) produces a fruit that is a drupe, with a bright red, cherry-like appearance.

Native cucumber - *see* PEPINO
Native gooseberry - *see* WILD GOOSEBERRY

NATIVE GUAVA - The small tree or shrub of Australia called the "native guava" (*Rhodomyrtus psidioides*) bears an edible fruit that is remarkably similar to the tropical American guava (*Psidium guajava*). The former has been used as food for millennia by the Aborigines.

NATIVE LIME - Australia has two citrus trees that bear fruits called "native limes." One is designated *Citrus australis*, and the other is *Microcitrus australasica*. In both cases, the fruit is very acidic and quite high in vitamin C.

Native myrtle - *see* BRUSH CHERRY
Native peach - *see* QUANDONG
Native potato - *see* WILD YAM

NAVY BEAN (*see also* BEANS) - Also called the "pea bean," the navy bean is any of several varieties of the kidney bean (*Phaseolus vulgaris*) that are cultivated for their nutritious white seeds. The name "navy bean" recalls former times when the beans were among the standard provisions of warships of the U.S. Navy.
Common names and synonyms: Kidney bean, pea bean.
See in addition: "Beans, Peas, and Lentils," Part II, Section C, Chapter 3; "Legumes," Part VIII.

Neapolitan medlar - *see* AZAROLE

NEBBIOLO (*see also* GRAPES) - The best of the red wine grapes of the Italian Piedmont, Nebbiolo grapes (*Vitis vinifera*) were named from the Italian *nebbia*, meaning "fog," because they are harvested during a time when the Langhe hills of the Piedmont are covered with mist. The Nebbiolo is used to produce the famed Barolo and Barbaresco wines and also to blend with other grapes. Nebbiolo grapes are expensive because, like the Pinot Noir variety, they are very difficult to grow.
See in addition: "Wine," Part III, Chapter 13.

Nebraska currant - *see* BUFFALO BERRY

NECTARINE (*see also* PEACH) - There are over 150 varieties of nectarines, with the name apparently derived from the Greek *nektar*, meaning "drink-of-the-gods." The nectarine is itself a variety of peach (*Prunus persica*), which it resembles in every way save that it is smaller, sweeter, and fuzzless - meaning that it looks more like a plum than a peach. The peach is an ancient fruit, but nectarines are hardly a newcomer to the dining table, having been known for more than 2,000 years. It is interesting, however, that little mention of nectarines can be found in the writings of the ancients.

In London in 1673, they were being grown for medicinal use by the Worshipful Society of Apothecaries, and by 1720, they were being cultivated among the peaches of Virginia. Like peaches, nectarines are either clingstone or freestone. They constitute one of the world's major fruit crops, with the United States and Italy the principal areas of cultivation. The fruit is grown in California, South America, and the Middle East for the American market, which makes them available year-round. Nectarines are eaten whole, made into juice, poached, baked, and grilled to accompany barbecued meats. Most are orange or yellow fleshed, but some are white fleshed. The orange-fleshed kinds in particular are an excellent source of vitamin A, and all are rich in vitamin C.

NEROLI (*see also* **CITRUS FRUITS**) – Also called "orange-flower water," neroli is the essential oil of bitter orange blossoms (*Citrus aurantium*), which is obtained by distillation. The oil is used in perfumery, and the perfumed essence is employed in making syrups and flavoring liqueurs. The process was introduced in France during the late seventeenth century by Anna Maria de la Trémoille, Princess of Neroli.

Common names and synonyms: Neroli oil, orange-flower oil, orange-flower water.

See in addition: "Spices and Flavorings," Part II, Section F, Chapter 1.

NETTLE(S) – Everyone knows these perennial herbs of the genus *Urtica* (especially *U. dioica*), which are naturalized worldwide. They bear "toothed" leaves that are covered with tiny, hollow hairs containing a number of irritating substances, which inflict a sting and a rash on those who accidentally touch them. But the young tips, picked as they broke through the ground in the spring, were frequently cooked and eaten as a vegetable by our foraging forebears, who may well have been on the lookout for greens to rid themselves of the first symptoms of scurvy after a winter of vitamin-C deprivation. The young leaves of nettles are often prepared much like spinach, are included in other dishes, and have been brewed into tea and even beer. Nettle seeds have been gathered for food as well. Indeed, many people still gather nettles today; the medicinal uses of the plant are as well known as its nutritional capacity. Nettles are rich in vitamins and minerals, particularly vitamin C, iron, sulfur, potassium, and sodium.

Common names and synonyms: Burning nettle(s), stinging nettle(s).

NEW MEXICO CHILLIES (*see also* **CHILLI PEPPERS**) – There are quite a number of chillies called New Mexico – all of the *Capsicum annuum* species, including the Anaheim, which is one of many New Mexico varieties. The major ones are the New Mexico Green (also called the "long green chilli") and the New Mexico Red (the mature form). Between 6 and 10 inches in length, and close to 2 inches in diameter, these peppers are only moderately hot and are favorites for roasting and stuffing. The red form is also used in a number of sauces, including barbecue sauces. When peeled and dried, New Mexico green and red chillies are sometimes called dried California chillies, and the red is also called *chilli colorado*. The latter is used to make chilli sauces and ground chilli powders. Other New Mexico chillies – the "NuMex" Eclipse, Sunrise, and Sunset – are, respectively, purple, goldish, and bright orange in color and are used mostly for decorative purposes, as are the newly developed New Mexico "Miniatures."

Common names and synonyms: Chilli colorado, dried California chilli, long green chilli, New Mexico Green, New Mexico Miniature, New Mexico Red, NuMex Eclipse, NuMex Sunrise, NuMex Sunset.

See in addition: "Chilli Peppers," Part II, Section C, Chapter 4.

NEW ZEALAND SPINACH – Although not actually a spinach (indeed, it is a member of a different botanical family), "New Zealand spinach" (*Tetragonia expansa*) has a spinach-like appearance and flavor, goes well in salads, and is also cooked like spinach. Native to New Zealand and Australia, this vegetable has diffused around the world and grows well in those warmer places where real spinach does not. Like spinach, New Zealand spinach is rich in beta-carotene, folacin, and other vitamins and minerals.

NIGELLA – A member of the buttercup family and native to the northern Himalayan mountains, the Middle East, and eastern Europe, nigella (*Nigella sativa*) consists of tiny dried black seeds, quite similar to black caraway seeds, with which they are sometimes confused. Today, the plant that yields them in swollen pods is most extensively cultivated in India, where nigella is used in numerous dishes. In the United States, it is carried in gourmet shops under the Indian name *kalonji* and, as in the Middle East, is sprinkled on breads. In fact, black nigella seeds are often encountered atop Jewish rye bread, pumpernickel, and the like.

Common names and synonyms: Black caraway, black cumin, black nigella, *charnushka,* devil-in-the-bush, fennel-flower, *kalonji,* love-in-a-mist, Russian caraway.

See also: "Spices and Flavorings," Part II, Section F, Chapter 1.

Niger – *see* **NIGER SEED**

NIGER SEED – Originating in West Africa and now grown extensively in Ethiopia and India, niger seed (*Guizotia abyssinica*) is cultivated as an oil crop, although the seeds are also used by humans as a condiment and as a food for birds. The oil has a number of industrial applications, but it is edible as well and is employed in the usual culinary ways – for cooking and in salads - especially in Ethiopia, where the seed is called "noog," and its oil is the most important edible oil in the country. In addition, niger-seed oil serves as an adulterant in other oils.

Common names and synonyms: Niger, nog, noog, nug, ramtil.

NIPA PALM - Palms of the genus *Nypa* (or *Nipa*) have leaves that are used locally for thatching, basket weaving, and making hats, whereas the stems are employed to fashion arrows. The Chinese eat the raw fruits of this tree for their sweetness or candy them as preserves. Sugar extracted from the fruit is used to make alcohol and vinegar, and the alcoholic beverage is also called "nipa."

Common names and synonyms: Mangrove, nypa palm.

Nispero - *see* **LOQUAT, SAPODILLA**
Nitta tree - *see* **PARKIA**
Noblecane - *see* **SUGARCANE**
No-eye pea - *see* **PIGEON PEA**
Nog - *see* **NIGER SEED**
Noisette - *see* **HAZELNUT AND FILBERT**
Nona - *see* **CUSTARD APPLE**
Noog - *see* **NIGER SEED**
Nopal - *see* **NOPALES, PRICKLY PEAR**
NOPALES (*see also* **PRICKLY PEAR**) - Also named *nopalitos* and "cactus pads," nopales are the leaves (called "paddles") of certain varieties of Mexican cacti (genus *Opuntia*). (In addition, the cochineal plant [*Nopalea cochenillifera = N. coccinellifera*] is called nopal, and its young joints are often sold as nopales.) These vegetables are fleshy yet slippery (they exude a mucilaginous substance similar to that in okra), have a crunchy texture, and when fresh have a delicate taste somewhere between that of green pepper and asparagus. Nopales can be eaten raw (once the spines are removed) but more often are cooked in boiling water until tender. They are frequently cooked with eggs, are often steamed for a vegetable dish, and (after cooling) can be added to salads. Nopales that are purchased in jars have a tart and pickle-like taste; they are called for in many "Tex-Mex" dishes. Nopales have been consumed by Native Americans of Mesoamerica and the southwestern portion of North America for millennia and have often served as a famine food. They are a fine source of beta-carotene, vitamin C, and some of the B-vitamins as well.

Common names and synonyms: Cactus pad, cactus paddle, cochineal plant, nopal, *nopalitos.*

Nopalitos - *see* **NOPALES**
Nori - *see* **LAVER, SEAWEED**
Northern pine - *see* **WHITE PINE**

Nug - *see* **NIGER SEED**
NuMex Eclipse - *see* **NEW MEXICO CHILLIES**
NuMex Sunrise - *see* **NEW MEXICO CHILLIES**
NuMex Sunset - *see* **NEW MEXICO CHILLIES**
Nut(-)grass - *see* **CHUFA**
NUTMEG (*see also* **MACE**) - A kernel of the fruit of a tropical tree (*Myristica fragrans*), the dried nutmeg berry is called "nutmeg" because of its nutlike appearance. Nutmeg and mace are the only spices that come from the same fruit, with mace the aril of the dried seed. The nutmeg berry can be as small as an apricot or as large as a peach. An ancient spice, nutmeg is native to the Moluccas (the "Spice Islands") and was employed in South Asian cuisines for many centuries before it found its way to Rome, where Pliny wrote of a tree that bore a nut with two different tastes. Its subsequent history is that of mace. Like mace, nutmeg has been used in the West primarily in sweet beverages and desserts. Many grate it at home, as needed, with a small grater. But nutmeg can also be purchased already ground. A sprinkle works well in stews and numerous sauces. The oil derived from nutmeg has medicinal applications and is also a component of nutmeg butter. Today, nutmeg is grown primarily in Grenada and Indonesia.

See in addition: "Spices and Flavorings," Part II, Section F, Chapter 1.

Nut pine - *see* **PINE NUT**
Nux gallia - *see* **WALNUT**
Nypa palm - *see* **NIPA PALM**

Oak tongue - *see* **MUSHROOMS AND FUNGI**
OAT(S) - One of the last of the wild grasses to be domesticated and cultivated, oats (*Avena sativa*) have served humans principally as a feed for domestic animals. Historically, oats achieved only a relatively minor status as a food for humans - perhaps because the crop was a latecomer among the domesticated grains - and today only about 5 percent of the world's crop is consumed in this way. Developed from wild grasses of eastern Europe and Asia, oats were despised by the Egyptians and others of the Middle East and were viewed as animal fodder by the Greeks and Romans. Indeed, it may be the case that the plant, which existed mostly as a weed in wheatfields, was not domesticated until after the Christian era had begun.

Some time after this, oats became a staple food in Scotland (mostly in the form of porridge) and by 1600 the grain was adapted as an important crop to the wet climate of northern Europe. By 1650, oats had crossed the Atlantic to be planted in Massachusetts, and in 1877 the Quaker Mill Company was founded in Ravenna, Ohio. Beginning in 1884, "Quaker Oats" - one of the first packaged foods to be marketed – were sold in the now-famous card-board canisters. "Steel-cut" oats are cracked-oat kernels, whereas "rolled" oats have been put through a roller to flatten them into thin flakes. Oats are a good source of manganese, folacin, iron, zinc, and vitamin E and an excellent source of dietary fiber. Oat bran is said to be an effective cholesterol reducer and thus was the focus of a health-food craze for a period in the latter part of the twentieth century. Today, we know that oats can help to lower LDL (the "bad" cholesterol), but not by enough to justify the claims of the faddists.

Common names and synonyms: Rolled oat(s), steel-cut oat(s).

See also: "Oat," Part II, Section A, Chapter 6.

OCA – An important crop in the Andean highlands, oca (*Oxalis tuberosa*) has edible leaves and young shoots, but its tubers are the most important parts nutritionally. They are wrinkled and come in a variety of sizes and shapes, not to mention colors, which range from red and orange to yellow and white. There are two kinds, sweet and bitter. The sweet variety is eaten raw, cooked, and dried (by the sun). More intensive drying produces a product that tastes like dried figs and has been used as a sweetener by native populations.

Bitter oca is freeze-dried and stored for later use. After the potato, it was oca that sustained Native American highland populations for millennia, and it remains a staple of Peruvian and Bolivian Indians living at high altitudes. Around 1830, oca reached the British Isles, where it served as a food, especially in Wales. In France, the plant grows wild and is gathered to make a dish called Peruvian soup. In the 1860s, oca was carried to New Zealand by an English immigrant who acquired some of the tubers in Chile, and the plant has recently become popular there as a misnamed "yam" that is boiled, baked, and fried.

Common names and synonyms: Bitter oca, occa, oka, sweet oca, ulluco.

Occa - *see* **OCA**

Ochro - *see* **OKRA**

OGEN MELON (*see also* **MELON**) – This cultivar of the green-fleshed muskmelon was developed in Israel. Smaller than most melons, the Ogen melon (*Cucumis melo*) averages from 3 to 4 pounds and has a golden yellow skin with attractive vertical green stripes. When ripe, its creamy flesh has an appealing aroma and is deliciously sweet, which may explain why the chefs of many acclaimed restaurants offer the melon on their menus. The Ogen melon is featured in appetizers, salads, and desserts, often in tandem with other fruits or sorbets. An enticing combination is Ogen melon, raspberries, and port.

See in addition: "Cucumbers, Melons, and Watermelons," Part II, Section C, Chapter 6.

OIL-BEAN TREE – A tropical West African native, the oil-bean tree (*Pentaclethra macrophylla*) has seeds that are rich in an oil (owala oil) used locally for cooking purposes. The seeds, high in protein, are also employed as a condiment.

Common names and synonyms: Owala-oil tree.

Oil nut - *see* **WALNUT**

Oil palm - *see* "An Overview of Oils and Fats," Part II, Section E, Chapter 1; "Palm Oil," Part II, Section E, Chapter 3

Oka - *see* **OCA**

OKARI NUT – This nut (*Terminalia okari*) belongs to the family Combretaceae. Native to Papua New Guinea, it is now grown in Southeast Asia as well as in Hawaii and Florida. The nut has a shiny dark outer skin but is white inside. It is eaten raw or roasted and is pressed into oil.

OKRA – A member of the mallow family, and called "gumbo" and "lady-fingers" along with a host of other common names, okra (*Abelmoschus esculentus = Hibiscus esculentus*) is often thought of as a vegetable but is actually a fruit. A native of Africa (most likely tropical Africa), okra was used by the Egyptians, was known to the Spanish Moors in the twelfth century A.D., and in the late seventeenth century was carried by slaves to the Americas. According to legend, okra was introduced in southeastern North America by the "Cassette Girls" – 25 young Frenchwomen who landed at Mobile in 1704 in search of husbands. They had with them okra that had been obtained from slaves in the West Indies, and which they used to invent "gumbo," which is a soup or stew thickened with okra. Okra has played a major role in the cuisines of ex-slave societies in the Americas, where it continues to be especially popular. It is also cultivated in Africa and East and South Asia. Okra has been commonly used in gumbo, but the pods are also cooked (especially fried) as a vegetable. The plant is often found in home gardens and produces seeds that can be saved and used the following year. Much of the okra crop is frozen and canned, and in Asia a dried okra powder is also used. Okra is a good source of calcium, magnesium, and potassium as well as vitamin C, folacin, and some of the other B-vitamins.

Common names and synonyms: Bamia, *bendi,* bhindee, bhindi, bindi, cantarela, gombaut, gombo, gumbo, lady('s)-finger(s), mesta, ochro, okro, quiabo, quimbambo, quingombo, rosenapfel, vendakai.

Okro - *see* **OKRA**

Olallieberry - *see* **BLACKBERRY**

Old-man - *see* **SOUTHERNWOOD**

Oleaster - *see* **ELAEAGNUS**

OLIVE (*see also* **ELAEAGNUS, OSMANTHUS**) – A very old fruit – actually a berry – the olive grows on gnarled and twisted evergreen trees (*Olea europaea*) that are apparently eastern Mediterranean in origin and were under cultivation by Semitic peoples some 5,000 years ago. Phoenician colonists, who carried olive trees to the Iberian Peninsula about 800 B.C., may have introduced them throughout much of Mediterranean Europe and Africa as well. Ancient Hebrew texts mention olives, and they were known in Greece by about 900 B.C. The olive tree - called the "king of trees" in the Bible - was further spread by the Romans about those regions of Europe that could grow it. In the first century A.D., Pliny recorded a number of varieties under cultivation as far away as Gaul (France) and Iberia, and any areas in the Mediterranean basin that the Romans may have missed were later filled in with olive trees by the conquering Arabs. Olives reached the New World with the Spaniards in the first decades of the sixteenth century and were later carried to California by the Franciscans, who planted the trees in San Diego. And just prior to the American Revolution, Thomas Jefferson tried unsuccessfully to grow olives at Monticello.

Olives have been cultivated mostly for their oil. Those that are consumed are too bitter to be eaten fresh and are first pickled - cured in lye, brine, or dry salt, with the majority brine-cured. Olives come in all shapes and sizes but are sometimes misleadingly categorized as "green" and "ripe." In fact, the green ones are actually the ripest, whereas the black, so-called ripe olives from California are really unripe green olives that have been processed with lye and oxidized to turn them brownish black. Black olives that have been picked when truly ripe will appear shriveled. Among the best-known olive varieties that are pickled are the Queen (especially the Sevillano of Spain), the Mission (California's most important variety), and the Manzanillo (an Old World variety), which is the largest of the pickling olives. In the United States, olives have long been stuffed with pimento and more recently with tiny onions, almonds, hot peppers, and anchovies. In Europe, olives have an important place in cooking, especially in the Mediterranean cuisines of Greece, Italy, and Provence in France. They are also frequently permitted to ferment a bit, then served as an appetizer. Spain, Italy, Greece, and Portugal are the world's leading olive producers. California accounts for about 5 percent of the world's crop. Delicious as olives can be, the reason they are pressed for oil is because they are loaded with fat. After processing, they are also loaded with sodium.

Common names and synonyms: Black olive, green olive, king-of-trees, Manzanillo, Mission, pickling olive, Queen, ripe olive, Sevillano.

See in addition: "An Overview of Oils and Fats," Part II, Section E, Chapter 1.

Olivo - *see* **ACEITUNA**

Olluco - *see* **ULLUCO**

Omam - *see* **AJOWAN**

Omum - *see* **AJOWAN**

ONION (*see also* **ONION TREE, RAKKYO, WELSH ONION, WILD LEEK(S)**) - Cultivated since prehistoric times, the onion (*Allium cepa*) is a native of central or western Asia that has become indispensable to cuisines the world over. This plant was used by the ancient Egyptians, Babylonians, Romans, and Greeks, who believed it to have curative powers. In addition, onions - along with garlic and chickpeas - reportedly made up the bulk of the food rations for the 100,000 or so laborers who built the Great Pyramid of Cheops around 2900 B.C. The ancients interpreted the layered internal structure of the onion as a symbol of eternity, and later the onion-shaped towers which became part of the architecture of Russia and Eastern Europe were so constructed to (hopefully) ensure that the buildings would stand forever. During the Middle Ages in Europe, physicians prescribed onions for people's ills, and even today they are a part of many home remedies.

The most common of the onions is the yellow onion, which accounts for more than 75 percent of the world's production. Sweet onions include the Spanish, the Bermuda, the California Italian Red, the Vidalia (from the area around Vidalia, Georgia), the Walla Walla (from Washington State), and the Maui (from Hawaii). "Scallions," used in salads and vegetable trays, are also called salad or green onions. Red onions (known to some as Italian red onions), purple onions, and tiny "pearl onions" (used for pickling and added whole to soups and stews) round out the list of the cultivated varieties.

In addition, there are many wild varieties around the world, including those of North America. Onions are common in salads, and both raw and fried onions are used in sandwiches and a great variety of other dishes. They are made into soups and are baked, boiled, and sautéed. Onions can be purchased frozen and canned, and they are also dehydrated to become onion flakes, onion powders, and onion salt. Onions are high in vitamin C and were long important to sea and desert travelers as a means of preventing scurvy.

Common names and synonyms: Bermuda onion, California Italian Red onion, common onion, green onion, Italian red onion, Maui onion, pearl onion, purple onion, red onion, salad onion, scallion, Spanish onion, spring onion, sweet onion, Vidalia onion, Walla Walla onion, white onion, wild onion, yellow onion.

See in addition: "The *Allium* Species," Part II, Section C, Chapter 2; "Spices and Flavorings," Part II, Section F, Chapter 1.

ONION TREE (*see also* **ONIONS**) - An unusual plant, the onion tree (*Allium cepa*) has no bulb at the base of the stem. Rather, the bulb, bulbils, or bulblets are located at the top of the plant, and as the top becomes too heavy for the stem, the latter bends - so that the bulbils may root several inches away from the main plant. Because of this, the onion tree is sometimes called a "walking onion." The top bulblets are generally pickled, but the stems and tops are also used as scallions.

Common names and synonyms: Egyptian onion, Egyptian tree onion, perennial onion, walking onion.
See in addition: "The *Allium* Species," Part II, Section C, Chapter 2.

ONZA (*see also* **CHILLI PEPPERS**) – Although called for in many soup and sauce recipes, the onza pepper (*Capsicum annuum*) is difficult to find even in its native Mexico. It is a small chilli that looks like a bright red jalapeño and delivers a medium amount of heat.
See in addition: "Chilli Peppers," Part II, Section C, Chapter 4.

Oolong - *see* **TEA**

ORACH – The various plants of the genus *Atriplex,* especially *A. hortensis,* are called orach. Orach has edible green leaves that resemble those of spinach and are used in the same ways. Although naturalized in America, orach is a Eurasian native that has doubtless been a quarry of foragers for millennia. It is also an ancient cultivar that continued to be widely grown until the eighteenth century. Today, however, like other plants such as "Good-King-Henry," orach has returned to the wild.
Common names and synonyms: Garden orach, green orach, mountain spinach, orache, red orach.

Orache - *see* **ORACH**

ORANGE (*see also* **BLOOD ORANGE, CITRUS FRUITS, MANDARIN ORANGE, TANGOR**) – One way to categorize this fruit of the genus *Citrus* is to distinguish bitter oranges (*C. aurantium*) from sweet oranges (*C. sinensis*). The bitter orange (also known as Sevilla, sour orange, and Bigarade) is a native of Southeast Asia and was cultivated in the Indus Valley some 6,000 years ago. The sweet orange (also known as the China sweet orange and – in India – the Malta orange) may also have originated in Southeast Asia, although many believe it to be a native of southern China, as is evidenced by its scientific name. Both fruits were slow to find their way to the Mediterranean basin; the bitter orange eventually arrived with the Arabs around A.D. 1000, but the Western advent of the sweet orange came more than 400 years later, perhaps with the help of Genoese traders or Portuguese explorers.

Sweet-orange trees were planted at Versailles in 1421, and later (1548) in Lisbon. Meanwhile, in 1493, the second voyage of Christopher Columbus is said to have carried sweet-orange seeds (along with lemon seeds) to Hispaniola, and Spaniards stationed in Florida were reportedly growing oranges there in 1565, the year St. Augustine was founded. A couple of centuries later, the Franciscans began planting orange groves at their mission of San Diego in California. In western North America, however, California trailed behind Arizona, which saw its first groves at the beginning of the eighteenth century. By the end of the Civil War, Florida was already shipping large quantities of oranges to the rest of the country, and today that state produces about 70 percent of the U.S. crop, practically all of which (some 90 percent) is made into juice.

Sweet oranges can be further divided into the varieties that have been developed. In the United States, only sweet oranges are grown commercially. The Valencia – a major representative of the sweet orange, sometimes called the "common orange" – accounts for about half of the oranges produced annually. The popular "navel oranges" constitute another variety that is easily identified by thick skins and navel-like scars. Most of California's orange crop is from Washington navel orange trees (which were developed in Bahia, Brazil, and ripen for Christmas holiday sales) or from those of the Valencia variety. Still other varieties are the virtually seedless Hamlins (grown mostly in Florida), "Pineapple oranges" (good for juicing but with many seeds), and Jaffa oranges (developed in Israel), which are sweeter than Valencias. Still other sweet oranges, such as the blood oranges and the Mandarin oranges (Clementine, Tangelo, Tangerine, Temple) are treated in separate entries in this work.

There is less to say about sour-orange trees, which are grown mostly as rootstock for other *Citrus* species, and produce fruits that are too sour to be eaten raw. Their major use is for marmalades and preserves, although the bergamot orange is grown for its oil, and others, such as the myrtle-leafed orange, have small fruits that are candied. Oranges contain much in the way of vitamin C, and in fact, orange juice is the most important supplier of this vitamin for many Americans.
Common names and synonyms: Bergamot orange, Bigarade, bitter orange, China sweet orange, Chinese orange, Clementine, common orange, Hamlin, Jaffa orange, Malta orange, Mandarin orange, myrtle-leafed orange, navel orange, Pineapple orange, Sevilla, sour orange, sweet orange, tangelo, tangerine, Valencia, Washington navel orange.

Orange-flower oil - *see* **NEROLI**
Orange-flower water - *see* **NEROLI**
Orange gooseberry - *see* **GOOSEBERRY**
Orange milkweed - *see* **BUTTERFLY WEED**
Orange pekoe - *see* **TEA**

ORANGEQUAT (*see also* **CITRUS FRUITS**) – A cross between the kumquat and the Mandarin orange, the orangequat (genera *Citrus* and *Fortunella*) is another hybrid resulting from a program of research, sponsored by the U.S. Department of Agriculture, designed to breed the resistance to cold of the kumquat into plants of other genera that have desirable qualities. The orangequat has a good, kumquat-like flavor.

Orange root - *see* **BUTTERFLY WEED**
Oregano - *see* **MARJORAM AND OREGANO**
Oregon grape - *see* **BARBERRY**
Organ-pipe cactus - *see* **PITAHAYA**
Oriental garlic - *see* **CHINESE CHIVE(S), CHIVE(S)**
Oriental melon - *see* **BITTER MELON, MELONS**

Oriental pear - *see* ASIAN PEAR

Oriental pickling melon - *see* GHERKIN

Oriental radish - *see* DAIKON

Orris root - *see* IRIS

OSMANTHUS - Also called "devilwood" and "wild olive," *Osmanthus* is a widely distributed genus of evergreen shrubs or trees with small, olive-like fruits that are softened in brine and used like green olives. In addition, the flowers of *O. americanus* are employed to add aroma to black teas.

Common names and synonyms: Devilwood, wild olive.

Ostrich fern - *see* FIDDLEHEAD FERN

Oswego tea - *see* BEE BALM

Otaheita-apple - *see* GOLDEN APPLE

OTAHEITE GOOSEBERRY - Also known as the "gooseberry tree," the Otaheite gooseberry (*Phyllanthus acidus*) is a small tropical tree, native to Africa and South Asia, that is now naturalized in the Caribbean and southern Florida. It produces a small, round, acidic fruit that is edible but is too sour to be eaten raw. Rather, it is pickled, made into chutney, and used to produce a syrup and jams.

Common names and synonyms: Chermai, gooseberry tree, grosella, Indian gooseberry, Malay gooseberry.

OTAHEITE ORANGE (*see also* CITRUS FRUITS) - Otaheite was the former name of Tahiti, and the Otaheite orange (*Citrus taitensis*) has retained the old name while also going by the name "Tahiti orange." The fruit is the size of an apple, has the shape of a lemon, and is colored like an orange. The pulp tastes something like pineapple.

Common names and synonyms: Tahiti orange.

Oudo - *see* UDO

Oval-leaf - *see* PEPEROMIA

Owala-oil tree - *see* OIL-BEAN TREE

Owe kola - *see* KOLA NUT

OYSTER MUSHROOM (*see also* MUSHROOMS AND FUNGI) - Raised mostly in California, Canada, and the southeastern United States, the oyster mushroom (*Pleurotus ostreatus*) grows in wooded areas and forms clusters on the stumps of dead trees. The 2- to 6-inch cap resembles a seashell and is moist and spongy; the color is usually brown to gray and fades with age. The gills run down the stem and are widely separated; they have a creamy beige or white color. The stem, which may be absent, is white, short, and firm (not as soft as the cap). The oyster mushroom is very much in demand but is only good as long as it is immature.

Common names and synonyms: Oyster fungus, pleurotte, shimeji, tree mushroom, tree oyster.

See in addition: "Fungi," Part II, Section C, Chapter 7.

OYSTERNUT - A native of tropical Africa and cultivated in East and Central Africa, the oysternut (*Telfairia pedata*), also called the "Zanzibar oil vine," is cultivated mostly for its large, edible, nut-like seeds, which are very high in protein. They are generally roasted before consumption and are also pressed to yield an oil similar to that from olives.

Common names and synonyms: African pumpkin, fluted cucumber, Zanzibar oil-vine.

Oyster-plant - *see* SALSIFY

Pacura - *see* BAKUPARI

Pai - *see* ALOCASIA

Paiko - *see* CHENOPODIUM, EPAZOTE

PAKCHOI AND KAI CHOY (*see also* CHINESE CABBAGE) - Both pakchoi (*Brassica chinensis*) and kai choy (*B. campestris*) are variations of Chinese cabbage with many synonyms. Pakchoi looks like tiny Swiss chard, whereas the leaves of kai choy are cupped.

Common names and synonyms: Celery mustard, Chinese chard, gaai chow, gaai choy, gai chow, gai choy, Japanese white celery mustard, mustard cabbage, pak choy, pak choy sum, pak toy, spoon cabbage.

See in addition: "Cruciferous and Green Leafy Vegetables," Part II, Section C, Chapter 5.

Pak choy - *see* PAKCHOI AND KAI CHOY

Pak choy sum - *see* PAKCHOI AND KAI CHOY

Pak toy - *see* PAKCHOI AND KAI CHOY

Palmetto - *see* HEART(S) OF PALM

Palm heart(s) - *see* HEART(S) OF PALM

Palm lily - *see* CABBAGE TREE

Palm oil - *see* "An Overview of Oils and Fats," Part II, Section E, Chapter 1; "Palm Oil," Part II, Section E, Chapter 3

Palmyra - *see* WINE PALM

PALOMINO (*see also* GRAPES) - A grape grown mostly in Spain, the Palomino (*Vitis vinifera*) accounts for 90 percent of the grapes planted to make sherry (*jerez*), the renowned fortified wine of that country.

See in addition: "Wine," Part III, Chapter 13.

Palta - *see* AVOCADO

Pana de pepita - *see* BREADFRUIT

Panama berry - *see* CAPULIN

Panama orange - *see* CALAMONDIN

PANDANUS - There are a number of species of palm-like trees and shrubs of the genus *Pandanus* (also called "screw-pines") that are found in southeastern Asia and the Pacific region. Most are utilized for fiber to weave mats and other such articles. Some, however, are used as a food source by Pacific Islanders in places like Papua New Guinea. The terminal bud of the branch, or "heart," is eaten along with the tips of roots, the young leaves, and the seeds and fleshy part of the fruit, which in cultivated varieties can weigh upwards of 30 pounds. In addition, the heart can be made into a flour that is high in carbohydrates. Eaten raw, pandanus is a good source of vitamins A and C.

Common names and synonyms: Fruited pandanus, pandanus fruit, pandanus heart(s), pandanus key(s), pandanus nut, screw(-)pine.

Panic(oid) grass(es) - *see* **MILLET**

Papa - *see* **WHITE POTATO**

PAPAW - Also called "pawpaw" and "custard apple," the papaw is a small, fleshy, edible fruit from the tree designated *Asimina triloba*. These trees reach from 30 to 40 feet in height and grow wild in North America along the East Coast of the United States and from New York State through the Midwest. The fruit, which is shaped like a thick, short banana, turns black as it ripens, at which point the yellowish pulp has the taste of an overripe cantaloupe. Papaws can be eaten raw, but many people find the taste more agreeable when the fruit is cooked. Generally mentioned as one of the many foods that sustained Native Americans, the papaw is central to a muddle of nomenclature because its names, "papaw" and "pawpaw," probably came from "papaya," a fruit to which it is not related. Nor is "custard apple" an appropriate nickname, because it is generally one of the names given to the cherimoya – also not a relative.

Common names and synonyms: Custard apple, paw(-)paw.

PAPAYA (*see also* **BABACO, CHAMBURO, MOUNTAIN PAPAYA**) - The papaya tree (*Carica papaya*) is an evergreen with a palmlike appearance. It is native to tropical Mesoamerica, is related to the gourd, melon, and pumpkin family, and may represent an ancient fusion of two or more species of the genus *Carica,* native to Mexico and Central America. The first Spaniards to reach Yucatán were welcomed by Mayans bearing gifts of fruit, among them papayas. At that time, the papaya was known only from Mexico to Panama, but shortly afterward, the Spaniards began moving the fruit via their Manila galleons westward across the Pacific to the Philippines and beyond, and the Portuguese carried it around the globe in the other direction.

The result is that the papaya is now cultivated throughout the tropical world – especially in Hawaii, Africa, and South Asia – for its fruit and for its milky latex. The latex contains the proteolytic enzyme papain, which is used as a meat tenderizer, to clear beer, and also for medical purposes. The yellow, orange, or pinkish somewhat sweet fruit is usually eaten raw (often for breakfast) but is also candied, converted into juice, put into pies and salads, and used to make sherbets. The unripe fruit is cooked like squash.

The papaya is sometimes wrongly called "pawpaw" or "papaw." Although papayas are grown throughout the world's tropical regions, most of those reaching U.S. consumers are the pear-shaped Solo varieties from Hawaii (introduced there from Barbados). These are about 6 inches in length and have either pink or yellow flesh. Papayas are a fine source of vitamin C.

Common names and synonyms: Green papaya, melon fruit, melon pawpaw, papaw, paw(-)paw, Solo (papaya).

Papdi - *see* **SUGAR PEA**

PAPER MULBERRY - This tree (*Broussonetia papyrifera*) is called "paper mulberry" because its bark is used to make paper in China and Japan. The tree also produces a sweet, red fruit, which is eaten raw, and leaves that are also edible. The paper mulberry is a native of East Asia that is now naturalized in southeastern North America.

Paper-reed - *see* **PAPYRUS**

Paper-rush - *see* **PAPYRUS**

Papoose root - *see* **BLUE COHOSH**

PAPRIKA (*see also* **CHILLI PEPPERS, SWEET PEPPERS**) - Because paprika, like cayenne, is made from dried American red peppers (*Capsicum annuum* and *C. frutescens*), it is a relative newcomer to the world's spice rack. As a rule, the chillies made into paprika are less potent than those used for cayenne. Chilli peppers were carried by the conquistadors from Mexico to Spain. The peppers subsequently found their way to Poland (the name "paprika" comes from the Polish *pierprzyca*) and then to Hungary, where they became a vital ingredient in Hungarian goulash – and, in due course, as the Hungarians perfected it, paprika became the national spice.

Paprika comes as sweet, mild, and hot (only the seeds are used for the mild type; the hot version is made from the whole fruit), and the best is made in Hungary; paprika made elsewhere is without much flavor and used mostly for the color it imparts. Paprika both flavors and adorns many Hungarian dishes, and it also spices and colors the sausages of Spain – another country that produces large quantities of paprika for its own national dishes.

Common names and synonyms: Paprika pepper, paprika plant.

See in addition: "Chilli Peppers," Part II, Section C, Chapter 4.

PAPYRUS - A tall sedge of the Nile Valley, papyrus (*Cyperus papyrus*) has also been called "paper-rush" and "paper-reed" because it was used by the ancient Egyptians, Greeks, and Romans to make a sheet or roll of material to write on. Practically forgotten is the food value of the plant, which provided tender shoots and rhizomes for the cooking pot.

Common names and synonyms: Paper-reed, paper-rush.

Paradise nut - *see* **SAPUCAIA NUT**

Paradise tree - *see* **ACEITUNA**

Paraguay(an) tea - *see* **YERBA MATÉ**

Para nut - *see* **BRAZIL NUT**

Paris mushroom - *see* **MUSHROOMS AND FUNGI**

Parish's yampah - *see* **INDIAN POTATO**

PARKIA - Named for the eighteenth-century Scottish explorer and surgeon Mungo Park, *Parkia* is a genus of leguminous, Old World tropical trees with pods that contain edible seeds and pulp. Among the species are the nitta tree (*P. biglobosa*) and the petai tree (*P. speciosa*). The latter has large, edible beans that hang down on the outside of the tree.

Common names and synonyms: Nitta tree, petai tree.

Parry pinyon pine - *see* **PINE NUT**

PARSLEY (*see also* **HAMBURG PARSLEY, LOVAGE)** - The aromatic leaves of parsley (*Petroselinum crispum*), a native of southern Europe, are employed for flavoring, although some parsley varieties are boiled and their roots consumed as a vegetable. The use of parsley dates from at least the time of the ancient Greeks, and because the plant has been introduced into most areas of the globe, it is one of the world's best-known herbs. According to the Sardinians, it is native to their island, although other regions also claim parsley as their own; regardless, it has been used in the Mediterranean region for thousands of years. The Greeks, who made crowns of it to honor athletes at ceremonies and themselves at banquets, also had medical uses for the herb. The Romans utilized parsley as an herb and introduced the plant throughout Europe.

There are three basic kinds of parsley. One is the familiar, bright-green curly parsley; another, sometimes called Italian parsley, has flat leaves and a stronger flavor than the curly type. The third is Hamburg parsley, also called turnip-rooted parsley, which is grown for its long white root, that when cooked tastes something like celeriac. Both curly and Italian parsley lend taste and eye appeal to salads and other dishes. Parsley also comes in dried flakes, but these have virtually no taste. The fresh kinds are rich in vitamins A and C, calcium, and iron.

Common names and synonyms: Curly parsley, Italian parsley.

See in addition: "Spices and Flavorings," Part II, Section F, Chapter 1.

PARSNIP - The parsnip (*Pastinaca sativa*), a native of Europe and western Asia, has been cultivated for its long, yellowish brown, carrot-shaped edible taproot since at least the time of the ancient Greeks. In the Middle Ages, physicians credited parsnips with medicinal properties, and in parts of England and Ireland (where parsnips have long enjoyed considerable popularity), many different ways of preparing the vegetable have evolved, and even a kind of wine has been made from its fermented roots.

Parsnips were introduced into the West Indies during the sixteenth century and North America at the beginning of the seventeenth century, whereupon their use spread rapidly among Native Americans. The vegetable also served as an important staple in the diet of the European colonists until the potato finally replaced it in the nineteenth century. Parsnips are usually boiled, then sometimes mashed or pureed, but they can also be fried and baked and go well in stews. The taste of parsnips is best only after the first frost; indeed, it was long customary to leave much of a crop in the ground over the winter to let the action of frost improve the flavor even more.

Such a practice, however, was not without controversy; some people insisted that parsnips became poisonous when left in the ground, whereas others held that the vegetable was not safe to eat until after it had weathered the first frost. Both sides have been pronounced wrong for various reasons, but very recently, medical science has suggested that parsnips may be toxic after all - because they contain psoralens, which have been linked to the development of cancer and mutations in laboratory animals. Unlike their relative the carrot, parsnips contain little beta-carotene, but they are rich in vitamin C.

Common names and synonyms: Wild parsnip.

Pasado - *see* **ANAHEIM**

PASILLA (*see also* **CHILLI PEPPERS)** - In Spanish, *pasa* means raisin, and thus *pasilla* translates as "little raisin." However, there is nothing raisin-like about the size of this chilli pepper (*Capsicum annuum*), which when fresh is called *chilaca* and averages about 6 inches in length. And even though it does have a wrinkled skin when dried, its other name, chilli negro, inspired by its dark color, seems more appropriate. Fresh *chilacas* are seldom available - in part, one suspects, because of the considerable demand for the dried fruit, which is regarded as crucial to many Mexican mole sauces. Other pasilla relatives that are smoked and dried are the *Pasilla de Oaxaca* (so called because it is grown only in Oaxaca) and the *Pátzcuaro*, both of which are relatively hot. *Pasillas* are also employed in salsas and are available in both dried and powdered forms. They are moderately hot.

Common names and synonyms: Chilaca, chilli negro, *Pasilla de Oaxaca, Pátzcuaro.*

See in addition: "Chilli Peppers," Part II, Section C, Chapter 4.

PASSION FRUIT - Native to southern Brazil, the passion fruit (*Passiflora edulis* or *P. quadrangularis*) is so named because early Spaniards in the New World thought that they saw in its flowers the symbols of the passion of Christ. However, they also called it a *granadilla*, representing the more mundane observation that the fruit resembled a small pomegranate. The fruits are yellow or purple berries, which can be either sour or sweet. They are eaten raw (including the edible seeds), the pulp is used to make cold drinks, and immature fruits are sometimes boiled as a vegetable.

Most passion fruits, however, become passion-fruit juice, which is used in numerous beverages and sauces. Passion fruits are grown commercially in California, Australia, South Africa, New Zealand, Hawaii, Kenya, and especially Colombia. There are some 350 other types of passion fruits, among them the "yellow granadilla" and the "wild water lemon" of Brazil and the "sweet granadilla" of Central America. Passion fruits are an excellent source of vitamins C and A and iron.

Common names and synonyms: Granadilla, maracuja, purple granadilla, purple passionfruit, sweet granadilla, wild passion-flower, wild water lemon, yellow granadilla, yellow passionfruit.

Patate aquatique - *see* **SWAMP CABBAGE**

PATAUÁ - A palm tree (*Jessinia bataua*) that is native to the Americas and is, indeed, the most common palm in the Amazon region, patauá has a huge fruit that provides both an edible oil (patauá oil) and a beverage. The oil, similar to olive oil, is used in cooking. The beverage, *chicha de seje,* tastes like chocolate.

Common names and synonyms: Seje ungurahuay.

Pátzcuaro - *see* **PASILLA**

Paw(-)paw - *see* **PAPAW, PAPAYA**

PEA(S) (*see also* **BEACH PEA, CHICKLING VETCH, LEGUMES, PEA LEAF, SUGAR PEA**) - Technically legumes, "peas" are the edible seeds enclosed in the elongated green pods of the vine *Pisum sativum.* Peas comprise a large group that can be divided into those that are "edible-podded" and those that are "tough-podded." Foremost among the latter are "green peas," also known as "garden peas" and "English peas" - the large, bulging sweet peas, fresh from gardens or found in produce markets. Other varieties - often canned or frozen - include baby green peas (*petits pois*) and the larger "early" or "June" peas. The edible-podded peas include "sugar" or "snow" peas, the sugar snap pea (*mange-tout*), and the Chinese pea pod. Historically, however, by far the most important peas in a nutrition sense were those that were preserved and consumed throughout the year.

Like so many of our foods, there is confusion over the origin of the pea, which may have occurred in central or southern Asia or in the Middle East. In any event, the wild forms must have been tasty seasonal items on the menus of hunter-gatherers, and peas were among the first plants to be domesticated - about 8,000 years ago (following the beginning of agriculture), after which they spread quickly to the Mediterranean region and to India and China.

Peas were an important food of the Egyptians, Greeks, and Romans - indeed, the word "pea" is from the Latin *pisum,* which was in turn derived from the Greek *pison.* The ancient Greeks mostly ate peas dried, as did the Europeans of the Middle Ages. The Old English *pise* became *pease* to remind us that "pease porridge" hot, cold, or nine days old was a bulwark of the English diet. In the sixteenth century, tender varieties of green peas (designed to be eaten fresh) entered the diet as the *mange-tout* or sugar pea was developed in Dutch gardens, and *petits pois* became a part of French cuisine.

Meanwhile, peas had made their way with the earliest settlers to the New World, becoming part of the diet of North America, and in 1870 the vegetable was among the first to be canned by what

would become the Campbell Soup Company. And while dwelling on the subject of peas and their history, we should mention the famous experiments during the 1860s in which the Austrian monk Gregor Mendel employed peas to deduce two fundamental laws of genetic inheritance.

Chickpeas, black-eyed peas ("cowpeas"), and pigeon peas are not true peas and are treated in other entries.

Common names and synonyms: Baby green pea, chickling vetch, Chinese pea pod, early pea, edible-podded pea, English pea, field pea, garden pea, green pea, June pea, *mange-tout, petits pois,* snow pea, sugar pea, sugar snap pea, sweet pea, tough-podded pea.

See in addition: "Beans, Peas, and Lentils," Part II, Section C, Chapter 3.

Pea apple - *see* **EGGPLANT**

Pea aubergine - *see* **EGGPLANT**

PEACH - Apparently a native of China despite its scientific name, *Prunus persica,* the peach spread to the Middle East and then to Greece. The Romans introduced the fruit in Europe, and the Spaniards carried it to the New World. In fact, peaches were growing so widely in eastern North America by the time of the American Revolution that many assumed the fruit to be an American native. Peaches are one of the stone fruits (drupes) and are classified as freestone or clingstone, depending on how easily the flesh separates from the pit. Modern peaches, the result of centuries of selective breeding, have either white or yellow flesh. Yellow-fleshed freestone types are the most preferable, and the "Bonanza" is the most popular of these. Peaches that are sold fresh or frozen are almost always freestone (as, for example, the Rio Oso Gem); clingstones (like the Red Haven) are generally used for canning. Peaches are a fine source of vitamins A and C.

Common names and synonyms: Bonanza peach, clingstone peach, freestone peach, Red Haven peach, Rio Oso Gem peach.

Peach palm - *see* **PEJEBAYE**

PEA LEAF (*see also* **PEA**) - In China, the tender leaves of the garden pea (*Pisum sativum*) are prevented from flowering or fruiting, which allows them to grow. Sold fresh, they are stir-fried and used in soups, generally on special occasions.

See in addition: "Beans, Peas, and Lentils," Part II, Section C, Chapter 3.

PEANUT (*see also* **HOG PEANUT**) - Native to South America, the peanut (*Arachis hypogaea*) is actually not a nut but a legume that develops belowground (hence the name "groundnut") and is very soft before it is dried. Peanuts dating from around 800 B.C. have been found in archaeological excavations in Peru. Native Americans ate the nuts fresh as a vegetable but also roasted them and crushed them into a nutritious, oily paste. Peanuts were being grown by the Tainos on Hispaniola when the Spaniards first arrived in the West Indies, and were later carried to the Philippines and the East on the Spanish Manila galleons.

The Portuguese accomplished the same thing, heading in the other direction. From Brazil, they introduced peanuts into Africa, where the crop became an important staple almost immediately. They also carried them to India, which today is the largest producer of peanuts, followed by China and the United States (with Nigeria the biggest exporter). In fact, the peanut is now a crop of tremendous commercial importance the world over.

Until World War II, peanuts were used mostly as livestock feed, but since then their importance in the human diet has increased enormously, although peanut meal continues to be used for animal feed. Peanuts are salted in the shell by soaking in a brine solution. They are dry-roasted, boiled, and made into peanut butter (which accounts for about half of the U.S. crop) and peanut brittle. Peanuts are also pressed to yield an oil for cooking, preserving, and use at the table and are made into flour for bread baking. Indonesians, Indians, Africans, and the Chinese prepare wonderful dishes that include peanuts, but this is generally not the case in the plant's home hemisphere, save for the West African cookery of the Brazilian northeast. Peanuts are higher in protein than any other nut and are a fine source of the B-vitamins, magnesium, and iron.

Common names and synonyms: Earth nut, goober (pea), groundnut, *mani,* monkey nut, runner peanut, Spanish peanut, Valencia peanut, Virginia peanut.

See in addition: "Peanuts," Part II, Section D, Chapter 2; "An Overview of Oils and Fats," Part II, Section E, Chapter 1.

Peanut-butter fruit - *see* **BUNCHOSIA**

PEAR - Indicative not so much of the millennia over which the pear (*Pyrus communis*) has been cultivated but rather of grafting done over the past few centuries, there are now some 5,000 varieties of the fruit. Native to the Middle East, pears today also grow wild across much of Europe and Asia. They do not seem to have been known to the ancient Greeks or Egyptians, but were to the Romans, who spread pear cultivation throughout their empire.

Pear trees were brought by early European visitors to North America, where the bell-shaped, yellow-skinned Bartlett, a summer pear, has emerged as the most widely grown and a pear much used in canning. The Anjou is the most abundant winter pear. Other varieties that can be found in markets include the Bosc, which is firm and thus is good for cooking and baking; the Comice, perhaps the sweetest of pears; the tiny Seckel; the juicy, sweet Clapp; and the Nellis, a late-winter pear. A pome fruit, the pear is related to the apple, and like apples, pears are frequently baked or otherwise

cooked as well as eaten raw, especially as dessert pears. In addition, they are turned into cider ("perry"), although not so often today as in the past. Pears are also canned and made into pear nectar. Most of the vitamin C and fiber that raw pears supply in good quantity is contained in the skins.

Common names and synonyms: Anjou, Bartlett, Bosc, Clapp, Comice, common pear, Nellis, perry, pome(-fruit), Seckel, summer pear, Winter Nellis, winter pear.

Pear haw - *see* **HAW**

Pearl moss - *see* **CARRAGEEN AND CARRAGEENIN**

Pear(-)melon - *see* **PEPINO**

Pearson bean - *see* **SWORD BEAN**

PECAN - A North American nut (actually a kind of hickory nut) sometimes said to be a native of Oklahoma, the pecan (*Carya illinoinensis*) is really indigenous to an area extending from the U.S. Midwest throughout the South and Southwest into Mexico - a region where it still grows wild today. Pecans are commercially cultivated in the band of states running from Georgia west to New Mexico, as well as in Mexico, Brazil, and, outside of the Western Hemisphere, in Israel, South Africa, and Australia.

The first recorded instance of pecan cultivation is said to have been when Thomas Jefferson carried the trees from the Mississippi Valley back to Virginia and gave them to George Washington. But long before this - eons before the Europeans arrived - pecans were an important item in the diet of Native Americans living in the south-central region of North America. The name "pecan" comes from the Algonquian *paccan,* which is similar to the Ojibwa *pagân,* meaning "hard-shelled nut."

The shells of wild pecans are indeed hard, but those that are cultivated have been bred for thinner shells that are easier to crack. The nuts are eaten raw, roasted, dry-roasted, and fried. They flavor stuffings for poultry as well as numerous desserts, including pecan pie. Unfortunately, as a nut, the pecan is high in fat and low in protein, but it does deliver a respectable amount of the B-vitamins, vitamin E, and numerous minerals.

Common names and synonyms: Carya pecan.

PEDRO XIMÉNEZ (*see also* **GRAPES**) - The best of the grapes planted to make sherry, the Pedro Ximénez (*Vitis vinifera*) is named for Peter Siemons, who carried the grape from Germany to Spain. Pedro Ximénez grapes are also employed to make white wines.

See in addition: "Wine," Part III, Chapter 13.

PEJEBAYE - Also known as the "peach palm," the pejebaye (*Bactris gasipaës* = *Guilielma utilis* = *G. gasipaës*) is a palm tree of the western Amazon region that was domesticated by Native Americans. It bears a fruit (largely unknown outside of Brazil) that somewhat resembles an apricot, although it is triangular in form. It is cooked before eating - usually by roasting. In addition, the fruit is dried and ground into flour and is also pressed for vegetable oil. But the tree's main culinary function (at least recently) has been to provide fresh palm hearts for Latin American and North American markets.

Common names and synonyms: Peach palm.

Peking cabbage - *see* **CHINESE CABBAGE**

Pekoe souchong - *see* **TEA**

PENNYCRESS - Plants of the genus *Thlaspi* are called "pennycress" along with a host of other names. Their leaves are edible, and the seeds can be employed as a condiment, like mustard seed. There are native species in North America that were a part of the diet of Native Americans. In Asia, Eurasian pennycress species have also long been cultivated.

Common names and synonyms: Fanweed, field pennycress, French weed, penny grass, thoroughwort pennycress.

Penny grass - *see* **PENNYCRESS**

Pennyroyal - *see* **MINT**

PENNYWORT - Any of several plants of the genus *Centella* (and the closely related *Hydrocotyle*) are called "pennywort," including Indian pennywort (*C. asiatica*). Also known as "coinworth" and *gota kola*, Indian pennywort has round green leaves that historically have been considered a stimulant to brain activity in India. They are eaten raw, cooked as a vegetable, and made into tea. Sometime in the past, the plant reached the eastern United States, where it grows as a weed.

Common names and synonyms: Asiatic pennywort, coinworth, *gota kola*, Indian pennywort.

PEPEROMIA - A large genus of tropical herbs, *Peperomia* belongs to the family Piperaceae - the same family as *Piper nigrum*, which provides the white and black peppercorns used at the table. Today, species of *Peperomia* are grown as ornamentals, but in the past some, like "oval-leaf" (*Peperomia obtusifolia*), were cultivated for their leaves, which were eaten as a vegetable.

Common names and synonyms: Oval-leaf.

Pepinella - *see* **CHAYOTE**

Pepinito - *see* **GHERKIN**

PEPINO - Also called "melon-shrub," "melon-pear," and "pear-melon," and often mistaken for a melon because of its taste and shape, the pepino (*Solanum muricatum*) is a native of the Andean region of South America and, like peppers and tomatoes, a member of the nightshade family. It was domesticated in pre-Columbian times and was widely cultivated when the Spaniards first arrived. For reasons that remain obscure, they named it *pepino de la tierra*, or "native cucumber." Although the pepino comes in many varieties, none of them resemble a cucumber. The most common are reddish, with stripes of varying color. The fruit is quite sweet and watery, like the cantaloupe. Outside of the American tropics, pepinos are cultivated in California and

New Zealand, which together meet most North American demand.

Common names and synonyms: Kachun, melon (-)pear, melon(-)shrub, native cucumber, pear (-)melon, *pepino de la tierra, pepino dulce.*

Pepino de la tierra - *see* **PEPINO**

Pepino dulce - *see* **PEPINO**

Pepitas - *see* **PUMPKIN**

Pepo - *see* **SQUASH AND PUMPKIN**

Pepper - *see* **CHILLI PEPPERS, INDIAN LONG PEPPER, JAVANESE LONG PEPPER, MELEGUETA PEPPER, PEPPER(CORNS), SICHUAN PEPPERCORN, SWEET PEPPERS**

PEPPERCORN - *Piper nigrum* is a vine - native to the East Indies - that has a small berry-like fruit called a peppercorn. Peppercorns, from which pepper is ground, come in colors. Underripe berries are green. When the full-grown but unripe fruit is dried, it is black. If the berries are allowed to mature further, they turn red or pink. White pepper - which commands a higher market price - is the result of drying the ripe fruit, then removing the outer shell. Lampong and Tellicherry are black peppercorns; Muntok and Sarawak are white. These pungent condiments are among the most important of the East Indian spices that have been eagerly sought since ancient times.

The Greeks and Romans accepted peppercorns as tribute, and the spice was certainly the basis for much of the "lure of the East" that impelled first the Portuguese and then other European explorers around Africa toward the fabled Spice Islands. Although both are called "pepper," *Piper nigrum* should not be confused with the American chilli peppers of the *Capsicum* genus. Major producers of pepper(corns) today include Indonesia, India, Malaysia, and China; white pepper is preferred by the majority of people in the latter country. In addition, white pepper yields an oil that is used in perfumes and medicines.

Common names and synonyms: Black pepper(corn), green pepper(corn), Lampong, long pepper, mignonette pepper, Muntok, pepper, pink pepper(corn), *pippah,* red pepper(corn), Sarawak, Sichuan pepper(corn), Tellicherry, white pepper(corn).

See also: "Spices and Flavorings," Part II, Section F, Chapter 1.

Pepper(-)grass - *see* **CRESS**

Pepperidge - *see* **BARBERRY, BLACK GUM**

Peppermint - *see* **MINT**

Pepper of Calicut - *see* **CHILLI PEPPERS**

PEPPERONCINI (*see also* **CHILLI PEPPERS**) - An orange-red chilli that is also known as "pepperoncino," the pepperoncini (*Capsicum annuum*) is a favorite in Italy, Sicily, and Sardinia. When dried, it is wrinkled, curved, and about 2 to 3 inches in length. A moderately hot pepper, the pepperoncini is used in sauces and cooked dishes and is often bottled in olive oil. It is also grown in Louisiana for the production of hot sauces.

Common names and synonyms: Pepperoncino.

See in addition: "Chilli Peppers," Part II, Section C, Chapter 4.

Pepper-root - *see* **TOOTHWORT**

Pepper tree - *see* **MASTIC TREE**

Pequín - *see* **TEPÍN CHILLIES AND RELATIVES**

Perennial goosefoot - *see* **GOOD-KING-HENRY**

Perennial onion - *see* **ONION TREE**

Perennial pea - *see* **EVERLASTING PEA**

Périgord (truffle) - *see* **TRUFFLE(S)**

PERILLA - Native to the Himalayan mountains between India and China, perilla (*Perilla frutescens* and *P. ocimoides*) is a plant grown for its fruit and leaves. The fruit seeds contain an oil that is employed in cooking and has industrial applications as well. The leaves are dried and used as an herb in cooking.

PERIWINKLE - Periwinkle is comprised of several Old World vetchlike herbs of the genus *Vinca*. *Vinca major*, a trailing foliage plant, is called "large periwinkle," whereas *V. minor*, a trailing evergreen herb, is known as "common periwinkle," "myrtle," "running myrtle," and "creeping myrtle." A third plant - this of the Old World tropics - is *V. rosea* (= *Catharanthus roseus*), which is called "cape periwinkle," "red periwinkle," and "Madagascar periwinkle." These plants are cultivated mostly for fodder, but their seeds have also served humans as food, especially during times of hardship.

Common names and synonyms: Cape periwinkle, common periwinkle, creeping myrtle, large periwinkle, Madagascar periwinkle, myrtle, red periwinkle, running myrtle.

Perry - *see* **PEAR**

Persian lime - *see* **LIME**

Persian walnut - *see* **WALNUT**

PERSIMMON - Although there are persimmon trees that are native to North America, the orange-red persimmon (*Diospyros kaki*) that North Americans usually consume originated in Asia. This persimmon is native to China but is known as the Japanese persimmon because it has been cultivated mostly in Japan. Today, however, the fruit is also cultivated in the south of France and some of the Mediterranean countries, where it was introduced in the early nineteenth century, and in the southern United States and California, where it arrived in 1870.

The American persimmon (*Diospyros virginiana*) is native to the eastern and southern United States, and the name "persimmon" - deriving from the Algonquian *pessemin* - is American, too. The Algonquians ate persimmons raw and also dried the fruits for winter consumption. American persimmons are smaller than those from Japan, which are about the size of a tomato. Both varieties may be yellow, orange, or red, although the American persimmon can be a darker red, almost purple. The trees of the *D. kaki* species grow to between 20

and 30 feet in height, whereas *D. virginiana* reaches 30 to 60 feet. A mature tree will yield 75 to 100 pounds of persimmons annually.

The Hachiya variety, which accounts for the overwhelming bulk of the commercial crop in the United States (grown mostly in California), is an astringent variety, meaning that it is bitter until it is ripe. Another variety, Fuyu (crisper and lighter in color), is more common in Japan and Israel. When ripe, persimmons are soft, and their brown or orange pulp has a sweet taste. They are a good source of beta-carotene and potassium as well as vitamin C.

Common names and synonyms: American persimmon, Chinese fig, common persimmon, date plum, Fuyu, Hachiya, Japanese persimmon, *kaki,* Oriental persimmon.

Peruvian carrot - *see* **ARRACACHA**

Peruvian groundcherry - *see* **CAPE GOOSE-BERRY**

Peruvian parsnip - *see* **ARRACACHA**

Petai tree - *see* **PARKIA**

Petanga - *see* **PITANGA**

PETITE SIRAH (*see also* **GRAPES**) - Not the true Syrah (also Shiraz) grape, the Petite Sirah (*Vitis vinifera*) makes a wine that is dark red to almost purple, with a peppery taste. Although in California the Petite Sirah grape was at one time believed to be the Syrah, it is now generally thought that it is the Durif Rhône grape, which is no longer grown in France. Once used to make a blending wine, the Petite Sirah has become an important varietal in the California wine industry.

See in addition: "Wine," Part III, Chapter 13.

Petits pois - *see* **PEA(S)**

Pe-tsai - *see* **CHINESE CABBAGE**

Pfifferling - *see* **CHANTERELLE, MUSHROOMS AND FUNGI**

PHALSA - Also known as "pharsa," phalsa (*Grewia asiatica*) is a shrubby tree of India and the East Indies. It produces a small red berry that is used to make sorbets and syrups but is too tart to eat out of hand.

Common names and synonyms: Pharsa.

Pharsa - *see* **PHALSA**

Philippine orange - *see* **CALAMONDIN**

Philippine spinach - *see* **TALINUM**

PHYSIC NUT - A small tree, originally of the American tropics, *Jatropha curcas* produces the "physic nut," which yields curcas oil. The oil has medicinal uses, especially as a purgative, but is toxic in high doses. When roasted, however, the nuts are said to be relatively harmless and are apparently consumed by many in India as well as the Americas. The young leaves of the tree are cooked like greens, and ashes of the burned root are used as a substitute for salt.

Common names and synonyms: Curcas oil, purging nut.

Piasa - *see* SUDAN POTATO
Pico de Pajaro - *see* CAYENNE PEPPER
Piedmont truffle - *see* TRUFFLE(S)
Pie-plant - *see* RHUBARB
Pigeon berry - *see* POKEWEED
PIGEON PEA (*see also* BEANS, LEGUMES) - Called by literally scores of names including "Congo pea," "no-eye pea," "red gram," and "gandul," the pigeon pea (*Cajanus cajan* or *C. indicus*) is probably native to South Asia and perhaps tropical Africa. Actually a bean that grows on a perennial shrub, it is one of the oldest cultivated plants and now is widespread throughout the tropical world, with India a center of diversity. In the Americas, it is a very important crop in Jamaica and is naturalized in South Florida and Mexico.

The fresh leaves are often used as a vegetable, as are the immature pods. The seeds are dried and used in the same ways as lentils or split peas in soups, stews, and so forth. Like other dried beans, pigeon peas are rich in nutrients. They are high in calcium, iron, protein, the vitamin-B complex, and folacin.

Common names and synonyms: Alverja, Bengal bean, Congo pea, dhal(I), gandul, goongoo pea, gray pea, Gungo pea, Indian dhal, Indian pea, no-eye pea, pois cajun, pois d'Angole, red gram, yellow dhal(I).

See in addition: "Beans, Peas, and Lentils," Part II, Section C, Chapter 3.

PIGEON PLUM (*see also* PLUM) - An American plant that (like its close relative the sea grape) grows on the seacoasts of the southern United States, Mexico, and the Caribbean, the pigeon plum (*Coccoloba diversifolia* = *C. floridana*) is a drupaceous fruit that is quite astringent until ripe, after which it has a pleasant sweet-and-sour taste. Additionally, there is the edible fruit of an African tree (*Chrysobalanus ellipticus*) that is also called "pigeon plum."

Common names and synonyms: Snailseed.

Pignoli - *see* PINE NUT
Pignolia - *see* PINE NUT
Pignon - *see* PINE NUT
Pignut - *see* EARTH NUT
Pigweed - *see* AMARANTH, CHENOPODIUM, GOOSEFOOT, LAMB'S-QUARTER, PURSLANE, QUELITES, QUINOA
PILI NUT - A tropical evergreen tree of the Philippines, the pili nut (*Canarium ovatum*) has a number of uses. Its nuts are eaten both raw and roasted and in either case are said to have a very pleasant flavor. Additionally, pili nuts are used in baked goods and ice cream, and the kernel is pressed for an edible oil of high quality. The pulp of its fruit is also pressed for oil but can be eaten, as can the young shoots, which frequently appear in salads. Most of the nuts are harvested from trees growing in the wild, which means that the crop has remained a relatively minor one.

Pimenta - *see* ALLSPICE

Pimento - *see* ALLSPICE, SWEET PEPPERS
Pimiento - *see* SWEET PEPPERS
Pimiento - *see* CHILLI PEPPERS
Pimiento dulce - *see* SWEET PEPPERS
Pimiento morrón - *see* SWEET PEPPERS
Pimpinel - *see* BURNET
Piña - *see* PINEAPPLE
Pina anona - *see* MONSTERA
Pinang - *see* BETEL NUT
Pindo palm - *see* JELLY PALM
PINEAPPLE - A native of the New World, the pineapple (*Ananas comosus*) is now cultivated in frost-free areas around the world. The Tupi-Guarani Indians of South America have been credited with its domestication, although this is in some dispute. It would seem, however, that the origins of the pineapple are definitely in lowland South America. The earliest written references to the fruit were made by Spanish chroniclers, including Christopher Columbus, who is alleged to have named the fruit, calling it the "pine of the Indies" because of its resemblance to a pinecone. It is still called *piña* in Spanish today, whereas the Portuguese word for "pineapple," *ananás* (also part of the scientific name), derives from an Indian term for the fruit.

After their discovery, pineapples were used to provision ships and spread from the Americas by two routes: One was across the Pacific in Spain's Manila galleons to the Philippines and from there to China; the second was in Portuguese ships from Brazil to Africa and beyond to India. Before the end of the sixteenth century, pineapple cultivation had spread across much of the tropical world, and the plant had found its way to some of the Pacific Islands. In the late eighteenth century, pineapples were introduced in Hawaii, where they have since become that state's most important fruit crop. Pineapples are mostly canned and made into juice, although some are eaten fresh. They are an excellent source of vitamins A and C and potassium.

Common names and synonyms: Anana, *ananás*, Cayenne pineapple, Hawaiian pineapple, nana, *piña*.

Pineapple guava - *see* FEIJOA
Pineapple orange - *see* ORANGE
Pineapple quince - *see* QUINCE
Pinecone mushroom - *see* MOREL, MUSHROOMS AND FUNGI
PINE NUT - Also called pignoli, pignolia, pignons, piñon nuts, and Indian nuts, these ivory-toned seeds come from the pinecones of several trees of the genus *Pinus* and rank alongside macadamias and pistachios as the most expensive nuts on the market. The European term for pine nuts is pignolia, indicating that they come from the Italian stone pine, which grows in Italy, Iberia, and North Africa. They are especially used in Mediterranean cooking, and Italian pignolia (from the Italian term for Pinocchio) are a vital ingredient in making pesto. But although the European pine nut has a higher oil

content and is the one most widely available in the United States, there are American varieties – and some from South America are much larger than their European counterparts. In the American Southwest, the piñon or Indian nut from the Colorado piñon tree has been consumed for thousands of years and was assiduously gathered and stored by many Native American tribes. Pine nuts go well in soups, salads, and desserts, in addition to pesto sauce, and they are also eaten roasted, salted, and raw. Like other nuts, pine nuts are a good source of thiamine, magnesium, and iron.

Common names and synonyms: Indian nut, Mexican nut pine, nut pine, Parry pinyon pine, pignoli, pignolia, pignon, pinolia, piñon (pine) (nut), pinyon (pine) (tree), silver pine, stone nut.

PINGUIN – A plant of the American tropics, and a relative of the pineapple, the pinguin (*Bromelia pinguin*) is used for hedges but also has a crowded head of berries that are plumlike and edible. Another of its names is "wild pineapple," and the fruit is employed mostly for juice. Similar fruits – such as *B. balansae* and *B. karatas* – also grow in South America. These, too, are used mostly for juice, although the yellow fruit of *B. karatas* is good to eat out of hand when ripe.

Common names and synonyms: Maya, piñuela, wild pineapple.

Pink-bottom (mushroom) – *see* **MUSHROOMS AND FUNGI**

Pink ginger-bud – *see* **TORCH GINGER**

Piñon (pine) (nut) – *see* **PINE NUT**

Pinot Bianco – *see* **PINOT BLANC**

PINOT BLANC (*see also* **GRAPES**) – A white wine grape grown mostly in the Alsace region of France, the Pinot Blanc (*Vitis vinifera*) yields an affordable, all-purpose, dry wine. It has been confused with the Chardonnay grape (which also makes a dry, white wine) to the extent that a number of Australian wines that are called Pinot Blanc are actually Chardonnay. Pinot Blanc grapes are also used in the production of sparkling wines and are grown in California.

Common names and synonyms: Beli Pinot, Clevner, Pinot Bianco, Weissburgunder, Weisserburgunder, Weisser Klevner.

See in addition: "Wine," Part III, Chapter 13.

PINOT MEUNIER (*see also* **GRAPES**) – A black wine grape that yields a white juice and is heavily planted in the Champagne region of France, Pinot Meunier (*Vitis vinifera*) is one of the three wine grapes (along with Chardonnay and Pinot Noir) used to make champagne. In the Australian state of Tasmania, Pinot Meunier grapes are now grown to fuel an ever-increasing production of sparkling wine "down under."

See in addition: "Wine," Part III, Chapter 13.

PINOT NOIR (*see also* **GRAPES**) – A black grape that yields a white juice and is sometimes regarded

as the "headache" grape by growers because of the difficulties (fragility and genetic changeability) in working with it, the Pinot Noir grape (*Vitis vinifera*) is nonetheless the grape responsible for the revered red wines of Burgundy. Indeed, Appellation Contrôlée laws prescribe that all red burgundies (save for Beaujolais) be made from Pinot Noir grapes, which are also one of the three principal grapes used to fashion French champagne. Pinot Noir grapes have also been adapted for growing in California. Needless to say, because of the difficulties in growing them, wines made from these grapes are generally on the expensive side.

See in addition: "Wine," Part III, Chapter 13.

Piñuela – *see* **PINGUIN**

Pinyon (pine) (tree) – *see* **PINE NUT**

Piperina – *see* **MINTHOSTACHYS**

Pippah – *see* **PEPPER(CORNS)**

PIPSISSEWA – Plants with many more common names than uses, pipsissewa are two species of weeds, *Chimaphila umbellata* and *C. maculata*, that grow in northern and eastern North America, respectively. Found in wooded areas, they are small herbs with bitter leaves that have long been employed in folk remedies and to make teas. More recently, pipsissewa has been used as one of the ingredients in root beer. *Chimaphila maculata* is known, among other things, as the striped or spotted pipsissewa, ratsbane, and dragon's-tongue. *Chimaphila umbellata* is called common pipsissewa and, more colorfully, king's-cure and love-in-winter.

Common names and synonyms: Common pipsissewa, dragon's-tongue, king's-cure, love-in-winter, ratsbane, spotted pipsissewa, striped pipsissewa.

Pisong jacki – *see* **BANANA**

Pistache – *see* **PISTACHIO NUT**

PISTACHIO NUT – A native of central Asia and member of the cashew family, the pistachio nut (*Pistacia vera*) has been cultivated for some 3,000 years and has a long history of popularity in the Mediterranean world. But it was not until the 1930s, with the advent of vending machines, that pistachio nuts (also called pistache) imported from Italy became something of a rage in the United States as a snack food. Their red-dyed, bony shells split naturally, making them easy to crack by hand or with the teeth. Following World War II, the evergreen trees that bear pistachios were imported to California, and although the imported nuts are still dyed, most American-grown pistachios are sold without dye, in naturally tan shells. The name "pistachio" is the Italian version of the Persian word *pistah,* meaning "nut." In the Middle East, pistachio nuts are an accompaniment for roast lamb, and many Mediterranean dishes also call for them. The characteristically green kernels are a good source of thiamine and iron.

Common names and synonyms: Pistache.

PITAHAYA (*see also* **SAGUARO**) – The cerus type of cacti is divided into *pitayos* – tall columnar cacti (like the saguaro [*Carnegia gigantea*]) with large fruits called *pitayas* – and *pitahayos,* which are smaller cacti with smaller fruits (*pitahayas*). Pitahayas were a staple of Native Americans, have been cultivated commercially in Mexico and Central America since colonial times, and are today grown in Texas, Florida, and the desert Southwest of the United States.

The flavorful, generally red to purple fruits are eaten fresh, made into drinks, preserves, jams, ice cream, and other desserts, and frozen and dried for later reconstitution. Some of the fruits also contain a natural oil, which is thought to improve the functioning of the digestive tract. Pitahayas are regularly shipped to Europe, but the United States – for health reasons – prohibits entry to those grown in certain countries, save in the form of a frozen puree. Among the fruit-bearing cacti are the "tree cactus" (genus *Cephalocereus*) and, in the genus *Echinocereus,* the *pitahaya de Agosto* (*E. conglomeratus*), the "Mexican strawberry" "(*E. stramineus*), and the "clear-up cactus" (*E. triglochidiatus*). The pitahayo or *pitahayas de agua* (genus *Heliocereus*) is another, as are the *pitahaya* (*Hylocereus undatas*) and the *pitayo dulce* (*Lemaireocereus queretaroensis*), also called the "organ-pipe cactus."

Common names and synonyms: Clear-up cactus, Mexican strawberry, organ-pipe cactus, *pitahaya de Agosto, pitahayas de agua, pitahayo, pitayo dulce,* tree cactus.

Pitahaya de Agosto - *see* **PITAHAYA**
Pitahayas de agua - *see* **PITAHAYA**
Pitahayo - *see* **PITAHAYA**
PITANGA – Also known as the "Surinam cherry," pitanga (*Eugenia uniflora*) is native to Brazil but now can be found throughout the world's tropics and subtropics. Given room, the tree will reach 20 feet or so in height, but generally it is grown as a bush or shrub. The fruits vary in size, color, and flavor but are usually oblate and, when ripe, maroon or nearly black. The taste is tart, very much like that of a sour cherry. In addition to being simply popped in the mouth, the fruits are used in salads, jellies, and pies.

Common names and synonyms: Brazilian cherry, Cayenne cherry, petanga, pitanga cherry, Surinam cherry.

Pitanga cherry - *see* **PITANGA**
Pitaya - *see* **SAGUARO**
Pitaya - *see* **CACTUS APPLE**
Pitayo - *see* **SAGUARO**
Pitayo dulce - *see* **PITAHAYA**
Pitchiri - *see* **PITURI**
PITHECELLOBIUM – Some species of the genus *Pithecellobium,* such as *P. dulce* (otherwise known as the "Manila tamarind" and guamochil), are native to the Americas in general, whereas a few New World species (like *P. flexicaule*) are native to North America (Texas, South Florida, and Mexico). Other species are native to tropical Asia. The young pods and shoots are edible and are cooked as a vegetable. The seeds are also eaten, after roasting, and the pulp that surrounds the seeds of *P. dulce* is made into a beverage.

Common names and synonyms: Guamochil, Manila tamarind.

Pito - *see* **CORAL BEAN**
PITOMBA – A relative of the guava, the pitomba (*Eugenia luschnathiana*) is a small yellow or orange fruit that grows on a small tree or bush. The fruit, a native of Brazil and grown almost exclusively there, is sometimes eaten raw but more often is made into juice and preserves.

PITURI – Of the family Solanaceae, pituri (*Duboisia hopwoodii*) is a perennial shrub of Australia. It produces a black berry, but its main use involves the leaves, which traditionally were dried, powdered, and mixed with other "power plants" by the Aborigines, then made into a quid and chewed. This preparation – called *pituri* or *pitchiri* – was commonly thought to be a narcotic by the first European visitors. A high nicotine content, however, seems to have been the reason for its use.

Common names and synonyms: Pitchiri.

PLANTAIN (*see also* **HAWAIIAN PLANTAIN**) – A herbaceous plant of the tropics, the plantain (*Musa × paradisiaca*) is a fruit similar to the banana (and a close relative), but it is larger, is green (although some varieties undergo the same changes of color as bananas), has more starch, and is not eaten raw. Plantains are believed to have originated in Southeast Asia but are now grown throughout the tropics of Asia, the New World, Africa, and the Pacific. They are fried, roasted, baked, boiled, and also dried and ground into a flour. In addition, in Africa plantains are used to make beer. Plantains (*plátanos*) are a favorite in the diets of many West Indian and Latin American populations, in which they replace potatoes or yams as the most important starch. Like bananas, plantains are a good source of potassium and vitamin C, and they are a better source of beta-carotene than bananas.

Another group of plants with the name "plantain" belongs to the genus *Plantago*. These are weeds with broad leaves that, when young, serve as a potherb. The plants were used by Native Americans for food and for medicine, and the leaves can also be boiled to make a tisane.

Common names and synonyms: Plátano.

See in addition: "Bananas and Plantains," Part II, Section B, Chapter 1.

Plantain lily - *see* **DAYLILY**
Plátano - *see* **PLANTAIN**
Pleurisy root - *see* **BUTTERFLY WEED**
Pleurotte - *see* **OYSTER MUSHROOM**

PLUM (*see also* **BEACH PLUM, CHERRY PLUM, DAMSON PLUM, JAPANESE PLUM, SLOE**) - A pitted fruit, or drupe, and related to peaches and apricots, the plum is the most widely distributed of all the stone fruits, growing on every continent save Antarctica. Certainly wild plums would have been a favorite of our hunting-and-gathering ancestors. Plums appear to have been cultivated by the ancient Egyptians and definitely were raised by the Romans, who encouraged the establishment of orchards throughout their empire.

Europeans brought their own plum (*Prunus domestica*) to the New World, with the result that American plum varieties have not been produced commercially. The plums of *P. domestica* are frequently dried (thus becoming prunes) and are also stewed and made into preserves. Then there is *P. salicina* - often called the "salicina" plum or the Japanese plum - which found its way from China to Japan about 300 years ago and subsequently reached North America. Salicina plums, with juicy, reddish to yellow flesh, are not turned into prunes but rather are eaten fresh, and a few varieties can be used in cooking. European plums, especially the California French variety with its high sugar content and firm flesh, make the best prunes. Plums that become prunes are generally freestone, and the drying process consolidates the nutrients, making the dried fruits a good source of vitamins A and E and a fair source of the vitamin-B complex. Prune juice is naturally very sweet, and pitted prunes are frequently cooked with poultry and lamb. Prunes, of course, are well known for their laxative properties, as is prune juice. Plums are a good source of vitamin C.

Common names and synonyms: California French, common plum, garden plum, greengage, Japanese plum, prune, prune plum, Red Beauty, red plum, Reine Claude, salicina plum, Santa Rosa, wild plum.

POBLANO (*see also* **CHILLI PEPPERS**) - Appearing something like a dark-green or almost black (or red in the mature form) bell pepper with a point, this member of the genus *Capsicum* is said to be one of the most popular peppers in Mexico, doubtless in no small part because of its versatility. Fresh, the poblano - a usually mild pepper - is often roasted, and its relatively large size makes it a favorite for stuffing (*chiles rellenos*). In addition, fresh poblanos are used in a number of cooked dishes. Dried, the poblano is called an ancho or a mulato. Ancho means "broad" or "wide" in Spanish and refers to the dried pepper's appearance, which is flat and wrinkled with a color ranging from oxblood to nearly black. The mulato is chocolate brown in color, and both impart a smoky flavor vital to mole sauces, with that of the mulato said to be superior.

Common names and synonyms: Ancho, mulato.

See in addition: "Chilli Peppers," Part II, Section C, Chapter 4.

Pocan - *see* **POKEWEED**

POHOLE - A fiddlehead fern native to Hawaii, the pohole (genus *Athyrium*) grows on the volcanic slopes of Maui, and its tender shoots have been a part of the Hawaiian diet for centuries. Their taste has been described as a blend of the flavors of asparagus and artichoke. Pohole shoots are steamed, sautéed, and added to salads.

Poi - *see* **TARO**

Pointed gourd - *see* **TANDOORI**

Pointleaf manzanita - *see* **HEATHER**

Pois cajun - *see* **PIGEON PEA**

Pois d'Angole - *see* **PIGEON PEA**

Poke - *see* **POKEWEED**

Pokeberry - *see* **POKEWEED**

Pokeroot - *see* **POKEWEED**

Poke salad - *see* **POKEWEED**

POKEWEED - Its blackish red berries are just one of the products of pokeweed (*Phytolacca americana*), a tall North American plant. In the U.S. South, the young shoots and tender tops of the plant are boiled to make "poke salad" in the early spring, and for many in the past - especially slaves - this dish was (despite the boiling) an important source of vitamin C after a winter of meat and meal. The root is poisonous but, with processing, has medicinal uses. The seeds of the berries are also toxic, but the flesh is not, and it is often pressed into a juice. The word "poke" comes from the Algonquian *pocan,* and doubtless the shoots, leaves, and berries of pokeweed were consumed by red men long before white and black men ever reached North America.

Common names and synonyms: Gorget, inkberry, pigeon berry, *pocan,* poke, pokeberry, pokeroot, poke salad, scoke, skoke, Virginian poke.

Polecat weed - *see* **SKUNK CABBAGE**

Poleo - *see* **MINTHOSTACHYS**

POLYNESIAN CHESTNUT - This edible kidney-shaped nut of the Polynesian chestnut tree (*Inocarpus edulis*) is called the Polynesian chestnut by everyone except the Maori of New Zealand (who call it *rata*) and others who prefer the name "Tahitian chestnut." The taste of the nuts is similar to that of chestnuts. They are boiled, roasted, and baked; in addition, some puree the seeds and flavor them with coconut cream.

Common names and synonyms: Rata, Tahitian chestnut.

POMEGRANATE - The pomegranate tree (*Punica granatum*), which reaches a height of 15 to 20 feet, is an ancient tree native to the Middle East (probably Iran). Along with olives, figs, dates, and grapes, the pomegranate was (some 5,000 to 6,000 or more years ago) among the first fruits to be cultivated. Because pomegranates are hardy and easily transported, they were widely known in early times, even in regions where they could not be grown. From Mesopotamia, the pomegranate spread out to be cultivated in ancient Egypt, India, Afghanistan, and China, and it reached Europe at a very early date. The fruit became important in ancient Greek mythology and was mentioned in early literature, including the Bible. It is now grown in all of the drier subtropical areas of Europe and Asia, and in the Americas from the warmer parts of North America (especially California) to Chile.

The name "pomegranate" translates literally as "apple with many seeds." The fruit is round and about the size of a large orange, with a smooth, leathery skin that varies in color from brownish yellow to red. Inside, the fruit is filled with edible, juicy pulp and hundreds of small seeds that are also edible. The rind is tough, which has permitted the pomegranate to serve as a kind of natural canteen for those navigating desert areas. The fruit is eaten fresh, made (including the seeds) into sauces, and is a part of various desserts. Pomegranate juice is highly regarded and is also used commercially to make grenadine syrup, which is employed around the world to flavor milk drinks, desserts, sodas, lemonades, and cocktails. The seeds (which some use as a meat tenderizer) figure prominently in the making of chutneys.

Common names and synonyms: Chinese apple, dalima, granada, grenade, grenadine.

POMELIT (*see also* **CITRUS FRUITS, GRAPEFRUIT**) – A cross between the pomelo and the grapefruit, the pomelit (genus *Citrus*) was developed in Israel for export. Its fruit is sweeter than the grapefruit and juicier than the pomelo.

POMELO (*see also* **CITRUS FRUITS, GRAPEFRUIT**) – The progenitor of the grapefruit, the pomelo (also pummelo) (*Citrus maxima* or *C. grandis*) probably originated in southeastern Asia, where it grew wild in the Indochinese peninsula and Indonesia (although the West Indies has also been proposed as a place of origin). The pomelo is the largest of the citrus fruits and is also known as "pumelo" and "shaddock" because it (or the grapefruit) was brought to the Caribbean by Captain James Shaddock. The aromatic fruit is very large and oval shaped with a thick skin. The pulp is sweet and a light-colored pink or red, the outside ranging from green to yellow to pink. Usually the pomelo is eaten raw, but in Asia the peel is candied, and an alcoholic beverage is made from the fruit. Today, pomelos are grown in California, China, and Japan. They differ from other kinds of citrus fruits in that the white pith is not edible. Pomelos have a high content of vitamin A and are a fine source of vitamin C.

Common names and synonyms: Chinese grapefruit, pumelo, shaddock, sweet pomelo.

Pomi di mori – *see* **TOMATO**
Pomme d'amour – *see* **TOMATO**
Pompion – *see* **PUMPKIN**
Poor-man's-asparagus – *see* **LEEK(S)**
Poor-man's-caviar – *see* **EGGPLANT**
Poor-man's-food – *see* **FIG**

Poor-man's-meat – *see* **BEANS**
Popcorn – *see* **MAIZE**
POPLAR – Mostly native to North America, poplar trees (genus *Populus*) grow from Alaska to the mountains of Kentucky and westward through the Rockies to California and Mexico. The inner bark of most species can be eaten raw, and the bark was also boiled or dried and ground into meal by Native Americans. In addition, the bark was used to make a tea and cut into strips to be cooked like noodles. Whites on the frontier learned to rely on the poplar for sustenance – even the sugary sap was collected and drunk. Because the use of the poplar provided much in the way of vitamin C, it was a scurvy preventive during the winter months.

POPPY SEED – The opium poppy (*Papaver somniferum*), which yields a latex that provides the drug opium (and the opiate derivatives morphine and codeine), has a botanical name that means "sleep-bearing." Fortunately for poppy-seed consumers, the latex comes from unripe seedpods, whereas the tiny, kidney-shaped, edible seeds form in ripe pods and thus have no narcotic effect. Asia Minor seems to be the plant's native region, and doubtless its "magical" effects attracted the attention of hunter-gatherers early on. Its medicinal properties have been put to work for humans at least since the time of the ancient Egyptians. Despite the minuscule size of the seeds – it takes close to a million of them to make a pound of weight on the scales – at some time in the distant past it was discovered that oil could be pressed from them. Their nutty taste was also appreciated, so that today poppy seeds are widely grown (the Netherlands is a major producer) and widely used in baked goods, from India through the Middle East to Europe and North America.

Common names and synonyms: Maw seed.
See also: "Spices and Flavorings," Part II, Section F, Chapter 1.

Porcini – *see* **BOLETE, MUSHROOMS AND FUNGI**
Porcino – *see* **BOLETE**
Poro – *see* **CORAL BEAN**
Portabello (mushroom) – *see* **MUSHROOMS AND FUNGI**
POSHTE – Perhaps the least known of the Annonaceae, the poshte (*Annona scleroderma*) is mostly cultivated in southwestern Guatemala and is prominent in the markets of that part of the world. Unlike its relatives – the cherimoya, the soursop, and the sugar apple – the poshte has a very tough skin, which means that it is less likely to be damaged in handling and transportation. But like the others it has a delicious pulp that is easily removed with a spoon.

Common names and synonyms: Anana del monte, cawesh, chirimoya.

Potato bean – *see* **APIOS, JÍCAMA**
Potato(es), sweet – *see* **SWEET POTATO**
Potato(es), white – *see* **WHITE POTATO**

Potato yam – *see* **AIR POTATO, LESSER YAM**

Pot marjoram – *see* **MARJORAM AND OREGANO**

Poussee-pied – *see* **GLASSWORT**

Prague Special – *see* **KOHLRABI**

PRAIRIE CLOVER – A number of species of the genus *Petalostemon* are called prairie clover, among them *P. candidum* (the white-tassel-flower) and *P. oligophyllum.* Native Americans ate the roots and young leaves as well as the flowers.

Common names and synonyms: White-tassel-flower.

Prairie potato – *see* **BREADROOT**

Prairie sunflower – *see* **SUNFLOWER OIL AND SEED**

Prairie turnip – *see* **BREADROOT**

Premier – *see* **LOQUAT**

Preserving melon – *see* **CITRON**

Prickly ash tree – *see* **SICHUAN PEPPERCORN**

PRICKLY LETTUCE – A wild Eurasian lettuce naturalized in North America, prickly lettuce (*Lactuca scariola* = *L. serriola*) reaches as many as 7 feet in height, with large lower leaves that can approach a foot in length. The upper ones are much smaller, but they, along with the bigger leaves, are eaten in salads and cooked as a vegetable.

Common names and synonyms: Wild lettuce, wild opium.

PRICKLY PEAR – The prickly pear is the edible fruit of various cacti of the genus *Opuntia.* Native to the Americas, where varieties can be found from South America to Canada, prickly pear cacti produce fruits that are pear shaped and bristle with sharp spines that require careful removal before eating or cooking. Also called cactus pears or Indian pears, the fruits (actually large berries) come in an estimated 300 species – often incredibly colored (inside and out) – with some sweet, some sour, some that can be eaten raw, and others that need cooking. About the size of large eggs, the berries contain a multitude of hard, black seeds.

The Aztecs used the berry juice to make an alcoholic beverage, and also boiled the juice down for its sugar. Indeed, the prickly pear was an important dietary item in Mexico long before the Spaniards arrived and until well into the twentieth century constituted the bulk of the diet of entire communities. When the Spaniards were adapting to their newly conquered Mexico, they called the pears *tunas* and delighted in encouraging new arrivals to eat one particular *tuna* that caused the urine of the consumer to turn bright red. Today, prickly pears are greatly appreciated for their sweet taste, and not just in Mexico and Central and South America but throughout much of the world, including all of the countries ringing the Mediterranean, southwestern Asia, Australia, and South Africa.

In the latter two areas, where the cacti were introduced by early European explorers, they had no natural parasites or competitors and have prospered to the point of becoming more nuisance than food. In Israel, the word *sabra* (meaning prickly pear) has given rise to the nickname "sabras" for the Israelis themselves – prickly on the outside, sweet on the inside! Prickly pears are crushed to make punches and cocktails, sliced into salads as well as eaten raw, and preserved or pickled with other fruits, such as lemons. The juice is sometimes used as a drink mixed with vodka or rum. In addition, prickly pears have served as a handy cattle feed in times of shortage. The prickly pear is a fine source of vitamin C, potassium, and fiber.

Common names and synonyms: Barbary fig, Burbank's spineless, cactus fig, cactus pear, Indian fig, Indian pear, *nopal, sabra,* spineless cactus, *tuna.*

Princess-feather – *see* **AMARANTH**

Princess pea – *see* **WINGED BEAN**

Proboscis-flower – *see* **UNICORN PLANT**

Provision tree – *see* **MALABAR NUT**

Prune – *see* **PLUM**

Puffball – *see* **MUSHROOMS AND FUNGI**

PULASAN – A tree native to the Malay Archipelago, pulasan (*Nephelium mutabile*) is related to the litchi. Pulasan trees grow wild. Those that are cultivated are grown mostly for their fruits, which are oblong, about 2 inches in length, and dark red when ripe. The skin is thin and leathery but not attached to the tart flesh, which comes out easily. The fruits are eaten raw and stewed, and made into jams and preserves.

Pulla chilli – *see* **GUAJILLO AND PULLA CHILLIES**

Pulse – *see* **CHICKPEA**

Pumelo – *see* **POMELO**

Pummelo – *see* **POMELO**

Pumpion – *see* **PUMPKIN**

PUMPKIN (*see also* **PUMPKIN SEED, ROUGE VIF D'ÉTAMPES [PUMPKIN], SQUASH AND PUMPKIN**) – Known in Old English as "pumpions" or "pompions," pumpkins (or calabazas) make up several species of the genus *Cucurbita,* and considerable confusion exists about the differences between them and winter squashes. From the standpoint of the consumer, pumpkins generally have orange-colored skins (although there are both black and white pumpkins as well) and are the more strongly flavored of the two. Pumpkins, which were domesticated in Mexico some 6,000 years ago, were probably initially cultivated for their edible seeds. Called *pepitos,* these were dried for consumption as a snack and also became vital ingredients in sauces, moles, and enchilada-type dishes.

Pumpkins spread northward and across North America long before the Europeans arrived to become one of the most important foods of the Native Americans of eastern North America. Later on, they were a chief factor in saving the Pilgrims of Plymouth Plantation from starvation during the winter of 1622–3. Today, pumpkins are far less important as a food than they were during colonial times, and in the United States the bulk of the pumpkin crop is grown for use at Halloween.

Most of the Halloween pumpkins belong to *C. pepo*, but *C. moschata* and *C. mixta* are also represented, as well as very large specimens of *C. maxima*. As a rule, those pumpkins used for decoration are too big and stringy to eat. How big? In 1900, a 400-pound pumpkin earned first prize at the World's Fair, but since then 800-pound pumpkins have been raised, which makes them the largest fruits of the plant kingdom. Such a behemoth would make quite a pie if used in this fashion, but it is generally the smaller and sweeter pumpkins (usually *C. pepo*) that are made into pie fillings and soups and used for other cooking purposes.

Perhaps the world's best pumpkin for use in this regard escaped from the Americas to be developed by the French. This is their famous *Rouge Vif d'Étampes* – also known as the "Cinderella pumpkin" – the flesh of which is very thick and is traditionally used for soups.

Pumpkin for cooking is available in canned (and frozen) form, which most people prefer to fresh. The taste is no different but there is considerably less mess. Pumpkin seeds are still eaten as a snack, and pumpkins themselves are cultivated worldwide.

Common names and synonyms: Calabaza, New England pie pumpkin, pepitas, pompion, pumpion, sugar pumpkin.

See in addition: "Squash," Part II, Section C, Chapter 8.

PUMPKIN SEED (*see also* **PUMPKIN, SQUASH AND PUMPKIN**) – The roasted and boiled seeds of other winter squashes as well as those of pumpkins (*Cucurbita pepo*) were a staple in the diets of Native American peoples for many millennia. In fact, pumpkins may well have started out as gourds raised for their edible seeds. Even today, pumpkin seeds are regarded as a tasty snack after they are dried, salted, and toasted – with a little oil – until golden brown. Indeed, on the street corners of Mexico City, *pepita* vendors are ubiquitous, as they are in many other cities of the world. Pumpkin seeds also yield an edible oil and are made into a paste used for thickening soups and other culinary purposes. In addition to their fine flavor, pumpkin seeds are low in fat, high in protein, and a good source of iron.

See also: "Squash," Part II, Section C, Chapter 8.

PUNCTURE VINE – Called the puncture vine because its prickly fruits can pierce tires, the feet of humans, and the hooves of livestock, this annual weed (*Tribulus terrestris*) is a Mediterranean native now naturalized in southwestern North America. The fruit separates into five nutlets that have been pounded into a meal for consumption during hard times. In addition, the leaves have been cooked as a vegetable.

Common names and synonyms: Punctureweed.

Punctureweed – *see* **PUNCTURE VINE**
Punk tree – *see* **CAJEPUT**

PUNTARELLE – A member of the genus *Cichorium* and a close relative of chicory, puntarelle (*C. intybus*) is an Italian vegetable with a name meaning "little points" – presumably because of the tiny points on its feathery leaves. Also known as "Roman chicory" or "wild Roman chicory," it is available only in the winter months. The typical head of puntarelle has bitter green leaves borne on less bitter, hollow, white stalks – the whole appearing much like endive. There is also a variety called "puntarelle red-rib," with bright red stalks and dark green leaves. Puntarelle stalks are used in salads (often with anchovy dressing), braised and eaten with fava beans, sautéed with garlic, and wilted in soups.

Common names and synonyms: Puntarelle red-rib, Roman chicory, wild Roman chicory.

Puntarelle red-rib – *see* **PUNTARELLE**
Purging nut – *see* **PHYSIC NUT**
Purple-goat's-beard – *see* **SALSIFY**
Purple granadilla – *see* **PASSION FRUIT**
Purple nutgrass – *see* **CHUFA**
PURPLESTEM ANGELICA – Also called "American angelica," "great angelica," and "masterwort," purplestem angelica (*Angelica atropurpurea*) is a North American native, found in the eastern half of that continent (as far west as Minnesota). It reaches from 4 to 6 feet in height and has an aromatic odor. Its roots (said to be poisonous when fresh) have been candied, and its stems and leaves were eaten by Native Americans and by early European settlers.

Common names and synonyms: American angelica, great angelica, masterwort.

Purple Vienna – *see* **KOHLRABI**
PURSLANE – Also called "pussley," purslane (*Portulaca oleracea*) is a trailing weed that has small yellow flowers, reddish stems, and leaves that are sometimes used in salads and stews and are also cooked like spinach as a side dish. Like okra, purslane has the ability to thicken dishes in which it is cooked. A relative – winter purslane (*Montia perfoliata*), also known as "miner's-lettuce" – is used in much the same manner.

Common names and synonyms: Cuban spinach, miner's-lettuce, miner's-salad, pigweed, pussley, winter purslane.

Pussley – *see* **PURSLANE**

Qat – *see* **KHAT**
Qhat – *see* **KHAT**
Quack grass – *see* **COUCH GRASS**
Quamash – *see* **CAMAS**
Quandang – *see* **QUANDONG**
QUANDONG – Also known as quondong, quandang, and native peach, the quandong tree (*Fusanus acuminatus* or *Elaeocarpus grandis*), of the family Santalaceae, is a

native of Australia. It produces round and red edible drupes, called "native peaches." The stone also contains an edible seed called the quandong nut. Both drupes and nuts were food for the Aborigines.

Common names and synonyms: Native peach, quandang, quandong nut, quondong.

Quañiwa - *see* CAÑIHUA

Queen-Anne's-lace - *see* CARROT

Queensland arrowroot - *see* ACHIRA

Queensland nut - *see* MACADAMIA NUT

QUELITES - The generic Spanish term *quelites* refers to a wide variety of edible greens gathered by the indigenous inhabitants of Mexico and Central America. Some prominent examples of the more than 2,000 species that have been identified are pigweed (genus *Amaranthus*), shrubby wound-wort (*Liabum glabrum*), violeta (*Anoda cristata*), chipiles (*Crotalaria pumila*), yerba de conejo (*Tridax coronopifolium*), and beldobes (*Galinsoga parviflora*). Native cultivators allowed these plants to grow freely in their *milpa* fields and harvested them young to eat raw, to boil in soups, or to spice mole sauces and tamales. Mature specimens were fed to animals along with maize leaves. Although many of these varieties are considered famine foods, used to extend maize after crop failures, they also provide an important source of vitamin A in the diets of many peasants. However, their consumption has declined in recent years in favor of European vegetables, which are considered more prestigious. The spread of modern agricultural methods, particularly the use of herbicides, has also decreased the importance of these herbs in Mexican diets.

Common names and synonyms: Beldobes, chipiles, pigweed (amaranth), shrubby wound-wort, *violeta, yerba de conejo.*

Quetembilla - *see* CEYLON GOOSEBERRY

Quiabo - *see* OKRA

Quick grass - *see* COUCH GRASS

Quihuicha - *see* QUINOA

Quimbambo - *see* OKRA

QUINCE - An aromatic fruit, quince (*Cydonia oblonga*) is yellow, small, and pear shaped, with very tough flesh. It is not eaten raw, but when cooked, its orange pulp turns a deep pink and becomes very sweet. The quince - a native of western Asia (Iraq and Iran) - grows on a small, twisted tree that rarely reaches a height of more than 12 to 15 feet. It is an old fruit that was very popular among the ancient Greeks and Romans (it was reportedly introduced in Rome in 65 B.C. by Pompey), and both Pliny and Columella were well acquainted with it.

Because of its sweetness, the quince became very popular around the Mediterranean during the Middle Ages. The Portuguese called the fruit *marmelo,* and the preserve they made from it *marmelada.* In fact, because of the great amount of pectin the quince yields, it is ideal for marmalade, jelly, jam, and candies and shares with the guava, the apple, and a few others the distinction of being among the best jelly fruits. However, beginning with the advent of cane sugar (and continuing through the fairly recent loss of interest in preserving), the quince has been reduced from a near-essential item in Western kitchens to a specialty fruit. Quince production is now principally located in the United States and a few European countries. The quince is a good source of vitamin C and fiber.

Common names and synonyms: Coines, coing, Cydonian apple, elephant apple, maja pahit, ma-tum, pineapple quince, quitte, vilvam.

Quingombo - *see* OKRA

QUINOA (*see also* CHENOPODIUM) - Pronounced "keen-wah," quinoa (*Chenopodium quinoa*) is an annual herb of the tropical American highlands and a native of Chile and Peru. Also known as quinua and sometimes as "goosefoot," quinoa is and historically has been the most important of the cultivated chenopods. Like amaranth, it is technically not a grain, meaning that it is not one of the cultivated grasses. Also like amaranth, quinoa helped sustain a great American civilization - in this case the Incas. After maize, it was the most utilized grain in the Andes region at the time of the Spanish conquest. It was used to make beer (*chicha*) as well as soups, stews, and porridges, and its leaves were employed as a potherb.

Quinoa does well in poor soils at high altitudes; indeed, it flourishes at 13,000 feet above sea level. One reason for this is its content of saponin, a bitter, soaplike coating that discourages birds and insects and protects the seeds from the greater radiation of sunlight at high altitudes. A closely allied species called *huauzontle* (*C. nuttalliae* = *C. berlandieri*) was developed in pre-Columbian Mexico, and a third, less important chenopod - *cañihua* (*C. pallidicaule*) - was also cultivated in the Altiplano regions of Peru and Bolivia.

Quinoa is cultivated today throughout the Andes from Ecuador to Bolivia and at one time was grown in England, where the leaves were consumed as greens and the seeds given to poultry. It is superior to the true grains in nutritional quality, with a better yield of riboflavin, folacin, magnesium, and zinc. Quinoa is employed in soups and gruels and is also toasted and ground into flour for breads, cakes, and biscuits. Quinoa can be found in health-food stores and even supermarkets. The bitter - and perhaps toxic - saponin must be washed away before consumption.

Common names and synonyms: Goosefoot, huauzontle, Inca wheat, pigweed, *quihuicha,* quinua.

Quintonil - *see* AMARANTH

Quinua - *see* QUINOA

Quitte - *see* QUINCE

Quondong - *see* QUANDONG

R'accacha - *see* **ARRACACHA**
Radicchio - *see* **CHICORY**
RADISH (*see also* **DAIKON**) – Technically referring to any of a number of plants belonging to the genus *Raphanus* and the mustard family, the term "radish" is usually taken to mean the thickened edible ends of *R. sativus*, which are used in salads and eaten as snacks and appetizers. Radishes come in innumerable varieties, colors (especially red, white, purple, and black), and shapes (ranging from round, to oblong, to long and finger-like). The most common in U.S. produce markets are red and round and are eaten raw, often in salads. Black radishes, common in Eastern Europe and found in a number of Russian dishes, have a very strong flavor and consequently are usually mixed with other foods. The white varieties are sometimes cooked and eaten like the turnips they resemble in taste. Additionally, in East Asia there is a giant white radish called a daikon, which is grated and cooked and used in salads and stir-fries.
Common names and synonyms: Clover radish.
See in addition: "Cruciferous and Green Leafy Vegetables," Part II, Section C, Chapter 5.

Ragi - *see* **FINGER MILLET, MILLET**

RAGWEED – A group of mostly North American plants, viewed as chief culprits in emitting a profuse pollen that provokes allergenic symptoms among hay-fever and asthma sufferers, ragweeds nonetheless belong to a genus called *Ambrosia* – a term from ancient Greek mythology meaning "food for the gods." The weeds' more appropriate common name derives from the ragged shape of their leaves, although the plants are also called "tansy ragwort," "bitterweed," and just plain "ragwort." The plants do have a food use, however, because an edible oil (oil of ragweed) can be obtained from their achenes, and the leaves of some species have reportedly been used as a flavoring.
Common names and synonyms: Bitterweed, ragwort, tansy ragwort.

Ragwort - *see* **RAGWEED**

RAIN TREE – So called because of a belief that it somehow exudes water from its leaflets, the rain tree (*Pithecellobium saman*) is a native of the American tropics that now also grows in the Old World tropics. It is widely used as a shade tree for crops such as coffee, cacao, and nutmeg, but it also produces sweet-pulp pods that serve as cattle fodder as well as a snack food for humans, especially children. A beverage is also made from the pulp.

RAISIN (*see also* **GRAPES**) – Doubtless, wild grapes that had dried on the vine were consumed by our hunting-and-gathering ancestors for hundreds of thousands of years. These were the first raisins (genus *Vitis*). With vine cultivation came the more conscious process of picking grapes and spreading them out to be sun-dried. Raisins were an important item of trade in the Near East and were highly prized by the Romans, who introduced grapes and the knowledge of raisin making to the rest of Europe. The Spaniards brought grapes and raisin-making techniques to the New World, and Spanish missionaries introduced them in California, where today, in the San Joaquin valley, about half of the world's raisins are produced. Like prunes, raisins have concentrated nutrients and are a good source of the B-vitamins – thiamine and B_6 – along with iron.

RAKKYO (*see also* **ONION**) – A relative of the onion, rakkyo (*Allium chinense*) is a small onion bulb that resembles garlic. Rakkyo is cultivated in China, Japan, and Thailand (and by Asian-Americans in the United States) and is used mostly for pickling, although it is also occasionally employed in cooking.
See in addition: "The *Allium* Species," Part II, Section C, Chapter 2.

RAMBAI – A widely cultivated native of Indonesia, the rambai tree (*Baccaurea motleyana*) is adorned with strings of rambai fruits that hang from its branches. The fruits are about the size of a hen's egg, brownish yellow, and soft to the touch when ripe. They are eaten fresh, stewed and made into jam.

Ramboutan - *see* **RAMBUTAN**

RAMBUTAN – A native of the Malay Archipelago, rambutan (*Nephelium lappaceum*) is a member of the soapberry family, a relative of the litchi and the longan, and one of the most common fruits of Southeast Asia. The fruit is bright red and oval, is about the size of a small egg, is covered with long, soft spines, and has a sweet, acid flesh that combines the tastes of pineapple and apricot. It grows on trees that can reach 60 feet in height and generally fruit twice a year. Rambutan has been cultivated in the Southeast Asian region since prehistoric times and figured prominently in early trade with the Arabs, who took the fruit to Zanzibar, where it is still cultivated. Rambutan is normally eaten raw but is also stewed and made into jams. Rambutans are high in vitamin C.
Common names and synonyms: Ramboetan, rambotan, ramboutan, rambustan, ramtum.

Ramón - *see* **BREADNUT**
Ramontochi - *see* **GOVERNOR'S PLUM**
Ramp - *see* **WILD LEEK(S)**
Rampion - *see* **CAMPANULA**
Ram's-horn - *see* **UNICORN PLANT**
Ramtil - *see* **NIGER SEED**
Ramtum - *see* **RAMBUTAN**

RANGPUR AND KUSAIE (*see also* **LIME**) – Both of these fruits are called "limes," but neither wholly deserves the name. Rather, both are probably hybrids of the Mandarin orange (*Citrus reticulata*) and the true lime (*C. aurantiifolia*). The rangpur develops a deep orange color that the kusaie does not. Both are acid in taste, although not so much as the lime, and the ease with which the segments separate is suggestive of the Mandarin orange. In the Western Hemisphere, the fruits are grown in the West Indies and California.

RAPE – An annual herb of European origin, rape (*Brassica napus*) looks like a cabbage but is cultivated mostly for its seeds, which yield an edible oil (rapeseed oil, called "canola oil" in the United States). The oil (also called "colza") is used for cooking and in salads, and the leaves of the young plants serve as a vegetable, in much the same way as spinach.

Common names and synonyms: Canola oil, colza, rapeseed oil.

See in addition: "An Overview of Oils and Fats," Part II, Section E, Chapter 1; "Cruciferous and Green Leafy Vegetables," Part II, Section C, Chapter 5.

Rapini – *see* **BROCCOLI RAAB**

RASPBERRY (*see also* **BERRIES**) – A number of shrublike, prickly plants of the genus *Rubus* have fruits that we call raspberries. Among them are *R. strigosus* (= *R. leucodermis*), which is a purple and black berry (the "black-cap") native to eastern North America, and *R. idaeus,* which is native to Europe. The latter species bears red raspberries, and most varieties cultivated today are a cross between the two. Pliny the Elder mentioned raspberries as a wild fruit, and they were probably not cultivated much before the seventeenth century. The apothecary and botanist John Parkinson – in his 1629 *Paradisi in sole paradisus terrestris* – wrote of red, white, and thornless varieties, indicating that some were under cultivation at that point.

The raspberry has a range that extends from the polar regions down through temperate North America, Asia, and Europe. One berry appears like a group of tiny berries lumped together. In addition to flavoring desserts and ice cream, raspberries are turned into wine, jams, and jellies, and the fruit is also used to flavor certain liqueurs. In the past, raspberries were among the berries gathered regularly and ritually by the Native Americans. Raspberries provide a good amount of vitamin C.

Common names and synonyms: American red raspberry, black-cap, black raspberry, purple raspberry, thimbleberry.

Rata – *see* **POLYNESIAN CHESTNUT, RATA VINE**

RATA VINE – A Maori word, *rata* indicates New Zealand trees of the genus *Metrosideros*. Some are hardwood trees that the Maori employed to make paddles and weapons such as war clubs. One (*M. fulgens*) has a vine that the Maori exploited as a sweetener. *Rata* can also mean the Polynesian chestnut.

Ratsbane – *see* **PIPSISSEWA**
Rattlebush – *see* **YELLOW WILD-INDIGO**
Red bell pepper – *see* **SWEET PEPPERS**
Redberry – *see* **BUCKTHORN**
Red-fleshed radish – *see* **DAIKON**
Red Globe – *see* **GRAPES**
Red gram – *see* **PIGEON PEA**
Red gum – *see* **SWEET GUM**

Red haw – *see* **HAWTHORN BERRY**
Red-in-snow – *see* **CHINESE AMARANTH**
Red Kuri (squash) – *see* **BUTTERCUP SQUASH**
Red pepper – *see* **CHILLI PEPPERS**
Red mombin – *see* **HOG PLUM, SPANISH PLUM**
Redroot – *see* **AMARANTH**
Red sorrel – *see* **ROSELLE**
Red vine spinach – *see* **MALABAR SPINACH**
Reed-mace – *see* **CATTAIL**
Rheumatism root – *see* **WILD YAM**

RHUBARB – Chinese rhubarb (*Rheum officinale*) is used mostly for medical purposes. Garden rhubarb (*R. rhabarbarum*) is grown for its edible stalks. The plant is native to southwestern Russia, southern Siberia, and China, where it was grown in ancient times for the alleged medicinal value of its roots. Rhubarb was cultivated in Europe from at least the seventeenth century and reached North America shortly after the American Revolution. The leaves are highly toxic, and only the reddish pink and celery-like stalk is consumed as a "fruit" in pies and sauces. Rhubarb, which has a bitter taste, contains much oxalic acid, which can adversely affect the absorption of calcium and iron.

Common names and synonyms: Chinese rhubarb, garden rhubarb, pie-plant, wild rhubarb.

Ribier – *see* **GRAPES**

RICE (*see also* **AFRICAN RICE, WILD RICE**) – Rice (*Oryza sativa*) is the most "super" of all the "superfoods" in that it helps to sustain more than half of the world's population. It is an ancient grain that has been cultivated for around 5,000 years and now comes in some 2,500 varieties. Most rice species are native to the Indian subcontinent – save for a minor species with red grains that is native to Africa. (The wild rice of North America is not actually a rice but rather an aquatic oat.) A plant of hot climates, rice only became important in China when agriculture developed in the southern provinces. Some have credited Alexander the Great with introducing the grain in Europe, but it was not until the eighth century that the Muslims grew large quantities of it in Spain. "Carolina rice" came into being in 1685, when rice was introduced into South Carolina.

Today, rice is divided into long-, medium-, and short-grained varieties, and various cultures prize one or another of these over the rest. Long-grained rice is preferred in most Western kitchens and in India. Medium-grained rice is more appreciated in some Asian countries, whereas short-grained rice, with its starch that makes the grains stick together, is the favorite of those who use chopsticks, such as the Japanese and Chinese.

In most industrialized countries, white rice is enriched to replace the nutrients stripped from the grain by milling. Brown rice is far more nutritious because it has only had the husk removed during milling and retains the bran on its outer coating. Parboiled or converted rice is soaked and steamed before milling to drive nutrients into the grain. Instant rice has been fully cooked and then dehydrated. In addition, there are special rices, such as Arborio, which absorbs much water as it cooks and plumps up well for dishes like Italy's specialty, risotto, and Spain's paella. *Basmati* rice, grown in India and Pakistan, elongates rather than plumps and is commonly featured in Indian cooking, whereas Jasmine rice is a traditional rice of Thailand.

Common names and synonyms: Arborio, *Basmati,* brown rice, Carolina rice, dry rice, *gohan,* hill rice, instant rice, Jasmine rice, long-grained rice, medium-grained rice, *meshi,* polished rice, short-grained rice, white rice.

See in addition: "Rice," Part II, Section A, Chapter 7.

RICE BEAN (*see also* **BEANS**) - A native of Asia, the rice bean (*Phaseolus calcaratus = Vigna umbellata*) grows wild from the Himalaya Mountains through central and southern China to Malaysia. It is cultivated to some extent in Asia and in the East Indies for its seed, although the young pods and leaves are also cooked as a vegetable. The seeds are generally eaten with rice, hence the name.

Common names and synonyms: Frijol arroz, haricot riz.

See in addition: "Beans, Peas, and Lentils," Part II, Section C, Chapter 3.

RICEGRASS - Also called "Indian ricegrass" because it was an important food for Native Americans, ricegrass (*Oryzopsis hymenoides* and *O. aspera*) is a bunch grass that grows throughout central North America. Its grain was ground into meal for bread and porridges.

Common names and synonyms: Indian ricegrass.

Rice wheat - *see* **EMMER**

RIESLING (*see also* **GRAPES**) - A white wine grape, the Riesling (*Vitis vinifera*) makes the great wines of Germany's Rhine and Mosel valleys as well as many of those from Alsace in France. The grape is also one of the two major white grapes grown in Washington State. In California, the grape is called Johannisberg Riesling. Oregon is also a major producer. Rieslings can vary from very dry to sweet, dessert-type wines, although most tend to the dry side.

Common names and synonyms: Johannisberg Riesling, white Riesling.

See in addition: "Wine," Part III, Chapter 13.

Rigani - *see* **MARJORAM AND OREGANO**
Robusta - *see* **COFFEE**
Rocambole - *see* **GARLIC**
Rock cranberry - *see* **LINGONBERRY**
Rocket - *see* **ARUGULA, YELLOW ROCKET**
Rocket salad - *see* **ARUGULA**
Rockweed - *see* **SEAWEED**
Rocky Mountain grape - *see* **BARBERRY**
Rocotillo - *see* **HABANERO AND SCOTCH BONNET PEPPERS**

Rocoto - *see* **HABANERO AND SCOTCH BONNET PEPPERS**
Roka - *see* **ARUGULA**
Roma - *see* **MUSHROOMS AND FUNGI**
Roman chicory - *see* **PUNTARELLE**
Roquette - *see* **ARUGULA**
ROSE (*see also* **ROSE HIPS**) - Roses (genus *Rosa*) are ancient plants that grew wild in Asia and have found culinary uses for thousands of years. The petals are used in salads, candied in desserts, and made into syrups and jams. Rose water (and rose essence, a more concentrated distillation of rose water) adds flavor and aroma to various dishes - especially curries and rice dishes - and has long been used to flavor milk drinks, desserts, and cakes.

Common names and synonyms: Rose essence, rose water, wild rose.

See in addition: "Spices and Flavorings," Part II, Section F, Chapter 1.

ROSE APPLE - Often confused with the Java apple because of similar scientific as well as common names, the rose apple (*Eugenia jambos* or *Syzygium jambos*) belongs to the family Myrtaceae, which includes myrtle, clove, and allspice. The fruits of an evergreen tree native to Southeast Asia, rose apples grow in clusters of four or more. When ripe, they are about 2 inches long, white or yellow with pink streaks, with a relatively large seed and the aroma of rose water (hence their name). The quality of the fruits varies considerably, and many are not juicy enough to deliver an excellent flavor. Those that are juicy are sometimes eaten raw, but as a rule rose apples are made into jams and jellies.

Common names and synonyms: Jambos, jambu, wax apple.

Rose-essence - *see* **ROSE**

ROSE HIP(S) (*see also* **ROSE**) - The red- to orange-colored, urn-shaped fruits of the rose that appear in late summer and early fall, rose hips (*Rosa canina* and *R. rugosa*) are actually the bases to which the flower's petals are attached. Once considered sacred, the hips were used by Catholic believers during the Middle Ages to count prayers or series of prayers - hence the name of the string of beads called a "rosary." Most rose hips are gathered from wild rose bushes and are utilized to make tea, jellies, and preserves and, in parts of Europe, a syrup used as a tonic. Rose hips are extremely high in vitamin C.

Common names and synonyms: Dog rose, wild rose.

Rosella - *see* **ROSELLE**

ROSELLE - Probably a native of West Africa (it is a close relative of okra), roselle (*Hibiscus sabdariffa*) is also called "rozelle," "Indian sorrel," "red sorrel," "Jamaican sorrel," and just plain "sorrel." The young shoots and leaves of the plant are eaten raw or as a cooked vegetable, and the flowers (actually the calyx), which constitute the main reason for the cultivation of roselle, are used to make beverages, jellies, sauces, preserves, and chutneys.

Roselle was introduced in Brazil in the seventeenth century but may have reached the West Indies even earlier - both of these introductions probably occurring via the slave trade. In addition, the plant has been under cultivation in Asia for some three centuries; extensive roselle cultivation was begun in Australia at the turn of the twentieth century and in the Dutch East Indies during the 1920s. Today, India, Java, and the Philippines are major producers.

Common names and synonyms: Indian sorrel, Jamaican sorrel, Java jute, red sorrel, rosella, rozelle, sorrel.

ROSEMARY - An aromatic herb, rosemary (*Rosmarinus officinalis*) is a Mediterranean native whose Latin name means "dew of the sea," presumably because it was frequently found growing close to the coast. The plant was known to the Romans, who used it mostly for medicinal purposes. Early in the Middle Ages, however, although its medical applications continued, rosemary joined a host of other herbs employed for culinary reasons, especially in the kitchens of the European royal and noble courts. Today, rosemary is more utilized in Italian cooking than in any of the other Mediterranean cuisines; in northern Europe, it is sometimes used in sausage making. The needle-like leaves of the rosemary plant are used both fresh and dried, but they have to be crushed, crumbled, or chopped to release their bold flavor and (especially in the case of fresh rosemary) to avoid spearing the consumer. Rosemary is wonderful with poultry, beef, lamb, and fish, and goes well in sauces. It is also used in salads, salad dressings, soups, and stews, and to make tisanes.

See also: "Spices and Flavorings," Part II, Section F, Chapter 1.

Rosenapfel - *see* **OKRA**
Rose water - *see* **ROSE**
Rosinweed - *see* **SILPHIUM**
Rosso di Verona - *see* **CHICORY**
Roucou - *see* **ANNATTO**
ROUGE VIF D'ÉTAMPES (PUMPKIN) (*see also* **PUMPKIN, SQUASH AND PUMPKIN**) - The French crafted this elegant pumpkin variety, the *Rouge Vif d'Étampes* (*Cucurbita maxima*), from more basic American stock. Also called the "Cinderella pumpkin," it is a heavily fleshed pumpkin that is generally regarded as the best of all pumpkins for baking, and especially for soup making.

Common names and synonyms: Cinderella pumpkin.
See in addition: "Squash," Part II, Section C, Chapter 8.
ROUGH BINDWEED - A European plant, rough bindweed (*Smilax aspera*) has roots that yield a kind of sarsaparilla.

Common names and synonyms: Bindweed, bindweed root.

ROUND GOURD - Known also as the "round melon," the round gourd (*Praecitrullus fistulosus*) is grown primarily in India and is practically unknown in the West. The round gourd is cooked as a vegetable while immature, and its seeds can be roasted.

Common names and synonyms: Round melon.
Round melon - *see* **ROUND GOURD**
ROWANBERRY (*see also* **BERRIES**) - The rowan tree (*Sorbus aucuparia*) is a small, attractive native of Europe and western Asia that produces orange-red rowanberries. The species name *aucuparia* means "bird-catching," referring to the trees' ancient use as bait. The berries have a long history of magical as well as culinary uses. Ancient northern Europeans comforted themselves with the belief that rowanberries guarded against the spells of witches, demons, and the like. The berries' juice makes a fine jelly that historically was eaten with game or cold meats. Rowanberries have also been fermented and used for distilling liquor. A similar species yields the whitebeam berry, which is like the rowanberry and was once used to make wine. Another, the service tree, yields serviceberries, which are now less common.

Common names and synonyms: Serviceberry, whitebeam berry.
Rozelle - *see* **ROSELLE**
Rucola - *see* **ARUGULA**
RUE - A Eurasian plant, rue (*Ruta graveolens*) has been used for many centuries in medicines and as a disease preventive. Indeed, rue was once credited with warding off the plague known as the Black Death and was called "herb-of-grace." The bitter, pungent leaves have also been employed as a potherb - first in Europe and later, after the plant became naturalized, in the southern United States.

Common names and synonyms: Herb-of-grace.
Rugala - *see* **ARUGULA**
Rugela - *see* **ARUGULA**
Rugula - *see* **ARUGULA**
Rukam - *see* **INDIAN PRUNE**
Rukam manis - *see* **INDIAN PRUNE**
Runner nut - *see* **PEANUT**
Running myrtle - *see* **PERIWINKLE**
Rush nut - *see* **CHUFA**
Russian caraway - *see* **NIGELLA**
Russian olive - *see* **ELAEAGNUS**
RUTABAGA - Closely related to the turnip, the rutabaga (*Brassica napobrassica*) is a relatively modern vegetable that resulted from a cross between a Swedish turnip and a cabbage. Called a "Swede," the rutabaga spread from Sweden to central Europe and had reached England by 1800. It was grown in the United States by the beginning of the nineteenth century. However, many rutabagas come to the United States from Canada, which has led to the nickname "Canadian turnip." The rutabaga's flesh is yellowish, and its taste is milder than that of the turnip.

Common names and synonyms: Canadian turnip, swede, Swedish turnip, yellow turnip.

See also: "Cruciferous and Green Leafy Vegetables," Part II, Section C, Chapter 5.

RYE – A native of central Asia, rye (*Secale cereale*) is a widely cultivated cereal grass with seeds that are used for flour, for making whiskey, and as livestock feed. The grain has been cultivated for millennia, but not always deliberately. Beginning some 4,000 years ago, rye started a westward movement, generally as a weed in fields of wheat (a close relative) and barley. Rye came to be appreciated when its hardiness kept it standing while the more valued crops failed. However, in the Mediterranean region, a mild climate prevented rye from displaying its quality of hardiness, and the grain was reportedly despised by the ancient Greeks.

Rye expanded during Roman times – but apparently not with the assistance of the Romans – and was cultivated mostly outside the empire, especially in northern Europe (from about the first century A.D.), where the climate was colder and the plant could grow in soils too poor for wheat. It was brought to North America by European colonists, and became an important staple in early New England, where it may also have played a disruptive role. Rye is especially prone to infection by ergot, a fungus that can cause hallucinations, convulsions, and even gangrene and death, and some historians suspect that ergot-poisoned rye may have been behind the strange behavior of the Salem "witches."

Certainly ergotism was a deadly disease in Europe for hundreds of years, and today rye is carefully inspected for the ergot fungus. Although generally thought of as "poor man's flour," rye remains popular in Scandinavia and eastern Europe. Rye flour is normally mixed with wheat flour to make rye bread. In addition, rye flakes, cracked rye, and whole rye "berries" are used in breakfast cereals, muffins, soups, and casseroles. A major product of rye over the last few hundred years has been the excellent malt it furnishes for the brewing and distillation of alcoholic beverages. The relatively small crop produced in the United States is divided between food and alcohol production on the one hand, and animal feed on the other hand.

See also: "Rye," Part II, Section A, Chapter 8.

RYEGRASS – Any of several species of the genus *Lolium* are called ryegrass. They are European plants that have become naturalized throughout North America. Some, such as Italian ryegrass (*L. multiflorum*), which is much used for hay, or English ryegrass (*L. perenne*) probably served as food for Old World humans in the past. In the New World, the grains of darnel (*L. temulentum*) were consumed by some Native American groups.

Common names and synonyms: Darnel, English ryegrass, Italian ryegrass.

Saba – *see* **BANANA**
Saba nut – *see* **MALABAR NUT**
Sabra – *see* **PRICKLY PEAR**
Sacred datura – *see* **MOONFLOWER**
SAFFLOWER – A thistle-like herb, the safflower plant (*Carthamus tinctorius*) is native to Asia or perhaps Egypt but is now cultivated throughout the world. The plant has red and yellow flowers that were once used as a seasoning (a saffron substitute), whereas its seeds have served for millennia in India as the base of medicines, paints, and cosmetics. But the main use of the seeds is to press them for an oil employed in cooking. Safflower oil is light, with a neutral taste, and is used in salads and for stir-frying.

SAFFRON – This spice comes from a species of crocus (*Crocus sativus*), in the form of saffron "threads," which are the stigmas (the parts that catch pollen for the ovary) of the flower. It has been estimated that, at three stigmas per plant, upwards of 250,000 of these crocus flowers are required to yield a pound of saffron. These numbers, coupled with the fact that the work is all done by hand, serve as a powerful explanation for saffron's distinction as the world's most expensive spice.

Native to the eastern Mediterranean, saffron was used in cooking for thousands of years before the Romans built their empire. Indeed, some credit Phoenician traders with introducing it in Spain – the country that today is the leading producer for the commercial market.

The word saffron comes from the Arabic word for "yellow," and its distinctive color and taste grace Spanish, Cuban, French, and Indian cuisines, especially their rice dishes. It is a vital ingredient in an authentic bouillabaisse or paella as well as the saffron bread of a traditional Swedish feast. Saffron also goes well with poultry, in tomato-based sauces and stews, and in liqueurs such as Chartreuse. The spice is marketed as dried threads and in ground form. Unfortunately, much adulteration of ground saffron occurs, including its near-total replacement with turmeric – a crime that in fifteenth-century Germany drew a penalty of execution by burning or burying alive.

See also: "Spices and Flavorings," Part II, Section F, Chapter 1.

Sagaloo – *see* **CALLALOO**

SAGE – The aggressive flavor and smell of sage (*Salvia officinalis*) doubtless helped to convince numerous peoples – from the ancient Greeks, Arabs, and Romans to the Europeans of the Middle Ages – of its medicinal properties. There are numerous varieties of this small Mediterranean native, with its long and narrow, not to mention pungent, leaves. Exactly when sage became more important in cooking than curing is not clear. Its leaves were brewed into a tea that was used as a spring tonic, and during the Middle Ages the plant gained a reputation (and its common name) for imparting wisdom and improving memory.

But for many centuries, sage has also been flavoring Italian veal, German eels, and French sausages, along with other meats such as pork. In the United States, the herb is a vital ingredient in many seasoned poultry stuffings; fresh sage leaves are universally employed in flavoring pickles, salads, and cheeses and are sometimes made into a tisane. Sage can be purchased in whole leaves (fresh or dried), and in dried and crumbled form (rubbed sage). Today it is cultivated in eastern and western Europe, around the Mediterranean, in the United States, and to a limited extent in West Africa and the West Indies at altitudes of over 1,500 feet.

Common names and synonyms: Common sage, garden sage, rubbed sage.

See also: "Spices and Flavorings," Part II, Section F, Chapter 1.

Sage tree - *see* **CHASTE TREE**

SAGO - Sago is a starch taken in large quantities from several varieties of tropical (sago) palms of the genus *Metroxylon*. The palms grow wild in low-lying, swampy areas of Southeast Asia, Oceania, and northern South America. When mature (at about 10 to 15 years of age), the tree is felled, the trunk split open, and the pith scooped and rasped out to be made into a powdery starch. A single tree may yield from 600 to 800 pounds of starch, which is cooked like rice pudding (it resembles tapioca) and used as a food thickener. "Pearl" sago, produced by putting a sago paste through a sieve and then drying the "pearls," is often used for desserts. Pearl sago is generally the only kind of sago available outside of the tropics. Sago provides much in the way of carbohydrates but lacks most other important nutrients and must be supplemented with foods containing protein, such as fish and local vegetable foods.

Common names and synonyms: Pearl sago.

See also: "Sago," Part II, Section B, Chapter 4.

Sago fern - *see* **TREE-FERN**

SAGUARO (*see also* **PITAHAYA**) - A giant columnar cactus of northern Mexico and southern Arizona, the saguaro (*Cereus giganteus* or *Carnegiea gigantea*) served as a staple food for Native Americans of the region, who often gathered saguaro fruits that had fallen to the ground and had been naturally dried by the sun. These they stored for later use. The red pulp of the fruit can also be eaten fresh, pressed into juice, and made into a syrup. In addition, the seeds can be turned into a paste. The fruits are sometimes called *pitayas,* and the saguaro cactus a *pitayo*.

Common names and synonyms: Pitaya, pitayo.

SAIGON CINNAMON (*see also* **CINNAMON AND CASSIA**) - Like its relatives cinnamon and cassia, "Saigon cinnamon" (*Cinnamomum loureirii*) is a

tree cultivated for its bark, which is processed into a spice. Probably a native of Southeast Asia, the tree is now grown primarily in China, Japan, and Java. Also known as "cassia" (which promotes some confusion), Saigon cinnamon is sold as cinnamon and is widely used in industrial baking and food processing in the United States.

Common names and synonyms: Cassia.

Saint-John's-bread - *see* **CAROB**

SAINT-JOHN'S-WORT - A Eurasian plant, now growing in North America and known throughout the world for its alleged antidepressant properties, "Saint-John's-wort" (*Hypericum perforatum*) produces lemon-scented leaves that have served humans as food for thousands of years and have also been used to make a tea. In addition, the flowers have been consumed, as have the flower buds and leaves of "great Saint-John's-wort" (*H. pyramidatum*).

Common names and synonyms: Great Saint-John's-wort.

Salad pear - *see* **ASIAN PEAR**

Salad savory - *see* **KALE**

SALAK - Salak (*Salacca edulis*) is the native name in Malaya for a fruit that grows on a palm, looks like a pear, and tastes like a pineapple.

SALAL - A close relative of wintergreen, salal (*Gaultheria shallon*) is a shrub of the northwestern Pacific coast of North America. It bears fruits that are dark, sweet, juicy, and about the size of the common grape. When these berries ripened in the autumn, they were consumed in great amounts by Native Americans of the region, who also dried them for use in the winter.

Salamander tree - *see* **BIGNAY**

SALEP - A starchy powder, ground from the dried roots of various Old World orchids of the genera *Orchis* and *Eulophia,* salep is employed in Asian cookery. When mixed with boiling milk, it makes a kind of pudding that is enjoyed by children. In a diluted form, salep was formerly sold on the streets to London laborers as an early-morning drink. Salep stalls, however, long ago gave way to coffee stalls.

SALMONBERRY (*see also* **BERRIES, CLOUDBERRY**) - This edible berry grows on a prickly shrub (*Rubus spectabilis*) that is a native of the coastal regions of the U.S. Northwest. Actually a raspberry, the fruit is a yellow-pink "salmon" color, hence its name. Both the berries and the young shoots of the plants were eaten by Native Americans.

Common names and synonyms: Thimbleberry.

Saloop - *see* **SASSAFRAS**

SALSIFY (*see also* **SCORZNERA**) - A perennial plant, thought by some to have a taste similar to that of an oyster (and consequently nicknamed "oyster-plant" and "vegetable-oyster"), salsify (*Tragopogon porrifolius*) is native to the Mediterranean region, where it has been cultivated since at least the sixteenth century. It is a parsnip-like root vegetable with light brown skin and a whitish flesh that is much more appreciated in Europe than in the Americas, although the plant has existed in North America for a couple of centuries and is grown commercially there.

At the top of the seed heads of this interesting plant grows a fluffy tuft that has prompted another nickname – "purple-goat's-beard." (A black variety of salsify is known as *scorzonera*.) Salsify has edible leaves that grow upwards of 2 feet in length and are used in salads or cooked as a vegetable. After the roots (an excellent winter vegetable) are unearthed, they are normally scraped, then prepared – like parsnips – by steaming or parboiling and sautéeing. Salsify provides the consumer with some measure of the B-vitamins and vitamin C.

Common names and synonyms: Oyster-plant, purple-goat's-beard, vegetable-oyster, white salsify.

SALTBUSH – A member of the goosefoot family (Chenopodiaceae), the four-wing saltbush (*Atriplex canescens*) has foliage that tastes salty. Native Americans used its seeds for meal and ate the new shoots and leaves as greens. Several other species of *Atriplex* were similarly employed. Another plant called saltbush – desert holly (*A. hymenelytra*) – may or may not have ever served as human food.

Common names and synonyms: Desert holly, four-wing saltbush.

SAMPHIRE (*see also* **GLASSWORT**) – A plant that inhabits Old World coastal areas from the British Isles along the shores of western Europe to the Mediterranean, samphire (*Crithmum maritimum*) has fleshy leaves that are used in salads. A member of the parsley family, saphire is also called "glasswort." Another plant with the name samphire is *Philoxerus vermicularis,* which is common along the beaches of the southeastern United States. It also has fleshy, edible leaves.

Common names and synonyms: Glasswort.

SAND CHERRY (*see also* **CHERRY**) – One of the many wild cherries of eastern North America, the "sand cherry" (*Prunus pumila*) is a low-growing cherry that likes sandy soil. The fruit is black, with a taste that ranges from sweet to very acidic. Native Americans pounded sand cherries (including the pits) into a jelly-like mass that could be shaped, dried, and stored for the winter. There is also a "western sand cherry" (*P. besseyi*) – of western North America – which bears a large fruit that is generally quite sweet.

Common names and synonyms: Western sand cherry.

Sand leek - *see* **GARLIC**

San Domingo apricot - *see* **MAMMEE**

Sand pear - *see* **ASIAN PEAR**

SANGIOVESE (*see also* **GRAPES**) – A red wine grape of central Italy (especially Tuscany), the Sangiovese (*Vitis vinifera*) is the primary grape used to make Chianti – the most popular wine of Italy. It is also used to make some of the other Tuscan red wines as well as medium-bodied reds in California.

See in addition: "Wine," Part III, Chapter 13.

Santa Fe Grande - *see* **WAX PEPPERS**

SAPODILLA – A tropical American species, the sapodilla (*Manilkara zapota*) is a tree that seems to have had its origins in southern Mexico, Central America, and perhaps northern South America, but it is now widespread from the West Indies to the East Indies – and with good reason. The bark contains a milky latex, widely known as "chicle" (an ingredient of chewing gum), and the tree bears fruits that are both juicy and sweet when ripe. The latter (also called "naseberries") are small, round, and reddish brown, with a yellowish pulp that can be spooned out of the skin. In addition to being eaten out of hand, sapodillas are used in salads and desserts.

Common names and synonyms: Chicle (tree), chico, chico sapote, chico zapote, chiku, dilly, mammee sapota, marmalade plum, naseberry, nispero, zapote, zapotillo.

Sapota - *see* **BLACK SAPOTE, MAMEY SAPOTE, WHITE SAPOTE**

SAPUCAIA NUT – Several trees of the genus *Lecythis,* which are native to Brazil, Guiana, and Trinidad, produce sapucaia nuts. Also called the "paradise nut," it is a sweet, oily nut that resembles the Brazil nut in taste, although some find that of the sapucaia to be superior. Like Brazil nuts, sapucaia nuts are formed inside an urn-shaped container. But this vessel – commonly called a "monkey pot" – is considerably larger than that of the Brazil nut. The problem is that unlike Brazil nuts, the sapucaia is not protected by a hard shell, and at maturity the cap of the "monkey pot" loosens, scattering the nuts over the jungle floor to be consumed by monkeys and other animals, and those that are not consumed are difficult to find. Thus, only a very small portion of sapucaia nuts are ever consumed by humans, and those reaching U.S. markets tend to be expensive.

Common names and synonyms: Paradise nut.

Sara chulpi - *see* **MAIZE**

Sarawak (pepper) - *see* **PEPPER(CORNS)**

SARSAPARILLA – The dried roots of American tropical plants of the genus *Smilax* yield an extract that was used in London for one of the first "soft drinks" – "Dr. Butler's Ale," first made around the turn of the seventeenth century. Sarsaparilla was later a common base for soft drinks made in the United States.

Saskatoon berry - *see* **SERVICEBERRY**

Saskatoon serviceberry - *see* **SERVICEBERRY**

SASSAFRAS – The spicy bark of both the trunk and roots of the North American tree *Sassafras albidum* is dried and used for flavorings. Sassafras tea has long been employed for medicinal purposes, and "saloop" – a kind of sassafras tea – not only was considered a remedy for many ailments but also, like salep, was sold on the streets of London to working men, much as coffee is now. In addition, sassafras twigs and leaves contain much mucilaginous matter, which is utilized in filé to flavor and thicken gumbos and other soups.

Common names and synonyms: Filé, saloop, sassafras tea.

Sassafras tea - *see* SASSAFRAS

Sativa - *see* ALFALFA

Satsuma - *see* MANDARIN ORANGE

Sauerkraut - *see* CABBAGE

Sauvignon - *see* SAUVIGNON BLANC

SAUVIGNON BLANC (*see also* GRAPES) - Also called Fumé Blanc, Sauvignon Blanc is a white wine grape (*Vitis vinifera*) that is employed to make some of the great dry wines of the Graves region of Bordeaux and the Loire Valley (important wine-producing areas of France) as well as many that are produced in California and Washington State. The wine Pouilly Fumé, of the Loire Valley, is 100 percent Sauvignon Blanc, as is Sancerre, and the grape is a major variety used in the production of Sauternes. Sauvignon Blanc grapes have been grown in California for over a century. The name Fumé Blanc was an invention of California wine maker Robert Mondavi that was intended to stimulate sales of his Sauvignon Blanc wine. To say simply that he succeeded is a colossal understatement.

Common names and synonyms: Blanc Fumé, Fumé Blanc, Sauvignon.

See in addition: "Wine," Part III, Chapter 13.

SAVORY - Summer savory (*Satureja hortensis*) and winter savory (*S. montana*) are both herbs that are native to the Mediterranean region. Their leaves have served to flavor foods since the time of the ancient Romans. Both have a faintly peppery taste, but that of summer savory is milder. Savory leaves are available both fresh and dried and go well with tomato-based dishes, legumes, stuffings, fish, salads, sauces, and sausages - to name but a few of the various foods this herb enhances.

Common names and synonyms: Summer savory, winter savory.

See also: "Spices and Flavorings," Part II, Section F, Chapter 1.

Scallion - *see* ONION

Scariole - *see* ENDIVE AND ESCAROLE

Scarlet haw - *see* HAWTHORN BERRY

Scoke - *see* POKEWEED

SCORZONERA - This vegetable (*Scorzonera hispanica*) was once believed by the Spaniards to cure snakebites as well as to just make people feel happy. Scorzonera is native to central and southern Europe, where it has been cultivated since at least the sixteenth century. The root is shaped like a carrot and is black skinned with white flesh. The flowers are yellow and the oblong leaves are hairy. A member of the Compositae family, scorzonera can be either eaten raw (often in salads) or boiled as a vegetable. The taste is often described as being

similar to that of an oyster. Scorzonera is an annual plant and popular in Europe. It grows wild over much of the continent, from Spain in the south and west, north to Germany, and east to the Caucasus. Scorzonera is also commonly known as black salsify.

Common names and synonyms: Black oyster-plant, black salsify, viper-grass.

Scotch bonnet - *see* HABANERO AND SCOTCH BONNET PEPPERS

Scotch gale - *see* BOG MYRTLE

Scotch spearmint - *see* MINT

Screwbean - *see* MESQUITE

Screw(-)pine - *see* PANDANUS, STRIPED SCREWPINE

Screwpod - *see* MESQUITE

Scuppernong - *see* MUSCADINE, GRAPES

SCURVY GRASS (*see also* ANGELICA, MOUNTAIN SORREL) - There are a number of plants called "scurvy grass." These plants were generally those that appeared early in the spring and were consumed by humans after a winter of vitamin-C deprivation. This "official" scurvy grass (*Cochlearia officinalis*) is a denizen of northern regions that has extremely bitter foliage. It is also called spoonwort because of the shape of its leaves; needless to say, it does contain some vitamin C.

Common names and synonyms: Spoonwort.

Scutch - *see* COUCH GRASS

Seabeach sandwort - *see* SEA PURSLANE

Sea bean - *see* GLASSWORT

SEA BUCKTHORN - A shrub found on the coasts of Europe and Asia, the sea buckthorn (*Hippophae rhamnoides*) has silver leaves and produces orangish red, edible berries.

SEA GRAPE - Also called the shore grape, the sea grape (*Coccoloba uvifera*) is a tropical American native found on sandy beaches from Florida throughout the West Indies to Venezuela. Not a grape (despite its name), the sea grape is a bushy, salt-tolerant, evergreen plant with clusters of purplish red fruits that are sweet. They are eaten raw, juiced, and made into jelly and wine.

Common names and synonyms: Shore grape.

Seagrass - *see* GLASSWORT

SEA HOLLY - A plant common in southeastern Europe (which has been introduced in North America) and credited over the centuries with medicinal properties, the sea holly (*Eryngium maritimum*) is also often called "eringo" or "eryngo." The plant was once believed to be an aphrodisiac. Its leaves were brewed to make a kind of tea, and the roots went into various concoctions. But the roots have served as a food, too; when cooked, they have a taste that is said to resemble that of chestnuts. The young shoots were also sometimes eaten. Candied sea holly roots are called "eryngo."

Common names and synonyms: Eringo, eryngo.

SEAKALE - A summer vegetable, seakale (*Crambe maritima*), which looks a bit like broccoli, grows wild along the coasts of western and northern Europe and has been cultivated in England and the United States. Despite its name, seakale is not related to the kale of the cabbage family. The stems and leaf tips are generally blanched, dipped into melted butter, and enjoyed like asparagus for their nutlike flavor.

SEA LETTUCE (*see also* **SEAWEED**) - Bright green seaweeds of the genus *Ulva* - especially *U. lactuca* - are collectively called "sea lettuce." These are gathered from rocks along seacoasts and added to soups, salads, and the like.

See in addition: "Algae," Part II, Section C, Chapter 1.

Sea moss - *see* **DULSE, SEAWEED**

Sea pickle - *see* **GLASSWORT**

SEA PURSLANE - Also called "seabeach sandwort," sea purslane (*Atriplex halimus* or *A. hastata*) has small edible leaves that are boiled and eaten as a vegetable. The plant is native to the Mediterranean, where its leaves have probably been consumed since the days of the hunter-gatherers.

Common names and synonyms: Seabeach sandwort.

Seaside plum - *see* **TALLOW WOOD PLUM**

Sea tangle - *see* **SEAWEED**

Sea vegetable(s) - *see* **SEAWEED**

Seaving - *see* **SOUARI NUT**

SEAWEED - Seaweeds - or more appetizingly, "sea vegetables" - consist of certain species of marine algae (belonging to genera like *Chondrus, Fucus, Macrocystis, Nereocystis, Laminaria,* and *Porphyra*) such as kelp, rockweed, gulfweed, and laver. When such algae are fresh, their taste is that of salty greens; when they are dried, however, the taste is just salty. Although (save for some people in the British Isles) Westerners from the time of the ancient Greeks have steadfastly ignored seaweed as a food, the Japanese have long appreciated it. They use kelp such as *nori* (in English, "laver" - *Porphyra laciniata, P. tenera,* and *P. umbilicalis*) for wrapping sushi; *kombu* (*Laminaria japonica* - known as giant sea kelp) for broths and stocks and for wrapping dried fish; *wakame* (*Undaria pinnatifida*) for soups and salads, and to sprinkle over rice dishes; *hijiki* (*Cystophyllum fusiforme*) for sautéing as well as deep-frying tempura; and agar as an agent for jelling. In the West, "Irish moss," or *carrageen*, is a seaweed that is the source of *carrageenin* and is instrumental in thickening salad oils, cottage cheese, and the like. Laver has been traditionally cooked into flatcakes (laverbread) by the Irish, and green laver is used as a cooked vegetable. In the past in the United States, one kind of edible kelp was called "bladder weed" because of its streamer-like leaves (or "giant bladder weed" when the streamers averaged 30 to 40 or more feet in length).

Depending on the variety, seaweed can be high in beta-carotene and vitamin C, and all types are packed with a host of minerals.

Common names and synonyms: Agar, alga(e), bladder weed, carrageen moss, dulse, giant bladder weed, giant sea kelp, green laver, green sloke, gulfweed, *hijiki,* Irish moss, *karenga,* kelp, *kombu,* laver, *limu, nori,* rockweed, sea lettuce, sea moss, sea tangle, sea vegetable(s), *tecuitlatl, wakame.*

See also: "Algae," Part II, Section C, Chapter 1.

Seckel - *see* **PEAR**

SEDGE - Plants of the sedge family (Cyperaceae) and of the genus *Carex* are called "sedges"; they resemble grasses but have sharp stems that are solid rather than hollow. Various species are found worldwide, and their stems, corms, and grains have served as food for many thousands of years. Examples include the tender, whitish bases of the leaves of *C. aquatilis,* a plant that grows in North America and Europe and has long been consumed. The grains of an East Asian species (*C. kobomugi*) are also eaten.

Seje ungurahuay - *see* **PATAUA**

SÉMILLON (*see also* **GRAPES**) - This white grape (*Vitis vinifera*) is used to produce dry white wines, usually in combination with another grape such as Sauvignon. However, it is also used to make sweet Sauternes wines and is found mainly in the Graves and Sauternes regions of France.

See in addition: "Wine," Part III, Chapter 13.

Seminole bread - *see* **ZAMIA**

Sencha - *see* **TEA**

SENNA - Any of the various plants of the genus *Cassia* are called senna. The leaves of many of these, such as *C. angustifolia,* have been used medicinally especially in Asia. In North America the leaves, young shoots, and green pods of others, such as *C. occidentalis,* were used as food by Native Americans and settlers.

SENTUL - The fruit of a tall tree native to Indonesia, the sentul (*Sandoricum koetjape* formerly *indicum*) is round, yellow, 2 to 3 inches in diameter, and sweet and juicy. The fruit is generally eaten raw but is also made into jam. In addition, there is a red sentul - called *kechapi* - that is smaller and sour tasting.

Common names and synonyms: Kechapi.

SERENDIPITY BERRY - An edible red berry, the serendipity berry (*Dioscoreophyllum cumminsii*) is found in west-central Africa. It belongs to a large genus of mostly tropical fruits and is a relative of both the American black sapote and the Japanese persimmon.

Serpolet - *see* **THYME**

SERRANO (*see also* **CHILLI PEPPERS**) - A very popular pepper in Mexico and the southwestern United States, the serrano (meaning "mountain" or "highland"), a *Capsicum annuum,* is a very hot pepper, about 1 to 2 inches in length, with a torpedo-like shape. Serranos come in the colors green and red; both kinds are used interchangeably in salsas and other dishes. They are also canned, pickled, and packed in oil. When dried, serranos are called *chilli seco* or *serrano seco*, remain intensely hot, and are available both whole and in powdered form.

Common names and synonyms: Chilli seco, serrano seco.

See in addition: "Chilli Peppers," Part II, Section C, Chapter 4.

SERVICEBERRY (*see also* **BERRIES, ROWANBERRY**) – Growing in most of the world's temperate zones on a number of small trees and shrubs of the genus *Amelanchier*, the serviceberry is also known in North America as "shadbush" (because its white flowers appeared at about the same time that shad did in the rivers) and as "juneberry." The brownish or purple to black serviceberries were an important food for Native Americans such as the Chippewa. This was especially true of the fruits of *A. alnifolia* (a plant of North America called "Saskatoon" in the Cree language) and the western serviceberry, which resembles the blueberry more than do other serviceberries. Serviceberries were of particular significance in the American West, where they were sometimes the only food available to nourish the Mormons and other pioneers. Today, the fruits are sought for their "serviceability" in pies, jams, jellies, and sauces. Serviceberry is also a name sometimes applied to closely related berries of the mountain ash family. Equally confusing is the name bilberry, sometimes given to serviceberries.

Common names and synonyms: Juneberry, Saskatoon berry, Saskatoon serviceberry, shadblow, shadbush, western serviceberry.

Sesaban - *see* **SESBAN**

SESAME – A small seed with a nutty flavor that comes in a variety of colors (white, black, red, and brown), sesame (*Sesamum indicum*) is far more important in other parts of the world than it is in North America, where the white or black seed is used mostly atop breads and buns. The plant is alternatively said to be native to East Africa and to India (as the Latin name would have it), but there is no reason that it cannot have originated in both locations. Sesame is probably the oldest crop grown for its oil: It was cultivated in the Tigris and Euphrates valleys some 5,000 years ago and has competed with olive oil in the Mediterranean and India ever since its production began.

Sesame oil is also the oil for many in Asia: The seeds are a basic ingredient in the *tahina* of the Middle East and the *halvah* of Turkey, and in the Far East pastry cooks have long mixed sesame seeds with wheat flour. The seeds traveled in the holds of slave ships to reach the New World and today are commercially grown in South America.

The darker, unhulled seeds (in contrast to the whitish, hulled seeds) are rich in calcium and iron.

Common names and synonyms: Benne, ben(n)iseed, gingelly, sim(-)sim, til(seed).

See also: "Sesame," Part II, Section E, Chapter 4; "Spices and Flavorings," Part II, Section F, Chapter 1.

SESBAN – Also known by numerous common names such as "sesaban," "sesnania," "white spinach," "West Indian pea," "corkwood tree," and "agati," sesban (*Sesbania grandiflora*) – now naturalized in the United States – is a small tree of Southeast Asia and Australia, where it is called the "Australian corkscrew tree." Its white wood is very soft, which lends it to the same uses as cork. The fruit is a green pod (growing up to 2 feet in length), which is cooked and eaten along with the leaves, the buds, and the very large, white flowers. In many cultures, the flower petals are battered and fried. The tree has provided nourishment for humans for thousands of years, and even today is cultivated in India as a food plant. A related North American plant is the "coffee weed" (*S. cavanillesii*), the roasted seeds of which have served Mexicans as a coffee substitute.

Common names and synonyms: Agati, Australian corkscrew tree, coffee weed, corkwood tree, sesaban, sesnania, West Indian pea, white spinach.

Sesnania - *see* **SESBAN**

Setar - *see* **KUNDANGAN**

Seychelles cinnamon - *see* **CINNAMON AND CASSIA**

Shadblow - *see* **SERVICEBERRY**

Shadbush - *see* **SERVICEBERRY**

Shaddock - *see* **GRAPEFRUIT, POMELO**

Shagbark - *see* **HICKORY**

SHALLOT(S) – Shallots, once thought to be a species (*Allium ascalonicum*) distinct from the onion (although related to it [as for example, are chives and garlic, also members of the genus *Allium*]), are now considered to be a variety of the onion species (*A. cepa*). In fact, because shallots do not exist in a wild state, they may actually be a mutation of the onion.

The name "shallot" comes from the Greek name of a trading town in southern Palestine (*Askalon*) that was associated with the vegetable, which was carried to western Europe by returning Crusaders. A shallot is generally the size of a large head of garlic, grows in clove form, has a flavor more subtle than onion, and is less pungent than garlic. Chopped fine, shallots are indispensable in numerous classic sauces; sliced, they are an ingredient in many fine dishes; and they are roasted whole as an accompaniment for meats and poultry. In the Far East, shallots are pickled for use in salads, as a snack, and as a side dish. In Louisiana, scallions are frequently (and incorrectly) called shallots, doubtless because the French settlers there substituted scallions for the shallots of their homeland.

Common names and synonyms: White shallot.
See also: "The *Allium* Species," Part II, Section C, Chapter 2.

Shantung cabbage - *see* **CHINESE CABBAGE**

Shattercane - *see* **SORGHUM**

Shea-butter - *see* **SHEA TREE**

SHEA TREE - A West African native, the shea tree (*Butyrospermum parkii*) has large seeds with kernels that yield a fat called "shea-butter." The fat is utilized locally in cooking and is also exported to Europe, where it is used to make margarine and employed as a cooking fat.
Common names and synonyms: Shea-butter.

Sheepberry - *see* **BLACK HAW**

Sheep sorrel - *see* **SORREL**

Sherbet-fruit - *see* **CHERIMOYA**

Shiitake - *see* **MUSHROOMS AND FUNGI**

Shimeji - *see* **OYSTER MUSHROOM**

Shiraz - *see* **SYRAH**

Shiso - *see* **BEEFSTEAK PLANT**

Shore grape - *see* **SEA GRAPE**

Shore plum - *see* **BEACH PLUM**

Shrubby wound-wort - *see* **QUELITES**

SHUM - A life-saving tree during India's great famine of 1868–9, the bark of the shum (*Prosopis cineraria*) was used to make a flour that kept many from starving to death.

Siberian cherry - *see* **CORNUS**

Siberian hazel - *see* **HAZELNUT AND FILBERT**

SICHUAN PEPPERCORN (*see also* **PEPPERCORN**) - An ancient spice in China but not actually a peppercorn, the "Sichuan peppercorn" (*Zanthoxylum piperitum*) was in use (especially in the province of Sichuan) long before true peppercorns arrived. It is a small, aromatic, reddish brown seed from the prickly ash tree and, when ground, is frequently blended with salt to make pepper-salt – a fragrant dip for grilled and fried foods – and is also blended with other ingredients as in China's "five spices." In Japan, the leaves of the prickly ash tree (which have a peppery-lemon taste) serve as a garnish.

Sicilian corn - *see* **MAIZE**

Silk-cotton tree - *see* **KAPOK TREE**

Silk Fig - *see* **BANANA, BANANA FLOWER**

Silkweed - *see* **MILKWEED**

Silphion - *see* **SILPHIUM**

SILPHIUM - An extinct plant of the genus *Ferula,* silphium was well known to the ancient Greeks and utilized as a condiment by the Romans. It was grown in North Africa and was used as a medicine as well as in cooking. There are other plants of a genus now called *Silphium* that have been employed as foods. One such food is the sap of an eastern North American plant (*S. laciniatum*) called "rosinweed" or "compass plant." Another is the roots of *S. laeve* (also called "compass plant"), which reportedly were consumed by Native Americans. These peoples also used the sap of the cup plant (*S. perfoliatum*), but apparently mostly as a medicine.
Common names and synonyms: Compass plant, cup plant, rosinweed, silphion.
See also: "Spices and Flavorings," Part II, Section F, Chapter 1.

SILVANER (*see also* **GRAPES**) - A grape known as "sylvaner" in Austria and France, the Silvaner (*Vitis vinifera*) originated in eastern Europe and moved west to become well known in medieval Germany. It remained one of Germany's most important wine grapes until about the middle of the twentieth century but now accounts for only about 7 percent of that country's wine. It is regarded today as a specialty grape of Franken (Franconia) in western Germany, although it is also grown in Alsace.
Common names and synonyms: Sylvaner.
See in addition: "Wine," Part III, Chapter 13.

Silver beet - *see* **SWISS CHARD**

Silverberry - *see* **ELAEAGNUS**

Silver ear - *see* **CLOUD EAR**

Silver pine - *see* **PINE NUT**

Silverthorn - *see* **ELAEAGNUS**

Sim(-)sim - *see* **SESAME**

Sing li mei - *see* **DAIKON**

SKIRRET - A Eurasian herb, skirret (*Sium sisarum*) is a member of the parsley family. It was cultivated in the past for its small, sweet, fleshy, edible roots, which can be boiled and buttered and eaten like potatoes or parsnips.
Common names and synonyms: Skirret-root(s).

Skoke - *see* **POKEWEED**

SKUNK CABBAGE - An offensive-smelling, swamp-dwelling herb of eastern North America, "skunk cabbage" (*Symplocarpus foetidus*) has a host of less-than-elegant common names, such as "polecat weed," "swamp cabbage," and "stinking poke." Its purple flowers are among the first of the New Year to appear and announce the impending arrival of spring. Skunk cabbage has long been used medicinally and even – despite its rank smell – culinarily. Native Americans boiled its young shoots as a vegetable and also cooked the root, after which it could be dried and made into a flour.
Common names and synonyms: Polecat weed, stinking poke, swamp cabbage.

SLIPPERY ELM - A tree of eastern North America, the slippery elm (*Ulmus fulva = U. rubra*) has unappetizing leaves and a rough outer bark but a fragrant, mucilaginous inner bark. Native Americans ate the inner bark raw and boiled it as a vegetable in both fresh and dried form. The bark continues to be harvested and dried (generally under pressure so that it remains flat); when reconstituted, it is employed as a food for babies and for adults with digestive problems.

Slip-skin grape - *see* **FOX GRAPE**

Sloak - *see* **LAVER**

SLOE (*see also* **PLUM**) - Also called "sloes," "black sloe," and "blackthorn," the sloe (*Prunus spinosa*) is a Eurasian and North African plum that is sometimes viewed as the ancestor of the Damson plum and other cultivated varieties. The fruit is berry sized, pale blue to black in color, and - as a rule - too astringent to be eaten raw. It is, however, made into juice, jellies, syrups, and preserves. Perhaps the most notable use of sloes is in the flavoring of liquors and liqueurs such as "sloe gin."

Common names and synonyms: Black sloe, blackthorn, sloes.

Sloes - *see* SLOE

Slook - *see* LAVER

Smallage - *see* LOVAGE

Small gourd - *see* IVY GOURD

Smartweed - *see* KNOTWEED AND SMARTWEED

Smokeweed - *see* KNOTWEED AND SMARTWEED

Smooth loofah - *see* ANGLED LUFFA

SMOOTH SUMAC - Also known as "mountain sumac," "upland sumac," and "vinegar tree" (among other common names), the smooth sumac (*Rhus glabra*) is a shrub of eastern North America. It is a relative of poison oak, poison ivy, and poison sumac, but it produces edible red berries that were dried and used as food by Native Americans.

Common names and synonyms: Mountain sumac, upland sumac, vinegar tree.

Snailseed - *see* PIGEON PLUM

Snake bean - *see* WINGED BEAN

Snake cucumber - *see* ARMENIAN CUCUMBER, CUCUMBER, SNAKE GOURD

SNAKE GOURD - Also called "snake melon," the snake gourd has long been thought of in terms of two species (*Trichosanthes anguina* and *T. cucumerina*), but it is now generally acknowledged that both names refer to the same species. Yet, as the two names remain, so do distinctions. *Trichosanthes anguina* is mostly intended to mean wild snake gourds, whereas *T. cucumerina* ("cucumber-like") refers to the cultivated vegetable. Unquestionably, the suggestion of a snake-like appearance seems appropriate - at least for the wild gourds, which can grow up to 5 or even 6 feet in length, sometimes remaining straight, sometimes curling, but in either case resembling a snake. The snake gourd is most appreciated in India and southeastern Asia, where the immature fruits, with a zucchini-like taste, are usually harvested at 10 to 12 inches in length and are boiled to be eaten whole or used in curries. The mature fruits, which become bitter, are cut into pieces for soups.

Common names and synonyms: Snake cucumber, snake melon.

Snake melon - *see* ARMENIAN CUCUMBER, SNAKE GOURD

Snapping hazel - *see* WITCH-HAZEL

Snow pea - *see* PEA(S), SUGAR PEA

SOAPBERRY - Any of several (mostly tropical) plants of the genus *Sapindus*, which produce berries that lather like soap in water, are called "soapberries," especially *S. saponaria* (the southern soapberry). Indeed, the berries contain sufficient saponin that they are sold as soap in some places. There are, however, other species, like *S. marginatus*, which Native Americans employed as food.

Common names and synonyms: Indian soap, southern soapberry.

SOLOMON'S-SEAL - Plants of the genus *Polygonatum* are called "Solomon's-seal" because of the resemblance of scars on their rootstocks to that mystical symbol of two interlaced triangles that make a six-pointed star. The plants are native to both Europe and North America, where their rhizomes have served humans as food for millennia. However, those rootstocks are toxic and consequently required processing. Native Americans sometimes dried them, then ground them into flour. In Europe, the rhizome was boiled and the starch made into a bread. The rootstocks and fresh shoots of some species are still consumed in East Asia.

SONCOYA - As its scientific name indicates, the soncoya (*Annona purpurea*) is a close relative of the cherimoya. The tree - a native of tropical and subtropical America - is relatively small (rarely reaching more than 22 feet in height), but the brown fruit is large. Its pulp is orange and sweet, and some have likened the taste to that of a papaw. The fruit is mostly eaten fresh.

SORB APPLE - The astringent fruit of the service tree, the "sorb apple" (*Sorbus domestica*) is a native of Asia Minor that was once fairly popular but is now uncommon. Like medlars, sorb apples are made edible by "bletting" (storage until they are on the verge of decomposing). A frost also helps to improve the texture and taste of these pear- and apple-shaped, brownish green fruits. Rowanberries and serviceberries are close relatives of the sorb apple, and their names are sometimes used interchangeably.

SORGHUM (*see also* **MILLET**) - There are several varieties of this Old World grass (*Sorghum vulgare* = *S. bicolor*) that are cultivated for grain, for forage, and as a source of syrup. Sorghum is native to East Africa, where it was being cultivated around 5,000 to 6,000 years ago. Sometime in the distant past (at least 2,000 years ago), the grain crossed the Indian Ocean to India and subsequently made its way to China. More recently, various sorghums reached the New World via the slave trade. Today, grain sorghums are grown extensively in Africa and Asia for use as human food and in the Americas as animal food.

Some sorghums in North America - like "Johnson grass" and "Mississippi chicken corn" - probably arrived as the seeds of important cultivars, only to escape from cultivation and become annoying weeds. The juices of sorghums have provided humans with syrup for sweetening, and in Asia and Africa the plant supplies malt, mash, and flavoring for alcoholic beverages, especially beers. Sorghum grains are made into flour (for unleavened breads) and into porridges, and they are also prepared and consumed much like rice. In addition, they can be popped in hot oil like popcorn. Despite these many uses, however, when available, the major grains like wheat, rice, and maize are chosen before sorghum, which means that its major role has been that of a famine food.

Common names and synonyms: Broomcorn, grain sorghum, great millet, Guinea corn, Johnson grass, Kaffir corn, Mississippi chicken corn, shattercane, sorgo, Sudan grass, sweet sorghum.

See also: "Sorghum," Part II, Section A, Chapter 9.

Sorgo - *see* **SORGHUM**

SORREL (*see also* **ROSELLE, WOOD SORREL**) - Species of the genus *Rumex* are called either sorrel or "dock." Garden sorrel (*R. acetosa*), also known as "sheep sorrel," and French sorrel (*R. scutatus*) are the two most important species that are cultivated for use as vegetables or herbs. Another type, *R. patientia*, known as "spinach dock," is less widely used. The name "sorrel" is derived from a Germanic word meaning "sour"; the plant's oxalic acid content contributes to its sour or bitter taste. Sorrel is related to rhubarb.

Many species of sorrel were native to Eurasia, and it was an herb used by the ancient Egyptians, Greeks, and Romans. These Old World species subsequently became naturalized in North America alongside native species that had been employed as food by Native Americans and were often cultivated as a vegetable. *Rumex articus* is an Arctic species that is still utilized by the Inuit, who boil and eat the leaves and also ferment them for later use. "Water dock" (*R. hydrolapathum*) and several other species are simply sorrels that grow in wet places.

The French employ *R. scutatus,* which is somewhat less acidic than garden sorrel, for their sorrel soup and famous *soupe aux herbes.* Other uses are in salads and egg dishes, and sorrel was a key ingredient in the old English green sour sauces that accompanied a roasted goose or pig. Last, sorrel leaves are often cooked and eaten like spinach, which they resemble. Sorrel is very high in vitamins A and C and is a good source of potassium.

Common names and synonyms: Dock, French sorrel, garden sorrel, round(-leaved) sorrel, sheep sorrel, sour(-)dock, sour grass, spinach dock, water dock, wild sorrel.

SORVA (*see also* **SERVICEBERRY**) - A tree of South America, sorva (*Couma utilis*) yields an edible, sweet fruit that is sold in local markets. Its main product, however, is a latex that serves as a substitute for chicle gum. "Sorva" is also a common name for the serviceberry.

SOTOL - Also known as the "spoonplant," "desert-spoon," and "cactus-spoon," the sotol (*Dasylirion wheeleri*) is a member of the agave family. Native Americans ate the heart and young stalks of the plant. Its head contains a sugary sap that when fermented becomes a potent beverage also called sotol.

Common names and synonyms: Cactus-spoon, desert-spoon, spoonplant.

SOUARI NUT - A native of Guiana, the souari nut (*Caryocar nuciferum* or *C. amygdaliferum* - also called "butternut") is an edible nut that grows on very tall trees that have been much used in ship-building. In addition to its consumption raw, the souari nut yields an oil used in cooking. This nut with white meat is seldom seen in North American markets.

Common names and synonyms: Achotillo, butternut, seaving.

Souchong - *see* **TEA**

SOUR CHERRY (*see also* **CHERRY**) - A member of the rose family, the sour cherry (*Prunus cerasus = Cerasus vulgaris*), a stone fruit, is mostly cultivated in North America but is said to be native to southwestern Asia. Its tree has been cultivated since antiquity. Indeed, there is a story that its Latin name refers to the city of Cerasus in Pontus, an ancient kingdom in the northeast of Asia Minor. After defeating its king, Mithradates, the Roman general Lucullus carried the tree back to Italy and called it *cerasus.*

The sour cherry tree is small and rarely reaches over 8 feet in height, but it is known to spread out quite a bit. Sour cherries, which are bright red to almost black in color, can be eaten raw and are often cooked in various dishes, most notably cherry pie. In addition, they yield a colorless juice, which can be used to advantage in certain culinary applications. There is also an Australian tree (*Eugenia corynantha*) with sour-tasting red fruits that are called "sour cherries." Both sour cherries are rich in vitamin C.

Sour(-)dock - *see* **CURLED DOCK, SORREL**

Sour finger carambola - *see* **BELIMBING**

Sour grass - *see* **SORREL**

Sour gum - *see* **BLACK GUM**

SOUR PLUM - *Ximenia caffra* is a small tree or shrub common in southern Africa. Its greenish blossoms are followed by oval orange to scarlet fruits that are about 1 inch in diameter. The fruit envelops a seed that yields an oil used in the tanning of leather. The pulp, rich in vitamin C and potassium, is made into jelly and marmalade.

Common names and synonyms: Emu apple, Natal plum.

SOURSOP - Native to the Caribbean region and now also grown in Madeira and the Canary Islands, the soursop (*Annona muricata*) is a spiny fruit with a white, tart, edible pulp. Also called "guanabana," it is a big fruit that can easily weigh 4 or 5 pounds. It is used for making syrups, it is often served as a frozen dessert resembling ice cream, and its juice is sold commercially as a soft drink. The soursop is a very close relative of the sweetsop (custard apple) and the cherimoya.

Common names and synonyms: Dutch durian, guanabana.

SOURWOOD - A tree of eastern North America, the sourwood (*Oxydendrum arboreum*) has longish and slightly sour-tasting leaves that, when young and tender, constituted one of the many wild foods gathered by Native Americans. Indigenous peoples also braved bees in seeking the honey made from the sourwood's small white flowers, which blossom in June and July.

Sousous - *see* **CHAYOTE**

South American apricot - *see* **MAMMEE**

South American lupin - *see* **ANDEAN LUPIN**

Southern curled mustard - *see* **MUSTARD GREENS**

Southern fox grape - *see* **GRAPES, MUSCADINE**

Southern pea - *see* **COWPEA**

SOUTHERNWOOD - A shrubby European wormwood sometimes called "old-man," southernwood (*Artemisia abrotanum*) has become naturalized in North America. In Europe, its leaves have been employed to flavor beers.

Common names and synonyms: Old-man, southern wormwood.

Southern wormwood - *see* **SOUTHERNWOOD**

Southwestern barrel cactus - *see* **BARREL CACTUS**

Sowfoot - *see* **COLTSFOOT**

SOW THISTLE - A number of coarse, often spiny herbs comprise the genus *Sonchus*. *Sonchus arvensis* (perennial sow thistle), *S. asper* (spiny sow thistle), and *S. oleraceus* (annual sow thistle) were known to the ancient Romans and doubtless to the hunter-gatherers who preceded them by thousands of years. Today, this plant, a native of Europe but now naturalized throughout the world, is a weed that grows best in cultivated soils. Its roots can be eaten raw or cooked, and the young shoots and leaves make a fine salad.

SOYBEAN (*see also* **BEANS, LEGUMES**) - Legumes are by far the best plant sources of protein, and soybeans (*Glycine max*) are the best of the legumes because they are the only plant food to contain a complete protein. Equally remarkable, the soybean is the most widely consumed plant in the world. According to legend, soybeans were under cultivation in China close to 5,000 years ago, and we know that the plant had emerged as a domesticate in the eastern part of northern China by about 3,000 years ago. The Chinese have had myriad uses for this green, pea-sized legume that comes in a hairy pod. It provides vegetable milk, vegetable oil, bean sprouts, meal, flour, paste, various sauces, a curd (tofu) that substitutes for meat, and the beans themselves, which are eaten both fresh and dried.

Many of these uses were expanded with the widening range of the plant. In the sixth century, soybeans accompanied Chinese Buddhist missionaries to Korea and Japan and became a staple food and a nutritional cornerstone for the teeming populations of these parts of East Asia. Soybeans were also introduced (by the migration of tribes, and by trade along the Silk Road and by sea) into Indonesia, the Philippines, Vietnam, Thailand, Malaysia, and northern India. Through Portuguese, Dutch, and (later) English traders and travelers, the West was made aware of soybeans, but, aside from acquisitions by botanical gardens, there was little interest in the plant. Indeed, this attitude persisted even after the turn of the eighteenth century, when Engelbert Kaempfer, a medical officer of the Dutch East India Company who had lived in Japan, published a book that explained the varied foodstuffs made possible by soybean cultivation.

In 1765 and again in 1803, soybeans were introduced in North America from England, and later on, after U.S. naval officer Matthew Perry had opened Japan to the West in 1854, germ plasm was acquired directly from Japan (as well as from China and Korea). However, those who grew the crop in the United States did so mostly for forage, and it was only in the late nineteenth and early twentieth centuries that soybeans began to receive scientific evaluation. In 1922, the first major soybean processing plant was built in Decatur, Illinois, and when enough such plants had come into being (about a decade later), the National Soybean Processors Association was formed.

During World War II, soybean oil was employed to replace imported fats and oils, and the meal found use as a feed to help expand the production of meat animals. After the war, soybeans played a major role in feeding the destitute population of Europe. Soybean production in the United States skyrocketed, and the nation quickly became the world's leading producer. Production in 1940 had been 78 million bushels, and in 1945 it was 193 million bushels. But by 1984, U.S. production had hit almost 2 billion bushels annually and was still climbing a decade later. Much of the U.S. crop is used for cattle feed, but soybean oil is also a mainstay of margarines, vegetable oils, salad dressings, and a host of processed foods. In addition, soy flour has many food-processing uses.

See in addition: "Soybean," Part II, Section E, Chapter 5; "Beans, Peas, and Lentils," Part II, Section C, Chapter 3; "An Overview of Oils and Fats," Part II, Section E, Chapter 1; "Spices and Flavorings," Part II, Section F, Chapter 1.

Spadic - *see* **COCA**

SPAGHETTI SQUASH (*see also* **SQUASH AND PUMPKIN**) - Also called "vegetable spaghetti," the spaghetti squash (*Cucurbita pepo*) is an exception to the rule that stringiness in squash is bad. This relatively new squash variety – the origin of which is uncertain – is so stringy that it can be baked (or "microwaved") and then its flesh raked with a fork into spaghetti-like strands that can be eaten like pasta. Moreover, spaghetti squash packs far fewer calories than pasta. Recipes abound combining this vegetable – spaghetti-like – with garlic, with vinaigrette dressing, with meat sauce, and with any of the other favorite pasta toppings.

Common names and synonyms: Vegetable spaghetti.

See in addition: "Squash," Part II, Section C, Chapter 8.

SPANISH BAYONET – There are several plants of the genus *Yucca* (and especially *Y. aloifolia = Y. elephantipes*) that are called "Spanish bayonet" because of the formidable appearance of their stiff, pointed leaves. The plants have a redeeming feature, however, in an edible pod-like fruit that ripens in clusters and is generally cooked rather than eaten raw. These fruits were among the many that sustained Native Americans in the southern part of North America.

Spanish cherry – *see* **MIMUSOPS**

Spanish chervil – *see* **CICELY**

SPANISH LIME – Also called "ginep," and *mamoncilla* in Cuba, the Spanish lime (*Melicoccus bijugatus*) is a popular tropical American green berry, about an inch in diameter and resembling a plum in appearance, with a grape-like taste. The fruit is eaten raw, although its pulp must be popped out of its tough skin; it is also made into drinks and cooked. In addition, Caribbean peoples roast the seeds of the Spanish lime and eat them like chestnuts. The tree is grown as far north as southern Florida.

Common names and synonyms: Genip, genipe, ginep, ginip, honeyberry, *mamoncilla*.

Spanish okra – *see* **JEW'S-MALLOW**

Spanish pine – *see* **AZAROLE**

SPANISH PLUM (*see also* **HOG PLUM, PLUM**) – Also called the "red mombin," the Spanish plum (*Spondias purpurea*) is a native of tropical America and a distant relative of cashews and pistachios. It is a red, edible fruit that is both eaten raw and employed in cooking. In addition, its stone is sometimes roasted and eaten like a chestnut.

Common names and synonyms: Red mombin.

Speedwell – *see* **BROOKLIME**

SPELT (*see also* **WHEAT**) – The place of origin of spelt (*Triticum spelta*), a hardy wheat, is a matter of some debate, with some experts suggesting Iran about 6000 to 5000 B.C.; others arguing for two independent sites, one in Iran and the second in southeastern Europe; and still others who would have spelt emerging only in Europe and at a later date. In any case, spelt was cultivated throughout the Near East, Europe, and the Balkans during the Bronze Age (4000 to 1000 B.C.) and, along with

einkorn and emmer, it is another of the ancestors of modern wheat. Spelt was probably an important cereal of the ancient Egyptians and Greeks and seems to have been a staple of the Romans, in which case the latter people may have facilitated the grain's spread northward to Germany and Switzerland and westward to Spain, where it was still being grown at the beginning of the twentieth century.

Complicating the picture, however, are the finds of spelt remains dating from 3800 to 2800 B.C. in Neolithic sites in Spain, western Germany, the Netherlands, and Belgium – but whether these are the remains of domesticated spelt is another matter. Also confounding the problem is that invading Vandals have been credited with introducing spelt in Europe around the fifth century A.D.

But, whenever and wherever spelt was established, the grain became a major cereal crop in Europe and joined einkorn and emmer in sustaining multitudes during the Middle Ages. Around the middle of the nineteenth century (if not before), spelt was carried to North America, where production (much of it for fodder) peaked in the early decades of the twentieth century. Spelt is grown today on a small scale in isolated parts of Germany and Switzerland, and it seems to be making a comeback in the United States and Canada because of the health-food market.

See in addition: "Wheat," Part II, Section A, Chapter 10.

Spice birch – *see* **SWEET BIRCH**

SPICEBUSH – "Spicebush" refers to a number of plants but the name is mostly intended to mean the eastern North American spicebush (*Lindera benzoin*). Also called the "Benjamin bush," it produces red or yellow berries. Native Americans dried and powdered the berries and used them as a spice. The bark from the roots and stems – along with the leaves – were employed to make a tea.

Common names and synonyms: Benjamin bush.

Spikenard – *see* **UDO**

SPINACH – A green leafy vegetable, spinach (*Spinacia oleracea*) is a native of southwestern Asia. The plant reached China as a gift from Nepal during the first years of the Tang dynasty (the early seventh century A.D.) and was introduced in Sicily in 827 by invading Saracens from North Africa – they having first encountered the plant in Persia. However, spinach seems to have been in no hurry to spread out over the rest of Europe, although it may well have done so without recorded mention during those centuries of the Middle Ages that food historian Reay Tannahill has called "The Silent Centuries." The vegetable probably reached Spain with the invading Moors, but it was not until the very end of the Middle Ages that spinach showed up in a cookbook published anonymously in Nuremberg in 1485. After this it caught on rather quickly on the Continent, probably in no small part because spinach made its appearance in early spring, when other fresh vegetables were still scarce yet human bodies were desperate for vitamin C after a winter of deprivation. Spinach was first planted in England in 1568, and within a century it had become one of the few vegetables that appeared on the tables of the wealthy. Presumably, the plant was carried to North America long before 1806, when seed catalogs mentioned three varieties. However, it was only after another century had elapsed that a food encyclopedia stated that the vegetable was becoming "increasingly popular."

Part of the difficulty in tracing the history of spinach is that there are so many spinach-like vegetables (such as the amaranth of India and Japan, the kang kong or water spinach of Southeast Asia, and New Zealand spinach) that one is not always certain which "spinach" is being confronted, and even "real" spinach comes in two basic types. The fresh spinach encountered in most markets is the crinkle-leafed Savoy kind, but there is also the flat, smooth-leafed variety that is generally employed for freezing or canning. In addition, there is a sort of "semi-Savoy" spinach that is a cross between the two basic types. Young, tender spinach leaves make fine salads. Sautéing and steaming are great ways to prepare the vegetable so that it does not become overcooked and develop a characteristic limp and washed-out appearance. Spinach also makes splendid soufflés; oysters, broiled on the half shell with a mixture of spinach, some other ingredients, and a sauce become "Oysters Rockefeller"; and when foods are served on a bed of spinach, they are known collectively as *florentine.*

With apologies to "Popeye the Sailor-Man" (whose appearance as a cartoon character in 1929 increased spinach consumption by 33 percent among children), spinach is not a "miracle food" – not even a particularly good source of iron. But it is rich in beta-carotene, calcium, folacin, and a number of important minerals.

Common names and synonyms: Savoy spinach.

Spinach beet - *see* **BEET, SWISS CHARD**
Spinach dock - *see* **SORREL**
Spinach-grass - *see* **AMARANTH**
Spinach tree - *see* **CHAYA**
Spineless cactus - *see* **PRICKLY PEAR**
Spirulina - *see* **TECUITLATL**
Sponge gourd - *see* **ANGLED LUFFA**
Spoon cabbage - *see* **PAKCHOI AND KAI CHOY**
Spoonflower - *see* **MALANGA**
Spoonleaf yucca - *see* **YUCCA**
Spoonplant - *see* **SOTOL**
Spoonwort - *see* **SCURVY GRASS**
Spotted alder - *see* **WITCH-HAZEL**
Spring kale - *see* **HANOVER KALE**
SPRUCE - The young shoots as well as the inner bark of spruce trees (genus *Picea*) were eaten by Native Americans, and the shoots are still employed in

Europe for various dishes. In addition, the shoots of some species have served to make "spruce beer" (at one time thought to be effective against scurvy), and the leaves can be made into a tea. Finally, spruce trees have been a source of balsam used as "chewing gum" since Paleolithic times.

Sqamash - *see* **CAMAS**
SQUASH AND PUMPKIN (*see also* **PUMPKIN, SQUASH FLOWERS**) - Squashes, pumpkins, and some gourds are all American natives and members of the Cucurbitaceae. However, further division can sometimes be confusing, especially when a common name embraces more than one species. There are five species of the genus *Cucurbita* that were domesticated in the Americas, four of which subsequently became good food for people the world over. But squashes are gourds, and domestication probably came about initially at the hands of those seeking hard shells to employ as containers and utensils. From that point on, however, it was only a matter of time until the seeds and, later on, the flesh of the various squashes began playing an important role in the Native American diet.

Moving from north to south, *C. pepo* may have been domesticated in what is now the eastern United States as well as in Mexico, where it has reportedly been grown for over 7,000 years. Most varieties of this species, such as zucchini, yellow straightneck, yellow crookneck, and pattypan (also called cymling or scallop), fall under the rubric of summer squash. The summer squash are eaten while still soft and immature, as are winter varieties of *C. pepo* (like the acorn squash and most pumpkins), which otherwise mature into hard, starchy fruits (the very large pumpkins, however, belong to *C. maxima*). Chayote, although thought of as a summer squash, is another plant entirely, albeit "squashlike."

The other species of *Cucurbita* provide winter varieties. *Cucurbita mixta* is the cushaw or calabaza – a pear- or crookneck-shaped squash – developed in an area extending from the U.S. Southwest to Costa Rica. The species that came into being at the intersection between the Northern and Southern Hemispheres is *C. moschata*, the major representative of which is the Butternut squash. *Cucurbita maxima* was apparently domesticated in Peru, and out of this emerged the Hubbard and banana squashes, as well as varieties developed outside the Americas, like the Australian Blue and the *Rouge Vif d'Étampes* squashes. Native Americans, who cultivated squashes and pumpkins, ate the vegetables roasted or boiled and preserved the flesh as *conservas* in syrup. They also ate the young shoots, leaves, flowers, and especially the seeds. Since the arrival of the Europeans, usage has been expanded to include employing the flesh in pies, in soups (especially in France), and even as pickles.

A species that was domesticated in the Americas but did not travel to other lands (although it was long thought to be a native of Asia) is *C. ficifolia*, sometimes known as the Malabar gourd or the fig-leafed gourd. Of all the cucurbits, this is the only species adapted to high altitudes, and it is a food for many in the highlands of Mexico and South America, where its fruits, appearing on the outside like small watermelons, can often be seen on rooftops, drying in the sun. In addition, there are wild cucurbits with flowers and seeds that served Native Americans as food; these include the buffalo gourd (*C. foetidissima*) and the coyote melon (*C. palmata*), and in southern Florida *C. okeechobeensis,* named for the lake, was consumed by Native Americans.

The yellow and orange flesh of winter squashes (especially the Hubbard and the Butternut) is rich in beta-carotene and not a bad source of vitamin C and folacin. Summer squashes are high in water content and, consequently, low in calories. They, too, are a fair source of vitamin C and folacin.

Common names and synonyms: Acorn squash, Australian Blue, banana squash, buffalo gourd, Butternut, calabaza, courge, courgette, coyote melon, crookneck, cushaw, cymling, fig-leafed gourd, gourd, Hubbard, Malabar gourd, pattypan squash, *pepo*, pumpkin, *Rouge Vif d'Étampes,* scallop squash, straight crookneck, summer squash, turban squash, vegetable marrow, winter squash, yellow crookneck, yellow straightneck, zucchini.

See in addition: "Squash," Part II, Section C, Chapter 8.

Squash blossom(s) – *see* **SQUASH FLOWER(S)**

SQUASH FLOWER(S) (*see also* **SQUASH AND PUMPKINS**) – The orangish yellow, mostly male flowers (so the vines will still bear fruit) that appear on summer squash (*Cucurbita pepo*) vines are frequently picked for consumption. They are edible and considered a delicacy by many. In fact, it is probably no coincidence that they are available in the markets of Mexico and are added most to the dishes of that land, where many, perhaps most, of the squashes originated. Squash flowers are sometimes added to *quesadillas* and sautéed, but they are generally battered and deep-fried. The flowers are a good source of beta-carotene and also – if the cooking is brief – of vitamin C.

Common names and synonyms: Squash blossom(s).

See also: "Squash," Part II, Section C, Chapter 8.

Squash pepper – *see* **HABANERO AND SCOTCH BONNET PEPPERS**

Squaw bush – *see* **HIGHBUSH CRANBERRY**

Squawroot – *see* **BLUE COHOSH, INDIAN POTATO, TRILLIUM**

Squirrel-tail barley – *see* **WILD BARLEY**

Stagbush – *see* **BLACK HAW, HAW**

Star – *see* **KUNDANGAN**

STAR-ANISE – Despite the names "star-anise" and "Chinese anise," *Illicium verum* is not, in fact, a member of the magnolia family and not related to true anise. Doubtless, the reason for the "anise" part of its name is that it has a licorice-like flavor, very similar to that of anise. As the rest of its name implies, star-anise has star-shaped yellow flowers, with each point of the star containing a shiny, oval seed. The leaves and seeds (which have a taste somewhat stronger than that of anise) are dried and added whole, broken, or ground to various dishes, especially in the cuisines of China and Vietnam. This spice has never been much used in the West, save as a flavoring for liquors such as anisette.

Common names and synonyms: Badian anise, Chinese anise.

See also: "Spices and Flavorings," Part II, Section F, Chapter 1.

STAR-APPLE (*see also* **CARAMBOLA**) – A tropical American fruit of the sapodilla family, and native to the West Indies and Central America, the star-apple (*Chrysophyllum cainito*) is a purple-brown, sweet fruit about the size of an apple. It grows on a large evergreen tree and fascinated early Spanish explorers, who discovered that when it was cut in two, it had a star shape in the middle.

Common names and synonyms: Caimito (fruit), *caymito*.

Starch wheat – *see* **EMMER**

Starchy breadroot – *see* **ZAMIA**

Star fruit – *see* **CARAMBOLA**

Steinpilz(e) – *see* **BOLETE, MUSHROOMS AND FUNGI**

STEVIA – An herb of South America (especially southern Brazil and Paraguay), stevia (*Stevia rebaudiana*) has leaves that have long been employed locally as a natural sweetener. Dried and ground, they are said to be infinitely sweeter than sucrose, and one suspects that we will hear more of this plant as a sugar substitute.

Common names and synonyms: Sugar-leaf, sweet-herb-of-Paraguay.

See also: "Spices and Flavorings," Part II, Section F, Chapter 1.

Stinking gum – *see* **ASAFETIDA**

Stinking poke – *see* **SKUNK CABBAGE**

Stitchwort – *see* **CHICKWEED**

STONECROP – A number of species of the genus *Sedum* are collectively called "stonecrop." *Sedum roseum* of North America has fleshy roots that have served as food for millennia. In Europe, the young leaves and shoots of *Sedum reflexum* are eaten in soups and salads, especially by the Dutch. They may be consumed cooked or raw and have a slightly astringent taste. The sharp taste of *S. acre* is sometimes employed for seasoning in Asia. The plant is also known as "Jenny-stonecrop" and "ditch-stonecrop."

Common names and synonyms: Ditch-stonecrop, Jenny-stonecrop.

Stone mint – *see* **DITTANY**

Stone nut - *see* **PINE NUT**

Stopper - *see* **MYRTLE**

Straight crookneck (squash) - *see* **PUMPKIN, SQUASH AND PUMPKIN**

STRAWBERRY (*see also* **BERRIES, WILD STRAWBERRY**) - The garden strawberry (*Fragaria ananassa*) is probably the best known of the berries and certainly the most versatile. It is a hybrid - between the Chilean berry (*F. chiloensis*) and *F. virginiana* of eastern North America that is now cultivated worldwide. There are myriad other strawberry species, however, that grow wild in the Americas and Eurasia. Indeed, although strawberries have been planted in gardens since Roman times, berries gathered from the wild were generally the only kind available to most people until the fifteenth century, when Europeans began to cultivate them in earnest. Most of the European names for these berries poetically suggest their fragrance, although the English name comes from the layers of straw that were placed around the plants to keep the berries off the ground. Strawberries were probably also cultivated by the Indians of North and South America, which may account for the fact that two of the American species produce the largest fruits.

Strawberries are now available fresh most of the year, making it possible to avoid frozen strawberries, which tend to disintegrate when thawed. Strawberries are mostly eaten raw but are also made into jams, preserves, and pies and are used to flavor everything from ice cream to chewing gum. They contain more vitamin C than any other berry.

Common names and synonyms: European strawberry, garden strawberry, Virginia strawberry.

STRAWBERRY GUAVA - Also known as the "Cattley guava," the strawberry guava (*Psidium cattleianum*) grows on a bush that is much more resistant to cold and frost than the common guava. But the reddish fruits are much smaller and lack the common guava's flavor. They are generally used for jelly.

Common names and synonyms: Cattley guava, purple guava.

STRAWBERRY-RASPBERRY (*see also* **JAPANESE WINEBERRY**) - This real "strawberry-raspberry" (*Rubus illecebrosus*), which is sometimes confused with the Japanese wineberry, is a low bramble that is frequently used in Japan as a ground cover to hold the soil on the banks of rivers and streams. It also produces showy, red, edible fruits that are generally made into preserves.

Common names and synonyms: Balloonberry.

Strawberry tomato - *see* **CAPE GOOSEBERRY**

STRAWBERRY TREE - A native of the Mediterranean region, the strawberry tree (*Arbutus unedo*) is a small evergreen tree with fruits that are strawberry-like in appearance but not in taste. The tree was known to the ancient Greeks, but its fruits have never really been developed. The most common variety is the "Killarney strawberry tree," whose berries are made into liqueurs, sherbets, confections and the like but are not eaten raw.

Common names and synonyms: Killarney strawberry tree.

Straw mushroom - *see* **MUSHROOMS AND FUNGI**

STRIPED SCREW-PINE - A native of the tropics of the Old World, and an important food tree for Pacific Islanders, the striped screw-pine (*Pandanus veitchii*) is also known as the "Veitch screw-pine." It has fruits and nuts that are both edible.

Common names and synonyms: Veitch screw-pine.

Succory - *see* **CHICORY**

Sudan grass - *see* **SORGHUM**

SUDAN POTATO - Also called "Hausa potato" and "piasa," the Sudan potato (*Coleus tuberosus = C. parviflorus = Solenostemon rotundifolius*) is a tuber - probably a native of tropical Africa - that is grown and used like a white potato. It is still cultivated in Africa and also in Southeast Asia. As a rule, the tubers (and sometimes the leaves) are boiled for consumption.

Common names and synonyms: Hausa potato, piasa.

Sugar apple (tree) - *see* **CUSTARD APPLE, SWEETSOP**

Sugar beet - *see* **BEET, SUGARCANE**

Sugarberry - *see* **HACKBERRY**

SUGARCANE - There are several species of sugarcane (genus *Saccharum*) in Southeast Asia, which probably gave rise to cultivated cane (*S. officinarum*), with a juice or sap high in sugar. This giant grass was used as a medicine - and possibly to sweeten foods and beverages - in ancient India and China. Sugar became known to the Persians and probably to the Greeks around 500 B.C., when, during a foray into the Indus Valley, the Persian king Darius reported finding reeds that produced honey although there were no bees. A couple of centuries later, an emissary of Alexander the Great learned that the "honey" in question was actually cane juice evaporated by boiling, and sometime after that the Persians themselves began making sugar.

Sugarcane was introduced in southern Europe in the ninth and tenth centuries A.D. by the Arabs, who had captured Persia and revived its sugar industry. Venice became a "middleman" that imported sugar, then exported it again to central Europe and the Slavic countries, and plantations were established in the West by the Arabs around Valencia in Spain. Medieval Europeans called sugar "white salt" but never tasted it save in medications destined mostly for the wealthy. Yet demand was sufficient that in the fifteenth century, the Iberians transferred sugar cultivation to Madeira and the Canary Islands, and slaves were imported from nearby Africa to work in the fields - all a dreadful harbinger of things to come in the Americas in the wake of Christopher Columbus. By 1518, the Spaniards were operating a number of sugar plantations on Hispaniola, and in that year began the transatlantic slave trade.

Europe, however, was closer to the sugar of the Middle East than it was to that of the West Indies, and a voracious European demand for sugar (other than as a medicine) had to wait for the consumption of tea, coffee, and chocolate to become widespread, which it did during the course of the seventeenth and eighteenth centuries. The Dutch seized northeastern Brazil in 1635 and moved into the sugar industry there. After being driven out a few years later, they began providing the secrets of sugar production to English colonists on Barbados, along with the financing to help them switch from tobacco to sugar cultivation. Such behavior was hardly altruistic; the Dutch made great profits supplying Barbados with slaves from Africa and carrying the sugar away to Europe.

This activity at about the midpoint of the seventeenth century is generally viewed as the beginning of the "sugar revolution," during which on island after island in the Caribbean saw lands devoted to sugar monoculture and gathered into the hands of a relatively few whites, surrounded by huge black slave populations. The French island of Martinique was caught up in the sugar revolution in 1655 – the same year that the British seized Jamaica from Spain. By the end of the seventeenth century, Jamaica had emerged as a major sugar producer, but by the end of the following century French St. Domingue was producing about half of the world's sugar. The slave revolution in that country (which created the new nation of Haiti) and British abolition of first the slave trade and then slavery itself (during the first third of the nineteenth century) led next to the rise of Cuba as the Caribbean's biggest sugar grower and a competitor of Brazil for dominance of the world market – a competition that Cuba won because of the willingness of its planters to embrace railroads and other new technologies.

Meanwhile, in North America sugar had been grown in Louisiana by French colonists throughout most of the eighteenth century, albeit with little success until experts on the crop, fleeing from the revolution in Haiti, arrived to take a hand. By the time of the American Civil War, Louisiana sugar held a position of world importance that it would never regain after the war's end and the abolition of slavery.

Despite the avalanche of sugar from sugarcane that was reaching the Old World from the New, beet sugar had been experimented with, and during the Continental blockade around the turn of the nineteenth century, Napoleon ordered that thousands of hectares of French land be planted with sugar beets to avoid dependence on imports from the New World. Although French production faltered after the war in the face of resumed imports of cane sugar, beet-sugar production continued to constitute worrisome competition for cane-sugar producers, and by 1845 beet sugar had captured some 15 percent of the world market.

In the United States, sugar beets were being raised on a commercial scale in the last two decades of the nineteenth century but accounted for only a fraction of the country's sugar needs. It was at about this time (1878) that London sugar magnate Henry Tate introduced the sugar cube to the world. Its effect on demand is not known, but about a century later – during the last decades of the twentieth century – the world was producing more sugar than it could use, despite the heavy demands made by the food-processing and beverage industries. Thus, in addition to its use as a sweetener with myriad applications, its employment in raw form in many tropical countries, and its by-products, such as molasses, rums, and other cane spirits, there have been efforts to convert sugar into fuel for automobiles, and even into wax. In the face of health concerns as well as competition from artificial sweeteners (such as saccharin and aspartame, which are now in use, and a vast number of others on the horizon), the future of sugar, after four centuries or more of prosperity, seems uncertain.

Common names and synonyms: Noblecane, white salt.

See also: "Sugar," Part II, Section F, Chapter 2.

Sugar-leaf - *see* **STEVIA**

Sugar maple (tree) - *see* **MAPLE SYRUP AND MAPLE SUGAR**

Sugar melon - *see* **CANTALOUPE AND MUSKMELON**

SUGAR PEA *(see also* **LEGUMES, PEA)** - Peas were domesticated about 6000 B.C. in the Near East, but the sugar pea (*Pisum sativum* var. *macrocarpon*) has only been around since the sixteenth century. Also known as the "snow pea," *mange-tout,* and "edible pod pea," the sugar pea is often said to have originated in China, but there is some evidence to indicate that the plant was first cultivated in Europe and taken to China by the Dutch. Moreover, the extent to which the sugar pea is employed in Asian cuisine today appears to be a matter of contention (in India there is a similar flat legume called *papdi*), although there is no question of its prominence in Asian dishes served in the West.

"Snow pea" seems something of a misnomer because the plant grows no earlier in the season than other peas. But the name "sugar pea" is quite appropriate, as it is a sweet legume. It appears similar to a garden pea except that it has a skin so thin and delicate that the entire pod can be eaten. Or at least this is the case if the sugar pea is picked when the immature peas inside are only just discernible, but if it reaches maturity, the pod becomes tough, and the sugar content decreases. The sugar snap pea, which has recently been developed, is an interesting legume that permits large sweet peas to grow inside a pod that remains sweet and edible. Sugar peas are high in vitamin C and iron.

Common names and synonyms: Chinese pea, Chinese pea pod, Chinese snow pea, edible-podded pea, edible pod pea, *ho loan, mange-tout, papdi,* podded pea, snow pea, sugar snap pea.

See in addition: "Beans, Peas, and Lentils," Part II, Section C, Chapter 3.

Suico - *see* **ANISILLO**

Sukun - *see* **BREADFRUIT**

Sultana - *see* **THOMPSON SEEDLESS (GRAPE)**

Sumac - *see* **SMOOTH SUMAC, SUMAC BERRY**

SUMAC BERRY (*see also* **BERRIES**) - There are countless varieties of shrubs and trees of the genus *Rhus,* with one in particular - "Sicilian sumac" (*R. coriaria*) - noted for its red, slightly sour-tasting berries that can impart a cherry color to dishes. These are dried and used whole, ground for sauces, or combined with other spices to sprinkle on meat dishes. The Romans employed sumac berries for their fruity sourness before lemons reached Europe, and they remain popular in the Middle East. In Europe, however, they are no longer in common use. In North America, *R. typhina* produces a sumac berry that was doubtless used by Native Americans for flavoring foods and liquids. Also doubtless, Native Americans quickly learned to stay clear of some other members of the sumac family, such as poison sumac, poison ivy, ;and poison oak.

SUMPWEED - A plant with an interesting history and a harsh name, sumpweed (*Iva annua*) has also been more pleasingly called the "marsh-elder." It is a weed that inhabits the central United States, is generally around 2 or 3 feet in height, and yields an oily seed that is as nutritious as the seeds of its domesticated relative, the sunflower. In fact, archaeobotanists have discovered that sumpweed was also domesticated some 2,000 years ago. Yet by the time the Europeans arrived, the plant had returned to the wild. The most likely explanation for this is that sumpweed was displaced by the maize-beans-and-squash triumvirate that had moved northward from Mexico and then across all of North America by A.D. 1200 or so.

Common names and synonyms: Marsh-elder.

Sunberry - *see* **WONDERBERRY**

Sunchoke - *see* **JERUSALEM ARTICHOKE**

SUNFLOWER OIL AND SEED (*see also* **JERUSALEM ARTICHOKE**) - The sunflower (*Helianthus annuus*), with its daisy-like head bristling with oil-rich seeds, is North America's only native plant to become a major world crop (the second most important oilseed crop in the world). Wild sunflower seeds were an important food gathered by Native Americans that could be dried and used throughout the winter. But many tribes in the western and especially the southwestern parts of what

is now the United States had gone beyond the gathering stage to domesticate and cultivate sunflowers long before the Europeans arrived. After that arrival, sunflowers - then thought of as a decorative plant - were carried to Europe around 1510, beginning what would be a world tour.

Two centuries later, the plants were being grown for their oil on a large scale in France and Bavaria, and following this development, they moved farther eastward into eastern Europe and especially Russia, where - as a previously unknown food - sunflower oil was not on the proscribed list for the many fasting days observed by the Orthodox church. As a result, today Russia is by far the world's largest producer of sunflower oil, accounting for about three-quarters of the total despite vast tracts of land given over to sunflowers in Argentina (which is a distant second), Uruguay, the United States, and some of the other eastern European countries. Turkey, Morocco, Tanzania, and Ethiopia are the most important producers in the tropics and subtropics.

With its low unsaturated-to-saturated fat ratio, sunflower oil has become ever more important as an oil for cooking, and the oilseeds (the black-shelled kind) are also popular as a feed for birds. Dried sunflower seeds make a fine snack that is high in protein, the B-vitamins, and calcium.

Common names and synonyms: Common sunflower, giant sunflower, prairie sunflower, single-headed sunflower.

See in addition: "Sunflower," Part II, Section E, Chapter 6; "An Overview of Oils and Fats," Part II, Section E, Chapter 1.

SUNSAPOTE - Native to the lowland tropics of central-northern South America, the sunsapote (*Licania platypus*) is a tall wild or semicultivated tree that produces a large fruit of the same name. The pulp of the fruit is sweet and generally is eaten raw. The sunsapote can be important locally but is not really a commercial crop.

SUNSET HIBISCUS - Also called "edible hibiscus" and "aibika," the sunset hibiscus (*Abelmoschus manihot = Hibiscus manihot*) is a relative of okra and probably a native of China. It is widely cultivated for its leaves in the islands of the South Pacific and in areas of tropical Asia. The usually sweet leaves are harvested when fully developed and are eaten raw, cooked as greens, and used in stews.

Common names and synonyms: Aibika, edible hibiscus.

Surinam amaranth - *see* **CALLALOO**

Surinam cherry - *see* **ACEROLA, PITANGA**

Surinam spinach - *see* **AMARANTH**

Susumber - *see* **EGGPLANT**

SWAMP CABBAGE (*see also* **HEART(S) OF PALM, SKUNK CABBAGE**) - Not to be confused with hearts of palm, which can also go by this name, this real swamp cabbage (*Ipomoea aquatica*) is a green-leafed vegetable and not a cabbage, grows in or near water, and is a member of the Convolvulaceae (sweet potato) family. "Kang kong" and "water spinach" are two common names for the plant, and both Africa and tropical Asia have been put forward as its place of origin. Swamp cabbage is grown throughout Southeast Asia, in some parts of Africa, and in Australia. A land form of the plant is grown in Indonesia. Both the water and land forms are raised for their tender stems and leaves, which are used in salads and cooked as a vegetable. The leaves are a good source of calcium and a fair source of vitamin C.

Common names and synonyms: Espinaca acquatica, kang(-)kong, karamta, kang kung, patate aquatique, swamp morning-glory, water convolvulus, water spinach.

Swamp morning-glory - *see* **SWAMP CABBAGE**

Swamp potato - *see* **ARROWHEAD**

Sweating plant - *see* **BONESET**

Swede - *see* **RUTABAGA**

Swedish turnip - *see* **RUTABAGA**

Sweet anise - *see* **FENNEL**

Sweet balm - *see* **LEMON BALM**

Sweet bay - *see* **BAY LEAF**

Sweet bean - *see* **HONEY LOCUST**

SWEET BIRCH - A tree that is native to eastern North America, the sweet birch (*Betula lenta*) is known to many as the "black birch." Its inner bark was eaten by Native Americans, who consumed it fresh and also dried it for later use. The twigs and leaves of the sweet birch (along with the inner bark) contain an oil similar to wintergreen and were used to brew a tea; the sap of the tree was also drunk. Later, European settlers made "birch beer" by steeping the bark in water.

Common names and synonyms: Black birch, cherry birch, spice birch.

SWEET CLOVER - This biennial herb (*Melilotus officinalis*) is native to Europe, temperate Asia, and North Africa. It was introduced into North America around 1700 and is grown for erosion control and for fodder. In Europe, it is often used as an herb. In France, sweet clover is an ingredient in the stuffing for a cooked rabbit. In Switzerland, the flowers and seeds of the plant are used to flavor Gruyère and Sapsago cheeses. The roots are also edible, and in Iceland they are cooked and eaten like other root vegetables. In many places throughout Europe, the leaves and flowers of sweet clover flavor soups, stews, and marinades. Its flowers are also a good source of nectar for honey production.

Common names and synonyms: Melilot, melist, yellow melilot, yellow sweet clover.

Sweet-corm-root - *see* **GUINEA ARROWROOT**

Sweet cumin - *see* **ANISE**

SWEET DUMPLING (SQUASH) (*see also* **SQUASH AND PUMPKIN**) - Like the Delicata and the Golden Nugget, the Sweet Dumpling squash (*Cucurbita pepo*) is a small squash that serves only one person. It is generally light colored with green stripes, and its sweet flesh makes a good soup. The small cavity of the squash can also be hollowed out for stuffing.

See in addition: "Squash," Part II, Section C, Chapter 8.

SWEET FERN - A shrub that grows throughout eastern North America, the sweet fern (*Comptonia peregrina*) has a pleasing, sweet-scented odor. Its leaves have been steeped to make a tea, and the leaves and tops can be chopped and used as a condiment.

Common names and synonyms: Canada sweetgale, fernbush, ferngale, meadow fern, sweet bush.

SWEET FLAG - Also known as "calamus," sweet flag (*Acorus calamus*) grows in eastern North America in moist areas such as swamps, the shores of lakes, and riverbanks. It has fernlike foliage and an aromatic root with a sharp taste, which in the past, at least, was sometimes candied. The rhizome is also used for flavoring alcoholic beverages, including beer, and has been sold commercially as a breath freshener. Native Americans ate the young shoots of the plant both raw and after cooking.

Common names and synonyms: Calamus, calamus root, flag root, myrtle flag.

Sweet gale - *see* **BOG MYRTLE**

Sweet granadilla - *see* **PASSION FRUIT**

SWEET GUM - The hardy tree *Liquidambar styraciflua* is native to North and Central America. Also known as "red gum," "American sweet gum," and "bilsted," the tree yields a resin that is called American styrax or storax. The resin has been chewed both to freshen the breath and to clean the teeth. It has also been used to flavor tobacco and beverages.

Common names and synonyms: American storax, American styrax, American sweet gum, bilsted, red gum.

Sweet haw - *see* **BLACK HAW**

Sweet-herb-of-Paraguay - *see* **STEVIA**

Sweet laurel - *see* **BAY LEAF**

Sweet-leaf bush - *see* **SWEET-SHOOT**

Sweet lemon - *see* **LIMETTA**

Sweet lime - *see* **LIMETTA**

Sweet locust - *see* **HONEY LOCUST**

Sweet pea - *see* **BEACH PEA, PEA, SUGAR PEA**

SWEET PEPPERS (*see also* **CHILLI PEPPERS**) - These Capsicums (*C. annuum* var. *annuum*) are called sweet because they do not impart the heat that their more aggressive relatives are noted for (although the "Mexi-Bell" - a cross between a sweet bell pepper and a hot pepper - has a bit of a bite). Bell peppers, which constitute one category of sweet peppers, are so called because of their bell-like shape. Although most commonly found in the color green, bell peppers also come in variations of red, yellow, orange, and black. Such variety makes bell peppers a colorful ingredient in salads and any number of other dishes and sauces. They are also grilled, roasted, and in many cultures have traditionally been stuffed.

A large, dark, heart-shaped red pepper (although not actually a red bell pepper, with which it is often confused), grown in the U.S. South, in Spain, and in Hungary, is called variously a pimento (or pimiento), a *chilli pimiento,* a *pimiento dulce,* or a *pimiento morrón.* The flesh of this chilli is roasted to become pimento or pimiento (not allspice, which the Jamaicans call pimiento), which is packed in jars and can be used for decorating dishes such as paella. Its major uses, however, are in stuffing olives and the production of paprika. A similar pepper is the Hungarian sweet chilli, which is elongated in shape but fairly thick, crimson in color, and sweet, with a flavor quite like that of the pimento.

Cubanelle peppers (also called *chawa*) are also sweet and have more taste than bell peppers. They are relatively long (about 4 inches), tapered, and range in color from pale yellow to light green; in other words, they have the characteristics of the banana or Hungarian wax peppers, including just a touch of heat. Of the sweet peppers, which are all natives of the Americas, bell peppers are the most popular in the United States and are extensively grown in California and Mexico as well as in the Mediterranean countries, Hungary, and the Netherlands.

Holland peppers, grown hydroponically in the Netherlands for the Dutch export trade in specialty produce, come in all of the bell pepper's many colors and act as expensive substitutes. In addition, the "sweet purple pepper" is cultivated by the Dutch. Sweet peppers are a good source of vitamin C, and those that tend toward red in color are rich in beta-carotene.

Common names and synonyms: Bell pepper, *chawa, chile pimiento, chilli pimiento,* cubanelle pepper, green bell pepper, green pepper, Holland pepper, Hungarian sweet chilli, mango (pepper), Mexi-Bell, pimento, pimiento, *pimiento dulce, pimiento morrón,* red bell pepper, sweet purple pepper.

See in addition: "Chilli Peppers," Part II, Section C, Chapter 4.

SWEET POTATO (*see also* **BONIATO**) - Not to be confused with the potato of the genus *Solanum,* nor with the yam of the genus *Dioscorea,* the sweet potato (*Ipomoea batatas*), with the Caribbean Indian name *batata,* is a member of the morning-glory family and a native of tropical America (probably western South America but possibly also southern Mexico and Central America). It was cultivated in Peru some 5,000 years ago for its sweet and starchy tubers, while at the same time there were many other wild *Ipomoea* species whose tubers and leaves constituted gathered

foods for other Native Americans in North, Central, and South America.

But the sweet potato did not confine its range to the Western Hemisphere. Rather, it wandered far and mysteriously - reaching Australia, New Zealand, and Polynesia long before (about 1,500 years before) the Europeans stepped ashore in the New World. By the time Christopher Columbus arrived, sweet potato cultivation had spread over much of the Americas and certainly across the Caribbean, and sweet potatoes were among the items he carried back to Spain at the end of his first voyage. A few years later, Hernando Cortés reintroduced sweet potatoes in Spain, and in 1564 John Hawkins is said to have taken the tubers from the Caribbean to England. Unlike the potato, which took a while to catch on, the sweet potato was received enthusiastically from the beginning by Europeans, who appreciated its sweet taste and were titillated by the reputation it quickly acquired as an aphrodisiac.

From the New World, sweet potatoes traveled on the Manila galleons of Spain to the Far East, while the Portuguese also spread the plant about as they tended their empires in Africa and the East Indies. The sweet potato was a staple for many in colonial America, including those soldiers in the War for Independence against Great Britain. Today, sweet potatoes are widely cultivated in the world's tropics and subtropics, especially in Latin America, the southern United States, Southeast and East Asia, and Oceania.

Sweet potatoes come in moist- and dry- (or mealy-) fleshed forms. The moist-fleshed variety is the one often (and wrongly) called a yam. Most people in the United States eat sweet potatoes only on the Thanksgiving and Christmas holidays, which means that save for these special occasions, they are depriving themselves of one of the most nutritious of the world's foods. Sweet potatoes are an excellent source of vitamin A, the B-vitamins, and vitamin C. They can be boiled, baked, and fried – indeed, they are used in the same ways as white potatoes, which includes starring in potato salad. Sweet potatoes come canned and frozen as well as fresh, but those that are canned and frozen suffer a substantial loss of nutrients.

Common names and synonyms: Batata, batata dulce, camote, common potato (archaic), *kumara,* wild sweet potato.

See in addition: "Sweet Potatoes and Yams," Part II, Section B, Chapter 5.

SWEET-SHOOT - Found in Southeast Asia, the sweet-shoot (*Sauropus androgynus*) has leaves that are used to flavor soups and stews. They are also consumed as a vegetable, act as a green dye in pastries, and as an ingredient in the alcoholic beverage "brem bali." The fruits of the plant are made into sweetmeats.

Common names and synonyms: Chekkurmanis, katook, katuk, sweet-leaf bush.

SWEETSOP - The sweetsop is a tropical American tree (*Annona squamosa* - sometimes called the "sugar apple tree") with a sweet, edible, yellowish green fruit about the size of a baseball (often called a "sugar apple"). The tree can reach upwards of 20 feet in height and (like its relative the papaw) belongs to the custard-apple family - so called because the taste of their fruits resembles that of custard. Although widely cultivated in warm regions, where it is used for making jellies and preserves, the sweetsop is quite perishable and thus is far from commonplace in northern markets.

Common names and synonyms: Anon, custard apple, sugar apple (tree).

Sweet wood - *see* **CINNAMON AND CASSIA**

SWISS CHARD (*see also* **BEET**) - Also called chard, "silver beet," and "spinach beet," Swiss chard (*Beta vulgaris* var. *cicla*) is a kind of beet, native to the shores of the Mediterranean (it may have originated in Sicily), that is grown for its greens rather than its roots. The leaves of both red (the leaf stalks and veins are red) and green Swiss chard are large and fleshy and are used in salads or prepared like spinach. The thick white or, occasionally, red stalks that can reach between 1 and 2 feet in length not only may be eaten but, in some countries of Europe, are viewed as the best part of the plant and a very satisfactory asparagus substitute. The small root, however, is not edible. Like other greens, Swiss chard is high in vitamin C, calcium, and especially vitamin A.

Common names and synonyms: Chard, green chard, green Swiss chard, leaf beet, red chard, red Swiss chard, seakale beet, silver beet, spinach beet, white beet.

Swiss-cheese plant - *see* **MONSTERA**

SWORD BEAN (*see also* **BEANS, JACKBEAN**) - Sometimes called the "wonder bean" or "Pearson bean" in the United States, and the "Babricorn bean" in the West Indies, the sword bean (*Canavalia gladiata*) is a native of tropical Asia and Africa but is now cultivated throughout the tropical world. It is very similar to the jackbean - so similar, in fact, that a common ancestor is suspected. The young pods and seeds are eaten as a cooked vegetable, and the seeds are also used in dried form.

Common names and synonyms: Babricorn bean, Pearson bean, wonder bean.

See in addition: "Beans, Peas, and Lentils," Part II, Section C, Chapter 3.

Sword fern - *see* **GIANT HOLLY FERN**

Sylvaner - *see* **SILVANER**

SYRAH (*see also* **GRAPES**) - Not to be confused with Petite Sirah, the Syrah (*Vitis vinifera*) is a grape with a pepper-like taste that has long been grown in the northern Rhône valley of France and more recently in Australia (where the popular wine it yields is called "Shiraz"). In California, Syrah is used to make spicy red wines.

Common names and synonyms: Shiraz.

See in addition: "Wine," Part III, Chapter 13.

Szechwan pepper(corn) - *see* **SICHUAN PEPPERCORN**

Common names and synonyms: Anise-pepper, fagara, prickly ash tree.

See also: "Spices and Flavorings," Part II, Section F, Chapter 1.

TABASCO PEPPER (*see also* **CHILLI PEPPERS**) - In the aftermath of the American Civil War, a wild pepper from Mexico (presumably from the state of Tabasco) was brought to Avery Island, Louisiana, where it was put under cultivation to make the now-famous McIlhenny "Tabasco" brand sauce. This bright orange to red and very pungent variety of *Capsicum frutescens* (the species name means "brushy") is now grown commercially in Central America as well. In addition to serving as the base of "Tabasco" sauce, the dried tabasco goes well in stir-fries and makes a lively salsa.

See in addition: "Chilli Peppers," Part II, Section C, Chapter 4.

TACOUTTA - Known also as "wing sesame," tacoutta (*Sesamum alatum*) is a West African tree that yields oil-rich seeds. The oil is used in cooking, and the seeds are often ground into a flour.

Common names and synonyms: Wing sesame.

Tacu - *see* **ALGARROBO**

TAGAL MANGROVE - An evergreen tree of East Africa and South and Southeast Asia, the tagal mangrove (*Ceriops tagal*) provides a bark that has a multitude of uses in folk remedies. It also has a leathery, berry-like fruit that is edible if not very tasty.

Tahitian chestnut - *see* **POLYNESIAN CHESTNUT**

Tahiti apple - *see* **MALAY APPLE**

Tahiti lime - *see* **LIME**

Tahiti orange - *see* **OTAHEITE ORANGE**

TAILED PEPPER - Also called the "Java pepper" as well as "cubeb," the tailed pepper (*Piper cubeba*) is a native of the Indonesian islands, where it is grown mostly in Java. The "pepper" in question is a brownish berry that grows on a tree-like vine. The berry was a commodity in the early spice trade and became popular in the West as both a medicine and a spice (it substituted for the peppercorn) until about 1600. That popularity, however, began to dissipate as real peppercorns became more available, and today the tailed pepper is once more confined to its native habitat. A member of the same genus as the common black and white peppercorns, the tailed pepper does not have the same taste, but rather one more like that of allspice.

Common names and synonyms: Cubeb, Java pepper.

Taioba - *see* **COCOYAM**

Takenoko - *see* **BAMBOO SHOOT(S)**

TALINUM - One of the edible plants of the genus *Talinum* is the fameflower (*T. aurantiacum*), the roots of which were cooked and eaten by Native Americans in southwestern North America. Another (*T. triangulare*) is called both fameflower and waterleaf; although probably a tropical American native, it is also cultivated in tropical Asia and Africa. Its other common names, such as "Ceylon spinach" or "Philippine spinach," correctly suggest that the plant is grown for its leaves, which sometimes are cooked to be eaten alone as a vegetable but more frequently are added to soups and stews.

Common names and synonyms: Ceylon spinach, fameflower, Philippine spinach, waterleaf.

Tallon - *see* **CHAYOTE**

Tallote - *see* **CHAYOTE**

Tallow tree - *see* **CHINESE TALLOW TREE**

TALLOW WOOD PLUM - Also known as "false sandalwood," "seaside plum," and - somewhat contradictorily - "mountain plum," the tallow wood plum (*Ximenia americana*) is borne on a small, spiny, tropical tree or shrub. It grows in tropical and subtropical America but, despite its scientific name, seems to be a native of Africa. The "plums" in question are plumlike, edible, yellow to orange fruits, which are eaten both raw and cooked and sometimes pickled when unripe. Inside the fruit is a seed containing a nutlike kernel that is edible raw or roasted and also yields an oil sometimes used for cooking. The young leaves of this plant can be eaten as well, after cooking.

Common names and synonyms: False sandalwood, mountain plum, seaside plum.

Tamar - *see* **TAMARIND**

Tamar-hindi - *see* **TAMARIND**

TAMARILLO - Sometimes called the "tree tomato," the tamarillo (*Cyphomandra betacea*) is a member of the eggplant family. The fruit comes from an evergreen tree that was originally native to Peru or Brazil but has been grown commercially in Jamaica and is now cultivated mostly in New Zealand. The tamarillo is about the size of a small, oval-shaped tomato - and, in fact, is a very distant subtropical relative of the tomato - with a skin color ranging from yellowish to purple to crimson. Within the tough peel, which is not eaten, is an orange flesh and rows of purple seeds. The fruits, which tend to be sour, are generally stewed, although they can be eaten raw. The tamarillo tree is noted for the attractive fragrance of its foliage and flowers, and its fruit contains high amounts of vitamins A and C.

Common names and synonyms: Tomate de arbol, tree tomato.

TAMARIND - The tamarind, a basic ingredient in Worcestershire sauce, has a Latin name (*Tamarindus indica*) that certainly suggests an Indian origin, but East Africa also claims this plant. Its name, which comes from the Arabic *tamar-hindi,* means "Indian date." The tamarind has been cultivated since ancient times in India, where it retains a place in formal Hindu ceremonies. It must have reached Europe sometime before the Spaniards moved into the Americas, because they carried the plant to the West Indies and Mexico.

The tamarind is classified as a spice and looks like a fruit but is actually a "bean" that grows on a tree. Tamarinds can be acquired fresh, dried, and in concentrated and block form. Their sticky black pulp has a sour, acidic taste, is used in curries and chutneys, and is made into tamarind paste, which is much appreciated in the dishes of India. In addition, the flowers and leaves of the plant are eaten in salads, and the fruit pulp is sometimes made into a sherbet. The tamarind has a prominent place in many Caribbean and South American recipes as well.

Common names and synonyms: Indian date, *tamar, tamar-hindi.*

Tampala - *see* **CHINESE AMARANTH**

Tanaka - *see* **LOQUAT**

TANDOORI - Also called "ivy gourd," the tandoori (*Trichosanthes dioica*) seems to be native to South Asia. These vegetables look like miniature light or dark green cucumbers and are used in curries.

Common names and synonyms: Ivy gourd, pointed gourd, tindola, tindoori.

Tangelo - *see* **MANDARIN ORANGE, ORANGE**

Tangerine - *see* **MANDARIN ORANGE, ORANGE**

Tango - *see* **LETTUCE**

TANGOR (*see also* **CITRUS FRUITS**) - The most important American tangor is the "Temple" orange, which is a cross between the Mandarin orange (*Citrus reticulata*) and the sweet orange (*C. sinensis*). Tangors have segments that separate more easily than those of sweet oranges, which makes them an important hybrid.

Common names and synonyms: Temple orange.

Tania - *see* **MALANGA**

Tanjong tree - *see* **MIMUSOPS**

Tannia - *see* **MALANGA**

Tansey - *see* **TANSY**

TANSY - A wild-growing herb native to Europe, tansy (*Tanacetum vulgare*) has small, yellow flowers and very green, aromatic leaves with a bitter taste. Nonetheless, the leaves (always used fresh) can give a pleasant flavor to desserts and in the past were much used in confections. Tansy is also added sparingly to salads, omelettes, and ground meats.

Common names and synonyms: Bitter button(s), cow bitter(s), golden button(s), mugwort, tansey.

TANSY MUSTARD - Also called "mountain tansy mustard," this plant (*Descurainia pinnata*), a member of the mustard family, is found throughout the desert Southwest of the United States. It has bright yellow flowers and long, slender, seed-containing pods. Native Americans employed the seeds for making "pinole," a ground meal. Another species, *D. richardsonii,* was similarly used (and is also called "tansy mustard"); in addition, its leaves served Native Americans as a vegetable.

Common names and synonyms: Mountain tansy mustard.

Tansy ragwort – *see* **RAGWEED**

Tapèra – *see* **CAPER(S)**

TAPEREBÁ – Also known as cajá, taperebá (*Spondias lutea*) is a distant relative of cashews and pistachios and a very popular fruit in the Brazilian northeast. The pulp is generally sour, but it is readily turned into a sweetened juice of excellent flavor.

Common names and synonyms: Cajá.

Tapioca-plant – *see* **MANIOC**

Tara – *see* **TARO**

Tare vetch – *see* **VETCH**

TARO (*see also* **CALLALOO, COCOYAM, MALANGA**) – A tropical root, taro (*Colocasia esculenta* or *Colocasia antiquorum*) belongs to the arum family. It is a shaggy, large, brown-colored tuber that has a number of smaller (or side) tubers. The flesh is white and very starchy, with a nutty flavor, and is used much like that of potatoes. The origin of the plant was probably in South Asia, but it reached Egypt about 2,000 years ago. From there, taro was introduced into Europe, and the Spaniards carried it to the New World, and it probably reached West Africa from there. Meanwhile, taro had spread outward from India to the Pacific, and consequently this plant has long served as a common staple throughout much of Asia and the islands of the Pacific as well as in Africa and parts of the Americas. In Hawaii, taro is made into *poi,* a sticky, paste-like substance that has a lengthy tradition of use. In the West Indies, taro is known as "dasheen" or "eddo." Apparently, "dasheen" is a corruption of *de chine* ("from China") – the name deriving from the belief that the plant was imported from China into the West Indies to feed slaves. Taro remains important in many Chinese dishes, and in the West Indies taro leaves are called "callaloo." Given taro's plethora of names and geographic range, it is little wonder that it is frequently confused with malanga – and even with manioc. The so-called Egyptian taro (*C. antiquorum*), which is also apparently native to India, is regarded as inferior to other taro varieties.

Common names and synonyms: Callaloo, cocoyam, dasheen, eddo, eddoe, eddy root, Egyptian taro, elephant's-ear, *poi,* swamp taro, tara, tarro, tarrow, true taro.

See in addition: "Taro," Part II, Section B, Chapter 6.

Taro de chine – *see* **COCOYAM**

TARRAGON – French tarragon (*Artemisia dracunculus*) and Russian tarragon (*A. dracunculoides*) are two closely related forms of the same herb. Native to western Asia, tarragon reached Europe with Arab traders. The Arabs seem to have been the first to use the herb for cooking (in the thirteenth century), and by the fifteenth century it was in common use throughout Europe. Tarragon's scientific name, *dracunculus,* means "little dragon," and apparently the herb was so called because in the Middle Ages it was thought that tarragon was an antidote for the bites of poisonous snakes and insects. Like anise – and fennel, for that matter – tarragon has a licorice flavor; the French variety (now called "true tarragon") possesses the more delicate taste, whereas the Russian type is more pungent and bitter. In the West, most people prefer French tarragon, which makes a great contribution to flavoring vinegars, salad dressings, and cooked vegetables. The French use the herb to flavor numerous meat, egg, and fish dishes as well, not to mention classic sauces such as béarnaise.

Common names and synonyms: French tarragon, Russian tarragon, true tarragon.

See also: "Spices and Flavorings," Part II, Section F, Chapter 1.

Tarro – *see* **TARO**

Tarrow – *see* **TARO**

Tartar cherry – *see* **CORNUS**

Tarvi – *see* **ANDEAN LUPIN**

TAWA BERRY – Native to New Zealand, the fruits and seeds of the evergreen tree *Beilschmiedia tawa* (much used for timber) are among the many "bush foods" that have long sustained the Maori.

TEA – Tea (*Camellia sinensis*) – the most commonly consumed drink in the world after water – is an ancient beverage that was enjoyed in China for at least 1,600 years before Europeans ever tasted it (Chinese legend would have it almost 4,500 years). But it was only about 1,000 years ago, during the Song dynasty, that tea drinking started to become widespread and the government began to supervise the production of tea, regulate its trade, and collect tea taxes. Buddhist monks, who were not permitted alcohol and needed stimulation to stay awake during meditation, are given much credit for helping to popularize the beverage, as well as for carrying tea culture to Korea and Japan.

The Portuguese reached the South China coast in 1514 and become the first Europeans to gain the right to trade with China and the first to drink tea. They were also the first to introduce tea in Europe, and in the following century tea became one of the prizes sought in the three-way tug-of-war between the Portuguese, Dutch, and English for control of the China trade.

Tea – along with coffee and cacao – caught on in Europe during the seventeenth century, which in turn increased demand for slave-grown sugar to sweeten the new beverages. In London, "coffee-houses" that served these beverages began to multiply, and some - such as that owned by Edward Lloyd, which served a specialized clientele (in this case, individuals concerned with maritime shipping and marine insurance) - blossomed into other businesses like Lloyd's of London. Others, such as "Tom's Coffee House," opened by Thomas Twining, became major tea importers.

Tea was a staple of the English colonists in North America and, because of a British tax, became one more source of friction between the thirteen colonies and Parliament, which ultimately resulted in the Boston Tea Party - one in a succession of steps that seem to have led inexorably to the American Revolution.

It was only in the nineteenth century that Europeans discovered the secrets of tea cultivation, thus dispelling an ignorance that until then had meant monopoly for China. It was during the first half of that century that the British established the great plantations of Assam and Ceylon in India, and the Dutch created tea plantations in their East Indian colonies. But China nonetheless continued to dominate the markets of the world, and Britain continued to buy huge amounts of Chinese tea, even though, as a rule, the tea had to be paid for in specie. The stubborn insistence by the Chinese that they needed nothing from the West but precious metals had always been a major irritant to the English, who now saw opium (grown in British India and smuggled into China) as a solution to the trade imbalance. The Chinese government became increasingly outraged at the wholesale addiction of its people, and its attempt to stop the traffic triggered the Opium Wars (1840-2), during which Britain triumphed militarily and effectively "opened" China to the trade of the world while wrangling huge territorial and trade concessions for itself.

The half century or so following the Opium Wars saw much competition in the China trade, and, with a Western public convinced that the fresher the tea the better, speed in transport became critical. For a few romantic decades, that speed was supplied by the famous clipper ships, which could rush tea from China to London or New York in 90 to 120 days instead of the earlier 6 to 9 months - effectively cutting the sailing time in half.

Tea reached the height of its popularity in the 1880s, but subsequent events served to sustain demand for the beverage. One was the introduction of iced tea to a thirsty crowd at the St. Louis World's Fair of 1904, which, although hardly constituting the invention of the drink (as has been claimed), certainly did help to popularize it. Another such event was the inadvertent invention of the "tea bag" by Thomas Sullivan in 1908. Sullivan was a tea merchant who began distributing his samples in

hand-sewn silk bags rather than in tin boxes and was suddenly swamped with orders by customers who had discovered that they could brew the tea right in the bag.

It has been said that there are more kinds of tea in China than there are wines in France. To this it might be added that the classification of teas is every bit as complicated as that of wines. All tea starts as "green," and it must be rolled, withered, fired, and dried to deactivate an enzyme present in the leaves. If, however, the rolled and cut leaves are permitted to stand (and ferment) for one to three hours before heating, the tea becomes "black." If the leaves are semifermented, the tea is called "Oolong." Tea grading is by leaf size. Young, soft shoots make the best tea, and thus only the bud and the top leaves are plucked from the bush. With black tea, the leaf bud is called "pekoe tip"; the youngest fully opened leaf is "orange pekoe"; the next leaf is "pekoe," then "pekoe souchong"; and finally there is "souchong" - the largest leaves that are used. The corresponding green tea grades are "twanky" for the bud, then "gunpowder," "imperial," "young hyson," and "hyson." The very small pieces, called "dust," generally go into tea bags.

The most famous of China's black teas is Keemun (or Keemum), known for its winelike quality. Darjeeling tea, from the foothills of the Himalayas, is one of India's contributions to the ranks of rare and prestigious black teas. Assam tea (from the same region but a lower elevation) is another. The Ceylon teas, from Sri Lanka, run the gamut - from the mild Flowery Orange Pekoe to the full-bodied Broken Orange Pekoe Fannings. The highest-grade Oolongs and the smoky Lapsung Souchongs come mostly from Taiwan.

In truth, however, most commercial teas are blends of several of these individual teas. Green teas are consumed mostly in Japan and some of the Arab countries, whereas black teas constitute the overwhelming bulk of the tea drunk in the West.

Common names and synonyms: Assam, black tea, Broken Orange Pekoe Fannings, *ch'a,* Darjeeling, dust, Flowery Orange Pekoe, green tea, gunpowder, hyson, iced tea, imperial, Keemun, Keemum, Lapsung Souchong, leaf pekoe, Oolong, orange pekoe, pekoe souchong, pekoe tip, *sencha,* souchong, *tsocha,* twanky, women's-tobacco, young hyson.

See also: "Tea," Part III, Chapter 11.

Teaberry - *see* WINTERGREEN

Tear-grass - *see* JOB'S-TEARS

Tea-tree oil - *see* CAJEPUT

TECUITLATL - A blue-green algae (*Spirulina geitleri*), *tecuitlatl* grew profusely in pre-Hispanic times on the surface of Lake Texcoco and was harvested and eaten by the residents of Tenochtitlan, the island capital of the Aztec empire. The Indians used fine nets to gather it, then spread it out to dry. After a few days, they cut it into loaves, which kept for up to a year. The Spanish naturalist Francisco Hernández described *tecuitlatl* as being like cheese "with a certain muddy smell." The Indians ate it on tortillas, often spiced with tomato-and-chilli sauce.

Tecuitlatl is 70 percent protein, with a blend of amino acids similar to that in a chicken egg, and is also an excellent source of the B-vitamin complex. Some scholars have speculated that the profuse growth of *tecuitlatl* indicates that the Mexicans dumped raw sewage into Lake Texcoco, and consequently would have suffered widespread gastrointestinal disease. Other sources, however, relate that wastes from the island city were carried by canoe to fertilize the raised-field *chinampas* of Lake Chalco-Xochimilco. Following the Spanish conquest, the lakes of the central valley were drained and *tecuitlatl* gradually declined. The algae was recently rediscovered on the shores of Lake Chad in central West Africa, where it was called *dihe* and was harvested and eaten in much the same manner as in pre-Hispanic Mexico.

Common names and synonyms: Dihe, dihé, douhé, tecuilatl.

See also: "Algae," Part II, Section C, Chapter 1.

TEF - Tef (*Eragrostis tef* = *E. abyssinica*), a plant native to Ethiopia, is an ancient grain that was cultivated long before recorded history. It is the basic ingredient in *injera,* the popular unleavened bread that is a major component of Ethiopian cuisine. *Injera* is a large, round, somewhat sour-tasting, spongy, flat bread from which pieces are torn to pick up mouthfuls of the stews that are generally the main course of the meal.

Both the bread and the grains from which it is made are cherished. But tef is costly, and thus only those with sufficient means can enjoy the bread regularly. Tef is also an important ingredient in *kita* (a sweet bread), in *muk* (a nutritious gruel), and in a number of homemade beverages. In addition, it can serve as a thickener for all sorts of foods. Nutritionally, tef is a superior cereal. It is a good source of protein and is rich in lysine, iron, calcium, potassium, and phosphorus; moreover, because the entire kernel is consumed, none of the important nutrients are lost. Free of gluten, tef provides an attractive alternative for persons allergic to wheat.

Despite its immense popularity in Ethiopia, *Eragrostis tef* has been a neglected crop in most other parts of the world. Exceptions are Yemen, Kenya, Malawi, and India, where it has been included in the traditional diet, and Australia and South Africa, where it has been cultivated as animal fodder. This is likely to change, however, as more and more people around the globe (particularly in Western cultures) come in contact with tef and enjoy it either as an exotic ethnic food or as a nutritious health food, or both. Because the plant is ideally suited to grow in arid regions and under conditions in which many other plants fail, it is not surprising that other countries, including the United States, have started production, albeit on a small scale.

Common names and synonyms: Annual bunch grass, lovegrass, t'ef, teff, toff, warm-season annual bunch grass.

T'ef - *see* **TEF**

Teff - *see* **TEF**

Tellicherry (pepper) - *see* **PEPPER(CORNS)**

Temple orange - *see* **TANGOR**

TEMPRANILLO (*see also* **GRAPES**) - A red-wine grape grown mostly in Spain, the Tempranillo (*Vitis vinifera*) is the dominant grape in the Spanish wine regions of Rioja, Navarra, Toro, and Ribera del Duero.

See in addition: "Wine," Part III, Chapter 13.

Ten-months-yam - *see* **WATER YAM**

TEPARY BEAN (*see also* **BEANS**) - An annual twining bean, the tepary bean (*Phaseolus acutifolius*) is a native of the southwestern United States and Mexico. It has been cultivated since ancient times by Native Americans (especially the Papagos, who are known as the "bean people") and is now also grown by white farmers because of its adaptability to arid conditions. In the past, the green, immature pods were sometimes eaten raw or cooked as a vegetable, but the bean's main food use was as dried seeds that were ground or parched.

See in addition: "Beans, Peas, and Lentils," Part II, Section C, Chapter 3.

TEPÍN CHILLIES AND RELATIVES (*see also* **CHILLI PEPPERS**) - Present in the archaeological record of Mexico from some 8,000 years ago, the wild varieties of the *Tepín* chilli (*Capsicum annuum*) still exist in a region extending from the southern United States, through the West Indies and Central America, to northern South America, and they are still collected and sold in the markets of Central America, where they are called *chilli pequín.* These are tiny (about a quarter of an inch in diameter), orange-red, oval-shaped peppers, which pack a huge punch when used in salsas, soups, and other cooked dishes.

Chilli pequín is also the name of a cultivated pepper that looks like the wild variety but is somewhat elongated. A close relative is the Macho pepper, which is cultivated and, as the name implies, is extremely hot - indeed, it is a close second to the fiery Scotch Bonnet and Habanero in pungency. Machos are tiny like the *pequín,* are both green and red, are generally used fresh, and are grown almost exclusively in Mexico. Another type of *pequín* is the *tuxtla,* an orangish, pointed chilli that is slightly larger and slightly less hot than its fiery relatives. Collectively, these are also known as "bird peppers" because birds eat the fruits.

Common names and synonyms: Bird pepper, chilli pequeño, *chilli pequín,* Macho pepper, *pequín,* Tepín pepper, *tuxtla.*

See in addition: "Chilli Peppers," Part II, Section C, Chapter 4.

Teposote - *see* MORMON TEA
Terong - *see* EGGPLANT
Teufelsdreck - *see* ASAFETIDA
Thai chilli (pepper) - *see* ASIAN CHILLIES
Thales - *see* LOQUAT
Thick-shell shagbark - *see* HICKORY
Thimbleberry - *see* RASPBERRY, SALMONBERRY
Thin-shell shagbark - *see* HICKORY

THISTLE - There are many species of thistle (genus *Cirsium*) as well as plants of the genera *Carduus* and *Onorpordum*, some of which are natives of the New and others of the Old World. However, today, as the result of humans transporting them about, they are found mixed together all around the globe. Native Americans ate the boiled or roasted roots of many different kinds of these prickly plants, along with the stems, which were peeled and cooked like greens. Other species have been consumed in Asia and Europe since the days of the hunter-gatherers. The dried flowers are employed to curdle milk, and the seeds can be dried and roasted or ground into meal.

THOMPSON SEEDLESS (GRAPE) (*see also* GRAPES) - Originally a wine grape from Turkey called the "Sultana," and further named for William Thompson, the first person to grow Sultana grapes in California around the turn of the twentieth century, the Thompson Seedless (*Vitis vinifera*) has been giving ground to the French Colombard and Chenin Blanc grapes since 1983 and now is mostly a table grape. In the past, however, it was an important grape in the California wine industry.
Common names and synonyms: Sultana (grape).
See in addition: "Wine," Part III, Chapter 13.

THORNLESS RUKAM - The thornless rukam (*Flacourtia inermis*) is easier to work with than most trees of the genus *Flacourtia*, which are, as a rule, very thorny. It is a native of Malaysia (and perhaps also of India) that produces bright red fruits about the size of cherries. Although there are sweet varieties, most are sour and are used to make pies, jams, and chutneys.
Common names and synonyms: Lovi-lovi.

THYME - Thyme, a strongly flavored herb that comes in many varieties, has leaves that are used both fresh and dried. The three most important kinds of thyme are *Thymus vulgaris, T. × citriodorus,* and *T. serpyllum.* The first - common or garden thyme - grows as a bush and has tiny, dark green leaves. The second - lemon thyme - has a citrus-like aroma and flavor and spreads out by growing horizontally. The third kind - creeping thyme, also called *serpolet* - is a wild French thyme that flavors Provençal dishes.

Thyme is a Mediterranean plant that, like so many herbs, was put to use medicinally before it was employed for culinary purposes. The name comes from the Greek "to make a burnt offering," meaning presumably that the spice was burned as a fumigant. But oil of thyme has been used since antiquity for gargles and mouthwashes as well. In culinary usage, thyme is one of the requisite herbs for a bouquet garni, and it joins sage in poultry stuffings and basil and oregano in tomato sauces. Thyme is an important ingredient in the Creole cookery of Louisiana as well as in the liqueur Benedictine.
Common names and synonyms: Common thyme, European wild thyme, French thyme, garden thyme, lemon thyme, *serpolet.*
See also: "Spices and Flavorings," Part II, Section F, Chapter 1.

Ti - *see* CABBAGE TREE
Tickbean - *see* FAVA BEAN
Tien-tsin (chilli pepper) - *see* ASIAN CHILLIES
Tientsin - *see* CHINESE CABBAGE

TIGER LILY - Native to East Asia, but now grown in gardens throughout the world for its black-spotted, reddish-orange flowers, the tiger lily (*Lilium tigrinum*) also has a starchy bulb that resembles a garlic bulb, cloves and all. Tiger lily bulbs are sold in both fresh and dried form and are added to simmered and stir-fried dishes.

Tigernut - *see* CHUFA
Ti leaf - *see* CABBAGE TREE
Til (seed) - *see* SESAME
Tindola - *see* TANDOORI
Tindoori - *see* TANDOORI
Tipo - *see* MINTHOSTACHYS
Tipsin - *see* BREADROOT
Tlilxochitl - *see* VANILLA
Toadback - *see* CALABAZA (SQUASH)

TOBACCO - An American herb, tobacco is a plant of the genus *Nicotiana*, now cultivated worldwide. Its leaves are dried and prepared for smoking, chewing, and "snuffing." Tobacco was used by the Indians of the Antilles when Christopher Columbus first reached them, and the word "tobacco" is probably from the Taino meaning a "roll of (tobacco) leaves." The name for the genus is in honor of Jean Nicot, who introduced tobacco plants at the French royal court. Tobacco use speeds up the metabolic processes and thus helps to hold down a person's weight, although at a considerable risk to health.

Tobacco-root - *see* VALERIAN
Toddy palm - *see* WINE PALM
Toff - *see* TEF
Togarashi (chilli pepper) - *see* ASIAN CHILLIES
To-kumquat - *see* CALAMONDIN
Tomate - *see* TOMATO
Tomate de arbol - *see* TAMARILLO
Tomate de bolsa - *see* TOMATILLO
Tomate de cascara - *see* TOMATILLO
Tomate verde - *see* TOMATILLO

TOMATILLO - A member of the tomato family, the tomatillo (*Physalis ixocarpa*) is a large berry (about the size of a cherry tomato) native to Mexico and used in a number of Mexican dishes including *salsa verde* and guacamole. Also called the "husk tomato," the tomatillo (which means "little tomato" in Spanish) has a compact, green pulp covered by a dry, parchment-like skin that is easily removed. The tomatillo has been cultivated in Mexico for thousands of years. The Aztecs used the term *tomatl* (meaning something round and plump) for several fruits, including a number of tomatoes of the Solanaceae family, which today are regarded as true tomatoes. But it was the tomatillo that was preferred, even after the tomato (*Lycopersicon esculentum*) – a South American native – reached Mexico to fit nicely into a system of cultivation already long established for *Physalis ixocarpa*. Indeed, even today in the Mexican highlands, the tomatillo is preferred for cooking, but it has only recently traveled out of Mexico to find a place in the cuisines of other cultures. Tomatillos can be grown in most gardens and can be purchased fresh or canned. Canned tomatillos work about as well in sauces as fresh ones. They are high in vitamins A and C.

Common names and synonyms: Chinese lantern, *fresadilla,* green tomato, husk tomato, jamberry, Mexican green tomato, Mexican husk tomato, *miltomate, tomate de bolsa, tomate de cascara, tomatillo enteros,* tomatillo ground cherry, *tomatitos verdes, tomatl, tomatoe verde.*

Tomatitos verdes – *see* TOMATILLO
Tomatl – *see* TOMATILLO, TOMATO
TOMATO – The tomato (*Lycopersicon esculentum*) is an American plant with an American name. In Nahuatl, the language of the Aztecs, *tomatl* indicates something round and plump, and this fruit (rather than vegetable) was almost certainly domesticated in Mexico, even though the presence of its numerous wild relatives (consisting of at least seven species) in South America suggests that it originated there. Apparently, however, tomatoes were not much used in the Andes region.

Meanwhile, to the north in Mexico, the tomatillo or "husk tomato" of the genus *Physalis*, which is also round and plump, was being cultivated, and as a consequence, there was already a cultivation tradition into which the newest round and plump fruit was fitted after its arrival. How the tomato made the voyage from South America to Mexico is not known with certainty, but it is probable that the seeds of wild tomatoes were carried by birds and that tomatoes began their career in Mexico as weeds in tomatillo fields. By the time Hernando Cortés reached Mexico in 1519, careful cultivation had brought forth a number of tomato varieties that were utilized for sauces, mixed with chillies, and eaten with beans along with numerous other dishes.

Before the sixteenth century was out, the tomato had been introduced in Europe, where its reception was far from enthusiastic. In part, this was because no one knew what it was or what to do

with it, and nomenclature was such that no one could be certain that they were talking about the same plant. The sudden introduction of several American foods had left Europeans a bit confused about where all of these new items were coming from. As a rule, new foods had arrived from across the Mediterranean with the Moors. Thus, in a number of languages, the tomato became a *pomi di mori* ("apple of the Moors") or some variation thereof. In addition, there arose corruptions, such as the French *pomme d'amour* ("love apple") – although the tomato had no reputation as an aphrodisiac – and the Italian *pomodoro* ("golden apple"), which has wrongly been taken by some as an indication that the first tomatoes in Europe were of an orangish or yellowish variety. The Spanish, who continued to call the tomato a *tomate,* readily incorporated it into their diets and introduced it as well in their territories in Italy, where it was destined to make its largest impact.

However, tomatoes caught on more slowly elsewhere, probably in part because of the rank smell of the plant, in part because it was known to be a relative of "deadly nightshade," and partly because the tomato was adapted to warm climates, and new varieties were needed for northern climates. Thus, in Great Britain and the United States (even though Thomas Jefferson had grown tomatoes), the acceptance of the tomato was a late-nineteenth-century or even twentieth-century phenomenon. This was also the case in China and much of the East, even though tomatoes were introduced in Asia by the Spaniards and the Portuguese as early as the sixteenth century.

Tomatoes come in numerous varieties, ranging from bite-sized cherry tomatoes (used in salads and as appetizers); to egg-shaped plum tomatoes, also called Italian or Roma tomatoes (good for sauces, stews, and other cooked dishes); to round tomatoes (such as the "beefsteak" or "sunny") that are sliced and diced or left whole for everything from sandwiches to salads to stewing. Tomatoes are red or yellow in color when ripe but are also breaded when green for frying. In the past, tomatoes were stored in cellars to ripen for winter use.

In the United States, California produces most of the tomatoes (about 85 percent) to be used for processing. These are field grown and mechanically picked and result in catsup, salsa, juice, and any of the other tomato products, such as tomato paste, puree, sauce, and soup. Tomatoes destined for the table, however, are still picked by hand, and increasingly, those grown in greenhouses in either soil or water (hydroponically) have become available for home consumption. In addition, tomatoes are sun-dried, just as Native Americans processed them for storage centuries ago. Ripe tomatoes contain large quantities of vitamin C and respectable amounts of beta-carotene.

Common names and synonyms: Beefsteak tomato, cherry tomato, Italian tomato, plum tomato, *pomi di mori, pomme d'amour,* pomodoro, Roma tomato, sunny tomato, *tomate, tomatl.*

See also: "Tomatoes," Part II, Section C, Chapter 9.

TONKA BEAN - Also called *cimaru,* which is the name of the mostly wild tropical American tree that it grows on, the tonka bean (*Dipteryx odorata*) has been cultivated to a limited extent in Venezuela and Trinidad. The bean is used mostly to flavor tobacco and in perfumery, but it is also employed to flavor liqueurs and to make artificial vanilla extracts.

Common names and synonyms: Cimaru.

TOOTHWORT (*see also* **COOLWORT**) - "Toothwort" is a common name for members of the genus *Dentaria.* These are wildflowers with edible tubers that are native to Europe, Asia, and eastern North America. In the latter region, the roots of *D. diphylla* (known as well as two-leaved toothwort, pepper-root, and crinkleroot) also served Native Americans as a spice. The roots have a horseradish-like flavor and are employed in salads and eaten raw like radishes. In addition, the leaves were eaten, both raw and cooked as a vegetable. This toothwort is not to be confused with a European plant, *Lathraea squamaria,* which is parasitic on hazel and beech trees.

Common names and synonyms: Crinkleroot, pepper-root, two-leaved toothwort.

Topee-tambu - *see* **GUINEA ARROWROOT**

Topiro - *see* **COCONA**

TORCH GINGER - A perennial herb of the East Indies that probably originated in southern Asia, torch ginger (*Phaeomeria magnifica*) has thick stems that can reach 15 feet in height and are topped with red or pink flower heads in the shape of cones, all of which gives the impression of a cluster of "torches." The plant is cultivated for its young shoots, which are used to flavor curries in Indonesia and Malaysia, and for its edible buds, which are often shredded as a garnish and added to soups and salads.

Common names and synonyms: Ginger bud, pink ginger bud.

Torfbeere - *see* **CLOUDBERRY**

Tornillo - *see* **MESQUITE**

Tossa jute - *see* **JEW'S-MALLOW**

Touch-me-not - *see* **JEWELWEED**

Tous-les-ois - *see* **ACHIRA**

TRAILING ARBUTUS - A plant of eastern North America, the trailing arbutus (*Epigaea repens*) spreads on the ground. Fragrant, waxy, pink flower clusters appear in the spring, and these were eaten raw by Native Americans.

Common names and synonyms: Gravek-plant, mayflower.

Trailing mahonia - *see* **BARBERRY**

Traminer - *see* **GEWÜRZTRAMINER**

Trapa - *see* **WATER CHESTNUT**

TREBBIANO (*see also* **GRAPES**) - Said to be the most widely planted of the white grapes in Italy, Trebbiano (*Vitis vinifera*) is used in the production of Italian white wines and is one of only two white grapes that can be used in making Chianti. Trebbiano is also blended into other wines of Italy.

See in addition: "Wine," Part III, Chapter 13.

Tree cactus - *see* **PITAHAYA**

Tree ear - *see* **CLOUD EAR, MUSHROOMS AND FUNGI**

TREE-FERN - The genus *Cyathea* encompasses a number of Australian and New Zealand tree-ferns with stems that yield a starch that has been consumed by aboriginal peoples for millennia. In New Zealand, one of these, the black tree-fern - also called the silver tree-fern - was heavily exploited by the Maori.

Common names and synonyms: Black-stemmed tree-fern, black tree-fern, sago fern, silver tree-fern.

Tree gourd - *see* **CALABASH**

Tree mushroom - *see* **OYSTER MUSHROOM, MUSHROOMS AND FUNGI**

Tree oyster - *see* **OYSTER MUSHROOM**

Tree tomato - *see* **TAMARILLO**

TRIFOLIATE ORANGE (*see also* **CITRUS FRUITS**) - A native of central and northern China, the trifoliate orange tree (*Poncirus trifoliata*) is planted for its rootstock, which is used in grafting *Citrus* species. The tree produces small, intensely bitter fruits that cannot be eaten directly, but their rinds are employed to flavor beverages and desserts.

Trifoliate yam - *see* **BITTER YAM**

TRILLIUM - There are a number of plants of the genus *Trillium* that have served as food in the past, although the roots of most species have generally been employed medicinally. The roots of *T. pendulum,* for example, are known as "birthroots" and were used by Native Americans as an aid in childbirth. But these peoples also cooked the young leaves of *T. grandiflorum* as a vegetable. In addition, the reddish berries of some *Trillium* species were consumed in northwestern Asia. The many species of *Trillium* have an incredible number of common names, among them "wake-robin," "Indian balm," and "squawroot."

Common names and synonyms: Birthroot, Indian balm, squawroot, wake-robin.

TRITICALE - Triticale is a hybrid grain (*Triticum secale*), the result of cross-breeding wheat (genus *Triticum*) and rye (genus *Secale*). Such a cross was first attempted in 1875 by a Swedish botanist in an effort to develop a grain that would combine the baking qualities and high yield of wheat with the durability and protein content of rye. The few seeds that did germinate, however, were sterile, and it was only in the late 1930s that a fertile cross was achieved. This engineering of a brand new species that is hardier and more nutritious than both of its parent strains became part of the stimulus for the "Green Revolution." Triticale combines the taste of rye with the nutrition of wheat and has a better balance of amino acids than either of the two. It can be purchased cracked, in flakes, and as whole berries, most usually in health-food stores. The grain has not yet proven as useful or important as had been anticipated, and although it is increasingly employed in the baking industry, most triticale is used as livestock feed. It is a good source of the B-vitamins, thiamine, and folacin.

See also: "Rye," Part II, Section A, Chapter 8; "Wheat," Part II, Section A, Chapter 10.

Tropical almond - *see* **MALABAR ALMOND**
Tropical cherry - *see* **CAPULIN**
TRUFFLE(S) (*see also* **MUSHROOMS AND FUNGI**) - A number of fleshy subterranean fungi of the genus *Tuber* are called truffles, which today, depending on the kind, can cost between $800 and $1,500 a pound, ranking them among the most expensive food items in the world, and certainly making them the world's most expensive vegetable. Truffles are also among the oldest vegetables in the historical record. Food historian Reay Tannahill reports that they were known to the Babylonians and the Romans and that truffles were secured from the Arabian Desert in ancient times, just as today some of the richest truffle mines known are located in the Kalahari Desert.

Truffles gained European attention in fourteenth-century France, where they had developed a reputation as an aphrodisiac. In the late fifteenth century, their popularity as a flavoring agent was on the rise and by the seventeenth century, they were known in England. The late eighteennth and nineteenth centuries saw truffles become something of a rage – with their desirability considerably enhanced by French gastronome Jean-Anthelme Brillat-Savarin's declaration in 1825 that without them there could be no truly gastronomic meal.

In France, the truffle of note (and the most famous variety) is the Périgord (*Tuber melanosporum*), a truffle that is black both inside and out, which Brillat-Savarin called a "black diamond." Another truffle – black on the outside but white on the inside – is the so-called cook's-truffle (*T. aestivum*). As the name implies, this fungus, found in the United Kingdom, is not as highly regarded. By contrast, the white truffle of the Italian Piedmont (*T. magnatum*) is a serious rival of the French Périgord, especially in the minds of the Italians. Spain, although not known for it, joins France and Italy as a major truffle producer, and in a given year any of the three countries may outproduce the other two.

"Mysterious" is a word often used in writings on truffles. Truffles vary in size from that of a walnut to that of a fist (belying the species name of the Piedmont truffle), are round shaped, and have a rough exterior. They live in clusters close to (and on) the roots of a host tree – especially the *truffier* or truffle oak – and, like mushrooms, they use spores to propagate. Truffles are gathered from October to late fall on the Continent (in the United Kingdom, the season is in late spring). Actually they are hunted, because they never break ground and thus must be smelled out, although a clue to their presence is that little else grows near the host tree – the truffles in providing their chosen tree with so much in the way of important nutrients from the soil discourage other growth. A sow, straining on a leash held by her owner, is a vivid portrait of a truffle-hunting team provided by art – the sow sniffing them out apparently because of a musky chemical exuded by truffles that mimics a sex hormone given off by hogs. Dogs (and other animals) are also used to hunt truffles but must be more rigorously trained for a task that the sow does happily.

The quarry is equally mysterious as a comestible. All truffles have a distinctive and powerful odor (something like garlic), which some find unpleasant and others think wonderful – and the Piedmont truffles have a garlicky taste. Yet somehow both aroma and taste transfer to whatever they are cooked with and enhance those foods in unbelievable fashion.

This quality helps to account for the cost of truffles. Another reason is scarcity. At the beginning of this century, the most costly truffles imported into the United States sold for upwards of $4 a pound – expensive in those days but nothing like the $1,000 or more charged today. This increase in cost reflects both the loss of forest lands and the overharvesting that make truffle production today only about 10 percent of what it was a century ago. In 1978, France harvested its first commercially cultivated truffles, but such production was fraught with so many difficulties that planned cultivation on a large scale remains a dream, and truffle prices continue to rise.

Because of the nearly prohibitive price of truffles (as well as the intense flavor they impart), they are used sparingly, frequently grated raw over hot foods (creamy fettuccine, for example) and employed to enliven the taste of pâté de foie gras. Truffles are also available canned and in tubes as a paste.

Common names and synonyms: Black diamond, cook's-truffle, Périgord, Piedmont truffle, white truffle.

See in addition: "Fungi," Part II, Section C, Chapter 7.

TRUMPET TREE - Also known as "trumpetwood," the trumpet tree (*Cecropia peltata*) has large leaves with hollow stems. It is native to the Caribbean, where its young buds have served the people of the region as a cooked vegetable for millennia. The tree also produces a sweet, edible fruit.

Common names and synonyms: Trumpetwood.

Trumpetwood - *see* **TRUMPET TREE**

Tsocha - *see* **TEA**

Tsumamina - *see* **DAIKON**

Tuberroot - *see* **BUTTERFLY WEED**

Tucum - *see* **TUCUMA**

TUCUMA - *Astrocaryum* is a genus of chiefly Brazilian palm trees, many species of which are found in the Amazon region. Some, especially *A. tucuma*, produce fruits that yield an edible oil. The fruits are also eaten for their pulp, but the taste is reportedly bitter and not much appreciated by people from outside of the region.

Common names and synonyms: Tucum, tucum palm.

TUFTED VETCH - A species of *Vicia*, tufted vetch (*V. cracca*) is cultivated locally in Europe and Asia and is now naturalized in the eastern United States. Like many other vetches, the tufted vetch has edible seeds, pods, shoots, and leaves. In the past, the plant was cultivated in Europe for its seeds, whereas other, New World species of *Vicia* served as a gathered food for Native Americans.

Common names and synonyms: Bird vetch, boreal vetch, Canada pea, cow vetch, Gerrard vetch.

Tuhu - *see* **TUTU**

Tukahoe - *see* **ARROW ARUM**

Tumeric - *see* **TURMERIC**

Tuna - *see* **PRICKLY PEAR, TUNA DE AGUA**

TUNA DE AGUA - This cactus of Mexico (*Pereskiopsis aquosa*) has fruits that are called "water tunas" or *tunas de agua*. They are used for making beverages and also are boiled to be eaten as a vegetable.

Common names and synonyms: Water tuna.

Tung sun - *see* **BAMBOO SHOOT(S)**

Tupelo - *see* **BLACK GUM**

TURKEY FRUIT - Sometimes called the "bull-dog," this wild, edible fruit of Australia (*Grewia retusifolia*) is a drupe, and red to red-brown when ripe. *Grewia* is a large genus of Old World tropical shrubs that produce such fruits.

Common names and synonyms: Bull-dog.

Turkish coffee - *see* **COFFEE**

Turkish wheat - *see* **MAIZE**

Turk's cap - *see* **MELON CACTUS**

Turk's head - *see* **MELON CACTUS**

TURMERIC - A major ingredient in curry powders, turmeric (*Curcuma longa*) is a member of the ginger family and, like ginger, is rhizomatous. Although it originated in India, the Chinese, Arabs, and Persians were all cultivating turmeric thousands of years ago. Turmeric was never very popular as a spice in western Europe, but its bright yellow color has been employed as a dye for clothing, margarine, and cheeses. Turmeric can be purchased whole or dried but - unlike ginger - is rarely available fresh. In addition to its use in curry powder, the spice goes well in chutneys, in rice and poultry dishes, and with cooked vegetables.

Common names and synonyms: Curcuma, Indian saffron, tumeric.

See also: "Spices and Flavorings," Part II, Section F, Chapter 1.

TURNIP AND TURNIP GREENS (*see also* **RUTABAGA**) - Members of the mustard family, wild turnips (*Brassica rapa*), which apparently are native to Asia Minor, were dug up and eaten by Old World hunter-gatherers millennia before such vegetables were cultivated - and they have been under cultivation in Eurasia for at least 4,000 years. Turnips, which are among the cruciferous vegetables, can grow in even poor soil and are so cheap to cultivate that they have often been grown for animal feed. Turnips were known to the Romans, became a staple of the European poor during the Middle Ages, and reached the Americas with colonists from both England and France. Turnip roots are generally white but can be other colors as well. They are used in stews and soups and are baked, fried, and boiled.

Perhaps more useful these days than turnip roots are the tops of turnips, eaten as a popular green, especially in Europe, the Orient, and the southern United States. They are tough and have very coarse leaves that are mostly light green, thin, and have a covering of hair. For tenderness and the best taste, turnip greens are harvested when they are very young. At one point in American history, this vegetable was a common part of the diet consumed by slaves and - consequently - today is a part of the cuisine called "soul food." Some varieties of turnips that are especially grown for their edible foliage are known as "Seven Top" and "Shogun."

Common names and synonyms: Seven Top, Shogun.

See in addition: "Cruciferous and Green Leafy Vegetables," Part II, Section C, Chapter 5.

Turnip broccoli - *see* **BROCCOLI RAAB**

Turnip cabbage - *see* **KOHLRABI**

Turnip chervil - *see* **CHERVIL**

Turnip-rooted celery - *see* **CELERY AND CELERY ROOT**

Turnip-rooted chervil - *see* **CHERVIL**

TURTLE BEAN (*see also* **BEANS**) - The turtle bean (*Phaseolus vulgaris*) is the small black bean that is the *frijol negro* of Mexico and of Cuba - indeed the main ingredient for the black-bean soup enjoyed by residents of that island and Cubans in Florida. Turtle beans are also much consumed in Brazil and are the foundation of that country's famous *feijoada*.

Common names and synonyms: Black bean, *Feijâo-prêto, frijol negro*.

See in addition: "Beans, Peas, and Lentils," Part II, Section C, Chapter 3.

Tussa jute - *see* **JEW'S-MALLOW**

Tutong - *see* **DURIAN**

TUTU BERRY - *Tutu* is a Maori word for a group of New Zealand shrubs or small trees of the genus *Coriaria*. Some, such as *C. ruscifolia*, produce a berry-like fruit that the Maori have made into a wine known as *tutu* or *tuhu*. Although the berries are edible, the rest of the parts of the tree (i.e., the shoots and seeds) are poisonous.

Common names and synonyms: Tuhu, wineberry.

Tuxtla - *see* **TEPÍN CHILLIES AND RELATIVES**
Twanky - *see* **TEA**
Tyfon - *see* **HOLLAND GREENS**

UDO - A stout Japanese herb, udo (*Aralia cordata*) is a perennial that annually produces edible shoots from its roots. Cultivation generally involves keeping the young shoots totally covered with soil to blanch them. The result is an asparagus-like vegetable that is briefly boiled to remove a resin, then added to salads or cooked further in various dishes.

Common names and synonyms: Oudo, spikenard.

UGLI FRUIT (*see also* **CITRUS FRUITS**) - A far-from-handsome fruit, as its name might suggest, the ugli fruit, of the genus *Citrus,* is a cross between the tangerine and the grapefruit. Also known as "hoo-gly," the fruit was developed in Jamaica but is now grown commercially in Florida as well. Although the ugli looks like a badly mistreated grapefruit, it has a delicious, sweet, and juicy taste, which seems to combine the flavors of grapefruit, bitter orange, and tangerine. Moreover, because it has the loose skin of the tangerine, it is easy to peel, and the orange-yellow pulp is practically seedless. Like all citrus fruits, the ugli fruit is high in vitamin C.

Common names and synonyms: Hoogly.

Ugni - *see* **CHILEAN GUAVA MYRTLE**

ULLUCO (*see also* **OCA**) - Also known as *olluco* and *ullucu, ulluco* (*Ullucus tuberosus*) is another of the ancient Andean root crops that have been cultivated for their edible tubers. A staple of the Inca diet, these multicolored (white, yellow, green, magenta) tubers are still grown commercially today and, indeed, are increasing in importance and thus in their geographic range, which now extends from Venezuela to Chile and northwestern Argentina. The plants, which form tubers both above and below the ground, are frost resistant and, along with potatoes, generally constitute a major source of carbohydrates for those who consume them. The tubers, which are used like potatoes, can be eaten fresh or dehydrated.

Common names and synonyms: Melloco, *olluco, ullucu.*

Ullucu - *see* **ULLUCO**

UMBÚ - A native of the Brazilian Northeast, the *umbú* (*Spondias tuberosa*) grows on a medium-sized tree. When ripe, the oval fruit is about 10 inches in length and has a sweet flesh that is almost liquid in consistency. The umbú is eaten raw and made into preserves and into juice - the latter is often mixed with

milk to become *imbuzada.* This drink of the Northeast has historically played an important role in the health of the people of the region.

UNICORN PLANT - Also called "martynia" and "devil's-claws," unicorn plants (*Proboscidea louisianica, P. parviflora,* and *P. fragrans*) are natives of the southern United States and Mexico. The elongated pods of these plants were eaten by Native Americans, and until recently people cultivated them in gardens and pickled the pods in much the same way as cucumbers are pickled.

Common names and synonyms: Devil's-claws, martynia, proboscis-flower, ram's-horn.

Upland cress - *see* **YELLOW ROCKET**
Upland sumac - *see* **SMOOTH SUMAC**
Urd - *see* **MUNG BEAN**

VALERIAN - A few plants of the genus *Valeriana* are called valerian. The "common valerian" (*V. officinalis*), a native of Europe and western Asia (and now naturalized in North America), has leaves that are used as greens and flowers that can flavor sauces. But its main use - and the reason for its cultivation in northern and eastern Europe - lies in its roots and rhizomes that have been used medicinally since the days of the Greeks. They contain an essential oil, which is employed mostly in the pharmaceutical industry but is also used to flavor beverages. Another valerian (this one a native of North America) called "tobacco-root" (*V. edulis*) has a large, fleshy, edible root, which was used as food by Native Americans.

Common names and synonyms: Bitterroot, common valerian, tobacco-root.

VANILLA (*see also* **CAROLINA VANILLA**) - Of the great number of orchid family members, *Vanilla planifolia* (= *V. fragrans*) is one of the few to be prized for something other than its flowers. The vanilla bean is the pod fruit of this climbing orchid, which is native to that part of the New World that also gave chocolate to the whole world. Indeed, when Hernando Cortés and his men first reached Mexico, the Aztecs offered them *chocolatl,* a chocolate drink flavored with *tlilxochitl* - the Aztec name for "vanilla" (the word "vanilla" itself is from the Spanish diminutive for *vaina,* which means "pod").

However, it was not the Aztecs who first discovered the secret of vanilla, which was one of nature's better-guarded secrets in that neither the vanilla flower nor its fruit have a telltale aroma that might have demanded further investigation. Rather, it was the Totonacs, in what has become the Mexican state of Vera Cruz, who discovered at least 1,000 years ago that if the initially tasteless beans were "sweated" in the sun for two or three weeks, and then slowly dried for several months, this process would force the development of *vanillin,* the major flavor component of the beans.

It is interesting to note that although the Totonacs were subsequently conquered by the Aztecs, they in turn joined forces with the newly arrived Spaniards to overturn the Aztec empire. And this meant that they continued to have a monopoly on vanilla. For although the Spaniards carried vanilla and chocolate back to Europe with them, and sugar produced in the New World became more and more plentiful (bringing on something of a revolution in beverages and desserts as well as baked goods), until the nineteenth century the Europeans were totally unsuccessful in growing vanilla elsewhere.

This was because of an intricate system of pollination involving hummingbirds, bees, ants, and butterflies within an ecosystem not found elsewhere in the world. But, during the eighteenth century, French colonists in Mexico cultivated vanilla, and in the nineteenth century the French introduced bees from Vera Cruz into their own tropical islands; combined with intensive hand-pollination techniques, this effort finally established vanilla production outside of Mexico. Recently, another plant (*V. tahitensis*) was promoted in French Polynesia to lessen reliance on the original vanilla orchid. And back in 1874, German chemists synthesized vanilla in an effort to free the flavor from the plant itself. Because of the high cost of real vanilla, there is plenty of false vanilla on the market today, although synthetic vanilla is easily detected because of a flat aroma and an unfortunate aftertaste. United States law insists that "vanilla extract" be true vanilla. In addition to extract, whole beans and powdered vanilla are available.

Common names and synonyms: Tlilxochitl.

See in addition: "Spices and Flavorings," Part II, Section F, Chapter 1.

Vanilla lily - *see* **YAM DAISY**

Vegetable beefsteak - *see* **MUSHROOMS AND FUNGI**

Vegetable brains - *see* **ACKEE**

VEGETABLE-FERN - The leaves of the vegetable-fern (*Diplazium esculentum*) are cooked and eaten as a vegetable in Java and other parts of tropical Asia.

Vegetable marrow - *see* **MARROW, SQUASH AND PUMPKIN, ZUCCHINI**

Vegetable meat - *see* **MUSHROOMS AND FUNGI**

Vegetable-oyster - *see* **SALSIFY**

Vegetable pear - *see* **CHAYOTE**

Vegetable spaghetti - *see* **SPAGHETTI SQUASH**

Vegetable sponge - *see* **ANGLED LUFFA**

Vegetable tallow - *see* **CHINESE TALLOW TREE**

Veitch screw-pine - *see* **STRIPED SCREW-PINE**

Velvet apple - *see* **MABOLO**

Velvet stem - *see* **ENOKITAKE**

VELVET TAMARIND - There are two trees of the genus *Dialium* that are called "velvet tamarind."

One is a large East Indian tree - *D. indicum* - that is used for timber and produces a small fruit with a blackish, velvety rind and a sweet pulp that is eaten raw. The other (also called the "black tamarind") is a West African tree - *D. guineense* - that produces velvety black pods that have an acid pulp. They are chewed to relieve thirst and are soaked in water to make a beverage.

Common names and synonyms: Black tamarind.

Vendakai - *see* **OKRA**

Verbain - *see* **BLUE VERVAIN**

Verbena - *see* **BLUE VERVAIN, LEMON VERBENA**

Vermont snakeroot - *see* **WILD GINGER**

VETCH (*see also* **BITTER VETCH, CHICKLING VETCH, LEGUMES, TUFTED VETCH**) - The common name vetch is the general label for the 150 species of *Vicia,* a genus of the legume family, the members of which are cultivated throughout the world. The most notable of the vetches is *V. faba* - the fava bean. Then there is the common vetch (*V. sativa*), native to the Mediterranean region and western Asia. Also known as "tare vetch" or "spring vetch," it is cultivated as a cover crop or for use as fodder. However, the young shoots as well as the pods and seeds of spring vetch, along with those of many other *Vicia* species, are edible. In North America, both *V. americana* and *V. gigantea* served as food for Native Americans.

Common names and synonyms: Common vetch, field vetch, spring vetch, tare vetch.

Viburnum - *see* **HIGHBUSH CRANBERRY**

Vilvam - *see* **QUINCE**

Vinegar tree - *see* **SMOOTH SUMAC**

Vine spinach - *see* **MALABAR SPINACH**

VIOGNIER (*see also* **GRAPES**) - A white grape from the Rhône valley of France, the Viognier (*Vitis vinifera*) is extremely susceptible to disease and thus difficult to grow. It is grown nonetheless because it yields a fine wine, and indeed, two of the most famous (and expensive) wines of the Rhône Valley are made from Viognier grapes. The grape has recently been planted in California, where presumably it will prosper and add even more diversity to the California wine industry.

See in addition: "Wine," Part III, Chapter 13.

Violeta - *see* **QUELITES**

Viper-grass - *see* **SCORZONERA**

Virginian poke - *see* **POKEWEED**

Virginian tukahoe - *see* **ARROW ARUM**

Virginian wake-robin - *see* **ARROW ARUM**

Virginia potato - *see* **APIOS, WHITE POTATO**

Virginia strawberry - *see* **STRAWBERRY**

Virginia wheat - *see* **MAIZE**

Visnaga - *see* **BARREL CACTUS**

Voandzou - *see* **BAMBARA GROUNDNUT**

Waferash - *see* HOPTREE
Waiawi-'ula'ula - *see* GUAVA
Wakame - *see* SEAWEED
Wake-robin - *see* TRILLIUM
Waldin - *see* AVOCADO
Waldmeister - *see* WOODRUFF
Walking onion - *see* ONION TREE

WALNUT - There are some 15 species of walnuts native to Asia, Europe, and the Americas, of which two - both with a green, leathery husk - are the best known. By far the most important of these commercially is the smooth-shelled and tan-colored Persian (or English, or Italian) walnut (*Juglans regia*), with its easy-to-crack shell. The Persian walnut was reportedly sent to ancient Greece by the Persians and found its way throughout Europe with the Romans. It is interesting to note that although one of its names is the English walnut, *wealhhnutu*, the Old English translation of the Latin *nux gallia*, means "Gaulish nut" or "foreigner's nut." Today, these nuts are grown in orchards and sold commercially, with California one of the leading producers. Historically, oil pressed from the Persian walnut has been highly prized. It was much used in the Middle Ages by those without a taste for - or access to - olive oil and was common in the cooking of central France until the middle of the nineteenth century. Today, some consider walnut oil to be one of the greatest salad oils because of its nutty flavor.

Another walnut is the black walnut (*J. nigra*), a North American native. It comes in a rough and very hard to crack shell but nonetheless is much used (in its native land, at least) in breads, cakes, candies, and ice cream. Still a third walnut is the little-known butternut (*J. cinerea*), another North American native, which many claim to be the best tasting of all nuts. Walnuts provide the consumer with some vitamin B$_6$ as well as iron, and the butternut has an incredibly high protein content - close to 30 percent.

Common names and synonyms: American black walnut, black walnut, butternut, California black walnut, Carpathian walnut, cordate walnut, demon walnut, eastern black walnut, English walnut, heartnut, Hind's walnut, Italian walnut, Juglans, *nux gallia*, oil nut, Persian walnut, Siebold walnut, walnut oil, *wealhhnutu*.

Walnut oil - *see* WALNUT

Wampee - *see* WAMPI

WAMPI - Native to southern China, the wampi (*Clausena lansium*) belongs to the family of plants that also includes oranges and lemons. Unlike these more familiar fruits, however, wampi are small and grow in clusters, much as grapes do. They are pale yellow and have a hard rind enclosing flesh with a consistency reminiscent of Jell-O. Their taste is sweet yet slightly acidic. Wampi are eaten as fresh fruit, made into preserves, used in desserts, and added to curries.

Common names and synonyms: Wampee.

Wapata - *see* ARROWHEAD

Wapato(o) - *see* ARROWHEAD

WASABI - A perennial crucifer, native to Japan and sometimes called "Japanese horseradish" or "mountain hollyhock," the wasabi plant (*Wasabia japonica*) has a gray-green-colored root that, when grated, becomes a searingly hot condiment used with dishes such as sushi and sashimi. A traditional but now very expensive seasoning in Japanese cuisine, wasabi is available fresh and in powdered form in most Asian markets. New Zealand now grows wasabi for the Japanese market and it is also cultivated in Oregon in the United States.

Common names and synonyms: Japanese horseradish, mountain hollyhock.

See also: "Spices and Flavorings," Part II, Section F, Chapter 1.

WATER BAMBOO - Also called Manchurian wild rice, water bamboo (*Zizania latifolia*) is a close relative of the wild rice (*Z. aquatica*) of North America. A gathered food in prehistoric times, water bamboo has been cultivated for its succulent stems since the beginnings of agriculture in paddy-like East Asian fields from Manchuria to Taiwan.

Common names and synonyms: Manchurian wild rice.

Water caltrop - *see* WATER CHESTNUT

WATER CHESTNUT - An Asian vegetable, the Chinese water chestnut (*Eleocharis dulcis*) is the edible bulb of a Chinese water plant that has been cultivated for thousands of years. The firm, white flesh is covered by a brown, shaggy coat that is not eaten. These bulbs are a paddy crop, grown in the mud, and require plenty of water. A similar but unrelated aquatic plant is the "caltrop" or European water chestnut (*Trapa natans*), which provided food for hunter-gatherer bands and has been fried, roasted, and made into flour in both Europe and Asia since antiquity. It is, however, the starchy and somewhat sweet Chinese water chestnut that provides crispness for so many Asian dishes.

Another vegetable called water chestnut is the water caltrop (*Trapa bicornis*), which is used like a water chestnut. Most water chestnuts available outside of Asia are canned, although they can be found fresh in some ethnic markets. There is also water-chestnut powder, available in many Chinese markets. Water chestnuts are a good source of carbohydrates as well as vitamin B$_6$ and riboflavin.

Common names and synonyms: Caltrop, Chinese water chestnut, European water chestnut, Jesuit nut, *trapa* nut, water caltrop, waternut.

Water convolvulus - *see* SWAMP CABBAGE

WATERCRESS - Native to Eurasia, watercress (*Nasturtium officinale*) is a cruciferous vegetable that now grows wild in freshwater ponds and streams the world over. But watercress is also produced commercially and is available in bunches in the produce sections of U.S. supermarkets as well as in the markets of Europe. The pungent, deep green leaves make a wonderful garnish and give a peppery taste to salads and sandwiches. Watercress is high in vitamin C and calcium.

See also: "Cruciferous and Green Leafy Vegetables," Part II, Section C, Chapter 5.

Water dock - *see* **SORREL**

WATERLEAF (*see also* **TALINUM**) - Any North American plant of the genus *Hydrophyllum* is called a waterleaf and is identifiable by its clusters of white or purplish flowers. The roots, leaves, and shoots of *H. canadense* served as food for Native Americans (and, later, white settlers) in the eastern part of the continent, whereas *H. occidentale* was similarly exploited in the West.

Water lily - *see* **LOTUS**

WATERMELON (*see also* **MELON**) - A native of Africa, this ground-hugging vine (*Citrullus lanatus = C. vulgaris*), cultivated for its melons, managed early on to get around the globe with a great deal of agility. It reached the Middle East, India, and what is now Russia in prehistoric times, was consumed in Egypt and ancient Persia some 6,000 years ago, and was later cultivated by the ancient Greeks and Romans. The Chinese were growing the fruit by the tenth century A.D.; it entered Europe through Spain with the Moors and reached the Americas via the slave trade.

Wild watermelons, which grow throughout Africa around water holes in the savannas and oases in the deserts, are not much larger than apples. Those that are cultivated (there are some 50 varieties) grow larger, ranging from "icebox" varieties that fit in the refrigerator to the "picnic" sizes that can be large enough to feed a crowd. Watermelons are cultivated worldwide in subtropical, tropical, and temperate climates; in the United States, they have flourished in the warm soils of the southern states as well as those of New Jersey. Most watermelons have red flesh, but some are orange and yellow fleshed, and all contain about 90 percent water and about 10 percent sugar. Watermelon rinds - especially those that are white inside - have traditionally been turned into sweet pickles. Juice from the fruit is bottled commercially and drunk fresh as well as reduced to syrup or sugar. Another use is as watermelon wine.

Watermelon seeds are consumed by humans after drying, roasting, and salting. In Iran and China, such snacks are thought to control hypertension. The seeds are 30 to 40 percent protein, are rich in the enzyme urease, and yield an edible oil (20 to 45 percent) that is used for cooking and illumination. Livestock animals are fed the expressed oilseed cakes and benefit from the high protein content. Like nuts, however, watermelon seeds are high in fat, whereas the flesh is low in calories. Seedless varieties have been developed and are very popular, although more expensive than the traditional

seeded varieties. Watermelons provide their consumers with some vitamin C.

Common names and synonyms: American watermelon, Jubilee, seeded watermelon, seedless watermelon.

See in addition: "Cucumbers, Melons, and Watermelons," Part II, Section C, Chapter 6.

Waternut - *see* **WATER CHESTNUT**

Water oat(s) - *see* **WILD RICE**

Water pepper - *see* **KNOTWEED AND SMARTWEED**

Water spinach - *see* **SWAMP CABBAGE**

Water tuna - *see* **TUNA DE AGUA**

WATER YAM (*see also* **YAMS**) - Also called "white yam," "greater yam," "Asiatic yam," and "winged yam" (among numerous other common names), the water yam (*Dioscorea alata*) is a native of Southeast Asia but is now grown throughout the tropical regions of the world, including the Caribbean and especially Australia and Polynesia. The plant is a climbing vine usually planted at the beginning of the rainy season, and its tubers are generally mature by the season's end. The large tubers, with a fine white flesh, are baked or boiled as a vegetable or cooked with coconut milk, although they can also be roasted and fried.

Common names and synonyms: Asiatic yam, greater yam, ten-months-yam, white yam, winged yam.

See in addition: "Sweet Potatoes and Yams," Part II, Section B, Chapter 5.

Wattle(s) - *see* **ACACIA**

Wax(-)apple - *see* **JAVA APPLE, ROSE APPLE**

Wax gourd - *see* **FUZZY MELON**

WAX PEPPERS (*see also* **CHILLI PEPPERS, SWEET PEPPERS**) - Also known generically as banana chillies (and in Spanish as *güero* - meaning "blond"), wax peppers (genus *Capsicum*) include the banana pepper, the Hungarian yellow wax pepper, and the Santa Fe Grande. They are all relatively large - about 3 to 5 inches in length and about an inch and a half in diameter. As a rule, the banana pepper is sweet with a generally mild taste; Hungarian wax peppers are hotter; and the Santa Fe Grande has just a touch of heat. A problem is that all three may be generically labeled "yellow wax" in supermarkets, which gives no clue as to the degree of heat they might deliver. Another pepper with the characteristics and color of waxed peppers is the Chawa, which is found mostly in stores in California. Wax peppers go well in salads, are pickled, and are used to make yellow mole sauces.

Common names and synonyms: Banana chilli, banana pepper, Chawa, *güero*, Hungarian wax pepper, Hungarian yellow wax pepper, Santa Fe Grande, yellow wax pepper.

See in addition: "Chilli Peppers," Part II, Section C, Chapter 4.

Wealhhnutu - *see* **WALNUT**

Weissburgunder - *see* **PINOT BLANC**

Weisser Burgunder - *see* **PINOT BLANC**

Weisser Klevner - *see* **PINOT BLANC**

WELSH ONION (*see also* **ONION**) - An important ingredient in the cuisines of China and Japan, the Welsh onion (*Allium fistulosum*), also known as the "Chinese onion," grows in clusters, which accounts for another of its many common names, "Japanese bunching." Actually a kind of scallion, with dark green, hollow, cylindrical leaves and a white end that does not develop a bulb, the Welsh onion is widely used in stir-fries.

> *Common names and synonyms:* Chinese onion, Japanese bunching, spring onion.
> *See in addition:* "The *Allium* Species," Part II, Section C, Chapter 2.

West African sorrel - *see* **JEW'S-MALLOW**
Western wheatgrass - *see* **BLUE-STEM**
West Indian cherry - *see* **ACEROLA**
West Indian elm - *see* **MUTAMBA**
West Indian gherkin - *see* **GHERKIN**
West Indian pea - *see* **SESBAN**
Weymouth pine - *see* **WHITE PINE**

WHEAT (*see also* **EINKORN, EMMER, KAMUT, SPELT**) - The wheat now growing in vast fields stretching across the Great Plains of North America had its beginnings in the eastern Mediterranean region, where the wild grass *Triticum aestivum* originated to become one of the first of the domesticated grains and ultimately one of the world's two most important superfoods. Wheat was probably first domesticated in the Middle East many thousands of years ago. The ancient Egyptians made bread from it, but only later did the Greeks adopt wheat in preference to emmer. Later still, one of the reasons for the expansion of Rome was the need for wheat, and the Romans turned Egypt into a wheat-growing breadbasket for their empire.

Wheat reached northern China later than it reached the West, and in eastern Asia it joined millet as a major crop. The plant does poorly in warm and humid climates because it is very susceptible to disease. But although it likes cool climates, it does not grow as far north as do rye and oats. In Europe, wheat lost ground to other grains (such as barley and rye) after the fall of the Roman Empire and did not regain its prominence until the nineteenth century. The grain reached the Americas in the early seventeenth century with the Spaniards and was first planted on the Great Plains at about the time of the American Civil War.

Wheat comes in some 30,000 varieties, which in part is testimony to its longevity as a domesticated plant which people tinkered with. The varieties, however, can be fitted into a relatively few classifications, such as "hard red spring," "hard red winter," "soft red winter," "durum," and "white" wheat. The hard varieties (hardness measured according to the strength of the kernel) provide more protein and are most valued for the production of all-purpose and baking flours. The even harder durum wheat is

employed for making semolina and pasta, whereas the soft wheats are preferred for flours utilized to bake pastries.

As a grain, wheat has a special characteristic that provides humankind with raised breads: When it is ground and combined with water, its protein forms gluten - a sticky, adhesive mass that can be rolled and pummeled yet still holds together and expands to contain rather than release the gases produced by yeast. Bulgur is made by steaming and drying whole wheat kernels, then cracking them. The coarsest wheat grains are used for pilafs, the medium for cereals, and the finest for the various forms of tabbouleh - a cold grain salad. Farina (also called "Cream of Wheat"), which has most of the bran and germ removed, usually comes as a breakfast cereal. Wheat can also be purchased as whole "berries," as cracked wheat, as rolled wheat, and as wheat flakes.

> *Common names and synonyms:* Alaska wheat, bearded wheat, bread wheat, bulgur, common wheat, cone wheat, cracked wheat, durum wheat, English wheat, farina, hard wheat, macaroni wheat, Mediterranean wheat, non-bearded wheat, Poulard wheat, red wheat, river wheat, rivet wheat, rolled wheat, soft wheat, spring wheat, wheat flakes, white wheat, wild wheat, winter wheat.
> *See in addition:* "Wheat," Part II, Section A, Chapter 10.

Wheat grass - *see* **COUCH GRASS**
Whitebeam berry - *see* **ROWANBERRY**
White beet - *see* **SWISS CHARD**
White carrot - *see* **ARRACACHA**

WHITE CINNAMON - An aromatic tree, the white cinnamon (*Canella alba* or *C. winteriana*) is native to southern Florida and the West Indies. It is also known as the wild cinnamon tree, and its bark, which is marketed rolled up in tubes, is referred to as "canella," "Bahama whitewood," and "white cinnamon," as well as "wild cinnamon." The bark's aromatic qualities make it useful as a spice. It is also employed to flavor tobacco and for medicinal purposes.

> *Common names and synonyms:* Bahama whitewood, canella, wild cinnamon (tree).
> *See also:* "Spices and Flavorings," Part II, Section F, Chapter 1.

WHITE PINE - Also known as the northern pine and the Weymouth pine, the white pine (*Pinus strobus*) - along with other species of *Pinus* - provides an inner bark that served as food for Native Americans of eastern North America. The bark was eaten fresh and was also dried over a fire, whereupon it was fashioned into cakes.

> *Common names and synonyms:* Northern pine, Weymouth pine.

WHITE POTATO - An enlarged tip of an underground stem that stores energy in the form of starch, the potato (*Solanum tuberosum*) may have been domesticated in the highlands of Peru as many as 10,000 years ago. Certainly it was a well-established crop some 5,000 to 6,000 years ago and, along with other tubers, maize, and quinoa, served as the foundation of the Andean diet. There were hundreds of varieties – some sweet, some bitter, some red, some blue, and some black – that were baked, boiled, used in soups and porridges, and even eaten for dessert. In addition, the ancient Peruvians discovered how to preserve potatoes by a process of freezing and drying, with the resulting product called *chuño*.

Outside of the Andean region there were and are a great number of species of wild potatoes, the tubers and leaves of which served as food for other Native Americans from North through Central to South America. But apparently it was only in the Andes that the potato was domesticated, and the Spaniards reaching Peru in the 1530s who had never seen one before thought at first that potatoes were truffles. The Incas called the potato a *papa*, a name the Spanish adopted. However, because they also adopted the Caribbean Indian name for the sweet potato, *batata*, sufficient confusion ensued that the potato (*papa*) was eventually given the name of the sweet potato (*batata*).

Potatoes were carried back to Spain in 1539 by returning conquistadors and followed the same route as the tomato to reach Spanish territory in Italy, where a hungry peasantry quickly embraced them. They reached the British Isles more circuitously, bringing about even more semantic confusion in the process. The story is that the confusion began when Francis Drake in 1586 picked up some potatoes at Cartegena in the Caribbean, then went to Virginia before returning to England. This created the impression that the potato had originated in Virginia. It also gave rise to the name "Virginia potato," which received "scientific" blessing in John Gerard's *Herbal* of 1597, and neither the impression nor the name was fully dispelled until the 1930s work of Russian geneticist Nikolai Vavilov established or reestablished an American origin for the potato.

Hardy and easy to grow, potatoes were therefore an inexpensive food that caught on quickly enough that the poor of Ireland were planting them in "lazybeds" by the early 1640s. The timing was fortunate, because at the end of that decade the English, under Oliver Cromwell, began killing and transporting thousands of Irish, and those who survived the English depredations did so on potatoes. Potatoes were also planted for the poor relatively early on in England but were not much appreciated there. On the Continent, potatoes were regarded with even less enthusiasm because they were thought to cause leprosy – a suspicion that lingered on in France until well into the eighteenth century. Moreover, potatoes were denounced by religious fundamentalists because the vegetable had not been mentioned in the Bible. Nonetheless, beginning in

about 1650, potatoes started to gain acceptance in the Netherlands and then became widespread throughout the Low Countries by the middle of the following century.

Elsewhere, in Germany and Russia, rulers compelled the peasantry to plant potatoes, sometimes at gunpoint, and by the end of the eighteenth century even the French were eating them. Resistance to the tubers, however, continued well into the nineteenth century in Russia, where (in the aftermath of two famines) they were at last uniformly adopted. By the beginning of the twentieth century, Russia was among the leading potato-producing countries of the world, with a good bit of that production becoming vodka.

Meanwhile, the peripatetic potato, which had left the New World to become the "Virginia potato" in the British Isles, returned to the Americas as the "Irish potato," reaching Boston in 1718 with Irish immigrants. The following year, potatoes were planted in New Hampshire, although another century elapsed before they really caught on in North America. Elsewhere, the Spaniards and Portuguese had carried potatoes to Africa and disseminated them throughout the East. By the middle of the seventeenth century they were grown in even the most remote regions of China and, along with sweet potatoes, were helping to fuel a population explosion. Because potatoes produce far more calories per acre than cereal crops, they were also to some immeasurable extent responsible for the population explosion in Europe during the eighteenth and nineteenth centuries.

The Irish potato famine – which began in 1845 with the loss of half the potato crop and saw its total loss in 1846, causing the death or migration of millions – was, in retrospect, inevitable. The Irish potato crop had failed numerous times during the previous 100 years, each time encouraging tenant farmers to select potato varieties that were the highest yielding. But in so doing, they narrowed the genetic base and bred potatoes with little resistance to fungal diseases. Perhaps ironically, the fungus (*Phytophthora infestans*) that caused the potato famine reached Ireland from North America, probably on potatoes imported for breeding purposes.

The devastating blight that killed one million persons was a stark reminder of the dangers of too much reliance on a single crop, yet at the same time it galvanized plant breeders to develop potatoes that not only were disease resistant but also stored and shipped well. Unfortunately, their product has turned out to be not particularly tasty. The relatively few potato varieties available outside of the Andean region are often divided into the dry and mealy kinds, such as Idaho or russet potatoes, utilized for baking and mashing, and the moist and waxy kinds (new potatoes, for example), which are scalloped and made into potato salads.

In addition to these uses, there are french fries, born in the mid–nineteenth century on the streets of Paris, where they were peddled by pushcart vendors. Beginning in 1864, french fries were increasingly united with fried fish, on sale in London streets since the seventeenth century, to become the famous English "fish and chips." It is interesting to note that as U.S.-based restaurant chains such as McDonald's and Burger King have become worldwide operations, french fries are now known in many places as "American fries."

Potato chips, however, are the true American fries. They are said to have been invented in 1852 in Saratoga Springs by a chef mischievously responding with humor to a customer's complaint that his french fries were too thick. In 1925, an automatic potato-peeling machine was introduced, allowing potato-chip production on a massive scale, which in turn permits Americans to consume a per capita average of 6 pounds of potato chips annually. Other breakthroughs have seen potatoes dehydrated for "instant" products, and french fries, hash browns, and even mashed potatoes are now frozen. Consequently, almost 65 percent of the potatoes grown in the United States are used for these processed products, including, of course, potato chips.

Potatoes constitute the fourth most important crop in the world - after rice, wheat, and maize - and are by far the healthiest. Potatoes are a good source of vitamin C (in fact, they are a leading source in the American diet because of the vast quantities consumed), potassium, niacin, vitamin B_6, and iron.

Common names and synonyms: American fry (fries), common potato, European potato, french fry (fries), Idaho potato, Irish potato, new potato, *papa,* potato chip(s), red potato, round potato, Russet Burbank, russet potato, Virginia potato.

See also: "Potatoes (White)," Part II, Section B, Chapter 3.

White salt - *see* **SUGARCANE**

WHITE SAPOTE - The white sapote (*Casimiroa edulis*), a native of Central America and Mexico, is now cultivated in California (since the nineteenth century), Florida, Hawaii, and Puerto Rico. It is about the size of an orange with a green to yellow skin and white pulp. This fruit's sweet yet simultaneously bitter taste is not appreciated by some, which helps to explain why the white sapote has been a somewhat neglected fruit.

Common names and synonyms: Custard apple, Mexican apple, sapota, *zapote, zapote blanco.*

White snakeroot - *see* **BONESET**

White spinach - *see* **SESBAN**

White sweet potato - *see* **BONIATO**

White-tassel-flower - *see* **PRAIRIE CLOVER**

White Vienna - *see* **KOHLRABI**

White wax-berry - *see* **CHINESE TALLOW TREE**

WHITE WILLOW - A large tree of Eurasia and North Africa, the white willow (*Salix alba*) was long ago introduced into North America. Its inner bark is edible, as are its young shoots, leaves, and flower clusters. The leaves, which are rich in vitamin C, were doubtless discovered to be a scurvy preventive sometime in the distant past.

Whitewood - *see* **AMERICAN LINDEN**

WHITE YAM (*see also* **YAMS**) - One of several yams that long ago lured West Africans into the forests to cultivate the tubers in clearings, the white yam (*Dioscorea rotundata*) has other common names, such as "Guinea yam" and "Eboe yam," which speak to its West African origin. The white yam is considered by many to be the premier yam grown in the region, and it is this yam that generally is used to make "foo-foo," the famous West African dish.

Common names and synonyms: Eboe yam, Guinea yam, white Guinea yam.

See in addition: "Sweet Potatoes and Yams," Part II, Section B, Chapter 5.

Whortleberry - *see* **BILBERRY, BLUEBERRY, HUCKLEBERRY**

Wild angelica - *see* **ANGELICA**

Wild apple - *see* **CRAB APPLE**

WILD BARLEY - Barley (*Hordeum vulgare*) - a Middle Eastern native - was domesticated in early Neolithic times. But many other species of the genus *Hordeum* continued to grow wild. In the Americas, one of these wild species was "little barley" (*H. pusillum*), which was widespread in western and southern North America as well as tropical America. Another was "foxtail barley" or "squirrel-tail barley" (*H. jubatum*). Both provided food for Native Americans.

Common names and synonyms: Foxtail barley, little barley, squirrel-tail barley.

See also: "Barley," Part II, Section A, Chapter 2.

Wild bean - *see* **APIOS**

Wild black cherry - *see* **CHERRY, CHOKECHERRY**

Wild blite - *see* **AMARANTH**

Wild cherry - *see* **CHOKECHERRY**

Wild cucumber - *see* **KORILA**

WILD CUSTARD APPLE - Native to West Africa, the wild custard apple (*Annona senegalensis*) now enjoys a wide distribution across all of that continent's tropical regions. Although it does well even in poor, sandy soils of those hot climates, the small tree (or shrub) prefers low, moist places, such as along a stream or in a boggy wooded area. With such optimal conditions, it may grow to a height of 19 feet. The leaves, lush and green year-round, are enjoyed by monkeys and bushpigs. The tree bears fruits that are barely 2 inches in diameter. When young, they are green with light spots and, depending on the variety, turn yellow or red when ripe.

Opinions on their flavor range from "limited appeal" to "the best indigenous fruit in parts of tropical Africa." Some have likened their taste to that of an apricot and their aroma to that of a pineapple. Their sweet pulp is consumed fresh and the fruits are also pickled.

WILD GINGER - The reference here is not to the wild form (*Zingiber zerumbet*) of the Old World's common ginger (*Z. officinale*). Rather, it is to two species of the genus *Asarum* that are called "wild ginger." By far the best known is Canada wild ginger (*A. canadense*), which is also named "Canada snakeroot," "Vermont snakeroot," "heart snakeroot," and so forth. It is a small plant with kidney- or heart-shaped leaves and is found in the forests of and along roadsides in eastern North America. The other "wild ginger," *A. caudatum,* is a lesser-known denizen of western North America. Both have a fragrant, spicy-tasting rootstock - with a flavor somewhat reminiscent of ginger - that is used either fresh or dried and powdered as a spice. Native Americans made a tea from the roots. There is also a perennial Australian plant, *Alpinia coerulea,* which grows wild and is related to the common ginger.

Common names and synonyms: Black snakeroot, Canada ginger, Canada snakeroot, Canada wild ginger, heart snakeroot, Vermont snakeroot.

WILD GOOSEBERRY (*see also* **BERRIES**) - Also known as the "native gooseberry" - although it is not a true gooseberry (genus *Ribes*) at all - the wild gooseberry (*Physalis minima*) is an edible berry of Australia and one of the many foods that were gathered by the aboriginal populations.

Common names and synonyms: Native gooseberry.

Wild grape - *see* **FOX GRAPE**

WILD GUAVA (*see also* **GUAVA**) - Also known as the "Costa Rican guava," the wild guava (*Psidium friedrichsthalianum*) is a tree of Central America that produces greenish (or yellowish) fruit. As with other guavas, the flesh of the fruit (in this case, white in color) is good to eat raw if one does not mind the numerous hard seeds. The latter can, however, be ground into an edible paste. A refreshing beverage is derived from the juice of the fruit, and jellies and jams are made from it as well.

Common names and synonyms: Costa Rican guava.

Wild hyacinth - *see* **CAMAS**

Wild hyssop - *see* **BLUE VERVAIN**

WILD LEEK(S) (*see also* **ONION**) - Actually not a leek but rather a North American wild onion, the "wild leek" (*Allium tricoccum*) is one of about 500 members of the genus *Allium*. This plant - frequently called a ramp - resembles the leek, in that it has a long stalk and flat tapering leaves. But unlike the leek, which has a mild taste, the wild leek is noted for its strong, garlic-like flavor. Native Americans gathered ramps, and they are still eagerly sought out by many in springtime.

Common names and synonyms: Ramp.

See also: "The *Allium* Species," Part II, Section C, Chapter 2.

Wild lettuce - *see* **PRICKLY LETTUCE**

Wild lime - *see* **KAFFIR LIME**

Wild mango - *see* **DUIKA**

Wild marigold - *see* **ANISILLO**

Wild olive - *see* **ELAEAGNUS, OSMANTHUS**

Wild opium - *see* **PRICKLY LETTUCE**

Wild Oregon grape - *see* **BARBERRY**

Wild parsley - *see* **LOVAGE**

Wild passion-flower - *see* **MAYPOP, PASSION FRUIT**

WILD PEACH - The "wild peach" (*Landolphia kirkii*) is a member of the Apocynaceae family of mainly tropical trees, shrubs, and herbs. The fruit, highly esteemed by the Zulu people, grows on shrubs or woody climbers in southern Africa and matures between November and March. Rich in carbohydrates, it lends itself to the preparation of refreshing drinks and delicious jams.

Wild peanut - *see* **HOG PEANUT**

Wild pepper - *see* **CHASTE TREE**

Wild pineapple - *see* **PINGUIN**

Wild potato - *see* **APIOS**

Wild prune - *see* **WONGAY**

WILD RICE - This tall, annual, grain-producing aquatic grass (*Zizania aquatica*) is actually not a rice at all. Rather, it is a native of the northern Great Lakes region of North America, where it grows in the shallow water of marshes and lakes and along riverbanks. It has been harvested by Native Americans from their canoes for millennia. They used the ripened, dark brown grains - now considered a delicacy - as a staple food. Recently, however, commercial producers have begun growing "wild rice" in paddies and employing mechanical harvesters - making the grain considerably less wild, although (so far at least) not less expensive.

Common names and synonyms: Indian rice, water oat(s).

Wild Roman chicory - *see* **PUNTARELLE**

WILD STRAWBERRY (*see also* **BERRIES, STRAWBERRIES**) - Wild strawberries (*Fragaria vesca* and numerous other species) have been an important food collected by humans since the days of the hunter-gatherers. One of these fruits is the "alpine strawberry" (*F. vesca* var. *monophylla*), which grows in the northern latitudes of Asia, Europe, and North America right up to the Arctic Circle. The *hautbois* (*F. moschata*), a native of central Europe, is another important wild strawberry, as were several American species (such as *F. vesca* var. *americana*, the "woodland strawberry"; and *F. chiloensis*) that provided vitamins A, B, C, and E for Native Americans. Today, wild strawberries are gathered mostly for making jams and jellies.

Common names and synonyms: Alpine strawberry, *hautbois,* woodland strawberry.

Wild tamarind - *see* **LEUCAENA**

WILD TRIGA - Also called "intermediate wheatgrass" when used as a forage crop, wild triga (*Agropyron intermedium* × *A. trichophorum* or *Elytrigia intermedia* ssp. *barbulata*) is an Old World perennial grain that can be cooked whole as a cereal or ground into flour for baking. It is a relative of wheat and may have been a staple crop in western Asia in ancient times. Today, wild triga is grown commercially in North America and elsewhere for hay and forage.

Common names and synonyms: Intermediate wheatgrass.

Wild water lemon - *see* **PASSION FRUIT**

WILD YAM (*see also* **YAMS**) - Also known as the "native potato," "devil's-bones," "rheumatism root," and "colicroot," the wild yam (*Dioscorea villosa*) grows throughout what is now the eastern and central United States. The rootstock was usually gathered in the fall and was one of the many foods that carried Native Americans through the winter. It is probably not the case (as has been suggested) that the plant's various common names, indicating pain, were occasioned by the backbreaking pain involved in digging up these slender tubers because the plant was also used medicinally.

Common names and synonyms: Colicroot, devil's-bones, native potato, rheumatism root.

See in addition: "Sweet Potatoes and Yams," Part II, Section B, Chapter 5.

Wild yam bean - *see* **AFRICAN YAM BEAN**

WILLOW - The majority of the 300 species of the genus *Salix* have practical uses and are planted for erosion control, windbreaking, or ornamental purposes, or are grown for their flexible branches, which can be woven into baskets and employed in light construction. But in the culinary realm, the leaves of the white willow (*S. alba*) are edible raw and are used as a tea substitute, whereas the inner bark and the young shoots of some Alaskan species are consumed raw or with seal oil by Eskimos. The leaves contain a fair measure of vitamin C.

Windberry - *see* **BILBERRY**

Windsor bean - *see* **FAVA BEAN**

Wineberry - *see* **JAPANESE WINEBERRY, TUTU BERRY**

WINE PALM - "Wine palm" refers to any of the various palm trees that yield sap or juice from which wine is made. Mostly, however, the name is intended to mean *Borassus flabellifer,* which has other common names such as "toddy palm," "lontar palm," and "palmyra." The wine palm also serves as a source of sugar in the drier portions of tropical areas where it grows best, especially in parts of India. In addition to providing sugar and toddy, the nuts of this palm contain a liquid that makes a refreshing drink, and the kernel of the fruit is eaten as a vegetable.

Common names and synonyms: Borassus palm, lontar palm, palmyra, toddy palm.

WINGED BEAN (*see also* **BEANS, LEGUMES**) - An annual herb, with names like "winged pea," "four-angled bean," "asparagus bean," "Goa bean," and "Manila bean" among its many aliases, the winged bean (*Psophocarpus tetragonolobus*) is a very close relative of the cowpea. It is usually said to have originated in tropical Asia - probably in India, although China may have been another center of origin. But some believe the winged bean to be an African plant because it grows wild in many parts of that continent. One explanation for this, however, is that it originally reached Africa from the East as a cultivated food crop but some plants managed a return to the wild.

The winged bean is now cultivated in all of the world's tropics, including those of South America and the Caribbean, which it presumably reached via the slave trade. The leaves, pods, seeds, shoots, and tubers of the plant are all edible and high in protein. The young and tender pods, which grow to a much greater length than string beans, are usually green, are eaten like string beans, and are known for their asparagus-like flavor as well as for their four longitudinal wings.

Once the seeds of the winged bean have reached maturity, they are either dried or eaten after roasting. In many places, the flowers of the winged bean are fried and yield a taste similar to that of mushrooms. Winged beans are very important in the cuisines of many peoples of Southeast Asia and southern China. The vegetable not only is a good source of protein but also provides some calcium, iron, and a fair amount of the vitamin-B complex. Today, in addition to the uses already mentioned, parts of the winged bean plant can be dried and used as a cereal and as feed for livestock, and the oily seeds make a cooking oil.

Common names and synonyms: Asparagus bean, asparagus pea, four-angled bean, Goa bean, long bean, long-podded cowpea, Manila bean, princess pea, snake bean, vegetable cowpea, winged pea.

See in addition: "Beans, Peas, and Lentils," Part II, Section C, Chapter 3.

Winged pea - *see* **WINGED BEAN**

Winged yam - *see* **WATER YAM**

Wing sesame - *see* **TACOUTTA**

WINTERBERRY - Like yaupon, the winterberry is a member of the holly family (genus *Ilex*). The leaves of this evergreen shrub are widely used for tea. Common winterberry is comprised of the species *I. verticillata* and *I. glabra*. The former is also called black alder, dogberry, and fever bush; the latter is called gallberry, bitter gallberry, inkberry, and Appalachian tea. In addition to the use of the leaves for tea, the flowers of *I. glabra* are a good source of nectar, which, after the bees finish their work, becomes honey.

Common names and synonyms: Appalachian tea, bitter gallberry, black alder, common winterberry, dogberry, fever bush, gallberry, inkberry.

Winter cherry - *see* **CAPE GOOSEBERRY**

Winter cress - *see* **YELLOW ROCKET**

WINTERGREEN - A native of eastern North America, wintergreen (*Gaultheria procumbens*) has aromatic leaves and spicy, edible, red berries. Oil of wintergreen is extracted from the leaves for flavoring a variety of foods, candies, chewing gum, and drugs. The berry is also called "checkerberry" and "teaberry" and it exudes the wintergreen aroma as well.

Common names and synonyms: Checkerberry, teaberry.

See also: "Spices and Flavorings," Part II, Section F, Chapter 1.

Winter melon - *see* **CASABA (MELON), HONEYDEW (MELON), MELONS**

Winter mushroom - *see* **ENOKITAKE, MUSHROOMS AND FUNGI**

Winter squash - *see* **SQUASH AND PUMPKIN**

WITCH-HAZEL - This tall shrub (which can reach 25 feet in height) is a native of eastern North America. Historically, it has been known as the plant that provided witch-hazel extract to relieve the itching bites of insects, other skin irritations caused by plants, and even burns. But witch-hazel (*Hamamelis virginiana*) also has culinary uses. Its small, shiny, black seeds - contained in a seed capsule that bursts open - were reportedly eaten by Native Americans, who also used the leaves of the witch-hazel plant to make a tea.

Common names and synonyms: Snapping hazel, spotted alder, wych-hazel.

Witloef - *see* **CHICORY**

Witloof - *see* **BELGIAN ENDIVE, CHICORY**

Wolf currant - *see* **GOOSEBERRY**

Women's-tobacco - *see* **TEA**

Wonder apple - *see* **BALSAM APPLE**

Wonder bean - *see* **SWORD BEAN**

WONDERBERRY (*see also* **BERRIES**) - Also known as "garden huckleberry," "sunberry," "morella," and "black nightshade," the wonderberry (*Solanum nigrum*) is closely related to the poisonous nightshades. Nonetheless, the leaves of the plant - which is probably Eurasian in origin - are cooked and eaten in Asia and southern Europe. The fruits - ripe black berries - can be eaten raw but are more often used in pies and preserves. Wonderberries grow mostly wild (in Africa and the states of the U.S. South as well as Europe and Asia), although they have been cultivated on occasion.

Common names and synonyms: Black nightshade, garden huckleberry, morella, sunberry.

WONGAY - Also called the "wild prune," the wongay (*Pouteria sericea*) is an Australian fruit that grows wild and was one of many gathered foods of the Aboriginal population.

Common names and synonyms: Wild prune.

Wong bok - *see* **CHINESE CABBAGE**

Wood ear - *see* **CLOUD EAR, MUSHROOMS AND FUNGI**

Woodland strawberry - *see* **WILD STRAWBERRY**

WOODRUFF - Several plants of the genus *Asperula*, and especially *A. odorata* (= *Galium odoratum*), are called woodruff, *Waldmeister*, and sweet woodruff. Although a native of Eurasia, woodruff is naturalized in North America. It has small, white flowers with an aroma when dried that is used for flavoring May wine, other drinks, and in Europe a variety of foodstuffs as well.

Common names and synonyms: Sweet woodruff, *Waldmeister.*

WOOD SORREL - Any of the approximately 850 species of the genus *Oxalis* may be labeled "wood sorrel," although the term is technically limited to *O. acetosella* and *O. violacea*. A perennial herb found in Europe and North America, *O. acetosella* - also known as "European wood sorrel" or "Irish shamrock" - bears leaves that have been eaten as a vegetable. *Oxalis violacea*, also a perennial herb, and sometimes called "violet wood sorrel," is another American plant that was eaten by Native Americans.

Common names and synonyms: European wood sorrel, Irish shamrock, violet wood sorrel.

Wormseed - *see* **EPAZOTE**

WORMWOOD - There are a number of plants of the genus *Artemisia* called wormwood, especially *A. absinthium.* The latter is a native of Europe and is now naturalized in North America. Its leaves were employed in Europe in centuries past for flavoring sauces. The plant also yields a bitter extract used for flavoring vermouth. It was employed in making absinthe, which has been outlawed in many countries since World War I because the combination of wormwood's essential oil and alcohol was not only highly addictive but could and did produce hallucinations and convulsions that sometimes led to death.

See also: "Spices and Flavorings," Part II, Section F, Chapter 1.

Wych-hazel - *see* **WITCH-HAZEL**

XICALLI (*see also* **CALABASH**) - *Xicalli* is the Nahuatl name for a gourd of the tree *Crescentia cujete;* in Spanish, the gourd became *jicara* and the tree became *jicaro*. When the Spaniards first reached the New World, *xicalli* was used by the Aztecs to fashion vessels for drinking chocolate and bailing out canoes. Doubtless in the process of making such cups and pails, the seeds of the gourd were sometimes retained to be roasted, and perhaps even the pulp was consumed. It is probably the case, however, that these squashes were initially cultivated for the manufacture of liquid containers, and only later were the edible seeds and flesh exploited.

Common names and synonyms: Güiro, higüero, jicara, jicaro.

Xuxu - *see* CHAYOTE

Ya - *see* COCOYAM
Ya bené - *see* COCOYAM
YACÓN - Also called "leafcup," yacón (*Polymnia sonchifolia*) - like ajipa - is often confused with jícama and, in fact, is called jícama in parts of South America. The plant originated in the Andes, was domesticated long before the Europeans reached the New World, and today is cultivated from Venezuela to northeastern Argentina and in New Zealand and the United States as well. The plant's purple roots (which are orange colored on the inside) are sweet tasting and generally eaten raw, but only after several days of exposure to the sun, so that the peel shrivels.

Common names and synonyms: Leafcup.

YAM(S) (*see also* AIR POTATO, BITTER YAM, BONIATO, CHINESE YAM, CUSH-CUSH YAM, LESSER YAM, WATER YAM, WHITE YAM, WILD YAM, YELLOW YAM) - There are several species of yams (genus *Dioscorea*) grown in the world's tropical and subtropical regions, some of which are used solely for medicinal purposes. Among the most common edible species are the water yam or greater yam (*D. alata*), a native of Southeast Asia, and the yellow yam (*D. × cayenensis*) and white yam (*D. rotundata*), both of which are natives of Africa. In the New World, the major species is *D. trifida*, with common names such as Barbados yam, yampie, *ñame*, and cush-cush.

Yams evolved separately in Asia, Africa, and the Americas, and although they may have been cultivated as many as 10,000 years ago in Asia, for most who ate them they were a gathered food for many more years than that. Indeed, until relatively recently, the wild yam was a valued food for some Native American groups in North America. Yams are cultivated for their tubers, which are between 15 and 40 percent starch. These can reach upwards of 100 pounds in weight, and many average some 30 pounds, although most are about the size of the sweet potatoes they resemble.

Depending on the kind, flesh color can range from white to orange to orange-red to purple. Some Old World yams contain a poisonous alkaloid and must be carefully peeled and then boiled to be safe. In addition to use in stews and soups, yams are baked, fried, and boiled like potatoes. In Japan, yams are also battered and deep-fried.

See in addition: "Sweet Potatoes and Yams," Part II, Section B, Chapter 5.

Yam bean - *see* AFRICAN YAM BEAN, AJIPA, JÍCAMA

YAM DAISY - With daisy-like flowers aboveground and yam-like tubers below, it is not difficult to understand how the yam daisy (*Microseris lanceolata*, formerly *M. scapigera*, and also called *murnong*) got its name. The tubers constituted an important food of the southeastern Australian Aborigines, whose women dug up the roots with digging sticks, then roasted them in baskets in earth ovens. The appearance of the plant's flowers was the signal to the gatherers that the roots were fully developed. Other important flowering plants with roots that were dug and consumed by the Aborigines were the "bulbine lily" (*Bulbine bulbosa*), the "vanilla lily" (*Arthropodium milleflorum*), and the "milkmaid" (*Burchardia umbellata*).

Common names and synonyms: Bulbine lily, milkmaid, murnong, vanilla lily.

Yamp - *see* INDIAN POTATO
Yampa - *see* INDIAN POTATO
Yampah - *see* INDIAN POTATO
Yampi - *see* CUSH-CUSH YAM
Yang tao - *see* KIWI FRUIT
Yard-long bean - *see* COWPEA

YARROW - Known as "milfoil" in Europe, yarrow (*Achillea millefolium*) is a pungent Eurasian herb now widely naturalized in North America. Its strongly flavored leaves enliven salads and soups; a tisane is also made from the plant, and it has been employed to flavor beer. Yarrow's genus is named for Achilles, who was said to have discovered its healing powers, and its medicinal uses have subsequently been myriad. A variety called western yarrow (*A. millefolium* var. *lanulosa*), which grows in the desert Southwest of North America, was much used by Native Americans.

Common names and synonyms: Milfoil.

YAUPON - Also known as cassina, the "Christmas tea-bush," and the "Carolina tea-tree," this holly (*Ilex vomitoria*) is found throughout the southeastern United States. The plant is a woody shrub that reaches 5 to 10 feet in height, with gray bark, dark green leaves, and yellow or orange berries. Native Americans made a ceremonial tea from the leaves by first toasting and then boiling them. This was the "black drink," the consumption of which might be followed by vomiting. The Muskogee (Creek) Indians as well as the related Seminoles of Florida were enthusiastic users, and indeed, the name of the Seminole war chief Osceola (1804?-38), which translates as "black water," was given to him because of his ritual position in the black-drink ceremony. Europeans who drank the black drink, however, experienced no emetic effect, and tests done in the twentieth century have established that yaupon is not an emetic. Thus, the vomiting seems to have been the result of a cultural practice. But yaupon *is* a natural source of caffeine, similar to *Ilex paraguariensis,* the yerba-maté tea of South America. The white residents of North Carolina's Outer Banks continued to drink yaupon until the twentieth century, as did residents of Charleston, South Carolina. The Europeans who first encountered the tea sent some of the leaves back to Europe, but this and subsequent efforts to establish yaupon tea as a commercial product have met with no success.

Common names and synonyms: Black drink, Carolina tea-tree, cassina, Christmas tea-bush.

Yautía - *see* **MALANGA**

YEHIB - Native to the arid regions near the Horn of Africa, this evergreen shrub (*Cordeauxia edulis*) is now an endangered species. It produces pods embracing a seed that weighs between 2 and 3 grams. Rich in starch and sugars, the pleasant-tasting nut is used by nomads in the region as a staple food.

Yellow bedstraw - *see* **LADY'S BEDSTRAW**
Yellowberry - *see* **CLOUDBERRY**
Yellow chives - *see* **CHINESE CHIVE(S)**
Yellow cleavers - *see* **LADY'S BEDSTRAW**
Yellow dhal(l) - *see* **PIGEON PEA**
Yellow dock - *see* **CURLED DOCK**
Yellow ginseng - *see* **BLUE COHOSH**
Yellow gram - *see* **CHICKPEA**
Yellow granadilla - *see* **PASSION FRUIT**
Yellow melilot - *see* **SWEET CLOVER**

YELLOW MOMBIN - A native of northern South America and Central America, the yellow mombin (*Spondias mombin*) is now grown throughout most lowlands of tropical America, although not with much enthusiasm, and it is not highly commercialized. The fruits are oblong, average about 10 inches in length, and vary greatly in taste, with some sweet but others harsh and unpleasant. They are consumed raw, made into preserves, and used as a flavoring.

Yellow nutsedge - *see* **CHUFA**

YELLOW ROCKET - Although considered a weed by some, this biennial herb (*Barbarea vulgaris*) has leaves that, when young, have occasionally been used in salads, whereas older leaves have been cooked as a vegetable. Native to Europe, the plant can now be found in North Africa, Asia, North America, New Zealand, and Australia. It is also known as "rocket," "upland cress," and "winter cress" and is rich in vitamins A and C.

Common names and synonyms: Rocket, upland cress, winter cress.

Yellowroot - *see* **GOLDTHREAD**
Yellow salsify - *see* **MOONFLOWER**
Yellow turnip - *see* **RUTABAGA**

YELLOW WILD-INDIGO - An herb with countless common names, ranging from "American indigo" to "rattlebush," yellow wild-indigo (*Baptisia tinctoria*) is found across eastern and central North America,

its native territory. Its young shoots were cooked and eaten by Native Americans.

Common names and synonyms: American indigo, rattlebush.

YELLOW YAM (*see also* **YAMS**) - Also known as "Guinea yam" and "yellow Guinea yam," the yellow yam (*Dioscorea × cayenensis*) is a West African native that was carried to the West Indies via the early-sixteenth-century slave trade. It continues to be widely cultivated in West Africa, where it is perhaps the most important yam species. It is of much less importance in the Caribbean and is not grown in other tropical regions of the world. The yellow yam is one of those yams used to make the famous West African "foo-foo," and is also roasted, boiled, and fried.

Common names and synonyms: Guinea yam, twelve-months yam, yellow Guinea yam.

See in addition: "Sweet Potatoes and Yams," Part II, Section B, Chapter 5.

Yerba de conejo - *see* **QUELITES**

YERBA MATÉ - Also called maté and Paraguay(an) tea, yerba maté is a tea made from the dried leaves and young shoots of the evergreen tree *Ilex paraguariensis*. It is mildly stimulative and was being consumed throughout the day and evening by males in what is now Paraguay and Brazil long before the Spaniards and Portuguese ever arrived in the New World. Most likely, then as now, the natives were drinking the tea out of dried gourds – actually sucking it through a tube called a *bombilla* with a strainer attached.

Common names and synonyms: Maté, Paraguay(an) tea.

YERBA SANTA - Common along the Pacific coast from Oregon to California, yerba santa (*Eriodictyon californicum*) is an evergreen shrub with leaves that are covered with a fragrant resin. They have long been chewed to alleviate thirst and also are made into a tea.

Common names and synonyms: Bear's-weed, gum-plant, mountain balm.

YOUNGBERRY (*see also* **BERRIES**) - Developed by B. M. Young, a twentieth-century fruit grower, the youngberry (genus *Rubus*) is a hybrid between a blackberry and a dewberry. A juicy and very large berry, the youngberry is mostly cultivated and available in the western United States.

Young hyson - *see* **TEA**
Ysaño - *see* **MASHUA**
Yuca - *see* **MANIOC**

YUCCA - There are various members of the genus *Yucca* with white flowers that in the American Southwest are sometimes added to salads. *Yucca filamentosa* has been a perennial favorite of the region and was exploited by Native Americans, who boiled or roasted its flower stalks and buds and ate its plumlike fruits.

Common names and synonyms: Adam's-needle, spoonleaf yucca.

Yuen sai - *see* **CILANTRO, CORIANDER**
Yun er - *see* **CLOUD EAR**
Yuquilla - *see* **ARROWROOT**
Yu-tao - *see* **COCOYAM**
YUZU - A golden yellow citron, the yuzu (*Citrus medica*) is about the size of a small orange. It is a very sour Japanese fruit, which is cultivated for its aromatic rind. The Japanese carve the rind into traditional shapes and use it as a garnish. The yuzu can sometimes be found in Asian markets in the United States.

Zahidi date - *see* **DATE**

Z

ZAMIA - Of the cycad family (and looking something like palm trees except for their fern-like as well as palmlike leaves), these tropical American members of the genus *Zamia* (including *Z. integrifolia* in southeastern North America) have underground roots that Native Americans of the West Indies and southern North America pounded, grated, dried, ground, boiled, mashed, washed with plenty of water, and drained and dried (again) to obtain starch for making bread and porridges. These rigorous methods were necessary to render the vegetable safe; without such efforts, the roots are toxic - even deadly. The seeds from the cone-like fruits, as well as the zamia stems, are also toxic and must be cooked or otherwise processed before they become edible. Almost from the time they reached the island of Hispaniola, Columbus and his men began dining on zamia bread prepared by the Taino Indians.

Common names and synonyms: Coontie, cycad, Florida arrowroot, Florida sago, Seminole bread, starchy breadroot.

Zanzibar oil-vine - *see* **OYSTERNUT**
Zapote - *see* **BLACK SAPOTE, SAPODILLA, WHITE SAPOTE**
Zapotillo - *see* **SAPODILLA**
ZINFANDEL (*see also* **GRAPES**) - This red wine grape (*Vitis vinifera*) has been something of a surprise in California, where it was earlier employed to make "jug" wines. In the past two decades, however, it has been developed into one of the best of the red varietal grapes and is the most widely grown grape in the state. Although the Zinfandel is of obscure European origin, it has become known as "California's grape," in part because it has been grown in that state since the late nineteenth century, and Zinfandel wines have been a major American contribution to the world of wine. There are both red and white Zinfandels (actually, the "white zinfandel" is a "blush" wine, and one only recently made available), or "Zins," as they are popularly known.

See in addition: "Wine," Part III, Chapter 13.

ZUCCHINI (*see also* **SQUASH AND PUMPKIN**) - Although winter squashes do not enjoy the popularity they once did, the same is not true for summer squashes, and especially not for the versatile zucchini. An American summer squash, the zucchini (*Cucurbita pepo*) bears an Italian name that is the diminutive of *zucca,* meaning "gourd." As a rule, this vegetable has a smooth, shiny, green, very thin rind - reminiscent of that of its cousin, the cucumber. But the flesh is firmer. The zucchini also comes with a deep yellow skin - this is called a "golden zucchini" - and there is another variety called "Italian squash" or *cocozelle.* Zucchini goes well with tomato sauce and is worked into numerous main and side dishes. On its own it can be steamed, fried, boiled, broiled, simmered, stuffed, and eaten raw as an appetizer and in salads.

Common names and synonyms: Cocozelle, courgette, golden zucchini, Italian squash, vegetable marrow.

See in addition: "Squash," Part II, Section C, Chapter 8.

Zula nut - *see* **CHUFA**
ZULU MILKBERRY - A southern African tree or shrub, *Manilkara concolor* varies in height from 9 to 23 feet and bears Zulu milkberries - egg-shaped fruits that range from yellow to bright red in color. Deliciously sweet, the fruits are good when eaten fresh but also are fermented to make alcoholic beverages. Zulu milkberries are highly prized and are frequently reserved for village chiefs.

Zuttano - *see* **AVOCADO**

Sources Consulted

Allen, Betty Molesworth. 1967. *Malayan fruits.* Singapore.

Andrews, Jean. 1984. *Peppers: The domesticated capsicums.* Austin, Tex.

Arbizu, C., and M. Tapia. 1994. Andean tubers. In *Neglected crops: 1492 from a different perspective,* ed. J. E. Hernándo Bermejo and J. León, 149-63. FAO Plant Production and Protection Series No. 26. Rome.

Arkcoll, David. 1990. New crops from Brazil. In *Advances in new crops,* ed. J. Janick and J. E. Simon, 367-71. Portland, Ore.

Ayerza, Ricardo, and Wayne Coates. 1996. New industrial crops: Northwestern Argentina Regional Project. In *Progress in new crops,* ed. J. Janick, 45-51. Alexandria, Va.

Bailey, L. H. 1976. *Hortus third: A concise dictionary of plants cultivated in the United States and Canada initially compiled by Liberty Hyde Bailey and Ethel Zoe Bailey.* Revised and expanded by the staff of the Liberty Hyde Bailey Hortorium. New York.

Bartlett, Jonathan. 1996. *The cook's dictionary and culinary reference.* Chicago.

Beauthéac, Nadine, ed. 1992. *The book of tea,* trans. Deke Dusinberre. Italy.

Bender, A. E., and D. Bender. 1995. *A dictionary of food and nutrition.* Oxford.

Brothwell, D., and P. Brothwell. 1969. *Food in antiquity: A survey of the diet of early peoples.* London.

Burkill, I. H. 1966. *A dictionary of the economic products of the Malay Peninsula.* 2 vols. Kuala Lumpur.

California Rare Fruit Growers. 1995. Online, CRFG Publications 1969-89, World Wide Web, Jan. 9, 1999.

Campbell, Richard J. 1996. South American fruits deserving further attention. In *Progress in new crops,* ed. J. Janick, 431-9. Alexandria, Va.

Cantwell, Marita, Xunli Nie, Ru Jing Zong, and Mas Yamaguchi. 1996. Asian vegetables: Selected fruit and leafy types. In *Progress in new crops,* ed. J. Janick, 488-95. Alexandria, Va.

Carpenter, Kenneth J. 1986. *The history of scurvy and vitamin C.* Cambridge, London, and New York.

1994. *Protein and energy: A study of changing ideas in nutrition.* Cambridge, New York, and Melbourne.

Chandler, William H. 1950. *Evergreen orchards.* Philadelphia, Pa.

Coe, Sophie D. 1994. *America's first cuisines.* Austin, Tex.

College of Agricultural Sciences. Ongoing project; last update Mar. 17, 1998. Commercial vegetable production guides. Online, Oregon State University, World Wide Web, Nov. 3, 1998.

Collins, Wanda W. 1993. Root vegetables: New uses for old crops. In *New crops,* ed. J. Janick and J. E. Simon, 533-7. New York.

Considine, John A. 1996. Emerging indigenous crops of Australia. In *Progress in new crops,* ed. J. Janick, 26-36. Alexandria, Va.

Couplan, François. 1998. *The encyclopedia of edible plants of North America.* New Canaan, Conn.

Densmore, Frances. 1974. *How Indians use wild plants for food, medicine and crafts.* New York.

Douglas, James A. 1993. New crop development in New Zealand. In *New crops,* ed. J. Janick and J. E. Simon, 51-7. New York.

Duke, James A. 1983. *Handbook of energy crops.* Online, Purdue University Center for New Crops and Plant Products, World Wide Web, Oct. 27, 1998.

Dunmire, William W., and Gail D. Tierney. 1997. *Wild plants and native peoples of the Four Corners.* Santa Fe, N. Mex.

Ensminger, Audrey H., et al. 1983. *Foods and nutrition encyclopedia.* 2 vols. Clovis, Calif.

Epple, Anne Orth, and Lewis E. Epple. 1995. *A field guide to the plants of Arizona.* Helena, Mont.

Facciola, Stephen. 1992. *Cornucopia, a source book of edible plants.* Second edition. Vista, Calif.

Felker, Peter. 1996. Commercializing mesquite, leucaena, and cactus in Texas. In *Progress in new crops,* ed. J. Janick, 133-7. Alexandria, Va.

Flowerdew, Bob. 1995. *The complete book of fruit.* New York.

Foster, Nelson, and Linda S. Cordell. 1992. *Chilies to chocolate: Food the Americas gave the world.* Tucson, Ariz., and London.

Freedman, Robert, comp. Ongoing project; last update March 10, 1998. Famine foods. Online, Purdue University Center for New Crops and Plant Products, World Wide Web, Oct. 19, 1998.

Giacometti, D., and E. Lleras. 1994. Subtropical Myrtaceae. In *Neglected crops: 1492 from a different perspective,* ed. J. E. Hernándo Bermejo and J. León, 229-37. FAO Plant Production and Protection Series No. 26. Rome.

Gray, Patience. 1987. *Honey from a weed: Fasting and feasting in Tuscany, Catalonia, the Cyclades and Apulia.* New York.

Griffith, Mark. 1994. *Index of garden plants.* Portland, Ore.

Grigson, Jane, and Charlotte Knox. 1986. *Cooking with exotic fruits and vegetables.* New York.

Hamilton, Philip, et al. Ongoing project; last update July 5, 1998. Edible fruit. Online, *UW Oykangand and UW Olkola dictionary,* World Wide Web, 1 Sept. 1998.

Harlan, Jack R. 1993. Genetic resources in Africa. In *New crops,* ed. J. Janick and J. E. Simon, 65-8. New York.

Heiser, Charles B., Jr. 1979. *The gourd book.* Norman, Okla., and London.

    1981. *The story of food.* San Francisco.

    1985. *Of plants and peoples.* Norman, Okla.

Hymowitz, Theodore. 1990. Grain legumes. In *Advances in new crops,* ed. J. Janick and J. E. Simon, 54-7. Portland, Ore.

Kiple, Kenneth F., ed. 1993. *The Cambridge world history of human disease.* New York and Cambridge.

Janson, H. Frederic. 1996. *Pomona's harvest: An illustrated chronicle of antiquarian fruit literature.* Portland, Ore.

Lamberts, Mary, and Jonathan H. Crane. 1990. Tropical fruits. In *Advances in new crops,* ed. J. Janick and J. E. Simon, 337- 55. Portland, Ore.

Mabberley, D. J., ed. 1997. *The plant book: A portable dictionary of the vascular plants.* Second edition. Cambridge and New York.

MacNeish, Richard S. 1991. *The origins of agriculture and settled life.* Norman, Okla., and London.

Magness, J. R., G. M. Markle, and C. C. Compton. 1971. *Food and feed crops of the United States.* Interregional Research Project IR-4, IR Bulletin 1 (Bulletin 828, New Jersey Agricultural Experiment Station). Online, Purdue University Center for New Crops and Plant Products, World Wide Web, Sept. 22, 1998.

Mahdeem, H. 1994. Custard apples. In *Neglected crops: 1492 from a different perspective,* ed. J. E. Hernándo Bermejo and J. León, 85-92. FAO Plant Production and Protection Series No. 26. Rome.

Margen, Sheldon, and the editors of the University of California at Berkeley. Wellness letter. 1992. *The wellness encyclopedia of food and nutrition.* New York.

Martin, Franklin W., Carl W. Campbell, and Ruth M. Ruberté. 1987. *Perennial edible fruits of the tropics: An inventory.* USDA Agriculture Handbook No. 642. Washington, D.C.

Matossian, Mary Kilbourne. 1989. *Poisons of the past: Molds, epidemics, and history.* New Haven, Conn., and London.

McGee, Harold. 1984. *On food and cooking: The science and lore of the kitchen.* New York.

McHargue, Lawrence T. 1996. Macadamia production in southern California. In *Progress in new crops,* ed. J. Janick, 458-62. Alexandria, Va.

McKean, Steve. Unpublished; ongoing project. Edible fruits of Zululand. Online, World Wide Web, Jan. 8, 1999.

Miller, Orson K., Jr. 1979. *Mushrooms of North America.* New York.

Mizrahi, Y., and A. Nerd. 1996. New crops as a possible solution for the troubled Israeli export market. In *Progress in new crops,* ed. J. Janick, 37-45. Alexandria, Va.

Mujica, A. 1994. Andean grains and legumes. In *Neglected crops: 1492 from a different perspective,* ed. J. E. Hernándo Bermejo and J. León, 131-48. FAO Plant Production and Protection Series No. 26. Rome.

Nagy, Steven, and Philip E. Shaw. 1980. *Tropical and subtropical fruits.* Westport, Conn.

National Research Council. 1996. *Lost crops of Africa.* Vol. 1: *Grains.* Washington, D.C.

Nerd, Avinoam, James A. Aronson, and Yosef Mizrahi. 1990. Introduction and domestication of rare and wild fruit and nut trees for desert areas. In *Advances in new*

crops, ed. J. Janick and J. E. Simon, 355-63. Portland, Ore.

Ng, Timothy J. 1993. New opportunities in the Cucurbitaceae. In *New crops,* ed. J. Janick and J. E. Simon, 538-46. New York.

Noda, H., C. R. Bueno, and D. F. Silva Filho. 1994. Guinea arrowroot. In *Neglected crops: 1492 from a different perspective,* ed. J. E. Hernándo Bermejo and J. León, 239-44. FAO Plant Production and Protection Series No. 26. Rome.

Novak, F. A. 1966. *The pictorial encyclopedia of plants and flowers,* ed. J. G. Barton. London and New York.

O'Hair, Stephen K. 1990. Tropical root and tuber crops. In *Advances in new crops,* ed. J. Janick and J. E. Simon, 424-8. Portland, Ore.

Ortiz, Elisabeth Lambert. 1992. *The encyclopedia of herbs, spices and flavorings.* London.

Passmore, Jacki. 1991. *The encyclopedia of Asian food and cooking.* New York.

Peet, Mary. Last update Jul. 1, 1998. *Sustainable practices for vegetable production in the South.* Online, Hort Base, North Carolina State University, World Wide Web, Nov. 3, 1998.

Purseglove, J. W. 1968. *Tropical plants - dicotyledons.* London.

    1972. *Tropical crops - monocotyledons.* London.

Rhodes, David. Ongoing project; last update Oct. 2, 1998. Potatoes - general introduction. Online, Purdue University Center for New Crops and Plant Products, World Wide Web, 17 Nov. 1998.

    Ongoing project; last update Oct. 10, 1998. Squash, pumpkins and gourds - general introduction. Online, Purdue University Center for New Crops and Plant Products, World Wide Web, Nov. 3, 1998.

Roecklein, John C., and PingSun Leung. 1987. *A profile of economic plants.* New Brunswick, Canada.

Rosengarten, F. 1984. *The book of edible nuts.* New York.

Royse, Daniel J. 1996. Specialty mushrooms. In *Progress in new crops,* ed. J. Janick, 464-75. Alexandria, Va.

Saade, R. Lira, and S. Montes Hernández. 1994. Cucurbits. In *Neglected crops: 1492 from a different perspective,* ed. J. E. Hernándo Bermejo and J. León, 63-77. Plant Production and Protection Series No. 26, FAO. Rome.

Salaman, R. N. 1940. Why "Jerusalem artichoke." *Journal of the Royal Horticultural Society* 95: 338-48, 376-83.

Schneider, Elizabeth. 1986. *Uncommon fruits and vegetables: A commonsense guide.* New York.

Schneider, M. 1990. Acorns as a staple food - different types and change of exploitation through time. *Bodenkultur* 41: 81-8.

Sievers, A. F. 1930. *The herb hunters guide.* USDA Miscellaneous Publication No. 77. Washington, D.C.

Simmons, N. W., and J. Smartt, eds. 1995. *Evolution of crop plants.* Second edition. London.

Simon, J. E., A. F. Chadwick, and L. E. Craker. 1984. *Herbs: An indexed bibliography, 1971-1980. The scientific literature on selected herbs, and aromatic and medicinal plants of the temperate zone.* Hamden, Conn.

Stallknecht, G. F., K. M. Gilbertson, and J. E. Ranney. 1996. Alternative wheat cereals as food grains: Einkorn, emmer, spelt, kamut, and triticale. In *Progress in new crops,* ed. J. Janick, 156-70. Alexandria, Va.

Stephens, James M. 1994. Guar - *Cyamopsis tetragonolobus* (L.) Taub. Online, University of Florida Horticultural Sciences Department, World Wide Web.

Tannahill, Reay. 1988. *Food in history.* New York.

Terrell, Edward E., Steven R. Hill, John H. Wiersema, and William E. Rice. 1986. *A checklist of names for 3,000 vascular plants of economic importance.* USDA Agriculture Handbook No. 505. Washington, D.C.

Thames, Shelby F., and Thomas P. Schuman. 1996. New crops or new uses for old crops: Where should the emphasis be? In *Progress in new crops,* ed. J. Janick, 8–18. Alexandria, Va.

Tindall, H. D. 1983. *Vegetables in the tropics.* Westport, Conn.

Tous, Joan, and Louise Ferguson. 1996. Mediterranean fruits. In *Progress in new crops,* ed. J. Janick, 416–30. Alexandria, Va.

Toussaint-Samat, Maguelonne. 1992. *History of food,* trans. Anthea Bell. Cambridge, Mass.

Trager, James. 1995. *The food chronology.* New York.

Ukers, William H. 1936. *The romance of tea: An outline history of tea and tea-drinking through sixteen hundred years.* New York and London.

Uphof, J. C. Thomas. 1968. *Dictionary of economic plants.* New York.

Vaughan, J. G., and C. A. Geissler. 1997. *The new Oxford book of food plants.* Oxford, New York, and Tokyo.

Wagoner, Peggy. 1995. Wild triga intermediate wheatgrass. Online, New Crop Factsheet, Purdue University Center for New Crops and Plant Products, World Wide Web, Sept. 27, 1998.

Walton, Stuart. 1996. *The world encyclopedia of wine.* New York.

Ward, Artemas. 1848–1925. *The grocer's encyclopedia.* New York.

Watson, L., and M. J. Dallwitz. 1992 ff. The families of flowering plants: Descriptions, illustrations, identification, and information retrieval. Online, World Wide Web, May 8, 1998.

Westland, Pamela. 1987. *The encyclopedia of herbs and spices.* London.

Yamaguchi, Mas. 1990. Asian vegetables. In *Advances in new crops,* ed. J. Janick and J. E. Simon, 387–90. Portland, Ore.

Zohary, D., and M. Hopf. 1993. *Domestication of plants: The Old World.* Oxford.

Index of Latin Names

Abelmoschus esculentus – see **Okra**
Abelmoschus manihot – see **Sunset Hibiscus**
Aberia caffra – see **Kai Apple**
Abies balsamea – see **Balsam Fir**
Acacia angustissima – see **Acacia**
Acacia greggii – see **Acacia**
Acacia senegal – see **Acacia**
Acer saccharum – see **Maple Syrup and Maple Sugar**
Achillea millefolium – see **Yarrow**
Achillea millefolium var. *lanulosa* – see **Yarrow**
Acorus calamus – see **Sweet Flag**
Acrocomia, genus – see **Macaw Palm**
Actinidia chinensis – see **Kiwi Fruit**
Adansonia digitata – see **Baobab**
Aegle marmelos – see **Bael Fruit**
Aesculus, genus – see **Buckeye**
Aesculus hippocastanum – see **Chestnut**
Aframomum melegueta – see **Melegueta Pepper**
Agaricus bisporus – see **Mushrooms and Fungi**
Agaricus campestris – see **Mushrooms and Fungi**
Agaricus rodmani – see **Mushrooms and Fungi**
Agave americana – see **Agave**
Agave lecheguilla – see **Lecheguilla**
Agave tequilana – see **Agave**
Agropyron intermedium var. *trichophorum* – see **Wild Triga**
Agropyron repens – see **Couch Grass**
Aleurites moluccana – see **Candlenut**
Alkanna tinctoria – see **Alkanet**
Alliaria officinalis – see **Garlic-Mustard**
Alliaria petiolata – see **Garlic-Mustard**
Allium ascalonicum – see **Shallot(s)**
Allium canadense – see **Garlic**
Allium cepa – see **Onion, Onion Tree**
Allium cepa – see **Shallot(s)** (mentioned)
Allium chinense – see **Rakkyo**
Allium fistulosum – see **Welsh Onion**
Allium oleraceum – see **Garlic**
Allium porrum – see **Leek(s)**
Allium sativum – see **Garlic**
Allium schoenoprasum – see **Chive(s)**
Allium tricoccum – see **Wild Leek(s)**
Allium tuberosum – see **Chinese Chive(s)**
Allium vineale – see **Garlic**
Alocasia cucullata – see **Alocasia**
Alocasia indica – see **Alocasia**
Alocasia macrorrhiza – see **Alocasia**
Alpinia coerulea – see **Wild Ginger**
Alpinia galanga – see **Galangal**

Alpina officinarum – see **Galangal**
Althaea officinalis – see **Mallow**
Amaranthus, genus – see **Callaloo, Goosefoot, Quelites**
Amaranthus caudatus – see **Amaranth**
Amaranthus cruentus – see **Amaranth**
Amaranthus hypochondriacus – see **Amaranth**
Amaranthus tricolor – see **Chinese Amaranth**
Ambrosia, genus – see **Ragweed**
Amelanchier alnifolia – see **Serviceberry**
Amomum cardamomum – see **Cardamom**
Amphicarpa bracteata – see **Hog Peanut**
Amygdalus communis – see **Almond**
Anacardium occidentale – see **Cashew**
Ananas, genus – see **Bromelia**
Ananas comosus – see **Pineapple**
Andropogon furcatus – see **Blue-Stem**
Anemone flaccida – see **Anemone Greens**
Anemone hepatica – see **Anemone Greens**
Anemone hupehensis Hort. Lemoine – see **Anemone Greens**
Anemone narcissiflora – see **Anemone Greens**
Anemone patens – see **Anemone Greens**
Anethum graveolens – see **Dill**
Angelica archangelica – see **Angelica**
Angelica atropurpurea – see **Purplestem Angelica**
Annona, genus – see **Atemoya**
Annona cherimola – see **Cherimoya**
Annona diversifolia – see **Ilama**
Annona muricata – see **Soursop**
Annona purpurea – see **Soncoya**
Annona reticulata – see **Custard Apple**
Annona scleroderma – see **Poshte**
Annona senegalensis – see **Wild Custard Apple**
Annona squamosa – see **Sweetsop**
Anoda cristata – see **Quelites**
Anthemis nobilis – see **Chamomile**
Anthriscus cerefolium – see **Chervil**
Antidesma bunius – see **Bignay**
Antidesma ghaesembilla – see **Bush Currant**
Apios americana – see **Apios**
Apios tuberosa – see **Apios**
Apium graveolens – see **Celery and Celery Root**
Apium graveolens var. *dulce* – see **Celery and Celery Root, Celery Seed**
Apium graveolens var. *rapaceum* – see **Celery and Celery Root**
Apocynum cannabinum – see **Hemp Dogbane**
Arachis hypogaea – see **Peanut**

Dioscorea villosa - see **Wild Yam**
Dioscoreophyllum cumminsii - see **Serendipity Berry**
Diospyros digyna - see **Black Sapote**
Diospyros discolor - see **Mabolo**
Diospyros kaki - see **Persimmon**
Diospyros virginiana - see **Persimmon**
Diplazium esculentum - see **Vegetable-Fern**
Dipteryx odorata - see **Tonka Bean**
Dolichos biflorus - see **Horse Gram**
Dolichos erosus - see **Jícama**
Dovyalis caffra - see **Kai Apple**
Dovyalis hebecarpa - see **Ceylon Gooseberry**
Duboisia hopwoodii - see **Pituri**
Durio zibethinus - see **Durian**

Echinacea, genus - see **Coneflower**
Echinocactus grandis - see **Barrel Cactus**
Echinocereus conglomeratus - see **Pitahaya**
Echinocereus stramineus - see **Pitahaya**
Echinocereus triglochidiatus - see **Pitahaya**
Echinochloa frumentacea - see **Japanese Millet**
Elaeagnus angustifolia - see **Elaeagnus**
Elaeagnus commutata - see **Elaeagnus**
Elaeagnus philippinensis - see **Elaeagnus**
Elaeagnus pungens - Elaeagnus
Elaeagnus umbellata - see **Elaeagnus**
Elaeocarpus denatus - see **Hinau Berry**
Elaeocarpus grandis - see **Quandong**
Eleocharis dulcis - see **Water Chestnut**
Elettaria cardamomum - see **Cardamom**
Eleusine coracana - see **Finger Millet**
Eleusine indica - see **Goosegrass**
Elytrigia intermedia ssp. *barbulata* - see **Wild Triga**
Elytrigia repens - see **Couch Grass**
Ensete ventricosum - see **Ensete**
Ephedra nevadensis - see **Mormon Tea**
Ephedra trifurca - see **Mormon Tea**
Ephedra viridis - see **Mormon Tea**
Epigaea repens - see **Trailing Arbutus**
Equisetum arvense - see **Horsetail Plant**
Eragrostis abyssinica - see **Tef**
Eragrostis tef - see **Tef**
Eremocitrus glauca - see **Australian Desert Lime**
Erica, genus - see **Heather**
Erica tetralix - see **Bog Heather**
Erigeron canadensis - see **Horseweed**
Eriobotrya japonica - see **Loquat**
Eriodictyon californicum - see **Yerba Santa**
Erioglossum rubiginosum - see **Mertajam**
Eriogonum longifolium - see **Indian Turnip**
Eruca sativa - see **Arugula**
Ervum ervilia - see **Bitter Vetch**
Eryngium foetidum - see **Long Coriander**
Eryngium maritimum - see **Sea Holly**
Erythrina berteroana - see **Coral Bean**
Erythrina fusca - see **Coral Bean**
Erythrina poeppigiana - see **Coral Bean**
Erythrina rubinervia - see **Coral Bean**
Erythroxylum coca - see **Coca**
Eucalyptus viminalis - see **Manna Gum**
Euchema, genus - see **Agar**
Eugenia brasiliensis - see **Grumichama**
Eugenia capensis - see **Myrtle Apple**
Eugenia corynantha - see **Sour Cherry**
Eugenia cumini - see **Jambolan**
Eugenia dombeyi - see **Grumichama**
Eugenia jambolana - see **Jambolan Plum**

Eugenia jambos - see **Rose Apple**
Eugenia javanica - see **Java Apple**
Eugenia luschnathiana - see **Pitomba**
Eugenia malaccensis - see **Malay Apple**
Eugenia myrtifolia - see **Brush Cherry**
Eugenia polyantha - see **Duan Salam**
Eugenia stipitata - see *Acraçá-Boi*
Eugenia uniflora - see **Pitanga**
Eulophia, genus - see **Salep**
Eupatorium, genus - see **Boneset**
Eupatorium dalea - see **Boneset**
Eupatorium perfoliatum - see **Boneset**
Eupatorium rugosum - see **Boneset**
Euphorbia esula - see **Leafy Spurge**
Euphoria longana - see **Longan**
Exocarpus cuppressiformis - see **Native Cherry**

Fagopyrum esculentum - see **Buckwheat**
Fagus grandifolia - see **Beechnut**
Fagus sylvatica - see **Beechnut**
Feijoa sellowiana - see **Feijoa**
Ferocactus wislizenii - see **Barrel Cactus**
Feronia limonia - see **Indian Wood-Apple**
Ferula, genus - see **Silphium**
Ferula assa-foetida - see **Asafetida**
Ficus carica - see **Fig**
Fistulina hepatica - see **Mushrooms and Fungi**
Flacourtia indica - see **Governor's Plum**
Flacourtia inermis - see **Thornless Rukam**
Flacourtia rukam - see **Indian Prune**
Flammulina velutipes - see **Enokitake, Mushrooms and Fungi**
Foeniculum vulgare - see **Fennel**
Fortunella, genus - see **Citrangequat, Limequat, Orangequat**
Fortunella crassifolia - see **Kumquat**
Fortunella japonica - see **Kumquat**
Fortunella margarita - see **Kumquat**
Fragaria, genus - see **Berries**
Fragaria ananassa - see **Strawberry**
Fragaria chiloensis - see **Wild Strawberry**
Fragaria moschata - see **Wild Strawberry**
Fragaria vesca - see **Wild Strawberry**
Fragaria vesca var. *americana* - see **Wild Strawberry**
Fragaria vesca var. *momophylla* - see **Wild Strawberry**
Frasera speciosa - see **Gentian**
Fucus, genus - see **Seaweed**
Fusanus acuminatus - see **Quandong**

Galega officinalis - see **Goat's-Rue**
Galinsoga parviflora - see **Quelites**
Galipea officinalis - see **Angostura**
Galium aparine - see **Goosegrass**
Galium odoratum - see **Woodruff**
Galium verum - see **Lady's Bedstraw**
Garcinia atroviridis - see **Asam Gelugur**
Garcinia bombroniana - see **Assam Aur Aur**
Garcinia livingstonei - see **Imbé**
Garcinia mangostana - see **Mangosteen**
Gaultheria procumbens - see **Wintergreen**
Gaultheria shallon - see **Salal**
Gaylussacia, genus - see **Huckleberry**
Gelidium, genus - see **Agar**
Genipa americana - see **Genipap**
Gentiana lutea - see **Gentian**
Geum urbanum - see **Herb Bennet**
Gigartina mammillosa - see **Carrageen and Carrageenin**
Ginkgo biloba - see **Ginkgo Nut**

Glechoma hederacea - see **Ground Ivy**
Gleditsia triacanthos - see **Honey Locust**
Glycine max - see **Beans, Bean Sprouts, Soybean**
Glycyrrhiza glabra - see **Licorice**
Glycyrrhiza Lepidota - see **Licorice**
Gossypium, genus - see **Cottonseed Oil**
Grewia asiatica - see **Phalsa**
Grewia retusifolia - see **Turkey Fruit**
Grindelia robusta - see **Gum Plant**
Grindelia squarrosa - see **Gum Plant**
Guazuma ulmifolia - see **Mutamba**
Guilielma gasipaës - see **Pejebaye**
Guilielma utilis - see **Pejebaye**
Guizotia abyssinica - see **Niger Seed**
Gyrophora esculenta - see **Manna**

Hamamelis virginiana - see **Witch-Hazel**
Hancornia speciosa - see **Mangaba**
Harpephyllum caffrum - see **Kaffir Plum**
Helianthus annuus - see **Sunflower Oil and Seed**
Helianthus giganteus - see **Indian Potato**
Helianthus tuberosus - see **Jerusalem Artichoke**
Heliocereus, genus - see **Pitahaya**
Hemerocallis fulva - see **Day Lily**
Heracleum sphondylium - see **Cow Parsnip**
Hibiscus esculentus - see **Okra**
Hibiscus manihot - see **Sunset Hibiscus**
Hibiscus moscheutos - see **Amberseed**
Hibiscus sabdariffa - see **Roselle**
Hippophaë rhamnoides - see **Sea Buckthorn**
Hordeum jubatum - see **Wild Barley**
Hordeum pusillum - see **Wild Barley**
Hordeum vulgare - see **Barley, Wild Barley**
Hosta, genus - see **Day Lily**
Hovenia dulcis - see **Japanese Raisin Tree**
Humulus lupulus - see **Hop(s)**
Hydrangea macrophylla - see **Big-Leafed Hydrangea**
Hydrocotyle, genus - see **Pennywort**
Hydrophyllum canadense - see **Waterleaf**
Hydrophyllum occidentale - see **Waterleaf**
Hylocereus undatas - see **Pitahaya**
Hypericum perforatum - see **Saint-John's-Wort**
Hypericum pyramidatum - see **Saint-John's-Wort**
Hyphaene thebaica - see **Dom Palm**
Hyptis albida - see **Hyptis**
Hyptis emoryi - see **Hyptis**
Hyptis suaveolens - see **Hyptis**
Hyssopus officinalis - see **Hyssop**

Ilex cassine - see **Dahoon Holly**
Ilex glabra - see **Winterberry**
Ilex opaca - see **Hollyberry**
Ilex paraguariensis - see **Hollyberry, Yerba Maté**
Ilex verticillata - see **Winterberry**
Ilex vomitoria - see **Yaupon**
Illicium verum - see **Star-Anise**
Impatiens capensis - see **Jewelweed**
Inga vera - see **Ice-Cream Bean**
Inocarpus edulis - see **Polynesian Chestnut**
Inula helenium - see **Elecampane**
Ipomoea aquatica - see **Swamp Cabbage**
Ipomoea batatas - see **Boniato, Sweet Potato**
Iridaceae germanica - see **Iris**
Irvingia gabonensis - see **Duika**
Iva annua - see **Sumpweed**

Jasminum, genus - see **Jasmine**

Jatropha curcas - see **Physic Nut**
Juglans cinerea - see **Walnut**
Juglans nigra - see **Walnut**
Juglans regia - see **Walnut**
Juniperus communis - see **Juniper Berry**

Kaempferia galanga - see **Galangal**
Kerstingiella geocarpa - see **Hausa Groundnut**

Lablab niger - see **Hyacinth Bean**
Lablab purpureus - see **Hyacinth Bean**
Lactuca sativa var. *capitata* - see **Lettuce**
Lactuca sativa var. *crispa* - see **Lettuce**
Lactuca sativa var. *longifolia* - see **Lettuce**
Lactuca scariola - see **Prickly Lettuce**
Lactuca serriola - see **Lettuce, Prickly Lettuce**
Lagenaria siceraria - see **Bottle Gourd, Calabash**
Laminaria japonica - see **Kelp, Seaweed**
Landolphia kirkii - see **Wild Peach**
Laninaria, genus - see **Seaweed**
Lansium domesticum - see **Langsat**
Larrea mexicana - see **Creosote Bush**
Larrea tridentata - see **Creosote Bush**
Lathraea squamaria - see **Toothwort** (mentioned)
Lathyrus, genus - see **Everlasting Pea**
Lathyrus latifolius - see **Everlasting Pea**
Lathyrus maritimus - see **Beach Pea**
Lathyrus odoratus - see **Beach Pea**
Lathyrus sativus - see **Chickling Vetch**
Lathyrus tuberosus - see **Earth Nut**
Laurus nobilis - see **Bay Leaf**
Lavandula angustifolia - see **Lavender**
Lavandula officinalis - see **Lavender**
Lecanora esculenta - see **Manna**
Lecythis, genus - see **Sapucaia Nut**
Lemairocereus queretaroensis - see **Pitahaya**
Lens esculenta - see **Lentil(s)**
Lentinus edodes - see **Mushrooms and Fungi**
Lepidium meyenii - see **Maca**
Lepidium sativum - see **Cress**
Leucaena leucocephala - see **Leucaena**
Leucopogon richei - see **Australian Currant**
Levisticum officinale - see **Lovage**
Lewisia rediviva - see **Bitter Root**
Liabum glabrum - see **Quelites**
Licania platypus - see **Sunsapote**
Lilium tigrinum - see **Tiger Lily**
Limonia acidissima - see **Indian Wood-Apple**
Lindera benzoin - see **Spicebush**
Linum usitatissimum - see **Flax Seed**
Lippia citriodora - see **Lemon Verbena**
Liquidambar styraciflua - see **Sweet Gum**
Litchi chinensis - see **Litchi**
Lolium multiflorum - see **Ryegrass**
Lolium perenne - see **Ryegrass**
Lolium temulentum - see **Ryegrass**
Lonicera japonica - see **Honeysuckle**
Lotus tetragonolobus - see **Asparagus Pea**
Luffa acutangula - see **Angled Luffa**
Luffa aegyptiaca - see **Angled Luffa**
Lupinus albus - see **Beans**
Lupinus angustifolius - see **Beans**
Lupinus luteus - see **Beans**
Lupinus mutabilis - see **Andean Lupin**
Lycium andersonii - see **Matrimony Vine**
Lycium chinense - see **Matrimony Vine**
Lycopersicon esculentum - see **Tomato**

Macadamia integrifolia – see **Macadamia Nut**
Macadamia tetraphylla – see **Macadamia Nut**
Macrocystis, genus – see **Seaweed**
Macrocystis pyrifera – see **Kelp**
Madhuca longifolia – see **Mahua**
Malpighia glabra – see **Acerola**
Malus coronaria – see **Crab Apple**
Malus domestica – see **Apple**
Mammea americana – see **Mammee**
Mandragora officinarum – see **Mandrake**
Mangifera foetida – see **Horse Mango**
Mangifera indica – see **Mango**
Mangifera odorata – see **Kuini**
Manihot esculenta – see **Manioc**
Manilkara bidentata – see **Mimusops**
Manilkara concolor – see **Zulu Milkberry**
Manilkara discolor – see **Forest Milkberry**
Manilkara zapota – see **Sapodilla**
Maranta arundinacea – see **Arrowroot**
Marasmius oreades – see **Mushrooms and Fungi**
Marlierea edulis – see **Cambucá**
Marrubium vulgare – see **Horehound**
Matteucia struthiopteris – see **Fiddlehead Fern**
Medeola virginiana – see **Indian Cucumber**
Medicago sativa – see **Alfalfa**
Melaleuca cajuputi – see **Cajeput**
Melaleuca quinquenervia – see **Cajeput**
Melia azedarach – see **Chinaberry**
Melicoccus bijugatus – see **Spanish Lime**
Melilotus officinalis – see **Sweet Clover**
Melissa officinalis – see **Bee Balm, Lemon Balm**
Melocactus communis – see **Melon Cactus**
Mentha arvensis – see **Corn Mint**
Mentha piperita – see **Mint**
Mentha rotundifolia – see **Mint**
Mentha spicata – see **Mint**
Mentzelia pumila – see **Moonflower**
Menyanthes trifoliata – see **Bog Myrtle**
Mesembryanthemum crystallinum – see **Ice Plant**
Mespilus germanica – see **Medlar**
Metrosideros fulgens – see **Rata Vine**
Metroxylon, genus – see **Sago**
Microcitrus australasica – see **Native Lime**
Microseris lanceolata – see **Yam Daisy**
Microseris scapigera – see **Yam Daisy**
Mimusops elata – see **Mimusops**
Mimusops elengi – see **Mimusops**
Mimusops parvifolia – see **Mimusops**
Mimusops sieberii – see **Mimusops**
Minthostachys mollis – see **Minthostachys**
Minthostachys verticillata – see **Minthostachys**
Mirabilis expansa – see **Mauka**
Momordica balsamina – see **Balsam Apple**
Momordica charantia – see **Bitter Melon, Melons**
Monarda, genus – see **Bergamot**
Monarda didyma – see **Bee Balm**
Monstera deliciosa – see **Monstera**
Montia perfoliata – see **Purslane**
Morchella deliciosa – see **Morel**
Morchella esculenta – see **Morel, Mushrooms and Fungi**
Morinda, genus – see **Morinda**
Morinda citrifolia – see **Morinda**
Moringa oleifera – see **Benoil Tree**
Moringa pterygosperma – see **Benoil Tree**
Morus alba – see **Mulberry**
Morus nigra – see **Mulberry**
Morus rubra – see **Mulberry**

Muntingia calabura – see **Capulin**
Murraya koenigii – see **Curry Leaf**
Musa ensete – see **Ensete**
Musa paradisiaca – see **Banana, Banana Flower, Plantain**
Musa sapientum – see **Hawaiian Plantain**
Myrciaria cauliflora – see **Jaboticaba**
Myrica cerifera – see **Bayberry**
Myrica gale – see **Bog Myrtle**
Myrica pensylvanica – see **Bayberry**
Myristica fragrans – see **Mace, Nutmeg**
Myristica officinalis – see **Mace**
Myrrhis odorata – see **Cicely**
Myrtus communis – see **Myrtle**
Myrtus ugni – see **Chilean Guava Myrtle**

Nasturtium officinale – see **Watercress**
Nelumbo lutea – see **Lotus**
Nelumbo nucifera – see **Lotus**
Nepeta cataria – see **Catnip**
Nephelium lappaceum – see **Rambutan**
Nephelium mutabile – see **Pulasan**
Nereocystis, genus – see **Seaweed**
Nicotiana, genus – see **Tobacco**
Nigella sativa – see **Nigella**
Nipa, genus – see **Nipa Palm**
Nopalea coccinellifera – see **Nopales**
Nopalea cochinellifera – see **Nopales**
Nuphar, genus – see **Lotus**
Nymphaea lotus – see **Lotus**
Nypa, genus – see **Nipa Palm**
Nyssa sylvatica – see **Black Gum**

Ocimum americanum – see **Basil**
Ocimum basilicum – see **Basil**
Ocimum minimum – see **Basil**
Oenothera biennis – see **Evening Primrose**
Olea europaea – see **Olive**
Onorpordum, genus – see **Thistle**
Opuntia, genus – see **Nopales, Prickly Pear**
Orbignya cohune – see **Cohune Palm**
Orchis, genus – see **Salep**
Origanum dictamnus – see **Dittany**
Origanum marjorana – see **Marjoram and Oregano**
Origanum onites – see **Marjoram and Oregano**
Origanum vulgare – see **Marjoram and Oregano**
Orontium aquaticum – see **Golden Club**
Oryza barthii – see **African Rice**
Oryza glaberrima – see **African Rice**
Oryza sativa – see **Rice**
Oryzopsis aspera – see **Ricegrass**
Oryzopsis hymenoides – see **Ricegrass**
Osmanthus americanus – see **Osmanthus**
Oxalis acetosella – see **Wood Sorrel**
Oxalis tuberosa – see **Oca**
Oxalis violacea – see **Wood Sorrel**
Oxydendrum arboreum – see **Sourwood**
Oxyria digyna – see **Mountain Sorrel**

Pachira aquatica – see **Malabar Nut**
Pachyrhizus ahipa – see **Ajipa**
Pachyrhizus erosus – see **Jícama**
Pachyrhizus tuberosus – see **Jícama** (mentioned)
Paliurus spina-christi – see **Christ's-Thorn Fruit**
Palmaria palmata – *see* **Dulce**
Panax quinquefolium – see **Ginseng**
Panax schinseng – see **Ginseng**

Panax trifolium - see Ginseng
Pandanus, genus - see Pandanus
Pandanus veitchii - see Striped Screw-Pine
Panicum, genus - see Millet
Papaver somniferum - see Poppy Seed
Parkia africana - see African Locust
Parkia biglandulosa - see African Locust
Parkia biglobosa - see Parkia
Parkia filicoidea - see African Locust Bean
Parkia speciosa - see Parkia
Parmentiera aculeata - see Cuajilote
Parmentiera edulis - see Cuajilote
Passiflora edulis - see Maypop, Passion Fruit
Passiflora incarnata - see Maypop
Passiflora quadrangularis - see Passion Fruit
Passiflora quandrangularis - see Giant Granadilla
Pastinaca sativa - see Parsnip
Paullinia cupana - see Guaraná
Peltandra virginica - see Arrow Arum
Pentaclethra macrophylla - see Oil-Bean Tree
Peperomia obtusifolia - see Peperomia
Pereskia aculeata - see Barbados Gooseberry
Pereskiopsis aquosa - see Tuna de Agua
Perideridia parishii - see Indian Potato
Perilla arguta - see Beefsteak Plant
Perilla frutescens - see Perilla
Perilla ocimoides - see Perilla
Persea americana - see Avocado
Petalostemon candidum - see Prairie Clover
Petalostemon oligophyllum - see Prairie Clover
Petroselinum crispum - see Parsley
Petroselinum crispum var. *tuberosum* - see Hamburg
    Parsley
Phaeomeria magnifica - see Torch Ginger
Phalaris canariensis - see Maygrass
Phalaris caroliniana - see Maygrass
Phaseolus, genus - see Beans, Legumes
Phaseolus aconitifolius - see Moth Bean
Phaseolus acutifolius - see Beans, Tepary Bean
Phaseolus angularis - see Azuki Bean, Beans
Phaseolus aureus - see Beans, Bean Sprouts, Lentil(s),
    Mung Bean
Phaseolus calcaratus - see Rice Bean
Phaseolus coccineus - see Beans
Phaseolus lunatus - see Beans
Phaseolus mungo - see Lentil(s)
Phaseolus trinervius - see Jerusalem Pea
Phaseolus vulgaris - see Beans, Cannellini Bean,
    Legumes, Navy Bean, Turtle Bean
Philoxerus vermicularis - see Samphire
Phoenix dactylifera - see Date
Phoradendron juniperinum - see Juniper Mistletoe
Phragmites australis - see Common Reed
Phragmites communis - see Common Reed
Phyllanthus acidus - see Otaheite Gooseberry
Phyllanthus emblica - see Amalaka
Physalis, genus - see Cape Gooseberry, Tomato
Physalis ixocarpa - see Cape Gooseberry, Tomatillo
Physalis minima - see Wild Gooseberry
Physalis peruviana - see Cape Gooseberry
Physalis pubescens - see Capulin
Phytolacca americana - see Pokeweed
Picea, genus - see Spruce
Pimenta dioica - see Allspice
Pimpinella anisum - see Anise
Pinus, genus - see Pine Nut, White Pine
Pinus strobus - see White Pine

Piper cubeba - see Tailed Pepper
Piper longum - see Indian Long Pepper
Piper methysticum - see Kava
Piper nigrum - see Peperomia (mentioned),
    Pepper(corns)
Piper officinarum - see Javanese Long Pepper
Piper retrofractum - see Javanese Long Pepper
Pistacia lentiscus - see Mastic Tree
Pistacia vera - see Pistachio Nut
Pisum arvense - see Pea(s)
Pisum sativum - see Lentil(s), Pea(s), Pea Leaf
Pisum sativum var. *macrocarpon* - see Sugar Pea
Pithecellobium dulce - see Pithecellobium
Pithecellobium flexicaule - see Pithecellobium
Pithecellobium jiringa - see Jering
Pithecellobium saman - see Rain Tree
Planchonella pohlmaniana - see Big Green Plum
Plantago, genus - see Plantain
Platonia esculenta - see Bacurí
Platonia insignis - see Bacurí
Plectranthus esculentus - see Kaffir Potato
Pleiogynium solandri - see Burdekin Plum
Pleiogynium timoriense - see Burdekin Plum
Pleurotus ostreatus - see Mushrooms and Fungi, Oyster
    Mushroom
Podophyllum peltatum - see Mayapple
Polygonatum, genus - see Solomon's-Seal
Polygonum bistorta - see Knotweed and Smartweed
Polygonum bistortoides - see Knotweed and Smartweed
Polygonum coccineum - see Knotweed and Smartweed
Polygonum convolvulus - see Knotweed and Smartweed
Polygonum cuspidatum - see Knotweed and Smartweed
Polygonum douglasii - see Knotweed and Smartweed
Polygonum hydropiper - see Knotweed and Smartweed
Polygonum persicaria - see Knotweed and Smartweed
Polygonum viviparum - see Knotweed and Smartweed
Polymnia sonchifolia - see Yacón
Polystichum munitum - see Giant Holly Fern
Poncirus trifoliata - see Citrangequat, Trifoliate Orange
Populus, genus - see Poplar
Porphyra laciniata - see Laver, Seaweed
Porphyra tenera - see Laver, Seaweed
Porphyra umbilicalis - see Laver, Seaweed
Porphyra vulgaris - see Laver
Portulaca oleracea - see Purslane
Potentilla anserina - see Goosegrass
Poterium sanguisorba - see Burnet
Pouteria caimito - see Abiu
Pouteria campechiana - see Canistel
Pouteria obovata - see Lucuma
Pouteria sapota - see Mamey Sapote
Pouteria sericea - see Wongay
Pouteria viridis - see Green Sapote
Praecitrullus fistulosus - see Round Gourd
Primula veris - see Cowslip
Proboscidea fragrans - see Unicorn Plant
Proboscidea louisianica - see Unicorn Plant
Proboscidea parviflora - see Unicorn Plant
Prosopis alba - see Algarrobo
Prosopis cineraria - see Shum
Prosopis juliflora var. *glandulosa* - see Mesquite
Prosopis juliflora var. *juliflora* - see Mesquite
Prosopis pallida - see Algarrobo
Prosopis pubescens - see Mesquite
Prosopis velutina - see Mesquite
Prunus americana - see Hog Plum
Prunus amygdalus - see Almond

Prunus armeniaca – see **Apricot**
Prunus avium – see **Cherry**
Prunus besseyi – see **Sand Cherry**
Prunus capollin – see **Capulin**
Prunus capuli – see **Capulin**
Prunus cerasifera – see **Cherry Plum**
Prunus cerasus – see **Cherry, Sour Cherry**
Prunus domestica – see **Cherry Plum, Plum**
Prunus dulcis – see **Almond**
Prunus ilicifolia – see **Chimaja**
Prunus insititia – see **Damson Plum**
Prunus laurocerasus – see **Cherry Laurel**
Prunus maritima – see **Beach Plum**
Prunus persica – see **Nectarine, Peach**
Prunus pumila – see **Sand Cherry**
Prunus salicifolia – see **Capulin**
Prunus salicina – see **Japanese Plum, Plum**
Prunus serotina – see **Capulin**
Prunus spinosa – see **Haw, Sloe**
Prunus virginiana – see **Cherry, Chokeberry** (mentioned),
     Chokecherry
Psidium angulatum – see **Araçá-Pera**
Psidium cattleianum – see **Strawberry Guava**
Psidium friedrichsthalianum – see **Wild Guava**
Psidium guajava – see **Guava, Native Guava** (mentioned)
Psophocarpus tetragonolobus – see **Asparagus Pea**
     (mentioned)
Psophocarpus tetragonolobus – see **Beans, Winged
     Bean**
Psoralea, genus – see **Indian Turnip**
Psoralea esculenta – see **Breadroot**
Ptelea trifoliata – see **Hoptree**
Pteridium aquilinum – see **Bracken Fern**
Pueraria lobata – see **Kudzu**
Pueraria thunbergiana – see **Kudzu**
Punica granatum – see **Pomegranate**
Pyrus communis – see **Pear**
Pyrus malus – see **Apple**
Pyrus pyrifolia – see **Asian Pear**
Pyrus ussuriensis – see **Asian Pear**

Quercus alba – see **Acorn**

Raphanus sativus – see **Daikon, Radish**
Ratibida columnifera – see **Coneflower**
Rhamnus carolinianus – see **Buckthorn**
Rhamnus crocea – see **Buckthorn**
Rheedia brasiliensis – see **Bakupari**
Rheedia macrophylla – see **Bacuripari**
Rheum officinale – see **Rhubarb**
Rheum rhabarbarum – see **Rhubarb**
Rhizophora mangle – see **Mangrove**
Rhizophora mucronata – see **Mangrove**
Rhodomyrtus psidoides – see **Native Guava**
Rhodymenia palmata – see **Dulse**
Rhus corioria – see **Sumac Berry**
Rhus glabra – see **Smooth Sumac**
Rhus typhina – see **Sumac Berry**
Ribes, genus – see **Berries, Currant(s)**
Ribes grossularia – see **Gooseberry**
Ribes nigrum – see **Black Curran, Currant(s)**
Ribes pinetorum – see **Gooseberry**
Ribes rubrum – see **Currant(s)**
Ribes sanguineum – see **Currant(s)**
Ribes sativum – see **Currant(s)**
Ribes uva-crispa – see **Gooseberry**
Ribes wolfi – see **Gooseberry**

Ricinodendron rautanenii – see **Mongongo**
Ricinus communis – see **Castorbean**
Robinia pseudoacacia – see **Locust**
Rollinia deliciosa – see **Biribá**
Rosa canina – see **Rose Hip(s)**
Rosa rugosa – see **Rose Hip(s)**
Rosmarinus officinalis – see **Rosemary**
Rubus, genus – see **Berries, Blackberry Boysenberry,
     Bramble(s), Raspberry, Youngberry**
Rubus caesius – see **Dewberry**
Rubus chamaemorus – see **Cloudberry**
Rubus hispidus – see **Dewberry**
Rubus idaeus – see **Raspberry**
Rubus illecebrosus – see **Strawberry-Raspberry**
Rubus leucodermis – see **Raspberry**
Rubus loganobaccus – see **Boysenberry, Loganberry**
Rubus phoenicolasius – see **Japanese Wineberry**
Rubus spectabilis – see **Salmonberry**
Rubus strigosus – see **Raspberry**
Rudbeckia laciniata – see **Coneflower**
Rumex acetosa – see **Sorrel**
Rumex articus – see **Sorrel**
Rumex crispus – see **Curled Dock**
Rumex hydrolapathum – see **Sorrel**
Rumex patientia – see **Sorrel**
Rumex scutatus – see **Sorrel**
Ruta graveolens – see **Rue**

Sabal palmetto – see **Heart(s) of Palm**
Saccharum officinarum – see **Sugarcane**
Sagittaria latifolia – see **Arrowhead**
Sagittaria sinensis – see **Arrowhead**
Salacca edulis – see **Salak**
Salicornia europaea – see **Glasswort**
Salicornia herbacea – see **Glasswort**
Salicornia stricta – see **Glasswort**
Salix alba – see **White Willow, Willow**
Salvia columbariae – see **Chia**
Salvia hispanica – see **Chia**
Salvia officinalis – see **Sage**
Salvia sclarea – see **Clary**
Sambucus canadensis – see **Elderberry**
Sambucus coerulea – see **Elderberry**
Sambucus nigra – see **Elderberry**
Sandoricul indicum – see **Sentul**
Sandoricum koetjape – see **Sentul**
Sanguisorba officinalis – see **Burnet** (mentioned)
Sapindus marginatus – see **Soapberry**
Sapindus saponaria – see **Soapberry**
Sapium sebiferum – see **Chinese Tallow Tree**
Sassafras albidum – see **Sassafras**
Satureja hortensis – see **Savory**
Satureja montana – see **Savory**
Satureja vulgaris – see **Basil**
Sauropus androgynus – see **Sweet-Shoot**
Schinus molle – see **Mastic Tree**
Scirpus fluviatilis – see **Bulrush**
Sclerocarya caffra – see **Marula Plum**
Scorzonera hispanica – see **Scorzonera**
Secale, genus – see **Triticale**
Secale cereale – see **Rye**
Sechium edule – see **Chayote**
Sedum acre – see **Stonecrop**
Sedum collinum – see **Stonecrop**
Sedum reflexum – see **Stonecrop**
Sedum roseum – see **Stonecrop**
Sesamum alatum – see **Tacoutta**

Turnera diffusa - see **Damiana**
Tussilago farfara - see **Coltsfoot**
Typha, genus - see **Cattail**
Ullucus tuberosus - see **Ulluco**

Ulmus fulva - see **Slippery Elm**
Ulmus rubra - see **Slippery Elm**
Ulva lactuca - see **Sea Lettuce**
Undaria pinnatifida - see **Seaweed**
Urtica dioica - see **Nettle(s)**
Ustilago maydis - see **Huitlacoche**

Vaccinium, genus - see **Berries, Blueberry**
Vaccinium angustifolium - see **Blueberry**
Vaccinium corymbosum - see **Blueberry**
Vaccinium macrocarpum - see **Cranberry**
Vaccinium myrtillus - see **Bilberry**
Vaccinium oxycoccus - see **Cranberry**
Vaccinium vitis-idaea - see **Lingonberry**
Valeriana edulis - see **Valerian**
Valeriana officinalis - see **Valerian**
Valerianella, genus - see **Cornsalad, Goosefoot**
Valerianella locusta - see **Cornsalad**
Valerianella olitoria - see **Cornsalad**
Vanilla fragrans - see **Vanilla**
Vanilla planifolia - see **Vanilla**
Vanilla tahitensis - see **Vanilla**
Vaupesia cataractarum - see **Mahawasoo**
Verbena hastata - see **Blue Vervain**
Veronica americana - see **Brooklime**
Veronica beccabunga - see **Brooklime**
Viburnum prunifolium - see **Black Haw**
Viburnum trilobum - see **Highbush Cranberry**
Vicia, genus - see **Tufted Vetch, Vetch**
Vicia americana - see **Vetch**
Vicia cracca - see **Tufted Vetch**
Vicia ervilia - see **Bitter Vetch**
Vicia faba - see **Beans, Fava Bean, Vetch**
Vicia gigantea - see **Vetch**
Vicia sativa - see **Vetch**
Vigna aconitifolia - see **Moth Bean**
Vigna lancelota - see **Maloga Bean**
Vigna sesquipedalis - see **Cowpea**
Vigna sinensis - see **Cowpea**
Vigna subterranea - see **Bambara Groundnut**
Vigna umbellata - see **Rice Bean**
Vigna unguiculata - see **Beans, Catjang, Cowpea**
Vinca major - see **Periwinkle**

Vinca minor - see **Periwinkle**
Vinca rosea - see **Periwinkle**
Vitex, genus - see **Chaste Tree**
Vitex agnus-castus - see **Chaste Tree**
Vitis, genus - see **Grape Leaf, Grapes, Raisin**
Vitis labrusca - see **Catawba (Grape), Concord Grape, Fox Grape, Grapes**
Vitis rotundifolia - see **Muscadine**
Vitis vinifera - see **Alicante Bouschet, Cabernet, Chardonnay, Cinsault, French Colombard, Gamay, Gewürztraminer, Grapes, Grenache, Lambrusco, Malvasia, Mavrodaphne, Merlot, Muscat, Nebbiolo, Palomino, Pedro Ximénez, Petite Sirah, Pinot Blanc, Pinot Meunier, Pinot Noir, Riesling, Sangiovese, Sauvignon Blanc, Sémillon, Silvaner, Syrah, Tempranillo, Thompson Seedless (Grape), Trebbiano, Viognier, Zinfandel**
Voandzeia geocarpa - see **Hausa Groundnut**
Voandzeia subterranea - see **Bambara Groundnut**
Volvariella volvacea - see **Mushrooms and Fungi**

Wasabia japonica - see **Wasabi**

Xanthium commune - see **Cocklebur**
Xanthium strumarium - see **Cocklebur**
Xanthosoma atrovirens - see **Malanga**
Xanthosoma sagittifolium - see **Malanga**
Xanthosoma violaceum - see **Malanga**
Ximenia americana - see **Tallow Wood Plum**
Ximenia caffra - see **Sour Plum**

Yucca aloifolia - see **Spanish Bayonet**
Yucca elephantipes - see **Spanish Bayonet**
Yucca filamentosa - see **Yucca**

Zamia integrifolia - see **Zamia**
Zanthoxylum piperitum - see **Sichuan Peppercorn**
Zea mays - see **Maize**
Zingiber mioga - see **Myoga Ginger**
Zingiber officinale - see **Ginger, Wild Ginger** (mentioned)
Zingiber zerumbet - see **Wild Ginger** (mentioned)
Zizania aquatica - see **Water Bamboo** (mentioned), **Wild Rice**
Zizania latifolia - see **Water Bamboo**
Zizia aurea - see **Alexander**
Ziziphus spina-christi - see **Christ's-Thorn Fruit**
Ziziphus jujuba - see **Jujube**
Ziziphus mauritiana - see **Desert Apple**

Name Index

Subject Index

About This Index

All plant and animal species appear under both their common name and their scientific (Latin) name. For example, the common pea is listed under *pea(s)* as well as *Pisum sativum*. The page citations given under the common names are for the major discussions of the food. Detailed subentries are found under the common name only and generally will not be duplicated under the scientific name.

The common name for any one species, such as *pea*, may also refer to many other species that are not *Pisum sativum*. In these cases the species most widely known by the common name is indicated by the subheading *common* before the Latin name. For example, under the main entry *pea(s)* are also such subheadings as *beach* (*Lathryus maritimus*), *blackeyed* (*Vigna* spp.), as well as the *common* (*Pisum sativum*).

In addition, the index subsumes entries under both individual countries and geographical regions. Thus, there are entries for Italy as well as for Europe, southern. Regions may also sometimes overlap, such as *Oceania*, *Pacific Islands*, and *Hawaiian Islands*. This is because of differences in the way the various essays discussed geographical regions and also because of changes in the names and boundaries of geographical regions over time.

A

abaca fiber (*Musa textilis*), 176
abalone
    in Chile, 1258
    farming of, modern, 467
    in Japan, 464
        culture of, 462
    in Korean archeological sites, 1187
    in North America (post-Columbian), 1312
abalong (cocoyam, *Colocasia esculenta*), 1760. *See also* cocoyam
abata kola (kola nut, *Cola acuminata*), 1797. *See also* kola nut
Abbassids, 1143
Abelmoschus esculentus (okra), 1824. *See also* okra
Abelmoschus manihot (= *Hibiscus manihot*, sunset hibiscus), 1861
Abies balsamea (balsam fir), 1726

abiu (*Pouteria cainito*), 1713
abóbora (*calabaza*, *Cucurbita moschata*), 1742
abol, 205
Aboriginal Australians (Aborigines). *See* Australian Aborigines
abortion
    iodine deficiency and, 803–804
    spontaneous, vitamin E in, 772
Abrégé du dictionnaire des cas de conscience, 630
absinthe, 661
    hyssop in, 1788
absorption, intestinal. *See* intestinal absorption
Abu Hureyra site (northern Syria), 84, 163
Abydos site, 397
Abyssinian banana (ensete, *Musa ensete*), 1771–1772
acacia (*Acacia* spp.), 1713
    in Australia, 1339
    seeds of, 1340
Acacia angustissima (prairie acacia), 1713

Acacia greggii (catclaw acacia), 1713
Acacia senegal (gum arabic), 1713
academic institutions, lobbyists on, 1636
Académie de Gastronome, 1213
Académie Française, 1213
Académie Royale de Médecine, 1582
Acanthopleura sp. (marine cockroach), 1271
Acanthuridae (surgeonfishes), 54
An Account of Foxglove and Some of its Medical Properties, 846
aceituna (*Simarouba glauca*), 1713
Acer spp. (maple syrup, maple sugar), 1810
    in North America
        post-Columbian, 1310
            19th cent., 1315
        pre-Columbian, 1289, 1296
Acer saccharum (sugar maple), 1810
acerola (*Malpighia glabra*, etc.), 1713. *See also* cherry
acesulfame K, 1679
Acetaria, a Discourse on Sallets, 1222

devilwood (osmanthus, *Osmanthus*), 1827

dewberry (blackberry, *Rubus* spp.), 1733, 1768

dhal (pigeon pea, *Cajanus cajan, C. indicus*), 1834. *See also* pigeon pea

Dhar Tichitt site, 1331

Dharma-Sutra, 1504–1505

Dhina, yam in, 215

Día de los Muertos, 1249

diabetes mellitus, 1078–1084
  adult-onset, in primitive societies, 69
  in ancient history through Middle Ages, 1078–1079
  in celiac disease, 1016
  chromium supplementation for, 859
  and diets
    in the age of insulin therapy, 1081–1082
    current issues of, 1082–1084
  in Pacific Islands, 1363
  in Pima Indians, 1065
  in Renaissance to 1920s, 1079–1081

diabetic diet, exchange system in, 1081

diagenesis, 16
  in isotopic analysis, 17, 59, 61

Dialium guineense (velvet tamarind), 1875

Dialium indicum (velvet tamarind), 1875

Diamante citron (citron, *Citrus medica*), 1757–1758

diamondback terrapin (*Malaclemys terrapin*), in North America
  pre-Columbian, 1290, 1297
  Spanish colonial, 1300

Dianthus spp. (gillyflower), 1778

diarrhea
  E. coli in, 1039–1040
  from fecal contamination, 1033
  geophagia and, 970
  infant, infant formulas in, 1448–1450
  and infectious disease, malnutrition, 1397–1398, 1401
  in marasmus, 979
  from parasites, 66
  in protein-energy malnutrition, 983
  sodium loss in, 852

Diary of a Country Parson, 1370

diasatyrion, 1526

diastases, 619, 623

Dickson Mounds site (Illinois), 68, 924, 1444–1445

Dicksonia antarctica (tree ferns), 1341

Dictamnus albus (dittany, gas plant), 1769

dictionaries, and culinary history, 1372

Dictionary (Johnson), 392

Dictionnaire Encyclopédique des Sciences Médicales, 988

Dictyopteris (*limu lipoa*), essential oils in, 245

Didelphis virginiana (opossum)
  in Caribbean (pre-Columbian), 1263, 1279
  in North America
    pre-Columbian, 1291, 1295, 1297
    Spanish colonial, 1300

Die Natürliche Lebensweise, 1490

Dier-el-Medina site, 1508

diet(s). *See also* specific types, e.g., Rastafarian diet
  of affluence, 739
  of Benedictine monks, 1204–1205
  and cancer, 1086–1087, 1089–1093
  of Catharsusian monks, 1205
  of Cistercian monks, 1205
  complexion and, 1206
  culture in, 1200
  and dental decay, 1569
  direct transference in, 1206
  disease and, 1193
  docrine of signatures in, 1206
  education in, 1200
  European monastic, 1204, 1205
  evolutionary phases of, 13–15
  food-balance data and, 1199
  of Franciscan monks, 1205
  of Gesuati monks, 1205
  healthful, 1193
  humoral theory of, 1205–1207
  of hunter-gatherer (*see* hunter-gatherers)
  as medicine (*see also* medicine/ medications, food as)
    in China (premodern), 1165–1166
  Mediterranean, 1193–1201 (*see also* Mediterranean diet)
  modern, risks of, 1474
  in Near East (ancient-medieval), social status on, 1126, 1127
  and obesity, 1066–1067, 1073
  paleolithic, salt in, 853
  plant-based, 1200 (*see also* Mediterranean diet; vegetarian diet)
  plant carcinogens in, 1474
  of prehistoric agriculturalists, 15
  protein content of, 886–888
  rachitogenic, 764

research methods and, 1198–1199
southern European, 1203–1209 (*see also* Europe, southern)
supplementation of (*see* specific supplements, e.g., vitamin E)
temporary changes in, 60
vegetarian, 1199 (*see also* vegetarian diet)

Diet, Nutrition, and Cancer, 1638

diet books, *Regimen Sanitatis* (1160), 1205

diet-breadth model, 1267–1268

The Diet Death, 1565

Diet for a Small Planet, 1321, 1491, 1563

diet-induced thermogenesis (DIT), 895

diet industry, 1493

dietary allowance, recommended, 1606–1619. *See also* Recommended Dietary Allowance (RDA)

dietary fiber hypothesis, 1689. *See also* fiber

Dietary Fibre in Human Nutritition, 1688

Dietary Goals for the United States, lobbyists on, 1636–1637

dietary gratification, democratization of, 1580

Dietary Guidelines for Americans, 1200
  1980, 1638
  1985, 1638–1639
  1990, 1639
  1995, 1640

dietary reconstruction
  chemical approaches in, 58–62
    anthropological, 60–61
    general approaches and assumptions, 58–59
    samples, instrumentation, and variables, 59–60
    statistical analysis, 62
  cultural taboos in, 58
  from human remains, 16–20
  seasonal availability in, 58
  skeletal remains in, 58, 67–68
    bone chemistry and isotopes, 16–17, 58–62, 163
    dental caries, 19–20, 28, 35, 69
    elements, 16, 59–60
    tooth wear, 17–19, 58
  temporary changes in, 60

dietary supplements
  definitions in, 1685–1686
  multivitamin/minerals, on mental development, 1457
  nonfoods as, 1685–1693
    bioflavonoids, 1686–1688

H

habanero pepper (*Capsicum chinense*), 1716, 1783. *See also* chilli pepper(s)
babichuela (hyacinth bean, *Lablab niger = L. purpureus*), 1788
Hachiya (persimmon, *Diospyros kaki, D. virginiana*), 1833. *See also* persimmon
Hacienda Grande site (Puerto Rico), 1270
haciendas, in coffee production, 650
Hacinebi Tepe site (Turkey), 620
hackberry (*Celtis* spp.), 1783
   C. occidentalis, 1289, 1293, 1294
haddock
   in the Netherlands (1300–1500), 1233
   propagation and release of, in Britain, 461
Hadith, 1503–1504
Hadza (Tanzania), diet in, 64, 65
baidi (*Laminaria japonica*), in China, 232
hairy melon (fuzzy melon, *Benincasa bispida = B. cerifera*), 1775–1776
Haiti. *See also* San Domingue; St. Domingue
   dietary liquids in
      cacao, 638, 643
      coffee, production of, 652
      rum, 660
   infant mortality in, 1285
   malnourishment in, 1285
   pig in, 541
   plant foods in
      chilli pepper (pre-Columbian), 281
      ginger, 1778
      rice (post-Columbian), 1286
      sugar and rum, 660
   population growth in, post-colonial, 1285
   revolution for independence in, 1284
Hajji Firuz site, 730, 1126
hake, in British Isles (1700–1900), 1224
bakusai (Chinese cabbage, *Brassica pekinensis*), 1754–1755
Hallan Cemi site (Turkey), 537
Halmahera, sugarcane in, 438
Hamamelis virginiana (witchhazel), 1883
Hamburg celery (celery, *Apium graveolens*), 1748–1749. *See also* celery
Hamburg parsley (*Petroselinum*

crispum var. *tuberosum*), 1783. *See also* parsley
Hamlin orange (orange, *Citrus sinensis*), 1826. *See also* orange(s), common
Hamwith site (England), 519–520
Hancornia speciosa (mangaba), 1809
Handbook of Geographical and Historical Pathology, 917, 988
Handbook of Vitamins, 1687
Handlist of Italian Cookery Books, 1374
Hanover kale (*Brassica napus*), 1783. *See also* cabbage; kale
Hanover salad (Hanover kale, *Brassica napus*), 1783
Harappa site (Indus Valley), 413, 496, 497, 593
Haratua's pa site, 210
harbor seal, 1298. *See also* seal(s)
hard clam (*Mercenaria* spp.), 1290
hard wheat (wheat, *Triticum aestivum*), 1878. *See also* wheat
hardhead catfish (*Arius felis*), in North America
   pre-Columbian, 1290
   Spanish colonial, 1300
hare. *See also* rabbit
   arctic, 1324
   in British Isles (Roman period), 1218
   Christian prohibitions of, 1503
   as forbidden food, 1499
   in North America (pre-Columbian), 1299
harebell (campanula, *Campanula*), 1743
   in British Isles (prehistoric), 1217
baricot (beans, *Phaseolus* spp.), 1729, 1799–1800
baricot riz (rice bean, *Phaseolus calcaratus =* Vigna umbellata), 1844
harlock (burdock, *Arctium lappa*), 1740
Harpephyllum caffrum (kaffir plum), 1795
Harper Hybrid melon, 308
Harris lines, 22–23, 41
Harvard beet (beet, *Beta vulgaris*), 1730–1731. *See also* beet
Harvard growth standards, 984
Harvard University, 1374, 1491, 1678
harvest moon festival, in Korea, 1187
Haselnuss (hazelnut, *Corylus avellana, E. maxima*), 1784. *See also* hazelnut
Hass avocado (avocado, *Persea*

americana), 1724–1725. *See also* avocado
Hastinapura site (India), 594
Haugh Units, 504
Hausa groundnut (*Kerstingiella geocarpa = Macrotyloma geocarpa*), 1783–1784
Hausa potato
   Plectranthus esculentus, 1795
   Sudan potato (*Coleus tuberosus = C. parviflorus =* Solenostemon rotundifolius), 1859
haute cuisine, southern European courtly, 1208
Haven of Health, 1688
Haversian canals, 22
haw (*Crataegus* spp., hawthorn berry), 1784. *See also* black haw; hawthorn berry; sloe
haw tree (hawthorn berry, *Crataegus* spp.), 1784
Hawaiian Islands
   diabetes mellitus in, 1363
   dietary colonialism in, 1361
   dietary liquids in, kava, 664, 665, 668
   famine in, 1413
   fish farming in, tribal, 457–458
   plant foods in
      banana, 178
      macadamia nut, 1805
      papaya, 1828
      pineapple, 1834
      rice, 139
      sugarcane, 444
      sweet potato (pre-Columbian), 210
      taro, 223, 224, 226, 227, 1866
      watermelon (post-Columbian), 306
Hawaiian Kona coffee (coffee, *Coffea arabica*), 1761. *See also* coffee
Hawaiian pineapple (pineapple, *Ananas comosus*), 1834
Hawaiian plantain (*Musa × sapientum*), 1784. *See also* plantain
hawk, broad-winged (*Buteo platypterus*), 1291
hawksbill turtle (*Eretmochelys imbricata*), 567
hawthorn
   black haw (*Viburnum prunifolium, Crataegus douglasii*), 1734
   Crataegus spp., 1784
      in North America (pre-Columbian), 1289
hawthorn berry (*Crataegus* spp.), 1784

I

I cinque libri di plante, 356
Iberian Peninsula (*see also* Spain, Portugal)
  animal foods in
    chicken, 496
    rabbits, 566
    sheep, 576
  plant foods in
    chickpea, 1728, 1752
    chilli peppers, 1753
    lemon, 1800
    maize, 1806
    olive oil (ancient-medieval), 378
    olives, 1825
    taro, 224
    tomato, 354
  wine (ancient-medieval), 732
ibope (*algarrobo, Prosopis pallida*), 1716
icaco (cocoplum, *Chrysobalanus icaco*), 1759-1760
icaco plum (cocoplum, *Chrysobalanus icaco*), 1759-1760
ice, compulsive consumption of, 972
ice cream, 699
  marketing of, 700
ice-cream bean (*Inga vera*), 1788
ice-cream soda, 707
ice plant (*Mesembryanthemum crystallinum*), 1789
iceberg lettuce (lettuce, *Lactuca sativa* var. *capitata*), 1801. *See also* lettuce
iced tea (tea, *Camellia sinensis*), 1866-1867. *See also* tea(s)
Iceland
  algae in, 233
  dulse in, 233
  sheep in, 578
Iceland lichen (Iceland moss, *Cetraria islandica*), 1789
Iceland moss (*Cetraria islandica*), 1789
Ictalurus spp. (freshwater catfish), 1290
Ictiobus spp. (buffalo), 1290
Idaho potato (white potato, *Solanum tuberosum*), 197, 1878-1880. *See also* potato(es)
idiopathic spasmophilic diathesis, 829-830
IgE antibodies, 1027, 1048
Iglulki people, 1327
igope (*algarrobo, Prosopis pallida*), 1716
iguana
  Cyclura spp.

    in Caribbean (pre-Columbian), 1263, 1266, 1267
    in Dominican Republic, 1271
    rock (*C. carinata*), 1267
  Iguana spp.
    in Caribbean (pre-Columbian), 1263, 1266
IITA (International Institute for Tropical Agriculture), 100
ilama (*Annona diversifolia*), 1789
Iles Turtues, 568
Ilex spp. (hollyberry), 1786
Ilex cassine (dahoon holly), 1766
  in North America (pre-Columbian), 1289
Ilex glabra (winterberry), 1882-1883
Ilex paraguariensis (yerba maté), 1786, 1885
Ilex verticillata (winterberry), 1882-1883
  in North America (pre-Columbian), 1289
Ilex vomitoria (yaupon), 1884-1885
  in North America (pre-Columbian), 1289, 1296
Illicium verum (star anise), 434, 1858
  in China, 1858
  in Vietnam, 1858
Ilynassa obsoleta (mud nassa), 1290
imbé (*Garcinia livingstonei*), 1789
immune system
  and circulatory system, 1110
  iron on, 812, 816-817
  malnutrition on, 1398-1400
  protein-energy malnutrition on, 983
  zinc on, 872-873
immunization(s)
  Guinea-Bissau research on, 1391-1392
  and iron metabolism, 922-923
  McKeown on, 1390-1391
  and mortality, 1382
immunoglobin E (IgE), 1027, 1048
Impatiens spp. (jewelweed), 1793
  in North America (pre-Columbian), 1289, 1296
Impatiens capensis, 1793
imperial tea (tea, *Camellia sinensis*), 1866-1867. *See also* tea(s)
Improved Aerated Liquid, 707
inanga (trout), 1344
Inca empire
  food production and distribution in, 1260
  plant foods in
    maize, 197, 1750, 1806, 1841
    potato, 187, 188-190
    tomato, 352, 1248, 1249

Inca wheat (quinoa, *Chenopodium quinoa*), 1841
Incaparina, 982
indentured servants, in Caribbean, 1284
India
  animal foods in
    buffalo milk, 588
    precolonial, 596
    camel, 468-469, 470
    cattle, 493
    chicken (prehistoric), 499
    native, 496
    fish (farmed), 461-462
    goat, 533
    locusts, 550
    pig, 539
    sea turtle, 568
    eggs of, 573
    sheep, 578
    yak, 608
    yak milk, 610
  caste in, 1514
  dietary culture and history in, 1148-1151
  dietary liquids in
    coffee
      precolonial, 642
      production of, 648
    milk and buttermilk (precolonial), 715
    tea, 714, 715-716
      British cultivation of, 1867
  diseases in
    aflatoxicosis in, 1698
    cancer, of oral cavity, pharynx and esophagus, 1089-1090
    celiac disease, 1010
    diabetes (ancient), 1078-1079
    gastrodisciasis, 1046
    geophagia, 969
  famine in, 1412-1413
    of 1868-9, shum tree and, 1852
    Bengal 1943, 1415
    on migration, 1418
    naming of, 1414
    policy toward, 1423
    subsistence ethic in, 1417
  fish farming in, early, 461-462
  fish hatcheries in, early, 460
  food subsidies in, 1596, 1598
  horse sacrifice in, 542
  nutrition in
    anemia and, 928
    beriberi and, 915
    iodine deficiency and cretinism, 801
    in neonates, 804

goitrogens in, 801
hardiness of, 182
nutritive value of, 182
origins of, 182–183
in Pacific, 186
in Paraguay, 1258
plant of, 181
preparation of, 801
products from, 1810
in Saladoid culture, 1271
slavery and, 183
in South America, 1255
spread of, 1810
toxins in, 181–182, 1697–1698, 1810
uses of, 182
varieties of, 181
yields of (cal), 1265
Manioc in Africa, 186
manna (*Lecanora* spp., *Gyrophora esculenta*), 1810
medicinal use of, 1541
manna eucalyptus (manna gum, *Eucalyptus viminalis*), 1810
manna gum (*Eucalyptus viminalis*), 1810
manna lichen (manna, *Lecanora* spp., *Gyrophora esculenta*), 1810
Manuel des Amphitryon, 1212
manuscript sources, in culinary history, 1370
"many foods-single aliment concept," 889, 901
Manyoshu, 316
manzana (*Capsicum pubescens*), 1810. *See also* chilli pepper(s)
Manzanillo olive (olive, *Olea europaea*), 1824–1825. *See also* olive(s)
manzanita (*Arctostaphylos uva-ursi*)
heather, 1785
pointleaf, 1785
manzano
Capsicum pubescens (manzana), 1810
Musa paradisiaca (banana), 1726
mao tai, 662
Maori peoples, 1339
diet of, 1343–1344
European contact on, 1345
farming of
colonial, 1346
precolonial, 1343
map turtle (*Graptemys* spp.), 1290, 1297
maple sugar (*Acer* spp.), 1810
in North America (pre-Columbian), 1289, 1296

maple syrup (*Acer* spp.), 1810
in North America
post-Columbian, 1310
19th cent., 1315
pre-Columbian, 1289, 1296
maracuja (passion fruit, *Passiflora edulis, P. quadrangularis*), 1829–1830
in South America, 1256
Maranta arundinacea (arrowroot), 1721–1722
in Caribbean (post-Columbian), 1284
in Garifuna diet, 1273
Marasmius oreades (fairy-ring mushrooms), 1819
marasmus, 41, 632
breastfeeding on, 1451
in Jamaica, 1285
as protein–energy malnutrition, 910–911
marc, 657
marconi wheat (wheat, *Triticum aestivum*), 1878
marcottage, of kola nut, 687
mare's tale (horseweed, *Erigeron canadensis = Conyza canadensis*), 1787
margarine, 700, 1677–1678
coconut oil in, 390–391
palm oil in, 397, 405
soybean oil in, 424
sunflower oil in, 429
Mariana Islands, plant foods in
coconut, 394
taro, 223
Mariculture, Ltd., 573
marigold
Calendula officinalis, 433, 1810
wild (anisillo, *Tagetes minuta*), 1719
marijuana (*Cannabis sativa*), in Garifuna diet, 1273
marine algae (seaweed), 1850. *See also* individual species, e.g., *Spirulina geitleri*
in North America (pre-Columbian), 1299
Marine Biological Association of England, 461
marine cockroach (*Acanthopleura* sp.), 1271
marine fats, 385–387
marine foods. *See also* specific foods, e.g., turtle(s), sea
elements in, 16
isotopes in bone with, 16–17
marine hatcheries, early, 461
marine oils, in cardiovascular disease, 1104
Marine Turtle Newsletter, 573

marine turtles. *See* turtle(s), sea
marjoram (*Origanum majorana, O. onites*), 433, 1811
in mead and small beers, 703
medicinal use of, 1540
market economy
and new product introductions, 1645
and nutrition policy, 1626–1627
Marlierea edulis (cambucá), 1743
marmalade box (genipap, *Genipa americana*), 1777
marmalade plum (sapodilla, *Manilkara zapota*), 1848
marmelo (bael fruit, *Aegle marmelos*), 1725
marmosets, 1570
Marmota monax (woodchuck, groundhog)
in British Isles (Medieval), 1220
in North America (pre-Columbian), 1291, 1295, 1297
Marquesas
kava in, 664, 667
taro in, 223
marron (chestnut, *Castanea sativa*), 362. *See also* chestnut
marrow (*Cucurbita pepo, C. maxima*), 340, 341, 342, 1811. *See also* squash
cultivars of, 347
marrow bean, 1730
marrow squash (marrow, *Cucurbita pepo, C. maxima*), 1811. *See also* squash
marrow stem (kale, *Brassica oleracea* var. *acephala*), 1795
Marrubium vulgare (horehound), 433, 1786–1787
marsh clam (*Polymesoda caroliniana*), 1290
marsh elder (sumpweed, *Iva annua*), 1861
marsh grapefruit (grapefruit, *Citrus* × *paradisi*), 1780
marsh mallow (mallow, *Althaea officinalis*), 1808
medicinal use of, 1541
marsh marigold (cowslip, *Caltha palustris*), 1764
marsh salad (cornsalad, *Valerianella* spp.), 1763
marsh samphire (glasswort, *Salcornia europaea, S. herbacea*), 1778
marsh trefoil (bog myrtle, *Myrica gale*), 1735
Marshall Islands, coconut in, 394
marshelder (*Iva ciliata*), 1289
Marsicam (onion), 250. *See also* onion(s)

organic foods
in Australia and New Zealand,
1349
in South America, 1259
Organic Gardening and Farming,
1491
Organization of Economic Cooperation and Development
(OECD), 1115–1117
food-balance data of, 1199
organotherapy, 1004
Orgeat, 704
Oriental eggplant (eggplant, *Solanum
melongena*), 1770
Oriental garlic (Chinese chive,
Allium tuberosum),
1755–1756
Oriental melon (*Cucumis*), 1813
Oriental mustard (*Brassica juncea*),
1819–1820
Oriental pear (Asian pear, *Pyrus
ussuriensis, P. pyrifolia*),
1723
Oriental persimmon (persimmon,
*Diospyros kaki, D. virgini-
ana*), 1833
Oriental pickling melon (gherkin,
Cucumis melo var.
conomon), 300, 1777
Oriental radish (daikon, *Raphanus
sativus*), 1767. *See also*
daikon
Origanum dictamnus (dittany),
1769
Origanum majorana (marjoram,
sweet marjoram), 433, 1811
in mead and small beers, 703
Origanum onites (pot marjoram),
1811
Origanum vulgare (oregano), 433,
1811
in southern Europe, 1209
Origin of Cultivated Plants, 98, 273
oris root (*Iris germanica*), 1790
Orkney Islands
algae in, 233
in bladderlocks (*Alaria esculenta*),
233
ornamental gourds (*Cucurbita pepo
ssp. ovifera* var. *ovifera*),
339–341
ornamental kale (kale, *Brassica oleracea* var. *acephala*), 1795
Ornithorhynchus anatinus (duck-
billed platypus), 1339, 1341
Orontium aquaticum (golden club),
1779
in North America (pre-Columbian),
1289, 1296
Oryctolagus (rabbit), 565. *See also*
rabbit(s)

Oryctolagus cuniculus (European
wild rabbit), 565
Oryza barthii, 134, 1714
Oryza glaberrima (African rice), 133,
1331, 1333, 1714–1715
in Africa, West, 134
Oryza perennis, 133
Oryza sativa, 133, 1714. *See also* rice
Oryza sativa (rice). *See* rice
Oryzopsis aspera (ricegrass), 1844
Oryzopsis hymenoides (ricegrass),
1844
osmanthus (*Osmanthus*), 1827
osteomalacia. *See also* rickets
in ancient populations, 36–37, 68
in Korea, 1190
vitamin D deficiency on,
763–764, 768, 786
osteomyelitis, in prehistoric hunter-
gatherers, 67
osteoporosis, 22, 947–960
alcoholism and, 793
in anorexia nervosa, 1001
bone fragility in, 950–951
bone mass in, 950
bone remodeling in, 949–950
calcium intake and, 958
boron and, 858
calcium in, 787–788
and bone remodeling, 958
homeostasis of, 949–950
and life, 947–948
regulation of, bone in, 948
requirement of
bases for, 952–954
definition of, 952
dermal losses in, 954
during growth, 954–956
intestinal absorption in,
953–954
during maturity, 956–957
during postmenopause, 957
RDA in, 954
renal losses in, 954
during senescence,
957–958
and terrestrial vertebrate diet,
948–949
as treatment for, 959
cereal-based diets and, 1473
definition of, 950
and disability recovery, 959
ethnicity in, 959–960
expression of, 950
fatigue damage in, 951, 958
flouride and, 791, 860
glucocorticoids and, 793
and illness/injury recovery, 959
as nutrient reserve disorder,
951–952
premature, 68

vitamin K and, 779
Ostrea edulis (oysters), 1156
Ostrea rivularis (oysters), 1156
ostrich eggs, 499
ostrich fern (*Matteuccia
struthiopteris*), 1773
Oswego tea (bee balm, *Melissa officinalis*), 1730
Otaheite gooseberry, 1159
Phyllanthus acidus, 1827
Otaheite orange (*Citrus taitensis*),
1827
Otolithes ruber (croaker), 1155
otter
in British Isles (prehistoric), 1217
Lontra canadensis, 1291, 1297
in North America (pre-Columbian),
1291, 1295, 1297, 1298
sea, 1298
Ottoman empire, tomato in, 357
Ottoman period, of Turkey, 282, 1148
oudo (udo, *Aralia cordata*), 1874
*Our Digestion; or My Jolly Friend's
Secret*, 1543
oval-leaf (peperomia, *Peperomia
obtusifolia*), 1832
ovarian cancer, 1092
ovens
in Mesopotamia (ancient-
medieval), 1141–1142
in Middle East (modern), 1143
in North America
19th cent., 1314
20th cent., 1319
in Pacific Islands, 1358
overweight. *See* obesity
ovines. *See* sheep
Ovis spp. (sheep), 574–578. *See also*
sheep
Ovis ammon f. aries, 1227. *See also*
sheep
Ovis aries (sheep), 574–578. *See
also* sheep
Ovis orientalis (urial, wild sheep),
574, 575. *See also* sheep
ovulation, lactation and, 627–628
owala-oil tree (oil-bean tree, *Pentaclethra macrophylla*), 1824
owe kola (kola nut, *Cola* sp.), 1797
owl, barred (*Strix varia*), 1291
ox liver, 297
ox (oxen), 492. *See also* cattle
in Korea, 1188
wild, in British Isles (prehistoric),
1217
Oxalis acetosella (wood sorrel), 434,
1883
Oxalis tuberosa (oca), 1255, 1824
Oxalis violacea (wood sorrel), 1883
Oxfam Lutheran World Federation,
1425

Japanese (*P. salicina*), 1792, 1848

Mexican wild (capulin, *P. capollin*), 1745

Myrobalan (cherry plum, *P. cerasifera*), 1751

P. americana, 1289

tart Damson (*P. insititia*), 1767

seaside (tallow wood plum, *Ximenia americana*), 1865

sour (*Ximenia caffra*), 1854

Spanish (*Spondias purpurea*), 1785

tallow wood (*Ximenia americana*), 1865

white (*Planchonella pohlmaniana*), 1732

wild (*Planchonella pohlmaniana*), 1732

plum tomato (tomato, *Lycopersicon esculentum*), 1870–1871. *See also* tomato(es)

plumbophagia, 968

PMR 45 melon, 308

poblano (*Capsicum*), 1837. *See also* chilli pepper(s)

in Mexico, 1837

pocan (pokeweed, *Phytolacca americana*), 1837

pocket gopher (*Geomys* spp.), 1291, 1295

podded pea (sugar pea, *Pisum sativum* var. *macrocarpon*), 1860–1861

Podilymbus podiceps (pied-billed grebe), 1291

Pogonias cromis (black drum), in North America

pre-Columbian, 1290

Spanish colonial, 1300

Pohnpei, kava in, 664, 665, 667, 668

pohole (*Athyrium*), 1837

poi (taro, *Colocasia esculenta, C. antiquorum*), 224, 226, 227, 1866. *See also* taro

in Pacific Islands, 1358

pointed cabbage

Brassica oleracea (cabbage), 1741

Brassica pekinensis (Chinese cabbage), 1754–1755

pointed gourd (tandoori, *Trichosanthes dioica*), 1865

pointleaf manzanita (heather, *Arctostaphylos uva-ursi*), 1785

poire brandy, 657

pois cajun (pigeon pea, *Cajanus cajan, C. indicus*), 1834

pois d'Angole (pigeon pea, *Cajanus cajan, C. indicus*), 1834

poison. *See* toxins

poke (pokeweed, *Phytolacca americana*), 1837

in North America (pre-Columbian), 1289, 1293, 1294, 1296

poke salad (pokeweed, *Phytolacca americana*), 1837

pokeberry (pokeweed, *Phytolacca americana*), 1837

medicinal use of, 1540

pokeroot (pokeweed, *Phytolacca americana*), 1837

pokeweed (*Phytolacca americana*), 1837

in North America (pre-Columbian), 1289, 1293, 1294, 1296

Poland

animal foods in

chicken (ancient-medieval), 497

duck, 518

pig, 539

food policy in, 1625

North American emigration from, 1313

plant foods in

buckwheat, 90

chilli peppers, 1828

cucumber, 309

oat, 125, 126

paprika, 1828

spices, 435

sugar, beet, 447

pole bean (*Phaseolus coccineus*), 1729

polecat weedskunk (skunk cabbage, *Symplocarpus foetidus*), 1852

poleo (*Minthostachysi* spp.), 1815

Polinices duplicatus (shark eye), 1290

poliomyelitis, 1043

polished rice (rice, *Oryza sativa*), 1843–1844. *See also* rice

beriberi from, 751, 915 (*see also* beriberi)

Political Action Committees (PACs), 1634–1635

The Political Economy of Hunger, 1591

pollack, 1188

pollen

coconut, 395

in coprolites, 45–46, 47–48

polyantha bean (*Phaseolus polyanthus*)

in Mexico and Central America, 275

origin and domestication of, 273, 275

polychlorinated biphenyls (PBCs), 1696, 1702

Polydontes sp. (land snail), 1271

polyethylene terephthalate (PET), 711

Polygonatum (Solomon's-seal), 1853

Polygonum (knotweed, smartweed), 1797

Polygonum bistorta (bistort, smokeweed), 1797

Polygonum bistortoides (bistort, smokeweed), 1797

Polygonum coccineum, 1797

Polygonum convolvulus, 1797

Polygonum cuspidatum (Japanese knotweed, Mexican bamboo), 1797

Polygonum douglasii, 1797

Polygonum erectum (erect knotweed), 1289, 1294, 1295, 1297

Polygonum hydropiper (water pepper), 1797

Polygonum persicaria, 1797

Polygonum viviparum, 1797

Polymesoda carolinana (marsh clam), 1290

Polymnia sonchifolia (yacón), 1883–1884

Polynesia

agriculture in, 1357

fish farming in, tribal, 457–458

plant foods in

air potato, 1715

banana, 178, 180, 1726

coconut, 394

limu (seaweed), 1358

sweet potato, 210

taro, 223, 224

water yam, 1877

yam, 213, 215

sea turtles in, 568

Polynesian arrowroot (*Tacca leontopetaloides*), 1722

Polynesian chestnut (*Inocarpus edulis*), 1837

Polypodium vulgare (common fern), 1680

Polyporus durus, 327

polysaccharides

in algae, 240–241

principal dietary source of, 893

Polystichum munitum (giant holly fern), 1777

in North America (pre-Columbian), 1299

polyunsaturated fatty acids (PUFA), and vitamin E, 771

poma amoris (tomato, *Lycopersicon esculentum*), 355. *See also* tomato(es)